6305
vol. IX

CAROLINA
COMMUNITY COLLEGES
at
MAYLAND COMMUNITY COLLEGE

DICTIONARY OF AMERICAN BIOGRAPHY

AMERICAN
COUNCIL
* OF *
LEARNED
SOCIETIES
*

D1418461

DICTIONARY
OF AMERICAN BIOGRAPHY

The *Dictionary of American Biography* was published originally in twenty volumes. Supplementary volumes were added in 1944 and 1958. This edition of the work combines all twenty-two volumes.

The present Volume I (Abbe–Brazer) contains Volumes I and II of the original edition, but these are now denominated "Part 1" and "Part 2" of the Volume. Volumes II through XI are arranged similarly, the Second Part in each instance representing a volume of the original series. For ease in reference, although the articles follow one another in strict alphabetical order, each Second Part is preceded by a half-title page which relates that Part to its place in the original numbering of the volumes.

The Errata list at the head of Volume I contains corrections of fact and additional data which have come to the attention of the Editors from the first publication of the work up to the present. Minor typographical corrections have been made in many instances directly on the plates.

PUBLISHED UNDER THE AUSPICES OF

THE AMERICAN COUNCIL OF LEARNED SOCIETIES

AMERICAN PHILOSOPHICAL SOCIETY

AMERICAN ACADEMY OF ARTS AND SCIENCES

AMERICAN ANTIQUARIAN SOCIETY

AMERICAN ORIENTAL SOCIETY

AMERICAN NUMISMATIC SOCIETY

AMERICAN PHILOLOGICAL ASSOCIATION

ARCHAEOLOGICAL INSTITUTE OF AMERICA

SOCIETY OF BIBLICAL LITERATURE AND EXEGESIS

MODERN LANGUAGE ASSOCIATION OF AMERICA

AMERICAN HISTORICAL ASSOCIATION

AMERICAN ECONOMIC ASSOCIATION

AMERICAN FOLKLORE SOCIETY

AMERICAN PHILOSOPHICAL ASSOCIATION

AMERICAN ANTHROPOLOGICAL ASSOCIATION

AMERICAN POLITICAL SCIENCE ASSOCIATION

BIBLIOGRAPHICAL SOCIETY OF AMERICA

ASSOCIATION OF AMERICAN GEOGRAPHERS

AMERICAN SOCIOLOGICAL SOCIETY

COLLEGE ART ASSOCIATION OF AMERICA

HISTORY OF SCIENCE SOCIETY

LINGUISTIC SOCIETY OF AMERICA

MEDIAEVAL ACADEMY OF AMERICA

AMERICAN MUSICOLOGICAL SOCIETY

ASSOCIATION FOR ASIAN STUDIES

AMERICAN SOCIETY FOR AESTHETICS

DICTIONARY

OF

American Biography

VOLUME IX

SEWELL - TROWBRIDGE

═══

Edited by

DUMAS MALONE

Charles Scribner's Sons *New York*

Prompted solely by a desire for public service the New York Times Company and its President, Mr. Adolph S. Ochs, have made possible the preparation of the manuscript of the Dictionary of American Biography through a subvention of more than $500,000 and with the understanding that the entire responsibility for the contents of the volumes rests with the American Council of Learned Societies.

VOLUME IX, PART 1
SEWELL - STEVENSON

(VOLUME XVII OF THE ORIGINAL EDITION)

CROSS REFERENCES FROM THIS VOL-
UME ARE MADE TO THE VOLUME
NUMBERS OF THE ORIGINAL EDITION.

CONTRIBUTORS
VOLUME IX, PART 1

Thomas P. Abernethy	T. P. A.	Louise Fontaine Catterall	L. F. C.
James Truslow Adams	J. T. A.	Zechariah Chafee, Jr.	Z. C., Jr.
Nelson F. Adkins	N. F. A.	Hope S. Chamberlain	H. S. C—in.
Robert Greenhalgh Albion	R. G. A.	Joseph Edgar Chamberlin	J. E. C.
William F. Albright	W. F. A.	Henry S. Chapman	H. S. C—an.
Edward E. Allen	E. E. A--n.	Wayland J. Chase	W. J. C.
William H. Allison	W. H. A.	Arney R. Childs	A. R. C.
Gertrude L. Annan	G. L. A.	Francis A. Christie	F. A. C.
George B. Arbaugh	G. B. A.	Arthur E. Christy	A. E. C.
John Clark Archer	J. C. A.	Jane Clark	J. C.
Newton Arvin	N. A.	Oral Sumner Coad	O. S. C.
Edwin Ewart Aubrey	E. E. A—y.	Frederick W. Coburn	F. W. C.
John Bakeless	J. B.	Fannie L. Gwinner Cole	F. L. G. C.
Frank Collins Baker	F. C. B.	Fay-Cooper Cole	F-C. C.
Thomas M. Balliet	T. M. B.	Rossetter G. Cole	R. G. C.
Thomas S. Barclay	T. S. B.	Florence Converse	F. C.
Adriaan J. Barnouw	A. J. B.	E. Merton Coulter	E. M. C.
Harold K. Barrows	H. K. B.	Jesse H. Coursault	J. H. C.
Clarence Bartlett	C. B.	William C. Covert	W. C. C.
Ernest Sutherland Bates	E. S. B.	Isaac J. Cox	I. J. C—x.
William G. Bean	W. G. B—n.	Esther Crane	E. C.
C. C. Benson	C. C. B—n.	Katharine Elizabeth Crane	K. E. C.
S. Stillman Berry	S. S. B.	Edward E. Curtis	E. E. C.
Julius August Bewer	J. A. B.	Stuart Daggett	S. D.
William C. Binkley	W. C. B.	Arthur Kyle Davis, Jr.	A. K. D., Jr.
Robert Emory Blackwell	R. E. B.	Clive Day	C. D.
Edith R. Blanchard	E. R. B.	Richard E. Day	R. E. D.
Wyndham B. Blanton	W. B. B.	D. Bryson Delavan	D. B. D.
Willard Grosvenor Bleyer	W. G. B—r.	Herman J. Deutsch	H. J. D.
Louise Pearson Blodget	L. P. B.	Bernard DeVoto	B. D-V.
Louis H. Bolander	L. H. B.	Edward H. Dewey	E. H. D.
Charles K. Bolton	C. K. B.	Everett N. Dick	E. N. D.
Robert W. Bolwell	R. W. B.	Mary LeGrand Didlake	M. L. D.
Sarah G. Bowerman	S. G. B.	Irving Dilliard	I. D.
Julian P. Boyd	J. P. B.	Charles A. Dinsmore	C. A. D.
John E. Briggs	J. E. B.	Frank Haigh Dixon	F. H. D.
Robert C. Brooks	R. C. B.	Eleanor R. Dobson	E. R. D.
Robert Preston Brooks	R. P. B.	Leonidas Dodson	L. D.
C. A. Browne	C. A. B.	Randolph C. Downes	R. C. D.
G. MacLaren Brydon	G. M. B.	William Howe Downes	W. H. D.
Solon J. Buck	S. J. B.	Carl S. Driver	C. S. D.
C. C. Burlingame	C. C. B—e.	Edward A. Duddy	E. A. D.
Edmund C. Burnett	E. C. B.	Andrew G. Du Mez	A. G. D-M.
William H. Burnham	W. H. B.	B. A. Dunbar	B. A. D.
Lester J. Cappon	L. J. C.	Harold H. Dunham	H. H. D.
Charles F. Carey	C. F. C.	George Matthew Dutcher	G. M. D.
Irving J. Carr	I. J. C—r.	Edward Dwight Eaton	E. D. E.
William Glasgow Bruce Carson	W. G. B. C.	Walter Prichard Eaton	W. P. E.
		Edwin Francis Edgett	E. F. E.

Contributors

Everett E. Edwards	E. E. E.	Leland Ossian Howard	L. O. H.
Clara Egli	C. E—i.	Harrison E. Howe	H. E. H.
Elizabeth Breckenridge Ellis	E. B. E.	Edward Buell Hungerford	E. B. H.
Milton Ellis	M. E.	J. Ramsay Hunt	J. R. H.
Carl Engel	C. E—l.	Ray W. Irwin	R. W. I.
Amos A. Ettinger	A. A. E.	Joseph Jackson	J. J.
Paul D. Evans	P. D. E.	Edna L. Jacobsen	E. L. J.
John O. Evjen	J. O. E.	T. Cary Johnson, Jr.	T. C. J., Jr.
Ellsworth Faris	E. F.	Horace Leonard Jones	H. L. J.
Paul Patton Faris	P. P. F.	Rufus M. Jones	R. M. J.
Hallie Farmer	H. F.	Louis C. Karpinski	L. C. K.
Ethel Webb Faulkner	E. W. F.	Paul Kaufman	P. K.
Harold U. Faulkner	H. U. F.	Herbert Anthony Kellar	H. A. K—r.
James Waldo Fawcett	J. W. F.	Howard A. Kelly	H. A. K—y.
Felix Fellner	F. F.	Rayner W. Kelsey	R. W. K.
Norman Fenton	N. F.	John Kieran	J. K.
Robert S. Fletcher	R. S. F.	Marie Goebel Kimball	M. G. K.
Harry W. Foote	H. W. F.	James O. Knauss	J. O. K.
Jeremiah D. M. Ford	J. D. M. F.	Ernst C. Krohn	E. C. K.
W. Freeman Galpin	W. F. G.	Leonard B. Krueger	L. B. K.
Paul N. Garber	P. N. G.	William Palmer Ladd	W. P. L.
Winfield R. Gaylord	W. R. G.	Gordon J. Laing	G. J. L.
George Harvey Genzmer	G. H. G.	William G. Land	W. G. L.
W. J. Ghent	W. J. G.	William Chauncy Langdon	W. C. L.
Blake-More Godwin	B-M. G.	Herbert S. Langfeld	H. S. L.
Armistead Churchill Gordon, Jr.	A. C. G., Jr.	Conrad H. Lanza	C. H. L.
Herbert H. Gowen	H. H. G.	Fred V. Larkin	F. V. L.
Dorothy Grafly	D. G.	Kenneth S. Latourette	K. S. L.
William Creighton Graham	W. C. G.	Edwin A. Lee	E. A. L.
Virginia Gearhart Gray	V. G. G.	Anna Lane Lingelbach	A. L. L.
Fletcher M. Green	F. M. G.	Walter Lee Lingle	W. L. L.
Anne King Gregorie	A. K. G.	Charles Sumner Lobingier	C. S. L.
Berenice Elaine Grieves	B. E. G.	Warfield T. Longcope	W. T. L.
Frank W. Grinnell	F. W. G.	Ella Lonn	E. L.
Charles Burton Gulick	C. B. G.	Frederic B. Loomis	F. B. L.
Sidney Gunn	S. G.	Harry Miller Lydenberg	H. M. L.
Le Roy R. Hafen	L. R. H.	Thomas McCrae	T. M.
Gordon S. Haight	G. S. H.	Roger P. McCutcheon	R. P. M.
J. Evetts Haley	J. E. H.	W. J. McGlothlin	W. J. M.
Courtney R. Hall	C. R. H.	Reginald C. McGrane	R. C. McG.
J. G. deR. Hamilton	J. G. deR. H.	Seth Shepard McKay	S. S. M.
Talbot Faulkner Hamlin	T. F. H.	Blake McKelvey	B. McK.
Joseph Mills Hanson	J. M. H.	Edward McMahon	E. M.
Edward Rochie Hardy, Jr.	E. R. H., Jr.	William McNamara	W. M.
Alvin F. Harlow	A. F. H.	T. F. McNeill	T. F. M.
Ralph V. Harlow	R. V. H.	John H. T. McPherson	J. H. T. M.
George McLean Harper	G. M. H.	Carey McWilliams	C. McW.
Ida Husted Harper	I. H. H.	Helen Jo Scott Mann	H. J. S. M.
Samuel G. Hefelbower	S. G. H.	Asa Earl Martin	A. E. M.
Samuel J. Heidner	S. J. H.	Jean West Maury	J. W. M.
Elizabeth Wiltbank Heilman	E. W. H.	William R. Maxon	W. R. M.
J. F. Hellweg	J. F. H.	Robert Douthat Meade	R. D. M.
John L. Hervey	J. L. H.	Franklin J. Meine	F. J. M.
John Donald Hicks	J. D. H.	Clarence W. Mendell	C. W. M—l.
John Haynes Holmes	J. H. H.	A. Howard Meneely	A. H. M.
Walter Hough	W. H.	Newton D. Mereness	N. D. M.
John Tasker Howard	J. T. H.	George P. Merrill	G. P. M.
		Raymond C. Miller	R. C. M.

Contributors

Broadus Mitchell	B. M.	William M. Robinson, Jr.	W. M. R., Jr.
Stewart Mitchell	S. M.	Nicholas R. Rodionoff	N. R. R.
Carl W. Mitman	C. W. M—n.	Victor Rosewater	V. R.
Frank Monaghan	F. M.	Earle Dudley Ross	E. D. R.
Robert E. Moody	R. E. M.	Henry Kalloch Rowe	H. K. R.
Charles Moore	C. M.	William Sener Rusk	W. S. R.
George T. Moore	G. T. M.	Verne Lockwood Samson	V. L. S.
Louise M. Moore	L. M. M.	David J. Saposs	D. J. S.
Warren King Moorehead	W. K. M.	Joseph Schafer	J. S.
Theodore H. Morgan	T. H. M.	Israel Schapiro	I. S.
Samuel Eliot Morison	S. E. M.	Richard C. Schiedt	R. C. S.
Richard B. Morris	R. B. M.	A. Arthur Schiller	A. A. S.
Frank Howard Neff	F. H. N.	Louis Bernard Schmidt	L. B. S.
Allan Nevins	A. N.	H. W. Schoenberger	H. W. S.
Clinton Andrew Neyman	C. A. N.	Hamilton Schuyler	H. Sc—r.
Jeannette P. Nichols	J. P. N.	Louis Martin Sears	L. M. Se—s.
Robert Hastings Nichols	R. H. N.	Robert Francis Seybolt	R. F. S.
W. A. Noyes	W. A. N.	Fred A. Shannon	F. A. S.
A. J. Olmsted	A. J. O.	William Bristol Shaw	W. B. S.
Francis R. Packard	F. R. P.	William E. Shea	W. E. S—a.
John McAuley Palmer	J. McA. P.	Solon Shedd	S. S.
Mildred B. Palmer	M. B. P.	William R. Shepherd	W. R. S—d.
John I. Parcel	J. I. P.	Guy Emery Shipler	G. E. S.
Stanley M. Pargellis	S. M. P.	Lester B. Shippee	L. B. S.
Arthur C. Parker	A. C. P—k—r.	Eleanor M. Sickels	E. M. S.
Edd Winfield Parks	E. W. P.	Kenneth C. M. Sills	K. C. M. S.
Charles O. Paullin	C. O. P.	Francis Butler Simkins	F. B. S.
Frederic Logan Paxson	F. L. P.	St. George L. Sioussat	St. G. L. S.
James H. Peeling	J. H. P.	Theodore Sizer	T. S.
Dexter Perkins	D. P.	Constance Lindsay Skinner	C. L. S.
Frederick T. Persons	F. T. P.	William Adams Slade	W. A. S—e.
A. Everett Peterson	A. E. P.	David Stanley Smith	D. S. S.
Caroline S. Pfaff	C. S. P—f.	Edward Conrad Smith	E. C. S.
James M. Phalen	J. M. P.	William E. Smith	W. E. S—h.
Francis S. Philbrick	F. S. P.	William Roy Smith	W. R. S—h.
Ulrich B. Phillips	U. B. P.	Harriet Smither	H. Sm—r.
John E. Pomfret	J. E. P.	Herbert Solow	H. So—w.
David deSola Pool	D. deS. P.	E. Wilder Spaulding	E. W. S.
Alfred C. Potter	A. C. P—t—r.	Oliver L. Spaulding, Jr.	O. L. S., Jr.
Charles Shirley Potts	C. S. P—s.	Thomas M. Spaulding	T. M. S.
Richard J. Purcell	R. J. P.	Robert E. Spiller	R. E. S.
Lowell Joseph Ragatz	L. J. R.	James Duane Squires	J. D. S.
James Garfield Randall	J. G. R.	C. P. Stacey	C. P. S.
Belle Rankin	B. R.	Harris Elwood Starr	H. E. S.
Albert G. Rau	A. G. R.	J. M. Steadman, Jr.	J. M. S., Jr.
P. O. Ray	P. O. R.	Bertha Monica Stearns	B. M. S.
Thomas T. Read	T. T. R.	Wendell H. Stephenson	W. H. S.
Herbert S. Reichle	H. S. R—e.	John A. Stevenson	J. A. S.
J. E. Retherford	J. E. R.	Tracy E. Strevey	T. E. S.
Charles Dudley Rhodes	C. D. R.	Lionel M. Summers	L. M. Su—s.
Edward E. Richardson	E. E. R.	William A. Sumner	W. A. S—r.
Leon B. Richardson	L. B. R.	William U. Swan	W. U. S.
Robert E. Riegel	R. E. R.	William W. Sweet	W. W. S.
Donald A. Roberts	D. A. R.	Charles S. Sydnor	C. S. S.
James Alexander Robertson	J. A. R.	Thomas E. Tallmadge	T. E. T.
Burr Arthur Robinson	B. A. R.	Lucy Lucile Tasher	L. L. T.
Herbert Spencer Robinson	H. S. R—n.	Ernest Trice Thompson	E. T. T.
William A. Robinson	W. A. R.	Frederic L. Thompson	F. L. T.

Contributors

R. P. Tolman . . . . R. P. T.
Harrison A. Trexler . . . . H. A. T.
Alonzo H. Tuttle . . . . . A. H. T.
Leonard Twynham . . . . . L. T.
Roland Greene Usher . . . R. G. U.
George B. Utley . . . . . G. B. U.
Carl Van Doren . . . . . . C. V-D.
Henry R. Viets . . . . . . H. R. V.
Harold G. Villard . . . . H. G. V.
Alexander J. Wall . . . . A. J. W.
D. D. Wallace . . . . . . D. D. W.
James Elliott Walmsley . . J. E. W.
Edith E. Ware . . . . . . E. E. W.
Robert A. Warner . . . . R. A. W.
Charles H. Warren . . . . C. H. W.
W. Randall Waterman . . . W. R. W.
Francis P. Weisenburger . . F. P. W.
Allan Westcott . . . . . . A. W.

Courtland Y. White, III . . . C. Y. W., III
Jerome K. Wilcox . . . . . . J. K. W.
Walter F. Willcox . . . . . W. F. W—x.
Mary Wilhelmine Williams . M. W. W.
Samuel M. Wilson . . . . . S. M. W.
Albert T. Witbeck . . . . . A. T. W.
Allen E. Woodall . . . . . A. E. W.
Robert H. Woody . . . . . R. H. W.
Thomas Woody . . . . . . T. W.
John W. Wright . . . . . . J. W. W.
Walter L. Wright, Jr. . . . . W. L. W., Jr.
Lawrence C. Wroth . . . . . L. C. W.
William F. Wunsch . . . . . W. F. W—h.
Mary Alice Wyman . . . . . M. A. W.
Kimball Young . . . . K. Y.
Casimir Douglass Zdanowicz . C. D. Z.
Adolf Edward Zucker . . . . A. E. Z.

DICTIONARY OF

AMERICAN BIOGRAPHY

Sewell—Stevenson

SEWELL, WILLIAM JOYCE (Dec. 6, 1835–Dec. 27, 1901), soldier, railroad executive, politician, was born in Castlebar, County Mayo, Ireland, the son of William and —— (Joyce) Sewell, and came to America as an orphan in 1851. After working in a New York shipping office, he was a clipper-ship officer (Prowell, *post*) and then engaged in business in Chicago. In 1860 he moved to Camden, N. J., which was thereafter his home. Commissioned captain in the 5th New Jersey Infantry, Aug. 28, 1861, he became lieutenant-colonel of his regiment after the Seven Days and colonel after Second Bull Run. On the morning of May 3, 1863, at Chancellorsville, he led his regiment against three heavy Confederate attacks, and then led his brigade in counter attacks, capturing eight colors and a thousand prisoners, but finally having to retire when ammunition gave out (*War of the Rebellion: Official Records*, 1 ser. XXV, 392, 473–76). Sewell was wounded there and at Gettysburg and was invalided after Spotsylvania, but returned to duty shortly as colonel of the 38th New Jersey Infantry and served until June 30, 1865. He was brevetted brigadier-general of volunteers for his gallantry at Chancellorsville.

For the rest of his life, he was prominently associated with the railroads of southern New Jersey, first with the Camden & Amboy Railroad and particularly with its subsidiary the West Jersey, which grew from thirty-seven miles in 1867 to 309 miles in 1896. After 1870, it was an autonomous part of the Pennsylvania system, controlling several subsidiaries of its own. Sewell was its general superintendent until 1881, when he succeeded A. J. Cassatt [*q.v.*] as vice-president, becoming a director in 1885. In 1899 he was made president of the West Jersey & Seashore Railroad, formed in 1896 by consoli-

dating the West Jersey and its subsidiaries. The Pennsylvania Railroad was a real power in New Jersey politics at that time. It was particularly interested in checking charters to rival lines and preventing local taxation. As state senator from Camden County from 1872 to 1881 and president of the Senate in 1876, 1879, and 1880, Sewell showed tactical skill in the events leading up to the general railroad law of 1873 and in time became virtual Republican boss of New Jersey. In 1873 he was a member of Governor Parker's staff with the rank of major-general, and that same year he secured a charter for the Camden Safe Deposit & Trust Company, of which he was an incorporator and thereafter a director. In 1881 he was elected to the United States Senate in place of Theodore Fitz Randolph [*q.v.*]. He sought reëlection in 1887, opposing Gov. Leon Abbett [*q.v.*], but after weeks of deadlock the choice fell on a dark horse, Rufus Blodgett. Sewell returned to the Senate in 1895, however, and was a senator until his death. It is interesting to note that he voted for the Interstate Commerce Act in 1887. He enjoyed considerable influence in Washington, particularly with President Harrison. During these years he retained his interest in military affairs. He commanded a brigade of the National Guard and ably handled the situation at Phillipsburg, N. J., in the railroad strike of 1877. In 1898 he was appointed major-general of volunteers, but did not see active service.

Sewell was married twice; his first wife died in 1861 and at the close of the war he married Helen L. Heyl, who with five children survived him. Two of his sons became army officers. He died at his home in Camden. His portrait, showing a mild expression and drooping moustache, gives no indication of the overbearing, masterful and vehement disposition sometimes ascribed to him. He had the faculty of summing up a complicated situation in a few words; he seldom made orations, and was doubtless at his best in the informal gatherings where the real decisions were made.

[E. C. Stokes, *Memorial Address upon Wm. J. Sewell* (1902); W. E. Sackett, *Modern Battles of Trenton* (1895); H. V. Poor, *Manual of the Railroads of the U. S.*, 1867–1901, esp. under "West Jersey"; J. Y. Foster, *N. J. and the Rebellion* (1868); *Manual of the Legislature of N. J.*, 1901; G. R. Prowell, *The Hist. of Camden County, N. J.* (1886); *Who's Who in America*, 1901–02; *Social Register, Phila.*, 1902; *Biog. Dir. Am. Cong.* (1928); *N. Y. Times, N. Y. Tribune, Daily State Gazette* (Trenton), *Daily True American* (Trenton), *Pub. Ledger* (Phila.), Dec. 28, 1901.]   R. G. A.

SEYBERT, ADAM (May 16, 1773–May 2, 1825), physician, scientist, congressman, was born in Philadelphia, the son of Sebastian and Barbara Seybert. After receiving instruction in the classics privately, he was prepared by Caspar Wistar [*q.v.*] for the medical department of the University of Pennsylvania, which granted him the degree of M.D. in 1793. His inaugural dissertation was an attempt to disprove experimentally the theory that in certain diseases the blood of living animals undergoes putrefaction. In his experiments Seybert used dogs, subjecting them to all the conditions, so far as he could simulate them, which famous physicians, among them, Herman Boerhaave of Leyden, had asserted induced the deterioration of the blood composition. This work, published in 1793 under the title *An Inaugural Dissertation, Being an Attempt to Disprove the Doctrine of the Putrefaction of the Blood of Animals*, attracted some attention and was reprinted in a collection of outstanding theses of American medical institutions, published by Charles Caldwell in 1805; it appeared, also, in a German translation in 1816.

Seybert continued his studies at London, Edinburgh, and Göttingen, but most intensively, in mineralogy, at the Ecole des Mines, Paris, under the Abbé Hauy, the "father of crystallography." Returning to Philadelphia in 1797, Seybert was that year elected to membership in the American Philosophical Society. To the sessions of the Society he contributed pioneer papers upon marsh air, and land and sea air, which were published in its *Transactions* (vol. IV, 1799). In 1799 he became one of the secretaries of the Society, serving as such until 1808; in 1810 and 1811 he was elected a counselor. He married, in 1798, Maria Sarah, daughter of Henry Pepper. Two children were born to them, a daughter who died in infancy and Henry Seybert [*q.v.*].

To his interest in chemistry, Seybert added a striking ability to analyze minerals correctly, becoming in this respect perhaps the earliest American expert. To the Philadelphia Academy of Sciences he sold his collection of European minerals, enabling that institution to begin, in 1814, a series of lectures upon mineralogy and crystallography. Upon the death, in 1809, of James Woodhouse, professor of chemistry at the University of Pennsylvania, Seybert was strongly recommended for the position by his old teacher, Caspar Wistar, but the position eventually went to John R. Coxe [*q.v.*] through the influence of Benjamin Rush [*q.v.*]. During the first few years of the century, Seybert ran a drug and apothecary shop in Philadelphia, to which was attached a laboratory for the manufacture of chemicals. In this early commercial laboratory were manufactured, it is claimed, the first mercurials in America (Scharf and Westcott, *post*, III, 2273).

In 1809 Seybert was elected to fill the congressional seat made vacant by the resignation of Benjamin Say [*q.v.*] and served as a Democratic member from 1809 to 1815 and again from 1817 to 1819. During this period he interested himself chiefly in the collection of elaborate statistical data concerning the revenues and expenditures of the federal government, publishing in 1818 *Statistical Annals . . . of the United States, 1789–1818*. Careful tables accompanied the book, tabulating the expenditures for the mint, the army, the navy, and other governmental departments; the national revenues and expenditures and the public debts were also summated therein. This work was translated into the French in 1820, and its appearance was noted in the British Isles by an article in the *Edinburgh Review* (January 1820) from the pen of Sydney Smith. Upon the conclusion of his last term in Congress Seybert returned to Europe for a two-year period, and again in 1824. He died in Paris and was buried in Père La Chaise cemetery.

The versatility of Seybert's mind is reflected by the breadth of his interests and activity. To whatever he turned his attention he brought the patience and persistence which exhibited the true scientist and friend of humanity. In chemistry and mineralogy he was one of the American pioneers, worthy to rank with Silliman, Hare, Woodhouse, and Mitchill. In his will he bequeathed the sum of $1000 for the education of the deaf and dumb, $500 to start a fund for discharged prisoners, and other sums to the Philadelphia Dispensary and to its Orphan Asylum. It was his belief, expressed in his will, that the poor unfortunates leaving the penitentiary might be prevented from the commission of further crimes by the donation to them of funds for two days' food and two nights' lodging; hence his provision for discharged prisoners. Besides the American Philosophical Society, he was a member of the American Medical Society, of the Chemical Society of Philadelphia, and of the Royal Scientific Society of Göttingen.

[J. T. Scharf and Thomson Westcott, *Hist. of Phila.* (1884), vols. II, III; E. J. Nolan, *A Short Hist. of the Acad. of Natural Sci.* (1909); W. S. W. Ruschenberger, *A Notice of the Origin, Progress and Present Condition of the Acad. of Natural Sci. of Phila.* (1852); E. P. Oberholtzer, *Phila.: A Hist. of the City and Its People* (1912), vol. II; E. F. Smith, "Early Scientists of Phila.," in *Pa. Mag. of Hist. and Biog.*, Jan. 1923 and "Early Science in Phila.," *Ibid.*, Jan. 1927; *Autobiog. of Charles Caldwell, M.D.* (1855), ed. by H. A. Warner; *Nat. Gazette* (Phila.), July 8, 1825; parents' names derived from Abstract of Federal Census of 1790 and Abstracts of Phila. wills.]   C.R.H.

SEYBERT, HENRY (Dec. 23, 1801–Mar. 3, 1883), mineralogist, philanthropist, was born in Philadelphia, the son of Adam [*q.v.*] and Maria Sarah (Pepper) Seybert. His early education was supervised by his father, whose traveling companion and scientific assistant he became. Later he studied at the École des Mines at Paris, and upon his return to Philadelphia he was made, at the early age of twenty-one, a member of the American Philosophical Society.

Having acquired a keen interest in science, he began a short but productive period as a contributor to the *Transactions of the American Philosophical Society*, the *Journal of the Academy of Natural Sciences of Philadelphia*, and Silliman's *American Journal of Science and Arts*. In his papers he analyzed tourmalines, manganesian garnets, glassy actynolite, crysoberyls, pyroxene, tabular spar, chromite, colophonite, fluosilicate of magnesia, and bog iron ore. In communications to Silliman's *Journal* (January, May 1823) he engaged in a controversy with Thomas Nuttall [*q.v.*] and other mineralogists over the identity of certain specimens previously classified by Cleaveland and Bruce. In the chondrodite of New Jersey he independently discovered fluorine (*American Journal of Science and Arts*, April 1883, p. 320). Though after his father's death in 1825 he seems to have lost something of the eager interest in mineralogy which had formerly characterized him, occasional papers by him appeared. He analyzed (*Ibid.*, January 1830) the meteorite which was first described by Bowen, and his analysis of the hydraulic lime used in the construction of the Erie Canal is historically interesting (*Transactions of the American Philosophical Society*, n.s., vol. II, 1825).

For the last half of his life Seybert devoted his attention and a large fortune to the promotion of human welfare and to the encouragement of an interest in science. In 1876 he gave to the city of Philadelphia the clock and bell for Independence Hall. He never married and became greatly concerned as to the proper disposal of his wealth, consulting on this question a number of the high church dignitaries of Europe. The mysteries of the future awakened in him a keen interest in psychical research and led him to bequeath to the University of Pennsylvania the sum of $60,000 to endow a chair of philosophy, on the condition that an additional sum be used to support the activities of a commission of the University appointed to investigate modern spiritualism. The condition was duly met, and the commission, which included such prominent persons as S. Weir Mitchell, William Pepper, and H. H. Furness [*qq.v.*], published a preliminary report of their findings four years after the donor's death, exposing many of the common frauds practised by the slate writers and invokers of spirits. Seybert was not a "blind believer in spiritualism," but "his desire was to have a fair, searching, and, as far as possible, scientific examination" of its claims (Pepper, quoted by Thorpe, *post*, p. 232).

His will contained 160 specific bequests to individuals and welfare or educational institutions. The negro, the Indian, prisoners, the sick and aged, poor children, and indigent families all received recognition. The residue of the estate was given to the city of Philadelphia to assist in providing clothing, maintenance, and practical education to the poor children of the community, until they could by their own labor enter the trades or engage in other useful employment. By 1906 this residual sum had increased to more than $1,000,000 and was at first used to support charities already established. In 1914, however, the Adam and Maria Sarah Seybert Institution for Poor Boys and Girls was established, which in addition to independent activities cooperates with all private, state, and city institutions.

[*A Living Hand: Ten-Year Report of the Seybert Institution* (1930); *Preliminary Report of the Commission . . . to Investigate Modern Spiritualism in Accordance with the Request of the Late Henry Seybert* (1887); F. N. Thorpe, *William Pepper* (1904); W. S. W. Ruschenberger, *A Notice of the Origin, Progress and Present Condition of the Acad. of Natural Sci. of Phila.* (1852); E. P. Oberholtzer, *Phila.: A Hist. of the City and Its People* (1912), vol. II; *Am. Jour. Sci.*, Apr. 1883; *Proc. of the Am. Philosophical Soc.*, vol. XXI (1884); Max Meisel, *Bibliog. of Am. Natural Hist.*, vol. II (1926).]   C.R.H.

SEYBERT, JOHN (July 7, 1791–Jan. 4, 1860), bishop of the Evangelical Association, was born at Manheim, Lancaster County, Pa., the eldest of the four children of Henry and

Susan (Kreuzer) Seybert. His mother was a native of Württemberg. His father, a boy of fifteen at the time, came to the United States as a German conscript in the British army and was captured and interned at Lancaster, where he may have heard the Rev. J. A. C. Helffenstein [*q.v.*] preach his famous sermon to the prisoners on Isaiah, LII, 3. At the close of the Revolution he refused to be exchanged and was "redeemed" for $100 by a man named Schaffner, who taught him the tailor's trade.

John Seybert inherited a little property from his father, who died in 1806, and became a cooper. He was troubled intermittently by religious incertitude until on June 21, 1810, through the instrumentality of Matthias Betz, an Evangelical preacher, he felt himself converted fully to the life eternal—"*tief ins ewige Leben hinein bekehrt.*" He joined the Evangelical Association, was licensed as an exhorter by John Dreisbach, and was elected class-leader for Manheim and Mount Joy, but for ten years he continued to work at his trade. Then, on Sept. 12, 1820, he set out as an itinerant preacher on the York circuit and devoted the rest of his laborious life to proclaiming the gospel as taught by his sect. He traveled other circuits in Pennsylvania and Ohio, was ordained a deacon in 1822 and an elder in 1824, was elected presiding elder in 1825 and assigned to the Canaan district, was reëlected in 1829 and assigned to the Salem district, and in 1833 was sent at his own request to do missionary work in the northwestern counties of Pennsylvania. At the General Conference of 1839 he was elected to the office of bishop, which had been vacant since the death of Jacob Albright [*q.v.*] in 1808. He had won and continued to hold the complete confidence of his fellows, and was reëlected unanimously every four years until his death. Under his leadership the Association became a vigorous missionary sect, extending its lines constantly to the west and north along the paths followed by German emigration.

Unencumbered by wife or child or by any concern for merely secular affairs, Seybert devoted himself to the work with apostolic singleness of purpose. He lived in the saddle. His biographer, tabulating the records of his scrupulously kept journal, found that in forty years he had traveled 175,000 miles on horseback, had preached 9,850 sermons, had held about 8,000 prayer and class meetings, and had made about 46,000 pastoral visits besides some 10,000 other calls on the sick and distressed. Like his prototype, Francis Asbury, he was an almost perfect circuit rider; even his eccentricity and uncouthness were elements of his power. In his sermons he dwelt

chiefly on the doctrine of entire sanctification in this life and denounced the sins of the world, or such of them as came to his notice, with a picturesqueness of objurgation that has been called "indescribable." He was especially hard on ostentatious dress, and such words as *Modesucht, Putzsucht, Hurenschmuck, Teufelsputz,* and *Sündenstrich* flared like rockets through the smoke of his discourse. In his fashion he was

student and became deeply read not only in the Bible but in the great devotional classics. Transparent simplicity and kindliness of character were his most winning traits. He died at the house of Isaac Parker near Bellevue, Ohio, and was buried in the village cemetery at Flat Rock. The last entry in his diary was "One soul saved."

[Solomon Neitz, *Das Leben und Wirken des seligen Johannes Seybert* (1862); S. P. Spreng, *The Life and Labors of John Seybert* (1888); Reuben Yeakel, *Hist. of the Evangel. Asso.* (2 vols., 1892–95).]

G. H. G.

SEYFFARTH, GUSTAVUS (July 13, 1796–Nov. 17, 1885), archeologist, theologian, the son of Traugott August Seyffarth, clergyman, was born at Uebigau near Torgau, Germany. He received an excellent classical training at St. Afra, the *Fürstenschule* at Meissen, and then continued his studies at the University of Leipzig from 1815 to 1819, where he passed examinations for the ministry and obtained the Ph.D. degree. Later he was appointed *Docent* in his alma mater and given the charge of completing, since he was the only one in the city who knew Coptic, the two volumes of F. A. W. Spohn's *De lingua et literis veterum Ægyptiorum . . .* (1825–1831). In order to equip himself better for the task, he visited public and private collections in numerous cities, particularly in southern Europe, from 1826 to 1828, and made more than 10,000 separate copies and impressions from Egyptian monuments and Coptic manuscripts. This material, "Bibliotheca Ægyptiaca Manuscripta," in fourteen royal folio volumes and an index in quarto, became in 1885 the property of the New York Historical Society, to which he willed it. In 1830 he was promoted to the first professorship of archeology at the University, and soon became involved in a lifelong controversy with the school of the French archeologist, Champollion. It was contended by Champollion that the ancient language of Egypt was modern Coptic and that Egyptian writing was mainly ideologic. Seyffarth claimed that Egyptian literature was based on ancient Coptic, related to Hebrew, the mother of all languages; that hieroglyphic signs were mainly phonograms, or syllabic writing; that the hieroglyph represented a syllabic composite derived from the alphabet of Noah, which consisted of eighteen consonants and seven vowels representative of the zodiac; and that all other alphabets were derived from this one.

Seyffarth was a man of vast erudition, with a marvelous memory for languages, but a speculative-dogmatic mentality was his bane. Since the Champollionists were given the curatorships in large museums, and Seyffarth found it increasingly difficult to publish his works and gain a following for his views, he resigned from the University in 1854 and emigrated two years later to the United States, thereby terminating at the same time unhappy domestic relations. He taught for three years gratuitously in Concordia College, St. Louis, Mo., and moved in 1859 to New York, where he preached at Yorkville. Together with other ministers he tried in vain to establish a theological seminary at Dansville. His theology was severely orthodox, championing verbal inspiration and Saxon Lutheranism. He agreed with the older "Missouri Lutherans" except that he attacked slavery. He favored the chronology of the Septuagint and of the Church Fathers, which he regarded as confirmed by mathematical fact and differing by 2,000 years from the vocalized Hebrew text of the Old Testament. In all of his interpretations there was an unwarrantable regard for unusual astronomical constellations. His views on Roman Chronology are partly expressed in the *Quarterly Review of the Evangelical Lutheran Church,* January 1872.

Seyffarth was a busy polyhistor, maintaining an extensive correspondence, and writing much for publication. Twelve pages in his autobiography, *The Literary Life of Gustavus Seyffarth* (1886), catalogue the titles of his publications in Latin, German, and English, devoted mainly to classical and Oriental philology, archeology, astronomy, chronology, and apologetics. Two pages list his manuscripts, not including his "Thesaurus Copticus" in four volumes, 1829, and twelve minor manuscripts, 1827–40, which are in the library of the University of Leipzig. The New York Historical Society possesses also his "Clavis Ægyptiaca," a collection of bilingual and some other hieroglyphic inscriptions translated and explained, with the syllabic alphabet in hieroglyphic, hieratic, and demotic characters, glossaries, and indexes. This "Clavis" was his most mature effort in Egyptology. One of his manuscripts is a treatise on aviation, with numerous designs for the construction of a dirigble airship. He also contributed articles to the *Evangelical Review,* July 1856, and July 1857; *Quarterly Review of the Evangelical Lutheran Church,* July 1886; and the *Transactions of the Academy of Science of St. Louis,* volume IV

(1886). He contended throughout his whole life that he had discovered that Egyptian literature was syllable writing, and had made known this discovery in his *Rudimenta Hieroglyphices* (1826), which he later regarded as juvenile, here and there absurd, but nevertheless substantially correct. He repeatedly accused the followers of Champollion (Brugsch, Lepsius, and De Rougé) of appropriating the substance of his own theory, and was zealously defended in his crusade by his pupils Prof. M. Uhlemann and Heinrich Wuttke. The latter in his *Geschichte der Schrift und des Schriftums* (1872) credits him with the discovery of the syllabic hieroglyphs (see p. 497). Knortz claims that the first translation of the Rosetta Stone was made possible by the use of Seyffarth's system. Seyffarth completely overlooked the brilliant contributions of the school he combated. His own translations possessed a certain beauty, but were frequently fantastic. Among theologians having a high regard for Seyffarth's knowledge of Semitics was Franz Delitzsch, once his pupil in Hebrew. The last nine years of Seyffarth's life were spent in New York City.

[In addition to references cited above, see: Karl Knortz, *Gustav Seyffarth, Eine Biographische Skizze* (1886); Georg Ebers, a critical estimate of Seyffarth's work, in *Zeitschrift der Deutschen Morgenländischen Gesellschaft,* vol. XLI (1887); Curt Wachsmuth, *Einleitung in das Studium der Alten Geschichte* (1895); *Festschrift zur Feier des 500 Jährigen Bestehens der Universität Leipzig* (1909), vol. IV, part 1; *Der Lutheraner,* Dec. 1, 1885; and the *N. Y. Herald,* Mar. 8, 1886.]   J.O.E.

SEYMOUR, GEORGE FRANKLIN (Jan. 5, 1829–Dec. 8, 1906), Protestant Episcopal bishop, was born in New York City, the son of Isaac Newton and Elmira (Belknap) Seymour. He graduated from Columbia College with distinction in 1850, and from the General Theological Seminary in 1854. Bishop Horatio Potter ordained him deacon on Dec. 17 of the same year in the Church of the Annunciation, New York, and priest in Zion Church, Dobbs Ferry, N. Y., on Sept. 23, 1855. His first cure was at Annandale-on-Hudson, Dutchess County, where he organized a church and incidentally trained students for the seminary, the latter work resulting in the establishment of St. Stephen's College, of which he was the first warden (1860). From 1861 he was rector in succession of St. Mary's, Manhattanville (now a part of New York City), Christ Church, Hudson (1862), and St. John's, Brooklyn (1863–67). In 1865 he was elected professor of ecclesiastical history at the General Seminary, New York, and in 1867 became chaplain of the House of Mercy, an institution in charge of the Community of St. Mary, founded in 1865 and one of the first religious orders in the Episcopal Church.

Seymour was an ardent Anglo-Catholic, in full agreement with the principles taught by Pusey. He broke with the more conservative high churchmen by defending the expression of doctrine in ritual, promoting the rise of monastic communities, and pleading for toleration for those who held more advanced opinions than he did. His argumentative temper made him willing to stand for his principles, but also gave a certain personal character to the controversies in which he was engaged. The first permanent dean of the General Seminary, John Murray Forbes, installed in 1869, had returned to the Episcopal Church from the Roman communion. In several points of policy and in his attempt to discipline certain Anglo-Catholic students, he was opposed by Seymour alone among the faculty. In 1871 Seymour published *A Defence of the Professor of Ecclesiastical History against the Assault of the Dean and the Other Professors of the General Theological Seminary*; nevertheless, on Forbes's retirement, Seymour was made, in 1872, acting dean, and in 1875 was formally elected to the deanship. Meanwhile, in 1874, he had been elected bishop of Illinois. His views and actions were widely attacked, and at the General Convention the House of Deputies, after a week in executive session, refused, by a close vote, to confirm the election. As dean of the Seminary, Seymour established a refectory and made a number of minor improvements in the plant. He secured the maintenance of the institution in New York—an achievement to which he attached great importance; restored its inclusive character; and left it prepared for future progress.

In December 1877 he was elected Bishop of Springfield, one of the three dioceses into which Illinois had been divided. After confirmation of the election and a second request from the diocesan convention he finally accepted in May 1878. He was consecrated in Trinity Church, New York, on June 11, and at once went West for a visitation of his diocese. At the end of the following academic year he resigned his positions in New York and moved permanently to Springfield. After ten years he was able to report that the diocese had doubled in almost all respects capable of statistical statement. The rest of his life saw a solid, if gradual, expansion. In 1892 Seymour obtained a coadjutor, Bishop Charles Reuben Hale [*q.v.*], but after his death in 1900 resumed the entire charge of the work.

Seymour was considered to be an effective teacher, and learned in church history and canon law. His scholarly productions, however, were all controversial or occasional—often pamphlets written at a sitting to meet a particular occasion. He lived to see the Catholic principles for which he had fought everywhere tolerated and widely accepted, and many advanced practices of his youth (*e.g.*, weekly communion) common to the whole church. Towards the end of his life, however, he was inclined to take a dark view of the state of the Church, and was seriously alarmed by the rise of the broad church party. He was one of those who conscientiously opposed the consecration of Phillips Brooks [*q.v.*]. Although he had been suspicious of the revision, the Prayer Book of 1892 included much which he had supported; but the movement for changing the name of the Protestant Episcopal Church, of which he was one of the chief promoters, remained unsuccessful. In 1904 a coadjutor, Edward William Osborne, was elected and consecrated, but Seymour remained active almost until the end, performing his last official acts a month before his death, which occurred at Springfield. He was survived by his wife, Harriet Atwood (Downe) Aymar, whom he married on July 23, 1889.

[W. S. Perry, *The Bishops of the Am. Church* (1897); *Living Church*, Dec. 15, 1906; "Mother Harriet of the Sisterhood of St. Mary," in the *Church Eclectic*, June 1896; *Jour. of the Proc. of the Conventions of the Protestant Episcopal Church in the Diocese of N. Y.*, 1855–77; *Proc. of the Board of Trustees of the Gen. Theological Sem.*, 1866–79; *Diocese of Springfield, Convention Jour.*, 1879–1906; *Who's Who in America*, 1906–07; *Ill. State Reg.* (Springfield), Dec. 9, 1906.]

E. R. H., Jr.

SEYMOUR, HORATIO (May 31, 1810–Feb. 12, 1886), governor of New York, was born in the frontier village of Pompey Hill, Onondaga County, N. Y., and was named for his father's elder brother, Horatio, later (1821–33) United States senator from Vermont. His father, Henry Seymour (1780–1837), a native of Litchfield, Conn., and a descendant of Richard Seamer or Seymour who emigrated from Hertfordshire to New England in 1638 and went the next year to Hartford, Conn. (Wall, *post*, p. 1), settled at Pompey Hill about 1800, as the keeper of the first store. He was one of the political lieutenants of Martin Van Buren and his election as canal commissioner was the decisive factor in the scheme to take the patronage of the Erie Canal from DeWitt Clinton [*q.v.*]. After thirteen years in this office, in 1835 Henry Seymour became president of the Farmers' Loan and Trust Company of New York. During the panic of 1837 he committed suicide while on a summer visit to Utica, which had been his home since 1819. His widow, Mary Ledyard (Forman), mother of his six children, survived until 1859.

She was the daughter of Jonathan Forman and the niece of William Ledyard [*q.v.*]. Although Horatio Seymour owed the better part of his education to reading, his schooling was as good as the community afforded. Under Joshua Leonard, the academy at Pompey Hill was the nursery of more than one notable man. After the move to Utica, Horatio attended the Utica Academy, Oxford Academy, and the Geneva Academy, until he was entered in the military academy which Alden Partridge [*q.v.*] then conducted at Middletown, Conn. There he remained for two years. In 1826 he returned to Utica and learned law in the office of Greene C. Bronson and Samuel Beardsley, being admitted to the bar in 1832. The business cares of the involved estate of his father drew him away from his profession after 1837.

In January 1833 Seymour became the military secretary of Gov. William L. Marcy [*q.v.*], a post he held for six years. He lived in Albany and learned the ropes of the Regency. For twenty-four years Marcy remained his closest political friend: Seymour was his lieutenant at the Baltimore convention in 1852, and was in close touch with him during his two periods of service in the cabinet. While living in Albany, Seymour met, and married on his twenty-fifth birthday, Mary, the youngest daughter of John Rutger Bleecker, head of an old Dutch land-holding family and part owner of the site on which the city of Utica grew up. The match was childless. After living together over fifty years, Seymour and his wife died within a month of each other.

William H. Seward [*q.v.*] defeated Governor Marcy in the fall of 1838, and Seymour retired to Utica, just about the time that Van Buren's independent treasury policy was splitting the New York Democrats into the factions that came to be known (1844–46) as Hunkers and Barnburners. The interests of Seymour's friends and his family lay with the conservatives (later the Hunkers). In the autumn of 1841 he was elected to the Assembly and served there in 1842. In the spring of 1842 he was elected mayor of the Whig city of Utica after an exciting campaign, but a year later he was defeated by sixteen votes (*Utica Weekly Herald*, Feb. 16, 1886). He served again in the Assembly in 1844 and 1845. As chairman he brought in his famous "Report of the Committee on Canals" (*New York Assembly Documents,* 1844, No. 177), and forced its recommendations through the legislature by skill and logic, over the opposition of the strict-constructionist Democrats, under the lead of Michael Hoffman. The Erie Canal became a tradition in the Seymour family. In the fifties

and sixties, he helped promote a scheme to unite the Great Lakes and the Mississippi by means of the Fox and Wisconsin Rivers, investing heavily in the land of that region. Waterways, he always argued, would regulate the rates of railways better than laws could ever do.

Seymour's success with his canal bill led to his election as speaker in 1845, after a fierce contest among the Democrats. After Polk's nomination for president the Van Buren Democrats were disgruntled, and Silas Wright [*q.v.*] had been nominated for governor to appease them. He was duly elected, serving 1845–47, but quarrels over the canal, anti-rent riots, a new state constitution, and the Mexican War wrecked Seymour's legislative program. Wright was defeated for reëlection in 1846, allegedly by the defection of Hunker votes, and his death in 1847 added a martyr to the Barnburner cause. Thereafter there were actually two Democratic parties in the state, and it was Seymour's success at effecting working compromises between them that made him important. Though as early as 1845, according to Silas Wright, he declared for free soil in the southwestern territory which might be gained from Mexico (R. H. Gillet, *The Life and Times of Silas Wright,* 1874, vol. II, 1625), his dislike for abolitionists was equaled only by his suspicion of Southern extremists. He always opposed federal interference with slavery, which was certain to succumb, he thought, to the competition of free labor as strengthened by immigration. His intelligent distrust of both sides of the argument partly accounts for his unwillingness ever to hold federal office.

Democratic quarrels over offices in Polk's cabinet and the election of Senators John A. Dix and Daniel S. Dickinson [*qq.v.*] seem to have determined Seymour to retire from politics. He withdrew to Utica and took no part in the constitutional convention in 1846, although he kept in touch with Marcy at Washington. After the Democratic schism of 1848, Marcy persuaded him to help repair the damage by accepting the first of his six nominations for governor in 1850. His narrow defeat by Washington Hunt that year was followed by his victory over the same opponent in 1852. He was an industrious, conscientious governor, taking particular care to improve the administration of the penal system. But the first of his two terms coincided with the high tide of prohibition sentiment in the legislature, as evidenced in the famous Maine Law Bill, which he courageously vetoed in the spring of 1854. He was defeated for reëlection by a handful of votes in a field of four candidates. In 1856 a second Maine Law was thrown out as unconstitutional. Seymour never relented in his uncompromising hostility to prohibition and anti-Catholicism, both of which played a part in the confused campaign of 1854. Two years later, on July 4, 1856, at Springfield, Mass., campaigning for Buchanan, he uttered the first of his once-famous denunciations of abolition, prohibition, and nativism (*Public Record,* pp. 1–21). For four years thereafter he devoted himself to private business.

By the spring of 1860 Dean Richmond hoped to nominate Seymour for the presidency as a compromise candidate at the Charleston Democratic Convention (Alexander, *post,* II, 276, 298). Seymour remained at Utica, withdrawing his name on June 5 (*New York Tribune,* June 6, 1860) from consideration by the Baltimore convention, which met June 18. He voted for Douglas, having helped to organize the fusion electoral ticket. He was prominent at the Tweddle Hall convention which met at Albany, Jan. 31, 1861, and, although he agreed with Tilden that Lincoln's victory without a single electoral vote from the South was a political disaster, he urged loyal acceptance of the constitutional fact, begging both North and South to compromise their quarrel and submit the Crittenden Compromise to popular vote. At first he thought the conquest of the South impossible; he never thought it wise.

During the first year of the war, Seymour helped Gov. Edwin D. Morgan [*q.v.*] to raise troops and money for the Union armies. When, in 1862, the radical Republicans of the state forced the nomination of General James Wadsworth for governor, Seymour's candidacy consolidated the conservative vote, and his election expressed not only disgust with abolitionists, but also disappointment with the progress of the war. The Democratic victories of 1862 probably spared Lincoln political pressure from the most noisome supporters of the Union, but Seymour found himself pushed into the precarious position of the national leader of the opposition. Although he opposed the Emancipation Proclamation (*Public Record,* pp. 99, 369) and denounced the arrest of Vallandigham as an outrage (McCabe, *post,* pp. 136–38; Wall, p. 94), he was tireless at filling up the state's quotas in the Union armies. Assistant-Secretary of War Dana testified to his unimpeachable loyalty (New York *Sun,* Feb. 13, 1886). To the end of his life, he insisted that the extra-constitutional powers assumed by the Lincoln administration were the most serious problem arising from the Civil War (see his article, "The Political Situa-

tion," in *North American Review,* February 1883).

Seymour's participation in the most notorious incident of his whole career was clouded by partisan politics. He had opposed the enrollment act of March 1863 as both unconstitutional and unwise, believing that the raising of troops belonged to the states. The inequalities of the statute and the tactlessness of its application encouraged discontent. When the riots of July 1863 broke out, Seymour hastened to New York from a vacation in New Jersey, and directed the rapid restoration of order. The famous "My Friends" speech (*Public Record,* p. 127) was addressed, at noon, to an orderly crowd in front of the city hall, at a time when the rioters were no nearer than three miles. But Greeley denounced him as a temporizing "Copperhead," and the legend of his disloyal language followed him to the grave. Careful examination of the evidence shows that the draft riots were grossly exaggerated : claims for property damage were corruptly padded, once it was discovered that the state was liable; and the traditional estimate of a thousand deaths is sheer fiction.

In 1864 he urged the Democrats to name a civilian candidate for president (Brummer, *post,* pp. 403–04; N. Y. *World,* Aug. 29, 1864), but he presided at the Chicago convention and campaigned for McClellan. To aid the ticket in New York he unwillingly accepted his fifth nomination for governor. The manipulation and suppression of the soldier vote cast a shadow of doubt, if not dishonesty, over his defeat. After the Civil War, Seymour retired to the country home he had built at Deerfield, just north of Utica, and devoted his leisure to reading, to farming, and to the reconstruction of the Democratic party. His nomination for president in 1868, in the convention of which he was again the presiding officer, resulted from a union of eastern Democrats who would not have George H. Pendleton [*q.v.*], with western Democrats who would not have Thomas A. Hendricks [*q.v.*]. Seymour was working for Chief Justice Chase, but his second choice was Hendricks. In the end, the West got the platform and the East the candidate. The final outcome was utterly against his will, and his acceptance, he always believed, was the great mistake of his life. When he was pushed out of the hall, he supposed the convention would adjourn until the following day, when he could persuade it to reconsider its vote, but the Democrats completed their ticket with Francis Preston Blair, Jr. [*q.v.*], and went home.

Seymour's showing in the campaign astonished even as astute a politician as Blaine. Although President Johnson threw his support against Grant, Blair's utterances were made to seem to threaten a reopening of the Civil War. Seymour was described as the insane son of a suicide. Partly to offset the influence of Blair, Seymour spoke with vigor and ability throughout the North and West. Although the electoral result was overwhelmingly against him, an analysis of the popular vote makes it not improbable that he was the choice of the white voters of the nation. Mississippi, Texas, and Virginia did not take part in the election, and Alabama, Arkansas, and South Carolina were "carried" by the Republicans; yet Grant received a majority of only 300,000. The Democratic victory in New York raised the cry of fraudulent naturalization, but Seymour himself was never unready to contradict the calculations of the Republicans by means of their own figures.

After 1868 Seymour became an elder statesman of the Democratic party, opposing centralization and protection. In the seventies he helped Tilden drive Tweed from power and took part in one of the early efforts to reform Tammany Hall (Alexander, III, 270–71; *N. Y. Times*, Oct. 9, 1871). Tweed, he liked to point out, was the creature of rich men who were too selfish and negligent to share the burden of government (see his article, "The Government of the United States," in the *North American Review*, November-December 1878). In 1876 he was nominated for governor a sixth time, but he forced the state convention to re-assemble and name another candidate. In 1875 he declined to be a candidate for senator and managed the election of Francis Kernan [*q.v.*]. He was a presidential elector in 1876–77, and spoke publicly against the seating of Hayes. It was fear of his influence on his brother-in-law, Roscoe Conkling [*q.v.*], which probably cost the latter a seat on the electoral commission. Although a sunstroke and increasing deafness took him out of public life, he supported Hancock for president in 1880 and lived to see his disciple, Grover Cleveland, in the White House. Among writings of his not already mentioned the following may be cited: *A Lecture on the Topography and History of New York* (1856, reprinted in 1870), evincing his lifelong interest in the geography of his state; "Crime and Tramps," in *Harper's New Monthly Magazine*, December 1878; and "The Influence of New York on American Jurisprudence," in the *Magazine of American History*, April 1879.

Though Seymour denounced the "leprosy of hypocrisy" all his life, his own diffidence about public office laid him open to the charge of insincerity. In manners and appearance he resembled his father, the memory of whose mental breakdown haunted him throughout life; thus the "great decliner," as enemies called him, was earnest in his love of private life, in spite of his power as a public speaker and the dignity and fascination of his presence. George Clinton alone excels him in number of nominations for governor. His name was a tower of strength: twice during the seventies his nephew, Horatio Seymour, Jr., was the only Democrat elected on the state ticket. Seymour's practical failure as a statesman can fairly be attributed to his gentlemanly scorn for extreme opinions. He was, in the genuine sense, a Jeffersonian, for he always insisted on the supreme importance of local government. If his faith in the Democratic party approached religious fervor, he nevertheless made and maintained friendships with distinguished Republicans like Hamilton Fish and Andrew D. White. Yet, wide as were his cultural interests, he never visited Europe, and, aside from trips to conventions and campaigns, he made only one extensive tour of the United States. His opposition to prohibition caused this respectable "teetotaling" Episcopalian to be charged with drunkenness; attacks of dyspepsia were said to be insanity. Yet Seymour, always outwardly serene, liked to remark that the longer he observed men the less he thought of their heads, and the better he thought of their hearts. None of his bitter enemies, it is significant to notice, ever knew him.

[The chief manuscript sources are the Horatio Seymour Papers and Scrap Books, an extensive collection in the State Library, Albany, N. Y.; and a collection of letters and notes in N. Y. Hist. Soc. Better than the two campaign biographies, J. D. McCabe, Jr., *The Life and Public Services of Horatio Seymour* (1868), and D. G. Croly, *Seymour and Blair* (1868), is the *Public Record . . . of Horatio Seymour* (1868), a careful compilation of his speeches and papers from 1856 to the spring of 1868, ed. by T. M. Cook and T. W. Knox. This volume, largely financed by August Belmont and Tilden, is one of the earliest examples of a reliable campaign textbook. A. J. Wall, *A Sketch of the Life of Horatio Seymour, 1810–1886* (1929), with bibliography of his speeches and articles; and C. H. Coleman, *The Election of 1868* (1933) are valuable studies of Seymour's character and career. See also Stewart Mitchell, "Horatio Seymour of New York: A Political Biography," a doctoral dissertation in the Harvard Coll. Lib.; C. Z. Lincoln, *State of N. Y. Messages from the Governors*, vol. V (1909); D. S. Alexander, *A Pol. Hist. of the State of N. Y.*, vols. II, III (1906–09); S. D. Brummer, *Pol. Hist. of N. Y. State During the Period of the Civil War* (1911). An excellent collection of pictures of Seymour is in the N. Y. Hist. Soc. The portrait commonly published is very poor.]
S. M.

SEYMOUR, HORATIO WINSLOW (1854–Dec. 17, 1920), editor, was born in Cayuga County, N. Y. His parents, Andrew

Milliken and Louisa Maria (Goodyear) Seymour soon removed to the state of Wisconsin; where, in the public schools of Racine, the boy received his early education and where he met Annie E. Jones to whom he was married in 1876. After serving an apprenticeship in Racine as a printer, he served as a reporter, city editor, and news editor of the *Milwaukee Daily News*. While connected with the *Milwaukee Daily News* his work attracted the attention of Wilbur Storey [*q.v.*], who offered him a position with the *Chicago Times,* then a radical Democratic newspaper. From 1875 until 1879 Seymour was telegraph editor, and from the latter date until 1883 he served as night editor of the Storey paper. While on the *Chicago Times* he wrote the headline "Jerked to Jesus" concerning the hanging of a religiously fanatical negro. Severing his connection with the *Times* he immediately became connected with the *Chicago Herald* and held the position of editor and managing editor until 1895. Under the direction of James W. Scott [*q.v.*], one of the owners, and Seymour, the *Herald* became an independent Democratic paper and enjoyed growing prosperity and an enviable reputation. Seymour's editorials gave him distinction as an expert on the tariff. Among the more important of his editorials that gained national fame were those attacking the protectionist policies of the Republican party. Among them were "Protectionism Exposed and Doomed," "Pauperizing and Brutalizing Labor," "Coining Money out of Blood," "Monopoly-Ridden Agriculture," and "Republicanism and Robbery," which with twenty-two others he wrote during the campaign of 1892 were published as *The Chicago Herald, Editorials that Won* (copr. 1892). In all of them he advanced the doctrine of competitive tariffs and advocated revision downward. In 1895 he became editor and publisher of the *Chicago Chronicle,* owned by John R. Walsh, with which he remained until 1907. In that year, with the crash of several of Walsh's banks, owing to the panic, the *Chronicle* was suspended, and Seymour went to New York City as editorial writer and supervisor of the *World*. He served for ten months as editor of the *St. Louis Republic,* and then returned in 1912 as editorial contributor for the *World*.

He was the author of one book, *Government and Co., Limited* (1895), which dealt with his ideas of free trade and democratic government. In both the campaigns of 1892 and 1896 he was active in attacking the hard money and high tariff policies of the Republican party, and he assumed a position of leadership in the western states. Among his colleagues he was noted for his new and startling use of headlines, a feature that found its way into many papers throughout the nation. He died in New York City.

[*Chicago Herald and Examiner, Chicago Daily Tribune, N. Y. Times,* Dec. 18, 1920; *Who's Who in America,* 1918–19; Eugen Seeger, *Chicago, the Wonder City* (1893); *A Hist. of the City of Chicago* (1900).]

T. E. S.

SEYMOUR, THOMAS DAY (Apr. 1, 1848–Dec. 31, 1907), classicist, was born in Hudson, Ohio, the son of Nathan Perkins and Elizabeth (Day) Seymour. He was a direct descendant of Richard Seymour (or Seamer) who came from England to Hartford, Conn., in 1639; on his mother's side he was the grandson of Thomas Day of Hartford, secretary of state in Connecticut for twenty-five years. His great uncle was Jeremiah Day [*q.v.*], president of Yale College. Thomas Seymour grew up in the college atmosphere of Western Reserve, where his father's home was on the New England Green which served Hudson and the College as a reminder of their origin. His father was a professor of Greek and Latin. Seymour matriculated at Western Reserve in 1866 and graduated with the degree of bachelor of arts in 1870, being given at the same time the unusual distinction of an honorary B.A. by Yale. He was valedictorian of his class and something of a leader both in social and literary affairs. Music, however, was his greatest interest outside the curriculum, and to the development of musical activities in the college he made a permanent contribution.

Nathan Seymour resigned his professorship in 1870 and the work he had been conducting was divided. Thomas was elected professor of Greek with leave of absence for two years to study in Europe in preparation for the position. These two years were spent at Leipzig, Berlin, and Athens, and during this period he developed still further a remarkable power of concentration which was his throughout life. He began his service at Western Reserve in the fall of 1872. On July 2, 1874, he married Sarah Melissa, daughter of Henry L. Hitchcock, the president of Western Reserve; they had three children. In 1880 he was called to a professorship of Greek in Yale College, which he held until his death. He taught a wide range of courses in Greek literature to the undergraduates and took an important part in developing the graduate school. He was always actively interested in the American schools for classical studies at Athens and at Rome and played a large rôle in their foundation and development. He was chairman of the managing committee of the school at Athens from 1887 to 1901, the period during which it attained real importance and recognition from the scholars of other nations. In 1903 he was elected president of the Archæological Institute of America, which position he held until his death. He was active in the American Philological Association and its president in 1888–89, was an honorary member of the Archæological Society of Athens, to which he was elected in 1895, and in 1900 was made an associate fellow of the American Academy of Arts and Sciences. He died in New Haven, Conn.

Throughout the years of his professional activity his leading interests were the fostering of the undergraduate life of the college, the development and strengthening of the graduate work of the University in his own field, and the furthering of the closely allied activities of the Archæological Institute and the American School at Athens. In all three fields he was distinctly a leader. Publication was to him rather a means of serving his ends in these directions than an end in itself. Instead of publishing all the material that he gathered and all of his original interpretations of classical texts, he used them in his teaching or to help others to publish, while he spent himself in gathering more knowledge, producing more scholars, and improving the conditions under which classical scholars develop. His own most notable publication was *Life in the Homeric Age* (1907), an exhaustive presentation of the body of evidence presented in the Iliad and the Odyssey. It is a masterpiece of thoroughness and clarity. He edited *Selected Odes of Pindar* in 1882 and published his *Introduction to the Language and Verse of Homer* in 1885. He was for many years one of the editors of Ginn & Company's College Series of Greek Authors and himself prepared a number of the volumes. He was an editor, also, of the *Classical Review*. An excursion which he made into the field of genealogy resulted in *The Family of the Rev. Jeremiah Day*, published in 1900.

[J. W. White, *Thomas Day Seymour, 1848–1907, Memorial Address* (1908); *Who's Who in America,* 1906–07; Yale Univ. records; *Nation,* Jan. 9, 1908; *Am. Jour. of Archæology,* Jan.-Mar. 1908; *Classical Jour.,* Feb. 1908; *Classical Philology,* Apr. 1908; personal acquaintance.]   C. W. M—l.

SEYMOUR, THOMAS HART (Sept. 29, 1807–Sept. 3, 1868), governor of Connecticut, congressman, minister to Russia, was born in Hartford, Conn., the only child of Maj. Henry and Jane (Ellery) Seymour. His father, a broker of means and a man of liberal education, was descended from Richard Seymour (or Seamer) who settled in Hartford in 1639, while his mother was descended from William Ellery of Gloucester, Mass., whose grandson had come to Hartford about 1742. Both families were so-

cially prominent and noted for their military spirit. After some schooling in Hartford, Thomas was sent to Capt. Alden Partridge's military academy at Middletown, Conn., from which he graduated in 1829. Subsequently, he studied law in Hartford and was admitted to the bar in 1833, but as he was too active by nature to settle down to the routine of the profession it was not until 1839 that he appeared on the register of practising attorneys.

Meanwhile he interested himself in politics and military affairs, becoming an active member of the Hartford Light Guard and serving as its commander from 1837 to 1841. When the Democrats came into power in 1836, he was elected probate judge for the Hartford district, and showed both legal and political acumen during the three years that he held office. In 1837 and 1838 he also edited the *Jeffersonian,* and in 1842 was clerk of the superior court. Elected to the Twenty-eighth Congress (1843–45), he was as active on the floor of the House as any of his age and standing. Though renominated by his party in 1844 he declined to run and returned to Hartford.

With the advent of the Mexican War, he again became active in military affairs. In 1847 he sailed with General Scott's forces to Vera Cruz as a major of Connecticut Volunteers. On Apr. 9, he was commissioned a major in the 9th United States Infantry, and on Aug. 12, lieutenant-colonel of the 12th Infantry. In the battle of Chapultepec he led his regiment after its commander had fallen, and, with his command, was first to enter the fortress. For gallant and meritorious service in this engagement he was brevetted colonel on Sept. 13, 1847.

Acclaimed for his part in the campaign, he was nominated for governor of Connecticut in 1849, but failed of election by a small margin. He was chosen, however, in 1850 and in 1851, when the elections were thrown into the legislature, and in each of the two years following he was re-elected by popular vote. He resigned in April 1853, the month after his fourth election, since, as a reward for his active support of Pierce in the presidential election of 1852, he had been tendered the appointment as minister to Russia, but he did not relinquish the governorship until Oct. 13, and did not sail for his post until Dec. 24. His duties at St. Petersburg were neither onerous nor difficult, and after four years of residence there he resigned in 1858, toured the Continent for nearly a year, and then returned to Hartford. His years abroad had separated him from events at home and from anti-slavery propaganda. His sympathies had turned toward the

South and he thus became the leader of the Connecticut Peace Democrats. When feeling became extreme in 1862, the Connecticut Senate voted to remove his portrait until his loyalty to the Union should be affirmed. He ran for governor in 1863, but defeat was inevitable. At the National Democratic Convention at Chicago in 1864 he received thirty-eight votes on the first ballot for the presidential nomination. He died, unmarried, in Hartford four years later, and was buried there in Cedar Hill Cemetery. Throughout his life he was noted for his courtesy and his military bearing.

[F. C. Norton, *The Governors of Conn.* (1905), first printed in the *Conn. Mag.*, ser. of 1902, vol. VII, nos. 3–4; Forrest Morgan, *Conn. as a Colony and as a State* (1904), vols. III, IV; J. H. Trumbull, *The Memorial Hist. of Hartford County, Conn.* (1886), vol. I; S. F. Bemis, *The Am. Secretaries of State and Their Diplomacy*, vol. VI (1928); *Biog. Dir. Am. Cong.* (1928); F. B. Heitman, *Hist. Reg. and Dict. U. S. Army* (1903).]   W.G.L.

SEYMOUR, TRUMAN (Sept. 24, 1824–Oct. 30, 1891), soldier, was born in Burlington, Vt., the son of Truman and Ann (Armstrong) Seymour. His father was a Methodist minister. After two years, 1840–42, at Norwich University he was appointed a cadet in the United States Military Academy; he was graduated and appointed brevet second lieutenant, 1st Artillery, July 1, 1846. He served with distinction in the Mexican War and received the brevets of first lieutenant and captain for gallant and meritorious conduct at Cerro Gordo, Contreras, and Churubusco. From 1850–53 he was assistant professor of drawing at West Point. During this period he was married to Louisa, daughter of Robert W. Weir, professor of drawing at the academy. Rejoining his regiment at Fort Moultrie, S. C., he participated in the operations against the Seminole Indians in Florida, 1856–58.

As captain of artillery he took part in the defense of Fort Sumter, and was brevetted major for gallant conduct. He commanded a training camp at Harrisburg, Pa., in the autumn of 1861, served in the defenses of Washington as regimental commander and divisional chief of artillery, and was appointed brigadier-general of volunteers on Apr. 28, 1862. In the Peninsular campaign, he was engaged at Mechanicsville, bore an important part in the defensive battle at Beaver Dam Creek, and skillfully covered the withdrawal to Gaines's Mill. He commanded a division at Malvern Hill, was engaged at Manassas, at South Mountain executed the decisive enveloping movement, and at Antietam led the advance of Hooker's corps in opening that battle. He was brevetted lieutenant-colonel and colonel of the regular army for gallantry at South Mountain and Antietam respectively. Transferred in November 1862 to the Department of the South, he commanded the assaulting column in the unsuccessful attack on Battery Wagner, Charleston harbor, July 18, 1863, and was severely wounded. Early in 1864 he was placed in command of the expedition to Florida and on Feb. 20 was badly defeated near Olustee Station. On May 5, having been relieved and ordered north, he took command of a brigade of Sedgwick's corps during the battle of the Wilderness, and on the following day he was taken prisoner. Because of his kindness to Confederate wounded after Antietam President Davis directed that provision be made for his comfort. The order, however, was not fulfilled; Seymour was exposed, as a retaliatory measure, to the fire of the Federal batteries bombarding Charleston and was otherwise harshly treated (*War of the Rebellion: Official Records, Army,* 1 ser., vol. XXXV, pt. 2, p. 164; 2 ser., vol. VII, pp. 135, 185, 571). Exchanged on Aug. 9, 1864, he commanded a division of the VI Corps in the operations in the Shenandoah Valley during November and December 1864, in the Richmond campaign, and in the siege of Petersburg. He handled his division at the battle of Sailor's Creek, Apr. 6, 1865, with an energy and ability that won the commendation of General Sheridan. He was present at the capitulation of General Lee. He received three brevet commissions dated Mar. 13, 1865, as major-general of volunteers, and brigadier- and major-general, United States army. After the war he reverted to his regular army rank of major of the 5th Artillery, and served in command of various posts along the Atlantic coast. After he was retired from active service at his own request, Nov. 1, 1876, he lived at Florence, Italy, where he died, survived by his wife. He was an artist of considerable talent. Brave and steady as a leader, he was modest and unaggressive in the promotion of his own ambitions. He won the regard of his subordinates by uniform courtesy and unfailing care for their welfare. He was, however, a man of strong prejudices with a tendency to impulsive action, which retarded the advancement his training, experience, and devotion would otherwise have merited.

[G. M. Dodge and W. A. Ellis, *Norwich Univ., 1819–1911* (1911), vol. II; *Twenty-third Ann. Reunion, Assoc. Grads. of U. S. Mil. Acad.*, 1892; W. L. Haskin, *The Hist. of the First Regiment of Artillery* (1879); G. W. Cullum, *Biog. Reg. Officers and Grads. U. S. Mil. Acad.*, vol. II (1891); *War of the Rebellion: Official Records (Army)*; obituaries in *Army and Navy Jour.*, Nov. 7, 1891, and *N. Y. Times*, Nov. 5, 1891; unpublished records of the War Department, 1840–91.]   T.F.M.

SEYMOUR, WILLIAM (Dec. 19, 1855–Oct. 2, 1933), actor, stage director, theatre manager, was born in New York City, the son of James Cunningham, who had changed his name to Seymour when he ran away from his home in Belfast, Ireland, to become an actor. He came to America in 1849 and acquired a high reputation as a comedian, his adopted name having since been retained by all members of his family. In the same year he married Lydia Eliza Griffiths of Philadelphia, who acted under the name of Mrs. Seymour for some thirty years thereafter. In 1857 in New Orleans the infant William made his first appearance on the stage in his mother's arms. His first speaking part was on his seventh birthday in *To Parents and Guardians*; afterwards he appeared occasionally with visiting stars. During this period he was receiving an elementary education in the New Orleans schools.

Returning to New York in 1865 with his mother (his father had died in 1864), he later was engaged at Booth's Theatre, being cast for the Player Queen in *Hamlet* and other rôles. After two seasons there, he went to the Globe Theatre in Boston in the fall of 1871, and on Apr. 2, 1872, he acted François in *Richelieu* with Edwin Forrest [q.v.] on that actor's last appearance on the stage. Following engagements at the Union Square Theatre in New York, with Lawrence Barrett on tour, with John McCullough [qq.v.] in San Francisco, and other actors, he joined the stock company at the Boston Museum in August 1879 where he remained for ten seasons, acting an occasional part such as the First Grave Digger in *Hamlet*. In 1889, after brief engagements in New York and elsewhere, he became house manager of the newly opened Tremont Theatre in Boston, where he remained until 1897, when he went on tour with Sol Smith Russell [q.v.]. He was manager of the Metropolitan Opera House, New York, in 1900–01, and in 1904 he joined the forces of Charles Frohman [q.v.], remaining with him for years as general stage director, actor, and historian. During his later years he lived in semi-retirement at South Duxbury, Mass., where he had long maintained a summer home, going thence frequently to Boston and New York to engage temporarily in such activities as a tour with George Arliss as actor and stage director, to appear in the all-star production of *The Two Orphans* in 1925–26, and to serve as stage director of the annual productions of the Players Club.

During many years his friends received a cordial welcome at South Duxbury and had the pleasure of looking over his notable collection of books, autograph letters, manuscripts, playbills, and other memorabilia. He was an efficient actor and an able producer of plays, whose training led many actors to success. He was of short stature and portly figure, a genial companion whose conversation was delightful and whose devotion to his family was one among his many admirable traits. On Jan. 8, 1882, he married May Davenport, daughter of Edward Loomis Davenport and younger sister of Fanny Lily Gypsy Davenport [qq.v.]. She had a brief career as an actress in the Boston Museum Stock Company and elsewhere, and died suddenly in New York in 1927. He died after a brief illness at the Jordan Hospital in Plymouth, Mass. Of their five children only one permanently adopted the family profession.

[M. J. Moses, *Famous Actor-Families in America* (1906); *Who's Who in America*, 1928–29; *Who's Who in the Theatre*, 1933; J. B. Clapp and E. F. Edgett, *Players of the Present*, pt. III (1901); Kate Ryan, *Old Museum Days* (1915); *N. Y. Dram. Mirror*, Dec. 24, 1898; *Boston Daily Globe*, Aug. 16, 1923; *Boston Herald*, Jan. 21, 1929; H. I. Jackson, in book section, *Boston Transcript*, Jan. 10, 17, 1931; obituaries in *Boston Transcript*, *N. Y. Times*, Oct. 3, 1933, and *Boston Herald*, *N. Y. Herald Tribune*, Oct. 4, 1933; personal acquaintance; information from Seymour's daughter, Mrs. May Davenport Seymour Eckert, who is the authority for the spelling of Lydia Eliza Griffiths' surname.]
            E. F. E.

SHABONEE (c. 1775–July 1859), Potawatomi chief, was born into the Ottawa tribe, possibly near the Maumee River in what is now the state of Ohio. It is said that his father was a nephew of Pontiac [q.v.]. His name was spelled variously as Shabbona, Shabonee, Shobonier, Shaubena, and sometimes Chambler or Chambly. It seems to have been pronounced in two syllables with the accent on the first, as though spelled Shabney. He married the daughter of a Potawatomi chief and on the death of the old chief succeeded to his place of influence in that tribe. For a time he lived in a Potawatomi village on the Illinois River near the mouth of the Fox but soon removed to a place that became known as Shabbona Grove, now in southern Dekalb County, Ill. About 1807 he became attached to the rising power of Tecumseh [q.v.], in 1810 went with the leader to visit the Indian villages in the northern Illinois country and on the Wisconsin River, and the next year accompanied him south to try to persuade the southern tribes to join the confederation. When war was declared between Great Britain and the United States he was loath to join in the bloody business of killing and scalping American settlers and, with Sauganash [q.v.], was active in saving the lives of the family of John Kinzie [q.v.] and others in the Chicago massacre of August 1812; but he fought at Tecumseh's side in the battle of the Thames.

After the War of 1812 he never wavered in his allegiance to the government of the United States and in various ways rendered important aid to the settlers. In the Winnebago outbreak of 1827 he opposed the desire of Big Foot and other Potawatomi to join the Winnebago, was made prisoner at Big Foot's Lake, now Geneva Lake, Wis., and narrowly escaped death in his efforts to protect the American settlers. When Black Hawk undertook active opposition to white encroachment in 1832, Shabonee again protected the settlers. He sent his son and nephew to warn the settlers at Holderman's Grove and on the Fox River, and himself set out on a desperate ride to the settlements near Bureau and Indian creeks. For this exploit the descendants of the settlers raised a monument in 1903 and in 1906 set aside a park to his memory, but in his own lifetime his reward was neglect and poverty. Although the treaties of July 29, 1829, and Sept. 26, 1833, seemed to grant him two sections of land at his own village, he became involved in technicalities of the white man's law of ownership and lost his lands to encroaching settlers. However, a small group of settlers bought for him a small farm in Grundy County, Ill. There in his old age he ate the bitter bread of charity and pondered on the white man's gratitude.

[G. S. Hubbard, "Addresses Delivered . . . 1868 . . . Sketches of . . . Shabonee," *Fergus' Hist. Series*, no. 10 (1877); L. A. Hatch, *The Indian Chief Shabbona* (1915); N. B. Wood, *Lives of Famous Indian Chiefs* (copr. 1906); Nehemiah Matson, *Memories of Shaubena* (1878); *Wis. State Hist. Soc. Colls.*, vol. VII (1876); *Ill. State Hist. Lib. Pubs.*, no. 12 (1908); H. L. Boies, *Hist. of De Kalb County, Ill.* (1868); *The Public Statutes at Large of the U. S.*, vol. VII (1846); *Niles' Weekly Register*, Sept. 15, 1827.]   K. E. C.

SHAFER, HELEN ALMIRA (Sept. 23, 1839–Jan. 20, 1894), educator and college president, was born in Newark, N. J., the daughter of Archibald and Almira (Miller) Shafer. In her girlhood, her father, a Congregational minister of Scotch and German ancestry, moved with his family to Ohio, and Helen entered Oberlin College, where she was graduated in 1863. After two years of teaching in New Jersey, she went to St. Louis, Mo., as teacher of mathematics under William Torrey Harris [q.v.], then superintendent of the St. Louis public schools and later United States commissioner of education. In 1877, her ability and distinction as a teacher of mathematics fully established, she was offered the chair of mathematics at Wellesley, two years after the founding of the college. The department of mathematics was hers to create, and under her leadership it became one of the strongest in the college. When as yet no adequate text-

books existed in English, she gave courses in the history of geometry and in determinants, Wellesley being one of the first colleges to offer such work. In her scholarship, as later in her administrative work, there was a masculine strain; justice, integrity, intellectual vision, and practical insight were her outstanding qualities.

In 1888 she succeeded to the presidency of the college. The administration of her predecessor, Alice Elvira Freeman Palmer [q.v.], had been brilliant, and in its nature extensive. Helen Shafer's work as scholar and administrator was intensive. Under her stimulus and guidance the curriculum was completely remodeled, the requirements for admission were altered to meet the exigencies of the new plan, and sixty-seven new courses of study were opened to the students. Although there have since been further modifications of the elective system, her work, wise, far-seeing, and modern, was the basis of Wellesley's later academic instruction. But she was no pedant. The social life of the undergraduate gained in dignity and freedom during her term of office; she fostered the beginnings of the college periodicals and furthered the reestablishment of the local Greek-letter societies. In the last ten years of her life she was constantly fighting a tendency to tuberculosis. In 1890–91 she spent a winter in Thomasville, Ga., for her health. Undoubtedly her life might have been prolonged had she chosen to retire, but she gave the college two more years and died at Wellesley of heart failure following upon pneumonia. Tall and slender, with a grave and rather severe exterior, she had the kindliness of a Christian gentlewoman and an unexpected sense of humor. A Scotch keenness of mind and a German thoroughness characterize all her work. The impress of her high standards, wise leadership, and clear vision in the formative years of the college remains a part of its permanent heritage.

[Florence Converse, *The Story of Wellesley* (1915); *Wellesley Mag.*, Feb. 1894; Wellesley Coll. reports, 1888–94; *Boston Transcript*, Jan. 20, 1894.]   F. C.

SHAFROTH, JOHN FRANKLIN (June 9, 1854–Feb. 20, 1922), representative, senator, governor of Colorado, was the youngest of the six children of John and Anna (Aull) Shafroth, of Swiss and German birth respectively. He was born at Fayette, Mo., where his father was a merchant. He received his primary education in the Fayette public schools and at Central College, and graduated from the University of Michigan in 1875. He then studied law in the office of Samuel C. Major of Fayette, was admitted to the Missouri bar in 1876, and practised with his preceptor until 1879, when he moved to Denver, Colo.

After some years of private practice here he was chosen city attorney in 1887 and again in 1889. Five years later he was elected to Congress on the Republican ticket. A strong advocate of free coinage of silver, he bolted the Republican National Convention of 1896 and with Senator Henry M. Teller helped found the Silver Republican Party. As a candidate of this party, and indorsed by the Democrats, he was reëlected in 1896 and 1898, and with the disappearance of the Silver Republicans he was again returned in 1900 by the Democrats. His election in 1902 was contested and the ballot boxes were taken to Washington. He requested permission to examine them, found that in certain districts frauds had been committed in behalf of the entire Democratic ticket, and immediately resigned (Feb. 15, 1904), asserting that he would not hold a tainted seat. He was generally praised for this act, which was practically unprecedented. Later that same year he ran again for Congress, but was defeated. While in the House his efforts had been largely devoted to the problems of the West. His battle for the Reclamation Act was successful, though his dream of free silver was not attained. He repeatedly introduced and supported a constitutional amendment for woman's suffrage. He also introduced (Mar. 27, 1897) a resolution to abolish the session of Congress held after the election of the succeeding Congress, popularly known as the "lame duck" session.

In 1908 and again in 1910 he was elected governor of Colorado. In the latter year he called the legislature in special session in an effort to force the enactment of the Democratic platform pledges of the previous year, and it was at that session that the direct primary, initiative, and referendum were adopted. Under him also the Highway Commission was started on its good-roads program. In January 1913 he was chosen by the legislature to the United States Senate, where he supported President Wilson in nearly all matters. He drafted and had charge of the bill providing constitutional government for Puerto Rico. In the Banking and Currency Committee, as a supporter of the President's plan, he helped frame and adopt the Federal Reserve Act. He clashed with the President, however, as he had with President Theodore Roosevelt, on the question of conservation; his speech in the Senate, Mar. 21, 1914, is the classic presentation of the Western viewpoint on that problem (*Congressional Record*, 63 Cong., 2 Sess., pp. 5224–31). During the World War,

with three sons in the service, he stood vigorously by the administration, and at its close became an advocate of the League of Nations. After his defeat for reëlection in 1918, he was for two years administrator of the War Minerals Relief Act.

On Oct. 26, 1881, Shafroth married Virginia Morrison of Fayette, Mo., who exerted a marked influence on his life and character; they had four sons and one daughter. One son and the daughter died before their father, whose death occurred in Denver in his sixty-eighth year.

[Biog. sketch by Senator C. S. Thomas in *Cong. Record*, Feb. 28, 1923 (67 Cong., 4 Sess., pp. 4944–47); Dawson Scrapbooks (State Hist. Soc. of Col.), LXI, 445–95, and LXIV, 21–47; *Portrait and Biog. Record of the State of Col.* (1899); J. C. Smiley, *Semi-Centennial Hist. of the State of Col.* (1913), vol. II; *Who's Who in America*, 1920–21; *Rocky Mountain News* (Denver), Feb. 21, 1922; data from the sons of Senator Shafroth.]   L. R. H.

SHAFTER, WILLIAM RUFUS (Oct. 16, 1835–Nov. 12, 1906), soldier, said to have been the first white male child born in Kalamazoo County, Mich., was the son of Hugh Morris and Eliza (Sumner) Shafter, who went west from Windsor, Vt. He attended the common schools of Galesburg, Mich., and at odd times helped on his father's farm and taught school. In 1861, while attending Prairie Seminary in Richland County, he enlisted for three years' Civil War service, and was commissioned first lieutenant, 7th Michigan Infantry. He took part in the battle of Ball's Bluff on Oct. 21, 1861, and in the Peninsular campaign of 1862. He was brevetted lieutenant-colonel and years later (June 12, 1895) was granted a Medal of Honor for distinguished gallantry at Fair Oaks. He was promoted major, 19th Michigan Infantry, on Sept. 5, 1862, saw service in the affair at Thompson's Station in March 1863, was taken prisoner and exchanged in the following May, and became lieutenant-colonel of his regiment on June 5, 1863. On Apr. 19, 1864, he was appointed colonel, 17th United States Colored Infantry, and took part in the battles of Dec. 15–16, 1864, in front of Nashville. He received, on Mar. 13, 1865, the brevet of brigadier-general of Volunteers. With post-war reorganization, he was assigned to frontier duty with the 24th United States Infantry, Apr. 14, 1869, with the rank of lieutenant-colonel, and ten years later was promoted colonel, 1st Infantry. He became brigadier-general, in 1897, and with the outbreak of the Spanish War was advanced to major-general of Volunteers.

Largely because of his rugged aggressiveness and ability to meet difficult situations, Shafter was given command of the important expeditionary force to Santiago de Cuba, and on Apr. 29, 1898, established his headquarters at Tampa, Fla. On June 14 he sailed for Cuba, with a fleet of thirty-two transports, carrying some 819 officers and 15,058 enlisted men, in addition to teamsters, packers, clerks, and correspondents. A landing was effected at Daiquiri on June 22, the town of Siboney was taken the next day, and the engagement of Las Guasimas was fought June 24. After a more or less hasty reconnaissance of the Spanish defenses in front of the city of Santiago, the main attack was begun against the city, July 1, with a secondary attack by the division of Henry W. Lawton [q.v.] upon the outlying suburb of El Caney. The battle was continued, July 2–3, with considerable loss to the American forces, and on the latter date Shafter demanded of Gen. José Velazquez Toral, the Spanish commander, the surrender of the city. This demand was refused, but owing to the almost total destruction of the Spanish fleet on July 3 Toral formally capitulated July 17. The surrender included some 23,500 combatants. During the armistice that preceded the final negotiations, the morale of the American troops was so seriously impaired by malaria and yellow fever that Shafter considered the advisability of withdrawing his troops to high ground, five miles from the city. However, Aug. 8–25, he embarked some 25,000 men for Montauk Point, L. I., of which about eighty per cent. were ill upon landing in the United States. A man of large size, Shafter was so ill during certain critical days of the Santiago campaign as to be able to maintain contact with his advanced troops only through his staff-officers. Although he was subjected to considerable criticism from the press of the country in regard to alleged deficiencies in subsistence and equipment, much of this may be justly charged to the country's unpreparedness for an overseas expedition in the tropics, and to the world's ignorance of tropical diseases.

In October 1898 Shafter was assigned to command the Department of the East at Governors Island, N. Y., but in a few days was transferred to his old command, the Department of California and Columbia. He remained at San Francisco until retired from active military service as a brigadier-general, Oct. 16, 1899, but retained command under his volunteer commission as a major-general, until June 30, 1901. By a special act of Congress, Feb. 2, 1901, he was advanced to the grade of major-general on the retired list, July 1, 1901. After retirement, he made his home with a daughter, on a ranch near Bakersfield, Cal., where his death occurred on

Nov. 12, 1906, after but a week's illness. His funeral and interment with high military honors took place Nov. 15, 1906, at the Presidio of San Francisco, and was attended by many distinguished persons and representatives of patriotic societies. His wife, Harriet Amelia Grimes, of Athens, Mich., to whom he was married Sept. 11, 1862, had died in 1898. On Aug. 22, 1919, there was unveiled at Galesburg, Mich., a bronze bust of Shafter, erected by the state of Michigan.

[H. H. Sargent, *The Campaign of Santiago de Cuba* (3 vols., 1907); Stephen Bonsal, *The Fight for Santiago* (1899); J. D. Miley, *In Cuba with Shafter* (1899); John Bigelow, *Reminiscences of the Santiago Campaign* (1899); George Kennan, *Campaigning in Cuba* (1899); S. W. Durant, ed., *Hist. of Kalamazoo County, Mich.* (1880); *Michigan History Magazine*, Apr.-July 1920, p. 485; *Who's Who in America*, 1906–07; *Army and Navy Journal*, Nov. 17, 1906; *San Francisco Examiner*, Nov. 13, 1906; *San Francisco Call* and *San Francisco Chronicle*, Nov. 13, 16, 1906; information supplied by Shafter's daughter, Mrs. Mary Shafter McKittrick, of Los Olivos, Cal., and by Dr. G. N. Fuller, Sec. Mich. Hist. Commission.]   C.D.R.

SHAHAN, THOMAS JOSEPH (Sept. 11, 1857–Mar. 9, 1932), Roman Catholic prelate and educator, was born in Manchester, N. H., to Maurice Peter and Mary Ann (Carmody) Shahan, Irish immigrants of some culture, who amassed a small competence in the mill towns of New England without acquiring a slavish obsequiousness to their "Yankee betters." Trained in the public school of Millbury, Mass., he developed a priestly vocation through association with an uncle, the Rev. Peter Shahan of Norwich, Conn. In the Sulpician College of Montreal, Shahan was thoroughly grounded in philosophy, the classics, and French literature before going to the American College and the Propaganda in Rome, where he won a doctorate in sacred theology in 1882 and was ordained to the priesthood, June 3, 1882. He was a brilliant student of prodigious memory and great versatility. He returned to Connecticut, where as a curate in St. John's Church, New Haven, chancellor of the diocese, and secretary to Bishop L. S. McMahon of Hartford, 1883–88, he obtained experience in ecclesiastical administration and an acquaintance with men and affairs in New England. Though essentially a priest, he took time to delve into the history of the diocese and its immigrant population, and supplied invaluable notes for J. H. O'Donnell's *History of the Diocese of Hartford* (1900). When in 1888 he was invited by Monsignor John Joseph Keane [q.v.] to lecture at the pontifical Catholic University at Washington in church history, Roman law, and patrology, he continued his studies at the Sorbonne and the Catholic Institute in Paris, at the Roman Seminary, which awarded him a licentiate in canon law in 1889, and at the University of Berlin, where he specialized in history and learned German. In 1891 he began his lectures. An enthusiastic and emotional teacher of vivid imagination, generous nature, and broad culture, he made history a living subject for his students. While he emphasized the German seminar method in training students, he was himself an interpretative historian whose religious intensity drove him into apologetic channels and whose Celtic fervor and fancy made his written style somewhat redundant. A voluminous writer of historical and apologetic essays for Catholic magazines over a period of forty years, author of *The Blessed Virgin in the Catacombs* (1892), *The Beginnings of Christianity* (1903), *The Middle Ages* (1904), *St. Patrick in History* (1904), *The House of God* (1905), and translator of Otto Bardenhewer's *Patrology; the Lives and Works of the Fathers of the Church* (1908), he exercised considerable influence over American Catholic thought. As a founder and an editor of the *Catholic Encyclopedia* (1907–13) to which he contributed over two hundred articles, he became known to Catholic scholars the world over.

In 1909 he was appointed a domestic prelate of the pontifical court and rector of the Catholic University. Five years later he was consecrated titular bishop of Germanicopolis, and in February 1928 he was named an assistant to the papal throne by Pius XI, with whom he had labored in the Roman archives. As head of the university, he was paternalistic but tactful; he led a harmonious, self-sacrificing faculty, protected freedom of teaching, maintained the principle of security of tenure, and popularized the university in critical circles. His vision was of a national medieval university, enriched by modern methods and science, and energized by American influences and rivalries, which should be a center for national Catholic activities and for a revival of Catholic culture. Yet he had a certain Puritan shrewdness about him. During his régime, the faculty increased fourfold; the endowment was raised to over $3,000,000; superior departments of theology, canon law, and Oriental studies were fostered; several buildings were constructed; and a score of religious communities were encouraged to establish houses of study near the university. He may be considered one of the founders or promoters of the Catholic Sisters' College, of the original summer school for teaching nuns (1913), of the Shrine of the Immaculate Conception in whose crypt he has found his tomb, of the Catholic Educational Association (1904), of the National Conference of

Catholic Charities (1910), of the American Catholic Historical Association (1917), and of the International Federation of Catholic Alumnae. With his assistance the *Catholic University Bulletin*, a literary magazine he had founded and edited, 1895–1909, gave way to the *Catholic Educational Review* (1911), the *Catholic Charities Review* (1917), the *Catholic Historical Review* (1915), and the *New Scholasticism* (1927). In 1928, having left an indelible mark on the cultural life of the Catholic Church in America, he retired from the rectorship to a quiet retreat at Holy Cross Academy.

[Ann. Reports of the Rector of Cath. Univ., 1909–28; files of *Cath. Univ. Bull.*, 1895–1909; *The Cath. Encyc. and Its Makers* (1917); *Am. Cath. Who's Who*, 1911; *Who's Who in America*, 1932–33; Speer Strahan, *The Spirit of Bishop Shahan* (1932) of which a part is printed in *Commonweal*, June 1, 1932; *Baltimore Cath. Rev.*, Mar. 11, 18, 1932; *Cath. Transcript* (Hartford), Mar. 1932; *Cath. Charities Rev.*, Apr. 1932, the *Cath. Educ. Rev.*, Apr., May 1932; *Cath. World*, Apr. 1932; obituary in *Evening Star* (Washington, D. C.), Mar. 9, 1932; personal information.]

R. J. P.

SHAIKEWITZ, NAHUM MEIR [See Schomer, Nahum Meir, 1849–1905].

SHAKALLAMY [See Shikellamy, d. 1748].

SHALER, NATHANIEL SOUTHGATE (Feb. 20, 1841–Apr. 10, 1906), geologist, educator, was born at Newport, Ky., the second child of Nathaniel Burger and Ann Hinde (Southgate) Shaler. An elder brother had died in infancy; three younger children lived to maturity. The father, son of a Connecticut sea-captain and nephew of William Shaler [*q.v.*], was a graduate of Harvard College and Medical School; the mother was the daughter of a Virginian who had built up a comfortable estate in Kentucky through the practice of law and the purchase of land.

Because Nathaniel was a frail child he had little formal schooling but spent most of his time out-of-doors with imaginary companions or with older people. He was familiar with the life of the village and of the military post at Newport, and from contact with people of all degrees gained considerable acquaintance with human nature; his father encouraged his interest in plants and animals; his grandfather Southgate, during the child's long visits on Sunday afternoons, gave him "counsel and instruction," and a certain guidance in interpreting the things he saw. After he was ten he acquired the rudiments of Latin and mathematics in the garrison school, took drawing lessons from a master in Cincinnati, and a little later received a thorough training in the use of sword and pistol. In his middle teens, a German clergyman stored his receptive mind with the Greek and Latin classics, introduced him to the philosophy of Hegel and Kant, and developed in him "a way of looking . . . upon the doings of men with an amused interest which kept me then and ever since much in the attitude of spectator" (*Autobiography, post,* p. 209). Mentally mature for his years but unsystematically schooled, he was sent at seventeen to Cambridge to be prepared for Harvard College. Here he resented being required to memorize rules for scanning the Latin verse he loved, and turning away from the humanities enrolled in 1859 in the Lawrence Scientific School as a student of geology and zoölogy under Agassiz. He was a favorite pupil of Agassiz, to whom throughout his life he was devoted, although after graduation he soon broke away from his preceptor's anti-Darwinianism to uphold the theory of evolution. Mentally stimulated, and with "the inquiring motive" planted in him for all time, he took the degree of B.S. *summa cum laude* in 1862.

After two years in the Union army as captain of the 5th Kentucky Battery, his health gave way and he returned to Cambridge. In 1862 he had married Sophia Penn Page, whom he had known since childhood. For two years he was assistant to Agassiz in paleontology, then spent nearly two years abroad in study and exploration. In 1868 he returned to Harvard as lecturer and the next year was made professor of paleontology; in 1888 his title was changed to professor of geology. From 1891 until his death he was also dean of the Lawrence Scientific School.

In his nearly forty years of teaching at Harvard, Shaler left an impression upon thousands of students. His elementary course, "Geology 4," was one of the most popular in the University. His teaching "was as a rule more broadening and inspiring than minutely systematic and instructive" (Davis and Daly, *post,* p. 319). Like his master Agassiz, he had a broad conception of the purpose of science study, and was more concerned with awakening the student's mind than with imparting information. He conducted a summer school of geology in 1875 and 1876 at "Camp Harvard" in Cumberland Gap and subsequently, as director, was instrumental in developing the Harvard summer school at Cambridge. As dean, he revivified the Lawrence Scientific School which had been overshadowed by the development of the College, secured the bequest (1903) from Gordon McKay [*q.v.*] for the teaching of applied science, and fought (1904–05) the proposed merger with Massachusetts Institute of Technology. He took a keen personal interest in individual problems of the students under his care; he made a practice of

visiting the infirmary, often gave financial aid, and was never too busy to receive, at home or office, a student seeking encouragement or counsel.

Characterized by William James as a "myriad-minded and multiple-personalitied embodiment of academic and extra-academic matters" (Davis and Daly, p. 320), Shaler had many activities outside the University. From 1874 to 1880 he was state geologist of Kentucky, spending most of his summer vacations with parties of students in the field. He was a member of Massachusetts state commissions on a topographic survey, the destruction of the gypsy moth, the development of a metropolitan park system, and the building of state highways; he established one of the first laboratories in the country for testing road materials. From 1884 to 1900 he was in charge of the Atlantic Coast Division of the United States Geological Survey, and in this connection traveled almost the whole length of the coast from Maine to Florida on foot. He was called into consultation in a number of mining ventures; on the basis of personal investigation advised Gordon McKay in his investments in mining properties, and himself was president of the Conroy mine in Montana.

Throughout his life Shaler was handicapped by frequent headaches, and his health was at no time robust; nevertheless, he was incessantly active. In the intervals between lectures, field trips, and the performance of administrative duties, he wrote prolifically, producing "books and essays on many subjects, in which his exceptional powers of observation, reflection, and imagination were blended" (Davis and Daly, p. 320). Besides the reports published by the Kentucky Survey, the United States Geological Survey, and the Museum of Comparative Zoölogy at Harvard, he contributed to the *Atlantic Monthly, Scribner's,* and many other periodical papers on "earthquakes, whales, the moon, climate, hurricanes, metal-mining, floods, red sunsets, altruism, the silver question," dreams, the negro problem, and other topics. He published *A First Book in Geology* (1884), *Aspects of the Earth* (1889), and a number of popular volumes on geological subjects. Most notable of his nongeological writings is a history, *Kentucky: A Pioneer Commonwealth* (copr. 1884), in the American Commonwealths series. Other titles which suggest the range of his interests are *Thoughts on the Nature of Intellectual Property* (1878); *The Interpretation of Nature* (1893), lectures delivered at Andover Theological Seminary; *Domesticated Animals: Their Relation to Man* (1895); *The Individual: A Study of Life* and Death (1900) ; *The Neighbor: The Natural History of Human Contacts* (1904) ; *The Citizen: A Study of the Individual and the Government* (1904) ; *Man and the Earth* (1905), an attempt to forecast the future from a study of the past. As a test of the theory, which he challenged, that scientific study impairs the imaginative faculty, he wrote *Elizabeth of England* (5 vols., 1903), a series of five romantic dramas in blank verse. A collection, *From Old Fields; Poems of the Civil War* (1906), was published after his death.

Shaler was thoroughly human. A ready speaker and brilliant conversationalist with a strong sense of humor, at times nervous and irascible, occasionally blunt and outspoken, he was generous of spirit and kind in his dealings, and was universally liked and respected. "In appearance he was striking . . . tall and well-proportioned, neither slender nor stout, . . . with erect, active carriage" (Wolff, *post*, p. 597). "If he hears you call him old man," said one of his students, "he'll walk your d—d legs off" (Memoir, in *Autobiography*, p. 369). In his later years, from the nervous intensity of his life at Cambridge he escaped at intervals to his "alleged farm" on Martha's Vineyard, where he found relaxation in exterminating field thistles with a hoe. Although he planned to retire from teaching and to write in this loved retreat, he died in harness, of pneumonia following an operation for appendicitis. His widow and two married daughters survived him.

[*Autobiography of Nathaniel Southgate Shaler with a Supplementary Memoir by His Wife* (1909); J. E. Wolff, in *Bull. Geol. Soc. of America*, vol. XVIII (1907), with extensive bibliog.; W. R. Thayer, in *Harvard Grads. Mag.*, Sept. 1906; *Science*, June 8, 1906; *Nature* (London), July 5, 1906; W. M. Davis and R. A. Daly, "Geology and Geography, 1858–1928," and other references, in *The Development of Harvard University . . . 1869–1929* (1930), ed. by S. E. Morison; G. P. Merrill, *The First One Hundred Years of Am. Geol.* (1924) ; *Boston Transcript*, Apr. 10, 1906.]
G. P. M.
E. R. D.

SHALER, WILLIAM (*c.* 1773–Mar. 29, 1833), sea captain, consul, and author, was born in Bridgeport, Conn., the son of Sibbel (Warner) and Capt. Timothy Shaler, who commanded the sloop *Lyon,* a privateer during the American Revolution (L. F. Middlebrook, *History of Maritime Connecticut During the American Revolution,* 1925, vol. II, p. 148). He first appears in 1800 in Mauritius, where he met Richard Jeffry Cleveland [*q.v.*] and sailed with him to Copenhagen as partner in a venture to sell coffee. At Copenhagen they purchased the *Lelia Byrd,* a brig of Portsmouth, Va., of which, by a toss of a coin, Shaler became captain. After various adventures in South America, they bought furs for the China trade in Mexico and on the Pacific coast of North America, and reached Canton in 1803. Returning alone in 1804 to collect more furs, Shaler visited the Hawaiian Islands and gained the confidence of the brilliant native king, Kamehameha I, whom he aided in negotiating the peaceful annexation of the last independent island of the archipelago. Having sold his brig to the king, he freighted his furs on another vessel, which took him to Canton as a passenger. His "Journal of a Voyage Between China and the North-Western Coast of America" (published in the *American Register,* vol. III, 1808, pp. 137–75) gives a valuable account of his experiences and observations during more than a year of trading with Indians and Spaniards.

During the summer of 1810 he was appointed consul and agent for commerce and seamen at Havana, whither he went in September; in January 1812, he left Havana for Louisiana and Natchitoches as an official agent to report on the filibustering activities of the Mexican revolutionist, Alvarez de Toledo. He returned to New York in February 1814 and in August made a journey to Ghent, having been commissioned by President Madison to attend as observer any general European peace congress. When a quarrel arose between Henry Clay and John Quincy Adams over his function, he returned disgustedly to America in December. As joint commissioner with Commodore Stephen Decatur, 1779–1820 [*q.v.*], to negotiate a peace with Algiers, he set sail from New York in May 1815 with the squadron which Decatur was taking to chastise that state for declaring war on the United States in 1812. The American commissioners secured at the cannon's mouth the most liberal treaty ever made with Algiers by a Christian power, and Shaler immediately went ashore as consul general. The treaty of 1815 remained in force until December 1816; on Dec. 23, though the Dey wished to renew the treaty of 1795, by which the United States paid tribute, he was forced to accept the American terms and signed a treaty embodying the provisions of the treaty of 1815. After this, though he had a leave of absence from April 1821 to the summer of 1822, Shaler remained at Algiers for twelve years, enjoying great prestige with both foreigners and natives. He wrote an article, "On the Language, Manners, and Customs of the Berbers, or Brebers, of Africa" (*Transactions of the American Philosophical Society,* vol. II, n.s., 1825); and in 1826 he published *Sketches of Algiers,* a volume which contains his remarkably accurate observations of the country, its government, and its history during his residence there; the book is said to have served as guide to the French expedition of 1830. In 1828 he visited the United States on account of ill health, and resigned the Algiers consulate to accept appointment, confirmed Mar. 29, 1830, to that at Havana, where, being a bachelor, he lived with R. J. Cleveland and his wife until he died of cholera in an epidemic. A man of "superior talents, . . . calm dignity of manner, and immoveable firmness" (A. S. Mackenzie, *The Life of Commodore Oliver H. Perry*, 1840, vol. II, p. 123), he achieved success in a position more diplomatic than consular, and through his writings added much to contemporary knowledge of unfrequented countries.

[C. O. Paullin, *Diplomatic Negotiations of American Naval Officers* (1912); G. W. Allen, *Our Navy and the Barbary Corsairs* (1905); *Memoirs of John Quincy Adams*, vol. III (1874), pp. 35, 47–58, 91, and vol. V (1875), p. 393; R. J. Cleveland, *Narrative of Voyages and Commercial Enterprises* (2 vols., 1842); H. W. S. Cleveland, *Voyages of a Merchant Navigator* (1886); review of *Sketches of Algiers* in *North Am. Rev.*, Apr. 1826; *Proc. Mass. Hist. Soc.*, vol. XLIV (1911), p. 316; obituary in *Daily Nat. Intelligencer*, Apr. 15, 1833; MSS. in the archives of the State Department and in the possession of Mrs. Willoughby Webb; information on Shaler's parentage and birth from Roy F. Nichols.]   W. L. W., Jr.

SHANNON, WILSON (Feb. 24, 1802–Aug. 30, 1877), lawyer, politician, diplomat, was born at Mount Olivet in Belmont County, Ohio Territory, the ninth and youngest child of George and Jane (Milligan) Shannon. After spending his boyhood on a farm he was sent to Ohio University at Athens, 1820–22, by his elder brothers. In 1823 he went to live with two of them, George and James, at Lexington, Ky., where he read law in their office and studied at Transylvania University. He returned to Ohio in 1826, was admitted to the bar in 1830, and began to practise at St. Clairsville. In 1832 he was defeated for Congress on the Democratic ticket, but the next year he was elected state's attorney. He was chosen governor of Ohio in 1838, being the first native to attain that office. He was defeated for reëlection two years later by the popular Thomas Corwin [*q.v.*] but in the contest of 1842 he defeated Corwin. Shannon resigned the governorship in 1844 to become minister to Mexico (appointed Apr. 9). In that position he "blustered, blundered, threatened and undertook to argue" (J. H. Smith, *The War with Mexico*, 1919, vol. I, 86), and although Calhoun disapproved his tactless course he was not recalled until the last of March 1845 (G. L. Rives, *The United States and Mexico*, 1913, vol. I, 702). Upon his return Shannon practised law at Cincinnati, but abandoned his profession to lead an

expedition of "Forty-Niners" from eastern Ohio and western Virginia to California. Returning to Ohio in two years, he served without distinction in Congress, 1853–55, and voted for the Kansas-Nebraska bill.

Shannon was commissioned governor of Kansas Territory on Aug. 10, 1855. He was welcomed at Westport and Shawnee by members of the Missouri party, with whom he became confidential. Free-State men aroused his suspicions, however, and he accused them of maintaining a secret military organization to resist the laws and assail Southern immigrants. The first few months of his administration passed quietly as opposing factions were perfecting their plans. Shannon himself presided at a pro-slavery meeting at Leavenworth Nov. 14 which organized a "Law and Order" party. A crisis arose two weeks later with the outbreak of the Wakarusa War. Free-State men rescued one of their number whom Sheriff Samuel J. Jones of Douglas County had arrested, and that officer requested 3,000 men of the Governor to enforce the laws. The militia which Shannon ordered to report for service was only partially organized, but some 1,200 Missourians responded and assembled on the Wakarusa River, eager to destroy Lawrence. Free-State emissaries soon convinced Shannon that such was the purpose of the "border ruffians," and he sought aid of Col. E. V. Sumner, commander of federal forces at Fort Leavenworth. The Missourians, Shannon admitted, *"are beyond my power, or at least soon will be"* (quoted in W. E. Connelley, *A Standard History of Kansas and Kansans*, 1918, vol. I, 507). Sumner refused to move without orders from Washington, and Shannon went to Lawrence to prevent a collision. He signed a "treaty" with Charles Robinson [*q.v.*] and James H. Lane, 1814–66 [*q.v.*], in which the two Free-State leaders pleaded ignorance of any organization to resist the laws, and Shannon denied that he had called the Missourians to assist him. He then persuaded both factions to disband their forces. Disturbances on a smaller scale continued sporadically during the winter. When guerrilla bands again assembled before Lawrence in May 1856, Shannon refused to intervene, and on the 21st they pillaged the town and destroyed the Free-State hotel and printing presses. On June 4 he issued a proclamation commanding that armed combinations organized to resist the laws disband. Later in June he left Kansas for an official visit to St. Louis, but directed Colonel Sumner to disperse the "pretended" Topeka legislature, by force if necessary, should it reassemble on July 4. In August, Lane invaded the territory with his "Army of the North" and attacked pro-slavery strongholds. Shannon again played the rôle of peacemaker and effected a settlement which constituted his last official act. On Aug. 18 he forwarded his resignation to the President; three days later he received notice of his removal. The problems of bleeding Kansas would have perplexed any statesman; to the time-serving politician the difficulties were insuperable.

Although Shannon was frequently a delegate to state and national Democratic conventions, he never again sought office. He resumed the practice of law, first at Lecompton, later at Topeka, and finally at Lawrence, and became a leading member of the Kansas bar. He was twice married; his first wife, Elizabeth Ellis, lived only a short time after their marriage; his second, Sarah Osbun of Cadiz, survived him four years. In 1885 a son and two daughters were living.

["Biography of Governor Wilson Shannon," and "Executive Minutes," in *Transactions of the Kansas State Hist. Soc.*, vol. III (1886), pp. 279–323; "Administration of Governor Shannon," *Ibid.*, V (1896), pp. 234–64; valuable notes in A. T. Andreas, *Hist. of the State of Kansas* (1883), and D. W. Wilder, *The Annals of Kansas* (1886); for Ohio career, "Hon. Wilson Shannon," in *The U. S. Magazine and Democratic Review*, Aug. 1849, pp. 173–78; A. T. McKelvey, *Centennial Hist. of Belmont County, Ohio* (1903); death notice in *Daily Leavenworth Times*, Aug. 31, 1877; obituary, *Ibid.*, Sept. 2, 1877, and *N. Y. Times*, Sept. 1, 1877.]   W. H. S.

SHARKEY, WILLIAM LEWIS (July 12, 1798–Mar. 30, 1873), chief justice and provisional governor of Mississippi, was born in the Holston valley of eastern Tennessee. Patrick Sharkey, his father, was of Irish descent; his mother was the daughter of Robert Rhodes. Together with an older cousin who, to the confusion of several writers, was William's guardian and also bore the name of Patrick, William entered the War of 1812 and was with Jackson at New Orleans. While returning to Tennessee at the close of the war, Patrick was favorably impressed with the country and in 1816 removed to Mississippi and settled on land now covered by the southern part of Vicksburg. William did not emigrate at this time but remained in Tennessee to attend school in Greeneville and then to read law at Lebanon before following his relatives to Mississippi. After continuing the study of law under Judge Edward Turner in Natchez, he was admitted to the bar in 1822, opened his office at Warrenton, and removed to Vicksburg three years later. During 1828 and 1829 he was a member of the state House of Representatives. In 1832 he was made circuit judge but served only a few months before being elected one of the

three judges of the high court of errors and appeals. This is noteworthy because just before the election he had vigorously opposed the part of the constitution of 1832 that subjected the judiciary to popular election. His two associates on the bench at once chose him chief justice. He was reëlected at the expiration of each term, although immediately before one election he resisted the popular demand for the repudiation of the Union Bank bonds. His opponent had promised the voters a decision against the validity of the bond issue. Though Sharkey knew a good deal of law, precedents influenced his decisions less than sound judgment and common sense. This was perhaps fortunate in view of his long term of service in the formative years of the state. He declined a seat in Taylor's cabinet in 1848. In November 1851 financial pressure drove him to resign his judgeship and to resume his private practice. He settled in Jackson.

He was elected president of the Nashville convention of 1850, and with great skill he strove to block the efforts of the extreme Southern party to capture that body. He worked in the same direction in 1859, when the opening of the African slave-trade was proposed in the Vicksburg convention. Fillmore appointed him to represent the United States as consul at Havana, but he soon resigned. He refused the secretaryship of war tendered by the same president. A task more to his liking came with his selection by the Mississippi legislature to be a member of a commission to compile *The Revised Code of the Statute Laws of Mississippi* (1857). A charter member of the board of trustees of the University of Mississippi, he served from 1844 to 1865. Although in his early political life he was a state-rights Whig, before 1861 he was probably the most active anti-secession man in Mississippi. In 1863 he took the oath of allegiance to the Union. These facts, together with his birth in east Tennessee, made him an unusually suitable person to negotiate with President Johnson concerning the reconstruction of Mississippi. Following a successful conference in Washington, he and his fellow commissioner returned home. Shortly afterward, in June 1865, he was appointed provisional governor, and he served until after the election of Benjamin G. Humphreys in the fall of that year. In spite of clashes of opinion over the well-known reconstruction problems and of Sharkey's own pre-war and war records, he evidently retained the confidence of the people of the state for he was chosen United States senator, but was denied a seat in that body, when Congress repudiated Johnson's plan of reconstruction. In 1867 he and Robert J.

Walker unsuccessfully endeavored to obtain a decision of the federal Supreme Court on the constitutionality of the Reconstruction activities of Congress (*State of Mississippi* vs. *Johnson,* 4 *Wallace,* 475). He died before the close of Reconstruction, survived by his widow, Minerva (Hyland) Wren Sharkey. He was buried in the Greenwood Cemetery at Jackson.

His wisdom, friendly manner, and upright life, as well as his religious convictions, enabled him to remain a trusted leader of a constituency from which he differed politically on many of the outstanding issues of the day. After his death Henry S. Foote (*post,* p. 62), who had known him forty years, wrote: "I never knew a person of more integrity and honor; nor one whose general course of life was more blameless and more worthy of commendation."

[Official papers relating to governorship in Miss. Dept. of Archives and Hist.; "Judge Sharkey Papers," ed. by F. G. Davenport, *Miss. Valley Hist. Rev.,* June 1933; recollections and manuscript geneal. of Clay Sharkey, Glen Allan, Miss.; *Amer. Rev.,* May 1852; J. S. Morris, *Miss. State Cases,* vol. I (1872), pp. iii–v; H. S. Foote, *The Bench and Bar of the South and Southwest* (1876); *Hist. Cat. of the Univ. of Miss.* (1910); J. D. Lynch, *The Bench and Bar of Miss.* (1881); J. F. H. Claiborne, *Mississippi* (1880); J. W. Garner, *Reconstruction in Miss.* (1901); Dunbar Rowland, *Mississippi,* vol. II (1907); *Miss. Hist. Soc. Pubs.,* vols. IV, XIV (1901–14); date of birth from tombstone.]   C. S. S.

SHARP, DALLAS LORE (Dec. 13, 1870–Nov. 29, 1929), author, educator, naturalist, was born in Haleyville, N. J., the son of Reuben Lore and Mary Den (Bradway) Sharp. Receiving his early education in the public schools of his native district, he graduated from the South Jersey Institute in Bridgeton, N. J., before he was eighteen. He made an attempt to become a surveyor, which was unsuccessful because his interest in nature distracted his attention from his duties as chain bearer, and he also went to Georgia to engage in business. However, he decided that he needed a college education and entered Brown University, a natural choice since his interest in nature study had already brought him into contact with J. W. P. Jenks of Brown. He supported himself at college by working in the biological laboratory and by acting as pastor of a Methodist Episcopal Church at Wakefield, R. I., receiving ordination as deacon in 1895. He did not neglect undergraduate activities, including track athletics, and he was class poet on graduation in 1895. On Aug. 4 of that year he was married to Grace Hastings, of Detroit, Mich. They had four sons. He entered the theological school of Boston University and completed the course for the S.T.B. degree in 1899,

while acting as pastor for churches in Brockton and East Weymouth, Mass. In 1899, however, he became assistant librarian of the college of liberal arts of Boston University and the next year he was also an instructor in English. As assistant professor of English after 1902 and professor after 1909, he was probably the best known man in the institution both to the student body and the outside public. He gave up his regular teaching in the university in 1922 but was again scheduled to teach a non-credit course for the year 1929–30.

In 1900 he joined the editorial staff of the *Youth's Companion,* and he remained on it three years, still continuing his academic work and literary activities. In 1901 he published his first book, *Wild Life Near Home,* and this and succeeding volumes and articles gave him a considerable reputation that was not affected when President Roosevelt fulminated against "nature fakers," for John Burroughs indorsed him as a true naturalist, and the public found his work attractive and convincing. He was very thrifty in the employment of his material, using magazine articles to make books and combining published matter to make new volumes; but he has more than twenty distinct volumes to his credit, and his contributions to periodicals run into the hundreds, while two of his books, *A Watcher in the Woods* (1903) and *Beyond the Pasture Bars* (1914), are said to have been sold to the extent of more than 100,000 copies each. He wrote many striking articles for the *Atlantic Monthly,* the most characteristic one, perhaps, being "Turtle Eggs for Agassiz," published in the issue of February 1910 (also in *The Face of the Fields,* 1911), which is probably the best example of his ability to present effectively aspects of nature or the study of nature for which he had enthusiasm. In the August 1925 issue of *Harper's Magazine* he published "Five Days and an Education," which was his comment on his own educative process. He had other than literary and academic prominence. He was for years a vigorous advocate of the democracy of the public school, and, as such, disapproved of private schools, attacking them repeatedly as educationally ineffective and undemocratic. He also entered politics in 1922, seeking the Democratic nomination for federal senator, but he was defeated in the primaries. He made a trip to California by automobile, lecturing along the way, and he has left an account of this in his book, *The Better Country* (1928). The last seven years of his life were devoted to public lecturing and literary work. He died at his farm, "Mullein Hill," in Hingham, Mass., from a tumor on the brain.

[*Current Literature*, Sept. 1904; *House Beautiful*, Nov. 1921; *Bostonia*, Mar. 1931; *Year-Book of the New England Southern Ann. Conference of the M. E. Church* for 1895 to 1900; *Who's Who in America*, 1928–29; *Boston Evening Transcript*, May 5, 1928, Nov. 30, 1929; *Boston Herald*, May 27, 1916, June 6, 1920, Apr. 28, Nov. 30, 1929.]   S. G.

SHARP, DANIEL (Dec. 25, 1783–June 23, 1853), Baptist clergyman, was born in Huddersfield, Yorkshire, England, son of the Rev. John Sharp, a Baptist minister. The boy grew up under favorable home and community influences. His first church connection was with the Congregationalists, but he became a Baptist by conviction. Because he was known as a youth of ability and integrity, he was appointed American agent of a Yorkshire mercantile firm, and he became a resident of New York at the age of twenty-two. His interest in religion associated him with a Baptist church, and he engaged occasionally in lay preaching, revealing personal qualities that led his friends to urge him to enter his father's profession. Deciding at length to do so, he placed himself under the tutelage of the Rev. William Staughton of Philadelphia, and on May 17, 1809, was ordained to the ministry in Newark, N. J., where he became pastor of the Baptist Church. Three years later, he accepted a call to the Third Baptist Church of Boston, afterward known as the Charles Street Church, and there he remained until his death.

He did not draw the attention of people to himself by any tricks of publicity. He was never sensational in his methods. His preaching was deliberate and impressive. As he warmed to his theme he turned aside from his manuscript, laid his glasses on the pulpit, and with vivid gesture and kindling energy spoke extemporaneously. Not only did he gain the regard and support of his own people, he won as well the respect of the community. Baptists were not yet on a legal equality with Congregationalists in the old Puritan capital, but Sharp was invited to preach the annual election sermon in 1824 before the governor and legislature, and in 1840 he was asked to preach to the Ancient and Honorable Artillery Company. A number of his sermons were printed, and his *Recognition of Friends in Heaven* (3rd ed., 1844) was widely read.

Sharp was a leader among the Baptists of his day. He had executive ability which fitted him for such responsibilities as came to him with the presidency of the American Baptist Foreign Mission Society and of the board of trustees of the Newton Theological Institution. He was concerned with the organization of the Northern Baptist Education Society, was elected a fellow of Brown University, and Harvard made him

one of its Overseers. In his later years his noble courage and white locks gave him an air of distinction. He was always dignified, and rather stern in manner as he was conservative in disposition, but he was gracious in friendliness. A biographer said of him: "God made him a perpendicular gentleman, of the noblest class, and we never expect to see him voluntarily assume, in any sense, the air and attitude of a curved and sycophantic charlatan" (*Knickerbocker*, August 1849, p. 95). He carried the responsibilities of his parish easily, and so was able to give large service to his denomination. As he approached the age of seventy his constitution weakened and he went South to visit friends and recuperate. He died near Baltimore, leaving a widow, Ann (Cauldwell), whom he had married Jan. 1, 1818, and nine of his eleven children.

[W. B. Sprague, *Annals of the Am. Pulpit*, vol. VI (1860); a collection of sermons and pamphlets in the library of the Andover Newton Theological School; Thomas Armitage, *A Hist. of the Baptists* (1895); *Christian Watchman and Reflector*, July 7, 1853; *Christian Rev.*, Oct. 1853; *Boston Transcript*, June 24, 1853.]   H. K. R.

SHARP, JOHN (Nov. 9, 1820–Dec. 23, 1891), Mormon pioneer, known as the "railroad bishop," was born in Clackmannanshire, Scotland, the son of Mary (Hunter) and John Sharp, the first Mormon convert in Scotland. At the age of eight he was sent to work in the coal pits, and he received little or no formal education. In 1847 he joined the Mormon Church and the next year left for America, although he did not finally reach Salt Lake City until August 1850. He secured work in the church quarries nearby, was shortly made superintendent, and managed the difficult task of quarrying great blocks of granite to construct the foundation of the Mormon Temple. On Oct. 7, 1856, Brigham Young [*q.v.*] ordained him bishop of the Twentieth Ward in Salt Lake City, a position he held for nearly thirty years. He was major and later colonel in the Nauvoo Legion, the Mormon militia. When federal troops under Gen. Albert Sidney Johnston [*q.v.*] threatened the Mormon settlements, he managed the removal of church property from Salt Lake City to points of safety. In 1872 he sponsored the formation of a local "institute" of young people which later gave birth to the Mutual Improvement Association, one of the most important organizations fostering social and religious solidarity among the Mormons. He held various local political offices and became intimately associated with many Mormon commercial enterprises: banking, manufacturing, merchandising, and telegraph service.

He is best known, however, as a railroad builder. In 1867, when Brigham Young took a contract to construct ninety miles of roadbed for the Union Pacific Railroad from Echo Canyon to Ogden, Sharp was one of the principal sub-contractors, and under his direction the heavy stone abutments and the tunnels in Weber Canyon were constructed. Later with Young he undertook other contracts for both the Union Pacific and the Central Pacific. Out of the financial settlement between the Union Pacific and Brigham Young, in which Sharp played an important rôle, the Utah contractors obtained a large amount of rolling stock and other railroad materials with which they developed the Utah Central Railroad, organized in 1869 to connect Salt Lake City with the transcontinental lines at Ogden. Sharp was at first assistant superintendent, later superintendent, and in 1873 president. In January 1871, when the Utah Southern Railway was incorporated, he was chosen vice-president. He later became one of the directors of the Union Pacific.

He had three wives. His first, Jean Patterson, he married in 1839; later in Utah he married two polygamous wives, Anne Wright Gibson and Sophie Smith. He was among the many Mormons brought to trial under the Edmunds Act forbidding polygamy, and when he was arraigned, Sept. 18, 1885, he was one of the first to plead guilty to "unlawful cohabitation," for which he was fined three hundred dollars and costs. Tall and impressive, with great physical endurance, he was a hard-headed man of affairs and although an ardent Mormon was never a fanatic; as one official Mormon biographer naïvely puts it, "He had a very common-sense type of mind, was, in fact, a 'man of the world,' notwithstanding he was a Bishop" (Jenson, *Biographical Encyclopedia, post,* p. 678). He possessed great tact in dealing with non-Mormons in business relations and thus admirably helped to bridge the gap of prejudice that had developed between the Mormons and the "gentile world" outside. He was survived by five sons and eight daughters.

[See H. H. Bancroft, *Hist. of Utah* (1889); O. F. Whitney, *Hist. of Utah,* vols. I, II, III (1892–98); Andrew Jenson, *Latter-Day Saint Biog. Encyc.,* vol. I (1901), and *Church Chronology* (2nd ed., 1914); obituaries in *Deseret Evening News* (Salt Lake City), Dec. 23, 1891, and *Salt Lake Tribune,* Dec. 24, 1891. For Sharp's connection with railroads, see also his testimony before the U. S. Pacific Railway Commission, *Sen. Doc. 51,* 50 Cong., 1 Sess. (1888), pts. IV, V, pp. 2154–89. Information on certain points has been supplied by relatives.]   K.Y.

SHARP, KATHARINE LUCINDA (May 25, 1865–June 1, 1914), librarian, library-school director, was born at Elgin, Ill., the daughter of John William and Phebe (Thompson) Sharp. After preparing for college at Elgin Academy and the Oakland, Cal., High School, she entered Northwestern University, Evanston, Ill., and graduated in 1885. Four years later she was awarded the master's degree. She taught school at Elgin for a couple of years, but without remarkable success, the unavoidable problems of discipline being distasteful to her. In 1888, accordingly, she accepted the proffered librarianship of the public library at Oak Park, a suburb of Chicago, and soon found that she had discovered a congenial life work. Better to equip herself for it she resigned her position after two years and took a course at the New York State Library School. Just as she graduated in 1892, Chicago was busily engaged in assembling and arranging the various exhibits for the World's Columbian Exposition, and she was placed in charge of the exhibit of the American Library Association. Her conspicuously excellent work, brought thus prominently to the attention of Chicago educators, resulted in her appointment as director of the newly established department of library science, opened in the fall of 1893 at Armour Institute of Technology. When, four years later, the library school was transferred to the University of Illinois, she continued as director and became also librarian of the University.

The founding of this school and her signally successful management of it for fourteen years brought her into the front rank of American librarians and gave her a deserved place of influence and leadership. In 1894–96 she was grand president of her college sorority, Kappa Kappa Gamma. She was director of the summer school of library science at the University of Wisconsin in 1895 and 1896, and lecturer on library economy at the University of Chicago in 1896. From 1895 to 1905 she was a member of the council of the American Library Association and in 1898 and 1907 was vice-president; she was elected a fellow of the American Library Institute in 1906 and was president of the Illinois Library Association in 1903–04. She wrote frequently for library periodicals, and her 800-page monograph, *Illinois Libraries* (5 vols., 1906–08), remains the foundation work on that subject. In the years before the establishment of a state library extension commission in Illinois, she gave much time and thought to library extension matters, she and her school serving practically as an informal bureau.

In 1907, because of impaired health, she left the professional library field—temporarily, as she thought—and became second vice-president and an executive in the Lake Placid Club in the

Adirondacks, then rapidly developing under the presidency and leadership of Melvil Dewey, who had been state librarian of New York and director of the New York State Library School when Katharine Sharp was a student there. She had been actively and happily engaged in this enterprise for seven years when she died as the result of an automobile accident. She had pronounced qualities of leadership, a well-balanced though perhaps not brilliant intellect, and an animated personality that compelled attention and recognition. She had rare administrative ability, an exceptional faculty for making wise decisions, and a happy combination of tact and forcefulness. In 1922 a portrait tablet, executed in bronze in low relief by Lorado Taft, was presented to the University of Illinois by her former students.

[*Semi-Centennial Alumni Record of the Univ. of Ill.* (1918); *Who's Who in America,* 1914–15; Frances Simpson, *Katharine L. Sharp, an Appreciation* (1914), a paper read before the Ill. Lib. Asso.; *Library Journal,* July 1914; *Public Libraries,* July 1914, May 1922; *Chicago Daily Tribune,* June 2, 1914.]   G.B.U.

SHARP, WILLIAM GRAVES (Mar. 14, 1859–Nov. 17, 1922), ambassador to France during the World War, was the son of George Snider and Mahala (Graves) Sharp of Mount Gilead, Ohio, and the great-grandson of John Sharp who emigrated from England and settled in Frederick, Md., at the end of the eighteenth century. He graduated from the high school at Elyria, Ohio, and, in 1881, from the law department of the University of Michigan. Like his father and grandfather, he first turned to journalism and edited a paper at Fargo, S. D., but he soon returned to Elyria and the bar, where at the age of twenty-five he was elected as a Democrat to the office of prosecuting attorney. However, the law was losing its attractions, so he refused a renomination and turned to manufacturing. He made a fortune in pig-iron, chemicals, and charcoal, and he built the large Lake Superior Iron and Chemical Company. In 1895 he was married to Hallie M. Clough. They had five children. He was a Cleveland elector in 1892, opposed Bryan and free silver in 1896, was nominated for Congress by the Democrats in 1900, was elected to that body in 1908, and reëlected for two succeeding terms by increasing majorities. In the House he became ranking member of the committee on foreign affairs; he introduced a pioneer air mail bill, supported the income tax and a substantial duty on the raw wool in which his own state was interested, and, more important for his own career, he spoke vigorously, on Dec. 13, 1911, in favor of denouncing the commercial treaty of 1832 with Russia be-

cause of Russian discriminations against Jewish-American citizens (*Congressional Record,* 62 Cong., 2 Sess., p. 316). In consequence he could not become ambassador to Russia some months later, when offered that post by President Wilson.

Appointed ambassador to France, to succeed Myron T. Herrick [*q.v.*], on June 19, 1914, he resigned from the House on July 23 and arrived in France in early September, while the Germans were threatening Paris and the French government was at Bordeaux. The American embassy, then representing German interests, remained at Paris. Because of the crisis Herrick remained at his post, and Sharp stayed in Paris unofficially until Nov. 28, when he was instructed to assume his duties. He spent four and a half useful years in Paris, conducting the business of the embassy, visiting German prison camps and Allied, and later American, army encampments, keeping his eye on developments in aviation, which always interested him, directing or encouraging relief work of various kinds, and ironing out the difficulties that arose between his own and the French governments. He made, for instance, a number of protests to the French authorities against the drafting of naturalized American citizens of French birth into the French army, but with meager results. However, with a French diplomat of Jusserand's experience and ability at Washington, it was only natural that many of the most important problems involving Franco-American relations should be settled directly between the state department and the French embassy, instead of through Sharp at Paris. Although a novice at diplomacy when appointed, he remained at his post until Apr. 14, 1919, long enough to become the first American dean of the diplomatic corps at Paris. An address he made at the presentation of a collection of French drawings and autographs to the American people was published in *Le Secours Américain en France* (1915), and after his death was published *The War Memoirs of William Graves Sharp* (1931). In 1919 he returned to Elyria, where he died.

[*War Memoirs, ante,* with a biographical introduction by Warrington Dawson; Beckles Willson, *America's Ambassadors to France* (1928); *Foreign Relations of the United States,* 1914–1918; *Register of the Department of State,* 1918; *Who's Who in America,* 1922–23; *N. Y. Times,* Nov. 18, 1922.]   E.W.S.

SHARPE, HORATIO (Nov. 15, 1718–Nov. 9, 1790), governor of colonial Maryland, was born near Hull, Yorkshire, England, one of a numerous and celebrated family. He had, before his appointment as governor, held a commission as captain of marines and as lieutenant-colonel of foot in the West Indies. His appointment was probably due in part to family influence and partly to the obvious expediency of placing a military man in office on the eve of a threatened attack by the French. Upon his arrival in Maryland on Aug. 10, 1753, he was immediately confronted by problems both numerous and serious. As a crown officer he had to provide men and supplies for the approaching war; as the representative of the proprietary he must resist every encroachment on his rights; but as the governor of the province he was equally bound to protect the citizens against injustice. The most immediately pressing of his problems was the French and Indian War. His correspondence shows how keenly he felt the gravity of the situation, and he promptly put himself in communication with the other governors. Commissioned royal commander-in-chief, he exerted himself with the greatest energy, consulting his colleague, Governor Dinwiddie, gathering supplies, and descending the Potomac in a canoe to inspect the military posts. When Braddock arrived to displace him in the midst of these preparations, he cooperated loyally. Upon the news of that officer's disaster, Sharpe seemed to increase his efforts, animating the people with his own courage. He strengthened Fort Cumberland and erected four small forts, and he also found time to attend military councils in New York and Philadelphia in 1755 and 1757.

In his conflicts with the lower house, he faithfully performed his duty to the proprietary under very trying circumstances. Probably the greatest tribute to his ability is the grudging admission of the Assembly that his inclination led him toward a due regard for the interest of the province. The delegates clung to their determination to pass no appropriation bills unless the revenues of the proprietor were included in the taxation proposed. In his private correspondence he deprecated the action that loyalty obliged him to take; and, when the government tried to punish the colonists for their niggardly support of the war by quartering troops in Annapolis, he remonstrated against punishing citizens instead of the real offenders, the burgesses. Some historians credit him with first suggesting the Stamp Act; certain it is that in 1754 in a communication to Lord Baltimore he outlined concisely a plan that is a prototype of the famous act (*Archives, post*, VI, 99). Yet, faced with open resistance to parliamentary taxation, his native good sense led him to warn the ministry that the act could be enforced only by troops. Especially charged to determine the boundaries of his province, he set men at work surveying the line in dispute with

Virginia and by 1760 arrived at an agreement that eventuated in the Mason and Dixon's line. In 1769, in spite of the tact he had exercised toward Lord Baltimore, he was replaced by a brother-in-law of the proprietor.

So wedded had he become to his province that he settled at "Whitehall," the country home he had created near Annapolis, to manage his estate, dispense a generous hospitality, and indulge his passion for agriculture until summoned to England in 1773 by family affairs. Though obliged to renounce the management of his estate to his friend and secretary, John Ridout, he watched the Revolution with interest and sorrow from his home in London. "Whitehall," one of the most beautiful examples of eighteenth-century architecture in the colonies, passed to John Ridout, who had married the daughter of Samuel Ogle [*q.v.*], Mary Ogle, for whom it is said that "Whitehall" was built and for whom its first master, Sharpe, remained a bachelor. On the wall of its dining-room still hangs (1935) a portrait of Sharpe painted probably by John Hesselius [*q.v.*].

[Some letters and transcripts in the Lib. of Cong.; "The Correspondence of Governor Horatio Sharpe," *Archives of Md.*, vols. VI, IX, XIV (1888–95); "Correspondence of Governor Sharpe," *Md. Hist. Mag.*, Dec. 1917; Lady Edgar, *A Colonial Governor in Md.* (1912); Jonathan Boucher, *Reminiscences of an Am. Loyalist* (1925); M. P. Andrews, *Tercentenary Hist. of Md.* (1925), vol. I; J. M. Hammond, *Colonial Mansions of Maryland and Delaware* (1914).]   E. L.

SHARPLES, JAMES (*c.* 1751–Feb. 26, 1811), portrait painter, was born in England but spent his youth in France studying for the priesthood until he realized that his bent was for art. Returning to England, where he settled after several moves at Bath, he began in 1779 to exhibit his pictures at the Royal Academy. He displayed some ability as an inventor as well. A design of his for a "steam carriage" is registered in the patent office of Great Britain (*Subject-Matter Index . . . of Patents of Invention*, 1857, pt. II, p. 761). In 1791 he published a pamphlet on *Reducing Friction in Machinery*, said to have been reprinted in 1856, and in 1804 one on *Apparatus for Surveying, Etc.* (Knox, *post*, p. 4). He was married three times. Of the first two wives little is known except that by the first he had a son, George, and by the second a son, Felix Thomas. His third wife was Ellen Wallace, a young lady of fashion and good family, whom he met through an art class he conducted in Bath. Their son James was born probably in Liverpool in 1788, and their daughter Rolinda in Bath in 1793. That year, with Felix, James, and Rolinda, they set out for America, but the journey was a difficult one and it was not until after their vessel had been captured by a French privateer and they had been interned at Brest for seven months that they finally arrived.

Sharples was soon painting portraits of men high in the military, civil, literary, and social life of the country. Noted for his ability to catch a likeness, he charged fifteen dollars for a profile and twenty dollars for a full face, and could finish a portrait in two hours. Although in England he had used oils, he now used pastels, crayons which he powdered and applied with a camel's hair pencil on a thick gray paper of soft grain and woolly texture. Making practical use of his inventive powers, he constructed a traveling carriage into which he packed his wife, the three children, and his drawing materials, and set out to travel as an itinerant painter through the New England states and into the South. In 1796 he settled in Philadelphia. There, according to Mrs. Sharples' diary, he "was generally engaged drawing in crayons the portraits of the most distinguished Americans, foreign Ministers and other distinguished visitants from Europe" (*Ibid.*, p. 13). About this time he made portraits of Washington and his wife. Copies of many of the portraits being in demand, his wife turned her talents to duplicating his efforts. The copying of their own portraits and of portraits by each other soon became a matter of course in the family, for James at fifteen and Felix at seventeen began professional art careers, and somewhat later Rolinda also turned to art. They did not sign their works, and in consequence much confusion and controversy have arisen in attempts to authenticate the work of the father. The Washington portraits were many times copied by Ellen and the two sons.

In 1798 the Sharples family were living in New York; in 1801, because of the unsettled state of English finances, they returned to Bath and three years later went to London, where the father turned again to his mechanical pursuits. Soon, however, they were in Bath again. In 1806, they started for America, but when their vessel foundered they turned back. Felix and James, however, landed in the autumn of 1806; on July 22, 1809, the others finally arrived. Sharples portraits known to have been executed in America between those dates are unquestionably by the sons (*Ibid.*, p. 25). After the return to America Sharples made his headquarters in New York but wandered through New York, Pennsylvania, and New Jersey, and often visited his son James in Albany; Felix, who was something of a rover but loved the South, seldom left that part of the country for long. The elder Sharples died of a heart attack in New York, his

last wish being that his family should settle permanently in England. His wife advertised the Sharples collection of portraits for sale and in late spring sailed for England. She had a second collection of the Sharples paintings there, which she left in 1849 to the Bristol Academy for the Promotion of the Fine Arts (later the Royal West of England Academy). Felix, in the South, was after 1811 the only member of the family in America. He too had a collection of pastels which he is said to have left as security for a loan with his friend Winder of "Yardley," Northampton County, N. C., intending to reclaim his property. He was never heard of again. The collection thus left, including portraits of many patriots of the time, was subsequently sold and is thought (*Ibid.*, p. 49) to be the nucleus of the Sharples collection in Independence Hall, Philadelphia.

[In the course of the Sharples family's wanderings in America their name sometimes became Sharpless. The most detailed biog. is that of Katharine McCook Knox, *The Sharples, Their Portraits of George Washington and His Contemporaries* (1930), with bibliog. See also *The Dict. of Nat. Biog.*; J. T. Scharf and Thompson Westcott, *Hist. of Phila.* (1884), vol. II, p. 1045; William Dunlap, *A Hist. of the Rise and Progress of the Arts of Design in the U. S.* (rev. ed., 3 vols., 1918); H. T. Tuckerman, *The Character and Portraits of Washington* (1859); J. W. Palmer, in *Lippincott's Mag.*, Dec. 1871; death notice in *Public Advertiser* (N. Y.), Feb. 28, 1811; *Cat. of the Independence Hall Coll. of Paintings*; *Cat. of the . . . Loan Exhibition of Portraits of George Washington . . . at the Corcoran Gallery of Art, Mar. 5, 1932*. The diary of Ellen Sharples is in the Royal West of England Acad., Bristol.]

                                      D.G.

SHARPLESS, ISAAC (Dec. 16, 1848–Jan. 16, 1920), college president, Quaker leader, was born on his father's farm in Birmingham Township, Chester County, Pa., the son of Aaron and Susanna (Forsythe) Sharpless and the descendant of John Sharples who became a Quaker and, with his son Joseph and other children, emigrated from England to Chester, Pa., in the seventeenth century. He has told with penetration and humor of his early training, in his *Quaker Boy on the Farm and at School* (copr. 1908). He attended the little Friends' school at Birmingham and later Westtown Boarding School near West Chester, Pa. He received the B.S. degree from Harvard College in 1873, specializing in bridge building. He taught mathematics for a few years at Westtown School, and in 1875 he began his long and fruitful service at Haverford College. On Aug. 10, 1876, he married Lydia Trimble Cope, of West Chester, Pa., who survived him with six children. He held the positions of instructor in mathematics, 1875–79, professor of mathematics and astronomy, 1879–84, dean, 1884–87, and president, 1887–1917.

After 1917 he consented to continue for a time under a lighter burden and served as dean of the T. Wistar Brown Graduate School of Haverford College until his death.

He was the author of several textbooks such as *Astronomy for Schools* (copr. 1882) and *An Elementary Plane Geometry* (copr. 1879), and he wrote many articles in mathematics and astronomy. He was a founder, in 1904, and the first president of Friends' Historical Society of Philadelphia, later Friends' Historical Association. He was also the first editor of its official *Bulletin*. His writings on early Pennsylvania, especially *A Quaker Experiment in Government* (1898), are marked by a maturity of understanding and a reserve of statement that give them peculiar value. It was followed in 1899 by "The Quaker in The Revolution" as vol. II of *A History of Quaker Government in Pennsylvania*, and in 1900 the two volumes were again published under the title *A History of Quaker Government in Pennsylvania*. In 1905 he published a volume of essays *Quakerism and Politics* and in 1915 *The American College*. He was a leader of an educational revival among Friends, especially in Philadelphia and the vicinity, that resulted in progress of thought and broadening of interests. His insistent advocacy of progress was always steadied by his respect for the past. In connection with a Quaker anniversary he once wrote: "The lack of historic background, while compatible with much Christian goodness and zeal . . . seems . . . to lead to opportunism, and to destroy that continuity of principle so essential to the preservation of the type" (*Friends Meeting House, Fourth and Arch Streets, Philadelphia, A Centennial Celebration*, 1904, pp. 8–9). He was active in local projects for community betterment and in the larger civic interests of state and nation. He strongly supported the peace movement and government reform. He was appointed shortly before his death on a state commission for revising the constitution of Pennsylvania but could not serve because of failing health.

In his later years his contributions were sought for educational conventions and periodicals. By that time he was one of the most eminent exponents in the United States of the efficient small college. At Haverford College, during his administration of thirty years, he wrought a great transformation. He relieved a difficult disciplinary situation by the adoption of student government, improved physical equipment, increased the general endowment tenfold, improved faculty standards by increased salaries, by the establishment of an independent pension fund, and

by a liberal system of tenure, and provided for the requirement of entrance examinations for all applicants, which was a rather courageous move for a small college. Resisting the clamor for technical and vocational courses, he held to the ideal of a liberal arts college. His own description of those years is contained in his *Story of a Small College* (1918). He was once introduced to a convention of educators as "the college President who does not lie." His great sense of justice was always impressive to his students who, though never coddled by him, came to regard him with a devotion bordering on worship. Part of his appeal lay in his inimitable humor, which frequently relieved a difficult and even a dangerous disciplinary situation. A tablet to his memory, in the science building named for him at Haverford College, bears the following inscription: *Magister amatus, dux sapiens, administrator fidelis.*

[Some unpublished MSS. at Haverford College, including "George Keith," and "Friends and Slavery"; *Quaker Biog.*, ser. 2, vol. V (1926); R. M. Jones, *Hist. of Haverford College* (1933); Gilbert Cope, *Geneal. of the Sharpless Family* (1887); *Bulletin of Friends' Hist. Soc. of Philadelphia*, May 1920, with bibliography of writings.]   R. W. K.

SHARSWOOD, GEORGE (July 7, 1810–May 28, 1883), judge, was born in Philadelphia, the posthumous son of George Sharswood, a lumber dealer, and Esther (Dunn). His paternal ancestors were English and old Philadelphians, though the first of the name in America, George Sharswood, settled in New London, Conn., *c.* 1665 (Hart, *post*, p. 34). He was graduated from the University of Pennsylvania with highest honors in 1828, and was admitted to the bar on Sept. 5, 1831. His practice soon became primarily that of a counselor. Nominated by the governor an associate judge of the district court of Philadelphia, and immediately and unanimously confirmed by the Senate, he served on that court, with a distinction rivaled only by that of his colleague, J. I. Clark Hare [*q.v.*], for twenty-two years (beginning Apr. 9, 1845); from 1848 onward he was president judge. In 1851 he was indorsed by five political parties for continuance on the court when the office became elective; and was reëlected in 1861 for another ten-year term; but before its expiration was elevated to the supreme court of the state. On that bench he served fifteen years (Jan. 6, 1868–Dec. 31, 1882), and then retired. From Jan. 6, 1879, onward he was chief justice by seniority.

He accomplished marvels in expediting business in the district court under rules compelling promptitude in trials. He had never been active in trial work before going on the bench, but he had prepared American editions of two English works on that field of practice, and proved to be, in the opinion of most competent lawyers, a *nisi prius* judge of unusual powers. Of immense yet exact learning, quick to grasp facts, full of practical wisdom, naturally judicial, rigidly impartial, decisive yet extraordinarily prompt in rulings, firm in controlling arguments, and remarkably lucid in his jury charges, he was unquestionably a great judge. His judgments were very sound; out of some 4,000 cases only 156 were appealed and only thirty-two reversed. In the main this extraordinary record was due to his accuracy; in part, doubtless, to his conservatism, for he was a stict constructionist, a great admirer of the common law, and little disposed to weaken the rule of *stare decisis.* Partly because of the hurry of an overburdened court, but probably also from choice, his opinions were succinct and devoid of any display of learning. Marked cooperation and mutual respect characterized his relations with the bar. His administrative talents were no less needed, and were similarly exercised, on the supreme court.

Appointed professor of law in the University of Pennsylvania in 1850, he reorganized and revivified its law school, serving it for eighteen years (as dean after May 4, 1852). Not only in private but also in public law, in politics, economics, and other fields he was continuously an earnest student, and as a teacher his ideal was "to teach young men how to study and to excite them to love to study" (Dickson, *post,* p. 123). He preserved throughout life his command of the classics. Before assuming judicial duties he served a term in the state legislature (beginning December 1837), and two terms in the select council of Philadelphia (1839–1840). A follower of Adam Smith and Thomas Jefferson, he cherished a strong antipathy to governmental interference with personal liberty and action (see, in particular, *An Address Upon the Rights of the States, delivered before the State Rights Association of Pennsylvania . . .,* 1834). His hatred of fiat money was embodied in a dissent to a decision of the district court (*Borie* vs. *Trott,* 5 *Philadelphia Reports,* 366) which held constitutional the Legal Tender Act of 1862. His report, for a stockholders committee, on the United States Bank (*The United States Gazette,* Philadelphia, Apr. 8, 1841) was a masterly legal production, quoted by Thomas H. Benton in his *Thirty Years' View* (II, 1856, pp. 365–69).

He was long a trustee of the University of Pennsylvania (1872–83), president of an institution for the deaf and dumb, a trustee of the

General Assembly of the Presbyterian Church, and a director of its theological seminary at Princeton. Sharswood was companionable and hospitable, despite a laborious life and poor health. For friends he spared no trouble; it is said that he learned Hebrew to aid one who was blind. His kindness to students and young lawyers was notable. On Nov. 27, 1849, he married Mary Chambers (d. Nov. 8, 1857), and by her had one son who predeceased him.

His opinions are in the *Philadelphia Reports,* vols. I–VI (covering 1850–68) and the *Pennsylvania State Reports,* vols. LVII–CII. His many other publications (for which see S. A. Allibone, *A Critical Dictionary of English Literature and British and American Authors,* vol. II, 1870, and Hart, Biddle, and Dickson, *post*) included: *A Compendium of Lectures on the Aims and Duties of the Profession of Law* (1854), better known by the half-title, *Professional Ethics,* and several times republished as *An Essay on Professional Ethics; Popular Lectures on Commercial Law* (1856); *Lectures Introductory to the Study of the Law* (1870); and various articles and addresses, among them *The Common Law of Pennsylvania* (1855). For three years (1843–46) he edited the *American Law Magazine.* His other editorial work included American issues, several in repeated editions, of eight English law textbooks, and of some twenty-nine volumes of collected English cases; and two volumes of United States statutes.

[*Legal Intelligencer,* June 1, 1883, vol. XL, 220; C. H. Hart, *Memoir of G. Sharswood* (1884); G. W. Biddle, *A Sketch of the Professional and Judicial Character of the late George Sharswood* (1883), also printed in 102 *Pa. State Reports,* 601–30; *Hon. George Sharswood, the Nominee for Judge of the Supreme Court of Pennsylvania. By a Member of the Philadelphia Bar* (n.d.); *Complimentary Reception and Dinner by the Philadelphia Bar to Hon. George Sharswood . . . Dec. 20, 1882* (1883); *Bar Meeting* [May 31, 1883]: *Stenographically Reported by R. A. West* (1883), also in *Legal Intelligencer,* June 8, 1883, vol. XL, pp. 230–32; H. L. Carson, "Historical Sketch of the Law Department," in *Catalogue of the Alumni of the Law Department of the University of Pennsylvania . . . 1790–1882* (1882), pp. 23–28; Samuel Dickson, "George Sharswood," in W. D. Lewis, ed., *Great American Lawyers,* vol. VI (1909), pp. 123–61; obituary in *Philadelphia Press,* May 29, 1883. In Hart, Biddle, and Dickson will be found analyses of important cases.]

F. S. P.

SHATTUCK, AARON DRAPER (Mar. 9, 1832–July 30, 1928), painter, was born at Francestown, N. H., the seventh of nine children of Jesse and Harriet (Williams) Shattuck. His grandfather, Stephen Shattuck, a Revolutionary pensioner, had settled at Francestown, but the family came originally from Massachusetts, the earliest settler having been William Shattuck, who was born in England about 1621 and died in Watertown, Mass., in 1672. Jesse Shattuck, a stone mason, worked at his trade in Francestown, at Lowell, Boston, and Worcester, Mass., and at Hartford, Conn. After having been educated in the public schools at Lowell, where his father's name appears in directories between 1844 and 1851, Aaron in 1851 began to paint portraits in the Boston studio of Alexander Ransom, later accompanying his master to New York. There he continued his art education at the National Academy of Design, perhaps through Ransom's advice. By 1855 he was already established as a portrait painter in New York. He was elected a member of the National Academy in 1861 (*Commemorative Exhibition by Members of the National Academy of Design, 1825–1925*, 1925, p. xx). He married, June 4, 1860, Marian, daughter of Samuel and Pamela (Chandler) Colman and sister of Samuel Colman [*q.v.*], the landscape painter, with whom he was closely associated. They had three sons and three daughters.

Shattuck's landscapes were specially commended in his New York period for the fidelity with which he rendered foreground objects. "He is exact, graceful, and often effective," says Tuckerman (*post*, p. 560). "There is a true pastoral vein in him; his best cattle and water scenes, with meadow and trees, are eloquent of repose . . ." He painted during the summers in the White Mountains, on Lake Champlain, and in the Housatonic valley. In 1868 he "discovered" Granby, Conn., and two years later he bought there a farm which became his permanent home during the rest of his very long life. He became a stock-breeder as well as a painter and often portrayed his own cattle and sheep in his landscapes. French (*post*, p. 144) especially commends his large painting, "Sunday Morning in New England," as "direct, simple, and truthful, without attempt to surprise by novel effects, or feats of elaborate realism." Among Shattuck's Academy pictures were "Hillside, Lake Champlain" and "Morning Light," 1869; "Lake Champlain," 1870; "The New England Farm" and "A Group of Sheep," 1871; "White Hills in October," 1872; "Sheep," 1873; "Sheep and Cattle," 1874; "The Old Homestead" and "Haying Time," 1875; "The Road to Simsbury" and "Autumn near Stockbridge," 1876; "Granby Pastures," 1877. "Down in the Meadows" became the property of the Albright Art Gallery, Buffalo, N. Y. He once devised a stretcher frame for painters' canvases which had a large sale. His later years were uneventful. He died at Granby, Conn. In the commemorative exhibition of the National Academy of Design, 1925,

he was represented by "Sheep near the Sea." His art was that of the nineteenth century academicians—scholarly, able, carefully finished; it has no considerable vogue among collectors of the twentieth century.

[The best evaluation of Shattuck as a painter is in H. T. Tuckerman, *Book of the Artists* (1867). See also Lemuel Shattuck, *Memorials of the Descendants of William Shattuck* (1855); H. W. French, *Art and Artists in Conn.* (1879); Clara E. Clement and Laurence Hutton, *Artists of the Nineteenth Century and their Works* (1879), vol. II; *Who's Who in America*, 1930–31; obit. in *Am. Art Ann.*, 1928; vital records, Granby, Conn.]

F. W. C.

SHATTUCK, FREDERICK CHEEVER (Nov. 1, 1847–Jan. 11, 1929), physician, was born in Boston, Mass., the son of George Cheyne Shattuck, 1813–1893 [*q.v.*], and Anne Henrietta (Brune) Shattuck. With his brother, George Brune Shattuck [*q.v.*], he was a member of the first class to graduate from St. Paul's School. A few months at the Boston Latin School were followed by four years at Harvard College in the class of 1868. He was very popular as a student although not a first-rate scholar. In view of the family tradition, a career in medicine naturally appealed to him and he was graduated from the Harvard Medical School in 1873. Work and research in hospitals in London, Paris, and Vienna occupied the next three years until he settled in Boston to practise in 1875. On June 19, 1876, he was married to Elizabeth Perkins Lee, the daughter of Henry Lee, of Brookline, Mass. Of his four children, one son, George Cheever Shattuck, became a physician, the fifth in direct line to practise medicine in Boston. After many years of indifferent practice, serving as an instructor in the Harvard Medical School and as a junior physician at the Massachusetts General Hospital, Shattuck was appointed James Jackson professor of clinical medicine in 1888. His private patients soon increased to a large number and, at the height of his career, he was the most noted physician in Boston. He was never primarily interested, however, in caring for patients. Teaching at the Medical School or on the wards of the Hospital, pleasant hours spent in the Massachusetts Historical Society room, at social gatherings at his beautiful manor-house in Brookline or in one of his clubs, or the writing of papers on historical subjects, were all of more importance to him. Nevertheless, he was a brilliant diagnostician, a useful consultant and a physician of wide influence. He read many papers of worth at medical meetings. Usually interpretive rather than creative, he was, nevertheless, an early advocate of adequate feeding in typhoid fever and, under his direction, the first drainage of the pericardium was successfully accomplished in Boston. He retired from his professorship in 1912. From 1913 to 1919 he was an overseer of Harvard College and for many years a trustee of St. Paul's School. An original member of the Association of American Physicians in 1886, he served as president in 1898.

In early life his youthful appearance and misunderstood levity kept him from rapid advancement, but later his sterling worth, his wit and his thorough knowledge of medicine gave him great popularity as a teacher from Maine to California. The picture of the doctor on the back seat of his small Victoria, being driven rapidly behind a pair of fast horses, and without regard for traffic rules through the streets of Boston, is one not easily forgotten. His favorite dachshund and a pile of medical journals were beside him, a cigarette was between his lips, a carnation was in his buttonhole, and a bright waistcoat and a cheery smile for all lent vivid color to the picturesque ensemble. Without revolutionizing medicine or adding greatly to the body of medical knowledge, Shattuck set a distinct stamp of vigorous scholarship and high standards upon the profession, largely through his influence on others.

[*Who's Who in America,* 1928–29; J. T. Morse, Jr., biog. sketch in *Harvard Grads. Mag.,* Mar., 1929; G. G. Sears and R. I. Lee, sketches in *New England Jour. of Medicine,* July 4, 1929; *Harvard Coll., Class of 1868, Fortieth Anniversary* (1909); *Index-Cat. of the Lib. of the Surgeon-General's Office, U. S. Army,* vol. XII (1891); 2 ser., vol. XV (1910); *Boston Evening Transcript,* Jan. 11, 14, 1929.]   H. R. V.

SHATTUCK, GEORGE BRUNE (Aug. 18, 1844–Mar. 12, 1923), physician and editor, the son of George Cheyne and Anne Henrietta (Brune) Shattuck, was born in Boston, Mass. His father, George Cheyne Shattuck, 1813–1893, his grandfather, George Cheyne Shattuck, and his brother, Frederick Cheever Shattuck [*qq.v.*], were all physicians of note in Boston. He was graduated in the first class of the St. Paul's School along with his brother and Horatio R. Bigelow, and then entered St. James College, Md., transferring to Harvard College in 1861, where he received the B.A. degree in 1863, the M.A. in 1867, and the M.D. in 1869. Before beginning practice in Boston Shattuck traveled in Italy and voyaged around Cape Horn in a sailing ship. On his return, he established a connection with the Boston City Hospital. Later made visiting physician, he served with distinction up to the time of his death. Judicious, conservative and unusually formal on his wardrounds, his common sense never deserted him; his comments, trenchant and discriminating,

were tempered by a pervasive humor. Particularly interested in typhoid fever, he wrote a number of papers on the subject. Teaching did not appeal to him and he served the Harvard Medical School for only a short time.

Shattuck was never vitally interested in the actual practice of medicine. He served as overseer of Harvard College for twenty-one years, president of the board of managers of the Massachusetts Eye and Ear Infirmary, president of the Boston Medical Library, director of the Boston Athenaeum, trustee of the Massachusetts Humane Society, and charter member of the Association of American Physicians. Shattuck was influential in establishing the Massachusetts State Board of Health in 1869, the first in the United States, and through the Massachusetts Medical Society rendered valuable service in influencing state and national legislation on public health measures.

Becoming a member of the board of editors of the *Boston Medical and Surgical Journal* in 1879, and editor-in-chief in 1881, he gave the greater part of his time to this publication until his resignation in 1912. He was an able editor, not always appreciated by his contemporaries, with a "rare capacity for literary expression, through which ran a vein of subtle humor, rendering his writings as it did his conversation, altogether charming" (Taylor, *post,* p. 780). The younger members of his staff, in whom he took a lively interest, were greatly influenced by his kindliness and sympathetic understanding of their problems. He wrote few papers, the most important being "Influenza in Massachusetts," a Shattuck Lecture given before the Massachusetts Medical Society in 1890, at the height of an influenza epidemic. In this lecture Shattuck gave an important account of his family and their influence on medicine in New England, his description of his grandfather being especially notable. He was married to Mrs. Amalia (Schutte) de La Valle, the daughter of William Schutte of Paris, on June 6, 1872. Two daughters survived him.

[The chief reference is the article by E. W. Taylor in the *Boston Medic. and Surgic. Jour.,* May 17, 1923. See also, *Who's Who in America,* 1922–23; *Report of the Secretary of the Class of 1863, Harvard College* (1913); and the *Boston Evening Transcript,* Mar. 13, 1923.]   H. R. V.

SHATTUCK, GEORGE CHEYNE (July 17, 1783–Mar. 18, 1854), physician and philanthropist, was born in Templeton, Mass., the youngest son of Benjamin and Lucy (Barron) Shattuck. The Shattuck family, many of whom have become distinguished in New England life, have a common ancestor, William Shattuck,

who was born in England and died in Watertown, Mass., in 1672. Shattuck's father, a graduate of Harvard College in 1765, a pioneer physician in Massachusetts, deeply religious, and
greatly respected by his contemporaries, was a
member of the fifth generation in America. He
named his son for George Cheyne of Bath, England, a physician whom he greatly admired. At
Dartmouth College George Cheyne Shattuck received the degree of A.B. in 1803, and M.B. in
1806. While there he was greatly influenced in
medicine by Nathan Smith, 1762–1829, and Lyman Spalding [qq.v.]. He also studied for a
short period at Harvard College, and finally
spent a year in medicine at the University of
Pennsylvania where he received the degree of
M.D. in 1807. Thus equipped with the best medical teaching of his day, he started a general
practice of medicine in Boston, living in a fashionable section of the city. He soon became the
leading physician and one of the most important
citizens. His practice was very large and he had
little time to devote to public interests, but he
served for a short period as consulting physician
to the city of Boston, as president of the Massachusetts Medical Society from 1836 to 1840, and
as president of the American Statistical Association, 1845–51.

Philanthropy was essentially a part of Shattuck's nature, but he gave without public acclaim. There are many stories about his kindness, especialy to needy students of Andover and
Harvard College. Many of his fees were remit-
ted, although in the best years his practice
amounted to about $10,000, collected at a time
when fees were $1.50 a visit. His larger gifts in-
cluded a donation toward the building of an astronomical observatory at Dartmouth College,
many books and portraits to the library, funds to
Harvard College, the endowment of what is now
the Shattuck Professorship of Pathological Anatomy in the Harvard Medical School, numerous benefactions to the American Statistical Association, and a grant to the Massachusetts Medical Society for the foundation of the Shattuck
lectures. He assisted James Thacher [q.v.]
financially with his *American New Dispensary*
(1810) and his *American Medical Biography*
(2 vols., 1828), and John James Audubon [q.v.]
with the *Birds of America* (1827–38). Shattuck,
himself, wrote little. Soon after he returned
from the University of Pennsylvania, he won the
Boylston medical prize two years in succession
for a series of essays, published in Boston in
1808. This was his only contribution of note
except "A Dissertation on the Uncertainty of
the Healing Art," published in *Medical Disser-*

*tations read at the Annual Meetings of the Mas-
sachusetts Medical Society* (vol. IV, 1829), a
stirring plea for hygienic measures "to prolong
and render more comfortable human existence"
(see p. 163), and a lengthy correspondence with
Nathan Smith. Several honorary degrees were
bestowed upon him, including one of M.D. by
Dartmouth College in 1812.

He was married on Oct. 3, 1811, to Eliza
Cheever Davis, the daughter of Caleb Davis of
Boston. They had six children, only one of
whom survived, the oldest son, George Cheyne
Shattuck [q.v.]. After the death of his first wife
in 1828, he was married to Amelia H. Bigelow
of Cambridge, on Aug. 17, 1835. From his first
wife he received a large fortune, part of which
he dispensed, along with his annual income, to
various charities.

[The chief references to Shattuck are a sermon by
C. A. Bartol, published in Boston in 1854, and *Memoir of the Life and Character of G. C. Shattuck*, by Edward Jarvis, M.D., read before the American Statistical Association, April 12, 1854, and published as a
pamphlet in that year. See also, Lemuel Shattuck,
Memorials of the Descendants of William Shattuck
(1855); H. A. Kelly and W. L. Burrage, *Am. Med.
Biog.* (1920); W. L. Burrage, *A Hist. of the Mass.
Med. Soc.* (1923); E. A. Smith, *The Life and Letters
of Nathan Smith* (1914); and the *Boston Evening
Transcript*, Mar. 18, 20, 27, 1854. Shattuck's diaries,
the catalogue of his library, and his account-books, are
now deposited in the Boston Medical Library.]
                                                    H. R. V.

SHATTUCK, GEORGE CHEYNE (July
22, 1813–Mar. 22, 1893), physician and philanthropist, the son of George Cheyne Shattuck
[q.v.] and Eliza Cheever (Davis) Shattuck, was
born in Boston, Mass. He enjoyed exceptional
educational opportunities, attending the Boston
Latin School, "Round Hill School" in Northampton, Mass., under Joseph Green Cogswell [q.v.],
Harvard College, where he received the degree
of B.A. in 1831, one year at the Harvard Law
School, and four at the Harvard Medical School,
receiving the M.D. degree in 1835. After he was
graduated in medicine, he spent nearly three
years studying in Europe. In Paris he fell under
the spell of P. C. A. Louis, one of the best medical teachers of his day, whose American pupils
were to influence the course of medicine in the
United States to a marked degree. Louis entrusted Shattuck with the translation of his
*Anatomical, Pathological and Therapeutic Re-
searches on the Yellow Fever of Gibraltar of
1828* (1839) and sent him to England to study
typhus fever at the London Fever Hospital.
Shattuck's report of thirteen cases in which he
differentiated typhoid from typhus fever was
read before the Medical Society of Observation
of Paris in 1838 and published in the *Medical
Examiner*, Philadelphia, Feb. 29 and Mar. 7,

1840. It is one of the early and important contributions to the subject, contemporary with the work of Gerhard, Pennock and Stillé.

Shattuck returned to Boston in 1840 to begin to practise with his father. Although at first without hospital or school appointment, he was so imbued with the spirit of Louis that he established a private clinic, or *ambulatorium,* in his home to train young men in clinical medicine. Eminently practical, like his famous teacher, he would not tolerate medical hypothesis or "system makers." With Oliver Wendell Holmes, Henry Ingersoll Bowditch, and James Jackson, 1777–1867, [*qq.v.*], he founded the Boston Society of Medical Observation, which had a lasting influence on Boston medicine. Official recognition came at last in 1849 when he succeeded Holmes as visiting physician to the Massachusetts General Hospital. A few years later, in 1855, he succeeded Jacob Bigelow as professor of clinical medicine at the Harvard Medical School, and in 1864 he was made dean of the school. The school at this time was a private undertaking for which the faculty were entirely responsible. Shattuck woke it out of lethargy, kept the best teachers, added new ones, extended the teaching outside of the regular courses to the hospitals and to the physicians' offices, and introduced clinical conferences.

In addition to his work in medical education, Shattuck made an important contribution to general education when he founded St. Paul's School in Concord, N. H., in 1855. The school was built upon the Cogswell formula, so successful at Round Hill: "Physical and moral culture can best be carried on where boys live with, and are constantly under the supervision of the teachers, and in the country" (Coit, *post,* p. 14). To this end he gave his country estate as a site for the school, with an adequate endowment. The school and the Protestant Episcopal Church, in which he was considered the foremost layman of his time, were Shattuck's greatest interests outside of medicine, throughout the rest of his life. He was a founder and active supporter of the Church of the Advent in Boston, and a trustee of the General Theological Seminary. A simple and sincere man, Shattuck endeared himself to Boston by his sturdy and selfless devotion to the welfare of others. His death was considered almost a public calamity. Stillé felt that "perhaps no one in Boston had done more good to a greater number of people" than Shattuck, an opinion shared by many of his contemporaries (Stillé, *post,* p. lxxiv). He was married on Apr. 9, 1840, to Anne Henrietta Brune, the daughter of F. W. Brune of Baltimore, Md. She and their three children survived him. Two sons became Boston physicians, George Brune Shattuck and Frederick Cheever Shattuck [*qq.v.*].

[*Boston Medic. and Surgic. Jour.,* Apr. 6, 1893; Alfred Stillé, sketch in *Trans. Coll. of Physicians, Phila.,* 3 ser., vol. XV (1893); Samuel Eliot, *Proc. Am. Acad. Arts and Sci.,* vol. XXVIII (1893); H. A. Coit, *A Sermon in Memory of the late George C. Shattuck* (1893); C. D. Bradlee, *New-England Hist. and Geneal. Reg.,* July 1894; *Boston Evening Transcript,* Mar. 23, 1893; diaries and note books, Boston Medical Library; personal reminiscences in "Memorials of St. Paul's School" (1891); portrait in Boston Medical Library.]

H. R. V.

SHATTUCK, LEMUEL (Oct. 15, 1793–Jan. 17, 1859), statistician, genealogist, son of John and Betsy (Miles) Shattuck and descendant of William Shattuck who died in Watertown, Mass., in 1672, was born in Ashby, Mass., and brought up in or near New Ipswich, N. H. He supplemented brief formal schooling at Appleton Academy by private study, then taught school at Troy and Albany, N. Y., and later in Detroit, where he organized the first Sunday school in Michigan. At the age of thirty, he became a merchant at Concord, Mass., in partnership with his brother Daniel. As a member of the school committee he reorganized the schools of Concord, introducing annual school reports, the first of which he presented and published. This practice, required by law throughout the state as a result of his suggestion as a member of the legislature in 1838, did much to improve the school system. About 1834 Shattuck removed to Cambridge and some two years later, to Boston, where he became a publisher and bookseller. At the age of forty-six he retired to devote the rest of his life to public service.

His first publications, appearing in a newspaper, were papers on the two hundred years of Concord's history. Finding that they kindled local interest, he added to them and in 1835 published *A History of the Town of Concord,* a great improvement upon preceding town histories. In studying local genealogy he found that the Concord records of births, marriages, and deaths had been greatly neglected; accordingly, he joined in founding the American Statistical Association, 1839, and not long afterward, the New-England Historic Genealogical Society. He helped to persuade the Massachusetts Medical Society and the American Academy of Arts and Sciences to propose a more effective system of registering births, marriages, and deaths, and was thus instrumental in securing the passage in 1842 of a law requiring such registration, passed in 1842. Shattuck furnished material for the early registration reports and alone prepared the fourth report, on a novel plan. As a member of the legislature in 1849 he became chairman of a special committee on registration which through its report brought about a thorough revision of the state's registration laws.

To utilize the statistics of births, marriages, and deaths as Shattuck desired to do, further information about various classes of the population was necessary. Accordingly, he persuaded the Boston Common Council, of which he had been an active member in 1837–41, to take a census of that city in 1845, and was chosen by the committee to execute the project. His method of procedure made this census primarily one of persons rather than of families. For the first time in the United States the record included "the name and description of every person enumerated . . . among other characteristics specifying the birth place of each, and thus distinguishing the native from the foreign population" (Shattuck's autobiography, *post*, p. 308). Shattuck also wrote an interpretative introduction to the report, another innovation that later became standard practice. The federal census of 1840 had been widely and justly criticized; when it was time for the federal census of 1850, Shattuck was called to Washington for consultation. He persuaded those who were organizing it to introduce many improvements based on his Boston experience, and as a result that census marked a longer advance over its predecessor than has been made at any other date.

He became chairman in 1849 of the commission to make a sanitary survey of Massachusetts, and its *Report* (1850), written entirely by him, is a milestone in the development of public health work throughout the country. Dr. Henry I. Bowditch [q.v.] said of it long afterwards, "The ideas contained therein germinated slowly but surely . . . Shattuck . . . as a layman, did more towards bringing Massachusetts to its present status than all the efforts made by the Massachusetts Medical Society in its corporate capacity or by members" (*Public Hygiene in America*, 1877, pp. 31–32). Of this same report, which led to the creation twenty years later of the Massachusetts State Board of Health, another writer said in 1917, "One is amazed, first, at the far-sightedness of Shattuck, and, second, at the way in which his ideal slowly fulfilled itself; there is hardly one of his fifty recommendations which has not in one way or another been carried out in Massachusetts, and there is hardly a public health measure put into practice which was not anticipated by Shattuck, save only those relating to bacteriology—a science then unborn" (George C. Whipple, *State Sanitation*, I, 170).

Shattuck was somewhat above the medium height, precise in dress, slightly pompous in manner. He married Clarissa Baxter of Boston, Dec. 1, 1825, and they had five daughters, of whom three survived him. In 1855 he published *Memorials of the Descendants of William Shattuck*, a genealogy of his own family.

[Autobiographical sketch in *Memorials*, mentioned above; *New-England Hist. and Geneal. Reg.*, Apr. 1860; *Memoirs of the Members of the Social Circle in Concord* (2 ser., 1888); *Memorial Biogs. of the New-England Hist. Geneal. Soc.*, vol. III (1883); *Boston Daily Advertiser*, Jan. 18, 1859.]   W. F. W—x.

SHAUBENA [See SHABONEE, *c*. 1775–1859].

SHAUCK, JOHN ALLEN (Mar. 26, 1841–Jan. 3, 1918), jurist, was the son of Elah and Barbara (Haldeman) Shauck, of Swiss-English and German ancestry, respectively. He was born near Johnsville in Richland (now in Morrow) County, Ohio, to which state his paternal grandfather had migrated from Pennsylvania in 1816. John worked on the farm, attended the common schools, and entered Otterbein University at Westerville, Ohio, where he received the degree of A.B. in 1866. A year later he was graduated in law at the University of Michigan. He began practice in Kansas City, Mo., but in 1869 returned to Dayton, Ohio, where he formed a partnership with Samuel Boltin. This association lasted for fifteen years, becoming especially well known in the field of probate and estate practice. On June 1, 1876, Shauck married Ada May Phillips of Centralia, Ill.

Upon the creation of the circuit courts in Ohio in 1884, Shauck was elected a judge of the second, soon recognized as one of the ablest in the state. After ten years' service on this bench he was elected, in 1894, a member of the supreme court of Ohio, and served for nineteen years, being chief justice three times, through the system of rotation. He was without question one of the greatest of the Ohio supreme court judges. His opinions are distinguished not only for their broad scholarship and clear legal reasoning, but also for their literary style. This same command of language appeared in his occasional addresses, particularly in that delivered in Cleveland in 1910 as a tribute to his intimate friend, William McKinley. As a judge he stood firmly for what he believed to be the most important of the fundamental principles of constitutional law. He held that the state legislatures are limited to powers governmental in nature and that it is the duty of courts to declare void all acts of state legislatures which are non-governmental in character even though not forbidden by express constitutional provision. This belief, fortified by a naturally conservative attitude of mind, led him to be more than willing to declare void legislation which to his mind was subversive. As a result, the supreme court of Ohio under his dominating leadership declared void many laws passed for social betterment, including an eight-hour law and a progressive inheritance tax. Many of the amendments proposed by the constitutional convention of 1921 were framed for the purpose of making such laws constitutional and thus rendering possible in Ohio legislation which had all along found favor in the eyes of the United States Supreme Court. Shauck's most useful contribution to Ohio jurisprudence was his courageous insistence upon the unconstitutionality of various acts of special legislation, passed for local partisan purposes. Such acts had been upheld by the supreme court over a long period of years, but soon after coming to the bench Shauck set out to have these many decisions overruled, and was finally successful in having a unanimous court concur with him.

From 1900 to 1915 he taught the subject of equity in the College of Law at the Ohio State University. As a teacher of law he belonged to the old school; a textbook, supplemented with a few selected cases, was his material. After his fashion, however, he was an excellent teacher, noted for his clarity of exposition and the deep personal interest he took in each student's development. Failing in 1913 of renomination for a fourth term on the supreme court, largely because of the opposition to his conservative views, he associated himself with Edgar L. Weinland in Columbus, in the practice of law. In July 1917 the Ohio State Bar Association elected him its president. The following year he died in Columbus, survived by one daughter.

[Shauck's decisions appear in 52–91 *Ohio Reports* and 1–8 *Ohio Circuit Court Reports*. Biographical information has been drawn from 96 *Ohio Reports*, xli–xlviii; A. W. Drury, *Hist. of the City of Dayton and Montgomery County* (2 vols., 1909); *Hist. of Morrow County and Ohio* (1880), p. 831; *Biog. Annals of Ohio*, 1902–03 (n.d.); *Who's Who in America*, 1916–17; *Proc. Ohio State Bar Asso.*, 1918; *Ohio State Journal* (Columbus), Jan. 4, 1918; family records and recollections.]   A. H. T.

SHAW, ANNA HOWARD (Feb. 14, 1847–July 2, 1919), reformer, physician, minister, was born in Newcastle-upon-Tyne, England, of Scotch-English parents, Thomas and Nicolas (Stott) Shaw. Her father was descended from the "fighting Shaws" of Scotland, and from her mother's side of the family as well she inherited courage and persistence. In 1849 in the hope of recouping his fortunes her father sailed for America, followed in 1851 by his wife and their six children. They lived in Lawrence, Mass., until 1859, when the visionary Thomas Shaw

put his small savings into 360 acres of unbroken wilderness in Michigan. Having cleared a spot large enough for a cabin, he continued for a time his trade of designing wall papers in Lawrence and sent out his wife and five of the children to hold the claim. Anna, who was twelve at the time, faced with characteristic courage the difficulties of these years in the wilderness, of which there is a vivid account in her autobiography, *The Story of a Pioneer* (1915). Though she had only the rudiments of an education, she read eagerly everything that was available and at fifteen became a school teacher at two dollars a week and board among her patrons. The years of the Civil War, in which her father and older brothers served, were particularly hard, but after the war, living with a married sister in Big Rapids, she entered the high school to prepare for college.

She was now about twenty-three. Her desire to become a preacher, an ambition she had cherished from childhood, was first realized when she was invited to preach in a Methodist Church by the presiding elder of the district, who later asked her to follow him during the year in his circuit of thirty-six appointments. Her family, strict Unitarians, who objected not only to her Methodism but to her preaching, considered that she had disgraced them, and for some time there was a marked breach between them. At twenty-four she was given a license to preach by the annual conference. From the fall of 1873 until February 1876, she was a student at Albion College, Albion, Mich., where she was soon in the midst of a battle to maintain the rights of the women students, and where, though she earned a little by giving an occasional temperance lecture or preaching in the neighboring villages, her financial problems were serious. After deep consideration, however, she decided to go on to the theological school of Boston University, an act which she later described as "an instance of stepping off a solid plank and into space" (Shaw, *post*, p. 82). Living in a little attic room on Tremont Street with no light but a skylight, no heat, and no water, she cooked her food over a coal-oil lamp and almost starved. At last the Woman's Foreign Missionary Society arranged that she should have an allowance of three dollars and a half a week; with this and the two dollars granted to licensed preachers for rent, she finished the year. During the summers she served as a substitute preacher on Cape Cod and was temporary pastor at Hingham. After finishing at the university in 1878 she became pastor of a church of the Wesleyan Methodist denomination at East Dennis, where she spent seven years. Since she was not an "ordained" but only a "licensed" minister, she could not administer the sacraments or baptize or receive members into the church, although she could perform the marriage service and bury the dead. When the Methodist Episcopal denomination twice refused to ordain her, she applied to the Methodist Protestant Church, and after a rigorous examination she was ordained, Oct. 12, 1880, against strong opposition. While she was at East Dennis she not only conducted three services a Sunday, did all the necessary parish work, and often lectured in Boston, but began and completed a course in the Boston University Medical School, where she received the degree of M.D. in 1886.

During her years in Boston she made many friends, among them such prominent figures as Mary R. Livermore, Julia Ward Howe, Anna Garlin Spencer, Lucy Stone and Henry Brown Blackwell, Ralph Waldo Emerson and his wife, Amos Bronson Alcott and his daughter Louisa, John Greenleaf Whittier, and Wendell Phillips [qq.v.]. Partly through them she had come to desire a wider field for her efforts. She had become interested not only in the temperance movement but in woman's suffrage, which she saw as a requisite in all reform work for women. In 1885 she became lecturer for the Massachusetts State Suffrage Association, of which Lucy Stone was president, and until the end of her life was actively associated with the effort to secure suffrage for women. In 1886, at the urging of Frances E. Willard [q.v.], she became superintendent of franchise of the national Woman's Christian Temperance Union, a position she held, for the most part without payment, for many years. About 1887 she began to lecture independently. She was soon in constant demand; night after night the year around she lectured, at "Chautauquas" and conventions during the summer and all over the country during the winter. She later wrote of all-night journeys in freight-cars, engines, and cabooses as "casual commonplaces," and of thirty- and forty-mile drives across the country in blizzards and bitter cold.

Although she knew well the prominent reformers of New England, she did not meet Elizabeth Cady Stanton, Susan Brownell Anthony, Lucretia Coffin Mott [qq.v.], and others of that branch of the suffrage movement in New York until she had been actively engaged in it for several years. After 1888, when she and Susan B. Anthony first met at the International Council of Women in Washington, they were intimate friends; for eighteen years they campaigned together for woman's rights, attended conventions, appeared before committees of Congress, and went to conventions in Europe. From 1892, when Miss Anthony became president of the National American Woman Suffrage Association, Anna Shaw was vice-president at large, and in 1904 she became president, an office she held for eleven years. After 1909, when national suffrage headquarters were opened in New York, she made the city the point of her going and coming. She attended the now frequent conventions for amending state constitutions and was greatly assisted in her work by Jane Addams and Katharine Dexter McCormick, who became officers of the national suffrage association. In 1915, recognizing that her object was nearly achieved, she resigned the presidency, becoming honorary president for life. Had it not been for the World War she might now have been free of some of her heaviest responsibilities. In April 1917, however, she was appointed by the Council of National Defense chairman of the women's committee, and from then until the middle of March 1919, when the committee ceased to exist, she devoted herself to it. She received the highest tributes for this work and was awarded the Distinguished Service Medal. She now saw an opportunity to take up the work for the federal suffrage amendment, which was at its most critical stage in Congress, and had arranged a long list of speaking engagements in various constituencies until May. But at the urging of William Howard Taft and of A. Lawrence Lowell, president of Harvard University, she joined them on a tour of the country to advocate the League of Nations and the treaty of peace under the auspices of the League to Enforce Peace. She surpassed the eloquence of all her former speeches, and vast crowds came out to hear her. Ill from over-exertion, she was obliged to enter a hospital in Springfield, Ill., where she was found to have pneumonia. She died several weeks later at her home in Moylan, Pa.

Her personal life was centered upon her home, her friends, and members of her family; with her lived Lucy E. Anthony, a niece of Susan B. Anthony, who was her private secretary, friend, and companion for over thirty years. As a lecturer she had no equal among women, a distinction that was acknowledged not only in the United States but abroad. Her voice was rich and musical, and she could speak for several hours without any apparent strain. The word, the phrase, the quotation she needed were always at her command, and she was mistress of all the arts of oratory. She was only five feet tall and was rather stout. Her hair, worn in a pompadour, grew white at an early age, but her black eyes sparkled and her smile won an audience immediately. Her humor, courage, and practical sense, which gave her the balance so conspicuously absent in many reformers, were invaluable aids to her in public activities. A vivid and forceful personality, she made friends and won admiration wherever she went. At the time of her death there were messages of regret from the most distinguished men and women of many countries, and many editorial tributes in the newspapers. Memorial foundations were later established at Barnard, Bryn Mawr, and the Women's Medical College of Pennsylvania.

[*Who's Who in America,* 1918–19; Anna H. Shaw, *The Story of a Pioneer* (1915); Susan B. Anthony and Ida H. Harper, eds., *The Hist. of Woman Suffrage,* vols. IV–VI (1902–22); Emily N. Blair, *The Woman's Committee, U. S. Council of Nat. Defense, An Interpretative Report* (1920); obituary in *N. Y. Times,* July 3, 1919.]   I. H. H.

SHAW, EDWARD RICHARD (Jan. 13, 1850–Feb. 11, 1903), educator, was born at Bellport, Long Island, N. Y., the son of Joseph Merritt and Caroline Amanda (Gerard) Shaw. His early education was received at Bellport Academy and the Port Jefferson High School. On July 10, 1876, he married Hulda Maria Green, by whom he had one child, a son, who died in 1889. Shaw was graduated from Lafayette College, Easton, Pa., in 1881, with the degree of Ph.B. and in 1887 received that of M.A. from the same institution. He entered the Graduate School of New York University while teaching, attending lectures and seminars after public-school hours, and in 1890 was made a doctor of philosophy.

Shaw's first teaching was done in the high school at Greenport, Long Island. In 1883 he was elected principal of the Yonkers high school. Here he made important reforms, especially in the teaching of physics and mathematics. He developed and introduced an inductive approach to geometry, which was widely adopted, and wrote two textbooks, *Physics by Experiment* (1891), and *English Composition by Practice* (1892). In his writings for educational journals he emphasized the significance of the motor factor in education, and the importance of studying educational problems in the light of biology and the theory of evolution. During his nine years at Yonkers he became known as one of the ablest high school principals in the country.

His experience in this position convinced him that teachers in secondary schools needed professional training on a higher level than that then given in normal schools, and he further believed that such training could be given only by universities, in departments established especial-

ly for the purpose. Largely through his efforts and advice, in 1887 New York University established a professorship of pedagogy in its Graduate School and in October 1890 expanded this professorship into the School of Pedagogy, a professional school on an equal basis with the Law School and the Medical School. A faculty of four full professors and three lecturers was appointed. This was the first university school of education, in distinction from a mere professorship, established in the United States, and is now one of the largest. Shaw became a professor in this school in 1892, and in 1894 was promoted to the position of dean, which he held until his resignation in 1901. In November 1902 he was elected superintendent of schools of Rochester, N. Y., but while preparing for his new duties was taken ill, and died in February following.

Shaw was deeply interested in the new educational movements of his day and appraised them with keen judgment and an unbiased mind. He made repeated journeys to Europe and to many parts of America and was thus able to bring to his students in New York University the best current thought on education in all progressive countries. He was a man of rare ability as a classroom instructor, exercising a marked influence over his students, who were mature young men and women, most of whom had had some experience in teaching. In 1901 he published *School Hygiene,* a textbook which was a standard work and widely used for many years. He also translated and edited Wilhelm Ostermann's *Das Interesse* (1895), under the title *Interest in Its Relation to Pedagogy* (1899), and published a purely literary volume, *Legends of Fire Island* (1895). A posthumous work entitled *A New Course of Study,* and containing a biographical sketch of him by Earl Barnes, was published in 1904.

[Biog. sketch by Earl Barnes, mentioned above; *The Men of Lafayette* (1891); *Universities and Their Sons: N. Y. Univ.* (1901), ed. by J. L. Chamberlain; *N. Y. Univ., 1832–1932* (1933), ed. by T. F. Jones; *Who's Who in America,* 1901–02; *N. Y. Times,* Feb. 12, 1903; records of N. Y. Univ.; correspondence with relatives and friends.]   T. M. B.

SHAW, ELIJAH (Dec. 19, 1793–May 5, 1851), pioneer minister of the Christian Connection, was born in Kensington, Rockingham County, N. H., of Scotch descent, the son of Elijah and Deborah (Nudd) Shaw. He was a farmer's boy, and the only formal education he received was that afforded by winter terms in the local school. The Shaws were Congregationalists, but partly through the influence of the father's second wife—Elijah's mother died when he was fourteen—the family became connected with the movement for a vital, undenominational Christianity inaugurated in New England by Abner Jones [q.v.]. Elijah was converted at the age of seventeen and almost immediately became an active religious worker. In the first half of the following year, 1811, he visited Newburyport, Mass., and Saratoga Springs, N. Y., to receive medical treatment, for, in addition to other infirmities, he had an affection of the right hip which incapacitated him for farm labor and gave him more or less trouble throughout his life. During the next three years he made frequent tours as an exhorter, not only in his native state but also in Maine, Vermont, and Massachusetts. On Mar. 31, 1814, he was ordained to the ministry at the "Christian" meeting house in Kensington.

From this time on his labors in behalf of the developing religious body he had joined were incessant and varied. On July 16, 1818, he married Lydia True of Andover, N. H., and soon afterward they removed to Cayuga County, N. Y., and settled at Brutus. For eight years or more Shaw cared for the congregation there and for those in surrounding towns, also making numerous missionary tours, some of which extended into Ohio and northward into Canada. Returning with his family to New England in the spring of 1828, he took charge of a church in Salisbury, Mass., but in 1830 accepted an invitation to become pastor of a church in Portland, Me. He was away much of the time, however, on preaching tours that carried him throughout New England. In 1834 he resigned and, after making his home in Amesbury, Mass., for a brief period, removed to Exeter, N. H., to take editorial charge of the *Christian Journal*. This paper was a continuation of the *Herald of Gospel Liberty*, the earliest religious newspaper in the United States, started in 1808 by Elias Smith [q.v.]. From 1818 to 1835 it was published as the *Christian Herald* by Robert Foster, from whom it was taken over by the Eastern Christian Publishing Association, organized Jan. 1, 1835, with Shaw as one of its executive committee. Shaw was sole editor of the *Journal* from 1835 to 1840 and associated with it till the end of his life. First issued as a bi-weekly, it later became a weekly. In 1840, when relieved of office work in connection with the paper, he removed to Lowell, Mass. The remaining eleven years of his life he spent in untiring labors, especially in behalf of education and organized missionary activity. For brief periods he had pastoral care of churches in Lowell, Mass., Durham, N. H., Franklin and Fall River, Mass.; he also continued his itinerant preaching. For a time (1842–43) he was agent to secure funds for the establishment of Durham (N. H.) Academy. He published *Sentiments of the Christians* (1847), a brief work setting forth succinctly the history, beliefs, and ecclesiastical polity of the Christian Connection. The preceding year he had served as president of its General Conference. In 1840 he began in the columns of the *Christian Herald* a series of articles urging a "missionary system," and partly as a result of these articles and other efforts of his the New England Missionary Society was formed in 1845, of which Shaw was appointed agent. He traveled in its interests chiefly in New England, but in 1850 made a tour from Massachusetts to Michigan and back. This was his last great effort; for some time his health had been failing, and in May of the following year he died.

[Letitia J. S. Brown, *Memoir of Elder Elijah Shaw, by His Daughter* (1852), reprints *Sentiments of the Christians* and other of Shaw's writings; see also E. W. Humphreys, *Memoirs of Deceased Christian Ministers* (1880), and M. T. Morrill, *A Hist. of the Christian Denomination in America* (1912).]   H. E. S.

SHAW, HENRY (July 24, 1800–Aug. 25, 1889), founder of the Missouri Botanical Garden, was born at Sheffield, England, the eldest of the four children of Sarah (Hoole) and Joseph Shaw, both natives of Leicester. His father was a manufacturer of grates and fire-irons. Between the ages of ten and sixteen he attended Mill High School, near London, which a hundred years before had been the home of Peter Collinson, a merchant who was the friend and correspondent of Linnæus, John Bartram [q.v.], and other well-known botanists. Here he acquired a good knowledge of French and received excellent training in mathematics.

Emigrating to Canada with his father in 1818, he was sent to New Orleans to learn the cotton business but he remained less than a year. In May 1819 he went to St. Louis. There he set up a small hardware and cutlery business in a second-story room, where for a time he slept, cooked, and ate his meals as well as sold his goods. Social life had little attraction for him, but he read widely and applied himself diligently to his work. By the time he was forty he had accumulated what he regarded as a fortune, and he retired from business to enjoy it. Most of the next ten years he spent in travel abroad, improving his knowledge of languages and becoming, though his tastes remained sober, a thoroughly cosmopolitan gentleman. He had a great interest in plants and with advice from such men as Asa Gray, Dr. George Englemann [qq.v.], and Sir William Jackson Hooker, then the director of Kew Gardens, he established a garden in St. Louis that was in reality a scientific institution for the study of plants. Work was begun in 1857, and about 1860 "Mr. Shaw's garden," as it was popularly known, was opened to the public. There he built up the nucleus of one of the best botanical libraries, as well as one of the largest herbariums, in the United States and provided in his will for the maintenance of a scientific staff which was to conduct "scientific investigations in botany proper, in vegetable physiology, the diseases of plants, the study of the forms of vegetable life . . ." Through a special act of the legislature, the Missouri Botanical Garden, as he named it, was established under a self-perpetuating board of trustees, the income from Shaw's estate being its only source of revenue. He also endowed what came to be known as the Henry Shaw School of Botany of Washington University. After 1851 he scarcely left St. Louis but devoted his time to the development of his garden and to the planning and planting of Tower Grove Park, his gift to the city. He never married. He died in St. Louis and was buried in the garden in a place he had chosen. During his lifetime the institution he founded was the only one of its kind in the United States, and after his death it continued to be one of the important botanical gardens of the world.

[Shaw's diaries and MSS. are in the library of the Mo. Botanical Garden. See *Mo. Botanical Garden Bull.*, Sept. 1918, Apr. 1921, June 1926, May 1931, and esp. Jan. 1921, which contains a series of portraits, and Nov. 1924, which reprints a biog. sketch from *First Ann. Report Mo. Botanical Garden*, 1890; obituary in *St. Louis Globe-Democrat*, Aug. 26, 1889.] G. T. M.

SHAW, HENRY WHEELER (Apr. 21, 1818–Oct. 14, 1885), humorist, better known by his pseudonym Josh Billings, was born in Lanesboro, Berkshire County, Mass., the son of Henry and Laura (Wheeler) Shaw. His grandfather, Samuel Shaw, a Vermont physician, was sent to jail for libelling John Adams and afterward, apparently for the same reason, to Congress. His father, for many years a henchman of Henry Clay's, ended his career in the House of Representatives by voting for the Missouri Compromise, which was unpopular in the Berkshires. A maternal uncle, John Savage, after holding various political offices, was for fourteen years chief justice of New York. Shaw attended an academy kept by John Hotchin in Lenox and entered Hamilton College in 1832, but neglected his books and was dismissed in his sophomore year for removing the clapper from the chapel bell. The records of his next twenty years are scanty. Armed with letters of recommendation from John Quincy Adams, Henry Clay, and Martin Van Buren [*qq.v.*], he went west and at St. Louis joined a party of young men who proposed to explore the Rocky Mountains, but when one of his companions died on the Kansas prairie the ill-considered expedition broke up. For a year or more he sojourned in Norwalk, Ohio, where he was remembered as a practical joker. One of his reputed hoaxes was a public lecture, "On Milk," a device to which he reverted when he became a professional humorist. After some years' absence he returned home and was married on Feb. 18, 1845, at Lebanon, N. Y., to Zilpha Bradford (Palmer, *post*, p. 165), daughter of Levi Bradford of Lanesboro, by whom he had two daughters. For a few years he lived as a farmer in his native township and then set out again for the West. After a harrowing experience as proprietor of a ramshackle Ohio river steamboat, which he tried to navigate in midwinter, Shaw decided that he had been a rolling stone long enough and settled in Poughkeepsie, N. Y., as an auctioneer and dealer in real estate.

He was forty-five years old before he began to write. His earliest attempts were printed in the New Ashford, Mass., *Eagle* and in Poughkeepsie newspapers, but until he rewrote his "Essay on the Mule" in grotesque misspelling he attracted no attention. Through the kindness of Charles Farrar Browne [*q.v.*], better known as Artemus Ward, he secured a publisher for his first book, *Josh Billings, His Sayings* (1865). Similar collections followed: *Josh Billings on Ice, and Other Things* (1868); *Josh Billings' Farmer's Allminax for the Year 1870* (1869–70) —a success that he repeated each year until 1880; *Twelve Ancestral Sighns in the Billings' Zodiac Gallery* (1873); *Josh Billings, His Works Complete* (1876); *Everybody's Friend* (1874); *Josh Billings' Trump Kards* (1877), *Complete Comical Writings* (1877); *Josh Billings Struggling with Things* (1881); and *Josh Billings' Spice Box* (1881). His books were pirated extensively in England. The range of his gift was narrow. "With me," he once observed, "everything must be put in two or three lines." He had no knack for story-telling or character portrayal, and his satire was too kindly to have much edge; but as a crackerbox philosopher, issuing bucolic aphorisms by the hundred, he had no equal among his contemporaries and has been surpassed only by Edgar Watson Howe. His best work is in the *Allminax*. Like other humorists of his day, he early ventured upon the lecture platform, but success came slowly. Once he gained a reputation, he removed from Poughkeepsie and made his headquarters in New York. He was fond of travel, and the discomforts of a lecturing tour were for him excitement and pleasure. He was tall and corpulent. Long hair—a fashion he detested—concealed a birthmark on his neck. In his maturity the harum-scarum, shiftless youth had long since disappeared in the thrifty, kindly moralist. He was unaffectedly domestic in his habits, was fond of driving and of trout-fishing, and read little except the newspapers and the Bible. His fame was largely popular, but a few earnest pursuers of the autochthonous in American literature thought they saw in him a Yankee Rochefoucauld. He died of an apoplectic stroke at Monterey, Cal., while sunning himself on a hotel veranda, and was buried in Lanesboro.

[Cyril Clemens, *Josh Billings, Yankee Humorist* (Webster Groves, Mo., 1932), and Jennette R. Tandy, *Crackerbox Philosophers in Am. Humor and Satire* (1925) are the most useful references. Both have bibliographies. See also W. P. Trent, "A Retrospect of Am. Humor," *Century Mag.*, Nov. 1901; E. P. Thomson, in *New England Mag.*, Feb. 1899; F. S. Smith, *Life and Adventures of Josh Billings* (1883); *Appletons' Ann. Cyc.*, 1885; obituaries in *Evening Post* (N.Y.) and *Boston Transcript*, Oct. 15, 1885; C. J. Palmer, *Hist. of Town of Lanesborough, Mass.* (1905).]

G. H. G.

SHAW, HOWARD VAN DOREN (May 7, 1869–May 6, 1926), architect, was born in Chicago, Ill. His father was Theodore Andrews Shaw, a wholesale dry-goods merchant of Madison, Ind., whose Scotch Presbyterian ancestry went back to the settlement of Pennsylvania. His mother was Sarah Van Doren of Brooklyn, a descendant of Pieter Van Doorn, who emigrated to America from Holland in 1659 and settled at New Amsterdam. After preparing for college at the Harvard School in Chicago Shaw went to Yale College, where he graduated in 1890. After studying architecture at the Massachusetts Institute of Technology (1890–91), he spent about a year abroad and returned to Chicago and entered the office of William LeBaron Jenney [*q.v.*] and William B. Mundie, pioneers in the design and erection of the skyscraper. On Apr. 20, 1893, he married Frances Wells, daughter of a prominent Chicago merchant, who with their three daughters survived him at the time of his death. When, sometime in the following year, he opened an office of his own, his work consisted at first in designing houses for his friends. His practice soon increased, however, and as his performance and his reputation grew together he became probably the most highly regarded architect in the sphere of domestic, ecclesiastical, and noncommercial architecture in the Middle West.

His work, particularly in domestic architecture, exerted a powerful influence on younger architects and on taste in general. Though reminiscent often of English or Austrian precedent, his style was very personal. He never used French and seldom Italian motives. The buildings he erected, for the most part, were of such character and magnitude that neither his ideals nor his talents had to suffer restrictions. He designed many town houses in Chicago, and country houses in Lake Forest and other fashionable suburbs. His other buildings include the Market Square in Lake Forest; a model town, built by the Clayton Mark Manufacturing Company, Indiana Harbor, Ind.; and in Chicago the Lakeside Press buildings; the Mentor Building; the Fourth Presbyterian Church (with Cram, Goodhue, and Ferguson); the University Church of the Disciples of Christ; the Quadrangle Club, University of Chicago; the Kenneth Sawyer Goodman Memorial Theatre; apartments at 1130 Lake Shore Drive, 2450 Lakeview Ave., and 191 E. Walton Place. Of all these and a great many others it can be said that each exemplified originality, taste, and learning at its best. It is to be regretted that Shaw designed so few churches, for he was an excellent Gothicist. In his last days he was awarded the gold medal of the American Institute of Architecture for service to American architecture.

About 1898 he built a beautiful house, "Ragdale," in Lake Forest, Ill., where he lived until his death. The estate became an experimental laboratory for the testing of his taste and craftsmanship. Here, in his spare hours, he became an excellent carpenter, bricklayer, tree-surgeon, gardener, and painter; he also designed the setting, lighting effects, and scenery for an outdoor theatre, and did much of the work upon it. Throughout his life he sought recreation in travel, often in Europe. Although he was of a markedly retiring disposition, behind the scenes he exerted a powerful influence in many civic and charitable activities. He was a trustee of the Art Institute of Chicago from 1900, chairman of the state art commission, a trustee of the United Charities and of Illinois College, Jacksonville, Ill. He was a Fellow of the American Institute of Architects and active in its councils. Shortly before his death, too late for him to serve, he was appointed a member of the United States battle monument commission, and was directed to design the United States naval monument at Brest and the memorial chapel in Flanders Field. He died of anemia in Baltimore, Md.

[Shaw's work is discussed in *Architectural Record*, Apr. 1913; *Western Architect*, Oct. 1917; and *House Beautiful*, Mar. 1927. See also *Who's Who in America*, 1924–25; *Yale Univ. Obit. Record of Grads.* (1926); *Forty Year Record, Class of 1890, Yale Coll.* (1933), ed. by L. S. Haslam; *Brickbuilder*, Jan. 1916; *Western Architect*, Sept. 1926; *Am. Architect*, May 20, 1926; *Jour. Am. Inst. of Architects*, July 1926; *Architectural Forum*, June, July 1926; *Architectural Record*, July 1926; obituaries in *Sun* (Baltimore), *Chicago Daily News*, May 7, 1926; poem in *Poetry*, July 1926.]

T. E. T.

SHAW, JOHN (1773–Sept. 17, 1823), naval officer, was born at Mountmellick, Queen's County, Ireland, the son of John and Elizabeth (Barton) Shaw, and died at Philadelphia, Pa. His paternal grandfather was an English army officer who entered Ireland on service in 1690 and later married and settled there. His father also became an army officer and served in Ireland and Germany. In 1763 he returned from the Continent, married Elizabeth Barton, a member of an English family which had become established in Kilkenny, and in 1779 retired to a farm where he subsequently eked out a meager livelihood and reared a large family. Poverty ultimately led to the emigration of two sons, John and an elder brother, to America. Reaching New York in December 1790, they soon proceeded to Philadelphia to seek employment. Apparently in consequence of his recent voyage, John immediately began a seafaring career. Between March 1791 and the autumn of 1797 he made four voyages to the East Indies. He also was employed in Philadelphia counting-houses and served with the Macpherson Blues, a volunteer military organization which in 1794 helped to suppress the insurgents in western Pennsylvania. Becoming master of a brig in 1797, he spent the next year in making a voyage to the West Indies and in trying to evade French privateers. Immediately after returning to Baltimore he entered the United States navy and on Aug. 3, 1798, was commissioned lieutenant. Until October 1799 he served aboard the *Montezuma,* which was engaged in convoying merchantmen throughout West Indian waters, and displayed such marked abilities that he soon received command of the schooner *Enterprise.* With her Shaw made a brilliant record; within a few months the *Enterprise* captured eight French privateers and fought five sharply-contested actions, of which two were "with vessels of superior force" (Cooper, *post,* vol. I, p. 139).

His activities during the ensuing years were exceedingly varied. In 1801 he commanded the *George Washington* on a voyage to Algiers with tribute to that regency; the following year, having been placed on half pay, he obtained a furlough that enabled him to make a voyage as master of a merchantman to Canton. In 1804, while he was absent, he was promoted to the rank of commander and upon his return volunteered to lead a flotilla of gunboats against Tripoli. In 1805 he was placed in command of the frigate *John Adams* and, accompanied by three gunboats, sailed to the Mediterranean but soon returned to America, peace with Tripoli having been declared in the meantime. He was ordered

to New Orleans in 1806 to construct gunboats for coastal defense, and Aug. 27, 1807, he was promoted to the rank of captain. Learning about Aaron Burr's intrigues in the Southwest, he prepared to frustrate them by mobilization of a naval force in the lower Mississippi. Later he served as a witness at Burr's trial. From May 1808 until August 1810 he was in charge of the navy yard at Norfolk, Va.; from 1811 until the spring of 1814 he was actively engaged in fortifying New Orleans and in helping to capture Mobile. In 1814 he took command of the naval squadron which was being blockaded by the British in the vicinity of New London, Conn., and there remained until the end of the war. Soon after he joined Commander William Bainbridge's squadron, ordered to the Mediterranean to settle accounts with Algiers, and when peace was made he remained behind in command of a squadron to protect American interests. After December 1817, when he returned to America, he did not go to sea. During his last years he was for a time in charge of the Boston navy yard and later of the naval station at Charleston, S. C. He was twice married. His first wife was Elizabeth Palmer, a Philadelphia Quakeress; she bore him a number of children, but only two daughters reached maturity. His second wife, whom he married Oct. 13, 1820, and by whom he had no issue, was Mary Breed of Charlestown, Mass., a member of the family after which Breed's Hill, of Revolutionary fame, was named.

[R. W. Irwin, *The Diplomatic Relations of the U. S. with the Barbary Powers, 1776–1816* (1931), and G. W. Allen, *Our Navy and the Barbary Corsairs* (1905) contain numerous references to Shaw's Mediterranean activities. See also J. F. Cooper, *Lives of Distinguished Am. Naval Officers* (1846), vol. I; *Nat. Gazette and Lit. Reg.* (Phila.), Sept. 20, 1823; T. B. Wyman, *Geneal. and Estates of Charlestown . . . Mass., 1629–1818* (1879), vol. II; brief obituary in *Poulson's Am. Daily Advertiser,* Sept. 18, 1823.]   R. W. I.

SHAW, JOHN (May 4, 1778–Jan. 10, 1809), physician, poet, was born at Annapolis, Md. He entered St. John's College in that city at its opening in 1789 and graduated as Latin salutatorian in October 1796, in the same class with his close friend, Francis Scott Key. His first published poem, apparently, was "The Voice of Freedom" in the *Baltimore Telegraphe* for May 13, 1795. For two years he remained at Annapolis studying medicine under Dr. John Thomas Shaaff and reading widely in Greek and medieval medical literature. In November 1798 he went to Philadelphia to continue his studies at the University of Pennsylvania, but a boyish freak led him to take the post of surgeon on a squadron about to sail for Algiers, and on Dec. 23 he embarked with James Leander Cathcart and William Eaton [*qq.v.*] on the brig *Sophia*. For a few months he was Eaton's secretary at Tunis and was then sent to London to confer on diplomatic business with the elder Rufus King [*q.v.*]. He visited Italy, Gibraltar, and Lisbon, and learned not only Portuguese, Spanish, and Italian but also some Arabic. He returned to Annapolis in the spring of 1800 but sailed again in July 1801 to take up his medical studies at Edinburgh. In 1803 he accompanied the colony sent out by Thomas Douglas, fifth Earl of Selkirk, to Prince Edward Island, where he had to cope with a severe epidemic. Early in 1805 he returned once more to Annapolis and took up practice with his old teacher Shaaff, but after his marriage on Feb. 12, 1807, to Jane Selby (or Telby) of Annapolis he removed to Baltimore. There he gained immediate recognition. In 1807 he joined with James Cocke and John Beale Davidge [*q.v.*] to secure a charter from the state legislature for the College of Medicine of Maryland, the fifth medical school in the United States, and the forerunner of the University of Maryland. The three founders and their colleagues gave instruction in their own houses, Shaw taking charge of the work in chemistry. He taught and worked with enthusiasm. One experiment that he conducted obliged him to immerse his arms in cold water at frequent intervals throughout an entire night; this exposure brought on an attack of pleurisy, and after it tuberculosis set in. In accordance with the practice of the time, he set out for the South. He died at sea while voyaging from Charleston, S. C., to the Bahamas. He had contributed poems to Joseph Dennie's *Port Folio* between 1801 and 1805 under the name of Ithacus (A. H. Smyth, *The Philadelphia Magazines and their Contributors,* 1892), and in 1810 *Poems by the Late Doctor John Shaw* was published at Philadelphia and Baltimore, with a memoir, including selections from his journal and letters, by John Elihu Hall [*q.v.*]. His poems reveal no conspicuous talent or originality, yet they were sufficiently pleasing to gain a place in nineteenth-century anthologies of American verse from Samuel Kettell's in 1829 to E. C. Stedman's in 1900. The best of them stand comparison with the work of Francis Hopkinson and with all but the finest of Philip Freneau's.

[Hall's memoir in *Poems by the Late Dr. John Shaw* (1810) is the only authority for Shaw's life but is generally inaccessible. The best secondary account is John Ruhräh, "John Shaw—A Medical Poet of Md.," *Annals of Medical Hist.*, Sept. 1921. See also H. A. Kelly and W. L. Burrage, *Am. Medic. Biogs.* (1920); E. F. Cordell, *Hist. Sketch of the Univ. of Md. School of Medicine* (1891); E. A. and G. L. Duyckinck, *Cyc. of Am. Lit.* (1875), vol. I.]

G. H. G.

SHAW, LEMUEL (Jan. 9, 1781–Mar. 30, 1861), jurist, was born in Barnstable, Mass., the second son of Oakes Shaw and his second wife Susanna, who was a daughter of John H. Hayward of Braintree. The Shaws were descendants of Abraham Shaw, who left Halifax, England, in 1636 and settled in Dedham, Mass. Oakes Shaw (a Congregationalist minister, was pastor of the West Church in Barnstable forty-seven years. Lemuel was named for his uncle, Dr. Hayward of Boston, father of George Hayward [*q.v.*], the surgeon. Taught at home by his father except for a few months at Braintree he entered Harvard in 1796. There he taught school in winter vacations. After graduating with high rank in 1800, he taught for a year in a Boston public school, and wrote articles and read proof for the *Boston Gazette,* a Federalist newspaper. In August 1801 he began studying law in Boston under David Everett [*q.v.*]. Meanwhile he learned French proficiently from a refugee, Antoine Jay, afterwards a founder in France of the liberal *Constitutionnel*. In 1802 he moved with Everett to Amherst, N. H., where besides doing legal work he contributed a poem on dancing and translations from French to the *Farmers' Cabinet,* a local newspaper. He became engaged to Nancy Melville, daughter of Maj. Thomas Melville of Boston, the original of Holmes's "The Last Leaf," but she died soon afterwards.

Admitted to the bar in Hillsboro County, N. H., in September 1804, and in Plymouth County, Mass., in November, he began practice in Boston. When his associate left Boston after being acquitted of murder in a political quarrel, he practised alone for fifteen years; about 1822 he took Sidney Bartlett, an able trial lawyer, as his junior partner. His practice gradually became large, but he was less known as an advocate than as the adviser of important commercial enterprises. On Jan. 6, 1818, he married Elizabeth Knapp, daughter of Josiah Knapp of Boston. She died in 1822, leaving a son and a daughter, who became the wife of Herman Melville [*q.v.*], nephew of Shaw's former fiancée. On Aug. 29, 1827, he married Hope Savage, daughter of Dr. Samuel Savage of Barnstable; they had two sons. He was admirably prepared for his judicial career by numerous public positions. He was a representative in the General Court in 1811–14, 1820, and 1829, a state senator in 1821–22, and a member of the constitutional convention of 1820. He also held many offices in Boston. In 1822, with few precedents to guide him, he drew the first charter of the city, which lasted until 1913. On the death of Chief Justice Isaac Parker [*q.v.*], Gov. Levi Lincoln,

1782–1868 [*q.v.*], offered Shaw the appointment. Though it meant giving up a practice of $15,000–$20,000 a year for a salary of $3500, he accepted. His commission was issued Aug. 30, 1830, and he served thirty years, resigning Aug. 21, 1860.

His exceptionally long judicial career coincided with the development of many important industries, so that his great abilities had full scope for making the law on such matters as water power, railroads, and other public utilities. Probably no other state judge has so deeply influenced commercial and constitutional law throughout the nation. Almost all the principles laid down by him have proved sound, although his remarkable skill in expounding the unfortunate fellow-servant rule considerably delayed the replacement of that rule by workmen's compensation. An opinion by Shaw rarely lends itself to isolated quotations; its strength lies in the entire solidity of its reasoning. "His words had weight rather than brilliancy or eloquence" (Chase, *post*, p. 278), and his greatness came from his personality as well as from his intellectual powers. He was no mere writer of opinions but preëminently a magistrate. In Shaw's time the chief justice sat often at trials. In such work he was thorough, systematic, very patient, with a remarkable power to charge juries so that they understood the exact questions before them. Among his cases that excited great public interest were the trial in 1834 of the anti-Catholic rioters who destroyed the Ursuline convent in Charlestown (*Commonwealth* vs. *Buzzell*, 33 *Mass. Reports*, 153) and that in 1850 of Prof. John White Webster [*q.v.*] for murdering Dr. George Parkman (*Commonwealth* vs. *Webster*, 59 *Mass. Reports*, 295). A notable example of his courage and integrity was his refusal in 1851 to release Sims, the fugitive slave, on *habeas corpus* (61 *Mass. Reports*, 285); he was strongly opposed to slavery, but he felt bound by the Constitution and the law, and disregarded both the violence of the mob and the denunciations of the respectable.

Widely read in English literature, he was also attracted by new mechanical processes and was a member of many learned and charitable societies. He was fellow of Harvard College from 1834 until his death, and an overseer from 1831 to 1853, two offices rarely united. In politics he was a Federalist and a Webster Whig, but remained all his life a free-trader. He attended Unitarian services, though he was never a communicant. Fond of entertaining and dining out, he was simple and affectionate in his home life, his interest in the social events of his household extending to the minutest details. After his resignation from the bench, his health failed, and

he died within a few months. He was buried in Mt. Auburn cemetery.

[The best biog. is that of F. H. Chase, *Lemuel Shaw, Chief Justice of the Supreme Judicial Court of Mass., 1830–1860* (1918), reviewed by E. H. Abbot, *Harvard Law Rev.*, Dec. 1918. A pamphlet, *Lemuel Shaw, Chief Justice of the Supreme Judicial Court of Mass.* (1885), reprints articles by S. S. Shaw and P. E. Aldrich in *Memorial Biogs. New England Hist. Geneal Soc.*, vol. IV (1885) and by B. F. Thomas in *Am. Law Rev.*, Oct. 1867. See also J. H. Beale, in *Great Am. Lawyers*, vol. III (1907), ed. by W. D. Lewis; C. G. Loring, in *Proc. Am. Acad. of Arts and Sci., 1860–1862*, vol. V (1862); *The Proc. at the Meeting of the Bar at the Birthplace of Chief Justice Shaw, West Barnstable, Mass., Aug. 4, 1916* (n.d.); W. T. Davis, *Hist. of the Judiciary of Mass.* (1900); obituaries in *New England Hist. and Geneal. Reg.*, July 1861, *Boston Daily Advertiser*, Apr. 1, 1861, *Boston Transcript*, Mar. 30, 1861, *Daily Evening Traveller* (Boston), Mar. 30, Apr. 1, 9, 1861. Shaw's opinions appear in 27–81 *Mass. Reports*. The proceedings of the bench and bar on his resignation are in 15 *Gray*, 599, and on his death in 1 *Allen*, 597.]

Z. C., Jr.

SHAW, LESLIE MORTIER (Nov. 2, 1848–Mar. 28, 1932), governor of Iowa, secretary of the treasury, banker, typified in his entire career Yankee business genius developed and modified by a midwestern, frontier environment. He was born at Morristown, Vt., but his parents, Boardman O. and Lovisa (Spaulding) Shaw, soon removed to a farm in Stowe township. His youthful ambition was to become a Western landowner, and after graduating from the village academy he taught school only long enough to secure the funds to go out, in 1869, to an uncle's farm in eastern Iowa. Two years later he entered the neighboring Cornell College, where, after supporting himself by farm labor, schoolteaching, and selling fruit trees, he graduated in 1874. Meanwhile his interest had shifted to the law, and in 1876 he completed the course at the Iowa College of Law, Des Moines, and started practice at Denison, where he had made friendships as a salesman. The following year, Dec. 6, 1877, he married Alice Crawshaw of Clinton County, the daughter of a pioneer farmer. They had three children, a son and two daughters.

Shaw's legal business was at first so light that he was forced to continue selling apple trees. He recognized that the chief need of his productive agricultural region was credit, and in 1880, with his partner, organized a bank and a mortgage loan business with branches in neighboring towns. For funds he turned to Vermont savings banks, persuading some of their officials to view the region at first hand. The result was the investment of several millions to the advantage of all concerned. Shaw was active in community business, educational, and religious organizations. His Methodist connections were an especial asset. His leadership in Sunday school work attracted state-wide attention, while his lay membership in four General Conferences (1888–1900) gave him national prominence in ecclesiastical circles. His political career began in 1896 when he was invited by fellow businessmen to reply to one of William Jennings Bryan's preconvention speeches. His presentation of his argument, illustrated by charts of price and currency trends, was so convincing that he was called upon for speeches throughout the campaign. The reputation thus gained was responsible for his nomination for governor after a deadlock in the Republican convention the next year. He was elected and served two terms (1898–1902), giving particular attention to institutional expansion and reorganization, especially of the state school system in all its branches.

Shortly after his retirement, in January 1902, President Theodore Roosevelt unexpectedly named him to head the Treasury Department. The selection, remarkable in view of Shaw's small-city background and the fact that Iowa already had a cabinet member in James Wilson, the secretary of agriculture, was due to Shaw's conspicuous position as a champion of the gold standard in the campaign of 1896, as permanent chairman of the International Monetary Convention in 1898, and as a campaigner for Roosevelt in 1900, as well as to political expediency in the removal of a potential rival in 1904. As secretary, Shaw resorted to unprecedented expedients for dealing with the pressing credit stringency—liberalizing the security and waiving the reserve requirement for government bank deposits; withholding funds, for deposit in time of need; artificially stimulating gold importation; and regulating note issues by executive decree —that were condemned by unfriendly critics as legally unwarranted and economically unsound. At the same time his ultra-protectionist views made the President uneasy. Nevertheless, when the Secretary desired to resign in 1905, Roosevelt persuaded him to remain until March 1907.

Shaw then spent a few years in metropolitan banking. He was head of the Carnegie Trust Company of New York in 1907–08 and of the First Mortgage Guarantee & Trust Company of Philadelphia, 1909–13. He was an avowed candidate for the presidential nomination in 1908, but received no serious consideration. Until 1918 he retained a New York City business address, but his residence after 1913 was in Washington, where he devoted himself to writing and lecturing. As a speaker he had a quaint, racy humor and a fund of apt anecdotes, drawn largely from personal experiences, that made him effective on Chautauqua circuit and political stump. His basic ideas, national dependence upon high protection and domestic *laissez-faire*, were well summarized in his books, *Current Issues* (1908) and *Vanishing Landmarks: The Trend Toward Bolshevism* (1919). He wrote and spoke for party measures and candidates until within a year of his death, which occurred in Washington, D. C.

[*The Messages and Proclamations of the Govs. of Iowa*, vol. VII (1905), ed. by B. F. Shambaugh; *Ann. Reports of the Secretary of the Treasury*, 1902–06; *Selections from the Correspondence of Theodore Roosevelt and Henry Cabot Lodge* (1925), vol. II; H. H. Kohlsaat, *From McKinley to Harding* (1923); G. E. Roberts, "Leslie M. Shaw," *Independent*, Jan. 16, 1902; A. P. Andrew, "The Treasury and the Banks under Secretary Shaw," *Quart. Jour. of Econ.*, Aug. 1907; *Who's Who in America*, 1930–31; *N. Y. Times*, Mar. 28, 29, 1932; *Des Moines Register*, Mar. 29, 1932.]

E. D. R.

SHAW, MARY (Jan. 25, 1854–May 18, 1929), actress, was born in Boston, the daughter of Levi W. and Margaret (Keating) Shaw, her father being a native of New Hampshire and her mother of Ireland. After being educated in the public schools of Boston, she taught there from 1873 to 1878. Obtaining an engagement as a minor member of the Boston Museum Stock Company, she made her début there in a small part in an extravaganza and remained during the season of 1879–1880. In 1881 she appeared as Lady Sneerwell in New York and for a brief period was with Augustin Daly's company, her first real opportunity coming when she joined the company of Madame Helena Modjeska [*q.v.*] in the fall of 1883. She remained with Modjeska four seasons, acting Celia in *As You Like It,* Mariana in *Measure for Measure,* Hero in *Much Ado About Nothing,* and other important rôles. She is described by Modjeska (*post,* p. 463) as "a studious, intellectual young woman, with a great deal of talent." In 1890 she supported Julia Marlowe.

She made her first starring tour in the spring of 1890 in *A Drop of Poison,* adapted from the German, but it was only a *succès d'estime.* A reviewer in the *Boston Transcript* (May 6, 1890) said that "her exquisitely trained voice, her Delsartian truth and facility of gesture, her easy mastery of the technique of her art, assure her permanent occupancy of the high position to which she has won her way by such worthy effort." Although she remained a hard-working actress for many years, this prophecy was scarcely fulfilled. Many of the plays in which she was obliged to act were of very little merit, and she was obscured in inconsequential characters; other excellent plays that she brought out had in them no marked elements of stage popularity. She soon returned to the support of stars and to acting secondary parts in traveling companies.

She acted Roxy in *Pudd'nhead Wilson* with Frank Mayo, Gretchen in *Rip Van Winkle* with Joseph Jefferson [*qq.v.*], Marian in *Tess of the D'Urbervilles* with Minnie Maddern Fiske, and she was the original Amrah in the dramatization of Lew Wallace's novel, *Ben Hur*.

In 1899 she produced Ibsen's *Ghosts,* and acted Mrs. Alving then and on future occasions during the following twenty years or more. Her interpretation of that part and of the part of Hedda Gabler brought her much praise but little substantial encouragement. In October 1905 she appeared in New York as Mrs. Warren in George Bernard Shaw's *Mrs. Warren's Profession,* which was immediately suppressed by the municipal authorities because of what they called its immorality. Feeling that the play and its motive had been misunderstood, she later revived it several times. She was twice married. Her second husband was M. de Brissac, a stage manager of French origin, but their life together was neither long nor happy. By her first marriage she had one son. She took an active part in feminist, suffragist, and humanitarian movements. She died in New York in retirement.

[Boston vital records; *Boston Museum . . . An Interesting Retrospect . . . Issued for Season of 1880–81* (pamphlet) ; J. B. Clapp and E. F. Edgett, *Players of the Present* (1901) ; T. Allston Brown, *A Hist. of the New York Stage* (1903), vol. III; Helena Modjeska, *Memories and Impressions* (1910) ; Eugene Tompkins and Quincy Kilby, *The Hist. of the Boston Theatre* (1908) ; William Winter, *The Wallet of Time* (1913), vol. II ; John Parker, *Who's Who in the Theatre,* 1925 ; *Who's Who in America,* 1928–29 ; *N. Y. Dramatic Mirror,* June 26, 1897 ; July 15, 1899 ; Oct. 26, 1910 ; obituaries in *N. Y. Times,* May 19, 1929, and *Boston Transcript,* May 20, 1929.]   E.F.E.

SHAW, NATHANIEL (Dec. 5, 1735–Apr. 15, 1782), a leading merchant of New London, Conn., acted during the Revolution as naval agent both for Connecticut and for the Continental Congress. His father, Nathaniel, a native of Fairfield, Conn., settled in New London before 1730, became a sea-captain in the Irish trade, founded a mercantile house, and married Temperance Harris. The younger Nathaniel took over his father's business and by the early 1760's was an established merchant in the West Indian trade. Occasionally he transacted business in London and the Mediterranean, but commonly his brigs and sloops took lumber, cattle, or provisions to the West Indies and brought back sugar and molasses, either to be landed at his wharves and warehouses in New London or shipped direct to his correspondents, Peter Vandervoort of New York, Thomas and Isaac Wharton of Philadelphia, and George Erving or William Miller of Boston. A typical Connecticut Yankee, shrewd, close, a stickler for his bond, a

curt letter-writer, he adhered rigidly to the high ethical code prescribed by the commerce of his age. Generous as a citizen, he presented his native town in 1767 with a fire engine, the "Compleatest ever Imported into this Continent," and was a proprietor of the Union School. He was married, July 20, 1758, to Lucretia, daughter of Daniel Harris and widow of Josiah Rogers.

The British Acts of Parliament of the 1760's found Shaw unwaveringly on the colonial side. The Sugar Act made him an avowed enemy of those "cruizing Pyrates," the revenue sloops, and as hard money became scarcer, he landed more and more cargoes without clearing at the custom house, "for In Short brown Sugars will not bear to pay dutys on" (Rogers, *post,* p. 226). In 1769 Boston custom commissioners accused him of aiding in the destruction of the revenue sloop *Liberty* and of rescuing his own vessel with prohibited goods. His safe reply was an offer to maintain his innocence before any jury in the colonies. During these troubled years he participated as a leading figure in every form of organized colonial action against British restrictive measures. By December 1774 he was negotiating the purchase of powder for the general assembly; a year later he mournfully acknowledged the end of all trade, "no Bussiness now but preparation for Warr, Ravaging Villages, Burning of Towns" (Rogers, p. 278). New duties awaited him, however. The Council of Safety of Connecticut named him agent for the colony, with the task of fitting and supplying ships and caring for sick sailors, while the Continental Congress appointed him its agent in Connecticut to take charge of prize vessels and purchase necessaries for the fleet. He procured provisions, blankets, and tents for the Continental troops, cannon and powder, pilots to guide the French fleet into the Sound; he acted as commissary for the exchange of naval prisoners; he examined the accounts and sold the prizes of colony captains. He was the man in Connecticut to whom everyone turned to get business done. In 1778 the general assembly gave him additional authority, the management and direction, as marine agent, of all armed vessels belonging to or fitted by the state. He corresponded with Washington, who once honored him with a visit. He served two terms as deputy to the assembly. Meanwhile, beyond the commissions he took on the naval business he transacted, he had an eye to his own advantage. Where once he ran a fleet of trading vessels, he now owned a string of privateers, the most pretentious, the *General Putnam,* being a brig of twenty guns. His gains by these means scarcely compensated, however, for the losses he sustained when Benedict Arnold's attack on New London in 1781 destroyed his wharves and warehouses. In that same year he opened commercial connections with Amsterdam merchants. In December his wife died from an infection caught from the sick prisoners she nursed. The following April, while hunting ducks off Lester's Rocks, Shaw was accidentally wounded by a discharge from his own gun. Three days later he died, confessing the "emptiness of this world, and the Vanity of all its Glory" (Rogers, p. 330). He left no children.

[The only full account of Shaw is in E. E. Rogers, "Connecticut's Naval Office at New London during the War of the American Revolution," *New London County Hist. Soc. Colls.*, vol. II (1933), which contains many documents, including Shaw's mercantile letter book, from the Nathaniel and Thomas Shaw Letters and Papers in the Yale Library. See also F. M. Caulkins, *Hist. of New London, Conn.* (1852); *The Pub. Records of the Colony of Conn.*, vol. XV (1890) and *The Public Records of the State of Conn.*, vols. I, II (1894–95), III (1922); *Naval Records of the Am. Revolution* (1906), ed. by C. H. Lincoln; *Conn. Hist. Soc. Colls.*, vols. XVI (1916), XVIII–XX (1920–23).] S. M. P.

SHAW, OLIVER (Mar. 13, 1779–Dec. 31, 1848), musician and composer, was born at Middleboro, Mass., one of eight children of Hannah (Heath) and John Shaw. As a young boy, he lost the sight of his right eye through an accident. When he was seventeen he attended the Bristol Academy at Taunton, Mass., and shortly after his graduation joined his father in seafaring enterprises. At twenty-one, when he was not fully recovered from yellow fever, he helped in taking nautical observations from the sun; this affected his remaining eye, and he was totally blind for the rest of his life. Blindness determined him to become a musician rather than a mariner. He first studied with John L. Berkenhead, a blind organist of Newport, R. I.; in 1803 he had lessons with Johann Christian Graupner [q.v.] in Boston, and some instruction on the clarinet from Thomas Granger. In 1807 he settled in Providence, R. I., where he remained until his death. He became organist of the First Congregational Church and gave music lessons in the homes of his pupils, led from house to house by a boy employed for the purpose. In 1809 he gathered a group of fellow musicians in Providence, among them Thomas Webb, and founded the Psallonian Society, "for the purpose of improving themselves in the knowledge and practice of sacred music, and inculcating a more correct taste in the choice and performance of it" (quoted in *Memorial, post*, p. 21). The society remained in existence until 1832, and in its twenty-three years gave thirty-one concerts. On Oct. 20, 1812, Shaw married Sarah Jenckes, daughter

of Caleb Jenckes, who bore him two sons and five daughters. His son, Oliver J. Shaw, was also a composer.

Shaw was important to his time not only for his compositions, which were characteristic of the sacred music of his day and were forerunners of the work of Lowell Mason [q.v.], but for his teaching and his interest in the betterment of church music. As a composer he represented the emergence of the native musician after the great immigration of foreigners in the latter eighteenth century. His best known hymn-tunes were "Taunton," "Bristol," and "Weybosset." One of his most popular sacred songs was "Mary's Tears," "sung at the oratorio performed by the Handel & Haydn Society in Boston, July 5th, 1817, in presence of the President of the United States" (Howard, *post*, p. 141). This program also contained Shaw's duet, "All Things Bright and Fair Are Thine." Others of his sacred songs were "Arrayed in Clouds of Golden Light," "The Missionary Angel," "There's Nothing True But Heaven," and works which show the trend of non-liturgical church music toward the ballad type. His secular compositions include "Bristol March," "Governor Arnold's March," and "Washington's Grand Centennial March," performed at the Providence Centennial Celebration in 1832. Several libraries have copies of Shaw's *For the Gentlemen* (Dedham, Mass., 1807): "A favourite selection of instrumental music . . . consisting principally of marches, airs, minuets, etc. Written chiefly in four parts, viz: two clarinets, flute and bassoon; or two violins, flute and violoncello."

[The most complete account of Shaw's career is given in the *Memorial of Oliver Shaw* (1884), ed. by Frederic Denison, A. A. Stanley, and E. K. Glezen. See also Thomas Williams, *A Discourse on the Life and Death of Oliver Shaw* (Boston, 1851); F. J. Metcalf, *Am. Writers and Compilers of Sacred Music* (1925); J. T. Howard, *Our Am. Music* (1931); death notice in *Newport Mercury*, Jan. 6, 1849.] J. T. H.

SHAW, PAULINE AGASSIZ (Feb. 6, 1841–Feb. 10, 1917), philanthropist, the youngest child of Cècile (Braun) and Jean Louis Rodolphe Agassiz [q.v.], was born in Neuchâtel, Switzerland. She lived there with her grandmother from the death of her mother in 1848 until she joined her father at Harvard College in 1850. As she grew up, her father formed the habit of inviting the more intimate companions of herself and her sister to his library for an afternoon each week, and she continually met his distinguished friends. She also assisted in the school for girls that her step-mother conducted in their home. In this environment she developed the charm and lovable personality that were to characterize her through life. When she was eighteen she accompanied her father on a trip to Europe, where he was entertained by scholars in England and France. On Nov. 30, 1860, she married Quincy Adams Shaw, president of the Calumet and Hecla Mining Company. He was the traveling companion and friend to whom Francis Parkman dedicated his *California and Oregon Trail* (1849) and was one of the first Americans to recognize the merits of the French landscape painters and to buy their works, particularly those of Millet. They had five children. Both before and after her husband's death in 1908 she interested herself in various philanthropies.

She did not use the fortune acquired by her husband merely to support long accepted types of educational and social service; instead, she was an educational and social pioneer, who, in three separate instances, saw the possibilities of some form of education that was too new and unproved to be supported by public funds, maintained it through the experimental period, and directed it so successfully that it came to be recognized and supported on a large scale at public expense. Thus she supported more than thirty kindergartens in and near Boston, after the school committee of Boston had, in September 1879, discontinued for lack of funds the public kindergartens established by the efforts of Elizabeth Peabody [*q.v.*] and others. By 1887 she had organized these kindergartens so fully and had so thoroughly demonstrated their usefulness that the school committee consented to reconsider the question. It examined her kindergartens, decided to reëstablish public kindergartens in Boston, and accepted fourteen kindergartens she had been supporting, together with the furniture and materials required in the instruction. She gave similar support to the manual training movement during its experimental period. After 1883 she provided the funds to give free normal instruction in various manual arts to teachers of the public schools and to support children's classes of manual arts in the public schools as well as in her North Bennet-Street Industrial School. Finally, in 1894, the school committee provided for manual training as a regular part of the school work. She also financed the Vocation Bureau of Boston, where Frank Parsons [*q.v.*] initiated work in vocational guidance, being its only annual contributor from March 1908 to June 1917, when the bureau was taken over by Harvard University. She founded and supported many other philanthropic and civic works, such as the Ruggles Street Neighborhood House, the Civic Service House, and the North Bennet-Street Industrial School.

[*Pauline Agassiz Shaw: Tributes paid her memory at the Memorial Service held April 8, 1917* (1917); *Ann. Report of the School Committee of . . . Boston, 1887* (1888), pp. 18–22; *Ibid. . . . . 1888* (1889), pp. 10–12; *Ibid. . . . 1892* (1893), pp. 9–20; *Ibid. . . . 1894* (1894); p. 31; *Documents of the School Committee of the City of Boston . . . 1887* (1887), no. 21; *Ibid. . . . 1891* (1892), no. 15; *Pioneers of the Kindergarten in America* (copr. 1924); L. A. Paton, *Elizabeth Cary Agassiz* (1919); *Fifty Years of Boston* (copr. 1932); Justin Winsor, *The Memorial History of Boston, 1630–1880*, vol. IV (1881), pp. 247, 405; J. M. Brewer, *The Vocational-Guidance Movement: its problems and possibilities* (1918), p. 23; *Arena*, July 1908, pp. 5, 6; Nov. 1908, p. 499; *Boston Evening Transcript*, June 10, 1908, June 12, 1908, Feb. 10, 1917; *New York Times*, Feb. 11, 1917; information from John M. Brewer, Graduate School of Education, Harvard University.]
E. C.

SHAW, SAMUEL (Oct. 2, 1754–May 30, 1794), Revolutionary officer, was born in Boston, Mass., the son of Francis and Sarah (Burt) Shaw. It is said that his grandfather, Thomas Shaw, emigrated from Scotland the third quarter of the seventeenth century. Samuel's father was a prosperous merchant, and the boy entered the counting-house early, but at the outbreak of the Revolution he obtained a commission as second-lieutenant in the artillery. He served during the siege of Boston and at its conclusion accompanied the army to New York. For a time he was stationed at Fort Washington. He participated in the battles of Trenton, Princeton, Brandywine, Germantown, and Monmouth, and shared in the sufferings of Valley Forge. During the remainder of the war, he served principally in New York and New England. He was promoted to the rank of first lieutenant in the 3rd Continental Artillery on Jan. 1, 1777, and became captain on Apr. 12, 1780. During much of the war he was aide-de-camp to General Knox. It was his fortune in the latter capacity to be present when Washington took possession of New York after its evacuation by the British and to assist in arranging for the disbandment of the Continental Army. He was secretary of the committee of officers that formed the Society of the Cincinnati. On retiring to civil life, he was commended by Washington for intelligence, activity, and bravery.

His capacity for business, demonstrated while in the army, led a group of merchants, bent upon establishing commercial relations with the Orient, to offer him the post of supercago on the *Empress of China,* the first American vessel dispatched to Canton. He set sail in February 1784 and returned in May 1785. He was appointed by General Knox to a place in the war department. He had in the meantime addressed a letter to John Jay, the secretary of foreign affairs, describing his voyage, and in 1786 he had the honor of being elected by Congress the first American consul in China. Resigning his position in the war department, he set sail for Canton in February 1786. After an absence of three years he returned to the United States. His appointment as consul was renewed by President Washington. He sailed for China again in 1790 on board the *Massachusetts,* one of the finest merchantmen of the day, which had been built at his direction near Quincy, Mass. After selling the vessel to agents of the Portuguese government in the East Indies, he invested the proceeds in a return cargo and arrived in the United States in January 1792. On Aug. 21 of that year he married Hannah Phillips, the daughter of William Phillips of Boston. The following year he embarked on his third and last voyage to the Orient. While visiting Bombay, he developed a disease of the liver. Finding no cure at Canton, he took passage for America and died near the Cape of Good Hope.

[*The Journals of Major Samuel Shaw,* with a life of the author by Josiah Quincy (1847) ; *Memorials of the Mass. Soc. of the Cincinnati,* ed. by J. M. Bugbee (1890) ; F. B. Heitman, *Hist. Register of Officers of the Continental Army* (1893) ; *Mass. Soldiers and Sailors of the Rev. War,* vol. XIV (1906) ; Amasa Delano, *A Narrative of a Voyager and Travels* (1817) ; J. W. Foster, *Amer. Diplomacy in the Orient* (1903) ; I. N. P. Stokes, *The Iconography of Manhattan Island,* vol. V (1926) ; mother's name from family Bible.] E. E. C.

SHAW, THOMAS (May 5, 1838–Jan. 19, 1901), inventor, was the son of James and Catherine (Snyder) Shaw, and was born in Philadelphia, Pa., where his first American ancestor had settled in 1694. Shaw was compelled to go to work at a very early age when his father, a merchant, lost everything in a coal-mining venture. This was not a hardship, for he disliked going to school and much preferred to invent and construct useful things, his favorite occupation in his spare time. He worked in grocery stores and other such places until he was sixteen, when he apprenticed himself to a machinist. His mastery of the machinist's trade was rapid and he soon began serious invention, his first patent (Apr. 27, 1858) being for a gas meter. Other inventions that he patented the following year included a press mold for glass, a gas stove, and a sewing machine. About this time he began working in the Cyclops Machine Works in Philadelphia, and in a comparatively short time became superintendent. When the William Butcher (later Midvale) Steel Works was organized in 1867, Shaw took over the superintendency of this plant as well. By this time he had a number of other inventions to his credit, including steam gages, a stone crusher, and a grinding machine. Now he turned his attention to iron and steel manufacture. In the course of the succeeding three years he devised a process for rolling and applying steel tires to cast-iron and invented the bolster and semi-elliptic spring for railroad cars, a centrifugal shot-making machine which eliminated the usual shot tower, and a steam-power hammer, as well as several other valuable devices of general utility. One of the simplest, yet most useful of these was the spring-lock nut washer patented in 1868 and put to immediate and almost universal use on railroads.

About 1871 Shaw gave up his connections with the Midvale and Cyclops companies to devote his whole time to the development and introduction of his own inventions. He established a manufacturing plant in Philadelphia, which he maintained until his death. The scope of his inventions, which was unusually wide, involved almost two hundred patents and included tools, engineers' special appliances, oil burners, United States standard mercury pressure gages, hydraulic pumps, noise quieting nozzles and mufflers for locomotives and steamships, steam engine and pump governors, pile drivers, power hammers, miners' safety lamps, and apparatus for testing and recording mine gases. Shaw's pile driver, patented in 1868 and 1870, was unique in that it made use of the explosive force of gunpowder and in one operation could drive a forty-foot wood pile, fourteen inches in diameter, its entire length into firm ground without injuring the timber. It was successfully used in driving most of the piles for the United States Naval Station at League Island, Philadelphia. Another very original and valuable invention was an apparatus to detect and record deadly gases in mines, for which he received a series of patents between 1886 and 1890. With it gases could be automatically tested throughout the mine at five-minute intervals by a tester above ground and, through a system of high pressure air signals in the mine, workers could be warned of danger in time to seek safety. The Shaw gas tester, as it came to be known, was capable of detecting inflammable gases to within one one-hundredth of one per cent., and was officially adopted by Pennsylvania and Ohio, as well as by Germany and Russia. During his later years Shaw received many offers for his services from foreign governments, all of which he declined. He married Matilda Miller Garber, who, with a daughter, survived him at the time of his sudden death at Hammonton, N. J. He was buried in Philadelphia.

[*Biog. Album of Prominent Pennsylvanians, Phila.,* 3 ser. (1890) ; J. W. Jordan, *Encyc. of Pa. Biog.,* vol. I (1914) ; *Index to Jour. of Franklin Inst., 1826–1885* (1890) ; Patent Office records ; obituary in *Pub. Ledger* (Phila.), Jan. 21, 1901.] C. W. M—n.

SHAW, WILLIAM SMITH (Aug. 12, 1778–Apr. 25, 1826), librarian of the Boston Athenaeum, was born in Haverhill, Mass., son of the Rev. John Shaw and Elizabeth (Smith) Shaw, the sister of Abigail Adams [q.v.]. Sickly and lame, he graduated at Harvard in 1798 and became for two years private secretary to President John Adams in Philadelphia. At Washington's death, in his official capacity he carried the resolution of Congress to the widow. From 1801 to 1804 he studied law in Boston with William Sullivan and became a member of the bar. His aunt, Abigail Adams, stimulated his love for books, and he soon resolved to improve the plane of American literature. He also began a collection of pamphlets that became notable. He was active in promoting literary enterprises, procuring subscriptions for a new periodical, *The Port Folio,* and for John Marshall's *Life of Washington* (5 vols., 1804–07). For Hannah Adams [q.v.] he worked unceasingly, by carrying books to her door, introducing new friends, procuring subscriptions to her writings, and, when age and infirmities overtook her, he raised an annuity for her support and attended to all her affairs. In 1805 he helped to found the Anthology Society, which took over *The Monthly Anthology,* a magazine of bookish miscellany founded in 1803. The Society's editors met weekly for supper, and, as treasurer, he was very active, although he seems to have retired at eleven o'clock each evening. For volumes I and II he wrote on trial by jury; and elsewhere in the first six volumes, of the ten, he had occasional contributions of minor note. An example of his style appears in his review of an oration where he says that the orator "added potency to omnipotence ... soared above the empyrean, till his wings were melted in the blaze of his own eloquence, and then tumbled and descended below the bottom of the abyss of bathos" (Aug. 1806, p. 444).

The society, having opened an Anthology Reading Room, transferred it in October 1806 to five trustees. This library the next year became the Boston Athenaeum and was so ardently fostered by Shaw as librarian from 1807 to 1822 that he became known as "Athenaeum Shaw." He gave his services. Judge William Tudor pictured his activities: "That dog Shaw goes everywhere. He knows everybody. Everybody knows him. If he sees a book, pamphlet, or manuscript —Oh Sir! The Athenaeum must have this. Well, have it he will and have it he must" (Tudor's comment on back of manuscript presented to the Library of the Boston Athenaeum). He was also secretary until 1823. He had an accurate knowledge of the value of books, coins, and medals.

Appointment as clerk of the federal district court for Massachusetts in 1806 relieved him from the strain of active practice of the law. He held the office for twelve years and devoted his leisure to building up the Athenaeum library. He aided neighboring organizations with gifts and money, being a member of many historical, scientific, and literary societies. His last years were afflicted with illness, and he died, unmarried, in Boston.

[J. B. Felt, *Memorials of William Smith Shaw* (1852) with correspondence and notes; Josiah Quincy, *The Hist. of the Boston Athenaeum* (1851) ; the *Journ. of the Proceedings of the Society which Conducts the Monthly Anthology,* with introduction by M. A. DeWolfe Howe (1910).]   C. K. B.

SHAYS, DANIEL (c. 1747–Sept. 29, 1825), soldier, insurgent, is generally said to have been born at Hopkinton, Mass., where Patrick Shay married Margaret Dempsey in 1744, although the birth records for that town do not contain his name (*Vital Records of Hopkinton, Mass.,* 1911). Most accounts give the year of his birth as 1747, but the *New York Evening Post,* Oct. 15, 1825, states his age at death as eighty-four. His origin was humble and his early life obscure. On July 18, 1772, the marriage intentions of Daniel Shay and Abigail Gilbert were recorded at Brookfield (*Vital Records of Brookfield, Mass.,* 1909). At the outbreak of the Revolution, Shays responded to the alarm at Lexington and served for eleven days. He was in the battle of Bunker Hill and was cited and promoted for gallant conduct. He also served at Ticonderoga, Saratoga, and Stony Point, and on Jan. 1, 1777, was commissioned captain in the 5th Massachusetts. He was very popular with his men, having the reputation of being considerate of his subordinates and at the same time a brave and efficient officer (Sanderson, *post,* pp. 177, 180; Warren MS.). Toward the end of the war a handsome sword was presented to him by Lafayette, which poverty led him to sell. In 1780 he resigned from the army, settling in Pelham, Mass., where in 1781 and 1782 he served as a member of the Committee of Safety. He was subsequently elected to various town offices.

Following the prosperity after the signing of peace, an acute economic depression, felt throughout all the rural districts, swept over the country. The wide-spread demand for redress of grievances, met by the obstinate non-compliance of the legislature, resulted in western Massachusetts in a resort to force, and in this phase of the movement Shays became so prominent that his name is given to the whole uprising— "Shays's Rebellion"—although others were as active as he. On Aug. 29, 1786, the insurgents prevented the sitting of the court of common pleas and general sessions, intending merely to prevent their giving judgments in debt cases before grievances were redressed; but the leaders soon began to fear that indictments would be brought against them, and they therefore determined to prevent the sitting of the supreme court at Springfield on Sept. 26. Major-General William Shepard [q.v.] of the Hampshire militia prepared to defend the court. On the day appointed, 800 militia faced about the same number of insurgents, and Shays made his first historical appearance as leader. He was chairman of a committee which drew up resolutions that the court should be allowed to sit, provided it dealt with no case involving indictments of insurgents or concerning debts. An agreement was reached by which both militia and insurgents disbanded, and the court adjourned.

Outbreaks continued, however, and the legislature made no real redress of the grievances, although it enraged the insurgents by suspending the writ of *habeas corpus*. By January 1787 the insurgents had given up hope of peaceful reform, and the legislature had chosen Gen. Benjamin Lincoln [q.v.] to suppress what had become an armed rebellion. Shays, as the leader of a force of insurgents at Wilbraham, and Luke Day, head of another band near by, intended to make a combined attack on the arsenal at Springfield, but owing to a failure of communication, Shays's force attacked alone. It was defeated by the militia under Shepard and dispersed. Lincoln, who had arrived after the attack, then marched against Day and broke up his force. Shays, with what was left of his band, at once retreated to Amherst, where he was joined by stragglers from the other party. Lincoln followed, and Shays fell back to Pelham, then to Hadley, and Hatfield. On Jan. 29, Lincoln sent word that he would recommend to the General Court for pardon any insurgents who would lay down their arms and take the oath of allegiance. He wrote to Shays offering the same terms. Shays replied that the rebellion was due to real grievances but that the people would disperse if given a general pardon, and asked for an armistice until petitions could be presented to the legislature. Lincoln, however, was without authority to delay operations, and on the night of Feb. 2, 1787, marched with his men through a snow storm, fell on Shays's troops at Petersham, and completely routed them. Shays fled to Vermont, and was one of the few exempted from the general pardon given later in the year. He was condemned to death by the supreme court, but in February

1788 petitioned for pardon, which was granted June 13.

Some time afterward, Shays moved to Schoharie County, N. Y., where he lived for a number of years, then moved on to western New York, settling in Sparta, where he died. In his old age he was allowed a federal pension for his services in the American Revolution. He was a man of no cultural background, little education, and not much ability, but he was brave and honest, and convinced that in the rebellion of 1786–87 he was fighting the same battle of the people which he had fought in the Revolution.

[The earlier general histories, such as J. G. Holland, *Hist. of Western Mass.* (2 vols., 1855), and G. R. Minot, *The Hist. of the Insurrections in Mass.* (1810), take an unfavorable view of Shays. One of the most important accounts is in the paper by Jonathan Smith, "Features of Shays' Rebellion" (1903), in *Hist. Papers Read at Meetings of the Clinton Hist. Soc.*, vol. I (n.d.). See also Grindall Reynolds, "Concord during the Shays Rebellion," in *A Collection of Historical and Other Papers* (1895); S. A. Green, "Groton during Shays's Rebellion," *Proc. Mass. Hist. Soc.*, 2 ser., I (1885); H. K. Sanderson, *Lynn in the Revolution* (1909); C. O. Parmenter, *Hist. of Pelham, Mass.* (1898); J. P. Warren, "The Confederation and the Shays Rebellion," *Am. Hist. Rev.*, Oct. 1905, and "The Shays Rebellion" (MS.), in the Harvard Library. Contemporary newspapers are cited in J. T. Adams, *New England in the Republic* (1926). There is much manuscript material in the Mass. Archives.]   J. T. A.

SHEA, JOHN DAWSON GILMARY (July 22, 1824–Feb. 22, 1892), historian and editor, son of James and Mary Ann (Flannigan) Shea, was born in New York City. His father came from Ireland in 1815, tutored in General Schuyler's household, established a private school with Eber Wheaton, taught English in Columbia College, served as a captain of militia and as a Tammany chieftain, and became a leader in Irish and Catholic affairs, though he fought Bishops Dubois and Hughes on the trustee question. His mother traced a maternal descent from Nicholas Upsall, one of Boston's earliest settlers, and also from Thomas McCurtin, an Irish schoolmaster, who established a classical school at Mount Holly, N. J., in 1762. Baptized John Dawson, Shea adopted the name Gilmary when he became a novice in the Society of Jesus. He early showed a liking for books and received his first training in the Sisters of Charity school, Mulberry Street, and in the Columbia Grammar School, graduating from the latter in 1837. Friendly connections procured him a position in the counting-house of Don Tomas, a Spanish merchant, where he gained a knowledge of Spanish and wrote a life of Alvarez Carrillo de Albornoz, but apparently learned little about the acquisition of money, if one may judge from his life of unprofitable scholarship and penury. When only fourteen years old he contributed an article to the *Children's Catholic Magazine*.

Tiring of trade, he studied law and in 1846 was admitted to the bar, but found himself more interested in reading history than in preparing briefs. Fascinated by George Bancroft's *History of the United States,* he became a member of the New York Historical Society and wrote a series of articles on "Our Martyrs" for the *United States Catholic Magazine* (1846–47), which may have led him, in 1848, into the Society of Jesus. As a novice, he studied at St. John's College, Fordham (1848–50), and at St. Mary's College, Montreal (1850–52), where he learned enough canon law to be consulted in later years by various prelates and acquired a fluent command of French. Of more vital importance was his association with the trained Jesuit historian, Felix Martin, whose biography of Father Jogues he translated in 1885. During this period he also came under the influence of the historical editor, Edmund Bailey O'Callaghan [*q.v.*]. In 1852, the year he gave up thoughts of a religious life, Shea published *Discovery and Exploration of the Mississippi Valley,* which he dedicated to Jared Sparks. This work won him the favor of contemporary historians and invitations to become a corresponding member of the historical societies of Wisconsin, Maryland, and Massachusetts—at the time a rare honor for a Catholic.

Meanwhile, he had commenced to write the innumerable articles which appeared through succeeding years in the *United States Catholic Magazine,* the *Catholic World,* the *United States Historical Magazine,* the *American Catholic Quarterly Review,* the Boston *Pilot,* and similar publications. While most of these contributions were of a popular nature, they were far better than the ordinary article of the same type, and added something to Shea's fame. Lack of money and his marriage in 1854 to Sophie Savage, of old Puritan lineage, by whom he had two daughters, compelled him to form a connection with E. Dunigan & Brother, publishers. For this firm he compiled *First Book of History* (1854), *A General History of Modern Europe* (1854), and *A School History of the United States* (1855), which were adopted rather widely in Catholic schools. Other works of his were published by D. & J. Sadlier, including *An Elementary History of the United States* (1855) and *The Catholic Church in the United States: A Sketch of Its Ecclesiastical History* (1856), a translation of the work by Henri de Courcy, revised and enlarged in 1879.

Shea, under pressure, found time to do many things: to contribute several chapters to Justin Winsor's *Narrative and Critical History of America*; to compile articles for encyclopedias; to edit Sadlier's *General Catholic Directory* (1858–90); to assist James Lenox [*q.v.*] in collecting Americana; to serve Archbishop Hughes as a diocesan historiographer with a resultant volume, *The Catholic Churches of New York City* (1878); to edit the *Library of American Linguistics* (1860–74), including some fifteen Indian grammars and dictionaries; to work on the *Historical Magazine* (1855–67); to edit without credit a pocket Catholic Bible and a patriotic volume of sketches, *The Fallen Brave* (1861); and to join John Ireland, R. H. Clarke, and Charles G. Herbermann in founding the United States Catholic Historical Society, of which he was editor (1887–89) and president (1890). Despite all these varied enterprises, he continued to work in his own field, compiling *History of the Catholic Missions among the Indian Tribes of the United States, 1529–1854* (1854); editing twenty-six volumes of Jesuit relations (published in a very small edition as Shea's Cramoisy Press Series, 1857–87) which had not been included in the collection issued by the Canadian government; publishing *History and General Description of New France* (1866–72), a translation in six volumes of P. F. X. de Charlevoix's work; and writing his monumental, critical, and impartial *History of the Catholic Church in the United States* in four large volumes (1886–92), for which he received some financial assistance from a committee of the hierarchy which had been instructed by the Plenary Council of Baltimore (1884) to cooperate with him.

An outstanding historian and the greatest American Catholic historical writer, Shea found little contemporary appreciation for his work. Catholic colleges were not teaching history beyond a stilted drill in questions and answers; American history was not recognized; the hierarchy was more interested in building churches and charitable institutions than in records and historical scholarship. The Jesuits gave him some support when he prepared the *Memorial of the First Centenary of Georgetown College* (1891), and on his death took over his rich collection of Americana. Impoverished, he wrote to Archbishop Corrigan in 1889, asking for a clerkship in the chancery office or even in Calvary Cemetery office, for he was too proud to become a pensioner. When the Catholic University at Washington was established, he vainly hoped for a call to the chair of history. Instead, he was given an editorship on Herman Ridder's *Catholic News* (1889), which enabled him to support his family in a humble home in Elizabeth, N. J., and to complete his great historical work. In that city he died.

[Peter Guilday, in *U. S. Catholic Hist. Soc. Hist. Records and Studies*, vol. XVII (July 1926); M. F. Vallette, "Dr. John Gilmary Shea," *Ibid.*, vol. I, pt. 1 (Jan. 1899); bibliog. of Shea's works, *Ibid.*, vol. VI, pt. 2 (Dec. 1912); R. H. Clarke, in *The Illustrated Catholic Family Annual* (1893); *Catholic News*, Mar. 2, 1892; *Cath. World*, Apr. 1892; *Am. Catholic Quart. Rev.*, Apr. 1913; *New York Freeman's Jour.*, Feb. 26, 1887; *The Sun* (N. Y.), Feb. 23, 1892.]   R.J.P.

SHEARMAN, THOMAS GASKELL (Nov. 25, 1834–Sept. 29, 1900), lawyer and economist, son of John and Sarah Shearman, was born in Birmingham, England, and at the age of nine was brought to New York by his father, his mother arriving later. His father, who was by turns a physician, writer, and preacher, soon became an invalid, and young Shearman at the age of twelve was obliged to shift for himself. His formal education ceased at thirteen; at fourteen he was a messenger boy, earning a dollar weekly and buying books with his savings; and at twenty-four he was an expert bookkeeper in a dry-goods store. He married Ella Partridge of Brooklyn in 1859. Almost immediately afterward he determined to become a lawyer and began studying in the office of Austin and Benjamin Vaughan Abbott [*qq.v.*]. Within six months he passed his examinations and was admitted to the bar.

While a student he began writing on procedure, and in 1861 he published, with John L. Tillinghast, the first volume of *Practice, Pleadings, and Forms in Civil Actions in the Courts of Record in the State of New York*. A second volume (1865), written wholly by Shearman, completed a reference work widely used until the law was changed in 1877. In 1860 he was employed by David Dudley Field [*q.v.*] of the New York code commission to prepare a book of forms, which he completed the following year. He then assisted with the proposed civil code (which was not adopted), preparing the part relating to obligations. With Amasa R. Redfield [*q.v.*] he wrote *A Treatise on the Law of Negligence* (1869), a pioneer work which was frequently cited in judicial opinions and greatly influenced the law on the subject. It reached its sixth edition in 1913.

In 1868 Shearman, with little practical experience but with a great store of legal learning, became a partner of Field and the immediate legal adviser of the officers and directors of the Erie Railroad, then under the control of James Fisk, Jr., and Jay Gould [*qq.v.*]. In the violent legal struggles of the "Erie war" the unusual methods of the partners, particularly the invention of injunctions by telegraph and the revival of writs of assistance, provoked much adverse criticism. In 1873, as a result of friction with Field's son, Shearman withdrew from Field & Shearman and with John W. Sterling established a new firm which specialized in corporate reorganizations and the management of large estates. Beginning in 1874 he gave most of his attention for nearly two years, without compensation, to defending his pastor, Henry Ward Beecher [*q.v.*], in civil and ecclesiastical proceedings resulting from the famous suit brought by Theodore Tilton. He successfully defended Jay Gould in every one of nearly a hundred damage suits growing out of the Black Friday gold panic of 1869. His firm was counsel for the National City Bank, for James J. Hill [*q.v.*], for the builders of the Canadian Pacific Railway, and for several important railroad and industrial companies.

By nature a reformer, Shearman succeeded Field as the foremost exponent of codification in New York and kept a number of clerks employed in preparing an annotated edition of the proposed civil code, which he would have published if the code had been adopted. An active free-trader, he assembled data to prove that protective tariffs had not even nominally raised the standard of wages. In 1881 he became converted to the fiscal measures of Henry George [*q.v.*] and in 1887 suggested to him the name "single tax" (Henry George, Jr., *The Life of Henry George*, 1900, p. 496 n.). In numerous pamphlets and in his *Natural Taxation* (1895) he presented statistics to prove inductively the conclusions that George had arrived at by deduction. Shearman estimated that half the proceeds of ground rent would pay all the expenses of government; and he was opposed to having more collected because of his fear of governmental extravagance. His particular theory, which proposed the collection of ground rents for purely fiscal rather than social purposes, became known as the "single tax limited." His *Natural Taxation* went through five editions. Besides its contribution to single tax theory, it contains one of the strongest indictments of the general property tax ever written. Shearman appeared on the platform more than seven hundred times in behalf of the Indian, the Armenian, the negro, and of the poor in coal fields, factories, sweat shops, and city tenements. He frequently gave his legal services without compensation to poor clients. Most of his large earnings were used in dispensing charity, and at his death in Brooklyn, his estate amounted to but little more than

$300,000. For all his humanitarian endeavors, however, he was never popular. His lack of tact and his habit of speaking in paradoxes alienated many who might have been his friends.

[*Memorial: Thomas Gaskell Shearman* (1900), recording various services held by Plymouth Church, Brooklyn, contains several personal estimates. The 1915 edition of *Natural Taxation* has an introductory sketch by C. B. Fillebrown, which is substantially the same as an article, "Thomas G. Shearman and His Natural Taxation," in the *National Magazine*, Mar. 1915, reprinted in pamphlet form. See also J. A. Garver, *John William Sterling* (1929); A. N. Young, *The Single Tax Movement in the U. S.* (1916); H. R. Stiles, *The Civil . . . Hist. . . . of the County of Kings and the City of Brooklyn, N. Y.* (1884); *Who's Who in America*, 1899-1900; *Brooklyn Daily Eagle*, Sept. 30, 1900. For criticisms of his conduct of the Erie litigations see C. F. Adams, *Chapters of Erie* (1871); and *High Finance in the Sixties* (1929), ed. by F. C. Hicks.]
E. C. S.]

SHECUT, JOHN LINNAEUS EDWARD WHITRIDGE (Dec. 4, 1770–June 1, 1836), physician, author, and botanist, was born in Beaufort, S. C. His father, Abraham Shecut, and his mother, Marie (Barbary) Shecut, were French Huguenots who were refugees first to Switzerland and later to America. In Shecut's early childhood his parents moved to Charleston, S. C., and there he made his home until his death. In 1786 he began the study of medicine under Dr. David Ramsay [*q.v.*]; later he is said to have gone to Philadelphia to study. He had an extensive practice in Charleston and was prominently identified with the cultural life of the city. As a physician, he was best known for his early experiments with the use of electricity in the treatment of disease. He had an electric machine which he used widely, and with much apparent success in cases of withered or paralyzed limbs; a number of these cases are fully described in *Shecut's Medical and Philosophical Essays* (1819). Having conceived the idea that yellow fever was in part caused by lack of electricity in the atmosphere, he wrote widely on the subject and sustained his contention by elaborate meteorological and thermometrical observations. The first of his essays on the subject was reviewed and warmly commended in the *New York Medical Repository* (vol. XIX, no. 3, 1818). He was in advance of his time in limiting the letting of blood and the use of mercury as a drug. In connection with yellow fever he said in 1819: "I have, as it regards this disease, long since sheathed my lancet. . . . Along with the lancet I have rejected mercury" (*Shecut's Medical and Philosophical Essays*, p. 128).

With unusual versatility he added to his medical practice an extensive study of botany and the publication of a number of books and pamphlets. His *Flora Carolinaeensis* (1806), of which only one volume was published, was the most extensive work on the botany of South Carolina up to that time and was intended to promote a taste for the study of botany by simplifying the Linnaean system. It is said to have cost him twenty months of work and, although it was published by subscription, over eighteen hundred dollars. In addition he wrote a number of pamphlets, *Sketches of the Elements of Natural Philosophy* (1826), and two novels, *Ish-noo-ju-lut-sche; or The Eagle of the Mohawks* (2 vols., 1841) and *The Scout; or the Fast of St. Nicholas* (1844). He is also said to have written a treatise on medicine called "Elements of Medicine." In 1813 he organized the Antiquarian Society of Charleston, which was incorporated a year later as the Literary and Philosophical Society of South Carolina, its primary purpose being the collection and preservation of specimens in natural history. The museum of the society became the nucleus of the Charleston Museum, one of the earliest public museums in the United States. In 1808 he became connected with the South Carolina Homespun Company, perhaps the earliest cotton mill in South Carolina (*Ibid.*, p. 26), which was sold at a loss about four years later. He was twice married. His first wife was Sarah Cannon, of Edisto Island, S. C., whom he married Jan. 26, 1792. He was married for a second time, Feb. 7, 1805, to Susanna Ballard, of Georgetown, S. C. He had nine children, four by the first marriage and five by the second. His books indicate that he was a man of broad culture and wide reading. His professional altruism was high, and he was eager to promote the welfare of humanity through his books and his work in medicine.

[Wilson Gee, "South Carolina Botanists: Biog. and Bibliog.," *Bull. Univ. of S. C.*, Sept. 1918; W. G. Mazÿck, *The Charleston Museum: Its Genesis and Development* (1908); *Am. Medic. Biogs.* (1920), ed. by H. A. Kelly and W. L. Burrage; death notice in *Charleston Courier*, June 2, 1836.]
A. R. C.]

SHEDD, JOEL HERBERT (May 31, 1834–Nov. 27, 1915), hydraulic and sanitary engineer, was born in Pepperell, Mass., the eldest of eight children of Joel and Eliza (Edson) Shedd. He was descended from Daniel Shed, who settled in Braintree, Mass., about 1642; his great-grandfather, Joel Shedd, was a soldier of the Revolution. After his education in the public schools and at Bridgewater Academy, Shedd began his professional life in 1850 as a student in the office of Thomas and John Doane in Charlestown, Mass. He made rapid progress and before his three years of study were completed went to Indiana to engage in railroad work in a responsible capacity.

ın 1856 he opened an office in Boston which he maintained for forty years. Many young engineers who later became prominent began their studies in his office. He soon became well known in the field of hydraulic engineering; in 1860 he was appointed by Gov. John A. Andrew of Massachusetts as commissioner on the Concord and Sudbury rivers and in 1876 he was made chairman of the newly established Board of Harbor Commissioners of Rhode Island, a position he retained for the rest of his life. He was later identified with many other state commissions in Rhode Island, serving as commissioner to the exposition at Paris in 1878, on the Rhode Island-Connecticut Boundary Commission and the Pawcatuck River Commission in the middle eighties, and on the Sakonnet River Stone Bridge Commission, 1902-10. His best-known works are probably those for the city of Providence, R. I. As early as 1866 he began investigations for a water supply, in 1869 he was appointed chief engineer in charge of construction, and in 1877, having completed the task, resigned, retaining a connection as consulting engineer. In 1871, while in charge of the water works, he designed and began the construction of a sewerage system which was completed between 1890 and 1897, while he was city engineer of Providence.

After this time he closed his Boston office and practised as a hydraulic and sanitary engineer in Providence for the remainder of his life. His wide reputation and proven skill in his profession brought him many important assignments. He gave special attention to damage caused by the diversion of water for public supplies, which field became an important part of his practice. Some of his notable water diversion cases included the Abbott Run–Pawtucket case; the Tatnuck and Kettle Brook diversion cases of Worcester, Mass.; and the Wachusett Reservoir cases on Nashua River in Massachusetts. He was commissioned to investigate the failure of the Diamond Hill Reservoir dam in the great freshet of 1886, which caused much damage in the valley of Abbott Run, near Pawtucket, R. I. He designed and developed the water-power project at Rumford Falls, Me., one of the larger early works of this kind. He devised and established systems for the measurement of water used for power purposes at various places in New England, including Norwich and Windsor Locks, Conn., and Lewiston, Me. In his later years he was engaged chiefly as an expert in valuation of water power and water works, and in this field, as an expert witness, he has rarely been equaled. His frankness of manner and pleasant personal-

ity were an asset when he was called to give testimony before a jury.

Shedd devised and patented the Shedd water meter (Sept. 7, 1880) and in connection with his work on the Providence sewerage project devised and patented a trap for house drains and waste pipes (Apr. 9, 1878). Later patents issued to him were for a movable dam (with O. P. Sarle, Jr.), Dec. 3, 1901, and a hydraulic air compressor, Sept. 8, 1903. He married in Medford, Mass., Aug. 26, 1856, Julia Ann, daughter of Thomas Clark of Newport, Me. She contributed widely upon art to various publications and was the author of several books, including *Famous Painters and Paintings* (1876) and *Famous Sculptors and Sculpture* (1881). She died in 1897, having borne two sons and a daughter, and on June 29, 1905, Shedd married Sarah Marble of North Smithfield, R. I., who with one son of his first marriage survived him. He died in Providence.

[*Trans. Am. Soc. Civil Engineers*, vol. LXXX (1916); *Representative Men and Old Families of R. I.* (1908), vol. III; *Who's Who in America*, 1914–15; *Who's Who in New England* (1916); F. E. Shedd, *Daniel Shedd Geneal.* (1921); *Providence Sunday Journal*, Nov. 28, 1915.]   H. K. B.

SHEDD, JOHN GRAVES (July 20, 1850– Oct. 22, 1926), merchant and philanthropist, was born on a farm near Alstead, N. H. Descended from Daniel Shed, who settled in Braintree, Mass., in 1642, he was the youngest son among the eight children of William and Abigail (Wallace) Shedd. He left the farm at seventeen to work in a small fruit store in Bellows Falls, Vt., with the prospect of receiving seventy-five dollars a year and his board. He soon entered the general store first of one Timothy Tufts and then of James H. Porter, both in Alstead. While with Porter he was induced in 1870 to go to Rutland, Vt., to work in a general store at a salary of one hundred and seventy-five dollars a year and his board. Soon after, he had an opportunity to visit Chicago in a vacation. There he sought an interview with Marshall Field [*q.v.*], who had already established himself in the retail dry-goods business. Having secured employment with Field, Leiter & Company, in 1872 he returned to Chicago to begin work as stock boy and salesman in the linen department of the wholesale house at ten dollars a week.

He was a natural salesman, a keen judge of merchandise, and a faithful worker. It was not long before he had worked out an analysis of sales as a basis for ordering goods; this drew him to the attention of his departmental superior, and from then on his rise was rapid. More intimately than anyone but Field himself, Shedd knew the conditions in the western country which were making possible the rapid expansion of the Field business. On May 15, 1878, he married Mary Roenna Porter of Walpole, N. H., daughter of Dr. Winslow Burroughs Porter, by whom he had two daughters. In 1893 he was taken into partnership, the firm having then become Marshall Field & Company by the withdrawal of Levi Z. Leiter. He had by this time made himself so essential both to the wholesale and retail branches of the business through his skill in buying that when Marshall Field died in 1906 he was chosen president. As the major executive of the company he not only continued the Field tradition of careful credit extension, quantity buying, and quality merchandise, but introduced ideas of counter display, specially built showrooms, and conveniences for customers which gave the Field organization prestige and reputation throughout the country. In order to control the quality of merchandise and to increase the earnings of the company, he embarked on a manufacturing program which led successively to the development of textile mills in North Carolina and Virginia, a rug-making factory in Philadelphia, and a lace-making industry at Zion City, Ill. In December 1922, when he retired from the presidency to become chairman of the board of directors, the Field organization had grown to proportions at which its founder might well have been amazed. He took an active interest in civic and business affairs. He was the first president of the Chicago Association of Commerce, a director in a number of insurance companies, banks, and railroads, and a member of the Chicago Plan Commission. He made liberal gifts to the Young Men's Christian Association and to the Art Institute of Chicago. In 1924 he established a fund of $2,000,000 to build the Shedd Aquarium in Grant Park, Chicago, with an additional $1,000,-000 as an endowment. He died in Chicago.

[F. E. Shedd, *Daniel Shed Geneal.* (1921); *Who's Who in America,* 1926–27; S. H. Ditchett, *Marshall Field and Company: the Life Story of a Great Concern* (1922); obituary in *Chicago Daily Tribune,* Oct. 23, 1926.]
E. A. D.

SHEDD, WILLIAM AMBROSE (Jan. 24, 1865–Aug. 7, 1918), Presbyterian missionary to Persia, was born at Mount Seir, Urmia (Urumiah), Persia, son of the Rev. John Haskell and Sarah Jane (Dawes) Shedd. His first American ancestor was Daniel Shed who settled in Braintree, Mass., about 1642. William graduated at Marietta College in 1887, and after two years in Persia entered Princeton Theological Seminary, where he graduated with the highest

honors in 1892. Ordained as an evangelist by the Presbytery of Athens, Ohio, June 23 of the same year, he returned to Persia and resumed work at his father's mission to the Nestorian Christians at Urmia. He was treasurer of the mission, superintendent of schools, and teacher of theology as well as editor of a paper in Syriac. He made many friends among the Mohammedans, although able to do little mission work among them. In 1904, however, he established a school for Moslem boys which became a part of Urmia College. He was a leader in the movement for the union of the old Nestorian and Evangelical churches and effected a working agreement under which there was a free interchange of pulpits, he himself preaching constantly in both churches.

He was a frequent contributor to various periodicals and was the author of two books: *Islam and the Oriental Churches* (1904), consisting of his lectures at various American seminaries, and a biography of Dr. J. H. Cochran in Persian (1907). He was also a leading collaborator in the Syriac Concordance to the Peshitta. This labor of years, existing only in manuscript but well known to scholars, perished with the destruction of the mission in 1918.

Although his work on the Syriac Concordance gave evidence of scholarship of the first rank, it is primarily as a statesmanlike leader of men that Shedd will be longest remembered. In 1905 he became the head of the legal board of the Evangelical Church, which was the court recognized by the government for the trial of all cases between Christians except those purely criminal. He became an authority on Persian law and an arbitrator of wisdom and power. The World War brought him into marked prominence. On the withdrawal of the Russian troops from the province in January 1915, the Christian population of the entire region flocked into Urmia, where they were besieged for five months by the Turks and Kurds. Shedd's cool-headed management of the situation was a factor in saving thousands from starvation and epidemic. After a year in America in 1916, he added to his other duties the chairmanship of the Urmia Relief Committee. In 1917 he was made a member of the food commission, at the request of the Persian government. On the final withdrawal of the Russians, Jan. 1, 1918, he became honorary vice-consul of the United States, and the mission compound became the American consulate. For many months during the ensuing siege by Turks and Kurds, Shedd was the chief defender of the Christians, and when some seventy thousand of them left the city, July 31, 1918, to flee to Hamadan, he followed them and protected the rear. Most of the refugees reached the British lines, but Shedd died of cholera on Aug. 7 at Sain Kala.

He was married three times: on June 21, 1894, to Adela Ludlow Myers, who died Nov. 30, 1901; on Apr. 24, 1903, to Louise Wilbur, who had been appointed to the mission in 1900 and died of typhus May 17, 1915; and on July 5, 1917, to Mary Edna Lewis, who accompanied him in the flight from Urmia and, with two daughters of the first marriage and two of the second, survived him.

[M. L. Shedd, *The Measure of a Man; the Life of William Ambrose Shedd, Missionary to Persia* (1922), with portr.; *The Eighty-Second Ann. Report of the Board of Foreign Missions of the Presbyt. Ch. in the U. S. A.* (1919), pp. 271–72; *Marietta Coll. Biog. Record* (1928); *Princeton Theol. Sem. Necr. Report*, 1919; *Princeton Theol. Sem. Biog. Cat.* (1909); W. T. Ellis, "A Yankee Cadi," *Century Mag.*, Feb. 1919; E. A. Powell, "Unsung Heroes I Have Known," *Am. Mag.*, Nov. 1926; F. E. Shedd, *Daniel Shed Geneal.* (1921); *N. Y. Times*, Aug. 21, 1918.]   F.T.P.

SHEDD, WILLIAM GREENOUGH THAYER (June 21, 1820–Nov. 17, 1894), theologian and author, sixth in descent from Daniel Shed who settled in Braintree, Mass., in 1642, was largely a product of New England Puritan ancestry, birth and education. His father, Marshall Shedd, who had entered preparatory school at twenty-one and graduated at Dartmouth as valedictorian, was pastor of the Congregational church at Acton, Mass., when his son William was born. The boy's mother, Eliza (Thayer), was the daughter of Obadiah Thayer, a wealthy Boston merchant who, making his home with her, constantly encouraged the grandson in his ambitions. William was named in honor of a friend of the Thayer family, William Greenough, a well-known New England philanthropist. His grandfather's companionship and his father's determination that the boy should have an adequate education exerted a decisive influence on the future religious leader.

The family having moved in 1831 to Willsboro, in northeastern New York, where Obadiah Thayer owned extensive property, William was prepared for college at Westport, N. Y., and at fifteen entered the University of Vermont. The greatest personal influence he felt there was that of James Marsh [q.v.], professor of philosophy, who made him an ardent disciple of Coleridge, Kant, and Plato. After graduation from college in 1839 he taught school for a year in New York City. There he united with a Presbyterian church and determined to enter the ministry. After three years in Andover Theological Seminary, where he graduated in 1843, he served the

Congregational church at Brandon, Vt., 1843–45, being ordained Jan. 4, 1844. Except for eighteen months (1862–63) at the Brick Presbyterian Church, New York City, as co-pastor with the venerable Dr. Gardiner Spring [q.v.], he devoted the remainder of his life to teaching and writing. He was professor of English literature at the University of Vermont, 1845–52; of sacred rhetoric at Auburn Theological Seminary, 1852–54; and of church history at Andover Seminary, 1854–62. He then entered upon the most notable phase of his career as a professor at Union Theological Seminary, New York City. For eleven years he taught sacred rhetoric, but in 1874 succeeded Henry Boynton Smith in the chair of systematic theology. Then began his greatest service, which continued until failing strength forced his resignation in 1893. His impact on his generation was felt in his vigorous lectures to his students, his public addresses, his writings for the religious press, and especially in his *Dogmatic Theology,* issued in two volumes in 1888, to which he added a third in 1894. This work was at once widely recognized for its close logic, intellectual power, earnest sincerity, and cogent defense of Calvinism.

Although Shedd attained high rank among American systematic theologians of his time, he became increasingly conservative in a day of progress in theological thinking, and during his last years was an active opponent of the higher criticism represented by his famous seminary colleague, Charles A. Briggs [q.v.], which since then has generally won its way throughout the Church. Nevertheless, by those who knew him best, however widely they differed with him, he was revered and loved for the simplicity and sincerity of his character and for the delightful charm of his personality. Of his many published works those which attracted most attention, besides his *Dogmatic Theology,* were his *Lectures upon the Philosophy of History* (1856), *Discourses and Essays* (1856), and *Literary Essays* (1878), and his editions of *The Confessions of Augustine* (1860) and *The Complete Works of Samuel Taylor Coleridge* (7 vols., 1853), which he issued with his own introductions. He published several other translations and commentaries and contributed frequently to religious and theological periodicals. In general his writings were characterized by vigor, beauty, and clearness of style. He married, Oct. 7, 1845, Lucy Ann Myers of Whitehall, N. Y., who with their two sons and two daughters survived him. He died in New York City.

[John De Witt, in *Presbyterian and Reformed Review,* Apr. 1895; G. L. Prentiss, *The Union Theol.*

Seminary (1899); F. E. Shedd, *Daniel Shed Geneal.* (1921); *N. Y. Observer*, Nov. 22, 1894; *N. Y. Tribune*, Nov. 18, 1894.]   P. P. F.

SHEEDY, DENNIS (Sept. 26, 1846–Oct. 16, 1923), stockman, merchant, capitalist, organizer, had a career that gives him a place in the early history of almost every state west of the Missouri River. He was born in Ireland, youngest of the twelve children of John and Margaret (Fitzpatrick) Sheedy. Both parents were educated. The father, who was a middle-class farmer, brought his family to the United States when Dennis was an infant. After settling near Rockport, Mass., they moved in 1858 to Lyons, Iowa, where the father soon died. Dennis began work by clerking in a store, but at sixteen he determined to seek his fortune farther west. He first went by wagon train to Denver, where he obtained employment in a store; two years later he was in Montana, engaged in placer mining and then in merchandising. He was very successful with freighting and trading in Utah and Montana and at nineteen had accumulated $30,000. After a winter in a commercial school in Chicago, he bought a wagon train and loaded it with stoves, which he freighted to Salt Lake City and sold at a handsome profit, taking produce in trade. This he took to the Montana mines and sold for gold dust. In 1870, after having been in Nevada, California, and Arizona, he went through New Orleans to Texas, bought 2,000 head of cattle, and drove them north to Abilene. A year later he bought 7,000 more. Having driven them north, with narrow escapes from outlaws, he sold all but 3,000. These he drove to Humboldt Wells, Nev., where he established a ranch that he held three years while he increased his stock and ran other herds in Texas, Nebraska, and Colorado. In 1878 the Cheyennes under Chief Dull Knife raided some of his herds and caused him much trouble and loss; the next year he consolidated his cattle interests on the North Platte River. He was now buying 10,000 head annually and branding 3,000 calves each year, but cold winters entailed heavy losses, about thirty per cent. in 1883. Foreseeing the end of the free range, he sold out his cattle interests—32,000 cattle and 400 horses—in 1884.

Furthermore, having been married, Feb. 15, 1882, to Catherine V. Ryan of Leavenworth, Kan., he desired to lead a more settled life. Going to Denver, he bought stock in the Colorado National Bank of Denver and became vice-president. When in 1886–87 the Holden Smelting Works of Denver, upon which the bank had made heavy loans, had financial difficulties, he was asked to work out a solution. His work in this shows his versatility. Being entirely unfamiliar with the methods and problems of smelting he set about to learn with the help of a teacher and by private study. He reorganized the smelting company, effected economies, and placed it on a paying basis. As president and general manager of the Globe Smelting and Refining Company he rebuilt and enlarged the plant, increased the annual production from $20,000 to $16,000,000, and founded the town of Globeville, Colo. His work with the railroads for favorable rates and with Congress for a protective tariff on lead ores contributed to the success of the company, with which he retained his connection until 1910. In 1894 he became president and general manager of the Denver Dry Goods Company, which under his management became the largest department store in Colorado. After the death of his first wife in 1895, he married Mary Teresa Burke of Chicago on Nov. 24, 1898. The two children born to her died in their youth. His widow and two of the six children of the first marriage survived him. He died in Denver. His record of his experiences, *The Autobiography of Dennis Sheedy*, was privately printed in 1922.

[The principal source of information about Sheedy's life is *The Autobiog. of Dennis Sheedy* (1922). A sketch of his early years appears in J. G. McCoy, *Hist. Sketches of the Cattle Trade of the West and Southwest* (1874). See also *Who's Who in America*, 1922–23; W. N. Byers, *Encyc. of Biog. of Colo.* (1901); J. C. Smiley, *Hist. of Denver* (1901); obituaries in *Denver Post*, Oct. 16, and *Rocky Mountain News*, Oct. 16, 17, 1923.]   L. R. H.

SHEFFIELD, DEVELLO ZELOTES (Aug. 13, 1841–July 1, 1913), missionary to China, was born in Gainesville, N. Y., the son of Asa Campbell Sheffield, a farmer, and Caroline (Murry). His early education was obtained in Warsaw, Middlebury, and Alexander academies. In 1861 he enlisted in the Union army, serving for two years. He was invalided home and to the end of his days bore the traces of his illness. He taught for about three years and for a time served as principal of the high school at Castile, N. Y. Apparently he passed through a religious crisis in his middle twenties; having been skeptical, he was converted, and united with the Presbyterian Church in Castile in 1866. In that same year he entered Auburn Theological Seminary, where he graduated three years later. On May 2, 1869, he was ordained to the ministry by the Cayuga Presbytery; on July 27 he married Eleanor Woodhull Sherrill of Pike, N. Y.; and soon afterward he sailed for China as a missionary of the American Board of Commissioners for Foreign Missions. On arriving in China he was assigned to Tungchow, a small city thirteen miles from Peking, where he spent most of the remainder of his life. He had three daughters and two sons, one of whom died in infancy.

Sheffield's achievements were mainly in education, literature, and administration. He was early attached to the school which his mission had established in Tungchow and had no small part in its development into a high school. He taught a wide variety of subjects, including courses in the affiliated Gordon Theological Seminary. When to the high school was added North China College (organized in 1892–93) he became the president of the new institution, and continued as such when by the cooperation of other missions (1902–03) the scope of the college was enlarged and its name changed to North China Union College. He retired in 1909 only because of advancing years. As president he taught and also for a long period did most of the preaching in the college church. He continued to teach until the year before his death. He had the reputation of being an excellent instructor, a strict disciplinarian, and an impressive preacher.

By dint of the persistence, diligence, and thoroughness which were characteristic of him he achieved a remarkable knowledge of the Chinese language. He was the author of several books in Chinese—on systematic theology, political economy, ethics, psychology, political science, church history, and general history—which largely grew out of his teaching. His *Universal History*, published in 1881—a pioneer in introducing modern China to that field—had a wide circulation. He devoted a large proportion of his time to the translation of the Bible into Chinese. He did much of the work on the standard Protestant cooperative revision of the New Testament in classical style, and was engaged in a similar revision of the Old Testament when, in 1912, failing health compelled him to give up his accustomed activities. He had also assisted in preparing the International Sunday School lessons in Chinese and in the revision of S. Wells Williams' Chinese-English dictionary. In addition to his exacting labors as a teacher and author he found time to serve in many administrative capacities —on the many committees which are a concomitant of Protestant missions, as secretary of his mission, and as president of the (Protestant) Educational Association of China (1896–99). He had not a little mechanical ability, and constructed a typewriter for the Chinese language as well as much of the apparatus required in college teaching.

He was slight of build and not of robust physique. He was wise in counsel, logical of mind, of a masterful spirit, ripe in judgment, and in his later years tolerant and possessed of a certain childlike simplicity. He died at Peitaiho, in North China.

[*Chinese Recorder*, Aug., Sept., 1913; *Missionary Herald*, Aug. 1913; *Ann. Report, Am. Board of Commissioners for Foreign Missions*, 1861–1912; archives of the American Board; *Who's Who in America*, 1908–09, 1910–11; *Gen. Biog. Cat. Auburn Theol. Sem.* (1918); C. H. Sherrill and L. E. deForest, *The Sherrill Geneal.* (1932).]   K.S.L.

SHEFFIELD, JOSEPH EARL (June 19, 1793–Feb. 16, 1882), merchant financier, philanthropist, was born in Southport, Conn., the son of Mabel (Thorp) and Paul King Sheffield. His father, who had moved from Stonington, had seen service on a privateer fitted out by his family during the Revolution; his mother was also a member of a seafaring family, a daughter of Capt. Walter Thorp of Southport, engaged in the West India trade. Sheffield completed his formal education at the age of fourteen, leaving the village school on a voyage to New Bern, N. C., in a vessel of his uncle's. He entered as clerk a store in that town, transferring the next year to the drug store of Dr. Thomas Webb, under whom he continued his studies. On a visit at Southport when the War of 1812 broke out, he undertook in the following spring to act as supercargo of a small vessel which ran the British blockade at Sandy Hook and brought back naval stores from New Bern. Remaining at New Bern, he conducted several similar and very profitable enterprises. In 1814, before he was twenty-one, he became the partner in New Bern of a large dry-goods firm in New York. Faced by the disastrous fall in prices after the peace of 1815, he boldly sold the dry goods below cost but turned loss into profit by the quick shipment of naval stores. On a horseback trip of over a thousand miles, which he made in 1816–17 in search of an outlet for the remainder of the stock, he was impressed by the prospects of Mobile, Ala., then a town of about a thousand inhabitants, still lacking a bank or any extensive trade, but at the outlet of two great rivers reaching into a rich cotton country. He entered the cotton trade, established important business connections in New Orleans, New York, Liverpool, and Havre, and became the largest exporter of this important port, in one year shipping 20,000 bales. He had judgment and courage, and in addition an appreciation, very unusual in that day, of the importance of accurate statistics as a basis of forecasting. He secured as detailed information as possible not only on the cotton crop but also on the harvests in Europe, and ascribed to this practice the fact that of twenty years in a very speculative trade only two were unsuccessful.

He had married on Aug. 22, 1822, Maria, daughter of Col. John T. St. John of Walton, N. Y., who bore him nine children. In 1835, influenced by considerations of health and social environment, he removed to New Haven. He gradually retired from the cotton trade, but found a larger field for his wealth, his business ability, and his craving for substantial accomplishment in the development of means of transportation. In close cooperation with an able engineer, Henry Farnam [q.v.], he helped to finance the completion of the New Haven-Northampton canal, the railroad which succeeded it, and the railroad from New York to New Haven. Although he lost money in these enterprises, he contracted with Farnam to complete the unfinished part of the Michigan Southern Railroad, about 170 miles, over which the first train from the East entered Chicago in 1852; in that year he contracted to build 182 miles for the Chicago & Rock Island Railroad completed in 1854 and extended by a bridge across the Mississippi the next year. The contractors were paid for their work on the Rock Island in bonds and stock at par; Sheffield raised all the cash, about five million dollars, and divided the profits equally with Farnam. He then retired from active business connections and devoted his energy to benefaction.

He gave a generous part of a large fortune to education. Impressed through his engineering experience with the importance of science, and with his interest probably quickened by the marriage of his daughter to Prof. John Addison Porter [q.v.], he gave steadily and wisely to the scientific department of Yale College. Without him its success would have been impossible; though it had been founded in 1847 and made a separate school in 1854, its resources were meager. His gifts and bequests to it, for which in 1861 it was renamed the Sheffield Scientific School, amounted to over a million dollars. In 1871, fifteen years before Yale College assumed the larger title of university, he expressed in a deed of gift the "hope and belief that New Haven is to be the seat of a true university, made up of many colleges having distinct though harmonious aims" (Chittenden, post, vol. II, p. 577). He also gave liberally to Trinity College, Hartford, Conn., to the Berkeley Divinity School, Middletown, Conn. (later in New Haven), and to local New Haven institutions. He died in New Haven, survived by his wife and six children.

[H. W. Farnam, in Papers of the New Haven Colony Hist. Soc., vol. VII (1908); memoir in Bernard's Am. Jour. of Educ., July 15, 1878; R. H. Chittenden, Hist. of the Sheffield Sci. School of Yale Univ., 1846–1922 (2 vols., 1928); obituary in New Haven Evening Reg., Feb. 16, 1882.]   C. D.

SHELBY, EVAN (1719–Dec. 4, 1794), soldier and frontiersman, was baptized in October 1719 at Tregaron, Cardiganshire, Wales. He came to America with his parents, Evan and Catherine (Davies?) Shelby, about 1734, the family first settling in what is now Antrim Township, Franklin County, Pa. In 1739, they moved into Prince George's (later Frederick) County, Md., where the father died in June 1750. Evan, Jr., continued to reside in Maryland, near the North Mountain, Frederick County, in which locality, now a part of Washington County, he acquired, by deed or patent, nearly 24,000 acres of land. He also became interested in the Indian fur trade and was concerned in trading-posts at Michilimackinac and Green Bay. He was in Braddock's campaign in 1755, and laid out part of the road from Fort Frederick to Fort Cumberland. Having served as first lieutenant in Capt. Alexander Beall's company in 1757–58, he was commissioned by Governor Sharpe of Maryland captain of a company of rangers and also held a commission as captain under the government of Pennsylvania. He was in the advance party of the force under Gen. John Forbes [q.v.] which took possession of Fort Duquesne in 1758, and crossed the Ohio with more than half his company of scouts, making a daring reconnoissance of the fort. On Nov. 12, 1758, near Loyalhanna, in a personal ecounter, Shelby is said to have slain with his own hand one of the principal Indian chiefs (Banvard, post). In this same war, he served later as major of a detachment of the Virginia regiment. For several years he was a justice of the peace. In May 1762 he was chosen one of the managers for Maryland of the Potomac Company. He sustained heavy losses in the Indian trade from the ravages growing out of Pontiac's Conspiracy of 1763, and most of his property in Maryland was subjected to the satisfaction of his debts.

Hoping to better his fortune he moved, probably in 1773, to Fincastle County, in Southwest Virginia, which he had previously visited, where he engaged in farming, merchandising, and cattle-raising, became again a prosperous landowner and a conspicuous and influential frontier leader. In 1774 he commanded the Fincastle Company in Dunmore's War, and in the battle of Point Pleasant, Oct. 10, 1774, he succeeded near the close of the action to the chief command in consequence of the death or disability of his superior officers. In 1776 he was appointed by Governor Henry of Virginia a major in the troops commanded by Col. William Christian against the Cherokees, and on Dec. 21 he became colonel of the militia of the newly created county of Washington, of which he was also a magistrate. In 1777, he was entrusted with the command of sundry garrisons posted on the frontier of Virginia, and in association with Preston and Christian negotiated a treaty with the Cherokees near the Long Island of Holston River. In 1779 he led a successful expedition of two thousand men against the Chickamauga Indian towns on the lower Tennessee River, for which service he was thanked by the Continental Congress.

By the extension of the boundary line between Virginia and North Carolina it was ascertained that his residence lay in the latter state, and in 1781 he was elected a member of its Senate. Five years later, the Carolina Assembly made him brigadier-general of militia of the Washington District of North Carolina, the first officer of that grade on "the Western Waters." In March 1787, as commissioner for North Carolina, he negotiated a temporary truce with Col. John Sevier [q.v.], governor of the insurgent and short-lived "State of Franklin." In August 1787, he was elected governor of the "State of Franklin," to succeed Sevier, but declined the honor. Having resigned his post as brigadier-general on Oct. 29, 1787, he withdrew from public life. He married first, in 1744, Lætitia Cox, a daughter of David Cox of Frederick County, Md. She died in 1777. His second wife, whom he married early in 1787, was Isabella Elliott, who survived him. He is buried in East Hill Cemetery, Bristol, on the Tennessee-Virginia line.

Shelby was of a rugged, stocky build, somewhat low in stature and stern of countenance. He possessed great muscular strength and unbounded energy and powers of endurance. He was straightforward and, at times, rather blunt in speech, absolutely fearless, and always prompt to take the aggressive in any action or enterprise, civil or military, in which he engaged. For a man of his day, he was well educated, and he was noted for his probity and patriotism. He left many descendants, of whom the most celebrated was his son, Isaac Shelby [q.v.], the first governor of Kentucky.

["Correspondence of Gov. Horatio Sharpe" (3 vols.), being Archives of Md., vols. VI (1888), IX (1890), XIV (1895); J. T. Scharf, Hist. of Western Md. (2 vols., 1882); Joseph Banvard, Tragic Scenes in the Hist. of Md., and the Old French War (1856); J. G. M. Ramsey, The Annals of Tenn. (1853); L. P. Summers, Hist. of Southwest Va. (1903) and Annals of Southwest Va. (1929); R. G. Thwaites and L. P. Kellogg, Doc. Hist. of Dunmore's War (1905); G. N. Mackenzie, Colonial Families of the U. S. A., II (1911), 652–57; Zella Armstrong, Notable Southern Families, vol. II (1922); S. C. Williams, Hist. of the Lost State of Franklin (1924); T. W. Preston, Hist.

Sketches of the Holston Valleys (1926); Cass K. Shelby, A Report on the First Three Generations of the Shelby Family in the U. S. (privately printed, 1927); A. M. Moon, Sketches of the Shelby, McDowell, Deaderick and Anderson Families (1933); D. C. Rees, Tregaron Historical and Antiguardian (Llandyssul, 1934).]
S. M. W.

SHELBY, ISAAC (Dec. 11, 1750–July 18, 1826), soldier, first governor of Kentucky, was born near the North Mountain, in Frederick (now Washington) County, Md., the son of Evan [q.v.] and Lætitia (Cox) Shelby. Brought up to the use of arms, he early became inured to the dangers and hardships of frontier life. He received a fair English education, worked on his father's plantation, was occasionally employed as a surveyor, and served as a deputy sheriff of the county. About 1773 the Shelby family moved to the Holston region of Southwest Virginia, now East Tennessee, where they established a new home.

Isaac Shelby served as a lieutenant in his father's Fincastle Company, at the battle of Point Pleasant, Oct. 10, 1774, distinguishing himself by his skill and gallantry; his report of the action is one of the best contemporary accounts now in existence (printed in Thwaites and Kellogg, post). He remained as second in command of the garrison of Fort Blair, erected on the site of the battle, until July 1775, when he visited Kentucky and surveyed lands for the Transylvania Company. The following year he returned to Kentucky and marked and improved lands on his own account, and also perfected military surveys previously selected and entered by his father. In July 1776 he was appointed by the Virginia committee of safety captain of a company of minute men. In 1777, Governor Henry made him commissary of supplies for a body of militia detailed to garrison frontier posts. He attended the Long Island Treaty with the Cherokees, concluded at Fort Patrick Henry, on July 20, 1777, at which his father was one of the Virginia commissioners. In 1778, he aided in furnishing supplies for the Continental Army and for the expedition projected by General McIntosh against Detroit and the Ohio Indians. The following year, he provided boats for Clark's Illinois campaign and collected and furnished supplies—mainly upon his own personal credit—for the successful campaign waged about the same time against the Chickamauga Indians. In the spring of 1779 he was chosen a member for Washington County of the Virginia legislature, and, the ensuing fall, Governor Jefferson made him a major in the escort of guards for the commissioners appointed to run the western boundary line between Virginia and North Carolina. Early in 1780, he became colonel of the militia of Sullivan County, N. C. In the spring and summer of the same year he was again in Kentucky, supervising the surveying of lands for himself and others.

News of the fall of Charleston (May 12, 1780) having reached him, he hurried home and found an urgent summons for help from Col. Charles McDowell [q.v.]. He at once organized a force and about July 25 joined McDowell at the Cherokee Ford, S. C. On July 30, 1780, at the head of a detachment, Shelby captured a formidable Loyalist stronghold, Thicketty Fort (or Fort Anderson), on the headwaters of the Pacolet River. In the second battle of Cedar Springs, Aug. 8, 1780, his command successfully repulsed a strong party sent against it by Major Ferguson, and on Aug. 18, he was largely responsible for the victory won over a superior force at Musgrove's Mill, on the north side of the Enoree River.

The report of General Gates's defeat at Camden on Aug. 16 halted further operations by the patriot forces under McDowell and Shelby. The term of enlistment of Shelby's volunteer regiment being about to expire, he proposed that an army of volunteers be raised on both sides of the mountains. A threatening message dispatched by Ferguson, instead of intimidating Shelby, fired him with greater resentment and determination. In consequence, he initiated and, in concert with John Sevier [q.v.] and others, organized and conducted the expedition against Ferguson, whose combined Provincial and Loyalist force was overwhelmingly defeated in the decisive battle of King's Mountain, Oct. 7, 1780. To Shelby, also, has been accorded credit for the scheme of attack, which led to the battle of the Cowpens, Jan. 17, 1781. In February 1781, the legislature of North Carolina adopted resolutions of thanks to Shelby and his compatriots for their services at King's Mountain, similar resolutions having been adopted by the Continental Congress on Nov. 13, 1780.

Repeated uprisings and depredations by Cherokee Indians along the western borders of North Carolina, during the first half of the year 1781, rendered it impracticable to send any considerable force from that quarter to assist General Greene. A treaty with the Cherokees having been negotiated on July 20, 1781, however, Shelby, in October, upon receipt of a delayed message of appeal from Greene, raised 500 mounted riflemen and, accompanied by Col. John Sevier in command of 200 more, marched to join Greene, by whose order they reported to General Marion on the Santee. Shelby, in joint command with Col. Hezekiah Maham, of the Carolina dragoons,

rendered conspicuous service in the capture of a strong British post at Fair Lawn, near Monck's Corner, S. C., on Nov. 27, 1781. While on this expedition, he was elected a member of the North Carolina legislature, and, obtaining leave of absence, attended its sessions in December. Many years later, he declared: "For myself, for the whole services of 1780 and 1781, both in camp and in the Assembly, I received a liquidation certificate which my agent in that country, after my removal to Kentucky, sold for six yards of middling broadcloth, and I gave one coat of it to the person who brought it out to me—indeed I was proud of receiving that" (*North Carolina Booklet*, July 1918, pp. 50–51, footnote 62). Reelected to the North Carolina Assembly in 1782, he attended the legislative sessions held at Hillsboro, in April. He was appointed one of three commissioners to superintend the laying off of the land south of the Cumberland River allotted by North Carolina for military service in the Revolution. This task was performed in the early months of 1783.

Shortly thereafter, he removed to Kentucky, where, at Boonesborough, he was married, on Apr. 19, to Susannah Hart, a daughter of Capt. Nathaniel Hart, by whom he had eleven children. In 1783 he was appointed a trustee of Transylvania Seminary (later Transylvania University). He was chairman of the convention of militia officers held at Danville on Nov. 7–8, 1784, called to consider an expedition against the Indians and separation from Virginia; he was also a member of the succeeding conventions (1787, 1788, 1789), which prepared the way for independent statehood. He helped to organize the Kentucky Society for Promoting Useful Knowledge, formed at Danville, Dec. 1, 1787. In January 1791, he was appointed a member of the board of war, created by Congress for the District of Kentucky, with power to provide for the defense of the frontier settlements and to prosecute punitive expeditions against the Indians. For several years he served as high sheriff of Lincoln County. He was a member of the convention (Apr. 2–19, 1792) which framed the first constitution of Kentucky, and in May he was elected governor, taking office on June 4, and serving four years. During his administration many events of importance to the infant commonwealth occurred, not the least being the part it took, under Shelby, in supporting Wayne's campaigns against the Indians in the Northwest Territory. At the close of his term, he declined reëlection, and for the next fifteen years gave attention to his private affairs.

The imminence of war with Great Britain

called him from retirement, and in August 1812 he was a second time elected governor. He co-operated vigorously in the prosecution of the war, and in 1813 assembled and led in person 4,000 Kentucky volunteers to join General Harrison in the Northwest for the invasion of Canada, an expedition which resulted in the decisive defeat of the British, Oct. 5, 1813, at the battle of the Thames. For his patriotic and heroic services he was awarded a gold medal by Congress on Apr. 4, 1818. In March 1817, he was tendered the portfolio of War by President Monroe, but de-clined the honor on the score of age. The year following he was commissioned, with Gen. An-drew Jackson, to hold a treaty with the Chicka-saw Indians for the purchase of their lands west of the Tennessee River, and performed this serv-ice most acceptably. He was president of the first Kentucky Agricultural Society, formed at Lexington in 1818, and was chairman of the first board of trustees of Centre College, founded in 1819 at Danville, Ky. At his death he was buried at his historic home, "Traveller's Rest," and a monument was erected over his grave by the state of Kentucky. Counties in nine states have been named Shelby in his honor.

In person, Shelby was of a sturdy and well-proportioned frame, slightly above medium height, with strongly marked features and florid complexion. He had a hardy constitution cap-able of enduring protracted labor, great priva-tions, and the utmost fatigue. Habitually dignified and impressive in bearing, he was, how-ever, affable and winning. A soldier born to command, he nevertheless evidenced a high de-gree of political sagacity and executive ability. Numerous difficulties confronted him during his first administration, when the new government was passing through its formative stage, and much depended on the choice of officials then made by the executive. Shelby exhibited rare selective intelligence and an extraordinary mas-tery both of men and measures. Kentucky at this time experienced constant dread of the occlusion by Spain of the Mississippi River, and use was made of this situation by designing men to pro-mote speculative ventures and political schemes hostile to the true interests of both Kentucky and the Union. Through it all, Shelby pursued a wise and moderate course which baffled the plots of all conspirators and held Kentucky firmly to her federal moorings. During his second admin-istration, the pressure of the war with Great Britain fell with extraordinary and unremitting severity upon the state, and he showed himself not only a prudent and farseeing counselor, but an active, resourceful, and patriotic leader. His

energy, determination, and perseverance knew no bounds, and his devotion to duty was unflag-ging.

[James Herring and J. B. Longacre, *The Nat. Por-trait Gallery of Distinguished Americans,* vol. I (1834); Autobiog. of Isaac Shelby (MS.), in Durrett Collec-tions, Univ. of Chicago; R. B. McAfee, *Hist. of the Late War in the Western Country* (1816); W. T. Barry, *Speech on the Deaths of Adams, Jefferson, and Shelby* (1826); John Haywood, *Civil and Pol. Hist. of the State of Tenn.* (1823); Mann Butler, *A Hist. of the Commonwealth of Ky.* (2nd ed., 1836); J. T. More-head, *An Address in Commemoration of the First Set-tlement of Ky.* (1840); Lewis and R. H. Collins, *Hist. of Ky.* (1874); J. G. M. Ramsey, *The Annals of Tenn.* (1853); L. C. Draper, *King's Mountain and Its Heroes* (1881); John Watts de Peyster, in *Mag. of Am. Hist.,* Dec. 1880, and *The Battle or Affair of King's Mountain* (1881); J. B. O. Landrum, *Colonial and Revolutionary Hist. of Upper S. C.* (1897); Edward McCrady, *The Hist. of S. C. in the Revolution* (2 vols., 1901, 1902); B. H. Young, *The Battle of the Thames* (1903), Filson Club Pubs., no. 18; R. G. Thwaites and L. P. Kellogg, *Doc. Hist. of Dunmore's War* (1905); C. H. Todd, in *Jour. of Am. Hist.,* vol. II (1908), no. 2; V. A. Lewis, *Hist. of the Battle of Point Pleasant* (1909); A. C. Quisenberry, *Ky. in the War of 1812* (1915); Archibald Henderson, *N. C. Booklet,* Jan. 1917, July 1918; Sam-uel M. Wilson, *A Review of "Isaac Shelby and the Genet Mission," by Dr. Archibald Henderson* (1920); "Hist. Statements Concerning the Battle of King's Mountain, and the Battle of the Cowpens, S. C.," *House Doc. 328,* 70 Cong., 1 Sess.; H. J. Berkley, in *Md. Hist. Mag.,* June 1932; *Ky. Gazette* (Lexington), July 21, 28, Aug. 25, 1826; a few MSS. in Lib. of Cong.]   S. M. W.

SHELBY, JOSEPH ORVILLE (Dec. 12, 1830–Feb. 13, 1897), Confederate soldier, the son of Orville Shelby and his second wife, Anna M. Boswell, was born in Lexington, Ky. He was a descendant of the fourth generation from Evan Shelby, who came to America from Wales about 1734, and a kinsman of Evan and Isaac Shelby [*qq.v.*] When Shelby was about five years old his father died and the boy received his early schooling from his step-father, Benjamin Grantz. He entered Transylvania University at the age of fifteen and remained there for three years. After an additional year's study in Philadelphia, he returned to Lexington to engage in rope man-ufacturing. In 1852 he moved to Berlin and later to Waverly, Mo., where he established a rope factory. During the Kansas-Missouri border troubles, Shelby, favorable to slavery, raised and commanded a company of Kentuckians. He then returned to his business pursuits and by 1861 was accounted one of the wealthiest slave and land owners in Missouri.

When Fort Sumter was fired on, Shelby, re-fusing a Federal commission, joined the Con-federacy and in three years rose from the rank of captain to that of brigadier-general. His cavalry force was prominently identified with the campaigns of Gen. Sterling Price [*q.v.*] in the West, fighting at Carthage, Wilson's Creek, Lexington, Springfield, Mo., Pea Ridge, St.

Charles, and Duvall's Bluff, Ark. In June 1862 he joined the forces of Gen. James E. Rains at Van Buren, Ark., to invade Missouri. Shelby's men swore at this time never to lay down arms until the war ended. At Newtonia, Mo., he organized a cavalry brigade, and during the fall of 1862 remained near Huntsville, Ark., operating throughout the winter against Gen. James Gillpatrick Blunt [q.v.]. The Confederates broke camp in Arkansas in December 1862, dashed into Missouri, captured the outer defenses of Springfield, and then retreated to Batesville, Ark. Here they rested until spring, when the ill-starred Cape Girardeau expedition was organized. This project was abandoned in favor of an attempt to interrupt Grant's communications and they attacked Helena, Ark., on July 4, 1863, not knowing that Vicksburg had fallen. Shelby was wounded in this action, but upon his recovery he raided Missouri, captured Booneville, Neosho, Bower Mills, Warsaw, Tipton, Stockton, and Humansville, and then withdrew to Camden, Ark., for winter quarters. Shelby was ordered on Mar. 3, 1864, to garrison Princeton, on the Saline River line, and to cover all roads leading into Camden. In the ensuing action, his thousand cavalrymen restrained Steele's force of fifteen thousand throughout an entire day. This engagement as well as the remarkably successful Missouri raid of the following summer demonstrated the devotion with which his men followed him and justified fully the respect he commanded from friend and foe alike. His personal courage and his mastery of cavalry tactics carried him to a conspicuous place among Confederate cavalrymen. The Confederates invaded Missouri again in the summer of 1864 to divert Grant from his hammering campaign. Shelby and Price attacked at Lexington and at the Little Blue River, then moved to Westport, Mo., where they engaged heavily late in October 1864. When Price was forced to withdraw to Newtonia, Shelby ably covered the movement. After an engagement with Blunt at Newtonia, Shelby retired to Clarksville, Tex., where he learned of Lee's surrender.

When General Buckner surrendered at Shreveport, La., Shelby urged his men to cross into Mexico, there to join forces either with General Juarez or Emperor Maximilian. Shelby's command buried their battle flag in the Rio Grande River on July 4, 1865, and crossed the border. Against Shelby's judgment, his men voted to support Maximilian, but the Emperor, suspicious of the proffered aid, held aloof. Later he repented of his folly, and gave Shelby some land upon which a colony, named Carlotta for the Empress,

was formed. As the French withdrew from Mexico, Juarez struck and Maximilian finally called for Shelby's aid, but his hour had passed and the unhappy monarch soon faced a firing squad. Shelby returned to Bates County, Mo., to rebuild his fortunes, but steadfastly refused to capitalize politically on his great personal popularity until 1893, when President Cleveland appointed him United States marshal for the western district of Missouri. While carrying out the duties of this office, he contracted an illness which resulted in his death at Adrian, Mo. He was buried in Forest Hill Cemetery, Kansas City, Mo. In 1858 he was married to Elizabeth N. Shelby, a remote cousin. They had seven children, of whom a daughter and several sons survived their parents.

[Correspondence with a member of the family; Zella Armstrong, *Notable Southern Families*, vol. II (1922); J. N. Edwards, *Shelby and His Men* (1867); B. H. Young, *Confed. Wizards of the Saddle* (1914); *Confed. Mil. Hist.* (1899), vol. IX; W. L. Webb, *Battles and Biographies of Missourians* (1900); W. R. Hollister, Harry Norman, *Five Famous Missourians* (1900); W. B. Stevens, *Centennial Hist. of Mo.* (1921), vol. II; J. N. Edwards, *Shelby's Expedition to Mexico* (1872); *St. Louis Globe-Democrat*, Feb. 14, 1897.]
                                            C. C. B—n.

SHELDON, EDWARD AUSTIN (Oct. 4, 1823–Aug. 26, 1897), educator, was born near Perry Center, N. Y., the son of Eleazer and Laura (Austin) Sheldon. He was a descendant of Isaac Sheldon, who emigrated to America, probably in 1634, and later settled in Windsor, Conn. As a boy he worked on his father's farm and in the winters attended a district school nearby. After preparing for college at the newly established Perry Center Academy, he matriculated in 1844 at Hamilton College but withdrew in 1847 to recuperate from an attack of pleurisy and for several months lived outdoors with Charles and Andrew Jackson Downing [qq.v.], well-known horticulturists of Newburgh, N. Y. The experiences of this period influenced him to enter into a partnership in the fall of 1847 in the nursery business at Oswego, N. Y., but the venture failed. Unsuccessful as well in his search for employment in New York City in 1848, he returned to Oswego.

Moved to sympathy by conditions among the poor people of the city and learning that many were illiterate, he succeeded in bringing about the organization, on Nov. 28, 1848, of the Orphan and Free School Association of Oswego and was appointed to take charge of it. Though he saw the need and importance of making all the public schools of the city free and urged it at this time, public interest in the "Ragged School," as it was called, waned, and in 1849 he resigned to open a private school for boys and girls, in partnership with J. D. Higgins. On May 16, 1849, he married Frances Ann Bradford Stiles, daughter of Ezra and Anna (Spear) Stiles of Syracuse, N. Y. In 1851 he again urged the establishment of free schools in Oswego and had the satisfaction of seeing his suggestions embodied in a bill which became a law in 1853. In the meantime he became superintendent of public schools in Syracuse, where he improved the classification and gradation of schools, established a system of evening schools, and organized school libraries. In 1853 he returned to Oswego as secretary of the board of education, a position corresponding to that of superintendent, and organized the first system of free schools there. As in Syracuse, he reorganized courses of study, graded and classified schools, and secured better qualified teachers. His accomplishments were recognized by other educators in the state and in 1860 he was elected president of the state teachers' association; in the same year he became one of the editors of the *New York Teacher*.

In May 1861, as a result of his recommendations, the Oswego Primary Teachers' Training School was opened, the first city training school in the United States. After the first year Sheldon became principal, a position he held until the year of his death. In 1863 he secured state recognition and financial aid for the school, which in 1866 became the Oswego State Normal and Training School. His success as head of the school was immediate. Under his direction it became the most important center of Pestalozzianism and objective instruction in the United States. His methods of practice-teaching were studied widely, and many of his graduates were called to organize and take charge of city training schools. In 1866–67 six additional state normal and training schools were established in New York on the plan of the Oswego school. His publications include several spelling books, a series of readers, *A Manual of Elementary Instruction* (1862), *Teachers' Manual of Instruction in Reading* (copyright 1875), and *Autobiography of Edward Austin Sheldon* (copyright 1911). At the time of his death he was survived by a son and four daughters, one of whom was Mary Downing Sheldon Barnes [*q.v.*].

[See esp. *Autobiog. of Edward Austin Sheldon* (copr. 1911), ed. by Mary Sheldon Barnes; N. H. Dearborn, *The Oswego Movement in Am. Educ.* (1925); A. P. Hollis, *The Oswego Movement* (1898). See also *Am. Ancestry*, vol. IV (1889); H. R. Stiles, *The Stiles Family in America* (1895); W. S. Monroe, *Hist. of the Pestalozzian Movement in the U. S.* (copr. 1907); *Am. Jour. Educ.*, Sept. 1865, pp. 484–85; *Proc. Nat. Educ. Assoc.*, 1898 (1898); obituary in *N. Y. Tribune*, Aug. 27, 1897.]

R. F. S.

SHELDON, EDWARD STEVENS (Nov. 21, 1851–Oct. 16, 1925), philologist, lexicographer, was born at Waterville, Me., a son of the Rev. David Newton and Rachel Hobart (Ripley) Sheldon, and a brother of Henry Newton Sheldon [*q.v.*]. After preliminary studies at the Waterville (later Coburn) Classical Institute and at Colby College, Waterville, where he spent one year, Sheldon went to Harvard College and graduated in 1872. Soon after, he was appointed proctor in the College, at the same time teaching Greek in a school for young ladies in Boston, and in the spring of 1873 he was instructor in Spanish and Italian at Harvard. Later he received a traveling fellowship, which enabled him to develop an already large linguistic equipment by three years' work at the Universities of Berlin, Leipzig, and Paris, 1874–77. During this sojourn he prepared himself for his life work in English lexicology and the teaching of Romance linguistics; he also gave much attention to Germanics and the history of the Greek and Latin languages. In Germany he profited particularly by his relations with the noted professor of Romance philology, Adolf Tobler. Returning to the United States, he became in 1877 an instructor in modern languages and then a tutor in German at Harvard University. With the year 1884, when he was appointed assistant professor of Romance philology, his labors at Harvard were fixed for good and all. In that year, on Apr. 2, he married Katherine Hamlin Hinckley of Poughkeepsie, N. Y., by whom he had one daughter. In 1894 he became professor of Romance philology, a position he held until his retirement in 1921. His activities brought him very naturally into connection with various learned societies. He was a fellow of the American Academy of Arts and Sciences; and he served as president of the American Dialect Society, which he had helped to found, in 1894–95, of the Modern Language Association of America in 1901, and of the Dante Society from 1909 to 1915.

Over a stretch of years Sheldon performed scholarly work of a monumental sort, which is represented by his revision of the etymologies in *Webster's International Dictionary* for its issues of 1890 and later. For this useful learning, in which his individuality is submerged, the world will never give him the reward merited by his patient and fruitful research, which often meant invaluable correction of errors present in anterior lexicons, not excluding the great *Oxford English Dictionary* (1888–1928). His writings, apart from minor articles in various learned reviews, include *A Short German Grammar* (1879), which went through several editions,

"Some Specimens of a Canadian French Dialect Spoken in Maine" (*Transactions and Proceedings of the Modern Language Association of America*, vol. III, 1888), "The Origin of the English Names of the Letters of the Alphabet" (*Studies and Notes in Philology and Literature*, 1892), "Further Notes on the Names of the Letters" (*Ibid.*, 1893); *Concordanza delle opere italiane in prosa e del Canzoniere di Dante Alighieri* (1905), in collaboration with A. C. White, and "Some Remarks on the Origin of Romance Versification" (*Anniversary Papers by Colleagues and Pupils of George Lyman Kittredge*, 1913). He was one of the best informed of all the specialists who have ever studied the general subject of French contributions to the English vocabulary. Unfortunately, in spite of the efforts of his friends to secure a permanent record of his knowledge of Anglo-French, he died without preparing the study of the subject he had promised. The agony of his last years, in which he suffered from an extremely painful ailment, explains his failure to leave such a tangible memorial of his erudition. He died in Cambridge, Mass.

[*Who's Who in America*, 1924–25; reports of Harvard Coll. Class of 1872 esp. those published in 1898, 1912, 1917, and 1924; C. H. Grandgent, in *Harvard Graduates' Mag.*, Dec. 1925; *Harvard Univ. Gazette*, Dec. 12, 1925; obituary in "Notes and Comments," *Modern Philology*, Feb. 1926; death notice in *Boston Transcript*, Oct. 16, 1925.]   J. D. M. F.

SHELDON, HENRY NEWTON (June 28, 1843–Jan. 14, 1926), jurist, was born in Waterville, Me., son of Rachel (Ripley) and David Newton Sheldon, a Unitarian clergyman who was at one time president of Waterville (later Colby) College, and brother of Edward Stevens Sheldon [*q.v.*]. Educated in the public schools of Bath and Waterville, he went first to Bowdoin for a year and then entered the sophomore class at Harvard, where he obtained a scholarship and, partly working his way, graduated first scholar in the class of 1863. He taught school and studied law for about a year and then entered the 55th Massachusetts Regiment (colored) as a lieutenant on June 28, 1864. After active service in South Carolina and Georgia, he returned to Boston at the close of the war and was admitted to the bar in 1866. On Dec. 31, 1868, he married Clara P. Morse of Hubbardston, Mass., by whom he had two children. Until 1894 he practised law in Boston, being associated for about twenty years with Gen. Wilmon W. Blackmar. During this period he edited Joseph Bateman's *A Practical Treatise on the Law of Auctions* (1883) and published *The Law of Subrogation* (1882), which became the standard work on the subject.

In 1894 the judicial office "sought the man" in a way that shows the value to the public of the Massachusetts system of judicial appointment. Being exceptionally modest, quiet, and scholarly in his habits, Sheldon would never have attracted political attention for a position on an elective bench; he was appointed to the superior court by Gov. Frederic Thomas Greenhalge [*q.v.*], a lawyer himself and a friend of Sheldon's in college. Though he had been comparatively obscure, he quickly became a leading figure on the court, where he served for ten years, and was known for his scholarship, his quick perception, his balanced judgment, his power of clear statement, his knowledge of men, his firmness, and his natural courtesy. When he was promoted to the supreme judicial court of Massachusetts in 1905, there was general gratification at the bar throughout the commonwealth. He excelled both as a *nisi prius* and as an appellate judge, and had the ability to make the loser feel that his case had been fairly considered. During his ten years of service on the appellate court he wrote almost six hundred opinions. Although he resigned in 1915, his work was not ended. That year he was chosen president of the Massachusetts Bar Association. Under his supervision the *Massachusetts Law Quarterly* was established, and he served as a member of its publication committee until the fall of 1921. While still on the superior court, he had rendered an important service as chairman of a special commission to simplify criminal procedure, and in 1919, when he was more than seventy-five years of age, he was drafted for two important public services. He served as chairman of an investigating committee of the Boston Bar Association, a most difficult and trying task which led to the removal of two district attorneys. He also served during a period of fourteen months as chairman of the judicature commission, which was created to study and report on the entire judicial system of Massachusetts. The work of this commission resulted among other things in the creation of the first statewide "small claims" procedure in the United States, and in the recommendation of a judicial council composed of representatives of both bench and bar for the continuous study of the judicial system, a plan which was later adopted not only in Massachusetts but in about twenty other states. In 1921 Sheldon retired from active service; five years later he died, survived by a son.

[See *Who's Who in America*, 1924–25; *Mass. Law Quart.*, Jan. 1926; *Proc. in the Supreme Judicial Court of Mass. in Memory of Henry Newton Sheldon* (1927), reprinted in *Bar Bull.* (Boston), Dec. 1927; obituary in *Boston Transcript*, Jan. 14, 1926; personal acquaintance. Sheldon's opinions appear in 189–220 *Mass. Reports.*].   F. W. C.

SHELDON, MARY DOWNING [See BARNES, MARY DOWNING SHELDON, 1850–1898].

SHELDON, WALTER LORENZO (Sept. 5, 1858–June 5, 1907), leader in the ethical culture movement, was born in West Rutland, Vt., first of three sons of Preston and Cornelia (Hatch) Sheldon. His father, a lumber dealer, was a descendant of Isaac Sheldon, who lived in Windsor, Conn., as early as 1652. Intended by his father for the Episcopalian ministry, Sheldon spent two years at Middlebury College, 1876–78, and then went to the College of New Jersey (Princeton), where he took an attitude, he wrote later, that put him "far outside the pale of its theology." Graduated in 1880, he studied philosophy in Berlin, Leipzig, and Paris until 1883; the next two years he passed in New York, a disciple of Felix Adler, who in 1876 had established the first Society for Ethical Culture. In 1886, after another winter in Germany, he went to St. Louis, Mo., where he organized the Ethical Society of St. Louis and became its lecturer. Regarding ethical culture as the means of freeing people from outmoded creeds, he nevertheless looked on it as universal religion, the societies as churches, and its lecturers as the clergy. Although he was young and retiring, he was soon recognized as an intellectual leader in a community widely known for its group of Hegelian philosophers, including William Torrey Harris and Henry C. Brokmeyer [*qq.v.*], and for the *Journal of Speculative Philosophy*, to which he contributed an article on "Agnostic Realism," in July 1886.

In 1888 he founded the Self-Culture Hall Association for wage-earners, an early attempt of settlement work in the United States, for which he won the services of educators and ministers of various faiths, and the support of such citizens as William Taussig and Nelson Olsen Nelson [*qq.v.*]. Sheldon described this venture in *Ethical Addresses* (1900, 7 ser.) and in an article in *Charities and the Commons,* Sept. 5, 1908. He organized classes for negroes, whose educational needs had been neglected, and he was also so keenly concerned with the training of children that he gave much time to lessons in citizenship, ethical Sunday schools, and ethical literature for children. He established a Greek Ethics Club for discussion of current problems, which survived as the Contemporary Literature Circle of St. Louis. In 1904 he directed the social science department of the congress of arts and sciences at the Louisiana Purchase Expo-

sition. Throughout his years in St. Louis he wrote prolifically. His publications include *Ethics and the Belief in a God* (1892), *Ethics for the Young* (1894), *Story of the Life of Jesus for the Young Told from an Ethical Standpoint* (1895), *An Ethical Movement* (1896), *The Story of the Bible from the Standpoint of Modern Scholarship* (1899), *An Ethical Sunday School* (1900), *Class Readings in the Bible* (1901), *Lessons in the Study of Habits* (1903), *Citizenship and the Duties of a Citizen* (copyright 1904), *Duties in the Home and the Family* (1904), and *The Divine Comedy of Dante* (1905). Posthumously appeared *Thoughts from the Writings and Addresses of Walter L. Sheldon* (1919), edited by Cecilia Boette. After celebrating his society's twentieth anniversary, he went to Japan for his health, but he accepted so many invitations to lecture that when he returned he was worse. Bedridden, he directed his society for another season, and then died of chronic myocarditis and arterio-sclerosis in his forty-ninth year. On May 18, 1892, he had married Anna Hartshorne of Philadelphia; there were no children. His widow later married Percival Chubb, his successor in the society. Sheldon's ashes were sealed in the cornerstone of the building of the Ethical Society of St. Louis, dedicated in 1912 and named the Sheldon Memorial in his honor, a personal recognition he unquestionably would have opposed. A handsome man with scholarly brow and pointed beard, he fully looked the intellectual leader. Probably no St. Louisan has enjoyed greater esteem in both extremes of society.

[See George Sheldon, *A Hist. of Deerfield, Mass.* (2 vols., 1895–96); *Who's Who in America,* 1908–09; William Hyde and H. L. Conard, *Encyc. of the Hist. of St. Louis* (1899), vol. IV; *Centennial Hist. of Mo.* (1921), vol. V; *The Book of St. Louisans* (1906), ed. by J. W. Leonard; *Sexennial Record of the Class of 1880, Princeton College* (1887); *St. Louis Post-Dispatch,* June 5, and *St. Louis Republic,* June 7, 1907; memorial addresses in *Ethical Addresses and Ethical Record* (1908, 15 ser.). The Sheldon Memorial contains his library, his published writings, several portraits, and many unpublished MSS. Information on certain points has been supplied by Mrs. Martha E. Fischel, an associate, Percival Chubb and George R. Dodson of St. Louis, and Rex Preston Sheldon of Salisbury, Vt., a nephew.]   I. D.

SHELDON, WILLIAM EVARTS (Oct. 22, 1832–Apr. 16, 1900), educator, was born in Dorset, Vt., the son of Julius King and Harriet Newell (Sheldon) Sheldon. His earliest years were spent on his father's farm. After attending local district schools, in 1847 he entered Burr Seminary in Manchester, Vt., where he remained for a year, earning his expenses by teaching during the winter quarter in West Rupert, Vt. Apparently he undertook too much and so undermined his health that he was obliged to resign and seek a milder climate. From 1848 to 1850 he lived in Virginia and in 1849–50 taught school near Richmond. In 1850 he reëntered Burr Seminary, where he graduated in 1853. He then matriculated at Middlebury College but withdrew to become principal of the high school in East Abington (later Rockland), Mass. Here he effected important reforms in methods of instruction and in administration, and succeeded in bringing about a reclassification and gradation of schools in the town. His achievements brought him many invitations to address teachers' institutes and societies. In 1857 he was elected president of the Plymouth County Teachers' Association; in the same year in Philadelphia he helped to organize the National Teachers' Association, of which he was elected secretary. He married, July 30, 1854, Mary Ames Soule of East Abington, daughter of Josiah and Sophronia (Jenkins) Soule, who with a daughter survived him.

From 1858 to 1864 he was principal of the high school at West Newton and became increasingly active in improving conditions in public schools. He was president of the Middlesex County Teachers' Association, 1861–62, an editor of the *Massachusetts Teacher*, 1860–65, president of the Massachusetts Teachers' Association, 1862–64, and of the American Institute of Instruction, 1867. As an organizing member in 1862 of the Society of Arts (one of the three divisions of the institution that became the Massachusetts Institute of Technology), he took an active part in the intellectual life of Boston. In 1864 he became principal of the Hancock School in Boston. Appointed supervising principal of the primary schools at the same time, he succeeded in reorganizing instruction on the basis of Pestalozzian principles, of which he was an untiring advocate. The organization of the kindergarten department of the National Education Association was due chiefly to his efforts.

In 1867 he resigned to join the firm of Bailey, Jenkins, and Garrison, wool merchants of Boston, but this proved to be an unhappy adventure, from which he withdrew two years later to become principal of the Waltham Grammar School. Somewhat later he became business manager of the *Boston Daily News,* and in 1875 he helped to establish the *Journal of Education,* acting as advertising manager, a position he held until the end of his life. He was also co-editor of the *American Teacher* from 1883 to 1887. He was secretary of the National Education Association in 1882–83 and 1885–86, and president in 1887. During these years he published many articles on educational topics and gave numerous addresses before teachers' organizations. Throughout his professional life he was nationally known as a leader of progressive educational movements and reforms.

[Vital records of Dorset, Vt.; records of Burr Seminary; *Am. Jour. Educ.,* Sept. 1865, pp. 525–26; *Jour. of Educ.,* Apr. 19, 1900; *Mass. Teacher,* Jan. and Apr. 1858, May and Sept. 1861; C. Northend, *The Annals of the Am. Inst. of Instruction* (1884); *Proc. Nat. Educ. Assoc., 1900* (1900); obituary in *Boston Transcript,* Apr. 17, 1900.]   R. F. S.

SHELEKHOV, GRIGORIĬ IVANOVICH (1747–July 31, 1795), Russian merchant, the founder of the first Russian colony in America, was born in Rylsk, in the government of Kursk, Russia. His name was also spelled Shelikhov, Shelikof, and Schelechof. Nothing is known about his education, his childhood and youth. He was the son of a merchant, Ivan Shelekhov, lived with his parents in Rylsk until their death, and about 1775 left his birthplace for Siberia. He settled in Kamchatka region, the base from which Russian merchants carried on a trade in arctic furs, began to send out his boats after furs, usually in partnership with other merchants, to the Kurile and Aleutian Islands, and was successful in his very first ventures. In 1781 he was married to a wealthy merchant-woman in Irkutsk, a person of great courage, energy, and business ability. Her first and middle names were Natal'ïa Aleksîeevna, her last name before her marriage to Shelekhov being unknown. In 1783 he organized in Irkutsk a fur-trading and exploring expedition to Alaska in partnership with Ivan Larionovich Golikov, a merchant of Kursk, and his nephew, Capt. Mikhail Sergîeevich Golikov. Near the harbor of Okhotsk the company built and equipped three vessels, armed them with several cannon, engaged a crew of 192 men, and on Aug. 27, 1783, set sail with Shelekhov at the head of the expedition. His wife was with him on board the vessel, *The Three Saints,* the first white woman to sail Alaskan waters. Not until a year later, on Aug. 14, 1784, did Shelekhov reach Kadiak Island, where he founded the first Russian colony in America, naming the harbor "The Three Saints." He conquered the native tribes with ease by the use of diplomacy and with the aid of his well-armed crew.

Soon afterward Shelekhov expanded his activities and conquests to the other islands and to the mainland of Alaska. He spent about a year and eight months in the new colony, and, leaving it in charge of one of his company's employees, Samoïlov, who was later replaced by Delarov, sailed back to Siberia, where he submitted a report of his achievements to the local governor-general, followed by a petition to Empress Catharine II for financial and military assistance for his company, and, especially, for a trade monopoly in the new Russian territories discovered by the company. In spite of the very favorable support and recommendations of the governor-general and the special commerce commission in St. Petersburg, the petition was not granted by the Empress, although she gave Shelekhov and I. L. Golikov special gold medals, silver swords, and a laudatory charter, which permitted them to continue their exploits for the benefit of Russian commerce. The petitioner, however, was explicitly denied a trade monopoly (see Complete Collection of Laws, *post,* vol. XXII, p. 1106). Bancroft in his history of Alaska, *History of the Pacific States* (vol. XXVIII, 186, p. 309), and C. L. Andrews in *The Story of Alaska* (1931, p. 39), are both in error in stating that the Shelekhøv-Golikov company was granted exclusive privileges by the Empress in 1788. Shelekov established his headquarters in Irkutsk and managed his enterprises quite successfully from there, organizing several Russian fur-trading companies. In 1790 he appointed Alexander Andreevich Baranov [*q.v.*] to the position of general-manager of the new colony. The keen and ruinous competition with other Russian as well as foreign fur traders caused Shelekhov to stick to his idea of the organization of a single powerful, monopolistic colonial company, protected and assisted by the Russian imperial government. He died in Irkutsk, however, before his plans materialized, and they were carried out by his widow, his son, Ivan, and his two sons-in-law, Nikolaĭ Petrovich Rezanov [*q.v.*] and Mikhail Matvĭeevich Buldakov. Thus in 1799 the famous Russian-American Company came legally into being, and Emperor Paul ordered that the principal director of the company be selected from the members of the Shelekhov family. The Emperor prior to that had granted rank of nobility to Shelekhov's widow and children (see The General Armorial, *post,* part 4).

Shelekhov wrote and published an account of his own voyage and of the expedition in Alaskan waters of his agents, Izmaĭlow and Bocharov, in 1788, under two long titles, of which the first words are: *Rossïiskago kuptsa Grigor'ïa Shelekhova stranstvovanie v 1783 godu Iz Okhotska po Vostachnomu Okeĭanu k Amerikanskim beregam* (The Voyage of Grigoriĭ Shelekhov, a Russian Merchant, in the Year 1783, from Okhotsk over the Eastern Ocean to the American Shores), and *Rossïiskago kuptsa Grigor'ïa Shelekhova prodolzhenie stranstvovanïĭa po Vostochnomu Okeanu k Amerikanskim bere-*

gam v 1788 godu (A Sequel to the Voyage of Grigoriĭ Shelekhov, a Russian Merchant, on the Eastern Ocean to the American Shores in the Year 1788). The first editions of these works, published in St. Petersburg, appeared in 1791 and 1792. Bancroft considered Shelekhov's account of these two expeditions one of the chief authorities for that period of Alaskan history, although V. M. Golovnin, a Russian naval officer, writer, and explorer, in the report of 1818 of his official investigation of the Russian-American Company's activities during the first years of its existence pointed out striking misstatements and misrepresentations in Shelekhov's books. This report was published in the official naval magazine, *Morskoĭ Sbornik,* St. Petersburg, 1861, as a supplement to the first number. Shelekhov was undoubtedly one of the outstanding leaders of Russian commerce, a shrewd business man who organized new enterprises under extremely severe physical conditions. He can hardly be considered a statesman, for he risked his life and suffered hardships primarily for the sake of gain; but he did help to make Russia's dominion over Alaska a fact. Until his coming her control was merely nominal, endangered by other powers, especially Great Britain. Had Alaska fallen under British dominion, the opportunity for its acquisition by the United States would probably never have come.

[All dates in this article are new style. For reference see: the Russian manuscripts in the Library of Congress referring to the Russian-American Company; *Polnoe Sobranie Zakonov Rossïiskoĭ Imperii* (Complete Collection of Laws of the Russian Empire), vol. XXII, pp. 1105–07, vol. XXIII, pp. 440, 478; vol. XXIV, pp. 670, 725, vol. XXV, pp. 699–718, 931; *Obshchiĭ Gerbovnik Dvorĭanskikh Rodov Vserossïiskïĭa Imperii* (The General Armorial of the Noble Families of the All-Russian Empire, St. Petersburg, 1798–1836); R. J. Kerner, "Russian Expansion to America. Its Bibliographical Foundations," *The Papers of the Bibliog. Soc. of America,* vol. XXV (1931); Avrahm Yarmolinsky, "Shelekhov's Voyage to Alaska, A Bibliographical Note," *Bull. of the N. Y. Pub. Lib.,* Mar. 1932; *Russkiĭ Biograficheskiĭ Slovar'* (The Russian Biog. Dict.), vol. "Shebanov-Shiuts" (1911); V. N. Berkh, *Khronologicheskaĭa istorïïa otkrytïĭa Aleutskikh ostrovoĭ* . . . (A Chronological Hist. of the Discovery of the Aleutian Islands, St. Petersburg, 1823); F. A. Golder, *Guide to Materials for Am. Hist. in Russian Archives* (1917); J. V. Farrar, *An Elementary Syllabus of Alaskan Hist.* (1924).]

N. R. R.

SHELTON, ALBERT LEROY (June 9, 1875–Feb. 17, 1922), missionary of the Disciples of Christ in West China and Tibet, was born in Indianapolis, Ind., the son of Joseph Oscar Shelton, at that time a carpenter, and of Emma Rosabelle (Belles) Shelton. When he was five years of age the family moved to Kansas, and his boyhood was spent there on a farm. Camp meetings and a country church were the background of his religious development and his elementary education was acquired in the district school. His first thought of becoming a missionary seems to have dated from a reading of *Ben Hur*. When he was seventeen he taught his first school, and at the age of twenty went to the Kansas State Normal College at Emporia. His course there was interrupted by a few months of service in the army during the Spanish-American War, but he resumed it after being mustered out. In 1899 he married Flora Beal, a fellow student. In 1900 he entered the medical department of Kentucky University, at Louisville, and graduated in 1903, the financial means for his course coming in part from a scholarship, in part from his wife's earnings as a teacher, and in part from his own labor.

On completing his medical course he was appointed a missionary to China by the Foreign Christian Missionary Society of Cincinnati. Shortly before sailing, in the autumn of 1903, he was ordained to the Christian ministry. The Society asked him to help Dr. Susie Rijnhart with a mission on the Tibetan border. She had lost her husband and child while undertaking a mission in Tibet, but wished to return and for two years had been looking in vain for a physician to accompany her. They arrived in Tachienlu, in Szechwan, near the Tibetan border, in 1904. Here Shelton studied Tibetan and Chinese and in due course began the varied life of a pioneer missionary, preaching, practising medicine, taking charge of a school, and itinerating, chiefly to care for the sick or for those wounded in the border skirmishes of the region. In 1908 he moved to Batang, farther inland and nearer his ultimate objective, Tibet. Here, with his colleagues, he established a mission station. Here, too, with his associates, he introduced new fruits and vegetables, partly to enlarge the menu of the staff, and partly to assist the people among whom he lived. From Batang he made long journeys in the difficult mountain region, healing and preaching. He was an ardent sportsman and an excellent shot. He won the confidence and respect of Tibetans and Chinese, partly by his friendliness and bluff manliness, partly by his sense of humor, partly by his commanding physique, but chiefly by his sterling character. He and his adventurous life made a marked appeal to the churches of his denomination in America, and during his two furloughs he spoke widely among them. Early in 1920, in Yünnan, while on the way out from Batang for one of these furloughs, he was captured by bandits, was held by them for over two months, and suffered greatly before his escape. While in America he published *Pioneering in Tibet* (1921). A few months after his return to his post, when he was hoping that his dream of reaching Lhasa was about to come true, he was shot by robbers a few miles from Batang and died as a result of the wound.

[Flora Beal Shelton, *Shelton of Tibet* (1923) and *Sunshine and Shadow on the Tibetan Border* (1912); annual reports of the Foreign Christian Missionary Society, some printed in the *Missionary Intelligencer,* and some in the *Annual Reports of the Constituent Boards of the United Christian Missionary Society*; *World Call,* Apr., May 1922; *Missionary Review of the World,* Aug. 1921, May 1922; *N. Y. Times,* Mar. 5, 7, 1922.]

K.S.L.

SHELTON, EDWARD MASON (Aug. 7, 1846–May 9, 1928), agriculturist, was born in Huntingdonshire, England, and came to America with his parents in 1855. The family settled first in New York, but removed in 1860 to Michigan, where Edward worked his way through the Michigan Agricultural College, teaching in country schools during the winters and graduating in 1871. In this year he joined as agriculturist the commission headed by Gen. Horace Capron which had been appointed by President Grant to advise the Japanese government in matters pertaining to stock raising and agriculture. It was at first intended to establish an agricultural school at Hokkaido, but that project apparently had no great chance of success from the first, and the commissioners confined themselves to operations in the neighborhood of Tokyo, where they accomplished work of value in the selection of machinery, horses, cattle, sheep, and swine for the imperial farms. In September 1872 Shelton was much gratified to see, at the ceremonial opening of the first Japanese railway, that the Emperor rode behind a pair of bay geldings which he had himself purchased in Coldwater, Mich.

Shelton returned to America in 1872 and, after a brief experience with the Greeley Colony in Colorado, took the degree of M.S. at the Michigan Agricultural College (1874), and accepted the position of professor of agriculture at the Kansas State Agricultural College. Here he remained till 1890, in which year he was called by the government of Queensland, Australia, to go thither as agricultural adviser and instructor. In this capacity he did much excellent work, achieved considerable fame locally, and in 1897 founded and was appointed the first principal of an agricultural school, Gatton College, one hall of which has been named in his honor. In 1899 he returned to the United States and settled with his family in Seattle, Wash. Here he continued his horticultural pursuits, including successful experiments in orcharding at Cashmere, Wash. By correspondence and the reading of a large literature he kept in contact with his old interests in various parts of the world and this interest he retained to the end of his life. Till his last illness, his vigor was apparently undiminished. He died in Seattle, in his eighty-second year, survived by his wife, Elizabeth (Sessons), whom he had married in 1890, together with two sons and five daughters.

[Letters and material made available by Shelton's family; *Queensland Agric. Jour.*, June 1928; *College Symposium of the Kan. State Agric. Coll.* (1891); H. H. Gowen, "An American Pioneer in Japan," *Wash. Hist. Quart.*, Jan. 1929; *Seattle Post-Intelligencer*, May 10, 1928.]   H. H. G.

SHELTON, FREDERICK WILLIAM (May 20, 1815–June 20, 1881), Protestant Episcopal clergyman, author, was born at Jamaica, Long Island, N. Y., the son of Nathan Shelton, M.D., and Eliza Henrietta, eldest daughter of Frederick William and Mary (Dundas) Starman. On his father's side he was descended from Daniel Shelton who was in Stratford, Conn., as early as 1687. He received his early education at the hands of Dr. Eigenbrodt and Professor Mulligan of Union Hall Academy, Jamaica, and graduated from the College of New Jersey in 1834. He married Rebecca, daughter of David S. and Isabella (Fletcher) Conkling, by whom he had six children, of whom only two sons survived him.

Shelton early wrote humorous sketches, but his first published work was *The Trollopiad; or, Travelling Gentleman in America* (1837), a satire by "Nil Admirari, Esq." In it he joined J. K. Paulding, J. Fenimore Cooper [*qq.v.*], and others in resenting the aspersions upon American manners and character which were then coming in great numbers from such English travelers as Capt. Basil Hall, the Rev. Isaac Fidler, and Mrs. Trollope. Both the preface and the poem itself, written in facile couplets, reveal more bitterness than humor. An admiration for Washington Irving, however, seems to have turned his pen into gentler channels. In 1838 he became a regular contributor to the *Knickerbocker*, then edited by Lewis Gaylord Clark [*q.v.*]. To this journal over a period of years he sent a series of sketches known as "The Tinnecum Papers," although they were not announced by that title. Among these were "Hans Carvel" (November 1838), "Rural Cemeteries" (December), "Peter Cram, or The Row at Tinnecum" (January 1841), "The Country Doctor" (February 1841–Jan. 1842), "Morus Multicaulis" (May 1845), and others. He contributed to the same magazine essays on the Latin poems of Vincent Bourne (October 1844) and on the writings of Charles Lamb (June 1850), and to

The Knickerbocker Gallery (1855), "Gentle Dove, an Indian Legend," a tale of Christianized Indians.

In the fall of 1844 he entered the General Theological Seminary, New York City, to prepare for the Protestant Episcopal ministry. He graduated June 25, 1847, and two days later was ordered deacon by the Rev. W. H. DeLancey, bishop of Western New York. He filled a temporary vacancy at Christ Church, Montpelier, Vt., for a few months, then served St. John's Church, Huntington, Long Island, 1848–52, being ordained priest, Dec. 3, 1848, by Bishop Whittingham. In 1852 he was appointed to Trinity Church, Fishkill, N. Y. Two years later he returned to Christ Church, Montpelier, as its rector, remaining until 1866, when he resigned. For about a year thereafter he was at St. Thomas's Church, East Somerville, Mass., and from 1869 to 1881 he was rector of St. Mark's Church, Carthage Landing, N. Y.

After his ordination, his literary work took a secondary place in his interests, but he continued to write essays somewhat in his earlier style, although more formal and moralistic in tone. Two collections of these were published: *Up the River* (1853), a series of letters, dated from Fishkill, N. Y., which run through the seasons with observant and friendly comments on men and nature; and *Peeps from a Belfry; or, The Parish Sketch Book* (1855), a record of his first winter in Vermont which reveals kindly humor and a considerable facility in the use of dialect. It also contains an essay in appreciation of Jeremy Taylor. In addition, he wrote three tales: *Salander and the Dragon, A Romance of the Hartz Prison* (1850), an allegory modeled on Bunyan's *Pilgrim's Progress*; *The Rector of St. Bardolph's* (1853), a simple tale of a country parson, similar in many respects to his sketches, and *Crystalline, or, The Heiress of Fall Down Castle* (1854), a conventional romance. The second is his most characteristic and popular work; it was reprinted in 1856 and again in 1882. Other published writings are "Clarence, A Domestic Story" (included in the volume with *Crystalline*); *Lectures before the Huntington Library Association* (1850); an historical sermon on the Montpelier parish (published posthumously in the *Vermont Historical Gazetteer*, vol. IV, 1882, pp. 413–19); and several poems (*Ibid.*, pp. 420–21). Among his unpublished manuscripts at his death were translations of several of the dialogues of Plato.

As a clergyman he was much loved by his parishioners for his gentle character, and as a writer he received extravagant praise from his contemporaries. Although his style was in the tradition of Irving, he stamped everything, but particularly his rural sketches, with the imprint of his personality. He liked best a life of semi-retirement, and seems to have devoted much of his time to miscellaneous reading and writing.

[A. M. Hemenway, *Vt. Hist. Gazetteer*, vol. IV (1882) ; E. N. Shelton, *Reunion of the Descendants of Daniel Shelton* (1877) ; E. A. and G. L. Duyckinck, *Cyc. of Am. Lit.* (1875), vol. II ; *Boston Transcript*, June 22, 1881, and *Churchman*, July 23, 1881 ; portrait in *The Knickerbocker Gallery* (1855).]

R. E. S.

SHEPARD, CHARLES UPHAM (June 29, 1804–May 1, 1886), mineralogist, was born in Little Compton, R. I., the son of Rev. Mase and Deborah (Haskins) Shepard, and a descendant of Thomas Shepard, who was living in Malden, Mass., before 1658. Most of his early education was received in the schools of Providence. In 1820 he entered Brown University but at the end of the freshman year left that institution to join the group which made up the original student body of Amherst College.

Shepard was primarily a mineralogist and his collection, or cabinet as he terms it, was the interest which determined much of his life. He began to collect minerals when he was fifteen years old, and carried his collection first to Brown University and then to Amherst. At the latter college he found disappointingly little science but came under Amos Eaton [*q.v.*], a distinguished botanist and geologist of that period. Shepard at once began making excursions to the various mineral localities, and found the tourmalines at Chester and Goshen. Eaton used Shepard's collection to illustrate his lectures, for the college had none of its own at that time. With these minerals, while still a student, Shepard began making exchanges, dealing with the Imperial Museum at Vienna and other institutions. Graduating from Amherst in 1824, the next year he accepted the position of teacher of natural science in the Boston schools, and at the same time began studying under Thomas Nuttall [*q.v.*], a botanist and mineralogist.

During the three years Shepard lived in Boston he collected in nearby places and one summer made a most profitable trip to Maine, where he discovered that the locality around Paris furnished the finest pink and green tourmalines then known. In this period, also, he began writing articles for the *American Journal of Science and Arts,* and through these he became acquainted with its editor, Benjamin Silliman [*q.v.*]. In 1827 he became Silliman's assistant at New Haven, and in 1830–31 was a lecturer in botany at Yale. The next two years he was in charge

of the Brewster Scientific Institute, New Haven, and in 1833 was appointed lecturer in natural history at Yale, which position he held until 1847. As Silliman's assistant he engaged in an investigation of the sugar industry for the Southern states, work which led to his appointment, in 1834, as professor of chemistry in the South Carolina Medical College. Since his duties there required but part of his time, he continued his lectures at Yale and in 1835 assisted in making the Connecticut geological survey. He also visited all the known mineral localities east of the Mississippi River and found the rutile locality on Graves Mountain, Ga. These rutiles and the Paris, Me., tourmalines became the means by which he was able to build up his great collection. In 1839 he began a long series of trips to Europe for making exchanges.

Accepting a call to be lecturer in natural history at Amherst under Edward Hitchcock [*q.v.*] in 1844, he made an arrangement with the college for housing his collection in a fireproof building and its eventual purchase. Accordingly, such a building having been provided, in 1847 his specimens were moved to Amherst and his Yale lectureship terminated. As early as 1828, he had collected meteorites, and by the end of his life this collection was the largest in America. During the Civil War he resigned his professorship at South Carolina Medical College, but was called back at the end of the war, serving until 1869, when he was succeeded by his son. In 1877 he retired from teaching at Amherst and the college purchased his collection as agreed, though he continued to collect until his death. After his retirement the collection was moved to another building, and in 1880 a fire destroyed a large part of it. The rarest minerals and the meteorites were stored in a vault, however, and so escaped the fire. After Shepard's death his supplementary collection was given to the college, and the collection as a whole was rebuilt.

Shepard wrote some forty papers for the *American Journal of Science and Arts,* partly on new minerals discovered and partly on mineral occurrences. He also wrote a textbook, *Treatise on Mineralogy* (1832), a second part to which appeared in 1835. He was a member of many learned societies, among them the Imperial Society of Natural Science in St. Petersburg, the Royal Society of Göttingen, and the Society of Natural Science of Vienna. His scholarship was everywhere recognized, and while his methods of teaching were far from conventional, his enthusiasm and kindliness attracted many students. On Sept. 23, 1831, he was married to Harriet, daughter of Robert Taylor of New Braintree, Mass.; they had three children.

[W. S. Tyler, *A Hist. of Amherst Coll.* (1895); Edward Hitchcock, *Reminiscences of Amherst Coll.* (1863); *Amherst Coll. Biog. Record of Grads.* (1927); *Popular Science Mo.,* Aug. 1895; *Am. Jour. of Sci. and Arts,* June 1886, pub. also in *Proc. Am. Acad. Arts and Sciences,* vol. XXI (1886); W. J. Youmans, *Pioneers of Sci. in America* (1896); *New Eng. Hist. and Geneal. Reg.,* Apr. 1869; *News and Courier* (Charleston, S. C.), May 2, 1886.]   F. B. L.

SHEPARD, EDWARD MORSE (July 23, 1850–July 28, 1911), lawyer, political reformer, was born in New York, the son of Lorenzo Brigham and Lucy (Morse) Shepard. His father, an able lawyer and active Democrat, died when Edward was six years old, and Abram S. Hewitt [*q.v.*] became guardian of the Shepard children. From early childhood Edward lived in Brooklyn, spending his summers at Lake George, near his mother's birthplace. He received his early education principally in the schools of Brooklyn and New York, and in 1869 was graduated with the highest distinction from the College of the City of New York. After reading law in the office of his father's former partner, he was admitted to the bar in 1871, and immediately entered upon a legal career distinguished by unusual ability and the highest ethical standards.

Although a specialist in civil practice, he, nevertheless, displayed professional mastery as special deputy attorney general in the criminal prosecution of John Y. McKane in 1893–94 for flagrant election frauds, and also in his defense of Dr. Algernon C. Crapsey [*q.v.*], whose case involved canon law. In his own field he rendered his most memorable service as counsel to the New York Rapid Transit Commission and to the Pennsylvania Railroad. His legal ability combined effectively with his concern for the public welfare in the intricate negotiations he directed for the building of the first subway and for the erection of the Pennsylvania Terminal.

A disciple of Jefferson and Van Buren, Shepard was a power in the Democratic party. The "bosses" both feared him and tried to make use of him. At a price he would not pay he might have attained high place, but at the demand of principle he readily subordinated self-interest, as his part in organizing the Young Men's Democratic Club of Brooklyn and the fact that in 1895 he was independent Democratic candidate for mayor of Brooklyn indicate. In 1896, as a "Gold Democrat," he supported John M. Palmer [*q.v.*] for president in preference to Bryan, but in 1900, believing imperialism the most important issue, he supported Bryan. He accepted nomination for mayor of New York on the regular Democratic ticket in 1901, running against Seth Low [*q.v.*]. Many criticized him for allowing himself to be used as a respectable head for the ticket by Tammany, but his action was due to his belief in party regularity and his feeling that reform should come from within. He was one of the leaders in the movement that brought about the nomination for governor of John A. Dix in 1910, and it was expected that the Democratic legislature would, in 1911, elect Shepard to the United States Senate, but opposition within the party arose and Shepard and his opponent withdrew in favor of James A. O'Gorman. By appointment he served as forestry commissioner of New York in 1884–85, a member of the Brooklyn water commission in 1889–90, and a commissioner of the Saratoga Springs Reservation in 1909. In collaboration with Everett P. Wheeler [*q.v.*], he drew the bill that applied the principles of civil service reform to New York. Upon its passage in 1883 he was appointed to the Brooklyn civil service commission, serving from 1883 to 1885 and, as chairman, from 1888 to 1890. When the application of the system became mandatory in municipalities in 1884, Shepard wrote the regulations for Brooklyn. He embodied his views in a paper, *The Competitive Test and the Civil Service of States and Cities* (1884), published by the New York Society for Political Education.

Shepard had part in several educational endeavors, but rendered his most continuous service to the College of the City of New York. A trustee from 1900 to 1911, and chairman of the board from 1904 to 1911, he gave to every detail of college business the most thorough consideration, and to larger matters of policy both vision and practical wisdom, at a time when, largely through his initiative, the college underwent basic educational as well as physical changes. Though an effective speaker and a man of broad contacts, he cherished a quiet life devoted to work, study, and the close fellowship of friends. This fact, however, indicated no inaccessibility of nature; for he was as democratic in spirit as he was patrician in manner. He never married, but enjoyed the life of the home in intimate association with his married brother and sister and their children. Although he wrote much on law and politics for periodicals he produced only one book, *Martin Van Buren* (1888), a minor classic of political biography which appeared in the American Statesmen series. He died at Lake George, N. Y., where he had been accustomed to spend his summers; he is commemorated there by a memorial park and a monument.

[*Who's Who in America*, 1910–11; *City Coll. Quart.*, Dec. 1911, Oct. 1912; *Nation*, Nov. 7, 1901, Aug. 3, 1911; *Current Lit.*, Jan. 1911; *Review of Reviews*, Nov. 1901; *Outlook*, Aug. 12, 1911; *N. Y. Times*, July 29, 1911; D. S Alexander, *Four Famous New Yorkers* (1923), pp. 361–71.]   D. A. R.

SHEPARD, FRED DOUGLAS (Sept. 11, 1855–Dec. 18, 1915), physician and missionary, was born on a farm at Ellenburg, Clinton County, N. Y., the son of Rufus George and Charlotte (Douglas) Shepard. At fourteen he became practically an orphan through the death of his father and the permanent invalidism of his mother. After several years on the farm of an uncle at Madrid, N. Y., he went to live with his mother and sisters at Malone, where he attended Franklin Academy and distinguished himself both in studies and sports. After graduation he taught in a district school for a year before entering the civil engineering course at Cornell in 1876, paying his way largely with his earnings as a farm workman. After two years of study he determined to take up medicine and transferred to the University of Michigan, where he graduated in 1881, second in a class of a hundred. The next year he spent fitting himself for the varied work of medical missionary by serving as clinical assistant in the New York Ophthalmic and Aural Institute under Herman Knapp [*q.v.*] and in taking a course in practical dentistry.

On July 5, 1882 (Riggs, *post*, p. 18), he married Fanny Perkins Andrews, who had been one year behind him in medical school and was the daughter of Lorrin Andrews [*q.v.*], missionary in Hawaii. Sailing the same year for Turkey, he went to Aintab as professor of surgery in the newly opened medical department of Central Turkey College, an institution founded by American Board missionaries. In 1888 lack of funds led to the closing of this department after twenty-one students, who became the leading Armenian physicians of southern Asia Minor, had been graduated, but Shepard continued his connection with the college as physician in charge of the small Azariah Smith Memorial Hospital. Meanwhile he carried on an extensive practice in the town and surrounding country, often traveling on horseback to Marash, Aleppo, or even Diyarbekir when called for serious illness. He played an important part in relief work after the massacres of 1895 and quelled a cholera epidemic among the Armenians of Zeitun, whose desperate revolt had provided the excuse for widespread attacks on their co-religionists. After similar outbreaks in 1909 in Cilicia and the Amanus Mountains, he was appointed chairman of the committee for relief and rebuilding set up by Jemal Pasha, the powerful "Young Turk" governor of Adana. For energetic and fearless work in distributing funds and fighting disease among the refugees he was decorated by the sultan and given the medal of merit of the American Red Cross. When deportation threatened the Armenians of Aintab in 1915, he went to Constantinople in an effort to avert it. The government granted his request for Protestant and Catholic Armenians, and he stayed at the capital for two months, working in a Red Cross hospital among Turks wounded at Gallipoli. When he returned to Aintab in October, however, he found deportation in full swing. He spent the remaining months of his life in heroic work among plague-stricken refugees, from whom he contracted a fatal attack of typhus.

A man of short stature but unusual strength, Shepard was a great hunter and tireless rider, who was dismayed by no obstacle of road or weather. Famed throughout the wide provinces between the Mediterranean and the Tigris, he obtained from wealthy officials and nobles fees which helped support his hospital. Though he was whole-heartedly an evangelical missionary, patients of every faith sought his services and honored him as a surgeon of outstanding ability, strong character, and loyal friendships, and as one who sought always to promote mutual understanding among the embittered peoples of Turkey. Working under the grave handicaps of primitive equipment and insufficient helpers, he operated with remarkable skill and success on many thousands of cases. He was one of the outstanding missionaries of his generation, and one who practised both medicine and Christianity.

[*Who's Who in America*, 1912–13; Alice Shepard Riggs, *Shepard of Aintab* (copr. 1920); W. N. Chambers, in *Missionary Herald*, Mar. 1916; *Mich. Alumnus*, Feb. 1916; J. K. Greene, *Leavening the Levant* (1916); brief obituary in *N. Y. Times*, Jan. 11, 1916; manuscript records, Am. Board of Commissioners for Foreign Missions, Boston, Mass.]   W. L. W., Jr.

SHEPARD, JAMES HENRY (Apr. 14, 1850–Feb. 21, 1918), chemist, was born in Lyons, Ionia County, Mich., the son of Daniel Ensign and Lydia Maria (Pendell) Shepard. In his early childhood both his parents died and, although he was cared for by his friends, he soon undertook his own support and secured his elementary schooling by doing any work obtainable. As a mere boy he recognized his proper career to be that of a scientist. His early struggles to this end account for his plain, rugged, uncompromising character, which prompted him later to reject many financial and professional offers that he regarded as savoring of bribery or compulsion. He was largely self-educated in the basic branches. After two years at Albion College, Albion, Mich., he went to the University of Michigan, where he was graduated in 1875 with the degree of B.S. As opportunity offered, he studied chemistry at Michigan until 1881 but was financially unable to complete work for a graduate degree. Later he refused offers of honorary degrees, since he regarded as meaningless a degree not based upon resident study. He was superintendent of public schools at Holly, Marquette, and Saline, Mich., 1875–80, and instructor in science in the high school at Ypsilanti, Mich., 1882–88, where he married Clara R. Durand on June 28, 1888.

In that year he became head of the department of chemistry in the South Dakota State College of Agriculture and Mechanic Arts, and chemist of the South Dakota agricultural experiment station. He also served as vice-president of the college, 1890–1900; as director of the experiment station, 1895–1901; and as chemist of the South Dakota pure food commission, 1901–18. He was a contributing member of many scientific societies. His homely, practical, and extremely effective methods of instruction reflected his early experience as a secondary teacher. His publications, likewise, are marked by forceful and concrete presentation, and an avoidance of pure theory. He was the author of *Elements of Inorganic Chemistry, Descriptive and Qualitative* (1885), the pioneer text in placing laboratory experimentation in the hands of the student; *A Record of Laboratory Work* (1886); *Notes on Chemistry* (1886), and many bulletins and brochures. As director of the South Dakota agricultural experiment station, he conducted a survey of the surface waters of the state, a chemical analysis of its forage plants, and developed sugar beets to a sugar content in excess of 25 per cent., as capable of profitable production in South Dakota (reported in the bulletins of the United States Office of Experiment Stations). In his researches upon bleached flour, whiskey constants and food adulterants, in his exhibit of adulterated foods at the Louisiana Purchase Exposition, St. Louis, Mo., and as an expert witness in the courts of the United States and England in pure food and whiskey trust prosecutions, he won an international reputation. In 1916 failing health caused his partial retirement from active work. He died in St. Petersburg, Fla.

[*Who's Who in America*, 1916–17; U. S. Dept. of Agriculture, *Experiment Station Record*, Mar. 1918; obituary in *Daily Argus Leader* (Sioux Falls, S. D.), Feb. 23, 1918; personal acquaintance.]   B. A. D.

SHEPARD, JESSE [See GRIERSON, FRANCIS, 1848–1927].

SHEPARD, SETH (Apr. 23, 1847–Dec. 3, 1917), jurist, was born at Brenham, Tex., the son of Chauncey Berkeley and Mary Hester (Andrews) Shepard. He was trained in Texas private schools and served in the Confederate army during the last months of the Civil War. He then entered Washington College, now Washington and Lee University, and was graduated in law in 1868, began the practice of law in Brenham, and became a state senator from Washington County. During the sessions of 1874 and 1875, he was an active leader in the "Democratic readjustment" under Gov. Richard Coke [*q.v.*], and he supported the movement for a constitutional convention in 1875. He led the fight against the compromise measure proposing an award of $3,000,000 in state bonds to the International Railroad, when the radical legislature in 1870 had voted the road a bonus of $8,000,000 to build across the state, and succeeded in substituting the Coke-Shepard plan of land gifts in 1875. In 1874 and the two following election years he failed by a narrow margin to obtain the Democratic nomination for Congress, and in 1880 he was nominated unanimously in convention but was defeated by the Greenback candidate. He had removed to Galveston and was attorney for the Gulf, Colorado and Santa Fé Railroad. He made Dallas his home in 1886 and continued the practice of law. As a member of the board of regents of the University of Texas from 1883 to 1891, he worked for improvement of the high schools and for a better system of correlation and affiliation with the university, and he was a spokesman for the regents, especially upon public occasions. He wrote the introduction and a chapter on "The Siege and Fall of the Alamo" in the first volume of D. G. Wooten's *Comprehensive History of Texas* (1898).

He was a leading speaker in the fight against state prohibition in 1887, arguing against the "paternalism in government" involved, opposed establishment of the railroad commission, and in 1892 advocated the change from an appointive to an elective commission. When in the Democratic split at the state convention of 1892 the Hogg group followed the Populist doctrine of "free coinage of silver" and repudiated the demands of the National Democratic Convention, Shepard, who had been a member of the committee of resolutions of the Chicago convention to write the party platform in June, adhered to the Clark faction that declared for the Cleveland policy of a gold standard. He always insisted that the Hogg men were the bolters. Hogg was elected after an exciting campaign, and the Texas Democrats were soon reunited. Cleveland appointed him as an associate justice of the court of appeals of the District of Columbia in 1893. He was made chief justice by Theodore Roosevelt in 1905. The Texas bar association unanimously urged his appointment to the United States Supreme Court after the death of Samuel Blatchford (*Galveston Daily News,* July 28, 1893), and he was even more seriously considered in 1895 after the death of Howell Jackson (letter of Cleveland to Shepard, Dec. 2, 1895, in possession of family). He retired from the court of appeals in the spring of 1917 and died the following December. Although a member of the Protestant Episcopal Church he became lecturer in law at Georgetown University in 1895 and served twenty-one years. He was married three times, on Jan. 18, 1882, to Caroline Nelson Goree, of Alabama, who died in 1889, on Mar. 25, 1890, to Etta K. Jarvis, of Louisville, Ky., who died in 1909, and subsequently to Mrs. Julia (Bones) Towsley, of Washington, who with four children survived him.

[Shepard Papers in the possession of Nelson M. Shepard, Chevy Chase, Md.; *Who's Who in America,* 1916–17; D. C. Wooten, *A Comprehensive History of Texas* (1898), vol. II; *Galveston Daily News* and *Evening Star* (Washington), Dec. 4, 1917.]   S. S. M.

SHEPARD, THOMAS (Nov. 5, 1605–Aug. 25, 1649), New England divine, was born in Towcester, England. In his autobiography he stated that his birth occurred on Gunpowder Day, Nov. 5, 1604 (Young, *post,* p. 499). Since the gunpowder plot culminated just a year later, there is uncertainty whether he was born in 1604 or 1605. His father, William, had been apprenticed to a grocer by the name of Bland, whose daughter he married, and Thomas was the youngest of their nine children. Both parents died during his childhood and he was brought up by an elder brother. He was admitted pensioner at Emmanuel College, Cambridge, on Feb. 10, 1619/20, received the degree of B.A. in 1623/24, and that of M.A. in 1627. On July 12 of the latter year he was ordained deacon, and the following day, priest. He was an occasional lecturer at Earles-Colne in Essex, and was silenced by Laud, then bishop of London, for non-conformity in 1630. He then became tutor and chaplain in the family of Sir Richard Darley of Buttercrambe, Yorkshire, and in 1632 married Darley's cousin, Margaret Tauteville. Soon after his marriage he went to Heddon, near Newcastle, Northumberland, but was not allowed to preach publicly by Bishop Morton of Durham "because Laud had taken notice" of him earlier.

In October 1634 he sailed for Boston but was driven back by a storm and remained in hiding

in England until August of the next year, when he sailed again, reaching his destination on Oct. 3, 1635. Soon after, his wife fell ill of consumption following a cold contracted on the ship and died in February 1635/36. She left one son, Thomas, another son having died in England. About this time Shepard was chosen pastor of the church at Newtown (Cambridge) constituted after Thomas Hooker [*q.v.*] had moved with his congregation to Connecticut. In 1636 a plan for an institution of learning was brought before the General Court, and there was some question as to its location. In the meantime Shepard had established his ministry so firmly that Edward Johnson [*q.v.*], in his *Wonder-Working Providence (post,* p. 201), speaks of it as "soul flourishing," and for this reason, as well as the fact that Shepard's congregation had been "preserved from the contagion of Antinomianism" (Albro, *post,* p. 224), Cambridge was chosen as the site. Shepard was an admirer and almost surely a friend of John Harvard, and in 1636 Harvard College became an actuality.

He took immediate and active part in the early controversies of his day. His theology was that of Calvin, and most of his early sermons illustrate the doctrine of salvation by grace. Important is his definition of Congregationalism as a *via media* between Brownism on the one hand, which placed the entire church government in the hands of the people, and Presbyterianism on the other, which lodged all power in the presbytery of the individual churches, or the combined presbytery of all of them. In his opposition to the Antinomians he was unswerving, and he was one of the active leaders in the Synod at Cambridge in 1637 which condemned them. He was particularly concerned with the education of the young. In 1644 he asked the Commissioners of the United Colonies of New England to approve a plan of his whereby each family able and willing should give "yearely but the fourth part of a bushel of Corne, or something equivolent" for "the dyett of divers such students as may stand in neede" ("Acts of the Commissioners of the United Colonies," *Records of the Colony of New Plymouth,* vol. IX, 1859, pp. 20–21). Thus he founded the tradition of scholarships in America. The last important contribution to the institutions of his time was his urgent instigation of a public confession of faith and a plan of church government which, after delays, was realized in the synod of 1647, and became part of the laws of the Commonwealth of Massachusetts and a platform for Congregational churches in America. He showed a constant interest in the conversion of the Indians, and kept a friendly guard over the first Indian mission in Cambridge, established by his friend John Eliot. In 1637 he married Joanna Hooker, daughter of Rev. Thomas Hooker, who bore him four children, one of whom died at birth, and another in infancy; Samuel and John survived their father. After the death of his second wife he married, Sept. 8, 1647, Margaret Boradel, who bore him one son, Jeremiah.

Shepard's diary was first published in *Three Valuable Pieces, Viz., Select Cases Resolved: First Principles of the Oracles of God; ... And a Private Diary; Containing Meditations & Experiences Never Before Published* (1747); in 1832 Nehemiah Adams [*q.v.*] edited and published *The Autobiography of Thomas Shepard*. These works furnish, in addition to the usual introspective jeremiad of the Puritan, an informal narrative of hardships and hopes in the earliest Colonial days. Of particular interest among his many published works is his *Theses Sabbaticæ* (1649), which is an account of the Sabbath, its origin and observance. His *Church Membership of Children and Their Right to Baptism* (1663) bears testimony to yet another of his varied interests, the advocacy of infant baptism. Another work, *The Sincere Convert* (1641), went through twenty-one editions between 1641 and 1812, and represents most of the popular religious tenets of the early Congregational churches. Jonathan Edwards made wide use of *The Parable of the Ten Virgins Opened and Applied* (1660) in his *Treatise Concerning Religious Affections* (1746). Among Shepard's more notable tracts are a sermon on the conversion of the Indians, *The Clear Sun Shine of the Gospel Breaking Forth Upon the Indians of New England* (1648), and *New Englands Lamentation for Old England's Present Errours* (1645). Characteristic of his dogma is his *Certain Select Cases Resolved* (1648), which, while it can scarcely interest the modern student, displays the learning and careful method of the author. He was a tireless worker and preacher. Samuel Mather said of his preaching that it was "close and searching with abundance of affection and compassion to his hearers" (Preface to Shepard's *Subjection to Christ*, 1652). If in his sermons he dwells at too great length upon the wickedness and worthlessness of men, it is without contempt. He was of humble mind and had the Puritan willingness to submit himself completely to the Divine Will.

[In addition to Shepard's diary and published writings, see Cotton Mather, *Magnalia Christi Americana* (ed. of 1853), I, 380–94; Alexander Young, *Chronicles of the First Planters of the Colony of Mass. Bay* (1846), which contains Shepard's autobiography; J. F. Jameson, ed., *Johnson's Wonder-Working Providence* (1910); G. L. Shepard, *A Geneal. Hist. of William Shepard and Some of His Descendants* (1886); J. A. Albro, *The Life of Thomas Shepard* (1847); W. B. Sprague, *Annals of the Am. Pulpit*, vol. I (1857); S. E. Morison, *Builders of the Bay Colony* (1930); Alexander Whyte, *Thomas Shepard, Pilgrim Father and Founder of Harvard* (1909); M. C. Tyler, *A Hist. of Am. Lit. During the Colonial Time* (ed. of 1897), I, 204–10; *Cambridge Hist. Soc. Pubs.*, vol. III (1908); John and J. A. Venn, *Alumni Cantabrigienses*, pt. 1, vol. IV (1927).]
E.H.D.

SHEPARD, WILLIAM (Dec. 1, 1737–Nov. 16, 1817), Revolutionary officer and representative in Congress from Massachusetts, was born in Westfield, Mass., the son of Elizabeth (Noble) and John Shepard, a tanner and a deacon of the Congregational Church. He was the grandson of John Shepard who emigrated from Suffolk County, England, to Westfield about the end of the seventeenth century. There the boy attended the local school and at seventeen enlisted as a private in the French and Indian War, from which he emerged with the valuable experience of six years of warfare and the rank of captain. Settling down on a farm in Westfield with his wife, Sarah (Dewey) Shepard, to whom he was married on Jan. 31, 1760, he was chosen selectman, took his part in the agitation against Great Britain, and was a member of the local committee of correspondence. In May 1775 he became lieutenant-colonel of Timothy Danielson's Massachusetts Regiment and served through the siege of Boston. Made lieutenant-colonel of the 3rd Continental Infantry in January 1776 and in October colonel to rank from May, he was present in the fighting around New York and distinguished himself in the important but little-known battle at Pell's Point (Pelham Manor). He fought at Saratoga, endured the winter at Valley Forge, and, as colonel of the 4th Massachusetts Infantry, did recruiting service at Springfield, Mass.

When he retired on Jan. 1, 1783, he returned to Westfield, where his wife was managing the farm and taking care of the younger children in their family of nine. In 1785 and 1786 he sat in the lower house of the state legislature and in 1786 was appointed major-general of militia for Hampshire County. In that capacity he found himself responsible for the defense of the federal arsenal and the protection of the federal court in Springfield at the time of Shays's Rebellion. His judgment in dealing with the insurgents and his skill in delaying them, as well as his decision to remove arms and ammunition from the arsenal without specific authority, were important in deciding the outcome of that difficult situation. On Jan. 25, 1787, before the arrival of Benjamin Lincoln [*q.v.*], he repulsed the attack on the

arsenal by a force under Daniel Shays [*q.v.*].
Under the new federal Constitution he was one
of the first presidential electors and enjoyed that
honor again in the election of 1793. Elected to
the governor's council in 1792 he served five
years and then sat for three terms, Mar. 4, 1797,
to Mar. 3, 1803, in the federal House of Representatives. He spent the last fifteen years of his
life quietly in Westfield, a deacon of the First
Congregational Church and the town's most
distinguished citizen. He had never gathered
any considerable fortune, and his means were
even more narrow because he was not reimbursed
for all of his own money that he had spent for
expenses and supplies at the time of Shays's Rebellion and because sympathizers with the uprising afterward wilfully destroyed his property
for revenge. He died in Westfield.

[A few papers in Lib. of Cong.; Isaac Knapp, *A
Sermon, Delivered . . . Nov. 18, 1817; at the Funeral
of Maj. Gen. Wm. Shepard* (1818); J. H. Lockwood,
Westfield (2 vols., copr. 1922); *The Hist. of the Cele-
bration of the . . . Anniversary . . . of the Incorporation
of . . . Westfield, Mass. . . . 1919* (n.d.); J. M. Bugbee,
Memorials of the Mass. Soc. of the Cincinnati (1890);
Wm. Abbatt, *The Battle of Pell's Point* (1901); J. P.
Warren, "The Confederation and the Shays Rebellion,"
Am. Hist. Rev., Oct. 1905; F. B. Heitman, *Hist. Register of Officers of the Continental Army* (1893); *Mass.
Hist. Soc. Colls.*, 7 ser., vol. VI (1907); *Columbian
Centinel*, Nov. 22, 1817; spelling of name from facsimile, *Proc. Mass. Hist. Soc.*, vol. XLIII (1910), p.
654, and death date from records of First Church, West-
field, through the courtesy of J. Chambers Dewey, city
clerk of Westfield.]
                        K. E. C.

SHEPHERD, ALEXANDER ROBEY (Jan.
31, 1835–Sept. 12, 1902), territorial governor of
the District of Columbia, was born in Washington, the eldest of seven children. His parents,
Alexander Shepherd and Susan Davidson (Robey), were of English extraction and natives of
Maryland; the former was a lumber merchant.
After his father's death, Alexander withdrew
from school and, as store boy, carpenter's apprentice, and plumber's assistant in turn, contributed to the support of the family. He ultimately opened his own plumbing establishment
and did a lucrative business, engaging also in
real estate and building operations. On Jan. 30,
1862, he married Mary Grice Young, daughter
of Col. W. P. Young; they had ten children, three
of whom died early in life.

Shepherd was a strong Republican and a
Union man. He served as a three months' volunteer at the opening of the Civil War and then
entered municipal politics, being elected to the
common council for three successive years and
holding the presidency in 1862. His public career
began at a time when Washington was a squalid
village with unpaved streets, poor lighting, a
primitive system of water supply, and open sew-

ers. Agitation for the removal of the Capital to
a more fitting center soon gained ground and,
whether from selfish motives or civic pride,
Shepherd became the ardent champion of an extensive program of modernization as a means of
averting the catastrophe. In October 1867 he
joined Crosby S. Noyes [*q.v.*] and three other
friends in purchasing the *Evening Star,* which
thereafter served as his organ. In physique, he
was a giant of a man. He had indomitable courage and was never daunted by criticism of the
means employed for the attainment of his objectives.

He was appointed to the levy court in 1867
and again in 1869. In 1870 he was chosen president of the Citizens' Reform Association and
became alderman in the same year. He advocated a centralized government, closely connected with Congress, as a means of carrying out a
broadly conceived plan of urban improvement,
and his efforts bore fruit in the act of Feb. 21,
1871, creating a territorial government for the
District of Columbia and constituting a board
of public works with extensive powers. President Grant named him a member of the latter
body and he was elected vice-president at its
first meeting. He quickly overshadowed his colleagues and won the name "Boss Shepherd" by
assuming complete control. Imbued with the
callous philosophy of a notoriously corrupt era
and carried away by his enthusiasm, he spent
millions beyond the legally authorized expenditures and hopelessly involved District finances.
His custom of awarding contracts to friends in
casual fashion without competitive bidding led
to accusations that he was sharing in the spoils.
Upon the resignation of Henry D. Cooke [*q.v.*]
as governor in 1873, Grant bestowed the position upon Shepherd. He expanded his projects
despite mounting opposition, and transformed
Washington into a metropolis with paved streets,
good sidewalks, adequate water and sewerage
facilities, gas lights, and spacious parks; but at
staggering cost. His recklessness and unscrupulous methods led to congressional investigation
and the passage of the act of June 20, 1874,
which replaced territorial government by commission rule. Grant thereupon named him commissioner, but the Senate refused to confirm
the appointment, although he had been found innocent of personal dishonesty.

Long neglect of private affairs had left Shepherd a poor man, but determined to start life
anew, he became interested in a silver mine at
Batopilas, Chihuahua, Mexico, moved there in
1880, and converted the property into a highly
valuable one. Meanwhile, the importance of his

old undertakings had come to be recognized and, on Oct. 6, 1887, upon a visit home, he was fêted as a public benefactor. He died of appendicitis at Batopilas fifteen years later. His remains were returned to Washington and interred in Rock Creek Cemetery.

[U. S. Statutes at Large, XVI, 419–29, XVIII, 116–21, XX, 102–08; Senate Executive Jour., Mar. 21, 1867, Apr. 3, 1867, Dec. 15, 20, 1869, Mar. 2, 1871, Dec. 2, 8, 1873, June 23, 1874; Report of the Joint Select Committee of Cong. Appointed to Inquire into the Affairs of the Govt. of the District of Columbia (3 vols., 1874), being Sen. Report 453, 43 Cong., 1 Sess.; William Tindall, "A Sketch of Alexander Robey Shepherd," in Records of the Columbia Hist. Soc., vol. XIV (1911); U. S. Grant, 3d, Territorial Govt. of Washington, D. C. (1929); The Unveiling of a Statue to the Memory of Alexander R. Shepherd (1909); War Hist. of the "National Rifles" (1887); F. C. Adams, Our Little Monarchy: Who Runs It, and What It Costs (1873); W. De Wintton, Who Is Alexander R. Shepherd? (1874); N. Y. Times, Sept. 13, 1902; Evening Star (Washington), Jan. 13, 15, 1870, and Sept. 13, 1902; Boston Transcript, Sept. 13, 1902.]
L. J. R.

SHEPLEY, ETHER (Nov. 2, 1789–Jan. 15, 1877), United States senator, jurist, the second son of John and Mary (Gibson) Thurlow Shepley, was born in Groton, Mass. He was descended from John Shepley (Sheple) who was in Salem, Mass., as early as 1637 and later settled at Chelmsford. After attending the academy in Groton conducted by Caleb Butler, he entered Dartmouth College, where he was graduated in 1811. Ill health caused him to abandon his ambition to become a physician and he turned to the study of the law, for two years in the office of Dudley Hubbard of South Berwick, Me., then with Zabdiel B. Adams in Lunenburg and Solomon Strong in Westminster. On being admitted to the bar in 1814, he opened an office in Saco, Me., where he practised for a time with William Pitt Preble [q.v.], and later alone. His rise in his profession was rapid, owing both to close application and to practical experience.

An ardent advocate of the separation of Maine from Massachusetts, Shepley entered politics as Saco's representative to the Massachusetts General Court in 1819. The same year he took an active part in the deliberations of the Maine constitutional convention. In February 1821 he succeeded William Pitt Preble as United States attorney for Maine, an office which he held until his election to the Senate in 1833 as the successor of John Holmes [q.v.]. As senator he was a vigorous supporter of Andrew Jackson, defending the removal of government deposits from the United States Bank, particularly in a long speech beginning Jan. 14, 1834, wherein he spoke warmly in favor of his college classmate, Amos Kendall [q.v.]. His greatest effort, however, was probably his speech on the French spolia-

tions (Register of Debates in Congress, 23 Cong., 2 Sess., p. 36). When Albion Keith Parris [q.v.] resigned from the Maine supreme court, Gov. Robert P. Dunlap [q.v.], on Sept. 23, 1836, appointed Shepley to the vacancy. Twelve years later, by appointment of Governor Dana, he became chief justice, a position he occupied for the seven years allowed by the state constitution. His decisions are recorded in 14–40 Maine Reports.

More suited to law than to politics, Shepley refused to return to political office, preferring to aid in clearing the docket of its deluge of land cases proceeding from the collapse of the speculative boom in Maine. Shortly after his retirement from the bench, he was appointed by legislative resolve, Apr. 1, 1856, sole commissioner to revise and cause to be printed—before Nov. 15 of the same year—the public laws of the state. The haste thus injudiciously forced upon him prevented The Revised Statutes of the State of Maine (1857) from being the complete work which his experience had prepared him to produce.

During the Civil War he took over the practice of his son, George Foster Shepley [q.v.], who was serving with the army. He had married, June 10, 1816, Anna Foster of Hanover, N. H., who died in 1868. They had five sons, two of whom died young. In 1822 Shepley joined the Congregational Church in Saco and thereafter took an active interest in religion. He was a trustee of Bowdoin College from 1829 to 1866. A fractured hip, resulting from a fall, caused his death early in 1877.

[William Willis, A Hist. of the Law, the Courts, and the Lawyers of Me. (1863); G. T. Chapman, Sketches of the Alumni of Dartmouth Coll. (1867); J. W. Patterson, in Memorials of Judges Recently Deceased, Graduates of Dartmouth Coll. (1881); E. Y. Hincks, Sermon upon the Life and Character of Chief Justice Ether Shepley (1877); Israel Washburn, Jr., in Me. Hist. Soc. Colls., vol. VIII (1881); Biog. Encyc. of Me. of the Nineteenth Century (1885); M. C. C. Wilson, John Gibson . . . and His Descendants (1900); Biog. Dir. Am. Cong. (1928); Daily Press (Portland, Me.), Jan. 16, 1877.]
R. E. M.

SHEPLEY, GEORGE FOSTER (Jan. 1, 1819–July 20, 1878), Union soldier, military governor of Louisiana, federal judge, son of Ether [q.v.] and Anna (Foster) Shepley, was born in Saco, Me. At the age of fourteen he entered Dartmouth College, graduating in 1837. After reading law for a time with his father and at Harvard, he began practice in Bangor in 1839 as the partner of Joshua W. Hathaway. In 1844 he moved to Portland where he became successively the partner of Joseph Howard and of John W. Dana. He was appointed, Nov. 8, 1848, United States district attorney for Maine, but lost the position the following year with the change in national politics. President Pierce in 1853 and President Buchanan in 1857 reappointed him to the office, which he held until June 1861. As district attorney he attracted much attention in the murder case of *United States* vs. *Holmes* (26 *Federal Cases,* 349), when competent observers stated that his prosecution of the case suffered nothing from comparison with the defense conducted by George Evans [*q.v.*].

Shepley was a delegate at large to the National Democratic Convention in Charleston in 1860 and attended its adjourned session in Baltimore, supporting Douglas in the campaign. An acquaintance, begun at this convention, with Benjamin F. Butler, 1818–1893 [*q.v.*], led, after the outbreak of the Civil War, to the inclusion of the 12th Regiment of Maine Volunteers, of which Shepley was colonel, in Butler's New England division in the New Orleans campaign. After the capture of that city, May 1, 1862, Butler appointed Shepley its military commandant; in June 1862 he became military governor of Louisiana, and in July was promoted to the rank of brigadier-general. He must in some measure share with Butler the responsibility for whatever dishonesty there may have been in the army's administration of New Orleans ("Letters from George S. Denison to Salmon P. Chase," *Annual Report of the American Historical Association, 1902,* vol. II, 1903). After the election of Georg Michael Decker Hahn [*q.v.*] to the governorship, by the Unionist portion of the state, Shepley was assigned to the command of the district of Eastern Virginia, in May 1864. In 1865 he was chief of staff of the XXV Army Corps under General Weitzel and when the latter occupied Richmond, was appointed military governor of that city. Years afterward he contributed an article on "Incidents of the Capture of Richmond," to the *Atlantic Monthly* (July 1880). He resigned his commission July 1, 1865, and returned to the practice of law in Portland. On Dec. 22, 1869, he was appointed circuit judge of the United States court. Equity and patent cases made up a large proportion of those in which he gave decisions. He had a quick comprehension of the intricacies of patents but his decisions contain for the most part merely a discussion of the case at hand rather than a thorough review of principles. He was vehement and impetuous, and did not possess an exploring mind.

Shepley married on July 24, 1844, Lucy A. Hayes, who died in 1859; and on May 23, 1872, he married Helen Merrill. In 1877 he joined St. Luke's Episcopal Church in Portland. He died

the following year of Asiatic cholera, after an illness of four days. His wife and two daughters survived him.

[*Proc. of the Bench and Bar of the Circuit Court of the U. S., Dist. of Me., Sept. 28, 1878, upon the Decease of Hon. George Foster Shepley* (1878); Daniel Clark, in *Memorials of Judges Recently Deceased, Grads. of Dartmouth Coll.* (1881); G. T. Chapman, *Sketches of the Alumni of Dartmouth Coll.* (1867); A. F. Moulton, *Memorials of Me.* (1916); James Parton, *Gen. Butler in New Orleans* (17th ed., 1882), pp. 590–92; B. F. Butler, *Autobiog. . . . Butler's Book* (1892); *Private and Official Correspondence of Gen. Benj. F. Butler* (5 vols., 1917); M. C. C. Wilson, *John Gibson . . . and His Descendants* (1900); *Daily Press* (Portland, Me.), July 22, 1878.]   R. E. M.

SHERIDAN, PHILIP HENRY (Mar. 6, 1831–Aug. 5, 1888), Union soldier, was the third of six children of John and Mary (Meenagh) Sheridan, who emigrated to America from County Cavan, Ireland, about 1830. They lived for a time in Albany, N. Y., where, according to his own account, Philip was born. Hoping to provide a better maintenance for his growing family, the father took them to Somerset, Perry County, Ohio, where he sought work upon the canals and roads then under construction. The village school provided Philip with the most rudimentary kind of an education, and even this was interrupted when he became a clerk in a county-store at the age of fourteen. He was too young to follow the youths of Somerset when they enlisted for the Mexican War, a bitter disappointment which was mitigated only by his appointment to the United States Military Academy. On the day of registration, July 1, 1848, Sheridan gave his age as eighteen years and one month, which would indicate that he had been born in 1830. With the aid of his roommate, Henry Warner Slocum [*q.v.*], he succeeded in passing the examinations, but his pugnacious tendencies soon brought him to grief. An altercation with a cadet-officer, who, Sheridan believed, treated him unjustly, reached a climax when Sheridan stepped from the ranks and pursued his superior with bayonet fixed. He was suspended from the Academy for a year, but subsequently was graduated with the class of 1853, number thirty-four in a class of forty-nine.

As a brevet second lieutenant, 1st Infantry, he served for a year along the Rio Grande River, and then, with the 4th Infantry, he saw arduous service against hostile Indians in the Northwest. In the spring of 1861, he received his captaincy in the 13th Infantry, and began his war service as quartermaster and commissary of Union troops in southwest Missouri and as General Halleck's quartermaster during the Corinth campaign. His aggressive spirit chafed, however, under the restrictions of staff duty, and he therefore welcomed his appointment as colonel of the 2nd Michigan Cavalry on May 25, 1862. In a little over a month, he won the stars of a brigadier-general for his signal victory at Booneville, Mo., where he commanded a brigade. His subsequent service was brilliant; at Perryville, commanding an infantry division, he succeeded where others failed, and at Stone River, he practically saved the army of Rosecrans by his stubborn resistance to the Confederate advance. His well-merited promotion to the rank of major-general of volunteers followed on Dec. 31, 1862. In the fall of the following year, Sheridan again distinguished himself in command of the XX Corps, Army of the Cumberland, at the sanguinary battle of Chickamauga. Some two months later in the battle of Chattanooga, his command swept up the heights and over the crest of Missionary Ridge in a magnificent charge which contributed largely to Grant's defeat of Bragg and brought Sheridan into favor with Grant. Accordingly, with the latter's promotion to the rank of lieutenant-general, he gave Sheridan command of all the cavalry of the Army of the Potomac, a corps consisting of three divisions, with about 10,000 men for duty.

Sheridan initiated a complete reorganization of his cavalry command with characteristic energy, and in a little over a month was actively engaged in the battles of the Wilderness, Todd's Tavern, Spotsylvania Court House, and Cold Harbor. Beginning on the morning of May 9, 1864, and continuing until May 25, Sheridan's corps raided the Confederate communications around Richmond, destroyed about ten miles of track on three important railroads, broke up telegraph communication, captured many trains of stores, and caused great alarm and apprehension in the Confederate capital. On May 28, he fought the battle of Hawes's Shop and, soon after, the battle at Trevilian Station. During the months of May, June, and July, he was engaged in successive raids against the Confederate lines, performing brilliant service and securing decisive results. Early in August 1864, Sheridan was placed in command of the Army of the Shenandoah, and received Grant's personal instructions to drive the enemy south and to destroy all supplies in the fertile Shenandoah Valley which might enable them to use it again as a base of operations. Sheridan prepared his plans with a caution which seemed almost dilatory to his superiors at Washington, and then, with forceful initiative, accomplished the defeat of Jubal Anderson Early [q.v.], at Winchester (Opequon) on Sept. 19, and again at Fisher's Hill on Sept. 22. As a reward, he was promptly

promoted brigadier-general in the regular army. He then proceeded to lay waste the Valley, driving out its herds of domestic animals and virtually reducing its non-combatants to the state of starvation. For this, Sheridan was severely censured by Southern sympathizers, but in his eyes it was a matter of military necessity, the means calculated to be the most effective in bringing the war to an early end. For three years the Valley had sustained Confederate forces which had dealt out defeat after defeat to the Federal armies and it had supported the so-called "guerrilla bands," such as Mosby's Men, which had wrought so much damage within the Union lines.

Sheridan's little army was, however, surprised by Early at Cedar Creek, and all but routed on Oct. 19, 1864. The commander, resting at Winchester en route to his army, was twenty miles from the scene. He made his famous ride to the battle-field—immortalized in verse by Thomas Buchanan Read [q.v.]—rallied his demoralized troops, reformed his retreating lines, and decisively snatched victory from defeat. As a fitting climax to this series of accomplishments, Sheridan was made a major-general in the regular army on Nov. 8, 1864, and, with his veteran troops, received the thanks of Congress for their achievements in the Valley of the Shenandoah, and especially for the victory at Cedar Run. "Little Phil" as Sheridan was known to his soldiers, was indefatigable. He was actively engaged from Feb. 27 to Mar. 24, 1865, in a great raid from Winchester to Petersburg, in which he again defeated Early at Waynesboro. He cut three railroads and two canals, destroyed important Confederate depots of supplies, and left Lee's army with but a single line of railroad communication with the South. Of even greater military importance, perhaps, the strategic concentration of Sheridan's forces at Five Forks upon the successful conclusion of this raid, enabled him, on Apr. 1, 1865, to turn the flank of the Confederate army, force it to evacuate Petersburg and to initiate the ill-fated retreat to Appomattox. In the resultant final operations of the War, which included Sheridan's successful engagement at Sailor's Creek, his command was thrown squarely across Lee's line of retreat, and the surrender of the Confederate army to General Grant followed.

After the war, Sheridan was entrusted with the highly responsible problem of administering the military division of the Gulf, fraught with unsettled conditions along the Mexican border. He combined considerable material and moral support to the Mexican liberals with strong demonstrations of American troops north of the Rio Grande River, and practically forced the French government to withdraw its support of Maximilian (see *Memoirs, post,* II, pp. 210 ff.). Early in 1867, the Reconstruction Acts were passed, and Sheridan was made military governor of the fifth military district, Louisiana and Texas, with headquarters at New Orleans—an appointment entailing many difficult as well as delicate problems of administration, incident to the bitterness engendered by post-war conditions. His policies were characterized by severely repressive measures in the interest of Reconstruction in the South, a cause to which Sheridan was thoroughly, if sternly, devoted, and although he was strongly supported by General Grant, the disapproval of President Johnson eventually brought about his relief from this duty and his transfer to the department of the Missouri. In this new sphere of action, he embarked upon military operations against the Cheyennes, Comanches, Arapahoes, and Kiowas, and finally forced these hostile Indians to settle upon the reservations which by treaty had been allotted them. On Mar. 4, 1869, President Grant appointed him lieutenant-general, and assigned him to command the division of the Missouri.

Sheridan went abroad in 1870–71, during the Franco-Prussian war, to visit the German armies in the field, met Bismarck, von Moltke, and the German emperor, and witnessed the great battle of Sedan. After a year's absence, he returned to resume command of his military division, with headquarters in Chicago. He was tentatively selected by the president to command the American forces in 1873, when an invasion of Cuba was seriously considered in connection with the *Virginius* affair. Two years later he was again sent to the city of New Orleans to settle disturbed conditions which culminated in political rioting. He was placed in command of the western and southwestern military divisions in 1878, and in 1884 he succeeded General Sherman as commander-in-chief of the army. On June 1, 1888, Congress bestowed upon him the highest military rank, that of general. The last months of his life were occupied by the writing of his *Personal Memoirs* (2 vols., 1888), the preface being signed only three days before his death at Nonquitt, Mass., where he had gone with his family in the hope of restoring his failing health. His funeral, with imposing military and civil honors, took place in Washington, D. C., and he was interred in the National Cemetery at Arlington. He was survived by his widow and by four children, three daughters and

a son. He had been married to Irene the daughter of Gen. D. H. Rucker, later quartermaster-general of the army, June 3, 1875, while stationed in Chicago.

Sheridan was a short, slight man, of unprepossessing bearing in his later years, and even of ungainly appearance in his earlier. A pronounced reserve which characterized him at all times did not affect the magnetic quality of his personality which so impressed his military subordinates. Always just and considerate in his dealings with his men, and assiduous in promoting the health, personal comfort, and general welfare of his troops, he won from them a complete and enthusiastic confidence. When the battle waged hottest, Sheridan was at his best—cool, exact, self-possessed, the dashing and brilliant leader of men willing to follow him anywhere. He was never a profound student of military science, but his natural aptitude for command led him always to execute with great success the two rules upon which he acted: to take the offensive whenever possible, and to wring the last possible advantages from a defeated enemy. It may be noted, however, that Sheridan rose to his conspicuous military position only near the end of the war, and that his greatest successes were won from a numerically inferior and poorly mounted foe.

[*Personal Memoirs of P. H. Sheridan* (2 vols., 1888); Joseph Hergesheimer, *Sheridan* (1931); W. H. Van Orden, *Gen. Philip H. Sheridan* (1896); John McElroy, *Gen. Philip Henry Sheridan* (1896); G. W. Cullum, *Biog. Reg. . . . U. S. Mil. Acad.* (1891); J. H. Wilson, biog. sketch in *Twentieth Ann. Reunion, Asso. Grads., U. S. Mil. Acad.* (1889); *The Centennial of the U. S. Mil. Acad. at West Point, N. Y.* (1904), vol. II; Adam Badeau, *Mil. Hist. of U. S. Grant* (1881), vol. III; Horace Porter, *Campaigning with Grant* (1897); *Washington* (D. C.) *Post,* Aug. 6, 1888.]   C. D. R.

SHERMAN, FRANK DEMPSTER (May 6, 1860—Sept. 19, 1916), poet, architect, mathematician, and genealogist, was born in Peekskill, N. Y., the son of John Dempster Sherman, an educator and dealer in books, and his first wife, Lucy (MacFarland) Sherman. The eldest of his father's nine children, he was a descendant of Elder William Brewster [*q.v.*] of the *Mayflower* and of Philip Sherman, who emigrated to New England about 1633, settled at Roxbury, Mass., and in 1638 was banished to Rhode Island with the adherents of Anne Hutchinson [*q.v.*]. For the most part he was educated at home by his parents, though he studied for one year at the Peekskill Military Academy. After serving for a period as secretary to William de Caindry of Washington, he entered Columbia College in October 1879, matriculating in the mechanical engineering course but transferring in February 1881 to architecture. After being graduated from Columbia with the degree of Ph.B. in June 1884, he enrolled for graduate study at Harvard, where he took courses in philosophy, Italian, Latin, and Greek, contributed to the *Harvard Advocate* and the *Harvard Lampoon,* and became an intimate friend of Clinton Scollard [*q.v.*], the poet, who later described him as "walking at twilight under the Cambridge elms," improvising "sonnet, rondeau or ballade with an ease that was the despair of those less versatile" (*Columbia University Quarterly,* March 1917, p. 162). His father's ill health limited his life at Harvard to one year, and he was obliged to return to Peekskill to look after the family business of book dealing. On Nov. 16, 1887, he married Juliet Mersereau Durand of Peekskill, N. Y., daughter of the Rev. Cyrus Bervick and Sarah Elizabeth (Mersereau) Durand. In 1887–88 he became assistant in architecture at Columbia. He was instructor in architecture, 1889–91, adjunct professor, 1891–1904, and professor of graphics, 1904–16. Known as an extraordinarily brilliant lecturer on mathematical subjects (*Columbia Alumni News, post,* p. 123), he was able also to write several volumes of poetry and to carry on the tireless research that bore fruit in an exhaustive genealogy of the Sherman family in America.

His publications include *Madrigals and Catches* (1887), *New Waggings of Old Tales* (1888), which was written in collaboration with John Kendrick Bangs [*q.v.*], *Lyrics for a Lute* (1890), *Little-Folk Lyrics* (1892), *Lyrics of Joy* (1904), and *A Southern Flight* (1905), written with Clinton Scollard. In 1917 Scollard published, with an appreciative introduction, *The Poems of Frank Dempster Sherman,* a collected edition. Contemporaries regarded Sherman as not quite equal to Sidney Lanier, Richard Hovey [*qq.v.*], or Bliss Carman, but as nevertheless on a high plane. He possessed a graceful, cheerful muse, his poetic ancestors clearly being Herrick, Lovelace, and Carew; among the moderns he owed much to Thomas Bailey Aldrich [*q.v.*] and Austin Dobson. Living long in New York society, he expressed many sides of its life in delightful *vers de société,* but his catholic and warm humanity also found expression in poems for children, which many readers have placed on library shelves beside those of Robert Louis Stevenson. Much of his lighter verse was written under the name of Felix Carmen. Manuscripts of some unpublished fugitive verse became the possessions of his descendants. His work on the genealogy of his family, which began in 1904 in a modest way,

became his greatest hobby; after his death his manuscripts were deposited in the New York Public Library. He was also interested in designing bookplates, and in collecting stamps and coins. He was a member of the National Institute of Arts and Letters. He died in New York City, survived by his wife and a son. On June 9, 1932, the Friendly Town Association of Peekskill, N. Y., dedicated a sculptured monument and a park as a memorial to him in the village where he was born.

[F. D. Sherman, "The Sherman Geneal.," unpublished MSS. in N. Y. Pub. Lib.; *Who's Who in America,* 1916–17; *Who's Who in N. Y.,* 1914; official records, Harvard and Columbia Universities; *N. Y. Geneal. and Biog. Record,* Apr. 1917; *New England Hist. and Geneal. Reg.,* supp. to Apr. 1917; *Columbia Univ. Quart.,* Sept. 1932; *Columbia Alumni News,* Oct. 27, 1916; *N. Y. Evening Post,* Dec. 3, 1904; *Herald Tribune* (N. Y.), June 10, 1932; obituaries in *N. Y. Times* and *Boston Transcript,* Sept. 20, 1916, and *Journal* (Richmond, Va.), Sept. 21, 1916.]   A. E. C.

SHERMAN, JAMES SCHOOLCRAFT (Oct. 24, 1855–Oct. 30, 1912), vice-president of the United States, the son of Richard Updike and Mary Frances (Sherman) Sherman, was of the seventh generation in descent from Philip Sherman, who came to Massachusetts about 1633 and later settled in Portsmouth, R. I. His grandfather, Willett Sherman, accumulated a small fortune as a glass manufacturer. His father was a newspaper editor, a Democratic politician, and the holder of several minor appointive offices under the state government and at Washington. James Schoolcraft Sherman was born at Utica, N. Y., and received his early education in the public schools and at Whitestown Seminary. He then entered Hamilton College, where he won some honors in debating, made many enduring friendships, and fulfilled the requirements for the degrees of A.B. in 1878 and LL.B. in 1879. In the latter year he was admitted to the bar and entered the Utica law firm of his brother-in-law, Henry J. Cookinham. Business and politics soon claimed his attention, and, though his practice was long continued, it was confined to advising clients in business matters. He became president of the New Hartford Canning Company on the death of his father in 1895, and was president of the Utica Trust and Deposit Company from its organization in 1900.

Against his father's advice Sherman entered politics, as a Republican. He was mayor of Utica in 1884 and member of the national House of Representatives in 1887–91 and 1893–1909. He early became a close friend of Thomas Brackett Reed, Joseph G. Cannon [*qq.v.*], and others of the "regular" Republican group, and throughout his congressional career acted and voted in accord with their policies. Considering his twenty years' service, his contributions to legislation were few. He introduced the false-branding bill which protected American manufacturers of cheese; he presented a committee report in 1896, strongly advocating government aid in constructing an interoceanic canal in Nicaragua; he proposed numerous measures to ameliorate the condition of the Indians; and he sponsored bills to construct a cable to the Philippines and to reform the revenue-cutter service. Apparently he had no desire to identify his name with important measures on the statute book. He preferred to give his attention to parliamentary management, for which he was conspicuously gifted. It was popularly supposed that he evolved most of the measures proposed by the committee on rules. He was made chairman of the committee of the whole in important debates like those on the Dingley tariff and the Cuban war revenue bills, when the Speaker would entrust the gavel to no one else. His firmness and dignity made him, next to Reed, the best presiding officer in the House during his service. Upon Reed's retirement, he was an unsuccessful candidate for the speakership. He presided over three New York state Republican conventions, and in 1906 was chairman of the congressional campaign committees.

In 1908, after Theodore Roosevelt had dictated Taft's nomination for the presidency, congressional leaders agreed upon Sherman for the vice-presidency to balance the ticket. Speaker Cannon spoke for him in the convention, and he was nominated on the first ballot. During the campaign, it was insinuated (*Current Literature*, August 1908) that Sherman had diverted congressional campaign funds in 1906 to secure his own reëlection and that he was interested in dummy corporations to exploit Indian oil lands; these insinuations he ignored. After his election he presided over the Senate to the satisfaction of members of both parties. He was renominated in 1912, but died before the close of the campaign. He was married, Jan. 26, 1881, to Carrie Babcock of Utica, and had three sons.

[*James Schoolcraft Sherman: Memorial Addresses Delivered at a Joint Session of the Senate and the House* (1913); *Memorial Service . . . James Schoolcraft Sherman . . . Republican Club of the City of New York* (1913); *Biog. Dir. Am. Cong.* (1928); *Who's Who in America*, 1910–11; F. D. Sherman, *The Ancestry of John Taylor Sherman* (1915), p. 58; H. J. Cookinham, *Hist. of Oneida County, N. Y.* (1912), vol. I; *Independent*, May 28, 1908; *Review of Reviews*, Aug. 1908; *N. Y. Times*, June 21, 1908; *N. Y. Tribune, N. Y. Herald*, Oct. 31, 1912.]   E. C. S.

SHERMAN, JOHN (Dec. 26, 1613–Aug. 8, 1685), Puritan clergyman, mathematician, was born in Dedham, England, the son of Edmund and Joan (Makin) Sherman. He matriculated sizar from St. Catharine's College, Cambridge, in 1631, but declined to subscribe to the Thirty-nine Articles of the established faith and left without a degree. In 1634 he emigrated to Massachusetts Bay, where he became assistant to the Rev. George Phillips [*q.v.*] at Watertown, but in 1635, with five others, was dismissed to the church at Wethersfield in Connecticut, where settlement had begun the previous year. In April 1636, with these associates he organized the Wethersfield church. He was one of the "Free Planters" of Milford, listed Nov. 20, 1639, and was invited to become teacher of the church there as a colleague of the Rev. Peter Prudden, but declined. In 1643 when Milford came under the jurisdiction of the New Haven Colony, he was sent as a deputy to the General Court.

After 1644 he preached and taught at Branford (then Totokett) and other places in the colony, but without being regularly settled. His reputation as a preacher was spreading, for not only did he win unstinted praise from Thomas Hooker and many other New England divines, but a recall came from England, which he promptly rejected. If the eulogistic pen that wrote his epitaph is to be trusted, he was "as a preacher a veritable Chrysostom." (W. T. Harris, *Epitaphs from the Old Burying Ground in Watertown*, 1869, p. 48). Invited to return to the Watertown parish after the death of Phillips, he was dismissed from the Milford church, Nov. 8, 1647, and became pastor at Watertown, where he remained for the rest of his life.

After returning to Massachusetts, Sherman became an occasional lecturer at Harvard College on mathematics, one of the few non-religious subjects to be encouraged in the early college. His fortnightly lectures continued over a period of thirty years, during which time he published for at least three years (1674, 1676, 1677) *An Almanack of Cœlestial Motions*. In the fashion of the time, pious reflections were added to these almanacs, lest in the fascination of the sciences, attention be withdrawn from the staff of the spiritual life. When his most active days were over, he was given honorary posts at Harvard which he filled with some difficulty. On May 19, 1669, he was made a freeman of the Bay Colony. In 1672 he became an Overseer of the College and in 1677, a fellow of the Corporation. The honor of bestowing degrees was given him in 1681, but, according to the College records, because "by reason of the Infirmitys attending his Age" he might not be able to do so, Increase Mather [q.v.] was authorized to act in his stead. In the spring of the following year, Sherman delivered a discourse before the convened Congregational ministers of Massachusetts, his being the first recorded sermon on such an occasion. While preaching at Sudbury on July 5, 1685, he was stricken with a fever, of which he died a month later. After the death of his first wife, Mary, at Milford in 1644, he married Mary Launce, a ward of Governor Hopkins, who survived him until 1710. Cotton Mather credits him with twenty-six children, but only thirteen are mentioned in his will.

[Cotton Mather, *Magnalia Christi Americana* (1702); W. B. Sprague, *Annals Am. Pulpit*, vol. I (1856); T. T. Sherman, *Sherman Geneal.* (1920); Henry Bond, *Geneals. of Watertown* (1855), II, 935; Convers Francis, *An Hist. Sketch of Watertown* (1830); J. B. Felt, *The Ecclesiastical Hist. of New England* (2 vols., 1855–62); C. J. Hoadly, *Records of the Colony and Plantation of New Haven*, vol. I (1857); S. W. Adams and H. R. Stiles, *The Hist. of Ancient Wethersfield* (1904), vol. I; *1639: Proc. at the Celebration of the Two Hundred and Fiftieth Anniversary of the First Church ... Milford ... 1889* (1890), p. 10; J. R. Simonds, *A Hist. of the First Church ... of Branford* (1919), p. 12; "Harvard College Records," vol. I, *Pubs. Col. Soc. Mass.*, vol. XV (1925); John and J. A. Venn, *Alumni Cantabrigienses*, Part I, vol. IV (1927); C. L. Nichols, "Notes on the Almanacs of Mass.," *Proc. Am. Antiq. Soc.*, n.s., XXII (1912), 23; *New England Hist. and Geneal. Reg.*, Jan. 1870, Apr., Oct. 1896, and esp. July 1897, pp. 309–13.]   E. H. D.

SHERMAN, JOHN (May 10, 1823–Oct. 22, 1900), statesman, born at Lancaster, Ohio, was the eighth child of Charles Robert and Mary (Hoyt) Sherman, and a younger brother of William Tecumseh Sherman [q.v.]. His father, a descendant of Edmund Sherman who came from England to Massachusetts probably in 1634 or 1635 and later settled in Connecticut, removed from the latter state in 1811 to Ohio, where he practised law. Charles Robert Sherman rose to the bench of the state supreme court, but his untimely death in 1829 required his widow to share the responsibility of educating some of their eleven children with various friends and relatives. The famous brothers, Tecumseh and John, were bound by rare ties of mutual understanding and affection. John had a lively, careless disposition, that was trying alike to teachers and foster parents; and his education, divided between Lancaster and Mt. Vernon, where he lived for four years with John Sherman, a cousin of his father, gave him little taste for the college life that was planned for him. He developed a liking for mathematics and surveying, left school at fourteen to work on canal improvements, and at sixteen had grown men working under him, constructing a dam. Fortunately for him, defeat of the Whigs by the Democrats in 1839 led to his

dismissal. After a few months of roistering, a change came over him. Helped by material influences, dormant ambitions, inherited from six generations of paternal ancestors addicted to the law and public service, were awakened; a new Sherman emerged —one who realized that Ohio, lush with expansion, was a fertile field for well-directed purpose. He substituted extreme self-control for careless abandon, and in 1840 set himself studying law under his uncle, Judge Jacob Parker, and his eldest brother, Charles Taylor Sherman, at Mansfield. In this field, his father's repute and his wide family connections proved stimulating and useful.

Thus arbitrarily shortening his period of immaturity and dependence, Sherman gained an early start on his career. Before formal admission to the bar, May 10, 1844, he was doing much of a full-fledged lawyer's work. Also he launched into business, proving competent as partner in a lumber concern and buying real estate wisely. His rise to local prominence was attested by his marriage, on Aug. 31, 1848, to Margaret Sarah Cecilia, the only child of a prominent Mansfield lawyer, Judge James Stewart. The Shermans had no children, but adopted a daughter. Not content with country-town law and business, Sherman entered state politics. Loss of a job at Democratic hands in 1839 had scarcely cooled his ardor for Whiggery in 1840; thereafter he presented himself faithfully at Ohio Whig conclaves, and he attended the national conventions of 1848 and 1852. He ran for no elective office until 1854, when the wave of anti-Nebraska sentiment carried him into the federal House of Representatives, along with many other comparatively unknown young men.

Unlike most of these, however, Sherman of Ohio remained an official part of the Washington scene continuously through nearly a half century; as representative, 1855–61; as senator, 1861–77; as secretary of the treasury, 1877–81; as senator, 1881–97; as secretary of state, 1897–98. This was an astounding feat, considering the fact that during these years Ohio four times elected a Democratic governor and thrice sent Sherman a Democratic colleague in the Senate. The explanation lies in Sherman's temperament and situation. His heritage, his mother's oft-repeated precepts, his victory over youthful excesses, and his quick success in local law and business combined to overlay his naturally hot temper with a cautious reserve that was excellently adapted to Ohio's uncertainties. Economically, the conservative, creditor point of view became his personal preference; but, politically, he understood the radical, debtor psychology that flourished among his constituents during the three major and four minor depressions that punctuated his tenure of office. He carefully studied the attitude of the Middle West and helped to stamp national legislation with the influence of that section. While he was compromising his conservative personal preferences with more radical demands from the Ohio electorate, the East was compromising with the West on each piece of major legislation. Thus he and his work in some sense became typical of his political generation.

He had been elected in 1854 because he was a compromise candidate on whom warring factions could agree; and, at Washington, his more moderate utterances on slavery, contrasted with those of men like Joshua R. Giddings and Owen Lovejoy [qq.v.], quickly aided his rise. Membership on a House committee investigating unsavory Kansas affairs was exploited; Sherman wrote a report, scoring the Democracy and all its Kansas works, which was used effectively in the 1856 campaign (*House Report No. 200,* 34 Cong., 1 Sess., "Kansas Affairs"). He became a hardworking and effective laborer in the young Republican vineyard and at the beginning of his third term (Dec. 5, 1859) was the caucus nominee for speaker. A forgotten indorsement carelessly given Helper's *Impending Crisis* deprived him of the coveted honor, and increased thereafter his leaning toward compromise and caution in legislative matters. The successful candidate, William Pennington [q.v.], adopted Sherman's committee slate and named him chairman of the ways and means committee. Here his tariff convictions insured equable relations with Eastern Republicans. From loyalty to party he never deviated.

Campaign labors of 1860 fortified Sherman further, making him, in spite of Ohio's Republican factions, the successor to Senator Chase, whom Lincoln elevated to the Treasury. On a widened stage the tall, spare, impressive junior senator was ready to play his part, especially in his favorite field of finance, for he at once became a member, and in 1867 became chairman, of the finance committee. In the din of war, with its necessities, he helped give the greenbacks the status of legal tender; but he never completely forgot that there must be a day of reckoning, that order must be wrought out of a chaotic currency. He sometimes tried to encourage a policy of "paying as you go" and led in planning, with Secretary Chase, the national banking system (embodied in the act of Feb. 25, 1863). If Sherman's program of economies and rigorous taxation, especially income taxes, had seemed politi-

cally expedient, fewer bond and greenback issues might have sprouted during the war. As it was, he quieted his uneasiness over the greenbacks by reiterating the popular doctrine that the country would "grow up to" the expanded currency.

On the reconstruction issue, war between Sherman's personal preferences and popular dicta waged unremittingly, for political rivalries in Ohio, as elsewhere, imposed irrational tests of party loyalty and defined patriotism without humanity. His desire for moderation was sufficiently well known for many Southerners to write him concerning tolerance, and he spoke out against the fiery Sumner's program. But he did not carry his efforts at moderation so far from the radical path as to stray outside the confines of dominant Republicanism. Opposing Thaddeus Stevens' drastic military reconstruction plan, he advanced a substitute little less rigorous, which became law Mar. 2, 1867; and he voted for most of the radical program. For his former friend, Andrew Johnson, Sherman openly expressed sympathy; he admired Johnson's "combative propensity," and asserted his right to remove Stanton (*Congressional Globe,* 39 Cong., 1 Sess., Appendix, p. 129). But, knowing the ostracism suffered by the President's supporters, he voted to convict him. When seven other Republicans prevented conviction, he felt "entirely satisfied" (*Recollections,* I, 432).

On post-war finance Sherman dominated national policy, because of his Senate chairmanship, his interest, and his ability; like most congressmen he was swayed by the strong tide of inflationist sentiment, although as a private individual he cherished anti-inflationist desires. He saw in cancellation of greenbacks the most direct route to specie resumption and declared that a beneficial fall in prices must mark resumption; yet on these very grounds he opposed McCulloch's currency contraction policies of 1866 and 1868. The Middle West being then strongly inflationary, he claimed that resumption would speedily come if the government merely met current obligations. The greenbacks outstanding, he thought, were not too much for the condition of the country. When public opinion blamed McCulloch's contraction policy for the stringency of 1868, Sherman said contraction should cease in deference to that opinion. It did. He realized that national credit must be safeguarded by resumption as soon as political conditions permitted; and he entertained dreams of financial reforms international in scope, aiding Emperor Napoleon III's scheme for a stable, unified currency among the great trading nations (*Recollections,* I, 406–12). His work on the funding act of July 14, 1870, reduced the burden of public interest and helped restore national credit. While the dollar was still at a premium, he pushed the mint-reform bill which ended the coinage of silver dollars, so that after silver fell he was labeled the arch marplot of the "Crime of '73." On the resumption act of Jan. 14, 1875, he had to yield his own excellent plan, of funding greenbacks into bonds, for the substitute of George F. Edmunds. His preëminence in financial matters, and his aid to Hayes's candidacy, made him the natural choice for the Treasury in 1877.

As secretary of the treasury, Sherman occupied a congenial place, for responsibility for the national finances gave rein to his native skill at economical management and deafened him to inflationist outcry. He strengthened the resumption act by his interpretation of it, declaring that it empowered the secretary to issue bonds after, as well as before, resumption (a position for which John G. Carlisle had reason to be grateful in 1893) ; and, in the face of congressional clamor, he convinced hard-headed bankers that the government would redeem its bonds in gold, thus immensely enhancing the national prestige. He disappointed bankers who were confidently expecting concessions from the government and amazed them by discarding their advice and achieving sale abroad at a bond price above that of the open market. Thoroughly informing himself beforehand, he coolly bargained with London and New York syndicates and bankers, playing them off against one another, even when they fought him in the gold market and when exchange rates and London discounts went against him. He facilitated direct sales to investors, independent of syndicates. The loans of 1878 and 1879 were especially skilful.

Sherman's statesmanship while secretary was proved by the political obstacles he surmounted. The political odds against him in Hayes's administration were terrific. Hayes's title to office was uncertain; the House was Democratic for four years, and the Senate for two; and the populace was discouraged by a wearisome depression. Business failures, especially in the West, increased in Sherman's first and second years, magnifying opposition to resumption, while mine-owners and inflationists joined hands in a concerted effort to obtain "free silver." With both parties torn sectionally on this issue, it appeared late in 1877 that inflation politics would prevent Sherman from attaining his main objectives, resumption of specie payments and funding of the public debt. The House stopped resumption operations temporarily by passing two

bills: Bland's for a silver dollar with unlimited legal tender and unlimited coinage, and Ewing's for indefinite postponement of the date of resumption (Nov. 5, 23, 1877). While these bills awaited Senate action, Sherman's Republican successor, Stanley Matthews, fathered a concurrent resolution (which lacks the force of law) declaring government bonds payable in silver; and both Houses passed it, thus humiliating Sherman.

However, divisions among inflationists ultimately gave Sherman sufficient support to defeat the more extreme objectives of Bland and Ewing. The Bland-Allison Act (Feb. 28, 1878) stipulated a limited coinage of silver, rather than free coinage; and instead of postponing resumption indefinitely Congress, on May 31, 1878, forbade further retirement of greenbacks. Sherman has been severely criticized for failure to oppose the Matthews resolution originally or to support Hayes's veto of the Bland-Allison bill finally. Faced by a fiscal and political exigency, he labored to obtain maximum concessions from the extremists. He judged resumption and funding might be achieved, in spite of Bland-Allison dollars and of 348,000,000 outstanding greenbacks; and they were.

After the passage of the silver bill, Sherman helped to rally conservative support behind the administration, and the insurgents were somewhat discredited in the 1878 elections. Henceforward comparatively free from the opposition that had been hounding him, and aided by favorable trade developments, he carefully protected the final preparations for resumption. He had the New York sub-treasury made a member of the clearing houses at Boston and New York, and made payments to the government receivable in either legal tenders or coin. Consequently, the premium on gold disappeared (Dec. 17, 1878) after nearly seventeen years; and on Jan. 2, 1879, specie payments were smoothly resumed, to the general astonishment.

Whether or not Sherman could continue specie payments thereafter depended upon the demand for gold. The law of May 31, 1878, to which he had agreed, not only had stopped cancellation of legal tenders redeemed in gold but also had directed their reissue. Later, realizing the potential drain, he fabricated a theory that notes once redeemed need not be reissued when the gold reserve became less than 40 per cent. of outstanding notes. Fortunately for him, rainswept Britain and Europe in 1879 had to buy huge quantities of American wheat, corn, and cotton, paying in gold. Trade rebounded beautifully, and specie payments seemed so secure that the Secretary described legal tenders as "the best circulating medium known" (*Annual Report of the Secretary of the Treasury . . . 1880*, p. xiv). Not so the Bland-Allison dollars. They soon worried Sherman, since their intrinsic worth was declining, business men were forcing them back on the government, and treasury channels were so choked with them as to threaten the placing of the United States on the silver standard. The Secretary made a futile plea to Congress to impose new limitations on their coinage. Then a rise in interior trade temporarily removed his apprehension and he soon returned to the Senate and to his political point of view on silver. As the end of his cabinet service approached, the United States still stood on the gold standard. Resumption was an admitted success.

The most distinguished phase of Sherman's career was closing, but he did not suspect it. He planned further achievements in the White House: refunding the public debt at lower interest, perfecting disbursements, settling the silver question without banishing gold or displacing paper, reducing taxes, freeing the civil service from "infernal scramble," breaking down sectionalism in party politics, and turning politics from outworn war issues to "business and financial interests and prosperity" (Sherman, to Richard Smith June 14, 1880, Sherman MSS.). His dreams were of the stuff that made the inner man, but his success at resumption had made him a failure as a candidate for the presidential nomination. He felt that the business class in general and the party in particular owed him the office; but the unparalleled prosperity that he had helped to create made Republican victory in 1880 so certain as to insure bitter competition for the nomination. Poorly organized Sherman forces, although they helped defeat the unit rule, could not rout the Grant phalanx, or match the Blaine magnetism. Worse, ten Ohio delegates stubbornly refused to vote for Sherman. The nomination fell to the popular and available Garfield, whose presence at Chicago Sherman had thought essential to his own success. In 1880, as in 1888 and to a less degree in 1884, Sherman failed of the nomination because he lacked unscrupulousness in the use of patronage, color in personality and appeal, cordial unity in the Ohio delegation, and skill in manipulating politicians, and because he had an abundance of inflationist opposition. In 1888 he reached the exciting total of 249 votes on the second ballot; but the thread of Ohio intrigue, tortuously unwinding through the correspondence of Foraker, Garfield, Hanna, Hayes, McKinley, and Sherman, shows how futile was his dearest hope.

Through his second period of sixteen years in the Senate (1881–97) Sherman played the rôle of prominent politician, so cast by his adaptation to the plot of the play in Ohio and in the nation at large. Ohio gave him Garfield's seat only after a contest and he had to keep watch lest he should be shelved, in 1879 and later, with the governorship. Democrats won the state thrice, but luckily Republicans controlled when he came up for reelection in 1885 and in 1892 he succeeded in postponing the candidacy of Foraker (until 1896). In national politics, also, the atmosphere was one of continual uneasiness. Neither Republicans nor Democrats obtained simultaneous control of the House, the Senate, and the presidency for more than a single period of two years during this time (Republicans, 1889–91; Democrats, 1893–95); and all the political veterans were confused by uncertainties rising from the economic revolution and by cleavages between East and West that were disruptive of party strength. In such a situation Sherman's services seemed indispensable, because of his long experience in legislative compromise, his understanding of Western demands, and his reputation for astuteness in estimating reactions. The newer group of Senate managers—Nelson W. Aldrich, Eugene Hale, O. H. Platt, and John C. Spooner [*qq.v.*]—left Sherman out of much of their basic planning, for he, unlike William B. Allison [*q.v.*], never joined them on terms of close intimacy; but when the time came to compromise with the West, they leaned heavily on him. He functioned most strikingly in connection with the anti-trust and silver-purchase laws of 1890. The final draft of the first came from the pen of Edmunds and the important purchase provisions of the second never had Sherman's hearty approval; but on the one he carried the responsibility, for the finance committee, of initiating tentative drafts during two experimental years (1888–90), and on the other he so adjusted a conference committee stalemate between the two Houses as to save his party from a silver veto and from the defeat of the McKinley tariff. Then, as often during his legislative career, the immediate political exigency faced by him and his fellow partisans warped his judgment on "sound" currency and the protection of the Treasury.

Republican colleagues honored Sherman with the position of president *pro tempore* (1885–87) and listened deferentially whenever the famous ex-Secretary spoke on finance. He was important in campaigns as keynoter on currency and tariff subjects. Insistence of Ohio wool-growers on protection led him into yeoman's service regimenting Middle-Western Republicans behind a high tariff. His assignment (1886) to the chairmanship of the foreign relations committee proved none too congenial. On minor issues he shifted his position, not always in conformity with popular trends. His economic philosophy always remained basically conservative; for example, he favored general regulation of interstate commerce but questioned the right of Congress to establish maximum and minimum rates and opposed the prohibition of pooling. After he recovered from his nomination fiasco of 1888, Sherman was content in the familiar Senate environment. There were leisure for profitable business undertakings, a never-forgotten sense of service, long evenings alone in his peaceful study and, latterly, preoccupation with the work, published in two volumes in 1895 as *John Sherman's Recollections of Forty Years in the House, Senate and Cabinet.* In 1879 he had published *Selected Speeches and Reports on Finance and Taxation, from 1859 to 1878.* Things might have drifted into the usual peaceful Senate demise if Hanna and the embarrassed McKinley had not translated Sherman to the State Department to give Hanna a Senate seat. In the unaccustomed place, under stress of Cuban excitements, it became all too evident that Sherman had a growing and humiliating weakness of memory which incapacitated him for functioning out of his usual routine. The fur-seal, Hawaiian, and Spanish negotiations were taken out of his hands. When the cabinet decided for war with Spain he rose to the defense of his anti-expansionist views, and resigned in protest. Two years of unhappy private life ensued before his final release.

[John Sherman MSS. (*c.* 110,000 letters), and William Sherman MSS., Lib. Cong.; *House Executive Document No. 9,* 46 Cong., 2 Sess., "Specie Resumption and Refunding of National Debt." containing many letters; *Annual Reports of the Sec. of the Treasury,* 1877–80; *Papers Relating to the Foreign Relations of the U. S.,* 1897–98; S. A. Bronson, *John Sherman; What He Has Said and Done* (1880); T. E. Burton, *John Sherman* (1906); W. S. Kerr, *John Sherman, His Life and Public Services* (2 vols., 1908); R. S. Thorndike, *The Sherman Letters* (1894); M. A. DeW. Howe, *Home Letters of Gen. Sherman* (1909); J. G. Randall, "John Sherman and Reconstruction," *Miss. Valley Hist. Rev.,* Dec. 1932; E. G. Lewis, "Contributions of John Sherman to Public and Private Finance" (unprinted thesis, U. of Ill., 1932); L. M. Sears, "John Sherman," in S. F. Bemis, ed., *The Am. Secretaries of State and Their Diplomacy,* IX (1929); T. T. Sherman, *Sherman Genealogy* (1920). A biography by J. P. and R. F. Nichols is in process of preparation.]   J.P.N.

SHERMAN, ROGER (Apr. 19, 1721 O.S.–July 23, 1793), statesman, the son of William and Mehetabel (Wellington) Sherman, was born in Newton, Mass. He was descended from Capt. John Sherman of Dedham, Essex, who settled in Watertown, Mass., about 1636 and became a freeman the next year (T. T. Sherman, *post*).

William Sherman purchased land and moved in 1723 to the part of Dorchester that was incorporated in 1726 as Stoughton (Boutell, *post,* p. 18). Roger lived there until 1743, learning the trade of cordwainer from his father and helping on the farm. He received no formal education save that offered by the common schools, but he doubtless came under the influence of the classically trained Rev. Samuel Dunbar and early acquired a habit of study that led him to read widely in theology, history, mathematics, and particularly law and politics. A plausible tradition pictures him at his cobbler's bench with an open book always before him. Surprisingly, because of his deep interest in theology, Sherman did not join the church until early manhood; this was probably due to a characteristic caution in making weighty decisions. His father died in 1741. In 1743 Roger moved to New Milford, Conn., where his elder brother William had already settled, and tradition has it that he walked the entire distance with his cobbler's tools on his back. Two years later he was appointed surveyor for New Haven County, and he continued in office when Litchfield County was organized in 1752, serving until 1758 (Boutell, pp. 24–26). This position was unusually lucrative and Sherman became a considerable owner of lands. He began at once to take an active part in town affairs, serving as juryman, gauger, town clerk *pro tem.,* clerk of the church, deacon, school committeeman, and agent to the Assembly on town business. In 1756 he became sole owner of New Milford's first store, which he and his brother had been operating. Amid all these duties he found time to publish in 1752 *A Caveat Against Injustice, or an Enquiry into the Evil Consequences of a Fluctuating Medium of Exchange,* a strong argument denying that bills of credit of neighboring provinces were legal tender in Connecticut in contracts not specifically mentioning them, and incidentally inveighing against imported luxuries and urging an excise on rum to discourage its use. More remarkable than this performance was his publication of a series of almanacs between 1750 and 1761 which were based upon his own astronomical calculations and contained, with quotations from Milton, Dryden, Pope, and others, some verse apparently of his own composition (Paltsits, *post*). In February 1754 he was admitted to the Litchfield bar and in May 1755 he represented New Milford in the General Assembly, which appointed him a justice of the peace; in 1759 he became a justice of the county court. At each election from 1755 to 1761, except in 1756–57, he was reëlected to the legislature. His experience in that body prepared him for legislative duties during the Revolution, especially in matters of military finance and supply; in 1755 he was on a committee to consider how to finance the colony's part in the Crown Point expedition and in 1759 he was appointed commissary for the Connecticut troops, his depot being in Albany.

At forty, a man of property and some political standing, he gave up his law practice and embarked upon wider mercantile enterprises by moving to New Haven. Here he imported merchandise as well as books for Yale students, and he began another store at Wallingford. In 1761 he contributed liberally to the building of the college chapel, and from 1765 to 1776 was treasurer of Yale, receiving the honorary degree of M.A. in 1768. The pressure of public duties compelled his retirement from business in 1772. From October 1764 to May 1766 he was a representative, or deputy, of New Haven in the lower house of the legislature. He was elected to the upper house, as an assistant, in May 1766, and held office in that body for nineteen years. He became a justice of the peace in May 1765, a member of the county court in October 1765, and in May 1766 he was made a judge of the superior court of Connecticut, being annually reappointed for twenty-three years. When these are added to his later offices, Sherman becomes outstanding even in a day when multiple office-holding was not uncommon. These public duties came to him during disturbances over the Stamp Act, possibly in recognition of his moderate support of the Sons of Liberty in their early phases, though he disapproved of their later "proceedings [which] tend to weaken the authority of the government" (L. H. Gipson, *Jared Ingersoll*, 1920, p. 207). When radicalism made its appearance in New Haven, Sherman issued a warrant for the arrest of the leader, Benedict Arnold. However, he served as head of the New Haven committee of correspondence in securing the non-importation agreements, and presided at a meeting of merchants who resolved to boycott New York traders for failing to uphold them (*Connecticut Journal*, Aug. 3, 1770). Though apparently not a member of the Susquehannah and Delaware companies, Sherman, as a member of Governor Trumbull's party, supported in the newspapers, in the legislature, and in the Continental Congress the idea of asserting Connecticut's charter claims to western territory (*Ibid.*, Apr. 8, 1774). Though belonging to the conservative wing of the Revolutionary party, he, with Jefferson, Wythe, and James Wilson, was one of the first to deny the supremacy of Parliament. John Adams noted in 1774 that Sherman

"thought the reverse of the declaratory act was true, namely, that the Parliament of Great Britain had authority to make laws for America in no case whatever" (C. F. Adams, ed., *The Works of John Adams*, II, 1850, p. 343). As a member of the First Continental Congress in 1774, and as a member of the committee on the Declaration of Rights, Sherman also voiced these sentiments in that body, where he spoke "often and long, but very heavily and clumsily" (*Ibid.*, II, 396). A devout Congregationalist as well as a merchant, he found additional reason to support the Revolution in his fear of an Anglican bishopric in the colonies.

Serving in the Continental Congress from 1774 to 1781, and again in 1783–84, always with faithful attention to the burdensome committee duties, Sherman gained a larger legislative experience than any other member. As a member of the committee appointed to draft the Declaration of Independence, of ways and means committees, of the board of war and ordnance, of the treasury board, and of the committee on Indian affairs, he applied himself with such characteristic industry that he was forced to write Governor Trumbull in 1777: "I must leave Congress soon . . . for my Constitution will not admit of so close an application to business much longer" (Boutell, p. 100). It was about this time that John Adams spoke of him as "an old Puritan, as honest as an angel and as firm in the cause of American Independence as Mount Atlas" (C. F. Adams, ed., *Familiar Letters of John Adams and His Wife*, 1876, p. 251). Being a member of the committee on the Articles of Confederation, he, as well as Franklin, proposed a plan of union; according to Adams, "Mr. Sherman's was best liked, but very little was finally adopted from either" (*Works of John Adams*, vol. III, 1851, p. 220). He consistently fought any attempts to weaken the credit of the new government by fiat currency or excessive loans. With a courage born of lofty indifference to popular clamor, he urged the frequent levying of high taxes by Congress and by the states (Boutell, p. 104). In 1777 he attended a convention of New England states called to consider the currency, and that body gave expression to his ideas concerning taxation and paper money. Early in 1778 he was a delegate to the New Haven convention on prices, helping to draft its detailed report. His last important actions in Congress had to do with the Connecticut cession of western lands. In making the transfer with a provision for the Western Reserve, he was accused by his old Susquehannah Company friends of abandoning them in their distress, and by others, with perhaps equal inaccuracy, of making a cession that was "nothing but a state juggle contrived by old Roger Sherman to get a side wing confirmation to a thing they had no right to" (William Grayson to James Madison, May 28, 1786, Madison Papers, Library of Congress). At all events, he was toward the end of the Revolution perhaps the most influential figure in Congress, and, according to Jeremiah Wadsworth, "as cunning as the Devil" in managing legislation (C. R. King, ed., *The Life and Correspondence of Rufus King,* I, 1894, p. 221). During his service in Congress he was also a member of the Council of Safety of Connecticut from 1777 to 1779 and again in 1782. In May 1783 he was appointed with Richard Law to revise the statutory law of Connecticut, a codification which was completed in five months (*Acts and Laws of the State of Connecticut,* 1784). From 1784 to 1786 he enjoyed comparative repose for the first time since the outbreak of the Revolution, his chief offices being those of judge of the superior court and mayor of New Haven.

In the latter part of his service in Congress, Sherman had drawn up a series of amendments designed to strengthen the Confederation, the chief of which provided that Congress should have power to regulate commerce, levy imposts, establish a supreme court, and make laws binding on the people. In 1787 he entered the Federal Convention still "disposed to patch up the old scheme of Government" but he soon saw the need of creating a new system (King, I, 221; Farrand, *post,* I, 34–35). Although he was a leading member of the compromise group in the convention, his leanings were toward a national government. On June 11 he introduced the so-called "Connecticut Compromise" (Farrand, I, 196), providing for a dual system of representation, a device he had hinted at eleven years earlier (*Works of John Adams,* II, 499); in the struggle for the adoption of this essential compromise, Sherman took a leading part. Reflecting his Connecticut background rather than an admiration for the British system, he favored an executive dominated by the legislature. His opposition to democratic tendencies was illustrated in his stand for election of congressmen and senators by state legislatures and in his opinion that popular ratification of the Constitution was unnecessary. When Sherman affixed his signature to the Constitution, he achieved the distinction of being the only person to sign that and three other great documents of the Republic— the Articles of Association of 1774, the Declaration of Independence, and the Articles of Confederation. He took a prominent part in the

campaign for ratification of the Constitution. Writing under the pseudonym of "A Countryman," he contributed a series of cogent letters addressed "To the People of Connecticut" (*New Haven Gazette,* Nov. 15, 22, 29; Dec. 6, 20, 1787; reprinted in P. L. Ford, *post,* where the first letter is misdated). These letters drew him into a notable correspondence with John Adams on the nature of the government (*Works of John Adams,* VI, 1851, pp. 427–42).

In 1789 he was elected a member of Congress, and in order to take his seat he reluctantly gave up his position as judge of the superior court. He took an active part in the debates of the first session, favoring the impost and opposing amendments to the Constitution, a subject he had already discussed in the press (*New Haven Gazette,* Dec. 18, 1788). In the second session he urged the use of western lands to extinguish the national debt and favored sale to settlers rather than to speculators. He had fought since 1776 for a sound system of credit and voted for Hamilton's measure for the assumption of state debts, but he opposed the measure for locating the government on the Potomac. In 1791 he was elected to fill the place of William Samuel Johnson [*q.v.*] in the Senate, an office which he held until his death.

Always illustrating at its best the Puritan combination of piety and a desire to succeed in practical affairs, Sherman opposed the granting of commissions to "foreign Papists" (*American Historical Review,* April 1896, p. 499) during the Revolution, and likewise opposed confirmation of Gouverneur Morris as minister to France because of an inherent distrust of irreligious natures (Boutell, p. 271). In 1789 he published *A Short Sermon on the Duty of Self-Examination Preparatory to Receiving the Lord's Supper,* which gained the commendation of Ezra Stiles and others. He corresponded with various New England theologians, and his discussion, with the Rev. Samuel Hopkins, of the doctrine of disinterested submission reveals his delight in theology (*Proceedings American Antiquarian Society,* n.s., vol. V, 1889, pp. 437–61). His contemporaries fully recognized his ability, honesty, and adroitness in legislative councils, but they were also fond of recording his personal awkwardness and a certain rusticity of manner. There is a crude but masterly portrait of him by Ralph Earl in the Yale Gallery of Fine Arts. His record attests industry, integrity, devotion to public duty, even moral grandeur. He was twice married: on Nov. 17, 1749, to Elizabeth Hartwell, by whom he had seven children before her death in 1760; and on May 12, 1763, to Rebecca (or Rebekah) Prescott, by whom he had eight. His second wife survived him.

[Sherman left a large mass of MSS. but they are thought to have been destroyed; some are in the Mass. Hist. Soc., in the Trumbull MSS. in the Conn. State Lib., and in the series called "Revolutionary War, 1763–1789" in the same place. A forthcoming biography by Roger Sherman Boardman is the best study, but at present L. H. Boutell, *The Life of Roger Sherman* (1896) is the standard. In addition to sources cited in the text and the usual standard works for the period, the following are useful: *Century Mag.*, Apr. 1889, pp. 803–33; *New England Quart.*, Apr. 1932, pp. 221–36; *Yale Law Journal*, Dec. 1908, pp. 75–84; John Sanderson and Robert Waln, Jr., *Biography of the Signers to the Declaration of Independence*, III (1823), pp. 197–306; V. H. Paltsits, "The Almanacs of Roger Sherman," in *Proc. Am. Antiquarian Soc.*, n.s., vol. XVIII (1907), pp. 213–58; *N. Y. Gazette*, Jan. 22, 1749/50; *Conn. Journal*, July 31, 1793 (obituary); records of the superior court of Conn., in office of secretary of state, vols. XIII–XVIII; *Am. Lit. Magazine*, June 1849, p. 697; P. L. Ford, ed., *Essays of the Constitution . . . 1787–1788* (1892), pp. 211–41; F. B. Dexter, ed., *The Lit. Diary of Ezra Stiles* (3 vols., 1901); Max Farrand, ed., *The Records of the Federal Convention* (3 vols., 1911); E. C. Burnett, ed., *Letters of Members of the Continental Cong.*, vols. I–VI (1921–33); S. E. Baldwin, *Two Centuries of New Milford, Conn. . . .* (1907), 232–55; **G.** F. Hoar, *Autobiog. of Seventy Years* (1903), I, pp. 7–19; Henry Bond, *Geneals. of the Families and Descendants of the Early Settlers of Watertown, Mass.* (1855), I, p. 431; T. T. Sherman, *Sherman Genealogy* (1920).] J. P. B.

SHERMAN, STUART PRATT (Oct. 1, 1881–Aug. 21, 1926), literary critic, educator, son of John and Ada Martha (Pratt) Sherman, belonged to an old New England family tracing its descent from Edmund Sherman who came to Massachusetts about 1634. His father, a lover of music and poetry, was, ironically, a druggist who had wandered out to Anita, Iowa, where Stuart was born. In 1882 the family moved to Rolfe, Iowa, and in 1887 to Los Angeles, seeking a more healthful climate for the father, who died in 1892. The family later returned to New England, where Sherman attended Troy Conference Academy at Poultney, Vt., and subsequently the high school in Williamstown, Mass. Entering the sophomore class of Williams College in 1900, he won prizes in Latin, French, and German, and succeeded Harry James Smith [*q.v.*] as editor of the *Williams Literary Monthly*. Graduating in 1903, he did graduate work in English at Harvard, where he was profoundly influenced by Irving Babbitt. He received the degree of Ph.D. in 1906, with a brilliant thesis on John Ford, expanded and published in 1915 as an introduction to his edition of Ford's *'Tis Pity She's a Whore, and The Broken Heart*. In September 1906 he became an instructor at Northwestern University and on Dec. 25 was married to Ruth Bartlett Mears, daughter of Leverett Mears, a

chemistry professor at Williams. In 1907 he accepted a call to the University of Illinois. A letter which he published in the *Nation*, May 14, 1908, attacking the formalism of graduate instruction in English, attracted wide attention. During the summer of 1908 he served as an editorial writer for the *Nation* and was offered a position on its staff, but the University of Illinois countered by raising him to the rank of associate professor. For the next ten years, however, he was a frequent contributor to the *Nation,* with whose policy, under the editorship of Paul Elmer More, he was for a time in almost complete sympathy. He was made a full professor in 1911 and permanent chairman of the English department in 1914. With a group of devoted colleagues, he made it one of the strongest in the Middle West. A natural teacher, he combined sound scholarship with a persuasive emphasis on the living values of literature. His best course, on Matthew Arnold, resulted in the publication of *Matthew Arnold: How to Know Him* (1917), acclaimed by the caustic Irving Babbitt as "the first good book" on the subject (*Nation*, Aug. 2, 1917). In the same year he published *On Contemporary Literature,* an application of Arnold's principles to the chief contemporary writers with devastating results.

The entrance of the United States into the World War fired his patriotism, and in an address on "American and Allied Ideals," delivered on Dec. 1, 1917, before the National Council of Teachers of English, he attacked the philosophy of Nietzsche, particularly as expressed by H. L. Mencken. This assault began an exhilarating literary quarrel with Mencken, which continued intermittently for nearly a decade, with much expenditure of wit by both combatants. Under the influence of the emotions bred by the war, Sherman for a time became almost chauvinistic in his nationalism. Believing intensely in democracy, he thought that contemporary American literature had gone astray through lack of loyalty to the national ideal and that the "spiritually alien strain in our recent literature" was due to "the later importations of European blood and culture." In "Is There Anything to be Said for Literary Traditions?" (*Bookman,* October 1920) he attacked the whole group of modernist critics. The controversy thus begun raged for several years, with a plentiful amount of misunderstanding on both sides. The younger critics in their assault on conventional moral and literary standards were led to adopt the non-moral estheticism of Benedetto Croce as a rallying-point, while Sherman confused his defense of the ethical content of literature with a defense of traditional emotion, nationalism, and Puritanism. In his polemical writings, he used to good effect Arnold's weapons of irony, understatement, and the edged epithet, and he had also acquired from Arnold the exasperating habit of rising to moral altitudes where he became invisible to his adversaries, but his victories, while sometimes real, were often merely rhetorical. He ended by being largely converted to the position of his opponents, confessing that he had erred in trying to make men good instead of happy.

His gradual turning to the left may be followed in *Americans* (1922), *The Genius of America* (1923), and *Points of View* (1924). In 1924 he contributed a series of critical essays to an edition de luxe of *Men of Letters of the British Isles: Portrait Medallions from the Life,* edited by Theodore Spicer-Stimson, and published *My Dear Cornelia,* a series of imaginary conversations with a lady of old-fashioned tastes, in defense of modernism, some of which had appeared in the *Atlantic Monthly.* In April 1924 he became editor of *Books,* the literary supplement of the *New York Herald Tribune,* and thenceforward by his weekly impressionistic essays made it the leading American critical journal of the day. Some of these essays were reprinted in 1926 under the title *Critical Woodcuts.* His death came as the result of a heart attack while swimming ashore from an overturned canoe near his summer cottage at Dunewood on Lake Michigan. He was survived by his wife and a son.

[Jacob Zeitlin and Homer Woodbridge, *Life and Letters of Stuart P. Sherman* (1929), with full bibliog.; see also, G. E. DeMille, *Lit. Criticism in America* (1931); Carl Van Doren, in *Century Mag.,* Aug. 1923; S. J. Kunitz, *Authors Today and Yesterday* (1933); *The Bookman,* June 1922, June 1926; *N. Y. Times,* Aug. 23, 1926; *N. Y. Herald Tribune: Books,* Sept. 26, 1926.]
E. S. B.

SHERMAN, THOMAS WEST (Mar. 26, 1813–Mar. 16, 1879), soldier, was born in Newport, R. I., the son of Elijah and Martha (West) Sherman. He was a descendant of Philip Sherman, who emigrated to America about 1633 and moved in 1638 to Rhode Island, where he settled at Portsmouth. After attending the public schools, Sherman saw no prospect of further education, since his parents were in humble circumstances. At eighteen, when his father disapproved of his centering his hopes on West Point and a soldier's career, he walked to Washington and appealed to President Jackson, who was so impressed by this show of determination and self-reliance that Sherman got his cadetship. He was graduated, July 1, 1836, and commissioned second lieutenant, 3rd Artillery.

In 1838, after two years' active service in the Florida War, he became first lieutenant and served in the Indian Territory, assisting the Cherokee transfer. Then came four more years of the Florida hostilities, service at Fort Moultrie, S. C., and recruiting duty. Promoted captain in May 1846, he served with Taylor's army in the Mexican War, in which he commanded a battery at Buena Vista, rendered conspicuous service, and received the brevet of major. He served at Fort Trumbull, Conn., and Fort Adams, R. I., from 1848 to 1853, when he was assigned to frontier duty in Minnesota. In 1857–58 he assisted in quelling the disturbances in Kansas. While there he married Mary, daughter of Gov. Wilson Shannon [*q.v.*]. Returning to Minnesota, he commanded an expedition to Kettle Lake in 1859 whereby the Sioux were restrained from war.

At the outbreak of the Civil War he was ordered to duties in connection with the defense of Washington. He was promoted major and lieutenant-colonel in the regular army, and brigadier-general of volunteers in rapid succession, and was placed in charge of an expedition to take and hold bases on the southern coast for the use of the blockading fleet. He occupied Port Royal Harbor, S. C., after a naval bombardment, Nov. 7, 1861, and later seized Bull's Bay, S. C., and Fernandina, Fla. His management of this enterprise was marked by skill and judgment. In 1862 he was assigned to the command of a division of Halleck's army, then operating against Corinth. His manner of exercising authority, however, resulted in complaints from some of his subordinates which led to his relief and assignment to the Department of the Gulf. After serving in command of troops above New Orleans from the fall of 1862 to January 1863, he commanded a division in the expedition against Port Hudson, La. On May 27, 1863, he was wounded while gallantly leading an assault on the Confederate works and afterwards lost his right leg by amputation. Promoted colonel, 3rd Artillery, he returned to duty after nine months' sick leave in command of a reserve brigade of artillery and of Forts Jackson and St. Philip, La. From 1864 to 1866 he was successively in command of the defenses of New Orleans, of the Southern Division of Louisiana, and of the Eastern District of Louisiana. All these duties he performed with marked energy and efficiency in spite of his physical handicap. He was brevetted brigadier-general, United States Army, for gallant and meritorious service at the capture of Port Hudson, and major general of volunteers for like services during the war. He was mustered out of volunteer service in 1866. After the war he served in command of his regiment at different stations on the Atlantic seaboard until November 1870; soon afterward he was retired from active service as major-general. He died at his home in Newport, R. I., his wife's death having preceded his by a few days; one son survived them. He was an officer of unquestioned ability, but his long career in the old regular army of the Indian frontier in some ways unfitted him for handling volunteers not inured to its iron discipline, and his ingrained training and positive personality sometimes produced friction that lessened the value of his military knowledge and experience.

[*New England Hist. and Geneal. Reg.*, vol. XXIV (1870), p. 163; G. W. Cullum, *Biog. Reg. Officers and Grads. U. S. Mil. Acad.*, vol. I (1891); *Battles and Leaders of the Civil War* (4 vols., 1887–88); *War of the Rebellion: Official Records (Army)*, esp. 1 ser., vol. VI (1882), vol. XVI (1886), pt. 2; *Harper's Weekly*, Nov. 30, 1861; W. E. Birkhimer, "The Third U. S. Artillery," *Jour. Mil. Service Inst.*, Mar. 1893; J. H. Smith, *The War with Mexico* (2 vols., 1919); *Army and Navy Jour.*, Mar. 15, 22, 1879; *Appletons' Ann. Cyc.*, 1879; *N. Y. Tribune*, Mar. 17, 1879.] T. F. M.

SHERMAN, WILLIAM TECUMSEH (Feb. 8, 1820–Feb. 14, 1891), Union soldier, was born at Lancaster, Ohio, the third son and sixth child of Charles Robert and Mary (Hoyt) Sherman. The family had been in America since about 1634 when Edmund Sherman came from Dedham in Essex, England, to Boston, Mass., with his son, Samuel, and a cousin, the progenitor of Roger Sherman [*q.v.*]. Another son was John Sherman, 1613–1685 [*q.v.*]. Tecumseh's grandfather, Taylor Sherman, of Norwalk, Conn., had served as a commissioner to settle land titles in the Western Reserve, receiving some Ohio lands as compensation. Attracted by these lands, his son, Charles Robert, moved West in 1811, and entered upon the practice of law at Lancaster. He became judge of the state supreme court in 1823 and served until his sudden death in 1829. Most of his eleven children were then distributed among relatives, friends, and neighbors to be cared for, and Tecumseh was welcomed into the family of Thomas Ewing, 1789–1871 [*q.v.*], who was indebted to the boy's father for helping him begin his career as a frontier lawyer. The red-haired lad, known intimately as "Cump," had been named by his father after the noble Shawnee chief, Tecumseh [*q.v.*], but under the influence of his devout Catholic wife, Thomas Ewing permitted him to be baptized with the name of William Tecumseh. Ewing never formally adopted him.

A sound education at a local academy was interrupted suddenly when the boy was "notified" to prepare for West Point (*Memoirs, post*, I, 14). Ewing secured an appointment for his charge in 1836, and Sherman was graduated number six in the class of 1840. He was assigned as second lieutenant, 3rd Artillery, on field service in Florida, and became a first lieutenant in 1841. The following year he was stationed at Fort Moultrie, S. C., where his duties left ample time for him to begin the study of law. During his first leave in 1843 in Lancaster, he became engaged to Eleanor Boyle Ewing (called Ellen), the daughter of his guardian. Returning from this leave, he traveled down the Mississippi River and began an acquaintance with Georgia which, supplemented by a tour of three months in 1844 and a detail at the Augusta arsenal in 1845, provided him a valuable knowledge of the countryside. During the Mexican War he was aide to Philip Kearny and later adjutant to Richard Barnes Mason [*qq.v.*], but he saw so little action that he submitted his resignation and was persuaded to withdraw it only when Persifor Frazer Smith [*q.v.*], in command of the new division of the Pacific, made Sherman his adjutant-general. He was relieved in January 1850 to carry dispatches east for General Scott. On May 1, after an engagement of seven years, he was married to Ellen Ewing in Washington, D. C., an event of great social importance in the capital because of the position of the bride's father.

Sherman served as captain in the subsistence department for a year and a half, and then resigned his commission on Sept. 6, 1853, to become a partner in a branch bank of a St. Louis concern in San Francisco, Cal. Business prospered for a while, but the period of severe depression caused the bank to close in the spring of 1857. He then represented the firm in New York for a short time, but the parent bank itself failed in October, and Sherman voluntarily assumed a heavy personal financial responsibility for losses to friends who had given him money to invest for them. His efforts to return to the army failed and he established a partnership with Thomas and Hugh Boyle Ewing [*q.v.*], practising law in Leavenworth, Kan. He lost the only case he tried. Contact with the garrison at Leavenworth increased his eagerness to rejoin the service, but after other attempts failed he applied for and received the post of superintendent of a new military college about to be opened at Alexandria, La., now Louisiana State University. He was conspicuously successful in this work, in which he was engaged from October 1859 until Jan. 18, 1861, endearing himself to his co-workers, and winning many friends.

Before the secession of Louisiana compelled him to resign he was even offered a high commission in the Confederate army. He later accepted the presidency of a St. Louis street railway. This was a very trying time for Sherman. Failure had dogged his footsteps; his industry, his honesty, his recognized abilities for mastering innumerable details had—in the army, in finance, in education, in industry—availed him nothing. He had been forced, time after time, to accept the tactful hospitality of the Ewing household for his family, and had often held off with some difficulty his particular *bête noir*—the management of the Ewing salt-works in Ohio, a means of livelihood which Thomas Ewing had offered him again and again out of genuine kindness.

The prospect of war between the Union and the South caused Sherman real anguish. He regarded the preservation of the Union and the integrity of the Constitution with the same fervor—almost religious—as did Thomas Ewing, from whose fire it had probably been kindled. He also loved the South and her people. Everything must be done to avert war; if it came, it must be brought to a conclusion as swiftly as possible, and the South must be returned to the fold with no further punishment than the sufferings which the actual conflict would mete out to her. Here lies the spring of Sherman's action from the day he parted from his Southern friends; the key to his prophetic views on the proportions of the war, to the ruthless march through Georgia, to his liberal peace terms, and to his consistent opposition to Congressional reconstruction.

At last when the regular army was increased in May 1861, Sherman was appointed colonel of the new 13th Infantry, and in July was assigned to command a brigade in General McDowell's army. With this command he shared in the disaster of Bull Run. He was advanced to the rank of brigadier-general of volunteers a month later, and became second in command in Kentucky to Robert Anderson [*q.v.*], inheriting the thankless job of trying to hold the state with little more than home guards when Anderson's poor health forced him to relinquish it. His anxiety over the raw recruits for whose lives he was responsible preyed upon his mind at this time, and his nervous temperament led him to overestimate the difficulty of his position, the forces of the enemy, and the number of troops required—although, as it was proved later, the last was moderate enough. His efforts to keep newspaper reporters out of his lines in the belief that the enemy learned valuable information from this source unfortunately aroused the enmity of the press, so that the rumour that Sherman's mind was giving way spread quickly to officials and to the public. Buell was sent to assume command in Kentucky and Sherman went to Missouri to report to Halleck. He was received with coldness and suspicion and so bitter was his resentment that he even contemplated suicide. Shortly after he returned from leave, he was assigned to the District of Cairo, Grant's former command. After the capture of the forts, he joined Grant with a division of volunteers and took a prominent part in the battle of Shiloh and the advance to Corinth. The frightful carnage at Shiloh again gave the newspapers a chance to strike at Sherman, and they reported that the Federals had been surprised in their camps. True it is, that sufficient preparation had not been made, and it may be supposed that Sherman's experience in Kentucky made him very wary of the camp rumour that Johnston's army was moving against him (see Lewis, *post*, p. 218 ff.). Sherman's command, however, was vigorous and he had four horses shot from under him during the battle. He was promoted major-general of volunteers with rank from May 1, 1862.

In July 1862, Grant succeeded Halleck in charge of the western armies and sent Sherman to Memphis to place it in a state of defense. Sherman suppressed guerrilla warfare, established civil authority on a firm basis, organized a charity drive, and would have brought the cotton trade under control had not Federal authorities obstructed him. Pillaging was strictly forbidden to his soldiers. The Mississippi was now open as far down as Memphis, and as far up from the mouth as Port Hudson. The only strong points remaining were Vicksburg, on the first high ground below Memphis, and the fortified naval base at Fort Hindman, or Arkansas Post, on the Arkansas River, which threatened the western flank of any advance. Grant proposed to move against Vicksburg. He, himself, was to hold Pemberton at the Yalobusha where the general advance of Nov. 24 had pushed him, and Sherman was sent down the river to take Vicksburg. Raids on his communications, however, forced Grant to fall back and release Pemberton, and rendered Sherman's expedition hopeless. After fruitless attempts at an assault he reëmbarked his troops on Jan. 2, 1863, and turned them over to General McClernand, who had arrived with orders from the president to command the forces on the river. These forces were reorganized into the Army of the Mississippi, with two army corps, one of which Sherman commanded. At Sherman's suggestion, McClernand, with the assistance of Porter's gunboat flotilla, proceeded to the capture of Arkansas Post, then returned to the Mississippi. Grant reorganized the whole force into the Army of the Tennessee, with four corps, Sherman retaining his own, the XV, and moved down the river to open his amphibious campaign which led to the surrender of Vicksburg on July 4, 1863. For his distinguished service in this campaign Sherman was made brigadier-general in the regular army.

In September, Sherman, with his own corps and other troops, was sent back to Memphis and thence eastward to the relief of Chattanooga. Grant's advancement to supreme command in the west placed Sherman in command of the Army of the Tennessee, but strong forces had to remain at Vicksburg and Memphis, so that he could assemble for the Chattanooga operation but little more than he had with him. His command was moved across the rear of Hooker's and Thomas' troops, already in position, and formed the left element of the general movement of Nov. 24, which raised the siege of Chattanooga. The next day Sherman's advance had reached Ringgold, when he was recalled to move to the relief of Knoxville. Starting at once, without waiting for his transport to join him, he reached Knoxville on Dec. 6 only to find that Longstreet had raised the siege and gone back to Virginia. He then placed his troops in winter quarters along the Tennessee River. This campaign, for which he received the thanks of Congress, had been fought under conditions extraordinarily distressing to Sherman. His son and namesake, nine years old, who had been with him during the quiet period after Vicksburg, died of typhoid fever at Memphis as the expedition was starting. In January he went down to Vicksburg to conduct an expedition against the Confederate base at Meridian. Arranging with Banks at New Orleans for a feint toward Mobile, he moved out with four divisions to Meridian, which he reached without serious opposition. After destroying the arsenal and depots he returned to Vicksburg.

The great event of the spring of 1864 was the appointment of Grant as lieutenant-general commanding all the armies. He went east in March, turning over his command to Sherman; McPherson succeeded to the command of the Army of the Tennessee. Grant's opinion of these two great lieutenants was expressed in a letter thanking them as "the men to whom above all others" he was indebted for his successes (Sherman, *Memoirs*, 1875, I, 399). The combined plan for 1864 called for an advance by Meade's Army of the Potomac against Lee and Richmond, and an advance by Sherman against Johnston and Atlanta. Sherman issued orders for a concentration about Chattanooga, and moved his headquarters to that place late in April. His field force consisted of the Armies of the Cumberland (Thomas), the Tennessee (McPherson) and the Ohio (Schofield)—in all about 100,000 men. Opposed was Johnston with some 60,000. His first care was to assure his supply. His base was Nashville, 150 miles north, with one single track railway, open to raids, and poorly supplied with rolling stock. He took complete possession of this road, cut off all civilian traffic, reduced military supplies to the strictest essentials, impounded all rolling stock coming in from the north, in spite of the complaints of the northern railways, and reduced field equipment and rations to a minimum. By these stringent measures he succeeded in accumulating a reserve of supplies sufficient to permit him to commence operations by May 5, the date set by Grant.

Johnston was at Dalton, holding Buzzard-Roost Gap, where the railway crossed Rockyface ridge. Sherman moved Thomas and Schofield directly against Buzzard-Roost, and McPherson around Johnston's left through Snake Creek Gap. McPherson passed through the Gap on May 9, but failed to take Resaca or to cut the railway. Johnston then fell back upon Resaca. Leaving a detachment of the railway, Sherman moved around by McPherson's route and on May 15 took Resaca and reopened his rail communications. He then followed on to Kingston and established an advanced depot there. Johnston fell back into the rugged hills behind Allatoona Pass. Sherman moved westward off the railway again and pushed up toward the Allatoona-Kenesaw Mountain line. Allatoona Pass was occupied on June 1. Progress was now slow. Johnston was entrenched in a strong position. Every advance against it was covered by hasty field works—not as a defensive, but as an offensive weapon. Violent assaults upon Kenesaw at the end of June failed, but a new extension of Sherman's right forced the abandonment of that position. Johnston fell back to the Chattahoochee. Schofield effected a crossing beyond Johnston's right, which forced him to give up the river line on July 9 and retire to the line of Peachtree Creek, immediately covering Atlanta. Here Johnston was relieved by Hood. Sherman extended his left, swinging around Atlanta by the north and east and drew violent attacks from Hood. The defenses of Atlanta being too strong for an assault, Sherman opened a regular siege, then worked his force around by his own right, west of the city, and cut the railways to Montgomery and Macon. Hood evacuated Atlanta on the night of Sept. 1. This victorious campaign won Sherman his promotion to the rank of major-general in the regular army, Aug. 12, 1864. He at once ordered the removal of the civil population from Atlanta, and proposed to Hood an armistice for this purpose. After some correspondence, in which Hood attempted without success to represent the proceeding as barbarous, it was carried out (*Memoirs*, II, 117 ff.).

Sherman had in mind from the first a further movement from Atlanta to some point on the seacoast. After correspondence with Grant, the plan took definite shape. Thomas and Schofield were sent back to hold Hood and to protect Tennessee. On Nov. 15, after destroying installations of military value, the army of 62,000 men marched out of Atlanta, breaking all communications, and disappeared for a month. The "march through Georgia" centered upon Sherman one of the bitterest controversies of the Civil War. His purpose was to break the resistance of the South by cutting off the supply of her armies and Georgia was the only untouched source of supply. The army was under orders to live off the country, to destroy war supplies, public buildings, railroads, and manufacturing shops. Foraging was strictly defined, and the destruction of private property was authorized only upon the order of the highest commanders and when some act of violence impeded the progress of the army. The execution of the orders, however, was extremely difficult to control. The army was in the pink of condition and in a holiday mood. Thousands of stragglers, negro and white, so-called "bummers," or soldiers detached from their own regiments, fringed the marching ranks and considered themselves under no orders. Wheeler's Confederate cavalrymen, also, committed acts for which the Federals were held responsible by an undiscriminating countryside. Many acts of pillage did occur, and it appears obvious that Sherman's discipline was not strict enough, a judgment which his own men rested upon him (see Hitchcock, *post*, p. 86). Under no illusions whatsoever as to the terrible effects of his march (see *Home Letters*, p. 298), Sherman contended that wanton destruction was prevented in so far as possible, and that there was no serious personal violence to noncombatants. The principle that the war could be terminated soon by bringing it home to a civilian population by the destruction of goods rather than life was a tenet to which Sherman clung. Aside from condemnation and acclaim, it is on the basis of his deliberate exploitation of this principle that he has been called the first modern general (see Hart, preface). On Jan. 10, 1865, Sherman received for the second time the thanks of Congress.

The city of Savannah was occupied on Dec. 21. On the first of February began the march northward through the Carolinas—a march in comparison to which, as Sherman said, that through Georgia was child's play. In seventeen days the army reached Columbia, forcing the evacuation of Charleston. That night Columbia was burned, and Sherman was charged with having ordered the burning. His orders were, however, to destroy only war materials and public buildings (see Lewis, *post*, p. 501). The evidence, reviewed by a nonpartisan, indicates that the evacuating troops set cotton on fire, that a high wind fanned it, that the citizens distributed liquor too liberally, that negroes and released Union prisoners itching for revenge applied the torch further, but that the officers adopted drastic measures to save the city (see Hart, *post*, p. 366 ff.). Johnston, commanding the Confederate forces in the Carolinas, was unable to make any effective resistance. On Mar. 22 Sherman effected a junction at Goldsboro with Schofield's corps. While his troops were being resupplied, he made a hasty trip by sea to visit Grant's headquarters at Citypoint on the James River, and there held the consultation with President Lincoln which so impressed upon him the government's plan for a liberal peace (*Home Letters*, p. 336). Sherman then moved upon Raleigh, but Lee had surrendered on Apr. 9, and now Johnston also made overtures for surrender. On Apr. 17 the two generals met, and liberal terms were granted by Sherman. In his eagerness to put an end to the war he inserted in his draft terms which were political in their nature and beyond his province. This fact, however, was explicitly recognized in the agreement signed, which, in effect, was merely an engagement by the generals to do their utmost to secure approval by their respective governments. But the feeling at Washington was bitter by reason of the assassination of Lincoln, and the agreement was repudiated with a vigor and discourtesy which deeply offended Sherman. At the final grand review in Washington, he publicly refused to shake hands with Secretary Stanton, although he became reconciled later.

Sherman took up his first post-war station at St. Louis in command of the Division of the Mississippi. He lent great assistance in the construction of the transcontinental railway and in controlling and mollifying the Indian opposition accomplished, in his own opinion, more of permanent value than during the war (Hart, p.

420). In the reorganization of the army, Grant became general and Sherman succeeded him as lieutenant-general on July 25, 1866. Soon afterward, he was called to Washington to take temporary command of the army, the President proposing to send Grant on a diplomatic mission to Mexico, escorting the minister accredited to President Juarez. Grant objected to this, considering it a political maneuver to get him out of Washington and Sherman was designated for the mission. The mission went to Mexico but failed to find Juarez; it constituted, however, a part of the diplomatic pressure exerted upon France for withdrawal of support to Maximilian. Upon Grant's inauguration as president, Sherman became general commanding the army on Mar. 4, 1869. Schofield, then still secretary of war, issued an order the next day to settle the long-standing quarrel of the commanding general and the heads of the staff departments, by placing them under his orders. Rawlins, however, who now became secretary of war, saw this as a diminution of the importance of his office, and rescinded the order. Although he had favored the system announced by Schofield, Grant refused to interfere. Sherman was deeply hurt by this and after a year spent on leave in Europe, 1871–72, moved his headquarters to St. Louis in 1874. A compromise having been reached, he returned to Washington in 1876, although the political chaos of Washington had always distressed him. He was untiring in the exercise of his command up to the moment of his retirement. One of his most important contributions to the army was his establishment of the school at Fort Leavenworth in 1881 which, under various names and forms, has had a continuous existence ever since, and has developed into the most influential agency of the service in shaping doctrine and training methods.

He retired from active service on Nov. 1, 1883, established himself in St. Louis, and remained there until 1886, when he moved to New York City. Repeated efforts were made to draw him into political life, especially in the Republican convention of 1884, when only his positive veto prevented a definite move for his nomination for the presidency. He established no business connections, but lived quietly and at leisure. His correspondence was very large, and he was in frequent attendance at military reunions and celebrations, besides being in constant demand at private social affairs. He died of pneumonia in New York City at the age of seventy-one and was survived by six of his eight children. At the end, while unconscious, Sherman received the last rites of the Catholic church,

but had never been a member. Ellen Sherman had died three years before, deeply absorbed to the last in her Catholic charities. Sherman was tall and erect, with sharp, dark eyes, reddish hair and beard, and deeply lined face. His features were grave and severe in repose, but animated and expressive in conversation, of which he was no mean master. His mind was extraordinarily quick; it flashed from premise to conclusion so rapidly that his associates could not follow, and even he himself seemed unconscious of the process. This rapidity, together with his nervous temperament, gave him the reputation of an erratic, even of a mentally unbalanced, genius—a reputation totally foreign to the fact. He was a cordial and devoted friend, his relations with Grant, in particular, being of the most intimate and confidential character. In public as well as in private address, in his letters and in the *Memoirs,* first published in 1875, his characteristics were strikingly displayed. The famous statement, "war . . . is all hell," was made by Sherman in a speech at Columbus, Ohio, on Aug. 11, 1880, and was reported in the *Ohio State Journal* of the following day. Augustus Saint-Gaudens [*q.v.*] modeled a bust of Sherman during the last years of the testy old general's life. The magnificent equestrian statue in Central Park, New York City, grew out of the first effort.

[Sherman and Ewing papers, Manuscript Division, Lib. of Cong.; T. T. Sherman, *Sherman Geneal.* (1920); *Memoirs of General William T. Sherman* (2 vols., 2nd ed. revised, 1886); M. A. DeWolfe Howe, ed., *Home Letters of General Sherman* (1909); R. S. Thorndike, ed., *Sherman Letters, Corresp. between General and Senator Sherman* (1894); Lloyd Lewis, *Sherman—Fighting Prophet* (1932); B. H. Liddell Hart, *Sherman—Soldier, Realist, American* (1929); W. L. Fleming, *General W. T. Sherman As College President* (1912); Henry Hitchcock, *Marching with Sherman* (1927); J. F. Rhodes, "Sherman's March to the Sea," *Am. Hist. Rev.,* Apr. 1901; Ferdinand von Meerheimb, *Sherman's Feldzug in Georgien* (1869, Berlin); *Boston Evening Transcript,* Feb. 14, 1891. See also a critical estimate of the *Memoirs* in an article by W. B. Stevens in *Mo. Hist. Rev.,* Jan. 1931.]   O. L. S., Jr.

SHERRY, LOUIS (1856–June 9, 1926), restaurateur, was born probably in St. Albans, Vt. His father was a carpenter, born in France; his mother was of New England Anglo-Saxon stock. Young Sherry, forced by circumstances to seek work at an early age, found a place as boy of all work in a hotel in Montreal, Canada. A year or two later he went to New York and, after a period of hardship, obtained a place as "bus boy" in a large hotel. There he was so punctual and efficient that he was presently promoted to be a waiter. In this position he still further distinguished himself by careful attention to every complaint and suggestion, and by his study of the patrons' personal and gustatory eccentricities. He was about twenty-two when he was hired by a large hotel at Elberon, N. J., then a very fashionable seaside resort, to take charge of its kitchen and dining room during its summer season. He was by this time planning a restaurant and catering business of his own, and during his two summers at Elberon he was promised the patronage of many wealthy New Yorkers, guests at the hotel. At the end of the second season he had saved $1,300, and with this capital he opened his first restaurant and confectionery at Thirty-eighth Street and Sixth Avenue, New York, in 1881. From the first he insisted upon the finest of materials and the most careful workmanship in every product of his house, and his motto was, "Never disappoint a patron." After he had prospered a little, he made journeys to Paris to perfect himself in culinary lore. A rapidly growing business encouraged him to move in 1890 to a larger and finer place at Thirty-seventh Street and Fifth Avenue. Here the aristocracy of the city favored him so greatly with patronage that in 1898 he moved to still more sumptuous quarters at Forty-fourth Street and Fifth Avenue, where he remained twenty years. This last place, with its costly paintings and tapestries and its cellar full of fine wines, represented an investment of $2,000,000. Frank A. Munsey, the publisher, lived in a luxurious suite in the building throughout Sherry's tenure. During some thirty years, many of the most elaborate dinners, balls, débuts, and other social, business, and political functions took place at Sherry's. The Seeley dinner in 1896, C. K. G. Billings' dinner on horseback in 1900, and other noted and bizarre affairs were given in his rooms. To prepare a dinner for 300 guests, given by a millionaire, he once went to Savannah, Ga., traveling with his staff in a Pullman sleeper and two baggage cars, carrying all china, linen, food, and decorations with him. On another occasion he sent a staff of twenty to San Francisco, where they took over a private residence for the elder J. P. Morgan's use, and he prepared some elaborate entertainments at which Morgan was host. When the national prohibition laws went into effect he disposed of his stock of wines to favored customers and closed his restaurant in 1919. He then opened a confectionery and catering business on Park Avenue, which he operated until his death. He was survived by his widow, Marie Bertha Sherry and by their son.

[Edward Hungerford, *The Story of Louis Sherry* (1929); A. S. Crockett, *Peacocks on Parade* (1931), esp. pp. 170–71, 184–93; I. N. P. Stokes, *The Iconography of Manhattan Island* (5 vols., 1926); *Where and How to Dine in New York* (copr. 1903); *New York Times* and *World* (N. Y.), June 10, 1926; death certificate, Bureau of Records, Dept. of Health, 139 Centre St., N. Y. C.]   A.F.H.

SHERWIN, THOMAS (Mar. 26, 1799–July 23, 1869), educator, was born in Westmoreland, N. H., only son of David Sherwin and Hannah (Pritchard) Sherwin, both of whom were natives of Boxford, Mass. His father, originally a farmer, had gone into business but had failed. Seeking to retrieve his losses, he went to New Hampshire, where he lived in Westmoreland, New Ipswich, and Temple. For six years, 1807–13, Thomas lived in the home of his uncle, Dr. James Crombie, in Temple, where he earned his board by small services. He was educated in the local district school and had some private lessons from his friend, Solomon P. Miles, a Dartmouth student. In 1813 he was apprenticed to Messrs. Samuel and Sewell Rockwood, a firm of clothiers in Groton, Mass. In 1819 his employers released him from his contract so that he might teach in a district school in Harvard, Mass. A year later an appointment as teacher in the Central School in Groton enabled him to enter the academy there in the spring. In March 1821 he entered the academy at New Ipswich and, after a few months of intensive preparatory study, matriculated at Harvard College, where he earned his college expenses by teaching school each winter.

Upon his graduation in 1825 among the ten best scholars in his class he was elected headmaster of the academy in Lexington, Mass. A year later he became tutor in mathematics at Harvard, where he spent his spare time in reading Blackstone and Coke with Elias Phinney, an attorney of Charlestown. Giving up his intention of becoming a lawyer, he tried engineering and in 1827 was employed under Col. Loammi Baldwin, 1780–1838 [*q.v.*], on the dry docks and other works at Charlestown and at Portsmouth. Later in the same year a pulmonary affection obliged him to withdraw from this work. In December 1828 he opened a private school for boys in Boston; in the following year he was elected sub-master of the English High School, which was then under the charge of his friend, Solomon P. Miles, and in May 1836, in recognition of his important contributions to the improvement of secondary school instruction, he was elected a member of the American Academy of Arts and Sciences. On June 10 of that year he married Mary King Gibbens, daughter of Daniel L. and Mary (King) Gibbens of Boston. Upon the resignation of Miles in 1837, he became principal of the school, a position he held until his death. Under his highly efficient administration, the English High School, the first to be called high school in the United States (established 1821), became the leading educational institution of its grade in the country. He staffed it with a remarkably able group of instructors, himself teaching mathematics. As its reputation grew, it attracted many visitors from other states, and inspired the establishment of similar schools elsewhere. Sherwin was one of the founders of the American Institute of Instruction in 1830, of the Massachusetts State Teachers' Association in 1845, and of the *Massachusetts Teacher* in 1847. He was one of the original editors of the *Massachusetts Teacher* and served as a member of the editorial board at intervals throughout his life, and he was a frequent contributor to the *American Annals of Education*. He was active in the establishment of the Massachusetts Institute of Technology, of which he was a director and counselor until the year of his death. His best known works are *Elementary Treatise on Algebra* (copyright 1841) and *Common School Algebra* (1845), for many years standard textbooks.

[R. C. Waterston, *Address on the Life and Character of Thomas Sherwin* (1870); *Am. Jour. of Educ.*, June 1860, Sept. 1865; C. Northend, *Annals Am. Inst. of Instruction* (1884); J. D. Philbrick, in *Memoirs of Several Deceased Members New England Hist. Geneal. Soc.* (1878); obituary in *Boston Transcript*, July 24, 1869.]   R. F. S.

SHERWOOD, ADIEL (Oct. 3, 1791–Aug. 18, 1879), Baptist clergyman, educator, was born at Fort Edward, N. Y. His father, Adiel, who had married a second cousin, Sarah (Sherwood), was a descendant of Thomas Sherwood who had emigrated to Boston in 1634 and in 1645 had settled in Stratford, Conn. The elder Adiel was a farmer, Revolutionary soldier, member of the New York legislature, and a personal friend of George Washington. The son entered Middlebury College, Vermont, in 1813, but after three years transferred to Union College, Schenectady, N. Y., where he was graduated in 1817. He then spent one year at Andover Theological Seminary.

Threatened with tuberculosis, on the advice of physicians he removed to Georgia, taking with him recommendations to leading Baptist ministers of that state. He landed in Savannah in 1818, and was soon the ardent and effective helper of every progressive movement in the Baptist denomination. Ordained at Bethesda Church, Green County, Mar. 20, 1820, he at once began a ministry that was long and apostolic in its zeal and effectiveness. Amid the pioneer conditions of that day he devoted much time to itinerant preaching over wide areas of Georgia. He organized churches and advocated missions, Sunday schools, and Bible societies. His laborious service is evinced by the fact that in 1828 he preached 333 sermons in forty different counties. He was at different times, and for longer or shorter periods, pastor of many country and town churches, a number of which he had established. In his church at Eatonton, in 1827, there started a revival, which spread over much of the state and resulted in the addition of 16,000 members to the churches of three Baptist associations. As a speaker he was clear, logical, and forceful.

Though first of all a preacher, he was also an organizer of ability. In 1820 he prepared a resolution, adopted by Sarepta Association, which led to the founding of the Baptist State Convention in 1822. In 1823 he introduced a resolution into the Triennial Convention, urging all the states to organize state conventions. He was clerk and treasurer of the Baptist State Convention of Georgia for many years. Greatly interested in education, he taught several years in Georgia academies and started a manual labor school and a theological school at Eatonton. He was instrumental in the establishment of Mercer Institute (later Mercer University); was a professor in Columbian College (now George Washington University), Washington, D. C., in 1837–38; taught sacred literature at Mercer from 1838 to 1841; and was president successively of Shurtleff College, Illinois, 1841–46, Masonic College, Lexington, Mo., 1848–49, and Marshall College, Griffin, Ga., from 1857 until the Civil War. From 1852 to 1857 he was pastor at Cape Girardeau, Mo.

A diligent and instructive writer for the religious press, he also published several pamphlets and books, the most important of which were *A Gazetteer of the State of Georgia* (1827), *The Jewish and Christian Churches* (1850), and *Notes on the New Testament* (2 vols., 1856). He was a vigorous friend of foreign and home missions, steadily opposing anti-mission propaganda, and serving as secretary of the American Indian Missionary Association. In 1865 he settled in St. Louis, Mo., where he resided until his death. He had a genius for friendship with important men, was intimate with the leading ministers of America, and was personally acquainted with many prominent national officials. He was twice married; first, May 17, 1821, to Anne Adams Smith, widow of Gov. Peter Early [*q.v.*]; she died in November 1822 and in May 1824 he married Emma Heriot of Charleston, S. C., who with one son, Thomas Adiel Sherwood [*q.v.*], and four daughters survived him.

[J. H. Campbell, *Ga. Baptists: Hist. and Biog.* (1847); *Hist. of the Baptist Denomination in Ga.* (1881); B. D. Ragsdale, *Story of Ga. Baptists* (copr. 1932); minutes of Ga. Baptist associations and of the Baptist State Convention; William Cathcart, *The Baptist Encyc.* (1881); Julia L. Sherwood, *Memoir of Adiel Sherwood, D.D.* (1884); *Mo. Republican* (St. Louis), Aug. 20, 1879.]   W.J.M.

SHERWOOD, ISAAC RUTH (Aug. 13, 1835–Oct. 15, 1925), editor, soldier, congressman, was born in Stanford, Dutchess County, N. Y., the son of Aaron and Maria (Yeomans) Sherwood. He was of English and Scotch ancestry, a descendant of the eighth generation from Thomas Sherwood who came to America about 1634. His father enlisted for service in the War of 1812, and both grandfathers and a great-grandfather were under arms in the American Revolution. He attended the Hudson River Institute at Claverack, N. Y., Antioch College, Yellow Springs, Ohio, then under the presidency of Horace Mann, where he studied from 1854 to 1856 and the Ohio Law College, Poland, Ohio. He early developed an interest in journalism, and while a law student, he purchased a weekly paper, the *Williams County Gazette,* in Bryan, Ohio. The most distinguished episode of Sherwood's editorial career occurred when, after having dared to give a favorable review to Walt Whitman's *Leaves of Grass* in his newspaper, he received a note of gratitude from the author and an autographed portrait. He was elected mayor of Bryan and probate-judge of Williams County. Enlisting in the Civil War as a private in the 14th Ohio Infantry, he participated in one of the first engagements of the war at Philippi, W. Va. After his three months' term had expired, he joined the 111th Ohio Volunteers, and rose to the rank of lieutenant-colonel in 1864. Thereafter he was continually in command of the regiment, and in February 1865 he was brevetted brigadier-general for his gallant services at Resaca, Ga., and at Franklin and Nashville, Tenn. The explosion of a shell near him while in East Tennessee destroyed the hearing in one ear. He was then transferred to the East and served through the North Carolina campaign.

After the cessation of hostilities he resigned his commission and returned to newspaper work on the *Toledo Commercial* and then on the *Cleveland Leader.* He served as secretary of state of Ohio from 1869 to 1873, and during his incumbency organized the bureau of statistics. He was a Republican congressman from the Toledo district from 1873 to 1875, but because of his financial views did not receive a renomination. He then purchased the *Toledo Journal* which he edited for nine years. From 1878 to 1884 he was also probate-judge of Lucas County, an office to which he was first elected by the National Greenback Party in whose ranks he was a prominent leader until he joined the Democrats in 1879. He edited the Canton *News-Democrat* from 1888 to 1898, but subsequently returned to Toledo. In 1906 he was somewhat unexpectedly elected to Congress where he served seven successive terms. For many years he was chairman of the House committee on invalid pensions. He was an aggressive advocate of large appropriations for that purpose, and sponsored the Sherwood "Dollar-a-Day" law for Civil War veterans, 1912. Nevertheless he became inclined toward pacifism before America's entrance into the World War and bitterly opposed large expenditures for preparedness (see the *New York Times,* January 5, March 8, 1916). Upon the passage of the war resolution of Apr. 6, 1917, he was the only Ohioan in Congress to vote in the negative. He was defeated in the Republican landslide of 1920 but was elected again in 1922. Failing to be returned two years later he retired from public life when almost ninety years of age, just fifty years after the completion of his first congressional term.

He was an ardent sportsman and the author of a popular humorous poem, *The Army Grayback* (1889), and his *Memories of the War* (1923). An orthodox Presbyterian and a total abstainer from the use of tobacco and liquor, he denounced the Volstead Act and the Anti-Saloon League in his later years. He was overcome by smoke during a fire in 1925 in the apartment house in which he lived in Toledo. Pernicious anemia developed afterward, and he died a few months later, survived by a son, a daughter, and a grand-daughter whom he had adopted. His wife Katharine Margaret Brownlee Sherwood [*q.v.*], to whom he had been married on Sept. 1, 1859, preceded him in death.

[Information from R. Lincoln Long, Toledo, Ohio; *Who's Who in America,* 1924–25; *Biog. Dir. Am. Cong.* (1928); Clark Waggoner, ed., *Hist. of the City of Toledo and Lucas County* (1888); Harvey Scribner, *Memoirs of Lucas County and the City of Toledo* (1910), vol. II; N. O. Winter, *A Hist. of Northwest Ohio* (1917), vol. II; Whitelaw Reid, *Ohio in the War* (1868), vol. I; B. J. Hendrick, "Pork-Barrel Pensions," *World's Work,* Mar., Apr. 1915; *Review of Reviews* (N. Y.), June 1912; *Toledo Blade, Toledo News-Bee,* Oct. 16, 1925.]   F.P.W.

SHERWOOD, KATHARINE MARGARET BROWNLEE (Sept. 24, 1841–Feb. 15, 1914), writer, reformer, known as Kate Brownlee Sherwood, was the daughter of Judge James Brownlee, a well-educated Scotsman who rose to distinction in eastern Ohio, and Rebecca

(Mullen) Brownlee, a member of a Pennsylvania family active in public affairs. She was born in Poland, Ohio, and spent her youth there. She received her early education in the local schools and in the Poland Union Seminary. She was married to Isaac Ruth Sherwood [q.v.] on Sept. 1, 1859, and went with him to Bryan, Ohio, where he was editing the *Williams County Gazette*. With youthful enthusiasm she promptly began to act as his assistant on this country newspaper. She learned every part of a printer's trade, wrote up the local news, and often supplied editorials. During the Civil War, while her husband was serving in the army, she continued to publish the paper. They moved to Toledo, Ohio, in the period following the war and thereafter Mrs. Sherwood identified herself with many civic activities. She continued her journalistic work, contributing to Cleveland and Toledo dailies, and, after 1875, when her husband purchased the *Toledo Journal,* she assisted in the editorial management of that paper for about nine years. From 1883 to 1898 she edited the woman's department of the *National Tribune,* the official organ of the Grand Army of the Republic. After General Sherwood became congressman from Ohio she acted as Washington correspondent for a newspaper syndicate. She was an active worker in the Women's Press Club of Toledo, and in her later years was elected honorary president of the Ohio Newspaper Women's Association. In addition to her journalistic writings she published patriotic playlets for use in schools, translations from the French and German, several books of selections, and two volumes of verse: *Camp-Fire, Memorial-Day, and other Poems* (1885), and *Dream of the Ages, a Poem of Columbia* (1893). One of her compositions, "The Flag that Makes Men Free," was often used at patriotic gatherings and had a circulation of over one hundred thousand copies.

Mrs. Sherwood became most widely known for her work in national associations of women. In 1879 she organized a number of societies auxiliary to the G. A. R. in the West. In 1883 these were united with the New England societies to form the Woman's Relief Corps, of which she became the first national secretary and the second national president. She did her most important work in this organization as chairman of the committee on pensions for soldiers' widows. She was also a member of the National Council of Women, and a worker on national committees of the D. A. R. In her own city she did pioneer work for women's clubs and for suffrage. Especially valuable was her cooperation in the Education League of Toledo and in the Centre University Extension Society. The breadth of her local interests is attested by the fact that she was at the same time a member of the Presbyterian church, an honorary member of the Council of Jewish Women, and the patroness of a Catholic hospital. In the midst of an active public career she found refreshment in wide reading and in domestic life. Her home, always a center of gracious hospitality, her two children and one adopted grandchild, remained absorbing interests. She was warmly admired by her contemporaries for her beauty, her forceful public speaking, and her work for civic betterment. At the funeral service held for her in Washington, D. C., Secretary of State Bryan, a valued personal friend, read a selection from his lecture "The Prince of Peace." Her tolerant spirit, free from all animosity, received due recognition in 1887 when she was asked to write a poem for the unveiling of a memorial to Albert Sidney Johnston [q.v.] at New Orleans.

[Information from a grand-daughter; *Who's Who in America,* 1912–13; N. O. Winter, *A Hist. of Northwest Ohio* (1917); Harvey Scribner, ed., *Memoirs of Lucas County and the City of Toledo* (1910), vol. II; *Toledo Times,* Dec. 1, 1912; *Evening Star* (Washington, D. C.), Feb. 16, 1914.]   B. M. S.

SHERWOOD, MARY ELIZABETH WILSON (Oct. 27, 1826–Sept. 12, 1903), author, was born in Keene, N. H., the eldest of seven children of James and Mary Lord (Richardson) Wilson. Her great-grandfather, Robert Wilson, a Presbyterian, came to America from Ireland in the first migration of Scotch-Irish to America and fought in the Revolution. Her grandfather, James Wilson, and her father were both members of Congress. Mary attended a private school but was not a good student and was reported to her parents by the village librarian as reading too many novels. Her first story, sent anonymously to the *Social Gazette,* brought her mother's reproof. After the family became Unitarians, she was sent to the school conducted by George Barrell Emerson [q.v.] in Boston. In driving there from Keene in winter on the outside of the stage coach she contracted the rheumatism that tormented her through life. When her father went to Iowa as surveyor-general about 1842, she accompanied him, meeting Charles Dickens in Washington on the way. During her father's term in Congress, 1847–50, she acted as his housekeeper and hostess in Washington, her mother having died. She was married in Keene on Nov. 12, 1851, to John Sherwood, a New York lawyer.

After her marriage she contributed to New York and Boston newspapers, to the *Atlantic Monthly, Scribner's Monthly, Appletons' Jour-*

nal, the *Galaxy, Harper's Magazine,* and *Frank Leslie's Weekly* (Willard and Livermore, *post*). Many verses appeared under the initials M. E. W. S. Her published volumes include *The Sarcasm of Destiny, or Nina's Experience* (1878), *Amenities of Home* (1881), *Home Amusements* (1881), *Etiquette* (1884), *Manners and Social Usages* (1884), which went through many editions, *Royal Girls and Royal Courts* (1887), *Sweet-Brier* (1889), *The Art of Entertaining* (1892), and *Poems by M. E. W. S.* (1892). Her stories and verse are not noteworthy. Her popularity was due to her books on social life and etiquette, which her experience in Washington official life, in New York society, and in Europe fitted her to write. Long considered authoritative, these are practical and not uninteresting, in spite of their continual insistence on the "fashionable" and the "proper." As was perhaps natural in a social arbiter, she was very conservative. In one of her books she remarks apropos of the extravagant balls of the Four Hundred in New York: "Whose business is it how rich people spend their money?" Her *An Epistle to Posterity; Being Rambling Recollections of Many Years of My Life* (1897) and *Here and There and Everywhere; Reminiscences* (1898) show her to have felt the importance of her social opportunities and of the prominent people who were her friends or acquaintances. Her style is vivacious, conversational, often humorous.

After her marriage she lived in New York but made frequent visits to Washington, Boston, and Europe. She numbered among her acquaintances Daniel Webster, W. H. Prescott, George Bancroft, J. L. R. Agassiz, James T. Fields, Oliver Wendell Holmes, Julia Ward Howe, the poets Longfellow, Bryant, and Lowell [*qq.v.*], Thackeray, Lord Houghton, Sir John Millais, and Sir Frederic Leighton. She was presented at many European courts and was decorated in France with the insignia of Officier d'Académie on account of her literary work (*Ibid.*). In New York she engaged in much philanthropy, and was especially interested in hospitals and work for women and children. During the Civil War she worked with the Sanitary Commission. Though an invalid for some years before her death, she continued to write and was a contributor to the *N. Y. Times Saturday Review of Books.* Of her four sons, two survived her. She died in New York City.

[See C. H. Bell, *The Bench and Bar of N. H.* (1894) for information on M. E. W. Sherwood's father and grandfather. See also *Vital Statistics of the Town of Keene, N. H.* (1905); M. E. W. Sherwood, *An Epistle to Posterity* (1897), *Here and There and Everywhere; Reminiscences* (1898); Frances E. Willard and Mary A. Livermore, *Portraits and Biogs. of Prominent Am. Women* (1897), vol. II; *Who's Who in America,* 1903-05; *N. Y. Times,* Sept. 15, 1903.]
S. G. B.

SHERWOOD, THOMAS ADIEL (June 2, 1834–Nov. 11, 1918), jurist, was born at Eatonton, Putnam County, Ga., the son of the Rev. Adiel [*q.v.*] and Emma (Heriot) Sherwood. After excellent training under the guidance of his scholarly father, he entered Mercer University, transferring later to Shurtleff College, Alton, Ill. After his graduation from the Cincinnati Law School in 1857, he was admitted to the bar in Mississippi County, Mo., and began practice at Neosho, in the southwestern section of the state. The region was virtually a frontier community and he rode the circuit, with few *Reports* and fewer books to assist him. During the Civil War he moved to Springfield, which had an able local bar, forming a partnership with his brother-in-law, H. C. Young. He disliked trial work and was at his best as counsel and before appellate courts. By 1870, he was well known throughout the judicial circuits of southwestern Missouri and a leader of its bar.

A conservative Democrat, he was in thorough accord with the party group which came into power in the state during the early seventies. Sectional influence and the support of certain party leaders resulted in his nomination in 1872 for judge of the supreme court. He was reëlected in 1882 and in 1892, serving thirty years. His entire official life was spent upon the bench and his political and social philosophy must be gleaned from his judicial opinions. These indicate clearly that he was a strict constructionist, opposing subsidies, grants, and all forms of "federal encroachment," and fearing executive "usurpation" and governmental "interference" in private enterprise. Confronted by problems of constitutional construction, he relied upon a series of fixed and rigid principles. Temperamentally a controversialist and an advocate, he frequently dissented, but had the satisfaction subsequently of having many of his dissenting opinions accepted by the majority (*Proceedings of the Missouri Bar Association, post,* pp. 220-21). His most significant contributions were in constitutional law, criminal law, and equity (74 *Mo.,* 237; 159 *Mo.,* 410; 168 *Mo.,* 133). He was an earnest defender of civil liberty and of constitutional guarantees, never hesitating to overrule in terse and vigorous language the civil and criminal verdicts of lower courts. Supported alike by important politico-legal leaders and by the party rank and file, his reëlections were marked by increased majorities. He was ambitious for a fourth term, being mentally alert and physically active (*Boonville Advertiser,* May 30, 1902). The legal and political influences of the then dominant railroad interests were very active in his support, but these were nullified by innumerable personal and professional animosities developed during a long career because of his aggressive and provocative personality, and by the contention that a younger man should be designated for the ten-year term.

Following his unwilling retirement from the bench, he practised law in Springfield for a few years, published a polemical work, *Commentaries on the Criminal Law of Missouri* (1907), and retained great interest in public affairs. He was a stanch advocate of judicial reform, both administrative and procedural. Officially, he was austere and dignified, utterly impervious to what he considered public clamor, but his intimate friends knew him as a genial companion, with a knowledge and a keen appreciation of history and of literature. He married, in June 1861, Mary E. Young, of southwestern Missouri, who, with four children, survived him. He died in California of the infirmities of age.

[50–171 *Mo. Reports* (1873–1903); A. J. D. Stewart, *The Hist. of the Bench and Bar of Mo.* (1898); H. L. Conard, *Encyc. of the Hist. of Mo.* (1901), vol. V; *Proc. of the . . . Mo. Bar Asso.,* 1919; J. O. Boyd, "Thirty Years a Justice," *Am. Law Rev.,* July–Aug. 1914; *Jefferson City Tribune,* Feb. 26, 1873; Dec. 7, 1892, Nov. 25, 1893, Nov. 26, 1918; *St. Louis Republic,* Mar. 16, 1909.]   T. S. B.

SHERWOOD, WILLIAM HALL (Jan. 31, 1854–Jan. 7, 1911), pianist, teacher, composer, was born in Lyons, N. Y., the eldest of seven children of the Rev. Lyman Hinsdale and Mary (Balis) Sherwood. On his father's side he was descended from Thomas Sherwood, who emigrated from London to Ipswich, Mass., in 1634, and settled in Fairfax, Conn., and on his mother's side from John Balis, a farmer with a large grant of land between Cairo and Catskill, N. Y. Lyman Sherwood was a man of culture, an accomplished linguist, an excellent pianist and organist. He supported his family by teaching music, being so successful that he founded Lyons Musical Academy in 1854, the second music school founded in America.

William Sherwood showed musical talent at the age of four and received his first training from his aunt who was a teacher in the Academy. At the age of seven he came under the careful training of his father, with whom he studied for ten years, taking a full course in piano, harmony, and composition. Between the ages of nine and eleven he frequently appeared in concert in New York, Pennsylvania, and Canada. From 1866 to 1871 he taught in the Academy and at the same

time acquired a literary education under his father, especially in French and German. For a short time he studied piano with Edward Heimburger in Rochester, N. Y., and Jan N. Fychowski in New York City, but in 1871 he began studying with William Mason, 1829–1908 [*q.v.*], who was conducting a normal institute at Binghamton, N. Y. In the autumn of that year, upon Mason's advice, he went to Germany, where he remained five years, at first studying piano with Kullak and theory with Weitzmann in Berlin. Within seven months he was one of the students chosen to play at the annual Kullak concert at the *Singakademie,* at which he gave a brilliant performance of the Chopin fantasia in F. Other students who took part—Scharwenka, Moszkowski, Nicodé—all became famous pianists. He studied with Deppe for a time and then went to Stuttgart, where he studied organ with Scotson Clark and composition with Doppler, but he returned to Kullak and Weitzmann. The next season he played the Beethoven E flat concerto with an orchestra conducted by Richard Wüerst before an audience of four thousand, and repeated this concerto several times that season in Berlin. In 1875 he went to Weimar to study with Liszt, who was enthusiastic over the abilities of the young artist. Sherwood had studied the Grieg concerto with the composer and his performance of it with the philharmonic orchestra in Hamburg received an ovation. This success opened the door for performances with other great orchestras of Germany. While in Berlin he was organist of the English Chapel and while in Stuttgart, of the English Church.

Sherwood returned to America in 1876 and taught for a few years in the New England Conservatory, Boston, and then moved to New York. From 1889 until his death he lived in Chicago, being connected for the first eight years with the Chicago Conservatory of Music. He resigned in 1897 and established the Sherwood Music School, and devoted himself wholly to teaching and giving concerts. He was one of the first Americans to play with the great European orchestras, but in spite of his great success abroad, was always far more interested in the appreciation of his own countrymen. After one of his European trips, Karl Reinecke, conductor of the Gewandhaus concerts, invited him to appear as soloist with this orchestra in Leipzig, at that time the musical center of Europe. But Sherwood declined the invitation in order to fulfill an obligation that he always placed above all else—the development of musical life in America. He was the first to play the Grieg concerto in America, and was the first soloist to appear with the Boston Symphony Orchestra under George Henschel. Besides making several tours with the Theodore Thomas and the symphony orchestra of New York he played with all the important American orchestras. He possessed a flawless, brilliant technique, delicacy and refinement of expression, and thorough musicianship. He rarely gave a recital without including one American composition. He had a large following as a teacher, especially through his summer courses at Chautauqua, N. Y., where for twenty-two years, from 1889 till his death, he was head of the piano department.

Essentially an interpretative artist Sherwood was not deeply drawn to composition. His best works are *Scherzo Caprice,* Opus 9, two suites, Opus 5 and 14, *Scherzo Symphonique,* and two sets of *Gypsy Dances.* He possessed a lovable nature, very affable, simple, and unpretentious. His first wife, Mary Fay, of Williamsburg, N. Y., to whom he was married in 1874 while a student in Berlin, was also a gifted student of Kullak, and they often played together successfully. His second wife, Estelle F. Abrams, of Monongahela, Pa., to whom he was married in 1887, was his student in Boston. He had three daughters by the first marriage, and two by the second. He died in Chicago. Sherwood published two articles on his European studies in the *Étude,* May and July 1908.

[Information from the family; *Who's Who in America,* 1910–11; Andrew Sherwood, *Daniel Sherwood and his Paternal Ancestors* (1929); G. L. Howe, *A Hundred Years of Music in America* (1889); J. M. Green, *Musical Biog.* (1908), vol. II; *Grove's Dict. of Music and Musicians, Am. Supp.* (1930); biographical articles in *Musician,* Apr., May 1911, July 1913; *Chicago Tribune,* Jan. 15, 1911, *Musical America,* June 27, 1925; obits. in *Étude,* Feb. 1911, *Chautauquan Weekly,* Jan. 12, 19, 1911, and *Democrat Chronicle,* Rochester, N. Y., Jan. 8, 1911.] F. L. G. C.

SHICK CALAMYS [See SHIKELLAMY, d. 1748].

SHIELDS, CHARLES WOODRUFF (Apr. 4, 1825–Aug. 26, 1904), clergyman, university professor, author, was born at New Albany, Ind., the son of James Read and Hannah (Woodruff) Shields, and grandson of Patrick Henry Shields. His paternal forebears, of Scottish descent, were settled for some time in Delaware, Maryland, and Virginia. His maternal ancestors, originally from Yorkshire, England, lived for several generations at Elizabeth, N. J. He was prepared for college at the Newark Academy, graduated from the College of New Jersey in 1844, and from Princeton Theological Seminary in 1847. On Nov. 22, 1848, he married Charlotte Elizabeth Bain of Galway, N. Y. For a time he lived in Brooklyn, supplying various pulpits, but on Nov.

8, 1849, he was ordained to the Presbyterian ministry and became pastor of a church at Hempstead, Long Island. The year following he accepted a call to the Second Presbyterian Church, Philadelphia, in the service of which he remained for fifteen years. His first wife died in 1853, and in 1861 he married Elizabeth Kane, of Philadelphia, sister of the Arctic explorer, Elisha Kent Kane [q.v.].

In 1861 he published a little book, *Philosophia Ultima,* which changed the course of his life. All his subsequent writing and lecturing was really an effort to substantiate the challenge uttered in the pages of that pamphlet. It advocated as an attainable and desirable object of intellectual endeavor the production of a work which should be a survey of the whole field of science, a statement of Christian theology, and a reconcilement of their apparent conflicts. This project attracted much attention. Some of his wealthy friends in Philadelphia raised a fund to enable him to develop his idea in the free atmosphere of an undenominational college, and in 1865, he was made professor of the harmony of science and religion in the College of New Jersey, at Princeton. The subject had been taught more or less irregularly in many institutions, but the chair was new and created expressly for Shields. His lectures were finished literary productions, and it was not long before they took shape as a book, *The Final Philosophy* (1877). This work was republished with two additional volumes under the title *Philosophia Ultima* (1888–1905). The title was misunderstood in some quarters, but a sentence in the preface explains it perfectly: "The construction of the final philosophy itself, it need scarcely be said, can only be the common work and reward of many minds through coming generations."

Believing that the credal statements of Christian orthodoxy were essentially the same in all those Protestant churches which have preserved historic continuity in doctrine and polity, Shields was devoted to the cause of reunion, and wrote many essays on the subject. As a step towards union, he urged the adoption of a book of common prayer by non-liturgical churches and published, in 1864, *Liturgia Expurgata, or The Book of Common Prayer amended According to the Presbyterian Revision of 1661,* and in 1893, the Presbyterian *Book of Common Prayer.*

His two great ideals, the reconcilement of science with revealed religion, and the reunion of Protestantism on a basis of ancient practices, Shields pursued with a passion which could not be discouraged. Though he frequently conducted the plain religious services which were traditional in the college chapel, he found ritual more congenial, and on Dec. 14, 1898, he was ordained deacon of the Protestant Episcopal Church, and on May 28, 1899, priest. He held his active professorship from 1865 to 1903, when he became professor emeritus. For thirteen years, 1869–82, he conducted courses in history, while continuing to lecture in philosophy.

He was one of the last of that venerable band of clerical professors in the Eastern endowed colleges who regarded themselves and were regarded by others as no less defenders of Christian orthodoxy than teachers of literature, philosophy, and science. They were expected to dominate and color university instruction. He was extremely serious, though mild, modest, and urbane. His lectures were subtle and refined in style, with a fiery undercurrent of earnestness that showed itself in outbursts of eloquence. He was fair-minded and not at all contentious. His survey of the conflicts between religion and the sciences is candid and remarkably full, though the reconcilement for which he yearned could not have been accomplished even by a modern Aquinas combined with a modern Bacon. He died at his summer home in Newport, R. I., survived by two sons and a daughter; his second wife had died in 1869.

[Personal recollections; information from the family; W. M. Sloane, "Charles Woodruff Shields," in *Philosophia Ultima*, vol. III (1905); H. W. Rankin, *The Philosophy of Charles Woodruff Shields: An Estimate* (1905); *Necrological Report, Princeton Theological Sem.*, 1905; *Biog. Cat. Princeton Theological Sem.* (1913); *Who's Who in America*, 1903–05.] G. M. H.

SHIELDS, GEORGE HOWELL (June 19, 1842–Apr. 27, 1924), politician, jurist, born at Bardstown, Ky., was descended on both sides from Scotch-Irish Presbyterians. His father, George W. Shields, came of ancestry that had early settled in Pennsylvania, moving thence to Ohio; his mother, Martha Howell, belonged to a pioneer Kentucky family. The Shields household removed in 1844 to Hannibal, Mo., where the father, as a civil engineer, surveyed turnpikes and subsequently railroads, invested in the packing business, and amassed a comfortable fortune. Shields was educated in the schools of Hannibal, and then spent two years, 1859–60, at Westminster College, Missouri.

The Civil War interrupted his education, caused the loss of his father's fortune, and disrupted the family. George became a Republican; his father and brother remained stanch Democrats. He served as a captain in the militia, protecting the local community against bushwhackers and guerrillas, and between raids studied law in Hannibal. Graduating from the Louisville

Law School in 1865, he returned home, married Mary H. Leighton on Feb. 1, 1866, and entered practice. For several years he served as city attorney and participated as counsel in many contested election cases in an era of bitter partisanship. A strict believer in party regularity, he refused to join the Liberal Republicans in 1870, but was elected to the legislature from Marion County. He was prominent in the session as a minority member of important committees, and as spokesman for his party. Following his defeat for judge of the supreme court by Thomas A. Sherwood [q.v.] in 1872, he moved to St. Louis and formed a partnership with John B. Henderson [q.v.].

His subsequent career was a successful combination of law and politics. His lucrative practice included many cases involving the rights of bondholders in connection with defaulted county and township bond issues; he was also active in the "Whiskey Ring" prosecutions and in important public-utility litigation. He served for many years as master of chancery in the federal court of the eastern district of Missouri. An intelligent organizer, he was chairman of the Republican state committee from 1876 to 1880, and was one of the few Republicans in the constitutional convention of 1875. His demonstrated ability and integrity made him the choice of his Democratic associates for the chairmanship of the Board of Freeholders, under whose auspices the city of St. Louis was separated from the county and the first home-rule charter in the United States was framed in 1876. As assistant attorney-general assigned to the Department of the Interior during the Harrison administration, he was successful in the solution of complicated legal issues concerning Indian lands, forest reserves, and conflicts with railroads and land-hungry settlers. He enjoyed the complete confidence and respect of the secretary, John W. Noble [q.v.]. From 1893 to 1895 he practised law in Washington and served as counsel of the United States before the Chilean Claims Commission. Encouraged by the Republican landslide of 1894, he returned to Missouri where he formed a partnership with John W. Noble and reëntered state politics. He continued in private practice until 1906, when he was elected to the circuit bench. During his two terms, 1906–12 and 1914–20, he acquired a reputation for fairness and for wise use of judicial power. A leading member of the Presbyterian church, deeply interested in many patriotic and veterans' organizations, he was highly esteemed both by the bench and bar and by the general public. He died in St. Louis of the infirmities of age, survived by two sons and a daughter.

[*Hist. of Marion County, Mo.* (1884); A. J. D. Stewart, *The Hist. of the Bench and Bar of Mo.* (1898); William Hyde and H. L. Conard, *Encyc. of the Hist. of St. Louis* (4 vols., 1899); W. B. Stevens, *Centennial Hist. of Mo.* (1921), vol. III; *Who's Who in America,* 1922–23; *St. Louis Globe-Democrat, St. Louis Post-Dispatch,* Apr. 28, 1924.]   T. S. B.

SHIELDS, GEORGE OLIVER (Aug. 26, 1846–Nov. 11, 1925), editor, author, and pioneer in the conservation of wild life, was born in Batavia, Ohio, the son of John F. and Eliza J. (Dawson) Shields. He obtained his entire formal education, three months in public school, in Delaware County, Iowa. He enlisted in the Union Army in February 1864, was wounded in action at Resaca, Ga., in May 1864, and was discharged in July 1865. After 1865 he seems not to have returned to his home for many years. For a short time after his discharge he was an immigration agent for the Pecos Irrigation and Improvement Company at Eddy (later Carlsbad), N. Mex. About this time he began writing for newspapers and periodicals. He had successfully hunted nearly every kind of game in North America south of the arctic circle, but soon after starting his career as a writer he became an ardent conservationist. Coquina, his pseudonym, was taken from the trade name of the Florida fossil-coral building material he described in his first book, *Rustlings in the Rockies* (1883). Like the first book, *Cruisings in the Cascades* (1889), made up of articles written for periodicals, is a simple narrative in which hunting and fishing play an important part. He also wrote *The Battle of the Big Hole* (1889), a valuable account of the Nez Percé Indian battle in Montana, *Camping and Camp Outfits* (1890), and *The Blanket Indian of the Northwest* (1921); he edited *The Big Game of North America* (1890), *The American Book of the Dog* (1891), and *American Game Fishes* (1892).

In 1894 he founded the popular magazine *Recreation,* through which he carried on vigorous campaigns, first against the excessive taking of game and later against the use by sportsmen of the automatic shotgun. From 1897 until 1902 he was the tireless but autocratic head of the Camp-Fire Club of America, the idea of which originated with Dr. William T. Hornaday. In 1898 he formed the League of American Sportsmen, which appointed game wardens in a great many states; through it he also encouraged animal photography and was awarded a bronze medal by the National Photographic Society. Early in 1905 he was forced into bankruptcy by his printers, though *Recreation* itself went on. Largely through the efforts of Dr. Hornaday, the New York Zoological Society soon raised money to establish *Shields' Magazine,* which was published until August 1912. Shields now devoted his whole time to lecturing. He was influential in having game laws enacted in many states and in securing the passage of the Lacey Act, the first federal law regulating interstate commerce and importation of birds and game. A man of remarkable energy and enthusiasm, too sincere in his belief in the importance of his work to adopt politic methods in presenting his views, he unfortunately made enemies of many people who might have helped him. Yet he has been called "unquestionably our most eminent and successful pioneer in the cause of the conservation of wild life" (*Outdoor Life, post,* p. 31). In his later years he was frequently given the title of colonel, evidently merely by courtesy. He married but separated from his wife in 1892; they had no children. He spent his last years in straitened circumstances in New York, where he died in St. Luke's Hospital in the early hours of the morning, Nov. 11, 1925.

[*Who's Who in America,* 1920–21; *Who's Who in N. Y.,* 1924; *Who's Who Among North Am. Authors,* 1921; W. T. Hornaday, *Our Vanishing Wild Life* (1913), *Thirty Years' War for Wild Life* (1931); G. O. Shields, in *Shields' Mag.,* Mar. 1905; *Outdoor Life,* Nov. 1931; *Back-Log,* May 1930; obituary in *N. Y. Times,* Nov. 13, 1925; information from Miss Myra Emmons, A. L. A. Himmelwright, Dr. W. T. Hornaday, T. Gilbert Pearson, and Mrs. Sadie Latimer, Shields's niece.]   E. W. H.

SHIELDS, JAMES (May 12, 1806–June 1, 1879), soldier, senator from Illinois, Minnesota, and Missouri, was born in Altmore, County Tyrone, Ireland, the son of Charles and Katherine (McDonnell) Shields. Trained in a hedge school and later in an academy and by a retired priest from Maynooth, he received a good classical education, supplemented by some teaching in tactics and swords play. Probably in 1822 he sailed by way of Liverpool for Quebec and was wrecked on the Scottish coast with only two other survivors. As a tutor, he earned a livelihood in Scotland until he obtained a berth on a merchantman and about 1826 arrived in New York harbor. He settled in Kaskaskia, Ill., where he taught French, read law, fought in the Black Hawk War, and practised Democratic politics and law. In 1836 he was elected a member of the legislature. As state auditor, he helped correct the disordered finances of the state brought to the verge of bankruptcy by the panic and canal building, but not without sharp criticism in the Whig press. As a result of anonymous charges in the newspaper, traced to the Misses Todd and Jayne, later the wives of Abraham Lincoln and Lyman Trumbull, he challenged to a duel Lincoln, who shouldered some responsibility. The matter was compromised on explanations from the latter, and the principals became permanent friends. In 1843 Shields was named to the supreme court by Gov. Thomas Ford, whose manuscript *History of Illinois* he edited and published later, in 1854. As a jurist, he was honest, industrious, and surprisingly detached in delivering decisions that were marked by common sense and some legal erudition. He was renamed by the legislature for a full term in 1845, but he resigned soon to accept President Polk's appointment to the commissionership of the general land office in Washington.

With the outbreak of the Mexican War he resigned and was commissioned brigadier-general of Illinois volunteers on July 1, 1846. At Cerro Gordo he was dangerously wounded, was brevetted a major-general, and cited by General Scott for his gallant conduct there. At Churubusco, after initial mistakes of some importance (Smith, *post*, pp. 115–17, 384), he led the charge of New York Irish and South Carolina volunteers that is commemorated in the painting in the national Capitol. In July 1848 his brigade was disbanded, and he returned to Kaskaskia and Belleville to build up his law practice, but he was soon appointed governor of Oregon Territory. This position he resigned immediately to accept an election to the federal Senate. A Whig Senate found a technicality in that he had not been a citizen the required number of years and declared his election void. He, however, was reëlected for the same term and served from Oct. 27, 1849, to Mar. 3, 1855. Martial in carriage, scrupulously neat, urbane and courteous of manner, graceful and humorous in debate, he was well informed because of his ability, experiences, and his command of Latin, French, and Spanish. In temper he was sharp and somewhat arrogantly independent. Something of a demagogue, he was intentionally candid. A strict party man, he had the courage to disagree with fanatics on either side of the slavery issue and to fight for a free California, land grants for veterans, railroad construction, and agricultural education. In 1855 he was defeated for reëlection by Lyman Trumbull in a legislature in deadlock between himself and Lincoln.

A Douglas appointee to distribute Sioux half-breed scrip, he went to Minnesota Territory, where he settled down on his land grant. He did much to stimulate an Irish movement into the region by organizing the townships of Shieldsville, Erin, Kilkenny, and Montgomery in Lesueur and Rice counties and by establishing with Alexander Faribault the town of Faribault. Elected to the federal Senate, on the admission of Minnesota, he drew the short term that expired Mar. 3, 1859, and a Republican legislature failed to reëlect him. He went to San Francisco, where in 1861 he married Mary Ann Carr, the daughter of an old friend in Armagh, Ireland, by whom he had three surviving children. Settled in Mazatlan, Mexico, as manager and part owner of a mine, he sold his interest and offered his services to Lincoln, when he learned that Fort Sumter had surrendered. Appointed as a brigadier-general of volunteers on Aug. 19, 1861, he campaigned in the Shenandoah Valley, where he won recognition at Winchester and at Port Republic. He resigned his commission on Mar. 28, 1863, and retired to San Francisco, where he was appointed a state railroad commissioner. In 1866, he was in Carrollton, Mo. There he entered politics again, campaigning against the "ironclad oath," losing an election to Congress when a canvassing board cast out the votes of two counties, and supporting the Liberal-Republican candidates of 1872. He lectured for religious, Irish, and charitable causes such as Southern relief during the cholera epidemic. Serving in the legislature, he promoted an act for a railroad commission to which he was afterward appointed. He was elected to fill out an unexpired term in the federal Senate from Jan. 27, 1879, to Mar. 3, 1879, but lack of health forced him to decline being a candidate for reëlection. He died at Ottumwa, Iowa, while on a lecture tour, and was buried with simple Roman Catholic rites at St. Mary's Cemetery in Carrollton, Mo., where in 1910 a colossal statue was erected to his memory. In 1893 his statue was placed in Statuary Hall in the national Capitol by Illinois and, in 1914, Minnesota, at the insistence of the Grand Army of the Republic, raised a memorial in the state capitol.

[W. H. Condon, *Life of Major-General James Shields* (1900); H. A. Castle, "Gen. James Shields," and John Ireland, "Address at the Unveiling of the Statue of General Shields," *Minn. Hist. Soc. Colls.*, vol. XV (1915); *N. Y. Freeman's Jour. and Catholic Register*, May 4, 1861, June 7, 14, 1879, Jan. 1, 1887; *Jour. of the Am.-Irish Hist. Soc.*, vol. IX (1900), vol. XIV (1915); *Studies* (Dublin), Mar. 1932; W. W. Folwell, *A Hist. of Minnesota* (1924), vol. II; J. H. Smith, *The War with Mexico* (2 vols., 1919); date of birth from statement concerning original family records in Castle, *ante*, p. 711.]   R. J. P.

SHIELDS, THOMAS EDWARD (May 9, 1862–Feb. 15, 1921), Roman Catholic priest, educator, son of John and Bridget (Burke) Shields, immigrants from Ireland, was born and reared on a farm near Mendota, Minn. He developed physically at a rate which retarded mental growth and was regarded by his unlettered parents and by his neighbors as a hopeless dullard or "omadhaun." Dominated by an elder brother, he became a powerful farmhand who spoke brokenly and shrank from all associations. Suddenly, however, there came a revolt from paternalistic control, and an awakening of his mind which resulted in his inventing a grubbing machine. He laboriously made his way through a book and thus learned to read. Realizing at length that he was not unlike other men, he began to display an undaunted self-confidence which he retained through life, often to the annoyance of less imaginative associates. Only his confessor, an able but odd Irishman, had faith in his ability; the bishop turned from the farm boy who knew no Latin when he presented himself as a candidate for the seminary. Shields applied himself to his books, and, untrammeled by formalism and bad teaching, his mind opened amazingly. In 1882 he gained admission to St. Francis College in Milwaukee, where he prepared for St. Thomas Seminary, which he entered in 1885. As a seminarian, his talent in philosophy and science was recognized, especially when he invented in 1888 a filing system for the accumulation of information under the title *Index Omnium.*

Ordained a priest, Mar. 14, 1891, by Archbishop Ireland, who admired his rugged integrity and brilliant mind, he was sent, after fourteen months as a curate at St. Paul's Cathedral, to St. Mary's Seminary, Baltimore, where he took a master's degree, and was permitted to take graduate work in biology at Johns Hopkins University, in recognition of which he was given the degree of Ph.D. in 1895. Such a course was a radical departure for a priest, and Shields attracted the attention of teachers and fellow students as one who correlated scholastic philosophy with science. His thesis, *The Effect of Odours, Irritant Vapours, and Mental Work Upon the Blood Flow,* a thorough piece of research, was published in 1896. As a lecturer in psychology and biology at St. Paul's Seminary, he proved an independent thinker and an inspiring teacher who sympathized with his students; but in 1898 he was removed to St. Joseph's Church, St. Paul, as second assistant. In this field of service he also showed marked ability, and incidentally invented a shoe polish.

Archbishop Ireland finally released him in 1902 to accept an instructorship at the Catholic University in Washington, D. C. A magnetic teacher, if somewhat informal, he was advanced to a professorship in education and psychology in 1909. He found time, in addition to his teaching at the University and Trinity College, to prepare scientific articles for encyclopedias and magazines; to perfect a plethysmograph (see

American Journal of Experimental Medicine, vol. I); and to write a number of books. Among his publications are *Psychology of Education* (1904), a series in mimeograph; *The Teaching of Religion* (1907), in multigraph; *The Education of Our Girls* (1906), with a preface by Cardinal Gibbons which disarmed critics; *The Making and Unmaking of a Dullard* (1909), which was annoyingly autobiographical; *Teachers' Manual of Primary Methods* (1912); *Philosophy of Education* (1917); and, with E. A. Pace, a couple of elementary books in religion as a protest against the stereotyped method of memorizing catechism. While his system of religious instruction was logical and practical, it found more criticism than acceptance in the parochial schools. Always a promoter, he founded and directed a Catholic Correspondence School (1904–09), apparently with the hope of bringing modern, secular methods to Catholic teachers. In 1911 he established the *Catholic Educational Review,* the first journal of its kind. As its editor for ten years, he formulated theories of teacher and child training which contributed to the improvement of methods employed in parochial and high schools. In an effort to assist nuns in meeting the higher requirements which he foresaw would be demanded by state boards of education and accrediting agencies, he started at the University with the sympathetic assistance of the rector, Bishop Thomas J. Shahan [q.v.], a summer school for sisters, with branches at San Francisco and at Dubuque; he was also instrumental in founding in 1911 the Catholic Sisters College as an affiliated school of the University. Both institutions were novel departures, and as such they were roundly criticized for drawing nuns from their convents. Soon, however, other Catholic universities followed the example thus set and began holding summer sessions for sisters, while various religious orders adapted themselves to teaching women and even to co-education. Shields also put into operation a scheme whereby colleges, high schools, and novitiates throughout the country were affiliated with the Catholic University as a means of improving their standards and securing uniformity without loss of school autonomy. As dean of the Sisters College, he rendered one of his most important services. He bought the site, interested influential patrons in the project, and found a faculty among his lay and clerical associates who were willing to sacrifice for an ideal. Believing that the time was ripe for a series of Catholic textbooks, he established the Catholic Educational Press (1908). Not until 1913 did he find time to visit Europe; his travels had been confined to visiting Mother Houses and schools, attending conventions, and holding institutes.

A genius and a crusader, erratic but sociable, careless of dress, uncanny in vision and hence regarded as a radical and as impractical, a hard and not unwilling fighter, Shields faced difficulties, misunderstanding, and a general lack of sympathy; but he went his way refusing to be discouraged by obstacles. For his ideals, he sacrificed personal comfort and even friends who could not follow him. Aggressively he forced his way until finally he burned himself out and died from a valvular disease of the heart. His estate went to the Sisters College, and his remains repose in a mausoleum on its campus.

[*Catholic Educ. Rev.*, Apr. 1921 (memorial number), Jan. 1929; *Am. Catholic Who's Who*, 1911; *Who's Who in America*, 1920–21; *The Catholic Encyc. and Its Makers* (1917); *Evening Star* (Washington, D. C.), Feb. 15, 1921; *Irish Monthly* (Dublin), Apr. 1934; personal knowledge and notes from a number of Shields's associates.]   R. J. P.

SHIKELLAMY (d. Dec. 6, 1748), Oneida chief, was born probably into the Cayuga tribe and early adopted by the Oneida, among whom he became a chief. John Bartram [*q.v.*] described him as a *"Frenchman,* born at Mont-real," although he also wrote that "his son told me he was of *Cayuga* nation" (*Observations, post,* p. 17). His name was spelled in various ways, such as Schickillemy, Shakallamy, Shick Calamys, Shikellamy, and sometimes after the Latin form of the Moravians, Shikellemus or Sicalamous. He was also called Swataney. About 1728 he was sent by the Six Nations to assert the right of Iroquois dominion over the conquered tribes of Pennsylvania, principally Delaware and Shawnee, and to prevent their selling land to the white governments. He established himself in a strategic position near the forks of the Susquehanna; at first he was probably about ten miles above the forks on the west branch and later at the Indian town of Shamokin, where Sunbury now stands, in Northumberland County.

He was soon engaged in the general oversight of Indian relations with the white people. Again and again he made the difficult journey through the wilderness of the upper Susquehanna Valley. To Onondaga, the seat of council for the Iroquois confederation, he took messages from the white governments, guided emissaries, and from time to time went to obtain instructions from the Six Nations concerning their subject tribes to the south. He kept the English informed of French advances of friendship to the Indians and was ever ready to discourage Iroquois participation in French plans. Through Conrad Weiser and James Logan [*qq.v.*], for whom his son James

Logan [*q.v.*] was named, he was able to influence the Pennsylvania government to support the claims of the Six Nations against the Delaware and the Shawnee. He was active in negotiating the two treaties of 1736 by which Pennsylvania agreed to pay the Iroquois an indemnity for lands already ceded by their subject tribes and to acknowledge Iroquois claims to Delaware lands on the lower Delaware River. Since the confederation had not hitherto exerted right of control over these lands, this action constituted a precedent to deny Delaware claims to any lands. His influence was important in obtaining the treaties of 1744 at Lancaster with Maryland and Virginia, which provided for the payment of indemnities and acknowledgment of Iroquois land claims within the borders of those states. Pennsylvania, actuated by the conviction of the power and importance of the Six Nations, represented by Shikellamy, continued to court that confederation and to offend the Delaware and Shawnee, thus avoiding an Iroquois war at the cost of the sullen resentment of the Delaware and Shawnee—a resentment that broke forth to ravage Pennsylvania after Braddock's defeat.

Apparently Shikellamy spoke more English than he generally acknowledged (Bartram, *post,* p. 43). He possessed a sympathy for white men, which he manifested over a period of years by protecting their personal safety, by his response to the Moravians, and by his personal relations to such men as Count Zinzendorf, Conrad Weiser, and David Zeisberger. In early life he had been baptized by a Jesuit in Canada, was for years interested in the Moravian way of life, and in his last year went down to Bethlehem to be received into that communion. Stricken with mortal illness he went home to Shamokin, where the Moravian missionaries watched with him until he died.

[C. H. Sipe, *The Indian Chiefs of Pa.* (1927); W. M. Beauchamp, "Shikellimy," *Am. Scenic and Hist. Preservation Soc., 21st . . . Report* (1916), pp. 599–611; J. S. Walton, *Conrad Weiser* (1900); *Minutes of the Provincial Council of Pa.*, vols. I–V (1852–51); *Pa. Archives*, vols. I, II (1852–53), ed. by Samuel Hazard; John Bartram, *Observations* (1751), pp. 17, 20, 43; G. H. Loskiel, *Hist. of the Mission of the United Brethren* (1794), trans. by C. I. Latrobe; E. A. De Schweinitz, *The Life and Times of David Zeisberger* (1870); W. C. Reichel, *Memorials of the Moravian Church* (1870), pp. 84–93; Witham Marshe, "Journ. of the Treaty . . . at Lancaster, Pa., June 1744," *Mass. Hist. Soc. Colls.*, vol. VII (1801), pp. 195–96.]
                                                      K. E. C.

SHILLABER, BENJAMIN PENHAL-LOW (July 12, 1814–Nov. 25, 1890), humorist, newspaperman, poet, was born at Portsmouth, N. H., one of six children of William and Sarah Leonard (Sawyer) Shillaber. He was a descendant of John Shillaber who emigrated from

Devonshire to Salem, Mass., toward the end of the seventeenth century. Educated in the district schools, he served his apprenticeship years as printer's devil in the Dover offices of the *New Hampshire Palladium and Strafford Advertiser*, 1829–31, and in the Portsmouth offices of the *Portsmouth Courier* and the *Christian Herald*. In the spring of 1833 he became a book-compositor with the printing firm of Tuttle & Weeks on School Street, Boston, who printed the popular Peter Parley tales of Samuel Griswold Goodrich, the *New England Farmer,* and some of the anti-slavery poetry of John Greenleaf Whittier [*qq.v.*]. At twenty-one he was rated as journeyman printer. In October 1835 violent nasal hemorrhages forced him to the tropics, where for about two years he served as compositor on the *Royal Gazette of British Guiana* (Demerara). Restored to health, he returned to Boston in July 1838 and there on Aug. 15 married Ann Tappan de Rochemont. They had eight children, of whom three daughters and one son survived their father.

Shortly thereafter he joined the *Boston Post,* then under the editorship of Charles Gordon Greene, an outstanding journalistic figure of the forties. Until 1847 he was a "manipulator of the stick and rule" without any aspirations for a literary career, when a squib he set up in the *Post* chanced to make a great hit. In this a certain imaginary Mrs. Partington, who had been described by Sydney Smith as vainly mopping back the ocean, was reported to have said that it "made no difference to her whether flour was dear or cheap, as she always had to pay just so much for a half-dollar's worth." The sayings and doings of the old lady soon made her a national figure and Shillaber an outstanding American humorist. In 1850 he became editor of the *Pathfinder and Railway Guide,* distributed by "news-butchers" on railroads and steamboats; a year later he began to edit a humorous weekly, the *Carpet-Bag,* through whose columns the nationally popular sayings of Mrs. Partington continued. Although the *Carpet-Bag* boasted the best humorous writers of the day, including in addition to the older established men the youthful Charles Farrar Browne, S. L. Clemens, Charles Bertrand Lewis, and Charles Graham Halpine [*qq.v.*], it died prematurely in 1853 after two years' struggle. It remains, however, one of the most important American humorous papers, developing as it did a whole school. To the *Boston Post* Shillaber returned that year as local reporter, remaining until 1856; from 1856 to 1866.he was on the staff of the *Saturday Evening Gazette,* and subsequently he spent two years on

the lyceum circuits giving humorous lectures. Later he retired to his home in Chelsea, Mass., where he died. Although he abandoned direct connection with the press, he was an occasional correspondent and contributor, wrote his Ike Partington juveniles, and continued the writing of poems, always referring to them as "rhymes" and to himself as a "rhymist." He was large of build, jovial, ever ready of wit, with a plain, frank face.

Chief among his separately published works are *Rhymes With Reason and Without* (1853), *Life and Sayings of Mrs. Partington* (1854), of which thousands of copies sold in a short time, *Knitting-Work* (1859), *Partingtonian Patchwork* (1872), *Lines in Pleasant Places* (1874), and the Ike Partington juveniles. His reminiscences, "Experiences During Many Years," appeared in the *New England Magazine,* June 1893–May 1894. Between the old school of American humor, which preceded the Civil War, and the new, he served as the chief connecting link. As a young newspaperman under Greene on the *Boston Post* he met and knew the humorists of the forties; as editor of the *Carpet-Bag,* 1851–53, he came into contact with and stimulated the coming generation of humorists. It was to the *Carpet-Bag* that Artemus Ward and Mark Twain sent their first contributions; and it was through Shillaber that they readily became a part of the ever-broadening stream of American humor.

[The chief source is B. P. Shillaber, "Experiences During Many Years," *New England Mag.,* June 1893–May 1894. See also *Geneal. of the Cutts Family in America* (1892), comp. by C. H. C. Howard; *A Family Souvenir: Record of Proc. at the First Gathering of Descendants of John Shillaber* (1877); *Proc. N. H. Press Assoc.* (1895); S. A. Allibone, *A Critical Dict. of Eng. Lit.,* vol. II (1870); G. W. Bungay, *Off-Hand Takings* (1854); *Appletons' Ann. Cyc.,* 1890; *Lit. World,* Dec. 20, 1890; obituaries in *Boston Post, N. Y. Tribune,* Nov. 26, 1890.]   F.J.M.

SHINN, ASA (May 3, 1781–Feb. 11, 1853), Methodist clergyman, one of the founders of the Methodist Protestant Church, was born in New Jersey, the son of Jonathan and Mary (Clark) Shinn, and a descendant of John Shinn, who emigrated from England to America and was in New Jersey as early as 1680. Both of Asa's parents were Quakers. When he was seven years of age they moved to one of the inland counties of Virginia, and seven years later to what is now Harrison County, West Virginia. In these frontier communities the boy's only schooling was received from a former sailor who wandered through the country conducting schools as opportunity afforded. In 1798, under the preaching of Rev. Robert Manly, a Methodist circuit rider, Shinn professed conversion and three years later, influenced by the scarcity of ministers in the West, he joined the Baltimore Conference of the Methodist Episcopal Church, and was assigned to the Redstone circuit in southwestern Pennsylvania. In 1803 he was transferred to the Western Conference, which included all the territory west of the Alleghany Mountains. Here he remained until 1807, serving circuits in western Virginia, southern Ohio, and Kentucky. He returned to the Baltimore Conference in 1807 and about the same time married Phebe Barnes of western Virginia, by whom he had two sons and two daughters. Until 1816, when he was forced by mental derangement temporarily to discontinue his work, he had charge of circuits in Maryland and the District of Columbia.

During the course of his life Shinn suffered four periods of insanity, resulting from a fracture of the skull in his boyhood. The first three of these, in 1816, 1820, and 1828, were of short duration; from the last, in 1843, he never recovered, and he died in an asylum for the insane at Brattleboro, Vt. Except for the short periods of inactivity caused by his ailment, Shinn continued to hold important circuits and stations in the Baltimore Conference until his transfer to the Pittsburgh Conference in 1825, where he served as presiding elder of the Pittsburgh district and as minister at Washington, Pa.

In 1824 he became greatly interested in the agitation for certain reforms in the government of the Methodist Episcopal Church. The reformers established a monthly paper in 1824 called *The Mutual Rights of Ministers and Members of the Methodist Episcopal Church,* for which Shinn became one of the most voluminous and effective contributors. He also wrote several controversial pamphlets, among them, *An Appeal to the Good Sense of the Citizens of the United States* (1826), *A Finishing Stroke to the High Claims of Ecclesiastical Sovereignty* (1827). When the Baltimore Conference in 1827 expelled a minister for circulating *Mutual Rights,* Shinn became active in his defense. Other reformers were also suspended. At the General Conference of 1828 the great issue was the appeal of these persons for restoration. Shinn presented their case in an eloquent speech which won the admiration even of his opponents, and had the vote been taken at once, the reformers would probably have been reinstated; but it was delayed until the next day and their cause was defeated.

Convinced that all chance at conciliation was past, the leading reformers now proceeded to form separate congregations and Conferences, and on Nov. 2, 1830, a convention of delegates from the disaffected groups met in the city of Baltimore and there formed the Methodist Protestant Church. Shinn took a leading part in its organization, was chosen president of the Ohio Conference when it was constituted, and in 1833, was elected president of the Pittsburgh Conference. From 1834 to 1836 he was in Baltimore, editing with Nicholas Snethen [*q.v.*], the new denominational paper, *Mutual Rights and Methodist Protestant,* and thereafter for the next ten years held important pulpits in Cincinnati, Pittsburgh, and Allegheny City. At the General Conference of 1838 the slavery issue brought on an acrimonious debate in which Shinn took the anti-slavery view and defended that position in a speech of great power.

He was the author of two considerable books on theology. The first, published in 1812, was entitled *An Essay on the Plan of Salvation;* the second, *On the Benevolence and Rectitude of the Supreme Being,* appeared in 1840. He possessed a logical mind and was particularly impressive in public address. After the death of his first wife he married Mary Bennington (Wrenshall) Gibson, widow of Woolman Gibson, and daughter of John Wrenshall, by whom he had one son.

[J. H. Shinn, *The Hist. of the Shinn Family in Europe and America* (1903); E. J. Drinkhouse, *Hist. of Methodist Reform* (1899); W. B. Sprague, *Annals Am. Pulpit,* vol. VII (1859); A. H. Bassett, *A Concise Hist. of the Methodist Protestant Church* (2nd ed., 1882); R. F. Shinn, *A Tribute to Our Fathers* (1853); Matthew Simpson, *Cyc. of Methodism* (1878); *Daily Commercial Jour.* (Pittsburgh), Feb. 18, 1853.]

W. W. S.

SHIPHERD, JOHN JAY (Mar. 28, 1802–Sept. 16, 1844), home missionary, one of the founders of Oberlin College, was born near Granville, N. Y., the third son of Zebulon Rudd and Betsy (Bull) Shipherd. His father, a successful lawyer, served for many years as a trustee of Middlebury College and, for one term (1813–15), as a Federalist member of Congress. When John was seventeen "the Lord mercifully revealed Himself to his mind" and he determined to become a minister. He was at that time attending Pawlet Academy, Pawlet, Vt., from which he soon transferred to Cambridge Academy, Cambridge, N. Y. He planned to complete his education at Middlebury College, but an accidental dose of poison so weakened his eyes and voice and so undermined his health generally that he was forced, for a time, to abandon the prospect of further study. After two years spent in unsuccessful ventures in the marble and whetstone industries at Vergennes, Vt., however, he entered the household of Rev. Josiah Hopkins at New Haven, Vt., to prepare for ordination.

Here he spent a year and a half, depending largely upon the eyes of others for his reading.

He was ordained as an evangelist by a Congregational council at Blanton, Vt., Oct. 3, 1827, but after preaching for a year at Shelburn, in the autumn of 1828 he accepted the general agency of the Vermont Sabbath School Union and removed to Middlebury. For the next two years he traveled about the state, founding and inspecting Sunday schools; he also published a semi-annual, *The Sabbath School Guide,* and a tiny juvenile religious magazine, *The Youth's Herald.* Middlebury College granted him an honorary master's degree in 1830. Already, however, he had decided to go as a home missionary "to Mississippi's vast valley."

Accordingly, in the autumn of 1830, without waiting to secure an appointment, he went West, stopping at Rochester, N. Y., to receive the advice and blessing of Charles G. Finney [*q.v.*]. Upon reaching Cleveland he was promptly assigned to the missionary pastorate of a Plan-of-Union Presbyterian church in the village of Elyria, Lorain County, Ohio. His experience here was checkered but generally disappointing to him, and in the summer of 1832, in collaboration with a classmate of Pawlet days, Philo P. Stewart [*q.v.*], he formulated a scheme for the evangelization of the West through a Christian colony and manual-labor school to be founded in the wilderness, far from the polluting influence of established communities. The new enterprise was christened Oberlin in honor of the philanthropist and educator, Jean Frédéric Oberlin, a life of whom had recently been published by the American Sunday School Union. In 1832–33 Shipherd traveled through New York and New England, securing money, teachers, pious settlers, and title to a tract of land nine miles from Elyria; while Stewart and other associates forwarded the enterprise on the spot. The first settlement was made in April 1833. Shipherd returned in September and presided at the opening of the preparatory and "infant" departments of the Oberlin Collegiate Institute, Dec. 3, 1833. A full staff of teachers was secured the following spring, and in the fall, the first students of college grade appeared. The initial report of the Institute, published in December 1834, was optimistic, but Shipherd knew that the funds available were insufficient to guarantee the long continuance of the enterprise.

The rebellion of the students at Lane Seminary, near Cincinnati, furnished the means of saving Oberlin. Lane, also, had been founded to promote the evangelization of the West and for this purpose had been liberally endowed by

Arthur and Lewis Tappan [*qq.v.*]. Under the leadership of Theodore Weld [*q.v.*] the students had begun the discussion of the slavery question and formed an anti-slavery society. The trustees, mostly conservative Cincinnati business men, prohibited further debate of this dangerous issue and the students walked out, almost to a man. Shipherd read of the situation in the religious periodicals and hastened to Cincinnati, where he discussed with the "rebels" and Rev. Asa Mahan [*q.v.*], one of the friendly minority of the Lane trustees, the possibility of their coming to Oberlin. His proposition was favorably received, but final acceptance was conditioned upon securing the support of the Tappans and the appointment of Charles G. Finney to teach theology at Oberlin. Shipherd and Mahan therefore proceeded to New York, where they won over the Tappans and persuaded Finney to accept the appointment if the Oberlin trustees would agree to leave the internal administration of the school exclusively to the faculty. Shipherd persuaded his reluctant associates to accept this condition. In the spring of 1835 Mahan became president of the Institute and the Lane "rebels" arrived to study theology under Finney in the newly founded theological department. Oberlin was now firmly established as a center of reform and revival piety.

After 1835, the leadership having passed to Finney and Mahan, Shipherd turned to the founding of other colonies and schools. His Grand River Seminary in Michigan, announced in 1836, and his Lagrange Collegiate Institute, proposed in the spring of 1838, were stillborn. In 1844 he led personally the little group of people who established the colony and school at Olivet in Michigan. There, early in the autumn of the same year, he died. In 1824 he had married Esther Raymond of Ballston, N. Y., by whom he had a daughter who died in infancy, and six sons.

[Letters and other manuscripts in the possession of Oberlin College and privately owned; D. L. Leonard, *The Story of Oberlin* (copr. 1898); *N. Y. Evangelist,* June 18, 1831, Jan. 30, 1832, Sept. 7, 1833, Mar. 21, July 18, 1835, Sept. 17, 1836, Mar. 31, Apr. 22, 1837; *Ohio Observer* (Hudson, Ohio), June 12, July 17, 1834, Feb. 5, July 9, 1835; W. B. Williams, *A Hist. of Olivet College* (1901), and "Two Early Efforts to Found Colleges in Mich.," *Hist. Coll. . . . Mich. Pioneer and Hist. Soc.,* vol. XXX (1906); R. S. Fletcher, "Oberlin, 1833–1866," in MS.]   R. S. F.

SHIPMAN, ANDREW JACKSON (Oct. 15, 1857–Oct. 17, 1915), scholar and lawyer, son of John James and Priscilla (Carroll) Shipman, was born in Springvale, Fairfax County, Va., and reared in the desperate days of the Civil War and Reconstruction. With his father in the

Confederate forces, the boy was dubbed a "little rebel Zouave" by Unionist soldiers who occupied the region. On his father's side his ancestry was English, while the Carrolls traced their descent from Thomas, an Irishman, who settled in Maryland in 1725. Taught by his learned grandfather, Bennett Carroll, and by a succession of stranded schoolmasters, the boy Andrew was amply prepared for Georgetown Academy, Washington, where he was sent upon the recommendation of one of his teachers, a Roman Catholic and a former officer in the Austrian army, from whom he had learned some German and considerable European history. He completed the preparatory course in 1874, and four years later was graduated from Georgetown College. While a student, he joined the Roman Catholic Church, to which his mother returned. In 1879, he was back in Fairfax County, editing the *Vienna Times* and learning Czech from Stefan Melzer, who like other wandering foreigners had sought temporary refuge with the Shipmans. The following year Shipman found employment as a superintendent of the coal mines of W. P. Rend & Company in Hocking Valley, Ohio. Here he took a deep interest in the welfare of the foreign laborers and undertook to learn a number of the Slavic dialects. Among the miners were many Catholics of the Greek and Ruthenian rites, to whom the Roman Catholic service seemed as strange as that of another creed. Shipman feared that they would lose the faith if priests of their own rite and race were not provided. Hence, at a time when Catholics were woefully unconscious of the problem, he entered with a convert's zeal upon a lay apostolate in their behalf.

In 1884 he acquired a competitive clerkship in the New York Custom House, where he challenged attention as an investigator of the sugar frauds and during his free time acquired, in 1886, a degree in law from the University of the City of New York. In 1891 he became a law partner of Edmund Mooney—whose sister, Adair, he married two years later—and in 1893 the firm of Blandy, Mooney, & Shipman was formed. Shipman won recognition as a forceful, diligent advocate, and a respected counselor in labor cases, in the St. Stephen's Protestant Episcopal Church cases (1891–1900, 11 *New York Supplement*, 669), which compelled a study of ecclesiastical law, and in the business of the Greek, Ruthenian, and Slavic peoples, in whose native lands he spent all his vacations. A Democrat of influence without desire for office, he was a member of numerous clubs, president of the board of Mohansic State Hospital, a member of the Board of Regents of the University of the State of New York (1913), an associate manager of the Sevilla Home for Children, a member of the state constitutional convention of 1915, a leader in the Catholic Theatre movement, and a promoter of the Marquette League for Indian missionaries. His keenest interest remained, however, in the problem of the Eastern-rites Catholic immigrants.

No other American Catholic knew and served the Greek, Syrian, Slavic, Hungarian, and Ruthenian Catholics as did Shipman, and few Americans knew so well the peoples and languages of Eastern Europe. He persistently labored to bring about a sympathetic union between Roman and Orthodox Greek Catholics, to urge upon Catholic prelates an appreciation of the importance of this religious issue, to secure European churchmen to care for the hundreds of thousands of Eastern-rite Catholics in the industrial centers and mining regions of America, and to Americanize these immigrants in a worthy sense. He wrote of these Eastern peoples and their religious forms in the *Catholic Encyclopedia,* the *Century, McClure's Magazine,* the *Messenger,* and *Pravoslavny Viestnik,* and he spoke of their problems from numerous platforms. In 1911, he translated into English, for the first time, *The Holy Mass According to the Greek Rite.* In 1895, he was associated with Rev. Joseph Chaplinski in organizing a Ruthenian Greek Church in New York; he brought a stone from Jerusalem for the Church of St. Joachim which the Syrians were building; he was the friend and prized adviser of Bishop S. S. Ortynsky [q.v.] when uninformed Catholic priests were suspicious of the orthodoxy of their Ukrainian brethren; he exposed the attempts of Orthodox priests to proselytize by using Greek ceremonials; and he prevented the legislative sanction sought by the Russian Orthodox bishop for the use of the term Russian Greek Catholic Church. On his sudden death, of acute Bright's disease, he was buried from St. Patrick's Cathedral, where, after the Roman Mass, Bishop Ortynsky read the burial service according to the Greek rite, and the Ukrainian choir, which Shipman had assisted in forming, chanted the dirge.

[*A Memorial of Andrew J. Shipman: His Life and Writings* (1916), ed. by C. B. Pallen; *The Am. Cath. Who's Who* (1911); *The Cath. Encyc. and Its Makers* (copr. 1917); Coleman Nevils, *Miniatures of Georgetown* (1934), pp. 352–53; *Records of the Am. Cath. Hist. Soc.,* Dec. 1917; *Proc. N. Y. State Bar Asso.,* 1916; *N. Y. Times,* Oct. 18, 1915.]   R. J. P.

SHIPP, ALBERT MICAJAH (June 15, 1819–June 27, 1887), Methodist Episcopal clergyman, educator, was born in Stokes County,

N. C., the son of John and Elizabeth (Oglesby) Shipp. Converted at Rock Spring camp meeting in August 1835, he joined the Methodist Church. In 1840 he was graduated at the University of North Carolina and in January of the following year was admitted on trial to the South Carolina Conference of the Methodist Episcopal Church. In 1843 he was ordained deacon by Bishop Andrew, and in December 1844, elder by Bishop Soule. He served two years on circuits, four years on stations, and one as presiding elder. He was a member of every General Conference of the Methodist Episcopal Church, South, from 1850 to 1886 inclusive, and of the Centennial Conference, held at Baltimore in 1884.

He early became one of the outstanding preachers in his denomination, but in 1848 his voice weakened under a chronic throat affection, making regular pulpit service thereafter impossible. His intellectual ability and his thorough scholarship pointed naturally to educational work as an alternative, and in 1848–49 he served as president of Greensboro Female College, North Carolina. For ten years (1849–59) he was professor of history in the University of North Carolina, and for the next sixteen years president of Wofford College, Spartanburg, S. C. From 1875 to 1885 he held the chair of exegetical theology in Vanderbilt University, for three years of the time serving as dean of the theological department and vice-chancellor of the University. Bishop Holland N. McTyeire, then powerful in the affairs of the institution, bluntly demanding a head of the theological department of greater ability, Shipp resigned in 1885, and was at his own request superannuated by the South Carolina Conference. The remaining two years of his life he spent at his home "Rose Hill," Marlboro County, near Cheraw, S. C.

As a teacher he won the respect and affection of his students. He was a man of correct literary taste and broad scholarship. In December 1876, his Conference requested him to prepare a history of Methodism in South Carolina. Pressure of his new duties at Vanderbilt University caused him to delay the project until the summer and fall of 1880, and the work, *The History of Methodism in South Carolina,* was published in 1883. Comprising a large amount of valuable data regarding both institutions and persons, it is still the most copious single body of information on the subject. It is less systematic, though more extensive, than Dr. A. M. Chreitzberg's *Early Methodism in the Carolinas* published in 1897. The effort expended in its preparation was a labor of love, and any profits from the pub-

lication were directed to the support of worn-out preachers and their widows and orphans. Though marked by hasty composition, it shows a realization of the part that Methodism has played in the life of the state and of its people, not neglecting the remarkable service rendered the slaves.

Dr. Shipp reared a large family; his wife was Mary, daughter of Samuel Gillepsie, a planter of Cheraw. An illness which the aged minister brought on by aiding a neighbor to fight a forest fire terminated in his death, at Cleveland Springs, N. C., where he had gone in quest of health.

[*Minutes of the . . . S. C. Ann. Conference of the M. E. Church,* 1887; *Southern Christian Advocate* (Columbia, S. C.), July 7, 14, 1887; *Christian Advocate* (Nashville), July 2, 16, 1887; K. P. Battle, *Hist. of the Univ. of N. C.* (2 vols., 1907–12); R. E. Grier, *S. C. and Her Builders* (1930), p. 335; *News and Courier* (Charleston), June 30, 1887; names of parents from Shipp's daughter.]

D. D. W.

SHIPP, SCOTT (Aug. 2, 1839–Dec. 4, 1917), soldier, educator, was born in Warrenton, Va., the son of John Shipp and Lucy (Scott) Shipp. After the death of his father in 1849, his mother married Henry Clarkson, a physician of Boone County, Mo., and the family removed there. He went to Westminster College at Fulton, Mo., and then found employment with a railroad. Attracting the attention of one of the officials of this railroad, Robert E. Rodes [*q.v.*], a graduate of the Virginia Military Institute, he was persuaded by Rodes to enter that institution, from which he graduated in 1859. From 1859 until the outbreak of the Civil War he was an assistant professor of mathematics and tactics there. He accompanied a detail of cadets to Harpers Ferry in December 1859 to witness the execution of John Brown. He was ordered in April 1861 with the entire corps of cadets to Camp Lee near Richmond to assist in the drilling of recruits for the Confederate army. Commissioned major in the 21st Virginia Infantry in July 1861, he participated in the West Virginia campaign in the late summer of 1861 under the command of Robert E. Lee and later served in the Romney campaign with Stonewall Jackson, his former preceptor and colleague. Upon the reopening of the Virginia Military Institute in 1862 he was ordered to report there as commandant of the cadets with the rank of lieutenant-colonel. He led the cadets into the field on five occasions, the most notable being the Valley campaign when the Federals under Hunter invaded the Valley of Virginia. In this campaign the cadets formed a part of Breckinridge's army and won fame at the battle of New Market in May 1864, where, though wounded, Shipp skilfully conducted the battalion of cadets across an open field against the Federals under the terrific fire of their batteries. Throughout the war he chafed at the inactive service imposed upon him and twice sought unsuccessfully to be relieved of his duties at the institute in order to join Lee's army. After the battle of Gettysburg, he obtained a two months' furlough, joined as a private the famous Black Horse Troop (4th Virginia Cavalry) and skirmished with it during July and August.

After the war he resumed his duties as commandant of the cadets, though he contemplated for a time the practice of law and in 1866 was graduated from the Lexington Law School (later the law department of Washington and Lee University. On Aug. 19, 1869, he was married to Anne Morson of Richmond. They had three children. For many years he was a vestryman of the Robert E. Lee Memorial Church in Lexington. He refused in 1880 the proffered honor of the presidency of the newly created Virginia Agricultural and Mechanical College (Virginia Polytechnic Institute), when he found himself restricted in the selection of his faculty. In spite of his denunciation of the Readjuster party he survived the proposed general change of the officers of the institute at the hands of a Readjuster board of visitors. Upon the resignation of Gen. Francis H. Smith in 1889 Shipp was elevated to the superintendency of the Virginia Military Institute in January 1890 and served in this capacity until his retirement in June 1907. As commandant and superintendent, he was noted as a strict disciplinarian. He dismissed his own son for a violation of military discipline, for which a lesser penalty than dismissal had been inflicted in the past, and he opposed, though not successfully, the boy's reinstatement later by the board of visitors. In educational matters, he was very conservative and emphasized the military feature of the institute against the wishes of a group of the alumni. Materially, his administration witnessed many changes, freedom from debt, increased appropriations from the state, an enlarged corps (to which he was on the whole opposed), and more buildings. During this period he was a member of the board of visitors at the United States Military Academy in 1890, and at the United States Naval Academy in 1894.

[J. C. Wise, *Personal Memoir of . . . Scott Shipp* (1915) and *The Military Hist. of the Va. Mil. Institute* (1915); *War of the Rebellion: Official Records (Army)*, 1 ser., XXXVII, pt. 1; F. H. Smith, *The Va. Mil. Institute* (1912); *Cat. of the Officers and Alumni of Washington and Lee Univ.* (1888).] W.G.B—n.

SHIPPEN, EDWARD (1639–Oct. 2, 1712), mayor of Philadelphia, speaker of the Assembly, president of the provincial council, and acting governor of Pennsylvania, was born at Methley in Yorkshire, England, and was baptised in the parish church on Mar. 5, 1639. He was the son of Mary (Nunes) and William Shippen, a prosperous yeoman and an overseer of the poor and of the highways. In 1668 he emigrated to Boston, Mass., where he soon became a wealthy merchant and owner of real estate. He joined the Society of Friends about 1671 and was severely persecuted on account of his faith until about 1694, when he removed his family and his business to Philadelphia. In 1695 he was elected to the provincial Assembly of Pennsylvania and was chosen speaker. He served as an elective member of the provincial council from 1696 until the constitution was changed in 1701 and then as an appointive member until 1712. He was president of the council from 1702 to 1712 and acting governor from April 1703 until February 1704. He also served again as a member of the Assembly in 1700–01 and 1705–06. In the charter of Philadelphia, granted by William Penn on Oct. 25, 1701, he was named as mayor and held that post until October 1703. He was also city treasurer from 1705 until 1712. The tradition that he was chief justice of Pennsylvania in 1698 is probably erroneous, but he was justice of the peace for many years, presiding justice of the county courts of Philadelphia, 1698–1701, and an associate justice of the supreme court, 1699–1703 (Martin, *post*, p. 14). He died at his home in Philadelphia.

He has been described as "a man of courage, energy, integrity, intelligence and sagacity" (*Letters and Papers, post*, p. xvii). Penn was favorably impressed by his business ability, and he served as one of the proprietary commissioners of property from 1701 until his death. He was famous in his day as the biggest man and the owner of "the biggest house and the biggest coach" in Philadelphia. His home, near the northwest corner of Spruce and Second streets, was called "the Great House" or "the Governor's House." It was surrounded by "extraordinary fine and large Gardens abounding with Tulips, Pinks, Carnations, Roses (of several sorts), Lilies" and many other flowers and shrubs (Gabriel Thomas, *An Historical and Geographical Account of Pensilvania*, 1698, p. 43, spelling the name Shippey). He was married three times: at Boston in 1671 to Elizabeth Lybrand, who died on Oct. 25, 1688; on Sept. 4, 1689, to Rebecca (Howard) Richardson of New York, who died in February 1705; and in Philadelphia, about Aug. 1, 1706, to Esther (Wilcox) James, who died in August 1724. His first wife probably converted him to the Quaker faith, but the story that he withdrew from the Quakers and retired from public life because of his third marriage (*Letters and Papers, post,* p. xviii) has no foundation. The manuscript records of the Society of Friends show, however, that Shippen was subjected to discipline, because he had anticipated the marriage relation with his third wife. He was finally pardoned and was a member of the Society in good standing at the time of his death. There is also evidence that the comparative inactivity of his later years was due to lack of health ("Correspondence," *post,* I, 304, II, 302, 307). He had eleven children, of whom Joseph became the grandfather of Edward Shippen (1729–1806) and William Shippen [*qq.v.*].

[Thomas Balch, *Letters and Papers Relating chiefly to the Provincial History of Pennsylvania* (1855); "Correspondence between Wm. Penn and James Logan," ed. by Edward Armstrong, *Memoirs of the Hist. Soc. of Pa.,* vols. IX, X (1870–72); J. H. Martin, *Martin's Bench and Bar of Philadelphia* (1883); C. P. Keith, *Provincial Councillors of Pa.* (1883); T. W. Balch, *The English Ancestors of the Shippen Family and Edward Shippen of Philadelphia* (1904); material in the Shippen, Penn and Logan manuscripts in the possession of the Pa. Hist. Soc. and in the manuscript records of the Society of Friends in Philadelphia; portrait, painted by an unknown artist, in possession of family and reproduced in J. T. Scharf and Thompson Westcott, *Hist. of Philadelphia* (1884), vol. I, p. 158.]

W. R. S—h.

SHIPPEN, EDWARD (Feb. 16/26, 1728/29– Apr. 15 1806), chief justice of Pennsylvania, was the son of Sarah (Plumley) and Edward Shippen of Lancaster and the great-grandson of Edward Shippen [*q.v.*]. He was born and went to school in Philadelphia. He went to London, probably not before 1748 (letter of Feb. 25, 1748, concerning "seeing all the curiosities," Balch, *post,* p. 15), read law in Middle Temple, and was called to the English bar on Feb. 9, 1750. He also studied law in the office of Tench Francis [*q.v.*], to whose daughter Margaret Francis he was later married, on Nov. 29, 1753. They had nine children, one of whom, Margaret, married Benedict Arnold [*q.v.*]. On Sept. 25, 1750, he was admitted to practice before the supreme court of Pennsylvania, and he soon became one of the leaders of the provincial bar. He was a member of the common council of Philadelphia, 1755–56, and on May 27, 1758, was elected clerk of the council and clerk of the city court. He was prothonotary of the supreme court from about 1762 until 1776 and a member of the provincial council from 1770 to 1775. We owe to his pen the earliest published law reports of the supreme court of Pennsylvania (A. J. Dallas, "Reports of Cases . . . in Pennsylvania," printed in the first

volume of Dallas' *United States Reports,* pp. 1– 7, 29. See also vol. II–IV for Shippen's opinions). He was also a judge of the court of vice admiralty from 1752 until 1776, although the position had "little or no value" after the court was reorganized in 1768 (*Pennsylvania Archives,* ser. 1, vol. IV (1853), ed. by Samuel Hazard, p. 600).

He was a moderate Loyalist during the Revolution and for a time was practically interned on his country estate near the falls of the Schuylkill. In a letter of July 12, 1777, he pled the Test Act as an excuse for not visiting his father at Lancaster (Shippen Mss. VIII, 13). On Aug. 15, 1777, however, he and several other Loyalists who were willing to maintain an attitude of neutrality had "the bounds prescribed in their respective paroles enlarged to the whole state of Pennsylvania" (*Minutes of the Supreme Executive Council of Pennsylvania,* vol. XI, 1852, p. 269). He must have been successful in the rôle of neutral because he and his family were prominent in the social life of Philadelphia during both the British occupation and the military administration of General Arnold. His career was not seriously handicapped even by the treason of his son-in-law. He was president of the court of common pleas of Philadelphia County, 1784–91, justice of the peace, 1785–86, and president of the court of quarter sessions and general jail delivery, 1785–86. On Sept. 14, 1784, he was also appointed a judge of the high court of errors and appeals, which was at that time the highest appellate court in Pennsylvania, and he served on this court as a special judge until 1791. He was a member of the supreme court from 1791 until 1805, as an associate justice until 1799 and then as chief justice. Although he was a Federalist, he did not take an active part in politics, and his opinions were free from political bias. He and two of his associates were, however, impeached by the Democratic assembly in 1804 under charges growing out of the Passmore case, but they were acquitted by the Senate of the Commonwealth in January 1805 (William Hamilton, *Report of the Trial and Acquittal of Edward Shippen* (1805). His health was failing at this time, and later in the year he resigned from the bench. He died at his home in Philadelphia. He was noted for his kindness and generosity and for the courtesy and dignity of his manners. His conservative attitude at the time of the Revolution was probably due partly to his religious affiliations and partly to the fact that he was a member of the governor's executive council. He was born and bred in a Presbyterian atmosphere, his father being one of the founders of the College of New Jersey (Princeton), but in his early manhood he joined the Church of England.

[Letters in possession of the Pa. Hist. Soc.; sketch by Lawrence Lewis, Jr., in *Pa. Mag. of Hist. and Biog.*, Apr. 1883; *Ibid.*, Jan. 1901–Dec. 1902 with some letters to his daughter Margaret; Thomas Balch, *Letters and Papers Relating Chiefly to the Provincial Hist. of Pa.* (1855); C. P. Keith, *Provincial Councillors of Pa.* (1883); E. A. Jones, *Amer. Members of the Inns of Court* (1924); date of birth from records of First Presbyterian Church of Philadelphia and date of death from *Poulson's Am. Daily Advertiser* (Philadelphia), Apr. 17, 1806; his portrait painted by Gilbert Stuart in the Corcoran Gallery of Art, Washington, D. C.]

W. R. S—h.

SHIPPEN, WILLIAM (Oct. 21, 1736–July 11, 1808), physician and pioneer teacher of anatomy and midwifery, was born in Philadelphia, the cousin of Edward Shippen, 1729–1806, and the great-grandson of Edward Shippen, 1639–1712 [*qq.v.*]. He was the son of Susannah (Harrison) and William Shippen, who was one of the prominent medical men of his day and a member of the Continental Congress. After attending the academy kept by Samuel Finley [*q.v.*] at Nottingham, the boy went to the College of New Jersey (Princeton), from which he graduated in 1754. He then studied medicine with his father until 1757, when he went abroad to study. About 1760 he was married in London to Alice Lee, the sister of Francis Lightfoot, William, Richard Henry, and Arthur Lee [*qq.v.*]. He studied especially under William Hunter and Colin McKenzie. He won the esteem and friendship of John Fothergill, who became greatly interested in his plans to establish courses in midwifery and anatomy in Philadelphia. From London he went to Edinburgh, where he received the degree of M.D. in 1761, with a thesis *"De Placentae cum Utero Nexu"* (1761). In spite of the fact that Great Britain and France were at war, through the good offices of Sir John Pringle, the physician-general of the British Army, he was able to take an English lady suffering from tuberculosis to southern France for her health and to see something of the medical schools at Paris and Montpellier.

When he returned to Philadelphia in 1762, Fothergill sent, in his care, to the Pennsylvania Hospital a number of anatomical drawings and casts that he desired the managers to permit Shippen to use in his teaching. The pictures had been made by Jan Van Rymsdyk, the celebrated Dutch painter residing in London, who made most of the pictures for William Hunter's great work on the gravid uterus. They are still preserved in excellent condition in the hospital. Shippen began his courses on Nov. 16, 1762, in the State House. Although he made use of the

Fothergill pictures and casts, he utilized chiefly the dissection of human bodies, a method taught by Hunter. This aroused the animosity of the populace, his dissecting rooms were mobbed on several occasions, and once he narrowly escaped with his life; but his courses were very successful, and the number of students increased year by year. Somewhat later he began giving courses on midwifery, not only to medical students but also to women who intended to practise midwifery. When John Morgan [*q.v.*] succeeded in getting the trustees of the College of Philadelphia to organize a medical school in connection with the college in 1765, Shippen was appointed professor of surgery and anatomy. In 1776 he was appointed chief physician and director general of the hospital in the Continental Army in New Jersey. In October of the same year he was appointed by Congress director general of all the hospitals in the west side of the Hudson River, and, after John Morgan was displaced by Congress, was appointed on Apr. 11, 1777, chief physician and director-general of the Continental Army hospital in his stead. Morgan in his published *Vindication of his Public Character* (1777) accused Shippen of having procured his discharge by underhand means in order that he might get the position. In March 1777 Shippen had submitted to Congress a plan for the reorganization of the army medical department, which had been adopted practically in its entirety; and this brought him prominently to the notice of Congress and, no doubt, had much to do with his obtaining the appointment (copy of this plan in Shippen's handwriting in the Library of Congress). Shippen himself was later subjected to a court martial on charges of financial irregularity in his department. He was acquitted and remained chief of the medical department of the Continental Army until his resignation in 1781. In 1778 he was elected physician to the Pennsylvania Hospital, but he resigned in the following year owing to the pressure of his military duties.

In 1791 he again became a member of the staff of the hospital, on which he continued to serve until 1802. He was one of the founders of the College of Physicians of Philadelphia and was president from 1805 to 1808. When the legislature repealed the charter of the College of Philadelphia in 1779 and created the University of the State of Pennsylvania, he accepted a chair in the new school. In 1791, when the University of Pennsylvania was established, he was appointed professor of anatomy, surgery, and midwifery. After the death of his only son, a young man of great promise, in 1798 he seems to have lost interest in life. His health gradually declined, his practice fell off, and he seldom lectured. He died in Philadelphia.

[A few papers and letters in Lib. of Cong.; Caspar Wistar, *Eulogium on Doctor Wm. Shippen, Delivered . . . 1809* (1818) and reprinted in *Philadelphia Journ. of the Medical and Physical Sciences*, vol. V (1822); Charles Caldwell, *Extract from an Eulogium on Wm. Shippen* (1818); G. W. Norris, *The Early Hist. of Philadelphia* (1886); J. F. Watson, *Annals of Philadelphia* (1844); T. G. Morton, *The Hist. of the Pa. Hospital* (1895); W. S. W. Ruschenberger, *An Account of . . . the College of Physicians of Philadelphia* (1887); Joseph Carson, *A Hist. of the Medical Department of the Univ. of Pa.* (1869); Roberdeau Buchanan, *Geneal. of the Descendants of Dr. Wm. Shippen* (1877); date of birth from E. W. Balch, *The Descendants of Edward Shippen* (1883).]   F.R.P.

SHIRAS, GEORGE (Jan. 26, 1832–Aug. 2, 1924), jurist, was born in Pittsburgh, Pa., one of four sons of George and Eliza (Herron) Shiras. His paternal ancestry was of Scotch origin, but American since 1750, when an earlier George Shiras settled at Mount Holly, N. J.; his maternal ancestors had also long been in the country. His general education was completed at Ohio University (Athens) and at Yale College, where he was graduated in 1853. After studying law in the office of Judge Hopewell Hepburn of Pittsburgh and in the Yale Law School, though he was not graduated therefrom, he was admitted to the Pittsburgh bar, Nov. 7, 1855. He practised first for a year in Dubuque, Iowa, in partnership with his brother, Oliver Perry Shiras [*q.v.*], then in Pittsburgh as a partner of Judge Hepburn (1858–62), and thereafter independently. He attained eminence as a lawyer and was constantly employed for many years in cases involving the railroad, banking, oil, coal, and iron interests of western Pennsylvania. In 1882 he was offered, as a compromise selection of the Pennsylvania legislature by a very close vote, an opportunity to represent his state in the Senate of the United States, but, apparently because of his own slight interest, he was not nominated.

On July 19, 1892, he was nominated by President Harrison as an associate justice of the Supreme Court of the United States. Though favored by the bar, he was opposed by the senators of his state, apparently only because, both being very insecure in office and at outs with the President, they were anxious about patronage, and Shiras was too little of a politician for them (A. K. McClure, *Old Time Notes of Pennsylvania*, 1905, II, 572–73, 579–81, 584; Carson, *post*, II, 560–63). Because of this situation, the Judiciary Committee of the Senate reported the nomination without recommendation, but it was nevertheless speedily confirmed, July 26, 1892. His wide experience and his personal qualities of courtesy, dignity, quick apprehension, clarity of thought, and restrained judgment, well qualified Shiras for judicial service. Unquestionably, also, he was a very able man and a lawyer of ample experience and technical acquirements. Yet his work as a member of the Court, while entirely creditable, was not remarkable, unless for one unfortunate incident. In the Income Tax Case (1895, *Pollock* vs. *Farmers' Loan & Trust Co.*, 157 *U. S.* 429, 158 *U. S.*, 601), one of immense importance and historical interest, Shiras was long supposed to have changed his vote on reargument, thus, by a vote of five to four, causing reversal of the first decision and nullification of the federal statute as unconstitutional (Warren, *post*, II, 700). Violent criticism followed, but since the grant of a reargument concedes the propriety of changed opinions, personal criticism was necessarily unjust, particularly so if it was in truth, as intimated by Chief Justice Hughes, another of the justices who changed his vote (C. E. Hughes, *The Supreme Court*, 1928, p. 54). The criticisms directed against him Shiras met with silence. He resigned on Feb. 23, 1903, under the statute of 1869 permitting voluntary retirement on full pay at the age of seventy, after ten years of service. He had married, Dec. 31, 1857, Lillie E. Kennedy, daughter of Robert T. Kennedy, a manufacturer of Pittsburgh. Two sons, both lawyers, survived him. He died in Pittsburgh, as the result of a fall.

[Shiras' opinions are to be found in 146–188 *U. S. Reports*. For biog. data and comment see H. L. Carson, *The Hist. of the Supreme Court* (1902), II, 560–64; Charles Warren, *The Supreme Court in U. S. Hist.* (rev. ed., 1926), II, 699 and index; *Yale Univ. Obit. Record*, 1925; *Who's Who in America*, 1922–23; *Report of the . . . Pa. Bar Asso.*, 1925; *N. Y. Times*, Aug. 3, 1924.]   F.S.P.

SHIRAS, OLIVER PERRY (Oct. 22, 1833–Jan. 7, 1916), jurist, brother of George Shiras [*q.v.*], was one of four sons of George and Eliza (Herron) Shiras. The home of the family during his youth was on a farm near the Ohio River about twenty miles from his birthplace, Pittsburgh. At the age of fifteen he entered the preparatory department of Ohio University at Athens, where he graduated in 1853. Thence he went to Yale. After a year of scientific study, he decided to be a lawyer and in 1856 obtained the degree of LL.B. Attracted by the bustling character of Dubuque, Iowa, while exploring the West for professional opportunity, he was easily persuaded by old friends, the Herron brothers, to settle there in preference to Chicago.

On Aug. 9, 1856, he was admitted to the Iowa bar. Confident of the future, in February 1857 he married Elizabeth Mitchell of Springfield, Ohio, by whom he had four children. In August 1862 he was commissioned first lieutenant and quartermaster of the 27th Iowa Volunteer Infantry, but was transferred to staff duty as an aide to Brigadier-General F. J. Herron [*q.v.*] before his own regiment was mustered in. Service as judge advocate took him campaigning with the Army of the Frontier, but he resigned in December 1863 and returned to resume the practice of law at Dubuque. His firm maintained an enviable reputation until it was dissolved by political preferment. When the federal judicial district of northern Iowa was created, Shiras was appointed judge, in August 1882. Thereupon he made one of his partners clerk of the court, and in November of the same year the other partner, D. B. Henderson [*q.v.*], was elected to Congress.

On the federal bench Shiras was known for his wisdom, integrity, and precise reasoning. His little manual, *Equity Practice in the United States Circuit Courts* (1889), is perhaps as much an evidence of his own interests as it is an attempt to aid the busy practitioner and the novice. One of the most important disputes to come before him was an action in equity—the final episode in the long stream of litigation flowing from the ambiguous Des Moines River improvement land grant. The government presented a bill to confirm the title of certain settlers to land they were supposed to have obtained from the United States, but Shiras, following the precedents of previous cases, dismissed the claim, though he recognized the injustice of deciding the dispute in favor of either party and recommended that Congress compensate the injured settlers for the loss of their homesteads (43 *Federal Reporter*, 1). The Supreme Court sustained this judgment, and Congress eventually followed his advice (142 *U. S.*, 510; 28 *U. S. Statutes at Large*, 396). The occasion for his principal judicial contribution, however, arose in connection with the attempt of the railroads to avoid regulation of interstate traffic before Congress assumed control in 1887. In opposition to the doctrine of a legal vacuum created by the failure of Congress to exercise its power (*Swift* vs. *Railroad Companies*, 58 *Federal Reporter*, 858), Shiras in 1894 enunciated the conception of a national common law subject to independent application by the federal courts irrespective of state interpretation. He held that the binding force of the general system of jurisprudence as applied to the whole country by the federal gov-

ernment was not derived from action by the states or subject to abrogation by them. In the absence of congressional legislation, the common rules of the common law prevail. Thus the railroads could not escape responsibility in a sphere of anarchy. His elaborate opinion in *Murray* vs. *Chicago & North Western* (62 *Federal Reporter*, 24) was cited with approval by Justice Brewer of the Supreme Court (181 *U. S.*, 92), and has become the accepted view.

On Oct. 11, 1888, in St. Paul, Minn., Shiras married his second wife, Hetty E. (Spaulding) Cornwall. He retired from the bench at the age of seventy, in November 1903, and thereafter devoted his attention to civic affairs until his death in 1916.

[E. H. Stiles, *Recollections and Sketches of Notable Lawyers and Public Men of Early Iowa* (1916), 167–69; *Who's Who in America*, 1914–15.; *Proc . . . Iowa State Bar Asso.*, 1916; *Yale Univ. Obit. Record*, 1916; *Dubuque Times-Journal*, Jan. 7, 16, 1916.]

J. E. B.

SHIRLAW, WALTER (Aug. 6, 1838–Dec. 26, 1909), genre, portrait, and mural painter, and engraver, was born at Paisley, Scotland. His father was an inventor, and a maker of the hand-looms used in the weaving of Paisley shawls. Before Walter was three the family came to America and settled in New York, where at the age of twelve he left school and entered the employ of a firm of real-estate agents. Soon afterward he was apprenticed for a term of five years to an engraver of banknotes, and during that time succeeded in saving about $800 with which to begin a career as a painter. His first picture was hung at the National Academy exhibition of 1861, but a few years later he found it expedient for economic reasons to return to engraving for a livelihood. For five years, until 1870, he was with the Western Bank Note and Engraving Company of Chicago. He was active in the founding of the Art Institute of Chicago, which was conceived about this time. In 1870 he went to Munich, where for about seven years he studied and painted. His first teacher was George Raab, in whose class he obtained a sound knowledge of drawing; later he came under the instruction of Alexander Wagner, A. G. Von Ramberg, and Wilhelm Lindenschmit, the younger. It was at Munich that he painted his two best pictures, "Toning the Bell" (1874) and "Sheep-Shearing in the Bavarian Highlands" (1876). Returning in 1877 to New York, where he exhibited his "Sheep-Shearing" at the National Academy, he became one of the founders and the first president of the Society of American Artists, taught in the Art Students' League, and occupied a studio in the old university building in Washington Square. In 1880 he married Florence Manchester. That year at the Doll and Richards gallery, Boston, he opened a notable "one-man show" containing fifty-eight oil paintings and a large collection of water colors and drawings. About ten years later he held another important exhibition in Boston. He became an Academician in 1888.

When mural decorations became popular he was commissioned to execute a frieze symbolizing peace and plenty for Darius Ogden Mills [q.v.] of New York. In this rich composition, which is excellent in design and felicitous in mood, he employed not only human figures but animals, birds, flowers, and fruits. A still more important decoration from his hand is the ceiling painting, "The Sciences," in the entrance pavilion of the west corridor in the Library of Congress, Washington, a series of eight female figures whose symbolic value is obvious enough but not over-emphasized. The design is conspicuously good, the play of line in the draperies being exceptionally fluid and rhythmical. He was one of the group of painters who decorated the dome of the Manufactures and Liberal Arts building of the Columbian Exposition in Chicago in 1893. He also did some minor decorative work for the house of William Thomas Evans [q.v.], including two stained-glass windows, "The Rainbow" and "The Lost Chord." He traveled much, and everywhere recorded his impressions. He made a considerable number of illustrations, usually in charcoal, for such magazines as the *Century* and *Harper's Monthly*. He was a master designer, a serious and weighty painter, an influential teacher, a man of culture and intelligence, and his success, though not phenomenal, was fairly commensurate with his merits. In the summer of 1909 he went to Spain; in December in Madrid he became ill and died after three weeks. He was buried in the English cemetery there. Soon after his death memorial exhibitions of his pictures were held in New York, Buffalo, Boston, Washington, Pittsburgh, Chicago, and St. Louis. His pictures are in museums in St. Louis, Buffalo, Chicago, Washington, and Indianapolis; and in the Century, Lotos, and Salmagundi Clubs, New York. The examples in St. Louis and Buffalo are of his best, but "Toning the Bell," probably his masterpiece, is privately owned (1934) in Chicago.

[*Who's Who in America*, 1908–09; T. H. Bartlett, in *Am. Art Rev.*, July and Aug. 1881, a full account of Shirlaw; W. H. Downes and F. T. Robinson, "Later Am. Masters," in *New England Mag.*, Apr. 1896; Royal Cortissoz, "Color in the Court of Honor at the Fair," *Century Mag.*, July 1893; A. J. Searle, in *Internat. Studio*, May 1911; S. G. W. Benjamin, *Our Am. Artists* (1879); Samuel Isham, *The Hist. of Am.*

Painting (1905); Clara E. Clement and Laurence Hutton, *Artists of the Nineteenth Century* (1885); *Handbook of the New Lib. of Congress* (1897), comp. by Herbert Small; Art Inst. of Chicago, *A Memorial Coll. of Works by Walter Shirlaw, N. A.* (1911); *Cat. of Am. Paintings Belonging to William T. Evans* (1900); *Cat. of the Private Art Coll. of T. B. Clarke* (1899); obituaries in *Am. Art News*, Jan. 1, 1910, *N. Y. Times*, Dec. 30, 1909.]
W. H. D.

SHIRLEY, WILLIAM (Dec. 2, 1694–Mar. 24, 1771), colonial governor, was born at Preston, in Sussex, the son of William Shirley, a London merchant, and Elizabeth, daughter of John Godman of Ote Hall, Wivelsfield, Sussex. When he was seven years old his father died, leaving him with comparatively little property but with aristocratic tastes and connections. From the Merchant Taylors' School, London, he was admitted pensioner at Pembroke College, Cambridge, and received the degree of A.B. in 1714/15. On July 3, 1720, he was called to the bar. Meanwhile he had married Frances, daughter of Francis Barker of London. Five daughters and four sons were born to them. For eleven years Shirley practised law in London, gaining a substantial reputation and influential friends, but not much money. A crisis in his financial affairs decided him to emigrate to America, and with his family he landed at Boston, Oct. 27, 1731, bearing a letter from his kinsman and lifelong patron, Thomas Pelham-Holles, Duke of Newcastle, to Gov. Jonathan Belcher [q.v.].

Shirley was by nature a "prerogative man" and his earliest case in Boston of a controversial sort aligned him with that party. While Belcher yielded more and more to the colonial view of business matters, Shirley upheld the imperial. He was appointed judge of admiralty in 1733, a post he soon exchanged for that of advocate-general. He labored faithfully to enforce the Molasses Act and other measures relative to trade, while in his private capacity he became counsel for Samuel Waldo [q.v.], a large operator in timber lands and one of the richest capitalists of Boston. Unsympathetic toward Belcher's policy of permitting the exploitation of the King's Woods by colonial business men, Shirley sent to England by the hand of his wife a report which tended to weaken the confidence of the government in Belcher's administration. Frances Shirley also improved the occasion to plead her husband's cause. He had already asked for several offices without success; she now pressed the Duke of Newcastle for a salary for the Advocate-General, or for her husband's appointment as collector of customs or naval officer at Boston, and finally, for his appointment as governor. In 1739 she was joined in England by Waldo, who was anxious to be rid of Belcher. The Governor for the moment was still too strong to be displaced, but in 1740 Shirley's opportunity arose, with the necessity for raising troops in New England for the English expedition to the West Indies. Acting on Newcastle's suggestion, he was much more successful in enlisting recruits than the unpopular Belcher, and this success enabled him to supersede his rival. He was commissioned governor of Massachusetts on May 25, 1741.

One of the first difficulties he had to meet was the problem of the land bank, left to him by his predecessor. This agrarian scheme for cheap money had created much ill feeling in the colony, but Shirley handled his share in it with adroitness, winning the respect even of the defeated land bankers. On his accession to office he also found the colonial defense in a precarious condition, but eventually persuaded the General Court to make fairly liberal appropriations for the repair of Castle William and other fortifications. By the time that war with the French, which he had foreseen, was declared in 1744, he had put the colony into a fair state of defense, and adjusted the problem of paper money.

With the outbreak of hostilities he at once showed himself alive to the economic importance of the war from the standpoint of the colonies, particularly as concerned the fisheries. To protect these and to provide themselves a naval base, the French, at vast expense, had fortified Louisbourg on Cape Breton Island, but as Shirley knew, the garrison there was in a weak condition, owing to the neglect and venality of the authorities. After the beginning of war, the French governor made an attack on an outpost of New England fishermen on Canso Island which, though ineffectual, aroused the ire of New England, and Shirley conceived the desire to capture Louisbourg. Undismayed by the failure to receive encouragement from the government in England, he matured his plans and laid the proposition before the General Court of Massachusetts. That body at first would have nothing to do with it, but the governor had gained the confidence of prominent merchants and with their help succeeded in winning the Court to the support of his plans, provided the other New England colonies would cooperate in the audacious project. The other governors promptly consented, and the expedition was set under way.

Shirley ably handled the negotiations with the other governments, the Court, and the English authorities. Carefully side-stepping trouble with the touchy governor of New Hampshire, Benning Wentworth [q.v.], who desired to lead the expedition, Shirley appointed William Pepperrell [q.v.] to the command. Meanwhile Newcastle in England had been more active in their behalf than the colonists knew, and Commodore Peter Warren [q.v.], in command of the fleet cruising in the West Indies, had been ordered to cooperate with the colonial forces. After some delay, Shirley was able to dispatch some thirty-three hundred men from Massachusetts, who with the smaller forces sent by New Hampshire, Connecticut, and Rhode Island, arrived at Louisbourg a few days after the fleet had taken up its position there. The undertaking was completely successful, and the capture of the weakly defended fortress on June 17, 1745, was the one great English victory of the war. Shirley wrote an account of it which was published in *A Letter ... to ... the Duke of Newcastle: with a Journal of the Siege of Louisbourg* (1746). The government rewarded his services by making him colonel of a British regiment to be raised from the New England provincial troops, and used him as a clearing house in examining the claims of the northern colonies for reimbursement of expenditures growing out of the war. Massachusetts' share of the amount allowed by Parliament in 1748 was approximately £183,649. With this unprecedented amount in hard cash the colony was enabled to retire its paper money and place its finances on a sound basis.

Meanwhile, in 1749, Shirley had gone to England on leave. While there he was appointed a member of the commission sitting in Paris to determine the boundary line between French North America and New England. The negotiations were spun out to interminable length and it was not until 1753 that he returned to his post in Boston. His first wife had died there in September 1746, and in Paris he married a young Frenchwoman, Julie ——, the daughter of his landlord.

Shirley foresaw that war must soon begin again between England and France, and as early as January 1754, writing to the authorities in England, urged the importance of uniting the colonies and the strategic significance of Crown Point. He also did what he could to establish friendly relations with the Indians. In February 1755 he was appointed major-general and in April was one of the five governors who attended a council of war with Gen. Edward Braddock [q.v.] at Alexandria, Va., to bring about concerted action. Here he argued the importance of controlling the Great Lakes, and when the council decided to move against Niagara, Crown Point, and the forks of the Ohio, Shirley was given command of the Niagara expedition. After the death of Braddock in July, he was the acknowledged commander of all the British forces on the continent and in August he was formally appointed to that position, although "his friends saw the risk he was running, and wished he had contented himself with his civil station" (Hutchinson, *post*, III, 38). His plans were sound, and that they were unsuccessful must be attributed in great measure to bickerings among the colonies, their failure to provide men and supplies, and jealousy and lack of cooperation on the part of individuals which Shirley had neither the capacity nor the prestige to overcome. He himself took the field with the Niagara expedition, which got no further than Oswego; confronted by a strong French force at Kingston, he left a garrison—inadequately provisioned—and turned back to Boston. His eldest son, secretary to Braddock, had been killed in Pennsylvania with his chief; his second son, a captain, died of fever on the Oswego expedition.

Meanwhile, the Governor's political enemies had been increasing in numbers and strength, and with the failure of his military venture they accused him of gross mismanagement and of intermeddling in Indian affairs, the sole province of William Johnson [q.v.]. At the same time a number of letters from some officer in the British colonies to the French were intercepted; in England it was believed these letters might have been written by Shirley, and the home authorities suspected him of treason. He was replaced as commander in chief temporarily by James Abercromby and then by John Campbell, Earl of Loudoun [qq.v.]. The latter, irritated by the evidences of Shirley's inefficiency as a military man and carelessness in financial matters, took an intense dislike to him and for a while seemed to be intent on destroying him. Shirley was ordered to England early in 1756 and after unwarranted delay sailed in October, arriving as his patron's ministry fell and was followed by that of Pitt. Officials of the War Office wished to have him court-martialed, but for lack of evidence against him the matter was dropped in the fall of 1757. Meanwhile, he had been succeeded as governor of Massachusetts by Thomas Pownall [q.v.]. He was given the rank of lieutenant-general and was promised the post of governor of Jamaica but did not receive it; in 1761 he was made governor of the Bahama Islands. This post he relinquished to his only surviving son, Thomas, in 1767. Two years later he returned to Massachusetts and took up his residence in his mansion, "Shirley Place," at Roxbury, where in March 1771 he died.

Shirley with reason has been called a "place-hunter"—even after he became governor of Massachusetts he expressed a desire for other, perhaps more comfortable, appointments. Nevertheless, as an executive he showed ability and tact, and although he steadily upheld what he believed to be the rights of the Crown, he became one of the most popular of colonial governors. In spite of his straitened circumstances and loose handling of army contracts and finances, his personal integrity was unimpeachable. Although as a military commander he was neither a tactician nor an organizer, he had more than any other contemporary governor a broad grasp of the whole imperial problem.

[The major published source is *Correspondence of William Shirley . . . 1731–1760* (2 vols., 1912), ed. by C. H. Lincoln. See also Wm. Alexander, *The Conduct of Maj. Gen. Shirley . . . Briefly Stated* (1758), a vindication by his private secretary; "Aspinwall Papers," *Mass. Hist. Soc. Colls.*, 4 ser. IX–X (1871); "The Belcher Papers," *Ibid.*, 6 ser. VI–VII (1893–94); "The Pepperrell Papers," *Ibid.*, 6 ser. X (1899); *Acts of the Privy Council of England, Colonial Ser.*, vols. III–VI (1910–12); John and J. A. Venn, *Alumni Cantabrigienses*, pt. 1, vol. IV (1927); Thomas Hutchinson, *The Hist. of the Province of Mass. Bay*, vol. III (1828); H. L. Osgood, *The Am. Colonies in the Eighteenth Century* (1924), vols. III, IV; S. M. Pargellis, *Lord Loudoun in North America* (1933); J. T. Adams, *Revolutionary New England* (1923); E. P. Shirley, *Stemmata Shirleiana* (1873); H. W. Foote, *Annals of King's Chapel* (2 vols., 1882–96); G. A. Wood, *William Shirley* (1920) is an administrative study covering the years 1731–49. The sketch by J. A. Doyle in *Dict. Nat. Biog.* is not very satisfactory.]   J. T. A.

SHOBONIER [See Shabonee, c. 1775–1859].

SHOLES, CHRISTOPHER LATHAM (Feb. 14, 1819–Feb. 17, 1890), printer, journalist, inventor, the son of Orrin Sholes, was born on a farm at Mooresburg, Pa. His ancestors, who came from England, settled in the vicinity of Groton, Conn. He is said to have been a lineal descendant of John and Priscilla Alden, and to have had several ancestors who served with distinction in the Revolutionary War. When Sholes was young his parents moved to Danville, Pa., where he attended Henderson's school until he was fourteen. When he had completed an apprenticeship of four years on the *Danville Intelligencer*, his parents moved to Wisconsin and settled at Green Bay. Although he was in rather delicate health, young Sholes went to work immediately at his trade; within a year he had become state printer and had taken charge of the house journal of the territorial legislature, carrying it to Philadelphia to be printed. At twenty he left home to follow his brother Charles to Madison, Wis., where the latter had acquired a substantial interest in the *Wisconsin Enquirer*. After service for a year as editor of this paper and as journal clerk of the legislature, he married Mary Jane McKinney at Green Bay on Feb.

4, 1841, and moved to Southport (later Kenosha), Wis., to become editor of the *Southport Telegraph* for four years, resigning when he was appointed postmaster of Southport, by President Polk. Through his activities as a journalist and postmaster, he was eventually drawn into politics in spite of the fact that he was very poorly fitted for it by character and temperament. He served, however, with credit to his constituents, two terms as state senator, and one term in the state assembly. In 1860 he moved with his family to Milwaukee, where he had accepted the editorship of the *Milwaukee News*. Subsequently he served as editor of the *Milwaukee Sentinel* but gave up this position to become collector of the port of Milwaukee, an appointment made by President Lincoln.

That Sholes was possessed of inventive genius in addition to his journalistic and political ability is evidenced by the fact that at an early date in his newspaper work he devised a method of addressing newspapers by printing the names of subscribers on the margin, but his extremely busy life at this time prevented his following closely his inventive bent. His less arduous duties as collector of customs presumably gave him the opportunity of exercising these talents again, for he and a machinist friend, Samuel W. Soulé, were granted a patent for a paging machine on Sept. 27, 1864, and one for a machine numbering serially the pages of blank books on Nov. 13, 1866; on Apr. 30, 1867, Sholes alone received patent No. 64,375 for an improvement on the numbering machine. Both men had space to work in a small machine-shop where there was also a third inventor, Carlos Glidden. The latter one day suggested to Sholes that as he had devised a numbering machine he ought to be well fitted to perfect a letter-printing machine, and referred him to a published account of a writing machine newly invented in London by John Pratt [*q.v.*]. The suggestion so much appealed to Sholes that he devoted the rest of his life to the perfection of the typewriter, which he lived to see definitely established and in use throughout the world. Sholes, Glidden, and Soulé were granted a patent for a typewriter, No. 79,265, on June 23, 1868, and another, No. 79,868, a month later. For the next five years Sholes struggled unsuccessfully to make and market the machine. In August 1871 he obtained a third patent for improvements. His partners one at a time relinquished their rights in the patents for working capital, and on Mar. 1, 1873, he gave up his rights to the Remington Arms Company for $12,000. This company, with its complement of fine machinery and expert mechanics, perfected the Sholes typewriter and successfully introduced it as the Remington typewriter. Sholes continued making typewriter experiments with the help of two sons, giving all of the results to the Remington company. His last patent was granted Aug. 27, 1878. The strain told on his naturally frail constitution, however; he became consumptive, and spent the last nine years of his life in search of health, though he continued to work on inventions even when he was too weak to be about. He was survived by his wife, six sons, and four daughters.

[Waldemar Kaempffert, *A Popular Hist. of Am. Invention* (1924), vol. I; C. E. Weller, *The Early Hist. of the Typewriter* (1918); H. W. Roby, *The Story of the Invention of the Typewriter* (1925), ed. by M. M. Quaife; Herkimer County Hist. Soc., *The Story of the Typewriter, 1873–1923* (1923); obituary in *Milwaukee Sentinel*, Feb. 18, 1890; correspondence with family, U. S. Nat. Museum.]   C. W. M—n.

SHONTS, THEODORE PERRY (May 5, 1856–Sept. 21, 1919), railroad executive, chairman of the second Isthmian Canal Commission, was a son of Dr. Henry Daniels and Margaret Nevin (Marshall) Shonts. He was born in Crawford County, Pa., where members of the Shonts (or Shontz) family, coming from Lancaster County, had settled about 1800. As a boy he went with his parents to Appanoose County, Iowa, and there he grew to manhood Dependent on the district schools of a new country for his education, he was a schoolmaster himself at sixteen and then passed four years at Monmouth College, Monmouth, Ill., where he was graduated in 1876. Upon his return to Iowa, the distinction of his work as comptroller for an investment company at Centerville, Iowa, soon led to a demand for his services as accountant for banks in the state, but he had decided to be a lawyer and after studying in the office of Gen. Francis M. Drake [*q.v.*], later governor of Iowa, he was duly admitted to the bar and made a partner in the firm. Drake, however, was an aggressive and successful organizer and builder of railroads and after a time he persuaded Shonts to give up the law as a profession for a railroad career. The first challenge to the younger man's mettle came from the Iowa Construction Company, financed in the East, which made him responsible for building within ninety days 100 miles of road to connect with the Central Iowa Railway (later Iowa Central). Although fifty-one of the ninety days were rainy, the job was completed in the stipulated time, so that the rails could receive locomotives and trains. In 1882 Shonts was married to Harriet Amelia Drake (called in his will Milla), daughter of his senior partner in the law firm. His advance in railroading was rapid. He was general superintendent of the Indiana,

Illinois & Iowa Railroad from 1882 to 1886, when he became general manager; from 1898 to 1902 he was also president. In time he succeeded to the presidency of the Chicago & Alton Railroad (1907–12), the Iowa Central Railway (1910–11), the Minneapolis & St. Louis Railroad (1909–11), and the Toledo, St. Louis & Western ("Clover Leaf") Railroad (1904–12). He was known in the Middle West among railroad men as an outstanding example of pluck and efficiency in management, an executive who could give and take hard knocks, who somehow succeeded most completely when the odds were against him.

In 1905, at the moment of beginning work on the Panama Canal, President Theodore Roosevelt was seeking a chairman for the second Isthmian Canal Commission. He was advised by his secretary of the navy, Paul Morton [q.v.], that Shonts (of whom Roosevelt had never heard) had many of the qualities demanded by that position. An interview, in which Shonts made his acceptance conditional on his being given a free hand and absolute authority, convinced the President that he was the man for the place and the appointment was made. Shonts, who cheerfully admitted his ignorance of the technique of canal building, was saved by Roosevelt from a disastrous error at the start when he was persuaded to reverse his intention to supplant Col. William C. Gorgas [q.v.], whose supervision of sanitation on the Isthmus led to most brilliant results and so made possible the completion of the canal with the minimum loss of life. Shonts cooperated most effectively with Gorgas, putting at his disposal a force of 3,500 men as a sanitary corps. In this, as in other features of his brief canal administration, Shonts acted on the assumption that full preparation must be made before the actual digging could be started. He did this work of preparation so thoroughly that when construction was begun, under other direction, it went forward with marvelous speed.

Just what led Shonts to resign from the Canal Commission in 1907 may never be known. He was committed to the contract system of construction and when Roosevelt decided against that procedure he may have thought it impossible to continue (W. J. Abbot, *Panama and the Canal*, 1914, pp. 188–90). He was at once made president of the Interborough Rapid Transit Company (and of its parent company, the Interborough-Metropolitan) of New York City, where a consolidation of subway, elevated, and surface lines had just been effected. Although the problems of city passenger traffic were as new to Shonts

as those of canal-digging had been two years before, he faced them with no lack of confidence; by dint of hard work and intense application he mastered some of the most serious of them, but the rapid growth of demand for transportation facilities outran even the expansion that he was able to achieve. Yet the same executive ability that he had developed when a young man in western railroading scored successes for him in New York.

Shonts died of pneumonia on Sept. 21, 1919. For more than ten years he had been estranged from his wife. His will made provision for her, but a clause leaving the residuary estate to Mrs. Amanda C. Thomas gave rise to litigation extending over two years (*New York Times*, Sept. 21, Nov. 8, 1919; Apr. 11, 1920; Apr. 9, 1921). In the end the higher courts confirmed the will, but many of the securities comprising the testator's property were found to be worthless. Two married daughters shared in the bequests.

[Walter Wellman, "The New Executive of the Panama Canal," in *Am. Monthly Review of Reviews*, May 1905; letter from Roosevelt, Jan. 22, 1907, printed in W. L. Pepperman, *Who Built the Panama Canal* (1915), pp. 238–39; J. B. and Farnham Bishop, *Goethals: Genius of the Panama Canal* (1930), pp. 129–30; *The Biog. Directory of the Railway Officials of America*, 1913; *Who's Who in America*, 1918–19.] W. B. S.

SHOOK, ALFRED MONTGOMERY (July 16, 1845–Mar. 18, 1923), Southern industrialist, the eldest son of James Keith and Eliza Herndon (Green) Shook, was born near Winchester, Franklin County, Tenn. The Shooks, of German descent, had moved Westward before 1800 and finally settled in Middle Tennessee; the Greens were more recent comers from Virginia. Alfred grew up on his parents' farm and attended the country school. He joined the Confederate cavalry in June 1862 but his military career was cut short when, in February 1863, he was wounded and captured at Fort Donelson. Held as a prisoner in the North until the end of the war, he returned to Tennessee in January 1866.

Through an uncle, he was soon placed in charge of the Tennessee Coal & Railroad Company's store at Tracy City, where he rapidly worked his way to a position of responsibility in the company. The mineral resources of the South were looked upon as a possible means of economic recovery from the effects of the Civil War and attracted many an enterprising Southerner from the impoverished agricultural districts. Shook, like his older associates, engaged in coal mining without any scientific training, but his capabilities were recognized by the new manager of the company, James C. Warner [q.v.], who appointed him superintendent in 1868. Shook's account of the struggles and discouragements of these early years portrays in realistic fashion the industrial pioneering of the "New South," where the margin between success and failure was narrow indeed (see Armes, *post*). The growth of the company's business during the seventies, however, justified a venture into the manufacture of coke and convinced Shook that the future of the enterprise would be assured by utilizing this fuel in the company's furnaces. Under his management the Sewanee Furnace was built at Cowan, Tenn., in 1881, and the following year the Tennessee Coal, Iron & Railroad Company, as it was now called, absorbed a rival English concern, The Southern States Coal, Iron & Land Company, operating a furnace near Chattanooga. Shook as general manager until 1886 was in direct touch with both the metallurgical and the accounting problems of the business; he mastered the intricacies of the blast furnace and saved the company many a dollar in operating expenses.

As the business was expanded and the stock increased to $10,000,000, the control passed from the hands of the Tennessee group to speculators on the New York Exchange, and a reorganization early in 1886 cost Shook his position. At this critical moment, however, industrial affairs in Birmingham, Ala., worked to his advantage and transferred the principal activity of the Tennessee Company to that city. The Pratt Coal & Iron Company of Enoch Ensley [*q.v.*], representing the largest iron interests of that region, was suddenly brought under the control of the Tennessee company by Shook and his Tennessee associates, who enlisted enough capital to secure options previously issued on the Pratt corporation. The Tennessee company, with its prestige so suddenly enhanced, underwent another reorganization, and Shook was reinstated as general manager. Closely associated with Ensley now, he worked to carry out the latter's dream of a new industrial city near Birmingham, and in 1889 the fourth up-to-date iron furnace went into blast. The ultimate goal, however, was the manufacture of steel, if it could be made from the South's high-phosphorus ore. Shook's faith in experiments by the Southern Iron Company, in which he had been interested in Chattanooga in 1890, was justified when the first heat of steel was poured at Ensley on Thanksgiving Day 1899, and the Tennessee company's steel works began a new era in Southern industrial developments. His connection with the company was almost continuous from the time of its revival in 1866 until 1901, and no one contributed more in sound judgment and able management to establishing its preëminence in the Southern iron and steel industry.

Shook married Teresa Estill on July 17, 1871, and had five children. He was a Presbyterian and deeply interested in education. The school which he built and furnished at Tracy City at a cost of $40,000 is but one example of his widespread benefactions. He lived in Nashville during most of his life, and died there in his seventy-eighth year.

[*Tracy City News*, supplement, 1895; *Nashville Tennessean*, Mar. 19, 1923; *Who's Who in America*, 1920–21; Ethel Armes, *The Story of Coal and Iron in Alabama* (1910); Crawford Perkins, *The Industrial Hist. of Ensley Ala.* (1907); information as to certain facts from Shook's son, P. G. Shook.]   L. J. C.

SHOREY, PAUL (Aug. 3, 1857–Apr. 24, 1934), classicist, born in Davenport, Iowa, was the son of Daniel Lewis and Maria Antoinette (Merriam) Shorey. His parents moved to Chicago when he was a boy and he received his secondary education at the Chicago High School. He took his A.B. degree at Harvard in 1878. After graduation he studied law in his father's office and was called to the bar in Illinois in 1880. He practised law for a brief period in Chicago, but not caring for the life went to Europe to pursue his classical studies. From that time to the day of his death in Chicago he never swerved from his devotion to the classics or wavered in his belief that in them the world could find its best literature, its most satisfying philosophy, and its most effective instrument of education.

After attending the University of Leipzig (1881–82), the University of Bonn (1882), and the American School of Classical Studies at Athens (1882–83), he took his Ph.D. degree in Munich in 1884. His first academic post in America was at Bryn Mawr College, where he was professor of Latin and Greek from 1885 to 1892. His edition of *Horace: Odes and Epodes* (1898, 1910) was the direct outcome of one of his courses there. It is unique in the aptness and range of the illustrative material drawn from Latin, Greek, French, and English literature. He was one of the group of scholars whom President William Rainey Harper [*q.v.*] called to the University of Chicago at its founding (1892). Coming as professor of Greek, he was made head of the department in 1896 and remained in that position till 1927. In 1901–02 he was annual associate director of the American School of Classical Studies at Athens. He became professor emeritus in 1927 but was invited to continue his courses and he held classes till the summer of 1933. He was one of the founders of the periodical, *Classical Philology*, and was its editor from 1908 to 1934. In June 1895 he married Emma L. Gilbert of Philadelphia, who survived him; there were no children.

Shorey's greatest contribution to scholarship was in the field of Platonic studies. His knowledge of philosophy, his faculty of keen analysis of philosophic concepts, and his command of Greek were the chief elements in his effectiveness. His first monograph in the subject was his doctoral dissertation at Munich, *De Platonis idearum doctrina atque mentis humanae notionibus commentatio* (1884). Later appeared *The Idea of Good in Plato's Republic* (1895); *The Unity of Plato's Thought* (1903); a translation of Plato's *Republic* in the Loeb Classical Library in two volumes (1930–35); and the outstanding work, *What Plato Said* (1933). The philosophic implications of other Greek authors are considered in "The Implicit Ethics and Pyschology of Thucydides," *Trans. Am. Philological Assoc.*, vol. XXIV (1893), 66–88, and in the more general essay, "The Abiding Power of Greek Philosophy" in *Culture of the Classics* (1910).

He had no patience with modern pedagogical methods. He often said that knowledge of the subject and some degree of common sense in the organization of courses and the handling of students constituted the only equipment that a teacher needed. In his hands a course in Homer or Pindar or Plato was not merely an exercise in translation; it was a study of epic or lyric poetry or of some phase of philosophy. His intimate knowledge of French and English literature and his pertinent and witty application of ancient ideas to modern times gave his lectures a zest that is too often lacking in academic classrooms. He supervised more than fifty doctoral dissertations and many of his students became teachers of Greek and Latin in the colleges and universities of the United States and Canada. He was convinced that the movement against the classics in education was a mistake, and frequently expressed his views in essays. The best known of these are "The Case for the Classics" (*School Review*, November 1910) and "The Assault on Humanism" (*Atlantic Monthly*, June, July 1917), but there are many others.

He was a member of the American Philosophical Society, the American Philological Association (president 1910), the American Institute of Archaeology, the American Academy of Arts and Letters, and associé de l'Académie Royale de Belgique. He had unusual gifts as a public speaker. He gave the Turnbull Lectures on Poetry at Johns Hopkins and the Lane Lectures at Harvard in 1912; the Harris Lectures at Northwestern University in 1916; the Sather Lectures at the University of California (twice); the Lowell Lectures in Boston; and the Martin Lectures at Oberlin. In 1913 he was Roosevelt

Exchange Professor at the University of Berlin, and in 1924 he lectured on Aristotle at four of the universities of Belgium. Honorary degrees were conferred on him by many universities. Shorey had a rare combination of qualities: he had erudition and yet fine literary appreciation; he was interested in research, but was also a teacher of unusual effectiveness; he was a classicist and a stanch protagonist of the classics as a medium of education, but his study of the ancients never dulled the edge of his interest in contemporary life.

[R. J. Bonner, "Paul Shorey," in *Classical Jour.*, June 1934; George Norlin, "Paul Shorey—The Teacher," in *Classical Philology*, July 1934, where there is also an unsigned obituary article; *Who's Who in America*, 1932–33; personal acquaintance.] G. J. L.

SHORT, CHARLES (May 28, 1821–Dec. 24, 1886), classical philologist, was born in Haverhill, Mass., the second of the twelve children of Charles and Rebecca (George) Short, and the seventh in descent from Henry Short, who emigrated to Ipswich in 1634 and later removed to Newbury. At Phillips Academy, Andover, 1837–40, he studied Greek and Latin with passionate ardor. "I used to open my eyes very early in the morning," he said later, "waiting impatiently for daylight, that I might rise and be at my books" (*Memoir, post*, p. 4). Once, when neither his teachers nor the available books could satisfy him as to a difficult passage in a Greek author, he tramped the twenty miles to Cambridge to settle the matter in the Harvard library. After two years of teaching he entered Harvard College in 1842 and graduated fourth in the famous class of 1846. While a sophomore he acquired renown by a translation into Greek hexameters of H. H. Milman's "The Belvidere Apollo." He tarried a year at Cambridge as a pupil of Prof. Evangelinus Apostolides Sophocles [*q.v.*]. He became an assistant master at his old school in 1847, was headmaster of the Roxbury Latin School, 1848–53, and conducted a school of his own in Philadelphia, 1853–63. In 1849 he married Anne Jean, daughter of Elihu Lyman of Greenfield, Mass., who with three sons and a daughter survived him. In 1860 he visited England; he went to Europe again in 1881 and in 1884. In 1862 he and his wife were confirmed in the Episcopal Church in the first class presented by Phillips Brooks [*q.v.*]. A year later, several clergymen having declined, he was elected to the presidency of Kenyon College, at Gambier, Ohio, in succession to the late Lorin Andrews [*q.v.*]. He retained the strong faculty that his predecessor had gathered, made the beginnings of a college library, and attracted worthy students to the institution, but in 1867, as the result of squabbles among the teachers and trustees, he resigned. Almost immediately he was called to succeed Henry Drisler [*q.v.*] as professor of Latin in Columbia College, New York, where he remained for the rest of his life. On its organization in 1872 he was made a member of the American Committee on the Revision of the English Authorized Version of the Bible, to serve in the New Testament Company. Of his scholarly productions the most notable were the monograph on "The Order of Words in Attic Greek Prose," prefixed to Drisler's edition of Charles D. Yonge's *An English-Greek Lexicon* (1870); his work on the letter *a* in *Harper's Latin Dictionary* (1879); and his minute textual study, "The New Revision of King James' Revision of the New Testament, as Illustrated by the Gospel of St. Matthew," in the *American Journal of Philology* (vols. II–VII, 1881–86). Brander Matthews described him as "a man of many amusing peculiarities, but possessed of real learning and inspired by a genuine love of letters" (*These Many Years*, 1917, p. 110). Until the steady inroads of nephritis began to make life burdensome for him, he was an able teacher and lecturer, and he remained a conscientious one to the end. He died at his home in New York and was buried in Sleepy Hollow Cemetery.

[C. L. Short, *Memoir of the Life of Charles Short, M.A., LL.D.* (privately printed, 1892), with list of his pubs.; *Cat. of the Biblical, Classical, and Miscellaneous Lib. of the late Charles Short* (auctioneer's cat., 1887); G. F. Smythe, *Kenyon Coll.: Its First Century* (1924), with portrait; *N. Y. Daily Tribune*, Dec. 25, 1886.]

G. H. G.

SHORT, CHARLES WILKINS (Oct. 6, 1794–Mar. 7, 1863), was a physician, teacher, and botanist, who collected, preserved, classified, and generously distributed to other naturalists the plants of the little explored country west of the Alleghanies. A nephew of William Short [*q.v.*], he was born at "Greenfield," Woodford County, Ky., the country place of his parents, Peyton Short and his first wife, Maria (or Mary), daughter of John Cleves Symmes [*q.v.*]. Charles attended Joshua Fry's celebrated school in Mercer County, and later, Transylvania University, Lexington, where he was graduated with honor in 1810. He began the study of medicine with his uncle, Dr. Frederick Ridgely, and in 1813 went to Philadelphia to become the private and beloved pupil of Dr. Caspar Wistar, 1716–1818 [*q.v.*]. The University of Pennsylvania bestowed upon him the degree of doctor of medicine in the spring of 1815, his thesis being on the medicinal virtues of *Juniperus Sabina*. In November of the same year he married his step-sister, Mary Henry Churchill, only daughter of Armistead and Jane (Henry) Churchill, the latter having become Peyton Short's second wife. The young couple soon returned to Kentucky, making the entire trip in a spring wagon and botanizing along the way.

After a short stay in Lexington and some years in Hopkinsville, combining the practice of his profession with botanical researches, he accepted, in September 1825, a call to the chair of materia medica and medical botany at Transylvania University, which he filled with distinction, serving as dean of the faculty from 1827 to 1837. With Dr. John Esten Cooke [*q.v.*], he started the publication, in 1828, of the *Transylvania Journal of Medicine and the Associate Sciences,* one of the first periodicals of its kind in the West. In this, most of his writings—descriptions of certain medical cases and contributions to botany—were published. Notable among the latter was "A Catalogue of the Native Phaenogamous Plants and Ferns of Kentucky," which he prepared in cooperation with Robert Peter and H. A. Griswold (December 1833, supplemented in the issues of December 1834, December 1835, September 1837). As an illustration of the zeal of himself and his associates, he states that within five years they had prepared and distributed 25,000 specimens among correspondents in Europe and America, who gave valuable and acceptable material in exchange (*Transylvania Journal of Medicine,* April 1836, p. 348).

In 1838 Short left Transylvania University to fill a similar position in the young Medical Institute of Louisville. After ten years more of teaching and while still in the prime of life, his own fortune having been augmented by an inheritance from his distinguished uncle, William Short [*q.v.*] of Philadelphia, he decided to retire, bought Col. George Hancock's beautiful estate "Hayfield" near Louisville, and indulged himself in promoting botanical research and in the enjoyment of his family, his gardens, his library, his herbarium and his correspondence. Here he died of typhoid pneumonia in the sixty-ninth year of his age, and was buried in Cave Hill Cemetery. One son and five daughters survived him. His valuable herbarium of over 15,000 species belongs to the Academy of Natural Sciences, Philadelphia. Dignity and modesty were perhaps his most noticeable qualities. A love of accuracy led him always to write out his lectures and read them to his pupils. Learned Latin phrases were frequent in his addresses. He was a member of the Presbyterian Church, and urged upon his students that "strict, unswerving, religious regard for truth which should be the prime object in every investigation."

[S. D. Gross, in *Proc. Am. Philosophical Soc.*, vol. X (1869) ; Asa Gray, in *Am. Jour. Sci.*, July 1863 ; *Louisville Jour.*, Mar. 18, 1863 ; Robert Peter, *The Hist. of the Medic. Dept. of Transylvania Univ.* (1905), Filson Club Pub. No. 20 ; H. A. Kelly, *Some Am. Medic. Botanists* (1914) ; Max Meisel, *A Bibliog. of Am. Natural Hist.*, vol. II (1926), pp. 455–57 ; *Transylvania Jour. of Medicine*, vols. I–XII (1828–38) ; Minutes Transylvania Medic. Faculty; information from grand-daughters and the curator of the dept. of botany, Acad. of Nat. Sci., Phila.]   M. L. D.

SHORT, SIDNEY HOWE (Oct. 8, 1858–Oct. 21, 1902), electrical engineer, inventor, was the son of John and Elizabeth (Cowen) Short and was born in Columbus, Ohio, where his father was engaged in manufacturing. Like many inventors, he displayed remarkable mechanical ingenuity as a child, and was so interested in electricity that at the age of fourteen years he was an expert telegrapher and had equipped his home with a burglar alarm and many other electrical devices. After completing grade school and spending a short time at Capital University, Columbus, he entered Ohio State University, where he was a student assistant in physics and graduated with the degree of B.S. in 1880. Immediately following his graduation he accepted the position of professor of physics and chemistry and vice-president of the University of Denver, Denver, Colo., and began with enthusiasm his professional career. His departments developed rapidly; in 1882 the work had become so great that he was relieved of chemistry to devote his whole time to teaching and research in physics. Although his earliest interests in electricity were the telegraph and the telephone —he perfected, patented, and sold a telephone transmitter in 1879—he turned his attention to arc-lighting and electric traction soon after going to Denver, and made important discoveries and improvements, many of which he patented.

After five years at the university he resigned and became associated with the United States Electrical Company, Denver, Colo., to develop and manufacture his inventions. At first he worked on improved equipment for electric arc-lighting, but about 1886 he invented a double reduction electric motor for street railways and soon engaged in building electric railways incorporating his inventions. After completing several installations and patenting additional improvements in his system, in 1889 he removed to Cleveland, Ohio, where with the financial help of Charles F. Brush he organized the Short Electric Railway Company and began the manufacture of his railway machinery. He was very successful in this but in 1892 sold his company

to the General Electric Company. In 1893 he became connected with the Walker Manufacturing Company of Cleveland, which immediately entered the electric traction field with an entirely new system of apparatus of Short's design ; by 1898 it had become such a formidable competitor of both the General Electric and Westinghouse companies that the latter felt compelled to purchase a controlling interest in it. Meanwhile Short had started negotiations with Messrs. Dick, Kerr & Company, Ltd., in England for the manufacture of his patented electric railway machinery and system. Accordingly late in 1898 he went to London, and within eighteen months the production of all kinds of equipment was under way at a new factory erected at Preston. He then became technical director of the English Electric Manufacturing Company, Ltd., organized a technical staff to undertake research and development work, and had practically completed the work he had gone to England to do when he died at the age of forty-four.

In his brief career he was granted over five hundred patents for improvements in electrical machinery both by the United States and foreign countries, and was widely recognized as an authority in electric railways and continuous current motors. He was a pioneer in the use of a conduit system of concealed feed rail to avoid the use of the overhead wire and trolley, and was also very successful with gearless motors in which all the gears between the electric motor armature and the driven car-axle were eliminated. He was a member of engineering societies in England and the United States, and was a fellow of the American Association for the Advancement of Science. He married Mary F. Morrison of Columbus, Ohio, in Washington, D. C., on July 26, 1881, and at the time of his death was survived by his widow and four children.

[*Electrical Rev.*, Nov. 1, 1902 ; *Electrical Rev.* (London), and *Electrician* (London), Oct. 31, 1902 ; Waldemar Kaempffert, *A Popular Hist. of Am. Invention* (1924), Patent Office records ; death notice in the *Times* (London), Oct. 23, 1902.]   C. W. M—n.

SHORT, WILLIAM (Sept. 30, 1759–Dec. 5, 1849), diplomatist, was born at "Spring Garden," Surry County, Va., the son of William Short, a well-to-do planter, and his wife Elizabeth, daughter of Sir William Skipwith. He was graduated in 1779 at the College of William and Mary, where he had been one of the founders of Phi Beta Kappa and was president of that society from December 1778 to January 1781. In 1783–84 he was a member of the Executive Council of Virginia, then followed Jefferson on his mission to France. Soon after his arrival in Paris, he was sent by Jefferson, Adams, and Franklin to arrange with the Prussian envoy at The Hague for a commercial treaty between Prussia and the United States. Upon the successful conclusion of this business he returned to Paris, where he acted as Jefferson's private secretary and later as secretary of legation. Of a sensitive, appealing personality, with the easy charm of the South in his manner and a perfect command of the French language, he achieved an enviable position in the highest circles of French society. Upon Jefferson's return to America in 1789, Short became chargé d'affaires, and during the next two years was busy attempting to negotiate a commercial treaty with France, handling the business of American loans in Amsterdam, and sending full reports to Jay and Jefferson on the political developments in France. An enthusiastic witness of the events of 1789, he became more doubtful of the benefits of revolution as the Jacobins rose to power, and his outburst against them after the August and September massacres of 1792 brought him a rebuke from Jefferson (*Short Papers*, 1789–92; Jefferson, *Writings*, Ford ed., VI, 153–55).

After Jefferson became secretary of state, Short nursed every hope of being appointed to succeed him as minister to France, but despite the weight of Jefferson's influence, the post went to Gouverneur Morris [*q.v.*], early in 1792, and Short reluctantly accepted appointment as minister at The Hague. With a heavy heart he set out from Paris. By this time he had become the devoted admirer of Alexandrine Charlotte de Rohan-Chabot, familiarly known as Rosalie, the young wife of the Duc de la Rochefoucauld. It was a profound attachment on both sides that was destined to last for nearly fifty years, but when the assassination of the Duke, in September 1792, left his widow free to marry again, she was restrained by an ideal duty to the aged Duchesse d'Anville, her mother-in-law. Her decision was one in which Short was bound to concur, but it added another to the list of disappointments that marked his life.

In February 1793 he went from The Hague to Madrid as joint commissioner with William Carmichael [*q.v.*] to negotiate a treaty concerning boundaries, navigation, and commercial privileges in regard to Florida and the Mississippi, and after Carmichael's recall in the spring of 1794, he was made minister resident with sole power to carry on the negotiations. Just as success was about to crown his labors, Thomas Pinckney [*q.v.*] was sent to Spain as envoy extraordinary and commissioner plenipotentiary

to conclude the treaty. The appointment for this task of Pinckney, still minister at London, was the result of the objection of the Spanish court, as a pretext for delay, that Short and Carmichael were not of sufficient rank to be acceptable; before Pinckney's arrival, however, Spain had become ready to negotiate. Although chagrined at being superseded, Short continued to handle affairs until Pinckney's arrival and then loyally cooperated with him in securing the treaty which bears Pinckney's name, signed Oct. 27, 1795. Leaving Spain the next day, he lived in Paris until 1802, when he returned to the United States. In March 1809 he was destined to receive one more rebuff. Commissioned by Jefferson in the previous August as minister to Russia, he had proceeded as far as Paris when he received word that a hostile Senate had rejected his appointment, declaring a permanent minister to Russia unnecessary.

Short remained in France until 1810, when he returned to America, settling in Philadelphia, and for the remainder of his life devoted himself to his private affairs. He had made profitable investments through the Dutch bankers with whom he had become acquainted in Amsterdam, and had made extensive purchases of land in Kentucky and northern New York. During the next years he built up a large fortune, but he never again interested himself in public office. Slightly world-weary, he seemed satisfied to look upon the realm of action from the heights of a bitter experience.

[The best account of Short's career yet published appears in S. F. Bemis, *Pinckney's Treaty* (1926). Sources include Short Papers and Jefferson Papers, Lib. of Cong.; MSS. in the possession of the Short family; *The Writings of Thomas Jefferson* (20 vols., 1903–04), ed. by A. A. Lipscomb and A. E. Bergh; *The Writings of Thomas Jefferson* (10 vols., 1892–99), ed. by P. L. Ford; *Am. State Papers, For. Rel.*, vol. I (1832). The account in L. G. Tyler, *Encyc. of Va. Biog.* (1915), II, 153, is brief and inaccurate. Marie G. Kimball, "William Short, Jefferson's Only 'Son'," *North Am. Rev.*, Sept., Oct., Nov. 1926, contains extracts from Short's correspondence with Madame de la Rochefoucauld. See also *Wm. and Mary Coll. Quart.*, Apr. 1896; *Pennsylvanian* (Phila.), Dec. 7, 1849.]

M. G. K.

SHORTER, JOHN GILL (Apr. 23, 1818–May 29, 1872), jurist, representative in the Confederate Congress, governor of Alabama, was born in Monticello, Ga., the son of Reuben Clark and Martha (Gill) Shorter. His father was a physician and planter who came originally from Virginia, settled in Georgia in his young manhood, and became a leader in the Democratic party in the state. John Gill was one of three sons who attained prominence in Alabama political life, the other two being Henry Russell, who served for some years as state railroad commissioner, and Eli Sims, who was a congressman.

John graduated from Franklin College (now the University of Georgia) in 1837 and immediately went to Eufaula, Ala., where he studied law and in 1838 was admitted to the bar. He spent four years in practice and was then appointed solicitor for the district in which he lived. He held this post until 1845, when he was elected to the state Senate. After two years in that body he declined to serve again and returned to his law practice. In 1851 he was elected to the lower house of the state legislature, but gave up his seat to accept an appointment to the circuit bench. Completing his term, he was elected to the office in 1852, and reëlected six years later without opposition.

He was an enthusiastic supporter of secession, and when Governor Moore appointed him Alabama's commissioner to the secession convention of the state of Georgia, he resigned his position on the bench to accept the appointment. Later he was chosen to represent his district in the provisional Confederate Congress, in the work of which he took an active part. An unwavering supporter of President Davis, he voted to sustain all of Davis's vetoes and favored all measures which he recommended. He was also active in the work of framing the Confederate constitution.

In August 1861, while he was in Richmond attending the third session of the provisional Congress, he was elected governor of Alabama, his election being an expression of the loyalty which the voters of Alabama accorded the Confederate government. Entering upon the duties of his office in a trying time, he was at first given enthusiastic support by the people. He exerted every effort to construct defenses where they were needed and tried especially to defend the port at Mobile. He was tireless in raising and equipping troops and in caring for the families of soldiers. Gradually, however, he lost popular support. Union troops invaded the state and devastated many parts of it. The tax burden became increasingly heavy as the war progressed. As loyal men went into the army, only the lukewarm or indifferent were left behind, and these were unwilling to endure the demands made upon them by the governor. Shorter, moreover, was stanch in his support of the Davis government and much of its unpopularity reacted upon him. His support of conscription, also, and his collection of the tax in kind brought him much criticism. In the election of 1863 he was defeated by a vote of more than three to one. He then returned to Eufaula and resumed the practice of

law, taking no further part in political life. On Jan. 12, 1843, he married Mary Jane Battle of Eufaula, by whom he had one daughter.

[A. K. Walker, *Old Shorter Houses and Gardens* (1911); T. M. Owen, *Hist. of Ala. and Dict. of Ala. Biog.* (1921), vol. IV; B. F. Riley, *Makers and Romance of Ala. Hist.* (n.d.); William Garrett, *Reminiscences of Public Men in Ala.* (1872); A. B. Moore, *Hist. of Ala. and Her People* (1927); W. L. Fleming, *Civil War and Reconstruction in Ala.* (1905); *Mobile Daily Reg.*, May 30, June 1, 1872.]   H. F.

SHOUP, FRANCIS ASBURY (Mar. 22, 1834–Sept. 4, 1896), Confederate soldier, educator, clergyman, was born in Laurel, Ind., the eldest son of the nine children of George Grove Shoup, a well-to-do merchant, and Jane (Conwell) Shoup. His father was a member of the Indiana constitutional convention and served for many years in the state legislature. His maternal grandfather, James Conwell, was also a member of the legislature, and was founder of the town of Laurel. After attending Asbury University (now De Pauw), in Greencastle, Ind., Shoup entered the United States Military Academy at West Point, N. Y., where he was graduated in 1855. He was commissioned second lieutenant of artillery and served in Florida on garrison duty and during a campaign against the Seminole Indians. In 1860 he resigned from the army, studied law, and was admitted to the Indianapolis bar. During the excitement following the John Brown raid, he organized a company of zouaves in the city and was chosen captain, but in 1861 he returned to Florida and was admitted to the St. Augustine bar. Moved by his aristocratic inclinations and admiration for the South, he volunteered for service with the Confederate army.

Upon the order of the governor of Florida, Shoup erected a battery at Fernandina. He was appointed lieutenant of artillery and in October 1861 was promoted to the rank of major. After a campaign in Kentucky, he became chief of artillery under Hardee, and at Shiloh, by effective massing of his guns, he played an important part in the capture of Prentiss' command. Subsequently, he fought under Beauregard and Hindman and was commended by the latter for his conduct at Prairie Grove, Ark. On Sept. 12, 1862, he was promoted to the rank of brigadier-general and, after service at Mobile, commanded a Louisiana brigade at Vicksburg. He was captured upon the fall of the city, but was soon exchanged and served with distinction as chief of artillery to Joseph Johnston [*q.v.*]. In the retreat from Dalton to Atlanta, Shoup did not lose a single gun, and the works constructed under his supervision at the Chattahoochee River were

highly praised. When a court of inquiry reported regarding the loss of stores to Sherman at
Atlanta in September 1864, he received mild censure. Perhaps because of his Northern birth,
he seems to have been much criticized, but Jefferson Davis wrote that "the only very clear information" communicated to him regarding the
establishment of munition manufactures in the
Trans-Mississippi "was in the report of that
much-abused officer, Brigadier-General Shoup"
(*War of the Rebellion: Official Records, Army,*
1 ser., LIII, 880). After the removal of Johnston, Shoup served as chief-of-staff under Hood.
He wrote a pamphlet urging the enlistment of
negro troops which was submitted to the Confederate Congress.

Upon the reorganization of the University of
Mississippi, Oxford, Miss., in 1865, Shoup was
elected professor of applied mathematics. In
1868 he took orders in the Episcopal church,
which he had joined while the Confederate army
was at Dalton, and served as rector of St. Peter's in Oxford, in addition to his university
duties. In 1869 he was chosen professor of
mathematics at the University of the South in
Sewanee, Tenn., assuming also the duties of
chaplain. He became rector at Waterford,
N. Y., in 1875, and later served churches at
Nashville, Tenn., and New Orleans, La. He
was recalled to Sewanee in 1883 as professor of
engineering and physics, and later, of mathematics, remaining here until his death. As a
professor, Shoup was "very stimulating upon
occasion," but was unable to raise the average
student to the level of his metaphysical thought
and soon gave up the effort (Du Bose, *post*). He
had marked intellectual ability and was the author of *Infantry Tactics* (1862), *Artillery Division Drill* (1864), *The Elements of Algebra*
(1874), and *Mechanism and Personality* (1891).
He was of distinguished military bearing, over
six feet tall. He was married in 1870 to Esther
Habersham Elliott of Sewanee, Tenn., the
daughter of Bishop Stephen Elliott, grand-
daughter of Stephen Elliott, and sister of Sarah
Barnwell Elliott [*qq.v.*] She and three children
survived him when he died at Columbia, Tenn.

[Information from Miss Laurel Conwell Thayer, In-
dianapolis, Ind., Bishop T. F. Gailor, and a former
student of Shoup's, the Rev. W. H. Du Bose; G. W.
Cullum, *Biog. Reg. . . . U. S. Mil. Acad.* (1891); *Hist.
Cat. of the Univ. of Miss.* (1910), including a bio-
graphical sketch by Shoup's wife; G. R. Fairbanks,
Hist. of the Univ. of the South (1905); *Nashville Am.,*
Sept. 5, 1896.]

R. D. M.

SHOUP, GEORGE LAIRD (June 15, 1836–
Dec. 21, 1904), first governor of Idaho, was born
at Kittanning, Pa., the son of Henry and Mary

Jane (McCain) Shoup. His father was of Dutch
and his mother of Scotch-Irish descent. He obtained his education in the public schools of his
native state before he started with his parents
for Illinois when about sixteen years of age. The
financial panic of 1857 broke soon after the family had settled and they were left with little or
nothing, the parents in poor health. In 1859
George went into the territory of Colorado to do
some mining and merchandising in the neighborhood of Pike's Peak and helped carve out of
the rugged Rocky Mountains the future state
of Colorado. When the Civil War began he enlisted in September of 1861 in a company of independent scouts working in New Mexico, Colorado, and Texas. Promotion came rapidly for
him and when the 3rd Colorado Cavalry was
formed he was commissioned colonel. He took
part in many sanguinary skirmishes, among
them, Apache Cañon and Sand Creek. He was
given a leave of absence from his command long
enough to act as a member of the constitutional
convention when Colorado made an attempt to
enter the Union in 1864.

After the war he was again in the mercantile
business. He took a stock of goods to Virginia
City, Mont., in 1866, and maintained a store
for a short time but later in the year moved on
to help found Salmon, Idaho, which he thenceforth claimed as his home. Here he was married
in January 1868 to Lena Darnutzer, of Swiss descent. Three sons and three daughters were born
to them. Here, also, a political career began with
his appointment as commissioner to organize
Lemhi County, from which, in 1874, he was
elected to the territorial legislature. In 1878 he
was a member of the territorial council, and in
the eighties served on the Republican National
Committee for Idaho. He represented Idaho at
the cotton centennial at New Orleans in 1884
where he spent $35,000 of his own money to ad-
vertise the resources of Idaho. President Harrison appointed him governor of the territory
of Idaho on Apr. 1, 1889. He at once repeated
a call issued by his predecessor for a constitutional convention which met on July 4, 1889.
When the document was finished, Shoup accompanied it to Washington to work for its ratification by Congress. In the elections that followed
ratification he became governor of Idaho. The
metamorphosis of Idaho from territory to state
then absorbed him. He called the legislature to
meet in December 1890, and was elected by this
body to be the first United States senator from
Idaho.

His policy in the Senate was to give a general support to all Republican measures, and a

special support to those dealing with the welfare of his state. He opposed the repeal of the "purchasing clause" in the Sherman silver bill by one of his two notable speeches in the Senate, and then supported the Republican measure in 1900 to establish the gold standard (*Congressional Record*, 53 Cong., 1 Sess., pt. II, p. 1440; 56 Cong., 1 Sess., pt. II, p. 1825). He was an opponent of "free silver" in spite of the fact that Idaho was a great producer of that metal. His great interest in the territories brought him the position as chairman of the Committee on Territories, member of committees on Military Affairs, Indian Affairs, Indian Depredations, Pensions, and Education. He advocated a liberal and just treatment of the Indians, was a firm believer in a liberal pension law and introduced many of the personal bills that President Cleveland vetoed. He believed in the popular election of United States senators. He held his place in the Senate continuously for ten years, being defeated in 1901, probably because of his stand on the silver question. He died at Boise, Idaho. His statue was placed in Statuary Hall at the national capitol by his state in 1910.

[*Who's Who in America*, 1903–05; *Biog. Dir. Am. Cong.* (1928); W. B. Mathews, *Sketch of the Life and Services of the Hon. George L. Shoup* (1900); Byron Defenbach, *Idaho, The Place and its People* (1933), vol. I; J. H. Hawley, ed., *Hist. of Idaho* (1920), vol. I; *Idaho Daily Statesman*, Dec. 22, 1904; *Idaho Statesman*, Jan. 16, 18, 1910.]   J. E. R.

SHRADY, GEORGE FREDERICK (Jan. 14, 1837–Nov. 30, 1907), surgeon and medical journalist, was the son of John and Margaret Beinhauer) Shrady. His father, a schoolmate of Washington Irving and Dr. John Wakefield Francis [*qq.v.*], was the son of John Shrady, active Revolutionary patriot, and grandson of Johan Schrade of Württemberg, who came to America about 1715 and twenty years later made his permanent home in New York city. His mother was the grand-daughter of Dr. John W. Zeiss of Amsterdam and daughter of Frederic Beinhauer of Vienna. (See *New York Genealogical and Biographical Record*, Oct. 1875, p. 198.) His brother John also practised medicine in New York. Educated in both private and public schools in New York, in 1858 he received the degree of M.D. from the College of Physicians and Surgeons of New York. His appointments were many; he was connected with St. Francis Hospital, New York Cancer Hospital, Columbus Hospital, Red Cross Hospital, Home for Incurables (Fordham), Vassar Hospital (Poughkeepsie), and the Hudson River State Hospital for the Insane, and he was physician in chief of the New York health department. During the Span-

ish-American War he was assistant surgeon of the Central Park Hospital, New York, and was detailed for field duty as well. His attention was early turned towards journalism. From 1860 to 1864 he edited the *American Medical Times*; from 1866 to 1904, the *Medical Record*, which he had helped to found. As an editor he championed many important and worthy causes. He advocated the abolition of sects in medical practice, the improvement of professional education, the extension of clinical instruction, and the establishment of state examinations for license to practice.

In spite of this work, which was his most important contribution to his profession, he did not neglect his practice. He was called to attend Pres. James Abram Garfield when he was shot and Pres. Ulysses S. Grant [*qq.v.*] in his last illness, and was consulted by Sir Morell Mackenzie on the illness of the Emperor Frederick III of Germany. He served as president of the American Medical Editors Association, the New York Pathological Society, the Practitioners Society of New York, and was a member of a number of other organizations. A calm, agreeable person, with an unusual gift for mimicry and a kindly sense of humor, he won many friends. Although a skilful operator, he was inclined to be conservative and very much opposed operations except when they were absolutely necessary. His work lay mostly in the field of plastic surgery; he wrote a number of articles on that subject and in other branches of surgery. His touching account of *General Grant's Last Days* (1908), his "Surgical and Pathological Reflections on President Garfield's Wound" (*Medical Record*, Oct. 8, 1881), and the satirical "Pine Ridge" papers in the *Medical Record* directed against medical charlatanism, are perhaps among the most important. In 1860 he was married to Mary Lewis of New York City, who died in 1883; he was married again on Dec. 19, 1888, to Hester Ellen Cantine of Ulster County, N. Y. He died in 1907 from sepsis following an attack of gallstones. He was survived by his wife, two daughters, and three sons (*New York Herald, post*), of whom one became a doctor and another, Henry Merwin Shrady [*q.v.*], a well-known sculptor.

[*Who's Who in America*, 1906–07; *Am. Medic. Biogs.* (1920), ed. by H. A. Kelly and W. L. Burrage; *The Coll. of Physicians and Surgeons, N. Y. . . . A Hist.* (n.d.), vol. I, ed. by John Shrady; *Medic. Record*, Dec. 7, 1907; obituary in *N. Y. Herald*, Dec. 1, 1907.]
         G. L. A.

SHRADY, HENRY MERWIN (Oct. 24, 1871–Apr. 12, 1922), sculptor, was born in New York City, the son of Mary (Lewis) and George

Frederick Shrady [*q.v.*]. Taking the degree of A.B. at Columbia in 1894, he was diverted from a legal career into business and for five years was with a match company, 1895–1900. After an illness and the failure of the company, he began to do sketching and modeling. One of his sketches, sent to the National Academy of Design exhibition without his knowledge, was sold, and a jeweler offered to take all the small animal bronzes he would make. What little technical instruction he had, he got from Karl T. F. Bitter [*q.v.*], who invited him to share a studio. Lack of early instruction prolonged all his labors and accounts for the small number of his works, of which he himself was a severe critic. He enlarged figures of a moose and a buffalo for the Pan-American Exposition of 1901 at Buffalo, and modeled a group of Indians in relief on a bronze panel for the pedestal of the Robert Fulton monument at Spuyten Duyvil. In 1901 he won a competition with his equestrian Washington at Valley Forge, placed in Brooklyn near the Williamsburg Bridge. He was elected a member of the National Sculpture Society in 1902, became an associate of the National Academy of Design in 1909, and was a member of the National Institute of Arts and Letters.

His preëminent achievement in sculpture is the Grant memorial in Union Square, forming the Capitol end of the Mall in Washington. In 1902, twenty-three sculptors and associated architects submitted designs (*The Grant Memorial, post,* p. 19). Those of Shrady and Edward Pearce Casey were chosen unanimously by a jury made up of two of Grant's officers, Generals John McAllister Schofield and Wesley Merritt; Augustus Saint-Gaudens [*qq.v.*] and Daniel Chester French, sculptors; Daniel Hudson Burnham and Charles Follen McKim [*qq.v.*], architects. The memorial represents a sweeping cavalry charge. In the center of the marble platform, 252 feet in length, rises the colossal figure of Grant, garbed according to his custom in the uniform of a soldier, without side arms. The horse, two and a half times life-size, is alertly intent, while his rider calmly watches the battle. This monument, in which there are thirteen horses in the round, places Shrady among the most prolific equestrian sculptors of all time. He spent twenty years laboring on details of action and equipment, which have passed the scrutiny of military men as well as artists, and suffered a financial loss as the result of such prolonged work. The panels on the memorial were executed by Sherry Fry from sketches made by Shrady. As a relief from his exacting labors on the Grant memorial he accepted commissions for the equestrian statue of Gen. Alpheus Starkey Williams in Belle Isle Park, Detroit, Mich., and the seated figure of Jay Cooke at Duluth, Minn. He made the bust of Grant in the New York University Hall of Fame, and for the Holland Society of New York he modeled the equestrian statue of William the Silent on Riverside Drive, New York City. His last work was on the equestrian statue of Gen. Robert E. Lee at Charlottesville, Va., which was modified and executed by Leo Lentilli. He died two weeks before the elaborate ceremonies of dedication of the Grant Memorial on Apr. 27, 1922. On Nov. 18, 1896, he had married Harrie E. Moore, with whom he made his home at Elmsford, N. Y., in a house that had been built before the Revolution. He had a daughter and three sons, all of whom, with his widow, survived him.

[*Who's Who in America*, 1920–21; R. E. Jackman, *Am. Arts* (1928); Lorado Taft, *The Hist. of Am. Sculpture* (1924); H. P. Caemmerer, *Washington, the Nat. Capital* (1932); *The Grant Memorial in Washington* (1924); Mrs. B. S. Church, in *Jour. of Am. Hist.*, Apr.–June 1913; C. H. Garrett, in *Munsey's Mag.*, July 1903; William Walton, in *Scribner's Mag.*, Mar. 1911; Helen Wright, in *Art and Archaeology*, Apr. 1922; obituary in *N. Y. Times*, Apr. 13, 1922; information from the family.]   C. M.

SHREVE, HENRY MILLER (Oct. 21, 1785–Mar. 6, 1851), steamboat captain on the Mississippi River and its tributaries, was a descendant of Thomas Sheriff [*sic*] who was in Massachusetts as early as 1641. He was born in Burlington County, N. J., where his great-grandfather, Caleb, had settled about the beginning of the century; his parents were Israel and Mary (Cokely) Shreve. The father, though a Quaker, served as colonel in the Revolutionary War, and having suffered the loss of home, crop, and stock at the hands of the British, joined the westward movement of the post-war period. Henry, scarcely three years old at the time of their migration to Fayette County, Pa., became acquainted with the frontier life and the hardships of the pioneer which rapidly developed youth into maturity. After the death of his father in 1799, he began to make trading journeys by keelboat, pirogue, or barge, down the Monongahela and the Ohio into the West. His successful fur-trading expedition, by barge, to St. Louis in 1807, started the trade between that city and Philadelphia, by way of Pittsburgh. His next new venture lay in the Upper Mississippi Valley, where the lead trade monopolized by the British had attracted his attention, and in 1810 he took a cargo of lead from the Fevre (Galena) River to New Orleans, thus inaugurating a lucrative trade. On Feb. 28, 1811, at Brownsville, Pa., he married Mary Blair, and for four years thereafter carried on a thriving trade between Pittsburgh and New Orleans by means of a 95-ton barge which he had built at Brownsville. After the death of his first wife, he married Lydia Rogers; a son and daughter of the first marriage and one daughter of the second died before their father; two daughters survived him.

In 1814, his ambition fired by the success of the *New Orleans,* Fulton's first steamboat on the Mississippi, Shreve became a stockholder in the steamboat *Enterprise,* an eighty-foot stern-wheeler, built at Brownsville under the patents of Daniel French. In this vessel, laden with supplies for Jackson's army, he went from Pittsburgh to New Orleans in December of that year. While the vessel was at New Orleans, December 1814–May 1815, Shreve gave valuable service to General Jackson, running the British batteries with supplies for Fort St. Philip and later being sent to the Gulf to exchange prisoners with the British fleet. By special permission, he helped man a twenty-four-pound gun in the battle of New Orleans. In May 1815 Shreve attempted successfully to ascend the Mississippi and Ohio rivers to Louisville; the *Enterprise* was the first steamer to accomplish that trip, but it remained for his second steamboat, the *Washington,* to establish the practicability of steam navigation on the Mississippi and Ohio route. The *Washington,* built at Wheeling under Shreve's direction, differed from its predecessors in that it had a flat, shallow hull and a high-pressure engine which it carried on the main deck instead of in the hold; it was also the first of the river boats to have a second deck. Just prior to its maiden trip, an accident to one of the cylinders of the *Washington* caused the first of the western steamboat explosions in which lives were lost, but despite this catastrophe, Shreve made the voyage from Pittsburgh to New Orleans and back to Louisville in 1816, and in 1817 made the round trip between Louisville and New Orleans in the record time of forty-one days. From this time on, boats modeled upon the *Washington* continued in increasing numbers to ply the western rivers. Shreve had interests in many other boats; his *Post Boy* (1819) was one of the first steamers to carry mail on western waters. His success as a steamboat builder and operator brought him into conflict with the Fulton-Livingston interests, to which monopoly of steam navigation of its waters had been granted in 1811 by the Territory of Orleans, but he won the lawsuit brought against him by the holders of the monopoly and thus opened the navigation of the Mississippi and its tributaries to competitive enterprise.

As superintendent of western river improvements, by appointment of the President, from Jan. 2, 1827, until his retirement 1841, Shreve designed the first steam snagboat (the *Heliopolis*), by means of which he drew from the river the sunken tree-trunks—sawyers, snags, and planters—that had for so many years menaced navigation in the early days of river trade. "Uncle Sam's tooth-pullers," as the snagboats were commonly designated at the time, not only broke the logs from their moorings, but drew them on board the boat, where they were used as fuel to continue the operation of removing their fellows still in the stream. In the thirties Shreve removed the famous Red River raft, an obstruction which had encumbered its waters for hundreds of years and had prevented the development of North Louisiana. His camp, established at Bennett's Bluff during the progress of the work, had grown by 1839 to such an extent that it was incorporated under the name Shreveport. After his retirement, Shreve spent the rest of his life on a plantation in St. Louis County, Mo. He died in St. Louis.

[L. P. Allen, *The Geneal. and Hist. of the Shreve Family from 1641* (privately printed, 1901); "Journal of Col. Israel Shreve," *Mag. of Am. Hist.,* Dec. 1878; "Henry Miller Shreve," in *U. S. Mag. and Democratic Rev.,* Feb., Mar. 1848; Caroline S. Pfaff, "Henry Miller Shreve: A Biog.," *La. Hist. Quart.,* Apr. 1927; E. W. Gould, *Fifty Years on the Mississippi* (1889); Herbert Quick, *Mississippi Steamboatin'* (1926); M. L. Hartsough, *From Canoe to Steel Barge on the Upper Mississippi* (1934); *Louisiana Gazette,* Oct. 9, 24, 1816, and Mar. 3, Nov. 15, 1817; Henry McMurtie, *Sketches of Louisville* (1819); J. T. Scharf, *Hist. of St. Louis City and County* (1883), vol. II; *Daily Missouri Republican* (St. Louis), Mar. 7, 1851.]

C. S. P—f.

SHREVE, THOMAS HOPKINS (Dec. 17, 1808–Dec. 22, 1853), writer and editor, was born in Alexandria, Va., the only son of Thomas and Ann (Hopkins) Shreve. On his father's side he was descended from a Thomas Sheriff (Shreve), who first appears in the records of a suit at law in New England in 1641, and who headed a line of Shreves numerous and prominent in colonial New Jersey. His grandfather, Caleb Shreve, served in the New Jersey assembly during and after the Revolution. His granduncle, Israel Shreve, father of Henry Miller Shreve [*q.v.*], was a colonel in Washington's army. His mother, who died in 1815, was closely related to Johns Hopkins [*q.v.*], founder of the Johns Hopkins University. Both Shreves and Hopkinses were Quakers. Shreve was educated in Alexandria and in Trenton, N. J., to which his father, after the failure of his calico mills, removed in 1821. About 1830 he followed his father and sisters to Cincinnati, where they had gone in 1827.

There he promptly entered upon a literary career in which he was associated with the literary pioneers of Cincinnati: William Davis Gallagher, James Handasyd Perkins [*qq.v.*], Otway Curry, James B. Marshall, and others. With Gallagher he published the *Cincinnati Mirror*, 1833–35, and in 1835 his own firm, T. H. Shreve and Company, brought out the first five numbers of a Unitarian magazine, the *Western Messenger*. Until the spring of 1836 he and Gallagher edited the *Cincinnati Mirror*, begun in 1831. For the *Mirror* he wrote about thirty essays, tales, and sketches, and a dozen poems. His essays and poems appeared also in the *Western Messenger*, 1835; the *Western Literary Journal and Monthly Review*, 1836; the *Western Monthly Magazine and Literary Journal*, 1837; the *Knickerbocker, or New-York Monthly Magazine*, 1837–38; the *Hesperian*, 1838–39; and the *Western Literary Journal and Monthly Magazine*, 1844. In 1838, with a brother-in-law, Joshua B. Bowles, he established in Louisville, Ky., the wholesale dry goods firm of Bowles, Shreve & Company, but he continued his contributions to magazines. On Apr. 16, 1840, he was married to Octavia Bullitt, daughter of Benjamin Bullitt, of Louisville, who survived him for many years; they had three daughters, all of whom died unmarried. Two years later he gave up his interest in an agricultural warehouse—the partnership with Bowles had been previously dissolved—to become assistant editor of George Dennison Prentice's powerful newspaper, the *Louisville Daily Journal*, a position he held until his death from tuberculosis. His work on the *Louisville Journal* won him the high esteem of Prentice and other editors of his day. He made a collection of his essays which never appeared in book form, though parts of it were published in the *Knickerbocker;* he also wrote "Betterton: A Novel," unpublished, and *Drayton: A Story of American Life* (1851). He died in Louisville and was buried in Cave Hill Cemetery. His best work is to be found in his genial and lively essays, often Addisonian in style and content. *Drayton*, while it reflects something of the life of the latter eighteenth century and the current social and political cleavages, is better proof of his ability as an essayist than as a novelist. Some of his few fugitive poems (reprinted in W. D. Gallagher's *Selections from the Poetical Literature of the West*, 1841) show native poetical capacity which was never fully developed. Though his contemporaries regarded him as a highly gifted writer whose talents would gain him an important place in western American letters, he is most interesting as a member of the group that brought Cincinnati and Louisville cultural rec-

ognition during the early decades of the nineteenth century.

[L. P. Allen, *The Geneal. and Hist. of the Shreve Family from 1641* (1901); W. T. Coggeshall, *The Poets and Poetry of the West* (1860); F. L. Mott, *A Hist. of Am. Mags.* (1930); W. H. Venable, "William Davis Gallagher," *Ohio Archaeogolical and Hist. Quart.*, Mar. 1888; J. S. Johnston, *Mem. Hist. of Louisville*, vol. II (n.d.); C. A. Neyman, unpublished monograph on Shreve, lib., George Washington Univ.]   R. W. B.
                                                                    C. A. N.

SHUBRICK, JOHN TEMPLER (Sept. 12, 1788–July 1815), naval officer, was born on Bull's Island, near Charleston, S. C., son of Col. Thomas Shubrick, a veteran of the American Revolution, and his wife Mary, daughter of Ezekiel Branford of Charleston. After attending school at Charleston and at Dedham, Mass., he began law study at Charleston under Col. William Drayton [*q.v.*], but soon felt a stronger call for the navy, in which he was commissioned midshipman on June 20, 1806. It was typical of his extraordinarily eventful service career that his first cruise brought him under fire in the surrender of the *Chesapeake* under Capt. James Barron [*q.v.*] to the British frigate *Leopard*, June 22, 1807. He served subsequently under Stephen Decatur, the younger [*q.v.*], in the *Chesapeake* and the *Argus*, and after challenging a fellow midshipman to a duel underwent the obviously lenient punishment of transfer to the brig *Viper*, where he became at once acting lieutenant (1810). In 1811 in the *Siren* he lost both thumbs by a single pistol shot fired by a New Orleans ropewalk superintendent whom he was about to strike with a stick for insults to himself and his men. These affairs apparently reflect merely the temper of his period and profession, for he was reputed to be of quiet, even melancholy spirit, so mild as to give a false impression of weakness.

Commissioned lieutenant in May 1812, he was in the *Constitution* in her celebrated escape from Broke's squadron, July 17–20, and in her victory over the *Guerrière*, Aug. 19; he commanded the quarter-deck guns and was in the thick of the mêlée when his ship's stern fouled the enemy. He was third lieutenant in the *Constitution's* defeat of the *Java*, Dec. 29, off Bahia. Sailing homeward in the *Hornet* under James Lawrence [*q.v.*], he was acting first lieutenant in a third famous victory on Feb. 24, 1813, the capture of the *Peacock*, which he boarded upon her surrender. Lawrence commended him highly, remarking that previous commanders could also testify to "his coolness and good conduct" (*The Naval Monument*, 1816, p. 42). After a relatively inactive period in the *United States* at New London, he shifted with Decatur to the

President, and was captured in her, Jan. 15, 1815, when she was attacked off New York by the British blockading squadron. After the death of his next superior early in the battle, Shubrick had become second in command. Through all these actions he came unscathed but with the reputation of bringing fighting to any ship in which he served. He received three medals from Congress and a sword from his native state. As first lieutenant in Decatur's flagship *Guerrière* against Algiers, he participated in the capture of the Algerian frigate *Mashuda,* June 17, 1815. After the peace he was given command of the *Epervier* to carry home the treaty. His ship passed Gibraltar early in July but was never again seen; it is believed to have gone down in a gale off the American coast.

Of the younger officers of the 1812 period none served more gallantly or gave brighter promise. He is described by Cooper as being five feet eleven in height, of strong frame, with grey eyes and brown hair, a man of intelligence and culture beyond the ordinary in his profession. His death was made more tragic by his marriage in 1814 to Elizabeth Matilda Ludlow of New York. His son, Edward Templer Shubrick, rose to lieutenant in the navy, resigning in 1852. Of the sixteen children in Col. Thomas Shubrick's family, six sons served in the War of 1812, four in the navy. Of these latter, Edward Rutledge became a captain and was lost at sea (1844); Irvine died a commander (1849); and William Branford [*q.v.*] became a rear admiral.

[See biog. sketch in *Analectic Mag. and Naval Chronicle,* Sept. 1816, reprinted in the *Portfolio,* May 1825; J. F. Cooper, *Lives of Distinguished Am. Naval Officers* (1846), vol. I, pp. 147–70; additional material in a sketch of W. B. Shubrick by Susan Fenimore Cooper, *Harper's Mag.,* Aug. 1876. For accounts of battles in which Shubrick took part, see E. S. Maclay, *A Hist. of the U. S. Navy from 1775–1893* (2 vols., 1894).]   A. W.

SHUBRICK, WILLIAM BRANFORD (Oct. 31, 1790–May 27, 1874), naval officer, son of Thomas and Mary (Branford) Shubrick [*q.v.*], and brother of John Templer Shubrick [*q.v.*], was born on his father's plantation, "Belvidere," Bull's Island, S. C. After schooling at Charleston and later at Dedham, Mass., he spent a year at Harvard and then in 1806 entered the navy as midshipman. Following a short Mediterranean cruise in the *Wasp,* he was on the American coast until 1810, serving under James Lawrence and as shipmate with James Fenimore Cooper [*qq.v.*], with whom he formed a lifelong friendship. Cooper dedicated to him *The Pilot* and *The Red Rover,* took brief cruises with him, and much enjoyed his seaman's comment on the lee

shore passage in the *Pilot,* "It's all very well, but you have let your jib stand too long, my fine fellow." A brief cruise in the *Hornet* early in the War of 1812 was followed by promotion to lieutenant, Jan. 5, 1813, and duty in the *Constellation* at Norfolk, during which he led a detachment of seamen in the successful defense of Craney Island, June 22, 1813, against a British boat attack. Later that year he joined the *Constitution* at Boston; he served in her as third lieutenant in her brilliant capture of the *Cyane* and *Levant,* Feb. 20, 1815, and as first lieutenant when she escaped from two ships of the line and a frigate, Mar. 11–12, near the Cape Verde Islands. His part in this cruise won him a congressional medal and mention in the vote of thanks to Commodore Charles Stewart [*q.v.*] and crew.

The next thirty years was a period of faithful routine service, marked by a cruise in the *Washington,* 1815–18; command of the *Lexington* and then the *Natchez,* 1826–29, in the latter of which he brought the body of Oliver Hazard Perry [*q.v.*] from Trinidad; promotion to captain, 1831; command of the West Indies Squadron, 1838–40; and administration of the bureau of provisions and clothing, 1845–46. At the opening of the Mexican War he applied for sea duty and sailed in the *Independence* to relieve John Drake Sloat [*q.v.*] in command of forces on the California coast. These orders unfortunately conflicted with similar ones to his senior, James Biddle [*q.v.*], who arrived at Monterey with the East Indies Squadron Jan. 2, 1847, a week later, and assumed control. Though chagrined, Shubrick remained, took charge of the Mazatlán blockade, Apr. 17–June 1, and was then recalled to California, where Biddle restored the command to him on July 19. The vigorous operations that followed included a hazardous night entry of Shubrick's squadron into Mazatlán harbor on Nov. 10, the landing of 600 men next day, and the occupation or blockade of other coastal towns. Relieved in May 1848, he became in 1849 head of the Philadelphia navy yard and later of the bureau of construction and repair, finding leisure in the summer of 1851 to visit Cooper during his last illness. In August 1852 he was made chairman of the lighthouse board, an office he held during the next nineteen years. In the ensuing summer he went to Halifax with a small squadron and made temporary arrangements with Admiral Sir George Seymour, R.N., for a fisheries treaty.

His name is now chiefly remembered through his command of the imposing expedition of nineteen ships and 2500 men sent to settle commercial and other difficulties with Paraguay. The fleet sailed in October 1858, and on Jan. 25 following reached Asunción, where Shubrick and the American commissioner, Mr. Bowlin, secured a treaty settling all points in dispute. "To the zeal, energy, discretion, and courteous and gallant bearing of Flag-officer Shubrick and the officers of his command," wrote Isaac Toucey (*Report of the Secretary of the Navy,* 1859, pp. 1137–38), "is the country largely indebted not only for the success of the enterprise, but for the friendly feeling . . . in that part of South America." His selection for these missions bears out the opinion expressed by Samuel Francis Du Pont [*q.v.*], that "he represented us abroad with men of high rank better than any officer we ever had" (S. F. Cooper, *post,* p. 406). He was a man of cultivated manners and fine presence; "feature, form, and carriage were all manly and distinguished" (*Ibid., post,* p. 403). In December 1861 he was retired after fifty-five years' service, less than ten of which were unemployed. Promoted to rear admiral (retired) in July 1862, he lived subsequently in Washington, in his last years nearly blind. His marriage in September 1815 to Harriet Cordelia, daughter of John Wethered of the Eastern Shore of Maryland, continued happily for over fifty years. His only daughter married Dr. George Clymer of the navy, and a grand-daughter became the second wife of Thomas Francis Bayard [*q.v.*].

[Susan Fenimore Cooper, in *Harper's Mag.,* Aug. 1876; *Commodore Shubrick, Speech of Hon. Andrew P. Butler of S. C. in the Senate, Mar. 18, 1856* (1856); *Correspondence of James Fenimore Cooper* (1922), containing frequent references to Shubrick and several of his letters; material on the Mexican war in *House Exec. Doc. 1,* 30 Cong., 2 Sess. (1848), on the fisheries treaty in *House Exec. Doc. 21,* 33 Cong., 1 Sess. (1854); Captains' Letters, Navy Dept. Lib., Washington, D. C., for the periods of his important activities; editorial in *Army and Navy Jour.,* May 30, 1874; obituary in *Evening Star* (Washington), May 27, 1874.]
A. W.

SHUCK, JEHU LEWIS (Sept. 4, 1812–Aug. 20, 1863), missionary to the Chinese, was born in Alexandria, then in the District of Columbia. His father died in 1816 and later his mother moved to Lewisburg, Greenbrier County, in what is now West Virginia. Here he studied privately and at the Lewisburg Academy. He read law for a time, but, after a deep religious experience, decided to enter the ministry and was licensed to preach by the Lewisburg Baptist Church on May 13, 1832. He prepared for his calling at the Virginia Baptist Seminary in Richmond. It was while there, apparently, that he determined to be a missionary. On Sept. 8, 1835, he was married to Henrietta Hall, who was then not quite eighteen years of age, and that same month sailed from Boston under the American Baptist Board of Foreign Missions as a missionary to the Chinese.

At that time Westerners—except a few Russians at Peking—were allowed in China only secretly or in the Portuguese colony of Macao and in a restricted district at Canton, so that it was uncertain where Shuck could settle permanently. For several months in 1836 he was in Singapore studying Malay and Chinese, and in 1836 he removed to Macao. Here, with the exception of one fruitless effort to reach the island of Hainan and occasional visits to Canton and Hongkong, he remained until 1842, studying the language and, in time, preaching to the Chinese in private houses or on the streets. He and his wife were the first Baptist missionaries to reside in China. His years at Macao were not altogether happy, for his first convert apostatized after a few months and he had misunderstandings with the board which supported him. In 1842 he removed to Hongkong, which had recently come into the possession of the British. There, within the next few years, he organized a church and shared in the organization of another, built three chapels, a mission house, and a school, and baptized several Chinese. His wife died Nov. 27, 1844, and several years later, 1852, a work she had prepared, *Scenes in China; or, Sketches of the Country, Religion, and Customs of the Chinese,* was published.

In 1845 Shuck returned with his children to the United States, bringing a convert and a Chinese nurse with him. Here he spoke extensively on China, and here, in October 1846, married Lizzie Sexton. Transferring his connection to the newly formed Board of Foreign Missions of the Southern Baptist Convention, he returned to China in 1847 and after a short visit at Hongkong removed to Shanghai, where he had a share in establishing a mission of his board. In 1851 his second wife died and not long afterward he again returned to the United States, this time to remain permanently. On June 5, 1854, he married Anna L. Trotti. Appointed by the Board of Domestic and Indian Missions of the Southern Baptist Convention to carry on work among the Chinese in California, he began a Chinese church in Sacramento. For at least part of the time he served as general secretary of his denomination in the state, and organized a number of churches and edited a paper. Resigning Jan. 1, 1861, he removed to South Carolina, where he was pastor of churches at Blackville and Steel Creek. He died at Barnwell Court House, S. C. In his earlier years, at least, he was decidedly intolerant and was at times blunt in presenting his own convictions, especially to the non-Christians whom he met in the Far East. He was the author of a number of tracts in Chinese, and in English of a volume published under the title *Portfolio Chinensis* (Macao, 1840).

[Alexander Wylie, *Memorials of Protestant Missionaries to the Chinese* (Shanghai, 1867), pp. 90, 91; T. S. Dunaway, *Pioneering for Jesus, The Story of Henrietta Hall Shuck* (1930); J. B. Jeter, *A Memoir of Mrs. Henrietta Shuck* (1846); *Ann. Reports of the Am. Baptist Board of Foreign Missions; Proc. of the Southern Baptist Convention*, 1861, p. 35; *Baptist Missionary Mag.*, 1836–44; G. B. Taylor, *Va. Baptist Ministers —Third Series* (1912), pp. 45–47; manuscript files of the Am. Baptist Foreign Mission Soc.]   K. S. L.

SHUEY, EDWIN LONGSTREET (Jan. 3, 1857–Sept. 27, 1924), business man, director of factory welfare work, author, was born in Cincinnati, Ohio, the son of Sarah (Berger) and William John Shuey [*q.v.*], a minister of the United Brethren in Christ. In 1865 the family removed to Dayton, where the son received his early education. In 1874 he entered Otterbein College at Westerville, Ohio, where he majored in Latin and Greek, and three years later received the degree of B.A. Following a year devoted to the study of law, he turned to teaching in academies in Indiana and northwestern Ohio, and in 1881 was invited to Otterbein to organize a preparatory department, of which he became the principal. On Aug. 15, 1882, he married Effie Mitchell of Springfield, Ohio, by whom he had two daughters and a son.

In 1885, prompted by the urgings of his father, he returned to Dayton to assume charge of the retail bookstore of the denominational publishing house. Through this work he became interested in advertising, in which he afterwards became a national expert. Asked by a Bible publishing company in Philadelphia to organize commentaries on the Scriptures from an American point of view, he obtained contributions from British and American experts and secured the compilation of a "word book" for assistance to readers of the Bible; these helps were sold as the Bible Readers' Aids of the International Bible, the compiler appearing only as the American editor. After his removal to Dayton he became active in the work of the Young Men's Christian Association as chairman of a local committee with the task of arranging evening study classes for young men. Although in New York cultural subjects had been taught in free evening sessions, in Dayton technical courses were offered with a charge for tuition and were so successful that Shuey was appointed in 1893 to the International Y. M. C. A. Committee; for over thirty years a member of this committee, he assisted in the development of its educational policies. In 1899 he was president of the International Convention; from 1917 to 1920 he was a member of the National War Work Council; and in 1923 he was active in devising a new plan for the national administration of the organization.

In 1897 he became head of the welfare department of the National Cash Register Company. His success in this work led to his writing *Factory People and Their Employers* (1900) and to his being consulted by other prominent corporations interested in welfare programs. In 1900 he associated himself with the Lowe Brothers Company of Dayton, paint manufacturers, to develop advertising and promote an effective sales policy; he achieved conspicuous success and remained with the company until his retirement in 1918. In 1915–16 he served as president of the Association of National Advertisers, whose declaration of ethical standards was due in part to his efforts. A delegate to several quadrennial conferences of the Church of the United Brethren, he was a successful advocate at the last one he attended of a liberalization of the Book of Discipline. For five years he was president of the board of trustees of Otterbein College. He was an imaginative, quietly dynamic man, whose decided opinions made enemies as well as friends. He died of cancer a few months after the death of his wife.

[D. B. Shuey, *Hist. of the Shuey Family in America* (2nd ed., 1919); *Who's Who in America*, 1924–25; N. R. Best, *Two Y Men: David A. Sinclair, Secretary*; Edwin L. Shuey, *Layman* (1925), based on Shuey's personal papers; *Daily News* (Dayton), Sept. 28, 29, Oct. 1, 1924.]   F. P. W.

SHUEY, WILLIAM JOHN (Feb. 9, 1827– Feb. 21, 1920), clergyman of the United Brethren in Christ, was born in Miamisburg, Montgomery County, Ohio, the son of Adam and Hannah (Aley) Shuey. He was of Huguenot lineage, a descendant of Daniel Shuey who emigrated to Pennsylvania in 1732 and settled in what is now Lebanon County. William attended the public schools of his native town and of Springfield, his parents having moved to a farm in the latter place in 1836. A brief period of study at the Ohio Conference High School of the Methodist Church, Springfield, completed his formal education. In 1848 he was admitted to the Miami Conference of the Church of the United Brethren and the same year, Mar. 7, he married Sarah Berger, by whom he had four sons, one of whom was Edwin L. Shuey [*q.v.*].

From the beginning of his ministry Shuey displayed, in addition to religious zeal, unusual administrative and business ability. He was quick to see and to indicate lines of advance, and no little of the progress of his denomination during the last half of the nineteenth century was due to his wisdom and energy. After serving on the Lewisburg Circuit (1849–51), he became pastor of the First Church, Cincinnati. In 1854, having been prominent in stimulating organized missionary activity, he was appointed by the newly constituted Home, Frontier, and Foreign Missionary Society to go to Africa and select a site for its first work abroad. Accompanied by D. C. Kumler and Daniel K. Flickinger [q.v.], he sailed in January 1855. The three fixed upon what seemed a suitable location, and Kumler and Shuey returned. Until 1864 he was engaged in pastoral work in Cincinnati and Dayton, and was for three terms presiding elder of the Miami Conference. During this period he published in collaboration with Flickinger, *Discourses on Doctrinal and Practical Subjects* (1859). In 1864 he was elected assistant publishing agent, and in 1865, agent. His more than twenty years' service in this position is regarded as an epoch in the history of the denomination. Taking charge of the publishing concern at Dayton when it was in a precarious condition, he put it on a permanent basis and greatly extended its activities. "More than any Bishop, editor, or other Church leader . . . Shuey in his position as Publishing Agent was for an entire generation the strategic center for the activities and progress of the United Brethren in Christ" (Drury, *post*, p. 581). He was an important member of the commission that formulated the revised confession of faith and constitution adopted in 1889, and in the long court contest for possession of the publishing house, inaugurated by those who held to the old constitution and separated from the majority, he carried the burden of the defense which kept the property in the hands of the latter. He was instrumental in the founding of Union Biblical Seminary (Bonebrake Theological Seminary), the first theological school of the United Brethren. Many of the institutions of the Church profited by his abilities; he was for twenty-two years a trustee of Otterbein College, for more than a quarter of a century a member of the board of missions, one of the first directors of the Church Extension Society, and a member of the Board of Education. For years he edited *The Yearbook of the United Brethren in Christ*; he prepared several editions of the denominational *Handbook*, and, with others, *A Collection of Hymns for the Use of the United Brethren in Christ* (1858); he published also, *An Outline of Our Church Troubles* (1881), and *A Manual of the United Brethren Publishing House* (1892). In 1897 he relinquished his position as publishing agent

and became business manager of Bonebrake Theological Seminary, retiring from official church service in 1901. During his long residence in Dayton he was active in civic affairs and was for many years a director of the Fourth National Bank.

[D. B. Shuey, *Hist. of the Shuey Family* (1919); Daniel Berger, *Hist. of the Ch. of the United Brethren in Christ* (1897); A. W. Drury, *Hist. of the Ch. of the United Brethren in Christ* (1924); *Who's Who in America*, 1918–19.]

H. E. S.

SHUFELDT, ROBERT WILSON (Feb. 21, 1822–Nov. 7, 1895), naval officer, was born at Red Hook, N. Y., son of George Adam Shufeldt, a prominent lawyer, and his wife Mary (Wilson) Shufeldt, and a descendant of George Shufeldt, who emigrated to New York from Holland in 1710. Entering the navy as midshipman, May 11, 1839, he cruised in the Brazil and Home Squadrons, was commissioned passed midshipman on July 2, 1845, after a year's study at the Philadelphia naval school, and then served a year in the coast survey and two years in African and Mediterranean waters. In 1849–51 he was chief officer of the mail steamers *Atlantic* and *Georgia*. He was made lieutenant in October 1853 but resigned from the navy the following June, and commanded first the Collins Line steamer *Liverpool* for two years and then the *Black Hawk* and *Catawba* between New York and New Orleans. At the opening of the Civil War, he was appointed consul general to Cuba and continued in this duty until April 1863, going to Mexico in 1862 on a hazardous secret mission at the time of the French invasion. He then rejoined the navy, his commander's commission dating from Nov. 19, 1862, and commanded first the *Conemaugh*, which participated in the capture of Morris Island, S. C., and in other operations off Charleston, and later the *Proteus* of the East Gulf Squadron, in which he was senior naval officer in joint operations, Mar. 23–27, 1865, at St. Marks, Fla. His post-bellum service included command of the *Hartford* and *Wachusett* in the Orient, with promotion to captain in 1869; of the *Miantonomah*, 1870; and of an expedition surveying the Isthmus of Tehuantepec canal route, 1870–71, his report of which was published in 1872 (*Senate Executive Document 6*, 42 Cong., 2 Sess., 1872). After a brief Mediterranean cruise in the *Wabash* and duty at the Brooklyn navy yard, he was chief of the bureau of equipment and recruiting, 1875–78; during this service he reorganized the naval apprentice system and also commanded naval forces at New Orleans during the election troubles of '76.

Having advocated the use of the navy in extending American commerce (in *The Relation of the Navy to the Commerce of the United States*, 1878) and persuaded James Gillespie Blaine [*q.v.*], then secretary of state, of the possibilities of a treaty with Korea, which had just made trade concessions to Japan but had not yet opened relations with any western power, he sailed in the *Ticonderoga* in 1878 on a combined commercial and diplomatic mission. After acting as American and British representative to settle a Liberian boundary dispute, and making a treaty with the king of Johanna, he sailed to Japan, reaching Nagasaki, Apr. 15, 1880, and Fusan, Korea, May 4. Finding Japanese mediation of very doubtful value, he secured from the Chinese viceroy Li Hung Chang a promise of aid with Korea in exchange for help in organizing a Chinese navy. After a trip home, Shufeldt was back in China in June 1881 as naval attaché and with full power to negotiate a treaty, which was finally drawn up, signed May 22, 1882, and subsequently ratified. Much more comprehensive than any previous American treaty with eastern nations, it established diplomatic relations, extraterritoriality, and privileges to Americans of trade and residence in open ports. The treaty was wholly the result of Shufeldt's initiative, pertinacity, and genuine diplomatic skill; it was the great achievement of his career. Subsequently he was president of the Naval Advisory Board, 1882–84, during the beginnings of the "White Squadron," and superintendent of the naval observatory, reaching rear admiral's rank in 1883, and retiring Feb. 21, 1884. Of gigantic frame and strong physique, he succumbed finally to pneumonia in his Washington home. His burial was at Arlington. His wife, whom he married Oct. 16, 1847, was Sarah Hutchins Abercrombie, daughter of the Rev. James Abercrombie of Philadelphia. They had six children, of whom three sons survived their parents.

[See G. N. Mackenzie, *Colonial Families of the U. S. A.*, vol. V (1915); L. H. Hamersly, *Records of Living Officers of the U. S. Navy* (4th ed., 1890); R. W. Shufeldt, *The Relation of the Navy to the Commerce of the U. S.* (1878); C. O. Paullin, *Diplomatic Negotiations of Am. Naval Officers* (1912); obituaries in *Army and Navy Jour.*, Nov. 9, and *Evening Star* (Washington), Nov. 7, 1895. The Shufeldt Papers, temporarily deposited in the Navy Dept. Lib., Washington, D. C., include a manuscript history, "The Cruise of the *Ticonderoga*," and many other docs. relating chiefly to the Korean mission.]   A. W.

SHULZE, JOHN ANDREW (July 19, 1775–Nov. 18, 1852), governor of Pennsylvania, was born in the township of Tulpehocken, Berks County, Pa. His father, Christopher Emanuel Shulze, a distinguished clergyman of the Lutheran Church, was a native of Saxony, Ger-

many, educated at the University of Halle, who emigrated to America in 1765; and his mother, Eva Elizabeth, was the daughter of Henry Melchior Mühlenberg [*q.v.*]. The boy received a classical and theological education, studying in Lancaster, York, and New York City under the guidance of some of the most eminent educators and divines of the day. He was married to Susan Kimmell, by whom he had at least two children. In 1796 he was ordained to the ministry, was admitted to the German Lutheran Synod of Eastern Pennsylvania, and preached in Berks County. In 1802 he retired from the active ministry on account of serious rheumatism. In 1804 he established himself in the mercantile business in Myerstown, then in Dauphin County, and within a decade had accumulated a moderate fortune.

In 1806 he served in the House of Representatives of Pennsylvania. He was reëlected for the two succeeding years but refused to become a candidate for a fourth term. A stanch advocate of Republican principles in government, he played a very active and influential part in the proceedings of the legislature during his three-year tenure in that body. In 1813 he was appointed to the office of surveyor-general of the state but declined this position. He was induced, however, to accept the duties of register, recorder, prothonotary, clerk of the orphans' court, and clerk of the sessions court of Lebanon County. After serving eight years in these capacities he was elected again to the House of Representatives in 1821 and the next year was chosen a state senator from Dauphin and Lebanon counties. In 1823 he received the Republican nomination for governor and was elected by a majority of more than 25,000. Upon the expiration of his term of three years he was returned to the governorship by the unprecedented majority of approximately 72,000 votes to about 2,000 for his opponent. In dispensing the patronage, grown to enormous proportions by the public works in which the state was then engaged, he proved himself a keen judge of men and a politician of no mean merit. Although questioning at first the wisdom of having the state embark on a program of internal improvements, the chief feature of which was the construction of a canal from Columbia on the Susquehanna River to Pittsburgh with side branches to act as feeders to the main canal, he bowed to the wishes of the people and gave the project his hearty support. Before the expiration of his second term of office more than $6,000,000 had been expended on the canals alone, and a considerable portion of the program had been completed.

Especially interested in the extension of the system of public elementary education to all classes throughout the state, he repeatedly appealed to the legislature on the subject. Although the legislation enacted in response to his requests did not measure up to his expectations, something was accomplished; and the publicity given the subject paved the way for the establishment of the system of public education on a sound basis during the decade of the thirties. After the expiration of his second term in December 1829, he retired from public life and devoted himself to farming, though he continued his interest in politics and public questions in general. In 1839 he was a delegate to the state convention that assembled in Harrisburg and the following year was chosen a member of the electoral college of the state, of which he was elected president. In 1846 he removed to Lancaster, where he resided until his death.

[*Pa. Archives*, ser. 4, vol. V (1900); W. C. Armor, *Lives of the Governors of Pa.* (1872); J. B. Sutherland, *An Impartial View of the Respective Claims of Mr. Shulze and Mr. Gregg to the Office of Governor of Pa.* (1823); W. H. Egle, *Hist. of the Counties of Dauphin and Lebanon* (1883); H. M. M. Richards, "Descendants of H. M. Mühlenberg," *Proc. and Addresses Pa.-Ger. Soc.*, vol. X (1900) p. 21 giving his name as John Andrew **Melchior** Shulze.] A.E.M.

SHUNK, FRANCIS RAWN (Aug. 7, 1788–July 30, 1848), governor of Pennsylvania, was born at Trappe, Montgomery County, Pa., the son of Elizabeth (Rawn) and John Shunk, a farmer. His two grandfathers, Francis Shunk and Caspar Rawn, had emigrated to America early in the eighteenth century from the Palatinate of the Rhine. Because of the poverty of his parents the boy's formal education was limited to the country school, and at the age of fifteen he became a teacher. Soon afterward he was placed in charge of the village school at Trappe, a position he continued to fill for nine years. When the school was not in session he worked on the neighboring farms and studied as much as he could. In 1812 he was appointed by Andrew Porter, the surveyor-general of the state, as a clerk. He also studied law in the office of Thomas Elder of Harrisburg and in 1816 was admitted to the bar. In 1814 he marched as a private in a local company of the state militia to the defense of Baltimore against the invasion of the British. Soon after his return he became assistant and then principal clerk of the House of Representatives. In 1820 he married Jane Findley. Nine years later he was appointed clerk to the canal commissioners and in 1839 became secretary of the commonwealth. In 1842 he began the practice of law in Pittsburgh, but in 1844

he was elected as a Democrat governor of the state. In 1847 he was reëlected by an increased majority.

He was essentially a self-made man. Though not brilliant, he was honest, industrious, and devoted. During his administration the Mexican War made many demands upon the resources of the state as did also a variety of complicated domestic problems of major importance, some of which had been inherited from the preceding decade. Especially troublesome was the serious plight of the public treasury on his accession to office. Not only had the debt of the state reached the then staggering sum of approximately $40,000,000, much of which had been accumulated in the construction of canals and other public works, but also the revenues were insufficient to meet the regular obligations of the government. Indeed, for a period of two years the interest on the state debt had not been paid, and the credit of the state was otherwise seriously impaired. To the question of balancing the budget and restoring the credit of the state he gave his constant attention throughout his entire administration with the result that he improved conditions measurably. His early labors gave him a hearty sympathy with the poor and unfortunate, and he steadfastly opposed all measures tending to the aggregation of property in the hands of the few or to the extension of special privileges and concessions to vested interests by legislative action. He vetoed many acts of the legislature granting concessions to corporate business enterprises. Among other measures which he commended to the legislature for favorable consideration were: state control of inheritance by laws preventing entailed estates, a more careful scrutiny on the part of the legislature of the increasingly large numbers of pleas for divorce presented to that body annually, and the extension and improvement of the system of public education. On July 9, 1848, however, on account of the failure of his health he resigned his office in a simple farewell message (*Archives, post*, pp. 275–76). He died of tuberculosis three weeks later.

[*Pa. Archives*, ser. 4, vol. VII (1902); W. C. Armor, *Lives of the Governors of Pa.* (1872); Moses Auge, *Lives of the Eminent . . . of Montgomery County, Pa.* (1879); *Commemoration Biog. Encyc. of Dauphin County, Pa.* (1896).] A.E.M.

SHURTLEFF, NATHANIEL BRADSTREET (June 29, 1810–Oct. 17, 1874), mayor of Boston and antiquary, was born in Boston, the descendant of William Shurtleff who was in Plymouth as early as 1634. He was the son of Sally (Shaw) and Benjamin Shurtleff, a physician of Carver, Mass., who had removed to

Boston to acquire a professional reputation and a fortune. The boy graduated at the Boston Public Latin School in 1822 and then went to the Round Hill School at Northampton, under Joseph G. Cogswell and George Bancroft [*qq.v.*]. At Harvard College, where he received the A.B. degree in 1831, he was an indifferent student. He took the medical degree at Harvard in 1834 and soon succeeded to his father's practice. He married on July 18, 1836, Sarah Eliza, the daughter of Hiram Smith of Boston, and had six children. Some twenty years after graduation he enhanced his growing reputation as an antiquary by editing with scrupulous care the *Records of the Governor and Company of the Massachusetts Bay in New England* (5 vols. in 6, 1853–54). He said that every word and letter in the proof sheets had been compared with the original by himself. *Records of the Colony of New Plymouth in New England* (8 vols., 1855–57) followed, and to these David Pulsifer added four volumes (1859–61) after Shurtleff's expensive methods were discontinued (see *Mass. Col. Soc. Pubs.*, vol. III, 1900, pp. 104, 114–17). His most important work was *A Topographical and Historical Description of Boston* (1871) from articles written in the midst of years of professional and political activity. It is a minute account of Boston places, well written and readable. He wrote on everything that interested him: phrenology, a perpetual calendar, a study of the Bay Psalm Book, maps, a decimal system for the arrangement of books in libraries, and accounts of the Shurtleff, Leverett, and Beal families. His list of *The Passengers of the Mayflower* (printed in *New England Historical & Genealogical Register,* Jan. 1847 and privately printed in 1849), compiled from sources known before Bradford's *History* was found, is an example of his thoroughness. He failed to mention nine minor passengers out of one hundred and one, and he included one woman and several children not on board.

He was mayor of Boston for three terms, 1868–70, as a Democrat, being reëlected by increasing pluralities. His administrations were marked by the annexation of Dorchester and Roxbury, by street improvements, and by unsuccessful attempts to economize. He was not, it was said, a good judge of character, and he knew little of the proper methods of government. His addresses, however, reveal high purposes and wide sympathies. He took pride in being the first life-long democratic mayor. His party opposed a third term but an aroused electorate returned him to office. He was chosen a member of the Massachusetts Historical Society in 1847 and held of-

fice in that society nearly all the years following until his death. He belonged to several other societies in the United States and in England. From 1854 to 1874 he served as secretary to the board of overseers of Harvard College, having been a member of the board, 1852–61, 1863–69. He was also a trustee of the public library. He lived at No. 2 Beacon Street, where his apartments were crowded with books. His library, which was sold at auction in the fall of 1875, had 1790 items, a first rate local historical and genealogical collection (*Catalogue of the Library of Dr. N. B. Shurtleff to be Sold at Auction . . . Nov. 30, 1875,* 1875).

[C. C. Smith, in *Proc. Mass. Hist. Soc.,* ser. 1, vol. XIII (1875); *New-England Hist. and Geneal. Register,* July 1878; J. M. Bugbee, "Boston Under the Mayors," *The Memorial Hist. of Boston,* ed. by Justin Winsor, vol. III (1881); Benjamin Shurtleff, *Descendants of Wm. Shurtleff* (2 vols., 1912); *Ballou's Pictorial Drawing Room Companion,* Jan. 5, 1856, with portrait.]
C. K. B.

SHURTLEFF, ROSWELL MORSE (June 14, 1838–Jan. 6, 1915), landscape painter, born at Rindge, N. H., was the fourth and youngest child of Asahel Dewey and Eliza (Morse) Shurtleff. He was a descendant of William Shurtleff, who was born in the West Riding of Yorkshire, England, and was in Plymouth, Mass., in 1634. He went to Dartmouth College with the class of 1857 but did not graduate. He took charge of an architect's office in Manchester, N. H., 1857; worked in a lithographer's shop in Buffalo, N. Y., 1858–59; went to Boston in 1859 and made drawings on wood for John Andrew, the engraver, in the meantime studying drawing in the evening classes of the Lowell Institute; and in 1860–61 was in New York, where he attended the school of the National Academy of Design and made magazine illustrations. Upon the opening of the Civil War he enlisted, as a private; in a short time he was promoted to a lieutenancy, and later he became adjutant. On July 19, 1861, he was wounded and captured. After nearly eight months in Southern hospitals and prisons, he was finally released on parole. He returned to New York, and busied himself with drawing illustrations for magazines and books. On June 14, 1867 (*Who's Who in America, post*), he married Clara Eugenia Halliday, daughter of Joseph B. and Eleanor C. Halliday, of Hartford, Conn. From 1869 to 1875 he had a studio in Hartford.

It was in 1870 that he began to paint in oils and in 1872 that he first exhibited at the National Academy. At first he specialized in such pictures of animal life as "The American Panther" (1876), "A Race for Life" (1877), "The Still Hunter," and "On the Alert" (1879), and "The

Wolf at the Door," all of which were shown at the Academy in the seventies. "The Race for Life," which depicted a pack of wolves dashing through the winter woods in pursuit of some unseen prey, was considered by contemporaries (*New York Tribune*, Apr. 28, 1877) a most remarkable picture. About 1880 Shurtleff turned to landscapes, and he won his greatest success through his paintings of the northern woods and forests. He usually went to the Adirondacks in the summer and autumn, and had a cottage and studio at Keene Valley, where he produced many excellent forest interiors that showed both thorough knowledge and fine feeling. He became an Academician in 1890. Characteristic examples of his work have been hung in several public museums. In the Corcoran Gallery, Washington, is "The First Snow." The Metropolitan Museum, New York, owns "A Mountain Stream," in which a brook flows between banks crowded by trees. The Museum of Springfield, Mass., also has a good landscape. Shurtleff regularly exhibited his wood interiors at the Academy for many years and was successful in finding a market for them. He died in New York, survived by his wife. There were no children.

[Benjamin Shurtleff, *Descendants of William Shurtleff* (2 vols., 1912); *Who's Who in America*, 1914–15; G. W. Sheldon, *Am. Painters* (1879); H. W. French, *Art and Artists in Conn.* (1879); Clara E. Clement and Laurence Hutton, *Artists of the Nineteenth Century* (1885); *Nat. Acad. Notes* and cats., 1881–1913, C. M. Kurtz, ed.; *Cat. of Am. Paintings Belonging to William T. Evans* (1900); *Met. Mus. of Art Cat. of Paintings* (1926); *Nat. Gallery of Art, Cat. of Colls.* (1926); obituaries in *Am. Art Ann.*, 1915, *Am. Art News*, Jan. 9, *N. Y. Times*, Jan. 7, 1915.]   W. H. D.

SHUTE, SAMUEL (Jan. 12, 1662–Apr. 15, 1742), colonial governor of Massachusetts, was the son of Benjamin Shute of London and his wife, a daughter of the Rev. Joseph Caryl, a distinguished nonconformist minister. Samuel received his preliminary schooling from the Puritan schoolmaster Charles Morton [*q.v.*], and was admitted to the Middle Temple, Nov. 23, 1683. On Dec. 12 of the same year he was admitted fellow commoner at Christ's College, Cambridge, but apparently took no degree. He obtained a captaincy in the army, fought in Marlborough's campaigns, was wounded at Blenheim, and in 1712 became lieutenant-colonel of the 3rd Dragoon Guards. He was selected for the governorship of Massachusetts Bay and New Hampshire in April 1716 and reached Boston on Oct. 4.

Although he was well received by Judge Samuel Sewall and the Rev. Cotton Mather [*qq.v.*], his administration was one of the stormiest suffered by any royal governor. He was insulted by the Assembly in their treatment of the salary question, a perennial cause of hostility between the executive and legislative powers. He opposed the issues of paper money, acting within his instruction and also in the light of sound business principles, but was over-powered by the Assembly, which was largely composed of men of "Small fortunes & Meane Education" (Perry, *post*, III, 121). The Assembly attempted to encroach upon the governor's rights to adjourn the General Court and to designate its place of meeting, claiming that the right of adjourning the court did not include the right of adjourning the lower House. They quarrelled with him over his right to negative the choice of a speaker, and as a result the colony was obliged in 1725 to accept an explanatory charter defining this right of the governor. There had been much trouble with the Indians on the northern frontier, and a further quarrel with the Assembly occurred when they refused to provide the fortifications which Shute considered necessary. In 1717, Shute met the Indians in a conference at Arrowsick Island, where, although he handled the negotiations without great ability, a new and useful treaty of friendship was signed, but by 1720 the relations with the more northern Indians, stirred up by French machinations, had become so serious as to necessitate war, and in connection with the military operations the Assembly made absurd and unwarranted claims to authority.

Finally, despairing of conducting the government in the face of these and other claims, Shute sailed, on Jan. 1, 1723, for England. There he presented a memorial to the Privy Council and laid his grievances before them. These were so obvious that the colony's agent, Jeremiah Dummer [*q.v.*], and other friends in England wrote to the Assembly that they were doing themselves and their cause much harm by the way they had treated Shute. The only answer that body made to their agent's candor was to refuse him an allowance (Palfrey, *post*, IV, 428, note). Shute remained in England, endeavoring to collect his arrears of salary. In the spring of 1727, when he was about to return to Massachusetts, his commission was vacated by the death of the king. He was not reappointed, but was consulted about the instructions for his successor, William Burnet [*q.v.*], and was awarded a pension of £400 a year. He remained thereafter in private life until his death.

[Inaccurate account by J. A. Doyle, in *Dict. Nat. Biog.*; J. T. Adams, *Revolutionary New England* (1923), with additional references; J. G. Palfrey, *Hist. of New England*, vol. IV (1875); W. S. Perry, *Hist. Colls. Relating to the Am. Colonial Church*, vol. III (1873), containing Shute's memorial to the King; *The Report of the Lords of the Committee upon Gov. Shute's Memorial* (1725); *George Town on Arrowsick Island*

. . . *A Conference of His Excellency the Governour with the Sachems and Chief Men of the Eastern Indians* (1717), repr. in *Me. Hist. Soc. Colls.,* vol. III (1853); *Jour. of the Commissioners for Trade and Plantations,* 1714–28 (1924–28); *Cal. of State Papers, Col. Ser., America and West Indies, 1716–21* (1930–33); *Mass. Hist. Soc. Colls.,* 5 ser. VII (1882), 6 ser. II (1888), 7 ser. VIII (1912).]   J.T.A.

SIAMESE TWINS [See CHANG and ENG, 1811–1874].

SIBLEY, GEORGE CHAMPLAIN (Apr. 1, 1782–Jan. 31, 1863), Indian agent, explorer, was born in Great Barrington, Mass., the descendant of John Sibley who emigrated from England to Plymouth about 1629 and later settled in Salem, Mass., and the son of John Sibley [*q.v.*] and Elizabeth (Hopkins) Sibley, the daughter of Samuel Hopkins, 1721–1803 [*q.v.*]. The boy was reared and educated in Fayetteville, N. C. Appointed a clerk in the Indian bureau, he went to St. Louis and in 1808 accompanied the military detachment sent up the Missouri to a point near the site of the present Sibley, Jackson County, Mo., to build Fort Osage. At this establishment, known also as Fiery Prairie Fort and Fort Clark, which included a government trading factory for the Indians and which for a decade was the furthermost outpost of the frontier, he was stationed as factor, and later as Indian agent, until about 1826. In June and July 1811, escorted by a band of Osage warriors, he explored the Grand Saline, in the present Woodward County, Okla. (see John Bradbury, *Travels in the Interior of America,* 1817, and H. M. Brackenridge, *Views of Louisiana,* 1814), and in August he made a tour of investigation among the Kansas Indians. Though his services in the War of 1812 seem not to have been conspicuous, they brought him the unofficial title of major, by which he was ever afterward known.

On Aug. 19, 1815, in St. Louis, he was married to Mary, the accomplished daughter of Rufus B. Easton, who accompanied him to the fort. Here the Sibleys, in a large log building, furnished with many of the conveniences and some of the luxuries of city life brought by the bride on her wedding voyage, kept open house for all voyagers and wanderers who passed that way. In 1825 Sibley served as one of the three commissioners to mark the Santa Fé trail from Council Grove to the Mexican boundary. A year or two afterward he retired from government service and made his home near St. Charles, where he developed a large and beautiful estate. In 1844 he was a delegate to both the state and the national Whig conventions and also an unsuccessful candidate for the state Senate. Though a semi-invalid in his later years, he maintained a lively interest in political and social questions. Both of the Sibleys held somewhat advanced views for their time and place, and Mrs. Sibley was one of the first avowed advocates of woman's suffrage. In 1827 they established a school for girls on a nearby tract named by them Lindenwood. This school, subsequently taken over by the presbytery of St. Louis and endowed with the gift of Sibley's estate, became Lindenwood College. Sibley died at his home. Though his criticism of the fur traders, whom he charged with swindling and corrupting the Indians, brought upon Sibley some abuse, he is generally praised for his honesty and good judgment, his hospitality and helpfulness, and his tactful relations with his savage wards.

[Sibley Papers in possession of Mo. Hist. Soc., and of Lindenwood College; R. G. Thwaites, *Early Western Travels,* esp. vols. V, VI (1904), XIV–XVII, XX (1905); J. C. Luttig, *Journal* (1920), ed. by S. M. Drumm; L. deL. Templin, *Two Illustrious Pioneers in the Education of Women in Mo. The Sibleys* (1926); Louis Houck, *A Hist. of Mo.* (1908) vols. I, III; C. J. Taylor, *Hist. of Great Barrington, Mass.* (1882); W. A. Benedict and H. A. Tracy, *Hist. of the Town of Sutton, Mass.* (1878), p. 722.]   W.J.G.

SIBLEY, HENRY HASTINGS (Feb. 20, 1811–Feb. 18, 1891), fur trader, territorial delegate, governor of Minnesota, was born in Detroit, Michigan Territory. He was the descendant of John Sibley who emigrated from England to Plymouth about 1629 and later settled in Salem, Mass., and the son of Solomon and Sarah Whipple (Sproat) Sibley. His mother was the granddaughter of Abraham Whipple [*q.v.*], and his father was territorial delegate to Congress and judge of the territorial supreme court. The boy's education at the local academy was supplemented by two years of tutoring in the classics and two years of law study. In June 1828 he became a clerk in the sutler's store at Fort Brady at Sault Ste. Marie. In the spring of 1829 he entered the employ of the American Fur Company at Mackinac as clerk, a position he held for five years. During the last two winters of this service he was stationed at Cleveland, Ohio, charged with the important duty of purchasing the company's supplies of flour, corn, pork, tobacco, and other produce. In the summer of 1834 Hercules L. Dousman and Joseph Rolette, veteran fur traders in the Northwest, invited him to join them as a partner in operating one of the outfits of the American Fur Company and to assume exclusive management of the trade with the Sioux from Lake Pepin to the Canadian boundary and west to the Rocky Mountain divide. On Oct. 28 (*Autobiography, post,* p. 29, footnote), after an arduous journey by canoe and horse, he arrived at Mendota, beneath the walls of Fort Snelling.

In 1835 he built himself "a substantial and commodious stone dwelling ... the first ... private residence, in all of Minnesota, and Dakota" (*Autobiography, post,* p. 35) ; and here many explorers, travelers, missionaries, Indians, and other visitors to the region were entertained. His influence among the Sioux was extensive, not alone because of his position as head of the fur trade, but because of his firm and commanding personality, his remarkable physique, and his skill as a huntsman. On May 2, 1843, he was married to Sarah Jane Steele, sister of Franklin Steele.

In 1848 he was elected delegate to Congress by the inhabitants of that part of the Territory of Wisconsin not included in Wisconsin state. He promoted the organization of Minnesota Territory in 1849 and was promptly elected as delegate to Congress. When Minnesota became a state in May 1858 he took office as the first governor, having been elected as a Democrat. His administration was marked by his interest in the state militia and in the public school lands, a premature sale of which he prevented by veto. He was not a candidate for reëlection in 1859. As territorial delegate he had urged on Congress a change in Indian policy but in vain, and in the Sioux uprising in Minnesota of 1862 he led the military forces of the state against the Indians. With an ill equipped command and practically no cavalry he marched from St. Paul to the relief of the frontier posts, reënforced the soldiers and settlers after the battle of Birch Coulee, and fought the battle of Wood Lake on Sept. 23. His influence among the Indians was no doubt partly responsible for the return of the white captives after this battle. In 1863 and 1864 he commanded punitive expeditions against the Sioux in the Dakota region, and in 1865–66 he was one of the commissioners to negotiate peace treaties with the Sioux.

He removed to St. Paul, Minn., and thereafter was concerned with more prosaic public service and private business. He was president of a gas company, an insurance company, and a bank in St. Paul; he was for one term a representative in the state legislature, 1871, and was for many years president of the board of regents of the University of Minnesota and of the Minnesota Historical Society, for which he wrote several addresses and sketches (see *Minnesota Historical Society Collections,* vols. I, III, *post*). These, with *The Unfinished Autobiography of Henry Hastings Sibley, together with a Selection of ... Letters* (1932) ed. by T. C. Blegen (also in *Minnesota History,* Dec. 1927) give a picture of his early life and of his character. He was perhaps the most striking figure among his contemporaries in Minnesota. For years after his retirement from politics he remained an important and influential figure in the state.

[W. W. Folwell, *A Hist. of Minn.* (4 vols., 1921–30) ; *Minn. Hist. Colls.,* vols. I (1872), III (1880), VI (1894) ; *Autobiog. ante,* and in *Minnesota Hist. Bull.,* Aug. 1919 ; Nathaniel West, *The Ancestry, Life, and Times of Hon. Henry Hastings Sibley* (1889) ; and W. P. Shortridge, *The Transition of a Typical Frontier, with Illustrations from the Life of Henry Hastings Sibley* (1922) ; W. A. Benedict and H. A. Tracy, *Hist. of Sutton, Mass.* (1878) ; *Daily Pioneer Press* (St. Paul), Feb. 17, 19, 1891 ; an important collection of Sibley's papers in possession of the Minnesota Historical Society.]

S. J. B.

SIBLEY, HIRAM (Feb. 6, 1807–July 12, 1888), business man and promoter, was born at North Adams, Mass., the son of Benjamin and Zilpha (Davis) Sibley. His education was what the village school could supply. At an early age, having already practised the shoemaker's trade, he left North Adams, and went to the village of Lima, N. Y., where he entered a cotton factory. At twenty-one, he started a machine-shop in the nearby town of Mendon, and there he built up a successful business, of which he was able to dispose at a profit. He also carried on at this time an extensive wool-carding business at Sparta and Mount Morris.

In 1838, with the beginnings of a fortune already in hand, he moved to Rochester, N. Y. Here he engaged in banking and real estate, and acquired sufficient popularity to be elected sheriff of Monroe County in 1843. During his period of office he came into contact with Royal Earl House [*q.v.*], the inventor of the House printing telegraph, then in financial difficulties. With this contact began Sibley's interest in the telegraph itself. He was instrumental the next year in obtaining an appropriation from Congress for the support of the experiments carried on by Samuel F. B. Morse [*q.v.*], and in 1851 he bought up the House patents and organized the New York & Mississippi Valley Printing Telegraph Company. Before the end of the year he had built 100 miles of line. He early formed the conviction, however, that there were too many small companies, and that consolidation was demanded. Accordingly, in 1854 he formed an association with Ezra Cornell [*q.v.*], who had valuable grants under the Morse patents, and the two agreed to form the so-called Western Union Telegraph Company, which was chartered in 1856, with Sibley as president. This position he held for the next ten years. Under his administration the number of telegraph offices increased from 132 to 4,000, and the value of the property from $220,000 to $48,000,000. He was the earnest advocate of a transcontinental telegraph line, and, failing to secure the support of his co-directors in the Western Union, he undertook the project on his own account, securing from Congress in 1860 an annual subsidy of $40,000 for ten years and shrewdly coming to terms with a California rival. The line was a success from the beginning and was amalgamated with the Western Union in 1864. He now dreamed of telegraphic communication with Europe via Bering Strait and Siberia. He had thoughtfully played a leading part in the entertainment of the Russian naval squadron in 1863, and when he visited Russia, soon afterward, was cordially received by the Czar. Wires were actually strung in Alaska and Siberia when the laying of the transatlantic cable led to the collapse of the project at heavy loss.

Retiring from the Western Union Company in 1869, Sibley started an extensive seed and nursery business. He had also a large interest in railroads in the South and West, and made extensive investments in both sections. He bought a 40,000-acre farm in Illinois, and much farm land elsewhere, usually letting it out to tenants, and was in 1888 the largest owner of improved lands in the United States. He also owned timber lands and salt mines. The scale of his agricultural enterprises has hardly been appreciated. He took an active interest in experiments of all kinds for the improvement of plants; he was much interested in reclamation, as in the case of the Fox Ridge Farm, formerly a swamp, in Central New York; he cultivated the largest farm in that state. In industry and agricultural pursuits alike, he was a man of extraordinary capacity.

With his friend Ezra Cornell, he was one of the incorporators of Cornell University, and to the new institution he gave at various times the sum of $150,000 for the foundation of the Sibley College of Mechanic Arts (now Sibley College of Mechanical Engineering). He also built and presented Sibley Hall to the University of Rochester, for use as a library. To Rochester hospitals and other charitable institutions he gave at least $100,000. His personality was an agreeable one. He had much humor, and was an excellent raconteur. In his business operations he practised the methods of diplomacy rather than those of coercion. He was simple in his habits and broad in his interests. His wife was Elizabeth M. (Tinker) who, with a son and daughter, survived him. He died in Rochester.

[Encyc. of Contemporary Biog. of N. Y. (4 vols., 1878–85), vol. II; Rochester Hist. Soc. Pub. Fund Series, vol. II (1923); J. D. Reid, The Telegraph in America (1879); North Adams Transcript, July 19, 1888; N. Y. Tribune, July 13, 1888.] D. P.

SIBLEY, JOHN (May 19, 1757–Apr. 8, 1837), physician, Indian agent, Louisiana politician and planter, was descended from John Sibley who came from England in 1629 and settled at Salem, Mass. Born at Sutton, Mass., the son of Timothy and Anne (Waite) Sibley, he studied medicine with Dr. John Wilson of Hopkinton, served in the Revolution with the Continental troops as surgeon's mate, and settled for practice at Great Barrington, where in 1780 he married Elizabeth Hopkins, daughter of the Rev. Dr. Samuel Hopkins [q.v.]. After her death in 1790 at Fayetteville, N. C., to which place he had moved with his family and where he had established the *Fayetteville Gazette,* he married on Nov. 10, 1791, Mrs. Mary White Winslow. In September 1802 he moved to Louisiana, leaving his family in North Carolina but keeping up a correspondence with them until the death of his wife in 1811. Two years later he married as his third wife Eudalie Malique, a resident of Louisiana. On his arrival in New Orleans, Sibley presented letters of introduction to prominent officials, and soon became a familiar visitor to the homes of some of the élite of the colony. At Natchez, where he visited many times, he met W. C. C. Claiborne [q.v.], later governor of Orleans Territory, who was impressed with Sibley's knowledge of Louisiana and of the Indian tribes and recommended to President Jefferson that he be sent into the colony to gather information. Leaving Natchez by boat and proceeding up Red River, he arrived at Natchitoches in March 1803. Upon the arrival of the United States troops after the transfer of that post from the Spanish, he was appointed contract surgeon to the army. In 1805 he was appointed Indian agent for Orleans Territory and subsequently visited most of the tribes within the area now covered by the state of Louisiana. Reporting on their condition to both Claiborne and Jefferson, he began the gathering of a vocabulary of the tribes within the territory. Whether this was ever completed is not known, but a considerable fragment of the Caddo vocabulary is printed in the *American Naturalist* for December 1879. Sibley's reports to Jefferson were unusually complete, and are an important source of information regarding Louisiana.

Summarily removed from the office of Indian agent late in 1814 for political reasons, he entered politics himself, becoming parish judge and serving in the legislature of the state for many years. His military training served him in good stead, for he soon became colonel of militia and joined Col. James Long's raid on the province of Texas in 1819. After the capture of Nacagdoches, he was made a member of the supreme council governing the latter post (D. G. Wooten, *A Comprehensive History of Texas*, 1898, I, 97; J. H. Brown, *History of Texas*, 2 vols., 1892–93). Returning to Natchitoches, he retired to his plantation at Grande Ecore, and engaged in the manufacture of salt at Postlewaite's salt works, a few miles away, and in the planting of cotton, in which occupations he became very prosperous. At his death he left many descendants, of whom the most prominent was his son, George Champlain Sibley [*q.v.*].

[Sibley left many diaries covering his experiences in Louisiana, and many letters, in some of which he recounts the events of his early life. See Sibley Manuscript Books, parts I, 5, 6, 7, at Lindenwood College, St. Charles, Mo.; letters of John Sibley in Jefferson Papers at Lib. of Cong., in the Mo. Hist. Soc., St. Louis, in the American Antiquarian Soc., Worcester, Mass., and elsewhere. Some of his reports appear in *Am. State Papers; Indian Affairs*, vol. I (1832). See also *A Report from Natchitoches in 1807 by Dr. John Sibley* (1922), ed. by A. H. Abel; *Official Letter Books of W. C. C. Claiborne* (6 vols., 1917), ed. by Dunbar Rowland; *Early Western Travels*, ed. by R. G. Thwaites, V (1904), 129, XVII (1905), 63–68; G. P. Whittington, in *La. Hist. Quart.*, Oct. 1927; W. A. Benedict and H. A. Tracy, *Hist. of the Town of Sutton* (1878), 722–23; C. J. Taylor, *Hist. of Great Barrington* (1882).]   A. T. W.

SIBLEY, JOHN LANGDON (Dec. 29, 1804–Dec. 9, 1885), librarian, was born in Union, Me., the eldest child of Dr. Jonathan and Persis (Morse) Sibley. After studying two years at Phillips Exeter Academy, he entered Harvard, where he partly supported himself by working in the library. On his graduation in 1825 he was appointed assistant librarian at an annual salary of $150. Resigning at the end of a year to continue studying for the ministry, he graduated from the Harvard Divinity School in 1828 and became pastor of the church in Stow, Mass., where he was ordained in 1829. In 1833 he returned to Cambridge to devote himself to various literary pursuits and for three years edited the *American Magazine of Useful and Entertaining Knowledge*, an illustrated monthly journal. In March 1841, just before the removal of the Harvard College Library to Gore Hall, he was reappointed assistant librarian; fifteen years later he became librarian, succeeding Thaddeus William Harris [*q.v.*]. He married on May 20, 1866, Charlotte Augusta Langdon Cook, daughter of Samuel Cook, a Boston merchant, with whom he lived in great happiness.

At the beginning of his long term of service in the library the number of volumes was about 41,-000 and the annual income from invested funds $250; when he retired in 1877 the number of books had increased to 164,000 and the investments to $170,000. According to Sibley himself, he made so many pleas for gifts of books that he "acquired the name of being a sturdy beggar," and there must have been many a book-hunting expedition like that of Nov. 18, 1862, recorded in the "Librarian's Diary," a detailed account of the work of the library which he kept with care for years, when he "spent four hours with a lantern and cloak in the chilly cellar and found many things not in the College Library" (A. C. Potter and C. K. Bolton, *post*, p. 40). Gore Hall, which had been confidently expected to hold the accessions for the rest of the century, became inadequate, and in the last year of his librarianship, a large addition was erected which contained a book stack of six floors, said to be the first example of this familiar form of library architecture. But Sibley's service to the library was by no means confined to fostering its accessions; he introduced many administrative improvements and in every way made the books more accessible. Though at the beginning of his term the public could use only the printed catalogue of 1830, in 1861 there was begun a public card catalogue, indexed according to author and subject, in which there were introduced for the first time many features later in common use. Although he had scant sympathy for the desultory reader and has usually been pictured as a typical example of the old-style librarian, only interested in increasing his hoard of books and in protecting them from the profane touch of the reader's hands, he gave generous help to the genuinely serious seeker after knowledge and freely granted access to the alcoves, a most unusual privilege in those days.

Failing eyesight finally obliged him to resign, but he continued with his most important literary work, his *Biographical Sketches of Graduates of Harvard University* (3 vols., 1873–85), covering the lives of graduates through the class of 1689. He left to the Massachusetts Historical Society his accumulated material for later classes and a fund for the continuation of the work. He also published *A History of the Town of Union, Me.* (1851). During his librarianship he prepared twelve triennial catalogues of Harvard, 1842–75, and one quinquennial catalogue, 1880, and for twenty years, 1850–70, edited the annual catalogues. He was also an occasional contributor to magazines and to the publications of the Massachusetts Historical Society. Not a rich man, he gave to many charities, and many needy students came to him both for advice and for financial help. At Phillips Exeter Academy, in memory of his father, he established a fund of nearly fifteen thousand dollars for the aid of meritorious students; one gift to Exeter of five thousand dollars for this fund, it is reported, represented more than half of his entire property. He died after a long illness, survived by his wife.

[*Proc. Am. Acad. Arts and Sci.*, vol. XXI (1886); F. O. Vaille and H. A. Clark, *The Harvard Book* (1875), vol. I, with portrait; *Lib. Jour.*, July–Aug. 1879; *Letters of James Russell Lowell* (1893), vol. II; *Proc. Mass. Hist. Soc.*, 2 ser., vol. II (1886), with portrait; A. P. Peabody, *Harvard Reminiscences* (1888); A. C. Potter and C. K. Bolton, "The Librarians of Harvard Coll.," *Lib. of Harvard Univ., Bibliographical Contributions*, no. 52 (1897); J. L. Sibley, librarian's diary and ann. reports, MSS. in Harvard Coll. Lib.; obituary in *Boston Daily Advertiser*, Dec. 10, 1885.]
           A. C. P—t—r.

SIBLEY, JOSEPH CROCKER (Feb. 18, 1850–May 19, 1926), oil refiner, congressman from Pennsylvania, was born in Friendship, Allegheny County, N. Y., the son of Lucy Elvira (Babcock) and Joseph C. Sibley, a physician. He was the descendant of John Sibley who emigrated from England and settled in Salem, Mass., about 1634. In 1866, while he was at the Friendship academy preparing for college, his father died, and until 1871 the boy was variously occupied as school-teacher, farm worker, drugstore clerk, medical student, and, toward the end of the period, as clerk in the drygoods-store of his brother-in-law, Charles Miller, of Franklin, Pa. On Mar. 17, 1870, he was married to Metta Evalina Babcock of Friendship, N. Y. They had two children. When Miller's business failed, Sibley became Chicago agent of the Galena Oil Works of Franklin, in which Miller was a partner. In 1873, after having lost his possessions in the Chicago fire, he returned to Franklin. There, after many trials, he made a signal oil superior in several respects to the oils then in use, and in 1875 he organized the Signal Oil Works, with himself as president, and arranged to have the new oil manufactured by the Galena Oil Works. By 1879 the controlling interest in both these companies had been acquired by the Standard Oil interests. Sibley also made a new valve oil for locomotives, which, under the Standard Oil management, came into use on most of the railroads in the United States and on many in South America and Europe. When in 1902 the Galena-Signal Oil Company was formed by a merger of the two companies, Sibley became a director of the new company, and he was chairman of its board of directors from 1905 to 1910 and remained on the board until 1913.

In 1879 Sibley, then a low-tariff Republican, was elected mayor of Franklin. In 1884 he left the party on the tariff question and began to vote the Prohibition ticket. He had apparently no political ambitions until in 1892 a combination of Democrats, Populists, and Prohibitionists nominated him for congressman. Elected in a district normally Republican, he voted and spoke in Congress for free silver, becoming sufficiently prominent in its support to be mentioned by members of the Bimetallic League as a possible presidential candidate in 1896. After his first term he was twice defeated for Congress, but in 1898 he was elected as a Democrat, and for three subsequent terms he was elected as a Republican. In 1906 he declined renomination; in 1910 he was nominated but was unable to campaign because of illness. Throughout his career his interest in business and politics was paralleled by a passion for agriculture and stock-breeding. Miller and he owned jointly a large farm near Franklin, on which they conducted a profitable business. Sibley was a pioneer in breeding Jersey cattle for milk-producing records and was regarded in the nineties as one of the best judges of Jerseys in the United States. On the stock farm were probably the first silo built west of the Alleghanies and the second DeLaval separator in the United States. He was active in national agricultural and breeding associations, was for a time a member of the state board of agriculture, and in later years, by demonstrations of methods at his "River Ridge Farm" three miles from Franklin, helped to spread agricultural science among the farmers of northwestern Pennsylvania. In 1910 he retired from business and devoted himself to study and experimental agriculture at his farm. After the death of his first wife in 1911 he was married, on Dec. 6, 1913, to Ida L. Rew. He died on his farm.

[Sketches by a brother in *Hist. of Venango County, Pa.* (1890), pp. 211–17, 792–94; C. A. Babcock, *Venango County, Pa.* (1919), vol. I; J. W. Jordan, *Geneal. and Personal Hist. of the Allegheny Valley, Pa.* . . . (1913) I; H. M. Irwin, "Presidential Possibilities: Hon. Joseph C. Sibley," in *Am. Mag. of Civics*, June 1895; *Biog. Directory of the Am. Cong.* (1928); *Who's Who in America*, 1926–27; *Gazette-Times* (Pittsburgh), May 20, 1926; information from J. French Miller, secretary of the Galena Oil Corporation of Franklin, Pa., and from *U. S.* . . . *vs. Standard Oil Co. (N. J.)* . . . *In Circuit Court of U. S. for Eastern Division of Eastern Judicial District of Mo.*, esp. "Brief for Defendants on the Facts," 3 vols. (1909), "Defendants' Exhibits," vol. XIX (1909), and "Petitioner's Exhibits," vol. XXI (1909).]
           S. J. B.

SICALAMOUS [Shikellamy, d. 1748].

SICARD, MONTGOMERY (Sept. 30, 1836– Sept. 14, 1900), naval officer, was born in New York City, son of Stephen and Lydia (Hunt) Sicard. His father, of a French *émigré* family settled in Philadelphia, was engaged, before his marriage, in a mercantile business that necessitated considerable residence in Mexico; his mother was a daughter of Montgomery Hunt of Utica, N. Y., and sister of Justice Ward Hunt [*q.v.*] of the United States Supreme Court. After Stephen Sicard's death, in 1840, the family moved to Utica, where Montgomery lived until his appointment to the Naval Academy, Oct. 1, 1851.

Following cruises after graduation on the Mediterranean and China stations, he was promoted to lieutenant, May 31, 1860, and saw active service throughout the Civil War. He was executive in the *Oneida* of Farragut's squadron during the engagements with the forts and flotilla below New Orleans and the ensuing campaign around Vicksburg; then, having been promoted to lieutenant commander, July 1862, in the *Susquehanna* off Mobile, from the spring of 1863 until late in 1864 he served in the *Ticonderoga,* hunting Confederate cruisers. He commanded the gunboat *Seneca* in both attacks on Fort Fisher, and had charge of the left wing, Second Naval Division, in the severe fighting of the final land assault, Jan. 15, 1865. After post-war duty as head of the Ordnance Department, Naval Academy, he commanded the *Saginaw* in the Pacific, and was wrecked, Oct. 29, 1870, on Ocean Island, remaining there two months with his crew while Lieutenant Talbot and four men—of whom but one survived—sailed for aid 1200 miles to Hawaii in the ship's gig.

Subsequently, his distinctive achievements were in the field of ordnance, and to his patient work and scientific attainments is chiefly credited the development of modern high-power naval guns before the war with Spain. He was on ordnance duty at the New York Navy Yard, 1871–72, and afterward at Washington until 1877, designing and constructing the first steel breech-loading guns for the navy (see his pamphlet, *Description of Naval 3-Inch Breech-Loading Howitzers,* 1876). With Richard W. Meade [q.v.] he also prepared a revised edition of the *Ordnance Instructions for the United States Navy* (1880). Having been advanced through the grade of commander (Mar. 2, 1870) to that of captain in 1881, he was head of the Bureau of Ordnance for ten years following, during which period the Washington Gun Factory was established and rapid progress made in ordnance manufacture. He was president of the Steel Inspection Board, 1890–91, and in command of the monitor *Miantonomah,* 1891–93. On July 10, 1894, he was made commodore, and subsequently his duties included administration of the New York Navy Yard, 1894–96, and, after his promotion to rear admiral, April 1897, command of the North Atlantic Squadron until March 1898. Despite his declining health, he had hoped to retain the squadron in the impending war with Spain, but on the adverse verdict of a medical survey he was forced to relinquish it to his senior captain, William T. Sampson [q.v.]. The sacrifice was bitter; "I remember no more pathetic scene," writes a newspaper correspondent (W. A. M. Goode, *post,* p. 15), "than the hurried departure from Key West of this white-haired old man." Regaining strength in the North, he was made president, with A. T. Mahan [q.v.] and A. S. Crowninshield as associates, of the strategy board which largely directed the naval war.

He was retired for age Sept. 30, 1898. By his marriage, May 20, 1863, to Elizabeth Floyd, great-grand-daughter of William Floyd [q.v.], a signer of the Declaration of Independence, he had three children. After his retirement, his winters were spent in Washington and his summers in the old Floyd home at Westernville, near Utica, N. Y. His death from apoplexy occurred at Westernville, and he was buried in the Westernville cemetery. The departmental special order announcing his death spoke of him as "one of the most able, upright, and conscientious officers of the service," whose "courage, coolness, and presence of mind in time of danger were proverbial and unquestioned."

[L. R. Hamersly, *Records of Living Officers of the U. S. Navy* (1898); *War of the Rebellion: Official Records (Navy)*; G. H. Read, *The Last Cruise of the Saginaw* (1912); W. A. M. Goode, *With Sampson Through the War* (1899); J. D. Long, *The New Am. Navy* (1903); further material in annual reports of the Secretary of the Navy; *Washington Post,* Sept. 15, 1900; information from family.]
A. W.

SICKELS, FREDERICK ELLSWORTH (Sept. 20, 1819–Mar. 8, 1895), inventor, was born in Gloucester County, N. J., not far from Camden, and was the son of John and Hester Ann (Ellsworth) Sickels. He had a grade-school education in New York City, where his father, who was a practising physician, had established his residence. His chief interest in his youth was in engineering and mechanical work, and at the age of sixteen he went to work as rodman for the Harlem Railroad. A year later he began an apprenticeship as machinist in the Allaire Works in New York City and at the same time, because of his great interest in invention, studied physics and mechanics in his spare moments. In 1841, he perfected his first invention. This was the first successful drop cut-off for steam engines devised in the United States, the basic patent for which was granted him on May 20, 1842. With this mechanism the admission of steam to an engine cylinder was stopped or cut off before the end of the piston stroke, and the expansive force of the steam in the cylinder was utilized. The immediate adoption by steam-engine builders of this device, with the three improvements patented between 1843 and 1845, brought him a considerable fortune, all of which he subsequently lost in fighting infringers.

In 1846 he turned his attention to the study of steering vessels by steam engines, and on July 2, 1849, he applied for a patent on his "mode of steering ships," presenting his steam-steering apparatus. While this patent was pending (a matter of eleven years) he proceeded with the construction of a full-size steam-steering unit, and at the same time tried to find some ship owner who would permit his vessel to be used to try out the apparatus. Having been unsuccessful in this at the time the machinery was completed in 1854, he placed it as a working exhibit in the Crystal Palace, New York. At last in 1858 he succeeded in having the equipment installed on the coastwise steamer *Augusta,* plying between Savannah, Ga., and Fernandina, Fla. Two years' demonstration proved its practicability, but Sickels found no purchasers, and after he received his patent, No. 29,200, on July 17, 1860, he took the unit to England. His success there was no better than at home, although he was granted three British patents, and in 1867 he returned to the United States. His brother meanwhile had made installations on a Hudson River steamer, a United States frigate, and the steamer *Great Eastern.* During the succeeding six years Sickels continued his fruitless efforts to interest ship builders and owners. In the end, financially ruined, he abandoned the project. Turning to civil engineering, he went west to engage in railroad and bridge construction. About 1890 he was made consulting engineer of the National Waterworks Company of New York and in 1891 was detailed as chief engineer of its operations at Kansas City, Mo. In this service he died suddenly at the age of seventy-six years. He was married to Rancine Shreeves, and was survived by his widow and five children. He was buried at Paterson, N. J.

[E. W. Byrn, *Progress of Invention in the Nineteenth Cent.* (1900); R. H. Thurston, *A Hist. of the Growth of the Steam-Engine* (1891); orig. data, U. S. Museum; E. H. Knight, *Am. Mechanical Dict.* (3 vols., 1874); *Nautical Gazette,* Nov. 5, 1881; obituaries in *Kansas City Star,* Mar. 8, 1895, *Kansas City Jour.,* Mar. 8, 9, 1895, *N. Y. Tribune,* Mar. 9, 1895; Patent Office records; correspondence with family.]

C. W. M—n.

SICKLES, DANIEL EDGAR (Oct. 20, 1825–May 3, 1914), congressman, Union soldier, diplomat, was born in New York City, the son of George Garrett and Susan (Marsh) Sickles, and a descendant of Zachariah (Zacharias) Sickels, of Vienna, Austria, who entered the service of the Dutch West India Company and settled ·in America about 1656. He attended the

University of the City of New York and later engaged in the printing trade, but changed to study law under Benjamin Franklin Butler, 1795–1858 [*q.v.*]. Admitted to the bar in 1846, he was elected to the state legislature in 1847. He was married to Theresa Bagioli, the seventeen-year-old daughter of an Italian music teacher, in 1853. The same year he was appointed corporation counsel for the city of New York, but resigned to become secretary of the United States legation at London. He held this position for two years, and then he was elected to the state Senate. He served as a Democrat in Congress from 1857 to 1861, residing with his wife and little daughter in Washington, D. C. On Feb. 27, 1859, he shot and killed Philip Barton Key, the son of Francis Scott Key [*q.v.*], on account of attentions to Mrs. Sickles. In a celebrated trial in which, for the first time, the defense pleaded temporary aberration of mind, Sickles was acquitted (see *Harper's Weekly,* Mar. 12, 19, Apr. 9, 23, 1859). Sickles subsequently forgave his young wife, who died a few years later.

Although a Democrat, Sickles offered his services to President Lincoln early in March 1861, and was authorized by him to raise troops for the Federal service. Sickles organized in New York, the Excelsior Brigade, becoming first a colonel, then brigadier-general and led it, participating in the Peninsular campaign. He was promoted to the rank of major-general early in 1863, commanding the III Corps, and had an important part in the Chancellorsville campaign. It was the III Corps that, on May 2, discovered the march of Stonewall Jackson around the Federal army. Sickles reported this fact, and after some delay was instructed to attack the enemy cautiously. He did so, but arrived too late, and was surprised by the Confederate attack launched against the XI Corps, posted on his right, which broke. Falling back with his men well in hand, Sickles attacked the victorious Jackson, and after bloody fighting stopped his advance.

The last campaign of Sickles was Gettysburg. Arriving on July 2, 1863, the second day of the battle, the III Corps was stationed by George Gordon Meade [*q.v.*] to cover the Round Tops, two hills on the left. Sickles decided he could best do this by advancing to the famous peach orchard salient in front of the Round Tops. This decision later aroused a bitter controversy (see *Battles and Leaders, post,* vol. III). Meade personally examined the new line, which Sickles had assumed without specific orders, and suggested retreat, but the discussion was interrupted by a violent Confederate attack on Sickles' forces led by James Longstreet [*q.v.*]. By nightfall the III Corps had lost one-half its men, but with belated reënforcements had stopped the enemy after slight loss of ground. At the very end of the battle, Sickles was struck by a shell, which resulted in the hasty amputation of his right leg on the field. Sickles' position would have been advantageous if an offensive battle had been contemplated, but, in the opinion of Meade, the battleground at Gettysburg favored a defensive contest for the Union forces, and he later criticized Sickles in his reports. His military career now at an end, Sickles was sent on a confidential mission to South America in 1865. He returned the same year and was appointed military governor of the Carolinas, but President Johnson found him too strenuous in the execution of his duties and relieved him in 1867. He was mustered out of the volunteer army on Jan. 1, 1868, reverting to the rank of colonel in the regular army. In 1869 he was retired as a major-general.

In May 1869 he was appointed minister to Spain where the complications of the Cuban problem and the *Virginius* affair proved too much for him. His actions were so vigorous that he was called the "Yankee King," but they were not diplomatic and he resigned in December 1873, leaving to his successor, Caleb Cushing [*q.v.*], the fruits of his efforts. Senorita Carmina Creagh became his second wife on Nov. 28, 1871, at the American legation in Madrid. Sickles then lived abroad for seven years, and when he returned to the United States his wife refused to come with him. They were reconciled more than three decades later at his deathbed, through the efforts of their son. A daughter by this marrige had died in New York City. Sickles became chairman of the New York state monuments commission in 1886, but was relieved in 1912 because of mishandling funds (see *New York Times*, Jan. 23, 26, 28, 1913). He served another term in Congress from 1893 to 1895. Separated from his family, continually involved in financial troubles and altercations, the "old, irresponsible and cantankerous" gentleman spent his last years in New York City (*Literary Digest*, May 16, 1914). His one claim to honor which remained undisputed was his successful effort in 1852 to obtain Central Park for New York City. He related some of his experiences in an article "Leaves from My Diary," in the *Journal of the Military Service Association of the United States*, June and September, 1885.

[*Who's Who in America*, 1914–15; S. A. Merriam, *The Ancestry of Franklin Merriam Peabody* (1929); *Trial of the Hon. Daniel E. Sickles* (1859); *War of the Rebellion: Official Records* (Army), 1 ser., vols. XIII, XXXIX, XLIII; *Battles and Leaders of the Civil War* (1887–88), vol. III; G. G. Meade, *With Meade at Gettysburg* (1930); Francis Marshal, *The Battle of Gettysburg* (1914); *Harper's Weekly*, Sept. 14, 1867; S. F. Bemis, *The Am. Secretaries of State*, vol. VII (1928); *Nat. Tribune* (Washington, D. C.), Mar. 31, 1910; *N. Y. Times*, May 4, 1914.]   C. H. L.

SIDELL, WILLIAM HENRY (Aug. 21, 1810–July 1, 1873), engineer and soldier, son of John Sidell, was born in New York City. He received an appointment to the United States Military Academy from New York on July 1, 1829, and was graduated four years later, standing sixth in a class of forty-three. He was commissioned brevet second lieutenant of the 1st Artillery, but, disappointed at not having been assigned to the engineer corps, he resigned from the army on Oct. 1, 1833, and took up the profession of civil engineer.

For four years he served successively as city surveyor in New York City, as assistant engineer on the Croton aqueduct, as division engineer of the Long Island Railroad, and as assistant engineer on projected dry docks in New York harbor. From 1837 to 1839 he was an engineer on the United States hydrographic survey of the delta of the Mississippi, and subsequently, until 1846, served as a civil engineer of various railroads in New York and Massachusetts. During the Mexican War he accepted a captaincy in the 4th New York Volunteers, but his regiment was never mustered into the federal service. From 1846 to 1849 he was with the Isthmus (of Panama) Railroad, becoming during the last year of his service its chief engineer. For the next two years he was in the United States service, exploring for a railroad route from the Mississippi to the Pacific. In 1851–52 he was engaged in the surveying of a railroad route across the isthmus of Tehuantepec in Mexico. Thereafter he was chief engineer of various railroads in Illinois and Missouri until 1858, when he returned to Mexico as chief engineer of the Louisiana Tehuantepec Company, to complete the difficult survey of the transisthmian railroad route on which he had been engaged some years earlier.

When the Civil War broke out, he at once offered his services to the Union, and, May 14, 1861, was commissioned major of the 15th Infantry in the regular army and assigned to recruiting duty in Kentucky and Tennessee. In 1862 he was appointed acting assistant adjutant-general of the department of the Cumberland, and in 1863, acting assistant provost-marshal-general for Kentucky and general superintendent of recruiting and chief mustering and disbursing officer at Louisville, Ky., which positions he held to the end of the war. On May 6, 1864, he was promoted to lieutenant-colonel, 10th Infantry. Though Sidell's accomplishments in the war were inconspicuous, they were of the greatest importance. He organized a system by which 200,000 men were mustered in and out of the armies without delay or confusion and with an exact record of each man's service. He was brevetted colonel, May 13, 1865, for meritorious and faithful services in the recruitment of the armies of the United States, and on the same date, brigadier-general for faithful and efficient services during the war. He was on frontier duty in the Dakotas and in Kansas for the most of the time until 1870, when he was retired from active service for disability contracted in line of duty. He died at the home of his sister, Mrs. Jasper Grosvenor, in New York City.

[G. W. Cullum, *Biog. Reg. Officers and Grads. U. S. Military Acad.* (1891); *Bull. Asso. Grads., U. S. Mil. Acad., Ann. Reunion, June 1873; War of the Rebellion: Official Records (Army)*; *Am. Ann. Cyc. 1873* (1874); *Army and Navy Jour.*, July 5, 1873; *N. Y. Times*, July 2, 1873; records at headquarters U. S. Mil. Acad., West Point, N. Y.; records of Pension Bureau, Washington, D. C.]   S. J. H.

SIDIS, BORIS (Oct. 12, 1867–Oct. 24, 1923), psychopathologist, was born in Kiev, Russia, the son of Moses and Mary or Elizabeth (Marmor) Sidis. His family was in comfortable circumstances, and he was tutored at home under the direction of his father until the age of seventeen, when he was sent to a government school at Kishinev in southern Russia. While there he was arrested for political reasons along with a number of other students, subjected to solitary confinement, and then sent home where he remained under police surveillance for several years. He finally came to the United States in 1887 and settled in New York City. Being without funds, he worked in factories and gave private lessons for a living, and in his spare moments studied in the public libraries. In 1892 he entered Harvard as a special student. In 1893 he was regularly enrolled, and received the A.B. degree in 1894, the A.M. in 1895, and the Ph.D. in 1897. He was married in 1894 to Sarah Mandelbaum, and they had two children. At Harvard he attracted the attention of William James [*q.v.*], and it was undoubtedly due to James and Hugo Münsterberg [*q.v.*] that he became interested in psychology. In 1898 he published his first book, *The Psychology of Suggestion,* an attempt to explain the nature of the subconscious, especially in relation to personality. The ideas he formulated on the subject of dissociation formed the basis of his future work. William James wrote a complimentary preface to the book, describing it as an original work, although he could not agree with all of Sidis' contentions.

Sidis returned to New York to accept the position of associate psychologist and psychopathologist in the recently established Pathological Institute of the New York State Hospitals from 1896 to 1901. While there he developed the method of treatment of functional psychoses and obtained some interesting cures. In 1901 he became director of the psychopathic hospital and laboratory of the New York Infirmary for Women and Children. He published his *Psychopathological Researches, Studies in Mental Dissociation* in 1902, contributions by Drs. G. M. Parker and W. A. White being included. He advanced the theory that psychoses were due to mental dissociations. One of his most interesting cases, the reassociation of the Rev. Mr. Hanna, who was suffering from amnesia and who had acquired a second personality, is described in his book *Multiple Personality,* written in collaboration with Dr. S. P. Goodhart, and published in 1905. In 1904 Sidis returned to Massachusetts and settled in Brookline where he spent five very active years, studying medicine at the Harvard Medical School, practising psychotherapy, and continuing scientific research. Among the papers he published was "Studies in Psychopathology," in the *Boston Medical and Surgical Journal,* Mar. 14, to Apr. 11, 1907, in which he described his theory of nerve energy in connection with psychotherapeutic cures. *An Experimental Study of Sleep* (1909), based on research performed in part at the Harvard Medical School through the friendly cooperation of Dr. W. B. Cannon, attempted to prove that monotony and limitation of voluntary movements tend to raise the threshold of psychomotor activities, and thus cooperate in the induction of sleep. In 1908 he received the M.D. degree from Harvard.

In 1909 he established the Sidis Psychotherapeutic Institute at Portsmouth, N. H., where he continued to practise until his death. *The Psychology of Laughter* appeared in 1913, and expounded the Freudian idea that forms of inferiority excite laughter. In his *Symptomatology, Psychognosis, and Diagnosis of Psychopathic Diseases* (1914), however, he takes issue with the Freudian doctrine. In the same year he published *The Foundations of Normal and Abnormal Psychology,* and in 1916, *The Causation and Treatment of Psychopathic Diseases.* Sidis had a very active and forceful mentality. In addition to his special subject, he was an ardent student of political economy, philosophy, and languages. He possessed a genial and kindly nature, but was apt to express his opposition to what he considered fraudulent or dishonest with abruptness and vigor. He was of a retiring disposition, and did not seek a following of pupils. He made few contacts with his colleagues, but the few friends he did make, among them Morton Prince [*q.v.*], were his loyal admirers.

[Information from the family: *Who's Who in America*, 1922–23; *Harvard Coll., Class of 1894* (privately printed, 1919); H. Addington Bruce, "Boris Sidis— An Appreciation," *Jour. of Abnormal and Social Psychology*, Oct.–Dec. 1923.]   H. S. L.

SIDNEY, MARGARET [See LOTHROP, HARRIETT MULFORD STONE, 1844–1924].

SIGEL, FRANZ (Nov. 18, 1824–Aug. 21, 1902), soldier and editor, the son of Franz Moritz and Maria Anna (Lichtenauer) Sigel, was born in Sinsheim, Baden, Germany. His father was chief magistrate of a district. After completing his studies in the Gymnasium of Bruchsal, Franz entered the military academy of Karlsruhe from which he graduated in 1843 to become a lieutenant in the grand ducal service. His liberal political views brought him into conflict with the existing régime, and in 1847, after severely wounding an opponent in a duel, he resigned from the service. In the insurrection in Baden in 1848, as an associate of Friedrich Karl Franz Hecker [*q.v.*], he led an army of 4,000 revolutionists against the government but was defeated and compelled to flee to Switzerland. The next year, when a revolutionary government succeeded in establishing itself in the duchy, he was recalled and became minister of war. He took the field against the Prussian army sent to restore the old order, but his inferior force was soon overpowered and he was again forced into exile in Switzerland. His reminiscences of these years were published in Germany in 1902 under the title, *Denkwürdigkeiten aus den Jahren, 1848 und 1849.* He spent the year 1851–52 in England and then emigrated to America and settled in New York City, where he became an instructor in the private school of Dr. Rudolph Dulon. He maintained an interest in military affairs and became a major in the 5th Regiment of the New York militia. He accepted a position as instructor in mathematics and history in the German-American institute of St. Louis, Mo., in the fall of 1857 and subsequently became a director of schools in that city.

When the Civil War broke out, Sigel organized the 3rd Missouri Infantry and, on May 4, 1861, became colonel. He performed efficient service in saving St. Louis, with its important arsenal, for the Union, and was soon assigned to command the 2nd Missouri Brigade, being appointed brigadier-general of volunteers to date from May 17, 1861. During the remainder of the year he took part in a number of battles in the struggle for the possession of Missouri. At the battle of Pea Ridge, Ark., Mar. 7–8, 1862, Sigel commanded two divisions in Frémont's army, and by his gallantry and skill contributed greatly to the decisive Union victory which settled the fate of Missouri. He was promoted to the rank of major-general of volunteers on Mar. 21, 1862, and in June became commander of the I Corps in Pope's army of Virginia. In this capacity he took a prominent part in the second battle of Bull Run. In September 1862 his corps was transferred to the Army of the Potomac as the XI Corps. Later, when Burnside divided that army into grand divisions, Sigel was given the reserve grand division, consisting of the XI and XII Corps, but in February 1863, he reverted to the command of the XI Corps. Owing to bad health he gave up his command temporarily in the spring of 1863, and when he returned to duty in the summer he was given a subordinate command in the department of the Susquehanna. He was assigned to command the department of West Virginia in March 1864, but a serious defeat at the hands of Breckinridge at New Market in the Shenandoah Valley, on May 15, 1864, cost him his command and he was removed to Harpers Ferry.

When Early's raid threatened Washington in July 1864, Sigel, by skilfully occupying a strong position on Maryland Heights, delayed Early's greatly superior force. The authorities, however, at no time had considered him sufficiently aggressive and now removed him from command. He resigned his commission in May 1865 and became for two years an editor of the *Baltimore Wecker,* a German newspaper in Baltimore, Md. In 1867 he moved to New York City where he spent the remainder of his life. His great influence with the German element soon brought him into politics. From 1866 to 1869 he was pension agent in New York, and two years later he was appointed collector of internal revenue for the city, later being elected register. He was a prominent lecturer and kept himself in the public eye as publisher and editor of the *Neu Yorker Deutsches Volksblatt,* and from 1897 to 1900 as editor of the *New York Monthly.* A love for free government had been the ruling motive of Sigel's life. His military successes were not of the greatest, but his prompt and ardent espousal of the Union cause was a great factor in uniting the large German population of the North, with which he was extremely popular, solidly behind the Union. In October 1907, a bronze equestrian statue of Sigel, by Karl Bitter [*q.v.*], was unveiled with impressive ceremonies on Riverside Drive in New York City. He had been married to Elise Dulon, the daughter of his first employer, in January 1854. She and their five children survived him when he died in New York City.

[Who's Who in America, 1901–02; C. W. Schlegel, Schlegel's German-Am. Families in the U. S., vol. I (1916); F. K. F. Hecker, Die Erhebung des Volkes in Baden (1848); War of the Rebellion: Official Records (Army), see index; Battles and Leaders of the Civil War (1887–88), vol. IV; N. Y. Times, Aug. 22, 23, 1902, Oct. 20, 1907; New-Yorker Staats-Zeitung, Aug. 22, 23, 24, 1902, Oct. 13, 20, 1907.]   S. J. H.

SIGMAN, MORRIS (May 15, 1881–July 20, 1931), labor leader, was born in Costesh, Bessarabia, Province of Hatino Uezd, the son of Samuel and Rebecca (Sikernetsky) Sigman. The son of a farmer in a small Bessarabian-Russian village, he received little schooling, and as a Jew and a subject of the czar of Russia he lived in an atmosphere of persecution and hate. At twenty-one he emigrated to London, where for a year he worked in a men's clothing shop. Initiated into the ideals of the labor movement, he journeyed to New York in 1903 and found employment on the East Side as a presser in a cloak shop, where he soon formed the Independent Cloakmakers' Union. Joining at first with those in the labor movement who favored opposition of "dual unions," he was led into the Industrial Workers of the World when it was formed in 1905; by 1908 he had come to believe that destroying existing unions by founding opposition unions was detrimental to the interests of the workers, and he helped to induce his and other I.W.W. locals of ladies' garment workers to affiliate with the International Ladies' Garment Workers' Union of the American Federation of Labor.

When the International Ladies' Garment Workers' Union undertook to control cut-throat competition and deplorably bad working conditions, the employers resisted, and the union became involved in a series of bitter strikes. In the historic strike of 1910, which established the union on a firm foundation, Sigman honorably acquitted himself in the difficult and dangerous position of chairman of the picket committee. When the employers consented to negotiate with the union he was selected as a member of the joint conference committee. This established the famous "Protocol," signed Sept. 2, 1910, which created permanent machinery consisting of representatives of labor, capital, and the public to supervise and regulate all relations in the industry. But permanent peace was not attained. During a strike in 1915 Sigman and seven other leaders were arrested and confined to jail while awaiting trial on charges of murder; with the others, he was later acquitted by a jury. In his own Pressers' Union, Local No. 35, he served in every important post from member of the executive board to business agent and manager. He was also the organizer and manager of the Boston unions in their formative period; the organizer, 1909, and manager, 1917–21, of the New York Joint Board of Cloakmakers' Unions (the coördinating body of the local unions of this trade); and vice-president, 1920–22, secretary-treasurer, 1914–15, of the International Union. He was in charge of establishing the New York Joint Board of the Dressmakers' Unions, and acted as its first manager. In February 1923 he became general president, a position he held to October 1928, when ill health caused him to resign. During his term as president two events shook the union to its very foundations. Before the World War a difference of opinion, later known as the Left and Right controversy, had developed within the ranks; after the Bolshevik revolution the Communists assumed leadership of the Lefts and organized themselves under the auspices of the Trade Union Educational League, formed in 1920. Sigman condemned this procedure as a dual union movement which aimed to disrupt the International Union and succeeded in disbanding the opposing Lefts, but the union suffered severe losses in membership. At the same time economic conditions in the industry once more became chaotic through the appearance of the jobber, who controlled the markets. Under Sigman's leadership a new economic program for the industry was devised. Failing to win the employers through negotiation, the union induced the governor to appoint an advisory committee, which succeeded in reconciling the two elements, and temporarily at least conditions were improved.

Sigman died in Storm Lake, Iowa, survived by his wife, Mathilda Sikernetsky, who was his cousin and whom he had married on Mar. 17, 1912. Although neither an orator nor a "showman," he was an effective and logical speaker. He showed little trace of vanity and remained to the end the simple but intelligent worker. Like most Jewish labor leaders he retained his socialist ideology, but reversed the emphasis. In his youth he stressed ultimate ideals; in his later years he fostered immediate reforms, with the hope that in addition to improving the conditions of the time they might ultimately bring about the overthrow of the wage system.

[Report of Proc. . . . Ann. Convention Internat. Ladies' Garment Workers' Union, 1908–31; Ladies' Garment Worker, 1910–18, Justice, 1919–31, official pubs. of the union; L. L. Lorwin, The Women's Garment Workers (1924); N. Y. Times, July 21–24, 1931;

information from Sigman's widow through the courtesy of Miss F. M. Cohn, Executive Secretary, Educ. Dept., Internat. Ladies' Garment Workers' Union.] D. J. S.

SIGOURNEY, LYDIA HOWARD HUNTLEY (Sept. 1, 1791–June 10, 1865), author, the only child of Ezekiel Huntley and his second wife Zerviah (Wentworth) Huntley, was born at Norwich, Conn., in the house of Mrs. Daniel Lathrop, by whom her father was employed as gardener. On her father's side she was of Scotch descent, her grandfather having emigrated from Scotland as a young man. For old Mrs. Lathrop she formed a sentimental attachment that inspired scores of youthful poems and left its impress on her whole life. She was educated in Norwich and Hartford. From 1811 to 1813 she conducted a school in Norwich with a friend, and in 1814 went to Hartford to establish a small school for girls. For their use she wrote much of her first book, *Moral Pieces, in Prose and Verse* (1815), and her persuasive teaching and kindly personality had an enduring influence upon her young pupils. But the promising career was interrupted by her marriage, June 16, 1819, to a widower with three children, Charles Sigourney, who had come from Boston in 1800 to open a hardware business in Hartford. A man of good classical education, he was inclined to be a little over-precise and pedantic, but he commanded general respect, and Mrs. Sigourney's friends believed that the humble school mistress had made a very fortunate marriage.

Finding, however, that her husband's affluence had been exaggerated, she turned to writing to supplement her means—anonymously at first, since her husband bitterly opposed her writing under her own name. Her success was marked. By 1830 she was contributing regularly to more than twenty periodicals, and three years later she dropped her anonymity. The volumes of prose and verse that appeared regularly each year and her constant contributions to the magazines and the newly risen annuals—she herself edited *The Religious Souvenir* for 1839 and 1840 —soon brought her a good income. Such edifying volumes as *How To Be Happy* (1833) and *Letters to Young Ladies* (1833), were followed by numerous poems and sketches, reading books for children, several memoirs, even by a *History of Marcus Aurelius, Emperor of Rome* (1836). She was so popular that she was paid well by Louis Godey [*q.v.*] for the mere use of her name as an editor of the *Lady's Book*; her contributions at the same time to the rival *Ladies' Companion* brought strong protests from him. It is almost impossible to find a number of one of the popular magazines of the thirties or forties that does not contain a poem or an article by her, and though Edgar Allan Poe [*q.v.*] in a review in the *Southern Literary Messenger* for January 1836 accused her of too direct imitation of other writers he continued to solicit her contributions.

By 1840 "the American Hemans" was sufficiently prosperous to go to Europe to secure new literary material, of which she was in urgent need. Toward the end of her two months' stay in Paris, she was presented to Louis Philippe; most of the time, however, she lived in England, attending to the publication of *Pocahontas, and Other Poems* (1841), *Poems, Religious and Elegiac* (1841), and a new edition of her *Letters to Young Ladies,* cultivating "literary friendships," calling on Samuel Rogers, the Carlyles and the Wordsworths, and distributing presentation copies of her poems with a lavish hand. On her return to America the inclusion in *Pleasant Memories of Pleasant Lands* (1842) of extracts from a letter of Mrs. Robert Southey gave the world its first intimation of the Poet Laureate's mental disintegration and precipitated a storm of recrimination. Mrs. Sigourney, who had never seen Mrs. Southey, was accused of having interpolated in the letter "phrases implying intimacy and ejaculations of pathos," and in spite of the warm defense of her friends the affair was never satisfactorily explained.

She spent the rest of her life quietly in Hartford, writing, busying herself with charities, receiving the visiting celebrities who stopped to pay their respects. Her fellow citizens were proud to think that this demure lady who sewed and knitted and chatted like one of themselves was at the same time "the recipient of costly gifts from Royalty in honor of her Muse" and "the most famous of the female bards of her country." In her later years she was described as a short little woman in a full dress of black satin and a fine lace cap with wide satin ribbons, her hands soft and patrician, and her flaxen curls carefully arranged (Louise J. R. Chapman, "A Visit to Mrs. Sigourney," *Connecticut Quarterly,* Jan.–Mar. 1895, p. 47). Regularly, year after year, appeared the sentimental volumes. Among the number of pious memoirs she wrote is *The Faded Hope* (1853), an account of her son Andrew, who died in 1850, not yet twenty. The death of her austere husband in 1854 and the marriage of her daughter left her quite alone, but there was no cessation in the steady stream of books—sixty-seven all told—which her unimpeachable morality and tuneful echoing of conventional sentiments made popular. Vigorous at its best, her prose style, like her poetry, is too often spoiled by absurd circumlocutions and an affected elegance. The theme of most of her writing is death. The inevitable regularity with which her poetic tribute followed the demise of any prominent person led a wag to declare that she had added a new terror to death. She herself died in Hartford, survived only by her daughter. Her autobiography, *Letters of Life* (1866), was published after her death.

[The chief source is the correspondence of Lydia H. Sigourney, Conn. Hist. Soc., Hartford. Her letters to Theodore Dwight are in the N. Y. Pub. Lib. See also her autobiography, *Letters of Life* (1866), *Sketch of Conn.*, *Forty Years Since* (1824), *Pleasant Memories of Pleasant Lands* (1842), and *The Faded Hope* (1853); R. W. Griswold, *The Female Poets of America* (1874); J. S. Hart, *The Female Prose Writers of America*, (1852); S. A. Allibone, *A Crit. Dict. of Eng. Lit. and British and Am. Authors*, vol. II (1870); Gordon S. Haight, *Mrs. Sigourney, The Sweet Singer of Hartford* (1930), with portraits and bibliog.; obituary in *Hartford Daily Courant*, June 12, 1865.]   G. S. H.

SIGSBEE, CHARLES DWIGHT (Jan. 16, 1845–July 19, 1923), naval officer, son of Nicholas and Agnes (Orr) Sigsbee, was born in Albany, N. Y. Appointed to the United States Naval Academy in 1859, he was graduated in 1863, made ensign, and assigned to the *Monongahela* and, later, to the *Brooklyn* of the West Gulf Blockading Squadron. He participated in the battle of Mobile Bay, Aug. 5, 1864, and was given special mention for his gallant conduct by his commanding officer, Capt. James Alden. Transferred to the North Atlantic Blockading Squadron, he took part in both attacks on Fort Fisher. In 1865 he was assigned to the Asiatic Squadron, and in 1869 was ordered to duty as an instructor at the Naval Academy. Here he served, in all, three tours of duty, 1869–71, 1882–85, and 1887–90, besides commanding the *Dale* and *Constellation* in three midshipmen practice cruises.

His most notable peace-time achievement was his work while in command of the Coast Survey steamer *Blake*, 1875–78. During these years, associated with Alexander Agassiz [*q.v.*], he was engaged in deep-sea explorations, principally in the Gulf of Mexico, where he made a complete deep-water survey of the Gulf. In recognition of this work its deepest area was named Sigsbee Deep. While on this duty he invented a deep-sea sounding machine, based on the wire sounding apparatus of Sir William Thomson; a water specimen cup for collecting specimens at various depths at a single haul; a gravitating or collecting trap for obtaining animal specimens from intermediate ocean depths; and a detaching apparatus to be used with a specimen-collecting cylinder originally devised by Commander George E. Belknap [*q.v.*]. These appliances practically revolutionized deep-sea sounding and dredging. For his contributions to the advance of scientific exploration Emperor William I of Germany bestowed upon him the decoration of the Red Eagle of Prussia; a gold medal, also, was given him at the International Fisheries Exhibition of London. He spent a total of ten years in the hydrographic office at Washington, and from 1893 to 1897 was chief hydrographer to the Navy Department.

Having been advanced through the preceding grades, he was commissioned captain Mar. 21, 1897, and was in command of the battleship *Maine* from April 10 of that year until she was blown up and destroyed in Havana Harbor, Feb. 15, 1898. The naval court of inquiry exonerated him and his officers and crew from all blame for the disaster. Sigsbee's temperate, judicious dispatches at the time did much to avert a popular demand for immediate reprisal against Spain. On May 25, 1898, in command of the *St. Paul*, he captured the British collier *Restormel* laden with coal for Cervera's squadron. On June 22 he engaged and defeated the Spanish destroyer *Terror* and the cruiser *Isabella II* off San Juan, Puerto Rico. For his services during the war he was advanced three numbers in rank with the citation: "For extraordinary heroism displayed during War with Spain and on the occasion of the wreck of *Maine*."

Commissioned rear-admiral Aug. 11, 1903, after a year at the League Island Navy Yard, he was given command of the Caribbean Squadron. On June 18, 1905, he sailed for Cherbourg, France, with a fleet of four ships and brought back the body of John Paul Jones in his flagship, the *Brooklyn*, arriving at Annapolis, July 23, 1905. After commanding the second squadron of the Atlantic Fleet for two years, he was retired Jan. 16, 1907. He wrote *Deep Sea Sounding and Dredging* (1880), and *The Maine, an Account of her Destruction in Havana Harbor* (1899). A veteran of two wars, in both of which he won the recognition of his superiors, Admiral Sigsbee achieved greater distinction for his services as an inventor and scientist than as a warrior, though his conduct at the time of the destruction of the *Maine* won him great popular acclaim. In November 1870 he married Eliza Rogers Lockwood, by whom he had one son and three daughters.

[*Army and Navy Jour.*, July 28, 1923; *Army and Navy Reg.*, July 28, 1923; L. R. Hamersly, *The Records of Living Officers of the U. S. Navy and Marine Corps* (1898); *Message from the President of the U. S. Transmitting the Report of the Naval Court of Inquiry Upon the Destruction of the U. S. Battleship Maine* (1898), being *Sen. Doc.* 207, 55 Cong., 2 Sess.; *John Paul Jones Commemoration at Annapolis* (1907), being *House Doc.* 804, 59 Cong., 1 Sess.; J. R. Spears, *Our Navy in the War with Spain* (1898); reports of the U. S. Coast and Geodetic Survey, 1877, 1878, 1879;

Ann. Report of the Chief of the Bureau of Navigation, 1898, Appendix; Who's Who in America, 1922–23; War of the Rebellion: Official Records (Navy); N. Y. Times, July 20, 1923.]   L. H. B.

SIKES, WILLIAM WIRT (Nov. 23, 1836–Aug. 18, 1883), journalist and author, was the son of Dr. William Johnson and Meroe (Redfield) Sikes. Born in Watertown, N. Y., where he lived as a boy, he attended the local schools. At the early age of sixteen he threw himself whole-heartedly into the temperance movement and lectured frequently in Watertown and its vicinity. When his youthful enthusiasm subsided, as it did soon, he entered the office of a local paper, where he learned the printing trade, and for a time conducted a sheet of his own. In 1855 he married Jeannette A. Wilcox, by whom he had a son and daughter, and in the following year became employed on the *Utica Morning Herald*. During the past few years he had frequently contributed to home and out-of-town papers tales and poems, some of which he collected in 1858 under the title *A Book for the Winter-Evening Fireside*. A more active mode of life now presenting itself, in 1861 he accepted the position of state canal inspector of Illinois, but two years later he was working on the *Chicago Evening Journal*. A life of wandering had become a habit with him, and in 1865 he removed to New York, where in the course of the next few years he contributed to such papers as the *Youth's Companion, Oliver Optic's Magazine, Harper's New Monthly Magazine,* and the *Sun* (N. Y.). It was at this time that he also established the Authors' Union. Settling in Nyack, N. Y., about 1868, for a few years he edited *City and Country* (Nyack) and the Rockland County *Journal* (Piermont, N. Y.), in both of which he possessed a financial interest. While working in Chicago he had given much time to the study of social conditions among the lower classes, and during his residence in New York and elsewhere he continued his investigations of city slums. This interest in social problems is reflected in a number of magazine articles, but especially in two novels, "The World's Broad Stage" published serially in the *Toledo Weekly Blade,* beginning Jan. 2, 1868, and *One Poor Girl* (1869). In 1870 he was divorced from his first wife and on Dec. 19, 1871, was married in New York to the well-known actress and lecturer, Olive Logan [*q.v.*], with whom he had been previously associated as a business manager (*Evening Post,* N. Y., Dec. 20, 1871). Among his varied hobbies at this time was an interest in art. A visit he made to the Wiertz Museum, Brussels, early in the seventies resulted in a biographical and critical sketch of Antoine Wiertz, contributed to *Harper's New Monthly Magazine* for May 1873, which was deemed worthy of being prefixed to the *Catalogue of the Wiertz-Museum . . .* (1899), a pamphlet published in English at Brussels. During his journalistic career he published much anonymously, employing, it is said, some twenty-two pseudonyms.

In June 1876 he was appointed United States consul to Cardiff, Wales. In his newly acquired leisure he turned his attention to the region surrounding Cardiff, rich in old Welsh folklore. "I have tramped the green lanes and roads of rural and the streets of urban South Wales so persistently during my residence at Cardiff," he writes, "that I almost know them inch by inch" (*Rambles and Studies in Old South Wales,* p. vii). The results of these excursions found ample expression in two interesting works, certainly the most enduring of his literary labors: *British Goblins: Welsh Folk-Lore, Fairy Mythology, Legends, and Traditions* (1880), favorably noticed in the English *Saturday Review* (Nov. 22, 1879), and *Rambles and Studies in Old South Wales* (1881). His last book, *Studies of Assassination* (1881), was a work of little permanent importance. He died at Cardiff, while still acting as consul, at the age of forty-six; he was buried in London.

[Much information has been furnished by Sikes's son, George P. Sikes. See G. P. Sikes, *By the Name of Sikes or Sykes* (1927); J. H. Redfield, *Geneal. Hist. of the Redfield Family in the U. S.* (1860); *Index to Harper's New Monthly Mag.,* vols. I–LXX (1886), for a list of Sikes's contributions; obituary by G. P. Sikes in *Sunday News* (Buffalo), Aug. 26, 1883; brief death notices in *Harper's New Monthly Mag.,* Nov. 1883, *Times* (London), and *Evening Post,* (N. Y.), Aug. 20, 1883.]   N. F. A.

SILL, ANNA PECK (Aug. 9, 1816–June 18, 1889), pioneer in women's education, youngest daughter of Abel and Hepsibah (Peck) Sill, was born in Burlington, Otsego County, N. Y. She was a descendant of Puritan ancestors, John and Joanna Sill, of England, who settled at Cambridge, Mass., about 1637; later the family removed to Connecticut and thence in 1789 to Otsego County. Her father was a farmer, quiet, industrious, and intelligent, and her mother, the daughter of Judge Jedediah Peck, a woman of great energy of character. Anna attended the district school. The early discipline of domestic duties, the inspiration of nature, and above all a "thirst for knowledge and religion" constituted the mainsprings of her life. To prayer she was so early accustomed that she regarded it as innate; the Bible and the Book of Common Prayer constituted her earliest books; and yet, she says, her soul "cried out for its God," and she "groped in the dark but did not find Him." Thus she continued till 1831, when, apparently, the "wind from the Holy Spirit" which blew over New England and surrounding territory, producing great revivals, touched her soul with peace.

At twenty she left Burlington to teach a district school at Barre, N. Y., near Albion, for which she received two dollars a week. In the vacation she attended school at Albion and entered the Phipps Union Seminary, a pioneer among institutions for girls' education. A year later she became one of the teachers at Phipps, where she continued till 1843. After considering the foreign missionary field in India, she turned to the great West, which was itself coming to be considered a fruitful field for missionary activity. Failing to find an opportunity there at the time, she went alone to Warsaw, N. Y., and in 1843 opened a seminary for ladies which, though it seems to have been an immediate success, was discontinued three years later. Between 1846 and 1849 she had charge of the female department of Cary Collegiate Institute, Oakfield, N. Y., and then accepted the invitation of Rev. Lewis H. Loss to open a school for girls at Rockford, Ill. On July 11 (*Memorials, post,* p. 15) she noted in her journal: "Today commenced school, and laid the foundation of Rockford Female Seminary. Opened with fifty-three scholars. O Lord, fit me for my work and glorify Thyself thereby." For the first two years, only preparatory work was done. The first seminary class entered in 1851, and a new building, begun in 1852, was crowded at once. To secure funds and regain failing strength, she went East and returned in 1854 with a fund of $5,000. In that year a three-year collegiate course was begun, which after 1865 became a four-year course. After 1882 collegiate degrees were conferred, and in 1892 the name of the institution was changed to Rockford College. In her work Anna Sill sought to reach the less favored classes, to combine domestic training with intellectual culture, to infuse a moral and religious culture through the school, and to foster a "missionary spirit" and "self-denying benevolence" toward all. The education of women, because of their influence in the family, she regarded as not less but more important than that of men. Though she retired from active service in 1884, she continued as principal emerita until her death, which occurred in Rockford.

[The birthplace is taken from Miss Sill's tombstone in Rockford, Ill. See G. G. Sill, *Geneal. of the Descendants of John Sill* (1859); *Memorials of Anna P. Sill, First Principal of Rockford Female Seminary* (1889); Hazel P. Cederborg, "The Early Hist. of Rockford Coll." (master's thesis, Wellesley Coll., 1926); official records of Rockford Female Seminary, 1849–84; C. A. Church, *Hist. of Rockford and Winnebago County, Ill.* (1900); Thomas Woody, *A Hist. of Women's Educ. in the U. S.* (2 vols., 1929); obituaries in *Rockford Daily Register,* June 18, 1889, and *Rockford Morning Star,* June 21, 1889.]   T. W.

SILL, EDWARD ROWLAND (Apr. 29, 1841–Feb. 27, 1887), poet and teacher, was born at Windsor, Conn., the son of Theodore and Elizabeth Newberry (Rowland) Sill. On his mother's side he was descended from a line of New England clergymen, one of whom, the Rev. David Sherman Rowland, as pastor in Providence, R. I., had taken an active part in the Revolution; and on his father's from John Sill, who emigrated from England to Cambridge, Mass., about 1637. Theodore Sill, like his father before him, was a physician widely beloved in the little community. After the death of his older son in 1847 and of his wife in 1852, he removed to Cleveland with his one child, and there, not long after opening an office, he too died in 1853. The boy now went to live with his uncle, Elisha Noyes Sill, at Cuyahoga Falls, Ohio. After a year at Phillips Exeter Academy and one at the preparatory school of Western Reserve College at Hudson, Ohio, he entered Yale in the fall of 1857, to graduate four years later with the class of 1861, in spite of the fact that at the end of his freshman year he was removed from college for neglecting his studies and was away for over a year. It was an hour of ebbing tides in the intellectual history of Yale, and he appears to have rebelled against the uninspired routine of college discipline; his poverty, however, and his native fastidiousness together imposed strict limitations on his protestantism, and he was remembered by his college contemporaries chiefly for his fine seriousness and brilliant literary promise. In his senior year he was on the editorial board of the *Yale Literary Magazine,* and the class poem he read at Commencement was long famous as one of the finest in Yale history.

On leaving college he was led, partly by the delicacy of his health, to make a sea voyage round the Horn to California. It was scarcely a nourishing atmosphere for a young poet of his type. The career of letters, if he had ever envisaged it practically, soon receded into the far distance, and, with characteristic plainness and freedom from self-pity, he turned his hand to such tasks as offered themselves. For some time he acted as clerk in the post-office at Sacramento; later he worked in a bank at Folsom. All the while he was casting about restlessly for a permanent profession. After fruitless attempts at reading law and then medicine he returned to the East in 1866, revisited Cuyahoga Falls for a few months, and in 1867 spent the early part of the year as a student at the Harvard Divinity School. It was the last of his experiments to give negative results. "Emerson could not preach," he wrote to his classmate, Henry Holt [q.v.], in August 1867, "and I now understand why." Strong as the hereditary bias was and constant as his own preoccupation was with essentially religious speculations, he could not ally himself with the institutionalized Protestantism of nineteenth-century America. "On religion," he wrote many years later to a young correspondent, "I doubt your ever agreeing with me that the church is a great fraud and nuisance. I am convinced it is doing infinitely more harm than good, every day and week."

He now spent several rather obscure months in New York making trial of journalism on the *New York Evening Mail*; and in the spring of 1868 he published *The Hermitage and Other Poems*, the one volume of his verse to appear publicly in his lifetime, and *Mozart, a Biographical Romance*, a translation from the German of Heribert Rau. In 1867, however, he had married his cousin, Elizabeth Newberry Sill, daughter of Elisha Noyes Sill, and he soon abandoned so unpredictable a calling, no doubt partly for economic reasons. Moreover, the desire to play a useful rôle in society was as strong in him as the desire to express himself in ideal form. He now returned to an old purpose, that of becoming a teacher. After three years of apprenticeship in Ohio, during the latter two years of which he was superintendent of schools at Cuyahoga Falls, he taught the classics and English at the high school in Oakland, Cal., 1871–74. From 1874 to 1882 he held the chair of English at the University of California, having been invited there by Daniel Coit Gilman [q.v.]. Undoubtedly one of the great teachers of his generation, without being a scholar in the strict professional sense, he had made himself a man of wide intellectual culture; his interest in exact science, for instance, was almost more continuous than his interest in letters, and his teaching was illuminated by his concern both for general ideas and for the realization of values in experience. Not that he substituted "inspiration" for less beguiling appeals: he is said to have been methodical even to austerity and exacting enough to antagonize the faint-hearted. But his personal distinction was so great and his high-mindedness so easily borne that only the dullest could resist his influence. Part of his impressiveness depended, superficially, on his striking appearance. Tall and very slender, he carried himself with an easy elegance; the pure and delicately cut outline of his features, the grave beauty of his dark blue-gray eyes, which

everyone spoke of as they spoke of Hawthorne's, the rich flexibility of his voice, the expressive responsiveness of his whole manner were outward facts that seemed in harmony with his essential spirit. The administrations that followed upon Gilman's were far from being so sympathetic to the humanities as his had been; the pressure from outside toward emphasis on technology and vocationalism was organized and truculent; and Sill was not happy during his last two or three years at Berkeley. Partly on this account, partly for family reasons, he resigned from his chair in March 1882, and the following year, after issuing privately a small volume of poems, *The Venus of Milo and Other Poems* (1883), he returned to his father-in-law's home in Cuyahoga Falls. He now contributed frequent anonymous essays to the *Atlantic Monthly*, as well as poems to it and other magazines, often under the pseudonym of Andrew Hedbrooke, but his last years were troubled by intellectual isolation, by private anxieties, and by ill-health. He died prematurely, following a minor operation, in a hospital in Cleveland.

As a prose-writer he can hardly be said to have an important place in literature. His essays, collected in 1900 as *The Prose of Edward Rowland Sill*, have a certain tenuous charm, and through some of them his fastidious humor shines pleasantly and mildly, but their substance is mostly of the slightest. Nor can even the best of his poetry (*The Poems of Edward Rowland Sill*, 1902) be said to loom imposingly on the horizon. It suffers from his own refusal after his earliest youth to take himself quite seriously as a writer. Nevertheless his gifts, if limited, were delicate and true, and his verse has a warm undercurrent of thoughtfulness and deep feeling. Mainly this is due to the sense it conveys of the spiritual conflicts that lay behind it. More than any other American verse of the time except that of Herman Melville [q.v.], it is colored by metaphysical doubt and perplexity and fatigue. Unable to accept the certainties of the Christian religion without scrutiny, he was unable also to dispense with spiritual assurance, and in consequence he is one of the authentic voices of the age's malady. Yet he was not merely a poet of low spirits, and many of his finest poems, such as "The Fool's Prayer" and "Opportunity," give expression to a humane and even humanitarian idealism which is the worthy American equivalent of Matthew Arnold's modern stoicism. The purity of his language and imagery, moreover, —its freedom, at its best, from the literary honey of his day,—accounts very largely for the pleasure with which it can still be read.

[H. R. Stiles, *The Hist. and Geneal. of Ancient Windsor, Conn.*, vol. II (1892); A. P. Stokes, *Memorials of Eminent Yale Men* (2 vols., 1914); *Obit. Record Grads. Yale Univ.* (1890); *The Twenty-Five Years' Record . . . Class of 1861, Yale Coll.* (1888), with bibliog.; W. B. Parker, *Edward Rowland Sill: His Life and Work* (1915); *A Memorial of Edward Rowland Sill . . . Together with Extracts from His Correspondence* (1887); *The Prose of Edward Rowland Sill* (1900), introduction; correspondence with Milicent W. Shinn, J. C. Rowell, and Eloise Hersey; correspondence and interview with Anna M. Sill; obituary in *Appletons' Ann. Cyc.*, 1887; death notice in *Cleveland Plain Dealer*, Mar. 1, 1887.]   N. A.

SILLIMAN, BENJAMIN (Aug. 8, 1779–Nov. 24, 1864), professor of chemistry and natural history in Yale College from 1802 to 1853, was the most prominent and influential scientific man in America during the first half of the nineteenth century. There is a tradition that his paternal ancestors were of Italian origin, Sillimandi by name, but long domiciled in Switzerland, and that from there, by way of Holland, the first of the family came to America at the time of the great Puritan migration, settling eventually near what is now Fairfield, Conn. In the records of Fairfield County he appears as Daniel Sillivant. By 1690 the name of the family had been changed to Silliman and its members were becoming people of substance and prominence. Benjamin's grandfather, Ebenezer Silliman, graduated from Yale College in 1727, as did his son, Benjamin's father, Gold Selleck Silliman, in 1752. Both followed the law as a profession. The former was a member of the Governor's Council and a judge of the superior court; the latter was a general in the Continental Army in charge of the defense of Connecticut against the British. On the side of his mother, Mary, daughter of Rev. Joseph and Rebecca (Peabody) Fish of North Stonington, Conn., Benjamin Silliman was descended from Puritan stock through the Peabodys of Rhode Island, who derived from John and Priscilla Alden.

He was born in a part of what is now Trumbull, Conn., and brought up at Fairfield. His early education was secured in the local schools. He was prepared for college by the Rev. Andrew Eliot and entered Yale in 1792 at the age of thirteen years, the youngest but one in his class. He graduated in 1796 and after two years spent partly at home and partly teaching in a private school at Wethersfield, Conn., returned to New Haven and began the study of law under Simeon Baldwin and David Daggett [*qq.v.*], leaders of the Connecticut bar. He was admitted to the bar in 1802. Meanwhile, from September 1799 he had served as a tutor in Yale College.

In September 1802, at the age of twenty-three, he was appointed to the newly established professorship of chemistry and natural history in Yale College. The next two years he devoted largely to study in preparation for his new duties, chiefly in Philadelphia, where he attended lectures in chemistry, botany, anatomy, and surgery at the medical school. Of greater importance to him, however, was an opportunity to work in the laboratory of the able chemist and physicist Robert Hare [*q.v.*], and of more value still were occasional visits to Dr. John Maclean [*q.v.*], professor of chemistry at Princeton, a very able and scholarly man from whom he learned much and received many valuable suggestions regarding the teaching of that science.

He began the duties of his new position in April 1804 with a course of experimental lectures in chemistry, the first ever given at Yale. In the spring of 1805 he sailed for England, partly for the purpose of purchasing books for the college library and scientific apparatus for his laboratory, but chiefly to extend his knowledge of science through study and association with foreign scholars. He traveled through England, Wales, and Scotland, and also visited Holland, but the disturbed condition of the Continent prevented him from visiting other countries. The greater part of his time was spent in London and Edinburgh, where he met on intimate and informal terms the most distinguished scholars of the times, among them Sir Humphrey Davy, Sir David Brewster, Dr. John Murray, and Dr. Thomas Hope. His associations with the last two and his attendance on their lectures in geology were especially significant in their influence on his subsequent career as a scientist. Murray and Hope were ardent supporters, respectively, of the then current and radically opposed theories of Werner and Hutton regarding the origin of rock formations of the earth's crust. Their discussions provided Silliman's first real contact with geology, and the interest thus aroused in him continued throughout his life, with a far-reaching and important effect on the development of the science in America. His analysis of the merits of these two rival theories, as given in his personal journal (Fisher, *post*, I, 167–72), bears evidence of his remarkable powers of observation, criticism, and sound judgment. Although he was still in his twenties, his scholarly attainments, his character, and his great personal charm did much to produce in the British seats of learning a favorable impression of Americans. He remained abroad a year. In 1810 he published, in two volumes, *A Journal of Travels in England, Holland and Scotland*, a full account of his visit with many interesting observations on British and Scottish university life and customs and the characteristics and achievements of the scholars he met. This book, celebrated in its day and still well worth reading, went through three editions and was widely and favorably read in both England and America.

On his return to New Haven he resumed his lectures in chemistry, enriched in material and scope by his studies abroad. He was now desirous of giving a new and full course of lectures in mineralogy and geology for which he had collected some illustrative material. During the summer of 1807, which he spent in Newport, R. I., he became acquainted with Col. George Gibbs [q.v.], a gentleman much interested in mineralogy and the possessor of what was then the finest mineral collection in America; later Colonel Gibbs lent his collection to Yale College for Silliman's use. Arranged and catalogued in rooms specially provided for it in South Middle College, the Gibbs Collection excited wide interest and also made it possible for Silliman to begin (1813) the full course of illustrated lectures in mineralogy and geology which he had planned. It was a significant event in American science. Later (1823) this celebrated collection was purchased by the College from funds raised for the purpose through Silliman's efforts.

During the period immediately following his return from abroad he was made a member of a committee representing the college to consider the organization of a school of medicine at Yale. If not, indeed, the originator of this proposal, Silliman was the one who worked out most of the details, won the cooperation of the state and local medical associations, and in the end secured a charter for the new medical school from the state legislature. The Yale Medical School was formally opened in 1813 with a faculty consisting of four professors of medicine and Silliman as professor of chemistry.

As early as 1808 Silliman introduced what was an innovation for a professor in the college when he began to give occasional scientific lectures open to the public of New Haven. In succeeding years he delivered similar lectures in New York and various New England cities. During March and April 1835 he delivered by invitation a series of geological lectures before the Boston Society of Natural History. He was at this time at the height of his powers as a lecturer and the Boston series created nothing less than a sensation and firmly established his reputation as a public speaker; he thenceforth experienced an ever increasing demand for his services. In 1836 he lectured in Boston on chemistry and in New York on geology. In 1838 he was invited to open the Lowell Institute, newly founded by John Lowell of Boston, and in the winter of 1839–40 he delivered the first series of lectures on this celebrated foundation. These dealt with geology and were followed during the next three years with lectures on chemistry. Although he spoke in the Odeon, seating 1500 people, the largest auditorium in the city, the demand for tickets was so great that each lecture was repeated. During his entire stay he received marked attentions from the intellectually and socially prominent people of Boston and Cambridge. It is doubtful if any series of scientific lectures has ever aroused greater interest, and Silliman justly regarded them as the crowning success of his professional life. Subsequently he lectured in all of the important centers of the country, going as far south as New Orleans and as far west as St. Louis. He had become a national scientific figure.

His college courses, interesting and stimulating as they were, with their wealth of experiments and material illustration, were nevertheless essentially cultural in character. There was no opportunity for advanced study or for laboratory work for any except those whom the professor employed as his personal assistants. Incidentally, the position of assistant was eagerly sought after by young men attracted by Silliman's reputation, and to mention the names of these assistants would be to enumerate many of the leaders of American science and education in the following generation. Silliman was particularly anxious to extend the opportunities for scientific study in the college, but it was not until 1847 that he succeeded, aided by his son, Benjamin Silliman, Jr. [q.v.], and his son-in-law, James Dwight Dana [q.v.], who had by this time taken over part of the instruction in geology, and doubtless also by some pressure from outside sources, in persuading the Corporation to establish a "Department of Philosophy and the Arts," under which the natural and physical sciences could be studied intensively. Even then he, his friends, and associates had to support the work of the department unaided by the college. From this modest beginning, however, within a few years, grew the Yale Scientific School which subsequently, aided by the generous support of Joseph E. Sheffield [q.v.], became the Sheffield Scientific School. This school, which rapidly became a center of scientific culture and perhaps Yale's most distinctive contribution to American education, was the direct fruitage of Silliman's influence.

In July 1818, Silliman issued the first number of *The American Journal of Science and Arts*, of which he was the founder, proprietor, and first editor. Devoted to the publication of original papers, notices, and reviews in the broad field of the natural and physical sciences, it became, under his skilful management, one of the world's great scientific journals. It brought him wide recognition throughout the scientific world and is one of his most enduring monuments. In the first hundred years of its history it had only four editors—Silliman himself, his son, his son-in-law, and his grandson.

In addition to the heavy burden of work entailed by the many activities already mentioned, Silliman found time for numerous scientific investigations and for writing. He edited, with some additions of his own, *The Elements of Experimental Chemistry* (2 vols., 1814), an American edition of William Henry's standard English textbook; he edited (1829) Robert Bakewell's *An Introduction to Geology*; and in 1830–31 he published his own excellent treatise, *Elements of Chemistry,* in two volumes. All of these went through several editions. In 1820 he published *Remarks Made on a Short Tour between Hartford and Quebec in the Autumn of 1819,* a volume which contained much of both general and scientific interest. This was widely read and went through two editions. Some sixty papers contain the results of his scientific investigations, among which may be mentioned one written in 1806 on the geology of New Haven and vicinity, a paper describing exhaustively the celebrated "Weston Meteor" (Conn.) of the fall of 1807, and several dealing with his experiments with the "Voltaic" current produced by a powerful deflagrator which he had developed with improvements along lines of one earlier made by his lifelong friend, Robert Hare. He also investigated gold deposits in Virginia and coal in Pennsylvania, and directed an investigation for the government on sugar culture. It is probably true, however, that the results of his original researches were less important than the contributions included in the vast scientific correspondence with distinguished scientists throughout the world which he carried on independently or in connection with his editorial work for *The American Journal of Science.* The influence of this correspondence, although difficult to measure, was very great. His letters also contain much of value dealing with public, political, and religious questions.

In 1805 he had been made a member of the American Philosophical Society; in the spring of 1840 he was elected the first president of the Association of American Geologists, forerunner of the American Association for the Advancement of Science; and in 1863 he became an original member of the National Academy of Sciences.

On Sept. 17, 1809, Silliman married Harriet Trumbull, second daughter of the second Governor Trumbull of Connecticut. He thus allied himself with one of the most distinguished and talented families of New England, a matter of no small importance to the rising young scholar. Incidentally it was through this connection that he secured for Yale College the historical paintings of Col. John Trumbull [*q.v.*] which now form the Trumbull Gallery of the Yale School of Fine Arts. Of the nine children of this marriage, one son and four daughters lived to maturity. Mrs. Silliman died on Jan. 18, 1850, and on Sept. 17, 1851, he married a relative of hers, Sarah Isabella (McClellan) Webb, who survived him.

In 1849 he indicated his desire to withdraw from his teaching duties at the close of the year, but was persuaded to continue in active service until 1853, when he retired as professor emeritus, having served the college for nearly fifty-four years, fifty-one as professor. During a considerable part of this period he had been the most distinguished and influential member of the Yale faculty. It can be said that he had established science at Yale and had exerted a most profound influence on collegiate education. After his retirement he enjoyed another decade of life, during which he made a second visit to Europe—an account of this trip was published in book form, *A Visit to Europe in 1851* (2 vols., 1853)—and occupied himself with compiling memoirs covering his life and work, with editorial work, and with his extensive correspondence. He died suddenly after a brief and painless illness at his home in New Haven, in his eighty-fifth year.

Benjamin Silliman was as richly endowed by nature physically as he was mentally. Tall, well-proportioned, and of vigorous physique, with handsome face and animated expression, he was a man of striking appearance. His unfailing dignity and courtesy of demeanor, his gentleness, kindliness, and generosity, and his noble integrity of character brought him a degree of regard and affection both at home and abroad seldom accorded to any man. His counsel and help in both public and private matters were constantly sought and freely given. To the members of his immediate family and to his intimate friends he appears to have been an object of love that was almost worship. Throughout his life he was deeply and sincerely religious. This was apparent in his daily life and is strikingly evident in his writings. Indeed, it was this combination of a scientific mind with deep, religious conviction that enabled him to exert such a profound influence in the interests of science on a generation that itself was dominated by strong religious convictions.

Silliman was an able scientific investigator and as such would doubtless have attained even greater distinction than he did, had he not chosen instead to be before all else the interpreter, promoter, and defender of science. To study science was, to him, to learn of the wonderful manifestations of God in the natural world, which it was man's duty to interpret reverently and by which it was his privilege to improve the conditions of his life; as told by him the story of the earth, revealed by geology, was a profoundly moving picture of the work of God. When he lectured, he conveyed much of his enthusiasm to his hearers. Speaking always extemporaneously, he drove home his point with a dignified but compelling eloquence. The experiments which were an important part of his chemistry lectures were ingenious, carefully prepared, and performed with remarkable elegance and skill. A rare and gifted teacher, whether in the college classrooms or on the public platform, he opened up new vistas of thought and inspired others with his own love of knowledge. In the course of his lifetime, despite vigorous opposition on the part of many who regarded scientific investigations and teaching as a menace to sound learning and even to morality and religion itself, he established the study of science on an equality with the older traditional educational culture, and made a whole nation conscious of its value to mankind.

[The major source is G. P. Fisher, *Life of Benjamin Silliman* (2 vols., 1866). Fisher was a student of Silliman's and later a warm personal friend and associate on the Yale College faculty; his biography is chiefly a compilation from reminiscences, diaries, and correspondence, suitably selected, arranged, and connected by brief biographical comments; a great part of the extensive original material is to be found in the Yale University library. See also Alexis Caswell, in *Nat. Acad. Sci. Biog. Memoirs*, vol. I (1877); J. M. Hoppin, in *Memorial Biogs. of the New Eng. Hist. Geneal. Soc.*, vol. VI (1905); *Proc. Am. Acad. Arts and Sci.*, vol. VI (1866); F. B. Dexter, *Biog. Sketches Grads. Yale Coll.*, vol. V (1911); R. H. Chittenden, *Hist. of the Sheffield Scientific School of Yale Univ.* (1928), vol. I; E. H. Schenck, *The Hist. of Fairfield, Fairfield County, Conn.*, vol. I (1889); *Morning Journal and Courier* (New Haven), Nov. 26, 1864.]

C. H. W.

SILLIMAN, BENJAMIN (Dec. 4, 1816–Jan. 14, 1885), chemist, was born and died in New Haven, Conn. His father was Benjamin Silliman [*q.v.*], for more than fifty years professor of chemistry and geology at Yale; his mother was Harriet (Trumbull), daughter of Jonathan Trumbull, governor of Connecticut, 1798–1809, and grand-daughter of Jonathan Trumbull [*q.v.*], governor of Connecticut during the Revolution. On May 14, 1840, Silliman married Susan Huldah Forbes of New Haven, who died in 1878. Of their seven children, four daughters and a son survived them.

Probably because of the influence of his distinguished father, Silliman's major interests throughout a very active life were scientific. Graduating from Yale in 1837, he began teaching immediately as assistant to his father. In 1838 he became an associate editor of the *American Journal of Science,* founded by his father twenty years earlier, and he continued in this capacity, or as editor, later assisted by his brother-in-law, James D. Dana [*q.v.*], until his death, a period of almost fifty years. Nearly all his scientific publications, numbering over fifty and concerned chiefly with chemistry and mineralogy, appeared in this journal, beginning in 1841. His best-known books were two college texts, *First Principles of Chemistry* (1847) and *First Principles of Physics* (1859). Both went through several editions. In 1846 he was appointed professor of practical chemistry and the following year, with John P. Norton [*q.v.*], he established a school of applied chemistry at Yale in the new Department of Philosophy and the Arts which later became the Sheffield Scientific School. In 1853 he was appointed to succeed his father, who had just retired, in the professorship of chemistry in the Yale Medical School and Yale College. He maintained his connection with the Scientific School until 1869, with Yale College until 1870, and with the Yale Medical School until his death. For a number of years also (1849–54) he spent a portion of his time in Kentucky as professor of chemistry in the medical department of the University of Louisville. He was one of the fifty original members of the National Academy of Sciences, incorporated in 1863.

Silliman frequently acted as a consultant in chemical and mining problems, and in this capacity made one major contribution to the petroleum industry the importance of which has not been generally appreciated. This was his *Report on the Rock Oil, or Petroleum, from Venango County, Pennsylvania* (1855), based on an investigation made for the company which owned the land on which Edwin L. Drake [*q.v.*] later drilled the first oil well in Pennsylvania. In this report, printed as a copyrighted pamphlet at the time and some years later republished in full in the *American Chemist* (July 1871), Silliman showed from his own researches that petroleum was essentially a mixture of hydrocarbons, entirely different in character from vegetable and animal oils, and that it could be separated, by fractional distillation and simple means of purification, into a series of distillates making up about ninety per cent. of the whole. He estimated that about fifty per cent. of the distillate (the intermediate fractions) could be used for illuminating purposes, and he found by quantitative measurements with a photometer devised for the purpose that the light was superior to that from any other of a number of illuminants. From the high-boiling oily fraction he extracted paraffine, purified it, and found it made excellent candles. The high-boiling oil he characterized as valuable for lubrication because it did not become rancid, did not freeze, and did not tend to form a gum. Finally, he found that crude petroleum, when passed through heated coke, decomposed into a gas of very high illuminating power suitable to enrich illuminating gas. In short, in this investigation Silliman discovered the chief uses which were to be made of petroleum products for the next fifty years and outlined the principal methods of preparing and purifying those products. Adequate uses for the low-boiling (gasoline) fraction were not discovered by Silliman, or by anyone else, until the development of the internal combustion engine, but the rapid growth of the industry along the lines laid down by Silliman is ample testimony to the usefulness of his discoveries.

[For biographical data, see *Am. Jour. of Sci.*, Feb. 1885; *Nat. Acad. Sci. Biog. Memoirs*, vol. VII (1913); *Record of the Class of 1837 in Yale Univ.* (7th ed., 1887); *Obit. Record Grads. Yale Coll.*, 1885; R. H. Chittenden, *Hist. of the Sheffield Scientific School of Yale Univ.* (1928), vol. I; *New Haven Evening Register*, Jan. 15, 1885. A copy of the rare pamphlet: *Report on the Rock Oil, or Petroleum, of Venango County, Pa.* (1855), is in the Yale Univ. Library.]

H. W. F.

SILLS, MILTON (Jan. 12, 1882–Sept. 15, 1930), actor, was born in Chicago, Ill., the son of William Henry and Josephine Antoinette (Troost) Sills. His full name was Milton George Gustavus Sills, the middle part of which he later dropped. He was graduated from the University of Chicago in 1903 with the degree of A.B., and for a year and a half remained there as a scholar and fellow in philosophy. His experiences in college dramatic performances prepared him to some extent for his professional début at New Palestine, Ohio, in 1906, in an old melodrama entitled *Dora Thorne*. A season of barnstorming through towns of the Middle West followed, and then he went to New York, where he was soon playing conspicuous rôles under the Frohman, Shubert, Belasco, and other managements. An engagement with Charles Coburn's repertory company gave him valuable experience in Shakespearian plays. He was for a time

leading man with Blanche Bates in *The Fighting Hope*. During this period he acted for the most part in plays of the hour that soon vanished from the stage; among them were *This Woman and This Man, Just Married, The Governor's Lady, The Law of the Land,* and *A Happy Marriage,* the last mentioned being one of the minor comedies of Clyde Fitch [q.v.]. In 1914 he deserted the stage for the screen, and in 1916, after preliminary experience in the ill-equipped studios of New York, he went to Hollywood, and there began a new era of success as a motion picture star. His first appearance on the screen was made in association with Wilton Lackaye in a motion picture version of Frank Norris's novel, *The Pit*. Later he played leading characters in *The Barker, Burning Daylight, The Sea-Hawk, Men of Steel* (of which he was part author), and *Paradise*. All of these were marked by the forceful acting in which he excelled both on the screen and the stage. He was, it is said, far removed from the popular idea of the film idol when he was outside of the studios. His library contained books in Greek, French, and Russian, all of which he read; his chess game was well above the average, and his talk ranged from philosophy or the experimental sciences to the fine points of tennis or golf (*New York Herald Tribune, post*).

He was tall, of fine figure, and with a resonant voice that served him well when the silent screen became vocal. His marriage to Gladys Edith Wynne in London on May 26, 1910, resulted in divorce in 1925, and on Oct. 12, 1926, he married an actress, Doris Margaret Kenyon. He died suddenly while playing tennis with his wife at their home in Santa Monica, Cal. With her survived a daughter by the first marriage and a son by the second. His work as an actor and motion picture performer did not fill all his active hours, for he remained interested in philosophy and art. He never abandoned his academic studies, and delivered occasional lectures at colleges and universities on various subjects connected and unconnected with the stage; in 1927 he spoke at the Harvard school of business administration on conditions in the motion picture world. He was the co-author with Ernest S. Holmes of a book, published (after his death) in 1932, entitled *Values: a Philosophy of Human Needs*, and he was one of the organizers of the Academy of Motion Picture Arts and Sciences. Unlike most actors, he became a wealthy man and left an estate of several hundred thousand dollars.

[*Who's Who in America*, 1930–31; obituaries in *Variety*, Sept. 17, 1930, in *Boston Transcript, Sun*

(N. Y.), *N. Y. Times,* and *N. Y. Herald Tribune,* Sept. 16, 1930.]   E. F. E.

SILSBEE, NATHANIEL (Jan. 14, 1773–July 14, 1850), seaman, merchant, statesman, was born in Salem, Mass., and was the oldest of the eight children of Nathaniel and Sarah (Becket) Silsbee. Both his parents, all of his grandparents, and all of his great-grandparents were born in Salem of English stock. His father, fourth in descent from Henry Silsbee who was in Salem in 1639, was a prominent and prosperous sea captain who met with financial reverses that forced his eldest son to withdraw from school and in 1787 to go to sea to assist the family, of which he became the sole support on his father's death in 1791. His first voyages were as clerk or supercargo, but in 1790 he was second mate of a brig, and the next year he commanded a sloop which he brought safely back from the West Indies after a survey there had declared her unseaworthy. Before he was twenty-one, and with a chief mate who was also a minor, he took command of the ship *Benjamin,* and in her completed one of the outstanding voyages in Salem annals, modifying the plan of the owners to take advantage of conditions arising from the outbreak of war between England and France, and by transactions in foreign exchange and merchandise bringing back a profit of over one hundred per cent. He made other noteworthy voyages to the Orient, the Mediterranean, and Russia. On one occasion, when brought as a prize into Malaga, he remained in the office of the French consul for forty hours continuously, refusing to leave till his case was decided, and secured by this means not only immediate trial but the release of both ship and cargo; in another instance, through determination and skillful bargaining, he prevented his ship's being conscripted to carry Napoleon's troops to Egypt. So uniformly successful was he that he accumulated a sufficient fortune to retire from the sea in 1801 to become a ship-owner and leading figure in the commercial and financial activities of Salem and Boston.

Silsbee was a Jeffersonian in a strong Federalist section, but the Era of Good Feeling made a man of his moderation and prominence politically strong. Against his wishes he was nominated for the federal House of Representatives in 1816 and induced to serve two terms as a public duty. On retiring from Congress, he was drafted for one term in the lower house of the Massachusetts legislature, 1821–22, and three terms in the upper house, 1823–26, acting as president of the latter body while he was in it. In 1826 he was made United States senator by

legislative election, and in 1829 was elected for a six-year term by the legislature. His senatorial colleague from 1827 was Daniel Webster, and he somewhat overshadowed Silsbee, who, however, was a member of the committees on finance and commerce, and acted as chairman of the latter from 1833 to 1835. In the House, too, he exerted influence on legislation affecting the navy, merchant marine, and other matters on which he had special knowledge, and in the Senate he had a good deal to do with a bill, passed Mar. 2, 1833, that marks a stage in the development of the customs service. He served continuously as a director of the Boston branch or the main division of the Bank of the United States in Philadelphia, 1816–32; he was a presidential elector, 1824 and 1836; and he was regarded as more important in both political and economic circles than the offices he held would indicate.

On Dec. 12, 1802, he was married in Salem to Mary Crowninshield, who died in 1835; one of his daughters was the second wife of Jared Sparks [*q.v.*], and his son Nathaniel held such offices as mayor of Salem, representative in the Massachusetts legislature, and treasurer of Harvard University. He died in Salem, survived by three of his children. His autobiography appeared as "Biographical Notes" in the *Essex Institute Historical Collections,* January 1899.

[M. W. F. Duren, *Three Generations of Silsbees and Their Vessels* (privately printed, 1924); J. A. Emmerton, in *Essex Inst. Hist. Colls.,* July 1880; Nathaniel Silsbee, *Ibid.,* Jan. 1899; R. J. Cleveland, *A Narrative of Voyages and Commercial Enterprises* (2 vols., 1842); R. D. Paine, *The Ships and Sailors of Old Salem* (1909); *Biog. Directory Am. Cong. 1774–1927* (1928); obituary in *Salem Reg.,* July 18, 1850; death notice, *Boston Daily Jour.,* July 22, 1850.]   S. G.

SILVER, THOMAS (June 17, 1813–Apr. 12, 1888), civil engineer, inventor, was of American Quaker parentage and was born at Greenwich, Cumberland County, N. J. It is recorded that he was educated in Greenwich and Woodstown, N. J., and in Philadelphia, Pa., and then engaged in civil engineering practice in Philadelphia. He became well known locally as a young man because of the unusual mechanical ingenuity he displayed in designing such contrivances as a grain-dryer, a gas-burner, a stove, and a window-tightening device to prevent rattling, patented June 13, 1854, No. 11,092. In 1854 the loss of the United States steamship *San Francisco,* bound to California with troops, turned his attention to devising a governor for marine engines. The ordinary steam engine governor was slow in action. When it was used with marine steam engines driving side-wheel steamships, it was unable to control the speed of the engine quickly, consequently, when a ship rolled, one of the paddle wheels was brought out of the water, and often much damage was caused. The first patent to correct this condition, No. 13,202, was issued to Silver on July 3, 1855. The contrivance was a very simple one, like the ordinary two-ball governor except that it was kept from being affected by the force of gravity by the use of four balls of equal weight placed at equal distance from the axis of motion. Furthermore, it could be used in any position—horizontal, vertical, or inclined. In 1856 Silver succeeded in having his governor installed on the United States mail steamship *Atlantic,* as well as on the engines of the United States mint at Philadelphia, the *Public Ledger* (Philadelphia) and the *New York Tribune,* where they operated with entire success. He failed to interest the United States navy, however, and in 1857 went to Europe in the hope of introducing his governor there. After obtaining an English patent on May 23, 1857, he went to France and succeeded in having it adopted by the French navy. He obtained a second United States patent on Apr. 26, 1859, a reissue of his original patent on July 25, 1865, and still another improvement patent on Oct. 2, 1866. Meanwhile, in 1864, he succeeded in having his governor ordered into general use in the British navy. This was followed by its adoption by most of the naval authorities of the world, though not by the United States. About 1870 he returned to take up residence at Nyack, N. Y., where he lived for the rest of his life. He obtained four additional patents between 1871 and 1885, one for a hoisting apparatus and three for a completely inclosed oil lamp, in which air was furnished to the burning oil by a revolving fan operated by a clock movement. He became a member of the Franklin Institute, Philadelphia, in 1855. He was awarded the James Watt medal by the Royal Polytechnic Society, London, in 1866, and received a medal from Napoleon III for his "regulateur marine." In 1887 he published a pamphlet on *The Scientific Explanation of the Polar Tides, and the Formation of Icebergs.* He married the daughter of James M. Bird, Philadelphia, and at the time of his death in New York was survived by his widow and a daughter.

[E. H. Knight, *Knight's Amer. Mech. Dict.,* vol. II (1875); *Sci. Amer.,* Apr. 28, May 19, 1888; *Jour. of Franklin Inst.,* June 1855, Mar. 1857; obituaries in *N. Y. Times, N. Y. Tribune,* Apr. 14, 1888; Patent Office records.]   C. W. M—n.

SILVERMAN, JOSEPH (Aug. 25, 1860–July 26, 1930), rabbi, was born at Cincinnati, Ohio, the son of Michael Henry and Ulrika (Piorkowsky) Silverman. His parents came to America from Russia, and his early surroundings were poor and humble. He was educated in the public schools, at the University of Cincinnati (A.B. 1883), and at the Hebrew Union College (Rabbi 1884, D.D. 1887). On Dec. 5, 1886, in Galveston, Tex., he married Henriette Block, by whom he had four daughters. After serving as minister of Temple Emanu-El in Dallas (1884–85) and Congregation B'nai Israel in Galveston (1885–88), he was called to the leading reform Jewish congregation of the country, Temple Emanu-El, New York, as junior rabbi, and on the retirement of Gustav Gottheil [*q.v.*] in 1897, he was elected rabbi. He filled this position for thirty-four years, becoming, in 1922, rabbi emeritus. He died in New York at the age of seventy.

Besides articles in the press, Silverman published some Jewish religious textbooks, pamphlets, and a volume of sermons, *The Renaissance of Judaism* (1918); he was also a contributing editor of the *Jewish Encyclopedia.* His strength, however, lay less in homiletic and literary work than in his community service. He was the founder (1903) and first president of the Emanu-El Brotherhood, and served as secretary of the Emanu-El Theological Seminary Association and as president of the Central Conference of American Rabbis (1900–03), the New York Board of Jewish Ministers (1906–07), the Order B'nai Brith, District I (1913–15), the Eastern Council of Reform Rabbis (1917–19), and the Association of Reform Rabbis of New York and Vicinity (1919–21). He also served as a governor of the Hebrew Union College and as a member of the American Jewish Committee. The breadth and variety of his interests is suggested by the fact that he was a member of the Congress of Religions at the World's Columbian Exposition, Chicago, in 1893; vice-president of the International Peace Forum; a member of the executive committee of the Lake Mohonk Peace Conference on International Arbitration (1912), and of the executive committee of the National Association for the Advancement of Colored People (1909–12). In 1892, and again in 1904, he delivered the opening prayer in the House of Representatives at Washington.

Though a liberal in religion, he was conservative in his social and political views. He was opposed to the feminist movement, and held that socialism was based on false theories and constituted a menace to American institutions. In the last eight years of his life, he allied himself with Zionism, energetically throwing himself into the work of raising funds and securing adherents. His conversion to this movement after many years of uncompromising opposition to it attracted wide attention. He became an honorary vice-president of the Palestine Foundation Fund, and a member of the national executive committee of the Zionist Organization of America.

Silverman was a good-looking man, especially in his later years, when his silvery hair and full beard added a venerable impressiveness to his appearance. His was a kindly and sympathetic nature, and he took real delight in participating in philanthropic movements. He is remembered as a man who was steadfast in his friendship, loyal to his convictions, and a messenger of intercreedal good-will.

[*N. Y. Times,* July 27–30, 1930; *Am. Hebrew,* Aug. 1, 1930; *Reform Advocate,* Aug. 2, 9, 1930; *Central Conference of Am. Rabbis, Year Book,* vol. XLI (1931); *Am. Jewish Year Book* (1903–04), p. 100; *Who's Who in Am. Jewry,* 1928; *Who's Who in America,* 1929–30.]   D. deS. P.

SILVERMAN, SIME (May 18, 1873–Sept. 22, 1933), editor and publisher, was born in Cortland, N. Y., son of George and Rachel (Ganz) Silverman. His mother was a native of Bristol, England, and a life-long lover of music. Educated in the public schools of Cortland and Syracuse, N. Y., and at a business college, he began active life with his father in business in Syracuse, but his interest in the theatre led him to New York, where he secured work with the *Morning Telegraph,* a racing and theatrical daily. On Mar. 1, 1898, he married Hattie Freeman, daughter of George Freeman of Syracuse. When he lost his job in 1905 because of some adverse criticism he wrote of a variety performance, he immediately borrowed enough money from his father-in-law to start his own paper, a weekly which he named *Variety.* It started humbly with sixteen pages and a total staff of three, Silverman and two assistants. Incidentally, it was written in correct English. When its founder died nearly thirty years later it was often issued with 100 pages, had 225 employees, and was almost entirely written in the worst, as well as often the most entertaining and lively English to be found anywhere in print. From 1905 until his death Silverman's story was entirely the story of his paper. He gave his entire time and life to it. Its success was due to his labors and to the qualities he put into it. It was honest, it kept well abreast of the times, and it was remarkably vivid. Unlike theatrical trade papers which had gone before, *Variety* never changed an opinion out of consideration for its advertisers or the influence of those whom it criticized, and the editor supported his staff against every outside pressure so well that there was general respect for the paper's opinions and reliance on its statement of facts. It was first, largely because of Silverman's foresight, in what turned out to be the highly remunerative fields of motion picture and radio reviewing, and made other innovations that were highly successful. Its style, furthermore, came to be one that reflected with curious fidelity the argot of Broadway—its slang, its verbal short cuts, and its "hard-boiled" humor. Though Silverman meant only to make his paper more effective with his professional readers, more and more people in the outside world bought it, and read and studied it to try the flavor of its odd language, which was often astonishingly effective in its brevity and vividness. In *Variety* verbs became nouns and nouns verbs; an actor "vowed" or "panicked" an audience.. Its headline on its story of the great financial debacle of 1929 was "Wall St. Lays an Egg" (Oct. 30, 1929); "Went for a Grand on Dust" meant that the producer had lost $1000 on a play called "Watch my Dust." *Variety* became, and remained, a place where philologists could study the popular language in evolution. In 1922 Silverman bought the old *New York Clipper;* he published it separately until 1924, when some features were absorbed by *Variety,* and then sold the name to the *Billboard* (Cincinnati). In 1923 he attempted to issue a daily paper of Broadway news, the *Times Square Daily,* but this soon failed. He did succeed, however, with a daily issue of *Variety* in Hollywood, Cal., begun Sept. 6, 1933. He died in Los Angeles a few weeks later.

After his death it was found that he had left fifty-one per cent. of *Variety* to his wife and son, and forty-nine per cent. to his employees, a gift of great value. The act was characteristic. Tall, spare, with white hair in later years, modest to a degree, even shy of any public appearance, but blunt and slangy and "hard-boiled" of speech, he yet possessed a strong strain of sentiment for his paper, for the world of Broadway, and for the men who worked with him. He tolerated no reporters he did not like, but those he kept found him raising their pay unasked, looking after their investments, and backing them up in all critical controversies. His staff, consequently, had for him unlimited devotion, which they expressed in the same Broadway lingo that he used; the old man was a "swell egg" to them. Though his paper so vividly reflected Broadway, he was not a Broadway playboy. He found his recreation in work and in convivial meetings with his staff late at night after work. He lived simply and left a large estate, with his son well trained for the editorial chair he vacated.

[Allene Talmey, in *Stage*, Mar. 1935; *Variety*, Sept. 26, 1933; *N. Y. Times*, *N. Y. Herald Tribune*, Sept. 23, 1933; information from Mrs. Silverman.] W. P. E.

SIMMONS, EDWARD (Oct. 27, 1852– Nov. 17, 1931), mural painter, was born at Concord, Mass., where his father, George Frederick Simmons, was a Unitarian minister. He was a descendant of Moses Simmons, who arrived in America in 1621. His mother, Mary Emerson (Ripley) Simmons, was a grand-daughter of Ezra Ripley [*q.v.*] and through her grandmother, Phoebe (Bliss) Emerson Ripley, was connected with the family of Ralph Waldo Emerson [*q.v.*]. Edward's name was originally Edward Emerson Simmons, but in his later life he dropped the middle name. Only three when his father died, he was reared at the Old Manse in Concord under the supervision of his mother and his grandmother Ripley, who knew some Sanskrit and read Greek and Latin with ease. In his boyhood he was a naturalist companion of Henry David Thoreau [*q.v.*]. Prepared in the local schools and by relatives for college, he went to Harvard, where he studied under Francis James Child and Asa Gray [*qq.v.*], and could have led his class but saw no reason to do so. He was a founder of the *Harvard Crimson* and, according to his autobiography, one of those who introduced Rugby football as an intercollegiate sport in the United States. Graduated in 1874, he first became an oil salesman in Cincinnati and then a clerk in a store in San Francisco, where he also wrote dramatic and literary criticisms for the *San Francisco Chronicle*. After teaching school in Strawberry Valley, Cal., 1876–77, and teaching painting in Bangor, Me., 1877–78, he studied painting at the Boston Museum of Fine Arts, where he came under the influence of Dr. William Rimmer [*q.v.*].

In 1879, assured of a small income, he took steerage passage to Europe, registered at the Académie Julian, and studied under Gustave C. R. Boulanger and Jules Joseph Lefebvre. His portrait of a highlander was in the Salon, 1881, and in 1882 his "La Blanchisseuse" had honorable mention. He joined the artist colony at Concarneau, Brittany, during 1881–86, where he had as friends Jules Bastien-Lepage and Marie Bashkirtseff. The novel *Guenn: a Wave on the Breton Coast* was written by Blanche Willis Howard [*q.v.*] in his Brittany studio, and a legend of his being its hero persists. In London, on Dec. 4, 1883, he married Vesta Schallenberger, author of several books of fiction. He later had a studio at St. Ives, Cornwall, for several years.

In 1891 a commission to design a window for Harvard University brought him back to the United States, where in 1893 he painted with great success the decorations of the dome of the Manufactures and Liberal Arts Building at the World's Columbian Exposition in Chicago, assigned him by Francis Davis Millet [*q.v.*]. Later he painted murals for the appellate division of the supreme court of New York; the criminal court building, courts of oyer and terminer, New York; the state capitols of Minnesota and South Dakota; court houses at Des Moines, Ia., and Mercer, Pa.; the Waldorf-Astoria Hotel, New York; the residences of John D. Rockefeller at Pocantico Hills and Frederick Vanderbilt at Hyde Park, N. Y.; and the Panama Pacific International Exposition at San Francisco in 1915. For the Library of Congress, Washington, D. C., he painted the nine muses in the corridor leading to the north from the entrance hall; for the Massachusetts State House, representations of "Concord Bridge, Apr. 19, 1775" and "The Return of the Colors . . . Dec. 22, 1863." Resident at New York from 1891 onward, he enjoyed social as well as professional popularity, for he was picturesque in person, an entertaining speaker and writer, and a clever amateur actor. He was of the group who called themselves Ten American Painters. In September 1903 he married Alice Ralston Morton. He died in Baltimore after a brief illness, survived by two sons by his first marriage and one by his second.

His autobiography, *From Seven to Seventy, Memories of a Painter and a Yankee* (1922), tells his story brilliantly and wittily, with many anecdotes of his celebrated contemporaries. His article on "The Fine Arts Related to the People," a statement of his philosophy of art which appeared in the *International Studio* for November 1917, lacks the vividness of the autobiography. Strong and direct, his paintings had both simplicity and dignity. He was what is called a "clean painter," not given to fumbling or hesitant strokes, but he lacked profound originality whether in composition or execution. His panels for the Massachusetts State House were criticized when unveiled as somewhat wanting in dramatic appeal and in unusual motivation, and when they are compared with the work in the same building of Robert Reid [*q.v.*], more poignantly interesting, that criticism may still appear just. He was at his happiest in the decorations of the Waldorf-Astoria ballroom, in which the gaiety and brilliance of his own personality are reflected.

[H. S. Bradford, *One Branch of the Bradford Family* (1898); L. A. Simmons, *Hist. of the Simmons Family* (1930); *Who's Who in America*, 1930–31; *Seventh*

Report . . . Class of 1874 of Harvard Coll. (1899); Samuel Isham, *The Hist. of Am. Painting* (1905); *Handbook of the New Lib. of Cong.* (1901), compiled by Herbert Small; Ellen M. Burrill, *The State House, Boston, Mass.* (1907); Arthur Hoeber, in *Brush and Pencil,* Mar. 1900; obituaries in *Art News,* Nov. 21, 1931, *Art Digest,* Dec. 1, 1931, and *N. Y. Times,* Nov. 18, 1931.]
F. W. C.

SIMMONS, FRANKLIN (Jan. 11, 1839–Dec. 6, 1913), sculptor, was born in Lisbon (later Webster), Me., the son of Loring and Dorothy (Batchelder) Simmons. John and Priscilla Alden of Plymouth, as well as Samuel Simmons, a Revolutionary veteran, were among his ancestors. He spent his boyhood at Bath and early showed an interest in art. He undertook modeling while he was employed in a mill at Lewiston, eventually reached the Boston studio of John Adams Jackson [*q.v.*], and later opened a studio of his own in Lewiston. "The Newsboy," modeled from life, was one of his early works. He studied at the Lewiston Falls Academy and, for a time at least, at the Maine State Seminary (later Bates College). Becoming an itinerant artist, he went from Waterville, the seat of Waterville (later Colby) College, where several of his early busts are preserved, to Brunswick, where he received the patronage of the Bowdoin faculty; in 1859 or 1860 he went to Portland, where he portrayed leading citizens in medallions and busts, and received his first commission for a statue, that of Maj.-Gen. Hiram Gregory Berry [*q.v.*] at Rockland. On Dec. 27, 1864, he married Emily J. Libbey of Auburn, Me. In the winters of 1865 and 1866 he was in Washington, making portraits of such leaders in political and military life as Ulysses S. Grant, William Tecumseh Sherman, and David Glasgow Farragut [*qq.v.*]. He also designed the war memorial for Lewiston. As a result of securing a commission for a statue of Roger Williams [*q.v.*], which was later placed by Rhode Island in Statuary Hall, Washington, he went to Italy with his wife, probably in the latter part of 1867, and thereafter lived in Rome, though he made occasional visits to America. A replica of the Williams statue was unveiled in Providence in 1877, with the addition of a figure representing history. Simmons' other works in Washington include the Naval Monument at the foot of Capitol Hill, erected in 1877; an equestrian statue of John Alexander Logan; statues of William King, the first governor of Maine, and Francis Harrison Pierpont, governor of the "restored" state of Virginia [*qq.v.*]; and the heroic Grant, which was placed in the rotunda of the Capitol in 1900. Meanwhile he made for Portland, Me., in 1888 the seated Longfellow in bronze and in 1891 the

Civil War monument, "The Republic." Of his ideal works the "Penelope" in marble, of which four replicas were made, is considered his best; it is now in the Portland Society of Art.

His first wife died in 1872; twenty years later, June 9, 1892, he married Ella, Baroness von Jeinsen, daughter of John F. Slocum of Providence, who died in 1905. There were no children. During his last years he traveled much of the time and worked on his symbolic group, "Hercules and Alcestis," which he finished not long before his death. He died suddenly in Rome just as he was about to return to America, and was buried in the Protestant Cemetery there, the grave marked by a replica of his "Angel of the Resurrection." He left his estate to the Portland Society of Art, where a collection of his works is preserved as the Franklin Simmons Memorial. Other examples are to be seen in the Portland public library, the Maine Historical Society, and the Greenleaf Law Library in Portland. His statues are distinguished by an idealism that at its best becomes simple and sculptural, as in the Roger Williams and the equestrian Logan, which in spite of its heavy bronze base has both grace and power. Possessed of tireless energy, he executed about a hundred portrait busts, about fifteen public monuments, and a number of ideal figures.

[*Who's Who in America,* 1912–13; *Maine Hist. Memorials* (1922); W. D. Spencer, *Maine Immortals* (1932); Lorado Taft, *The Hist. of Am. Sculpture* (1924); "A Veteran Sculptor," *Outlook,* May 27, 1911; Lilian Whiting, in *Internat. Studio,* May 1905, supp.; C. E. Fairman, *Art and Artists of the Capitol of the U. S. A.* (1927); obituary in *La Tribuna* (Rome), Dec. 10, 1913.]
W. S. R.

SIMMONS, THOMAS JEFFERSON (June 25, 1837–Sept. 12, 1905), soldier, jurist, was born at Hickory Grove, Crawford County, Ga., the son of Allen G. and Mary (Cleveland) Simmons. His grandfather, William Simmons, was a native of North Carolina. Poverty prevented Thomas from receiving even the scanty educational advantages afforded by the county schools, but with borrowed money he was at length enabled to attend Bromwood Institute at Lagrange, in Troup County. Later he studied in the law office of A. D. Hammond, of Forsyth, and in August 1857 was admitted to the bar and began practice at Knoxville in his native county. In 1859 he married Pennie Hollis.

At the beginning of the Civil War he entered the Confederate army. Enlisting in the Crawford Greys, the first troops to leave the county, he was made a lieutenant. His company became a part of the 6th Georgia Infantry under Col. A.

H. Colquitt [*q.v.*], and Simmons was soon in Virginia, where he fought until Lee's surrender. He was attached to the 45th Georgia Infantry in the 3rd Brigade in A. P. Hill's division of Longstreet's corps; in 1862, he was promoted to lieutenant-colonel; and near the end of the year he was made a colonel. He was recommended by General Lee for a brigadier-generalship, but the surrender came before his commission could be delivered. At the battle of Seven Pines, he received a severe wound which disabled him for six months.

After the war, he returned to Georgia and soon thereafter was chosen a delegate to the constitutional convention which met in November 1865. Under the new government set up, he was elected to the state Senate. In 1867 he became solicitor of the Macon circuit; but, being a Conservative, he was replaced with a Republican a few months later by the incoming Radicals. He then moved to Macon and in 1871 served again in the state Senate. With the Radicals now displaced from power, he played a conspicuous part as chairman of the committee on finance and bonds. By proving many of the Reconstruction bonds to be fraudulent, he prevented their validation and thereby saved the state millions of dollars. The amount the legislature repudiated was $7,957,000. He was reëlected to the Senate in 1873, and in 1875 he was made its president. In 1877 the Conservatives, having the state securely in their hands, called a constitutional convention, to which Simmons was elected and in which he became the chairman of the committee on finance. He reported the financial provisions of the new document and saw them adopted without material change.

The next year he was elected to the superior court of the Macon circuit, where he continued as judge for nine years. In 1887 he was elected to fill a vacancy on the state supreme court, and the following year was elected to a full term. In 1894, when the chief justice, Logan E. Bleckley [*q.v.*], retired, Simmons succeeded him and continued in that position until his death eleven years later. It is for his work as a judge, extending over a period of twenty-seven years, that he is best remembered. He was an indefatigable worker, as is well attested by the large number of decisions which he wrote. Though not brilliant, he had a tenacious memory and was a patient listener. In religion he was a Primitive Baptist. After the death of his first wife, in 1864, he married, in 1867, Lucille Peck, who died in 1882. Six years later he married Mrs. Nannie R. Renfro, who with three of his children, survived him.

[A. D. Candler and C. A. Evans, *Georgia* (1906), vol. III; W. J. Northen, *Men of Mark in Ga.*, vol. IV (1908); *Who's Who in America*, 1903–05; A. O. Park, *Report of the Twenty-Third Ann. Session of the Ga. Bar Assoc.* (1906); *War of the Rebellion: Official Records (Army)*; 79–123 *Ga. Reports*; "In Memoriam," 124 *Ga.*, 1083–98; *Jour. of the Senate of the State of Ga.*, 1871–77; I. W. Avery, *The Hist. of the State of Ga. from 1850 to 1881* (copr. 1881); *Weekly Banner* (Athens, Ga.), Sept. 15, 22, 1905; *Atlanta Constitution*, Sept. 13, 1905.]

E. M. C.

SIMMS, WILLIAM ELLIOTT (Jan. 2, 1822–June 25, 1898), lawyer, soldier, congressman, Confederate senator, was born near Cynthiana, Harrison County, Ky. His parents were William Marmaduke Simms, born in Henry County, Va., who emigrated to Kentucky in 1809, fighting in the War of 1812 under the command of William Henry Harrison, and Julia (Shropshire) Simms, a daughter of James Shropshire, a Kentucky pioneer. He had one brother, Edward, who died in 1840. His father died in 1844, and his mother, in her twenty-first year. The family had moved in 1828 to Bourbon County, with which Simms was thereafter identified. He received a scanty education in the county schools, and after his father's death began reading law in Lexington in the office of Judge Aaron K. Wooley. In 1845, he entered the law department of Transylvania University, and the next year he completed his course of study with distinction. He had scarcely begun the practice of his profession in Paris, the county seat of Bourbon, before war with Mexico broke out. Raising a company of the 3rd Kentucky Regiment of Infantry and becoming its captain, he served in Mexico under Gen. Winfield Scott, and at the end of the war brought back at his own expense the bodies of his comrades who had fallen. As was true of many other veterans of this war, he capitalized in politics his military career. In 1849, he was elected as a Democrat to the Kentucky House of Representatives, where he served one term, and then returned to his law practice in Paris.

In 1857 he began editing the *Kentucky State Flag,* largely to promote the election to Congress of James B. Clay. Two years later he was nominated by the Democrats to succeed Clay, in the famous Ashland district, and after a heated campaign he succeeded in defeating John Marshall Harlan [*q.v.*] by sixty votes. In this campaign he became embroiled with Garret Davis [*q.v.*], who challenged him to a duel, but mutual friends were able to prevent their meeting. In the Thirty-sixth Congress Simms took an active part in the bitter sectional debate, showing unusual ability as an orator, both in the selection of effective words and phrases and in delivery. He strongly opposed the election of John Sherman to the speakership, and he solemnly charged the North with a fanaticism which had already expressed itself in the Kansas struggle and in the John Brown raid and which was about to drive the South from the Union. He also opposed polygamy in Utah and spoke against sectional tariff measures which, he argued, protected the capital of the New England states but ignored labor in the South and the West. On Christmas Day, 1860, he issued a message to the citizens of his district, *To the People of the Eighth Congressional District of Kentucky,* advising Kentucky to be ready to join the South if coercion should be used against any Southern state. On Feb. 9, 1861, after the Southern Confederacy had been formed, he delivered a powerful attack against the Republican party, in which he charged it with being the author of all the woes which were besetting the country. Apparently his Southern sympathies were too much for the Ashland district, for he was defeated for reëlection by John J. Crittenden [*q.v.*].

Being unable longer to remain neutral, he joined, in September 1861, the Confederate forces of Humphrey Marshall, 1812–1872 [*q.v.*], and as a colonel fought through eastern Kentucky and western Virginia. In November he was selected by the Confederate government of Kentucky to be one of the three commissioners to treat with the Confederacy for the admission of the state, and upon its entry into the Confederacy, he was elected to the Confederate Senate, where he served until the end of the war. At the close of hostilities he fled to Canada and there remained a year before returning to Kentucky. Laboring under political disabilities, which were not removed until about three years before his death, he henceforth eschewed politics and devoted himself to agriculture. In his new occupation he became one of the wealthiest men in Bourbon County, living on his estate near Paris, which he called Mount Airy. On Sept. 27, 1866, he married Lucy Ann Blythe, a daughter of James Blythe of Madison County, and to them were born three children.

[For biog. data, see *The Biog. Encyc. of Ky.* (1878); Lewis and R. H. Collins, *Hist. of Ky.* (2 vols., 1882); *Daily Leader* (Lexington, Ky.), June 25, 1898. The *Biog. Dir. Am. Cong.* (1928) gives Simms's middle name as Emmet, but James Blythe Anderson, Esq., of Lexington, Ky., in a letter to Dr. Allen Johnson, Aug. 17, 1929, stated that the name is recorded as Elliott, in the handwriting of Simms's father, in the family Bible in Mrs. Anderson's possession. In most other places only the initial appears.]   E. M. C.

SIMMS, WILLIAM GILMORE (Apr. 17, 1806–June 11, 1870), novelist and man of letters, was born in Charleston, S. C., the son of a Scotch-Irish William Gilmore Simms who had come from Ireland shortly after the Revolution, and of Harriet Ann Augusta (Singleton) Simms, a member of a family which had left Virginia for South Carolina before the Revolution. On neither side was the child allied by birth with the ruling class in South Carolina, then the most compactly governed as well as the most feudal of the American states. There was, moreover, no wealth to bring him such advantages as it could. His father, an unsuccessful merchant, lost everything during the winter of 1807–08 and his mother died at almost the same time. The elder Simms turned his disheartened back on Charleston to wander and settle in what was still the territory of Mississippi, and to be a volunteer soldier in the forces of Andrew Jackson. The younger, brought up in Charleston by his maternal grandmother, a widow who had remarried and was now Mrs. Gates, was sent to public and private schools, all of which he later remembered as useless, and was apprenticed to a druggist at some unknown date. At eighteen he was called upon to decide between South Carolina and Mississippi, to which he had gone to visit his father. Much as the youth seems to have been impressed by the rough humors and violences of the frontier, and strongly as he was urged by his father to give up Charleston, he chose to be loyal to a more venerable tradition. He studied law in his native city, married Anna Malcolm Giles there on Oct. 19, 1826, and the next year was admitted to the bar.

Law from the first was for Simms only a way to literature. Beginning with Byronic impulses, he wrote and published a good deal of verse, of which his fifth volume was *Atalantis* (1832), a kind of epic-romance concerned with the fabulous lost continent. A journalist almost as soon as he was a poet, he gave his energy also to magazines and newspapers, and as editor of the *City Gazette* of Charleston took a vigorous, unpopular stand against nullification. Though too much a South Carolinian not to insist upon state rights, he was too much an American, as late as 1832, to look with favor on disunion. That year saw the breakup of his life as he had so far planned it. His wife died, soon after the deaths of his father (1830) and his grandmother, and he was left without money or a newspaper and with a small daughter. Having nothing but literature to sustain him, he set out for the North, where in New York he formed a permanent friendship with Bryant and a new taste for the theatre, and in New Haven wrote a tale of crime, *Martin Faber* (1833), which by 1837 appeared in the customary two volumes. It was so well received that he followed it with *Guy Rivers*

(1834) and *The Yemassee* (1835), much as Cooper a dozen years before had followed his first experiment with more successful and more characteristic ventures. Simms, however, could not feel at home in the North. Again he returned to Charleston, which took hardly a greater interest in the novelist than it had taken in the boy.

Circumstances aided him. In 1836 he married Chevillette Roach, the daughter of Nash Roach of "Woodlands" plantation, in Barnwell County, and thereafter for a quarter of a century lived in a handsome house on a dignified plantation from October to May of every year, and spent the summers in Charleston with his family or in New York on his own literary business. As Nash Roach trusted his son-in-law, and increasingly depended upon him, Simms was soon in effect the master of the household. He passed long mornings in his library, but by dinner he was at the disposal of the guests who were likely to be present, and his afternoons and evenings were spacious and genial. Charleston, as conservative in its literary inclinations as in its social standards, still largely disregarded him. In Barnwell County he was a man of mark and influence. For six or seven years after his second marriage he felt himself free to be a romancer, and he produced ten substantial novels and a collection of short stories. *Richard Hurdis* (1838) had its melodramatic scene in Alabama, *Border Beagles* (1840) in Mississippi, *Beauchampe* (1842) in Kentucky. Others went still further afield, most of all *Pelayo: A Story of the Goth* (1838). But Simms was unmistakably at his best when he kept at home in South Carolina, as in *The Partisan* (1835), *Mellichampe* (1836), and *The Scout*, originally called *The Kinsmen* (1841).

Writing romances, however, was not enough for a story-teller who had a strong bent toward public affairs, a warm local patriotism, and a passion to defend South Carolina, with the whole South, against those who, he thought, maligned or misunderstood them. To say that Simms from being a beneficiary of slavery became an apologist for the institution is to speak, no doubt, with a logic too cold and short to be entirely true. But he did lose all his union sentiments, chiefly because he held that slavery was "an especially and wisely devised institution of heaven" which the North, without true consideration for the negroes, would destroy. Both the South and slavery must be saved. Simms was not satisfied to be the formal advocate of a doctrine, though he did contribute an essay, published as a pamphlet in 1838, to the influential volume, *The Pro-Slavery Argument, as Maintained by the Most Distinguished Writers of the Southern States*

(1852). With a powerful if uncritical industry he undertook to do whatever a man of letters could do for South Carolina, not only by compiling a *History* (1840) and a *Geography* (1843) of the state but by delivering orations, writing poetry, tragedies, criticism, biographies of Francis Marion (1844), Captain John Smith (1846), the Chevalier Bayard (1847), and Nathanael Greene (1849), and even editing the apocryphal plays of Shakespeare (1848). By the quantity and diversity of his output he made himself an impressive figure in whom many of his contemporaries saw a Southern Cooper and some an American Scott. In all Simms wrote there was something generous, earnest, and high-minded. If nothing of his miscellaneous work survives it is because such moral qualities are less lasting than the literary qualities which he did not have or use. The most ardent local patriotism cannot make a good general man of letters of a man who is untrained, formless, diffuse, and extravagant in conception and execution.

From 1842 to 1850 Simms wrote comparatively little fiction, employing what then seemed the heavier guns of history, biography, oratory, and disquisition in his literary siege of Charleston. During the decades before the Civil War he turned again to romantic novels, the best of them, as before, celebrating the valors and endurances of South Carolina in the Revolution. To the *Partisan* series he added *Katharine Walton* (1851), *The Sword and the Distaff* (1853), later (1854) known as *Woodcraft, The Forayers* (1855), and its sequel *Eutaw* (1856), and half a dozen other novels, among them the sensational *Charlemont* (1856), and the neglected but stirring and varied romance of seventeenth-century Carolina, *The Cassique of Kiawah* (1859).

Simms experienced to the full the cataclysm of the war. In 1856 he undertook to explain the South to the North in lectures delivered in New York, and found his audiences first hostile and then absent. His tour was abandoned. That same year, when a convention at Savannah appointed a committee to prepare for the South a "series of books in every department of study, from the earliest primer to the highest grade of literature and science" (Trent, *post*, p. 246), his name was omitted from the list, though in the North Simms was regarded as the leading Southern man of letters. He seemed to himself, at times, a man without any true country, and he declared that he should long ago have followed his father's advice and left Charleston altogether. Yet during the war he was as Southern in his sympathies as in his adversities. His house at "Woodlands" was burned by accident in 1862.

His wife died in 1863, and two more of the nine children whom he survived had died in 1865. That part of his house which had been rebuilt was destroyed by Sherman's raiders, and Simms witnessed the dreadful burning of Columbia in which he had taken refuge. Though a young Northern officer who admired Simms's novels protected him and his family in Columbia, it cast but a momentary light upon his black fortunes. And after the war was over Simms could do nothing to restore himself and his lost country but edit the *War Poetry of the South* (1867), busy himself with helpless journalism, and write bad serials for worse magazines in New York and Philadelphia. He died in Charleston.

Only the curious now read Simms's poetry or plays or criticisms or biographies or consult any of the varied books by which he showed himself a man of letters if not of genius. Though certain of his novels have continued to be read, and a collection of *Border Romances* has been several times reprinted, the selective process had been much stricter in his case than in, say, Cooper's. His novels with a foreign setting, *Pelayo, The Damsel of Darien* (1839), *Count Julian* (1845), and *Vasconselos* (1853), are practically extinct. His novels of the Southern Border, like *Richard Hurdis, Border Beagles, Beauchampe,* and *Charlemont,* have been kept half-alive, at best, by a sporadic interest in their materials. The novels of South Carolina alone still have such vitality as may be felt in the romances of an outmoded fashion.

Little of course is to be gained by insisting that romances which most people find unreadable deserve to be read or by accusing an indifferent posterity of unjustly overlooking a writer who did not please many even of his contemporaries. Yet, Simms's novels dealing with the frontier are full of a rich picaresque energy, of the rogues whom he magnificently enjoyed drawing to the life with all their eccentric vulgarity and swaggering ruthlessness. If the young man could only have left Charleston and its traditions, he might in the Southwest, fugitive and rebel like his father who somehow appears the younger of the two, have made himself the realist which the region called for and which he was fitted by a whole set of impulses to become—although in the Southwest he might not have written at all. Dealing with South Carolina, he could seldom forget the stiffening presence of its aristocracy. His gentlemen and ladies are generally too great to be convincing. He was obliged to assign to a lower class most of the characters who still remain alive because they were created lifelike rather than correct and noble and eloquent. On the whole a more veracious novelist than Cooper, Simms wrote almost no novels which seem so clearly to be of the same material throughout as some of Cooper's. This is because Cooper's actions take place in the forest where none but the persons of the story live at all. Simms's novels are crowded with life, and a life which besides being romantic is often robust and comic.

His best-remembered novel, *The Yemassee,* happens to be perhaps his most romantic. It is a chronicle of the Yemassee War of 1715, hardly known except for Simms's story. He chose to give his Indians a dignity and courage which he thought becoming to their heroic age. He invented a mythology for them. He made the action turn upon a high dramatic moment in which a renegade Indian, having betrayed his tribe, is denounced by his father and with a more than Roman fortitude is killed by his mother who thus saves him from a final shame which could be inflicted only upon a living man. All the changes of taste since 1835 have not been able to deprive this episode of its moving power. But *The Yemassee,* however well remembered, displays a narrower range of Simms's abilities than is to be found in the *Partisan* series.

The first of the series, itself called *The Partisan,* was designed as the first member of a trilogy which was to celebrate the Revolution in South Carolina. Simms did not keep to his scheme, and though he finally called *Mellichampe* and *Katharine Walton* the other members of the trilogy, he used more or less the same material in four more novels which belong to the same cycle. *The Partisan* traces events from the fall of Charleston to Gates's defeat at Camden; the action of *Mellichampe,* which is nearly parallel to that of *Katharine Walton,* the real sequel to *The Partisan,* takes place in the interval between Camden and the coming of Greene; *The Scout* illustrates the period of Greene's first victories; *Woodcraft* furnishes a kind of comic afterpiece to the series. Simms later returned to the cycle and produced *The Forayers* and *Eutaw* to do honor to the American successes of the year 1781. Of these seven *The Scout* is perhaps the worst, because of the terrific melodrama into which Simms always tended to run. *Woodcraft* is on many grounds the best, by reason of its close-built plot and the high spirits with which it tells of the pranks and courtship, after the war, of Captain Porgy, the most truly comic character produced by this school of American romance.

But neither of the two books is quite representative. Neither has the full dignity which Simms imparted to his work when he was most under the spell of Carolina. That always warmed him. He had a tendency to overload his tales with fact in a passionate antiquarianism which made him forget his own belief that "the chief value of history consists in its proper employment for the purposes of art." He was too much stirred by actual events in the history of Carolina to perceive that they needed to be colored into fiction. Simms never looked upon his art as a mere contemporary enterprise. He held that "modern romance is the substitute which the people of the present day offer for the ancient epic," and he aspired to be another Homer. The *Partisan* novels are his epic of the Revolution. Marion, "the Agamemnon of these wars," had already become a legend in the popular memory with the help of Weems's fantastic life; Simms exhibited the whole society of South Carolina as engaged in Marion's task.

Simms relied too often upon one plot for his tales—a partisan and a loyalist as rivals in love —and he repeated stock scenes and characters over and over. But he handled warfare with interest and power and he managed to multiply episodes with a rich invention. His epic was decidedly nearer to Froissart than to Homer. He was both sanguinary and sentimental. His women, at least his gentlewomen, seem now almost all of them fragile and colorless. His comedy is successful chiefly in the words and deeds of the gourmand Porgy and such rowdy playboys. Simms could be admirable in dealing with landscapes. His natural descriptions are full of reality and gusto but have agreeably little to say about the "poetry" or "philosophy" of nature.

All the students of Simms's character, as a man and as an author, have found themselves admiring him for his integrity and force and deeply regretting his misfortunes. His misfortunes were not all external, not all the result of the strife which led to the Civil War, not all the consequences of his allegiance to a state which refused to recognize him or admit him to the rank which he deserved. He suffered most from the conflict in him between his nature and the tradition which he inherited. By nature a realist, with the heartiest appetite for general human life seen with his own eyes, he let himself be limited by a romantic tradition which did not call for all his powers and which indeed gave him over to inflation and often to sensationalism. It was in spite of his conscious aims and his deliberate theories that he now and then wrote about convincing characters and situations through vivid pages in a simple, nervous, racy style. The most accomplished and typical man

of letters of the Old South was often, though perhaps not often enough, a good writer judged by any standard.

[The *Border Romances* were collected in an edition of 17 vols. in 1859 and were several times reprinted, but little of his miscellaneous work survives. The standard biography is that by W. P. Trent, *William Gilmore Simms* (1892). Bibliographies are A. S. Salley, Jr., "A Bibliography of William Gilmore Simms," in *Pubs. Sou. Hist. Asso.*, vol. I, Oct. 1897, and "Additional Simms Bibliography," *Ibid.*, vol. XI, Nov. 1907; Oscar Wegelin, *A List of the Separate Writings of William Gilmore Simms of South Carolina* (1906); *The Cambridge Hist. of Am. Literature*, vol. I (1917), pp. 540–44. An excellent critical discussion of his work appears in V. L. Parrington, *Main Currents in Am. Thought*, vol. II (1927), pp. 125–36. An obituary appeared in *Charleston Daily Courier*, June 13, 1870.]
C. V—D.

SIMONTON, CHARLES HENRY (July 11, 1829–Apr. 25, 1904), soldier, jurist, was born in Charleston, S. C., of Scotch-Irish parents, Charles Strong and Elizabeth (Ross) Simonton. His father was a merchant of Charleston and his mother had emigrated from Ireland. Educated at the public high school, the College of Charleston, and South Carolina College (October 1846–December 1849), from which he was graduated with first honor, he served for one year as assistant in the private academy of William J. Rivers, Charleston; meanwhile, he studied law in the office of William Munro and was admitted to the bar in 1851. In 1852 he married Ella, daughter of Thomas W. Glover.

For a brief period (1851–52) Simonton was assistant clerk of the House of Representatives, and from 1858 to 1860 he was a member of that body. An ardent secessionist, he entered the service of his state as captain of the Washington Light Infantry; for a few weeks during the summer of 1861 he was acting adjutant and inspector general of South Carolina. On Feb. 24, 1862, he was mustered into the Confederate service as commander of the Eutaw Battalion, which soon afterwards was consolidated with the 25th Regiment, South Carolina Volunteers, with Simonton as colonel. Until April 1864 he saw service on the islands commanding the approaches to Charleston. He then rejoined his regiment in Virginia, but was again detached and placed in command of Fort Caswell. After the forced evacuation of that post, Simonton was captured at Town Creek, N. C., Feb. 20, 1865. He was sent first to a Washington prison, and then to Fort Delaware, where he remained until Aug. 6, 1865.

He was a member of the South Carolina constitutional convention of 1865 and of the legislature of 1865–66, and on Dec. 18, 1865, was elected speaker of the House to fill an unexpired term. He was chairman of the state Democratic convention of 1868 which declared for a "white man's government," and, the same year, was a member of the Democratic national committee and a delegate to the national convention. In the decisive political campaign of 1876, he was chairman of the important executive committee of Charleston County. With the overthrow of Radical rule, he again became a member of the House, 1877–86; in 1882 he was one of the codifiers of the general statutes of the state.

In 1865 Simonton became the senior partner in a very successful law practice with Theodore G. Barker of Charleston, a connection which continued until he was commissioned judge of the United States district court of South Carolina, in September 1886. This position he occupied until his elevation to the circuit court of appeals, Dec. 19, 1893. He was assigned to the fourth circuit and served until his death. In 1857 he compiled and published, with James Conner, *A Digest of the Equity Reports of the State of South Carolina*, covering decisions of the court of chancery from 1784 to 1856. In 1896 he delivered some lectures before the law school of Richmond College, which were afterwards published as *The Federal Courts, Their Organization, Jurisdiction and Procedure* (1896).

As a lawyer, legislator, and judge, he was distinguished for his calm and even temperament; tact and common-sense and a pleasing personality rather than eloquence or brilliance accounted for his professional advancement. In politics he was essentially conservative and was noted for his ability to effect compromises. Combined with unusual industry and a great love for the law, he had a quick and logical mind with a gift for clear expression. A life-long resident of Charleston he was greatly interested in civic and educational improvements. He died in Philadelphia, survived by his widow and daughter, and was buried in Magnolia Cemetery, Charleston.

[*Who's Who in America*, 1903–05; Edward McCrady and S. A. Ashe, *Cyc. of Eminent and Representative Men of the Carolinas of the Nineteenth Century* (1892), vol. I; U. R. Brooks, *S. C. Bench and Bar*, vol. I (1908); *Memorial Proc. on the Life and Character of Charles Henry Simonton Had in the U. S. Circuit Court of Appeals* (1904); *Relics, Mementos, Etc., of the Washington Light Infantry* (n.d.), catalogue of a display in the W. L. I. armory; *War of the Rebellion: Official Records (Army)*; memorial proceedings of the Washington Light Infantry Veterans (MS.) and memorial resolutions of Camp Sumter No. 2, United Confederate Veterans (MS.) in possession of Simonton's grand-daughter, Caroline S. Alston; *House Journals* of the S. C. General Assembly; *Jour. of the Convention of the People of S. C. Held in Columbia, S. C., Sept. 1865* (1865); *House Misc. Doc. 31*, 44 Cong., 2 Sess., pt. 2, pp. 125–30; 28–119 *Federal Reporter*; *News and Courier* (Charleston), Apr. 26, 1904.]   R. H. W.

SIMONTON, JAMES WILLIAM (Jan. 30, 1823–Nov. 2, 1882), journalist, was born in Co-

lumbia County, N. Y. His family moved to New York City when he was a boy, and there he attended the public schools until the poverty of the family obliged him to become apprenticed to a tailor. He was eager for a journalistic career, however, and at the age of twenty he secured a position as reporter on the *Morning Courier and New-York Enquirer*. For this work he displayed such aptitude that in the next year he was sent by his paper to Washington with Henry Jarvis Raymond [*q.v.*] as congressional correspondent. He remained until 1850, steadily winning the respect and confidence of leading statesmen in the capital. With the opening of California in the fifties he conceived the plan of establishing a Whig paper in San Francisco, and he accordingly set out across the continent with a complete printing-press outfit. On his arrival, finding that he had been anticipated in his purpose, he joined the staff of the *California Daily Courier*. When the *New York Times* was founded in 1851 he became one of the proprietors, and soon afterward returned to Washington to serve as correspondent for the *Times* and for papers in New Orleans, San Francisco, and Detroit. His weekly letters entitled "The History of Legislation," 1855–58, which were almost a political history of these years, won for him wide recognition. In 1857 he performed the most distinguished feat of his career: an exposure in the *Times* for Jan. 6, 1857, of a congressional bill ostensibly granting public lands for the provision of necessary rights of way to the Pacific railroad but actually surrendering a large part of the territory of Minnesota. The congressional investigation that resulted ended in the expulsion of four members from the House of Representatives. In the course of the hearings before the investigating committee Simonton, subpoenaed as a witness, steadfastly refused to disclose the sources of his information, resting upon the principle of journalistic ethics that the origin of facts revealed to a representative of the press in confidence must not be divulged. Piqued by this persistent stand, the committee forthwith excluded him as reporter from the floor of the House.

In 1859 he became part owner of the *San Francisco Evening Bulletin* and afterwards of the *Morning Call*. In 1867 he was recalled to New York as the general agent of the Associated Press, a capacity in which he served fourteen years. During this period he was instrumental in exposing some of the corruption of Grant's administration through the press, but not without arousing bitter attacks upon his own integrity. In 1873 appeared an anonymous pamphlet of forty-seven pages, *One of the Reasons for*

Telegraphic Reform. Power and Tyranny of the Associated Press. The Character of its ... Manager James W. Simonton ... Shall He Continue to be the Sole Telegraphic Historian of the Country? Quoting at length from the record of the hearings of the investigating committee in 1857, but interlarding this text with distorted scurrilous headings, this broadside accused Simonton of perjury and of admitting that he had acted as a paid lobbyist. He was called the "sole telegraphic historian of the country" because of the preference which the Associated Press enjoyed in transmission of dispatches through the Western Union Telegraph Company. Says the discreetly anonymous author of his pamphlet, "The object of its publication is to arouse ... the people generally to the real character of this small and vicious tyrant who prepares for the public the only telegraphic record they can have of the hurrying events of the times ..." (*One of the Reasons,* p. 4). But apparently the public remained apathetic, for the "tyrant" came through the ordeal unscathed. Retiring in 1881, Simonton purchased a large tract of land in the Sacramento valley and devoted his time to various agricultural and civic enterprises. He died suddenly in the following year on his estate at Napa. About a year and a half before his death he married Minnie Bronson, who was his second wife. He was survived by his widow, two sons, and a daughter.

[*Frank Leslie's Illustrated Newspaper,* Sept. 10, 1859; J. P. Young, *Journalism in Cal.* (1916); Augustus Maverick, *Henry J. Raymond and the N. Y. Press* (1870); E. H. Davis, *Hist. of the N. Y. Times, 1851–1921* (1921); J. M. Lee, *Hist. of Am. Journalism* (1917); *Cong. Globe,* 34 Cong., 3 Sess., pp. 274–77, for land-grants investigation; editorial in *San Francisco Call* and obituary in *N. Y. Times,* Nov. 4, 1882.]
P. K.

SIMPSON, ALBERT BENJAMIN (Dec. 15, 1843–Oct. 29, 1919), clergyman, founder of the Christian and Missionary Alliance, was born at Bayview, Prince Edward Island, of Scottish ancestry, the son of James and Jane (Clark) Simpson. The father, a miller, shipbuilder, and exporter at Bayview and, after 1847, an Ontario farmer, was a Presbyterian elder deeply interested in foreign missions. Sensitive and imaginative, Albert was early molded by the religious training of his home, nine miles from Chatham, Ontario, and at fourteen he determined to enter the ministry. After a few months in the Chatham high school and of study under tutors, he taught for a term, and in 1861 entered Knox College, Toronto, graduating in 1865. On Sept. 12 of that year he was ordained by the Hamilton Presbytery as pastor of Knox Church, Hamilton. In 1874 he accepted a call to the Chestnut

Street Church, Louisville, Ky. In this city he led a united evangelistic campaign and later conducted Sunday evening services of his own in public halls. A deepening of his own spiritual life led to his emphasizing sanctification in his preaching. Dissatisfaction in his congregation followed, and this, together with his desire to reach a larger number with his message, resulted, late in 1879, in his undertaking the pastorate of the Thirteenth Street Church, New York City. For two years he endeavored to lead his new congregation into evangelistic work for neglected people, but in November 1881 he asked to be released, and soon embarked on the independent movement which he was to carry on until his death.

He first held meetings in a hall, preceding his evening services with street preaching. Growing attendance soon compelled him to utilize a, theatre and later, Steinway Hall. Within eight years twelve places of worship were used until, in 1889, a tabernacle, with which were connected a book store, the six-story Berachah Home of divine healing, and quarters for his missionary training college, was opened at Eighth Avenue and Fourteenth Street. Here he continued an increasing work until the end of his life, at which time five additional buildings were also in use, at Nyack, N. Y. In 1882 he organized an independent church, especially for people of the middle class who had no church connection; later he added many rescue mission activities to his work.

His outstanding achievement was the founding, in 1887, of the Christian Alliance, which, in 1897, was combined with the International Missionary Alliance, under the name Christian and Missionary Alliance. Of this organization Simpson became president and general superintendent. At his death it reported between 300 and 400 branches and connected churches in the United States and Canada, with about 200 pastors and local superintendents and twenty-five evangelists. In the foreign mission field it was active in sixteen countries. More than 1,000 missionaries had been sent out, who had been educated, with nearly 3,000 other Christian workers, at the Bible and missionary training schools of the Alliance.

A feature of Simpson's ministry was the conducting of conventions, with the aid of numerous associates, throughout the United States and in several foreign lands. These combined characteristics of camp meeting, Bible conference, evangelistic campaign, Second Coming retreats, and missionary conventions. In 1871 he visited Europe for his health; in 1885 he attended a conference in Great Britain on the spiritual life; and beginning in 1893 made many tours which took him to Europe, Asia, Africa, and South America, to visit mission fields and recruit new supporters.

Literary work consumed much of his energy. He published more than seventy religious books, including poems, some of which have had wide and continued circulation. Among the best known were *The Fullness of Jesus* (1886), one of many sermon volumes; *The Christ Life* (1892), the second of four small books explaining the Alliance movement; *The Holy Spirit in the Old and New Testaments* (1899); and *Christ in the Bible* (1888–1909), a sixteen-volume commentary. He also composed words and music of many hymns. Periodicals which he founded and edited included *The Gospel in All Lands* (1881–1903), a pioneer illustrated missionary monthly, and *The Word, Work and World*, a monthly first issued in 1882, which later became *The Alliance Weekly*.

He was no extremist, whatever follies or fanaticisms some of his followers may have fallen into. Though a believer in divine healing, he gave first place to his evangelistic message. He was a man of commanding personality, and his resonant voice and gracious manner gave added force to the intellectual and spiritual power of his preaching and of his spoken prayers. He took little sleep, usually working from twelve to fifteen hours a day. When he died he left no estate. Having voluntarily surrendered all his business affairs to others in 1918, he lived on an allowance from the Alliance. On Sept. 13, 1865, he married Margaret, daughter of John Henry of Toronto, by whom he had six children.

[A. E. Thomson, *The Life of A. B. Simpson* (1920) quotes from a brief manuscript autobiog. of Simpson's earlier years, and includes appraisals of his life by religious leaders; it also gives evidence that his birth was in 1843 rather than in 1844 as stated elsewhere; see also *Who's Who in America*, 1918–19; *N. Y. Times*, Oct. 30, 1919.]

                                     P.P.F.

SIMPSON, EDMUND SHAW (1784–July 31, 1848), actor, theatrical manager, was English born. Although educated for a mercantile life, he had, as he phrased it, " 'a soul above buttons,' " so he "ran away, and took to the stage" (Dunlap, *post*, p. 356). He made his bow in May 1806, with a barn-storming troupe in the village of Towcester, Northamptonshire, England, appearing as the Baron in August F. F. von Kotzebue's then famous play, *The Stranger*. He soon shifted his allegiance to a company at Buckingham, where he wrote, "we had the pleasure of playing in a larger stable" (*Ibid.*, p. 356). Subsequently he acted at Dover, Margate, and Brighton, and then undertook an engagement at

Dublin, whence he was brought to the United States by Thomas Abthorpe Cooper and Stephen Price [*qq.v.*], managers of the Park Theatre, New York. His American début occurred at that house on Oct. 25, 1809. On this occasion, as Harry Dornton in *The Road to Ruin* by Thomas Holcroft, and later in such rôles as Jack Absolute in *The Rivals* and Joseph Surface in *The School for Scandal* he gave convincing evidence of distinct gifts for high comedy. He was at once warmly received by the playgoers and praised by the critics, who pronounced him "easy, natural, and graceful," with a "modulant and sonorous" voice (*Ramblers' Mag., post*, pp. 103, 104) and a "glowing and animated expression of . . . countenance" (Odell, *post*, II, 351). That he displayed ability also in other departments of the theatre is seen in his appointment as "acting manager" by 1812 (*Ibid.*, p. 387), and some half dozen years later he replaced Cooper as Price's partner. Because of the latter's frequent absences abroad much of the burden of management fell upon Simpson, but, despite a disastrous fire at the Park on May 24, 1820, and increasing competition, he kept the theatre in a prosperous state for several years. The popularity of the house was greatly enhanced by the many celebrities of the British stage brought over by the partners for brief starring visits, and by the introduction of Italian opera to New York in 1825 through the engagement of the admirable Garcia company.

Perhaps because of permanent lameness, resulting from a serious stage accident in December 1827, and because of his waning popularity as a player, Simpson practically withdrew from acting about 1833 and confined himself largely to his duties as director. As a result of the panic of 1837 and of the enterprise of young and progressive competitors, the fortunes of the Park and its managers declined so much that when Simpson became sole lessee of the theatre upon the death of Price in 1840 he found himself master of a tottering house. For some years he struggled on doggedly and not always hopelessly, thanks to the efforts of a good company. But it was a losing battle. His methods were outmoded, the building was in an advanced state of dilapidation because of the proprietors' niggardliness, and the public had formed the habit of going elsewhere. On June 5, 1848, the ruined manager surrendered, forfeiting his interests to Thomas Sowerby Hamblin [*q.v.*] of the Bowery Theatre for a small annuity. Less than two months later he died—of a broken heart, his contemporaries believed. He left a widow—the former actress Julia Elizabeth Jones, whom he married Mar. 9, 1820—and several children, one of them Edward Simpson [*q.v.*]. For their relief a highly profitable benefit was held at the Park on Dec. 7, in which many leading actors of the day participated. This was followed by five other dramatic benefits in the city, indisputable testimony to the high esteem in which Simpson was held by his fellow-townsmen for his long years of able public service in the theatre, his valiant struggle against adversity, and his unblemished character.

[William Dunlap, *A Hist. of the Am. Theatre* (1832); G. C. D. Odell, *Annals of the N. Y. Stage,* vols. II, III, IV, V (1927–31); T. A. Brown, *Hist. of the Am. Stage* (1870) and *A Hist. of the N. Y. Stage* (1903), vol. I; J. N. Ireland, *Records of the N. Y. Stage,* vols. I, II (1866–67); *Ramblers' Mag., and N. Y. Theatrical Reg.,* vol. I (1809–10?); Joseph Cowell, *Thirty Years Passed Among the Players in England and America* (1844); newspaper notices in the *Albion* (N. Y.), June 10, Aug. 5, 1848, and in *Evening Post,* (N. Y.), Aug. 1, 1848; date of marriage from records of Grace Church, N. Y. City.] O. S. C.

SIMPSON, EDWARD (Mar. 3, 1824–Dec. 1, 1888), naval officer, was born in New York City, son of Edmund Shaw Simpson [*q.v.*] and Julia Elizabeth (Jones) Simpson. The mother was of Welsh parentage, the father an Englishman who had come to New York in his twenties and was for years manager of the Park Theatre. The son entered the navy as midshipman on Feb. 11, 1840, served five years in the Brazil and Mediterranean Squadrons, and after nine months' study at the United States Naval Academy, then just established at Annapolis, was made passed midshipman, July 1846. Through the Mexican War he was in the small steamer *Vixen* "whereever a shot was fired on the east coast" (Harrington, *post*), including the attacks on Tabasco, Tampico, and Túxpan, and the siege of Vera Cruz, where the *Vixen* made a celebrated reconnaissance under the guns of the fort, remaining there till ordered back by Perry. During the next decade he was in the coast survey, 1848–49 and 1855–56; in the *Congress,* Brazil Squadron, 1850–53; instructor in gunnery, Naval Academy, 1853–54; and after promotion to lieutenant in 1855, in the *Portsmouth,* Asiatic Squadron, participating under Andrew Hull Foote [*q.v.*] in the capture of the barrier forts below Canton. From September 1858 to May 1862 he had charge of ordnance instruction at the Naval Academy, being made first head of that department in 1860. His *Treatise on Ordnance and Naval Gunnery* (1859) was long an academy textbook. After promotion to lieutenant commander in 1862 and another year at the academy as commandant of midshipmen, he secured sea service in command of the *Wabash,* and

shortly afterward of the ironclad *Passaic,* which figured in the attacks on Forts Wagner and Sumter and in the whole arduous 1863 campaign off Charleston, S. C. He commanded the steamer *Isonomia* on the southeast coast, May–December 1864, and subsequently joined the West Gulf Squadron, with promotion to commander, March 1865, acting as fleet captain under Rear Admiral Henry Knox Thatcher in operations below Mobile until after its capitulation. His generous, kindly nature is illustrated by his loan of $100 to surrendered Confederate officers, his former students, with the words "Repay it when you are able; never, if not" (Harrington, *post*). His post-bellum sea commands included the *Mohican* and *Mohongo* in the Pacific, 1866–68, *Franklin* and *Wabash* in the Atlantic, 1873–74, and *Omaha* in the south Pacific, 1875–77. More noteworthy, in view of his eminence in the field of ordnance, were his shore assignments, especially as assistant chief of the ordnance bureau, 1869–70. In 1873 he published his *Report on a Naval Mission to Europe Especially Devoted to the Material and Construction of Artillery,* in two volumes. Made captain in 1870, commodore in 1878, and rear admiral in 1884, he commanded the New London, Conn., station, 1878–80, and the League Island navy yard, 1880–83. He was president of the gun foundry board, 1883–84, for which he wrote a report of a mission abroad (*House Executive Document 97,* 48 Cong., 1 Sess.); president of the naval advisory board, 1884–85; and president of the board of inspection and survey from October 1885 until his retirement Mar. 3, 1886. His publications include "A Proposed Armament for the Navy" (*The Proceedings of the United States Naval Institute,* vol. VII, 1881), "The Navy and its Prospects of Rehabilitation" (*Ibid.,* vol. XII, 1886), and *Modern Ships of War* (1888), with Sir Edward Reed. His high service reputation is evidenced by his selection as president of the United States Naval Institute, 1886–88, and of the association of naval academy graduates from its organization until his death. His wife was Mary Ann, daughter of Gen. Charles Sterett Ridgely, whom he married at Oak Ridge, Md., in 1853, and by whom he had a son, who became a rear admiral, and four daughters. His death from Bright's disease occurred at Washington; he was buried in Cypress Hills Cemetery, Long Island.

[L. H. Hamersly, *Records of Living Officers . . . U. S. Navy* (4th ed., 1890); obituaries in *Army and Navy Jour.,* Dec. 8, 1888, and *Evening Star* (Washington, D. C.), Dec. 1, 1888; papers in the possession of Simpson's grandson, E. R. Simpson, Ruxton, Md., including a biog. sketch in MS. by Rear Admiral P. F. Harrington.] A. W.

SIMPSON, JAMES HERVEY (Mar. 9, 1813–Mar. 2, 1883), soldier, engineer, author, was born in New Brunswick, N. J., the son of John Neely and Mary (Brunson) Simpson. After a common-school education he entered the United States Military Academy, West Point, N. Y., at fifteen and graduated creditably in 1832. Commissioned in the artillery, he served as aide to Gen. Henry Lawrence Eustis during the Seminole War, 1837–38, and was in action at Locha-Hatchee. In 1838 he was transferred to the topographical engineers, and during the following ten years was engaged in engineering projects in the East and the South. In 1849 he was in charge of the exploration of a route from Fort Smith, Ark., to Santa Fé, N. Mex. (*Report from the Secretary of War Communicating the Report and Map of the Route from Fort Smith, Ark., to Santa Fé, N. Mex.,* 1850), serving as chief topographical engineer, Department of New Mexico. About this time, too, he reconnoitered a route from Santa Fé to the Navajo Indian country, which he reported in *Journal of a Military Reconnaissance from Santa Fé, N. Mex., to the Navajo Country* (1852). He was promoted captain, Mar. 3, 1853, and served five years on road construction in Minnesota and two years on coast survey duty. In 1858 he accompanied the Utah Expedition, and submitted a valuable report on a new route from Salt Lake City to the Pacific coast.

With the outbreak of the Civil War he attained the rank of major and for a few months was chief topographical engineer, Department of the Shenandoah, when he was commissioned colonel, 4th New Jersey Volunteers. With his regiment he saw service in the Peninsular campaign, and was engaged at Westpoint, Va., and at Gaines's Mill, where he was taken prisoner. After being exchanged he resigned his volunteer commission on Aug. 27, 1862, and served as chief topographical engineer and chief engineer, Department of the Ohio, 1862–63. Until the end of the war he was in general charge of fortifications and engineering projects in Kentucky. For faithful and meritorious services during the war, he was brevetted colonel and brigadier-general, Mar. 13, 1865. He became chief engineer, Department of the Interior, 1865–67, and was charged with general direction and inspection of the Union Pacific Railroad (*Report on the Union Pacific Railroad and Its Branches,* 1865), as well as of all government wagon-roads. He was promoted colonel of engineers on Mar. 7, 1867. His subsequent active military service covered road construction, river and harbor improvements, and lighthouse supervision in the South and the Middle West. At his own request he retired on Mar. 31, 1880, and made his home in St. Paul, Minn., where he died of pneumonia, and where he was buried with military honors. He was married first to Jane Champlin, and second, in 1871, to Elizabeth Sophia (Borup) Champlin, widow of Raymond Champlin. He was survived by his wife, two daughters, and two adopted daughters. He published a number of interesting reports, descriptive of his explorations in the West (listed in *Centennial of the United States Military Academy,* 1904, vol. II, p. 356), including *Route From Fort Smith, Ark., to Santa Fé, N. Mex.* (1850), *The Shortest Route to California* (1869), *Coronado's March in Search of the Seven Cities of Cibola* (1871), and *Exploration Across the Great Basin of the Territory of Utah* (1876).

[G. W. Cullum, *Biog. Reg. Officers and Grads. U. S. Mil. Acad.* (3rd ed., 1891), vol. I; *Fourteenth Ann. Reunion Assoc. Grads. U. S. Mil. Acad.* (1883); C. L. Andrews, *Hist. of St. Paul, Minn.* (1890); obituaries in *Army and Navy Jour.,* Mar. 17, 1883; *N. Y. Times, Daily Globe* (St. Paul), Mar. 3, 1883.]   C. D. R.

SIMPSON, JERRY (Mar. 31, 1842–Oct. 23, 1905), congressman from Kansas, was born in the old Scotch settlement in Westmoreland County, New Brunswick, Canada, the son of Joseph Simpson. His mother's maiden name was Washburn. He was probably named Jeremiah. His father, a sawmill owner and sailor, decided in 1848 to remove the family to Upper Canada, and, though the journey was interrupted near Syracuse, N. Y., by 1852 they were established east of the Saint Clair River. Probably they subsequently removed to Indiana. The boy had almost no formal education, but home influence and books in part compensated. At the age of fourteen he became cook on a lake boat and ultimately became captain. At the opening of the Civil War he enlisted for three months in Company A, 12th Illinois Infantry. After 1869 his home was in Porter County, Ind., where he met Jane Cape, a native of Cumberlandshire, England, whom he married on Oct. 12, 1870, at Buffalo, N. Y. About 1879 he abandoned the Lakes for a farm and sawmill near Holton, Kan.; after five years he took advantage of increased prices to sell out and invested his savings, about $15,000, in a cattle ranch near Medicine Lodge, Kan. His hopes for speedy profits from this new "boom" were ended, when an especially severe winter wiped out his herd, and he found himself under mortgage and without resources. He was glad to accept appointment as marshal of Medicine Lodge at forty dollars a month. In a sense, his prosperity, his disaster, and his courageous efforts at recovery were typical of the big majority of his fellows. Ruinous prices made the mortgage burden impossibly large, and "booming" gave way to despair; in 1888–89, the Farmers' Alliance swept through the state until, with its allies, it numbered a third of the voters, and in 1890 as the People's Party it entered politics. Simpson was named for Congress from the seventh district.

He was prepared to lead such a movement. Originally a Lincoln Republican, he had deserted that party to work for Peter Cooper and his monetary program. He had followed his principles into the newer Union Labor party and was twice defeated for the state legislature, 1886 and 1888, in spite of Democratic support. In this campaign for Congress, his wit and clever, telling illustrations were very effective before audiences that accepted agrarian doctrines and needed only the emotional stimulus to break past allegiances. A reporter twisted a statement to mean that, in contrast to his wealthy banker opponent who wore silk socks, he, Simpson, wore none, and the name "Sockless Jerry" was his for life. The Populist state ticket was narrowly defeated in 1890, but Simpson was elected. In 1892 the Democrats were eager to draw Kansas from the Republican presidential column, and their indorsement gave victory to the state ticket; he was again elected. In 1894 the allies divided, and he went down with his ticket in defeat. National fusion in 1896 meant the practical absorption of the Populists by the Democrats, and, after his reëlection of that year, he called himself a Demo-Populist. In 1898 he was defeated for the second time by Chester I. Long, whom he had twice defeated, and, after a vain attempt to obtain Populist convention indorsement for senator, he retired to private life. He accepted Populist doctrine completely and combined with it a belief in the single tax. In Congress he delivered few speeches and proposed few bills; his weapon was a shrewd question or witty comment directed at effort that he thought false or insincere, and he was a feared and respected opponent. He advocated a paper money system and accepted free silver coinage as only a step. His belief in simple democracy and his monetary program are the two consistent threads through his career. On the Spanish War he was uncertain, but he was an ardent opponent of army expansion and imperialism. After retirement he lived a short time in Wichita and Kansas City. On May 8, 1899, he began to publish *Jerry Simpson's Bayonet,* which he continued to publish until Sept. 17, 1900. In 1902, partly on account of his health, he removed to Roswell, N. Mex., where he associated with a land and colonization corporation. His health grew steadily worse, and he returned to Wichita, where he died and was buried. He was survived by a wife and one son.

[A. L. Diggs, *The Story of Jerry Simpson* (copr. 1908), a slight memoir by a co-worker assisted by Simpson's wife; *Biog. Directory Am. Cong.* (1928); T. A. McNeal, *When Kansas was Young* (1922); Hamlin Garland, "The Alliance Wedge in Congress," *Arena,* Mar. 1892; S. J. Buck, *The Agrarian Crusade* (1920); J. D. Hicks, *The Populist Revolt* (1931); *Leavenworth Times,* Oct. 24, 1905.]
　　　　　　　　　　　　　　　　　R. C. M.

SIMPSON, JOHN ANDREW (July 4, 1871–Mar. 15, 1934), farm leader, was born near Salem, Nebr., the son of William J. and Sarah Catharine (Cornell) Simpson; his father died when John was seven years old. He attended the district school and later the Auburn high school, where he completed the four years' course in one year and graduated as the honor student of his class. After some teaching he entered the University of Kansas, from which he received the degree of LL.B. in 1896. On June 21 of the same year he married Millie Berlet.

He began the practice of law in Auburn, but the political upheaval of the nineties brought him into the ranks of the Populist party and in 1897 he was appointed accountant in the state auditor's office in Lincoln, a position which he held for four years. He then resumed the practice of law in Auburn, but within a year the pioneer spirit that led his father and mother to move westward impelled him to go to Oklahoma, which had been opened to settlement, and in 1901 he drew a claim at the El Reno drawing. Taking possession of his land, which lay near the town of Alfalfa in Caddo County, for some nine years he engaged in farming and also became a country banker. He was a member of the Oklahoma legislature in 1915–17, the only official position he ever held in public life, except that of membership on the school board.

About this time he became interested in the Farmers' Union, joining that organization in Custer County, Okla., in 1916. The following year he became state president and held this office until 1930, during which period the membership increased from 500 to 200,000, and more than 200 cooperative institutions were established with headquarters and warehouses in Oklahoma City valued at $100,000. Meanwhile, he founded and edited the *Oklahoma Union Farmer.* In 1930 he was elected president of the Farmers' Educational and Cooperative Union of America, which office he held until his death. His twenty years of farm leadership were characterized by bitter controversies, activity in political campaigns, attacks on the national administrations, and numerous stumping tours. He advocated violence in the form of farm strikes and holidays when such measures were deemed necessary. He was a caustic critic of the Hoover administration; advocated the election of Smith to the presidency in 1928; was one of Franklin Roosevelt's earliest supporters for that office in the Southwest; and was mentioned for the secretaryship of agriculture in the Roosevelt cabinet. He was a zealous champion of the enactment of a law to guarantee cost of production prices for farm products consumed in the country, and stressed the impossibility of regulating the production of 30,000,000 farm occupants. He maintained that the government should treat agriculture as it treats industry, and that it should refinance the farmer's mortgage indebtedness on as favorable terms as it accords to industry. He urged currency inflation, the remonetization of silver, and paper money. The national Farmers' Union, under his influence, put forward the Swank-Thomas bill, which provided that the farmer should be guaranteed cost of production plus a reasonable profit for his products consumed in the home market; the Frazier-Lemke bill, to refinance the farmer at 1½ per cent.; and the Wheeler free coinage bill. To the furtherance of these measures he devoted practically all his time. He died in Washington, survived by his wife, two sons, and four daughters. After his death a collection of excerpts from his speeches and writings, *The Militant Voice of Agriculture* (1934), was published.

[*Who's Who in America*, 1932–33; *N. Y. Times*, Mar. 16, 1934; *N. Y. Herald Tribune*, Mar. 16, 1934; *Cong. Record*, Apr. 2, 1934; *Okla. Union Farmer*, Feb. 1, Mar. 1, Apr. 1 and 15, 1934; data supplied by Mrs. John A. Simpson of Oklahoma City.]   L. B. S.

SIMPSON, MATTHEW (June 21, 1811– June 18, 1884), bishop of the Methodist Episcopal Church, was the son of James Simpson, who at the time of Matthew's birth was manufacturing weaver's reeds and running a store in Cadiz, Ohio, of which town he had been one of the first settlers. His widowed mother had migrated with her family from Ireland to the United States in 1793 and settled in Huntington County, Pa., whence her sons later moved westward. James died when Matthew, the youngest of three children, was a year old, and the latter was brought up by his mother, Sarah, a native of New Jersey, daughter of Jeremiah Tingley. He had little schooling, but, naturally inclined to books, mastered with practically no other aid the ordinary school subjects, German, and Latin; acquired some knowledge of Greek during a summer term at an academy in Cadiz; and spent two

months at Madison College, Unionville, Pa., being unable financially to stay longer. He also learned something of the printing business in the office of an uncle who was editor of the county paper, of the law by frequenting the court of which another uncle, Matthew Simpson, was a judge, and of public affairs from the same uncle, who was for ten years a member of the Ohio Senate. He supported himself by reed-making, by copying in the office of the county court, of which a third uncle was clerk, and by teaching. In 1830 he began the study of medicine under Dr. James McBean of Cadiz and after three years qualified as a practitioner.

In the meantime, having been reared under strong Methodist influences, he had become active in religious work and had been licensed to preach. Deciding at length to devote himself to the ministry, he was received into the Pittsburgh Conference on trial in 1834, and in 1836 admitted into full connection. On Nov. 3 of the preceding year he had married Ellen Holmes Verner, daughter of James Verner of Pittsburgh. On the Cadiz circuit, in the neighborhood where he had been reared, a tall, plain-faced, somewhat ungainly and diffident young man, he began a career of swiftly increasing responsibility and prominence which culminated in his being the best known and most influential Methodist of his day in the United States, a counselor of statesmen, and a public speaker of international reputation. His promise was soon recognized and after a year on the Cadiz circuit he was stationed at Pittsburgh (1835–36), and then at Williamsport (Monongahela). Elected professor of natural sciences in Allegheny College in 1837, he entered the educational field and in 1839 became president of Indiana Asbury University, now De Pauw, Greencastle, Ind., chartered in 1837. During the nine years he served in this capacity he did valuable pioneer work in the development of the institution. Invitations to the presidency of Northwestern University, Dickinson College, and Wesleyan University, Middletown, Conn., were later declined.

As a member of the General Conferences of 1844 and 1848 he became prominent in the deliberations of his denomination. The General Conference of 1848 elected him editor of the *Western Christian Advocate*. Through this medium his frank and forceful utterances on public questions, especially those relating to slavery, attracted wide attention and brought him to the favorable notice of Salmon P. Chase. A delegate to the General Conference of 1852, he was by that body elected bishop. His patriotism was as deep and sincere as his religious convictions and during the Civil War he was a tower of strength for the Union cause. Both his knowledge and his oratorical powers were employed in behalf of the Union, and his address on "The Future of Our Country," delivered in many places, had great effect on large audiences. Already known to Secretary Chase, he soon stood high in the esteem of Secretary Stanton, and was consulted by both Stanton and Lincoln. He preached a notable sermon in the House of Representatives the day after Lincoln's second inauguration and delivered the eulogy at his burial in Springfield, Ill. His episcopal residence was first Pittsburgh, later Evanston, Ill., and finally Philadelphia, but his duties carried him all over the United States, to Mexico, Canada, and Europe. In 1857 he was a delegate to the British Wesleyan Conference, Liverpool, attended the Conference of the Evangelical Alliance at Berlin, and visited the Holy Land. In 1870 and again in 1875 he made official visits to Europe, and in 1881 he delivered the opening sermon at the Ecumenical Methodist Conference, London. His address in Exeter Hall at a meeting in commemoration of President Garfield, presided over by James Russell Lowell, evoked an unusual response from an audience of three thousand, the most of whom were English.

The high place which he held both officially and in popular esteem was due to the character of the man himself, to a well balanced if not brilliant endowment, and particularly to his extraordinary power over audiences. He was not preëminent as a theologian, as a scholar, or as an innovator, but he was well informed and combined conservatism, open-mindedness, practical wisdom, ability to discern the adjustment conditions called for, and unadulterated religious devotion in an exceptional degree. While remaining strictly orthodox, he was sympathetic toward science and in general progressive. He early favored higher education for Methodist ministers, and was influential in the movement to secure lay representation in the General Conference. Judged by the effect upon the hearers, few public speakers of the day were his equal. Having remarkable facility of expression and an imagination of wide sweep, he took great subjects and portrayed them on a big canvas with a fervid evangelical earnestness. His aim was not to instruct but to persuade. Thoroughly sincere, he felt profoundly the truths which he expounded, so that his preaching had in it the note of testimony. People believed in him and surrendered themselves to him. Such was his power over them that frequently large numbers rose to their feet, clapped their hands, laughed, or

wept. Too busy with many things for much literary work, he nevertheless wrote *A Hundred Years of Methodism* (1876) and edited the *Cyclopædia of Methodism* (1878). His *Lectures on Preaching Delivered before the Theological Department of Yale College* was published in 1879. After his death *Sermons* (1885), from shorthand reports by G. R. Crooks, appeared.

[H. A. Simpson, *Early Records of the Simpson Families* (1927); *Minutes of the Annual Conferences of the M. E. Church* (1884); E. A. Smith, *Allegheny—A Century of Education, 1815–1915* (1916); G. R. Crooks, *The Life of Bishop Matthew Simpson* (1890); E. M. Wood, *The Peerless Orator* (1909); C. T. Wilson, *Matthew Simpson* (1929); *National Mag.,* Oct. 1855; *Meth. Quart. Rev.,* Jan. 1885; *Zion's Herald* and *Western Christian Advocate,* June 25, 1884. Many of Simpson's MSS. have been deposited in the Lib. of Cong.]

H. E. S.

SIMPSON, MICHAEL HODGE (Nov. 15, 1809–Dec. 21, 1884), capitalist, manufacturer, inventor, was born in Newburyport, Mass., the son of Paul Simpson and his wife, Abigail (Johnson), widow of J. S. Hodge; his father was a sea-captain who became a merchant. Michael was educated in the schools of Newburyport until he was fifteen, when he went to Boston and entered the employ of a shipping firm. In the small ventures clerks were allowed to make, he and a fellow employee named Coffin were so successful that before either was twenty-one they owned one-third of the cargo of a ship bound for Calcutta and had established their own business. Much of it consisted in the importing of wool from South America. This wool was cheap but not suitable for spinning because of the dirt and burrs embedded in it, and constant efforts were being made to devise machinery for combing out these foreign materials. By 1831 Simpson had bought out his partners, and later he disposed of the business to the New England Worsted Company, of Saxonville, Mass.

His contacts with this concern brought the mechanical problems of manufacture more directly to his attention, and in 1833 he happened to see a machine for burring wool designed by a French inventor named Samuel Couillard. This he bought and improved, patenting the improvements July 7, 1837. The English rights to it he then sold for ten thousand pounds. The panic of 1837 threw the Saxonville mills into the hands of their creditors, of whom he was one, and he became their agent, commencing, in 1839, the manufacture of bunting, in addition to blanket and worsted yarns. On July 4, 1848, at the inauguration of work on the Washington Monument at the capital, he presented the Washington National Monument Society with what is said to have been the first American bunting flag made in the United States. The mills did not prosper, however, and so Simpson bought a two-thirds interest and assumed their management and most of the financial responsibility for their operation. With machinery improved or invented by him they gradually became extremely profitable, and in 1854 he bought a carpet factory in Troy, N. Y., moved it to Roxbury, Mass., equipped it with machinery that gave it an advantage over its competitors till the patents had expired, and conducted it in conjunction with the Saxonville mills. As an employer of labor he was remarkably considerate and generous, allowing the grounds of his extensive Saxonville estate to be used as a park by his employees, and on one occasion, when the mills were burned down, paying wages to all of his force who applied for work, even when there was nothing for some of them to do.

He gave liberally to educational and civic enterprises. He contributed $50,000 in 1880 to build a jetty at the mouth of the Merrimac River; to Wellesley College he donated in 1881 an infirmary, Simpson Cottage; he made by far the largest donation towards the building of an addition to the Newburyport Public Library, which was opened in 1882 and called The Simpson Annex; he also gave sums for the construction of roads, the sprinkling of the streets in summer, and other public purposes. He was married, Dec. 24, 1832, to Elizabeth Kilham, of Boston, by whom he had several children; after her death, he married, June 1, 1882, Evangeline Marrs, of Saxonville. He died in Boston.

[*Boston Morning Jour.*, and *Boston Post*, Dec. 22, 1884; J. J. Currier, *Hist. of Newburyport, Mass.*, 1764–1909 (2 vols., 1905–09); A. H. Cole, *The Am. Wool Manufacture* (1926), vol. I; J. L. Hayes, *Am. Textile Machinery* (1879); M. D. Leggett, *Subject-Matter Index of Patents for Inventions Issued by the U. S. Patent Office . . . 1790 to 1873* (1874).]   S. G.

SIMPSON, STEPHEN (July 24, 1789–Aug. 17, 1854), author and editor, was born, lived, and died in Philadelphia. Following the occupation of his father, George Simpson, who had been an official in the Bank of North America, the Bank of the United States, and Girard's Bank, Stephen became a note clerk in the second Bank of the United States and afterwards cashier of Girard's Bank. His father had been assistant commissary-general in the Revolution; Stephen enlisted for the War of 1812 and distinguished himself at the battle of New Orleans, at the same time forming an admiration for Andrew Jackson which motivated much of his political writing a decade later. After the war, with his brother-in-law Tobias Watkins, he founded the *Portico*, Baltimore, a miscellany discussing every topic

from Russian literature to nervous diseases, of which he was joint editor from January 1816 to June 1817. The financial failure of this magazine did not deter him from becoming co-proprietor with John Conrad in 1822 of the weekly *Columbian Observer*, Philadelphia, in which Jackson was as extravagantly praised as Calhoun was extravagantly condemned. He wrote for the *Aurora* and contributed an essay on "The Waywardness of Genius" to *The Philadelphia Book; or Specimens of Metropolitan Literature* (1836). He was the first, but unsuccessful, candidate for Congress of the initial political organization of workers in the United States, the Workingmen's Party of Philadelphia; paradoxically, for he was opposed to several leading principles of the old Hamiltonians, he was at the same time (1830) the candidate of the Federal Party.

The chief expression of his views is to be found in *The Working Man's Manual: a New Theory of Political Economy on the Principle of Production the Source of Wealth* (Philadelphia, 1831). This was written at the time of his political candidacy, and is informed by the philosophy of Robert Owen as made specific in the advocacies of Robert Dale Owen and Frances Wright [*qq.v.*]. It owed much also to the nationalist economic demands of Mathew Carey [*q.v.*] and others among the Philadelphia protectionist writers. Simpson's "American Theory" discountenanced "the profound dissertations of [European] writers bewildered in the fogs of Gothic institutions," and gave place "to the elucidation of obvious principles, of practical utility or equitable application" (p. 4). In holding that "all wealth is produced by labor" (p. 67) he borrowed from Adam Smith, but in amplifying the doctrine to the contention that labor should therefore receive the whole of its production he placed himself among the important anticipators of Marx. The chief filchers of labor's just rewards were the fund holders and the land-monopolists, upheld by outworn legal sanctions. He wanted, instead of "personal parties," political division according to economic allegiance. "The party of the producers," he maintained, opposing "the party of stockholders and capitalists" and gaining the ascendency, "could not fail to shed a genial, and prosperous beam upon the whole society. Such a party would merely exhibit the interest of society, concentrating for the true fulfilment of the original terms of the social compact" (p. 23). Simpson resembled in America the Chartists in England. He desired to improve the condition of labor through parliamentary means. "Let the producers . . . but once fully comprehend their injuries, and fully appreciate their strength at the polls," he said, "and the present oppressive system will vanish" (p. 20). Political action by the workingmen, however, required a system of free public education. Simpson resented the economic exploitation of workers hardly less than the cultural patronage to which they were treated by the rich and learned, although, unlike Frances Wright, he opposed literary education for women because he thought it would take them from the circle of the family and make them labor competitors of men. Simpson was an economic optimist, as befitted one viewing the productivity of a new country; it was not the niggardliness of nature, but the injustice of social institutions which held down the standard of living. He espoused the protective tariff to encourage manufactures. In an appendix to his *Manual* he retreated from his former objections to the United States Bank and its notes, thus losing influence among the working men whom he had led. In 1832 he published a *Biography of Stephen Girard* which displayed the financier's foibles with more humor than hostility, and the following year issued *The Lives of George Washington and Thomas Jefferson: with a Parallel* (1833); the biographies contained in the latter volume were reprinted separately in 1844.

[Besides the publications mentioned above, see J. R. Commons and others, *Hist. of Labour in the U. S.* (1918), vol. I; Henry Simpson, *The Lives of Eminent Philadelphians, Now Deceased* (1859); F. L. Mott, *A Hist. of Am. Mags.* (1930); *Pennsylvania* (Phila.), Aug. 19, 1854.]   B. M.

SIMPSON, WILLIAM DUNLAP (Oct. 27, 1823–Dec. 26, 1890), governor and chief justice of South Carolina, was born in Laurens District, S. C. He was the son of Elizabeth (Saterwhite) and John W. Simpson, a successful physician, and the grandson of John Simpson, a Scotch-Irish Presbyterian who emigrated from Belfast, Ireland, to Laurens shortly after the American Revolution and became a wealthy planter and merchant. After studying at the Laurens academy he entered South Carolina College, now the University of South Carolina, and graduated in 1843. He entered the Harvard Law School but withdrew after a single session and returned home, where he continued his studies in the office of Henry Young. Admitted to the bar in 1846, he became Young's partner and in March 1847 married his daughter Jane. They had eight children. He was successful in law and was elected to the state legislature. Appointed an aide to M. L. Bonham [q.v.] at the secession of South Carolina, he participated in the siege of Fort Sumter and the first battle of Manassas. He aid-

ed Samuel McGowan [q.v.] in the organization of the 14th South Carolina Volunteers, which became a part of Gregg's Brigade, became a major and subsequently lieutenant-colonel, and fought in important battles in Virginia. He was slightly wounded at Germantown, and the bow of his cravat was shot away at Cold Harbor. His popularity among the soldiers and the men at home led to his election in 1863 to the Confederate Congress, in which he served until the end of the war.

After the war he practised law at Laurens with his brother, John Wistar Simpson. In 1868 he was a delegate to the National Democratic Convention and was elected to the federal Congress but was denied a seat on the grounds that he was disqualified under the Fourteenth Amendment. In 1876 he became Democratic candidate for lieutenant-governor and accompanied Wade Hampton [q.v.] on a memorable tour of the counties of South Carolina. As the presiding officer of the Senate he refused to take the oath of office a second time at the behest of the Republican majority of the Senate, and he engineered the organization of that body in such a way as to obtain a Democratic majority. In 1878 the Democrats obtained his reëlection without serious opposition. Immediately thereafter he became acting governor as a result of the illness of Governor Hampton and became governor, when Hampton resigned at the beginning of the following year to become United States senator. In his messages to the legislature he urged educational progress, and he aided in the creation of a state agricultural bureau (for his principal address as governor see *Journal of the House of Representatives of S. C. . . . 1879*, 1880, pp. 11–30). In August 1880, two months before his term as governor expired, he resigned to become chief justice of the state and served until his death. Although well trained in the knowledge of adjudicated cases he sought also to analyze the underlying principles of the law. During his service on the supreme court his convictions and example were important in upholding the constitutional provision that forbade circuit judges to instruct juries as to their own opinions on the facts in any case. His career was like that of many other Southerners of his class and age. Well born and handsome, pious and patriotic, competent but not brilliant, he accepted the opinions of his class and justified the series of honors conferred upon him because of conscientious service.

[*Cyc. of Eminent and Representative Men of the Carolinas* (1892), vol. I; J. F. J. Caldwell, *The Hist. of . . . "Gregg's" and subsequently . . . "McGowan's Brigade"* (1866); "Tribute of Respect," 33 *S. C. Reports*, app. pp. 613–27; *Confederate Military Hist.* (1899) by C. A. Evans, vol. V, pp. 841–45; *News and Courier* (Charleston), Dec. 27, 1890.]   F. B. S.

SIMPSON, WILLIAM KELLY (Apr. 10, 1855–Feb. 6, 1914), laryngologist, was born at Hudson, N. Y., the youngest of nine children of George Nicholas and Caroline (McCann) Simpson. He attended school at Hudson and at the Episcopal Academy (later the Cheshire School), Cheshire, Conn., and graduated from Cornell in 1876 with the degree of B. A. and from the College of Physicians and Surgeons, New York, in 1880. After serving as interne in the Presbyterian Hospital until 1882, he became a specialist in laryngology through the influence of Dr. Clinton Wagner [*q.v.*], the celebrated laryngologist. On Oct. 25, 1882, he married Anna Farrand of Hudson, N. Y., who with a daughter and a son survived him. He early identified himself with dispensary and hospital practice. He was attending surgeon to the Northern Dispensary, and to the throat department of the Presbyterian Hospital and of the New York Eye and Ear Infirmary. As attending physician to the outdoor department of the New York Foundling Asylum, he became associated with Dr. Joseph O'Dwyer [*q.v.*] in his work on intubation; he was among the first after O'Dwyer to advocate the method in the application of intubation to chronic stenosis of the larynx. He was assistant surgeon to the Metropolitan Throat Hospital and instructor in laryngology in the New York Post-Graduate Medical School, in association with Dr. Wagner, 1885–87. He became an assistant in the throat department of the Vanderbilt Clinic in 1887, chief of clinic and instructor in 1898, and in 1904 succeeded Dr. George Morewood Lefferts [*q.v.*] as professor of laryngology at the College of Physicians and Surgeons, Columbia University, a position he held until his death. He was consulting laryngologist to a number of hospitals, a fellow of the American Laryngological Association, of the New York Academy of Medicine, and of the Hospital Graduates' Club, and secretary of the executive committee of the Congress of American Physicians and Surgeons.

An excellent practitioner and lecturer, his contributions to the literature of his specialty were of distinct value. The most important are *Sequelae of Syphilis of the Larynx* (1896), "A Study of . . . Intubation in Chronic Stenosis of the Larynx" (*Transactions of the American Laryngological Association*, 1901), "A Case of Laryngeal Diphtheria in an Adult" (*Ibid.*, 1905), "Stenosis of the Trachea" (*Ibid.*, 1906), "Laryngeal Stenosis in the Adult" (*Ibid.*, 1908), and

"Two Cases of White Exudative Laryngeal Growths" (*Ibid.*, 1912). He was a lover of music and excelled as a vocalist; he was a leading member and one of the best tenors of the Musurgia Society for many years. He was a man of attractive personality and highly social nature.

[*Who's Who in America*, 1914–15; *The Coll. of Physicians and Surgeons, N. Y.* (n.d.), vol. I, ed. by John Shrady; H. A. Kelly and W. L. Burrage, *Am. Medic. Biogs.* (1920); *Trans. Am. Laryngological Assoc.* (1914); *Medic. Record*, Feb. 14, 1914; obituary in *N. Y. Times*, Feb. 7, 1914.]   D. B. D.

SIMS, CHARLES N. (May 18, 1835–Mar. 27, 1908), Methodist Episcopal clergyman, college president, was born in Fairfield, Ind., the son of John and Irene (Allen) Sims. He had no middle name, but for some reason used the initial N. Brought up on a farm, he obtained his early education in neighboring district schools. Itinerant preachers of the Methodist Church stopping at his father's house acquainted him in his boyhood days with religious and ecclesiastical matters. One of these, the zealous John P. Durbin [*q.v.*], took an interest in the lad and urged him to prepare for the ministry. At the age of seventeen he began to teach school and two years later he entered Indiana Asbury University (De Pauw University), from which he graduated in 1859. During the latter part of his course he served as principal of Thorntown Academy and was admitted on trial (1857) to the Northwest Indiana Conference of the Methodist Episcopal Church, being ordained deacon the year of his graduation, and elder in 1861. In 1860 he was made president of Valparaiso College, but the outbreak of the Civil War hampered its work and he remained but two years. Entering the active ministry, he was in charge of churches in Indiana and Illinois until he was called East in 1870, where he held important pastorates in Baltimore, Newark, and Brooklyn. In 1881 he was elected chancellor of Syracuse University.

This institution at that time was poorly equipped and in financial straits. "The indomitable perseverance of Chancellor Sims, his tireless industry, his undying faith in the college and its future saved the plant, and an upward progress was slowly begun" (*The Golden Jubilee*, post, p. 12). He virtually "lived in a carpet bag," and his pursuit of funds was notably successful. During the twelve years of his administration the indebtedness of the college was decreased, its endowment enlarged, and a building era inaugurated. He was instrumental in securing from John Crouse funds for the erection of Crouse Memorial College at a cost of approximately

$250,000; and a library, an observatory, and a gymnasium were erected. He was also active in denominational affairs, being a member of the General Conferences of 1884 and 1888, and one of the speakers at the Centennial Conference held in Baltimore in 1884. The state of New York utilized his abilities by making him one of a commission of three, established by the legislature in 1882, to investigate the condition of the Onondaga Indians, and his name heads the report presented in 1883 (*Documents of the State of New York . . . 1883, No. 35*). A commission was appointed to negotiate a new treaty with the Indians, upon which, also, he served.

After resigning the chancellorship of the University in 1893, he was pastor of the Meridian Street Church, Indianapolis (1893–98), and of the First Church, Syracuse (1898–1904). Two years later, having in the meantime been general secretary for the Methodist Hospital, Indianapolis, he retired to Liberty, Ind., where he died. Of his several publications the most important was *The Life of Rev. Thomas M. Eddy* (1879). On Aug. 12, 1858, he married Eliza A. Foster of Tippecanoe County, Ind.

[C. A. Martin, *Alumnal Record, DePauw Univ.* (1910); *The Golden Jubilee of Syracuse Univ., 1870–1920* (n.d.), ed. by Frank Smalley; *Minutes of the Seventy-seventh Session of the Ind. Ann. Conf. of the M. E. Ch.* (1908); obituary in *Christian Advocate* (N. Y.), Apr. 9, 1908.]   H. E. S.

SIMS, JAMES MARION (Jan. 25, 1813–Nov. 13, 1883), gynecologist, was born in Lancaster County, S. C. His father, John Sims, descended from the English colonists of Virginia, was a tiller of the soil, the village hotel keeper and sheriff, a great hunter and cock fighter; his mother was Mahala (Mackey), of Scotch-Irish origin. Marion grew up in a variety of schools and attended the South Carolina College, Columbia, during the presidency of Thomas Cooper [*q.v.*], a man of remarkable learning, who, Sims thought, "exerted a very bad influence," because he was a pronounced infidel and denied the Mosaic authorship of the Pentateuch. Graduating in 1832, Sims reached home two months after his mother's death. She had counted on his entering the Presbyterian ministry, while his father wanted him to study law. He therefore turned to medicine, although his father reckoned it a profession "for which I have the utmost contempt" (Sims, *post*, p. 116).

With the local Dr. Churchill Jones as preceptor, Sims entered the Charleston Medical School in November 1833, where John Edwards Holbrook [*q.v.*], celebrated herpetologist, was his professor of anatomy. Here he found his billet

and pitched in zealously. The following October, in true medical peripatetic fashion, he traveled by stage to Philadelphia and matriculated in the Jefferson Medical College. While he was there smallpox broke out, contracted from a dissecting-room subject, and several of the students died; Sims, who nursed one of them, was protected by a vaccination he had forgotten. He graduated in May 1835, and returned home with a full set of surgical instruments.

Settling in Mount Meigs, Ala., he attracted attention, after eight or nine other doctors had been consulted to no avail, by urging an abdominal incision for an abscess, although a consultant had diagnosed cancer. A layman-arbiter siding with Sims, he performed the operation, and the patient recovered. In 1840, Sims moved to Montgomery. One of his early achievements here was the complete rectification of a cleft palate with a hideous snout-like protrusion; the patient came to him wearing a double-thick blue veil to hide her face even from her own family, but the new presentable mouth effected by the operation made of her a really pretty woman. Chapin A. Harris [*q.v.*], of the Baltimore College of Dental Surgery, visiting Montgomery, insisted on the publication of the case, and although Sims protested that he had never written anything in his life, the article appeared in the *Journal of Dental Surgery* for September 1845.

In June of that year a call to a colored girl of seventeen, Anarcha, three days in labor, proved the turning point in Sims's life. Impaction and extensive sloughing resulted in a large bladder fistula and a wreck of a patient, unfit for all social relationships—a burden for life on her master's hands. This was his first fistula case, but two others shortly appeared, all being regarded as incurable. In spite of strenuous objections, the third patient was sent to Sims's small negro hospital. At that very juncture, an accident to a patient causing a uterine displacement revealed to him a new approach and suggested a way of treating his fistula patients, on whom, with a newly devised speculum, he now inaugurated a long-drawn-out series of operations. Anesthesia was not yet known; doctor friends, enthusiastic coadjutors in holding the patients so long as there was a bright hope of relieving the incurable malady, could no longer be commandeered when weeks and months brought only slight improvement, and Sims had to depend upon the poor sufferers themselves for any assistance. After many failures, his brother-in-law, Dr. Rush Jones, pleading the waste of time and labor and the consequent injustice to his family, begged him to drop the whole matter. Sims replied: "I am as sure that I shall carry this thing through to success, as I am that I now live. . . . I am going on with this series of experiments to the end. It matters not what it costs, if it costs me my life" (Sims, pp. 242–43). Subsequently, in a moment of inspiration, he had a local artisan make some silver wire for sutures which were passed and tightened with perforated shot. This was the crucial step; the thirtieth operation on Anarcha was crowned with success. The silver sutures and the unparalleled deftness and skill the surgeon had acquired in the long, patient years of repeated efforts had transformed the situation. This operation took place in the late spring of 1849; two weeks later, Betsey and Lucy were also cured. Sims was now fully justified in declaring, "Then I realized the fact that . . . I had made, perhaps, one of the most important discoveries of the age for the relief of suffering humanity" (*Ibid.*, p. 246).

Six weeks later he collapsed with an old intestinal complaint and had to quit work and spend several years moving from place to place in search of relief. His weight dropped to ninety pounds. Lying in bed at home, desperately ill, in the fall of 1850, he wrote the history of the vesicovaginal fistula operation, which appeared in the *American Journal of the Medical Sciences* for January 1852 and was reprinted separately in 1853. At the time he thought it "my last free-will offering to the medical profession, before I should quit this world" (Sims, p. 259). In 1853, dismissing his negro servants and selling out all his interests in Montgomery, he journeyed to New York with his family and bought a house on Madison Avenue. Valentine Mott, Francis, Stevens, Delafield, and other leaders of his profession, astounded by his claims, began to seek him out. The first New York fistula cases brought no remunerative practice, since some of his colleagues even borrowed his instruments for their own use. This situation finally forced him to consider the establishment of a hospital, where poor patients could be received and visiting doctors instructed. Henri L. Stuart assisted at the beginning of the project by using the city papers to invite the physicians of New York to hear Sims speak on the need of a woman's hospital. When the day arrived in the spring of 1854, no less than 250 doctors filled the hall. From that time on, with the further effective cooperation of the leading women of the city, chief among them Mrs. William E. Dodge, the hospital plan advanced to its inauguration at 83 Madison Avenue, May 1, 1855, with about thirty beds—all charity. The state charter for the Woman's Hospital of the State of New York was obtained in 1857, the city bargaining for fifty free beds and giving in exchange the old Potter's Field with its memories of the cholera epidemic of 1832.

In June 1861, Sims, never vigorous physically, sailed for Europe for a rest. Wherever he went he was royally received. Sir James Y. Simpson of Edinburgh was especially interested in his work. In Paris, he met Jobert de Lamballe, writer of the *Traité de Fistules* (1852), and Velpeau and Nélaton. The elderly Civiale complimented him before a group of students; the King of the Belgians made him a Knight of the Order of Leopold I. In Paris, he cured one of Jobert's patients after sixteen futile efforts. Doctor Mungenier brought him a woman with an enormous fistula of more than twenty years' duration, whom he cured by a single operation; some seventeen or eighteen of the leaders in the profession were present at this *tour de force*. These, with five previous successful operations in Paris within three or four weeks, "created a furore among the profession."

He returned to New York in January 1862, but, unhappy there because of his sympathy with the South, took his family back to Paris in July to find abundant work awaiting him. In 1863, the Empress Eugénie was under his care for several weeks, and for the next two years Paris yielded him a comfortable living. In London, in 1866, he published his *Clinical Notes on Uterine Surgery* (brought out in an American edition the same year). This book was a potent factor in the formation of the nascent specialty of gynecology. Hearing of the destitution in his native county following Sherman's march to the sea, he sent five thousand francs to relieve the most needy, later giving enough to buy a large house and sixty acres of land for the helpless indigent, to be known as The J. Marion Sims Asylum for the Poor.

After the Civil War he returned to New York, but upon the outbreak of the Franco-Prussian War in 1870, went again to France to organize and become surgeon-in-chief of the Anglo-American Ambulance Corps. For distinguished professional services, France bestowed on him the Order of the Commander of the Legion of Honor. In 1872, again in New York, he was made a member of the board of surgeons of the Woman's Hospital, where work had been maintained efficiently by Thomas Addis Emmet [*q.v.*], but two years later he resigned, offended by the ruling of the managers limiting to fifteen the spectators admitted to any operation. In 1876, he was president of the American Medical Association. His last visit to the South, in March 1877, was the occasion of a triumphal entry into

Montgomery where he was met by the medical and surgical societies, his old friend W. O. Baldwin delivering a notable address (published with Baldwin's memorial tribute, *post*). In 1880, he presided over the American Gynecological Society. Happy memories and many friendships drew him to revisit Paris in 1882. On returning, in August 1883, he bought a building lot in Washington, where he intended to settle, but pneumonia claimed him on the morning of Nov. 13, three days after the execution of the title deed.

Sims's wife was Eliza Theresa Jones of Lancaster, to whom he had been devoted since they were respectively eleven and nine years old. She took him in spite of strong parental opposition, married him while poor (Dec. 21, 1836), lived in log cabins with him and the rapidly arriving children, guided him in all but his professional activities, and cared for and clung to him through years of harassing, exhausting illnesses, herself ill part of the time. Repeatedly she made the crucial decisions of life. With a son and four daughters, she survived him. Sims's autobiography, *The Story of My Life*, edited by his son, was published in 1884.

[J. M. Sims, *The Story of My Life*, mentioned above; W. O. Baldwin, *Tribute to the Late James Marion Sims* (1884); Ely van de Warker, in *Trans. Am. Gyn. Soc.*, vol. IX (1885); J. A. Wyeth, in H. A. Kelly and W. L. Burrage, *Am. Medic. Biogs.* (1920); *Boston Medic. and Surgic. Jour.*, Nov. 22, 1883; *Am. Jour. Obstetrics*, Jan. 1884; *N. Y. Times*, Nov. 14, 1883.]
H. A. K—y.

SIMS, WINFIELD SCOTT (Apr. 6, 1844–Jan. 7, 1918), inventor, was born in New York City, the son of Capt. Lindsay D. and Catherine B. Sims. He was graduated from the Newark, N. J., high school in 1861; soon after this he enlisted in the 37th New Jersey Regiment and served in the Civil War, 1861–65. On June 11, 1867, he married Lida Leek of Newark, who died in 1888; on June 27, 1891, he married Mrs. Josephine Courter French of Newark. He invented various devices in electro-magnets. In 1872 he constructed a small electric motor for light work, with a battery of twenty half-gallon Bunsen cells, which would propel an open boat sixteen feet long, with six persons on board, at four miles an hour. He was the first to apply electricity for the propulsion of torpedoes. His "fish torpedo," on which he secured patent No. 319,633 in 1882, was a submarine boat with a cylindrical hull of copper, conical ends, and a screw propeller and rudder. Within it was a coil of cable two miles long, by means of which it was propelled, guided, and exploded, the power being electrically generated on shore or shipboard. Ten

of these, purchased by the United States government in 1885, were experimented with for a number of years by army officers, and for a time were seriously considered for adoption as a principal means of coast defense. These torpedoes were twenty-eight feet long, twenty-one inches in diameter, and attained a speed of eleven miles an hour when tested by the government in 1885. Subsequently he designed a boat with a speed of twenty-two miles an hour, capable of carrying a five hundred pound charge of dynamite.

He also invented an apparatus for coiling ropes and for preventing ropes from kinking and twisting while they were being paid out, patent No. 374,209, and the Sims-Dudley powder pneumatic gun, patent No. 619,025, which was used by the Cuban insurgents and by the Rough Riders at the battle of Santiago. This was a very light field gun, intended to be drawn by one horse, or by three or four men, and consisted of two tubes, one of which carried the projectile and the other the powder charge of from six to eight ounces of powder. The projectile was a vaned cylinder with a Merriam fuze and a charge of explosive gelatin, pencil of gun cotton, and fulminate of mercury; when the projectile struck an object, a steel ball, acting as a hammer, was driven forward by the sudden retardation of the flight of the shell and struck one or more percussion caps, which ignited the charge. He also invented a breech mechanism for cannon, patent No. 619,026; the Sims-Merriam projectile, patent No. 667,407; a wireless dirigible torpedo, of which he sold five to the Japanese government in 1907; a dynamite gun for use with dirigibles, and a dynamite gun for aeroplanes. At the time of his death he was engaged in designing a dynamite cruiser to carry one hundred tons of high explosive, controlled by an operator on shipboard or on shore. He died in Newark, where he had made his home for years.

[See *Who's Who in America*, 1916–17; obituary in *N. Y. Times*, Jan. 8, 1918. Sims's "fish torpedo" is treated in *Harper's Mag.*, Nov. 1885, *World* (N. Y.), Dec. 19, 1885, and *Iron Age*, Dec. 31, 1885.]
C. F. C.

SINGER, ISAAC MERRIT (Oct. 27, 1811–July 23, 1875), inventor, was born in Pittstown, Rensselaer County, N. Y., the son of a millwright, who a few years later moved to Oswego, N. Y., to work at his trade. Here Singer spent his boyhood and received a bit of schooling. At twelve he left home, went to Rochester, N. Y., and for seven years worked at all sorts of unskilled labor. He finally entered a machine shop as an apprentice machinist, but after four months he left and began nine years of wandering from state to state, making a good living because of his mechanical cleverness and gaining wide experience. On May 16, 1839, while he was living in Lockport, Ill., he obtained his first patent, for a rock-drilling machine; however, he soon squandered the money he made when he sold it. In 1849, when he was in Pittsburgh, he secured a patent on a wood and metal-carving machine that he had begun five years before in Fredericksburg, Ohio. He went immediately to New York and secured the help of A. B. Taylor & Company to finance the development of his invention. After unavoidable delays lasting over a year, he completed a machine that was commercially practicable and operated it for a short time. Then a boiler explosion in the manufactory completely destroyed it and left him penniless.

In 1851 he was at work in a machine shop in Boston when a Lerow and Blodgett sewing machine was brought in for repairs. He was called upon for suggestions and was told incidentally that if he could make a practical sewing machine his fortune would be made. Within twelve hours he had prepared a rough sketch and within eleven days had built a machine incorporating his ideas. He immediately applied for a patent, which was granted Aug. 12, 1851, patent No. 8294, and with a few hundred dollars borrowed from friends he organized the I. M. Singer & Company and began the manufacture of his machine. Though the sewing machine of Elias Howe [q.v.] was supreme at that time Singer's had one feature that Howe's lacked, the ability to do continuous stitching; because of this his machine came into immediate demand. When Howe brought suit for $25,000 because he refused to pay royalties, Singer fought it for three years, but in July 1854, losing the case, he was forced to pay $15,-000 in settlement. By that time, however, his company had reached a commanding position in the sewing-machine industry, and took a leading part in bringing about the subsequent combination of manufacturers and the pooling of patents. Singer received twenty patents between 1851 and 1863 for improvements on his machine; the most important were the continuous wheel feed, the yielding presser foot, and the heart-shaped cam as applied to moving the needle bar. His greatest service, however, was in developing the first practical domestic sewing machine and in bringing it into general use. In 1863, with forty per cent. of the stock in his name, he withdrew from active connection with the company and went to Europe to live. Early in life he married Catherine Maria Haley, from whom he was divorced in 1860; in 1865 he married Isabella Eugenia Summerville in New York. At the time of his death at his home in Torquay, Devonshire,

England, he was survived by his widow and two daughters.

[F. L. Lewton, "The Servant in the House," *Ann. Report . . . Smithsonian Inst.*, 1929; Henry Howe, *Adventures and Achievements of Americans* (1858); *Genius Rewarded or the Story of the Sewing Machine* (1880); *N. Y. Atlas*, Mar. 20, 1853; obit. in *N. Y. Tribune*, July 26, 1875; Patent Office records.]
C. W. M—n.

SINGERLY, WILLIAM MISKEY (Dec. 27, 1832–Feb. 27, 1898), editor and publisher, the eldest of five children of Joseph and Catherine (Miskey) Singerly, was born in Philadelphia, Pa., where his father was a successful carpenter and builder. Graduating from high school in 1850, he secured a job with a produce commission house on the water front. After ten years in this school of long hours and hard work, he became associated with his father in the development of street railways, especially in Germantown, Pa. In 1870 he removed to Chicago to engage again in the commission business, but he was soon recalled. During this period of interest in street railways he dipped into politics, and in 1877 he purchased the *Public Record,* buying it very cheaply at a time when its circulation had ebbed to 5,200. Though he then knew nothing of newspaper publishing, he improved paper and typography, introduced display headlines, added new departments, and enlarged the Saturday issue. In 1879 he changed the name to *Philadelphia Record,* cut the price in half, and made it the pioneer morning daily in Philadelphia sold at one cent and giving complete news. In 1882 he launched a Sunday edition. He went roughshod after the theft of bodies by the coroner's underlings, exposed bogus medical colleges, laid bare registration frauds, assailed corruption in office. Warring against excessive coal prices, he organized a direct sales scheme in 1881 that undercut the established rate by seventy-five cents a ton and saved hard-pressed householders thousands of dollars. In 1882 he moved the *Philadelphia Record* into a new building that was among the first in which incandescent electric lighting was used. The circulation of the paper grew rapidly from the start and rose to nearly 200,000 during his lifetime. To assure the necessary supply of paper, he ran his own paper mill at Elkton, Pa.

He was soon the recognized Democratic leader of Pennsylvania. He championed Cleveland in each of his presidential campaigns, espoused tariff reform when that doctrine was particularly unpopular in Pennsylvania, and helped to secure the election of Robert Emory Pattison [q.v.], the only Democrat chosen governor in Pennsylvania after the Civil War until 1934. In

1894 he himself was nominated for governor but was not elected; otherwise he refused office except honorary appointment to the Fairmount Park Commission. In 1896 he withdrew his support from Bryan and gave it to John McAuley Palmer and Simon Bolivar Buckner [qq.v.]. His boundless energy found many other outlets. In 1878 he inherited his father's shares in the Germantown Passenger Railway, appraised at $750,000, which he subsequently sold for $1,500,000. In addition to the paper mill, he owned a gleaner and binder factory at Norristown and knitting mills in Philadelphia, at one time the largest producer of "jerseys" in the land, and had a model stock farm, which was his suburban home. In the biggest single building operation in Philadelphia to that date, he erected over a thousand dwellings. After the destruction by fire of the Temple Theatre he erected a building on its site for the Chestnut Street National Bank and its savings fund affiliate, which he had organized under the presidency of Ex-Governor Pattison and of which he became president in 1891. The disastrous collapse of these banks in the aftermath of the 1893–96 depression gave his brilliant career a tragic ending. Struggling to meet his obligations, he arranged to divert the earnings of his *Record* holdings equitably to his creditors. His signature on the indenture scarcely dry, he died suddenly in Philadelphia from an aneurism ascribed to "tobacco heart." Of imposing appearance, with the air of one born to command, Singerly was reckless of consistency and fearless of consequences, the embodiment of enterprise and open-handedness. He was twice married, first on June 4, 1854, to Pamelia Anna Jones of Philadelphia and second on Aug. 12, 1872, to Mary Ryan of Chicago, both of whom died. He was survived by one of his two daughters.

[T. W. Bean, *Hist. of Montgomery County, Pa.* (1884); J. T. Scharf and Thompson Westcott, *Hist. of Phila., 1609–1884* (1884), vol. III; George Morgan, *The City of Firsts* (1926); J. R. Young, *Memorial Hist. of the City of Phila.*, vol. II (1898); *A Gallery of Eminent Men of Phila.* (copr. 1887), ed. by E. C. Savage and William Anderson; obituaries in *Phila. Record, Public Ledger* (Phila.), Feb. 28, 1898.]   V. R.

SINGLETON, ESTHER (Nov. 4, 1865–July 2, 1930), author, editor, and music critic, was born in Baltimore, Md., the daughter of Martha Colgate (Morling) and Horace Leonard Singleton. Her father was a grandson of John Singleton of Norfolk, who fought in Daniel Morgan's rifle regiment and in the Virginia line under Washington, and a direct descendant of Edward Rawson, secretary of the Massachusetts Bay Colony, and Nathaniel Reynolds, a captain in King Philip's War. Her mother was the daughter of a near relative of Jane Austen. Educated in private schools and by private teachers in Baltimore, for several years she studied with Sidney Lanier [q.v.], who was a friend of her parents. In her early teens she spent much time in the Naval Observatory studying with her cousin, Edward Singleton Holden [q.v.], the astronomer. In 1887 she went to New York to prepare for a musical career. Although she became a proficient violinist, she lacked confidence in her ability and turned to writing for a living; music, however, remained one of the chief enthusiasms of her life. One of her earliest books is *A Guide to the Opera* (1899); later appeared *A Guide to Modern Opera* (1909) and *The Orchestra and Its Instruments* (1917).

The subtitle of her first book, *Turrets, Towers and Temples: The Great Buildings of the World as Seen and Described by Famous Writers* (1898), suggests the nature of most of her books: prose anthologies of love, famous women, notable pictures, statues, cathedrals, various interesting cities, countries, natural wonders, and the world's great events. The vogue for collecting antiques stimulated her own lively interest in the historical associations of things, and led her to write several books and numerous articles on antiques. In *The Furniture of our Forefathers* (1900), *Social New York under the Georges* (1902), and *Dutch New York* (1909), she built up historical backgrounds, reconstructed homes, and gave glimpses of the family and social life of the times by quoting freely from old inventories, wills, newspaper advertisements, letters, diaries, and travel books, and by describing and giving illustrations of heirlooms and museum treasures of those periods. Her careful research, historical insight, and artistic selection make the books both interesting and authentic. From 1923 until 1930 she was editor of the *Antiquarian*. The writing of *The Shakespeare Garden* (1922) gave her keen satisfaction, for she knew, word for word, most of the comedies and the greatest of the tragedies. Her last published book, *Shakespearian Fantasia: Adventures in the Fourth Dimension* (1929), and a story for girls, *A Daughter of the Revolution* (1915), are the only ones that are not the result of research, compilation, or translation. She was an ardent French student and used the language with facility. In addition to translating from the French many of the selections in her anthologies, she published two translations, *Musical Education* (1903) and *The Music Dramas of Richard Wagner* (1898), from the French of Albert Lavignac. She also wrote *États-Unis d'Amérique* for the first part of the *Encyclopédie de la Musique et Dictionnaire du Conservatoire* (1922).

During 1904 she traveled abroad, but she did not welcome either change or motion and lived in New York almost continuously for over forty years. She enjoyed the society of brilliant people and was herself a gifted conversationalist. Her interest in music, art, literature, and history was keen, her memory remarkable, and her appetite for reading omnivorous. In searching out facts for her books and articles she was both accurate and indefatigable. She contributed to many magazines, among them the *Saturday Evening Post, Garden and Home, International Studio,* and the *Musical Courier.* She died at Stonington, Conn., where she was spending the summer.

[*Who's Who in America,* 1930–31; *Woman's Who's Who of America,* 1914–15; Esther Singleton, preface to *The Shakespeare Garden* (1922) and "Die Meistersinger" under Anton Seidl," *Musical Courier,* Feb. 1, 1930; *N. Y. Times,* Aug. 31, 1930, pt. VIII (appreciation) and July 5, 1930 (obituary); obituary in *Musical Courier,* July 12, 1930; correspondence with Charlotte Austen Carrington, a sister.]   V. L. S.

SINGLETON, JAMES WASHINGTON (Nov. 23, 1811–Apr. 4, 1892), congressman, was an Illinois political leader of Southern antecedents. He was born at "Paxton" in Frederick County, Va., the estate of his father, Gen. James Singleton, who served in the Revolutionary War and the War of 1812. Through his mother, Judith Throckmorton (Ball), he had ancestral connections in common with George Washington. After attending the academy in Winchester, Va., he struck out for the West, "read medicine," practised as youthful physician, then turned to legal studies, and became a circuit-riding lawyer. About 1834 he settled at Mount Sterling, Ill. In the "war" against the Mormons (1844) he served as brigadier-general of militia. He also served his state in constitutional conventions, 1847 and 1862, and in the legislature, 1850–54, 1860–62. Having removed to Quincy about 1854, he lived on a large estate, "Boscobel," combining the grand life of a gentleman planter with law and politics and being widely known as a gracious Southerner at whose mansion prominent men gathered. In 1862 he served on an international commission to investigate water communication between the United States and Canada.

During the Civil War he labored persistently for peace. Pursuing the political aims of the "Sons of Liberty," he opposed Lincoln's arbitrary measures and took prominent part in peace conventions at Peoria and Springfield in August 1864. In November 1864 he was in Canada conferring with Clay and Tucker, Confederate "commissioners." Seeking interviews with Lincoln for his plans to end the war, he reached the President both directly and through intermediaries and claimed to have been told by Lincoln that abolition would not be demanded as a condition of peace (O. H. Browning, *post,* I, 694, 699), though this was inconsistent with Lincoln's terms as given in the Greeley peace episode. Late in the war he made several trips to Richmond bent on peace projects and being associated with O. H. Browning and James Hughes [*qq.v.*] in a scheme to buy Southern products with greenbacks, get them through Grant's lines with presidential permission, and sell them in the North at enhanced prices. Lincoln approved this scheme as a means to shorten the war by getting federal money into Southern hands. As to the peace efforts, however, Lincoln withheld official sanction while standing ready to step in if satisfactory Confederate proposals should emerge from Singleton's informal "negotiation." After the war Singleton continued his political activities, serving as a Democrat in Congress from 1879 to 1883, but gave increasing attention to railroad promotion. Interested particularly in transportation advantages for his own city, he directed the building of two roads, the Quincy & Toledo, which merged with the Wabash, and the Quincy, Alton & St. Louis, which was absorbed by the Chicago, Burlington & Quincy. Political animosities did not mar his friendships, and "Boscobel" remained during this period a scene of generous entertainment. He was married three times: first probably to Catherine McDaniel, second to Ann Craig of Kentucky, and third, in 1844, to Parthenia McDonald, who bore him seven children. About 1891 he removed to Baltimore, where he died.

[Information from his daughter, Mrs. Lily Singleton Thomas Osburn of Charles Town, W. Va.; "The Diary of Orville Hickman Browning," ed. by T. C. Pease and J. G. Randall, *Ill. State Hist. Colls.,* vols. XX, XXII (1927–33); *The Biog. Encyc. of Ill.* (1875); E. C. Kirkland, *The Peacemakers of 1864* (1927); *Hist. Encyc. of Ill. and Hist. of Schuyler County* (1908), ed. by Newton Bateman; "The Constitutional Debates of 1847," ed. by A. C. Cole, *Ill. State Hist. Colls.,* vol. XIV (1919); P. H. Redmond, *Hist. of Quincy* (1869); D. F. Wilcox, *Quincy* (1919), vol. I; H. E. Hayden, *Va. Geneal.* (1891); *Ill. State Jour.* (Springfield), Aug. 6–25, 1864; editorial, *N. Y. Tribune,* Jan. 13, 1865; M. P. Andrews in *N. Y. Times,* Feb. 12, 1928; *Whig* (Quincy, Ill.), Apr. 5, 1892; *Sun* (Baltimore, Md.), Apr. 5, 1892.]   J. G. R.

SIRINGO, CHARLES A. (Feb. 7, 1855–Oct. 19, 1928), cowboy, detective, and author, was born in Matagorda County, Tex. His father, an Italian emigrant, died when the boy was only a year old, and his mother, herself an emigrant from Ireland, brought up the little family. At the age of four Charlie started to school. At twelve he rode out as a full-fledged cowboy, accoutred in all the habiliments of the range. He worked on the coast for the colorful "Shanghai" Pierce, drove on the trail with cattle in 1876, spent some time in the Kansas cowtowns, and in the spring of 1877 helped, as a cowboy, to establish the LX's, an extensive ranch in the Texas Panhandle fostered by eastern capital. There he remained until sent to New Mexico in the fall of 1880 with a posse of Texas cowboys to help run down "Billy the Kid." He took the company money to Las Vegas for the purpose of buying provisions, fell into a game of monte, lost all, and rejoined the posse with an empty chuck-wagon. Leaving the search for the Kid to bolder spirits, he turned south to the mining camp called White Oaks and back to the LX range after the outlaw band was dispersed. After a mercantile venture at Caldwell, Kan., he drifted into Chicago. Probably in the summer of 1882 at Wellington, Kan., he was married to Mamie Lloyd of Shelbyville, Ill., who died six years later leaving one daughter.

In 1885, "being in need of money," and he was always in need, he published his first book, a racy little volume called *A Texas Cowboy, or Fifteen Years on the Hurricane Deck of a Spanish Pony.* Bound in paper and peddled by "butcher boys" upon the trains, its sale is said to have run to near a million copies. The next year he joined the Pinkerton detective agency in order "to study the world" and record his "experiences in book form." After about twenty-two years he had collected the necessary copy. *A Cowboy Detective,* the stirring account of his connection with the agency, resulted in the raising of legal barriers to publication by his former employers. The text was modified, the Pinkertons fictitiously alluded to, and in 1912 the volume appeared —an account of the suppression of Haymarket riots, strikes, express banditry, cattle rustling, and anarchical outbreaks—though the agency later obtained a permanent injunction and suppressed the book. In 1915 he issued a homely little pamphlet in a glowing paper cover called *Two Evil Isms: Pinkertonism and Anarchism,* merely outlining the *Cowboy Detective* and telling what he first wanted to tell about his late employers and a good deal he had thought of since. In 1919 he published *A Lone Star Cowboy* to take the place of his first book, then out of print, and issued a pamphlet of ballads called *The Song Companion of a Lone Star Cowboy.* Next year he compiled his *History of "Billy the Kid"* (1920). In 1927 he saw the best of his stories on cowboys and detectives issued in dignified format by a standard publisher under the title of *Riata and Spurs.* Again the Pinkertons objected, and the volume was radically revised

(1927), eleven chapters being replaced with fresh material from what was to have been Siringo's last book, "Bad Men of the West." The "Bad Men" failed to appear. He left no fluent narrative or polished works, but he traced honest chronicles in a simple and direct style. Though he was uncritical of careless sources, his works will probably live for their vivid portrayal of the cattle range and cowboy characters, and for their rollicky cowboy style. No single writer typifies the achievement of cowboy literature, from the plane of the dime novel to one of character and distinction, so well as Charlie Siringo. Much of his later life was spent in New Mexico, at Roswell and Santa Fé, though he died at Hollywood, Cal.

[Letters of Siringo to author, Mar. 4, 1928, Jas. H. East to author, 1927, and letters from Siringo in the East Collection in possession of author; Harrison Leussler to author, May 17, 1934; writings, *ante*; *Publishers' Weekly*, Nov. 17, 1928; *Fort Worth Star-Telegram*, Oct. 20, 1928; *Houston Post-Dispatch*, Oct. 21, 1928.]

J. E. H.

SITTING BULL (1834?–Dec. 15, 1890), a Hunkpapa Sioux chief, leader in the Sioux war of 1876–77, was born on Grand River, S. D. His father, also named Sitting Bull, was a subchief. The son earned a reputation as a warrior in the sixties, but at a comparatively early age he retired to the safer and more lucrative occupation of medicine man and political leader. Always hostile to the whites, he spent most of his time off the reservation. His camp in the buffalo country became the rallying point for all Sioux, Cheyenne, and Arapaho hostiles; and as he had become wealthy, in an Indian way, he was enabled to make presents that greatly extended his influence throughout the Sioux confederacy and the allied tribes. Though not a war chief, he had become by 1875 the head of the war council. The certainty of war, in the spring of 1876, brought to his camp numbers of well-armed warriors until he had a fighting force estimated at from 2,500 to 4,000 men and boys. When, on June 25, George A. Custer [*q.v.*] made his disastrous attack on the consolidated Indian village at the Little Big Horn, Sitting Bull did no fighting but spent the time in "making medicine," while Gall and Crazy Horse [*qq.v.*] took the leading parts. His following soon afterward broke up into small bands, and, under the relentless pursuit of the military, thousands returned to the reservations. By the end of the year his own band had been pushed across the Canadian border. He remained there until the defection of all his leaders and the increasing destitution of his people caused him to return. At Fort Buford, in July 1881, with 187 men, women and children, he surrendered. He was taken to Fort Randle and was later settled on the Standing Rock reservation. To the end he remained a bitter irreconcilable. In 1890 he took an active part in the Messiah agitation. On Dec. 15 he was arrested by Indian police and in the fight that followed was shot and killed. He was buried in the military cemetery at Fort Yates.

He was a heavy-set, muscular man, about five feet eight inches in height. James McLaughlin, who was Indian agent at the Standing Rock reservation during the Messiah agitation of 1890, credited him with a knowledge of men and a deep insight into affairs among Indians, but wrote that he was wily, untrustworthy, and in his rôle of medicine man "had all the tricks of the fake spiritualist" (*My Friend . . . post*, pp. 180–81, 203). His fame during the years from 1875 to 1881 had a disturbing effect on the unstable imaginations of a number of whites, and many fantastic myths about him were created. He was asserted to be a white man, a graduate of West Point, as well as of other institutions, a linguist, a scholar, a Mason, and a Catholic; and much was written and published in support of these assertions. A book that appeared in 1878, *The Works of Sitting Bull*, credited him with the authorship of French and Latin poems. In reality his sole achievement in letters, won by him during his exile in Canada, seems to have been the ability to write his name, which he spelled "Seitting Bull."

[Jas. McLaughlin, *My Friend the Indian* (1910) and his report in *Sixtieth Ann. Report of the Commissioner of Indian Affairs, 1891* (1891), pp. 325–38; James Mooney, "The Ghost Dance Religion and the Sioux Outbreak of 1890," *14th Annual Rept. of the Bureau of Ethnology*, pt. 2 (1896); W. F. Johnson, *The Red Record of the Sioux* (1891); J. M. Hanson, *The Conquest of the Missouri* (1909); unsigned sketch in *Handbook of Am. Indians* (1910), ed. by F. W. Hodge; a wholly different interpretation of character and achievement in Stanley Vestal, *Sitting Bull* (1932) and *New Sources of Indian Hist.* (1934); C. A. Eastman, *Indian Heroes* (1918).]
W. J. G.

SIZER, NELSON (May 27, 1812–Oct. 18, 1897), phrenologist, was descended from Anthony de Zocieur, a French sailor from the island of Terceira, who took the name Sizer after he settled in Middletown, Conn., in 1726. His grandfather, William Sizer, was an ingenious Jack-of-all-trades whose most notable exploit occurred during the Revolution when he inoculated four men with a jack-knife, and carried them through smallpox with butternut physic made into pills by boiling the juice. His father, Fletcher Sizer, was married to Lydia Bassett, of Westfield, Mass., and moved to Chester, Mass., where Nelson was born. Reared among the Berkshire Hills, he wrote for country news-

papers until he came under the influence of the phrenologist, J. G. Spurzheim, who came to the United States in 1832. He studied phrenology, lecturing after 1839 in the South and East, and in 1849 he became examiner in the famous phrenological cabinet of Orson Squire Fowler and Samuel Roberts Wells [*qq.v.*] in New York City. He examined the heads of nearly three hundred thousand persons. From 1859 to 1863 he edited the *American Phrenological Journal*, which, under his editorship, was a dignified periodical. He became president of the American Institute of Phrenology, founded in 1866, with Amos Dean and Horace Greeley among the corporate members. Sizer was the principal lecturer at the Institute, which, at the time of his death, had graduated 731 students.

He was the author of many articles in the *Phrenological Journal*, and of ten pamphlets on phrenology and related subjects, published in the *Human-Nature Library*. His first known publication was *An Address on the Life and Character of Washington* (1842). The most important of his many books expounded the principles of phrenology, and developed the phrenological theses in respect to the reading of character, education, vocational choice, and marriage. Of the first sort are *Heads and Faces, and How to Study Them* (1885), and *How to Study Strangers by Temperament, Face, and Head* (1895). On education, he published *How to Teach According to Temperament and Mental Development* (1877). On vocational guidance, he contributed *What to Do, and Why* (1872), and *The Road to Success* (1885). His contributions on marriage were *Thoughts on Domestic Life* (1850), and *Right Selection in Wedlock* (n.d.). His *Forty Years in Phrenology* (1882) is a volume of recollections of his life work. Although not so important a figure in the history of phrenology as Gall, Spurzheim, the Combes, and the Fowlers, Sizer was one of the leading popularizers and practitioners of the pseudo-science. The basic assumptions of the phrenologists were unsound, but their efforts to analyze character, their discussions of the problems relating to sex, vocational choice, prison reform, and educational reform, stimulated progressive thought. Their influence was felt by such men as Edgar Allan Poe, Walt Whitman, Horace Mann, and Henry Ward Beecher. There is ample testimony that Sizer exerted a helpful influence on the men and women whom he advised. Perhaps the same skill which permitted his grandfather to cure smallpox with butternut physic aided the phrenologist to cure souls by measuring the cranial protuberances. He was married at Suffield,

Conn., on Mar. 12, 1843, for the second time, and had two children by his first wife, and one by his second.

[On the Sizer family, see bound manuscript data in the Newberry Library, C. W. Hayes, *William Wells of Southold and His Descendants* (1878), F. W. Bailey, *Early Conn. Marriages*, vol. II (1896), and *Vital Records of Chester, Mass.* (1911). For Nelson Sizer, see his *Forty Years in Phrenology* (1882), obituaries in the *N. Y. Times* and *N. Y. Daily Tribune*, Oct. 19, 1897, and the *Phrenological Jour. of Sci. and Health*, Dec. 1897.]   E. B. H.

SKANIADARIIO (*c.* 1735–Aug. 10, 1815), Seneca sachem, religious leader, was born at the village of Ganawaugus, on the west side of the Genesee River opposite the present town of Avon, N. Y. He was also known to his own people as Ganiodaiio, and his name is translated Handsome Lake. He led a dissolute life until about 1796, when he suffered a severe illness brought about by his dissipation. According to native accounts he wasted away in a hut near the present Warren, Pa., and passed into a condition of coma. Arising from this, he declared that he had been visited by four messengers of the Creator of Life and had been instructed in certain principles that were to constitute a new religion to be called the Gaiwiio. According to the code that he later proclaimed, he afterward had other revelations. His great work was in recrystallizing a declining faith and giving it new vigor by means of his revelations, thus giving to the Iroquois a new philosophy and religion about which to rally. Wandering from one Indian village to another he preached his doctrine with considerable success, demanding that his people abstain from drunkenness, witchcraft, and infidelity, practise industry and thrift, and hold faith in his revelations. For fifteen years, from 1800 to 1815, he conducted his ministry, at one time visiting Thomas Jefferson to whom he explained his teachings. He succeeded in blotting out much of the older religion of the Iroquois and in blocking missionary efforts, but during his last years he seems to have been assailed with doubts, for he had obtained a clearer view of Christianity. He died at Onondaga, near Syracuse. In 1900 the followers of his religion among the Iroquois of New York and Ontario numbered more than one fourth of all these people, and at the present time (1935) there are groups of his followers meeting in "long houses" on every reservation of the Iroquois except at Tuscarora, Saint Regis, and Caughnawaga.

[A. C. Parker, "The Code of Handsome Lake," *N. Y. State Museum Bull.*, no. 163 (1913); L. H. Morgan, *League of the . . . Iroquois* (1851); F. W. Hodge, *Handbook of Am. Indians*, pt. II (1910).]
       A. C. P—k—r.

SKENANDOA (1706?–Mar. 11, 1816), Oneida chief, was said to have been born into some other tribe, possibly the Conestoga, and adopted by the Oneida at an early age. His name is often written differently, Scanondo, Schenandoah, Shenandoa, and even Johnko' Skeanendon. Traditionally, he was a drunkard until about 1755, when, finding himself to have been robbed in a drunken stupor, he resolved to change his way of life and succeeded in doing so. Shortly after that he was converted to Christianity by Samuel Kirkland [*q.v.*]. A firm friend of the colonists, he fought against the French in the French and Indian War, and at the outbreak of the Revolution, with Samuel Kirkland and Thomas Spencer, he was responsible for keeping the Oneida and Tuscarora from joining the rest of the Iroquois Confederation in fighting for the British. Instead, he was able to persuade the Oneida to adopt an address of neutrality in May 1775 and, when they abandoned neutrality, to influence many of the Oneida and Tuscarora to join the Americans. He is said to have prevented the massacre of many settlers at German Flats, now in Herkimer County, N. Y.

After the war he shared the fate of the rest of his people, living on year after year in a situation gradually becoming more narrow and more uncomfortable. He grew to be a very old man, perhaps past the century mark, blind and feeble, "an aged hemlock . . . dead at the top" (Campbell, *post*, App. p. 30), and he died at his home near Oneida Castle strong in the white man's faith. According to his often expressed wish he was buried by the side of his friend Samuel Kirkland in the latter's garden at Clinton, N. Y., and later removed with Kirkland to lie in the graveyard of Hamilton College. There the Northern Missionary Society erected a monument to him, who, "wise, eloquent and brave . . . long swayed the Councils of his Tribe . . . remained a firm friend of the United States . . . and . . . adorned by every Christian virtue . . . fell asleep in Jesus."

[Consult: obituary from Utica *Patriot*, Mar. 19, 1816, reprinted as Note D in App., W. W. Campbell, *Annals of Tryon County, N. Y.* (1831); *Documentary Hist. of Hamilton College* (1922); Wm. Gordon, *The Hist. of the . . . Independence of the U. S.* (3rd Am. ed., 1801), I, 359–61; S. K. Lothrop, "Life of Samuel Kirkland," *The Lib. of Am. Biog.*, ser. 2, vol. XV (1848), ed. by Jared Sparks; Pomroy Jones, *Annals and Recollections of Oneida County* (1851), pp. 865–68; H. R. Schoolcraft, *Hist. of the Indian Tribes* (1857), pt. 6. p. 136; "Skenandoah" was a pseudonym used by Lewis H. Morgan, see his *League of the . . . . . . Iroquois*, new ed. (2 vols. in 1, 1904), ed. by H. M. Lloyd, II, 164, 195.]
       K. E. C.

SKENE, ALEXANDER JOHNSTON CHALMERS (June 17, 1837–July 4, 1900), pioneer gynecologist, was born in Fyvie, Aberdeenshire, Scotland, of a family well known in Scottish history (see W. F. Skene, *Memorials of the Family of Skene of Skene,* Aberdeen, 1887). His parents were Johnston and Jean (McConachie) Skene. He spent his boyhood in his native village, acquired an education in the local schools, and began to study medicine at Kings College. At nineteen years of age he left home and came to America. He studied medicine in Toronto in 1860 and attended the University of Michigan in 1861 and 1862. The following year he received the M.D. degree from the Long Island College Hospital Medical School. His practice, begun in Brooklyn in 1864, was interrupted by active duty in the Federal army as assistant surgeon in the volunteer corps. He taught gynecology at the New York Post-Graduate Hospital from 1883 to 1886, and was consultant to a number of dispensaries and hospitals. He was for many years attached to the Long Island College Hospital, where he served as teacher, operator, dean, and president. He was a founder of the American Gynecological Society (president, 1886–87), and the International Congress of Gynecology and Obstetrics (honorary president, Geneva, 1896), and acted as president of the Medical Society of Kings County, 1874–75, the New York Obstetrical Society, 1877–79, and the Brooklyn Gynecological Society, 1891–92. He was associate editor of the *Archives of Medicine,* 1883–84, the *American Medical Digest,* 1884–89, and the *New York Gynaecological and Obstetrical Journal,* 1891–1900. He has to his credit more than one hundred medical papers (see Browning and Schroeder, *post*), and he was the author of *Diseases of the Bladder and Urethra in Women* (1878); *Education and Culture as Related to the Health and Diseases of Women* (1889); *Electro-haemostasis in Operative Surgery* (1889); *Medical Gynecology* (1895); and *Treatise on the Diseases of Women* (1888). One mediocre novel, *True to Themselves,* published in 1897, came from his pen.

He entered the field of gynecology at a critical moment, when great leaders were in demand to direct the investigations which were bringing about startling and important developments. His discovery in 1880 of what are now called Skene's urethral glands gave him an international reputation and an assured place in the history of gynecology. He also is known to have devised thirty-one surgical instruments. He opened a private sanitarium in 1884 in Brooklyn with Dr. W. M. Thalon, and, in 1899, Skene's Hospital for Self-supporting Women.

His tremendous physique, his ruddy face, glowing with a kindly heartiness, his firm chin, and compelling eyes, reflected a vigorous and commanding personality. Intense in his work, he was equally so in his emotions, a stanch friend and formidable enemy. His lectures were lucid, terse, and to the point, and he never missed an opportunity to assist and encourage younger men in special lines of work. A skilful operator, the leading physician of Brooklyn of his time, he rose early, operated all morning, and saw as many as fifty patients in the afternoon. He never became resigned to city life and resorted frequently to his country home in the Catskills where he enjoyed to the full the freedom of outdoor life. Here he could devote himself to his artistic talents, for had he not been a physician, he might well have made a name for himself as a sculptor. Many examples of his work may be seen at Kings County Medical Society. He was married to Annette Wilhelmine Lillian Van der Wegen of Brussels, Belgium. They had no children but adopted a daughter. After completely disregarding repeated warnings, he succumbed to an attack of angina pectoris at a comparatively early age and at the height of his career. A bust of him stands in Prospect Park, Brooklyn, an unusual honor and tribute to a physician.

[Some obituaries and biographies give 1838 as Skene's birth date, see, however, *Who's Who in America,* 1899–1900. For further data, consult: H. A. Kelly and W. L. Burrage, *Am. Med. Biogs.* (1920); William Browning, "Alexander . . . Skene," *Brooklyn Med. Jour.,* Apr. 1897; R. L. Dickinson, "Alexander . . . Skene," *Trans. Am. Gynecological Soc.,* vol. XXVI (1901); J. C. MacEvitt, "Alexander . . . Skene," *Am. Jour. of Surgery,* Mar. 1928; William Schroeder, "Alexander . . . Skene," *Brooklyn Med. Jour.,* Sept. 1900; *Brooklyn Daily Eagle,* July 5, 9, 1900.]   G. L. A.

SKILLERN, ROSS HALL (Nov. 13, 1875–Sept. 20, 1930), laryngologist, was born in Philadelphia, Pa., the son of Dr. Samuel Ruff Skillern and his wife, Sarah Hall Ross. He received his preliminary education in George F. Martin's academy, studied in the school of biology at the University of Pennsylvania, 1892–93, then entered the medical department, from which he was graduated in 1897. After practising general medicine for several years with his father he began to specialize in laryngology. In 1905 he suffered an attack of epidemic cerebrospinal meningitis which he had contracted from a patient. He recovered after a prolonged illness and then went abroad to study rhinology and laryngology in Vienna for a year and a half. He returned to Philadelphia in 1907 and began giving private courses in the anatomy and pathology of the nasal accessory sinuses. In 1913 he was professor of laryngology in the Medico-Chirurgical College of Philadelphia and continued to serve in that capacity after the institution became part of the graduate school of medicine of the University of Pennsylvania in 1919. He was an enthusiastic and gifted teacher, and an excellent operator, and his classes attracted many students. He was a frequent contributor to current medical literature, his bibliography enumerating the titles of forty-six contributions to medical journals. His most important work, *The Catarrhal and Suppurative Diseases of the Accessory Sinuses of the Nose,* was published in 1913 and reached four editions within ten years.

During the World War he served first as a major in the medical corps, chief of the division of surgery of the head, in the base hospital at Camp Sheridan, Ala. He was promoted to the rank of lieutenant-colonel in July 1918, and acted as commanding officer of United States base hospital No. 89, American Expeditionary Force, at Mésves-sur-Loire, France. In 1912 he organized the Philadelphia Laryngological Society and became the first president. He was a member of the American Academy of Ophthalmology and Otolaryngology, and served as president in 1926; he was chairman of the section on otolaryngology of the American Medical Association in 1920, and president of the American Laryngological, Rhinological and Otological Society in 1929. He was a member of the American Laryngological Association, and when the American Board of Examiners in Otolaryngology was organized in 1924, was chosen as one of the delegates to represent the Association on the Board, a position to which he was reëlected every year until his death. He was also a fellow of the College of Physicians of Philadelphia and of other local medical societies. He was married to Eliza Michler Porter, of Hackettstown, N. J., on June 3, 1903. She, with two daughters and two sons, survived him when he died suddenly in Philadelphia.

[*Who's Who in America,* 1930–31; *Who's Who in Am. Med.,* 1925; memoir by G. M. Coates, M.D., in *Trans. . . . of the Am. Laryngological Asso.* (1931); personal acquaintance; *Public Ledger* (Phila.), Sept. 21, 1930.]   F. R. P.

SKINNER, AARON NICHOLS (Aug. 10, 1845–Aug. 14, 1918), astronomer, was born at Boston, Mass., the son of Benjamin Hill and Mercy (Burgess) Skinner. He attended the schools in the vicinity of his home, and early developed habits of study which in his later life became dominant characteristics. He continued his education at Beloit College, Beloit, Wis., and pursued a special course in astronomy at the University of Chicago from 1868 to 1870. He was married to Sarah Elizabeth Gibbs, of Framingham, Mass., on Feb. 9, 1874, and they had two children, a daughter and a son. While studying at the University of Chicago, he held a position as assistant at the Dearborn Observatory, and after completing his course he became assistant astronomer at the United States Naval Observatory, a position which he held for twenty-eight years. He then passed a competitive examination and in 1898 was commissioned in the naval service as a professor of mathematics. From 1893 to 1902 he was in charge of the twenty-six-inch equatorial. From 1903 until his detachment from the Naval Observatory in 1909, he had charge of the equatorials.

He discovered four variable stars in the course of his observations with the meridian circles. The transit circle observations of the sun, moon, planets, and meridian stars were carried out under his direction, first as an assistant astronomer and then as a professor. From these observations he determined the places of approximately 8824 stars in the zone from 14 degrees, south declination, to 18 degrees, south declination, as a contribution to the *Katalog der Astronomischen Gesellschaft* of Leipzig, Germany. This work was published as the Washington Zone Catalogue in 1908 under the title: *Catalogue of 8824 stars between 13° 50' and 18° 10' south declination.* He was placed in charge of the expedition which was sent to the island of Sumatra to observe the total eclipse of the sun on May 18, 1901. He took with him six members of the Observatory staff and five scientists from other observatories in the United States. The expedition was ably handled by Skinner, who carefully arranged to cover all possible contingencies. In addition to the observations made of the total solar eclipse, observations were made at newly erected, outlying stations; at Solok one member of the expedition (W. W. Dinwiddie) discovered a bright comet on the night of May 3.

Skinner was retired from the United States naval service with the rank of commander, United States Navy, Professor Corps, in 1907, but remained in active service in the Naval Observatory until 1909. He was a member of the American Association for the Advancement of Science, the Astronomische Gesellschaft of Leipzig, Germany, and of the Astronomical and Astrophysical Society of America. His writings, in addition to the Washington Zone Catalogue, include results of observations, published by the United States Naval Observatory, the *Naval Observatory Expedition to Sumatra* (1902), printed first in *Popular Astronomy,* January 1902, and numerous articles on variables and minor planets for scientific periodicals. He died at Framingham, Mass.

[*Who's Who in America*, 1918–19; *Pubs. of the U. S. Naval Observatory*, 2 ser., vol. VI (1911); *Washington Post*, Aug. 15, 1918.]   J. F. H.

SKINNER, ALANSON BUCK (Sept. 7, 1886–Aug. 17, 1925), anthropologist and ethnologist, was born in Buffalo, N. Y., the son of Frank Woodward Skinner, a civil engineer, and Rachel Amelia (Sumner) Skinner. When he was a small boy, the family moved to Staten Island, where Alanson became interested in natural science and made collections of Indian relics. During a school vacation (1902) he worked for the American Museum of Natural History, New York, in the excavation of an ancient shellheap near Shinnecock Hills, Long Island, and two years later accompanied an archeological expedition of the Peabody Museum of Harvard to western New York, where he made his first visit to an Indian reservation. After finishing his high school course, he occupied a position in a commercial establishment for a time, but ultimately devoted himself to scientific work.

From 1907 to 1913 he was connected with the American Museum of Natural History, finding opportunity in the meantime to take courses at Columbia and Harvard. During this period he led two expeditions (1908, 1909) to Hudson Bay, to study the Cree Indians; carried on investigations in Wisconsin; visited the Florida Everglades to make collections from the Seminoles; and spent much time in explorations on the archeological sites of the Algonquian Indians in New York State. This last work led him to make studies of the material culture of these Indians and of the Siouan tribes in contact with them, in which field he became an authority. In 1916 he joined the staff of the Museum of the American Indian, Heye Foundation, and took charge of an archeological expedition to Costa Rica. Two years later he accepted the position of curator of anthropology at the Public Museum of Milwaukee. Returning to the Museum of the American Indian in 1924, he remained with that institution until his death in an automobile accident near Tokio, N. Dak., the following year.

Beginning in 1903, he published rapidly the results of his investigations; a bibliography of his writings contains more than a hundred titles. Among these papers may be mentioned the following: "A Short Account of the Algonkin Indians of Staten Island" (*Proceedings of the Natural History Society of Staten Island*, Jan. 6, 1904); "Notes on the Eastern Cree and Northern Saulteaux" (*Anthropological Papers of the American Museum of Natural History*, vol. IX, 1911); with Max Schrabisch, a preliminary chapter on the types of Indian remains found in New Jersey (*Geological Survey of New Jersey, Bulletin IX*, 1913); "Social Life and Ceremonial Bundles of the Menomini Indians" (*Anthropological Papers of the American Museum of Natural History*, vol. XIII, 1913); *The Indians of Greater New York* (1915); "Exploration of Aboriginal Sites at Throgs Neck and Clasons Point, New York City" (*Contributions of the Museum of the American Indian, Heye Foundation*, vol. V, 1919); in collaboration with John V. Satterlee, "Folklore of the Menomini Indians" (*Anthropological Papers of the American Museum of Natural History*, vol. XIII, 1915); *Ethnology of the Ioway Indians* (1926); *The Mascoutens or Prairie Potawatomi Indians* (3 parts, 1924–27), and a posthumous work in which Skinner returned to archeology, *Certain Mounds and Village Sites of Shawano and Oconto Counties, Wisconsin* (1932), all published as bulletins of the Milwaukee Public Museum.

He was a man of athletic figure, but suffered from ill health. During the World War he tried several times to enlist, but was rejected on physical grounds. As a member of the New York Guard, however, he served in the 9th Coast Artillery. His good nature and friendliness won him the confidence of the Indians. His wife, Dorothy Preston, who, with a small daughter, survived him, was part Wyandotte. He confined his work to the observational field and did not undertake the intangibles, yet the gatherings of his short but busy life are of the greatest value and importance to anthropology.

[*Am. Anthropologist*, vol. XXVIII (1926); M. R. Harrington, in *Indian Notes* (New York), Oct. 1925; *Explorers Jour.*, July–Dec. 1925; *N. Y. Times* and *N. Y. Herald Tribune*, Aug. 19, 1925.]   W. H.

SKINNER, CHARLES RUFUS (Aug. 4, 1844–June 30, 1928), politician, educator, librarian, was born on a farm in Union Square, Oswego County, N. Y., the son of Avery and Charlotte Prior (Stebbins) Skinner. Educated in the district school and at Mexico Academy and Clinton Liberal Institute, both in Oswego County, he went to New York City in 1867 and spent three years there in business. From 1870 to 1874 he was city editor and manager of the *Daily Times*, Watertown, N. Y. He married, Oct. 16, 1873, Elizabeth Baldwin of Watertown, daughter of David W. and Laura (Freeman) Baldwin. In 1876 he published *Watertown, N. Y., A History of Its Settlement and Progress.* He served on the Watertown board of education, 1875–84. A member of the state legislature from 1877 to 1881, he was chairman of the committee on railroads and advocated a five-cent fare on the New York elevated railway. In 1881 he was elected as representative to Congress, succeeding Warner Miller, who had resigned in order to fill the unfinished term of Thomas Collier Platt [qq.v.]; he was reëlected and served until 1885, his chief interest being in postal matters. He originated and secured the passage of a bill providing for special delivery letters.

After another year of editorial work, he became deputy state superintendent of public instruction in 1886, supervisor of teachers' institutes and teachers' training classes in 1892, and state superintendent of public instruction in 1895. During these years he compiled and edited a teachers' manual, books on school libraries and school architecture, an *Arbor Day Manual* (1890), and a *Manual of Patriotism* (1900). He also compiled *The Bright Side* (copyright 1909), a scrapbook of quotations. He was president of the National Education Association, 1896–97. To the end of his life he believed that the state should concentrate its educational efforts on the elementary schools, leaving the high schools and colleges to private enterprise and endowment. In 1904, when the department of public instruction was merged with the state board of regents through legislation that Skinner himself sponsored, his position ceased to exist.

From 1906 to 1911 he was assistant appraiser of merchandise for the port of New York. He was librarian of the state assembly, 1913–14, and in 1915 was given the newly created post of legislative librarian. Under him the legislative library became a quick reference library in which everything was arranged alphabetically, apple orchard cultivation and arbitration in labor disputes following each other in the same section. The librarian personally knew where material could be found, and there he ruled, tall, handsome, and commanding, until Oct. 31, 1925, when he reached the legal retiring age. Not quite three years later he died while he was visiting his son in Pelham Manor, N. Y. He was survived by three sons and a daughter.

[*Who's Who in America*, 1928–29; *Biog. Directory of the Am. Cong., 1774–1927* (1928); C. E. Fitch, *The Pub. School; Hist. of Common School Educ. in N. Y., 1633 to 1904* (n.d.), prepared for N. Y. State Dept. of Pub. Instruction; N. Y. (State) Univ., *Bull. to the Schools*, Sept. 15, 1928, p. 10; obituaries in *Watertown Daily Standard*, June 30, 1928, *N. Y. Times*, July 1, 1928.]   E. E. W.

SKINNER, HALCYON (Mar. 6, 1824–Nov. 28, 1900), inventor, the son of Joseph and Susan (Eggleston) Skinner, was born in Mantua,

Ohio, where his parents had gone from Massachusetts upon their marriage. When he was eight years old his parents removed to Stockbridge, Mass., and there he received a common school education, working at the same time on neighboring farms and in his father's shop. After his parents removed to West Farms, N. Y., in 1838, he helped his father in the making of violins and guitars for seven years. He then engaged in general carpentry work for himself until 1849, when he was hired by Alexander Smith, a carpet manufacturer in West Farms, to design and construct a hand loom that would weave figured carpet instead of the striped sort prevailing at the time. The machine, which was completed in a year, was so successful that by 1851 Smith had one hundred looms at work to supply the demand for the new "tapestry ingrain" carpet. For forty years Skinner was retained by Smith as mechanical expert and consultant. In 1856 he devised and patented jointly with Smith a power loom to weave Axminster or tufted carpets, but it was not until 1860 that a satisfactory machine was put into operation. He then turned his attention to inventing and patenting a power loom for weaving ingrain carpets and developed a very successful machine, first installed in 1864 in Smith's new manufactory at Yonkers, N. Y., and used until ingrain carpet weaving was discontinued. Around 1870 Smith began the manufacture of tapestry carpet, using looms imported from England; these, however, were not satisfactory until after Skinner had completely altered them and had doubled their output.

Probably his most important invention was a power loom for weaving moquette carpets, first conceived in 1876 and patented on January 16, 1877. In the course of five or six years, Skinner and his two sons secured a series of patents. The machines built in accordance with these placed Smith's company in the lead among American manufacturers of moquette carpets. It is said that the origination of the moquette loom stamped Skinner as a creative genius and placed him in a high position among the inventors of the world. In 1889 he severed his connections with the Smith company and lived more or less in retirement in Yonkers. He perfected some further improvements of the moquette loom, however, and occasionally served his former employer in an advisory capacity. He was twice married; his first wife, Eliza Pierce, died in 1869, and subsequently he married Adelaide Cropsey of Brooklyn, N. Y. His death occurred when he was struck by a train. He was survived by his widow, and two sons and three daughters, all by his first marriage.

[J. T. Scharf, *Hist. of Westchester County, N. Y.* (1886), vol. II; *Am. Carpet and Upholstery Jour.*, Dec. 1900; *Carpet and Upholstery Trade Rev.*, Dec. 1, 1900; obituaries in *N. Y. Times* and *N. Y. Herald*, Nov. 29, 1900; Patent Office records.]   C. W. M—n.

SKINNER, HARRY (May 25, 1855–May 19, 1929), representative from North Carolina, was born in Perquimans County, N. C., and came of a family prominent in state affairs through several generations. His parents were Elmyra (Ward) and James C. Skinner, a prosperous planter. He received his preparatory education at the Hertford academy, and in 1875 he received the LL.B. degree from Kentucky University. He returned to North Carolina and, having been admitted to the bar in 1876, began practice in Greenville. On June 5, 1878, he was married to Lottie Monteiro of Richmond, Va., who died ten years later leaving four children. Devoting himself to his profession for some years, he was very successful. He was also interested in politics as a rather uncompromising Democrat, and in 1891 he was a member of the lower house of the legislature. Already well and favorably known, he was prominent in spite of inexperience, was chairman of the committee on internal improvements and of the house branch of the committee on redistricting the state, advocated the appointment of a committee to codify the corporation laws, and worked enthusiastically for the establishment of a state college for women and for other educational improvements.

His mind had for some years been much occupied with the problem of improving the condition of the farmer and laborer, and he had become convinced that the evils which oppressed them were due chiefly to a faulty financial system. He joined the Farmers' Alliance and was prominent in its political councils. In *Frank Leslie's Illustrated Newspaper*, for Nov. 30, 1889, he published "The Hope of the South," an exposition of a plan for the federal government to fix the price of cotton at thirteen cents a pound by providing warehouses and issuing negotiable warehouse certificates to the cotton growers. He always claimed that his ideas formed the basis for the "sub-treasury" plan that the Alliance and, later, the People's party advocated. Later he introduced a bill in Congress providing for the establishment of the system and a somewhat similar plan to care for the cotton crop of the South. His name was proposed to the Democratic state convention for lieutenant-governor, but he refused to let it be considered because he thought his financial views made his selection unwise and nothing must be done to endanger party success, since he was strongly opposed to the plan of separate party organization. When the Populists elected him a delegate to the Omaha Convention in 1892, he repudiated their action. He also declined the Populist nomination by acclamation for governor and for Congress.

However, in 1894 he was elected by the Populist party to the Fifty-fourth Congress and reelected two years later. In that year he was permanent president of the Populist state convention and, as a "middle-of-the-road" Populist, opposed further fusion with the Republicans. He split with the leaders of his party who wanted to break the agreement made in 1895 to reëlect Jeter C. Pritchard to the federal Senate, and he helped obtain the election. In Congress Skinner was true to his party faith. He labored under the handicap of belonging to a minority, but, an eloquent speaker, able debater, and an impressive figure, he gave a good account of himself (for his financial and tariff theories see such speeches as *The Coin Redemption Fund. Remarks . . . in House . . . Dec. 27, 1895*, 1896, and *Equitable Protection and Bimetallism . . . Speech . . . in the House . . . Mar. 25, 1897*, 1897). Apart from his work for Populist policies, he was active in his support of a system of inland waterways. He was defeated in 1898 and returned to the practice of law. In 1900 he was still a Populist and a supporter of Bryan, and he favored the ratification of the constitutional amendment disfranchising the bulk of the negroes; but shortly thereafter he became a Republican. In 1902 he became federal district attorney and served ably for eight years. He was president of the North Carolina Bar Association in 1915 and for several years vice-president for North Carolina of the American Bar Association. He was a member of the Episcopal Church. He died in Greenville survived by three children and by his second wife, Ella (Monteiro) Skinner, to whom he was married on Oct. 26, 1895.

[*Cyc. of Eminent and Repres. Men of the Carolinas* (1892), vol. II; *N. C. Bar Ass. Proc. . . . 1929* (1929), pp. 77–79; J. G. deR. Hamilton, *Hist of N. C.* (1919), vols. III and IV ed. by special staff; J. D. Hicks, *The Populist Revolt* (1931); *Greensboro Daily Record*, Mar. 14, 1892; *News and Observer* (Raleigh), May 20, 1929.]   J. G. deR. H.

SKINNER, JOHN STUART (Feb. 22, 1788– Mar. 21, 1851), agricultural editor and writer, was born in Calvert County, Md., and spent his early years on the family plantation established by Robert Skinner, who emigrated from England in the early part of the seventeenth century. His father, Frederick, was an officer in the American Revolution and later managed his own plantation and one inherited by his wife, who was a sister of the well-known "Jack" Stuart, companion of Lafayette. Skinner was educated in local schools and at Charlotte Hall, a classical academy in St. Mary's County. At eighteen he became an assistant to the clerk of the county court and later began to study law at Annapolis. Here he was appointed reading clerk in the legislature and made a notary public for Annapolis by Governor Wright. At the age of twenty-one he was admitted to the bar.

Following the outbreak of the War of 1812, President Madison made him inspector of European mail at Annapolis, and he was also designated an agent for prisoners of war. Skinner successfully performed these responsible duties, incidentally making life-long friends among the British officers. In 1813 his headquarters were removed to Baltimore, where, Mar. 26, 1814, he was commissioned a purser in the navy, a position held throughout the war and for a number of years thereafter. While visiting the fleet of Admiral Cockburn, Skinner and Francis Scott Key [q.v.] were detained during a furious night bombardment of Fort McHenry, Sept. 13–14, 1814, following which they were released and returned to Baltimore. They then went to the "Fountain Inn," where Key wrote "The Star Spangled Banner." Skinner, impressed with the beauty of the song, took the manuscript and arranged to have it printed. From 1816 to 1837 he was postmaster at Baltimore. In 1841 President Harrison appointed him third assistant postmaster general, in which capacity, through his attention to detail he was able, it is said, to reduce by $200,000 the expenditures of the United States post office department. In 1845, under President Polk, he was removed from office for political reasons.

Perceiving the worn-out state of much of the soil in Maryland and stimulated by the writings of John Taylor of Caroline [q.v.], Skinner decided in 1819 to establish an agricultural paper, with a view to disseminating knowledge respecting the best methods of farm practice. Accordingly, on Apr. 2, he offered to the public the initial number of the *American Farmer*, the issue being held over a day lest the paper be taken for an April Fool joke. Although David Wiley published the *Agricultural Museum* at Georgetown in 1810, to Skinner belongs the honor of establishing the first continuous, successful agricultural periodical in the United States. The *American Farmer* quickly became the principal organ of expression for all those who took an active interest in agricultural improvement. In its pages one finds communications from such men as John Taylor of Caroline, Thomas Jefferson, Timothy Pickering, John Hare Powel, James Garnett, James Madison, Richard Peters, John H. Cocke,

and others of like standing. Among foreign contributors were Sir John Sinclair, Thomas W. Coke, and General Lafayette. Throughout the twenties the paper offered the best available information on field crop cultivation, fertilization of soil, horticulture, new agricultural machines, agricultural organizations, fairs, prices, internal improvements, and similar subjects. In August 1829 Skinner started the monthly publication of the *American Turf Register and Sporting Magazine*, devoted to the improvement of American thoroughbred horses, and to veterinary knowledge, racing, shooting, hunting, fishing, and the habits of American game. It was the first magazine of its kind in the United States and was more influential than any other factor of its day in improving the breed of American horses. Finding the dual editorship too great a demand upon his time, he sold the *American Farmer* in 1830 for $20,000, remaining thereafter an occasional contributor. In 1835 the *American Turf Register* was sold for $10,000 to Gideon B. Smith, who, four years later, sold it to William Trotter Porter [q.v.]. Greeley and McElrath, proprietors of the *New York Tribune*, engaged Skinner in 1845 to edit, in New York, the *Farmers' Library and Monthly Journal of Agriculture*, the first issue of which was dated July of that year. A portion of each number consisted of a reprint of some celebrated agricultural work, frequently foreign; the remainder was devoted to material on domestic and foreign farming, experiments, new machines, inventions, and similar subjects. The publication eventually proved too technical for popular subscription and at the conclusion of a three-year contract, Skinner bought the rights and established, at Philadelphia, a periodical of his own entitled *The Plough, the Loom, and the Anvil*, the first number of which appeared in July 1848. Its pages were devoted to domestic agriculture and industry, and to advocating a protective tariff for both. The magazine soon attained wide popularity and Skinner continued as editor until his death.

In cooperation with officials of the Maryland Agricultural Society he established a stock farm a few miles from Baltimore, where the Society observed the scientific breeding of horses and mules, various types of cattle, Tunis sheep, and other animals. He was also active in developing the Western Shore branch of the Maryland Agricultural Society, and a society to improve the breed of horses. At the time of General Lafayette's visit to Baltimore in 1824, Skinner arranged a special meeting of the Maryland Agricultural Society which Lafayette attended. The two became friends, corresponded extensively, and Skinner acted as business agent for Lafayette in the United States, and later for the Lafayette family. In the course of his career he became an honorary member of practically every important agricultural organization in his own country and abroad. Several of these presented him with costly sets of silver, and the South Carolina Agricultural Society voted him a gold medal. Making use of his extensive acquaintance among officers in the United States Navy, he was instrumental in having brought into the United States useful plants, improved livestock, and valuable agricultural books from various parts of the world. As early as 1824 a quantity of guano was thus introduced, but he did not succeed in popularizing this type of fertilizer.

Skinner wrote *The Dog and the Sportsman* (1845), and a number of monographs on agricultural subjects. He also contributed agricultural articles to leading newspapers such as the *Albion* (New York), and the *Philadelphia Courier,* and edited a number of agricultural works. Among the latter were *Memoirs of the Pennsylvania Agricultural Society* (1824); *The Horse* (1843) by William Youatt; *Every Man His Own Cattle Doctor* (1844) by Youatt and Francis Clater; *Every Man His Own Farrier* (1845) by Clater; and *Mason's Farrier and Stud Book* (1848), by Richard Mason. He also added supplementary material to François Guénon's *A Treatise on Milch Cows* (1846), and John Badcock's *Farriery* (1848); and subsequently printed, with a preface written by himself, *Sheep Husbandry in the South* (1848) by H. S. Randall [q.v.], which had appeared in the *Farmers' Library* in 1847. Skinner's activities as an agricultural publicist were chiefly carried on for over twenty-five years outside of his working hours as a public official. On Mar. 10, 1812, he married Elizabeth G. Davies, by whom he had three sons, one of whom, with his widow, survived him. Skinner's death, at the height of his powers, was occasioned by an accidental fall in the post office at Baltimore.

["Memorial of J. S. Skinner, Praying the Establishment of an Agricultural Department of Government," *Senate Misc. Doc. 120*, 30 Cong., 1 Sess.; *The Plough, the Loom, and the Anvil* (N. Y.), Apr., Dec. 1851, July 1854; B. P. Poore, *Biog. Sketch of John Stuart Skinner* (repr. 1924); *Am. Farmer* (Baltimore), Apr. 1851; *Ohio Cultivator* (Columbus), Apr. 1, 1851; *Prairie Farmer* (Chicago), May 1851; *Am. Agriculturist* (N. Y.), May 1851; *Cultivator* (Albany), May 1851; *Am. Hist. Rev.*, Jan. 1928; *Minn. Hist.*, Dec. 1933; W. E. Ogilvie, *Pioneer Agricultural Journalists* (1927), privately printed; E. G. Swem, "A Contribution to the Bibliog. of Agriculture in Va.," *Bull. Va. State Lib.*, Jan.–Apr. 1918; *Baltimore Clipper*, Mar. 22, 1851; Myrtle Helfrich, "A Baltimore Pioneer of Farm and Turf," in *The Sun* (Baltimore), Feb. 17, 1935.]
H. A. K—r.

SKINNER, THOMAS HARVEY (Mar. 7, 1791–Feb. 1, 1871), Presbyterian clergyman, educator, and author, seventh of the thirteen children of Joshua and Martha Ann Skinner, was born at Harvey's Neck, N. C. The mother, reared an Episcopalian, became a member of the Baptist Church, and her husband, a Quaker, followed her into that communion. Their dwelling served as the neighborhood schoolhouse, the elder Skinner employing the schoolmaster. Here Thomas received his early education; later, he attended two other schools, and eventually enrolled as a student at Edenton Academy. The rapid progress which he made induced his eldest brother, Joseph, an Edenton attorney, to assume in 1804 the direction of Thomas' further education, and for three years the boy was a member of the brother's home. Entering the College of New Jersey in 1807, he won distinction in mathematics, and was graduated in 1809. For a year and a half he read law in his brother's office, serving also as clerk of the superior court.

About to be admitted to the bar, he decided in 1811, partly as a result of the death in a shipwreck of his youngest brother, John, to enter the Presbyterian ministry. Accordingly, he studied theology at Princeton, N. J., under President Samuel Stanhope Smith [q.v.] of the College of New Jersey; at Savannah, Ga., under Dr. Henry Kollock; and at Elizabethtown, N. J., in the home of Dr. John McDowell [q.v.]. On June 10, 1813, he was ordained at Philadelphia and became co-pastor with Dr. Jacob J. Janeway of the Second Presbyterian Church. He served in this capacity until 1816, vigorously preaching New School theology. Opposition developing, he resigned, and became pastor of the Fifth Church, to which small congregation on Locust Street about seventy members of the Second Church followed him. Seven years later a new edifice was dedicated at a more desirable location on Arch Street. Here his doctrinal sermons attracted crowded evening audiences. He remained with this congregation, except for a few months when he was in charge of the Pine Street Church, Boston, for nearly sixteen years.

After repeated invitations, in 1832 he accepted the professorship of sacred rhetoric in Andover Theological Seminary. Here he labored arduously in the then new task of teaching homiletics. His love of active preaching, however, together with the fact that his health had become impaired, led him in 1835 to undertake the pastorate of the new Mercer Street Presbyterian

Church, New York. Here he remained more than twelve years, a period in the church's history characterized by able preaching and religious revival. He also gave much aid in the work of establishing and stabilizing Union Theological Seminary. From its founding, in 1836, he was a director, and in 1848, when poor health compelled him to relinquish his pastorate, a parishioner endowed a chair of sacred rhetoric there, with special reference to its occupancy by Skinner.

He remained connected with Union until his death, at New York, twenty-three years later. In 1854 he was elected moderator of the General Assembly (New School). He had earlier published several books, of which *Aids to Preaching and Hearing* (1839) was perhaps the most notable, and during his years at Union he issued several others, among them *Pastoral Theology* (1853) and *Homiletics* (1854), both editions of Alexandre R. Vinet's works, prepared with much care and evidence of learning. He was also the author of *Discussions in Theology* (1868) and of a biography of his brother, *The Life and Character of the Late Joseph B. Skinner* (1853). During his career he did noteworthy work in systematizing the teaching of homiletics and in promoting broader theological views and closer interdenominational relations. Personally he was a man of cultivation, sincerity, simplicity, and deep spirituality. He was married and one of his children, Thomas Harvey Skinner (1820–92), was professor of theology at McCormick Seminary, Chicago.

[G. L. Prentiss, *A Discourse in Memory of Thomas Harvey Skinner* (1871); E. F. Hatfield, *The Early Annals of Union Theological Sem.* (1876); *Gen. Cat. of the Coll. of N. J.* (1896); *Princeton Theological Sem. Biog. Cat.* (1909); *N. Y. Observer*, Feb. 9, 1871; *N. Y. Tribune*, Feb. 2, 1871.]   P. P. F.

SKINNER, WILLIAM (Nov. 14, 1824–Feb. 28, 1902), silk manufacturer, the son of John and Sarah (Hollins) Skinner, was born in London, England. He received some private instruction, but at an early age went to work in the silk dyeing establishment where his father was employed. In 1843 his employer's son, who had started a dyeing establishment in Florence, Mass., sent to England for a foreman and William came to the United States to take the position. When his employer failed, Skinner took over the business, out of which grew the Nonotuck Company. In 1848, with Joseph Warner, he started the manufacture of sewing silk. This partnership was short-lived, however, and Skinner then built a mill between Haydenville and Williamsburg, Mass., on a site later called Skinnersville. There his business flourished and of-

fices were opened in New York and other cities. He built houses for his employees and a substantial home for himself, but all were destroyed, with the exception of his own home, when, in the flood of 1874, the Mill River dam gave way. Undaunted by this disaster, he set about looking for another location and finally decided upon Holyoke, Mass., where the Holyoke Water Power Company offered him a large tract of land if he would erect a mill. His credit being good and his personal integrity well known, he had no difficulty in reëstablishing his business. When his two sons were taken into partnership in 1883, the name of the concern became William Skinner & Sons. The firm gave special attention to broad-silk weaving, and its cotton-back satins and linings were popular throughout the country, "Skinner's Satin" being accepted as the hallmark of excellence in lining material.

Skinner was married on Apr. 12, 1848, to Nancy Edwards Warner of Northampton, Mass., the sister of his partner. She died about two years later and on May 15, 1856, he married Sarah Elizabeth Allen, daughter of Capt. Joseph Allen of Northampton. They were the parents of seven children, five daughters and two sons. He took a keen interest in the affairs of the city in which he lived, was president of the Manufacturers Association of Holyoke, and of the board of directors of the Holyoke City Hospital, which he founded and in which he took a keen interest until his death. He gave generously to the Holyoke Young Men's Christian Association and to the public library, and made gifts to Vassar College and to Mount Holyoke College, of which he was a trustee. From the time of its formation in 1872 he was a director of the Silk Association of America. Known as the "Old Roman" to his intimates, he had a rugged personality and his word was never questioned.

[*Am. Silk Jour.*, Apr. 1902; *XXX Ann. Report of the Silk Asso. of America* (1902); *Hist. of the Conn. Valley in Mass.* (1879), II, 926; *Springfield Daily Republican*, Mar. 1, 1902; information as to certain facts from Joseph A. Skinner, a son.]   B. R.

SLADE, JOSEPH ALFRED (c. 1824–Mar. 10, 1864), reputed "bad man," variously known as "Jack," "Alf," and "Cap" Slade, was born at or near Carlyle, Clinton County, Ill. The earliest available record concerning him is of May 22, 1847, when he enlisted in the army. After more than a year's uneventful service in New Mexico, he was mustered out at Alton in October 1848. He is next heard of, in the late fifties, as a freighter and wagon-train boss in the employ of Russell, Majors & Waddell. In the spring of 1860, after the firm had organized its overland stage service, he was made a division agent at

Julesburg, in what is now Colorado, with instructions to rid the region of bandits preying upon the company's property. In an encounter with "Old Jules" Reni (or Réné Jules, as one writer insists) Slade shot his antagonist to death, cut off his ears, and nailed them up to dry, later, it is said, wearing one of them as a watch-charm.

Transferred to a more westerly division, he continued to prove a scourge to evil-doers. Mark Twain, who in August 1861 met him at a Wyoming station, says that he then bore the reputation of having killed twenty-six men. In 1862 the stages were withdrawn to a more southerly line, and Slade was transferred to a new station, Virginia Dale, a hundred miles north of Denver. Unaccountably, he had by this time become a brawling drunkard, and in the fall of the year was discharged. With his companion, a dashing and attractive frontier woman whose given name was Maria Virginia and whose surname may have been Dale, he set out in the spring of 1863 at the head of a small freighting outfit for the Montana gold diggings. Settling on a small ranch near Virginia City, he conducted a number of freighting expeditions and for a time was peaceful. Later, he again began drinking heavily and indulging in outbursts of drunken rowdyism. When arrested, in March 1864, he defied the People's Court, and subsequently, revolver in hand, made threats against the judge. A joint meeting of the Vigilantes of Virginia City and the miners of the adjoining camp of Nevada decreed his execution, and though he begged pitifully for his life, he was promptly hanged. The body was embalmed in alcohol and buried in Salt Lake City.

Slade was of sturdy build. When sober he was genial and friendly, according to Mark Twain "the most gentlemanly-appearing, quiet and affable officer" found along the road (*post*, p. 87); but when drunk he was a ferocious ruffian. Though the accounts of his numerous killings have been disputed by some writers, they were fully accepted by Frank A. Root, who entered the company's service in Colorado only a few months after Slade's departure and who had every opportunity to learn the facts.

[*Record of the Services of Ill. Soldiers in the Black Hawk War . . . and in the Mexican War* (1882); Granville Stuart, *Forty Years on the Frontier* (1925), I, 151; F. A. Root and Wm. E. Connelley, *The Overland Stage to Cal.* (1901); N. P. Langford, *Vigilante Days and Ways* (1890), vol. II; T. J. Dimsdale, *The Vigilantes of Mont.* (2nd ed., 1882); Emerson Hough, *The Story of the Outlaw* (1907); Hoffman Birney, *Vigilantes* (1929); E. L. Sabin, *Wild Men of the Wild West* (1929); Mark Twain (S. L. Clemens), *Roughing It* (1872).]
W. J. G.

SLADE, WILLIAM (May 9, 1786–Jan. 16, 1859), statesman and educator, was born at Cornwall, Vt., the son of Capt. William Slade, a veteran of the Revolution, who had moved to Vermont from Washington, Conn., about 1783. He was a descendant of William Slade who was in Lebanon, Conn., as early as 1716. The youngest William's mother was Rebecca (Plumb). After preparatory work in the Addison County grammar school at Middlebury and four years at Middlebury College, where he was graduated in 1807, Slade studied law in the office of Judge Joel Doolittle of Middlebury. Admitted to the bar in the summer of 1810, he at once opened an office in the same village. Clients, however, were few, and the excitement of a bitter political contest in his state drew him into politics.

Like his father he was an ardent Democrat and he now devoted himself heart and soul to the interests of his party. Speeches and pamphlets were puny weapons against the Federalist press of Middlebury; Slade, therefore, in 1813, helped to found the *Columbian Patriot,* a weekly newspaper, which two years later became the *National Standard* (*Proceedings of the American Antiquarian Society,* n.s. vol. XXXV, 1925, p. 125). Soon he was its proprietor and editor, conducting in connection with it a book printing and selling establishment. The *Patriot* was a decided political success and it was partly responsible for the Democratic triumph in Vermont in 1815; as a business venture, however, it was a failure and by 1817 Slade was ruined. Refusing bankruptcy, he was saddled with a heavy debt which he struggled the rest of his life to repay; hence, in part, his eager search for political office.

Fortunately, the Democratic triumph of 1815 carried him into the office of secretary of state, a post which he filled with credit until 1823. Meanwhile (1816–22), he was judge of the court of his county. Having relinquished his state offices, he served as a clerk in the Department of State, at Washington (1824–29), until discharged at the beginning of Jackson's administration. He had married Abigail Foote of Middlebury, Feb. 5, 1810, by whom he had nine children, and he now sought to support his family by resuming his practice of law; but politics remained his prime interest and the main source of his livelihood. While serving as state's attorney for Addison County he was elected in 1830 to Congress, where he sat for twelve years, in the course of time joining the Whig party. He distinguished himself as an uncompromising opponent of slavery, and with John Quincy Adams fought tenaciously against the gag rules. Though not a great orator, he was a quick-witted and a ready debater with a command of searing phrases which enraged the Southern representatives. With an eye to the Vermont woolen industry he was a persistent champion of protective tariffs.

For one year (1843–44) after his retirement from Congress he was reporter of the state supreme court, resigning to become governor, in which office he served from 1844 to 1846. Under his leadership the legislature provided for a geological survey of the state and for a thorough reorganization of the public school system. He bitterly opposed the admission of Texas to the Union and the policy which led to war with Mexico. Before the end of his second term as governor he had lost the support of many influential Whig leaders, partly because of his bitter public controversy with Samuel S. Phelps, Whig senator from Vermont, whom, it was charged, Slade wished to supersede. His political career ended, he became corresponding secretary and general agent of the Board of National Popular Education. Indefatigable in this congenial work, which he continued until a few weeks before his death, he traveled through most of the Northern states, founding local societies and recruiting teachers in the East for service along the Western frontier. Besides many speeches in and out of Congress and his annual reports to the educational board, he published the *Vermont State Papers* (1823), a volume of documents on the early history of the state, and *The Laws of Vermont of a Publick and Permanent Nature* (1825). He died in Middlebury.

[T. B. Peck, *William Slade of Windsor, Conn., and His Descendants* (1910); *Cat. of the Officers and Students of Middlebury Coll.* (1928); Lyman Matthews, *Hist. of the Town of Cornwall, Vt.* (1862); Samuel Swift, *Hist. of the Town of Middlebury* (1859); M. D. Gilman, *The Bibliog. of Vt.* (1897); J. M. Comstock, *A List of the Principal Civil Officers of Vt.* (1918); J. G. Ullery, *Men of Vt.* (1894); W. H. Crockett, *Vermont*, vol. III (1921); *Biog. Dir. Am. Cong.* (1928); *Memoirs of John Quincy Adams*, vols. VII, IX, X (1876).]   P. D.·E.

SLAFTER, EDMUND FARWELL (May 30, 1816–Sept. 22, 1906), Protestant Episcopal clergyman, author, was born at Norwich, Vt., the seventh of the ten children of Sylvester and Mary (Johnson) Slafter, and a descendant of John Slaughter (Slafter) who emigrated from England to Massachusetts in 1680, and later went to Connecticut. Edmund's great-grandfather, Samuel, was one of the original proprietors of Norwich, Vt. The boy grew up on his father's farm in Thetford, preparing for college at the local academy. He graduated from Dartmouth in 1840, and studied at the Andover Theological Seminary in 1840–41 and 1842–44. On

July 12, 1844, he was ordained a deacon of the Protestant Episcopal Church, and on July 30 of the following year, priest. He served as rector of St. Peter's Church, Cambridge, Mass. (1844–46), and of St. John's Church at Jamaica Plain (1846–53). Meanwhile, he had married, Aug. 16, 1849, Mary Anne Hazen of Boston, who brought him sufficient wealth to permit him to retire from pastoral work when his health weakened in 1853. His vigor restored by 1857, he became superintendent, for his denomination, of the American Bible Society. This post he held for twenty years. Since its duties were not burdensome, he had ample leisure for the quiet activities of the scholar which he pursued for the rest of his long life.

From the time he joined the New England Historic Genealogical Society in 1861 he was one of its most active members. From 1867 to 1887 he was its corresponding secretary; from 1867 to 1889, a director; from 1879 to 1889 a member of its committee on publication; and to the end of his life a frequent contributor to its *Register*. His interest in genealogy, evinced by the study of his own family, *Memorial of John Slafter* (1869), soon ripened into historical research. The results of his labors appeared in the publications of the Prince Society, an organization formed in 1858 to preserve and extend the knowledge of American history by editing and printing important source material. Slafter served as its secretary in 1865–66 and as its vice-president from 1866 to 1880, when he became its president, which position he held until his death. Of its monographs he edited *Sir William Alexander and American Colonization* (1873), *Voyages of the Northmen to America* (1877), *Voyages of Samuel de Champlain* (3 vols., 1878–82), and *John Checkley, or, The Evolution of Religious Tolerance in Massachusetts Bay* (2 vols., 1897). He also contributed a well documented chapter on Champlain to the fourth volume (1885) of Justin Winsor's *Narrative and Critical History of America*. Among his minor publications were contributions to the journals of other New England societies.

Slafter maintained an active interest in the work of his Church long after he gave up preaching. From 1884 until his death he was registrar of the diocese of Massachusetts; and to him is due the foundation and development of the rich diocesan library. During a considerable period he was also assistant to the rector of Trinity Church, Boston. Absorbed as he was in historical and religious work, he yet found time for the successful management of his moderate fortune, which he increased considerably. Having no children, he bequeathed his estate to various educational and charitable institutions. The portrait of himself, which he left to the Massachusetts Historical Society, shows a kindly, sensitive face, and a strong, firm chin. He died at Hampton, N. H.

[*Who's Who in America,* 1906–07; C. K. Bolton in *New England Hist. and Geneal. Reg.,* Apr. 1907; M. D. Gilman, *The Bibliog. of Vt.* (1897); *The Prince Society,* 1903; *Boston Daily Advertiser,* Sept. 24, 1906.]
P. D. E.

SLATER, JOHN FOX (Mar. 4, 1815–May 7, 1884), manufacturer, philanthropist, was born in Slatersville, R. I. His father was John Slater who emigrated from England to the United States about 1804 after having familiarized himself with machinery for the making of yarns and cloths. His mother was Ruth (Bucklin) Slater of Pawtucket, R. I., where Samuel Slater [*q.v.*], an uncle, had established the first cotton mill in the United States. Young Slater received a good education and attended academies in Plainfield, Conn., and at Wrentham and Wilbraham, Mass. When he was seventeen, he began work in his father's woolen mill at Hopeville, Conn., of which he was placed in full charge by the time he was twenty-one. He was next entrusted with the management of his father's cotton mill in the nearby village of Jewett City. About 1842 he removed to Norwich, Conn., where he died some forty years later. On May 13, 1844, he married Marianna L. Hubbard, by whom he had six children. On the passing away of his father in 1843 he came into a modest fortune. He at once formed an equal partnership with his brother William S. Slater to manufacture cotton and woolen goods. In the course of a few decades he became very wealthy. When he and his brother dissolved their partnership in 1872 he retained the Jewett City mill and also an interest in the Ponemah mill at Taftville, a suburb of Norwich. This cost $1,500,000 to build and when opened on Nov. 16, 1871, was probably the second largest plant of its kind in the world.

He was of a devout disposition and contributed liberally both to the erection and upkeep of the Park Congregational Church of Norwich, of which he was a member. Always interested in educational questions, he in 1868 helped to found and endow the Norwich Free Academy. Influenced by the successful working of the Peabody Education Fund for negroes he finally decided, probably without any outside suggestion, to give a million dollars toward conferring Christian education upon the lately emancipated population of the Southern states. On Apr. 28, 1882, the New York legislature passed an act incorporating the John F. Slater Fund, and in the following month he transferred the promised million to its first board of trustees, of which the president was Rutherford B. Hayes. This munificent gift was widely acclaimed, and Congress passed a resolution thanking the donor and bestowing on him a gold medal. Slater, disliking publicity, did not even strive for the perpetuation of his own name. He expressly directed that his fund might be wound up after thirty-three years should there be no serious need for it. However, the fund still (1935) exists and in the fifty years following its establishment it distributed nearly four million dollars, mainly in aiding the training of teachers for the colored race.

[*Documents relating to the origin and work of the Slater Trustees 1882 to 1894* (1894); S. H. Howe, "A Brief Memoir of the Life of John F. Slater," *The Trustees of the John F. Slater Fund Occasional Papers,* No. 2 (1894); D. C. Gilman, *Memorial Sketch of John F. Slater* (1885); *Proc. of the Trustees of the John F. Slater Fund, 1884* (1885); *Vital Records of Norwich,* pt. 2 (1913), p. 907; *Appletons' Ann. Cyc. . . . 1884* (1885); *N. Y. Daily Tribune,* Mar. 8, 1884.]
H. G. V.

SLATER, SAMUEL (June 9, 1768–Apr. 21, 1835), founder of the American cotton industry, was born at "Holly House" in Belper, Derbyshire, England, where his father William Slater, a respected, educated independent farmer, lived and tilled his own land. His mother was Elizabeth (Fox) Slater. Young Slater received the ordinary English education, in which he manifested a particular interest in mathematics. Appreciating this, his father arranged that upon the completion of his education Samuel should enter the employ of a neighbor, Jedediah Strutt, who was in partnership with Richard Arkwright in the development of cotton manufacturing machinery. When he was fourteen his father died suddenly, and on Jan. 8, 1783, he was apprenticed to Strutt for six and a half years. Strutt's natural interest in his friend's son, coupled with Slater's unusual aptitude, created an affection between the two which Strutt showed in advice and help. Although Strutt believed that cotton manufacturing in England would always yield a living to the individual manufacturer, he saw no great future for it. Influenced by this opinion and by the advertisements of bounties offered by the state legislatures in America for experienced textile men and machines, Slater decided to go to America. Since at that time the exportation from England of any data relative to textile machinery was prohibited, he set out first to acquaint himself thoroughly with cotton machinery as made by Arkwright, James Hargreaves, and Samuel Crompton. After completing his apprenticeship when he was a little over twenty-one, he remained for a short time to supervise Strutt's mill and the erection of new works, and to get a general knowledge of the business, and then in September 1789 embarked for America—in disguise, since the emigration of textile workers was forbidden—carrying all of his information in his head. He reached New York in November and was first employed by the New York Manufacturing Company. In January 1790 he met Moses Brown in Providence, R. I., and on Apr. 5, 1790, signed a contract with Almy & Brown to reproduce Arkwright's cotton machinery for them. Brown had a wooden spinning-frame that was not satisfactory and was quite ready to agree to the building of new machinery. Almost a year passed before the first machines were put into operation, for Slater was handicapped by lack both of skilled mechanics and of tools, but sales of American-made cotton yarn began almost immediately thereafter. In 1793 they built their first factory in Pawtucket under the firm name of Almy, Brown & Slater. On Oct. 2, 1791, Slater married a daughter of Oziel Wilkinson, Hannah Wilkinson, who is said to have conceived the idea of making sewing-thread of fine cotton yarn instead of linen and to have produced thread so satisfactory that her brothers established a factory to make it. In 1798, still continuing his relationship with Almy & Brown, he formed a partnership with his father-in-law and brothers-in-law, known as Samuel Slater & Company. Manufacturing their own machinery, they erected their first cotton manufacturing plant near Pawtucket; subsequently they began the spinning of yarn in Smithfield, R. I. (later called Slatersville), and at East Webster, Mass. They reëstablished a defunct cotton mill at Jewett City, Conn., and finally erected a mill at Amoskeag Falls, N. H., on the Merrimac River, which was the foundation of the great manufacturing industries now located at Manchester. Besides these large mill operations, which he directed until his death, Slater was an incorporator and for fifteen years president of the Manufacturers' Bank in Pawtucket. After the death of his first wife in 1812, he married Esther, widow of Robert Parkinson of Philadelphia, Nov. 21, 1817. There were nine children by the first marriage (White, *post*, p. 242), of whom six sons were living in 1817.

[G. S. White, *Memoir of Samuel Slater, the Father of Am. Manufactures* (1836); Henry Howe, *Memoirs of the Most Eminent Am. Mechanics* (1844); W. R. Bagnall, *Samuel Slater and the Early Developments of the Cotton Manufacture in the U. S.* (1890); F. L. Lewton, "Samuel Slater and the Oldest Cotton Machinery in America," *Ann. Report Smithsonian Inst., 1926*; *The Slater Mills at Webster* (n.d.); *The Biog.*

Cyc. of Rep. Men of R. I. (1881); J. D. Van Slyck, *Representatives of New England* (2 vols., 1879); Massena Goodrich, *Hist. Sketch of the Town of Pawtucket* (1876); "The Slater Cotton Centennial, 1790–1890," *Providence Daily Jour. and Evening Bull.*, Sept. 29, 1890; obituary in *Manufacturers and Farmers Jour.*, Apr. 23, 1835.]
C. W. M—n.

SLATTERY, CHARLES LEWIS (Dec. 9, 1867–Mar. 12, 1930), bishop of the Protestant Episcopal Church, was born at Pittsburgh, Pa., son of the Rev. George Sidney Leffingwell and Emma McClellan (Hall) Slattery. He was a descendant of Thomas Slattery who emigrated from Ireland and was in Westerly, R. I., some time before 1780. Charles's father, a clergyman of the Episcopal Church, died in early life, leaving his family little more than an inspiring tradition. Returning to Maine with his widowed mother, young Slattery grew up in an environment of culture and natural beauty. The Rev. Harry P. Nichols of Brunswick, and, later, Bishop Phillips Brooks, were the mentors of his youth. He graduated with honors from Harvard in 1891 and from the Episcopal Theological School, Cambridge, in 1894. On June 20 of the same year he was ordained deacon by Bishop Lawrence, and on June 8, 1895, priest.

From 1894 to 1896 he was a master at Groton School and rector of St. Andrew's Church, Ayer, Mass. In the latter year he became dean of the Cathedral of Our Merciful Saviour, at Faribault, Minn., while Bishop Henry B. Whipple [*q.v.*], "Apostle to the Indians," was still living. In 1907 he was called to Christ Church, Springfield, Mass., where he served until 1910, when he became rector of Grace Church, New York City, in succession to the Rev. William R. Huntington [*q.v.*]. He was elected bishop coadjutor of Massachusetts on May 3, 1922, and was consecrated at Trinity Church, Boston, on Oct. 31, of the same year. When Bishop Lawrence retired, May 30, 1927, Bishop Slattery automatically succeeded him. He died at his home in Boston after a brief illness, and he was buried in Mount Auburn Cemetery, Cambridge.

Slattery was preëminently a scholar and a pastor. "He had a consuming love of books and of sound learning. He combined a sensitiveness to truth with a fine appreciation of beauty" (*Churchman*, Apr. 5, 1930, p. 10). During the thirty-five years of his busy ministry he wrote a total of some twenty-five volumes as well as countless occasional papers for the periodical press. Among his best known works were: *The Master of the World: A Study of Christ* (1906); *Life beyond Life: A Study of Immortality* (1907); *The Historic Ministry and the Present Christ: An Appeal for Unity* (1908); *The Au-*

thority of Religious Experience (1912); *Why Men Pray* (1916); *The Holy Communion* (1918); *The Ministry* (1921); *Following Christ* (1928), and biographies of Felix Reville Brunot, Edward Lincoln Atkinson, Alexander Viets Griswold Allen, William Austin Smith, and David Hummell Greer. To the Church at large his supreme contribution was his devoted labor during fifteen years toward the revision and enrichment of the Book of Common Prayer, a task which he lived to complete and the fruits of which he saw generally accepted. In all his work he combined liberality of outlook with great spirituality. As a parish priest and guide he showed real genius. Equipped with an abundant natural love for pastoral duty, he conceived it a privilege to maintain close personal touch with his people, and was tireless in his endeavor to be a true shepherd to his flock.

The calls made upon him, however, were numerous and varied. For many years he was general chairman of the Church Congress in the United States. He served on the Church commissions on the hymnal and the lectionary, and was chairman of the commission on the revision of the Book of Common Prayer. He lectured at the Seabury Divinity School, 1905–07, and at the Berkeley Divinity School, 1909–10, and gave the Paddock lectures at the General Theological Seminary, 1911–12, and the West lectures at Stanford University, 1915. He was an overseer of Harvard College, a trustee of Boston University and of Brooks School, Andover, and president of the board of trustees of Wellesley College. On Nov. 19, 1923, he was married to Sarah, daughter of Bishop Lawrence, by whom he was survived.

[H. C. Robbins, *Charles Lewis Slattery* (1931); *Boston Transcript,* Mar. 13–15, 1930; *N. Y. Times,* Nov. 20, 1923, June 2, 1927, Mar. 13, 1930; *Churchman,* Mar. 22, Apr. 5, 1930; *Living Church,* Mar. 22, 29, 1930; the files of *Church Militant,* 1922–30; *Who's Who in America,* 1928–29; and information from personal friends.]

J. W. F.

SLAUGHTER, PHILIP (Oct. 26, 1808–June 12, 1890), Episcopal clergyman, historian, was born at his father's home, "Springfield," in Culpeper County, Va., a descendant of a family that had been prominent in Culpeper County since the earlier years of its settlement; his parents were Philip Slaughter, a captain in the American Revolution, and his wife, Elizabeth, daughter of Col. Thomas Towles, of Lancaster County, Va., and widow of William Brock. After preliminary training at an academy in Winchester, in 1825 the younger Philip entered the University of Virginia, finishing his course in 1828. For five years he practised law, giving up this profes-

sion in order to prepare himself for the ministry of the Protestant Episcopal Church at the Theological Seminary in Virginia, at Alexandria.

Ordained deacon in May 1834 and advanced to the priesthood in July 1835, he was in active pastoral work for about twelve years, serving the Church in Middleburg, Va.; Christ Church, Georgetown, D. C.; Meade and Johns parishes, Fauquier County; and for the last five years of this period, St. Paul's Church, Petersburg.

He quickly came into prominence as a remarkably effective preacher of the intensely evangelical type, and his services were in constant demand in series of meetings, called "Associations." In connection with these, he preached in many of the city churches and rural parishes of Virginia. Though brief, writes a biographer, his active ministry was "brilliant and effective. He had all the personal magnetism, the fire and spiritual power of Whitefield. Great crowds attended on his ministry and conversions were numbered by the hundred" (Brock, *post,* p. xii).

His health failing, he spent the years 1848 and 1849 in travel in Europe, and was then compelled to give up the hope of further continuous pastoral work. Returning to Richmond, he established in 1850 the *Virginia Colonizationist,* a periodical published in the interests of the colonization of negro slaves in Africa. For five years he edited this periodical with signal ability, and was successful in enlisting the interest of the Virginia legislature and in securing large appropriations for the project. He then removed to his own home on Slaughter's Mountain in Culpeper County. With the aid of friends he erected a church building upon his father's farm in which he preached as his health permitted. The church was destroyed during the Civil War. Driven from his home by invading forces, he found refuge with his family in Petersburg. While sojourning here he published a religious paper, the *Army and Navy Messenger,* for distribution among the soldiers of the Confederate army. At the close of the war he returned to his home in Culpeper County and devoted the remainder of his life to historical and genealogical studies, in which from early life he had been interested.

In 1846 he published *A History of Bristol Parish,* and the following year, *A History of St. George's Parish,* both of which were revised and republished, the former in 1879 by Slaughter himself, and the latter in 1890 by Dr. R. A. Brock. The publication of these doubtless did much to arouse interest in the preservation of the original records of many other parishes and the protection of the historic records of the state.

Slaughter had formulated a plan for the preparation of a general history of the old parishes and families of Virginia and for years had been gathering material, but his declining health compelled him to relinquish the task and to turn over the material to Bishop William Meade [*q.v.*], who after years of research published in 1857 his monumental work, *Old Churches, Ministers, and Families of Virginia.* Slaughter himself wrote *A History of St. Mark's Parish* (1877) and had practically completed, at the time of his death, *The History of Truro Parish,* which was published in 1908 by Rev. Edward L. Goodwin. In addition to his parish histories, Slaughter was the author of many historical books, pamphlets, and addresses, among the most important being: *The Virginian History of African Colonization* (1855); *A Sketch of the Life of Randolph Fairfax* (1864); *Memoir of Col. Joshua Fry* (1880); *Christianity the Key to the Character and Career of Washington* (1886). His more significant monographs include his address at the semi-centennial celebration of the Theological Seminary in Virginia (1873); a paper on historic churches of Virginia printed in W. S. Perry's *The History of the American Episcopal Church* (1885); "The Colonial Church in Virginia," published in *Addresses and Historical Papers Before the Centennial Council of the Protestant Episcopal Church in Virginia* (1885); and a biography of the Rt. Rev. William Meade, in *Memorial Biographies of the New England Historic and Genealogical Society* (vol. IV, 1885).

The Diocese of Virginia elected him historiographer of the diocese in 1879, and after his death honored him by giving his name to a parish in that part of Culpeper County in which he lived. On June 20, 1834, he married Anne Sophia, daughter of Dr. Thomas Semmes, of Alexandria, Va., who with one daughter survived him.

[Biog. sketch by R. A. Brock in Slaughter's *History of St. George's Parish* (2nd ed., 1890); *Southern Churchman,* June 19, 26, July 10, 1890; *Richmond Dispatch,* June 15, 1890; reports of the historiographer and other records in the council journals of the Diocese of Va.]

G. M. B.

SLEEPER, JACOB (Nov. 21, 1802–Mar. 31, 1889), merchant, philanthropist, son of Jacob and Olive (Dinsdale) Sleeper, was born in Newcastle, Me. He received his early education in the common schools and at Lincoln Academy. When he was fourteen, his parents died and he was placed in the care of his uncle in Belfast, where he worked in the latter's store and subsequently in a store of his own. Seeking medical relief from a lameness which troubled him all through life, though it did not noticeably affect

him, in 1825 he went to Boston, where he was a bookkeeper for True & Brodhead, dealers in naval supplies. Here he received the business training which in 1835 led him to form a partnership with Andrew Carney, a clothier. Carney's contracts for furnishing clothing to the navy, made before the panic of 1837, proved especially profitable in a period of falling prices and the firm prospered steadily. When Sleeper withdrew from business in 1850, his fortune was estimated to be $250,000, a sum which investments in real estate increased considerably.

After his retirement he became interested for a brief time in politics. He was a member of the state House of Representatives in 1851 and 1852; of the Governor's Council from 1859 to 1861 inclusive; and an alderman of Boston in 1852 and 1853. As candidate for mayor in the latter year on the Young Men's League ticket, he was defeated. His greatest interest, however, was the Methodist Episcopal Church, of which he became a member at the age of twenty-one. For fifty-nine years he was superintendent of the Sunday School of the Bromfield Street Methodist Episcopal Church, in Boston, and for forty-six years treasurer of the church's board of trustees. He was an original member of the Boston Wesleyan Association, frequently serving as its president, and was a liberal supporter of the New England Methodist Historical Society, of which, also, he was president. As a trustee of Wesleyan University from 1844 to 1878, and as an overseer of Harvard from 1856 to 1868, he became greatly interested in education, and devoted much time to the study of it, both in the United States and in England. This interest led to his becoming, in 1869, one of the three founders of Boston University, the other two being Lee Claflin and Isaac Rich [*q.v.*]. Sleeper's total benefactions to this university exceeded $500,000, nearly all of it given during his lifetime. He was its treasurer, 1869–73, and vice-president of its corporation, 1875–89. Among his other educational interests were Wilbraham Academy, Wilbraham, Mass., the New England Female Medical College, which in 1873 united with the Boston University School of Medicine, and the New England Conservatory of Music. His private philanthropies were innumerable, his practice being to give away yearly the bulk of his income. He himself followed the advice he proffered a friend, "Do as much good as you can, and don't make a fuss about it." He was married twice; first, May 7, 1827, to Eliza Davis; and second, Apr. 7, 1835, to her sister Maria. He had three daughters and a son. His death occurred in Boston.

[Boston Jour. and Boston Transcript, Apr. 1, 1889;
Zion's Herald, Apr. 3, 1889; Abner Forbes and J. W.
Green, The Rich Men of Mass. (1851); The Twenty
Years of Boston Univ. 1869–1889. Fifteenth Ann. Re-
port of the President (1890); John C. Rand, One of a
Thousand (1890); Methodist Rev., Sept.-Oct. 1889;
D. L. Marsh, The Founders of Boston University
(1932).]   R. E. M.

SLICER, THOMAS ROBERTS (Apr. 16,
1847–May 29, 1916), Unitarian clergyman, was
born in Washington, D. C., the son of Henry and
Elizabeth Coleman (Roberts) Slicer. His father, of Scotch descent, was a prominent minister of the Methodist Episcopal Church and several times chaplain of Congress. Thomas was
educated in the public schools of Baltimore and
in Baltimore City College. When he was twenty
years old he was admitted on trial to the East
Baltimore Conference of the Methodist Church;
he was ordained deacon in 1869 and elder in
1871. He then transferred to the Colorado Conference and was pastor at Denver (1871) and
Georgetown (1872). Returning East, he became a member of the New York Conference in
1873. After serving churches within its bounds
for several years, he was impelled by changes in
his theological views to sever his Methodist connections and to unite with the Unitarians. Pastorates in Providence, R. I. (1881-90), and Buffalo, N. Y. (1890-97), were followed by one at
All Souls Church, New York City, which continued until his death. On Apr. 5, 1871, he married Adeline E. Herbert, daughter of Theodore
C. Herbert of the United States Navy.

Slicer achieved prominence in three ways:
through his preaching, through his writings, and
as a civic reformer. He had the ability, though
speaking extemporaneously, to express ideas co-
gently, consecutively, and in a manner that held
the close attention of his hearers. Many of his
sermons and addresses, stenographically reported, appeared in print, and his church is said to
have been one of the few to which strangers
in New York City asked to be directed. His
theological views are set forth in such publications as The Great Affirmations of Religion
(1898), The Foundations of Religion (1902),
One World at a Time (1902), and The Way to
Happiness (1907). They are an attempt to guide
those emancipated from the bonds of orthodoxy
to a rational religion, and the fundamental ideas
they elaborate are that religion is a natural function of the human soul, since the mind is so constituted that it cannot conceive of the causeless;
that, consequently, the assumption that what is
best in man's mind and feeling has its counterpart at the heart of the universe, is inescapable;
and that the religious life consists in the devel-

oping of this best to its perfection in the individual and in society. There was a poetic strain
in his temperament and his interest in the field
of literature led him to publish Percy Bysshe
Shelley, an Appreciation (1903) and From Poet
to Premier: the Centennial Cycle 1809–1909
(1909), which offers commentaries on Poe, Lincoln, Holmes, Darwin, Tennyson, and Gladstone,
all born in 1809. After his death, a volume of selections from his writings, which he himself had
put together as an aid to devotion, was published
under the title, Meditations: a Message for All
Souls (1919).

Although convinced that an ideal society can
be achieved only through the regeneration of the
individual, he believed that those who sought that
ideal were called to combat social evils. To many,
therefore, he was best known as a militant leader
of civic reform. While at Buffalo he was in the
thick of the fight for clean politics and better
municipal institutions. Upon going to New
York, he became a member of the City Club, organized to aid in securing permanent good government for the city, and was later placed on its
board of trustees. As chairman of one of its committees he formulated the charges against District Attorney Asa Bird Gardiner in 1900. These
were dismissed by Gov. Theodore Roosevelt,
who, however, later in the year removed Gardiner from office (Public Papers of Theodore
Roosevelt, Governor, 1900, pp. 186–87, 200–05).
Slicer also carried on a warfare against gambling institutions, which brought him much publicity. He was chairman of the National Commission on Prison Labor, a member of the council of the Immigration League, and a trustee of
the People's Institute, to which he was especially
devoted. His varied exertions broke down his
health and for two or three years before his
death, in New York City, he was comparatively
inactive.

[Minutes of the East Baltimore, Colorado and N. Y.
Conferences of the M. E. Ch.; Who's Who in America,
1916–17; obituary of Henry Slicer in Christian Advocate (N. Y.), Apr. 30, 1874; Christian Register, June
8, 22, 1916; N. Y. Times, Sun (N. Y.), and Buffalo
Express, May 30, 1916.]   H. E. S.

SLIDELL, JOHN (1793–July 29, 1871), Louisiana politician, diplomat, was born in New
York City. His mother, Margery (called May)
Mackenzie, was a Scotswoman; his father, for
whom he was named, became a respected merchant and president of the Tradesmen's Insurance Company and the Mechanics' Bank. His
younger brother, Alexander Slidell Mackenzie
[q.v.], adopted the name of a maternal uncle,
and his sister Jane married Matthew C. Perry
[q.v.]. After graduating at Columbia College

in 1810, John went into a mercantile business with James McCrea, but this was ruined by the Embargo policy and the War of 1812. In 1819, partly because of this failure, and partly because of the scandal resulting from a duel (Scoville, *post*, pp. 258–60), he removed to New Orleans, equipped with a knowledge of law and commercial principles; by 1833 he boasted that his practice yielded him $10,000 annually. Two years later he was married to Mathilde Deslonde, a Creole girl of twenty.

Slidell was defeated for Congress on the Jackson ticket in 1828, but he was appointed district attorney at New Orleans the following year. His rival, Martin Gordon, soon procured his dismissal, and neither Jackson nor Van Buren was sympathetic when he suggested a diplomatic post in 1833, though he continued to support Van Buren for a decade longer. In 1834 and again in 1836 he was an unsuccessful candidate for the United States Senate. As a member of Congress from 1843 to 1845, he advocated the use of the civil law in federal courts in Louisiana, a reduction of the tariff, except the duty on sugar, and remission of the fine levied against Jackson in 1815. In the election of 1844 he and other Democrats transported "floaters" from New Orleans to Plaquemines parish under doubtful legal authority, and thereby assured a majority for Polk in Louisiana (*Congressional Globe*, 28 Cong., 2 Sess., pp. 233, 243; Greer, *post*, p. 31). Late in 1845 he was appointed commissioner to Mexico to adjust the Texan boundary and Mexican claims, and to purchase New Mexico and if possible California. Although the Mexican government had agreed to receive an agent, it refused to treat with him upon the technical ground that his credentials were faulty. Withdrawing to Jalapa to wait and observe, he remained until April without accomplishing his major object, and apparently without justifying the American cause to other powers. His mission did, however, help to prepare the American conscience for a war to secure what could not be acquired through diplomatic channels. In 1853 he declined the Central American mission but accepted an agency to sell bonds of the New Orleans and Nashville Railroad in London.

Slidell had a twofold ambition, to attain a seat in the Senate for himself and the presidency for Buchanan. His rival in the Louisiana Democracy, Pierre Soulé [*q.v.*], whose ultra-Southern position contrasted with his own rôle as a moderate national Democrat, defeated him for the Senate in 1848, but Soulé's appointment as minister to Spain in 1853 opened the way for Slidell's entrance into that body, where he remained

until 1861. He favored repeal of the Missouri Compromise, credited Buchanan with the Ostend Manifesto, and blamed Pierce with the failure of the movement to acquire Cuba. After two unsuccessful attempts to secure the Democratic nomination for Buchanan, he widened his activities as campaign manager in 1856 and materially promoted Buchanan's nomination and election. Accepting responsibility for the success of the incoming administration, he recommended numerous cabinet and diplomatic appointments though he himself preferred to remain in the Senate as its spokesman. In 1858 he presented a resolution to grant the president limited authority to suspend neutrality laws, with a view to promoting filibustering, and the next year he introduced a bill to appropriate thirty millions to purchase Cuba (*Congressional Globe*, 35 Cong., 1 Sess., pp. 461–62; 35 Cong., 2 Sess., p. 277). He urged admission of Kansas under the Lecompton constitution as a test of the abstract principle of non-intervention, and questioned whether the Union would long endure if the bill should fail to pass. Never a friend of Douglas, he headed the movement to read him out of the party in 1858, managed the redistribution of the federal patronage in Illinois, and opposed his nomination at the Charleston convention. Although Slidell supported the Breckinridge-Lane ticket in 1860, he was a moderate Union man until Lincoln's election was interpreted as a cause for secession. Returning to Congress for the session of 1860–61, he found himself at odds with the administration, though he did not break with Buchanan until John B. Floyd was replaced in the War Department.

Slidell's Mexican mission and residence in Louisiana made him a logical appointee to represent the Confederacy in France. He reached Nassau safely and, with James M. Mason [*q.v.*], newly appointed agent to England, took passage on the British mail steamer *Trent*. Their removal and detention at Fort Warren, Boston, caused a tense diplomatic situation and delayed their arrival in Europe until Jan. 30, 1862. Reaching Paris early in February, Slidell was enthusiastically greeted by Confederate sympathizers. Napoleon III received him cordially at Vichy in July, and avowed sympathy for the Confederacy, but found difficulty in giving it material expression. Slidell proposed recognition of independence and a Franco-Confederate treaty which would admit French products duty free and provide a cotton subsidy for naval convoys of merchant vessels. He left with the impression that if Great Britain did not soon favor joint action, France would move by herself. In

a second interview at St. Cloud on Oct 28, Napoleon proposed a six months' armistice with Confederate ports open, which if refused by the
North would justify recognition and perhaps intervention. The Emperor also suggested a Confederate navy and implied that vessels might be
built in French shipyards. In 1863 Slidell and
James D. Bulloch [q.v.] arranged with Arman
and Voruz for the construction of two ironclads
and four corvettes at Nantes and Bordeaux. Although the scheme had the approval of the Emperor, protests from William L. Dayton [q.v.]
led to official notification that the vessels could
not enter Confederate service. Meanwhile it
appeared that the rams for which Bulloch had
contracted at Liverpool would not be delivered.
An ingenious scheme was concocted with Bravay
& Company of Paris to purchase them for delivery to the Sultan of Turkey, but this plan also
failed. Early in 1863 a contract was arranged
with Emile Erlanger, whose son married Slidell's daughter, to lend the Confederacy £3,000,-
000 secured by cotton to be delivered within six
months after the war closed. The sale of bonds
netted little more than one-sixth of the amount
because of high commissions and discounts and
the necessity for "bulling" the market. On numerous occasions Slidell approved Napoleon's
Mexican venture and attempted unsuccessfully
to use it, along with a belated offer of emancipation, as leverage to secure recognition of the
Confederacy.

Slidell and his family continued to reside in
Paris with occasional visits to England until the
Empire fell. He had a son, two daughters—both
of whom married Frenchmen, and possibly another daughter. Although he did not seek pardon, he applied to President Johnson in 1866 for
permission to visit Louisiana, but received no
reply. Mrs. Slidell died in 1870, and he died at
Cowes the following year. As a diplomat Slidell performed creditably, although with few exceptions Confederate agents in Europe distrusted him. As a politician he was a shrewd manager and skilful wire-puller. His control of men
came from great capacity for political intrigue
rather than from oratorical effort. He possessed
more ingenuity than ability, but shallowness was
in part offset by good breeding. From the thirties he wielded a potent influence in Louisiana
politics; in the fifties he was political boss of
his state; and during the first three years of Buchanan's administration he was the power behind
the presidency.

[L. M. Sears, *John Slidell* (1925), contains much
material published earlier in *Am. Hist. Rev.*, Jan. 1921,
July 1922, and in *So. Atlantic Quart.*, Jan. 1913.
Valuable notes are available in Beckles Willson, *John
Slidell and the Confederates in Paris* (1932); F. L.
Owsley, *King Cotton Diplomacy* (1931); J. H. Smith,
The War with Mexico (1919), vol. I; S. F. Bemis, ed.,
The American Secretaries of State and their Diplomacy,
vol. V (1928); Pierce Butler, *Judah P. Benjamin*
(1907). The Buchanan Papers in the Pa. Hist. Soc.
Lib. and the James M. Mason Papers in the Lib. of
Cong. contain Slidell letters. For his Mexican corres.
see Washington *Union*, Apr. 18, 1846, *et seq.* See also
John Bigelow, *France and the Confederate Navy*
(1888); J. A. Scoville, *The Old Merchants of N. Y.
City*, II (1863); J. K. Greer, *Louisiana Politics, 1845–
1861* (1930), reprinting articles in *La. Hist. Quart.*]
W. H. S.

SLOAN, JAMES FORMAN (Aug. 10, 1874–
Dec. 21, 1933), popularly known as "Tod"
Sloan, the most celebrated jockey of the early
twentieth century, was born at Bunker Hill, near
Kokomo, Ind., and died at Los Angeles, Cal.
Like that of most followers of his calling, his
origin was humble and obscure, his father having been a barber. James was so small a child
that his father called him "Toad," a name which
was transformed into "Tod" by his playmates.
In later life he signed himself James Todhunter
Sloan, in order more ornamentally to account for
the nickname which was his universal designation. He was the youngest of three children and
his mother died when he was five; soon after, the
father, a veteran of the Civil War and no longer
able to support himself or keep his family together, was placed in a soldiers' home. The boy
was adopted by a woman named Blauser, of
Kokomo, where he lived until he was about fifteen. He then ran away and joined the troupe
of a so-called "Professor" Talbot, who made
balloon ascensions at county fairs. After varied
adventures he finally joined fortunes with an
elder brother, Cassius, who had become a professional jockey. According to Sloan's own
statement he was as a child much afraid of horses
and did not overcome this fear entirely for a long
while. Eventually, however, he was able to master powerful and rebellious horses and became
celebrated for his ability to win the confidence
and obedience of his mounts.

For a number of years he knocked about in
the lower circles of the turf, making little progress, until he obtained employment from John S.
Campbell, of Kansas City, Mo., one of the ablest
trainers of his time, who encouraged him to per-
severe. A boy of quick mentality, he was attracted by the problem of wind-resistance, then
just becoming a moot one among athletes, and in
view of it adopted the seat in the saddle that was
to revolutionize modern race-riding. Lying
along the neck and shoulders of his mounts, he
rode in what was jeered at as a "monkey-on-a-
stick" attitude until his success became so great
that imitation followed and finally his way of

riding was everywhere adopted. Being ambitious, daring, and of unlimited self-confidence and egoism, after several seasons of glittering success in America, he decided to go abroad, where he made his first appearances in the saddle in England in 1897. There, on account of his peculiar seat, he was the subject of unlimited ridicule, but after he had ridden twenty-one winners in his first season the ridicule ceased. At home he had become the principal rider for William C. Whitney, then the owner of the most powerful racing stable in America. In England he was employed by the leading turf magnates and finally was selected to ride the horses of King Edward VII. He also became a spectacular figure upon the Parisian courses. Thereafter he was seen in America but seldom until his career came to a sudden and sensational end by the announcement in 1901 that he had been refused a license to ride in England by the Jockey Club, an action which led to his being banned by all other turf bodies of repute the world over.

The reasons assigned for the action of the Jockey Club were his activities in the betting ring and other conduct "prejudicial to the best interests of the sport." Many and powerful efforts were made to have him restored to good standing but they were unsuccessful. In the perspective of time it has become the impression that the extreme and severe punishment allotted him was out of all proportion to any misdemeanors that he may have committed. Prior to his disgrace, Sloan had accumulated a fortune said to have approximated $300,000, but it was dissipated in a few years of prodigal living and futile efforts to establish himself in various enterprises. He returned to America and thereafter until his death led a hand-to-mouth existence, finally dying penniless after a long illness. Always a diminutive personage, at his death he was reported to have weighed but sixty pounds. He was twice married, in each case to an actress: first, in 1907 to Julia Sanderson, from whom he was divorced in 1913; second, in 1920, to Elizabeth Saxon Malone, from whom he was divorced in 1927. By his second wife he had one daughter. Sloan is generally accorded, by the best authorities, the credit of being an epochal man in his profession, not only because of his peculiar seat (in which he had been anticipated by an earlier American jockey, Edward H. Garrison), but also because he introduced the practice of forcing the pace from the fall of the starter's flag, instead of "waiting to win," the system consecrated by immemorial custom previously. In 1915 he published, in London, *Tod Sloan by Himself*, an autobiography, written in collaboration with A. Dick Luckman.

[In addition to his autobiog. sources include: L. H. Week, *The Am. Turf* (1898); George Lambton, *Men and Horses I Have Known* (1924); *Idler*, Apr. 1899; *Times* (London), Dec. 22, 1933; *N. Y. Times*, Dec. 22, 1933; data in author's possession.]   J. L. H.

SLOAN, RICHARD ELIHU (June 22, 1857–Dec. 14, 1933), judge, governor, author, was born on a farm in Preble County, Ohio, the son of Dr. Richard and Mary (Caldwell) Sloan. His ancestors on both sides were of Scotch-Irish origin, and settled first in South Carolina. After graduating A.B. at Monmouth College, Illinois, in 1877, he taught in a preparatory school for about a year, meanwhile beginning the study of law in an office at Hamilton, Ohio. He then went to Denver, Colo., where he worked as a reporter on the *Daily Rocky Mountain News* while continuing his law studies. From 1879 to 1882 he tried his fortune in the mining regions of Leadville and Breckenridge, Colo., but in the last-named year returned to his native state and entered the Law School of the Cincinnati College (now University of Cincinnati), where he received the degree of LL.B. two years later.

Planning to practise in the West, he went to San Francisco, but upon the advice of a friend to "try Arizona," opened an office, with a classmate, at Phoenix, where he was enrolled as a member of the territorial bar in January 1885. After about two years he removed to Florence, distant some seventy-five miles, upon the promise of appointment as district attorney of Pinal County, an office which he held for two years. In 1887 he returned to Ohio and married, Nov. 22, Mary Brown of Hamilton, by whom he had three children, a son who predeceased his father, and two daughters who survived him. In 1888 he was a delegate from Pinal County to the Republican territorial convention, where he was chosen temporary chairman and made the "keynote speech." Later in the same year he was elected a member of the Territorial Council and served one term, being on several committees and chairman of that on the judiciary.

His most noteworthy service began in October 1889, when he was appointed by President Benjamin Harrison as a judge of the territorial supreme court—the first *bona fide* resident of Arizona to receive such an appointment. He thereupon removed to Tucson and, like his associates, exercised *nisi prius* as well as appellate jurisdiction. In his appellate court work, his first important opinion was in *Cheyney* vs. *Smith* (3 *Ariz.*, 143), Mar. 24, 1890, holding that the limit of "sixty days duration" fixed by the federal statute for territorial legislative sessions, meant sixty working, but not necessarily consecutive, days. In *Porter* vs. *Hughes* (4 *Ariz.*, 1), he held that the governor's affixing of his signature to an appropriation bill constituted approval of the whole measure, even though he disapproved a specific item; and in *Carroll* vs. *Byers* (4 *Ariz.*, 158), he held unconstitutional a territorial statute authorizing verdicts by nine jurors in civil cases and misdemeanor prosecutions. Toward the close of his term he was obliged to commit for contempt an editor and his attorney for falsely charging in the former's paper that the judge was closeted with the prosecuting attorney following the argument of a demurrer to the editor's indictment for criminal libel. Friends of the convicted parties thereupon sought Judge Sloan's removal; but President Cleveland not only permitted him to serve the balance of his term but for some eight months thereafter (until June 1894), before he appointed a successor. Sloan then reëntered the practice of his profession, at Prescott; but, after three years he was restored to the bench by President McKinley (July 8, 1897), and was twice reappointed by President Theodore Roosevelt. He served in all seventeen years—longer than any other Arizona judge up to his time. His first important opinion during his second period was that in *Gage* vs. *McCord* (5 *Ariz.*, 227), wherein he construed the federal act authorizing the obligations of the territory and its subdivisions to be refunded. In 1908 he was elected a delegate to the Republican National Convention, where he secured the adoption of a plank favoring statehood for Arizona. In the following year he was tendered by President Taft the post of governor, which he accepted, qualifying May 1, 1909. Thus within a quarter century he served with distinction in all three branches of the Arizona government—legislative, judicial, and executive—and was its last territorial governor. In March 1911 he presided at the dedication of the Roosevelt Dam and in February 1912 he surrendered his office to the recently elected governor of the new state.

The remaining years of his life were devoted to professional and literary labors. He will be long remembered as the supervising editor of the four-volume *History of Arizona* (1930) as well as for his *Memories of an Arizona Judge* (Stanford University Press, 1932). He died at Phoenix as the result of a fall.

[*Memories* above mentioned; *Journals of the Fifteenth Legislative Assembly of the Territory of Ariz.* (1889); 3–12 *Ariz. Reports*; *Portrait and Biog. Record of Ariz.* (1901); *Hist. of Ariz.*, mentioned above, III, 10–13; *Who's Who in America*, 1932–33; *Arizona Independent Republic* (Phoenix), Dec. 15, 1933; middle name from a daughter, Mrs. Blake C. Wilbur.]

C. S. L.

SLOAN, SAMUEL (Dec. 25, 1817–Sept. 22, 1907), railroad executive, was a son of William and Elizabeth (Simpson) Sloan of Lisburn, County Down, Ireland. When he was a year old he was brought by his parents to New York. At the age of fourteen, the death of his father compelled Samuel to withdraw from the Columbia College Preparatory School, and he found employment in an importing house on Cedar Street, with which he remained connected for twenty-five years, becoming head of the firm. On Apr. 8, 1844, he was married, in New Brunswick, N. J., to Margaret Elmendorf, and took up his residence in Brooklyn. He was chosen a supervisor of Kings County in 1852, and served as president of the Long Island College Hospital. In 1857, having retired from the importing business, he was elected as a Democrat to the state Senate, of which he was a member for two years.

Sloan at forty was recognized in New York as a successful business man who had weathered two major financial panics, but it could hardly have been predicted that twenty years of modest achievement as a commission merchant would be followed by more than forty years of constructive and profitable effort in a wholly different field—that of transportation. As early as 1855 he had been made a director of the Hudson River Railroad (not yet a part of the New York Central system). Election to the presidency of the road quickly followed, and in the nine years that he guided its destinies (including the Civil War period), the market value of the company's shares rose from $17 to $140. Resigning from the Hudson River, he was elected, in 1864, a director, and in 1867, president, of the Delaware, Lackawanna & Western Railroad, then and long after known as one of the small group of "coal roads" that divided the Pennsylvania anthracite territory. Beginning in the reconstruction and expansion era following the Civil War, Sloan's administration of thirty-two years covered the period of shipping rebates, "cut-throat" competition, and hostile state legislation, culminating in federal regulation through the Interstate Commerce Commission. Sloan's immediate job, as he saw it, was to make the Lackawanna more than a "coal road," serving a limited region. Extensions north and west, and, finally, entrance into Buffalo, made it a factor in general freight handling. Readjustments had to be made. It was imperative, for example, that the old gauge of six feet be shifted to the standard 4' 8½". This feat was achieved in 1876, with a delay to traffic of only twenty-four hours. The total cost of the improvement was $1,250,000. Great changes in the road's traffic ensued. In the decade 1881–90, while coal shipments increased thirty-two per cent., general freight gained 160 per cent. and passenger traffic, eighty-eight per cent. Dividends of seven per cent. were paid yearly from 1885 to 1905.

Although Sloan resigned the presidency in 1899, he continued for the remaining eight years of his life as chairman of the board of directors. At his death, in 1907, at the age of ninety years, he had been continuously employed in railroad administration for more than half a century and had actually been president of seventeen corporations. He died in Garrison, N. Y., survived by his wife and six children.

[*Evening Post* (N. Y.), and *N. Y. Tribune,* Sept. 23, 1907; *Railroad Gazette,* Oct. 11, 1907; *Who's Who in America,* 1906–07; J. I. Bogen, *The Anthracite Railroads* (1927); annual reports of the Del., Lackawanna & Western Railroad Company; information as to certain facts from a son, Benson Bennett Sloan.]

           W. B. S.

SLOAN, TOD [See SLOAN, JAMES FORMAN, 1874–1933].

SLOANE, WILLIAM MILLIGAN (Nov. 12, 1850–Sept. 11, 1928), historian and educator, was born at Richmond, Ohio, where his father, a native of Topsham, Vt., was principal and half the faculty of a combined academy and college. His parents, James Renwick Willson Sloane and Margaret Anne Wylie (Milligan), were of Scotch Covenanter ancestry; both his grandfathers were Presbyterian ministers. When William was five years old, his father became pastor of the Third Reformed Presbyterian Church in New York City, and here the boy received his early education. A graduate of Columbia College (1868) at the age of eighteen, he taught for some five years in a private school. He became interested in history while acting (1873–75) as private secretary and research assistant to George Bancroft [*q.v.*], who for a part of that time was American minister at Berlin. From the University of Leipzig he received the degree of doctor of philosophy in 1876. In the same year he was called to the College of New Jersey at Princeton. There he taught Latin from 1877 until 1883, when he was appointed professor of history and political science. In 1896 he accepted the Seth Low professorship of history at Columbia, continuing in that position until his retirement with the title of professor emeritus twenty years later. In 1912–13 he held the Roosevelt exchange professorship at Berlin and also gave lectures at Munich. Among the other honors he received were election to the presidency of the National Institute of Arts and Letters, the American Historical Association (1911), and

the American Academy of Arts and Letters (1920).

Of his writings, that which attracted most attention was his *Life of Napoleon Bonaparte.* It was published originally in the form of a serial in the *Century Magazine,* beginning in November 1894, was enlarged into four massive volumes in 1896, and appeared in a revised edition in 1910. The product of many years of elaborate investigation, it was sumptuously illustrated and composed in a fashion to appeal to the general reader rather than the historical student. His other works include: *The French Revolution and Religious Reform* (1901); *Party Government in the United States of America* (1914); *The Balkans: A Laboratory of History* (1914); *The Powers and Aims of Western Democracy* (1919); and *Greater France in Africa* (1924). He also published *The Life of James McCosh* (1896) and his father's autobiography, with supplementary material, *Life and Work of J. R. W. Sloane* (1888).

Powerful in build, hearty in manner, genial, urbane, Sloane resembled the diplomat and man of affairs rather than the typical professor. To the duties of presiding officer on public occasions he imparted a gracious dignity. Fluent in conversation, abounding in pithy anecdote and witty allusion, possessed of an extraordinary knowledge of unusual things, he moved always in a circle of friendship and appreciation. He was married, Dec. 27, 1877, to Mary Espy Johnston and they had two sons and two daughters. He died at his home in Princeton, N. J.

[*Who's Who in America,* 1928–29; *Columbia Univ. Quart.,* Sept. 1911; *A Bibliog. of the Faculty of Political Science of Columbia Univ., 1880–1930* (1931); commemorative tribute by Henry van Dyke, in *The Am. Acad. of Arts and Letters: Publication No. 67* (1929); *New Eng. Hist. and Geneal. Reg.,* July 1929; *N. Y. Times,* Sept. 12–16, 1928; critical reviews of Sloane's *Napoleon* in the *Nation* (N. Y.), Nov. 25, 1897; *Am. Hist. Rev.,* Jan. 1898, Apr. 1911, and of other works of his in *Am. Hist. Rev.,* July 1902, Jan., Apr. 1915, Apr. 1925; obituary note, *Ibid.,* Oct. 1928.]   W. R. S—d

SLOAT, JOHN DRAKE (July 26, 1781–Nov. 28, 1867), naval officer, was the posthumous son of Capt. John Sloat, an officer of the Revolution, who was accidentally killed by a sentinel. His father's family was of Dutch stock; that of his mother, Ruth (Drake) Sloat, English. He was born near Goshen, N. Y., where he attended the country schools. Appointed a midshipman in the navy, Feb. 12, 1800, he served until the end of the naval war with France, chiefly in the West Indies on board the *President,* flagship of Commodore Thomas Truxtun [*q.v.*]. Discharged from the navy under the peace establishment of 1801, he entered the merchant service as commander of his own vessel and made several voyages, losing heavily on his ventures. On Jan. 10, 1812, he returned to the navy with the rank of master and went to sea on board the frigate *United States* under the younger Stephen Decatur [*q.v.*], participating in that ship's successful fight with the *Macedonian*. This cruise ended his active service in the War of 1812, however, for on the arrival of his ship at New London she was blockaded there and kept in port until the end of the war. On July 24, 1813, he was commissioned lieutenant. On Nov. 27, 1814, he was married to Abby Gordon (1795–1878), who bore him two sons and a daughter.

Obtaining a furlough, he made a voyage to France in 1815 as master of the schooner *Transit*. It is said that there he was a party to a plan that miscarried to convey Napoleon and his suite to the United States. Returning to the navy in 1816, he was on duty alternately at the New York navy yard and the Portsmouth navy yard until 1820–21. In 1821–22 he served in the Pacific on board the *Franklin,* and in 1822–23 in South American waters on board the *Congress.* At the age of forty-two he received his first naval command, the schooner *Grampus,* and in 1824–25 he cruised among the Windward Islands, engaged in the hazardous work of suppressing piracy. On Mar. 21, 1826, he was promoted master-commandant and on Mar. 6, 1837, captain, taking rank from Feb. 9. A period of service at the New York naval rendezvous was interrupted in 1828–31 by a tour of duty in the Pacific as commander of the *St. Louis.* At Callao during a revolution in Peru he gave refuge to several leading Peruvian officials. In 1840–44 he was commandant of the Portsmouth navy yard.

On Aug. 27, 1844, he was chosen commander of the Pacific Squadron, a position of much responsibility by reason of the uncertain relations between the United States and Mexico. He arrived at Mazatlán, Mexico, on Nov. 18, 1845, and remained there seven and a half months with his flagship *Savannah.* In February 1846, he received from George Bancroft [*q.v.*], secretary of the navy, secret and confidential orders, dated June 24, 1845. These were decidedly unwarlike. The ships of the squadron were to be assiduously careful to avoid any act that might be construed as an act of aggression. In case of a declaration of war by Mexico, however, he was to occupy San Francisco and blockade or occupy such other ports as his force might permit (Sherman, *post,* p. 51). Later he was ordered, in the event of hostilities, to dispose of his whole force so as to carry out most effectually the objects specified in the earlier instructions. Receiving word on June

7 that the Mexicans had invaded Texas and had attacked the American forces there, he sailed for California the next day on board the *Savannah,* convinced that the hostilities of the Mexicans would justify "commencing offensive operations on the west coast" (*Ibid.,* p. 82). He arrived at Monterey on July 2; five days later, after consulting with the American consul, who counseled the postponing of action (Smith, *post,* vol. I, p. 334), and after examining the defenses of the town and preparing various official documents, he landed a detachment of seamen and marines under Capt. William Mervine [*q.v.*], who hoisted the American flag over the custom-house and read a proclamation taking possession of California and extending over it the laws of the United States. Sloat has been severely criticized for delaying action for five days, but it has also been held that in annexing California he exceeded his orders (*Ibid.,* vol I, p. 531). On July 6 he sent one of his officers to take possession of San Francisco; a few days later all California north of Santa Barbara was in the possession of the Americans. Suffering from ill health, he turned over the squadron to Commodore Robert Field Stockton [*q.v.*] on July 23 and returned to the United States by way of Panama, arriving at Washington in November. His conduct of affairs in the Pacific was warmly commended by Bancroft, who described the military movements of Sloat and his successor as "ably conceived and brilliantly executed" (Sherman, p. 85). He was commandant of the Norfolk navy yard, 1848–51; on special duty, 1852–55, with the bureau of construction and repair, part of the time in charge of the building of Stevens' Battery at Hoboken, N. J.; and on Sept. 27, 1855, he was placed on the reserved list. In 1862 he was promoted commodore and in 1866 rear-admiral, both on the retired list. He died at Staten Island and was buried in Greenwood Cemetery, Brooklyn. There is a statue to his memory, unveiled in 1910, at the Presidio, Monterey, Cal.

[E. A. Sherman, *The Life of the Late Rear-Admiral John Drake Sloat* (1902), an amateurish book, contains most of the essential facts. See also J. H. Smith, *The War with Mexico* (2 vols., 1919); G. L. Rives, *The U. S. and Mexico, 1821–1848* (1913), vol. II; J. C. Frémont, *Memoirs of My Life,* vol. I (1887); Record of Officers, 1798–1871, Bureau of Navigation; obituary in *Army and Navy Jour.,* Mar. 7, 1868; death notice in *N. Y. Tribune,* Nov. 29, 1867. Sloat's official dispatches for July 1846 appear in *House Executive Doc. I,* 30 Cong., 2 Sess., pp. 1006–34.]   C. O. P.

SLOCUM, FRANCES (Mar. 4, 1773–Mar. 9, 1847), Indian captive, was born in Warwick, R. I., the descendant of Anthony Slocum who was one of the early settlers at Taunton, Mass., in 1637, and became the ancestor of Samuel,

Henry Warner Slocum and Margaret Olivia (Slocum) Sage [*qq.v.*]. She was the daughter of Jonathan and Ruth (Tripp) Slocum. In 1777 the Slocums with their seven children removed to the upper Susquehanna frontier near Wyoming, Pa. Disregarding the warning of the Wyoming massacre in July 1778, the Slocums fell victims to an attack by Delaware on Nov. 2, when, in the absence of the adult males, Frances was captured. She was adopted by a Delaware family to take the place of a dead daughter, Weletawash, whose name Frances was given. Her home changed with the fortunes of the Delaware, and she accompanied her family from the Sandusky, to Niagara, to Detroit, and finally at the close of the Revolution to the Maumee on the site of what became Fort Wayne. At the latter place she married a Delaware named Little Turtle. When he went west after the defeat of Wayne, she remained behind. She then married a Miami named Shepancanah, or Deaf Man, by whom she had four children. She spent the rest of her life at Deaf Man's Village on the Wabash near what is now Peru, Ind., to which she and her husband moved about the year 1810.

The country of the defeated Miami nation was gradually surrounded by white settlements, and by the treaty of St. Mary's in 1818 the tribe was confined to a reservation on the Wabash; and she and her family shared in the annuities paid by the United States to her adopted nation. In 1835 a chance traveler found her living among the Miami, communicated with the postmaster at Lancaster, Pa., and established her identity. When visited by her white relatives in 1837, she and her family were not dependent upon the hunt and the chase but lived the agricultural life. They had over fifty horses, one hundred dogs, seventeen head of cattle, and many geese and chickens. Although she knew no English and spoke the Miami tongue and adhered to the Miami ways of life, she preferred, with the permission of the United States government, to remain with her family on the Wabash, when the tribe was removed to the west in accordance with the treaty of 1840. She would not, however, return to her relatives on the Susquehanna. Mentally alert, she was an able administrator of her home establishment both before and after her husband's death. Although short of stature, she was exceedingly sturdy, a fact symbolized by her Miami name, Maconaquah, which means "little bear." She died among her Indian children and grandchildren.

[John Todd, *The Lost Sister of Wyoming* (1842); J. F. Meginness, *Biog. of Frances Slocum* (1891); M. B. Phelps, *Frances Slocum* (1905); C. E. Slocum, *Hist. of Frances Slocum* (1908) and *A Short Hist. of the*

Slocums (1882); date of birth from monument; photograph of monument in Phelps, *ante*, p. 146.] R. C. D.

SLOCUM, HENRY WARNER (Sept. 24, 1827–Apr. 14, 1894), Union general, was born at Delphi, Onondaga County, N. Y., the son of Matthew Barnard and Mary (Ostrander) Slocum. He was of the eighth generation in descent from Anthony Slocombe, who came from Taunton in England to Taunton, Mass., in 1637. His early education was in the local district school and in Cazenovia Seminary. For several years he taught school, attending the state normal school during some of his vacations. An early interest in military reading was stimulated by the Mexican War, and he sought an appointment to the United States Military Academy. He secured it in 1848 and was graduated in 1852, number seven in a class of forty-three, being commissioned second lieutenant in the 1st Artillery. He went first to Florida, then, in 1853, to Fort Moultrie. On Mar. 3, 1855, he was promoted first lieutenant, but resigned on Oct. 31, 1856, to engage in the practice of law, for which he had been preparing himself while at Moultrie. He was admitted to the bar in 1858 and established himself at Syracuse, N. Y. He soon gained local prominence; in 1859 he was a member of the New York assembly, and, in 1860, treasurer of Onondaga County. He also served as colonel and artillery instructor in the New York militia.

On May 21, 1861, he became colonel of the 27th New York Infantry. At the battle of Bull Run on July 21, he was severely wounded, but won promotion as brigadier-general of volunteers, on Aug. 9, 1861. Reporting for duty again in September he was assigned to the command of a brigade in Franklin's division, and went with it to the Peninsula. This division became part of the VI Corps; Franklin was assigned to command the corps, and Slocum succeeded him in the division, which he commanded through the rest of the campaign. On July 4, 1862, he was promoted major-general of volunteers. Upon the withdrawal of McClellan's army from the Peninsula, Slocum's division was transported to Alexandria. From there it moved forward to assist in covering Pope's withdrawal. Slocum remained in command during the ensuing campaign in Maryland, and was engaged at South Mountain and Antietam. In October he assumed command of the XII Army Corps, which took part in the Fredericksburg campaign, but was not engaged in the battle. In the following spring it bore a very active part in the campaign and battle of Chancellorsville. At Gettysburg Slocum had command of the extreme right of the

Union line—the "point of the fish-hook," from Culp's Hill southward. Until Meade's arrival early in the morning of July 2, Slocum exercised command, as senior officer present, of all the troops as they arrived, and supervised the formation of the lines.

In the autumn of 1863, after the battle of Chickamauga, it became necessary to reënforce Rosecrans by troops from the east. On Sept. 24, Howard's XI Corps and Slocum's XII were designated to move by rail to Tennessee. General Hooker was assigned to command the two corps. Slocum had been hostile to Hooker ever since the battle of Chancellorsville, and now, rather than serve under him, tendered his resignation. This was not accepted, but dispositions were made so as to avoid in so far as possible personal contact between the two officers. This transfer of troops was the largest ever made by rail up to that time. It involved the transportation of 24,000 men, with artillery and trains, for a distance of 1200 miles, with three changes of trains, and was completed in nine days. Slocum with half his corps was stationed on the Nashville-Chattanooga Railway; the rest of the corps served directly under Hooker. In April 1864, he was assigned to command the district of Vicksburg. The XI and XII Corps were consolidated into the XX Corps under Hooker. In July, after McPherson's death, Howard was assigned to command the Army of the Tennessee in his place. Hooker, being senior to Howard, asked to be relieved, and Slocum returned to his old command as now enlarged. He joined it before Atlanta on Aug. 26, and his troops were the first to enter the city on Sept. 2. On the march to the sea and up through the Carolinas, Slocum commanded the left wing of Sherman's army, consisting of the XIV and XX Corps. Toward the end of the campaign the two wings became separate armies, Howard's resuming its old title as the Army of the Tennessee, and Slocum's, taking that of the Army of Georgia.

At the end of the war Slocum was assigned to command the department of the Mississippi with headquarters at Vicksburg. He resigned on Sept. 28, 1865, and returned to Syracuse. He was nominated as Democratic candidate for secretary of state of New York, but was defeated by Francis Channing Barlow [q.v.]. In the spring of 1866 he moved to Brooklyn, and began the practice of law in that city. He was a Democratic presidential elector in 1868. He was elected to Congress in 1868, and again in 1870. In 1876 he was commissioner of public works in Brooklyn. In 1882 he was returned to Congress, and served until March 1885. He was active in

the case of Fitz-John Porter [q.v.], and in that officer's interest delivered one of his strongest speeches in Congress on Jan. 18, 1884. Slocum maintained an active interest in military matters, and was a member of the Board of Gettysburg Monument Commissioners. His wife, Clara Rice, of Woodstock, N. Y., to whom he had been married on Feb. 9, 1854, survived him, with three of their four children, when he died in New York City.

[C. E. Slocum, *A Short Hist. of the Slocums, Slocumbs and Slocombs of America*, vol. I (1882), vol. II (1908), *The Life and Services of Major-General Henry Warner Slocum* (1913); *In Memoriam, Henry Warner Slocum 1826–1894* (1904); G. W. Cullum, *Biog. Reg.... U. S. Mil. Acad.* (1891); *Biog. Dir. Am. Cong.* (1928); *War of the Rebellion: Official Records (Army)*, see index; *Brooklyn Daily Eagle*, Apr. 14, 16, 1894.]   O. L. S., Jr.

SLOCUM, JOSHUA (Feb. 20, 1844–c. 1910), mariner, author, lecturer, was born in Wilmot Township, Nova Scotia, on a little farm close to the Bay of Fundy, the son of Sarah Jane (Southern) and John Slocomb [*sic*]. His father came from a line of mariners but was himself a farmer. His earliest American ancestor was apparently Simon Slocomb, who was in Boston in 1701, but the Slocombs, Loyalists at the time of the Revolution, had been in Nova Scotia for three generations. While he was still a boy Joshua shipped as cook on a fishing schooner and later made deep-sea voyages that carried him to many parts of the world. Except for some later studies in navigation and marine architecture his schooling was scanty, but he took advantage of his leisure at sea to become widely read. On the California coast in 1869 he secured his first command. For several years he sailed from San Francisco to China, Japan, Australia, and other parts of the Pacific. In January 1871 he was married at Sydney, Australia, to Virginia A. Walker, by whom he had three sons and a daughter. In 1874 he built an eighty-ton steamer at Subig Bay in the Philippines; about that time, too, he secured command of the *Northern Light*, which he maintained to be one of the finest ships of her day; and he had a career as a shipmaster that was on the whole successful and prosperous until 1886. At that time he invested his savings in the purchase of a 326 ton bark, the *Aquidneck*, and set out with his second wife, Henrietta M. Elliott, whom he had married in Boston in February 1886, and two of his sons to trade along the South American coast. In the last days of 1887 the *Aquidneck* was wrecked on a Brazilian sandbar. From the wreckage Slocum built a thirty-five foot sailing canoe that he called the *Liberdade*, and in this he sailed with his wife and sons all the way to New York. For the next few years he tried various ventures without success. In December 1893 he took the Ericsson *Destroyer* from New York to Brazil for use against the revolutionists, but the Brazilians sank her at Bahia and Slocum was not paid for his services.

His chief adventure started when he acquired the dilapidated hulk of a sloop at Fairhaven, near New Bedford, Mass., and rebuilt it almost completely. In the *Spray,* which now was nearly thirty-seven feet long and measured nine tons net, he started from Boston on Apr. 24, 1895, for what he asserted to be the first solitary cruise around the world. The *Spray,* built like a fisherman, was such a good sea boat that in normal weather he could lash the tiller and sleep soundly while she made good progress through the night; for a tender, he carried a dory sawn in half. From Boston he sailed to Nova Scotia and then to Gibraltar by way of the Azores. He had at first intended to go through the Suez Canal but, being warned of Red Sea pirates, recrossed the Atlantic to Pernambuco and worked his way down the coast, encountering his roughest weather in the Straits of Magellan. Finally clear, he reached Juan Fernandez and, after forty-three days on the Pacific, Nukahiva. He spent nine months in Australia, crossed the Indian Ocean to Durban and Cape Town, and spent three months visiting South Africa. After leaving St. Helena and Ascension, he met the *Oregon* on her famous run and finally reached Newport, June 27, 1898, by way of the Leeward Islands, having covered 46,000 miles. Although he had started the trip with no capital at all, he received generous gifts and assistance throughout the voyage. In Australia he began to reap substantial profits by lecturing and charging admission to the *Spray.* In 1900 he published *Sailing Alone Around the World,* which had appeared in the *Century Magazine,* Sept. 1899–Feb. 1900.

He had become a naturalized American citizen early in his life and now, retiring for a while from the sea, he made his home at West Tisbury, Martha's Vineyard, Mass. His writings include *Voyage of the Liberdade* (1890), which also appeared in *Outing,* Nov. 1902–Apr. 1903, as "The Voyage of the Aquidneck"; "The Voyage of the 'Destroyer' from New York to Brazil," in *McClure's Magazine,* March 1900; "Lines and Sail-Plan of the Spray," in *Century Magazine,* March 1900; and "Bully Hayes, the Last Buccaneer," in *Outing Magazine,* March 1906. On Nov. 14, 1909, he sailed in the *Spray* once more and was never heard from again. Rumors occasionally drifted back that he had been seen on a South American river, but he was finally declared legally dead as of the date on which he sailed. Bald-headed and bearded, he looked like a typical shrewd Yankee skipper.

[C. E. Slocum, *A Short Hist. of the Slocums, Slocumbs and Slocombs of America* (2 vols., 1882–1908); *Who's Who in America,* 1908–09; Clifton Johnson, in *Outing,* Oct. 1902; private correspondence.]

R. G. A.

SLOCUM, SAMUEL (Mar. 4, 1792–Jan. 26, 1861), inventor, manufacturer, was the son of Peleg and Anne (Dyer) Slocum and was born on Canonicut Island, Jamestown Township, Newport County, R. I. He was a descendant of Anthony Slocum (or Slocombe), one of the first purchasers of Cohannet, New Plymouth (later Taunton, Mass.), in 1637. After a rudimentary education, he learned the trade of carpentry and for upwards of twenty years engaged in construction work in various parts of Rhode Island. He apparently accumulated in the course of these years quite a sum of money. Shortly after his marriage in 1817 to Susan Stanton in Richmond, Washington County, R. I. (Slocum, *post,* p. 291) he accepted the office of justice of the peace of Richmond. His movements after this are not clear. Probably about 1823 he removed from Richmond to Bristol, but just what his occupation was there is not known. Some eight or ten years later he sailed with his family for England and for upwards of five years lived in London and in Newport on the Isle of Wight. Although up to this time he had given no indication of an interest or talent in invention, in 1835 he perfected and patented in London a machine to make wrought-iron nails, and the same year devised and patented a machine for making pins with solid heads.

It is thought that, being unable to find a financial backer in England, he returned to the United States shortly after obtaining his pin-machine patent, and after establishing his residence in Providence, R. I., sought a partner to engage in making pins for the market. At all events, the firm of Slocum and Jillson was a going concern in 1840 at Poughkeepsie, N. Y., and was one of the two pin-making companies in the United States. Meanwhile the question of packaging pins held Slocum's attention, and on Sept. 30, 1841, he obtained patent No. 2,275 for a machine for sticking pins in paper. Shortly after this Slocum and Jillson joined forces with John Ireland Howe [*q.v.*], and from Slocum's pin-sticking machine and Howe's paper-crimping device evolved a sticking machine superior to that of their competitor, Fowler Brothers of Northford, Conn. The latter, however, had the better pin-making machine, and in 1842 this organization was purchased by Brown and Elton of Waterbury, Conn., who subsequently purchased a third interest in Slocum and Jillson's works and acquired control of Howe's paper crimper as well. Slocum continued operating his plant at Poughkeepsie for the succeeding four years, however, and then sold out to the newly established American Pin Company. This company retained Slocum for some years, and he secured an extension and reissue of his patented machine for sticking pins on paper, Oct. 1 and Dec. 4, 1855. About this time he retired to his native Rhode Island and lived first in Smithfield, and last in Pawtucket, where he died. He was survived by his widow and three sons.

[C. E. Slocum, *A Short Hist. of the Slocums* . . . *of America* (1882); *Vital Record of R. I., 1636–1850,* vol. IV (1893); W. G. Lathrop, *The Brass Industry in Conn.* (1909); J. L. Bishop, *A Hist. of Am. Manufactures* (1864), vol. II; Patent Office records.]

C. W. M—n.

SLOSS, JAMES WITHERS (Apr. 7, 1820–May 4, 1890), industrialist, the son of Joseph and Clarissa (Wasson) Sloss, was born at Mooresville, Limestone County, Ala. His father, an immigrant to Virginia in 1803 from County Derry, Ireland, had served in the War of 1812. James's education was limited. At fifteen he was working as bookkeeper for a butcher, which position he held for seven years. He married Mary Bigger, Apr. 7, 1842, and opened a store in Athens, Ala., that same year. His business grew, and by the fifties he had mercantile establishments at several points in northern Alabama. He continued to prosper and bought a number of plantations in the Tennessee Valley about Decatur. From early years he was deeply interested in railroads, seeking to extend them through southern Tennessee and northern Alabama, and after the Civil War he combined a number of short lines into the Nashville & Decatur Railroad, becoming the president of the combine in 1867. This line now forms that portion of the Louisville & Nashville system which connects the Cumberland and Tennessee rivers. His ambitions drove him to encourage the extension of the line southward, through the new and booming coal and iron center of Birmingham, to Montgomery, where it made connection with a line from the Gulf.

Thus brought into contact with the rising Birmingham district, Sloss, in 1876, together with James Thomas, leased the Oxmoor iron furnaces, a few miles south of the new industrial city. In January 1878, with Truman Aldrich and H. F. De Bardeleben [*q.v.*], he formed the Pratt Coal & Coke Company, the first big concern organized in the Birmingham district. The Company exploited the Browne Seam, a large body

of coal just west of Birmingham, later called the Pratt Seam in honor of Daniel Pratt [*q.v.*]. In 1879 Sloss withdrew from this company and concentrated his interests in the Eureka Mining Company, the first concern to make pig iron with coke instead of charcoal in the Birmingham district.

In 1881 he organized the Sloss Furnace Company and put up two furnaces on the eastern edge of the growing city. His plant was well located with relation to the railroads, and prospered. After some years of operation he sold his control, in 1886–87, to J. W. Johnston of the Georgia Pacific Railway and others having New York capital, and the plant later became one of the units of the Sloss-Sheffield Steel & Iron Company.

By his first wife, Mary Bigger, Sloss had nine children, of whom six died young; and by his second, Martha Lundie, he had three, all of whom survived him. He was highly respected as one of the great men of the Birmingham district in the days when it had to find its own capital, and his railroad enterprises were of inestimable value to that growing industrial center of the South.

[T. M. Owen, *Hist. of Ala. and Dict. of Ala. Biog.* (1921), vol. IV; E. M. Armes, *The Story of Coal and Iron in Ala.* (1910); G. M. Cruikshank, *Hist. of Birmingham and Its Environs* (2 vols., 1920); *Daily Register* (Mobile), May 6, 1890.]

H. A. T.

SLOSS, LOUIS (July 13, 1823–June 4, 1902), San Francisco capitalist and philanthropist, was born in Bavaria, of a Jewish family. Endowed with ambition and self-reliance, he left the overcrowded community of his birth and emigrated to America in 1845. He first settled in Mackville, Ky., where he opened a country store. In 1849 he joined the gold-seekers, crossed the plains, and reached Sutter's Fort, Cal., on Sept. 13. He traded in some of the flourishing mining towns for a time, but early in the fifties moved to Sacramento and for ten years (1852–61) was engaged in the wholesale grocery business with Lewis Gerstle [*q.v.*], another Bavarian emigrant, and Simon Greenewald, under the firm name of Louis Sloss & Company. The great flood of 1861 brought heavy losses and led the firm to move to San Francisco early in 1862, where they opened a stock brokerage office. In 1866, Sloss obtained a seat on the San Francisco Stock and Exchange Board, and soon acquired a commanding position as a broker, especially in connection with the silver discoveries in Nevada. During the period of frenzied mining speculation and widespread business dishonesty and treachery in the seventies, he commanded universal public confidence as "the most honest man that ever handled mining shares" (*San Francisco Chronicle*).

Leaving the Stock Exchange in 1873, the firm engaged in the wool, fur, hide, and commission business, and became one of the most extensive shippers in the port of San Francisco. Their tannery became the largest in the city, manufacturing more sole leather than any other establishment of its kind on the Pacific coast. Along with his partners, Sloss was one of the prime movers in the organization of the Alaska Commercial Company, and for many years was a director and the president of the company. In 1869 or 1870, he went to Washington and negotiated the lease from the government of the exclusive right for twenty years, beginning May 1, 1870, to conduct seal-fishing on the Pribilof Islands. After the discovery of gold in Alaska, the company developed into a great trading enterprise.

Among the notable commercial investments of Sloss was the Alaska Packers Association, owning large salmon canneries in Alaska. He was also interested in fire and marine insurance and served as first president of the Anglo-Nevada Assurance Association. Directly or indirectly, he had a substantial interest in numerous mercantile enterprises, as well as extensive landholdings in Southern California. A handsome fortune resulted from his varied activities, and after it had reached a certain amount, he systematically endeavored to prevent its attaining huge proportions by means of pensions and charities to carefully selected individuals and societies. He took especial delight in helping worthy persons to start in business and become permanently self-sustaining. The orphans and sick, the aged and feeble, also elicited his special interest and care; he actively supported almost every charity and philanthropy in San Francisco. He was a member of the Congregation Emanu-El, twenty-eighth president of the Society of California Pioneers (1884–85), treasurer of the Republican state central committee, trustee of the Free Public Library, and treasurer of the University of California (1885–1902). On July 19, 1855, in Philadelphia, he married Sarah Greenebaum, whose sister later married his partner, Gerstle. Mrs. Sloss, with five of their six children, survived her husband, who died at his summer home in San Rafael and was buried in Home of Peace cemetery, San Mateo County. Although he was a business genius of the first order, the *San Francisco Chronicle* said of him at the time of his death, "Modesty was his ·cardinal virtue, and [he] knew no distinction between rich and poor, the favored and un-

fortunate. . . . No man was ever more considerate of his fellow-beings."

[See *San Francisco Call,* June 5, 1902; *San Francisco Chronicle,* June 5, 1902; W. F. Swasey, *The Early Days and Men of Cal.* (1891), pp. 277–82; J. A. Graves, *My Seventy Years in Cal.* (1927), pp. 87–88; A. W. Foster, "Louis Sloss," in *Univ. Chronicle* (Univ. of Cal.), July 1902; J. S. Hittell, *The Commerce and Industries of the Pacific Coast* (1882), p. 493. On the early history of the Alaska Commercial Company, see "Hist. of Alaska, 1730–1885," *The Works of H. H. Bancroft,* XXXIII (1886), 637–59, 746–47; "Fur Seal Fisheries of Alaska," *House Report No. 3883,* 50 Cong., 2 Sess. (1889); *Reply of the Alaska Commercial Company to the Charges of Gov. Alfred P. Swineford, of Alaska, against the Company in his Annual Report for the year 1887* (n.p., n.d.). This reply is signed by Louis Sloss as president of the Company and Appendix 3 is a letter of Sloss to U. S. Treasury Agent George R. Tingle, dated Dec. 10, 1887.]   P. O. R.

SLOSSON, EDWIN EMERY (June 7, 1865–Oct. 15, 1929), chemist, author, lecturer, was born at Albany, later called Sabetha, Kan., the son of William Butler Slosson and Achsa (Lilly) Slosson. His father, of Puritan ancestry, had moved from Maine, N. Y., to what was then a border community and became a pioneer merchant. Slosson attended the high school at Leavenworth, Kan., and then chose a European trip rather than to attend college. He managed, however, to enter the University of Kansas when he returned and received the B.S. degree in 1890 and the M.S. degree in 1892. He became an assistant professor in chemistry at the University of Wyoming, but continued his studies, spending his summers studying organic chemistry at the University of Chicago, where he received the Ph.D. degree in 1902. On Aug. 12, 1891, at Centralia, Kan., he was married to May Gorsline Preston, the first woman to receive a Ph.D. from Cornell University. While teaching at the University of Wyoming, Slosson began to write, and many of his contributions appeared in the *Independent.* So successful was this effort, and he derived such pleasure from it, that he soon combined journalism with his study of the natural sciences, and in this unique field achieved his greatest distinction. In 1903 he became the literary editor of the *Independent,* serving that organization in various capacities until 1921, when he became director of Science Service of Washington, D. C. He remained in this position until his death in Washington. His interests were of the broadest, and by dint of hard study, he equipped himself to discuss advances in numerous fields of science, as well as in philosophy, politics, and religion, and to write on various cultural topics.

He was a man of more than average size, being almost six feet in height and of rather heavy build, blond, broad-featured, energetic, restless. He was a keen observer, an excellent reviewer, a successful reporter, an experimentalist in politics and social theory, a philosopher, and a humorist who enjoyed any play on words, including puns. He had a unique knack of associating ideas in his discussions in an unexpected way which emphasized his points and crowded his sentences full of facts. He was humble, almost diffident or shy, and yet, besides his achievement as a writer and an editor, he was in great demand as a lecturer. His engagements were limited only by his physical strength which was affected by an ailing heart. As an editor he was fearless, always telling the whole truth frankly as he found it, while his humor enabled him to place telling emphasis on important points and to retain always the interest of his audience. He was especially prolific in ideas for books, articles, and projects so numerous that he was physically unable to carry them all to completion. He was fond of the library as well as the laboratory, the theatre, the museum, and the opera. His amazing interest in all things made it a pleasure for him to search out details, and this always led to a number of suggestions for still further writing. He was a kindly, generous soul, and interested in promising youths, several of whom he assisted in obtaining a college education.

At his death, Slosson was easily the outstanding interpreter of sciences to the non-technical public. He was able to interest anyone, not only in the accomplishments of science, but in science itself, without offending the purest of the scientists. A bibliography of his works includes eighteen books, more than eighty pamphlets of reprinted articles and addresses, twenty technical bulletins based on his research in chemistry, and about 2,000 articles, editorials, and essays. The best known of his books, some based upon his articles, are *Major Prophets of Today* (1914), *Six Major Prophets* (1917), *Creative Chemistry* (1919), *Easy Lessons in Einstein* (1920), *The American Spirit in Education* (1921), *Plots and Personalities* (1922), *Chats on Science* (1924), *Sermons of a Chemist* (1925), *Snapshots of Science* (1928). In addition to his doctorate, he held many honorary degrees, and when he died had been about to accept the title of "Professor of Things in General" at Rollins College, Winter Park, Fla. One of his two sons, Preston William Slosson, survived him.

[Private correspondence with the family; *Who's Who in America*, 1928–29; C. H. Preston, *Descendants of Roger Preston* (1931); biographical memoir by Preston W. Slosson in E. E. Slosson, *A Number of Things* (1930); *Bibliog. of the Writings of Edwin E. Slosson*, compiled by Science Service (1929); *Jour. of the Washington Acad. of Sci.*, Nov. 4, 1929; Hamilton Holt, memorial article in *Book League Monthly*, Dec. 1929; *Washington Post*, Oct. 16, 17, 1929.] H. E. H.

SMALL, ALBION WOODBURY (May 11, 1854–Mar. 24, 1926), sociologist, teacher, university administrator, was born at Buckfield, Me., the eldest son of the Rev. Albion Keith Parris Small, a Baptist minister, and Thankful Lincoln (Woodbury) Small. He was a descendant of Edward Small who emigrated from England, probably before 1640, and settled at Kittery, Me. The family at first owned by title from the Indians all the northern part of the county of York. On his mother's side he was descended from Samuel Lincoln of Hingham, Mass., the earliest American ancestor of Abraham Lincoln. After ten years at Bangor, the family moved in 1868 to Portland. Graduated from the high school in Portland, Small entered Colby University (later Colby College), Waterville, Me., where he was an outstanding figure. Receiving the degree of B.A. in 1876, he entered Newton Theological Institution the next year and was graduated in 1879. At Newton, under the influence of Ezra P. Gould, he developed an ambition for a life of scholarship. Devoting himself to history and political economy, he spent a year at the University of Berlin and another at Leipzig, and then returned to take the chair of history and political economy at Colby, where he taught from 1881 to 1888. Before returning to America he married, June 20, 1881, the daughter of a German general, Valeria von Massow, who died in 1916. In 1889 he received the degree of Ph.D. at Johns Hopkins University in the graduate school of history and political economy. In the same year he became president of Colby University.

As college presidents in those days were also teachers, Small began a course in the new field of sociology, his interest in the subject due chiefly to the conviction that history was tending to be a mere chronicle of events and that economics was neglecting essential aspects of social life. In 1892 he became head of the department of sociology at the new University of Chicago, the first department of its kind. He served also as dean of the College of Liberal Arts, and from 1904 to his retirement in 1924 as dean of the Graduate School of Arts, Literature and Science. He was vice-president of the Congress of Arts and Sciences at the Louisiana Purchase Exposition at St. Louis in 1904, president of l'Institut International de Sociologie at Paris, one of the leaders in the organization of the American Sociological Society in 1905, and its president, 1912–14. He exerted his strongest influence, however, through the *American Journal of So-*

ciology, which he founded, and of which he was editor from July 1895 to March 1926. The first journal devoted exclusively to the subject, it became the forum for sociological discussion for America and Europe, and Small admitted to its pages all shades of opinion. He himself was for years the most prolific contributor not only of articles but of reviews of sociological literature.

The bibliography of his writings includes some three hundred titles. His *General Sociology* (1905) is a systematic treatment that shows the influence of the Germans, especially of Gustav Ratzenhofer, and reveals the profound ethical interest which characterized his whole life and work. In *Adam Smith and Modern Sociology* (1907) and *The Meaning of Social Science* (1910) he set forth his conviction of the unity of the social sciences, one of his ruling passions. In *The Cameralists* (1909), his most scholarly volume, he discussed with profound insight the application of social theory to political institutions. It was in 1913 that his most remarkable book appeared, *Between Eras: From Capitalism to Democracy.* This brilliant discussion was published as a dialogue, which may account for its lack of influence in academic circles, but perhaps its indictment of capitalism is sufficient reason for the relatively scant attention it received. His last book was *Origins of Sociology* (1924), a history of tendencies in social science in Germany during the nineteenth century.

As a teacher he was distinguished for the rare charm of his personality. His whimsical humor never deserted him, even during the last years when he was suffering from a painful malady. As a scholar he possessed the outstanding merit of intellectual hospitality. At Chicago he built up a large and important department, purposely assembling men of divergent views, and he is one of four men who may be said to have founded American sociology. He died in retirement at Chicago, survived by a daughter. He bequeathed his estate to the University of Chicago to found a journal devoted to the application of moral and Christian principles to society.

[L. A. W. Underhill, *Descendants of Edward Small of New England* (rev. ed., 1934), vol. I; *Who's Who in America,* 1924–25; articles by T. W. Goodspeed, H. E. Barnes, Annie M. Maclean, and F. N. House, in *Am. Jour. of Sociology,* July 1926; T. W. Goodspeed, in *Univ. Record* (Univ. of Chicago), vol. XII (1926); E. C. Hayes, in *Social Forces,* June 1926; *Am. Masters of Social Sci.* (1927), ed. by H. W. Odum; obituary in *Chicago Daily Tribune,* Mar. 25, 1926.]   E.F.

SMALL, ALVAN EDMOND (Mar. 4, 1811– Dec. 31, 1886), homeopathic physician, was born in Wales, Me. His father was Joseph Small, who served several terms in the state legislature. His mother was Mary (Jackson) Small, the daughter of Bartholomew Jackson, a Revolutionary soldier. Small was one of a large family of children, and received his earliest education in the public schools of his state. He then entered the Monmouth Academy, Monmouth, Me., and at the age of sixteen began to teach in the district schools. After four years he was made principal of one of the city schools of Bath, Me., a position which he held for two years. During this period he was a private pupil of Benjamin Randall under whom he pursued studies in the classics and in English literature. He started the study of medicine in the office of Dr. Israel Putnam, of Bath, in 1831, continuing his studies later under the preceptorship of Dr. H. H. C. Greene, of Saco, Me. In 1834 he was married to Martha Mary Sloan of Bath. In 1840 he entered the Pennsylvania Medical College from which he was graduated in 1842. He began his practice in Upper Darby, Delaware County, Pa., but moved to Philadelphia in 1845. When the Homoeopathic Medical College of Pennsylvania was organized in 1848, he was appointed professor of physiology and pathology.

He moved to Chicago in 1856 to take over the practice of Dr. David S. Smith. The Hahnemann Medical College of Chicago was organized three years later and Small was elected the first dean. From 1850 to 1869 he served as professor of theory and practice of medicine. In accordance with the peculiar educational methods in medical colleges of the period, he was forced at times to teach unrelated subjects during the same session. He resigned as dean in 1865 and became president of the institution in 1869. The same year he was elected a life member of the Chicago Historical Society. He delivered his last lecture to the students of Hahnemann Medical College in 1885, but maintained his private and other institutional activities and interests to the day before his death. In addition to his private and institutional work, he possessed intense literary interests. He was general secretary of the American Institute of Homoeopathy, 1849–50, and president in 1850. He was co-editor of the *Philadelphia Journal of Homoeopathy,* 1854–60, and of the *United States Medical and Surgical Journal* from 1870 to 1874. His contributions to medical literature were numerous. In 1854 he published a *Manual of Homoeopathic Practice,* for the use of families and private individuals, which went through fifteen editions and was translated into German by K. J. Hempel in 1856. In 1856 he published *Diseases of the Nervous System,* and in 1886 appeared his voluminous work of 900 pages, *A Systematic Treatise on the Practice of Medicine.* He was survived by his wife, and three of their four children. Two sons became homeo-pathic physicians.

[H. H. Cochrane, *Hist. of Monmouth and Wales* (1894), vol. I; *Biog. Sketches of the Leading Men of Chicago* (1868); T. L. Bradford, *Hist. of the Homoeopathic Med. Coll. of Pa.* (1898); *Trans. . . . Am. Inst. of Homoeopathy, 1887* (1887); *Med. Visitor,* and *Hahnemannian Monthly,* Feb. 1887; *U. S. Med. and Surgical Jour.,* Oct. 1872; *Chicago Tribune,* Jan. 1, 1887.]   C. B.

SMALLEY, EUGENE VIRGIL (July 18, 1841–Dec. 30, 1899), journalist, editor, was the son of Jared Frost Smalley and his wife, Cordelia Lewis, who moved from New York to settle on the Western Reserve. He was born at Randolph, Portage County, Ohio, but after the death of the father returned with the family to Blackrock and then Fredonia, N. Y. At the age of eleven, he started to learn the printer's trade and at fourteen went to Painesville, Ohio, where he was joined by his mother a year later. Between 1856 and 1861 he wandered east as far as New York City and west to Louisville and Harrodsburg, Ky. Between short periods of formal education, he set type or taught school, and, on the eve of the Civil War, bought, with a friend, two papers in Painesville, which they consolidated and published. Smalley enlisted in the 7th Ohio Infantry and remained in service until he was wounded at Port Republic. Letters from the field, written to his paper and copied in others, opened a place for him on the Cleveland *Herald.* In 1863 he was in Washington, D. C., holding a minor clerkship in the treasury department. He made the acquaintance of James A. Garfield, whom he much resembled in appearance and who was responsible for his obtaining the clerkship of the House Committee on Military Affairs. In 1868 he bought the *Mahoning Register,* a paper published in Youngstown, Ohio, but after a short time he sold it and became a free-lance journalist. He traveled in Europe in 1869–70, and then began contributing articles to the *New York Tribune,* becoming a regular member of the staff in 1871. During this period he investigated Ku Klux Klan activities in North Carolina, reported the Vienna world's fair in 1873 and the Centennial Exhibition at Philadelphia for the *Tribune,* and wrote extensively for the periodicals, *Forum, Atlantic Monthly,* and *Century.* For the last of these he made a trip west from Lake Superior and wrote about northwestern states and territories.

Henry Villard, when he was preparing for the formal opening of the Northern Pacific Railroad, engaged Smalley to edit the *History of the Northern Pacific Railroad* (1883), and thus began a long connection with the advertising department of that road. In 1883 he started *The Northwest Illustrated Monthly Magazine* designed to acquaint people with the resources of the region traversed by the railroad. In 1884 Smalley and the magazine moved from New York to St. Paul, Minn., where the editor resided until his death. He traveled in the Northwest and wrote profusely of the area he knew so well. In 1889 he published *The Great Northwest; a Guide Book and Itinerary.* He took an active part in Republican politics through his writings, publishing in 1880 *The Republican Manual; . . . with Biographical Sketches of James A. Garfield and Chester A. Arthur,* and, in 1884, *A Brief History of the Republican Party,* the latter being elaborated in 1896 to include a history of Republican Minnesota and Minnesotians. He also wrote *American Journalism—An Appendix to the Encyclopædia Britannica* (1884). He was a member and, for many years, president of the St. Paul Chamber of Commerce. He was also active in G. A. R. circles and the Sons of the American Revolution. At his death he was survived by his wife, Mrs. Josephine M. Conday, to whom he had been married in 1873, a son and a step-son.

[*Who's Who in America,* 1899–1900; St. Paul *Daily Pioneer Press,* St. Paul *Globe,* Dec. 30, 1899; *Memoirs of Henry Villard* (2 vols., 1904); *Northwest Magazine,* Jan. 1900.]   L. B. S.

SMALLEY, GEORGE WASHBURN (June 2, 1833–Apr. 4, 1916), journalist, was born at Franklin, Norfolk County, Mass., "of good Old Colony stock," and grew up there and at Worcester, Mass., whither he went with his parents, the Rev. Elam and Louisa Jane (Washburn) Smalley, in 1840. In 1849 he entered Yale University, where he won his chief laurels as an athlete, rowing stroke in the first Yale-Harvard race on Lake Winnepesaukee. He received the A.M. degree in 1853, and read law for a year at Worcester in the office of George Frisbie Hoar [*q.v.*]. He studied at the Harvard Law School, 1854–55, was admitted to the bar in 1856, and practised law in Boston until 1861. In Boston he became closely associated with Wendell Phillips [*q.v.*], with whom he several times shared the danger of mob violence. When Smalley wished to go South in the autumn of 1861, partly for his health and partly to see something of the war, Phillips obtained for him an assignment from the *New York Tribune* to do a series of papers on South Carolina negro life. From November 1861 to October 1862 he served as war correspondent at the front, notably with Frémont in the Shenandoah Valley and with the Army of the Potomac. On the field of Antietam, Sept. 17, 1862, he acted as impromptu aide to "Fighting

Joe" Hooker, carrying orders for him under fire. After the battle Smalley commandeered a horse (his own had two bullets in it), rode in the night thirty miles to the nearest telegraph, and wired in a summary of the engagement. The operator, on his own initiative, sent the dispatch to Washington instead of to New York. Smalley then took a night train to New York and wrote his longer story standing under a dim oil lamp. This earliest account of Antietam, which appeared on Sept. 19, was a notable triumph for the *Tribune,* and Smalley's feat was, in the opinion of Henry Villard [*q.v.*], the greatest single journalistic exploit of the war (*Memoirs of Henry Villard,* 1904, I, 335). Smalley was married to Phoebe Garnaut, adopted daughter of Wendell Phillips, on Dec. 25, 1862. She was the "only child of an estimable friend of Welsh birth who had married a native of France and come to Boston, where her husband soon died" (Lorenzo Sears, *Wendell Phillips, Orator and Agitator,* 1909, p. 87n). They had five children, two boys and three girls. In October 1862 Smalley took a regular place on the *Tribune* staff in New York, and when the *Tribune* building was attacked by the draft rioters in 1863 he was prominent among the armed defenders.

The beginning of Smalley's distinguished career as a foreign correspondent came in 1866, when he was sent to Europe on two days' notice to report the Austro-Prussian War. Although the fighting was practically over when he arrived, he made use of the newly-laid transatlantic cable to send from Berlin what was probably the first of all cabled news dispatches. In 1867 he was again sent abroad to organize a London bureau which should receive and coordinate all European news. This move marked a revolution in journalism. At the outbreak of the Franco-Prussian War in 1870 Smalley formed the first international newspaper alliance, with the London *Daily News,* and organized his bureau on the basis of a free use of both telegraph and cable hitherto unknown on either side the Atlantic. Combining this policy with an adaptation of his own procedure at Antietam, he scored, through the exploits of his correspondents with both armies, triumph after triumph, notably the famous "scoop" of Sedan. Smalley remained in charge of the *Tribune's* European correspondence until 1895, when he returned to America to act as American correspondent of the London *Times.* This position he held for ten years (1895–1905), living either in New York City or in Washington, D. C. Then, retiring from active journalism except for weekly letters to the *Tribune* and occasional contributions to reviews, he

made his home in London until his death in 1916.

Smalley's letters to the *Tribune,* both before and after the *Times* interlude, added greatly to the reputation he had gained by his revolutionary handling of war news. The initialed signatures G. W. S. became widely familiar, and without doubt Smalley did excellent service to the cause nearest his heart, the cementing of Anglo-American friendship and understanding. His style is vigorous and lucid. Moving freely in the upper strata of English society, he knew everybody of importance in both England and America, and was, perhaps, even too eager to let his high connections be known. He is at his best in his brief portrait sketches, always chatty and anecdotal but invariably discreet. Indeed, many readers have been distinctly annoyed by his rather ostentatious discretion, his attitude of "I could an I would." This somewhat superior air, his violent likes and dislikes, his "cold irony," and his toryism, made him numerous enemies on both sides of the ocean. Yet he won the respect of people as diverse as Gladstone, Lowell, Whistler, and Arnold. The best of the *Tribune* letters, with some other material, were collected in a series of books which still hold considerable interest: *A Review of Mr. Bright's Speeches* (1868); *London Letters* (2 vols., 1891); *Studies of Men* (1895); and *Anglo-American Memories* (1911, second series, 1912). He also published in 1909 *The Life of Sir Sydney H. Waterlow, Bart.*

[There is incidental autobiographical material in most of Smalley's books, notably *Anglo-American Memories,* in particular the first series. Other sources include: *Who's Who in America,* 1906–07; *Who Was Who,* 1916–28 (London, 1929); *Worcester Births, Marriages and Deaths* (1894); obituaries in the London *Times,* the N. Y. *Tribune,* N. Y. *Herald, Evening Post, Sun,* and *World,* Apr. 5, 1916; N. Y. *Tribune,* Apr. 6, 1916; N. Y. *Jour.,* May 29, 1900; N. Y. *Herald,* Oct. 1, 1895; *Mail and Express* (N. Y.), Apr. 20, 1898; F. L. Bullard, *Famous War Correspondents* (1914); *Obit. Record of Grads. of Yale Univ.,* July 1, 1916.]
E. M. S.

SMALLS, ROBERT (Apr. 5, 1839–Feb. 22, 1915), negro congressman from South Carolina, was born at Beaufort, S. C., the son of Robert and Lydia Smalls and a slave of the McKee family. He was kindly treated by his master and allowed to acquire a limited education. In 1851 he moved with his master to Charleston and became successively a hotel waiter, a hack driver, and a rigger. In 1856 he married his first wife, Hannah, who died in 1883. In 1861 the Confederate authorities impressed him into service and made him a member of the crew of *The Planter,* a dispatch and transportation steamer doing service in Charleston Harbor. In the early morning of May 13, 1862, taking advantage of the absence of the white officers, with his wife, two children, and twelve others aboard, he carried *The Planter* beyond the Charleston forts into the lines of the blockading Federal squadron outside the harbor. This daring exploit gave him national fame. He was made a pilot in the United States Navy and given a share of the prize-money. His knowledge of Charleston Harbor and its fortifications was of great service to the Federals. On Dec. 1, 1863, when the commander of *The Planter* deserted his post under Confederate fire, Smalls took command of the steamer and led it out of danger. For this act he was promoted to the rank of captain and placed in command of *The Planter*, holding this post until September 1866, when his craft was put out of commission.

His rise to political importance in South Carolina during Reconstruction was inevitable. He was good-humored, intelligent, fluent, and self-possessed. His moderate views and kindness toward the family of his former master made him to the whites the least objectionable of the freedmen with political aspirations. The fact that he was the pet of their liberators led the freedmen to believe that he was "the smartest *cullud* man in Souf Car'lina" (*The Trip of the Steamer Oceanus to Fort Sumter and Charleston*, 1865, p. 86). His modesty and lack of education were the only circumstances which prevented him from becoming preëminent among the directors of the state during Reconstruction. As early as May 1864, a meeting of negroes and northerners at Port Royal elected him a delegate to the National Union Convention. He was one of the less prominent delegates to the state constitutional convention of 1868. From 1868 to 1870 he served in the state House of Representatives and in the latter year was elected to the state Senate, where he served through the session of 1874. From 1875 to 1887, except during 1880 and 1881, he served in Congress.

His congressional career was not notable. His most important speeches were attacks on the election tactics of the South Carolina Democrats and in support of a bill to provide equal accommodations for the races on interstate conveyances. A thorough partisan, he opposed civil service reform and favored pension bills. He made an unsuccessful attempt to have $30,000 voted him as additional compensation for his part in *The Planter* escapade. He was a conspicuous figure in the Republican national conventions of 1872 and 1876. From 1865 to 1877 he served in the state militia, rising to the rank of major-general. In December 1889 he was appointed collector of the port of Beaufort, holding this position until 1913 except during Cleveland's second term. In 1877 he was convicted of accepting a bribe of

$5,000 while state senator and was sentenced to three years in prison, but while his case was under appeal he was pardoned by Gov. William Dunlap Simpson [*q.v.*] as part of the policy of amnesty which the state Democratic administration deemed wise. His last conspicuous service was as one of the six negro members of the state constitutional convention of 1895. Before that body he made a vain but gallant attempt to prevent the practical disfranchisement of his race. The last twenty years of his life were spent quietly at Beaufort, where he enjoyed the confidence of both races, cooperating with white leaders in efforts to advance the material interests of the community. On Apr. 9, 1890, he was married a second time, to Annie E. Wigg.

[The best sketches of Smalls are in *Who's Who in America*, 1912–13; J. H. Brown, *The Cyc. of Am. Biogs.*, VII (1903), 103–04; and the *Union Herald* (Columbia, S. C.), Nov. 1, 1873. The episode of *The Planter* is described in *War of the Rebellion: Official Records (Army)*, 1 ser. XIV, 13–14, and in *Report of the Secretary of the Navy*, 1862, pp. 227–28. His political career is traced in F. B. Simkins and R. H. Woody, *S. C. during Reconstruction* (1932); S. D. Smith, "The Negro in Congress, 1870–1901" (MS.), the library of the Univ. of N. C.; A. A. Taylor, *The Negro in S. C. during the Reconstruction* (copr. 1924); *Biog. Dir. Am. Cong.* (1928). An obituary appeared in *News and Courier* (Charleston, S. C.), Feb. 25, 1915. Sir George Campbell, *White and Black; the Outcome of a Visit to the U. S.* (1879), pp. 346–47, 356–57, and *Letters and Diary of Laura M. Towne* (1912), ed. by R. S. Holland, pp. 240–41, give personal impressions. Mr. William Elliott of Columbia, S. C., and Mr. and Mrs. Niels Christensen of Beaufort, S. C., have furnished information concerning Smalls's relations with the whites.]   F. B. S.

SMALLWOOD, WILLIAM (1732–Feb. 12, 1792), soldier and governor, was the great-grandson of James Smallwood, who arrived in Maryland in 1664, settled in Charles County, became a large planter, served as sheriff and as county commissioner, received the rank of colonel with authority to raise a regiment for fighting Indians, and during nearly the entire period of the royal government of Maryland, 1692–1715, was a representative of his county in the Maryland Assembly. William Smallwood's father was Bayne Smallwood, a delegate for Charles County in the Maryland Assembly in 1738 and several succeeding years. His mother was Priscilla (Heaberd), who was born in Virginia. William, born in Charles County, is said to have been sent to school in England. He began his military career as a soldier in the French and Indian War. He took his seat in the Maryland Assembly in 1761 as a delegate for Charles County and became one of the liberal leaders of that body, speaking and voting on important questions with Thomas Johnson and William Paca [*qq.v.*]. He joined the Maryland non-importation association in June 1769, and as a delegate to the Maryland

Convention of 1775 he joined the Association of the Freemen of Maryland which advocated "opposition by arms, to the British troops, employed to enforce obedience to the late acts and statutes of the British parliament, for raising a revenue in America" (*Proceedings of the Conventions of the Province of Maryland, 1774, 1775 & 1776,* 1836, pp. 17–18).

In January 1776, commissions were issued to raise a regiment of Maryland troops under Smallwood's command. The Maryland Convention withdrew its objections to a declaration of independence June 26, and five days after the famous declaration by the Continental Congress, Smallwood marched northward with a battalion of nine companies. Reinforcements followed, and in the battle of Long Island, although Smallwood was absent, the Maryland line established a reputation for valor. Under Smallwood the survivors covered Washington's retreat. They fought with like valor at White Plains, where Smallwood was wounded. The Continental Congress elected him a brigadier-general Oct. 23, 1776, and two months later he was ordered to Maryland to promote the raising of new levies. His men fought at Fort Washington, Trenton, Princeton, and Germantown. In 1778–79 he was at Wilmington, Del., covering Washington's stores at the head of the Elk River, watching for operations of the enemy on the Chesapeake, and suppressing a Tory uprising on the Eastern Shore of Maryland. He was ordered to the South in April 1780, was promoted to the rank of major-general in September of that year, and for brave fighting near Camden he and his men received the thanks of Congress. Upon the death of Baron de Kalb [*q.v.*] three days after the battle of Camden, Smallwood was placed in command of a division, but when Horatio Gates [*q.v.*] was removed, his position was that of a subordinate to Baron Steuben [*q.v.*]. He protested and threatened to resign rather than serve under a foreigner, but Washington expressed his displeasure at this attitude, Congress was firm, Greene sent him to Maryland to aid in procuring supplies and reinforcements, and he continued in the service until Nov. 15, 1783.

Smallwood made himself disagreeable by repeated complaints that he was not promoted as rapidly as he deserved, by complaints that his state was not accorded recognition in proportion to its services, and by his offensive attitude toward foreigners. The sacrifice of his men during battle seemed not to disturb him. His greatest service in the war was as a drill master, in raising men and supplies, and in administering other military affairs of his state. When the war had ended, he enjoyed some of the usual popularity of a military hero. The Maryland Assembly elected him a delegate to the Continental Congress (Dec. 4, 1784), but he declined to serve. He was elected governor the following year and served three consecutive terms of one year each. As governor he called the convention in which Maryland ratified the constitution of the United States, and he promoted the movement for the improvement of the navigation of the Potomac. Smallwood never married. He died in Prince George's County and was buried in Charles County.

[*Archives of Md.,* vols. XII, XVI, XXI, XLIII, XLV, XLVII, XLVIII (1893–1931); *Md. Hist. Mag.,* Sept. 1924, June 1927; *Papers Relating Chiefly to the Md. Line during the Revolution* (1857), ed. by Thomas Balch; H. E. Buchholz, *Governors of Md.* (1908), critical but inaccurate; M. P. Andrews and H. F. Powell, *Tercentenary Hist. of Md.* (1925), vols. I, IV; *Maryland Journal and Baltimore Advertiser,* Feb. 1792.]

N. D. M.

SMART, JAMES HENRY (June 30, 1841– Feb. 21, 1900), school superintendent, president of Purdue University, was born at Center Harbor, N. H., the son of Dr. William Hutchings Smart, a successful physician, and Nancy (Farrington) Smart, of old New England stock. Educated at home and at the Concord high school, he began his career as a teacher when he was eighteen years of age. After one year in a district school he became the principal of a graded school at Laconia, N. H., in 1860 and taught in this and other local schools for three more years, becoming meanwhile an associate editor of the *Journal of Education* published at Manchester, N. H. He removed in 1863 to Toledo, Ohio, where he was so successful as a school principal that in 1865 he was named superintendent of schools at Fort Wayne, Ind. Here he successfully dealt with problems involving the relations of public and parochial schools, and thereby confirmed a reputation as an able administrator. On July 21, 1870, he married Mary H. Swan, daughter of a professor in Grinnell College, Iowa. In swift succession he now harvested the honors of his profession. He was president of the Indiana State Teachers' Association, 1871; state superintendent of public instruction, 1874– 80; president of the National Education Association, 1880; a trustee of Indiana University at Bloomington, 1882; and president of the American Association of Agricultural Colleges and Experiment Stations, 1890. He was a trustee of the state normal school for six years and a member of the Indiana state board of education for twenty-seven years. In 1873 he was assistant commissioner of Indiana to the Vienna exposition; in 1878 United States commissioner to the Paris exposition; and in 1891 commissioner from the United States Department of Agriculture to the argricultural congress at The Hague.

In 1883 he became president of Purdue University, a land-grant college that had been established nine years before. Its initial years had been weak and struggling, but under its new administrator it gained new lease of life. Though not indifferent to agriculture, its teaching and research, Smart fostered especially the schools of engineering, which henceforth were subdivided. The university became widely known in the field of locomotive testing, and new housing, the finest of the time, was provided for the school of mechanical engineering. A school of pharmacy was started. There were notable increases in faculty, student body, and corporate income. Smart worked so indefatigably to build up the university that he brought on his own death by overwork. Among his publications are *The Indiana Schools and the Men Who Have Worked in Them* (n.d.), which he edited, and *Commentary on the School Law of Indiana* (copyright 1881).

[*Who's Who in America*, 1899–1900; *Encyc. of Biog. of Ind.*, vol. I (1895), ed. by G. I. Reed; *A Biog Hist. ... of the State of Ind.* (1880), vol. II; W. M. Hepburn and L. M. Sears, *Purdue Univ.: Fifty Years of Progress* (1925); *Purdue Exponent* (Lafayette, Ind.), Mar. 1, 1900; obituaries in *Nat. Educ. Asso. Jour. of Proc. and Addresses*, 1900, and *Indianapolis Jour.*, Feb. 23, 1900.]
          L. M. Se—s.

SMEDLEY, WILLIAM THOMAS (Mar. 26, 1858–Mar. 26, 1920), portrait painter and a leading illustrator of his time, was born in West Bradford, a township of Chester County, Pa., of Quaker stock. He was the second of six children of Peter and Amy Anna (Henderson) Smedley, and a descendant of George Smedley, who emigrated from Derbyshire, England, about 1682. His father was a miller and had operated mills in various places. At fifteen Smedley left school to enter a newspaper office. After studying for a time at the Pennsylvania Academy of the Fine Arts, he went to New York in 1878 as a draftsman for the illustrated periodicals; later he went to Paris and studied painting under Jean-Paul Laurens. From about 1880, when he opened a studio in New York, until 1906, when he turned to portrait painting, he divided his time between painting and illustrating. His work in black and white for *Harper's Monthly Magazine* and other illustrated magazines soon brought him a well-earned reputation for subtle interpretation of character, and he became one of the most important illustrators of contemporary social life. Not even Charles Dana Gibson portrayed the social characteristics of his day more lovingly and completely than Smedley. In 1882, commissioned by the publishers of *Picturesque Canada*, he traveled through the western part of the dominion for the purpose of making a series of illustrations, and in 1890, after several sketching tours in the United States, he went around the world, pausing in Australia long enough to make some interesting drawings for an illustrated publication on that country. At the exhibition of the American Water Color Society in the same year, his "A Thanksgiving Dinner" was awarded the William T. Evans prize and with his "One Day in June" became part of the Evans collection. On Nov. 27, 1892, he married May Rutter Darling, daughter of Edward Payson Darling of Wilkes-Barre, Pa., by whom he had two daughters and one son. A member of the National Institute of Arts and Letters, the American Water Color Society, and the National Academy of Design (1905), he received medals at the International Exposition at Paris in 1900; at the Pan-American Exposition, Buffalo, 1901; and at the National Academy exhibitions, 1906 and 1907. A book of his drawings was published in 1899 under the title, *Life and Character*. He died on the sixty-second anniversary of his birth at his home in Bronxville, N. Y. A large collection of his original drawings is in the Library of Congress, Washington, D. C.; other examples of his work are in the Metropolitan Museum of Art, New York, and the National Gallery of Art, Washington.

Prolific as he was, his work never suffered from lack of thought or preparation. His portraits were satisfying likenesses, skilfully and pleasingly done in academic style, but he was preëminently the illustrator and the historian of the middle class. His water-color drawings exhibited at the Avery Galleries, New York, in 1895 included many diverting glimpses of fashionable life at Bar Harbor, Narragansett Pier, Washington, and New York. As records of the American scene in the nineties such drawings as his "Afternoon at the Country Club," "Christmas Shopping on West Twenty-Third Street" and "The Meadowbrook Races" have an undeniable authenticity and historical value. "The pretty girls . . . in wonderful toilettes, and the well-groomed old gentlemen in their offices or clubs," his customary types, were depicted admirably, with a faint touch of humor. Perhaps no American illustrator has understood better than he the manners and customs of his period as exemplified by typical groups of the genteel class.

[Gilbert Cope, *Geneal. of the Smedley Family* (1901); *Who's Who in America*, 1918–19; *Who's Who in N. Y.*, 1917–18; W. T. Smedley, *Life and Character* (1899), preface by Arthur Hoeber; P. G. H., Jr., in *Book Buy-*

er, Mar. 1895; F. H. Smith, *Am. Illustrators* (1892); Ripley Hitchcock, *Some Am. Painters in Water Colors* (1890); Frank Weitenkampf, *Am. Graphic Art* (1912); C. M. Kurtz, *Am. Acad. Notes* (1883); Samuel Isham, *The Hist. of Am. Painting* (1905); obituaries in *Am. Art News*, Apr. 3, 1920, *Am. Art Ann.*, 1920, and *N. Y. Times*, Mar. 27, 1920; information from William Patten, Rhinebeck, N. Y.]   W. H. D.

SMIBERT, JOHN (1688–Apr. 2, 1751), one of the earliest artists of any importance to settle in America, was born in Edinburgh, Scotland, where his baptism was recorded in the Southwest District on the "First Aprill 1688." He was the son of John Smibert, a "litster" or dyer, and his wife Alison (Bell) Smibert. Endless confusion has arisen over the spelling of his name, which has been given as Smibert, Smybert, and even Simbert. The first of these alone appears in the Edinburgh records, in all contemporary Boston newspaper notices, in the dozen or more paintings the artist signed, and in his letters. His father was a lay member of the ecclesiastical council, and it is said that he destined his son for the ministry. His friend George Vertue (1684–1756) says he was "first apprentice at Edenbourough servd 7 years to a house painter and plaisterer. in all that time tho' he had a strong inclination to drawing and studying but no oppertunity to improve came to London" (*Proceedings of the Massachusetts Historical Society*, vol. XLIX, 1915–16, p. 25). There he was first employed in coach painting and later in copying pictures for dealers. He attended an academy, probably the original and short-lived one which opened in the autumn of 1711 on Great Queen Street. After three or four years he went to Edinburgh to try his hand at portraiture, but finding little demand for it and feeling the need of further training he returned to London and left for Italy in 1717.

In Florence, where he came under the protection of the gloomy and degenerate Medician grand duke, Cosimo III, he spent three years in copying portraits of Raphael, Titian, Rubens, and Van Dyck, and thus acquired a feeble Venetian technique and a certain facility at "face painting" in the grand manner. In Rome he painted several persons from life. It was during this Italian sojourn that he met George Berkeley, later bishop of Cloyne, then a tutor of Trinity College, Dublin. Leaving Italy in 1720 he returned probably to Edinburgh, and thence to London with something of a reputation. Although he soon found employment as a portrait painter, only a few examples of this period are known. He was a member of the Rose and Crown Club (usually confused with the Society of Virtuosi of St. Luke and referred to as Van Dyck's Club) of which he did, according to Vertue, a "large painting peice"; this has disappeared, though a rough sketch of it exists in the Vertue manuscripts. The painter's studio, to quote Berkeley (letter to Thomas Prior, Fraser, *post*, p. 132), was "next door to the King's Arms tavern, in the little piazza, Covent Garden." Berkeley, then dean of Derry, often used his friend's quarters as a convenient place to stop when in London, and it was during these visits that he induced Smibert to accept the post of professor of drawing, painting, and architecture in the proposed "universal college of science and arts in Bermudas" (Walpole, *post*, IV, 29). Smibert, "a silent and modest man, who abhorred the finesse of some of his profession, was enchanted with a plan that he thought promised him tranquility and honest subsistence in a healthful Elysian climate ... glowing with scenery, which no pencil had yet made cheep and common" (*Ibid.*).

After four years of preparation Berkeley, accompanied by his wife and friends, embarked at Gravesend early in September 1728, landed in Virginia, and thence proceeded to Newport, R. I., Jan. 23, 1729, where he intended to remain until the £20,000 voted by Parliament for the college in Bermuda was forthcoming. The little company was painted by Smibert in Newport shortly after landing; the picture, which is at Yale, is one of the earliest group portraits painted in America. It is said that on shipboard Smibert taught Berkeley's wife, Anne Forster, to paint passable portraits. If this was so, she was among the first woman artists in British America. The "indifferent wooden house" on Berkeley's farm, "Whitehall," three miles from Newport, is sometimes said to have been designed by Smibert, but it had been built more than five years before the dean's arrival. Both philosopher and artist were much interested in the Narraganset Indians and in the strange signs on Dighton Rock. The story of their visit to the Indians, which has been called the first ethnological anecdote in American history, has been often cited, but a careful drawing which Smibert is said to have made of the pictograph writing on Dighton Rock is unfortunately lost. (See *Colonial Society of Massachusetts Publications*, vol. XVIII, 1916, p. 27.) In the fall of 1731, after waiting well over two years for the promised funds, the disappointed Berkeley returned to London.

Smibert had settled in Boston early in 1730, living first in the house of Capt. James Gooch in Green Lane, whose portrait and that of his wife he painted (now in the Brooklyn Museum with a third painting by Smibert, that of Gooch's second wife). On July 30, 1730, he married Mary, the twenty-three year old daughter of Dr. Nathaniel Williams [q.v.], physician and schoolmaster. She brought her husband a dowry of £400 and a residence in the west half of the Williams mansion, which with the land was valued at £3,000. In 1743 the Smiberts acquired the whole house, which was "in Queen Street, between the Town House and the Orange Tree" (*Bostonian Society Publications*, vol. II, 1917, p. 113). With the best location that the town afforded, a foreign reputation, and local social prestige, Smibert began to paint the "best" people in the Bay Colony—colonial officials, divines, eminent magistrates, prosperous merchants and their wives. He must have turned out some two hundred canvases in his nineteen or twenty active working years in America. Many are, of course, lost; others are miscatalogued and are masquerading under the names of other painters. The large group portrait of Berkeley and his fellow passengers, and a painting in the Essex Institute, Salem, Mass., of Sir William Pepperrell [q.v.], done about 1745, are his most ambitious pieces. One of his London portraits, of his friend Allan Ramsay, the author of *The Gentle Shepherd*, was engraved by Vertue. Some half-dozen of those painted in America were engraved by Peter Pelham, the step-father of John Singleton Copley [qq.v.].

Discovering in spite of his success that portraiture did not bring him sufficient income for his rapidly growing family, Smibert opened a store in his house for the sale "of Colours, dry or ground, with Oils and Brushes," and "the best Metzotinto, Italian, French, Dutch and English Prints, in Frames and Glasses, or without, by Wholesale or Retail, at Reasonable Rates . . ." (Dow, *post*, p. 3). The next year he advertised "a collection of valuable PRINTS, engrav'd by the best Hands, after the finest Pictures . . . done by Raphael, Michael Angelo, Poussin, Rubens, and other the greatest Masters . . ." (*Ibid.*). Judging from his correspondence with Arthur Pond, business prospered. About 1740 he took in his nephew, John Moffatt, as a partner. He had a number of copies of pictures in European galleries, besides "a collection of good busts and statues, most of them antiques, done in clay and paste, among the rest Homer's head and a model of the Venus of Medicis" (Hamilton, *post*, p. 139). The great tradition of the Renaissance was thus carried to American shores.

On May 31, 1735, Berkeley, who had been elevated to the bishopric of Cloyne, wrote and suggested to Smibert "to embark with your busts, your prints, and your drawings, and once more cross the Atlantic," and settle in Cork, a "city four times as populous as Boston, and a hundred times as rich" (*Gentleman's Magazine*, Feb. 1831, p. 100). He remained, however, in the Bay Colony, continuing with the shop and his painting. His name occurs occasionally upon the Boston town records. He furnished the designs for Faneuil Hall, which was built in 1742 from funds provided by Peter Faneuil [q.v.], whom he painted. (The picture is now in the collections of the Massachusetts Historical Society; a copy is in Faneuil Hall). Because of his failing eyesight his professional career ended about 1748. In a letter to Arthur Pond in 1749 he says, "my eyes has been sometime failling me, but is stil heart whole and hath been diverting my self with something in the Landskip way which you know I always liked" (*Proceedings of the Massachusetts Historical Society, op. cit.*, p. 34), which places him as one of the earliest landscape painters in America. Unfortunately, no examples remain or have been identified. Thirteen were listed in the inventory of his estate, though some of these might have been his copies after European masters. He died at sixty-three and was buried in the tomb of his father-in-law in the Granary Burying Ground. The grave, however, no longer bears his name but has the inscription, Thomas and John Bradlee'[s] Tomb 1816 (*Proceedings of the Massachusetts Historical Society, op. cit.*, p. 38). There is a self-portrait of Smibert in the left-hand corner of the group picture at Yale, and a portrait of his wife in the collections of the Massachusetts Historical Society.

His estate was appraised by a fellow-artist, John Greenwood, ten months later at £1,387 4s. 9d. (*Proceedings of the Massachusetts Historical Society*, vol. IX, 1866–67, pp. 208–09). His wife and his nephew, John Moffatt, succeeded to his artist's materials and print business, which they conducted for many years. About his children there is much uncertainty. According to Walpole, he left a widow with two children. Smibert himself wrote in 1743, "I am happy in 4 clever Boys . . .," and four sons are named in the records of Suffolk County, in which Nathaniel is listed as the fourth. He is also said to have had "nine children, two daughters and seven sons, the second, Nathaniel" (*Antiques, post*, p. 120). Nathaniel or Nathanael (Jan. 20, 1734– Nov. 3, 1756) is given as "the second son of the late Mr. John Smibert" in a contemporary obituary notice. The son showed considerable promise as a painter; three portraits are known by his hand, those of John Lovell at Harvard, Pres.

Ezra Stiles [qq.v.] at Yale, and Dorothy Wendell in a private collection in Boston.

Smibert's influence persisted long after his death. Charles Willson Peale [q.v.] visited his "painting-room" in 1765 and heard there of young Copley. It is doubtful if Copley received any instruction from Smibert, "but it is very probable that he was the recipient of some attention, if not information" (Proceedings of the Massachusetts Historical Society, IX, 209). John Greenwood occupied the premises, which had already become Boston's art center, and was followed by John Trumbull [q.v.] after he resigned from the Continental Army in 1777. Succeeding generations of artists—Samuel King [q.v.], John Mason Furnass, John Johnston, and Samuel Minot, the goldsmith—continued to occupy the celebrated Smibert House. (See W. K. Watkins, "The New England Museum and the Home of Art in Boston," Bostonian Society Publications, 2 ser., vol. II, 1917.) Smibert's style was much like that of the best of his contemporaries in England, which was none too good. A provincial painter in spite of his European training, he is often awkward, but there is a sincerity, honesty, and vitality about his work which many regard as peculiarly characteristic of early American painting. His importance is due to his precise, faithful, and often grim records of New England worthies, and to the fact that his work served as an early link between the art of Europe and that of the colonies.

[The chief source concerning Smibert's life in England is Horace Walpole's Anecdotes of Painting in England (2nd ed., 4 vols., 1765–71), an abridged and not wholly exact version of the Vertue papers in the British Museum (Add. MSS. 23,076, fol. 13, 18), which are being published by the Walpole Society of London; portions of the Vertue papers have appeared in the Proc. Mass. Hist. Soc., vol. XLIX (1915–16) and in W. T. Whitley, Artists and Their Friends in England, 1700–1799 (1928), vol. I. See Alexander Hamilton, Itinerarium Being a Narrative of a Journey . . . 1744 (privately printed, 1907), ed. by A. B. Hart, for a description of Smibert's studio; G. F. Dow, The Arts & Crafts in New England 1704–1775, Gleanings from Boston Newspapers (1927) for Smibert's advertisements in Boston Gazette, Oct. 21, 1734, and Sept. 16, 1746, and in Boston News-Letter, Oct. 10/17, 1734, May 15/22, and June 5/12, 1735, and Sept. 4, 1746, as well as for obituaries of Smibert from Boston News-Letter, Apr. 4, 1751, and of Nathaniel Smibert from Boston Gazette, Nov. 8, and Boston News-Letter, Nov. 11, 1756; Proc. Mass. Hist. Soc., vol. XLIX (1915–16), for five of Smibert's letters and for obituaries from the Boston Gazette, Apr. 9, Boston Evening Post, Apr. 8, and Boston Post-Boy, Apr. 8, 1751. Later sources are William Dunlap, A Hist. of the Rise and Progress of the Arts of Design in the U. S. (3 vols., 1918), ed. by F. W. Bayley and C. E. Goodspeed; Justin Winsor, ed., The Memorial Hist. of Boston, vol. II (1881), for Smibert's signature and a map showing the location of his house; Wilkins Updike, A Hist. of the Episcopal Church in Narragansett, R. I. (3 vols., 1907), ed. by Daniel Goodwin; F. W. Bayley, Five Colonial Artists of New England (privately printed, 1929); H. W. Foote, Robert Feke, Colonial Portrait Painter (1930); Dict. of Nat. Biog. Among articles in periodicals are "Am. Artists and Am. Art," Mag. of Art, vol. II, 1879; R. R. Wilson, in New England Mag., Mar. 1902; Lawrence Park, in Bull. Worcester Art Museum, Oct. 1917; L. P., in Bull. Cleveland Museum of Art, Jan. 1921; F. W. Coburn, Art in America, June 1929; Cuthbert Lee, in Antiques, Aug. 1930; Theodore Sizer, in Parnassus, Feb. 15, 1929; Handbook of the Gallery of Fine Arts, Yale Univ. (1931), and Bull. of the Associates in Fine Arts, June 1934; H. W. Foote, New Eng. Quart., Mar. 1935. For Berkeley's connection with Smibert, see A. C. Fraser, Life and Letters of George Berkeley, D.D. (1871); Noah Porter, The Two-Hundredth Birthday of Bishop George Berkeley (1855); Benjamin Rand, Berkeley's Am. Sojourn (1932); and Theodore Sizer, "Bishop Berkeley as a Patron of Art," MS. in Yale Univ. Lib.; Andrew Burnaby, Travels through the Middle Settlements in North-America, In the Years 1759 and 1760 (1775). For lists of Smibert's work see A. T. Perkins, in Proc. Mass. Hist. Soc., vols. XVI (1878) and XVII (1879–80), incomplete, and Theodore Bolton, in Fine Arts, Aug. 1933. There are a number of contemporary portraits (probably English) bearing the forged signature of Smibert. A new list is being prepared by the Rev. Henry Wilder Foote, Belmont, Mass., who is also preparing a book on Smibert.]   T. S.

SMILEY, ALBERT KEITH (Mar. 17, 1828–Dec. 2, 1912), educator, humanitarian, was born in Vassalboro, Me., the son of Daniel and Phebe (Howland) Smiley. From his early boyhood on his father's farm his life was closely linked with that of his twin brother, Alfred Homans Smiley (d. Jan. 25, 1903). In their infancy the resemblance between the two was so strong that even their mother found it difficult to distinguish them, and they retained a striking similarity of feature throughout their lives. After attending a local academy the brothers went to Haverford College, where in 1849 they constituted the graduating class. They remained at Haverford as instructors in English and mathematics until 1853, when they established an English and classical academy in Philadelphia. After four years in this school Albert K. Smiley returned to Maine to serve as principal of the Oak Grove Seminary near his birthplace. In 1860 he went to Friends' School in Providence, R. I., and as teacher and principal remained until 1879. On July 8, 1857, at a Friends' meeting-house in New York City, he married Eliza Phelps Cornell. A few years after their marriage they were greatly saddened by the death of their only child.

In 1869, while Smiley was teaching in Providence, he bought a tract of land on Lake Mohonk in Ulster County, N. Y. He made over an old inn on the tract and in 1870 it was opened to guests under the management of his brother. Smiley continued to teach, in order to pay for the property, until 1879, when he left Providence to devote himself to the hotel project, taking pride, especially, in developing the natural scenery about the establishment. The unwritten regulations concerning guests, which included a ban on card-playing and the use of liquor as well as a strict observance of Sunday, apparently did not lessen the popularity of the place, which became a well-known resort.

In 1879 Smiley was appointed to the Board of Indian Commissioners by President Hayes. He remained a member of the board until his death. Of humane spirit and interests, he entered seriously into the work of the commissioners and served on various special committees within the organization. In the fall of 1883, in an effort to bring together groups and individuals concerned with Indian problems, he invited legislators, administrators, and persons interested in the welfare of the American Indians to attend a conference at Lake Mohonk. The meetings thus begun, known first as the Lake Mohonk Conferences of Friends of the Indian, were held annually, and the scope of the discussions in time widened to include the negro and inhabitants of the dependencies of the United States. Annual reports of the meetings were published from 1883 to 1913. Smiley also identified himself with the movement for world peace and in the spring of 1895 instituted another series of discussions, similar in organization to the Indian conferences, known as the Lake Mohonk Conferences on International Arbitration. The meetings were held annually, and reports of the proceedings were published.

In 1889 Smiley was appointed by the Secretary of the Interior to serve as chairman of a commission delegated to select reservations for the Mission Indians of California. In the same year he bought about two hundred acres of land south of Redlands, Cal., where he and his brother built winter homes. They were generous in their benefactions to the community and allowed their property, beautified by many rare and exotic plants, to be used as a public park. The Albert K. Smiley Library, named for its donor, and a park adjoining the library property, were gifts of permanent value to Redlands. After the death of the brothers the little city began to celebrate Smiley Day, Mar. 17, in affectionate remembrance of the two. Albert Smiley retained his interest in education throughout his life. He served as a trustee of Brown University, Bryn Mawr College, and Pomona College, and at the time of his death was president of the board of trustees of the New York State Normal School at New Paltz. He died at his California home at the age of eighty-four. His wife survived him by only a few days.

[*The Golden Day*, a memorial published upon the celebration of the fiftieth wedding anniversary of Albert K. Smiley and his wife, July 8, 1907; Lyman Abbott, *Silhouettes of My Contemporaries* (1921); *Hist.*

of San Bernardino and Riverside Counties (3 vols., 1922), ed. by John Brown, Jr., and James Boyd; J. S. McGroarty, *California of the South* (4 vols., 1933); L. A. Ingersoll, *Ingersoll's Century Annals of San Bernardino County* (1904); F. E. Partington, *The Story of Mohonk* (1911; 2nd ed., 1932); *Biog. Cat. of the Matriculates of Haverford Coll., 1883–1900* (1900); *Phi Beta Kappa Gen. Cat.* (1922); *Bull. of the Pan American Union*, Jan. 1913; scrapbooks of newspaper clippings at the Albert K. Smiley Library, Redlands, Cal.]   M.B.P.

SMILLIE, GEORGE HENRY (Dec. 29, 1840–Nov. 10, 1921), landscape painter, was born in New York, son of Katharine (Van Valkenbergh) and James Smillie [q.v.], and younger brother of James David Smillie [q.v.]. He was educated in private schools, received his first lessons in art from his father, and later became the pupil of James MacDougal Hart [q.v.], who, like himself, was a landscapist of Scotch descent. He spent his professional life in New York, where he had his studio, but sought his subjects from New England to Florida and west to the coast. On June 28, 1881, he married Nellie Sheldon Jacobs, a painter of genre pictures, who had been a pupil of James D. Smillie and was a member of the American Water Color Society. A year later he was made a member of the National Academy of Design. In 1884, with his wife, he made an extended tour of Europe. He was recording secretary of the National Academy from 1892 to 1902, and treasurer of the American Water Color Society for four years. With James D. Smillie, he and his wife shared a studio in East Thirty-sixth street; their home was in Bronxville, N. Y.

The merits of his pictures were recognized by amateurs of discernment. Three good specimens were included in the famous collection of Thomas B. Clarke, "Low Tide," "From Grindstone Neck," and "Landscape, Easthampton, L. I."; in the collection of William T. Evans [qq.v.] were his "Long Island Farm" and "Gray Autumn." The museums were not slow in following the example of the collectors. "A Long Island Farm" and "Autumn on the Massachusetts Coast" were acquired by the Corcoran Gallery, Washington, D. C.; other examples are to be seen in the Metropolitan Museum of Art, New York; the Rhode Island School of Design, Providence, R. I.; the Lotos Club, New York; and the Union League Club of Philadelphia, which owns his "Light and Shadow along Shore."

Among his important works is the "Lake in the Woods," first shown at the National Academy in 1872, and subsequently exhibited at the Centennial Exhibition, Philadelphia, 1876, together with several water colors. The summing-up of his qualities as a landscape painter in the catalogue of the Clarke collection is fair: "His pictures combine artistic skill and poetic feeling in a high degree and are marked by agreeable cheerfulness of color . . ." He won the first prize of the American Art Association, New York, 1885, and received medals at the Louisiana Purchase Exposition, St. Louis, 1904, and from the Society of American Artists, 1907. He died of heart disease at his home in Bronxville in his eighty-first year, leaving his wife and three sons.

[*Who's Who in America*, 1920–21; *Who's Who in N. Y.*, 1917–18; Clara E. Clement and Laurence Hutton, *Artists of the Nineteenth Century* (1885 ed.); Samuel Isham, *The Hist. of Am. Painting* (1905); catalogues of the Corcoran Gallery of Art, 1908, the Thomas B. Clarke collection, 1899, and the William T. Evans collection, 1900; obituaries in *Am. Art News*, Nov. 19, 1921, and *N. Y. Herald*, Nov. 11, 1921.]

W. H. D.

SMILLIE, JAMES (Nov. 23, 1807–Dec. 4, 1885), engraver, was born in Edinburgh, Scotland, the son of David and Elizabeth (Cummins) Smillie. His father was an amateur lapidary and is said to have been an authority on the flora and fauna of the Hebrides. James was apprenticed to James Johnston, a silver-engraver, with whom he worked for nearly a year; later he worked for a time with an engraver on steel, Edward Mitchell. In 1821 the Smillie family moved to Quebec, Canada, where the father and an elder brother William, also an engraver, are believed to have carried on a jewelry business. James worked with them as an engraver until 1827, when he went to London and thence to Edinburgh, returning to Quebec only to proceed to New York about 1829. At the outset he had some difficulty in obtaining employment, but Robert Walter Weir and Asher Brown Durand [*qq.v.*] lent him their assistance and influence to such good effect that by 1830 he was settled there permanently as a busy banknote engraver, a pioneer in this work. As opportunity offered, he also engraved on steel the works of some of the leading figure painters and landscapists of the period. During the early years in New York he was associated with George W. Hatch; among other things they reproduced some views of New York City (1831), after C. Burton, and a plate in one of the annuals, "The Equinoctial Storm," which William Dunlap [*q.v.*] considered "of exceeding beauty."

The first of his line engravings to attract favorable notice was "The Convent Gate," after the painting by Robert W. Weir. Other excellent reproductive plates are "Dover Plains," after Durand; "Evening in the New York Highlands," after Weir; "The Bay and Harbor of New York," after John Gadsby Chapman; "Mount Washington from Conway Valley," after John

Frederick Kensett; "American Harvesting," after Jasper Francis Cropsey; and "The Land of the Cypress," after Daniel Huntington [*qq.v.*]. But the most important undertaking of all was the series of large plates after the "Voyage of Life," of Thomas Cole, a set of four allegorical paintings that met with great popularity and drew an eloquent eulogy from William Cullen Bryant [*qq.v.*]; few were the genteel parlors of the fifties that were not adorned with one or more of these works. It was the period of the gift books known as annuals, and Smillie from time to time contributed line engravings to these flowery publications. He supplied prints after sketches by Thomas Addison Richards [*q.v.*] for a volume called *Georgia Illustrated* (1842), engraved the landscape background for Durand's historical picture entitled "The Capture of Major André" (1845), in collaboration with Robert Hinshelwood, and for the American Art Union reproduced "The Dream of Arcadia" after Thomas Cole's painting. Another important plate which elicited much commendation was "The Rocky Mountains," after one of the big scenic compositions of Albert Bierstadt [*q.v.*] which was famous in its day (1864).

Smillie was outstanding among engravers of landscape; it is therefore difficult to explain why, after 1861, he should have devoted all his time to engraving banknote vignettes, with the exception of 1864, when he was working on the Bierstadt. It may have been due to prudential considerations, or possibly to changes in the public taste for landscape work. He was elected a member of the National Academy of Design in 1851, one of the few engravers to have won that distinction. He married Katharine Van Valkenbergh of New York in 1832. Three of their sons, James David, George Henry [*qq.v.*], and William Main, following in their father's footsteps, became engravers of note. He died at Poughkeepsie, N. Y., survived by his widow, four sons, and two daughters.

[Frank Weitenkampf, *Am. Graphic Art* (1912), *How to Appreciate Prints* (1921 ed.), and "The Evolution of Steel Engraving in America," *Book Buyer*, Sept. 1901; W. S. Baker, *Am. Engravers and Their Works* (1875); Clara E. Clement and Laurence Hutton, *Artists of the Nineteenth Century* (1885 ed.); William Dunlap, *A Hist. of the Rise and Progress of the Arts of Design in the U. S.* (1918), ed. by F. W. Bayley and C. E. Goodspeed; D. M. Stauffer, *Am. Engravers upon Copper and Steel* (1907), vol. I; obituaries in *Appletons' Ann. Cyc.*, 1885, and *N. Y. Tribune*, Dec. 6, 1885; family information from Smillie's grand-daughter.]

W. H. D.

SMILLIE, JAMES DAVID (Jan. 16, 1833–Sept. 14, 1909), engraver and etcher, born in New York, the eldest son of Katharine (Van Valkenbergh) and James Smillie [*q.v.*] and the brother of George Henry Smillie [*q.v.*], was educated in private schools and the academic department of the University of the City of New York (later New York University). Under his father's tutelage he began work in engraving very early, and became one of the most finished masters of the craft in America. He made his first plate when he was only eight years old, and until 1864, when he turned to painting, he collaborated with his father in much of his work, which included the making of banknote vignettes for the American Bank Note Company. But Smillie was not satisfied to confine his efforts to the mechanical phases of engraving, and he soon turned from line engraving on steel to etching, dry point, aquatint, mezzotint, and lithography, achieving in all of them originality, freedom, and richness of effect. His first oil painting to be exhibited was a landscape sent to the National Academy of Design in 1864. Two years later he helped to found the American Society of Painters in Water Colors (later the American Water Color Society), of which he was treasurer, 1866–71, and president, 1871–77. He was elected an Academician in 1876, and served both as a member of the council and as treasurer. During the seventies and eighties he was foremost in the movement to promote painter-etching as an art, and with a few other artists he organized the New York Etching Club in 1877. The catalogue of its first exhibition, 1882, contains an interesting account by Smillie of the making of the first little etched plate, now in the collection of the New York Public Library. On May 7, 1881, he married Anna Clinch Cook (d. 1895) of New York, by whom he had two sons. Throughout his life he continued to engage in the most diverse artistic activities. For his landscape subjects he traveled widely, paying special attention to mountain scenery in both the eastern and western United States. He died in New York.

His engravings include illustrations for the novels of Charles Dickens and James Fenimore Cooper [q.v.] after the vignettes by Felix O. C. Darley [q.v.]. They have been called "the most pleasing and satisfactory examples of the employment of steel-engraving for book-illustration" (Weitenkampf, post, p. 101). He also made a series of line engravings for The National Gallery of American Landscape (copyright, 1869), illustrations of the Saguenay River and the Yosemite Valley for Appletons' Picturesque America (2 volumes, 1872–74), some small plates after artists of the day for the American Art Review, 1880, and a reproduction of "The Goldsmith's Daughter" of Daniel Huntington [q.v.], 1884. Typical examples of his landscapes are "Evening, High Sierras, California," exhibited at the

National Academy, 1876, "Cathedral Rocks, Yosemite," 1883, and "The Lifting of the Clouds, White Mountains." His "Cliffs of Normandy," which belongs to the Corcoran Gallery, Washington, D. C., dates from 1907. His etchings, dry points, and aquatints, however, are his most personal contributions to the art of his day, and reveal great versatility and technical mastery. Complete collections may be seen in the print departments of the Boston Museum of Fine Arts and the New York Public Library.

[Who's Who in America, 1908–09; Who's Who in New York, 1909; Frank Weitenkampf, Am. Graphic Art (1912); Samuel Isham, The Hist. of Am. Painting (1905); S. R. Kochler, in Am. Art Rev., Oct. 1880; obituaries in Am. Art News, Sept. 20, 1909, and N. Y. Times, Sept. 15, 1909.]   W. H. D.

SMITH, ABBY HADASSAH (June 1, 1797– July 23, 1878), and her sister, Julia Evelina (May 27, 1792–Mar. 6, 1886), advocates of woman's rights, were born in Glastonbury, Conn., where their earliest American ancestor, Benjamin Smith, had settled about 1693. Their father, Zephaniah Hollister Smith, a graduate of Yale, was at first a Congregationalist minister, but, becoming a Sandemanian, he soon decided it was wrong to preach for hire and turned to the law, which he practised the rest of his life. He was an abolitionist. Their mother, Hannah Hadassah (Hickock) Smith, was acquainted with Latin, Italian, mathematics, and astronomy, and wrote verse. The sisters were well educated. Julia, like her mother, had a scholarly bent. She knew Latin, Greek, and Hebrew, and made a translation of the Bible from the original, which was published in Hartford, Conn., in 1876. For a time she taught in the Emma Willard school in Troy, N. Y., but spent most of her life with her sister on the family homestead at Glastonbury. After the death of their parents and three other sisters, Abby, practical, spirited, and energetic, became manager of the home and farm, while Julia, who was rather dependent and retiring, devoted more time to scholarly pursuits. They lived simply, did their own housework, made butter and cheese, and in speech and manner reflected rural New England. Locally they were noted for their geniality, kindliness, and honesty, their hatred of slavery, and their many deeds of charity.

Their interest in woman's suffrage began about 1869 when, indignant at having to pay a highway tax twice, they went to a suffrage meeting in Hartford. In 1872–73 they were again aroused by having their taxes and those of some other women increased, while men's were not, and in October 1873 Abby, then seventy-six, attended the Woman's Congress in New York. The next month she spoke at the Glastonbury town-meeting against taxing unenfranchised women; later, denied another hearing by that body, she mounted an ox-cart outside and addressed the crowd. From 1873 until her death she refused to pay local taxes without a vote in town-meeting, and Julia joined her in resisting. A tract of their land worth $2,000 was once disposed of at public sale for a $50 assessment, and repeatedly their cows were sold at the sign-post for delinquent taxes. In 1877 Julia published *Abby Smith and Her Cows, with a Report of the Law Case Decided Contrary to Law.* The sisters became active also in general work for woman's suffrage. They wrote letters to the press, and spoke at local meetings and at suffrage conventions; almost annually they petitioned the Connecticut legislature for the vote, and in January 1878 they attended a hearing on the equal suffrage amendment before a committee of the United States Senate, at which Julia spoke. The Smith sisters and their cows soon became known in foreign lands as well as throughout the United States, and gave new publicity and added impetus to the cause of woman's rights. After the death of Abby, Julia, who had leaned on her in many ways, on Apr. 9, 1879, married Amos A. Parker, aged eighty-six (with whom she had become acquainted when he wrote to sympathize with her over her sister's death), and soon thereafter went to Hartford to live.

[F. B. Dexter, *Biog. Sketches of the Grads. of Yale Coll.*, vol. IV (1907), for Zephaniah Smith's life and family background; L. W. Case, *The Hollister Family of America* (1886); *Hist. of Woman Suffrage*, vol. III (1887), ed. by Elizabeth C. Stanton, Susan B. Anthony, and Matilda J. Gage; journal of the Conn. State House of Representatives and of the Conn. State Senate, 1874–79; *Woman's Jour.*, Jan. 26, Mar. 2, Apr. 20, Aug. 3, 1878, and Mar. 13, 1886; *Hartford Daily Courant*, Dec. 11, 1873, July 25, 1878, Mar. 8, 1886; *Boston Daily Advertiser*, July 27, 1878; private information.]

M. W. W.

SMITH, ALBERT HOLMES (July 19, 1835–Dec. 14, 1885), obstetrician and gynecologist, was born in Philadelphia, Pa., a descendant of Quakers from Yorkshire who settled in Pennsylvania in 1685. He was the youngest of seven children of Moses B. and Rachel (Coate) Smith, his father being a prominent physician. He was educated at the Friends' school at Westtown and in private schools in Philadelphia. Although he passed the entrance examinations of the University of Pennsylvania at the age of thirteen years, he did not enter at once; he was graduated with the degree of A.B. in 1853 and of M.D. in 1856, his preceptor being Prof. George Bacon Wood [*q.v.*]. He was assistant physician in the Frankford Asylum for eighteen months, and then an interne in the Pennsylvania Hospital for an equal

period of time; in 1859, after finishing his term there, he began practice.

He soon showed a decided skill in obstetrics, to which he gave especial attention. Appointed in 1859 assistant physician to the Philadelphia Lying-in Charity, he was promoted in 1862 to be attending physician, a position he held for over twenty years. For a short time he was obstetrician to the Philadelphia Hospital. In 1867 he became consulting physician to the Woman's Hospital of Philadelphia. He was also a manager of the Wills Ophthalmic Hospital, 1863–71. His interest in obstetrics led to the invention of various instruments and to the modification of others, among them a pessary that bears his name. His modification of the Hodge pessary, known as the Smith-Hodge pessary, probably did more to extend his reputation than his writings; among other inventions were a uterine speculum, urethral dilators, and modifications of obstetrical forceps. His writings dealt almost entirely with obstetrical and gynecological subjects, and he was regarded as one of the leading obstetricians of his day. He was a founder of the Philadelphia Obstetrical Society and its president, 1874–76; a founder of the American Gynaecological Society and its president in 1884; an honorary member of the British Gynaecological Society; president of the Philadelphia County Medical Society, 1880–81; and a member of the American Philosophical Society. He seems to have gained his eminence rather by patient study and hard work than by brilliance or genius; he was evidently a safe reliable man in all that he did.

He played a prominent part in advocating the recognition of women in medicine at a time when support of this view was unpopular with the majority of men in the profession. His acceptance of the post of consulting physician to the Woman's Hospital exposed him to much criticism and alienated some of his friends; the feeling was so strong that it was even suggested that he be expelled from the College of Physicians. A particularly bitter controversy arose over the proposal to admit women physicians to membership in the county medical society, for which Smith carried on an active but unsuccessful campaign. He taught for many years in the Lying-in Charity, which students of both sexes attended, and the statements of his contemporaries bear testimony to the soundness and value of his instruction. In 1860 he married Emily Kaighn, daughter of Charles Kaighn of Camden, N. J.; they had seven children, five of whom survived him. His death occurred from malignant disease of the prostate after an illness of several years, during part of which he carried on his work despite the handicaps of pain and weakness.

[H. A. Kelly and W. L. Burrage, *Am. Medic. Biogs.* (1920); *Medic. News*, Dec. 19, 1885, with bibliog.; *Am. Jour. of Obstetrics*, Feb. 1886; *Trans. Am. Gynaecological Soc.*, vol. XI (1887); *Proc. Am. Philosophical Soc.*, vol. XXIII (1886); *Trans. Coll. of Physicians of Phila.*, 3 ser., vol. IX (1887); *Phila. Enquirer*, Dec. 15, 1885.]
                                            T. M.

SMITH, ALEXANDER (Sept. 11, 1865–Sept. 8, 1922), chemist, educator, author, was born in Edinburgh, Scotland, the son of Alexander and Isabella (Carter) Smith. His grandfather was a sculptor and his father a musician. In preparation for the University of Edinburgh he studied for seven years at the Edinburgh Collegiate School. While he received the degree of B.S. in chemistry in 1886, he devoted a good part of his four years at the university to the study of astronomy and published four semipopular articles on it before he was graduated. Finding that there was little prospect of a successful career in that subject, however, he turned to the study of chemistry under Adolph Ritter von Baeyer at the University of Munich, where his principal subject was organic chemistry. After securing the degree of Ph.D. at Munich in 1889, he was assistant in analytical chemistry at Edinburgh for a year and gave a course of lectures on organic syntheses. During a visit to the United States in the summer of 1890 he was appointed professor of chemistry and mineralogy at Wabash College, Crawfordsville, Ind., a position he held for four years. He also continued his researches in organic chemistry, following the lines of his work in Munich. In 1891 he became a member of the Royal Society of Edinburgh.

In 1894 he was invited by John Ulric Nef [*q.v.*] to take charge of the work in elementary inorganic chemistry at the University of Chicago. He was assistant professor, 1894–98; associate professor, 1898–1904; and professor, 1904–11. From 1900 to 1911 he was dean of the junior colleges. Partly because of his field of teaching, but quite as much because he thought it wise to devote his energies to inorganic and physical chemistry rather than to compete with the brilliant work Nef was doing in organic chemistry, he very soon began important investigations on quite other topics than those on which he had been working. Thoroughly trained in physics and mathematics, he soon made for himself a distinguished name in physical chemistry, which was rapidly coming into vogue in America through the influence of chemists who had received their inspiration in the laboratory of Wilhelm Ostwald in Leipzig. His most important studies in the new field were on the forms of sulfur, for which he was awarded the Keith prize and medal by the Royal Society of Edinburgh in 1912, and on vapor pressure measurements at comparatively high temperatures. In a series of masterful, experimental researches, he threw a flood of light on the conditions for the formation and existence of the different solid and liquid forms of sulfur. He also devised new methods for the determination of vapor pressures and through them demonstrated that the vapor above solid calomel consists of a mixture of metallic mercury and mercuric chloride. As a teacher he made a very careful study of the best methods for presenting chemistry to beginners. His ideas were crystallized in a book on *The Teaching of Chemistry and Physics in the High School* (1902), written with Edwin H. Hall. In 1906 he published his *Introduction to General Inorganic Chemistry*, which probably had a greater success than any other textbook of inorganic chemistry published during the first quarter of the twentieth century. It was translated into German, Italian, Russian, and Portuguese. Its phenomenal success was due to the fact that it presented adequately for the first time in a textbook written in English the theories of ionization and equilibria which lay at the foundation of the rapid advances then in progress in physical chemistry.

On Feb. 16, 1905, he married Sara (Bowles) Ludden, daughter of William Bowles of Memphis, Tenn.; they had a son and a daughter. Six years later, in 1911, he became head of the department of chemistry at Columbia University, a position he held until 1919, when he retired because of failing health. He became president of the American Chemical Society, 1911; a member of the Society of Physics and Chemistry of Madrid, 1911, and a member of the National Academy of Sciences, 1915. He died in Edinburgh.

[*Who's Who in America*, 1920–21; *Am. Men of Sci.* (3rd ed., 1921), ed. by J. M. Cattell and D. R. Brimhall; W. A. Noyes, "Biog. Memoir of Alexander Smith, 1865–1922," *Memoirs of the Nat. Acad. of Sci.*, vol. XXI (1926), with bibliog.; James Kendall, in "*Proc. Am. Chem. Soc.*," issued with *Jour. Am. Chem. Soc.*, Dec. 1922; obituaries in *Weekly Scotsman* (Edinburgh), Sept. 16, 1922, and *N. Y. Times*, Sept. 10, 1922; personal acquaintance.]
                                            W. A. N.

SMITH, ALFRED HOLLAND (Apr. 26, 1863–Mar. 8, 1924), railroad president, was born on a farm near Cleveland, Ohio, the son of William and Charlotte (Holland) Smith. He attended the Rockwell Grammar School until he completed its course. At the age of fourteen, because of his father's death, he obtained employment as a messenger out of school hours with the

Lake Shore & Michigan Southern Railway. Entering upon regular employment in 1879, he continued with the railroad for forty-five years. After advancing to a chief clerkship he sought relief from the narrowing restraints of office work by joining a bridge gang. He became bridge foreman, then general foreman of construction work; in 1890, reports of his energy, resourcefulness, and gift for leadership having reached headquarters, he was made superintendent of the Kalamazoo division of the Lake Shore. After a series of similar positions, in April 1901 he was made assistant general superintendent with headquarters at Cleveland, and in a few months general superintendent. Transferred in 1902 to the New York Central and Hudson River Railroad as general superintendent, less than two years later he became general manager; by 1912 he had become vice-president; and by 1913 senior vice-president of the railroad and its subsidiary lines in charge of operation, construction, and maintenance. In 1913, because of his generally recognized sense of fairness, he was made a member of the arbitration board that settled the controversy with conductors and trainmen in Eastern territory. When the railroad and its subsidiaries were amalgamated as the New York Central Railroad, he became president, taking office on Jan. 1, 1914.

He was then in his fifty-first year, the chief executive of a system of 13,000 miles, serving the richest traffic territory in the country. Under his guidance widely scattered and loosely joined lines were welded into an efficient and smoothly operating system. At the time the problem of railroad regulation was an acute public question. He was frequently a witness before the Interstate Commerce Commission, and, although he was not enthusiastic over the steady increase in the commission's powers, he was not an obstinate opponent, for he felt regulation to be politically unavoidable. In 1916 he was made chairman of a royal commission on railways and transportation in Canada. Following the recommendation of the majority of this body Canada entered upon its experiment in government ownership, but Smith's minority report suggested a plan of relief that would have left the railroads in private hands. His counsel was again sought in aid of the problem of consolidation of the Cuban railroads, and he was engaged upon the problem at the time of his death. With the outbreak of the World War he was faced with the need of swift mobilization for war service. Under national control of individualized railroad systems he was made assistant director general of railroads in trunk-line territory east of Chicago and north of

the Ohio, and in January 1918 he was appointed regional director of the eastern district. When he assumed charge the port of New York was blocked as a result of freezing weather and a series of blizzards that made water transport impossible, and there was great congestion on the railroads. Taking personal direction of the situation, he finally cleared up the confusion in a way that showed plainly his indomitable energy and persistence, and his leadership in the face of difficulties.

After the war he handled new problems with a grasp of their significance that amounted to genius. He dealt successfully with matters of equipment, rehabilitation, electrification, and grade-crossing elimination in New York City, re-location of lines, consolidation, and the problem of terminals in New York and Chicago, and at the time of his death he was completing for his company the most favorable annual report in its history. His manifold accomplishments as a railroad executive were due to his abundant energy, his vision and imagination, his intimate knowledge of all phases of railroading, and a remarkable understanding of people. He died as the result of a fall from a horse which he was riding in Central Park, New York City. He was survived by his wife, Maude Emery of Adrian, Mich., whom he had married Sept. 9, 1885, and one son.

[*Who's Who in America*, 1922–23; *Railway Age Gazette*, Dec. 12, 1913; *Railway Age*, Mar. 15, 1924; *Railroad Trainman*, Apr. 1924 (editorial tribute); *N. Y. Central Lines Mag.*, Apr. 1924, memorial issue; obituaries in *N. Y. Herald, N. Y. Times, N. Y. Tribune*, Mar. 9, 1924; information from Smith's wife.]

F. H. D.

SMITH, ANDREW JACKSON (Apr. 28, 1815–Jan. 30, 1897), soldier, was the son of Samuel Smith, who had been a lieutenant under Montgomery at the assault on Quebec and a captain at the siege of Yorktown. Samuel Smith married a daughter of one John Wilkinson and spent the rest of his life as a farmer in Bucks County, Pa., except while commanding a brigade of militia during the War of 1812. When his youngest son was born in the township of Buckingham soon after the battle of New Orleans, he "had no other means in his power of Showing his regard for the Hero, who achieved the Victory, than calling his son for him" (War Department records, *post*). This son, who is described as "intelligent and sprightly" (*Ibid.*), was appointed a cadet at West Point, July 1, 1834, and on his graduation, July 1, 1838, was commissioned second lieutenant in the 1st Dragoons (now the 1st Cavalry). His early service was practically all in the West, including some minor Indian campaigns. He was promoted first lieutenant, Mar. 4, 1845; captain,

Feb. 16, 1847; and major, May 13, 1861, all in the 1st Dragoons.

At the outbreak of the Civil War he was stationed in California. He was appointed colonel of the 2nd California Cavalry, Oct. 2, 1861, but resigned, Nov. 3, 1861, and was sent to Missouri, where he became chief of cavalry under Henry Wager Halleck [q.v.] and served as such through the Corinth campaign in 1862. He was appointed brigadier-general of volunteers, Mar. 17, 1862. He commanded a division in the expeditions against Chickasaw Bluffs and Arkansas Post in the following winter, and throughout the Vicksburg campaign in 1863. In the Red River campaign, March to May, 1864, he had a command made up of troops drawn from the XVI Corps (his own) and the XVII Corps. He was appointed major-general of volunteers, May 12, 1864. He spent the next few months in Tennessee and Mississippi in service which, overshadowed by the great Atlanta campaign, would have been as inconspicuous as it was necessary, had it not been illuminated by his defeat of Nathan Bedford Forrest [q.v.] at Tupelo, July 14, 1864. His command was then sent to Missouri for the defense of that state, and returned in haste to reinforce George Henry Thomas [q.v.] and take part in the battle of Nashville in December. Its wanderings had become so extensive that Smith now referred to his troops as the "lost tribes of Israel." As commander of the XVI Corps he took part in the Mobile campaign of 1865. He was mustered out of the volunteer service, Jan. 15, 1866, and reverted to his regular army rank of lieutenant-colonel, to which he had been promoted, May 9, 1864; but on July 28, 1866, he was appointed colonel of the 7th Cavalry. He resigned from the army, May 6, 1869, when he was appointed postmaster at St. Louis, Mo.; he was city auditor from 1877 to 1889, and commanded a brigade of militia during the strikes in St. Louis in 1877. Under a special act of Congress he was appointed colonel on the retired list of the regular army, Jan. 22, 1889. His wife was Ann Mason Simpson, daughter of Dr. Robert Simpson of St. Louis. Smith "was of small stature, with rather brusque, abrupt manners, sometimes verging on irascibility, yet was popular with his troops, and shunned none of the hardships to which they were subjected" (Perry, Twenty-Eighth Annual Reunion (post, p. 53). Constantly shifted from place to place to meet emergencies, he did not remain long enough with any one army to become identified with it, and as a consequence the confidence his superiors had in him did nothing to enhance his popular reputation.

[War of the Rebellion: Official Records (Army); Battles and Leaders of the Civil War (1887–88), vols. III, IV; G. W. Cullum, Biog. Reg. Officers and Grads. U. S. Mil. Acad. (3rd ed., 1891); L. J. Perry, in Twenty-Eighth Ann. Reunion . . . Assoc. Grads. U. S. Mil. Acad. (1897) and N. Y. Sun, Feb. 21, 1897; St. Louis Globe-Democrat, Jan. 28, 31, 1897; unpublished records in the War Dept.]   T. M. S.

SMITH, ARCHIBALD CARY (Sept. 4, 1837–Dec. 8, 1911), marine painter, designer of yachts, commonly known as Cary Smith, was born in New York City, one of several children of the Rev. Edward Dunlap Smith, a Presbyterian minister, and Jane B. (Cary) Smith. After a grammar-school education he learned boat building at Pamrapo, N. J., in the shop of Robert Fish, a designer of large fast yachts, and under W. W. Bates, a shipwright of the old school. He built for himself several small boats, including the Comet in 1860, and came to be regarded as the best racing helmsman and handler of small yachts on New York Bay (Outing, post, p. 227). Later, however, he gave this up for marine painting, which he studied under Mauritz F. H. de Haas in New York. By 1867 he had produced his first picture, "Off Little Gull," a lighthouse scene on eastern Long Island Sound. This was followed by "Sunrise" (1869), "The Last of the Old Ships" (1871), "Nor' Wester, Coast of Maine" (1871), "Windy Day" (1876), and "Perils of the Sea" (1878). He also made paintings of five large schooner yachts, "Columbia," "Sappho," "The Wanderer," "The Yacht Dauntless" (1877), and "Peerless."

One of his first efforts in naval architecture resulted in the building of the cutter Vindex in 1871, among the first deep-craft iron yachts to be built in America. The next year he designed the sloop Vision for J. Joseph Alexandre. About this time he discarded the long accepted method of whittling out the model in wood, and began to work out his ideas on a drawing-board. For some years he was known scornfully as a "paper boatman," but his methods of yacht and boat design have become standard. After 1877 he seems to have done little painting. A few years later he designed the sloop Mischief (1879), said to have been the first scientifically designed yacht employed for cup defense, an example of what was called the "compromise" type. He designed well over a hundred yachts. Among the most notable were the schooners Prospero (1877), Intrepid (1878), Fortuna (1882), Meteor (1902), built for the German emperor, Wilhelm II, and Enchantress (1911); the sloops Mischief (1879), which was the successful defender of the America's Cup in 1881, Priscilla (1885), and Banshee (1887); the cutters Kestrel (1882), Rajah (1884), and Vera (1885); the auxiliary schooners *Free Lance* (1895) *Genesee* (1900), *Tekla* (1902), *Vergemere* (1903), and *Resolute* (1903); the steam yachts *Cayuga* (1899), *Twinkle* (1901), and *Continental* (1905). His principal commercial productions were the Long Island Sound steamers *Richard Peck, City of Lowell,* and *Chester W. Chapin,* and the pilot boats *New York* and *Espadon;* in these he increased both speed and economy of operation. He was a member of the New York Yacht Club, and of the Society of Naval Architects and Marine Engineers. In September 1904 he published "Yacht-Racing Recollections and Reflections" in *Scribner's Magazine.* A confirmed vegetarian, he was a man of medium height and somewhat spare build, quick and nervous in his movements. He died at his home in Bayonne, N. J., of Bright's disease, the oldest and best-known naval architect in America. He had been married and was survived by a daughter.

[*Who's Who in America,* 1910-11; Clara E. Clement and Laurence Hutton, *Artists of the Nineteenth Century* (ed. of 1885); W. P. Stephens, *Am. Yachting* (1904) and "The Evolution of the Yacht Designer: Pt. II—The Am. Designers," *Outing,* Nov. 1901, with portrait; W. M. Thompson and T. W. Lawson, *The Lawson Hist. of the America's Cup* (1902); H. G. Peabody, *Rep. Am. Yachts* (1893); obituaries in *Evening Post* (N. Y.) and *Newark Evening News,* Dec. 9, 1911.]   W. U. S.

SMITH, ARTHUR HENDERSON (July 18, 1845–Aug. 31, 1932), missionary to China, author, was born in Vernon, Conn., the son of the Rev. Albert Smith, a Congregational minister, and of Sarah Tappan (Stoddard). As a boy he went with his parents to Illinois. From May to September 1864, he served as a member of Company B, 40th Wisconsin Infantry and in 1867 he graduated from Beloit College as valedictorian of his class. While in college, he publicly declared himself a Christian and about the same time decided to become a foreign missionary. At Beloit he met his future wife, Emma Jane Dickinson, to whom he was married Sept. 8, 1871. There, too, he formed an intimate friendship with a classmate, Henry Dwight Porter, with whom he later spent many years in China. From 1867 to 1869 he was a student in Andover Theological Seminary; in 1870 he graduated from Union Theological Seminary, New York City; and during the following winter, 1870–71, he attended lectures at the College of Physicians and Surgeons, New York, in further preparation for his work as a missionary. The next year, for short terms, he supplied churches in Ann Arbor, Mich., Appleton, Wis., South Chicago, and Clifton, Ill.

On May 29, 1872, he was ordained to the Congregational ministry and in July sailed for China as an appointee of the American Board of Commissioners for Foreign Missions. The Smiths and the Porters were first stationed in Tientsin, where they remained eight years; in 1880 they were sent to a pioneer post in a rural community at P'ang Chia Chuang in Shantung. Here Smith spent most of the next quarter-century helping to found a Christian community. While on a furlough to the United States in 1885–86 he was acting pastor of the First Congregational Church of Pasadena, Cal. During the Boxer storm in 1900, he and his wife were among those who were in the besieged legations in Peking. Later, in 1906, in an interview with President Theodore Roosevelt, he made a suggestion which possibly contributed toward the remission by the United States, in 1908, of a portion of its share of the Boxer Indemnity and the allocation of the funds so released to the education of Chinese youths (*American Historical Review,* October 1926, p. 65). From 1906 until his retirement from active service, in March 1925, he was missionary-at-large under his board, a position which left him free to interpret the missionary movement by voice and pen and to share in interdenominational cooperation, but with his assignment still to North China and his residence usually in T'ungchow near Peking (Peiping). In 1926 he made his home in Claremont, Cal.

One of the most widely and highly esteemed missionaries in the China of his day, Smith was prominent in denominational and interdenominational activities. He was the American chairman of the notable China Centenary Conference (of Protestant Missions) in 1907; he attended the epoch-making (Protestant) World's Missionary Conference at Edinburgh in 1910; was a member of the important China Continuation Committee, which coordinated most of the Protestant activities in China and prepared the way for the National Christian Council of China; and served on the editorial board of the *Chinese Recorder.* He was alert, quick of observation, rapid of speech, and possessed a keen sense of humor. His pungent witticisms were extensively quoted and he was very popular as a speaker. Humble and devoted, he made many friends among both the lowly and the powerful. He was probably most distinguished for his books on China. Some of these went through many editions and had large sales, two of them over a considerable space of time; two were translated into a number of foreign languages. His first venture was *Proverbs and Common Sayings from the Chinese* (Shanghai, 1888). His next two, *Chinese Characteristics* (1890) and *Village Life in China* (1899), depicted life in North China as he had observed it, the former probably being his most famous work; *China in Convulsion* (1901) was an account of the Boxer outbreak. His *Rex Christus, An Outline Study of China* (1903) and *The Uplift of China* (1907) were primarily texts for mission study classes in the churches. His *China and America Today* (1907) and *A Manual for Young Missionaries to China* (Shanghai, 1918) which he edited and to which he was the chief contributor were not so widely known. He died in Claremont, his wife and three children having predeceased him.

[*Who's Who in America,* 1932–33; *Chinese Recorder,* Dec. 1932; *North-China Herald* (Shanghai), Sept. 21, 1932; *Missionary Herald,* Sept. 1924, Jan. 1925, Nov. 1932; *The Year Book of the Congregational and Christian Churches,* 1932; *N. Y. Times,* Sept. 2, 1932; annual reports and manuscript files of the American Board of Commissioners for Foreign Missions.]
K. S. L.

SMITH, ASA DODGE (Sept. 21, 1804–Aug. 16, 1877), Presbyterian clergyman, college president, was born in Amherst, N. H., the son of Dr. Rogers and Sally (Dodge) Smith. Most of his childhood was spent at Weston, Vt., but at sixteen he was apprenticed to a printer in Windsor. During his apprenticeship his religious interests were aroused and he began to look forward to a career in the ministry. At the age of twenty he entered Kimball Union Academy; in 1830 he graduated from Dartmouth College; and in 1834, from the Andover Theological Seminary. At once he accepted a call to the only pastorate he ever held, that of the newly formed Brainerd Presbyterian Church in New York City. During his leadership of twenty-nine years this church came to be one of the important organizations of the city, building successively two edifices and receiving fourteen hundred new members. In addition to his pastoral work, Smith was active in the affairs of his denomination, serving as a trustee of the Union Theological Seminary and as a member of the controlling boards of several Presbyterian societies.

In 1863 he became seventh president of Dartmouth College. At that time the institution was at a low ebb both with respect to student attendance and to finances. It was also in some disrepute on account of the pro-slavery attitude of its retiring president, Nathan Lord [*q.v.*]. In meeting these conditions Smith was in many respects successful. Feeling against the institution was assuaged by his tact, the student attendance more than doubled, and the Thayer School of Engineering and the New Hampshire College of Agriculture were established in accord with the president's policy of making the institution a university—a policy which was abandoned by his successors. Financially, however, the administration was less fruitful. The scholarship

funds were substantially increased and large donations were received for other purposes, but many of the gifts were restricted to special uses and were in the form of accumulating funds not immediately available; consequently, the institution had the utmost difficulty in meeting current obligations. The burden on the president increased from year to year, and finally, Mar. 1, 1877, his health having given way, he resigned his office.

Tall, erect, of great dignity and urbanity of manner, he looked the part of the college president. He was remarkably fluent of speech, self-possessed, and never at a loss for a telling phrase. He was genuinely solicitous for the students and sincerely charitable, his personal donations being large in proportion to his income. Withal, he was not soft as an administrator and there was no relaxation of discipline during his term of office. Most striking was his tact, which tided over many difficult situations, but was thought by some to be overdone, and brought upon him the reproach of insincerity. His point of view was ultra-conservative, and no innovations from established practice marked his administration. While he was a student at Andover he published *Letters to a Young Student* (1832), many of his sermons and addresses appeared in pamphlet form, and he was a frequent contributor to the periodical press. On Nov. 9, 1836, he married Sarah Ann Adams of North Andover, Mass. His death occurred at Hanover, N. H.

[For biographical information, see E. B. Coe, *An Address in Commemoration of Asa Dodge Smith* (1882); J. K. Lord, *Hist. of Dartmouth Coll.* (1913); L. B. Richardson, *Hist. of Dartmouth Coll.* (1931); *Concord Daily Monitor* (Concord, N. H.), Aug. 18, 1877. The greater part of Smith's correspondence during his presidency is deposited in the library of Dartmouth College.]
L. B. R.

SMITH, ASHBEL (Aug. 13, 1805–Jan. 21, 1886), surgeon-general and secretary of state of the Republic of Texas, was born in Hartford, Conn., the son of Moses and Phoebe (Adams) Smith. Through his father he was descended from Richard Seymour who came to Hartford in 1639; through his mother, from George Adams who died in Watertown, Mass., in 1696, and from René Cossitt, who settled at Granby, Conn., about 1720. He graduated at Yale in 1824 with Phi Beta Kappa honors, and four years later received his medical degree. Having taught school in Salisbury, N. C., from 1824 to 1826, he returned to that place to begin the practice of medicine. He continued his medical studies in Paris in 1831–32, and in March 1832 began his attendance at Neckar Hospital during an epidemic of Asiatic cholera. For his services during this plague he was publicly thanked by the director of the hospital. Returning to North Carolina in 1832, he continued his practice and became identified with political affairs as editor and part owner of the *Western Carolinian,* a Nullification paper.

In 1837, Ashbel Smith went to Texas and was made surgeon-general of the new republic. He was one of the commissioners to negotiate a treaty with the Comanches in 1838 and was minister to England and France, 1842–44. In 1843, he made known to his government certain plans of the British and Foreign Anti-Slavery Society for the abolition of slavery in Texas and in the Southern states (Garrison, *post,* vol. II, pt. 2, pp. 1098–1103, 1116–19). These facts he also communicated to the Texan minister at Washington, who placed them in the hands of Calhoun and other Southern leaders. On the basis of the evidence thus revealed, President Tyler, in 1844, offered annexation to Texas in the form of a treaty, which was rejected by the Whig Senate. Texas desired to secure annexation if possible by honorable means, and if not, to secure peace and permanent independence. To the latter end, Ashbel Smith, appointed secretary of state by President Anson Jones [*q.v.*] in February 1845, negotiated with Mexico the Smith-Cuevas Treaty by which that nation acknowledged the independence of its former province. Tyler, meanwhile, signed on Mar. 1, 1845, the joint resolution offering annexation to Texas. The issue now rested with the people of Texas, who voted overwhelmingly in favor of annexation. A torrent of abuse swept upon Smith because of the Smith-Cuevas Treaty and twice he was burned in effigy.

After a brief period of service in the Mexican War, Smith retired to his plantation. In 1848, he was appointed on the board of visitors to West Point. As a member of the legislature in 1855, he sponsored legislation aiding railroad construction within the state, the common schools, and the payment of the public debt. During the Civil War he served as captain of the Bayland Guards and as lieutenant-colonel and colonel of the 2nd Texas Volunteer Infantry. He was cited for gallantry at Shiloh and at Vicksburg. As brevet brigadier-general he commanded the forces at the head of Matagorda Peninsula which saved the rich coast counties from invasion, and later was placed in command of the defenses of Galveston. When the war closed he was one of the commissioners sent to New Orleans to surrender the district.

Smith was elected to the Texas legislature in 1866 and again in 1878. Regarded as a leader in all movements for the advancement of education in the state, he was president of the board of trustees of the Galveston Medical School and was one of the commissioners to locate the Agricultural and Mechanical College for colored youths. As president of the board of regents in 1881, he undertook the chief labor of organizing the University of Texas, endeavoring to get the best men that could be induced to go to Texas in order that the institution might start with an established reputation for scholarship. After his entrance into political life, he practised his profession for the most part only in times of emergency, such as the epidemics of yellow fever in Houston and Galveston. He was the author of several scientific and historical treatises: *The Cholera Spasmodica as Observed in Paris in 1832* (1832); *An Account of the Yellow Fever which Appeared in the City of Galveston, 1839* (1839); and *Reminiscences of the Texas Republic* (1876). He died, unmarried, at "Evergreen," his plantation home, and was buried in the State Cemetery at Austin.

[J. D. Lynch, "Life and Character of Ashbel Smith," *Daniel's Texas Medic. Jour.,* Apr. 1886; A. G. Clopton, *An Eulogy on the Life and Character of Dr. Ashbel Smith* (1886); *Obit. Record Grads. Yale Univ. . . . 1880–90* (1890); E. D. Adams, *British Diplomatic Correspondence Concerning the Republic of Texas, 1838–1846* (1917); G. P. Garrison, "Diplomatic Correspondence of the Republic of Texas," *Ann. Report Am. Hist. Asso.* for 1907 and 1908 (3 vols., 1908–11); Anson Jones, *Letters Relating to the History of Annexation* (1848; 1852) and *Memoranda and Official Correspondence of Texas* (1859); E. D. Adams, *British Interests and Activities in Texas, 1838–46* (1910); J. H. Smith, *The Annexation of Texas* (1911); "The Service of Texan Troops in the Armies of the Southern Confederacy," in D. G. Wooten, *A Comprehensive Hist. of Texas* (1898), vol. II; J. J. Lane, *Hist. of the Univ. of Texas* (1891); *Western Carolinian* (Salisbury, N. C.), 1826–36; *Journal of Commerce* (New York), 1845; *Telegraph and Texas Register* (Houston), 1839–46; *Houston Telegraph,* 1860–69; *Houston Daily Post,* 1881–86; *Galveston News,* 1875–86; *Austin Statesman,* 1884–86; Ashbel Smith Papers, and O. M. Roberts Papers in the Univ. of Texas Lib.; W. D. Miller Papers and Official Records of the Republic and State of Texas in the Texas State Lib.]   H. Sm—r.

SMITH, AZARIAH (Feb. 16, 1817–June 3, 1851), medical missionary, first cousin of Judson Smith [*q.v.*], was born at Manlius, Onondaga County, N. Y., where his father, Azariah, was proprietor of a cotton-spinning factory. His mother, Zilpah, was a daughter of David Mack of Middlefield, Hampshire County, Mass. After studying at local schools, Smith attended Yale College and graduated in 1837. During a memorable revival at the College in March 1835 he decided to become a medical missionary and thenceforth devoted himself to preparation for this work. From September 1837 to May 1839 he attended the Geneva Medical College at Geneva, N. Y., then spent several months at a dispensary and hospital in Philadelphia, and in the autumn of 1839 returned to Yale for a final year in medicine (M.D. 1840) and for theological training. While studying in the Divinity School, from which he graduated in 1842, he also attended lectures on law, astronomy, and meteorology, besides finding time to write for the *American Journal of Science and Arts* an article on "Electricity in Machinery" (April–June 1840, pp. 134–36), based on observation in his father's factory.

On Aug. 30, 1842, he was ordained by the Presbytery of Onondaga at Manlius, and on Nov. 19 sailed from Boston for Constantinople, as a missionary of the American Board of Commissioners for Foreign Missions. From the first his work was primarily among the Gregorian Armenian and Nestorian Christians, and from 1843 to 1845 he traveled extensively throughout Asiatic Turkey, preaching and practising medicine in Trebizond, Brusa, Smyrna, and many interior cities, including Mosul. In 1844 he visited the pioneer Assyriological excavations of Botta and described them in an article, "Ruins of Nineveh," in the *American Journal of Science and Arts,* April–June 1845. In 1845 he settled in Erzurum, where in the following year an Armenian mob plundered his house and seized a Gregorian priest with Protestant leanings who had sought refuge there. John Porter Brown [q.v.] of the American legation in Constantinople was sent with a Turkish commissioner to investigate the incident and obtained for Smith a payment for damages and a formal apology from the Gregorian Patriarch.

In 1847 Smith was transferred to Aintab, and in the following spring returned to America to marry, on July 6, his first cousin, Corinth Sarah Elder of Cortlandville, N. Y. Accompanied by his wife, he immediately returned to Aintab, where he devoted himself and his small private fortune to such missionary activities as preaching, writing tracts, and practising medicine. One of his last accomplishments was the organization under the Ottoman law of a civil community for the Protestant Armenians of Aintab. On a journey in the spring of 1851 to Arabkir, Malatya, and Diyarbekir, where he founded a Protestant church, he contracted typhoid fever, of which he died shortly after his return to Aintab.

Always a careful student and the possessor of an immense fund of general information, Smith excelled as a writer and organizer rather than as a linguist and evangelist. His continuing interest in science is attested by "Abstract of Thermometrical Records Kept at the Missionary Stations of the American Board of Commissioners for Foreign Missions in Western Asia" (*American Journal of Science and Arts,* July 1846), which comments on records kept by a number of mission stations. The present mission hospital at Aintab is a memorial to him and bears his name.

[*Record of the Class of 1837 in Yale Univ.* (7th ed., 1887); F. B. Dexter, *Biog. Notices Grads. Yale Coll.* (1913); *Eighth Gen. Cat. of the Yale Divinity School* (1922); G. S. S. Martin, *Mack Geneal.* (1903); many long letters from Smith, in the *Missionary Herald, passim;* brief biography, *Ibid.,* Jan. 1852.]

W. L. W., Jr.

SMITH, BENJAMIN ELI (Feb. 7, 1857–Feb. 24, 1913), editor, was born at Beirut, Syria, the posthumous son of Eli Smith [q.v.] by his third wife, Hetty Simpkins (Butler) Smith, a native of Northampton, Mass. After the birth of her son Mrs. Smith returned home and established herself at Amherst as keeper of a boarding-house. Smith attended the local high school and graduated in 1877 from Amherst College. Julius Hawley Seelye [q.v.] evidently thought well of his pupil, for he engaged him to prepare a revised, extended edition (1880) of his translation of Albrecht Schwegler's *A History of Philosophy in Epitome.* Smith remained at Amherst as a postgraduate student, 1877–78, and as instructor in mathematics, 1878–80, and then went to Germany for a year of university study. After spending a term at Göttingen, as was still all but obligatory for Americans, he went to Leipzig to hear Wilhelm Wundt. He was an assistant in philosophy in the Johns Hopkins University for another year before joining, in 1882, the staff of *The Century Dictionary and Cyclopedia,* which was then organizing under the supervision of William Dwight Whitney [q.v.]. His original appointment he probably owed to his family connection with Roswell Smith [q.v.] of the Century Company, but he soon discovered an extraordinary aptitude for the work, and to it the rest of his life was devoted. Credit for the plan and scope of the *Dictionary,* and for the high standard of scholarship set for it, belongs primarily to Whitney, but as managing editor Smith had direct charge of the endless details involved in the preparation, revision, and publication of the *Dictionary,* which began to appear in 1889. He also had a large share in the work of defining terms, an undertaking for which he was well qualified by his wide knowledge, logical habits of thought, and command of a clear, terse English. On Whitney's death in 1894 he succeeded him as editor-in-chief. He had charge of *The Century Cyclopedia of Names* (copyright 1894), *The Century Atlas* (1897), the *Century Dictionary* supplement (2 vols., 1909), and the successive issues of the *Dictionary,* culminating in a thorough revision of the *Dictionary,* the *Cyclopedia of Names,* and the *Atlas* in twelve volumes in 1911. As recreation from this strenuous and illimitable task, he edited a series of pocket-size volumes of wisdom literature: a translation of Cicero's *De Amicitia* (1897); Franklin's *Poor Richard's Almanack* (1898); *Selections from the Meditations of Marcus Aurelius* (1899); *Epictetus: Selections from His Discourses* (1900); and *Selections from the Thoughts of Pascal* (1902). Smith was married Oct. 13, 1883, to Cora (Shelton) Cheesman, daughter of George Wellington Shelton of Derby, Conn., who with one daughter survived him. He made his home in New Rochelle, N. Y., and took an active part in civic affairs as a member of the board of education and of the public library board. Years of intense work on the *Dictionary* resulted in a breakdown of his health in 1911; a fatal disease of the kidneys developed; and he died at his home in New Rochelle at the beginning of his fifty-seventh year.

[*Who's Who in America,* 1912–13; *Obit. Record of Grads. of Amherst Coll.* (1913); *Amherst Coll. Biog. Record ... 1821–1921* (1927); obituary in *N. Y. Times,* Feb. 25, 1913.]   G. H. G.

SMITH, BENJAMIN MOSBY (June 30, 1811–Mar. 14, 1893), Presbyterian clergyman, educator, was born at "Montrose," Powhatan County, Va., the son of Josiah and Judith Micheau (Mosby) Smith. He was educated by private tutors and at Hampden-Sidney College, from which he graduated with first honors in 1829. For two years he taught in an academy at Milton, N. C., where he organized one of the first educational associations in the South. From 1832 to 1834 he was a student at Union Theological Seminary in Virginia and spent the next two years there as an assistant instructor. In the meantime, Apr. 19, 1834, he was licensed to preach by the West Hanover Presbytery, and on Oct. 19, 1835, he was ordained. After leaving Union Seminary he traveled abroad for two years, chiefly in Prussia, making a special study of Semitic languages.

Returning to America, he held pastorates in Danville, Va. (1838–40), Tinkling Spring and Waynesboro—where he also taught a classical school (1840–45), and at Staunton (1845–54). At the end of this last pastorate he served for a year as secretary of the Presbyterian Board of Publication, in Philadelphia. He then accepted a call to Union Theological Seminary, at Hampden-Sidney, Va., as professor of Oriental literature, which position he occupied until 1889, when he became professor emeritus. He has been called with some justification the second founder

of the seminary, for during the Civil War the school's endowment was largely destroyed and the rapid recovery of the institution and its subsequent prosperity was due to him more than to any other single individual. For sixteen years (1858–74) he was co-pastor with Robert L. Dabney [*q.v.*] of the college church. In 1876 he was elected moderator of the General Assembly of the Southern Presbyterian Church (Presbyterian Church in the United States).

Smith also rendered a large service to puolic education in Virginia, of which he was one of the earliest and most active advocates. In 1839 his thoroughgoing report on the Prussian primary school system, which he had studied at first hand, was submitted by Governor Campbell to the Virginia House of Delegates (Document 26, *Journal of the House of Delegates ... of Virginia,* 1839). This report is recognized as one of the most significant educational documents of the period. With Thomas Ritchie and R. G. Scott, he presented a report on primary schools to the Richmond Educational Convention of December 1841. This report was published the following year in the form of an appeal, "To the People of Virginia" (*Richmond Enquirer,* Nov. 22, 1842). He took an active part in the Educational Association of Virginia (organized 1863), and sought unsuccessfully in 1869 to have it indorse the system of common schools inaugurated by the unpopular Underwood Reconstruction Convention of that year. At the initial meeting of the new board of education (1870), twelve county superintendents were chosen, of whom the first to take the field was Smith. He continued to serve as superintendent of Prince Edward County, in spite of many annoying difficulties, till 1882, when a political revolution in Virginia swept Dr. William H. Ruffner [*q.v.*], state superintendent, and his appointees out of office.

Smith wrote frequently for the papers and for religious and educational journals. A report of his, "The Merits and Defects of Prevailing Schemes of Common School Education in the United States," appeared in *The Educational Journal of Virginia* (August 1870). He published *Family Religion* (1859); *The Poetical Books of the Holy Scriptures* (1867), prepared in cooperation with A. R. Fausset, a reprint in large part from the Jamieson, Fausset, and Brown series of commentaries; and *Questions on the Gospels* (1868). On Oct. 31, 1839, he married Mary Moore Morrison, a daughter of Rev. James Morrison of New Providence. Five daughters and one son survived him.

242

[Autobiog. fragment covering the years 1811–32 and a diary in possession of a daughter, Mrs. A. J. McKelway; published sermons and addresses in library of Union Theological Sem. in Va., and in library of Presbyterian Foundation at Montreat, N. C.; *Union Sem. Mag.,* V (1893–94), 73–84; *Minutes of the Synod of Va.,* 1893, pp. 266–68; minutes of board of trustees of Washington and Lee Univ., Jan. 19, 1894; *Gen. Cat. of Union Theological Sem. in Va.,* 1807–1924 (1924); W. A. Maddox, *The Free School Idea in Va. before the Civil War* (1918); R. L. Morton, *Hist. of Va.,* vol. III (1924).]

E. T. T.

SMITH, BUCKINGHAM (Oct. 31, 1810– Jan. 5, 1871), lawyer, politician, antiquarian, was born on Cumberland Island, Ga., the son of Josiah and Hannah Smith (cousins), of Watertown, Conn. He was christened Thomas Buckingham Smith. His father had moved to East Florida during the British occupation, and after the cession of Florida to the United States, went to Mexico on business, leaving his wife, Buckingham, and a daughter, in St. Augustine, where Buckingham received his early education. He visited his father in Mexico when he was about fourteen years of age after the latter had been appointed United States consul in Mexico. At the death of the elder Smith in 1825, Buckingham became the ward of his uncle, Robert Smith, and was placed in Washington (later Trinity) College in Hartford, Conn., where he remained three years. In 1836 he was graduated from the Harvard Law School and then spent some time in the law office of Judge Fessenden of Portland, Me. On his return to St. Augustine, he practised law for a time and in 1839–40, acted as secretary to Gov. Raymond Reid. He was a member of the Florida territorial legislature in 1841, serving one term. On Sept. 18, 1843, he was married to Julia G. Gardner of Concord, N. H.

Through the influence of Senator Jackson Morton, he was appointed secretary of legation in Mexico on Sept. 9, 1850, and served until February 1852. On June 5, 1855, through the influence of William Pitt Fessenden [*q.v.*], he was appointed secretary of legation in Spain, where he formed a lasting friendship with the great Americanist, Pascual de Gayangos, and other influential men of letters. He continued the archival research begun in Mexico, with special reference to the history of Florida, and aided various American historians, including Sparks, Bancroft, and Parkman. He was recalled in 1858 and returned to St. Augustine two years later. Although a slave owner, he sided with the North during the Civil War, and in May 1864 was a delegate to the Democratic convention held in Baltimore, Md. Shortly afterwards he went again to Spain to make further investigations in the archives and to select improved stocks for his orange grove. He returned to Florida in 1868 and was appointed tax commissioner. In 1870–71, he resided in New York City, but the northern climate did not agree with him and it is said that he contracted tuberculosis. On Jan. 4, he suffered a stroke near his home and never regained consciousness. A policeman, thinking him intoxicated, locked him in a cell at the police station. In the morning he was taken to Bellevue Hospital, where he died. His body was removed to the morgue and was about to be buried in the potter's field when it was identified by an acquaintance. He was buried at St. Augustine.

He bequeathed his valuable papers to the New York Historical Society, and his library was purchased for the Society by John David Wolfe. He left his property to be administered for the negroes of St. Augustine by the Buckingham Smith Benevolent Association. He was a large portly man, somewhat overbearing in his manner, but his opinions were highly regarded by his friends. An Americanist of note, he stimulated study in the early history of Florida and nearby regions. His writings and books are many and varied, ranging from studies of the Everglades of Florida, and the expedition of Verrazano, to Indian linguistics, and a geographical description of Sonora (the first publication in its original or any language of a Spanish document of the eighteenth century). In 1852 he supplied extracts translated from three unpublished Spanish journals to the third volume of the monumental work on the American Indian by Henry Rowe Schoolcraft [*q.v.*]. His most important publications were: *The Narrative of Alvar Nuñez Cabeça de Vaca* (1851), translated from the Spanish with a revised translation in 1871 and published after his death by Henry C. Murphy, and the *Narratives of the Career of Hernando de Soto in the Conquest of Florida, as told by a Knight of Elvas,* translated from the Portuguese, first published as a whole in 1866. This translation was republished in two volumes under the editorship of E. G. Bourne in 1922. A de luxe edition of the de Vaca narrative based on the 1871 edition of Smith's translation was privately printed in 1929. Of considerable importance also are his *Letter of Hernando de Soto and Memoir of Hernando de Escalante Fontaneda* (privately printed, 1854), and his *Colección de Varios Documentos para la Historia de la Florida y Tierras adyacentes* (1857). With his Elvas he published also the memoir by Luis Fernandez de Biedma (written about 1544) and other materials. A number of his books were published in small editions under the patronage of George W. Riggs, Jr., of Washington, D. C.

[J. G. Shea, Introduction to the 1871 edition of the narrative of Alvar Nuñez Cabeza de Vaca; R. H. Rerick, *Memoirs of Florida* (1902), vol. I (to be used with caution); *A Jour. of the Proc. of the Legislative Council of the Territory of Fla. at its Nineteenth Session* (1841); various items in contemporary newspapers of Florida, especially the *St. Augustine Examiner*; manuscript notes received from J. C. Yonge of Pensacola, Fla.; letter from A. J. Wall, librarian, New York Historical Society; letter written in 1823 by Andrew Anderson of Florida (in the possession of Mr. Yonge); some letters and other MSS. in Lib. of Cong.; *N. Y. Times*, Jan. 9, 1871.] J. A. R.

SMITH, BYRON CALDWELL (Aug. 28, 1849–May 4, 1877), philologist, was born at Island Creek, Jefferson County, Ohio, the eldest child of George P. and Margaret (Caldwell) Smith. He was of German descent on his father's side and of Scotch-Irish on his mother's. His father was colonel of the 129th Illinois Volunteers at the outset of the Civil War and later was proprietor of newspapers in various towns in Illinois and Kansas. Byron entered Illinois College at Jacksonville, Ill., as a preparatory student in 1863 and remained in residence until 1868. His father's means permitting, he then went to Germany, intending to study Greek philology, philosophy, and other subjects for six years and to take the degree of Ph.D. as the preliminary to an academic career. He studied at Heidelberg, Berlin, and Munich, lived for a short period in Vienna, and finally spent six months at Athens. His plans were disrupted by the death of his only sister, and in the spring of 1872 he returned to the United States and joined his parents at Humboldt, Kan. The next autumn he was appointed instructor in Greek at the recently founded University of Kansas. He was a brilliantly successful teacher and was advanced the next year to the rank of professor. Meanwhile he became engaged to Kate Stephens, who was one of his pupils. In the winter of 1874 he went to Philadelphia to be treated for an ailment there diagnosed as renal neuralgia. Regaining his health, but losing his position at the University, he joined the editorial staff of the Philadelphia *Press* and devoted his leisure to the study of economics. He developed tuberculosis after an attack of pneumonia and died, in his twenty-eighth year, at Boulder, Colo., where he had gone in hope of benefiting by the mountain air. He was buried at Humboldt.

His friends mourned him as an heir of unfulfilled renown, and his scholarly attainments and gracious personality have become something of a legend. Two collections of his letters have been published: *A Young Scholar's Letters: Being a Memoir of Byron Caldwell Smith* (1897), edited by D. O. Kellogg, consists of the letters written to his parents from Europe; his letters to his fiancée were first published as *The Professor's Love-Life: Letters by Ronsby Maldclewith* (1919), with various alterations in the text, and were republished, without the alterations, as *The Love-Life of Byron Caldwell Smith* (1930). At the University of Kansas he showed some kindness to Frank Harris (1855?–1931), who praised him extravagantly and maligned him obscenely.

[Besides the published letters, see A. I. Tobin and Elmer Gertz, *Frank Harris: A Study in Black and White* (1931); Hugh Kingsmill Lunn, *Frank Harris* (1932); Kate Stephens, *Lies and Libels of Frank Harris* (1929), ed. by Gerrit and Mary Caldwell Smith. Dean R. L. Lacey of Illinois College has supplied some additional information.] G. H. G.

SMITH, CALEB BLOOD (Apr. 16, 1808–Jan. 7, 1864), lawyer, congressman, cabinet officer, was born in Boston, Mass., but when six years old was taken by his parents to Cincinnati, Ohio. He was enrolled as a student at the College of Cincinnati, 1823–25, and at Miami University, 1825–26, but did not graduate. Commencing the study of law in Cincinnati, he soon removed to Connersville, Ind., where he continued his law studies in the office of Oliver H. Smith [*q.v.*]. He was admitted to the bar, and commenced practice in the fall of 1828. His eloquence before juries contributed no little to his advancement in his profession.

Entering politics, he was an unsuccessful candidate for a seat in the Indiana House of Representatives in 1831, but the following year he purchased an interest in the *Political Clarion*, changed its name to the *Indiana Sentinel*, used it as a medium for the publication of his Whig policies, and was elected. He was reëlected each year until 1837 and was again elected in 1840. In the sessions of 1835–36 and 1836–37 he was speaker of the House and in 1840–41, chairman of the committee on canals. During his legislative career he was one of those who took the lead in procuring an order for the survey, by the federal government, of routes in Indiana for canals and railroads, and in otherwise promoting projects for internal improvements. When those projects were more or less wrecked by the panic of 1837, Smith was appointed a commissioner to collect assets and adjust debts. He accepted and served, but not without a temporary loss of popularity. In a triangular election in 1840 he was defeated as a candidate for a seat in Congress, but he won in a clear field in 1842, was reëlected in 1844, and again in 1846. In the Twenty-ninth Congress (1845–47) he was a member of the committee on foreign affairs, and in the Thirtieth (1847–49), chairman of the committee on the Territories. At a Whig caucus preceding the opening of the Thirtieth Congress he was proposed for nomination as speaker of the House, but failed of nomination by fifteen votes. His first speech in the House was made Feb. 8, 1844, in favor of excluding from membership the men who, in four states, had been elected by general ticket. He participated in debates on the Oregon question, the independent treasury bill, slavery in the Territories and the District of Columbia, the tariff, and the Dorr rebellion, but his principal efforts were directed against the annexation of Texas and the war with Mexico. He supported Taylor in the presidential campaign of 1848, and was proposed for the position cf postmaster general in Taylor's cabinet, but was given, instead, a seat on the board of commissioners to adjust claims against Mexico, serving in that capacity until 1851, when he removed to Cincinnati and resumed the practice of law. Three years later he was made president of the Cincinnati & Chicago Railroad Company, which was soon in financial difficulties, and in 1859 he removed to Indianapolis, Ind.

Smith was one of the leaders of the Indiana delegation to the Republican National Convention in Chicago in 1860, and when, in behalf of that delegation, he had seconded the nomination of Lincoln, the convention broke into its greatest demonstration. In the campaign that followed, he was one of the most effective speakers, especially in Indiana, a doubtful state. In recognition of his services or in fulfillment of a promise, Lincoln appointed him Secretary of the Interior, but when failing health would no longer permit his administration of that office, the President accepted his resignation, December 1862, and immediately appointed him judge of the United States district court for Indiana. A little more than a year later he was fatally stricken while in the court house in Indianapolis, and died the same day. On July 8, 1831, he married Elizabeth B. Walton, daughter of William Walton, a pioneer from Ohio; they had three children.

[L. J. Bailey, "Caleb Blood Smith," in *Ind. Mag. of Hist.*, Sept. 1933; Charles Roll, "Indiana's Part in the Nomination of Abraham Lincoln for President," *Ibid.*, Mar. 1929; G. J. Clarke, "The Burnt District," *Ibid.*, June 1931; *Biog. and Geneal. Hist. of Wayne, Fayette, Union and Franklin Counties, Ind.* (1899), vol. I; C. W. Taylor, *Biog. Sketches and Review of the Bench and Bar of Ind.* (1895); *Biog. Dir. Am. Cong.* (1928); *Am. Whig Rev.*, Dec. 1850; *Indianapolis Daily Jour.*, Jan. 9, 1864; Caleb Blood Smith Papers (8 vols.), MSS. Div., Lib. of Cong.]   N. D. M.

SMITH, CHARLES ALPHONSO (May 28, 1864–June 13, 1924), educator and author, was born at Greensboro, N. C., the son of the Rev. Jacob Henry Smith, Presbyterian minister, and his second wife, Mary Kelly (Watson) Smith,

both Virginians. His father's family, though of German ancestry, had been in Virginia for several generations, and Jacob Smith had been educated at Washington College (later Washington and Lee University, of which another of his sons afterwards became president). In the Greensboro public schools Smith was prepared for Davidson College (Davidson, N. C.), and meanwhile became a friend of the Greensboro drug clerk, William Sydney Porter [*q.v.*], better known as O. Henry. From Davidson he received the degrees of A.B., 1884, and A.M., 1887. After four years of teaching in three little North Carolina towns, he went to Johns Hopkins in 1889 and in 1893 received the degree of Ph.D., his dissertation being on *The Order of Words in Anglo-Saxon Prose* (1893). At Louisiana State University, 1893–1902, his gifts as lecturer and teacher clearly emerged. Two small books, *Repetition and Parallelism in English Verse* (1894) and *An Old English Grammar* (1896), with various articles, represent the literary and scholarly output of these years. In 1902 he became a professor in the University of North Carolina and soon after first dean of its graduate department. Here he founded and edited *Studies in Philology*, published by the university, to encourage graduate scholarship. He married, Nov. 8, 1905, Susie McGee Heck, of Raleigh; they had two daughters and a son. During these years he produced a series of grammars for school use, a thin volume of *Studies in English Syntax* (1906), *An English-German Conversation Book* (1902), with Dr. Gustav Krüger, and performed editorial work for the *Library of Southern Literature* (17 vols., 1907–23).

A superb raconteur and a very able and stimulating lecturer, he reached the fullness of his power and popularity as first Edgar Allan Poe Professor of English in the University of Virginia, 1909–17. On leave of absence for 1910–11, he served as Roosevelt Professor of American History and Institutions at the University of Berlin, lecturing on American literature in German and conducting a seminar on Poe. Back in Virginia, he was not merely the genial professor. He lectured widely; he wrote his most characteristic and widely circulated little book, *What Can Literature Do for Me?* (1913), and his most ambitious literary work, the *O. Henry Biography* (1916); and he founded in 1913 the Virginia Folk-Lore Society, which under his enthusiastic leadership brought together an exceedingly rich collection of genuine folk ballads, published after his death under the editorship of A. K. Davis, Jr., as *Traditional Ballads of Virginia* (1929). This ballad quest has been termed "the activity for which in the long run he may be best remembered" (Barr, *post*, p. 10). In 1917 he left Virginia to become head of the English department at the United States Naval Academy at Annapolis, Md. There he employed his gifts as expounder and interpreter of literature in winning future naval officers to the love of letters. He also continued his editorial and literary activities. In 1924, suffering a comparatively sudden illness, he died at Annapolis, survived by his wife and children, and was buried in Greensboro. His *Southern Literary Studies* (1927) was published after his death under the devoted anonymous editorship of his widow (d. Apr. 24, 1933). He was a member of the Modern Language Association and of the American Dialect Society. His eminence was not primarily that of the critical scholar; though he illuminated many fields and greatly stimulated graduate study in the South, the very diversity of his interests limited his achievement in pure scholarship. He was essentially the apostle of letters and, in the better sense, the popularizer of literature. The basis of his power lay in the fact that he was a delightful human being and that a sure psychological instinct enabled him to communicate his enthusiasms vividly. In the words of his memorial tablet at Annapolis, truer than most, "He gave back as rain what he received as mist."

[C. A. Smith, *Southern Lit. Studies* (1927), contains bibliog. and biog. study by F. S. Barr. See also *Who's Who in America*, 1924–25; Archibald Henderson, in *Greensboro Daily News*, Nov. 20, 1927; J. C. Metcalf, in *Va. Jour. of Educ.*, Feb. 1925; J. E. Routh, in *Alumni Bull. Univ. of Va.*, Apr. 1911; bibliog., *Ibid.*, Apr. 1924; Susie M. H. Smith, *The Love that Never Failed* (1928); A. K. Davis, Jr., intro. to *Traditional Ballads of Va.* (1929); Julian Street, *Am. Adventures* (1917), pp. 165–68; K. P. Battle, *Hist. of the Univ. of N. C.*, vol. II (1912); P. A. Bruce, *Hist. of the Univ. of Va.*, *1819–1919*, vol. V (1922); obituary in *Greensboro Daily News*, June 14, 1924. A large collection of letters and newspaper clippings is in the possession of Smith's daughter, Mrs. L. Dee York, Charlottesville, Va.]   A. K. D., Jr.

SMITH, CHARLES EMORY (Feb. 18, 1842–Jan. 19, 1908), journalist, diplomat, postmaster-general, was a son of Emory Boutelle and Arvilla Topliff (Royce) Smith, representatives of old New England families. He was born at Mansfield, Conn., but when he was seven years old his father, a manufacturer of silk, moved to Albany, N. Y. Charles attended the public schools and Albany Academy, from which he was graduated at the age of sixteen. While still in school he began his journalistic career by writing for the *Albany Evening Transcript*. In 1859 he entered Union College as a junior, graduating in 1861. His college years were chiefly noteworthy for his leadership in student jour-

nalism and in an organization formed to promote the success of the Republican party in the election of 1860. At the beginning of the Civil War he became military secretary to Brigadier-General John F. Rathbone, assisting him in the administration of the recruit depot at Albany and later was in the office of the adjutant-general. Toward the end of 1862, he resigned and became an instructor in Albany Academy, at the same time contributing two columns of editorials daily to the *Albany Express*, the staff of which he joined in 1865. Five years later he became associate editor of the *Albany Evening Journal*, the leading Republican newspaper of up-state New York, and in 1874, editor. During the next six years he wrote nearly all the state Republican platforms and in 1876, most of the national platform. In 1879 he was elected a member of the board of regents of the University of the State of New York.

He was called to Philadelphia in 1880 to become editor of the Philadelphia *Press*, which had declined considerably in circulation and influence after the retirement of John W. Forney [*q.v.*]. Chiefly by his own efforts he reëstablished it within four years as the leading Republican newspaper of the city and the state. The editorial page, written from his wide acquaintance with men and affairs, presented clear interpretations of the course of public events. Toward local matters his attitude was progressive; but he was generally conservative in his discussions of national questions. He advocated the nomination and election of Blaine in 1884 and stressed the benefits of the protective tariff, the gold standard, and other favorite measures of the Eastern Republicans.

The position of the *Press*, combined with first-rate skill in estimating the movement of public opinion and in political management, gave him an important influence in state and national affairs. For two years, beginning Feb. 14, 1890, he was minister to Russia, and won popularity both there and in the United States by his distribution of American relief funds to famine sufferers. In 1898 President McKinley appointed him postmaster-general in order, it was supposed, that he might have his advice on the political problems of the Spanish-American War period. According to one of his colleagues, he contributed to the cabinet counsels "generous and progressive views on all political questions" (John D. Long, *The New American Navy*, 1903, II, 146). In the management of his department he was active in preventing the use of the mails by vendors of quack remedies and worthless securities, and for fraudulent purposes generally.

He greatly extended and popularized the rural free delivery service, with which the previous administration had experimented. Though admitting its expensiveness, he justified it as a means of promoting good roads, enhancing farm values, and making rural life less isolated and more attractive. He supported the efforts of a subordinate to stamp out corruption in the postal service which his department had established in Cuba. Unfortunately, some irregularities of long standing in the service at home were allowed to continue and become a serious problem for his successor.

During his absence in Washington his business interests suffered and he resigned in 1901 to give them his full attention. In person he was described as a man of medium height and slender build with a round face and piercing black eyes. He won a considerable reputation as an effective and accomplished public speaker. He was married first, June 30, 1863, to Ella Huntley; after her death he was married, Oct. 3, 1907, to Nettie Nichols. He died in Philadelphia.

[*Leslie's Hist. of the Republican Party* (n.d.); *The New International Year Book . . . 1908* (1909); *Who's Who in America*, 1908–09; Charles Morris, *Makers of Phila.* (1894); S. W. Pennypacker, *The Autobiog. of a Pennsylvanian* (1918); J. T. Scharf and Thompson Westcott, *Hist. of Phila.* (1884), vol. III; *Press* (Phila.), *N. Y. Times*, Jan. 20, 1908.]   E. C. S.

SMITH, CHARLES FERGUSON (Apr. 24, 1807–Apr. 25, 1862), soldier, was born in Philadelphia, Pa., the son of Samuel Blair Smith, surgeon in the United States Army, and Mary (Ferguson) Smith. He was admitted to the United States Military Academy as a cadet, July 1, 1820, and was graduated and appointed second lieutenant, 2nd Artillery, July 1, 1825. After four years of garrison service he returned to the Military Academy as an instructor in 1829, and remained there for more than thirteen years as instructor of infantry tactics, adjutant, and finally commander of cadets. It was there, under Sylvanus Thayer [*q.v.*], that the qualities of discipline and precision, and the martial bearing and spirit that so distinguished his later career were developed and fixed. He was promoted first lieutenant in 1832 and captain in 1838. He was married, Mar. 24, 1840, to Fanny Mactier of Philadelphia. After 1842 he served at Fort Columbus, Governors Island, N. Y., and the arsenal at Frankford, Pa., until 1845, when impending war with Mexico called him to duty with Gen. Zachary Taylor's army in Texas. In command of a battalion of artillery serving as infantry he participated in the battles of Palo Alto and Resaca de la Palma, Tex., and was brevetted major for gallant conduct in those battles, May

9, 1846. With the same "red-legged infantry" at Monterey he stormed the works on Loma Federacion, a key position commanding the city. For this action he was brevetted lieutenant-colonel, Sept. 23, 1846. Transferred to Gen. Winfield Scott's army in command of an independent battalion composed of two artillery and two infantry companies, which became known as Smith's Light Infantry, he took prominent part in all the operations of that army from the siege of Vera Cruz to the capture and occupation of Mexico city. For gallant and meritorious conduct at Contreras and Churubusco he received his third brevet, that of colonel, Aug. 20, 1847.

From 1849 to 1855, in addition to garrison duties, he served on important boards dealing with the training and administration of the army. Promoted major, 1st Artillery, Nov. 25, 1854, and lieutenant-colonel, 10th Infantry, Mar. 3, 1855, in 1856 he led an expedition to the Red River of the North. The next year he served in the Utah expedition, and was in command of the Department of Utah, 1860–61. At the outbreak of the Civil War, after temporary service in Washington, he was appointed brigadier-general of volunteers (and colonel, regular army) and assigned to command the District of Western Kentucky. He commanded the 2nd Division of Grant's army in the operations against Fort Henry, Tenn., Fort Heiman, Ky., and Fort Donelson, Tenn. At a critical stage of the battle at Fort Donelson he personally led an assault against the Confederate outworks and secured a position within the defenses, the immediate cause of the surrender of the garrison. For this he was promoted major-general of volunteers, Mar. 21, 1862. He was placed in command of the expedition up the Tennessee River, but an injury resulting from an accident developed into an illness that caused his death at Savannah, Tenn., a month later. He was survived by his wife and three children.

[G. W. Cullum, *Biog. Reg. . . . Officers and Grads. U. S. Mil. Acad.* (1891), vol. I; J. H. Smith, *The War with Mexico* (2 vols., 1919); *War of the Rebellion: Official Records (Army)*; *Battles and Leaders of the Civil War*, vol. I (1887); unpublished records of the War Dept., 1845–62; records of U. S. Pension Office, for name of wife and date of marriage; J. H. Wilson, *Under the Old Flag* (1912), vol. II, for remarks about Smith attributed to Sherman and Grant; obituaries in *Phila. Inquirer*, *Pub. Ledger* (Phila.), and *Daily Nat. Intelligencer* (Washington, D. C.), Apr. 28, 1862.]   T. F. M.

SMITH, CHARLES FORSTER (June 30, 1852–Aug. 3, 1931), professor of Greek and classical philology, born in that part of Abbeville County which is now Greenwood County, S. C., came of fine colonial stock. His father, James Francis Smith, was a Methodist clergyman; his mother, Juliana Forster, was the daughter of a distinguished preacher and educator of the same denomination. His grandfather, John Smith, was a wealthy planter and merchant of the Abbeville section, to which region his father, William Smith, had emigrated from Virginia about 1790.

Fifth of eleven children, of whom the youngest, James Perrin Smith [q.v.], became a well-known professor of geology, Charles Forster was reared in a cultured home, attended the neighboring schools described in his *Reminiscences and Sketches,* and entered Wofford College at the age of sixteen. There he came under the inspiring influence of President James H. Carlisle, "the best man I have ever known and most potent human influence in my life" (Dedication of *Reminiscences and Sketches*). Receiving the degree of A.B. in 1872, he taught at Greenwood, S. C., until January 1874, then had a semester at Harvard University and a year at Leipzig, returning in 1875 to teach classics and German at Wofford. In 1879 he had saved money enough to go back to Leipzig with his bride, Anna L. Du Pré of Spartanburg, S. C., and in 1881 he obtained the degree of Ph.D., offering as his dissertation *A Study of Plutarch's Life of Artaxerxes, with Especial Reference to the Sources,* published (1881) in English at Leipzig.

After a year as assistant professor of Latin and Greek at Williams College, he went in 1882 to Vanderbilt University, Nashville, Tenn., as professor of modern languages, taking the chair of Greek the following year. His sound scholarship and stimulating influence on his students brought reputation as a teacher, and he was a leader in the intellectual life of the city. He formed lasting friendships, and, in later years, looked back on this period as the happiest in his life. In 1893 his wife died, leaving him with five small children. The next year he accepted the chairmanship of the Department of Greek and Classical Philology at the University of Wisconsin. Becoming professor emeritus in 1917, he regretfully relinquished active teaching, for he believed profoundly in the dynamic effect of the personality of the teacher and was eager to fire young minds with his own enthusiasm. The declining interest in the classics and their omission from the list of required studies caused him bitter regret, and he voiced his opinions with outspoken frankness.

He was president of the American Philological Association in 1902–03, and associate editor of *Classical Philology* from its founding in 1906 until his death. Although retired, he was, by exception, appointed annual professor for 1920–21 at the American School of Classical Studies in Athens. His leisure was employed in completing his accurate and very readable translation of Thucydides for the Loeb Classical Library, and his biography, *Charles Kendall Adams* (1924), for the University of Wisconsin. Besides editions of college texts (Thucydides, Bks. III, VI, VII, Xenophon's *Anabasis,* Herodotus, Bk. VII) and contributions to classical journals, marked by thoroughness and learning, he published many essays on various subjects in other periodicals, especially studies of favorite authors or great personalities; some of these were collected in the volume *Reminiscences and Sketches* (1908). In them appear his love of poetry, his fondness for the mountains, where he liked to tramp, his appreciation of character and personality, and his strong attachment to his friends. His style was decidedly personal and subjective. A citation from the introduction by President E. A. Birge to a volume of studies published in his honor by his colleagues, in 1919, fittingly portrays him: "We recognize in him one who lives among us the life of letters, who has made literature—not only Greek but all great literature—a vital influence for us as well as for his students."

He died at the home of a daughter in Racine, Wis. During his last years he was working on an unfinished book on the Old South, of which he was an excellent representative.

[*Who's Who in America,* 1930–31; *Classical Studies in Honor of Charles Forster Smith* (1919, Univ. of Wis. Studies in Lang. and Lit.); R. G. Thwaites, *The Univ. of Wis.* (1900); family records; faculty minutes of Univ. of Wis.; personal acquaintance of more than forty years.]   C. D. Z.

SMITH, CHARLES HENRY (June 15, 1826–Aug. 24, 1903), journalist, humorist, known as Bill Arp, was born at Lawrenceville, Ga., the son of Asahel Reid Smith, a native of Vermont, and Caroline Ann (Maguire) Smith, whose father had emigrated from Dublin, Ireland, and settled in Georgia. He attended a manual labor school, clerked in his father's store, and at nineteen entered Franklin College (later the University of Georgia). In 1848 his father's illness forced him to return home and manage his father's store. In the following year he married Mary Octavia Hutchins, daughter of Judge Nathan L. Hutchins, of Lawrenceville. After a brief study of law he was admitted to the bar. Moving to Rome, Ga., in 1851, he formed a partnership with John W. H. Underwood. He enlisted in the Confederate Army in 1861, served on the staffs of Gen. Francis S. Bartow and Gen. George Thomas Anderson [q.v.], and in 1864 became judge advocate at Macon. In the early years of the war there appeared in the *Southern*

Confederacy (Rome, 1861–62) four letters, addressed to "Mr. Abe Linkhorn" and signed "Bill Arp," written in the illiterate dialect employed by many early American humorists. Bill Arp—the name was that of a local wag—was first portrayed as a sympathizer with the North (*Bill Arp: From the Uncivil War to Date,* 1903), but the later sketches dropped the rôle of Yankee sympathizer and transformed Bill Arp into the uneducated but wise, humorous rustic philosopher. Dialect was gradually used less and less, and Bill Arp became more like his creator in his language, thoughts, feelings, and experiences. The popular reception accorded these letters encouraged Smith later to devote most of his time to writing. For over twenty-five years he contributed to the *Atlanta Constitution* weekly letters, which were reprinted in *Home and Farm* (Louisville, Ky.), the *Sunny South* (Atlanta), and other papers. These were a blend of humor, genial but forceful satire, and common-sense philosophy. After the war he formed a law partnership with Joel Branham, served as state senator, 1865 and 1866, acted as mayor of Rome, 1868–69, and for a time edited the *Rome Commercial.* Meanwhile he published *Bill Arp, So Called* (1866) and a little later *Bill Arp's Peace Papers* (1873), collections of the weekly letters in the *Constitution.* About 1877, giving up the practice of law, he moved to "Fontainebleau," his farm near Cartersville, Ga. Eleven years later he moved into Cartersville, where he spent the rest of his life in study and writing. His later books were *Bill Arp's Scrap Book* (1884), *The Farm and Fireside* (1891), and *Bill Arp: From the Uncivil War to Date* (1903). He also wrote *A School History of Georgia* (1893). He died at his home in Cartersville after an emergency operation following an illness of several weeks. He was survived by his wife and ten of his thirteen children.

He was a man both witty and tolerant, and his lovable personality appears plainly in his writings. Through lecture tours he widened his circle of friends and won for himself the title of "the best loved man in all the Southland"; the *Savannah Press* once said of him, "In the dark days he kept southern hearts from breaking" (quoted in *Atlanta Constitution,* Aug. 28, 1903). For many reasons his writings continue to be interesting. His handling of the negro and the Georgia cracker dialects is trustworthy and accurate. His war-time sketches are valuable for the facts presented and for the insight they give into Southern attitudes and sentiments. The outspoken courage and the vigor of his satire are blended with good-humored tolerance. "I joined

the army and succeeded in killing about as many of them as they of me," he once remarked (*Scrap Book,* p. 378). At times he shows a remarkable gift for narration and for character delineation, as in "Uncle Tom Barker" in *The Uncivil War.* His opinions on woman's suffrage, the graduated income tax, the one-crop system of farming, and the negro question are still worthy of consideration.

[*Who's Who in America,* 1903–05; C. H. Smith, *Bill Arp: From the Uncivil War to Date* (1903) and *Bill Arp's Scrap Book* (1884); Marian C. Smith, *I Remember* (privately printed, 1931), and biog. sketch in memorial ed. of *Bill Arp: From the Uncivil War* (1903); L. L. Knight, *A Standard Hist. of Ga. and Georgians* (1917), vol. III, pp. 1416–20 and 1761; G. H. Aubrey, in *Men of Mark in Ga.* (1911), vol. III, ed. by W. J. Northen; *Atlanta Constitution,* Aug. 25–28, 1903; obituary in *N. Y. Tribune,* Aug. 30, 1903; family papers.]
J. M. S., Jr.

SMITH, CHARLES HENRY (Nov. 1, 1827–July 17, 1902), soldier, the son of Aaron and Sally (Gile) Smith, was born in Hollis, Me. He was graduated from Waterville (now Colby) College at Waterville, Me., in 1856, and three years later received the A.M. degree from that institution. From 1856 to 1860 he was principal of the high school at Eastport, Me., and studied law there. When the Civil War broke out he volunteered and became a captain in the 1st Maine Cavalry. His regiment was assigned to the Army of the Potomac early in 1862, and during that year he fought on a reconnaissance to Front Royal, Va., in the battle of Cedar Mountain, and in the second battle of Bull Run. From September 1862 to January 1863 he was provost-marshal at Frederick, Md., remaining thereafter on almost continuous duty with the cavalry of the Army of the Potomac. He was rapidly promoted in 1863 through the grades of major and lieutenant-colonel to colonel. During this year he commanded the 1st Maine Cavalry on Stoneman's raid into Virginia, in the Gettysburg campaign where he was cited for distinguished conduct, and in the Mine Run campaign.

The year 1864 was an active one for the cavalry; skirmishes, reconnaissances, raids, and long marches were the order of the day. Two horses were shot from under him at St. Mary's Church, Va., on June 24, 1864, and Smith was himself shot through the thigh early in the afternoon, but he did not relinquish command of his regiment until the day was over. For his heroism on this occasion he was brevetted brigadier-general of volunteers, and was awarded the Congressional medal of honor in 1895. He commanded a cavalry brigade through most of the Richmond campaign from August to December 1864 and again received special mention for distinguished service. In 1865 he fought through the Appomattox campaign to the end of the war and won renown at Sailor's Creek, Va., on Apr. 6, for a bold attack with his brigade against the flank of a retreating Confederate column. He was mustered out of the army on Aug. 11, 1865, returned to Machias in his native state, was admitted to the bar, practised law, and in 1866 became a state senator. On July 28, 1866, he accepted the appointment of colonel of the 28th Infantry in the regular army. He served at various posts in Missouri, Louisiana, Colorado, and Texas until Nov. 1, 1891, when he retired from active duty and settled in Washington, D. C. He was married to Mary Richards Livermore of Eastport, Me., on July 28, 1864. Besides the brevet rank already mentioned, he was brevetted major-general of volunteers in 1865, brigadier-general in the regular army, 1867, for his action in the battle of Sailor's Creek, and major-general for gallant service during the war. This modest officer fought in sixty-three battles and skirmishes and was three times wounded. He died in Washington, D. C., and was survived by a son and a daughter.

[*Who's Who in America*, 1901–02; W. E. Thwing, *The Livermore Family of America* (1902); *Gen. Cat. of Officers and Grads. of Colby Univ.* (1882); *War of the Rebellion: Official Records (Army)*, see index; F. B. Heitman, *Hist. Reg. and Dict., U. S. Army* (1903); *Men of Progress . . . State of Me.* (1897); *Army and Navy Reg.*, July 19, 1902; *Washington Post*, July 18, 20, 1902.]   S. J. H.

SMITH, CHARLES PERRIN (Jan. 5, 1819–Jan. 27, 1883), New Jersey politician, editor, genealogist, was born in Philadelphia. His father was George Wishart Smith, of distinguished Virginia ancestry, and his mother, Hannah Carpenter (Ellet) of Salem County, N. J. The former died shortly after Charles was born and the child was taken by his mother to her home in Salem. Here, in the common schools, he received a rudimentary education, richly supplemented later by his own efforts. At the age of fifteen he entered the printing office of the *Freeman's Banner,* where he learned the practical work of newspaper publishing. In 1840, having reached his majority and inherited some property, he bought the *Banner* and renamed it the *National Standard.* This paper he edited for eleven years in the interests of the Whig party. Later, he also edited the *Harrisonian,* a campaign periodical. In 1843 he married Hester A. Driver of Caroline County, Md. He held several local offices, was active in advocating the construction of a railway in West Jersey for the development of that section of the state, and was interested in improving the life-saving stations on the Jersey coast, toward which

end he was instrumental in securing action by Congress. In 1851 he retired permanently from regular newspaper work and thenceforth devoted his time to travel, political activities, and literary and antiquarian pursuits.

Elected to the state Senate from Salem County in 1855, he served two years, and then was appointed clerk of the supreme court of New Jersey, which office he held for three terms of five years each, meanwhile making his home in Trenton. His political activities during this period were strenuous and, according to his own estimate, important. In 1856 he was appointed a member of the National American state committee and also the same year was a delegate to the Fusion Convention and a member of the committee to select permanent officers. He nominated William L. Dayton [*q.v.*] as president of the convention and secured his election, thus bringing him into national prominence and so preparing the way for his subsequent nomination by the Republican party for the vice-presidency of the United States. In 1859 Smith was appointed a member of the "Opposition" state executive committee and was successively reappointed for ten years with the exception of one year, when he declined the position. For part of the time he was chairman, and he was active in securing the election as governor of Charles S. Olden [*q.v.*]. He was opposed to the candidacy of William H. Seward for the presidency in 1860 and through his efforts induced the state convention to indorse Dayton with a view to blocking Seward's nomination at the national convention, by withholding the New Jersey vote until it could be thrown to a more eligible candidate. During the Civil War period he was active in bringing New Jersey into line with the policies of the Federal government. He advocated the nomination of General Grant for president in 1867 and arranged for a great mass meeting in Trenton, at which Grant was enthusiastically indorsed.

Retiring from office in 1872, Smith continued to live in Trenton until his death eleven years later, devoting much of his time to travel and writing. He prepared "The Personal Reminiscences of Charles Perrin Smith, 1857–1875," a large folio volume in manuscript, which was given to the New Jersey state library after his death by his daughter, Elizabeth A. Smith. This work includes his autobiography, with full genealogical records of his ancestry, and comments on political events in the state and nation with which he was actively concerned or personally familiar. Based apparently upon a carefully kept diary, it is notable for its accuracy, urbanity, and fair-mindedness. Besides narratives of his travels, political writings, and speeches, his publications include *Lineage of the Lloyd and Carpenter Family* (1870, 1873), privately printed; and *Memoranda of a Visit to the Site of Mathraval Castle, Powys Castle, Valle Crucis Abbey, Pilar of Elisig, with a Genealogical Chart of the Descent of Thomas Lloyd* (1875). He died at Trenton, N. J., survived by his wife and two daughters.

[*Report of the Proceedings of the Numismatic and Antiquarian Society of Phila. for . . . 1883* (1884); Thomas Cushing and C. E. Sheppard, *Hist. of the Counties of Gloucester, Salem, and Cumberland, N. J.* (1883); E. M. Woodward and J. F. Hageman, *Hist. of Burlington and Mercer Counties, N. J.* (1883); C. M. Knapp, *N. J. Politics During the Period of the Civil War and Reconstruction* (1924); Hamilton Schuyler, *A Hist. of St. Michael's Church, Trenton . . . 1703 to 1926* (1926); *Daily True American*, Jan. 29, 1883.]
H. Sc—r.

SMITH, CHARLES SHALER (Jan. 16, 1836–Dec. 19, 1886), bridge engineer, was born in Pittsburgh, Pa., the son of Frederick Rose and Mary Anne (Shaler) Smith. During his childhood his father died; and his mother, when he was sixteen. He attended private schools in Pittsburgh until his mother's death, when his formal education ended. After serving as rodman with a surveying party on the Mine Hill & Schuylkill Haven Railroad in 1852, and subsequently with a railroad survey in the mining regions of Lake Superior, he was made assistant engineer under George McLeod, chief engineer of the Louisville & Nashville Railroad, in 1855. The next year he became resident engineer on the Memphis branch of the Louisville & Nashville, and in 1857, he was transferred from the field to the office as assistant to Albert Fink [*q.v.*], engineer of bridges and buildings for the line. This early association had an important effect in shaping Smith's career. In 1859, he was placed in charge of track and bridge construction for the Memphis division, but he left shortly to become chief engineer of bridges and buildings for the Wilmington, Charlotte & Rutherford Railroad in North Carolina. Here he remained until the outbreak of the Civil War, when he entered the Confederate army as captain of engineers, serving with distinction throughout the conflict. One of his outstanding achievements was the building, in the Augusta district, of a powder mill with a daily capacity of 17,000 pounds—one of the largest ever built up to that time.

Immediately after the war, he built a number of bridges in the South, among them Fink truss spans over the Catawba and Congaree rivers on the Charlotte & South Carolina Railroad. In 1866, he entered partnership with Benjamin H. and Charles H. Latrobe [*qq.v.*] under the style

Smith, Latrobe & Company, soon changed to Baltimore Bridge Company. Smith was the bridge expert of the firm, which built a number of the most important structures in the country. Among these were a series of iron trestles on the Louisville, Cincinnati & Lexington and the Elizabethtown & Paducah railroads, the first metal viaducts of modern type to be built; a large bridge over the Missouri River at St. Charles, Mo.; one over the Kentucky River at Dixville, Ky.; one over the Mississippi River at Minneapolis for the Chicago, Milwaukee & St. Paul Railroad; and one over the St. Lawrence River at the Lachine Rapids (near Montreal) for the Canadian Pacific Railway. In addition, Smith served as consultant to James Buchanan Eads [*q.v.*] on the great St. Louis arch bridge, and as consulting engineer in an advisory capacity on difficult bridge problems for nearly every important Western railroad.

The Kentucky River bridge, built for the Cincinnati Southern Railway in 1876–77, was probably his greatest engineering achievement. At the point of crossing, the river was over twelve hundred feet wide, running through a canyon 275 feet deep and subject to tremendous freshets, during which a rise of as much as forty feet in one day had been recorded. Smith's plan originally contemplated spanning the three main openings of 375 feet each by a fully continuous Whipple truss, but in deference to the opinion of L. F. G. Bouscaren, chief engineer of the Cincinnati Southern, the plan was modified to the extent of providing hinges in the outside spans, thus transforming the structure into a cantilever bridge. Cantilever construction on this scale had at the time no precedent anywhere in the world, and by most engineers was viewed with profound suspicion, so that Smith (who assumed the duties of contractor as well as designer) staked both his professional reputation and his fortune on the venture. Carried through to completion strictly according to plans, without the use of falsework in the cantilever spans, and without serious mishap, it was a technical achievement second to none of its time, and the cantilever soon was widely adopted and became the dominant type for long-span construction.

Smith began preparing plans for the Lachine Bridge in 1880, using a deck truss over two side spans of 270 feet and through trusses over the two 408-foot central spans. The transition from deck to through truss was achieved by graceful lines which gave the structure an unusually beautiful appearance. It was erected largely without falsework by the cantilever method and was designed to function as a cantilever under dead load and as a full continuous truss under live load. The actual construction of this bridge was begun about the time Smith was stricken with his fatal illness, but he retained direction of the work until the critical stages were past. It was completed a few months after his death, and remained for many years the only continuous bridge of importance in America. Later (1917) this type of design was revived and became widely adopted.

Smith died in his early prime, accepted as the foremost bridge engineer in America and one of the greatest of the century. This judgment rested less upon the number of great bridges he had built (brilliant as this record was) than upon the boldness and originality of the ideas he introduced. Though his comparatively brief professional life was too crowded to allow much time for writing, he prepared a short treatise, *Comparative Analysis of the Fink, Murphy, Bollman, & Triangular Trusses* (1865), and contributed several important papers to the *Transactions of the American Society of Civil Engineers,* including "Draw-Spans and Their Turn-Tables" (vol. III, 1874), "Proportions of Eye-bar Heads and Pins, as Determined by Experiment" (vol. VI, 1877), and "Wind Pressure upon Bridges" (vol. X, 1881).

Smith moved to Missouri in 1868 to supervise the construction of the St. Charles Bridge, and upon its completion in 1871 established his home in St. Louis, where he resided until his death. He was married on May 23, 1865, to Mary Gordon Gairdner, of Augusta, Ga., who with several children survived him. He possessed a nobility of character matching his intellectual gifts. His courtesy, his utter frankness and honesty, his generosity in all matters, won him the complete loyalty of all who served with him (or for him) in any capacity.

[*Proc. Am. Soc. Civil Engineers,* vol. XIII (1887); J. A. L. Waddell, *Bridge Engineering* (1916), vols. I, II; J. B. Johnson, C. W. Bryan, and F. E. Turneaure, *The Theory and Practice of Modern Framed Structures* (augmented ed., 1904); *Railroad Gazette,* Dec. 31, 1886; *St. Louis Globe-Democrat,* Dec. 20, 1886.]
J. I. P.

SMITH, CHARLES SPRAGUE (Apr. 27, 1853–Mar. 30, 1910), educator, was born at Andover, Mass., the son of Charles and Caroline Louisa (Sprague) Smith. His childhood and youth were precocious. He graduated from Phillips Academy, being valedictorian and class poet, at the age of fifteen, but delayed his entrance to college for two years. In 1874 he received the degree of bachelor of arts from Amherst College. Going abroad in 1875, he spent five years in the study of languages and literature: first at the University of Berlin, where he delivered a "Centenary Poem" at a gathering of American students and residents, then at the Sorbonne; later at various institutions in Italy and Spain; and finally at Oxford University, from which he received a certificate stating that "No one of his years had accomplished as much as he in his chosen field of language and literature."

In 1880 he returned to the United States to become an instructor at Columbia, where he gave the first course in Icelandic ever offered in an American university. In the same year he was raised to the Gebhard professorship of German, a position which he retained for eleven years. On Nov. 11, 1884, he was married to Isabella Jane, daughter of Benjamin Woodbridge Dwight [q.v.] of Clinton, N. Y. After resigning from Columbia in 1891, he continued to lecture there occasionally, as well as at Harvard and elsewhere, but he was more and more impressed with the inadequacy of the American educational system in so far as the cultural development of the masses was concerned. In 1895 he organized the Comparative Literature Society in an effort to maintain and integrate the different racial cultures of immigrants to the United States. A more important undertaking was his founding, in 1897, of the People's Institute, at Cooper Union, an institution established by Peter Cooper [q.v.] in 1857–59 for the education of the working classes but until Smith's time never effectively organized to that end. Smith succeeded in making the People's Institute a community center which exercised great influence, by its example, on like movements in other places, while in New York City itself it was the parent of many similar local enterprises. Lecture courses were offered, and work in music and drama; the Cooper Union Forum, the People's Church, the People's Lobby, and the Wage Workers' Social Club were established within the Institute.

Although keenly alive to questions of social justice, Smith was humanitarian rather than socialistic in his outlook. He was a fervent patriot and intensely religious in an unorthodox manner, being considerably affected by Hindu literature. He considered that the United States possessed a divine cosmic mission to realize the gospel of liberty and fraternity. Idealistic and romantic, he exerted an influence based more upon generosity and sweetness of character than upon intellectual power. He published *Barbizon Days* (1902), the record of a summer in the Forest of Fontainebleau with sketches of Millet, Corot, and others; *Working with the People* (1904), an account of the People's Institute;

and *Poems* (1908), a collection of mediocre verse mostly written in earlier years. In addition to his work at the People's Institute, in 1908 he organized the Ethical Social League and served on the Wall Street Commission to investigate the stock exchange, and in 1909 organized the National Board of Censorship of Motion Pictures, acting as its executive chairman until his death in the following year.

[R. S. Fletcher and M. A. Young, *Amherst Coll. Biog. Record* (1927); *Civic Jour.*, Apr. 30, 1910; *Who's Who in America*, 1908–09; J. A. Riis, "The People's Institute of N. Y.," *Century Mag.*, Apr. 1910; John Collier, "The People's Institute," *Independent*, May 30, 1912; records of the People's Institute, through the courtesy of Everett Dean Martin, director.]
E. S. B.

SMITH, CHAUNCEY (Jan. 11, 1819–Apr. 5, 1895), lawyer, was born at Waitsfield, Vt., the son of Ithamar and Ruth (Barnard) Smith, and a descendant of Samuel Smith who emigrated to Wethersfield, Conn., in 1634. While Chauncey attended the village school and, for a time, an academy at Gouverneur, N. Y., working and teaching to pay his expenses, it was the daily life on his father's farm that supplied the chief factor in his early development. After two years at the University of Vermont, 1845–47, he left college to study law in the office of Henry Levenworth in Burlington. He was admitted to the bar in 1848, and soon thereafter in Boston formed a partnership with Samuel W. Bates, which continued for many years. On Dec. 10, 1856, he married Caroline E. Marshall of Cambridge. They had three children, and lived for many years at 121 Brattle Street, Cambridge, adjoining the home of the poet Longfellow. During the 1850's Smith edited *English Reports in Law and Equity* (40 vols., 1851–58), the first thirty volumes in collaboration with E. H. Bennett; these reports covered the period 1850–57. Smith also edited, with Samuel W. Bates, *Cases Relating to the Law of Railways, Decided in the Supreme Court of the United States and in the Several States* (2 vols., 1854–56), and compiled *Digest of the Decisions of the Courts of England, Contained in the English Law and Equity Reports* (1857); and in 1853 he prepared an American edition of James Stamford Caldwell's *Treatise of the Law of Arbitration*. During the Civil War he held a confidential position with the War Department, acting as counsel to the provost marshal in Washington. After the war he returned to his practice in Boston.

His most eminent service was as one of the lawyers of the Bell Telephone Company and its successors in the great telephone litigation of 1878 to 1896. In 1877 he had approved as counsel the policy of Gardiner G. Hubbard [*q.v.*] to rent telephones instead of selling them and to issue all licenses subject to that condition. This policy was an essential factor in the development of the Bell System. The telephone litigation comprehended four groups of legal proceedings. Practically though not technically a part of it were the telephone interferences (1878–89), cases to determine whether the two telephone patents issued to Alexander Graham Bell in 1876 and 1877 interfered with the patent rights of certain other claimants. Smith and his associate James J. Storrow [*q.v.*] took an active part as counsel in these cases and all were decided in favor of the Bell patents.

The telephone litigation itself consisted of about 600 cases in the United States courts. The first of these stands in a class by itself. This was *Bell Telephone Company* vs. *Peter A. Dowd,* the so-called Western Union Case. Smith and James J. Storrow were the counsel for the company, which, on Sept. 12, 1878, sued Dowd, the agent of a telephone subsidiary of the Western Union Telegraph Company, for infringement. That company contended that Bell had simply invented an instrument and that the instruments invented by Elisha Gray, Amos E. Dolbear, and Thomas A. Edison, which it was using, were not infringements of the Bell patents. As the evidence was put in, George Gifford, the chief counsel for the Western Union, became convinced that the Bell patents were valid and that they covered any use of electricity in the transmission of speech. He so advised his clients, and Smith and Gifford spent most of the summer of 1879 negotiating a settlement, with the result that on Nov. 10, 1879, the court approved an agreement by which the field of electrical communications was divided between the two companies, each undertaking not to encroach on the field of the other.

There soon sprang up a great many infringing telephone companies, whose chief purpose was to break or circumvent the Bell patents. It became a matter of unavoidable routine to sue every one of these companies. The resulting tangled network of litigation finally reached the United States Supreme Court in the form of five cases, which were considered together and decided in favor of the Bell Company on Mar. 19, 1888 (*The Telephone Cases*, 126 *U. S.,* 1). These cases demanded of Smith and Storrow the utmost skill in meeting the devious technicalities of the opposing attorneys, and here Smith's penetration, forensic ability, and caustic wit had full play. In a fourth group of cases the infringing companies, beginning in 1885, assumed the offensive and attacked the telephone company in a series of suits, culminating in the so-called Government Case, *United States of America* vs. *American Bell Telephone Company et al.,* to annul the Bell patents. This dragged through the courts until, in 1896, the managing counsel for the infringers died, and the case was abandoned.

For Smith and his associates the long contest had been a triumphant but also a life-draining struggle. In his latter years recurrent attacks of rheumatism frequently prostrated him, and before the litigation had ended, he himself died in a heart attack at his home in Cambridge. Smith was of heavy build, nearly six feet tall, square-shouldered, round-headed, and square-jawed. He wore his heavy hair cut round and long like an old-fashioned wig. His expression was belligerent but the frequent twinkle in his blue eyes gave assurance of a very kindly disposition and sense of humor. He was actively interested in civil service reform and in a lower tariff. His attitude toward industry and science amounted to reverence. He advanced considerable sums of money to inventors to enable them to work out their ideas, frequently declining to accept repayments of these loans even when himself financially embarrassed. It was his conviction, in his own words, that "the inventor is the chief agent in the progress of the world."

[M. B. Jones, *Hist. of the Town of Waitsfield, Vt., 1782–1908* (1909); autobiographical fragment by Chauncey Smith (MS.) and Julia M. Caverno, "Reminiscences of my Uncle" (MS.), in the Chauncey Smith Collection, Am. Telephone Hist. Library, N. Y. City; C. H. Swan, "Narrative Hist. of the Litigation on the Telephone Patents, 1878–1896" (MS. 1903), in the same library; *Boston Journal,* Apr. 6, 1895; *Boston Transcript,* Apr. 6, 1895; information as to certain facts from the family.]   W. C. L.

SMITH, DANIEL (Oct. 29, 1748–June 16, 1818), soldier, Tennessee official, was born in Stafford County, Va., the son of Henry and Sarah (Crosby) Smith. He received his education at the College of William and Mary, and became a surveyor. On June 20, 1773, he was married to Sarah Michie of the Eastern Shore of Maryland. After his marriage he settled in Augusta County, Va., on the Clinch River at Fort Christian, and received an appointment as a deputy surveyor in 1773. In 1774 he fought as company commander at the battle of Point Pleasant and in other engagements with the Indians. On Jan. 20, 1775, he signed the Fincastle County Resolutions, protesting against the oppressions of the British government. In 1777 he aided in the organization of Washington County and became a major in the county militia. In 1779 he and Thomas Walker [*q.v.*] acted as representatives of Virginia who, with Richard Henderson [*q.v.*] and two others from North Carolina, extended the boundary between the two states. This resulted in the establishment of the disputed Walker's Line. Smith advanced rapidly in the Washington County militia, becoming a colonel in 1781. He was appointed sheriff of the county in 1780 and also participated in the battle of King's Mountain. As a surveyor, he acted as attorney for Thomas Walker in the sale of lands.

In 1783 he moved to the Cumberland settlements and settled in what is now Sumner County near the present town of Hendersonville, Tenn. The North Carolina Legislature appointed him a director for laying out the town of Nashville in 1784, and, the next year, trustee of Davidson Academy. In 1787 the North Carolina Assembly made him a commissioner for the new county of Sumner, and in 1788 elected him brigadier-general of the Mero District militia. He was a member of the North Carolina convention which ratified the United States Constitution in 1789. He served as the secretary of the territory southwest of the Ohio under the governorship of William Blount [*q.v.*], and, as acting governor during Blount's absences from the territory, he promoted the interests of the westerners in their conflicts with the Indians. He also made the first map of Tennessee, which was published in 1794 in the *General Atlas for the Present War,* by Mathew Carey [*q.v.*], and wrote *A Short Description of the Tennessee Government* (1793), and a journal of his experiences on the boundary commission. The original manuscript of the journal and the map are in the Draper collection of the Historical Society of Wisconsin. The journal was printed in the *Tennessee Historical Magazine,* March 1915.

In 1796 he was a member of the convention which drew up the first constitution of Tennessee, and, in 1798, he succeeded Andrew Jackson in the United States Senate. Although he served only a short time, he was later returned to that body for a term from 1805 to 1809. In ability, education, and usefulness Smith ranked with the ablest men who moved to the West in this early period. He engaged in business as a planter and distiller, but he always evinced a primary interest in public affairs. He died at his home, "Rock Castle," in Sumner County. He had two children; his daughter married Samuel Donelson and was the mother of Andrew Jackson Donelson [*q.v.*].

[*Biog. Dir. of the Am. Cong.* (1928); J. G. Cisco, *Historic Sumner County* (1909); R. G. Thwaites, L. P. Kellogg, *Doc. Hist. of Dunmore's War* (1905); R. G. Thwaites, *Early Western Travels,* vol. III (1904); L. P. Summers, *Hist. of Southwest Va.* (1903), and *Annals of Southwest Va.* (1909); *Annals of Congress,* 1797–1810; *Colonial and State Records of D. C.,* see index; "Papers of General Daniel Smith," *Am. Hist. Mag.*, July 1901.] C. S. D.

SMITH, DANIEL B. (July 14, 1792–Mar. 29, 1883), pharmacist, philanthropist, educator, was born in Philadelphia, Pa., the son of Benjamin Smith and Deborah (Morris) Smith, and a descendant of Daniel Smith who emigrated from Bramham, Yorkshire, England, to New Jersey in 1691, one of the first of several brothers who settled there. Smith's baptismal certificate gives his name simply as Daniel; he evidently inserted the initial later. When Daniel was about a year old his father died, and his mother moved to Burlington, N. J. There he attended the school conducted by John Griscom [*q.v.*], a distinguished Quaker educator, who had a liking for the sciences. It was his influence, no doubt, that led young Smith to take up pharmacy as a career. After leaving school he returned to Philadelphia and entered the drug store of John Biddle on Market Street between Fourth and Fifth Streets. On the completion of his term of apprenticeship, he was taken into partnership under the firm name of Biddle & Smith. About a year later, in 1819, he opened his own store at the corner of Arch and Sixth Streets. He was married in 1824 to Esther Morton, daughter of John Morton, a merchant of Philadelphia. They had one daughter. In 1828 he took in William Hodgson, Jr., a young English apothecary, as a partner, and the firm thus established remained in existence until 1849, when the property was sold. He was actively associated with the movement that resulted in the establishment of the Philadelphia College of Pharmacy (incorporated, Mar. 30, 1822) and served it as secretary, 1821–27; as vice-president, 1828; as president, 1829–54; and as chairman of the committee on publications. On Mar. 28, 1826, about nine months after he assumed this chairmanship, there was published the first issue of the *Journal of the Philadelphia College of Pharmacy* (later the *American Journal of Pharmacy*), to which he was a liberal contributor of original articles until 1857. Through his position in the college and his contributions to its journal he attained national reputation, and when the pharmacists of the country met in Philadelphia in 1852 to organize the American Pharmaceutical Association he was unanimously chosen to be its first president. His early business life as an apothecary was contemporaneous with an era of great progress in chemistry and pharmacy, and he took a keen interest in the various discoveries made, reading the foreign reports as soon as they became available. His interest in these records of progress was scientific rather than commercial,

and was not limited to the field of pharmacy and chemistry.

Having a strong interest in education and in social problems, he was an originator of the Apprentices' Library, 1820, one of the corporators of the Philadelphia Savings Fund, 1819; of the Historical Society of Pennsylvania, 1826, of which he was the first corresponding secretary, and of the House of Refuge, 1828. He was actively associated with the Franklin Institute. In 1834 he accepted the chair of moral philosophy, English literature, and chemistry at Haverford School (later College), where he taught for twelve years. During this time he prepared and published *The Principles of Chemistry for the Use of Schools, Academies and Colleges* (1837) and numerous lectures on ethics, and the lives and doctrines of the early members of the Society of Friends. He resigned his position at Haverford in 1846 to return to the practice of pharmacy, from which he did not retire fully until 1853. In 1849 he removed to Germantown, Pa., where he lived until his death. One of the most learned and public-spirited pharmacists of his day, he was outstanding for the versatility of his attainments.

[R. M. Smith, *The Burlington Smiths* (1877); *Am. Jour. of Pharmacy*, July 1883; *The First Century of the Phila. Coll. of Pharmacy* (1922); *Proc. of the Am. Pharmaceutical Assoc.*, vol. XXXI (1884); obituary in *Pub. Ledger* (Phila.), Mar. 31, 1883.] A. G. D–M.

SMITH, EDGAR FAHS (May 23, 1854–May 3, 1928), chemist, provost of the University of Pennsylvania, was born in York, Pa., the son of Gibson and Susan (Fahs) Smith, of Dutch and German ancestry. After preparing at York County Academy, he entered Pennsylvania (later Gettysburg) College at Gettysburg, where he received the degree of B.S. in 1874. Here he came under the influence of Samuel Philip Sadtler [*q.v.*], who stimulated his interest in chemistry and encouraged him to complete his education under Friedrich Wöhler at the University of Göttingen, Germany. He received the degree of Ph.D. from Göttingen in 1876 and again in 1926, according to the custom at Göttingen, upon the fiftieth anniversary of his promotion to the doctorate. From 1876 to 1881 he was assistant in analytical chemistry to Prof. Frederick Augustus Genth [*q.v.*] of the University of Pennsylvania. He told charmingly of his experiences during this period in his article on mineral chemistry in "A Half-Century of Chemistry in America, 1876–1926" (*Journal of the American Chemical Society; Golden Jubilee Number*, Aug. 20, 1926). On Apr. 10, 1879, he married Margie A. Gruel of Gettysburg, Pa. He was professor of chemistry at Muhlenberg College, Allentown,

Pa., 1881–83, and at Wittenberg College, Springfield, Ohio, 1883–88. It was during this period that he published *A Text-Book of Inorganic Chemistry* (1883) and *Chemistry of the Carbon Compounds, or Organic Chemistry* (1886), both translations from the German of Victor von Richter, which were used for several decades as textbooks in American colleges.

In 1888 he returned to the University of Pennsylvania to accept the professorship of analytical chemistry, from which Genth had retired; four years later he became head of the department of chemistry. During his years at Pennsylvania he carried on with his pupils a large number of investigations upon methods of electrochemical analyses, in which he was a pioneer, upon atomic weight determinations, compounds of the rarer metals, and complex salts of various inorganic acids. His *Electro-Chemical Analysis* (1890) went through six editions and was translated into several foreign languages. He won wide attention for his work upon molybdenum, and upon tungsten and its compounds; his research on tungsten led to its extensive use in scientific and artistic work. Appointed vice-provost of the university in 1898 and provost in 1911, he carried on a very successful administration; not only were millions of dollars raised, but there was a great quickening of the intellectual and spiritual life of the university. Resigning as provost and teacher in 1920, he devoted the remainder of his life to promoting an interest in the humanistic and cultural aspects of chemistry, which he felt were being neglected in the industrial stress of American civilization. He was influential in establishing the divisions of chemical education and historical chemistry in the American Chemical Society. He wrote numerous biographical sketches of prominent American chemists and amassed a private collection of prints, autograph letters, medallions, rare books, and other memorabilia of prominent chemists that was one of the most extensive ever assembled; endowed by his wife after his death, it is preserved intact as the Edgar Fahs Smith Memorial Collection of the University of Pennsylvania. His writings include thirteen chemical textbooks, five of which were translations, seven volumes and thirty-six brochures upon historical-chemical subjects, and 169 chemical papers. He died of pneumonia in Philadelphia, survived by his wife; there were no children. Among the chemists of his time he was unsurpassed as a conversationalist, lecturer, and public speaker. His genial, affable personality and strong capacity for friendships made him loved in every circle.

He won many distinctions for his scientific and educational work. He was president of the American Chemical Society, 1895, 1921, and 1922; of the American Philosophical Society, 1902–08; and of the History of Science Society at the time of his death. He was a member of the National Academy of Sciences, an officer of the Legion of Honor of France, and an honorary member of the American Chemical Society, the American Electrochemical Society, the Société de Chimie Industrielle de France, and the American Institute of Chemists. He was awarded the Elliott Cresson medal by the Franklin Institute in 1914, the Chandler medal by Columbia University in 1922, and the Priestley medal by the American Chemical Society in 1926. From 1914 to 1920 he was a trustee of the Carnegie Foundation, and from 1917 to 1922 president of the Wistar Institute of Anatomy. He served upon the jury of awards of the Columbian Exposition at Chicago in 1893 and was a member of the United States Assay Commission, 1895 and 1901–05. In 1917 and in 1925 he was a member of the Electoral College, serving as its president in the latter year; in 1919 he was a member of the commission for the revision of the constitution of Pennsylvania, and in 1921 was appointed by Pres. Warren Gamaliel Harding a member of the board of technical advisors to the disarmament conference.

[*Who's Who in America*, 1926–27; *Jour. of Chem. Educ.*, Apr. 1932, a memorial number with bibliog. and photographs; C. A. Browne, in *Ibid.*, June 1928, and in *Isis*, Dec. 1928; W. T. Taggart, in *Science*, July 6, 1928; F. X. Dercom, M. T. Bogert, and J. H. Penniman, in *Memorial Service for Edgar Fahs Smith . . . Dec. 4, 1928*, Univ. of Pa.; obituary in *Pub. Ledger* (Phila.), May 4, 1928; information from Miss Eva V. Armstrong.]   C. A. B.

SMITH, EDMUND KIRBY [See KIRBY-SMITH, EDMUND, 1824–1893].

SMITH, EDMUND MUNROE (Dec. 8, 1854–Apr. 13, 1926), professor of legal history, editor, and writer, nephew of Henry Boynton Smith [*q.v.*], was born in Brooklyn, N. Y., the son of Dr. Horatio Southgate and Susan Dwight (Munroe) Smith. He received the degree of A.B. from Amherst in 1874, and subsequently did graduate work in politics and jurisprudence under Prof. John W. Burgess who was then teaching there. Entering the Columbia Law School, he received the degree of LL.B. in 1877. At the suggestion of Burgess, who had become professor at Columbia, he then began to prepare himself for a proposed chair of Roman law and comparative jurisprudence by going abroad and attending the lectures of Jhering, Bruns, Windscheid, Gneist, and other famous jurists, at the universities of Göttingen, Berlin, and Leipzig.

His manuscript notes (now at Columbia) attest a thorough comprehension of the ancient and modern fields of law which these scholars presented. In 1880 he received the degree of doctor of civil and canon law at Göttingen. From 1880 to 1883 he was instructor, and from 1883 until 1891, adjunct professor, of history and political science at Columbia. On Apr. 17, 1890, he married Gertrude, daughter of Gen. Henry Shippen Huidekoper, of Philadelphia; one daughter of this marriage survived him. The following year he was appointed to the chair for which he had prepared himself, that of Roman law and comparative jurisprudence, and in 1922 he became Bryce Professor of European Legal History, retiring in 1924 as professor emeritus. From its establishment in 1886 he was for many years managing editor of the *Political Science Quarterly*. Among honors that he received were the presidency of the American Political Science Association (1917) and the vice-presidency of the International Academy of Comparative Law (1924).

Munroe Smith will be remembered by his contemporaries as one of the leaders in the development of Columbia from a college to a university, as a guiding spirit in the early years of the *Political Science Quarterly*, and by his students, as an inspiring lecturer; but posterity must look to his written works to evaluate him. His first work of merit was "State Statute and Common Law," which first appeared in the *Political Science Quarterly* (March 1887–March 1888) and was reprinted in *A General View of European Legal History and Other Papers* (1927). It is a severe criticism of codification when applied to the common law system. Another early work of significance comprised a series of articles entitled "Four German Jurists" which also appeared in the *Quarterly* (1895–1901) and was reprinted in *A General View*. It presents a study of the interrelation of the juristic thoughts of his four teachers mentioned above. Smith had studied in Germany at a time when Bismarck towered over Europe; in his *Bismarck and German Unity* (1898, 3rd ed. 1923), which soon became a classic, youthful impressions are substantiated by careful scholarly thought. In fact, Bismarck influenced Smith's later writings, particularly his war books, and it can be said that no American knew Bismarck as well as did Smith. The first years of the twentieth century he devoted to various studies in constitutional law, Roman law, legal education, and jurisprudence generally. Of his writings in these fields, "Customary Law" (*Political Science Quarterly*, June 1903) and "The Japanese Code and the Family" (*Law Quarterly Re-*

view, January 1907), both reprinted in *A General View*, well illustrate his wide scholarly interests. With the outbreak of the World War, he became an anti-German propagandist, and though his writings reflect careful thinking, they are of less scientific value than his earlier works. The volume *Militarism and Statecraft* (1918) incorporates the best of the articles of this period; in addition he compiled *Out of Their Own Mouths* (1917), a collection of statements by Prussian officials and others revealing the principles by which their political activities were governed. After the war Smith perfected his lectures in Columbia Law School, published posthumously as *The Development of European Law* (1928), which with his *A General View of European Legal History* (1927) are among the best treatises upon this subject in English. These works, in which he stresses the homogeneity of European law, place his name among those of the great legal scholars.

[C. M. Fuess, "Edmund Munroe Smith," *Amherst Grads. Quart.,* Nov. 1926; *Obit. Record of Grads. and Non-Grads. of Amherst Coll.,* 1925–26; F. J. Goodnow, Foreword, in *A General View,* etc.; H. F. Stone, "Edmund Munroe Smith," *Actorum Academiae Universalis Iurisprudentiae Comparativae,* vol. I (1928); L. B. Chapman, *Monograph on the Southgate Family of Scarborough, Me.* (1907); J. B. Moore, Foreword, in Smith's *The Development of European Law* (1928); *A Bibliog. of the Faculty of Political Sci. of Columbia Univ., 1880–1930* (1931); *Who's Who in America,* 1926–27; *N. Y. Times,* Apr. 14, 1926.]   A. A. S.

SMITH, ELI (Sept. 13, 1801–Jan. 11, 1857), missionary and Orientalist, was born at Northford, Conn., the son of Polly (Whitney) and Eli Smith, who was a farmer and a manufacturer of tools, shoes, and leather. In 1821 he was graduated from Yale, after which he taught for two years in Georgia. Entering Andover Theological Seminary, he was graduated in 1826 and was ordained in Springfield, May 10, 1826. Several months before graduation, he was appointed by the American Board of Commissioners for Foreign Missions (Congregational) as associate editor of its publishing house at Malta, then the center of all printing operations carried on by the American missionary societies working in the Mediterranean. He arrived in Malta after a two months' journey from New York, which he had left in May. A few months later he left for Syria in order to study Arabic and prepare himself for translating the Bible into Arabic, but after the battle of Navarino in October 1827 he was forced to leave Syria with other American missionaries, and he returned to Malta. In early 1829 he made a tour through Greece, and in March 1830 with Harrison Gray Otis Dwight [q.v.], who had recently arrived from America, he undertook an extended journey of exploration through Asia Minor, Armenia, and Georgia into Persia, from which he returned by way of Constantinople early in 1831. The results of the journey, made with a view to opening mission stations, were published by the two travelers under the title *Researches of the Rev. E. Smith and Rev. H. G. O. Dwight in Armenia: Including a Journey through Asia Minor and into Georgia and Persia, with a Visit to the Nestorian and Chaldean Christians of Oormiah and Salmas* (2 volumes, 1833). In this journey the two missionaries explored much unknown territory and gave an extremely valuable account of conditions in Armenia, about which little was then known to the West. Their description of the poverty and ignorance of the Nestorian Christians led to the establishment of the American mission at Urumiah, one of the most important in the Near East.

Shortly after his return from this journey, Smith went back to America. There he prepared the account of his travels for publication and published a volume of *Missionary Sermons and Addresses* (1833). On July 21, 1833, he married Sarah Lanman Huntington, daughter of Jabez Huntington, who accompanied him to Syria that fall and died at Smyrna in September 1836. In January 1838 at Cairo he joined Edward Robinson, 1794–1863 [q.v.], who had been his teacher at Andover, and accompanied him on his epoch-making explorations in Sinai, Palestine, and southern Syria. Robinson's critical and scholarly training was supplemented by Smith's knowledge of the East and its people, and his thorough familiarity with Arabic; without these Robinson could have accomplished but little. In the fall Smith accompanied his friend to Germany, where he arranged for the casting of fonts of Arabic type for the mission press at Beirut, and then went back to America. In 1841 he returned to Beirut, accompanied by his second wife, Maria Ward Chapin, a daughter of Judge Moses Chapin of Rochester, N. Y., whom he married Mar. 9, 1841, and who died the following year. They had one son. Since his own health was now seriously undermined, he was forced to leave for America again in 1845. About a year later, after his recovery from a dangerous illness, he married his third wife, Hetty Simpkins Butler of Northampton, Mass., on Oct. 23, 1846, and returned with her to Syria in January 1847. They had two daughters and three sons, one of whom, Benjamin Eli Smith [q.v.], was born after his father's death. Smith devoted the last decade of his life to the translation of the Bible into Arabic, for which everything else had been preparatory. He was well equipped for this work both by his wide linguistic training and by his long experience in Arabic presswork. Besides knowing Greek, Latin, and Hebrew, and the principal European languages, he was well acquainted with Turkish and knew Arabic so well that it had become almost a second vernacular to him. In 1856 ill health compelled him to give up his work, and he died of cancer at Beirut the following January.

[S. W. Phoenix, *The Whitney Family of Conn.* (1878), vol. I, pp. 685–88; F. B. Dexter, *Biog. Notices Grads. of Yale Coll.* (1913); Edward Robinson, *Biblical Researches in Palestine, Mount Sinai and Arabia Petraea* (3 vols., 1841); *Am. Congreg. Year-Book,* 1858; obituary in *Missionary Herald,* July 1857.]
W. F. A.

SMITH, ELIAS (June 17, 1769–June 29, 1846), clergyman, associated with the movement that led to the establishment of the Christian Connection, author, editor of the first religious newspaper in the United States, was born in Lyme, Conn., a son of Stephen and Irene (Ransom) Smith. In his fourteenth year the family moved from a Connecticut farm to the much harder conditions of the frontier settlement of South Woodstock, Vt. Elias' meager educational advantages ended with this change, but he was a thoughtful boy and fond of reading. His father was a Baptist, but the mother was a "strict" or "separatist" Congregationalist, a fact which accounted for his being baptized by "sprinkling"—to his lasting resentment—in his eighth year. At the age of eighteen he attended school for a few weeks and then began teaching, which occupation he followed for two years. About this time he experienced a profound religious awakening and, after much mental conflict over the subject of baptism, joined the Baptist Church in 1789. He now devoted himself to the study of the Bible and theology and, though greatly distrustful of his own worthiness and ability, began to preach in 1790. His success was marked and he was ordained by the Baptists as an evangelist at Lee, N. H., in August 1792. On Jan. 7 of the following year he married Mary Burleigh, established his home in Salisbury, N. H., and became a successful itinerant preacher throughout the towns of New Hampshire and Massachusetts. In 1798 he was installed pastor of the Baptist church in Woburn, Mass., but was unhappy in the relations of the settled pastorate, largely because he found no precedent for the installation in the New Testament.

Meanwhile his theological opinions underwent a radical change. He rejected the Calvinistic system held by the Baptists, repudiated the doctrine of the Trinity, and disowned all systems of church order and all denominational names not found in the New Testament. After a brief business venture which failed, he moved to Portsmouth and founded a church acknowledging no creed but the Bible and having no denominational name but Christian. He was unsparing in his criticism of other churches with their settled and tax-supported clergy and their theological systems, which he regarded as having no Biblical foundation. His denunciations, coupled with his strong anti-Federalist political views, created for him a host of enemies who pursued him for many years, and often he narrowly escaped mob violence. In order to reply more effectively to his opponents, he began to write, and his *History of Anti-Christ* (1803? 1811), *The Clergyman's Looking-Glass* (1803), *The Whole World Governed by a Jew* (1805), *A Short Sermon to the Calvinist Baptists of Massachusetts* (1806), only added fuel to the flames. In 1805 he began a quarterly, *The Christian's Magazine, Reviewer and Religious Intelligencer,* which continued for two years. On Sept. 1, 1808, he issued the initial number of the *Herald of Gospel Liberty,* the first weekly religious newspaper in the United States. This organ of the growing Christian fellowship was published in Portsmouth, Portland, and Philadelphia during Smith's residence in these places and was later continued under various names. In 1818 Smith sold the paper, and became a Universalist. He formed a business connection with Dr. Samuel Thomson [*q.v.*] of Boston, originator of the Thomson system of medicine and therapeutics, mastered the system, and soon built up a lucrative practice, establishing, about 1830, a private sanitarium. In 1823 he renounced Universalism, but his restoration to the Christian fellowship was only partial.

In addition to the works already mentioned and several volumes of sermons and hymns, Smith's more important books were: *Twenty-Two Sermons on the Prophesies* (1808); *The New Testament Dictionary* (1812); *The American Physician and Family Assistant* (1832); *The People's Book* (1836). In 1816 he published an autobiography, *The Life, Conversion, Preaching, Travels and Sufferings of Elias Smith.* His first wife died in Philadelphia, Feb. 27, 1814, and in the latter part of the same year he married Rachel, daughter of Samuel Thurber of Providence, R. I. There were a number of children by the first marriage.

[In addition to Smith's autobiog., see J. P. Barrett, *The Centennial of Religious Journalism* (2nd ed., 1908); Charles Burleigh, *The Geneal. of the Burley or Burleigh Family of America* (1880); M. T. Morrill, *A Hist. of the Christian Denomination in America* (1912); E. W. Humphreys, *Memoirs of Deceased Christian Ministers* (1880); F. L. Mott, *A Hist. of*

Am. Mags. (1930); *Portsmouth Jour.* (N. H.), July 11, 1846. A résumé of Smith's teachings from a hostile viewpoint is found in Thomas Andros, *The Scriptures Liable to be Wrested to Men's Own Destruction, and an Instance of this Found, in the Writings of Elias Smith* (1817).]

F. T. P.

SMITH, ELIHU HUBBARD (Sept. 4, 1771–Sept. 19, 1798), physician, author, and editor, was the only son of Dr. Reuben Smith, a Yale graduate and a prominent and public-spirited citizen of Litchfield, Conn., and Abigail (Hubbard) Smith. His American ancestry went back to William Smith, who settled in Wethersfield, Conn., about 1644, and to George Hubbard of Hartford, Conn., born in England in 1601 (Bailey, *post,* p. 11). From a cultured home in a town of unusual intellectual and humanitarian activities he entered Yale in 1782. Only a youth of fifteen, at graduation, he was sent for two years' further study at the academy at Greenfield Hill, Conn., under Dr. Timothy Dwight, the elder [*q.v.*], later president of Yale. At seventeen he had written, among other things, a group of five sonnets that are nearly the earliest extant in American literature. He next returned to Litchfield for two years' medical study with his father, supplemented by attendance on the medical lectures of Dr. Benjamin Rush [*q.v.*] in Philadelphia during the winter and spring of 1790–91. Here he became intimate with Joseph Bringhurst, Jr., and Charles Brockden Brown [*q.v.*], on whose life and work he exerted a continued and helpful influence. With Bringhurst he carried on for several months during 1791 in the *Gazette of the United States* a fanciful verse correspondence modeled on that of Robert Merry and Mrs. Hannah Parkhouse Cowley (Bailey, *post,* pp. 44–50).

As a practising physician at Wethersfield from the fall of 1791 to the spring of 1793, he became associated with the literary group at Hartford, which then comprised Richard Alsop, David Humphreys, and Theodore Dwight, and his fellow physicians Lemuel Hopkins [*qq.v.*] and Mason Fitch Cogswell. To the "Echo" series of satiric skits produced by the group between 1791 and 1800, and published in the *American Mercury* (Hartford), Smith contributed one number, "Extracts from Democracy, an Epic Poem, by Aquiline Nimblechops," and unidentified portions of others. Withdrawing from Wethersfield in the spring of 1793, he spent several happy months at Litchfield in the company of Brockden Brown, who may have assisted him in publishing during the summer the first volume of *American Poems,* the earliest anthology of American poetry. Of its 304 pages, 188 were devoted to the verse of his Connecticut friends, especially John Trumbull (1750–1831), Joel Barlow [*qq.v.*], Dwight, and Humphreys. Several other volumes were projected but never published.

Instead, early in September, he settled as a physician in New York City, and despite his years soon won an enviable professional reputation, strengthened by the publication in 1795 of his *Letters to William Buel on the Fever . . . in New-York in 1795,* in which he contended that the disastrous series of yellow-fever epidemics in Philadelphia and New York was due to crowded and unsanitary living conditions. After 1794 he lived with a fellow bachelor and lover of letters, a young lawyer, William Johnson. Their house, at first on Cedar Street, later on Pine, became the headquarters of the Friendly Club, with William Dunlap, Dr. Samuel Latham Mitchill, Edward and Samuel Miller, 1769–1850, James Kent [*qq.v.*], William Walton Woolson, George Morrison Woolson, and Anthony Bleecker as members. His closest friends, besides Johnson, were Dunlap, the dramatist and theatre manager, and Brockden Brown, whose *Alcuin* he saw through the press in March 1798, with a preface of his own writing. Dunlap staged Smith's *Edwin and Angelina,* originally written as a drama but revised as a ballad opera, at the John Street theatre, Dec. 19, 1796; it had a moderate success and was published by Swords in New York the following year and later republished in London, with a collection of other plays. Smith in turn assisted Dunlap in the publication of *André* (1798) and wrote the address for the opening of the Park Theatre, Jan. 29, 1798. He was also active as a member of the New York Society for Promoting the Manumission of Slaves, a trustee of the colored school in the city, and one of the organizers of the American Mineralogical Society in 1798. With Dr. Mitchill and Dr. Edward Miller he projected the first American medical journal, the *Medical Repository,* and edited it with them from the summer of 1797 to his death, contributing extensively to it himself.

His last literary ventures were his American edition of Erasmus Darwin's *The Botanic Garden* (1798), prefaced with a long verse epistle to Darwin, and a noteworthy series of critical and biographical sketches of contemporary American writers in the *Monthly Magazine* (London), July–October, 1798. With Brown, who became an occupant of his home in the summer of 1798, he was planning a magazine and review to be undertaken in New York. The disastrous yellow fever epidemic of 1798, however, intervened. Smith, already exhausted with con-

scientious attendance upon many patients, took into his household Dr. Joseph B. Scandella, an Italian physician dying with the disease, contracted it himself (as did Brown also), and died on Sept. 19, 1798, about a fortnight after his twenty-seventh birthday. He is described by his contemporaries as a man of lovable character and great talents, and his zeal and enthusiasm for literature, science, and the advancement of humanity knew virtually no limit.

[See Marcia Edgerton Bailey, *A Lesser Hartford Wit, Dr. Elihu Hubbard Smith* (1928), Univ. of Me. Studies, 2 ser., no. 11, with portrait and bibliog.; *Diary of William Dunlap* (3 vols., 1930), N. Y. Hist. Soc. Colls.; William Dunlap, *The Life of Charles Brockden Brown* (2 vols., 1815), and *A Hist. of the Am. Theatre* (1832); biog. sketches in *Medic. Repository,* vol. II (1798), and *Am. Medic. and Philosophical Reg.,* Jan. 1814; F. B. Dexter, *Biog. Sketches Grads. of Yale Coll.,* vol. IV (1907); obituary in *Commercial Advertiser* (N. Y.), Sept. 20, 1798. Some of Smith's letters are in the Yale and Harvard Univ. libraries. For a discussion of *Am. Poems,* see Milton Ellis, "Aaron Stockwell's Book," *Tex. Rev.,* Oct. 1917; for Smith's influence on Brown's work see D. L. Clark, *Charles Brockden Brown, a Crit. Biog.* (1923).]   M. E.

SMITH, ELIZA ROXEY SNOW [See SNOW, ELIZA ROXEY, 1804–1887].

SMITH, ELIZABETH OAKES PRINCE (Aug. 12, 1806–Nov. 15, 1893), author, lecturer, reformer, was born at North Yarmouth, Me., the second daughter of David and Sophia (Blanchard) Prince. On her father's side she was a descendant of John Prince, who was in Watertown, Mass., before 1633; Thomas Prince [*q.v.*], the colonial chronicler of New England, was a member of the same family. Her ancestors on her mother's side were French Huguenots, and her grandfather was a prosperous ship owner in the East India trade. Her early childhood was dominated by strong religious discipline, against which she later rebelled. After her father's death her mother remarried, and in 1814 the family moved to Portland. There, in deference to her mother's wishes, she abandoned her hopes for a higher education and a career as head of a school for girls, and married, Mar. 6, 1823, Seba Smith [*q.v.*], editor of the *Eastern Argus.* Her husband had her admiration and respect, but there is a pathos in her statement that he was "nearly twice my age, wore spectacles," and was very bald." They had five sons. Apropos of her lack of daughters she once said, "Mr. Smith rather prefers boys," but her autobiography reveals that, too well aware of the limitations imposed on women, she was secretly glad not to produce daughters.

During the early years of her marriage she devoted her energies chiefly to her home and young children. When their fortune was lost in the speculation that culminated in the panic of 1837, the family moved in 1839 to Charleston, S. C., where Smith hoped to sell cotton-cleaning machines to planters. The venture failing, they went after a short time to New York, where they lived until 1860. To assist her husband Mrs. Oakes Smith, as she was known, contributed sketches, essays, and poems to such popular periodicals of the day as the *Ladies' Companion,* the *Southern Literary Messenger, Godey's Lady's Book,* and *Graham's American Monthly Magazine.* One Wordsworthian poem, *The Sinless Child* (1843), evoked surprisingly laudatory comment from such critics as Edgar Allan Poe and Rufus Wilmot Griswold [*qq.v.*]. She edited several annuals or Christmas gift books, had two plays produced, and wrote seven novels, in addition to numerous didactic books for children. Four of the novels—*The Western Captive* (1842), *Black Hollow* (1864), *Bald Eagle, or the Last of the Ramapaughs* (1867), and *The Sagamore of Saco* (1868)—show the influence of James Fenimore Cooper [*q.v.*] and probably owed some of their popularity to his fame; her *Bald Eagle* was one of the best sellers in Beadle's dime novel series. Her interest in the supernatural is revealed in *The Salamander, A Legend for Christmas* (1848); *Bertha and Lily* (1854), romantic and sentimental, shows her concern with social, moral, and religious questions, while her sentimental story, *The Newsboy* (1854), seems to have done much to arouse concern in New York over conditions in the slums. A considerable amount of her work appeared under the name Ernest Helfenstein. Some articles on woman's suffrage written for the *New York Tribune* in 1850 led her into lyceum lecturing, 1851–57, at which she was very successful. In 1851 these articles were published, with some of her speeches, as *Woman and Her Needs,* a plea for the recognition of the abilities of women. Her autobiography, part of which has been published as *Selections from the Autobiography of Elizabeth Oakes Smith* (1924), is filled with personal observations and anecdotes of the leading figures of public life before the Civil War. Because of the illness of Seba Smith the family moved about 1860 to Patchogue, Long Island. After his death in 1868, Mrs. Oakes Smith lived much of the time with her eldest son in Hollywood, N. C. In 1877 she became for a year pastor of the Independent Church at Canastota, N. Y. She died in North Carolina and was buried at Patchogue. Her children bore the name Oaksmith, the change having been made legally in their childhood.

[The autobiog. of Elizabeth Oakes Smith is in the manuscript dept. of the N. Y. Pub. Lib., N. Y. City. See Mary A. Wyman, *Selections from the Autobiog. of Elizabeth Oakes Smith* (1924) and *Two Am. Pioneers, Seba Smith and Elizabeth Oakes Smith* (1927) with bibliog.; *Old Times in N. Yarmouth, Me.,* Mar. 1877, Apr. 1879, Jan. 1882; E. A. Poe, in *Godey's Lady's Mag.,* Dec. 1845; R. W. Griswold, *The Female Poets of America* (1848); E. A. and G. L. Duyckinck, *The Cyc. of Am. Lit.* (1855); obituary in *Appleton's Ann. Cyc.,* 1893); editorial in *Daily Eastern Argus* (Portland, Me.), Nov. 21, 1893. The date of death has been supplied by Miss Geraldine Oaksmith, Newport, N. C., grand-daughter of Mrs. Oakes Smith.]
L. M. M.
R. W. B.

SMITH, ERASMUS DARWIN (Oct. 10, 1806–Nov. 11, 1883), jurist, was the son of Hubbard Smith, a physician, and Eunice (Jones) Smith, who moved about 1801 from Rensselaer County to Madison County, N. Y., while it was still part of the frontier. He was born at De Ruyter, N. Y., and obtained his early education in the district schools. At the age of fifteen he began to teach, using his earnings for further schooling. Completing his preparatory studies at Hamilton Academy in three summers, he entered Hamilton College in 1826, but did not remain for graduation. In 1829 he went to Rochester and began studying law in the office of Gregory & Humphrey. The next year he was admitted to the bar, and began practising in partnership with Ebenezer Griffin, whose daughter, Janet Morrison, became in 1831 his first wife.

He held the minor positions of master of chancery, 1832–35; injunction master for the eighth district, 1840; and chancery clerk for that district, 1841–47. The Democratic party nominated him for the Assembly and for Congress but, the districts being strongly Whig, he was defeated. For a short time in 1849 he was the political editor of the Rochester *Daily Advertiser.* In 1855 he was elected justice of the supreme court and served by subsequent reëlections until he was retired on account of age, Jan. 1, 1877. After 1872 he was a general term justice of the fourth department. The state constitution then provided that supreme court justices might be designated to sit on the court of appeals, and Smith was so designated in 1862 and again in 1870. With these exceptions his judicial service was wholly in the inferior courts of the state.

During his tenure of twenty-two years he had an important influence upon the development of the law. His decision in *Clarke* vs. *The City of Rochester* (24 *Barbour,* 446), a case involving many millions in investments, settled the right of cities to subscribe to the stock of railroad corporations after a referendum to the people. In 1863 he upheld the legal tender act as an incident to the war powers of Congress and the right of the national government to preserve its existence (*Hague* vs. *Powers*, 39 *Barbour*, 427). Secretary Chase said that the decision was, in its influence on the credit of the government, equal to a victory in the field (Peck, *post*, p. 680). His best-known decision was in the case of *People* vs. *Albany & Susquehanna R. R.* (55 *Barbour*, 344) in which he settled the main point involved in the "Erie War," a controversy that had menaced the state's police authority and the reputation of its courts.

He had a ready and extensive acquaintance with legal principles and authorities which he supplemented when occasion required by industrious research. The tendency of his decisions was to uphold legislative acts whenever possible. In both law and equity cases he was unsympathetic toward artificial rules. He approached every inquiry in a large spirit. Having arrived at a conclusion, it was his custom to write his opinions with great vigor and positiveness. Sometimes his enthusiasm led him into dicta which the higher courts would not approve. After his retirement from the bench he was frequently employed as a referee. His death followed an apoplectic stroke in his seventy-eighth year. He was survived by his second wife, Emilie Maria (Perkins), widow of Erastus T. Smith, whom he married June 6, 1879, and by several children.

[For sources, see W. F. Peck, *Semi-Centennial Hist. of the City of Rochester* (1884); *Appletons' Ann. Cyc. ... 1883* (1884); *Landmarks of Monroe County, N. Y.* (1895); C. E. Perkins, *The Descendants of Edward Perkins* (1914); *Rochester Post Express*, Nov. 12, 1883; *Rochester Morning Herald*, Nov. 12, 14, 1883. An extended discussion of Smith's decision in the Albany & Susquehanna case may be found in *High Finance in the Sixties* (1929), ed. by F. C. Hicks.]

E. C. S.

SMITH, ERMINNIE ADELLE PLATT, (Apr. 26, 1836–June 9, 1886), geologist, ethnologist, was born at Marcellus, N. Y., the daughter of Joseph Platt. She attended the Troy Female Seminary at Troy, N. Y., and was graduated in 1853. Within a year she was married to Simeon H. Smith, of Jersey City, N. J., and became absorbed in a rigid and exacting domestic routine. Her interest in geology and botany, which she had demonstrated from childhood, did not wane, however, and received new impetus when she took advantage of an opportunity to study geology, mineralogy, crystallography, and other branches of science, while educating her four sons in Germany. She studied crystallography at Strasburg, German language and literature at Heidelberg, and visited and investigated the amber industry on the coast of the Baltic Sea. Mineralogy interested her and she gathered one of the largest collections of her time. She also pursued courses in the famous Bergakademie at Freiberg and was graduated from that institution. Upon her return to the United States she lectured on scientific and cultural subjects and attained a reputation for lucid and eloquent address.

She became interested in the New York Indians of her neighborhood, and was led to study ethnology. In 1880 she received an appointment on the staff of the Bureau of American Ethnology of the Smithsonian Institution, Washington, D. C. The director, John Wesley Powell [*q.v.*], detailed her to study the language, customs, and myths of the Iroquois Indians. She spent two summers among the Tuscaroras in Canada and completed an Iroquois-English dictionary, now with her papers in the archives of the Smithsonian Institution. The Tuscaroras adopted her as a member of the tribe, giving her the name "Beautiful Flower." Her book, *Myths of the Iroquois,* published in the *Second Annual Report of the Bureau of Ethnology* in 1883, was an outgrowth of these studies of tales which she obtained from older informants possessing the fast-fading lore of the tribe. A complete bibliography of her contributions is to be found in J. C. Pilling's *Bibliography of the Iroquoian Languages, Bulletin 6, Bureau of American Ethnology* (1889). In recognition of her attainments she was the first woman to be elected a fellow of the New York Academy of Sciences, and also became a member of the American Association for the Advancement of Science. She held the secretaryship of the section of anthropology at the time of her death. She founded the Aesthetic Society of New Jersey and became the first president. One of the pioneers of the woman's movement, she was very active in promoting the organization of cultural societies and clubs. She was a member of the London Scientific Society, Numismatic and Antiquarian Society of Philadelphia, and others. In 1883 a geological prize was founded in her honor at Vassar College.

[Information from Mrs. Everett Griffith, Forest Glen, Md., and J. N. B. Hewitt, Bureau of Am. Ethnol., Smithsonian Institution, Washington, D. C.; *In Memoriam. Mrs. Erminnie A. Smith, 1837–1886* (privately printed, 1890); *Emma Willard and Her Pupils or Fifty Years of Troy Female Seminary* (1898); *N. Y. Times*, June 10, 1886.]

W. H.

SMITH, ERWIN FRINK (Jan. 21, 1854–Apr. 6, 1927), botanist and bacteriologist, was born at Gilberts Mills, Oswego County, N. Y., the son of R. K. and Louisa (Frink) Smith, and spent his boyhood and young manhood on farms in New York and Michigan. Since he was forced to work his way through both high school and college, it was not until 1886 that he received the degree of B.S. from the University of Michigan, where three years later he received the degree of Sc.D. In 1886 he joined the scientific staff of the United States Department of Agriculture and began the remarkable career that was terminated only by his death. In 1901 he became pathologist in the bureau of plant industry, and in 1902 pathologist in charge of the laboratory of plant pathology, a position he held until 1927. His early work dealt with yellows and other obscure peach diseases, and while he did not solve these problems completely he labored with such thoroughness that little of importance has since been added to the sum of his studies on the subject. Turning to the fungus diseases of other economic plants, he gave attention to the *Fusaria* as plant parasites and carried out fundamental studies on which other workers later based the development of disease-resistant varieties of melons, cotton, cowpeas, potatoes, cabbage, and other crops. He early became interested in what was then the very new field of the bacterial diseases of plants and advanced the theory that bacteria caused plant diseases, an idea that was rejected in scorn by European workers, Alfred Fischer and Robert Hartig in particular. With his usual thoroughness and persistence, however, Smith soon firmly established the truth of his statements and completely silenced his critics.

About 1904 he took up the study of plant tumors and the so-called crown-gall disease. His paper, "A Plant Tumor of Bacterial Origin" (*Science*, Apr. 26, 1907), written in collaboration with C. O. Townsend, established the latter disease as of bacterial origin, and was followed by many publications dealing with the etiology and other phases of the disease. His conviction that there was a striking analogy between crown-gall of plants and cancer of animals was not only accepted by plant pathologists but by the medical profession as well, as was evidenced by his election to the presidency of the American Association for Cancer Research in 1925. His work on plant tumors included studies of formative stimuli, conditions of growth, the mechanism of tumor formation, and problems of histogenesis. In the course of his professional career he contributed to American and foreign scientific journals over a hundred and fifty original papers and many reviews. His outstanding scientific publications are the exhaustive treatise, *Bacteria in Relation to Plant Diseases* (3 vols., 1905–14), of which there were other volumes in preparation at the time of his death; his textbook, *An Introduction to Bacterial Diseases of Plants* (1920);

and the series of crown-gall and cancer papers published in English, French, and German in a wide range of technical journals.

On Apr. 13, 1893, he married Charlotte M. Buffett of Cleveland, Ohio, who died Dec. 28, 1906. In 1914, on Feb. 21, he married Ruth Annette Warren of Springfield, Mass., who survived him. He died in Washington. He was a member of the National Academy of Sciences, the American Academy of Arts and Sciences, the American Philosophical Society, as well as numerous other American and European learned societies in several fields. His non-scientific interests were wide. Music and art had a great appeal for him, and he was a skilled linguist, reading French, German, Italian, Greek, and Latin. His literary ability is evidenced by his poems, by his *Pasteur, the History of a Mind* (1920), translated (with Florence Hedges) from the French of Émile Duclaux, and by his translation of the sonnets of José Maria de Heredia. By temperament an artist as much as a scientist, he stands out as a creative genius who not only did the work of a pioneer but throughout a lifetime acted as a leader in the development of the science of plant pathology. In his field he was without an equal; what Louis Pasteur and Robert Koch were to animal pathology, he was to bacterial plant pathology.

[*Who's Who in America*, 1926–27; J. M. Cattell and D. R. Brimhall, *Am. Men of Sci.* (3rd ed., 1921); R. H. True, in *Phytopathology*, Oct. 1927, with portrait and full bibliog.; L. R. Jones and F. V. Rand, in *Jour. of Bacteriology*, Jan. 1928; F. V. Rand, in *Mycologia*, July–Aug. 1928, with portrait; E. W. Brandes, in *Science*, Oct. 28, 1927; *Evening Star* (Washington, D. C.), Apr. 7, 1927.]   J. A. S.

SMITH, EUGENE ALLEN (Oct. 27, 1841– Sept. 7, 1927), state geologist of Alabama for fifty-four years, was born in Washington, Autauga County, Ala., the son of Samuel Parrish and Adelaide Julia (Allen) Smith, both of New England ancestry. The boy's early training was obtained at a private school in Prattville, Ala., but in 1856, at the age of fifteen, he entered the Central High School of Philadelphia where he remained until the autumn of 1859. The year following he entered the University of Alabama, Tuscaloosa, with advanced standing, graduating with the degree of A.B. in 1862. Throughout the Civil War he served as drill master and instructor in tactics at the University. In 1865 he went to Europe and for the next three years was in attendance at various German universities, including Berlin, Göttingen, and Heidelberg, receiving from the last named the degree of Ph.D. *summa cum laude* in 1868.

Returning to America in that year, he was

appointed assistant professor of chemistry in the University of Mississippi, where he came under the influence of Professor Eugene W. Hilgard [q.v.], from whom he apparently derived his first special interest in geology. In 1871 he was elected professor of chemistry and mineralogy in the University of Alabama, with the proviso that he was to devote such of his time as could be spared from his teaching to investigating the natural resources of the state. This arrangement led naturally to his appointment as state geologist in 1873, though with no immediate increase in salary. In this position he served continuously during the remaining fifty-four years of his life, a term as state geologist believed unequaled in America; for forty years he also retained his University professorship, resigning it in 1913 to give his whole time to the survey.

Smith was of a modest and retiring disposition, devoted to the interests of the state and of the survey, and with no thought of personal gain. He was of slight stature and build, wiry, and very active both physically and mentally. As a geologist he made no startling discoveries and was not given to theory, but worked steadily and faithfully, respected and loved by all who knew him. He was president of the Geological Society of America in 1913. Of the more than 100 titles given in his bibliography, many were the regular reports of progress of the survey; other papers worthy of mention are "The Iron Ores of Alabama," in *Proceedings of the American Association for the Advancement of Science* (vol. XXVII, 1879); "The Iron Ores of Alabama in Their Geological Relations" (*Mineral Resources of the United States, 1882,* 1883); "Physicogeographical and Agricultural Features of the State of Alabama," in *Report on Cotton Production in the United States,* being vol. VI (1884) of the Reports of the Tenth Census; *On the Phosphates and Marls of Alabama* (1892), a bulletin of the state survey. To the study of the coastal region he gave most of his personal energies after 1880, noteworthy papers in this field being "The Post-Eocene Formations of the Coastal Plain of Alabama" (*American Journal of Science,* April 1894); *Report on the Geology of the Coastal Plain of Alabama* (1894), published by the Alabama survey; and "On Some Post-Eocene and Other Formations of the Gulf Region of the United States" (*Proceedings of the American Association for the Advancement of Science,* vol. LV, 1906). His most original contribution was perhaps a short paper, "Underthrust Folds and Faults," published in the *American Journal of Science* for April 1893.

Smith was married, July 10, 1872, to Jane

Henry Meredith Garland, daughter of Landon Cabell Garland [q.v.], a professor at the University of Mississippi and subsequently first chancellor of Vanderbilt University. Smith died in Tuscaloosa, survived by his widow and three sons.

[Charles Butts, "Memorial of Eugene Allen Smith," with bibliography, *Bull. Geol. Soc. of America,* Mar. 1928; W. B. Jones, in *Engineering and Mining Journal,* Dec. 17, 1927, and in *Science,* Jan. 6, 1928; *Who's Who in America,* 1926–27; *Montgomery Advertiser,* Sept. 8, 1927.]

G. P. M.

SMITH, FRANCIS HENNEY (Oct. 18, 1812–Mar. 21, 1890), soldier and educator, was the son of Francis Smith, merchant of Norfolk, Va., and Ann (Marsden) Smith. Commissioned 2nd lieutenant, 1st artillery, Nov. 30, 1833, after his graduation from the United States Military Academy in July, he was on garrison duty for a year and then taught geography, history, and ethics at the Academy for a year. In 1834 he married Sarah Henderson, daughter of Thomas Henderson; they had seven children. Resigning his commission in 1836 to accept the professorship of mathematics at Hampden-Sidney College in Virginia, in June 1839 he became principal professor and after 1840 superintendent of the newly organized Virginia Military Institute at Lexington, to the service of which he devoted the remainder of his life. On Nov. 11, 1839, the Institute was opened with two instructors, Smith and John T. L. Preston, and twenty-eight cadets. The six thousand dollars appropriated annually by the legislature for its support was a sum so far from sufficient to warrant the adoption of the full course of instruction of West Point, as had been intended, that a system of exchange of instruction was arranged with Washington College (later Washington and Lee University), also at Lexington. In 1846 the system of cooperation with Washington College was discontinued. The growth of the Institute was accompanied by many difficulties. Local merchants resented the establishment of a commissary; Washington College sought to circumscribe its instruction; and Presbyterian Lexington not only looked with disfavor upon the founding by Smith of an Episcopal church in the community but also charged him with sectarian favoritism in the administration of the Institute. So unfriendly was local sentiment that in 1849 the legislature contemplated the removal of the Institute to another location, whereupon the local attitude toward the Institute changed. In the fifties appropriations for buildings were increased, and the faculty was enlarged; in 1859, after a six months' inspection of scientific schools in Europe, Smith recommended the expansion of the

Institute into a general scientific school, publishing a report of his trip as *Special Report of the Superintendent of the Virginia Military Institute: Scientific Education in Europe* (1859). But before final action was taken the Civil War was upon the country.

When, alarmed by the invasion of John Brown (at whose execution Smith was the commanding officer), the state appropriated one-half million dollars for armament, Smith was a member of the commission to supervise the expenditure of the money. With the cadets called into active service at the outbreak of the war, he was appointed a member of the governor's advisory board. At its dissolution in the summer of 1861 he was placed in command of Craney Island, near Norfolk, with the rank of major-general of Virginia Volunteers; he remained there until the reopening of the Institute, January 1862. Although in June 1864 the Institute was burned by the army of Gen. David Hunter [*q.v.*], for part of 1864–65 he carried on its work in Richmond, and in October 1865 saw it reopened in Lexington. In September 1865, just before its reopening, he urged the immediate rebuilding and reorganization of the institution. When a promise of an annual appropriation for current expenses had been secured from the legislature, bonds were issued to the amount of fifty thousand dollars, for the security of which Smith pledged his small estate and the faculty agreed to contribute one-third of its meager salaries. By 1870 the restoration was completed upon a scale superior to that existing before 1864, and in 1884 the bonded debt was assumed by the legislature. After fifty years as superintendent, Smith retired, Dec. 31, 1889. As an educator he attacked the classical type of education prevalent in the South before the war, emphasized the utilitarian aspects of education, and advocated military organization because of its system of discipline. Intensely religious, he presented every graduate with a Bible along with his diploma. He published a series of mathematical textbooks, *An Elementary Treatise on Analytical Geometry* (1840), translated from the French of J. B. Biot, *Best Methods of Conducting the Common Schools* (1849), and *College Reform* (1851). He died in Lexington.

[G. W. Cullum, *Biog. Reg. Officers and Grads. U. S. Mil. Acad.* (1891), vol. I; *In Memoriam: Francis H. Smith, Father and Founder of the Va. Mil. Inst.* (1890); *Reg. Officers and Cadets Va. Mil. Inst., 1860–1873*; F. H. Smith, *The Va. Mil. Inst., Its Building and Rebuilding* (1912); J. C. Wise, *The Mil. Hist. of the Va. Mil. Inst. from 1839 to 1865* (1915); obituaries in *Richmond Dispatch*, Mar. 22, 1890, and *Rockbridge County News* (Lexington, Va.), Mar. 27, 1890.]

W. G. B—n.

SMITH, FRANCIS HOPKINSON (Oct. 23, 1838–Apr. 7, 1915), engineer, artist, writer, was born in Baltimore, Md., the son of Francis and Susan (Teackle) Smith, and a great-grandson of Francis Hopkinson [*q.v.*], poet and signer of the Declaration of Independence for New Jersey. His father, whom he later portrayed in the character of Richard Horn, was a student, a musician and inventor of a musical instrument, a mathematician, and a philosopher. Smith was brought up in the society of quiet Baltimore and received an academic education in preparation for college, but reverses in the family fortunes sent him to work instead, first as a shipping clerk in a hardware store and then as an assistant superintendent in an elder brother's iron foundry. Then came the Civil War, and he removed to New York, where again he worked in the office of a foundry until the unmerciful treatment accorded an unfortunate contractor by his employer so outraged his sense of fair play that he left without the formality of a written resignation. The act was characteristic; years later he sympathized with another under-dog, and after the Dreyfus case refused to exhibit his pictures in Paris. After leaving the foundry he set up independently as an engineer, soon taking as a partner one James Symington, who like himself dabbled in art. Shortly afterwards, on Apr. 26, 1866, he married Josephine Van Deventer of Astoria, N. Y. For about thirty years the firm was engaged in construction work, the greater part of which was for the government. For this exacting client they built the Race Rock lighthouse (an experience later recorded in *Caleb West, Master Diver*), the Block Island breakwater, the sea wall at Tompkinsville, Staten Island (where their contractor was Mary Morgan, the original of the heroine of *Tom Grogan*), and the foundations for the Statue of Liberty, and filled many other marine contracts. Of them all Smith considered the Race Rock lighthouse his greatest achievement. Eight miles out at sea, at a point where the rip raced seven miles an hour, it was enough to stimulate every ingenuity and tax the courage of the engineer. Smith began work on it in 1871; on Jan. 1, 1879, it was finally completed (*Annual Report of the Light-House Board*, 1879, p. 19), a monument to the pertinacity and resourcefulness of its builder.

All this time, in the few spare moments his profession allowed him, he pursued his hobby of painting. He was thankful for whatever time he could snatch, for he believed that a man who has "a passion for art for its own sake and not as a mere means of making money" should enter an occupation that would earn him a livelihood, and should then "in his evenings and on his Sundays . . . take down his Aladdin's lamp and give it a rub," for in this way he kept his art "high and noble, his worthiest and best expression" (*Literary World, post*, 246). He had always had an interest in painting, though except for a few lessons while he was still a schoolboy he was substantially self-taught. In New York he readily made friends among the younger artists and became a member of the famous Tile Club, which included such men of prominence as Edwin Austin Abbey, Elihu Vedder, and William Merritt Chase [*qq.v.*]. He had already illustrated verse from Lowell, Holmes, and Whittier in *Old Lines in New-Black-and White* (copyright 1885), and to *A Book of the Tile Club* (1886), published anonymously, he contributed not only sketches, as did his fellows, but also stories of their adventures. More important than these, since it led directly to his literary life, was *Well-Worn Roads of Spain, Holland, and Italy* (1887), in which he first supplemented his drawings by recollections of the varied life before his canvas. Asked by his publishers for a similar accompaniment to his second series of travel sketches, he produced *A White Umbrella in Mexico* (1889), delightful both in its prose and in its pictures of Mexican life. With the recognition that came to him through these books he found more and more time for painting, and with his wife and daughter spent summers in Spain, in Italy, in Constantinople, always in search of the picturesque. He worked with a rapidity amazing even to professional artists; one summer in Venice, working ten hours a day, he painted a picture a day for fifty-three days (*Ibid.*, p. 245), yet his execution was sure and confident. Haste, of course, was principle to one who believed that the artist must finish his picture before the sun, or his mood could change. His water-colors, especially those of Venice, are wholly charming, and in their delicate tints buoyant with sunny luminescence. But if his most popular work was in water-color—he seldom used oils—perhaps his most effective was in such charcoal studies as those in *Charcoals of New and Old New York* (1912), *In Thackeray's London* (1913), and *In Dickens's London* (1914). These compositions in the contrast of light and shade, faithful to the architecture yet not conventionalized by it, interesting in their deep blacks, and vividly suggestive of the character of the cities, are among the best things he ever did.

Some promise of his literary work is to be found in the descriptions of people and places, and in the stories of tourist luck recorded in an early journal that tells of a trip made through the Virginia mountains in the summer of 1857, when he was eighteen years old. He was over fifty, however, when he published his first book of fiction. The writing of *Colonel Carter of Cartersville* (1891) grew almost by accident out of a decision to put into print some of the after-dinner stories for which he was famous. This delightful story of the old Virginia gentleman, impoverished but not disheartened by the war, was so successful that he abandoned his engineering career as one whose risks and hazards were hardly suited to a man of his advancing years, and the Aladdin's lamp so carefully polished on Saturday afternoons and Sundays now took the place of sea-walls and lighthouses. There followed in a succession quick for one no longer young a long line of travel books, of tales, of short stories, and of longer works of fiction. He was by no means restricted for subject matter to the post-war life of the South but found in his wide experience great variety. The picturesque scene as the traveling artist saw it he portrayed in *A Day at Laguerre's* (1892), *Gondola Days* (1897), and *The Veiled Lady* (1907); artist life in *The Fortunes of Oliver Horn* (1902), partly autobiographical, and *The Wood Fire in No. 3* (1905); the romance of the engineer's profession in *Tom Grogan* (1896), and *Caleb West, Master Diver* (1898); the problem of the effect of divorce upon children in *The Tides of Barnegat* (1906); the Old South during the thirties and forties in *Kennedy Square* (1911); and social contrasts in *The Other Fellow* (1899). His special talent lay in the anecdote, the local-color sketch, and the tale, forms he handled with a sure sympathy for what was picturesque and human. Even his longer stories —save *The Tides of Barnegat*, which alone among them has a tight construction—are simply extensive developments of these forms. Among his many well-rounded characters Colonel Carter, symbol of the patrician Southerner, generous, lovable, genuine, will live as one of the great figures of American literature.

His achievements in such varied fields as engineering, painting, writing, and lecturing—he was one of the most popular lecturers of his time —would have been impossible to one less versatile, less vigorous of mind and body. Thomas Nelson Page [*q.v.*], his old friend, speaks of him as ever in his prime, a man to whom fatigue was unknown and to whom the "infinite capacity for taking pains" was second nature. Revealed in "The Virginia Mountains: A Journal," as a normal, healthy boy, fond of society, yet quite independent, in later life he not only was capable of easy friendliness toward any fellow being but also had the ability to retreat into himself in crowded railway stations or in busy London streets. Beneath his distinguished appearance, which suggested the banker or the prosperous merchant more than the artist or author, beneath the brilliance and the wit, he was a steadfast friend, invincibly cheerful, hearty in frequent and breezy laughter, possessed of a quality that was like the sunlight he loved and reflected in all his work. He died in New York, survived by his wife and two sons (*American Art News, post*, p. 5).

[*Who's Who in America*, 1914–15; F. H. Smith, "The Virginia Mountains: A Journal," MS. in the possession of H. V. D. Moore, N. Y. City, and *Capt. Thomas A. Scott* (1908); T. N. Page, in *Scribner's Mag.*, Sept. 1915; E. F. Harkins in *Lit. World*, Sept. 1904; Clara E. Clement and Laurence Hutton, *Artists of the Nineteenth Century* (1885); Buffalo Fine Arts Acad., *Acad. Notes*, Apr. 1915; *Bookman*, May 1915, with portrait; *Outlook*, Apr. 21, 1915; *Am. Art News*, Apr. 10, 1915 (by Smith's son); *Am. Art Ann.*, 1915; *N. Y. Times*, Apr. 8 (obituary), Apr. 9 (editorial), Apr. 13, 1915 (letter); G. E. Schilling, in *Publisher's Weekly*, Dec. 2, 1922.]   C. Y. W., III.

SMITH, FRANCIS MARION (Feb. 2, 1846– Aug. 27, 1931), capitalist, known as "Borax" Smith, was born at Richmond, Wis., the son of Henry G. and Charlotte (Paul) Smith, who had moved to Wisconsin from Rochester, N. Y., in 1842. After attending Milton Academy (later College) at Milton, Wis., in 1863, he remained on his father's farm until 1867, when with a few hundred dollars he went West and for about five years followed mining camps from Montana to Idaho, and then to Nevada and California. In 1872, while cutting timber for mines at Columbus, Nev., he and his partner, William Tell Coleman [*q.v.*], discovered in Teel's Marsh the mineral (colemanite) from which borax is derived. These mines soon became and for many years remained the world's chief source of borax. It was then used mainly by blacksmiths and druggists, and cost between thirty and thirty-five cents an ounce. The partners organized the Pacific Coast Borax Company and through it succeeded in controlling the borax market for a long period. By greatly reducing the price they made borax a household staple. Later Smith acquired colemanite deposits in Death Valley, Cal. From there the product was hauled by mules 164 miles to Mojave, Cal., and the "twenty-mule-team" became a familiar borax trade-mark. In 1910 he settled in Oakland, Cal. There, investing his great profits in public utilities, he brought about a merger of all street-car lines in Alameda and Contra Costa counties, which with the addition of a ferry system from Oakland to San Francisco became the Key Route system. He also opened up large tracts of land for residen-

tial and industrial uses in East Bay cities. In these new activities, however, he soon met financial disaster, and the $20,000,000 fortune that he had accumulated rapidly disappeared. Owing to his crude financial methods and reckless borrowing on short-time notes, he became involved in extended litigation that ended in his bankruptcy. Between 1921 and 1925 he strove, with only partial success, to recoup his fortunes through the acquisition of a newly discovered deposit of colemanite in Clark County, Nev. He also became a political storm center in Oakland and Berkeley through his attempts to acquire rights upon the waterfronts of those cities.

He married Mary R. Thompson of New Jersey in 1875, and in 1901 established in her name the Mary R. Smith Trust to maintain a home for Friendless Girls in Oakland; she died on Dec. 31, 1905. They had no children of their own but had adopted several. Two years later, Jan. 23, 1907, he married Evelyn K. Ellis of Oakland, by whom he had one son and three daughters. For some years he was a trustee of Mills College in Oakland. He founded a magazine, the *Blue Mule*, edited by H. A. Laffler, which flourished for a time. In politics he was a Republican, and served as a presidential elector in 1904 and 1908. He took an active interest in outdoor sports and was a devotee of yachting, especially when at his New York home at Shelter Island; in 1906 he won the cup offered by King Edward VII in the national race off Newport, R. I. He was believed to be on the way to new wealth at the time of his death in Oakland.

[*Who's Who in America*, 1924–25; J. E. Baker, *Past and Present of Alameda County, Cal.* (1914), vol. II; J. M. Guinn, *Hist. of the State of Cal. and Biog. Record of Oakland and Environs* (copr. 1907), vol. II; H. G. Hanks, in *Cal. State Mining Bureau. Third Ann. Report . . . State Mineralogist* (1883), pt. II; *San Francisco: Its Builders, Past and Present* (1913), vol. II, pp. 107–09; obituaries in *San Francisco Chronicle*, Aug. 28, and *Oakland Tribune*, Aug. 27, 1931.]
                                         P. O. R.

SMITH, GEORGE (Feb. 10, 1806–Oct. 7, 1899), banker and financier, was born in the parish of Old Deer, Aberdeenshire, Scotland. He appeared in the village of Chicago about the year 1834 and invested what little money he had in lots and wild lands. Following the boom in land values in 1835 and 1836, he had the sagacity to sell his holdings before the slump came in 1837. In 1836 he became associated with, and was in a sense the founder of, the Chicago Marine and Fire Insurance Company. The following year he went back to Scotland and organized the Scottish Illinois Land Investment Company. On his return to America in 1839, he found that the legislature of Illinois had passed a law which suppressed the banking operations of his Chicago corporation. He therefore went to Wisconsin and prevailed upon some friends in the legislature to charter a similar organization. Following the panic of 1837, nearly all the legislatures in the Midwest were dominated by Jackson Democrats, and it was therefore necessary for Smith to obtain a bank charter by stealth. It contained nearly all the powers usually conferred upon insurance companies, but contained a clause that the "corporation may receive money on deposit, and loan the same on 'bottomry, respondentia,' or other satisfactory security, at such rates of interest as may be done by individuals by the law of this territory." The same section, however, contained a proviso that nothing therein contained should give the said company banking privileges. The Wisconsin Marine & Fire Insurance Company was chartered Feb. 28, 1839.

Smith made Alexander Mitchell [q.v.], then a young Scotchman twenty-two years of age, secretary of the company. He soon became the active managing head of the organization. From the beginning the company began doing a general banking business. Its certificates of deposit, which were in fact bank notes, totaled $11,918 in June 1840, but by Dec. 1, 1852, the total outstanding amounted to $1,470,235. Throughout the forties the territorial legislature endeavored to repeal its charter. Mitchell's contention that the legislature could not determine the rights of a company while "acting in the three-fold capacity of a party interested, a jury, and a court" did not fall upon deaf ears, and the matter was never carried to the courts. After Wisconsin became a state, in 1848, the attorney general began *quo warranto* proceedings to test the legality of the charter, but on the promise of either Smith or Mitchell to incorporate as a state bank in the event that the Wisconsin free-banking law was adopted by a vote of the people, proceedings against the company were dropped. In 1853 the Wisconsin Marine & Fire Insurance Company became a state bank. Under the Wisconsin law no bank could issue notes in excess of its capital stock. Smith soon saw that this provision would deprive him of the enormous profits he had made under the old charter, and in 1854 he sold his stock to Alexander Mitchell, and proceeded to Georgia. Here he obtained from the state a charter incorporating a bank of issue located at Atlanta, a rather inaccessible place at that time. He had hoped to make his Chicago institution and Mitchell's bank at Milwaukee the fountainhead of his Atlanta bank, but following the adoption of free-banking in Midwest states, "George

Smith's money" could no longer win the field, and in 1856 he closed out his banking business.

Between that date and the outbreak of the Civil War he made several trips to Scotland. On his last return to America in 1860 he invested his huge fortune in Chicago real estate and the securities of the Rock Island, Northwestern, and St. Paul railroads, which at the time were greatly depreciated, and retired from active business life. His investments were wisely chosen, for at his death in 1899 estimates of his fortune ran as high as $100,000,000. None was lower than $50,000,000. Although a man's fortune may be no test of his worth to society, Smith's contributions to the development of the West were very great. During the troublesome days of wildcat money, the credit of George Smith & Company was as good as the government's and better than that of most states. The rapid economic expansion of Wisconsin and Illinois in the forties would not have been possible without the aid of "George Smith's money." From 1860 to his death, he divided his time between his castle in the Scottish Highlands and the Reform Club of London. He never married and had no close relatives. He died at the Reform Club in London.

[Horace White, "An Elastic Currency," in *Proc. of the Nineteenth Ann. Convention of the Am. Bankers' Asso.* (1893); *Milwaukee Sentinel*, Aug. 18, 1893, Oct. 9, 1899; *Chicago Tribune*, Oct. 9, 1899; A. T. Andreas, *Hist. of Chicago*, vol. I (1884); J. D. Butler, "Alexander Mitchell, the Financier," in *Colls. of the State Hist. Soc. of Wis.*, vol. XI (1888); J. J. Knox, *A Hist. of Banking in the U. S.* (1900); E. B. Usher, *Wis. Its Story and Biog.* (1914); original record books of the Wis. Marine & Fire Insurance Company in State Hist. Library, Madison.]   L. B. K.

SMITH, GEORGE HENRY (Oct. 20, 1873–Jan. 9, 1931), newspaper writer and author of humorous juvenile stories, was born at Knoxville, Tenn., the son of George Henry Smith, a jeweler, and his second wife Annie (Ramage) Smith. He was a grandson of the Rev. Richard and Maria (Stribley) Smith of London, England, who settled in Horseheads, N. Y., about 1828, and is said to have been a descendant of Sir Richard Grenville. His grandparents on his mother's side were Mary (Cowan) and Joseph Ramage of Philadelphia, the latter a descendant of French Huguenots who settled in the north of Ireland. When he was three years old his father died; five years later his mother remarried, and he was sent to boarding school. He later attended University School, Knoxville, studied under private tutors, traveled in America and the British Isles, and after four years at Yale received the degree of B.A. in 1899. At seventeen he was a reporter on the *Knoxville Journal*, and before he entered college he was writing for the

Knoxville Sentinel and the *Chattanooga News.* He became traveling representative for the Lyman D. Morse Advertising Agency of New York, 1899, and a year later established an independent advertising and publishing business. He founded and was president of the Writer's Aid Association, 1901–03. For four years, 1903–07, he was solicitor for schools with the advertising department of the *New York Times.* He then became New York representative of the Chronicle Publishing Company of Orange, N. J., 1907–09.

On Apr. 8, 1901, in New Haven, Conn., he married Harriet Clarke Sanford, daughter of Rev. Elihu Turney Sanford and Harriet Ford (Clarke) Sanford. His success in entertaining the eldest of his four children with droll bedtime stories disclosed an unsuspected talent for interesting children and led him directly into a special field of newspaper work. His stories, which first began to appear in the *Globe* (New York) in 1909, were syndicated and appeared daily in many newspapers throughout America under the pen name of "Farmer Smith" and "Uncle Henry." He became children's editor on the *Globe*, 1909–15, and held similar posts successively on the *New York Evening Mail*, 1915; the *Public Ledger* (Philadelphia), 1915–17; the *Philadelphia Record*, 1918–19; the *Newark Ledger*, 1920–23; the *Daily Graphic* (New York), 1925–27; and the *Brooklyn Standard-Union*, 1928–31. During these years he also contributed special articles to the *Evening World* (New York), 1905–30, and reviewed motion pictures for the *Newark Ledger*, 1923–25. He published three collections of his early stories: *Daddy's Goodnight Stories* (1910), *Oh, Look Who's Here* (1911), and *The Dollie Stories* (1912). In 1915, while he was children's editor of the *Ledger*, he formed the "Farmer Smith Rainbow Club," which he developed from a clever advertising stunt into an organization providing wholesome occupation and amusement for its many thousands of youthful members. At the entrance of the United States into the World War he was asked to aid in the mobilization of children in war work. In 1917 he founded the National Children's Committee and assisted in the organization of the Junior Red Cross; in 1918 he conducted a speaking campaign in the South to increase membership in the Junior Red Cross. He died in Maplewood, N. J., of heart disease, survived by his wife, two daughters, and one son.

[*Hist. of Class of Eighteen Hundred Ninety-Nine, Yale Coll.*, vol. IV (1919); *Obit. Record Grads. of Yale Univ.*, 1930–31; *Editor & Publisher and the Journalist,* Apr. 22, 1916; obituary in *N. Y. Times*, Jan. 10, 1931; unpublished diaries, 1890–94, and undated newspaper clippings in the possession of Mrs. R. H. Smith; correspondence with Mrs. Smith.]   V. L. S.

SMITH, GERALD BIRNEY (May 3, 1868–Apr. 3, 1929), theologian, was born at Middlefield, Mass., the son of Metcalf John and Harriet Louise (Eldredge) Smith, and a descendant of Matthew Smith who emigrated to Massachusetts from England in 1637. He was a nephew of Judson Smith [*q.v.*]. His early training was in the public schools of Middlefield, and in the home of his father, a man of college education, with advanced views but trusted in his community, given to philosophizing. After graduating with the degree of A.B. from Brown University in 1891, he taught Latin in Oberlin Academy for one year, and mathematics and foreign languages at Worcester Academy for three years. On July 10, 1894, he married Inez Michener of New Sharon, Iowa. Entering Union Theological Seminary, he was graduated with the degree of B.D. in 1898 and awarded a traveling fellowship for the next two years in Europe. These years of study took him to Berlin, Marburg, and Paris. Upon his return he was called to the divinity school of the University of Chicago, where he passed through the ranks from instructor to professor. On Nov. 23, 1902, he was ordained to the Baptist ministry.

In his early years, following the German study, he was greatly influenced by the Ritschlian point of view, especially as that was infused with the mystical piety of his own teacher, Herrmann. His stress upon experience rather than on Biblical teaching as a basis for theology led him, however, more and more into a recognition of the claims of scientific and democratic ideals. In a monograph entitled *Practical Theology* (1903) he still insisted that the interests of science and of practical religion are in conflict and urged a new department to adapt the scientific findings of critical theology to the religious needs of men. He made an essay in this direction, collaborating with two Biblical scholars, E. D. Burton and J. M. P. Smith, in a study of the Atonement (*Biblical Ideas of Atonement: Their History and Significance,* 1909), in which he wrote the final section on the value of these critical findings for vital religious experience.

In 1912 he delivered the Taylor Lectures at Yale, published the following year under the title *Social Idealism and the Changing Theology* (1913), the purpose of which was "to show how and why the change from aristocratic to democratic ideals has taken place, and to indicate wherein an understanding of the significance of this ethical evolution may aid in the reconstruction of theology" (p. x). Here he threw down the glove to authoritarianism, and from that time on his efforts were constantly to find a vital religion which should not rest upon authoritative dogma. He initiated the project of the volume which he edited, *A Guide to the Study of the Christian Religion* (1916), in order to help pastors "to keep in sympathetic touch with the latest scholarship." Later, he brought this task up to date by editing what in a way was a supplementary volume, *Religious Thought in the Last Quarter-Century* (1927). His own chapter in the *Guide* is really a systematic prolegomenon to an empirical theology which is throughout set over against the method of authority. What this chapter does for theology his *Principles of Christian Living* (1924) does for Christian ethics. "The ethical life," he affirms, "is one of inquiry as well as one of obedience to formal principles" (p. 4). His last book was a brief but meaty work called *Current Christian Thinking* (1928), in which, after a trenchantly critical survey of various contemporary appeals to authority, he offered a thoroughly empirical approach to theological reconstruction.

As a theologian Smith was scrupulously honest in research and penetrating in his grasp and criticism of controversial literature, but he always united these qualities with a rare sense for spiritual power from which he ever feared that scholarship might be divorced. He never developed a system of theology, feeling that the fluid state of scientific research did not permit this; and he sought to give his students a method of critical and constructive thinking rather than a body of conclusions. As a teacher he was systematic and incisive, patient but intolerant of humbug, and inspired his students to do independent thinking. As a man he was genial and endowed with a rich sense of humor, extremely broad in his interests and always conveying the impression of balance and humaneness. He was very fond of sports. For several years he was chairman of the University Orchestral Association; he was president of the board of the University of Chicago Settlement, a sponsor of a history of his native town, and adviser to the Religious Education Association. With Shailer Mathews, in 1921, he edited *A Dictionary of Religion and Ethics*. As managing editor of the *American Journal of Theology* from 1909 to 1920, and editor of the *Journal of Religion* from 1921 until his sudden death at the height of his powers, he struck a balance between sound scholarship and concern for popular religious needs. He was survived by his wife and one son.

[Sources include P. M. Smith and E. C. Smith, *A Hist. of the Town of Middlefield, Mass.* (1924); S. S. Martin, *Mack Geneal.* (2 vols., 1903–04); *Alumni Cat. of the Union Theological Seminary* (1926); *Hist. Cat. of Brown Univ.* (1905); *Who's Who in America,* 1928–29; *Baptist* (Chicago), Apr. 13, 1929; *The Divinity Student* (Univ. of Chicago Divinity School), vols. VI (1929), VIII (1931). For revelation of Smith's personality see his article, "The Professor and the Fundamentalist," *Christian Century,* Nov. 11, 1926.]
E. E. A—y.

SMITH, GERRIT (Mar. 6, 1797–Dec. 28, 1874), philanthropist and reformer, was born at Utica, N. Y., the grandson of James Livingston [*q.v.*] and the son of Elizabeth (Livingston) and Peter Smith [*q.v.*]. In 1806 the family moved to Peterboro, Madison County, N. Y., where Smith spent the greater part of his adult life. He graduated from Hamilton College in 1818 and helped his father manage the substantial fortune, the product of shrewd land purchases. On Jan. 11, 1819, he married Wealthy Ann Backus, the daughter of Azel Backus [*q.v.*]. She died the next August, and on Jan. 3, 1822, he married Ann Carroll Fitzhugh. Of their four children, only two lived to maturity. In 1826 he became a member of the Presbyterian Church.

He succeeded to the entire control of his father's property, which, real and personal, was valued at about $400,000, and was able to increase it in amount and in value. His father, melancholy and later estranged from his second wife who had gone back to Charleston, S. C., to live, withdrew into himself more and more. Smith used his wealth, in so far as he could find guidance on the subject from prayer and from his own conscience, for what he considered the good of mankind. For a time he helped to build churches, and he gave generously to several theological schools and to various colleges. He experimented with systematic charity on a large scale, giving both land and money to needy men and women throughout his own state (see sketch of James McCune Smith); but his carefully selected "indigent females" made poor farmers, and the blacks whom he tried to colonize in the Adirondack wilderness found the environment unsuited to their needs. Much of the property he disposed of in this work was subsequently sold for non-payment of taxes.

His greatest reputation was made in the field of reform. He labored in the cause of the Sunday School and of Sunday observance; he was an anti-Mason; he advocated vegetarianism; and he opposed the use of tobacco and alcoholic beverages; he joined the national dress reform association and the woman's suffrage cause; he believed in prison reform and in the abolition of capital punishment. He contributed to home and foreign missions and to the causes of the oppressed Greeks, the Italians, and the Irish. Through his influence his cousin, Elizabeth Cady Stanton [*q.v.*], was interested in temperance and abolition movements. He was vice-president of the American Peace Society and advocated compensated emancipation of slaves. He joined the anti-slavery crusade in 1835 with his customary enthusiasm, and he became one of the best-known abolitionists in the United States. Although on terms of intimate friendship with William Lloyd Garrison, he never went to the extremes of the Garrison group; but he was always ready to help escaped slaves to Canada and in 1851 participated in the "Jerry rescue" in Syracuse. After the enactment of the Kansas-Nebraska law he joined the Kansas Aid Societies in New York, and he helped Eli Thayer's New England Emigrant Aid Company in Massachusetts. This work cost him at least fourteen thousand dollars; how much more it is difficult to determine. In spite of his advocacy of peace, he urged the use of force against the pro-slavery contingent in Kansas, and forcible resistance to the federal authorities there, because, as he said, the federal government upheld the pro-slavery cause. In February 1858 John Brown went to Smith's home in Peterboro, not to plan his campaign in Virginia but to obtain Smith's moral and financial support for plans already made. On this occasion, at a second visit in April 1859, and in several letters, Smith gave Brown assurance of his approval and some money. After the raid at Harpers Ferry, Smith became temporarily insane. He made a quick recovery, however, and six months later he was in his usual good health. From then on to the end of his life he denied complicity in Brown's plot, but the available evidence bears out newspaper charges made at the time, that he was an accessory before the fact.

Unlike the Garrisonians, he believed in political action as a means of reform, and for a full fifty years, from 1824 to 1874, he took an active part in politics. He was one of the leaders in forming the Liberty party; in 1840 he was its candidate for governor. In 1848 the "true" Liberty party men, those who refused to indorse the Free Soil "heresy," nominated him for the presidency, though he declined. In 1852 he was elected a member of Congress on an independent ticket and served from Mar. 4, 1853, to Aug. 7, 1854, when he resigned. In 1858 he ran for governor on the "People's State Ticket," advocating temperance, anti-slavery, and land reform. During the Civil War he wrote and spoke often in support of the Union cause. This work led him gradually into the Republican party, so that he campaigned for Lincoln's reëlection in 1864

and for Grant in 1868. In reconstruction he advocated a policy of moderation toward the Southern whites with suffrage for the blacks. In 1867 he was one of the signers of the bail bond to release Jefferson Davis from captivity. He published many of his speeches and letters on important subjects. Of his published books the more important are: *Religion of Reason* (1864), an exposition of his later religion of Nature or Rationalism; *Speeches of Gerrit Smith in Congress* (1856); and the two volumes (1864–65) of his *Speeches and Letters of Gerrit Smith on the Rebellion*. He died in New York City.

[Family papers in Lib. of Syracuse Univ.; O. B. Frothingham, *Gerrit Smith* (1878); 2nd ed. (1879) "corrected" by Smith's daughter in order to bring it into harmony with the family belief that Smith was not an accomplice of John Brown; C. A. Hammond, *Gerrit Smith* (1900); K. W. Porter, *John Jacob Astor* (2 vols., 1931); *Appletons' Ann. Cyc.*, 1874; R. V. Harlow, "Gerrit Smith and the John Brown Raid" and "Rise and Fall of the Kansas Aid Movement," *Am. Hist. Rev.*, Oct. 1932, Oct. 1935; *N. Y. Tribune*, Dec. 29–30, 1874.]   R. V. H.

SMITH, GILES ALEXANDER (Sept. 29, 1829–Nov. 5, 1876), Union soldier, was born in Jefferson County, N. Y. He was the son of Cyrus and Laura (Wales) Smith and a brother of Morgan Lewis Smith [*q.v.*], and was descended from Ignatius Smith, who emigrated to Cape Cod probably in the first half of the eighteenth century. About 1847 he went to London, Ohio, but soon afterwards moved to Cincinnati, where he engaged in the dry-goods business. Shortly after his marriage, July 31, 1856, to Martha McLain of London, Ohio, he removed to Bloomington, Ill., continuing in the dry-goods business until 1859, when he became the proprietor of a hotel. On June 4, 1861, he entered the military service as captain of Company D, 8th Missouri Volunteers, his brother's regiment, and took part in the capture of Forts Henry and Donelson, in the battle of Shiloh, and in the siege of Corinth. He was promoted lieutenant-colonel, June 12, 1862, and, on the promotion of his brother to brigadier-general, succeeded him, June 30, as colonel of the regiment. In Sherman's expedition against Vicksburg, December 1862, the command of a brigade devolved upon Smith during the assault on Chickasaw Bluffs, and he retained that command during the operations terminating in the capture of Arkansas Post, his soldierly conduct in that capacity drawing commendation from Sherman. In Grant's operations against Vicksburg he particularly distinguished himself by the rescue of the gunboat flotilla which, while trying to force a passage to the Yazoo, had been trapped in Steele's Bayou by the Confederates. He was promoted brigadier-general of volunteers, Aug. 4, 1863, for gallant and meritorious conduct in the field. On Nov. 24, 1863, at Chattanooga, he seized a position on the south bank of the Tennessee River by a skilful maneuver and covered the crossing of Sherman's corps. Later in the day, in the first assault on Missionary Ridge, he was severely wounded. In the Atlanta campaign he distinguished himself at Resaca, and on July 20, 1864, he was transferred to command the 2nd Division, XVII Corps. When two days later the battle of Atlanta was fought, the brunt of the attack fell on his division, and the repulse of the Confederates was largely due to its heroic conduct. He led his division in the march to the sea and in the Carolina campaign, and was brevetted major-general of volunteers, Sept. 1, 1864. After the collapse of the Confederacy he was stationed in Texas. He was promoted major-general of volunteers, Nov. 24, 1865. When the volunteer forces were disbanded he declined a commission as colonel of cavalry in the regular army and returned to his home in Bloomington.

He was appointed second assistant postmaster general in 1869 but resigned in 1872 because of failing health. Though he removed to California in 1874 in the hope of checking the progress of disease, he returned to his old home in Bloomington two months before his death. He possessed a natural soldierly aptitude. Under the tutelage of his brother and the experience of war he advanced rapidly by merit alone, and won esteem for his gallantry and completeness as an officer. His superiors generally took it for granted that any mission assigned him would be well performed, and there was no occasion when this confidence was not justified by the result.

[F. A. Virkus, *The Compendium of Am. Geneal.*, vol. V (1933); F. B. Heitman, *Hist. Reg. and Dict. of the U. S. Army* (1903); *Report of Proc. Soc. of the Army of the Tenn. Eleventh Ann. Meeting, 1877* (1885); *Memoirs of Gen. W. T. Sherman* (2 vols., 2nd ed., revised, 1886); *War of the Rebellion: Off. Records (Army)*; *Battles and Leaders of the Civil War* (4 vols., 1888); U. S. Pension Office records, for name of wife and date of marriage; obituaries in *St. Louis Globe-Democrat* and *Daily Inter Ocean* (Chicago, Ill.), Nov. 6, 1876; family records.]   T.F.M.

SMITH, GUSTAVUS WOODSON (March 1822–June 24, 1896), civil and military engineer, Confederate officer, was born in Georgetown, Scott County, Ky., the son of Byrd and Sarah Hatcher (Woodson) Smith. His grandfather, John Smith, had emigrated to Kentucky from Virginia with Daniel Boone. On the maternal side he was a descendant of John Woodson who came to America before 1679. He entered the United States Military Academy from Virginia and was graduated in 1842 as a second lieuten-

ant, Corps of Engineers. He was assigned to duty at New London, Conn., where he served two years as an assistant engineer on the construction of fortifications, and was then ordered to West Point as an instructor in civil and military engineering. On Oct. 3, 1844, he was married to Lucretia Bassett, the daughter of Capt. Abner Bassett, of New London, Conn. They had no children. Upon the outbreak of the Mexican War, he was detailed to assist Capt. Alexander J. Swift to recruit and train the sole company of engineers in the army. Shortly after reaching Mexico, Captain Swift was invalided and the command devolved upon Smith. The engineer-soldiers were employed in converting the infamous mule paths of northern Mexico into passable roads until March 1847, when they joined Scott's expedition at Vera Cruz. Smith was cited for distinguished services at Vera Cruz, Cerro Gordo, Contreras, Churubusco, and Mexico City, and was brevetted, successively, first lieutenant, captain, and major, the last brevet being disapproved by the war department. Upon the conclusion of peace he returned to West Point as assistant professor of engineering.

He resigned on Dec. 18, 1854, to join, it is said, the Cuban filibustering expedition of John Anthony Quitman [*q.v.*]. This expedition proved still-born, and Smith accepted a treasury department appointment to supervise the repairs to the mint and the construction of the marine hospital in New Orleans, La. A year later he became associated with the engineering firm of Cooper and Hewitt in New York City, and served them as chief engineer of the Trenton Iron Works. He was appointed street commissioner for New York City in 1858, served until 1861, and soon achieved prominence in the councils of the Democratic party. He served on a board to revise the program of instruction at West Point in 1860. He participated in the Pine Street meeting of citizens of New York to devise measures to avert civil war, and favored the Crittenden Compromise. In the late summer of 1861, having been stricken with paralysis in April, he set out for Hot Springs, Ark., upon the advice of his physician. At Lexington, Ky., he learned that his arrest as a disloyal person had been ordered from Washington. This determined him to join the Confederacy, and he proceeded at once to Richmond, where he was appointed, Sept. 19, 1861, a major-general in the provisional army.

He commanded one wing of the Army of the Potomac until the conclusion of the Peninsular Campaign. After General Johnston was wounded during the battle of Seven Pines on May 31, 1862, he commanded as senior officer until General Lee's arrival on June 1. On June 2, he suffered another attack of paralysis. His relief by Lee caused the renewal of a quarrel with President Davis, which had originated over the appointment of his aide-de-camp the previous year. In August 1862 he was placed in command of the sector from the right of Lee's theatre of operations on the Rappahannock to the Cape Fear River, with headquarters in Richmond. He acted as secretary of war from Nov. 17 to Nov. 20. In consequence of the promotion of six officers over his head and presidential interference with details of his command, he resigned on Feb. 17, 1863. He served a short time as a volunteer aide to Beauregard in Charleston, and then became superintendent of the Etowah Mining and Manufacturing Company in north Georgia. In June 1864, he accepted an appointment as major-general to command the 1st Division, Georgia Militia, which was attached to the Army of Tennessee. After the fall of Atlanta, his division was employed in observation of Sherman's army, falling back before it during the famous march to the sea. On Dec. 30, 1864, he was assigned a sector in the defenses of the department of South Carolina, Georgia, and Florida. He surrendered to the Wilson raiders at Macon, Ga., in April 1865.

After the war, he gave testimony on Jan. 30, 1867, before the Congressional committee investigating the affairs of Southern railroads. He was employed as general manager of the Southwestern Iron Company at Chattanooga, Tenn., from 1866 until 1870, when he was appointed as the first insurance commissioner of Kentucky. He held this office for five years, and then moved to New York City, where he resided until his death. He was the author of *Notes on Life Insurance* (1870), *Confederate War Papers* (1884), *The Battle of Seven Pines* (1891), *Generals J. E. Johnston and G. T. Beauregard . . . at Manassas* (1892), and *Company "A," Corps of Engineers, U. S. A., . . . in the Mexican War* (1896).

[H. M. Woodson, *Hist. Geneal. of the Woodsons* (1915); G. W. Cullum, *Biog. Reg. . . . U. S. Mil. Acad.* (1891); *U. S. Army Register*, 1839; C. S. Stewart, in *Ann. Reunion, Asso. Grads., U. S. Mil. Acad., 1897* (1897); C. M. Wilcox, *Hist. of the Mexican War* (1892); *War of the Rebellion: Official Records (Army)*, see index; M. J. Wright, *Gen. Officers of the Confed. Army* (1911); *Confed. Mil. Hist.* (1899), vol. I; *House Report No. 34*, 39 Cong., 2 Sess. An obituary article in *Appletons' Ann. Cyclop., 1896* (1897), gives June 23 as the date of Smith's death. See, however, the *Augusta Chronicle*, June 26, 1896.]　　　W. M. R., Jr.

SMITH, HAMILTON (July 5, 1840–July 4, 1900), mining engineer, was the grandson of Valentine Smith, a judge at Durham, N. H.,

where the family had been established for over a century. His father, also named Hamilton Smith, was trained in the law and went to Louisville, Ky., where he practised with brilliant success. He married Martha, daughter of William Hall of Bellows Falls, Vt., and their son, the second Hamilton Smith, was born near Louisville. His mother died when he was small, his father married again, and at the age of six the boy was sent back to his grandfather at Durham, where he attended the village school. Meanwhile his father had established a cotton factory and coal mines at Cannelton, Ind., and there Hamilton was sent, in his fourteenth year, to acquire a mastery of those enterprises through experience in their engineering and accounting departments. Industrious, competent, and with unusual aptitude for mathematics, he soon demonstrated his ability, and at an early age was recognized as the chief of the engineering and accounting departments of the Cannelton coal mines.

During the sixties, he was engaged in developing other collieries in Kentucky and Indiana, but in 1869 was attracted to the Pacific Coast by its apparently greater opportunities. His first work there was as engineer and manager of the Triunfo mine in Lower California, but his most notable was at the North Bloomfield and Milton gold mines in Nevada County, Cal., which were worked by hydraulic methods. There he became the recognized authority on hydraulics in California. He was also active in efforts to reduce the cost of high explosives and in the establishment of the Vulcan Powder Works. Attracting the favorable attention of Baron Rothschild, who made a visit of inspection to the properties, he became consulting mining engineer for the Rothschild interests. For them he reported on the El Callao mine, Venezuela, in 1881, and then developed it and supervised its operation. In 1885 he opened a consulting office in London, in partnership with Edmund de Crano, and there in 1886 published his notable treatise, *Hydraulics: The Flow of Water through Orifices, over Weirs, and through Open Conduits and Pipes.* The same year he married Mrs. Charles Congreve (*née* Jennings, of New Orleans), and also, with his partner, organized the Exploration Company, Ltd. His paper, "Costs of Mining and Milling Free Gold Ores," published in the *Engineering and Mining Journal*, Sept. 4, 1886, attracted wide attention, and the Exploration Company soon became an important factor in the development of mines throughout the world, but notably in South Africa, where gold had been discovered in 1885. Many of the engineers who built up the gold industry in Africa entered that field through their previous association with Hamilton Smith's earlier mining ventures. His own work was done mostly in London, but he visited South Africa in 1892 and 1895, and was the author of important papers on conditions there, especially on the possibility of mining at deep levels. Subsequent events showed his views to be sound. He introduced into the British market the securities of notable American mining enterprises, he participated in the organization of many important mines, formed the Fraser & Chalmers mining machinery company, at Erith, England, and also organized the Central London Railway. After the death of Edmund de Crano in 1895, he took H. C. Perkins into partnership and soon moved the firm's offices to New York, though he spent much time in Washington, D. C., California, and New Hampshire. At the time of his death at Durham, N. H., from accidental drowning, he was engaged in attempting to develop the Mariposa grant in California, acquired by John Charles Frémont [q.v.] a half-century before, but long in litigation. Besides his treatise on hydraulics, he contributed three important papers on hydraulics to the *Transactions of the American Society of Civil Engineers:* "The Flow of Water through Pipes" (vol. XII, 1883), "Water Power with High Pressures and Wrought-Iron Water-Pipe," and "Temperature of Water at Various Depths in Lakes and Oceans" (vol. XIII, 1884). An accomplished engineer himself, he is perhaps more notable as an outstanding factor in bringing about the employment of American engineers at mines in the British dominions and in securing the participation of British capital in financing mines in the United States and Alaska.

[*Trans. Am. Soc. Civil Engineers,* vol. XLVI (1901); *Minutes of Proc. of the Inst. of Civil Engineers* (London), vol. CXLII (1900); *Trans. Am. Inst. Mining Engineers,* vol. XXXI (1901); *Engineering and Mining Journal,* July 7, 14, 28, 1900; *Manchester Union* (Manchester, N. H.), July 5, 1900.]   T. T. R.

SMITH, HANNAH WHITALL (Feb. 7, 1832–May 1, 1911), author, religious interpreter, reformer, was born in Philadelphia, Pa., the daughter of John Mickle and Mary (Tatum) Whitall. Her first known American ancestor was James Whitall, who in 1688 was living near Philadelphia. Both branches of her family had for many generations been members of the Society of Friends (Quakers). Her home was characterized by a blending of broad culture with spiritual piety of an unusual depth, the double effect of which was apparent in her throughout her life; her biography is in large degree the story of the development of an interior life. In 1848 at the age of sixteen she had a mystical awakening which she described in her "spiritual autobiography" as the "first epoch" in her religious life, and which she later came to regard as a period of "morbid self-introspection." It lasted until her marriage, June 25, 1851, to Robert Pearsall Smith of Philadelphia, son of John Jay Smith [q.v.]. He was a glass manufacturer who also had a deep interest in religion and in later life became a noted religious leader and widely read author. Their children, in addition to a daughter who died young, were Franklin Whitall, Logan Pearsall, Alys, who married Bertrand Russell, and Mary Logan, who married Bernhard Berenson. The death of her son Franklin Whitall in 1872 was the occasion of her writing *The Record of a Happy Life: Being Memorials of Franklin Whitall Smith* (1873). In 1858, after a period of scepticism, she passed through the second epoch of her religious life. Coming under the influence of the Plymouth Brethren she entered into an "assurance of faith," which at the time gave her peace and serenity, and freedom from self-examination. In her "third epoch," not many years later, she made a momentous discovery, which she described as the discovery of "the unselfishness of God." It carried with it for her a belief in a final restitution of all things and every person, and gave her a temporary reputation of being a heretic. In 1865, when the family moved from their home in Germantown, Pa., to a small New Jersey town, Millville, where they were cut off from the associations they had enjoyed, she went through a period of great dissatisfaction and unhappiness. This in 1865 brought her to the fourth and final "epoch," a religious stage which she called the "higher life" or the "life of faith," a life of "absolute consecration, entire obedience, and simple trust" (*The Unselfishness of God,* p. 276). It was out of this ripe experience that she produced somewhat later the book that was always associated with her name, *The Christian's Secret of a Happy Life* (1875). Translated into every language of Europe and into a number of Oriental languages, it went through numerous editions, had an almost fabulous circulation, and made the writer known around the world. A few years later she published *John M. Whitall, the Story of His Life* (1879).

She and her husband had both begun to preach. They now had remarkable non-sectarian meetings "for the deepening of the spiritual life" in America, in England, and on the continent of Europe, their work in Europe reaching its highest point during the years of 1873 and 1874. As a preacher she was practical, explicit, and simple. Throughout her life she had a marked capacity, based largely on the practical character of her own nature, for recognizing what was insincere, fanatical, perverted, or misguided in religious enthusiasm, and she left an interesting collection of papers in which she recorded her observations, published in 1928 as *Religious Fanaticism: Extracts from the Papers of Hannah Whitall Smith*. She was an ardent reformer, working zealously for peace, for temperance, and for the widening of the sphere and scope of the influence of women. In 1886 the family settled permanently in England, and there she continued to live after the death of her husband in 1898. In 1903 she published her book on *The Unselfishness of God and How I Discovered It,* ner "spiritual autobiography." Growing in breadth and wisdom with the years, she came to see that it was a mistake to expect all persons to pass through any one path of religious experience. The later years of peace and tranquillity were marked by an influence not less impressive than in the period of prominent public service at home and abroad. She died at Iffley, where she had lived since 1905.

[C. E. Pearsall, H. M. Pearsall, and H. L. Neall, *Hist. and Geneal. of the Pearsall Family* (1928), vol. II; R. M. Smith, *The Burlington Smiths* (1877); H. W. Smith, *The Unselfishness of God and How I Discovered It* (copr. 1903), John M. Whitall, *the Story of His Life* (1879), and *The Christian's Secret of a Happy Life* (1875); Ray Strachey, *A Quaker Grandmother: Hannah Whitall Smith* (copr. 1914) and *Religious Fanaticism: Extracts from the Papers of Hannah Whitall Smith* (1928), ed.; *Am. Friend,* May 11, 1911; death notices in *Pub. Ledger* (Phila.), May 4, and the *Times* (London), May 3, 1911.]   R. M. J.

SMITH, HAROLD BABBITT (May 23, 1869–Feb. 9, 1932), electrical engineer, educator, was born in Barre, Mass., the son of Samuel Francis and Julia Asenath (Babbitt) Smith. He claimed descent in the sixth generation from Capt. Joseph Smith who led a company of Sudbury Minutemen at Lexington, and in the ninth, from Richard Smith who settled in Ipswich, Mass., about 1640. From the Barre High School, Smith went to Cornell University and was graduated in 1891 with the degree of mechanical engineer. After further study at Cornell, he became in 1892 professor of electrical engineering at the University of Arkansas, but resigned after about a year to become head designer and electrical engineer for the Elektron Manufacturing Company of Springfield, Mass. A few months later he was appointed professor of electrical engineering at Purdue University, where he founded the department and served as director of the School of Engineering until 1896. In that year he joined the faculty of Worcester Polytechnic Institute, where he established the elec-

trical engineering department and continued as its head until his retirement on account of ill health in January 1931. Under his able direction this department flourished and received national recognition; the electrical engineering laboratories constructed and installed at Worcester under his supervision were the finest of their kind in the country. Smith was a pioneer in electrical engineering education; a number of his students became heads of electrical engineering departments in other institutions, and many achieved distinction in the engineering field.

While successfully carrying on his academic work, Smith became prominent in the electrical manufacturing industry. He maintained an active practice as consulting engineer and traveled extensively. From 1905 to 1913 he held the double position of engineer and designer for the Westinghouse Electric & Manufacturing Company of Pittsburgh, Pa. An innovator in the development of high-voltage power transmissions and equipment, he carried on extensive research in dielectric phenomena and electric stress distribution. He was also concerned with the design of direct-current generators and motors and alternating-current transformers, and held many patents. During the World War he was an associate member of the Naval Consulting Board, and a consulting engineer for the special board on anti-submarine devices.

Smith's was a strong character, ambitious, and sometimes considered ruthless. He made bitter enemies and loyal friends. He was chosen president of the American Institute of Electrical Engineers in 1929, the highest honor his national society could confer upon him. He was a member of the American Engineering Council and belonged also to a number of other professional organizations. He was the author of numerous monographs and shorter articles contributed to engineering societies and periodicals, one of his best-known papers being "The Development of a Suspension-Type Insulator" (*Journal of the American Institute of Electrical Engineers,* August 1924). He was twice married: first, at Ithaca, N. Y., June 15, 1894, to Laura Bertha, daughter of Samuel and Ann (Saunders) Smith, and after her death in April 1910, to Persis Helen Smith of New York City, Sept. 28, 1911. The second marriage was ended by a divorce in 1930. There were three children. Smith was a member of the Unitarian Church.

[*Jour. Am. Inst. Elec. Engineers,* July 1929; *Electrical World,* Sept. 24, 1927 and Dec. 15, 1928; *Jour. Worcester Polytechnic Inst.,* Feb., Apr. 1932; *Who's Who in America.* 1930–31; *Who's Who in Engineering,* 1931; *N. Y. Times,* Feb. 10, 1932; information from friends and associates in Worcester.] T. H. M.

SMITH, HARRY JAMES (May 24, 1880–
Mar. 16, 1918), playwright, novelist, seventh of
nine children of John B. and Lucy F. (Nichols)
Smith, was born in New Britain, Conn. He attended the public schools there, taught for a few
months in the district school at Cornwall Hollow, Conn., and in 1898 entered Williams College. There he specialized in biology, studied
one summer at Woods Hole, and the year after
graduation (1902–03) was assistant in the biological laboratory. This scientific training was
far from wasted, as it served later to balance his
romantic zest in life and to supply an underlying
realistic attitude in his writing. After a year's
post-graduate work in English at Harvard,
where he received the degree of M.A. in 1904,
he became instructor in English composition
(1904–05) at Oberlin. He proved to be a brilliant teacher, intuitively dramatizing his work
and carrying his classes with him by his spontaneous enthusiasm. His purpose was set toward writing, however, and after a year he gave
up teaching and declined every later inducement
to return to it. A year of free lancing in New
York City was followed by one on the editorial
staff of the *Atlantic Monthly* and several more
in New York. In 1909, however, after a severe
illness, he retired from the city, whose thrill he
loved while its din tormented his exacerbated
nerves, to the peaceful surroundings of home in
Berlin, Conn. Here, while still near enough to
permit frequent visits to the metropolis, he was
able to be with his family, to which his unusually
tender devotion drew him all the closer through
the fact that he never married.

Meanwhile, in 1908 appeared his first novel,
Amédée's Son, an idyllic tale of the Cape Breton
coast which he had visited, to escape from severe hay fever, nearly every summer after boyhood. This was followed in 1910 by *Enchanted
Ground,* a novel of New York City, turning on
the contrast between the bleak morality of New
England and the morally dissolvent fascination
of New York. Then, in 1910–11, came the extraordinary success of his comedy, *Mrs. Bumpstead-Leigh,* written for Mrs. Fiske. After this
there were lean years; partially because of managerial incompetence, his plays *Blackbirds, Suki,*
and *Oh! Imogen* were not successful; but in
1917 *A Tailor-Made Man* repeated the success of
Mrs. Bumpstead-Leigh—two of the wittiest
comedies America has produced—and *The Little Teacher,* produced in 1918, was also successful.

These dramas were all comedies of manners,
the flash of wit playing over not too profound
situations of human interest. While Harry

Smith could appreciate Ibsen and Shaw, in his
own work he deliberately avoided every semblance of the problem play. Battling with constant ill health, he had won a degree of fame
and fortune, and, what was more dear to him,
a command of the playwright's craft, when the
World War interrupted his career. Always an
intense admirer of French culture from the days
of a bicycle trip through France in the summer
of 1903, a constant reader of French literature,
with Molière, whose picture he kept above his
desk, as his dramatic ideal, he sympathized from
the outset with the Allies. Soon after the entrance of the United States into the war he gave
up writing and, incidentally, an early opportunity
to have *The Little Teacher* produced, in order to
devote himself to the study of Nova Scotian
sphagnum moss for use in surgical dressings. As
a result he became convinced of the utility of this
material and, almost single-handed, secured its
adoption. He "employed helpers, found and prepared the moss, arranged hospital demonstrations, raced to Washington at every chance of a
hearing, and finally won out" (Tompkins, *post,*
p. xiii). Having investigated Canadian resources, at his own expense, he discovered several fields of the moss in British Columbia, harvested it, and shipped it to France where it was
used in military hospitals. While engaged in
this work, he was killed near Murrayville, B. C.,
in a collision between his automobile and a train.
Altogether characteristic of the charm of his
conversation was the testimony of his chauffeur
that he had not noticed the train because he was
listening to what Smith was saying.

[*Letters of Harry James Smith* (1919) with an introduction by Juliet Wilbor Tompkins, and a brief
sketch; *Who's Who in America,* 1916–17; *The Record
of the Twenty-fifth Reunion of the Class of 1902, Williams College* (n.d.); obituaries in the *N. Y. Times,
N. Y. Herald, N. Y. Tribune.* Mar. 18, 1918; personal
acquaintance.]   E. S. B.

**SMITH, HENRY AUGUSTUS MIDDLE-
TON** (Apr. 30, 1853–Nov. 23, 1924), jurist,
local historian, born in Charleston, S. C., was
descended through his father, John Julius Prin-
gle Smith, from Robert Smith, 1732–1801 [*q.v.*],
the first Protestant Episcopal bishop of South
Carolina, and through his mother, Elizabeth
(Middleton), from Thomas, brother of Arthur
Middleton [*q.v.*], a signer of the Declaration of
Independence, whose famous seat, "Middleton
Place," came into Smith's possession. Much of
his early childhood was spent at "Beech Hill
Plantation." A schoolboy during the Civil War,
he witnessed the chaos that it brought; he was in
Columbia the morning that Sherman's army en-
tered, and he never forgot the destruction of the

Old South into which he had been born. After some years in Aiken, he returned to Charleston for his later education, and was graduated from the College of Charleston in 1872. Having read law in the office of McCrady & Sons, he was admitted to the bar in 1874, and for thirty-four years (1877–1911) was one of the leading lawyers of Charleston in the firm of Mitchell & Smith. On June 24, 1879, he married Emma, daughter of Maj. Arthur Middleton Rutledge of Franklin County, Tenn. She, with a son, survived him.

Although a consistent Democrat and never an office-seeker, in 1911 he was appointed by President Taft judge of the United States court for the Eastern District of South Carolina, in which capacity he served till 1923. Tending always to independence, his decisions in admiralty and citizenship cases were noteworthy, and he attracted considerable attention when he denied citizenship to a Syrian on the ground that the applicant was not white within the meaning of the law. Although he was austere and exacting on the bench, and reserved with those whom he had not admitted to intimacy, he possessed a subtle sense of humor and his judgments were mellowed by a secret vein of human sympathy. As a sportsman, he loved the out-of-doors; and as owner of several plantations, he planted successfully both rice and sea-island cotton. He was also a good botanist, and during several years of poor health made a hobby of studying the grasses of the coast. Always modest and unassuming, he frequently amazed specialists with his knowledge of widely diverse subjects, for he was an expert accountant, delighted in Italian and other languages, and was widely read in literature, theology, ethnology, anthropology, and Egyptology. He also wrote creditable verse. Always interested in history, he was an organizer and member of the South Carolina Historical Commission, and for twenty years a vice-president of the South Carolina Historical Society.

It is for his contributions in the field of South Carolina history that he is chiefly remembered. A lover of the land—and himself one of the largest land-owners in the state—he constituted himself its historian. His writings might well be called the Domesday Book of the South Carolina tidewater. Beginning with "The Colleton Family in South Carolina" in the first volume of the *South Carolina Historical and Genealogical Magazine* (October 1900), they concluded with "Goose Creek" in the twenty-ninth volume (October 1928). Drawn from manuscript sources, they all dealt with the land, tracing the original plans and following the histories of the settlers of early towns and baronies, and the chain of ownership of river seats and settlements. All were illustrated with maps the author had constructed from ancient plats. Of most general interest, perhaps, was his series, "The Baronies of South Carolina" (April 1910–January 1917), reprinted by the South Carolina Historical Society in 1931. Often legal in style and detailed in evidence, sometimes repetitious, but always clear and painstaking, his writings are a mine of information to the student of social history and second only to the original records in value.

[Recollections of Mabel L. Webber and Langdon Cheves; *Charleston Evening Post*, Nov. 24, 1924; *S. C. Hist. and Geneal. Mag.*, Jan. 1928; for genealogy, *N. Y. Geneal. and Biog. Record*, Oct. 1897; *Who's Who in America*, 1924–25; *News and Courier* (Charleston), Nov. 24, 1924.]   A. K. G.

SMITH, HENRY BOYNTON (Nov. 21, 1815–Feb. 7, 1877), Presbyterian clergyman and theologian, was born at Portland, Me., the son of Henry Smith, a merchant, and Arixene, daughter of Judge Robert Southgate of Scarborough, Me., and niece of Rufus King, 1755–1827 [q.v.]. He was descended in the fourth generation from John Smith who was married in Plainfield, Conn., in 1699. In his senior year at Bowdoin College, Henry Boynton Smith went through a religious experience which caused him to forsake Unitarianism, in which faith he had been reared, and to decide to be a minister. Graduating in 1834, he spent a year at Andover Theological Seminary and the following year at Bangor Seminary. After a year's teaching at Bowdoin (1836–37), he went to Europe because of ill health. Here he studied philosophy, theology, and church history at Halle and Berlin, laying the foundation for the knowledge of German thought and historical criticism by which he contributed much to American intellectual life. Returning in 1840, he taught another year at Bowdoin, and at length, on Dec. 29, 1842, was ordained to the Congregational ministry in West Amesbury, Mass. On Jan. 5, 1843, he was married to Elizabeth Lee Allen, daughter of William Allen, 1784–1868 [q.v.], sometime president of Bowdoin. His effective ministry to the congregation at West Amesbury ended in 1847 with his appointment to the professorship of philosophy in Amherst College. During the last two years of his pastorate he had also been instructor in sacred literature at Andover Seminary.

Smith's chief work began in 1850, when he went to Union Theological Seminary to teach for twenty-four years, first in the field of church history and after 1854 in that of theology. His reputation, steadily heightened by his writing, gave prestige to the young institution. He greatly enriched its library, of which he had charge during his whole service. By his teaching, character, and personal interest he deeply impressed the students. In theology he was of the school of Jonathan Edwards, but his encyclopedic knowledge, his contact with the intellectual currents of the world, his reconciling temper, and his endeavor to develop independent thought in his students made his influence broadening and awakening, so that he became a conspicuous representative of an orthodoxy of liberal tendencies. His conversation, abounding in original views, learning, and quaint humor, quickened the thinking of a wide circle of friends. The acknowledged intellectual leader of the New School Presbyterian Church, he was moderator of its General Assembly in 1863. To him more than any other was due the reunion of the two branches of the Presbyterian Church in 1869.

Much of Smith's best writing appeared in periodicals. For many years he contributed regularly to the *New York Evangelist*. From its establishment in 1859 he was editor of the *American Theological Review*, later published under several different titles. His many essays and reviews greatly enlarged his influence. One of his best-known articles was that ironically entitled "British Sympathy with America," published in the *Review* in July 1862, and later separately, which expressed the indignant disappointment of Northerners over what they considered British desertion of the cause of human freedom for financial gain, and powerfully vindicated the course of the United States in the Civil War. The most important examples of his service in introducing German theological work to Americans were his *Textbook of Church History* (5 vols., copr. 1855–79), a translation and revision of Johan K. L. Gieseler's work, and *A Textbook of the History of Doctrines* (2 vols., 1861–62), a revision and enlargement of C. W. Buch's translation of Karl R. Hagenbach's work. In his *History of the Church of Christ in Chronological Tables* (1859) much excellent writing on church history is obscured by a cumbrous form. From his manuscripts there were compiled *Apologetics* (1882), *Introduction to Christian Theology* (1883), and *System of Christian Theology* (1884).

In 1869–70 Smith was in Europe in search of health. He taught and carried on the *Review* under difficulties until 1874, when he resigned his professorship. Three years later he died in New York City, survived by his wife and four children.

[H. S. Munroe and A. D. Smith, *Ancestry of Henry Boynton Smith, Frederick Southgate Smith, and Horatio Southgate Smith* (1922); L. B. Chapman, *Mono-graph on the Southgate Family of Scarborough, Me.* (1907); E. L. Smith, *Henry Boynton Smith: His Life and Work* (1881); L. F. Stearns, *Henry Boynton Smith* (1892); G. L. Prentiss, *Union Theological Sem. in the City of N. Y.* (1889); R. E. Thompson, *Hist. of the Presbyt. Churches in the U. S.* (1895); *New York Evangelist*, Feb. 15, 1877; *Presbyterian Quart. and Princeton Rev.*, Apr. 1877; *N. Y. Tribune*, Feb. 8, 1877.]

R. H. N.

SMITH, HENRY PRESERVED (Oct. 23, 1847–Feb. 26, 1927), clergyman, Biblical scholar, was born at Troy, Ohio, the son of Preserved Smith and Lucy (Mayo) Smith, and the brother of Richmond Mayo-Smith [*q.v.*]. He was of Puritan descent, on his father's side going back to the Rev. Henry Smith, a graduate of Cambridge University, who came to New England about 1637 and a few years later became the first settled pastor at Wethersfield, Conn.; on his mother's side, to the Rev. John Mayo, first pastor of Second Church, Boston, 1650. His parents, who were New England Congregationalists, moved to Ohio, where they joined the New School Presbyterians. After his graduation from Amherst College in 1869 he studied theology at Lane Theological Seminary in Cincinnati, Ohio, where he graduated in 1872. He was licensed to preach in 1871 and was ordained in 1875 by the Presbytery of Dayton. He studied at the University of Berlin, Germany, in the winters of 1872–73 and 1873–74, with a trip to Palestine in the intervening spring. On his return to America he first taught church history at Lane Seminary for a year; in 1875 he became an instructor in Hebrew, and in 1876–77 went to the University of Leipzig in order to prepare himself more thoroughly for his professorship. On Dec. 27, 1877, he married Anna Macneale of Cincinnati. They had four children, two of whom survived their father. From 1877 to 1893 he was professor of Old Testament at Lane. Conservative by nature and training—even in Germany he had selected conservative teachers—he did not at first touch Biblical criticism in his teaching. But inevitably his study led him to see that the Bible text was corrupt, the Bible itself not infallible, the tradition about it untenable, and the use of textual, literary, and historical criticism inescapable. In order not to disturb the peace of the church he did not publish these views at once; although his article on "The Critical Theories of Julius Wellhausen" in the *Presbyterian Review* for April 1882 aroused some suspicion of his orthodoxy, nothing came of it. For himself it was momentous, for he had become convinced by Wellhausen's brilliant exposition of the truth of higher criticism. It was not till he felt impelled to speak out publicly in the General Assembly of the Presbyterian Church in defense of Charles

Augustus Briggs [*q.v.*], the great protagonist of higher criticism in the United States, that he was to feel the opposition of the conservatives. In November 1892 he was tried for heresy by the Presbytery of Cincinnati and suspended from the Presbyterian ministry because he denied the doctrine of the verbal inspiration and inerrancy of the Bible; the decision was upheld on appeal to the General Assembly of 1894. He gave up his professorship and his home at Cincinnati, and from 1893 to 1898 was without official position. He now wrote his *A Critical and Exegetical Commentary on the Books of Samuel* (1899) for the celebrated International Critical Commentary on the Holy Scriptures and gave the Ely Lectures at Union Theological Seminary on *The Bible and Islam* (1897). From 1898 till 1906 he was professor of Biblical literature and associate pastor at Amherst College; from 1907 to 1913 he taught the history of religions at Meadville Theological School; and from 1913 to 1925 he was chief librarian at Union Theological Seminary. In 1917 he was also made professor of Hebrew and cognate languages at Union, but he gave little of his time to teaching. After his resignation he lived in Poughkeepsie till his death.

His position in the history of American scholarship is secure not only because he was one of the pioneers who introduced modern Biblical criticism into the United States but also because he made important contributions to it. His *Samuel, Old Testament History* (1903), and *The Religion of Israel* (1914) are standard works; his *The Bible and Islam* and *Essays in Biblical Interpretation* (1921) rank high. In the bibliography appended to his autobiography, *The Heretic's Defense* (1926), there are sixty-five titles, many of great value. He had a singularly charming spirit. Though he was not eloquent or inspiring as a speaker or teacher, he was always clear and keen in thought and speech. A fearless fighter for truth and liberty, he dealt chivalrously, fairly, and sincerely with his opponents.

[H. R. Stiles, *The Hist. of Ancient Wethersfield* (1904), vol. II; *Who's Who in America*, 1926–27; H. P. Smith, *The Heretic's Defense* (1926); J. A. Bewer, in *Am. Jour. of Semitic Languages and Literatures*, July 1927, with portrait; obituary in *N. Y. Times*, Feb. 27, 1927.]   J. A. B.

SMITH, HEZEKIAH (Apr. 21, 1737–Jan. 24, 1805), Baptist clergyman, was born in Hempstead, Long Island, the son of Peter and Rebecca (Nichols) Smith (F. C. Torry, *The Ancestors and Descendants of Humphrey Nichols of Newark, New Jersey*, 1917, pp. 11–12, 18–19). In his youth the family moved to Morris County, N. J. Here, in 1756, he was baptized by John Gano

[*q.v.*] and immediately began to contemplate entering the ministry, notwithstanding the opposition of his father, who, however, yielded his consent at the solicitations of an older son and Gano. After preparatory studies at Hopewell Academy, he entered the College of New Jersey as a sophomore, graduating in 1762. Partly in the interest of his health, he started southward on horseback, preaching constantly during an itinerancy of fifteen months, during which time he covered over four thousand miles. At Charleston, S. C., he united with the Baptist Church, where he was ordained Sept. 20, 1763.

After his return north, he accompanied James Manning [*q.v.*] to Newport, R. I., and became associated with the founding and development of Rhode Island College (Brown University). Continuing his itinerant preaching, on July 27, 1764, he reached Haverhill, Mass., which was to become his home. After preaching for some weeks at a Congregational Church, he was invited to become its pastor. He thereupon acknowledged his views as to baptism, which terminated negotiations; but he had already stimulated the New Light elements in the community, and soon there was organized the First Baptist Church of Haverhill. On Nov. 12, 1766, he was installed as its pastor. According to his diary (Guild, *post*), he was married to Hephzibah Kimball of Boxford on June 27, 1771, though the vital records of Haverhill give the year as 1770. Four of their six children lived to maturity.

Smith exerted a wide and varied influence. His pastorate at Haverhill was distinguished by evangelistic preaching and pastoral ministration of marked effectiveness. Its routine was frequently interrupted by missionary journeys, especially into southern New Hampshire and the province of Maine, where he was instrumental in the organization of many churches. In the developing life of his denomination he was a positive factor, notably in the counsels of the Warren Association, of which he was one of the organizers (1767). Through his membership on its committee of grievances he played a part second only to that of Isaac Backus [*q.v.*] in the persistent effort of Baptists to secure separation of church and state. He was selected to go to England to confer with eminent Baptists there, with a view to obtaining from the British government relief from the intolerable situation in which the Baptists felt themselves placed, but other responsibilities compelled him to decline this mission. In the field of education, his great work was done for Rhode Island College. From his own student days the intimate friend of President Manning, he was one of the first fellows appointed and for some forty years attended assiduously to his duties. He devoted eight months, including the winter of 1769–70, to traveling in the South in behalf of the college, securing for its needs about $2,500. At the last meeting of the Corporation which he attended, only a few months before his death, Asa Messer [q.v.], one of several young men whom Smith had in part prepared for college while carrying on his ministerial duties at Haverhill, was elected to the presidency. As regimental (1775–78) and later as brigade chaplain (1778–80) in the Continental Army, Smith gained a wide fame and thereafter was generally known as Chaplain Smith. His character and ability won for him the esteem of the higher officers, including Washington himself. Evidences of his contemporary significance abound, justifying the epithet so often used, "the great man of Haverhill," an allusion to his place of residence rather than to his sphere of influence.

[R. A. Guild, *Chaplain Smith and the Baptists* (1885), gives copious selections from Smith's journal and from other papers, most, if not all, of which are now at the Lib. of Cong.; the account in W. B. Sprague, *Annals Am. Pulpit*, vol. VI (1860), which is largely followed in William Cathcart, *The Baptist Encyc.* (1881), records family tradition, which, as Guild points out, is incompatible with the statements in the journal. See also, A. S. Train, *Centennial Discourse . . . on the One Hundredth Anniversary of the Organization of the Baptist Church, Haverhill, Mass.* (1865); A. E. Vanderpoel, *Hist. of Chatham, N. J.* (1921); F. B. Heitman, *Hist. Reg. Officers of the Continental Army* (1914).]   W. H. A.

SMITH, HIRAM (Feb. 19, 1817–May 15, 1890), agriculturist, was a descendant of a long line of Quaker colonial ancestors, the first of whom came to America with William Penn. He was born in Tinicum, Bucks County, Pa. In 1820 his father, Jonas Smith, moved to New York state. Until 1847 Hiram and his brother A. J. Smith, who later became associate editor of *Hoard's Dairyman*, carried on the business of farming, foundry work, and plow-making at the family home in Lowville, N. Y. On Mar. 20, 1845, Hiram married Catherine A. Conover, by whom he had a son and a daughter. Two years later he moved to Sheboygan Falls, Wis., where he spent the rest of his life.

Buying a tract of government land, he ultimately developed it into one of the outstanding dairy farms of the state, being among the first in that section to turn from wheat farming to dairying. By the time of the Civil War, he had become one of the leading dairymen in Wisconsin. He was active in the early history of the Wisconsin Dairymen's Association, the group most largely responsible for the shift from grain farming to dairying. He was its president for

two years, 1875–76, and its vice-president from 1878 until his death. He was also influential in starting the Dairy Board of Trade at Sheboygan Falls in 1872 and was its first president, serving a second time in that capacity in 1889. In 1871–72 he was a member of the state legislature. He was appointed a regent of the University of Wisconsin in 1877 by Gov. William E. Smith, taking office the next year, and served continuously by successive appointments until his death. He was chairman of the agricultural committee of the regents and vice-president of the board in 1889–90.

While listening to a talk which Smith was giving before the farmers at the Manitowoc county fair, Assemblyman Charles E. Estabrook conceived the idea of having a series of talks given by successful farm leaders at gatherings similar to teachers' institutes. Accordingly, he introduced into the legislature and secured the passage, in 1885, of a bill providing for the establishment of farmers' institutes. The establishment at the University of Wisconsin of the first dairy school in the United States was also largely the work of Smith while one of the regents. The school opened in 1890, the year of his death, with two students; the next winter the enrollment reached seventy, partly as a result of reports of the famous milk tests made at the University under the direction of Stephen M. Babcock. A new dairy building was opened in January 1892 and was later named Hiram Smith Hall. Besides helping to establish the dairy school, Smith took an active part in forming the Wisconsin Agricultural Experiment Station and in building up the Wisconsin College of Agriculture.

[*Sheboygan County News*, May 21, 28, 1890; *Hoard's Dairyman*, May 23, 30, 1890; R. G. Thwaites, *The Univ. of Wis., Its Hist. and Its Alumni* (1900); J. F. A. Pyre, *Wisconsin* (1920); H. C. Adams, "In Memoriam," *19th Ann. Report of the Wis. Dairymen's Asso.* (1891); "Seven Wise Men of Wis.," in *Dairy Farmer*, Aug. 1, 1919; *Milwaukee Sentinel*, May 16, 1890; records of Univ. of Wis. Board of Regents, Doc. No. 101.]   W. A. S—r.

SMITH, HOKE (Sept. 2, 1855–Nov. 27, 1931), secretary of the interior, governor of Georgia, United States senator, was born in Newton, N. C., his parents being Hosea Hildreth Smith and Mary Brent (Hoke) Smith. Hosea Smith was a native of New Hampshire and a graduate of Bowdoin College; his wife was a North Carolinian; both were of Revolutionary ancestry. The elder Smith went to North Carolina in 1850 to become president of Catawba College at Newton. Six years later he was made professor of Greek and Latin at the University of North Carolina. Forced out during the troublous Reconstruction time, he set up a private school at

Lincolnton, N. C., in 1868, and in 1872 removed to Atlanta, where he was connected with the public-school system. The son, Hoke, growing up during the Civil War and Reconstruction period, received little formal education, but having a first-class mind and the advantage of the tutelage of such a father, he suffered little handicap from lack of conventional schooling. He read law in the offices of Collier, Mynatt, & Collier of Atlanta, and was admitted to the bar in 1873.

Smith took naturally to politics. Before reaching his majority he was chairman of the Fulton County Democratic executive committee. With the purchase in 1887 of the *Atlanta Journal,* he acquired an organ, edited and managed personally, which enabled him to build up a wide following for the liberal and reform movements associated with his name. In Cleveland's third contest for the Democratic presidential nomination (1892), Smith carried Georgia for him against David B. Hill. Smith was a delegate that year to the National Democratic Convention. In recognition of this service, Cleveland appointed him secretary of the interior. As secretary (1893–96), Smith was active in furthering the cause of conservation of natural resources in the West and in purging the pension list of fraud. In the silver agitation of the nineties, he upheld Cleveland's effort to maintain the gold standard. In the summer of 1896, before Bryan's nomination at Chicago, Smith stumped the state of Georgia in opposition to the candidacy of Congressman Charles F. Crisp [*q.v.*], a leading silverite, for a seat in the Senate. However, with the subsequent nomination of Bryan for the presidency, Smith took the position that preservation of white control in the South demanded that his section support the regular Democratic nominees. Feeling uncomfortable in Cleveland's cabinet, he resigned on Sept. 1, 1896.

Ten years elapsed before Smith was again in politics. During those years he advocated, in the columns of the *Journal* as long as he controlled it (until 1900) and later through his friend and supporter, James R. Gray, the new owner, the more effective control of railways, and the extension of the powers of the railroad commission. He urged the establishment of a highway department, denounced the convict-lease system, and in general allied himself with and became the leader of the progressive and reform element in the state. In 1906 he offered himself as a candidate for governor, along with four others, including Clark Howell, editor of the rival daily, the *Atlanta Constitution.* Smith appealed against ring rule and railroad domination of politics. The state railroad commission, he held, was

serving the railroads instead of the people and was stifling the state by maintaining excessive intrastate rates, especially between Atlanta and other interior points and the Georgia ports. With a view to the elimination of a purchasable element in the electorate, he advocated what amounted to the disfranchisement of negroes. In the Democratic primary, which was equivalent to election, he carried 122 of the 145 counties, and received a larger popular vote than all the other aspirants combined. He had two non-consecutive terms as governor, from July 1907 to July 1909, and from July 1911 to November 1911. In the primary of 1908 he was defeated by Joseph M. Brown, son of the war-time governor, Joseph E. Brown [*q.v.*], whom he had suspended from his office as state railroad commissioner. Smith and Brown again contested for the Democratic nomination in 1910 and Smith was victorious by a narrow margin. His two terms were marked by legislation of a distinctly progressive type. He accomplished more in extending the scope of social control in Georgia than any other governor in recent times. Under his leadership the General Assembly created the highway department and inaugurated the good-roads movement; it established the Department of Commerce and Labor; it uprooted the convict-lease system, long a reproach to the state; it passed a new suffrage law, imposing educational and property qualifications for the privilege of voting—a law which for many years operated principally to deprive negroes of the suffrage; and it increased the railroad commission from three to five members, and extended its jurisdiction over power, telephone and telegraph, express, street railway, and dock and wharf companies. The legislature also passed the first Southern state-wide prohibition law, though Smith preferred local option.

Shortly after Smith's second inauguration (July 1, 1911) he was elected by the legislature to fill the unexpired term of United States Senator A. S. Clay, who had died in the preceding fall. He did not, however, vacate the governorship until November, preferring to continue in office until his reform program could be enacted into law. In 1914 he was reëlected for the long senatorial term, defeating his old opponent, Joseph M. Brown. He served until 1921, being defeated for renomination in 1920 by Thomas E. Watson [*q.v.*]. Watson was an uncompromising opponent of the League of Nations; another candidate, Hugh M. Dorsey, supported the Wilson position; Smith favored the Senate reservations. Hoke Smith's prime interest as a senator was in furthering the cause of education, and more especially education of the vocational type. He was chairman of a Commission on National Aid to Vocational Education created by joint-resolution of Congress on Jan. 20, 1914. This commission made an exhaustive survey (published in 1914) out of which developed the Smith-Lever bill (May 8, 1914), which resulted in a nation-wide extension service devoted to the improvement of rural life; and the Smith-Hughes bill (Feb. 23, 1917), which provided for instruction in the common schools in agriculture, home economics, trade, and industry, and for the vocational rehabilitation of disabled civilians. He also secured the passage of a bill setting up a division of markets in the Department of Agriculture. While the country was still neutral in the World War, Smith made a fight to force all belligerents to respect American rights in the matter of international trade. After the entrance of the United States into the war, he was a powerful and effective supporter of all measures making for the more efficient conduct of the struggle. He disagreed with President Wilson on a number of issues, notably with reference to the League of Nations.

Hoke Smith was a man of impressive characteristics. He was uncommonly large and strong; as a public speaker he was forceful, even eloquent; as a leader he was fearless; in manner he was kindly and agreeable; he made friends easily and held them securely. Throughout his long career he played an important part in the civic development of Atlanta. He served for years as chairman of the Board of Education; he and his associates organized the Piedmont Hotel and the Fulton National Bank; it was largely through his efforts that the Federal Reserve Bank was located in Atlanta. On his death, the *Constitution*, which so long opposed him, said in an editorial (Nov. 28, 1931): "In going Senator Smith leaves an indelible imprint upon the history of the State which he served long and well." On Dec. 19, 1883, he married Birdie Cobb, daughter of Gen. Thomas R. R. Cobb [*q.v.*]. They had four children, a son and three daughters. Mrs. Smith died in 1919, and on Aug. 27, 1924, he married Mazie Crawford of Cordele, Ga. He was an elder in the North Avenue Presbyterian Church in Atlanta.

[A. D. Candler and C. A. Evans, ed., *Georgia* (1906), vol. III, 315–16; Clark Howell, *Hist. of Ga.* (1926), vol. I; *Who's Who in America*, 1930–31; *Who's Who in the South*, 1927; platform of first gubernatorial contest, *Atlanta Journal*, Sept. 5, 1906; Smith's address outlining his accomplishments as governor, *Ibid.*, July 1, 1911; obituary articles, in *Atlanta Journal*, Nov. 27, 1931, and *Atlanta Constitution*, Nov. 28, 1931; his gubernatorial messages in *Jour. of the Senate of the State of Ga.*, 1908, pp. 10–42; 1909, pp. 12–58; 1911, pp. 172–98; A. C. True, *A Hist. of Agric. Educ.* in the U. S., 1785–1925 (1929), pp. 281–82, 361–62, 365, 368; "Report of the Commission on National Aid to Vocational Education," *House Document No. 1004*, 63 Cong., 2 Sess. (2 vols., 1914).] R. P. B.

SMITH, HORACE (Oct. 28, 1808–Jan. 15, 1893), inventor, manufacturer, was born in Cheshire, Mass., and was the son of Silas and Phoebe Smith. When he was four years old his father, who was a carpenter by trade, moved with his family to Springfield, Mass., where he found work in the United States armory. Upon completing the public school curriculum in Springfield young Smith, then sixteen years old, entered the armory as a gunsmith's apprentice and spent eighteen years there becoming an expert gun maker. He then went to Norwich, Conn., and worked for a year with Charles Thurber [*q.v.*], the noted manufacturer of small arms. After spending a number of months in the armory of Eli Whitney at New Haven, Conn., making tools for the manufacture of rifles, he returned to Norwich and worked three years, 1843–46, in the pistol factory of Allen and Thurber. For three years he was in business for himself, manufacturing guns, but in 1849 gave it up to work for Oliver Allen in Norwich manufacturing whaling guns.

About this time he turned his attention to invention, particularly to the improvement of the breech-loading rifle, and obtained his first patent, No. 8317, Aug. 26, 1851. Before undertaking its manufacture, however, he took a position with Allen, Brown & Luther, manufacturers of rifle barrels in Worcester, Mass. While there, about 1852, he met Daniel Baird Wesson [*q.v.*], a gunsmith like himself, with whom he worked successfully, in spare time, on perfecting a repeating rifle. In 1853 they entered into partnership to manufacture the rifle in Norwich, and secured a patent on it, Feb. 14, 1854. In 1855 they were induced to sell out to the Volcanic (later the Winchester Repeating) Arms Company of New Haven. Smith returned to Springfield and for two years operated a livery stable with his brother-in-law. Meanwhile Wesson worked on the construction of a revolver to use a central-fire metallic cartridge he and Smith had devised and patented Aug. 8, 1854, which contained not only the requisite charge of powder but also a lubricant placed within the case between the powder and ball. In 1857 the two men reëstablished their partnership to make the new firearm and cartridge in Springfield, applying the principle of interchangeable parts in the manufacture. They produced their first revolvers late in 1857, before receiving their patents, which were issued July 5, 1859, and Dec. 18, 1860, respectively. From the beginning the demand for their revolver in the United States was very great, for it was adopted by the Federal military authorities; to meet it the partners were compelled to build a new plant in 1860, which had to be further enlarged periodically thereafter as the business grew. After 1867, when they exhibited their products at the international exposition at Paris, they secured large contracts with Japan, China, England, Russia, Spain, France, and most of the South American countries. In the succeeding years Smith and Wesson worked continually to better their revolver and cartridge, and not only patented a number of improvements of their own invention but also purchased the improvements of others—notably the invention of W. C. Dodge for extracting empty shells from the revolver cylinder, which they bought in 1869. Smith continued as executive head of the business for upwards of sixteen years. In July 1873 he sold his interest to Wesson and retired. He served two terms as an alderman of Springfield and was a director of a number of industrial enterprises; at the time of his death he was president of the Chicopee National Bank. He was married three times: first, to Eliza Foster, who died in 1836; second, to Mrs. Eliza Hebbard Jepson, who died in 1872, and third, to Mary Lucretia Hebbard, of Norwich, Conn., who died in 1887. He died leaving no direct descendants.

[C. W. Chapin, *Sketches of the Old Inhabitants and Other Citizens of Old Springfield* (1893); C. B. Norton, *Am. Inventions and Improvements in Breech-Loading Small Arms* (1880); J. W. Roe, *Eng. and Am. Tool Builders* (1926); obituary in *Springfield Republican*, Jan. 16, 1893; Patent Office records.]   C. W. M—n.

SMITH, ISRAEL (Apr. 6, 1759–Dec. 2, 1810), lawyer, politician, was born in Suffield, Conn., the son of Daniel and Anna (Kent) Smith, and during his childhood moved with his parents to Rupert, Vt. The family apparently was interested in securing adequate education and Israel graduated in 1781 at Yale, where an older brother, Noah, also to be prominent in the early politics of Vermont, had graduated three years before. After reading law with this brother in Bennington, Israel was admitted to the Vermont bar in 1783, and began practice in Rupert. Between 1785 and 1790 he served four terms in the legislature, its journals showing that he was active in the routine work of that body but throwing little light on his character or interests. In 1789 he served on a joint commission for adjusting boundary and title disputes with New York, and two years later took part in the convention which ratified the Constitution of the United States.

In 1791 he was elected to the federal House of Representatives, having removed to the larger and more prosperous town of Rutland in the same year. His term of service, extending from Oct. 17, 1791, to Mar. 3, 1797, was not characterized by any notable achievements. Party alignments were still fluctuating and Smith, in spite of his Yale training, moved into the Jeffersonian ranks, supporting the opponents of the administration in their effort to block the Jay Treaty by withholding the necessary appropriation. Throughout the remainder of his career he was identified with the Republican party. Defeated for Congress in 1797, he returned to Rutland, resumed practice, reëntered the legislature, and became chief justice, being ousted as a result of the Federalist victory of 1798. With the growth of Republican sentiment in Vermont he was elected to the Seventh Congress, serving from Mar. 4, 1801, to Mar. 3, 1803, when he entered the United States Senate, serving until Oct. 1, 1807. The scantily reported debates of that era fail to show the extent of his activity in the latter body, although he spoke with ability and vigor in support of Jefferson's foreign policy, denouncing British aggressions on neutral commerce (*Annals of Congress*, 9 Cong., 1 Sess., cols. 94–96). He resigned from the Senate in 1807 upon being elected governor, but held this office for one term only. His message to the legislature showed that in one matter, a more humane treatment of convicts, he was somewhat in advance of public sentiment. A year later his strength, mental and physical, having begun to deteriorate, he retired from public life. His unfortunate condition and early death deprived the state of a leader whose ability and temperate views would have been very useful in the disturbed era which accompanied the War of 1812.

Smith was married in his twenties and had two sons, one of whom died in childhood. His widow, Abiah, was married in 1811 to Col. William C. Harrington.

[*Records of the Gov. and Council of the State of Vermont*, esp. V (1877), 147–48, 393–96; W. H. Crockett, *Vermont*, V (1923), 70–71; F. B. Dexter, *Biog. Sketches Grads. Yale Coll.*, vol. IV (1907); A. M. Hemenway, *The Vt. Hist. Gazetteer*, III (1877), 1061–62; *Biog. Dir. Am. Cong.* (1928); *Rutland Daily Herald*, Oct. 12, 1867; date of birth and names of parents from the Suffield Vital Records through the courtesy of the Connecticut State Library; information concerning Smith's marriage from American Antiquarian Society, Worcester, Mass.]   W. A. R.

SMITH, JAMES (c. 1719–July 11, 1806), signer of the Declaration of Independence, was born in northern Ireland, the second son in a large family. His father, John, was induced to migrate to Pennsylvania (c. 1729) by his brothers, who had settled previously in Chester County. John Smith purchased a tract of land west of the Susquehanna in York County and became an enterprising farmer. James attended school in Philadelphia under the Rev. Francis Alison [*q.v.*], studying Latin, Greek, and surveying, and then read law in the office of his elder brother, George, at Lancaster. Shortly after his admission to the bar in 1745 he moved to Cumberland County, near Shippensburg, where he engaged in surveying and practised law when chance offered. After four or five years on the frontier he returned to York, which became his residence for the rest of his life. Although the only resident practising lawyer in town until 1769, he found little business during his early years there. Possibly it was this fact that encouraged him to take up iron manufacturing on the Codorus Creek in 1771. The venture cost him £5,000 before he sold out in April 1778. Of the two managers who brought about this loss he once remarked, with his accustomed drollery, that "the one was a knave, and the other a fool" (Carter and Glossbrenner, *post,* p. 172).

From the outbreak of trouble with the mother country, Smith assumed a rôle of leadership in the backcountry. In the provincial conference, July 1774, he read an "Essay on the Constitutional Power of Great Britain over the Colonies in America" (mentioned in *Three Signers, post*) and urged the non-importation of British goods and a general congress of the colonies as a means of securing redress for colonial grievances. Inspired by the proceedings of the conference, he returned to York and the following December raised a volunteer company of which he was chosen captain. The company later grew to a battalion, and he accepted the honorary title of colonel, leaving active command to younger men. He was a delegate to the provincial convention at Philadelphia in January 1775 and to the provincial conference, June 18–25, 1776. An ardent exponent of backcountry protests against the hegemony of the eastern counties, in the latter revolutionary body he helped to draft resolutions recommending independence and to set the wheels in motion for improving provincial defenses and for securing a new government. In the constitutional convention of 1776 he was a member of the committee to draft a new frame of government. Before the convention had been in session a week he was elected to Congress (July 20), and thus became a signer of the Declaration of Independence. Although left out of the delegation sent to Congress in February 1777, he was reëlected, Dec. 10, 1777, and served for the following year, declining election after that term.

He was a state-rights man, vigorously opposing all measures which might interfere with domestic police. While Congress met in York the meetings of the board of war were held in his office. After retiring from Congress he held but few political posts: he served one term in the assembly (1779); as judge of the Pennsylvania high court of errors and appeals (Nov. 20, 1780–May 10, 1781); as brigadier-general of militia (1782); and as counselor for Pennsylvania in the Wyoming controversy. In 1785 the assembly again honored him by electing him to Congress, but he declined on account of his age. From 1781 to 1801 he was chiefly engaged in the practice of law, and by the time of his retirement in 1801 he had acquired a substantial estate. Fire destroyed his office and practically all of his papers in the fall of 1805. Though regarded as somewhat eccentric, Smith was noted for his sharp wit, lively manner, and unusually retentive memory. An excellent conversationalist with a large store of anecdote, he drew around him many friends, especially prospective lawyers who read law in his office. He was married about 1760 to Eleanor, daughter of John Armor of New Castle, Del., who with two of their five children survived him.

[An adequate appraisal of Smith's life remains to be written. Material bearing on his career may be found in the following: W. C. Carter and A. J. Glossbrenner, *Hist. of York County* (1834), new ed. (1930), ed. by A. M. Aurand; W. H. Egle, in *Pa. Mag. of Hist. and Biog.,* IV (1880), 362–64; J. R. Harris, "The Peculiar Mr. Smith," in *Pa. Soc. Sons of the Am. Rev.: Papers . . . 1912–13–14 upon Pa. Signers of the Declaration of Independence* (n.d.); J. C. Jordan, "York, Pa., in the Revolution," *Pa. Mag. of Hist. and Biog.,* Oct. 1908; *James Wilson, James Smith and George Ross, Three Signers of the Declaration of Independence* (pamphlet, 1902); *Pa. Archives,* 2 ser., III (1875); and *Minutes of the Supreme Exec. Council of Pa.,* vols. XI, XII (1852–53).]　　　　　　　　　　J. H. P.

SMITH, JAMES (*c.* 1737–*c.* 1814), pioneer, soldier, and author, was born in the Conococheague settlement in what is now Franklin County, Pa. He received only a limited education, but was well versed in woodcraft and hardened to the rigors of frontier life. While helping to cut a road from Shippensburg to join Braddock's road at the Youghiogheny in 1755, he was captured by Indians and adopted into one of their families. He subsequently accompanied his captors in their wanderings through the Ohio country until his escape, near Montreal, in 1759. Early in 1760, he returned to the Conococheague region, settled at his old home, and engaged in farming.

Following his marriage, in 1763, he entered upon an adventurous career, embracing leadership in 1763, 1765, and 1769 of the so-called "Black Boys"—self-constituted rangers whose purpose was to defend the frontier settlements against Indian attacks, service as an ensign in

1763, and service as a lieutenant in Bouquet's expedition against the Ohio Indians in 1764. In 1766-67, with a small party, he made an exploration into southern Kentucky and Tennessee, which, with the exception of tours made by Henry Scaggs, a hunter, is said to have been the first made by Anglo-Americans into the country west of the Cumberland Mountains in Tennessee. About 1769 Smith removed to a farm on Jacob's Creek, a branch of the Youghiogheny, in the region that became first Bedford, then Westmoreland County, Pa. He was a member of the board of commissioners of Bedford County in 1771, and of Westmoreland in 1773, and was a captain of militia in 1774; he was a member of the Westmoreland County convention in 1776, and of the Pennsylvania Assembly, 1776-77. During the next two years he was engaged in fighting Indians in western Pennsylvania, in 1778 being commissioned colonel of militia.

After the close of the war, he spent most of the summer of 1785 in Kentucky, looking after some land claims, and thither he removed in 1788, settling on Cane Ridge, in Bourbon County, about seven miles from Paris. That same year he was elected a member of the convention which sat at Danville, Nov. 4, 1788, to deliberate about separation from Virginia. He was a member of the constitutional convention of 1792, and afterwards, until 1799, with the exception of the session of 1796, he represented Bourbon County in the General Assembly of Kentucky.

Smith was somewhat of a religious enthusiast and for some time took an active part in the reform movement headed by Barton W. Stone [q.v.] but he eventually returned to the Presbyterian Church, from which he had withdrawn, and, receiving licensure, spent much time in his later years as a missionary among the Indians. On returning from one of his missionary excursions into Tennessee, he found that his son James had joined the Shakers and had taken his family to the Shaker settlement on Turtle Creek, near Lebanon, Ohio. After sojourning for a short time with that sect, the father poured out his wrath upon their leaders in a pamphlet entitled *Remarkable Occurrences Lately Discovered among the People Called Shakers; of a Treasonous and Barbarous Nature; or Shakerism Developed* (1810), of which a second edition soon appeared. This brought a rejoinder from Richard McNemar, one of the Shaker leaders; Smith again appeared in print, in a pamphlet entitled *Shakerism Detected; Their Erroneous and Treasonous Proceedings ... Exposed to Public View* (1810); and was answered by McNemar in the following year.

The book which constitutes Smith's chief title to fame as an author, however, was *An Account of the Remarkable Occurrences in the Life and Travels of Col. James Smith, During His Captivity with the Indians, in the Years 1755, '56, '57, '58 & '59,* printed and published by John Bradford in Lexington, Ky., in 1799. This valuable work has been reprinted several times, and much or all of it has been reproduced in various publications relating to the Indians and pioneers of the Ohio Valley. In 1812, Smith published *A Treatise on the Mode and Manner of Indian War, Their Tactics, Discipline and Encampments,* drawn largely from his previous *Account.*

Smith was a man of quiet and taciturn character, and much given to religious study and meditation. He had the courage of his convictions, however, and, when roused, displayed more than ordinary talent in debate. In May 1763, he married Anne Wilson, by whom he had seven children. She died about 1783, in Pennsylvania, and some two years later he married Margaret (Rodgers), widow of Abraham Irvin. She died in 1800, in Bourbon County, Ky., survived by her husband and several children born of her first marriage.

[Biog. sketch by Robert Clarke and notes by W. M. Darlington, in the 1870 edition of *An Account of the ... Travels of Col. James Smith;* biog. introduction to 1834 edition; Lewis and R. H. Collins, *Hist. of Ky.* (2 vols., 1874); Henry Howe, *Hist. Colls. of Ohio* (3 vols., 1891); J. N. Boucher, *Hist. of Westmoreland County, Pa.* (1906); P. G. Thomson, *A Bibliog. of the State of Ohio* (1880).]   S. M. W.

SMITH, JAMES (June 12, 1851–Apr. 1, 1927), United States senator, Democratic boss of New Jersey, was born in Newark, N. J., the son of Irish immigrants, James and Mary (Lyndon) Smith. After attending private schools and St. Mary's College, Wilmington, Del., he embarked upon a business career. Beginning as a clerk in his father's grocery store, he subsequently became a member of the J. H. Halsey & Smith Company, engaged in manufacturing patent and enameled leathers, and built up one of the largest establishments of its kind in the country. In 1904 he became president of the Federal Trust Company of Newark, and for several years owned the *Newark Advertiser* and its successor, the *Star.* These and other important financial interests gave him prominence in the business community, but it was chiefly through his position as Democratic overlord that he became a powerful influence in the affairs of New Jersey.

He rose to this estate as a result of many years of participation in local, state, and national politics. Beginning as an alderman (1883-87), he served as president of the board of works of

Newark and was chairman of the state's delegations to the Democratic National Convention in 1884, 1892, and 1896. In 1892 he swung his delegation from David B. Hill to Cleveland, and the following year, "with money as plentiful as ugly rumors" (Kerney, *post*, p. 20), he was elected to the United States Senate. There during his single term his services were undistinguished. He spoke infrequently and in voting generally reflected the views of "big business." The belief that he, along with other senators, had speculated in sugar stocks while the Wilson tariff bill was pending resulted in a Senate investigation. Smith denied the accusation (*Senate Report 606,* 53 Cong., 2 Sess.), but a strong suspicion against him remained long after he left the Senate.

Although his close alliance with the vested interests of New Jersey was well known and subject to much criticism, it was not until 1910 that his domination of the Democratic organization was threatened. Then he was prevailed upon by George Harvey [*q.v.*] to accept Woodrow Wilson as the Democratic candidate for governor, and by "steam-roller" methods in the state convention he forced Wilson's nomination. After the party's triumph at the polls in November, Smith put himself forward as a candidate for the Senate, despite previous assurances that he would not enter the contest. Wilson stood by the winner of the September primary, however, and succeeded in defeating Smith when the legislature balloted in January 1911. In revenge the latter fought the Governor's legislative program, but without much success. Another effort in 1912 to return to the Senate also failed, when he was beaten in the primary by Wilson's choice, William Hughes. These reverses, together with the collapse of his private business interests in 1915, destroyed his power and forced his retirement from public life.

In 1874 Smith was married to Katherine R. Nugent of Newark, who died in 1910. Ten children were born to them, of whom six survived their father. His death occurred in Newark, in his seventy-sixth year.

[*Biog. Dir. Am. Cong.* (1928); *Who's Who in America,* 1926–27; James Kerney, *The Political Education of Woodrow Wilson* (1926); R. S. Baker, *Woodrow Wilson,* vol. III (1931); R. E. Annin, *Woodrow Wilson* (1924); *N. Y. Times, Newark Star-Eagle, Newark Evening News,* Apr. 2, 1927; name of Smith's mother from his daughter.]   A. H. M.

SMITH, JAMES ALLEN (May 5, 1860–Jan. 30, 1924), political scientist, was born at Pleasant Hill, Mo., the son of Isaac James and Naomi (Holloway) Smith. His ancestors were Virginians and Kentuckians who became large land

owners and slave-holders in Missouri. As a boy he grew up amid the bitter political and social antagonisms growing out of the Civil War and Reconstruction. He prepared for college in the schools of Kansas City and graduated from the University of Missouri in 1886. As an undergraduate he took a prominent part in discussion groups interested in economic and political subjects, and was influenced by the writings of Henry George.

Immediately after graduation he entered the law school, received the degree of LL.B. in 1887, and then began practice in Kansas City. He was not happy in his profession, however; the narrow limits of the legal life annoyed him. On Nov. 26, 1890, he married Doris J. Lehmann, of Kansas City, who appreciated his scholarly abilities and urged him to pursue work in the social sciences. Entering the University of Michigan, he came under the influence and guidance of Henry Carter Adams [*q.v.*]. Smith's dissertation for the doctorate was a theoretical study of money which refuted many of the basic contentions of the gold standard advocates; fundamentally it was an exposition of the ideas since made familiar by Irving Fisher's "Compensated Dollar." The thesis was vigorously opposed by some members of the faculty but Smith successfully defended his view and received the degree of Ph.D. in 1894. In 1895 he was elected professor of economics and sociology at Marietta College. In March 1896 his dissertation was published, under the title "The Multiple Money Standard," in *Annals of the American Academy of Political and Social Science.* It at once became the subject of controversy in the bitter monetary discussions of that year, and the following year he was dropped from the faculty, ostensibly for reasons of economy, although a successor was immediately elected in his place. In 1897 he became professor of political science at the University of Washington, with which institution he remained until his death. He was dean of the graduate school from 1909 to 1920, relinquishing the duties because of declining health.

On the eve of another political upheaval he published his best-known work, *The Spirit of American Government* (1907), which profoundly influenced Theodore Roosevelt, LaFollette, and many of the leading Progressives. It is a presentation of the underlying principles of American government which emphasizes the undemocratic features, laying particular stress on the arrangement of checks and balances, party organization, judicial review, and the general confusion and irresponsibility of political parties. Because of his views Smith became the storm center of hostile criticism, and repeated efforts were made to remove him from his professorship; but all were unsuccessful. Personally he was a large, handsome man, but extremely modest and retiring except among intimate friends. He never sought a quarrel but having been engaged in one he pursued it to the bitter end. In his classroom he was an inspiring, fearless, and stimulating teacher. He was at his best, as his students soon learned, when his views were stiffly opposed. Repeatedly denounced as a radical, he was, in fact, a Jeffersonian democrat who insisted upon teaching the truth as he saw it, in his own field, irrespective of criticism. He more than once declined administrative college positions; in 1912, he could have been nominated for governor of Washington by the Progressive party; in 1922, he was urged to become a candidate for the United States Senate; none of these opportunities appealed to him; he was a scholar interested in teaching.

Despite recurring attacks of heart trouble, he worked steadily to complete his last book, to which, with the aid of his daughter, he was giving final revision at the time of his death. This volume, *The Growth and Decadence of Constitutional Government* (copr. 1930), is a protest against the centralization of administration in the federal government, and against the concept of the modern state as a dominating influence rendering popular control ineffective; it is also a plea for increased freedom of initiative and authority on the part of the local government.

[V. L. Parrington, *Main Currents in Am. Thought,* vol. I (1927), and introduction to *The Growth and Decadence of Constitutional Government*; *Am. Pol. Sci. Rev.,* Feb. 1909, p. 138, May 1930, p. 524; *Who's Who in America,* 1923–24; T. S. Barclay, in *Mo. Alumnus,* Apr. 1931; *Seattle Daily Times,* Jan. 30, 1924; *N. Y. Times,* Jan. 31, 1924; private letters and papers.]
E. M.

SMITH, JAMES FRANCIS (Jan. 28, 1859–June 29, 1928), soldier, lawyer, colonial administrator, was a native of San Francisco, Cal., the son of Patrick and Ann Smith. After a common-school education, he graduated from Santa Clara College in 1877 with the degree of B.S.; in 1878 he received the degrees of B.A. and M.A. After studying law at Hastings College of the Law, San Francisco, he was admitted to the bar in January 1881 and began the practice of his profession. On Aug. 13, 1885, he married Lillie A. Dunnigan of Santa Clara (d. March 1910). During early manhood he became actively interested in local military affairs, and on May 6, 1898, was commissioned colonel, 1st California Volunteer Infantry, and commanded that regiment in the early expedition to the Philippine

Islands that followed the outbreak of the War with Spain. His regiment played a brilliant part in the first day's fighting at the capture of the city of Manila (Blount, *post,* pp. 193–94). Upon occupation of the city by the American forces, he was appointed deputy provost marshal, and in October was placed in command of the 1st Brigade, 1st Division, VIII Army Corps. Early in January 1899 he was appointed a member of the military commission to confer with commissioners designated by Emilio Aguinaldo regarding peace between the American forces and the Filipino insurgents. Soon afterward he took part in the engagement at Santa Ana, Feb. 5, and in the subsequent fighting at San Pedro Macatí, Pateros, and Taguig, Feb. 15–Mar. 1, 1899. He was officially commended in dispatches for gallantry in these actions, and was placed in command of the island of Negros as a sub-district of the insular military government.

Advanced to the grade of brigadier-general, United States Volunteers, Apr. 24, 1899, he was designated military governor of Negros and subsequently military governor of the Visayas. So successful was he in winning the good-will and the respect of the Filipinos that during the so-called Philippine Insurrection the island groups under his control gave little or no trouble to the American authorities (Blount, *post,* p. 557; Le Roy, *post,* II, 108–10). Rather against his personal wishes, he was made collector of Philippine customs at Manila, and applied to a troublesome problem of the new American government administrative methods that were both wise and efficient. With the inauguration of civil government in the islands under William Howard Taft, he was discharged from the military service and appointed an associate justice of the supreme court of the Philippines, June 17, 1901, an office he filled most creditably. In January 1903 he resigned to accept the portfolio of secretary of public instruction. A member of the Philippine Commission, which was virtually the cabinet of the governor-general, he was appointed as vice-governor in January 1906. On Sept. 20, 1906, he succeeded Henry Clay Ide [*q.v.*] as governor-general and served with great ability and marked success until May 1909, when he went to the United States. During this visit he resigned to practise law in the United States, his resignation taking effect Nov. 11, 1909. It was during his term of office that the Philippine legislature met for the first time, Oct. 16, 1907, and it was largely due to his tactful as well as practical assistance that the two houses that formed the legislature worked in comparative harmony (Worcester, *post,* I, 353). In March

1910 he was appointed an associate justice, United States court of customs appeals, an office he held for some eighteen years. (For his reports see *Court of Customs Appeals Reports,* vols. I–XVI, 1911–1929.) He served also as relief justice for the District of Columbia supreme court and court of appeals. He died at Washington after a severe heart attack that occurred while he was on the bench in an important case. He was survived by his son (*Evening Star,* Washington, *post*).

[*Who's Who in America, 1928–29; Eighth Ann. Report of the Philippine Commission to the Sec'y of War, 1907* (3 pts., 1908); *Report of the Philippine Com. to the Sec'y of War, 1908* (2 pts., 1909); J. A. LeRoy, *The Americans in the Philippines* (2 vols., 1914); D. C. Worcester, *The Philippines Past and Present* (1914), vol. I; J. H. Blount, *The Am. Occupation of the Philippines, 1898–1912* (1912); *Court of Customs Appeals Reports,* vol. XVI (1929), pp. 1–14; obituary in *Evening Star* (Washington, D. C.), June 30, 1928.]

C. D. R.

SMITH, JAMES McCUNE (Apr. 18, 1813–Nov. 17, 1865), negro physician and writer, was born in New York City, the "son of a slave, owing his liberty to the Emancipation Act of the State of New York and of a self-emancipated bondswoman" (Frederick Douglass, *My Bondage and My Freedom,* 1855, see the introduction by Smith). Both were of mixed blood. In the *Matriculation Albums of the University of Glasgow* (1913) is the notation in his own hand, "*Filius natu maximus Samuelis, Mercatoris apud New York.*" He was educated in the African Free School on Mulberry St., between Grand and Hester. Here, on Sept. 10, 1824, Lafayette addressed the pupils and young Smith, aged eleven, was chosen to make the reply. He entered the University of Glasgow in 1832, receiving the degrees of B.A. in 1835, M.A. in 1836 and M.D. in 1837. Following a short period in the clinics of Paris, he returned to New York City to practise medicine, and shortly thereafter opened a pharmacy on West Broadway, said to be the first in the country to be operated by a negro.

For twenty-five years he was a skilful and successful practitioner of medicine and surgery but his claims to remembrance rest upon his writings and his public service in the interest of his race. For twenty years he was on the medical staff of the Free Negro Orphan Asylum. In 1846 Gerrit Smith [*q.v.*], of Peterboro, N. Y., donated 120,000 acres of land in that state for distribution among the negroes of New York City. Smith, with two prominent negro clergymen, was chosen to select the names of about 2,000 heads of families to receive plots of land. The committee issued an address in pamphlet form (1846) extolling the project and the generosity of the donor. For a variety of reasons the venture was not a success. He was a consistent opponent of the American Colonization Society, formed for the purpose of repatriating negroes in Africa. In 1852 at a meeting of colored people in Albany, N. Y., he induced the assembly to adopt a resolution of protest against Governor Hunt's proposal to the state legislature for an appropriation in support of the colonization project. Interested in every phase of negro welfare, he was prominent in New York activities of the Underground Railroad. As early as 1833 Smith was a contributor to *Emancipator* and from January to May 1839, he was an editor of the *Colored American.* To this journal he contributed "Abolition of Slavery and the Slave Trade in the French and British Colonies," June 9, 1838. In 1841 he issued in pamphlet form *A Lecture on the Haytien Revolutions; with a Sketch of the Character of Toussaint L'Ouverture,* and in 1844, "Freedom and Slavery for Africans" in the *New York Tribune* (reprinted in the *Liberator,* Feb. 16, 23, 1844). During the short life of the *Anglo-African Magazine* (1859–60) he contributed: "Civilization: Its Dependence on Physical Circumstances," January 1859; "The German Invasion," an article on waves of immigration and their effects upon American life, February 1859; "Citizenship," a discussion of the Dred Scott decision, May 1859; and "On The Fourteenth Query of Thomas Jefferson's Notes on Virginia," a discourse upon the comparative anatomy of the white and black races, August 1859. Throughout his career he was engaged in controversy in support of the physical and moral equality of the black race. He contributed to *Hunt's Merchants' Magazine,* April and May 1846, an article on "The Influence of Climate upon Longevity" in reply to an attack upon the race by John C. Calhoun. He wrote one essay for each of the two volumes of the collection, *Autographs for Freedom* (1853, 1854). His writings show high scholarship, with a knowledge of the sciences, of history, and of foreign languages and literature. He was thought to be the most scholarly negro writer of his day by Henry Highland Garnet [*q.v.*]. At the request of the congregation of the Fifteenth Street Presbyterian Church of Washington, D. C., he wrote the introduction on the "Life and Labors of Rev. Henry Highland Garnet" for Garnet's *A Memorial Discourse* (1865). In 1863 he accepted an appointment as professor of anthropology at Wilberforce University, but failing health prevented his teaching, and he died after a prolonged illness from heart disease at his home in Williamsburg, Long Island, whither he had moved in 1864. He left a widow and five children.

[*Medic. Reg. of the City of N. Y.*, 1866; *Jour. of Negro Hist.*, Apr. 1916, Apr. 1921; G. W. Williams, *Hist. of the Negro Race in America* (2 vols., 1882); C. G. Woodson, *The Negro in Our History* (5th ed., 1928); D. A. Payne, *Recoll. of Seventy Years* (1888); Vernon Loggins, *The Negro Author* (1931); *New York Tribune*, Nov. 18, 1865.]   J. M. P.

SMITH, JAMES PERRIN (Nov. 27, 1864–Jan. 1, 1931), paleontologist, geologist, and teacher, was born near Cokesbury, Abbeville County, S. C., the son of the Rev. James Francis and Juliana (Forster) Smith. The Smith family was of English origin and had settled in Virginia, moving later to South Carolina. The boy received his early education at home until the family moved to Spartanburg where he entered the preparatory school of Wofford College. From 1876 to 1879 he was tutored by his brother, Charles Forster Smith [*q.v.*], and in 1884 was graduated with the B.A. degree from the college. Two years later he received the M.A. degree from Vanderbilt University, Nashville, Tenn. He then taught in the Nashville high school until 1888 when he was appointed assistant chemist and geologist for the newly organized Arkansas Geological Survey.

A desire for further study led him to resign his position and to go to Germany in 1890. He worked at the University of Göttingen in paleontology under Professor von Koenen and in mineralogy under Professor Liebisch, receiving the Ph.D. degree in 1892. After a brief period of study under von Zittel at Munich he returned to the United States to accept a position as the associate of John Casper Branner [*q.v.*] in the department of geology at Leland Stanford University, Palo Alto, Cal. He taught historical geology, paleontology, mineralogy, crystallography, and petrography until 1905 when he was made professor of paleontology. The study of the ammonites particularly absorbed his interest while at Stanford. He made numerous collecting trips to study the stratigraphy of various parts of western United States. He also came to be regarded as an authority on the geology of California and in 1916 superintended the compilation of a geological map of the state and prepared a descriptive report to accompany it.

From 1895 to 1906 he was assistant geologist in the United States Geological Survey and, from 1906 to 1924, geologist. His life-time work on the ammonites group culminated in the publication of a notable series of studies by the Survey: *The Carboniferous Ammonoids of America, Monographs of the United States Geological Survey*, volume XLII (1903); *The Triassic Cephalopod Genera of America, Professional Paper 40* (1905); *The Middle Triassic Marine Invertebrate Faunas of North America, Professional Paper 83* (1914); *Upper Triassic Marine Invertebrate Faunas of North America, Professional Paper 141* (1927); and *Lower Triassic Ammonoids of North America, Professional Paper 167* (1932). He published more than fifty other papers in various scientific journals and collections. In 1925 he was elected to membership in the National Academy of Sciences, and on Apr. 24, 1928, received the Mary Clark Thompson Gold Medal for his work in geology and paleontology. During thirty-seven years of teaching, Smith built up a solid following of students and took an intimate part in the life of the university. The social as well as the academic atmosphere of the college classroom appealed to him; he was fond of sports and possessed an unfailing sense of humor. At his death he was survived by his wife, Frances Norris Rand, to whom he had been married on Aug. 19, 1896, a daughter and three sons.

[Personal knowledge; information from the family; *Who's Who in America*, 1930–31; *Science*, Apr. 10, 1931; *Stanford Illustrated Rev.*, Feb. 1931; *San Francisco Examiner*, Jan. 2, 1931.]   S. S.

SMITH, JAMES YOUNGS (Sept. 15, 1809–Mar. 26, 1876), manufacturer, governor of Rhode Island, was born in Poquonoc village, in the town of Groton, Conn., the son of Amos Denison and Priscilla (Mitchell) Smith, the latter a descendant of Priscilla Mullins who came to Plymouth in the *Mayflower*. Born in humble surroundings, Smith rose to positions of prominence and responsibility by reason of native ability, indefatigable industry, and a securely founded reputation for unquestionable integrity. His formal education was such as could be obtained by intermittent attendance at a district school, and it ended when he was thirteen years old. At that time he became a clerk in the general store of his native town. In 1826, having exhausted the opportunities of this limited position, he moved to Providence and entered the counting-room of Aborn & Smith, lumber dealers. In 1830 he had made himself sufficiently important in the business to be admitted to partnership, and in 1837 he assumed full proprietorship. On Aug. 13, 1835, he married Emily Brown, daughter of Thomas Brown of Providence. They had three children, a son who died young, and two daughters. Brown was a successful cotton manufacturer and through him Smith began to turn his attention and his investments from the lumber business to that of cotton. In 1843 he entered into a partnership with his brother Amos, under the firm name of A. D. & J. Y. Smith, and engaged in the manufacture of cotton goods, and in carrying on a wholesale merchandise business. To these enterprises, as to all his financial ventures, he gave the most careful and constant personal attention. Some of the mills being at a considerable distance from Providence, he frequently made long journeys at night to avoid encroaching on the working hours of the day. In 1862 he withdrew from partnership with his brother and organized the James Y. Smith Manufacturing Company, which, with the admission of his sons-in-law, became James Y. Smith, Nichols & Rogers.

Smith found time for official public service. He was long a member of the Providence school committee, and for two years (1855, 1856) he was mayor of the city. In 1861 he was nominated for governor by the Republican party but was defeated in the election. Two years later he was renominated and this time was successful. He held the office from 1863 to 1866, declining to serve longer. In 1865 he had established an unequaled record when he received a majority vote in every town and ward of the state. His period of service as governor fell within the difficult period of the Civil War, and though he gave himself unsparingly to furthering the purposes and orders of the federal government, he did not escape criticism. Rhode Island had refused to draft its citizens to complete the quotas required of it, and it was necessary to hire recruiting officers and offer bounties, a method which required the raising and handling of large sums of money. In some instances fraudulent practices developed and Governor Smith's political enemies endeavored to lay upon him a certain measure of responsibility. It proved impossible to attach any real blame to him, however, and his reputation as a disinterested leader in public affairs was undisturbed.

To an unusual degree he enjoyed the respect and confidence of his fellow citizens, evidenced, among other ways, by the frequency with which his services as director were sought by local banks and insurance companies and as a member of committees to carry out public works. He was a man of sensitive sympathies, and his philanthropies were extensive. No intermediary was permitted to act for him, his contacts with those whose poverty or distress had brought them to his notice were always personal. For years he was the outstanding figure of Rhode Island.

[*Representative Men and Old Families of R. I.* (1908); *The Biog. Cyc. of Representative Men of R. I.* (1881); Charles Carroll, *R. I.: Three Centuries of Democracy* (1932), vol. II; *Providence Jour.*, Mar. 27, 1876.]
                                        E. R. B.

SMITH, JEDEDIAH STRONG (June 24, 1798–May 27, 1831), trader, explorer, was the son of Jedediah Smith, a native of New Hampshire. Born in Bainbridge, Chenango County, New York, he received a fair English education, acquired a little Latin, and learned to write a good hand. At thirteen he became clerk on a Lake Erie freighter, learning business methods and presumably meeting traders returning from the Far West to Montreal from whom he imbibed an ambition for adventurous wilderness trade. Testimony concerning the time of Smith's arrival at the frontier is conflicting. He may have been in St. Louis as early as 1816, or he may have gone there several years later.

Gen. William Henry Ashley [q.v.], who organized his Rocky Mountain trade in 1822, probably had Smith in his employ from the first. It is certain that the latter was on the upper Missouri with Ashley in 1823, and continued with him thereafter until, at Great Salt Lake in the summer of 1826, Ashley sold his business to Smith, David E. Jackson, and William L. Sublette, all trusty lieutenants of the previous years' campaigns. These three men now carried on the Rocky Mountain trade till the summer of 1830, when they sold out to other mountain men, among them James Bridger [q.v.].

It was in the period 1826–30 that Smith made the journeys on which his fame as an explorer rests. He had already become familiar with the trade of the Columbia region, contested by the British, and he now proposed to investigate the Southwest and the practicability of penetrating the Oregon country from California. Leaving Great Salt Lake in August 1826, with seventeen men, he passed through the nations of the Utes, the Paiutes, and the Mohaves, and entered California from the Mohave desert, on Nov. 27, reaching the Mission San Gabriel, where he was kindly received. The governor of California was suspicious of him, however, and it was only through the intercession of Capt. W. H. Cunningham of the ship *Courier*, of Boston, that he escaped imprisonment and received permission to lead his party back across the mountains. His plan to go north into Oregon was temporarily frustrated.

Smith proceeded eastward and northward to the valley of King's River whence, in February 1827, he tried to cross the mountains and failed. He then moved farther north, to the American River, established camp for his main party, and, taking with him two companions, in May crossed the mountains, probably on the line of the present railway (Merriam, *post*). He did not chance upon the Humboldt River, and made his dreary way to Salt Lake over the unrelieved desert. About a month later he retraced the previous year's route, this time with a company of eighteen men, but the Mohave Indians, probably instigated thereto by the Californians, attacked the party treacherously, killing ten and plundering goods and papers.

With the remaining eight, Smith reached San Gabriel Mission, secured a few necessaries, and turned northeast to join the men left on the American. He found them in sad plight, which he was unable to relieve. Jeopardizing his own liberty, which would have been lost had not a group of American skippers at Monterey come to his aid, he now put himself in the hands of Governor Echeandía and finally gained permission to purchase supplies and leave the country. He wintered in the Sacramento Valley, but in April 1828, instead of crossing the mountains eastward or directly northward, he headed northwest and on June 8 reached the seacoast at the mouth of Klamath River. On July 14, he had already crossed the Umpqua on the way to the Willamette, his chosen route to the Columbia, when the Umpqua Indians massacred all his men save two. Smith and John Turner followed the Willamette route to Fort Vancouver, where they found Arthur Black, the other survivor. Dr. John McLoughlin [q.v.] aided Smith to recover his property, kept him as guest till March, and gave him a passage up the river to the Spokane, whence he made his way, over ground already familiar, to Pierre's Hole, the new rendezvous.

Smith retired from the Rocky Mountain trade the following year. In 1831 he entered the Santa Fé trade and toward the end of May, at a water hole near the Cimarron, he was surrounded by a body of hostile Comanches and killed. He was the first explorer of the Great Basin, the first American, so far as is known, to make his way into California from the east and out of California from the west. His road to Oregon is in part identical with the modern Roosevelt Highway along the coast. Smith was a gentlemanly character and a devout Christian, reared under Methodist influences.

[The chief source is H. C. Dale, *The Ashley-Smith Explorations and the Discovery of a Central Route to the Pacific, 1822–1829* (1918); M. S. Sullivan, *The Travels of Jedediah Smith* (1934), prints a more recently discovered transcript of a narrative of Smith's, and a fragment of his journal, together with other previously unpublished documents; see also H. D. Fisher, "The First Smith of California," *Am. Mercury*, Sept. 1928. For Smith's route east from California, this sketch follows the interpretation of C. H. Merriam in "First Crossing of the Sierra Nevada: Jedediah Smith's trip from California to Salt Lake in 1827," *Sierra Club Bull.*, vol. XI, no. 4 (1923), which differs from that of Dale and Sullivan. The date of birth given above is from a eulogy in the *Illinois Magazine*, June

1832; another date, Jan. 6, 1799, appears in a photographic facsimile of a family Bible record, dated 1834, printed in Sullivan, *ante*.]   J.S.

SMITH, JEREMIAH (Nov. 29, 1759–Sept. 21, 1842), congressman, governor of New Hampshire, jurist, was born in Peterborough, N. H., one of the younger members in a typical pioneer family of ten children. His parents were William Smith, an emigrant from the North of Ireland, and Elizabeth (Morison) Smith. From his Scotch-Irish ancestry Jeremiah derived habits of thrift, capacity for hard work, caustic wit, and a tendency to hardness and austerity. His early education was scanty but he possessed a native fondness for books and profited from such opportunities as the itinerant teachers of the day provided. After further study under more competent preceptors he entered Harvard College in 1777 and remained two years, his studies interrupted by a tour of duty with the New Hampshire contingent sent to oppose Burgoyne's invasion. During this term of service he was wounded at Bennington. Because of the unsatisfactory conditions at Harvard, due to the Revolution, he completed his course at Queen's College (Rutgers College), graduating in 1780.

For some years thereafter he served as a teacher in various localities in New Hampshire and Massachusetts, studying law meanwhile. In 1786 he was admitted to the bar at Amherst, in Hillsborough County, N. H. The unsettled conditions following the war and the opportunities afforded by the establishment of new institutions provided a rare opportunity for constructive work. He spent ten years at Peterborough, during which period he entered political life through the familiar school of town government. In 1790 he was elected to the Second Congress and a year later served in the New Hampshire constitutional convention which did so much to establish the governmental system of the state. He was an industrious but not particularly prominent member of Congress until his resignation, July 26, 1797. He took advantage of the enlarged opportunities for study provided by Philadelphia, followed the work of courts and government departments, became an intimate of many of the great Federalist leaders, imbibed a fair share of their distrust of democratic institutions, learned to hate French influence and Jeffersonian doctrines, and on Mar. 8, 1797, married Eliza Ross of Maryland, whom he met at the capital.

He gave up his congressional career to accept appointment as United States attorney for the New Hampshire district, and bought a home at Exeter. In 1800 he became judge of probate for Rockingham County, and his legal knowledge enabled him to improve and clarify the unsatisfactory administration of this branch of New Hampshire law. He prepared a treatise on probate law, which, while it was not published, had considerable influence, being frequently consulted, it is said, by members of the New Hampshire bar. On Feb. 20, 1801, on the recommendation of John Marshall, he was appointed circuit judge by President Adams, but his tenure of office was soon terminated by the repeal of the act establishing these courts by the Jeffersonian majority in Congress. On May 17, 1802, he became chief justice of New Hampshire and for the next seven years rode on circuit, studied indefatigably, and worked to raise the standards of bench and bar in what was, in many respects, a pioneer community. Jeremiah Mason testified that Smith had done much to remedy the "most intolerable evil of a bad administration of justice" resulting from vague and uncertain judicial decisions, "by establishing and enforcing a more orderly practice, and by strenuous endeavors to conform all judicial decisions to known rules and principles of law" (Morison, *post*, p. 210); and the competent historian of the New Hampshire bar declares that "Judge Smith did more, perhaps, for the improvement of the jurisprudence of the State than any other man" (C. H. Bell, *post*, p. 61).

In 1809 he resigned the chief justiceship to serve a single term as governor, but without satisfaction either to the Federalist party, the state at large, or himself, his talents being judicial rather than political. He then resumed private practice but again served as chief justice from 1813 to 1816 during a stormy period when the courts were undergoing a reorganization, of dubious constitutionality, at the hands of the Federalist majority. With the defeat of the Federalists he returned to private life. Immediately he became associate counsel—with Daniel Webster and Jeremiah Mason [*qq.v.*]—for the trustees of Dartmouth College in his most celebrated case, *The Trustees of Dartmouth College* vs. *Woodward.* (For Smith's argument before the superior court of New Hampshire see Timothy Farrar, *Report of the Dartmouth College Case*, 1819.) In 1820 he retired from practice.

He had lived frugally and accumulated a competence sufficient to maintain him comfortably according to the modest standards of the time. His life in retirement was saddened by the death of his wife and the last of their five children. On Sept. 20, 1831, he married, second, Elizabeth Hale of Dover, N. H., and a son, Jeremiah [*q.v.*], was born on July 14, 1837. In his declining years Smith showed no diminution of mental vigor,

and he gave time and energy to local enterprises and causes, rendering valuable service to Phillips Exeter Academy, and attracting interest and attention as one of the last surviving Elder Statesmen of the Washington era. In 1842 he sold his Exeter estate, in order to lighten the responsibilities of his executors and dependents, and moved to Dover, where his death occurred a few months later.

[J. H. Morison, *Life of the Hon. Jeremiah Smith, LL.D.* (1845), based on original sources; some copies of letters in the William Plumer Papers, Lib. of Cong.; Jeremiah Smith, Jr., *Decisions of the Superior and Supreme Courts of N. H., from 1802 to 1809 and from 1813 to 1816 . . . with Extracts from Judge Smith's Manuscript Treatise on Probate Law* (1879), reviewed in *Granite Monthly*, Mar. 1879; C. H. Bell, *The Bench and Bar of N. H.* (1894); Albert Smith, *Hist. of the Town of Peterborough*, . . . *N. H.* (1876); C. H. Bell, *Hist. of the Town of Exeter, N. H.* (1888); *Biog. Dir. Am. Cong.* (1928); *Boston Daily Advertiser*, Sept. 24, 1842.]

W. A. R.

SMITH, JEREMIAH (July 14, 1837–Sept. 3, 1921), jurist and law teacher, was born in Exeter, N. H., son of Jeremiah Smith [*q.v.*], then in his seventy-eighth year, and his second wife, Elizabeth Hale, daughter of William Hale of Dover. His father had been a congressman, governor of New Hampshire, and chief justice of the New Hampshire supreme court. In 1843 the widowed mother settled on a farm in Lee, N. H., where the boy was taught by her and at a district school. From 1849 to 1853 he attended Phillips Exeter Academy. Entering Harvard College as a sophomore, he graduated in 1856 with high rank. He studied law under Daniel M. Christie of Dover and for a year at Harvard Law School, 1860–61. After admission to the bar in Strafford County, N. H., in 1861, he practised in Dover. On Apr. 5, 1865, he was married to Hannah M., daughter of Daniel K. Webster of that city. She died in 1904, leaving a daughter and a son.

On Oct. 16, 1867, when only thirty, Smith was appointed associate justice of the supreme court of New Hampshire, then a very strong court which included Ira Perley [*q.v.*] as chief justice and Charles Doe [*q.v.*]. Smith's decisions often dealt with questions on which there was little precedent. Instead of limiting himself to the immediate issue, he endeavored to solve general problems. His mind was greater than his task. As he said later to his students, "I know judges make law—I've done it myself." His decision, for example, in *Eaton* vs. *Boston, Concord & Montreal Railroad* (51 *N. H. Reports*, 504) established the meaning of "taking" by eminent domain. His opinions are "learned without prolixity, full of common sense, but searching first for legal principles, lawyer-like, convincing, sane" (Beale, *post*, pp. 2–3).

The heavy, confining trial work then required of his court so wore upon Smith that he was threatened with tuberculosis and resigned on Jan. 26, 1874. He restored his health by several winters in Minnesota. Meanwhile, he prepared his father's judicial opinions for the press and occasionally participated in legal consultations and briefs. In 1882 he reopened his office in Dover and at once became a leader of the state bar, frequently acting as referee and arguing many cases before the supreme court.

In 1890, at the age of fifty-three, chance brought an abrupt change in his work. A lecture he gave on Legal Ethics to Harvard students so impressed President Eliot, who happened to be in the audience, that a month later, Mar. 31, Smith was appointed Story Professor of Law. In September 1890 he settled at 4 Berkeley St., Cambridge, a house formerly owned by Richard H. Dana [q.v.], and began twenty years of teaching at the Harvard Law School. His subjects were torts, agency, corporations (then a new course), persons, and interpretation of statutes. He had a wide experience in the application of law and an illuminated common sense which checked the excess of mere theory. The personality of "Jerry" Smith furnished as large an inspiration to his pupils as his direct instruction. "The beauty of his character and the charm of his kindly smile and noble face attracted all with whom he came in contact. He was simple and direct of speech and manner, courteous and unfeignedly democratic in his dealings with all" (Williston, post, p. 158). "A class, however large, was never to him merely a collective unit" (Williston, quoted by Beale, post, p. 5). He had a remarkable gift for remembering persons, and he recognized and cultivated the separate individualities of his students. Precise and thorough as he was in defining legal rights and duties, he had little respect for the man who always insists on those legal rights, and will not do more than law requires. It was his wont each year, after showing how few positive acts were demanded by law, to recommend the students to read the last part of the twenty-fifth chapter of St. Matthew, and thus to call to mind the obligations above and beyond law. His case books in torts and other subjects display sagacity in finding significant decisions. His numerous legal articles broke new ground on several important questions, particularly "Crucial Issues in Labor Litigation" (Harvard Law Review, February–April 1907).

In the summer of 1910 he retired from teaching but not from work. Several hours of each day he spent in the Law School library, "learning the law all over again." Several of his best articles were written in this period. Though he taught students no longer, his younger colleagues delighted in learning from him. His powers remained unbroken until past the age of eighty-four. After a week's illness he died at St. Andrews, New Brunswick, which had long been his summer home. His son Jeremiah (1870–1935) was a noted lawyer, prominent in international affairs, whose work as financial adviser to Hungary after the World War is regarded as saving that country from the consequences of financial ruin.

[J. H. Beale, "Jeremiah Smith," Harvard Law Rev., Nov. 1921; Samuel Williston, "Jeremiah Smith," Harvard Graduates' Mag., Dec. 1921; Boston Transcript, Sept. 6, 1921; Eugene Wambaugh, "In re J. S.," Green Bag, Dec. 1904; secretary's reports, Harvard Coll., Class of 1856; The Centennial Hist. of Harvard Law School (1918); Who's Who in America, 1920–21; Smith's opinions in 47–54 N. H. Reports.] Z. C., Jr.

SMITH, JOB LEWIS (Oct. 15, 1827–June 9, 1897), physician, was born in the township of Spafford, Onondaga County, N. Y. He was descended from John Smith, one of the founders of Milford, Conn.; his grandfather, Job Smith, and his father, Lewis Smith, served as officers in the Revolution; the latter was also active in the political life of Onondaga County and was a member of the state legislature in 1829. He married Chloe Benson, a descendant of a Massachusetts Puritan, and she bore him five children, one of whom, Stephen Smith [q.v.], was later a distinguished surgeon in New York City. Job Lewis Smith was the youngest child.

The boy passed the early years of his life on his father's farm and attended the village school. Thence he went to Homer Academy in Homer, Cortland County, N. Y., to prepare for Yale College, where he obtained the degree of B.A. in 1849. In accordance with the custom of his times, he entered a medical apprenticeship under the tutelage of a practising physician, and attended lectures at the Buffalo Medical College, coming under the influence of the famous clinician, Austin Flint, 1812–86 [q.v.]. Through him Smith obtained an interneship in the Buffalo Hospital of the Sisters of Charity, spent one year there, and then entered the College of Physicians and Surgeons in New York City, receiving his degree of doctor of medicine in 1853. He immediately began a private practice which he pursued with great devotion for forty-four years. His first office was at 137 West Forty-ninth Street, then considered far uptown in New York, and his first patients were the poor, from whom he received little or no material remuneration but to whom he gave faithful service even at the height of his career. In the course of general practice, he developed an especial interest in the diseases of children. He is an excellent example of the specialist of the nineteenth century to whom a special field was often merely one chapter, albeit one more affectionately studied, in the book of general medicine. In 1869 he incorporated the fruit of his studies and personal experience in a textbook, *A Treatise on the Diseases of Infancy and Childhood,* which passed through eight editions in the next twenty-seven years. It is apparently one of the earliest of American publications dealing with the diseases of children in their entirety and as a specialty, and sixty years later is still interesting because its shrewd observations of disease were drawn from a wealth of personal experience controlled and amplified by an intimate contact with scientific literature. Its many editions were not merely reprints, but followed faithfully, though critically, the essential changes in medical opinion.

Smith's skill as a clinician and teacher brought him fame as one of America's leading pediatricians, a preëminence which he shared with Abraham Jacobi [*q.v.*]. He was called to the service of eight prominent New York hospitals, lectured on the diseases of children at the Bellevue Hospital Medical College, was professor of morbid anatomy there in 1871–72, and in 1876 became clinical professor of the diseases of children at Bellevue, sixteen years after the first special chair of pediatrics had been created for Jacobi at the New York Medical College. Smith held his professorship for twenty years, retiring in 1896 as professor emeritus. He was a founder of the American Pediatric Society, and in 1890 was elected its second president. He married, Apr. 22, 1858, Mary Anne, daughter of George Hannah, by whom he had seven children. A son died in 1889, shortly after entering upon the practice of medicine; four daughters survived their father.

[F. H. Garrison, "History of Pediatrics," in I. A. Abt, *Pediatrics,* vol. I (1923); E. H. Grandin, in H. A. Kelly and W. L. Burrage, *Am. Medic. Biogs.* (1920); Ellsworth Eliot, in *Trans. N. Y. Acad. of Medicine, 1896–1901* (1903); John Shrady, in *Trans. N. Y. State Medic. Asso.,* vol. XIV (1897), with portr. and bibliog. of Smith's publications; *Obit. Record Grads. Yale Univ.,* 1897; *Record of the Graduated Members of the Class of 1849 of Yale Coll.* (1875); *Gen. Alumni Cat., N. Y. Univ. . . . Medic. Alumni* (1908); *Archives of Pediatrics,* July 1897; *N. Y. Times,* June 10, 1897.]

H. S. R—e.

SMITH, JOEL WEST (Sept. 17, 1837–May 9, 1924), educator of the blind, was of New England stock and was born in East Hampton, Conn., to Delia Elliot (West) Smith, a minister's daughter, and John William Burke Smith, a

farmer. He was educated in the public schools and at a local academy. Having a bent for business, he became postmaster and manager of the village store. At the age of twenty-four, while celebrating the Fourth of July, he was blinded for life. Entering the Perkins Institution for the Blind, he learned piano tuning and became instructor in that subject there in 1866. In 1872 he was called to London to open a department of tuning in the new Royal Normal College for the Blind. After three years he returned to Perkins, where he so built up his department that he secured and held for it the yearly contract of keeping in tune and repair the pianos of the Boston public schools. Being an ingenious mechanic he worked out such devices for the use of the blind as tangible maps and improved writing appliances, one of which was a machine for typewriting in Braille letters. His scientific revision of Braille's alphabet, known as American Braille, received increasing recognition until the demand for world-wide uniformity caused it to be superseded. For four years he edited, published, and largely financed the *Mentor,* 1891–94, the first magazine published in the United States for the blind. He introduced the use of the typewriter at Perkins, working out for himself the now common touch method of using it.

In 1894 he left Massachusetts permanently for his native East Hampton, where he owned property and where he voted. A public-spirited citizen, he served repeatedly on church and village improvement committees, was one of the prominent men of his town, and became a trustee of the Connecticut School for the Blind. His geniality and humor made people forget that he was blind, and at Perkins he was counselor and popular leader. He had, however, a mercurial temperament, his periods of depression becoming pronounced as distressing disabilities came upon him. In one of these he took his own life, an act said by his intimates to be due to his morbid fear of becoming a burden to his friends. His death occurred at Middletown, Conn. He left an estate of some $25,000, partly inherited but mostly accumulated through thrift and careful investment. Some of this was left to his relatives and friends, some to church and town enterprises, and some to organizations for the blind.

[Perkins Institution and Mass. School for the Blind, ann. reports for 1872, 1895, and 1924; *Ann. Reports Board of Educ. of the Blind* (Conn.), 1924; *State of Conn. Pub. Doc.,* No. 35 (1924); *The Outlook for the Blind,* June 1924, Dec. 1928; obituary in *Hartford Courant,* May 10, 1924; autobiog. notes, letters, and other data, Perkins Inst.; personal acquaintance.]

E. E. A—n.

SMITH, JOHN (1579/80–June 21, 1631), adventurer, explorer, author, is popularly one of the best and historically one of the least known figures in early American history. With regard to many events in his life the evidence is still conflicting. Born in Willoughby, Lincolnshire, England, and baptized there Jan. 9, 1579, o.s., he was the son of George Smith, a member of the Smith family of Crudley, Lancashire, and his wife Alice. John's father died in 1596 and left him a modest property. After a grammar-school education he was apprenticed to a prominent merchant, Thomas Sendall of Lynn, whom he soon left to seek adventure. Four years of soldiering on the Continent followed. After a brief visit to Scotland, he went to the Continent again to engage in the war against the Turks. After various unverifiable adventures he succeeded in joining the military forces on the Hungarian and Transylvanian frontier. He claims that he fought three single combats with leading Turkish warriors and that his military exploits so impressed Prince Sigismund Bathori that that leader granted him a coat of arms and a pension of three thousand ducats annually. In the subsequent fighting in Transylvania, he says that he was taken prisoner and was sent to Constantinople as a present for the Turkish Pasha's wife, Tragabigzanda; she fell in love with him and, in order to protect him, sent him to her brother who ruled over a somewhat vaguely defined country between the Caspian and Black seas. There, however, he was made a slave. He killed his master, Timor, and escaped, finding his way back to Transylvania and to Bathori, who gave him a safe-conduct. With this in his possession, he claims to have wandered over a large part of Europe, with his customary adventures. He returned to England, probably in 1604. With his other travels, real or imaginary, before his connection began with American history, we need not be concerned. (For a severe analysis of Smith's story, see L. L. Kropf, *Notes and Queries,* 7 ser., vol. IX, 1890, and *American Historical Review,* July 1898, pp. 727–38; for a more favorable estimate, see Fletcher and Wroth, *post.*)

In 1606 the Virginia Company of London received its patent and Smith claims to have taken an active part in the promotion and organization of the enterprise. In December of that year three ships set sail for Virginia with 144 colonists, among them Smith. They proceeded by way of the Canaries and West Indies, entering Chesapeake Bay Apr. 26, 1607. Only 105 disembarked at Jamestown, May 24. When the instructions from England were opened it was found that the government for the first year was to consist of a council of seven, including Smith.

Owing to charges of mutiny on the voyage, he was not permitted to serve on the council until June 20, but from the first he engaged in exploration. Wingfield was chosen as president. Trouble began soon after the ships sailed back for England, leaving the colonists. There was great sickness and within the first seven months nearly two-thirds of the settlers died. Feeling ran high against the local government for various reasons. The leaders fell out among themselves, and Smith was never good at acting in concert with others. He showed at his best in the expeditions he made among the Indians to procure corn and other food for the half-famished colony. On one of these he and his companions were taken prisoner by some of the savages and, according to his story in the *Generall Historie* (1624), he was condemned to death. It was on this occasion that he is supposed to have been saved by the intercession of Pocahontas [*q.v.*], the young daughter of the chief Powhatan [*q.v.*]. Around this incident, as around most of the more spectacular adventures of Smith, controversy has long raged. Such intercession, however, was quite in accord with the customs of Indian life and there is nothing inherently improbable in the story. In any case, Smith returned to Jamestown in January 1608 to find his enemies, John Ratcliffe and Gabriel Archer, in command of the turbulent settlement; he was promptly arrested, tried for the loss of two of his men, and condemned to be hanged. Fortunately for him, Captain Christopher Newport [*q.v.*], with supplies and new settlers from England, arrived that evening. Smith was released and restored to his place in the council.

He spent much of the summer in exploring the Potomac and Rappahannock rivers and Chesapeake Bay. Newport sailed back to England after three months. In June, on the *Phoenix,* Smith sent to England the account published that year as *A True Relation of Such Occurrences and Accidents of Noate as Hath Hapned in Virginia since the First Planting of That Collony.* The "sickly season" again took its toll at Jamestown and about forty-five men out of ninety-five died. On his return on July 21 from one of his exploring trips, which interested him much more than administration at Jamestown, he effected the deposition of President Ratcliffe, and, leaving in charge Matthew Scrivener, started out again. In the autumn, however, elected president by the council, he settled down to governing the colony. That winter, 1608–09, starvation again faced the settlers and Smith saved them by getting corn from the Indians. He had a far clearer notion of the value of a colony than the company in England, which wished the settlers to waste themselves in trying to find gold, but unfortunately he was not always practical; as spring came it was found that rats had been allowed to eat a large part of the stores. Smith divided the colony into three parts, each to go where food might be found. In 1609, following the granting of a new charter, some supplies and new colonists, with whom came Ratcliffe and Archer, reached Virginia. After much wrangling about authority, Smith, who had been wounded by an explosion, sailed for England in October 1609. George Percy [q.v.] succeeded him. Complaints, mostly unfounded, were made against him at home, and in London he severely criticized the Virginia Company and its methods. In 1612 he published *A Map of Virginia, With a Description of the Countrey, the Commodities, People, Government and Religion.*

In comparison with Smith's brief, spectacular career in Virginia, the substantial contributions that he made in his later years to the founding of New England have not been sufficiently stressed. In March 1614 he was sent to the region by London merchants and, though he failed to take whales or discover gold, he brought back a valuable cargo of fish and furs. More valuable still was his map, which was printed in *A Description of New England* (1616) and several of his later works and served to establish the name of the region. He emphasized the importance of fishing and continued to the end of his life to proclaim the favorable prospects of New England for permanent settlement. Sent by Sir Ferdinando Gorges and others of the "west country," as well as the London merchants, he started on another voyage, but was captured by pirates and then by the French, and spent months at sea until landed at La Rochelle in November 1615. He managed to get back to Plymouth, where he had been given up for dead. Except for the sending of fishing vessels, his hopes of another venture were disappointed. The Pilgrims made use of his books and maps, but had no desire that he should join them (*Generall Historie*, 1907 ed., vol. II, 182). In 1620 he published *New Englands Trials* (republished later, with additional matter on the Pilgrims), and in 1624 *The Generall Historie of Virginia, New-England, and the Summer Isles,* in which much of his early writing and narratives by others were incorporated. On seamanship and his own adventures he published *An Accidence or the Path-way to Experience* (1626), which he republished in an enlarged edition as *A Sea Grammar* (1627); and *The True Travels, Adventures, and Observations of Captaine John Smith, in Europe, Asia, Affrica,*

and America (1630). The year of his death there appeared his *Advertisements for the Unexperienced Planters of New England, or Anywhere* (1631), which is full of sound and sometimes amusing suggestions based on his own experiences. Apparently he had gained, as he deserved, high repute among those engaged in American colonization.

[The best collection of Smith's writings is Edward Arber, *Capt. John Smith . . . Works* (1884), reprinted with the same pagination and with some corrections as *Travels and Works of Capt. John Smith* (2 vols., 1910), with introduction by A. G. Bradley. Valuable also are J. G. Fletcher and L. C. Wroth, eds., *The True Travels, Adventures, & Observations of Captaine John Smith* (1930), with introduction by Fletcher and bibliographical notes by Wroth; and Wilberforce Eames, *A Bibliography of Capt. John Smith* (1927), reprinted from Sabin, *Dict. of Books Relating to America.* None of the biographies is thoroughly satisfactory from the scholarly point of view. The two latest are E. K. Chatterton, *Capt. John Smith* (1927), which is strongly biased in his favor; and J. G. Fletcher, *John Smith— Also Pocahontas* (1928). J. A. Doyle, in *Dict. Nat. Biography,* is a good brief account. The strong skeptical criticism of Smith and his adventures started by Charles Deane in his ed. of E.-M. Wingfield, "A Discourse of Va.," in *Am. Antiquarian Soc. Trans.,* vol. IV (1860), was continued by him in his ed. of *A True Relation* (1866); by Henry Adams, in *No. Am. Review,* Jan. 1867, a review of Deane's ed.; by Alexander Brown, in *The Genesis of the U. S.* (2 vols., 1890), and other writings; and by Justin Winsor, in *Narrative and Critical Hist. of America,* vol. III (1885). The danger of impugning all of Smith's writings because of the extravagance of some of them, however, has been pointed out by recent scholars and there is an increasing recognition of the value of his services; see, especially, C. M. Andrews, *The Colonial Period of Am. Hist.,* vol. I (1934), p. 142 n., and Fletcher and Wroth, *ante.*]   J. T. A.

SMITH, JOHN (*c.* 1735–*c.* 1824), clergyman, merchant, United States senator, was supposedly born in Virginia. In 1790 he was ministering to a Baptist congregation on the forks of the Cheat River, in what is now West Virginia. The following year he moved to Columbia, Ohio, later a part of Cincinnati, where he took charge of a recently organized church, and for several years combined preaching with the more lucrative operations of merchant and farmer. His gifts as a speaker early brought him into public life. In 1798 he entered the first legislative assembly of the Northwest Territory and in this and the succeeding assembly was noted for his opposition to Governor St. Clair (Burnet, *post,* p. 288). As a reward for his activity in promoting statehood he was selected, in April 1803, as one of the two senators from Ohio. In addition to local connections, Smith expanded his trading and speculative activities into West Florida, where he followed the usual practice of taking an oath of allegiance to the Spanish king, and where for a time Reuben Kemper [q.v.] represented him. Smith took his seat in the Senate in the fall of 1803. He was credited with one speech only, but conferred frequently with President Jefferson, whom he had consistently supported, concerning claims to West Florida (Pickering Papers, *post*; also Burnet, *post*, pp. 294–95). He busied himself principally with army contracts, land deals, and the interest of his constituents.

Smith is best known for his association, altogether too intimate, with Aaron Burr [*q.v.*]. He furthered the latter's project for a canal around the falls of the Ohio and when the former vice-president visited the West in 1805, entertained him at Cincinnati; and again, in 1806. When contemporary reports concerning Burr's purpose aroused the Western country, Smith became alarmed and obtained from Burr a statement specifically denying any intention to separate the Western states from the Union. Smith later visited Frankfort while a grand jury was investigating Burr's conduct, and his prompt departure indicated a wish to avoid witnessing against his former associate. To the measures taken by Jefferson and the local authorities to break up Burr's project he contributed freely the necessary provisions and credit and thus helped keep the Ohio militia in the field. Later he went to New Orleans to provide Gen. James Wilkinson [*q.v.*] with provisions for his forces there. While in that city Smith learned that he also had been indicted for complicity with Burr. He immediately withdrew to West Florida and later surrendered himself to the governor of the Mississippi territory, and was allowed to go to Richmond, under escort, by way of Cincinnati. When Burr was acquitted in the Virginia court, the bill against Smith was quashed.

Rumors of Smith's complicity with Burr and his obvious neglect of his senatorial duties had stirred up his enemies in the Ohio assembly and in Cincinnati to demand his resignation. When he arrived in Washington, January 1807, his colleagues in the Senate appointed a committee headed by John Quincy Adams to investigate the charges against him. He was able to explain most of the charges acceptably but not to clear himself of the suspicion that he and his sons knew more of Burr's plans than they chose to divulge. The committee favored his expulsion but its recommendation failed of passage by one vote less than the required two-thirds. Smith thereupon resigned his seat. For a time he carried on his business operations in Cincinnati and vicinity but the notoriety gained in connection with Burr led to delay in settling his government contracts and ultimately forced him into bankruptcy. Removing to West Florida in 1812, he resided for a time in Pensacola and later retired to St. Francisville (now in Louisiana), where

he carried on his clerical and business activities until his death.

[A number of letters written by Smith in his own defense are to be found in the Pickering Papers of the Mass. Hist. Soc. (see "Hist. Index to the Pickering Papers," *Mass. Hist. Soc. Colls.*, 6 ser. VIII, 1896); many facts relating to his life and his connection with the Burr conspiracy are brought out in "Testimony in Connection with Investigation of Senator John Smith . . . Queries Addressed by the Committee, Dec. 9, 1807, to Mr. Smith," ordered printed Dec. 31, 1807; *Annals of Cong.*, 10 Cong., 1 Sess., pt. 1, contain the proceedings in the Senate against him, and should be supplemented by *Memoirs of John Quincy Adams*, vol. I (1874); see also William Plumer's *Memorandum of Proceedings in the United States Senate, 1803–1807* (1923), ed. by E. S. Brown; Jacob Burnet, *Notes on the Early Settlement of the North-Western Territory* (1847); C. T. Greve, *Centennial Hist. of Cincinnati*, vol. I (1904); I. J. Cox, *The West Florida Controversy, 1798–1813* (1918).]

I. J. C.—x.

SMITH, JOHN AUGUSTINE (Aug. 29, 1782–Feb. 9, 1865), physician, college president, teacher, author, and editor, was born in Westmoreland County, Va., the second son of the Rev. Thomas Smith of Cople Parish and Mary Smith, who was the daughter of John Smith of Shooter's Hill, a member of the House of Burgesses and cousin of George Washington. After graduating from the College of William and Mary, Williamsburg, Va., in 1800, he went abroad for a medical education and studied at St. Thomas' Hospital, London. On his return to the United States he practised first in Gloucester County, Va., but shortly moved to New York City. In 1809 he married Letitia Lee, by whom he had nine children. He was assigned a place on the first faculty of the College of Physicians and Surgeons in 1807 as adjunct lecturer on anatomy; he became professor of anatomy and surgery in 1808, and professor of anatomy, surgery, and physiology in 1811. When the school was merged with Columbia College (later Columbia University), he and Wright Post [*q.v.*] became joint professors of these subjects. In 1814 he was elected to the presidency of the College of William and Mary. The faculty of the college consisted of but four professors, including the president, who in addition to performing the duties of his office taught moral and political philosophy. It was not a prosperous period in the history of the college, which reached its low ebb in 1824. Not unnaturally some of the opprobrium was heaped on Smith. His enemies said he had injured the college by abolishing the honor system and instituting a plan of discipline too harsh for Virginia youths; it was alleged that he was a Deist, and that he was fonder of hunting than of teaching. But the opposition to Smith at this time was chiefly due to his attempt to move the college to Richmond. Before the legislature in 1824 he cited the alarming shrinkage in the student body of the college and predicted that the expected opening of the University of Virginia would seriously reduce even this small number; he proposed not only to move the college but to enlarge it by the creation of theological and medical departments, declaring that they "would give utility, dignity and importance to the institution" (*Journal of the House of Delegates of the Commonwealth of Virginia*, 1824, p. 4). As there was no medical school in Virginia at this time his proposal was warmly supported by the physicians of the state. The scheme, however, ran athwart the maturing plans of Thomas Jefferson for a great state university at Charlottesville, incurred his opposition, and failed.

Fortunately at this juncture (1825) a reorganization of the faculty of the College of Physicians and Surgeons in New York was in process. Invited to resume his old chair, Smith accepted, and six years later, 1831, he succeeded John Watts as president. After Valentine Mott [q.v.] joined the faculty in 1834 as professor of anatomy, Smith confined himself to the teaching of physiology. Three years later he was influential in moving the college to a new location on Crosby Street. The curriculum of the college was now materially broadened, and many new features were introduced which have continued to the present time. In 1841 he inaugurated a spring course of clinical lectures with the cooperation of such men as Willard Parker [q.v.] and Alonzo Clarke. One unpleasant incident occurred. A controversy with James R. Manley, lecturer on obstetrics, whose appointment Smith had opposed, and whose eviction from the faculty he secured, led in 1841 to the sharp strictures of a forty-eight page pamphlet entitled *Exposition of the Conduct and Character of Dr. Smith.* Smith retired to private life in 1843, devoting his leisure to a philosophical work entitled *Prelections on Some of the More Important Subjects Connected with Moral and Physical Science* (1853). His other published works consist of an *Introductory Discourse at New Medical College, Crosby Street* (1837), *Select Discourses on the Functions of the Nervous System in Opposition to Phrenology, Materialism and Atheism* (1840), *The Mutations of the Earth* (1846), *Moral and Physical Science* (1853). In 1809 he was editor of the *Medical and Physiological Journal,* and in 1828 co-editor of the *New York Medical and Physical Journal.*

[L. G. Tyler, *Encyc. of Va. Biog.*, vol. II (1915), and *Coll. of William and Mary in Va.* (1907); John Shrady, ed., *The Coll. of Physicians and Surgeons, N. Y.* (n.d.), vol. I; J. J. Walsh, *Hist. of Medicine in N. Y.* (1919), vol. II; *Am. Medic. and Philosophical Reg.*, Apr., July, 1813; *William and Mary Coll. Quart.*, Jan. 1932; *Circulars of Information Bureau of Educ.*,

no. 1 (1887); death notice in *N. Y. Times*, Feb. 10, 1865; Family records in the possession of Miss Ellen Bagby, Richmond, Va.]   W. B. B.

SMITH, JOHN BERNHARD (Nov. 21, 1858–Mar. 12, 1912), entomologist, was born in New York City of German parentage. His father was John and his mother Elizabeth (Scheuerman) Smith; the father came to America in 1853, from Bavaria. The younger John was educated in the public schools, studied law, and was admitted to the bar. He established himself as a lawyer in Brooklyn, where he practised between 1880 and 1884. As a young man he became interested in the study of insects and joined the Brooklyn Entomological Society. At first *Coleoptera* attracted him, but later he took up the *Lepidoptera* and became especially interested in the large group known as the owlet moths (*Noctuidae*). In 1882 he became an editor, and later sole editor, of the *Bulletin of the Brooklyn Entomological Society,* which afterwards developed into a journal known as *Entomologica Americana.* The latter journal, which he edited from April 1885 to September 1890, was for a time the most prominent American periodical in its field for the publication of short papers and notes. Giving up his law in 1884, Smith became a field agent of the United States Department of Agriculture and spent two years in investigating insects affecting the hop and the cranberry. In 1886 he was made assistant curator of insects in the United States National Museum, and held this post until 1889, when, with the founding of the state agricultural experiment stations, he was appointed entomologist of the New Jersey station. Here he began his most important economic work, which lasted until his fatal illness.

Smith took a high rank among the rapidly growing body of state entomologists, was given the honorary degree of Doctor of Science by Rutgers in 1891, and was president of the Association of Economic Entomologists in 1895, and the Entomological Society of America in 1910. He was prominent in the early work against the San Jose scale, and conducted many other important investigations of injurious insects. His greatest triumph, however, was in the discovery of the breeding habits of the salt-marsh mosquitoes, a discovery which made it possible for summer resorts and other communities near large areas of salt marsh greatly to improve conditions. On the basis of his early biological work with these forms, he succeeded in impressing the New Jersey people, and especially the New Jersey legislature, with the possibility of the control of the salt-marsh mosquitoes, and started a movement which has gone on ever since and

came rector of St. John's Church, Bangor, Me., and two years later, 1852, was appointed assistant minister of Trinity Church, Boston, Mass. In 1860 he was instituted rector of the Church of the Ascension, New York, where he remained until his death. In 1867 he became associate editor of *The Protestant Churchman,* later *Church and State*—of which he subsequently became editor in chief, serving in that capacity until his periodical was absorbed by *The Churchman.*

Smith was distinguished as a scholar, theologian, preacher, and philanthropist. During the years of his ministry there were four major issues in the religious field, all of which enlisted his active interest, as editor, author, and preacher —foreign missions, social problems, adjustment of new knowledge in theological and scientific fields to traditional theological concepts, and church union. For twenty-two years he was a member of the foreign committee of the board of missions of the Episcopal Church. In the field of social problems his chief interest lay in the direction of tenement-house reform. He was a stanch and pioneer advocate of model housing and it was under his auspices that the first model tenement was erected in New York City. His book, *Improvements of the Tenement House System of New York* (1879), consisting of extracts from the report of the Ascension Association, created a sensation. In considering the socalled conflict between science and theology, his motto was, "What is true is safe." The adaptability of his mind to new knowledge is indicated by an earlier and a later essay on evolution— the second revealing a marked change in point of view from the first—published by him in his volume, *Miscellanies, Old and New* (1876). His interest in church union was evinced by his assertion that his devotion to the Episcopal Church came from his conviction that "it offered the best available basis for the unifying of American religion." In the earlier years of his ministry in New York he took the position that reunion would be possible only through purging the church of non-Protestant characteristics, *i.e.* as represented by the high church party. Later he modified this position, convinced that such a solution was impractical. From then on he emphasized the comprehensive character of the Episcopal Church, stressing his conviction that there must be room in it for all three parties (high, broad, and low). This point of view he emphasized in a sermon preached before the diocesan convention of New York, later published in his *Briar Hill Lectures* (1881). His influence with clergymen of Christian bodies outside his own gave him a strong position of leadership among

the clergy of New York. He was a delegate to the General Convention of the Episcopal Church of 1880, served as a trustee of General Theological Seminary, and for twenty years was a member of the Protestant Episcopal Society for the Promotion of Evangelical Knowledge. He was one of the early promoters of the Church Congress, an annual meeting of members of the Church, lay and clerical, to discuss matters religious, moral, and social. While the rector of a wealthy parish, he was emphatically a pastor of the poor. He was known as an earnest, attractive preacher, giving impressive delivery to strong thoughts clearly expressed. Among his published works not already mentioned were *A Plea for Liberty in the Church* (1865); *The Church's Law of Development* (1872); *Limits of Legislation as to Doctrine and Ritual* (1874); *The Church's Mission of Reconciliation* (1880). He was married, Dec. 19, 1849, in Portland, Me., to Harriette, daughter of Gen. James Appleton [*q.v.*]. Two sons and four daughters survived him; one of the sons, Roland Cotton Smith (1860–1934), was for a number of years rector of St. John's Church, Washington, D. C.

[Wm. R. Huntington, *The Counsellor of Peace: A Sermon Commemorative of the Late Rev. John Cotton Smith* (1882); Bayard Tuckerman, *A Sketch of the Cotton Smith Family of Sharon, Conn.* (1915); W. S. Perry, *A Memorial of the Rev. Thomas Mather Smith, D.D.* (1866); Nehemiah Cleaveland, *Hist. of Bowdoin Coll.* (1882), ed. by A. S. Packard; *Churchman,* Jan. 14, 1882; *Living Church,* Jan. 21, 1882; *N. Y. Tribune,* Jan. 10, 1882.]   G. E. S.

SMITH, JOHN EUGENE (Aug. 3, 1816– Jan. 29, 1897), soldier, was born in the canton of Berne, Switzerland. His father, John Banler Smith, was an officer in one of the Swiss regiments which accompanied Napoleon from his ill-fated Moscow campaign to Waterloo. Before John Eugene was a year old his parents emigrated to America and settled in Philadelphia, Pa. There he received an elementary education and learned the jeweler's trade. In 1836, after having followed his trade for a few years in St. Louis, Mo., he removed to Galena, Ill., and established a jewelry business. During the same year he was married to Aimee A. Massot of St. Louis. In 1860 he was elected treasurer of Jo Daviess County, Ill. When the Civil War broke out he at once offered his services to Governor Yates, and, after serving on the staff of the latter for a few months, he organized the 45th Illinois Infantry, known as the "Washburne Leadmine Regiment," and became colonel on July 23, 1861. During 1862 he led his regiment with bravery and distinction in the operations against Forts Henry and Donelson, was in the thickest of the fight at Shiloh, and temporarily commanded a brigade at the siege of Corinth. He was appointed brigadier-general of volunteers on Nov. 29, 1862.

In the spring of 1863 he was given command of a division, under General Grant, which he led ably throughout the Vicksburg campaign, participating in the expedition to Yazoo Pass, the battles of Port Gibson, Raymond, Jackson, Champion's Hill, Big Black River, and the final siege and capture of Vicksburg. Smith, with his division, was then transferred to the Army of the Tennessee, made a brilliant charge at Missionary Ridge, Tenn., and accompanied General Sherman on his march to the sea. A prompt and effective deployment of his division at Savannah, Ga., on Dec. 20, 1864, was instrumental in causing the Confederates to evacuate the city. In June 1865 he was assigned to command the district of western Tennessee where he remained until he was mustered out of the service on Apr. 30, 1866. The following July he was commissioned colonel of the 27th Infantry in the regular army. He served at various frontier posts, and by his coolness and prompt action at Fort Laramie, Wyo., helped to quell an outbreak of the Sioux Indians under Spotted Tail [q.v.]. Smith retired from active service in May 1881, and settled in Chicago, Ill., where he died. His body was taken to his old home at Galena for interment. He had been three times honored with brevet rank: in 1865, as major-general of volunteers for service and gallantry in action; in 1867, as brigadier-general in the regular army for gallantry at the siege of Vicksburg; and again in the same year, as major-general in the regular army for action at Savannah, Ga. He was survived by three sons.

[*War of the Rebellion: Official Records (Army)*, vols. I, VII, X, XVII, XXII, XXIV, XXX–XXXII, XXXVIII, XXXIX, XLIV, XLVII–XLIX, LII; F. B. Heitman, *Hist. Reg. . . . U. S. Army* (1903); *Memorials of Deceased Companions . . . Commandery of the State of Ill., Mil. Order of the Loyal Legion* (1901); *The Forty-Fifth Ill.* (1905); Newton Bateman, Paul Selby, J. S. Currey, *Hist. Encyc. of Ill.*, vol. I (1925); *Army and Navy Reg.*, Feb. 6, 1897; *Chicago Tribune, Chicago Times-Herald*, Jan. 30, 1897.]   S.J.H.

SMITH, JOHN GREGORY (July 22, 1818– Nov. 6, 1891), railway organizer and executive, governor of Vermont, was born at St. Albans, Vt., the eldest son of John and Maria (Curtis) Smith, and a cousin of William Farrar Smith [q.v.]. Established position and affluence were his birthright. For nearly two centuries his paternal ancestors had flourished in Massachusetts. His grandfather, Samuel, a pioneer settler in St. Albans (1789), had acquired a leading position in the community and during the lad's youth his father gained success alike in law, business and politics. Educated at the local grammar school and at the University of Vermont, where he was graduated in 1838, young Smith then studied law in his father's office and at Yale until 1841. The next year he was admitted to the bar and joined his father in legal practice.

Soon thereafter a period of railway building in Vermont began. The Vermont Central Railroad, commenced in 1846, was completed to Burlington in 1849. Meanwhile, the elder Smith was promoting the Vermont & Canada Railroad to connect the Central near Burlington with Canada. The new line, built as far as Swanton between 1848 and 1851, was leased before completion to the Central, the elder Smith subsequently holding positions with both roads. The son early joined his father on the legal staff of the railways and after his father's death in 1858, he became president of the Vermont Central, or rather of the board of trustees which was managing the road for the bondholders. He took control at a time when the physical condition of the railroad demanded heavy expenditures for rebuilding. During the boom period following the Civil War he succeeded in financing this work by large issues of trust bonds. These necessitated increased revenue, which Smith endeavored to obtain by extending his line to the Canadian border (1863) and persuading Canadian capitalists to build the connecting link to Montreal (1868). By 1872 the railroad property was undoubtedly in much better shape than a decade before, but it was in serious financial difficulties. Some of these Smith hoped to overcome by the formation in that year of a new corporation, the Central Vermont Railroad Company, which in 1873 became receiver for the Vermont Central and the Vermont & Canada companies. Smith was its president from the beginning until his death in 1891. Harrowed by interminable legal suits and constant financial difficulties, he succeeded, by leases and otherwise, in extending his line into an imposing system with terminals at Ottawa and New London and with dependent freight lines on the St. Lawrence and on Long Island Sound. Though the original investors in the Vermont railroad companies complained bitterly, Smith at least kept the lines in operation and augmented his own fortune. His enemies charged that he manipulated the state legislature and courts with entire lack of scruple.

His vision of the Vermont lines as a part of a great system which should tap the developing resources of the West undoubtedly accounts for his interest in the Northern Pacific Railroad. He succeeded Josiah Perham [q.v.] as president of that embryo concern in 1866. It was largely due to his initiative and his determination that the company was broadened, in 1867, to include most of the leading railroad men of the East. Though much occupied at home, he found time to devote to the building of the new line. He was doubtless over-optimistic and extravagant in the enterprise, and has been charged with neglect and the intrusting of important matters to incompetent and dishonest persons, but by the time friction between him and Jay Cooke brought about his resignation in 1872, nearly 500 miles of the railroad had been built and the main lines of its development fixed.

His multifarious business enterprises did not exhaust his abounding energy. He found time to play a leading part in the politics of his state; indeed, his political activity was a counterpart of his business in a day when the state legislature could make or break the railroads within its borders. After two years in the Senate (1858–59) and three in the lower house (1860–62), of which he was speaker in 1862, he served as governor of the state in 1863 and 1864. An ardent Republican and protectionist, he gave warm support to Lincoln's administration. For many years after his retirement from office he remained a power in state politics. He married, Dec. 27, 1843, Ann Eliza Brainerd of St. Albans, who with five of their six children survived him.

[L. A. Brainard, *The Geneal. of the Brainerd-Brainard Family in America* (1908), vol. II, pt. 4, pp. 162–63; J. G. Ullery, *Men of Vt.* (1894); *Gen. Cat. of the Univ. of Vt.* (1901); *Burlington Daily Free Press,* Nov. 7, 9, 1891; E. V. Smalley, *Hist. of the Northern Pacific Railroad* (1883); E. P. Oberholtzer, *Jay Cooke, Financier of the Civil War* (1907).]   P. D. E.

SMITH, JOHN JAY (June 16, 1798–Sept. 23, 1881), editor and librarian, a grand-nephew of Richard Smith [*q.v.*], was a grandson of John Smith, one of the founders of the Philadelphia Contributionship (1752), the first fire-insurance company instituted in America, and of Hannah (Logan) Smith, daughter of James Logan, 1674–1751 [*q.v.*]. Born on a farm at Green Hill, Burlington County, N. J., the sixth of seven children of John and Gulielma Maria (Morris) Smith, John Jay attended the Friends' boarding school at Westtown, Pa., and was given some courses in languages at an early age. He was then apprenticed to a druggist in Philadelphia. After a brief partnership with Solomon Temple in the wholesale drug business, he entered business on his own account, and on Apr. 12, 1821, married Rachel Collins Pearsall, of Flushing, L. I., daughter of a New York merchant. About this time he was active in the establishment of a line of Conestoga wagons, operating as regular carriers between Philadelphia and Pittsburgh, but the enterprise was short-lived.

From his early years he was interested in literature, and occasionally wrote short pieces for the local newspapers. In 1827, in partnership with George Taylor, who had published a newspaper in Mount Carbon, Pa., he inaugurated the *Pennsylvania Gazette,* purchasing the subscription list of the *Aurora* from John Norvell. Two years later he withdrew from this firm to become librarian of the Library Company of Philadelphia; he was a hereditary trustee of the Loganian Library, one of its component parts. Through his taste and industry, he gathered for the institution a large collection of autographs and manuscripts relating to the history of New Jersey and Pennsylvania.

In the early thirties Smith suggested to Adam Waldie, a Philadelphia printer, the republication of important foreign books in the form of a cheap weekly, which could be circulated through the mails; this project was realized on Oct. 1, 1832, when the first issue of *Waldie's Select Circulating Library* appeared, under Smith's editorship. This was the first effort in America to take advantage, on an extensive scale, of the absence of international copyright. Within three months the work had a circulation of 6,000 copies a week, and for some years it enjoyed great success. The covers of *Waldie's* carried literary news, edited by Smith, under the title, "The Journal of Belles-Lettres." During 1835, for Eliakim Littell [*q.v.*], he also edited the *Museum of Foreign Literature, Science, and Art.* He was treasurer of the Philadelphia Museum and a founder of the Girard Life Insurance, Annuity, and Trust Company and of Laurel Hill Cemetery. During the laying out of the cemetery, his interest in landscape gardening was deepened, and he afterwards edited (1850–51) *The North American Sylva* by François André Michaux [*q.v.*], and the eleventh edition (1857) of *The American Gardener's Calendar* by Bernard McMahon [*q.v.*]. He also published *Designs for Monuments and Mural Tablets . . . With a Preliminary Essay on the Laying Out, Planting, and Managing of Cemeteries* (1846) and *Guide to Laurel Hill Cemetery* (1844), which went through seven editions in his lifetime.

To *The National Portrait Gallery of Distinguished Americans* (1834–39), edited by James Herring and J. B. Longacre [*q.v.*], Smith contributed articles on Benjamin Franklin, David Rittenhouse, William Augustine Washington, and Simon Kenton. In 1847, assisted by John F. Watson [*q.v.*], he edited *American Historical and Literary Curiosities,* of which, in 1860, a second series was issued in New York, under Smith's editorship. Meanwhile, in 1845, his son, Lloyd Pearsall Smith [*q.v.*], had begun the publication of *Smith's Weekly Volume,* a successor to *Waldie's,* and this publication was edited by the elder Smith from January 1845 to Mar. 25, 1846. He made four trips to Europe, describing one in *A Summer's Jaunt across the Water* (2 vols., 1846). In 1851 he retired from his librarianship so that his son Lloyd might be appointed to the place. His later literary work included the editing of *Letters of Dr. Richard Hill* (1854) and the authorship of a volume of entertaining gossip, written for his children, which was edited by his daughter and privately printed in 1892 under the title, *Recollections of John Jay Smith Written by Himself.* His paper, "The Penn Family" (1867), was used as an introduction to the first volume (1870) of *Correspondence between William Penn and James Logan.* Smith died at his estate, "Ivy Lodge," Germantown, at the age of eighty-three. He had had four sons and three daughters; Hannah Whitall Smith [*q.v.*] was his daughter-in-law.

[Smith's *Recollections,* ed. by E. P. Smith; J. T. Scharf and Thompson Westcott, *Hist. of Phila.* (1884), II, 1183–85, III, 2359; autobiographical touches in Smith's "Journal of Belles-Lettres"; G. M. Abbot, *A Short Hist. of the Library Company of Phila.* (1913); *Centennial Meeting of the Phila. Contributionship* (1852); Thompson Westcott, *The Historic Mansions and Buildings of Phila.* (1877); R. M. Smith, *The Burlington Smiths* (1877); *Public Ledger* (Phila.), Sept. 24, 1881.]
J. J.

SMITH, JOHN LAWRENCE (Dec. 17, 1818–Oct. 12, 1883), chemist and mineralogist, was born near Charleston, S. C. His father, Benjamin Smith, born in Virginia, was a merchant of Charleston. Prepared in private schools and in the College of Charleston, he entered the University of Virginia in 1835 and for two years studied chemistry, natural philosophy, and civil engineering under John P. Emmet, W. B. Rogers, and Charles Bonnycastle. After leaving the University, he was for a year an assistant engineer on the projected Charleston and Cincinnati railroad and then entered the Medical College of South Carolina, where in 1840 he was graduated with the degree of M.D. For several years after graduation he studied abroad. Liebig, Orfila, Dumas, and Élie de Beaumont were perhaps his most influential teachers.

In 1844 he returned to Charleston to establish himself as a medical practitioner and as a lecturer. In January 1846, with Dr. S. D. Sinkler, he founded the *Southern Journal of Medicine and Pharmacy,* which later became the *Charleston Medical Journal and Review.* Meanwhile he had

published some researches on certain soils of South Carolina, which led to his selection by James Buchanan, then secretary of state, to go to Turkey in response to the request of the Turkish government for an adviser on cotton culture. In this capacity he sailed, but was soon appointed to investigate the mineral resources of the Empire, and spent three years thus engaged. His discovery of emery and coal deposits made his services profitable to his employer; moreover, his observations regarding the minerals found in association with emery and corundum, communicated to the younger Benjamin Silliman [*q.v.*], resulted in the discovery of several emery deposits in the United States. He published several papers on his findings, notably "Memoir on Emery" in two parts (*American Journal of Science,* November 1850, January 1851).

In the summer of 1850, while in Paris, Smith conceived the idea of the inverted microscope, which he later perfected (*American Journal of Science,* September 1852). By December 1850 he was back in the United States. For the next two years he lived in New Orleans, studying, and lecturing before a group of scientific students, and enjoying the titular professorship of chemistry in the University of Louisiana, an institution which then existed largely on paper. On June 24, 1852, he married Sarah Julia, daughter of James Guthrie [*q.v.*] of Louisville, Ky. They had no children.

In the fall of 1852, Smith succeeded Robert E. Rogers [*q.v.*] as professor of chemistry at the University of Virginia. Here he and his assistant, George J. Brush [*q.v.*], prepared their "Reexamination of American Minerals," an important contribution to the study of the chemistry of minerals, published as a series of papers in the *American Journal of Science,* 1853–55. His own means and his wife's now made him independent, and in 1853 he resigned his professorship. The following winter he passed in Washington as the guest of his father-in-law, now secretary of the treasury. Here Smith spent his time working and lecturing in the Smithsonian Institution. In 1854 he succeeded Benjamin Silliman, Jr., as professor of medical chemistry and toxicology in the University of Louisville, holding this chair until 1866. Although he traveled frequently, visiting Europe many times, he made his home in Louisville until his death.

During his years there, Smith was especially interested in meteorites. His collection of meteoric stones, one of the finest in America, was sold, just before his death, to Harvard University. During these years he was also something of a man of affairs. He was for a time president of the Louisville Gas Works, was associated with E. R. Squibb [*q.v.*] in a pharmaceutical laboratory, and was the founder and a liberal benefactor of the Baptist Orphanage of Louisville. For more than forty years, from the time of his graduation from medical college in 1840 until his death, he was a frequent contributor to scientific journals. His bibliography (Marvin, *post*) lists 145 separate papers. Many of these were collected and published in 1873 as *Mineralogy and Chemistry: Original Researches*. Benjamin Silliman the elder considered Smith the first noteworthy organic chemist in America (*Journal of the Elisha Mitchell Scientific Society*, June 1906, p. 33). He was president of the American Association for the Advancement of Science in 1872, was a member of the National Academy of Sciences, in 1879 succeeded Sir Charles Lyell as corresponding member of the Academy of Sciences of the Institute of France, and was decorated by the governments of France, Russia, and Turkey. Although he was neither magnetic, charming, nor eloquent, and never a great teacher, he was a bold thinker and one of the ablest American chemists of his time.

[Smith's *Mineralogy and Chemistry* (1873) was reprinted as *Original Researches in Mineralogy and Chemistry by Prof. J. Lawrence Smith* (1884), ed. by J. B. Marvin, with a list of Smith's published papers prepared by Marvin, and biographical sketches by Marvin, B. Silliman, Jr., and Middleton Michel. See also *Popular Science Monthly*, Dec. 1874; H. A. Kelly and W. L. Burrage, *Am. Medic. Biogs.* (1920); *Year Book of the City of Charleston, S. C., 1883* (1884); *Louisville Medic. News*, Dec. 6, 1879; *Proc. Am. Acad. Arts and Sci.*, vol. XIX (1883); *Nat. Acad. Sci. Biog. Memoirs*, vol. II (1886); *Proc. Am. Asso. for the Advancement of Science*, vol. XLVIII (1899); *Am. Jour. Sci.*, Nov. 1883; *Courier-Journal* (Louisville), Oct. 13, 1883.]
                                        T. C. J., Jr.

SMITH, JOHN MERLIN POWIS (Dec. 28, 1866–Sept. 26, 1932), Biblical scholar, was born in London, England. His parents, William Martin Smith and Anne (Powis), were natives of Shropshire. The boy's early education was obtained in private schools at Leominster, Hereford, and at Dawlish, Devon. In 1881 he successfully passed the entrance examination for Cambridge. Throughout his life he displayed an extraordinary tenacity of purpose. During adolescence he had chosen a scholarly career as his goal and his interest had turned to Bible study. Finding further progress blocked in his native land, he emigrated in 1883 to Denison, Iowa. Here he worked for a time on the farm of an uncle but soon became teacher of the local school. In 1889 he found his way to Des Moines College, where he joined the Baptist Church. Here he

supported himself by teaching Greek to beginners and by arduous manual toil; yet he took a prominent part in extra-curricular activities and graduated with the degree of A.B. in 1893.

With his ultimate goal still in mind he became instructor in Greek in Cedar Valley Seminary, Osage, Iowa, but in the summer of 1894 enrolled as a graduate student in Semitics in the first summer session of the new University of Chicago. A year later he gave up his teaching post and enrolled at Chicago as a candidate for the degree of Ph.D. in Semitics. On July 1, 1899, he was awarded that degree *cum laude* and was appointed to the teaching staff of the department of Semitics as docent. His marriage to Catherine McKlveen of Chariton, Iowa, followed on Sept. 19 of the same year. Already the "tawny-haired young Englishman" had attracted the attention of President William Rainey Harper [*q.v.*], who shortly made him his literary secretary. He now entered upon a period of approximately seven years devoted almost exclusively to research under the direction of this brilliant scholar and commanding personality. The fruitful association which ensued came as a direct result of Smith's tenacity of purpose and devotion to exact knowledge in which he had schooled himself during the early years of his rigorous self-discipline. Soon the personnel of the original Semitics group at Chicago was tragically and rapidly depleted by the untimely deaths of George S. Goodspeed, the Oriental historian, President Harper, and his brother, the Assyriologist, Robert Francis Harper [*q.v.*]. These calamities made Smith's rapid advancement imperative. He became assistant professor in 1908, associate professor in 1912, and in 1915 was made professor and charged with the editorship of the *American Journal of Semitic Languages*, in succession to R. F. Harper. He fulfilled the duties of both positions with distinction till the day of his death.

His contribution to Biblical scholarship was of a double order. He developed into a highly stimulating classroom teacher who played a most important part in undermining the foundations of obscurantism and prodding the religious leadership of his generation to adjust itself, morally and intellectually, to expanding horizons. His contribution to the scientific literature of his field was also notable. His more important works include commentaries on Micah, Zephaniah, Nahum, and Malachi in the International Critical Commentary Series; *The Prophet and His Problems* (1914); *William R. Harper's Elements of Hebrew* (1921) and *Harper's Hebrew Method and Manual* (1921); *The Religion of the Psalms*

(1922); *The Moral Life of the Hebrews* (1923); *The Prophets and Their Times* (1925); *The Old Testament: An American Translation* (1927), of which he was general editor as well as translator of large sections of the text; and *The Origin and History of Hebrew Law* (1931). More than seventy technical and popular articles also came from his pen. Nor was his productivity significant in bulk alone; it was a positive and stimulating contribution to the reconstruction of the history of Hebrew life and thought. Smith had a fine command of the historical background of the whole ancient Near Eastern world, and he displayed great insight in relating the Hebrew experience to the total picture of the development of civilization in that world. Better still, he made his public conscious of the contribution of that world to the life of the West.

His standing was recognized by the fraternity of Orientalists in his appointment in 1927 as annual professor in the American School of Oriental Research in Jerusalem and by his election in 1931 as president of the Society of Biblical Literature and Exegesis and vice-president of the American Oriental Society. His death occurred as the vessel which carried him home from a sojourn in England and Europe was docking in New York harbor.

[*Am. Jour. of Semitic Languages and Literatures,* Jan. 1933; *Univ. Record* (Chicago), Jan. 1933; *Who's Who in America,* 1932–33; *N. Y. Times,* Sept. 28, 1932.]

W. C. G.

SMITH, JOHN ROWSON (May 11, 1810– Mar. 21, 1864), painter of panoramas, was born at Boston, Mass., the son of Elizabeth Pepperal (Sanger) and John Rubens Smith [*q.v.*]. After the family's removal in 1814 to Brooklyn, N. Y., John Rowson studied at a private school and in his father's drawing academy, which was later moved to Philadelphia, Pa. While living there he made sketches at Pottsville which his father engraved and published, but because of a family misunderstanding he left home and apprenticed himself to the scenic artist of the National Theatre, Philadelphia. Although he painted much scenery for theatres in New Orleans, La., St. Louis, Mo., and other cities from 1832 on, he became interested in experimenting with the panorama, invented probably by Robert Barker, an Edinburgh artist, about 1787. His panorama of Boston, designed to give people of interior towns successive views of a seaport, was mechanically but not financially successful; in "The Conflagration of Moscow," his next attempt, he used transparent colors on muslin and ingenious devices to simulate fire. Meantime, he had made carefully detailed sketches of Missis-

sippi river scenes, which were worked up at Boston into a huge panorama. It was burned after a brief exhibition in Boston in 1839, but the artist cherished the idea of repainting it. He married in Philadelphia, Jan. 5, 1841, Emma Louise Broughton, and in 1843 he became scenic artist at Castle Garden Theatre, New York, where he had prosperous years. He was one of those interested in the socialistic plans of Robert Dale Owen [*q.v.*], serving as president of the New York society for their furtherance.

In 1844 he completed his panorama of the Mississippi from the Falls of St. Anthony to the Gulf of Mexico. Shown at Saratoga, it earned $20,000 in six weeks, and, after touring the United States with it, in 1848 in partnership with John Risley, acrobat, he took it abroad. In London the work was in spirited competition with another Mississippi panorama, painted by John Banvard [*q.v.*], who had credentials as to its fidelity to nature from a United States engineer, the mayor of Louisville, Ky., and many steamboat men (*Description of Banvard's Panorama of the Mississippi River,* 1847). Smith in turn secured letters, which are extant, from Baron Friedrich Wilhelm von Humboldt and George Catlin [*q.v.*] affirming the scientific and artistic superiority of his panorama. By invitation of Queen Victoria he showed the piece at Balmoral, and thereafter to huge audiences in England and on the Continent. This panorama has been credited with greatly stimulating emigration toward the Mississippi Valley. While showing his panorama in Europe he made for American use a "Panorama of the Tour of Europe," which inspired a long poetic tribute in the *Philadelphia Inquirer,* Nov. 11, 1853. To it was added, in 1854, "The Siege of Sebastopol." After his return from Europe, he bought and occupied a large farm at Carlstadt, N. J., where he entertained many guests. According to Smith, he was the originator of the moving panorama in America. A brilliant and industrious artist, he painted scenery for a number of New York theatres: the Broadway in 1847, the Bowery and the National in 1856, and the Bowery again in 1862. He also had much employment winters at southern theatres. Thus employed at Mobile in 1861 at the outbreak of the Civil War, he escaped via New Orleans on the last boat carrying northerners home. In 1864, while at work at the Arch Street Theatre of Louise Lane Drew [*q.v.*] in Philadelphia, he fell victim to pneumonia. He was buried at Laurel Hill Cemetery, Philadelphia. From the nature of scene painting little of his work has been preserved, but it was highly esteemed by managers and theatre-goers of his time. A few examples of his painting and of his early engraved work are in the possession of his son, also trained in scenic art. The panorama, however, in the making of which he was a past master, was his great contribution to American social history.

[The chief source for the life of John Rowson Smith is the MS., "Recollections of John Rowson Smith" by his son, Edward S. Smith, a copy of which is in the N. Y. Pub. Lib.; this contains biog. data, announcements of panoramas, press notices, and photographs. See also Wilberforce Eames's continuation of Joseph Sabin, *A Dict. of Books Relating to America*, vol. XX (1927), pp. 298–99; G. C. D. Odell, *Annals of the N. Y. Stage*, vols. IV–VII (1928–31); death notice in *Pub. Ledger* (Phila.), Mar. 23, 1864. For a complete story of Am. panoramas, dioramas, and cycloramas consult the extensive coll. of documents in the Boston Pub. Lib.]

F. W. C.

SMITH, JOHN RUBENS (Jan. 23, 1775–Aug. 21, 1849), drawing master, engraver, painter, was born in Covent Garden, London, a son of John Raphael and Hannah (Croome) Smith, and a grandson of Thomas Smith, known as "Smith of Derby," landscape painter. From his father, an eminent mezzotinter, John Rubens learned sound draftsmanship, and between 1796 and 1811 he had nearly fifty paintings in the annual exhibitions of the Royal Academy. He came to America at least as early as 1809, for on Apr. 14, 1809, he married Elizabeth Pepperal Sanger in Boston, Mass. (*A Volume of Records Relating to the Early Hist. of Boston*, 1903, p. 273). Like other English artists, he probably emigrated because of the depression caused in Great Britain by the Napoleonic wars. In Boston, where he lived in Milk Street, he made a series of topographical water colors of local landmarks, these including Beacon Hill, then in process of partial demolition, the Old South Church, and Pawtucket Falls in the Blackstone River.

An assertive personality is said to have made him unpopular in Boston, and he presently removed (1814) to New York, where, as well as for a time in Philadelphia, Pa., he gained the reputation of being a good teacher and a quarrelsome person. He is described as being a man of "short figure, large head, peculiar one-sided gait, and indescribable expression of countenance" (*Crayon*, Nov. 7, 1855, p. 287). Among his pupils were Eliab Metcalf, Anthony De Rose, Thomas Seir Cummings [*q.v.*], George Washington Tyler, and Frederick Styles Agate [*q.v.*]. His alleged unethical attacks upon the work and character of John Vanderlyn and his shabby treatment of Francis Alexander [*qq.v.*] were indignantly denounced by Dunlap. Even the tolerant Cummings, who characterized him as "a teacher of the highest order of excellence," could

not forgive his master for "his untiring animosity and open hostility to the [National] Academy of Design and its members" (Cummings, *post*, p. 32), evidently provoked by the fact that he was not invited to become a member. Twenty years or more after these misunderstandings of the Academy's first period, Smith expressed deepest regret for his scurrilous writings and admitted that throughout life "his own temper had been his worst enemy and ruin" (*Ibid.*, 33). It is also on record (*Ibid.*, 174) that in 1843 he applied for a professorship of perspective at the Academy and that, though his request was not granted, he was offered three months' use of a room in which to exemplify some apparatus he had invented.

His last days were rendered uncomfortable by poverty which, as Cummings relates, was "in some degree alleviated by those who had suffered most from his pungent pen." He died in New York. One of his children was John Rowson Smith [*q.v.*]. During his years as a teacher of art in America he published *The Juvenile Drawing-Book* (8th ed., 1847), *A Compendium of Picturesque Anatomy* (1827), and *A Key to the Art of Drawing the Human Figure* (1831), besides engaging under the pseudonym of "Neutral Tint" in many literary controversies. His extant works, such as his mezzotints of portraits of Benjamin Lincoln [*q.v.*] and James Patterson, and his aquatint of the fire that nearly destroyed the Old South Church, Boston, are the work of an able draftsman who had an acute perception of individual character and dramatic effect; their antiquarian interest is considerable.

[Julia Frankau, *An Eighteenth Century Artist and Engraver, John Raphael Smith* (1902); William Dunlap, *A Hist. of the Rise and Progress of the Arts of Design in the U. S.* (1918), vols. II, III, ed. by F. W. Bayley and C. E. Goodspeed; T. S. Cummings, *Historic Annals of the Nat. Acad. of Design* (1865); "Saving the Old South," *Boston Sunday Globe*, Sept. 1, 1929, Frank Weitenkampf, *Am. Graphic Art* (1912); Boston Museum of Fine Arts, *A Descriptive Cat. of an Exhibition of Early Engraving in America* (1904); D. M. Stauffer, *Am. Engravers upon Copper and Steel* (2 vols., 1907); letter from Edward S. Smith, New York, a descendant, who has many unpublished documents concerning J. R. Smith.]

F. W. C.

SMITH, JONAS WALDO (Mar. 9, 1861–Oct. 14, 1933), civil engineer, son of Francis and Abigail Prescott (Baker) Smith, was born at Lincoln, Mass. At the age of fifteen he had his first engineering experience upon the small water-works system of his home town, showing such aptitude that at the age of seventeen he became chief engineer of the plant, acting as operator and general superintendent of outside work. He graduated from Phillips Academy, Andover, in 1881 and then for some three years was an assistant in the office of the Essex Company at Lawrence, proprietors of the water power of the Merrimac River at that place. In 1887 he graduated in the civil engineering course at the Massachusetts Institute of Technology. During his course, he had spent two summer vacations with the Holyoke Water Power Company, and after graduation he served from 1887 to 1890 as their assistant engineer.

In 1890 Smith became assistant engineer for the East Jersey Water Company, and for the next dozen years was engaged in the construction or maintenance of a succession of water-supply systems in northern New Jersey; he was made principal assistant engineer of the company in 1891 and ultimately chief engineer. In this capacity, in 1901, he directed the design and construction of the Little Falls mechanical filtration plant, a pioneer, and, at the time of its completion, the largest of its kind. The following year he supervised the completion of the new $7,500,000 water-supply system for Jersey City, including the Boonton dam, a concrete aqueduct, and pipe lines.

In 1903 Smith accepted the position of chief engineer of the Aqueduct Commission of New York City, taking charge of the construction of the new Croton dam then under way—in that day the largest masonry dam in the world. At this time he also made surveys for the Cross River and Croton Falls reservoirs, which were subsequently constructed. Two years later, when the Board of Water Supply of the City of New York was created to provide an additional water supply for that city, Smith became its chief engineer and began the most important work of his life as director of the Catskill Water Supply System. The initial program for this project included the Ashokan Reservoir, of 128,000,000,000 gallons capacity, upon Esopus Creek, about ninety miles from New York City, controlled by a masonry dam some 250 feet high and 1,000 feet long, and the Catskill Aqueduct, capable of supplying 500,000,000 gallons of water daily from the reservoir to the city. One of the most difficult problems was the crossing under the Hudson River near Storm King Mountain. Shafts were sunk on each side of the river to a depth of 1,114 feet below river level, and 14-foot tunnels were bored through solid rock to meet under the river. The Aqueduct, which is large enough for a railroad train to pass through, terminated at Kensico Reservoir, thirty miles from the city, where another masonry dam 307 feet high was completed in 1918.

As the demand for water by the city increased it became necessary in 1916 to commence the second step in this great project, developing an added supply from Schoharie Creek, north of Esopus Creek. Here the Gilboa dam, another massive masonry structure, was constructed, to form another large reservoir from which by the Shandaken tunnel—some eighteen miles long, the longest tunnel in the world when it was built —the waters of Schoharie Creek are taken into Esopus Creek and Ashokan Reservoir to supplement the initial supply and bring it up to the planned amount of 500,000,000 gallons a day. In 1922, when the project was nearing completion, Smith resigned as chief engineer of the Board of Water Supply, but he continued to act as its consultant and also as consulting engineer upon new water supply systems for Boston, Hartford, Providence, Kansas City, San Francisco, Kingston, Ont., and Vancouver, B. C., as well as upon the Moffat Tunnel near Denver. He continued actively engaged in his work until his sudden death, from heart disease, at his residence in New York City.

In 1918 Smith was awarded the John Fritz Medal—the highest honor in the engineering profession—by the four national engineering societies, for "achievement as engineer in providing the City of New York with a supply of water." He was also made an honorary member of the American Society of Civil Engineers, the American Water Works Association, and the New England Water Works Association. His exceptional abilities and character were well epitomized by the *Engineering News-Record* in an editorial at the time of his death: "Engineering judgment and intuition of highest order were essential parts of his equipment, of course, but to these he joined a great power over men— an almost magical ability to inspire loyalty and affection in all who worked for him, and at the same time to disarm and convince his opponents. Integrity, simplicity and justice, and a homely New England shrewdness combined to create this power. . . . The Catskill aqueduct stands as a monument to Smith, one of the greatest engineers of his time and a master of human arts."

[*Civil Engineering*, Nov. 1933; *Engineering News-Record*, Oct. 19, 1933; *N. Y. Times*, Oct. 16, 1933; *New York's Catskill Mountain Water Supply* (Report of Board of Water Supply, 1928); *Who's Who in America*, 1920–21, 1932–33; *Who's Who in Engineering*, 1931.]

H. K. B.

SMITH, JONATHAN BAYARD (Feb. 21, 1742–June 16, 1812), merchant, member of the Continental Congress, was born in Philadelphia, the second of three sons of Samuel Smith, a native of Portsmouth, N. H., and a prominent Philadelphia merchant. Jonathan received a liberal education, graduated from the College of

New Jersey in 1760, and entered business. One of the first of the younger Philadelphia business men to voice emphatic protests against the measures of the mother country, he played a prominent part in the movement leading up to separation. He was a member of the provincial conference of June 1774, secretary to the provincial convention, January 1775, and secretary to the provincial conference of June 18–25, 1776. In this last capacity he helped to engineer the overthrow of the old provincial government. In the meantime he was appointed a member of the committee of safety (1775) and later of the council of safety (1777). A believer in firm measures to insure independence, when Howe's army approached Philadelphia in the fall of 1776 he presided at a meeting of "Real Whigs" (Dec. 1) which passed resolutions recommending that every man between sixteen and fifty be ordered under arms for the defense of the state until the assembly should pass a militia law. On Feb. 5, 1777, he was elected to Congress, but on Sept. 13 following, with the British again approaching Philadelphia, he resigned to assist actively in the defense of the city. At first a captain (1775), later colonel, he was now made lieutenant-colonel of a battalion of "Associators" and participated in the Brandywine campaign, winning recognition as an "intrepid militia officer."

Smith was reëlected to Congress on Dec. 10, 1777, and served for the following year. He was made a member of the board of war on Jan. 14, 1778, and was a member of the committee to supervise publication of the journals of Congress. He stanchly defended the Articles of Confederation, prosecuted with zeal measures designed to eradicate irregularities and inefficiency in government boards and the army, and while belonging to the more liberal Whig faction, favored a minimum of acts of force as a means of keeping Whigs solidly together. An indefatigable worker, he was constantly in the heart of things in Congress, despite the handicap of serious illness during the spring and summer of 1778. From Apr. 4, 1777, to Nov. 13, 1788, he was prothonotary of the court of common pleas for the city and county of Philadelphia, and on July 6, 1778, he was commissioned justice of that court. Beginning with 1792 he served two years as alderman of Philadelphia and in the latter year was auditor-general of Pennsylvania under Gov. Thomas Mifflin [q.v.].

After 1800 Smith aligned himself with the Republicans of the more moderate stamp in Pennsylvania's factional politics, and in 1805 threw in his lot with the group opposing a constitutional convention. While no longer in public

office, he continued his interest in civic affairs and politics. Throughout his life, especially in the Revolutionary period, he earned an enviable reputation for keeping records with scrupulous care. William Findley [q.v.], commenting in 1812 on the need for an accurate history of Pennsylvania, declared that years before he had fixed on Smith as the man to write it (*Pennsylvania Magazine of History and Biography*, October 1884, p. 345), but though Smith apparently at one time considered writing such a history, he abandoned the idea in later life. He was a member of the Society of the Sons of St. Tammany, a grand master of Masons of Pennsylvania, a trustee of the University of Pennsylvania and of the College of New Jersey, and a member of the American Philosophical Society. His wife was Susannah, daughter of Col. Peter Bayard of Maryland and cousin of John Bubenheim Bayard [q.v.]; after his marriage he adopted Bayard as his middle name. His son, Samuel Harrison Smith [q.v.], was the founder of the *National Intelligencer* of Washington, D. C.

[Jonathan Bayard Smith and Samuel Harrison Smith Papers in Lib. of Cong.; J. G. B. Bulloch, *A Hist. and Geneal. of the Families of Bayard, Houstoun of Ga., and the Descent of the Bolton Family* (1919); F. V. Cabeen, "The Society of the Sons of St. Tammany, of Phila.," in *Pa. Mag. of Hist. and Biog.*, Oct. 1902; J. H. Martin, *Martin's Bench and Bar of Phila.* (1883); E. C. Burnett, *Letters of Members of the Continental Cong.*, vols. II–IV (1923–28); *Pa. Archives*, 1 ser., V, VI (1853), XI (1855), 2 ser., III (1875); *Minutes of the Supreme Exec. Council of Pa.*, vols. XI, XII (1852–53); J. G. Wilson, "Col. John Bayard (1738–1807) and the Bayard Family," *N. Y. Geneal. and Biog. Record*, Apr. 1885; *Poulson's Am. Daily Advertiser*, June 17, 1812.]   J. H. P.

SMITH, JOSEPH (Mar. 30, 1790–Jan. 17, 1877), naval officer, was born in Hanover, Mass., second son of the nine children of Albert and Anne Lenthall (Eells) Smith. He was a descendant of John Smith of Barnstable and Sandwich, Mass., who came to America before 1640, and his great-grandfather was the Rev. Thomas Smith of Pembroke, Mass. On the maternal side he was descended from John Eells who was in Massachusetts as early as 1634, but who later returned to England and is reported to have fought in Cromwell's army. At an early age Joseph learned shipbuilding, his father's business. On Jan. 16, 1809, he entered the navy as a midshipman and was soon ordered to the *Chesapeake,* then at Boston. Later in the same year he was furloughed in order that he might make a voyage in the merchant service. On Oct. 13, 1812, he was ordered to Lake Champlain and in the following year, on July 24, he was commissioned lieutenant. As first lieutenant of the *Eagle,* he assisted her commander, Robert Henley [*q.v.*], in building and manning that vessel, and in the battle of Lake Champlain there fell to him the duty of winding ship and bringing to bear on the enemy an uninjured broadside. Although wounded he stayed at his post, and was commended by Henley for his gallantry and voted a silver medal by Congress.

In the war with Algiers he served on board the frigate *Constellation* and participated in engagements with the Algerines. During the long period of peace following the war, he was often on leave from the navy because there were not enough billets for his continuous employment. He was several times stationed at the Boston or Portsmouth navy yard, occasionally as commander of a receiving ship. He was a lieutenant on board the *Guerrière* in the Mediterranean in 1818–19, and, in 1828–31, again served on that vessel when it was attached to the Pacific Squadron. On Mar. 3, 1827, he was promoted master commandant. He became a captain—at this time the highest rank in the navy—on Feb. 9, 1837. The same year he aided in fitting out the Wilkes exploring expedition. From 1838 to 1840 he commanded the *Ohio* of the Mediterranean Squadron and from 1843 to 1845 he commanded that squadron with the *Cumberland* as his flagship—his last sea duty. From 1846 until 1869 he was chief of the Bureau of Navy Yards and Docks, one of the longest terms of service for a bureau chief in the history of the navy department and exceedingly important by reason of the revolution in naval construction and the naval activities of the Civil War. On Aug. 8, 1861, President Lincoln chose him as the ranking naval officer of a naval board authorized to examine plans relating to ironclad vessels. From many competing drawings the board chose three, of which one was the plan of the *Monitor,* submitted by John Ericsson [*q.v.*]. This choice of the board, made in opposition to naval tradition and expert naval opinion, proved to be epoch-making. Secretary of Navy Welles wrote that Smith beyond any other person in the department was deserving of credit for the *Monitor* (*Diary of Gideon Welles,* 1911, vol. I, p. 214).

Smith was placed on the reserved list in 1855, but was restored to the active list in 1858, being made a rear-admiral on the retired list in 1862. From 1870 to 1871 he was president of the retiring board. For many years before his death he resided in Washington, D. C., where he was a regular attendant at St. John's Episcopal Church, serving as senior warden for twenty-one years. On Mar. 1, 1818, he was married to Harriet Bryant of Nobleboro, Me. They had two sons and two daughters. One of the sons,

Joseph Bryant Smith, commanded the *Congress* when she was attacked by the *Merrimac* in March 1862, and was killed in the battle.

[S. A. Smith, *A Memorial of Rev. Thomas Smith* (1895); F. F. Starr, *The Eells Family of Dorchester, Mass.* (1903); W. H. Brooks, *A Sermon Commemorative of the Life and Character of Joseph Smith* (1877); Jedediah Dwelley, J. F. Simmons, *Hist. of the Town of Hanover, Mass.* (1910); *New-Eng. Hist. and Geneal. Reg.,* Oct. 1877; Bureau of Navigation, *Record of Officers,* 1809–78; *Navy Register,* 1815–77; *Army and Navy Jour.,* Jan. 20, 1877; *Evening Star,* Washington, D. C., Jan. 18, 19, 1877.]   C. O. P.

SMITH, JOSEPH (Dec. 23, 1805–June 27, 1844), Mormon prophet, was born at Sharon, Windsor County, Vt., the fourth of ten children of Joseph Smith and Lucy (Mack) Smith. Both families, established in New England since the middle of the seventeenth century, had declined to the status of frontier-drifters when Smith's parents were married at Tunbridge, Vt., in 1796, and they made at least ten moves in nineteen years. They went to Palmyra, N. Y., in 1816 and remained in that general vicinity till Joseph was grown. His boyhood was spent among a footloose class, excitable, semi-illiterate, and superstitious, in a part of the country (frontier New England and New York) that produced a great many of the irregular sects and experimental societies of the first half of the century.

An attack of melancholy in his fifteenth year, coincident with one of his family's periodic conversions, conditioned his whole life. His first vision occurred in the spring of 1820 (*History,* I, 5), and was followed by similar experiences on Sept. 21, and 22, 1823. The accounts of them we possess are based on one which he wrote for the *Times and Seasons* in 1842 and represent an evolution, fragments of contradictory versions being on record. The burden of the visions, conveyed to him by the angel Nephi (later corrected to Moroni), was that no existing sect represented God's will, that the church of Christ had been withdrawn from the earth, and that God had selected Smith to restore it. The vision was renewed annually and on Sept. 22, 1827, he was allowed to take from their repository at the Hill Cumorah (near Manchester, Ontario County, N. Y.) certain "plates" of gold which recorded the history of the true church on the American continent, following its migrations from Jerusalem. The history was written in ancient characters, which he contradictorily described, and during the next three years he was engaged in translating it by miraculous means. The result was published at Palmyra, N. Y., in July 1830, as *The Book of Mormon.* This volume with *A Book of Commandments* (Jackson, Mo., 1833, later and now *Doctrine and Covenants,* 1835, consisting of sermons by and divine relations to Smith) forms the basis of the Mormon Church.

That *The Book of Mormon* was based on a historical novel by Solomon Spaulding was long a favorite theory but cannot be established. That it could be work of so ignorant a man as Smith appears strange and yet he cannot be shown to have met Sidney Rigdon [*q.v.*], the most likely source of its doctrinal matter, until after its publication. It contains much autobiographical matter and its entire material is indigenous to the society in which he grew up. Probably the book is in the main Smith's composition, slowly built up from fantasy, an anthology of religious and historical ideas to which all of his associates contributed. It is a "catch-all" of frontier Protestant doctrine and touches on practically every controversial belief of the time. It also deals with many social questions that excited his neighbors, and it capitalized the wide current interest in the origins of the American Indians. It is crammed with anachronisms and, as a literary production, was summed up by Mark Twain in the epithet, "chloroform in print."

Before its publication Smith had founded the Church of Jesus Christ of Latter-Day Saints on Apr. 6, 1830, at Fayette, Seneca County, N. Y. The communicants were Smith's relatives and neighbors; not until the baptism, on Nov. 14, 1830, of Sidney Rigdon, did the extraordinary growth begin. Borrowing from most ephemeral sects of the age, the church was "at once millenial, restorationist, and perfectionist" (De-Voto, *post,* p. 12). It took over much material from contemporary communistic experiments and much theology, also, from the Campbells. Both its organization and its doctrines, however, represent an evolution over a good many years. In this evolution and in the extension of his kingdom, the prophet Joseph was the dominant personality but by no means the leading intelligence or even the chief architect. He was a dynamic despot holding authority from God, to whose service the energies of better minds were devoted. It is certain that much of the doctrine and most of the ecclesiastical organization must be ascribed to Rigdon, W. W. Phelps, and similar minds; and that such exegetes, apologists, organizers, and propagandists as Phelps, Heber C. Kimball [*q.v.*], and Brigham Young [*q.v.*] were decisive influences in its spread and preservation. The church became a cooperative society ruled by an ecclesiastical oligarchy. It was a system excellently adapted to success on the farthest frontier but one which brought the Mormons into continual conflict with their neighbors in the communities they occupied during Smith's lifetime.

The growth of Mormonism, essentially a frontier phenomenon, made Smith an important force in frontier life. He very early contemplated removal to the Rocky Mountains or beyond, but first, in 1831, took his flock to Kirtland, Ohio, where Rigdon had a church. A fugitive from justice as the result of "wildcat" banking, Smith in 1838 fled to Missouri, where he had already established an outpost on what he declared to be the site of the Garden of Eden. Political and social friction with the Missourians drove the Mormons from Jackson County to less settled parts of the state and eventually (1839) to Commerce, Ill., which Smith renamed Nauvoo. Converts from Europe as well as America swelled the population of the settlement, and, owing to the desire of both political parties to gain the solid Mormon vote, the city was chartered and the Nauvoo Legion authorized by the state legislature. Extraordinary powers were granted the local government and practical independence was permitted the military establishment. The growing church was vouchsafed five years of prosperity, and Smith ruled gaudily, enjoying power, publicity, and worship, one of the most famous Westerners of his day, a prophet, an author, a lieutenant-general of the Nauvoo Legion, and finally a candidate for the presidency of the United States. Formal announcement of his candidacy was made Feb. 15, 1844, and Mormon campaigners were scattered through the country at the time of his sudden death (Linn, *post,* pp. 253–54). His increasing megalomania had enhanced the unpopularity of his sect, and with the scandal of his business affairs and the gradual discovery of polygamy (foreshadowed as early as 1831, declared as a revelation July 12, 1843), it produced schism within the church. On June 7, 1844, appeared the first and only issue of the *Nauvoo Expositor,* containing a vigorous attack on Smith. On June 10, in compliance with his order as mayor backed by his authority as lieutenant-general, the printing-press was tyrannically destroyed. The flight of his critics was followed by an uprising among the non-Mormons in neighboring districts. Smith and his brother were arrested and lodged in the jail at Carthage, Ill., whence they were taken on June 27 and then shot. Had he lived much longer it is likely that his church would have split up; his martyrdom, however, served the usual function of consolidating his followers.

Smith had intense religious suggestibility and a jovial earthy ebullience, both of which were important elements in his leadership, but the mania of his later years seems to have been less religious than egoistic. He ruled quite as much by personality as by the acknowledged divinity of his message. He was witty, athletic, vigorous, and virile; in appearance he was tall, light-haired, blue-eyed, distinguished. He was at his best in situations that could be personalized and dramatized, but he lacked intelligence and his judgment was almost uniformly bad. He was married to Emma Hale of Harmony, Pa., on Jan. 18, 1827. She bore him five children, among them Joseph Smith, 1832–1914 [q.v.]. The number of his polygamous wives is officially set at twenty-seven; unofficial claims have been made on behalf of several others. No polygamous issue has been proved. Joseph Fielding Smith [q.v.] was his nephew.

[Mormonism has called forth an enormous litera-ture, practically all of it controversial. The prophet's autobiography, "The History of Joseph Smith," is available in B. H. Roberts, ed., *Hist. of the Church of Jesus Christ of Latter-Day Saints,* vols. I–IV (1902–08). *Biographical Sketches of Joseph Smith,* by Lucy Smith, his mother (Liverpool, 1853), was not edited, as the autobiography was, but is only of indirect value. E. D. Howe, *Mormonism Unveiled* (Painesville, 1834), the earliest of the anti-Mormon books, is almost unique in containing trustworthy source material. J. H. Evans, *Joseph Smith* (1933), the work of a devout Mormon, is important because of its study of Smith's ancestry; see also M. A. S. Anderson, *Ancestry and Posterity of Joseph Smith and Emma Hale* (1929). The best mod-ern biography is contained in M. R. Werner, *Brigham Young* (1925), though it does not supersede that of W. A. Linn in *The Story of the Mormons* (1902). I. W. Riley, *The Founder of Mormonism* (1903), is unac-ceptable as an interpretation but contains much valu-able material. H. M. Beardsley, *Joseph Smith* (1931) is comprehensive but superficial. For a discussion of Smith's mental state and the relation of his church to contemporary social movements see Bernard DeVoto, "The Centennial of Mormonism," in *The American Mercury,* Jan. 1930. This is criticized by G. B. Ar-baugh, *Revelation in Mormonism* (1932), app. II.]
B. D—V.

SMITH, JOSEPH (Nov. 6, 1832–Dec. 10, 1914), Mormon prophet, president of the Reor-ganized Church·of Jesus Christ of Latter Day Saints, son of Joseph Smith, 1805–1844 [q.v.], was born at Kirtland, Ohio, while that place was the headquarters of the Church of Jesus Christ of Latter Day Saints which his father had founded two years before. Both his father and his mother, Emma (Hale) Smith, were of New England ancestry. The boy's early years were spent at Kirtland; he then experienced the Mor-mons' brief and stormy sojourn in Missouri and saw the mushroom growth of Nauvoo, Ill. His father thrice "blessed" him, though appar-ently not to prophetic succession. After the elder Smith's death at the hands of a mob in 1844, the mother, instead of going west with the followers of Brigham Young [q.v.], remarried and continued to operate the Nauvoo hotel. Jo-

seph studied law, but soon gave it up and turned to farming. On Oct. 22, 1856, he married Emme-line Griswold.

In this same year he was asked to head the Reorganized Church of Jesus Christ of Latter-Day Saints (later known as "non-polygamous Mormons"), started in 1852 by Mormons who had left the sect of James Jesse Strang [q.v.]. These claimed that the presidency of the Church must pass from father to son, realizing that only thus could their branch be popularized. Smith hesitated, but through "divine direction" timidly accepted office in 1860. In 1865 he moved to Plano, Ill., as editor of the *Saints' Herald.* His wife died in 1869 and on Nov. 12 of that year he married Bertha Madison. This period was filled with zealous activity; most Mormons in the Mid-dle West joined his church. Smith always op-posed polygamy, refusing to admit that his fa-ther had ever preached or practised it and main-taining that the doctrine had been fastened on the Church by Brigham Young [q.v.]. He did not actively defend his father's memory until many of the founders of the Church were no longer living. When, however, in 1879 his mother, on her deathbed, apparently to satisfy her son's hopes, said that to her knowledge Joseph Smith had neither practised nor taught polygamy, Smith went to Utah, challenged any one to prove his father's guilt, and insisted that even if his father were responsible for introducing the doc-trine, the practice was not thereby justified. He denounced it in tracts and periodicals, one of his chief opponents in the controversy being his cousin, Joseph Fielding Smith [q.v.]. With H. C. Smith he also wrote a large, apologetic trea-tise, *History of the Church,* in several volumes, the first issued in 1897. He fostered legal sup-pression of polygamy and convinced two courts that the Utah church had become heterodox. His lesser writings on polygamy and other subjects include: *Who Then Can be Saved?* (1866); *One Wife, or Many* (n.d.); *Reply to L. O. Lit-tlefield, in Refutation of the Doctrine of Plural Marriage* (1885); and articles in the *Arena* (August 1902, May 1903) and the *North Amer-ican Review* (March 1903).

In 1881 the church leaders moved to Lamoni, Iowa. Here Smith strengthened his church, fought alcohol, tobacco, tea, and coffee (in con-formance with "revelation"), helped found Grace-land College, and opposed Mormonism's late doctrines of polytheism and baptism for the dead. Physically strong, he enjoyed plowing and hay-ing and continued to farm. Though color-blind he was a close observer of nature. His second wife died in 1896 and on Jan. 12, 1898, he married Ada Rachel Clark. By each wife he had several children. His private life was cheerful but his friendship was not quickly extended. He had a clear, untrained tenor voice and loved familiar melodies but cared nothing for classical music. He wrote several hymns. He was a poor financial administrator but by personality and appearance was fitted for his patriarchal position. He was of large frame, and his white hair and beard lent his unusual face impressiveness. In advancing his positions he was cautious and yet firm. He disliked flattery, ostentation, and dispute, and was at times more coldly logical than persuasive; his straightforwardness of speech caused some to think him unapproachable. Under his leadership the church grew from a handful to 70,000, and he was able to visit missions in England and Hawaii. As a prophet—to the disappointment of his church, which expects continuous revelation—he translated no "hidden books" but merely explained former scriptures or designated persons for office. In 1906 he moved to Independence, Mo. During his last years he was blind and quite deaf, though he remained an interesting companion, drawing on a wealth of remembered poetry and wit. After his son and successor, Frederick, had relieved him of actual church leadership, he dictated his "Memoirs," publication of which was begun in the *Saints' Herald*, Nov. 6, 1934. Until his death the charge on his father's honor was his heaviest cross.

[*Saints' Herald*, Dec. 16, Dec. 23, 1914; *Journal of History* (pub. by the Reorganized Church), 1908–25, esp. Jan. 1915, and Oct. 1918 ff., Apr. 1925; "My Father's Letters," *Vision*, Jan. 1932 ff.; E. W. Tullidge, *Life of Joseph the Prophet* (1880); S. W. Traum, *Mormonism Against Itself* (1910); G. B. Arbaugh, *Revelation in Mormonism* (1932); M. A. S. Anderson, *Ancestry and Posterity of Joseph Smith and Emma Hale* (1929); information from M. A. (Smith) Anderson of Lincoln, Nebr., Smith's daughter.] G. B. A.

SMITH, JOSEPH FIELDING (Nov. 13, 1838–Nov. 19, 1918), sixth president of the Utah branch of the Mormon church and nephew of Joseph Smith, 1805–1844 [*q.v.*], the founder of Mormonism, was born in the town of Far West, Mo., the son of Hyrum and Mary (Fielding) Smith. His father and uncle, with other Mormon leaders, were in prison at the time. His whole childhood was spent during the period of the violent and bitter conflict between Mormons and non-Mormons in Missouri and Illinois. He had little or no schooling beyond that given him by his mother. In the crisis following the death of his father and uncle at the hands of a mob in June 1844, his mother followed the majority of the Mormons under the leadership of Brigham Young [*q.v.*], migrating to Utah in 1848.

Two months before Joseph Fielding was fourteen he was left an orphan by the death of his mother. At fifteen he was sent on a mission for his church to Hawaii. Recalled in the autumn of 1857 because of the impending "invasion" of Utah by federal troops under General Albert Sidney Johnston [*q.v.*], he enlisted in the "Nauvoo Legion" and served in the so-called "Utah War" until a truce was concluded between the Mormons and federal officials. In April 1860, he set out on a mission to Great Britain, where he served until 1863. In March 1864, with other Mormon leaders, he was dispatched on a special mission to Hawaii, where he remained for nearly a year in charge of church interests.

Rising rapidly in the hierarchy of Mormondom, he was made an apostle July 1, 1866, a few months before he was twenty-eight years old. He had been active in various home missions or colonization schemes in Utah for a decade when in 1874–75 he was sent to England to be president of the European mission; in 1877 he filled this position again for some months. Upon his return in September of that year, he was sent to take charge of the Mormon interests in the eastern part of the United States. In October 1880, he was made second counselor to John Taylor [*q.v.*], the president of the church.

In the early sixties he became active in politics. He served on the municipal council of Salt Lake City, and for seven consecutive terms (1865–74) was a member of the lower house of the territorial legislature. In 1880 and again in 1882 he sat in the upper house, during the second term being president. In 1882, also, he presided over the constitutional convention of Utah, but was legally disqualified under the Edmunds law because of his plural marriages. During his lifetime he had six wives, of whom the five polygamous ones bore him forty-two children. In September 1884, chiefly to prevent his prosecution for polygamy under the federal law, he was sent to Hawaii on another mission and remained there in voluntary exile until the summer of 1887. The next year he was busy in Washington with other Mormon leaders, urging Congress to grant Utah her statehood. On Apr. 7, 1889, he became second counselor to president Wilford Woodruff, and nine years later, on Sept. 13, 1898, second counselor to Lorenzo Snow [*q.v.*], who had become president. On Oct. 4, 1901, he moved into the position of first counselor to Snow, and on Oct. 17, a week after the death of the latter, Smith was chosen president and "Prophet, Seer. and Revelator" of his church.

The agitation concerning Mormon polygamy did not cease in spite of official pronunciamentos by Mormon officials following the so-called "Manifesto" of 1890, and in February 1904, as president of his church, Smith was subpœnaed to appear in Washington, D. C., before the Senate Committee on Privileges and Elections, then sitting on the Reed Smoot case (*Senate Document No. 486*, 59 Cong., 1 Sess., vol. I, pp. 80 ff.). He contended that, contrary to hearsay, the Mormon church no longer sanctioned plural marriages; and at the annual conference of the church on Apr. 3 he issued an official statement to this effect. In the decade that followed, the conflict of the Mormon church with the federal government and with sectarian elements having been dissipated, Smith turned his attention to strengthening its work in various Mormon communities and in foreign countries. He made two trips to Europe (1906, 1910), several trips to Hawaii, and one to Canada in 1913, when he dedicated a site for the first Mormon temple to be erected outside the United States. In his eightieth year his health became enfeebled, and he died six days after his eightieth birthday. He was buried in Salt Lake City.

Joseph Fielding Smith was the first among the presidents of the Utah Mormons to be born within his own church, and, as the official eulogy put it, "to have spent every day of his life under its ægis and influence" (*Deseret Evening News*, Salt Lake City, Nov. 19, 1918). Rather than the initiation of any important changes in the church, his chief contribution was the strengthening of the organization itself, and, through his kindly spirit of compromise, the fostering of more friendly relations with non-Mormons both in Utah and outside. In 1919, the year after his death, *Gospel Doctrine: Selections from the Sermons and Writings of Joseph F. Smith* was published.

[Andrew Jenson, *Latter-Day Saint Biog. Encyc.*, I (1901), 66–74, III (1920), 781–84; *Hist. Record* (Andrew Jensen, editor), VI (1887), 183–95; B. H. Roberts, *A Comprehensive Hist. of the Church of Jesus Christ of Latter-Day Saints* (1930), vols. V, VI; O. F. Whitney, *Hist. of Utah*, vol. IV (1904); Noble Warrum, *Utah Since Statehood* (1919), II, 66–70; *Improvement Era*, vol. XXII, Dec. 1918, Jan. 1919.]

K. Y.

SMITH, JUDSON (June 28, 1837–June 29, 1906), educator, missionary secretary, was born at Middlefield, Mass., where his parents, Samuel and Lucina (Metcalf) Smith, reared a family of seven sons and three daughters on a farm among the Berkshire hills. He was a descendant of Matthew Smith who settled at Woburn, Mass., in 1637, and a first cousin of Azariah Smith [*q.v.*]; Gerald Birney Smith [*q.v.*] was his nephew. Judson was fitted for college at home and at Williston Seminary, Easthampton, Mass., and

after taking part of his college course at Oberlin, graduated at Amherst in 1859. He taught in 1862 at Monson Academy, Mass. He graduated at Oberlin Theological Seminary in 1863, having also had a year at Union Seminary, New York. He was tutor in Latin and Greek at Oberlin, 1862–64, and instructor in mathematics and mental and moral philosophy at Williston Seminary, 1864–66. On Aug. 1, 1865, he married Jerusha Augusta, daughter of Seth A. Bushnell of Hartford, Ohio.

In 1866 Smith was called to Oberlin as professor of Latin, and on Oct. 17 of that year was ordained a Congregational minister. In 1870 he was transferred to the chair of ecclesiastical history in Oberlin Seminary, which he held until 1884. He also was lecturer on modern history at Oberlin, 1875–84, and lecturer on history at Lake Erie Seminary, Painesville, Ohio, 1879–84. From 1871 to 1884 he served as president of the Oberlin board of education. During the early eighties he was largely instrumental in the founding in China of the Shansi Mission of the American Board, which was at the outset manned by his pupils, several of whom lost their lives during the Boxer uprising of 1900.

In 1884 Smith was called from Oberlin to Boston as a secretary of the American Board of Commissioners for Foreign Missions, where he served with widening influence throughout the rest of his life. Entering upon his new duties at a time when the educational work of the Board was rapidly expanding, he brought much valuable experience to aid in this development, with which he was in hearty sympathy, as he was also with the quickening sense of the responsibility of missions for social service. He visited the missions of the Board in Turkey in 1888, and was chairman of a deputation inspecting its missions in China in 1898. He was of dignified bearing, punctilious courtesy, and abounding enthusiasm. His statement when chairman of the General Committee of the Ecumenical Conference of Foreign Missions at Carnegie Hall, New York, in 1900, that the story of missions is "a record more thrilling and more significant than any epic which man has produced," was characteristic of his habitual attitude. He served as trustee of Oberlin and of Williston Seminary and was president of the board of trustees of Mount Holyoke College. He lectured on missions at Oberlin and Hartford seminaries and was associate editor of the *Bibliotheca Sacra*. He was author of *Lectures in Church History and the History of Doctrine* and *Lectures in Modern History*, both published in 1881.

[*Ecumenical Missionary Conf., N. Y., 1900: Report of the Ecumenical Conference on Foreign Missions (2*

vols., 1900); *Amherst Coll. Biog. Record* (1927); *Who's Who in America*, 1906–07; *Missionary Review of the World*, Aug. 1906; *Congregationalist*, July 7 and 14, 1906; *Bibliotheca Sacra*, Oct. 1906; *Missionary Herald*, Aug. 1906; *Boston Transcript*, June 30, 1906.]
E. D. E.

SMITH, JULIA EVELINA (1792–1886) [See SMITH, ABBY HADASSAH, 1797–1878].

SMITH, JUNIUS (Oct. 2, 1780–Jan. 22, 1853), lawyer, merchant, promoter, has been called the "father of the Atlantic liner." He was born in Plymouth, then part of Watertown, Conn., third of the four sons of David and Ruth (Hitchcock) Smith. His father, a major in the Revolution and a general in the Connecticut militia, was a prosperous storekeeper. Junius was prepared for college at Bethlehem near by, and went as a sophomore to Yale. After graduating in 1802, he became a fellow student of John C. Calhoun at Tapping Reeve's law school, Litchfield, and in 1804 opened a law office in New Haven. Sent to London in 1805 by his brother's firm, he secured from the Court of Admiralty Appeal the award of liberal damages for the seizure of the New Haven ship *Mohawk*. He settled in London as a merchant, making his home there, except for a brief sojourn in Liverpool, until 1843. On Apr. 9, 1812, he married Sarah, daughter of Thomas Allen of Huddersfield, Yorkshire. She died in 1836, leaving one daughter. Smith dealt chiefly with New York, corresponding with his nephew Henry Smith, and constantly suggesting additional articles of export, clover seed being a favorite. In spite of reverses during the War of 1812, he became quite prosperous.

Smith's principal distinction arises from his share in establishing regular steamship service across the ocean. The single voyage of the *Savannah* in 1819, sponsored by Moses Rogers and William Scarborough [*qq.v.*], had been premature. In 1829, the *Curaçao* had made several trips from Holland to the Dutch West Indies, and in 1833 the *Royal William* went from Quebec to England, but none of these ventures developed into regular permanent service. The "liners" of the day were the highly efficient New York sailing packets. Smith seems to have conceived the idea of a line of transatlantic steamers about the time of his fifty-four-day voyage to New York in a British sailing vessel in 1832. He actively devoted the next few years to creating public opinion and raising capital for the support of his project. Kind, generous, and very hospitable, the little man, barely five feet six, went at the task with great energy of purpose and perseverance. Rebuffed in New York, he returned to London and in February 1833 proposed his idea to the directors of the London & Edinburgh Steam Packet Company without success. He issued several prospectuses, with no immediate response. In 1836, however, having secured a powerful ally in Macgregor Laird [see *Dictionary of National Biography*] of the great Birkenhead shipbuilding family, he organized the British & American Steam Navigation Company.

Great Britain's conversion to ocean steamships, once Smith had overcome the prevailing skepticism, was rapid, and in quick succession a number of rival companies were formed. Smith and Laird, in fact, had only a few hours to spare in being the first to reach New York. Isambard K. Brunel [*Ibid.*], engineer of the Great Western Railway, persuaded its Bristol backers in 1836 to form a transatlantic steamship company. Their 1340-ton steamship, *Great Western*, was launched July 19, 1837. Smith and Laird, in the meantime, were encountering disheartening delays. They had ordered a 1700-ton steamship in October 1836, but the failure of the contractor postponed even the laying of the keel until Apr. 1, 1837. Eager to be the first across the Atlantic, they decided not to wait for this vessel to be completed, so chartered from the Cork Steamship Company the little 700-ton *Sirius*, which left Cork on Apr. 4, 1838, and reached New York, on the voyage that marked the start of permanent transatlantic steam service, on the evening of Apr. 22, a few hours ahead of the *Great Western*, which had left Bristol on Apr. 7. Smith's vessel, the *British Queen*, was finally launched on May 24, 1838, and first reached New York July 27, 1839. Smith was the hero of the hour. It was declared in *Hunt's Merchants' Magazine* (October 1840, p. 298) that to him "more than to any other individual, is the final and successful accomplishment of this great enterprise doubtless to be attributed." Yale gave him the degree of LL.D. in 1840 and he had visions of knighthood (Pond, *post*, p. 187).

Then came reverses. Under Laird's supervision, his company, in December 1839, launched the *President*, the "largest ship in the world." She sailed on a return voyage from New York Mar. 11, 1841, and disappeared without a trace. This disaster, coupled with the successful competition of the line established by Samuel Cunard, who received the lucrative British mail subsidy in 1839, soon brought the British & American Steam Navigation Company to a close, and Smith in 1843 ended his long London residence. Back in America, he purchased a plantation near Greenville, S. C., and tried to relieve the country from dependence upon China for tea by growing it in the Southern states. The idea apparently came to him through his daughter, who was married to an army chaplain in India. He wrote numerous articles on the domestic growing of tea, celery, and broccoli, and made experiments which, according to later reports of the Department of Agriculture, indicated promise of a successful American supply of tea. This work, however, came to a tragic close. Smith's anti-slavery sentiments aroused his neighbors, and on Dec. 23, 1851, he sustained a fractured skull from a beating at the hands of "patrollers." These injuries hastened his death, which occurred at Bloomingdale Asylum, after some months of illness in his nephew's home, Astoria, L. I.

Smith's publications included: *An Oration, Pronounced at Hartford, before the Society of the Cincinnati, for the State of Connecticut* (1804); *Letters upon Atlantic Steam Navigation* (1841); *Essays on the Cultivation of the Tea Plant, in the United States of America* (1848); agricultural papers in the reports of the commissioner of patents; articles in the *Merchants' Magazine,* notably "Origin of Atlantic Ocean Steam Navigation" (February 1847); "Letters on Atlantic Steam Navigation" and "Steam Ships, and Steam Navigation," in *American Journal of Science and Arts* (January, July 1839).

[E. L. Pond, *Junius Smith, A Biog. of the Father of the Atlantic Liner* (1927), utilizing source material and reproducing much correspondence between Smith and his nephew; F. B. Dexter, *Biog. Sketches Grads. Yale Coll.,* vol. V (1911); *Hunt's Merchants' Mag.,* Oct. 1840; W. S. Lindsay, *Hist. of Merchant Shipping and Ancient Commerce,* vol. IV (1876); *Brief Memoirs of the Class of 1802* (1863); article by Henry Smith in *Evening Post* (N. Y.), June 24, 1882; *Evening Post* (N. Y.), Jan. 24, 1853; *Jour. of Commerce* (N. Y.), Jan. 25, 1853.]   R. G. A.

SMITH, JUSTIN HARVEY (Jan. 13, 1857–Mar. 21, 1930), historian, was born at Boscawen, N. H., the youngest of the three sons of Ambrose and Cynthia Maria (Egerton) Smith. On the death of the father, a Congregational minister, the family moved first to Pembroke, N. H., and then to Norwich, Vt. From Norwich, Justin walked each day the three miles to Hanover, N. H., where he attended Dartmouth as his father had done; he graduated in 1877, the valedictorian of his class. He was a serious student, keeping somewhat to himself. After graduation he visited the Paris Exposition, accompanying as private secretary, John D. Philbrick, who was in charge of the United States educational exhibit. Perhaps this experience implanted in young Smith that love of journeying abroad which later made of him a world traveler. The years 1879–81 he spent at the Union Theological

Seminary; but, instead of proceeding to the ministry, he entered the employ first of Charles Scribner's Sons and then of Ginn & Company. After holding positions of responsibility, both on the business and on the editorial side, he became in 1890 a member of the latter publishing firm, highly valued by his associates. His marriage, May 22, 1892, to Mary E. Barnard of Chico, Cal., the daughter of Allyn and Sarah Barnard, who, like Smith himself, had entered into the musical circle of Boston, was followed after two years by a separation and later by a divorce in Paris (private information).

In 1898 Smith, now possessed of ample means, retired from the publishing business. He became next year professor of modern history at Dartmouth College. One of his students recalled him as "a man of flexible dignity, kindness, judgment, and scholarly taste," whom "the classroom never succeeded in narrowing" (private letter to author). Here began his work as a productive scholar with the publication in 1899 of *The Troubadours at Home* (reviewed in *American Historical Review,* April 1900). All of his later work lay in the field of American history. *Arnold's March from Cambridge to Quebec* appeared in 1903, as did also *The Historie Booke,* edited by Smith for the Ancient and Honorable Artillery Company of Massachusetts. For this he wrote the historical narrative. He also published *Our Struggle for the Fourteenth Colony: Canada and the American Revolution* (1907). In 1908 he resigned his professorship to devote his time entirely to historical research. *The Annexation of Texas,* appeared in 1911. In respect to this it has been said, "Few books of history have more decisively settled controversy on their subject" (*American Historical Review,* July 1930, p. 942). His *magnum opus, The War with Mexico* (2 vols., 1919) brought to Smith the Pulitzer Prize for 1920 and the first Loubat Prize (1923) for the best book in English published during the previous five years on the history, geography, archeology, ethnology, philology, or numismatics of North America. Both books evidenced the author's characteristics as a scholar: a tireless searching for all possible sources, consultation of the originals themselves, knowledge through travel of the regions to be described, critical discernment, and a cumulative presentation of voluminous footnotes. Smith wrote also many articles in historical journals. For the Historical Manuscripts Commission of the American Historical Association, of which he was chairman from 1917 to 1923, he edited "Letters of General Antonio López de Santa Anna Relating to the War Between the United

States and Mexico, 1846–1848" (*Annual Report of the American Historical Association for the Year 1917*, 1920). In his many reviews of books, his trenchant criticism occasionally elicited controversy, as with Prof. E. D. Adams (*American Historical Review*, Oct. 1910, pp. 151–54; Jan. 1911, pp. 402–06; Apr. 1911, p. 683).

Tall, with a somewhat ruddy countenance and keen eyes, and, at least in later life, a full beard, Smith presented a commanding figure. He was a member of many societies and clubs, professional and social, and received several honorary degrees. He derived pleasure from cruising in power boats, constructed after plans of his own which resulted in more comfort than beauty. To house what he had collected in his extensive travels he built on Parker Hill, Boston, a bungalow where, at a huge three-sided desk, constructed for the purpose, he did much of his writing. In November 1929, he was shocked and weakened by a taxicab accident. On Mar. 21, 1930, having returned from the South, where of late years he had spent his winters, he reached New York, and late that afternoon, while taking a walk in Brooklyn, where he lived, he suffered a heart attack in front of Borough Hall and died instantly. After some delay his body was identified by his friend and former associate, George A. Plimpton of Ginn & Company. The funeral service was held at Trenton, N. J., where one of his nephews lived. His remains were buried in the town of his birth.

[Sketches in *Who's Who in America*, 1901–02, and later editions; obituary in *N. Y. Herald Tribune*, Mar. 24, 1930; biographical sketch in *Dartmouth Alumni Magazine*, May 1930; *Semi-Centennial Record of the Class of 1877. Dartmouth College 1877–1927* (n.d.); letters from friends and associates; personal knowledge.]   St. G. L. S.

SMITH, LLOYD PEARSALL (Feb. 6, 1822–July 2, 1886), librarian, publisher, editor, eldest child of John Jay Smith [*q.v.*] and Rachel Collins (Pearsall) Smith, was born in Philadelphia. After his graduation from Haverford College in 1837, he was placed in the counting house of Walm & Leaming, importers, to learn the business. In 1845 he began publishing *Smith's Weekly Volume*, edited by his father, a successor of *Waldie's Select Circulating Library*. This publication continued until the spring of 1846, and during part of this period young Smith also published *The Medical Library* and some law books. In 1847 he issued *A Plan of the District of Spring Garden, Philadelphia*.

In 1849 he became assistant librarian of the Library Company of Philadelphia, of which his father was librarian, and two years later succeeded him. With this ancient library, founded

by Franklin and his friends, he remained identified until his death. Under his direction the third volume of *Catalogue of the Books Belonging to the Library Company of Philadelphia* was issued in 1856, for which work he supplied a copious index. When the Confederate forces invaded Pennsylvania in 1863, Smith enlisted for three months in a volunteer regiment, and closing the library, went forth to the defense of Gettysburg. During the war, he also joined with others in collecting money for the relief of those in East Tennessee who remained loyal to the Union, and published a report of a commission that was sent there to investigate conditions. He was the first editor of *Lippincott's Magazine*, conducting that periodical from January 1868 to December 1869. Under his editorship the magazine published Anthony Trollope's novel, "The Vicar of Bullhampton"; one by Robert Dale Owen, "Beyond the Breakers"; also contributions from Bayard Taylor and from George H. Boker.

In 1876 he contributed to *Public Libraries in the United States of America*, issued by the United States Bureau of Education, the section entitled "Public Libraries of Philadelphia." A paper of his read before the American Library Association and published in 1892 under the caption *On the Classification of Books*, was a pioneer discussion of the subject. Another paper, read before the Germantown Science and Art Club appeared in 1885 as *Symbolism and Science*. That same year he published *A Bibliography of that Ancient and Honourable Order, the Society of the Cincinnati*. Upon the appearance of the first volume of *Histoire de Jules César*, by Napoleon III, in 1865, Smith reviewed it in the *United States Service Magazine*, later issuing the review in pamphlet form—*Remarks on the Apology for Imperial Usurpation Contained in Napoleon's Life of Caesar* (1865). He was regarded as a most scholarly man and as better acquainted with library management than any one else of his time. He was one of the original associate editors of the *American Library Journal*, begun in September 1876. As an after dinner speaker he was much in demand. On Oct. 13, 1844, he married Hannah E. Jones, daughter of Isaac C. Jones, a Philadelphia merchant engaged in the East India trade; no children were born to them, but they adopted a daughter.

[G. M. Abbot, "Some Recollections of Lloyd P. Smith," *Library Journal*, Dec. 1887; *Public Ledger* (Phila.), July 3, 1886; J. T. Scharf and Thompson Westcott, *Hist. of Phila.* (1884), II, 1185; G. M. Abbot, *A Short Hist. of the Lib. Company of Phila.* (1913); *Biog. Cat. of the Matriculates of Haverford Coll.* (1922); information from a member of the family.]   J. J.

SMITH, MARCUS (Jan. 7, 1829–Aug. 11, 1874), actor, better known as Mark Smith, was the son of the well-known comedian and theatre manager, Solomon Franklin Smith [q.v.], and his first wife, Martha (Mathews) Smith. He was born in New Orleans, La., but was educated chiefly in schools in and near St. Louis, Mo., the family home. As a child he was sometimes seen on the stage of the Ludlow and Smith Theatre in St. Louis, playing Tom Thumb in Henry Fielding's burlesque, *Tom Thumb,* as early as 1836. But his father was opposed to his adopting the stage as a profession, and sought to train him first as a printer, then as a navigator, and later as a mechanic. In 1848, however, he went to New York, where he secured a position in the Chatham Theatre. A year later he joined his father's company at the St. Charles in New Orleans, making his début as Diggory in *Family Jars.* He continued at this theatre under the management of Ben De Bar after the dissolution of the firm of Ludlow and Smith in 1853. After a season under Joseph M. Field in Mobile he became a member of the stock company of William Evans Burton [qq.v.] in New York. There he soon began to make a name for himself as an interpreter of the "good old English gentlemen" in the "good old English comedies" and became a great favorite. He remained with Burton until the closing of his theatre in 1858 (Odell, *post,* VII, 163–64).

After this he at different times supported such stars as Laura Keene, Edwin Forrest, and Edward Loomis Davenport [qq.v.]. In March 1862 he first appeared with the company of Lester Wallack, playing Sir William Fondlove in J. S. Knowles's comedy of *The Love Chase.* During the summer of 1863 he managed with Emily Thorne a brief season at the Winter Garden. After another year with Wallack he again tried his hand at management, becoming in 1866 joint-manager with Lewis Baker of the New York Theatre. February 1869 found him stage-manager for Edwin Booth [q.v.] at the latter's theatre, and the following year, after supporting Mme. Franziska Janauschek [q.v.] and Mrs. Scott-Siddons, he went abroad, there to play at the St. James's Theatre, London, under Mrs. John Wood. But he soon returned to the United States and, for a time, to Booth's Theatre in New York. The season of 1872–73 he spent under Albert Marshman Palmer [q.v.] at the Union Square Theatre. There he scored such a success in *One Hundred Years Old* that he bought the acting rights to the piece and toured the country as the centenarian. The following spring he went abroad to attend the operatic début of his daugh-

ter, and died after a stroke in Paris, Aug. 11, 1874. His death elicited many eulogies both of his artistry and of his personal character. When Mark Smith was playing one of his old gentlemen, wrote William Winter [q.v.], "the observer of him felt that every trait of manliness, kindly worth, gracious serenity, and human feeling that warmed and beautified the fictitious character had its native source in the heart of the man himself" (*Vagrant Memories,* 1915, p. 131). He was survived by his widow, Elizabeth McKenney, his daughter Kate (who as Catarina Marco became a successful opera singer), and two sons, Mark and Percival.

[See T. A. Brown, *Hist. of the Am. Stage* (1870); Laurence Hutton, *Plays and Players* (1875) and *Curiosities of the Am. Stage* (1880); S. F. Smith, *Theatrical Management* (1868), pp. 221–22; N. M. Ludlow, *Dramatic Life As I Found It* (1880); G. C. D. Odell, *Annals of the N. Y. Stage,* vols. V–VII (1931); obituary in *N. Y. Times,* Aug. 27, 1874. Many of Smith's letters to his father are in the estate of his nephew, the late Sheridan S. Smith, Webster Groves, Mo.]

W. G. B. C.

SMITH, MARGARET BAYARD (Feb. 20, 1778–June 7, 1844), society leader, author, was the daughter of John Bubenheim Bayard [q.v.] and his wife, Margaret Hodge. On Sept. 29, 1800, she married her second cousin, Samuel Harrison Smith [q.v.]. Soon after her husband became President Jefferson's political editor, she found herself a leader in Washington society. In this capacity she was hardly excelled. She was a charming hostess, happy in her married life, capable, intelligent, vivacious, energetic, sympathetic, and positive. She read the best books, and conversed with distinguished men on subjects of domestic, national, and international import. Among her guests were statesmen, philosophers, poets, musicians, and diplomats. Although the wife of a stanch Jeffersonian, she remained true to her Federalist rearing, and welcomed Whigs to her home. Men of opposite political faith associated there on friendly terms. Although she professed to think little of balls and parties, she played well at chess and whist, and participated gaily in the whirl of society during the winter season when she had left her country seat, "Sidney," for her city residence.

In addition to her social activities she baked her own bread, took great pride in making her own butter, reared four children, aided the poor, attended church regularly, and won a contemporary reputation as an author. She contributed to Godey's *Lady's Book,* the *Southern Literary Messenger, Peter Parley's Annual,* and Herring and Longacre's *National Portrait Gallery,* and wrote a novel in two volumes entitled, *A Winter in Washington; or, Memoirs of the Seymour*

Family (1824), and another tale, *What Is Gentility?* (1828). Her "Domestic Sketches" and other stories in Godey's *Lady's Book* were pitched high in moral tone, as were all her contributions to magazines; her novel is valuable to history for its true stories of Washington characters. Her most valuable contribution to literature, however, lies in her delightfully refreshing, informative, and truthful letters to her friends. These, edited by Gaillard Hunt [*q.v.*] and published in 1906 under the title, *The First Forty Years of Washington Society,* form a record, by a keen observer, of events from Jefferson to Harrison. They also reveal the writer's personal opinions. She saw no incompatibility between politeness and republicanism, but she believed that democracy was more jealous of power and privilege than despotism. Influenced undoubtedly by Jackson's fight against the United States Bank, of the Washington Branch of which her husband was president, she deplored the influence of Jackson's "Kitchen Cabinet," and the spoils system, and finally decided that the old General was in his dotage when he championed Peggy O'Neale [*q.v.*] against the ladies of the cabinet.

[In addition to Mrs. Smith's letters, ed. by Hunt, mentioned above, see: J. G. Wilson, "Col. John Bayard and the Bayard Family," *N. Y. Geneal. and Biog. Record,* Apr. 1885, repr. separately (1885); Helen Nicolay, *Our Capital on the Potomac* (1924); W. B. Bryan, *A Hist. of the National Capital,* vol. I (1914); *Daily National Intelligencer* (Washington), June 8, 1844. The important Margaret Bayard Smith Papers (28 vols., covering the period 1798–1845) are in the Library of Congress.]   W. E. S—h.

SMITH, MARTIN LUTHER (Sept. 9, 1819–July 29, 1866), Confederate soldier, was born at Danby, Tompkins County, N. Y., to which place his father, Luther Smith, had removed from Maine. He entered West Point as a cadet in 1838, and upon his graduation in 1842 was commissioned in the topographical engineers, then a separate corps of the army. His service was entirely in the Southern states, except for a brief period in Mexico, when he reconnoitered and mapped the valley of the city of Mexico. He executed surveys of several rivers and harbors in Florida and Georgia, and examined into the possibilities of a projected ship-canal across the Florida peninsula. For five years, 1856–61, he also acted as chief engineer of the Fernandina & Cedar Key Railroad. In 1846 he married Sarah, daughter of John and Harriet (Cooper) Nisbet of Athens, Ga. He was promoted first lieutenant in 1853 and captain in 1856.

Owing to his marriage and his long residence in Florida and Georgia, "his associations, feelings and interests are with the South" (Senator Yulee to Jefferson Davis, Mar. 1, 1861, War Department records); and he tendered his resignation from the army, hoping to serve the Confederacy but determined in any event not to serve against it. His resignation was accepted, Apr. 1, 1861. He had already, Mar. 16, 1861, been appointed a major of engineers in the Confederate regular army, being recorded as a citizen of Florida. Though occasionally commanding troops in the field—at one time a division —it was as an engineer that he was chiefly employed. He had a large part in the planning and construction of the fortifications of New Orleans and those of Vicksburg, and commanded troops in the defense of both of those places when they were taken in 1862 and 1863. He was appointed colonel, 21st Louisiana Infantry, in February 1862; brigadier-general (provisional army) in April 1862; and major-general in November 1862. After the surrender of Vicksburg in July 1863 he was a prisoner on parole until his exchange some seven months later. From April to July 1864 he was chief engineer of the Army of Northern Virginia, and from July to October, of Hood's Army of Tennessee. In that capacity he was responsible for the construction of the fieldworks used in the campaigns of those armies. Thereafter he was chief engineer to Beauregard, who was in administrative command in the western theatre; his principal service there was in the preparation of the defenses of Mobile to receive the attack which was delivered against them in the last days of the Confederacy. He was paroled at Athens, Ga., in May 1865 and took up the practice of engineering as a civilian for the few remaining months of his life. He died in Savannah.

[*War of the Rebellion: Official Records (Army)*; *Battles and Leaders of the Civil War* (4 vols., 1887–88); G. W. Cullum, *Biog. Reg. Officers and Grads. U. S. Mil. Acad.* (3rd ed., 1891); C. A. Evans, *Confed. Mil. Hist.* (1899); unpublished records in the War Dept.]   T. M. S.

SMITH, MELANCTON (May 7, 1744–July 29, 1798), merchant, lawyer, member of the Continental Congress, son of Samuel and Elizabeth (Bayles) Smith, was born at Jamaica, L. I. His education was home training of a sort to reflect credit upon his obscure parents. At an early age he was placed in a retail store at Poughkeepsie. He soon owned land in various parts of Dutchess County, and had acquired a reputation for wide reading, honesty, and ability. He early manifested a life-long interest in metaphysics and religion; in 1769 he helped organize the Washington Hollow Presbyterian Church and purchased one of the pews. He was one of ten delegates from Dutchess County in the First Provincial Congress in 1775 and was made a member of a committee to raise a regiment of the line in Dutchess County. He also organized and was captain of the first company of Rangers of that county, a home guard so effective in controlling Loyalists that the First Committee for Detecting Conspiracies adopted it as a model and on Dec. 20, 1776, appointed Smith, with the rank of major, to the command of all such companies.

On Feb. 11, 1777, he was made one of three members of a commission for "inquiring into, detecting and defeating all conspiracies . . . against the liberties of America" (*Journals, post,* I, 803), under which broad phraseology he served almost daily for the next six months at twelve shillings *per diem,* administering oaths of allegiance, arresting suspects, informing upon and examining Loyalists. While wielding this powerful civil and military authority, he was also serving as high sheriff of Dutchess County, to which position he was elevated in 1777 and again in 1779. He extended his land holdings by purchasing some of the forfeited Loyalist estates (Ledger of Forfeited Estates in Dutchess County, MS., New York Public Library).

As a merchant and as one enjoying the confidence of Gov. George Clinton [*q.v.*], he naturally gravitated to the commissary department in the last years of the Revolution, and, though he came out of the war a man of considerable property, one whose word is usually reliable said he was "as pure a man as ever lived" (Hammond, *post,* I, 61). In 1782 Washington appointed him to a commission to settle disputes between the army and contractors at West Point and elsewhere (Washington Papers, Library of Congress, vols. LV–LVII, *passim*). Smith charged contractors with bad faith and in turn was charged with inducing soldiers to spend their pay in his store (*Ibid.,* LXIII, 146, 150; B. XVI, pt. 2, p. 47). He shared the indignation of other patriots over the decision in *Rutgers* vs. *Waddington* which in 1784 invalidated an act of the legislature proscribing Loyalists.

About 1785 he moved to New York City and entered upon extensive mercantile enterprises and a lucrative law practice, though it is not known where he secured his legal training. He served in the Continental Congress from 1785 to 1788. His most conspicuous public service was in the Poughkeepsie convention called in 1788 to consider ratification of the Federal Constitution. Basing his campaign on an anti-Loyalist issue, he was unable to secure election in Federalist New York County but represented Dutchess County in the convention as an Anti-

Federalist. In the convention he bore the brunt of the Federalist attack and was so successful in opposing even Hamilton that he has been characterized as "one of the ablest debaters in the country" (Alexander, *post,* I, 34). He held out for a Bill of Rights until Hamilton's eloquence and news of Virginia's ratification impelled him to announce his support of the Constitution, an action which broke the Anti-Federalist ranks and brought down Clinton's wrath upon his head. Although he was one of the few important landowners and merchants among the Anti-Federalists, Smith continued in the Clintonian party and helped in 1789 to sponsor a movement for a second constitutional convention. He was elected to the legislature in 1791 and canvassed the state for Clinton in 1792. He was one of the first victims of the yellow fever epidemic in New York City in 1798. Melancton Smith [*q.v.*], distinguished naval officer, was his grandson.

[Surprisingly few records of Smith exist for one who played such an able part among the Anti-Federalists. A few letters are in the N. Y. Hist. Soc., the N. Y. Pub. Lib., the N. Y. State Lib., and among the Force Transcripts in the Lib. of Cong. See also *Journals of the Provincial Cong. . . . of the State of N. Y.* (1842), vol. I; *Minutes of the Committee and of the First Commission for Detecting and Defeating Conspiracies* (2 vols., 1924–25); *The Debates and Proc. of the Convention . . . at Poughkeepsie* (1788); J. W. Poucher, "Melancton Smith," *Year Book Dutchess County Hist. Soc.,* 1925; *N. Y. Hist. Soc. Colls.* for 1906; *Names of Persons for Whom Marriage Licenses Were Issued by the Secretary of the Province of N. Y. Previous to 1784* (1860); D. S. Alexander, *A Pol. Hist. of the State of N. Y.,* vol. I (1906); A. C. Flick, *Loyalism in N. Y. during the Am. Rev.* (1901); J. D. Hammond, *The Hist. of Pol. Parties in the State of N. Y.* (1842), vol. I; Frank Hasbrouck, *The Hist. of Dutchess County, N. Y.* (1909); C. E. Miner, *The Ratification of the Federal Constitution by the State of N. Y.* (1921); E. W. Spaulding, *N. Y. in the Critical Period* (1932). The year of Smith's birth is often given as 1724; Poucher, *ante,* is authority for the date here given.]   J.P.B.

SMITH, MELANCTON (May 24, 1810–July 19, 1893), naval officer, was born in New York City, the third of his name, his grandfather, Melancton Smith [*q.v.*], having been prominent in early New York politics and his father, a colonel in the War of 1812. His mother was Cornelia Haring Jones. On Mar. 1, 1826, he entered the naval service, and after three years in the Pacific and study at the naval school in New York he was made passed midshipman in April 1832. During the next decade his sea duty was chiefly in the West Indies and his shore duty in New York, with promotion to lieutenant in 1837 and active participation (June 1839–March 1840) in the Seminole War in Florida. He was in the Mediterranean, 1841–43; in the *Vandalia,* Home Squadron, 1844–46; executive of the Pensacola yard during the Mexican War;

and again in the Mediterranean in the *Constitution*, 1848–51. In 1855 he was made commander, but save for a few months as executive of the *Potomac* in 1855 he had no further sea service until the opening of the Civil War, when he was sent to the mouth of the Mississippi in command of the *Massachusetts*. Here he had a long-range cannonade with Confederate batteries on Ship Island, July 9, 1861, and another with the *Florida* on Oct. 19. Speaking of his "efficient service," the Navy Department ordered him north at the close of 1861, but soon sent him back to command the side-wheeler *Mississippi* in Farragut's force against New Orleans. The *Mississippi*, as third ship of the first division, was heavily engaged in the night passage of the forts below New Orleans on Apr. 23–24, 1862, had a seven-foot gash cut in her side by the ram *Manassas*, and at daybreak drove the ram ashore and riddled it with two broadsides.

Continuing in Farragut's squadron through the ensuing year, the *Mississippi*, on the night of Mar. 14, 1863, participated in the attempt to pass the batteries at Port Hudson. At a bend in the narrow channel she grounded directly under the enemy guns, and after desperate efforts to save his ship Smith was forced to fire and abandon her, drifting with his men in boats to the Union vessels below. Admiral George Dewey [*q.v.*], who as a youthful officer was executive under Smith throughout this period, pictures vividly in his *Autobiography* (*post*, p. 51) the personality of his commander, whom he greatly esteemed. "He was a pronounced character," writes Dewey, "absolutely fearless, with something of Farragut's grim determination in the midst of battle. He smoked continually, lighting one cigar with the butt of another, whether shells were bursting around him or he was lounging on the deck. . . . His hobby, except in the matter of cigars, was temperance." An earnest, religious man, without humor, he was a dogged fighter, and when he went north in June, after some further service in the *Monongahela*, Farragut wrote, "I hope the department will appreciate your services as highly as I do" (June 23, 1863, Personnel Files, Navy Library). In the monitor *Onondaga* he was afterward a divisional commander in the James River, and in May–June 1864 he commanded a half dozen or more wooden gunboats in Albemarle Sound during efforts to destroy the ram *Albemarle*. His flotilla on May 5 had a desperate mêlée with the ram, in which, though driven back up the Roanoke River, the latter suffered somewhat less than her light-built opponents. The department congratulated him on "this remarkable contest"

and on his "vigilant and gallant use of the means" at his disposal (*Official Records, post*, 1 ser., IX, 761). He commanded the *Wabash* in Porter's fleet against Fort Fisher, and was warmly commended by Porter for his handling of his ship during the two heavy bombardments in December–January 1864–65. Made captain in 1862, commodore in 1866, and rear admiral in 1870, he was chief of the Bureau of Equipment and Recruiting, 1866–70, and was subsequently in charge of the New York Navy Yard until shortly after his retirement, May 24, 1871. He was governor of the Philadelphia Naval Asylum, 1871–72. In 1837 he married Mary Jackson, daughter of Thomas Jones of Long Island, N. Y.; she died at South Oyster Bay, Long Island, Apr. 4, 1885, and Smith died some eight years later at Green Bay, Wis.

[L. H. Hamersly, *Records of Living Officers of the U. S. Navy* (4th ed., 1890); *Autobiog. of George Dewey* (1913); Personnel Files, Navy Dept. Lib.; *Official Records of the Union and Confederate Navies in the War of the Rebellion* (see general index); *Army and Navy Journal*, July 22, 1893; *N. Y. Tribune*, July 21, 1893.]   A. W.

SMITH, MERIWETHER (1730–Jan. 24, 1794), statesman, was born at "Bathurst," Essex County, Va., the son of Col. Francis and Lucy (Meriwether) Smith. His father, grandson of Nicholas Smith of Petsworth Parish, Gloucester County, was a member of the House of Burgesses, 1752–58. Meriwether Smith was one of the signers of the Westmoreland Association (Feb. 27, 1766) in opposition to the Stamp Act and wrote "several spirited pieces" relating to that and other British measures (Rind's *Virginia Gazette*, Aug. 24, 1769). From 1774, when he became a member of the Essex County Committee, he was seldom out of public office during the period of the Revolution. He was a member of the Virginia House of Burgesses in 1775, of the conventions of 1775 and 1776, of the House of Delegates in 1776, 1778, 1781–82, 1785–88, of the convention of 1788, occasionally of the council, and he was three times (1778, 1779, 1780) elected a delegate to the Continental Congress.

In the Virginia convention of 1776 he was chosen to the important committee on privileges and elections and second on the committee to prepare a declaration of rights. On May 15 he was one of three members, the other two being Edmund Pendleton and Patrick Henry, who drafted resolutions of independence; Pendleton's draft, however, was accepted. Although Madison recorded a tradition (Rives, *post*, I, 164) that Smith prepared a first draft of the Virginia constitution of 1776, the weight of evidence assigns the authorship of that document to George Mason (K. M. Rowland, *The Life of George Mason*, 1892, I, 228, 254–56). John Augustine Washington classed Smith among the five best speakers in the convention (*Southern Literary Messenger*, November 1858, p. 330).

In the Continental Congress, in which he took his seat Sept. 28, 1778, he played an active, and at times a conspicuous, part in the proceedings. Like several other Virginia delegates he declined to espouse the cause of the Lees in the notorious Deane-Lee controversy, and his course in that fiery contest brought down upon him the sharp criticism of Richard Henry Lee and those aligned with him. "Mr. Smith (alias Dogberry)," Lee wrote to Henry Laurens (from Virginia, June 13, 1779), "has been famous here for being a very vain and a very troublesome man" (Ballagh, *post*, II, 70). Marbois said of him, "He has much sagacity but too much subtlety, and in seeking to penetrate he misses the goal" (*Affaires Étrangères, États-Unis, Mem. et Doc.*, 1). He impressed members of Congress no less than his Virginia contemporaries with his eccentricities, and was dubbed with such nicknames as "the Oddity of Virginia," "Fiddle," "Fiddlehead," "Base Viol," "Ugly Instrument," etc., the origin of which remains in obscurity. For his part he was by no means averse to throwing fat into the fire when occasion offered; accordingly, when a letter of Henry Laurens severely criticizing Congress was intercepted and printed in Rivington's *New York Royal Gazette* (May 5, 1779)—he and Laurens had already more than once crossed swords—Smith eagerly brought the matter to the attention of Congress (*Journals of the Continental Congress*, May 14, 15, 18; Burnett, *post*, IV, 212–15). Friendly to the French alliance, he was of course at odds with the whole anti-Gallican party.

Although reëlected to Congress in June 1779, he did not take his seat. On his return to Virginia in the autumn of that year he became involved in a controversy with the Assembly over his account as a delegate, a controversy revolving, in part at least, around his commercial connections, but engineered no doubt by his political opponents. In June 1780, however, he was for a third time elected to Congress and attended from February to September 1781. Some of his colleagues feared that he would again indulge in trouble-making, but his course appears to have been one of acceptable placidity. Always interested in the financial problems of Congress, in April 1781 he offered a "Scheme of Finance," to which was appended this injunction: "Let Congress adopt and pursue this plan and be great

and happy." Congress honored the scheme with a first reading but chose to seek greatness and happiness by other means.

In the Virginia House of Delegates in 1785 Smith opposed the proposition to grant Congress control over commerce, and again, in 1786, he was among the irreconcilable opponents of the Annapolis convention; nevertheless, he was chosen a delegate, but declined to attend. Characteristically, in the convention of 1788 he opposed the adoption of the Federal Constitution, aligning himself with his former political enemy, Richard Henry Lee.

He was twice married: first, about 1760, to Alice, daughter of Philip Lee of Maryland and widow of Thomas Clarke; second, Aug. 3, 1769, to Elizabeth, daughter of Col. William Daingerfield of Essex. There were two children by each marriage; a son by the first, George William Smith, succeeded James Monroe as governor of Virginia (Dec. 5, 1811), but lost his life when the Richmond theatre was burned on Dec. 26 following. Meriwether Smith died at "Marigold," Essex County.

[*William and Mary Coll. Quart. Hist. Mag.*, July 1897 (which contains authority for date of death), July 1916, July 1903; H. B. Grigsby, *The Hist. of the Va. Federal Convention of 1788* (2 vols., 1890–91); J. C. Ballagh, *The Letters of Richard Henry Lee* (2 vols., 1911); E. C. Burnett, *Letters of Members of the Continental Cong.*, I–VII (1921–34); W. C. Rives, *Hist. of the Life and Times of James Madison* (3 vols., 1859–68); E. G. Swem and J. W. Williams, *A Reg. of the Gen. Assembly of Va., 1776–1918* (1918); W. G. and M. N. Stanard, *The Colonial Va. Reg.* (1902); some letters in Lib. of Cong.; Smith's accounts for services in Congress (MSS.), Va. State Lib.]
E. C. B.

SMITH, MILTON HANNIBAL (Sept. 12, 1836–Feb. 22, 1921), railroad official, spent over half a century in the employ of the Louisville & Nashville Railroad, of which, for almost forty years, he was chief executive. The son of Irulus and Almira (Blakeslee) Smith, he was born in Windham Township, Greene County, N. Y., and at the age of fourteen accompanied his family to Cook County, Ill. After a meager common-school education he went South in 1858 to make his fortune. In 1860 he became an operator for the Southwestern Telegraph Company at Oxford, Miss.; later the same year he became telegraph operator and assistant agent for the Mississippi Central Railroad at Jackson, Tenn. In 1861 he was transferred to the superintendent's office at Holly Springs, Miss., as telegraph operator and chief clerk. He was drawn into the Civil War in connection with the Federal military railroad service, being stationed successively at Stevenson, Ala., Chattanooga, Tenn., Huntsville, Ala., Knoxville, Tenn., and Atlanta, Ga. After the war (1865) he worked for a time for the Adams

Express Company at Louisville and then (1866) as division superintendent of the Alabama & Tennessee River Railroad.

Smith's connection with the Louisville & Nashville began in August 1866, when he went to Louisville as the local agent of that road. In 1869 he became general freight agent, and in 1878 he resigned because of a disagreement with his superiors in which his orders had been over-ruled. He was not one to accept interference kindly. Immediately after his resignation he be-came assistant to vice-president John King of the Baltimore & Ohio Railroad, and in the fol-lowing year was made general freight agent. For a short time late in 1881 he was general agent of the Pennsylvania Railroad at New York City. In 1882, however, he returned to the Louisville & Nashville, to renew an association which was to continue unil his death. His first position upon his return was one created special-ly for him—that of third vice-president in charge of traffic. On July 6, 1882, he became the chief executive, a position which he retained for approximately forty years, even though the title changed from time to time. At first he was called vice-president; in 1884 he was made president; from 1886 to 1891 he was again titled vice-president so that one of the New York officers could be given the higher official rank; from 1891 to 1921 he was again president, except for the period of the World War, during which he was federal manager.

When Smith took charge of the Louisville & Nashville it was in poor condition, not having recovered from the effects of the Civil War and the panic of 1873. By an immense amount of effective work he converted his road into one of the stronger and more important railroad prop-erties of the country. Personally he was rough in appearance, a hard but fair fighter, a hard worker who took almost no recreation, and averse to publicity. He was interested primarily in the construction and operation of his railroad and apparently but little concerned with its finan-cial control (H. D. Dozier, *A History of the At-lantic Coast Line Railroad*, 1920, pp. 147–51). He was proud of the great expansion of the road, of the improvement of its properties, and of the excellent dividend record. As a nineteenth-cen-tury railroad man he was an exponent of prac-tices which came to be questioned in later years. Between 1914 and 1917 he had difficulties with the Interstate Commerce Commission over its investigation of the use of passes and the par-ticipation in politics of the Louisville & Nash-ville. Abuses had certainly existed, but Smith insisted, with earnest conviction, that the com-

mission should not have access to his records and that the railroad's activities were entirely proper. Upon his death he was justly mourned as one of the last members of the group respon-sible for the rapid expansion of the American railroad net during the last half of the nineteenth century. He died in Louisville, survived by his wife, Annette (Jones) Smith, and by two sons and two daughters.

[Obituary in *Railway Age*, Mar. 4, 1921, based on Smith's dictated statements; *Who's Who in America*, 1920–21; obituaries in *Courier-Journal* and *Evening Post* (both of Louisville, Ky.), Feb. 23, 1921; *Railroad Gazette*, Oct. 25, 1878, p. 518; *Railway Age*, Feb. 6, 1879, p. 66, Mar. 22, 1883, p. 162; *Railroad Gazette*, Mar. 13, 1891, p. 188; *Railway Age Gazette*, Feb. 20, 1914, p. 393, July 17, 1914, p. 103, Mar. 5, 1915, p. 413, Oct. 6, 1916, p. 607, Dec. 15, 1916, p. 1101, Nov. 9, 1917, p. 849; *Railway Age*, Mar. 1, 1918, p. 446; 31 *Interstate Commerce Commission Reports*, 261; 33 *I. C. C.*, 168; 245 *U. S.*, 33; 49 *I. C. C.*, 320; *Poor's Manual, passim.*]   R. E. R.

SMITH, MORGAN LEWIS (Mar. 8, 1821– Dec. 28, 1874), Union soldier, was born in the town of Mexico, Oswego County, N. Y., the son of Cyrus and Laura (Wales) Smith, and elder brother of Giles Alexander Smith [*q.v.*]. His father, a farmer, soon afterwards moved to Jef-ferson County, N. Y., with his family. Leaving home in 1842, Smith settled in Meadville, Pa., but before long went to New Albany, Ind., and there taught school for about two years. He enlisted in the United States army in July 1845 under the name of Mortimer L. Sanford, and served for the five-year period of his enlistment as sergeant and drill instructor at the recruit depot, Newport, Ky. From 1850 to 1861 he held various positions on steamboats running between Cincinnati, Ohio, St. Louis, Mo., and New Orleans, La., and at the outbreak of the Civil War he organ-ized the 8th Missouri Volunteer Infantry, com-posed mainly of rivermen and recruits from the rough element in the population of St. Louis. Appointed colonel, July 7, 1861, he soon brought his regiment to a high state of discipline, train-ing, and combat efficiency. After conducting an expedition against guerrillas in southern Mis-souri, he joined the army of Ulysses Simpson Grant [*q.v.*], and at Fort Donelson, Tenn., in command of a brigade composed of his own and another regiment, he successfully stormed a strong position held by the enemy. Gen. Lew Wallace, in reporting Smith's conduct of this attack, wrote: "Words cannot do justice to his courage and coolness" (*War of the Rebellion: Official Records (Army)*, 1 ser., vol. VII, p. 240). He commanded a brigade in the expe-dition up the Tennessee River, and in the Shiloh and Corinth campaigns. His command bore the principal part in the battle at Russell's House, May 17, 1862, where his conduct won commendation from Gen. William Tecumseh Sherman [*q.v.*]. He was appointed brigadier-general of volunteers, July 16, 1862. He took part in Sherman's expedition against Vicksburg after active service in Tennessee and northern Mississippi. While reconnoitering the enemy's position on Chickasaw Bluffs, Dec. 28, 1862, he received a gunshot wound that disabled him until Oct. 6, 1863. On that date he returned to duty as commander of the 2nd Division, XV Corps, and bore a distinguished part in the assault and capture of Missionary Ridge, and the subsequent movement for the relief of Knoxville. He further distinguished himself for skill and gallantry in the operations against Atlanta, and was temporarily in command of the XV Corps, July 23–28, 1864. The rigors of this campaign caused such irritation of his old wound as to permanently incapacitate him for field service. He was on sick leave from Aug. 17 to Sept. 27, 1864, when he was placed in command of the District of Vicksburg. There his firm administration of martial law quickly stopped the disorders that had become prevalent. He remained at Vicksburg until the close of the war, resigning his commission, July 12, 1865.

For about two years after his marriage to Louise Genella, Dec. 18, 1866, he was United States consul general in Honolulu. Resigning, he declined the governorship of the Colorado Territory and engaged in business in Washington, D. C. He acted as counsel for the collection of claims, held contracts for the delivery of United States mails on various southern and western routes, and at the time of his death was connected with a building association. He died suddenly at Jersey City, N. J., where he was a visitor. He was survived by two daughters. He was a natural leader, magnetic, resolute, and extraordinarily brave and cool in battle, and he had in an unusual degree the ability to establish discipline in volunteer troops. The official records show that such distinguished generals as Grant, Sherman, and Wallace held him in high esteem as an able and dependable officer.

[F. A. Virkus, *The Compendium of Am. Geneal.*, vol. V (1933); *War of the Rebellion: Off. Records (Army)*; unpublished records of the War Dept.; *Report of Proc. Soc. of the Army of the Tenn.* . . . *Sept. 29, 1875* (1877); *Battles and Leaders of the Civil War* (4 vols., 1888); U. S. Pension Office records; obituaries in *Evening Star* (Washington, D. C.), *Washington Chronicle*, and *Nat. Republican* (Washington), Dec. 30, and *N. Y. Times*, Dec. 31, 1874; family records.]
T. F. M.

SMITH, NATHAN (Sept. 30, 1762–Jan. 26, 1829), surgeon, physician, professor of theory and practice of physic and of surgery in Yale College, was born at Rehoboth, Mass., the son of John Smith by his second wife, Elizabeth (Ide) Hills, widow of Benjamin Hills. The Smith family had lived at Rehoboth for four generations, Henry Smith, the great-great-grandfather of Nathan, having come to the colonies from England in 1638. Shortly after Nathan's birth the family moved to Chester, Vt., where the boy helped his father farm, received meager education in the district schools, and served in the militia towards the end of the Revolutionary War. While still a youth he was called upon to help Dr. Josiah Goodhue at an operation. The experience, it is said, made such an impression upon him that he determined to be a surgeon. After a year's preparation with the Rev. Dr. Whiting of Rockingham, Vt., and three years as pupil, assistant, and apprentice to Dr. Goodhue, he began to practise in 1787 at Cornish, N. H. Soon realizing the inadequacy of his training, he spent the year 1789–90 at the institute of medicine at Harvard College, under John Warren, Benjamin Waterhouse [*qq.v.*], and Aaron Dexter. At the termination of the year 1790, having presented a dissertation on "The Circulation of the Blood," he received the degree of bachelor of medicine. Shortly after resuming his practice in Cornish, he married, Jan. 16, 1791, Elizabeth, daughter of Gen. Jonathan Chase of Cornish; two years later she died without issue, and in September 1794 he married her half-sister, Sarah Hall Chase.

Though Smith's practice grew, he was not entirely content. He gave some private instruction, one of his pupils being Lyman Spalding [*q.v.*], but wished to teach more extensively. He was only too well aware of the difficulties of obtaining an education in medicine. At that time the only three medical schools in the United States were at Harvard, Columbia, and Pennsylvania, all at a considerable distance from the center of New England. Dartmouth College was not far from Cornish, and he became imbued with the idea that he might himself teach students medicine and surgery at this institution. With a directness which characterized many of his actions, he applied to the trustees, asking their approval and support "of a plan he had devised to establish a Professorship of the Theory and Practice of Medicine in connection with Dartmouth College" (Hubbard, *post*, p. 12). His plan in general was approved by President John Wheelock, but final action by the trustees was postponed for one year. Undaunted by this delay, he proceeded to fit himself for the post which he fully intended to occupy and spent a year abroad in study, traveling at considerable financial sacrifice, during the winter of 1796–97, to Glasgow, Edinburgh, and London. In the autumn of 1797 he returned with books for the library at Dartmouth and apparatus for anatomy, surgery, and chemistry.

Promptly thereafter, at the age of thirty-five, he delivered a course of lectures on medicine at the College, although it was not until August 1798 that the trustees formally approved his plan and elected him professor. It was his duty "to deliver public lectures upon Anatomy, Surgery, Chemistry and the Theory and Practice of Physic." He was the entire medical faculty; as Oliver Wendell Holmes expressed it, he filled a "Settee of Professorships" (quoted in *Life and Letters of Nathan Smith, post,* p. 97). Among his students was George C. Shattuck [*q.v.*] of Boston, with whom he formed an intimacy that lasted through his entire life. In 1801 Dartmouth conferred upon Smith the degree of M.D., rarely given in those days, and in 1811 he received that degree from Harvard College.

These years were crowded with many activities. From his letters one gathers that he expended much thought upon the preparation of his lectures and devoted much time to teaching. He traveled from Worcester, Mass., to Brattleboro, Vt., and from Concord, Mass., to Wethersfield, Conn., couching for cataract with great success; performing operations for necrosis of bone; attending children with "spotted fever," a disease which ravaged the Connecticut Valley in 1811; and caring for patients with "Typhus Fever." He practised vaccination shortly after Waterhouse first introduced it into the United States in July 1800. He went to state medical meetings and was elected president of the Vermont State Medical Society in 1811. He was constantly writing to his friend Shattuck in Boston for new books to add to his rapidly growing library; for chemicals; for apparatus, which he wanted built according to pattern; and for "air thermometers," for the construction of which he gave directions. He engaged Dr. Alexander Ramsay [*q.v.*] to give a course in anatomy in 1808. He visited the legislature repeatedly in efforts to obtain funds for the medical school, and was so far successful as to obtain a grant of $600 for chemical apparatus in 1803, and, after much perseverance, $3,450 for a medical building, for which he himself donated the land. He became exasperated at the slowness of the legislature to act, at its lack of support, and at proposed laws which, if passed, would restrict dissections and thus materially hamper the teaching of anatomy. He wrote to Shattuck in May

1810 of his discouragement and, finally, of his determination to leave Hanover.

It was at about this time that President Timothy Dwight, 1752–1817 [*q.v.*], of Yale College became actively engaged in a project, long under contemplation, to furnish instruction in medicine to students at Yale. In 1811 the lieutenant governor of Connecticut, Professor Silliman of Yale, and Dr. Nathan Strong were appointed a committee to act with the medical convention in establishing a chartered medical school (Steiner, *post,* p. 24). The previous year Jonathan Knight, 1789–1864 [*q.v.*], a tutor at Yale, had received a letter from Timothy L. Gridley, who was then a student under Smith, in which the writer pointed out the desirability of appointing Smith to the professorship of surgery in the proposed institute of medicine at Yale. He wrote of his originality of mind, of his success in operative surgery, of his "general information," and of his "dignified deportment," adding "in fact, wherever he is known he is admired and beloved" (*Ibid.*). Gridley had learned from Smith that should Yale College require his services, he would accept a position there without hesitation. The corporation and president were convinced, however, that his religious beliefs were unorthodox, and, since they could not countenance the appointment of an "infidel," the committee selected Dr. Mason F. Cogswell of Hartford as professor of anatomy and surgery. Cogswell was loath to accept the appointment and asked that it be reconsidered. There ensued a correspondence between Cogswell and Smith, and between Silliman and Smith, with the result that the committee was assured that Smith "had fully renounced his infidelity"; whereupon he was elected professor of theory and practice of physic, surgery, and obstetrics. Although instruction in medicine at Yale College began in the autumn of 1812, Smith was unable to leave Dartmouth until the autumn of 1813 and his resignation was not actually accepted until 1814. He was reëlected professor there in 1816 and, though he declined, he gave a final course of lectures at Dartmouth that year, so that it was not until 1817 that he permanently removed with his family to New Haven.

Smith went to Yale at the age of fifty-one, vigorous, energetic, and with wide clinical experience. He was known throughout New England as an able surgeon; he had acquired a wide reputation as a teacher, and had gained the admiration and respect of his associates. He rapidly assumed a position of importance in the community. It was largely through his personal efforts that the Connecticut legislature in 1814 appropriated $20,000 to the institute for the purchase of land, the erection of a new building, and the development of a botanical garden. In addition to his teaching, he practised medicine and surgery throughout the state and in the neighboring parts of New England. He showed an ability and resourcefulness in his methods of practice which were unsurpassed in that day. In 1821 he performed successfully ovariotomy, unaware of the fact that Ephraim McDowell [q.v.] of Kentucky had previously done that particular form of operation for the first time in the United States. It is said that he had never lost a patient from post-operative hemorrhage. In 1821 he assisted President Allen of Bowdoin College in the organization of a medical department, where he delivered a course of lectures each summer until 1826. He also lectured during the summer months at the medical department of the University of Vermont in Burlington, where his son, Nathan Ryno Smith [q.v.], had been active in developing a department of medicine.

Smith's reputation does not rest entirely either on his success as a practical surgeon and physician or on his ability as a teacher. These were what gave him eminence in his day, but for succeeding generations the importance of his work is to be found in the fresh and original manner in which he attacked problems in medicine and surgery. His approach to them is indicated by the following statements in his letters: "However we may class diseases we must study them in detail"; and in reference to theorizing, "This mode of proceeding tends to substitute idleness for industry and dogmatism for patient inquiry" (*Life and Letters*, pp. 35, 36). Dr. William H. Welch said of Smith: "Famous in his day and generation, he is still more famous today, for he was far ahead of his times, and his reputation, unlike that of so many medical worthies of the past, has steadily increased, as the medical profession has slowly caught up with him. We now see that he did more for the general advancement of medical and surgical practice than any of his predecessors or contemporaries in this country. He was a man of high intellectual and moral qualities, of great originality and untiring energy, an accurate and keen observer, unfettered by traditions and theories, fearless, and above all blessed with an uncommon fund of plain common sense" (*Yale Medical Journal*, November 1901, pp. 141–42). His writings attest the fact that he had a conception of disease which is eminently modern. In a day when the etiology of infectious diseases was unknown, when speculation as to the classification of disease processes was rife, and when doubt was being cast upon the specific nature of many diseases, he let no

opportunity pass to emphasize his belief in their specific character. He dwelt with emphasis upon the necessity of accurate observation and the importance of factual experience as opposed to thin-spun theory. Elaborate hypotheses, not susceptible to practical test, aroused his sharp criticism, for he looked upon them as obscuring clear vision. His *Practical Essay on Typhous Fever* (1824) is a classic. Typhoid fever, for it is that disease which he describes, had never before been so clearly defined or so accurately depicted. His statement, "I consider Typhous fever a disease *sui generis,* arising from a specific cause, and that cause contagion, and seldom affecting the same person more than once," is entirely modern. He also had the courage to pronounce it a self-limited disease, unaffected in its course by drugs. "His "Observations on the Pathology and Treatment of Necrosis" (*Medical and Surgical Memoirs, post,* pp. 97 ff.) is of almost equal importance.

In 1816 he published an edition of *A Treatise on Febrile Diseases,* by A. P. Wilson Philip, with an introduction, notes, and additions. He commented especially in these notes on typhous and spotted fever; devoted some attention to an epidemic of "pneumonia typhoidea"; described in all probability an epidemic of German measles; and wrote on dropsy. He also gave an account of experiments which he seems to have devised to determine whether the cutaneous surfaces absorb fluid. Two of his students immersed themselves for several hours in a warm bath of water colored with madder, and afterwards examined their urine for the coloring matter. The urine was in small degree colored with madder, but Smith concluded that this slight effect might have been caused by conditions other than absorption of the dye through the skin. From 1824 to 1826, with his son Nathan Ryno and others, Smith edited the *American Medical Review.*

He had four sons and six daughters; all his sons became practitioners of medicine. There is a striking portrait of him, by Samuel F. B. Morse [q.v.], in the possession of the Yale Medical School. He appears as an elderly gentleman, dignified in his mien, with keen penetrating eyes and a sensitive mouth. When President Woolsey of Yale was a child, he saw much of Smith in his father's house and said of him, "He was the most delightful, unselfish and kind-hearted man I ever knew, and we children all loved him" (*Life and Letters,* p. 90). He died in his sixty-seventh year and was buried in New Haven.

[E. A. Smith, *The Life and Letters of Nathan Smith, M.B., M.D.* (1914), with an introduction by Dr. William H. Welch; O. P. Hubbard, *The Early Hist. of the N. H. Medic. Institution, with a Sketch of Its Founder*

Nathan Smith, A.M., M.D. (1880); W. R. Steiner, "The Evolution of Medicine in Conn., with the Foundation of the Yale Medic. School as its Notable Achievement," *Memorial of the Centennial of the Yale Medic. School* (1915); W. H. Welch, "The Relation of Yale to Medicine," *Yale Medic. Jour.*, Nov. 1901; S. C. Harvey, "The Education of Nathan Smith," *Yale Jour. of Biology and Medicine*, May 1929; H. S. Burr, "The Founding of the Medic. Institution of Yale Coll.," *Ibid.*, Jan. 1934; William Allen, *An Address Occasioned by the Death of Nathan Smith, M.D.* (1829); N. R. Smith, *Medic. and Surgic. Memoirs of Nathan Smith, M.D.* (1831); J. A. Spalding, *Dr. Lyman Spalding* (1916); H. A. Kelly and W. L. Burrage, *Am. Medic. Biogs.* (1920).]
W.T.L.

SMITH, NATHAN (Jan. 8, 1770–Dec. 6, 1835), Connecticut jurist and politician, United States senator, son of Richard and Annis (Hurd) Smith, was born in Woodbury, Conn. On account of the poverty of his parents, he received little formal schooling. A shrewd trader and a wandering Yankee peddler in his younger days, he soon followed in the footsteps of his brother Nathaniel [*q.v.*] and read law with Judge Tapping Reeve [*q.v.*] at Litchfield. Overcoming the obstacles of poverty and a fragmentary knowledge of books, he was admitted to the Litchfield County bar in 1792, and commenced the practice of law in New Haven. He soon won a reputation as an able lawyer of sound judgment, and a clever politician, but was recognized as a man of high principle who would not plead an obviously unrighteous case. In 1808 he was given the honorary degree of M.A. by Yale College. A prominent Episcopalian, a vestryman of Trinity Church in New Haven, a participant in the sturdy fight for a charter for Washington (later Trinity) College in Hartford, of which he became an incorporator, Smith was an outstanding Tolerationist who fought stoutly for the separation of Church and State in the tedious campaign leading to the defeat of the Congregational-Federalist ascendency in 1817. The following year he was one of the framers of the reformed constitution of 1818. He disagreed, however, with the policy of popularizing the state judiciary, for he was no democrat and was completely unsympathetic with the experiments of the radical group.

He was prosecuting attorney for New Haven County from 1817 to 1835, an unsuccessful candidate for the governorship against Oliver Wolcott in 1825, and United States attorney for Connecticut by appointment of President John Quincy Adams in 1828, removed in the following year by President Jackson. In May 1832 he was chosen as a Whig to the United States Senate, to succeed Samuel A. Foot [*q.v.*], but his senatorial career was cut short by a heart attack, in Washington, three years later. President Jackson and his cabinet attended the funeral

services in the Senate chamber, and in New Haven his obsequies at Trinity Church, presided over by the Rev. Harry Croswell [*q.v.*], brought together state and local officials and officers of Yale College, regardless of their political affiliations, for Smith had not been so aggressive a partisan as to arouse personal hostility. It was generally agreed that he deserved well of his community as a prudent counselor, a civic benefactor, and a Christian gentleman. He was the father of six children.

[*Proc. at New Haven, in Relation to the Demise of the Hon. Nathan Smith* (n.d.); R. J. Purcell, *Conn. in Transition* (1918); *Biog. Dir. Am. Cong.* (1928); G. H. Hollister, *The Hist. of Conn.* (1855), II, 655; P. K. Kilbourne, *A Biog. Hist. of the County of Litchfield* (1851); Wm. Cothren, *Hist. of Ancient Woodbury*, vols. I (1854), III (1879); *Daily National Intelligencer* (Washington, D. C.), Dec. 7, 1835; year of birth supported by most reliable accounts, although others give 1769.]
R.J.P.

SMITH, NATHAN RYNO (May 21, 1797–July 3, 1877), surgeon, teacher of anatomy and surgery, was born in Cornish, N. H., the second son of Dr. Nathan Smith [*q.v.*] by his second wife, Sarah Hall (Chase). The boy's middle name was selected by his mother from one of Ossian's poems, and throughout his life he was called Ryno by his family and intimate friends. He received his early education from tutors, but later was sent to school in Hanover. In 1813 he entered Yale College and in the autumn of the same year his father moved to New Haven, where he had been called to assume the duties of professor of theory and practice of physic, surgery, and obstetrics in Yale College.

Young Ryno, from contemporary accounts, was one of the leading members of his class, but appears to have been more attracted by literature than by medicine, for in 1816 he wrote a commencement play, "The Quixotic Philosopher," in which he also acted. After receiving the degree of A.B. in 1817, he went to Virginia as tutor for the family of Thomas Turner of Fauquier County. After about a year and a half, he returned to New Haven to study medicine under his father, and in 1823 he was graduated with the degree of M.D. from the medical school at Yale. A few months later he moved to Burlington, Vt., where, the following year, he married Juliette Octavia Penniman, daughter of Dr. Jabez Penniman. The intense interest which the father had always had in the education of young men for the medical profession soon became a predominant characteristic of the son; for one of the first matters to attract his attention was the possibility of establishing a medical school at the University of Vermont. With the aid of his father, this project was accomplished and, at the age of twenty-seven, Smith assumed the duties of professor of anatomy and physiology in the new institution.

Burlington was then a comparatively isolated community, however, and Smith soon realized that he needed wider experience than was afforded there. Accordingly, he spent the winters of 1825 and 1826 at the University of Pennsylvania, then the leading medical school in the United States, acquainting himself with methods of instruction and obtaining more knowledge of anatomy and surgery. Here he met the "bold, brilliant and energetic surgeon," Dr. George McClellan [q.v.], who gave private courses in anatomy and surgery. McClellan, who was not associated with the University of Pennsylvania, contemplated, in the face of much opposition, the formation of another medical school in Philadelphia. Impressed by the ability of young Smith, he invited him to take the chair of anatomy in the proposed institution and Smith became a member of the first faculty of Jefferson Medical College, teaching anatomy there for two sessions. Among his pupils were Dr. Samuel D. Gross [q.v.], who later became a well-known surgeon, and Washington L. Atlee [q.v.], the distinguished ovariotomist. During his short stay in Philadelphia, Smith devoted some time to writing; with his father and others he edited the *American Medical Review* and in 1825 he published *A Physiological Essay on Digestion.* He also founded, in 1827, and edited the *Philadelphia Monthly Journal of Medicine and Surgery,* which the following year was merged with the *American Journal of the Medical Sciences.*

His activities in Burlington and Philadelphia gave him more than a local reputation, and when the chair of anatomy became vacant at the University of Maryland, through the resignation of Prof. Granville Sharp Pattison [q.v.], Smith was asked, in 1827, to occupy it. Accepting the position, he soon became a leading member of the faculty and also engaged in the practice of medicine and surgery. In 1829, after the death of Dr. John B. Davidge [q.v.], founder of the school, Smith was transferred to the chair of surgery, which he held, except for one comparatively short interruption, for almost half a century. That same year he published *An Essay on the Diseases of the Middle Ear,* from the French of J. A. Saissy, with a supplement of his own on diseases of the external ear. He founded the *Baltimore Monthly Journal of Medicine and Surgery,* the first number of which appeared in February 1830 with Smith as editor; it survived for only a year, however. About the same time he collected and edited, with a biographical note,

addenda, and some of his own papers, the *Medical and Surgical Memoirs of Nathan Smith M.D.* (1831). In 1832 he published *Surgical Anatomy of the Arteries,* a second edition of which appeared in 1835.

Owing to his skill, ingenuity, and constant practice in the field of surgery, he gained national prominence in that branch of his profession. He made original contributions to the art of surgery that were of considerable practical importance, among them a new instrument for the operation of lithotomy. He wrote several papers on the management of fractures, the most important of which dealt with a new principle in the treatment of fractures of the thigh and leg. To put this principle into operation he constructed a form of splint, known as the anterior suspensory apparatus, or anterior splint, which was far superior to any device used for this purpose at that time and in modified form is in general use today. Begun at this period but not published until 1867 was his *Treatment of Fractures of the Lower Extremity by the Use of the Anterior Suspensory Apparatus.* He was also a pioneer in the extirpation of the thyroid gland.

In 1837 Smith was invited to give lectures on medicine and surgery at the Transylvania University, Lexington, Ky., and from 1838 to 1840 he acted as professor of surgery at this institution. Though he never relinquished his permanent residence in Baltimore, he severed his connection temporarily with the University of Maryland, since his new duties required him to spend about four months of every year in Lexington. While on one of his visits to Kentucky, he met Henry Clay and a friendship sprang up between them. He was frequently called to pay professional visits to Washington, and there formed an acquaintance with Daniel Webster, who became an occasional visitor at the Smith house in Baltimore. This house, in which he had his office and surgery, was, in fact, a center to which many visitors were constantly welcomed, and to which his students were in the habit of coming. He had eight children, one of whom, Alan Penniman Smith (1840–1898), became a prominent surgeon of Baltimore a.id was instrumental in obtaining from Johns Hopkins the gift to found the Johns Hopkins Hospital. Tall and impressive in appearance, Smith was called by his students "The Emperor," and the sobriquet soon gained such popularity that, in later life, he was known generally by this name. His imperial appearance was tempered, however, by a courtesy and charm of manner which endeared him to friends and patients. His duties as teacher and practitioner left him little time for other forms of occupation, but he took much pleasure in his country place "Wilton," not far from Baltimore, where he amused himself by conducting farming operations along original lines that proved expensive and entirely unsuccessful. When the press of work permitted, he read with pleasure Homer, Virgil, and Plutarch. In 1869 he published *Legends of the South,* containing tales connected with White Sulphur Springs, Mammoth Cave, and other places. After 1869 his connection with the University of Maryland was nominal, and in 1870 he became professor emeritus. Ill health forced him to reduce his practice but he did not relinquish it until shortly before his death. In 1867, at the age of seventy, he made his first journey to Europe, where he was received as a distinguished visitor by the surgeons of England and the Continent. On his return he began to write a treatise on surgery, which, however, was never completed.

[E. A. Smith, *The Life and Letters of Nathan Smith* (1914); S. C. Chew, *An Address Commemorative of Nathan Ryno Smith, M.D., LL.D.* (1878); E. F. Cordell, *Hist. Sketch of the Univ. of Md. School of Medicine* (1891), and *The Medical Annals of Md.* (1903); S. D. Gross, *Autobiog.* (1887), I, 385–87; H. A. Kelly and W. L. Burrage, *Am. Medic. Biogs.* (1920); Alexius McGlannan, "The Surgical and Anatomical Works of Nathan Ryno Smith," *Univ. of Md., Bull. of the School of Medicine,* Apr. 1925; *Sun* (Baltimore), July 4, 1877; letters of Nathan Ryno Smith in the possession of the author.]   W. T. L.

SMITH, NATHANIEL (Jan. 6, 1762–Mar. 9, 1822), Connecticut jurist, was born in Woodbury, Conn., the son of poor parents, Richard and Annis (Hurd) Smith. He received little formal schooling and began working in his early years, traveling as a Yankee peddler throughout New England. On one occasion while waiting for his brother, Nathan [*q.v.*], who was to join him in Rutland, Vt., he visited a court room and was so struck by the ineptitude of lawyer and judge that he was moved to test his own talents in a study of the law. Indomitable of will, he succeeded in gaining admission as clerk and student to the law office of Judge Tapping Reeve [*q.v.*]. After some time in hard study, he was admitted to the bar (1787) and began practice in Woodbury, rapidly demonstrating ability as a clever advocate and a magnetic stump-speaker.

Smith represented Woodbury in the General Assembly, 1790–95, taking an aggressive leadership in the gradual abolition of slavery and in the foundation of a common-school system financed in part by the sale of the state's western land claims. In recognition of his service, Yale College bestowed upon him an honorary master's degree in 1795. A stout Federalist, he was elected a representative in Congress for two terms (1795–99), but at the expiration of the second he declined to stand again as a candidate, since he had lost popularity by his support of the Jay Treaty. Returning to his practice in Woodbury, he represented that town in the state council from 1800 through 1804. In 1806 he was appointed associate judge of the superior court, in which capacity he served with considerable distinction until he was retired in 1819 after the overthrow of the Old Order in the Republican-Tolerationist sweep of the state. As an appointed member of the Hartford Convention (1814), he won the undying hostility of the Republican nationalists despite the fact that he was of the persecuted Episcopalian minority and assuredly of no disloyal turn of mind. The last three years of his life were marred by a painful illness bravely borne. He was survived by his wife, Ruth, daughter of the Rev. Noah Benedict, and by one son.

[Wm. Cothren, *Hist. of Ancient Woodbury,* vols. I (1854), III (1879); P. K. Kilbourne, *A Biog. Hist. of the County of Litchfield* (1851); D. C. Kilbourn, *The Bench and Bar of Litchfield County* (1909); R. J. Purcell, *Conn. in Transition* (1918); *Biog. Dir. Am. Cong.* (1928); *Conn. Courant* (Hartford), Mar. 19, 1822; *American Mercury* (Hartford), Mar. 18, 1822.]
                           R. J. P.

SMITH, OLIVER (Jan. 20, 1766–Dec. 22, 1845), philanthropist, was born at Hatfield, Mass., the son of Samuel and Mary (Morton) Smith. On his father's side, he was a descendant of Samuel Smith who emigrated from England on the ship *Elizabeth* in 1634, settled in Wethersfield, Conn., and later moved to Hatfield. Mary Morton's ancestry went back to George Morton [*q.v.*], one of the organizers of the voyage of the *Anne* and the *Little James* to Plymouth. The year after Oliver, the youngest of six sons, was born, his father died of an "apoplectic fit," occasioned by overwork in the hay field on a hot July day. The boys were brought up by their mother, a woman noted in the community for her frugality, vigor, and piety. One of them was Joseph, father of Sophia Smith [*q.v.*], founder of Smith College.

Oliver began life with a capital of $500; when he was middle aged, the boys of Hatfield expressed their ambition for wealth by saying they wished they could be as rich as Oliver Smith; at his death he left what for the place and time was a large fortune—almost $400,000. He engaged in farming, fattened cattle for market, and in his later years made profitable investments in Wall Street securities. He wasted nothing, spent little, and rarely gave anything away. A contemporary wrote regarding him: "During the thirty years or more of my recollection of him, he wore the same overgarments; but by reason of a certain trimness and neatness, he always appeared respectably dressed" (S. D. Partridge, in Wells, *post*, p. 263). When stoves were put in the meeting house, he was leader of a protesting group who withdrew from the ecclesiastical society. He was strictly honest in his dealings with others, but managed to avoid paying taxes on all his property, probably feeling that the money would be wasted. He was opposed to liberal education, believing it a hindrance rather than a help to success in life, and carried about in his pocket statistics to support his conviction. In politics he was originally a Jeffersonian Democrat, but later became a National Republican. He was a member of the Massachusetts constitutional convention in 1820, a presidential elector in 1824, voting for John Quincy Adams, and twice represented his town in the state legislature (1827–28). For many years he was a director of the bank in Northampton. He never married.

Penurious in the extreme throughout his life, he nevertheless provided that the greater part of his wealth should be devoted to charitable and educational purposes after his death. By his will —a remarkable document—he established an accumulating fund, which, when it had reached a certain amount, was to be used for three objects. Brought up by a widowed mother and mindful of the straitened circumstances of his early days, he directed that the major portion of the fund should be utilized to provide grants for indigent young people and widows. Boys selected by the trustees were to be bound out in good families, taught husbandry or a trade, and when twenty-one, if worthy, receive a grant of $500; similarly, girls were to be bound out, instructed in domestic duties, and given $300 as a marriage portion. Smaller amounts were to be given under certain conditions to young women about to be married, for household equipment, and to needy widows with dependent child or children. Smith's interest in agriculture led him to stipulate that another portion of the fund be used to establish an agricultural school in Northampton. The remainder, $10,000, was to go to the American Colonization Society. The will was contested by the heirs-at-law and a notable legal battle in the supreme judicial court of Massachusetts followed, opening July 6, 1847, with Rufus Choate counsel for the contestants, and Daniel Webster for the executor; but the will was sustained (54 *Mass.*, 34). The amount expended by the trustees in carrying out the terms of the will reaches into the millions, and on Mar. 15, 1907, the Smith's Agricultural School and Northampton School of Technology was established.

[D. W. and R. F. Wells, *A Hist. of Hatfield, Mass.* (copr. 1910), appendix containing portion of Smith's will; C. A. Wight, *The Hatfield Book* (copr. 1908); E. D. Hanscom and H. F. Green, *Sophia Smith and the Beginnings of Smith Coll.* (1926); Mass. Board of Educ., *Seventy-Third Ann. Report* (1910).] H. E. S.

SMITH, OLIVER HAMPTON (Oct. 23, 1794–Mar. 19, 1859), lawyer, representative and senator, was of Quaker descent. His ancestors accompanied William Penn to America; his grandparents occupied Smith's Island in the Delaware River about twelve miles above Trenton; and here, in Bucks County, Pa., Oliver, the son of Thomas and Letitia Smith, was born. He had six brothers and two sisters. He obtained an elementary education at a neighboring country school. When he was in his nineteenth year his father died, and Oliver soon lost the small fortune which he had inherited. In 1816 he set out for the West, and at Pittsburgh engaged to take two coal boats to Louisville. He struck a snag and lost one of them, but succeeded, in the spring of 1817, in reaching Rising Sun, Ind., where he engaged in a small business with seventy-five dollars as his capital. A year later he was in Lawrenceburg, studying law, and in March 1820 he was admitted to the bar.

He commenced practice at Versailles, but soon removed to Connersville, where he rapidly rose to prominence. In August 1822 he was elected to the Indiana House of Representatives. He was made chairman of the judiciary committee and served until 1824, when the governor appointed him prosecuting attorney for the third judicial district. During two years of service in this capacity he successfully prosecuted four notorious frontiersmen charged with the murder of Indians. In 1826 he was elected to Congress as a Jackson Democrat. He rode to Washington on horseback and took his seat at the opening of the Twentieth Congress, Dec. 3, 1827. He was a member of the committee on Indian affairs, and on Feb. 19, 1828, made a vigorous plea for an Indian policy "marked with justice, humanity, and a magnanimity of purpose, that will atone, as far as possible, for the great injustice which we have done them." In another address, Jan. 28, 1829, he presented cogent arguments in favor of appropriations for the construction of the Cumberland road. Defeated for reëlection to Congress, he was engaged in the practice of law and in farming when, in December 1836, the General Assembly elected him as a Whig to a seat in the United States Senate. He was a member of the committee on the militia in 1837, and of the committee on the judiciary in 1839, and was made chairman of the important committee on public lands in 1841. His principal speeches in the Senate were on measures relative to the public lands, banking, bankruptcy, the Cumberland road, and the abolition of slavery in the Territories. He rose to leadership in evolving a federal land policy in the interest of the actual settlers (*Congressional Globe, 27 Cong., 1 Sess.,* App., p. 456), and supported the Whig plan for the federal assumption of state debts to the extent of the proceeds of the sales of the public lands within the states.

Failing of reëlection to the Senate, Smith retired to private life in Indianapolis, projected the Indianapolis & Bellefontaine Railroad, became its first president, and subsequently participated in a project for a line from Indianapolis to Evansville. In July 1857 he commenced writing for the *Indianapolis Daily Journal* a series of sketches and reminiscences of frontier life in Indiana which in the following year was published in book form under the title, *Early Indiana Trials and Sketches* (1858). Although crude in style, the volume is a vivid presentation of various phases of early Indiana history.

Smith was a rough-hewn frontiersman, five feet ten inches in height, with standing black hair, shaggy eyebrows and a strong voice; he was diffuse but convincing in speech, and one of the most respected of Indiana pioneers. He married Mary Bramfield, a Quaker, in 1821, and they had three children. He died in Indianapolis and was buried in Crown Hill Cemetery.

[W. W. Woollen, *Biog. and Hist. Sketches of Early Indiana* (1883); *Biog. Dir. Am. Cong.* (1928); *A Biog. Hist. of Eminent and Self-Made Men of the State of Indiana* (1880), vol. II; *Indianapolis Daily Journal,* Mar. 21, 1859; *Lafayette Daily Journal,* Mar. 22, 1859.]
N. D. M.

SMITH, PERSIFOR FRAZER (Nov. 16, 1798–May 17, 1858), soldier, was born in Philadelphia, Pa., the son of Jonathan and Mary Anne (Frazer) Smith. He was a descendant of Joseph Smith who emigrated from Ireland to Chester County, Pa., probably in 1720, and of Persifor Frazer, 1736–1792 [q.v.]. Graduating from the College of New Jersey (later Princeton University) with the degree of A.B. in 1815, he studied law and toward the end of 1819 removed to New Orleans, La. There his ability and attractive personal qualities quickly won him success and popularity, and he held several civil and judicial offices. At the same time he commanded successively a company and a battalion of militia, and became adjutant-general of Louisiana. On Jan. 19, 1822, he was married to Frances Jeanette Bureau, daughter of François Bureau of New Orleans, by whom he had a son who became a physician in New Orleans. In 1836 he raised a regiment of Louisianians for the

Seminole War and served with distinction in the campaigns of 1836 and 1838. After his return he became judge of the city of Lafayette, and later of the parish of Jefferson.

At the outbreak of the Mexican War he was commissioned colonel, United States Army, May 27, 1846. After commanding a brigade in the army of Zachary Taylor [q.v.] in the battles around Monterey, in which he directed the successful attacks against the forts on the south flank of the city and for his gallant conduct was brevetted brigadier-general, Sept. 23, 1846, he was transferred to Winfield Scott's army in command of the new regiment of mounted rifles. During the siege of Vera Cruz he defeated near Vergara a Mexican force that advanced to harass the besiegers; on the advance to Mexico city he commanded the first brigade of the division under David Emanuel Twigg [q.v.], and at Contreras, assuming command of three American brigades trapped between the superior forces of Santa Anna and Valencia, he conceived and executed a surprise attack in the early morning of Aug. 20, 1847, which resulted in the destruction of Valencia's army. He further distinguished himself at Churubusco, Chapultepec, and the capture of the Belen gate of the Mexican capital, and was brevetted major-general for gallant and meritorious conduct. A member of the armistice commission that arranged for suspension of hostilities, he later served as military governor of Mexico city, and as commanding officer at Vera Cruz he prepared the embarkation of the American forces leaving Mexico, discharging all these difficult offices with characteristic efficiency. After the war he was assigned according to his brevet rank to command first the Pacific Division; then, 1850–56, the Department of Texas; and in 1856 the Western Department, with headquarters at St. Louis. The absence of civil authority in California, Indian uprisings in New Mexico, and border warfare in Kansas made each of these posts in turn difficult. He was commissioned brigadier-general, Dec. 30, 1856. In April 1858 he was assigned to command the Department of Utah, where the Mormons were opposing Federal authority, but he died in the early hours of the morning, May 17, at Fort Leavenworth, Kan., where he had gone to organize his forces. He was buried in Laurel Hill Cemetery, Philadelphia. After the death of his first wife in 1852, he married, Apr. 18, 1854, Anne Monica (Millard) Armstrong, widow of Maj. Francis W. Armstrong of the United States Army, whose son Frank C. Armstrong [q.v.] was a Confederate officer.

Although he was prepossessing and soldierly

in appearance, his remarkably magnetic personality was based on mental and moral qualities; few men have been able so to command the implicit trust of all ranks and classes of men. His arrival on the field of Contreras was welcomed by the soldiers with cries of "Here he is!" and "Now we'll have them!" (Smith, *post*, II, 108). Nicholas Philip Trist [*q.v.*] writes of him as "one of the most beautifully balanced characters that I have ever known" (*North American and United States Gazette*, May 25, 1858). Gen. Winfield Scott [*q.v.*] as early as Aug. 3, 1847, refers to him in a letter as "the gallant and judicious General Smith," and wherever he has occasion to refer to him does so in terms of affectionate admiration. Simple, scholarly, conciliatory, but vigilant and sure, he united daring with imperturbable composure and control of all his resources in the most critical circumstances.

[J. S. Harris, *Record of the Smith Family* (1906); F. B. Heitman, *Hist. Reg. . . . U. S. Army* (2 vols., 1903), *Gen Cat. Princeton Univ.* (1908); J. T. Sprague, *The Origin, Progress, and Conclusion of the Florida War* (1848); D. H. Maury, *Recollections of a Virginian in the Mexican, Indian, and Civil Wars* (1894), pp. 84–85; J. H. Smith, *The War with Mexico* (2 vols., 1919); G. L. Rives, *The U. S. and Mexico, 1821–1848* (1913), vol. II; *House Exec. Doc. 17*, 31 Cong., 2 Sess., pp. 703 *et seq.*, for reports of Smith on Cal.; *Gen. Scott and His Staff* (1848), pp. 117–24; War Dept. records, 1836–58; *Living Age*, June 5, 1858; *Pennsylvanian* (Phila.), May 29, 1858; *Daily Picayune* (New Orleans), May 20, 1858; some letters in Lib. of Cong.]   T. F. M.

SMITH, PETER (Nov. 15, 1768–Apr. 14, 1837), land-owner, was born near Tappan, N. Y., son of Gerrit P. and Wyntje (Lent) Smith, descendants of Dutch emigrants to America in the seventeenth century. At an early age Peter became a clerk in the New York house of Abraham Herring. From 1785 to 1788 he conducted a general store in New York selling books, library, school, and theatrical supplies. He met John Jacob Astor [*q.v.*] and formed a partnership in the fur trade that lasted only about a year. However, they cooperated in the purchase and sale of land in upstate New York for a number of years thereafter. In 1789 Smith moved to what is now Utica and established the first general store on the site of the old Baggs Hotel. There he lived for several years selling supplies and groceries to traders and Indians, receiving in return grain, pelts, and furs. At the same time he speculated in land. In 1794 he obtained a lease from the Oneida Indians for a large tract extending roughly over Oneida and Onondaga counties, and, after the state acquired title by the treaty of 1795, he was able to obtain ownership from the state. In the center of this holding he built the "Homestead," calling the village that

developed Peterboro and the township Smithfield. Further purchases increased his holdings to nearly a million acres, scattered through most of the counties of the state. He was also interested in agricultural activities, engaged in the manufacture and sale of grindstones, and for a time managed a glass factory at Peterboro. His relations with the Indians were cordial. He named his eldest son Peter Skenandoah in honor of Skenandoa [*q.v.*]. He was the second sheriff of Herkimer County and the first "first judge" of Madison County as well as holding other minor offices. He was a member and officer of the New York Tract Society.

He married twice. On Feb. 5, 1792, he married Elizabeth Livingston, the daughter of James Livingston [*q.v.*], who died in 1818. They had six children of whom the most important was Gerrit Smith [*q.v.*]. His second wife was Sarah Pogson of Charleston, S. C., though of English birth. This marriage ended in bitterness and separation. The wife returned to South Carolina, and the husband gave himself up to the religious and personal peculiarities of his earlier years. In 1819 he had made arrangements to hand over his business to his son Gerrit but retained the income from $125,000. His earlier letters and journals reflected his gloomy religious ideas, and his business dealings revealed both decided financial abilities and equally decided penurious tendencies. Growing more morose, he brooded morbidly over what he considered the neglected religious opportunities of his active years. He lived most of the time at his Schenectady home, "a trouble to himself and a vexation to those about him" (Frothingham, *post*, pp. 20–21). He died there.

[Family papers in Lib. of Syracuse Univ.; K. W. Porter, *John Jacob Astor* (2 vols., 1931); O. B. Frothingham, *Gerrit Smith* (1878); L. M. Whitney, E. C. and L. M. Hammond, *Hist. of Madison County* (1872); J. E. Smith, *Our County . . . Madison County* (1899); date of death from *Albany Argus*, Apr. 14, 1837, although Frothingham, *ante*, gives Apr. 13.]   W. F. G.

SMITH, RICHARD (Mar. 22, 1735–Sept. 17, 1803), lawyer, diarist, member of the Continental Congress, belonged to a Quaker family which was transplanted to America from its original home, Bramham in Yorkshire, by the migration of several brothers during the last decade of the seventeenth century. His grandfather, Samuel Smith, settled in West Jersey in 1694. Richard was born in Burlington, N. J., youngest of the five children of Richard and Abigail Rapier (or Raper) Smith. The elder Richard was a merchant and for many years sat in the colonial Assembly; his son Samuel, secretary and treasurer of the colonial council, published *The His-*

tory of the Colony of Nova-Caesaria, or New Jersey (1765), which is still a valuable source. Young Richard was educated by tutors and at a Friends' school, and later studied law with Joseph Galloway [*q.v.*] of Philadelphia. About 1760, he was admitted to the bar and became recorder of Burlington or clerk of the county; on June 5, 1762, he married Elizabeth Rodman, who bore him five sons. He apparently served as clerk of the colonial Assembly for several years. Following the Treaty of Fort Stanwix (1768), he was one of a group of proprietors who received a grant of land, the "Otego Patent" of 69,000 acres, in the present Otsego County, on the upper Susquehanna in New York. With several companions, Smith visited the tract in 1769, keeping a journal of the trip, with interesting observations on the valleys of the Hudson, Mohawk, Susquehanna, and Delaware. Smith helped to promote settlement in the grant, which he visited again in 1773, 1777, and 1783 before making his home there in 1790. In 1773 he built "Smith Hall" in what is now the town of Laurens.

On July 23, 1774, Smith was elected one of New Jersey's five delegates to the Continental Congress. He was twice reëlected and served until June 1776. He was a member of the committee on claims, but the chief interest attaching to his service in the Congress arises from his detailed diary of the proceedings from Sept. 12 to Oct. 1, 1775, and from Dec. 12, 1775, to Mar. 30, 1776. This diary supplies much information not available in the *Journals* or elsewhere, being more detailed than Samuel Ward's and covering periods when John Adams was absent. Smith signed the "olive branch" petition to the King (July 8, 1775) but evidently was not yet ready to consider independence. Burlington had Loyalist leanings, and on June 12, 1776, with ill health as a reason or an excuse, Smith resigned. Ten days later New Jersey sent to the Congress an entirely new delegation, more definitely in favor of independence. On Oct. 17, 1776, Smith was elected to the state treasurership, recently vacated through his brother's death, but after five months resigned that office and retired to "Bramham Hall" near Burlington.

In 1790, he moved from Burlington to the "Otego Patent," whither his son, Richard R. Smith, had already followed William Cooper of Burlington, founder of Cooperstown and father of James Fenimore Cooper [*q.v.*]. The younger Smith became the first sheriff of the new Otsego County. The father settled at "Smith Hall," remaining until 1799, when he removed to Philadelphia. Four years later, while traveling in the

Mississippi Valley, he died of fever at Natchez. His son described him as "a man of incorruptible integrity, of gentle and amiable manners, of almost unexampled temperance," with "a strong mind, enriched with a variety of knowledge, collected from judicious observations upon men and manners, and from intimate acquaintance with almost every author of note in the ancient or modern languages" (Halsey, *post*, p. xx).

[Smith's journal of his trip in 1769 was edited, with a biographical foreword, by F. W. Halsey, as *A Tour of Four Great Rivers* (1906). The Continental Congress journal (now in Lib. of Cong.) is reproduced, also with a biographical sketch, in *Am. Hist. Rev.*, Jan., Apr. 1896; and, in the form of extracts, in E. C. Burnett, *Letters of Members of the Continental Cong.*, vol. I (1921). See also R. M. Smith, *The Burlington Smiths* (1877), p. 115, table 26; V. L. Collins, *President Witherspoon* (1925), I, 212–13; R. E. Spiller, *Fenimore Cooper* (1931), 12, 18; H. W. Boynton, *James Fenimore Cooper* (1931), pp. 8–10; *Archives of the State of N. J.*, 1 ser. XIX (1897), XXIX (1919), XXXII (1924); *Biog. Dir. Am. Cong.* (1928); C. H. Jones, *Geneal. of the Rodman Family* (1886); *Poulson's Am. Daily Advertiser* (Phila.), Oct. 18, 1803.]

R. G. A.

SMITH, RICHARD PENN (Mar. 13, 1799–Aug. 12, 1854), lawyer, author, playwright, was born in Philadelphia, the son of William Moore Smith and his wife, Ann Rudulph. His grandfather, the Rev. William Smith, 1727–1803 [*q.v.*], had been the first provost of the College of Philadelphia; his father was a lawyer and a man of slight poetic gifts, interested in letters and the arts. Penn Smith, as the son was usually called, was reared in a home of refinement and culture. He received his early education under a private tutor, John Sanderson [*q.v.*], and at Joseph Neef's grammar school. When in his teens, he was placed under the care of John Johnson, a Presbyterian clergyman, who had established a school at Huntingdon, Pa., but in 1818 he returned to Philadelphia to study law in the office of William Rawle, and in 1821 was admitted to the Philadelphia bar. His inherited taste for letters now began to take possession of him, and in the columns of *The Union* he published a series of moral and literary essays under the title of "The Plagiary." He also contributed a biography of Francis Hopkinson to John Sanderson's *Biography of the Signers to the Declaration of Independence* (vol. II, 1822). Late in 1822, he purchased the Philadelphia *Aurora*, with which in 1824 he merged the *Franklin Gazette*, but in 1827, finding the duties of an editor too onerous, he sold the paper and resumed the practice of law.

He had already begun a period of unusual literary activity. In the decade 1825–35 he wrote twenty plays, of which fifteen were performed. He was a practical playwright who depended mainly upon foreign writers for his inspiration. Five of his acted plays were inspired by French originals: *The Eighth of January* (1829), a melodrama of the battle of New Orleans, is a clever adaptation of *Le Maréchal de Luxembourg* (1812), by Frédéric and Boirie; *The Disowned* (1829) is a slightly changed version of *Le Caissier* (1826), a drama by La Salle and Maurice; *The Sentinels* (1829, not published) is a faithful translation of a poor melodrama, *Les deux Sergents* (1823) by D'Aubigny; *Is She a Brigand?* (1833) is an adaptation of a French comedy, *Clara Wendel* (1827) by Theaulon, Dartois, and Francis; *The Actress of Padua* (1836) is an adaptation of Victor Hugo's romantic drama, *Angelo, Tyran de Padoue*; it was published by Smith as a narrative, with other tales, in 1836. Four of his five unacted plays also had French sources: *The Last Man, The Bombardment of Algiers, Shakespeare in Love,* and *The Daughter.* His first acted play, *Quite Correct* (1828, published 1835), is a comedy based upon an English story by Theodore Hook, who in turn borrowed the idea from a French comedy, *L'Hôtel garni,* by Désaugiers and Gentil. Besides *The Eighth of January,* his plays dealing with American history were *William Penn,* played in 1829 but not printed, and *The Triumph at Plattsburgh* (1830). Probably his two best plays are *The Deformed* (1830) based on the second part of *The Honest Whore* by Thomas Dekker, and *Caius Marius,* which was produced by Edwin Forrest in 1831. Contemporary criticism was high in praise of this last play, which unfortunately has not survived. Smith did not confine himself wholly to the writing of plays; he published a novel, *The Forsaken* (1831), his most pretentious literary production, and wrote a large number of tales and sketches and considerable verse. To him has also been ascribed *Col. Crockett's Exploits and Adventures in Texas* (1836), which purported to have been written by the gallant Tennessean prior to the massacre at the Alamo. In a single year over 10,000 copies were sold in the United States and in 1837 the book was reprinted in England and favorably received there. To Smith's early training in journalism was doubtless due his facility in composition, a facility which often resulted in serious blemishes in his work. His writings are marred by confusion of plot, unconvincing characterization, and a lack of ease.

Smith married, first, on May 5, 1823, his cousin, Elinor Matilda Blodget, daughter of Samuel [*q.v.*] and Rebecca (Smith) Blodget and widow of Abel Lincoln. Of the five children born to this union only one, Horace Wemyss

Smith, lived to maturity. Smith's first wife died in 1834, and two years later, in 1836, he married Isabella Stratton Knisell who also bore him five children. After this marriage, he retired to his family seat at the Falls of the Schuylkill, near Philadelphia, where he lived until his death.

[Smith's papers are in the library of the Hist. Soc. of Pa. The principal printed sources are Morton Mc-Michael, Introduction, in *The Miscellaneous Works of the Late Richard Penn Smith* (1856), ed. by H. W. Smith; H. W. Smith, *Life and Correspondence of the Rev. William Smith, D.D.* (2 vols., 1879–80); B. W. McCullough, *The Life and Writings of Richard Penn Smith, with a Reprint of His Play, "The Deformed," 1830* (1917), Univ. of Pa. thesis. See also *Burton's Gentleman's Mag.* (Phila.), Sept. 1839; *Daily Pennsylvanian* (Phila.), Aug. 14, 1854; and A. H. Quinn, *A Hist. of the Am. Drama from the Beginning to the Civil War* (1923), containing critical estimate and complete bibliography of Smith's plays.]   H. W. S.

SMITH, RICHARD SOMERS (Oct. 30, 1813–Jan. 23, 1877), soldier and educator, was born in Philadelphia, Pa. In early life he was commonly called, and called himself, Richard S. Smith, Jr., although the name of his father, a prominent merchant and city councilor, was Francis Gurney Smith. His mother was Eliza (Mackie) Smith. On his father's side he was descended from early settlers of Long Island. Entering the United States Military Academy at West Point in 1829, he graduated in 1834 and was commissioned in the infantry, but was employed on topographical duty until 1836, when he resigned from the army to take up engineering in civil life. He was employed by the Philadelphia and Columbia Railroad, 1836–37; by a projected Charleston-Louisville-Cincinnati railroad, 1837–38; and by the Chesapeake and Ohio Canal, 1839–40. Reappointed in the army as a second lieutenant of infantry, Dec. 31, 1840, he was promoted first lieutenant in 1846 and transferred to the artillery in 1848, but served only at West Point, where he was an instructor and assistant professor of drawing from 1840 to 1855, serving also as quartermaster, 1846–51, and treasurer, 1852–55. He resigned in 1856 to become professor of mathematics, engineering, and drawing in the Brooklyn Collegiate and Polytechnic Institute (later the Polytechnic Institute of Brooklyn) where he remained until 1859. During these years he published his *Manual of Topographical Drawing* (1853) and *Manual of Linear Perspective* (1857). He was teacher of freehand drawing and then director of Cooper Union, New York City, until 1861, when, after a few weeks' service as quartermaster with New York volunteers, he was for the third time appointed to the regular army, being commissioned as major in the 12th Infantry, a newly organized regiment. After being on detached service as a mustering and disbursing officer in Maryland and in Wisconsin until December 1862, he joined his regiment with the Army of the Potomac and remained with it until after the battle of Chancellorsville.

On May 30, 1863, he resigned from the army once more to accept the presidency of Girard College, Philadelphia, for which a man who was both an experienced educator and a strict disciplinarian had been sought. In some respects his administration was a success, but it was marred by lack of harmony and finally by violent contention. Eventually he was removed by the board of directors, Nov. 1, 1867. The city councils took a hand in the dispute, directed an investigation, and on Feb. 20, 1868, received a report, published at great length in the *Journals of Councils* of that year, which "probably gave aid and comfort to both sides in the controversy; it also probably satisfied neither side" (Herrick, *post*, p. 58). From 1868 to 1870 Smith was professor of engineering in the Polytechnic College of Pennsylvania in Philadelphia. In the latter year he was called to the United States Naval Academy and spent the rest of his life in Annapolis, Md., at first as professor of mathematics and after 1873 as professor of drawing. He married Ellen Clark, who died about fourteen months before him. They had six children.

[J. W. Jordan, ed., *Colonial and Revolutionary Families of Pa.* (1911), vol. II; G. W. Cullum, *Biog. Reg. Officers and Grads. U. S. Mil. Acad.* (2nd ed., 1891), vol. I; *Eighth Ann. Reunion Asso. Grads. U. S. Mil. Acad. . . . 1877* (1877); *Sixteenth Ann. Report Bd. of Directors, Girard Coll.* (1864); C. A. Herrick, *Hist. of Girard Coll.* (1927); obituaries in *Army and Navy Jour.*, Jan. 27, 1877, and the *Sun* (Baltimore, Md.), Jan. 24, 1877; unpublished records in the War Dept.]

T. M. S.

SMITH, ROBERT (*c.* 1722–Feb. 11, 1777), colonial architect and builder, is said to have been born in Glasgow, Scotland, and to have come to Philadelphia at an early age, but he emerges from obscurity only about the middle of the eighteenth century as a builder in Philadelphia and a member of the Carpenters' Company of that city. His first recorded commission was the construction of Nassau Hall, built to house the College of New Jersey at Princeton (later Princeton University). The trustees' minutes refer to the design of the building (begun in 1754) as the work of Smith and "Doct. Shippen" (possibly Dr. William Shippen, Sr., 1712–1801, who had family connections with the college), but *An Account of the College of New Jersey* (1764) gives the credit to Smith alone. Nassau Hall, one of the largest buildings in the colonies, served as a pattern for University Hall at Brown University and Dartmouth Hall at Dartmouth

College, and seems to have been the progenitor of a whole school of American college architecture. Only the walls of the building now standing at Princeton are Smith's work. The house he built for the president of the college still stands nearby. His next major task, the erection of St. Peter's Church, Philadelphia, was undertaken in 1758. In drawing the plans he probably had the collaboration of Dr. John Kearsley [*q.v.*], who was a member of the building committee. The church still exists, in almost its original condition save for the addition of a spire; it is notable for its fenestration and the beauty of its interior appointments, and may probably be considered its builder's masterpiece. From this time forward Smith's services seem to have been in constant demand. He submitted plans for a building for the Carpenters' Company in 1768, and when Carpenters' Hall was built two years later his name headed the list of the building committee. He appears to have designed the Zion Lutheran Church (1766) and the Walnut Street Prison (1773); these have been destroyed, while the Third (Old Pine Street) Presbyterian Church, also his work (1766), survives in a form altered beyond recognition. Though the statement that he built the spire of Christ Church is probably unfounded, he carried out large repairs on it about 1771. There is record of his having built dwelling houses.

In 1774 he was one of a committee chosen by the "mechanics" of Philadelphia to assist in organizing agitation against the coercion of Boston, and at a mass meeting of citizens on June 18 he was appointed to the committee of correspondence that was directed to take steps for a general colonial congress (*Pennsylvania Gazette*, June 15, 22, 1774). On July 24, 1775, the Pennsylvania committee of safety approved a plan he submitted for the construction of chevaux-de-frise to block the channel of the Delaware below Philadelphia, and accepted his offer to serve gratis in supervising the three lines that were placed in the river near Fort Mifflin. During 1776 he was employed in the preparation of similar defences, anl other works, at Billingsport, N. J., further down the river. The obstacles he devised were of a very massive nature (*The Annual Register . . . for the Year 1777*, 1778, p. 134) and embarrassed the British considerably in their efforts to open communication with Philadelphia by sea in the autumn of 1777 (*The Writings of George Washington*, edited by J. C. Fitzpatrick, vol. IX, 1933, p. 428). Smith died, however, without seeing his inventions tested in action.

In the greatest age of colonial building he was

Philadelphia's most eminent architect. Though his designs might be taxed with an excessive plainness amounting to severity (probably explicable by local circumstances), and with a tendency to repetition, he handled the contemporary Georgian style with admirable dignity combined with a sane regard for practical ends, and made a very distinguished contribution to the amenity of the city. He owned a country house as well as the one in town where he died, and the journal of his friend Jacob Hiltzheimer (*post*) testifies that in his later years he was fond of company and entertainment. He was a member of the American Philosophical Society from 1768. His wife, Esther or Hester, lived until 1783. The John Smith who was associated with her in administering her husband's estate (*Pennsylvania Gazette*, Apr. 9, 1777) may have been a son, and the Philadelphia records of the Society of Friends (*post*), to which Smith appears to have belonged, mention two girls, Martha and Rebecca, who died in 1758 and 1770 respectively, as "daughters of Robert Smith." These records give his age at his death as fifty-five; the *Pennsylvania Evening Post*, Feb. 13, 1777, states that he was in his fifty-fifth year.

[See Joseph Jackson, *Early Phila. Architects and Engineers* (1923); P. B. Wallace and W. A. Dunn, *Colonial Churches and Meeting Houses, Pa., N. J., and Del.* (1931); *Extracts from the Diary of Jacob Hiltzheimer of Phila., 1765–1798* (1893), ed. by J. C. Parsons; *Minutes of the Provincial Council of Pa.*, vols. X, XI (1852); *Pa. Archives*, 1 ser., vols. IV, V (1853); John Maclean, *Hist. of the Coll. of N. J.* (1877), vol. I; C. P. B. Jefferys, "The Provincial and Revolutionary Hist. of St. Peter's Church, Phila., 1753–1783"; *Pa. Mag. of Hist. and Biog.*, Oct. 1923; *An Act to Incorporate the Carpenters' Company of the City and County of Phila.* (1866), not reliable for dates prior to 1763; J. T. Scharf and Thompson Westcott, *Hist. of Phila., 1609–1884* (1884), vol. II; transcripts of vital records of Soc. of Friends, Hist. Soc. of Pa., Phila.; records of the Am. Philos. Soc. There are a few manuscript fragments by or relating to Smith in the possession of the Hist. Soc. of Pa. and the Princeton Univ. Lib.; several of his architectural books are preserved at Carpenters' Hall.]   C. P. S.

SMITH, ROBERT (Aug. 14, 1732–o.s. Oct. 28, 1801), Revolutionary patriot, first Protestant Episcopal bishop of South Carolina, was a native of Worstead, Norfolk, England, the second child of Stephen Smith, a grazier, and Hannah (Press) Smith. At the age of sixteen, having spent seven years at the Norwich grammar school under Timothy Bullimer, he was admitted sizar at Gonville and Caius College, Cambridge, matriculating in 1750. He received his bachelor's degree in 1754 and in 1755 was appointed a fellow. On Mar. 7, 1756, he was ordered deacon, and on Dec. 21 was ordained priest by the Bishop of Ely. The next year, upon the recommendation of William Mason, M.P., he was ap-

pointed assistant minister of St. Philip's Church in Charlestown, S. C., and arrived there Nov. 3, 1757. He became rector in 1759. On July 9, 1758, he married Elizabeth, the daughter of John Pagett. Ten years later, in the hope of restoring her broken health, he carried her to England, where they remained for eighteen months. She died June 8, 1771, however, some five months after their return to America. Early in 1774 he married Sarah, the daughter of Thomas Shubrick. She died July 7, 1779, and some years later he married Anna Maria (Tilghman) Goldsborough, daughter of Col. Edward Tilghman of Wye, and the widow of Charles Goldsborough, by whom she had a son Charles [*q.v.*]. She died Dec. 6, 1792. By his second wife Smith had one daughter, and by his third, two sons.

He was "a very sociable & polite clergyman" (*Publications of the Southern History Association*, vol. II, 1898, p. 138), a prodigious worker, and a powerful speaker. His position at St. Philip's also gave him importance, and in the years before the Revolution he acquired great influence. He was early an intense patriot and in November 1775 was elected to the second provincial congress, where he failed to take his seat, but became chaplain of an artillery company. Later he was chaplain of the 1st South Carolina Regiment, and also of the Continental Hospital in Charlestown. Still later, he was chaplain general of the Southern department of the Continental Army. During the siege of Charlestown he served as a private soldier, and so active was he in the American cause that his name headed the list, published Dec. 30, 1780, of those whose estates were sequestered under Cornwallis' proclamation of Sept. 6. When offered immunity if he would support the British cause, he replied, "Rather would I be hanged by the King of England than go off and hang myself in shame and despair like Judas" (letter in private hands). He had inherited the "Brabant" plantation of 3,600 acres from his first wife and had added to it by purchase, so that his loss was great; to cap his misfortune, moreover, he was imprisoned in Charlestown and later banished to Philadelphia. After a stay of some months there he went to Maryland, where he took charge of St. Paul's Parish, Queen Anne's County. He returned to Charleston in 1783.

Smith was active in many good works of peace. As rector of St. Philip's he had charge of a successful school for negroes. He was instrumental in founding the Society for the Relief of Widows and Orphans. After his return from Maryland he founded a school which in 1790 became the College of Charleston, of which he was principal until 1798. When the movement for the organization of the Protestant Episcopal Church in the United States began, Smith was chiefly responsible for the assembling of a convention in South Carolina, which sent delegates to the General Convention of 1785. He did not attend, but was present in 1786 and 1789. There was much opposition in the state to the selection of a bishop, but finally, in 1795, after the first minister chosen had declined, Smith was elected and was consecrated at Christ Church, Philadelphia, in September. He continued to be rector of St. Philip's until his death, and because of local prejudice he never administered the rite of confirmation. He is buried in St. Philip's Cemetery.

[John and J. A. Venn, *Alumni Cantabrigienses*, pt. 1, vol. IV (1927); John Venn, *Biog. Hist. of Gonville and Caius Coll.*, vol. II (1898), p. 63; *S. C. Hist. and Geneal. Mag.*, Jan. 1917, Apr. 1919, Jan., Apr., July 1920, Jan. 1924; Frederick Dalcho, *An Hist. Account of the Protestant Episcopal Church in S. C.* (1820); William Moultrie, *Memoirs of the Am. Revolution* (1802); Alexander Garden, *Anecdotes of the Am. Revolution* (1822), 2 ser. (1828); Elizabeth Poyas, *Days of Yore; or Shadows of the Past* (1870), pt. 2, pp. 1–24; H. H. Ravenel, *Charleston, the Place and the People* (1907); Edward McCrady, *The Hist. of S. C. in the Revolution, 1775–1780* (1901), *1780–1783* (1902); W. S. Perry, *The Hist. of the Am. Episc. Church, 1776–1883* (1885) and *Jours. of the Gen. Conventions of the Protestant Episcopal Church in the U. S., 1785–1833* (1874); W. B. Sprague, *Annals of the Am. Pulpit*, vol. V (1859); *News and Courier* (Charleston), Jan. 26, 1898; D. E. Huger Smith and A. S. Salley, Jr., *Reg. of St. Philip's Parish . . . 1754–1810* (1927).]   J. G. deR. H.

SMITH, ROBERT (Nov. 3, 1757–Nov. 26, 1842), secretary of the navy and secretary of state, brother of Samuel Smith [*q.v.*], was born in Lancaster, Pa. His parents were John Smith and Mary (Buchanan), daughter of Robert Buchanan. He was educated at the College of New Jersey, graduating in 1781. For a time he served as a private in the Revolution. Later, he studied law and was admitted to the bar in Baltimore. Ambitious, industrious, courteous, and amiable, he soon had the largest admiralty practice in the city. On Dec. 7, 1790, he married a distant cousin, Margaret, daughter of William Smith. Eight children were born to them, of whom only one, a son, lived to maturity.

From 1793 to 1795 Smith was a member of the Maryland Senate and then for some time a member of the House of Delegates; from 1798 to 1801 he sat in the Baltimore city council. By now he had become a loyal Republican and ardent admirer of Jefferson, who, in 1801, after first offering the post to his brother, appointed him secretary of the navy. At the beginning of Jefferson's second term Smith asked to be transferred to the attorney-general's office; and this was done, Jacob Crowninshield [*q.v.*] being tendered his place in the navy department. The Senate confirmed both appointments, but since Crowninshield would not accept the position, Smith continued to act as secretary of the navy and after a few months gave up the attorney-generalship, continuing at the head of naval affairs until March 1809 without being recommissioned or reconfirmed. Though greatly criticized by the secretary of the treasury, Albert Gallatin [*q.v.*], Smith seems to have been fairly efficient in this office. With very limited funds he maintained a blockading squadron in the Mediterranean during the war against the Barbary States; though opposed to the Embargo, he seems to have tried conscientiously to enforce it; and in 1808 it was he, and not the Secretary of State, who was Jefferson's intermediary with George Henry Rose, Canning's agent in the diplomatic discussions of impressment.

As president-elect, Madison wished Gallatin to be his secretary of state, but his desire was opposed by a faction headed by senators Samuel Smith, William Branch Giles, and Michael Leib [*qq.v.*]. In an effort to win their support he decided to give the treasury portfolio to Robert Smith, to be assisted in his duties by Gallatin from the State Department. Gallatin refused these terms, however, and Smith was made secretary of state. Friction developed inevitably between the Secretary and the President, for Smith sided with the Senate cabal, which continued its attack on Gallatin, and in his official capacity generally opposed the President's plans for commercial restrictions. The two men frequently disagreed over the policy to be pursued in the troubles growing from the Napoleonic wars; moreover, Madison could not endure the English in which the Secretary expressed his views, and therefore, was soon writing all of the important diplomatic communications of the administration.

Matters reached a climax when Gallatin handed in his resignation early in March 1811. Madison refused to accept it, and sent for Smith. In the ensuing interview he criticized Smith for inefficiency, breach of trust, and causing discord in administration circles. As a way out, he offered Smith the position of minister to Russia, but after some hesitation the latter refused the offer, resigned his portfolio, and returned to Baltimore. In June 1811 he published *Robert Smith's Address to the People of the United States,* an attempt at self-defense which further hurt his prestige. During the last thirty years of his life, spent in Baltimore, he filled offices in a number of private organizations. His ability was, on the whole, little more than average, and the high positions to which he attained came chiefly through the influence of his brother, Gen. Samuel Smith.

[C. C. Tansill, "Robert Smith," in S. F. Bemis, *The American Secretaries of State and Their Diplomacy*, vol. III (1927); Henry Adams, *Hist. of the U. S. A.* (9 vols., 1889–91); *Votes and Proc. of the Gen. Assembly of the State of Md.*, 1793–1800; G. E. Davies, "Robert Smith and the Navy," *Md. Hist. Mag.*, Dec. 1919; C. O. Paullin, "Naval Administration under Secretaries of the Navy Smith, Hamilton, and Jones, 1801–1814," *Proc. U. S. Naval Inst.*, vol. XXXII (Dec. 1906); *The Life and Correspondence of James McHenry* (1907), ed. by B. C. Steiner; *The Writings of Thomas Jefferson* (20 vols., 1903–04); *Letters and Other Writings of James Madison* (4 vols., 1865); *Aurora* (Phila.), May 4, 1811; *American and Commercial Daily Advertiser* (Baltimore), July 6, 1811, Nov. 28. 1842; *National Intelligencer*, Mar. 26, July 4, 6, 9, 11, 1811, Nov. 29, 1842; genealogical table of the Smith family, Wilson Miles Cary MSS. Coll., F 62, Md. Hist. Soc.; Smith Papers, MSS. Div. Library of Congress; information from the secretary of Princeton Univ.]   M. W. W.

SMITH, ROBERT ALEXANDER C. (Feb. 22, 1857–July 27, 1933), promoter, capitalist, dock commissioner, was born in Dover, England, the son of Gilbert and Emily Smith. His father was chief engineer of the Compañia Transatlantica, a steamship line operating between Spain and Cuba. From his second to his thirteenth year, Robert lived in Cadiz and then completed his education at Folkestone and London. In 1874, he came to New York. His knowledge of Spanish led him into the employ of Lyles & Gilson, who specialized in selling railroad supplies to Latin America, and for a time he was the firm's representative in Havana.

Cuba was the principal scene of Smith's activity for many years. Becoming a sort of contact man for the Ward Line and other American business interests, he was particularly active in railroads and shipping. In association with Henry G. Runkle, he is credited with the chief initiative in introducing gas, electric, and water systems to Havana. It is said that he and one J. J. McCook once formed a syndicate to free Cuba by purchase (*Herald Tribune*, July 28, 1933). During the Spanish-American War, he assisted with transport and shipping, having particular charge of the evacuation of Spanish prisoners. That same year, he organized and became head of the American Indies Company, a public utilities organization, and the American Mail Steamship Company, which secured a lucrative mail contract and soon leased its ships to the United Fruit Company. His financial activities were not limited to Cuba, however. In 1895, with Morgan backing, he and Alden M. Young formed the Gas Supply Company, later the Connecticut Railway & Lighting Company,

which secured control of some fourteen separate lighting and traction companies in that state. His interests also included sugar, coal, realty, and banking corporations and he was chairman of the board of the White Rock Mineral Springs Company.

Although through his exploits in economic imperialism he had built up a fortune and influenced the development of Cuba, his most distinctive service to his generation was his share in the development of the Port of New York. Because of his knowledge of shipping problems he was appointed chairman of a state commission "to investigate port conditions and pier extension in New York Harbor," and in 1913, before the publication of his report, he was made commissioner of docks and ferries of New York City. New York at the time was challenging London, Liverpool, and Hamburg for first place among world seaports. After the outbreak of the World War in 1914, it held a secure primacy. The port had grown, however, without any coordinated plan; something had to be done at once to accommodate the new thousand-foot liners, which were too large for the regular docks. The construction of a splendid group of North River (Hudson) piers was Smith's first achievement. In 1915, the ferries were operated at a profit for the first time in ten years of municipal ownership. Smith also urged the deepening and straightening of Hell Gate. A violent discussion arose in 1916 over the "West Side" problem, provoked by the privileges enjoyed by the New York Central, the freight tracks of which lay along the Hudson waterfront. Smith preferred improvements which would continue the Central's favored position as against those who sought more privileges for the railroads having their terminals on the New Jersey side of the river, but the question was still unsettled at the end of his administration in 1917. Smith wrote several vigorous pamphlets on various aspects of port problems. Among these were: *Commission to Investigate Port Conditions in New York Harbor . . . A Tabulation of Facts* (1915); *New York's Progress in Port Problems* (1915); *Report on the Operation of Municipal Ferries by the City of New York from 1905 to 1915* (1916); *The West Side Improvement and its Relation to all of the Commerce of the Port of New York* (1916); *Hell Gate* (1917). He was influential in calling attention to the needs which in 1921 led to the creation of the Port of New York authority.

Retiring as commissioner in 1917, he continued to serve as director in various corporations. After a period of ill health, he sailed for

England but died on board the *Majestic* just after the vessel's arrival at Southampton. In 1882 he had married Alice S. Williams of Brooklyn, who with two daughters survived him.

[*N. Y. Times* and *N. Y. Herald Tribune,* July 28, 1933; *N. Y. Times,* Aug. 17, 1933; *Directory of Directors in the City of N. Y.,* 1899–1933; *Ann. Reports of the Dept. of Docks and Ferries* (N. Y. City), 1913–17; *Joint Report with Comprehensive Plan and Recommendations: N. Y., N. J. Port and Harbor Development Commission* (1920); *Who's Who in N. Y.,* 1929.]
R. G. A.

SMITH, ROBERT BARNWELL [See RHETT, ROBERT BARNWELL, 1800–1876].

SMITH, ROBERT HARDY (Mar. 21, 1813–Mar. 13, 1878), lawyer, member of the provisional Congress of the Confederacy, was born in Camden County, N. C., the son of Robert Hardy and Elizabeth (Gregory) Smith. His grandfather, Joseph Smith, was a native of London, England; his maternal ancestors were also of English descent, but had served the American cause with distinction in the Revolutionary War. Robert received an appointment to West Point but he did not graduate. He taught school in various counties of Virginia and Alabama, studied medicine, and later turned to the law. Admitted to the bar in 1835, he settled for practice at Livingston, Ala. He was successful in his profession and was recognized as especially able in addresses to the jury. His style was clear and forceful, argumentative rather than oratorical.

In politics he was a Whig. He supported Harrison in 1840 and Clay in 1844. In 1849 he was elected to represent Sumter County in the legislature, being the only Whig chosen from that county. He was regarded as the leader of the Whigs in the Alabama House of Representatives during the session and in 1851 became a candidate for the state Senate on a platform of opposition to the Nashville Convention and defense of the compromise measures of 1850 against the State-Rights Democrats. The campaign was a bitter one and John A. Winston [*q.v.*] defeated Smith by one vote. For the next ten years he was actively interested in politics but held no office. In 1853 he moved to Mobile, where he continued the practice of law. Throughout the period he was one of the leaders of the opposition to William L. Yancey [*q.v.*] and was tireless in his efforts against the growing sentiment in the state for secession. He supported Bell and Everett in 1860 and appears to have originated the movement to fuse the Bell and Douglas forces in the state in order to defeat secession. The movement failed.

When Alabama withdrew from the Union, Smith accepted the decision loyally. He was Alabama's commissioner to confer with North Carolina on secession and was elected to the provisional Confederate Congress in 1861 as one of Alabama's two delegates at large. In the Congress he served on the committee which framed the permanent constitution for the Confederacy and took an active part in the debates. He was anxious that the wording of the constitution be clear and simple and most of his work was directed toward securing definiteness and clarity of statement. He also served on the judiciary committee and on the committee on naval affairs. In 1861 he published *An Address to the Citizens of Alabama on the Constitution and Laws of the Confederate States of America.* He organized, in 1862, the 36th Alabama Infantry and was elected colonel, but was compelled to resign before the end of the year because of poor health. Thereafter he practised law in Mobile until his death. He was married three times and had several children. His first wife, whom he married Jan. 12, 1839, was Evelina Inge. After her death in 1843, he married, Nov. 25, 1845, her sister Emily. A third wife, whom he married Apr. 9, 1850, was Helen Herndon.

[Dates are from family Bible and records; for published sources, see T. M. Owen, *Hist. of Ala. and Dict. of Ala. Biog.* (1921), vol. IV; Willis Brewer, *Ala.: Her Hist., Resources, War Record, and Public Men, 1540 to 1872* (1872); William Garrett, *Reminiscences of Public Men in Ala. for Thirty Years* (1872); *News* (Gainesville, Ala.), Sept. 3, 1870; article by Stephens Croom, in *Southern Law Jour.,* Jan. 1879, repr. in *Daily Register* (Mobile), Mar. 23, 1879; obituary in *Daily Register,* Mar. 15, 1878.]
H. F.

SMITH, ROSWELL (Mar. 30, 1829–Apr. 19, 1892), lawyer and publisher, was born at Lebanon, Conn., the son of Asher Ladd Smith and his second wife, Wealthy Pratt. Asher Smith, farmer and business man, wrote *How to Get Rich* (1856; 2nd ed., 1866), and his brother, Roswell Chamberlain Smith, was the author of numerous textbooks in grammar, arithmetic, and geography. The boy was named for this uncle, but in mature life rarely used his middle name. In 1843 he went to New York to enter the employ of his uncle's publishers, Paine & Burgess. Five years later he entered Brown University as a student in the two-year English and scientific course. The record books of the university show that his marks were consistently high; the lowest, 83, was in French. After honorable dismissal, May 6, 1850, he studied law in Hartford, under Thomas C. Perkins, and began practice in Lafayette, Ind. In 1852 he married Annie Goodrich Ellsworth, daughter of Henry Leavitt Ellsworth [*q.v.*].

In 1868, as a result of a successful practice and fortunate investments in real estate, Smith was

able to retire and go to Europe. He had conceived the idea of buying a newspaper or a magazine upon his return, and when, by arrangement,
he met Josiah Gilbert Holland [q.v.] at Geneva,
the two worked out plans for a new magazine to
encourage American art and literature. A warm
friendship developed between them and upon
their return to the United States in 1870, they
joined with Charles Scribner [q.v.], the publisher of Holland's works, in the corporation of
Scribner & Company, which in November 1870
published the first issue of *Scribner's Monthly*.
Holland, as editor-in-chief, was ably seconded
by Richard Watson Gilder [q.v.]. In 1873, Smith
proposed the publication of a high-class magazine for children, and accordingly *St. Nicholas*,
edited by Mary Elizabeth Mapes Dodge [q.v.],
was sponsored by the firm. In the face of the
financial panic of that year Smith held out for
the purchase and merging with the new magazine
of several juvenile periodicals, and the outcome
completely vindicated his judgment. In 1881,
Holland, in ill health, sold his interest in the
company to Smith, and later Smith also purchased the Scribner interest, which gave him
control of the magazine. This purchase, however, carried the requirement that he change the
name of the company and of the periodical, and
in this way *Scribner's Monthly* became the *Century*.

In 1882, Smith first conceived the idea of *The
Century Dictionary and Cyclopedia*, which was
his chief interest for the next ten years. That it
was completed before his death was, to him, a
great source of comfort. As work on it progressed, the project grew far beyond the proportions of the original design, which had been little
more than a revision for American use of Ogilvie's
Imperial Dictionary (2 vols., Glasgow, 1851);
but Smith refused to consider proposals of economy and enabled the editors to make the *Century*
the most comprehensive work of its kind in the
English language up to the completion of the
great Oxford Dictionary. Smith's behavior in
this instance was characteristic: whatever he
undertook he determined should be the best in
its field, regardless of expense. As a result of
this characteristic, his magazines, under Alexander Wilson Drake [q.v.] as art director, were
a major factor in stimulating the development
of American illustration. Holding the enthusiastic belief that American publications could
win praise and financial success in foreign countries, Smith demonstrated his faith by spending
large sums of money, personally arranging the
details involved in placing his magazines before
English readers. In addition to his activities as

president of the Century Company, he was interested in educational work, especially in the
South; Lincoln Hall, at Berea College, Ky., is
an example of his generosity.

Smith's own literary work was slight. It consists of a sixteen-line poem, "What the Devil
Said to the Young Man" (*Scribner's Monthly*,
May 1871), and two short stories in *St. Nicholas*: "The Boy Who Worked" (January 1874),
and "Little Holdfast" (January 1891). Of small
value in themselves, the stories illustrate, as
Smith intended, two principles that he followed
rigidly: work hard; and when you make a promise, hold fast to it, regardless of consequences.
Smith was tall, with a leonine head, and made a
commanding appearance. He loved his home, his
family, and a few friends, but he was not fond of
"social life." He felt that a man should be useful
in a public way, and he was too busy trying to be
useful to have time for trivial pleasures. He died
of Bright's disease and paralysis, at his home in
New York, after an illness of three years. For
eight weeks before his death he had been unable
to speak, as a result of a succession of paralytic
strokes. He was survived by his wife and by
one daughter.

[G. W. Cable, *A Memory of Roswell Smith* (1892);
Century Magazine, June 1892; *St. Nicholas*, June
1892; *Commercial Advertiser* (N. Y.), Apr. 19, 1892;
N. Y. Tribune, N. Y. Times, World (N. Y.), all of Apr.
20, 1892; Record Books in Brown Univ. Library; *Hist.
Cat. Brown Univ.* (1905); information from members
of the family.]   H. S. R—n.

SMITH, RUSSELL (Apr. 26, 1812–Nov. 8,
1896), painter, third in a family of four boys and
three girls, was born in Glasgow, Scotland. Although christened William Thompson Russell
Smith, he was known simply as Russell Smith.
His father, William Thompson Smith, and his
mother, Margaret (Russell) Smith, a practising
physician who had studied medicine in Glasgow,
emigrated to America with their children in
1819 because of their political views. They settled in Indiana County, Pa., but moved to Pittsburgh in 1824. There Russell's father, who is
said to have been "an ingenious mechanic, excelling in the manufacture of cutlery, artists'
tools, and mathematical instruments" (Tuckerman, *post*, p. 519), established a cutlery business,
and Russell began his art career by painting with
house paints life-sized portraits of Gen. William
Jackson, 1759–1828, and Lafayette [qq.v.]. He
also joined a dramatic society, for which he
played female parts and painted scenery. His
success at the latter led to four years of study
under the painter James Reid Lambdin [q.v.].
In 1833, when Francis Courtney Wemyss, manager of the Pittsburgh Theatre, took Edwin For-

rest [*qq.v.*] to Pittsburgh, Smith was asked in an emergency to paint the scenery, although actor and producer doubted the ability of so young a man. The result was a tent scene for *Metamora* so successful that Smith attached himself to Wemyss as professional scene-painter and began an active career that was spent partly in Boston, but mostly in Philadelphia, Baltimore, and Washington. On Apr. 7, 1838, at Milestown, Pa., he married Mary Priscilla Wilson. His wife, well educated and of a cultured family, had been a teacher of French and Latin, and was a painter of flowers. They had two children, Xanthus [*q.v.*] and Mary (Sept. 25, 1842–June 6, 1878), both painters.

The years 1851–52 the family spent in Europe, returning so that Smith could produce a panorama of Mexico and California, and a diorama of the Holy Land (both exhibited in Philadelphia) as well as much operatic scenery and a number of drop-curtains, including those for Welsh's old National Theatre in Philadelphia and for the Boston Museum. When the Philadelphia Academy of Music was built, 1855–56, he was commissioned to produce its landscape drop-curtain, scenery for its operas, and additional drop-curtains, a task that stretched through the years almost until the time of his death. He painted all the scenery for the American Academy of Music in Baltimore, and drop-curtains for the principal theatrical houses in Philadelphia, Boston, and Brooklyn. These large canvases, many of them fifty feet square or more, were ordinarily painted with no more assistance than that of a color grinder who also helped to raise and lower the frame that held them. Smith believed that unless he executed the entire project himself his individuality as an artist would suffer. In 1879, after the death of his daughter Mary, he founded the Mary Smith Prize of $100, given yearly to a resident woman artist exhibiting in the annual exhibition of oil paintings at the Pennsylvania Academy of the Fine Arts. In addition to his scene painting, he devoted considerable time to illustrations for scientific lectures, drawings for geological surveys, and occasional landscapes in oil. Always interested in observing nature closely, he made sketching trips to picturesque parts of Virginia, New England, and Pennsylvania, using the resultant material in composing such landscape drop-curtains as that in the Philadelphia Academy of Music. After a vigorous old age he died in his home in Glenside, Pa.

[See H. T. Tuckerman, *Book of the Artists* (1867); Clara E. Clement and Laurence Hutton, *Artists of the Nineteenth Century* (1885); *Appletons' Ann. Cyc.*, 1896; obituary in *Pub. Ledger* (Phila.), Nov. 9, 1896; *Cat. of the Forty-Ninth Ann. Exhibition Pa. Acad. of the Fine Arts* (1878) and *Descriptive Cat. of the Permanent Colls.* (1892). For Mary Smith see *A Brief Sketch of the Life of Mary Smith, the Painter* (privately printed, 1878). Information has been supplied by Mary B. Smith, wife of Xanthus Smith.]   D. G.

SMITH, SAMUEL (July 27, 1752–Apr. 22, 1839), soldier and statesman, was born in Carlisle, Pa.; but his parents removed to Baltimore, Md., when he was seven or eight years old. His mother was Mary Buchanan of Lancaster, Pa. His father, John Smith, a native of Strabane, Ireland, of Scotch-Irish descent, was brought to Pennsylvania by his parents in 1728. He removed to Baltimore in 1760, became one of the wealthiest merchants in that city, and was active in Revolutionary politics. After two years in an academy at Elkton, Md., Samuel, then fifteen, entered his father's counting house. He was sent to Europe in 1772, spent considerable time traveling there, and upon his return resumed his work with his father.

In 1775 he organized a company of volunteers and entered the conflict against Great Britain. He participated in the battle of Long Island, covered the rear of the American army in its retreat across New Jersey, and was with Washington at Valley Forge and at the battle of Monmouth. As commander of Fort Mifflin, in the Delaware, near Philadelphia, he held out for some forty days, helping keep Howe's fleet at bay and thus contributing towards Burgoyne's surrender, which marked the turning point of the war. For this service Congress gave him a vote of thanks and a sword. After the Revolution he continued his mercantile activities in Baltimore, and engaged in land speculation in various states, becoming very wealthy. In 1791 he commanded the Maryland quota of troops sent to suppress the Whiskey Rebellion. Three years later, when war threatened with France, he was made brigadier-general of the state militia.

Meanwhile, in 1792 he had entered politics, through being elected to Congress. He was re-elected four times, serving until 1803. For a few months (Mar. 31–June 13, 1801) at the beginning of Jefferson's administration, until the appointment of his brother Robert [*q.v.*], he acted as virtual secretary of the navy while Henry Dearborn was nominal secretary *ad interim*. In this capacity he began energetic action against Tripoli. In 1803 Smith was elected to the Senate, where he remained until 1815. During the War of 1812, with the rank of major-general, he headed the land and sea forces which defended Baltimore from the British. He returned to the House, Jan. 31, 1816, serving, by reëlections, until December 1822, when he resigned to fill a vacancy in the Senate caused by the death of William Pinkney [*q.v.*]. To this seat he was reëlected in 1826, serving until 1833, and thus completing forty continuous years in Congress.

At first Federalist in his leanings, Smith soon became a stanch Jeffersonian Republican. He was tall and handsome, of proud countenance and imperious bearing, and easily attracted attention. He was also self-confident, ambitious, industrious, intelligent, and an able and forceful debater. He quickly made his influence felt both on the floor of Congress and behind the scenes. Repeatedly he was president *pro tempore* of the Senate, and he did important work as chairman of the finance committees of both houses. He was given to cabals and intrigues, was one of the leaders in opposing the nomination of Madison, and, following it, headed a group which aimed, in vain, to eliminate nominating by congressional caucus. Nevertheless, in 1816 he was chairman of such a gathering, and in 1820 he made a futile effort to secure by caucus the nomination of Clay for vice-president because he himself aspired to Clay's position as speaker of the House (J. Q. Adams, *Memoirs, post*, V, 58–60). He was one of the leaders of the faction which fought Albert Gallatin [*q.v.*] as secretary of the treasury, and did much to embarrass the administration through holding up in Congress the financial measures advocated by Gallatin. Thus, in 1811, he opposed the rechartering of the United States Bank, although in 1816 he advocated the chartering of a new United States bank, and in 1830, as chairman of the Senate committee on finance, recommended its rechartering. He was chairman of the special committee which introduced the non-importation agreements in 1806; he opposed Macon's Bill, No. 1, in March 1810; and was a member of the faction which delayed by twelve days the declaration of war against Great Britain in 1812. He favored equalization of tariff duties but fought bitterly Clay's "American system" and in 1832 even suggested dividing the Union at the Potomac to escape it (Adams, *Memoirs*, VIII, 455). Perhaps his most constructive efforts were those for the recovery of trade with the British West Indies. He was the chief sponsor of the act of Congress approved May 29, 1830, authorizing the president to undertake negotiations for the opening of British ports in those islands to American vessels.

After his last term in the Senate, Smith lived in retirement in Maryland until 1835, when, as commander of the state militia, he was called upon to quell the riots in Baltimore resulting from the failure of the Bank of Maryland, precipitated by Jackson's withdrawal of deposits. As the "savior of the City," he was elected its mayor in 1835 on the resignation of Jesse Hunt. He was reëlected in 1836 and served until 1838, dying the following year in Baltimore. Smith married in 1778 Margaret Spear of Baltimore, by whom he had eight children. His wife's sister, Dorcas, was the wife of William Patterson [*q.v.*] and the mother of Betsy Patterson who married Jerome Bonaparte, and Smith made much of this family connection with Napoleon I. In 1819 a panic in the Baltimore branch of the United States Bank caused the failure of his firm, Smith & Buchanan, and the loss of his personal fortune. Some scandal attached to his partner, but none to Smith, whose public service was uninterrupted.

[*Biog. Dir. Am. Cong.* (1928); *Memoirs of John Quincy Adams*, vols. I, IV–VIII (1874–76); J. F. Essary, *Md. in National Politics* (2nd ed., 1932); *The Life and Correspondence of James McHenry* (1907), ed. by B. C. Steiner; Annie L. Sioussat, *Old Baltimore* (1931); Henry Adams, *Hist. of the U. S. A.* (9 vols., 1889–91); *Niles Weekly Register*, Sept. 10, 24, Oct. 27, 1814; J. T. Scharf, *The Chronicles of Baltimore* (1874); *Sun* (Baltimore), Apr. 23, 1839, Apr. 16, 1911; genealogical table of the Smith family, Wilson Miles Cary MSS. Coll., F62, Md. Hist. Soc.; Smith Papers MSS. Division, Lib. of Cong.; clippings, etc., in private hands.]   M. W. W.

SMITH, SAMUEL FRANCIS (Oct. 21, 1808–Nov. 16, 1895), Baptist clergyman, editor, poet, was born in Boston, Mass., the son of Samuel and Sarah (Bryant) Smith. He graduated from the Eliot School and from the Boston Latin School, receiving at the latter in 1825 both the Franklin medal and a prize medal for a poem. He entered Harvard College in what proved to be one of its most distinguished classes, 1829, its memory prolonged by Oliver Wendell Holmes's poem, "The Boys," in which are the lines:

> "And there's a nice youngster of excellent pith:
> Fate tried to conceal him by naming him Smith."

His studies for the ministry were pursued at Andover Theological Seminary, where he was graduated in 1832.

He had met some of the cost of his education by the translation of articles for the *Encyclopaedia Americana*, edited by Francis Lieber [*q.v.*]. During the latter part of his course in the seminary he was asked by Lowell Mason [*q.v.*] to translate or compose verses for a song book to be used in schools. Among the tunes placed in his hands was one which especially appealed to him. "Being pleased with its simple and easy movement," he later wrote, "I glanced at the German words, and seeing that they were patriotic, instantly felt the impulse to write a patriotic hymn of my own to the same tune. Seizing a scrap of waste paper, I put upon it, within half an hour, the verses substantially as they stand to-day" (*Poems of Home and Country*, 1895, p. xvii). This hymn, beginning "My country, 'tis of thee," was first published in Mason's *The Choir* (1832). As it then appeared it contained five stanzas, the third of which was later discarded. It speedily was popularly adopted as the national hymn, a status never needing the support of political action, but maintained by force of sentiment.

Smith attained fame by this one enduring poem, but his career was otherwise productive and influential. Ordained to the Baptist ministry on Feb. 12, 1834, he had two pastorates at important educational centers. The first of these was at Waterville, Me., 1833–42, where he was also professor of modern languages in Waterville College (now Colby); the second, at Newton Center, Mass., which was his home from January 1842. From 1842 to 1848, in addition to his pastoral work, he edited *The Christian Review*. On Sept. 16, 1834, he married Mary White Smith of Haverhill, a grand-daughter of Dr. Hezekiah Smith [*q.v.*]; six children were born to them, one of whom, Daniel Appleton White Smith, went in 1863 as a missionary to Burma and served for forty years as president of the Karen Baptist Theological Seminary. In 1854 Smith resigned his church at Newton Center and became editorial secretary of the American Baptist Missionary Union.

He wrote much both in verse and prose. While most of the former lacked distinction, it was the outpouring of a simple, wholesome idealism, as is suggested by the title of his collected poetry, *Poems of Home and Country* (1895). "The Morning Light is Breaking" became one of the most widely sung missionary hymns, and his poem, "The Lone Star," 1868, is generally conceded to have saved the Telugu mission at Nellore, India, and a dramatic reference to it in 1925 led, in a crisis, to the strengthening of the Baptist missionary efforts in the Orient. His prose works include *Life of the Rev. Joseph Grafton* (1849); *Missionary Sketches* (1879); *History of Newton, Mass.* (1880); *Rambles in Mission-Fields* (1883), based on a tour of mission fields in Europe and Asia. He also edited, with Baron Stow [*q.v.*], *The Psalmist* (1843), which for more than thirty years was the hymn book most widely used by Baptists. The April before his death, in recognition of his authorship of "America," a great public celebration was held in Boston. A tower and a chime of bells in the First Baptist Church, Newton Center, are a memorial to him.

He died suddenly in a train at the railroad station, Boston, as he was on his way to fill a preaching engagement.

[An autobiog. sketch appears in *Poems of Home and Country*, and another by G. H. W. Whittemore in *America! Our National Hymn* (1879). See also C. M. Fuess, in *Christian Science Monitor*, May 15, 1930; H. S. Burrage, *Baptist Hymn Writers and Their Hymns* (copr. 1888); H. K. Rowe, *Tercentenary Hist. of Newton* (1930); *Boston Transcript*, Nov. 18, 1895. Parents' names have been verified by Smith's granddaughter, Miss Anna Haven Smith, Newton Center, Mass. There are a few miscellaneous papers of Smith's in the Lib. of Cong.]   W. H. A.

SMITH, SAMUEL HARRISON (1772–Nov. 1, 1845), journalist, banker, author, was the son of a Philadelphia merchant, Jonathan Bayard Smith [*q.v.*], and Susannah (Bayard) Smith. He was educated in Philadelphia, graduating at the University of Pennsylvania in 1787, and early in his life became a journalist and author. He gained the recognition of Thomas Jefferson in 1797 by tying for the first prize offered by the American Philosophical Society for the best essay on a system of education and a plan for free public schools (*Remarks on Education,* 1798). In the late summer of 1796, however, he had begun the publication of a Jeffersonian newspaper, the *New World* of Philadelphia, which he published until Aug. 16, 1797. In September 1797 he bought the *Independent Gazetteer* of the elder Joseph Gales [*q.v.*], and three months later, Nov. 16, 1797, began to issue the *Universal Gazette*. Upon the invitation of Jefferson, he followed the government to Washington, D. C., in 1800, where he continued the *Universal Gazette* as a weekly and inaugurated a tri-weekly, the *National Intelligencer and Washington Advertiser,* issuing the first number Oct. 31, 1800. On Sept. 29 of this year he had married his cousin, the brilliant and versatile Margaret Bayard [see Margaret Bayard Smith], daughter of Col. John Bubenheim Bayard [*q.v.*]. They had a son and three daughters.

Smith was thoroughly a party editor, but his calm, sound, judicial temperament kept him from being as vitriolic as some of his Republican partisans desired. The Federalists dubbed the *Intelligencer* the "National Smoothing-Plane," and to some of the Jeffersonians he was known as "Silky-Milky Smith." His admiration for Jefferson, whom he often pronounced the greatest man in America, was unbounded, and he warmly advocated every measure which Jefferson proposed. The *Intelligencer,* being the official organ of the Jefferson administration, published Jefferson's *Manual of Parliamentary Practice* (1801), the executive proclamations, and public notices. It also received half of the congressional printing. Though unwavering in his adherence to Jeffersonian principles, in his personal relations Smith may have been influenced somewhat by his Federalist wife, to whom he was devoted; she never gave up her Federalist friendships. Thus, while Smith admired Calhoun and Madison, their opponent, Henry Clay, was often welcomed into his home. The Smiths often dined with Jefferson and visited him at Monticello. In 1804 Smith bought "Turkey Thicket," a country estate which later became part of the grounds of the Catholic University. This place he named "Sidney." Whether in the country or in town, his home was the rendezvous of statesmen, authors, musicians, politicians, and editors. He set a lavish table, filled his cellar with rare wines, attended an Episcopal church regularly, enjoyed chess and whist, and drove fine horses. He owned slaves, rejoiced in the purchase of Louisiana, opposed nullification, and advocated nationalism. He admired Madison, cared little for Monroe, disliked Adams, and tolerated and feared Jackson. He sympathized with labor and the poor, but feared the result of a government by the masses. Because of ill health, he sold the *Intelligencer*, Aug. 31, 1810, to the younger Joseph Gales [*q.v.*]. In July 1813 he was appointed commissioner of revenue, and in 1828 he was chosen president of the Washington Branch of the United States Bank. He served as a director of the Washington Library, as president of the Bank of Washington nearly a decade, as treasurer of the Washington National Monument Society, and as a public school trustee. He died in Washington and was buried in Rock Creek Cemetery.

[*The First Forty Years of Washington Society* (1906), ed. by Gaillard Hunt, being family letters of Mrs. Samuel Harrison Smith; Josephine Seaton, *Wm. Winston Seaton . . . A Biog. Sketch* (1871); *Daily National Intelligencer*, Nov. 3, 1845; W. B. Bryan, *A Hist. of the National Capital* (2 vols., 1914–16); J. G. B. Bulloch, *A Hist. and Geneal. of the Families of Bayard, Houstoun of Ga. . . .* (1919); C. S. Brigham, "Bibliog. of American Newspapers: Philadelphia," *Proc. Am. Antiquarian Soc.*, n.s. XXXII (1923); Jonathan Bayard and Samuel Harrison Smith Papers and Mrs. Samuel Harrison Smith Papers, MSS. Div., Lib. of Cong.]   W. E. S—h.

SMITH, SAMUEL STANHOPE (Mar. 16, 1750–Aug. 21, 1819), Presbyterian clergyman, college president, was born at Pequea, Lancaster County, Pa., the son of the Rev. Robert and Elizabeth (Blair) Smith; one of his younger brothers was John Blair Smith [*q.v.*]. At the age of six Samuel commenced the study of Latin and Greek at the academy conducted by his father at Pequea and was so well grounded in these essentials that he was admitted when sixteen to the junior class of the College of New Jersey, at Princeton. There mathematics awakened in him a life-long interest in natural science; there, also, he began to manifest the spirit of free inquiry that characterized ever afterward his intellectual activities. He had become infected "with the fanciful doctrines of bishop Berkeley" and it required the blandishments of a Witherspoon to wean him from the cloudy speculations of immaterialism to the clear light of common sense (*Sermons, post*, I, 7–16).

After graduating in 1769 he assisted his father at the academy for a time, but the following year was recalled to Princeton to teach the classics and to cultivate among the students a taste for belles-lettres. In 1773 he was licensed to preach by the New Castle Presbytery, and, partly because of ill health, he abandoned his books for the missionary field. In the western counties of Virginia, among his own Scotch-Irish people, he supplemented the work of his predecessor, Samuel Davies [*q.v.*], in strengthening the Presbyterian allegiance. So great was his influence that his humble adherents raised the sizable sum of $50,000 to found, in 1776, under his guidance, the Academy of Hampden-Sidney, rechartered in 1783 as the College of Hampden-Sidney. Meanwhile he married Ann, daughter of John Witherspoon [*q.v.*]; nine children were born to them. After serving as president of the Academy in addition to his pastoral work for two or three years, ill health compelled him to turn over the work to his brother John.

In 1779 he returned to the College of New Jersey as teacher of moral philosophy. Here for thirty-three years he labored, first as professor and after 1795 as president. In the absence of President Witherspoon, who was engaged in public affairs, much of the administrative work fell on Smith. The task that confronted him was herculean. Money had to be raised to repair the ravages of the Revolution; in 1802, after Smith had succeeded to the presidency, the work had to be done again, for Nassau Hall was practically destroyed by fire. Suspicion that wanton students were responsible for the damage led to the strengthening of discipline; and while the elders talked of irreligion and false notions of liberty, the students with Gallic fervor charged restraints upon their liberties. In 1807, just after the enrollment had reached 200 students, insubordination broke out. More than half the undergraduates were suspended. Smith never recovered from the strain of those days and from that time on his health waned; in 1812 he resigned. To the intellectual advancement of the college, however, he had contributed much. He raised funds for scientific apparatus and called to the college, in 1795, John Maclean [*q.v.*], the first undergraduate teacher of chemistry and natural science in the United States. For ten years a unique course that combined training in the sciences and the humanities was offered. All such innovations were bitterly opposed, however. Smith himself was subjected to hostile criticism because of his views. His position upon the subject of divine grace was not approved, and he was constrained to discontinue his original lectures upon the evidence of religion and moral philosophy.

He was a popular preacher, compounding "the sound sense and masterly argument of the English preachers," and "the spirit, fire, and vehemence of the French" (*Sermons*, I, 55). Though the three volumes of his sermons were widely read, his *Lectures on the Evidences of the Christian Religion* (1809) and his *Lectures . . . on the Subjects of Moral and Political Philosophy* (2 vols., 1812) have had a lasting influence. These works aided in perpetuating the common-sense realism of Witherspoon, which became so popular and so widely spread as to bear the legitimate claim of being distinctive American philosophy. Smith showed a willingness to liberalize many of the old and more strict data of moral philosophy. Discarding the theory of catastrophe in the affairs of men, he put forth the view, far in advance of that of his time, that "The minutest causes, acting constantly, and long continued, will necessarily create great and conspicuous differences among mankind" (*An Essay on the Causes of the Variety of Complexion and Figure in the Human Species*, 1787, p. 3). In the same essay he flatly contradicted the theory of the separate creation of the different races. Independently of revelation, he arrived at a belief in the genetic unity of mankind, ascribing the existence of racial types to the influences of climate and "the state of society." He gave much thought to the problem of slavery and devised a plan whereby, he believed, freedmen might become economically independent.

[A. J. Morrison, *Coll. of Hampden Sidney Dict. of Biog., 1776–1825* (1921); *Sermons of S. S. Smith* (1821); W. B. Sprague, *Annals Am. Pulpit*, vol. III (1858); John Maclean, *Hist. of the Coll. of N. J.*, vol. II (1877); V. L. Collins, *Princeton* (1914); Gladys Bryson, "Philosophy and Modern Social Sciences," *Social Forces*, Oct. 1932.]   J. E. P.

SMITH, SEBA (Sept. 14, 1792–July 28, 1868), political satirist under the pseudonym of Major Jack Downing, was born in a log cabin in Buckfield, Me., the son of Seba and Aphia (Stevens) Smith, and a descendant of Francis Smith, who emigrated to America in the seventeenth century and settled in Massachusetts. In 1799 his father moved with his family to Bridgton, some thirty-five miles north of Portland, and was for a time post-rider from Portland to Waterford. The toil of pioneer life left the boy Seba little time for book-learning. He worked in a grocery store, in a brick yard, and in a foundry for casting iron, but he managed to learn enough to teach school in Bridgton at eighteen. In 1815 he finally entered Bowdoin College as a sophomore, graduating in 1818 with honors. After teaching for a year in Portland he made a journey as far south as the Carolinas and across the Atlantic from Portland to Liverpool, in all probability working his passage as he went. Upon his return to Maine he assumed the assistant-editorship of the *Eastern Argus,* an important Democratic paper in Portland, and continued his connection with it until 1826. While he was editor of the *Argus,* on Mar. 6, 1823, he married Elizabeth Oakes Prince, a promising young woman of Portland who as Elizabeth Oakes Smith [*q.v.*] was later to win distinction both as a writer and as a lecturer on the lyceum platform.

In the fall of 1829 he launched the *Portland Courier,* a newspaper of his own with no political affiliation, and the first daily to be issued in Maine. This paper was the vehicle for his Downing letters, which first appeared in January 1830, written by a Yankee adventurer who had left his native village of Downingville with cheeses and other country products to trade in Portland. From bargaining Jack Downing turned to politics, wandered into the legislature, and, finding proceedings blocked by party animosities, wrote humorous accounts of the situation to the Downings at home. These letters were reprinted in Boston, and their wider circulation through New England led to a more ambitious program, suggested by two years of the spoils system under Andrew Jackson [*q.v.*]. Smith sent Jack Downing as an office-seeker to Washington, allowed him to become the confidant of the president, and viewed through his eyes the trend of national events, at the same time hinting through covert satire at the dangers threatening this emerging democracy. In the unexpectedness of such a spokesman, a threadbare hero shining in the reflected glory of Old Hickory, there was the welcome element of comedy. This plan resulted in the widespread popularity of the Downing letters and the reprinting of them in local newspapers throughout the Union. The irony of their vogue in the heyday of the new democratic era was obvious, and many spurious Jacks made political use of Seba Smith's device. Smith's freedom from party hostility sets him apart from his only serious rival among his imitators, Charles Augustus

Davis (Tandy, *post*, pp. 32–38 and Wyman, *Two American Pioneers, post*, pp. 70–82), and from such later satirists of the Jackson period as Nathaniel Beverly Tucker in *The Partisan Leader* (1836) and John Pendleton Kennedy [*q.v.*], in *Quodlibet* (1840). The popularity of the Davis letters, however, and the confusion of the public as to their true author hastened Smith's publication of his letters in 1833 as a book entitled *The Life and Writings of Major Jack Downing of Downingville*. His rather mild ridicule of parties, platforms, and national leaders is in distinct contrast to the sharp wit and pointed political application of Davis, who is more often quoted by historians. (See A. B. Hart, *American History Told by Contemporaries*, vol. III, 1901, p. 540.) But the creation of this Yankee critic— a racy figure against a rustic and picturesque New England background, yet shrewd enough to serve as counselor to the president of the United States—must be credited to Seba Smith alone.

Smith was one of the victims of the land boom that began in 1834. After a desperate and unsuccessful attempt in 1839 to retrieve his losses by going to South Carolina, where he hoped to sell cotton planters a machine for cleaning cotton, he returned from Charleston to New York with his wife and their four sons. There his wife joined him in supplying articles for the *Southern Literary Messenger* and other periodicals of the day. By 1843, however, he had resumed his rôle as editor, having connections first with the *Rover*, a weekly magazine of some dignity, 1843–45, and later for a long period of time, though intermittently, 1854–59, with Emerson's *United States Magazine*. In 1859 he established a monthly, the *Great Republic*, which lasted only a year. Of his published books, which ranged from a metrical romance, *Powhatan* (1841), to an original dissertation on geometry, *New Elements of Geometry* (1850), the one most widely circulated was a collection of quaint tales on Yankee customs and characters called *'Way Down East* (1854). In 1847 he had begun his second series of Downing letters, which were published in the *Daily National Intelligencer,* and in 1859 these appeared in book form with the best of the earlier letters under the title *My Thirty Years Out of the Senate,* a parody on Thomas Hart Benton's *Thirty Years' View* (1854–56). In 1860 Smith retired from active life to spend his last years in Patchogue, Long Island. In disposition shy and retiring, he was essentially conservative, regarding with apprehension extreme measures which might endanger the solidarity of the Union. He will be remembered as a political satirist who set a new pattern for American humor, and who led the way for a host of homely philosophers and critics from Sam Slick and Hosea Biglow to Mr. Dooley and Will Rogers.

[The date of death is from a manuscript note by Elizabeth Oakes Smith in the Colls. of the Me. Hist. Soc., Portland, Me. Smith's autobiog. in MS. is in the Bowdoin Coll. Lib., Brunswick, Me.; that of Elizabeth Oakes Smith is in the manuscript dept. of the N. Y. Pub. Lib., N. Y. City. See *Hist. of Bowdoin Coll. with Biog. Sketches of its Grads.* (1882), A. S. Packard, ed.; Mary A. Wyman, *Selections from the Autobiog. of Elizabeth Oakes Smith* (1924) and *Two Am. Pioneers, Seba Smith and Elizabeth Oakes Smith* (1927); W. P. Trent, *A Hist. of Am. Lit., 1607–1865* (1903); Jennette R. Tandy, *Crackerbox Philosophers in Am. Humor and Satire* (1925); Constance Rourke, *Am. Humor, A Study of Nat. Character* (1931); H. L. Koopman, in *Pine Tree Mag.* (Portland, Me.), Nov. 1906; death notice in *N. Y. Tribune*, July 31, 1868.]

M. A. W.

SMITH, SOLOMON FRANKLIN (Apr. 20, 1801–Feb. 14, 1869), comedian, theatre manager, generally known as Sol Smith, was born, the eighth of the eleven sons of Levi and Hannah (Holland) Smith, in Norwich, N. Y., but spent most of his early years in a log house in Solon, Cortland County, N. Y. His father, who had been a piper in a volunteer company in the Revolutionary War, at Solon was a goldsmith (Smith, *post*, p. 1). Such education as Smith obtained, except for three quarters of regular schooling, he owed to his mother. At the age of eight he was sent to work on a farm a few miles away. After staying there four years he made his way to Boston; there he worked in a store owned by one of his brothers, and in the fall of 1814 accompanied his brothers to Albany. It was then that his predilection for the stage manifested itself. He devoted his leisure hours to reading Shakespeare and many of his evenings to surreptitious visits to the theatre of John Bernard [*q.v.*], where he made the acquaintance of the actors, among them the later celebrated family of Samuel Drake [*q.v.*]. Having decided after frequent experiments that nature intended him for an actor, in 1817 he ran away and sought to join the company when it left Albany, but was compelled to return home disappointed. A year later his brothers decided to move to Cincinnati. When he failed to keep an appointed meeting with one of them, he floated alone down the river to Pittsburgh, whence he worked his way to Ohio. There he remained for a time, but he was too restless for a sedentary life, and the next three or four years he spent roaming about from town to town in Ohio, Indiana, and Kentucky, usually in pursuit of his friends the Drakes. For a time he served as a printer's apprentice in Kentucky and later as foreman of the *Western Sun and General Advertiser,* Vincennes, Ind. He joined an occasional Thespian society, acted with the Drakes, performed the duties of prompter in the Collins and Jones company in Cincinnati, and studied law. In 1822 he married Martha Therese Mathews, an amateur singer, daughter of Edwin Mathews, and in the same year started in Cincinnati the *Independent Press and Freedom's Advocate,* one of the first Ohio papers to support Andrew Jackson [*q.v.*]. But he soon tired of journalistic work, sold the paper, and, buying out Collins and Jones, embarked in 1823 on his managerial career.

During the next twelve years he traveled about the country, picking up a living as best he could, chiefly with itinerant theatrical troupes, some of which he managed. In 1827 he and his wife joined the company of James H. Caldwell of New Orleans, La., and with it made their first visit to St. Louis, Mo. After a "gagging tour" of the southern states Smith rejoined Caldwell in 1831 to play in the Mississippi river towns under the management of Noah Miller Ludlow [*q.v.*]. With four more years of independent trouping in the southeastern states, where he was by this time well known, he attained the dignity of a star, and in 1835 played engagements with Ludlow in St. Louis and at the Park Theatre in New York under Edmund Shaw Simpson [*q.v.*] and the Walnut Street Theatre in Philadelphia under Francis Courtney Wemyss. In the fall of 1835 he joined Ludlow in Mobile, Ala., and became junior partner in the firm of Ludlow & Smith, which developed rapidly into one of the most important in the West, if not in the country. For sixteen years it dominated the St. Louis stage, and in that city built the first real theatre west of the Mississippi, with scenery by John Rowson Smith [*q.v.*], the artist. It also controlled Mobile until 1840, when, having lost two theatres by fire and being threatened with the rivalry of Caldwell, the partners abandoned the town to him, but in turn invaded his home territory, New Orleans. A bitter war ensued, but in 1842 with the erection of the New St. Charles Theatre they finally drove their rival out of business. By 1851 Smith gave up the St. Louis Theatre; two years later the firm of Ludlow & Smith was dissolved. Settling in St. Louis he devoted himself to the law, which for some years he had practised occasionally, and in 1861 he was elected to the state convention which kept Missouri from secession. He died suddenly in 1869 after a paralytic stroke. He was survived by his second wife, Elizabeth Pugsley, whom he had married in 1839 after the death of his first wife, and seven sons, two of whom, Marcus [*q.v.*] and Sol, Jr., became actors. On the stage his forte

was low comedy, but one of his favorite rôles was that of Mawworm in Isaac Bickerstaffe's *The Hypocrite.* As an actor he was extremely popular, especially in the West. He was a man of the most upright character and occupied an honored place both on the stage and in the community. In his life-time he published three autobiographical works, *The Theatrical Apprenticeship* (1846), *The Theatrical Journey-Work* (1854), and *Theatrical Management in the West and South* (1868), a combination of the first two.

[The best source of information concerning Smith's life is his *Theatrical Management in the West and South* (1868), which is on the whole reliable, though dates are sometimes hard to determine. See also T. A. Brown, *Hist of the Am. Stage* (1870) ; G. C. D. Odell, *Annals of the N. Y. Stage,* vol. IV (1928) ; N. M. Ludlow, *Dramatic Life As I Found It* (1880), which is characterized by a hostile bias ; and *N. Y. Times,* Feb. 16, 18, 24, 1869. Many letters, diaries, and other records are part of the estate of Smith's grandson, the late Sheridan S. Smith, Webster Groves, Mo. ; a number of old programs and other papers are in the estate of Smith's daughter-in-law, the late Mrs. Thaddeus S. Smith, St. Louis, Mo.]   W. G. B. C.

SMITH, SOPHIA (Aug. 27, 1796–June 12, 1870), founder of Smith College, fourth of the seven children of Joseph and Lois (White) Smith, was born in Hatfield, Mass., a descendant of Samuel Smith who emigrated from England in 1634, and a niece of Oliver Smith [*q.v.*]. Her family was substantial, though not conspicuous except for excessive thrift. Sophia showed little of the initiative characteristic of the Smiths; her younger sister Harriet took charge of the household after their mother's death and directed activities for the shy and retiring Sophia. Harriet's death in 1859 left Sophia bereft indeed, but she leaned on her eldest brother Austin, whose parsimony and success in speculation enabled him to amass a fortune to which, on his sudden death in 1861, Sophia fell sole heir. Now sixty-five years old, diffident, deaf, she felt an overwhelming burden of loneliness and responsibility. Accustomed always to depend on others, she laid her problems before her young pastor, John Morton Greene. Hoping to give her introspective nature opportunity for expression, he advised her to keep a journal, the source now of what is known of her inner life. It reveals an anxious and suspicious spirit, battling with afflictions, bewailing her sins, praying for self-improvement and for greater perfection of character.

"This is no tale of a stout-hearted, single-minded woman, fired by great ambition, evolving a great ideal" (Hanscom and Greene, *post,* p. 10). The founding of Smith College is rather the tale of the conscientious young minister of the town Congregational Church, the loyal friend and far-sighted adviser to whom the perplexed woman turned. His was the vision, with which, through long years of thoughtful planning and consultation with educational authorities, he was to kindle the imagination of his parishioner. Unable to interest her in his own college, Amherst, or in Mount Holyoke Seminary, founded by Sophia Smith's distant cousin, Mary Lyon [q.v.], Greene proposed an academy and woman's college, or a deaf-mute institution. In 1862 she made a will omitting the woman's college but providing for a library, an academy, and an institution for the deaf at Hatfield. The foundation of the Clarke School for the Deaf in Northampton anticipated the latter provision, and Greene again (1868) urged her to endow a woman's college. At her request, he prepared a "Plan for a Woman's College," which was embodied in a new will providing for a college "with the design to furnish for my own sex means & facilities for education equal to those which are afforded now in our Colleges to young men" (Ibid., p. 61). The location of the college, originally planned for Hatfield, was changed in her fifth and final will in 1870 to Northampton. The bequest amounted to nearly half a million dollars by 1875, when the college was opened.

Sophia Smith's own education had been elementary, though she indulged a taste for reading, especially after she became deaf. She lived a quiet life enlivened by occasional trips to watering places and once to Washington, and by visits to and from friends. One of the few luxuries she allowed herself was the building of a fashionable but ugly mansard-roofed mansion, in which she spent her last three years.

[MSS. assembled by John M. Greene in Lib. of Smith College; Sophia Smith's journ., Greene's journ., and manuscript narrative in possession of Helen French Greene; E. D. Hanscom and H. F. Greene, *Sophia Smith and the Beginnings of Smith College* (1925); *Addresses at the Inauguration of Rev. L. Clark Seelye as President of Smith College* (1875); *The Centennial of the Birth of Sophia Smith* (1896); *Celebration of the Quarter-Centenary of Smith College* (1900); G. B. Stebbins, "The Home of Sophia and Oliver Smith," *New England Mag.*, Oct. 1898.]   E. W. F.

SMITH, STEPHEN (Feb. 19, 1823–Aug. 26, 1922), surgeon and pioneer in public health, was born on a farm near Skaneateles, Onondaga County, N. Y., the son of Chloe (Benson) and Lewis Smith, and a descendant of John Smith, of Oxfordshire, England, who settled in Milford, Conn., in the seventeenth century. Stephen, a delicate child, was forced to undergo long hours of arduous toil on the farm. With his brother, Job Lewis Smith [q.v.], he attended the village school and later the academy at Homer in Cortland County. He then took his first course of

lectures in the Geneva Medical College, his second course at the Buffalo Medical College, and later established residence as a medical student in the hospital of the Sisters of Charity in Buffalo, N. Y. In 1850 he went to New York City to study at the College of Physicians and Surgeons where he was graduated with the M.D. degree in 1851. He was selected from ten other candidates to be interne at Bellevue Hospital in New York. While there, he wrote his first medical paper, "A Contribution to the Statistics of Rupture of the Urinary Bladder," for the *New York Journal of Medicine,* May 1851. This made such a reputation for him that he was elected to the surgical society of Paris and in 1853 was made joint editor, and later editor, of the periodical in which his paper was published. He remained a member of the surgical staff at Bellevue until 1911.

It is impossible to list his numerous offices or his many notable achievements. He was a conservative surgeon but not afraid of progress. One of his early operations was the second Syme's amputation of the foot ever done in the United States. A great advance in modern conservative surgery was effected by his amputation at the knee-joint. His *Hand-book of Surgical Operations,* published in 1862, was invaluable to Civil War surgeons, and his *Manual of the Principles and Practice of Operative Surgery* (1879, revised in 1887) was used as a standard textbook. Well known as a teacher and surgeon, his name will be remembered first of all for his efforts in promoting legislation for public health. His work in making New York City a safe and sanitary place in which to live was of incalculable value. He prepared the draft of a public health bill passed in 1866 as the Metropolitan Health Law, which became the basis of civic sanitation in the United States; he was commissioner of the new Board of Health, 1868–75; in 1868, through his efforts, the Bureau of Vaccination was formed; he helped to organize the American Public Health Association, 1871, of which he was the first president; he was instrumental in founding training schools for nurses; he drafted bills for a national board of health and a state board of health in 1878 and 1880; he was state commissioner in lunacy, 1882–88; he drafted the original bill for the State Care Act, passed in 1890; he was sent by President Cleveland as one of the three delegates to the ninth International Sanitary Conference in Paris in 1894; and he contributed active support to the passage of the bill giving the State Board of Charities authority for licensing and supervising dispensaries in 1899. He assisted in planning the

Roosevelt Hospital, New York City, and the Johns Hopkins Hospital, Baltimore, Md. He was one of the first to propose organization of the Bellevue Hospital Medical College where he taught both anatomy and surgery, and he had the distinction of being the first to introduce Lister aseptic treatment of wounds into Bellevue Hospital.

Although the later years of his life were not spent in such active service, he was vice-president of the State Board of Charities from 1903 to 1913, and was a faithful and influential member of the Board until 1918. He was president of the thirteenth New York State Conference of Charities and Corrections in 1912. From 1918 until his death he lived in quiet retirement, occasionally giving public lectures. In the spare moments of his busy life, Smith found time to contribute numerous articles to medical literature. Among these should be mentioned the monographs, "The Evolution of American Surgery," in J. D. Bryant and A. H. Buck's *American Practice of Surgery* (8 vols., 1906–11), and his "History of Surgery," in T. L. Stedman's *A Reference Handbook of the Medical Sciences* (3rd edition, 8 vols., 1913–17). A vivid description of some of Smith's public health work may be found in his *The City that Was* (1911), and in *Who is Insane* (1916). For thirty years he was the New York correspondent of the London *Lancet*. The splendid care he took of his delicate constitution in youth helped to preserve him until he reached nearly the century mark. To the end his intellect remained unclouded and his memory bright. He held himself erect and square-shouldered, never seeming to lose the vitality and energy of his youth. A keen, disciplined mind and a genial sense of humor won him the esteem and admiration of his contemporaries. A painting of him hangs in the New York Academy of Medicine. He was married to Lucy E. Culver of Brooklyn, N. Y., on June 1, 1858. They had nine children, six daughters and three sons. Smith died at the home of his daughter at Montour Falls, N. Y., after a short illness.

[*Who's Who in America*, 1920–21, 1922–23; F. L. Colver, *Colver-Culver Geneal.* (1910); John Shrady, ed., *The Coll. of Physicians and Surgeons, New York* (1903–04, vol. I); F. H. Garrison, "Dr. Stephen Smith," *Annals of Med. Hist.*, Autumn Number, 1917; J. J. Walsh, *Hist. of Med. in N. Y.* (1919), vol. V; "Stephen Smith," *State Service*, June 1918; S. W. Francis, *Biog. Sketches of Distinguished N. Y. Surgeons* (1866); *Stephen Smith, M.D., Addresses in Recognition of his Public Services* (1911); *Dinner in honour of Dr. Stephen Smith* (1911); *N. Y. Times*, Aug. 27, 1922.]
G. L. A.

SMITH, THEODATE LOUISE (Apr. 9, 1859–Feb. 16, 1914), genetic psychologist, was born at Hallowell, Me., the daughter of Thomas and Philomela (Hall) Smith. She received the degrees of B.A., 1882, and M.A., 1884, at Smith College, and the degree of Ph.D. at Yale University, 1896. Before taking her degree at Yale she taught in Gardiner, Me., 1882–84; Brooklyn Heights (N. Y.) Seminary, 1884–86; and Mount Vernon Seminary, Washington, D. C., 1886–89. In 1895–96 she was a student at Clark University. Her special work as a student of child psychology she did at Clark, where she was research assistant to Granville Stanley Hall [*q.v.*] from 1902 to 1909, and lecturer and librarian at the Children's Institute from 1909 to the time of her death. She not only assisted Hall in his pioneer studies in genetic psychology but gave aid to many graduate students. As librarian she brought together a vast number of pamphlets and other publications on child welfare, one of the largest collections of its kind in the world, and made them available to teachers and others. She also did a large amount of independent work, wrote articles for such magazines as the *Pedagogical Seminary* and the *American Journal of Psychology* ("On Muscular Memory," July 1896; "The Psychology of Day Dreams," October 1904; "Note on the Psychology of Shame," April 1915), and collaborated with Hall in his *Aspects of Child Life* (1907).

Her most noteworthy contribution was her interpretation of Dr. Maria Montessori's psychology and methods of child-training, which she studied in Rome. In *The Montessori System in Theory and Practice; An Introduction to the Pedagogic Methods of Mme. Montessori* (1912) she explained Mme. Montessori's practical methods of will-training and called attention to her indebtedness to Edouard Seguin [*q.v.*], the great master in the training of the feebleminded. Doing her work in the scientific study of children at a time when rash practical applications based on unverified inferences were likely to be made, she not only took a sane view of the results in this new subject but applied them with caution, common sense, and an appreciation of their wider relationships. Of her Dr. Hall wrote, "As a scholar, thoroughgoing and widely read; as a psychologist and student of childhood, sane and conservative; as a teacher, clear and straightforward; as a colleague, modest, helpful and generous; one did not always realize the scope of her accomplishments on account of the fact that her training was so well balanced" (*Pedagogical Seminary, post*, p. 160).

[*Pedagogical Seminary*, Mar. 1914; *Smith Alumnae Quart.*, Apr. 1914; tribute by G. Stanley Hall, in *Scientific Papers of Theodate L. Smith* (1906–14), vol. II, Clark Univ. Lib.; *Obit. Record Grads. Yale Univ.*

(1914); obituary in *Boston Transcript*, Feb. 16, 1914; date of birth supplied by the registrar of Smith Coll.]

W. H. B.

SMITH, TRUMAN (Nov. 27, 1791–May 3, 1884), lawyer, congressman, was born at Roxbury, Conn., the eldest child of Phineas and Deborah Ann (Judson) Smith and a descendant of John Smith who was in Lancaster, Mass., as early as 1653. Two of his uncles, Nathan and Nathaniel Smith [*qq.v.*], were lawyers and members of Congress, and it is reasonable to suppose that their careers determined the direction of his ambitions. He was reared on his father's farm and completed his preparation for college under the Rev. Daniel Parker. In 1815 he was graduated from Yale. After studying at the Litchfield Law School he was admitted to practice in 1818 and gradually won his way to the front rank of the unusually able Litchfield bar.

A habit of cultivating the friendship of all classes laid the foundation of his political career. After an apprenticeship in the state legislature, 1831–32 and 1834, he was elected to the federal House of Representatives in 1838 and served until 1843, and from 1845 to 1849. He was a presidential elector on the Whig ticket in 1844. In the House he was chiefly interested in parliamentary management in behalf of the Whig party, in which activity he was conspicuously successful. He was one of the first of the party leaders to promote the presidential candidacy of Taylor in 1848, and, as the first chairman of the Whig national committee, he directed Taylor's campaign. He declined to accept the reward of appointment as secretary of the interior, preferring to take the seat in the Senate to which he had been elected in 1849.

In accordance with good Whig doctrine he obtained a land grant to assist in the construction of the Sault Sainte Marie canal, and urged the construction of a Pacific railroad "by the central route if possible." In the absorbing controversy over slavery he refused to become a leader either of the "Cotton Whigs" or of the active free-soil men. The sectional question, in his opinion, was "an offensive cesspool." It should be settled, he thought, on the basis of the climate and topography of the regions into which it was proposed to extend slavery. On most yea and nay votes he followed the predominant views of his own section. He vigorously opposed bills to grant $100,000 to Dr. W. T. G. Morton [*q.v.*] for having introduced anaesthesia in surgical operations, and in 1853 published *An Examination of the Question of Anaesthesia* (reprinted in later editions under various titles), in which he sought to prove that credit for prior discovery and application belonged to Dr. Horace Wells [*q.v.*] of Hartford. His speeches were straightforward presentations of facts, with sensible estimates of the effects of pending measures. He was at his best in informal colloquies.

On May 24, 1854, he resigned his seat for financial reasons and opened a law office in New York, commuting from Stamford, Conn. He appeared in a number of important cases, but resumed practice too late in life to attain the same relative rank as in his earlier professional career. In July 1862 President Lincoln appointed him a judge of the mixed court set up by the treaty with England of Apr. 7, 1862, for the trial of British and American vessels suspected of engaging in the slave trade. He served until the court was terminated in 1870. In the fall of 1872 he retired from active practice. He was twice married: first, June 2, 1832, to Maria Cook of Litchfield; she died in April 1849, and on Nov. 7, 1850, he married Mary A. Dickinson. By his first marriage he had a son and two daughters, and by his second, six sons; one of his daughters became the second wife of Orville H. Platt [*q.v.*].

[*Biog. Dir. Am. Cong.* (1928); W. R. Cutter and others, *Geneal. and Family Hist. of the State of Conn.* (1911), vol. II; William Cothren, *Hist. of Ancient Woodbury*, vol. I (1854); F. B. Dexter, *Biog. Sketches Grads. Yale Coll.*, vol. VI (1912); E. W. Leavenworth, *A Geneal. of the Leavenworth Family* (1873); D. C. Kilbourn, *The Bench and Bar of Litchfield County, Conn.* (1909); some MSS. in Lib. of Cong.]

E. C. S.

SMITH, URIAH (May 2, 1832–Mar. 6, 1903), religious leader, editor, was born in West Wilton, N. H., the son of Samuel and Rebekah (Spaulding) Smith, and the great-grandson of Uriah Smith, who was in Wilton as early as 1778. Samuel was a highway builder and contractor. As a youth of twelve, Uriah came into contact with William Miller [*q.v.*] and his followers, who expected Christ's return to earth on Oct. 22, 1844, and the religious excitement of those days made a profound impression on him. His mother embraced the views taught by the Adventists and continually strove to guide her children into a deep Christian experience. In early boyhood Uriah contracted a sickness resulting in a "fever sore" on his left leg above the knee, which, when he was fourteen, necessitated amputation of the leg. He studied at the academy at Hancock, N. H. (1846–47) and at Phillips Academy, Exeter (1848–51). Because of financial reverses which his father experienced, he was forced to relinquish his plan for a college education.

In the meantime his sister Annie had begun work in the office of the *Advent Review and Sabbath Herald,* a struggling little weekly, then being published at Saratoga, N. Y. In 1852 it was moved to Rochester and the following year Uriah also entered its employ. For their services they received only their board, room, and clothes. In 1855 the paper was again moved, this time to Battle Creek, Mich., and Smith became editor. With one slight interruption he continued in charge of it until 1898, and his editorial connection was not broken until his death. Under his direction it developed into a healthy church organ representing a growing constituency which numbered at his death over a hundred thousand. On June 7, 1857, he married Harriet Newell Stevens, an assistant in his office.

In addition to his editorial work, Smith played an important rôle in the organization of the Seventh-Day Adventist denomination. He was one of those who advocated the establishment of a General Conference, and upon its organization in 1863 he was made secretary. This important office he also filled on four subsequent occasions, serving twenty years in all. In 1874 he was ordained to the ministry and labored much in camp meetings and conferences from the Atlantic to the Pacific. Upon the establishment of Battle Creek College that same year he became lecturer on the Bible there. In 1877, in connection with editorial attention he was giving to *The Signs of the Times,* a newly founded Adventist paper on the Pacific coast, he established a Biblical Institute at Oakland, Cal., for the training of young ministers. As a General Conference official and editor of the church organ, he had a prominent part in the founding of the well-known Battle Creek Sanitarium.

Although his days were filled with various duties, he found time between nine in the evenings and midnight to write books. His most important work, perhaps, was *Thoughts Critical and Practical on the Book of Daniel and the Revelation* (1873); expanded and reprinted in 1882, and issued in subsequent editions. Another of his widely read works was *The Marvel of Nations* (1887), a history of the United States as an Adventist phenomenon. Among his other publications were *The Testimony of the Bible on the State of the Dead* (1873); *Modern Spiritualism* (1896); and *Here and Hereafter* (1897). Some of his poems appear along with his sister's in the volume published by their mother, *Poems: With a Sketch of the Life and Experiences of Annie R. Smith* (1871).

By trade Smith was a wood engraver. He had a mechanical turn of mind which enabled him to make some practical inventions. Since his cork leg caused him considerable difficulty in kneeling in prayer, he constructed an improved wooden

leg with movable foot. For this he received a patent (No. 39,361), July 28, 1863, and with the income he derived from the invention he bought a house. Later he invented a school desk with folding seat. In 1894, in the interests of his paper he visited Europe and the Near East. While in Syria he contracted a fever from the effects of which he never fully recovered. He died at Battle Creek, survived by his wife and five children.

[A. A. Livermore and Samuel Putnam, *Hist. of the Town of Wilton . . . N. H.* (1888); Harold Lincoln, "Uriah Smith," MS. in Union Coll. Lib., Lincoln, Nebr.; J. N. Loughborough, *Rise and Progress of the Seventh-Day Adventists* (1892); M. E. Olsen, *A Hist. of the Origin and Progress of Seventh-Day Adventists* (copr. 1925); *Advent Rev. and Sabbath Herald* files, 1851–1903; *Mich. Pioneer Colls.,* II (1880), 214–15, III (1881), 353, 363; *Detroit Free Press,* and *Detroit Tribune,* Mar. 7, 1903.]   E. N. D.

SMITH, WALTER INGLEWOOD (July 10, 1862–Jan. 27, 1922), congressman, jurist, was born in Council Bluffs, Iowa, the son of George Francis Smith, a building contractor, and Sarah Henrietta (Forrest). Having graduated from high school at the age of fifteen, he entered Park College, Parkville, Mo., but soon had to leave because of illness. During the following year he taught a country school and then began the study of law in the office of D. B. Dailey at Council Bluffs. Admitted to the bar in December 1882, before he was of legal age, he at once became a partner of his tutor. On July 10, 1890, he married Effie M. Moon, by whom he had four children. By November of the same year he had achieved sufficient professional distinction to be elected judge in the fifteenth judicial district of Iowa, to which office he was twice reëlected.

On Sept. 1, 1900, he resigned to accept the Republican nomination for the office of representative from the ninth congressional district, a position left vacant by the appointment of Smith McPherson [*q.v.*] to a federal judgeship. He won the seat for the unexpired term and was reëlected for the regular term by decisive majorities. Beginning his congressional career on Dec. 3, 1900, he served continuously until Mar. 15, 1911. Although he was on several special committees, including one to investigate the practice of hazing at West Point, he concentrated his attention mainly upon the work of the appropriations committee, of which he became a member in the Fifty-eighth Congress. For a number of years his chief activity was in connection with the fortifications appropriation bill. During his last term, as a member of the reorganized rules committee, he had a prominent part in the "revolution" of 1910. Even in his first term, Smith was acknowledged to be one of the ablest members of the Iowa delegation which had "a national reputation for strong men" (*Register and Leader,* Des Moines, July 24, 1902). He was not widely known at home, however. In the bitterly factional Republican state convention of 1901, though at first howled down, he later made such a sensible, good-humored speech that he won general admiration (*Dubuque Daily Times,* Aug. 8, 1901). The next year he was made temporary chairman and accomplished the difficult task of stating a tariff policy that was acceptable to both the conservatives and progressives (*Register and Leader,* Des Moines, July 31, 1902).

The elevation of Willis Van Devanter to the United States Supreme Court in December 1910, created a vacancy on the bench of the circuit court of appeals in the eighth circuit. Most of the Iowa congressional delegation signed a petition indorsing Smith for the position. Meanwhile, the Iowa legislature was deadlocked in the choice of a successor to J. P. Dolliver [*q.v.*] in the United States Senate, and Smith was mentioned for that office if insurgent opposition to his judicial appointment should develop (*Washington Post,* Jan. 18, 23, 1911). President Taft, however, was known to consider him qualified for the highest judicial position (*Shenandoah World,* Iowa, Jan. 28, 1922), and his appointment was confirmed on Jan. 31, 1911. His work on the federal bench was characterized by the same legal ability, honest judgment, and common sense that he exhibited throughout his public career. Though he rarely dissented, he wrote his share of the opinions of the court. Probably one of the most significant was his closely reasoned distinction between civil and criminal contempt of court (*Merchants' Stock and Grain Company* vs. *Chicago Board of Trade,* 201 *Federal Reporter,* 20). With the decision which held the Iowa sterilization act unconstitutional as applied to criminals he concurred, not because cruel and unusual punishment would be inflicted, but on the more technical ground of denial of due process (*Davis* vs. *Berry,* 216 *Federal Reporter,* 413). Since he dealt almost exclusively with appeals, it was natural that his judgments should be legalistic. Smith died at Council Bluffs of apoplexy, after a lingering illness.

[*Congressional Record,* 1900–11 ; *Federal Reporter,* 1911–22; H. H. Field, and J. R. Reed, *Hist. of Pottawattamie County, Iowa* (1907), I, 258, 259; *Proc. . . . Iowa State Bar Asso.,* 1922; Johnson Brigham, *Iowa: Its Hist. and Its Foremost Citizens* (1915), vol. II ; *Who's Who in America,* 1920–21 ; *Biog. Dir. Am. Cong.* (1928) ; *Des Moines Capital,* Feb. 1, 1922 ; *Dubuque Times-Journal,* Jan. 27, 1922.]   J. E. B.

SMITH, WILLIAM (Oct. 8, 1697–Nov. 22, 1769), jurist, was born at Newport-Pagnell, Buckinghamshire, England, the eldest son of Thomas and Susanna (Odell) Smith. His father, a tallow chandler, brought his family to New York in 1715, and shortly afterward William entered Yale College. He was graduated in 1719 and received the master's degree three years later, distinguishing himself as a scholar in Hebrew, classical languages, and theology. From October 1722 to April 1724 he served as a tutor at Yale.

Though admitted to the bar in 1724, Smith soon supplemented his colonial legal training by attendance at the Inns of Court, being admitted to Gray's Inn in 1727. On his return to America, he established a lucrative practice in New York City and attained considerable eminence at the bar, identifying himself throughout his career with the radical Presbyterian faction in provincial litigation and politics. The most noted cases with which he was associated were those in which he sought to curb the governor's prerogative. In 1733, in conjunction with James Alexander [*q.v.*], he was retained by Rip Van Dam [*q.v.*] to defend the action for a division of the emoluments of office brought by Gov. William Cosby [*q.v.*] before the judges of the supreme court sitting on the equity side of the exchequer. Smith at once proceeded to attack the legality of the court, and was sustained by Chief Justice Lewis Morris [*q.v.*], Justices James De Lancey [*q.v.*] and Philipse dissenting. Action was blocked; no decision on Cosby's claim was reached, but the efforts of the opposition to get rid of the court of exchequer continued unabated. On the strength of petitions from Queens and Westchester counties that courts might be established only by statute, William Smith and Joseph Murray, an eminent legal contemporary, were called before the Assembly in 1734 to argue the question of the legality of that court as established by the prerogative. Smith's learned plea (*Mr. Smith's Opinion Humbly Offered in General Assembly of the Colony of New York,* 1734) that both English and colonial courts rested upon statutory authority seems, at least on the colonial side, the more convincing, although Sir John Randolph, who agreed with Smith, was quick to point out that both parties had fallen into a common error in regard to the extension of British statutes to the plantations (William Smith, *History of New York,* 1829, I, 314–15, note).

In the feud between the Cosby and Morris factions, Smith was one of the stalwarts of the latter group and was associated with the founding of Peter Zenger's opposition paper, the *New York Weekly Journal*. It was thus only natural that in 1735 Smith, joined with Alexander, should appear in the supreme court to defend Zenger in his trial for seditious libel. Both attorneys at once attacked the validity of the appointment of De Lancey and Philipse as judges on the ground that their commissions were granted during pleasure and contrary to legal precedent. For this they were disbarred (Livingston Rutherfurd, *John Peter Zenger*, 1904, pp. 173–90); but they countered with a petition to the Assembly stating their grievances, which they followed up by personal pleas before the committee of the Assembly. Two years later the decree against them was set aside by the court and they were readmitted to practice.

Smith continued his fight against the prerogative party, and, in 1737, in the election dispute between Garret Van Horne and Adolph Philipse, challenged the latter's seating on the ground that Jews had been permitted to vote for him, whereas, he claimed, history and theology denied them the franchise. Although unsuccessful in preventing the seating of Philipse, his argument was followed by a resolution of the Assembly that the Jews "ought not to be admitted to vote for representatives in this colony" (*Journal of the General Assembly*, 1764, I, 712; Smith, *History*, 1829, II, 38–40).

Smith was associated as counsel in many of the leading cases in the mayor's court of New York City, frequently acted as proctor in admiralty, and practised extensively in neighboring colonies, serving in 1743–44 as counsel for Connecticut in a case against the Mohegan Indians (*Documents, post*, VI, 258). He was appointed attorney-general in 1751 and served one year, but was not confirmed by the royal authorities (*Ibid.*, VI, 737, 766). He was a member of the Provincial Council from 1753 to 1767, and as such attended the Albany Congress in 1754, being one of the members of the committee that formulated the plan of union, which he strongly advocated (*Ibid.*, 853, 860). In this same year he served as commissioner in the boundary controversy between New York and Massachusetts. He declined the office of chief justice of New York in 1760, but became an associate justice of the supreme court in 1763, and held office until his death. In this capacity, in the case of *Cunningham* vs. *Forsey* (1764), he stoutly denied the right of appeal in questions of fact, taking the popular position, bitterly opposed by Colden, but subsequently affirmed on appeal (*Ibid.*, VII, 685; *Acts of the Privy Council of England, Colonial Series*, IV, 1911, p. 740).

One of the few college-trained members of the early New York bar, Smith took a leading rôle in behalf of public education. He was associated with the founding of the first public school in New York in 1732, was one of the incorporators of the College of New Jersey, is believed to have been largely responsible for the phraseology of its first two charters (John Maclean, *History of the College of New Jersey*, 1877, I, 87), and was a founder and trustee of the New York Society Library (A. B. Keep, *The Library in Colonial New York*, 1909, p. 163). Foremost among the proponents of a non-sectarian college in New York, Smith vigorously protested against the establishment of King's College under Episcopalian auspices (Herbert and Carol Schneider, *Samuel Johnson . . . His Career and Writings*, 1929, IV, 208–12).

Smith was twice married: first, May 11, 1727, to Mary, daughter of René and Blanche (Du Bois) Het, by whom he had fifteen children, including William, 1728–1793 [*q.v.*], and Joshua Hett, whose career became tangled in the skein of Benedict Arnold's treason; and secondly to Elizabeth (Scott) Williams, widow of the Rev. Elisha Williams [*q.v.*], fourth rector of Yale College, and daughter of the Rev. Thomas Scott of Nithern, Herefordshire, England. By this second marriage there was no issue.

[Printed materials include *The New-York Gazette, or the Weekly Post-Boy*, Nov. 27, 1769; M. L. Delafield, "William Smith," *Mag. of Am. Hist.*, June 1881; E. A. Jones, *Am. Members of the Inns of Court* (1924); F. B. Dexter, *Biog. Sketches Grads. Yale Coll.*, vol. I (1885); *N. Y. Geneal. and Biog. Record*, Apr. 1873, Jan. 1879, July 1880; E. B. O'Callaghan, *Docs. Rel. to the Col. Hist. of the State of N. Y.*, vols. VI–VII (1855); I. N. P. Stokes, *The Iconography of Manhattan Island*, vol. IV (1922). Smith's pleadings in the Mayor's Court are available in the court files in the office of the Commissioner of Records, New York City.]
R. B. M.

SMITH, WILLIAM (Sept. 7, 1727–May 14, 1803), educator, clergyman, first provost of the College, Academy, and Charitable School of Philadelphia, was born in Aberdeen, Scotland, the son of Thomas Smith, a gentleman of means, and Elizabeth (Duncan) Smith. After attending the parish school he was taken in charge by the Society for the Education of Parochial Schoolmasters and educated under its care until 1741, when he entered the University of Aberdeen, from which he graduated A.M. in 1747. The next few years he seems to have spent in London as agent of the Society that had sponsored him, and also, for a time, as agent of the Society for the Propagation of the Gospel.

On Mar. 3, 1751, he sailed for New York as tutor to two sons of Colonel Martin of Long Island, who were returning to their native country. He was a member of the Martin household until August 1753, during which time he prepared and published *A General Idea of the College of Mirania . . .* (1753), addressed particularly to the trustees nominated by the legislature to receive proposals relating to the establishment of a college in New York. In it he outlined the kind of institution he thought best adapted to the circumstances of a new country. The making of good men and good citizens was to be its chief objective; history, agriculture, and religion were to be most emphasized; and it was to embrace a school to meet the needs of those who were to follow the "mechanic profession," for whom time spent on the learned languages would be thrown away. Smith sent a copy of his pamphlet to Benjamin Franklin and to the Rev. Richard Peters [*qq.v.*], trustees of the Academy and Charitable School, Philadelphia. Franklin wrote Smith, expressing interest in his ideas. Accordingly, the young man visited Philadelphia, with the result that he was invited to connect himself with the Academy. So impressed with the institution was he that he addressed to the trustees *A Poem on Visiting the Academy of Philadelphia, June 1753* (1753). Before entering upon his duties, he went back to England and was ordained deacon in the Established Church on Dec. 21, 1753; two days later he was elevated to the priesthood.

On his return to Philadelphia in May of the year following, he at once became teacher of logic, rhetoric, and natural and moral philosophy in the Academy. From that time until the Revolution he was the dominant influence in its affairs. In December 1754 the trustees requested Smith and Francis Alison [*q.v.*], the rector, to prepare a clause to be incorporated in the charter, empowering the Academy to grant degrees. They drew up what was practically a new charter, adding the word college to the title of the institution, and providing for a provost and vice-provost. The charter was approved and went into effect the next year, and Smith became provost of the College, Academy and Charitable School of Philadelphia. In 1756, he presented to the trustees at their request a curriculum, prepared some two years before, which was one of the most comprehensive schemes of education which up to that time had been devised for any American college.

His duties as provost and teacher, however, offered insufficient scope for his talents and ambitions. These required a large stage upon which he could play many parts. Accordingly, as time went on, his influence came to be felt in all the affairs of the province—social, religious, scientific, literary, and political. When in England for his ordination, he had addressed a long communication to the Society for the Propagation of the Gospel regarding the need of affording the Germans in Pennsylvania such educational facilities as would make them one with the other people. As a result, the Society appointed certain American gentlemen a board of trustees to establish and manage schools where the Germans were principally settled. Smith was made secretary of the board, and was active in its work. He was a member and official of the Masonic order, to which many of Philadelphia's most noted citizens belonged. An ardent churchman, he was prominent in ecclesiastical matters and in constant communication with Church officials in England. He strongly favored the appointment of an American bishop and undoubtedly hoped to occupy that position himself. Politically, he was a friend of the Penns and a leading supporter of the proprietary interests, by this affiliation, as well as by other actions, incurring the bitter enmity of Franklin. During the French and Indian War, he publicly condemned the Assembly for its failure to adopt aggressive military measures, publishing in 1755 *A Brief State of the Province of Pennsylvania.* As an easy plan to restore quiet and defeat the ambitions of the French, he suggested requiring members of the Assembly to take an oath of allegiance to the king declaring they would not refuse to defend their country against all his enemies, withdrawing the right to vote from the Germans until they were better acquainted with the English language, and forbidding the publication of any newspaper or periodical in a foreign tongue. The pamphlet drew forth caustic replies and in 1756 Smith published *A Brief View of the Conduct of Pennsylvania in 1755.* His enemies assailed his character in the newspapers, and accused him of teaching what was inconsistent with the charter of the college and even with religion itself. A committee appointed by the trustees of the College, July 5, 1756, investigated the charges and completely exonerated the provost.

Partly because of his interest in literature, but more especially to provide himself with a political weapon, Smith established in 1757 *The American Magazine and Monthly Chronicle of the British Colonies,* published by William Bradford, 1722–1791 [*q.v.*]. It supported the Crown against France and the interests of the Penns against the Quakers and Franklin, but also contained scientific and religious articles and papers on miscellaneous subjects. It was particularly notable for its encouragement of poetry, among its contributors being Francis Hopkinson, the younger Thomas Godfrey, and James Sterling

354

[*qq.v.*]. The genius of young Benjamin West [*q.v.*], also, was first announced to the public through this publication. Smith himself wrote for the magazine a series of papers entitled "The Hermit," and signed Theodore, which were religious in character. The periodical was issued for only a year, however, since in December 1758 Smith's political troubles compelled him to sail for England.

These troubles arose from his association with William Moore, 1699–1783 [*q.v.*], a Pennsylvania judge and an advocate of more aggressive opposition to the French. Moore had been charged with unjust and extortionate behavior in office, and the Assembly had petitioned Gov. William Denny to remove him. In reply, after the Assembly had adjourned, Moore presented a memorial to the governor which characterized the Assembly's petition as virulent and slanderous. It was published in the *Pennsylvania Gazette* and *Pennsylvania Journal,* and at Smith's behest translated and printed in a German paper, which he had been instrumental in establishing in connection with his educational work for the Germans. The next Assembly ordered the arrest of both Moore and Smith, which was effected Jan. 6, 1758. Smith was later brought before the bar of the House, charged with promoting and publishing seditious libels, and convicted. He was ordered committed to jail and confined until he had made satisfaction. He remained there until after the Assembly had adjourned, being released by order of the supreme court on Apr. 11; in the meantime he had taught his classes at the jail. On June 3, he married Moore's daughter, Rebecca. In September he was arrested for a second time and kept in jail until the House was dissolved. During his first confinement he had appealed to the King, and early in December 1758 he sailed for England to prosecute the appeal. Here his writings and activities had brought him into great favor. The Archbishop of Canterbury and several bishops recommended him to Oxford for the degree of D.D., which the University conferred; he also received the same degree from the University of Aberdeen. The law officers of the Crown, after hearing his case, reported to the Lords of the Committee for Plantation Affairs that in their opinion Moore's address was a libel, but that since it was published after the Assembly adjourned, no subsequent Assembly had a right to consider the offense. This opinion was approved by the Privy Council.

Vindicated in his contention that his arrest had been illegal, Smith was back in Philadelphia on May 3, 1759. In February 1762, however, he again sailed for England and was away from home more than two years engaged in collecting funds for the College. This work, in which he was highly successful, was carried on jointly with James Jay [*q.v.*] under a royal brief authorizing them both to solicit subscriptions, Jay being in England at that time in the interests of King's College, New York. The funds they secured were divided between the two institutions. While he was abroad, 1763, the University of Dublin honored Smith with the degree of doctor of divinity. Upon his return he speedily resumed his various activities. At the request of Henry Bouquet [*q.v.*] and from facts supplied by him he prepared *An Historical Account of the Expedition Against the Ohio Indians in 1764* (1765), which attained much popularity abroad. From 1766 to 1777 he acted as rector of Trinity Church, Oxford, Pa. He was elected a member of the American Philosophical Society, Jan. 2, 1768, and the following year was associated with David Rittenhouse [*q.v.*] and John Lukens at the former's Norriton observatory in observing the transit of Venus. The approach of the Revolution placed him in an embarrassing predicament. He opposed the Stamp Act as "contrary to the faith of charters and the inherent rights of Englishmen," but he did not favor independence. His *Sermon on the Present Situation of American Affairs* (1775), preached at Christ Church, Philadelphia, June 28, 1775, before Congress, created a great sensation. It went through many editions and was translated into several foreign languages. It opposed British measures and awakened patriotism, but in its preface Smith professed himself as "ardently panting for a return of those Halcyon-days of harmony" and as "animated with purest zeal for the mutual interests of Great-Britain and the Colonies." He is credited, moreover, with the authorship of *Plain Truth; Addressed to the Inhabitants of America* . . . (1776) and *Additions to Plain Truth* . . . (1776), signed Candidus, which endeavored to show that "American independence is as illusory, ruinous, and impracticable, as a liberal reconciliation with Great Britain is safe, honorable, and expedient." When General Howe was advancing on Philadelphia he was among those ordered apprehended because of conduct and conversation inimical to the American cause. He gave his parole and retired to Barbados Island, which belonged to an estate he had purchased on the Schuylkill. After the evacuation of the city he returned to Philadelphia and set to work rehabilitating the College.

In 1779 the General Assembly appointed a committee to examine into the state of the College. A majority of this committee reported that the corporation had shown hostility to the government and constitution of the State and that the original principle of the institution, which required it to afford equal privileges to all religious denominations, had not been observed. Accordingly, on Nov. 27, 1779, the Assembly passed an act making void the charter of the College and creating a new corporation to be known as the Trustees of the University of the State of Pennsylvania. Smith's activities were now transferred to Maryland. He became rector of Chester Parish, Chestertown, Kent County, and established Kent School, which had 142 pupils in 1782, when it was chartered as Washington College with Smith as president. Always successful as a money-raiser, he secured more than £10,-000 for the new institution. He was president of every convention of the Episcopal churches of Maryland during his residence there, and was invariably sent as a delegate to the General Conventions, where he was one of the leaders in the organization of the Protestant Episcopal Church. As chairman of the committee appointed in 1785 to adapt the prayer book to American conditions, he performed much of the work. His ambition to be bishop was never realized, however. The Maryland Convention of 1783 elected him to that office, but the General Convention did not confirm the election. For its failure to do so there were probably several reasons, but the decisive one, doubtless, was that given by the church historian Perry. Writing of the convention of representatives of the Church held in New York, October 1784, over which Smith presided, he says: "It was at this very convention, that he was destined, alas! to make shipwreck of a lifetime's honors, and by a public indulgence . . . in intemperate habits to close to himself the coveted episcopate none labored more to secure" (post, II, 29). He was opposed, Perry adds, by his oldest pupils and his dearest friends.

During his residence in Maryland, Smith had kept in close touch with Philadelphia and labored to have the rights of the old College restored. Finally, his efforts and those of others were successful, the Assembly on Mar. 6, 1789, declaring the act of 1779 repugnant to justice and restoring the former charter with all its privileges. In July Smith resumed his position as provost. The University of the State of Pennsylvania still existed, however, and on Sept. 31, 1791, the two were united, John Ewing [q.v.] becoming provost of the new institution. On Mar. 1 of that year, in behalf of the American Philosophical Society, Smith, ironically enough, had delivered an oration on the death of Franklin, in the German Lutheran Church, before the members of Congress and a great gathering of notable personages. According to a family tradition, his daughter Rebecca said to him afterward, "I don't think you believed more than one tenth part of what you said of Old Ben Lightning Rod" (H. W. Smith, post, II, 344) ; Smith made no reply. He spent the most of his remaining days on his estate at the Falls of the Schuylkill, engaged more or less in land speculation and in advocating the development of canal navigation in Pennsylvania. At the time of his death he was preparing his writings for publication in five volumes, two of which appeared in 1803. He died at the home of a daughter-in-law in Philadelphia, survived by five children.

In spite of the responsibilities that were intrusted to him and the honors he received, he never enjoyed the highest respect and confidence of many of his noted contemporaries. While this fact may be attributed in part to political and ecclesiastical differences, it was undoubtedly due, also, to defects in Smith's character. Upon meeting him for the first time, John Adams wrote, "There is an appearance of art" (C. F. Adams, The Works of John Adams, vol. II, 1850, p. 360). Learned and righteous Ezra Stiles [q.v.] had nothing but contempt for him. "Dr. Smith," he recorded in his diary, "is a haughty, self-opinionated, half-learned Character"; and on another occasion, "His moral character is very exceptionable and unbecoming a Minister of Christ, & it is even a doubt whether he is a Believer of Revelation. He is infamous for religious Hypocrisy" (F. B. Dexter, The Literary Diary of Ezra Stiles, 1901, vol. III, p. 350; vol. II, p. 528). Dr. Benjamin Rush [q.v.], who knew him well and attended him in his last illness, left a vivid portrait of him. "Unhappily," Rush says, "his conduct in all his relations and situations was opposed to his talents and profession. His person was slovenly and his manners awkward and often offensive in company . . . he early contracted a love for strong drink and became toward the close of his life an habitual drunkard. . . . His temper was irritable . . . and when angry he swore in the most extravagant manner. He seldom paid a debt without being sued or without a quarrel, he was extremely avaricious. . . . On his death bed he never spoke upon any subject connected with religion . . . nor was there a Bible or Prayer Book ever seen in his room. . . . He descended to his grave . . . without being lamented by a human creature. . . . From the absence of all his children not a drop of kindred blood attended his funeral" (A Memorial Containing Travels Through Life or Sundry In-

cidents in the Life of Dr. Benjamin Rush, 1905, pp. 175–79).

With all his faults, however, he was one of the ablest, most versatile, and most influential Pennsylvanians of his day. Rush himself admits that Smith possessed "genius, taste, and learning." He was a clear, forceful writer and an eloquent public speaker. The importance of his service for practically a quarter of a century during the formative period of what is now the University of Pennsylvania is incalculable, and his contribution to education in general, not inconsiderable. He imparted literary enthusiasm to a notable group of young men, aided in the publication of their work, and helped to make Philadelphia a literary center. Notwithstanding his Loyalist tendencies, he was an ardent supporter of liberty, and his political activities, while not uninfluenced by personal motives, were in the main directed by a passion for the best interests of his state and the country. Though more interested in its temporal than in its spiritual condition, he played no insignificant part in the organization of the Protestant Episcopal Church, the name of which he is said to have suggested.

[H. W. Smith, *Life and Correspondence of the Rev. William Smith, D.D.* (2 vols., 1880), is the best single source, but presents all Smith's activities in the most favorable light; for discussion of the Moore-Smith libel on the Assembly, consult W. R. Riddell, in *Pa. Mag. of Hist. and Biog.*, Apr., July, Oct. 1928; see, also, C. J. Stillé, *A Memoir of the Rev. William Smith, D.D.* (1869); J. L. Chamberlain, *Universities and Their Sons: Univ. of Pa.* (1901); F. N. Thorpe, *Benjamin Franklin and the Univ. of Pa.* (1893); H. M. Lippincott, *The Univ. of Pa.: Franklin's Coll.* (1919); W. B. Sprague, *Annals of the Am. Pulpit*, vol. V (1859); W. S. Perry, *The Hist. of the Am. Episcopal Church* (1885); C. C. Tiffany, *A Hist. of the Protestant Episcopal Church in the U. S. of America* (1895); J. T. Scharf, *Hist. of Md.* (1879); E. P. Oberholtzer, *The Lit. Hist. of Phila.* (copr. 1906); A. H. Smyth, *The Phila. Magazines* (1892); F. L. Mott, *A Hist. of Am. Magazines, 1741–1850* (1930); L. N. Richardson, *A Hist. of Early Am. Magazines, 1741–1789* (1931).]

H. E. S.

SMITH, WILLIAM (June 25, 1728–Dec. 3, 1793), jurist, historian, Loyalist, was born in New York City, the eldest son of William, 1697–1769 [*q.v.*], and Mary (Het) Smith. His legal career closely paralleled his father's. He attended Yale College, from which he was graduated in 1745, studied law in his father's office with Whitehead Hicks and William Livingston [*q.v.*], and was admitted to the bar in 1750. With Livingston as his partner, he soon established himself as a leading practitioner in the mayor's court, supreme court, and Court of Vice-Admiralty. In 1752 he and Livingston, at the request of the Assembly, published the first digest of the colony statutes in force at that time, *Laws of New York from the Year 1691 to 1751, Inclusive*; ten years

later a second volume, *Laws of New York . . . 1752–1762* (1762), appeared. Smith was concerned as counsel in some of the most important litigation in the middle colonies. One notable instance was his appearance in 1771 in behalf of Lord Dunmore in his suit against Lieut.-Gov. Cadwallader Colden [*q.v.*] for an accounting of the governor's emoluments (*Collections of the New York Historical Society, Publication Fund Series*, LVI, 1925, pp. 172–82; E. B. O'Callaghan, *Documents Relative to the Colonial History of the State of New York*, vol. VIII, 1857, p. 257). He was one of the founders and vice-president of The Moot, a select organization of the principal New York lawyers formed in 1770 for the discussion of legal problems (Moot Court Minutes, MS., New York Historical Society). His legal papers abundantly testify to his scholarship.

Prior to the Revolution Smith was a leader of the Whig Presbyterian forces in New York. With William Livingston and John Morin Scott [*q.v.*] he was one of the chief contributors to the *Independent Reflector*, 1752–53, and the *Occasional Reverberator*, September-October 1753 (see L. N. Richardson, *A History of Early American Magazines, 1741–1789*, 1931, pp. 78–84, 87–91). In 1757 the three collaborators published *A Review of the Military Operations in North America . . . 1753 . . . 1756* (reprinted in *Collections of the Massachusetts Historical Society*, 1 ser. VII, 1801). This was a defense of Gov. William Shirley [*q.v.*] of Massachusetts and contained a series of attacks on James De Lancey, Thomas Pownall, and Sir William Johnson [*qq.v.*]. Smith's chief literary contribution was *The History of the Province of New-York, from the First Discovery to the Year M.DCC. XXXII*, published in London in 1757; it was reissued in 1814, with a continuation, attributed to J. V. N. Yates, and was reprinted again, with Smith's own continuation bringing the narrative down to 1762, by the New York Historical Society in 1829, under the title, *The History of the Late Province of New York* (2 vols.). It is in large measure a political chronicle of the eighteenth century, probably the most valuable material being contained in an appendix of one hundred pages describing the economic, religious, and legal organization of the province. Smith's narrative is marred by inaccuracies and partisanship, and his adversaries were bitter in their comments. By far the most important part of the chronicle, however, both from the historical and the biographical point of view, was never published. These "Historical Memoirs," now in the New York Public Library, cover the period from the eve of the Revolution to 1783, and comprise six closely written volumes, indispensable to an understanding of New York's position during the Revolution.

Smith's career during the Revolution is unique in the annals of American Loyalism. Though an office-holder under the Crown, having become chief justice of the province in 1763 and succeeded his father as a member of the council in 1767, he was one of the foremost leaders of the popular party and a founder of the Whig Club. When violence broke out, he appears to have taken a position on the fence, gradually leaning toward the Loyalist side, never completely repudiated by the patriots, never completely accepted by his own party (*B. F. Stevens's Facsimiles of MSS. in European Archives Relating to America*, 1889, no. 487, in vol. V; *The Works of John Adams*, vol. II, 1850, pp. 353–54). Despite his anomalous position, he was the recipient of many honors, and therefore the *bête noire* of his envious colleague, Thomas Jones [*q.v.*], whose venomous *History of New York during the Revolutionary War* (edited by E. F. De Lancey, 2 vols., 1879) is devoted in no inconsiderable part to exposing his alleged duplicity. The attempts of his enemies to discredit him included the publication of a letter ascribed to him, later shown to be a forgery, conveying valuable information to General Howe in regard to the plans of the revolutionists (Peter Force, *American Archives*, 4 ser., IV, 1843, col. 1000; *Magazine of American History*, June 1881, pp. 423–24). In drafting the state constitution, the committee of the New York Provincial Convention freely consulted him, and in later years as an exile he claimed credit for influencing the federal constitutional program (Sabine, *post*, II, 312–13), apparently basing his claim on the parliamentary plan of union which he had put forth on the eve of the conflict and consistently advocated thereafter as a solution of the imperial issues (manuscript Diary, V, Oct. 31, 1777, July 17, 1778, July 1, 1780; *History of . . . New York*, 1829, I, xi–xiii). Refusing in 1777 to take the oath of allegiance to the state, he was ordered to Livingston Manor on parole. Refusing again the following year, he was banished by the commissioners for detecting and defeating conspiracies, under the act of June 30, 1778, and returned to New York City (Stokes, *post*, V, 1068, 1069, 1074; *New York Gazette*, Sept. 17, 1778), still maintaining a friendly correspondence with Gov. George Clinton [*q.v.*], although by this time he was confident that the Revolution would fail because of a popular uprising against it. Appointed chief justice of New York on May 4, 1779, to succeed

Daniel Horsmanden [*q.v.*], he took the oath of office in 1780 and strongly urged the restoration of civil government (Diary, VI, Aug. 1–5, 1779; VII, May 27, 1782; Smith MSS., fol. 194). He never actually served as chief justice, since the city remained under military control until the evacuation (Stokes, V, 1074, 1085, 1091, 1108). In the fall of 1780 he was one of the commissioners who visited General Washington in an attempt to save Major André.

On the evacuation of New York in 1783 Smith proceeded to England, remaining there until 1786, when he sailed to Canada to take the post of chief justice, to which he had been appointed on Sept. 1, 1785. This office he held until his death at Quebec, Dec. 3, 1793. Smith was married on Nov. 3, 1752, to Janet Livingston, daughter of James and Maria (Kierstedt) Livingston and first cousin of James Livingston [*q.v.*]. They had eleven children; the only son who survived infancy was William (1769–1847), the Canadian historian and jurist.

[For the unpublished chronicle and diary of Smith and other miscellaneous papers in the New York Public Library, see E. B. Greene and R. B. Morris, *A Guide to the Principal Sources for Early Am. Hist.* (1600–1800) *in the City of New York* (1929), pp. 102–03. Smith's pleadings in the mayor's court and supreme court are available in the office of the Commissioner of Records, New York City. Historians frequently confuse the elder William Smith with his son the historian. Useful biographical material will be found in M. L. Delafield, "William Smith—The Historian," *Mag. of Am. Hist.*, June 1881; Lorenzo Sabine, *Biog. Sketches of the Loyalists of the Am. Rev.* (1864), II, 312–13; F. B. Dexter, *Biog. Sketches Grads. Yale Coll.*, vol. II (1896); B. F. Butler, "Annual Discourse," *Trans. Albany Inst.*, I (1830), 154–56, 207–09; William Smith, "Memoir," prefixed to Smith's *Hist. of the Late Province of New-York* (1829), I, x–xvi. I. N. P. Stokes, *The Iconography of Manhattan Island*, vols. IV–VI (1922–28) makes considerable use of Smith's MSS.]
R. B. M.

SMITH, WILLIAM (c. 1754–Apr. 6, 1821), Episcopal clergyman, was probably born in Aberdeen, Scotland, for he is described as "a fellow countryman and townsman" of Dr. William Smith, 1727–1803 [*q.v.*] of Pennsylvania (H. W. Smith, *Life and Correspondence of the Rev. William Smith*, 1880, II, 274). He received a university education, possibly at Aberdeen, and was ordained in the Scottish Non-juring Episcopal Church before coming to America. From January to July 1785 he was in charge of Trinity Church, Oxford, and All Saints, Pequestan (now a part of Philadelphia). He then became minister of Stepney Parish, Somerset County, Md. Resigning this charge in 1787, he assumed, on July 7, the rectorship of St. Paul's Church, Narragansett, R. I. Ezra Stiles [*q.v.*] in his diary records a visit to his church on Oct. 21, 1788: "The Rev. Mr. Smith, late fr. Scotld., a non-Juror, has been about 1 y. inducted here by Dr. Seabury. He preached on Eccl.—all Vanity. An excellent Sermon" (F. B. Dexter, *The Literary Diary of Ezra Stiles*, 1901, III, 330). In 1789 Smith undertook occasional services at Trinity Church, Newport, and on Jan. 27, 1790, resigned his Narragansett charge to become rector of the Newport church. He was active in the organization of the diocese of Rhode Island, preaching the sermon (*A Discourse at the Opening of the Convention . . . the 18th of November, 1790*) at its first convention.

On Apr. 12, 1797, he resigned the Newport church to become rector of St. Paul's, Norwalk, Conn. That same year, Oct. 18, he preached at the consecration of the Rev. Abraham Jarvis [*q.v.*] as second bishop of Connecticut. The publication of his sermon (*A Discourse . . . Before the Ecclesiastical Convention . . . Assembled . . . To Witness the Consecrating of the Right Rev. Abraham Jarvis, 1797*) led to a controversy on episcopacy with the Rev. Samuel Blatchford, a Congregational minister of Bridgeport, who published *The Validity of Presbyterian Ordination Maintained, in a Letter to the Rev. William Smith, D.D.* (1798). To this Smith replied with *Dr. Smith's Answer to Mr. Blatchford's Letter* (1798). In 1800 Smith disagreed with his Norwalk flock over a proposal made by them that his tenure of office should be determined each year by the congregation, and resigned. He then went to New York City where he opened a grammar school. In 1802 the trustees of the Episcopal Academy at Cheshire, founded by Bishop Seabury, which was then undertaking work of college grade in order to prepare men for the ministry of the Episcopal Church, elected Smith as principal. The academy did not prosper under his direction, however. Following an investigation made by the diocesan convention, he resigned June 5, 1806, and returned to New York, where he engaged in private instruction. Afterwards, returning to Connecticut, he did supply work in various parishes, particularly Milford and West Haven. The frequent changes in Smith's ministerial work suggest that he did not possess the gift of commending himself to the people of his successive cures. The Hon. Gulian C. Verplanck [*q.v.*], who as a youth, in the home of his grandfather, Dr. William Samuel Johnson [*q.v.*], had seen Smith, says of him that he "was a man of extensive and diversified learning, of an ardent and fertile mind, a great and ready command of language, a flow of thought, as well extemporaneously and in conversation as on paper." He had moreover "deep religious feeling, unquestionable zeal and devotion to his duties,

whether in religious or secular instruction, and a frank, kind disposition. Yet, unhappily, he was never successful in either sphere of labour, in any proportion to his ability or acquirements" (Sprague, *post,* p. 346).

Smith was an accomplished musician and published several books intended for the use of organists and church choirs, which had a widespread and salutary influence in the development of church music, particularly in his own communion. Among them was *The Churchman's Choral Companion* (1809). He is said to have built with his own hands several small pipe organs (Updike, *post,* II, 352). His chief production, published in 1814, is entitled *The Reasonableness of Setting Forth the Most Worthy Praise of Almighty God, According to the Usage of the Primitive Church; with Historical Views of the Nature, Origin, and Progress of Metre Psalmody*. It is a refutation of eighteen objections to chanting in churches, and incidentally a violent attack on metre psalmody, the Scottish custom of singing the psalms in metrical and rhythmical versions, then prevailing throughout the Protestant churches of America. It approves, however, hymns such as those contained in the Methodist collection. Among his other publications were *Consolations from Homar, an Hermit of the East* (1789) and *The Convict's Visitor; or, Penitential Offices* (1791), the latter containing suitable devotions for use before or at the time of execution. Perhaps Smith's chief claim to remembrance is that he contributed the "Office of Institution of Ministers" to the Episcopal Book of Common Prayer. He composed this service originally at the request of the clergy of Connecticut where it was first used. Later it was adopted with slight modification by the General Convention of the Church. His wife was Magdalen Milne, by whom he had several children.

[W. B. Sprague, *Annals of the Am. Pulpit*, vol. V (1859); Wilkins Updike, *A Hist. of the Episcopal Church in Narragansett* (3 vols., 1907), ed. by Daniel Goodwin; G. C. Mason, *Annals of Trinity Church, Newport* (1890); E. E. Beardsley, *An Address . . . on Occasion of the Fiftieth Anniversary of the Episcopal Acad. of Conn.* (1844); C. M. Selleck, *Address at the Centenary of St. Paul's Church, Norwalk, Conn.* (1886).]   W. P. L.

SMITH, WILLIAM (*c.* 1762–June 26, 1840), lawyer, United States senator, is said to have been born in North Carolina. He always spoke of himself as a South Carolinian, however, and his grand-daughter believed that a change of boundary lines threw his birthplace in South Carolina into North Carolina (O'Neall, *post,* I, 112). His preliminary training is supposed to have been under the Rev. Mr. Alexander at Bullock's Creek, York County, S. C., and Andrew Jackson and William H. Crawford are said to have been his schoolmates there. It is certain that he knew them both from boyhood. Later he attended Mount Zion Society school at Winnsboro. His early life is reputed to have been "wild, reckless, intemperate, rude and boisterous" (*Ibid.*, I, 107). His reformation was attributed to his wife, Margaret Duff, who was fourteen years old when he married her in 1781; they had one child, a daughter. He studied law in Charleston and was admitted to the bar. Settling in York District, he was speedily successful.

He served in the state Senate, 1802–08, and was president of that body, 1806–08. In the latter year he was elected judge of the constitutional court of appeals. He filled that office with ability until 1816, but gained a reputation for great severity. On Dec. 4, 1816, he was elected by the legislature United States senator to fill the vacancy of John Taylor [*q.v.*] and on the same day was elected for the term beginning Mar. 4, 1817. In the Senate he gained reputation as a powerful speaker, though he was far from being an orator. He was a persistent defender of state rights and slavery and as persistent an opponent of banks, capitalism, internal improvements, and the tariff. The most important of his speeches was that in the Missouri debates, delivered Dec. 18, 1820. By building up a state-rights organization in South Carolina and aligning himself with Crawford in national politics, he won the enmity of Calhoun, who declared him "narrow-minded and . . . wedded to the Georgia politicians," and suggested Hayne as a suitable successor ("Correspondence of John C. Calhoun," *Annual Report of the American Historical Association . . . 1899*, vol. II, 1900, p. 204). Defeated for reëlection in 1823 he returned home, joining with William C. Preston, Thomas Cooper, and Stephen D. Miller [*qq.v.*] in organizing the group of "Radicals" who opposed the nationalism and latitudinarianism of Calhoun. He was elected to the lower house of the state legislature in 1824 and again in 1825, and led the so-called "Revolution" of 1825 by pushing through to passage a series of resolutions declaring a protective tariff and internal improvements unconstitutional.

In 1826 he was again elected by the legislature to the United States Senate to fill a vacancy. He took his seat Dec. 7, and during the four years he served he was twice elected president *pro tem*. In 1829 he declined to accept a proffered appointment to the Supreme Court. During this term he was increasingly a strict constructionist and on Apr. 11, 1828, made an elaborate speech in opposition to the system of in-ternal improvements as extravagant, unequal, and unjust in its operations in different sections, and as a "flagrant outrage . . . to the Constitution." He objected to the word "national" that had "crept into our political vocabulary," and declared it "a term unknown to the origin and theory of our government." On Feb. 10, 1829, he presented the protest of South Carolina against the tariff and in his speech said, "I, as Senator from South Carolina, can never consent to that doctrine, that dangerous principle that a majority shall rule. If a majority is to rule, away with your constitution at once." In 1829 he received the seven electoral votes of Georgia for vice-president.

Smith's state-rights views stopped short of nullification, however, which he thought a remedy as bad as the disease. He opposed a convention as unnecessary since the protective tariff and internal improvements system were, he thought, crumbling to destruction. He was reasonably consistent, but the same group of nationalists, who had thought him too radical in 1823, now, as the leaders of the nullification movement, thought him too broad and national, and in 1830 they secured his defeat for reëlection, Stephen D. Miller replacing him. In November he published a letter "To the Good People of South Carolina" (*Charleston Courier*, Nov. 13, 15, 1830, reprinted from the *Yorkville Pioneer*) against nullification, and was thereafter identified with the Union party as one of its strongest leaders. He hated Calhoun, who, so he said, had "sold the state twice; once for the tariff and again for internal improvements" (O'Neall, *post*, I, 119) and who wanted a grievance rather than tariff reduction. He also resented leadership in the state passing to Calhoun and to Hamilton, Hayne, and McDuffie [*qq.v.*], all of them his juniors, and thus his opposition to nullification was tinged with personal feeling.

In 1831 he was again in the state Senate and there ended his career in South Carolina. He had for years been buying land in the Southwest, and had become very wealthy. In 1833 he moved to Louisiana, and, after a brief residence there, to Huntsville, Ala. In 1836 Jackson again offered him an appointment to the Supreme Court, but he declined. In the same year he was elected to the lower house of the Alabama legislature and served until his death. A Jeffersonian Democrat of the straitest sect, able, industrious, fearless, with none of the evasions of the politician, Smith was a strong and outstanding figure. But he was a bitter and vindictive enemy, witheringly sarcastic and never conciliatory, inclined to be opinionated and prejudiced, and never gained the influence to which his talents and character entitled him.

[*Annals of Cong.*, 1817–1823, 1826–1831; *Jours. of the Senate of S. C.*, 1802–1808, 1831; *Jours. of the House of Representatives of S. C.*, 1824–1825; *Jours. of the House of Representatives of Ala.*, 1836–1839; "Diary of Edward Hooker, 1805–1808," in *Ann. Report of the Am. Hist. Asso., 1896*, vol. I (1897); Dumas Malone, *The Public Life of Thomas Cooper* (1926); B. F. Perry, *Reminiscences of Public Men* (1883); C. S. Boucher, *The Nullification Controversy in S. C.* (1916); J. B. O'Neall, *Biog. Sketches of the Bench and Bar of S. C.* (1859); D. F. Houston, *A Critical Study of Nullification in S. C.* (1896); William Garrett, *Reminiscences of Public Men in Ala.* (1872); Gaillard Hunt, *John C. Calhoun* (1907); W. M. Meigs, *The Life of John Caldwell Calhoun* (1917); *Biog. Dir. Am. Cong.* (1928); *Daily National Intelligencer* (Washington, D. C.), July 14, 1840; *Mobile Daily Commercial Register and Patriot*, July 3, 1840.]

J. G. deR. H.

SMITH, WILLIAM (Sept. 6, 1797–May 18, 1887), congressman, governor of Virginia, Confederate soldier, was born at "Marengo" in King George County, Va., the son of Col. Caleb and Mary Waugh (Smith) Smith. His parents, who were first cousins, claimed descent from Sir Sidney Smith who emigrated from England in the reign of George I. William attended school in King George County and at fourteen, after the death of his mother, was sent to an academy at Plainfield, Conn. Called home in 1812 to prevent his enlistment in the navy, he was sent after the death of his father in 1814 to Nelson's Classical School in Hanover County. He subsequently studied law in Fredericksburg and Warrenton, and spent a few months in the office of Gen. William H. Winder in Baltimore. In 1818 he began practice in Culpeper, and in 1821 was married to Elizabeth H. Bell.

In 1827 he organized a mail-coach service from Fairfax Court House to Culpeper Court House, and by 1834 had established a daily post service from Washington, D. C., to Milledgeville, Ga. From the rapid extension of his mail service and the frequent extra payments he received from the Post Office Department, came the sobriquet, "Extra Billy Smith," bestowed on him by Senator Benjamin Watkins Leigh [*q.v.*] of Virginia in the course of an attack on Postmaster-General William T. Barry [*q.v.*]. From 1836 to 1841 Smith served in the Virginia Senate and from 1841 to 1843, in Congress, being unsuccessful in his campaign for reëlection. In 1842 he moved to Fauquier County. He was elected governor of Virginia for the term 1846–49, and on Mar. 13, 1847, signed the act accepting the retrocession to Virginia of the part of the District of Columbia south of the Potomac River. In April 1849 he took up his residence in California, where two of his sons were living. He was sent as a delegate from San Francisco to the State Democratic

Convention, was unanimously elected its chairman, and was nominated for the United States Senate, but, unwilling to forfeit his Virginia citizenship, declined the nomination. Returning to Virginia in 1852, he was again elected to Congress and served from 1853 to 1861.

At the beginning of the Civil War he was offered by Governor Letcher a commission as brigadier-general, but declined it, saying that he was "wholly ignorant of drill and tactics" and became colonel of the 49th Virginia Infantry instead. He fought at Manassas and while with his troops was elected a member of the Confederate Congress. He attended its sessions during intervals between campaigns, rejoining his command on adjournment. When the regiment was reorganized as a part of the Confederate States Army in May 1862, he was reëlected colonel and resigned his seat in Congress. He subsequently took part in the operations on the Peninsula, about Yorktown, and around Richmond, was severely wounded at Sharpsburg, and promoted brigadier-general in command of the 4th Brigade near Fredericksburg. In May 1863 he was again elected governor of Virginia, serving from Jan. 1, 1864, until after the fall of the Confederacy. In August 1863 he had received the brevet rank of major-general. His energies as governor were largely given to securing food and supplies for the Confederate troops centered in Virginia. On the fall of Richmond, he led his government first to Lynchburg and then to Danville, but after Lee's surrender returned to Richmond, was paroled, and spent the remainder of his life in farming at his estate, "Monterosa," near Warrenton, Fauquier County. When he was eighty years old, still erect and active, he was elected to the Virginia House of Delegates, and served from 1877 to 1879. He died at "Monterosa" in his ninetieth year and was buried in Hollywood Cemetery, Richmond. Of his eleven children, one daughter and two sons survived him. His wife had died in 1879.

[Sketch by R. A. Brock, in *Hardesty's Hist. and Geog. Encyc.*, Va. edition (1884); J. W. Bell, *Memoirs of Gov. William Smith of Va.* (1891); M. V. Smith, *Virginia, 1492–1892 . . . With A History of the Executives* (1893); *Biog. Dir. Am. Cong.* (1928); L. M. S. Price, *The Sydney-Smith and Clagett-Price Geneal.* (1927); *Richmond Dispatch*, May 21, 1887.]

J. E. W.

SMITH, WILLIAM ANDREW (Nov. 29, 1802–Mar. 1, 1870), clergyman, author, college president, was born in Fredericksburg, Va., the son of William Smith, English immigrant, and Mary (Porter) Smith. He was left motherless at two and fatherless at eleven years of age, his father losing both his fortune and his life at the hands of faithless trustees. After his father's death the boy was befriended by Mr. Russell Hill, a merchant of Petersburg, Va., and was given a limited education. After teaching in Madison County several years he was admitted on trial as preacher in the Methodist Episcopal Church in 1825 and in full connection in the Virginia Conference in 1827. Thereafter he served churches in Petersburg, Lynchburg, Richmond, and Norfolk, acting also as joint-editor of the *Virginia Conference Sentinel*. He was one of the great preachers of his day. Few had more sons in the gospel, many eminent ministers among them and in various denominations. A delegate to every general conference of the Methodist Episcopal Church from 1832 to 1844, at the conference of 1844 he acted as counsel in the appeal case of the Rev. F. A. Harding, who had become a slave-holder by marriage and who had been suspended from ministerial work. Smith took the position that "slavery is a great evil, but beyond our control; yet not necessarily a sin" (*Report of Debates in the General Conference, 1844, post*, p. 28); at the same time he argued that it is no part of the work of a minister to "meddle with politics." At the same conference he was a leading participant in the more important extra-judicial trial of Bishop James Osgood Andrew [*q.v.*] which led to the division of the church. He was a member of the Louisville convention which organized the Methodist Episcopal Church, South, and was a delegate to all its general conferences until his death.

In 1846 he was elected president of Randolph-Macon College, Ashland, Va., then in the darkest period of its history. He had been one of its trustees from the beginning, 1830, and in 1833, while acting as its agent, had been crippled for life by the overturning of a carriage. Under his able administration the enrollment was increased, the quality of work was improved, and an endowment fund of $100,000 was secured, most of it swept away by the Civil War. As professor of "Moral and Intellectual Philosophy" he delivered to his students a series of lectures published in 1856 under the title *Lectures on the Philosophy and Practice of Slavery as Exhibited in the Institution of Domestic Slavery in the United States, with the Duties of Masters to Slaves,* which had considerable influence in the South. He undertook to show that philosophy, natural rights, and Holy Scripture all sustained the system of domestic slavery, which was intended to be perpetual. The book called forth a reply by J. H. Power under the title *Review of the Lectures of Wm. A. Smith, D.D., on the Philosophy and Practice of Slavery* (1859). Resigning the presidency of Randolph-Macon in

1866, he became pastor of Centenary Church, St. Louis, Mo. Two years later he was elected president of Central College, Fayette, Mo., for which he raised an endowment of nearly $100,000. Ill health prevented his continuing this work, and he returned to Virginia. He died in Richmond, Mar. 1, 1870, and was buried there in Hollywood Cemetery. He was married three times: first to Mahala Miller of Delaware, second to Laura Brooking of Richmond, and third to Mrs. Eliza V. Williams of Lynchburg. He had two children by his first wife and two by his second.

[See esp. J. R. Spann, in *John P. Branch Hist. Papers of Randolph-Macon Coll.*, June 1916. See also J. C. Granberry, in *In Memoriam: Rev. Bishop James Osgood Andrew, D.D. . . . Rev. William A. Smith, D.D.* (1871), compiled by W. T. Smithson; Richard Irby, *Hist. of Randolph-Macon Coll., Va.* (n.d.); *Jour. of the Gen. Conference M. E. Church . . . 1844* (1844); *Report of Debates in the Gen. Conference M. E. Church . . . 1844* (1844); obituaries in *Richmond Daily Whig, Richmond Christian Advocate, Daily Enquirer* and *Daily Dispatch* (Richmond), Mar. 2, 3, 1870.]   R. E. B.

SMITH, WILLIAM FARRAR (Feb. 17, 1824–Feb. 28, 1903), Union soldier, engineer, was born at St. Albans, Vt., the son of Ashbel and Sarah (Butler) Smith. Family tradition held that in colonial days the name had been Smithson, the last syllable having been dropped before the family moved to Vermont from Barre, Mass. John Gregory Smith [*q.v.*] was a cousin. William received a common school education and was graduated from the United States Military Academy in 1845 as a second lieutenant of topographical engineers, standing fourth in a class of forty-one members. He was engaged in making surveys and in teaching mathematics at West Point for the next fifteen years. During a tour of duty in Florida in 1855 he suffered a severe attack of malaria which shattered his health temporarily and made him subject to recurrent seizures which at various times during his life caused him great pain and mental depression.

At the beginning of the Civil War, he was commissioned colonel of the 3rd Vermont Volunteers, and was present in the Manassas campaign. In August 1861 he was promoted to the rank of brigadier-general and was assigned to the command of the 2nd Division of the IV Corps, Army of the Potomac, which opened the Peninsular campaign in 1862. He led his division in the battle of Williamsburg and the Seven Days' battles, and, in June 1862, was brevetted lieutenant-colonel in the regular army for his services at White Oak Swamp. In July he became a major-general, commanded the 2nd Division, VI Corps, at Antietam, and was brevetted colonel for this service. After the disasters of Fredericksburg, in which he had taken part, Smith indulged in the indiscretion of writing a letter, signed also by William Buel Franklin [*q.v.*], directly to President Lincoln, expressing the dissatisfaction of the subordinate officers and the common soldiers in their leadership, objecting to the proposed advance on Richmond as impracticable, and offering an alternative plan (*Official Records, Army,* XXI, 868). Lincoln saved him from being relieved from duty, but the incident occasioned his transfer to the IX Corps. The Senate having refused to sanction to the promotion of major-general on Mar. 4, 1863, he reverted to the rank of brigadier-general.

The great call for troops to rescue Rosecrans' army after the disaster at Chickamauga took Smith to Chattanooga, Tenn., in October 1863, as chief engineer. The problem of supplying the starving army by restoring a short line of communication with Bridgeport challenged Smith's extraordinary engineering skill. The unquestioned excellence of his work in constructing pontoon bridges won extravagant praise from Grant, Sherman, and Thomas, and led to a reappointment as major-general in March 1864, but made it especially difficult for Smith to bear with equanimity an acrid controversy which was later waged over the question as to whom credit was due for opening the famous "cracker-line." Rosecrans had been occupied with the problem before Smith's arrival, but, unfortunately, was relieved by Thomas before his plan could be executed. Consequently Smith, until his death, labored under the impression that the plan, as it was successfully carried out by Thomas, was original with him. The matter was finally disposed of for all but Smith with the publication of the findings of an investigating committee in 1901. Rosecrans was credited with having planned the recovery of Lookout Valley and was said to have been long aware of the strategic importance of Brown's Ferry. At Missionary Ridge Smith took charge of the preparations for the assault, of moving troops, and of building bridges and defenses.

Grant took Smith east with him in 1864 and assigned him to the XVIII Corps under Benjamin Franklin Butler [*q.v.*]. He participated in the bloody and fruitless action at Cold Harbor and was once more moved to criticize the actions of Meade to Grant. His complaints were justified in the light of later changes of policy, but struck too close to Grant to make him acceptable as a subordinate. Smith led the attack on Petersburg in June. His delay in pushing the movement because of the fatigue of his men, and

a sudden return of his old illness, lost for him some of the reputation he had justly earned and, on July 19, Grant relieved him of his command. The confidence which Grant had demonstrated toward Smith in the west was probably never shaken, but his hand was forced by the circumstances, particularly the difficulty of keeping Butler, who was very popular, and Smith, at peace with each other. Smith was brevetted brigadier-general and major-general on Mar. 13, 1865, for distinguished services at Chattanooga, and in the Virginia campaign of 1864.

Smith resigned as a major-general of volunteers in 1865 and, two years later, from the regular army. He had, meanwhile, become president of the International Ocean Telegraph Company which was operating a cable to Cuba, and remained in this position until the controlling interest was sold in 1873. He then spent two years in Europe with his family, and returned to the United States to become president of the Board of Police Commissioners in New York City. He resigned in 1881 and for the next twenty years was employed by the government on engineering projects for river and harbor improvements, being restored to the army with the rank of major in 1889. Smith wielded a vigorous pen in support of his "cracker-line" claims in his *Military Operations Around Chattanooga* (copyright 1886), his articles for *Battles and Leaders of the Civil War* (4 volumes, 1887–88), *The Relief of the Army of the Cumberland* (1891), and *From Chattanooga to Petersburg* (1893). The last ten years of his life were spent in Philadelphia. His wife was Sarah Ward Lyon, to whom he had been married on Apr. 24, 1861. Two of their five children survived their parents.

[*Who's Who in America,* 1901–02; J. H. Wilson, article in *Ann. Reunion, Asso. of Grads. U. S. Mil. Acad.* (1903), and *Heroes of the Great Conflict* (1904); G. W. Cullum, *Biog. Reg. . . . U. S. Mil. Acad.* (1891); *Report of a Board of Army Officers upon the Claim of Maj. Gen. William Farrar Smith* (1901); *Memoirs of Gen. W. T. Sherman* (2nd ed., 1886), vol. I; *War of the Rebellion: Official Records (Army),* 1 ser., vols. XI, XVIII, XIX, XXX, XXXI, XXXVI, XL; *House Report No. 1813,* 50 Cong., 1 Sess.; *Public Ledger,* Philadelphia, Mar. 2, 1903.]   C. H. L.

SMITH, WILLIAM HENRY (Dec. 4, 1806–Jan. 17, 1872), actor, was a native of Montgomeryshire, Wales, and is said to have been the son of an officer in the British army who was killed in Spain during the Peninsular War. At fourteen, after an unhappy childhood under the domination of a harsh stepfather, he ran away from home and joined a troupe of strolling players. On the stage he was known as W. H. Smith, but in private affairs he used his family name of Sedley. After acting in many provincial companies in theatres in Glasgow, Lancaster, and other cities of Great Britain, he came to the United States and made his début at once in Philadelphia at the Walnut Street Theatre in June 1827, appearing as Jeremy Diddler in *Raising the Wind* and as Lothair in *Adelgitha* (Wemyss, *post,* p. 130). Varied engagements followed both as actor and stage manager; in the latter capacity he revealed a skill that held him to that line of his professional work through his entire career, in Philadelphia, Boston, and other cities. It was not until 1840 that he ventured to New York, acting there for the first time in November of that year in support of Junius Brutus Booth [*q.v.*], playing Edgar to his Lear, Laertes to his Hamlet, Gratiano to his Shylock, and Mark Antony to his Brutus. His subsequent appearances on the New York stage were infrequent.

In 1843 he joined the new stock organization at the Boston Museum, becoming stage manager of the theatre, and remaining there in that capacity and also as actor for sixteen years. His making-over of *The Drunkard,* a manuscript play by another author, brought lasting popularity to the Boston Museum; after its first performance there on Feb. 12, 1844, it was acted continuously for an exceptionally long run of one hundred and forty times. Smith himself acted the rôle of Edward Middleton, the play remaining a favorite with American playgoers for several years. His life after he left Boston and the Museum in 1859 was for some time a wandering one. An interesting episode in this part of his career was his acting of David Deans in the dramatization by Dion Boucicault [*q.v.*] of *The Heart of Midlothian* at the Winter Garden in New York, May 6, 1865, at the benefit of his daughter, Mrs. Sedley Brown, who played Jeanie Deans. During his last years he was in San Francisco, and was connected with the California Theatre as actor and stage manager. He was a versatile actor in a wide range of parts, being equally successful in his younger days in juvenile characters and in his later years in the acting of comedy old men. Joseph Cowell, with whom he was associated when he first came to America, says that he was "one of those pink-looking men, with yellow hair, that the ladies always admire, and in his day was considered the best fop and light comedian on the continent" (Cowell, *post,* p. 81). Yet his art is said to have been "intellectual, truthful, conscientious, significant with thought and purpose, and warm with emotion" (Winter, *post,* p. 272). When in Boston he had married Sarah (Lapsley) Riddle of the Philadelphia theatrical family of that

name, who died in 1861 after a distinguished career on the stage. They had a son and a daughter who in later years became well known on the stage, first as Mrs. Sedley Brown, and later as Mrs. Sol Smith. His second wife, Lucy, survived him by many years.

[Joseph Sabin, *A Dict. of Books Relating to America,* pt. 122 (1930), continuation by R. W. G. Vail; F. C. Wemyss, *Wemyss' Chronology of the Am. Stage* (1852); Joseph Cowell, *Thirty Years Passed Among the Players in England and America* (1844); *Boston Museum, an Interesting Retrospect* (1880–81); W. M. Leman, *Memories of an Old Actor* (1886); William Winter, *Brief Chronicles,* pt. 3 (1890); T. A. Brown, *A Hist. of the N. Y. Stage* (1903), vol. I; G. C. D. Odell, *Annals of the N. Y. Stage,* vols. IV (1928), VII (1931); *Boston Transcript,* Mar. 6, 1915, pt. 3; obituaries in *N. Y. Times,* Jan. 20, and *Morning Bull.* (San Francisco), Jan. 19, 1872.]   E. F. E.

SMITH, WILLIAM HENRY (Dec. 1, 1833–July 27, 1896), journalist, was born at Austerlitz, Columbia County, N. Y., the son of William DeForest Smith. His father is said to have come from Litchfield County, Conn., where his ancestors settled about 1640, and his mother is said to have been a member of a family named Gott, which settled in Columbia County, N. Y., at the close of the Revolutionary War. He was taken by his parents as an infant to Homer, Ohio. After serving as a school teacher and a tutor, he began his journalistic career by acting as correspondent for Cincinnati newspapers. He early joined a group of young men—free soilers—that included Rutherford B. Hayes and John Brough [*qq.v.*]. In 1855 he was married to Emma Reynolds, who died in 1891. He became a member of the staff of the Cincinnati *Gazette,* but he gave up newspaper work for a time to act as private secretary to Governor Brough and from 1864 to 1866 to be secretary of the state of Ohio. After his second term as secretary of state, he edited the Cincinnati *Evening Chronicle.* In 1870 he took charge of the Western Associated Press, then a struggling organization with headquarters at Chicago. President Hayes, his old friend, appointed him collector of the port of Chicago, but he also continued his press association work. As collector he was instrumental in correcting certain abuses in the New York customs office that worked to the disadvantage of Chicago importers. In 1882 he effected a combination of the New York Associated Press and the Western Associated Press and was chosen general manager of the joint organization, a position he held until he was succeeded by Melville E. Stone [*q.v.*]. During his twenty-two years as head of these two press associations, a system of leased wires was established, and typewriters were used in receiving the telegraphic news reports. He also aided Whitelaw Reid [*q.v.*] in organizing and developing the Mergenthaler Linotype Company.

He was keenly interested in the history of the Middle West. He took an active part in the preservation of historical material pertaining to the Northwest Territory and was requested by the Ohio state legislature to edit the papers of Arthur St. Clair, the first governor of the territory. These were published in two volumes in 1882 under the title *The St. Clair Papers*. After 1892 he devoted his time to preparing a history of slavery in this country, particularly with reference to the anti-slavery movement in the Middle West, with which he had been identified. This work, practically completed at the time of his death, was finally published in two volumes in 1903 as *A Political History of Slavery*. He also collected some material for a volume on the life and times of President Hayes, which was to be a continuation of his history of slavery. This material was incorporated in the *Life of Rutherford Birchard Hayes* (2 vols., 1914) written by Smith's son-in-law, Charles Richard Williams [*q.v.*]. He died at his home in Lake Forest, Ill., survived by one son.

[Biographical sketch by Whitelaw Reid in *A Political History of Slavery, ante*; some details of his friendship with Hayes in Williams, *ante*; M. E. Stone, *Fifty Years a Journalist* (1921); *Ohio Arch. and Hist. Pubs.*, vol. IV (1895); *Chicago Daily Tribune*, July 28, 1896; *N. Y. Tribune*, July 28, Aug. 28, 1896.]

W. G. B—r.

SMITH, WILLIAM LOUGHTON (*c.* 1758–Dec. 19, 1812), congressman from South Carolina, diplomat, and political pamphleteer, was the great-grandson of William Smith who was in South Carolina as early as 1690 and the son of Benjamin Smith who held many provincial offices, made a fortune in trade, and gave generously to welfare work. His mother, Anne (Loughton) Smith, died when William was but two years old. At the age of twelve, a few months before his father's death, he was sent to London and entered at Hackney. On May 12, 1774, he was admitted to the Middle Temple, but from 1774 to 1778 he studied at Geneva. Returning to England in 1779, he studied law until the fall of 1782, when he left London to seek passage for America. A year later he reached Charleston, where he was admitted to the bar in January 1784 and in November was elected to the legislature. On May 1, 1786, he married Charlotte Izard, the daughter of Ralph Izard [*q.v.*]. She bore him a son and a daughter and died in 1792. After holding various local offices, he was elected to the First Congress, where his seat was contested by David Ramsay [*q.v.*] on the ground that he was not an American citizen, the first of

the congressional contested elections. He was seated and soon became a leading Federalist. A heavy speculator in government paper, he vigorously supported assumption of state debts by the federal government, and it is said that after the reading of Hamilton's report he was one of those who sent fast-sailing vessels down the coast to purchase all the certificates that could be had from discouraged holders. In the summer of 1790, he set out from New York with Washington's party for Rhode Island, an episode of which he has left an interesting journal (*post*). In 1792 he published his first pamphlet, which has been erroneously attributed to Alexander Hamilton (copy in Charleston Library Society with attribution in own handwriting, see Salley, *post*, p. 254), *The Politicks and Views of a Certain Party, Displayed*, an attack on Jefferson. In 1796 it was probably he who attacked Jefferson anonymously in *The Pretensions of Thomas Jefferson to the Presidency Examined* (originally published in *Gazette of the United States*, Oct., Nov. 1796). In the same year he received an honorary LL.D. from the College of New Jersey, now Princeton (*General Catalogue of Princeton*, 1908, p. 404, is mistaken; see Matthews, *post*, footnote 3, p. 29). His *Comparative View of the Constitutions of the Several States with Each Other, and with That of the United States* (1796) was much admired and is said to have been used as a text at Princeton. In the spring of 1794, his political enemies in Charleston expressed their dislike by burning him in effigy in the company of Arnold and the Devil. Although Hamilton rated him a man of abilities, information, industry, and integrity, both he and Washington felt that Smith's personal unpopularity debarred him from a conspicuous appointment.

However, he was elected to Congress five times and served until July 10, 1797, when he resigned to become minister to Portugal. There he entertained handsomely, worked smoothly with the British diplomats, and, as attested by voluminous letters, followed intelligently the progress of Napoleon in Europe. He was relieved on Sept. 9, 1801, but remained in Europe. Upon his return to Charleston in December 1803 he resumed the practice of law and at the next election was defeated for Congress. About this time he included his mother's name with his own to distinguish him from William Smith, *c.* 1762–1840 [*q.v.*], with whom he has usually been confused. On Dec. 19, 1805, he married Charlotte Wragg, the daughter of William Wragg [*q.v.*], by whom he had a son. In February 1806 under the name of "Phocion," he began a series of letters in the *Charleston Daily Courier* (reprinted in pamphlet form as *The Numbers of Phocion,* 1806, in Charleston and as *American Arguments for British Rights,* 1806, in London).

[Papers and letters in Lib. of Cong. and in Pickering Papers of the Mass. Hist. Soc.; some letters in *S. C. Hist. and Geneal. Mag.,* Apr. 1924–Jan. 1925, and *Sewanee Review,* Jan. 1906; sketches and bibliog. in A. S. Salley, "Wm. Smith and Some of his Descendants," *S. C. Hist. and Geneal. Mag.,* Apr. 1903, and in Albert Matthews, "Journ. of Wm. Loughton Smith, 1790–1791," *Mass. Hist. Soc. Proc.,* vol. LI (1918) and separately (1917); David Ramsay, *Observations on the Decision . . . Respecting the Eligibility of the Hon. Wm. Smith* (1789); E. A. Jones, *Am. Members of the Inns of Court* (1924); U. B. Phillips, "The S. C. Federalists," *Am. Hist. Rev.,* July 1909.] A. K. G.

SMITH, WILLIAM NATHAN HARRELL (Sept. 24, 1812–Nov. 14, 1889), representative from North Carolina and judge, was born at Murfreesboro, N. C. His father, William Lay Smith, a native of Lyme, Conn., and a half-brother of James Murdock [*q.v.*], was a Yale graduate and a physician. He removed to North Carolina in 1806, married Ann Harrell of Murfreesboro, and died in 1813. The son, prepared for college at Kingston, R. I., and Colchester, Conn., was graduated from Yale College in 1834, studied law there, and was admitted to the North Carolina bar. He immediately removed to Texas but remained there only six months. On Jan. 14, 1839, he married Mary Olivia Wise of Murfreesboro. They had three children. He was a good jury lawyer and successful in practice. Active in the campaign of 1840, he became a Whig member of the House of Commons. In 1848 he was a member of the Senate. In 1849 he was elected solicitor and served until 1857. In that year he accepted the nomination of the American party for Congress. He was, however, not a Know-Nothing, opposing frankly their proscriptive principles. He was defeated but, after serving in 1858 in the House of Commons, was elected to Congress and served from Mar. 4, 1859, to Mar. 3, 1861. In the long contest for speaker that grew out of John Sherman's indorsement of *The Impending Crisis,* Smith's election seemed certain, although he himself took no part in the contest. A believer in protection, he was apparently satisfactory to the Pennsylvania Republicans, several of whom voted for him. He received a majority of one, but, before the result was announced, E. Joy Morris of Pennsylvania demanded that the Pennsylvania delegation should dictate the organization of the ways and means committee. Smith refused to make any bargain, and, three Republicans changing their votes, he failed of election.

Intellectually and temperamentally opposed to secession, he was earnest in his efforts to obtain compromise, but the call for troops ended all discussion of the matter for him. One of the very few members to serve in all three Confederate congresses, he was a hard-working, useful member, always conservative, a supporter of the administration, though not a blind one. He voted, for example, uniformly against the suspension of the writ of *habeas corpus,* but he also voted to discontinue the exemption of those who had furnished substitutes. He declined to countenance the peace movement and voted against the peace resolutions of 1864. In 1865–66 he was again a member of the state House of Commons and was particularly active in promoting the liberal legislation concerning the freedmen. He favored President Johnson's policy and was a delegate to the National Union convention in 1866. He was a leader in organizing the Conservative party to oppose Radical control of the state and was a delegate to the National Democratic Convention in 1868. In 1869 he volunteered as counsel for the members of the bar, led by B. F. Moore [*q.v.*], who had been disabled from practice before the supreme court on account of their protest against the political activity of the judges. In 1870 he removed to Norfolk but two years later established himself in Raleigh, N. C. In 1871 he was one of Governor Holden's counsel in the impeachment trial and delivered what was generally regarded as the ablest argument of the trial. In 1873 the disabilities of the Fourteenth Amendment were removed.

In 1878 he became chief justice of the state supreme court and served until his death. Though not a great judge he was a prodigious worker and as executive of the court highly successful. His opinions are scholarly, relying heavily upon precedent, partly as a result of his temperament, but more, probably, because of his modesty. They were logically reasoned but were written in a very involved style. Personally he was a courteous, retiring gentleman with many friends and no enemies. He did not lack convictions, but there was in him no trace of undue partisanship. He was an able and fluent speaker, a learned lawyer in the best sense of the term.

[*Biog. Hist. of N. C.,* vol. VII (1908), ed. by S. A. Ashe and S. B. Weeks; *N. C. Reports,* vol. CIV (1890), App. pp. 955–66; *Hist. of the Class of 1834 in Yale College* (1875); F. B. Dexter, *Biog. Sketch of the Grads. of Yale College,* vol. V (1911); J. G. deR. Hamilton, *Reconstruction in N. C.* (1914); *News and Observer* (Raleigh), Nov. 15, 1889.] J. G. deR. H.

SMITH, WILLIAM RUSSELL (Mar. 27, 1815–Feb. 26, 1896), lawyer, congressman, author, was born in Russellville, Ky., the son of Ezekiel and Elizabeth (Hampton) Smith, descendants of old Virginia families. According to tradition, both of the boy's grandfathers fought in the battle of King's Mountain. Ezekiel, a planter, left his farm to fight in the Seminole War and shortly after his return he died. His widow moved to Huntsville, Ala., and in 1820, to Tuscaloosa. Before William was ten years old she died also, leaving her children to the care of strangers. William was befriended by George W. Crabb, who recognized his ability and financed his education. In 1834, having completed three years of college work at the University of Alabama, he entered the law office of his benefactor. He was soon admitted to the bar and opened an office in Greensboro, Ala.

Throughout his life he had a wide variety of interests and turned with bewildering rapidity from one to the other. He had been practising only one year when the outbreak of a Creek War led him to abandon law for arms. He raised a company and marched to the scene of conflict only to find that the uprising had been put down. His company then moved on toward Texas with the idea of aiding the Texans in their revolt against Mexico, but was stopped at Mobile by the news of the battle of San Jacinto. Smith stayed in Mobile and began the publication of a monthly, of which only six numbers were issued. In 1837 he returned to Tuscaloosa. He edited a Whig newspaper of some merit and served as mayor in 1839. Independent and an individualist, he found it difficult to work with a party, and he was severely criticized for his many shifts in party allegiance. In 1841 and again in 1842 he was elected to the Alabama general assembly as a Whig, but he was opposed to the Whig position on the tariff and left the party in 1843. In 1844 he moved to Fayette County and from 1850 to 1851 served as circuit judge. In 1850 he was elected to Congress as a supporter of the Union and served until Mar. 3, 1857. In 1855 he allied himself with the American party and was mentioned as a vice-presidential possibility in the election of 1856, but was defeated as an American candidate for Congress in that year. After retiring from Congress he moved back to Tuscaloosa. He supported Bell and Everett in 1860 and opposed secession in the Alabama state convention of 1861, but recruited and became colonel of the 26th Alabama Regiment. Before active fighting began, however, he was elected to the Confederate House of Representatives, where he served throughout the war. He was a candidate for governor in 1865 and for Congress in 1866 and in 1878. He was defeated in 1865 and in 1878, and in 1866 he withdrew from the contest. In 1870 he was elected president of the University of Alabama by the radical board of trustees, in an attempt to secure popular support for the university. The feeling between radicals and conservatives was so strong, however, that only a few students enrolled in 1871 and the president resigned. After his resignation he practised law in Tuscaloosa until 1879, when he removed to Washington, D. C., where he practised and devoted much time to writing.

He was a prolific writer in many fields. As early as 1833 he published a volume of poetry, *College Musings, or Twigs from Parnassus*. His best known poem, *The Uses of Solitude* (1860), was read to the Tuscaloosa chapter of Phi Beta Kappa. His *The Justice of the Peace* (1841), a book for the guidance of magistrates, appeared in two subsequent editions under the titles *The Jurisdiction of Justices of the Peace in Civil and Criminal Cases* (1859, 1860). In 1861 he published *The History and Debates of the Convention of the People of Alabama . . . 1861*. His *Reports of Decisions of the Supreme Court of the State of Alabama* (10 vols., 1870-79), covering the period 1820-46, with notes, was widely known. He also wrote *Reminiscences of a Long Life* (copr. 1889). In addition he published several volumes of poetry, plays, and essays. His first wife was Jane Binion of Tuscaloosa, to whom he was married in 1843 and who died less than two years thereafter. On Jan. 3, 1847, he married Mary Jane Murray of Fayette, Ala. After her death in 1853 he married June 14, 1854, Wilhelmine M. Easby of Washington. He had children by all three wives.

[Anne Easby-Smith, *William Russell Smith of Ala.* (1931); T. M. Owen, *Hist. of Ala. and Dict. of Ala. Biog.* (1921); William Garrett, *Reminiscences of Public Men in Ala. for Thirty Years* (1872); *Biog. Dir. Am. Cong.* (1928); Willis Brewer, *Alabama* (1872); *Washington Post*, Feb. 27, 1896.]   H.F.

SMITH, WILLIAM SOOY (July 22, 1830– Mar. 4, 1916), civil engineer, Union soldier, was born in Tarlton, Pickaway County, Ohio, the son of Sooy and Ann (Hedges) Smith. His father was a local magistrate. William worked his way through Ohio University, Athens, Ohio, graduating with distinction in 1849. He immediately obtained an appointment to the United States Military Academy at West Point, where he graduated in 1853, ranking sixth in his class.

On June 19, 1854, he resigned his commission to become an assistant on construction for the Illinois Central Railway, but his career was soon interrupted by a desperate illness and he subsequently spent two years teaching in Buffalo, N. Y. Resuming engineering practice in 1857, he organized the firm of Parkinson & Smith, and made the first surveys for an international bridge at Niagara Falls. In 1859 he began the construction of a large bridge over the Savannah River for the Charleston & Savannah Railroad. In connection with this structure he made the first use in America of the pneumatic process for sinking foundations, then but recently developed in France. Finding the method cumbersome and ill-suited to his requirements, he made many fundamental changes in the design of apparatus and in construction procedure.

The project was interrupted by the outbreak of the Civil War, whereupon Smith immediately returned to his native state and enlisted in the volunteer army. On June 26, 1861, he was commissioned colonel of the 13th Ohio Infantry, and on Apr. 15, 1862, he was made a brigadier-general. He served with distinction until 1864, when a serious attack of inflammatory rheumatism completely disabled him. Resigning from the army July 15, 1864, he regained his health slowly, occupied as a farmer at Oak Park, Cook County, Ohio, and it was not until 1866 that he again took up civil engineering practice. His next project was that of building a protection for the Wagoschance lighthouse on the Straits of Mackinac. In connection with this enterprise he further developed his pneumatic caisson process for sinking foundations, and later perfected it on several railroad bridges which he constructed in the early seventies. For this work he received a prize award from the American Centennial Exposition in 1876. In 1876 he prepared plans for a tunnel under the Detroit River, which he proposed to build by sinking a continuous series of pneumatic caissons across the river. His plan received the approval of the advisory board of engineers, but it was too far in advance of the times to secure financial support.

For the next twelve years, Smith specialized in bridge construction and deep foundations. He was successively engaged, either as chief engineer or consulting engineer, on important railroad bridges over the Missouri River at Omaha, Leavenworth, Boonville, Glasgow, Plattsmouth, Sibley, and Kansas City. During this period steel was perfected to the point of competing with wrought iron, and Smith was one of the first to champion the use of the new material. Owing to his influence, it was decided to use steel throughout in the trusses of the Glasgow bridge, which became the first all-steel truss bridge in the world.

About 1890 Smith settled in Chicago and gave most of his professional attention to the subject of building foundations, which presented an extraordinarily difficult problem in that vicinity because of the great depth of rock and bad soil conditions. He was one of the first to advocate carrying the piers of high buildings to rock instead of supporting them on rafts or grillages. He was consulted in regard to the foundations of nearly all the large buildings constructed in Chicago during the period from 1890 to 1910, in which year he retired from active practice. The remainder of his life he spent quietly in the village of Medford, Ore. His professional labors never ceased, however; at the time of his death, which followed an attack of pneumonia in his eighty-sixth year, he was completing plans for a new-type fireproof building. He was one of the founders of the Western Society of Engineers, of which he was president from 1877 to 1880, and thereafter for a number of years chairman of its committee on iron and steel. He was also an influential member of a similar committee of the American Society of Civil Engineers. To this society he contributed two important papers: "Pneumatic Foundations" (*Transactions*, vol. II, 1874) and "The Hudson River Tunnel" (*Ibid.*, vol. XI, 1882). He was married in 1854 to Elizabeth Haven of Buffalo, N. Y., by whom he had one son, Charles Sooysmith [q.v.]. His first wife died in 1860, and in 1862 he married Anna Durham of Bowling Green, Ky., who died in 1882; in 1884 he married Josephine Hartwell of St. Catharines, Ontario, by whom he had a son.

[G. W. Cullum, *Biog. Reg. Officers and Grads. U. S. Mil. Acad.* (1891); *Engineering News*, Mar. 30, 1916; *Jour. Western Soc. of Engineers*, Jan. 1917; *Who's Who in America*, 1914–15; *Morning Oregonian* (Portland), Mar. 6, 1916.]   J. I. P.

SMITH, WILLIAM STEPHENS (Nov. 8, 1755–June 10, 1816), Revolutionary soldier, was born in New York. His father, John Smith, was a wealthy merchant. His mother, Margaret Stephens, belonged to a Loyalist family. After graduating from the College of New Jersey (Princeton) in 1774, he studied law with Samuel Jones of New York. He entered the army at the outbreak of the Revolution, being appointed aide to General Sullivan with the rank of major in August 1776. He was present at the battle of Long Island, and when the American troops withdrew across East River on the night of Aug. 29, it is said that he was one of the last to leave, accompanying Washington in his barge. In October, although suffering from a wound received at Harlem Heights, he destroyed the bridge at Throgs Neck, and thus helped to prevent Howe from outflanking the American army. After participating in the battle of White Plains, he accompanied the Revolutionary forces on the retreat across New Jersey. Gallantry at Trenton won him a lieutenant-colonelcy in William R. Lee's regiment. In 1777 he served under Putnam in New York; in 1778, fought at Monmouth and

Newport; in 1779, marched with Sullivan against the Indians; and in 1780, took part in the battle of Springfield. After acting as inspector and adjutant to a corps of light infantry under Lafayette, he was honored in July 1781 by an appointment as aide to Washington, performed important duties at Yorktown and was charged with supervising the evacuaction of New York by the British in accordance with the treaty of peace.

He was appointed secretary of legation in London in 1785. There he met and was married, on June 12, 1786, to Abigail Amelia, daughter of the American minister, John Adams, 1735–1826 [q.v.]. In company with Francisco de Miranda, he toured the Continent, visiting Prussia in order to study the army organization of Frederick the Great, and was later sent on a diplomatic mission to Spain and Portugal. He returned to the United States in 1788 and plunged heavily into land speculation and politics. He held successively the offices of federal marshal, supervisor of the revenue, and surveyor of the port of New York. When war with France impended in 1798, Adams nominated him as adjutant-general, but the nomination was rejected by the Senate largely owing to the interference of Timothy Pickering (C. F. Adams, *The Life of John Adams,* 1871, II, 269), and Smith was obliged to content himself with the command of the 12th Infantry. In 1806 he was prosecuted for complicity in the fitting out of Miranda's filibustering expedition to South America and was acquitted but his political career was seriously affected. He returned to his farm in Lebanon, N. Y., where he devoted himself to agriculture until 1812 when he was elected to Congress as a Federalist, serving from 1813 until his death at Lebanon. He was one of the founders of the Society of the Cincinnati, succeeding his friend von Steuben as president of the order. He was the pattern of the eighteenth-century gentleman, handsome, brave, urbane, and equally at ease at camp or court. His wife preceded him in death. They had three children, two sons and a daughter.

[Letters to and from Smith are scattered through public and private collections, including those of his great-grandson, Mr. H. A. DeWindt, the New York and Massachusetts Historical Societies, the Library of Congress, and the Academia Nacional de la Historia (Caracas). See also *The Trials of William S. Smith and Samuel G. Ogden* (1807); *Jour. and Corresp. of Miss Adams* (2 vols., 1841, 1842); *The Lee Papers,* vol. III (1874); M. D. Raymond, in *N. Y. Geneal. and Biog. Record,* Oct. 1894; *Pubs. of the Southern Hist. Asso.,* vol. XI (1907); B. C. Steiner, *The Life and Corresp. of James McHenry* (1907); K. M. Roof, *Colonel William Smith and Lady* (1929); W. S. Robertson, *The Life of Miranda* (2 vols., 1929); *New-York Gazette & General Advertiser,* June 17, 1816.]

E. E. C.

SMITH, WILLIAM WAUGH (Mar. 12, 1845–Nov. 29, 1912), educator and college president, born at Warrenton, Va., was the son of Richard McAllister Smith and Ellen Harris Blackwell, both members of families connected with the educational development of Virginia. The father, a first cousin of Gov. William Smith, 1797–1887 [q.v.], was principal of the academy at Warrenton, editor of the Alexandria *Evening Sentinel* and subsequently of the *Richmond Enquirer,* and in his later life professor of natural sciences in Randolph-Macon College, Ashland, Va. Willie Waugh, as he was known in his youth, was educated in his father's academy and in the Quaker Academy at Alexandria, Va., until the outbreak of the Civil War. He was rejected twice for military service as a "little boy in knee pants," but in 1862 was accepted as a volunteer. He served in the Confederate army until 1865, acting in intervals as reporter of the Confederate Senate for his father's paper, the *Enquirer,* and rejoining his regiment at the beginning of each campaign. He was wounded at Seven Pines, at Sharpsburg and at Gettysburg, and kept through his later life the little diary, with embedded bullet, that saved his life on one occasion.

In 1867 he entered the University of Virginia and completed the course in Latin in one year, which according to accepted custom gave him the right to be a "graduate of the University of Virginia." The next year he went to Randolph-Macon College, and graduated in Greek in one year. He taught a year in Lane's University School in Richmond, returning to Randolph-Macon in 1870 and graduating with the degree of A.M. in 1871. From 1871 to 1874 he served as co-principal of Bethel Academy and as its principal from 1874 to 1878. Then called to Randolph-Macon College, he occupied there, successively, the chairs of mental and moral philosophy, Greek, and Latin. While professor of Latin in 1886 he was elected president of the college. He soon became convinced that honest college work was impossible while colleges in the South were admitting totally unprepared students with the sole requirement that they be sixteen years old. To prepare students especially for Randolph-Macon College, in 1890 he established an academy at Bedford City, Va., and another in 1892 at Front Royal. In scholastic requirements, in training of faculty, and in building and equipment, the two academies were the standard toward which the state moved and which in many particulars only the best of the modern Virginia high schools have equaled.

At the time of his inauguration as president

of Randolph-Macon College, the state had five colleges and two universities for men, but not a single standard college for women. He wrote in 1890: "We wish to establish in Virginia a college where our young women may obtain an education equal to that given in our best colleges for young men and under environments in harmony with the highest ideals of womanhood" (Harmanson, *post*, p. 6). With this end in view he launched plans that year for the erection of Randolph-Macon Woman's College at Lynchburg. Formally opened in 1893, this was the first woman's college in the South to be given general academic recognition. In the *Annual Report* of the Carnegie Foundation for 1907 it was named as one of the three Southern institutions on the accepted list. Serving as president until his death, Smith steadily enlarged the plant, secured an endowment, and saw the enrollment grow to nearly 600. From 1897 he was also chancellor of the Randolph-Macon System. That year he caused to be established an institute for girls at Danville. During his administration at the Woman's College he was bitterly attacked for having the college enrolled on the "accepted list" of the Carnegie Foundation, which required that trustees "should remain free from control of any other body." The college board of trustees was a self-perpetuating body, but had been closely identified with the Virginia conferences of the Methodist Episcopal Church, South. After enduring the attack of certain Methodist leaders for two years, Smith agreed to the passage of a resolution by the board itself that elections of trustees be approved by the Methodist conferences in Virginia. Accordingly, the college withdrew from the Carnegie list.

Smith was twice married, first, to Ella Jones, of Richmond, on Oct. 1, 1869; and after her death to Marion Love Howison of Alexandria, on Jan. 27, 1875. He had no children. Quick in thought and plan, physically and mentally energetic, he was tireless in work, devoted in purpose, inspiring in leadership. He even sold his own home to speed up an endowment subscription. He lived up to his own motto, "What must be done, can be done" (Harmanson, p. 40). He worked out for the South new standards of secondary education for boys and of higher education for women.

[Richard Irby, *Hist. of Randolph Macon Coll.* (1898?); S. T. M. Harmanson, "Recollections of Dr. W. W. Smith," in *Bulletin of Randolph-Macon Woman's Coll.*, Oct.–Dec. 1917 and "Randolph-Macon Woman's College," *Ibid.*, July–Sept., Oct.–Dec. 1923; R. E. Blackwell, "Dr. William Waugh Smith," in *Alumnae Bulletin of Randolph-Macon Woman's Coll.*, April 1931; Carnegie Foundation for the Advancement of Teaching, *Fourth Annual Report of the President and of the Treasurer* (1909); L. G. Tyler, ed., *Men of Mark in Va.*, vol. I (1906); *Who's Who in America*, 1912–13; *Times-Dispatch* (Richmond), Nov. 30, 1912; L. M. S. Price, *The Sydney-Smith and Clagett-Price Genealogy* (1927); family manuscripts in the possession of J. F. Howison, Richmond, Va., and R. C. Howison, Raleigh, N. C.]   J. E. W.

SMITH, WINCHELL (Apr. 5, 1871–June 10, 1933), playwright, director, was born in Hartford, Conn., son of William Brown and Virginia (Thrall) Smith. His father, a nephew of John Brown, 1800–1859 [*q.v.*], owned a flour, grain, and feed store. Educated in the Hartford public schools, young Winchell rejected college and enrolled in the school of acting at the Lyceum Theatre (later the American Academy of Dramatic Arts) in New York City. Upon completion of his course in 1892, he found sporadic employment for a decade as actor and stage manager, without attracting much attention, though he acted with William Gillette in *Secret Service*. It was not until 1904, when with Arnold Daly [*q.v.*] he produced in New York a series of plays by George Bernard Shaw, that he became prominent. The first, *Candida*, was produced with $1,000 lent by William Gillette and, with those that followed, started the Shaw vogue in America. Two years later, in collaboration with Byron Ongley, Smith tried his own hand at playwriting with a dramatization of George Barr McCutcheon's *Brewster's Millions*, which he also directed and which was a popular success. Thereafter he gave up acting entirely, and became a dramatist and director. His other original plays were *The Fortune Hunter* and *The Only Son*; all the rest were done in collaboration. With Victor Mapes he wrote *My Little Friend, The New Henrietta*, and *The Boomerang*; with Paul Armstrong [*q.v.*], *Via Wireless*; with John E. Hazzard, *Turn to the Right*; with Tom Cushing, *Thank You*; with Augustin McHugh, *Officer 666*; and with Frank Bacon [*q.v.*], the actor, *Lightnin'*, which was one of the greatest popular successes ever produced in America.

He also acted as "play doctor" for numerous other scripts and almost always directed any play he worked on, as well as plays by other authors, notably Frank Craven's *The First Year*, which ran for over 700 performances on Broadway. Because of his skill in gauging public taste and his ability as a director, the percentage of popular successes on his list was phenomenally high; in consequence, his services, at a high fee, were for twenty years in great demand, which no doubt explains why he wrote so few plays entirely alone. Practically all the plays he worked on, however, were comedies in the American tradition of character types, broad effects, brisk dialogue, a "wholesome" atmosphere, and a sentimental ending. They added nothing to the development of a serious native drama nor were they experimental in technique, but they were of their kind theatrically expert and unfailingly entertaining. Though he rose to fame as a producer of Shaw, Smith never in his own playwriting betrayed any Shavian influence. One of his quaintest character creations was "George Spelvin." In an early Smith production an actor who "doubled" was given a second name, George Spelvin, on the program; thereafter the name appeared in the cast of every play with which Smith was associated, till many theatre-goers thought there actually was such a person. Smith married Grace Spencer of Troy, N. Y., on Dec. 20, 1895. They had no children. After his successes began to mount he purchased an estate in Farmington, Conn., close to the town of his birth, and gave much time to its extensive development. His fortune was now ample, and he was with increasing difficulty tempted from his country acres to Broadway; the last play he staged was *The Vinegar Tree* in 1930. He died leaving an estate estimated at a million and a half, a share of which was willed as a trust fund for the care of needy actors and dramatists. Though so successful a man of the theatre, he never lost a boyish bright simplicity and a certain Yankee tang. His smooth, alert face, behind eyeglasses, was that of a keen and kindly observer, without an actor's wrinkle or a worried managerial scowl. He was soft and pleasant spoken, with a dry but kindly wit, and he was universally liked both by his colleagues in the theatre and his neighbors in the country. The writing of popular plays was easy for him, his worldly affairs were uniformly successful, and he lived pleasantly by giving pleasure.

[According to one account—W. R. Cutter, ed., *Geneal. and Family Hist. of the State of Conn.* (1911), vol. II, p. 617—Smith's name was originally William Brown Smith. See *Who's Who in America*, 1932–33; *Who's Who in the Theatre* (1933); *Christian Sci. Monitor* (Boston), Sept. 26, 1916; *N. Y. Times*, Mar. 26, pt. 2, Nov. 19, pt. 5, and Dec. 10, 1916, pt. 2; *Hartford Courant*, Apr. 19, 1931, pt. VI; obituaries in *Hartford Courant* and *N. Y. Times*, June 11, 1933.]

W. P. E.

SMITH, XANTHUS RUSSELL (Feb. 26, 1839–Dec. 2, 1929), painter, was born in Philadelphia, Pa., the son of Russell Smith [*q.v.*] and Mary Priscilla (Wilson) Smith. Educated at home and at the University of Pennsylvania, where he studied medicine from 1856 to 1858 and gave particular attention to anatomy, he had his art training at the Pennsylvania Acad-

emy of the Fine Arts, at the Royal Academy in London, and in Europe. He received his first commission for a landscape at sixteen.

Although listed in the family Bible as Xanthus Russell Smith he did not use his middle name until he enlisted at the outbreak of the Civil War, in which he served under Samuel Francis du Pont [*q.v.*] and took part in Farragut's operations during the capture of Mobile. After the war he painted pictures of many important naval engagements and land battles. Among these are "Surrender of the *Tennessee*," "Sinking of the *Cumberland*," and "Attack on Fort Fisher" in the permanent collection of the Pennsylvania Academy of the Fine Arts; "*Monitor* and *Merrimac*" and "*Kearsage* and *Alabama*" in the Union League of Philadelphia; and "Pickett's Last Charge at Gettysburg" in the John Wanamaker collection. He also painted a picture of "John Burns' July First at Gettysburg," a portrait of John Burns in civilian dress, and portraits from life of Maj. Francis Wister, Gen. Rush Shippen Huidekoper, and Joshua Lawrence Chamberlain [*q.v.*]. Among his other paintings are "The Treaty Elm" in the Bank of North America, Philadelphia, and portraits of Washington and Walt Whitman, and several of Lincoln, whom he greatly admired, one of them being in the possession of the Union League of Philadelphia. On June 19, 1879, he married Mary Binder, daughter of George A. Binder of Philadelphia, by whom he had a daughter and two sons. Private collectors acquired many of his landscapes and marines, the latter painted off the Maine coast, where he maintained a summer home on an island in Casco Bay. In winter he lived at Edgehill, Pa., and worked in his Philadelphia studio, turning especially to portraiture in his last years. After an illness of several years he died at his home in Edgehill and was buried in Ivy Hill Cemetery.

[Necrology in *The New Internat. Year Book*, 1929; Pa. Acad. of the Fine Arts, *Descriptive Cat. of the Permanent Colls.* (1902); obituaries in *Am. Art Ann.*, 1930, *Art Digest*, mid-Dec., 1929, *Pub. Ledger* (Phila.), Feb. 27, Dec. 4, 1929, and *N. Y. Times*, Dec. 4, 1929; information from Mary B. Smith, Smith's widow.]

D. G.

SMOHALLA (c. 1815–1907), Indian prophet and founder of the Dreamer religion, was chief of a small tribe related to the Nez Percés, the Wanapum or Sokulk, which inhabited the region around Priest Rapids on the Columbia River, Yakima County, Wash. Soon after 1850 he achieved local celebrity as a medicine man. In the Yakima War of 1855–56 the mystical belief in dreams that he was inspiring aided in encouraging the Indian hostility to the white man.

His new prominence brought him the jealous enmity of Moses, a neighboring chief, who provoked a quarrel. In the resulting fight Smohalla, badly wounded, was left on the field for dead. However, he partially revived, made his way to a boat on the Columbia River, and cast himself adrift. Rescued by white men, he was afraid to return to the hatred of his rival, so set out on romantic wanderings down the Pacific coast into Mexico and then through Arizona, Utah, Nevada, and back home. There he reappeared as one miraculously resurrected from the dead. The resulting prestige and his new knowledge he used with skilful oratory and canny prophecy to gain, by 1872, a wide following. Though short, bald-headed, and almost hunchbacked, he possessed a high forehead, bright, intelligent eyes, and above all a fluent tongue. The Dreamer religion developed by him and his apostles appealed to Indians who, circumscribed and regulated, harassed by white encroachments and attacks, and with a life of hunting and fishing ever harder, were near despair. It taught that the Indians alone were the real people, that the whites, the negroes, and the Chinese were later created by Saghalee Tyee, "The Great Chief Above," to punish them for their apostasy from ancient customs. They had only to live as their fathers had lived and to follow the Dreamer rituals in order to get the aid of cataclysmic forces of nature and the resurrection of the myriad hordes of Indian dead to drive out or to suppress these interlopers. The ritual, based on Indian custom with additions gathered from military parades, Roman Catholic ceremonial, and Mormon practices, so utilized the hypnotic influence of beaten drums, ringing bells, and rhythmic dancing, as to bring visions and exaltation. All the Indian conflicts with the government in this region derived inspiration from Dreamer doctrines. Chief Joseph and his people during the tension with authority that eventuated in the Nez Percé war of 1877 were greatly influenced, especially through Smohalla's apostle, Toohulhulsote, though Smohalla himself was persuaded to peaceful submission. Later this religion was considered to be the principal check to civilizing influences and the peaceful acceptance of land restrictions, and it maintained an important influence for some time after the death of Smohalla.

[James Mooney, "The Ghost Dance Religion," Fourteenth Ann. Report Bur. of Amer. Ethnology, pt. 2 (1896); Report of the Commissioner of Indian Affairs ... 1870 (1870), pp. 50, 54, report of A. B. Meacham of the Oregon superintendency; Ibid. ... 1892 (1892); O. O. Howard, Nez Percé Joseph (1881), esp. pp. 8–9. 45–48, 64–67, 81–83; J. W. MacMurray, "The Dreamers," Trans. Albany Institute, vol. XI (1887); E. L.

Huggins, "Smohalla," Overland Monthly, Feb. 1891; S. I. Crowder, "The Dreamers," Ibid., Dec. 1913.]
R. A. W.

SMYTH, ALBERT HENRY (June 18, 1863–May 4, 1907), educator, author, and editor, was born in Philadelphia, Pa., the son of William Clarke and Adelaide (Suplee) Smyth. He studied in the public schools of Philadelphia and graduated from the Central High School in 1882. After two years of desultory work on local newspapers, and some time as assistant librarian in the Mercantile Library, he was engaged in 1885 to catalogue books at the Johns Hopkins University, Baltimore, Md., where he found opportunity to pursue certain seminar courses in 1885–86, and in February 1887 received the degree of A.B. extra ordinem. Elected professor of English language and literature at the Central High School of Philadelphia in 1886, from 1893 till his death he was head of the department. He never married. Instead he showed a rare devotion to cultural pursuits. His active and versatile mind found an outlet in writing and in lecturing, especially in courses arranged by the Free Library of Philadelphia and by the University Extension Society. Enthusiasm for his subject, ready wit, a fine presence, a beautiful voice, and a natural gift of eloquence made him an unusually pleasing speaker. Among his earlier volumes were American Literature (1889), The Philadelphia Magazines and Their Contributors (1892), and Bayard Taylor (1896) in the American Men of Letters series; he edited Edmund Burke's Letter to a Noble Lord (1898) and Pope: the Iliad of Homer (1899). At the age of twenty he had become one of a small group of youths who founded Shakespeariana, which he continued to edit until 1886; later in his writing, teaching, and lecturing he did valuable service in encouraging a wider interest in Shakespeare and became known as a student of Shakespeare and his country. Every summer after 1886 he spent abroad, studying in foreign libraries and establishing lasting friendships with some of the leading scholars of the time. In addition to his Shakespeare's Pericles and Apollonius of Tyre (1898), a revision of seminar studies made at Johns Hopkins, he wrote a critical and historical introduction to a translation of Hamlet into modern Greek and published numerous reviews of modern Greek translations of Shakespeare. Upon invitation he even superintended a production of Hamlet at Phalerum, Greece.

In 1887 he was elected to the American Philosophical Society, as a delegate of which he delivered a Latin oration at Glasgow on the occasion of the 450th anniversary of the university. Two of his memorial addresses were published in the *Proceedings of the American Philosophical Society, Memorial Volume I* (1900), one on Henry Phillips, the other on Daniel Garrison Brinton [*qq.v.*]. It was undoubtedly through his interest in the Society that the most notable undertaking of his life developed, the publication of the *Writings of Benjamin Franklin* (10 vols., 1905–07). The American Philosophical Society had long had in its possession the most valuable collection in existence of Franklin's manuscripts, more than 13,000 documents in nine languages, and when plans were begun for the celebration of the bicentenary of Franklin's birth it was thought that "a revised and authoritative edition of his Works might be possibly the best and most enduring monument" to his memory (*Writings of Benjamin Franklin*, vol. I, p. viii). There had been three previous editions of Franklin's writings. William Temple Franklin in 1818 had produced an edition of his grandfather's works that was neither adequate nor satisfactory; Jared Sparks [*q.v.*] had saved many valuable papers from oblivion, but had tampered ruthlessly with spelling, grammar, style, and even substance; John Bigelow [*q.v.*] had not had available material that later came to light and occasionally accepted the defective transcripts of Sparks. Smyth's edition was made with assiduous and painstaking care that involved his personal examination of practically all the known documents in Europe and America, a careful study of eighteenth-century newspapers, and the examination of many of Franklin's private papers that had never before fallen into the hands of an editor. As a result of his extensive and thorough research he published 385 letters and 40 articles that had not appeared in previous editions, and from the discovery of many missing leaves was enabled to restore letters hitherto "mutilated" or "incomplete." Every document was faithfully reprinted from the original, "every point, capital letter, and eccentricity of spelling loyally preserved" in accordance with the desires of Franklin, who had urged his printer to observe "strictly the Italicking, Capitalling and Pointing" (*Ibid.*, p. ix). There were added a bibliography of printed material, an analysis of Franklin's writings, and an extensive index. In both the editing and annotating of this authoritative edition Smyth displayed great literary skill, historical accuracy, and good judgment. In 1906 he was decorated by the French government with the insignia of the Legion of Honor when he spoke with marked distinction as the representative of the United States at the dedi-cation of a statue of Franklin in Paris. His plans to write a life of Franklin and to edit the writings of George Washington were frustrated by his sudden death in Germantown, Pa., of Bright's disease. On the day of his funeral the schools of Stratford-on-Avon were closed as a mark of respect. A portrait of him, painted by James B. Sword, is in the Central High School, Philadelphia.

[See *Who's Who in America*, 1906–07; F. S. Edmonds, *The Early Life of Albert Henry Smyth, 78th Class* (1912), in Hist. Ser. of the Associated Alumni of the Central High School of Phila.; J. G. Rosengarten, in *Proc. Am. Philosophical Soc.*, vol. XLVI (1907); William Winter, *Old Friends* (1909), pp. 329–36; A. S. Henry, in *Book News Monthly*, July 1907; Albert Mordell, in *Barnwell Bull.*, Mar. 1934; R. E. Thompson, *Ibid.*, Oct. 1934; obit. notice in *Pub. Ledger* (Phila.), May 5, 1907. Smyth himself gives an excellent account of his editorship in *Writings of Benjamin Franklin*, vol. I (1905).]   A. L. L.

SMYTH, ALEXANDER (1765–Apr. 17, 1830), soldier, congressman, was born in the island of Rathlin off the coast of Ireland and was brought as a child to Virginia by his father, the Rev. Adam Smyth, who became rector of the Episcopal parish of Botetourt, at Fincastle, Botetourt County. Here Alexander grew up during the American Revolution. He completed his preparatory studies at home, read law, and was appointed deputy clerk of Botetourt County when he was twenty years old. He was licensed in 1789 and began practice at Abingdon, Va. In January 1791, he married Nancy Binkley of Wythe County, and the next year established his home there, where he maintained a practice until his death. He was the father of two sons and two daughters. In 1792, 1796, 1801–02, and 1804–08, he served in the Virginia House of Delegates, and in 1808–09 in the state Senate.

Meanwhile, July 8, 1808, President Jefferson had commissioned him colonel of the Southwest Virginia rifle regiment, and on July 6, 1812, upon the outbreak of war with Great Britain, he was appointed inspector-general with the rank of brigadier-general, United States Army. In this year he published *Regulations for the Field Exercise, Manoeuvres, and Conduct of the Infantry of the United States*. At his own request he was given command of a brigade of regulars ordered to Niagara for the projected invasion of Canada. Here he quarreled with his superior officer, Gen. Stephen Van Rensselaer [*q.v.*] of the New York militia, as to whether the crossing into Canada should be made above or below the Falls. Van Rensselaer, without the cooperation of Smyth, attempted to cross below, failed for lack of support by his own forces, and was relieved of his command at his own request. His force was then turned over to Smyth, who took command at Buffalo, Oct. 24, 1812, and issued a boastful and confident address promising immediate conquest of Canada. On Nov. 25 he gave orders to prepare for crossing, at Black Rock, above Buffalo. Two detachments crossed successfully on the morning of Nov. 28, but by that afternoon it was discovered that only 1,200 of the 4,500 men could be embarked on the boats from the navy yard; Smyth, probably correctly, refused to risk fighting with less than 3,000 men, and a council of war decided to abandon the project. After one more attempt to cross, Dec. 1, the ill-organized, untrained, and ill-equipped army dissolved. One of Smyth's subordinates, Peter B. Porter [q.v.], in command of volunteers, published a letter in the *Buffalo Gazette* (Dec. 8, 1812), attributing the failure to the cowardice of Smyth, who challenged him, but after an exchange of shots on Grand Island the two men shook hands and came back to Black Rock unhurt. Smyth suffered much just ridicule for his bombast and much unjust condemnation for his failure. His answer to a committee of citizens of western New York (dated Dec. 3, 1812; see Severance, *post*, p. 235), in which he laid the blame on the miserable condition of the army and the lack of soldierly spirit in the troops, described the conditions correctly.

He asked permission to visit his family in the winter of 1812–13, which was granted by Dearborn. Before his leave expired, by an act of Congress reorganizing the staff, he was "legislated out" of the army. He sent a petition to Congress, couched in somewhat sentimental terms, asking that his name be replaced on the list of officers, that he might "die, if Heaven wills it, in the defence of his country" (*Annals of Congress*, 13 Cong., 1 Sess., p. 807), but no action was taken in the matter. His own people in Virginia retained their confidence in him, however, and sent him to the House of Delegates, 1816–17 and 1826–27, and to every Congress, except the Nineteenth (1825–27), from 1817 until his death. In his later years he wrote *An Explanation of the Apocalypse, or Revelation of St. John* (1825). In 1811 had appeared *Speeches Delivered by Alexander Smyth, in the House of Delegates and at the Bar*. He died at Washington, and was buried in the Congressional Cemetery.

[For sketches of Smyth's career see Goodridge Wilson, *Smyth County Hist. and Traditions* (1932); F. H. Severance, "The Case of Gen. Alexander Smyth," *Buffalo Hist. Soc. Pubs.*, vol. XVIII (1914); and T. N. Parmelee, "Recollections of an Old Stager: Apocalypse Smythe," *Harper's New Monthly Mag.*, June 1874. The Niagara correspondence is printed in Hezekiah Niles's *Weekly Register*, Sept. 1812–Mar. 1813, and in *The Hist. Reg. of the U. S.*, pt. 2, vol. II (1814). The treatment of Smyth by the major historians is uniformly unfavorable; see Henry Adams, *Hist. of the U. S. A.*, vol. VI (1890); J. B. McMaster, *A Hist. of the People of the U. S.*, vol. IV (copr. 1895); James Schouler, *Hist. of the U. S. A.*, vol. II (copr. 1882); B. J. Lossing, *The Pictorial Field-Book of the War of 1812* (1868). See also *Biog. Dir. Am. Cong.* (1928); *Daily National Intelligencer*, Apr. 19, 1830; *Richmond Enquirer*, Apr. 23, 1830. Copies of Smyth's speeches and family MSS. are in the possession of R. P. Johnson, Wytheville, Va.]

J. E. W.

SMYTH, EGBERT COFFIN (Aug. 24, 1829–Apr. 12, 1904), Congregational clergyman, professor at Andover Theological Seminary, was born in Brunswick, Me., the son of William Smyth [q.v.], professor of mathematics at Bowdoin College, and Harriet Porter (Coffin); Newman Smyth [q.v.] was a brother. Egbert attended Dummer Academy at Byfield, Mass., and was graduated at Bowdoin College in 1848. He taught at Farmington, N. H., 1848–49, was tutor in Greek at Bowdoin, 1849–51, and graduated at Bangor Theological Seminary in 1853. The year following he studied theology at Andover and then for two years was professor of rhetoric and oratory at Bowdoin. He was ordained at Brunswick on July 22, 1856, and served as Collins Professor of Natural and Revealed Religion at Bowdoin from 1856 to 1862. After a year spent in the study of theology at Berlin and Halle he was appointed Brown Professor of Ecclesiastical History at Andover and so continued for the rest of his life. He was also lecturer on pastoral theology, 1863–68, and president of the faculty, 1878–96.

He was a leader in the foundation, in 1884, of the *Andover Review*, a magazine conducted by the faculty in the interest of the interpretation of the old theological standards in the light of modern scholarship. In 1886 he and four other professors were brought to trial by the board of visitors for ideas expressed in the *Review*, and Smyth was removed from his chair of instruction. The trustees, who sustained the faculty, appealed to the supreme court of Massachusetts, which, Oct. 28, 1891, set aside the verdict of the board of visitors on technical grounds. A second trial before the board, the following year, resulted in the case being dismissed. As a member of the prudential committee of the American Board of Commissioners for Foreign Missions Smyth steadily championed the right of liberal interpretation standards, during the controversies in the eighties over the qualifications of candidates for appointment to the mission field. He did not affirm, as he was charged with doing, the doctrine of "future probation," but he did believe and teach that no eschatology could stand which limited God's redemptive purpose. This controversy was finally ended in 1893 by the board's adoption of a modern policy.

His especial interest in the field of ecclesiastical history was the development of Christian thought, which he pursued by the historical rather than the dogmatic method. His favorite field was the first three centuries, through which he traced the growth of the doctrines of the Trinity and the divinity of Christ with great detail and scholarly thoroughness. The other major domain of his interest was the religious thought of the eighteenth century, with especial reference to Jonathan Edwards. While Smyth produced no books, he was the author of many published sermons and a large number of scholarly monographs, the more important of which are: *Value of the Study of Church History in Ministerial Education* (1874); "The Change of the Sabbath to the Lord's Day," in *Sabbath Essays* (1880), edited by W. C. Wood; *Recent Excavations in Ancient Christian Cemeteries* (1882); *Progressive Orthodoxy* (1886), and *The Divinity of Jesus Christ* (1893), in collaboration with the other editors of the *Andover Review*; *Some Early Writings of Jonathan Edwards,* reprinted from *Proceedings of the American Antiquarian Society* (n.s., vol. X, 1896); *The Prevalent View in the Ancient Church of the Purpose of the Death of Jesus Christ* (1900); "Influence of Jonathan Edwards on the Spiritual Life of New England," in *Jonathan Edwards; a Retrospect* (1901), edited by H. N. Gardiner. He also prepared, in collaboration with Prof. C. J. H. Ropes, *The Conflict of Christianity with Heathenism* (1879), a translation of Gerhard Uhlhorn's work, and edited *Observations Concerning the Scripture Œconomy of the Trinity and Covenant of Redemption* (1880), by Jonathan Edwards.

Smyth was a member of several historical societies, a trustee and overseer of Bowdoin College, and a trustee of Dummer and Abbot academies. His nature was rich and sympathetic and his manner, quiet and self-effacing; but his indomitable will caused him to stand firm for his convictions. His wife, whom he married Aug. 12, 1857, was Elizabeth Bradford, daughter of Rev. William Theodore Dwight of Portland, Me., and a descendant of Jonathan Edwards: they had no children.

[*Congregational Year-Book,* 1905; *Congregationalist,* Apr. 23, 1904; *Andover Theological Sem., Necrology,* 1903–04; *Proc. Mass. Hist. Soc.,* 2 ser., vol. XVIII (1905); *Proc. Am. Antiquarian Soc.,* n.s. vol. XVI (1905), with full list of Smyth's publications; E. Y. Hincks, "Rev. Egbert Coffin Smyth, D.D., LL.D.," *New Eng. Hist. and Geneal. Reg.,* Jan. 1905, also printed separately (1904); H. P. Dewey, *Address at the Presentation of the Portrait of Professor Smyth to Andover Theological Seminary* (1901); *The Andover Case* (1887); C. A. Bartol, *The Andover Bottle's Burst* (1882).]

F. T. P.

SMYTH, JOHN HENRY (July 14, 1844–Sept. 5, 1908), negro lawyer, diplomat, and educator, was born in Richmond, Va., the son of Sully and Ann Eliza (Goode) Smyth. His father was a slave who had been bought from his master for $1,800 by his free-born wife. Since she could not set her husband free under the Virginia law, she willed him to her son. When eight years old John was sent to Philadelphia to be educated. He attended Quaker schools until the death of his father in 1857, when he was obliged to go to work. He is said to have been the first colored newsboy in Philadelphia and he also did errands for a dry-goods store. In 1858, when only fourteen, he entered the Pennsylvania Academy of the Fine Arts, the first colored student admitted there; later, after he had met with fair success as a landscape and figure painter, he was made a member.

In 1859 he became a student in the Institute for Colored Youth, from which he was graduated on May 4, 1862. He then taught in the Philadelphia public schools and at Wilkes-Barre and Pottsville. In 1865 he went to England with the intention of studying for the stage under Ira Aldridge [*q.v.*], the negro actor. The latter died unexpectedly so that Smyth was unable to carry out his plan. While in London he supported himself by giving Shakespearian readings. Returning to the United States in 1869, he entered Howard University Law School, Washington, D. C., and became a clerk, first in the Freedmen's Bureau, and later, in the Census Bureau. On Dec. 24, 1870, he married Fannie E. Shippen, by whom he had a son and a daughter. In 1872 Smyth graduated from Howard University and was made cashier of the Wilmington (N. C.) branch of the Freedmen's Savings & Trust Company of Washington. After the failure of this institution in 1874, he practised law and in 1875 was a delegate to the state constitutional convention. In 1876 he worked for the nomination and election of President Hayes. As a reward for these activities he was appointed, May 23, 1878, minister resident and consul general in Liberia, which position, with one brief intermission, he held until Sept. 11, 1885. He proved himself a thoroughly competent diplomat, and wrote some excellent dispatches on conditions in Liberia (see *Foreign Relations of the United States,* 1879–83).

For some years following his return to the United States he was engaged in the real estate business in Washington. This he relinquished to become editor of the *Reformer,* of Richmond, Va. Learning that delinquent colored boys were being sent to penal institutions in Virginia where they soon became hardened criminals, as the crowning work of his life he secured the establishment in 1897 of the Virginia Manual Labor School at Hanover, the necessary funds being contributed by Northern and Southern philanthropists. It was opened Sept. 12, 1899, and until his death Smyth was in charge of the institution, which has always been conducted on the lines laid down by him (see his article, "Negro Criminality," in the *Southern Workman*, November 1900). He was a handsome member of his race, dark in color with a fine head and regular features. He was large and portly, wore a moustache and a short tufted beard, and was courtly in manners.

[W. J. Simmons, *Men of Mark* (1887); *News Leader* (Richmond, Va.), Sept. 5, 1908; *Times-Dispatch* (Richmond), Sept. 6, 1908; *Southern Workman*, Oct. 1908; data supplied by a daughter, Mrs. Clara Smyth Taliaferro.]　　　　　　　　　　　　H. G. V.

SMYTH, JULIAN KENNEDY (Aug. 8, 1856–Apr. 4, 1921), minister of the Church of the New Jerusalem, was born at New York City, the son of Joseph Kennedy and Julia Gabriella (Ogden) Smyth. He came of colonial stock, which on the paternal side was Loyalist, and on the maternal, Revolutionary. An ancestor, Francis Lewis [*q.v.*], was a signer of the Declaration of Independence. Julian's childhood years were spent in France; in America, he was educated under private tutors in his parents' home, "Boscobel," Fordham. Through his mother—her sister was Anna Cora (Ogden) Mowatt [*q.v.*] —the youth inherited dramatic talent, and was attracted about equally to the theatre, journalism, and the ministry. As a student at Urbana University, Urbana, Ohio, however, he decided for the ministry, and went there in 1877 to the New-Church Theological School, then situated at Waltham, Mass.

That same year he began his ministry at Portland, Me., and on Nov. 22 married Winogene Horr, of Urbana; two daughters were born to them. In 1882 he was called to the Roxbury (Mass.) Society of the New Church. During a ministry of sixteen years there he was also an editor (1894–98) of the *New-Church Review*, and published two books, *Footprints of the Saviour* (1886) and *Holy Names* (1891). A visit to Palestine and Egypt in the year 1892 added to his vividness as an expositor of the Bible. His abilities as an executive and his gift of leadership came to wider notice when, in 1898, he undertook the pastorate of the New York Society, where he served for the remaining twenty-three years of his life. He was elected presiding minister of the state association in 1909, and, in 1911, president of the General Convention of the

New Jerusalem in the United States of America, serving in both positions to the end of his life. In the latter office he exerted a marked constructive influence throughout the Church he served. Even in the disturbing years of the World War, his energy and spirit brought unprecedented solidarity to the organization. A national sustaining fund was established, the liturgy was made uniform, and a campaign launched for the more adequate endowment of Urbana University. He was instrumental in arranging for the preparation of a new hymnal for the Church, to which he himself made a number of contributions. In connection with his parish he directed a mission, "Kennedy House." He also found time for writing and published *Swedenborg* (1911), a stirring address he had delivered the previous year at the Swedenborg Congress in London; *Religion and Life* (1911), the best illustration of his varied powers as a preacher; *The Heart of the War* (1914); *Christian Certainties of Belief* (1916); and *The Gist of Swedenborg* (1920), with W. F. Wunsch. He died in White Sulphur Springs, W. Va.

[W. O. Wheeler, *The Ogden Family in America* (1907); *New-Church Messenger*, June 1, 1921; *New-Church Rev.*, July 1921; *Jour. of the . . . General Convention of the New Jerusalem in the U. S. A.*, 1909, 1911; *N. Y. Herald*, Apr. 6, 1921.]　　W. F. W—h.

SMYTH, NEWMAN (June 25, 1843–Jan. 6, 1925), Congregational clergyman, theologian, was born in Brunswick, Me., the son of William Smyth [*q.v.*], long professor of mathematics at Bowdoin College, and a brother of Egbert C. Smyth [*q.v.*]. His mother was Harriet Porter Coffin. Named by his parents Samuel Phillips Newman, he early dropped the first two appellations. At the age of twelve he entered Phillips Academy, Andover, and four years later, Bowdoin College, from which he graduated in 1863. After a brief period as librarian and assistant teacher of mathematics in the naval academy at Newport, R. I., he entered the Union army as a first lieutenant in the 16th Maine Volunteers and saw active service in the vicinity of Petersburg, Va., until the close of the Civil War. In 1867 he graduated from Andover Theological Seminary, and began his ministry in Providence, R. I., where he took charge of a mission connected with what was then the High Street Congregational Church, being ordained Jan. 29, 1868. A year later he went to Germany and pursued theological studies at the University of Berlin and the University of Halle. Upon his return he became pastor of the Congregational Church at Bangor, Me., continuing as such until 1875, and on June 20, 1871, marrying Anna M. Ayer. In 1876 he assumed charge of the

First Presbyterian Church, Quincy, Ill., in which relationship he remained until 1882, when he was called to the pastorate of the First Church of Christ (Congregational), New Haven, Conn. After serving for twenty-six years he became pastor emeritus. In 1899 he was elected a fellow of Yale University, and was active in the affairs of that institution until his death.

As a preacher Smyth's appeal was to the thoughtful. His sermons had literary style and were delivered with a quiet yet deep emotional intensity; but he had few oratorical gifts and never resorted to cheap expedients for popular effects. As a thinker and contributor to theological development, however, he exerted a strong influence both in the United States and abroad. He had a keen, logical mind and, even in his college days, a passion for reality not inhibited by fears of any kind. The New England theology as expounded by Prof. Edwards A. Park [q.v.] at Andover he repudiated as orthodox rationalism. His studies in Germany introduced him to modern Biblical criticism. He returned home to become one of the most constructive theological writers of his generation. His first book, *The Religious Feeling*, appeared in 1877. This was followed by *Old Faiths in New Light* (1878), *The Orthodox Theology of Today* (1881), *The Reality of Faith* (1884), *Christian Facts and Forces* (1887). In these his approach to spiritual truth is through a study of man in connection with his total environment, a method which, grounded in faith, "seeks to interpret results in mind and history by following with patient investigation the processes of life through which they have come to be what they are" (Smyth, "Orthodox Rationalism," *Princeton Review,* May 1882, p. 309). Upon the retirement of Professor Park from his chair at Andover in 1881, Smyth was chosen by the trustees to succeed him. Opposition to the appointment arose in the board of visitors, however, based on a statement in Smyth's writings regarding eternal punishment, and this opposition helped to precipitate the famous Andover controversy. His theological method caused him to welcome with enthusiasm the results of modern science, and he became a student in the Yale biological laboratory to gain better acquaintance with the scientific method and discoveries. The fruits of his studies appear in *The Place of Death in Evolution* (1897), *Through Science to Faith* (1902), *Modern Belief in Immortality* (1910), *Constructive Natural Theology* (1913), and *The Meaning of Personal Life* (1916). Another work, written earlier for the International Theological Library, *Christian Ethics* (1892), at once took rank

among the leading treatments of that subject. During his later years he devoted himself with a zeal that no adverse winds could chill to the cause of church union, serving on various commissions and, in 1913, as chairman of a delegation to the Non-Conformist Churches of Great Britain in the interest of a world conference. He welcomed the modernist movement in the Roman Catholic Church as suggesting a possible future means of approach for the Catholic and Protestant bodies; his own activities were directed particularly to the union of the Congregational and Episcopal denominations. In 1908 he published *Passing Protestantism and Coming Catholicism*; in 1919, with Williston Walker, *Approaches Towards Church Unity*; and in 1923, *A Story of Church Unity.* Shortly before his death, which occurred in New Haven, he finished an autobiographical work, *Recollections and Reflections* (1926).

[*Recollections,* to which are appended commemorative addresses by B. W. Bacon, Peter Ainslie, and J. DeW. Perry; *Gen. Cat. of Bowdoin Coll.* (1912); *Gen. Cat. of the Theological Sem. at Andover, Mass., 1808–1908* (n.d.); *Who's Who in America,* 1924–25; J. W. Buckham, *Progressive Religious Thought in America* (1919); *Congregationalist,* Jan. 22, 1925; *New Haven Journal-Courier,* Jan. 6, 7, 1925; personal acquaintance.]
H. E. S.

SMYTH, THOMAS (June 14, 1808–Aug. 20, 1873), Presbyterian clergyman and author, was born in Belfast, Ireland, one of twelve children. His father, Samuel Smyth, of English descent and a ruling elder in the Presbyterian Church, was a successful business man who accumulated a considerable fortune but lost it all. His mother, Ann (Magee) Smyth, of Scotch descent, belonged to a rather remarkable family, one of whom founded the Magee College in Londonderry, Ireland. After his marriage the father changed the spelling of his name to Smith, but Thomas resumed the "y" in 1837. He was a frail but precocious child and won many prizes in school. For five years he attended the Academic Institution of Belfast and in 1827 entered Belfast College, where he made a brilliant record. In 1829 he enrolled at Highbury College, London, continuing his classical course and at the same time beginning the study of theology.

Because of financial reverses his family moved to the United States in 1830, and Smyth spent the year 1830–31 in Princeton Theological Seminary. On Oct. 4, 1831, he was ordained to the ministry by the Presbytery of Newark. Soon after his ordination he was called to supply the pulpit of the Second Presbyterian Church of Charleston, S. C., and on Dec. 29, 1834, was installed as its pastor. In the meantime, on July 9, 1832, he married Margaret Milligan Adger, a member of his congregation; ten children were born to them. When he came to Charleston he was a frail but scholarly young man of twenty-five. He grew rapidly in scholarship and in power as a preacher and writer, until he was one of the leading ministers in his state and denomination.

Although his health was always precarious, he was an untiring worker. His sermons were prepared with the greatest care and he was also a diligent pastor. In addition to his regular duties he was an omnivorous reader and a prolific writer. Some time after his death his writings were collected and edited by his son-in-law, Rev. J. William Flinn, D.D., and his daughter Jean Adger Flinn, and published in ten volumes under the title *Complete Works of Rev. Thomas Smyth* (1908-12). In these writings Smyth discussed with great ability many questions which were before the Church in his day. Since the majority of them have been displaced by others, his discussions do not have the same interest or value for the present generation which they had for his own; yet they constitute a vast storehouse of information and thought. His *Autobiographical Notes, Letters and Reflections,* which was published in 1914, contains much that is of historical value.

In 1850 Smyth suffered a stroke of paralysis from which he never fully recovered, but he toiled on for twenty years. "I have lived from day to day as a tenant at will," he wrote, "looking any moment for an ejectment and change of residence" (*Autobiographical Notes,* p. 510). In 1870 another stroke came and he resigned the pastorate of his church. He continued to work, however, sorting and arranging his manuscripts. From time to time he would say to his physician: "Not ready yet, Doctor." Finally all the manuscripts were arranged, and when the physician came again, Smyth said: "Doctor, I have finished, I am ready" (*Ibid.,* p. 710). That afternoon the end came. While still a student in Highbury College, London, he had developed "a voracious appetite for books." This appetite grew with the years until he had what was probably the most complete collection of theological books to be found in any private library in America. Toward the close of his life his library was turned over to the Columbia Theological Seminary, then located at Columbia, S. C., and now at Decatur, Ga., and it is still kept intact by that institution. In his will he left an endowment for this library, and also an endowment for the Smyth Lectureship at Columbia Seminary.

[G. R. Brackett, *The Christian Warrior Crowned —In Memoriam* (1873); George Howe, *Hist. of the Presbyterian Church in S. C.,* vol. II (1883); *Semi-Centennial of Columbia Seminary* (1884); W. C. Robinson, *Columbia Theological Seminary and the Southern Presbyterian Church* (1931); H. A. White, *Southern Presbyterian Leaders* (1911); *News and Courier* (Charleston, S. C.), Aug. 21, 1873.]
W. L. L.

SMYTH, WILLIAM (Feb. 2, 1797–Apr. 4, 1868), professor of mathematics, was born at Pittston, Me., the son of Caleb and Abia (Colburn) Smyth. In William's childhood his father moved to Wiscasset; he was a shipbuilder and also taught music. During the War of 1812 young Smyth entered the army and gave his bounty to his mother. His service consisted in acting as secretary to his colonel; it is said he was never in his life able to fire a gun (Packard, *post,* pp. 7–8). After leaving the army he became a clerk at Wiscasset and prepared himself to teach. His parents died when he was eighteen and to support a younger brother and sister he opened and taught a private school, and at the same time fitted himself for college, often studying by the light of the fire. Two years later he became an assistant at Gorham Academy and continued studying with such good results that in 1820 he entered Bowdoin College as a junior. Here he pursued his course against great obstacles, for his sight had been so much impaired that he was obliged to have his lessons read to him by his roommate. He also supported a younger brother in college, though often at his wit's end even for the bare necessities of life. Nevertheless he took the lead of an able class and graduated with the English valedictory in 1822.

After graduation he spent a year at Andover Theological Seminary and then returned to Bowdoin as instructor in Greek. Although Greek was his specialty, he soon was obliged also to take on instruction in mathematics. It is recorded that he introduced the use of the blackboard and made his course so interesting that many requested the privilege of reviewing their algebra under the new method. On succeeding to the professorship of mathematics in 1828 he began a series of textbooks, many of which were used in the leading colleges of the country and won the commendation of the foremost American scientists of the day. The earliest of these were *Elements of Algebra* and *Elements of Analytic Geometry,* both published in 1830. They were followed by others on the same subjects and on trigonometry and calculus.

In his later life Smyth showed unusual public spirit. A devoted member and officer of the Congregationalist Church of Brunswick, on one occasion when the church edifice was being rebuilt he served as tender to a mason to save expense.

He also drew the working plan for the spire. He was a vigorous supporter of the temperance movement and an opponent of slavery, his home being a station on the "underground railroad" for forwarding escaped slaves to Canada. He was particularly devoted to the college, and by his personal efforts raised the larger part of the money required to build Memorial Hall in honor of Bowdoin men who fought in the Civil War; indeed, it was his arduous labors in connection with this enterprise that led to his sudden death. He was also much interested in public education. He introduced a system of graded schools at Brunswick and often appeared before the Maine legislature on school matters. What were then liberal educational movements had his earnest support. He was an admirable example of the college professor of the old school, a competent scholar, an able teacher, precise, simple, clear, a strong Christian, a man greatly interested not merely in his students but in his community and in his state. He was married in 1827 to Harriet Porter Coffin; they had six children, two of whom were Egbert and Newman [qq.v.].

[*Vital Records of Pittston, Me., to the Year 1892* (1911); G. A. and H. W. Wheeler, *Hist. of Brunswick, Topsham, and Harpswell, Me.* (1878); A. S. Packard, *Address on the Life and Character of William Smyth, D.D.* (1868); Newman Smyth, *Recollections and Reflections* (1926); L. C. Hatch, *The Hist. of Bowdoin Coll.* (1927); *Gen. Cat. of Bowdoin Coll.* (1912); *Bangor Daily Whig and Courier*, Apr. 6, 7, 1868.]

K. C. M. S.

SNEAD, THOMAS LOWNDES (Jan. 10, 1828–Oct. 17, 1890), soldier, author, was born in Henrico County, Va., the son of Jesse and Jane J. (Johnson) Snead, the daughter of Mary (Henley) and Benjamin Johnson. He went to Richmond College, then to the University of Virginia, where he studied law for two years, 1846–48. Although admitted to the bar of Virginia in 1850, he chose St. Louis, Mo., for his future home. There he practised law and became interested in newspaper work. He was on the staff of the *Bulletin* during 1860 and 1861. There also he met Harriet Vairin Reel, the only child of John W. and Harriet Louise (Shreve) Reel, to whom he was married on Nov. 24, 1852. At the outbreak of the Civil War, he set aside editorial and legal work to become aide-de-camp to Gov. Claiborne F. Jackson. Acting as the governor's secretary, he attended the Planters' Hotel conference in June 1861, the last futile attempt of Missourians for peace. Immediately thereafter he became acting adjutant-general, with rank of colonel, of the Missouri state guard and took part in the battles of Booneville, Carthage, Wilson's Creek, and Lexington. He acted as one of Missouri's two commissioners in a military convention with the Confederate States, which was signed on Oct. 31, 1861. In 1862 he became assistant adjutant-general of the Confederate army, serving with the rank of major, chief of staff to Gen. Sterling Price in the southwest. In 1864 he was elected representative from Missouri to the Second Confederate Congress and resigned his post in the army. A faithful supporter of Jefferson Davis, he was a member of the committees on foreign affairs and on impressments and also of a special committee on increasing the military force.

After the war, on account of the severe test oath of Missouri's radical Reconstruction, he made New York City his third and last home. In 1865 he became the managing editor of the *New York Daily News*. The following year he was admitted to the bar and devoted his time to the law and to writing. His best known work is a detailed history of the war entitled *The Fight for Missouri*, published in 1886 and covering the period from November 1860 to Aug. 10, 1861. He also wrote "The First Year of the War," "With Price East of the Mississippi," and "Conquest of Arkansas" in *Battles and Leaders of the Civil War* (vols. I–III, 1887–88, ed. by R. U. Johnson and C. C. Buel). He possessed a host of friends who were attracted by his buoyant optimism and sunny disposition. He was a member of the Union Club of New York and was a charter member of the New York Southern Society. His death came suddenly from heart disease in his rooms in the Hotel Royal, New York City, and he was survived by his wife, a daughter, and a son. He was buried in Bellefontaine Cemetery, St. Louis.

[E. A. Allen, "Thomas Lowndes Snead," *Library of Southern Literature*, XI (1907), ed. by E. A. Alderman and J. C. Harris; S. B. Paul, *Memorial of Thomas Lowndes Snead* (1890); Dunbar Rowland, *Jefferson Davis, Constitutionalist* (1923), vols. VIII, X; O. V. S. Hatcher, *The Sneads of Fluvanna* (1910), pp. 111–12; *War of the Rebellion: Official Records (Army)*, 1 ser., III, XVII, XXII, XLI, pt. 2, LII–LIII, 2 ser., I, 4 ser., III; H. E. Robinson, *Two Mo. Historians; a Paper . . . before the State Hist. Soc. Mo. . . . Dec. 5, 1901* (1912); *N. Y. Times, Richmond Dispatch*, and *St. Louis Globe-Democrat*, Oct. 19, 1890; *St. Louis Post-Dispatch*, Oct. 18, 1890; University of Va. records, information from I. Shreve Carter, St. Louis, Mo.]

L. L. T.

SNELLING, HENRY HUNT (Nov. 8, 1817–June 24, 1897), pioneer in photographic journalism, was born at Plattsburg, N. Y. He came of army stock—his father was Col. Josiah Snelling [q.v.]; his mother, Abigail, was the daughter of Col. Thomas Hunt—and his childhood was spent in army posts on the northern and northwestern frontiers, with Indian boys and girls and the children of other soldiers as his playfellows. Apparently his father expected him to follow a military calling, for in 1828 he was entered in a military academy at Georgetown, D. C., but upon his father's death soon afterward the family moved to Detroit, Mich., where the mother opened a boarding house, and here Henry completed his schooling and began a business career. In 1837 he married Anna L. Putnam, a sister of George Palmer Putnam [q.v.]. She was the author of *Kabaosa; or The Warriors of the West* (1842).

The year after his marriage Snelling moved with his wife to New York City, where he was employed for a while as librarian of the New York Lyceum and then for a time conducted a circulating library. In New York he met Edward Anthony, who was instrumental in awakening his interest in photography. When in 1843 Anthony started manufacturing and selling daguerrean supplies, Snelling became his general sales manager and devoted his energy to the forwarding of this business with such good purpose that it grew rapidly and was dominant in its field for many years. In 1849 Snelling made his first contribution to photographic literature, *The History and Practice of the Art of Photography*, published by his brother-in-law; this is said to have been the first bound volume on photography published in America. In 1850 Snelling sent out proposals for the issuance of the *Photographic Art Journal*, a pioneer in its field, and the first number appeared in January of the following year. Soon after its inception the magazine was increased to quarto size and its name was changed to *Photographic and Fine Art Journal*, the aim of the editor being to give artistic as well as technical instruction to photographers. In 1854 he published *A Dictionary of the Photographic Art*. During these years he was constantly experimenting with photographic processes. In 1852 he invented the enlarging camera; about the same time he devised a ray filter, eliminating the yellow rays by means of blue glass; in 1856 he announced a color process, but never published a description of it. In addition to his editorial and experimental labors he retained his active connection with the firm of E. & H. T. Anthony, often devoting sixteen hours a day to its business. Excessive work brought on nervous prostration, and, beginning in 1857, he was forced to spend three years in rest and idleness. About this time the *Photographic and Fine Art Journal* was sold to C. A. Seely, who had been a contributor to its pages.

Upon regaining his health, Snelling held clerical positions first with the Bureau of Internal Revenue and then with the immigration service, but suffered another breakdown, and was or-

dered to the country, where he experimented with farming for a period of two years. Later he moved to Newburgh, N. Y., but after a few months responded again to the lure of editorial work and, moving to Cornwall, N. Y., conducted the *Cornwall Reflector* for a period of eight years. Again illness overtook him, this time accompanied by blindness, which brought about his complete retirement in 1887.

Snelling was described by his nephew, George Haven Putnam, as "a good-natured 'Skimpole' kind of man, who was always in need of help from his brothers-in-law" (*A Memoir of George Palmer Putnam*, 1903, I, 87). Childless and left alone by the death of his wife, he spent his last years in the Memorial Home, St. Louis. In 1889-90 he published "Photographic Entertainments" in *Wilson's Photographic Magazine*. He died at the Memorial Home in his eightieth year. A manuscript autobiography—"Memoirs of a Life" —covering the years down to 1868, is in the Newberry Library, Chicago.

[*St. Louis and Canadian Photographer*, Aug. 1890; *Wilson's Photographic Mag.*, 1889-90, and Aug. 1893; *Minn. Hist. Soc. Colls.*, vol. V (1885); E. F. L. Ellet, *Pioneer Women of the West* (1852); A. J. Olmsted, "Snelling the Father of Photographic Journalism," *Camera* (Phila.), Dec. 1934; *St. Louis Globe-Democrat*, June 25, 1897.]   A.J.O.

SNELLING, JOSIAH (1782–Aug. 20, 1828), soldier, was born in Boston, Mass., and was married there, Aug. 29, 1804, to Elizabeth Bell, who died soon after the birth of a son, William Joseph Snelling [q.v.]. Snelling entered the army in 1808 as a first lieutenant in the 4th, later 5th) Infantry, then being organized, and was promoted captain in 1809. He fought at the battle of Tippecanoe, and was afterwards stationed at Detroit, becoming a prisoner of the British upon the capitulation of Gen. William Hull [q.v.], in August 1812. Years later he published *Remarks on "General Wm. Hull's Memories of the Campaign of the Northwestern Army, 1812"* (1825). Just prior to the surrender, Snelling had married his second wife, Abigail Hunt, daughter of Col. Thomas Hunt of the 1st Infantry. After his exchange he served as major (assistant inspector general), lieutenant-colonel of the 4th Rifles, and colonel (inspector-general), taking part in the Niagara campaign. At the close of the war he became lieutenant-colonel of the 6th Infantry, and in 1819 was promoted colonel of the 5th Infantry, the regiment in which he had originally served.

In that year the regiment was assembled at Detroit and dispatched into the unexplored West to establish three military posts which should serve as centers for the expected settlement of the new country. The chief of these, and the headquarters of the regiment, was Fort St. Anthony, adjacent to the present cities of St. Paul and Minneapolis. Construction was begun by Lieutenant-Colonel Henry Leavenworth [q.v.] in August 1820 and the cornerstone was laid by Colonel Snelling, with ceremony, on Sept. 10, 1820. Some of the buildings were occupied in 1821, though the group was not completed before 1823. The fort consisted of barracks, storehouses, and officers' quarters, with a parade ground, all enclosed by a wall ten feet high, built of stone quarried locally by the soldiers. Two of its towers still survive (1935). Although untenable against troops with artillery, it was impregnable against Indian attack, and was well designed for the purposes it was to serve.

During and after the building of the fort Snelling had to be not only a military commander and a constructing engineer, but also the virtual monarch of a remote and self-contained community, completely isolated from civilization; for it was to be many years before continuous settlement extended so far. He fulfilled his duties well. The perfect type of the rough and convivial old colonel of fiction, "improvident in his habits and usually in debt," "considerate and intelligent when not under the influence of drink," he was likewise a natural leader of men. Though ruthless in discipline, he was admired and liked by his soldiers, who among themselves called him "the Prairie Hen," in consideration of his red and scanty hair. It was with good reason that the War Department in 1825 changed the name of Fort St. Anthony to Fort Snelling in honor of its builder, who remained in command until January 1828. He died in Washington a few months later, while on leave of absence, survived by his wife and four of their children, one of whom was Henry Hunt Snelling [q.v.], together with the son of his first marriage. Snelling's own summary of his career (Hansen, post, p. 219) is modest and shrewd: "I have passed through every grade to the command of a regiment. I owe nothing to executive patronage, for I have neither friend or relation connected with the government: I have obtained my rank in the ordinary course of promotion, and have retained it by doing my duty."

[M. L. Hansen, *Old Fort Snelling, 1819–1858* (1918); Charlotte O. C. Van Cleve, *"Three Score Years and Ten"* (1888); E. D. Neill, *Fort Snelling, Minn.* (1888), repr. from *Mag. of Western Hist.*, June, Aug. 1888; *Minn. Hist. Soc. Colls.*, esp. vols. I (1872), II (1889), III (1880), V (1885), VI (1894); "Abigail Snelling," in Elizabeth F. L. Ellet, *Pioneer Women of the West* (1852); F. B. Heitman, *Hist. Reg. and Dict.*

U. S. Army (1903); *Daily National Intelligencer* (Washington, D. C.), Aug. 21, 1828.]   T. M. S.

SNELLING, WILLIAM JOSEPH (Dec. 26, 1804–Dec. 24, 1848), journalist, satirist, was born in Boston, Mass., the son of Josiah Snelling [q.v.] and his first wife, Elizabeth Bell. The mother died early, and the boy was left in the hands of relatives who sent him to Dr. Luther Stearns's classical school at Medford. In 1818 he entered the United States Military Academy, but was very unhappy there and left after two years to drift westward toward his father's army post. For some time he lived among the Dakota Indians and eventually became a trapper in the vicinity of Fort Snelling. He married a French girl of Prairie du Chien, but she died during the first winter in their prairie hut; he shared in putting down the Winnebago Indian revolt of 1827 (see his paper, "Early Days at Prairie du Chien," *Wisconsin Historical Society Collections*, vol. V); his life was altogether wild and adventurous.

After the death of his father, Snelling gravitated to Boston, where he appeared in 1828 as a writer. He engaged in hack work for a while, most often under the pseudonym Solomon Bell. Then in 1831 he published *Truth: A New Year's Gift for Scribblers,* a satire on contemporary poets that rocked the small literary world of Boston for a time. He next plunged into newspaper work and made a great many powerful enemies as a reformer and social satirist. His most remarkable exploit in this direction was his crusade against gamblers, undertaken while he was an editor of the *New-England Galaxy* (see his *Exposé of the Vice of Gaming as It Lately Existed in New England,* 1833, reprinted from the *Galaxy*). He was generally successful in his reform activities but he stirred up a wasps' nest against himself. The onslaughts of his political and literary foes, combined with personal misfortunes, gradually drove him to despair, and he took refuge in drink. To the great delight of his ill-wishers, he spent four months in the House of Correction, but he emerged broken rather in health than in spirit. He continued as an independent journalist and in 1847 became the editor of the *Boston Herald,* which he conducted with great vigor for one year before he died, in Chelsea, at the age of forty-four, burned out. He was survived by his wife, Lucy Jordan, whom he had married Mar. 2, 1838, and by three daughters.

Snelling is best remembered as a satirist of his times and especially as the author of *Truth,* which is one of the best verse satires ever written in America. He is represented as a poet by one long piece, "The Birth of Thunder" (R. A.

Griswold, *Poets of America,* 1842). His *Tales of the Northwest; or, Sketches of Indian Life and Character* (1830), have both charm and authenticity; and *The Rat-Trap; or, Cogitations of a Convict in the House of Correction* (1837), written during his term in prison, is a document of unique interest. Only a few of his lesser writings have survived, since he often wrote anonymously and under pen names. He was sincere, fiery, and uncompromising, ever a champion of the oppressed and a passionate advocate of his own high ideas of "truth" and "freedom," but he dissipated his energies, neglected his education, and ruined his health in a series of mad quixotic adventures. His publications reveal a man of great talent, perhaps of genius, who found neither the leisure nor the opportunity to be a great writer.

[G. C. Beltrami, *A Pilgrimage in Europe and America* (1828), vol. II; A. E. Woodall, *William Joseph Snelling* (1933), repr. from *Univ. of Pittsburgh Bull.*, Jan. 1933; Barbara A. S. Adams, "Early Days at Red River Settlement and Fort Snelling," *Minn. Hist. Soc. Colls.*, vol. VI (1894); E. D. Neill, *Fort Snelling, Minn.* (1888); E. A. Perry, *The Boston Herald and Its Hist.* (1878); *The Jordan Memorial* (1882); comments on Snelling's *Truth* in S. G. Goodrich, *Recollections of a Lifetime* (1856), vol. II, and O. W. Holmes, *A Mortal Antipathy* (1885), Introduction; *Boston Transcript*, Dec. 26, 1848; *Minn. Hist.*, June 1928; unpublished thesis by A. E. Woodall, Univ. of Pittsburgh.]

A. E. W.

SNETHEN, NICHOLAS (Nov. 15, 1769–May 30, 1845), clergyman, one of the founders of the Methodist Protestant Church, was born at Glen Cove, then known as Fresh Pond, Long Island, the son of Barak and Ann (Weeks) Snethen. On his father's side he was of Welsh descent. Barak Snethen cultivated a farm and operated a flour mill, sending his product to New York in his own schooner. Nicholas spent much of his early life on the farm and the schooner. Later, through private study he acquired a competent knowledge of English and a usable knowledge of Greek and Hebrew. When he was about twenty-one the family moved to Staten Island, and in 1791 to Belleville, N. J. Here Snethen came under the influence of Methodism and professed conversion.

In 1794 he entered the ministry of the Methodist Episcopal Church and for four years served circuits in New England. In 1799 he was appointed to Charleston, S. C., and was ordained elder there in 1800. The following year he preached in Baltimore and in 1801–02 was traveling companion of Bishop Asbury. For the next three years he preached in Baltimore and New York. In 1804 he married Susannah Hood Worthington, daughter of Charles Worthington of Frederick County, Md., and came into possession of a farm and some slaves. Between 1806 and 1809 he retired temporarily from the active ministry, but then, until 1814 he preached at Fells Point, Md., Baltimore, Georgetown, D. C., Alexandria, Va., and Frederick, Md. While at Georgetown he became chaplain of the House of Representatives. In 1814 he retired to his farm, and in 1816 became a candidate for representative in Congress, but was defeated.

During the controversy which followed the revolt of James O'Kelly [q.v.] against the episcopal authority of Asbury in 1792, Snethen took Asbury's side, issuing in 1800 *A Reply* to O'Kelly's *The Author's Apology for Protesting Against the Methodist Episcopal Government* (c. 1798), and, a year or so later, *An Answer* to O'Kelly's *Vindication of An Apology* (1801). At the General Conference of 1812, however, he identified himself with the faction favoring lay representation in the Conferences and limitation of the powers of the bishops, declaring in the course of the debate that he would not again appear on the floor of the General Conference until he was sent there by vote of the laity as well as the ministers. When, in 1820, the *Wesleyan Repository* (Trenton, N. J.) was established to further the cause of reform, Snethen was a frequent contributor, his articles later appearing in a volume under the title *Snethen on Lay Representation: Essays on Lay Representation and Church Government* (1835). He also contributed to the reform monthly, *Mutual Rights,* published at Baltimore beginning in 1824. He prepared the memorial to the General Conference of 1828 asking for reform. That body turned a deaf ear to the request, and in November 1828 the Reformers convened in Baltimore and projected the establishment of the Methodist Protestant Church. Snethen was the leading spirit in drawing up the Articles of Association for the new organization and was elected president of the Maryland Conference.

In 1829, freeing his slaves, he moved to Sullivan County, Ind. Subsequently he removed to Louisville, and later to Cincinnati, where he continued to labor in the ministry of the Church he had helped to establish. In 1834 he returned to Baltimore to edit *Mutual Rights and Methodist Protestant* in conjunction with Asa Shinn [q.v.]. In 1836 he conducted a theological school in New York founded by the Methodist Protestant Church. Moving West again in 1837, he became head of a manual labor college, founded by Ohio Conference at Lawrenceburg, Ind., which survived but a year. His last activities were spent in the Territory of Iowa, where he attempted to establish a school in Iowa City known as

Snethen Seminary. Before it was fairly under way, however, he died at the home of a daughter in Princeton, Ind. Besides the works already cited, he was the author of a *Funeral Oration on Bishop Asbury* (1816); *Lectures on Preaching* (1822); *Lectures on Biblical Subjects* (1836), and *Sermons* (1846), edited by W. G. Snethen.

[*Mutual Rights and Methodist Protestant*, July 12, 1845; Abel Stevens, *Hist. of the Methodist Episcopal Church* (1867), vol. III; Matthew Simpson, *Cyc. of Methodism* (1878); W. B. Sprague, *Annals Am. Pulpit*, vol. VII (1859); T. H. Colhouer, *Sketches of the Founders of the Methodist Protestant Church* (1880).]

W. W. S.

SNIDER, DENTON JAQUES (Jan. 9, 1841– Nov. 25, 1925), author, educator, was born on a farm near the village of Mt. Gilead, Ohio, the son of John R. and Catherine (Prather) Snider. His mother died when he was six years old, and the family was separated. The boy passed an arduous childhood but attended several schools and finally entered Oberlin College, where he received the degree of A.B. in 1862. He enlisted in the Union Army, rose to be second lieutenant, served for a time under William Starke Rosecrans [*q.v.*], and resigned after a year of service because of ill health. As soon as his strength was regained he began, March 1864, to teach Greek and Latin in the College of the Christian Brothers in St. Louis, Mo. There he soon fell in with William Torrey Harris and Henry C. Brokmeyer [*qq.v.*], under whose influence he devoted himself to a six years' study of the philosophy of Hegel, although at one time he became so impatient with it that he threw the sacred *Logic* across the room. In the fall of 1866 he entered Brokmeyer's law office, chiefly, as he said, in order to become "a pupil of the University Brokmeyer in person" (*The St. Louis Movement*, p. 11). He was one of the original members of the St. Louis Philosophical Society, founded in January 1866, and a frequent contributor to the *Journal of Speculative Philosophy*. Versed in five foreign languages—Greek, Latin, French, German, and Italian—he brought to the St. Louis movement a knowledge of literature and a catholicity of outlook lacking in the older leaders. But he had neither the originality of Brokmeyer nor the organizing ability of Harris; he was essentially a spectator and critic. Drawn by Harris into the St. Louis schools, where he taught from 1867 to 1877, he declined to be made assistant superintendent, refusing to sacrifice intellectual freedom to professional advancement. In August 1867 he was married to Mary Krug, who bore him three children before her death in 1874. The years 1877–79 he spent in Europe, mainly in Greece. He then returned to St. Louis

and resumed his position in the high school but resigned after a year, unable to stomach the formalized methods of instruction. Every summer for a number of years he lectured in Harris' Concord School of Philosophy, where he rather scandalized the natives by his lack of reverence for the Concord tradition. During the same period he taught Homer, Sophocles, Herodotus, and Thucydides to persons studying kindergarten methods in the kindergarten training-school of Susan Elizabeth Blow [*q.v.*] in St. Louis, this interesting experiment being terminated by a violent quarrel with Miss Blow, whose autocratic personality and Christian fervor resented both Snider's independence and his paganizing tendencies.

He spent the next thirteen years, 1884–97, in lecture tours, chiefly in the Middle West, centering about Chicago. His chief educational achievements during this period were the establishment of a few weeks' Goethe school in Milwaukee in 1886 (with the cooperation of Harris and Brokmeyer) and the establishment of a ten weeks' literary school in Chicago (again with Harris' aid), which ran for eight successive seasons. He proved a brilliant popular lecturer. Tall, slender, with black mustache and fiery manner, he would move impetuously about the stage, checking his flow of eloquence only to chide severely the late-comers. It was he more than any other who carried the idealism of the St. Louis movement to the intellectually starved and spiritually hungry cities of the Middle West. Thus it was fitting that he should finally return in 1897 to the birthplace of the movement and spend his long declining years there, devoting his energy mainly to writing. He lived, by preference, in a boarding-house in the Ghetto, where he enjoyed the society of the immigrants and was free to indulge his numerous eccentricities. Suffering from varicose veins, he always composed while standing or walking about his room, using the back of a chair as an improvised desk. His irregular habits were momentarily interrupted by his marriage on Oct. 21, 1916, to Mrs. Augusta (Siemon) Sander, an admiring disciple forty years his junior, but they lived together only a short time and he was soon happily back in the Ghetto. His last years were passed at the home of a friend, William H. Miner, where he died in 1925, survived by his widow and one daughter by his former marriage. His grave in Bellefontaine Cemetery was for many years annually visited by the Snider Association.

With the possible exception of Harris, he was the only one of the St. Louis group to produce literary work of some permanent value. Ever unwilling to commercialize his talent, he himself published (under the name of the Sigma Publishing Company) more than forty volumes at his own expense, none of which proved or was expected to prove at all remunerative. In fact, he was accustomed to give copies away at his lectures to any who would promise to read them. The more important of his writings fall into three groups: the earliest in inception, dealing with Greece and Rome, includes in prose *A Walk in Hellas* (2 vols., 1881–82) and in verse *Delphic Days* (1880), *Agamemnon's Daughter* (1885), *Homer in Chios* (1891) and *Prorsus Retrorsus* (1892); the chief product of his middle period was a series of nine volumes of commentaries, three on Shakespeare, two each on Homer, Dante, and Goethe, published between 1877 and 1897; his final period brought forth a number of volumes fitted into a grand philosophic or, as he preferred to call it, "psychologic" system, the most significant of these being *Psychology and the Psychosis* (1890), *Ancient European Philosophy* (1903), *Modern European Philosophy* (1904), *The American Ten Years' War, 1855–1865* (1906), *Cosmos and Diacosmos* (1909), *The Biocosmos* (1911), *Music and the Fine Arts* (1913). He also wrote two autobiographical books, *A Writer of Books in His Genesis* (1910) and *The St. Louis Movement in Philosophy, Literature, Education, Psychology, with Chapters of Autobiography* (1920). He remained essentially a Hegelian until the end, *a priori* in his methods, mistaking results for causes, and hypnotized by the triadic scheme which his extensive but far from profound classical and historical scholarship enabled him to impose superficially upon the facts; and, although he correctly estimated the growing importance of psychology, his own psychologic method was outworn, taking little account of current developments. On the other hand he was an esthetic critic of acumen, sensitive to beauty, and extraordinarily gifted in catching meanings and significances, in detecting hidden relations, and in suggesting principles of interpretation. His works, particularly those on Shakespeare and Goethe, form no unimportant addition to American esthetic criticism. Dear to his own heart, though less significant, were his poems, especially *Johnny Appleseed's Rhymes* (1895), which he used to read aloud with great gusto, his bright eyes shining, his long hair tossing, and his voice rolling with Homeric laughter.

[The chief sources of information about Snider's life are his autobiographies, *A Writer of Books* (1910) and *The St. Louis Movement* (1920). See also *Who's Who in America*, 1924–25; *The St. Louis Movement in Philosophy: Some Source Material* (1930), ed. by

C. M. Perry; *A Brief Report of the Meeting Commemorative of the Early Saint Louis Movement* (1922), ed. by D. H. Harris; Lilian Whiting, in *Theosophical Path*, Nov. 1914; J. G. Woerner, *The Rebel's Daughter* (1899), a novel in which Snider appears as Dr. Taylor; A. E. Bostwick, *List of Books Written by Denton J. Snider* (1924); obituary in *St. Louis Post-Dispatch*, Nov. 27, 1925.]   E. S. B.

SNOW, ELIZA ROXEY (Jan. 21, 1804–Dec. 5, 1887), Mormon poet and woman leader, sister of Lorenzo Snow [*q.v.*], was born in Becket, Berkshire County, Mass., the daughter of Oliver and Rosetta L. (Pettibone) Snow. When she was a small child her family migrated westward, settling at Mantua, Ohio, where she received the best available education of her day. As a young woman she showed considerable ability in the practical handicrafts and in writing verse. Her poems were well received by the frontier press, and she developed a certain local prominence. Early in 1835 her mother and elder sister Leonora joined the Mormon church, and in April of that year Eliza herself was baptized in the new sect. In December 1835 she removed to Kirtland, Ohio, where she lived with the family of the Mormon Prophet, Joseph Smith [*q.v.*]. She supported herself by teaching a "select school for young ladies." Later, under her mother's and her influence, her father and her favorite brother Lorenzo became converts to Mormonism.

In 1838 the Snow family joined the general exodus of the Saints to Missouri, remaining there until forced to flee to Illinois because of religious persecution. When Nauvoo was founded in 1840 she settled there and soon became prominent among the women of her church. In 1842, when the chief Mormon women's organization, the Relief Society, was founded, she was made its first secretary. At the dispersal of the Mormons from Illinois following the death of Joseph Smith she joined the faction under Brigham Young [*q.v.*] and migrated with them, first to Iowa and thence to Utah, arriving there late in the summer of 1847, in one of the early pioneer companies.

In May 1855, she was given the responsibility of managing the women's work in the Mormon Endowment House, where the secret religious rituals of the church were performed before any temples were built in Utah. In 1866 she became president of the general (central) church organization of the Women's Relief Society, which position she held until her death. During the year 1872–73 she was a member of a missionary party headed by her brother Lorenzo which visited Palestine. She died Dec. 5, 1887, after several years of feeble health. On June 29, 1842, at Nauvoo, she was secretly married to the Prophet Joseph Smith under the new "dispensation" of plural marriage or spiritual wifery, which he and other Mormon leaders had begun to practise. In 1849, in Salt Lake City, she married Smith's successor, Brigham Young, as one of his polygynous wives. She had no children by either husband.

From the very outset of her association with Mormonism, she began to pour out poems appropriate to various religious and public occasions, and throughout her long life many of the signal disasters or successes of her church led her to commemorate the events in verse. Contemporary Mormon hymnology owes much to her writing, and one of the most popular and typical Mormon hymns, "O My Father, Thou that Dwellest," was written by her. Eliza R. Snow, in fact, served the very important function of putting Mormon history into verse on many occasions, thus helping to build the folk beliefs so important in fostering group solidarity. In addition to *Poems, Religious, Historical, and Political* (vol. I, 1856; vol. II, 1877), she published in 1884 *Biography and Family Record of Lorenzo Snow.*

[Andrew Jenson, *Latter-Day Saint Biog. Encyc.*, vol. I (1901), pp. 693–96; obituary in *Deseret Evening News*, Dec. 5, 1887.]   K. Y.

SNOW, FRANCIS HUNTINGTON (June 29, 1840–Sept. 20, 1908), naturalist, educator, was born at Fitchburg, Mass., the son of Benjamin and Mary (Boutelle) Snow. One of his paternal ancestors was Richard Warren, who came over on the *Mayflower*; his earliest American ancestor with the surname Snow was Richard Snow, who emigrated from England in 1645 and settled in Woburn, Mass. He spent his youth at Fitchburg, and graduated from Williams College in 1862 and from the Andover Theological Seminary in 1866. When in the autumn of 1866 the University of Kansas was founded at Lawrence, Kans., he was appointed to the professorship of mathematics and natural science, one of three men who made up the faculty. About two years later, on July 8, 1868, he married Jane Appleton Aiken of Andover, Mass., a grand-daughter of Jesse Appleton [*q.v.*], president of Bowdoin College, and a descendant of Samuel Symonds, deputy governor of the Massachusetts Bay Colony in 1673.

It does not appear that he was especially interested in entomology until he began his teaching work in Kansas; wishing, however, to make his department useful to the farmers of the state, he took up entomology with enthusiasm. With the help of his students and collaborators, he made very large collections in entomology, bot-

any, and geology. The year after the elder Agassiz [*q.v.*] started his famous summer school of natural history on Penikese Island in 1873, he joined the group of distinguished workers there and returned to his Kansas work broadened and encouraged. In 1883 he was appointed consulting entomologist to the state board of agriculture, a position which he filled (afterwards under the title of state entomologist) for the greater part of the rest of his life. Later he induced the legislature of the state to appropriate funds for the erection of a museum of natural history (afterwards known as the Snow Hall of Natural History) on the campus of the university, an effective and attractive building that he himself planned. After 1886, at his own request, his work was restricted to botany and entomology. In 1889 he was made president of the faculties and in 1890 chancellor of the university. When his health began to fail after twelve years of very successful executive work, he resigned the chancellorship (1901) and for the rest of his life devoted himself largely to museum work, remaining emeritus professor of organic evolution, systematic entomology, and meteorology. As chancellor he played an important part in the building of a great university. He was in executive charge at a critical period in its history, when all the educational institutions of the state, even the Kansas State Agricultural College at Manhattan, suffered at the hands of the Populist legislature, and it is acknowledged that it was almost wholly by his efforts that the funds necessary to carry on the institution were appropriated. He had an extensive personal acquaintanceship with the people of the state and a high place in their respect and affection.

He was probably the pioneer naturalist of Kansas. His personal contributions to science were principally economic, systematic, and faunistic. In 1872 he published the first checklist of Kansas birds, to which he added from year to year, but his bibliography is not extensive, although he made many important contributions to entomology. In the early nineties, having secured special appropriations from the state legislature, he made some interesting experiments involving the artificial introduction of epidemic diseases among chinch bugs, the great enemy to wheat and corn at that time. The work itself was later abandoned, but among both farmers and entomologists it aroused great interest in scientific investigations of injurious insects, and it consequently had a wide value. Snow seems also to have been a remarkable teacher, attracting and holding strong students to scientific studies. He died at Delafield, Wis.

[*Who's Who in America*, 1908–09; *Fiftieth Anniversary Report Williams Coll. Class of '62* (1913); G. C. Brackett, in *First Biennial Report of the Kan. State Horticultural Soc. . . . 1887–88* (1889); A. R. Grote, in *North Am. Entomologist*, Dec. 1879; C. E. McClung, in *Entomological News*, Dec. 1908; V. L. Kellogg, in *Jour. of Econ. Entomology*, Feb. 1909; *Auk*, Oct. 1908; obituary in *Topeka State Jour.*, Sept. 21, 1908.]

L. O. H.

SNOW, LORENZO (Apr. 3, 1814–Oct. 10, 1901), fifth president of the Utah branch of the Mormon church, was born in Mantua, Ohio, the son of Oliver and Rosetta L. (Pettibone) Snow, who had migrated from Massachusetts to the Western Reserve in the early years of the century. As an undergraduate at Oberlin College, Lorenzo became thoroughly disillusioned regarding religion. He is quoted as saying, "If there is nothing better than is to be found here in Oberlin College, goodbye to all religions" (*Historical Record*, Feb. 1887, p. 141). Lorenzo left college in 1836. During a visit to his sister Eliza [*q.v.*], who had joined the Mormons in 1835 and who was living at Kirtland, Ohio, he was converted to the new faith and was baptized in June 1836. Some months later, in 1837, he was busy converting others throughout Ohio to Mormonism. In 1838 he moved to Missouri and in the same year undertook a second mission, this time traveling in Missouri, Kentucky, and southern Illinois. Later in the same year he returned to Portage County, Ohio, where he taught school for two winters. In the fall of 1840 he was sent out from Nauvoo, Ill., on his third mission, this time to England. After his return in the spring of 1843, he became active in local affairs and among other projects organized a new company of the Nauvoo Legion and became its captain. In the midst of intense conflict between the Mormons and other citizens of Illinois in the spring and summer of 1844, Joseph Smith [*q.v.*] offered himself as a candidate for the presidency of the United States, and Snow, like dozens of other zealots, entered into a vigorous political campaign in his behalf. In the controversy over leadership following the death of Joseph and Hyrum Smith, Snow supported the Brigham Young faction. When the Saints were finally forced to abandon Nauvoo, Snow, in company with others, on Feb. 12, 1846, moved across the Mississippi into Iowa; here he remained until the summer of 1848, when he trekked on westward to Salt Lake City.

On Feb. 12, 1849, Snow was made an apostle, thus taking a place among the dominant leaders of his church. In October 1849, Brigham Young [*q.v.*] sent out the first group of missionaries from Utah, and Lorenzo Snow was "set apart" to open the mission in Italy. In June 1850, Snow and his companions began their proselyting in Italy, chiefly among the Protestant Waldenses in the Piedmont. In 1851 Snow with T. B. H. Stenhouse carried this missionary work into Switzerland. He planned to open missions in Malta, Turkey, Russia, and India, but before he could fulfil all his plans he was released from his duties and returned to Utah in July 1852.

In the fall of 1852 he was elected to the territorial legislature, where he served for thirty years, for ten years being president of the upper house. After a year or so of school teaching in Salt Lake City, he was sent out to colonize in northern Utah and in 1853 he led fifty families to Brigham City, which became his residence for nearly forty years. During the winter of 1863–64, Snow, together with three others, organized the Brigham City Mercantile and Manufacturing Association, an example of the consumers' and producers' cooperative institution known in Mormondom as the "United Order." This organization grew to include more than 1500 members—almost the entire adult male population of the community. After a decade of flourishing activity it fell into competition with private industries and gradually shrank in scope and function until it disappeared.

After the passage of the Edmunds Bill early in 1882, Snow, like other prominent Mormons, was haled into court on charges of "unlawful cohabitation" with plural wives. He was convicted, disfranchised, and sent to prison in January 1886. Finally his case was reversed by the United States Supreme Court, and he was released on Feb. 8, 1887. On Apr. 7, 1889, he became president of the quorum of Twelve Apostles—a position that put him second in power in his church. On Sept. 13, 1898, shortly after the death of President Wilford Woodruff, Snow was chosen president of his church, but, already advanced in age, he died three years later. He was buried in Brigham City, Utah.

As a leader Lorenzo Snow represents a mixture of piety and a strong belief in "spiritual gifts" with a distinct practicality in managing men and affairs. He was one of the few early Mormon leaders who had any college training. He was an ardent missionary, and he will long be remembered for his efforts to make a success of the "United Order." His reaction to polygyny illustrates his loyalty to official dogmas. When Joseph Smith explained its principles to him, Snow decided to marry although he was at the time a bachelor of forty years. At his first matrimonial venture he took two wives on the same day, shortly thereafter marrying two more. Later he added five other wives to his household. Snow's principal contribution to Mormon theology is his aphorism: "As man now is, God once was; as God now is, man may be." This principle, later called "the doctrine of eternal progression," he announced privately in 1840 to his sister Eliza and to his close friend, Brigham Young. A year or so later Joseph Smith gave public approval to this idea, and the doctrine has become firmly intrenched in Mormon theology.

[Eliza R. Snow Smith, *Biography and Family Record of Lorenzo Snow* (1884); Andrew Jenson, *Latter-Day Saint Biog. Encyclopedia*, vol. I (1901), pp. 26–31; vol. III (1920), pp. 786–87; Andrew Jenson, comp., *Church Chronology*, 2nd ed. (1914); Andrew Jenson, ed., *The Historical Record*, vol. VI, no. 2, Feb. 1887, pp. 139–45; obituary in *Deseret Evening News*, Oct. 10, 1901.]

K. Y.

SNOWDEN, JAMES ROSS (Dec. 9, 1809–Mar. 21, 1878), numismatist, director of the United States mint, lawyer, was born in Chester, Pa., a son of the Rev. Nathaniel Randolph Snowden, curator of Dickinson College, and Sarah (Gustine) Snowden, daughter of Dr. Lemuel Gustine of Carlisle, Pa. He was a descendant of John Snowden, who emigrated from Nottinghamshire, England, about 1678 and settled on the site of the future Philadelphia; John Snowden is said to have been one of the few Europeans who welcomed William Penn when he made his first visit to his province. After attending Dickinson College for a time and studying law in an office in Carlisle, James Snowden was admitted to the bar at nineteen and in 1830 went to Franklin, Venango County, Pa., where he began practice. Shortly afterward he was appointed deputy attorney general (district attorney), in Venango County; from 1838 to 1844 he was a member of the Pennsylvania legislature, serving as speaker of the House of Representatives, 1842–44. Soon after his admission to the bar he became interested in the state militia and was elected colonel of a local regiment. In 1845 he presided at the state military convention at Harrisburg, Pa.

Elected treasurer of Pennsylvania in 1845, in a comparatively short term he succeeded in improving the character of state loans, and in 1848 was appointed treasurer of the United States mint and assistant treasurer of the United States in Philadelphia (appointment confirmed, Feb. 14, 1848). On Sept. 13, 1848, he was married to Susan Engle Patterson, a daughter of Gen. Robert Patterson [q.v.] of Philadelphia; they had two sons and three daughters. In 1850 he resumed practice as a lawyer in Pittsburgh, Pa., having been appointed solicitor of the Pennsylvania Railroad Company. From 1854 to 1861 he was director of the United States mint, Philadelphia, an appointment made by Pres. Franklin

Pierce (confirmed, Mar. 8, 1854). It was while he was actively connected with the mint that he developed an interest in numismatics, on which he wrote several books: *A Description of Ancient and Modern Coins in the Cabinet Collection at the Mint of the United States* (1860), *A Description of the Medals of Washington; of National and Miscellaneous Medals, and of Other Objects of Interest in the Museum of the Mint* (1861), *The Medallic Memorials of Washington in the Mint of the United States* (1861), and *The Coins of the Bible, and Its Money Terms* (1864). He contributed articles on the coins of the United States to the *National Almanac and Annual Record for the Year 1873*, and an article on international coinage to *Lippincott's Magazine*, January 1870, in which he urged that all nations be invited to adopt the dollar as a monetary unit, and advocated a single standard (gold) for all countries; he later published a pamphlet, *A Measure Proposed to Secure a Safe Treasury and a Sound Currency* (1857), in which he suggested the issuing of certificates on deposits of gold bullion at the mint, its branches, and the assay office, in convenient sums and payable to the bearer. As director of the mint he was instrumental in having the building made fireproof. In 1861 he was appointed prothonotary of the supreme court of Pennsylvania and held the office until 1873, when he resigned to resume the practice of law in Philadelphia. During the Civil War he was lieutenant-colonel of the 1st Regiment of the Philadelphia Home Guard. He died in his country home, Hulmeville, Bucks County, Pa.

[F. W. Leach, in *North American* (Phila.), July 14, and Dec. 8, 1912; Alfred Nevin, *Centennial Biog.: Men of Mark of Cumberland Valley, Pa., 1776–1876* (1876); *Hist. of Venango County, Pa.* (1890); C. A. Babcock, *Venango County, Pa., Her Pioneers and People* (1919), vol. I; *Proc. of the Celebration of the First Centennial of the Organization of the County of Venango, Pa., for Judicial Purposes* (1905); death notice in *Pub. Ledger* (Phila.), Mar. 23, 1878.]

J. J.

SNOWDEN, THOMAS (Aug. 12, 1857–Jan. 27, 1930), naval officer, son of Dr. Thomas Snowden and Catherine Clinton (Wood) Snowden, was born in Peekskill, N. Y. He was appointed to the United States Naval Academy in 1875 and was graduated in 1879. After five years spent in sea duty on the Atlantic, in 1884 he was ordered to the hydrographic office and in 1889 to the naval observatory. Commissioned junior lieutenant in 1892, he was assigned to the *Ranger* and spent over two years in coast survey work with her off the coast of Alaska. During the Spanish-American War he served on the cruiser *Dolphin* in the squadron under Admiral William

Thomas Sampson [*q.v.*], taking part in the bombardment of Santiago, June 6, 1898, and in the action near Caimanera, June 14. He was navigator of the battleship *Illinois* for three years, commanded the presidential yacht *Mayflower* from 1908 to 1910, and the battleship *South Carolina* in the Atlantic Fleet from 1911 to 1913. In this ship he was at Tampico and Vera Cruz for six months during the early disturbances under the Huerta régime in Mexico. He was then sent to the Naval War College for a year, after which he commanded the battleship *Wyoming*. When the United States entered the World War he was acting as hydrographer to the Navy Department; promoted to rear admiral July 1, 1917, he commanded a squadron of the battleship force of the Atlantic Fleet throughout the war, and at its close was awarded the Navy Cross "for exceptionally meritorious service in a duty of great responsibility as commander, Division Two, Battleship Force One, Atlantic Fleet" (*The Navy Book of Distinguished Service*, 1921, p. 131, edited by H. R. Stringer).

Soon after the armistice he was made military governor of Santo Domingo, with the additional duty of serving as military representative of the United States in Haiti. During his administration he worked indefatigably to place the republic on a safe and enduring foundation, establishing schools, and undertaking the construction of roads and public buildings. "No official ever served his country with greater fidelity, or an alien people . . . with a more lofty purpose than Admiral Snowden gave to the Dominicans" (*Times,* San Juan, Puerto Rico, Mar. 4, 1924). Ill health, however, forced him to relinquish his post in 1921, when he returned to the United States. He was assigned to duty on the general board of the navy but was retired on Aug. 12, 1921, and relieved of all active duty. Besides the Navy Cross he held the large cross of the order of El Sol de Peru, a decoration conferred by the Peruvian government. Though his career gave him no great opportunity for spectacular service, he was a highly capable seaman, an expert navigator, and an able administrator, and was highly popular throughout the service. He was twice married: first on June 2, 1881, to Adelaide Van Ness Smith of Peekskill, N. Y., and second on Jan. 14, 1911, to Helen Koerper of Washington, D. C., daughter of Col. E. A. Koerper, U. S. A. He had one son by his second marriage.

[*Who's Who in America*, 1928–29; H. W. Wilson, *The Downfall of Spain* (1900); Navy Dept. Registers, 1879–1921; Navy Dept., transcript of service record in archives of Bur. of Navigation; *Army and Navy Jour.,* Feb. 1, 1930; obituary in *N. Y. Times*, Jan. 29, 1930; information from correspondence with Snowden's widow and his brother.]   L. H. B.

SNYDER, EDWIN REAGAN (Sept. 2, 1872–Jan. 13, 1925), educator, was born in Scottdale, Pa., the son of Daniel and Catherine (Reagan) Snyder, of Pennsylvania German stock, whose characteristic tenacity of purpose he possessed. After spending his childhood and youth on his father's farm, at eighteen he entered the State Normal School of Colorado (later the State Teachers College) at Greeley at the same time that his brother, Zachariah Xenophon Snyder, became president of the college. Upon his graduation in 1895 he became principal of the public schools at Bald Mountain, Colo., and two years later of those in New Windsor, Colo. He became supervisor of manual training in the schools of Alameda, Cal., in 1900, and in 1902 head of the department of industrial arts in the State Normal School at San José (later the San José State Teachers College). During the year 1904–05 he served also as an assistant at Stanford University, where he received the degree of A.B. in 1905. He was research scholar at Teachers College, Columbia University, 1907–08, and fellow, 1908–09, and received the degree of Ph.D. in 1909, with a thesis on *The Legal Status of Rural High Schools in the United States* (1909), which reveals his belief in thoroughly democratic education. After two more years at San José he was elected in 1911 to the vice-presidency of the Fresno State Normal School (later Fresno State Teachers College), where he also served as assistant superintendent of city schools. For a few months in 1913 he served as superintendent of schools in Santa Barbara, but in January 1914 he became the first commissioner of vocational education in California. In this position he remained until the summer of 1923, when he became president of San José State Teachers College, a post he held until his death about a year and a half later at San José. He was married to Sara Llewellyn on Dec. 29, 1900, in San Francisco. They had a son and a daughter.

His greatest contributions to education came during his decade of service as commissioner of vocational education. His theory of education was given full expression in his first annual report to the state superintendent of public instruction: "We wish every child in the commonwealth to have the opportunity to secure such training in the school as will fit him to do as well as possible that work which he is, by nature and economic opportunity, best fitted to do" (*First Biennial Report of the State Board of Education of California*, 1915, p. 128). This lies at the root of his deep interest in vocational education and guidance, his belief in the part-time continuation school, his insistence that public high schools serve aims more democratic than the single one of preparation for higher institutions. In large measure his theory has since become practice, and no legislation which he proposed, whether it concerned vocational education specifically—he framed practically all the statutes for the administration of the vocational program in California —or the wider reaches of a state educational program, has been seriously modified. Essentially a philosopher, he was vigorously analytical and scientific in his approach to all problems; he had, too, an abiding faith in humanity and a sense of humor that never allowed the philosopher to become pedantic or the scientist to forget his limitations in dealing with human stuff.

[California State Board of Education, Reports of the Commissioner of Industrial and Vocational Education, 1914–22; *Industrial Educ. Mag.*, Sept. 1923; University of California, *Vocational Educ. News Notes*, Feb. 1925; *San José Evening News*, Jan. 14, 1925.]

E. A. L.

SNYDER, JOHN FRANCIS (Mar. 22, 1830–Apr. 30, 1921), physician, Confederate soldier, archaeologist, and author, son of Adam Wilson Snyder and Adelaide (Perry) Snyder, was born at Prairie du Pont, Saint Clair County, Ill., a mile south of Cahokia, in a log building erected in 1759 by the monks of Saint Sulpice. His mother, who was of French ancestry on both sides, was a grand-daughter of Capt. John Baptiste Saucier, the architect of Fort Chartres. His father, a son of Adam Snyder, a German soldier of the Revolution who was born in Alsace and settled in Reading, Pa., had come to Cahokia in 1817, penniless and afoot. Snyder was first educated at Belleville, Ill., at McKendree College, Lebanon, Ill., and at the St. Louis University. He was fond of books, a close observer of nature and natural history, and early began the collection of fossils, minerals, and archaeological relics. As a boy he played about the famous Cahokia mounds near his home, and in his maturer years his interest in archaeology developed and expanded. During the winter of 1849–50 he was a student at McDowell Medical College in St. Louis, and the following summer he crossed the plains to California; he visited the Sandwich Islands in 1852, returned home that year by way of the Isthmus of Panama, and arrived at Philadelphia in time to enter Jefferson Medical College, where he graduated in 1853. For a short period thereafter he was in government medical service in western territories and went over the old Santa Fé trail to Taos and Albuquerque, N. Mex.; then he resigned and began the practice of medicine at Bolivar, Mo., where on Sept. 27, 1854, he married Annie E. Sanders, daughter of

Landon Sanders of Lexington, Ky. He was admitted to the Missouri bar in 1859, but he never practised law. In June 1861 he joined the Confederates under Sterling Price [*q.v.*] and as colonel fought through the Civil War, taking active part in the battles of Wilson Creek, Lexington, Pea Ridge, Helena, Corinth, and Baldwin. Although he was reared in familiarity with a modified form of slavery (indenture of colored servants), served in the Confederate army, and was himself a slave-holder on a small scale, he always abhorred slavery, defending it only on the meager ground of expediency. Returning to Illinois after the war, he resumed the practice of medicine at Virginia. He was elected a member of the thirty-first Illinois legislature, where he gave a good account of himself, but declined further participation in party politics.

One of the founders of the Illinois State Historical Society in 1899, he became its president, 1903–05, and contributed many important papers to it. He was also affiliated with the St. Louis Academy of Sciences, the Illinois Academy of Science, and other organizations. He took part in the survey and mapping of the Cahokia mounds, 1880, and advocated their preservation. For many years he was a research correspondent of the Smithsonian Institution, which published several of his shorter papers. His most important writings are *The Field for Archaeological Research in Illinois* (1900); *Captain John Baptiste Saucier at Fort Chartres in the Illinois, 1751–1763* (1901), reprinted in *Transactions of the Illinois State Historical Society, 1919* (1920); *Adam W. Snyder and His Period in Illinois History, 1817–1842* (1903); "Prehistoric Illinois; Its Psychozoic Problems" (*Journal of the Illinois State Historical Society*, Oct. 1911), "The Kaskaskia Indians" (*Ibid.*, July 1912), and "The Great Cahokia Mound" (*Ibid.*, July 1917). He may well be considered the ranking pioneer in archaeology of the state of Illinois. He was the first to indicate cultural differences between prehistoric tribes of southern and central Illinois, and explorations by the University of Illinois in 1922–27 proved the correctness of his views. He died in Virginia, Ill., at the age of ninety-one years, in full possession of all his faculties.

[Newton Bateman and Paul Selby, eds., *Hist. Encyc. of Ill. and Hist. of Cass County* (1915), vol. II; *Jour. Ill. State Hist. Soc.*, Apr.–July 1921; *Belleville News-Democrat* (Belleville, Ill.), May 2, 1921; *Chicago Daily Tribune*, May 1, 1921.]

W. K. M.

SNYDER, SIMON (Nov. 5, 1759–Nov. 9, 1819), governor of Pennsylvania, was born at Lancaster, Pa., the son of Maria Elizabeth (Knippenburg) Kraemer Snyder and Anthony

Snyder, a mechanic who emigrated to America from the Palatinate. The boy's childhood was spent in poverty and hard work. At the age of seventeen he began an apprenticeship of four years as tanner and currier at York, where he also attended night school kept by John Jones, a Quaker. About 1784 he established himself at Selinsgrove in Northumberland, now Snyder, County. There he opened a general store, operated a mill, found frequent employment as a scrivener, and rose rapidly in the general estimation of the community. He was appointed a justice of the peace and, later, judge of the court of common pleas of Northumberland County, was a member of the state constitutional convention, 1789–90 and of the Assembly from 1797 to 1807. He was speaker three terms and, as a leader of the backcountry democracy, fought to liberalize the judiciary laws and to diminish the governor's powers. He was one of the principal agitators for the hundred-dollar act extending the jurisdiction of justices of the peace to cases not exceeding one hundred dollars and for compulsory arbitration legislation.

Tremendously popular in his district and among his faction, he was nominated for governor by the anti-judiciary Republicans in 1805, his chief mouthpiece being the *Republican Argus* in Northumberland edited by his close friend, John Binns [*q.v.*]. Unsuccessful by some five thousand votes in the bitter campaign that followed, he returned to the state house of representatives in 1806 to lead the abortive attempt to impeach Gov. Thomas McKean [*q.v.*]. In 1808 he was elected governor and was reëlected by overwhelming majorities in 1811 and 1814. He was the first representative of the German element or of the backcountry farming class to be elected governor of Pennsylvania. Unlike his predecessors he did not have a brilliant military or legal record. Exceedingly plain in his ways, he emulated Jeffersonian simplicity, and instead of delivering his message to the legislature in person sent it in writing. A state-rights man, he vigorously asserted the supremacy of the state in 1809 by calling out the militia to prevent a federal court from enforcing its decision in the Olmstead case, though he later yielded under protest to the federal government. He gave loyal support to the War of 1812, sponsored an act for public education, recommended abolition of the death penalty and modification of the law for imprisonment for debt, and advanced numerous schemes for internal improvements. In 1814 he vetoed over loud public protests "the forty bank bill" to establish banks over the state, on the grounds that it would give too much power to

"privileged orders," invite visionary speculation, and divert men from useful pursuits. The bill was passed over his veto. In 1817 he was elected to the state Senate. He was a member of the Moravian Church. He was married three times: first to Elizabeth Michael of Lancaster, second on June 12, 1796, to Catherine Antes, and third on Oct. 16, 1814, to Mary Slough Scott, a widow of Harrisburg, who survived him. He died from typhoid fever.

["Autobiographical Notes by Simon Snyder," *Pa. Mag. of Hist. & Biog.*, vol. IV (1880); M. K. Snyder, *Life of Gov. Simon Snyder* (n.d.); "Papers of Gov. Simon Snyder," *Pa. Archives*, 4 ser., vol. IV (1900); *Recollections of the Life of John Binns* (1854); J. B. Linn, *Annals of Buffalo Valley, Pa.* (1877); J. H. Peeling, "Governor McKean and the Pennsylvania Jacobins," *Pa. Mag. of Hist. & Biog.*, Oct. 1930; *Snyder Co. (Pa.) Annals*, vol. I (1919), compiled by G. W. Wagenseller; J. H. Peeling, "The Public Life of Thomas McKean, 1734–1817" (1929), doctor's thesis (MS.) at Univ. of Chicago; *Poulson's Am. Daily Advertiser*, Nov. 13, 19, 20, 1819.]   J. H. P.

SOBOLEWSKI, J. FRIEDRICH EDUARD (Oct. 1, 1808–May 17, 1872), conductor, composer, writer, was born in Königsberg, East Prussia, a descendant of an ancient Polish family. He received a fine musical education, eventually studying with Carl Friedrich Zelter and Carl Maria von Weber. In 1830 he was appointed director of music at the Königsberg theatre, and in 1835 became cantor at the *Altstädtische Kirche*. The *Philharmonische Gesellschaft*, a dilettante orchestra, was founded in 1838 and he was elected conductor, being similarly honored when the *Musikalische Akademie*, a mixed chorus, came into existence in 1843. In the course of his Königsberg period, he composed and produced the operas *Imogen* (1832), *Velleda* (1835), *Salvator Rosa* (1848), and *Der Seher von Khorassan* (1850). He developed literary activity, functioning as music critic of the *Ostpreussiche Zeitung*, and as correspondent, under the pseudonym J. Feski, of Robert Schumann's *Neue Zeitschrift für Musik*. Dubbed M. Hahnbüchn, he became a Davidsbündler, one of that redoubtable band gathered around Schumann to wage warfare upon the musical Philistines. He was appointed director of music at the Bremen theatre, presumably in 1854. During the Bremen period he published the pamphlets *Reaktionäre Briefe* (1854), *Oper, nicht Drama* (1857), *Debatten über Musik* (1857), and *Das Geheimniss der neuesten Schule der Musik* (1859). His opera *Komala* received its initial performance at Bremen in 1857 and was accorded the exceptional distinction of production at Weimar under the aegis of Franz Liszt the following year.

Apparently leaving Bremen at the end of the

season, Sobolewski took pasage for America, arriving in Milwaukee, Wis., before the end of July 1859. In an incredibly short time he composed the opera *Mohega*, which was given two performances by the Milwaukee *Musikverein*, Oct. 11, and Nov. 1, 1859. *Mohega* was probably the first operatic treatment of an episode from the Revolutionary War, the libretto celebrating the love and tragic end of Count Pulaski and the Indian maid Mohega at the siege of Savannah in 1779. Sobolewski became conductor of the short-lived Milwaukee Philharmonic Society, functioning at both concerts of the first (and last) season on Feb. 28 and Apr. 13, 1860. The St. Louis Philharmonic Society was organized in June 1860, and Sobolewski was engaged as conductor. He led his first concert a month before Hans Balatka directed the initial performance of the Chicago Philharmonic Society, both men laboring valiantly to prepare the way for the Messiah that was to come in the person of Theodore Thomas [*q.v.*] and his orchestra. Sobolewski conducted forty concerts of the St. Louis Philharmonic Society from Oct. 18, 1860, to Apr. 19, 1866, holding his organization together and achieving musical triumphs through the troubled years of the Civil War. He did missionary work of heroic dimensions, his orchestral programs constituting a liberal education in the appreciation of the classical and romantic schools. At the outset of the seventh season he resigned and devoted himself to teaching and composing. He remained professionally active until an apoplectic stroke cut him down in his sixty-fourth year.

Sobolewski was married three times. By his first wife, Bertha Dorn, he had four children, by his second wife, three, and by his third wife, Bertha von Kleist, six. He was an accomplished linguist, master of five languages. He contributed to the *Journal of Speculative Philosophy* the articles: "A Dialogue on Music" (1867), "The New School of Music" (1868), "Mendelssohn" (1873), and "Robert Schumann" (1874). He wrote an abundance of good music but his finest scores have become widely scattered if not irretrievably lost.

[Documentary material and data from Prof. Dr. Joseph Müller-Blattau, Königsberg, Rudolph Edward Sobolewski, Laddonia, Mo., Lillie Sobolewski Peterson, Loveland, Colo.; autograph letters of Sobolewski in the library of the author; the correspondence of Wagner and Liszt, *Gesammelte Schriften über Musik und Musiker von Robert Schumann* (5th ed., 2 vols., 1914); O. Burckhardt, *Der Musikverein von Milwaukee* (1900); E. E. Hipsher, *Am. Opera* (1927); E. C. Krohn, *A Century of Mo. Music* (1924), and *The Development of the Symphony Orchestra in St. Louis* (1924); *Mo. Republican*, May 18, 19, 20, 1872; *The Impressario*, June 1872.]   E. C. K.

SOLDAN, FRANK LOUIS (Oct. 20, 1842–Mar. 27, 1908), educator and scholar, was born in Frankfort-on-the-Main, Germany, the son of Johann Justin and Caroline (Elssman) Soldan. He attended German schools, emigrated in 1863 to the United States with his wife, Ottilie (Bernhard), settled in St. Louis, Mo., where he established a young ladies' academy, and in 1882 became a naturalized citizen.

In 1868 he began a notable career in connection with the St. Louis public school system. From instructor of modern languages in the high school, he was promoted to assistant superintendent in charge of instruction in German (1870); principal of the normal school (1871); principal of the combined normal and high schools (1887); and superintendent of instruction (1895), a position which he held until his death. Although a pioneer in city school administration, he saw clearly the principles effective in this work, and was largely influential in obtaining charter regulations which provided for appropriate and definite allocation of educational responsibilities together with the authority to meet them. The board of education was relieved of many details, and the initiative in administrative matters requiring professional insight was granted the superintendent. He revealed a surprising grasp of details, and tempered firmness of management with a tactful human interest in those under him.

Soldan's service to education was not confined to St. Louis. In 1880 he organized the first normal institute for teachers in South Carolina, thus contributing to a state-wide educational revival. From 1877 until his death, he was an active member of the National Educational Association, serving it in various official capacities. He lectured frequently and contributed numerous articles to educational periodicals and to *Western,* a journal of literature published in St. Louis. Closely associated with William Torrey Harris [*q.v.*] and others, he helped to make that city a center of culture. Among the subjects upon which he wrote were "The Darwinian Theory," "Goethe and Spinoza," "Law and Cause," "Goethe's Suleika," "Dante's Purgatorio," and "Culture and Facts." He published a couple of language books, *Grube's Method: Two Essays on Elementary Instruction in Arithmetic* (1881); and *The Century and the School, and Other Educational Essays* (1912). He was much interested in the writings of Horace, selections from which he translated. A turning lathe in his workshop and an excellent photographic equipment provided him means for gratifying other tastes. He died in the midst of his varied activities, falling dead in the street while on his way to attend a conference with his assistant superintendents. He was survived by his wife and one daughter. The St. Louis Soldan High School was named in his honor.

[*National Educ. Asso. Jour. of Proc. and Addresses* (1908); *A Memorial—Frank Louis Soldan* (1908); William Hyde and H. L. Conard, *Encyc. of the Hist. of St. Louis* (1899), vol. IV; James Cox, *Old and New St. Louis* (1894); *Mo. Hist. Rev.*, Oct. 1920, p. 92; *Outlook*, July 22, 1905, p. 739; *Educational Rev.*, May 1903, pp. 517–19, and May 1908; *St. Louis Globe-Democrat*, Mar. 28, 1908.]   J. H. C.

SOLEY, JAMES RUSSELL (Oct. 1, 1850–Sept. 11, 1911), teacher, naval writer, and lawyer, was born at Roxbury, Mass., son of John James and Elvira Codman (Dégen) Soley. He was a descendant of John Soley, an English settler at Charlestown, Mass., in the seventeenth century, and (through both parents) of Judge James Russell of Charlestown. After preparation in the Roxbury Latin School, he entered Harvard College and graduated in 1870. A year's instructorship in St. Mark's School, Southborough, Mass., was followed by his appointment, Oct. 1, 1871, as professor of ethics and English at the United States Naval Academy. Two years later, despite his youth and juniority to other instructors, he was made head of the department of English studies, history, and law, a position he held until 1882. From Aug. 18, 1876, until his resignation in 1890 he was a member of the naval corps of professors of mathematics, rising from lieutenant to commander. In 1878 he was abroad from April to December on duty connected with the American educational exhibit at the international exposition in Paris. He had also been commissioned to make a study of foreign systems of naval education, and his *Report on Foreign Systems of Naval Education* appeared as a government document in 1880. Between 1882 and 1890 he had duty in Washington, collecting and arranging the Navy Department library, and, as superintendent of the office of naval war records, supervising the publication of Civil War naval records. He also lectured on international law at the Naval War College, 1885–89, and was Lowell Institute lecturer in 1885 on American naval history and in 1888 on European neutrality in the Civil War. He had studied law in Annapolis and continued this work at Columbian (later George Washington) University, receiving his law degree in 1890. On July 16, 1890, he resigned his naval commission to become assistant secretary of the navy, and occupied this position until March 1893 with special administration of labor in naval shore establishments. Thereafter he practised law in

New York City with his former naval chief, Benjamin Franklin Tracy [*q.v.*], in the firm of Tracy, Boardman, and Platt (later Boardman, Platt, and Soley). His special field was international law, and his most notable legal service was as counsel for Venezuela in the boundary dispute with Great Britain, arbitrated at Paris in 1899. Until otherwise occupied after 1890, he was a prolific and able writer, chiefly on naval subjects. His books include a *Historical Sketch of the United States Naval Academy* (1876); *The Blockade and the Cruisers* (1883), in the series called Campaigns of the Navy in the Civil War; *The Rescue of Greely* (1885), with W. S. Schley; *The Boys of 1812* (1887); *Sailor Boys of '61* (1888); and *Admiral Porter* (1903). He also edited the *Autobiography of Commodore Charles Morris* (1880), contributed the naval chapters to Justin Winsor's *Narrative and Critical History of America* (1884–89), and wrote frequently on naval and legal themes for periodicals and works of reference. He was orator in 1890 at the unveiling of the monument in Annapolis commemorating the *Jeannette* expedition, and in 1891 at a memorial service for Admiral David Dixon Porter [*q.v.*] in Tremont Temple, Boston. He was married, Dec. 1, 1875, to Mary Woolsey Howland, daughter of the Rev. Robert Shaw Howland of New York; they had a son who died in infancy and two daughters. His burial was in the Church of the Heavenly Rest, New York City.

[*Who's Who in America*, 1910–11; *Tenth Report of the Class of 1870 of Harvard Coll.* (1920); *Army and Navy Jour.*, Sept. 16, 1911; *N. Y. Tribune*, Sept. 12, 1911; letter of R. S. Howland, recommending Soley to a professorship at Columbia Univ., Stauffer Coll., N. Y. Pub. Lib.]   A. W.

SOLGER, REINHOLD (July 17, 1817–Jan. 11, 1866), scholar, author, was born in Stettin, Prussia, the son of Friedrich Ludwig Wilhelm Solger, a member of the Prussian *Reichstag*, and his second wife, Auguste Amalie Jungnickel. His full name was Reinhold Ernst Friedrich Karl Solger. He received a careful education at home and later at a military school at Züllichau, a small town east of Berlin, a place to which he referred in his later writings as his "prison." In the fall of 1837, he entered the University of Halle to study theology but exchanged this field shortly afterward for philosophy and history. Three years later he transferred to Greifswald and was awarded a doctor's degree in 1842. He was an industrious student, very active in liberal political movements, contributing numerous poems to revolutionary papers. Through a friend of his father he received an appointment as *Referendar* in Potsdam and spent there and in Berlin one year of gay social activity which gave him the profound scorn for *Junker* and bureaucrats that is characteristic of his later writings. He then decided to emigrate to America but owing to a ticket fraud got only as far as Liverpool, England. He was offered the post of tutor in the home of a country gentleman, a sinecure that enabled him to continue his studies and to begin giving public lectures in English. He made the acquaintance of Carlyle, Dickens, and Lord Lytton, who became his friends and sponsors.

In 1847 he went to Paris and moved in the circle of the political exiles, Bakunin, Herzen, Herwegh, Bernays, and others. An attempt to establish himself in Berlin failed and he returned to Paris. Here, on Feb. 19, 1848, he married a young French girl, Adèle Marie Bémere, who was his constant companion throughout his later numerous changes of residence and the mother of his four children. After the February Revolution of 1848 Solger went to Berlin, espousing the Revolution as member of a democratic club, and later, during the fighting in Baden, serving as adjutant and interpreter to General Mieroslawski, commander of the revolutionary forces. When the Baden uprising was crushed Solger fled from Germany with a price on his head. He spent two years in Berne and Zürich, some time in Paris and London, and in the spring of 1853 emigrated to America, settling in Roxbury, a suburb of Boston, Mass. As in Switzerland and in England, he supported himself by his pen and by public lectures on history and modern German philosophy. In 1857 and 1859 he delivered a series of twelve lectures at the Lowell Institute of Boston where James Russell Lowell and Louis Agassiz [*qq.v.*] were among his hearers. He became an American citizen in May 1859, and interested himself in the political questions of the day as an enthusiastic member of the new Republican party. So effective was his speaking in the elections of 1856 and 1860 that John Albion Andrew, governor of Massachusetts, said of him that he had been as influential in bringing the Germans in the East to the Republican side as Carl Schurz had been in the West (letter to John Sherman, Nov. 29, 1865). President Lincoln appointed him to the newly created office of assistant register of the treasury, an interim position created with the purpose of making him register as soon as this post was vacated. In April 1864, he had suffered a stroke of paralysis which turned his last days into painful suffering.

Solger was twice awarded a literary prize. In 1859 the committee in charge of the New York

celebration of the centennial of Schiller's birth chose his eulogistic poem, "Erinnerung," for the prize. In 1862 his novel, *Anton in Amerika,* won the prize over twenty-two others in a competition arranged by the *Bellestristisches Journal* of New York. The novel, a satire of Gustav Freytag's best seller, *Soll und Haben* (1855), purports to be a sequel of this work; its theme is the problem of the adjustment of the cultured German in the American melting-pot. It was reworked and published again by Erick Ebermayer in 1928. Among other works by Solger are a humorous Byronic epic, *Hanns von Katzenfingen,* in part the story of the author's youth, and a farce in one act, *Der Reichstagsprofessor,* in which the inefficiency of the intellectual revolutionists of the Parliament of Frankfurt is pilloried. Solger was typical of the intellectual revolutionists of 1848 whose enthusiasm flowed through their pens. He was tall in stature and of very distinguished appearance.

[Personal information from Frederick R. Solger, Washington, D. C.; Friedrich Kapp, *Aus und Über Amerika* (1876), vol. I, and "Reinhold Solger," *Deutsch-Amerikanische-Monatshefte,* Feb. 1866; M. A. Dickie, *Reinhold Solger,* doctoral dissertation, 1930, see *Univ. of Pittsburgh Bull.,* Nov. 1930; S. A. Allibone, *A Critical Dict. of English Literature,* vol. II (1870); *Daily Nat. Intelligencer,* Washington, D. C., Jan. 13, 1866.]   A. E. Z.

SOLIS-COHEN, JACOB DA SILVA [See COHEN, JACOB DA SILVA SOLIS, 1838–1927].

SOLOMONS, ADOLPHUS SIMEON (Oct. 26, 1826–Mar. 18, 1910), philanthropist, was born in New York City, the son of John and Julia (Levy) Solomons. His father, who was of English birth, had emigrated to the United States in 1810, and was on the editorial staff of the *National Advocate* and the *Morning Courier and New York Enquirer*; his mother was of old New England stock. At fourteen he enlisted in the New York state militia and served for seven years. After his education in the public schools of New York City, he went into the stationery business. On June 25, 1851, he married Rachel Seixas Phillips, a descendant of the colonial patriot families of Seixas and Phillips, who bore him eight daughters and a son. In the same year Daniel Webster [*q.v.*], then secretary of state, appointed him special bearer of dispatches to Berlin. Moving his business to Washington, D. C., in 1859, he did government printing, added a book department, which became a literary headquarters for such men as Ulysses Simpson Grant and Chief Justice Salmon Portland Chase, and later established a photographic gallery in which pictures of many notable men, including the last photograph of Abraham Lincoln [*qq.v.*], were made. Characteristic of the esteem he enjoyed in Washington is the fact that when Schuyler Colfax [*q.v.*], vice-president of the United States, was prevented from making the address at the dedication of the Young Men's Christian Association building, Solomons, a Jew, was called upon to take his place. In 1871 he was elected to the house of delegates of the District of Columbia, and became chairman of the committee on ways and means. In 1873 Grant offered him the office of governor of the district, an honor Solomons refused, largely because his observance of the seventh-day Sabbath would be incompatible with the duties of the office. On giving up business in 1891, he served as general agent in America of the Baron de Hirsch Fund. At seventy-seven he retired and lived in Washington until his death.

Though never a man of ample means he was a creative philanthropist. He organized the first training school for nurses in Washington and the Washington Night Lodging-House Association, which supplied men with free lodging. He was an officer of the Provident Aid Society, of the Emergency Hospital, of the Society for Prevention of Cruelty to Animals, and director of the Providence Hospital, the Columbia Hospital for Women, and the Garfield Memorial Hospital, the last of which he had also helped to organize. In April 1881 the organization of the Associated Charities was projected at a meeting held in his house, and in May 1881 at another meeting there it was decided to organize the American Association of the Red Cross, of which he became an officer. In 1884 he was a representative of the United States at the Red Cross international congress in Geneva, Switzerland, and in 1903 he was one of the twelve petitioners on whose memorial Congress later reorganized the association. In New York his suggestion led to the organization of Mount Sinai Hospital and of the Montefiore Home for Chronic Invalids (later the Montefiore Hospital). A founder of the Jewish Protectory and Aid Society, and of the Russian Jews Immigration Aid Society (1881), he was acting president of the Jewish Theological Seminary Association when it was reorganized into the Jewish Theological Seminary of America, and its teachers' institute was formed solely through his initiative. His transparent sincerity, unassuming goodness, genial optimism, and willingness to serve made him a rarely beloved figure. His unswerving personal devotion was coupled with a beautiful tolerance. It has been said of him that, though he was "possessed of the grandeur of soul which pertains to a saint," he had "the simplicity of a child" and

lived a life "replete with moral beauty" (Marshall, *post*, pp. 169–70).

[Louis Marshall, in *Pubs. Am. Jewish Hist. Soc.*, no. 20 (1911); Cyrus Adler, *Ibid.*, no. 33 (1934); *The Jewish Encyc.*, vol. IX (ed. of 1925); Samuel Joseph, *Hist. of the Baron de Hirsch Fund* (1935), *passim*; *Am. Jewish Year Book*, 1904–05; *Jewish Comment* (Baltimore, Md.), Oct. 24, Dec. 12, 1902; *Evening Telegram* (N. Y.), Apr. 27, 1880; *Sunday Star* (Washington), Oct. 28, 1906; *Am. Hebrew*, Mar. 25, 1910; *Hebrew Standard*, Apr. 29, 1910; *Washington Post*, Mar. 19, 1910 (obituary), and Mar. 13, 1932 (mag. section).]

D. deS. P.

SOMERS, RICHARD (Sept. 15, 1778–Sept. 4, 1804), naval officer, was born at Somers Point, N. J. His great-grandfather, John Somers, came to America from England before 1693 and the family ultimately settled in Gloucester County, N. J., in the Great Egg Harbor region, acquiring a considerable amount of land. He was the youngest of six children of Richard and Sophia (Stillwell) Somers. The elder Richard was a colonel in the militia, a county judge, and an ardent Whig. It appears that because of the exposure of Egg Harbor to Loyalist attacks during the American Revolution, Colonel Somers moved to Philadelphia soon after the British evacuation of that city. There young Richard Somers received some elementary schooling, but later attended an academy in Burlington, N. J., where he remained until about the time of his father's death in October 1794. For some time he was apparently engaged in coastwise shipping between New York and Philadelphia, but on Apr. 30, 1798, along with Stephen Decatur, 1779–1820 [*q.v.*], he enlisted in the navy and served as midshipman aboard the frigate *United States*. Her cruise began in July 1798, and was continued, chiefly in West Indian waters, during the remainder of the year. Hardly more than a twelvemonth after his enlistment Somers received a promotion to the rank of third lieutenant; then, in the autumn of 1799, he sailed on board the *United States* for Europe in company with the American commissioners to France. The *United States* was laid up after the peace of 1801, and Somers was transferred, as first lieutenant, to the frigate *Boston* which, during the summer of 1801, sailed for France with Chancellor Livingston on board, and later proceeded to the Mediterranean where American warships were engaged in the war with Tripoli.

Soon after the return of the *Boston* to America near the end of 1802, Somers was given command of the schooner *Nautilus*, attached to the squadron of Commodore Edward Preble [*q.v.*]. It was employed in convoying merchantmen, in blockading Tripoli, and in obtaining supplies from Naples. In August 1804 Somers was placed in command of one of two divisions of gunboats which had been borrowed from Naples. In each of the ensuing attacks upon Tripoli, on Aug. 3, 7, 28, and Sept. 3, he displayed great coolness and courage, and earned the high commendation of Preble. In the meantime, plans were being made to send a fireship into the harbor at Tripoli. Somers, now a captain, volunteered to prepare the craft and to take her into the harbor. The vessel employed was a ketch which had been captured from the Tripolitans and renamed the *Intrepid*. About one hundred barrels of powder were stored in her magazine, and about 150 shells were placed on her deck. Fuses were installed which were expected to burn fifteen minutes before igniting the powder, and the thirteen men who accompanied the *Intrepid* were to escape to safety by means of two small boats. The ketch entered the harbor on the night of Sept. 4, but, before reaching her intended destination, she suddenly exploded, killing all hands, and apparently failing to injure the enemy.

Somers was of middle stature and sturdy of frame. Ordinarily mild and amiable, he was on occasion, given to heroic and dramatic action. While a very young man, he once fought three duels in one day with associates who had questioned his courage. After his death a number of vessels were named in his honor, and a resolution was passed by Congress on Mar. 3, 1805, expressing regret for the loss of the gallant men who had died in the *Intrepid* venture.

[J. E. Stillwell, *Stillwell Geneal.*, vol. III (1930); E. M. Hoopes, *Richard Somers* (1933); C. W. Goldsborough, *The U. S. Naval Chronicle*, vol. I (1824); J. F. Cooper, *Lives of Distinguished Am. Naval Officers* (1846), vol. I; G. W. Allen, *Our Navy and the Barbary Corsairs* (1905); J. F. Hall, *The Daily Union Hist. of Atlantic City and County, N. J.* (1900); *Records of Officers and Men of N. J. in Wars, 1791–1815* (1909); M. E. Seawell, *Decatur and Somers* (1894); *Naval Mag.*, Mar. 1836.]   R. W. I.

SONNECK, OSCAR GEORGE THEODORE (Oct. 6, 1873–Oct. 30, 1928), musician, librarian, historian, was born in Jersey City, N. J., the son of Georg and Julia (Meyne) Sonneck. He lost his father in early childhood and settled with his mother, a woman of wide culture and brilliant mind, in Frankfort-on-the-Main, Germany, where she had been called to direct the household of a widowed banker. From 1883 to 1889 young Sonneck attended the *Gelehrtenschule* at Kiel, and the *Gymnasium* at Frankfort. He spent one semester at the University of Heidelberg, and then matriculated at the University of Munich, which he left in 1897 without wishing to take a degree. His chief teachers were Adolf Sandberger in musicology, Carl Stumpf and W. H. Riehl in philosophy, Theodor Lipps

in psychology, and M. E. Sachs in musical composition. The letters dating from his student days and two small collections of German verses, *Seufzer* (1895), and *Eine Totenmesse* (1898), give early evidence of Sonneck's singularly self-analytical and pessimistic nature. These characteristics were strangely companioned by strong ambition, an indomitable will to work, and a keen sense of humor. After leaving Munich, Sonneck concentrated for a while on his technical development as a musician. He studied piano in Frankfort under James Kwast, composition and orchestration under Iwan Knorr, and conducting under Carl Schröder in Sondershausen.

Although Sonneck had composed and published several sets of songs and piano pieces between 1896 and 1899, he deliberately shunned a career as a creative musician, realizing that his talents, mentality, and capacity for assiduous application fitted him more particularly for scholarly pursuits. He spent part of 1899 in Italy, working mainly in the libraries of Padua, Bologna, and Venice. Upon his return to America, about the end of 1899, he embarked on his searching quest for data regarding American musical life in colonial and Revolutionary times. Old newspaper files, especially, yielded much information, with the aid of which Sonneck succeeded in giving the first methodical and correct picture of musical conditions in America prior to 1800. In 1902 he offered the manuscript of his *Bibliography of Early Secular American Music* (privately printed, 1905) without recompense to the Librarian of Congress as a government publication. The offer could not be accepted but it led to his appointment as the first chief of the music division in the Library of Congress, Aug. 1, 1902. As the creator and organizer of the division he devoted almost superhuman energy and perseverance to the development of the largest and most comprehensive collection of music and books on music in the country and one of the leading music libraries in the world. He resigned on Sept. 5, 1917, to join the G. Schirmer company, music publishers of New York, in a managerial position, which he held until his death. The Washington years, however, represent best "his life of high public importance" (Putnam, *post*, p. 1).

In 1904 the Library published his model "Classification" of music and books on music (adopted December 1902, revised April 1917). In 1905 he published privately his book on *Francis Hopkinson, the First American Poet-Composer, and James Lyon, Patriot, Preacher, Psalmodist*. Among his most important historical and critical publications are: *Early Concert-life in Amer-*

ica (1907), *Report on The Star-spangled Banner, Hail Columbia, America, Yankee Doodle* (1909, followed by an enlarged and revised monograph on *The Star Spangled Banner* in 1914), *Early Opera in America* (1915); two volumes of essays, *"Suum cuique"* (1916), and *"Miscellaneous Studies in the History of Music"* (1921). The actual manual labor, apart from the research, performed by Sonneck in cataloguing music, in preparing his various bibliographies on dramatic music (1908), orchestral music (1912), opera librettos (2 vols., 1914), and the works of Stephen C. Foster (1915) and Edward MacDowell (1917), is well-nigh incredible. He represented the government at the musical congresses in Rome and London in 1911, and was one of the three United States delegates to the Beethoven Centenary in Vienna in 1927, representing the Beethoven Association of New York, which, with Harold Bauer, he founded in 1919. When Rudolph Edward Schirmer [*q.v.*] founded *The Musical Quarterly* in 1914 Sonneck became the editor. He was elected vice-president of the Schirmer company in 1921. In his activity as music publisher he fostered American talents of promise and advocated "clean music in good taste," regardless of purpose. He himself resumed his composing and published several sets of highly personal and polished songs. His last important work of critical research was *Beethoven Letters in America* (1927). His wife, Marie Elisabeth Ames, to whom he had been married in Washington on Nov. 9, 1904, survived him.

[Sonneck papers in the Lib. of Cong.; *Who's Who in America,* 1928–29; Carl Engel, "O. G. Sonneck, Ein Charakterbild," *Studien zur Musikgeschichte. Festschrift für Guido Adler* (1930), "A Postscript," *Musical Quart.,* Jan. 1929; *Musical America,* Jan. 13, 1923, Nov. 10, 1928; Herbert Putnam, Rubin Goldmark, articles in *Musical Quart.,* Jan. 1929; Frank Patterson, "Personal Recollections of Oscar G. Sonneck," *Musical Courier,* Nov. 15, 1928; *Vol. of Proc. of the Music Teachers Nat. Asso.,* 1928 (1929); *Grove's Dict. of Music and Musicians, Am. Supp.* (1930); A. Eaglefield-Hull, *A Dict. of Modern Music and Musicians* (1924), *N. Y. Times,* Nov. 11, 1928.]   C. E—l.

SONNICHSEN, ALBERT (May 5, 1878–Aug. 15, 1931), war correspondent, author, was born in San Francisco, Cal. His father, Nicolai Sonnichsen, a native of Copenhagen, Denmark, was a soldier in the American Civil War and later a Pacific ship-owner and Danish consul at San Francisco; his mother, Bertha (Leichardt) Sonnichsen, was of German parentage. Albert attended public schools at San Francisco, Oakland, and San José, Cal., and also had some schooling at a Jesuit monastery, but at fifteen he ran away from school and went to sea, where he spent most of his time for the next five years, the first three of them before the mast. At one time he stopped off in Cuba for several weeks to aid the Cubans in their fight for independence from Spain; at another he spent several weeks in Tynemouth, England, studying painting, but decided that he had not the talent for it. Having a taste for knowledge, he did much reading on shipboard, and his years at sea gave him a liberal education. Some of their happenings are described in his book, *Deep Sea Vagabonds* (1903). With the beginning of the Spanish-American War in 1898, he became quartermaster on the United States transport *Zeelandia,* which sailed from San Francisco and reached Manila, P. I., in July. In the following January he was taken prisoner by the Philippine insurgents under Emilio Aguinaldo and was held for ten months, suffering greatly from privation and disease. He finally escaped in November 1899. While he was in prison he began writing the story of his experience, published as *Ten Months a Captive Among Filipinos* (1901).

Returning to the United States in 1900, he worked as a staff writer with the *New York Tribune* for six months in 1901–02. During 1903 he was employed by the New York publishing firm of McClure, Phillips & Company, and wrote special articles and feature stories for their news syndicate. War having broken out in southeastern Europe, he went to the Balkans in 1904 as special correspondent for the New York *Evening Post,* and was on the Bulgarian front for two years. Early in 1906, for the sake of adventure and of getting an "inside" story, he joined the Macedonian revolutionists, or brigands, as they were frequently called, in Turkey, being in effect one of them. In America it was reported that he had been slain by some of the rebel bands. He remained with them for nearly a year as soldier and peasant, then returned to America, and published his story as *Confessions of a Macedonian Bandit* in 1909. In 1907–08 he made a study of Slavic immigrants in the Middle West for the United States Immigration Commission, his work being embodied in the voluminous reports of the Commission, published in 1911. He had long been critical as to methods of distribution of products in the United States, and his study of the subject led to his serving as secretary of the Cooperative League of America (favoring production and distribution on the Rochdale system), 1910–15 and 1919–21, and as vice-president, 1924–26. He was editor of the *Co-operative Consumer* (later *Co-operation*) from 1914 to 1918. Meanwhile he wrote magazine articles on this and other subjects, and brought out his book, *Consumers' Coöperation,* in 1919. He spent the last ten years of his life near Willimantic, Conn., where he operated a successful poultry farm. In 1919 he married Gladys Brooks of San Francisco, who with two sons and a daughter survived him.

[See *Who's Who in America*, 1930–31; *Cooperation* (N. Y.), Sept. 1931; obituaries in *Sun* (N. Y.), *World-Telegram* (N. Y.), *N. Y. Evening Post*, Aug. 17, and *Hartford Courant*, Aug. 16, 1931. Some information has been supplied by Sonnichsen's family; his own books give details of the adventurous portions of his career.]   A. F. H.

SOOYSMITH, CHARLES (July 20, 1856–June 1, 1916), civil engineer, was born at Buffalo, N. Y., the son of William Sooy Smith [*q.v.*] and Elizabeth (Haven) Smith. His father determined to give him the best technical training available, and he was accordingly sent to Rensselaer Polytechnic Institute, at that time the most famous engineering school in America. After his graduation, at the age of twenty, he was sent to Europe for two years' study and travel, a considerable part of which he spent at the Polytechnic Institute in Dresden, Germany. Returning to America in 1879, he entered the service of the Atchison, Topeka & Santa Fé Railway as assistant superintendent of the department of track, bridges, and buildings, but left this position in 1881 to form with his father the firm of William Sooy Smith & Son, Engineers & Contractors. Six years of association with his father served to fix the son's interests in the field of subaqueous foundations, to which he was to devote the remainder of his professional life.

Withdrawing from the partnership in 1887, he formed his own organization, Sooysmith & Company, Contractors, of which he was president. This firm during the following ten years was engaged in many of the most difficult and important foundation projects in the country. Among these may be mentioned the piers for the bridges over the Mississippi River at Keithsburg, Ill., and at Fort Madison, Iowa; and over the Missouri River at Sioux City, Iowa, East Omaha, Nebr., Kansas City, Mo., and Sibley, Mo. His company also built the Manhattan Life, the American Surety, the Empire, and the Washington Life buildings in New York City. During this period, Sooysmith acted personally as chief engineer of construction on the Central Bridge over the Harlem River in New York City, and directed the foundation construction for the Baltimore & Ohio Railroad bridge over the Schuylkill River in Philadelphia, Pa.

Sooysmith retired from contracting in 1898 and opened an office as consulting engineer in New York City, where he resided until his death. He was consulting engineer to the Underground Rapid Transit Railway of New York and a member of the Metropolitan Sewerage Commission, and was widely consulted on difficult foundation problems. While William Sooy Smith was the first to introduce the pneumatic caisson into American practice, using it widely in bridge construction, his son appears to have been the first to make extensive use of this process in the construction of high buildings. His most important and original contribution to the profession, however, was the introduction into the United States of the so-called "freezing" process of excavation in unstable soils, already practised in England and Germany. The method consisted essentially of driving a series of pipes into the soil and freezing it by a process similar to that generally used in artificial refrigeration. It was thus made possible to carry foundations through strata of boulders and quicksand which defied all ordinary methods of excavation. Sooysmith took out many patents on improvements of the process, and shortly before his death he devised and patented a variation of the method, suitable for subaqueous tunnel construction, but although this method was one of great ingenuity, it does not appear to have been widely adopted in practice.

Sooysmith's professional career was limited to a narrow field, but within that field his knowledge was profound and his authority second to none. Outside his profession, his tastes were those of a scholar and his avocation the study of languages and literature. He wrote very little; one short paper—"Concerning Foundations for Heavy Buildings in New York City" (*Transactions of the American Society of Civil Engineers*, vol. XXXV, 1896)—and a few scattered discussions constitute the whole of his contributions to the technical press. He was married, Dec. 17, 1887, to Pauline Olmsted of Hartford, Conn.

[*Who's Who in America*, 1912–13; *Hartford Courant*, Dec. 19, 1887; *Trans. Am. Soc. Civil Engineers*, LII (1904), 449; *Engineering News*, June 8, 1916; *Engineering Record*, June 10, 1916; *N. Y. Times*, June 2, 1916; personal recollections of engineering acquaintances.]   J. I. P.

SOPHOCLES, EVANGELINUS APOSTOLIDES (*c.* 1805–Dec. 17, 1883), classicist and neo-Hellenist, one of the most picturesque figures in American education, was born between 1800 and 1808 (he concealed the exact date) in Tsangarada, Thessaly, near Mt. Pelion. Even the original form of his name is uncertain. According to one report he was christened Sophocles, to which he prefixed his grandfather's name, Evangelinus. The commoner explanation gives the latter as his baptismal name; in America he added the patronymic Apostolides (after his father) and finally the surname Sophocles, first bestowed upon him by his paternal uncle

Constantius. This uncle took him to Cairo, where he was educated in the establishment belonging to the monastery of St. Catherine, on Mt. Sinai. The trips which he made thither across the desert provided him with his most exciting boyhood experiences, and throughout life he maintained friendly relations with the Sinaitic monks. Returning to Greece, he endeavored to obtain a post as teacher, but for reasons not wholly clear he yielded to the advice of the Rev. Josiah Brewer, a missionary of the American Board of Commissioners for Foreign Missions, and emigrated to Massachusetts. After studying at Monson Academy, Monson, Mass., he entered Amherst College in 1829 but withdrew on account of ill health before the end of the year. For some years he taught at Mount Pleasant Classical Institute (later Amherst Academy) at Amherst; in 1834 he was instructor in mathematics at Hartford, Conn. The next year he brought out *A Greek Grammar for the Use of Learners,* often reissued during the next thirty years. Other textbooks followed quickly: *First Lessons in Greek* (1839), *Greek Exercises* (1841), *Greek Lessons* (1843), all marked by clarity and originality and a wide range of illustration. The year 1842 was signalized by his appointment as tutor in Greek at Harvard, and by the publication of *A Romaic Grammar,* with chrestomathy and vocabulary (omitted in the edition of 1857), in which he exploded the theory of an Aeolic-Doric origin of Modern Greek, and rightly traced it to the Byzantine. This work presented new and correct theories of morphology and syntax long before the treatises of Albert Thumb and Hubert Octave Pernot; its neglect by transatlantic scholars reveals the remoteness of America at that time from the learned centers of Europe. Another useful work was his *A Catalogue of Greek Verbs* (1844). Although ill health interrupted his teaching for a time, in 1847 he resumed his post as tutor. In 1848 his *History of the Greek Alphabet* proved to be far in advance of its time, anticipating in many details regarding pronunciation the work of Friedrich Wilhelm Blass. He revisited Greece in 1849 and 1860. In 1859 he had been appointed assistant professor, and in 1860 he was elected to a unique position as professor of Ancient, Byzantine, and Modern Greek. His "A Glossary of Later and Byzantine Greek" (published in the *Memoirs of the American Academy of Arts and Sciences,* vol. VII, n.s., 1860) was expanded into his greatest work, *Greek Lexicon of the Roman and Byzantine Periods* (1870), of which a memorial edition was published at Harvard in 1887.

If Sophocles was somewhat indifferent to the wealth of scholarship Western Europe had brought to bear upon Greek art and letters, this was because his own work lay in a field not yet explored by competent scholars. Humor and epigram, scorn of ignorance and superficiality, and a wide acquaintance with literature (except possibly German), characterized his teaching. He seems to have been disappointed in the results of the Greek Revolution; a Bavarian Greece had not been his ideal of a liberated Greece. His small body was surmounted by an Olympian head covered with a shock of white hair; his dark eyes gleamed almost ferociously. But under a brusqueness which terrified the stranger he cherished a tender sympathy for his intimate friends. Little children loved him; the chickens which he tended on the ground now occupied by Radcliffe College came at the call of their own names. With seeming parsimony he saved money to build a bridge and waterworks for his native village, and he left large sums to friends and to the Harvard library. His dignity, courtesy, and frugality suggested the Greek peasant, and the solitariness of the bare room in Holworthy Hall in which he died, the monk's cell.

[Frederick Tuckerman, *Amherst Acad., A New England School of the Past, 1814–1861* (1929), p. 219; J. L. Chamberlain, *Harvard Univ.* (1900); S. E. Morison, *The Development of Harvard University . . . 1869–1929* (1930), with portrait; *Ann. Reports of the Pres. and Treas. of Harvard Coll., 1883–84* (1885), p. 4; minutes of the Harvard Faculty of Arts and Sciences, Jan. 8, 1884; G. H. Palmer, in *Atlantic Monthly,* June 1891 (reprinted in Palmer's *The Teacher,* 1908), with some inaccuracies; George Batchelor, in *Harvard Grads.' Mag.,* June 1916; C. L. Jackson, in *Harvard Alumni Bull.,* Mar. 15, 1923; D. C. Hesseling, *Evangelinos Apostolidis Sophoclis néo-helléniste* (Amsterdam, 1925), reprinted from *Koninklijke Akad. van Wetenschappen,* Deel 59, no. 7, the best account of Sophocles' scientific attainments; *Nation,* Jan. 3, 1884; obituaries in *Boston Transcript,* and *Boston Daily Advertiser,* Dec. 18, 1883; private correspondence in the Harvard Univ. Archives; a MS. diary of Christos Evangelides of Syra for 1856–60 in the Harvard Univ. Lib.]   C. B. G.

SORGE, FRIEDRICH ADOLPH (Nov. 9, 1828–Oct. 26, 1906), socialist and labor leader, was born in Bethau bei Torgau, Saxony, the son of Georg Wilhelm and Hedwig Klothilde (Lange) Sorge. An early education received from his father, a clergyman, was supplemented by instruction at the Franckeschen Stiftungen at Halle. In 1848 he took part in the revolutionary activities at Torgau and Baden, and crossed the Swiss border with the revolutionary army. With others he was interned at Freiburg, but in September was released and went to Geneva, where he supported himself by teaching music. Here he first came in contact with liberal socialists through the German Workers Educational Society, of which Karl Liebknecht was the leader. He was forced to leave Geneva in the summer of 1851 and joined his brother at Liège, where he worked in a carpenter shop and taught German in a private school, being continually under police surveillance. In March 1852 he was expelled from Belgium, and, exiled from Germany because of a death sentence imposed by a military tribunal at Torgau, he went to London. Here he first met Karl Marx and renewed a passing acquaintance with Friedrich Engels. While suffering from an attack of the cholera, he took ship supposedly for Australia, but found himself instead landed in New York City on June 21, 1852. Here he eventually established a reputation as a musician and music teacher.

In 1858 he joined the Communist Club organized by Albert Komp in New York, and in 1868 was a member of the executive committee of the Union for German Freedom and Unity, organized to support the republican movement in Germany. He associated with the radical anti-slavery wing of the Republican party during the Civil War; was secretary of the Secularists, a freethinker group, in 1868; joined in the political activity of the Soziale Partei in 1868; and finally, in 1869, became a member of Section 1 of the International Working-Men's Association. From 1869 to 1876, he was not only the most active and influential, but also the clearest exponent of the German-American proletariat. He attended The Hague convention of the International in 1872, came into active opposition to Bakunin, the leading anarchist factor in the International and was instrumental in the expulsion of Section 12 of the American branch, which was advocating anarchism, free love, and other doctrines foreign to the purposes of the International. After the removal of the International headquarters to New York City, he was persuaded to undertake the office of general secretary. At The Hague he became more intimately acquainted with Marx and Engels, and until his death was the authoritative representative of Marx in America. In July 1876, Sorge and Otto Weydemeyer represented the North American Federation of the International Working-Men's Association, at a convention held in Philadelphia for the purpose of unifying the American labor and socialist movements. This meeting resulted in ultimate adherence to the Socialist Labor Party, with which Sorge had little to do.

Sorge was keenly interested in bringing about a national organization of the labor union movement, and to that end he associated in 1877 with Ira Steward [q.v.] in the Eight-Hour League at Boston. The following year with J. P. McDonnell, he was instrumental in organizing the textile workers of New Jersey. At that time he was living in Hoboken, N. J. In 1891 Samuel Gom-

pers requested Sorge to make for European publication a fair statement of the conditions under which the American Federation of Labor was being attacked by the American Socialists, and from 1891 to 1895 he contributed a series of articles in German to the Neue Zeit (Stuttgart) on the labor movement in the United States. He was also the author of many propaganda pamphlets, one of which, Socialism and the Worker, was reprinted in 1910 in London. Following the Philadelphia meeting, he gradually withdrew from public connection with the Socialist movement, owing to the development of tendencies with which he was not in sympathy. Sorge was a tall, stout man with a bullet-shaped head, full-bearded, the moustache not large enough to cover a hare lip. He was overbearing and dictatorial, often quarreling bitterly with his associates and his family. Shortly after coming to the United States he was married to a young German girl. They had a son and a daughter. In 1877 he moved temporarily to Rochester, N. Y., later returning to Hoboken, N. J., where he resided until he died.

[Samuel Gompers, Seventy Years of Life and Labor (1925); Morris Hillquit, Hist. of Socialism in the U. S. (1903); J. R. Commons, Hist. of Labour in the U. S. (1921), vol. I; Hermann Schlüter, Die Internationale in Amerika (1918), Heft 7; G. M. Stekloff, Hist. of the First International (1928); Neue Zeit, Nov. 3, 1906.]
W. R. G.

SORIN, EDWARD FREDERICK (Feb. 6, 1814–Oct. 31, 1893), Roman Catholic priest, educator, founder of the University of Notre Dame, was born at Ahuillé, near Laval, France. Having completed his collegiate studies with high honors, he entered the diocesan seminary and was ordained priest on May 27, 1838. The Abbé Basil Antoine Moreau, a professor in the seminary at Le Mans, had recently organized a community of priests of the diocese and to this band he later added a society of lay brothers, giving to the united group the title Congregation of Holy Cross. Attracted by the ideals of the new society, Father Sorin entered it and made his profession Aug. 15, 1840.

About this time Bishop Hailandière of Vincennes, Ind., then in France, asked the new community to send missionaries to his diocese. After due consideration, the community decided to send Father Sorin and six brothers. They sailed from Havre as steerage passengers on the packet Iowa and arrived in New York Sept. 13, 1841. Traveling mostly by water, they arrived at Vincennes about a month later. At first they settled at St. Peter's in Daviess County, about twenty-seven miles from Vincennes. The following year Bishop Hailandière offered to Sorin a plot of land near South Bend, in St. Joseph County, on condition that he start a college within two years. Accompanied by the brothers, Father Sorin started for the new site, called by Father Badin, the original owner, Sainte Marie des Lacs. Arriving Nov. 26, 1842, he set about at once to fulfil the condition laid down by the bishop. He sent back to France for more priests and brothers and began to build. In the meantime he had obtained from the General Assembly of Indiana, Jan. 15, 1844, a charter for Notre Dame University. The first college building was completed in time for the initial commencement exercises in June 1844. Father Sorin continued as president until 1865 and he, more than any one else, shaped the traditions and spirit of Notre Dame. He also acted as provincial superior and together with his fellow religious took care of the mission posts in northeastern Illinois, northern Indiana, and southern Michigan. The college progressed steadily under his guidance despite extreme financial difficulties, several fires, and even a plague of cholera which seriously depleted the ranks of the little community.

In 1843 Father Sorin brought to America from Le Mans some Sisters of Holy Cross and the following year established them at Bertrand, Mich., about five miles from Notre Dame. Under his direction, this band of zealous women grew rapidly into a large community conducting schools in all parts of the country. In 1854 he secured the site of the present motherhouse adjacent to Notre Dame and moved there the sisters' community house and academy. He was especially instrumental in bringing to that community Eliza Maria Gillespie, who, as Mother Angela [q.v.], became to the Sisters of Holy Cross, after their separation into a distinct community, what Father Sorin was to Notre Dame. In 1865 he began the publication of Ave Maria, a family magazine of influence and importance. Immediately following the outbreak of the Civil War he sent priests and sisters to care for the soldiers. In 1868 he was elected superior-general of the Congregation of Holy Cross and as such supervised the educational and missionary activities of the community in France, Canada, and Bengal as well as in the United States. He retained, however, his presidency of the trustees of Notre Dame. The French government conferred upon him, in 1888, the insignia of Officer of Public Instruction for his service to education. In 1883 he assisted in the deliberations of the Plenary Council of Baltimore. His voluminous and important correspondence shows an acquaintanceship with the Catholic leaders of America, clerical and lay; it was at his sugges-

tion, in 1883, that the custom was established at Notre Dame of awarding the Laetare Medal annually to a distinguished Catholic layman.

[Father Sorin's journal and "Missions Attended from Notre Dame," in the Provincial archives, Notre Dame; Timothy Howard, A Hist. of St. Joseph County, Ind., vol. II (1907); A Brief Hist. of the Univ. of Notre Dame du Lac, 1842–1892 (1895); Notre Dame Scholastic, vols. XVI, XXVII, XXXIX; South Bend Daily Times, Feb. 28, Mar. 7, 14, 1898; Indianapolis Sentinel, Nov. 1, 1893; Ave Maria, Nov. 4, 1893.]

W. M.

SOTHERN, EDWARD ASKEW (Apr. 1, 1826–Jan. 20, 1881), actor, was born in Liverpool, England, seventh child in the large family of John Sothern, prosperous ship and colliery owner. He made attempts in London to study surgery and then theology, finally ending in a Liverpool ship-broker's office, but he was drawn strongly to the stage, first as an amateur, and in 1849, in Guernsey, as a professional. Though there was no acting tradition in his family, and his first attempts were failures, he persisted, acting in provincial cities under the name of Douglas Stewart, and in 1852, still under that name, set out for America. After his first engagement at the National Theatre, Boston, as Dr. Pangloss, in The Heir at Law, a part to which he was unsuited and in which he failed, he went to the old Howard Athenaeum, Boston, and then to Barnum's Museum in New York, where he toiled twice a day for a year. By 1854 he had sufficiently improved to be engaged by Lester Wallack, in whose New York company he acted for four years. During this period he assumed his own name, and acted Armand to the Camille of Matilda Agnes Heron [q.v.]. At Laura Keene's theatre in 1858 he was cast for a small part in Our American Cousin. According to the story told by Joseph Jefferson, the younger [q.v.], to E. H. Sothern (The Melancholy Tale of "Me," post, pp. 172–73), Sothern had resolved to give up the trifling part and go back to England, but Jefferson, who wished him to continue to share the expense of a stable for their riding horses, persuaded him to stay, on condition that Miss Keene permit him to build up his part. Thus was born the rôle of Lord Dundreary, Sothern's most famous creation, little noticed for the first two weeks, but as time went on gradually usurping the whole play, so that Miss Keene and Jefferson took the original version, and let Sothern organize a new company for his version. The play was produced in America, Oct. 18, 1858. In 1861, when it was produced in London at the Haymarket, it became even more widely popular, and ran for 496 performances. The part was, as Andrew Carpenter Wheeler put it, "the elaboration of a negation," in which the actor showed "the rich fulness of a vacuum" (Pemberton, *post*, p. 32). There had never been a similar British silly ass on the stage before, nor has there been since. It was *sui generis,* at once a comical burlesque and a thing of quaint and inexplicable dignity. The character had a mythical Brother Sam, whom Sothern later caused to be dramatized, as a sort of sequel. He also produced, among other plays, Thomas W. Robertson's romantic *David Garrick,* and a version of Henry J. Byron's *The Prompter's Box,* called *A Crushed Tragedian,* in which his part of the old actor was a mingling of almost burlesque character-drawing and pathos. So firmly had Sothern's Dundreary fixed him in the public mind as a comedian, however, that the pathos seldom told at its true value. After the first long run of Dundreary in London, he divided his time almost equally between the United States and England, touring through both countries with vast success, and carrying with him his entire company instead of depending on local stock companies for support. He retained a home in London, however, and there he died of what was perhaps euphemistically called a nervous collapse, the result of a combination of hard professional labors and excessive conviviality. In spite of his twenty years of success, his estate was found to be less than $50,000.

He had plentiful equipment for an actor—nervous sensibility, keen powers of observation, a lithe figure and handsome face, with keen, dominating blue eyes, a magnetic sense of fun, and in his professional work capacity for concentrated labor and minute attention to detail. His Dundreary was elaborated with the utmost care; every least gesture and inflection was studied, often from life, and welded into the whole. Nothing was left to chance. But in his personal life he was spendthrift of his time and energies; he loved to ride and hunt and to be in convivial society, and he was perhaps the most noted practical joker of the day. The most engaging of his innumerable pranks is that related by his son in *The Melancholy Tale of "Me,"* when the elder Sothern arrived in Boston, drove to the home of his friend Mrs. Vincent, Boston's best loved actress, burst in on a party she was giving, picked her up, dashed with her back to his cab, and drove frantically off, with all the guests in full pursuit of the abductor. There was no end to his invention of these jokes, which were carried out with as much acting skill, when necessary, as his stage impersonations. He married Frances Stewart, an actress, daughter of the Rev. R. I. Stewart, County Wexford, Ireland (Moses, *post,* p. 97). She bore him four children, all of whom went on the stage: Lytton Edward, Eva Mary, George, and Edward Hugh Sothern [*q.v.*]. But Sothern's personal habits were not those conducive to domestic happiness, and long before his death his wife had separated from him. She died in 1882. In spite of his habits, which included laxities more common on the stage then than now, he retained almost to the end a fresh, rosy complexion and unwrinkled face, though his hair early turned white and his shoulders were bowed, and the charm and conviviality of his company continued to be much sought.

[*The Dict. of Nat. Biog.*; *Birds of a Feather Flock Together, or Talks with Sothern* (1878), ed. by F. G. De Fontaine; T. E. Pemberton, *A Memoir of Edward Askew Sothern* (1889); Brander Matthews and Laurence Hutton, *Actors and Actresses of Great Britain and the United States* (copr. 1886), vol. IV; M. J. Moses, *Famous Actor-Families in America* (1906); William Winter, *Other Days* (1908); E. H. Sothern, *The Melancholy Tale of "Me"* (1916); obituaries in *Times* (London) and *N. Y. Tribune,* Jan. 22, 1881.]
W. P. E.

SOTHERN, EDWARD HUGH (Dec. 6, 1859–Oct. 28, 1933), actor, son of Edward Askew Sothern [*q.v.*] and Frances (Stewart) Sothern, was born at 79 Bienville St., New Orleans, La., during one of his father's American tours. He was educated in England and intended to become a painter, but the inherited call of the stage was too strong. In 1879 he joined his father in America, and on Sept. 8, at the Park Theatre, New York, he made an unfortunate début as a cabman in the farce, *Brother Sam,* produced by the elder Sothern, in which, overcome by stage fright, he was unable to utter a sound. Sent to Boston to act with the Boston Museum stock company under the kindly eye of Mrs. Mary Ann Vincent, a family friend, in the next few months he found his confidence, and joined for a time the company of John McCullough [*q.v.*], Shakespearian actor, to which he returned in 1883 after nearly two years in England. After failing dismally in his attempt to star in *Whose are They?* in 1884, he joined the company of Helen Dauvray at the Lyceum Theatre, New York, and there was discovered by Daniel Frohman, who took over the Lyceum in 1886 and made Sothern a leading man in his stock company. In the next fourteen years he built up in this company a brilliant reputation as a light comedian and as a charming romantic actor in the "cloak and sword" dramas then so popular. His *Captain Lettarblair* and *Lord Chumley* are best remembered as comedy, and his *Rudolf,* the dashing hero of *The Prisoner of Zenda,* as romance. As *Rudolf,* he toured the country and won such wide recognition that after 1899 he became a star in his own right, and with his wife, Virginia Harned, whom he married Dec. 3, 1896, acted in *The King's Musketeers* (adapted from the elder Dumas), *The Song of the Sword, The Sunken Bell,* and *Drifting Apart.* On Sept. 17, 1900, at the Garden Theatre, New York, he acted *Hamlet* for the first time, and thereafter kept it in his repertoire, alternating it during the next three or four years with such plays as *Richard Lovelace, If I Were King,* with which he opened the new Lyceum Theatre, and *The Proud Prince.* From 1904 to 1907 under the management of Charles Frohman [*q.v.*], he formed an alliance with Julia Marlowe to act chiefly in Shakespeare. In the next two years Sothern alone produced Laurence Irving's *The Fool Hath Said, Richelieu, Don Quixote,* and a revival of his father's famous impersonation of Dundreary in *Our American Cousin.* On Nov. 8, 1909, Miss Marlowe rejoined him, acting Cleopatra to his Antony, to open the New Theatre, New York. They then resumed their tours, acting some of the more familiar plays of Shakespeare, *Jeanne d'Arc,* Sudermann's *John the Baptist,* Hauptmann's *The Sunken Bell,* and occasionally *When Knighthood Was in Flower.* The Shakespearian productions, carefully and elaborately staged, were everywhere enormously popular, and during that decade in America were perhaps the leading attraction in the theatres. On Aug. 17, 1911, in London, having been divorced by his first wife, Sothern married Julia Marlow (born Sarah Frances Frost), who had been married previously to Robert Taber. In 1916 ill health forced her to retire, and Sothern, after an appearance in *The Two Virtues,* devoted the next years to war work, appearing as an entertainer in soldiers' camps. After the war, in 1919, his wife once more attempted to act but was unable to continue steadily; he appeared from time to time, however, either in plays or public readings, his last theatrical appearance in New York being at the Lyceum Theatre, Jan. 29, 1927, with Haidee Wright, in *What Never Dies.* His readings and lectures, given widely throughout the country, continued for several years more. (See Arthur Ruhl's "Second Nights" in the New York *Herald Tribune,* Nov. 17, 1929.) In his later years, with his wife, he spent his summers in England and his winters, when he was not in America, at Luxor on the Nile. His autobiography, *The Melancholy Tale of "Me"* (1916), is one of the most delightful of theatrical reminiscences. It is plainly the work of a man of culture, wit, and literary skill, and suggests that if its author had not been an actor he might have made a career as a writer. He died in New York

City of pneumonia. He was survived by his wife.

Sothern's stage personality was sufficiently impressive to conceal the fact that he was a small man. He had a sensitive, handsome face, extremely fine eyes, much bodily grace and expressive body control, quickness and litheness of movement, and a well-trained voice. He developed and perfected "a distinct, authoritative, crisp style, not unique, but neat, expert in mechanism, and felicitous in assumption of nonchalant, lacka-daisical demeanor" (Winter, *Vagrant Memories, post,* pp. 433–34). He excelled in the give-and-take of comedy repartee, and in romantic sword play and dashing heroics and amours; as a stage director he was skilful in bringing out the melodramatic structure of a story or the swing of the narrative. He was not by natural endowment a tragic actor, but he was led by ambition and by devotion to the ideal of a classic repertoire to act Hamlet, Shylock, Macbeth and Antony and by dint of hard work and keen, sensitive intelligence he gave in nearly all cases an excellent account of himself. His best Shakespearian rôle, however, was probably Malvolio, where with no loss of comic effect he presented a pathetic picture of an inherent gentleman overcome by vanity. One of his irresistibly comical performances was his reincarnation of his father's Dundreary. Those who saw Sothern act in the nineties, however, especially those who saw him in *The Prisoner of Zenda,* will most fondly remember him as the dashing, charming, alluring symbol of that pseudo-romance which had such a brief and beautiful Indian summer before the realistic new century set in. Better than any other player on either continent Sothern embodied its humor and gaiety, its chivalric love, its delicate grace, its wistfulness.

[*Who's Who in America,* 1932–33; *Who's Who in the Theatre* (1933); E. H. Sothern, *The Melancholy Tale of "Me"* (1916), with portraits, and "Why I Produce Shakespeare Plays," *Dramatic Mirror,* Jan. 18, 1911; William Winter, *Vagrant Memories* (1915) and *The Wallet of Time* (1913), vol. II; Arthur Symons, *Great Acting in English* (priv. printed, London, 1907); W. P. Eaton, in *Sun* (N. Y.), Apr. 12, 1908; Winthrop Ames, in *N. Y. Times,* sec. 9, Nov. 12, 1933; *Sunday Herald* (Boston), Apr. 5, 1903, reproductions of pictures painted by Sothern as a boy; obituary in *N. Y. Times,* Oct. 30, 1933.]   W. P. E.

SOTO, HERNANDO DE [See DE SOTO, HERNANDO, *c.* 1500–1542].

SOUCHON, EDMOND (Dec. 1, 1841–Aug. 5, 1924), anatomist, surgeon, sanitarian, was born in Opelousas, Saint Landry Parish, La., the son of Eugene Souchon, "surgeon dentist," and Caroline (Pettit) Souchon, both natives of France. He was sent at first to private schools at Saint Martinville, La., Mobile, Ala., and New

Orleans, La., but later, when his father suffered ill health and financial reverses, he went to public school and sold papers to aid his family. Reviving fortune took him in 1860 to Paris, where he studied medicine, ranked fourth among three hundred and fifty in the grilling concours for internship in Paris hospitals, and served at Charité under the famous surgeon, Alfred Armand Velpeau. His acting as interpreter for Dr. James Marion Sims on the latter's visit to Paris brought him financial aid from Sims and a letter of introduction to Dr. Tobias Gibson Richardson [qq.v.] when he afterwards returned to New Orleans. Upon his graduation in 1867 from the medical department of the University of Louisiana (later the Tulane University of Louisiana), he became Richardson's prosector and later his chief of clinic at Charity Hospital of New Orleans, and assisted him in private practice for many years. On Dec. 6, 1869, he married Corinne Lavie of New Orleans; they had three children, a son, who became a surgeon, and two daughters.

He was demonstrator of anatomy in the medical department of the University of Louisiana (Tulane), 1873–76, and from 1885 until 1908 served as professor of anatomy and clinical surgery, his aim being to teach anatomy "in its direct practical application" to the needs of the medical practitioner. He invented ingenious mechanical devices that were applied in both anatomical and surgical practice, and for the preservation of anatomical dissections devised original methods of injection and coloration. His museum of anatomy, housed in the Richardson Memorial Building at Tulane (which in 1892 he planned for the Richardson family), contained four hundred dissections. His anatomical knowledge led to his association in hospital work with Dr. Andrew Woods Smyth, who first successfully ligated the innominate artery. As a surgeon he was typical of the operators drilled in the quick French school of the sixties, and in the surgical renaissance of the seventies and the eighties he evolved his own methods in keeping with antisepsis and asepsis. Led to study aneurisms and shoulder dislocations, he wrote many monographs that are "conspicuous landmarks" in the history of these subjects, "undoubtedly the most enduring literary monuments of his surgical career" (*Transactions of the American Surgical Association, post,* p. 974). His surgical and anatomical writings began in 1866 with "Aneurisms of the Arch of the Aorta" (*New Orleans Medical and Surgical Journal,* May 1867) and continued until late in his life, two of the later articles being "Original Contri-

butions of America to Medical Sciences" (*Transactions of the American Surgical Association,* vols. XXXV and XXXVIII, 1917–20). Many others are listed in the *Index Catalogue of the Library of the Surgeon General's Office, United States Army* (1 ser., vol. XIII, 1892; 2 ser., vol. XVI, 1911; 3 ser., vol. IX, 1931). As president of the Louisiana State Board of Health, 1898–1908, he prepared a sanitary code embodying all the health laws of the state, contributed actively to the "Atlanta Regulations" adopted by the Southern states in 1898 to regulate yellow fever quarantine, and in 1903 announced warfare on the *Stegomyia* mosquito. He served as an officer of the American Medical Association, the Southern Surgical and Gynecological Society, and the American Surgical Association (1899); he was a fellow of the American Association of Anatomists, honorary fellow of the American College of Surgeons (1914), and corresponding member of the Société Nationale de Chirurgie de Paris. A man whose very positive convictions were often tinged with abruptness, he possessed many peculiarities that lent themselves to anecdote. In spite of his dominating passion for punctuality and method, he was capable of great outbursts of enthusiasm, expressed with typical French volubility and gaiety. His life was marked by loyal friendships and devoted domestic ties.

[*Who's Who in America,* 1924–25; Rudolph Matas, in *Jour. Am. Med. Assoc.,* Aug. 16, 1924, in *Surgery, Gynecology, and Obstetrics,* May 1931, and in *Trans. Am. Surgical Assoc.,* vol. XLIII (1925); I. A. Watson, *Physicians and Surgeons of America* (1896); obituary in *Times-Picayune* (New Orleans), Aug. 6, 1924.]
V. G. G.

SOULÉ, GEORGE (May 14, 1834–Jan. 26, 1926), mathematician, educator, and lecturer, was born at Barrington, N. Y., the second son of Ebenezer and Cornelia Elizabeth (Hogeboom) Soulé. His father died in 1838, and in 1842 his mother took the family to Illinois, settling some fifty miles west of Chicago. For the next ten years George lived on a farm. In 1853 he was graduated from an academy at Sycamore, Ill., and went to St. Louis, where he attended some lectures on medicine and law. Financial considerations forced him to abandon professional study, however, and he entered Jones' Commercial College, from which he graduated in 1856.

That same year he went to New Orleans, where, discovering that there was no business school, he opened Soulé College in a single room. Almost from the first the institution prospered; in 1861 it was chartered. On Sept. 6, 1860, Soulé married Mary Jane Reynolds of Summit, Miss. He entered the Confederate army Mar. 5, 1862,

403

as captain of Company A, Crescent Regiment, Louisiana Infantry, was captured at Pittsburg Landing Apr. 7, and was exchanged Nov. 10. He then served in General Kirby-Smith's army as chief of the labor bureau. He was paroled in June 1865, at which time he was lieutenant-colonel of the Crescent Regiment.

Returning to New Orleans, he took personal charge of Soulé College. A pioneer in business education in the South, he tried to give his students something more than shorthand and book-keeping. His own interest in arithmetical processes and in systems of accounting led him to devise and to publish many textbooks. Among these were *Soulé's Analytic and Philosophic Commercial and Exchange Calculator* (1872); *Soulé's Intermediate Philosophic Arithmetic* (1874); *Soulé's New Science and Practice of Accounts* (1881); *Soulé's Introductory Philosophic Arithmetical Drill Problems* (1882); *Soulé's Philosophic Practical Mathematics* (1895); and *Soulé's Manual of Auditing* (6th ed., 1905). The most of these went through several editions. He was active in the National Commercial Teachers' Federation, before which he often spoke in behalf of better and more ethical standards. His success in commercial education was reflected in the rapid and steady growth of his college; during the seventy years of his presidency, some forty thousand students were enrolled. In the life of New Orleans he took a prominent part. He was a leader in Masonic activities, a prominent member of the Unitarian Church, and a most active and valuable member of the Rex carnival organization. He was king of the carnival in 1887 and wrote the history of the carnival for the golden anniversary of 1922. Tulane University conferred the degree of LL.D. on him in 1918.

In addition to annual addresses at Soulé College, he lectured frequently and widely. One of his chief interests was phrenology, which he enthusiastically believed to have a scientific basis in anatomy. In many respects he was far ahead of his times. He opposed child labor, favored more hygienic conditions for workers, and rebuked the city authorities for what he considered the shameful violation of architectural beauty and of hygienic principles and laws. When such subjects were taboo, he advocated studies in sex-hygiene and eugenics. To his success as a speaker, his striking appearance contributed. He was over six feet tall, erect, and keen-eyed; his hair fell down to his shoulders. Active in public affairs almost to the end of his life, he died after a brief illness, survived by four sons and two daughters.

[G. T. Ridlon, *A Contribution to the Hist., Biog., and Geneal. of the Families Named Sole, Solly, Soule, Sowle, Soulis* (1926); J. S. Kendall, *Hist. of New Orleans* (1922), II, 827–30; A. B. Booth, *Records of La. Confederate Soldiers* (1920), vol. III, bk. II, p. 651; *Who's Who in America,* 1924–25; *Times-Picayune* (New Orleans), June 6, 1918, Jan. 27, 1926; information from the Soulé family, and from Dr. Rudolph Matas.]   R. P. M.

SOULE, JOSHUA (Aug. 1, 1781–Mar. 6, 1867), bishop of the Methodist Episcopal Church, a lineal descendant of George Soule who came to America on the *Mayflower,* was born at Bristol, Me., the fifth son of Joshua and Mary (Cushman) Soule. Although his parents were Presbyterians, Joshua in 1797 joined the Methodist Episcopal Church, and in 1799, at the age of seventeen, was admitted on trial to the New England Conference. In 1802 he was ordained deacon and the following year, elder. He served as a pioneer itinerant and presiding elder in New England until 1816. In that year he was made book agent of the church and in 1818 became the first editor of the *Methodist Magazine.* Between 1816 and 1820 he was also active in the work of the American Bible Society and in 1819 he became a charter member and treasurer of the Missionary and Bible Society of the Methodist Episcopal Church in America, the pioneer missionary body of that denomination. From 1820 to 1824 he held pastorates in the New York and Baltimore conferences. He was elected bishop in 1824 and was assigned to the western and southern conferences, making his home in Lebanon, Ohio. In 1842 he was fraternal messenger to the British and Irish Wesleyan Conferences.

At the age of twenty-six, Soule wrote the constitution of the Methodist Episcopal Church. The early methods of vesting the legislative powers of the church in a quadrennial assembly of the preachers had become so unsatisfactory, that at the General Conference of 1808, a committee of which Soule was a member was appointed to prepare a more efficient plan. Without any assistance, he prepared a draft, which with only a few minor changes was adopted as the constitution of the church. His plan provided for a delegated and representative General Conference, which was, subject to six restrictive rules, to have legislative authority for the denomination. It also promoted the connectionalism of Methodism, and gave to Methodist polity democratic and stabilizing characteristics. Soule did his work so well as the "Father of the Constitution" that there has been only slight inclination on the part of Episcopal Methodism to devise new means of ecclesiastical law making. Subsequently, he affected the polity of Methodism by his views concerning the sub-episcopate. Until

1820 the presiding elders had been appointed by the bishops, but objections had arisen on the ground that this practice was undemocratic, and that it made the presiding elders amenable to the bishops and not to the preachers. Therefore, at the General Conference of 1820 it was decided that the annual conference should elect the presiding elders. At this same Conference Soule had been elected bishop, but when the vote on the sub-episcopate was announced he refused to be consecrated. He insisted that an elective presiding eldership was unconstitutional, since the fundamental law of the church instructed the bishops to oversee the business of the church. This function Soule asserted would be impossible if the presiding elders were not directly responsible to the bishops. His arguments were so pertinent that the delegates resolved to suspend the enforcement of the resolution for four years. By the time of the next General Conference (1824) the church had approved Soule's constitutional position, and he was again elected bishop. For twenty years he was a bishop of the Methodist Episcopal Church. He was an excellent administrator and was recognized as an authority on polity.

In 1844, when the General Conference sought to depose Bishop James O. Andrew [q.v.] for his connection with slavery, Soule held that it had violated the constitution which he himself had written. Therefore, when, at the Louisville Convention in 1845, the Methodist Episcopal Church, South, was organized, Soule was present and gave his approval to its work. At the first General Conference of that body in 1846 he formally adhered thereto, and thereby a man born in Maine became the senior bishop of the Southern branch of Episcopal Methodism. He now removed to Nashville, Tenn., later establishing his home on a farm outside the city. Soule was an active bishop until 1855. He died in Nashville and was buried in the old City Cemetery, but in October 1876 his remains were reinterred on the campus of Vanderbilt University. He was married in Providence, R. I., Sept. 18, 1803, to Sarah Allen, by whom he had eleven children. He was six feet tall and muscular, had wide cheek bones, a high forehead, and a head so large that it was necessary to have extra-size hats manufactured for him.

[G. T. Ridlon, *A Contribution to the Hist., Biog., and Geneal. of the Families Named Sole, Solly, Soule, Sowle, Soulis* (1926); H. M. DuBose, *Life of Joshua Soule* (1911); J. J. Tigert, *A Constitutional Hist. of Am. Episcopal Methodism* (1904); James Mudge, *Hist. of the New England Conference* (1910); J. B. McFerrin and others, *Hist. of the Organization of the Methodist Episcopal Church, South* (1845); *Republican Banner* (Nashville), Mar. 7, 1867.]   P. N. G.

SOULÉ, PIERRE (Aug. 31, 1801–Mar. 26, 1870), jurist, diplomat, was born at Castillon-en-Couserans in the French Pyrenees, the youngest son of Joseph and Jeanne (Lacroix) Soulé. His father, a brilliant Napoleonic officer, was for twenty years a magistrate; his mother came of distinguished native stock. Destined for the Church, Soulé at fifteen rebelled against the rigid Jesuit discipline of the Collège de l'Esquille at Toulouse and, turning to politics, became an anti-Bourbon conspirator at Bordeaux by choice and thus an exiled shepherd in Navarre by necessity. Pardoned in 1818, he returned to Bordeaux where, the next year, he took his bachelor's degree, and then proceeded to Paris to study law. A lawyer in 1822, he soon joined in the republican movement against Charles X, publishing with others the journal, *Le Nain Jaune,* and thereby inviting monarchical prosecution. Arrested in April 1825, he was convicted and sentenced to prison. Preferring exile, Soulé escaped to England and on Sept. 5, 1825, arrived at Port-au-Prince, Haiti. Finding conditions there unsatisfactory, he proceeded in October to the United States, landing at Baltimore.

A stranger in Baltimore, a wanderer in New York, Soulé in November found refuge in New Orleans. To perfect his English he traveled inland in 1827, receiving Andrew Jackson's hospitality at "The Hermitage" and, after an illness, requiting the kindness of Dominican monks at Bardstown, Ky., by acting as gardener. Returning to New Orleans, in 1828, he married Armantine Mercier, a belle of the Vieux Carré and a sister of Armand and Charles Alfred Mercier [q.v.]. She bore him a son. The next twenty years witnessed his rise in varied fields of endeavor: as criminal lawyer, orator, financier, and man of affairs. He was a generous friend of French refugees, a philanthropist toward his fellow citizens, and, politically, a notable accession to the Democracy. Having spoken for Van Buren in 1840, he was chosen a delegate to the convention of 1844 for revising the state constitution; there he early gained recognition as the unofficial leader of the New Orleans delegation, although Judah P. Benjamin shattered his constitutional arguments. In the first election ensuing under the revised constitution, New Orleans, on Jan. 19, 1846, sent Soulé to the state Senate where he led the successful struggle for the abolition of compulsory capital punishment.

On the death of United States Senator Alexander Barrow in December 1846, John Slidell [q.v.], Soulé's rival, preferring a full term of six years, encompassed the latter's election for the unexpired term of three months. Although mentioned as a possible colleague of Nicholas P. Trist as peace commissioner to Mexico, Soulé, in March 1847, retired from public affairs for a time, but in the senatorial election of 1848, utilizing a Whig majority and capitalizing his opponent's Plaquemines frauds of 1844, defeated Slidell, the regular Democratic candidate, for the six-year term and control of Louisiana. He served until his resignation, Apr. 11, 1853. As senator, Soulé succeeded Calhoun as leader of the state-rights wing of the Southern Democracy, but, except for his oratory, achieved no outstanding parliamentary distinction. His senatorial career was a paradox in that he was a leader in the state-rights movement, although a sincere proponent of the democratic form of American government; a pioneer in the American movement for world republicanism, yet a strong protagonist of slavery; a sponsor of international amity, yet, withal, a stanch partisan advocate of American imperialism.

Soulé preferred Stephen A. Douglas in the Democratic National Convention at Baltimore in June 1852, but rendered services to Franklin Pierce in the campaign. Although mentioned for the attorney-generalship, he was passed over by Pierce in selections for the cabinet, and thus sought solace in the diplomatic service. The English and French missions being closed to him, the former by Buchanan's claims, the latter because of his republican hatred of Louis Napoleon, who cordially reciprocated, Soulé dreamed of St. Petersburg, only to be thwarted by the Czar, to whom his republicanism was anathema. On Apr. 7, 1853, Soulé therefore accepted the mission to Madrid, thereby deliberately revoking a pledge to secure it for his brilliant Louisiana friend, the historian Charles Gayarré [q.v.]. Soulé's qualifications included linguistic ability, a knowledge of Gallic Europe, and Catholicism. He was in complete harmony with Pierce's annexationist program as to Cuba, but his very zeal made his appointment an insult to Spain and a source of mortification to the United States. Continual errors marred his career. He lauded the Cuban Junta in New York; he visited Continental republican exiles in London; he sought to seduce France from Great Britain and Spain in Paris. In Madrid, after his arrival on Oct. 14, the condescending tenor and impertinent advice of his proposed address to the Queen led to revision and rebuke from the Foreign Office; his sartorial vagaries and belligerent pride led to two notorious duels by him and his son, and to the ostracism of his family. Despite the express prohibitory instructions of Secretary William L. Marcy [q.v.], Soulé sought the ac-

quisition of Cuba by purchase, by favor of the Queen Mother, or as collateral for a royal loan. The *Black Warrior* episode in Havana led him to exceed instructions and attempt acquisition by threat of war. On Apr. 3, 1854, Marcy at last ordered him to attempt the purchase of Cuba and, failing that, to "detach" it from Spain. Finding purchase programs futile, Soulé, that summer, strove to "detach" Cuba, first, by aiding Spanish republican revolutions, and second, by conniving with Ledru-Rollin in engendering revolution in France, involving the assassination of Louis Napoleon. Failure in both plans caused Soulé's sudden and discreet withdrawal from Madrid to his Pyrenean château.

On Aug. 16, Marcy, cancelling the project of a commission to aid Soulé, which had led the latter to threaten his resignation, directed him, James Buchanan [q.v.], minister to Great Britain, and John Y. Mason [q.v.], minister to France, to confer on Spanish-American relations with particular reference to Cuba. Buchanan, seeking annexation on strict ethical and legal bases, posited the application of economic pressure on Spain through foreign bondholders; Mason, with passive complacence, would permit expediency to outweigh ethics, but demanded a semblance of legality; Soulé, militant and embittered by past failures, sought Cuba regardless of ethics or legality. Meeting first at Ostend and then at Aix-la-Chapelle, the triumvirate on Oct. 18, 1854, signed the Ostend Manifesto, a document largely Soulé's handiwork (Ettinger, *post,* pp. 364–68), which proposed the purchase of Cuba in "open, frank, and public" negotiations with the Spanish Constituent Cortes. Should Spain refuse to sell, and should Cuba, "in the possession of Spain, seriously endanger our internal peace and the existence of our cherished Union," then and then only must it be wrested from Spain (*House Executive Document No. 93,* 33 Cong., 2 Sess.). Unknown to Buchanan, Soulé sent his own militant interpretation of this document to Marcy, who received both the Manifesto and the interpretation at a time when he was confronted by evidence of Soulé's revolutionary machinations, his untimely encounter with French officials at Calais, and decisive Democratic defeats in the congressional elections of 1854. Sheer expediency led Marcy on Nov. 13 to reject the Manifesto, thereby repudiating his own instructions on Apr. 3 to "detach" Cuba. For the seventh time Soulé had failed and, on receipt of Marcy's negatory letter, he resigned on Dec. 17, returning as scapegoat for the *volte-face* of the administration.

Retiring to private law practice, Soulé in 1857

successfully defended William Walker, the Nicaraguan filibuster, and became interested in a projected transisthmian canal in Tehuantepec, Mexico. In politics, he supported Buchanan as delegate to the Democratic Convention of 1856, and finally lost Louisiana to Slidell in 1859. The next year, although now opposed to secession, he went with his state. General Benjamin Butler's notorious régime in New Orleans found Soulé the chief adviser of Mayor Monroe and Confederate provost-marshal. Arrested in June 1862, he was sent to Fort Lafayette, N. Y., and paroled in November to Boston, whence he fled to Nassau in the Bahamas and Havana in February 1863. Successfully running the blockade to New Orleans, he tendered his services to the Confederacy at Richmond from September 1863 to June 1864, but President Davis' hostility prevented his rise to position other than a somewhat honorary brigadier-generalship. In 1865 he joined ex-Senator William M. Gwin [q.v.] of California in a project to settle Confederate veterans in Sonora. Four years later his powerful intellect gave way, and he was declared interdict. He died on March 26, 1870.

[In his last two years Soulé systematically destroyed his private papers; only a few unimportant letters remain in the Lib. of Cong., and in the possession of his grand-daughters, Mrs. A. H. Denis of New Orleans and Mme. M. G. S. de Arias-Salgado, Havre, France. Important sketches are Alfred Mercier, "Biographie de Pierre Soulé, Sénateur à Washington" (Paris, 1848), a partisan account by his brother-in-law; Jean Signorel, Pierre Soulé (Toulouse, 1911), a stirring little narrative based on documents in the possession of Leon Soulé; Leon Soulé, Notice sur Pierre Soulé, avocat à la Nouvelle Orléans, sénateur de la Louisiane à Washington (Toulouse, 1901), a memoir by his last surviving nephew; and Commandant Trespaillé, "Pierre Soulé," Revue des Pyrénées et de la France Méridionale, vol. II, (1890), pp. 540–72, highly laudatory and not based on original material. For surveys of his mission to Spain, see J. A. Reinecke, Jr., "The Diplomatic Career of Pierre Soulé," an unpublished master's thesis at Tulane University, New Orleans, 1914; H. B. Learned, "William Learned Marcy," in S. F. Bemis, ed., The American Secretaries of State and Their Diplomacy, vol. VI (1928); and R. F. Nichols, Franklin Pierce (1931). The latest study, which in ch. 3 reviews Soulé's life and which contains a full bibliography, is A. A. Ettinger, The Mission to Spain of Pierre Soulé, 1853–1855 (1932).]   A. A. E.

SOUSA, JOHN PHILIP (Nov. 6, 1854–Mar. 6, 1932), bandmaster, composer, was born in Washington, D. C., the son of Antonio and Elizabeth (Trinkaus) Sousa. Antonio Sousa's parents had been driven from Portugal during the revolution of 1822, and had moved to Spain where Antonio was born. He left Spain as a youth and emigrated to America in the early 1840's. He was a gentleman of culture, an accomplished linguist, and an amateur musician. Elizabeth Trinkaus was a native of Franconia, Bavaria, and had met Sousa while visiting

friends in Brooklyn, N. Y. John Philip Sousa, one of ten children, showed an aptitude for music at an early age, and when he was six years old he entered the conservatory of John Esputa, receiving his first instruction on the violin, but later being taught to play a number of band instruments. At the end of his third year at the conservatory he won all five medals offered by the school, and while still with Esputa, organized a small orchestra to play for dancing. When he was thirteen years of age a circus manager offered him a position in his band, but his father, hearing of the plan, arranged that he enlist in the United States Marine Band, of which he himself had been a member. He played with the organization for about five years, and finally obtained a release in order to study violin, harmony, and theory with George Felix Benkert.

In the summer of 1872 he conducted an orchestra at Kernan's Théâtre Comique, a Washington variety house, and also played the violin in the orchestra of Ford's Opera House. By this time he had started to compose music, and had succeeded in publishing a few of his pieces. A march entitled "The Review," and a galop, "The Cuckoo," were sold outright by the composer to Lee & Walker, Philadelphia music publishers, for one hundred printed copies of each piece. In his early compositions he chose a form in which he was to earn international distinction; he became to the march what the Viennese, Johann Strauss, was to the waltz. About 1874 Sousa accepted an offer to join the Milton Nobles Comedy Company, as orchestra conductor on tour, but after a season returned to Ford's Opera House at Washington. When Matthew Somerville Morgan [q.v.] came to this theatre with his Living Pictures Company, the manager offered Sousa a position as conductor, and he again went on tour. His next engagement was as violinist in Jacques Offenbach's orchestra during the Philadelphia Centennial Exhibition in the summer of 1876. For Offenbach Sousa composed his "International Congress" fantasy. From 1876 to 1879 he made his headquarters in Philadelphia, playing at the Chestnut Street Theatre and at the Arch Street Theatre. During this period Sousa was invited to drill and conduct a group of Philadelphia society amateurs which became known later as the Philadelphia Church Choir Company. He composed for this organization his first comic opera, "The Smugglers," and through it met Jane Bellis, of Philadelphia, to whom he was married during the first week of 1880, while the bride was still in school.

On Sept. 30, 1880, he assumed the conductorship of the United States Marine Band, which he held for twelve years. He reorganized the band with vigor and vision and breathed the breath of life into a somnolent group. As the logical successor of Patrick S. Gilmore [*q.v.*] Sousa carried on the development of the wind band by devising an instrumentation which allowed effects as soft as those of a symphony orchestra. His leadership of the Marine organization brought fame to the band as well as to himself on tours throughout the nation. During these twelve years Sousa was active also as a composer, and wrote a variety of works including the famous "Washington Post March" (1889), "The High School Cadets" (1890), "The Gladiator" (his first great popular number, sold to the publishers for thirty-five dollars), and "Semper Fidelis" (1888), which became the official march of the United States Marine Corps. "Hands Across the Sea" (1899), "King Cotton" (1897), and the "Liberty Bell" (1893), were also well known wherever band music was played.

In the spring of 1892 Sousa accepted an offer from David Blakely which included a salary and financial backing for a band of his own. He accordingly secured a discharge from the Marine Corps, and gave the first concert of Sousa's Band in Plainfield, N. J., on Sept. 26, 1892. Although the first tour was not successful financially, Sousa, with more courage than his manager, insisted that they continue with their plans. After the first season the band proved an overwhelming success. It was engaged for important expositions, beginning with the Chicago World's Columbian Exposition, 1893, and toured the United States, visited Europe four times, and, in 1910–12, made one trip around the world. Sousa was one of few men to have the distinction of serving in three branches of military service: as musical director of the VI Army Corps during the Spanish-American War; as conductor of the United States Marine Band; and as lieutenant in charge of navy bands during the World War. In the last capacity he was a "dollar-a-year" man. He also toured the country with the Great Lakes Naval Training Station Band and drew millions of dollars into the government's treasury on Liberty Loan drives. A year after his discharge he received the rank of lieutenant-commander. Honors and decorations were showered upon him. He received the Royal Victorian Order of Great Britain, the Golden Palms and Rosette of the French Academy, and the Cross of Artistic Merit of the Academy of Arts, Sciences, and Literature of Hainault, Belgium.

Sousa composed more than a hundred marches, nearly all of them stamped with an individuality unmistakably his own. While some of the earlier marches were sold outright to Harry Coleman, Philadelphia music publisher, his later works were published on a royalty basis, and the composer derived handsome profits from their sale. From the famous "Stars and Stripes Forever," composed in 1897, he made about $300,000. He wrote ten comic operas, the best known being "The Bride-Elect" (1897), "El Capitan" (1896), and "The Free Lance" (1906). His works include more than fifty songs, six waltzes, two overtures, twelve suites, and a number of miscellaneous compositions. His vast library of music was bequeathed to the University of Illinois. Sousa also turned his hand to the writing of novels and produced *The Fifth String* (1902), *Pipetown Sandy* (1905), and *Transit of Venus* (1920).

Sousa's genial, gracious, robust wit, and handsome personal presence, always enhanced the dramatic performances of his band. Extravagant public applause followed in his wake around the world. He was an excellent horseman and trapshooter, and at one time was president of the American Trapshooter's Association. During his later years his helpful interest was widely solicited in the formation of amateur bands. He died suddenly in Reading, Pa., and his body was taken to Washington, where it lay in state until his burial in the Congressional Cemetery. His wife, a son, and two daughters survived him. The family home was at Sands' Point, Port Washington, L. I.

[*Who's Who in America*, 1930–31; J. P. Sousa, *Marching Along* (1928); *Through the Year with Sousa* (1910); *Grove's Dict. of Music and Musicians, Am. Supp.* (1930); *Music Trade News*, Mar. 1932; *Musical Courier*, Mar. 12, 1932; *Evening Star* (Washington, D. C.), Aug. 7, 1921; *Washington Post*, Mar. 6, 1932; *N. Y. Times*, Mar. 6, 1932; information from the family.]   J. T. H.

SOUTHACK, CYPRIAN (Mar. 25, 1662–Mar. 27, 1745), pioneer New England cartographer, privateer, was born in London, the son of Cyprian and Elizabeth Southack, of Stepney, Middlesex. The father was a naval lieutenant in the service of Charles II, and the son, at the age of ten, fought in the engagement at Southwold Bay (*Calendar of State Papers, Colonial Series, America and West Indies, 1689–92*, 1901, p. 337). In 1685 he came to Boston, Mass., where he resided for many years. Holding a commission from the Admiralty Board, he guarded the New England coast from the ravages of pirates and privateers. Among the vessels he commanded were the *Porcupine* (1689–90), *Mary* (1690), *William and Mary* (1692), *Friends Adventure* (1693), *Seaflower* (1703), and the Massachusetts Province Galley, between 1697 and 1714.

He was a member of Sir William Phips's unsuccessful expedition to Nova Scotia in the summer of 1690. By his heroic work on the night of Sept. 16 of that year the South Meeting House in Boston was saved when five neighboring buildings burned. In 1698 he commanded the Province Galley when it conveyed Maj. James Converse and Col. John Phillips from Boston to effect peace with the Indians at Casco Bay, and in 1704 he commanded the galley in an expedition under Col. Benjamin Church [*q.v.*] against the French and Indians in Maine and Nova Scotia. Sailing in August 1711 to carry supplies to Admiral Sir Hovenden Walker's ill-fated St. Lawrence River expedition, he met the returning transports and sailed back to Boston (*Ibid., 1711–12*, 1925, pp. 141–42). In 1717 Gov. Samuel Shute sent him out to take charge of a wrecked pirate fleet at Eastham on Cape Cod. On Feb. 18, 1718, he with several others was commissioned to inspect the plan of a lighthouse at the entrance to Boston harbor, to consider the proposal of a second light, and to report their findings to the governor and council; and in that same year he was one of the commissioners sent to adjust the boundaries of Nova Scotia (*Ibid., 1719–20*, 1933, pp. 67–69, 317–18). In 1720 he was selected by Governor Phillips to be a member of the Council in Nova Scotia (*Ibid., 1720–21*, 1933, p. 90). He served as a warden and vestryman of King's Chapel, Boston.

Apparently using only the log and compass, Southack made several charts during his numerous cruises along the northeast coast of North America. His *New England Coasting Pilot*, which appeared about 1720, was revised in 1734 and again about 1775. It was also issued as a map with the title, *An Actual Survey of the Sea Coast from New York to the I. Cape Briton*, about 1758 and 1770. On Feb. 26, 1694, he presented to King William III of England a copy of his *Draught of New England, Newfoundland, Nova Scotia and the River of Canada*, for which he received as reward a gold chain worth £50 and a medal. In the same year he issued *A Dravght of Boston Harbor*; in 1697, a map of the St. John River, since lost. About 1710 he drew a chart of the St. Lawrence River and in 1717 a chart of the English plantations from the mouth of the Mississippi to the St. Lawrence. In 1720 *The Harbour of Casco Bay and Islands Adjacent* and *Map of Canso Harbour* were published; in 1746, *A New Chart of the British Empire in North America*, and at an unestablished date a *Map of the Sea Coast of New England*. Southack died in Boston and was buried in the Granary Burying Ground. By his wife, Eliza-

beth, he had several children whose births are listed in the Boston records.

[*Proc. of the Bostonian Soc., Jan. 12, 1904* (1904); *Boston Weekly News Letter*, Mar. 28, 1745; *Records of the Court of Assistants of the Colony of the Mass. Bay*, vol. I (1901); J. P. Baxter, *Doc. Hist. of the State of Me.*, V (1897), 84–85, 127–30, 339–79; Thomas Hutchinson, *Hist. of the Province of Mass. Bay*, II (1767), 109; C. C. Sewall, *The Hist. of Woburn* (1868), p. 182; Benjamin Church, *The Hist. of the Eastern Expeditions . . . Against the Indians and French* (1867), ed. by H. M. Dexter, pp. 123, 175; Sir Hovenden Walker, *A Jour.: or Full Account of the Late Expedition to Canada* (1720); J. F. Jameson, *Privateering and Piracy in the Colonial Period* (1923); Justin Winsor, *The Memorial Hist. of Boston*, I (1880), 541; *Proc. Mass. Hist. Soc.*, 2 ser. VII (1892); *Mass. Hist. Soc. Colls.*, 5 ser. V (1878), 330; John Green, *Explanation of the New Map of Nova Scotia* (1755); Joseph Sabin, Wilberforce Eames, and R. G. Vail, *Bibliotheca Americana*, vol. XXII (1932); *Heraldic Journal*, July 1866, pp. 138–39, Jan. 1867, p. 47; catalogue of maps, plans and charts in the Library of the Colonial Office, London.]   C. E—i.

SOUTHALL, JAMES COCKE (Apr. 2, 1828–Sept. 13, 1897), journalist, was born at Charlottesville, Va., son of Valentine Wood Southall and his wife Martha (Cocke) Southall. He was a descendant of Darcy Southall, who came to America in 1720, and, through both his father and his mother, of Richard Cocke, who arrived in Virginia in 1634. Studious and apt from youth, upon graduating from the University of Virginia in 1846 with the degree of M.A. he was termed by Dr. James Lawrence Cabell [*q.v.*] "by long odds the most finished and promising student that had been educated at the University up to that time" (Ruffner, *post*, p. 99). After a year of travel in Europe, his observant impressions of which he communicated under the signature of "Solitaire" to the *Richmond Daily Whig*, he read law in his father's office and in 1849 was licensed to practise. He substituted for his father as commonwealth's attorney during part of 1850–51, performing with dignity and ability; but the law proved uncongenial, and in 1852, despite his prospects of success, he abandoned it as a profession. For several years following this he applied himself assiduously to an elaborate and far-reaching system of studies, which, as occasion permitted, he pursued throughout his active career; his deeply religious nature turned him towards theology and Biblical study, while his scholarly love of truth led him to familiarize himself with political and civil history, ethics, psychology, ethnology, biology, geology, and other related sciences. In 1858 he again went to Europe, returning in April 1860. A few months before the outbreak of war, with Green Peyton he started a newspaper called the *Charlottesville Review*. Originally a fervent Unionist, but after the gage of coercion had been cast an energetic supporter of the Confederacy, Southall contributed to the *Review* a notable series of editorials which attracted attention North and South, and more than seventy years later inspired a prominent historian to designate their author as a "Virginian Socrates and Quixote, rolled into one" (U. B. Phillips, "Southern Argument on Secession," *Virginia Quarterly Review*, Jan. 1932, p. 133). Never robust, he was bitterly disappointed at being rejected for military service but continued his journalistic labors until the *Review*, like the other Charlottesville papers, succumbed late in 1861 or early in 1862. About June 1865 he acquired the *Charlottesville Daily Chronicle* and conducted it with ability and vigor until 1868, when he was made chief editor of the *Richmond Enquirer*. In this rôle he furthered the conservative principles which he had maintained as a member of the Virginia constitutional convention assembled in December 1867, and his fearless, trenchant, and sagacious editorials helped to direct public opinion into channels beneficial to the state during the troubled reconstruction era.

At heart, however, he was a scholar rather than a journalist, and in 1874 he resigned his editorship to become assistant to the superintendent of public instruction, with shorter working hours and enlarged opportunity for study. The following year he published his important volume, *The Recent Origin of Man*, the erudition and logic of which evoked widespread scientific discussion, English and American; in 1878 he reissued this in a revised, more compact treatment, *The Epoch of the Mammoth*. Subsequent investigation and foreign travel led him to modify certain of the views set forth in these works and in his anti-evolutionary address, *Man's Age in the World* (1878), but they were provocative, influential, and for their time in many respects advanced. About 1880, with the Rev. William T. Richardson, he bought the Richmond *Central Presbyterian* and edited it until 1889; shortly after that time, his health failing, he settled in Norfolk, where on Nov. 10, 1869, he had married Eliza Frances Sharp, daughter of William Willoughby Sharp, who bore him a son and daughter. His last noteworthy publication was his "Genealogy of the Cocke Family in Virginia," printed in the *Virginia Magazine of History and Biography* in five installments between January 1896 and January 1898.

[For the Southall family, see R. A. Brock, in *Va. Hist. Soc. Colls.*, vol. V, n.s. (1886). See also W. H. Ruffner, in *Alumni Bull. of the Univ. of Va.*, Feb. 1898; *Univ. of Va.* (1904), vol. I, edited by P. B. Barringer, J. M. Garnett, and Rosewell Page; obituary in *Richmond Dispatch*, Sept. 14, 1897. Some information has been supplied by Southall's son.] A. C. G., Jr.

SOUTHARD, ELMER ERNEST (July 28, 1876–Feb. 8, 1920), neuropathologist, social psychiatrist, and teacher, was born in South Boston. Mass., the son of Martin Southard, a mill superintendent, and Olive Wentworth (Knowles) Southard. As a child he did not care for manual work but preferred books and chess, which his father taught him, a lifelong interest. Graduating from the Boston Latin School in 1893, he entered Harvard, where he received the degrees of A.B. (1897), M.D. (1901), and A.M. (1902). During his college years he played chess on the Harvard team and wrote occasionally for the *Harvard Monthly*, including in his contributions poems and short stories, forms to which he returned in his later years. Of the men at Harvard who had the most lasting influence upon him, two—William James and Josiah Royce [*qq.v.*]—stand out prominently. According to Southard, James was responsible for his interest in psychopathology and Royce for his constant effort toward logical writing and thinking; his scheme of diagnosis by orderly exclusion he attributed to the influence of Royce and to his reading of Francis Bacon. In the case of a man of his rare abilities, however, it is difficult to delineate the forces that played upon his personality and developed his motivation; essentially the exceptional drive came from his own personality, a unique combination of artist, philosopher, and scientist.

His greatest contribution to human welfare was in the field of neuropsychiatry and its social implications. His actual career began as interne in pathology in 1901 at the Boston City Hospital, where he was later an assistant physician. In 1902 he studied in Germany at Senckenberg Institute, Frankfort, and at Heidelberg. He was instructor in neuropathology at the Harvard Medical School, 1904–06, and assistant professor, 1906–09; in 1909 he was appointed to the newly created Bullard professorship, the youngest man ever to receive a full professorship there. From 1906 to 1909 he was also assistant physician and pathologist at the Danvers State Hospital, Danvers, Mass., and in 1909 he became pathologist to the Massachusetts Commission on Mental Diseases. At the opening of the Boston Psychopathic Hospital in 1912, he was made the first director and remained in this position until June 1919, when he was given the title of director of the Massachusetts Psychiatric Institute. Thus he had a rare combination of opportunities for research and teaching. His contacts with students in the Harvard Medical School and internes in the Boston Psychopathic Hospital also afforded him the means of influencing young neuropathologists and psychiatrists. Never throughout his professional life was he without a group of students under his guidance, many of whom later attained prominence. His first book, *Neurosyphilis*, written with H. C. Solomon, was published in 1917; his second, *Shell-Shock and Other Neuropsychiatric Problems*, in 1919. His publications, of which there are about two hundred, reveal his continued interest in the field of mental medicine, but in the later years show a growing concern with sociological problems. During the last four years of his life he wrote twenty-one papers in the field of social psychiatry, in which his posthumously published book, *The Kingdom of Evils* (1922), written with M. C. Jarrett, was the first textbook. He was responsible for the establishment of the out-patient clinic in psychiatric cases, and for the definition of the field of social psychiatry; it was at the Boston Psychopathic Hospital under his leadership that the term "psychiatric social work" and the program of training for such workers were evolved. He was also responsible for the establishment in 1918 of the Smith College School for Social Work. At the time of his death in New York City in 1920, he was engaged in a dozen or more comprehensive research projects of great potential scientific importance. As he was only forty-three years of age then, a man whose wealth of interests and joy in teaching and learning revealed an exuberance of spirit beyond that of ordinary men, it may be said that his was a genius never gleaned. On June 27, 1906, he married Mabel Fletcher Austin, a graduate of the Johns Hopkins School of Medicine and a lecturer in social hygiene, daughter of Horace Austin, once governor of Minnesota. They had two sons and a daughter.

[*Who's Who in America*, 1918–19; M. M. Canavan, *Elmer Ernest Southard and His Parents: A Brain Study* (priv. printed, 1925); R. C. Cabot, in *Harvard Grads.' Mag.*, June 1920; *Mental Hygiene*, July 1920; Norman Fenton, in *Jour. of Juvenile Research*, vol. XIII, 1929; William Healy, *Ibid.*; *Bull. Mass. Commission on Mental Diseases*, Feb. 1920; obituary in *Boston Transcript*, Feb. 9, 1920.]   N. F.

SOUTHARD, LUCIEN H. (Feb. 4, 1827–Jan. 10, 1881), musician, composer, was presumably born in Sharon, Vt., and according to the records of Trinity College, Hartford, Conn., which he entered in 1844, he was the "son of Dr. Alva Southard of Nantucket," Mass. The records also state that he was "dismissed for indolence" from Trinity in January 1846. Although he had originally intended to follow his father's career as a physician, he went to Boston to study music. From 1851 to 1858 he was general supervisor of music in the Boston public schools. For the next two or three years he lived in Norfolk, Va., but found it convenient to leave that city because of his Northern sympathies. The year 1861 he spent in Hartford, where he was organist of the North Congregational Church, being succeeded in 1862 by Dudley Buck [*q.v.*]. Southard then enlisted in the Union army and served as a captain of cavalry in the Army of the Potomac. In 1865 he was wounded, and, after receiving an honorable discharge, returned to Boston. Three years later (1868) he became the first director of the music conservatory of the Peabody Institute in Baltimore, Md., and organized an orchestra in the school. From 1871 to 1875 he was again in Boston, removing in the latter year to Atlanta, Ga., where he remained until his death.

Between the years 1850 and 1870 Southard was active as a composer. Among his works were two operas: *The Scarlet Letter* (1855), and *Omano* (produced in concert form in Boston, January 1858). He wrote numerous glees, organ pieces, and compositions for the church services, among them "Ave Maria" (1867?); "Te Deum and Jubilate" (1868); and three motets—"As the Hart Pants," "My Heart Doth Find," and "Praise Waiteth for Thee" (1872). He was also industrious as an editor and compiler of music books, among which were *A Collection of Organ Voluntaries* (1849); a number of volumes in collaboration with Benjamin F. Baker [*q.v.*], including *The Haydn Collection of Church Music* (1850), *A Complete Method for the Formation and Cultivation of the Voice* (1852), *The Union Glee Book* (1852), and *Classical Chorus Book* (1853); *The Bouquet* (1855), with G. W. Pratt; *Course of Harmony* (1855); *The School Bell* (1857), with Charles Butler; *Morning and Evening* (1865), for quartet choirs; *The Offering* (1866); *Two Masses* (1867); *The Standard Singing School* (1868). He died in Augusta, Ga., survived by his wife.

[The only complete account of Southard's life is found in *Grove's Dict. of Music and Musicians, Am. Supplement* (1920), based largely on information supplied by the late Nathan H. Allen of Hartford. The author of this article is indebted to Dr. Waldo Selden Pratt for added data.]   J. T. H.

SOUTHARD, SAMUEL LEWIS (June 9, 1787–June 26, 1842), jurist, secretary of the navy, senator, governor of New Jersey, was born at Basking Ridge, N. J., the son of Henry and Sarah (Lewis) Southard. His father, who had moved from Long Island as a boy, was a congressman from 1801 to 1811 and from 1815 to 1821. Samuel attended the school conducted by the Rev. Robert Finley [*q.v.*] at Basking Ridge and in 1804 was graduated with honors at the

College of New Jersey, where he shared a room with Theodore Frelinghuysen [*q.v.*]. He then went as a tutor to Virginia, became a friend of James Monroe, studied law at Fredericksburg, and was admitted to the bar in 1809. Returning to New Jersey in 1811, he was deputy sheriff for a while, married Rebecca Harrow, a Virginian, in June 1812, and moved to Flemington in 1814, becoming prosecutor of Hunterdon County. In 1815, he was elected to the Assembly, but after sitting for a few days was appointed associate justice of the supreme court and three years later, reporter also, serving in both capacities until 1820 and editing 4–5 *New Jersey Reports*. In 1817 he was an unsuccessful candidate for attorney-general and governor. He moved to Trenton about 1820 and in 1838, to Jersey City.

In 1820 he was a presidential elector for Monroe and was appointed to the United States Senate to succeed James J. Wilson, taking his seat on Feb. 16, 1821. A week later, he and his father, whose career in the House was just closing, were elected members of the joint committee on the Missouri question. It is claimed that Samuel drafted the compromise measure by which Missouri was finally admitted (Southard's reminiscences, quoted by Elmer, *post*, p. 213). His friend Monroe appointed him secretary of the navy in September 1823, to succeed Smith Thompson of New York, and he held the office until the close of John Quincy Adams' administration. As secretary he made several foresighted recommendations, the only one to bear immediate fruit being the building of the first naval hospitals in 1828. He also urgently advocated a naval academy, a thorough charting of the coast, a naval criminal code, a rank higher than captain, reorganization and increase of the marine corps, and the establishment of regular communication across Panama. The Pensacola navy yard was started in 1825, and Southard urged a more intelligent location of such bases. The navy increased from thirty-five to fifty-two vessels during his administration, though only about sixteen of these were regularly kept on duty; the personnel rose from some 3,400 to 5,-600, with an average of about 200 officers and 250 midshipmen, while the annual cost rose from about two million dollars to three. Southard also served *ad interim* as secretary of the treasury (Mar. 7–July 31, 1825) and as secretary of war (May 26–June 19, 1828).

Jackson's victory was a bitter blow to the Adams cabinet and Southard returned to Trenton in 1829, described as "very much broken . . . and . . . melancholy" (see Elmer, p. 227). He resumed his law practice and was at once made attorney-general of New Jersey, succeeding Frelinghuysen, who went to the Senate. Though he was by this time a Whig in a state that was rapidly turning to Jackson, he succeeded the Democrat Peter D. Vroom as governor in 1832. After three months in office, during which he vigorously attacked nullification before the legislature, he secured another election to the Senate, where he took his seat on Dec. 2, 1833, just as the Bank fight was approaching its climax. Strongly opposed to Jackson, he made a long speech on Jan. 8 and 10, 1834, opposing the removal of the federal deposits (*Congressional Globe*, 23 Cong., 1 Sess., pp. 87–88, 90–91). On Mar. 28, despite the fact that the New Jersey legislature had approved the presidential policy, he and Frelinghuysen were among the majority of twenty-eight voting to censure Jackson. He continued as a prominent member of the Whig minority but his relations with Clay were not always friendly. Reëlected in 1838, he became president *pro tempore* of the Senate on Mar. 11, 1841 and, after Tyler went to the White House, served as its president until his resignation, May 3, 1842, just before his death.

Never a profound scholar, Southard was a skilful advocate, earnest, lucid, and forceful. With a voice that was generally pleasing but sometimes pitched too high, he was capable of impassioned eloquence which when fully roused was "like a sea in a storm." Impressive in appearance, he thoroughly enjoyed society and was a constant favorite with the electorate, but he lacked the tact essential in a good political organizer. From 1822 until his death he was a trustee of the College of New Jersey and of Princeton Theological Seminary. After 1838, he was president of the Morris Canal & Banking Company. He died in Fredericksburg, Va., at the home of his brother-in-law, after a brief illness.

[Printed sources include L. Q. C. Elmer, in *N. J. Hist. Soc. Colls.*, vol. VII (1872); *Am. State Papers, Naval Affairs*, vols. I–III (1834–60); *Somerset County Hist. Quart.* (N. J.), Oct. 1914; J. P. Snell, *Hist. of Hunterdon and Somerset Counties, N. J.* (1881); W. H. Shaw, *Hist. of Essex and Hudson Counties* (1884), II, 1052; F. B. Lee, *N. J. as a Colony and as a State* (1902); *Biog. Dir. Am. Cong.* (1928); records in files of Gen. Biog. Cat., Princeton Univ.; *Newark Daily Advertiser*, June 28, 30, 1842; *Daily Nat. Intelligencer* (Washington, D. C.), June 28, 1842. Some miscellaneous papers of Southard are in the Lib. of Cong.]
R. G. A.

SOUTHMAYD, CHARLES FERDINAND (Nov. 27, 1824–July 11, 1911), lawyer, was born in New York, the son of Samuel Dwight Southmayd, a merchant, and Mary (Ogden) Southmayd. His formal education, begun in a private school, was terminated at the age of twelve and a half when his teacher "announced to his astonished father that he had taught the boy all that he knew and he had thoroughly mastered it" (Choate, *post*, p. 139). Fortunately a place was found for the precocious lad in the law office of Hurlbut & Owen, where he at once began his legal training. When Judge Elisha P. Hurlbut formed a partnership with Alexander S. Johnson [*q.v.*] the following year, Southmayd went with him. By dint of great diligence and the exercise of a remarkable power of concentration he soon attained such a proficiency in the law that he became known in the firm as the "Chancellor," and, in the course of time, entered into a partnership with Johnson. When this partnership was dissolved on the election of Johnson to the New York court of appeals in 1851, Charles E. Butler and William M. Evarts [*q.v.*], impressed by the legal ability Southmayd had displayed in the important case of *Iddings* vs. *Bruen* (4 *Sanford's Chancery Reports*, 223, 417) in which they were opposing counsel, asked him to join their firm. This association continued until the retirement of Butler in 1858—a resignation that proved premature since he later rejoined the firm. Some months later, Joseph H. Choate [*q.v.*] joined Evarts and Southmayd to make up the famous legal triumvirate of Evarts, Southmayd & Choate.

The brilliancy of these partners attracted to the firm many of the most important cases of that period. Although Southmayd detested trial work and never appeared in court unless the vital interests of his clients demanded his attendance, the clearness of his intellect and the soundness of his learning, as well as his unimpeachable integrity, contributed in no small measure to the deserved preëminence of the firm. Elihu Root describes him as "the typical solicitor, learned, logical, cautious, independent in judgment, stubborn in opinion, caustic in expression" (Choate, "Memorial," *post*).

Through careful savings Southmayd amassed a considerable fortune, and in 1884 he retired from practice. Unfortunately, law had absorbed him to such an extent that he had no interest to turn to during the remainder of his life. His days were filled with vague apprehensions and with the nursing of his innate conservatism, a conservatism that made him object to elevators, automobiles, elevated trains and electric street cars, and even led him to view a European trip by Choate's daughter as all nonsense. He sold his real estate holdings lest unbeknown to him his properties be used for immoral purposes and he be held accountable under the terms of a new law making landlords responsible in such cases.

Before he died, however, he was to frame one more great argument, that which he wrote in the case of *Pollock* vs. *Farmers' Loan and Trust Co.* (157 *U. S.*, 429; 158 *U. S.*, 601), resulting in the decision that held unconstitutional the income tax imposed in the Wilson-Gorman Tariff Act. Although he never appeared in court and others obtained the glory, Choate insists that it was Southmayd's brief which was the one to influence the Supreme Court in its opinion. It is characteristic that he wrote this brief ten years after he had retired from active practice, because he felt his own income threatened and that offended his conservative sense of property right. When he died in 1911 his name was already becoming a memory, for the busy world of New York had its new legal luminaries and recollected but poorly the stalwart figures of an earlier age.

[J. H. Choate, "Memorial of Charles F. Southmayd," *The Asso. of the Bar of the City of N. Y., Year Book*, 1913; reprinted separately (1912) and in *Arguments and Addresses of Joseph Hodges Choate* (1926), ed. by F. C. Hicks; *N. Y. Times*, July 12, 1911; T. G. Strong, *Landmarks of a Lawyer's Lifetime* (1914); E. S. Martin, *The Life of Joseph Hodges Choate as Gathered Chiefly from His Letters* (2 vols., 1920); B. W. Dwight, *The Hist. of the Descendants of John Dwight* (1874), vol. I; W. O. Wheeler, *The Ogden Family in America* (1907).]

L. M. Su—s.

SOUTHWICK, SOLOMON (Dec. 25, 1773– Nov. 18, 1839), journalist, was born in Newport, R. I., the son of Solomon and Ann (Gardner) Carpenter Southwick, and a descendant of Lawrence Southwick who settled in Salem, Mass., about 1630. The younger Solomon's mother, daughter of Lieutenant-Governor John Gardner of Rhode Island, died when the boy was about ten years old. His father, of Quaker ancestry, published the Newport *Mercury,* and for his ardent espousal of the cause of liberty suffered loss of property by Loyalist confiscation, so that from comfortable circumstances he and his family were reduced to poverty. Early in life Solomon went to sea. In 1791 he landed in New York City, where he became apprenticed to a printer, and in 1793 found employment in Albany as a journeyman with Robert and John Barber, who had established in 1788 the *Albany Register* to oppose Federalism. Robert Barber soon withdrew from the concern, and his brother, recognizing unusual talent in the young mechanic, promoted him to editorial duties and made him a partner. Southwick's prepossessing appearance, charming manner, and effective speech won for him the friendship and confidence of the leading Republicans, so that he held successively the positions of clerk of the Assembly, 1803–07; clerk of the Senate, 1807;

and sheriff of the city and county of Albany, 1809–10.

In 1800 he had relinquished formal connection with the *Register,* but when John Barber, whose sister Jane he had married on Mar. 31, 1795, died in 1808, Southwick became sole proprietor and editor, and was chosen state printer. He declared that no personal invective would appear in the *Register,* and that he would treat his enemies with "silent contempt." Such a policy was contrary to the prevailing journalistic style, however, and having a penchant for biting phrases and for apt allusions drawn from his wide reading, together with a vivid imagination but no sense of humor to hold it in check, he engaged in such scathing denunciation of political and editorial opponents that he became involved in a number of libel suits.

Always asserting his Republicanism, Southwick found difficulty in maintaining friendship with rival and ambitious party leaders. In 1805 he joined DeWitt Clinton and Ambrose Spencer [*qq.v.*] in opposing Morgan Lewis [*q.v.*] and the chartering of the Merchants' Bank in New York City. He supported George Clinton [*q.v.*], uncle of DeWitt, for president, to succeed Jefferson, in opposition to Madison, who was Spencer's choice. In 1812 he completely alienated Spencer by his conduct in connection with the "Six Million Bank" bill, which he upheld as vigorously as he had denounced the 1805 measure. Spencer, convinced that Southwick had been bribed to secure votes for the bill, set out to ruin his editorial influence by establishing a rival press. His first attempt, the *Albany Republican,* failed; but his purpose was accomplished when in 1813 the *Albany Argus* was inaugurated under the able and dignified editorship of Jesse Buel [*q.v.*]. In 1814 Buel supplanted Southwick as state printer. The following year Southwick was appointed postmaster at Albany. In 1817 he terminated his editorship of the *Register* in a state of political bankruptcy. He was financially insolvent as well, owing to overspeculation in Albany real estate and carelessness in keeping accounts, and for a time he was imprisoned for debt.

Twice Southwick aspired unsuccessfully to become governor; first, in 1822, when he was an independent candidate against Joseph C. Yates; and, again, in 1828, when he headed the Anti-Masonic ticket, which he supported as editor of the *National Observer.* From 1823 to 1826 he edited the *National Democrat.* In his later years he became a religious and moral enthusiast, and from 1831 to 1837 delivered lectures on the Bible, temperance, and self-im-

provement. In 1815–16 he edited the *Christian Visitant;* from 1819 to 1823, the *Plough Boy,* the first agricultural periodical in Albany County. In 1823 he published *The Pleasures of Poverty,* a long didactic poem; and in 1837, *Five Lessons for Young Men; by a Man of Sixty.* He and John Barber started in 1799 a circulating library of four hundred volumes, and he was one of the organizers of the Apprentices' Library. A favorite Fourth of July orator, he appeared in that rôle for the last time only a few months before his death, which came suddenly as the result of a heart attack. He was survived by four of his nine children.

[J. M. Caller and M. A. Ober, *Geneal. of the Descendants of Lawrence and Cassandra Southwick of Salem, Mass.* (1881); Joel Munsell, *The Annals of Albany,* vol. V (1854); DeAlva S. Alexander, *A Pol. Hist. of the State of N. Y.,* vol. I (1906); J. D. Hammond, *The Hist. of Pol. Parties in the State of N. Y.* (1842), vol. I; *Albany Evening Jour.,* Nov. 19, 1839; *Albany Daily Advertiser,* Nov. 22, 1839, copied from *N. Y. Commercial Advertiser.*]   E. L. J.

SOUTHWORTH, EMMA DOROTHY ELIZA NEVITTE (Dec. 26, 1819–June 30, 1899), novelist, was born near Capitol Hill, Washington, D. C., the elder daughter of Charles LeCompte Nevitte, a merchant of Alexandria, Va., and his second wife, Susanna George (Wailes) of Saint Mary County, Md. As Dorothy Emma Eliza Nevitt [*sic*] she was baptized a Roman Catholic (records of St. Peter's Church, Washington, D. C.). After the death of her father, her mother in 1826 married Joshua L. Henshaw of Boston, who about 1829 opened an academy which Emma and her sister attended. Following her graduation in 1835 she developed an insatiable interest in the traditions of Saint Mary County and acquired a thorough and sympathetic knowledge of southern life that served as a background for many of her stories later. She married Frederick H. Southworth of Utica, N. Y., on Jan. 23, 1840, and in 1841 moved with him to a farm near Prairie du Chien, Wis., where a son, Richmond, was born. The following year she taught in the public school at Platteville, Wis., and in 1843 (deserted by her husband, it was reported), she returned to Washington; her daughter, Charlotte, was born after this separation. Through friends she obtained a teaching position in the public schools of Washington, which she held until 1849 despite her own bad health and the sickness of her children.

During this period she wrote several short tales, published in the *Baltimore Saturday Visitor* and elsewhere, for the most part without compensation to her. In 1847 the *National Era* published, and paid for, her novel, *Retribution* (1849), and this success, together with the personal encouragement of John Greenleaf Whittier [*q.v.*], then a corresponding editor of the *National Era,* persuaded her to give up teaching and turn to writing. For many years she wrote serials for the *New York Ledger,* in which in 1859 appeared her great success, *The Hidden Hand* (copyright 1859). Shortly after its publication she made a visit to England, where she witnessed a theatrical production of *The Hidden Hand* with John Wilkes Booth [*q.v.*] in the rôle of Black Donald. In 1862 she returned to Prospect Cottage, her Georgetown house overlooking the Potomac, and lived there for the remainder of her life. About this time she suggested to Whittier the story that later became the ballad of Barbara Frietchie; when the poem was completed Whittier wrote her, "If it is good for anything, thee deserve all the credit of it" (S. T. Pickard, *Life and Letters of John Greenleaf Whittier,* 1894, vol. II, pp. 454–57). In 1877 a uniform edition of her novels in forty-two volumes was issued in Philadelphia. By this time she had become a celebrity and her home a rendezvous for the local literati; growing increasingly deaf, however, she spent the last busy years of her life in retirement. From being a communicant of the Episcopal Church, she turned in 1883 to Swedenborgianism. At the time of her death, which occurred in Georgetown, she had written more than sixty published novels, and she left much unfinished material in manuscript. Contemporary criticism praised her sentimental and melodramatic plots immoderately, and her large reading public, mostly women, encouraged her to an abundant production which she realized was not related to great literary art. In commenting on some unpublished work she revealed that she consciously had used materials and style "to please the taste of readers of the *Ledger*" and implied that she would have written differently if freed from financial pressure. Among the best known of her works, many of which are still reprinted in paper-back editions, are *Self-Raised* (copyright 1876), *The Fatal Marriage* (copyright 1869), *The Curse of Clifton* (copyright 1852), *The Maiden Widow* (copyright 1870), and *The Missing Bride* (1855).

[*Who's Who in America,* 1899–1900; T. H. Y., prefatory biog. sketch in Mrs. Southworth's *The Haunted Homestead* (1860); C. W. Stoddard, in *Nat. Mag.,* May 1905, with portrait; Sarah M. Huddleson, in *Records of the Columbia Hist. Soc., Washington, D. C.,* vol. XXIII (1920), with portrait; Edna Kenton, in *Bookman,* Oct. 1916; H. C. B., "A Noted Novel-Writer," *Washington Post,* Dec. 2, 1894; *Evening Star* (Washington), Sept. 6, 1890; obituaries in *Evening Star,* July 1, 1899, and in *Appletons' Ann. Cyc.,* 1899; information from the family.]
R. W. B.
B. E. G.

SOWER, CHRISTOPHER (1693–Sept. 25, 1758), printer and publisher, was born in Germany at Laasphe on the Lahn, which was then in the county of Sayn-Wittgenstein-Berleburg. Under its pious regent, the Countess Hedwig Sophia, this diminutive realm had become an asylum for sectarians and separatists from all Germany. Sower, who was of humble origin, grew to manhood buffeted by winds of doctrine blowing from every quarter and thoroughly enjoyed the gusty spiritual climate. Seeking greater economic with equal religious liberty, he emigrated to Pennsylvania in the autumn of 1724, bringing with him his wife, Maria Christina, and their three-year old son, Christopher, 1721–1784 [*q.v.*]. He worked as a tailor in Germantown until the spring of 1726 and then bought and began to farm a fifty-acre tract, now part of Leacock township, Lancaster County, in the Conestoga Valley. Here his proximity to Johann Conrad Beissel [*q.v.*], whom he had known in Germany, proved ruinous, for in 1730 Mrs. Sower was converted to Beissel's doctrines and left her husband in order to live as a hermit. As Sister Marcella she became sub-prioress of the Ephrata Community, but in 1744 she was at last persuaded to return to her family. Sower, his farming operations crippled by her desertion, went back to Germantown and formed an alliance with Christopher Witt, an English mystic, physician, and astrologer, the last survivor of the society founded by Johann Kelpius [*q.v.*]. Under Witt's tuition he learned clock-making, his principal occupation for the next few years, and tried his hand at concocting herbal medicines, but his religious scruples probably made him abstain from the darker arts practised by his master.

He bought six acres of land in Germantown, built a large house, and in 1738 began his notable career as the first German printer and publisher in America. Where he obtained his press, type, and other apparatus, and the skill to use them, is unknown. The first issue of the press was *Eine Ernstliche Ermahnung, an Junge und Alte* (1738) and was followed by *Der Hoch-Deutsch Americanische Calender . . . 1739,* his famous almanac, the last issue of which appeared in 1777. The first complete book from the press was the *Zionitischer Weyrauchs Hügel oder Myrrhen Berg* (1739), a huge hymnbook for the Ephrata Community, of which John Peter Miller [*q.v.*] was editor. The 400th hymn in the collection was the cause of a ludicrous controversy between Beissel and Sower. On Aug. 20, 1739 o.s., appeared the first number of the newspaper, *Der Hoch-Deutsch Pensylvanische Geschicht-Schreiber,* which, with various changes of title, had a career as long as the almanac. These two publications were sold throughout the colonies and made Sower and his son influential among the Germans of Pennsylvania and Maryland. Among the sectarians their influence was especially great. Very early Sower spoke out against war and slavery; in 1754, scenting a political plot in Provost William Smith's proposed charity schools among the Pennsylvania Germans, he waged a bitter, victorious war against the plan. As a result of Sower's propaganda, Michael Schlatter [q.v.], who had innocently accepted the superintendency of the schools, was thoroughly discredited and his usefulness among the German Reformed destroyed. The most famous and ambitious of all Sower's undertakings was his edition of the Bible, *Biblia; Das ist, Die Heilige Schrift Altes und Neues Testaments, Nach der Deutschen Übersetzung D. Martin Luthers* (1743). Except for the Indian version of John Eliot [q.v.], this was the first American edition of the Bible. Sower's son published editions in 1763 and 1776. His first publication in English was *Extract from the Laws of William Penn* (1740); from 1749 on, English as well as German publications regularly issued from the press. Most books bearing the Sower imprint were religious or educational. Sower made his own ink and may perhaps have cast type, although his best fonts came from the foundry of Dr. Heinrich Ehrenfried Luther at Frankfurt-am-Main; he is also said to have built a paper-mill in 1744 (Weeks, *post*, p. 31). For many years he continued to conduct a shop in which he sold medicines, clocks, and other wares. He was an agent for the Pennsylvania stoves invented by Franklin and manufactured by Robert Grace at Warwick Furnace. He was one of the leaders of the German Baptist Brethren. In his zeal for social reform and religious dissent, his thirst for practical information and handiness at many trades and crafts, and in his remarkable talent for popular journalism, he was, with certain variations, a German Daniel Defoe. He died at his home in Germantown and was buried on his own land behind his house.

[Sower's name is often spelled Saur or Sauer. See C. G. Sower, *Geneal. Chart of the Descendants of Christopher Sower, Printer of Germantown, Phila., Pa.* (1887); Oswald Seidensticker, "Die beiden Christoph Saur in Germantown," *Der Deutsche Pionier*, Apr. to June, Aug. to Dec. 1880, and Jan., Feb., Apr., June, and July 1881, reprinted with some abridgment in Seidensticker's *Bilder aus der Deutsch-pennsylvanischen Geschichte* (1885); J. F. Sachse, *The German Sectarians of Pa., 1708–1800* (priv. printed, 2 vols., 1899–1900); M. G. Brumbaugh, *A Hist. of the German Baptist Brethren in Europe and America* (1899); J. S. Flory, *Literary Activity of the German Baptist Brethren in the Eighteenth Century* (1908); J. Max Hark, tr., *Chronicon Ephratense* (1889), pp. 41–42; S. W.

Pennypacker, *Hist. and Biog. Sketches* (1883) and *Pa. in Am. Hist.* (1910); Isaiah Thomas, *The Hist. of Printing in America* (2nd ed., 2 vols., 1874); C. F. Huch, "Die erste Schriftgiesserei in den Vereinigten Staaten von Nordamerika," *Deutsch-Amerikanische Geschictsblätter*, July 1909; L. H. Weeks, *A Hist. of Paper-Manufacturing in the U. S., 1690–1916* (1916); John Wright, *Early Bibles of America* (3rd ed., rev. & enl., 1894); A. H. Cassel, "The German Almanac of Christopher Sauer," *Pa. Mag. of Hist. and Biog.*, vol. VI, No. 1 (1882); "Forges and Furnaces in the Province of Pa.," *Pubs. of the Pa. Soc. of the Colonial Dames of America*, vol. III (1914), p. 73.]

G. H. G.

SOWER, CHRISTOPHER (September 1721–Aug. 26, 1784), bishop of the Dunkers or German Baptist Brethren, printer and publisher, was born at Laaspfe, Westphalia, the only child of Christopher Sower, 1693–1758 [q.v.], and Maria Christina Sower, and was brought to Pennsylvania by his parents in 1724. As a boy he received his schooling from the celebrated Christopher Dock [q.v.], whose *Eine Einfältige und gründlich abgefasste Schul-Ordnung* (1770) he later took pride in publishing; heard the preaching of Alexander Mack, the founder of the Dunker sect; and learned printing, bookbinding, ink-making, and other trades from his father. He was baptized, Feb. 24, 1737 o.s.; was made a deacon of the Germantown congregation in May 1747; became an elder on trial in June 1748; and was ordained by Peter Becker, June 10, 1753. To the very end of his life he was the leader of his sect, exerting on it an influence that continued to be felt for several generations. The power and persuasiveness of his preaching, his insight into the human heart, and his humble, charitable way of life have been a tradition among his people. Meanwhile, on Apr. 21, 1751 o.s., he married Catharine Sharpnack of Germantown, who bore him nine children and died on Jan. 8, 1777. He early took charge of the bindery in his father's publishing house in Germantown, and beginning in 1754 the English publication of the Sower press bore his imprint. On his father's death in 1758 he fell heir to the whole establishment and carried on the business with the intelligence and energy that had distinguished his father. The most notable productions of the press under his management were the second and third editions (1763 and 1776) of the Sower, or Germantown, Bible. In 1773 he built a paper-mill on the Schuylkill. In his periodicals he was a steadfast opponent of negro slavery, and berated the Germans for allowing the evil practice to take root among them. His political support went to the proprietary party. With the outbreak of the Revolution his prosperity ceased and the evil days came upon him. Like the Quakers, Mennonites, Schwenkfelders, and Moravians, the Dunkers refused to take oaths or to bear arms. As the leader of the Dunkers, Sower was suspected all the more because his sons Christopher [*q.v.*] and Peter were avowed Loyalists; and suspicion ripened into conviction when it was realized that he was a man of wealth whose houses, lands, and goods would enrich more than one deserving patriot. In a proclamation of May 8, 1778, he was named as under suspicion of treason and given till June 25 to appear before a magistrate. On May 23, 1778, he was arrested, maltreated, and variously abused, and was released only by the intervention of Gen. John Peter Gabriel Muhlenberg [*q.v.*]. His property, except what clothes he wore and a little food, was ruthlessly taken from him and was disposed of "at auction" for a fraction of its actual value. Sower might later have obtained redress, but, true to his religious convictions, he refused to go to law. His one protest was against the ignominy of being called a traitor. The few remaining years of his life were spent at Methacton, a few miles above Norristown, where he found refuge in a friend's house, and was cared for by his daughter, Catharine. He earned what money he needed by working as a bookbinder. Two weeks before his death he went on foot the twelve miles to Skippack to preach at a meeting of the Brethren. He died and was buried at Methacton.

[Like his father, Sower for a time used the spellings Saur and Sauer. See Oswald Seidensticker, "Die beiden Christoph Saur in Germantown," *Bilder aus der Deutsch-pennsylvanischen Geschichte* (1885); C. G. Sower, *Geneal. Chart of the Descendants of Christopher Sower, Printer, of Germantown, Phila., Pa.* (1887); M. G. Brumbaugh, *A Hist. of the German Baptist Brethren in Europe and America* (1899); J. F. Sachse, *The German Sectarians of Pa., 1708–1800* (priv. printed, 2 vols., 1899–1900). Seidensticker gives the date of birth as Sept. 21; Sower as Sept. 26. The date of death is from the tombstone. Information has been supplied by the Germantown Hist. Soc.]   G. H. G.

SOWER, CHRISTOPHER (Jan. 27, 1754– July 3, 1799), Pennsylvania publisher and Loyalist, was born in Germantown, Pa., the son of the second Christopher Sower [*q.v.*] and his wife, Catharine (Sharpnack) Sower. Reared in a family who were leaders among the Dunkers, he naturally conceived a strong antipathy to those colonial leaders—among them Benjamin Franklin, Henry Melchior Mühlenberg, the leader of the German Lutheran Church in America, and John Henry Miller [*qq.v.*], the publisher of *Der Wöchentliche Pennsylvanische Staatsbote*—who were bitter critics of the German sectarians and of the beliefs they held. When these men favored the Colonial party in its disagreement with the mother country, the conservatism of young Sower, accentuated by his aversion to the opponents of his family, drove him early into the ranks of those who were loyal to the British government. On Jan. 8, 1775, he was married to Hannah Knorr, sister of the wife of Zachariah Poulson [*q.v.*].

His public life began toward the end of 1774, when his father, without any legal formality, transferred to him the ancestral home in Germantown and the famous Sower printing establishment. Sometime between Apr. 20, 1775, and Mar. 20, 1776, the name of the firm was changed to Christopher Sower and Son; between the latter date and February 1777 it became Christopher Sower, Jr., and Peter Sower, the young man thus publicly assuming full charge. During these momentous years he apparently published in his newspaper, *Die Germantowner Zeitung,* everything favorable to the royal cause so far as the Patriot authorities allowed him, and when the British took possession of Philadelphia in September 1777, he removed to that city and continued the paper under the title, *Der Pennsylvanische Staats Courier.* On Dec. 5 he was wounded and captured by a detachment of American troops in Germantown, and on Jan. 10 of the following year he was released by exchange. At the time of the evacuation of Philadelphia by the British in 1778, he had no safe alternative but to accompany them to New York. In August the estate of the entire family, variously estimated to be worth from ten thousand to thirty thousand pounds, was confiscated and sold. With the encouragement of Sir Henry Clinton he now entered into correspondence with various men in Pennsylvania for the purpose of obtaining information and of organizing Loyalist Associations, which in February 1780 in the counties of Lancaster, York, and Northumberland professed to have an enrollment of six thousand, probably an exaggeration. He also published and distributed in the spring of 1780 a sixteen-page pamphlet with the title, *Zuschrift an die Teutschen in Pennsylvanien und benachbarten Provinzen,* a publication that may be considered the valedictory of the family as colonial printers. A year later, in the spring of 1781, he was sent by Clinton on a secret mission to Virginia. After the defeat of Cornwallis he concentrated his efforts on futile attempts to induce the British government to grant such liberal terms to the Colonies that they would willingly remain in the empire. On the British evacuation of New York he went to England to push his claims for indemnification for the losses he had sustained, and was allowed the sum of 1,289 pounds. In 1785 he went to the province of New Brunswick, where he later became deputy postmaster-general and king's printer of the province, and published the

Royal Gazette and Weekly Adveriser. Leaving New Brunswick in 1799 he went to the home of his youngest brother, Samuel, in Baltimore, Md., where he died, survived by his wife and five of his six children.

[Like his father and grandfather, Sower also used the spellings Saur and Sauer, particularly when writing in German. There are two comparatively large collections of original source material on his activities: his records, gathered at the time when he laid claim to indemnity, in the Audit Office Records found in the Pub. Records Office (Class 13, Bundle 102), London, England; and the Clinton papers in the William L. Clements Lib. Some of the London material has been transcribed and is in the N. Y. Pub. Lib. A secondary source almost as valuable as the original sources is "William McCulloch's Additions to Thomas's Hist. of Printing," ed. by C. S. Brigham, *Proc. Am. Antiquarian Soc. . . . Apr. 13, 1921,* vol. XXXI, n.s., pt. 1 (1922). See also C. G. Sower, *Geneal. Chart of the Descendants of Christopher Sower, Printer, of Germantown, Phila., Pa.* (1887); M. G. Brumbaugh, *A Hist. of the German Baptist Brethren in Europe and America* (1899); J. O. Knauss, *Social Conditions among the Pa. Germans in the Eighteenth Century, as Revealed in German Newspapers Published in America* (1922), and "Christopher Saur the Third," *Proc. Am. Antiquarian Soc. . . . Apr. 15, 1931,* vol. XLI, n.s., pt. 1 (1931).]   J. O. K.

SPAETH, ADOLPH (Oct. 29, 1839–June 25, 1910), Lutheran clergyman, was born at Esslingen, Württemberg, the eldest of the seven children of Ernst Philipp Heinrich and Rosine Elisabeth (Boley) Spaeth, and was christened Philipp Friedrich Adolf Theodor. His father, a skilful and beloved physician, a liberal in politics, died in 1856; his mother died in 1902 at her son's home in Philadelphia. Both parents were deeply religious; and although Spaeth wavered for a while in his final choice of a career, there was never any real doubt as to his vocation. He was educated at the Lateinschule of his native town, the Klosterschule of Blaubeuren, and the University of Tübingen. Having been ordained Oct. 10, 1861, at Waiblingen, he served for about a year as vicar at Bittenfeld and then, partly for the sake of his health, spent the winter of 1862–63 as a private tutor in northern Italy. The next year, one of the happiest and most significant of his life, was passed in Scotland, where he was a tutor in the family of the Duke of Argyll. The Marquis of Lorne, governor-general of Canada, 1878–83, was one of his pupils. While in Scotland Spaeth was betrothed to Maria Dorothea Duncan, daughter of the Scotch theologian, John Duncan, who at first was reluctant to give her to a man who did not subscribe to the Westminster Confession.

Through a cousin who was a member of the church council, Spaeth received a tentative call as assistant to William Julius Mann [*q.v.*] at St. Michael's and Zion's in Philadelphia. Thinking that the experience of a few years in America would be good for him, he accepted. On Oct. 16,

1864, he was formally installed as Mann's colleague. For the rest of his life Philadelphia was his home and the center of his work and influence. On May 8, 1865, he married his betrothed, who bore him five sons and a daughter and died Dec. 21, 1878. His second wife, whom he married Oct. 12, 1880, and by whom he had four sons and a daughter, was Harriett Reynolds Krauth, daughter of Charles Porterfield Krauth [*q.v.*]; she survived him and wrote his biography. In 1867 Spaeth accepted a call to the newly organized St. Johannis Church, with which he remained, with an assistant after 1893, until his death. From 1873 until his death he was a professor in the Philadelphia Lutheran Theological Seminary, his principal subject being New Testament exegesis. He was president of the General Council of the Evangelical Lutheran Church in North America, 1880–88; of the Ministerium of Pennsylvania, 1892–95; and of the General Conference of Lutheran Deaconess Motherhouses in America, 1896–1910; and an active member of many boards and committees of his denomination. Especially notable was his work in liturgics and hymnology. The bibliography of his published writings occupies thirteen pages of his biography; his books were *Saatkörner* (1893), a collection of sermon outlines; *Erinnerungsblätter* (1895), a selection, held together by a thread of biographical narrative, from the writings of William Julius Mann; *Annotations on the Gospel According to St. John* (1896), in the Lutheran Commentary Series; *Charles Porterfield Krauth* (2 vols., 1898–1909); *Die Heilige Passion* (1897); and *Order of Lutheran Worship* (1906). He had the magnetic personality, the powerful, flexible voice, the kinship with the audience and sense of its needs, of a great public speaker, and as an orator he was most widely known. In his command of English he was often compared to Carl Schurz, for whom he had a warm admiration; and the clarity, simplicity, and music of his German diction were flawless. He visited Europe ten times and traveled much in the United States; few of the leaders of his denomination were so widely known or exerted so much personal influence. In temperament he was a true Swabian, working with a tremendous will and enjoying life heartily to its close. He died at his home at Mount Airy, Philadelphia, in his seventy-first year.

[H. R. Spaeth, *Life of Adolph Spaeth, D.D., LL.D.* (1916), with a list of his publications; L. D. Reed, *The Phila. Seminary Biog. Record* (1923); *Public Ledger* (Phila.), June 27, 1910.]   G. H. G.

SPAHR, CHARLES BARZILLAI (July 20, 1860–Aug. 30, 1904), editor and economist, was born in the Methodist parsonage on Town Street, Columbus, Ohio, the son of the Rev. Barzillai Nelson Spahr and Elizabeth Jane (Tallman) Spahr. The Spahr family was originally of Swiss descent and seems to have settled in Virginia well before the Revolution; Gideon Spahr, father of Barzillai Spahr, was born in Virginia in 1788. Prepared for college in the Columbus schools, Spahr entered Amherst College and graduated with honors in 1881. After teaching in the Columbus high schools for a short time, he studied at Leipzig, 1884–85, and then took the degree of Ph.D. at Columbia in 1886. On July 5, 1892, he was married in Princeton, N. J., to Jean Gurney Fine, daughter of the Rev. Lambert S. Fine and Mary (Burchard) Fine, and sister of Henry Burchard Fine [q.v.], later dean of Princeton University, who had been a fellow-student of Spahr's in Leipzig; for the three years immediately preceding her marriage she had been the first head-worker of the New York College Settlement, of which she was one of the founders. They had five daughters.

Soon after taking his degree at Columbia he joined the editorial staff of the Outlook (then the Christian Union), with which he remained until February 1904, an associate of Lyman Abbott, Hamilton Wright Mabie [qq.v.], and Lawrence Abbott, who had been his roommate at Amherst. He also lectured at Columbia for several years during this period and was for some time an editorial writer on the New York Commercial Advertiser. In his editorial work he was largely concerned with sociological and economic problems. Though his views often brought him into conflict with the papers for which he wrote, and though he refrained rigidly from writing against his convictions, he was remarkable for his ability to remain on friendly terms with his most convinced opponents. He had a tremendous sympathy for the humble. Once he remarked: "I can't find it in my heart to have any one black my boots. Somehow, it seems to me undemocratic. And as I don't have time often to do it, the result is they go unblacked" (In Memory of Charles B. Spahr, post, p. 13). It was characteristic of him that in politics he was usually on the side of the minority. He was fond of remarking that his only successful presidential vote was cast for Cleveland and that he later regretted it; he is credited with having cast one of the three Populist votes in his election district in New York City, and in 1896 and 1900 he gave enthusiastic support to Bryan, having been from his college days an ardent advocate of free silver as a benefit to the debtor class. He was active in the Social Reform Club of New York, which he

helped to organize in the Outlook office in 1894 and of which he was president, 1896–98; he was also one of the founders and chairman of the executive committee of the Anti-Imperialist League. His writings include An Essay on the Present Distribution of Wealth in the United States (1896), America's Working People (1900), and papers on "The Taxation of Labor" (Political Science Quarterly, Sept. 1886), "The Single Tax" (Ibid., Dec. 1891), and "Giffen's Case Against Bimetallism" (Ibid., Sept. 1893). In 1904 he became owner and editor-in-chief of Current Literature, and in his new position was compelled to add to his duties the work of a business manager, with which he was unfamiliar. The nervous strain so undermined his health that in July he went abroad for a rest, traveling from Trieste through Austria and Germany to the Rhine. His health had improved and the fits of depression from which he suffered had become less frequent, when on Aug. 30 he disappeared from the ship on which he had sailed from Ostend for Dover. His body was washed ashore near Broadstairs, Kent, Sept. 21.

[Who's Who in America, 1903–05; In Memory of Charles B. Spahr (1905), with portrait; Amherst Coll. Biog. Record of the Grads. and Non-Grads. (1927), ed. by R. S. Fletcher and M. O. Young; F. H. Parsons, Thirty Years After: A Record of the Class of Eighty-One, Amherst Coll. (1911), not altogether accurate; editorials in Outlook, Jan. 30, Sept. 10, and Oct. 1, 1904; obituaries in Current Lit., Oct. 1904, N. Y. Times, Sept. 2, and N. Y. Tribune, Sept. 2, 3, 1904; report of inquest in Times (London), Sept. 24, 1904.]
J. B.

SPAIGHT, RICHARD DOBBS (Mar. 25, 1758–Sept. 6, 1802), governor of North Carolina, representative in Congress, was born in New Bern, N. C. His father, Richard Spaight, a native of Ireland, married Margaret, the sister of Gov. Arthur Dobbs [q.v.], and was a member of the colonial council under him, secretary of the colony, and paymaster of troops during the French and Indian War. Both parents died when the boy was eight years old, and he was sent to Ireland to be educated. It is said that his advanced studies were completed at the University of Glasgow. In 1778 he succeeded in returning to North Carolina, where in 1779 he was a member of the House of Commons from the borough of New Bern. Afterward, as aide to Gen. Richard Caswell commanding the state militia, he was present at the battle of Camden. There his military career ended, for he was reelected to the Commons, where he represented either New Bern or Craven County from 1781 to 1787, except 1784, and again in 1792. Young as he was in these early sessions, he won reputation, but rather in committee service and in council than in debate. In 1785 he was chosen speaker, and on Jan. 1, 1787, when the House entered upon a sweeping investigation of the state judges and of alleged official corruption, he was selected as chairman of the whole. He was defeated for the Continental Congress, but he was appointed to fill a vacancy in 1783, was elected the next year, and served until 1785, during which time he was a member of the committee to frame a temporary government for the western territory and of the committee of the states. In political faith a democrat and a strict constructionist, he was opposed to what he regarded as the usurpation by the North Carolina courts of the power to declare an act of the legislature null and void, asking, perhaps with some point, who would control the judges.

In 1787 as an advocate of a stronger federal government, he was chosen a delegate to the federal constitutional convention, where he favored the election of senators by the state legislatures, a term of seven years for senators and president, the election of the president by Congress, and the filling of congressional vacancies by the president. He voted for the Constitution and signed it. In 1787 he was defeated for governor, but he was a member of the state convention of 1788, was active in explanation and defense of the Constitution, and, in spite of his well-known democratic views, voted with the Federalists. When North Carolina finally ratified in 1789, he was the Anti-Federalist candidate for federal senator but was defeated. His health had already failed, and for four years he withdrew from public affairs and traveled widely in search of a cure. In 1792 he was elected governor and served three terms. In 1793 he was a presidential elector. As governor in 1793 he issued a proclamation enjoining neutrality in the European war, and he had several French privateers, which were being fitted out in Wilmington, seized and held. In 1795 he married Mary Leach of Holmesburg, Pa., who with three children survived him.

He was a member of Congress from Dec. 10, 1798, to Mar. 3, 1801, but declined reëlection. A stanch Republican, he favored the repeal of the Alien and Sedition Acts and in the election of president by the House voted for Jefferson. He was, however, never a narrow partisan, and, always independent, he frequently voted differently from his party. After his retirement from Congress he was elected state senator in 1801 and 1802. In 1802 he was mortally wounded in a duel with John Stanly, a prominent Federalist leader, who has ever since been depicted as the aggressor, while Spaight has been regarded as a martyr. But in fact, as appears clearly in the cor-

respondence between them, Spaight forced Stanly to the duel (R. A. Spaight, *Correspondence,* 1802). It is difficult to conceive of him in such a light, for he was normally genial, affable, and good-tempered, and had few personal quarrels and fewer enemies. In politics he was notably dispassionate. His abilities, which do not seem very striking today, were measured highly by his contemporaries.

[S. A. Ashe, *Biog. Hist. of N. C.,* vol. IV (1906) ; J. H. Wheeler, *Sketch of the Life of Richard Dobbs Sperry* (1880) ; *The State Records of N. C.,* vols. XIII, XVII–XX, XXII (1898–1907) ; G. J. McRee, *Life and Correspondence of James Iredell* (1858), vol. II, esp. pp. 120–22, 168–70, 273.]   J. G. deR. H.

SPALDING, ALBERT GOODWILL (Sept. 2, 1850–Sept. 9, 1915), sportsman and merchant, was born on a farm in Byron, Ogle County, Ill., the son of James Lawrence and Harriet Irene (Goodwill) Wright Spalding and a descendant of Edward Spalding who became a freeman of the Massachusetts Bay Colony in 1640. He was educated in the public schools of Byron and Rockford, Ill., and at the Rockford Commercial College. His first employment was as a grocer's clerk. A crippled soldier, it is said, invalided out of the Civil War, taught the boys of Rockford how to play baseball and young Spalding became an apt pupil. At the age of seventeen his skill as a pitcher and batsman was such that he became an outstanding player with the Forest City team of Rockford. Largely through the prowess of Spalding and Ross Barnes, who also later became a National League player, this team attained a wide reputation. After the establishment of professional baseball, Spalding joined in 1871 the Boston team managed by Harry Wright [*q.v.*]. Spalding was pitcher and captain until 1875 and during that time the team won the championships of the National Association of Professional Base Ball Players from 1872 to 1875, inclusive.

In 1876 William A. Hulbert of Chicago, with Spalding as aid and adviser, formed the National League of Professional Base Ball Clubs, and Spalding became pitcher, captain, and manager of the Chicago team. In March of the same year he organized, with his brother James, a business firm to manufacture and sell baseball equipment and other sporting goods, under the name A. G. Spalding & Brother. Two years later his brother-in-law, William T. Brown, joined them and the firm name became A. G. Spalding & Brothers. In time the concern developed into the largest and most successful of its kind in the United States, with a capitalization in 1932 of $6,000,000. Spalding maintained a connection with the Chicago Club for many years, however.

Upon the death of William A. Hulbert in 1882 he became its president and continued as such until 1891, when he felt it necessary to give all his time to his sporting-goods business.

He was a big fellow physically, with a dominating personality, and a genius for organizing and directing. He was a great believer in baseball as a beneficial sport as well as an exciting public spectacle. As early as 1874 he made the arrangements for a tour of England and Ireland by two baseball teams, in an endeavor to impress the good points of the game on the followers of cricket and football. Again, in 1888–89, he organized and took personal charge of a trip around the world made by his Chicago team and another group known as the All-American players. They gave exhibitions of baseball in Australia, Ceylon, Egypt, Italy, France, and the British Isles. In Egypt a game was played on the sands near the pyramids. In these early days of professional baseball it was necessary to stamp out rowdyism and eliminate professional gamblers who sought to corrupt teams and players for their own ends. As a player and later as a club manager, president, and league official, Spalding was a forceful leader in the fight for honest play, honest players, and a wholesome and respectable atmosphere around the ball parks. He was chosen as director of the section of sports for the United States at the Olympic Games of 1900, held in connection with the World's Fair at Paris that same year. For his work in this capacity, he later received from France the rosette of the Legion of Honor. A powerful and colorful figure, he loomed large in the field of sports for many years and, through his enthusiasm, his energy, and his keenness of mind contributed largely to the success of baseball and to the spread of many other sports. From 1878 to 1880 inclusive he edited *Spalding's Official Baseball Guide,* and in 1911 published *America's National Game,* a comprehensive history of baseball. He spent the last fifteen years of his life as a resident of Point Loma, Cal., and it was there that he died of heart failure, at the age of sixty-five. His first wife, whom he married Nov. 18, 1875, was Sarah Josephine Keith and by her he had one son; she died in 1899 and in 1900 he married Mrs. Elizabeth Churchill Mayer, who survived him.

[Spalding's collection of books, pamphlets, pictures, and other material on baseball is in the N. Y. Pub. Lib. For sources of information see his *America's National Game* (1911); *Spalding's . . . Guide,* 1916; C. W. and S. J. Spalding, *The Spalding Memorial: A Geneal. Hist. of Edward Spalding . . . and His Descendants* (1897); *Who's Who in America,* 1914–15; *Literary Digest,* Sept. 25, 1915; *N. Y. Times,* Sept. 10, 11, 1915. Information as to certain facts was furnished by J. T. Doyle, Am. Sports Pub. Company.]   J. K.

SPALDING, CATHERINE (Dec. 23, 1793–Mar. 20, 1858), foundress and mother superior of the Sisters of Charity of Nazareth, was born of old Maryland stock in Charles County, Md. On the death of her father, Ralph, a kinsman of Martin J. Spalding and William H. Elder [*qq.v.*], Catherine and her sister Ann accompanied her mother and the Thomas Elder family to Kentucky. The mother died in 1801, and Catherine was reared by the Elders and their daughter, Mrs. Richard Clark, mother of the distinguished Father William E. Clark. When John B. M. David [*q.v.*] with the assistance of Bishop Flaget [*q.v.*] established the Sisters of Charity in Nazareth, Bardstown, Ky., with a rude cabin as a mother-house, Catherine Spalding and six other girls from Kentucky and Maryland joined as charter members (Jan. 21, 1813). Catherine was elected mother superior and directed the primitive community, which soon included her blood-sister, with rigid economy and noble courage. The nuns labored in the fields, spun and wove their own clothing, built a chapel (1816), and established a small boarding school at Bardstown (1818), one of the first academies on the Kentucky frontier. Under her successor, Mother Agnes Higdon (1819–25), Sister Catherine continued to be the guiding spirit of the growing community as mistress of novices, as foundress of St. Vincent's Academy in Union County, and as director of the Academy of St. Catherine's, founded in 1823 in Scott County and moved to Lexington in 1834.

She was chosen mother superior again in 1825, serving until 1831. In the latter year she established Presentation Academy, the first Catholic school in Louisville, and two years later, as a nurse in the cholera epidemic, she carried the stricken victims' orphans to her home, thus founding St. Vincent's Orphanage in Louisville, for which she obtained liberal support from Protestants as well as Catholics. In 1836 she founded St. Vincent's Infirmary at Louisville, which in 1853 was developed into the commodious St. Joseph's Infirmary. In 1850, she established the School of St. Frances at Owensboro, and in 1854 she rejoiced in the consecration of a Gothic chapel at Nazareth, then the largest church in the diocese. In her later years, although she served four more terms as mother superior, her primary concern was St. Vincent's Orphanage at Louisville. Here she died, as the result of a cold contracted while on a sick mission. Loved and revered as a humble servant of the destitute, Mother Catherine was as beautiful in character as in person.

[Biog. Sketch of Mother Catherine Spalding (1912);
a sketch of three and a half columns in the N. Y. Freeman's Journal, May 15, 1858, reprinted from the Louisville Guardian; B. J. Webb, The Centenary of Catholicity in Kentucky (1884), useful but inaccurate; Anna
B. McGill, Sisters of Charity of Nazareth (1917); annual Catholic directories.]   R.J.P.

SPALDING, FRANKLIN SPENCER (Mar.
13, 1865–Sept. 25, 1914), bishop of the Protestant Episcopal Church, was the son of Rev. John
Franklin and Lavinia Deborah (Spencer) Spalding and a descendant of Edward Spalding who
was made a freeman of Massachusetts Bay Colony on May 13, 1640. At the time of Franklin's
birth his father was rector of St. Paul's Church,
Erie, Pa., but in 1873 he was elected missionary
bishop of Colorado, Wyoming, and New Mexico.
The boy received his early education in the public schools of Erie and Denver, and prepared for
college at Jarvis Hall in the latter city. In 1883
he entered the College of New Jersey, Princeton, where he took only fair rank as a student
but was a prize debater and participated with enthusiasm in student activities, winning a place
on the baseball and football teams and on the
editorial board of the Princetonian. After graduating in 1887 he taught for a year in the Princeton Preparatory School and then entered the
General Theological Seminary, New York. Upon
completing the course in 1891, he returned to
Colorado and on June 3 was ordained deacon by
his father; the following year, June 1, he was
advanced to the priesthood.

His first charge was All Saints' Church, North
Denver, a newly formed parish, where, with
characteristic enthusiasm, he threw himself into
the work of organization and joined the communal activities. Incidentally he became known
and admired for his athletic prowess, especially
as the star fullback of the Denver Athletic Club's
football team. From 1892 to 1896 he was master
of Jarvis Hall, the diocesan school for boys. In
the latter year he was called to his father's old
parish, St. Paul's, Erie, Pa., where he remained
until 1904, when he was elected missionary bishop of Utah, a field which included, in addition to
Utah, parts of Nevada, Wyoming, and Colorado. He was consecrated in his own church on
Dec. 14, and immediately removed to Salt Lake
City, which was his residence until, ten years
later, he was killed by an automobile while crossing the street. He never married, but with regard
to the merits of celibacy expressed the opinion
that "to be the husband of some woman, or the
wife of some man took more grace than to be a
monk or a nun, and to walk the floor with a crying baby more Christianity than the vow to poverty" (Melish, post, pp. 90, 91).

The district of Utah offered peculiar difficulties

to an Episcopal bishop, but Spalding won the respect of all classes and displayed exceptional ability in adapting himself both to the problems of
Salt Lake City and to the rough conditions of the
outlying country. A thoroughgoing Churchman,
he was nevertheless broad in his sympathies,
progressive theologically, and not inclined to attach too much importance to elaborate ceremonials. He abhorred "begging," but was successful in raising money in the East for hospital
and educational work. Glimpses of his field are
given by him in articles in the Spirit of Missions
(October, December 1912, September 1914). It
was his conviction that the Church should not
only minister to the individual but also direct its
energies to the transformation of his environment, and outside his own communion Spalding
was best known perhaps as the "socialist bishop."
From the beginning of his career he took an active interest in social and political affairs. During the Presidential campaign of 1896 he made
speeches in Colorado in support of free silver.
At Erie he espoused the cause of the working
man in labor controversies. Believing that Christian ideals cannot be realized without a revolution in the social organization, he at length
avowed his belief in Marxian socialism, and in
sermons and lectures uncompromisingly set forth
his convictions, fearlessly challenging the Church
to array itself on the side of radical reform. His
views provoked opposition but his transparent
sincerity and devotion to human welfare won him
the regard of those who differed with him. He
was a public speaker of more than ordinary effectiveness, and his addresses at the Pan-Anglican
Congress, London, in 1908, and a sermon he delivered in Westminster Abbey, called forth much
favorable comment. He was a prison reformer,
a prohibitionist, and a pacifist, rewriting in 1914
such militant hymns as "Onward Christian Soldiers" and "Stand up, Stand up for Jesus" with
the warlike terms eliminated. He even went so
far as to suggest that the phrase "fight manfully
under his banner" in the baptismal service be
changed to "work faithfully for his cause." In
the Atlantic Monthly for May 1913 he set forth
his views on church unity. At the time of his
death he was characterized as a unique combination of hero and saint.

[C. W. Spalding, The Spalding Memorial: A Geneal.
Hist. of Edward Spalding . . . and His Descendants
(1897); J. H. Melish, Franklin Spencer Spalding, Man
and Bishop (1917); Christian Socialist, Nov. 9, 1911,
Nov. 1914; Spirit of Missions, Nov. 1914; Churchman,
Oct. 3, 10, 17, 1914; Living Church, Oct. 3, 10, 1914;
Outlook, Nov. 25, 1914; Salt Lake Tribune, Sept. 26,
27, Nov. 2, 1914.]   H. E. S.

SPALDING, JOHN LANCASTER (June 2,
1840–Aug. 25, 1916), Catholic prelate and edu-

cator, was born in Lebanon, Ky., a son of Richard Madison and Mary Jane (Lancaster) Spalding, a nephew of Martin John Spalding [*q.v.*], and a descendant of Thomas Spalding who settled in Maryland about 1650. Educated in local schools and St. Mary's College, from which he was graduated in 1859, Spalding, in answer to the priestly vocation so common in his family, entered Mount St. Mary's Seminary of the West in Cincinnati. Subsequently, he proceeded to the American College at Rome and to the American College at Louvain. Ordained a priest by dispensation on Dec. 19, 1863, he remained in Europe two years longer engaged in advanced studies. After his return to the United States, he served as a curate of the Cathedral in Louisville, organized St. Augustine's negro parish (1869), and acted as secretary to Bishop Peter J. Lavialle and William McCloskey and as chancellor of the diocese (1871). Recognized as a scholarly theologian, he accompanied his ordinary to the Second Plenary Council of Baltimore (1866), where he was invited to preach before the assembled prelates. In 1872 he left the Louisville diocese and was stationed as an assistant at St. Michael's Church in New York. While here he published a biography of his uncle, *The Life of the Most Rev. M. J. Spalding* (1873).

Named by Pope Pius IX to the see of Peoria, Spalding was consecrated bishop by John Cardinal McCloskey in St. Patrick's Cathedral, New York, on May 1, 1877. He was associated with the liberal leaders of the Church in the Third Council of Baltimore (1884); with John Ireland in the Irish colonization movement; and with the founders and promoters of the Catholic University of America at Washington, D. C., in the establishment of which he is regarded as the moving force (see *An Address Delivered at the Laying of Corner-Stone of the Catholic University*, 1888). As an ordinary, he managed his diocese with skill, promoted education, and founded in 1898 a model boys' high school, the Spalding Institute. He was largely responsible for the Catholic educational exhibit at the World's Columbian Exposition in Chicago. As an essayist he had no peer in the priesthood, although some critics feared that he leaned toward the philosophy of Kant and Hegel. His educational essays, which appeared in the *American Catholic Quarterly Review*, the *Catholic World*, and the *Educational Review*, received high praise from impartial critics. A voluminous writer, he published a number of books treating of philosophy, religion, education, and social problems; among them are *Essays and Reviews* (1876); *Religious Mission of the Irish People* (1880); *Lectures and Discourses* (1882); three volumes of verse— *America and Other Poems* (1885), *The Poet's Praise* (1887), *Songs Chiefly from the German* (1896)—under the pen name Henry Hamilton; *God and the Soul* (1901); *Education and the Higher Life* (1890); *Things of the Mind* (1894); *Thoughts and Theories of Life and Education* (1897); *Opportunity and Other Essays* (1898, 1900), which, translated by the Abbé Felix Klein, went through three French editions; *Means and Ends of Education* (1895); *Religion, Agnosticism and Education* (1902, 1903); *Socialism and Labor and Other Arguments* (1902, 1905); *Religion, Art, and Other Essays* (1905); *Aphorisms and Reflections* (1901); *Glimpses of Truth* (1903). In 1905 *The Spalding Year Book: Quotations from the Writings of Bishop Spalding* appeared, under the editorship of M. R. Cowan; and a long narrative poem, *A Kentucky Pioneer*, was published in 1932. A sermon touching upon Americanism which he preached at Rome in 1900 (published by the Ave Maria Press, Notre Dame University), challenged attention and was quoted at length in the *Independent* (Sept. 20, 1900), with the observation that "such a leader, who is a scholar, theologian, and poet, is an honor to his Church."

In 1902, at the suggestion of leaders of the striking miners, President Theodore Roosevelt, who believed that Spalding was "one of the very best men to be found in the entire country" (*Theodore Roosevelt: An Autobiography*, 1913, p. 509), appointed him to the anthracite coal commission (*Report to the President on the Anthracite Coal Strike of May-October 1902*, 1903). Since most of the striking miners were Catholics, Spalding's efforts and personality had great influence in bringing about a satisfactory solution of the difficulties involved. His active life was ended by a paralytic stroke in 1905. He resigned his see on Sept. 11, 1908, and lived in retirement as titular archbishop of Scitopolis until his death.

[P. H. Callahan, biographical introduction to Spalding's *A Ky. Pioneer* (1932); *Souvenir of the Episcopal Silver Jubilee of Rt. Rev. J. L. Spalding* (1903); *Ceremonies of the Golden Sacerdotal Jubilee of His Grace John Lancaster Spalding* (1913); *Catholic Univ. Bull.*, Jan. 1898; *Am. Catholic Who's Who* (1911); *Who's Who in America*, 1916–17; official Catholic directories, esp. 1917; M. F. Rutherford, *The South in Hist. and Lit.* (1906); F. J. Zwierlein, *The Life and Letters of Bishop McQuaid* (3 vols., 1925–27); J. F. Rhodes, *The McKinley and Roosevelt Administrations* (1922); Sister M. Evangela Henthorne, *The Irish Cath. Colonization Asso. of the U. S.* (1932); *Catholic Encyc.*, XI (1911), 602; *Harper's Weekly*, Oct. 25, 1902; *Dial*, Jan. 1, 1904; *Chicago Daily Tribune*, Aug. 26, 27, 1916; material from Msgr. E. L. Spalding, Alton, Ill.]

R. J. P.

SPALDING, LYMAN (June 5, 1775–Oct. 21, 1821), physician and surgeon, was born in Cornish, N. H., the son of Dyer Spalding and Elizabeth Cady (Parkhurst) Spalding, and a descendant of Edward Spalding who came to America from England before 1640. At the age of seven, he entered the academy at Charlestown, Mass., was graduated in July 1794, and almost immediately began the study of medicine under the tutelage of Nathan Smith, 1762–1829 [q.v.]. In the winter of the same year, he began to attend lectures at the Harvard Medical School, and the following year carried on the practice of Dr. Smith while the latter was away on a visit to Europe. He resumed his studies at Harvard and was graduated in 1797 with the degree of M.B. Later Harvard honored him with the M.D. degree and Dartmouth College with the M.B. and M.D. degrees. From 1797 to 1799, he lectured on chemistry and materia medica at the medical school which had just been organized at Dartmouth. During this time he prepared a translation of a French book on chemistry which he published in 1799 under the title *A New Nomenclature of Chemistry*. Realizing that he could not make a living by lecturing, he settled in Walpole, N. H., with the intention of establishing a practice there, but soon moved to Portsmouth where he served as a contract army surgeon for the troops stationed at the fort in the harbor. He rapidly built up an extensive private practice and was compelled to discontinue his lectures at Dartmouth. On Oct. 9, 1802, he was married to Elizabeth Coues, the daughter of Capt. Peter Coues. Five children were born to them.

Spalding practised in Portsmouth from 1799 to 1812. Early in this period, he founded a medical society which eventually became the Eastern District Branch of the New Hampshire Medical Society, and, later, an anatomical museum. He originated and distributed "bills of mortality" which gave the causes of death of all persons in Portsmouth from 1800 to 1813. He obtained a portion of the first shipment of smallpox vaccine from England to the United States and immediately began experimentation. His activity as an investigator during this period is further manifested by his invention of a galvanic battery for therapeutic use, the perfection of a method for the preparation of oxygen for inhalation, and the invention of a soda fountain. In 1810 Spalding formed a connection with an academy at Fairfield, N. Y., and lectured there on chemistry and surgery for seven years. In 1813 he was made president of the institution, which then became known as the College of Physicians and Surgeons of the Western District of New York, and filled most of the chairs until 1816. In the last year, he started the publication of a book in pamphlet form on the institutes of medicine but it was never completed. Following this period, he established a residence in New York City, practised his profession, pursued the investigations which interested him, and wrote until his untimely death. While walking down Pearl Street he was struck on the head by some rubbish thrown from a second-story window, and never fully recovered from the effects.

Spalding's most outstanding contributions to medicine during his later years were his studies on yellow fever, additional investigations in the field of vaccination, an extensive and thorough study of hydrophobia, and the founding of the United States pharmacopoeia. Of these, the last was undoubtedly his greatest achievement. As early as 1815 he had written to some of his friends, urging that a national pharmacopoeia be established, but did not receive any encouragement until two years later when he read a paper on the subject before the New York County Medical Society. A committee was appointed, with Spalding as chairman, to suggest measures for the elaboration of a national pharmacopoeia. The plan worked out by this committee provided that a national convention be held of delegates chosen from each of four sections into which the United States was divided. A convention was held in Washington, D. C., on Jan. 1, 1820, plans for the elaboration of the book were agreed upon, and Spalding was made chairman of the committee on publication. This committee set to work immediately and made such rapid progress that the book was completed and printed by Dec. 15, 1820. Spalding took an active interest in the public schools and served as a trustee of the schools of the city of New York during his residence there. He died in Portsmouth, N. H.

[S. J. Spalding, *Spalding Memorial* (1872); C. W. Spalding, *The Spalding Memorial* (1897); H. A. Kelly, W. L. Burrage, *Am. Medic. Biographies* (1920); J. A. Spalding, *Dr. Lyman Spalding* (1916), and *The Friendship of Dr. Nathan Smith and Dr. Lyman Spalding* (1906); H. M. Hurd, article in *Am. Jour. Pharmacy*, June 1919; *Proc. Am. Pharmaceutical Asso.*, vol. LII (1904); *New-Hampshire Gazette*, Nov. 6, 1821.]

A. G. D–M.

SPALDING, MARTIN JOHN (May 23, 1810–Feb. 7, 1872), Catholic prelate, was born at Rolling Fork, Ky., the son of Richard and Henrietta (Hamilton) Spalding, who had migrated with their families to Kentucky in 1790. He was a descendant of Thomas Spalding who settled in St. Mary's, Md., about 1650. Bishop John L. Spalding [q.v.] was a nephew. After the death of their mother, the Spalding children were reared by an unusually devout grandmother, whose influence doubtless accounts in part for the fact that two of them entered the priesthood and two others joined a convent. Martin attended a typical log-cabin school and St. Mary's College, near Lebanon, from which he was graduated in 1826. He then entered the seminary at Bardstown, where he came into contact with such Catholic pioneers as Bishop B. J. Flaget and his coadjutor, John B. M. David, and F. P. Kenrick [qq.v.]. Although delicate as a child, he developed into a large man of demonstrative spirit, with a merry ring in his laughter, a good speaking voice, and a frank, blunt address. Sent by Bishop Flaget to the Urban College, Rome, in 1830, Spalding ranked well in his examination for the doctorate in theology and won the friendship of John England [q.v.], the future Cardinals, Wiseman and Cullen, and Monsignor Capellari (Gregory XVI), connections which no doubt facilitated his later rise in the Church. Ordained, Aug. 13, 1834, by Cardinal Pedicini, he said his first mass at St. Peter's tomb and soon returned to Bardstown, Ky., as pastor of the cathedral and instructor in the seminary.

The young priest was active in making conversions, in ministering to the negroes, and in writing for the *St. Joseph's College Minerva,* a literary magazine, the forerunner of the *Catholic Advocate* (begun 1835) of which later he was editor and which was in turn succeeded (1858) by his *Louisville Guardian* under lay editors. In 1838, he was appointed to the rectorship of St. Joseph's College, from which he resigned in 1840, engaging thereafter in pastoral work in Lexington and, after the episcopal see was removed to Louisville in 1841, in the old Bardstown parish. About this time he commenced the career as a lecturer which brought him fame throughout the United States and Canada. He also contributed to such magazines as the *Religious Cabinet,* the *United States Catholic Magazine,* and *The Metropolitan,* serving the last named in an editorial capacity. In 1844 Bishop Flaget called him to Louisville to be vicar-general. Here, with Father John McGill [q.v.], he conducted a series of lectures, published as *General Evidences of Catholicity* (1847), and republished in several subsequent editions. At the suggestion of the aged Flaget, he was appointed by Pope Pius IX to the coadjutorship of Louisville with the right of succession as titular bishop of Lengone, though certain members of the hierarchy feared that he lacked the necessary energy and firmness for the office.

Consecrated bishop on Sept. 10, 1848, he took active charge of the diocese, although he did not formally succeed until Feb. 11, 1850. Leaving financial affairs to his brother, Rev. Benedict J.

Spalding (1812–68), whose patrimony was bequeathed to diocesan institutions, the Bishop gave zealous attention to administrative matters. He established schools, an orphanage, a house for Magdalens, and a conference of the St. Vincent de Paul Society (1854); he built churches and a cathedral (1852). In 1852 he went to Europe with aid for John Henry Newman, who was in financial difficulties because of the suit brought against him by Dr. Achilli; as a result of this trip he introduced into his diocese in 1854 the Xaverian Brothers from Bruges. He also introduced the Minor Conventuals, the Ursulines, and the Sisters of Notre Dame. In the Councils of Baltimore and Cincinnati he took an active part. His pastorals on the sacraments, on marriage, and on the school question attracted wide attention, as did his series of articles in *The Catholic Guardian* (1858) contrasting the liberal acceptance of religious schools in Europe with the hostility which they encountered in America. The bishop's greatest difficulty arose from the Know-Nothing agitation stirred up by the *Louisville Daily Journal,* then edited by George D. Prentice. A mob attacked the foreign quarters, murdered about a hundred Irish and German residents of Louisville on "Bloody Monday," Aug. 5, 1855, and drove many from town. Spalding bore himself with tactful force and displayed a courageous leadership of his people which deterred further violence (see *An Address to the Impartial Public on the Intolerant Spirit of the Times,* 1854, p. 45).

Interested in higher education, he and Bishop Peter Paul Lefevere [q.v.] of Detroit promoted in 1857 the American College of Louvain when most members of the hierarchy displayed little interest in the enterprise. Later, he was active in the establishment of the North American College in Rome and was one of the first prelates to urge a national Catholic university for higher studies in the United States. He found time, also, for considerable writing of an apologetic and historical nature: *Sketches of the Early Catholic Missions of Kentucky* (1844); *D'Aubigne's 'History of the Great Reformation in Germany and Switzerland,' Reviewed* (1844), which was expanded into *A History of the Protestant Reformation* (2 vols., 1860); *Sketches of the Life, Times, and Character of the Rt. Rev. Benedict Joseph Flaget* (1852); *Eight Days Retreat of Father David* (1864); *Miscellanea* (1855), a series of essays, in one of which, by a skilful use of historical evidence, he disposed of some of the charges against Catholicism brought by Samuel F. B. Morse; and an introduction and notes to *A General History of the Catholic Church* (4 vols., 1865–66), a translation from the French of J. E. Darras.

Though a Southerner, during the Civil War Spalding tried to be scrupulously neutral. In charities, he was assuredly so. He detailed Sisters of Charity and Sisters of Nazareth as nurses on the battle fields and in the Louisville hospitals. He visited and preached in camps; he advised against Archbishop Kenrick's proposal of a definition of the Church's position in the struggle; he influenced Governor Magoffin to veto the first test-oath bill which passed the Kentucky legislature, but when it became law he took the oath under protest that he held the act unconstitutional. His brochure, *Dissertazione nella Guerra Civile Americana* (1863), is said to have had considerable effect upon Continental opinion. After the death of Archbishop Kenrick, he was transferred on July 31, 1864, to the archepiscopal see of Baltimore, to the general satisfaction of Catholics throughout the country, despite apparent protests by Secretary Seward to Rome on the score of Spalding's doubtful loyalty to the federal cause. As archbishop, his régime was brief but noteworthy. The Second Plenary Council was held in 1866 and carried out much church legislation formulated by himself and Dr. James A. Corcoran of Charleston. He busied himself in collecting funds for the rehabilitation of the churches in the South, and displayed unusual activity in organizing conferences of the St. Vincent de Paul Society, the Catholic Protectory under the Xaverian Brothers, a home of the Good Shepherd, St. Francis School and Colored Orphanage, and the headquarters of Father Herbert Vaughan's Josephite Fathers for colored missions, which has since become an important community. He gave ample support to the Passionists, and to the Redemptorists and the Jesuits who were building their respective houses of study at Ilchester and Woodstock. In 1867–68, he was in Rome on papal invitation to celebrate the anniversary of St. Peter's martyrdom and in 1870 he took a leading part in the Vatican Council as a member of the commissions on Faith and Postulata. A strong supporter of the cause and definition of papal infallibility, he published *Pastoral Letter to the Clergy and Laity of the Archdiocese on the Papal Infallibility, Written in Rome, July 19, 1870* (1870), which has both theological and historical value, and *Lecture on the Temporal Power of the Pope and the Vatican Council . . . Philadelphia* (1870). Two years later he died and with fitting services was buried in his cathedral.

[J. L. Spalding, *The Life of the Most. Rev. M. J. Spalding* (1873), from papers left by the archbishop to his friend I. T. Hecker, C.S.P.; Spalding's printed pastoral letters; B. J. Webb, *The Centenary of Catholicity in Ky.* (1884); J. G. Shea, *Hist. of the Catholic Church in the U. S.*, vol. IV (1892); R. H. Clarke, *Lives of the Deceased Bishops of the Catholic Church in the U. S.*, vol. III (1888); *Cath. Encyc.*, vol. XIV (1912), p. 208; *Sun* (Baltimore), Feb. 8, 12, 1872.]

R. J. P.

SPALDING, THOMAS (Mar. 26, 1774–Jan. 4, 1851), planter, writer, legislator, and congressman, only child of James and Margery (McIntosh) Spalding, was born in Frederica, St. Simon's Island, Ga. His father, a noted Scotch student and trader, settled in Georgia in 1760 and built up an extensive Indian trade; being a Loyalist, he removed to Florida at the outbreak of the Revolution, but later returned to Georgia. His mother was a daughter of Col. William McIntosh, an officer in the Revolution, who had settled in Georgia in 1736. Spalding was educated in common schools in Florida and Georgia and a private school in Boston, Mass. He studied law under Judge Thomas Gibbons [*q.v.*] of Savannah and was admitted to the bar in 1795, but never practised. He married, Nov. 5, 1795, Sarah Leake, only child of the wealthy Richard Leake of Belleville, McIntosh County, Ga. He built a home on St. Simon's but soon sold his estate and spent several years in England, where he engaged in business and took great interest in Parliament. After returning to Georgia he bought a plantation on Sapelo Island and devoted himself to his family, politics, and agriculture. He was the father of sixteen children, of whom several died before reaching maturity. His home was noted, even after the death of his wife in 1843, for his lavish entertaining.

Spalding's political life was influential though not spectacular. Before going to England, he served in the constitutional convention of 1798 and as Glynn County's representative in the legislature. After his return, at several different times he represented McIntosh County in the state Senate. He successfully contested the election of Cowles Mead to Congress in 1805, but resigned in 1806. An ardent patriot, he secured arms from the federal government in 1812 and armed his slaves against the British. In 1815 he was sent by the government to Bermuda to investigate claims of American citizens against Great Britain for property destroyed and slaves carried away during the War of 1812 (for some of his letters as United States agent, see *Niles' Weekly Register*, Sept. 30, 1815). In 1826 he represented Georgia on the commission appointed to determine the boundary between Georgia and Florida; but he could not agree with the federal commissioner and the dispute remained unsettled until years later. As a member of the Milledgeville anti-tariff convention of 1832, he aided in drawing up its resolutions on the tariff. He took a moderate position on the sectional controversy over slavery. Elected president of the Georgia Convention of 1850, he favored the compromise measures of that year and was influential in getting Georgia to accept them.

Spalding had extensive agricultural interests. Owning hundreds of slaves, he was noted for his considerate treatment of them. He never sold a slave, and while in the legislature advocated a law prohibiting the sale of a slave from the estate on which he was born. He founded and was president of the Bank of Darien and its Milledgeville branch. One of the first to introduce sea island cotton into the South, he was the first to grow sugar cane and manufacture sugar in Georgia. He experimented with silk culture, imported wines, and developed vineyards and wine making. His contributions to agricultural journals were voluminous. Courteous and affable and with easy, unassuming manners, he was a fluent and energetic speaker, often in demand at the Agricultural and Sporting Club, of which he was a member. He liked neither art nor music, but loved books and collected one of the largest libraries in the South. Especially interested in history, he wrote "A Sketch of the Life of General James Oglethorpe," published in the *Collections of the Georgia Historical Society* (vol. I, 1840). Although tender, loving and generous, he was devoid of a sense of humor and sternly condemned dancing and card playing. He died at his son's home in Darien and was buried in St. Andrews Cemetery of Christ Church, Frederica.

[C. W. Spalding, *The Spalding Memorial* (1897); *Biog. Dir. Am. Cong.* (1928); L. C. Gray, *Hist. of Agriculture in the Southern U. S. to 1860* (1933), vol. II; L. J. Hill, *The Hills of Wilkes County, Ga.* (n.d.); L. L. Knight, *Georgia's Landmarks*, vol. II (1914); Caroline C. Lovell, *The Golden Isles of Ga.* (1932); W. J. Northen, *Men of Mark in Ga.*, vol. II (1910); George White, *Hist. Colls. of Ga.* (1854); C. S. Wylly, *The Seed that Was Sown in the Colony of Ga.* (1910); *Savannah Daily Republican*, Jan. 8, 1851.]   F. M. G.

SPALDING, VOLNEY MORGAN (Jan. 29, 1849–Nov. 12, 1918), botanist, was born at East Bloomfield, N. Y., the son of Frederick Austin and Almira (Shaw) Spalding, and a descendant of Edward Spalding, who came from England and settled in Massachusetts before 1640. His mother was of Scotch-Irish ancestry. He attended the public schools of Gorham, N. Y., and, after the removal of his family to a farm near Ann Arbor, Mich., in 1864, prepared for college at the Ann Arbor High School. In 1869 he entered the University of Michigan, and was graduated with the degree B.A. in 1873. The next three years he served as principal of high schools at Battle Creek and Flint, Mich. In 1876 he joined the faculty of the University of Michigan as instructor in zoölogy and botany (1876–79), and subsequently devoted himself wholly to botanical research and instruction, filling in succession the positions of assistant professor (1879–81), acting professor (1881–86), and professor of botany (1886–1904).

At intervals during his early career he studied plant physiology, anatomy, and histology at Harvard, the University of Pennsylvania, and Cornell, and later carried on advanced studies in European universities, receiving from Leipzig the Ph.D. degree in 1894. Admirably suited in character for teaching, and well-equipped by long and many-sided training in botanical fields until then little cultivated in America, he became noted for his earnest insistence upon the recognition of botany in its broadest sense as a science of the utmost utility to mankind and upon the requirement of thorough training for teachers of science in secondary schools. He was himself an uncommonly successful teacher, even-tempered, genial, and possessed to an unusual degree of the ability to impart his own deep enthusiasm to those who studied under him and went out as investigators and teachers. His textbook, *Guide to the Study of Common Plants: An Introduction to Botany* (1893), served an important purpose.

Among other subjects, forests early interested Spalding, and over the long educational period required to arouse public appreciation of their importance and value as an irreplaceable national asset he steadfastly advocated a detailed study of the manifold problems connected therewith and the development of a rational policy of forest conservation and utility. He assisted the federal government not only in planning forestry work but by carrying out extended experimental studies as well, and was the principal author of *The White Pine* (*Pinus Strobus Linnaeus*), a monograph published in 1899 by the United States Department of Agriculture. In later years his interest was directed primarily to ecology and the life relations of desert plants. Failing health compelled him to spend the winter of 1898–99 in southern California and later (1904) to resign his professorship at Michigan. The next year he joined the resident staff of the Desert Botanical Laboratory of the Carnegie Institution of Washington, at Tucson, Ariz., a region better suited to his condition. Of the results of his work here the volume *Distribution and Movements of Desert Plants* (1909) is the most important. Owing to increasingly severe rheumatism he removed in 1909 to a sanitorium at Loma Linda, Cal., where, cheerful and mentally alert although physically more and more helpless, he resided until his death. He was married in September 1876 to Harriet Hubbard of Battle Creek, Mich., and on Jan. 1, 1896, some years after her death, to Effie Almira Southworth, of Forestville, N. Y., who survived him. A bronze tablet erected at the University of Michigan in 1909 by former students fittingly commemorates his life and services.

[C. W. Spalding, *The Spalding Memorial: A Geneal. Hist. of Edward Spalding . . . and His Descendants* (1897); *Science*, Nov. 29, 1918; H. S. Reed, "Volney Morgan Spalding," in *Plant World*, XXII, 14–18 (Jan. 1919), portr.; B. A. Hinsdale, *Hist. Univ. Mich.* (1906); F. E. Bliss, *The Class of '73 of the Univ. of Mich.* (1923); *Mich. Alumnus*, May 1899; *Who's Who in America*, 1918–19; Regents' Proceedings Univ. of Mich., 1901–06; Univ. of Mich, alumni office records.]

W. R. M.

SPANGENBERG, AUGUSTUS GOTT-LIEB (July 15, 1704–Sept. 18, 1792), bishop of the Moravian Church, was the youngest of four sons of George Spangenberg, Lutheran pastor at Klettenberg-Hohenstein, and his wife, Elizabeth Nesen. He was left an orphan in 1714, with a small estate, most of which was wiped out by fire. All of the children had gymnasial and university training, however, by virtue of the patient industry of the older boys, and Augustus entered the university at Jena in 1722. Here he came under the influence of Francke, Breithaupt, Freylinghausen, and Buddeus, was made a member of Buddeus' family, and was assisted by a yearly stipend. Pietism was just beginning to divide Protestant sentiment into two schools and Spangenberg's young mind was laid open to the evangelical possibilities of the new spirit. Under the influence of his distinguished foster father, he abandoned the study of law for theology, receiving the M.A. degree in 1726, and becoming an assistant in theology in the university. An acquaintance with Count Zinzendorf and the Moravians of Herrnhut about this time attracted Spangenberg's interest to the practical application of pietistic ideas to everyday life. He visited Herrnhut in 1730 and found himself in such sympathetic comradeship that he looked upon the Moravians as brethren. He meanwhile refused a profitable lectureship at Copenhagen, but was persuaded two years later by the king of Prussia to accept the chair of religious education at the University of Halle. By this time the orthodox and separatist movements in the Lutheran Church had become more antagonistic and his adherence to the Moravians resulted in dismissal from his position. He went at once to Herrnhut as an assistant to Zinzendorf and the two became lifelong friends. He was responsible for carrying out the Zinzendorf plans for the establishment of missions in Surinam and in Georgia, and the negotiations in Amsterdam and in London proved him a patient and competent agent, and made for him strong friends in both countries.

In 1735 he started for America with some Swiss colonists and began a service of almost thirty years in Georgia and in Pennsylvania. His superlative qualities of leadership, his outstanding common sense, his vigorous but controlled evangelism, and his ability to restrain the extravagances of the pietistic attitude, made him the driving force in the organization of the Moravian work in America. He left Savannah in 1736 and went to Pennsylvania where he lived with the Schwenkfelders while he looked for a site for a Moravian mission center. In 1739, having made arrangements for the Georgia group to move north, he went to Marienborn and then to Herrnhaag, in Württemberg, where he was married to Mrs. Eva Maria (Zielgelbauer) Immig, on Mar. 5, 1740. In 1741 he founded at London the Society for the Furtherance of the Gospel to enlist the financial support of the Church of England for Moravian missions. He was consecrated bishop in 1744 at Herrnhaag and at once sailed for America to become overseer of the Bethlehem settlement, started in 1741 by Zinzendorf and David Nitschmann [*q.v.*]. An invasion from Canada had made the colonists fearful of the Indians as allies of the French, and his first move was to send all the New York converts to Bethlehem from the northern stations and to organize the American work with Bethlehem as a center. He divided his people into two alternating groups, the "Home" and the "Pilgrim" congregations, operating under a communistic order which he himself established and directed very effectively, notwithstanding the pressure of war conditions and much local opposition. In Europe, meanwhile, pietism had run wild in Moravian circles, carrying with it most of the men around Zinzendorf, and internal church politics caused Spangenberg to lose his influence. He was replaced at Bethlehem by Bishop John Nitschmann and returned to London, where, in 1750, he wrote a declaration in defense of Zinzendorf which appeared as the *Apologetische Schluss-Schrift* at Leipzig in 1752.

After the cross-fire of pietism had burned out, he was again selected to go to Bethlehem. He found his so-called "Economy" disrupted by laziness and lack of management, and he promptly began to plan a new scheme to separate family life that should supplant the former system. His wife had died in 1751 and, on May 19, 1754, he was married to Mrs. Mary Elizabeth (Jaehne) Miksch. A short visit to London in the spring of 1753 had convinced him that plans for America must be made in accordance with existing conditions, so when he returned in 1754, he promptly began to organize a new work in North Carolina on a large tract selected from the Granville grant in 1752 and hastened the break up of the Economy at Bethlehem. He also took active part in the colonial legislation that moved the Indians to the further side of the Ohio. The anxieties and privations of these proceedings, involving much laborious travel, so undermined his health that, at last, in 1762, when the new organization was complete, he returned to Herrnhut. Here he stayed for the rest of his life as the actual leader of the group of so-called elders, recognized not only by his own, but by all Christian groups in Europe, as the dominating figure in the work of missions. He was continually called into conference by rulers and ministries as an expert in matters of colonial control. During this period of his life he produced most of his literary work. His first efforts were *Leben des Herrn Nichlaus Ludwig Grafen und Herrn Zinzendorf* (three volumes, 1772–75), and his *Idea Fidei Fratrum* (Barby, 1779). His *Kurzgefasste Historsche Nachricht von der . . . Bruederunität* was published in Frankfort in 1774, the *Reden an Kinder*, in Barby, 1782; *Das Wort von Krenz* and *Vergebung der Sünde*, in Barby, 1791–92.

Spangenberg's second wife died at Bethlehem in March 1759. He had no surviving children from either marriage. He retired from active service in 1790, but remained in full strength of mind, even though feeble in body, until his death in Berthelsdorf. He was buried at Herrnhut.

[Spangenberg papers in the Moravian archives, Bethlehem, Pa., and Herrnhut, Saxony (also photostatic copies in the Lib. of Cong.) ; manuscript mission reports, and diary of the congregation, Bethlehem; K. F. Ledderhose, *The Life of Augustus Gottlieb Spangenberg* (London, 1855) ; Gerhard Reichel, *August Gottlieb Spangenberg* (Tübingen, 1906) ; Jeremiah Rissler, *Life of Spangenberg* (Barby, 4 vols., 1794) ; *Pubs. South. Hist. Asso.*, vol. I (1879) ; *Pa. Mag. of Hist. and Biog.*, no. 4, 1878, no. 1, 1879 ; A. L. Fries, *Records of the Moravians in N. C.*, *Pubs. N. C. Hist. Commission* (4 vols., 1922–30) ; J. T. Hamilton, *A Hist. of the Ch. Known as the Moravian Ch.*, *Trans. Moravian Hist. Soc.*, vol. VI (1900) ; J. M. Levering, *A Hist. of Bethlehem, Pa.* (1903) ; *Trans. Moravian Hist. Soc.*, vols. I, III, IV (1876, 1886, 1891).]

A. G. R.

SPANGLER, EDWARD [See BOOTH, JOHN WILKES, 1838–1865].

SPANGLER, HENRY WILSON (Jan. 18, 1858–Mar. 17, 1912), engineer, educator, author, was born at Carlisle, Pa., the son of John Kerr and Margaret Ann (Wilson) Spangler. While he was attending public school in Carlisle, the United States Navy inaugurated the four-year course for engineers at the Naval Academy, announcing that twenty-five cadets would be appointed annually on competitive examination. Spangler, viewing this announcement somewhat in the light of a divine dispensation, took the examination, passed it, and received his appointment to the United States Naval Academy at the age of sixteen. His career at the Academy was brilliant; his technical aptness led him into advanced work in mathematics, and he was graduated third in the class of cadet engineers in 1878.

At that time, it was the practice of the Navy to assign young officers to engineering colleges as teachers of engineering subjects. Spangler and two of his classmates, Ira Nelson Hollis [*q.v.*] and Mortimer Elwyn Cooley, were so detailed; all three later resigned from the Navy; and all three became noted educators in the field of engineering. From 1878 to 1889 Spangler retained his affiliation with the Navy, rising to the rank of assistant engineer, and returning in 1898 for service with the rank of chief engineer during the Spanish-American War. Meanwhile, on detached service he was instructor in marine engineering (1881) and assistant professor of dynamical (mechanical) engineering from 1882 to 1884 and from 1887 to 1889 at the University of Pennsylvania, where in 1889 he was made full professor, a merited promotion which had been delayed on account of his youth. It was during the twenty-three years of service that followed, as professor of mechanical engineering, holder of the Whitney professorship of dynamical engineering, and head of the department of mechanical and electrical engineering, that Spangler brought to mature fruition those qualities of precision, initiative, leadership, and executive ability which he had so ably developed at the Naval Academy, and made his noteworthy contribution to the development of engineering education.

As an author he published standard textbooks on several subjects: *Valve-Gears* (1890) ; *Notes on Thermodynamics* (1901) ; *Elements of Steam Engineering* (1903), jointly with A. M. Greene, Jr., and S. M. Marshall; *Graphics* (1908) ; *Aplied Thermodynamics* (1910) ; and contributed a wealth of papers and reports to technical periodicals. He maintained membership in the Franklin Institute and numerous professional societies. As a teacher he was endowed with an imposing personality, a quick and brilliant mind, a stern sense of discipline, and a scathing contempt for affectation and pretense. These qualities, coupled with his genuine regard for accurate and rigorous teaching, made him feared at first and later loved by an admiring student body who manifested their affection through the kindly nickname, "Pop." He was honored with membership on the advisory council of the Engineering Congress of the World's Columbian Exposition, 1893, and membership on the jury of awards of the Buffalo exposition of 1901. A painting of him hangs in the Engineering Building at the University of Pennsylvania.

Spangler married, Dec. 1, 1881, Nannie Jane Foreman of Carlisle, Pa., and they had three children. He died of heart disease at the age of fifty-four, survived by his wife and one son.

[*Who's Who in America*, 1912–13; *Trans. Am. Soc. Mech. Engineers*, vol. XXXIV (1913); *Science*, Mar. 29, 1912; *Old Penn* (Univ. of Pa.), Mar. 23, 1912; Edgar Marburg, in *Engineering News*, Mar. 28, 1912, repr. in *Proc. Engineers' Club of Phila.*, vol. XXIX (1912); *Pub. Ledger* (Phila.), Mar. 19, 1912; *Pennsylvanian* (Phila.), Mar. 19, 1912; letter from Dean Greene; conversations with Univ. of Pa. alumni.]
F. V. L.

SPARKS, EDWIN ERLE (July 16, 1860– June 15, 1924), college president, historian, was born near Newark, Licking County, Ohio. His father, Erastus Felton Sparks, a bridge contractor and farmer, traced his lineage from a Captain Sparks who came to Virginia with the second group of colonists sent out by the London Company; some of the descendants of this colonist emigrated later to the Ohio Valley. His mother, Jane Erle (Dodd) Sparks, a well-known evangelist, was descended from a Virginia family, one branch of which moved to Ohio in 1840. After his farm boyhood he worked at a variety of odd jobs and served as a reporter on a number of Ohio newspapers until he acquired enough money to go to college. He entered Ohio Wesleyan University, Delaware, Ohio, after a year in the preparatory department there, but in 1881 he transferred to the sophomore class at the Ohio State University, Columbus, where he received the degree of B.A. in 1884.

He was assistant in history at Ohio State University, 1884–85, and principal in the public schools of Portsmouth and Martins Ferry, Ohio, 1885–90. On Jan. 1, 1890, he was married to Katharine Cotton of Portsmouth, Ohio, by whom he had a daughter. During the next six years he held the position of administrative head of the preparatory department of the Pennsylvania State College at State College, Pa., where he also taught history. In 1891 he received the degree of M.A. from Ohio State University and in June 1900 the degree of Ph.D. in history from the University of Chicago, where he was a member of the faculty, 1895–1908, rising to a professorship of American history in 1904. He was also curator of the historical museum, 1905–08, and dean of University College, 1905–07. His

extension courses in history, an innovation in the field of higher education, attracted nationwide attention. In 1908 he was called to the presidency of the Pennsylvania State College, a position in which he showed marked capacity. He expanded the work of the institution both on the campus and, by extension service, throughout the state, and effected many reforms in the interest of educational efficiency and scholastic standards. At the same time the faculty of the college was enlarged from 114 to 518, and the student body increased from 1,147 to 4,316; ten new buildings were erected, and the administrative divisions of the institution were thoroughly reorganized. He served for several years on the executive council of the American Historical Association (1909–12) and was an active member of other historical organizations. In 1920 he resigned to devote his time to teaching American history, lecturing, and organizing chapters of the scholastic honorary society, Phi Kappa Phi. Throughout his entire career he displayed rare ability as a popular lecturer on historical, scholastic and administrative topics. Among his publications are *Topical Reference Lists in American History* (1893); *The Expansion of the American People* (1900); *The Men Who Made the Nation* (1901); *Formative Incidents in American Diplomacy* (1902); *The United States of America* (2 vols., 1904); *The Capture of William Johnston* (1906); *National Development, 1877–1885* (1907); *The English Settlement in the Illinois* (1907); *Worth-While Americans* (1921); and *Worth-While Europeans* (1923).

[*Who's Who in America*, 1924–25; *In Memoriam: Edwin Erle Sparks, Pres. of the Pa. State Coll.*, 1908–1920 (1925); obituaries in *N. Y. Times* and *Pub. Ledger* (Phila.), June 16, 1924; papers of E. E. Sparks in the Pa. State Coll. lib.]
A. E. M.

SPARKS, JARED (May 10, 1789–Mar. 14, 1866), editor and historian, was born at Willington, Conn., to Eleanor Orcutt, daughter of a substantial farmer. The date is found in his own "Biographical Memoranda" (Sparks Manuscripts, 141a). In the baptismal records of the First Church of Willington, the minister wrote "Jared son of [   ] by Elinor Orcut July 1789," but crossed out "son of" and wrote "born" in the blank space (*New England Historical and Genealogical Register*, Apr. 1913, p. 123; information from Town Clerk of Willington). On Dec. 24 of the same year Eleanor Orcutt married Joseph Sparks (Manuscript Vital Statistics, Town Clerk's office, Book B., p. 84), a young Willington farmer, and subsequently bore him nine children. Local tradition has it that Joseph was Jared's father. His maternal grandmother was something of a poet and local prophetess, and his mother a reader of history and philosophy; hence we have sufficient biological explanation of the boy's talents, without recourse to other theories of his paternity.

Just before his sixth birthday, when four or five younger children were straining the resources of the Sparks household, Jared was taken in charge by a childless uncle and aunt; and the next winter he had his first schooling. With the temporarily adopted parents, he emigrated to Camden, Washington County, N. Y., in 1800. Jared spent so much time helping his shiftless uncle, that little opportunity was found for schooling; he remembered reading Guthrie's geography while feeding logs into a saw-mill, and being greatly interested in Franklin's *Autobiography*. Returning to his parents at Willington in 1805, he so quickly exhausted the resources of the local schools as to be known as "the genius." The young boy became keenly interested in astronomy, and observed the comet of 1807 with a homemade cross-staff. At the age of eighteen he worked as a journeyman carpenter in summer and school teacher in winter; at twenty, he began the study of mathematics and Latin with the minister at Willington, the Rev. Hubbell Loomis, paying in part by shingling the parson's barn. Another nearby minister, the Rev. Abiel Abbot, was so favorably impressed with Jared as to obtain him a scholarship at the Phillips Exeter Academy, whither the young man repaired on foot. After two happy and fruitful years there, he entered Harvard College in 1811. Although several years older than his classmates, and forced to work his way, Sparks was a social as well as a scholastic success. He was the first member of his class to be chosen to the leading sophomore society and with two aristocratic classmates, John G. Palfrey [*q.v.*] and William H. Eliot, he formed lifelong friendships. In order to earn money he served during sophomore year as a private tutor at Havre de Grace, Md., where he witnessed the plundering of the town by Admiral Cockburn's expedition. His employer wished him to establish a private school; but he returned to Harvard, joined the Phi Beta Kappa, won the Bowdoin prize with an essay on Newton which was regarded as setting a new high mark for undergraduate work, and delivered a commencement part at his graduation in 1815. Jared Sparks loved people, his zest for improvement was combined with delightful social qualities, and in whatever community he found himself, from earliest youth, he took a leading part and made devoted friends.

Essentially roving and adventurous in disposition, the young graduate from rustic Connecticut longed to explore Africa. The travels of Mungo Park and of John Ledyard [*q.v.*] fascinated him; in college he was already planning to cross the Sahara, visit the mysterious city of Timbuktu, sail down the Niger, and circumnavigate Africa. It is true that after graduating he conventionally took up the study of divinity, but this may have been in the hope of reaching the Dark Continent as a missionary; for in 1816 he offered his services to the African Society of London. They were not encouraging; and during the two years 1817–19, Sparks served as science tutor at Harvard while studying at the Harvard Divinity School, and for a short period editing the *North American Review*. Although brought up a Calvinist, he yielded to the Unitarian influences at Harvard. On completing his studies and taking a master's degree, the young man received three offers: a comfortable parish in Boston, a professorship at a small college, and the pulpit of the First Independent Church (Unitarian) of Baltimore. The last appealed to his adventurous nature; and the famous ordination sermon of William Ellery Channing [*q.v.*] when Sparks was installed at Baltimore (May 5, 1819), made that occasion the "Pentecost of American Unitarianism." Sparks flung himself with youthful energy into his pastoral duties, and created new ones. Regarding himself as an apostle of liberal Christianity to the South, he engaged in pamphlet controversy with conservatives, and launched sundry schemes for religious propaganda and publication. His love of travel was gratified by invitations to preach in Southern cities as far as Savannah; and for a year, as chaplain to the House, he was much in Washington. But the ministry was never more than a stepping-stone for Sparks: in April 1823, greatly to the regret of his congregation, he resigned.

It so happened that Edward Everett, editor of the *North American Review,* was at odds with the "association of gentlemen" who owned it. Sparks first proposed to move the *Review* to Philadelphia, and let Everett start a rival periodical in Boston (Manuscript Diary, 1823–26, p. 12); but Everett's restless ambition turned elsewhere. Sparks then purchased the *Review* on credit for about $10,000, and edited it for six years, when he sold it for almost double the amount. Under his vigorous management the *North American* shook off the dilettante flavor of its youth, and became an equal to the great English and French reviews, remarkable for the quality and range, both geographical and intellectual, of its articles. The editor even subscribed to South American newspapers, and learned

Spanish in order to keep his readers in touch with Latin-American affairs; and he was constantly thinking up desirable subjects for articles, and getting them written. Sparks became a leading social and literary figure in the Boston group that revolved about Prescott, Ticknor, the Eliots, and the Everetts; and *The Life of John Ledyard* (1828), republished in England, and soon translated into German, gave him an independent literary reputation. The portraits of him by Rembrandt Peale (1826), Gilbert Stuart (1828), and Thomas Sully (1831), show him to have been remarkably handsome, with dark curly hair, brown eyes, and a Roman nose; robust in physique; and having the general air of an intelligent and alert aristocrat. His tastes, however, remained simple; he made no concealment of his humble origin, and kept in touch with childhood friends.

In the meantime Sparks had begun what was destined to be his greatest life work, the publication of the writings of George Washington. Justice Bushrod Washington, the owner of the Washington manuscripts, was won over by an offer to share the profits, through the friendly mediation of Chief Justice Marshall, who also consented to take an equal share, twenty-five per cent., with the owner (Bassett, *post*, p. 80). In January 1827, Sparks found himself alone at Mount Vernon with the manuscripts. An examination of them extending over three months showed that years would be required for the undertaking; and with the owner's consent, Sparks carried off the entire collection, eight large boxes, picking up on the way to Boston a box of diplomatic correspondence from the Department of State, and the Gates manuscripts from the New York Historical Society (Manuscript Journal, June 14, 1827). Not content with these, he searched or caused to be searched public and private archives for material, questioned survivors of the Revolution, visited and mapped historic sites. In 1830, for instance, he followed Arnold's route to Quebec. The first of the twelve volumes of *The Writings of George Washington* to be published (vol. II) appeared in 1834 and the last (vol. I, containing the biography) in 1837. In the meantime Sparks had become so enthusiastic over the literary possibilities of the Revolutionary period, as to begin and partially to complete several parallel publications. These included *The Life of Gouverneur Morris* (3 vols., 1832), *The Works of Benjamin Franklin* (10 vols., 1836–40), *The Library of American Biography* (first series, 10 vols., 1834–38), to which he himself contributed several lives, and *The Diplomatic Correspondence of the American Revolution* (12

vols., 1829–30). In order to obtain material for this last work he visited Europe in 1828–29, and spent several months copying documents in the archives of England and France, which he was probably the first American to enter. He was also a pioneer purchaser and collector of manuscript Americana. From 1837 to 1840 Sparks served on the Massachusetts Board of Education; but he took slight interest in politics and held no other public office.

Only by knowing the paucity and poverty of printed material on the American Revolution before 1830 can one realize the debt that American history owes to Sparks. All his work except that on the *Diplomatic Correspondence* was done on his own responsibility, and at his own risk, without subsidies or grants or a wealthy patron. The result proved that Sparks knew his public. These formidable sets of printed letters and documents sold to such an extent as to make a handsome profit for all concerned; and they were a boon to students and writers of history for the next fifty years. Yet Sparks's editorial methods were very bad; for he treated historical documents as if they had been articles or reviews submitted to the *North American,* using the editorial blue pencil freely. He made omissions without indicating them, standardized spelling and capitalization, and undertook to improve Washington's English. These methods are partly explained by Sparks's editorial experience, partly by his sense of social responsibility. He approached history as a gentleman in the "era of good feeling," rather than a scientific historian, resolved to tell the truth however unpalatable. He wished to spare the feelings of great men's descendants, and of those who lent him documents. Justice Washington enjoined him "to avoid giving offence to the writers [of letters to Washington], or their famileis [*sic*], by publishing any which have a reference to the state of parties, and alluding to particular indeviduals [*sic*] by name"; to which Sparks replied, "I am fully aware of the delicacy you mention, and trust my judgment will guard me against any indiscretion" (Apr. 9, 17, 1827, Sparks Manuscripts; Adams, *post*, II, 15). Observing that Washington in his old age completely rewrote his early letters, Sparks felt obliged to touch up later letters when they appeared to need it; and usually he had only the rough draft, not the letter actually sent, to work from. The harsh and hasty criticism of men and measures, in which the harassed General sometimes indulged, especially those that might arouse sectional animosities, Sparks thought best to gloss over or omit; but no sectional bias was shown in the omissions. Similarly, a strong secession passage was deleted from a letter of Gouverneur Morris, published in the critical year 1832. With Lord Aberdeen, who gained him access to the Public Record Office, Sparks had a gentleman's understanding that nothing would be published from that source tending to revive angry feelings between the two countries; and the same reticence was applied to documents from the French archives that might injure the traditional friendship (Justin Winsor, *Narrative and Critical History of America,* VIII, 1889, p. 414). It was customary, in his day, to edit very freely the letters of literary and historical figures before publication; and neither the English nor the American public had acquired a taste for seeing their heroes in the buff. Thus, in editing *The Works of Benjamin Franklin,* Sparks omitted the famous definition of chastity, and all other matters of the sort. But Sparks's carelessness respecting the Washington manuscripts is inexcusable. When George Corbin Washington, Justice Washington's heir, sold the "public" papers of the General to the United States, he allowed Sparks to keep "a few autographs" (Sparks's acknowledgment to G. C. Washington, Aug. 16, 1837, Sparks Manuscripts) of the "private" papers, and from these Sparks tore out and gave away leaves to friends who desired a specimen of the great man's handwriting (J. C. Fitzpatrick, *George Washington Himself,* 1933, p. 529; *The Diaries of George Washington,* 1925, vol. I, 211; IV, 295; Ellis, *post,* p. 254). It is not fair, however, to blame all cases of missing Washington manuscripts on Sparks, for Justice Washington gave away some of the diaries, and G. C. Washington mentions in a letter to Sparks (Dec. 27, 1848, Sparks Manuscripts) "some few unimportant autographs presented to friends."

These fifteen years (1823–38) of intense activity enlarged Sparks's circle of friends, brought him fame and money, and the opportunity for a change of occupation. On Oct. 16, 1832, he married Frances Anne Allen of Hyde Park, N. Y., and brought her to live in the historic Craigie House at Cambridge. She died in 1835, but he continued to reside at Cambridge, and in 1838 was offered the Whig nomination for Congress from that district. This he declined in favor of the McLean Professorship of Ancient and Modern History at Harvard, with a salary of $2,000; he had earlier declined the Alford Professorship of Philosophy. His first course, on the American Revolution, began in March 1839; and on May 21 he married an heiress twenty years his junior, Mary Crowninshield Silsbee, daughter of Senator Nathaniel Silsbee of Salem, and

brought her to live in a large house near the College Yard. Sparks was the first professor of history other than ecclesiastical in any university of the United States; and in the conditions that he laid down for accepting the chair, he showed prophetic insight into the form that history teaching was to assume in American universities fifty years later (Adams, II, 372–75). He proposed to discard recitations on set textbooks for the upper classes, to instruct by lectures, assigned reading, and essays; he insisted that he should "not at any time be called on to instruct in any other branch than that of history," and that he should not be expected to reside and lecture more than four months in the year. These conditions, which would be liberal even today, were accepted by the College Corporation. Sparks organized a department of history, using young graduates of no special training to teach the younger students out of textbooks, while he lectured to the upper classes and to law students, mostly on American, but occasionally on Greek, history. He seems to have impressed rather than interested the students; and although we find him lecturing on "the nature of historical evidence, and the rules of historical composition," he trained no disciples, and his professorship proved to be a false dawn for modern history in American universities. It was on one of his long absences to search European archives and collections, in 1841, that Sparks discovered the copy of D'Anville's map marked by Franklin, which subsequently figured in the "Battle of the Maps" that followed the Webster-Ashburton negotiations (Adams, II, 393–413). At that time Sparks was making researches for a "formidable history of the American Revolution" (Adams, II, 378) which was never completed. On returning to America he did much lyceum and other public lecturing, at New York and elsewhere, when not in residence at Cambridge. The stenographic reports of one of these courses, in the *New York Herald,* Nov. 8–Dec. 19, 1841, show that Sparks without sacrificing dignity was a lively and entertaining lecturer.

On Feb. 1, 1849, Sparks was chosen by the governing boards, president of Harvard University. His election was welcomed by the students as a return to the "Augustan Age" of Kirkland after the asperities of the Quincy and the inanities of the Everett administrations. Quite unexpectedly, Sparks attacked the elective system of studies in his inaugural address, which Professor Longfellow considered "very substantial, but retrograde." His object appears to have been to substitute definite alternative programs for indiscriminate groupings of course units; but the result was reaction toward the rigidly prescribed course, with recitation sections determined by alphabet rather than proficiency, that had prevailed at Harvard before the reforms associated with George Ticknor [*q.v.*]. Although he encouraged a greater use of lectures in instruction, notably in the case of Louis Agassiz [*q.v.*] and of two young scholars, Josiah P. Cooke and Francis J. Child [*qq.v.*], who owed their first professorial appointments to him, the McLean chair of history remained vacant; Professor Sparks's promising historical program became President Sparks's first victim. The Harvard Observatory, the only research unit of the University at that time, was furthered by his influence, and he had the satisfaction of seeing its new plant completed. Sparks was unhappy in the presidential office. By delegating petty disciplinary duties to a lower official he had hoped to find leisure for literary pursuits; and he did manage to finish his *Correspondence of the American Revolution* (4 vols., 1853) and to reply vigorously to Lord Mahon's strictures on his editorial methods. But new duties arose to fill up the time saved; and, fearing to become completely bogged in administrative routine, he resigned early in 1853.

Except for a year in Europe (1857–58) where he was much entertained, and had the pleasure of meeting David Livingstone, and reviving the African dreams of his youth, Sparks passed the remainder of his life quietly at Cambridge. For ten years he continued to collect material for his projected history of the Revolution, but nothing was written. Time slipped away rapidly and pleasantly with old friends and new, summer travels with wife and children, and answering the questions of correspondents. One gathers that the rôle of sage was not uncongenial to Sparks. He died of pneumonia at Cambridge on Mar. 14, 1866, and was survived by his widow, one son, and three daughters.

On account of Sparks's faulty editorial methods, no one of his documentary collections can be regarded as definitive, although every one was *editio princeps*. He has an assured place as an explorer and producer of American history. His energetic search for original documents, skill in selecting and annotating them, and success in getting them published, gave the American public a new conception of their history, and provided a host of writers with material. The fruits of his original or editorial labors amounted to over one hundred volumes. If Sparks dressed his subject with too much formal dignity, it was because she was young, and frontier manners would not have recommended her

to the family of Clio. His significance lies in the fact that he did obtain that recognition for American history.

[H. B. Adams, *The Life and Writings of Jared Sparks* (2 vols., 1893) is the official biography based on Sparks's own papers. Important appraisals of Sparks's work are in Justin Winsor, *Narrative and Critical Hist. of America*, VIII (1889), 416–24, and J. S. Bassett, *The Middle Group of American Historians* (1917), Ch. II. Bassett printed some *Correspondence of George Bancroft and Jared Sparks*, which throws light on his editorial methods, in *Smith College Studies in History*, II (1917), no. 2. The best memoirs by contemporaries are those of G. E. Ellis, in *Proceedings Mass. Hist. Soc.*, X (1869), 211–310; of Brantz Mayer, *Memoir of Jared Sparks, LL.D.* (1867); and of A. P. Peabody, in *Harvard Graduates Whom I Have Known* (1890). See also Ephraim Emerton, "History," in S. E. Morison, *The Development of Harvard Univ.* (1930). The pamphlet controversies with Lord Mahon and others are covered by the Adams biography and the Ellis memoir. The Sparks MSS. are in the Harvard Coll. Lib.; there is a brief calendar of the historical MSS. by Justin Winsor in *Harvard Univ. Lib. Bibliographical Contributions*, no. 22 (1889); but this does not include the several thousand pieces of private correspondence, journals, accounts, and other MSS. referring to Sparks's life, which were used by Adams and Bassett. These have been card-catalogued. The Peale portrait and several photographs of Sparks are owned by Harvard; the photographs of the Stuart and Sully portraits, owned by descendants, are in Adams' biography.]   S. E. M.

SPARKS, WILLIAM ANDREW JACKSON (Nov. 19, 1828–May 7, 1904), lawyer, congressman, and commissioner of the General Land Office, was born near New Albany, Harrison County, Ind., the youngest of ten children of Baxter and Elizabeth (Gwin) Sparks. His ancestors on both sides were English and early settlers in Virginia; his parents had moved to Harrison County about 1805 and when William was seven they moved again, settling in Macoupin County, Ill. In 1840 the father died but William was allowed to continue his schooling in a nearby log house during the winter months. The death of his mother, when he was fifteen, forced him to seek employment on a neighboring farm. For several years he worked by day and spent his evenings in study; then he turned to teaching school. By 1847 he had saved enough of his earnings to enter McKendree College at Lebanon, Ill., where he graduated in 1850. After studying law in the office of Sidney Breese [*q.v.*] at Carlyle, Ill., he was admitted to the bar in 1851 and immediately began practice. In 1853 he was appointed receiver in the federal land office at Edwardsville, Ill. Characteristic of him is the story that upon the discovery of an apparent error of three dollars in his accounts, when he relinquished his receivership after three years, he journeyed to Washington by stage, compelled a re-examination of his books, and had them found exactly correct. While at Edwardsville, Apr. 16, 1855, he married Julia E. Parker.

After resuming his law practice at Carlyle he served in the lower house of the legislature (1856–58), and in 1863, upon the death of J. M. Rodgers, succeeded him in the state Senate. He presided at many Democratic state conventions and was a delegate to the Democratic National Convention in 1868 and 1884. Meanwhile, in 1874, he was elected to Congress from a district regarded as Republican and was returned for three successive terms. In 1882 his district is said to have been gerrymandered and he declined to seek renomination. In the House he served on the Appropriations Committee and was later chairman of the Committee on Military Affairs. He was known as a "Jacksonian" Democrat with a contempt for Civil Service. Being an able speaker, he took a prominent part in discussions, especially those on the tariff, currency, and military affairs. He was a strong advocate of government regulation of the railroads. He became excited in debate, and at one time a physical encounter between Sparks and Representative James B. Weaver was narrowly averted (*Congressional Record,* Dec. 21, 22, 1880).

After Mar. 3, 1883, Sparks returned to Carlyle and developed a wide reputation as a jury lawyer. He had built up a "liberal fortune" when on Mar. 26, 1885, President Cleveland appointed him commissioner of the General Land Office. In this position he performed his most notable public service. Public opinion had come to feel that the Land Office was dominated by the land-grant railroads, syndicates, speculators, and cattle barons, to the detriment of actual settlers; moreover the Land Office was handicapped by considerable arrears of work. To aid him in his new duties Sparks had pugnacious honesty, good health, legal training, and an independent income. His attempts to reform the land service began with special reports on urgent cases, and his famous "April 3rd" order (Apr. 3, 1885; see his *Report* for 1886, p. 43) withheld the issue of patents for certain regions. He abolished the special privileges of the land lawyers of Washington. His thoroughly able reports of 1885, 1886, and 1887 set forth needed changes in land laws with cogent reasons therefor. He was stanchly supported by President Cleveland and Secretary L. Q. C. Lamar [*q.v.*], though Congress and the partisan press proved extremely hostile. As the result of a dispute with the Secretary regarding a railroad case, however, Sparks tendered his resignation, Nov. 15, 1887, which the President accepted, while expressing cordial sympathy with his accomplishments.

After a trip abroad, Sparks again practised law at Carlyle until about 1900, when he moved to St. Louis, where he died. He was taken to Carlyle for burial in St. Mary's Catholic Cemetery. He left no children.

[*Biog. Dir. Am. Cong.* (1928); *Ann. Reports of the Commissioner of the Gen. Land Office,* 1885, 1886, 1887; *Copp's Land Owner,* 1885–87; *Centennial McKendree Coll. with St. Clair County Hist.* (1928); *N. Y. Tribune, Index,* 1885–87; files of *N. Y. Tribune* and *N. Y. Times; N. Y. Tribune,* Mar. 25, 1885; *Washington Post,* Nov. 12, 13, 16, 17, 1887; St. Louis and Carlyle papers, May, 1904.]   H. H. D.

SPARROW, WILLIAM (Mar. 12, 1801–Jan. 17, 1874), Episcopal clergyman, educator, was born in Charlestown, Mass., the son of Samuel and Mary (Roe) Sparrow. His father's family had gone to Ireland from England in the time of Cromwell and settled in County Wexford. Because of participation in the rebellion of 1798, Samuel Sparrow had been obliged to leave his native land. He found refuge in Massachusetts, but in 1805 was permitted to return to Ireland, where his oldest son, William, was brought up in the home of his grandfather, William Sparrow, at Gorey. With a view to entering Trinity College, Dublin, he acquired an excellent classical education, but in 1816 his grandfather died and the following year William returned to the United States with his parents, who established themselves in Utica, N. Y. Here, in a competitive examination, he won a position as classical teacher in the academy. In 1819 he entered Columbia College, and apparently pursued studies there for two years. In the meantime his family moved to Huron County, Ohio, where his mother died in 1821, and whither he himself went the next year.

In Ohio he became associated with pioneer educational enterprises, especially with those initiated by Bishop Philander Chase [*q.v.*], whose wife's sister, Frances Greenleaf, daughter of Duncan and Susannah (Greenleaf) Ingraham, he married on Feb. 13, 1827. He first taught in the school at Worthington conducted by Bishop Chase's son and later in Cincinnati College, of which the Bishop was president. In November 1824, Miami University opened its doors with Rev. Robert H. Bishop as president and William Sparrow as professor of languages, both having been elected on July 6 preceding (*The Diamond Anniversary Volume . . . 1824–1899,* n.d., p. 80). The following year, however, Bishop Chase persuaded Sparrow that his duty to the Episcopal Church, in which he was about to take orders, required him to sacrifice his opportunity at Miami and assist in establishing a theological seminary. The school was opened on the Bishop's farm at Worthington, and upon his arrival Sparrow became principal and chief teacher. On June 7,

1826, he was ordained deacon and four days later was advanced to the priesthood. From the start the most of the work in the seminary was preparatory and collegiate, and out of it developed Kenyon College and Gambier Theological Seminary, Gambier, Ohio, whither the institution was moved in June 1828. Although Bishop Chase by virtue of his office was head of the institution, Sparrow, as vice-president, was its administrator. Interference by the former led to a controversy between him and the faculty and, in 1831, to his resignation as bishop. Changes in the organization of the institution, brought about by Bishop Charles P. McIlvaine [q.v.] in 1840, led Sparrow to accept a professorship in the Theological Seminary in Virginia, Alexandria, in 1841.

For more than ten years he had been a leading educator and official in the diocese of Ohio; now for thirty-three years he was to have a quieter but no less influential career in Virginia. Twice, in 1844 and in 1851, he was asked to return to Kenyon as president, but declined; he was also called to important churches in Boston, Cincinnati, Richmond, and Baltimore. His teaching in the Seminary, of which he was soon made dean, was chiefly in the field of theology and Christian evidences. He had great gifts as a teacher and his work was characterized by breadth of mind and the spirit embodied in his own advice to others: "Seek the truth; come whence it may, cost what it will" (Goodwin, *post*, p. 601). He was repeatedly a delegate to the diocesan Convention, and was regarded as one of the strongest representatives intellectually of the evangelical Low Churchmen. He died suddenly in the First National Bank of Alexandria, where he had gone to cash a check. His wife had died in the previous year; they had ten children.

[*The Gen. Cat. of Miami Univ.... 1809–1909* (n.d.); G. F. Smythe, *Kenyon Coll.: Its First Century* (1924); A. R. Goodwin, *Hist. of the Theolog. Sem. in Va.*, vol. I (1923); Cornelius Walker, *The Life and Correspondence of Rev. William Sparrow, D.D.* (1876); J. E. Greenleaf, *Geneal. of the Greenleaf Family* (1896); *The Sou. Rev.*, July 1876.]　　　　　　H. E. S.

SPAULDING, ELBRIDGE GERRY (Feb. 24, 1809–May 5, 1897), a substantial banker of Buffalo, N. Y., acquired the sobriquet "father of the greenbacks" during a brief period of service in the House of Representatives. He was born in Cayuga County, N. Y., whither his parents, Edward and Mehitable (Goodrich) Spaulding, had gone from New England as pioneers. His ancestor, Edward Spalding, had established the name in Massachusetts Bay by 1640. Spaulding studied law in offices at Batavia, Attica, and Buffalo, and began practice in Buffalo in the middle

thirties. He was immediately successful in his profession, and was actively concerned in the development of the city, handling business connected with its harbor, its sewage system, its gas works, and the enlargement of the Erie Canal. He married, Sept. 5, 1837, Jane Antoinette Rich, the daughter of an Attica banker, and in due course brought to Buffalo the Farmers' & Mechanics' Bank of Batavia. He served as mayor (1847), as assemblyman (1848), and as state treasurer (1853).

Spaulding's national career began with his election, as a Whig, to the Thirty-first Congress (1849–51). He declined reëlection, returning to his banking business, in which he laid the foundation of a large fortune. Turning Republican, he went again to Congress in 1859, sat on the Congressional Executive Committee, and had some part in the peace negotiations that attempted to avert the Civil War. Reëlected in 1860, he found himself in the Thirty-seventh Congress a member of the Committee on Ways and Means, and one of its sub-committee of three in charge of the problem of war loans. In the summer of 1861 the United States Treasury was on the verge of bankruptcy, with receipts from taxes inadequate and with the credit of the government too uncertain for the favorable placement of loans. Currency was scarce and in unusual demand, and on Monday, Dec. 30, 1861, the New York banks suspended specie payments (D. C. Barrett, *The Greenbacks and Resumption of Specie Payments, 1862–1879,* 1931, p. 14). On the same day Spaulding introduced into the House of Representatives a bill for the issuance of legal-tender treasury notes payable on demand (*Congressional Globe,* 37 Cong., 2 Sess., p. 181). "The bill before us is a war measure. . . ." he stated in debate upon his proposal; "We were never in greater peril than at this moment . . . the Treasury must be supplied from some source, or the Government must stop payment in a very few days" (*Ibid.,* p. 523 f., Jan. 28, 1862). He took pride in the resulting law of Feb. 25, 1862, authorizing the issuance of the legal-tender notes, or greenbacks, to the amount of $150,000,000. As financial needs became more pressing, there was a second authorization of $150,000,000 in July 1862; and before the Thirty-seventh Congress expired, on Mar. 3, 1863, another $150,000,000 had been made available. Spaulding called himself "a somewhat prominent though humble actor in originating and maturing" the law. Its legal-tender feature was distasteful to the Secretary of the Treasury and to the banks, and was accepted only as a measure of desperation. Thaddeus Stevens [q.v.], chairman of the Committee on Ways and Means, gave it his support, however, and in the Senate John Sherman and Charles Sumner [*qq.v.*] supported it.

This was Spaulding's only important work in Congress, and with it his political career came to an end. He was thenceforth content to be a benevolent local magnate. He brought his bank into the national banking system in 1864 as the Farmers' & Mechanics' National Bank of Buffalo, and managed it until, late in his life, he turned it over to his son. After his return from Washington he compiled a volume published in 1869 under the title, *A Resource of War—The Credit of the Government Made Immediately Available: History of the Legal Tender Paper Money Issued during the Great Rebellion: Being a Loan without Interest and a National Currency.* In 1875 he decorated a Buffalo park with a monument to the Spauldings, some of them his forebears, who fought at Bunker Hill. He was three times married; after the death of his first wife, Jane Rich, in 1841, he married, Sept. 5, 1842, Nancy Selden Strong, who died May 4, 1852, leaving two sons and a daughter; two years later, May 2, 1854, he married Delia (Strong) Robinson, sister of his second wife. There were no children by the first and third marriages.

[C. W. Spalding, *The Spalding Memorial: A Geneal. Hist. of Edward Spalding . . . and His Descendants* (1897), p. 395, which gives Spaulding's name a spelling that he did not follow; *Biog. Dir. Am. Cong.* (1928); *World* (N. Y.), May 6, 1897; *Buffalo Commercial,* May 5, 1897.]   F. L. P.

SPAULDING, LEVI (Aug. 22, 1791–June 18, 1873), missionary, was born in Jaffrey, N. H., the son of Phineas and Elizabeth (Bailey) Spaulding, and a descendant of Edward Spaulding (or Spalding) who was in Massachusetts before 1640. Levi received his early education from the Rev. John Sabin of Fitzwilliam, N. H., and graduated from Dartmouth College in 1815. Having decided during his senior year to enter the Christian ministry, he proceeded to Andover Theological Seminary, was graduated in 1818, and on Nov. 18 of that year was ordained by a Congregational Council at Salem, Mass. On Dec. 10, at Antrim, N. H., he was married to Mary, daughter of Samuel and Zebiah Warren Christie of that town. Under appointment of the American Board of Commissioners for Foreign Missions, he and his wife, in company with others designated for the India service, sailed from Boston, June 8, 1819, on the brig *Indus,* bound for Calcutta around the Cape of Good Hope. The ship arrived at Calcutta Oct. 19, whence the party took passage on Nov. 10 for Ceylon, finally reaching their destination, Jaffnapatem (Jaffna), Ceylon, on Feb. 18, 1820. The

following June they settled at Uduvil Ooaou-ville), a new station five miles from Jaffna. Except for residence in nearby Manepay, Aug. 25, 1821, to Aug. 25, 1828, and in Tellippallai, until Mar. 8, 1833, Uduvil was the permanent base of Spaulding's work until his death. He remained longer in active foreign service than had any other missionary sent out by the Board. Only once did he and his wife return on furlough to America. Coming home late in 1844 they were back again in Uduvil before the end of March 1847.

Spaulding distinguished himself as an educator and a Tamil linguist, in addition to faithful and effective service otherwise. At Manepay he received in 1823 his first convert to the Christian faith. There also he took charge of the Mission's Female Boarding School, transferred temporarily (1825–28) from Uduvil. At Tellippallai he conducted the boys' preparatory school which was united in 1832 with the Mission's seminary at Vaddukkoddai (Batticotta, in the old records). At Uduvil he was in charge of the church, the schools, and evangelistic work among the villages. Early in 1834, he made a two months' tour of southernmost India, commissioned to investigate a continental region for the extension of the Mission's Tamil work. The important Madura Mission·was the ultimate outcome. Toward the close of 1838 he began a significant service as translator, reviser, proof-reader, and tract and hymn writer. He prepared in Tamil more than twenty tracts and composed many of the choicest vernacular hymns. He compiled a Bible history and translated *Pilgrim's Progress.* For the sake, incidentally, of "settling" the orthography and the definition of Tamil terms, he compiled a Tamil dictionary and the revised and enlarged *English-Tamil Dictionary* (1852). He was one of the commission, from 1847, on the Scriptures published by the Bible Society, in Madras, being largely responsible for making the Tamil Bible "idiomatic and acceptable" (*Missionary Herald,* September 1849, p. 309); from 1865 to 1871 he served as a reviser of the Tamil Old Testament. He is described as "a shrewd man, a man of humor, utterly unostentatious, and quietly industrious" (*Ibid.,* October 1873, p. 308). He died in Uduvil, survived until Oct. 28, 1874, by his wife. They had two daughters and a son.

[Spaulding's journal, letters, and reports are scattered through *The Panoplist and Missionary Herald,* which in 1820 became the *Missionary Herald.* For other biog. material, see C. W. Spalding, *The Spalding Memorial: A Geneal. Hist. of Edward Spalding and His Descendants* (1897); *Gen. Cat. Theological Sem., Andover, Mass., 1808–1908* (n.d.); *Memoirs of Am. Mission-*

aries (1833); H. O. Dwight and others, *The Encyc. of Missions* (1904).]   J. C. A.

SPAULDING, OLIVER LYMAN (Aug. 2, 1833–July 30, 1922), soldier and civil official, was born in Jaffrey, N. H., the son of Lyman and Susan (Marshall) Spaulding. He was seventh in descent from Edward Spalding, who settled in Braintree, Mass., before 1640; his grandfather was a brother of Levi Spaulding [*q.v.*]. Oliver attended local elementary schools, and the Melville Academy in Jaffrey. In 1851 the family moved to Medina, Mich., and he received further education at Oberlin College, where he was graduated in 1855. After teaching school in Medina and reading law for two years, he moved, in 1857, to St. Johns, Clinton County, a new village just being laid out. There he studied in the law office of James W. Ransom and in 1858 was admitted to the bar. That same year he was elected a regent of the University of Michigan for a term of six years.

He entered the Union army in 1862 as captain in the 23rd Michigan Infantry, and passed through the intermediate grades to that of colonel (Apr. 16, 1864). With his regiment he took part in the Atlanta campaign, the battles of Franklin and Nashville, the capture of Fort Anderson, N. C., and the advance from Wilmington to Goldsboro and Raleigh, N. C. Toward the close of the war he commanded his brigade, and was mustered out in 1865 as colonel and brevet brigadier-general.

He then returned to St. Johns and to the practice of law. From 1867 to 1870 he was secretary of state of Michigan. In 1871 he declined appointment as federal judge in Utah; but in 1875 he accepted appointment as special agent of the Treasury at Detroit. This office he held most of the time until 1890, retaining his residence in St. Johns and his legal connections there. For one term, 1881–83, he represented his home district in Congress. For the greater part of 1883 he was chairman of a commission appointed to investigate the workings of the Hawaiian reciprocity treaty, a task which involved a visit to Honolulu and to other places in the Islands, then not at all easy of access. As special agent of the Treasury his duties included not only the ordinary inspections of his own district, which extended from Marquette to Rochester, but special investigations of customs and immigration matters from New York to San Francisco. From 1890 to 1893, and again from 1897 to 1903, he was assistant secretary of the Treasury, having supervision of Customs, Revenue Cutter, Marine Hospital, Life Saving and Immigration services, and the Seal Islands. He was charged also with the special arrangements for handling customs affairs at the World's Columbian Exposition, Chicago, and developed procedure which has served as precedent at subsequent expositions. He was president of the first Customs Congress of the American Republics, held in New York in January 1903. In that year he resigned as assistant secretary by reason of ill health, but continued to reside in Washington until his death, serving as special agent of the Treasury there until continued ill health forced his complete retirement.

He was regarded as the leading authority in the country on customs law and administration, and until he finally relinquished his residence in Michigan, was one of the leaders of the bar of the state. In politics he was a Republican, and when not in public office was active in Michigan political affairs. For several years he was chairman of the Republican state committee. He was an active Mason, and served as grand master of the Michigan Grand Lodge and Grand Commander of the Michigan Knights Templars. He was a communicant of St. John's Episcopal Church in St. Johns, and for nearly twenty-five years was senior warden. He married, May 29, 1856, Mary Jane Mead of Hillsdale, Mich., who died the next year, and on Apr. 12, 1859, he married her sister, Martha Minerva, who died in 1861; the following year, Aug. 12, he married Mary Cecilia, daughter of John Swegles, one of the leading figures in Michigan affairs and founder of the village of St. Johns. Spaulding died at his home in Georgetown, D. C., survived by his wife, four sons, and a daughter.

[C. W. Spalding, *The Spalding Memorial: A Genealogical Hist. of Edward Spalding . . . and His Descendants* (1897); *Biog. Dir. Am. Cong.* (1928); *Who's Who in America*, 1922–23; *Washington Post*, Aug. 1, 1922; *N. Y. Times*, Aug. 1, 1922; manuscript memoirs of General Spaulding; information from members of his family.]   J. W. W.

SPEAR, CHARLES (May 1, 1801–Apr. 13, 1863), Universalist minister, friend of prisoners, was born in Boston, Mass. As a child he was apparently nurtured in a religious atmosphere, for a younger brother (born in Boston, Sept. 16, 1804) was named after John Murray [*q.v.*], the founder of Universalism in America. Accordingly, although completing an apprenticeship as a printer, Charles likewise studied theology under the Rev. Hosea Ballou and was called to minister to the Universalist parish in Brewster (1828), then in Rockport (*c.* 1837), and finally in Boston (1839). On Dec. 22, 1829, he married Mrs. Frances King of Brewster. A little book, *Names and Titles of the Lord Jesus Christ,* which he compiled and printed in 1841, gained him a wider acquaintance, but his religious fervor was more a product of sentiment than of scholarship, and it was his sympathy for the fate of both condemned and discharged criminals that made his life significant. Printing his *Essays on the Punishment of Death* in 1844, Spear deserves some of the credit for the formation in that year of the Society for the Abolition of Capital Punishment, of which he became the faithful secretary. It was at this point that a squabble among the friends of prison reform in New England alienated a large faction from the dogmatic leadership of Louis Dwight of the Boston Prison Discipline Society, and Spear found the occasion propitious for the establishment of a thin weekly paper, *The Hangman,* the first issue appearing in January 1845; a year later the title was changed to *The Prisoners' Friend,* and in September 1848, on the occasion of a John Howard Festival in Boston, organized by Spear and a group of friends, the weekly was transformed into a monthly. Meanwhile, in its pages and subsequently in book form, Spear had published *A Plea for Discharged Convicts* (1846).

While Charles was issuing appeals against the irrevocable punishment of death and in behalf of the friendless discharged man, his younger brother, John Murray Spear, also a Universalist minister and collaborator in the journal, undertook a personal mission of visitation, befriending and assisting released convicts. The two brothers thus introduced Boston to the humanitarian activities later to be organized under parole laws, in which pioneering they had been preceded by Isaac Tatem Hopper [*q.v.*] in New York. Depending entirely on the philanthropy of their subscribers—numbering only 1,500 in 1845—and faced with the fact that "all do not pay up," they were fortunate in attracting a donation of $225 from Jenny Lind in 1850. Wider recognition was received in the same year when an official request from England for information concerning the laws of the states on capital punishment was referred by the authorities at Washington to Charles Spear. Interpreting this request as a providential command to go over and help Europe abolish capital punishment, he proceeded to Washington to gather information and to enlarge the circle of his backers. Securing a letter from Daniel Webster, he journeyed to England in time to attend the Congress of the Friends of Universal Peace at London in 1851, but his "Notes by the Way," sent back to his brother who was temporarily in charge of the *Prisoners' Friend,* naïvely reveal that his inspection of English and French prisons and his attempted conference with several British states-

men made very little stir in the Old World. His dream of a world association to safeguard the interests of convicts remained to be dreamed afresh by Enoch Cobb Wines [*q.v.*] in the late sixties.

Even back in Boston the friendless prisoner was becoming still more friendless as the fifties advanced, and Charles Spear, with many of his subscribers disgruntled over the cost of the editor's five-month "vacation," found the support for his paper steadily decreasing and was forced to discontinue publication in 1859 or shortly thereafter. Meanwhile John Murray Spear had been attracted to Spiritualism, and had become a medium in 1852. Perhaps because of his unorthodox interests, his later years are obscure, though publications of his indicate that he was still living in 1872. It is evident that Charles kept to the firmer path of the devout friend of the down-trodden, for in 1858, together with his second wife, Catharine Swan Brown, he engaged in missionary activities (*Missionary Labors of Mr. and Mrs. Charles Spear for the Year Ending January, 1859,* 1859), and soon after the outbreak of the Civil War he secured an appointment as hospital chaplain in Washington, where he contracted a disease and wasted away his remaining energies visiting wounded soldiers. His decease in 1863 was mourned by *The Liberator* (Apr. 24, 1863, p. 67) as that of a modest philanthropist who found "his chief happiness in laboring for others, especially for the neglected and most wretched classes of society."

[Charles Spear's publications are listed in Joseph Sabin, Wilberforce Eames, and R. W. G. Vail, *A Dict. of Books Relating to America,* XXII, 487–89; of these the volumes of the *Prisoners' Friend,* 1846–59, have the greatest value to the biographer, but see also J. G. Adams, *Fifty Notable Years: Views of the Ministry of Christian Universalism* (1882); *Boston Transcript,* Apr. 14, 22, 1863. For John M. Spear his *Labors for the Destitute Prisoner* (1851), *The Educator* (1857), and *Twenty Years on the Wing* (1873), as well as Frank Podmore, *Modern Spiritualism* (2 vols., 1902), are of assistance.]
B. McK.

SPEAR, WILLIAM THOMAS (June 3, 1834–Dec. 8, 1913), jurist, was born at Warren, Trumbull County, Ohio. He was named after a grandfather who was a soldier at Valley Forge, crossed the Delaware with the army of Washington, and was present at the surrender of Cornwallis at Yorktown. The boy's father, Edward Spear, a worker in wood, was a native of Pennsylvania; his mother, Ann (Adgate) Spear, was from Norwich, Conn. In 1819 they moved to Warren, Ohio. Here William received in the public schools and at a private academy his early education. Learning the trade of a printer, he worked as such on the local newspaper in Warren, in Pittsburgh, and in New York City. Returning to Warren, he became deputy clerk of the probate and common pleas courts and began the study of law, his preceptor being Jacob D. Cox [*q.v.*], later governor of Ohio and secretary of the interior in the cabinet of President Grant. In 1858 he was admitted to the bar and soon after went to the Harvard Law School, where he was graduated in 1859. He then formed a partnership in Warren with his old instructor, Cox, and on Sept. 28, 1864, was married to Frances E. York of Lima, N. Y. Having served as city solicitor of Warren for two terms, he was elected in 1871 prosecuting attorney of Trumbull County and reëlected for a second term. In 1878 he was elected a judge of the common pleas court, and while serving his second term in this office was in 1885 elected a member of the Ohio supreme court. He continued as such until 1912, when, on account of the "Progressive Party" split in the Republican organization, he was defeated for reëlection. This continuous tenure of over twenty-seven years as a supreme court judge was the longest in the history of the court. Leaving the bench at the age of seventy-nine, frail of body but keen of mind, he opened an office for the practice of law in Columbus, Ohio. Here within a year he died, survived by his wife and four children.

There was nothing spectacular about his career; his was the cloistered life of a deep student of the law who for thirty-four years served as a judge. He took no part in public affairs and wrote nothing of a lasting character save the 288 opinions, some of which are to be found in every volume of the *Ohio State Reports* from the 44th to the 87th inclusive, and which exceed in number those written by any other judge of the Ohio supreme court. He did not possess an unusually quick mind. "He is the hardest worker on the bench of any judge I ever knew" was the testimony of one who was for years the supreme court reporter (E. O. Randall, in *Ohio State Journal,* Dec. 9, 1913). This capacity for labor, combined with a remarkable fairness of judgment, liberality of view, and kindliness of manner, made him a truly great judge, and one of the ablest and most conscientious of those who have served on the Ohio bench.

["William T. Spear: A Memorial of His Life, Character, and Pub. Services," 89 *Ohio State Reports,* xlviii; *Western Reserve Chronicle,* Dec. 11, 1913; *Ohio State Jour.* (Columbus), Dec. 9, 1913; *Ohio Law Reporter,* May 27, 1912, Dec. 15, 1913, July 20, 1914; *Case and Comment,* May 1911; *Who's Who in America,* 1912–13.]

A. H. T.

SPEED, JAMES (Mar. 11, 1812–June 25, 1887), lawyer, federal attorney-general, was the descendant of James Speed who emigrated from England and settled in Surry County, Va., about the end of the seventeenth century. His grandfather, also James, settled near Danville, Ky., about 1783. His father, John, settled in Jefferson County, at "Farmington," five miles from Louisville, and married Lucy Gilmer Fry. There James was born. He attended school in the neighborhood, and then at St. Joseph's College in Bardstown, where he was graduated probably in 1828. The next two years he spent in the county clerk's office in Louisville. He then went to Lexington to the law department of Transylvania University. In 1833 he began the practice of law in Louisville and continued with a few interruptions as long as he lived. In 1841 he married Jane Cochran, the daughter of John Cochran of Louisville. They had seven sons. In 1847 he was elected to the state legislature. In 1849 he was defeated for the state constitutional convention by James Guthrie, on the emancipation issue. His grandfather, James, had suffered defeat for a seat in the Constitutional Convention of 1792 on the same issue, for hostility to slavery long characterized the Speed family. In 1849 Speed wrote a series of letters to the *Louisville Courier,* in which he boldly assumed a position against slavery that definitely limited his political career until the outbreak of the Civil War. For two years, from 1856 to 1858, in addition to his legal practice, he taught law in the University of Louisville.

In the secession movement he took the typical Kentucky attitude—a desire to preserve the Union and at the same time avoid war. He was a member of the Union central committee, which was set up to merge the Bell and Douglas forces, and which on Apr. 18, 1861, issued an address lauding Gov. Beriah Magoffin's refusal to respond to Lincoln's call for troops and advising the people to refuse aid to either side. In 1861 he was elected to the state Senate as an uncompromising Union man, and he continued in this position until 1863. He became a principal adviser of Lincoln on affairs in Kentucky, and in the latter part of 1864 was appointed attorney-general. He was the brother of Joshua Fry Speed, Lincoln's intimate friend. He was also a Southerner and a conservative, a man agreeing with the President's policy of moderation toward the Southern states, and a man for whom Lincoln had a personal affection. Lincoln could say of him in Washington, that he was "an honest man and a gentleman, and one of those well-poised men, not too common here, who are not spoiled by a big office" (Lord Charnwood, *Abraham Lincoln,* 1916, p. 404). As long as Lincoln lived Speed held true to the President's policy;

but when a strange fascination for the radicals developed, Charles Sumner was then able to say of him that he was the "best of the Cabinet" (J. F. Rhodes, *History of the United States*, 1904, V, 533). He favored military commissions to try the Lincoln conspirators and other persons not protected by their paroles (*Opinion of the Constitutional Power of the Military to Try and Execute the Assassins of the President*, 1865, and the *American Annual Cyclopaedia*, Appletons', 1866), though he consistently held that Jefferson Davis should be tried by the civil courts. He early began to advocate negro suffrage and was soon as critical as Stanton of President Johnson. He opposed Johnson's veto of the Freedmen's Bureau bill and favored the Fourteenth Amendment. As time went on he found himself increasingly out of harmony with Johnson, and on July 17, 1866, he resigned. The breaking point seems to have developed over the Philadelphia convention, when, in answer to a communication sent him by the committee in charge of promoting that convention, he declared that he thoroughly disapproved of it.

He then returned to Louisville and later bought a home near the city, "The Poplars." In September 1866 he attended the Southern Radical convention in Philadelphia and was made its permanent chairman. There he made a bitter speech against Johnson, characterizing him as the "tyrant of the White House"—an expression he later changed to "tenant" (J. G. Blaine, *Twenty Years*, 1886, II, 226; G. F. Milton, *Age of Hate*, 1930, p. 726, footnote 28). Back in Kentucky he took a prominent part in Radical Republican activities. In 1867 he received forty-one votes in the Kentucky legislature for senator but was defeated; the next year the Kentucky delegates gave him their votes for vice-president; in 1870 he ran for the national House of Representatives and was defeated. In 1872 and in 1876 he was a delegate to the Republican National Convention and each time served on the committee of resolutions. As he grew older he reverted to the ways and beliefs of his earlier life. He continued his practice of law in Louisville and from 1872 to 1879 he taught law again in the University of Louisville. In 1884 he supported Grover Cleveland for the presidency. A few years before his death he became an unwilling party to a controversy with Joseph Holt, over the question of President Johnson having received the recommendation for mercy in the Mrs. Surratt case. Against the almost frantic appeals of Holt to Speed to say publicly that Johnson saw the recommendation, Speed resolutely refused on the ground of the rule against divulging cabinet proceedings. Speed's last public appearance was at Cincinnati on May 4, 1887, when he addressed the Society of the Loyal Legion, *Address of Hon. James Speed before the . . . Loyal Legion* (1888). He died at "The Poplars" and was buried in Cave Hill Cemetery at Louisville.

[James Speed, *James Speed, A Personality* (1914); *Biog. Encyc. of Kentucky* (Cincinnati, 1878); *Diary of Gideon Welles* (1911), vol. II; A. J. Beveridge, *Abraham Lincoln* (1928), vol. I; *Appletons' Ann. Cyc. . . ., 1887* (1888); *War of the Rebellion: Official Records (Army)*, 2 ser., VII; Lewis and R. H. Collins, *Hist. of Ky.* (2 vols., 1874); Thomas Speed, *Records and Memorials of the Speed Family* (1892); *New York Herald*, July 17, 1866; *Louisville Commercial*, June 26, 1887; *North American Review*, July, Sept. 1888; letters in Joseph Holt Correspondence and Edwin M. Stanton MSS. in the Lib. of Congress and in the Charles Sumner MSS. in Harvard College Lib.]   E. M. C.

SPEER, EMORY (Sept. 3, 1848–Dec. 13, 1918), congressman, jurist, was born in Culloden, Ga., the son of the Rev. Eustace Willoughby and Anne (King) Speer. Both his grandfather and his father were Methodist divines of notable eloquence. The boy inherited much of their fine physique and power, and grew up alert and headstrong, moving with his parents from town to town as his father was sent to different churches. At sixteen he fell in with Lewis' Kentucky brigade of mounted infantry retreating before Sherman's advance, and volunteered enlistment in their ranks. The war over, he entered the University of Georgia and was graduated in 1869 with distinction in scholarship and oratory. The same year he was admitted to the bar. He served as state solicitor-general in 1873–76 and as congressman in 1879–83. Elected first as an Independent Democrat, and reëlected as an Independent, he affiliated with the Republicans before his second term expired, thus losing the good will of many of his constituents but gaining substantial reward. He was put on the Ways and Means Committee and on the conference committee on the tariff bill of 1883, and in that year was appointed district attorney of the North Georgia circuit by President Arthur. Despite vigorous Democratic opposition, he was promoted, Feb. 18, 1885, to the federal court of the southern district of Georgia, a position which he held until his death.

As judge he was distinguished by his dignity and formality and his ultra-courteous bearing. His enemies—and they were many—accused him of tyranny and pomposity, but politics and local interests were doubtless at the bottom of hostile criticism. In 1913 an attempt was made to divide the district, and upon its failure, a House resolution was secured appointing a committee to visit Georgia and conduct an *ex-parte* investigation of Speer's conduct, as a basis for impeachment. His defense was superb; the record fills a pamphlet of 331 pages (*House Resolution No. 234 . . . Statement and Reply of Judge Emory Speer,* n.d., probably privately printed). Upon recommendation of the investigating committee, the proceedings were dropped for lack of evidence. During the thirty-three years of his incumbency Judge Speer wrote pioneer decisions in many cases involving the expansion of federal powers. His opinions commanded respect not only for their lucidity and admirable marshaling of evidence, but for their literary excellence. They cover a wide range of cases, the most outstanding, *United States* vs. *Greene and Gaynor* (146 *Federal Reporter,* 803), being regarded as one of the greatest criminal trials ever conducted in a federal court. His later decisions proved a valuable support to the government in upholding vital statutes evoked by the World War.

Speer was dean of the Law School of Mercer University from 1893; in 1897 he published *Lectures on the Constitution of the United States.* His addresses on public occasions revealed his talents at their best, and were in constant demand; some of these were published under the title *Lincoln, Lee, Grant and Other Biographical Addresses* (1909). From 1877 to 1885 he served as alumni trustee of the University of Georgia. He was twice married; his first wife, Sallie Dearing of Athens, died while he was a member of Congress, leaving him with five small daughters, all of whom grew up, married, and survived him. While still in Congress and in his early thirties he married Eleanora D. Morgan, daughter of Dr. James E. Morgan of Washington. He began practice in Athens, removed to Atlanta in 1883, and in 1887 to Macon, where he established an attractive home, "The Cedars," identified with the rest of his life. He was buried in Riverside Cemetery at Macon.

[*Federal Reporter,* 1885–1918; *Investigation of the Behavior of Judge Emory Speer,* being *House Report No. 1176,* 63 Cong., 2 Sess.; *Conduct of Emory Speer: Hearings before a Subcommittee of the Committee on the Judiciary, House of Representatives, Sixty-third Cong.* (1914); O. A. Park, "Judge Emory Speer," *Report . . . Ga. Bar Asso.,* 1919; *Who's Who in America,* 1918–19; *Case and Comment,* Mar. 1912; *Savannah Morning News,* Dec. 14, 1918; *Atlanta Constitution,* Dec. 14, 1918; personal acquaintance.] J. H. T. M.

SPEER, WILLIAM (Apr. 24, 1822–Feb. 15, 1904), Presbyterian missionary, was born in New Alexandria, Westmoreland County, Pa. He was a great-grandson of James Speer who came from Ireland to Lancaster County, Pa., about 1759, and a grandson of the Rev. William Speer, who graduated from Dickinson College, Carlisle, Pa., and became the first chaplain at the seat of the new government of the Northwest Territory, Chillicothe, Ohio; his parents were Dr. James Ramsey Speer, a physician of Pittsburgh, and Hetty (Morrow) Speer. William spent a year at Jefferson College, Canonsburg, Pa., and then entered Kenyon College, Gambier, Ohio, from which he was graduated in 1840. He began the study of medicine in his father's office, but having been strongly influenced toward missionary work while he was at Jefferson by Walter M. Lowrie, later known as the "martyr missionary," he began the study of theology at Allegheny Seminary, now Western Theological Seminary, Pittsburgh. On Apr. 21, 1846, he was graduated and licensed to preach, and on June 16 of the same year he was ordained to the Presbyterian ministry. Married May 7, 1846, to Cornelia Brackenridge, he sailed at once, with his wife, for missionary work in China. A child was born to them there, but under the severe climatic conditions both mother and child died.

With two colleagues, Speer organized the first Presbyterian mission work in Canton and set the program for all subsequent work in that area. Broken by the death of his wife and child and in failing health, he returned to America in 1850. On Apr. 20, 1852, he was married to Elizabeth B. Ewing, a daughter of the Hon. John H. Ewing of Washington, Pa. Chinese from Canton Province were then pouring into California in search of gold, and Speer felt called to minister to the people with whom he had labored in their native land. Accordingly, he and his wife sailed for the Pacific coast by way of the Isthmus of Panama. Arriving there, he began a varied program of religious and social work among the rapidly increasing numbers of Chinese people, chiefly in San Francisco. He organized the first Chinese church on the Western Continent, and established a weekly paper, called *The Oriental,* printed in both Chinese and English and dealing with both secular and religious matters, which did much to soften the racial antipathy that made the life of the Chinese almost intolerable. He also led in the successful agitation for the repeal of legislation in the mining regions unfavorable to the Chinese.

With his educational and organizing experience, he was well qualified for the service he was called to render when, in 1865, he was chosen secretary of the board of education of the Presbyterian Church. To this work he gave ten years of active leadership during the disordered period following the Civil War. He developed higher standards of education for the ordained ministry, encouraged the building and maintenance of church colleges and academies, and enlarged the available scholarship funds devoted to the education of worthy candidates for the Presbyterian ministry. He constantly contributed to weekly and monthly periodicals, and was the author of a number of books; among them *Semicentenary Review: A Practical Summary of the Principles and Work of the Presbyterian Church* (1869), *The Oldest and the Newest Empire: China and the United States* (1870), *The Great Revival of 1800* (1872), *God's Rule for Christian Giving* (1875). Retiring from active service in 1876, he traveled extensively throughout the Orient, reviewing the progress of the work of which he was a pioneer. He died at Washington, Pa.

[David Elliott, *The Life of the Rev. Elisha Macurdy* (1848), pp. 269–71; William Rankin, *Memorials of Foreign Missionaries of the Presbyterian Church* (1895); *Who's Who in America*, 1903–05; F. A. Virkus, *The Compendium of Am. Geneal.*, vol. V (1933); Alfred Nevin, *Encyc. of the Presbyterian Church in the U. S. A.* (1884); *Presbyterian Banner*, Mar. 3, 1904; date of death from death notice in *Pittsburgh Dispatch*, Feb. 17, 1904.]   W. C. C.

SPEIR, SAMUEL FLEET (Apr. 9, 1838–Dec. 19, 1895), physician, was born in Brooklyn, N. Y., the son of Robert Speir, a New York merchant, and Hannah (Fleet) Spier, descendant of Capt. Thomas Fleet, a retired officer of the British navy who settled on Long Island about 1660. He was educated in the Brooklyn Polytechnic Institute and in the medical department of the University of the City of New York (later New York University), from which he graduated in 1860. The following two years he spent in attendance upon European clinics, mainly in Paris. There he became interested in the recently devised plaster of Paris splint, and, returning home, he brought it to the attention of the military authorities for use upon the battlefields of the Civil War. In 1862 the Sanitary Commission fitted up for him two boats, with which he assisted in caring for the wounded of the Army of the Potomac, then engaged in the Peninsular campaign. In 1865 he went again to Europe for post-graduate study in ophthalmology and otology, afterwards returning to his practice in Brooklyn, where he spent the remainder of his life. He was married to Frances S. Hegeman, daughter of Peter Hegeman of New York, in 1869. Possessed of a handsome face and figure, with a gracious manner, he attained a success in professional practice hardly equaled in Brooklyn; for many years he was the unquestioned leader of the medical profession of the city. He served on the surgical staff of the Brooklyn Eye and Ear Infirmary and of the Brooklyn Dispensary, held the posts of physician, curator, and microscopist at the Brooklyn City Hospital, and

for a time (1864–65) was demonstrator of anatomy at the Long Island College Hospital. In 1864 he attracted the attention of the local profession by a paper, "On the Pathology of Jaundice" (*Transactions of the American Medical Association*, vol. XV, 1865, pp. 311–36), which was awarded a gold medal by the American Medical Association, and he made a notable contribution to the literature of pathology in his *The Use of the Microscope in the Differential Diagnosis of Morbid Growths* (1871). For the control of arterial hemorrhage during operations he devised an ingenious instrument called an artery constrictor, which is noted in the standard surgical works of the day, though it was soon superseded by the artery forceps, and was awarded a prize by the Medical Society of the State of New York (*Medical Record*, Apr. 1, 1871). In 1875 he published *Going South for the Winter*, a volume on the climatic treatment of tuberculosis. In addition to his county and state medical societies and the American Medical Association, he was a member of the New York Pathological Society and a fellow of the New York Academy of Medicine. Though a skilful surgeon, he was loath to resort to surgery until the aid of therapeutics had been exhausted.

He was a leader in public charity work, with original ideas on the subject. He organized the seaside Home for Children and the Helping Hand Dispensary, two examples of intelligently applied charity. Of a different character was the Robins Island Club, which he organized as a "sportsmen's seaside home." He was a lover of nature, happiest when in the fields or upon the sea. On his estate on Gravesend Bay he maintained a refuge for wild animal life, grew flowers in profusion, and collected rare and exotic plants; here too he kept a kennel of prize-winning hunting dogs and a herd of Guernsey cattle. His later years were saddened by the death of a son and a daughter, and by a protracted period of invalidism which terminated suddenly with a gastric hemorrhage probably due to a malignant growth. He was survived by his wife and one daughter.

[W. B. Atkinson, *Physicians and Surgeons of the U. S.* (1878); *Jour. Am. Medic. Asso.*, Dec. 28, 1895; Robert Ormiston, W. H. Bates, and E. W. Wright, in *Brooklyn Medic. Jour.*, May 1896, pp. 325–31, with portrait; obituary in *N. Y. Tribune*, Dec. 20, 1895.]
J. M. P.

SPENCER, AMBROSE (Dec. 13, 1765–Mar. 13, 1848), congressman and jurist, second son of Philip and Abigail (Moore) Spencer, was born in Salisbury, Conn. He was descended from William Spencer, who came to New England with his brothers about 1630 and later was one of the first settlers of Hartford, Conn. Philip Spencer was an iron dealer and an ardent Whig in the Revolution who furnished cannon and supplies to the American armies. Ambrose, with his elder brother, was prepared for college under a Presbyterian minister in Canaan and in 1779 was admitted to Yale; in 1782 he transferred to Harvard, where he was graduated with honors in 1783. Until 1785 he studied law at Sharon, Conn., under John Canfield, whose daughter, Laura, he married, Feb. 18, 1784. After three years as clerk in law offices in Claverack and Hudson, N. Y., he was admitted to the bar in December 1788. In 1786 he was appointed clerk of the city of Hudson. In 1793 he was elected as a Federalist to the Assembly and in 1795 to the state Senate, where he served until 1802. In 1796 he was made assistant attorney general of Columbia and Dutchess counties, and in 1797 he was a member of the Council of Appointment. Spencer served loyally in the Federalist party until 1798, when he astounded his colleagues by announcing the transfer of his allegiance to the Republicans. Federalists attributed his action to disappointment at not being made comptroller, an accusation which Spencer denied with characteristic vehemence (*Albany Gazette*, Jan. 12, and Oct. 5, 1801; Hammond, *post*, I, 177).

Elected with DeWitt Clinton [*q.v.*] in 1800 to the all-powerful Council of Appointment, Spencer entered upon two decades of almost undisputed dictatorship of politics in New York. With a thoroughness rarely equaled in partisan politics, he and Clinton inaugurated the spoils system in New York by wholesale removals. The only high office untouched was that of attorney general; but the incumbent, Josiah Ogden Hoffman [*q.v.*], resigned in 1802 to make way for Spencer, no doubt by virtue of a bargain between the two (McBain, *post*, p. 111; Hammond, I, 182), though Spencer denied it emphatically. He was appointed to the supreme court bench, Feb. 3, 1804, and though he remained there until 1823, becoming chief justice in 1819, his power and activity in politics increased rather than abated.

His first wife, who had borne eight children, died in 1807, and shortly afterward he married Mary, sister of DeWitt Clinton and widow of Burrage Norton. She died a few months later, and in September 1809 he married her sister Catherine (Clinton) Norton, widow of Samuel, the brother of Burrage. In 1812 Spencer separated from Clinton on account of the latter's attitude toward the Bank of America, the reëlection of Gov. D. D. Tompkins [*q.v.*], and the war with Great Britain (see *The Coalition*, 1812, by Spencer and John Armstrong); possibly these

factors were augmented also by family differences occasioned by his third marriage (Spencer to James Clinton, Feb. 19, 1810, letter in New York Historical Society). To counteract the advocacy of the Bank by the *Albany Register*, Spencer established the *Albany Republican*, by means of which during the campaign he bitterly castigated Clinton, the Bank, and all those opposing him. With Clinton in retirement, Spencer's power in state politics from 1812 to 1816 was supreme. In 1816 he suddenly healed the breach with Clinton and forced him from retirement against the party's wishes. Dissatisfaction with Spencer's autocratic manner as well as his autocratic power, together with a growing feeling against judges in politics, produced a reaction against his rule which found expression in the New York constitutional convention of 1821 and in the person of Martin Van Buren. The amendments abolishing the Council of Appointment, extending the suffrage, and popularizing the judiciary were direct blows at Spencer, who, as a member of the convention from Albany, opposed them to the last. His regard for the sanctity of the eighteenth-century safeguards of property and privilege led him to refuse to sign the new constitution.

Subsequently he served two years (1824–25) as mayor of Albany, was an unsuccessful candidate for the United States Senate in 1825, was elected to Congress in 1829, saw his son John Canfield Spencer [*q.v.*] become secretary of war in Tyler's cabinet, and in 1844 served as president of the Whig Convention in Baltimore; but, as a factor to be reckoned with in New York politics, his career ended in 1823 when Gov. Joseph Yates [*q.v.*] nominated him for reappointment to the supreme court and the Senate rejected him by an almost unanimous vote.

Spencer's great ability as a jurist has been obscured by the prominence and fury of his political activities. With a trace of provincialism, Henry Adams declared that "Ambrose Spencer's politics were inconsistent enough to destroy the good name of any man in New England; but he became a Chief Justice of ability and integrity" (*History of United States*, vol. I, 1889, p. 112). Not a deep student of legal lore like James Kent [*q.v.*], he wrote brief opinions wherein citations were few and reasoning was based on commonsense realities. Frequently he disregarded settled dicta and often his dissent gave the first expression to what became accepted doctrine in New York courts, as in *Mann & Toles* vs. *Pearson* (2 *Johnson's Reports*, 37). He was accused of allowing politics to influence his decisions, as in *Tillotson* vs. *Cheetham* (3 *Johnson*, 56) and

In the Case of John V. N. Yates (4 *Johnson,* 317). His greatest contribution in the formative years of the New York judiciary was probably in domesticating the English Common Law (*e.g., Jackson* vs. *Brownson,* 7 *Johnson,* 227), wherein, with constructive foresight, he guided the jurisprudence of New York along lines he thought it should follow, rather than along channels marked out by judicial precedent. Somewhat in the manner of John Marshall and Theophilus Parsons [*qq.v.*], he created judicial law largely by the sheer force of his own reasoning and authority. He occasionally dissented from the opinions of Chancellor Kent and was sustained in the court of errors, as in *Anderson* vs. *Roberts* (18 *Johnson,* 515).

Of stately presence, with dark flashing eyes, energetic, domineering manner, and often vehement speech, Spencer was capable of inspiring fear, hostility, and admiration in his contemporaries. He retired in 1839 to Lyons, N. Y., where he took up agriculture, and formally accepted the Christian religion. This latter course he urged upon his lifelong friends, John Armstrong and Chancellor Kent, who, in obedience to a masterful voice, both accepted his advice.

[There are scattered letters in N. Y. State Lib., N. Y. Hist. Soc., Lib. Cong., and elsewhere. Printed sources include W. B. Sprague, *A Discourse Commemorative of the Late Hon. Ambrose Spencer* (1849); A. B. Street, *The Council of Revision of the State of N. Y. . . . and Its Vetoes* (1859); H. L. McBain, *DeWitt Clinton and the Origin of the Spoils System in N. Y.* (1907); J. D. Hammond, *The Hist. of Pol. Parties in State of N. Y.* (2 vols., 1842); D. S. Alexander, *A Pol. Hist. of the State of N. Y.,* vols. I, II (1906); D. D. Barnard, *A Discourse on the Life, Character and Public Services of Ambrose Spencer* (1849), a eulogy which is valuable for its estimate of Spencer's contribution to jurisprudence, but which, like that by W. B. Sprague, must be used carefully; Nathaniel Goodwin, *Geneal. Notes . . . of Some of the First Settlers of Conn. and Mass.* (1856); *Albany Law Jour.,* Apr. 29, 1876, Dec. 25, 1886; *Memorial of Ambrose Spencer* (1849), including resolutions and the eulogies by Sprague and Barnard as well as that by Horatio Potter, *Christian Suffering* (1849); *Pa. Law Jour.,* June 1848; C. E. Fitch, *Encyc. of Biog. of N. Y.,* vol. I (1916); L. B. Proctor, "Ambrose Spencer," *Am. Lawyer,* IV, 8–9 (1848); G. C. Verplanck, *Dick Shift or The State Triumvirate* (1819); "The Autobiography of Martin Van Buren," ed. by J. C. Fitzpatrick, *Ann. Report Am. Hist. Asso. . . . 1918,* vol. II (1920); L. B. Proctor, *The Bench and Bar of New York* (1870); N. H. Carter and W. L. Stone, *Reports of the Proc. and Debates of the Conv. of 1821 for the Purpose of Amending the Constitution of the State of New York* (1821); *Journal of the Convention* (1821); Joel Munsell, *The Annals of Albany* (10 vols., 1850–59); Wm. Johnson, *N. Y. Sup. Ct. Reports* (1804–23) and *N. Y. Chancery Reports* (1814–23); *Daily Albany Argus,* Mar. 14, 1848. A series of articles by M. D. Rudd, "Ambrose Spencer," in the *Lakeville Journal* (Lakeville, Conn.), Jan. 3, 10, 17, 23, 31, and Feb. 7, 1935, is based in part on local manuscript records.]   J. P. B.

SPENCER, ANNA GARLIN (Apr. 17, 1851–Feb. 12, 1931), journalist, minister, educator, reformer, was born in Attleboro, Mass. She came of fine old New England stock, her father, Francis Warren Garlin, being a descendant of Peter Garland [*sic*], who was in Charlestown, Mass., in 1637, and her mother, Nancy Mason (Carpenter) Garlin, a descendant of William Carpenter, one of the founders of Rehoboth, Mass., in 1643. Her education, according to her own statement, was "largely private." She began her career as a teacher in the public schools of Providence, R. I. (1870–71), and as a member of the staff of the *Providence Daily Journal* (1869–78). On Aug. 15, 1878, in Providence, she married William Henry Spencer, a Unitarian clergyman; they lived in parishes in Haverhill and Florence, Mass., and Troy, N. Y. As early as 1870 she had discovered and had begun using her remarkable abilities as a public speaker; now, under the influence of her husband, she occasionally preached in Unitarian and other liberal pulpits. On Apr. 19, 1891, she was ordained and installed as minister of the Bell Street Chapel (independent), Providence, and thus became one of the few women clergymen of America, among whom she was decidedly the most successful. Her ministry at the Bell Street Chapel, which began before her ordination, lasted fourteen years.

It was during these years that she began those multifarious labors in education, philanthropy, and humanitarian endeavor which made her a national figure. Her interests ran all the way from local charities to world movements of reform, such as woman's suffrage and international peace, and her ceaseless energies took her from pulpit and platform to college halls and administrative offices. The list of her activities is bewildering. Early in her career she enlisted in the moral education movement, and served as an officer of the American Purity Alliance, a federation of moral education societies later merged with the American Social Hygiene Association.

During the years 1903 to 1928 she lectured widely. She was associate leader of the New York Society for Ethical Culture, staff lecturer and associate director in the New York School of Philanthropy (later the New York School of Social Work), special lecturer on education and social service at the University of Wisconsin, director of the Summer School of Ethics of the American Ethical Union, director of the Institute of Municipal and Social Service, Milwaukee, Wis., acting professor of sociology and ethics at the Meadville Theological School, Meadville, Pa., lecturer at the University of Chicago, and at Teachers College, Columbia. Her offices in women's organizations for suffrage, temperance, child-labor reform, and world peace were numerous and important, and her labors for these causes nation-wide. She wrote many newspaper and magazine articles, pamphlets, hymns, and books, among them *The History of the Bell Street Chapel Movement* (1903), *Woman's Share in Social Culture* (1913), and *The Family and Its Members* (copyright 1923). In her seventy-ninth year she was serving as director of the family relations division of the American Social Hygiene Association, New York. On Feb. 10, 1931, after a full day at her desk, she attended a public dinner for world peace and was there stricken with a sudden heart attack. She died two days later, survived by her daughter. Physically diminutive, clad always in a Quaker-like garb of gray, with brilliant eyes shining beneath a crown of white hair, she was a person of exceptional intellectual and spiritual power, and her magnetism, kindled from an inner fire of moral conviction, was extraordinary. When she spoke, in a full, resonant voice that seemed to belie her tiny frame, she held attention and commanded allegiance. More strong than gentle, vibrant rather than serene, she demonstrated in many fields her capacity for public leadership.

[Anna Garlin Spencer's name appears in W. H. Spencer, *Spencer Family Record* (1907), as Anna Carpenter Garlin. See J. G. Garland, *Garland Geneal., the Descendants of Peter Garland, Mariner* (1897); *Who's Who in America*, 1901–02, and 1930–31; *Woman's Who's Who of America*, 1914–15; *Jour. of Social Hygiene*, Mar. 1931, with portrait; *Survey*, Mar. 15, 1931; *N. Y. Times*, Feb. 13 (obituary), 14, 15, 1931; manuscript bibliog. of Anna Garlin Spencer's writings, Teachers Coll., Columbia Univ.; personal acquaintance.]   J. H. H.

SPENCER, CHRISTOPHER MINER (June 20, 1833–Jan. 14, 1922), inventor, manufacturer, son of Ogden and Asenath (Hollister) Spencer, was born on his father's farm at Manchester, Conn. He attended school until he was fourteen and then entered the machine shop of the Cheney silk mills in Manchester. Upon completing his apprenticeship in 1849, he worked in the Cheney mills as a journeyman machinist until 1853, when he went to Rochester, N. Y., and found employment in a tool-building and locomotive shop with a view to acquiring familiarity with machinery other than that used in textile manufacture. For the succeeding seven years he worked successively in the Colt armory, Hartford, Conn., and in the Cheney silk mills. During this period he obtained his first patent, which was for an automatic silk-winding machine that was utilized by the Willimantic Linen Company.

By this time he had turned his attention to firearms, for which he had had a passion since boyhood, and on Mar. 6, 1860, he received patent No. 27,393 for a self-loading, or repeating, rifle.

This was immediately adopted by the United States government and a company known as the Spencer Repeating Rifle Company was organized to manufacture it. Before the Civil War was over, about 200,000 Spencer rifles had been produced. Meanwhile, he continued his inventions in firearms and in 1862 patented a breech-loader; in 1863, a magazine gun; and in 1866 obtained two additional patents for improvements on the latter. At the close of the war he went to Amherst, Mass., and became associated there with Charles E. Billings [*q.v.*] in the Roper Arms Company, established to manufacture Spencer's magazine gun. This venture was not a success, and in 1869 Spencer and Billings went to Hartford, Conn., formed the Billings & Spencer Company, and began the manufacture of drop forgings. It is said that the partners' work in this field did more for the art of drop forging, particularly with respect to the accuracy and application of the process, than that of anybody else. Spencer continued with his inventive work and perfected a machine for turning sewing machine spools. This suggested to him the idea of a machine for turning metal screws automatically. Working secretly, on Sept. 30, 1873, he obtained patent No. 143,306 for a machine for making screws. The great feature of this invention was the automatic turret lathe. Peculiarly enough, this feature, with its blank cam cylinder and flat strips adjustable for various jobs, was wholly overlooked by the patent attorney, with the result that Spencer could claim no patent rights to it. Convinced of the efficiency of his screw machine, he gave up active connection with the Billings & Spencer Company in 1874, and in 1876 formed with others the Hartford Machine Screw Company and, as superintendent, laid the foundation of one of the largest industrial enterprises in Hartford. He could not forget firearms, however, and in 1882 withdrew from the screw company in order to manufacture a new repeating shotgun that he had invented. He organized the Spencer Arms Company at Windsor, Conn., and although the gun was a success mechanically, the company failed and Spencer lost heavily. He then returned to the field of automatic lathes, and in 1893 organized the Spencer Automatic Machine Screw Company at Windsor, Conn., which, together with his directorship of the Billings & Spencer Company, consumed his entire attention until his retirement some years before his death. He was twice married: first, in June 1860, to Frances Theodora Peck, who died in 1881; second, July 3, 1883, to Georgette T. Rogers. He died in Hartford, survived by three children.

[E. S. Farrow, *Farrow's Military Encyc.* (1885), vol. III; J. W. Roe, *English and Am. Tool Builders* (1926); *Commemorative Biog. Record of Hartford County, Conn.* (1901); L. W. Case, *The Hollister Family* (1886); *Hartford Courant*, Jan. 15, 1922; Patent Office records; information from family.]

C. W. M—n.

SPENCER, CORNELIA PHILLIPS (Mar. 20, 1825–Mar. 11, 1908), author, was born in Harlem, N. Y. She was the daughter of Judith (Vermeule) and James Phillips. Her father was a teacher and Presbyterian minister who emigrated from England to the United States in 1818. Her mother (sometimes called Julia) was a member of Dutch families of distinction, whose settlement in New Jersey antedated the Revolution. Growing up in Chapel Hill, N. C., where in 1826 her father accepted the chair of mathematics at the University of North Carolina, she lived the life of that time and place though she was better educated than the average Southern girl. In addition to acquiring the customary ladylike accomplishments, she learned Latin, Greek, and mathematics, and her reading was both extensive and well-chosen. On June 20, 1855, she married James Munroe Spencer, a lawyer of Clinton, Ala., and removed to her husband's home, but after his death in 1861 she returned to Chapel Hill with her young daughter. Her first book, *The Last Ninety Days of the War in North Carolina* (1866), was written immediately after the Civil War at the request of her friend, Gov. Zebulon Baird Vance.

She distinguished herself in the years following the war by her efforts on behalf of the University of North Carolina, which was pitiably impoverished. In 1868 the reconstruction government of the state closed the institution, and then reorganized and reopened it; after a year or two this ill-advised experiment ended in failure, and the university was closed a second time. Through all these changes Mrs. Spencer remained in Chapel Hill, writing for the conservative papers of the state accounts of the inadequacy and dishonesty of the new régime. During 1869 she published a series of "Pen and Ink Sketches of the University of North Carolina As It Has Been" in the *Raleigh Sentinel* (Apr. 26–July 6, 1869). When the second closing of the university occurred she rallied the alumni, most of whom she knew personally, to the task of restoration, and by means of innumerable letters and many newspaper articles helped to crystallize public sentiment in favor of it. The reopening of the university was finally voted by the assembly of the state on Mar. 20, 1875, and soon she had the satisfaction of seeing it functioning usefully again under the presidency of Kemp

Plummer Battle [*q.v.*]. From 1869 through the seventies she contributed a weekly column to the *North Carolina Presbyterian* (Charlotte, N. C.) and in 1889 published *First Steps in North Carolina History*. During her last years she lived in Cambridge, Mass., with her daughter and son-in-law. Her journals, letters, and other papers which have been preserved reveal both her personal charm and her strength of character.

[K. P. Battle, *Hist. of the Univ. of N. C.* (2 vols., 1907–12); Hope S. Chamberlain, *Old Days in Chapel Hill: Being the Life and Letters of Cornelia Phillips Spencer* (1926); obituaries in *Boston Transcript*, Mar. 12, and *News and Observer* (Raleigh, N. C.), Mar. 13, 1908; Spencer papers in the possession of the N. C. Hist. Commission and the Univ. of N. C.]

H. S. C—in.

SPENCER, ELIHU (Feb. 12, 1721–Dec. 27, 1784), clergyman, was one of the group of sturdy Presbyterian ministers who helped to shape American religious and political history during the last half of the eighteenth century. Although his work was done in the middle colonies, he was of New England ancestry, birth, and education. His parents were Isaac and Mary (Selden) Spencer of East Haddam, Conn., where he was born; and he was a descendant of Jared or Garrard (the name is given under various spellings) Spencer, who came to Massachusetts about 1630, later went to Connecticut, and was one of the first settlers of Haddam. Elihu graduated from Yale College in 1746. David and John Brainerd [*qq.v.*] were his second cousins, and on David's recommendation the Boston commissioners of the Society for the Propagation of the Gospel appointed Spencer and Job Strong missionaries to the Indians. They passed the winter of 1747–48 with John Brainerd at Bethel, N. Y., and the following summer with Jonathan Edwards [*q.v.*] at Northampton, Mass., preparing for their work. On Sept. 14, 1748 Spencer was ordained at Boston as missionary to the Oneidas, and later proceeded to Onooguagua (Unadilla), Otsego County, N. Y. The difficulties of the work, augmented by an unfortunate choice of interpreter, so discouraged him that in the spring of 1749 he abandoned the enterprise. In the meantime he had made progress on a vocabulary of the Oneida language.

On Feb. 7, 1749/50 he was installed as pastor of the Presbyterian church, Elizabethtown, N. J., succeeding Jonathan Dickinson [*q.v.*], and on the fifteenth of October married Joanna, daughter of John and Joanna Eaton of Shrewsbury, N. J., where he also ministered to a congregation. During the early part of his pastorate at Elizabethtown, in 1752, he was elected to the board of trustees of the College of New Jersey, of which he was an active member till his death, being placed almost immediately on a committee to negotiate with the people of Princeton with regard to locating the college there. From 1756 to 1759 he served the church in Jamaica, L. I., as stated supply, and in 1758 was chaplain to the New York troops in the French and Indian wars. For six years he was in charge of the church in Shrewsbury and served smaller parishes, but when in May 1765 Rev. John Rodgers [q.v.] left St. George's, Del., Spencer was invited to supply the church there and the Forest Church, Middletown, and on Apr. 17, 1766, was installed over the two congregations. Resigning in 1769, he became pastor at Trenton, N. J., and continued as such until his death.

In addition to his parochial work his services were many and varied. In the ecclesiastical bodies to which he belonged he held important offices. With Alexander MacWhorter [q.v.], he was sent by the synod in 1764 to visit the scattered congregations of the South, especially those in North Carolina, as general adviser and counselor. They were to adjust bounds, administer the sacraments, ordain, and instruct in matters of discipline. His earlier interest in the Indians did not altogether pass, and he was an official visitor to Brainerd's Indian School. From 1770 to 1775 he was a delegate from the synod to the Congregational and Presbyterian Council. An ardent supporter of the Revolution, he was requested by the North Carolina delegates in the Continental Congress, December 1775, to visit, in company with MacWhorter, the more isolated portions of the South, inform the people there of existing conditions, and insure their support of the war. This mission they performed. His activities enraged the Loyalists, and a price of one hundred guineas was placed upon his head. During the British occupancy of Trenton he retired to St. George's, but his home and library were destroyed. On appointment of Congress he acted as chaplain to hospitals in the vicinity of Trenton from 1777 to 1781. His ability to deliver a sermon or address at short notice won for him the appellation "ready money Spencer." A letter of his to Ezra Stiles [q.v.] on Dissenting interest in the middle colonies in 1759 seems to have been printed. An addition to it is in the *Collections of the Massachusetts Historical Society* (2 ser., vol. I, 1814). His elder brother, Joseph [q.v.], was a general in the Revolution; one of his daughters married Jonathan Dickinson Sergeant [q.v.], and was the mother of John and Thomas Sergeant [qq.v.]. The inscription on the tombstone over his grave in the churchyard at Trenton describes him as "possessed of fine

genius, of great vivacity, of eminent and active piety," adding, "his merits as a minister and as a man stand above the reach of flattery."

[W. H. Spencer, *Spencer Family Record* (1907); S. S. Rogers, E. S. Lane, E. V. Selden, *Selden Ancestry* (1931); Nathaniel Goodwin, *Geneal. Notes ... of Some of the First Settlers of Conn. and Mass.* (1856); F. B. Dexter, *Biog. Sketches Grads. Yale Coll.*, vol. II (1896); E. F. Hatfield, *Hist. of Elizabeth, N. J.* (1868); John Hall, *Hist. of the Presbyt. Church in Trenton, N. J.* (1859); *A Hist. of Trenton, N. J., 1679–1929* (2 vols., 1929), pub. by the Trenton Hist. Soc.; Richard Webster, *A Hist. of the Presbyt. Church in America* (1857); W. B. Sprague, *Annals Am. Pulpit*, vol. III (1858); F. B. Heitman, *Hist. Reg. of Officers of the Continental Army* (1914).]   H. E. S.

SPENCER, JESSE AMES (June 17, 1816– Sept. 2, 1898), Episcopal clergyman, educator, author, was born at Hyde Park, N. Y. His father, Reuben, was a seafaring man of Connecticut stock; his mother, Mary (Ames), came from Sudbury, Mass. When Jesse was seven years old the family moved to Poughkeepsie, N. Y., and three years later, to New York City. Here he received his education and did most of his life's work. His mother died when he was thirteen and soon afterward he left school and was employed for two and a half years in a print shop in lower Manhattan, a training which was to influence his entire career. "I was steady and diligent and resolved to learn the trade thoroughly," he records in his autobiography (*Memorabilia*, p. 20). At the end of this experience he became assistant to his father, who had been appointed city surveyor. While in this position he decided to enter the Episcopal ministry. During the year 1833–34 he attended Trinity School, then entered Columbia College, where he was graduated in 1837, having received several medals for proficiency in Greek and English, and in the fall entered the General Theological Seminary, graduating in 1840. On Sept. 4 of that year he married Sarah J. E. Loutrel. Ordained deacon June 28, 1840, by Bishop B. T. Onderdonk, he became rector of St. James's Church, Goshen, N. Y., and while there he was ordained to the priesthood, July 28, 1841, by Bishop Onderdonk.

Resigning his rectorship in 1842 because of ill health, he made a tour of Europe, and on his return in 1843 supplied for several parishes, taught, wrote magazine articles, and did editorial work for publishers. In 1844 he published his first book, a volume of sermons, *The Christian Instructed in the Ways of the Gospel and the Church*. About this time he purchased the school of the Rev. C. D. Jackson, near Washington Square, New York, but for lack of capital gave it up within a few months. For several years, including this period, he edited Greek and Latin textbooks for D. Appleton & Company. In 1845 he founded a monthly magazine, *The Young Churchman's Miscellany,* which was suspended in 1848. In its pages appeared as a serial his *History of the Reformation in England,* published in book form in 1846. During these years he edited *The Four Gospels and Acts of the Apostles, in Greek, with English Notes* (n.d.; 1847?). Owing to another failure of his health, in 1848, he went abroad for two years. On his return, in 1850, he became professor of Latin and Oriental languages in Burlington College, Burlington, N. J., but resigned the following year and became editor and secretary of the General Protestant Episcopal Sunday School Union, New York, serving in this capacity until the Union, in 1857, transferred its publishing business to E. P. Dutton & Company. During the year 1856–57 he supplied the pulpit at St. Thomas' Church, New York, and in the following year assisted in Trinity Chapel, at the same time tutoring private pupils and doing editorial work for Appletons' *American Cyclopædia.* In 1863 he became rector of St. Paul's Church, Flatbush, but resigned two years later, returning to New York City and resuming his work of teaching, editing, and supplying various pulpits. He was elected secretary of the Corporation for the Relief of Widows and Children of Clergymen in the State of New York and in 1869 was appointed professor of Greek in the College of the City of New York, a position he held for ten years, on his retirement being made professor emeritus. Difficult years followed, owing to his advanced age. In 1883 he was appointed custodian of the Standard Bible of the Church.

Spencer was of the school of broad churchmanship. His point of view was established when, during his time as student at the seminary, the controversy over the Oxford Movement in England was raging. His evangelical position is emphasized in all his theological writings. His best known work was *History of the United States* (3 vols., copr. 1858), continued by B. J. Lossing, and copyrighted in 1878 as *The Complete History of the United States of America* (4 vols.). It was translated into German and Spanish. In addition to the works named, Spencer was the author of *The East: Sketches of Travel in Egypt and the Holy Land* (1850), *The Inspiration of the Holy Scriptures* (1865), *The Young Ruler Who Had Great Possessions* (1871), *Pronunciation of Ancient Greek* (1875), *Memorabilia of Sixty-five Years* (1890), *Papalism versus Catholic Truth and Right* (1896), and edited *The Woman of Early Christianity: a Series of Portraits, with Appropriate Descriptions by Several American Clergymen*

(1852). He died in his eighty-third year, survived by one son.

[Spencer's *Memorabilia of Sixty-five Years* (1890); *Churchman,* Sept. 10, 1898; *N. Y. Tribune,* Sept. 3, 1898.]
                                  G. E. S.

SPENCER, JOHN CANFIELD (Jan. 8, 1788–May 17, 1855), lawyer, congressman, cabinet officer, was born in Hudson, N. Y., the eldest son of Ambrose Spencer [q.v.] and Laura (Canfield) Spencer. His father soon afterward became established in Albany; and subsequently held many important public offices—a fact of considerable significance in relation to the public career of the son. John C. Spencer entered college at Williamstown, Mass., where he remained about a year; then transferred to Union College, Schenectady, N. Y. He graduated with high honors in 1806, and during the following year became the private secretary of Gov. Daniel D. Tompkins [q.v.]. He also began the study of law in Albany, and in 1809 was admitted to the bar. On May 20 of that year he married Elizabeth Scott Smith, daughter of J. Scott Smith of New York City, and soon thereafter moved to Canandaigua, Ontario County, N. Y., where, with very limited funds, he began to practise law.

His rise was rapid. Within two years he became a master in chancery, and in 1813 was appointed brigade judge-advocate in active service along the frontier. He was appointed postmaster at Canandaigua in 1814, and in 1815 became assistant attorney-general and district attorney for the five western counties of the state. While holding the last-named office, he was elected to Congress by the Clintonian faction. During his term in the House (1817–19), he served on a committee which investigated and reported unfavorably on the affairs of the Bank of the United States (*House Document 92,* 15 Cong., 2 Sess.). While still in Congress, he was nominated for United States senator by the Clintonian members of the legislature, but was defeated in the ensuing election. He was next elected to the General Assembly, serving three terms, 1820, 1821, 1822, in the first as speaker. He was a member of the state Senate during four sessions, 1825–28. In 1827 Gov. DeWitt Clinton [q.v.] appointed him with John Duer and B. F. Butler [qq.v.] on a committee to revise the statutes of the state. Spencer's abilities, including an amazing grasp of detail, eminently qualified him for this task and contributed greatly to the successful revision (*The Revised Statutes of the State of New York,* 3 vols., 1829).

Having in the meantime joined the Anti-Masonic party, Spencer, in 1829, became special prosecuting officer to investigate the abduction of

William Morgan [q.v.], and, despite attempts to assassinate him, pursued the investigation until lack of funds necessitated his resignation in 1830. His pamphlet, *A Portrait of Free Masonry* (1832), was reprinted in John Quincy Adams' *Letters Addressed to Wm. L. Stone . . . upon the Subject of Masonry* (1833). In 1831 and 1833 he was again a member of the state Assembly. In 1837 he moved to Albany, where he spent the greater portion of his remaining years. In 1838 he edited *Democracy in America,* translated by Henry Reeves from the French of De Tocqueville. Joining the Whig party, he became secretary of state of New York in 1839, and upon the reorganization of the cabinet following the death of President Harrison in 1841, he was appointed by President Tyler as secretary of war. His adherence to Tyler cost him the friendship of the Clay Whigs, and when in January 1844 Tyler nominated him to the United States Supreme Court, the Senate rejected him. He remained in the War Department from Oct. 12, 1841, until Mar. 3, 1843; then became secretary of the treasury, but resigned, May 2, 1844, because of his opposition to the annexation of Texas. After retiring from public life, his last important legal case was the successful defense of Dr. Eliphalet Nott [q.v.], president of Union College, against the charge of misappropriating college funds (*Argument in Defense of the Rev. Eliphalet Nott,* 1853).

In personal appearance Spencer has been described as tall and slender; with eyes "fierce and quick-rolling," and a face bearing "the line of thought and an unpleasant character of sternness." He was considered one of the ablest lawyers of his day, but his devotion to detail often prevented his taking a broad view of public problems. He was notoriously short-tempered, and his inability to yield to or work with others kept him from acquiring the political power he desired. He died in Albany, survived by his wife and three children. One son, Philip, serving as acting midshipman under Alexander Slidell Mackenzie [q.v.], was executed for attempted mutiny on the brig *Somers,* in 1842, while his father was secretary of war.

[L. B. Proctor, *The Bench and Bar of N. Y.* (1870); Joel Munsell, *The Annals of Albany,* vols. III (1852), VI (1855); W. A. Butler, *The Revision of the Statutes of the State of N. Y. and the Revisers* (1889); D. S. Alexander, *A Pol. Hist. of the State of N. Y.,* vols. I, II (1906); E. A. Werner, *Civil List . . . of N. Y.* (1889); *Evening Post* (N. Y.), May 21, 1855; *N. Y. Daily Times,* May 19, 1855; *Albany Evening Atlas,* May 18, 19, 1855; *Albany Argus,* May 19, 1855.]
R. W. I.

SPENCER, JOSEPH (Oct. 3, 1714–Jan. 13, 1789), Revolutionary soldier, was the son of Isaac and Mary (Selden) Spencer, the brother of Elihu Spencer [q.v.], and the great-grandson of Jared (Gerard) Spencer, an English emigrant who settled in Haddam, Conn., about 1662. In that part of the town which in 1734 became East Haddam Joseph was born, related by blood and marriage to half the countryside, as he was to his second cousins John and David Brainerd [qq.v.] and their sister Martha, to whom he was married on Aug. 2, 1738. Throughout his adult life he enjoyed official position in the community, was probate judge from 1753 to his death, deputy to the Assembly in most of the sessions between 1750 and 1766, and assistant after 1766. In 1767 he became deacon of the Millington Congregational Church. He was an officer in the last two of the colonial wars. In 1747 he was commissioned lieutenant of the company raised in Millington Parish, became a major in 1757, lieutenant-colonel in 1759, and colonel in 1766. At the outbreak of the Revolution he was chosen brigadier-general of the Connecticut forces and was stationed at Roxbury early in May 1775. Notwithstanding his experience, his military rank in the colony, and his civil position he found himself superseded, when on June 20, 1775, the Continental Congress raised Israel Putnam [q.v.] to the rank of major-general, while two days later it commissioned Spencer, his superior officer in the Connecticut line, as brigadier-general. In his disappointment and resentment Spencer left the army without leave or notice to the new commander-in-chief, George Washington, and returned to Connecticut, where opinion about the propriety of his conduct was divided. Silas Deane wrote to his wife that he "once had a good opinion of him, but his leaving the forces . . . shocks it very greatly . . . I wish him to resign at once and let another take his place" (*Connecticut Historical Society Collections, post,* p. 288). On the other hand, forty-nine of his fellow officers at Roxbury addressed a letter to the Connecticut Assembly asking it to take up the matter with the Congress. The governor and council drafted a letter and appointed two members to try to reconcile Spencer to the situation. This was arranged, and he served through the siege of Boston and in New York. On Aug. 9, 1776, he became major-general. In September he was one of the three officers who advised Washington to attempt to hold New York City. Ordered to New England in December, he took up headquarters at Providence and planned a movement against the enemy. When he was criticized for his failure in the autumn of 1777 he asked for and received a court of inquiry, which exonerated him. However, he resigned on Jan. 13, 1778.

At home in Connecticut he was at once appointed to the council of safety and in 1779 was chosen a member of the Continental Congress, in which he took his seat on Mar. 27, 1779. He was also elected to the Assembly, deputy in 1778 and assistant in 1779, and he again served on the council of safety, in 1780 and 1781. He died in East Haddam, survived by his second wife, Hannah (Brown) Southmayd Spencer, to whom he was married in 1756. Of his thirteen children, Martha became the mother of Spencer Houghton Cone [q.v.] and Joseph the father of Elizabeth Spencer who married Lewis Cass [q.v.].

[Some papers in the Lib. of Cong.; C. B. Whittelsey, *Hist. Sketch of Joseph Spencer* (1904) and also in *Decennial Register of the Soc. of the Sons of the Rev. in . . . Conn.* (1913); H. B. Niles, *The Old Chimney Stacks* (1887), pp. 118–22; *The Public Records of the Colony of Conn.*, vols. IX–XV (1876–90); *The Public Records of the State of Conn.*, vols. I–III (1894–1922); *The Writings of George Washington*, vols. IV–XI (1931–34), ed. by J. C. Fitzpatrick; *Conn. Hist. Soc. Colls.*, vol. II (1870); *Am. Archives*, 4 ser., II, cols. 1585–86 (1839), ed. by Peter Force; *Jour. of the Continental Cong.*, vol. XIII (1909), ed. by W. C. Ford; L. A. Brainard, *The Geneal. of the Brainerd-Brainard Family* (1908), vol. II, pt. 7, p. 70.]   K. E. C.

SPENCER, PITMAN CLEMENS (July 28, 1793–Jan. 15, 1860), surgeon and lithotomist, was born in Charlotte County, Va., the second son of Gideon Spencer, a lieutenant in the Revolutionary War, colonel of militia, and member of the Virginia General Assembly, and Catherine Clements (or Clemens, as her son seems to have spelled it), daughter of Dr. John Clements of Essex County. The family medical tradition descended to her sons, Pitman and Mace Clements Spencer. Pitman's early education was meager, a disadvantage which he overcame in later life by diligent study. For six or seven years, beginning in 1810 and interrupted only by a brief service as surgeon's mate to a detachment at Norfolk during the War of 1812, he studied medicine under his older brother, Mace. Then he went to Philadelphia for further training, became a pupil of Wistar, Chapman, and Physick, and in April 1818 received his M.D. degree from the University of Pennsylvania. Returning to Virginia, he practised with Dr. Archibald Campbell at Nottoway for several years; but in 1827 his eagerness for wider experience took him to Europe. For three years he traveled, studying surgery and anatomy in London and Paris especially. In Paris he laid the foundation for his later fame as a specialist in urinary surgery, studying under Dupuytren and observing the operations of Civiale, who had just made public a new method of lithotrity, or stone-crushing.

He acquired in Paris a fine set of crushing instruments, and devoted many hours to acquiring skill in their use.

Upon his return to Virginia he settled in Petersburg, where he remained the rest of his life, and rapidly acquired fame as a surgeon. In August 1833 his first published article appeared in the *American Journal of the Medical Sciences*, with the title, "Case of Urinary Calculus successfully treated by Lithotrity." However, he soon abandoned stone-crushing for lithotomy, which he first performed in 1833. His article, "Results of Fifteen Operations for Lithotomy," published in the same journal, July 1850, and reprinted in the *Stethoscope*, March 1851, shows the influence of his Paris training, for he "uniformly operated with the same instrument, viz. lithotome caché . . . of Baron Dupuytren" (*Virginia Medical Journal*, July 1858). By 1858 his lithotomies totaled twenty-eight, with only two deaths, the first two he performed, a mortality of one in fourteen. The rate in Philadelphia was one in eight, and in French hospitals one in six. He also wrote on other subjects, describing a remarkable case of tumor-removal for the *American Journal of the Medical Sciences*, January 1845; a successful operation for "Occlusion of the Vagina," for the *Stethoscope*, April 1851; and "A Case of Empyema," *Virginia Medical and Surgical Journal*, January 1855.

A contemporary spoke of Spencer as "a born surgeon . . . bold to recklessness in his operations, but his success was marvelous" (Claiborne, *post*, p. 121). The success was no doubt partly due to his great care of patients before and after operation and to his free use of soap and water. His name became a household word in Virginia and North Carolina and was well known nationally. He was president of the Petersburg Medical Faculty in 1851 and vice-president of the Medical Society of Virginia in 1855. He was unmarried and died in Petersburg.

[Will Books, Essex County, Va., nos. 12, 13; article by R. M. Slaughter, in H. A. Kelly, W. L. Burrage, *Am. Medic. Biog.* (1920); G. N. Mackenzie, *Colonial Families of the U. S.*, vol. VI (1917); L. A. Burgess, *Va. Soldiers of 1776*, vol. I (1927); J. H. Claiborne, *Seventy-Five Years in Old Va.* (1904); W. B. Blanton, *Medicine in Va. in the Eighteenth Century* (1931); *Md. and Va. Medic. Jour.*, Mar. 1860; *N. Am. Medico-Chirurgical Rev.*, May 1860; *Am. Medic. Recorder*, vol. I (1818), p. 304; *Daily Richmond Enquirer*, Jan. 18, 1860.]   L. F. C.

SPENCER, PLATT ROGERS (Nov. 7, 1800– May 16, 1864), penman, was born at East Fishkill, Dutchess County, N. Y., the youngest of the eleven children of Caleb and Jerusha (Covell) Spencer. His father, a farmer and a soldier in the Revolution, was of Rhode Island stock; his mother was a native of Chatham, Mass., on Cape Cod. The Spencers moved, when Platt was about three years old, to the vicinity of Wappingers Falls and thence to Windham, Green County, where after a few years the father died. Foot-loose and hopeful, however poor, the family set out for the West and on Dec. 5, 1810, after a wagon jaunt of fifty-one days, pulled up at Jef-ferson, Ashtabula County, Ohio. Except for short absences occasioned by his duties as a peripatetic teacher and for two others of some-what longer duration, Spencer lived the rest of his life in that county. From earliest child-hood he had a Chinese reverence for calligraphy, which, growing to a master passion, became his mission and his livelihood and made his name familiar, like Noah Webster's and Lindley Mur-ray's, in the schoolrooms of his country. As a small boy he studied and often criticized severely the handwriting of the notices posted on the vil-lage bulletin-board and practised his own chi-rography on sandbeds, snowbanks, and other available surfaces, for paper was scarce and ex-pensive in the back settlements. In later years he enjoyed telling the story, half humorous and half pathetic, of his first piece of writing paper. By the time he was twenty years old he had de-veloped his characteristic hand, a sloping, semi-angular style, rapid and legible, and easily lend-ing itself to embellishment with mazy capitals and shaded lines of the sort affected by old-time writing masters. His schooling having been of the scantiest, he was practically self-taught, but a dilute Rousseauism was in the atmosphere, and to Nature Spencer gave all credit for his art, maintaining in prose and rhyme that he had found his inspiration in the graceful forms of the feathered grass, the vine, and the undulating waves of Lake Erie's shore. After a little ex-perience as clerk in a store and supercargo on a lake vessel, he entered on his life-work as a teacher of penmanship. Besides conducting his own school in a log-house on his farm at Geneva, Ohio, he traveled around the country teaching in various academies and business colleges. His innocent, winning manner, the skill and enthusi-asm of his teaching, and the conviction with which he preached the moral, esthetic, and pe-cuniary benefits of the gospel of penmanship made him irresistible. In 1848 he first issued copy-slips with printed instructions; copy-books followed about 1855; and soon a whole series of textbooks began to appear. His five grown sons and a favorite nephew became his chief disciples, and continued and spread his work.

Spencer was married in 1828 to Persis Duty,

by whom he had six sons and five daughters. Despite his devotion to his profession, he took great delight in his family life and had several avocations. In spirit even more a reformer than a pedagogue, he was, like most reformers, too magnanimous to restrict himself to one line and gave himself generously to the temperance and anti-slavery causes. For a time he lived in Ober-lin in order to enjoy congenial society. He was treasurer of his county for twelve years and secretary, from its founding in 1838, of its his-torical society. His wife's death in 1862 was a great affliction to him, and he survived her by less than two years. He died at his home at Geneva, Ohio.

[Biog. sketch, with an introductory note by J. A. Garfield, in *Hist. of Ashtabula County, Ohio* (1878), ed. by W. W. Williams; R. C. Spencer, *Spencer Family Hist. and Geneal.* (Milwaukee, 1889); *The Am. Ann. Cyc.*, 1864.]

G. H. G.

SPENCER, ROBERT (Dec. 1, 1879–July 10, 1931), painter, was born at Harvard, Nebr., the son of Solomon Hogue Spencer, a Swedenborgi-an clergyman, and Frances (Strickler) Spencer. On his father's side he was descended from Sam-uel Spencer, who emigrated from England and settled in Upper Dublin, Pa., prior to 1699, and on his mother's from Hollanders who early set-tled in Virginia. His boyhood was enlivened by close association with his father, and by their common liking for reading and the classics. Be-cause of the movement of the family from Ne-braska to Kansas, Missouri, and Virginia, his early education was somewhat desultory, but they finally remained long enough in Yonkers, N. Y., for him to be graduated in 1899 from high school. He studied at the National Academy of Design in New York, 1899–1901, and at the New York School of Art, 1903–05, where he was encouraged by William Merritt Chase [*q.v.*], the painter. He worked also with Robert Henri [*q.v.*], Francis Coates Jones, and Frank Du-Mond. Except for one year spent in an engi-neering office, he never deviated from painting as a career. Although he traveled extensively abroad, he did not study there. After his early study in New York, where he developed an in-terest in slum dwellers as subjects for his sketch-es, he lived in Frenchtown, Point Pleasant, and Lumberville, Pa., studying with Daniel Garber and painting landscape direct from nature. About 1909 he settled in New Hope, Pa., where he made his home until the end of his life. There he turned to imaginative and philosophical compo-sition, or for subject matter drew upon the mills; in a later and final period he painted almost en-tirely from notes, again making use of the mills and reviving an earlier interest in portraiture. To eke out a living he tried potboilers for a time under the pseudonym of John St. John but without success. In 1914, however, his "Repairing the Bridge" was purchased by the Metropolitan Museum of Art, and he was elected an associate member of the National Academy of Design, of which he became a full member in 1920. On Feb. 27, 1914, he married a painter, Margaret A. Fulton, of Santa Barbara, Cal., by whom he had two daughters. Tall and spare, he was never robust, and suffered several nervous breakdowns that led to prolonged depression and culminated in his suicide in his home, July 10, 1931. He was survived by his wife and children.

He won numerous prizes, among them the second Hallgarten prize at the National Academy of Design (1913), the Jenny Sesnan gold medal of the Pennsylvania Academy of the Fine Arts (1914), the Inness gold medal of the National Academy of Design (1914), a gold medal at the Panama Pacific International Exposition (1915), the gold medal and purchase prize of the Boston Art Club (1915); third prize in the International Exhibition of the Carnegie Institute, Pittsburgh (1926); and a gold medal at the Sesquicentennial Exposition at Philadelphia (1926). One of his paintings, "Across the River," was purchased in 1928 by the National Academy of Design through the Ranger Purchase Fund. He is represented also in the National Arts Club, New York; the Corcoran Gallery of Art, Washington; the Art Institute of Chicago; Carnegie Institute, Pittsburgh; the Albright Art Gallery of the Buffalo Academy of Fine Arts; the Brooklyn Museum; the Detroit Institute of Arts, and the Phillips Memorial Gallery, Washington, where a number of his paintings ("The Evangelist," "Mountebanks and Thieves," "The Barracks," "Day in March," "The End of the Day," "The Seed of a Revolution," "Ship Chandler's Row," and "The Auction") may be seen.

[*Who's Who in America*, 1930–31; F. N. Price, in *Internat. Studio*, Mar. 1923, with portrait; *Am. Art Ann.*, 1929, biog. directory; E. A. Jewell, in *N. Y. Times*, July 5, 1931, sec. 9; Duncan Phillips, *A Collection in the Making* (copr. 1926); obituaries in *Art News*, Aug. 15, 1931, and *Pub. Ledger* (Phila.), July 11, 1931; information from Mrs. Robert Spencer.]

D. G.

SPENCER, SAMUEL (Mar. 2, 1847–Nov. 29, 1906), railway engineer and executive, was born in Columbus, Ga., the only child of Lambert and Vernona (Mitchell) Spencer. He was in the fifth generation of descent from James Spencer, who settled in Talbot County, Md., in 1670. Spencer obtained his early education in the elementary schools of Columbus and at the Georgia

Military Institute in Marietta, which he left in 1863 to enlist in the Confederate army. He served first as a private in the "Nelson Rangers," an independent company of cavalry, and later under Forrest, remaining in uniform until April 1865. Resuming his education, he entered the junior class of the University of Georgia at Athens, and was graduated B.A. in 1867 with first honors. He studied engineering at the University of Virginia in the two following years, and received the C.E. degree in 1869.

Spencer's lifelong railway career began with the Savannah & Memphis Railroad, on which he acquired practical engineering experience in various capacities between 1869 and 1872, ending as principal engineer. After his marriage on Feb. 6, 1872, to Louisa Vivian Benning, daughter of Henry Lewis Benning [*q.v.*], he went north and was for a few months clerk to the superintendent of the New Jersey Southern Railroad at Long Branch, N. J. He then spent four years in charge of one of the transportation divisions of the Baltimore & Ohio Railroad. For a brief period he was general superintendent of the Long Island Railroad, but in 1879 returned to the Baltimore & Ohio as assistant to the president. He rose through successive vice-presidencies to the presidency in December 1887. His incumbency of that office was brief and stormy. His central purpose was to reduce the floating debt, which had grown to over $8,000,000, by rewriting book values and by other drastic measures. In this program he met with considerable success, but his opponents forced his resignation after a year, fearing that Drexel, Morgan & Company were seeking through Spencer to gain control of the road.

In March 1889, Spencer became the railroad expert for Drexel, Morgan & Company, and by December 1890, had become a partner in the firm. In this capacity he had an important part in the Morgan railroad reorganization campaign, particularly in regard to southern railroads. He was appointed in 1893 one of the receivers for the Richmond & Danville Railroad, and for the East Tennessee, Virginia & Georgia Railway. In 1894 a Morgan reorganization created the Southern Railway out of the Richmond & Danville and other moribund southern railroads, and Spencer was made the first president. The twelve intervening years before his death saw efficient, conservative management and great expansion of this Morgan-controlled railroad. Between 1896 and 1906 the mileage of the system increased from 4,391 to 7,515, the number of passengers from 3,427,858 to 11,663,550, the tons of freight from 6,675,750 to 27,339,377, and the annual earnings from $17,114,791 to $53,641,438. The emphasis, however, had been placed on increase in volume of traffic, and the road's physical condition was not improved proportionately. In the two years preceding his death, Spencer was much in the public eye as an opponent of further legislation for rate-regulation. Although he agreed that secret, discriminatory rates were indefensible, and did not deny that the railroads were affected with a public interest, he characterized further government control as "commercial lynch law" (*New York Tribune,* Oct. 12, 1905, p. 9). He appeared before the House Committee on Interstate and Foreign Commerce as spokesman for the railroads, and carried on a vigorous campaign, public and private, against the passage of the Hepburn Act of June 29, 1906.

Spencer was one of seven persons killed in a rear-end collision of two fast passenger trains on his own road, near Lawyers, Campbell County, Va. He was survived by his wife, and by two sons and a daughter. He was regarded with affection by his employees, who erected a monument to him in front of the Southern Railway station at Atlanta. The railroad he administered was a vital factor in the economic development of the New South, and at Spencer's death he was perhaps the most outstanding southerner in the American business world.

[*In Memoriam Samuel Spencer* (1910); Rosewell Page, biog. ed., *Univ. of Va. Its History, Influence, Equipment and Characteristics* (1904), vol. I; Edward Hungerford, *The Story of the Baltimore & Ohio Railroad, 1827–1927* (1928), vol. II; Lewis Corey, *The House of Morgan* (1930); W. J. Northen, *Men of Mark in Ga.,* IV (1908); *Outlook,* Dec. 8, 1906; *Who's Who in America,* 1906–07; Samuel Spencer, "Railway Rates and Industrial Progress" in *Century Mag.,* January 1906; *Collier's,* May 4, 1917, p. 14; *Poor's Manual of the Railroads of the U. S.,* 1869–1906; *N. Y. Tribune,* Feb. 1, Oct. 12, 1905, Nov. 30, Dec. 1, 8, 1906; *Evening Star* (Washington, D. C.), Nov. 29, 30, Dec. 1, 2, 3, 1906.] L. P. B.

SPERRY, ELMER AMBROSE (Oct. 12, 1860–June 16, 1930), engineer, inventor, was born at Cortland, Cortland County, N. Y., the son of Stephen Decatur and Mary (Burst) Sperry and a descendant of Richard Sperry who came to America from England and settled in the New Haven Colony between 1640 and 1650. From his father, who was engaged in the production, transportation, and sale of lumber, Sperry may have inherited his leaning toward machinery, and from his mother, who died soon after his birth, his keen mathematical sense. He was brought up by his paternal grandparents in Cortland. During his school days he took every opportunity to examine and study the machinery in the various shops and factories there and in the laboratories at Cornell University, not far away. For a time

he worked in a book bindery after school hours, and with the money he saved, and through an arrangement made possible by the Young Men's Christian Association, he visited the Centennial Exhibition in Philadelphia in 1876. This visit, with the inspiration he received from the mechanical exhibits he saw there, he always regarded as having determined the direction of his career.

After completing his common-school education he spent three years at the State Normal and Training School, Cortland, and a year of casual attendance at Cornell, 1878–79. Here he had his first insight into dynamo electric machinery, particularly the Gramme type of dynamo built in the University shops. He immediately saw possibilities of increasing the production of electric current by making certain alterations in the dynamo, and succeeded in interesting a Cortland manufacturer, who financed him in the construction of his improved dynamo and an arc lamp as well. These were so successful that he was sent to Syracuse immediately to build a large dynamo capable of operating a series of arc lamps. Upon completing this work early in 1880, he went to Chicago, Ill., and there founded the Sperry Electric Company to manufacture dynamos and arc lamps, and also other electrical appliances. His factory was opened on his twentieth birthday, and in two or three years many industrial plants and municipalities in the Northwest were furnished with Sperry arc light equipment. One of his most notable installations was the 40,000 candle-power electric beacon on the Board of Trade tower, 350 feet high, the highest beacon in the world at that time.

In the middle eighties, Sperry turned his attention to the application of electricity to mining, and in 1888 organized the Sperry Electric Mining Machine Company to manufacture an electrically driven, undercutting, punching machine for use in soft coal mines. He subsequently perfected a continuous chain undercutter, and designed new electric generators and electric mine locomotives, the manufacture of which was undertaken by the Goodman Manufacturing Company of Chicago. From electric mine locomotives it was but a short step to electric street-railway cars, and in 1890 Sperry founded the Sperry Electric Railway Company and established a plant for the manufacture of his cars at Cleveland, Ohio. He operated this concern until 1894, adding constantly his own patented improvements to the equipment, and then sold the plant and all his patents bearing on street railway machinery to the General Electric Company. Turning next to electric automobiles, he was engaged from 1894 to 1900 in the manufacture of electric carriages of his own design, having as their particular feature an improved storage battery capable of operating a vehicle over the remarkable distance of one hundred miles. For the production of his patented storage battery the National Battery Company was organized, with works at Buffalo.

Meanwhile, Sperry had become interested in electro-chemistry, and about 1900 established in Washington, D. C., a research laboratory which he maintained for upwards of ten years. He had there as his associate C. P. Townsend, an electrochemist, and between them they evolved the so-called Townsend Process for manufacturing pure caustic soda from salt, accompanied by the production of hydrogen and chlorine compounds; this process has since been used extensively by one of the largest manufacturers of soda and chlorine products at Niagara Falls, N. Y. Another of their achievements was the chlorine detinning process, for recovering tin from old cans and scrap; this process, involving some thirty patents, was taken over by the Goldsmith Detinning Company. During these years Sperry also devised machinery for producing electric fuse wire, and established the Chicago Fuse Wire Company to manufacture it. As early as 1890 he began investigations and experiments looking toward the development of a compound internal combustion engine using low-grade fuel oil, in other words, a compound Diesel engine. This work was started in Chicago, continued in Cleveland, and after 1910, carried on in Brooklyn, N. Y.; at the time of Sperry's death eight distinct experimental engines had been produced, and the work was still in progress.

Sperry's most distinctive inventions, however, were those which put to practical use the principles of the gyroscope, which had been for several centuries merely an amazing toy. He began work on this project about 1896, and through tedious and expensive investigation and great ingenuity overcame the obstacles involved and successfully combined electrical and mechanical elements into gyroscopic compasses and stabilizers for ships and airplanes which have been great contributions to the safety and comfort of the navigation of the sea and air. The Sperry Gyroscope Company was established in Brooklyn in 1910, in which year Sperry's first compass was tried out on the battleship *Delaware* at the Brooklyn Navy Yard. The compass was shortly adopted by the United States Navy; during the World War it was used in the navies of the Allies, and subsequently by more than sixty steamship lines. The gyroscopic stabilizers for ships appeared in 1913, and in 1914 Sperry's airplane stabilizer was awarded a first prize of 50,000 francs by the French government, through the Aero Club, in a contest for safety devices for airplanes.

In 1918 Sperry produced his high-intensity arc searchlight, 500 per cent. brighter than any light previously made; at the time of his death, it was the standard searchlight of the principal armies and navies of the world. Because of its high actinic value, it proved useful also in a totally different sphere, making possible the taking of motion pictures indoors, without the sun. In 1929 Sperry disposed of the Sperry Gyroscope Company and organized Sperry Products, Inc., to continue investigation and research in other fields. Before he died he had just completed a device for detecting flaws in railroad rails.

Sperry possessed the very unusual combination of inventive ability and clever business sense. In the course of his life he founded eight companies to manufacture his inventions, with an aggregate annual business in excess of $8,000,-000. He obtained more than four hundred patents, both in the United States and in Europe, and for nearly fifty years was an unusually productive worker in a surprisingly wide field of both science and engineering. Many honors were conferred upon him. He was made a member in 1915 of the United States Naval Consulting Board, and chairman of the division of engineering and industrial research of the National Research Council. In addition to the award for his airplane stabilizer, he received in 1914 the John Scott Legacy Medal and Premium, awarded by the Franklin Institute of Philadelphia. He was awarded the Collier Trophy in 1915 and 1916; the John Fritz and the Holley medals in 1927; the American Iron and Steel Institute Medal and the Elliott Cresson Medal in 1929; two decorations from the Emperor of Japan; and two from the last Czar of Russia. Stevens Institute of Technology, Lehigh University, and Northwestern University gave him honorary degrees. He was a founder-member of the American Institute of Electrical Engineers and the American Electrochemical Society; a life member and president (1928–29) of the American Society of Mechanical Engineers; and a member of many other technical, engineering and scientific societies. He was intensely interested in promoting a better understanding between the peoples of the United States and Japan and devoted much of his time in his later years to this work. Throughout his life he was deeply grateful to the Cortland Y. M. C. A. for the opportunity afforded him to attend the Centennial

Exhibition, and in his will he bequeathed $1,-000,000 to the national organization of that body. He married Zula A. Goodman of Chicago on June 28, 1887, and at the time of his death in Brooklyn was survived by two sons and a daughter. Another son had lost his life in 1923, flying an airplane over the English Channel.

[Gano Dunn, W. L. Saunders, and B. A. Fiske, "The Engineering and Scientific Achievements of Elmer Ambrose Sperry," *Mechanical Engineering*, Feb. 1927; *Ibid.*, July, Sept. 1930; *Jour. Am. Inst. Elec. Engineers*, July 1930; *S. A. E. Jour.* (Soc. of Automotive Engineers), July 1930; *Dr. Sperry as We Knew Him* (Sperry Memorial Book Committee, Japan, 1931); *Who's Who in America*, 1926–27; H. F. Pringle, "Gadget-maker," in *New Yorker*, Apr. 19, 1930; *N. Y. Herald Tribune*, June 17, 1930; *N. Y. Times*, June 17, 1930.]   C. W. M—n.

SPERRY, NEHEMIAH DAY (July 10, 1827–Nov. 13, 1911), congressman and postmaster of New Haven, was born in Woodbridge, Conn., the third son of Enoch and Mary Atlanta (Sperry) Sperry and the descendant of Richard Sperry, an original settler in Woodbridge and one of those who aided the regicides in 1661. Nehemiah obtained a scanty education at the district school and later at a private school in New Haven, and while scarcely more than a boy taught successfully in various district schools. As a youth he learned the trade of mason and builder. In 1847 he was married to Eliza H. Sperry of Woodbridge who died in 1873 leaving two children. In 1847 also he began business as a building contractor in partnership with his brother-in-law. The firm, later known as Smith, Sperry & Treat, was successful from the start, and for more than a half century was a leading firm of contractors in New Haven. Early financial success led him into other lines of business, and he became prominent in many New Haven enterprises. He was particularly interested in transportation and among other projects organized the Fair Haven and Westville horse railroad, said to be the first street railroad in the state, obtained for it a charter from the state, and served as its president for ten years. He was also one of the promoters and incorporators of the New Haven and Derby railroad.

Although an able and successful business man, his primary interest was politics, and it is doubtful if, in length of years, his political career has been equaled in Connecticut. In 1853 he was a member of the New Haven common council, and an alderman in 1854. Originally a Whig, he threw himself into the new American or "Know-Nothing" party and was an important leader in Connecticut. As a candidate of that party he was elected secretary of state for 1855 and 1856, and only his lack of the requisite age prevented

his nomination for governor in 1855. In 1856 he was a member of the platform committee of the national convention of the American party that nominated Fillmore and was one of those who bolted the convention because of its refusal to take a strong anti-slavery stand. From then on his affiliations were with the Republican party, and for many years, as chairman of the state Republican committee, he dominated Republican politics in Connecticut. He was a member and secretary of the Republican National Committee during the Lincoln administration, and one of the executive committee in charge of his reëlection. Throughout most of his life Sperry's great influence in politics was as a committeeman behind the scenes rather than as an elected officeholder. In his later life, however, he consented to run for the federal House of Representatives and was elected to eight successive congresses, 1895–1911, when he retired. In Congress his chief interests were the tariff and the postal service. He was an ardent believer in high protection, which he frequently defended on the platform, and in an efficient postal service. His particular hobby was the rural free delivery. For a quarter of a century he advocated this system in season and out. As postmaster of New Haven, 1861–86 and 1890–94, he maintained the office at such high efficiency that it was long considered a model post-office. He was offered membership on a commission to study the postal systems of Europe but declined. He died at New Haven. His second wife, Minnie B. (Newton) Sperry, to whom he was married on Dec. 3, 1874, survived him.

[E. E. Atwater, *Hist. of the City of New Haven* (1887); *Biog. Dir. Am. Cong.* (1928); *Representative Men of Conn.* (1894); *Who's Who in America*, 1910–11; *Hartford Courant, Hartford Times, New Haven Register* and *Springfield Republican*, Nov. 14, 1911; dates of service as postmaster from *Journ. of the Exec. Proc. of the Senate*, vols. XXV, XXVII (1901), XXIX (1909).]   H. U. F.

SPICKER, MAX (Aug. 16, 1858–Oct. 15, 1912), musician, conductor, composer, was born in Königsberg, Germany, the son of Alexander Spicker and his wife, Doris. He received his first musical instruction from Robert Schwalm and Louis Köhler. His parents were anxious that he become a physician, but the boy insisted on entering the Royal Conservatory at Leipzig, where, from 1877 to 1879, he studied piano with Karl Reinecke and Ernst Ferdinand Wenzel, and theory with Solomon Jadassohn. He also attended Oscar Paul's lectures on the history and esthetics of music. On completing his studies he was engaged for a concert tour of Germany and Russia with the violin virtuoso, Miska Hauser. Following this engagement, he started his career as a conductor, and on Oct. 2, 1879, directed the performance of Beethoven's music to Goethe's *Egmont* at the *Stadt-Theatre* of Heidelberg. Subsequently he appeared as conductor in the opera houses of Cologne, Aix-la-Chapelle, Kiel, and at the royal theatres in Ghent, Belgium, and in Potsdam. His health, however, was not equal to the strenuous demands of the opera house, and, when he learned that the directorate of the New York Beethoven-Männerchor was vacant, he applied for the post and received the appointment over 161 rivals. Possibly the enthusiastic recommendation of Anton Rubinstein helped to win him the position.

He came to New York in 1882 and acted as conductor of the Beethoven-Männerchor until 1888, conducting the silver jubilee concerts in 1884. From 1888 to 1895 he was director of the Brooklyn Conservatory of Music, and in the summers of 1889–90 shared the conductorship of the Brighton Beach orchestra concerts with Anton Seidl [*q.v.*]. While he was at the Brooklyn Conservatory he also conducted each winter a series of symphony concerts at the Brooklyn Academy of Music, featuring such artists as Rafael Joseffy, Arthur Friedheim, and Lilli Lehmann. From 1895 to 1907 he was head of the theory department at the National Conservatory of Music in New York, and from May 1898 until 1910 he was music director of the Temple Emanu-El. He was also connected as a reader and editor with the G. Schirmer publishing company. In 1899 he was married to Isabel Sternthal, who, with a son, survived him.

Spicker was a man of simple tastes, sincere and unaffected. An estimate of his place in American music was attempted by A. W. Kramer in an obituary article in *Musical America,* Oct. 26, 1912: in all the many capacities in which he served a musical public, he ". . . won the approval of musicians and music-lovers throughout the length and breadth of the land . . . his compositions are not epoch-making in any sense, nor were they intended to be, but they show and show very conclusively that their creator was a musician of high rank, a man of culture and of deep and scholarly make-up. . . ." Spicker's published compositions include his incidental music to Schiller-Laube's *Demetrius; Suite Moderne,* for orchestra; an arrangement for men's chorus and orchestra of the first finale from Wagner's *Rienzi; The Pilot,* for men's chorus and orchestra; a *Festival-Overture*; and many songs and shorter choral works. He edited many editions of the classics—an *Operatic Anthology* (5 volumes, 1903–04); *Anthology of Sacred Song* (4 volumes, 1902); *The Masterpieces of Vocaliza-*

tion (6 volumes, 1896); a *Synagogical Service* (1901); and *Songs of Germany* (1904), a collection of folk-songs.

[The material for this sketch has been derived largely from an account of Spicker's career published in the *New-Yorker Staats-Zeitung,* Oct. 16, 1912. See also brief accounts in *Grove's Dict. of Music and Musicians, Am. Supp.* (1930), and *Baker's Biog. Dict. of Musicians* (3rd ed. 1919).]

J. T. H.

SPIERING, THEODORE (Sept. 5, 1871–Aug. 11, 1925), violinist, conductor, and teacher, was born in St. Louis, Mo., the elder of two sons of Ernst and Theresa (Bernays) Spiering. His father, an excellent violinist, who was born in Lübeck, Germany, was brought to the United States at the age of ten and for twenty-five years was concert-master of the St. Louis symphony orchestra, as well as first violin of the Beethoven String Quartet. His mother was born in Highland, Ill., the daughter of Charles L. Bernays, a prominent newspaper man. At the age of five the boy had his first lessons on the violin from his father and at seven made his first public appearance. He attended the public schools of St. Louis until he was fifteen, when he went to Cincinnati to study for two years with Henry Schradieck [*q.v.*] at the Cincinnati College of Music. The next four years, 1888–92, he spent in Berlin, where he studied with Joseph Joachim and during his last year was concert-master of the Joachim Hochschule Orchestra. After his return to America, he was married on Oct. 2, 1895, at Arlington, N. J., to Frida Mueller, daughter of Wilhelm Mueller, New York journalist and writer.

As a result of a letter from Joachim to Theodore Thomas [*q.v.*], Spiering in 1892 became a member of the Chicago Symphony Orchestra and remained with it until 1896. During this period he frequently appeared as soloist under Thomas, especially during the World's Columbian Exposition, and organized the Spiering Quartet, which during the twelve years of its existence, 1893–1905, gave over four hundred concerts. He founded and directed the Spiering Violin School in Chicago, 1899–1902, and was a director of the Chicago Musical College, 1902–05, where he was also instructor in violin. Going abroad, he established himself as a concert artist and teacher in Berlin, 1905–09, and made successful concert tours through Germany, England, and Holland. Having attracted the attention of Gustav Mahler, he was appointed concert-master of the New York Philharmonic Society, 1909–11, and during Mahler's prolonged last illness in 1911 conducted the seventeen remaining concerts of the season, each of which added new laurels to his brilliant record as conductor. The

New York press, with rare unanimity, was enthusiastic in his praise, and it was expected that he would be chosen Mahler's successor, but the American tradition prevailed of seeking conductors in Europe. Disappointed, Spiering returned to Berlin, where he was engaged as a conductor, 1911–14, and toured Germany, Scandinavia, and Switzerland as a soloist. He was also musical adviser of the *Neue Freie Volksbühne* in Berlin and conductor of their symphony concerts, besides appearing as guest conductor of the Philharmonic and Blüthner orchestras. Always on the outlook for worthy novelties, he gave the first Berlin performances of such works as symphonies by Georges Enesco and Paul Dukas, the "Concerto in Antique Style" of Max Reger, Frederick Delius' "In a Summer Garden," Emil Reznicek's "Der Sieger" (with unusual success), and Henry Hadley's "The Culprit Fay."

After the outbreak of the World War he made his permanent home in New York, devoting himself largely to teaching (he was a born pedagogue) and to extensive editorial work. In the New York season of 1918–19 he conducted performances of Maurice Maeterlinck's "The Betrothal" with music by Eric Delamarter; in September 1923 he was once more guest conductor in Berlin and Vienna, and won renewed praise. He was appointed conductor of the Portland (Ore.) Symphony Orchestra in 1925. Partly for rest—he had always worked under the handicaps of poor health and extreme nervousness— and partly to select new works for the coming season, he went abroad again, but he was taken ill in Munich and there died, survived by his mother, his wife, and two daughters. He was buried in St. Louis. Though he was a brilliant performer and possessed deep musicianship, he was modest and unassuming in his bearing and affable in his personal relationships. He was the recipient of many honors, among them the French decoration of Officier d'Académie, conferred by the French government in 1905 in recognition of his work in introducing French music, notably chamber music, in the United States.

[*Who's Who in America*, 1924–25; *International Who's Who in Music and Musical Gazetteer*, 1918; *Musical America*, Mar. 25, 1911, the material of which was verified by Spiering's wife and mother, and Aug. 22, 1925; *Sun* (N. Y.) and *Evening Mail* (N. Y.), Feb. 27, 1911; *World* (N. Y.), Feb. 27, Mar. 12, 18, 1911, and Aug. 14, 1925 (obit.); *Brooklyn Daily Eagle*, Mar. 20, 1911; Otto Taubmann, in *Berliner Börsen-Courier*, Sept. 29, 1923; Rudolf Kastner, in *Berliner Morgenpost*, Sept. 30, 1923; Paul Ertel, in *Berliner Lokal Anzeiger*, Oct. 4, 1923; obituaries in *Musical Courier* (N. Y.), and *Musical Leader* (Chicago), Aug. 20, *Münchener Neueste Nachrichten*, Aug. 12, *Münchener Zeitung*, Aug. 14, *Münchener-Augsburger Abend Zeitung*, Aug. 15, and *N. Y. Times*, Aug. 14, 1925.]

F. L. G. C.

SPILLMAN, WILLIAM JASPER (Oct. 23, 1863–July 11, 1931), scientist, agricultural economist, eleventh of fifteen children of Nathan Cosby and Emily Paralee (Pruitt) Spilman, was born in Lawrence County, Mo. His father, a farmer and judge, had little formal education but was a leader in the community. The son earned his way through the University of Missouri, graduating in 1886 as valedictorian and three years later receiving the degree of M.S. While at the university he changed the spelling of his name. On May 20, 1889, he married Mattie L. Ramsay, who with one son survived him.

After brief periods of teaching in state normal schools of Missouri and Oregon and at Vincennes University, Spillman in 1894 joined the staff of Washington State College, Pullman, and its experiment station. The need of a wheat better adapted to conditions in Washington led him to breed new varieties. His account of his work in hybridization contained essentially an independent statement of the two chief tenets of Mendelism ("Quantitative Studies on the Transmission of Parent Characters to Hybrid Offspring," *Proceedings of . . . the Association of American Agricultural Colleges and Experiment Stations . . . 1901,* 1902). His pleas for quantitative studies in plant breeding gave considerable impetus to this kind of research. Because of his work in genetics he was appointed in 1902 as agrostologist in charge of grass and forage plant investigations in the United States Department of Agriculture. In this capacity he instituted studies of types of farming and farming methods. An office of farm management was created in 1904, and to the direction of its work he gave his major efforts thenceforth until his resignation in 1918, as the result of friction with Secretary Houston (see *Senate Document 300,* 65 Cong., 2 Sess., and *House Resolution 611,* 65 Cong., 3 Sess.). After a three-year interim during which he was associate editor of the *Farm Journal,* he returned to the Department, where he remained until his death. From 1922 he was also professor of commercial geography in the Foreign Service School of Georgetown University.

Spillman "to a very unusual degree . . . combined practical organizing ability with penetrating power of abstract reasoning" (*Journal of Farm Economics,* January 1932, p. 1). His hobby was mathematics, but "his fertile mind suggested many more things than one man could do. . . . He was an inspirer of men, not only because of his own exuberance and fertile imagination but because of his personal relationships" (*Ibid.*). Among his important achievements were the development of farm management surveys and the extensive use of this method of approach to farm problems in representative areas. In 1903 he devised the dot-map method of presenting statistics graphically. He also directed historical and geographical studies, including the preparation of atlases on agriculture. Under his ægis demonstration work and the county-agent system were begun. He discovered the mathematical form of the law of diminishing returns with relation to the results of the use of fertilizers on farms. Later he completed a means of solving arithmetically for several variables the exponential yield curve or law of biological growth. The domestic allotment plan of farm relief was outlined in detail in his book, *Balancing the Farm Output* (1927). His leadership and pioneer efforts in the field of farm management were early recognized and he was chosen the first president of the American Farm Economic Association (1910–12). He was a member of the National Academy of Sciences and many other learned bodies, and spoke frequently before both scientific and popular audiences. His unusual record of accomplishment in many and diverse fields is reflected in his writings, over three hundred in number, ranging from popular articles for the farm press to highly technical mathematical treatises.

[*Who's Who in America*, 1930–31; *Experiment Station Record*, Nov. 1931; E. N. Bressman, "Spillman's Work on Plant Breeding," *Science*, Sept. 23, 1932; Lillian Crans, *A List of the Printed and Mimeographed Publications of Dr. W. J. Spillman* (U. S. Bureau of Agric. Economics, Aug. 1931); E. F. Gaines, "The Value of the Hybrid Wheats Produced by the State College of Washington," *Northwest Science,* Mar. 1933; Earl Godwin, "Steps Back to the Farm," *Country Life in America,* Mar. 15, 1911, portr.; F. C. Kelly, "A Wonderful Question Answerer," *Am. Mag.,* Jan. 1917, portr.; *Wash. Acad. Sci. Jour.,* vol. XXI, p. 346 (Aug. 1931); articles by C. B. Smith, E. H. Thomson, and G. F. Warren, in *Jour. Farm Econ.,* Jan. 1932; *Evening Star* (Washington, D. C.), July 12, 1931; *Memorial Honoring the Late Dr. W. J. Spillman* (Wash. State Coll., 1931); *The Official Record* (U. S. Dept. Agric.), July 25, 1931; biography of Spillman (MS., 1933) by his son, Dr. Ramsay Spillman, New York City.]
E. E. E.

SPILSBURY, EDMUND GYBBON (Dec. 7, 1845–May 28, 1920), mining engineer and metallurgist, son of Francis Gybbon Spilsbury, was born in London, England. He received most of his education in Belgium, attending a preparatory school at Liège and then pursuing technical studies at the University of Louvain, where he was graduated in 1862. After a post-graduate "practical course" at Clausthal, Germany, he was for three years in the employ of the Eschweiler Zinc Company of Stolberg, Germany, which was engaged on a large scale in mining and smelting lead and zinc. In 1865 he took

charge of its works in Sardinia, and subsequently was sent to the Atlas Mountains in Morocco. During his stay in Sardinia he had occasion to entertain, on behalf of the company, the Duke of Brabant, afterward King Leopold II of the Belgians, who was in the island on a hunting trip. This experience resulted in a lasting friendship. Returning to London, Spilsbury in 1867 entered the service of the British firm of McClean & Stilman, for whom he supervised construction of the iron gates for the Surrey Commercial Docks. In 1868, in the employ of J. Casper Harkort, he designed much of the detail work of the Keulenberg Bridge in Holland, and of bridges over the Danube in Vienna, and over the Rhine at Düsseldorf.

In 1870 he came to the United States in the employ of an Austro-Belgian metallurgical firm to investigate American lead and zinc resources. He spent two years in this work, then resigned to establish himself in private practice. As general manager of smelting works at Bamford, Pa., he introduced the Harz system of dressing zinc ores into Pennsylvania and New Jersey. In 1879 he built the Lynchburg Blast Furnace and Iron Works in Virginia, at about the same time acted as consulting engineer for the Coleraine Coal & Iron Company of Philadelphia, and subsequently (1883) became general manager of the Haile gold mine in South Carolina. From 1887 to 1897 he was in the employ of Cooper, Hewitt & Company of New York, serving from 1888 to 1897 as managing director of their Trenton Iron Company, Trenton, N. J. Here he introduced the Elliott locked wire rope and the Bleichert system of aerial tramways, publishing, in 1890, a thirty-five page brochure, *Wire Rope Tramways; with Special Reference to the Bleichert Patent System.* In 1893 he presided at sessions of the mining division of the International Engineering Congress, held in connection with the World's Columbian Exposition at Chicago. After 1897 he was in private practice as consulting engineer until his death, traveling in connection with his work into many parts of the world. He had but recently returned from Brazil when, in the spring of 1920, he submitted to an operation for cataract, in a New York hospital, and died of heart failure soon afterward. He had married Rosa Hooper, and was survived by three sons and a daughter.

During his career Spilsbury contributed a number of significant papers to the *Transactions of the American Institute of Mining Engineers,* among which were: "On Rock-Drilling Machinery" (vol. III, 1875); "A New Air Compressor" (vol. VIII, 1880); "Gold Mining in

South Carolina" (vol. XII, 1884) ; "Notes on the General Treatment of the Southern Gold Ores, and Experiments in Matting Iron Sulphides" (vol. XV, 1887) ; "The Chlorination of Gold-Bearing Sulphides" (vol. XVI, 1888) ; "Notes on a Novel Cable-Transfer for Railroad-Cars and the Use of the Patent Locked-Wire Rope" (vol. XX, 1892) ; "Improvements in Mining and Metallurgical Appliances during the Last Decade" (vol. XXVII, 1898) ; and "Improvement in Cyanide Process" (vol. XLI, 1911). To the *Mining and Scientific Press* he contributed two informal, entertaining articles on some of his professional experiences ("Technical Reminiscences," July 10, Aug. 28, 1915). He was active in the work of the numerous professional societies to which he belonged, being called upon frequently for service on various committees.

[*Who's Who in America*, 1920–21; *Trans. Am. Soc. Civil Engineers*, vol. LXXXIV (1921) ; *Trans. Am. Inst. Mining and Metallurgical Engineers*, vol. LXVI (1922) ; *Engineering and Mining Jour.*, June 5, 1920 ; *Mining and Scientific Press*, June 12, 1920 ; *N. Y. Times*, May 30, 1920.]

B. A. R.

SPINNER, FRANCIS ELIAS (Jan. 21, 1802–Dec. 31, 1890), treasurer of the United States, was born in that part of the town of German Flats, Herkimer County, N. Y., which afterwards became the village of Mohawk. He was the eldest son of the Rev. John Peter and Mary Magdalene Fidelis (Brument) Spinner. His father, a native of Werbach, Baden, had been a Roman Catholic priest in Germany, but in 1801 had renounced that faith and emigrated to America; at the time of Francis' birth he was pastor of the Reformed Dutch Church at German Flats. Francis was a pupil in four Mohawk Valley district schools and in his old age stated that he learned nothing in any of them (letter to F. G. Barry, in *College and School*, Utica, N. Y., April 1890; Hartley, *post*, pp. 192–95). His father apprenticed him to a confectioner at Albany and later to a saddler at Amsterdam, N. Y.; during his spare time he devoted himself to reading and formed an acquisitiveness of mind that persisted throughout his life.

As time went on he became a merchant in Herkimer, major-general of artillery in the state militia, cashier, director, and president of the Mohawk Valley Bank. In politics he was long known as an aggressive Democrat. He was appointed to supervise the building of the state insane hospital at Utica, and during the Polk administration was auditor of the Port of New York. Identifying himself with the anti-slavery wing of the Democratic party, he was elected to Congress from the Herkimer district in 1854. In the protracted speakership contest of 1855–56 he

refused to caucus with the House Democrats and was the only representative elected as a Democrat whose vote was cast for Nathaniel P. Banks [*q.v.*]. For the rest of that Congress he was affiliated with the Whig-Republican majority. He served on the committee that dealt with the Brooks-Sumner assault, and was a member of the conference committee in charge of the long-disputed army appropriation bill in the summer of 1856. To the two succeeding Congresses he was elected as a Republican by large pluralities. He became known as an outspoken and inflexibly honest representative who never left his colleagues long in doubt as to his stand on any public question.

A vigorous supporter of Lincoln, he was appointed treasurer of the United States in March 1861. In that capacity he served fourteen years, under three presidents. When he took office, the Treasury was paying out $8,000,000 a month; within sixty days the expenditure amounted to $2,000,000 a day. It was Spinner's task to guard the government's money chest in a time of perils and difficulties for which there was no precedent. In connection with the issue of Treasury notes during the Civil War years, Spinner's autograph signature—the despair of would-be forgers—came to be a kind of national symbol, known to all. In the expansion of his bureau and its personnel at a time when men were needed for military service he employed a few young women, at first to count currency bills and later to take over various clerical duties, so that by the end of the war women had a definite status in the civil service. For this innovation he has always been given the chief credit.

Following his resignation in 1875, caused by friction with the department head over responsibility for appointments, Spinner went to Jacksonville, Fla., where he lived much in the open for fifteen years. At eighty he took up the study of Greek as a mental recreation. He died in his eighty-ninth year of cancer of the face, after prolonged suffering. On June 22, 1826, he had married Caroline Caswell of Herkimer; one of three daughters survived him.

[*Biog. Dir. Am. Cong.* (1928) ; N. S. Benton, *A Hist. of Herkimer County* (1856) ; A. L. Howell, "The Life and Public Services of Gen. Francis E. Spinner," *Papers Read Before the Herkimer County Hist. Soc.*, vol. II (1902) ; W. R. Hooper, in *Hours at Home*, Sept. 1870 ; reports of Treasurer of U. S., 1861–75 ; I. S. Hartley, *Mag. of Am. Hist.*, Mar. 1891, pp. 185–200 ; Hugh McCulloch, *Men and Measures of Half a Century* (1882) ; J. C. Derby, *Fifty Years among Authors, Books and Publishers* (1884), pp. 644–46 ; M. C. Ames, *Ten Years in Washington* (1873) ; L. E. Chittenden, *Personal Reminiscences* (1893) ; S. P. Brown, *The Book of Jacksonville* (1895) ; *N. Y. Times*, Jan. 1, 1891 ; *Fla. Times-Union* (Jacksonville), Jan. 1, 1891.]

W. B. S.

SPITZKA, EDWARD ANTHONY (June 17, 1876–Sept. 4, 1922), anatomist and criminologist, son of Dr. Edward Charles Spitzka [q.v.] and Catherine (Watzek) Spitzka, was born in New York City. He was educated in the College of the City of New York and obtained his medical degree in 1902 from the College of Physicians and Surgeons, Columbia University. He was assistant demonstrator of anatomy at Columbia University, 1905–06, and then became professor of general anatomy at Jefferson Medical College, Philadelphia, Pa. On June 20, 1906, ne was married to Alice Eberspacher of New York. He was made director and professor of anatomy at the Daniel Baugh Institute of Anatomy at Jefferson Medical College in 1911, but in 1914 he resigned to take up the practice of nervous and mental diseases in New York. Upon the entry of the United States into the World War, he went to a medical officers' training camp at Fort Benjamin Harrison, Ind. After being assigned to duty at Camp Grant, Ill., he was promoted to the grade of lieutenant-colonel and in the summer of 1918 was sent to France in command of the sanitary train of the 86th Division. When he was discharged from the army in the following year he returned to practice in New York. A life full of early promise and of frustrated achievement had its tragic culmination three years later in his sudden death from cerebral hemorrhage at his home in Mount Vernon, N. Y. At the time of his death he held the position of medical referee with the United States Veterans' Bureau.

His most important contributions to medicine are his studies upon the human brain. These include notable studies of the size and structure of the brains of Japanese, Eskimos, and certain South Sea islanders, observations on electrocution and its effects, and studies of the brains of criminals and of noted men. He was particularly interested in the anatomical variations in the brains of criminals, and performed the autopsy on Leon F. Czolgosz, the assassin of Pres. William McKinley [q.v.], and made a detailed study of the brain. He had a special interest as well in the evolutionary development of the nervous system, which he studied comparatively in the primates and in the higher mammals. He made other notable studies upon the morphology of the ductless glands, wrote on Resuscitation of Persons Shocked by Electricity (1909), and edited the eighteenth American edition of Henry Gray's Anatomy, Descriptive and Applied (1910), which is a lasting monument to his memory. In his chosen work he had the accuracy and the zeal of the investigator together with the broader and deeper interest of the cultural scientist, and his studies show marked originality. He was tall and of heavy, powerful build. Though he was inclined to be melancholic and reticent of speech, with little inclination for ordinary social activities, he displayed when he was interested an unexpectedly good command of language, and had a gift for intimate friendships.

[Who's Who in America, 1922–23; Jour. Am. Medic. Assoc., Sept. 16, 1922; Jour. of Nervous and Mental Diseases (N. Y.), Jan. 1923; Am. Men of Sci. (3rd edition, 1921), ed. by J. M. Cattell and D. R. Brimhall; Dict. Am. Medic. Biog. (edition of 1928), ed. by H. A. Kelly and W. L. Burrage; bibliog. in Index Cat. Lib. of Surgeon Gen's. Office, U. S. Army, 2 ser., vol. XVI (1911); obituary in N. Y. Times, Sept. 6, 1922.]

J.M.P.

SPITZKA, EDWARD CHARLES (Nov. 10, 1852–Jan. 13, 1914), neurologist and psychiatrist, was born in the city of New York to Charles Anthony and Johanna (Tag) Spitzka. His father, a watch and clock maker of Germano-Slavonic origin, had been compelled to flee from Germany following the Revolution of 1848, a cause which he had espoused. The son was educated in the public schools, and after two years in the College of the City of New York entered the medical department of the University of the City of New York (later New York University), from which he graduated in 1873. He spent the following three years in post-graduate study in Europe, first in Leipzig and later in Vienna. In Vienna he came under the instruction of Theodor Meynert, the great anatomist and psychiatrist, and of Samuel Leopold Schenk, distinguished in the field of human and comparative embryology, whose influence had much to do with shaping his future career. On June 30, 1875, he married Catherine Watzek in Vienna. A year later he began a general practice in New York, but after a few years he limited his practice to nervous and mental diseases. Immediately after his return he took up neurological work at Mt. Sinai and St. Mark's hospitals and at the Northeastern Dispensary. From pathological material collected from public and private asylums of the vicinity he produced an essay on The Somatic Etiology of Insanity (1882) published as a supplement to the American Journal of Neurology and Psychiatry, which in 1878 won the W. and S. Tuke prize offered by the British Medico-Psychological Association. In the same year he was awarded the William A. Hammond prize of the American Neurological Association for his essay on "The Anatomical and Physiological Effects of Strychnia on the Brain, Spinal Cord, and Nerves" (Journal of Nervous and Mental Disease, April 1879). One of the pioneers of his specialty in America, he gained a nation-wide reputation as a consultant and as a medico-legal expert in cases involving insanity and injury to the nervous system. His most noted case was that of Charles J. Guiteau, the assassin of Pres. James Abram Garfield [q.v.], whom he considered insane.

He filled the position of professor of comparative anatomy at the Columbia Veterinary College at different times, and was professor of anatomy and physiology of the nervous system at the New York Post-Graduate Medical School, 1882–85. Working upon the comparative and human anatomy of the nervous system throughout his career, he made many notable contributions to the knowledge of this subject. He made exhaustive studies of the central nervous system of birds and reptiles, and is credited with being the original discoverer of the so-called Lissauer tract in the spinal cord; he also devoted himself to the morbid anatomy of organic diseases of the central nervous system and to the classification of mental disorders by clinical methods. He published a textbook on *Insanity, Its Classification, Diagnosis, and Treatment* (1883) and was the author of monographs on "The Chronic Inflammatory and Degenerative Affections of the Spinal Cord," and "Anaemia and Hyperaemia of the Brain and Spinal Cord," in William Pepper's *A System of Practical Medicine* (vol. V, 1886), and on brain histology and the spinal cord in *A Reference Handbook of the Medical Sciences* (vol. VIII, 1889), edited by A. H. Buck, popularly known as Woods' Reference Handbook. Among the subjects he treated in journal articles were the relation of race and heredity to insanity, the historic rôle of mental disorders, the misconceptions regarding physical abnormality of criminals, and the legal and biologic disabilities of illegitimate children. For three years (1881–84) he was editor of the *American Journal of Neurology and Psychiatry*; in 1883–84 he was president of the New York Neurological Society, and in 1890 president of the American Neurological Association. Tall and heavily built, with a rugged, smooth-shaven face, he was an impulsive man, quick in action, thought, and speech. A contemporary wrote of him that he was "a red headed, hot-headed man, but finely trained in anatomy . . . very scornful of American work and violently antagonistic to the state methods of caring for the insane at that time— as he had a right to be" (C. L. Dana, "Early Neurology in the United States," *Journal of the American Medical Association*, May 5, 1928, p. 1422) and adds that his critical attitude was of great benefit to New York neurology. He died suddenly as the result of a cerebral hemorrhage, leaving his wife and a son, Edward Anthony Spitzka [q.v.].

[*Who's Who in America*, 1912–13; E. A. Spitzka, in *Jour. of Nervous and Mental Disease* (N. Y.), Apr. 1914; *Am. Medic. Biogs.* (1920), ed. by H. A. Kelly and W. L. Burrage; N. E. Brill, *N. Y. Medic. Jour.*, May 9, 1914, with portrait; obituary in *N. Y. Times*, Jan. 14, 1914.]   J. M. P.

SPIVAK, CHARLES DAVID (Dec. 25, 1861–Oct. 16, 1927), physician, author, editor, was born in Krementchug, government of Poltava, Russia, the son of Samuel David Spivakowsky and his wife, Deborah Adel Dorfman. From his father and the Cheder, a Jewish school, he received the traditional Hebrew education, while he was self-educated in secular subjects. He took and passed successfully the examination of the local Gymnasium, and continued his private studies. In common with his revolutionary-minded contemporaries in Russia, he participated in illegal political activities, until the danger of imprisonment compelled him to leave the country. Joining the Kiev group, "Am Olam," a society of young intellectuals who planned to emigrate to America and establish themselves there as agriculturists on a communal basis, he arrived in the United States in March 1882. Ignorant of the language and without means, he started out as a laborer, loading and unloading freight in railroad yards, paving Fifth Avenue in New York City, working in wool and cotton mills in Maine, as a typesetter on the *Jewish Messenger*, and as a farm-hand in Alliance, N. J., where he later taught. Settling in Philadelphia, he studied medicine at the Jefferson Medical College, was graduated with the M.D. degree in 1890, and then attended lectures at the University of Berlin, 1891–92. Two years later he was appointed chief of the clinic for gastro-intestinal diseases at the Philadelphia Polyclinic. From 1896 to 1901 he was associate professor in the department of medicine of the University of Denver; professor of anatomy, 1897–98; and then professor of clinical medicine and chief of the clinical laboratory at Denver and Gross College of Medicine, 1900–07. He was president of the Colorado Medical Library Association, 1902; librarian of the Denver Academy of Medicine, and a member of numerous medical societies. In 1920 he was delegated by the Joint Distribution Committee of the American Funds for Jewish War Sufferers to study health and sanitation conditions among the Jews in the devastated war areas of Europe. His main achievement, however, was the founding of the Jewish Consumptives' Relief Society in 1904, for the care of tubercular patients without means, and the building of the Society's Sanatorium in Denver, Colo., acknowledged to be one of the best in the country. From the inception until his death Spivak acted as secretary and gastro-enterologist to the Sanatorium. The locality of the Sanatorium Buildings was named Spivak, Colo., in his honor after his death.

Notwithstanding his onerous professional and communal duties as physician and social worker, Spivak found time for a many-sided literary activity. He wrote with equal facility in Hebrew, Yiddish, Russian, and English. (His Hebrew and Yiddish writings appeared under his Jewish name Hayyim Spivak.) Even during his early years of struggle he contributed to the *Woskhod* (Russian) and *Hameliz* (Hebrew), both in St. Petersburg, as well as to Yiddish and Anglo-Jewish periodicals in the United States. The greater part of his writing, however, has been chiefly in the field of gastro-enterology, in which he won a national reputation (see the *Index-Catalogue of the Library of the Surgeon-General's Office, U. S. Army*, 2 ser., vol. XVI, 1911). Among his other interests were medical bibliography, linguistics, and the history of medicine, particularly of Jewish physicians and their achievements. His familiarity with the Hebrew sources led him to make many interesting contributions to the history of early medicine. He was editor of *Medical Libraries* from 1898 to 1902, and a *Longevity Almanach* (Yiddish) in 1921; compiler and editor of *Medical Coloradoana*; author of a number of bibliographies on medicine among the Jews; and a contributor to the *Annals of Medical History* and the *Jewish Encyclopedia*. Of special value were his articles on medicine in the Bible, the Talmud, and in Rabbinic literature. Two periodicals, the *Denver Jewish News*, 1915–18, and the *Sanatorium*, 1907–27, appeared in Denver under his editorship. For the *Jewish Daily Forward* of New York City he wrote a series of popular articles on hygiene and longevity from a Jewish standpoint. He had an insatiable curiosity for data bearing on medical notions in ancient Jewish folklore. Of his linguistic researches may be mentioned a *Yiddish Dictionary* (1911), compiled in collaboration with Solomon Bloomgarden [*q.v.*], containing all the Hebrew and Chaldaic elements of the Yiddish language illustrated with proverbs and idiomatic expressions.

Spivak was married to Jennie (Gittel) Charsky in Philadelphia in 1893. She survived him with one son and two daughters.

[*Who's Who in America*, 1926–27; *Who's Who in Am. Med.*, 1925; *Who's Who in Am. Jewry*, 1926; *Rocky Mountain News* (Denver, Colo.), Oct. 17, 1927; Zalmen Reisen, *Lexicon fun der Yiddisher Literatur*, vol. II (Vilna, 1927); *Am. Rev. of Tuberculosis*, Dec. 1927; A. Levinson, *Charles D. Spivak's Contribution to Medicine*, reprinted from *Medic. Life*, Jan. 1928.]
I. S.

SPOFFORD, AINSWORTH RAND (Sept. 12, 1825–Aug. 11, 1908), librarian, the son of the Rev. Luke Ainsworth and Grata (Rand) Spofford, was born in Gilmanton, N. H. He was a descendant of John Spofford who came to Massachusetts with the Rev. Ezekiel Rogers' company in 1638 and in 1643 settled in what became the town of Rowley, Mass. Ainsworth prepared under private tutors and at Williston Seminary for admission to Amherst College, but ill health prevented him from entering. Instead, he gave himself over to a course in books; through a long life they were his unnumbered and always unforgotten *almae matres*. At the age of nineteen he removed to Cincinnati, where he was successively a clerk in a bookstore, a bookseller and publisher, and, from 1859, associate editor of the *Cincinnati Commercial*. In 1856 he was a delegate to the convention in Philadelphia that nominated John C. Frémont for the presidency. Books appealed to him far more strongly than politics, however, and accordingly, while in Washington in 1861 after the battle of Bull Run, which his newspaper had sent him to report, he accepted an appointment as chief assistant to Dr. John G. Stephenson, then librarian of Congress. "With his entrance upon librarianship he put away the merely contemporary, and from that moment no one could find him partisan upon a current issue, nor, except after insistent effort, could discover his opinion upon it" (Putnam, *post*). Following Stephenson's resignation, Spofford, on Dec. 1, 1864, became the librarian-in-chief and directed the affairs of the Library of Congress until 1897. In that year, on the removal of the library from its old quarters in the Capitol to the building newly erected for it, he gave way to a younger man and once more took the chief assistant's position, continuing in that office until his death. On Sept. 15, 1852, he was married to Sarah Putnam Partridge of Franklin, Mass.; three children were born to them.

Spofford, in his day and land, was perhaps the most widely renowned of the librarians of the old school, those masters and servants at once of the books about them, who took, or seemed to take, all that was between the covers as their province, and who counted what they brought back with them from personal journeyings over endless printed pages as of greater importance in the administration of a library than bibliographical method. With Spofford, these journeyings were unceasing; his memory retained all that he found along the way, and nothing escaped him. So extraordinary was his memory that he has been likened to the celebrated Magliabecchi. For nearly half a century he was known as an unfailing source of factual knowledge to official and unofficial Washington and to an unnumbered constituency beyond. His ability to recall on the spur of the moment a fact which he had somewhere read made him a conspicuous and even unique member of various cultural and learned societies in Washington, and was an ever ready aid to him as the author and the compiler of numerous volumes. A list of his publications, brought together by his successor as chief assistant librarian, Appleton P. C. Griffin [q.v.], and printed in the pamphlet *Ainsworth R. Spofford, 1825–1908* (1909), contains no less than 184 titles. Of yet more importance to the Library, Spofford's memory seemed to carry within its recesses a complete record of the books needed in the Library collections, and never a title of the kind escaped him as he scanned the catalogues of dealers. His memory and industry together, and his astonishing success in the use of the fund for the purchase of books, which never amounted to more than $10,000 a year, enabled him to increase the collections he administered from some 60,000 items in 1861 to more than 1,000,000 items in 1897, and to lay the foundations for the National Library which he ever insisted the Library of Congress should be. Out of this notable achievement grew his other and more easily visible one, the establishment of a separate building to house the growing institution. After fully twenty years of opposition, discouragement, and delay, he prevailed upon Congress to provide for it, and in 1897 it was completed. This building (now greatly enlarged), and the many books in it which Spofford obtained are his lasting contributions to American cultural life. In choosing the quotations to be lettered here and there in the building, one that he took from Carlyle must have had its own special meaning to him: "The true university of these days is a collection of books."

[Knowledge of Spofford may be gained from his *A Book for All Readers* (1900) and from his "Washington Reminiscences," *Atlantic Monthly*, May, June 1898. See also Jeremiah and A. T. Spofford, *A Geneal. Record . . . Descendants of John Spofford* (1888); Herbert Putnam, in the *Independent*, Nov. 19, 1908, reprinted in the *Library Jour.*, Dec. 1908, presenting a striking picture of Spofford, "a soul aloof in a world ideal—the world of books"; *Records of the Columbia Hist. Soc., Washington, D. C.*, vol. XII (1909); *Evening Star* (Washington), Aug. 12, 1908. Certain facts in this sketch were supplied by Spofford's daughter, Miss Florence P. Spofford, Washington, D. C.] W. A. S—e.

SPOFFORD, HARRIET ELIZABETH PRESCOTT (Apr. 3, 1835–Aug. 14, 1921), author, was one of several children of Sarah Jane (Bridges) and Joseph Newmarch Prescott, a merchant. She was descended from John Prescott, who in 1643 was one of the first settlers of Lancaster, Mass. She lived in Calais, Me., her birthplace, until she was fourteen years of age. At about that time her father set out for the West, hoping to better his fortunes, and soon afterwards her mother removed to Newburyport, Mass., thereafter the permanent home of the family. Here Harriet Prescott attended the excellent Putnam Free School for three years. During this time one of her essays attracted the attention of Thomas Wentworth Higginson [q.v.], who encouraged her ambition to become a writer. Her formal education was completed by a brief period at the Pinkerton Academy in Derry, N. H. Her father having returned from the West fortuneless and broken in health, she began contributing to newspapers and periodicals before she was twenty in order to assist with the financial burdens of the household. She worked tirelessly but with little recognition and scant payment until her story "In a Cellar" was published in February 1859 by the newly established *Atlantic Monthly*. Mr. Higginson, proud of the "demure little Yankee girl," introduced her into the literary circles of Boston, and opportunity opened before her. In rapid succession during the next few years she published *Sir Rohan's Ghost* (1860), *The Amber Gods, and Other Stories* (1863), and *Azarian: an Episode* (1864), all characterized by highly romantic details, elaborate word-painting, and an absence of any definite moral purpose. On Dec. 19, 1865, she married Richard Smith Spofford, Jr., a talented young lawyer of Newburyport. She spent the winters of her early married life in Washington, D. C., where her husband was professionally associated with Caleb Cushing [q.v.]. One of her later works, *Old Washington* (1906), pleasantly reflects the interest she always took in the city. In 1874 Mr. Spofford bought picturesque Deer Island in the Merrimac River near Newburyport, and there, in a delightful old house of generous size, she continued her writing. During the next thirty years a succession of stories, articles, and poems made her name a familiar one to readers of the outstanding American magazines; many of these contributions were later collected into such volumes as *New-England Legends* (1871), *In Titian's Garden and Other Poems* (1897), and *Old Madame and Other Tragedies* (1900). Her interest in domestic life found expression in such works as *Art Decoration Applied to Furniture* (1878), and *The Servant Girl Question* (1881), published originally in *Harper's Bazar,* for which she wrote regularly. Her genius for friendship and her generous appraisal of others are charmingly revealed in *A Little Book of Friends* (1916), an account of eight literary contemporaries. Although she was best known to a popular audience by her fiction, she considered poetry her more significant work. The luxuriant fancy which led her to write over-opulent descriptions in her early prose finds a natural expression in the imagery of her verse.

During her later life, she spent many winters in Boston. One trip to Europe with her husband, and one after his death in 1888 were her only distant wanderings. New England and an imaginative world of romance were the regions she knew best. She took no active part in the reform movements of her time, although she was sympathetic toward them. The beauty of her island home and the companionship of congenial friends and kinsfolk brought her the great satisfactions of her life. In a poem written at the time of Richard Spofford's death ("R. S. S. at Deer Island on the Merrimac"), John Greenleaf Whittier [*q.v.*] reveals with quiet sensitiveness the happy hospitality of that home. Mrs. Spofford was a woman of distinguished presence, and all who saw her moving about in her garden, clothed in the trailing black garments she always wore as she grew older, were impressed by her serenity and grace. She died at Deer Island, in her eighty-seventh year. Her only child, a son, died in infancy.

[William Prescott, *The Prescott Memorial* (1870); *Who's Who in America,* 1920–21; Elizabeth K. Halbeisen, *Harriet Prescott Spofford* (1935), with portraits; Rose Terry Cooke, in *Our Famous Women* (1884); J. J. Currier, *"Ould Newberry"* (1896); Jeremiah Spofford, *A Geneal. Record . . . Descendants of John Spofford* (1888); review in *North Am. Review,* Jan. 1865, and one by P. E. More in *Atlantic Monthly,* Aug. 1897; obituary in *Boston Transcript,* Aug. 15, 1921; information from relatives and friends.]
B. M. S.

SPOONER, JOHN COIT (Jan. 6, 1843–June 11, 1919), senator from Wisconsin, born at Lawrenceburg, Ind., moved with his parents to Madison, Wis., in 1859. His father, Philip Loring Spooner, born in New Bedford of old Massachusetts stock, was married in 1839 to Lydia Lord Coit, of Plainfield, Conn., and lived for twenty years at Lawrenceburg, Ind. He was a lawyer, and the reporter of four volumes (XII–XV) of the *Wisconsin Reports.* John attended the University of Wisconsin, receiving his degree while on duty at the front in 1864. Mustered out with the brevet rank of major, he became colonel on the staff of Gov. Lucius Fairchild [*q.v.*], whose secretary he was; and in 1867

he was admitted to the Wisconsin bar. He married Anna E. Main of Madison, on Sept. 10, 1868, and moved in 1870 to Hudson, on the western border of the state, where he at once took rank as a brilliant lawyer. In due time he was elected to the Assembly (1872) and appointed as regent of the University of Wisconsin. His brief for the state in the case of *Schulenberg* vs. *Harriman* (21 *Wallace,* 44) helped establish the federal law as to railroad land grants, and pointed to the class of legal business for which he was fitted. As counsel for the Chicago, St. Paul, Minneapolis & Omaha Railway, and for the roads that were merged as the Chicago & Northwestern Railway, he developed marked talent, and as legislative adviser he watched proceedings at Madison, where he was described as "chief of the corporation lobbyists" (*Milwaukee Sentinel,* Jan. 16, 1885, p. 4). As a campaigner for Blaine in 1884 he established his reputation on the stump.

He was elected to the United States Senate in 1885, with the patronage of Philetus Sawyer [*q.v.*], defeating Lucius Fairchild in the caucus and William F. Vilas in the canvass. Spooner sacrificed a large private income when he became senator, but he acquired immediate reputation as an able debater, brilliant parliamentarian, and sound constitutional lawyer. When his term came to an end in 1891, Wisconsin was in the hands of the Democrats, who chose Vilas to succeed him. Spooner returned to Madison, resumed the practice of his profession without abandoning his activity in politics, and assisted as counsel in the gerrymander cases, whereby the supreme court of Wisconsin in 1892 twice set aside Democratic apportionment laws (81 *Wisconsin Reports,* 440; 83 *Wisconsin Reports,* 90). He offered himself for sacrifice in 1892 when he was defeated for governor by George W. Peck [*q.v.*]. In 1897 when the term of Vilas ended the Republicans were once more in complete control of Wisconsin, and Spooner was returned to his seat in the Senate. For the next ten years, "the day of the Elder Statesman" (Stephenson, *post,* p. 134), Spooner was a notable national figure, sharing with Nelson W. Aldrich, William B. Allison, and Orville H. Platt [*qq.v.*] the confidence of both McKinley and Roosevelt. He managed on the floor of the Senate the intricate matters of constitutional law relating to the new colonial ventures, and attached his name to the canal bill of 1902. He was essentially counsel for his party, rather than its leader, and never overcame a distaste for the manipulations of politics. So long as Henry C. Payne [*q.v.*] could direct the "stalwart" interests in Wisconsin, and could prevail over the attacks of the "half-breeds" led by Robert M. LaFollette [*q.v.*], Spooner remained the great ornament of his state in Washington, and "the most brilliant man in Congress" (Wellman, *post*, p. 167). In 1900 he talked of leaving the Senate to resume the law, but he was persuaded to accept reëlection in 1903, and he became, as caricatured, the mahout of the G. O. P. elephant, with Roosevelt on its back. In 1904 his intimacy with Roosevelt created a perplexing dilemma for the President, for LaFollette was selected as head of the regular delegation to the Republican National Convention, while Spooner was head of a bolting delegation, and Payne was both postmaster general and vice-chairman of the Republican National Committee. The Spooner delegation was seated, throwing LaFollette into bitter opposition that was dangerous even to Roosevelt. Lincoln Steffens chose this moment to attack the original election of Spooner to the Senate in 1885, as due to corrupt manipulation by Sawyer, and other "enemies of the Republic" (*McClure's Magazine*, October 1904) ; the death of Payne removed the local organizer of "stalwart" victory; and when LaFollette was elected to the Senate in place of Joseph V. Quarles in 1905, Spooner set the date at which he proposed to resume his practice. He had declined the offices of secretary of the interior and attorney general under McKinley and was later to decline the secretaryship of state under Taft. At the end of the Fifty-ninth Congress, Mar. 2, 1907, Spooner sent in his resignation, effective May 1. He left the Senate, with brevet from the *New York Times*, as "the ablest man in it" (June 12, 1919, p. 14), but without a client or an announced plan of operations. For the rest of his life his name appeared rarely in the news, but his office in New York was busy and profitable, for he was among the greatest lawyers of his day. He rarely returned to Wisconsin, and seems never to have reconciled himself to the reversal in politics that left his friends in a minority. He died in New York City, survived by his widow and three sons.

[The Spooner Papers, now in the Lib. Cong., have not yet been exploited, though some use of them was made in N. W. Stephenson, *Nelson W. Aldrich* (1930). Printed accounts are W. R. Bagby, in 174 *Wisconsin Reports* (1921), pp. lvii–lix ; Walter Wellman, "Spooner of Wisconsin," *Am. Monthly Review of Reviews*, Aug. 1902 ; obituaries in *Milwaukee Sentinel*, June 11, 1919, and *N. Y. Times*, June 11, 12, 1919. See also F. W. Chapman, *The Coit Family* (1874) ; *Biog. Directory of the Am. Congress 1774–1927* (1928) ; *Who's Who in America*, 1918–19.]   F. L. P.

SPOONER, LYSANDER (Jan. 19, 1808–May 14, 1887), lawyer and writer on political subjects, was born at Athol, Mass., the son of Asa and Dolly (Brown) Spooner and a descend-

ant of William Spooner who was in Plymouth, Mass., as early as 1637. Lysander remained on his father's farm until the age of twenty-five, and then read law in the office of John Davis and, later, in that of Charles Allen at Worcester, Mass. In defiance of the legal requirement that those not college graduates should read law for three years before practising, he opened an office. In 1835 he published a pamphlet, addressed to members of the legislature, which secured repeal of that requirement the following year. After six years' residence in Ohio, where he protested unsuccessfully against the draining of the Maumee River, he returned to the Atlantic seaboard and in 1844 established the American Letter Mail Company, a private agency carrying letters at the uniform rate of five cents each between Boston and New York. He soon extended the service to Philadelphia and Baltimore, but, faced with many prosecutions brought by the government, was forced to abandon the enterprise within the year. Thereupon he published a vigorous pamphlet, *The Unconstitutionality of the Laws of Congress Prohibiting Private Mails* (1844), in which he contended that the constitutional authority was permissive, not exclusive. It has been believed that Congress twice reduced postage rates within the following six years as a result of his activities.

Spooner was an uncompromising foe of slavery, and, believing that the institution had no constitutional sanction, advocated political organization with a view to its abolition. His *Unconstitutionality of Slavery* (1845, reprinted with a second part added, 1847, 1853, 1856, 1860) became campaign literature of the Liberty Party. Not only did slavery lack validation in the Constitution, he contended, but it "had not been authorized or established by any of the fundamental constitutions or charters that had existed previous to this time; . . . it had always been a mere abuse sustained by the common consent of the strongest party" (p. 65). His starting point was that "Law, . . . applied to any object or thing whatever, signifies a *natural*, unalterable, universal principle. . . . Any rule, not . . . flexible in its application, is no law" (p. 6). The last quotation discloses Spooner's dogmatic insistence upon natural rights. Gerrit Smith [*q.v.*] agreed with his legal contentions as to slavery as heartily as Wendell Phillips and William Lloyd Garrison [*qq.v.*] disapproved of them (see Wendell Phillips, *Review of Lysander Spooner's Essay on the Unconstitutionality of Slavery*, 1847). All admitted, of necessity, that he was an inexorable logician. His *A Defence for Fugitive Slaves, against the Acts . . . of 1793 and . . . 1850*

(1850) showed the same ingenuity in argument and the same intense moral purpose; the laws being unconstitutional, "it follows that they can confer no authority upon the judges and marshals appointed to execute them; and those officers are consequently, in law, mere ruffians and kidnappers" (p. 27). For his religion as for his political and legal theory, he sought a basis in nature, as is evidenced by his *The Deist's Reply to the Alleged Supernatural Evidences of Christianity* (1836). When Millerite laborers at Athol quit work to wait for the end of the world and were arrested as vagrants, he secured their release because of a flaw in the indictments. He was a bachelor and a recluse, spending much of his time in the Boston Athenaeum. Of strong convictions and positive utterance, he had few lasting friends. The range of his interests was wide, however, and his sympathies were warm. He defended the Irish against British tyranny and attacked American financiers for exploitation of the public. His *Essay on the Trial by Jury* (1852) maintained that jurors should be drawn by lot from the whole body of citizens, and that they should be judges of law as well as of fact. Among his other works were *Constitutional Law, Relative to Credit, Currency, and Banking* (1843), *A New Banking System* (1873), and *The Law of Intellectual Property* (1855).

[Thomas Spooner, *Records of William Spooner, of Plymouth, Mass., and His Descendants*, vol. I (1883); *Boston Sunday Globe*, May 15, 1887; *Boston Transcript*, May 16, 1887.]
                                                    B. M.

SPOONER, SHEARJASHUB (Dec. 3, 1809–Mar. 14, 1859), dentist, art editor, was one of the ten children of Paul and Deborah (White) Spooner. His earliest ancestor in America was William Spooner who came to New Plymouth in 1637 as an indentured apprentice. His father and grandfather were carpenters. He was born at Orwell, Vt., but his family, the following year, moved to the neighboring village of Brandon, where he attended school. For several years he worked on a farm, but at the age of eighteen he joined Dr. John Roach Spooner, one of his four brothers who became physicians, in Montreal and studied the classics and medicine. From general medicine he turned to dentistry, and in 1833 went to New York City to attend the New York Medical College. Two years later, in obtaining the degree of Doctor of Medicine from the College of Physicians and Surgeons, he presented and defended his thesis: *An Inaugural Dissertation on the Physiology and Diseases of the Teeth* (1835). The following year he published a *Guide to Sound Teeth, or A Popular Treatise on the Teeth*. His practice grew rapid-

ly and he became affluent. His last published work of importance on dentistry was *An Essay on the Art of the Manufacture of Mineral, Porcelain, or Incorruptible Teeth* (1838).

He was married, on Nov. 26, 1836, to Jane E. (Foot) Darrow, the widow of Allen Darrow. His wife possessed a modest competence and he had amassed a small fortune from his practice. Some time before 1842 he retired from dentistry to devote himself to art and to the promotion of art appreciation in America. While in Europe in 1842 he purchased the old copper plates of John Boydell's illustrations of Shakespeare. These plates were carefully restored and in 1852 he published a two-volume edition of them with original descriptions from his own pen under the title *The American Edition of Boydell's Illustrations of the Dramatic Works of Shakspeare*. He had observed in Paris in 1842 that the plates of two celebrated French works of art, the *Musée Français* and the *Musée Royal*, were for sale. He determined to make these works available to his countrymen, purchased the 522 "coppers" and brought them to New York, but found that he was unable to pay the heavy import duties. He petitioned Congress for an exemption, and finally offered them to the Smithsonian Institution, Washington, D. C., if it would agree to carry out his original plan. These appeals failed, the plates were shipped back to France, and the project collapsed. He published a pamphlet, remarkable for its elucidation of the state of the arts in contemporary America, during his fight to have the plates admitted free of duty: *An Appeal to the People of the United States, in Behalf of Art, Artists, and the Public Weal* (1854).

More successful were two other productions in the field of the arts: *Anecdotes of Painters, Engravers, Sculptors and Architects, and Curiosities of Art* (3 vols., 1850), and *A Biographical and Critical Dictionary of Painters, Engravers, Sculptors and Architects . . .* (1853). For some years these works were looked upon as standard authorities and they have not yet completely lost their value. It was in their preparation that Spooner contracted a nervous disorder which, aggravated by his difficulties in 1854, finally resulted in his death at Plainfield, N. J.

[Thomas Spooner, *Memorial of William Spooner . . .* (1871), and *Records of William Spooner, of Plymouth, Mass., and His Descendants*, vol. I (1883); *N. Y. Herald*, Mar. 18, 1859.]
                                                    F. M.

SPOTSWOOD, ALEXANDER (1676–June 7, 1740), lieutenant-governor of Virginia, son of Robert and Catherine (Mercer) Elliott Spotswood, was born in Tangier, where his father was physician to the English garrison. In 1693 he became an ensign in the Earl of Bath's regiment of foot, and, during the War of the Spanish Succession, served as lieutenant-quartermaster-general under Lord Cadogan, rising to the rank of lieutenant-colonel. He was wounded at Blenheim, and apparently captured at Oudenarde, since a month later Marlborough was negotiating his exchange. On June 23, 1710, he assumed office as lieutenant-governor of Virginia, under the nominal governor George Hamilton, Earl of Orkney. He entered upon his new duties with a vigor rather disconcerting to a people inclined to reduce governmental activity to a minimum. He sought to regulate and stabilize the fur trade and at the same time to finance an enlightened Indian policy by the erection, in 1714, of the monopolistic Virginia Indian Company with headquarters at Fort Christanna. In 1713 the governor obtained the passage of a measure requiring inspection of all tobacco designed for export or use as legal tender. Anathema to the producer and marketer of low-grade tobacco as well as to the debtor and taxpayer, who naturally favored "cheap money," the Tobacco Act, coupled in the popular mind with the Indian Act, led to a violent quarrel between governor and burgesses in 1715, a quarrel that continued, even after the Crown had repealed both acts. His land policy was designed to encourage the actual settler as opposed to the mere speculator, to render the quit-rents as profitable as possible, and to bring completeness and order to the public records. Here he achieved fair success, much that he proposed being accepted by the colony with tolerably good grace.

However, his reforms embroiled him with two prominent members of his council, William Byrd [q.v.] the receiver-general, and Philip Ludwell the deputy auditor, who resented interference and had little taste for the additional labors the governor thrust upon them. Shortly thereafter, he found himself at odds with the majority of the council, which had hitherto supported him against the burgesses. The councillors claimed that as members of the General Court they alone had the right to compose the newly created courts of oyer and terminer. The quarrel had many side currents, and underlying the specific points at issue was a struggle for power between governor and council. Similarly, the question of the governor's right to induct ministers seems to have cloaked a contest with Commissary James Blair [q.v.] for the paramount voice in church affairs. In 1718, with both council and burgesses hostile, the situation boded little good for the public life of the colony. Pressure was brought

to bear from England, and two years later harmony was restored.

From his first arrival in Virginia he was actively identified with the problems of the frontier. His name inevitably calls to mind the picture of the governor leading a company of colonial gentlemen, rangers, Indians, and servants over the Blue Ridge and down to the waters of the Shenandoah, which the Adventurers named the Euphrates. A peak of the Ridge was loyally named Mount George, and copious potations were drunk to the royal health. Romance and policy were nicely joined when Spotswood instituted the Order of the Golden Horseshoe with the evident object of cultivating among Virginians an interest in the West. The journey of 1716, however, was merely the most famous of Spotswood's excursions to and beyond the limits of settlement. He sought to protect the colony from Iroquois raids by establishing compact communities of friendly Indians, powerful enough to resist attack and convenient for the work of missionary and schoolmaster. When the repeal of the Indian Act left him unable to finance this scheme, he negotiated a treaty with the Iroquois at Albany whereby they were to keep north of the Potomac and west of the Blue Ridge. He watched with apprehension the difficulties with the Tuscarora in North Carolina in 1712 and with the Yamasee in South Carolina in 1715. The success of either of these attacks would have placed Virginia in a serious position, and the measure of assistance that he in both instances afforded the Carolinians was not pure altruism. Behind the Indians were the Spanish and the French, and Spotswood urged upon the British authorities the advisability of seizing Florida, and of taking possession of the Appalachians before the French did so. He was handicapped by a lack of precise geographical knowledge, and some of his proposals were quite impracticable. More practical was the policy of fostering settlement in the frontier districts by exempting the inhabitants from taxes and quit-rents.

During the closing years of his administration his attitude toward colonial self-assertion mellowed perceptibly. Doubtless due in part to the conviction, born of experience, that it was futile to contend against what amounted to a Virginia nationalism, the change was natural in one who had decided to make America his permanent home. Before he ceased to be governor he had acquired, by means not always above question, an estate of some eighty-five thousand acres in Spotsylvania County. In 1722, removed from office, he retired to Germanna, where he had founded, as early as 1714, a colony of Germans as part of the scheme of frontier defense, and where he was now actively engaged in the mining and smelting of iron. In the hope of adjusting his land titles that had been challenged, he went to England in 1724. He was married, the same year, to Anne Butler Brayne, the daughter of Richard and Anne Brayne of St. Margarets, Westminster, by whom he had four children. Six years later he returned with his family to Virginia, having obtained appointment as deputy postmaster-general for the American colonies. He extended the regular postal service as far south as Williamsburg. When war with Spain broke out in 1739, he proposed the recruiting of a regiment in the colonies. He was assigned the task of raising it, was made its colonel, and was appointed major-general and second in command of the expedition that Lord Cathcart was to lead against Cartagena. Entering upon such congenial duties with customary vigor, he was halted by death, the end coming at Annapolis.

[Letters and Papers, esp. in Lib. of Cong. and in Public Records Office, London; *The Official Letters of Alexander Spotswood* (2 vols., 1882–85), ed. by R. A. Brock; Leonidas Dodson, *Alexander Spotswood, Governor of Colonial Virginia, 1710–1722* (1932); *The Writings of "Col. Wm. Byrd"* (1901), ed. by J. S. Bassett, esp. intro. pp. li-lxxv; James Fontaine, *Memoirs of a Huguenot Family* (1907), ed. by Ann Maury; Hugh Jones, *The Present State of Va.* (1724); *Dict. of Nat. Biog.*; T. J. Wertenbaker, "The Attempt to Reform the Church of Colonial Va.," *Sewanee Rev.*, July 1917; Charles Campbell, *Geneal. of the Spotswood Family* (1868); *Wm. and Mary College Quart.*, Oct. 1901, pp. 143–44; mother's maiden name "Mercer" from *Va. Mag. of Hist.*, July 1905, p. 98.]
L. D.

SPOTTED TAIL (c. 1833–Aug. 5, 1881), a head-chief of the Lower Brulé Sioux, was born near Fort Laramie, Wyo. He had no hereditary claims on the chieftainship, and his advancement was due to his feats as a warrior. He was in the fight near Fort Laramie on Aug. 19, 1854, in which Lieut. John Grattan's command was annihilated, and after Harney's victory at Ash Hollow, Nebr., he was demanded of the tribe, with two others, for trial. To save the tribe from further punishment the three warriors voluntarily surrendered at Fort Laramie. Imprisoned for two years, they were released to find themselves acclaimed as heroes. At the Fort Laramie council in June 1866, he opposed the stand of Red Cloud [q.v.] and favored the government's proposals to open the road to the gold regions of Montana. He was one of the signers of the treaty of Apr. 29, 1868, providing for an Indian reservation of the western part of the present state of South Dakota and for the withdrawal of Indian opposition to railroad construction, and he was ever afterward distinguished for his friendliness to the whites. In the same year his tribe was settled on a reservation on the Missouri River,

near Fort Randall, but within a few years was moved to the newly created Spotted Tail reservation at Camp Sheridan in northwestern Nebraska, in the vicinity of the Red Cloud reservation. On the discovery of gold in the Black Hills in 1874, he joined with Red Cloud in an effort to sell the mineral rights to the government. When it was found, however, that Spotted Tail, who considered himself an astute business man, had set the price at $60,000,000, negotiations ceased, and the government permitted the miners to enter the Black Hills region without its opposition. Nevertheless, he stoutly resisted the efforts of agitators to bring his tribe into the war of 1876 and succeeded in holding most of his followers to the reservation. In the spring of 1877 he was influential in bringing about the surrender of Crazy Horse [q.v.], his nephew, and in the late summer was a leading figure in the dramatic episode that ended with that fiery chieftain's death. In 1880 he seems to have become for a time inflated with an undue sense of his importance and to have threatened serious trouble; but he was soon cured and, on Red Cloud's deposal from the chieftainship of the Oglalas, was recognized as head-chief at both agencies. He did not live to enjoy the honor. On leaving a council he was followed by Crow Dog, a prominent sub-chief, who shot and killed him.

According to Bourke, though a man of dignified bearing, with strong, melancholy features, he was at all times "easy and affable in manner ... sharp as a brier, and extremely witty. He understood enough English to get along at table," had good conversational powers, and his opinions, which were carefully considered, were clearly expressed. He was, in Bourke's opinion, one of the great men of this country, "bar none, red, white, black, or yellow" (*post*, pp. 400–01). Eastman, a Sioux, credited him with being one of the most brilliant of the Sioux leaders, but expressed the view that in manifesting so great a friendliness for the whites he was in some degree unfaithful to his people (*post*, pp. 35, 41).

[J. G. Bourke, *On the Border with Crook* (1891); Doane Robinson, "Hist. of the Dakota or Sioux Indians," *S. D. Hist. Soc. Colls.*, vol. II, pt. 2 (1904); Frank Huntington and Doane Robinson, *Handbook of Am. Indians*, pt. 2 (1910), ed. by F. W. Hodge; C. A. Eastman, *Indian Heroes and Great Chieftains* (1918); H. W. Wheeler, *Buffalo Days*, ch. xxiii (1925); Anson Mills, *My Story* (1918); report of J. M. Lee, agent at Spotted Tail Agency, Nebr., *Ann. Report of the Commissioner of Indian Affairs ... 1877* (1877), p. 462.]
W. J. G.

SPRAGUE, ACHSA W. (c. 1828–July 6, 1862) spiritualist, author, was born on a farm at Plymouth Notch, Vt., the sixth child of Charles (d. 1858) and Betsy Sprague (d. 1868). She was a connection of William Sprague, 1830–1915 [*q.v.*], and of the stepmother of Calvin Coolidge, who describes the family of Achsa Sprague as "very intellectual . . . but nervously unbalanced" (letter to the author). At twelve she began teaching in a rural school, but a scrofulous disease of the joints overtook her when she was about twenty, and though for a time she continued her duties in a crippled condition, she later became a bedridden invalid for about six years. In 1854, having been restored to apparently normal health through the agency of "angelic powers," she became a trance medium and later a lecturer on spiritualism, and addressed large audiences throughout the country. She is represented by tradition as having a personality of rare charm; it is plain that she had a wide following. Known as the "preaching woman," she opposed slavery, visited prisons in numerous cities and urged reforms, and condemned what she said was the contemporary belief that "woman must be either a slave or a butterfly." She abandoned the *materia medica* of the day, experimented with magnetizing processes, with galvanic bands, with hypnotism, and with sensational séances, and came finally to a belief in mental healing, which with no strange physical manifestations had raised her almost instantly from her sick bed and seemed to her "the voice of God."

She read widely in the poets and wrote voluminously, especially during the last few years of her life. Many of her compositions were produced by automatic writing—at the rate of 4,600 lines in seventy-two hours on the first draft of "The Poet"—in which she believed herself to be under the control of divine and mystic energies. Her poems, which display no careful craftsmanship, are spontaneous expressions of spiritual anguish and despair, appeals for economic justice and equality, or exultant affirmations of faith and hope. Only a very small part of what she produced is represented by her published books, *I Still Live, A Poem for the Times* (1862) and *The Poet and Other Poems* (1864). Among her unpublished writings, which include essays, journals, and a play, is an autobiographical poem of 162 pages, which she composed in six days in such a nervous state that spinning-wheel, latches, and roosters were muffled for her peace of mind. In 1861 she became a victim of her old affliction and died a year later at the age of thirty-four. She was buried at Plymouth.

[See biog. sketch by M. E. G. in A. W. Sprague, *The Poet and Other Poems* (1864); Athaldine Smith, *Achsa W. Sprague and Mary Clarke's Experiences in the First Ten Spheres of Spirit Life* (Oswego, N. Y., 1862); O. R. Washburn, in *Nat. Spiritualist*, Feb. 1, 1932; W. J. Coates, in *Drift-Wind*, Nov. 1927; death notice in *Rutland Weekly Herald*, July 24, 1862. The chief sources are materials in the possession of the author (clippings from *New England Spiritualist*, 1855-57, and other publications; diary, letters, poems, sermons, etc.), some of which are being prepared for publication.]

L. T.

SPRAGUE, CHARLES (Oct. 26, 1791–Jan. 22, 1875), banker and poet, was born in Boston, one of seven sons of Samuel and Joanna (Thayer) Sprague. His father, a native of Hingham, Mass., and a descendant of William Sprague who came to New England in 1628 and settled in Hingham in 1636, was one of the "Indians" of the Boston Tea Party. Young Sprague attended the Franklin School for a time, but his formal education was brief, and at the age of thirteen he was apprenticed to Messrs. Thayer & Hunt, importers of dry goods. At the age of nineteen he entered into partnership with a grocer; five years later, abandoning this project, he formed another partnership, which, however, lasted but four years. In 1819 he became a teller in the State Bank; with the establishment of the Globe Bank in 1824 he became its cashier, a position he held for the next forty years. As a business man, he was greatly respected and trusted. Almost never absent from his accustomed desk in the bank, "he occupied a foremost place in the financial circles of Boston" (Quincy, *post,* p. 41).

It is, however, as a poet that he will be chiefly remembered. A literary amateur in the sense that his best poetry was written in spare moments snatched from business duties, he held during the late twenties and thirties a significant place in the literary life of Boston. Like his contemporaries, William Cullen Bryant and Fitz-Greene Halleck [*qq.v.*], with whom he was frequently ranked by critics of that day, he disdained the subtleties of thought and mood which were becoming so popular in the work of Tennyson and Browning. Relying upon clarity and purity of diction, he found his chief inspiration in the poetic traditions of the preceding century. The heroic couplet is employed in five prize prologues which he wrote for the opening of new playhouses and in *Curiosity,* delivered at the Harvard Phi Beta Kappa exercises of 1829, which in recurring moods of humor, satire, and didacticism traces the course in human life of curiosity, "the power That masters man in every changing hour." A group of odes to be found in his collected works (*Writings of Charles Sprague, Now First Collected,* 1841, of which there were four later editions) is best represented by the one on Shakespeare, in which he affects with some success the dignity of Collins and Gray, and that delivered "at the Centennial Celebration of the Settlement of Boston," which introduces a panegyric on the American Indians and received the commendation of the London *Athenaeum* in the issue of Jan. 29, 1831 (reprinted in *Museum of Foreign Literature*, Apr. 1831). In many of his shorter pieces, such as "The Funeral" and "The Tomb of Emmeline," he relied too heavily on the morbid, graveyard sentimentality of Mrs. Lydia Howard Huntley Sigourney [*q.v.*], although even in some of these verses one finds at times a strain of genuine pathos. He was probably at his best, however, in the whimsical didacticism of the lines "To My Cigar," in the simple sincerity of "The Brothers," and in the quiet deism of "The Winged Worshippers." Undoubtedly much overrated as a poet by his contemporaries, he must to-day take his place among those minor authors without whom we should scarcely have had an early American literature.

Like Halleck, he wrote most of his poetry and achieved his greatest fame early in life. But, partly from ill health and partly from temperament, he became as time went on more and more retiring, hardly ever venturing outside the limits of Boston. His marriage on May 8, 1814, to Elizabeth Rand provided him with a happy home and four children, one of whom, Charles James, born in 1823, attained some note as a poet. Unable to leave his home during the last few years of his life, he had ample time for reading and reflection. Years before, his religious beliefs had acquired a tinge of rationalism which in later life he freely avowed to his friends.

[Hosea Sprague, *The Geneal. of the Sprague's* (*sic*) *in Hingham* (1828); W. V. Sprague, *Sprague Families in America* (1913); C. J. Sprague, in *The Poetical and Prose Writings of Charles Sprague* (1876), with portrait; Edmund Quincy, *Memoir of Charles Sprague* (1875); R. C. Waterston, *Remarks upon the Life and Writings of Charles Sprague* (1875); J. S. Loring, *The Hundred Boston Orators* (1853); E. A. and G. L. Duyckinck, *Cyc. of Am. Lit.* (1855), vol. II, pp. 132–35; R. W. Griswold, *The Poets and Poetry of America* (1850); E. P. Whipple, *Essays and Reviews* (1848), vol. I, pp. 38–44; J. T. Buckingham, *Personal Memoirs* (1852), vol. I, pp. 184–200; *New England Mag.*, Aug. 1832; reviews in *Littell's Living Age*, Jan. 12, 1850, and *North Am. Review*, July 1824, Apr. 1830; obituary in *Boston Transcript*, Jan. 22, 1875; date of death from Registry Dept., Boston, Mass.]   N. F. A.

SPRAGUE, CHARLES EZRA (Oct. 9, 1842– Mar. 21, 1912), banker, writer on accountancy, teacher, was born at Nassau, N. Y., the son of the Rev. Ezra Sprague and his second wife, Elisabeth Brown (Edgerton) Sprague. He was a descendant of Ralph Sprague who emigrated from Dorsetshire, England, and arrived in Salem, Mass., in 1628. At fourteen he entered Union College, Schenectady, N. Y., where he took all prizes for which he was eligible and was elected to Phi Beta Kappa at graduation in 1860. Later he received the degree of M.A. in course from Union University, for which he acted as

alumni trustee, 1894–98, and as life trustee from 1906 until he resigned shortly before his death. In 1862, after teaching at Greenwich Union Academy, he enlisted in the New York National Guard and saw active service in the Civil War until he was wounded at Little Round Top during the battle of Gettysburg. For meritorious service in that battle he was made a brevet colonel of the New York Volunteers. He served again in the New York National Guard, 1870–72, and 1897–1901; during the latter period he was assistant paymaster-general for the state of New York with the rank of colonel. From 1864 until 1870 he taught at Yonkers (N. Y.) Military Institute, Peekskill Military Academy, and Poughkeepsie Military Institute. He wrote numerous articles on military tactics, on which he became an expert, and because of his knowledge of British and Prussian methods was asked to aid the commandant of the United States Military Academy in revising the book of tactics used there.

In 1870 his career as a banker began. At that time his ability as an interpreter—he spoke sixteen languages, studying obscure ones and unusual dialects as a hobby—brought him a position as clerk with the Union Dime Savings Bank in New York City; seven years later he became secretary, then treasurer, and in 1892 president, the position which he held at his death. Becoming a skilled accountant during his clerkship, he was one of the first to qualify as a certified public accountant. He introduced from Great Britain the idea of having a board of examiners for public accountants and served as chairman of the New York board, 1896–98. Savings bank bookkeeping owes much to the systems which he devised or adapted. Always in search of new and more efficient ways of performing routine tasks, he introduced the use of the small check book and pass book, and loose-leaf ledger, designed the first machine (which he never patented) for the making of ledger entries, and worked out amortization methods that are widely used in savings banks. He was a moving spirit in the establishment of the New York University School of Commerce, Accounts, and Finance, and found time in the midst of numerous other activities to teach evening classes there as professor of accountancy from 1900 until his death. Since his subject was without methods, texts, or other materials, he himself provided them for his students. Between 1900 and 1910 he wrote *The Accountancy of Investment* (1904), *Extended Bond Tables* (1905), *Problems and Studies in the Accountancy of Investment* (1906), *Logarithms to 12 Places* (1910), *Amortization* (1908), *Tables of*

Compound Interest (1907), and *The Philosophy of Accounts* (1908), a fifth edition of which was published in 1922. His *The Algebra of Accounts* had appeared as early as 1880. Though he contributed articles on business to magazines and newspapers, he was interested also in such widely divergent matters as croquet, simplified spelling, Esperanto, Volapük, and the revival of Gaelic, and wrote occasional articles on them as well. His wife was Ray Ellison of New York City (d. May 17, 1931), whom he married Apr. 2, 1866. Of their four children, all daughters, two survived at his death. He died of pneumonia in New York City.

[*Who's Who in America*, 1912–13; *Who's Who in N. Y.*, 1911; Helen S. Mann, *Charles Ezra Sprague* (1931), with portraits; A. V. V. Raymond, *Union Univ.* (1907), vol. II; E. G. Sprague, *The Ralph Sprague Geneal.* (1913); obituary in *N. Y. Times*, Mar. 22, 1912.]   H. J. S. M.

SPRAGUE, HOMER BAXTER (Oct. 19, 1829–Mar. 23, 1918), educator, was born at South Sutton, Mass., the second child of Jonathan and Mary Ann (Whipple) Sprague, both of old Colonial stock. On his father's side he was descended from William Sprague, who emigrated from England with his brothers Ralph and Richard in 1628, and was one of the founders of Charlestown and later of Hingham, Mass. Although he worked as a boy in a cotton mill (where he was paid $1.50 for a sixty-six hour week), became a cobbler's apprentice, and had only desultory schooling, he entered Yale in September 1848 and graduated in 1852. After his graduation he taught Greek and Latin at Worcester, Mass., studied law, and in 1854 was admitted to the bar. On Dec. 28, 1854, he married Antoinette Elizabeth Pardee of New Haven, Conn., by whom he had four children. He served as principal of the Worcester High School from 1856 to 1859, but then returned to New Haven to practise law. At the opening of the Civil War he raised a volunteer company and was elected captain; his war experiences he described in two books, *History of the 13th Infantry Regiment of Connecticut Volunteers* (1867), and *Lights and Shadows in Confederate Prisons* (1915).

After the war he went back to educational work with renewed vigor. During 1866 and 1867 he was principal of the Connecticut State Normal School at New Britain, Conn., and in 1868 a member of the Connecticut House of Representatives, where he was chairman of the joint standing committee on education. In the fall of 1868 he became professor of rhetoric and English literature on the first faculty at Cornell University under Pres. Andrew Dickson White [*q.v.*]. Leaving Cornell in 1870, he became presi-

dent of Adelphi Academy in Brooklyn, N. Y., where his developing talents as a lyceum speaker brought him wide acclaim. He returned to New England in 1876 as headmaster of the Girls' High School of Boston, continued to lecture widely, and became a director of the Boston Watch and Ward Society. In 1879 he founded the Martha's Vineyard Summer Institute, the "first general summer school in the United States." But his spirit was not entirely content with the life of a New England headmaster. In 1885 he accepted the presidency of Mills College at Oakland, Cal., newly reorganized; two years later he assumed the same office at the University of North Dakota, which had recently been established at Grand Forks, Dakota Territory. When in 1889 North Dakota entered the Union, he prepared the article on education for the new constitution, at the unanimous request of the constituent assembly. A moderate Republican in politics and hence a member of the dominant political faction, it was only his unswerving opposition to the Louisiana lottery scheme that kept him from being elected the first United States senator from North Dakota. Retiring from active administrative work in 1891, he spent most of his later years in Newton, Mass. He gave occasional lectures at the University of Southern California, at Drew Theological Seminary, and at Cornell, and wrote a number of books, among them *Shakespeare's Alleged Blunders in Legal Terminology* (1902), *The True Macbeth* (1909), *Caesar and Brutus* (1912), *The Book of Job; the Poetic Portion Versified* (1913), which he prepared in his eighty-fourth year, and *Studies in Shakespeare, First Series* (1916). At the time of his death he left completed a second series of studies in Shakespeare. He wrote several autobiographical articles for the *Tomahawk*, published by Alpha Sigma Phi (February, May 1916), and one of reminiscences which appeared in the *Quarterly Journal of the University of North Dakota* (October 1916). In many respects he represented the best qualities in post Civil War America—its optimism, its moral earnestness, its devotion to education, and its intense belief in progress. His greatest joy was not in his personal achievement but in his friendships with those men and women all over the country who had been his "boys and girls" in their student days, and whom, with a kind of patriarchal dignity, to the day of his death he regarded as being in a peculiar sense his own.

[The principal source is Sprague's autobiog. in the *Tomahawk*, Feb., May 1916. See also his reminiscences in *Quart. Jour. of the Univ. of N. Dak.*, Oct. 1916; V. P. Squires, *Ibid.*, May 1928; *Who's Who in America*, 1916–17; *Obit. Records Grads. Yale Univ.* . . . *1918* (n.d.); *Records of the Class of 1852, Yale Coll.* (1878); A. B. R. Sprague, *Geneal. (in Part) of the Sprague Families in America* (1905); W. V. Sprague, *Sprague Families in America* (1913); obituaries in *Boston Transcript*, Mar. 23, *N. Y. Times*, Mar. 24, and *Grand Forks Herald*, Mar. 25, 1918. There is a collection of Sprague correspondence and other materials in the Alpha Sigma Phi alumni lib. at Yale Univ.]

J. D. S.

SPRAGUE, KATE CHASE (Aug. 13, 1840–July 31, 1899), political hostess, was born in Cincinnati, Ohio, the daughter of Salmon Portland Chase [q.v.] and his second wife, Eliza Ann (Smith) Chase. She was christened Katherine Jane. Her mother died in 1845, and seven years later her stepmother was dead, leaving a daughter. In the years that followed, the lonely father turned more and more to his elder daughter, whom he indulged greatly, and whose talents and personality he developed by participation in his own career. Her schooling was begun by him, and from 1847 to 1856 she was a pupil at the school kept by Henrietta B. Haines in New York City. In Columbus, when her father was governor of Ohio, she studied at Heyl's Seminary, where she specialized in music and languages and became proficient in French. Proficiency in German was to come later, from her travels and her residence abroad. From her sixteenth year she was her father's official hostess. At eighteen, according to Carl Schurz, "she had something imperial in the pose of her head," and "took a lively and remarkably intelligent part" in the conversation at her father's table (*The Reminiscences of Carl Schurz*, II, 1907, 169). With her pale auburn hair, white skin, pert nose, and graceful figure she was a beauty. Already she was thoroughly extravagant in clothes and personal expenditures. She went with Chase to the Republican convention in Chicago in 1860 and worked hard for his nomination as presidential candidate. When he became secretary of the treasury she established a salon in their home at Sixth and E streets. Her marriage on Nov. 12, 1863, to William Sprague [q.v.] was declared to be the most brilliant wedding Washington had ever seen. She was referred to as "the toast of the nation." What she wore, said, and did became national news. "The birth of her first baby,"—a son who in 1890 committed suicide—"was a national event, every woman in the country reading descriptions of the layette" (Bowers, *post*, p. 254). The Sprague country home, "Canonchet," built in 1868, became a showplace, where some of the country's greatest were entertained. The Sprague wealth became an instrument to further her political ambitions for her father. Jealous for her father's political future, she disliked Lincoln and was believed to

have known about the "Pomeroy Circular" even though Chase was ignorant until he saw it in print. From time to time newspapers noticed her political influence, and gossip was ever busy with the subject (*New York Herald*, Jan. 20, 1868; *Independent* (N. Y.), June 4, 1868; Warden, *post*, pp. 705–06). At the National Democratic Convention of 1868 in New York she waged a vigorous campaign for her father. "Competent judges have believed that had she been able to go into the convention and make her combinations on the spot she would have secured his nomination" (A. B. Hart, *Salmon Portland Chase*, 1899, p. 420).

By 1866 it had been whispered that her marriage was in difficulty, and with the stress due to Sprague's financial difficulties in 1873 the breach widened with a series of quarrels discussed in public print. In August 1879 Sprague in a jealous rage attacked with a gun his children's German tutor and Roscoe Conkling [q.v.]. Newspapers the next day and for days following described the scene and the details of what the parties to the quarrel said to reporters and to others. After divorce proceedings, scandalous and widely discussed, she was granted a divorce in 1882 and sailed for Europe with her three daughters. In 1886 she returned to Washington to take up a dreary existence at "Edgewood," her father's old home, where in her last years she struggled pitifully for mere existence, raising chickens, peddling milk, and always getting deeper in debt. In 1896 Henry Villard raised a fund sufficient to pay the mortage, and she died at "Edgewood."

[Consult bibliog. of sketches of father and husband; scrapbook kept by Zechariah Chafee, the estate trustee, and now in possession of Zechariah Chafee, Jr., Cambridge, Mass.; see also M. M. Phelps, *Kate Chase* (copr. 1935), inaccurate esp. in details of the financial failure and of Chafee's relations to the estate and to the family; V. T. Peacock, *Famous Am. Belles of the Nineteenth Century* (1901); C. G. Bowers, *The Tragic Era* (1929); R. B. Warden, *An Account of the Private Life and Public Services of Salmon Portland Chase* (1874); Benj. Knight, *Hist. of the Sprague Families* (1881), esp. appendix for divorce proceedings; J. C. Chase and G. W. Chamberlain, *Seven Generations of . . . Chase* (1928); *Ladies' Home Jour.*, June 1901; *N. Y. Times*, Nov. 15, 1863, Aug. 10–19, Nov. 27, 1879, Oct. 20, 29, Dec. 5, 20, 1880–Jan. 28, Feb. 26, 1881; *N. Y. Tribune*, Aug. 13, 15, May 28, 1882, Feb. 15, 1896, Aug. 1, 1899.]

J. W. M.
K. E. C.

SPRAGUE, PELEG (Apr. 27, 1793–Oct. 13, 1880), jurist, son of Seth and Deborah (Sampson) Sprague, was born in Duxbury, Mass., one of a large family of children. His father, a merchant of Duxbury and for many years a member of the Massachusetts legislature, was descended from William Sprague, who came from England to Salem in 1628 and finally settled at Hingham, Mass. Peleg Sprague graduated from Harvard

College in 1812, and, after studying law at Litchfield, Conn., was admitted to the bar in 1815 and practised first in Augusta and then in Hallowell, Me. In August 1818 he married Sarah, daughter of Moses Deming of Whitesboro, N. Y. They had three sons and one daughter.

Sprague was elected to the first legislature of Maine after its separation from Massachusetts and served in 1820–22. He represented Maine in the federal House of Representatives from 1825 to 1829, and in the United States Senate, 1829–35. He then entered the practice of law in Boston, was chosen a presidential elector as a Whig in 1840, and in the following year was appointed United States district judge for the district of Massachusetts. In this position he found his real vocation until his retirement in 1865.

From his college days, because of a nervous affection of the eyes, Sprague was unable to read much of the time. His trouble grew worse soon after he was appointed to the bench so that during most of his judicial career he was obliged to darken the courtroom and even to sit with eyes closed while listening to those addressing him. Nevertheless, he became a really great judge. His opinions, delivered orally, disclosed the full background of an exceptional mind trained in those powers of concentration which are sometimes characteristic of the blind. Upon his retirement a committee of the bar, headed by Benjamin R. Curtis and including Sidney Bartlett and Richard H. Dana, Jr. [qq.v.], paid merited tribute to his thorough legal knowledge, to his extraordinary "power of analysis . . . united with sound judgment to weigh its results," and to his possession of "that absolute judicial impartiality which can exist only when a tender and vigilant conscience is joined to an instructed and self-reliant intellect and a firm will" (2 Sprague's Decisions, 352).

In March 1851 he delivered a notable charge to the grand jury after a mob had broken into the federal courtrooms, and rescued a negro named Shadrach who had been arrested as a fugitive slave. Though himself regarding slavery as a great political and moral evil, he reminded the grand jury that the fact that human institutions are not perfect is no justification of forcible resistance to government and the introduction of anarchy and violence. In 1854 he delivered what has been described as an epoch-making opinion in maritime law, holding that "when a sailing vessel, going free, meets a steamer, the rule . . . requires the former to keep her course, and the latter to keep out of the way" (The Osprey, 1 Sprague's Decisions, at p. 256). This rule has survived all attacks as the guiding rule of the

sea in American courts. During the Civil War (March 1863) he delivered a charge to the grand jury on the doctrine of treason and the powers of the federal government in which he "allowed of no line beyond which the government could not follow a treasonable rebellion" (Dana, post, p. 10). This address, printed and circulated by the Union League, "did more to settle the minds of professional men in this part of the country . . . than anything that appeared, from whatever source, in the early stages of the controversy" (Ibid.).

Before his appointment as a judge, Harvard College had offered Sprague the chair of ethics and moral philosophy, which he declined. The law school repeatedly sought his services as a professor, without avail. He retired from the bench in 1865 because of failing health, and was entirely blind for the last sixteen years of his life. He died in Boston at the age of eighty-seven. His Speeches and Addresses (1858) contains, among others, his speeches in Congress and his charge to the grand jury in the Shadrach case; selections from his decisions were published as Decisions of Hon. Peleg Sprague, in Admiralty and Maritime Cases (cited as Sprague's Decisions), Vol. I appearing in 1861, Vol. II in 1868.

[Justin Winsor, A Hist. of the Town of Duxbury (1849), p. 319; Richard Soule, Jr., Memorial of the Sprague Family (1847); W. V. Sprague, Sprague Families in America (1913); Biog. Dir. Am. Cong. (1928); R. H. Dana, Jr., A Tribute to Judge Sprague (1864); New England Mag., June 1835; Chicago Legal News, Nov. 15, 1879; New Eng. Hist. and Geneal. Reg., Apr. 1881; Boston Daily Advertiser, Oct. 14, 1880; judicial traditions of Judge Sprague among his successors on the bench.]   F. W. G.

SPRAGUE, WILLIAM (June 5, 1773–Mar. 28, 1836), textile manufacturer, was the son of William and Isabel (Waterman) Sprague and was born on his father's farm in Cranston, R. I. He was descended from William Sprague who emigrated from England and died at Hingham, Mass., in 1675. After obtaining the education afforded by the district schools of the time and helping in the farm work, Sprague induced his father to erect a gristmill for him in Cranston because he then had but little interest in farming. He operated this for a number of years and at the same time widened his activities to include a sawmill that he erected in the same vicinity. Both of these enterprises were very successful, and about 1808 he ventured into the field of textiles, particularly the manufacture of cotton cloth. He first converted his gristmill into a factory to card and spin cotton yarn, using the crude machinery available for the purpose. As power weaving was then unknown, he arranged with the local farmers' wives and daughters to weave his yarn on their own hand looms and return the cloth to him. After bleaching it in the open air by the sun and water method he sold the finished product to merchants as far away as Baltimore, Md. This was one of the first cotton-cloth manufactories in Rhode Island, and under his management it was continued successfully for upwards of thirteen years. Meanwhile rapid developments in cotton-mill machinery had taken place, particularly in power machinery, and in 1821 he purchased one half of the water power at Natick Falls, Kent County, R. I., and erected there a forty-two-loom cotton mill as well as a building for carding and spinning. From that time the expansion of his business was phenomenal, as evidenced by the fact that five mills were constructed and put into operation in the succeeding fifteen years. Besides being one of the earliest cotton-cloth manufacturers he was also among the first calico printers of Rhode Island, for in 1824 he transformed his original mill at Cranston into a bleaching, dyeing, and printing factory and began to manufacture and market calicoes known as "indigo blues." The printing machines first used printed but two colors, additional colors being printed by hand with wood blocks. Besides his textile interests he carried on farming to a considerable extent, specializing in stock raising. He conducted, too, in the winter season quite a lumbering business. Until in his early thirties he evidenced little interest in politics. Then he became a violent anti-Mason and did everything he could to overthrow the Masonic order in Rhode Island, even running for governor in 1832 on the Anti-Masonic Ticket. He married Anna Potter of Cranston. They had five children. He died at his home in Cranston from the effects of a bone that was stuck in his throat.

[Charles Carroll, *Rhode Island* (1932), vol. I; Benj. Knight, *Hist. of the Sprague Family in R. I.* (1881); W. V. Sprague, *Sprague Families in America* (1913).]
C. W. M—n.

SPRAGUE, WILLIAM (Sept. 12, 1830–Sept. 11, 1915), governor of Rhode Island, senator, was born in Cranston, R. I., the son of Amasa and Fanny (Morgan) Sprague, the grandson of William Sprague, 1773–1836 [q.v.], and the descendant of William Sprague who emigrated from England and died at Hingham, Mass., in 1675. His father greatly increased the mill holdings and capital he had inherited and in 1843 was murdered, probably because he had influenced the town council to refuse a license to sell liquor near his factory. Owing to a general belief that the wrong man was convicted and executed for

his murder, capital punishment was abolished soon afterward in Rhode Island. The boy received an inadequate education in schools in East Greenwich and Scituate, R. I., and at Irving Institute, Tarrytown, N. Y. He was fifteen when he went to work in the factory store. The next year he became a book-keeper in the Sprague counting-house. When he was twenty-six, at the death of his uncle, he and his brother assumed control of the Sprague properties. He was a handsome young man, and his great wealth soon made him a prominent figure in the state. At this time he was an enthusiastic member of the Providence Marine Artillery, of which he later became colonel. In 1859 he went to Europe and returned home to find himself the Democratic nominee for governor in the impending election. After a vigorous contest, in which he was accused of astounding bribery, he won by a large majority. In 1861 he was reëlected.

The outbreak of the Civil War served to heighten his popularity and to increase fabulously his wealth from the family cotton mills. Owing to his energy and financial support, a Rhode Island regiment was one of the first to reach Washington after the call for troops. He himself served as an aide under General Burnside and in the battle of Bull Run proved his gallantry under fire. Later he was offered the rank of brigadier-general but declined. He was one of twelve war governors who met at Altoona, Pa., in 1862 to pledge themselves to support President Lincoln's policies. That same year he was reëlected governor but resigned to become federal senator. He took his seat on Mar. 4, 1863, and served until Mar. 3, 1875. On Nov. 12, 1863, Sprague was married to Kate Chase (see Sprague, Kate Chase), the very beautiful and much courted daughter of the secretary of war, Salmon P. Chase [q.v.]. They had four children. During his first term in the Senate he took little part in its business, but soon after his reëlection he delivered a series of five speeches (*National Affairs, Speeches . . . in the Senate . . . Mar. 15, 17, 24, 30 and Apr. 8, 1869*, 1869), attacking what he described as the grip of capital and industry upon the organs of government. Gideon Welles (*Diary*, 1911, III, 565) wrote that, in spite of efforts to answer him, "Sprague's remarks remain"; but the speeches angered many of his constituents, because of bitter personal attacks and because they thought that he betrayed a distinct lack of responsibility as a legislator. In December 1870 he introduced a resolution providing for an investigation of charges against him of illicit trading for cotton in Texas during the war. The committee appointed held the charges were not sustained by the evidence at their disposal and was discharged on the ground that the session was too short for going into the matter further (*Senate Executive Document 10*, pt. 4, 41 Cong., 2 Sess., 1871, vol. I; *Senate Report 377*, 41 Cong., 3 Sess., 1871).

About the same time his financial standing began to be questioned. With the panic of 1873, acrimonious complaints and litigation culminated in a failure involving some $20,000,000 that wiped out all but a fraction of the Sprague wealth. Domestic troubles developed also, and in 1882 he was divorced with a good deal of scandal for both sides. Moreover his name was constantly involved in the difficulties and litigation (citations, *post*) over the Sprague properties, of which Zechariah Chafee had accepted the responsibilities of trustee on Dec. 1, 1873, when the three trustees first chosen by the creditors refused to act unless the creditors should protect them against personal liability for their conduct of the business. On Mar. 8, 1883, Sprague married Dora Inez (Weed) Calvert. In 1883 he was again candidate for governor, but he was unsuccessful. He retired to "Canonchet," his large estate at Narragansett Pier, which remained a relic of his former splendor. After this house was burned to the ground, he went to live in Paris, his mind and health much shattered. He died there, and his body was brought back to his native state for burial.

[H. W. Shoemaker, *The Last of the War Governors* (1916); Charles Carroll, *Rhode Island* (1932), vol. I; Benj. Knight, *Hist. of the Sprague Families in R. I.* (1881); W. V. Sprague, *Sprague Families in America* (1913); *Latham vs. Chafee*, 7 *Fed. Reports*, 520, 525, *Quidnick Company vs. Chafee*, 13 *Rhode Island*, 367, 438, 442, and *Hoyt vs. Sprague*, 103 *U. S.*, 613 for litigation over estate; for divorce see bibliography of sketch of wife, Kate Chase Sprague; scrapbook kept by Zechariah Chafee, the estate trustee, and now in the possession of Zechariah Chafee, Jr., Cambridge, Mass.; W. H. Chaffee, *The Chaffee Geneal.* (1909), pp. 237–38 for brief review of trusteeship of Sprague estate; *Providence Daily Jour.*, Apr. 12, 1869, Sept. 12, 1915; *N. Y. Tribune*, Aug. 20, 1879, Dec. 25, 1882; *Sun* (N. Y.), Dec. 19, 1880.]

E. R. B.
K. E. C.

SPRAGUE, WILLIAM BUELL (Oct. 16, 1795–May 7, 1876), clergyman, biographer, collector, was a native of rural Connecticut, having been born in a part of Hebron which is now incorporated in the town of Andover, Tolland County. He was the youngest son of Benjamin Sprague and Sibyl, daughter of William and Sibyl (Post) Buell, and a descendant of Francis Sprague who came to Plymouth in 1623, later settling at Duxbury. Having prepared for college under Rev. Abiel Abbot, minister in the nearby town of Coventry, he entered Yale College, from which he graduated in 1815. The following year he spent at "Woodlawn," about two miles from Mount Vernon, Virginia, as tutor in the family of Maj. Lawrence Lewis, a nephew of George Washington, and the husband of Eleanor Parke Custis, grand-daughter of Martha Washington. He then entered Princeton Theological Seminary, where he was a student until 1819. On Aug. 25 of that year he was ordained and installed as a colleague of Rev. Joseph Lathrop, who just sixty-three years before had himself been installed pastor of the Congregational Church of West Springfield, Mass. Upon Dr. Lathrop's death, Jan. 31, 1820, his colleague succeeded him.

Sprague's active ministry covered a period of fifty years, ten at West Springfield, and forty at the Second Presbyterian Church, Albany, N. Y., of which he assumed the pastorate, July 26, 1829. During this time he became one of the most widely known American clergymen of his day—an able sermonizer, constantly called upon for addresses on special occasions; a scholar especially interested in history and biography; a prolific writer on a variety of subjects; and an enthusiastic collector of autograph manuscripts. A list of his publications includes more than 150 titles, to which must be added numerous contributions to periodicals. For the most part these writings are sermons and addresses, but they also include such works as *Letters on Practical Subjects From a Clergyman of New England to His Daughter* (1822); *Lectures to Young People* (1830); *Lectures on Revivals of Religion* (1832); *Lectures Illustrating the Contrast Between Christianity and Various Other Systems* (1837); *Letters to Young Men, Founded on the History of Joseph* (1844); "Life of Timothy Dwight," in Jared Sparks's *Library of American Biography* (2 ser., vol. IV, 1845); *Memoirs of the Rev. John McDowell, D.D., and the Rev. William A. McDowell* (1864), and *The Life of Jedidiah Morse, D.D.* (1874). He made two trips to Europe, the first in 1828 and the second in 1836. While on the former he wrote a series of letters which appeared in the *New York Observer* (May 17–Oct. 4), were published in book form under the title, *Letters from Europe* (1828), and reprinted in London. His *Visits to European Celebrities* appeared in 1856. Probably his most enduring work, however, is his *Annals of the American Pulpit* (9 vols., 1857–69), an invaluable compendium of information regarding Protestant ministers in America down to 1850.

Throughout his life he was an indefatigable collector, especially of pamphlets, manuscripts, and autographs. While a tutor at "Woodlawn," he was given permission by Bushrod Washington to select from General Washington's correspondence whatever letters he wanted on condition he would leave copies of them. He thus came into possession of some 1,500 letters. At his death he is said to have had the largest and most valuable collection of autographs in the United States, numbering some 40,000 (Draper, *post,* p. 15). He was the first to complete a set of autographs of the Signers of the Declaration of Independence, and later completed two more sets. His own opinion of collectors he once expressed as follows: "I would advise you to have as little to do with an autograph collector as possible, for though there are some honorable exceptions yet, as a class, I think they rank A No. 1 in point of meanness" (Joline, *post,* pp. 39–40). He himself had some reputation for fairness and even generosity, but Christopher C. Baldwin wrote regarding him: "He has so much fury about him in collecting autographs that he would carry off everything that had a name attached to it. I am heartily glad he has gone out of New England, for he is so much esteemed wherever he goes that people let him into their garrets without any difficulty, and, being a Doctor of Divinity, they never think to look under his cloak to see how many precious old papers he bears off with him" ("Diary," *post,* pp. 297–98).

After his resignation at Albany, Sprague made his home with a son at Flushing, Long Island, where he died. His first wife, to whom he was married on Sept. 5, 1820, was Charlotte Eaton of Brimfield, Mass., daughter of Gen. William Eaton [*q.v.*]. She died the following year, and on Aug. 2, 1824, he married Mary Lathrop of West Springfield, who died in 1837. His third wife was her sister, Henrietta Burritt Lathrop, to whom he was married on May 13, 1840. By the first marriage he had one child; by the second, four; and by the third, five.

[F. B. Dexter, *Biog. Sketches, Grads. Yale Coll.,* vol. VI (1912); Joel Munsell, in *Colls. on the Hist. of Albany,* vol. IV (1871); C. B. Moore, "Biographical Sketch of the Rev. William Buell Sprague, D.D., LL.D.," *N. Y. Geneal. and Biog. Record,* Jan. 1877; Albert Welles, *Hist. of the Buell Family* . . . (1881); B. W. Dwight, *The Hist. of the Descendants of John Dwight of Dedham, Mass.* (2 vols., 1874); W. V. Sprague, *Sprague Families in America* (1913); "Diary of Christopher Columbus Baldwin," *Trans. and Colls. Am. Antiquarian Soc.,* vol. VIII (1901); L. C. Draper, *An Essay on the Autographic Collections of the Signers of the Declaration of Independence and of the Constitution* (1889); A. H. Joline, *The Autograph Hunter and Other Papers* (1907); *Albany Evening Journal,* May 9, 11, 12, 1876; Sprague papers in Yale Univ. Lib.]
H. E. S.

SPRECHER, SAMUEL (Dec. 28, 1810–Jan. 10, 1906), preacher, scholar, educator, was born in Washington County, Md. His father, David Sprecher, was one of three brothers who emigrated to America from Germany before the Revolution; his mother was probably a native of Washington County. He was the youngest of ten children and of delicate constitution. He early showed unusual intellectual ability and was very religious. After clerking for a while in a store in Williamsport, Md., he entered the Gymnasium in Gettysburg, Pa., in 1830, and was a student when it was organized as Pennsylvania (now Gettysburg) College in 1832. In 1834 he entered the Lutheran Theological Seminary at Gettysburg from the junior year in college, and was under the tutelage of Samuel Simon Schmucker [*q.v.*]. He was graduated from the Seminary in 1836, and on Oct. 13 of that year he was married to Catharine, the daughter of John George Schmucker [*q.v.*]. They had nine children, six boys and three girls. He was pastor of Zion Lutheran Church, Harrisburg, Pa., from 1836 until 1840, when he resigned because of poor health and became principal of Emmaus Institute, Middletown, Pa. He was pastor at Martinsburg, W. Va., from 1842 to 1843, and at Chambersburg, Pa., 1843 to 1849. Before Dr. Ezra Keller, the first president of Wittenberg College, Springfield, Ohio, died in 1849, he chose Sprecher as his successor. The trustees acted in harmony with his suggestion, and Sprecher was president from 1849 to 1874, professor of theology and philosophy, 1874 to 1880, professor of systematic theology, 1880 to 1884, and professor emeritus until his death.

In 1849 Wittenberg College was still a pioneer educational venture and the new president acted also in the capacity of chief teacher and field agent. During his administration the first building, begun under his predecessor, was completed, the endowment fund was started, and the teaching staff and the student body were enlarged. Though he was small of stature, weak in voice, and without forceful manner, his presence was always felt. Through sheer power of personality, he exercised his peculiar talents to maintain an institution of admirable academic standing. He was a born teacher and was revered by his students in philosophy and theology. He was a persuasive and convincing preacher, though somewhat handicapped by his stature and voice. His message was conservatively evangelical; his methods were often sanely evangelistic. In spite of his aggressive intellectual urge, he was a mystic pietist, representing, as did S. S. Schmucker, the conservative movement of the American Lutheran Church, which a later generation came to consider too liberal. Administrative duties and a heavy teaching load interfered with his creative work. Early in life he planned a translation of I. A. Dorner's *Entwick-*

lungsgeschichte der Lehre von der Person Christi (1845), but this work was delayed by other more pressing tasks and was finally performed by others. Until he was in the late sixties he had published only articles in religious and theological journals. In 1879 he published *The Groundwork of a System of Evangelical Lutheran Theology,* the only volume that came from his pen. Sprecher lived to be ninety-five years of age. He spent his last years at the home of a daughter in San Diego, Cal., where he died, and is buried at Springfield, Ohio.

[P. G. Bell, ed., *Samuel Sprecher, In Memoriam* (1906) ; G. G. Clark, *Hist. of Wittenberg Coll.* (1887) ; W. H. Wynn, article in the *Luth. Quart.,* Apr. 1906 ; C. B. Stover, C. W. Beachem, *The Alumni Record of Gettysburg Coll.* (1932) ; *Ohio State Jour.* (Columbus), Jan. 12, 1906.]   S. G. H.

SPRECKELS, CLAUS (July 9, 1828–Dec. 26, 1908), sugar manufacturer and California capitalist, was born in Lamstedt, in Hanover, Germany, eldest of the six children of Diedrich and Garinna (Back) Spreckels. In 1846 he came to America and found employment in a grocery store in Charleston, S. C., eventually buying the business. Here, in 1852, he married Anna Christina Mangel. In 1855 he sold this business and removed to New York City, where he successfully ran a wholesale and retail grocery store. His brother Bernard, returning from California, induced him to dispose of his profitable New York enterprise and to move in 1856 to San Francisco. Here he again operated a grocery store, soon selling it, however, and engaging in the more profitable brewing business.

In 1863 Claus and his brother established the Bay Sugar Refining Company, getting their raw material from the Hawaiian Islands. Two years later he sold his interest, and went to Europe to study the manufacture of sugar in all its aspects. Returning to California in 1867 with new ideas and improved machinery, he organized the California Sugar Refinery, and within five years the plant had grown to large proportions, with an output of fifty million pounds a year. He invented and patented, July 28, 1874, a method of manufacturing hard or loaf sugar. Between 1881 and 1883, he completed the construction in San Francisco of the largest refinery on the Pacific Coast. Convinced of the commercial possibilities in the sugar-beet industry, he went to Europe and purchased machinery for a sugar-beet refinery, which he established at Salinas, Cal., near two large sugar-beet ranches which he had previously begun to develop. To connect these projects with San Francisco he financed the Pajaro Valley Railroad, opened in 1895 and completed in 1898 For many years he held a virtual monop-

oly of the manufacture and sale of refined sugar on the Pacific Coast, and was called the "Sugar King." Enraged at the competition and threats of the Sugar Trust, he dramatically carried the war into the enemy's country by constructing a three million dollar refinery in Philadelphia (1888–89), which he compelled the Trust to buy at his own price. He fought the transportation monopoly of the Southern Pacific Railroad by aiding in the financing of the San Francisco & San Joaquin Valley Railway, which later became a part of the Santa Fé system. By organizing the Independent Light & Power Company (1899) and the Independent Gas & Power Company (1903), he compelled the San Francisco Gas & Electric Company first to reduce rates and improve the service to the people of San Francisco and then to purchase the independent companies. By organizing a rival street railway company (1906), he attempted to prevent the United Railroads under Patrick Calhoun from setting up an overhead trolley system on San Francisco's principal streets.

Shortly after moving to California, Spreckels became deeply interested in the development of the sugar industry in the Hawaiian Islands, and eventually obtained from the King a concession of upwards of 40,000 acres. This he proceeded to develop through the Hawaiian Commercial Company. Over the control of this company and its rich plantations a family feud, which had been in existence for some time, came to a climax in 1899. After long and bitter financial and legal battles, the sons, Rudolph and Claus Augustus, defeated their father and their two brothers, Adolph and John Diedrich [*q.v.*]. They secured control of the company, reorganized its affairs, and sold their interests at a great profit. A family reconciliation was effected in 1905, and thereafter Rudolph became the active manager of his father's affairs. Claus at his death left a fortune of not less than $15,000,000, two-thirds of which was invested in real estate, including the Spreckels Building on Market Street, the first skyscraper in San Francisco. He owned several fine residences, the one on Van Ness Avenue being partially destroyed at the time of the great fire. He gave generously to the welfare of San Francisco and its institutions. He never sought office, though he was a presidential elector on the Republican ticket in 1872. He was a man of unusual force of character, endowed with boundless pluck, daring, and resourcefulness. He died in San Francisco, survived by his wife, four sons, and a daughter.

[Alonzo Phelps, *Contemporary Biog. of California's Representative Men* (1881) ; *The Bay of San Francisco* (1892) ; R. D. Hunt, *Cal. and Californians* (1926) ;

Who's Who in America, 1908–09; *San Francisco Call,* Mar. 24, 1906, Dec. 27, 1908; *San Francisco Chronicle,* Dec. 27, 1908; *San Francisco Bulletin,* Feb. 11, 1905; article in Los Angeles *Express,* May 19, 1906, repr. in B. K. Power, *William Henry Knight* (1832); *N. Y. Times,* Dec. 27, 1908.]   P.O.R.

SPRECKELS, JOHN DIEDRICH (Aug. 16, 1853–June 7, 1926), sugar merchant and California capitalist, was the eldest of thirteen children born to Claus Spreckels [*q.v.*] and Anna (Mangel). Three years after his birth in Charleston, S. C., his parents moved to San Francisco. He was educated in the public schools, and in Oakland College, Oakland, Cal., later studying chemistry and mechanical engineering in the Polytechnic College in Hanover, Germany. Upon his return to California, he became an apprentice in the technical and business departments of his father's sugar refinery, and at the age of twenty-two was made a plant superintendent. In 1876 he went to the Hawaiian Islands and devoted a year to sugar analysis, and later superintended the erection of a sugar mill and the development of his father's sugar plantations. In 1880 he founded the J. D. Spreckels & Brothers Company, shipping and commission merchants, which in December 1881 established the Oceanic Steamship Company, operating between San Francisco and the Hawaiian Islands. Subsequently, the firm's shipping interests were extended to Australia and New Zealand.

Visiting San Diego on a pleasure trip in 1887, he became captivated with the locality and made it the chief seat of his activities for the rest of his life, contributing in many ways to the development of the city and nearby Coronado. First he built a wharf and began supplying coal to the Santa Fé Railroad; in 1887 the Spreckels Brothers' Commercial Company was organized and soon practically controlled the import and export trade of San Diego. He promoted the erection of the Coronado Beach Hotel; bought the San Diego street railway and supplanted horsepower with electricity; aided the city in obtaining an adequate supply of pure water; erected modern office buildings, a theatre, and two more hotels. He generously aided in the success of the Panama-California Exposition (1915–16), and among his best known benefactions was the gift of the great organ in Balboa Park, dedicated on the eve of the opening of the Exposition. Another of his notable benefactions was a large gift which he, a 33rd degree Mason, made to Mercy Hospital, a Catholic institution, for a much needed addition. Through his efforts, the San Diego & Arizona Railway (later part of the Southern Pacific system) was built during the World War as a link between San Diego, the Imperial Valley, and the East. In most of these interests and activities he was closely associated with his brother Adolph B. Spreckels, who died in 1924.

He was president or vice-president of many business corporations, including the Oceanic Steamship Company, the Western Sugar Refining Company, the Spreckels Sugar Company, the San Diego Electric Railway, the Pajaro Valley Railroad, and the San Diego & Arizona Railway. He was a member of numerous clubs, including the Pacific Union and Bohemian Club of San Francisco and the San Francisco and San Diego yacht clubs. His magnificent yacht *Venetia* he turned over to the government during the World War. Yachting, music, and art were his favorite avocations. In 1897 he purchased the *San Francisco Call* and conducted it until 1913, when it became an evening paper, with Spreckels holding a minority interest. At one time he was a dominant figure in the Republican party of the state. In October 1877 he married Lillie C. Siebein of Hoboken, N. J.; four children were born to them. Although he owned a beautiful residence in San Francisco, his favorite home was in Coronado, where he lived during the last twenty years of his life and died.

[*Who's Who in America,* 1920–21; R. D. Hunt, *Cal. and Californians* (1926); *The Bay of San Francisco* (1892); *San Francisco Call, San Francisco Chronicle, San Francisco Examiner,* and *N. Y. Times,* June 8, 1926; *San Francisco Bulletin,* June 7, 1926; C. A. McGrew, *City of San Diego and San Diego County* (1922), II, 3–6; *San Francisco: Its Builders, Past and Present* (1913).]   P.O.R.

SPRING, GARDINER (Feb. 24, 1785–Aug. 18, 1873), Presbyterian clergyman, was born at Newburyport, Mass., descended from John Spring who settled at Watertown, Mass., in 1634. His father was Samuel Spring [*q.v.*] and his mother, Hannah (Hopkins) Spring, the daughter of Samuel Hopkins, for fifty-six years minister in Hadley, Mass. Spring graduated at Yale College in 1805, entered a New Haven law office, then went to Bermuda to teach, and remained until late in 1807, except for a visit during which he was married to Susan Barney of New Haven, on May 25, 1806. Resuming his legal studies, he was admitted to the bar in December 1808 and began practice in New Haven. Before long a religious experience that had begun in college caused his decision to become a minister. In the autumn of 1809 he entered Andover Theological Seminary, where he studied for eight months. Called to the pastorate of the Brick Presbyterian Church, then located on Beekman Street at Nassau, he was ordained and installed on Aug. 8, 1810, as colleague to the aged John Rodgers, 1727–1811 [*g.v.*].

He took up this pastorate, his life-work, with a concentrated devotion that remained constant with him. From the first, preaching was his chief concern. In his early ministry, as always, his sermons came out of diligent study and wide reading but were definitely intended to produce conversions. He believed firmly in the revival method, which then dominated the American churches. During the twenty years preceding 1834 his church experienced repeated awakenings, resulting in a steady religious earnestness. Thereafter his preaching had a larger element of instruction. Distinctly pastoral and ethical, it had a strong theological framework. He was a thorough Calvinist, with considerable liberality of spirit. He protested strongly against the exclusion of several synods from the Presbyterian Church in 1837 because of theological differences, but when the church divided he and his congregation joined the conservative branch. After the Brick Church had suffered for ten years because of its down-town location—meanwhile held together chiefly by loyalty to its pastor—a new building was dedicated in 1858, which still (1935) stands at Fifth Avenue and Thirty-seventh Street. He had now built up a congregation remarkable for the strength of its membership, which included many people influential in the city, and for its abundant philanthropies. He held a commanding position in the life of New York and was active in all sorts of religious and charitable enterprises, local and national, especially in missionary causes. The publication of many of his sermons and addresses increased the influence gained by his preaching. His most widely circulated books were *Essays on the Distinguishing Traits of the Christian Character* (1813), *Obligations of the World to the Bible* (1839), and *The Power of the Pulpit* (1848). In 1866 he published two volumes of *Personal Reminiscences of the Life and Times of Gardiner Spring*. His wife, the mother of his fifteen children, died on Aug. 7, 1860, and on Aug. 14, 1861, he was married to Abba Grosvenor Williams.

The Civil War stirred him to intense activity. He had sympathized strongly with the South, because he held that slavery was recognized in the Constitution and had opposed the Abolitionists. But when secession impended, he committed himself to the cause of the Union. In the Old School Presbyterian General Assembly that met in May 1861 he proposed the "Gardiner Spring resolutions." By adopting these, somewhat amended, after a strenuous debate, the Assembly gave its allegiance to the Federal government—an action memorable in the relations of church and state. In the General Assembly of 1869, in his own church, though eighty-four and almost blind, he pled powerfully at a critical point for the reunion of the two branches of the Presbyterian Church, the New School and the Old School, and he saw it accomplished. Four years later he died in New York.

[J. O. Murray, *A Discourse Commemorating the Ministerial Character and Services of Gardiner Spring* (1873); F. B. Dexter, *Biog. Sketches of the Grads. of Yale College*, vol. V (1911); Shepherd Knapp, *A Hist. of the Brick Presbyterian Church in the City of New York* (1909); L. G. VanderVelde, *The Presbyterian Churches and the Federal Union, 1861–1869* (1932); *New York Observer*, Aug. 28, 1873.]   R. H. N.

SPRING, LEVERETT WILSON (Jan. 5, 1840–Dec. 23, 1917), clergyman, professor of English, and historian, was born at Grafton, Vt., the son of Edward and Martha (Atwood) Spring, and a descendant of John Spring who came from England and settled at Watertown, Mass., in 1634. He received his elementary education in Manchester, Vt., and was graduated from the Burr and Burton Academy in 1858. After taking the degree of B.A. from Williams College in 1863, he entered the Theological Institute of Connecticut at Hartford, from which he was graduated in 1866; the following year he continued his studies at the Andover Theological Seminary, and began preaching. His formal education completed, he was married on Sept. 25, 1867, to Sarah Elizabeth Thompson, daughter of Prof. William Thompson of Hartford. They had two children, a daughter, who died in 1888, and a son. He was ordained as pastor of the Rollstone Congregational Church of Fitchburg, Mass., in 1868 and continued at that charge till 1875, when he moved to Lawrence, Kan., for his health. After serving as minister of the Plymouth Congregational Church of Lawrence, 1876–81, he became professor of belles-lettres and English literature at the University of Kansas, Lawrence. During these years he wrote the book for which he is best known, *Kansas: the Prelude to the War for the Union* (1885), which he based not only upon printed sources but upon personal reminiscences collected from surviving pioneers. In this book, the first nonpartisan account of the Kansas struggle, he was eminently fair to John Brown; however, he offended the admirers of that crusader who wanted nothing printed but panegyrics, and brought forth a storm of criticism by his account of the massacre of Dutch Henry's Crossing and other rash exploits of Brown. The book nevertheless has become the basis for later critical studies of the fight for Kansas. In 1886 Spring became Morris Professor of Rhetoric at Williams, a position he held till he was retired in

1909 in his seventieth year. The remainder of his life he spent in Boston, where he died.

His later works include *Mark Hopkins, Teacher* (1888); *Williams College, Williamstown, Mass., Historical Sketch and Views* (1904); and *A History of Williams College* (1917). He also wrote various other sketches of Williams College for college publications and cooperative works. To the proceedings of the Massachusetts Historical Society he contributed a sketch of Col. Samuel Walker's visit to John Brown (vol. XLVII, 1914), "A Case of Church Discipline in the Berkshires" (vol. XLIX, 1916), and "The Singular Case of a New England Clergyman" (vol. L, 1917), and to the *American Historical Review,* April 1898, "The Career of a Kansas Politician," the subject being James Henry Lane [*q.v.*].

[See *Who's Who in America,* 1916–17; T. C. Smith, in *Proc. Mass. Hist. Soc.,* vol. LI (1918), pp. 214–19; obituary in *Boston Transcript,* Dec. 24, 1917. Information has been supplied by Prof. C. L. Maxcy of Williams Col., Prof. E. M. Hopkins of the Univ. of Kan., and Romney Spring, Boston, Mass., Spring's son.]

F. A. S.

SPRING, SAMUEL (Feb. 27, 1746 o.s.–Mar. 4, 1819), Congregational clergyman, one of the founders of Andover Theological Seminary and of the American Board of Commissioners for Foreign Missions, was a native of that part of Uxbridge, Mass., that is now known as Northbridge. He was a descendant of John Spring who settled in Watertown, Mass., in 1634; his parents were Col. John, a wealthy farmer, deacon, and slave-holder, and Sarah (Read) Spring. His father's opposition to an academic education for his son having been overcome by his mother's influence, Samuel pursued preparatory studies under Rev. Nathan Webb of Uxbridge and graduated from the College of New Jersey in 1771. The next three years he spent in the study of theology under John Witherspoon at Princeton, and under Joseph Bellamy, Samuel Hopkins [*qq.v.*], and Stephen West. In 1775 he joined the Continental Army and was chaplain of Arnold's expedition to Canada. He left the army at the close of 1776 and on Aug. 6, 1777, was ordained pastor of the North (now Central) Congregational Church of Newburyport, Mass., where he served the remainder of his life.

Spring occupied a position of commanding influence among the Congregational churches of New England and was identified with the "Hopkinsian" or extreme Calvinist wing. He was a leader in the formation of the Massachusetts Missionary Society in 1779, an organization devoted to the promotion of his type of theology, and was an editor of its organ, *The Massachusetts*

Missionary Magazine, established in 1803. He was also one of the founders of the Massachusetts General Association in 1803, a union of the two Calvinistic parties with a view to opposing more effectually the rising tide of Unitarianism. Much interested in theological education and an instructor of students for the ministry, he was one of the first to conceive of a school of divinity for New England and in 1806 took the lead in securing an endowment for a seminary of strict Hopkinsian principles to be established at West Newbury. At the same time another school was being projected by the more moderate Old Calvinist party at Andover, and after much adjustment the two movements were finally brought together, with the result that the Andover Theological Seminary was opened in September 1808. The West Newbury group, known as the "Associate Founders," were perpetuated in the Board of Visitors and their creed, formulated by Spring and destined to be productive of much mischief in the subsequent history of the Seminary, was added to the standards of the institution. Though reluctant at first, he finally became a champion of the union and was a Visitor and a stanch supporter to the end of his life.

Although a wave of missionary interest had been rising in the churches and colleges, no attempt at an organization to carry on missionary work had been made till the meeting of the Massachusetts General Association at Bradford in June 1810, when the American Board of Commissioners for Foreign Missions was founded. Spring was in large measure responsible for the inauguration of the enterprise and was its vice-president, a member of its prudential committee, and its ardent champion till his death. He was the author of about twenty-five publications which were mostly sermons for various occasions. Typical of them were his *Christian Knowledge and Christian Confidence Inseparable* (1785); *The Exemplary Pastor* (1791); *Two Discourses on Christ's Selfexistence* (1805). He was a clear thinker, a forceful preacher, and noted for his practical wisdom. John Quincy Adams wrote of him: "His sentiments are extremely contracted and illiberal, and he maintains them with the zeal and enthusiasms of a bigot, but his delivery is very agreeable, and I believe his devotion sincere" (*Life in a New England Town . . . Diary of John Quincy Adams,* 1903, p. 63). On Nov. 4, 1779, he married Hannah, daughter of Rev. Samuel Hopkins of Hadley, Mass. Their family consisted of eleven children, one of whom was Gardiner Spring [*q.v.*].

[Henry Bond, *Geneals. of . . . the Early Settlers of Watertown, Mass.* (1855); W. B. Sprague, *Annals Am. Pulpit,* vol. II (1857); *Personal Reminiscences of the*

Life and Times of Gardiner Spring (1866); *A Memorial of the Semi-Centennial Celebration of the Founding of the Theological Sem. at Andover* (1859); Leonard Woods, *Hist. of the Andover Theological Sem.* (1885); W. E. Strong, *The Story of the Am. Board* (1910); Williston Walker, *A Hist. of the Congregational Churches in the U. S.* (1894); *Columbian Centinel* (Boston), Mar. 6, 1819.]   F.T.P.

SPRINGER, FRANK (June 17, 1848–Sept. 22, 1927), lawyer, paleontologist, son of Judge Francis and Nancy (Coleman) Springer, was born at Wapella, Iowa. He was educated in the local public schools and the state university at Iowa City, receiving the degree of B.S. in 1867. He then studied law in the office of Henry Strong, and in 1869 was admitted to the bar and given the position of prosecuting attorney for the Burlington district. In 1873 he left Burlington for New Mexico, settling at Cimarron in the northern part of the territory, whence in 1883 he moved to Las Vegas, retaining his residence there until his death, though spending much of his time in Santa Fé and in Washington, D. C.

Springer early became one of the leading lawyers of the state, and "during all the years of his active career at the bar, either as trial lawyer or as counsel, was consulted in every case of any consequence which was heard in the courts of New Mexico" (Twitchell, *post*, p. 159). In 1890 he was elected president of the New Mexico Bar Association, and became leader in a movement providing for the immediate settlement by Congress, through a proper tribunal, of titles under Spanish and Mexican land grants, the bill establishing the "Court of Private Land Claims" which finally became a law, being, it is stated, drafted by him. His most conspicuous legal effort was as counsel in the case of the celebrated Maxwell Land Grant, which he fought in the United States courts for some thirty years and finally won, becoming in 1891 president of the Maxwell Land Grant Company. In 1880 and in 1901 Springer was a member of the legislative council of New Mexico; in 1889, of the constitutional convention. He was for five years (1898–1903) president of the board of regents of the New Mexico Normal University at Las Vegas, and he took a prominent part in the building of the Eagle's Nest Dam and the St. Louis, Rocky Mountain & Pacific Railroad.

While a student at the University of Iowa he became interested in the natural sciences, and under the extremely favorable conditions there afforded entered upon paleontological studies that in the end placed him in the foremost rank of students of the great group of fossil crinoids. Even after his removal to New Mexico, he returned for a number of years each summer to Burlington, where he and Charles Wachsmuth [*q.v.*] built up what became known in later years as the Wachsmuth-Springer collection, comprising over 100,000 individual specimens. Springer was not, however, a mere collector. He became a leader along the lines of systematic and morphologic work and published, alone or with Wachsmuth, fifty-eight books and papers on crinoids. Their first great joint work, *Revision of the Palaeocrinoidea,* a three-part volume of 725 pages, was published during 1880–86. This was followed in 1897 by a three-volume work, *The North American Crinoidea Camerata*; in 1920, after the death of Wachsmuth, by *Crinoidea Flexibilia* in two volumes; and in 1926, by *American Silurian Crinoids,* all comprising "the most magnificent of monographs on invertebrate paleontology published in this country" (Schuchert, *post,* p. 74). Springer early became interested in archaeology, also, and was one of the founders and active promoters of the museum of New Mexico and the school of American research in Santa Fé. He was prominent in the councils of the Archaeological Society of America and was for some years sponsor for its publications.

In the spring of 1906 he developed an organic disease of the heart, which became a cause of frequent prostrations. In 1910 he retired from his law practice but continued his studies on his crinoid collections, which became the property of the National Museum at Washington, where he did most of his work. His last publication, *American Silurian Crinoids,* he completed and saw through the press while confined to his bed at the home of his son-in-law in Philadelphia. On Oct. 10, 1876, he was married to Josephine M. Bishop of Santa Fé, who, with three sons and four daughters, survived him.

[Charles Schuchert, "Memorial of Frank Springer," in *Bull. Geological Soc. of America,* Mar. 1928; Charles Keyes, "Springer of the Crinoids," in *Pan. Am. Geologist,* Dec. 1927; addresses by E. L. Hewett, R. E. Twitchell, and others on the occasion of the presentation to the state of a bronze bust of Springer, at Santa Fé, Oct. 2, 1922, reprinted in his *Am. Silurian Crinoids*; *Who's Who in America 1926–27*; *Santa Fé New Mexican,* Sept. 23, 1927.]   G. P. M.

SPRINGER, REUBEN RUNYAN (Nov. 16, 1800–Dec. 11, 1884), philanthropist, son of Charles and Catherine (Runyan) Springer, was born in Frankfort, Ky. His father, a farmer, fought under General Wayne at the battle of Maumee (1794) and was for many years postmaster of Frankfort. Springer was educated in the local schools and at thirteen entered the post office as a clerk, succeeding his father as postmaster upon the latter's death in 1816. Two years later, he secured a position as clerk on the *George Madison,* a river boat that ran between Louisville and New Orleans; later, he held a similar position on the *George Washington,* a boat owned by Kilgour, Taylor & Company, the largest wholesale grocery house in Cincinnati. On Jan. 30, 1830, he married Jane Kilgour, the daughter of the senior member of this firm. Springer was soon admitted to partnership in the concern and for the next ten years was engaged in mercantile pursuits. In 1840 he retired from active business on account of ill health. Two years later he went to Europe, and again in 1844–45, 1849, and 1851. During his travels abroad he spent much time in visiting the art centers and in collecting valuable works of art. As a result of prudent investments in real estate and railroads, he accumulated a fortune. He was a large stockholder and a director of the Little Miami and the Pittsburgh, Fort Wayne & Chicago railroads, and a director in numerous banks and insurance companies.

Springer is best remembered as a patron of music and art and as a liberal donor to the Catholic Church, of which he was a devoted member. He interested himself particularly in the education of young men for the priesthood. In connection with music, he was largely responsible for providing Cincinnati with a music hall and a college of music. The music festivals held in 1873 and 1875 created great enthusiasm and suggested the establishment of a permanent institution devoted to music. In May 1875 Springer addressed a letter to John Shillito offering to donate $125,000 for the purpose of building a music hall, on two conditions: first, that the lot on Elm and Fourteenth streets be secured from the city at a nominal rental and free from taxation for the perpetual use of a society formed for the purpose; and second, that a further sum of not less than $125,000 be donated by the citizens. The offer was received with much acclaim but subscriptions came in slowly. Many felt that preference was being extended to the music hall at the expense of the exposition building. "We are a mechanical people, not a race of fiddlers," was the argument advanced (*Cincinnati Enquirer,* Dec. 11, 1884). Several times when the success of the project seemed to be threatened Springer came to the rescue with supplementary propositions, and it is estimated that his donations amounted to $190,500. He also secured a lot and advanced funds for the erection of a suitable building for the College of Music; gave the institution a permanent endowment; provided for the construction of the Odeon—an adjunct to the college, for recitals and student concerts; and established a fund of $5,000 for gold medals to be awarded to pupils of superior merit. His do-

nations to the college amounted in all to $200,000. He was one of the incorporators in 1881 of the Cincinnati Museum Association, and left $20,000 to the Art School of Cincinnati. A quiet, unostentatious, modest man, he refused to have the Music Hall or the College of Music named after him. He had no children.

[*The Biog. Cyc. and Portrait Gallery . . . of the State of Ohio,* vol. II (1884); G. M. Roe, *Cincinnati: The Queen City of the West* (1895); C. T. Greve, *Centennial Hist. of Cincinnati* (1904), vol. I; *Cincinnati Enquirer,* Dec. 11, 12, 14, 16, 1884.]   R. C. McG.

SPRINGER, WILLIAM McKENDREE (May 30, 1836–Dec. 4, 1903), lawyer, congressman, was born in New Lebanon, Ind., the son of Thomas B. and Katherine Springer. When he was about twelve years old the family moved to Jacksonville, Ill. William attended the public schools in New Lebanon and Jacksonville and prepared for college under Dr. Newton Bateman [*q.v.*], who was then teaching in the latter city. He entered Illinois College, Jacksonville, but was dismissed in 1856 following some difficulty with the faculty. He immediately enrolled at Indiana University, where he was graduated in 1858. The following year he was admitted to the bar and began practising law in Lincoln, Ill. On Dec. 15, 1859, he married Rebecca, daughter of the Rev. Calvin W. Ruter of Bloomington, Ind. She became a writer of some note, publishing several novels and contributing poetry to current magazines. They had one son. In 1861 they moved to Springfield, Ill., where Springer entered into a law partnership with N. M. Broadwell and John A. McClernand [*q.v.*].

After the Civil War he admitted that he had not supported the war measures of the administration and took the position that the Southern states were never out of the Union. He further stated that he had been agreeably surprised by President Johnson's policies, having expected very little from him (speech reported in *Daily Illinois State Register,* Sept. 12, 1865). Springer's non-support of the war was not entirely passive, however; he was a member of two anti-administration organizations, the Sons of Liberty (*War of the Rebellion: Official Records, Army,* 1 ser., vol. XLV, pt. 1, p. 1083) and the Order of American Knights (*Ibid.,* 2 ser. VII, 298, 746). In 1862 he represented Logan County at a state constitutional convention held in Springfield and was chosen secretary. There was much bitterness between the northern and southern parts of the state at this time. Most of the convention officers were from the southern section and their attempt to force through a constitution led to increased animosity. The constitution finally accepted was defeated by vote of the people (Elliott Anthony, *Constitutional History of Illinois,* 1891; O. M. Dickerson, *The Illinois Constitutional Convention of 1862,* 1905). In 1868 Springer left his law practice to travel in Europe, partly for his wife's health and partly for pleasure. He returned to Illinois in 1870.

Ten years before he had been defeated on the Democratic ticket for representative in the state legislature, but in 1870 he was elected to represent Sangamon County. In 1874 he was elected to the Forty-fourth Congress from the twelfth district, and served continuously from Mar. 4, 1875, to Mar. 3, 1895. During these twenty years he was on many committees and chairman of some important ones—Claims, Territories, Elections, Ways and Means, Banking and Currency. He was always a friend of the territories and introduced bills under which Washington, Montana, and the Dakotas were admitted into the Union as states. He was interested in the tariff and as chairman of the Ways and Means Committee carried through several minor tariff revisions during the Fifty-second Congress. In the following Congress he used his influence in favor of the Wilson tariff measure which was passed in 1894. He was a parliamentarian, and as such was often more interested in the rules of procedure and debate than in the issues involved. "Uncle Joe" Cannon remarked that Springer had "a weakness for breaking into the limelight regardless of the inconvenience he caused other Members" (L. W. Busbey, *Uncle Joe Cannon: The Story of a Pioneer American,* copr. 1927, p. 342). Renominated for Congress in 1894, he was defeated. A friend, Henry Clendenin, editor of the *State Register* of Springfield, claimed that his defeat was due to his conversion to the gold standard after years of advocating the free coinage of gold and silver at the ratio of 16 to 1 (*Autobiography of Henry W. Clendenin,* 1926, p. 215). Upon the completion of his congressional career, Springer resumed his law practice in Washington, D. C., but was appointed in 1895 judge of the northern district of the Indian Territory and justice of the United States court of appeals in the Indian Territory. When his term expired, in December 1899, he again took up the practice of law in Washington. He died of pneumonia in his sixty-seventh year.

[*Hist. of Sangamon County, Ill.; Together with . . . Biogs. of Representative Citizens* (1881); biog. sketch in Springer's *Tariff Reform . . . Speeches and Writings* (1892); *Chicago Daily Tribune,* Dec. 5, 1903; *Ill. State Journal* (Springfield), Dec. 5, 1903; *Ill. State Reg.* (Springfield), Dec. 5, 1903; Joseph Wallace, *Past and Present of the City of Springfield and Sangamon County, Ill.* (1904); *Biog. Dir. Am. Cong.* (1928); *Who's Who in America,* 1901–02.]   E. B. E.

SPROUL, WILLIAM CAMERON (Sept. 16, 1870–Mar. 21, 1928), manufacturer, governor of Pennsylvania, was born at Octoraro, Lancaster County, Pa., the son of William Hall and Deborah Dickinson (Slokom) Sproul. On his father's side he was of Scotch-Irish ancestry, being descended from Charles Sproul, who came to America from Ireland in 1786; his mother's people were Quakers. When William was four years old the family removed to Negaunee, Mich., where he attended public schools. Returning to Lancaster County in 1882, the Sprouls decided soon after to settle in Chester, a rising industrial center of Delaware County, where their son completed the high-school course in 1887. He then entered Swarthmore College, and was graduated in 1891. As an undergraduate he interested himself in athletics, oratory, and journalism, among other distinctions achieving the editorship of the Swarthmore College *Phoenix.* Soon after leaving college he acquired an interest in the daily *Chester Times,* later extending his investments with unusual financial success to manufacturing, railroad, traction, real estate, and banking enterprises. On Jan. 21, 1892, he married Emeline Wallace Roach, grand-daughter of John Roach [*q.v.*] and daughter of John B. Roach who was the owner of a large shipbuilding concern on the lower Delaware River; they had two children.

Coincident with his entrance into business, Sproul engaged actively in local politics. In 1895, the first year he was eligible under the constitutional age requirement, he became a candidate for a seat in the Senate of the Commonwealth from the ninth (Delaware County) district, being elected thereto the following year and every four years thereafter to and including 1916. Early in his career as state senator (1896), he voted for John Wanamaker [*q.v.*], candidate for the United States Senate against Boies Penrose [*q.v.*]; the latter, however, was elected. He also opposed the reëlection to that body of Matthew S. Quay [*q.v.*], leader of the Republican state organization, who at the time was under indictment because of certain banking scandals. For these bold actions he was hailed as a reformer, destined perhaps to cleanse the Augean stables of Pennsylvania politics. After Quay's acquittal, in 1901, however, Sproul made his peace with the organization and supported its leader for the United States senatorship. Thereafter, while preserving, probably, as great a degree of independence as the boss-ridden condition of the state permitted, he remained essentially a regular Republican, at times making vigorous denials of the charge that he was an Insurgent or Progressive. While in the state Senate Sproul pushed highway construction vigorously, $100,000,000 being appropriated to that purpose during his long period of membership. In consequence he became widely known throughout the state as the "father of good roads."

As early as 1910 and again in 1914 Sproul's friends urged his candidacy for the governorship, his reply on both occasions being: "I have not cocked up my hay yet." In 1918, however, he entered the contest, winning the nomination in the direct primary by 205,000 votes. During the ensuing campaign he supported prohibition and woman's suffrage, both of which measures were opposed by the Democratic nominee, Eugene C. Bonniwell, whom he defeated by 247,222 votes. As governor from 1919 to 1923 Sproul continued his interest in good roads and secured a much needed reorganization of several branches of the state administration. He attracted wide attention by going outside the commonwealth for his superintendent of public instruction, appointing a well-known expert, Dr. Thomas E. Finegan, then deputy commissioner of education in New York. During the great steel strike of 1919 his administration was criticized severely by liberals because of the conduct of the state police in the areas affected. He pushed vigorously the proposal for a convention to revise the antiquated state constitution dating from 1874; but it was rejected by nearly 100,000 majority at the referendum of Sept. 20, 1921. At the Republican National Convention of 1920 Sproul was a "favorite son" candidate for the presidency, receiving the support of the entire Pennsylvania delegation and a total of eighty-four votes; after the ninth ballot he withdrew. Foregoing his own ambition, he had occasion as governor to appoint three men to vacancies caused by death in the United States Senate—William E. Crow *vice* Philander C. Knox, George Wharton Pepper *vice* Boies Penrose, and David A. Reed *vice* William E. Crow. After completing his term at Harrisburg, Sproul devoted himself to travel, to the interests of Swarthmore College—of the board of managers of which he was a member from 1902 onward and to which he had presented the Sproul Astronomical Observatory—and to the management of his large business interests. He died at "Lapidea Manor," the family residence, near Chester, Pa.

[*Smull's Legislative Handbook and Manual of the State of Pa.*, 1896–1916, 1919–25; *Address of Gov. William C. Sproul to the Gen. Assembly of Pa.* (1923); C. E. Slocum, *A Short Hist. of the Slocums, Slocumbs and Slocombs*, vol. I (1882); J. W. Jordan, *Encyc. of Pa. Biog.*, vol. IV (1915); G. F. Donehoo, *Pa.: A Hist.* (1926), vol. VII; *Who's Who in America*, 1926–27; *Pa. Mag. of Hist. and Biog.*, July 1928; *Evening Pub.*

Ledger (Phila.), Mar. 22, 1928; *Phila. Inquirer*, Mar. 22, 1928.]   R. C. B.

SPROULL, THOMAS (Sept. 15, 1803–Mar. 21, 1892), clergyman of the Reformed Presbyterian Church and theological teacher, was born near Lucesco, Westmoreland County, Pa. Thither his parents, Robert and Mary (Dunlap) Sproull, north of Ireland people and Covenanters, had moved from Franklin County in 1796. The Sproulls maintained covenanting principles alone in their neighborhood for twenty years, until they were joined by David Houston. From these families there sprang an influential Reformed Presbyterian or Covenanter congregation. Thomas Sproull conformed to the teaching of his Church by leading his life wholly within its associations. Because of his parents' poverty he had in boyhood only an elementary education. From the age of twenty-three he studied for two years with Jonathan Gill, minister of the church at Lucesco, and then entered the senior class of the Western University of Pennsylvania, graduating in 1829. After leaving college he read theology with John Black, minister of the Reformed Presbyterian Church of Pittsburgh. On Apr. 4, 1832, he was licensed to preach by the Presbytery of Pittsburgh, and on the same day of 1833 he was ordained as a home missionary. At the General Synod of 1833 the Reformed Presbyterian Church divided into Old School and New School—Synod and General Synod. The New School allowed church members to vote and hold civil office, thus departing from the disapproving attitude toward the government of the United States maintained by the Church. Sproull, who was present at this meeting, sided with the Old School. The Pittsburgh Reformed Presbyterian Church having joined the New School, a small Old School Church was formed in Allegheny (North Pittsburgh), over which he was installed pastor on May 12, 1834. During his ministry of thirty-four years this congregation grew to be the strongest in the denomination.

At the founding of the theological seminary of the Church in Allegheny in 1838 Sproull was chosen professor of theology, and served until 1845, the institution then being moved to Cincinnati. In 1856 it was reëstablished in Allegheny and he again became professor. Twelve years later, when he resigned his office because of pastoral duties, the Synod asked him to leave his church and devote himself to the seminary; to this request he acceded. He was made professor emeritus in 1874, but carried on some teaching for seventeen years longer. His theology appears in his *Prelections on Theology* (1882) as Calvinism according to Covenanter traditions.

He was a leader of his Church in all its affairs. In 1847 he was moderator of its Synod. He was especially interested in its missionary work in China and in behalf of negroes and Indians. For two years he was one of the editors of the *Christian Witness,* an early anti-slavery paper published 1836–40. He was editor of the *Reformed Presbyterian* from 1855 to 1863, and then of the *Reformed Presbyterian and Covenanter* until 1874. For these periodicals he wrote many articles, chiefly in support of the distinctive tenets of the Reformed Presbyterians, and a series of sketches of their early history in America. In 1859 he was appointed to compose a declaration of the Church regarding slavery and secret societies. While he held rigidly to the peculiar witness of his Church, his gracious Christian influence was widely acknowledged. After teaching until he was eighty-eight, he spent his last days in Allegheny. He was married on July 1, 1834, to Magdeline Wallace of Pittsburgh, and had three sons who were Reformed Presbyterian ministers.

[W. M. Glasgow, *Hist. of the Reformed Presbyterian Church in America* (1888) ; R. D. Sproull, in *Reformed Presbyterian and Covenanter,* June 1892, and other articles, *Ibid.,* May, July 1892 ; Minutes of the Synod of the Ref. Presbyt. Church in *Reformed Presbyterian and Covenanter;* O. H. Thompson, *Sketches of the Ministers of the Reformed Presbyterian Church of North America from 1888 to 1930* (1930) ; *Pittsburg Press,* Mar. 21, 1892.] R. H. N.

SPRUNT, JAMES (June 9, 1846–July 9, 1924), business man, author, and philanthropist, was born in Glasgow, Scotland, the son of Alexander and Jane (Dalziel) Sprunt. The family emigrated to Duplin County, N. C., in 1852, and two years later removed to Wilmington. James attended school in Glasgow, in Kenansville, N. C., and in Wilmington. He began preparation for college but the needs of the family compelled him to go to work at the age of fourteen, though he still attended a night school and studied navigation. During the Civil War, his father was captured while attempting to run the blockade and heavy responsibilities were thrown upon the boy. In 1863, however, he went to Bermuda to become purser of the *North Heath,* a blockade runner; later, he became purser of the *Lilian.* After several trips through the Federal fleet, the ship was captured in 1864 and Sprunt was imprisoned at Fort Macon. Taken to Fortress Monroe for transfer to another prison, he escaped through cool daring and made his way by Boston to Halifax, Nova Scotia. While returning he was wrecked on Green Turtle Cay, but was rescued and became purser of the *Susan Beirne,* on which he served until the fall of Fort Fisher. Setting out from Green Turtle Cay in a launch for Wilmington, he was wrecked off Cape

Canaveral in Florida. He walked to Fernandina and, avoiding Federal troops, finally reached Wilmington.

He had brought through the blockade as a personal venture ten barrels of sugar, the profits from which he invested in cotton. Five bales survived the Federal occupation of the city, and with the proceeds from these the exporting firm of Alexander Sprunt & Son, dealing in naval stores and later in cotton, was established. Direct connections were established with British customers and presently Sprunt went to the Continent and formed connections in Holland, Belgium, France, Germany, Russia, Switzerland, and Italy. Untiring effort, keen business sagacity, and unquestioned integrity brought success and the firm became the largest exporter of cotton in the country, with more than fifty foreign agencies. In 1884 Sprunt succeeded his father as British vice-consul, holding the post until his death and twice receiving the formal thanks of the British government. From 1907 to 1912 he was Imperial German Consul and upon his retirement was decorated with the Order of the Royal Crown. For many years he was chairman of the board of commissioners of navigation and pilotage and accomplished much in securing river and harbor improvement for Wilmington. He was president of the North Carolina Literary and Historical Association, and of the North Carolina Folk Lore Society. He wrote many valuable biographical and historical sketches and several books, among them : *Information and Statistics Respecting Wilmington, North Carolina* (1883) ; *Tales and Traditions of the Lower Cape Fear, 1661–1896* (1896) ; *Chronicles of the Cape Fear River* (1914; 2nd ed., 1916) ; and *Derelicts* (1920). In 1900 he established a fund at the University of North Carolina for the publication of the "James Sprunt Historical Monographs," known after 1910 as the "James Sprunt Historical Publications." In 1883 he married Luola, daughter of Kenneth McKenzie Murchison.

Sprunt had a genius for friendship ; he was the soul of hospitality, and his home in Wilmington and his beautiful colonial plantation "Orton," on the Cape Fear, were known and loved by many. A wide reader, rich in personal experience, a gifted conversationalist, he was an ideal host. He viewed wealth as a trust and poured it out in wise philanthropy and charity. A devoted Presbyterian, he was untiring in church work. He built several churches, maintained two schools in China; established a loan fund at Davidson College; founded a lectureship at Union Theological Seminary, Richmond, Va. He also gave much financial assistance to hospital activities.

Crippled by an accident in early manhood, he was ever eager to relieve suffering, and sent all deformed and crippled children in the mill sections of Wilmington to Baltimore for orthopedic treatment.

[*James Sprunt: A Tribute* (1925); *Wilmington Morning Star,* July 10, 1924; biog. sketch in *Chronicles of the Cape Fear River* (1914); Walter Clark, *Histories of the Several Regiments and Battalions from N. C. in the Great War 1861–'65* (1901), V, 353–451; personal acquaintance.]   J. G. deR. H.

SQUANTO (d. 1622), Indian of the Pawtuxet tribe, was called Tisquantum. He is by some authorities identified with the Tisquantum whom George Waymouth [*q.v.*], according to Ferdinando Gorges's *Briefe Narration* (1658, see Baxter, *post,* vol. XIX, p. 8), carried off from the Maine coast in 1605 and with the Tantum whom Capt. John Smith brought out from England and set on shore at Cape Cod in 1615 (John Smith, *The Generall Historie of New England,* 1624, p. 222). However that may be, he was one of the Indians kidnapped by Capt. Thomas Hunt at Pawtuxet (Plymouth) later in the same year and sold into slavery at Malaga in Spain. He escaped to England and lived at London two years with John Slany, treasurer of the Newfoundland company, who sent him to Newfoundland. Capt. Thomas Dermer took him back to England in 1618. The next summer Squanto acted as Capt. Dermer's pilot to the New England coast but left him before reaching Cape Cod. Squanto made his way home to Pawtuxet and found himself the only surviving member of his tribe. Introduced by Samoset to the Pilgrim Fathers in March 1621, he conducted Edward Winslow to Massasoit [*q.v.*] and acted as interpreter in concluding the treaty of Plymouth with that chief and the Pilgrims. "*Squanto* continued with them, and was their interpreter, and was a spetiall instrument sent of God for their good beyond their expectation. He directed them how to set their corne, wher to take fish, and to procure other comodities, and was also their pilott to bring them to unknowne places for their profitt, and never left them till he dyed" (Bradford, *post,* I, 202–03). The same year he took part in Winslow's hungry embassy to Massasoit, delivered the famous rattlesnake skin stuffed with bullets to Canonicus, and was rescued by Miles Standish from Corbitant. Squanto made himself obnoxious to the Indians by exploiting his friendship with the English and pretending a power to spread the plague. At Plymouth in the spring of 1622 he sounded a false alarm of impending treachery by Massasoit, who, when he heard of it, sent a messenger to demand Squanto, as one of his subjects. The Pilgrims were at the point of starvation, and Governor Bradford was about to deliver Squanto up, when a boat was seen at sea; and the Governor, thinking it might be Frenchmen in league with Massasoit, postponed his decision. By the time he had ascertained that it was an English boat, Massasoit's messengers had "departed in great heat." Squanto later made his peace with Massasoit. In November 1622 he served as guide and interpreter on Bradford's expedition around Cape Cod. At Chatham Harbor "Squanto fell sick of an Indean feavor, . . . and within a few days dyed ther; desiring the Gov[erno]r to pray for him, that he might goe to the Englishmens God in heaven, and bequeathed sundrie of his things to sundry of his English freinds, as remembrances of his love; of whom they had a great loss" (Bradford, *post,* I, 283).

[Wm. Bradford, *Hist. of Plymouth Plantation* (1912), vol. I, ed. by W. C. Ford; J. P. Baxter, "Sir Ferdinand Gorges," *Prince Soc. Pubs.,* vols. XVIII–XX (1890); L. N. Kinnicutt, "The Plymouth Settlement and Tisquantum," *Proc. Mass. Hist. Soc.,* vol. XLVIII (1914–15, pp. 103–18).]   S. E. M.

SQUIBB, EDWARD ROBINSON (July 4, 1819–Oct. 25, 1900), physician, pharmacist, and chemist, was born in Wilmington, Del., of Quaker parents, James R. Squibb and Catherine H. (Bonsal) Squibb. After his boyhood days in Wilmington, where he pursued his studies under the guidance of a tutor, he began an apprenticeship under Warder Morris, a druggist in Philadelphia, Pa., in 1837 and completed it under J. H. Sprague, another Philadelphia druggist, at the end of five years. Having graduated from Jefferson Medical College, Philadelphia, in 1845 with the degree of M.D., he practised medicine in Philadelphia for two years and held the positions of assistant demonstrator of anatomy, curator of the museum, and clerk of the clinic at Jefferson Medical College. On Apr. 26, 1847, he accepted a commission as assistant surgeon in the United States navy; he spent the next four years at sea as medical officer on the *Perry,* the *Erie,* and the *Cumberland* in Mexican and South American waters and on the Mediterranean. In 1851 he was assigned to duty at the naval hospital in Brooklyn, N. Y., where he began his career as a manufacturing pharmacist and chemist. It is believed that his experiences at sea with drugs and medicines of poor quality supplied to the navy were largely responsible for starting him on this career; it is known that he set about attempting to secure better supplies almost immediately after his arrival in Brooklyn. It was largely through his efforts that the Navy Department was authorized to establish its own laboratory, of which he became assistant director in 1852, for the manufacture of pharmaceuticals and chemicals. The equipment installed was for the most part crude, much of it having been designed and built by Squibb himself, yet the laboratory was a success from the start. Here ether was first manufactured by the use of steam heat instead of an open flame; the first Squibb still for the manufacture of anesthetic ether was built; processes were perfected for the manufacture of chloroform, fluid extracts, bismuth salts, calcium chloride, benzoic acid, aconite and ergot preparations, and methods were devised for the assay of opium, potent tinctures, and powdered extracts. From 1853 until 1857, when the laboratory was discontinued for lack of funds, Squibb was director. Within the same year he resigned from the navy and accepted the position of manufacturing co-partner in the firm of Thomas E. Jenkins & Company of Louisville, Ky., known as the Louisville Chemical Works. About this time the suggestion was made to him by Dr. Richard Sherwood Satterlee [q.v.], then chief medical purveyor of the army, that he start a laboratory of his own from which the army could purchase its drugs and chemicals with the assurance that they would be of high purity and strength. In 1858 he established in Brooklyn the first Squibb chemical and pharmaceutical laboratory under the name of Edward R. Squibb, M.D. Just as the work of the new establishment was getting well under way, it was completely destroyed by fire that resulted from an explosion of ether, and Squibb was severely burned. During his convalescence, however, he drafted plans for rebuilding, and a year later a new laboratory was erected. In 1892 he admitted his two sons to co-partnership and changed the name of the firm to E. R. Squibb & Sons. Shortly after his retirement in 1895, his health began to fail, and five years later he died at his home in Brooklyn, N. Y. He was survived by his wife, Caroline F. Lownds Cook of Philadelphia, to whom he was married on Oct. 7, 1852, and his three children, a daughter and two sons.

Squibb was a pioneer in the manufacture of pharmaceuticals and chemicals, and one of the leaders in independent chemical research in the United States. He differed from manufacturers generally in that he had no secrets in his business and was ready at all times to share with others the fruit of his ingenuity and labors. He was recognized as an authority on the *United States Pharmacopoeia,* in the revision of which he took a leading part, and he was an indefatigable investigator and writer. His studies and his work in improving the process of percolation were perhaps his greatest contribution to pure phar-

macy. Over a hundred of his papers on subjects of fundamental importance to pharmacy were published in the *American Journal of Pharmacy* alone; others appeared in various journals, including *An Ephemeris of Materia Medica, Pharmacy, Therapeutics, and Collateral Information,* published by Squibb at irregular intervals from 1882 until his death. (A list of his more important articles appears in *General Index to Volumes One to Fifty of the Proceedings of the American Pharmaceutical Association . . .,* 1904, compiled by H. M. Wilder.) He was a delegate to the pharmacopoeial conventions of 1860 and 1870, and served on the committee of revision of the *United States Pharmacopoeia* in 1880. From 1869 to 1872 he lectured at the College of Pharmacy of the City and County of New York (later part of Columbia University). He took an active interest in the affairs of the American Pharmaceutical Association, which he served as a member of various committees and as first vice-president, 1858–59, and was a member of numerous other scientific societies.

[*Proc. of the Am. Pharmaceutical Assoc.,* vol. XLIX (1901); *Am. Jour. of Pharmacy,* Dec. 1900; *Bull. of Pharmacy,* Dec. 1900; *Nat. Druggist,* Dec. 1900; obituary in *Brooklyn Daily Eagle,* Oct. 26, 1900; letters from Margaret R. Squibb of New York, grand-daughter of E. R. Squibb.]   A. G. D–M.

SQUIER, EPHRAIM GEORGE (June 17, 1821–Apr. 17, 1888), journalist, diplomat, and archaeologist, was born in Bethlehem, N. Y. His father, Joel Squier, minister of the village Methodist Church, was a descendant of Philip Squier, who emigrated from England to America after the Reformation, settling first in Boston and later in Connecticut; his mother, Catharine (Kilmer or Külmer) Squier, belonged to a prominent New York family, Palatine German in origin. He had little opportunity for formal schooling beyond the grades, but through study by himself he became a scholar of distinction. As a child he worked on a farm, and in his early youth taught school and studied civil engineering; but the panic of 1837 made engineering unprofitable, and he soon turned to journalism and literature. After some success as contributor to Albany papers, he launched the *Poets' Magazine* in Albany in the spring of 1842, but only two issues appeared. He was next associated with the *New York State Mechanic,* an organ for prison reform which ceased publication in 1843, and in 1844–45 was editor of the *Evening Journal,* Hartford, Conn., a Whig publication supporting Henry Clay [q.v.]. Through his efforts the party carried the state, but after Clay's national defeat he left the *Journal* and removed to Chillicothe, Ohio, where for some years he published the *Scioto Gazette.*

In 1847 and 1848 he was clerk of the Ohio House of Representatives. In Ohio, in collaboration with Edwin Hamilton Davis [q.v.], he studied the remains of the Mound Builders. The results of their researches appeared in the first publication of the Smithsonian Institution under the title, *Ancient Monuments of the Mississippi Valley* (Smithsonian Contributions to Knowledge, no. 1, 1847). Later he examined native remains in New York and published his chief work on the subject, *Aboriginal Monuments of the State of New-York* (1851), again through the Smithsonian Institution. These two studies were marked by observation and description so accurate and thorough that they became authoritative in their fields.

In April 1849, through the influence of William Hickling Prescott [q.v.], the historian, he was appointed for a term of about a year and a half chargé d'affaires to Central America. In this capacity he signed with Nicaragua an agreement for the American construction of an interoceanic canal. It was never ratified, but through being submitted to the Senate it caused considerable embarrassment to the British-American negotiations which finally resulted in the Clayton-Bulwer Treaty. In 1853, as secretary of the Honduras Interoceanic Railway Company, he visited Central America again to examine the proposed route for the road, which was never built. About 1860 he became chief editor of the publishing house of Frank Leslie [q.v.], and under his direction *Frank Leslie's Pictorial History of the American Civil War* (2 vols., 1861–62) was begun. From 1863 to 1865 he was United States commissioner to Peru and was successful in settling financial claims between the two countries. In 1868 he was made consul general of Honduras in New York City. Following his return from Peru he continued his work with *Leslie's* for some years, but gave it up when his health permanently failed and his mind became clouded. He died in Brooklyn, N. Y., after many years of hopeless illness. In 1858 he was married to Miriam Florence Folline [see Miriam F. F. Leslie] of New Orleans, La., who divorced him in 1873 and about a year later married Leslie.

The major results of his connection with Latin America were his published writings on the archaeological remains and the general conditions of the countries he visited. The best of these are *Nicaragua; Its People, Scenery, Monuments, and the Proposed Interoceanic Canal* (2 vols., 1852), *The States of Central America* (1858), and *Peru: Incidents of Travel and Exploration in the Land of the Incas* (1877). He wrote a number of other volumes and many arti-

cles of value, chiefly upon archaeological and ethnological subjects. He was honored at home and abroad as one of the most distinguished Americanists of the nineteenth century, and is perhaps the best single authority on the Central America of the period. He was handsome and distinguished in appearance, with waving hair, full beard, and fine features. He was sociable, somewhat fond of gayety, slightly vain, but had a saving sense of humor and a strong altruistic bent, and in the performance of duty was conscientious as well as energetic.

[C. H. Kilmer, *Hist. of the Kilmer Family in America* (1897); *Letters from Francis Parkman to E. G. Squier* (1911), edited by Don C. Seitz; *A List of Books, Pamphlets, and More Important Contributions to Periodicals, etc.*, by Hon. E. G. Squier (1876); Joseph Sabin, *A Dict. of Books Relating to America*, vol. XXIII (1932–33), continued under the editorship of Wilberforce Eames and C. W. G. Vail; I. D. Travis, *The Hist. of the Clayton-Bulwer Treaty* (1899); Mary W. Williams, "John Middleton Clayton," in *The Am. Secretaries of State and Their Diplomacy*, vol. VI (1928), ed. by S. F. Bemis; Squier MSS. in Lib. of Cong.; obituary in *N. Y. Times*, Apr. 18, 1888.] M. W. W.

SQUIER, GEORGE OWEN (Mar. 21, 1865–Mar. 24, 1934), soldier, scientist, electrical engineer, was born at Dryden, Mich., the son of Almon Justice and Emily (Gardner) Squier. He entered the army as a second lieutenant of artillery upon his graduation, seventh in his class, from the United States Military Academy in June 1887. For the next six years he was stationed at Fort McHenry, Md., during part of that time studying physics, mathematics, and chemistry at the Johns Hopkins University, where he received the degree of Ph.D. in 1893. After several brief assignments in various parts of the country, he attended the Artillery School at Fort Monroe, Va., 1894–95, and from November 1895 to April 1898 was instructor in its department of electricity and mines. During the Spanish-American War he served as a signal officer, attaining the rank of lieutenant-colonel of volunteers, and upon his return to the Regular Army was assigned to the signal corps as a first lieutenant. He was in command of the cableship *Burnside*, 1900–02, laying submarine cables in the Philippine archipelago, and was superintendent of telegraph lines in the Philippine Islands for a year thereafter. Promoted captain in 1901 and major in 1903, he was signal officer in San Francisco, 1903–05, and assistant commandant of the Army Signal School, Fort Leavenworth, Kan., 1905–07. While engaged in studying various methods of cable and radio communication he discovered that growing trees could be utilized as receiving radio antennae, and demonstrated absorption by vegetation-covered areas of some of the electro-magnetic waves passing over them. After brief service in the office of the chief signal officer at Washington, 1911–12, he became military attaché at the United States embassy in London, being promoted to lieutenant-colonel in 1913. In 1912 he was also a delegate to the International Radio Telegraphic Conference in London.

He had become interested in aviation as early as 1908, and while in England made a study of European military aviation, after the outbreak of the World War closely observing technical developments in radio and aviation in the British army. Recalled to Washington in May 1916, he had charge of the aviation section of the signal corps until his appointment, Feb. 14, 1917, as chief signal officer of the army, with the rank of brigadier-general. At this time he also became a member of the Joint Army and Navy Board on Aeronautics, serving until Sept. 6, 1918. As chief signal officer he organized the cable and radio communications between military headquarters in the United States and the American Expeditionary Forces abroad.

He was a representative of the War Department and technical adviser to the American delegation at the International Conference on Electrical Communications held in Washington, D. C., in 1920. During the following year he represented the Department of State at the sessions of the provisional technical committee at the International Conference on Electrical Communications in Paris, France, and in the fall of 1921 served as an expert assistant to the American commission at the conference on the limitation of armament held in Washington, D. C. He was an *ex-officio* member representing the War Department on the national committee of the International Electrotechnical Commission. He continued as chief signal officer of the army, with the rank of major-general after Oct. 6, 1917, until his retirement at his own request, Dec. 31, 1923.

Squier's administrative services during the World War won him the Distinguished Service Medal of the United States and appointment as Knight Commander of the Order of Saint Michael and Saint George (Great Britain), Commander of the Order of the Crown (Italy), and Commander of the Legion of Honor (France). His attainments as a scientist brought him election as a member of the National Academy of Sciences and a fellow of Johns Hopkins University. For his researches he was awarded the Elliott Cresson Gold Medal (1912) and the Franklin Medal (1919) of the Franklin Institute and the John Scott Legacy Medal of the City of Philadelphia (1896). His important contribu-

tions to science included his researches in connection with electro-chemical effects due to magnetization; the polarizing photochronograph; the sine-wave systems of telegraphy and ocean cabling; the absorption of electro-magnetic waves by living vegetable organisms; multiplex telegraphy and telephony; and tree telegraphy and telephony. His most significant papers were published in the *Transactions of the American Institute of Electrical Engineers,* the *Journal of the Franklin Institute,* or publications of the signal corps. He was the inventor of the monophone for broadcasting over telephone wires. Of his inventions, by far the best known is "wired wireless," which includes multiple telephony, wireless telephony, long-distance telephony, and practical telephony. He was the holder of a number of patents in these fields.

After his retirement from the army he made his home at Dryden, Mich., but spent a part of each year in Washington, D. C., where he died. He never married.

[Official records, Adjutant-General's Office and Office of the Chief Signal Officer, War Dept., 1888–1934; A. E. Kenelly, in *Science,* May 25, 1934; *Who's Who in America,* 1932–33; *Who's Who in Engineering* (1925); G. W. Cullum, *Biog. Reg. Officers and Grads. U. S. Mil. Acad.,* vols. III–VII (1891–1930); *Proc. Inst. Radio Engineers,* vol. XXII (May 1934); B. J. Hendrick, *The Life and Letters of Walter H. Page,* vol. III (1925); *Washington Post,* Mar. 25, 1934.]

I. J. C—r.

SQUIERS, HERBERT GOLDSMITH (Apr. 20, 1859–Oct. 20, 1911), soldier, diplomat, was born of American parents at Madoc, Canada, the son of John T. and Elizabeth J. Squiers. He attended Canandaigua Academy, Canandaigua, N. Y., and the Minnesota Military Academy at Minneapolis, graduating in 1877 and securing appointment as second lieutenant in the 1st United States Infantry. After two and a half years' service he obtained a transfer to the Artillery School at Fortress Monroe, Va. While here, Oct. 11, 1881, he married Helen Lacy Fargo, daughter of William George Fargo [*q.v.*]. On completing his course, May 1, 1882, he pleaded for and obtained assignment to the cavalry, but after three years again sought change and got himself assigned to St. John's College, Fordham, N. Y., as teacher of military science. A memorandum issued from the Adjutant-General's Office at this time (July 8, 1885) reveals the irritation Squiers' love of change provoked in the bosom of authority: "There is not probably a young officer in the service who has been more indulged in his personal requests than has Lieutenant Squiers. . . . He has not shown one particle of military spirit but rather the reverse." His wife, having borne a son and three daughters, died in 1886, and in 1889 he married Harriet Bard Woodcock of Bedford Hills, N. Y., daughter of Dr. William P. and Mary (Bard) Woodcock. To this marriage three sons were born.

Repeated endeavors to have Squiers return to active service proved unavailing and he remained at St. John's College until the fall of 1890, when an Indian uprising in South Dakota led him to ask for duty in the field. He was promptly ordered West, was promoted to first lieutenant, Dec. 17, and twelve days later took part in the battle of Wounded Knee. The following summer he was granted a month's leave, and after the month was up delayed returning to duty so long that finally he was ordered to return at once or resign. He resigned, Nov. 28, 1891, in a letter justifying his conduct on the ground of urgent private business.

In person Squiers was handsome and attractive, and despite his restlessness had superior qualities of mind and character, including a robust will to work. Throughout life he was a student, with a passion for history but interested in many fields. His personality and talents were much better adapted to the new career which opened for him on Nov. 15, 1894, with appointment as second secretary to the United States embassy at Berlin. Here he remained until May 1897, when he resigned. A year and a half later he reëntered the diplomatic service as secretary to the legation at Peking. During the Boxer uprising of 1900, his previous military training caused Sir Claude MacDonald to select him as chief of staff. The courage and competence with which he discharged his duties won for him the thanks of the British government and commendation by President McKinley. Lord Lansdowne, British foreign minister, in a note to the ambassador at Washington said: "Sir Claude mentions that his [Squiers's] earlier services in the U. S. Army were of great use in the defence and that he cannot speak too highly of his zeal and ability. The barricades on the Tartar Wall were designed and carried out by him and under Sir Claude's orders he drew the plan for the entry of the troops which was conveyed to General Gaselee by a messenger let down from the wall" (Dec. 11, 1900; State Department Archives).

From May 1902 until November 1905, Squiers filled with distinguished success the arduous and difficult post of United States minister to the newly constituted Republic of Cuba. At the outset he made clear his special status as the representative of the United States, claiming the right to deal with the president of Cuba directly instead of through the secretary of state. The treaty containing the Platt Amendment was ratified during his incumbency, and he was instructed to impress upon the Cuban government the dangers of insolvency and to urge the importance of carrying out the suggested sanitation plans. From 1906 until failing health caused by tropical fevers forced his retirement in 1910, he was minister to Panama. He died in London in 1911. One of his daughters married Harry Harwood Rousseau [q.v.]. His wife, Harriet B. W. Squiers, engaged actively in work for the wounded during the World War; she died in New York, June 18, 1935.

[Archives of the War and State departments; *The Times* (London), Oct. 19, 1900; *Outlook*, July 5, 1902; F. B. Heitman, *Hist. Reg. and Dict. U. S. Army* (1903); *Papers Relating to the Foreign Relations of the U. S.*, 1902–05; *Who's Who in America*, 1910–11; H. F. Guggenheim, *The U. S. and Cuba* (1934); *N. Y. Herald*, Oct. 21, 1911; correspondence with Squiers's son; obituary of Mrs. Squiers, *N. Y. Times*, June 19, 1935.]

W. E. S—a.

SQUIRE, WATSON CARVOSSO (May 18, 1838–June 7, 1926), capitalist, governor of the Territory of Washington, United States senator, was born at Cape Vincent, N. Y. His father, the Rev. Orra Squire, a Methodist Episcopal clergyman, and his mother, Erreta (Wheeler) Squire, were both of New England stock. He attended public schools, Falley Seminary, Fulton, N. Y., and Fairfield Seminary in Herkimer County. In 1859 he graduated from Wesleyan University, Middletown, Conn., and during the year following was principal of Moravia Institute at Moravia, N. Y. He began the study of law at Herkimer, but soon after the outbreak of the Civil War he enlisted as a private in Company F, 19th New York Volunteer Infantry, and was later promoted to first lieutenant. Mustered out in October 1861, he went to Cleveland, Ohio, graduated from the Cleveland Law School in 1862, and was admitted to the bar. He then organized the 7th Independent Company of Ohio Sharpshooters, of which he became captain. The company operated with the Western divisions during the remainder of the war. In 1864–65 Squire served as judge advocate on Rosecrans' staff. He had been promoted to major and was subsequently brevetted lieutenant-colonel and colonel.

After the war he returned to New York State and accepted a position with E. Remington & Sons, manufacturers of firearms. On Dec. 3, 1868, he married Ida, daughter of Philo Remington [q.v.]; they had four children. He soon attained managerial rank in the company and negotiated important sales to France, during the Franco-Prussian War, and to other powers. His business necessitated extensive travel in Europe, also a winter's sojourn in Mexico. In the spring of 1879, property interests took him to the Puget Sound country, and from that year Seattle became his permanent residence. Besides acquiring extensive real-estate holdings, he interested Eastern capitalists, chiefly Henry Villard [*q.v.*], in the Territory's railroads and coal mines.

Affiliated with the Republican party, he leaned toward the Stalwart or regular wing. Appointed governor of Washington Territory in 1884, he distinguished himself for his firmness in maintaining law and order during the anti-Chinese riots of 1885–86. In 1887 he resigned to devote himself to his private business, but in 1889 he was called to preside over the convention held at Ellensburg for the purpose of drafting a state constitution. Statehood attained, Squire was elected senator. As a member and twice as chairman of the committee on coast defenses, he secured material enlargements in these defenses. Among his other important interests were Alaska, for which he secured the government geological survey and special reconnaissances of its mineral resources; and the Isthmian canal, for which he favored the Nicaraguan route. For his state he secured the naval station and dry dock at Bremerton, extensive harbor and river improvements, and the initial appropriation for the Lake Washington Canal. When he first entered the Senate, drawing with the other new arrivals from the omnibus states, Squire secured a two-year term, but he was reëlected in 1891; in 1897, however, the strength of the free-silver movement eliminated him, a gold-standard man, from candidacy for reëlection. He returned to business and became president of the Union Trust Company and of the Squire Investment Company. He died in Seattle.

[*Alumni Record of Wesleyan Univ. . . . 1921* (n.d.); *Hist. of the Remington Armory. E. Remington & Sons* (1872); C. B. Bagley, *Hist. of Seattle from the Earliest Settlement to the Present Time* (1916), vol. III; F. J. Grant, *Hist. of Seattle, Wash.* (1891); W. F. Prosser, *A Hist. of the Puget Sound Country* (1903), vol. II; C. A. Snowden, *Hist. of Wash.* (1911), vols. IV, V; *Who's Who in America,* 1924–25; *Biog. Dir. Am. Cong.* (1928); *Seattle Daily Times,* June 8, 1926.] H. J. D.

STAGER, ANSON (Apr. 20, 1825–Mar. 26, 1885), telegraph pioneer, was born in Ontario County, N. Y., but was brought up in Rochester, where his father was engaged as an edged-tool maker. At the age of sixteen, upon completing his education in the public schools, he became a printer's devil in the office of the *Rochester Daily Advertiser,* owned and published by Henry O'Reilly [*q.v.*]. By 1845 Stager had become the *Advertiser's* bookkeeper. About this time O'Reilly contracted with Samuel F. B. Morse [*q.v.*] and

his associates to raise the capital to build a line of Morse's electro-magnetic telegraph from Philadelphia to the Middle West. His activities undoubtedly aroused Stager's interest, and while O'Reilly was constructing the first link of the telegraph line to Pittsburgh, the younger man was learning telegraphy in his spare time, and upon the opening of the telegraph office at Lancaster, Pa., in 1846, he was installed as operator. In the succeeding three months he was transferred to Chambersburg and from there to Pittsburgh, serving as manager of the latter office during most of 1847.

With the extension of the O'Reilly lines to Cincinnati late in that year, Stager was made manager of the operating department of the Pittsburgh, Cincinnati & Louisville Telegraph Company. During the succeeding four years he conducted the office skilfully and originated the system by which telegraph wires were worked from a common battery on a closed circuit. His reward came in 1852 when he was appointed general superintendent of the New York & Mississippi Valley Printing Telegraph Company. With the formation of the Western Union Telegraph Company in 1856, Stager was immediately appointed its general superintendent and assigned the work of rearranging the many telegraph lines, strengthening the organization, and establishing favorable relations with the great railroad interests. He was the originator of the cunningly devised contract which for many years gave the Western Union an iron-bound monopoly of the privilege of stringing wires along the railroads.

After 1856 Stager made his headquarters at Cleveland, Ohio, and upon the outbreak of the Civil War he was asked to take the management of the telegraphs in the military department of the Ohio. Appointed captain and assistant quartermaster general on Nov. 11, 1861, he was placed on duty in Washington as chief of the United States military telegraphs. On Feb. 26, 1862, he was promoted to colonel and subsequently assigned as aide-de-camp to General Halleck at the War Department. After 1864 his headquarters were in Cleveland, Ohio, and continued there until he was honorably mustered out Sept. 1, 1866. For his meritorious services, which included the originating and development of the military telegraph cipher system, he had been brevetted brigadier-general of volunteers on Mar. 13, 1865.

He had not broken his connection with the Western Union Telegraph Company, and upon its reorganization following the war he was tendered the general superintendency of the whole system. When he refused the offer, the system was divided into three great divisions, Central, Eastern, and Southern, and Stager accepted the superintendency of the Central Division, with headquarters at Cleveland. In 1869 these were transferred to Chicago, Ill., and there Stager lived for the remainder of his life. He became a vice-president of the Western Union, which office he resigned in 1881. He was the leading Western representative of the Vanderbilt interests, and took an active part in all electrical progress of the time. He helped found the Western Electric Manufacturing Company and was its president until a few months before his death. He was prominent in furthering the telephone business in Chicago and the Northwest generally, as well as in the introduction of the electric light, serving as president of the Western Edison Electric Light Company from its formation until his death. On Nov. 14, 1847, he married Rebecca Sprague of Buffalo, and at the time of his death in Chicago was survived by three children.

[J. D. Reid, *The Telegraph in America* (1879); W. R. Plum, *The Military Telegraph During the Civil War in the U. S.* (1882), vols. I and II; *Electrical World*, Mar. 28 and Apr. 4, 1885; *Electrician and Electrical Engineer*, Apr. 1885; *Journal of the Telegraph*, Apr. 20, 1885; records of Adjutant-General's Office, War Dept., Washington, D. C.; *Chicago Daily Tribune*, Mar. 26, 1885.]   C. W. M—n.

STAHEL, JULIUS (Nov. 5, 1825–Dec. 4, 1912), soldier and consular officer, son of Andreas and Barbara (Nagy) Stahel (Hungarian name Számvald), was born in Szeged, Hungary. He received a classical education at Budapest. In the struggle for Hungarian independence in 1848 he espoused the patriotic cause, became a lieutenant in the forces of Louis Kossuth, was wounded and decorated for bravery. With the triumph of Austrian arms in 1849, however, he was forced to flee the country. He then maintained himself in Berlin and London by teaching and journalism until 1856, when he came to America and settled in New York City. There he continued a journalistic career until the outbreak of the Civil War, at which time he was on the staff of the *New York Illustrated News*.

When Lincoln called for volunteers in April 1861, Stahel at once responded, helped organize the 8th New York Infantry, and became its lieutenant-colonel. On July 21, 1861, when the Union army was routed at Bull Run, Stahel, then in command of his regiment, was with a brigade in reserve at Centerville; ordered to cover the retreat, the brigade performed its task so well that the Confederate commander, General Johnston, in his report on the battle stated that "the apparent firmness of the U. S. troops at Centreville . . . checked our pursuit" (*War of the Rebellion:*

Official Records, Army, 1 ser. II, 478). The following month Stahel was promoted to colonel and soon thereafter assigned to command a brigade. On Nov. 12, 1861, he was appointed brigadier-general of volunteers. He fought under General Frémont in the Shenandoah Valley in the spring of 1862, particularly distinguishing himself at Cross Keys on June 8, when his brigade bore the brunt of the fighting. At the second battle of Bull Run, Aug. 30, 1862, he temporarily commanded a division and was commended for gallantry. In October 1862 he was assigned to command a division in the Army of the Potomac, and for a short time during the next winter he commanded the XI Corps. Promoted to major-general on Mar. 14, 1863, he was given command of the cavalry division in front of Washington. In the spring of 1864 he was transferred to a cavalry division in the department of West Virginia and led General Hunter's advance in the Shenandoah Valley gallantly until June 5, 1864, when he was badly wounded in the arm while personally leading a successful charge against the Confederate flank. For his bravery on this occasion he was awarded the Congressional Medal of Honor in 1893. After recovering from his wound he served on court-martial duty in Washington, and in the Middle Department until Feb. 8, 1865, when he resigned his commission. He was soon given opportunity to show his abilities in a new field of public service, being appointed in 1866 consul at the important post of Yokohama. He returned to the United States in 1869, and for the next eight years engaged in mining operations. On Oct. 25, 1877, he was nominated as consul to Osaka and Hiogo, the nomination being confirmed on Feb. 6, 1878. He held this post until 1884, when he was made consul at Shanghai, China. The next year he resigned because of ill health, thus ending an eventful public career which throughout was characterized by ability and the highest standards of honor and duty. He returned to New York, where for a number of years he held an executive position with the Equitable Life Assurance Company. He was never married.

[*War of the Rebellion: Official Records (Army)*; Eugene Pivany, *Hungarians in the Am. Civil War* (1913); *The Union Army* (1908), vol. VIII; *A Record of the Commissioned Officers, Non-Commissioned Officers, and Privates of the Regiments . . . Organized in the State of New York* (1864); F. B. Heitman, *Hist. Reg. and Dict. U. S. Army* (1903); *Military Order of the Loyal Legion of the U. S. . . . State of New York, Circular 19, Series of 1913*; *Who's Who in America,* 1912–13; *N. Y. Times,* Dec. 5, 1912; *New-Yorker Staats-Zeitung,* Dec. 5, 1912.]   S. J. H.

STAHLMAN, EDWARD BUSHROD (Sept. 2, 1843–Aug. 12, 1930), railroad official, publisher, was born at Güstrow, in the German grand duchy of Mecklenburg-Schwerin, the fourth son of Frederick and Christine (Lange) Stahlman. His only formal education was secured in the primary school taught by his father at Güstrow. In 1854 the family emigrated to the United States and settled at West Union, Doddridge County, Virginia (now West Virginia). Soon afterward the father died, leaving his wife and children destitute. In spite of the fact that a school-room accident had left him permanently crippled, Edward aided in supporting the family until the mother remarried. In 1863 he went to Nashville, Tenn., where he entered the employ of the Louisville & Nashville Railroad Company. Three years later he became the Nashville representative of the Southern Express Company, and in 1871 returned to the service of the Louisville & Nashville Railroad as freight agent. Rising rapidly, he was made a vice-president of the company in 1884, after having held a similar position with the Louisville, New Albany & Chicago Railway (Monon Route) from 1883 to 1884. Withdrawing from the Louisville & Nashville in 1890, he served until 1895 as commissioner for the Southern Railway and Steamship Association, in which capacity he was an important representative of the transportation interests of the South during the period of the creation and adjustment of the Interstate Commerce Commission.

His real life work began, however, in 1885, when he purchased the *Nashville Banner,* then a small paper with little influence and less financial standing. Throughout the next thirty-five years the editorial policy of this paper was a direct reflection of the personality and convictions of its owner, with the result that it became one of the best-known journals of the South. He was seldom neutral on an issue, making vigorous use of both news and editorial columns to promote any cause which he espoused. Thus he unhesitatingly threw himself into a fight to prevent the citizens of Nashville from voting a proposed bond issue for the Tennessee-Midland Railroad in 1885, and against a similar plan put forward by the Tennessee Central Railroad in 1901–02; into the fight to preserve an independent judiciary for the state in 1910; and into another in 1925 to protect the power resources of the state from seizure and exploitation by the power trusts. In such contests he fought both brilliantly and bitterly, arousing, as a result, an intense antagonism on the part of his opponents which usually led to recriminatory attacks.

Through his connection with transportation interests he became a powerful political factor in the state. Proceeding on an avowed belief that independence is essential to the highest usefulness of a paper, he was never willing to affiliate permanently with a political party or faction. He was, nevertheless, a shrewd worker in the field of practical politics, and participated in many state and local contests, frequently sponsoring the candidacy of a promising young leader only to turn against him as he later became absorbed into the regular party organization. Although he never held important public offices, he exercised a dominating influence in the municipal affairs of Nashville as a member of the board of education, as a promoter of chamber of commerce activities, and as a leader in real-estate and building development. He was twice married: first, Oct. 4, 1866, to Mollie T. Claiborne of Nashville, by whom he had three children; she died in 1915, and on Aug. 23, 1920, he married Sarah Shelton, of Erin, Tenn., by whom he had a son.

[*Who's Who in Tennessee* (1911); *Who's Who in America*, 1930–31; *Nashville Banner*, Aug. 12, 13, 1930, and *Nashville Tennessean*, Aug. 13, 1930.]

W. C. B.

STAHR, JOHN SUMMERS (Dec. 2, 1841–Dec. 21, 1915), clergyman, educator, was born near Applebachsville, Bucks County, Pa., the son of John and Sarah (Summers or Sommer) Stahr. The family name had been originally Stoehr, his ancestors having come from the Palatinate in 1739 to settle in Bucks County. He received his early education in the public schools and became a teacher when he was but sixteen years of age. He prepared for college during the summer months at the Bucks County Normal and Classical School and finally entered the junior class of Franklin and Marshall College, Lancaster, Pa., in 1865, graduating *summa cum laude* in 1867. He had then intended to enter the theological seminary of the Reformed Church at Mercersburg, Pa., but he was urged to accept a position as tutor in German and history at his alma mater, and, at the same time, to study theology under the direction of John Williamson Nevin [*q.v.*]. In 1868 he was made adjunct professor of the natural sciences and German, and in three years rose to a full professorship in the natural sciences and chemistry, with additional work in German and political economy. He held this position until 1887 when he became temporary financial agent for the college. In 1889 he was the acting president and professor of philosophy, and president from 1890 until he retired in 1909. He retained the professorship of philosophy, however, until he died.

In 1872 he was ordained to the holy ministry and served as assistant pastor of the First Reformed Church at Reading, Pa., but declined a call to the pastorate. He was a member of the Eighth Council of the Alliance of Reformed Churches which met at Liverpool in 1904, and at the Tenth Council at Aberdeen in 1913. In 1914 he was elected president of the General Synod of the Reformed Church. From 1890 to 1908 he served as a member of the International Sunday School Lesson Committee, representing it at a convention in Rome in 1907. His linguistic accomplishments led to an appointment to the editorial staff of the Funk & Wagnall Standard Dictionary, and for forty-five years he was a frequent contributor to the *Mercersburg Review* and its successors, the *Reformed Church Quarterly* and the *Reformed Church Review*, on which he served as a managing editor from 1906. Stahr spoke and wrote a pure English, and, with the same ease, a faultless German. He showed in his opening address of the college year of 1870 on "Pennsylvania German," *Mercersburg Review*, October 1890, its proper place in the realm of the Germanic languages. He wrote on education, science, philosophy, ethics, and theology, and when Darwin's *Origin of Species* was still vehemently opposed by the leading churchmen, he discussed in another opening address "Evolution Theories and Theology," in which he stoutly maintained that the theory of evolution and the tenets of genuine Christianity did not conflict (*Ibid.*, July 1872). His position became even more definite in his eloquent and profoundly scholarly refutation of A. Wilford Hall's *The Problem of Human Life Here and Hereafter* (1880), for the *Reformed Church Quarterly*, July 1883. His chief interest, however, was in the study of philosophy. He was the last of the master exponents of the Mercersburg Philosophy (see his article, "Philosophy as a Factor in the Educational System of the Reformed Church," *Reformed Church Review*, January 1898).

A recital of his experiences as administrator of college funds, "The Financial Development of Franklin and Marshall College" (*Reformed Church Review*, April 1903), reveals an infinite capacity for work and a zealous and practical interest in business matters. He procured for the college legacies and gifts, one immediate result of his financial mission being the building and equipment of the first chemical laboratory under his supervision. He was one of six men who founded the Pennsylvania-German Society in 1891 and he acted as president in 1903–04. On July 23, 1872, he was married to Francina Elmira Andrews, the daughter of Hugh Andrews of Lancaster County. She, with three of their five children, survived him.

[Information from the family; *Who's Who in America*, 1914–15; a brief autobiography in the *Student Weekly of Franklin and Marshall Coll.*, Feb. 3, 1916; Profs. Mull, Richard, and Herman, "In Memoriam," *Proc. and Addresses, Pa.-Ger. Soc.*, vol. XXVI (1918); J. H. Dubbs, *Hist. of Franklin and Marshall Coll.* (1903); *Public Ledger*, Philadelphia, Dec. 22, 1915.]
R. C. S.

STALEY, CADY (Dec. 12, 1840–June 27, 1928), civil engineer, the son of Harmanus and Evaline (Darrow) Staley, was born in Florida township, Montgomery County, N. Y., and spent his boyhood on a farm. He received his early education in a district school, in Jonesville Academy, and in the Classical Institute in Schenectady, then studied civil engineering at Union College, under Prof. William M. Gillespie [*q.v.*]. He was graduated A.B. with honors in 1865 and the following year received the degree of C. E. Soon afterward, he crossed the plains as an ox-driver with a wagon train, spent some months in prospecting for gold, then went to work for the Central Pacific Railroad as a civil engineer, being engaged in tunnel construction.

In 1867 he returned to Union College as an instructor in civil engineering, and the following year, upon the death of Gillespie, became professor of civil engineering and president of the faculty. In December 1869, at Waterford, N. Y., he married Kate, daughter of Elvin and Philetta (Hall) Holcomb. He was dean of the faculty from 1876 to 1886, when he resigned to become professor of civil engineering and president of the faculty of Case School of Applied Science, Cleveland, Ohio. Bringing to his new post well-defined ideas of organization and administration, the result of his years of experience at Union, he insisted upon assuming the direction of the work of the school, although he allowed the department heads full power in their several fields. His method proved eminently successful and Case School remains a monument to his administrative ability. In addition to his teaching, until some time after he went to Case, Staley practised his profession, specializing in sanitary engineering. He was a pioneer in promoting the separate system of sewerage; collaborated with George S. Pierson in publishing *The Separate System of Sewerage* (1886); and was associated with him in designing and superintending the construction of such systems in West Troy and Schenectady, N. Y., and in Dayton, Ohio. Because suitable textbooks on stresses in framed structures were lacking, he wrote *Notes on Bridge Engineering* (1875); *Strength of Materials and Stability of Structures* (1876); and *Elements of Truss Bridges* (1878). He edited Gillespie's *Treatise on Levelling, Topography, and Higher Surveying* (1870; 1877), and compiled

The Teachings of Jesus, Selected from the Gospels (copyright 1889).

As a teacher, Staley was informal and sympathetic; as an executive he had the welfare of the individual at heart, and never hesitated to make exceptions in general rules for the benefit of individuals. Thus in many cases he made it possible for a student who was slow or poorly prepared to achieve an engineering education.

In his prime Staley had a magnificent physique. He was tall, broad-shouldered, and heavily built. He was a great lover of horses, and for a time owned a stock farm in the West, where he hoped after his retirement to raise heavy draft horses from imported Percheron stock. A series of unsuccessful years discouraged him, however, and he disposed of his farm and stock. During his summer vacations, after going to Case, Staley and his wife traveled a great deal, and in 1902 Staley retired so as to spend more time in foreign travel. With his wife he made a trip around the world, then made his home on a farm at Minaville, N. Y., but continued to spend much time in travel. By 1907, however, he had tired of having no definite work to do, and from then until 1917 spent the fall term of each year at Case as professor of political economy. He died at Minaville, in his eighty-eighth year.

[*Proc. Am. Soc. Civil Engineers,* vol. LV (1929); *Who's Who in America,* 1920–21; *Who's Who in Engineering,* 1925; *Union College . . . Commemoration . . . of the One Hundredth Anniversary* (1897); *Cleveland Plain Dealer,* June 28, 1928; records of Case School of Applied Science; personal acquaintance.]

F. H. N.

STALLO, JOHANN BERNHARD (Mar. 16, 1823–Jan. 6, 1900), lawyer, scientist, minister to Italy, was born at Sierhausen, Oldenburg, Germany, the son of Johann Heinrich and Maria Adelheid (Moormann) Stallo. He was of Frisian descent, his ancestors for many generations having been schoolmasters. Under his grandfather's tutelage he learned to read and cipher before he was four years old, and later learned English and the classical languages, while his father taught him French. At the age of thirteen he entered the normal school at Vechta and then the Gymnasium, but his father lacked means for his further education, and to avoid becoming a village schoolmaster he emigrated to America at sixteen years of age. At Cincinnati, Ohio, where an uncle had settled previously, the studious boy procured a position as teacher in a Catholic school. He published a primer, *ABC, Buchstabier und Lesebuch, für die deutschen Schulen Amerikas* (1840), as well as some poems which betray a philosophical interest in nature, and until 1844 was a student at St. Xavier's College in Cincinnati, teaching German and the classical languages at the same time. He employed all his spare time in the study of chemistry and physics and was appointed professor of these sciences in St. John's College, Fordham, N. Y., from 1844 to 1847. Here he studied philosophy and prepared his *General Principles of the Philosophy of Nature* (1848), introducing American readers to the philosophical views of Kant, Hegel, Fichte, Schelling, and Lorenz Oken. While it served its purpose in this respect, Stallo later disavowed the book as having been written "under the spell of Hegel's ontological reveries" (see the introduction to *Concepts, post,* p. 11).

Stallo then returned to Cincinnati, studied law, and was admitted to the bar in 1849. After practising for some time he was appointed judge in the Hamilton County Court of Common Pleas from 1853 to 1855. One of his most famous cases was his defense of the Cincinnati School Board in a mandamus suit in which Protestant clergymen tried to force it to retain the singing of hymns and the reading of the Bible as part of the school curriculum. His brilliant plea before the superior court of Cincinnati won the day for religious freedom (see *The Bible and the Public Schools,* Cincinnati, 1870). Throughout the years of his law practice Stallo continued his study of philosophy, physics, and mathematics. He gave lectures on scientific subjects, was a frequent contributor to periodicals, and collected an enormous library containing some rare first editions of Kepler annotated by the scientist himself. For seventeen years he was examiner of candidates for teaching positions, was on the Board of Curators of the University of Cincinnati, and in many ways showed his interest in education. He published *The Concepts and Theories of Modern Physics* in Appleton's *International Scientific Series* (vol. XXXVIII, 1882), which was translated into French, German, Spanish, Italian, and Russian. It was primarily an essay in epistemology with results similar to Ernst Mach's, and attempted to define the contemporary position of science.

Stallo was a great admirer of Jefferson and belonged to the Democratic party until the question of slavery became acute, when he helped found the Republican party. In 1856 he was an elector for Frémont. At the outbreak of the Civil War he eloquently called on the Germans of Cincinnati to form a regiment, the 9th Ohio Infantry, sometimes called "Stallo's Turner Regiment." When corruption became rife within the Republican party he joined the group of reformers who attempted to nominate Charles Francis Adams at the convention in Cincinnati in 1872.

In speeches and letters Stallo always favored the interests of the people against monopolies, and was an opponent of the protective tariff. In 1885 in recognition of his activity in political reform, Cleveland appointed him minister to Italy. After four years in Rome he settled in Florence where he spent the remainder of his life with his books. He published his German writings under the title *Reden, Abhandlungen und Briefe* in 1893. Stallo's home was a seat of rare culture in letters, science, and music, and was open only to a few people. He was a born scholar, a keen and liberal thinker whose works anticipated the studies of Darwin. In 1855 he had been married to Helene Zimmermann, of Cincinnati, who survived him with two of their seven children.

[H. A. Rattermann, *Johann Bernhard Stallo* (1902); shorter accounts in Gustav Körner, *Das deutsche Element in den Vereinigten Staaten* (1880); T. J. McCormack, biographical article in *Open Court*, May 1900; *Popular Sci. Monthly*, Feb. 1889; Hans Kleinpeter, "J. B. Stallo als Erkenntniskritiker," *Vierteljahrsschrift für wissenschaftliche Philosophie*, Nov. 1901; autobiographical items in preface to Stallo's *Die Begriffe und Theorien der Modernen Physik* (1882); *Cincinnati Enquirer*, Jan. 7, 1900.]   A. E. Z.

STANARD, MARY MANN PAGE NEWTON (Aug. 15, 1865–June 5, 1929), Virginia historian, was born in Westmoreland County, Va., of prominent stock, daughter of the Rt. Rev. John Brockenbrough Newton and his wife Roberta Page (Williamson) Newton. She was a descendant of John Newton who emigrated from Hull, Yorkshire, first to Maryland and then to Westmoreland County about 1675. She attended first the ordinary schools near her home, later graduating from the Leache-Wood School in Norfolk, but she grew up in a literary atmosphere and early developed scholarly instincts; throughout her life, despite her sociable and companionable nature and her none too robust health, she remained essentially the student. On Apr. 17, 1900, she married William Glover Stanard [*q.v.*] of Richmond, Va., corresponding secretary of the Virginia Historical Society, and thereby associated herself permanently with the city whose history she was so lovingly to record. Reared to venerate Virginia's past and to believe in its present, her residence in Richmond enabled her to gratify her interest in both. From the creation of the office until her death she was historian of the Association for the Preservation of Virginia Antiquities; she served as vice-president of the Virginia Society of the Colonial Dames of America and as president of the Richmond Woman's club; and she was a member of the Virginia Writers' club, of the executive committee of the Edgar Allan Poe Shrine, and of the Virginia War History commission.

Her first volume was her original and meritorious study, *The Story of Bacon's Rebellion* (1907), although she had previously collaborated with her husband in the laborious and highly valuable compilation, *The Colonial Virginia Register* (1902); this she followed with *The Dreamer; a Romantic Rendering of the Life-Story of Edgar Allan Poe* (1909), in which particular emphasis was laid on the poet's early life in Richmond. More significant, and likely to prove her most enduring works, are her detailed and interesting social histories, *Colonial Virginia, Its People and Customs* (1917) and *Richmond, Its People and Its Story* (1923), both abounding in excellent word pictures of noteworthy and influential people and events. Besides numerous magazine articles and short stories, she published two other brief volumes, *John Marshall* (1913), and *John Brockenbrough Newton* (1924), first published serially in the *Virginia Churchman*, a biographical sketch of her father, at one time rector of Monumental Episcopal Church in Richmond and later bishop coadjutor of Virginia; she edited, most capably, the *Edgar Allan Poe Letters Till Now Unpublished, in the Valentine Museum, Richmond, Va.* (1925), and in 1928 published her last book, *The Story of Virginia's First Century*. She died in Richmond, survived by her husband. They had no children. While not primarily concerned with discovering new facts or correcting minutiae, she wrote enjoyable and authoritative books on Virginia history for the general reader, more than passingly accurate despite their disregard of footnotes or bibliographies. All of her work shows a sense of order and arrangement, of discriminating selection, graphic detail, and graceful charm; it is local history, definitely restricted in compass, but there is little of it that will need to be done again.

[*Who's Who in America*, 1928–29; Daniel Grinnan, in *Va. Mag. of Hist. and Biog.*, July 1929; obituary in *Richmond Times-Dispatch*, June 6, 1929; date of birth supplied by a relative of Mrs. Stanard.]   A. C. G., Jr.

STANARD, WILLIAM GLOVER (Oct. 2, 1858–May 6, 1933), editor and antiquarian, was born in Richmond, Va., of substantial and well-connected stock (the Stanard family had settled in Middlesex County before 1700), son of Capt. Robert Conway and Virginia M. (Cowan) Stanard. His father, who was a captain in the Confederate Army, died in 1861, and his mother later married William B. Wooldridge. Educated at McGuire's School, Richmond, at the College of William and Mary, 1875–76, and at Richmond College (later part of the University of Richmond), 1876–80, during his young manhood he worked at various occupations, including those of surveyor and of reporter for the *Richmond Daily Whig*, but early developed a taste for historical and genealogical study, and began to contribute occasional articles to the *Critic* (Richmond) and other periodicals. In October 1898 he succeeded Philip A. Bruce as corresponding secretary of the Virginia Historical Society and editor of the *Virginia Magazine of History and Biography*, continuing in this dual capacity until his death. Barring his marriage, Apr. 17, 1900 (see Stanard, Mary Mann Page Newton) and the publication of his two useful and meritorious volumes, *The Colonial Virginia Register* (1902), compiled with the assistance of his wife, and *Some Emigrants to Virginia* (1911), there were few milestones in the remaining portion of his career. The record of his later days was that of faithful and painstaking devotion to the routine tasks of collecting and preserving whatever bore upon the history of Virginia, as colony or as commonwealth, and of extending the sphere of the society whose efficient officer he was. He printed little in book form, despite his industry, his power of easy, direct composition, and the astonishing extent of his information—it has been said that "he knew more of the history of Virginia than any other man has ever known" (quoted in Munford, *post*); self-effacing and generous, he employed no little of his private research in supplying material for the narratives his wife wrote, while with gentle and patient courtesy he gave unstintingly of his time and knowledge to the numberless students who, seldom fruitlessly, sought historical or genealogical aid from him. The thirty-five volumes of the *Virginia Magazine of History and Biography* which he published, however, remain a monument to his scholarly and authoritative editorship at the same time that they abound in valuable contributions from his pen, most of them with characteristic modesty left unsigned.

[*Who's Who in America*, 1932–33; R. B. Munford, Jr., *In Memoriam: William Glover Stanard* (1934), with portrait, reprinted from the *Va. Mag. of Hist. and Biog.*, July 1933; obituaries in *Richmond Times-Dispatch*, May 7, 8, and *News-Leader* (Richmond), May 8, 1933.]   A. C. G., Jr.

STANBERY, HENRY (Feb. 20, 1803–June 26, 1881), lawyer, attorney-general of the United States, was born in New York City, the son of Dr. Jonas and Ann Lucy (Seaman) Stanbery. In 1814 his parents removed to Ohio and settled in Zanesville. Henry showed unusual gifts as a student and was graduated from Washington College (later, Washington and Jefferson) in Pennsylvania at the age of sixteen. He then read law with Ebenezer Granger and Charles B. Goddard and upon reaching his majority was admitted to the bar. That same year he was invited into partnership with Thomas Ewing [*q.v.*] of Lancaster, Ohio, one of the ablest attorneys in the state, and continued in association with him until Ewing entered the United States Senate in 1831. Stanbery early developed into a thoroughly well-rounded lawyer, learned in both the technicalities and the general principles of the law, and won for himself a place at the front rank of the Ohio bar, then renowned for its distinguished practitioners. His election to the newly created office of attorney-general of Ohio in 1846 necessitated his removal from Lancaster to Columbus, and for the next few years he was engaged in organizing the new department of justice and in expanding his practice in the United States courts and in the Ohio supreme court. He was among the most influential members of the constitutional convention of 1850 and ably contributed out of his broad learning and experience to the improvement of the organic laws of the state. In 1853 he transferred his law office to Cincinnati and continued his practice there until appointed attorney-general of the United States in 1866.

A handsome man of imposing presence, kindly manner, and unsullied character, Stanbery was universally respected. His clear and forceful reasoning, persuasiveness, and finished eloquence combined to make him effective on the stump as well as in the court room, but he was not an office-seeker and seldom took a conspicuous part in political campaigns. He identified himself with the Whig and later the Republican party and was an ardent supporter of the Lincoln administration. The moderate policy of reconstruction begun by Lincoln and carried forward by Johnson appealed to him strongly, and after entering the cabinet of the latter, July 23, 1866, he interpreted the reconstruction legislation as liberally as the language of the acts permitted. Gideon Welles thought him too much a man of precedents and too timid when action seemed appropriate (*Diary, post*, III, 221, 308–09), but Johnson placed a high estimate upon his judgment and wisdom and apparently relied much upon him in the preparation of his veto messages. When the impeachment proceedings against the President were begun, Stanbery resigned as attorney-general (Mar. 12, 1868) to serve as Johnson's chief counsel. After the opening days, in which he bore the main burden of the defense, illness forced him to withdraw, but he returned to make the final argument. His summation glowed with loyalty and praise for the harassed executive. At the close of the trial Johnson renominated him as attorney-general, but the Senate, as in the case of his nomination to the United States Supreme Court in April 1866, refused to confirm his appointment. In both instances the Senate's action was undoubtedly dictated by hostility to the President rather than by any question as to the nominee's fitness. After his rejection in 1868 Stanbery resumed his practice in Cincinnati with distinguished success, but failing sight obliged him to retire about 1878. He died in New York City. He was married twice: first, in 1829, to Frances E. Beecher of Lancaster, Ohio, who died in 1840 after having borne him five children; subsequently, he married Cecelia Bond, who survived him.

[G. I. Reed, *Bench and Bar of Ohio* (1897), vol. I; *Biog. and Hist. Cat. of Washington and Jefferson Coll.* (1902); *Trial of Andrew Johnson* (3 vols., 1868); *Diary of Gideon Welles* (1911), vols. II, III; Charles Warren, *The Supreme Court in U. S. Hist.* (1928), vol. II; E. P. Oberholtzer, *A Hist. of the U. S. Since the Civil War*, vol. II (1922); W. H. Safford, in *Ohio State Bar Asso. Reports*, vol. IV (1884); *N. Y. Times,* June 27, 1881; *Cincinnati Commercial,* June 27, 1881; information from grandson.]   A. H. M.

STANCHFIELD, JOHN BARRY (Mar. 30, 1855–June 25, 1921), lawyer, son of John King and Glorvina (Smith) Stanchfield, was a descendant of John Stinchfield who came to Gloucester, Mass., from Leeds, England, in 1735, and later settled at New Gloucester, Me. The boy's father was a native of Maine, a graduate of the medical department of Bowdoin College, and for thirty years a physician at Elmira, N. Y. Upon taking up his residence in that place, apparently, he changed his name from Stinchfield to Stanchfield. John the younger was born there and was educated at the Elmira Free Academy and at Amherst. His record in his studies was only average, but he excelled in debating, rowing, and baseball. He is credited with being one of the first to use the "curve ball" in pitching. After his graduation in 1876, he attended some lectures at the Harvard Law School and then, returning to Elmira, studied in the office of David Bennett Hill [*q.v.*], under whose guidance he learned much about law and acquired a taste for politics. He was admitted to the bar in 1878 and became Hill's partner the following year. He served as district attorney of Chemung County, 1880–86, and as mayor of Elmira, 1886–88. After a few years, during which he devoted himself exclusively to law and obtained a good practice throughout most of western New York, his ambition for a political career led him to enter the New York Assembly in 1895. He was minority leader the following year and in 1898 was the unsuccessful candidate of Hill's faction for the Democratic nomination for governor. He was nominated in 1900, but was defeated through the opposition of organized labor and the unpopularity of his party's national candidates.

The experience was at least valuable in making him well known throughout the state. After the election he opened an office in New York City, where he at once gained favorable reputation through his conduct of several criminal cases, notably the defense of members of the Metropolitan Turf Association charged with violating laws against bookmaking, and of F. A. Heinze, charged with misappropriating funds of the Mercantile National Bank. During the last ten years of his life he was engaged in probably more cases which attracted public interest than any other member of the New York bar. He was counsel for friends of Harry K. Thaw in obtaining his release from Matteawan, for Duveen Brothers in cases concerning duties on works of art, for forty-one individuals and sixty-nine corporations charged with conspiracy in restraining trade in bituminous coal, for the Assembly committee in the impeachment of Governor Sulzer, and in family lawsuits of the Goulds and the Guggenheims. Though often retained as advisory counsel, he was generally engaged for work in the courtroom, where his erect, imposing figure, resonant voice, power of concise statement, courage, and resourcefulness in emergencies showed to great advantage.

On public affairs his convictions were conservative; his expressions, positive. It was he who, at the Democratic National Convention of 1912, called Bryan a "money-grabbing, selfish, office-seeking, favor-hunting, publicity-loving marplot." In 1915 he was a delegate to the state constitutional convention, in which he took little part. He was active in the National Security League, publishing an address in 1916, entitled, *Some Suggestions on the Perils of Espionage,* in which he recommended that Congress create a new offense, which he called misprision of espionage or misprision of treachery, and extend protection to systems of communications, mines, and factories, as well as to government property. His last appearance in public proceedings was in 1920 as counsel for the New York Assembly in the expulsion of five Socialist members. On Sept. 2, 1886, he married Clara, daughter of Henry C. Spaulding of Elmira; they had a son and a daughter.

[J. C. Stinchfield, *Hist. of the Town of Leeds . . . Me.* (n.d.); *The Asso. of the Bar of the City of N. Y., Year Book,* 1922; D. S. Alexander, *Four Famous New Yorkers* (1923); *Who's Who in America,* 1920–21; *Obit. Record, Grads. . . . of Amherst Coll.,* 1922; Ausburn Towner, *Our County and Its People: A Hist. of the . . . County of Chemung* (1892); *N. Y. Times,* June 26, 1921; information as to certain facts from Stanchfield's son.]   E. C. S.

STANDERREN, ANN LEES [See LEE, ANN, 1736–1784].

STANDISH, MYLES (*c.* 1584–Oct. 3, 1656), Pilgrim father and captain, is said to have been born in Lancashire, England, and affirmed in his will that he was descended from the important Roman Catholic family, Standish of Standish, and had been fraudulently deprived of his inheritance, but no confirmation of this descent and no details of his early life have been discovered by extended modern research. He served in the Low Countries as soldier of fortune and in 1620 was hired by the Pilgrims to accompany them, sailing from London on the *Mayflower.* The only man with practical experience in camping, he was their mainstay in the first explorations of Cape Cod and was one of the small party who made the first landing at Plymouth on Dec. 11/21, 1620. During the general sickness of the first winter he was the only man except William Brewster, 1567–1644 [*q.v.*], who escaped, and with Brewster he rendered most important service to the sick. Probably it was this incident which made him one of the Pilgrims in fact and not merely their employee. Their first relations with the Indians he handled expertly, and, soon learning the Indian dialects, he became their chief resource in "foreign relations." Almost single-handed he suppressed the early conspiracies against them, designed and superintended the erection of the fort, and devised their measures of defense. So well did he work that after 1623 the colony experienced no real danger for half a century. This was one of the most important contributions to the welfare and success of Plymouth. In 1624 he became one of the five assistants then appointed for the first time. Four years later he broke up the settlement of Thomas Morton [*q.v.*] at Merry Mount and shipped the offender to England. Certainly by 1625 he was established as one of the Pilgrims, for at that time he was selected for a difficult mission. Isaac Allerton and Edward Winslow, 1595–1655 [*qq.v.*], had failed to complete satisfactory arrangements with the Merchant Adventurers or with the Council for New England, and the Pilgrims were as yet without rights in the new world to land or property. Standish was chosen to return to England bearing credentials to negotiate on their behalf. With the Council he had some success, with the merchants very little; but he did secure further loans and purchased supplies of great importance. He returned in April 1626. The following year he became one of the Undertakers who assumed the debts of the colony, and in 1630 was the attorney for the Council for

New England to deliver to the Pilgrims their land under the new grant. In later years he continued one of the chief men in all affairs, for six years treasurer and for twenty-nine an assistant. He and John Alden [*q.v.*] founded Duxbury in 1631, later set off as the first new town in their jurisdiction (1637), and there he lived for the remainder of his life.

His wife, Rose, having died in the sickness of the first winter, he married in 1624 his second wife, Barbara, who had come in the *Anne* in 1623. They had six children, of whom a son and a daughter died young. There is no historical basis for the story of John Alden's proposal to Priscilla on Standish's behalf or for other incidents in Longfellow's *The Courtship of Miles Standish* (A. E. Alden, *Pilgrim Alden,* 1902). There is some doubt whether he was ever a member of the Pilgrim church (Goodwin, *post,* p. 449), but the better view seems to be that he became a convert soon after reaching Plymouth. On his death in 1656 he left a considerable property in land and cattle, and one of the largest libraries at Plymouth. He was survived by his wife and four sons. Short, plump, and sturdy in appearance, he was called by Thomas Morton "Captaine Shrimp," a "quondam Drummer" (C. F. Adams, *The New English Canaan of Thomas Morton,* 1883, pp. 285–87), and by William Hubbard [*q.v.*], he was compared for his "very little stature" and his "hot and angry temper" to "a little chimney . . . soon fired" (*A General History of New England from the Discovery to MDCLXXX,* 1815, p. 111). He was nevertheless a man of great physical endurance and high courage.

[The chief authority is William Bradford, *Hist. of Plymouth Plantation, 1620–1647* (2 vols., 1912), ed. by W. C. Ford. See also R. G. Usher, *The Pilgrims and Their Hist.* (1918); J. A. Goodwin, *The Pilgrim Republic* (1888); Tudor Jenks, *Captain Myles Standish* (1905); T. C. Porteus, *Captain Myles Standish, His Lost Lands and Lancashire Connections* (1920); Myles Standish, *The Standishes of America* (1895), which gives Standish's will; C. E. Banks, *The English Ancestry and Homes of the Pilgrim Fathers* (1929).]
R. G. U.

STANFORD, JOHN (Oct. 20, 1754–Jan. 14, 1834), preacher, teacher, humanitarian, the son of William and Mary Stanford, was born at Wandsworth, in Surrey, England. He received his early education at a seminary in Wandsworth. At the age of sixteen he began to study medicine but his studies were interrupted by the death of his parents and he subsequently took charge of a boarding school in Hammersmith. Reared an Anglican he turned to the Baptist faith, began to write and distribute tracts before there were any Tract Societies, organized a Baptist church in Hammersmith, and was ordained as its first minister in 1781. Five years later he emigrated to the United States and, after a brief period of teaching in Norfolk, Va., and in New York City, he served as pastor of the First Baptist Church of Providence, R. I., in 1788–89, afterwards returning to teaching in New York City. In 1795 he erected a building for combined use as a church, school, and residence on Fair (now Fulton) Street, and acted as pastor until the yellow fever scourge of 1798 disrupted his congregation and a fire in 1801 reduced his church building to ashes. Stanford never held a fixed pastorate thereafter. For a decade he was known to his friends as a professor of theology although he preached frequently in Baptist churches in New York, New Jersey, Pennsylvania, and Connecticut. He spoke occasionally before the inmates of Bellevue Hospital and the New York State Prison, and in 1812 was appointed chaplain of the Prison. He called his charges at the latter institution his "Greenwich congregation." His services in a similar capacity in municipal institutions began the following year without formal appointment by any city authority, but he was compensated annually by the Common Council by special resolution. It was "for his zeal in administering to the spiritual wants of the poor and afflicted in the Alms House Gaol—and City Prison" (*Minutes Common Council, post*, VIII, 400), that the original annual stipend of $250 was increased to $300 in 1816, and to $500 in 1830.

Unfortunates of every description found a friend in Stanford, but the youthful inmates of institutions were particularly his concern. With a zeal reminiscent of John Howard he pled with the city magistrates to separate young offenders from the hardened criminals, and, as a result, the House of Refuge, called by Governor DeWitt Clinton the "best penitentiary institution . . . [which had] ever been devised by the wit and established by the beneficence of man" was dedicated by Stanford with a discourse in 1825 (*Journal of the Assembly of the State of New York*, 1826, p. 15). He organized the "Paupers' School" in the Alms House and drew up the necessary "regulations." He wrote a unique catechism for these children and persuaded the city to pay for the preparation and printing. In addition to many tracts and printed discourses, dedicated to the welfare of youth, Stanford wrote *The Aged Christian's Cabinet* (1829). He was married on June 16, 1790, to Sarah Ten Eyck who died during the fever scourge of 1798, leaving two sons and two daughters.

[Stanford's diary, 5 vols., manuscript, 1816–31, and his Letter Book, 1795–1821, autographed copies of his annual reports as Chaplain of the State Prison, 1819–26, and of New York City institutions, 1819–30, are preserved in the archives of the N. Y. Hist. Soc.; C. G. Sommers, *Memoir of the Rev. John Stanford, D.D.* (1835), with portrait, is based on the diary and Letter Book but contains many unfortunate changes in phraseology; "A Brief Sketch of the Life of the Rev. John Stanford, D.D.," is to be found in *Aged Christian's Companion* (1855, 4th edition of the *Cabinet*). See also Enoch Hutchinson's biographical sketch in *The Bapt. Memorial and Monthly Record*, vol. VIII (1849); *Minutes of the Common Council of the City of N. Y., 1784–1831*, 21 vols. (1917–30); original letters and reports in city clerk's archives; brief references in David Benedict, *A Gen. Hist. of the Bapt. Denomination* (1813), vol. I, and *A Brief Hist. of the Am. Tract Soc.* (1857); H. W. George, "The Ten Eyck Family in New York," *N. Y. Geneal. and Biog. Record*, July 1932; *New-York American*, Jan. 15, 1834.]   A. E. P.

STANFORD, LELAND (Mar. 9, 1824–June 21, 1893), railroad builder, governor of California, and United States senator, was born in Watervliet, N. Y. Originally his name was Amasa Leland (Clark, *post*, p. 14), but he never used the full form after he was mature. His father, Josiah Stanford, a native of Massachusetts and a man of means, was a descendant of Thomas Stanford who settled at Charlestown, Mass., in the seventeenth century. His mother was Elizabeth Phillips, whose parents were once residents of Boston, moving thence to Vermont, and later to New York. Leland Stanford was the fourth son of a family of seven sons and one daughter. The daughter died in infancy, and one son in early life. The remaining children were, in the order of their ages, Josiah, Charles, Asa Phillips, Leland, De Witt Clinton, and Thomas Welton. The boys helped their father upon the farm, and perhaps also with various contracts for road and bridge construction in which he was interested. Leland attended school until the age of twelve. He was then taught at home for three years. After an interval of two years he returned to school, attending Clinton Liberal Institute, Clinton, N. Y., and Cazenovia Seminary at Cazenovia, and at the age of twenty-one entered the law office of Wheaton, Doolittle and Hadley at Albany. Three years later he was admitted to the bar. He can thus be said to have received a fair education for his place and time. When the young man began the practice of the law in 1848 at Port Washington, Wis., his father presented him with a law library that was said to be the best in that part of the United States north of Milwaukee.

While Leland Stanford entered upon a professional career, his brothers migrated to California, attracted by the commercial opportunities in that rapidly developing community. Under the leadership of the younger Josiah, who led the way, the five brothers prospered in the mercantile business, with a wholesale house in Sacramento and retail stores at Mormon Island and Michigan Flat, all more or less connected, and one brother as a purchasing agent in New York (Clark, p. 51). It is not improbable that Leland may have considered joining them, for Port Washington was a small place, and his legal ability was in no way conspicuous. The change did not occur, however, until 1852. In the meantime, on Sept. 30, 1850, he married Jane Elizabeth Lathrop, daughter of a respected merchant at Albany, N. Y., Dyer Lathrop, and his wife, Jane Ann Shields. Two years later his office at Port Washington, with his law library, was burned. The newly married couple were jolted out of their accustomed routine, and, instead of settling down again, decided to follow the other younger members of the Stanford family to the Pacific Coast. They returned to Albany, where Mrs. Stanford remained with her father while her husband went ahead to prepare the way.

In 1852, accordingly, Leland Stanford was in California, visiting at first his brother in Sacramento. J. M. Bassett, who knew him well, and who was likely to be acquainted with the facts, says that he came to California poor as a church mouse, and that his brothers set him up in business in El Dorado County, at Cold Springs, with a stock of miners' supplies (San Francisco *Daily Report*, Mar. 21, 1896). Capt. Nicholas T. Smith, later treasurer of the Southern Pacific, was his partner. Bassett says, further, that Stanford was popular with the miners and did a good business. He and Smith thought they were making money until they found out that the San Francisco firm with which they dealt was charging them interest on unpaid balances. This absorbed their profit, and they went out of business with very little cash. Whether for this reason or because the mining at Cold Springs petered out, Stanford started a new store at Michigan Bluff the following spring, and is said to have done well.

Michigan Bluff was a central business point for the Placer County mining territory, and well located for the distribution of miners' supplies. Whether Stanford, in addition to merchandising, profited by successful mining operations at this time is not certain, but if he did engage in mining it was probably upon a small scale. In 1855 he returned to Albany for his wife and the next year he moved to Sacramento to join his brothers in business there. Meanwhile his attention had been drawn to politics. In Michigan Bluff he had been justice of the peace. During the state campaign of 1857 he was the Republican candidate for state treasurer, but went down to defeat with his party. In 1859 he was nominated for governor and made a thorough canvass, only to be decisively beaten by Milton S. Latham [*q.v.*]. In 1860 he was chosen delegate to the Republican National Convention, but did not attend. These various activities made him known, and in 1861 when the outbreak of the Civil War split the Democratic party of the state in two, the tenacious Stanford, again a candidate, was elected governor, although he received less than the combined vote of his two Democratic opponents. His success was due to his personal popularity, and to his strong Union and Republican convictions, for he had had no opportunity to distinguish himself in public service. In 1863 he was not renominated, and he held no other public office until his election as United States senator in 1885.

The chief task of Stanford's administration as governor was to hold California safely in the Union, and this he accomplished to the satisfaction of the Union party and of the state legislature. He had, in addition, to cope with difficulties caused by a serious flood upon the Sacramento at the very outset of his gubernatorial career. In addition to providing for sufferers from the flood of 1861, and promoting minor administrative and legislative reforms, Stanford approved, during his term of office, several public grants to the transcontinental railroad via Truckee, Cal. This was the enterprise which brought him wealth, and upon which his reputation chiefly rests. His connection with the transcontinental railroad project, like that of Collis Potter Huntington [*q.v.*], seems to have been due to the promotion activity of Theodore Dehone Judah [*q.v.*]. When he became interested, Stanford subscribed, with others, a sufficient amount to finance instrumental surveys which gave satisfactory evidence of the feasibility of the proposed railroad line, and then to permit the organization of the Central Pacific Railroad on June 28, 1861. Only a small amount of capital was available to the associates; most of the necessary funds for the building of the road were procured by means of subscriptions and grants of a public nature.

Ground was broken at Sacramento in January 1863, and in April Stanford as governor signed four acts affording considerable assistance to the new enterprise. One of these instructed the board of supervisors of Placer County to order a special election to consider a county subscription of $250,000 to the Central Pacific capital stock. A second provided for a similar election in the City and County of Sacramento to approve a subscription for 3,000 shares. A third act directed the supervisors of the City and County of San Francisco to submit a proposal to the voters to subscribe $600,000 to the stock of the Central Pacific and $400,000 to the stock of the Western Pacific Railroad. The last act authorized the comptroller of the state to draw warrants in favor of the Central Pacific to the extent of $10,000 per mile. The warrants were to be issued when the first twenty miles, the second twenty miles, and the last ten out of fifty miles were finished. They were to bear seven per cent. interest if the state proved unable to cash them when presented. It should be added that this law was repealed in the following year, when the legislature proposed, instead of drawing warrants, to assume the interest on 1,500 of the company's bonds bearing seven per cent. interest and running for twenty years. From these various acts the Central Pacific ultimately realized some $825,000, besides the interest payments contemplated by the act of 1864. Stanford had no scruples about taking official action as governor where his private interests as railroad president were engaged, or he overcame such as may have occurred to him by reflecting upon the public importance of a railroad connection with the East.

When his term of office expired in 1863, Stanford left the governorship to devote his whole time to railroad construction. He then occupied an important position in the little group that was responsible for the transcontinental railroad, and he worked hard during the next ten years to make this project a success. He was president and director of the Central Pacific Railroad from the beginning until his death in 1893. He was director of the Southern Pacific Company from 1885 to 1893, and president of the company from 1885 to 1890. He was director of the Southern Pacific Railroad in 1889 and in 1890. At all times he was a shareholder in and contributor to the resources of the construction companies, such as the Contract & Finance Company, which built the Central Pacific, the Southern Pacific, and their allied properties. The course pursued, in connection with the construction of the Central Pacific, was described by the Pacific Railway Commission as "indefensible" (*Report of the ... United States Pacific Railway Commission,* 1887, p. 72; see also Carman and Mueller, *post*). While Huntington was the financial representative, purchasing agent, and chief lobbyist in the East, and Charles Crocker [*q.v.*] took charge of construction, Stanford seems to have handled the financial affairs and looked after the political interests of the Central Pacific in the West. He was widely known and personally of good credit, and although he sold no Central Pacific stock in the early days, and never succeeded in persuading other men of wealth to join with him and his associates, he was able to borrow considerable sums when they were needed in anticipation of receipts, and so to insure the essential continuity of construction work.

The importance of the Central Pacific Railroad, the obvious difficulties of topography and of climate which it overcame, the dramatic speed at which the work was done, the picturesque personalities and subsequent great wealth of the promoters and their relations with national and local governments, have since attracted great attention to this particular exploit. The Central Pacific was not, at the beginning, particularly well built, and it was not located upon the easiest route over the Sierras. The present Feather River route of the Western Pacific Railroad has lower grades and less snow. While the engineering difficulties were serious, the railroad was built almost entirely with or on the security of public funds, so that Stanford and his friends risked less of their own capital in the undertaking than has sometimes been supposed. Nevertheless, the associates risked their own personal fortunes, whether large or small, in building a transcontinental railway, they assembled the force and created the organization with which the work was done, and they contributed energy and courage and assumed responsibility for decisions which determined the success of the undertaking.

After the completion of the Central Pacific Railroad on May 10, 1869, by its junction with the Union Pacific near Ogden, Utah, Stanford was definitely committed to a railroad career. His business life thereafter was devoted to the strengthening and expansion of his railroad properties. In this he continued to work in close cooperation with his former associates; indeed, the continued unity in management of Central Pacific and Southern Pacific affairs was an important element in the later success of these companies as operating organizations. This same unity makes it impossible to determine Stanford's separate contribution to Central Pacific policy except in a few special instances; but it permits one to assume that he had a fair share in whatever results his organizations achieved. Notable among these was the acquisition of satisfactory terminal facilities for the new company upon San Francisco Bay, the purchase in 1871 of the competing line of the California Pacific Railroad Company from Sacramento to Vallejo, the purchase of the San Francisco and San Jose Railroad, probably in 1868, and the organization of the Southern Pacific Railroad. This last named company was incorporated in October 1870, to construct and operate a railroad from San Francisco to the Colorado River. It eventually was built from Gilroy to Tres Pinos, and from Goshen in the San Joaquin Valley to Los Angeles, Fort Yuma, and to the Needles, all in California. With connecting companies under the same control it provided a through line from San Francisco to New Orleans. In 1884, on Stanford's suggestion, the Stanford-Huntington group organized the Southern Pacific Company under the laws of Kentucky and caused it, in 1885, as a holding company, to lease the Southern Pacific Railroad, the Central Pacific Railroad, and other system properties. After this, the Southern Pacific Company became the dominant unit in the organization. The principal object of the change was to continue undisputed control of the Central Pacific in the hands of the associates in spite of sales of considerable quantities of Central Pacific stock to English and other buyers.

There has never been a public accounting of the profits which Stanford and his friends drew from the construction of the Central and Southern Pacific Railroads. We know they were great, because the associates died very rich men. Mark Hopkins engaged in no important enterprises outside of his hardware business except in railroad construction and operation, and yet in 1878 he left an estate appraised at over $19,000,000. Eleven years later, Charles Crocker's estate was estimated at c. $24,000,000. Stanford's estate was not appraised in 1893, and Huntington did not die until long afterwards, but both shared equally with Hopkins and Crocker in the results of the tasks which they undertook together.

It was this great personal fortune, as well as the backing of the Southern Pacific, which enabled Stanford to indulge his tastes in matters not strictly connected with his business. In this he showed a wider range of interests than his colleague Huntington, who remained in harness until the end of his life. Stanford, on the other hand, bought land in Tehama County, where he maintained extensive vineyards, and a large ranch, "Palo Alto," where he bred and ran fine racing stock. He did much to raise the grade of California horses and achieved records in eastern fields. His original methods of training were widely adopted. He was interested in photography as a means of studying animal locomotion, and in this connection sponsored some of the first successful experiments with instantaneous photography (Clark, chs. x, xi).

He interested himself greatly in the education of his son, a bright affectionate boy, and suffered cruelly when the lad died in 1884 at the age of fifteen years and ten months. Stanford desired to raise a fitting memorial to his son, and out of this grew Leland Stanford Junior University, founded in 1885 and opened in 1891, an institution, generously endowed, which has acquired high standing among the universities of the United States. For ten years after his death, his wife devoted herself to the problem of caring for the young institution.

Stanford also turned to politics. In a sense, indeed, he had never left politics. After the expiration of his term as governor in 1863, he was naturally the man in the Central Pacific group best fitted to resist the attempts to pass hostile legislation, as well as the one most likely to be able to secure new favors at Sacramento and elsewhere. After the completion of the transcontinental line in 1869, he continued to observe the local situation. His attitude was, as might have been expected, entirely opposed to interference with railroad business by public bodies, for by character and training he was entirely unfitted to understand the movement for public control of quasi-public enterprises which began to gain momentum in the early seventies. Many of Stanford's expressions with respect to railroad regulation have been preserved. The California constitution of 1879 displeased him greatly. He declared that *Munn* vs. *Illinois* and the other Granger cases seemed to recognize the "communistic" idea of the distribution of property and the absolutism of control by a majority of the people, and he advocated a return to the "civilized" government of the fathers which gave protection to the individual and made him truly a free and independent citizen. Stanford justified certain types of discrimination; he defended consolidation; he alluded to the efforts of the railroad to build up the state; and he asserted its right to protect itself by political action when attacked. "There is no foundation in good reason," he said to his stockholders in his annual report for 1878, "for the attempts made by the General Government and by the State to especially control your affairs. It is a question of might, and it is to your interest to have it determined where the power resides" (*Annual Report of the Board of Directors of the Central Pacific Railway to the Stockholders . . . 1878,* 1879, p. 5.).

The general belief in California was that the Southern Pacific Company gave practical effect to Stanford's views by active and persistent interference in the politics of the state, and there is evidence in support of this opinion. Stanford himself held no political office until his return from a trip to Europe in November 1884, after the death of his son Leland. A Republican legislature was to assemble in January 1885, and was to elect a successor to James T. Farley, Democrat, chosen by the legislature of 1877–78. The logical candidate for the position was A. A. Sargent, previously a representative and senator from California, but Stanford allowed his name to be used and was elected by a strict party vote soon after the legislature convened. The decision to accept public office was, on Stanford's part, undoubtedly a mistake. In the first place, it profoundly offended Collis P. Huntington, who was a friend of Sargent and believed that the latter's interests had been betrayed. The difference between Huntington and Stanford remained concealed for several years, but it broke out openly in 1890, when Huntington bitterly criticized Stanford for his political activity, and succeeded in supplanting him as president of the Southern Pacific Company. In the second place, election to the senatorship projected Stanford into a field for which he had no proper training, and for which his abilities were inadequate. He was not an easy speaker, except perhaps on a limited range of subjects connected with his personal experience, he had little talent for sustained thought on difficult problems of a general sort, and his reading in economics seems rather to have confused than to have clarified his mind. In the Senate he found himself assigned, on the whole, to committees of minor importance. His most significant committee, that on naval affairs, dealt with a subject of which he knew nothing. Nor did he try to exert influence upon the floor of the Senate. Between March 1885, when Stanford first appeared in Congress, and June 1893, when he died, the national legislature passed laws providing for the regulation of interstate commerce, for the purchase of silver, for the revision of the tariff, and for the exclusion of Chinese. These were perhaps the most important subjects considered during this period. Stanford was absent from the Senate when the Interstate Commerce Act in its first form was voted on, and when the Senate finally approved the conference report upon the measure in January 1887 he was again absent, though paired against the bill. He was likewise absent when the tariff act of 1890 and the Silver Purchase bill of the same year were passed, although paired in favor of both measures. In neither of the two last-named cases did he participate in the debates, and his contributions to the consideration of the Interstate Commerce Act were unimportant. Stanford said nothing in the Senate with reference to

the exclusion of Chinese laborers in 1888, and the record fails to show whether or not he took part in the final vote. The one proposal in which he showed a real interest was a suggestion of his own, that the federal government issue paper money to borrowers on the security of mortgages upon real estate up to fifty per cent. of the assessed value of the property and at a rate of interest of two per cent. The economic theory underlying the scheme was complex but unsound, and Congress gave it scant attention; but the bill was approved by the National Grange of the Patrons of Husbandry as a step in the direction of cheap money, and brought Stanford some political backing. It is not too much to say that this legislative record shows lack of interest or lack of capacity—probably lack of both; his senatorship satisfied Stanford's vanity and increased his prestige in California, but it did not add to his reputation.

Stanford was five feet eleven inches tall, and in later years weighed as much as 268 pounds. During his prime he possessed unusual energy, working sometimes day and night without cessation, and enduring the hardships incident to railroad construction without complaint. Mentally he was slow, susceptible to flattery, and given to somewhat ponderous platitudes concerning human life and the economic conditions and organizations required for national success. He was elected by the California legislature to succeed himself in the United States Senate on Jan. 14, 1891, but by this time he was an ill man, more concerned with recovery of his health than with political or economic programs. He sought relief in America and abroad from various types of healers, but grew steadily worse, and at last died suddenly at his home in Palo Alto on June 21, 1893. The immediate cause of his death was paralysis of the heart, but the disease from which he had long suffered was diagnosed as locomotor ataxia. He left two brothers, Thomas Welton Stanford, then resident in Australia, and Asa Phillips Stanford, of New York, besides a number of nieces and nephews. The bulk of the estate passed to Mrs. Stanford, apart from a gift of $2,500,000 to Leland Stanford Junior University, and minor bequests to relatives and friends. Mrs. Stanford died in 1905.

[T. H. Hittell, *Hist. of California*, vol. IV (1897); H. H. Bancroft, *Hist. of California*, vol. VII (1890); Stuart Daggett, *Chapters on the Hist. of the Southern Pacific* (1922); Gustavus Myers, *Hist. of the Great American Fortunes*, vol. III (1910); G. T. Clark, *Leland Stanford* (1931); Bertha Berner, *Incidents in the Life of Mrs. Leland Stanford* (1934); Matthew Josephson, *The Robber Barons* (1934); G. C. Quiett, *They Built the West* (1934); H. J. Carman and C. H. Mueller, "The Contract and Finance Company and the Central Pacific Railroad," *Miss. Valley Hist. Rev.*, Dec.

1927; "Testimony Taken by the U. S. Pacific Railway Commission," *Senate Executive Document 51*, 50 Cong., 1 Sess. (1887), vol. V; *Report . . . of the U. S. Pacific Railway Commission* (1887); *California Hist. Soc. Quart.*, Oct. 1923, pp. 203–10; June 1926, pp. 178–83, containing reminiscences and letters; obituary notices in San Francisco *Daily Evening Bulletin* and *Morning Call*, June 21, and the San Francisco *Examiner*, June 21, 22, 23, 24, 1893; A. W. Stanford, *Stanford Genealogy* (1906).]   S. D.

STANG, WILLIAM (Apr. 21, 1854–Feb. 2, 1907), Roman Catholic prelate and educator, son of Francis Joseph and Frances (Bellm) Stang, was born in Langenbrücken, Baden, Germany, where he attended a local gymnasium. In the *petit séminaire* of Saint-Nicolas, Belgium, he prepared for his theological studies at the American College in Louvain. Ordained priest, June 15, 1878, he accepted the call of Bishop Thomas F. Hendricken (1827–86) to Providence, R. I., where he served as a curate in the Cathedral of SS. Peter and Paul. Six years later, he became rector of St. Anne's Church at Cranston, R. I., from which he was soon recalled to the rectorship of the cathedral and chancellorship of the diocese. In the latter capacity he largely inspired the erection of St. Joseph's Hospital in 1892. A thorough student and an exceptional linguist, he found time to publish *The Life of Martin Luther* (1883), *The Eve of the Reformation* (1885), *More about the Huguenots* (1886), and *Germany's Debt to Ireland* (1889). While not learned works, they evidenced wide reading on the part of the author, as well as a scientific spirit of toleration. In 1895 he was appointed vice-rector of the American College in Louvain, where he was honored by the Belgian hierarchy with election in 1898 to the chair of moral theology in the University of Louvain. During his tenure he wrote or compiled solid volumes, *Pastoral Theology* (1896), and *Historiographia Ecclesiastica* (1897). In 1899 he returned to Providence as superior of the diocesan apostolate, which included the direction of missions to non-Catholics, and in 1901 became pastor of St. Edward's Church as well.

Recognized as a spiritual priest and as a capable administrator who could handle racial questions intelligently and sympathetically, on Mar. 12, 1904, he was named by Pope Pius X as bishop of the newly created diocese of Fall River, which had over a hundred priests, of whom fifty were attending French, Polish, Italian, and Portuguese parishes. Consecrated on May 1, 1904, by Bishop Matthew Harkins of Providence (1845–1921), whom he had served so wholeheartedly, he began a brief episcopate. In 1907 he underwent an unsuccessful operation at St. Mary's Hospital, Rochester, Minn., on the eve

of which he gave orders for a simple and inexpensive funeral such as became an impoverished scholar. His later publications, aside from articles in the *American Ecclesiastical Review* (later the *Ecclesiastical Review*) and thoughtful pastoral letters on *Christian Marriage* and *Christian Education* (1907), included a handy *Business Guide for Priests* (1899), *The Devil: Who He Is and What He Is* (1900), *Spiritual Pepper and Salt* (1902), an apologetic treatise for missionaries, *Socialism and Christianity* (1905), *Medulla Fundamentalis Theologiae Moralis* (1907), and *The Holy Hour of Adoration* (1907).

[*Jour. American-Irish Hist. Soc.*, vol. VII (1907); *Cath. Encyc.*, vol. V (1909), p. 771; ann. official Cath. directories; F. J. Bradley and M. V. McCarthy, *A Brief Hist. of the Diocese of Fall River* (1931); sketch by Joseph Stang, *Pastoral-blatt* (St. Louis), Jan. 1920; obituary in *Boston Post*, Feb. 3, 1907.]   R. J. P.

STANLEY, ALBERT AUGUSTUS (May 25, 1851–May 19, 1932), educator, conductor, and composer, was born in Manville, R. I., the younger of two sons of Dr. George Washington and Augusta Adaline (Jefferds) Stanley. He was the seventh in line of descent from Matthew Stanley, founder of the second immigration of Stanleys from England and first mentioned in Lynn, Mass., in 1646. In 1856 his parents moved to Slatersville, R. I., where the father practised medicine for over thirty years and the son obtained his only formal schooling. As a child he exhibited unusual musical ability, doubtless inherited from his mother, who was fond of music and possessed a fine contralto voice. He early manifested a decided preference for the organ; at fourteen he became organist of the Congregational church in Slatersville, and at seventeen organist of the Church of the Mediator in Providence. Going to Germany in 1871, he studied at the Leipzig conservatory under Ernst Ferdinand Wenzel (piano), Benjamin Robert Papperitz (organ), Ernst Friedrich Richter (theory), Carl Heinrich Reinecke, and Oscar Paul. His scholarship was so excellent that during his last year he assisted Richter in the theory classes and was substitute organist at the Nikolai-Kirche. Upon his graduation in 1875, he returned to America, taught one year at Ohio Wesleyan College, Delaware, Ohio, and then went to Providence as organist of Grace Church (1876–88). In 1888 he was called to fill the chair of music at the University of Michigan, a position he retained till his death, becoming emeritus professor in 1921. A man of boundless energy, he displayed great ability for organization, combined with a contagious enthusiasm for whatever he had in hand. He welded together the various university and local musical activities, reorganized the earlier Ann Arbor School of Music as the University School of Music with well-rounded courses of study and a larger faculty, and in 1894 established the Ann Arbor May Festival. This annual music festival, which greatly broadened the cultural influence of the music department, under his energetic development (he was conductor until 1921) became one of the most influential of its kind. He was also conductor of the Choral Union (1888–1921), which from 1893 on maintained an average membership of about three hundred. He took an active interest in association work as well. He was secretary, treasurer, and in 1886 president of the Music Teachers' National Association, president of the Michigan Music Teachers Association, one of the founders of the American College of Musicians (1884) and of the American Guild of Organists (1896); president of the American Section of the Internationale Musikgesellschaft (1906–12), representing America at several important European musical congresses; and honorary vice-president of the Musical Association (Great Britain).

In his earlier years he was a brilliant organist, but he gradually abandoned this field for the more urgent activities of university life. His more important compositions include a symphony "The Soul's Awakening"; a symphonic poem, "Attis"; a choral work, "Chorus Triumphalis"; and three works for chorus and orchestra, "A Psalm of Victory" (1906), "Fair Land of Freedom" (1919), and "Laus Deo." For various academic performances in Ann Arbor he wrote incidental music, employing ancient modes and suggesting ancient instrumentation, to Percy Mackaye's *Sappho and Phaon* (first performed with Stanley's music, 1907), Euripides' *Alcestis* (1912) and *Iphigenia among the Taurians* (1917), and Plautus' *Menaechmi* (1916). The last four, with elaborate annotations, were published as *Greek Themes in Modern Musical Settings* (University of Michigan Studies, Humanistic Series, vol. XV, 1924). His love for details found expression in a scholarly and exhaustive *Catalogue of the Stearns Collection of Musical Instruments* (1918), a collection presented to the university in 1898. On Dec. 27, 1875, he married Emma F. Bullock, of Randolph, Mass., who died July 9, 1911. Their only child, Elsa, died May 14, 1910. His second wife was Dorothea Oestreicher of Ann Arbor, Mich., whom he married Dec. 1, 1921. He died in Ann Arbor, survived by his wife.

[*Who's Who in America*, 1932–33; *Grove's Dict. of Music and Musicians: Am. Supp.* (rev. ed., 1930); C. A. Sink, in *Mich. Alumnus*, June 4, 1932; obituary in *Detroit News*, May 19, 1932; Stanley's memoirs, in MS., in the School of Music of the Univ. of Mich.; information about ancestry from Stanley's widow.]

R. G. C.

STANLEY, ANN LEE [See LEE, ANN, 1736–1784].

STANLEY, DAVID SLOANE (June 1, 1828–Mar. 13, 1902), soldier, was born at Cedar Valley, Ohio, the son of John Bratton and Sarah (Peterson) Stanley, and a descendant of Thomas Stanley who came to Massachusetts from England in 1634. David was educated in a log school house until he was fourteen years old, when he was apprenticed to study medicine. In 1848 he entered the United States Military Academy, at West Point, N. Y., graduating in 1852 as second lieutenant of dragoons. His first assignments were in Texas and California. On Apr. 2, 1857, he married Anna Maria, daughter of J. J. B. Wright, an army surgeon. In 1856 he was active in the Kansas disturbances, and the next year in operations against Cheyenne Indians.

The commencement of the Civil War found him a captain of cavalry at Fort Smith, Ark. He was offered the colonelcy of an Arkansas regiment in the Confederate service, but declined and in May 1861 escaped from Southern territory by a hazardous march to Kansas. Later in the same year he served in the Missouri campaign, receiving and accepting a commission as brigadier-general of volunteers in October 1861. In November he broke his leg and was forced to quit the field. The following spring he took a prominent part in the battles of New Madrid and Island No. 10. He next participated in the capture of Corinth, Miss. When the Confederates attempted to retake that city in October, Stanley counter-attacked at the head of his troops, and drove the enemy back. For this victory, he was given command of a cavalry division in Tennessee, becoming a major-general in April 1863, his commission being dated Nov. 29, 1862. He ably seconded the campaigns of Rosecrans during 1863. At the end of that year, he was assigned to the 1st Division, IV Corps, guarding communications. In 1864 he took part in Sherman's Atlanta operations, being particularly commended for gallant conduct at Resaca, Ga. On July 27 he succeeded to the command of the IV Corps, and in September was wounded at Jonesboro, Ga. Although criticized by Sherman (see B. H. Liddell Hart, *Sherman*, 1930, p. 301), Stanley led his troops with vigor. In November 1864 his corps arrived at Pulaski, Tenn., just in time to save Thomas' army from the advance of Hood. Falling back, Stanley next fought the battle of Spring Hill, enabling the balance of the army to retreat north. On Nov. 30, Thomas was heavily attacked by Hood at Franklin, Tenn. Once again Stanley personally led a counter-attack, restoring the battle to the Federals. He was painfully wounded and his active career in the Civil War came to an end.

In June 1865 Stanley's IV Corps was sent to Texas to support diplomatic representations against French interference in Mexico. In February 1866 Stanley was mustered out of the volunteer service as a major-general, and on July 28, 1866, became colonel, 22nd Infantry, in the Regular Army. He was now sent to the Indian frontier. In 1873 he led the expedition into the Yellowstone area (see his *Report on the Yellowstone Expedition,* 1874), and between 1879 and 1882 he settled several Indian disturbances in Texas. On Mar. 24, 1884, he was promoted to the rank of brigadier-general, United States Army, and subsequently commanded in Texas until he retired, June 1, 1892. He was governor of the Soldiers' Home, Washington, from Sept. 13, 1893 to Apr. 15, 1898, and thereafter lived in Washington until his death.

His great service was his thirty-four years spent in the opening of the West. He was a master in handling Indians. He possessed the esteem of his associates, but was disliked by some on account of his deep prejudices, which his kindly appearance failed sometimes to conceal. He contributed an article to *Battles and Leaders of the Civil War* (vol. II, 1888), edited by R. U. Johnson and C. C. Buel, and an incomplete autobiography, *Personal Memoirs of Major-General D. S. Stanley, U. S. A.,* was published in 1917. His wife died in 1895, and of seven children four daughters and a son survived him.

[*War of the Rebellion: Official Records (Army)*; G. W. Cullum, *Biog. Reg. Officers and Grads. U. S. Mil. Acad.* (1891); I. P. Warren, *The Stanley Families of America* (1887); *Who's Who in America,* 1901–02; *Evening Star* (Washington), Mar. 13, 1902; *Washington Post,* Mar. 14, 1902; family information from Stanley's son, Col. D. S. Stanley.]   C. H. L.

STANLEY, FRANCIS EDGAR (June 1, 1849–July 31, 1918), inventor, manufacturer, was born in Kingfield, Me., the son of Solomon and Apphia (French) Stanley. His father was a teacher and a farmer, a descendant of Matthew Stanley who emigrated from England to Lynn, Mass., about 1646. Stanley attended public school in Kingfield and graduated in 1871 from the Farmington State Normal and Training School. For a number of years he taught school in various towns in Maine; at the same time, having a talent for crayon portraiture, he

built up a portrait business. In 1874 the demands of this work led him to give up teaching, and he removed to Lewiston, Me., where he believed a larger opportunity lay. In the course of the succeeding nine years, which were successful ones, he added photography to his business and became one of the leading portrait photographers of New England. Having begun about 1883 to experiment with photographic dry plates, he devised a formula for a dry-plate firm which seemed to have such possibilities that in partnership with his twin brother, Freelan O. Stanley, he organized the Stanley Dry Plate Company and established a manufactory in Lewiston. Their products, which were of very good quality, soon came into general use in the United States and foreign countries, and in 1890 the Stanleys established a new plant at Newton, Mass., where better railroad facilities were to be had. In 1905, the brothers sold their business to the Eastman Kodak Company of Rochester, N. Y.

Meanwhile Francis had become interested in steam automobiles, and early in 1897 began a series of experiments which resulted in the production by the brothers in that year of the first steam motor car to be successfully operated in New England. For this he designed a very efficient high-pressure steam boiler, light in weight and yet with ample storage capacity. This he combined with a new design of light weight, reversing, two-cylinder steam engine, and produced a very successful steam automobile. Having organized a company to manufacture their machine, the brothers in 1898 began the construction of one hundred cars, all with standard parts, but before completing them they sold the entire business, including the patents, to John Brisben Walker of New York, who subsequently organized the Mobile Company of America and was interested in the establishment of the Locomobile Company of America. In 1902, however, the Stanley brothers repurchased their original patents from the Locomobile Company and organized the Stanley Motor Carriage Company, with Francis as president, and continued to conduct the affairs of the company until their retirement in 1917. In the last years of his life Francis Stanley was engaged in developing a "unit steam engine" to be applied to the running of individual steam cars on interurban railroad lines. With his brother he also invented a process for manufacturing illuminating gas from gasoline. As an avocation he gave much attention to the theory and practical science of violin construction. He was an ardent student of economics, and was a member of economic associations and clubs, as well as of literary clubs. A collection of his addresses and essays presented to these organizations during his life was privately printed after his death under the title *Theories Worth Having* (1919). He married Augusta May Walker, daughter of William Walker of New Portland, Me., on Jan. 1, 1870, and at the time of his death, which occurred as the result of an automobile accident, was survived by his widow and three children.

[E. S. Stackpoole, *Hist. of Winthrop, Mass., with Geneal. Notes* (1925); biog. sketch in F. E. Stanley, *Theories Worth Having* (1919); *Automobile Trade Jour.*, Dec. 1, 1924; obituary in *Boston Transcript*, Aug. 1, 1918; Patent Office records.]   C. W. M—n.

STANLEY, HENRY MORTON (1841–May 10, 1904), explorer, was born at Denbigh, Wales, the son of a small farmer named Rowlands, who died soon after the boy's birth. His mother's maiden name was Parry. Until his adoption in America in 1859, he was known as John Rowlands. The confusion about the date of his birth, taken into consideration with the marked heartlessness of his mother and uncles toward him, has led some students of his history to suspect that he was illegitimate. He lived with his mother's father till the latter died in 1847; with him, departed the last vestige of humane treatment the child was to know. One day the son of the family with whom his uncles boarded him told him he would be taken on a journey to visit his Aunt Mary, whom he had never seen (*Autobiography*, p. 10). He set out happily and was delighted to see the imposing house where the cart finally stopped. He ran in looking for his aunt, to meet with mockery and taunts. The building was St. Asaph Union Workhouse. John now came under the discipline of the boys' schoolmaster, James Francis, a fanatically brutal man who ended his own days in a madhouse. Stanley has related briefly and movingly how he and a comrade stole into the room where a boy, who had been popular with all his companions, lay dead, and how one of them, presumably himself, turned down the sheet and saw the marks of the blows which had caused his death (*Ibid.*, p. 22). His treatment by his family and the years of horror at St. Asaph are described intimately and with much detail in his *Autobiography*, which was written, as he indicates, out of a desire to make his nature and character comprehensible to the world which knew him in the day of his fame. At St. Asaph his only comforter was the God revealed to him in his Bible as the Divine Father and the friend of the helpless. Out of his experiences with the scriptures and with prayer grew the faith in "A God at hand and not afar off" which so strongly influenced him in later years, and which infuses his narratives of his great exploits and some of his letters.

He was about fifteen years old when, one day, he turned on the brutal master and, to his own astonishment, worsted him in the bout. Seeing the tyrant laid low by his prowess brought a rush of conflicting emotions on the boy: fears for his life mingled with the sudden proud knowledge that he had had the courage to rebel and the muscular strength to conquer. He ran away from the workhouse in May 1856 and at last, tired and hungry, reached the house of his paternal grandfather, a well-to-do farmer, who callously showed him the door. He found refuge with a cousin, a schoolmaster at Brynford, who needed the help of a pupil-teacher, for which post Stanley's earnest application to study, while at St. Asaph, had qualified him. The same curious family resentment was evident here, too, and a year later he was sent to an uncle in Liverpool. This relative was not unkind but he was very poor. Stanley worked first for a haberdasher and then for a butcher, but he saw no prospect of advance in Liverpool so he shipped as cabin boy on a vessel bound for Louisiana in 1859. He found work in New Orleans with a merchant named Henry Morton Stanley, who became deeply interested in him, and presently adopted him rather informally and gave him his name (December 1859, *Autobiography*, p. 120). In the fall of 1860 he was sent to a country store in Arkansas to begin his experience as a merchant. Meanwhile, the elder Stanley went to Cuba on business and died there in 1861. He had made no legal provision for his adopted son, who did not even know of his death until some years later.

In 1861 Stanley enlisted in the Dixie Grays, and in April 1862 was taken prisoner at the battle of Shiloh. He has written a vivid description of the hardships endured by those Confederate prisoners, who did not die under them, at Camp Douglas, Chicago. After two months' experience of them, he enrolled in the Federal artillery but his physical condition was so bad as to render him useless, and he was discharged within the month. He worked his way back to England and sought out his mother, who showed him plainly that, like the rest of his relatives, she wanted nothing to do with him. He returned to America in 1863, enlisted in the United States Navy the next year and was present at the attack on Fort Fisher, N. C.

Given the talent for narration and description, the habit of close observation and the thoughtful mind, it was natural that Stanley should turn to journalism, after the war, at a time when so much American territory, and so many colorful phases of American life, were still undiscovered literary material. He crossed the plains to Salt Lake City, Denver, and other western parts, sending to various newspapers accounts of his journeys which were eagerly read by the public. Apparently there was a career for him as a press correspondent. In 1866 he was in Asia Minor; the next year the *Weekly Missouri Democrat* of St. Louis sent him with General Hancock's army against the Indians and his reports of this expedition brought him a commission from the *New York Herald* to accompany the British forces against the Emperor Theodore of Abyssinia in 1868. Stanley distinguished himself by sending through the first account of the fall of Magdala. This was, in newspaper parlance, a brilliant "scoop" for the *Herald*. The younger James Gordon Bennett, 1841–1918 [*q.v.*], took note of the young journalist and commissioned him to travel wherever matters of dramatic interest seemed to be looming and to report on them for the *Herald*. In 1868 Stanley went to Crete, then in rebellion, and later to Spain, where he reported the state of affairs following on Isabella's flight and the Republican uprising (1869).

In response to a wire he joined Bennett in Paris in October 1869, and was informed that his next task would be to lead an expedition into the heart of Africa to find David Livingstone (*Autobiography*, p. 245). There had been agitation in Great Britain for some time over the probable fate of the Scotch missionary, and the general belief now was that he had perished. Bennett may have shared this opinion, while still seeing the expedition as spectacular publicity for the *Herald,* for he gave Stanley other assignments which delayed him en route so that he did not reach Zanzibar till Jan. 6, 1871. Newspaper enterprise of this sort was new to England: it roused a storm of fury which was to break later about Stanley's head. The Royal Geographical Society was inspired to take up the search for Livingstone, subscriptions poured in, and an expedition was launched. Meanwhile, Stanley had seen the opening of the Suez Canal, visited Philae, Jerusalem, Constantinople, and the scenes of the Crimean War, had traversed the Caucasus and crossed Persia to the sea at Abu-Shehr, sailed thence to Bombay, and from Bombay to Africa. On Mar. 21 he set off for the interior. In this wild land, wholly strange to him, he was to go through hardships and perils for which his past experiences had little prepared him, and which would test his full equip-

ment of intelligence and moral force. But, in due course, he raised his helmet to a frail, gray-haired, white man in the native village of Ujiji, and spoke the greeting which has passed into the history of humor, as well as of exploration: "Dr. Livingstone, I presume?" The meeting occurred on Nov. 10. Livingstone's report of it is less restrained: "I am not of a demonstrative turn; as cold, indeed, as we islanders are usually reputed to be, but this disinterested kindness of Mr. Bennett, so nobly carried into effect by Mr. Stanley, was simply overwhelming. . . . Mr. Stanley has done his part with untiring energy; good judgment in the teeth of very serious obstacles" (*The Last Journals of David Livingstone,* 1874, vol. II, 156). Stanley had brought a tent and other comforts and necessaries for Livingstone, as well as a supply of trading goods. In company with Livingstone he explored the northern shore of Lake Tanganyika, where the discovery was made that the river Rusizi flowed into, not out of, the lake and therefore was not one of the Nile's headwaters. The discovery was of great importance at that time when the problem of the sources of the Nile was uppermost in the minds of geographers.

In 1872 Stanley was back in London, bearing Livingstone's journals and letters to his children and friends. In that year he published his account of the adventure, *How I Found Livingstone*. In the meantime the English expedition had come to nothing. The fury of resentment which burst upon the young explorer, from certain quarters, is difficult to understand, however much American newspaper methods may have been disliked by conservative Englishmen of that period. It was loudly asserted that Stanley was a cheat and his story a lie, that he had not found Livingstone, that he had not made the journey to Ujiji, which was a feat not possible of achievement by a young man of his total inexperience in Africa; as to Livingston's journals and letters, Stanley had forged them. Investigation brought to light these shocking facts as proofs of his fraudulence: his name was not Stanley, it was John Rowlands, and he was a "workhouse brat" from Wales. However, Livingstone's son verified his father's handwriting in the journals, the letters were declared genuine by himself and by friends who had received them; and Queen Victoria sent Stanley her thanks for the great service he had rendered, and a gold snuff box set with brilliants.

Later in the year Stanley lectured successfully in the United States; and in 1873 the *Herald* sent him as special correspondent with the army of Viscount Wolseley, on the Ashanti campaign.

He was at the island of St. Vincent, Cape Verde Islands, on his way home next year when he heard of Livingstone's death. Stanley went on to England and sought sympathy and support for plans, which he had been formulating, to carry on Livingstone's work against slavery and to settle geographical problems which his death had left unsolved. The latter were uppermost in his mind. John Hanning Speke, discoverer of Victoria Nyanza, the second largest lake in the world, believed rightly that he had discovered the source of the Nile but his conclusions were not yet considered final by geographers. He had not explored Victoria's shores, hence the point was still unsettled whether this was one vast body of water, or one of a group of lakes. Furthermore, there was Livingstone's belief that the Lualaba, or Congo, was the upper Nile. Such an expedition required a good deal of money to back it, as well as a spirit that was not looking chiefly to journalistic profits, since its purposes were purely scientific. Stanley discussed his project with Sir Edwin Arnold, the poet, then a writer on the staff of the London *Daily Telegraph,* a man keenly interested in Africa. Arnold's interest, happily for Stanley, was shared by his chief, Edward Levy (later Levy-Lawson and Lord Burnham), editor of the *Daily Telegraph,* who persuaded Bennett to join him in raising funds for an Anglo-American exploring expedition in Africa, under Stanley's command.

Stanley sailed for Africa in October of that same year, 1874, not to return until the fall of 1877, after a journey which was outstanding in its discoveries, and was to prove momentous in its commercial and political results. In short, on this exploration Stanley had accomplished more than had any other single expedition in Africa. From Jan. 17, 1875, to Apr. 7, 1876, he had been engaged in tracing the extreme southern sources of the Nile from the marshy plains and uplands, where they rise, down to the immense reservoir of Victoria Nyanza. He had circumnavigated Victoria's entire expanse, explored its bays and creeks by boat and, on foot, had traveled hundreds of miles along its northern shore, discovered Albert Edward Nyanza, and also explored the territory between Victoria and Edward. By proving that mighty Victoria was one single lake and not five, he insured to Speke, its discoverer, "the full glory of having discovered the largest inland sea on the continent of Africa" (*Through the Dark Continent,* 1878, vol. I, 482).

After his exploration of the Nile's headwaters, Stanley made as complete a survey of Lake Tanganyika and then turned his attention to the Congo. From Zanzibar he reached the Con-

go at Nyangwe, the place of Livingstone's death, and there launched upon the unknown stream of the second largest river in the world. He forced his way through the territory where Arab hostility had turned Livingstone back, and followed the long course of the river to its sea mouth at Boma, where he arrived in August 1877. The journey was one of terrible hardship owing to natural obstacles, fever, and unfriendly natives. Stanley's three white companions died in the jungle; his own powerful constitution was sapped, his face lined, and his hair nearly white, when he again reached civilization. The next year, 1878, he published *Through the Dark Continent* (2 vols.). His talent for the apt phrase gave Africa what amounted to a new name, for "Dark Continent" caught the imagination of scientists as well as of press writers and the general public. While the solution of geographical problems was of immense value, Stanley's journey resulted significantly in other ways. From Uganda he sent letters to England emphasizing the importance of sending missionaries to the court of Mtesa; and the immediate response was the first step in bringing the territory of the Nile's headwaters under British protection. During his stay with Livingstone, Stanley had adopted the missionary's recent conviction, namely, that it was impracticable to Christianize natives who were utterly at the mercy of the Arab slave traders, and never free from fear of raids. Protection in some form must be established first, and the cruel trade abolished, before the gospel could be preached. Also the new region which Stanley had traversed held immense commercial possibilities in its rubber and ivory; to open it up to commerce and civilization needed only swift-moving and stubborn enterprise. It was the American Stanley, the man who had seen the wheel-ruts of pioneer wagons on the western prairie and young sturdy towns on the recent Indian battle-grounds, who looked at the Congo region and saw nothing there to daunt determined men thoroughly equipped with the means and methods of civilization.

His news reached Europe ahead of him, and Leopold II of Belgium caught the vision, in its commercial hues at least; his commissioners were at Marseilles when Stanley's ship docked, with proposals that he return to the Congo in Belgian employ. Stanley refused and continued his journey home. He was worn out and needed to recuperate and also he wished Great Britain, not some other power, to make use of his discoveries. To his great disappointment British interest was not aroused. In November 1878, at Leopold's repeated request, Stanley went to

Brussels and agreed to lead an expedition for study of the region which he had discovered. He arrived on the river in August 1879. He remained for five years and established twenty-two stations on the Congo and its tributaries, put four small steamers on the upper river, and built a road past the long cataract of Stanley Falls. The natives, watching the arduous work of road-building go forward under the inflexible will of the white man, gave him a name meaning the strong one, the rock-breaker—"Bula Matari." It is carved on the rough stone pillar which marks his grave. On the basis of Stanley's work the Congo Free State was formed. In 1885 Stanley published his book, *The Congo and the Founding of Its Free State* (2 vols.). During the Berlin Conference of 1884–85, which dealt with African affairs, he acted as technical adviser to the American delegates. He lectured in several German cities, where he found the people much more interested in Africa than were the English, who remained curiously indifferent to the vast interests at stake—or, perhaps, blindly and stubbornly resentful against the "American journalist," still an American citizen, who trod on their traditions of good form and modesty and always finished successfully whatever enormous task he set himself. He was "Bula Matari" in a symbolic sense long before a group of wondering blacks so christened the first road-builder in their forest.

In 1887 Stanley sailed for Africa again on a three-fold mission. He was to further plans for the establishment of a British protectorate in East Equatorial Africa; to give help to the Congo Free State, which was seriously menaced by Tippu Tib and his Arab tribesmen from Zanzibar; and to proceed to the relief of Emin Pasha, governor of the Equatorial Province of Egypt, who was cut off after the fall of Khartoum (1885) by the fanatical force of the Mahdi. As to its outlined purposes, the expedition proved somewhat abortive. Seeing the strength of the wily Tippu Tib, Stanley resorted to the bold expedient of creating him governor of Stanley Falls station for the Congo Free State and then arranged with him for carriers on the march to relieve Emin, who, as it turned out, did not wish to be relieved, nor to abandon his province, and who felt that Stanley's arrival had caused him to lose face with his people. In achieving this unsatisfactory result Stanley crossed the densest area of the Ituri, or Great Congo, Forest three times. The expedition crawled at a snail's pace, covering only three or four hundred yards in an hour, among densely packed trees which rose a hundred and fifty feet with interlaced branches hung with vines that shut out the sun's rays. Underbrush twice a man's height clogged the path, which lay over swampy ground, the breeding place of innumerable insects and of fever. Stanley nearly died of fever himself and he brought out of the forest only a third of the men he took in with him. This adventure, with descriptions of the forest and its animal life, as well as both vivid and valuable ethnological data regarding the Pigmy tribes, forms the content of *In Darkest Africa* (2 vols.), which was published in 1890 in six languages. On his way from the vast shadow where so many of his men had met death Stanley discovered the Ruwenzori or "Mountains of the Moon." He also traced the Semliki River to its source in Albert Edward Nyanza.

He was greeted warmly in England. Among numerous honors he received the degree of D.C.L. from Oxford and of LL.D. from Cambridge and from Edinburgh. He was then about fifty years of age. On July 12, 1890, he married Dorothy, second daughter of Charles Tennant, at one time member of Parliament from St. Albans. He spent two years lecturing in Australia and New Zealand and in America, where he revisited the scenes of his youth. His roving career had been a long one and his African journeys had taken toll of his vitality, but his mind was as restless and eager as ever. Chiefly to provide an outlet for his mental energies, his wife persuaded him to run for Parliament as the Liberal-Unionist candidate for North Lambeth in 1892, after his renaturalization as a British subject in 1892; he was defeated by a small majority. In the next election, 1895, he was successful; but representing an English constituency failed to interest the former Congo State builder, and he did not campaign again in 1900. The year of his election he published *My Early Travels and Adventures in America and Asia* (2 vols., 1895). In 1897 Stanley went on his last journey to Africa, as the guest of the British South Africa Company, to speak at the opening of the railway from the Cape to Bulawayo. In his last volume, *Through South Africa* (1898), he described his tour to the Victoria Falls of the Zambezi, and enriched the gallery of vivid portraits which his books present with a lifelike and penetrating study of Paul Kruger. In 1899 he was made a Knight Grand Cross of the Bath. His health was failing and he retired to his small country estate called "Furze Hill," near Pirbright. He died on May 10, 1904, at his London house in Richmond Terrace, Whitehall, after a paralytic stroke. Services for him were held in Westminster Abbey, although the Dean refused him a resting place there. He was buried at Pirbright. He left one son, Denzil, apparently adopted. Three years later his widow married Henry Curtis, F.R.C.S.

The extent of his geographical discoveries alone places Stanley's name first among African explorers, even when one considers the great contribution made by Livingstone during his many years in Africa. In addition to his qualities as an explorer, Stanley possessed the vision and organizing ability of the true pioneer builder. He believed wholly in the superiority of his race and civilization; and, as organizer of the Congo Free State (Belgian Congo), never doubted that he was bringing good to the natives. He saw himself pushing on Livingstone's work and adding to it the benefits of a vast commerce. As a westerner he looked at the Congo and, as a westerner, he sped on to the tasks of Bula Matari in Leopold's employ when the British rejected the empire in embryo which he offered them. His disappointment over later developments in the Congo is suggested by his phrase, "a moral malaria." Moral force was strong in him. It was rooted deeply in his faith in God; and, in resisting the common vices to which he was early subjected, it was aided by his innate fastidiousness. In his teens he thought drunkenness and licentiousness both repulsive and stupid, and he never changed this opinion. His strong will was invoked not only to overcome external obstacles but, less happily, to suppress his naturally affectionate and trusting temperament and all desire for affection from others. Though he had to fight his way through hostile regions, at times, in Africa, he was generally successful in winning the friendship of the natives. But in civilized countries he had no tact. Self-schooled to live without illusions and emotional expression, he never understood the offended clamor aroused by his criticisms of the methods of other men in Africa who had perished and become heroes. He himself did not think that mistakes detracted from these men's personal nobility, and he believed that their errors should be seen and avoided by their successors; but the public called him a brute. To say that he was egotistical and ambitious is to state the obvious: his loneliness made him introspective and self-absorbed; and his energy and pride drove him on to win a fame that should wipe out the stigma of his despised origin. His total lack of humor possibly has been overstressed; it is a question whether humor develops later in any one whose youth has been without laughter. Three tragic episodes of his younger life were continuously with him: the day he entered St. Asaph's, his mother's cold

dismissal of him years later when he sought her out, and the treatment he received in England on his return from finding Livingstone. Harsh and narrow in his judgments of those who wronged him, he forgave nothing and his wounds were always fresh. A Welsh writer has said of his countrymen that they are "narrow, but dangerously deep," and Stanley was Welsh. His unfinished *Autobiography,* begun chiefly in the desire to make his character understood, shows him still bewildered by the chicaneries and cruelties he relates. He was preëminently the man of action, ever on the move from one exacting labor to another, yet there was a metaphysical cast to his mind that probed for answers beyond the actualities of his life and career. It may have shaped his last conscious thought. As the watchers by his bed heard Big Ben strike, Stanley opened his eyes and said, "How strange!— So that is time." He died two hours afterwards.

[*The Autobiography of Sir Henry Morton Stanley* (1909), ed. by his wife, Dorothy Stanley; J. S. Keltie, ed., *The Story of Emin's Rescue as Told in Stanley's Letters* (1890); H. M. Stanley, *My Dark Companions and Their Strange Stories* (1893); H. M. Stanley, *Slavery and the Slave Trade in Africa* (1893); A. J. A. Symons, *H. M. Stanley* (1933); J. S. Keltie, "Stanley and the Map of Africa," in *Annual Report of . . . the Smithsonian Institution . . . 1890* (1891), first published in *Contemporary Review,* Jan. 1890; Ethel Jameson, ed., *The Story of the Rear Column of the Emin Pasha Relief Expedition* (1891); W. G. Barttelot, *The Life of Edmund Musgrave Barttelot* (1890); A. J. M. Jephson, *Emin Pasha and the Rebellion at the Equator* (1890); Jakob Wassermann, *H. M. Stanley—Explorer* (1932), first pub. in Germany (1932) and in the U. S. (1933) as *Bula Matari;* Herbert Ward, *My Life with Stanley's Rear Guard* (1891); J. R. Troup, *With Stanley's Rear Column* (1890); S. J. Low, in *Dict. of Nat. Biography,* 2 supp. (1912), vol. III, with good bibliographical note; obituary and account of funeral, *Times* (London), May 11, 18, 1904.]   C.L.S.

STANLEY, JOHN MIX (Jan. 17, 1814–Apr. 10, 1872), painter of Indians, was born at Canandaigua, N. Y. He was orphaned when he was fourteen and spent his boyhood in Naples and Buffalo, N. Y., as apprentice to a wagon maker. At twenty he went to Detroit, where he painted portraits and landscapes; by 1838–39, when he lived in Chicago and Galena, Ill., he had begun painting the Indians near Fort Snelling. After spending the next few years in New York City, Troy, N. Y., Philadelphia, Pa., and Baltimore, Md., he went in 1842 with Sumner Dickerman of Troy to Arkansas and New Mexico, sketching and painting Indians and Indian scenes, and during the next ten or twelve years he traveled widely in the West, painting wherever he went. In June 1843, having gone with Pierce Mason Butler [*q.v.*] to a council with the chiefs of many Cherokee tribes, he made numerous sketches and paintings of the Cherokee chiefs, whose caprice and superstition made them at first somewhat unwilling to serve as subjects. After spending part of 1845 in New Mexico, with Dickerman he exhibited eighty-three canvases in Cincinnati and Louisville in January 1846, but returned to the West in May 1846. He visited Keokuk at his lodge, painted portraits of Sauk chiefs and of the wife of Black Hawk, and in the fall of 1846, at Santa Fé, joined the expedition of Stephen Watts Kearny [qq.v.] overland to California. Less than a year later he was on his way from California to Oregon, which he reached by July. There he journeyed nearly a thousand miles on the Columbia River by canoe, made sketches of Mount Hood and of scenes on the river, and later painted two pictures of Mount Hood. From San Francisco, to which he returned, he took ship for New York, but stopped at Honolulu and remained there during most of 1848. The portraits he painted at that time of King Kamehameha III and his queen hang in the government museum, Honolulu, formerly the royal palace.

In 1850 he exhibited about a hundred and fifty pictures at Troy and Albany, N. Y., and in 1851 at New Haven and Hartford, Conn., and Washington, D. C. This collection, which is described by the painter as containing accurate portraits painted from life of "forty-three different tribes of Indians, obtained at the cost, hazard, and inconvenience of a ten years' tour through the South-western Prairies, New Mexico, California, and Oregon," was deposited in the Smithsonian Institution in 1852. All but five of the pictures were destroyed by fire in 1865, but a full list (there seem to have been no additions) is given in the catalogue, *Portraits of North American Indians, with Sketches of Scenery, etc., Painted by J. M. Stanley, Deposited with the Smithsonian Institution*, which appeared in 1852. In 1853, when he was appointed artist of the expedition sent by the United States government to explore a route for the Pacific Railroad from St. Paul, Minn., to Puget Sound, he was sent on a special mission to the Piegan Indians and brought back about thirty of their chiefs to a council with Isaac Ingalls Stevens [q.v.] at Fort Benton. He had taken with him a daguerreotype apparatus (probably the first taken up the Missouri River), and made both daguerreotypes and paintings of the Indians, much to their pleasure and admiration. After spending nine years, 1854–63, in Washington, D. C., he went to Buffalo for a year. There he began "The Trial of Red Jacket," a picture containing about a hundred figures, his most important work. He died in Detroit, Mich., of heart disease. His work was characterized

by such spirit, accuracy of observation, and attention to detail that the destruction of the pictures in the Smithsonian was an irreparable loss to students of history and ethnology.

[D. I. Bushnell, Jr., in *Ann. Report of the Board of Regents of the Smithsonian Institution*, 1924, with portrait, reproductions of Stanley's paintings, and an account of his life written by his son; Bertha L. Heilbron, in *Minn. Hist.: A Quart. Mag.*, June 1926; obituaries in *Detroit Free Press*, Apr. 11, and *N. Y. Times*, Apr. 14, 1872.]   R. P. T.

STANLEY, WILLIAM (Nov. 22, 1858–May 14, 1916), electrical engineer, inventor, was the son of William and Elizabeth Adelaide (Parsons) Stanley, and was born in Brooklyn, N. Y., where his father practised law. He was a descendant of John Stanley who arrived in Boston in 1634. He was educated in the schools of Great Barrington, under private tutors in Englewood, N. J., which was his home during most of his boyhood, and at Williston Academy, Easthampton, Mass. At seventeen he entered Yale College with the class of 1881. The pre-law classical course, however, so irked him that he left in three months, went to New York, and obtained a job with a manufacturer of telegraphic apparatus. A while later, with money borrowed from his father, he purchased a partnership in a nickel-plating business and for a little more than a year did a thriving business. About 1880 he gave it up to become research assistant to Hiram Stevens Maxim [q.v.] in the United States Electric Lighting Company in New York. When the company purchased the Western Arc Light Company, he became assistant to Edward Weston and thus gained in two years an invaluable experience in both incandescent and arc electric-lighting. In 1882 he went to Boston to carry on experimental work for the Swan Electric Light Company. There he made his first invention, a perfected method of exhausting incandescent lamp bulbs. A year later he returned to Englewood and established his own research laboratory, where for two years he engaged in experimental work on storage batteries, on the manufacture of incandescent lamps, and on other electrical problems, obtaining three patents in these fields.

In 1885 he accepted the position of chief engineer of the Westinghouse Electric and Manufacturing Company of Pittsburgh, Pa., contracting at the same time to undertake certain investigations which were to be taken up as business enterprises by Westinghouse if successful. During his first year he devised the multiple system of alternating current distribution together with its equipment (patent No. 372,942 issued Nov. 8, 1887), but Westinghouse refused to finance its development until Stanley at his own expense had put the system into regular commercial service in Great Barrington, installing it in several stores. Thereupon in the fall of 1886 Westinghouse financed the installation of a similar plant at Buffalo, N. Y. In 1888 Stanley resigned his position of chief engineer, continuing, however, as a general consultant; in 1890 he severed this connection and established in Pittsfield, Mass., the Stanley Laboratory Company and the Stanley Electric Manufacturing Company in association with C. C. Chesney and J. F. Kelly. The partners together worked out the famous "S.K.C." system of long-distance transmission of alternating current from the inductor type of generator, and in 1894 put into operation a plant in which they had installed equipment of their own manufacture to supply electric power to textile mills at Housatonic and Great Barrington. In 1905, after directing the affairs of his company for eleven years, Stanley sold it to the General Electric Company. Among his many inventions were condensers, two-phase motors, generators, and an alternating-current watt-hour meter employing magnetic suspension of its moving parts, the manufacture of which was undertaken by the Stanley Instrument Company, established at Great Barrington in 1898. For his alternating-current system of long-distance transmission of electrical energy he was awarded the Edison Medal in 1912 by the American Institute of Electrical Engineers, of which he served as a vice-president from 1898 to 1900. He married Lila Courtney Wetmore of Englewood on Dec. 22, 1884, and at the time of his death in Great Barrington was survived by his widow and nine children.

[I. P. Warren, *The Stanley Families* (1887); *Who's Who in America*, 1916–17; Harry Douglas, *William Stanley, A Short Biog.* (1903), with a list of Stanley's patents; *Proc. Am. Institute Electrical Engineers*, vol. XXXV (1916); *Electrical Rev. and Western Electrician*, May 20, 1916; obituary in *Boston Transcript*, May 15, 1916.]   C. W. M—n.

STANLY, EDWARD (July 13, 1810–July 12, 1872), congressman, a native of New Bern, N. C., was the son of John Stanly, a Federalist leader and member of Congress, from whom he acquired the nationalistic opinions and intense hatred of the Democratic party which shaped his public life. His mother was the daughter of Martin Frank of Jones County. His education in the American Literary, Scientific, and Military Academy at Middletown, Conn., where he was a student from 1827 to 1829, tended to strengthen his Federalism. Having taken up the study of law, he was admitted to the bar in 1832 and began practice in Beaufort County, N. C.

Soon thereafter he married a daughter of Dr. Hugh Jones of Hyde County. She died about 1850, and some ten years later he married Cornelia, a sister of Joseph G. Baldwin [q.v.], then an associate justice of the supreme court of California.

Stanly was a successful lawyer, but his ambitions were almost wholly political, and in 1837 he was elected to Congress as a Whig. He served three terms, distinguishing himself by his eloquence, his readiness in debate, and his numerous quarrels. His temper was passionate, and his sarcastic and unrestrained tongue spared neither friend nor foe. He became, as John Quincy Adams expressed it, "the terror of the Lucifer party" (*Memoirs*, vol. XI, 1876, p. 19). Several times he engaged in personal encounters on the floor of the House, and he fought a duel with S. W. Inge of Alabama. By virtue of his ability, however, he became a leader of his party in the House. Defeated for reëlection to Congress in 1843, he was a delegate to the Whig convention in Baltimore in 1844, and was elected to the House of Commons, being reëlected in 1846. At both sessions he was speaker. In 1847 be became attorney general of the state, but resigned the next year to return to the legislature. Again elected to Congress in 1848, he supported the compromise measures of 1850. Making his campaign on the abstract issue of secession and declaring his readiness to vote men and money to whip any seceding state back into the Union, he was returned to Congress by an increased majority. Defeated for reëlection in 1853, he removed to California the following year, and in San Francisco won instant success in his profession. He supported Frémont in 1856 as a choice of evils, and in 1857, although he was still a slaveholder, and scarcely in accord with the party, he was nominated for governor by the Republicans, but was defeated.

Secession brought only anger and horror to Stanly's mind, and, unaware of the change of sentiment, he could not rid himself of the belief that the withdrawal of North Carolina from the Union was the result of Democratic deception of the people, and that, if they could be informed of the purposes of the North by one in whom they had confidence, they would renew their allegiance. He expressed to Lincoln his readiness to undertake such a mission, and to his amazement the latter in May 1862 made him military governor of the state, to foster Union sentiment and promote the establishment of a loyal civil government. Stanly assumed office on May 26, and quickly discovered that he had an impossible task. He could get no hearing and was despised as a traitor. Soon, moreover, he was in trouble with the abolitionists, and, through them, the ire of Charles Sumner, who had never forgiven Stanly for a bitter speech against him in 1852, was freshly aroused. He found himself unable to protect private property from what he characterized as "the most shameful pillaging and robbery that ever disgraced an army in any civilized land." The last straw was the Emancipation Proclamation, to which he was bitterly opposed, and on Jan. 15, 1863, he resigned, returning to California in March. After the war he opposed congressional reconstruction with his accustomed vehemence, and in 1867 left the Republican party to canvass the state against the policy. His death, following a stroke of apoplexy, occurred in San Francisco.

[S. A. Ashe, *Biog. Hist. of N. C.*, vol. V (1906); *A Military Governor among Abolitionists; a Letter from Edward Stanly to Charles Sumner* (1865); J. G. deR. Hamilton, *Reconstruction in N. C.* (1914); J. H. Wheeler, *Reminiscences and Memoirs of N. C.* (1884); C. C. Baldwin, *The Baldwin Geneal. Supp.* (1889); G. M. Dodge and W. A. Ellis, *Norwich Univ.* (1911), II, 226; *Biog. Dir. Am. Cong.* (1928); *Morning Bulletin* (San Francisco), July 15, 1872.]   J. G. deR. H.

STANSBURY, HOWARD (Feb. 8, 1806–Apr. 17, 1863), soldier, explorer, was born in New York City, the son of Arthur Joseph and Susanna (Brown) Stansbury, and a grandson of Joseph Stansbury [*q.v.*]. He was educated as a civil engineer. On Sept. 1, 1827, he married Helen Moody of Detroit. In October of the following year he was placed in charge of a series of surveys in connection with the project of uniting Lake Erie and Lake Michigan with the Wabash River by canals. Between 1832 and the end of 1835 he surveyed the route of the Mad River & Lake Erie Railroad and the mouths of the Cumberland, Vermilion, and Chagrin rivers, and had charge of a number of public works in Indiana. In 1836, as a preliminary to the project of improving the harbor of Richmond, Va., he surveyed the lower part of the James River, and in the early part of 1838 was engaged in the survey of a proposed railroad route from Milwaukee to the Mississippi.

He entered the army on July 7, 1838, as a lieutenant of topographical engineers, and on July 18, 1840, was made a captain. His work during the next eight years included various surveys of the lake regions and a minute survey of the harbor of Portsmouth, N. H. In 1849 he was put in command of an exploring and surveying expedition to the Great Salt Lake region. With a party of eighteen men, including Lieut. John Williams Gunnison [*q.v.*] as second in command, he left Fort Leavenworth on the last day of May and proceeded by South Pass to Fort Bridger.

Here he divided his party and, engaging James Bridger [*q.v.*] as his guide, explored a new route to the lake midway between the Bear River and the Echo Canyon trails. Reuniting the two sections of his party near Salt Lake City and dismissing Bridger, he marched northward and after some months circled the lake. For various reasons the work was not completed as planned, and in the summer of the following year he started on his return. At Fort Bridger, Sept. 5, 1850, again employing Bridger as guide, he determined upon the exploration of a route to the settlements more direct than that by way of South Pass. Proceeding directly eastward, he traversed the course subsequently followed by the Overland Stage and, in the main, by the Union Pacific Railway; and though not the first to use it was the first to recommend its feasibility and to make it widely known. His report, "Exploration and Survey of the Valley of the Great Salt Lake of Utah, Including a Reconnoissance of a New Route through the Rocky Mountains" (printed in 1852 as *Senate Executive Document 3, 32 Cong.*, special session of the Senate) won immediate popularity in England as well as in the United States, and during the next four years was several times reprinted by the Lippincotts. During the next ten years he was engaged in surveys in the lake region and in the construction of military roads in Minnesota. In 1861 he was ordered to Columbus, Ohio, as mustering officer for that locality, and on Aug. 6 was made a major. On Sept. 28, 1861, he was retired, but he later reëntered the service and was appointed mustering and disbursing officer for Wisconsin, with station at Madison, where he died. He was survived by his wife, a son, and a daughter.

[F. H. Wines, *The Descendants of John Stansbury of Leominster* (1895); F. B. Heitman, *Hist. Reg. and Dict. of the U. S. Army* (1903), vol. I; J. C. Alter, *James Bridger* (1925); *The Am. Ann. Cyc.*, 1863; obituary in *Wis. State Jour.* (Madison), Apr. 17, 1863.]
                                           W. J. G.

STANSBURY, JOSEPH (Jan. 9, 1742 o.s. ?–Nov. 9, 1809), Loyalist, was the son of Samuel and Sarah (Porter) Stansbury. He was born in London, where his father was a mercer and haberdasher. Joseph was a pupil at St. Paul's School, not on the foundation, but in 1753 he was withdrawn and apprenticed to a trade. On Apr. 2, 1765, he married Sarah Ogier, a Huguenot, and, embarking in 1767 for America, they landed at Philadelphia on Oct. 11. He at once opened a china store and entered with instant sympathy into the cultivated social life of the city. He was intelligent and vivacious and, among other talents, possessed the ability to write and to sing songs. When the Revolution impended, he sympathized with the colonists but opposed independence by writing songs about race kinship and race glory. In 1776 he suffered a brief imprisonment for his loyalty, but during the British occupation of Philadelphia he was held in favor and appointed to several minor offices. As his whole nature was opposed to war and violence, he steered a peaceful middle course, paid for substitutes in the Philadelphia militia, and even signed the oath of allegiance and abjuration. He was permitted to remain in the city until the end of 1780. Arrested then on the suspicion that he was carrying on a secret correspondence with the enemy, he sought and obtained permission to retire with his family within the British lines. The suspicions against him were well grounded; it was he who carried Benedict Arnold's first proposals to British headquarters and who, during the entire correspondence, was Arnold's go-between, as Jonathan Odell [q.v.] was André's ("André-Arnold Treason," Sir Henry Clinton Papers, William L. Clements Library). For his secret services he received lodgings in New York, rations, and a stipend. Meanwhile he continued to write festive political songs and to satirize with playful humor the inconsistencies of the Whigs. As a writer of satirical verse, free from hatred or bitterness, he was "without a rival among his brethren" (Tyler, *post*, II, 80). Many years later *The Loyal Verses of Joseph Stansbury and Doctor Jonathan Odell* was edited by Winthrop Sargent (1860).

His animosity ended with the war; he burned all his political poems he could find and tried to resume his old life in Philadelphia. Those he had satirized were not so tolerant; he was again imprisoned and forced to return to New York. In August 1783 he sought refuge in Nova Scotia, whose cold wilderness he found uninviting. The next year he spent in England seeking compensation for his secret services but, because of the oath of allegiance and abjuration, did not succeed. In 1786 he was permitted to resume his business in Philadelphia. However, not prospering as before, in 1793 he removed his family to New York. There he was for many years secretary of the United Insurance Company. He died in New York, survived by his widow and seven of their nine children. Caroline Matilda Kirkland and Howard Stansbury [qq.v.] were grandchildren and Joseph Kirkland [q.v.] was a great-grandson.

[MSS. of Mrs. V. C. Sanborn, Lake Forest, Ill., and Frederick S. Tyler, Washington, D. C.; Am. Loyalists Transcripts, N. Y. Pub. Lib.; manuscript biographical sketch by Arthur Joseph Stansbury, a son, Tyler Papers, Cornell Univ. Lib.; M. C. Tyler, *The Literary Hist. of the Am. Rev.* (2 vols., 1897); Malcolm Decker, *Benedict Arnold* (1932), p. 484; F. H. Wines, *The Descendants of John Stansbury of Leominster* (1895); F. S. Tyler, *The Hist. and Connection of the Stansbury-Tyler-Adee Families* (1933); *The Admission Registers of St. Paul's School from 1748 to 1876* (1884), ed. by R. B. Gardiner; *N. Y. Gazette & General Advertiser*, Nov. 11, 1809.]   J.C.

STANTON, EDWIN McMASTERS (Dec. 19, 1814–Dec. 24, 1869), attorney-general and secretary of war, a native of Steubenville, Ohio, was the eldest of the four children of David and Lucy (Norman) Stanton. His father, a physician of Quaker stock, was descended from Robert Stanton, who came to America between 1627 and 1638, and, after living in New Plymouth, moved to Newport, R. I., before 1645, and from the latter's grandson, Henry, who went to North Carolina between 1721 and 1724 (W. H. Stanton, *post*, pp. 27–34). His mother was the daughter of a Virginia planter. The death of Dr. Stanton in 1827 left his wife in straitened circumstances and Edwin was obliged to withdraw from school and supplement the family income by employment in a local bookstore. He continued his studies in his spare time, however, and in 1831 was admitted to Kenyon College at Gambier, Ohio. During his junior year his funds gave out and he was again obliged to accept a place in a bookstore, this time in Columbus. Unable to earn enough to return to Kenyon for the completion of his course, he turned to the study of law in the office of his guardian, Daniel L. Collier, and in 1836 was admitted to the bar. His practice began in Cadiz, the seat of Harrison County, but in 1839 he removed to Steubenville to become a partner of Senator-elect Benjamin Tappan.

Stanton's ability, energy, and fidelity to his profession brought him quick recognition and a comfortable income. To give wider range to his talents he moved to Pittsburgh in 1847 and later, in 1856 he became a resident of Washington, D. C., in order to devote himself more to cases before the Supreme Court. His work as counsel for the state of Pennsylvania (1849–56) against the Wheeling & Belmont Bridge Company (13 *Howard*, 518; 18 *Howard*, 421) gave him a national reputation and resulted in his retention for much important litigation. He was one of the leading counsel in the noted patent case of *McCormick* vs. *Manny* (John McLean, *Reports of Cases . . . in the Circuit Court of the United States for the Seventh Circuit*, vol. VI, 1856, p. 539) and made a deep impression upon one of his associates, Abraham Lincoln, because of his masterly defense of their client, Manny (A. J. Beveridge, *Abraham Lincoln*, 1928, vol. I, 581). Stanton's practice was chiefly in civil and constitutional law, but in 1859 in defending

Daniel E. Sickles [*q.v.*], charged with murder, he demonstrated that he was no less gifted in handling criminal suits. More important than any of these cases, however, was his work in California in 1858 as special counsel for the United States government in combatting fraudulent claims to lands alleged to have been deeded by Mexico to numerous individuals prior to the Mexican War. It was a task requiring prodigious and painstaking research in the collection of data and the most careful presentation, but Stanton proved equal to the occasion and won for the government a series of notable victories. It has been estimated that the lands involved were worth $150,000,000. His services in this connection were undoubtedly the most distinguished of his legal career. As a lawyer Stanton was capable of extraordinary mental labor; he was orderly and methodical, mastering with great precision the law and the facts of his cases, and he was able apparently to plead with equal effectiveness before judges and juries.

It was his success in the California land cases, together with the influence of Jeremiah S. Black [*q.v.*], that won for him the appointment of attorney-general on Dec. 20, 1860, when Buchanan reorganized his cabinet. Prior to that time Stanton had taken little part in politics and had held only two minor offices, those of prosecuting attorney of Harrison County, Ohio (1837–39), and reporter of Ohio supreme court decisions (1842–45). Jacksonian principles enlisted his sympathies while an undergraduate and he appears to have adhered quite consistently to the Democratic party from that time until his entrance into Lincoln's cabinet in 1862. He favored the Wilmot Proviso, however, and was critical of the domination of the Southern wing of the party during the two decades before 1860. Like his forebears he disapproved of the institution of slavery, but he accepted the Dred Scott decision without question and contended that all laws constitutionally enacted for the protection of slavery should be rigidly enforced. He supported Breckinridge's candidacy for the presidency in 1860 in the belief that the preservation of the Union hung on the forlorn hope of his election (Gorham, *post*, I, 79). Above all Stanton was a thorough-going Unionist.

In Buchanan's cabinet he promptly joined with Black and Joseph Holt [*q.v.*] in opposition to the abandonment of Fort Sumter and was zealous in the pursuit of persons whom he believed to be plotting against the government. Since he was of an excitable and suspicious temperament, his mind was full of forebodings of insurrection and assassination, and, while he hated the "Black Republicans," he collogued with Seward, Sumner, and others in order that they might be apprised of the dangers he apprehended to be afoot. The disclosure of this later resulted in the charge that he had betrayed Buchanan (*Atlantic Monthly* and *Galaxy, post*). If Stanton was at odds with the President at that time he gave him no indication of it for Buchanan wrote in 1862: "He was always on my side and flattered me *ad nauseam*" (G. T. Curtis, *Life of James Buchanan*, 1883, vol. II, 523).

During the early months of Lincoln's presidency, Stanton, now in private life, was utterly distrustful of him and unsparing in his criticism of "the imbecility of this administration" (*Ibid.*, II, 559). When George B. McClellan [*q.v.*] took over the control of the operations of the army in 1861, Stanton became his friend and confidential legal adviser and expressed to him his contempt for the President and his cabinet. Oddly enough, soon afterwards he also became legal adviser to Secretary of War Simon Cameron [*q.v.*] and aided in framing the latter's annual report recommending the arming of slaves (*Atlantic Monthly*, Feb. 1870, p. 239; Oct. 1870, p. 470). It was this proposal, offensive to Lincoln, which hastened Cameron's departure from the War Department and inadvertently helped to pave the way for Stanton's succession to the post. Although he had had no personal contacts of any kind with Lincoln since Mar. 4, 1861, Stanton was nominated for the secretaryship, confirmed on Jan. 15, 1862, and five days later entered upon his duties. Various plausible explanations for his selection by Lincoln have been given. Gideon Welles firmly believed that Seward was responsible for it, but Cameron claimed the credit for himself (*American Historical Review*, Apr. 1926, pp. 491 ff.; Meneely, *post*, pp. 366–68). The true circumstances may never be known.

Stanton was generally conceded to be able, energetic, and patriotic, and his appointment was well received. It presaged a more honest and efficient management of departmental affairs and a more aggressive prosecution of the war. In these respects the new secretary measured up to the public expectations. He immediately reorganized the department, obtained authorization for the increase of its personnel, and systematized the work to be done. Contracts were investigated, those tainted with fraud were revoked, and their perpetrators were prosecuted without mercy. Interviews became public hearings; patronage hunters received scant and usually brusque consideration; and the temporizing replies of Cameron gave way to the summary judgments of his successor. At an early date Stanton persuaded Congress to authorize the taking over of the railroads and telegraph lines where necessary, and prevailed upon the President to release all politicaı prisoners in military custody and to transfer the control of extraordinary arrests from the State to the War Department. Also he promptly put himself in close touch with generals, governors, and others having to do with military affairs, and especially with the congressional Committee on the Conduct of the War.

For a few months after entering office Stanton continued his friendly relations with McClellan and assured the general of his desire to furnish all necessary *matériel,* but he became impatient when McClellan proved slow in accomplishing tangible results. Despite the Secretary's professions of confidence and cooperation, McClellan soon became distrustful and suspected Stanton of seeking his removal. The withdrawing of McDowell's forces from the main army in the Peninsular campaign was attributed to Stanton and editorial attacks upon him began to appear in the New York press which were believed to have been inspired by McClellan (Gorham, I, 415–21). Both men were too suspicious, jealous, and otherwise ill-suited to work in harmony; trouble between them was inevitable. Stanton was particularly irked by McClellan's disobedience to orders and in August 1862 joined with Chase and others in the cabinet in seeking to have him deprived of any command (Welles, *Diary,* I, 83, 93, 95–101; "Diary and Correspondence of Salmon P. Chase," *Annual Report of the American Historical Association for the Year 1902,* 1903, vol. II, 62–63).

Although McClellan constantly complained of a shortage of men, supplies, and equipment, Stanton appears to have made vigorous efforts to meet his requisitions. The same was true with respect to other commanders in the several theatres of operations. His dispatch of 23,000 men to the support of Rosecrans at Chattanooga (September 1863) in less than seven days and under trying circumstances was one of the spectacular feats of the war. Quickness of decision, mastery of detail, and vigor in execution were among Stanton's outstanding characteristics as a war administrator, and he became annoyed when his subordinates proved deficient in these qualities. He was frequently accused of meddling with military operations and was probably guilty of it on many occasions; but Grant had no complaint to make of him in this respect. His severe censorship of the press was also a source of much criticism in newspaper circles, and his exercise of the power of extraordinary arrest was often capricious and harmful. Soldiers and civilians alike found him arrogant, irascible, and often brutal and unjust. Grant said that he "cared nothing for the feeling of others" and seemed to find it pleasanter "to disappoint than to gratify" (*Personal Memoirs,* vol. II, 1886, p. 536). A noted instance of his harshness was his published repudiation of General Sherman's terms to the defeated Johnston in May 1865. That Sherman had exceeded his authority was generally admitted, but the severity of the rebuke was as unmerited as it was ungrateful. Again, Stanton's part in the trial and execution of Mrs. Surratt, charged with complicity in Lincoln's assassination, and his efforts to implicate Jefferson Davis in the murder of the President were exceedingly discreditable (Milton, *post,* Ch. x; DeWitt, *post,* pp. 232–34, 272–76). His vindictiveness in both instances was probably owing in part to a desire to avenge the death of his chief, whose loss he mourned. Intimate association for three years had gradually revealed Lincoln's nature and capacities to Stanton, and while he was sometimes as discourteous to him as to others, there developed between the two men a mutual trust and admiration.

At the request of President Johnson, Stanton retained his post after Lincoln's death and ably directed the demobilization of the Union armies. At the same time he entered upon a course with respect to reconstruction and related problems that brought him into serious conflict with the President and several of his colleagues. During the war he appears to have been deferential and ingratiating in his relations with the radical element in Congress, particularly with the powerful congressional Committee on the Conduct of the War, and when peace came he began almost immediately to counsel with leading members of that faction as to the course to be pursued in reconstruction. Although he expressed approval in cabinet meetings of the President's proclamation of May 29, 1865, initiating a reasonable policy of restoration under executive direction, it was soon suspected by many of Johnson's supporters that Stanton was out of sympathy with the administration and intriguing with the rising opposition. In this they were not mistaken (Beale, *post,* pp. 101–06). When Charles Sumner in a speech on Sept. 14, 1865, denounced the presidential policy, insisted on congressional control of reconstruction, and sponsored negro suffrage, Stanton hastened to assure him that he indorsed "every sentiment, every opinion and word of it" (Welles, II, 394).

From the summer of 1865 onward, upon nearly every issue he advised a course of action which would have played into the hands of the Radicals and fostered a punitive Southern policy. He urged the acceptance of the Freedmen's Bureau and Civil Rights bills of 1866, and while he was evasive regarding the report of the Stevens committee on reconstruction, he subsequently expressed approval of the Military Reconstruction bill based upon it which was passed over the President's veto on Mar. 2, 1867 (Welles, III, 49; Gorham, II, 420). Stanton actually dictated for Boutwell [q.v.] an amendment to the army appropriation act of 1867 requiring the president to issue his army orders through the secretary of war or the general of the army and making invalid any order issued otherwise (G. S. Boutwell, *Reminiscences of Sixty Years in Public Affairs*, 1902, vol. II, 107–08; Milton, p. 378). He was also responsible for the supplementary reconstruction act of July 19, 1867, which exempted military commanders from any obligation to accept the opinions of civil officers of the government as to their rules of action (Gorham, II, 373). The one important measure in the rejection of which the Secretary concurred was the Tenure of Office bill which was chiefly intended to insure his own retention in the War Department. He was emphatic in denouncing its unconstitutionality and "protested with ostentatious vehemence that any man who would retain his seat in the Cabinet as an adviser when his advice was not wanted was unfit for the place" (Welles, III, 158; J. D. Richardson, *A Compilation of the Messages and Papers of the Presidents*, 1897, vol. VI, 587). He aided Seward in drafting the veto message.

For more than a year Johnson had been importuned by his supporters to remove Stanton and he repeatedly gave the Secretary to understand "by every mode short of an expressed request that he should resign" (Richardson, *ante*, VI, 584), but Stanton ignored them and with fatal hesitation the President permitted him to remain. In doing so he virtually gave his opponents a seat in the cabinet. By the beginning of August 1867, however, Johnson could tolerate his mendacious minister no longer. He had become convinced that the insubordination of General Sheridan and other commanders in the military districts was being encouraged by the Secretary and he was now satisfied that Stanton had plotted against him in the matter of the reconstruction legislation. Consequently, on Aug. 5, he called for his resignation, but Stanton brazenly declined to yield before Congress reassembled in December, contending that the Tenure of Of-

fice bill had become law by its passage over the veto and Johnson was bound to obey it. A week later he was suspended, but in January 1868 he promptly resumed his place when the Senate declined to concur in his suspension. Johnson then resolved to dismiss him regardless of the consequences and did so on Feb. 21, 1868. Stanton with equal determination declared that he would "continue in possession until expelled by force" (Gorham, II, 440), and was supported by the Senate. He ordered the arrest of Adjutant-General Lorenzo Thomas, who had been designated secretary *ad interim*, and had a guard posted to insure his own occupancy and protect the department records from seizure. For several weeks thereafter he remained in the War Department building day and night, but when the impeachment charges failed (May 26, 1868) he accepted the inevitable and resigned the same day.

Over-exertion during his public life, together with internal ailments, had undermined Stanton's health and he found it necessary after leaving the department to undergo a period of rest. During the fall of 1868 he managed to give some active support to Grant's candidacy and to resume to a limited extent his law practice, but he never regained his former vigor. He was frequently importuned to be a candidate for public office, but steadfastly refused. His friends in Congress, however, prevailed upon Grant to offer him a justiceship on the United States Supreme Court and this he accepted. His nomination was confirmed on Dec. 20, 1869, but death overtook him before he could occupy his seat.

With the gradual rehabilitation of Andrew Johnson's reputation Stanton's has suffered a sharp decline. His ability as a lawyer and his achievements as a tireless and versatile administrator during the Civil War have not been seriously questioned, but his defects of temperament and the disclosures of his amazing disloyalty and duplicity in his official relations detract from his stature as a public man. In 1867 he explained his remaining in the War Department by contending that his duties as a department head were defined by law and that he was not "bound to accord with the President on all grave questions of policy or administration" (Gorham, II, 421; J. F. Rhodes, *History of the United States*, 1920, VI, 210, note 3); but shortly before his death he is said to have admitted that "he had never doubted the constitutional right of the President to remove members of his Cabinet without question from any quarter whatever," and that in his reconstruction program Johnson advocated measures that had been favorably considered by Lincoln (Hugh McCulloch,

Men and Measures of Half a Century, 1888, pp. 401–02). Stanton was encouraged in his disloyalty and defiance by Republican politicians, newspapers, and Radical protagonists generally, but his conduct has found few defenders among modern students of the post-war period. Whether he was motivated by egotism, mistaken patriotism, or a desire to stand well with the congressional opposition is difficult to determine.

In appearance Stanton was thick-set and of medium height; a strong, heavy neck supported a massive head thatched with long, black, curling hair. His nose and eyes were large, his mouth was wide and stern. A luxuriant crop of coarse black whiskers concealed his jaws and chin. Altogether he was a rather fierce looking man; there was point to Montgomery Blair's characterization, the "black terrier." Stanton was twice married. Mary Ann Lamson of Columbus, Ohio, with whom he was united on Dec. 31, 1836, died in 1844. On June 25, 1856, he married Ellen M. Hutchison, the daughter of a wealthy merchant of Pittsburgh. Two children were born of the first union; four of the second. His biographers assure us that in his family life Stanton was a model husband and father, and for his mother, who survived him, he appears to have cherished a lifelong filial devotion.

[There is no satisfactory biography of Stanton. G. C. Gorham, *The Life and Public Services of Edwin M. Stanton* (2 vols., 1899), and F. A. Flower, *Edwin Mc-Masters Stanton* (1905) contain much useful data, but both are extremely laudatory. The *Diary of Gideon Welles* (3 vols., 1911), although hostile, is a very serviceable documentary source. The writings and biographical literature of other public men of the day contain numerous references to Stanton. Of especial value for the war period are J. G. Nicolay and John Hay, *Abraham Lincoln: A History* (10 vols., 1890), and *Complete Works of Abraham Lincoln* (12 vols., Gettysburg ed., 1905). See also A. H. Meneely, *The War Department—1861* (1928). G. F. Milton, *The Age of Hate: Andrew Johnson and the Radicals* (1931), and H. K. Beale, *The Critical Year* (1930) are the most scholarly of the recent studies of the reconstruction era. D. M. DeWitt, *The Impeachment and Trial of Andrew Johnson* (1903), is the standard book on the subject and has a sharply critical chapter on Stanton's public career. Revealing disclosures of his conduct while in Buchanan's cabinet are to be found in the Black-Wilson controversy in the *Atlantic Monthly,* Feb., Oct. 1870, and the *Galaxy,* June 1870, Feb. 1871, reprinted as *A Contribution to History* (1871). The papers of Stanton and many of his associates are deposited in the Lib. of Cong.; these, together with *War of the Rebellion: Official Records (Army),* and other government publications pertaining to the war and reconstruction problems are the basic sources for the study of Stanton's official life. Genealogical material is in W. H. Stanton, *A Book Called Our Ancestors the Stantons* (1922). For an obituary, see *N. Y. Daily Tribune,* Dec. 25, 1869.]
              A. H. M.

STANTON, ELIZABETH CADY (Nov. 12, 1815–Oct. 26, 1902), reformer and leader in the woman's rights movement, was born in Johnstown, N. Y. Her parents were Daniel Cady [q.v.] and Margaret (Livingston) Cady, daughter of Col. James Livingston [q.v.]. A stern religious atmosphere pervaded her home, and as a child Elizabeth feared rather than loved her parents, who seem to have had little positive influence upon the shaping of her personality and character. Simon Hosack, minister of the Presbyterian church to which the Cady family belonged, had a larger share in her affections and did much to give a serious, purposeful bent to her life. Her education was superior to that of most girls of her time. Encouraged by Simon Hosack, she studied Greek, Latin, and mathematics with classes of boys in the academy in Johnstown, where she spent several years, and took second prize in Greek. At the age of fifteen she was sent to the famous seminary of Emma Willard [q.v.] at Troy, N. Y., from which she graduated in 1832. For a time she studied law with her father. She early learned that she was living in an imperfect world. As a small child, hearing women in her father's law office pour forth recitals of wrongs supported by existing law, she was troubled by the handicaps and discriminations existing against her sex. In her young womanhood, under the influence of her cousin Gerrit Smith [q.v.] of Peterboro, N. Y., she likewise became deeply interested in temperance and anti-slavery, but it was not until somewhat later that she was fully launched as a reformer.

It is significant that on May 10, 1840, when she married Henry Brewster Stanton [q.v.], the word "obey" was at her insistence omitted from the ceremony. Stanton, who later became known as a lawyer and journalist, was already a noted abolitionist and immediately after his wedding went as a delegate to the world anti-slavery convention held in London in the summer of 1840. There his wife, who accompanied him, met Lucretia Coffin Mott [q.v.] and was much influenced by conversations with her. When Mrs. Mott and a few other American women who were delegates to the anti-slavery gathering were refused official recognition by the convention on the ground of their sex, Mrs. Mott and Mrs. Stanton resolved to hold a woman's rights convention upon their return to the United States. Though the execution of this resolve was delayed, Mrs. Stanton began to work for temperance and abolition, and used her influence for the passage of the married woman's property bill of New York State, which finally became a law in 1848. Two years before this she moved with her husband and their children from Boston, where they had been living, to Seneca Falls, N. Y., and the handicaps she was aware of in this small frontier-like community made her thoughts turn more seriously to the hard, circumscribed lot of woman. Her mind was full of the subject when, on July 13, 1848, she again met Lucretia Mott. To Mrs. Mott and a few others she poured out her indignation at the established order and succeeded in so rousing herself as well as the others that a week later, July 19 and 20, they held a woman's rights convention in the Wesleyan Methodist Church in Seneca Falls. Mrs. Stanton, who made the opening speech, read a "Declaration of Sentiments," modeled after the Declaration of Independence, setting forth the grievances of women against existing law and custom, and she was wholly responsible for a resolution demanding suffrage. When Lucretia Mott protested against the last, "Why, Lizzie, thee will make us ridiculous," the author of the resolution defended it as the key to all other rights for women, and with the help of Frederick Douglass [q.v.] it was adopted with ten other resolutions.

The Seneca Falls convention, which promptly became the object of sarcasm, ridicule, and denunciation from press and pulpit, formally launched the modern woman's rights movement. Other conventions devoted to the same purpose soon followed, and in many of them Mrs. Stanton played a leading part. In addition she gave much time to writing articles, protests, and petitions, lecturing in public, and speaking before legislative bodies in the interest of temperance, abolition, and woman's rights, but as the years passed she devoted more and more of her time to the cause of women. From 1851, when she first met Susan B. Anthony and induced her to enlist in the crusade for woman's rights, the two women worked together, a remarkably efficient pair whose association ended only with Mrs. Stanton's death. Together they planned campaign programs, organization work, and speeches and addresses; together they appeared upon public and convention platforms, and before legislative bodies and congressional committees to plead for woman's rights. Miss Anthony had the greater persistence and was the better organizer and executive, but her colleague was the more eloquent and graceful speaker and writer, and in general had a more charming and persuasive personality. Both were hard fighters and both were long considered rather dangerous radicals, though Mrs. Stanton was at first more conspicuous in this latter regard because of her pioneer stand for suffrage and her demand a little later that women be permitted to secure divorce on the grounds of drunkenness and brutality. Though she hated war as stupid and wicked,

she saw the Civil War as a struggle for the abolition of slavery, and helped to organize and became president of the Women's Loyal National League, which supported the Union and fostered the complete emancipation of slaves. The war ended, she and her colleagues first strove to secure suffrage for women in connection with the enfranchisement of negro men, but they later renewed and enlarged their earlier activities directly in behalf of woman's rights. When in May 1869 the National Woman Suffrage Association was founded, she was chosen president, an office which for the most part she held until 1890; at that time the organization was united with the American Woman Suffrage Association to form the National American Woman Suffrage Association, of which she was also elected president. These twenty-one years at the head of the more radical of the two woman's rights organizations covered the period of Mrs. Stanton's greatest activity for the cause to which she had dedicated herself. Partly from a suggestion of hers came the first International Council of Women, held in Washington in 1888 under the auspices of the National Woman Suffrage Association, and it was she who sent out the call, and made the opening and closing addresses before the Council.

In addition to her suffrage work, from 1869 to 1881 she devoted eight months annually to lyceum lecturing throughout the country, usually on family life and the training of children, of whom she had borne and reared seven. She also found time to write for publication. In 1868 she and Parker Pillsbury [q.v.] as joint editors started the *Revolution,* a weekly devoted especially to woman's rights, and many of the best articles and editorials appearing during her connection of about two years with the publication were from her pen. She was largely responsible, too, for the *Woman's Bible,* published in two parts in 1895 and 1898. To newspapers and magazines, especially the *North American Review,* she contributed many articles. In 1898 she published her reminiscences, *Eighty Years and More.* But her monumental undertaking was the compilation, in conjunction with Susan B. Anthony and Matilda Joslyn Gage [q.v.], of the first three ponderous volumes of the *History of Woman Suffrage* (1881–86). In the cause of woman's rights she was undoubtedly one of the most influential leaders of her day. Her strong and undaunted manner made her very impressive, though she was short in stature, not exceeding five feet three inches. Her skin was fresh and fair, and the good-natured expression of her face was accentuated by the merry twinkle rarely absent from her clear, light blue eyes. In youth her curly hair was black, but it began early to turn gray and by middle age was snowy white. She died at her New York City home when she was closing her eighty-seventh year. She was survived by six of her children.

[See O. P. Allen, *Descendants of Nicholas Cady of Watertown, Mass., 1645–1910* (1910), where Mrs. Stanton's name is given as Elizabeth Smith Cady; *Who's Who in America*, 1901–02; *Elizabeth Cady Stanton as Revealed in Her Letters, Diary and Reminiscences* (2 vols., 1922), ed. by Theodore Stanton and Harriot Stanton Blatch; *Hist. of Woman Suffrage* (6 vols., 1881–1922), ed. by E. C. Stanton, etc.; Alice S. Blackwell, *Lucy Stone, Pioneer of Woman's Rights* (1930); obituary in *N. Y. Times*, Oct. 27, 1902. In the Lib. of Cong., Washington, D. C., are some unpublished letters of minor importance.]   M. W. W.

STANTON, FRANK LEBBY (Feb. 22, 1857–Jan. 7, 1927), journalist, poet, son of Valentine Stanton, a printer, and Catherine Rebecca (Parry) Stanton, was born in Charleston, S. C. His formal education was interrupted by the death of his father. At the age of twelve he moved to Savannah, Ga., with his family and became copy-boy on the Savannah *Morning News*, edited by William Tappan Thompson [*q.v.*]. His verses, which he had begun writing at the age of eleven ("To Lizzie"), attracted the attention of Joel Chandler Harris [*q.v.*], then a member of the editorial staff, who encouraged him to write. He served as reporter and feature writer until 1887, when he became owner and editor of the weekly *Smithville News* of Smithville, Ga. He continued to write verses that were copied in many newspapers. On Jan. 15, 1887, he married Leona Jossey, who inspired some of his best poems and was a gifted reader of his poetry. A year later he joined the staff of the *Tribune of Rome,* published in Rome, Ga., under the editorship of John Temple Graves [*q.v.*], and a year after that, persuaded by Joel Chandler Harris, went to the *Atlanta Constitution.* After serving as reporter and feature writer for a short time, he began his "Just from Georgia" column, one of the first American newspaper columns, to which for nearly forty years he contributed daily anecdotes, brief essays, and poems, many of them in negro and Georgia cracker dialects. His philosophy was a simple, idealistic one, and he wrote unaffectedly about his own thoughts and feelings.

In 1892 his great popularity as a "scrap-book poet" encouraged him to publish a collection of his poems, *Songs of a Day and Songs of the Soil.* Other volumes, in which there is a wide range of lyrical forms, followed at intervals: *Comes One with a Song* (1898), *Songs from Dixie Land* (copyright 1900), *Up from Georgia* (1902), *Little Folks Down South* (1904), and

Frank L. Stanton's Just from Georgia (1927), a posthumous collection compiled by his daughter, Mrs. Marcelle Stanton Megahee. They are characterized by spontaneity, humor, kindly tolerance, and a bright, optimistic tone. These qualities, and his use of simple emotions and subjects of such universal appeal as love, beauty, childhood, nature, patriotism, and democracy endeared this "Riley of the South" to a wide circle of readers. He was honored at home by his appointment on Feb. 22, 1925, as poet laureate of Georgia, and abroad by the translation of his poems (as songs) into many languages. Ethelbert Woodbridge Nevin [*q.v.*], Carrie Jacobs Bond, and Edward Kneisel set some of his songs to music; his "Georgia Land" is a sort of unofficial state song. Since he wrote one or more poems every day for nearly forty years, they were naturally of unequal merit. But he wrote a surprisingly large number of good ones. He will be remembered, however, chiefly for a small group of poems in which his lyrical gift finds its happiest expression: "St. Michael's Bells," "A Song of Harvest," "One Country," "My Study," "Marcelle," " 'Nearer to Thee,' " "Oh, Christmas Skies in Blue December," on the death of Henry W. Grady, and "Going Home," a poem of stately repose of spirt. His last published poems appeared in his column on Christmas morning, 1926. He died on Jan. 7, 1927, after an illness of a few weeks. He was survived by his wife and three children.

[See *Who's Who in America*, 1916–17; *Lib. of Southern Lit.*, vol. XI (1909), edited by E. A. Alderman, J. C. Harris, and C. W. Kent; Mildred L. Rutherford, *The South in Hist. and Lit.* (copr. 1906); Walter Chambers, in *Am. Mag.*, Feb. 1925, with portrait; L. L. Knight, *Reminiscences of Famous Georgians*, vol. I (1907); "The Poet of Georgia," *Nation*, Jan. 19, 1927; "A Columnist of the South," *Outlook*, Jan. 19, 1927; papers in the Joel Chandler Harris collection, Emory Univ.; *Atlanta Constitution*, Jan. 8 (obituary), 9–11, 16, 1927. Information has been supplied by Mrs. Marcelle Stanton Megahee, Stanton's daughter.]   J. M. S., Jr.

STANTON, FREDERICK PERRY (Dec. 22, 1814–June 4, 1894), congressman and acting governor of Kansas Territory, was born in Alexandria, then a part of the District of Columbia, the son of Richard and Harriet (Perry) Stanton. Richard Henry Stanton [*q.v.*] was an older brother. The boy was taught the bricklayer's trade by his father, and attended the private school conducted by Benjamin Hallowell [*q.v.*]. Later he taught in this same school, and also at Occoquan and at Portsmouth Academy in Virginia. After receiving the degree of A.B. from Columbian College (now George Washington University) in 1833, he served for two years as principal of Elizabeth City Academy in North

Carolina. Meantime he read law, was admitted to the Alexandria bar, and joined the Democratic party. In 1835 he removed to Somerville, Tenn., and some two years later to Memphis, where he practised his profession and contributed political editorials to the *Gazette*. On Dec. 25, 1835, he married Jane Harriet Sommers Lanphier of Alexandria. They had nine children, five of whom died in infancy. In 1845 Stanton entered Congress from the Memphis district and served until Mar. 3, 1855. He was assigned to the committee on naval affairs, and became its chairman in December 1849. His speeches reveal a wealth of scientific nautical information. He contended that replacements rather than additions would promote efficiency in the navy, advocated the use of heavier ordnance and the screw propeller, and proposed regular itineraries for both the Atlantic and the Pacific fleets. In the speakership contest of 1849 he introduced the resolution to substitute the plurality for the majority rule which resulted in the election of Howell Cobb [q.v.]. During the crisis of 1850 he threatened secession unless a satisfactory compromise was effected, and he voted against the District of Columbia slave trade bill, and against the admission of California as a free state. In discussing the Kansas-Nebraska measure, he assured the North that slavery could not exist in either territory, and that the bill was of no practical importance to the South "except for the principle of non-intervention." During his last term he served as chairman of the judiciary committee.

After a decade in Congress Stanton retired voluntarily but continued to reside in Washington, where he practised law. On Mar. 10, 1857, President Buchanan appointed him secretary of Kansas Territory, and he went there with a natural pro-slavery prejudice. From his arrival at Lecompton on Apr. 15 until he was relieved by Robert J. Walker [q.v.] on May 27, he served as acting governor. He urged a general political amnesty, promised a safeguarded franchise, and pledged enforcement of the territorial laws. With inadequate information on conditions in Kansas, he apportioned delegates to the Lecompton convention under an incomplete and inequitable census. Practical experience in the territory developed open-mindedness, and in the summer of 1857 both Walker and Stanton promised a fair vote in the October election for members of a legislature. They redeemed their pledge by rejecting sufficient fraudulent votes to change the party character of both houses. This act cost Walker his position and Stanton again became acting governor (Nov. 16–Dec. 21). At the request of Free-State men he convened the newly chosen legislature in extra session to provide a referendum on the whole Lecompton constitution. His removal for this act completed his transition to the Free-State party, and in the winter of 1858 he toured the North to lay its cause before the people. After Kansas was admitted into the Union in 1861, Stanton was defeated for the United States Senate. A few months later, when Senator James H. Lane [q.v.] accepted a brigadiership, Gov. Charles Robinson appointed Stanton to the supposed vacancy; but the Senate decided that none existed.

Soon after his arrival in Kansas, Stanton purchased a tract of land near Lecompton and erected a commodious stone house. In 1862 he removed to "Farmwell," in Virginia, and resumed law practice in Washington. Years later (1886) he settled in Florida. At the height of his congressional career, Buchanan characterized him as persevering, industrious, faithful, and able, credited him with "practical sense and sound judgment," and designated him as "the most promising" young man in the lower house (U. B. Phillips, "The Correspondence of Robert Toombs, Alexander H. Stephens, and Howell Cobb," *Annual Report of the American Historical Association . . . 1911*, vol. II, 1913, p. 181). He died at Stanton, near Ocala, Fla.

[A few of Stanton's speeches are preserved in pamphlet form in the Lib. of Cong., and his correspondence with Cass while acting governor is available in *Sen. Ex. Doc. 8*, 35 Cong., 1 Sess.; see also *Cong. Globe*, 1845–55; *Trans. Kan. State Hist. Soc.*, vol. V (1896); D. W. Wilder, *The Annals of Kan.* (1875); W. E. Connelley, *A Standard Hist. of Kan. and Kansans* (1918), vol. II; *Frank Leslie's Illustrated Newspaper*, Mar. 27, 1858; *U. S. Mag. and Democratic Rev.*, June 1850; *Biog. Dir. Am. Cong.* (1928); *Florida Times Union* (Jacksonville), June 5, 1894; information concerning family and children from a descendant.]   W. H. S.

STANTON, HENRY BREWSTER (June 27, 1805–Jan. 14, 1887), lawyer, reformer, journalist, was born in Griswold, Conn. His father, Joseph, a woolen manufacturer and merchant, traced his ancestry to Thomas Stanton who emigrated to America from England, and about 1637 settled in Connecticut. He was Crown interpreter of the Indian tongues in New England and judge of the New London county court. Henry's mother, Susan Brewster, was a descendant of William Brewster [q.v.] who arrived on the *Mayflower*. After studying at the academy in Jewett City, Conn., Henry went to Rochester in 1826 to write for Thurlow Weed's *Monroe Telegraph*, which was then supporting Henry Clay for the presidency. In 1828 he delivered addresses and wrote for the *Telegraph* in behalf of John Quincy Adams. The next year he became deputy clerk of Monroe County, N. Y., and continued in that office until 1832, meanwhile studying law and the classics. Converted by Charles G. Finney [*q.v.*], and having come into contact with Theodore D. Weld [*q.v.*], he then entered Lane Theological Seminary, in Cincinnati, where in the fall of 1834 he helped organize an anti-slavery society. This the trustees, who tried to prevent all discussion of the question, opposed, and in consequence about fifty students left, including Stanton (*Liberator*, Jan. 10, 1835), who at once associated himself with James G. Birney [*q.v.*] in his anti-slavery work. Soon he was made agent of the American Anti-Slavery Society, and was later a member of its executive committee.

For many years thereafter he devoted practically all of his time to this reform. He wrote for the *Liberator* and other abolitionist journals, for religious publications, and for some political papers, including the *National Era* of Washington and the *New York American*. He also appeared before many legislative commissions, and made platform speeches from Maine to Indiana. As a speaker he was quick-witted, eloquent, and impassioned, capable of making his hearers laugh as well as weep, and was ranked by many as the ablest anti-slavery orator of his day. His handsome, distinguished appearance, personal charm, and rare conversational powers added to his general popularity. His thunderous denunciations of human bondage subjected him, however, to scores of mob attacks. From 1837 to 1840 he busied himself with trying to get the abolitionists to form a strong political organization, a project which William Lloyd Garrison [*q.v.*] opposed, thereby causing a permanent break in the relation of the two men. On May 10, 1840, he married Elizabeth Cady [see Elizabeth Cady Stanton], daughter of Judge Daniel Cady [*q.v.*] of Johnstown, N. Y.; seven children were born to them.

Immediately after his marriage Stanton sailed with his wife for London to attend the World Anti-Slavery Convention, to which he was a delegate. Later, he traveled through Great Britain and Ireland delivering many speeches on the slavery question. One result of this tour was his *Sketches of Reforms and Reformers, of Great Britain and Ireland* (1849). Upon his return to the United States he studied law with his father-in-law, was admitted to the bar, and began practising in Boston. Finding the Massachusetts winters too severe for his health, he removed about 1847 to Seneca Falls, N. Y., making this place his home for the next sixteen years. He was successful at the law, but his continued interest in abolition led him into increased political

activity. In 1849 he was elected to the state Senate from Seneca Falls. He was one of the senators who resigned to prevent a quorum in the Senate and the passage of the bill appropriating millions of dollars for the enlargement of the canals. In 1851 he was reëlected but was not again a candidate. He helped draft the Free-Soil platform at Buffalo in 1848; in 1855 he helped organize the Republican party in New York State; and in 1856 he campaigned for Frémont. He remained a Republican until Grant's administration, during which he joined the Democrats. After the Civil War he gave most of his time to journalism, being connected with the *New York Tribune* under the editorship of Greeley, and with the *Sun* from 1869 to his death. He died in New York City.

[H. B. Stanton, *Random Recollections* (3rd ed., 1887); *Elizabeth Cady Stanton, as Revealed in her Letters, Diary, and Reminiscences* (copr. 1922), ed. by Theodore Stanton and Harriot Stanton Blatch; *Letters of Theodore Dwight Weld, Angelina Grimke Weld and Sarah Grimke* (2 vols., copr. 1934); annual reports of the Am. Anti-Slavery Soc., 1835 ff.; N. Y. Senate *Journal* and *Documents*, 1850–51; William Birney, *James G. Birney and His Times* (1890); W. A. Stanton, *A Record . . . of Thomas Stanton, of Connecticut, and His Descendants* (1891); *Liberator* (Boston), Jan. 10, 1835; *N. Y. Tribune* and *N. Y. Sun*, Jan. 15, 1887.]
M. W. W.

STANTON, RICHARD HENRY (Sept. 9, 1812–Mar. 20, 1891), congressman, jurist, and legal writer, was born at Alexandria, D. C. (now Va.), the son of Richard and Harriet (Perry) Stanton; Frederick P. Stanton [*q.v.*] was a younger brother. He received his elementary education at the academy in Alexandria conducted by Benjamin Hallowell [*q.v.*]. In early youth he assisted his father in his occupation as a brick-mason, but devoted his spare time to reading law. In 1835 he moved to Kentucky, taking up his residence at Maysville the following year, and in 1839 was admitted to the bar. He was a ready writer and edited the *Maysville Monitor* until 1841, when he entered regularly upon the practice of law. In later years, in association with Thornton F. Marshall, he published the *Maysville Express,* and afterwards was for some time editor of the *Maysville Bulletin.*

Appointed postmaster at Maysville in 1845, he held the position until 1849. In that year he was elected to Congress and was twice reëlected. During his second term he was chairman of the committee on public grounds and buildings and was instrumental in advancing the construction and improvement of the Capitol. In his last term, he was chairman of the committee on elections and of the select committee on the military supervision of civil works. It was upon his motion and insistence that the territory (now the state) of Washington received its name by congressional enactment in February 1853. During his congressional career he is said to have been "the ablest and most popular Democrat in the district" (Collins, *post*, II, 117). Stanton, the county seat of Powell County (established in 1852) was named in his honor.

In 1857 he was appointed commonwealth's attorney for what was then the tenth judicial district of Kentucky. To this office he was elected in 1858, and retained the post until 1862, when he resigned. In 1868 he was elected judge of the circuit court for the fourteenth judicial (Maysville) district, and served the full term of six years. Always an ardent Democrat, he was a delegate to the Baltimore Convention of 1844, by which James K. Polk was nominated for the presidency, and was also a delegate to the Baltimore Convention of 1852, which nominated Franklin Pierce. In 1856 he was a presidential elector from Kentucky and cast his vote for James Buchanan. On account of his anti-administration attitude and outspoken Southern sympathies, in October 1861 he was arrested and temporarily confined in Camp Chase, at Columbus, Ohio, but was soon transferred to Fort Lafayette, New York City, where he remained a prisoner for some time. He was a member of the Union Convention which met in Philadelphia in 1866, and of the New York Convention of 1868, which nominated Horatio Seymour for president. In February 1867 he was an unsuccessful candidate for the Democratic nomination for governor of Kentucky, and, a year later, he failed to secure nomination for senator in the Democratic caucus of the Kentucky legislature.

As a newspaper editor and contributor, he was a writer "of marked versatility and vigor" (Collins, II, 561). Of his earlier speeches, that delivered at Maysville on Dec. 18, 1847, "In Defence of the Mexican War," is, perhaps, the best example, and his speech in the House of Representatives, on June 14, 1854, "Against Military Superintendency of Civil Works," is a good illustration, in style and substance, of his political sentiments. He ranked high as a jurist. He was methodical, painstaking, and laborious; solid, safe, and thorough, rather than original or brilliant. His works as a law-writer comprise the following publications, which were extensively used: *Code of Practice in Civil and Criminal Cases for the State of Kentucky* (1859); *The Revised Statutes of Kentucky* (2 vols., 1860); *The Revised Statutes of Kentucky* (2 vols., 1867); *A Practical Treatise on the Law Relating to the Powers and Duties of Justices of the Peace, Clerks of the Circuit and County Courts, Sher-

iffs, Constables, Jailers, and Coroners in the State of Kentucky* (1875); *A Practical Manual for the Use of Executors, Administrators, Guardians, Trustees . . . in Kentucky* (2nd ed., 1875); *A New Digest of the Decisions of the Court of Appeals of Kentucky* (2 vols., 1877).

In 1833 he was married, in Alexandria, to Asenath Throop, of Fairfax County, Va. She was a daughter of Rev. Phares and Elizabeth (Bonner) Throop. Nine children were born to them, of whom three sons and four daughters grew to maturity. The eldest, Maj. Henry Thompson Stanton (June 30, 1834–May 8, 1898), was a lawyer and journalist; he served as an officer in the Confederate army and achieved considerable reputation as a novelist and poet.

[*The Biog. Encyc. of Ky.* (1878); Lewis and R. H. Collins, *Hist. of Ky.* (2 vols. 1874); *Evening Bull.* (Maysville, Ky.), Mar. 21, 1891; *Maysville Bull.*, May 22, 1924; *Cong. Globe,* 32nd Cong., 2 Sess.; *Biog. Dir. Am. Cong.* (1928); information from Stanton's family and from family MSS.]   S. M. W.

STANWOOD, EDWARD (Sept. 16, 1841–Oct. 11, 1923), editor, historian, was born in Augusta, Me., the son of Daniel Caldwell and Mary Augusta (Webster) Stanwood. He came of a family long settled in Essex County, Mass.; his ancestor Philip Stanwood having been a citizen of Gloucester as early as 1652. His father, at the age of fourteen, went to Augusta to live with an uncle, who had moved thither from Massachusetts (Ethel S. Bolton, *post*). Daniel Caldwell Stanwood became a man of some mark in Augusta; he was a book-seller by occupation, and served as city clerk and as major in the state militia. Edward Stanwood was educated in the public schools of the city, and at Bowdoin College, from which he graduated in 1861. Among his fellow students at Bowdoin was Thomas B. Reed, in later years speaker of the House of Representatives. From boyhood, Stanwood was deeply interested in public affairs, and strongly drawn to the profession of journalism. At seventeen he was reporting the proceedings of the Maine legislature for the Augusta *Age*; and after his graduation from college he was similarly employed on the staff of the *Kennebec Journal*, of which James G. Blaine [*q.v.*] was for some years the editor. Blaine had married a cousin of Stanwood's and the relations of the two men were close for many years. For a time in 1863–64 he was Blaine's secretary in Washington, shortly returning to Augusta to continue his newspaper work.

In 1867 the attention of the editor of the Boston *Daily Advertiser* was attracted to Stanwood, and he offered the young man a position on the *Advertiser* staff. For sixteen years Stanwood was connected with this paper, rising to the post of editor-in-chief. During these years he contributed articles to many magazines, published a book called *Boston Illustrated* (1872), and wrote for Justin Winsor's *The Memorial History of Boston* a chapter on the topography and landmarks of the city (vol. IV, 1881). In December 1883 Stanwood resigned the editorship of the *Advertiser* and shortly afterward joined the staff of the *Youth's Companion*. First as managing editor and then, after the death of Daniel Sharp Ford [*q.v.*], as editor, he remained for twenty-seven years with this famous household weekly; and after his retirement from the editorship he continued to contribute to its editorial page almost to the end of his life. He was in responsible charge of its conduct during its period of greatest popularity and prosperity. He maintained faithfully the policies and traditions by which, under the direction of Ford, the *Youth's Companion* had become one of the journalistic institutions of the United States. Its carefully selected combination of wholesome and entertaining fiction with articles of information and reminiscence by eminent writers, and a great variety of anecdote, both humorous and instructive, amply justified the esteem in which the paper was held in half a million households all over the land.

In 1884, Stanwood published *A History of Presidential Elections*, a valuable political handbook, of which several editions appeared. In 1898 it appeared in enlarged form as *A History of the Presidency*, and under that title was several times reissued. In 1903 Stanwood published his *American Tariff Controversies in the Nineteenth Century* (5 vols.). Written by a convinced adherent of the policy of protection to industry through tariff duties, the book may be found to lack thorough impartiality; but it assembles a great body of facts not available elsewhere in collected form. In 1905 appeared Stanwood's *James Gillespie Blaine*, written for the American Statesmen series. The long and close friendship between the author and his subject gives this book a certain personal as well as biographical interest. As is natural from the circumstances of the case, it takes a view consistently favorable to Blaine. For years Stanwood was identified with the affairs of the cotton industry. He was secretary and treasurer of the Arkwright Club, special agent for cotton manufactures in the preparation of the census of 1900 (*Census Reports. Twelfth Census. . . . Manufactures, Textiles,* 1902); and for textiles in 1905 (*Department of Commerce and Labor. Bureau of*

the *Census. Bulletin 74. Census of Manufactures: 1905. Textiles,* 1907). For years he was a contributing editor to the *Statesman's Year Book,* dealing with American affairs. From 1903 to the year of his death he was a member of the Massachusetts Historical Society, and most of that time its recording secretary.

He was married on Nov. 16, 1870, to Eliza Maxwell Topliff of Boston, daughter of Samuel Topliff, and was the father of three children, two of whom, a daughter and a son, survived him. He died at his home in Brookline, Mass., on Oct. 11, 1923.

[This article is based in part on personal acquaintance. The best account of Stanwood's life is the memoir of his son-in-law, C. K. Bolton, in *Mass. Hist. Soc. Proceedings,* vol. LVII (1924). For genealogy and a list of his writings to 1899, see *A Hist. of the Stanwood Family* (1899) by his daughter, Ethel Stanwood Bolton. A character sketch, by Geoffrey Bolton, in manuscript, is in the library of the Boston Athenaeum. See also *The Class of 1861, Bowdoin College* (1897), compiled by Stanwood; obituary in *Boston Evening Transcript,* Oct. 11, 1923; and passages in E. P. Mitchell, *Memoirs of an Editor* (1924).]

H. S. C—an.

STAPLES, WALLER REDD (Feb. 24, 1826–Aug. 20, 1897), Confederate congressman, Virginia jurist, was born at Stuart, Patrick County, Va., the son of Col. Abram Penn and Mary (Penn) Staples. At sixteen he entered the University of North Carolina, and after two years there transferred to the College of William and Mary, where he was graduated with honors in 1846. He studied law under Judge Norbonne Taliaferro in Franklin County, and in 1848 began practice in Montgomery County, Va., as the junior associate of his kinsman, William Ballard Preston [*q.v.*]. Preston's appointment within a few months to the post of secretary of the navy under President Taylor was of great professional advantage to the younger man. He became a Whig in politics and served as a delegate from Montgomery County in the House of Delegates, 1853–54.

In the crisis of 1860–61 Staples opposed immediate secession and worked with the conservatives to avert the disruption of the Union, but when Virginia adopted the ordinance of secession he volunteered for service in the state forces. He was appointed to the staff of Col. Robert C. Trigg, but was soon chosen, together with W. C. Rives, R. M. T. Hunter [*qq.v.*], and John Brockenbrough on the commission sent to represent Virginia in the provisional Confederate Congress at Montgomery, Ala. He served in that body until the end of its existence in February 1862, and then, having been elected by a large majority, took his seat in the House of Representatives of the new Confederate Congress. He was reëlected in 1863 and served till the end of the war.

After the war he resumed his practice in Montgomery County, regained his place as a leader at the bar, and in 1870 was elected a justice of the Virginia supreme court of appeals. His most notable opinion as a member of this court was his dissent in the "Coupon Case" in 1878 (*Antoni* vs. *Wright*, 63 *Va. Reports*, 833) which led to the forming of the Readjuster party and to the partial repudiation of a portion of the state debt. Staples, dissenting, held that the Virginia law of 1871 making coupons of bonds issued in that year receivable for all state taxes was invalid as applied to school taxes for which a special fund had been set aside by the state constitution. After the Readjuster period his opinion on this point was upheld by the supreme court of Virginia (*Commonwealth* vs. *McCullough*, 90 *Va.*, 597) and by the United States Supreme Court (*Vashon* vs. *Greenhow*, 135 *U. S.*, 713). He sat on the supreme bench for a full term of twelve years, but when the Readjuster party secured a majority in the legislature he and his associates were not reëlected. During his judicial service he was offered at different times the Democratic nominations for governor, attorney-general, and United States senator, but he declined political office, though he canvassed the state for the nominees and was twice a Democratic presidential elector.

In 1884 Staples, Judge E. C. Burks, a former colleague on the bench, and Maj. John W. Riely, later a member of the same court, were appointed to prepare *The Code of Virginia,* approved and published in 1887. For two years Staples was counsel for the Richmond & Danville Railroad Company, resigning this position to devote himself to a lucrative practice as senior member of the Richmond law firm of Staples & Munford. During this same period he was president of the Virginia Bar Association. As attorney in two significant cases before the Virginia supreme court of appeals (*Fifield* vs. *Van Wyck*, 94 *Va.*, 557 and *Munford, Trustee,* vs. *McVeigh*, 92 *Va.*, 446), he won reversals of former decisions of the supreme court.

Above medium height, of strong, athletic build, with a persuasive voice, Staples was a polished orator but also enjoyed a "knock down and drag out" legal fight. He was never married. He died at his Christiansburg home, in Montgomery County, at the age of seventy-one.

[Frederick Johnston, *Memorials of Old Va. Clerks* (1888) ; 94 *Va. Reports,* xxi–xxvi ; *Va. Law Reg.,* Feb. 1898 ; *Report . . . Va. State Bar Asso.,* 1898 ; *Green*

Bag., Sept. 1893, pp. 407, 409 ; *Richmond Dispatch,* Aug. 21, 1897 ; parents' names from a nephew, Hon. A. P. Staples.]   J. E. W.

STAPLES, WILLIAM READ (Oct. 10, 1798–Oct. 19, 1868), historian, was born in Providence, R. I., the youngest son of Samuel and Ruth (Read) Staples. He graduated from Brown University in 1817. After reading law in the office of a local attorney, he was admitted to practice in 1819, and although at the bar and on the bench he maintained a successful association with the law for nearly half a century, he impressed one of his contemporary biographers as being "not especially fond of his profession" (Guild, *post,* p. xvii). He entered public life in 1832 as a member of the common council of Providence, served as a police justice of the city for two years, and in June 1835 took his seat by appointment as an associate justice of the supreme court of Rhode Island. Elected chief justice of that court in 1854, he was compelled through loss of health to resign his office in March 1856. Thereafter, except for a few months in 1856 as state auditor, he devoted himself largely to unofficial public service and to the development of his interest in the history of his native state. From the eulogies of his professional associates at the time of his death, one learns that it was not profound legal knowledge that gave him distinction among Rhode Island jurists so much as a faculty for dealing systematically and promptly with the business of the court and unusual readiness in discerning the bearing of general principles of law upon particular cases.

He was one of the incorporators of the Rhode Island Historical Society in 1822. He was chosen at once to act as its librarian and cabinet keeper, one of the several offices that he held in the society in the course of his long membership. He edited for the society an edition of *Simplicities Defence* by Samuel Gorton [*q.v.*] in *Rhode Island Historical Society Collections* (vol. II, 1935). His annotation of that confused narrative and his documentary additions to it indicate the possession of a more than respectable knowledge of early New England and a conception of editorial responsibility seldom attained by the untrained antiquarians of his day. In his *Annals of the Town of Providence,* published in 1843 (also in *Rhode Island Historical Society Collections,* vol. V, 1843), he claimed with too much modesty that his purpose was only "to collect facts for the future historian," but in that book he arranged economically a great store of facts, collected from numerous original sources, into a vigorous, reliable narrative covering two centuries of the city's life. At the instance of the Assembly he performed in his closing years a similar task of research and presentation in his *Rhode Island in the Continental Congress,* a work that was brought out by the state in 1870 under the editorship of Reuben Aldridge Guild [*q.v.*]. He edited also *The Documentary History of the Destruction of the Gaspee* (1845) and, at different periods of his life, certain works of legal utility of no general interest. His closest religious affiliation was with the Friends, though he does not seem to have been a member of that society. He was married in November 1821 to Rebecca M. Power who died in 1825. They had two children both of whom died in childhood. In October 1826 he was married to his second wife, Evelina Eaton of Framingham, Mass., who survived him with six of their eleven children.

[Preface" and the "Introductory Memoir" by R. A. Guild, in *Rhode Island in the Continental Congress, ante*; *Hist. Cat. of Brown Univ.* (1914); S. G. Arnold, *Greene-Staples-Parsons* (1869); *Providence Daily Journ.*, Oct. 20, 1868.]   L. C. W.

STARIN, JOHN HENRY (Aug. 27, 1825–Mar. 22, 1909), transportation owner, congressman, was of old Dutch stock, a descendant of Nicholas Ster, who emigrated from Holland to New Amsterdam in 1696 and about 1705 moved up the Mohawk Valley to a settlement called German Flats. He was born in Sammonsville, N. Y., fifth of the eight children of Myndert and Rachel (Sammons) Starin. His father developed extensive manufacturing interests in Sammonsville and was the founder of Fultonville. After attending Esperance Academy, he began to study medicine with Dr. C. C. Yates, an Albany doctor, but, preferring business, returned in 1845 to his brother's drug store at Fultonville, where he served also as postmaster, 1850–53. In 1856 he moved to New York and began to manufacture toilet articles. There the difficulties he met in shipping his products called his attention to the complete lack of system in handling freight around New York. The situation was a chaotic one, the result of the insular position of Manhattan, accentuated by the fact that several railroads started on the Jersey side of the Hudson. In 1859 he organized a general freight agency, the Starin City River and Harbor Transportation Lines, and soon won the support of Vanderbilt and other railroad officials, who realized that a centralized system would mean economy. At first he used canal boats for transshipping freight. During the Civil War the government relied on his organization for the moving of men, munitions, and supplies, and it is said that his quick work once saved a regiment from starvation. After the war he rapidly increased his equipment of lighters and tugs. In 1866 he in-

vented the car float, by which a freight train could be broken into parts and the cars carried across the harbor—a system that, with few modifications, is still extensively used. He was, in fact, responsible for most of the important solutions of the problem of handling freight down to the time of his death. He devised special facilities for handling grain and coal, and built up the largest "harbor marine" in the country, if not in the world. In addition, he owned and operated passenger and freight lines on Long Island Sound. Having purchased Glen Island (formerly Locust Island), off New Rochelle on the Sound, he made it into a summer resort intended to rival Coney Island and linked it to New York City with a line of excursion steamers, on which he annually gave free trips to war veterans, police, firemen, newsboys, poor women, and other groups from the city. To build and repair his "navy" he had a shipyard, iron works, and drydock on Staten Island. Until the very end he kept active daily control of his wide-spread activities from his office on Pier 13, North River.

He also deserves much credit for establishing New York's subway system. He was an original member of the Rapid Transit Commission of the city, 1894–1907, and served as vice president, 1895–1907. Opposed to the building of more elevated and surface lines, he fought hard for the subways, construction of which was begun on Mar. 24, 1900. It is said, too, that by his firm stand against all the rest of the board he prevented the traction interests from securing a monopoly of the franchises. A strong Republican, he sat in Congress for an upstate district from 1877 to 1881, declining a third term. More than once he was prominently mentioned for governor. He was president of the Saratoga Monument Association and its most active supporter, president of the Holland Society, 1901–02, vice president of the Union League Club, and a member of many other organizations. He had several estates, one at his old home in Fultonville, another in a remote part of the Adirondacks on Hamilton Lake, and a third, "Folly Island," on the South Carolina coast, where he had a herd of 4,000 Angora goats. He married Laura M. Poole of Oriskany, N. Y., on Jan. 27, 1846. He died in New York City. He was survived by a son and two daughters, his wife and two sons having predeceased him.

[See W. L. Stone, *The Starin Family in America* (1892), with portraits; *Who's Who in America, 1908–09*; *Biog. Directory Am. Cong., 1774–1927* (1928); J. H. Mowbray, *Representative Men of N. Y.* (1898), vol. II; *Year Book Holland Soc. of N. Y.*, 1909; *Report of the Board of Rapid Transit Railroad Commissioners ... City of N. Y. ... 1902* (1903). The N. Y. harbor transportation situation is best described, without specific reference to Starin, in *Joint Report with Comprehensive Plan and Recommendations; N. Y., N. J. Port and Harbor Development Commission* (1920).]

R. G. A.

STARK, EDWARD JOSEF (Apr. 29, 1858–Apr. 22, 1918), cantor, composer of synagogue music, was born at Hohenems, Austria, to Josef and Josepha (Pollak) Stark. From his father, a synagogue cantor who had been a pupil of the world-famed Salomon Sulzer, he derived his knowledge and love of Jewish religious music. After a childhood spent for the most part at Ichenhausen, Bavaria, he came with his parents in 1871 to the United States, where his older brothers were already in business. Young Stark received his musical education in New York City and in European conservatories, whither he was sent by a wealthy friend. On his return to America, he spent a short time in business before becoming cantor in the Beth Elohim Synagogue in Brooklyn, N. Y. This position he held until October 1893, when he was called to be cantor in Temple Emanu-El, San Francisco. He served in this capacity until, in August 1913, owing to failing health, he was made honorary cantor emeritus. On Apr. 1, 1884, in New York City, he married Rosa Weinberger, who bore him two sons and two daughters.

His was the uneventful life of a synagogue cantor and composer devoted to his calling. He possessed a rich, magnetic, baritone voice which he used with dramatic feeling. While his principal works are in the field of sacred music, he also wrote light operettas for the Progress Club (1884) and the Germania Quartett Club in New York (1885), and for celebrations in the Sunday School of Temple Emanu-El in San Francisco (1895 and 1906). Many of his numerous sacred compositions have gained wide recognition in American synagogues. They include the four collections (each under the Hebrew title *Sefer Anim Zemiroth) Musical Service for Sabbath Evening* (New York, 1911, third printing 1931), *Musical Service for Sabbath Morning* (1909, second printing 1926), *Musical Service for the Eve and Day of New Year* (1910, third printing 1930), *Musical Service for the Eve of Atonement and for the Day of Atonement* (1913), besides anthems, adaptations, and a number of unpublished works. His anthem "The Lord is my light" won the Schirmer prize in the national contest of 1905; "Day of God," sung on the eve of the Day of Atonement, is often regarded as his finest composition. He was a prolific worker, sometimes sitting all night composing at the organ. A feature of some of his work, which is unusual in synagogue music, is its orchestral setting for string and wind instruments.

"He was gifted with considerable creative talent, and with power and depth of Jewish expression" (Idelsohn, *post,* p. 326–27). His synagogue music, especially that for the New Year and the Day of Atonement, using Jewish modes and showing both the influence of Sulzer and of the classic oratorio, disciplines Jewish traditional motifs and modes by the constraints of the organ and of Western musical conventions. This combination of traditionalism and modernism makes his compositions particularly well adapted for reform Jewish temples. He aimed to preserve the traditional character of the synagogue service in which the main elements of the ritual are rendered by the cantor in recitatives and solos, with the choral and hymnal elements constituting a superstructure on this foundation. His influence in this direction was the greater and more needed because he came into the field at a time when the tendency in American reform Judaism had been towards the entire elimination of the plaintive, emotional Eastern Jewish traditional motifs in favor of operatic airs, or the stately devotional Western music borrowed, or at least copied, from that of the dominant Church.

[*Emanu-El* (San Francisco), Apr. 26, 1918; A. Z. Idelsohn, *Jewish Music* (1929); *The Am. Jewish Year Book . . . 1903–1904* (1903), p. 102, which gives date of birth as Mar. 29, 1863; unpublished records in possession of Stark's children.] D. deS. P.

STARK, JOHN (Aug. 28, 1728–May 8, 1822), Revolutionary soldier, was born at Londonderry, N. H., the son of Archibald Stark and his wife, Eleanor Nichols. The elder Stark was a Scotsman who, after residing some years in Ulster County, Ireland, emigrated to New Hampshire in 1720 with a party of compatriots. Brought up in a frontier community where fishing, hunting, and Indian-fighting were the chief occupations, Stark developed a physique well adapted to endure the risks and rigors of military life. He became familiar with the New Hampshire wilderness and guided exploring expeditions into remote regions. During the French and Indian War he saw extensive service with Rogers' Rangers and attained a captaincy by gallantry on the field. He took part in the operations resulting in the defeat of Baron Dieskau in 1755. In January 1757, en route with a scouting party to Lake Champlain, he distinguished himself by walking forty miles in deep snow, after a day's fighting and a night's marching, in order to bring succor to the wounded. He was present during Rigaud's attack upon Fort William Henry, and in 1758 participated in Abercromby's futile assault upon Ticonderoga. He concluded this chapter of his military career, by serving under Amherst at the reduction of Crown Point and Ticonderoga in 1759, and then returned to his farm and his mills, and devoted himself to the settlement of a new township, at first called Starkstown but later Dunbarton. On Aug. 20, 1758, he was married to Elizabeth, the daughter of Capt. Caleb Page.

When the news of the battles of Lexington and Concord came, he promptly mounted horse and set out for Cambridge, Mass. A regiment of New Hampshire patriots presently assembled at Medford and Stark was appointed colonel. In the battle of Bunker Hill his men defended the rail fence on the American left. After the siege of Boston, he assisted in planning the defenses of New York, and in May 1776 went to Canada and accompanied the American forces on their retreat southward. He played a conspicuous part in the battles of Trenton and Princeton, but resigned his commission in March 1777 because Congress had promoted junior officers over his head (see *Proceedings of the Massachusetts Historical Society*, LVII, 1924, p. 334).

When Burgoyne invaded the province of New York, the Vermont council of safety, anticipating a raid into the region west of the Connecticut River, largely unprotected after the fall of Ticonderoga, appealed to the authorities of New Hampshire for help. On July 18 the general court authorized the mobilization of a force to assist Vermont, and elected Stark to command it with the rank of brigadier-general. Within twenty days he raised and equipped a brigade of about 1,400 men, crossed the mountains, and arrived at Manchester, Vt., where he conferred with Seth Warner, Benjamin Lincoln [qq.v.], and the Vermont leaders. On Aug. 8, he moved southward to Bennington with the intention of cooperating with Schuyler in a movement to harass Burgoyne's flank. On the next day the British commander dispatched Colonel Baum with 500 men to test the sentiment of the Hampshire Grants and to secure supplies of cattle, horses, and wagons. On Aug. 16 Stark attacked Baum on the Walloomsac River, about five miles northwest of Bennington, and captured almost his entire force. As he led his men into action, he is alleged to have exclaimed, "There, my boys, are your enemies, the red-coats and tories; you must beat them or my wife sleeps a widow tonight" (Caleb Stark, *post*, p. 60). Later in the day, Stark and Warner repulsed reënforcements under Breymann hastening to Baum's assistance. Stark received the thanks of Congress three days later, after having been censored for disregarding orders for a different movement of his men.

On Oct. 4, 1777, he was promoted to the rank of brigadier-general in the Continental service. After capturing Fort Edward, he helped to effect the surrender of Burgoyne by blocking his line of retreat across the Hudson. His services during the remainder of the war were interesting and significant. He twice commanded the northern department; served with Gates in Rhode Island in 1779; participated in the battle of Springfield in 1780; and acted on the board of general officers appointed to try Major André. He was brevetted a major-general in September 1783.

After the war he retired to his estate, eschewing public office and devoting himself to the cares entailed by a large farm and a family of eleven children. He was buried with military honors in a cemetery upon his own land, the site being marked by a granite obelisk erected in 1829, on the anniversary of the battle of Bennington. He was a man of medium height, bold features, keen, light-blue eyes, and compressed lips. While the phraseology of his celebrated sayings in battle has been disputed, there is no doubt that he possessed a gift for picturesque expression which served to enhance the dramatic quality of his martial exploits.

[Sources include N. H. Hist. Soc. collection of published and unpublished letters and papers of John Stark; George Stark, *Origin of the Stark Family* (1887); C. E. Potter, *The Hist. of Manchester* (1856); Caleb Stark, *Memoir and Official Corres. of Gen. John Stark* (1860); Isaac Jennings, *Memorials of a Century* (1869); *N. H. State Papers*, vols. VII–VIII (1873–74); *Proc. in Cong. upon the Acceptance of the Statues of John Stark and Daniel Webster, Sen. Misc. Doc., 64, 53 Cong., 3 Sess.* (1895); Henry Boynton in *Granite Monthly*, Oct. 1902; F. B. Sanborn in *Proc. N. H. Hist. Soc.*, vol. III (1902); H. D. Foster & T. W. Streeter, *Stark's Independent Command at Bennington* (1918); John Spargo, *The Bennington Battle Monument* (1925); *Natl. Standard* (Middlebury, Vt.), May 28, 1822. Stark's stirring adventures among the Indians served as a basis for a novel, *The Hero of the Hills* (1901), by G. W. Browne.]   E. E. C.

STARR, ELIZA ALLEN (Aug. 29, 1824–Sept. 7, 1901), writer, lecturer on art, the second of four children of Oliver and Lovina (Allen) Starr, was born in a rangy old house at Deerfield, Mass. On both sides her family traced descent from early English emigrants to the Bay Colony and found satisfaction in their long residence in Deerfield. Her father, a dyer, was a descendant of Dr. Comfort Starr, who emigrated from Kent, England, to Boston in 1635. Uneducated but intelligent, the Starrs encouraged Eliza to go beyound the district school, and even the local academy, to Boston, where she took lessons in art and painting from the wife of Richard Hildreth [q.v.], the historian. In some way about 1845 her Unitarian beliefs were upset by a sermon of Dr. Theodore Parker [q.v.], and her religious yearnings were not satisfied until in 1854 she joined the Roman Catholic Church, influenced by her association with Bishops Francis Patrick Kenrick and John Bernard Fitzpatrick, and her cousin, George Allen [qq.v.], a convert and a professor of Latin and Greek at the University of Pennsylvania. Her conversion was the central fact in a life dedicated to painting, poetry, and writing where religion provided the motif. Finding the climate disagreeable in Boston, where she had a studio, she taught art in private schools in Brooklyn, N. Y., and Philadelphia, Pa., became a tutor in a wealthy family of Natchez, Miss., and finally settled in Chicago, Ill., about 1856 as one of its first teachers of art and the first to instruct her pupils from nature and casts.

Her early success was partly due to Bishop Kenrick, with whom she kept up a long correspondence, to Bishop James Duggan of Chicago, and to such pioneer patrons of art in Chicago as William Butler Ogden [q.v.], Walter Loomis Newberry [q.v.], Jonathan Young Scammon [q.v.], and Leander James McCormick [q.v.]. In addition to private teaching she gave for a score of years an annual series of lectures, which contributed to the cultural life of the first families of the city, on painting, architecture, and the great artists of the Renaissance. After her studio burned in the great fire of 1871, she spent a few years at St. Mary's Academy (later College), South Bend, Ind., under Mother Angela [q.v.], organizing an art department. She became widely known as a lecturer in Catholic circels and convent schools, and as a writer of poems and popular essays on art in the *Catholic World, Ave Maria, New York Freeman's Journal, London Monthly,* and other magazines. In 1875 she traveled extensively in Europe, drawing upon her experiences later for her *Pilgrims and Shrines* (2 vols., 1885). Other books, always devotional, which she herself usually illustrated, followed in rapid succession: *Patron Saints* (1 ser., 1871; 2 ser., 1881), *Songs of a Life-Time* (copyright 1888), *Isabella of Castile* (1889), *Christian Art in Our Own Age* (1891), *The Seven Dolors of the Blessed Virgin Mary* (1898), *The Three Archangels and the Guardian Angels in Art* (1899), and *Three Keys to the Camera Della Segnatura of the Vatican* (1895). She received a medallion from Pope Leo XIII in appreciation of her work; a Laetare Medal (1885), awarded annually by the University of Notre Dame to an outstanding Catholic contributor to the church and nation; and a gold medal at the World's Columbian Exposition of 1893 in Chicago for her work as a teacher. She died at the home of a brother in Durand, Ill., and was buried from the Cathedral of the Holy Name, Chicago, in Calvary Cemetery.

[See B. P. Starr, *A Hist. of the Starr Family* (1879), which gives Eliza Starr's name as Eliza Ann ('Allen') Starr; *Who's Who in America*, 1901–02; *The Cath. Encyc.*, vol. XIV (copr. 1912); J. J. McGovern, *Life and Letters of Eliza Allen Starr* (1905); *N. Y. Freeman's Jour.*, Sept. 3, 1887; W. S. Clarke, in *Cath. World*, Nov. 1897; W. S. Merrill, *Ibid.*, Feb. 1902; Frances E. Willard and Mary A. Livermore, *A Woman of the Century* (1893), with portrait; obituary in *Chicago Daily Tribune*, Sept. 9, 1901.] R.J.P.

STARR, FREDERICK (Sept. 2, 1858–Aug. 14, 1933), anthropologist, was born in Auburn, N. Y., the fourth of the seven children of the Rev. Frederick Starr, a Presbyterian minister, and Helen Strachan (Mills) Starr. He was a descendant of Dr. Comfort Starr, who emigrated from Kent, England, to Boston in 1635. He spent his boyhood in the East and in 1882 graduated from Lafayette College, Easton, Pa., where in 1885 he received the degree of Ph.D. He was professor of biology at Coe College, Cedar Rapids, Iowa, 1883–87, and registrar and professor of geography at Chautauqua University, Chautauqua, N. Y., 1888–89. From 1889 to 1891 he was engaged in arranging, labelling, and classifying the collections in the department of ethnology in the American Museum of Natural History, New York. In 1891 he became professor of geology and anthropology, and dean of the science department in Pomona College, Claremont, Cal., but in the following year he was called to organize the work of anthropology at the newly established University of Chicago, under William Rainey Harper [q.v.], where in 1895 he became associate professor. During his thirty-one years there he was probably the most popular instructor in the university. Though his classes were crowded and he was the only instructor in his subject, he refused to add others, remaining, as he said, "the Lone Star." He had numerous personal idiosyncrasies. He refused to wear an overcoat, never used a telephone, and usually walked about the campus with an open book in his hands, while his apartment was a labyrinth of books stacked on the floors of various rooms. His frankness and fearlessness in the expression of opinion often made him enemies; on the other hand, his informality and camaraderie in the classroom created a loyalty seldom met with between students and professor. When he retired from the university in 1923 his former students presented him with a large purse, which enabled him to purchase a house in Seattle, Wash., a location convenient for his frequent trips to Japan.

Throughout his career he traveled widely for the sake of making anthropological studies. In preparation for the Louisiana Purchase Exposition at St. Louis, Mo., in 1904, he visited northern Japan and brought back with him a representative group of Ainu; he also visited various parts of the United States and Mexico, the Philippines, Korea, and Africa, returning several times to the last two. During these visits he lived the life of the people, and in Japan, at least, he wore native dress. Keenly interested in the intimate life of those he met, he was always inclined to take the part of minority or unpopular groups. While the world was condemning the African policy of King Leopold II, he visited the Congo and came forward with a vigorous defense of Belgian rule; while "imperialism" was at its height in America he advocated Philippine independence. Mexico found in him an ardent advocate, and shortly before his death he defended Japan in the Manchukuo dispute. He was a chevalier of the Order of the Crown of Italy, a member of the Third Order of the Sacred Treasure of Japan, an officer of the Order of Leopold II (Congo), and had been awarded medals by Holland, Belgium, and Liberia, as well as the palms of Officer of Public Instruction by the French government. His best known writings are *Some First Steps in Human Progress* (1895), *American Indians* (copyright 1898), *Indians of Southern Mexico* (1898), *Strange Peoples* (1901), *Readings from Modern Mexican Authors* (1904), *The Truth about the Congo* (1907), *In Indian Mexico* (1908), *Philippine Studies* (1909), *Japanese Proverbs and Pictures* (1910), *Congo Natives* (1912), *Liberia* (1913), *Korean Buddhism* (1918), *Fujiyama, the Sacred Mountain of Japan* (1924). His greatest contribution to anthropology lies, however, in the wide interest he personally created in the subject, and in the appreciation of other peoples which he engendered in his students. In 1923 he went through the earthquake that devastated Tokio and claimed many of his closest friends. Ten years later he died of bronchial pneumonia in the same city. He was unmarried.

[B. P. Starr, *A Hist. of the Starr Family* (1879); *Who's Who in America*, 1932–33; *Am. Men of Sci.* (1933), edited by J. M. and Jaques Cattell; *Biog. Cat. of Lafayette Coll., 1832–1912* (1913); *Univ. Record* (Chicago), Oct. 1933; *Am. Anthropologist*, Apr.–June 1934; *Am. Jour. of Sociology*, Nov. 1933; obituaries in *Japan Advertiser* (Tokio) and *N. Y. Times*, Aug. 15, 1933, personal acquaintance.]   F.–C. C.

STARR, LOUIS (Apr. 25, 1849–Sept. 12, 1925), physician, was born in Philadelphia, Pa., the son of Isaac and Lydia (Ducoing) Starr. The line of his paternal ancestors was estab-lished in America by Isaac Starr, an English Quaker, who settled in Wilmington, Del., in 1710. Eight generations remained in the Quaker faith and married within the bounds of their religious convictions until Starr's father, a banker, took as his wife a French girl, Lydia Ducoing, who was a refugee from the slave insurrections of Santo Domingo and a descendant of a family which had originally come from Bordeaux, France. Louis graduated from Haverford College in 1868 with the degree of B.A., studied medicine at the University of Pennsylvania, and obtained the degree of M.D. in 1871. After acting as the resident physician for the Episcopal Hospital, he entered general practice in Philadelphia, where his personal charm, diligence, and, doubtless, his excellent social position made him a very successful practitioner. Nevertheless, he turned to a special field and by 1882 was recognized as a pediatrician of note. He was visiting physician to the Episcopal Hospital, 1875–84, and to the Children's Hospital, 1879, and held numerous other such appointments. In 1884 he became clinical professor of the diseases of children in the University of Pennsylvania, a position he held until 1890. For fifty years he was a fellow of the College of Physicians of Philadelphia, at various times a member of its council, and later a censor; he was also a fellow of the Royal College of Physicians of London. He first appeared in scientific literature in 1885–86 as an assistant to Dr. William Pepper [*q.v.*] in the editing of *A System of Practical Medicine* (5 vols., 1885–86). Subsequently he published several textbooks on pediatric subjects. His most successful publication was *Hygiene of the Nursery* (1888), one of the first popular expositions of nursery care, and his most ambitious *The American Text-book of Diseases of Children by American Teachers* (1894).

On Sept. 16, 1882, in Kent, England, he married Mary Parrish of Philadelphia, grand-daughter of Joseph Parrish [*q.v.*]. They had three children. At the age of sixty-two, when he was forced to retire from all official and professional activities because of serious cardiac disease, he took up residence with his family in England, but the leisure of his retirement was soon interrupted by the World War. When his younger son, Dillwyn, was killed in the battle of the Somme as a lieutenant of the Coldstream Guards, he sought respite from his sorrow in the cultivation of an artistic talent which had hitherto lain dormant. Some of his etchings were later shown at an exhibition of the Pennsylvania Academy of the Fine Arts in Philadelphia and are said to have won favor in authoritative circles. The death of his older son, Louis, in 1921 caused him to leave the scene of so much affliction, and he repaired to Dinard, on the coast of Brittany, where he spent the last years of his life in pursuit of his artistic inclinations. He died after a short illness, survived by his wife and daughter.

[*Who's Who in America*, 1914–15; T. S. Westcott, *Trans. Coll. of Physicians of Phila.*, 3 ser., vol. XLVIII (1926); *Jour. Am. Medic. Assoc.*, Oct. 10, 1925; obituary in *Pub. Ledger* (Phila.), Sept. 14, 1925.]

H. S. R—e.

STARR, MERRITT (Feb. 27, 1856–Aug. 2, 1931), corporation lawyer, was born at Ellington, Chautauqua County, N. Y. His father, James Comfort Starr, later a proprietor of the Moline Paper Company, was a descendant of Dr. Comfort Starr, of Ashford, Kent, who emigrated from England to Massachusetts in 1635; his mother, Cynthia Cordera (MacKoon), was a descendant of Roger Williams. Merritt Starr spent his boyhood in Rock Island, Ill. He attended Griswold College at Davenport, Iowa, for two years, and in 1873 entered Oberlin College as a junior, receiving the degree of A.B. from Oberlin in 1875 and from Griswold (*ad eundem*) in 1876. Ambitious for a legal career, he read law in the office of the attorneys for the Chicago, Burlington & Quincy Railroad Company, entered the Harvard Law School in 1878 and Harvard College, as a junior, in 1879, and was graduated A.B. and LL.B. in 1881.

Establishing residence in Chicago, he was admitted to the Illinois bar Jan. 11, 1882. He began his career by preparing briefs for his fellow attorneys and publishing valuable contributions to legal literature. In 1883 appeared his *Index-Digest of the Wisconsin Reports* and his chapters on practice in *A Treatise on the Law of Waters* by John Melville Gould. Shortly afterward he began a collaboration with R. H. Curtis in compiling *Annotated Statutes of the State of Illinois* (1st ed., 2 vols., 1885, with supplements 1887, 1892; 2nd ed., 3 vols., 1896). He also digested the *Illinois Cases* for the *Northeastern Reporter,* from 1885 to 1888.

Meanwhile he was becoming well known in the field of corporation law. During the suspension of the Indiana banks in 1883, he conducted the litigations in Chicago on behalf of their creditors and "established in the Supreme Court of Illinois the then novel doctrine that banks must hold the entire funds of the garnished depositor for the benefit of all the creditors who may thereafter perfect a claim" (*Chicago Legal News,* Jan. 18, 1896, p. 169). From 1890 until his death he was associated with John S. Miller, under a succession of firm names and with several other individuals as partners. In Washington, D. C.,

he maintained offices from 1925 to 1931, as a member of the firms of Hopkins, Starr & Hopkins, and (1926–29) Hopkins, Starr, Hopkins & Hamel.

Starr was a trustee of Oberlin College, 1893–1924, and a trustee of the National College of Education, Evanston, Ill., 1922–31, being president of its board, 1926–31. To the latter institution he gave most of his valuable library, and he contributed unstintingly of his time and legal counsel to both Oberlin and the National College of Education. He was a member of the board of managers of the Chicago Law Institute, 1888–90, and its president, 1896–97; a member of the executive committee of the Civil Service Reform Association of Chicago, 1884–1914; and president of the Chicago Literary Club, 1910–11. Much interested in local affairs, he was village attorney of Winnetka, Ill., 1894–95, a member of the Winnetka board of education, 1899–1907, and its president, 1900–05. On Sept. 8, 1885, he married Leila Wheelock, whom he had met at Oberlin College. They had four children, three of whom survived him.

[B. P. Starr, *A Hist. of the Starr Family of New England* (1879); *The Past and Present of Rock Island County, Ill.* (1877); J. M. Palmer, *The Bench and Bar of Ill.* (1899), I, 100; *Chicago Legal News,* Jan. 18, 1896; *Who's Who in Jurisprudence,* 1925; *Chicago Literary Club: Yearbook,* 1932–33; *Chicago Bar Asso. Record,* Jan.–Mar. 1932; *Our Guidon* (Nat. Coll. of Educ.), Aug. 1931; *Oberlin College Alumni Necrology,* 1930–31; *Who's Who in Chicago,* 1931; *Twenty-fifth Anniversary Report . . . Class of 1881 of Harvard College* (1906); *Ann. Report Ill. State Bar Asso.,* 1932; *Who's Who in America,* 1930–31; *Chicago Daily Tribune,* Aug. 4, 1931.]

J. K. W.

STARR, MOSES ALLEN (May 16, 1854–Sept. 4, 1932), neurologist, was born in Brooklyn, N. Y. He was the son of Egbert and Charlotte Augusta (Allen) Starr, of Middlebury, Vt. His first American ancestor was Dr. Comfort Starr of Ashford, County Kent, England, who came to Boston, Mass., in 1635 and settled in Warren, Conn. His early education was received in a private school in Orange, N. J., and he received the B.A. degree from Princeton University in 1876. During the whole period of his undergraduate study he was second honor man and after his graduation he was offered a professorship of history. With the intention of pursuing this subject he studied in Germany under Mommsen and Curtius, but he also attended the lectures of Helmholz and McCosh, developing a special interest in psychology and the functions of the nervous system, and upon his return to America he decided to prepare for a medical career. He entered the College of Physicians and Surgeons in New York City, received the M.D. degree in 1880, and spent the next two years as an interne in Bellevue Hospital. After this he again went to Germany and became a student of the renowned neurologists, Erb and Schultze, in Heidelberg, later continuing his studies in Vienna with Nothnagel and Meynert. His first important publication appeared soon after his return to America. The article, "The Sensory Tract in the Central Nervous System," was awarded the Alumni Association Prize of the College of Physicians and Surgeons in May 1884, and was published in the *Journal of Nervous and Mental Disease,* July 1884.

In 1884 he was appointed professor of anatomy and physiology at the New York Polyclinic Medical College and in 1886 was made Professor of Nervous Diseases. He retained this position for three years and then resigned to accept the professorship of diseases of the mind and nervous system in the College of Physicians and Surgeons, a chair which he held with distinction until 1915 when he became professor emeritus. His early work as an investigator was on cerebral localization, a field in which he was one of the American pioneers. He contributed to the localization of visual function, and of the senses of touch, pain, and temperature in the parietal region, and also to the problem of aphasia. He was one of the first in America to investigate brain tumors and with Dr. Charles McBurney published in 1895 an analysis of fifty brain tumors: *Tumor of the Corpus Callosum.* His *Atlas of Nerve Cells* (1896) received favorable reviews in all parts of the world. He also published one hundred special articles covering a wide range of neurological subjects and several important systematic works, *Familiar Forms of Nervous Disease* (1890), *Brain Surgery* (1893), *Organic and Functional Nervous Diseases* (1903). He held many important hospital positions as consultant, among them the Presbyterian Hospital, St. Vincent's, St. Mary's Free Hospital for Children, St. John's Hospital, Yonkers, the New York Eye and Ear Infirmary, and the Neurological Institute of New York. He was president of the New York Neurological Society, 1894–97, of the American Neurological Association, 1896–97, and was a vice-president of the New York Academy of Medicine, 1903–06. He was an honorary member of the Neurological Section of the Royal Society of London, and of French, German, and Austrian neurological and psychological societies. He also received many academic honors during his active career. Starr was particularly noted as a teacher, and his clinics at the College of Physicians and Surgeons were famous in a day when neurology was in its early evolution as a special

field of medicine. He was married to Alice Dunning on June 7, 1898, and one of their two children survived him.

[Personal acquaintance; *Who's Who in America,* 1930–31; B. P. Starr, *A Hist. of the Starr Family* (1879); Frederick Tilney, article in the *Jour. of Nervous and Mental Disease,* Feb. 1933; Frederick Peterson, in *Bull. of the N. Y. Acad. of Med.,* Nov. 1932; L. Casamajor, in *Arch. of Neurology and Psychiatry,* Dec. 1932; John Shrady, ed., *The Coll. of Physicians and Surgeons* (n.d.), vol. I; *N. Y. Times,* Apr. 5, 1912, Sept. 5, 1932.]   J. R. H.

STARRETT, LAROY S. (Apr. 25, 1836–Apr. 23, 1922), inventor, manufacturer, was born on his father's farm at China, Me., one of the twelve children of Daniel D. and Anna (Crummett) Starrett, both of Scotch ancestry. He worked on the farm in his youth, attended public school during the winter months, and developed a marked interest in mechanics. When he was seventeen years old he went to work on a stock farm at Vassalboro, Me., and later on a dairy farm at Newburyport, Mass., to help support the family. After about eight years he acquired for himself a six-hundred acre stock farm in Newburyport, which he operated for four years. He tried his hand at invention during this time and devised among other things a meat chopper, for which he was granted patent No. 47,875 on May 23, 1865. Shortly after obtaining the patent he made an arrangement with the Athol Machine Company, Athol, Mass., to manufacture his chopper while he undertook its sale in Maine. His success was so great that three years later he sold his farm, moved to Athol, purchased a controlling interest in the manufacturing company, and reorganized it for the special purpose of manufacturing his meat chopper, as well as a washing machine and a butter worker which he had patented in 1865 (patents No. 48,-458 and 49,953).

In the period of more than ten years in which he served as superintendent of the Athol Machine Company, he invented a number of hand tools useful in the building trades. The first of these was a combination square which contained a steel rule, graduated into small parts of an inch on both sides, with a sliding head capable of being moved along the rule or detached entirely from it; with the aid of the head it could be used as a square or mitre, as a bevel, and as a plumb bob. Shortly after patenting this (May 6, 1879), he established a business of his own on a small scale to manufacture it, and experienced slow but positive success. During the eighties he devised and patented a center try-square, a surface gauge, a bevelling instrument, a micrometer caliper square, and a new type of dividers, manufacturing each as it was patented.

Since the products were marketed and sold in increasing numbers, he was obliged to enlarge his plant a number of times. In 1882 the establishment of agencies in England, Germany, France, and other countries helped to increase his business materially and to establish his name the world over as a maker of fine tools. By 1906 he was employing about one thousand people in a great general manufacturing plant in Athol and in a caliper manufacturing plant at Springfield, Mass. He manufactured steel rules in a large variety of styles, and in both English and metric graduations; many different styles of squares; almost two hundred varieties of calipers and dividers; and such articles as bevels, surface and depth gauges, levels, steel tapes, plumb bobs, hacksaw frames and blades, as well as a number of unique precision instruments. In 1912 his company was incorporated with a capital stock of $3,500,000 as the L. S. Starrett Company, of which he was president until his death. His whole life was centered in his business and in the Methodist Church, his outstanding contribution to the latter being the gift of a new parsonage, a pipe organ, and a church building in Athol. He married Lydia W. Bartlett of Newburyport, Mass., on Apr. 20, 1861. At the time of his death at his winter home in St. Petersburg, Fla., he was survived by four children.

[L. B. Caswell, *Athol, Mass., Past and Present* (1899); D. H. Hurd, *Hist. of Worcester County, Mass.*, vol. II (1889); E. B. Crane, *Hist. of Worcester County, Mass.*, vol. II (1924); obituary in *Boston Transcript*, Apr. 24, 1922; Patent Office records.]   C. W. M.—n.

STARRETT, WILLIAM AIKEN (June 14, 1877–Mar. 26, 1932), engineer, financier, builder, architect, was born in Lawrence, Kan., one of seven children of William Aiken and Helen (Ekin) Starrett. His grandfather and great-grandfather (of Scotch origin) had been carpenters and stone masons in and near Pittsburgh and Allegheny, Pa. His father, Presbyterian minister though he was, did not lose touch with the building tradition; he had, it is said, built his church, shared in the building of the first structure of the University of Kansas, and not only built but designed his own house. All five of his sons in their turn became builders of importance. Educated in local schools, in Chicago, and at the University of Michigan (1893–95), Starrett worked for a time in a wholesale grocery house, became a timekeeper for the George A. Fuller Company, general contractors, of which his brother Paul was a member, and by 1899 had risen to the position of a superintendent. From 1901 to 1913 he was vice-president of the famous Thompson-Starrett Company, New York, found-

ed by his brothers Theodore and Ralph, for many years one of the two or three largest and most successful firms engaged in constructing skyscrapers, large commercial buildings, and factories. For five years, 1913–18, he was a partner in the architectural firm of Starrett and Van Vleck, which designed numerous commercial buildings, among them the Kaufmann and Baer department store in Pittsburgh (1915), and the Lasalle and Koch store in Toledo (1916).

In 1917 he was appointed head of the emergency construction section of the War Industries Board, charged with the construction of camps, hospitals, army bases, flying fields. With the building industry in a chaotic state, to build $150,000,000 worth of cantonments in three months seemed almost impossible; yet under his direction the buildings began to rise all over the country with amazing rapidity. Nominal profits of contractors were held within 3⅔ per cent., an extraordinary achievement. Construction under these conditions was of necessity extremely costly, however, and after the war was the subject of congressional investigation, in the course of which inexcusable and unwarranted accusations were made against Starrett, only to be proved groundless. After his discharge from the army, a colonel in the quartermaster corps, he became vice-president of the George A. Fuller Company, and directed the construction of a number of large office buildings in Tokio, especially designed to resist earthquakes. In 1922 with two of his brothers and Andrew J. Eken he founded the contracting firm of Starrett Brothers, Inc. (later Starrett Brothers and Eken, Inc.), builders of some of the most important American skyscrapers of the time, among them the nineteen-story Starrett Lehigh Terminal Building in New York, the Carew Tower in Cincinnati, Ohio, the forty-story Ramsey Tower in Oklahoma City, Okla., the seventy-story 40 Wall Street Building in New York, and the Empire State Building in New York. Starrett was perhaps the chief financial and business executive in this work. When the Starrett Corporation (N. Y.) was formed to handle the Starretts' large interests, which had branched out from pure construction to financing, he became president and as such coordinator of all their companies. He died in Madison, N. J., where he made his home. He was survived by his wife, Eloise Gedney of East Orange, N. J., whom he had married on June 14, 1900, and by a son and a daughter. He was a member of the Society of Military Engineers, the American Society of Civil Engineers, the American Society of Mechanical Engineers, and from 1914 to 1918 of the

American Institute of Architects. In 1917 he received the degree of B.S. in civil engineering as of the class of 1897 from the University of Michigan.

A gifted and persuasive writer, he contributed from time to time to magazines such things as "Marked 'Shop' " (*Atlantic Monthly,* July 1917), a story; "Building for Victory" (*Scribner's Magazine,* Nov. 1918), a description of his government work; and "New Construction in an Ancient Empire" (*Scribner's Magazine,* Sept. 1923), an account of his work in Japan. His *Skyscrapers and the Men Who Build Them* (1928) contains a brief history of the skyscraper, a vivid description of the tremendous complexity and the careful organization necessary in the building industry, and a simple exposition of the various trades and their part in the erection of a modern steel-frame structure. Perhaps the best popular exposition of the subject that has been produced, it is written with verve, drive, power. Of Starrett himself it reveals much. The chapters devoted to the financing of large buildings make strange and ironical reading in a time of depression. He seemed completely oblivious to all city-planning values except the financial, and quite overlooked the danger of unchecked speculation. Thus he writes, "There are opportunities in New York, Chicago, or any other large metropolis, for an enterprising operator to run a shoe-string into a fortune legitimately in one enterprise" (*Skyscrapers and the Men Who Build Them,* p. 110). He has been called "a great business executive with an engineering background" (*New York Times,* Mar. 27, 1932), and in all his connections—contracting, governmental, architectural—it was his power as an executive that distinguished him. As long as there was a job to do, to the doing of it he brought tremendous energy and clear vision; his imagination in his own line was vivid, his judgment acute and sure. But in the wider implications of the job, he had, apparently, little interest. He was essentially an executive, not a designer; a man of action rather than a man of thought.

[*Who's Who in America,* 1930–31; *Who's Who in Engineering,* 1931; A. R. Palmer, in *Trans. Am. Soc. of Civil Engineers,* vol. XCVIII (1933); "The Contributors' Column," in *Atlantic Monthly,* July 1917; *Architectural Record,* Apr. 1932, with portrait; letter signed G. C., in *N. Y. Times,* Mar. 31, 1932; obituary in *Herald Tribune* (N. Y.), Mar. 27, 1932; information from Ernest A. Van Vleck.]   T. F. H.

STATLER, ELLSWORTH MILTON (Oct. 26, 1863–Apr. 16, 1928), hotel owner, was born in Somerset County, Pa., the son of William Jackson and Mary (McKinney) Statler. His father, a German Reformed clergyman, tried to piece out his income by farming, but the family was large and the living was still hard. When Ellsworth was five his family moved to Bridgeport, Ohio, and at nine the boy went to work in a glass factory across the river in Wheeling, W. Va., where he endured intense heat for a wage of fifty cents—rising later to ninety cents—a day. At thirteen he found a position as bell-boy in a hotel in Wheeling, the McClure House. There he began polishing his manners and his language, taking the hotel bartender as his model at first, and advanced to the position of night clerk, then to that of day clerk; meanwhile he studied bookkeeping and the details of hotel management. He was not yet of age when he took over the billiard room and railroad-ticket concession in the hotel. A little later he opened a combination lunch room, billiard hall, and barber shop in Wheeling, from which he derived a comfortable yearly income.

In 1896 he bought the restaurant concession in the Ellicott Square Building, Buffalo, N. Y., and prospered with it. During the Pan-American Exposition in Buffalo, he built and operated a temporary frame hotel of 2,100 rooms near the exposition grounds. Though he made no profit on the venture, he acquired both reputation and experience, and in 1904 won the privilege of erecting the famous Inside Inn on the grounds of the Louisiana Purchase Exposition in St. Louis, Mo., upon which he cleared $280,000 profit. Before the summer was over he began building a hotel in Buffalo, the Statler (later the Buffalo), the first in the country in which each room had running ice-water and a bath. The cardinal rule of the house, and afterwards of his entire business, was "The guest is always right." He later built the New Statler in Buffalo and in rapid succession a Statler hotel each in St. Louis, Mo., Cleveland, Ohio, and Detroit, Mich., and took over the management of the Hotel Pennsylvania in New York. His last achievement was the Hotel Statler of Boston, opened in March 1927. He originated the practice of slipping a morning newspaper under the door of each guest's room, and is said to have been the first to install a radio connection in every room of a hotel. Several other devices to promote the ease and good will of guests were his, and his name became a symbol for comfort, courtesy, and efficient service. At his death his hotel properties were the largest owned by one man, their annual receipts being estimated at $25,000,000. In 1926 he was decorated by the French government with the Cross of the Legion of Honor. He was for several years president of the Hotel Men's Mutual Benefit Association of the United States and Canada. He was married twice: on Apr. 16, 1895, to Máry I. Manderbach (d. 1925) of Akron, Ohio, and on Apr. 30, 1927, to Alice M. Seidler, who had been his secretary for many years. He died in New York City of pneumonia, survived by his wife and by three of the four children he and his first wife had adopted.

[*Who's Who in America*, 1926–27; Walter Tittle, in *World's Work*, Nov. 1927; E. M. Statler, in *Am. Mag.*, May 1917, and *Mag. of Business*, Sept. 1927; *N. Y. Times*, May 1, 1927 (second marriage), Apr. 17, 18 (obituary and editorial), May 19 (will), 1928; obituaries and editorials in *N. Y. Herald Tribune* and *World* (N. Y.), Apr. 17, 1928.]   A. F. H.

STAUFFER, DAVID MCNEELY (Mar. 24, 1845–Feb. 5, 1913), civil engineer, editor, collector, author, was born in Richland, now the borough of Mount Joy, Lancaster County, Pa. His father, Jacob Stauffer, a patent lawyer and naturalist of reputation, was a descendant of John Stauffer, who emigrated from Switzerland to Pennsylvania in 1710; his mother, Mary Ann Knox McNeely, was of a Scotch-Irish family that settled in Pennsylvania about 1721. Graduating from the high school at Lancaster in 1862, at the head of his class, David was granted a scholarship in Franklin and Marshall College, but on Sept. 12, 1862, enlisted for service in the Civil War and saw action almost at once in the Antietam campaign. He subsequently attended classes for a while at the college, but could not remain out of the service, and early in 1864 was appointed a master's mate in the United States Navy and ordered to the *Alexandria* in the Mississippi Squadron under Rear Admiral David Dixon Porter [*q.v.*]. As mate he later commanded the same vessel, in May 1865 he was listed as acting ensign, and on Nov. 1, 1865, was honorably discharged.

At once he began his engineering career as rodman on surveys for the Columbia & Port Deposit Railroad in eastern Pennsylvania. He continued on surveys and construction work successively as assistant engineer of the Philadelphia & Reading Railroad and division engineer of the Allentown Railroad from 1868 until 1870, when the boom in railroad construction collapsed. Subsequently, from August 1870 until its completion in February 1876, he served as assistant engineer and consultant in the construction of the South Street Bridge over the Schuylkill River, Philadelphia. In this work he used compressed-air caissons in sinking foundations, a method which at the time was comparatively new to the United States, and his paper, "The Use of Compressed Air in Tubular Foundations" (*Journal of the Franklin Institute*, November

1872), based on study of the French and English practice, was used for a time as a textbook in several engineering schools. A fuller description of the work at South Street Bridge was published after its completion in the *Transactions of the American Society of Civil Engineers* (vol. VII, 1878). Meanwhile, as assistant chief engineer on the Bound Brook line of the Philadelphia & Reading Railroad, Stauffer had special charge of the construction of the Delaware Bridge, and upon its completion, June 1, 1876, he engaged in private practice, during which he made bridge plans for the City of Philadelphia. Beginning on Apr. 15, 1877, he was construction engineer for the Philadelphia Water Department, building the Frankford reservoir and pumping stations. Late in 1879 with the contractor R. A. Malone, he undertook the construction of the Dorchester Bay sewage tunnel at Boston, an inverted siphon some 9,000 feet long, with a bottom 180 feet below sea level. The seepage through the rock roof was so great that an enormous pumping plant involving large expense was necessary. The engineering problems he encountered are described in Stauffer's paper, "Shaft Sinking Under Difficulties at Dorchester Bay Tunnel" (*Transactions of the American Society of Civil Engineers*, vol. X, 1881). In December 1880, when the tunnel was nearly finished, he sold his interest in the contract to his partner, returned to Philadelphia, and was associated with the Philadelphia Bridge Works until September 1882, when he resigned and opened an office in New York as consulting engineer. In January 1883, he bought an interest in *Engineering News*, with which he was connected in an editorial capacity until he sold his interest in 1907. In addition to his contributions to the technical magazines and transactions of professional societies, he was the author of *Modern Tunnel Practice* (1906).

Stauffer will be remembered for his avocations almost as much as for his professional success. He traveled extensively and was an enthusiastic collector of autographic and illustrative material relating to the colonial and revolutionary history of America, and in connection with his collecting made thousands of pen-and-ink and watercolor drawings. He designed a number of bookplates (see *D. McN. Stauffer: His Bookplates*, n.d.). Many of the illustrations in *Engineering News* were from his pen. Early in his career he began a collection of thousands of prints illustrating the first four centuries of the art of engraving on wood and copper, and in his later years this hobby absorbed most of his time and energy. In 1907 he published *American Engrav-*

ers upon *Copper and Steel* (2 vols.), which remains a standard work in its field. He was also interested in public affairs, and was long a member of the Palisades Interstate Park Commission for the preservation of the Palisades of the Hudson River. On Apr. 19, 1892, he married Florence Scribner, daughter of G. Hilton Scribner, secretary of state of New York under Governor Dix. He died at his home in Yonkers.

[*Who's Who in America,* 1912–13; J. W. Jordan, in *Pa. Mag. of Hist. and Biog.,* Apr. 1913; *Engineering News,* Feb. 13, 1913; *Sun* (N. Y.), Feb. 7, 1913.]

B. A. R.

STAUGHTON, WILLIAM (Jan. 4, 1770– Dec. 12, 1829), Baptist minister and educator, was born at Coventry, Warwickshire, England, the oldest child of Sutton and Keziah Staughton. At seventeen he entered Bristol Baptist College, where he showed such promise that in 1793 he was called to the church at Northampton to succeed Dr. John Ryland, who became president at Bristol. He early looked to America as his future field of labor, so when Dr. Richard Furman [*q.v.*] wrote to Dr. John Rippon of London asking him to suggest "a young man of promise and character" (Lynd, *post,* p. 27) for South Carolina, he went supported by strong commendations. He arrived at Charleston, S. C., in the fall of 1793 and there married Maria Hanson before January 1794. They had six children. For about a year and a half he supplied at Georgetown, S. C., a church soon being formed. In the summer of 1795 he went to New York, became head of an academy at Bordentown, N. J., and on June 17, 1797, was ordained there. Moving in 1798 to Burlington, where there was a larger academy, he organized a small Baptist church which he served as pastor. He edited several works in the classics and for his talents received the degree of Doctor of Divinity from the College of New Jersey (later Princeton). After a tour in the West, where he considered settling, he was called in 1805 to the First Baptist Church in Philadelphia. Although several groups were dismissed to form other churches, there was a relatively large increase in membership. In 1811, partly on account of some internal tension over his English birth (superficially indicated by the remark of the sexton regarding a smoking stove, "There must be an Englishman in the stovepipe"), he became pastor of what was known as the Sansom Street Baptist Church, a new church in the western part of the city. In 1814 he took an active part in organizing the Triennial Convention and as its corresponding secretary until 1826, was concerned with the constant and varied problems of the foreign missionary enterprise.

As the need for better-trained ministers stirred the Baptists to provide schools for their education, it was to Staughton they turned for practical leadership. For many years he had been taking young men into his home in Philadelphia to begin their theological education; with the formation in 1812 of the Baptist Education Society of the Middle States, he was designated its tutor. So intimate was his connection with it that the educational institution could hardly be distinguished from his home. His reputation as a classical scholar was heightened by his editions of *The Works of Virgil . . . To Which is Added a Large Variety of Botanical, Mythological, and Historical Notes,* and of Edward Wetenhall's *A Compendious System of Greek Grammar,* both published in 1813. When the Triennial Convention took up its educational task more definitely in 1817, the incipient institution at Philadelphia was recognized as its theological department, with Staughton as principal and Irah Chase [*q.v.*] as professor of languages and Biblical literature. More definite plans for the organization of what was soon called Columbian College (later George Washington University) were adopted in 1818, but the transfer to Washington, D. C., was not made until September 1821. Staughton remained most of the time in Philadelphia until the fall of 1823, although he was installed as president on Jan. 9, 1822, with professorial responsibilities in "General History, Belles Lettres, Rhetoric and Moral Philosophy" in the classical department, and in "Divinity and Pulpit Eloquence" in the theological department. From the beginning he visualized a university of national scope rendering service broader than that required by denominational needs, a conception which found its correlate in the world-mission ideal so dominant in Luther Rice [*q.v.*], the chief financial agent for the college. The effective forces in the development of collegiate education during that period, however, were largely stimulated by denominational loyalties and local economic considerations, rarely entirely divorced from speculative land interests. Competing educational institutions were rapidly forming, financial complications arose, and in 1829 Staughton resigned the presidency. He was soon chosen president of Georgetown College in Kentucky. Starting for his new field, he died as he was passing through Washington. A few months before his death, on Aug. 27, 1829, he married Anna Claypoole Peale [*q.v.*], who survived him. Hampered as he was later at Columbian College, he nevertheless achieved a far-reaching and significant educational influence during the years at Philadelphia, when largely through his own direct personal instruction he trained young men who became outstanding leaders in religion and education.

[The standard work on Staughton is that by his son-in-law, the Rev. S. W. Lynd, *Memoir of the Rev. William Staughton, D.D.* (1834), which contains much source material; little is added in W. B. Sprague, *Annals Am. Pulpit*, vol. VI (1860), and William Cathcart, *The Baptist Encyc.* (1881). For a few other details, see a letter by Irah Chase, in *Baptist Memorial*, Apr. 15, 1842, and obituary in *Daily Nat. Intelligencer* (Washington, D. C.), Dec. 14, 1829.]   W. H. A.

STAYTON, JOHN WILLIAM (Dec. 24, 1830–July 5, 1894), jurist, was born in Washington County, Ky., the son of Robert G. and Harriet (Pirtle) Stayton, both descendants of early settlers of the state. When he was two years old the family removed to Paducah in the western part of Kentucky, a region then sparsely settled. The death of his father two years later placed the burden of his support and education on his mother. Her death in 1844 left him an orphan at the age of fourteen. The next four years were spent on his grandfather's farm, where he performed farm labor during the summer and attended the country schools in the autumn and winter. He also read all the books he could find.

At the age of seventeen he made up his mind to prepare himself for the bar. Since his guardian was unwilling that he should spend his meager resources on a college education, he left the farm and apprenticed himself to a blacksmith in order to learn the trade and earn the money to pay for his legal training. Upon attaining his majority he continued to work at his trade and at the same time carried on a systematic course of study. At twenty-four he began reading law under the written direction of his mother's brother, Henry Pirtle of Louisville, Ky. In the fall of 1855 he entered the law school of Louisville University, from which he was graduated the following March with the degree of bachelor of laws. In November 1856 he removed to Texas, settling the following year at Pleasanton, south of San Antonio, where for a time he operated a blacksmith shop and conducted a law office. His law practice, however, soon absorbed all his time and energies. In 1858 he was elected to the office of district attorney and was reëlected in 1860. At the end of his term of office he enlisted in the Confederate army as a private in Capt. Lewis Maverick's company, but later he was commissioned to raise a company of cavalry, which he commanded during the remainder of the war. Immediately after the war, since the courts were all closed, he earned a livelihood by teaching school for a year. In 1866, in partnership with Samuel C. Lackey, he opened a law office at Clinton, Tex., then the county seat of DeWitt County. In 1871 Maj. A. H. Phillips of Victoria was admitted to the partnership, the firm name becoming Phillips, Lackey & Stayton, and Stayton removed with his family to Victoria. Phillips in 1878 retired and two years later Stayton's son, Robert Weldon, and R. J. Kleberg joined the firm, which was thereafter known as Staytons, Lackey & Kleberg. In 1875 Stayton served as a member of the constitutional convention. Gov. O. M. Roberts appointed him associate justice of the supreme court in 1881 to fill the vacancy caused by the resignation of Chief Justice George F. Moore, and he was elected for a full term the following year. In 1888, upon the retirement of Asa H. Willie [*q.v.*], he became chief justice. In this position he served most acceptably until his death some six years later at the home of his daughter, at Tyler.

In 1856, immediately after his graduation from law school, he married Eliza Jane ("Jennie") Weldon, daughter of Abraham and Mary Jane (Rutter) Weldon, and grand-niece of United States Attorney-General Felix Grundy [*q.v.*]. They had one son and two daughters, all of whom survived him. A grandson, Robert Weldon Stayton, served for several years on the commission of appeals of the supreme court, and became professor of law at the University of Texas.

[87 *Texas Reports*, v–xviii; J. D. Lynch, *The Bench and Bar of Tex.* (1885); L. E. Daniell, *Personnel of Tex. State Gov., with Sketches of Representative Men of Tex.* (1892), pp. 80–81; J. H. Davenport, *The Hist. of the Supreme Court of the State of Tex.* (copr. 1917); *Dallas Morning News*, and *Houston Post*, July 6, 1894; information from grandson.]   C. S. P—s.

STEARNS, ABEL (Feb. 9, 1798–Aug. 23, 1871), California pioneer, was born in Lunenburg, Mass., the son of Levi and Elizabeth (Goodrich) Stearns, and a descendant of Isaac Stearns who emigrated from England to Salem, Mass., in 1630. About 1826 he went to Mexico, where he became naturalized. In July 1829 he arrived at Monterey, expecting to obtain a land grant. Suspected by the Mexican governor, Manuel Victoria, of some political design, he was banished, but in 1831 he returned and joined in the movement by which Victoria was overthrown. Two years later he settled in Los Angeles as a trader in hides and liquors, and grew prosperous, though he was often in trouble with the authorities because of alleged smuggling. He was chosen *sindico* (fiscal agent) of the village in 1836. Ordered by Gov. Mariano Chico to leave the country, he joined in a revolution which placed Juan Bautista Alvarado in power and made California for two years (1836–38) an independent republic. About 1840 he married Maria Francisca Paula Arcadia Bandini, a woman of great beauty and charm, and soon afterward acquired the extensive Los Alamitos ranch. In November 1842, more than five years before the discoveries on the American River, he sent to the Philadelphia mint twenty ounces of gold taken from the San Feliciano placers, near the present Newhall. He engaged in stock-raising, bought more lands, and by the time of the conquest was doubtless the wealthiest man in California. He built the most imposing residence in the village, which he named *El Palacio*, and entertained lavishly. In 1844–45 he took part in the revolution which expelled Gov. Manuel Micheltorena. Hating the Mexicans but admiring the Californians, he sided with the party that was attempting to bring California into the Union by peaceful means. With the outbreak of hostilities in 1846, however, he remained neutral, and in the following year, under American rule, became again the village *sindico*. He was a member of the constitutional convention of 1849. In 1858 he built the Arcadia block, the largest and most expensive structure south of San Francisco. Although during the drought of 1864 he suffered staggering losses, before his death seven years later he managed to recover much of his former wealth. He died suddenly at the Grand Hotel in San Francisco and was buried in Los Angeles. His wife survived him; there were no children.

He was a tall, well-formed man, with a homely visage which won him the nickname of *Cara de Caballo*, "Horse-Face." A personal encounter in 1835 had left him with a scar about the mouth and an impediment in his speech. He was quick-tempered, with strong prejudices, but was hospitable and generous. At various times he held local political office. He was deeply interested in education, and just before his death had planned to establish a foundation at the projected University of Southern California.

[A. S. Van Wagenen, *Geneal. and Memoirs of Isaac Stearns and His Descendants* (1901); H. H. Bancroft, *Hist. of Cal.*, vol. V (1886), pp. 732–33; *Sixty Years in Southern Cal.* (2nd ed., 1926), ed. by M. H. and M. R. Newmark; *A Hist. of Cal. and an Extended Hist. of Los Angeles and Environs* (1915), vol. III, ed. by J. M. Guinn; C. D. Willard, *The Herald's Hist. of Los Angeles City* (1901); H. D. Barrows, "Don Abel Stearns," *Hist. Soc. of Southern Cal. Pubs.*, vol. IV (1897–99); obituary in *Daily Alta California* (San Francisco), Aug. 24, 1871.]   W. J. G.

STEARNS, ASAHEL (June 17, 1774–Feb. 5, 1839), lawyer, descended from Isaac Stearns who became a freeman of Watertown, Mass., in 1631, was born in Lunenburg, Worcester County, Mass., the son of the Hon. Josiah and Mary (Corey) Stearns and a first cousin of Abel

Stearns [*q.v.*]. After graduating from Harvard College in 1797 he studied law in the office of Timothy Bigelow, of Groton. In 1800 he married Frances Wentworth (Whitney) Shepard, daughter of Benjamin Whitney of Hollis, N. H., and widow of Daniel Shepard. They had a son and a daughter who grew to maturity.

Settling after his marriage in that part of Chelmsford which is now Lowell, Mass., Stearns practised law there until 1815, when he moved to Charlestown. In 1813 he had been appointed district attorney for Middlesex County, in which position he served until 1832, except for the period 1815–17, when he represented his district in Congress. In 1817–18 he served also as representative in the General Court, and in 1830–31 as state senator.

By 1817 his character and attainments as a sound and scholarly lawyer had so impressed the community that when in that year the Harvard Law School was established under Chief Justice Isaac Parker [*q.v.*] Stearns was appointed University Professor of Law. He accepted the appointment with diffidence; the venture was an experiment, and in practice it amounted to the opening of an office by Stearns in connection with the university, in which he devoted part of his time to delivering lectures, conducting moot courts, and otherwise supervising the work of the students. Although he was not very successful, he retained the post of professor until the reorganization of the law school in 1829, when under Joseph Story and John Hooker Ashmun [*qq.v.*] its real history as an educational force began. Stearns's professorship was not wholly unproductive, however, for in connection with his teaching he prepared a series of lectures, the substance of which he published in 1824 under the title, *A Summary of the Law and Practice of Real Actions*. This work proved to be one of the notable early American law books and was welcomed by a bar in need of accurate available information on technical procedure.

While Stearns was not successful as a pioneer law professor, his reputation as a sound lawyer continued, and in 1832 he was appointed one of the commissioners under the chairmanship of Charles Jackson [*q.v.*] to make the first real revision of the Massachusetts statutes. Adopted, with few changes, by the legislature on Nov. 4, 1835, *The Revised Statutes of the Commonwealth of Massachusetts* (1836) set a standard for such work and, with the commissioners' notes accompanying their report, remains of great practical value to the courts and to the bar. Stearns had previously, as joint commissioner with Lemuel Shaw [*q.v.*], compiled the fourth and fifth volumes (1823) of *Private and Special Statutes of . . . Massachusetts.* His health began to fail about 1836 and although in 1837 he presided over a board of arbitration of an important case from the state of Maine, he gradually retired from active work and died in 1839. In addition to his professional activities, he was an officer in various banks and in 1833 was treasurer of the Society for Propagating the Gospel Among the Indians.

[A portrait of Stearns by Harding is in the possession of the Harvard Law School. For biog. data see *Law Reporter,* Apr. 1839; *The Centennial Hist. of the Harvard Law School, 1817–1917* (1918); A. P. Peabody, *Harvard Reminiscences* (1888); *Biog. Dir. Am. Cong.* (1928); A. S. Van Wagenen, *Geneal. and Memoirs of Isaac Stearns and His Descendants* (1901); *Boston Daily Advertiser,* Feb. 8, 1839.]   F. W. G.

STEARNS, EBEN SPERRY (Dec. 23, 1819–Apr. 11, 1887), educator, was born in Bedford, Mass., the youngest son of the Rev. Samuel and Abigail (French) Stearns. He was descended from a long line of clergymen and teachers, the original ancestor in America having been Isaac Stearns, who came from England and settled in Watertown, Mass., in 1630. Three of his brothers also became clergymen, one of whom was William Augustus Stearns [*q.v.*]. Eben, who gave up the use of his name Ebenezer for the shorter form early in youth, was graduated from the Phillips Academy, Andover, Mass., in 1837, and received the B.A. degree from Harvard in 1841. He taught in a school for young women at Ipswich, Mass., and at Portland, Me., before receiving the M.A. degree from Harvard in 1846. Afterwards he organized and acted as principal of the Newburyport, Mass., Female High School until 1849, when he succeeded Cyrus Peirce [*q.v.*] as principal of the normal school at West Newton. He remained as principal when the school, the first of its kind in the United States, was moved to Framingham in 1853. Two years later he was elected principal of the Albany (New York) Female Academy, where he remained until he was appointed the first president of the Robinson Female Academy at Exeter, N. H., in 1869. A strict disciplinarian, he often quoted to students and visitors that "order is heaven's first law." In addition to the usual normal and classical studies, he inaugurated and taught personally a class in household science.

In September 1875 he was selected by officials of the Peabody Fund as first president of the new State Normal School at Nashville, Tenn., and a few months later he was appointed, by the board of trust, Chancellor of the University of Nashville. At his inauguration the school had thirteen pupils; when he died it had over two hundred. At the beginning any prospective teacher, regardless of previous training, could enter the school if he could pass an elementary examination, but he soon raised that standard so that high school graduates only were admitted. Stearns was an ardent missionary of popular education, and emphasized in many speeches that free government was based on the intelligence of its people. He rapidly prepared teachers to meet the new demand in the South and kept in close touch, through correspondence and occasional tours, with Southern schools and county superintendents of education, all of his work being accomplished under the close supervision of the Peabody Fund. He also made a vigorous effort to beautify Southern colleges, and tree-planting became a yearly rite at Nashville. He prevented the removal of the State Normal College, as it came to be known in 1878, to Georgia in 1880, and secured from a reluctant legislature the first grant of aid to the state normal school. A colorless but efficient administrator, Stearns left small imprint of his own personality on the school. The first two years he taught didactics; after that he was concerned only with administrative problems. In that field he was highly successful, leaving the school in good financial condition. He was indefatigable in trying to raise educational standards throughout the South. He was married to Ellen Augusta Kuhn, of Boston, on Aug. 27, 1854; she died in 1873. He was again married in 1880 to Betty Irwin, of Marianna, Fla. Their only child died in infancy, but his widow and three children of his first wife survived him. He is buried at Boston, Mass.

[Information from the family; Stearns's scrapbook and correspondence in the Peabody College Library, Nashville, Tenn.; Avis Stearns Van Wagenen, *Geneal. and Memoirs of Isaac Stearns and His Descendants* (1901); R. C. Winthrop, *Tribute to Eben Sperry Stearns* (1887); C. M. Fuess, *Men of Andover* (1928); E. S. Stearns, *Hist. Sketch of the Normal Coll.* (1885); L. S. Merriam, *Higher Education in Tenn., Bur. of Education, Circular of Information, No. 5* (1893); R. H. White, *Development of the Tenn. State Educ. Organization* (1929); *Daily American,* Nashville, Apr. 12, 1887.]   E. W. P.

STEARNS, FREDERIC PIKE (Nov. 11, 1851–Dec. 1, 1919), civil engineer, son of William Henry Clark Stearns and Mary (Hobbs) Hill Stearns, was born at Calais, Me. He was a descendant of Isaac Stearns, who became a freeman of Watertown, Mass., in 1631. After attending the Calais public schools he worked for a short time for a local business concern, but when he was eighteen went to Boston, found a job with the city engineering department, and began to study civil engineering. Here he came under the influence of such able engineers as James B. Francis and Hiram F. Mills [*qq.v.*], and by his diligence and power of application gained proficiency in his field and laid a solid foundation for later achievement.

By 1872 he was engaged in responsible work upon the Sudbury River water supply of Boston and in 1880 he became division engineer on the sewage tunnel under Dorchester Bay. In 1886 Stearns was called by the State Board of Health to become its chief engineer. This board, newly reorganized, had been placed in charge of the state's inland waters, and empowered to advise the various municipalities with regard to sanitation and water supply. This was pioneer work, requiring great sense and soundness in making decisions, and the influence which the Board acquired was due largely to the good judgment, tact, and fairness of its chief engineer. His exhaustive studies of water supplies and the means of controlling and improving them have become the basis for practice in many other states. He also made plans for the sewerage of the Mystic and Charles River valleys which were adopted and carried out, and planned the improvement of the Charles River Basin—later carried out with his advice as consultant—by which the foul tidal estuary of the Charles was converted into a beautiful fresh-water basin.

His most notable piece of work as engineer for the State Board of Health was the design, utilizing the Nashua River, for the metropolitan water supply of Boston and its vicinity. When this plan was adopted in 1895, he became chief engineer of the new metropolitan water board which carried it to completion in 1907 at a cost of $40,000,000. These water works were widely recognized as examples of the best practice in this field. They included as an innovation a provision by which the fall of water into the aqueduct was utilized for the development of power, a feature productive of increased revenue for the metropolitan water district.

After completion of the Boston metropolitan water supply, Stearns withdrew as chief engineer and became consultant for the board as well as for many other municipalities. His more important projects included water-supply problems of New York City, Baltimore, Los Angeles, Hartford, Conn., Providence, R. I., Rochester, N. Y., Worcester, Mass., and Winnipeg, Manitoba, and sewerage for Baltimore, Chicago, and Pittsburgh. He also did much important consultation work upon dams and other difficult structures. In 1905 he was appointed by President Theodore Roosevelt as a member of the board of consulting engineers to consider plans for the Panama Canal. He was one of the minority who advocated a lock canal, the type which

was adopted. He later served upon another board appointed by President Roosevelt to accompany Secretary of War William H. Taft [q.v.] to Panama and subsequently to revise the plans for the Gatun dam.

Stearns published many important papers in the engineering field, among the more significant of which were the following: "Description of Some Experiments on the Flow of Water Made during the Construction of Works for Conveying the Water of Sudbury River to Boston," with Alphonse Fteley (Transactions of the American Society of Civil Engineers, vol. XII, 1883) ; "On the Current-Meter" (Ibid.) ; "Experiments on the Flow of Water in a 48-Inch Pipe" (Ibid., vol. XIV, 1885) ; "Disposal of Sewage in Massachusetts" (Ibid., vol. XVIII, 1888) ; "The Effect of Storage upon the Quality of Water" (Journal of the New England Water Works Association, March 1891) ; "The Selection of Sources of Water Supply" (Ibid., March 1892) ; "The Development of Water Supplies and Water-Supply Engineering" (Transactions of the American Society of Civil Engineers, vol. LVI, 1906). He also contributed many discussions of other papers and was chairman of the special committee of the American Society of Civil Engineers which reported upon methods of evaluating public utilities (Transactions, vol. LXXXI, 1918, p. 1311), as well as of the committee upon yield of drainage areas of the New England Water Works Association (Journal, December 1914), which presented a report of much value that has been widely used. He was active in professional organizations and served as president of the American Society of Civil Engineers and of the Boston Society of Civil Engineers.

On June 21, 1876, Stearns married Addie C. Richardson of Framingham, Mass., who died two years before her husband. He was survived by two sons, both engineers.

[A. S. Van Wagenen, Geneal. and Memoirs of Isaac Stearns and His Descendants (1901) ; Trans. Am. Soc. Civil Engineers, vol. LXXXIII (1921) ; Jour. of the New England Water Works Asso., Mar. 1920 ; Who's Who in America, 1920–21 ; Boston Transcript, Dec. 2, 1919.]   H. K. B.

STEARNS, GEORGE LUTHER (Jan. 8, 1809–Apr. 9, 1867), Free-Soiler, was born in Medford, Mass., the eldest son of Luther and Mary (Hall) Stearns and the descendant of Charles Stearns who became a freeman of Watertown, Mass., in 1646. Such formal education as the boy received was in a preparatory school for boys established by his father, a physician. At the age of fifteen he began his business career in Brattleboro, Vt., in 1827 entered a ship-chandlery firm in Boston, and in 1835 returned to Medford to manufacture linseed oil and to marry, on Jan. 31, 1836, Mary Ann Train. He became a Unitarian and was prominent in church activities. After the death of his wife in 1840, he reëntered business in Boston, at first with a ship-chandlery company but later, very successfully, as a manufacturer of lead pipe. By 1840 he felt strongly enough on the subject of slavery to support James G. Birney and the Liberty party. His marriage, on Oct. 12, 1843, to Mary Elizabeth Preston probably furthered his interest in the anti-slavery cause for his wife was a niece of Lydia Maria Child [q.v.]. In 1848, as a Conscience Whig, he liberally supported the Free-soil campaign with his money. He was greatly disturbed by the passage of the Fugitive Slave Law in 1850 and is known to have aided at least one slave to escape. He was among the leaders in the movement that put Charles Sumner in the federal Senate, and later, as a member of the famous Bird Club, he played a considerable part in the rise of the Republican party in Massachusetts, becoming particularly interested in the political fortunes of his friend John A. Andrew.

He was in the group that, in 1856, raised a subscription to equip the free state forces in Kansas with Sharpe's rifles. The subsequently successful operations of the Kansas committee of Massachusetts, of which he became chairman, were largely due to the willingness with which he contributed his time and money. In 1857 he met John Brown and made him the committee's agent to receive the arms and ammunition for the defense of Kansas and also aided in purchasing a farm for the Brown family at North Elba, N. Y. Indeed, from this time on Stearns practically put his purse at Brown's disposal. That he ever appreciated Brown's responsibility for the murders on the Potawatomi is doubtful, but in March 1858 Brown confided to him the general outline of his proposed raid into Virginia, an enterprise that Stearns approved, as did S. G. Howe, Theodore Parker, T. W. Higginson and Franklin B. Sanborn [qq.v.]. These five men constituted an informal committee in Massachusetts to aid Brown in whatever attack he might make on slavery. Stearns acted as treasurer for the enterprise in New England. Gerrit Smith of New York and Martin F. Conway of Kansas were also in the secret. Stearns, however, does not appear to have known just when and where Brown proposed to strike, and the blow at Harpers Ferry took him by surprise. On learning of Brown's capture he authorized two prominent Kansas jayhawkers to go to Brown's relief if they thought they could effect his rescue. Stearns

himself, becoming somewhat apprehensive of the attitude of the Federal government, fled with Howe to Canada. He soon returned, however, and appeared before the Mason committee of the Senate that was investigating the Brown conspiracy. No further action was taken by the government respecting Stearns.

During the Civil War, upon Governor Andrew's authorization he recruited many negro soldiers for the 54th and 55th Massachusetts regiments, especially from the middle and western states. So satisfactory were his efforts that in the summer of 1863 Secretary Stanton commissioned him as major with headquarters in Philadelphia and directed him to recruit colored regiments for the Federal government. A few months later he was sent to Nashville, where he successfully continued his work until a misunderstanding with Stanton led him to resign from the army early in 1864. In 1865 he established the *Right Way*, a paper that supported radical Republican policies, particularly negro suffrage, and attained a circulation of 60,000, largely at his expense. He died of pneumonia while on a business trip to New York.

[F. P. Stearns, *The Life and Public Services of George Luther Stearns* (1907) and *Cambridge Sketches* (1905); O. G Villard, *John Brown* (1910); J. F. Rhodes, *Hist. of the U. S.*, vol. II (1892); *Sen. Report, No. 278,* 36 Cong., 1 Sess. (1860); A. S. Van Wagenen, *Geneal. and Memoirs of Charles and Nathaniel Stearns, and Their Descendants* (1901).]   W. R. W.

STEARNS, HENRY PUTNAM (Apr. 18, 1828–May 27, 1905), physician, was born in Sutton, Mass., the son of Asa and Polly (Putnam) Stearns, and a descendant of Charles Stearns, who became a freeman in Watertown in 1646. He was fitted for college in Monson, Mass., and received the B.A. degree from Yale in 1853, the M.D. degree two years later, studied medicine at Harvard, and finally completed his medical studies at the University of Edinburgh, Scotland. He was married to Annie Elizabeth Storrier of Dumfries, Scotland, on Aug. 29, 1857, and they had three children. On his return to the United States Stearns established himself in private practice in Marlboro, Mass., and remained there for three years before going to Hartford, Conn., where he made his home until his death. He achieved some distinction as a general practitioner, and when the Civil War broke out he was made surgeon of the 1st Connecticut Regiment. After three months he became surgeon of volunteers, was on the staff of General Grant, and was discharged from service in August 1865. During the greater part of that period, he was medical director of United States hospitals, stationed for the most part at St. Louis, Mo., Nashville, Tenn., and Paducah, Ky.

He spent eight years in general professional work in Hartford after the war, and in 1874 was appointed to succeed Dr. J. S. Butler and Eli Todd [*q.v.*], as superintendent of the Hartford Retreat for the Insane. He went abroad to familiarize himself with theory and practice in France and Great Britain, and at Cheadle, England, observed the successes of the "cottage system" which he later established at the Hartford institution. This system permitted patients to be treated without unnecessary limitation of their activities. During his years at the Retreat, he found time for numerous reports and monographs on various phases of insanity, which attracted wide comment. *Insanity, Its Causes and Prevention* was published in 1883, and *Lectures on Mental Diseases* in 1893. *Physiology vs. Philosophy* (1880) appeared first as an article in the *New Englander*, July 1880; *The Care of Some Classes of the Chronic Insane* (1881), in the *Archives of Medicine*, February 1881; and *Heredity, a Factor in the Etiology of Insanity* (1897), in the *American Journal of Insanity*, October 1897. Stearns classified mental disease according to causes and pathology. He suggested the appointment of physicians to the National Board of Health, and advocated education of the public in the prevention of insanity. For eighteen years he lectured at Yale on mental disease. He was a member of the Connecticut Medical Society and served as president 1898–99; he was a charter member of the Hartford Medical Society and of the New England Psychological Society, a member of the Association of Medical Superintendents of American Institutions for the Insane, and honorary member of the British Psychological Society and the Boston Medico-Psychological Society.

[Unpublished notes on Stearns by Dr. Henry Barnard; *Who's Who in America*, 1906–07; A. S. Van Wagenen, *Geneal. and Memoirs of Charles and Nathaniel Stearns, and Their Descendants* (1901); H. A. Kelly, W. L. Burrage, *Am. Medic. Biographies* (1920); *Obit. Records of Grads., Bull. of Yale Univ.*, July 1905; G. W. Russell, article on Stearns in *Proc. Conn. State Medic. Soc.* (1906); *New England Medic. Monthly*, Aug. 1885; *Am. Jour. of Insanity*, Oct. 1890; *Hartford Times*, May 27, 1905.]			C. C. B—e.

STEARNS, IRVING ARIEL (Sept. 12, 1845–Oct. 5, 1920), mining engineer, was born in Rushville, Ontario County, N. Y., the son of George Washington and Miranda (Tufts) Stearns. He was a descendant of Charles Stearns, an Englishman, who was admitted a freeman at Watertown, Mass., May 6, 1646. His father, a farmer and county judge, moved to Michigan in 1867 and subsequently became editor of the Coldwater *Semi-Weekly Republican*. Stearns was educated at Rushville Academy, Benedict's Collegiate Institute, Rochester, N. Y., and Rensselaer Polytechnic Institute, Troy, where he was graduated in 1868. He remained at the Institute for one year as assistant in analytical chemistry, then spent two years in Wilkes-Barre, Pa., as engineer in the office of Richard P. Rothwell [*q.v.*]. In 1871 he became superintendent of the McNeal Coal & Iron Company of Schuylkill County, Pa., and the following year, when Rothwell moved to New York, succeeded to the latter's business. As consulting engineer he examined and reported on mining properties in Pennsylvania, Virginia, West Virginia, Arkansas, Colorado, California, Wyoming, Idaho, and Utah. He was concerned with the building of bridges at Shickshinny and Pittston, Pa., and surveyed and mapped a great number of mines in the anthracite region. He was in charge of designing and carrying out for the Lehigh Valley Railroad Company improvements at Buffalo, N. Y., including canals, docks, and coal-stocking plant.

His prominence as a mining engineer brought him appointment in 1885 as manager of the coal interests of the Pennsylvania Railroad. He managed these properties with great efficiency, installing at Shamokin the first high-pressure boilers in the anthracite region; introducing electricity for underground haulage at the Lykens Valley colliery in 1886—its first use for such a purpose in the United States; and introducing high pressure compressed air for haulage in 1895. He also made radical improvements in the processes of mining and preparing anthracite coal. He retained the managership of the Pennsylvania's coal properties until July 1897, when he was chosen president of the Cross Creek Coal Company, of Coxe Brothers & Company, Inc., of the Delaware, Susquehanna & Schuylkill Railroad Company, and of Coxe Iron Manufacturing Company. He headed these organizations until the Coxe properties were bought in 1905 by the Lehigh Valley Coal Company, of which he became a director.

Retiring at this time from active business, he accepted in November 1906 election as first president of the Wilkes-Barre Park Commission, throwing himself enthusiastically into its work and during his ten years' incumbency securing almost the entire park system through gifts to the city. He had been one of the organizers of the American Institute of Mining Engineers, and retained his membership until the end of his life. At Wilkes-Barre, Nov. 20, 1872, he married Clorinda Shoemaker, daughter of Lazarus Denison and Esther (Wadhams) Shoemaker. He had two sons and one daughter, but only the latter survived him. His death occurred at Wilkes-Barre in his seventy-sixth year.

[*Trans. Am. Inst. Mining and Metallurgical Engineers*, vol. LXVI (1921); *Mining and Metallurgy*, Nov. 1920; *Coal Age*, Oct. 28, 1920; A. S. Van Wagenen, *Geneal. and Memoirs of Charles and Nathaniel Stearns, and Their Descendants* (1901); *Proc. and Colls. Wyoming Hist. and Geol. Soc.* (Pa.), vol. XVIII (1923); *Public Ledger* (Phila.), Oct. 6, 1920.]   B. A. R.

STEARNS, JOHN NEWTON (May 24, 1829–Apr. 21, 1895), temperance reformer, born at New Ipswich, N. H., was the son of Jesse and Lucinda (Davis) Stearns and a descendant of Isaac Stearns who came to New England in 1630. Jesse Stearns was a school-teacher; many of his family became reformers. John graduated from New Ipswich Academy, but poor health prevented his attending college. At the age of seven he joined the celebrated "Cold Water Army," donned its blue and white uniform, and paraded the streets of New Ipswich singing "The Teetotalers Are Coming." This refrain became the battle-cry of his whole existence. He joined the Cadets of Temperance in 1839, the Band of Hope in 1842, and was among the first members of the Order of the Sons of Temperance in 1848. The last, a fraternal order designed to strengthen reformed (though backsliding) inebriates, sought to promote temperance by forbidding its members all alcoholic potations.

Thus far Stearns had taught school in his natal village, but about 1850 he settled in New York City and became a magazine salesman. He was soon conspicuous in Sunday school and temperance movements, especially in Brooklyn, liberally distributing buttons, badges, and temperance pledges. In December 1853 he purchased *Merry's Museum*, a children's magazine founded by S. G. Goodrich [q.v.], and the following year, while canvassing for his magazine in Utica, N. Y., he met and married Matilda C. Loring.

In 1865 he was chosen publishing agent of the National Temperance Society and editor of the *National Temperance Advocate*, the first issue of which appeared in January 1866. In that year he was made Most Worthy Patriarch of the National Division of North America, the highest office in the Sons of Temperance. During twenty-seven years he edited the *National Temperance Almanac and Teetotaler's Year Book*. Active in every prohibition group, he held from 1876 to 1878 the office of Most Worthy Templar of the Supreme Council of the Templars of Honor and of Temperance of North America. For thirty years he was responsible for a flood of prohibitionist propaganda: books, almanacs, hymn-books, pamphlets. All were paste-pot compilations, bombastic and vacuous. He estimated that $1,500,000 had been collected and spent in printing and distributing the publications which he edited. Among these were the *Temperance Hymn-Book* (1869); *The Temperance Speaker* (1869); *Water Spouts* (1878); *National Temperance Hymn and Song Book* (1880); *Prohibition Does Prohibit; or, Prohibition Not a Failure* (1882); *The Prohibition Songster* (1884); *Foot-Prints of Temperance Pioneers* (1885); *Temperance in All Nations* (2 vols., 1893), reprinting speeches delivered at the World's Temperance Congress at Chicago in June 1893, which he had eagerly organized. He died in Brooklyn of heart failure, resulting from bronchial asthma.

[*N. Y. Tribune*, Apr. 22, and *N. Y. Times*, Apr. 23, 1895; *A Noble Life . . . A Memorial Pamphlet* (undated, unsigned; copy in N. Y. Pub. Lib.); excellent collection of Stearns's works in N. Y. Pub. Lib.; J. A. Krout, *The Origins of Prohibition* (1925); A. S. Van Wagenen, *Geneal. and Memoirs of Isaac Stearns and His Descendants* (1901); information from Charles Montague of Ithaca, N. Y., and Frank Ryan of New York City.]   F. M.

STEARNS, OLIVER (June 3, 1807–July 18, 1885), Unitarian clergyman and theologian, born in Lunenburg, Mass., was through his father, Maj. Thomas Stearns, descended from Isaac Stearns, who was admitted freeman of Watertown, Mass., in 1631. Through his mother, Priscilla, daughter of Hon. Charles Cushing of Hingham, Mass., he was a descendant of Charles Chauncy [q.v.], the second president of Harvard College. He was a nephew of Asahel Stearns [q.v.], and uncle of Luther Stearns Cushing [q.v.]. Educated in the Lunenburg district school with added tutoring from the local clergyman and a term in the academy at New Ipswich, N. H., he entered Harvard College at the age of fifteen and graduated in 1826, ranking second in his class. After a year of teaching in a private school in Jamaica Plain, he was influenced by William Ellery Channing [q.v.] to enter the Harvard Divinity School, combining study there with the office, for two years, of tutor in mathematics in the college. Graduating in 1830, he was ordained pastor of the Second Congregational Society (Unitarian), Northampton, Mass., and remained there until Apr. 1, 1839, when, on account of ill health, he resigned. Unable, because of his health, to accept a call to Newburyport, he later became pastor of the Third Congregational Society in Hingham, Mass., where he was installed in April 1840, and where he remained sixteen years. As a minister Stearns won distinction by a profundity of thought matured in studious seclusion and by the ethical passion of his anti-slavery utterances. One of the earlier of his infrequent publications was *The Gospel as Applied to the Fugitive Slave Law* (1851). There were occasions when irritated listeners walked out while he was preaching.

During his Hingham pastorate he developed a theological method reconciling the older Unitarian thought with the newer Transcendentalism, and he found his truer vocation when, in 1856, he became president of the Meadville Theological School, Meadville, Pa. His eminent success in that office led in 1863 to his appointment to the Parkman Professorship of pulpit eloquence and pastoral care in the Harvard Divinity School, in succession to Convers Francis [q.v.], and to a lectureship in Christian theology in succession to George E. Ellis [q.v.]. Here, in association with Frederic Hedge and James Freeman Clarke [qq.v.], he modernized the older Unitarian tradition of the school. When President Eliot reorganized the school in 1870, Stearns was given the office of dean, and under the title of Parkman Professor of Theology, taught systematic theology and ethics. In 1878, aged seventy-one, he resigned, and lived in retirement in Cambridge until his death. On May 14, 1832, he was married to Mary Blood, daughter of Hon. Thomas H. and Mary (Sawyer) Blood of Sterling, Mass.; she died on June 10, 1871, and on July 2, 1872, he married Mrs. Augusta Hannah (Carey) Bailey. By his first wife he had six sons and two daughters.

Stearns was probably the first theologian in America to profess belief in evolution as a cosmic law, even before Herbert Spencer's adoption of the idea, though his own interest was in establishing a theory of historical development for Christian thought. His purpose was to unite the old dependence on Biblical revelation with the Transcendentalist reliance on present intuition, and at the same time, to find a relative justification of doctrines elaborated in stages of Christian history. After a preliminary effort in "Peace Through Conflict" (*Monthly Religious Magazine*, November 1851) he published further articles (*Christian Examiner*, September 1853, September 1856), in which he asserted that this progressive development is a story of intuitive reason interpreting revelation, with a safeguard against private aberration by the intention to seek truth in the light of the Holy Catholic Church. This development is more than a human process. The divine is immanent in it. Man's growing spiritual experience is an "evolution of the divine life through human nature." In support of this view, in 1856 he adopted from *Earth and Man* (1849), by Arnold Guyot [q.v.], the formulation due to von Baer, that "in the evolution of nature, the point of departure is a *homogeneous unit,* that the progress is *diversification,* that the end is an *organic* or harmonic unit" (*Christian Examiner,* September 1856, p. 174).

The same law, Stearns held, governed the history "not only of Christian theology, but of that Christian life which gives theology the law of its form and the sap of its growth" (*Ibid.*). In his Meadville instruction, he applied this thought with imperfect consistency and with a version of Christian beginnings now supplanted by modern criticism. In his Harvard period, ever receptive to new currents of thought, he assimilated some of that criticism, as is evidenced in a paper dealing with the Messianic consciousness of Jesus ("The Aim and Hope of Jesus," *Christianity and Modern Thought,* 1872), the last of his rare publications.

[A. S. Van Wagenen, *Geneal. and Memoirs of Isaac Stearns and His Descendants* (1901); A. P. Peabody, *Harvard Reminiscences* (1888); *Unitarian Rev.,* Oct. 1885; *Christian Reg.,* July 30, 1885; S. A. Eliot, *Heralds of a Liberal Faith* (1910), vol. III; F. A. Christie, *The Makers of the Meadville Theological School* (1927); *Boston Transcript,* July 20, 22, 1885.]

F. A. C.

STEARNS, ROBERT EDWARDS CARTER (Feb. 1, 1827–July 27, 1909), naturalist, was born in Boston, Mass., the son of Charles and Sarah (Carter) Stearns. His paternal grandfather was the Rev. Charles Stearns of Lincoln, mentioned by Holmes in *The Autocrat of the Breakfast Table,* and his first American ancestor was Charles Stearns who became a freeman at Watertown in 1646. His love of nature, intense from childhood, was fortunately appreciated and shared by his father and the two were frequently tramping and hunting companions. His education in the Boston public schools, often interrupted by poor health, was followed by mercantile training, but his artistic bent led him, in 1849, to paint a panorama of the Hudson River in a canvas 900 feet long and eight feet wide. He was married to Mary Ann Libby, the daughter of Oliver Libby of Boston, on Mar. 28, 1850. About this time he engaged in the investigation of certain Indiana coal fields, and in 1854 became resident agent for several copper mines in northern Michigan. But mining proved a passing interest, and after he lost his income in the panic of 1857, Stearns sold his Dover farm and migrated to California. He became a partner in a San Francisco printing business and later attempted independent publication, his first paper in 1859 being a prophetic article on the value of the sugar-beet for California. As acting editor of the *Pacific Methodist* he strongly upheld the Union cause in the Civil War and exerted an influence in the state said to have been far from negligible. Possessing considerable administrative capacity he became deputy clerk of the California supreme court, 1862–63, and secretary to the State Board of Harbor Commissioners, 1863–

68. Resigning because of ill health he spent the next two years in the East. Stearns returned to California to serve as secretary to the Board of Regents of the University of California in 1874, and supervised the dignified landscaping of the old campus until illness again impelled his retirement.

Even as a boy Stearns had become interested in collecting shells. His first zoölogical publication was a list of mollusks of Bolinas Bay (*Proceedings of the California Academy of the Natural Sciences,* vol. III, 1868). He likewise actively participated in the work of the young and struggling Academy of Natural Sciences, which he joined in 1864, holding many of its offices, and helping to prevent its dissolution after the earthquake of 1868. Thenceforth his scientific labors, particularly in the study of conchology, were unremitting. In 1869 he participated in a zoölogical expedition to Florida, and after another ten years again went east. In 1882 he was engaged in research for the United States Commission of Fish and Fisheries. In 1884 he was appointed paleontologist to the United States Geological Survey by John Wesley Powell, and assistant curator of mollusks in the National Museum by Spencer F. Baird [*qq.v.*]. In 1892 he settled in Los Angeles where he lived in semi-invalidism until his death. He was survived by one daughter.

Essentially a naturalist of the old school he will long be remembered as one of that group of earnest pioneer students of the Californian fauna which included Joseph Le Conte, James G. Cooper, William H. Dall [*qq.v.*], and others. A bibliography of his writings lists about 160 titles, mainly concerning molluscan systematics and distribution, but including several on coelenterates and others appertaining to ethnology, agriculture, and forestry. His was the foundational work on the interesting fossil land-snails of the John Day beds in Oregon. Although he suffered often from depression, Stearns's outstanding characteristics were vivacity, enthusiasm, versatility, a lively sense of humor, and a deep attachment to friends, especially exemplified in an intense and enduring love for his father. He became a fellow of the American Association for the Advancement of Science in 1874. Numerous mollusca and other animals, living and extinct, commemorate his name. His collection of mollusks was acquired by the National Museum.

[*Who's Who in America,* 1908–09; Avis Stearns Van Wagenen, *Geneal. and Memoirs of Charles and Nathaniel Stearns, and Their Descendants* (1901); M. R. Stearns, *Robert Edwards Carter Stearns,* privately printed (n.d.), and "Bibliography of Scientific Writings of R. E. C. Stearns," with a biographical sketch by W. H. Dall, *Smithsonian Misc. Colls.,* vol. LVI (1912):

W. H. Dall, "Dr. R. E. C. Stearns," *Nautilus,* Oct. 1909; *Los Angeles Daily Times,* July 29, 1909.]

S. S. B.

STEARNS, SHUBAL (Jan. 28, 1706–Nov. 20, 1771), Baptist clergyman, was born in Boston, Mass., the son of Shubael (*sic*) and Rebecca (Larrabee or Lariby) Stearns and a descendant of the Charles Stearns who was admitted a freeman of Watertown, Mass., in 1646. In 1715 the family moved to Tolland, Conn., where the father was one of the original land grantees and became the second town clerk. On Mar. 6, 1726/27, Shubal married Sarah Johnson of Lexington, Mass. Coming under the influence of the Great Awakening, he attached himself to the New Lights (Separatists) in 1745 and became a preacher among them. In 1751 he became convinced that believer's immersion was the New Testament baptism and was immersed by the Rev. Wait Palmer, who also participated on May 20, 1751, in his ordination as a Baptist minister. Although he continued to preach in New England for two years or more, he had a compelling inward conviction that he was called to a work outside that region.

Accordingly, with several married couples from the community, including some relatives, he went southward to Virginia, sojourning first at Opequon Creek and then at Cacapon. Here his brother-in-law, Daniel Marshall [*q.v.*], who had married Shubal's gifted sister, Martha, joined them and soon the group moved to Sandy Creek, N. C. There, in 1755, they organized a Baptist church, Stearns being chosen pastor, a position he retained during the rest of his life. Like the Regular Baptists of the Southern colonies, these Separate Baptists, as they were known, were Calvinists, but they had an evangelistic zeal which was their most distinctive character. Stearns himself as a preaching evangelist had been rated by some as next to Whitefield in effectiveness. The extent of his influence upon the Baptists of the wide area in which he and the ministers stimulated by him moved—the Carolinas, Georgia, and Virginia—is incalculable, but it was certainly dominant for a decade and was a primary factor in the astounding growth of the Baptists during the 1760's in those colonies. Both directly and indirectly he prepared the way for the union of the Regular and Separatist Baptists, producing the blend of Calvinistic orthodoxy and evangelistic fervor—particularly effective with the Scotch-Irish population—which has been a special mark of Southern Baptists. He was one of the principal founders of the Sandy Creek Association, in which churches of a wide area were united. Morgan Edwards has given the classic description of him: "He was but a little man but of good natural parts, and sound judgment. Of learning he had but a small share, yet was pretty well acquainted with books. His voice was musical and strong. . . . His character was indisputably good. . . . In his eyes was something very penetrating—there seemed to be a meaning in every glance" (Paschal, *post,* 286–87). He died in his sixty-fifth year.

[W. B. Sprague, *Annals of the Am. Pulpit,* VI (1860), 60; R. B. Semple, *Hist. of the Rise and Progress of the Baptists in Va.* (1810); David Benedict, *A Gen. Hist. of the Baptist Denomination in America* (2 vols., 1813); G. W. Purefoy, *A Hist. of the Sandy Creek Baptist Asso.* (1859); G. W. Paschal, *Hist. of N. C. Baptists* (1930); A. S. Van Wagenen, *Geneal. and Memoirs of Charles and Nathaniel Stearns, and Their Descendants* (1901).]   W. H. A.

STEARNS, WILLIAM AUGUSTUS (Mar. 17, 1805–June 8, 1876), Congregational clergyman, president of Amherst College, was born at Bedford, near Concord, Mass., his parents being the Rev. Samuel Horatio and Abigail (French) Stearns. Eben Sperry Stearns [*q.v.*] was a younger brother. Through his father his ancestry ran back to Isaac Stearns who emigrated to Salem in 1630 and was admitted freeman of Watertown, Mass., in 1631. Descended through both parents from distinguished leaders of the Congregational Church, he early felt himself destined to the ministry. The family consisted of eleven children who lived to reach adult estate and the problem of giving the five boys and six girls the benefit of "the New England system of education in ministers' families, viz: pure air, simple diet and a solid training in knowledge, human and divine" (Tyler, *Discourse, post,* p. 12) on an annual stipend which never exceeded five hundred dollars, in almost forty years of service, must have been a great one, but it was successfully met. The boys were all sent to Phillips Academy, Andover, Mass., and four of them were later graduated at Harvard College, William in the class of 1827. He then entered Andover Theological Seminary, where he became one of a group of unusually able young men, all of whom later fulfilled their early promise.

While he was still a student at Andover he preached occasionally to a small and weak congregation in Cambridgeport, and on his graduation he was invited to become its pastor. His friends protested that his talents entitled him to a more important charge, but, interpreting the call as evidence of divine will, he accepted it and was ordained Dec. 14, 1831. The pastorate lasted twenty-three years and was singularly successful, the weak and despised mission becoming one of the most prosperous and efficient of all the churches in the vicinity of Boston. The period was characterized by increasing heat over the slavery issue and the young clergyman brought much obloquy on himself by condemning the extreme measures of the abolitionists although he preserved a consistent attitude of opposition to slavery.

His success as a pastor and especially the fruitfulness of his work among his younger parishioners led, in 1854, to his selection as the fourth president of Amherst College, a call he was moved to accept in spite of many misgivings. Thus he began his long term of service in the field of education which was to last until his sudden death at Amherst twenty-two years later. His kindly and urbane manner and the very evident sincerity of his moral character combined to captivate and hold the affections of faculty and students alike. He proved to be an exceptionally strong administrator and greatly increased the material wealth of the College while at the same time the curriculum was enriched and broadened. He was in great demand as a preacher on notable occasions and his sermons were generally printed at the request and expense of his hearers. He also wrote a considerable number of pamphlets on educational and missionary affairs. His only books were: *Life of Rev. Samuel H. Stearns* (3rd and enlarged edition, 1846), *Infant Church-Membership, or the Relation of Baptized Children to the Church* (1844), and *Adjutant Stearns* (copr. 1862), a short life of a son, Frazar Augustus, killed in the Civil War. He was a member of the Massachusetts Board of Education, and a trustee of Phillips Academy, and of Andover Theological Seminary. He held the presidency of the Massachusetts Home Missionary Society from 1859 to 1876 and was influential in the counsels of the American Board of Commissioners for Foreign Missions.

On Jan. 10, 1832, he married Rebecca Alden Frazar of Duxbury, Mass., by whom he had three sons and three daughters; after her death, July 19, 1855, he married, in August 1857, Olive Coit Gilbert of Providence, R. I.

[A. S. Van Wagenen, *Geneal. and Memoirs of Isaac Stearns and His Descendants* (1901); W. S. Tyler, *Discourse Commemorative of the Late President Stearns* (1877) and *A Hist. of Amherst College* (1895); C. M. Fuess, *Men of Andover* (1928); *Springfield Daily Republican,* June 9, 1876; *Congregational Quart.,* July 1877, pp. 425–26; information from descendants.]   F. L. T.

STEBBINS, HORATIO (Aug. 8, 1821–Apr. 8, 1902), Unitarian clergyman, was born at South Wilbraham, Mass., the son of Calvin and Amelia (Adams) Stebbins, and a descendant of Rowland Stebbins who emigrated from England to Massachusetts in 1634 and settled successively in Roxbury, Springfield, and Northampton. Horatio's mother died when he was six years old and his father married again. The boy's early education, broken by periods of farm work and teaching, was completed at Phillips Academy, Exeter, N. H., in 1846. Entering Harvard, he graduated in the class of 1848. While there he made a hundred dollars by raising a crop of potatoes on a plot of ground where one of the college buildings now stands. He remained at Harvard as a student in the Divinity School until 1851, in which year, June 3, he married Mary Ann, daughter of Samuel and Mary (Bowman) Fisher of Northboro, Mass. On the fifth of the following November he was ordained and installed as colleague of Rev. Calvin Lincoln at the Unitarian Church, Fitchburg, Mass. After a successful ministry here, he became on Jan. 31, 1855, the associate of Dr. Ichabod Nichols at the First Church, Portland, Me., succeeding him as pastor when Nichols died in 1859.

After the death, in 1864, of Thomas Starr King [q.v.], one of the most influential and beloved men on the Pacific Coast, the members of the Unitarian Church in San Francisco chose Stebbins to succeed him. Accepting the call, Stebbins left his comfortable and well established Portland parish for the more primitive conditions of the Far West. Sailing for California by the way of Panama, he arrived on Sept. 7, 1864, and for the next thirty-five years was an acknowledged force in the development of the state. After more than three decades of service he said with truth: "I have not withheld my hand or my heart as a minister, a man, or a citizen from any human interest, within the reach of limited capacity and prescribed duty" (*Thirty-one Years of California*, 1895, pp. 21, 22). Though quite different from the magnetic King, he was himself a striking personality. His physical appearance attracted attention everywhere, for he was a big, towering man, dignified in bearing and polished in manners. Independent, intellectually honest, direct and forceful in speech, and possessing an organ-like voice, he was likely to be the principal speaker at any important gathering. He had, furthermore, the faith, the patience, the indifference to both praise and censure, and the broad culture needed in the California leaders of his time. His influence stands out most conspicuously in the educational field. The year after his arrival in San Francisco he was made a trustee of the College of California and soon became president of the board. He strongly supported the establishment of a state university, and when the Agricultural, Mining, and Mechanical Arts College was projected, the trustees of the College of California offered to cede its property to the state

with the condition that a college of liberal arts be maintained. Without Stebbins' "planning wisdom and public skill the acceptance of the proposals . . . would probably not have been gained from the State" (Ferrier, *post*, p. 467). He was given a place on the first board of regents of the University and had an important part in its management until 1894. He was a friend and adviser of Leland Stanford [q.v.], helped in the formation of Stanford University, and became one of its trustees. Named by the will of James Lick [q.v.] as a trustee of the California School of Mechanical Arts, he was for many years active in the affairs of that institution. A serious heart trouble compelled him to resign his pastorate in January 1900. Returning to the East, he died in Cambridge, Mass., a little more than two years later, his body being taken to Portland, Me., for burial. His first wife, by whom he had three children, died in February 1875 and on Nov. 9, 1876, he married Lucy Ward, daughter of Doliver and Eliza Ann (Wilbray) Ward of Chicago, by whom he had a son and a daughter. Several of his addresses were published and selections from his writings are contained in *Horatio Stebbins: His Ministry and Personality* (1921), by Charles A. Murdock.

[In addition to the two works mentioned above, see R. S. and R. L. Greenlee, *The Stebbins Geneal.* (1904); *Unitarian Year Book*, 1902; S. A. Eliot, *Heralds of a Liberal Faith* (1910), vol. III; W. W. Ferrier, *Origin and Development of the Univ. of Cal.* (1930); *Univ. Chronicle*, July 1902; *Christian Register*, Apr. 17, 1902; *San Francisco Chronicle*, Apr. 10, 1902.]   H. E. S.

STEBBINS, RUFUS PHINEAS (Mar. 3, 1810–Aug. 13, 1885), Unitarian clergyman, was a descendant of Rowland Stebbins, or Stebbing, a native of Cambridge, England, who in 1634 emigrated to Roxbury, Mass., and later moved to Springfield. A descendant, Stephen, became a farmer in South Wilbraham in 1741, and his great-grandson Rufus Phineas, second son of Luther and Lucina (Stebbins) Stebbins, was born there. Meager schooling with farm labor was the lot of his athletic and buoyant youth, when, as his cousin Horatio Stebbins [q.v.] reports, "he could spring up a horse's back from the ground, and ride like the wind without pad or saddle" (*Unitarian Review, post*, p. 437). After belated preparation in Wilbraham Academy, he graduated with distinction from Amherst College in 1834, and after three years in the Harvard Divinity School was ordained as pastor of the Congregational Church in Leominster, Mass., Sept. 20, 1837, nine days after his marriage to Eliza Clarke Livermore of Cambridge. In his own later words, he came to the parish "all ablaze with enthusiasm, flaming with zeal to correct all evils and perfect all good in a day . . . restless, dissatisfied, aggressive, belligerent" (*Reverend Calvin Lincoln: Sermon Preached . . . September 18, 1881,* 1882), and the energy of his denunciation of slavery, intemperance, and war provoked some temporary opposition. This vanished in view of his religious fervor and pastoral efficiency, and though austere in censure of innocent youthful amusements, he developed a crowded Sunday school, for whose forty-one teachers he conducted fortnightly training classes. He also received private pupils in his home, among them his cousin Horatio, and Thomas Hill [*q.v.*], afterwards president of Harvard University.

In 1844 Stebbins became the first president of the Theological School of Meadville, Pa., then founded in the interest of the Unitarians and the Christian Connection, serving also as pastor of the Meadville Unitarian Church until 1849. Robust energy of body and mind enabled him to accomplish a creative work in administration and teaching. He had a magisterial comprehension of the full range of knowledge, which found expression in an initial address in Meadville, Oct. 24, 1844, and in *Academic Culture* (1851), an address delivered before the students of Allegheny College. Resigning in 1856, he sought rest in Cambridge, but on Apr. 30, 1857, he began a new pastorate in Woburn, Mass. Here his notable public service on the school board of the town and the emotional power and ethical emphasis of his pulpit eloquence won adherents to his church, but for reasons now obscured he suddenly resigned, Nov. 28, 1863. He then took up his residence in Cambridge and devoted his time to preaching in various pulpits and to his duties as president of the American Unitarian Association. Early in 1865 he raised by personal effort over a hundred thousand dollars for the work of the Association—an amount unparalleled at that time—and in May accepted temporarily the administrative office of secretary. From 1871 to 1878 he built up the struggling Unitarian Church of Ithaca, N. Y., winning to its friendship Ezra Cornell [*q.v.*]; then, returning to New England, he organized, Apr. 21, 1878, the Unitarian Church of Newton Center, Mass., which he served until his death in Cambridge seven years later.

With little interest in philosophy, Stebbins based his thought solely on the Bible read with the Unitarian exegesis taught him by his Harvard teachers. He remained unaffected by the Transcendentalist movement of German Biblical criticism. In his *Study of the Pentateuch* (1881) he still upheld Mosaic authorship. The Bible, he maintained, was a revelation, even though

divine illumination of its authors was not always verbal inspiration and though the revealed truth was often expressed in poetical form with imaginative coloring and emotional rather than logical terms. Strenuous in denial of Trinitarian doctrine (see *Christian Examiner,* July 1851, June, September 1853), he found in Jesus, not only the Messiah commissioned to proclaim the Gospel, but an ever present agent in the affairs of the world, spiritually present when the bread was broken in the holy communion, and a constant saving presence to support and comfort men in the vicissitudes of life.

He contributed articles to the *Christian Examiner,* the *Christian Palladium,* the *Christian Repository,* of which he was one of the founders and editors, and the *Unitarian Review.* He also published, in addition to numerous sermons and other addresses, *An Historical Address Delivered at the Centennial Celebration . . . of the Town of Wilbraham* (1864), which comprises, with appendix and index, 317 pages.

[*Unitarian Rev.,* Nov. 1885; *Christian Reg.,* Aug. 20, 27, 1885; Joseph Allen, *The Worcester Asso. and Its Antecedents* (1865); S. A. Eliot, *Heralds of a Liberal Faith* (1910), vol. III; E. M. Wilbur, *A Hist. Sketch of the Independent Congregational Church, Meadville, Pa.* (1902); F. A. Christie, *The Makers of the Meadville Theological School* (1927); R. S. and R. L. Greenlee, *The Stebbins Geneal.* (2 vols., 1904).]
F. A. C.

STECK, GEORGE (July 19, 1829–Mar. 31, 1897), piano manufacturer, was born in Cassel, Germany. In his youth and early manhood he studied piano making with Carl Scheel of Cassel, who had worked for Erard, the Paris piano manufacturer, from 1837 to 1846. Steck emigrated to America in 1853, and after a period of employment by other piano makers in New York City founded his own business in 1857. The firm of George Steck & Company prospered almost immediately, and in 1865 retail warerooms were opened on Clinton Place, New York, under the name of Steck Hall. A larger establishment was opened on East Fourteenth Street in 1871. Steck was particularly interested in designing scales for pianos, and it is said that his scales for both grand and upright pianos were often copied and imitated by other manufacturers (Dolge, *post,* p. 318). In 1873 he was awarded the first prize of merit for pianofortes at the Great Vienna Exposition. He presented one of his grand pianos to Richard Wagner in 1876, and the manufacturers of the Steck piano exhibited this instrument in the United States, stating that it was the piano Wagner used at Villa Wahnfried, in Bayreuth, when he composed *Parsifal.* Steck was something of a philanthropist, concerned with the welfare of his employees. In 1884 he incorporated his business and alloted shares of stock to the men who worked for him. He retired from active participation in the firm in 1887, and devoted the last ten years of his life to experimentation in constructing a piano which would stay permanently in tune. In 1904 George Steck & Company was consolidated with the Aeolian Company of New York. A widow and two daughters survived him at his death in New York City.

[George Steck is briefly mentioned in *Grove's Dict. of Music and Musicians, Am. Supp.* (1930). The most complete account of his career is in Alfred Dolge, *Pianos and Their Makers*, vol. I (1911). An obituary is to be found in the *N. Y. Times*, Apr. 2, 1897.]

J. T. H.

STEDMAN, EDMUND CLARENCE (Oct. 8, 1833–Jan. 18, 1908), poet, critic, editor, was born in Hartford, Conn., the son of Maj. Edmund Burke Stedman and Elizabeth Clementine (Dodge) Stedman, who as Elizabeth C. D. Stedman Kinney [*q.v.*] became known as a poet and essayist. On his father's side he was descended from Isaac Stedman, a London merchant who came to Scituate, Mass., about 1637. His mother was the great-grand-daughter of the Rev. Aaron Cleveland [*q.v.*]. Edmund Stedman, who was a lumber merchant, died when his son was two years old, and the boy, until he was six, was brought up on his maternal grandfather's farm at Plainfield, N. J. He then passed under the care of his uncle, James Stedman, an austere and puritanical lawyer of Norwich, Conn., and received his early education at the "Old Brick Schoolhouse" and the "Old Academy" in Norwich. Although of small and frail physique, he showed boyish prowess in fighting, running, and swimming. He also wrote much juvenile poetry under the influence of the Romanticists and later of Tennyson, who became a lifelong admiration. He entered Yale in 1849, the youngest member of his class. Four principles of conduct were inscribed in his notebook: to obey all the rules and regulations of the institution; to come to every recitation with lessons carefully prepared; to abstain from profane swearing, gaming, drinking, or disorderly behavior; to follow duty in all things. These resolutions he carried out during his first year in college; in the second, beer, skittles, and other amusements caused his downfall. Although he won the sophomore prize in English composition with a poem, "Westminster Abbey," he neglected his class work and was rusticated at the end of the year to study under a tutor at Northampton, Mass., where instead of studying he fell in love with a neighboring damsel. He and another student started to tour New England as "the well-known tragedian Alfred

Willoughby, and his sister Miss Agnes Willoughby"; their exposure after the first performance caused his expulsion from Yale. He next studied law for several months in the office of his uncle, and then in 1852, in partnership with Charles B. Platt, bought the *Norwich Tribune*, which he edited for about half a year until it expired. Meanwhile he and Platt had fallen in love with the same woman, Laura Hyde Woodworth, daughter of a Norwich dyer, and wrote her a joint letter, offering her the choice of marriage between them. She chose Stedman, and they were married on Nov. 3, 1853. In Feb. 1854, in partnership with Stephen A. Hubbard, Stedman bought the *Mountain County Herald* at Winsted, Conn., which he edited until April 1855. Convinced by his experience that newspaper publishing was merely a form of business like any other and less profitable than most forms, he moved to New York and became a partner with E. A. Ingraham in the firm of Ingraham and Stedman, clockmakers. The partnership lasted for only one year, and there followed a financially precarious period for the Stedmans during which they lived at the "Unitary Home" on East Fourteenth Street, a cooperative venture inspired by Stephen Pearl Andrews [*q.v.*].

In the fall of 1859 the marriage of Frances Bartlett, a New York girl in her teens, to an aged but wealthy Cuban, Don Estaban de Santa Cruz de Oviedo, caused much unfavorable public comment, and Stedman made it the theme of a satiric poem, "The Diamond Wedding," which, published in the *New-York Daily Tribune*, Oct. 18, 1859, gained wide attention and commendation. Unwise threats of legal prosecution by the Bartlett family increased Stedman's *réclame*, further augmented by the publication of his popular "Ballad of Lager Bier," "John Brown's Invasion," and "Honest Abe of the West," thought to be the first Lincoln campaign song. These poems also brought him the acquaintance, ripening into intimate friendship, of Bayard Taylor, Richard Henry Stoddard, Thomas Bailey Aldrich, and William Winter [*qq.v.*]. He joined the staff of the New York *World* in August 1860, and during the same year published his first volume, *Poems Lyrical and Idyllic*. The outbreak of the Civil War sent him to the front as correspondent for the *World*, in which capacity he followed the campaigns of 1861. Being a violent partisan of the North, he thought he could do more efficient service for its cause by accepting a position in the attorney-general's office, in which he remained during 1862–63. Then, returning to New York, he entered the banking firm of Samuel Hallett and Company, but the next year opened his own brokerage office, which he retained for the rest of his life. Although he affected to regard the stock exchange as a mere means of livelihood, there can be no doubt that he had a real liking for business and thoroughly enjoyed the battles of the market. At the same time his love of literature was even more genuine, and after daily spending six hours on his feet in the stock exchange he devoted much of the night to writing.

His later life was uneventful, except for his successive publications: *Alice of Monmouth, an Idyl of the Great War, with Other Poems* (1864); *The Blameless Prince, and Other Poems* (1869), in which "Anonyma" caused an amusing attack on him for "immorality"; *The Poetical Works of Edmund Clarence Stedman* (1873), a complete edition; *Victorian Poets* (1875); *Poets of America* (2 vols., 1885); *A Library of American Literature from the Earliest Settlement to the Present Time* (11 vols., 1889–90); *The Nature and Elements of Poetry* (copyright 1892), the substance of lectures delivered on the Percy Turnbull Memorial Foundation at the Johns Hopkins University; *The Works of Edgar Allan Poe* (10 vols., 1894–95), edited in collaboration with George E. Woodberry; *Poems Now First Collected* (1897); *A Victorian Anthology, 1837–1895* (1895); and *An American Anthology, 1787–1899* (1900). Two trips to the Caribbean Sea, 1875 and 1892, inspired some of the best of his later poetry. In 1883 he bought an estate, "Kelp Rock," at Newcastle, N. H., as a summer residence, but he was rarely able to get away from his business to enjoy it. He took great delight, however, in his attractive colonial house in an artists' colony at Lawrence Park in Bronxville, N. Y. Generous, kindly, and idealistic, he was quick to join any efforts to promote the prestige of literature or alleviate the hard lot of authors. He was one of the founders of the Authors' Club, president of the American Copyright League, chairman of the American Committee of the Keats-Shelley Memorial Association, president of the National Institute of Arts and Letters, a member of the American Academy of Arts and Letters, and president of the New England Society. He died in New York, survived by one son and a grand-daughter. Always immaculately dressed, with fine features and beautiful white beard, he was easily the most popular and most highly esteemed member of the New York literary circle of his day. Time has dealt harshly with his poetry, which for all its technical merits was largely imitative, and with his works of criticism, which were narrowly Victorian in taste, but he brought an unusually thor-ough and conscientious scholarship to the task of editing, and through his numerous anthologies, as well as through his own writings, he exercised a great influence on the American culture of the period.

[*Who's Who in America*, 1906–07; *Obit. Record Grads. Yale Univ.* (1910); Laura Stedman and G. M. Gould, *Life and Letters of Edmund Clarence Stedman* (2 vols., 1910), with portrait and full bibliog.; *In Memory of Edmund Clarence Stedman, a Meeting Held at Carnegie Lyceum, N. Y.* (1909); Margaret W. Fuller, *A New England Childhood* (1916); Theodore Dreiser, in *Munsey's Mag.*, Mar. 1899; obituary in *N. Y. Times*, Jan. 19, 1908.]   E. S. B.

STEEDMAN, CHARLES (Sept. 20, 1811–Nov. 13, 1890), naval officer, son of Charles John Steedman and Mary (Blake) Steedman, was born in the Parish of Saint James, Santee, S. C. His grandfather, James Steedman, had emigrated from Scotland to America before the Revolution. Entering the navy as a midshipman, Apr. 1, 1828, he was promoted to the grade of passed midshipman, Jan. 14, 1834, and later, through successive grades, to that of rear-admiral, May 25, 1871. His early service, mainly in the West Indies, was without special incident. In 1835 he was ordered to the *Constitution*, and in her joined the Mediterranean Squadron, where he remained until June 1838. He spent the next four years largely in West Indian duty. In 1843 he was ordered to duty on the coast survey brig *Washington*. The next year he joined the corvette *St. Mary's*, and in her participated in the naval operations on the Gulf coast during the Mexican War, commanding the *St. Mary's* launch in the capture of the Mexican schooner *Pueblana* inside Tampico bar, Nov. 14, 1846. He also commanded an eight-inch gun of a naval shore battery in the bombardment of Vera Cruz and San Juan d'Ulloa, Mar. 24–27, 1847. After two years at the Naval Observatory, in 1850 he was again ordered to the Mediterranean Squadron. In the Paraguay expedition under William Branford Shubrick [*q.v.*] he commanded the brig *Dolphin*, returning to the United States in December 1860.

Though he was a South Carolinian, he remained loyal to the Union when the Civil War began. He was at once ordered to duty in Chesapeake Bay, keeping communications open and transporting troops from Havre de Grace to Annapolis while the railroad bridges between Baltimore, Md., and Philadelphia, Pa., were being repaired. Thence he was ordered to duty with Andrew Hull Foote [*q.v.*] on the Mississippi, but was soon recalled and given command of the *Bienville*, in which he participated in the Port Royal expedition of November 1861, his vessel leading the second attacking column. After the battle he blockaded the Georgia coast, participating in the capture of all the ports south of Savannah. In June 1862 he was transferred to the steamer *Paul Jones,* and with her silenced the batteries on St. John's Bluff, Fla. On Apr. 13, 1863, he was transferred to the *Powhatan,* doing blockade duty off Charleston, S. C., until September 1863, when he towed the captured ram *Atlanta* to Philadelphia. He was at once given command of the *Ticonderoga* and ordered to cruise against Confederate commerce raiders, particularly the *Florida.* After an unsuccessful search for this vessel off the Brazilian coast, he returned to Philadelphia in October 1864 in his ship with broken-down engines. In command of the same ship he took part in both attacks on Fort Fisher, N. C. In November 1865, after extensive repairs to the *Ticonderoga,* he joined the European Squadron of Louis Malesherbes Goldsborough [*q.v.*], returning home in the *Colorado* in September 1867. He was in charge of the Boston navy yard from 1869 to 1872, and of the South Pacific Squadron from Oct. 10, 1872, until Sept. 22, 1873, retiring Sept. 24, 1873. His record in two wars was an honorable one. His courtly bearing and polished manner were never disturbed amid the excitement of battle; a comrade said of him, "He was as cool under fire as on parade." He married Sarah Bishop of Philadelphia on Feb. 7, 1843, and had two sons and four daughters. After an extended tour of Egypt, Palestine, and Europe following his retirement, he settled in Washington, where he spent his declining years.

[*Memoir and Correspondence of Charles Steedman, with his Autobiog. and Private Journals* (1912), ed. by A. L. Mason; *War of the Rebellion: Official Records (Navy),* 1 ser., vols. I–IV (1894–97), VII (1898), XI–XVI (1900–03), XXII (1908); *Report of the Secretary of the Navy* (1859); G. F. Emmons, *The Navy of the U. S. from the Commencement 1775 to 1853* (1853); J. H. Smith, *The War with Mexico* (1919), vol. I; *Army and Navy Jour.,* Nov. 22, *Bangor Weekly Courier,* Nov. 21, *Evening Star* (Washington, D. C.), Nov. 14, and *Washington Sunday Herald,* Nov. 16, 1890.]

L. H. B.

STEEDMAN, JAMES BLAIR (July 29, 1817–Oct. 18, 1883), soldier and politician, was born in Northumberland County, Pa., the son of Mellum and Margaret (Blair) Steedman. He was left an orphan in childhood, and his education was limited to a few months in the district school. Learning the printer's trade, he worked in newspaper offices in Lewisburg, Pa., and Louisville, Ky.; later he served for a time in the Texan army and finally settled in Ohio. There he took an active part in politics; he was elected in 1847 to the state legislature, where he served two terms, and was frequently a delegate at party conventions. In the gold rush of 1849 he went to California but returned the next year to Toledo, where he made his permanent home, and resumed newspaper work. He was appointed public printer in 1857 during Buchanan's administration. A strong Douglas Democrat, he was a delegate at the Charleston and Baltimore conventions in 1860, and an unsuccessful candidate for Congress that year.

He entered the military service, Apr. 27, 1861, as colonel of the 14th Ohio Infantry, which he raised in Toledo; he was mustered out, Aug. 13, 1861, and again mustered in, Sept. 1, 1861. On Mar. 1, 1862, Lincoln nominated him to be brigadier-general of volunteers, but objection to his confirmation was made in the Senate on account of an editorial in his newspaper, the *Toledo Times,* which presented arguments in favor of the right of secession. Though these arguments were published only that they might be refuted in a later issue, the incident caused a long delay in Steedman's confirmation, and it did not take place until July 17, 1862. He commanded a brigade first in the (old) Army of the Ohio, and then in the Army of the Cumberland (Perryville and Murfreesboro), and finally a division in the latter (Tullahoma campaign). His greatest distinction was earned in the battle of Chickamauga, where he commanded a division of Granger's corps which came to the rescue of George Henry Thomas [*q.v.*], standing as the "rock of Chickamauga" when all the rest of the army had been swept away. In twenty minutes Steedman's division lost a fifth of its strength. Though his horse was shot under him and he was severely bruised, he retained command and himself headed the attack, carrying the colors of one of his regiments. One moment he gave to personal concerns, when he directed a staff officer to see that the newspaper obituaries spelled his name *Steedman* and not *Steadman,* a form he hated. He was appointed major-general of volunteers, Apr. 20, 1864. At the battle of Nashville he commanded a "detachment" of troops from various sources, the equivalent of a division. Resigning from the army, Aug. 18, 1866, he was collector of internal revenue at New Orleans, La., until 1869, when he returned to Toledo. He edited the *Northern Ohio Democrat,* served in the state Senate, was chief of police of the city, and was otherwise active in public affairs up to the time of his death. A man of great size and strength, he was aggressive, determined, fearless of responsibility, at his best in great emergencies. He was married three times: first, in 1838 at Napoleon, Ohio, to Miranda Stiles, recently of New Jersey; second, to Rose Barr; and third, Sept. 16, 1878, at Monroe, Mich., to Margaret, daughter of John Gildea.

[*War of the Rebellion: Official Records (Army)*; *Battles and Leaders of the Civil War* (4 vols., 1887–88); J. C. Smith, *Oration at the Unveiling of the Monument Erected to the Memory of Maj. Gen. James B. Steedman* (1887); J. M. Killits, *Toledo and Lucas County, Ohio* (1923), vol. I; Clark Waggoner, *History of the City of Toledo and Lucas County* (1888); Harvey Scribner, *Memoirs of Lucas County and the City of Toledo* (1910), vol. II; obituary in *Cincinnati Enquirer*, Oct. 19, 1883; unpublished records in the War Dept.; letter from Steedman's widow confirming statements as to full name, date of birth, parentage, and marriages.]

T. M. S.

STEELE, DANIEL (Oct. 5, 1824–Sept. 2, 1914), Methodist Episcopal clergyman, teacher, author, was born at Windham, N. Y., in the Catskills, a son of Perez and Clarissa (Brainerd) Steele and a descendant of George Steele who came to Massachusetts in 1631/32, later settling in Connecticut. During his entire preparatory course at Wesleyan Academy, Wilbraham, Mass., he supported himself by teaching school as he did also during his freshman year at Wesleyan University, Middletown, Conn., where he was graduated, second in his class, in 1848. For the next two years he was a tutor in mathematics at Wesleyan, and during this period, 1849, he joined the New England Conference of the Methodist Episcopal Church, of which he remained a member till 1906, when he assumed a retired relation. From his ordination in 1850 until 1861, he served churches in the following places in Massachusetts: Fitchburg, Leominster, Boston, Malden, Springfield, and Holliston. Leaving the pastorate in the latter year, he was from 1862 to 1869 professor of ancient languages in Genesee College, Lima, N. Y., and from 1869 to 1871 was acting president of that institution. When the college was moved to Syracuse and became Syracuse University in 1871, he held the chair of mental and moral philosophy there for a year and also served as vice-president of the college of liberal arts in 1871–72, and as acting chancellor of the university in 1872. Again resuming the pastorate, he ministered continuously to churches in Massachusetts from 1872 to 1888, serving in Boston, Auburndale, Lynn, Salem, Peabody, Reading, and again in Boston. While pastor in Reading in 1884 he became instructor in New Testament Greek and exegesis in Boston University. From 1886 to 1899 he taught in the New England Deaconess' Training School, and then devoted the remainder of his life to literary work.

He was the author of a commentary on the Book of Joshua which appeared in 1873 as the third volume in D. C. Whedon, *Commentary on the Old Testament*; and in addition published *Binney's Theological Compend Improved* (1875); *Love Enthroned* (1875), his most widely known and influential work; *Milestone Papers*

(1878); a commentary on Leviticus and Numbers (1891), in the Whedon Series; *Half-Hours with St. Paul* (1895); *Defense of Christian Perfection* (1896); *Gospel of the Comforter* (1897); *Jesus Exultant* (1899); *A Substitute for Holiness; or, Antinomianism Revived* (1899); *Half-Hours with St. John's Epistles* (1901); *Steele's Answers* (1912). He was a constant contributor to the religious press, was associate editor of *Divine Life*, 1889–93, and of the *Christian Witness*, 1896. His weekly contribution to *Zion's Herald*, known as "Daniel Steele's Column" was eagerly read for many years.

Steele was a leader in his denomination and active in the principal reform movements of his day. He was a stanch opponent of slavery and a persistent advocate of temperance and woman's rights. He was a man of scholarly attainments and saintly character; but with his earnest piety he combined the saving grace of a delightful sense of humor. His outlook was broad and he was in full sympathy with the liberal scientific and theological opinion of his time. He had a wide circle of friends both within and beyond the confines of his own denomination. He died at his home in Milton, Mass., in his ninetieth year. On Aug. 8, 1850, he was married to Harriet, daughter of Rev. Amos Binney of Wilbraham, Mass., and two sons and two daughters survived him.

[*Official Minutes . . . New England Conference of the Methodist Episcopal Church*, 1915; *Zion's Herald*, Sept. 9, 1914; *Boston Transcript*, Sept. 3, 1914; *Who's Who in America*, 1914–15; D. S. Durrie, *Steele Family* (1859); *Alumni Record of Wesleyan Univ.* (1911).]

F. T. P.

STEELE, FREDERICK (Jan. 14, 1819–Jan. 12, 1868), soldier, was born at Delhi, Delaware County, N. Y., the son of Nathaniel Steele, and a descendant of John Steele of Essex, England, who emigrated to Newtown (Cambridge), Mass., in 1631/32 and was later one of the founders of Hartford, Conn. Frederick was appointed a cadet at West Point, July 1, 1839, and upon his graduation, July 1, 1843, was commissioned second lieutenant in the 2nd Infantry, with which he served in the Mexican War, in action at Ocalaca, Contreras, Churubusco, Molino del Rey, and Chapultepec. He was twice brevetted for gallant conduct (Contreras and Churubusco). Promoted first lieutenant on June 6, 1848, he served in California for the next five years, and from 1853 to 1861 in Minnesota, Nebraska, and Kansas. He was promoted captain, 2nd Infantry, Feb. 5, 1855, and on May 14, 1861, was appointed major in the 11th Infantry, one of the new regular regiments created by presidential proclamation and later confirmed by act of Congress. (Out of it, in later reorganizations, were formed the

16th and 20th Infantry of the present army; the present 11th Infantry has no connection with the older regiment so designated.)

During the first year of the Civil War Steele commanded a brigade at the battle of Wilson's Creek and in the other operations in Missouri. He was appointed colonel, 8th Iowa Infantry, Sept. 23, 1861, and brigadier-general of volunteers, Jan. 29, 1862. As a division commander in Curtis' Army of the Southwest he participated in the Arkansas campaign of 1862, and was appointed major-general of volunteers, Nov. 29, 1862. He commanded a division of the XIII Corps in the operations against Chickasaw Bluffs and Arkansas Post, and a division of the XV (Sherman's) Corps in the Vicksburg campaign. Immediately after the surrender of the city he was placed in command of the forces in Arkansas and charged with completing the conquest of that state. This task he substantially accomplished within a few months, defeating or driving back the small Confederate forces which might have menaced the flank of the greater operations east of the Mississippi. The portion of the state remaining in Confederate hands was too remote to affect the course of the war in any respect. When Banks started on his Red River campaign, Steele was directed to assist by operating against the Confederate forces before him, which orders he carried out at a heavy cost in men and animals and without other result. In actual combat he was successful enough, but it was impracticable to maintain the long line of communications which was necessary. The responsibility rests with the superiors who ordered the impossible, and not with Steele. He remained in charge in Arkansas through 1864, and then took part in Canby's campaign against Mobile, which ended with the capture of that city in April 1865. Though a good division commander, Steele was never entrusted with a large command. The Army of Arkansas, though operating independently, never exceeded about fourteen thousand men.

After the war he commanded the Department of the Columbia, in the northwest, until shortly before his death. He was not mustered out as major-general of volunteers until Mar. 1, 1867, having meanwhile been promoted lieutenant-colonel in the regular army, Aug. 26, 1863, and colonel, July 28, 1866. While on leave at San Mateo, Cal., he was stricken with apoplexy, fell from the carriage in which he was driving, and died instantly.

[D. S. Durrie, *Steele Family* (1859); *War of the Rebellion: Official Records (Army)*; *Battles and Leaders of the Civil War* (4 vols., 1887–88); G. W. Cullum, *Biog. Reg. Officers and Grads. U. S. Mil. Acad.* (3rd ed., 1891); *Evening Bulletin* (San Francisco), Jan. 14, 1868; unpublished records in the War Dept.]

T. M. S.

STEELE, JOEL DORMAN (May 14, 1836– May 25, 1886), educator and textbook writer, son of the Rev. Allen and Sabra (Dorman) Steele, was born in Lima, N. Y., a descendant of John Steele, one of the founders of Hartford and Farmington, Conn. His early schooling was irregular, for his father was an itinerant Methodist minister, but he had two years under Charles Anthon [*q.v.*] at the Boys' Classical Institute in Albany, and two years at the Boys' Academy in Troy. After a year in clerical positions in New York City, he entered Genesee College (later part of Syracuse University) and was graduated in 1858. To defray his college expenses, he worked summers on his father's farm or taught district school. He became instructor (1858– 59), then principal at Mexico Academy, Mexico, N. Y. His marriage on July 7, 1859, to Esther Baker, teacher of music at the academy, daughter of the Rev. Gardner Baker, proved one of rare intellectual and spiritual companionship. In 1861 he resigned to raise the 81st New York Volunteers, of which he was captain. He was severely wounded at the battle of Seven Pines, Fairoaks, Va., and his life hung in the balance for weeks, but in the following autumn he was well enough to become principal of the high school at Newark, N. Y. In 1866 he became principal of the Elmira Free Academy, where he found discipline sadly demoralized; he soon had the situation under control, however, and introduced the honor system with extraordinary success. "I had become convinced," he said, "that the germinal idea of discipline was self-control; and that the true aim of the schoolmaster was not to teach the pupil how to be governed by another, but how to govern himself" (Palmer, *post*, p. xxvii).

At Elmira he taught only science, always his favorite subject. He took careful notes of effective classroom procedure, largely abandoned use of the cumbersome textbooks of the period, and substituted outlines of his own. These developed into his famous "Fourteen Weeks" series of textbooks in the sciences, the first of which was published in 1867. In 1872, at the insistent urging of his intimate friend and publisher, Alfred Cutler Barnes, he resigned his principalship to devote the rest of his life to writing textbooks. He had begun the year before, in collaboration with his wife, to write textbooks in history, known as the Barnes Brief History Series, the most popular of which was *A Brief History of the United States for Schools* (1871). No authors' names appeared on the history textbooks until after Steele's death, since he felt that to acknowledge the authorship of books in a field not his own would injure his prestige in science. His contribution in these scientific and historical textbooks lay in his ability to present facts comprehensibly and with interest; his success is attested by the fact that five of his science textbooks and two of his histories were still in print in 1928. Through them he popularized science as a secondary school subject, introduced simple laboratory exercises and the study of specimens, and urged departure from memoriter recitations. He had the advantage, as he often said, of a devoted wife who assisted him from the beginning in all his writing, and who continued to revise editions after his death. In his memory she erected the Steele Memorial Library in Elmira. He was all his life profoundly religious. His interest in reconciling science and religion is evidenced in his textbooks, in his bequest of $50,000 to Syracuse University to found a chair of "theistic science," and in the inscription his wife had placed on his tombstone: "His true monument stands in the hearts of thousands of American youth, led by him to 'look through Nature up to Nature's God.'"

[Anna C. Palmer, *Joel Dorman Steele: Teacher and Author* (1900) with autobiog. introduction; J. B. Pratt, *Seventy-five Years of Book Publishing* (1913); D. S. Durrie, *Steele Family: A Geneal. Hist. of John and George Steele (Settlers of Hartford, Conn.), 1635–36, and Their Descendants* (1859); obituary in *Jour. of Proc. and Addresses Nat. Educ. Asso., Session of 1886* (1887); *Appletons' Ann. Cyc.*, 1886.]　　　E. W. F.

STEELE, JOHN (Nov. 16, 1764–Aug. 14, 1815), congressman from North Carolina, comptroller of the treasury, the son of William and Elizabeth (Maxwell) Gillespie Steel or Steele, both from Pennsylvania, was born in Salisbury, N. C. There his parents, and after his father's death in 1773 his mother, kept a tavern well known in the Piedmont region of the Carolinas. The boy was educated in Salisbury and at "Clio's Nursery," conducted by James Hall [*q.v.*]. He then engaged in a mercantile business in Salisbury, establishing soon afterward a connection with Robert Cochran, a wealthy merchant of Fayetteville, whose daughter-in-law, Mary Nesfield, he married Feb. 9, 1783. Three daughters lived to adult life. In 1784 he was assessor of the town of Salisbury, in 1787 was a town commissioner, and in the same year was elected as a borough member to the House of Commons, where he served two terms. The legislature made him a commissioner to treat with the Cherokee and Chickasaw in 1788. He was a Federalist member of the Hillsboro convention, called to consider the federal Constitution, and attracted much favorable attention by his part in the debates. The convention failed to ratify, and he was a delegate to the Fayetteville convention of 1789 that carried the state into the Union. He was at once elected to the House of Representatives of the First Congress and served with some distinction for two terms. Nominally a Federalist, he showed considerable independence in his whole course, regarding with disfavor the powers granted the president, opposing, in spite of his admiration and personal friendship for Alexander Hamilton, the latter's plan of assumption of state debts, and objecting to the maintenance of a standing army of any size. Later he was warmly hostile to the extension of judicial power, criticizing Marshall's decision in the *Marbury* vs. *Madison* case as a usurpation of power. He was not reëlected in 1792 owing to the reaction against the Federalists, and he was the same year an unsuccessful candidate for the federal Senate.

Returning to North Carolina he was a member of the House of Commons in 1794 and 1795. In the last session he was the unsuccessful candidate of the Federalists for federal senator. In 1794 he was commissioned a major-general of militia. In 1796 Washington appointed him comptroller of the treasury, and he served in that office until 1802, when, over the earnest protest of Jefferson who desired to retain him in office, he resigned, chiefly on account of illness in his family. In 1805 and in 1812 he was a member of the commission to determine the boundary between North Carolina and South Carolina, and in 1807 of the commission to settle the boundary dispute between North Carolina and Georgia. An extensive land-owner, after his return from Washington he devoted the greater part of his time to agriculture and the breeding and racing of blooded horses. He was again a member of the House of Commons in 1806, 1811 to 1813, and he was elected in 1815 but died before taking his seat. He was chosen speaker in 1811 to fill a vacancy.

[Papers in possession of N. C. Hist. Soc. and N. C. Hist. Commission; "The Papers of John Steele," *N. C. Hist. Commission Pubs.* (2 vols., 1924), ed. by H. M. Wagstaff; "Letters of Nathaniel Macon, John Steele and Wm. Barry Grove," with sketches by K. P. Battle, *James Sprunt Hist. Monograph*, no. 3 (1902); E. H. Bean, "Gen. John Steele," *Davidson College Studies in Hist.*, vol. I (1898); Archibald Henderson, "John Steele" and "Elizabeth Maxwell Steel," *N. C. Booklet*, Jan., Apr. 1919, Oct. 1912; date of birth from intro. to "Papers," *ante*, p. xxv.]　　　J. G. deR. H.

STEENDAM, JACOB (1616–c. 1672), eulogist and first poet of New Netherland, was born in the Netherlands, perhaps in Amsterdam, perhaps in Enkhuizen. He signed his poems with the device *Noch Vaster*, meaning "still firmer"

Steendam

than a stone dam. According to the *Formulier-boek* of the Amsterdam Classis, Dec. 3, 1640, Jacob Jacobss. van Steendam was "to go to the West Indies as a comforter of the sick" (*De Indische Gids*, September 1907, p. 1461); but instead, he spent eight years on the Gold Coast, returning to Holland in 1649 with a large collection of poems, which he published under the title of *Den Distelvink* (3 vols., 1649–50). He was an industrious rhymester with a good memory for Bible texts, but his poems contained little that was worth preserving. During a brief residence in Amsterdam he married Sara de Rosschou, and in 1652 he was settled in New Netherland as a merchant and trader. In that year he bought a farmstead at Amersfoort (Flatlands), and in the following year two houses at New Amsterdam and a farm at Mespath. He contributed to the fund raised for the defense of New Amsterdam against the Indians in 1653 and 1655; in 1655 he was orphan master, and in 1660 he and other burghers petitioned the Governor and Council for a license to import slaves and other commodities from the Gold Coast (O'Callaghan, *post*, p. 210).

As a business man Steendam was interested in the prosperity of New Amsterdam. Accordingly, seeing its welfare neglected by the West India Company and its future imperiled by the scarcity of colonists, he published in 1659 *Klacht van Nieuw Amsterdam in Nieuw Nederlandt tot Haar Moeder* (Complaint of New Amsterdam in New Netherland to Her Mother), a poem addressed to the mother city in Holland. This poem was followed in 1661 by *'T Lof van Nuw Nederland,* an extravagant eulogy of the many attractions of the colony. The burgomasters of Amsterdam shortly afterward financed a scheme of Pieter Corneliszen Plockhoy to plant a Mennonite settlement on the South (Delaware) River. A pamphlet by Plockhoy, *Kort en Klaer Ontwerp* (1662), in which he set forth the conditions for participation in his enterprise, contained "*Prickel-Vaerzen*" ("Spurring Verses") by Steendam, descriptive of the advantages of settlement in that far country.

When this pamphlet saw the light, Steendam was evidently back in Holland. In April 1663 he petitioned for permission to fence in his land at Mespath Kil, but he never returned to New Netherland. Instead, resuming the profession of comforter of the sick, he sailed for the East Indies in 1666 in the company of his wife and children. The Consistory at Batavia sent him to Bengal, but on Aug. 16, 1667, appointed him orphan master at Batavia. Here, in 1671, he published *Zeede-Zangen voor de Batavische*

Steenwijck—Steenwyck

Jonkheyt (Moral Songs for the Batavian Youth). He died, evidently, before September 1673, for a resolution of the Governor-General and Council of Sept. 5 of that year states that, since J. Steendam's widow had died, it was resolved to employ her daughter Vredegund Steendam and her betrothed Cornelis Wadde of Ooltgensplaat, for a trial period of two or three months.

[A small portrait of Steendam by J. M. Quinkhard is in the Rijksmuseum at Amsterdam; another, engraved by Coomans, is reproduced in H. C. Murphy's memoir, *Jacob Steendam, Noch Vaster* (1861), which contains the three poems on New Amsterdam and New Netherland, in the original Dutch and in English translation. This work is reprinted in Murphy's *Anthology of New Netherland* (1865). See also *De Indische Gids*, Sept. Oct. 1907; *De Navorscher*, XIV (1864), 305–06; *De Nieuwe Taalgids*, vols. XIII (1919) and XIV (1920); Gerrit Kalff, *Geschiedenis der Nederlandsche Letterkunde*, IV (1909), 465–67; W. L. Andrews, *Jacob Steendam* (1908); Berthold Fernow, *The Records of New Amsterdam* (1897), vols. I–III; E. B. O'Callaghan, *Calendar of Hist. MSS. in the Office of the Secretary of State, Albany, N. Y.*, vol. I (1865).]

A. J. B.

STEENWIJCK, CORNELIS VAN [See STEENWYCK, CORNELIS, d. 1684].

STEENWYCK, CORNELIS (d. 1684), colonial merchant, was born in Holland, probably in Haarlem, and appeared in New Amsterdam as early as 1651, coming as mate of a trading vessel. He engaged in trade and rose to prominence, ultimately sending his vessels to Virginia and the West Indies. In 1655, when fear of English encroachment was aroused in New Netherland, he contributed 100 guilders for the defense of the city; in 1656 he was the victim of a piece of gossip which resulted in a suit for slander which in turn brought about an extension of the power of the lower courts (Stokes, *post*, IV, 174). He was one of those who signed a petition, dated May 3, 1660, in which a number of merchants of New Amsterdam sought permission to trade for slaves along the west coast of Africa (O'Callaghan, *Calendar, post*, p. 210). A schepen in 1658 and 1660, burgomaster in 1662 and at later periods, he was chosen in 1663 to represent the interests of the colony in the mother country, an honor which he felt obliged to decline. In 1664, however, he was engaged as a commissioner for the colony in the diplomatic transactions which foreshadowed the English conquest. His mental poise is conspicuous in his proceedings with the swashbuckling Capt. John Scott, who as a commissioner for Hartford, Conn., urged the English claim (O'Callaghan, *Documents, post*, II, 399–401). Steenwyck took part in the negotiations which followed the appearance of the English fleet in the harbor of New Amsterdam, and his name is one of those attached to the articles by which New Netherland was surrendered. His oath of allegiance to the new government rested on the assurance that the rights of Dutch subjects would be preserved as guaranteed by the articles. Trusted and honored by the English governors, he remained throughout a stanch defender of those rights.

Richard Nicolls [*q.v.*], the first English governor, made Steenwyck mayor of New York, an office in which he was retained for more than two years (1668–70). Gov. Francis Lovelace [*q.v.*] admitted him to his council; and, when the Governor was called away on public affairs, he chose Steenwyck and Thomas Delavall "to take ye managery of such Affaires as shall happen here within ye City of New Yorke or places adjacent."

The restoration of Dutch authority in the colony by no means excluded Steenwyck from places of trust. By Gov. Anthony Colve he was appointed councilor with executive functions; he commanded militia and was otherwise employed in preparations for the city's defense, being also custodian of the accounts and journals of the insolvent Dutch West India Company in New Netherland. He was one of three commissioners who visited the eastern towns of Long Island to present to the English inhabitants the oath of allegiance to the States General. The English settlers, viewing themselves as subjects of Charles II, rejected the demand, and had the bearers of the summons exercised their powers in the spirit of Captain Scott, tragic incidents must have been added to the annals of Long Island.

No hint of political pliancy appears in Steenwyck's second acceptance of English rule; for, if he welcomed Sir Edmund Andros, the new governor, he met imprisonment at Andros' hands by insisting on recognition of the treaty claims of Dutch subjects. A reconciliation followed, however, and Steenwyck thenceforth was granted a serene official life. In 1682–83 he was mayor once more, and in this capacity presided over the newly established court of general sessions.

Steenwyck's commercial activities brought him wealth. In 1674 his estate was appraised at 50,-000 florins, exceeded in the colony only by that of Frederick Philipse (*Documents,* II, 699). His house, at the corner of Whitehall and Bridge (Brugh) streets, was furnished in a style luxurious for that period and he was reputed the best dressed, most polite, and most popular man in New Amsterdam (Valentine, *post,* 1858, p. 512, 1874, pp. 662–64). On June 5, 1658, he married Margaretha de Riemer, by whom he had seven children, none of whom, apparently, lived to maturity. He was an elder in the Reformed Dutch Church in the city, and one of his last acts was to bequeath the Manor of Fordham to that communion.

[Berthold Fernow, *The Records of New Amsterdam* (7 vols., 1897) and *N. Y. State Lib. Bull. No. 58 . . . Calendar of Council Minutes, 1668–1783* (1902); V. H. Paltsits, *Minutes of the Exec. Council of the Province of N. Y.* (1910), vol. II; E. B. O'Callaghan, *Calendar of Hist. MSS. in the Office of the Secretary of State, Albany, N. Y.,* vol. I, Dutch (1865), vol. II, English (1866), and *Docs. Rel. to the Col. Hist. of the State of N. Y.,* vols. II (1858), III (1853), XI (1861); Berthold Fernow, *Docs. Rel. to the Col. Hist. of the State of N. Y.,* vol. XIV (1883); I. N. P. Stokes, *The Iconography of Manhattan Island* (6 vols., 1915–28); D. T. Valentine, *Manual of the Corporation of the City of N. Y.,* 1853, 1858, 1864; W. E. De Riemer, *The De Riemer Family* (1905); a portrait in the N. Y. Hist. Soc.]
R. E. D.

STEERS, GEORGE (July 20, 1820–Sept. 25, 1856), naval architect, yacht designer, inherited much of his ability from his father, Henry Steer, a successful British shipbuilder, who emigrated to the United States from Devonshire in 1819, added a final "s" to the family name, and became one of the leading naval constructors of his time. His third son, George, one of thirteen children, was born in Washington, D. C., and grew up in his father's shipyard at the foot of East Tenth Street, New York City. When ten years of age he built a scow which his brothers broke up as unsafe, and at sixteen he turned out a sloop whose success brought him to the attention of John C. Stevens, one of the leading citizens in New York, and his lifelong friend and patron. Steers's first larger boat, the twenty-seven-ton sloop, *Manhattan,* built in his father's yard in 1839, was followed by the fast pilot boat, *William G. Hagstaff,* the 250-ton schooner *St. Mary the First,* three steamers for the Great Lakes, and a small ship, *Sunny South,* which subsequently became a slaver.

In his early productions Steers adhered to the accepted "cod's-head-and-mackerel-tail" theory of design, but in 1849 he turned out a schooner, *Mary Taylor,* in which the forefoot was boldly rounded away, the bows moderately hollowed, with a clean afterbody and well balanced ends. The almost instantaneous success of the *Mary Taylor* as a fast pilot boat, and others of similar lines, soon made the New York pilot fleet the talk of the shipping world. Through his intimate acquaintance with the Stevens brothers, John Cox, Robert Livingston, and Edwin Augustus Stevens, Steers was enabled to keep in close touch with the most progressive ideas of the day in steam engineering, marine propulsion, railroading, and other mechanical devices. Under the name of Hathorn & Steers he had charge of a boatyard on the Williamsburg side of the East River from 1845 to 1849, when he formed a partnership with his brother, James R. Steers. They built a number of notable vessels including the steamship, *Adriatic,* for the Collins line, and the warship, *Niagara,* which helped to lay the first transatlantic cable.

Steers became well known as a builder of pleasure craft such as the schooners *Syren, Sybil, Una, Ray, Julia, Cygnet, Cornelia,* and *Haze*— all of which were prominent in yacht races before and even after the Civil War. But his most famous craft was the *America.* He received the order for this boat from a syndicate of six members of the New York Yacht Club, John Cox Stevens, Edwin Augustus Stevens, Col. James A. Hamilton, George L. Schuyler, Hamilton Wilkes, and John K. Beekman Finlay, while engaged in the yard of William H. Brown at the foot of East Twelfth St. Steers is credited with both her design and construction. His clients were sharp business men who held him to his contract to build an unbeatable boat and paid him twenty instead of thirty thousand dollars after the *America* had been defeated by the sloop *Maria,* a much larger craft, in her first test of speed. Unchagrined by the seeming failure, Steers crossed the ocean on the *America* and sailed her in the memorable race of Aug. 22, 1851, around the Isle of Wight. At one time during her course, no second boat was in sight of the American craft. Although the *America* revolutionized yacht design on both sides of the Atlantic, Steers seems to have been forgotten in the festivities which followed the winning of the 100 guinea cup of the Royal Yacht Squadron, and it was not until some years later that his great creations received their just due. His death at the early age of thirty-seven resulted from injuries received in a runaway accident near his home at Great Neck, L. I.

[W. M. Martin, W. P. Stephens, W. U. Swan, *The Yacht "America"* (1925); W. M. Thompson, *The Lawson Hist. of the America's Cup* (1902); H. L. Stone, *The "America's" Cup Races* (1914); Nigel Lindsay, *The America's Cup* (London, 1930), *N. Y. Herald,* Sept. 26, 27, 1856.]

W. U. S.

STEHLE, AURELIUS ALOYSIUS (Apr. 30, 1877–Feb. 12, 1930), Roman Catholic cleric, fourth archabbot of St. Vincent, Latrobe, Pa., was born at Pittsburgh, Pa., the fourth child of Richard Stehle of Binsdorf, Württemberg, Germany, and Rose (Niggel) Stehle of Butler, Pa. He received his early education at St. Paul's parochial school, Pittsburgh, and on Mar. 17, 1885, he was sent with his older brother Joseph to St. Vincent College, Latrobe, Pa. Here in spite of his youth he soon ranked high in his classes. After completing the Latin course in 1892, he decided to study for the church and to become a Benedictine. On July 11, 1893, following his year of probation, he made his first vows, and during the next five years studied philosophy and theology in St. Vincent Seminary. After a papal dispensation had been obtained because he had not reached his canonical age, he was ordained priest on Sept. 8, 1899, by Bishop Regis Canevin of Pittsburgh. Having always shown a great love for classical languages, he was appointed professor of Latin in the seminary, and he gradually achieved in that tongue such perfection that he could use it in daily conversation. He also became secretary to Archabbot Leander Schnerr [*q.v.*] and made special studies in the liturgy of the church, which resulted in the publication of *The Manual of Episcopal Ceremonies* (1914), a book extensively used by the prelates of the Catholic Church in the United States. In 1911 he was appointed vice-rector of St. Vincent Seminary. It was chiefly through his efforts that the institution in 1914 was raised by the Roman authorities to the rank of a pontifical seminary, with the right of granting all ecclesiastical degrees in philosophy and theology. On June 25, 1918, by the vote of the capitulars of St. Vincent Archabbey, he was chosen coadjutor-abbot of the monastery with the right of succession; on Sept. 3, 1920, upon the death of Archabbot Leander Schnerr, he became the fouth archabbot of St. Vincent.

His administration is noteworthy for the extension and perfection of the course of studies at St. Vincent College, and for the founding of the Catholic University at Peking, China. With the addition of pre-medical, pre-legal, educational, and aeronautical courses to the existing curriculum of St. Vincent College the number of students was nearly doubled. The plan for a university in China, which began in a very modest manner in 1918, grew by leaps and bounds to unexpected proportions. Believing that the founding of a Benedictine abbey in China would contribute much toward the conversion of that nation, Father Aurelius and Dr. Barry O'Toole, a professor in St. Vincent Seminary, by degrees arrived at the decision to found a Benedictine university there and in 1922 secured the approval of the Congregation de Propaganda Fide in Rome. Two years later, June 10, 1924, the first Benedictines left St. Vincent for the Far East. In 1925 Archabbot Aurelius, who had been appointed chancellor of the new institution by Rome, went to China and procured the perpetual lease of Prince Ts'ai T'ao's palace, which became the first building of the university. In 1929 a large modern structure in Chinese architecture was built. Meanwhile the educational board of ‹he Chinese republic also approved the course of studies and granted the institution the right of conferring academic honors. In 1929 the Archabbot went to Rome to consult the ecclesiastical authorities about the extension of the work and to obtain material assistance. His labors, especially those connected with this American foundation in the Far East, gradually sapped the strength of the affable, tireless, and talented churchman, whose health was never of the best. In January 1930, while addressing a meeting of churchmen in Cleveland on behalf of his beloved project, he was stricken with a nervous breakdown, and shortly thereafter died in St. Francis Hospital, Pittsburgh, Pa.

[Who's Who in America, 1930–31; files of St. Vincent Coll. Jour., 1892–1930, and Bull. of the Cath. Univ. of Peking, 1926–30; letters and docs. in archives of St. Vincent Archabbey; obituary in Pittsburgh Sun-Telegraph, Feb. 13, 1930.]   F. F.

STEIN, EVALEEN (Oct. 12, 1863–Dec. 11, 1923), poet, author, and artist, was born in Lafayette, Ind., and spent her entire life there. Her father, John Andrew Stein (1832–1886), a Pennsylvania farmer by birth, practised law in Lafayette from his twenty-third year until his death; as a member of the Indiana Senate he drafted the bill which founded Indiana Agricultural College (later Purdue University). Her mother, Virginia (Tomlinson) Stein (1840–1924), was born at Logansport, Ind., of a pioneer family that had moved westward from Virginia. After being educated in the public schools of Lafayette, she studied at the Art Institute of Chicago and did creditable work as a decorative designer, exhibiting illuminated manuscripts at the Society of Arts and Crafts in Chicago, and in other midwestern cities. It is, however, as a poet and as a writer of children's stories that she gained widest recognition. Her home associations stimulated literary ambitions. Her father contributed verse and essays to local newspapers; her mother was the author of a few short stories for children; and her brother, Orth, was a professional newspaper man and magazine writer. After her father's death, she became assistant to her mother, who for over thirty years was librarian of the Lafayette public library.

At twenty-three she began contributing verse to the Indianapolis Journal and the St. Nicholas magazine. Her first book of poetry, One Way to the Woods (1897) was followed five years later by a second, Among the Trees Again, and some years later by a book of verse for children, Child Songs of Cheer (1918), and two volumes of translations, Little Poems from Japanese Anthologies (1925) and Poems of Giovanni Pascoli (1923). The majority of her poems describe with accurate and keenly-observed detail the seasons and the moods of nature, and express a sincere and ardent joy in natural objects; the best of them have a lilting cadence, as in "By the Kankakee," or a rush and sweep of verse, as in "A Song of Thought." In January 1900 she published in St. Nicholas a Christmas story for children, entitled "Felix"; three years later she included it in Troubadour Tales, the first of a number of children's books. Her knowledge of the art of illuminating manuscripts is evident in the second of these, Gabriel and the Hour Book (1906), and her interest in medieval France, awakened by her study of the art of illumination, appears in A Little Shepherd of Provence (1910), The Little Count of Normandy (1911), Pepin: A Tale of Twelfth Night (1924), and several of her short stories. Many of her stories are legends and fairy stories retold with clarity, simplicity, and charm. In 1915 she published Our Little Norman Cousin of Long Ago, one of four books written for a series introducing young readers to the people and customs of vanished nations. Unfortunately in these books, written to instruct rather than to entertain, she failed to exhibit the artistry of the legends and her usual ease in story-telling. She also wrote The Christmas Porringer (1914), Rosechen and the Wicked Magpie (1917), When Fairies were Friendly (1922), and The Circus Dwarf Stories (1927). Gentle and quiet in manner, she spent her leisure among books, cultivating her garden, or enjoying the natural beauties of the countryside. In 1907 she traveled in Europe for a few months, but except for this tour and an earlier trip to California she scarcely left Indiana.

[R. P. De Hart, Past and Present of Tippecanoe County, Ind. (2 vols., 1909); Lafayette Jour. Courier, Dec. 12, 1923, and Nov. 8, 1924; undated newspaper clippings in the possession of Florence G. Ruger, librarian of the Albert A. Wells Memorial Lib., Lafayette, Ind.]   V. L. S.

STEINER, BERNARD CHRISTIAN (Aug. 13, 1867–Jan. 12, 1926), teacher, librarian, and historian, was born at Guilford, Conn., the son of Sarah Spencer (Smyth) and Lewis Henry Steiner [q.v.]. He was the descendant of Jacob Stoner or Steiner who settled in Frederick County, Md., before 1736. He prepared for college at the academy at Frederick, Md., received the degrees of A.B. and A.M. from Yale in 1888 and in 1890, and received the doctor's degree in history from The Johns Hopkins University in 1891. In 1894 he received the LL.B. degree from the University of Maryland. He began his active career as instructor of history at Williams College for the year 1891–92. Excellently fitted, through training and interest, for teaching or for the bar, he would doubtless have adopted one or the other as his profession but for his election in 1892 at the age of twenty-five to the librarianship of the Enoch Pratt Free Library in succession to his father. As instructor in history, and later as associate, he gave courses in constitutional history at Johns Hopkins from 1893 to 1911. During this period he acted also, 1897–1900, as dean and professor of constitutional law in the short-lived Baltimore University, and, 1900–1904, as dean and professor of public law in the Baltimore Law School. These academic interests were subordinate to his work as librarian of the Enoch Pratt Free Library, the municipal public library of Baltimore. His conduct of that institution was marked by conservatism in methods of administration coupled with extraordinary aggressiveness in broadening its field of influence through the establishment of branch libraries in every neighborhood of an expanding city, increasing the number of these in his thirty-three-year tenure of office from six to twenty-five. His creed, "The Library is the continuation school of the people" was frequently on his lips and constantly in his mind, and its strict application in practice gave an element of austerity to his administration that sometimes placed him at variance with popular conceptions of the function of a public library. He kept abreast of the departmental development of the modern public library, however, in spite of an equipment and income adapted to the simpler needs of the late nineteenth century.

His interest in historical study, especially in the history of Maryland and Connecticut, the history of education in America, and religious and constitutional history, found constant expression in authorship. From 1891 to 1926 he made almost ninety contributions in the form of books and articles to the history of Maryland alone, and, under the direction of the Maryland Historical Society, he edited for the state with comprehensive introductions, volumes XVIII, XXXVI–XLV of the *Archives of Maryland* (1900, 1916–27), displaying in this task skill in the handling of archival material and breadth in its interpretation. His biographies were, perhaps, his most significant productions. For the subjects of these books he chose deliberately men of real importance in their own times who, falling short of the highest achievement, were in danger of being forgotten. Of these the most important are "Life and Administration of Sir Robert Eden," *Johns Hopkins University Studies in History and Political Science*, 16 ser., nos. 7–9 (1898); *Life and Correspondence of James McHenry* (1907); *Life of Reverdy Johnson* (1914);

Life of Henry Winter Davis (1916); "Life of Henry Barnard," *U. S. Bureau of Education Bulletin*, no. 8 (1919); and *Life of Roger Brooke Taney* (1922). Other important writings are "History of Education in Connecticut," *U. S. Bureau of Education Circular of Information*, no. 2 (1893); "History of Education in Maryland," *Ibid.*, no. 2 (1894); *Citizenship and Suffrage in Maryland* (1895); *History of ... Guilford, Conn.* (1897); *Institutions and Civil Government of Maryland* (1899). Notable among his personal characteristics were his convinced Republicanism, his enthusiasm for civic and social service, and an intense religious conviction, expressed formally through active membership in the Presbyterian Church. All these interests were carried into his daily life and into his conversation, with the enthusiasm that was one of his noteworthy possessions. At his death he was survived by a son and by his widow, Ethel Simes (Mulligan) Steiner, to whom he was married Nov. 7, 1912.

[*Quarter-Century Record of the Class of 1888, Yale College* (1914), comp. by B. C. Steiner (1914); L. H. and B. C. Steiner, *The Geneal. of the Steiner Family* (1896); *Who's Who in America*, 1924–25; intro. by L. C. Wroth to *Archives of Md., ante*, vol. XLV with list of writings on Md. compiled by W. R. Steiner; *Proc. Am. Antiquarian Soc.*, Apr. 1926; *Sun* (Baltimore), Jan. 13, 1926.]   L. C. W.

STEINER, LEWIS HENRY (May 4, 1827–Feb. 18, 1892), physician and librarian, was born in Frederick, Md., the son of Christian Steiner, a general merchant, and Rebecca (Weltzheimer), his cousin. He was of German descent, his first American ancestor on his father's side being Jacob Steiner who was in Frederick County before 1736. Lewis was educated in Frederick Academy and in Marshall College at Mercersburg, Pa., where he was graduated in 1846. Three years later he took his degree in medicine at the University of Pennsylvania. He began practice in Frederick, but removed to Baltimore in 1852 to take a teaching position in a private medical institute. Always interested in the natural sciences, particularly in chemistry and botany, he decided in 1855 to give up the practice of medicine and devote his whole time to the teaching of these subjects.

He was professor of chemistry and natural history at Columbian College and of chemistry and pharmacy at the National Medical College, both located in Washington, D. C., from 1853 to 1855; lecturer on chemistry and physics at the College of St. James at Hagerstown, Md., from 1854 to 1859; and lecturer on applied chemistry at the Maryland Institute in 1855 and 1856. He was one of a group that, in 1856, reorganized the Maryland College of Pharmacy, in which he held

the chair of chemistry until 1861. With the outbreak of the Civil War he returned to Frederick
and entered the service of the United States
Sanitary Commission. He was chief of that
service with the Army of the Potomac during the
campaigns of 1863 and 1864. His experiences
are recorded in two reports issued in 1862 and
1863, and in 1866 he published a short history of
the Sanitary Commission.

He was chosen president of the Frederick
County school board, in 1865, in which capacity
he interested himself particularly in providing
school facilities for negro children. From 1871
to 1883 he represented his native county in the
state Senate as a Republican, delivering there,
Feb. 23, 1876, a notable address published under
the title, *The Louisiana Legislature and States
Rights* (1876). He was a delegate to the Republican National Convention in 1876, which
nominated Hayes for the presidency. From 1873
to 1884 he was political editor of the *Frederick
Examiner.*

When, in 1884, Enoch Pratt [*q.v.*] of Baltimore endowed and built the free library which
bears his name, he brought Steiner from Frederick to be its librarian. It was opened to the
public in 1886, and from that time until his sudden death from apoplexy in 1892 Steiner guided
its destinies. He was succeeded as librarian by
his son, Bernard Christian Steiner [*q.v.*], who
held the position for thirty-four years until he in
turn died in 1926. Steiner's publications were
numerous and varied. Among his pamphlets are
Physical Science (1851), *Report on the Progress of Medical Chemistry* (1855), *Report on
Strychnia* (1856), *The Medical Profession and
Modern Chemistry* (1856), *The Marvelous in
Modern Times* (1860), *The Divining Rod*
(1861), *Table Movings and Spirit Rappings*
(1861), and *Animal Magnetism and Hypnotism*
(1861). He was an elder of the Reformed Church
of Frederick and a member of the Potomac
synod. For its publishing house he made translations from the German of a number of children's
stories, notably *The Adventures of Leo Rembrandt* (1869), and *The Story of Father Miller*
(1869), both by Franz Hoffmann. He also published *Outlines of Chemical Analysis*, a translation, made in collaboration with David Breed,
from the German of Heinrich Will. As a member of the synod he collaborated in the preparation of a hymn-book, *Cantate Domino* (1859), *A
Catechism of Christian Religion; Commonly
Called the Heidelberg Catechism* (1860), and
Order of Worship (1866). From 1859 to 1861
he was assistant editor of the *American Medical
Monthly* of New York.

In addition to his affiliations with medical societies he was a member of the Maryland Academy of Science, the Philadelphia Academy of
Natural Science, the American Association for
the Advancement of Science, and the American
Public Health Association. He was one of the
founders in 1876 of the American Academy of
Medicine, and its president in 1878. On Oct. 30,
1866, he married Sarah Spencer Smyth, daughter of Judge Ralph D. Smyth of Guilford, Conn.;
they had three sons and three daughters. Steiner
edited and published a *History of Guilford, Connecticut* (1877) from manuscript left by his father-in-law.

[L. H. and B. C. Steiner, *The Geneal. of the Steiner
Family* (1896); E. F. Cordell, *Univ. of Md.* (1907);
Bull. Am. Acad. Medicine (1892), pp. 216–18; J. R.
Quinan, *Medic. Annals of Baltimore* (1884); H. A.
Kelly and W. L. Burrage, *Am. Medic. Biogs.* (1920);
Sun (Baltimore), Feb. 19, 1892.]   J.M.P.

STEINERT, MORRIS (Mar. 9, 1831–Jan. 21,
1912), collector of musical instruments, was born
of Jewish parents, Heyum Löb Steinert and
Esther Steinert, in Scheinfeld, a small Bavarian
village. His early education was necessarily
meager, but later he came under the influence of
a man named Kleinschrod and under his guidance
made extensive studies in the German classics
and philosophy. Moritz (his given name) showed
from the beginning an aptitude for music. He
first learned to play, not on the pianoforte, but on
the clavier, and grew naturally to understand the
older types of instruments and the music of the
Mozart-Haydn period written for them. This
affection for the antique in music led to the development of his taste for collecting instruments
in his later years. He learned also to play the
violoncello and many times his mastery of both
keyboard and bowed instruments served him well
in his struggle to make a living as a musician.
Music was not, however, his first profession. At
the age of twelve he worked in the shop of a
maker of optical instruments at Coblenz. He was
then sent out by his employer as a salesman at
Bad-Ems, where he remained for three years.
The interruption of business by the Revolution
of 1848 necessitated his return to his home for
a time, and thus the record of his life for a number of years thereafter is one of wandering from
city to city in an attempt to make his way as an
optician. His business took him first to Switzerland, then to Germany and Russia. He settled
for short periods in 1855 at Berlin, Helsingfors,
and St. Petersburg successively. His experiences
during this time of his career were not always
pleasant, for life in cold, police-ridden Russia
was exceedingly difficult, even hazardous.

Throughout these earlier years Steinert's love

for music became intensified as he heard the then "new" music of Beethoven, Schubert, and Schumann, and the German and Italian operas. Shortly after 1855 he emigrated to America, and after several years of selling optical instruments at Sharon Springs, N. Y., he settled in New Haven, Conn. The musical profession, however, gradually took the place of his trade, and the records show him as a violoncellist in Maretzek's orchestra in New York City, and as pianist with a traveling minstrel's troupe. After a short period of residence in Savannah and Thomasville, Ga., the opening of the Civil War sent him North and he settled permanently in New Haven. From 1861 until his death his work was identified with New Haven, and his most memorable activities were those that contributed to the musical development of that city. He founded the Mathushek Pianoforte Company, and later the M. Steinert and Sons Company, which maintained stores for the sale of pianos in Boston Providence, New Haven, and other cities.

In his later years Steinert became greatly interested in collecting old musical instruments, purchasing the first examples in and near his native village of Scheinfeld. His skill in discovering and restoring them was soon recognized, and he was invited to exhibit his collection at the Vienna exposition of music and drama in 1892, and at the World's Columbian Exposition in Chicago in 1893. He donated the greater part of the collection in 1900 to Yale University. There are few more important collections of the kind, containing as it does many rare examples of clavichords, harpsichords, early pianofortes, and viols (see Steinert's *The M. Steinert Collection of Keyed and Stringed Instruments*, 1893). In 1892 Steinert founded the New Haven Symphony Orchestra, one of the oldest symphonic organizations in America. He was married to Caroline Dreyfuss on Jan. 7, 1857, and there were nine children. Shortly before her death in 1899, he wrote *Reminiscences of Morris Steinert* (1900), a book which reflects in a delightfully natural way the rare good humor of its author and which gives a vivid picture of an unusually eventful life.

[Information from the family, and Steinert's *Reminiscences*. See also: *Grove's Dict. of Music and Musicians, Am. Supp.* (1930); W. S. Pratt, ed., *The New Encyc. of Music and Musicians* (1929); T. B. Willson, *Hist. Cat. of the M. Steinert Coll. of Musical Instruments* (1913); *New Haven Evening Register*, Jan. 22, 1912.]   D. S. S.

STEINITZ, WILLIAM (May 17, 1836–Aug. 12, 1900), chess player, was born at Prague, the son of middle-class Jewish parents. When he was twenty years old he registered as a student in the Polytechnicum in Vienna and there in the cafés became enamored of chess. Turning briefly to journalism as a means of livelihood, he perfected himself in the royal game. In 1862, when he participated in the international tournament in London, he placed sixth. In the same year he defeated Serafino Dubois in the first of some thirty important matches, all won except the final two of 1894 and 1896. By his defeat of Adolph Anderssen in 1866 he achieved general recognition as chess champion of the world, a title which he held for twenty-eight years and justified by a fine record of successes in matches and tournaments. He was never defeated in any even match until he met Emanuel Lasker; though he was not at his best in tournament play; in fifteen major tournaments he was nine times first and only once as low as sixth. He spent twenty years (1862–82) in England, where from January 1873 to August 1882 he edited the chess column in the English journal, *Field*. Though he had become a British citizen, in 1883 he came to America and a year later acquired American citizenship. In America he edited the *International Chess Magazine*, 1885–91, *The Book of the Sixth American Chess Congress . . . 1889* (1891), the chess column in the *New York Tribune* (Sunday edition), Oct. 19, 1890–Aug. 6, 1893, and for a brief time the columns in the *Sunday Herald* (Baltimore) and the *New York Herald*. His most notable literary achievement was *The Modern Chess Instructor* (2 pts. 1889–1895), which contributed to the theory of chess a somewhat new point of view. In chess tactics he represented the beginning of the modern school in which the accumulation of small advantages plays the greatest rôle. In 1894 and again in 1896 he was defeated by Emanuel Lasker in a match for the championship of the world. The defeat was a blow not only to his prestige but to his means of livelihood. Undoubtedly his mental troubles, which began shortly after this time, were due to the circumstances caused by his defeat. In 1897, while in Saint Petersburg (later Leningrad) at a tournament, he was adjudged insane and was confined for a time. Spells of insanity recurred until his death at the Manhattan State Hospital, Ward's Island, New York. In 1900 he published a small tract, an ill-natured appeal for money: *My Advertisement to Antisemites in Vienna and Elsewhere by "A Schacherjude" (Mercenary Jew): or, An Essay on Capital, Labor, and Charity.*

He was short in stature, heavy set, and slightly lame. His infirmity in later life gave him a hunchbacked and gnomelike aspect, to which his ruddy beard and large head contributed. In disposition he was inclined to be disagreeable, and the trait carried over into some of his chess commentaries.

He expressed himself vigorously and picturesquely, with less restraint as he grew older. He must early have appreciated that there was a possibility for him to attain in chess an eminence not likely in business. Certainly both his long career as champion of the world and his literary activity amply vindicated his choice of a career. By matches, by exhibitions, by play for money in clubs, by occasional engagements in the mechanical player at the Eden Museum in New York, and by literary work, he was able to make a living, albeit a somewhat precarious one, at the game of chess. He was twice married, once in England and once in America; his first wife, Caroline, died May 27, 1892 (dedication to *My Advertisement*). A daughter whom he had adopted in England died in New York in 1888; there was one son born to the American wife, who was much younger than her husband.

[The date of birth is from Devidé, who knew Steinitz long and intimately; it is given as May 18, 1837, by the Czechoslovakian legation, Washington, D. C. Sources include Charles Devidé, *A Memorial to William Steinitz* (1901); Ludwig Bachmann, *Schachmeister Steinitz: Ein Lebensbild des ersten Weltschachmeisters, dargestellt in einer vollständigen Sammlung seiner Partien* (vols. I–IV, 1910–20) and *Schachjahrbuch für 1900* (Ansbach, 1901), pp. 197–203; P. W. Sergeant, *A Century of British Chess* (1934); obituaries in *Deutsche Schachzeitung*, Sept. 1900, *British Chess Mag.*, Sept. 1900, *N. Y. Tribune*, Aug. 14, and *Times* (London), Aug. 15, 1900; correspondence with Charles Devidé and Hermann Helms; personal acquaintance.]

L. C. K.

STEINMETZ, CHARLES PROTEUS (Apr. 9, 1865–Oct. 26, 1923), mathematician, electrical engineer, the only child of Karl Heinrich Steinmetz and his first wife, Caroline (Neubert) Steinmetz, was born in Breslau, Germany, where his father was employed as a lithographer in the railroad office. His given name, which he used for about the first twenty-five years of his life, was Karl August Rudolf, but in his application for American citizenship he anglicized his first name to Charles and substituted for the other two the name Proteus, a nickname given him when he joined the student mathematical society in Breslau. Although deformed from birth, he was a normally inquisitive, mischievous boy but badly spoiled by his grandmother, who mothered the family after the death of Charles's mother when he was a year old. It was evident early in his school career that he had a keen mind, and when he had completed the course in the gymnasium his father willingly sent him to the University of Breslau instead of apprenticing him to a trade. He entered the university in 1883, his eager, penetrating mind just beginning to open to the stimulus of study and his whole nature a questioning one. He was decidedly versatile and had an astonishing capacity for study. During his six years at the university he never missed a class, took a prodigious number of notes, and even undertook independent investigations at home. From the very first he selected difficult technical subjects. Beginning with mathematics and astronomy, he expanded his studies so that in his sixth year he was taking theoretical physics, chemistry, electrical engineering, specialized work in higher mathematics, and medicine. In addition, he was a student of economics and kept up his reading of the classics. At the same time he was a friendly, sociable fellow who was ready to join in lively, carefree student parties at almost any hour. About 1884 he joined the student Socialist group and in the course of the succeeding four years became most active, serving for a time as ghost editor of the *People's Voice*, published by the Socialists of Breslau. This proved his undoing; for, as a result of a most daring editorial published early in 1888, he had to flee from Germany to avoid arrest and imprisonment just as he had completed his university work and his thesis for his doctor's degree, which was never conferred upon him. Fleeing to Switzerland, where he lived a year in Zürich in straitened circumstances, he spent six months in attendance at the Polytechnic School, and occasionally wrote an article on some phase of electrical engineering for a German technical journal.

In the late spring of 1889, on the spur of the moment, he sailed steerage for the United States, financed by a student friend who accompanied him. He landed in New York on June 1 and within two weeks found employment as a draftsman for Rudolf Eickemeyer [*q.v.*] at Yonkers, N. Y., to whom he had gone with a letter of introduction (Hammond, *post*, p. 155). Eickemeyer, who was then engaged in research and in the development of electrical machinery, soon found Steinmetz, with his keen mathematical and technical mind, of the greatest help, and before very long established him in an experimental laboratory of his own. Here he applied himself earnestly not only to the electrical problems given him but also, in characteristic fashion, to the problem of Americanizing himself. He mastered the language, applied for citizenship, and even joined the American Institute of Electrical Engineers and the New York (later American) Mathematical Society. At the time electrical engineers were concerned with reducing the losses of efficiency in electrical apparatus due to alternating magnetism (hysteresis). The laws of this power loss were entirely unknown, and many engineers doubted its existence. Steinmetz, however, having been given the task of calculating and designing an alternating current commutator motor, and wishing to calculate the hysteresis loss, derived the law of hysteresis mathematically from existing data. He followed this with an elaborate series of tests on any and every sample of iron obtainable to prove the law and simplify its application, and in 1892 read two papers on the subject before the American Institute of Electrical Engineers. These at once established his reputation as a new thinker possessed of a powerful, analytical mind. Publicly acclaimed on every hand, he became widely known among electrical scientists, and his mathematical genius was recognized as far above the ordinary. Shortly after the organization of the General Electric Company in 1892, he joined the staff of the calculating department and went first to Lynn, Mass., and then to Schenectady, N. Y. After completing his second year with the company he was made consulting engineer, a position he held throughout the rest of his life. While he was engaged in his studies of magnetism at Yonkers, he had begun studies of alternating electric current phenomena, which were then little understood and most complex. Through the application of pure mathematics involving a degree of intricate work bewildering to the layman, he found a mathematical method of reducing the alternating current theory to a basis of practical calculation, and presented a rather complicated outline of the new method to the International Electrical Congress in session at Chicago, Ill., in 1893. Lack of funds prevented its publication at that time, but four years later he published the original paper, as well as a series of articles bringing out the practical side of his method, as a textbook under the title, *Theory and Calculation of Alternating Current Phenomena* (1897), with Ernst J. Berg as co-author. He found himself in unapproachable intellectual solitude, however, for practically no one could understand his theory or use his method. Gradually, however, through the publication of several textbooks— *Theoretical Elements of Electrical Engineering* (1901), *Engineering Mathematics* (1911)— and the expansion of his first book into three volumes—*Theory and Calculation of Alternating Current Phenomena* (5th ed., 1916), *Theory and Calculation of Electric Circuits* (1917), and *Theory and Calculations of Electrical Apparatus* (1917)—he brought about a clear understanding of his symbolic method, which is now universally used in alternating current calculations. His third and last great research undertaking had to do with the phenomena which are centered in lightning. As electric transmission lines spread over the country, lightning, an old enemy,

became more formidable, and protection from lightning most important. In an effort to learn more about it, Steinmetz began a systematic study of the general equation of the electric current and of "transient electrical phenomena," as lightning is scientifically called, publishing the results periodically from 1907 onward. This work culminated in 1921 with the dramatic experiments yielding man-made lightning in the laboratory. Though this was not the end of the investigation, it was left uncompleted at Steinmetz's death.

In addition to his consulting work and his writing, he was professor of electrical engineering, 1902–13, and professor of electrophysics, 1913–23, at Union University, Schenectady, N. Y., and lectured on electrical subjects throughout the country. He served on the board of education of Schenectady, of which he was president for two terms, and on the common council. The numerous honors conferred on him included the presidency of the American Institute of Electrical Engineers, 1901–02; the award of the Elliott Cresson gold medal, made by the Franklin Institute, Philadelphia; and membership in the American Academy of Arts and Sciences and the American Philosophical Society. He patented a large number of inventions, many of them basic, and wrote several books in addition to those mentioned, among them *Theory and Calculation of Transient Electric Phenomena and Oscillations* (1909); *General Lectures on Electrical Engineering* (copyright 1908), compiled and edited by J. L. Hayden; *Radiation, Light and Illumination* (1909); and *Elementary Lectures on Electric Discharges, Waves and Impulses, and Other Transients* (1911), all of which went through several editions. He never married but legally adopted as his son and heir Joseph Le Roy Hayden, who survived him.

[*Who's Who in America*, 1922–23; *Who's Who in Engineering*, 1922–23; J. W. Hammond, *Charles Proteus Steinmetz, A Biog.* (copr. 1924); J. T. Broderick, *Steinmetz and His Discoverer* (copr. 1924); J. N. Leonard, *Loki: The Life of Charles Proteus Steinmetz* (1929), a popular biog.; and "Steinmetz, Jove of Science," *World's Work*, Feb. 1929; Mary V. Hun, in *Forum*, Feb. 1924; obituaries in *Trans. Illuminating Engineering Soc.*, vol. XVIII (1923), H. M. H., in *Jour. Institution of Electrical Engineers* (London), vol. LXII (1924), *Jour. Am. Inst. of Electrical Engineers*, Nov. 1923; obituary and editorial in *N. Y. Times*, Oct. 27, 1923.]   C. W. M—n.

STEINMEYER, FERDINAND [See Farmer, Father, 1720–1786].

STEINWAY, CHRISTIAN FRIEDRICH THEODORE (Nov. 6, 1825–Mar. 26, 1889), piano manufacturer, was born in Seesen, Germany, the eldest child of Henry Engelhard Steinway [*q.v.*] and Juliane (Thiemer) Steinway.

As a youth he was musically talented, and in 1839 sufficiently accomplished as a pianist to be given the task of demonstrating his father's pianos at a fair in Brunswick. He was educated at Jacobsohn College in Seesen, where he became interested in the study of acoustics and was commissioned by his instructor, who took a particular interest in his brilliant pupil, to make the models needed for the lectures. When he completed his college course and went to work at a bench in his father's piano factory, he brought his scientific training to bear on the design and construction of pianofortes. In 1851, when his father and brothers left Germany for America, he stayed in Seesen, ostensibly to close the family business affairs and later to follow his kin to New York. He remained in Germany, however, for fourteen years after the departure of his family. On Oct. 10, 1852, he married Johanna Frederika Karolina Magdalena Luederman, and moved the piano business to Wolfenbüttel. In 1858 he admitted Friedrich Grotrian to partnership, and in the following year moved the firm's headquarters to Brunswick. Following the death of two of his brothers in 1865, he received an appeal from his father to come to New York to assist in the conduct of the Steinway business in America (the family name, originally Steinweg, had been legally changed to Steinway in 1864). He accordingly sold his business at Brunswick to his partners, Grotrian, Helfferich, and Schulz, and departed for New York. He immediately took charge of the construction department of the factory of Steinway & Sons, by this time a flourishing enterprise, and while his brother William [*q.v.*] devoted himself to the business management and sales department of the firm, he applied modern science to the problems of piano building. He investigated and tested the relative qualities of various woods; he continued his study of chemistry to determine the best ingredients of glue, varnish, and oils; and he experimented in metallurgy to find a proper alloy for casting iron plates strong enough to bear the strain of 75,000 pounds from the strings of the concert grand piano he wished to build.

He remained in America for only five years. He never enjoyed his surroundings in New York and sincerely wished to return to Germany. Moreover, he was anxious to be near Hermann Ludwig Ferdinand von Helmholtz, the distinguished physicist who had established a sure physical foundation for the phenomena manifested by musical tones. After leaving America in 1870, however, he was continuously in the employ of the American firm until his death in

Brunswick. He continued his research and experiments, traveled extensively in Europe to meet and confer with eminent scientists, and made frequent trips to New York. Utilizing the discoveries of Helmholtz and of John Tyndall, the author of *Sound* (1867), he demonstrated that scientific study and research are as necessary to piano design and manufacture as empirical methods. A musician and pianist himself, he knew the demands made on the piano by the music of such composers as Franz Liszt and Anton Rubinstein, and he made it his business to construct an instrument which would meet the requirements of nineteenth-century virtuosi.

[In addition to the sources referred to in the article on Henry Engelhard Steinway, see William Geppert, in *Musical Courier*, Oct. 19, 1929, and *N. Y. Tribune*, Mar. 27, 31, 1889. Information has been supplied by Theodore Steinway.]   J.T.H.

STEINWAY, HENRY ENGELHARD (Feb. 15, 1797–Feb. 7, 1871), piano manufacturer, originally named Steinweg, was born in Wolfshagen, Germany. The names of his parents are not noted in the family records. In his boyhood and youth he endured many hardships. During the Napoleonic invasion of Germany several of his brothers were killed and the Steinweg house was burned, and when he was fifteen his father and remaining brother were killed in an accident. In 1815 he was drafted for the army and is said to have taken part in the battle of Waterloo. Though he was without musical training and manual instruction, he had a talent for craftsmanship and an interest in the making of musical instruments. His first instrument, made after his return from the war, was a zither. In 1818 he entered the shop of an organ builder at Seesen, and became the organist of the village church; two years later he became interested in piano-making. Though his first piano is given various dates between 1825 and 1835, one account relates that it was his wedding-gift to his bride (Dolge, *post*, p. 300). According to family records, his marriage occurred in February 1825, and the bride was Juliane Thiemer. Seven children were eventually born to the Steinwegs: Christian Friedrich Theodore [*q.v.*], Doretta, Charles, Henry, Wilhelmina, William [*q.v.*], and Albert.

Steinweg's piano business prospered. In 1839 he exhibited a grand piano and two square pianos at a fair in Brunswick, Germany, where he was awarded the first prize, a gold medal, but in 1848 and 1849 the revolutions in Central Europe ruined his business, and two years later he decided to emigrate to America, where his son Charles had already gone. With his wife and daughters, and all of his sons but Theodore, he embarked from Hamburg on the *Helene Sloman,* and arrived in New York, June 9, 1851. For about two years he and his sons worked in various piano factories in New York. On Mar. 5, 1853, they joined forces again to start their own business. A year later they were awarded a medal for a square piano they exhibited at the Metropolitan Fair in Washington, D. C. In 1855 Steinweg exhibited an innovation in piano-making at the American Institute, New York, a square piano with cross- or over-strung strings, and a full cast-iron frame. For five years after coming to America he concerned himself with building square pianos only, but in 1856 he manufactured a grand piano and in 1862 an upright. Meanwhile the factory quarters on Walker Street, New York, became too small for the growing business, and in 1860 a new factory was completed on Fourth (Park) Avenue at Fifty-third Street. On Apr. 30, 1861, he and his son signed their first co-partnership agreement, and in July 1864 had their name legally changed to Steinway.

Soon after this event tragedy visited the family, for in 1865 two of the sons died. The organization was so crippled that Steinway persuaded his eldest son, Theodore, to come to America and join the business, and aid him in the technical supervision of building pianos. In 1866 he built Steinway Hall on Fourteenth Street (formally opened in 1867), a building containing retail warerooms and offices for the firm, and a concert hall that became one of the centers of New York's musical life. A few years later he died in New York, survived by his daughters and three of his sons. In his piano business, which has continuously remained in the possession of his descendants and still bears his name, he established an enterprise in which manufacturing has been regarded in the old fashion: as a craft, not as a mere commercial undertaking.

[The most complete account of Steinway and his family appears in Alfred Dolge, *Pianos and Their Makers,* vol. I (1911). See also *The Steinways of To-day,* a pamphlet issued by Steinway & Sons, from which the date of birth is taken; "Lineal Descendants of Henry Engelhard Steinway" in *Clef* (Kansas City, Mo.), vol. III, no. 8, 1916; Elbert Hubbard, *The Story of the Steinways* (1911), an account that stresses the picturesque; *Fortune,* Dec. 1934, and *Music,* Jan. 1897. For an obituary see *N. Y. Tribune,* Feb. 8, 1871.]

J.T.H.

STEINWAY, WILLIAM (Mar. 5, 1835– Nov. 30, 1896), piano manufacturer, was born in Seesen, Germany, the sixth child and fourth son of Henry Engelhard Steinway [*q.v.*] and Juliane (Thiemer) Steinway. The family name was originally Steinweg. Like his eldest brother, Christian Friedrich Theodore [*q.v.*], he

studied at Jacobsohn College in Seesen, where his father was engaged in manufacturing pianos. He lacked the scientific mind of his brother, and his interest lay in the study of languages and music rather than in acoustics from the standpoint of the physicist. When the family moved to New York in 1851 he was offered the choice of studying music or of learning the piano-making craft. He chose the latter and was apprenticed to the firm of William Nunns & Company, one of the leading piano manufacturers of the time. In 1853 he joined his father in business. After several years at a workman's bench he turned his attention to the commercial side of the business, and at the death of two of his brothers in 1865 he was equipped to take full charge of the financial and commercial departments of the firm.

With his brother Theodore in full charge of the scientific and manufacturing departments, he was able to devote his attention to selling the pianos his father and brother made. Realizing that the more interested Americans became in music, the more likely they would be to buy pianos, he urged his father to build and open Steinway Hall on Fourteenth Street, inaugurated in 1867 with a concert given by Theodore Thomas [*q.v.*] and his orchestra; he became one of the financial backers of the Thomas orchestra, and interested himself in the opera at the Academy of Music; he encouraged distinguished foreign pianists and musicians to visit America, and often provided the funds to guarantee the success of their tours. He also started an aggressive advertising campaign that was revolutionary in the piano industry and shocking to some of his conservative competitors. Having won an international standing for the Steinway firm by inducing foreign artists to play Steinway pianos, he opened a Steinway hall in London in 1876, and in 1880 established a factory at Hamburg, Germany, to supply the European demand for the product of his firm. When Steinway & Sons was incorporated, May 17, 1876, he was elected president, and continued in that office until his death twenty years later.

Although he was primarily interested in the affairs of his business and in music, he was active also in public affairs. He was the first chairman of the Rapid Transit Commission of New York City, which planned the construction of New York's first subway. It was he who planned and started the subway under the East River from Forty-second Street to Long Island City, and when this project was later purchased and completed by August Belmont it was named the Steinway tunnel in his memory. In 1880 he purchased four hundred acres of land on Long Island Sound and established the town of Steinway, L. I., where the present factories of Steinway & Sons are. He was also a member of the German Turn Verein in New York, and for fourteen years president of Der Deutscher Liederkranz (New York). He was married on Apr. 23, 1861, in Buffalo, N. Y., to Johanna Roos, by whom he had a son and a daughter; and on Aug. 16, 1880, in Hamburg to Elizabeth Raupt, by whom he had a daughter and two sons. He died in New York City, survived by his five children.

[The date of Steinway's birth, which is sometimes given as 1836, has been supplied by the family. In addition to the sources referred to in the article on Henry Engelhard Steinway, see *N. Y. Tribune*, Dec. 1, 6, 11, 1896. Information has been supplied by Theodore Steinway.]   J. T. H.

STEPHENS, ALEXANDER HAMILTON (Feb. 11, 1812–Mar. 4, 1883), congressman, Confederate vice-president, was born on his father's farm in that part of Wilkes County, Ga., that later became Taliaferro County. Known by his constituents as "Little Ellick," he was of average stature, but in weight seldom if ever attained a hundred pounds. A shrill voice, a sallow complexion, recurrent illness, and occasional melancholia gave evidence of organic defects; but his mind was not often morbid, and his will was always robust. Alexander Stephens, an immigrant from England to Pennsylvania, said to have been a Jacobite who came after the failure of the rising in 1745, had married a ferryman's daughter on the Susquehanna before drifting to the Georgia Piedmont, where he lived and died as a farmer of small scale. His youngest son, Andrew Baskins Stephens, made his home nearby, supplementing the meager earnings of his farm by conducting a country school. Andrew's first wife, Margaret Grier, died after bearing a daughter and two sons, and her place was filled by Matilda Lindsey, who added five more to the tale of the Stephens children. The deaths of Andrew and Matilda in 1826 brought a dispersal of the brood into the homes of such relatives as could give them shelter. But Alexander, the youngest of the first group, managed in after years to set the feet of Linton [*q.v.*], youngest of all, upon the path to prominence as a jurist.

Before his father's death Alexander, despite his frail physique, was doing a plowman's work, with brief terms at school interspersed. The fate which sent him to an uncle's care was kind, for the schooling was better, and the youth's earnestness prompted a patron to send him to an academy in the Georgia village of Washington. Here his admiration for his teacher, the Rev. Alexander Hamilton Webster led the boy to adopt Hamilton as a middle name. Here also a Presbyterian educational society lent him funds for a course at the University of Georgia with a view to his preparation for the ministry should he so determine. After four happy years at Athens he graduated in 1832 at the head of his class, and having decided against a church career, cast about for a livelihood and the means to repay the charges of his education. A year and a half of rural teaching proved so full of rough episodes and so fatiguing that he read law, was admitted to the bar in 1834, and began practice at Crawfordville within a few miles of his birthplace.

The University of Georgia was in the time of Stephens' residence a place of lively debate among the students, with sentiment strong against protective tariffs and in favor of state rights. As a graduate Stephens was already primed to address his fellow-citizens on such themes; and this he did at Crawfordville on July 4, 1834, preceding his admission to the bar on July 22. Nullification he deprecated; but the right of a state to secede he upheld as a doctrine essential for keeping the central government within the bounds of constitutionality, moderation, and equity (Johnston and Browne, *post*, pp. 87–88). Within two years after that speech he was elected to the Georgia legislature; and, except for one term when he abstained from candidacy (1841), he was returned to one or the other of its houses until he went to Congress. His outstanding advocacy in this period was the project of the Western & Atlantic Railroad, to be built by the state as an avenue of commerce between Georgia and the grain region of the Northwest. The party with which Stephens had cast his lot embraced in the main the well-to-do folk whether on the seaboard or in the uplands. In its early phases a personal following successively of James Jackson, William H. Crawford, and George M. Troup [*qq.v.*], it adopted "State Rights" as its official designation in the later 'twenties, only to merge in the 'thirties with similar elements in other states under the Whig banner. The local opposition altered its name synchronously from Clark (see sketch of John Clark) to Union, then to Democratic, without material change of constituency. There were few substantial issues between the two except that on financial questions the Troup-State Rights-Whig party was the more conservative. It was not love of Henry Clay or indorsement of his nationalist program which led this group of Georgians into the Whig ranks, but rather a wish to link their local unit with a country-wide organization and to resist the Jacksonian surge. Stephens in particular sought in 1840 to promote the nomination of Troup for the presidency, and failing in this he declared for Harrison against Van Buren as "the choice of evils." Then and thereafter he found party restraint irksome.

Entering Congress in 1843, Stephens for a long time spoke only upon questions of large importance. His first notable speech was made at the beginning of 1845 on the Texas question. Annexation, he said, while tending to lessen the prosperity of the cotton states already in the Union, would give the South a greatly needed political weight, "thus preserving a proper balance between the different sections of the country" (Cleveland, *post,* pp. 301–02). He collaborated with Milton Brown of Tennessee to frame the resolution which prevailed against rival measures and was adopted. The next year he denounced the dispatch of troops to the Rio Grande and the consequent precipitation of war with Mexico; and in 1847, deprecating the Democratic project of expansion, he censured the Wilmot Proviso particularly, saying that if its policy were pursued the harmony of the Union would give place to a "prospect of desolation, carnage and blood" (*Ibid.,* p. 334). In July 1848, he said that had he "a voice that would echo from the mountain tops to the remotest plains and valleys of the country he would rouse the people from their slumbers to a sense of these outrages upon the great fundamental principles upon which their government was founded, and upon which their liberties rested" (*Congressional Globe,* 30 Cong., 1 Sess., p. 912). The occasion was a bill to deny to Texas the Santa Fé region although it lay within the Rio Grande limits. In the next month, without such lyricism but with great elaboration, he resisted the Clayton compromise bill, as a denial of Southern rights by indirection. This bill, to organize the territories of New Mexico and California with a reference of the question of slavery therein to the courts, was indorsed by the bulk of the Whigs, but Stephens caused enough defection to effect its defeat.

Thus the middle of the century came, with a miscellany of questions at loose ends. When Clay's plan for adjusting all these was before the House, Stephens contented himself in the main with votes of indorsement, though in August he blazed forth in defiance of the North: "Whenever this Government is brought in hostile array against me and mine, I am for disunion—openly, boldly and fearlessly, for *revolution.* . . . I am for conciliation if it can be accomplished upon

any reasonable and just principles. . . . You may think that the suppression of an outbreak in the southern States would be a holiday job for a few of your northern regiments, but you may find to your cost, in the end, that seven millions of people fighting for their rights, their homes, and their hearth-stones cannot be 'easily conquered' " (*Congressional Globe,* 31 Cong., 1 Sess., Appendix, pp. 1083–84).

Like Robert Toombs and Howell Cobb [*qq.v.*], Stephens was using strong words at Washington in order that if the result were favorable he might give soft counsel at home. In fact when the compromise measures were enacted, these three hastened to canvass Georgia in indorsement of the Union-saving legislation. For a convention which had been summoned with power to take unlimited action in the name of the state, Unionist delegates were now chosen at the polls in great majority; and the convention adopted the "Georgia Platform" approving the national compromise but with a threat of secession in case Congress or the Northern states failed to maintain it in letter and spirit. Stephens claimed the authorship of this platform, "on all turning points" (*Recollections,* p. 27). To improve the prospect of intersectional peace he, Toombs, and Cobb—two Whigs and a Democrat —undertook to discard their accustomed connections and launch jointly a Constitutional Union party. The lack of response in distant quarters brought a collapse of this project in Georgia and the return of Stephens and Toombs to an uneasy membership in their old party. When Winfield Scott was nominated as the Whig presidential candidate in 1852, Stephens framed a public letter which several other Southern Whig congressmen signed with him, repudiating the ticket on the ground of Scott's free-soil proclivities. The Know-Nothing movement soon captured a large part of the disintegrating Whig party; but Stephens, denouncing vigorously the proscription of immigrants and Catholics, made a shift to the Democratic organization without losing his seat in Congress.

In the welter of issues and the miscellany of men at Washington, Stephens found in Stephen A. Douglas a man to admire and indorse because of his urbane spirit, his fondness for "principles," and his opposition to congressional prohibition of slavery in the territories. The Kansas-Nebraska bill of course met his prompt approval; and when it reached the House he became the floor manager in its behalf. Not only did he share in the debates, but when these threatened to become interminable in committee of the whole, he procured closure by a shrewd motion to strike out the enacting clause. Under existing rules, as few but he were aware, this motion took precedence of pending amendments, and its adoption had the effect of causing the committee to report the bill unfavorably to the House. To get it reported in any manner without amendment was the essential purpose; and its friends who seemingly had killed the bill in committee promptly revived it by having the House disagree with the committee's report. Thereupon, by narrow margin, they promptly carried its enactment. Then and for years afterward Stephens was not merely proud of his personal feat but convinced that the bill was admirable (*American Historical Review,* October 1902, pp. 91–97). "The moral effect of the victory on our side," said he, "will have a permanent effect upon the public mind, whether any positive advantages accrue by way of the actual extension of slavery or not" (*Annual Report of the American Historical Association . . . 1911,* II, 344). Moreover, the bill embodied a principle; and however ambiguous and ineffective it might prove in operation, to the principle Stephens would cling.

But the disorders in Kansas, the party platforms, the Dred Scott decision, and the ceaseless wrangles over them gave even Stephens his fill of tweedledum and tweedledee; and he turned his thoughts mainly from the question of slavery in the territories to negroes and slavery at large. In 1845, denying that he was a defender of slavery in the abstract, he had said he would rejoice to see all men free "if a *stern necessity* . . . did not in some cases interpose and prevent" (Cleveland, p. 301). But within a decade he was praising the Southern system as the best in the world for the sustenance, advancement, and happiness of negroes (*Ibid.,* p. 429); in 1857 he was defending slavery on biblical grounds (*Ibid.,* pp. 557, 560); and in 1859 he was discussing with implications of approval the project of reopening the trade with Africa to procure more slaves in order to make more slave states. "African slavery with us," he now said, "rests upon principles that can never be successfully assailed by reason or argument" (*Ibid.,* p. 647). He was ready to meet Seward on his own ground: "I, too, believe in the higher law—the law of the Creator as manifested in his works and his revelation. . . . We must stand on the higher law, as well as upon the constitution." Since order is nature's first law, he continued, and gradations and subordination are essential in order, enslavement of an inferior race is right: "The principle will ultimately prevail. The wickedest of all follies, and the absurdest of all crusades are those

which attempt to make things equal which God in his wisdom has made unequal" (*Ibid.,* p. 649). These remarks of 1859 were made in a rather vainglorious speech at Augusta telling his constituents that he would represent them in Congress no longer. The main burden of this speech was the victory of the South at all important points, the placidity of the prospect within the Union, and the consequent lack of need for such watchmen as he at Washington. In his claim of all the virtues modesty was ignored; but if he had said merely that his conscientious best was always at call in the public service, none then or now could say him nay.

After his retirement from Congress, as previously between sessions, he plied a lucrative practice in the Georgia courts, and in leisure kept open house at "Liberty Hall" in Crawfordville, with a widowed sister presiding in default of a wife. He was a kindly master to his slaves, a generous patron of youths desiring college education, and a sociable companion when health permitted. Reciprocally, a multitude, including many negroes, held him in warmest esteem. Sometimes, however, his temper had proved brittle. Quarrels with William L. Yancey and Herschel V. Johnson brought him near to duels in the middle 'forties; and an affray with Judge Francis N. Cone in 1848, at a hotel in Atlanta, nearly cost him his life. In 1856 a joint debate with Benjamin H. Hill resulted in a challenge which Hill declined, saying privately that he had a family to support and a soul to save, while Stephens had neither. Stephens then posted Hill in the newspapers as "not only an impudent braggart but a despicable poltroon besides" (Pendleton, *post,* pp. 86–87).

Though he little thought it, Stephens was but a product of his time. A sensitive soul requiring himself to be high-minded, when he found a cause to champion he sought a principle to buttress every policy. This rationalizing of his conduct, while giving him great satisfaction, produced an exaltation of the technical and the trivial. Strategy was of little moment if his tactics were expert. His essential concern, often and sincerely proclaimed, was the preservation of Southern security within a placid Union of all the states; but his inability to yield on a detail or to suffer an opponent to score a point, his relish of victory for the sake of prestige and partisan morale, paralyzed him for the greater purpose. This is the more curious in the light of his complete lack of rancor and his essential kindliness toward all men.

The retirement to "Liberty Hall" and the courts of law could not divorce him from politics. As the campaign approached in 1860 he besought his correspondents to maintain Democratic solidarity. His preference for the presidency was R. M. T. Hunter [*q.v.*], with Douglas as a second choice. When the party split he clung to Douglas as against Breckinridge, and despite his own prior intention of abstinence, took the stump in a consciously forlorn effort to carry Georgia for the ticket. The Georgia legislature was in session when Lincoln was elected; and Gov. Joseph E. Brown promptly recommended that a convention be summoned for action upon the question of secession. In this crisis the Assembly invited several prominent citizens to give their advice. On the night of Nov. 12, Thomas R. R. Cobb spoke for secession forthwith. Toombs on the next evening proposed a quick plebiscite and secession by the legislature if the referendum should give warrant. Stephens took the rostrum on the third night, advocating not only a convention of Georgia but a conference of all the Southern states. Realizing that a policy of mere delay would be rejected, he proposed that the future convention demand of the several Northern states that they repeal their "personal liberty laws" and that Georgia retaliate in some manner upon such as might refuse. Beyond this he contemplated mere watchful waiting, with hope that the benefits of the Union might be retained but with readiness for drastic recourse if Lincoln or Congress invaded Southern rights or violated the constitution. Appealing to the spirit of Georgia's official motto, "Wisdom, Justice and Moderation," he said: "My position, then, in conclusion, is for the maintenance of the honor, the rights, the equality, the security, and the glory of my native state in the Union, if possible, but if these cannot be maintained in the Union, then I am for their maintenance, at all hazards, out of it" (*War Between the States,* II; 299). Toombs, seated on the platform, made interjections during the speech, and was answered in each instance. When Stephens ended he went to the desk and said with even more than his usual vigor: "Fellow citizens, we have just listened to a speech from one of the brightest intellects and purest patriots that now lives. I move that this meeting now adjourn, with three cheers for Alexander H. Stephens of Georgia!" (Pendleton, p. 163). The Damon-and-Pythias friendship of these twain was universally known; and this gesture of undiminished esteem during their brief divergence was received with great applause.

The publication of the speech brought Stephens a flood of letters, including one from Lin-

coln requesting a revised copy. In his reply Stephens alluded to the responsibility resting upon Lincoln in the crisis. To this Lincoln answered that he felt the weight of this, and said that any fears by the people of the South "that a Republican administration would directly, or *indirectly,* interfere with their slaves, or with them about their slaves" was groundless. He concluded: "I suppose, however, this does not meet the case. You think slavery is *right* and ought to be extended; while we think it is *wrong* and ought to be restricted. That I suppose is the rub. It certainly is the only substantial difference between us." Stephens rejoined, saying that the gravamen against the Republicans was their purpose "to put the institutions of nearly half the States under the ban of public opinion and national condemnation." He then turned to a more critical matter, for South Carolina had now seceded. Ultimate sovereignty residing always in the separate states, he said, "there is no rightful power in the general government to coerce a State in case any one of them should . . . resume the full exercise of her sovereign powers. Force may perpetuate a Union. That depends upon the contingencies of war. But such a Union would not be the Union of the constitution. It would be nothing short of a consolidated despotism" (Cleveland, pp. 150–54).

Meanwhile the Georgia legislature had summoned a convention, and the delegates elected were known to be secessionist in majority. When it met at the middle of January, Stephens, who was a delegate, spoke but once and briefly, supporting a resolution which as a substitute for a pending ordinance of secession proposed a Southern convention to consider the state of affairs and determine a course of action. Expressing a persistent hope of securing Southern interests within the Union, and urging negotiations to this end, he concluded: "My judgment, as is well known, is against the policy of immediate secession for any exciting causes. It cannot receive the sanction of my vote; but . . . if a majority of the delegates in this Convention shall, by their votes dissolve the compact of union . . . to which I have been so ardently attached, and have made such efforts to continue and to perpetuate on the principles upon which it was founded, I shall bow in submission to that decision." (Johnston and Browne, pp. 381–82. A fraudulent version was issued in 1863 by the Union League of Philadelphia in *The Rebuke of Secession Doctrines by Southern Statesmen,* and reprinted in many places after as well as before Stephens denounced it in his *War Between the States,* I, 23. L. L. Mackall discussed this forgery in the book section of the *New York Herald-Tribune,* Nov. 9, 1924.) When the convention rejected this resolution and adopted the ordinance, Stephens signed the document without further demur.

The project in hand was centripetal as well as centrifugal. The Georgia convention, pursuing a plan already prepared, elected delegates to a convention at Montgomery, Stephens among them, to form a union of the seceded states. In this assemblage he met no substantial opposition to his own specific desire to frame a government upon the model of that of the United States. Under the quickly devised Provisional Constitution, which converted the convention into a Provisional Congress and empowered that body to choose the executives, Jefferson Davis was elected as president of the Confederate States of America and Stephens as vice-president, both of these on Feb. 9, 1861, without overt opposition. The vice-president under this régime had no regular functions, for until the Permanent Constitution went into effect the next year there was no Senate over which he might preside. Stephens merely continued as a member of the single house and lent a hand in affairs outside as occasion invited. His most notable expression in this period was the "corner-stone speech" at Savannah, Mar. 21. In this he surveyed the conditions of the Confederacy, praised its Constitution, and appealed for wise and patriotic support of the cause. As to negro slavery, he said that the architects of American independence, as exemplified in Jefferson, had contemplated a theoretical equality of races; but, he continued: "Our new government is founded upon exactly the opposite idea; its foundations are laid, its corner-stone rests upon the great truth that the negro is not equal to the white man; that slavery—subordination to the superior race—is his natural and normal condition" (Cleveland, p. 721). In the same speech he said: "We are now the nucleus of a growing power, which if we are true to ourselves, our destiny, and high mission, will become the controlling power on this continent" (*Ibid.,* p. 726). But how to procure a prosperous or a peaceful future neither he nor any other Confederate could say. To solve the specific impasse concerning the seaboard forts, a cannonade reduced Sumter on Apr. 15, whereupon Lincoln called upon the several states for troops and Virginia, North Carolina, Tennessee, and Arkansas took steps for a junction with the original seven in the Confederacy. Stephens went as a commissioner and addressed the Virginia convention to hasten this process. This was his last official mission until the Hampton Roads Conference.

His fondness for scruples and constitutional restraint made Stephens an unhappy member of a wartime government, for exigencies were as naught in the face of his principles. Many of Davis' early appointments, and his course concerning cotton as a factor in foreign relations, were ill-judged in Stephens' opinion. But these were minor matters. The conscription of troops, the suspension of *habeas corpus,* and the establishment of military government in sundry localities all seemed to him outrageous invasions of civil rights. In 1862, when the Permanent Constitution gave him a Senate over which to preside, he became in a sense the leader of the opposition. His official duties, however, yielded him so little satisfaction that at one period he stayed away from Richmond for a year and a half. In public and private letters and occasional speeches he alternated censures of the administration and gloomy prognostications with appeals for support of the Confederate cause. In particular he stimulated Gov. Joseph E. Brown [*q.v.*] to challenge the power of Davis to conscript Georgia citizens.

The war itself was keenly distressing to Stephens, and particularly the sufferings of the wounded and the prisoners on both sides. He visited hospitals and stockades often, to give such relief or solace as he might, and he concerned himself zealously with promoting systematic exchange and parole of prisoners of war. In June 1863, Stephens procured a sanction from Davis to try to open negotiations with Lincoln to regularize exchanges and perhaps to reach some arrangement for ending the war. A refusal of Lincoln to receive such a mission killed the project for the time being. In September of the next year General Sherman, having captured Atlanta, sent oral messages to Stephens and to Brown inviting them to a conference with him with a view to possible arrangements for terminating the war. Stephens, while saying that he would gladly serve as a channel for an authoritative overture, declined the invitation to a personal conference (Johnston and Browne, p. 472). Brown answered to the same effect, and the war dragged on.

At the beginning of 1865 a bill to continue the suspension of *habeas corpus* passed the Confederate House and met a tie vote in the Senate. Stephens announced that it was his duty to cast the deciding vote, and said that before doing so he would state the reasons which influenced him. His right to make the proposed speech was challenged, and after sundry proceedings it was permitted only in secret session. The remarks he then made (summarized in *War Between the States,* II, 587–89) concluded with an expression of hope for independence through negotiation. Soon afterward Francis P. Blair, Sr., came from

Washington with Lincoln's permission to sound the Confederate authorities on a project of his for a truce and a joint expedition against Maximilian in Mexico. Davis broached this in confidence to Stephens, who leaped at the chance to confer with Lincoln. With R. M. T. Hunter and John A. Campbell [*qq.v.*] as fellow commissioners, he met Lincoln and Seward on shipboard near Fortress Monroe, Feb. 3, only to find an armistice unattainable and a basis of peace impossible between those who stipulated Confederate independence and those who required acquiescence to the Federal laws. The commissioners returned from Hampton Roads to Richmond in failure. Stephens went sadly home; and upon the collapse of the Confederacy he was not surprised when a detail of Federal troops arrested him, May 11, at "Liberty Hall." Taken eastward in custody, he was held prisoner at Fort Warren in Boston Harbor, diminishing the tedium by writing a narrative of recent events and a diary (printed in Avary, *Recollections*). Released on parole, Oct. 12, he was greeted warmly by throngs at New York, Washington, and Atlanta as he traveled homeward. At "Liberty Hall" he dwelt much as before, with former slaves of his continuing to serve him.

In January 1866 he was elected to the Senate of the United States, only to meet exclusion along with all others from the "rebel" states. On Washington's birthday he made a speech before the Georgia legislature in response to a request for his views on public affairs. In the deep adversity he counseled self-discipline, patience, and forbearance from recrimination. The total change in Southern internal polity, he said, ought to be given a fair trial, with the good will toward the negroes which their fidelity in times past had merited: "It is an ethnological problem, on the solution of which depends not only the best interests of both races, but it may be the existence of one or the other, if not both" (Johnston and Browne, p. 589). Specifically, he recommended support of the policies of President Andrew Johnson. In April he testified before the congressional joint committee on reconstruction. Questioned as to the sentiments prevailing among the people of Georgia, he said that they, while not repudiating the theoretical right of secession, were convinced by the failure of their effort and were cherishing no thoughts of such recourse in future. He described likewise a general acquiescence in the abolition of slavery and a somewhat surprising accord between the two races on the new legal and industrial basis. But as to pending projects of reconstruction by Congress he said the sentiments of Georgians, and his own, were

opposed to the vesting of the suffrage in the negroes or to any constitutional amendment while a number of states were deprived of representation. In fact he denied the constitutional power of the federal government to impose conditions precedent to the restoration of the late Confederate states to their functions in the Union (*Ibid.*, pp. 594–607). Congress proceeded with its drastic program; and Stephens accepted a publisher's invitation to write *A Constitutional View of the Late War Between the States.*

The first of these bulky volumes was published in 1868, the second in 1870. In an ill-judged attempt at enlivening its 1,200 pages of text, the book was cast in colloquies between Stephens and sundry men of straw whom he politely but continuously knocked down. It is a tedious rationalization, obscuring the historic problem of negro slavery by refinements of doctrine on the sovereignty of the states. Dull as the book may be to readers in the twentieth century, it was a sensation in its day, evoking attacks by Northern and Southern champions of causes upon which it impinged and yielding its author some $35,000 in royalties. Stephens not only replied to critics of every sort, but assembled the reviews, rejoinders, sur-rejoinders and rebuttals in a volume, *The Reviewers Reviewed* (1872), which is more dull than its predecessor. Afterward he wrote a school history of the United States (*A Compendium of the History of the United States,* 1872) which met some success, and a stout illustrated work (*A Comprehensive and Popular History of the United States,* 1882), which deservedly fell flat. In 1869 Stephens was offered a professorship of political science and history at the University of Georgia, but declined it. The next year he participated in a lease of the Western & Atlantic Railroad from the state of Georgia; but upon receiving a remonstrance from Toombs, pointing to the dubious quality of his colleagues and the questionable character of the procedure, Stephens transferred to the state his share of stock in the corporation. In 1871 he bought an interest in the *Southern Sun,* an Atlanta newspaper, and the next year filled its editorial page with endless arguments against the junction of the Democrats with the Liberal Republicans to support Horace Greeley. A few years of such ponderous journalism forced his withdrawal at a heavy loss.

Though reduced by rheumatism to crutches and a wheeled chair, Stephens in 1872 declared himself a candidate for the United States Senate. He was defeated by John B. Gordon, but before the end of that year he was elected to the lower house of Congress. At Washington a journalist described him as "an immense cloak, a high hat, and peering somewhere out of the middle a thin, pale, sad face." The writer continued: "How anything so small and sick and sorrowful could get here all the way from Georgia is a wonder. If he were to draw his last breath any instant you would not be surprised. If he were laid out in his coffin, he need not look any different, only then the fires would have gone out in those burning eyes. . . . That he is here at all to offer the counsels of moderation and patriotism proves how invincible is the soul that dwells in his shrunken and aching frame" (Pendleton, p. 387). This "queer-looking bundle," this pallid face, now seamed with "a thousand lines," remained in Congress for a decade, this cracked falsetto voice rising now and again to prove its owner still a master parliamentarian and a guardian of the public interest. In particular he counseled acquiescence in 1877 when the electoral commission decided the presidential contest in favor of Hayes, and he defended his own course, with fire on occasion, against criticism from all quarters.

Long since disabled for the practice of law, he resigned from Congress in 1882, only to find idleness a burden. He soon entered a successful candidacy for the governorship of Georgia; but he died a few months after inauguration. When his poor body lay in state "Little Ellick" had already become a tradition as one who had served his people through fair times and foul with conscience, eloquence, and unflagging zeal.

[A. H. Stephens, *A Constitutional View of the Late War Between the States* (2 vols., 1868–70), and M. L. Avary, ed., *Recollections of Alexander H. Stephens* (1910) are in part autobiographical. R. M. Johnston and W. H. Browne, *Life of Alexander H. Stephens* (1878), is a full biography, though not extending to his death; Louis Pendleton, *Alexander H. Stephens* (1908), is briefer. Henry Cleveland, *Alexander H. Stephens in Public and Private* (1866) is a collection of his principal speeches to the date of publication, preceded by a eulogistic sketch. "The Correspondence of Robert Toombs, Alexander H. Stephens, and Howell Cobb," ed. by U. B. Phillips, is in *Ann. Report of the Am. Hist. Asso. . . . 1911* (1913), vol. II, with a calendar of letters previously published. Certain letters alleged to have passed between Stephens and Abraham Lincoln in January 1860, were printed in a pamphlet by Judd Stewart, *Some Lincoln Correspondence with Southern Leaders before the Outbreak of the Civil War* (1909). The validity of these is effectively challenged by W. C. Ford in *Proc. Mass. Hist. Soc.*, LXI (1928), 183–95; but the Stephens-Lincoln correspondence at the close of that year, printed in crude facsimile in Cleveland's book, is of unquestioned authenticity. Eudora R. Richardson, *Little Aleck; A Life of Alexander H. Stephens* (1932), is a recent biography. See also J. D. Waddell, *Biog. Sketch of Linton Stephens* (1877); U. B. Phillips, "Georgia and State Rights," *Ann. Report of the Am. Hist. Asso. . . .1901* (1902), vol. II; R. H. Shryock, *Georgia and the Union in 1850* (1926); obituary in *Atlanta Constitution*, Mar. 4, 5, 1883.]   U. B. P.

STEPHENS, ALICE BARBER (July 1, 1858–July 13, 1932), illustrator, was born on a farm outside Salem, N. J., eighth of the nine children of Samuel C. Barber, a Quaker farmer whose forebears had emigrated to America from England more than three generations before, and Mary (Owen) Barber, of Welsh descent, whose ancestors had settled in Wading River, L. I., before the Revolution. She was educated in a New Jersey country school and in the public schools of Philadelphia, and studied art from an early age. At fifteen she began to earn her own living by selling wood engravings, which she had learned to make under Edward Dalziel. Intermittently between 1870 and 1876 she studied at the School of Design for Women in Philadelphia, where she later conducted life and portrait classes, and then worked under Thomas Eakins [q.v.] at the Pennsylvania Academy of the Fine Arts. Although her professional career began with wood engravings for *Scribner's Monthly, Harper's Weekly, Harper's Young People,* and other magazines, about 1876 she turned to illustrating. She spent the years 1886 and 1887 abroad, studying at the Académie Julian in Paris and in the studio of Filippo Colarossi, and traveling in Italy. In 1890 she won the Mary Smith prize at the Pennsylvania Academy of the Fine Arts for her "Portrait of a Boy." In June of the same year she married Charles Hallowell Stephens, artist and collector of Indian relics, by whom she had one child, a son. Her illustrations for George Eliot's *Middlemarch* and paintings for Dinah Maria Mulock Craik's *John Halifax, Gentleman* won a gold medal at the exhibition of women's work held at Earl's Court, London, in 1899; a year later she won a bronze medal at the Exposition Universelle in Paris and illustrated a special two-volume edition of Hawthorne's *The Marble Faun.* For fifteen months during the years 1901 and 1902 she traveled and studied in the art galleries of England and the Continent. Returning to Philadelphia, she settled with her husband and child in Rose Valley, Pa., where she lived for the rest of her life in a stone barn, "Thunder Bird," that she remodelled as a house and studio. Throughout her career she fought against ill health, often aggravated by pressure of work. By 1926 her active professional career was at an end, though she painted landscapes and still life until her last year. She died at Rose Valley and was buried in West Laurel Hill Cemetery.

During her career she illustrated books by George Eliot, Louisa May Alcott, Bret Harte, Sir Arthur Conan Doyle, and Hawthorne, and supplied illustrations for numerous periodicals. Though she used both oils and watercolors for these, after 1900 she worked almost exclusively in charcoal, sometimes with a color wash. She painted landscapes for recreation and executed a few portraits, and produced numerous sketches and paintings of Quakers and the Pennsylvania Germans. She excelled in pictures of quiet scenes and incidents, which are characterized by simplicity of expression and technical assurance. In 1929 a comprehensive exhibition of her work was held at the Plastic Club, Philadelphia, of which she had been a founder. About seventy original illustrations and sketches are in the possession of the Library of Congress, Washington, D. C., among them most of the *Middlemarch* and *Marble Faun* drawings as well as various magazine illustrations.

[See *Who's Who in America,* 1932–33; *Woman's Who's Who of America,* 1914–15; F. B. Sheafer, in *Brush and Pencil,* Sept. 1900, with portrait; *Press* (Phila.), Sept. 26, 1915; *Woman's Progress,* Nov. 1893; Julius Moritzen, in *Twentieth Century Home,* Dec. 1904; obituaries in *Art News,* Aug. 13, and *Evening Bull.* (Phila.), July 14, 1932. Information, including date of death, has been supplied by D. Owen Stephens, Mrs. Stephens' son. The statement made in various obituaries that Mrs. Stephens painted a portrait of the queen mother of Spain is false.]   D. G.

STEPHENS, ANN SOPHIA (1813–Aug. 20, 1886), author and editor, was born in the town of Derby, Conn., the daughter of John and Ann Winterbotham. Her father emigrated from England to America in 1806 at the request of David Humphreys [*q.v.*] to act as manager of the woolen mills newly established in this region. There she spent her childhood. She learned to read, sew, and knit at a tender age in a dame's school and later received further training in South Britain. She listened to her father read aloud to his large family in the evenings and early tried her own hand at composition. Occasionally she attended plays written by Humphreys for the operatives in his factory and was strengthened in her determination to become an author. In 1831 she married Edward Stephens of Plymouth, Mass. They removed to Portland, Me., which remained their home until 1837. There in 1834 they established a literary monthly, the *Portland Magazine,* especially directed to "the Ladies of Maine." For the next two years she acted as editor of this paper, contributing to it a large part of the poems, sketches, literary notices, and romantic historical tales that made up its contents. In 1836 she edited *The Portland Sketch Book,* a collection of material from the works of local writers. The following year after winning a prize for a story of pioneer life, she accepted an invitation to act as associate editor of the New York *Ladies' Companion.* Her historical tales, florid in style but always full of action, promptly increased the popularity of the periodical. During the forties she became one of the best known of the New York literati. She was often to be

met at literary soirées of Anne Lynch Botta [*q.v.*], much admired for her high spirits and lively conversation. Edgar Allan Poe described her at this time as "tall and slightly inclined to embonpoint," with brilliant blue eyes and masses of blonde hair (*post,* p. 63). In 1842 *Graham's Magazine* announced her as one of its editors, promising that her "life-like and thrilling stories should appear in its columns. *Brother Jonathan,* a weekly newspaper published by her husband, the *Lady's Wreath,* and the *Columbian Lady's and Gentleman's Magazine,* all featured her work during the decade. In 1843 she entered upon a connection with the magazine that later became *Peterson's Magazine.* This lasted until her death. She contributed to almost every number of the journal during the last twenty years of her life, and regularly supplied it with a new serial every January. From 1850 to 1852 she traveled in Europe, meeting many distinguished persons and enjoying the courtesies they extended to her. After her return she undertook a magazine of her own, *Mrs. Stephens' Illustrated New Monthly* (1856–58).

Between 1854 and 1880 she published more than twenty-five books in addition to the serials, poems, and articles constantly appearing in periodicals. Of these the most popular were *Fashion and Famine* (1854) and *The Old Homestead* (1855). Her publishers declared that her works were always successful because of her skill in "heightening, coloring, and enlarging nature." In novels like *The Rejected Wife* (1863) and many earlier works she dealt freely with American history, supplying strange episodes in the careers of notable personages. English history attracted her even more, and she delighted to portray royal figures in the midst of purple velvet, oriental pearls, ivory caskets, and snowy plumes. In 1860 she supplied Beadle & Company with the first of its famous "dime novel" series—*Malaeska,* an Indian tale, expanded from one of her early short stories. She contributed to this same series *Ahmo's Plot* (1863), *The Indian Queen* (1864), and other lively accounts of Western adventure. Stories from her pen continued to appear in *Peterson's* for several years after her death. Sir Walter Scott and Fenimore Cooper had no more devoted follower in America than this energetic romancer. She died in Newport, R. I., at the home of Charles J. Peterson [*q.v.*], her faithful friend and publisher. Her two children survived her.

[Samuel Orcutt and Ambrose Beardsley, *The Hist. of the Old Town of Derby, Conn.* (1880); E. A. Poe, *The Literati* (1850), ed. by R. W. Griswold, pub. first in *Godey's Mag.,* May–Oct. 1846; S. J. Hale, *Woman's Record* (rev. ed. 1876); *Frank Leslie's Illustrated*

Newspaper (with portrait), Aug. 16, 1856; *N. Y. Tribune*, Aug. 21, 1886.]
B. M. S.

STEPHENS, CHARLES ASBURY (Oct. 21, 1844–Sept. 22, 1931), author, was born in Norway Lake, Me., the only child of Simon and Harriet N. (Upton) Stevens. He adopted the spelling Stephens as being the ancestral form of his name. On both sides he was descended from a line of successful and keen-minded farmers; his paternal line went back probably to John Stevens, who settled in Andover, Mass., about 1645. He was fitted for college in the local school known as the Norway Liberal Institute and graduted from Bowdoin College with the degree of B.A. in 1869. For some time after his graduation he taught school. In college, however, he had been influenced by Elijah Kellogg [*q.v.*] to attempt the field of juvenile literature, and while he was still an undergraduate (1868) he contributed to *Our Flag of Boston* and wrote a serial called "Guess" for *Ballou's Monthly Magazine* (Boston). In 1870 he was engaged by Daniel Sharp Ford [*q.v.*] to write under a regular contract for the *Youth's Companion,* a connection that he maintained for more than sixty years. Under Ford's influence he traveled a great deal in Canada, the West Indies, Mexico, Panama, Europe, and Alaska for the sake of material; and attended the School of Medicine at Boston University, from which he graduated with the degree of M.D. in 1887. He once estimated that he had written more than three thousand short stories or sketches for the *Youth's Companion* and over a hundred serials. His knack of verisimilitude and circumstantiality was very great, and many of his stories were accepted as a true record of experience. His most popular contributions to juvenile literature were *Camping Out* (1872), *Lynx-Hunting* (1872), *Left on Labrador* (1872), *On the Amazons* (1872), *The Knockabout Club Alongshore* (copyright 1882) and others in the series, *When Life Was Young* (copyright 1912), and *Katahdin Camps* (1928).

In 1883 he removed from his birthplace, a farm at Upton's Ridge, to a site on Lake Pennesseewassee, Norway Lake, Me., where he erected a large laboratory, and began a systematic course of study and of original research in the field of cell life. Out of this study he developed a theory of the possibility of the indefinite extension or maintenance of cell life in the human being by systematic renewal of the biogen transmitted with the ovum by inheritance. Upon his researches at the Norway Lake laboratory he founded a series of books, beginning with *Living Matter: Its Cycle of Growth and Decline in Animal Organisms* (copyright 1888), asserting the possibility

of eventual human control of the conditions of life. He rejected all but material conditions, finding in the individual no soul apart from the tissues of living organisms. His scientific books include *Pluri-cellular Man* (1892); *Natural Salvation* (1903), later issued under the title, *Salvation by Science (Natural Salvation) Immortal Life on the Earth.* He was twice married: on Apr. 30, 1871, to Christine Stevens, his second cousin, by whom he had two daughters, and on Dec. 26, 1912, to Minnie Scalar Plummer. He died in Norway, survived by his second wife and one of his two daughters.

[Though *Who's Who in America*, 1914–15, gives the date of Stephens' birth as 1847, the town clerk of Norway, Me., reports it as 1844. Other sources are C. F. Whitman, *A Hist. of Norway, Me.* (1924); obituaries in *Publishers' Weekly*, Oct. 3, and *Boston Transcript*, Sept. 22, 1931; recollections of Don C. Seitz, New York City; information supplied by Mrs. Stephens; personal acquaintance.]
J. E. C.

STEPHENS, EDWIN WILLIAM (Jan. 21, 1849–May 22, 1931), editor, publisher, son of James Leachman and Amelia (Hockaday) Stephens, was born in Columbia, Mo., where he lived and died. His grandfather, Elijah Stephens, a Kentucky farmer, settled in Boone County, Mo., near Columbia, in 1819, and in 1843 Edwin's father, a dry-goods merchant, introduced a chain-store system in central Missouri, consisting of three cash mercantile establishments in as many county seats. The boy entered the University of Missouri soon after Union soldiers broke barracks on the campus. Graduated at the age of eighteen, he went to Jones Commercial College, St. Louis, and then reported speeches in a congressional campaign. In 1870 he purchased a half interest in the *Boone County Journal.* Within a year he bought out his associates, changed the paper's name to *Columbia Herald,* and edited it for thirty-five years. Trenchant writing and clean typography made it known as "America's Model Weekly" (*Missouri Historical Review, post,* p. 546). Meanwhile, he founded printing companies in Jefferson City and Columbia, which built up court and state record business of national proportions. In 1890 he was president of the National Editorial Association and of the Missouri Press Association; in 1905 he was elected vice-president of the International Press Congress at Liège. He performed an outstanding service to his state as chairman of the commission which had charge of the erection of the $4,000,000 Missouri capitol, completed in 1918 on a site overlooking the Missouri River. A Democrat appointed by a Republican governor, Herbert S. Hadley [*q.v.*], he was chosen chairman by his three fellow commissioners. The construction time, seven years, was shorter than that of any capitol of like size, and so scrupulously were the funds handled that it was possible to devote a large surplus to making the edifice a treasury of painting and sculpture.

Stephens was a leading Baptist layman and filled numerous offices in that denomination, including the chairmanship of the Missouri Baptist Board of Home and Foreign Missions for twenty-six years, of the Missouri Baptist General Association for twenty years, and of the Southern Baptist Association for three years. For almost half his life he headed the board of curators of Stephens College, Columbia, named for his father, and he served in the same capacity for the University of Missouri from 1885 to 1887. As early as 1896 he proposed that the state support a school of journalism and when it was opened in 1908, he had the pleasure of seeing as its dean Walter Williams, whom as a young man he had engaged to help him with the *Herald*. He had a deep interest in local history, dating from his youth when he wrote the story of Boone County, published as a series of articles in the *Boone County Atlas* in 1875, and in book form in 1882, with the title, *History of Boone County, Missouri*. He helped found the State Historical Society of Missouri in 1898 and was its first president, serving for six years. Hard roads and many other progressive enterprises had his enthusiastic support. Friends urged him to become a candidate for governor, senator, and other offices, but he always declined. In 1909 he published *Around the World*, an account of his own travel experiences. He died at his home in Columbia of the infirmities of age in his eighty-third year, survived by his widow, formerly Laura Moss, whom he married Sept. 26, 1871, together with three sons and a daughter, six children having previously died. His body lay in state at Stephens College and at the University of Missouri flags were lowered in his honor.

[“In Memoriam Edwin William Stephens, 1849–1931,” *Mo. Hist. Rev.*, July 1931; *St. Louis Post-Dispatch*, May 22, 23 (editorial), 1931; “The Story of a Columbian,” autobiographical, in *Columbia Missourian*, May 23, 25, 26, 27, 1931; autobiographical data in *Hist. of Boone County, Mo.* (1882); R. S. Douglass, *Hist. of Mo. Baptists* (1934); *Columbia Daily Tribune*, May 22, 1931; *State of Mo.: Official Manual*, 1923–24; *Who's Who in America*, 1930–31; information from a daughter, Mrs. Ashley Gray of St. Louis, and from friends.]   I. D.

STEPHENS, HENRY MORSE (Oct. 3, 1857–Apr. 16, 1919), historian and educator, was born in Edinburgh, Scotland, the son of John Edward Stephens, who belonged to an old army family and served as an army medical officer in India, and of Emma (Morris) Stephens, the daughter of John Carnac Morris, whose family was prominent in the Indian civil service. He entered Haileybury College, near Hertford, in 1871, and Balliol College, Oxford, in 1877, and he obtained a first class in modern history in 1880 and a third in jurisprudence in 1881. He was admitted to the degree of B.A. in 1882. In 1881 he was enrolled at Lincoln's Inn and later attended lectures at the universities of Bonn and Paris. For several years he was engaged in journalism, but historical studies were his prime interest, and when only twenty-eight years of age he published the first volume of his *History of the French Revolution* (1886), which established his reputation. After assisting William Wilson Hunter, the historian of India, with several works, he served from 1887 to 1890 as librarian of the Leeds library, of which he issued a printed catalogue. As one of the principal contributors to the *Dictionary of National Biography*, he provided for its first twenty volumes (1885–89) more than two hundred articles, principally of military biography. Besides numerous other items he furnished for the ninth edition of the *Encyclopaedia Britannica* the historical account of Portugal, which was later enlarged as a volume, *The Story of Portugal* (1891), in the Story of the Nations Series. The second volume of his *History of the French Revolution* (1891) was promptly followed by an edition of *The Principal Speeches of the Statesmen and Orators of the French Revolution, 1789–1795* (2 vols., 1892), and by *Europe, 1789–1815* (1893) as volume VII in A. Hassall's Periods of European History Series. Meanwhile he edited *India, a Journal for the Discussion of Indian Affairs*, 1890 to 1894, contributed to the Rulers of India Series a volume on *Albuquerque* (1892), and was teacher in Indian history at the University of Cambridge in connection with the Board of Indian Civil Service studies. After considerable earlier experience on the lecture platform, he served as a lecturer in the Oxford University extension system from 1890 to 1894. The extraordinary amount, scope, and high character of these scholarly contributions, produced in a little more than a dozen years after leaving Oxford, revealed his prodigious capacity for work and placed him in the front rank of historical scholarship in England.

He was chosen for the chair of modern European history at Cornell University, which he held from 1894 to 1902. In the latter year he accepted a call to the University of California as head of the department of history, where he remained until his death. From 1902 to 1909 he was also director of university extension and, from 1917 to 1918, dean of the faculty of letters and science. His methods of teaching were developed from his experience as an extension lecturer. He customarily prepared extended printed syllabi for his courses to recite the facts that were admirably illuminated in his lectures. To an unusual degree he became the confidant and trusted adviser of the students in both their individual and collective interests; he encouraged athletics and, at California, promoted the movement for student self-government. His generous and stimulating assistance to advanced students was given a new direction and a marked impetus as a result of his success in obtaining for the University of California the collection of works, relating to Spanish colonization and to the Pacific coast, gathered by Hubert Howe Bancroft [q.v.]. As an historian he was a thorough-going realist and insisted on a rigorous scientific method. His work, however, both as a writer and as a lecturer, was permeated by an intense interest both in individuals and in humanity in general. His heritage and training were reflected in his interest in military history and in the history of the British empire, especially in India. As early as 1898 he devoted one of his courses to the history of British colonization.

The heavy burdens of teaching, administration, and lecturing that he assumed in America hampered but did not stop his literary productivity. Only one of his several later publications, an essay on "History," contributed to the volume *Counsel upon the Reading of Books* (1900), may be selected for special mention because it expounds his own position as an historian. The scope of his activities, of his unusual gifts for friendship, and of his inspiring encouragement of younger scholars extended far beyond the precincts of his own university. He was a member of many clubs, notably the Bohemian Club of San Francisco, and of various historical societies, especially the American Historical Association in which he was one of the most prominent and active figures and of which he was president in 1915. He took an important part in founding the *American Historical Review* in 1895 and was a member of the board of editors during its first decade. An illness in December 1916 seriously undermined his health but did not lessen his devotion to his work, and his death came without warning. He left his estate, including his book collections, to the University of California, where he is commemorated by a memorial hall which is the center of student activities.

[*Who's Who in America*, 1918–19; *The Balliol College Register* (1914), ed. by Edward Hilliard; *Cornell Alumni News*, Mar. 19, 1902; *Nation* (N. Y.), Apr. 26,

1919; *American Historical Review*, esp. July 1919 and Oct. 1920; *University of California Chronicle*, esp. vol. XXI (1919), "Univ. Record," pp. 62–69; private information.]
G. M. D.

STEPHENS, JOHN LLOYD (Nov. 28, 1805–Oct. 12, 1852), traveler, author, steamship and railroad executive, was born in Shrewsbury, N. J., the son of Benjamin and Clemence (Lloyd) Stephens. He was graduated at Columbia College, in 1822, and then read law with Daniel Lord and attended the law school at Litchfield, Conn., then conducted by James Gould [q.v.]. At the age of twenty he gratified his incurable wanderlust for the first time by journeying to Arkansas, to visit an aunt. Returning to New York, he was soon admitted to the bar, practised law for eight years, and gained some repute as a Tammany orator.

The law bored him, however, and when in 1834 his doctor suggested a sea voyage as a cure for an affection of the throat, he gladly followed the prescription and spent the next two years seeking the unusual in the Mediterranean and in eastern Europe. Some of his letters, appearing in Hoffman's *American Monthly Magazine*, were so well received that in 1837 he published *Incidents of Travel in Egypt, Arabia Petraea, and the Holy Land*, in two volumes; this was followed by *Incidents of Travel in Greece, Turkey, Russia, and Poland* (2 vols., 1838). He was a born raconteur, had a zest for exploring the unusual, and wrote "with a quick and keen observation, an appreciative and good-natured sense of the ludicrous, and a remarkable facility of retaining vividly to the last the freshness of first impressions" (Hawks, *post*, pp. 66–67). Overnight, he became known as "the American traveler."

A Democrat, he was sent by Van Buren in 1839 on a confidential and rather hazy diplomatic mission to Central America. His friend Francis L. Hawks [q.v.] claims the credit for urging him to investigate the ancient civilizations reported by Antonio del Rio, Guillaume Dupaix and Frederick de Waldeck, in accounts published between 1822 and 1838. Accordingly, he took with him Frederick Catherwood, an English artist with experience in archeology. He "travelled over all Guatemala looking for the government to which he was accredited, and which he never could find" (Hawks, p. 67). His main interest was in the ruins in Honduras, Guatemala, and Yucatán. At Copán, Uxmal, Palenque, and elsewhere, Catherwood with his pencil and Stephens in words portrayed the ancient ruins. Stephens lacked the thorough scholarly background necessary for sound speculations upon their origin; his chief function was to advertise them in attractive form and thus arouse further interest. Always whimsical, he purchased all of Copán for fifty dollars and considered moving some of the monuments to New York. A result of this trip was his *Incidents of Travel in Central America, Chiapas, and Yucatan* (2 vols., 1841), with sixty-five plates by Catherwood. In 1841 they returned for a more intensive study and published in 1843 two further volumes, *Incidents of Travel in Yucatan.* It is said that by the time of Stephens' death, there had been published 21,000 copies of the *Egypt*; 12,000 of the *Greece*; 15,000 of the *Central America* and 9,750 of the *Yucatan* (*Ibid.*, p. 65).

Stephens next became a promoter and director of the Ocean Steam Navigation Company, which started a line to Bremen in 1847 and was the first to take advantage of the government subsidies to mail steamships. Stephens went to Bremen on the maiden voyage of the *Washington.* The company was soon eclipsed by the subsidy line of Edward K. Collins [*q.v.*]. Stephens was also an active supporter of the Hudson River Railroad. His last great work was in connection with the Panama Railroad, in the establishment of which William H. Aspinwall [*q.v.*], Henry Chauncey, and he were the prime movers. Elected vice-president of the company at its start in 1849, Stephens handled the necessary negotiations at Bogotá. He then succeeded Thomas W. Ludlow [*q.v.*] as president and threw himself wholeheartedly into the enterprise, spending two winters in personally supervising the surveys and the preliminary work. Returning in the spring of 1852, he was attacked by a disease doubtless contracted in that dangerous climate, and died in New York City. A monument to him was erected at the highest point on the railroad, which was opened early in 1855.

[In addition to his own works, and a biog. sketch by Catherwood in some editions of the *Incidents of Travel in Central America*, see F. L. Hawks in *Putnam's Monthly Mag.*, Jan. 1853; *No. Am. Rev.*, Oct. 1841, pp. 479–506; F. N. Otis, *Illustrated Hist. of the Panama Railroad* (1861); W. R. Scott, *The Americans in Panama* (1912), pp. 31–34; *N. Y. Herald* and *N. Y. Tribune*, Oct. 14, 1852.]   R. G. A.

STEPHENS, LINTON (July 1, 1823–July 14, 1872), legislator, jurist, and soldier, was born near Crawfordville, Ga., the grandson of Alexander Stephens who emigrated to Pennsylvania from England in 1746, was a captain in the Revolution, and removed to Georgia in 1795. His father, Andrew Baskins Stephens, was a farmer and teacher and his mother, Matilda S. (Lindsey) Stephens, was the daughter of John Lindsey, a Scotch-Irish Revolutionary soldier of Wilkes County, Ga. Linton was the youngest of his father's eight children. Both parents died in 1826, and the boy was reared by his maternal

relatives until 1837, when he went to live with his half-brother, Alexander Hamilton Stephens [*q.v.*], in Crawfordville. Having attended the Culloden and Crawfordville academies, he entered Franklin College, now a part of the University of Georgia, in 1839 and graduated in 1843. He spent the winter of 1843–44 in Washington visiting Congress and the Supreme Court. He studied law under Robert Toombs, received the degree of bachelor of laws at the University of Virginia in 1845, and attended Joseph Story's lectures at Harvard for a short time. Admitted to the bar in 1846, he immediately gained prominence and, as a partner of Richard M. Johnston [*q.v.*], was a leader of the bar.

As a Whig, he was elected to the legislature in 1849 from Taliaferro County and served until his removal to Sparta in 1852. An able and fearless speaker, he loved the Union and supported the compromises of 1850. He aided his brother, Toombs, and Cobb in organizing the Constitutional Union party but returned to the Whig party in 1852. Representing Hancock County in the Senate, 1853–55, he introduced the Nebraska resolution opposing the Kansas-Nebraska Bill. As a candidate opposed to the Know-Nothings, he was defeated for Congress in 1855 and again in 1857. As a Democrat he attended the Cincinnati convention of 1856 and helped to write the state Democratic platform of 1857. A delegate to the Southern Commercial Convention at Montgomery in 1858, he took an extreme position, favoring secession unless Kansas were admitted as a slave state. Governor Brown appointed him to the state supreme court in 1859, and he won recognition as an able jurist. Because of lack of health, he resigned in 1860. He supported Douglas in 1860, hoping to defeat Breckinridge in the South and thus avert revolution. A member of the convention of 1861, he voted against secession but, when the war began, raised a company and as lieutenant-colonel of the 15th Georgia Volunteers saw service in Virginia, 1861–62. Because of the failure of his health he resigned but was commissioned a colonel in the state cavalry in 1863 and served around Atlanta. A member of the legislature again in 1863, he opposed conscription and the suspension of the writ of *habeas corpus.* He introduced the famous resolutions justifying the Confederacy and the peace resolutions of 1864. He also opposed the grant of unconstitutional powers to Governor Brown.

After the war, he practised law and refused to reënter politics. He condemned the Radical party and aided in the overthrow of the bullock régime. He denounced the Fourteenth and Fifteenth admendments and the Reconstruction acts as nullities, subversive of American liberties. He resisted the Enforcement Act of 1870, was arrested and tried before a federal commission in Macon. Pleading his own case he denounced the entire Reconstruction program, and the case was dropped. In a famous speech in Atlanta he bitterly opposed Southern support for Horace Greeley in 1872. He was twice married: first, in January 1852, to Emmeline (Thomas) Bell, the daughter of James Thomas of Sparta, who bore him three daughters and died in 1857, and, second, in June 1867, to Mary W. Salter, the daughter of R. H. Salter of Boston, Mass., who also bore him three children. Devoted to his family, his brother, and his friends, he preferred home life to active politics. Positive, independent, and aggressive, he was unbending in his convictions; yet honest and sympathetic, he was loved and esteemed by the people of Georgia. He was an earnest student, a critic of literature, with a brilliant intellect, a scholar and philosopher rather than a man of action. Buried at his home in Sparta, he was reinterred in 1914 at "Liberty Hall," near Crawfordville, Ga.

[J. D. Waddell, *Biog. Sketch of Linton Stephens* (1877); L. L. Knight, *Reminiscences of Famous Georgians* (2 vols., 1907–08); I. W. Avery, *The Hist. of . . . Ga.* (1881); *Men of Mark in Ga.*, vol. III (1912), ed. by W. J. Northen; *Atlanta Daily Sun*, July 16, 1872].   F. M. G.

STEPHENS, URIAH SMITH (Aug. 3, 1821– Feb. 13, 1882), pioneer labor leader, was born near Cape May, N. J. It was his original intention to become a Baptist minister, but the panic of 1837 brought reverses to his family and terminated his studies. He was then indentured to a tailor, from whom he derived both a trade and mercantile wisdom. Meanwhile he became a student of economics, one of his teachers and companions being Rev. John L. Lenhardt. After completing his apprenticeship, he taught school for a short time in New Jersey. In 1845 he moved to Philadelphia, and in 1853 began an extended trip, through the West Indies, Central America, and Mexico, to California, where he remained nearly five years. After his return to Philadelphia he agitated for a westward workers' migration. An abolitionist, he supported Frémont in 1856 and Lincoln in 1860. In 1861 he was present at the national convention of workingmen opposed to the Civil War. He was a Mason, an Odd Fellow, and a member of the Knights of Pythias. There is no evidence to bear out the legend that he came under direct Marxist influence. His political interest was confined to Greenbackism.

In 1862 he helped organize the Garment Cut-

ters' Association of Philadelphia. The difficulties which that organization encountered from the pressure of the employers led Stephens and six others, upon its dissolution in 1869, to found the Noble Order of the Knights of Labor, an organization destined to become the most powerful labor body of its day, with a membership in 1886 of over three quarters of a million. After being defeated on the Greenback ticket for Congress from the fifth district of Pennsylvania in 1878, he resigned as Grand Master Workman of the Knights. He was reëlected *in absentia*, and resigned again in 1879. The principles which Stephens and his associates laid down for the Knights were secrecy, union of all trades, education, and cooperation. The secrecy aspect, with its attendant rituals, was introduced by Stephens. The practical unification of trades in a national organization was a unique and invaluable contribution to the labor movement. Unity was also an internal policy vigorously extended to include skilled and unskilled, women and men, negro and white. Education became agitation of the principles of cooperative organization. Cooperative ownership of the means of production was one of the ideas of the time, a facet of utopian socialism, and Stephens conceived of the Knights of Labor not simply as a trade-union, but as a nucleus for building a cooperative commonwealth. The lack of *class* consciousness which underlay the cooperative movement led to the use of the boycott (consumer action) rather than the strike as an economic weapon, though strikes occurred.

The ruthless crushing of the Molly Maguires after the great strikes of the middle seventies, the Knights' retarded growth, the active opposition of the Catholic Church (mainly in the person of Terence V. Powderly [*q.v.*], Stephens' successor), gave strength to an anti-secrecy faction which, soon after Stephens' resignation in 1879, overthrew District Assembly 1, which had controlled the General Assembly. In 1881, after a bitter fight between Stephens and Powderly, the principle of secrecy was repudiated. Stephens thus tasted defeat on his basic idea of labor organization, but he is nevertheless justly revered as one of the great pioneer labor leaders of America. After his death, in Philadelphia, the Richmond convention of the Knights (1886) granted $10,000 for his family.

[J. R. Commons and others, *Hist. of Labour in the U. S.* (1918), vol. II; G. E. McNeill, *The Labor Movement: The Problem of To-day* (1887); T. V. Powderly, *Thirty Years of Labor, 1859–1889* (1889); Selig Perlman, *A Hist. of Trade Unionism in the U. S.* (1922); N. J. Ware, *The Labor Movement in the U. S., 1860–1895* (1929); C. D. Wright, "An Hist. Sketch of the Knights of Labor," in *Quart. Jour. of Economics*, Jan.

1887; A. C. Stevens, *The Cyc. of Fraternities* (1899); *Pub. Ledger* (Phila.), Feb 15, 1882.]   H. So—w.

STEPHENSON, BENJAMIN FRANKLIN (Oct. 3, 1823–Aug. 30, 1871), physician, founder of the Grand Army of the Republic, was born on a farm in Wayne County, Ill., one of the eleven children of James Stephenson, a native of South Carolina, and Margaret (Clinton) Stephenson. The family early moved to a farm in Sangamon County, where Benjamin grew to manhood. He had had only the advantages of education in the local schools when he went to study medicine with an older brother at Mount Pleasant, Iowa. Later he attended lectures at Columbus, Ohio, and graduated from Rush Medical College in Chicago in 1850. He settled for practice at Petersburg, Ill., and on Mar. 30, 1855, he was married at Springfield to Barbara B. Moore, recently from Kentucky. From 1855 to 1857 he was lecturer on general, special, and surgical anatomy in the medical department of the State University of Iowa at Keokuk. In June 1861 he went to Jacksonville where the 14th Illinois Volunteers was being organized and was appointed surgeon of the regiment. He served three years in the western armies of Grant and Sherman, reached the grade of major, and was mustered out with the regiment on June 24, 1864. He is credited with having been a capable surgeon, held in high confidence by the regiment which he served. After his release from the army he joined a drug firm in Springfield, but the next year he formed a partnership with one of the leading physicians of the city.

During his war service he and the regimental chaplain, W. J. Rutledge, of Petersburg, had frequently discussed the project of forming a national association of Union veterans and he now commenced developing it. He originated the name and wrote the ritual and the constitution with some help from his old regimental friend. Though the early work of organization was done at Springfield, Stephenson's plans met with little favor there, and it was at Decatur, Ill., that Post No. 1 of the Grand Army of the Republic was formed on Apr. 6, 1866. Here the name, ritual, and constitution were adopted, and Stephenson mustered in the newly elected officers and gave the post a charter, signing himself commander of the department of Illinois. He was grievously disappointed when the representatives of the new society met in Springfield in July 1866 to form a department organization and selected another for the honor of department commander. As organizer of the order he had assumed the title of commander-in-chief and in this capacity he issued the call for a national convention to meet

at Indianapolis on Nov. 20, 1866. A second disappointment awaited him when Stephen A. Hurlbut [*q.v.*] was chosen as commander and he was given the subordinate place of adjutant-general. At the second national convention at Philadelphia on Jan. 15, 1868, he failed of election to any office. Though he had conceived and launched the new order it was generally realized that he was not one to make of it a great success. An enthusiast in a new enterprise, he lacked steadiness of purpose and had a distaste for routine duties and responsibilities. His administration as national adjutant-general was notably inefficient. Through these years the Grand Army had occupied his thoughts to the detriment of everything else. His usefulness as a physician had become seriously impaired without bringing him any substantial return for his sacrifices. Impoverished, and broken in health and spirit by repeated slights, he moved his family in the winter of 1870–71 to Rock Creek where he died, leaving a widow, a son, and two daughters.

His last years were further embittered by the thought that his labors had been fruitless, for at that time the Grand Army had almost ceased to exist in the section where it had originated. Years were to pass before it became the organization of his dreams, and he did not live to see that day. In 1882 his remains were moved from the village where he died to the soldiers' plot in Rose Hill Cemetery, overlooking the Sangamon River at Petersburg, by the Grand Army post of that town. A monument, erected to his honor in Washington, D. C., was dedicated in 1909.

[M. H. Stephenson, *Dr. B. F. Stephenson, Founder of the G. A. R., A Memoir* (1894); *Proc. . . . Stephenson Grand Army Memorial, Sen. Doc. 857,* 61 Cong., 3 Sess. (1911); H. A. Kelly and W. L. Burrage, *Am. Med. Biographies* (1920), a sketch by G. H. Weaver; O. M. Wilson, *The G. A. R.* (1905); R. B. Beath, *Hist. of the G. A. R.* (1888); J. A. M. Passmore, *Ancestors and Descendants of Andrew Moore* (1897), vol. I; *Ill. State Jour.* (Springfield), Sept. 1, 1871.]   J.M.P.

STEPHENSON, ISAAC (June 18, 1829–Mar. 15, 1918), pioneer lumberman, congressman, and United States senator, was born in Maugerville, New Brunswick, son of Isaac Stephenson, of Scotch-Irish descent, and Elizabeth (Watson). Isaac went to Milwaukee at the age of sixteen, already competent to cruise for timber and to manage gangs of workmen in the woods. He worked at odd jobs in eastern Wisconsin, made a farm at Janesville, filed claims in the Escanaba country, Michigan, contracted for the moving of logs up the lake, and acquired an interest in steamers on Lake Michigan. He settled at Marinette, Wis., in 1858 as a member of the firm of N. Ludington & Company, and thereafter he was connected with every operation in

the Menominee River valley. His fortune grew
with each phase of the industry in wood and
wood manufacture. He turned out railroad ties,
broom handles, pails, and other wooden articles
from his factories at Peshtigo, as well as saw-
logs and lumber for the Chicago and Milwaukee
markets. The profits from his industry were
turned into banks, mining companies, and railroads.

On Oct. 8, 1871, forest fires wiped away his
factory town of Peshtigo, and the way in which
he met this disaster established his reputation as
the strong man of his community. Already he
had held local office, and had twice been a member of the Wisconsin Assembly (1866, 1868).
Three times, in 1882, 1884, and 1886, he was
sent to Congress; but since his party was in the
minority, he had little chance to shine as a legislator. He watched local appropriations and took
care of private pension bills, but Senator Philetus Sawyer [q.v.] of Wisconsin was the more
striking figure. Stephenson declined renomination in 1888, and for a decade devoted himself to
his large private interests. In 1899 he coveted
the seat of John L. Mitchell in the Senate, but
was mortified when the regular Republican manager, guided as Sawyer wished, bestowed it
upon Joseph V. Quarles. Now, for the first
time, Stephenson said, he realized "the power
and devious ways of the 'machine'" (Recollections, post, p. 201). His feeling that he had been
betrayed led him to join forces with the rebellious half-breeds and to finance the campaign of
Robert M. LaFollette [q.v.] for governor in
1900. The Milwaukee Free Press (1901) was
launched with his money in their behalf. He
would have been pleased to take his reward when
Quarles retired in 1905, but LaFollette himself
then chose to go to the Senate. When John C.
Spooner [q.v.] resigned in 1907, Stephenson
announced his candidacy at once, and was elected with less help from Senator LaFollette than
he expected. In 1908, seeking reëlection, he dis-
bursed more than $107,000 in the primary cam-
paign, and before the legislature was ready to
ballot for senator he was under fire. The pro-
gessive associates of LaFollette, with John J.
Blaine in the lead, attacked his use of money;
while one of the stalwart leaders, E. L. Philipp
[q.v.], complained that "through the agency of
the primary the state of Wisconsin offers its
rich old men an opportunity to buy the senatorship as sort of a floral tribute to themselves"
(Wisconsin State Journal, Sept. 12, 1908, p. 1).
Stephenson was nevertheless elected after a fight
drawn out from Jan. 27 until Mar. 4, 1909. The
next legislature sent a resolution to Washington,

June 26, 1911, challenging his right to sit; but
the Senate declined to unseat him, Mar. 27, 1912,
after a debate in which Elihu Root characterized the case against Stephenson as "an extreme
of fantastical whimsicality" (Congressional Record, 62 Cong., 2 Sess., p. 3820). At the close
of his term he retired to Marinette. When he
died there he was survived by his widow (a third
wife), and six of his eight children.

[In his autobiography, Recollections of a Long
Life, 1829–1915 (1915), Stephenson defended himself
against an adverse view of his activities presented in
LaFollette's Autobiog.: A Personal Narrative of Political Experiences (1913). The materials upon his
senatorial contest are in Report of the Senate Members
of the Joint Senatorial Primary Investigation Committee (Madison, 1911), and "Election of Isaac Stephenson: Report of the Committee on Privileges and Elections, U. S. Senate," Sen. Doc. 312, 62 Cong., 2 Sess.
See also, Biog. Dir. Am. Cong. (1928); Who's Who in
America, 1916–17; Wis. State Jour. (Madison), Mar.
15, 1918; Madison Democrat, Mar. 16, 1918.]

F. L. P.

STEPHENSON, JOHN (July 4, 1809–July
31, 1893), pioneer street-car builder, was born
in County Armagh, Ireland, and was the son of
James and Grace (Stuart) Stephenson, who
were respectively of English and of Scotch descent. When he was two years old his parents
emigrated to the United States, settling in New
York City, and there he was educated in the public schools and in Wesleyan Seminary. At sixteen he became a clerk in a store but in 1828,
having developed a marked mechanical taste and
inclination, he apprenticed himself to a coach-
maker, Andrew Wade, of Broome Street, New
York. During his apprenticeship of two years
he devoted all of his evenings to learning mechanical drawing and tried his hand at the designing of vehicles. Upon the completion of his
apprenticeship he found employment as repair-
man for a liveryman, Abram Brower. A year
later, in May 1831, he opened his own shop to
engage in the repair of all kinds of vehicles, and
in the course of the year designed and built the
first omnibus made in New York. Brower purchased this and established the city's first omnibus line, which became so popular that he had
Stephenson build three additional busses immediately. In the same year he was employed to
build a horse-drawn car for the newly organized
New York & Harlem Railroad to use on its
Fourth Avenue line. His car was used when
the railroad was opened on Nov. 26, 1832, and
thus he gained the honor of designing and building the first car for the first street railway in
the world. The "'John Mason," as it was called
in honor of the president of the company, resembled a great omnibus mounted on four flange
wheels. So satisfactory was it that in the suc-

ceeding three years Stephenson received orders for cars not only for this original line but for newly established street-car lines in several cities in the East. The financial panic of 1837, however, was disastrous to him, and he was compelled to close down his factory. Nevertheless, in six years he had paid all his creditors and had once more undertaken manufacturing, this time of coaches and omnibuses exclusively. He continued in this profitably until 1852, when the establishment of horse-car lines in many cities of the world brought with it a great demand for cars. At that time he altered his plant for the manufacture of cars and for many years thereafter was recognized as the chief street-car builder of the world. He made horse cars, cable, electric, and open cars, his plant in 1891 employing five hundred men and producing about twenty-five cars a week. He directed all of the affairs of his company and devised many improvements in the design of cars. In addition to his initial patent of Apr. 22, 1833, he secured about ten others in the course of his life, all on street cars. During the Civil War his factory was devoted to the construction of gun carriages and pontoons for the government, and ran up a record of seventy completed pontoons in seventeen days. Stephenson, who was very fond of music, was an active member of the New York Sacred Music Society and the Harmonic Society of New York. In 1833 he married Julia A. Tiemann, and at the time of his death in New Rochelle, N. Y., where he had resided since 1865, he was survived by two sons and a daughter.

[Waldemar Kaempffert, *A Popular Hist. of Am. Invention* (1924), vol. I; *Am. Railroad Jour.*, Nov. 17, Dec. 1, 1832; *Am. Engineer and Railroad Jour.*, Sept. 1893; "The Original Carbuilder," *N. Y. Tribune*, May 10, 1891; obituaries in *N. Y. Tribune* and *N. Y. Times*, Aug. 1, 1893; Patent Office records.]   C. W. M—n.

STERETT, ANDREW (Jan. 27, 1778–Jan. 9, 1807), naval officer, and son of John and Deborah (Ridgley) Sterett, was born in Baltimore, Md. His paternal grandfather, also named Andrew, emigrated from Ireland to America, and settled temporarily at Bradford, Mass., but later moved to Lancaster, Pa., and eventually, to Baltimore, Md. John Sterett became active in public life, serving as captain of a company during the Revolution, and later, as a member of the Maryland state legislature. He was also a successful shipping merchant, was interested in iron-works, and owned a 1646 acre estate, together with a considerable number of slaves. Deborah (Ridgley) Sterett was a sister of Gen. Charles Ridgley, owner of the large country estate "Hampton" near Baltimore.

Beyond the facts that Andrew was the fourth of ten children, that he inherited a considerable amount of property from his father, and that at an early age he became interested in maritime affairs, little seems to be known about the first years of his career. His emergence from obscurity really begins with his entering the navy as a lieutenant on Mar. 25, 1798. For a time thereafter he served as the executive officer of the frigate *Constellation*, commanded by Thomas Truxtun [*q.v.*]. On Feb. 9, 1799, the *Constellation*, after a battle lasting one hour and fourteen minutes, captured the French frigate *Insurgente* off the island of Nevis, West Indies. In this engagement only two Americans were killed, and three wounded—one of the former being slain by Sterett himself. "One fellow," he said, "I was obliged to run through the body with my sword, and so put an end to a coward. You must not think this strange, for we would put a man to death for even looking pale on board this ship" (Frost, *post*, p. 130). The *Constellation* won another signal victory on Feb. 2, 1800, by capturing a powerful French frigate, *La Vengeance*. Sterett was at the time first lieutenant on board the *Constellation*, and took an active part in the action. Later in the year he was given command of the schooner *Enterprise*, and in December 1800 captured the *L'Amour de la Patrie*, a vessel of six guns and seventy-two men, in the West Indies.

He performed the most brilliant exploit of his career soon after the outbreak of war between the United States and Tripoli. He took the *Enterprise* to the Mediterranean in 1801, and on Aug. 1 of that year, while en route to Malta, sighted a Tripolitan polacca, the *Tripoli*. The latter vessel, finding escape impossible, finally resorted to boarding tactics, in which the Tripolitans were reputed to excel, but the skilful maneuvering of the *Enterprise* kept the enemy at a distance and enabled the Yankee gunners to fire sweeping broadsides which brought the captain of the polacca to throw his colors into the sea and to surrender his vessel after three hours of fighting (Allen, *post*, pp. 95, 96). Because of his victory Sterett received words of appreciation and a sword from Congress. He was also promoted to the rank of master commandant, and was placed in command of a brig which was under construction at Baltimore. On June 29, 1805, soon after the contest with Tripoli ended, he resigned his commission and entered the merchant marine (*Maryland Historical Magazine*, *post*, p. 246). One United States destroyer was named after Sterett in recognition of his contribution to the upbuilding of the morale and prestige of the navy.

[Materials relating to Sterett's ancestry have been provided by one of his collateral descendants, Mr. Wm. B. Marye, of Baltimore, who has the Sterett family records. See also G. W. Allen, *Our Navy and the Barbary Corsairs* (1905); C. W. Goldsborough, *The U. S. Naval Chronicle* (1824); H. H. Frost, *We Build a Navy* (1929); *The St. Mémin Coll. of Portraits* (1862); *Md. Hist. Mag.*, Sept. 1917.]   R. W. I.

STERKI, VICTOR (Sept. 27, 1846–Jan. 25, 1933), physician, conchologist, was born in Solothurn, Switzerland, the son of Anton and Magdalena (Müller) Sterki. His early education was received in a country school and at the Gymnasium. After two years in the college of Solothurn, he studied medicine at the University of Bern and, later, at the University of Munich. A serious illness during this period left its marks upon him for life. Having passed an examination at Munich which gave him the privilege of practising medicine, he served as polyclinical and clinical assistant in the hospital of the University of Bern, and in 1874 went into practice for himself. In 1878, at the age of thirty-two, he received the degree of doctor of medicine. He had been engaged in a careful study of the *Infusoria* (*Protozoa*), and his doctor's dissertation, *Beiträge zur Morphologie der Oxytrichinen* (1878), brought favorable comment from leading zoölogists of that time. On Feb. 2, 1875, he married Mary Lanz, of Huttwyl, Switzerland. Emigrating to the United States in 1883, he settled in New Philadelphia, Ohio, and engaged in the practice of medicine.

He was always keenly interested in the phenomena of nature and in his youthful days made extensive collections of the fauna and flora of his neighborhood. His study of the *Protozoa* in college and university was another expression of this interest. In America a new field opened to him, and all the time that he could spare from his medical practice he devoted to it. *Protozoa*, mosses, and other groups claimed some of his attention, but to the *Mollusca*, especially the smaller forms, he was chiefly attracted. The small gastropods, especially the *Pupillidae*, were the first he studied, and he at once began a systematic examination of the rich fauna of this group living in America, bringing to light many new species and races and providing the basis for a comprehensive nomenclature of the peculiar folds and plications found within the aperture of these tiny mollusks. A distinguished authority on the land fauna of the United States says of his work: "In 1888 Dr. Victor Sterki published the first of a long series of studies upon American *Pupidae*, which have marked a great advance in our knowledge of the group, not alone in the increased number of species, but in the more just appreciation of their interrelationships" (*Proceedings of the Academy of Natural Sciences of Philadelphia*, vol. LII, 1901, p. 582). Other small forms of mollusks, such as the *Zonitidae*, attracted his interest, as did also the great group of *Naiades*, or freshwater mussels, and to knowledge of the anatomy and physiology of these he made valuable contributions.

The group of *Mollusca* to which his name will be attached for all time, however, is the *Sphaeriidae*, small freshwater bivalves. These he began to study early in his American residence and they principally engaged his attention to the time of his death. He amassed the largest collection of this family ever assembled and studied literally hundreds of thousands of specimens from all parts of America as well as from other sections of the world. A hundred or more species have been added to the American fauna and many yet remain to be described. This collection, together with other mollusks acquired during his lifetime, has been deposited in the Carnegie Museum at Pittsburgh, Pa., in which institution he was an assistant (*in absentia*) in the department of invertebrates from 1909 until his death. Sterki was an able writer and more than 150 papers appeared under his name. His contributions were published in *The Nautilus*, the official organ of the conchologists of America; the *Proceedings of the United States National Museum* at Washington; *Proceedings of the Academy of Natural Sciences of Philadelphia*; *Proceedings of the Ohio State Academy of Science*; and the *Annals of the Carnegie Museum*.

One of Sterki's most notable characteristics was his willingness to help others, especially beginners in the science, and during his residence in America he examined thousands of specimens sent to him for determination by all classes of students—the adolescent amateur and the distinguished professional. He was a man of genial and hospitable nature, and always unpretentious in his manner. A son and two daughters survived him, a third daughter having predeceased her father by a few weeks.

[S. T. Brooks, in *The Nautilus*, Apr. 1933, and in *Annals of the Carnegie Museum*, vol. XXII (1934), with bibliog.; *Who's Who in America*, 1918–19; *N. Y. Times*, Jan. 27, 1933.]   F. C. B.

STERLING, GEORGE (Dec. 1, 1869–Nov. 17, 1926), lyric poet, was born in Sag Harbor, N. Y., the eldest of nine children of George Ansel and Mary Parker (Havens) Sterling. He was a descendant of William Sterling, an Englishman who settled in Haverhill, Mass., in 1662. From the Havens he inherited his splendid physique, handsome features (his resemblance to Dante was often noted), his sprightly and restless spirit. His maternal grandfather, Wickham

Sayre Havens, sailed from the port of Sag Harbor between 1820 and 1840 as captain of a whaling vessel. His paternal forefathers were men of some intellectual attainment, but the line carried a taint of emotional instability that was quite manifest in the elder Sterling, a physician. In middle life Sterling's father was converted to the Roman Catholic faith. An ardent proselyte, he induced his son to enter the second year of high school at St. Charles' College, Ellicott City, Md. At St. Charles', from which he graduated in 1889, Sterling came to know as instructor and friend Father John Bannister Tabb [q.v.]. Before completing his course, however, he renounced the church, and for the rest of his life he remained consistently irreverent. His philosophic views crystallized in the simple conviction that the total of human happiness is unalterably fixed, varying only in details actually irrelevant, and that the part of wisdom is to choose pleasure and avoid pain. After leaving school, he went to live in Oakland, Cal., where he was employed as private secretary by his uncle, Frank C. Havens, a wealthy man of affairs, from 1890 until 1908.

In the summer of 1892 he first met Ambrose Bierce [q.v.]. Promptly proclaiming Bierce his master, he submitted to him for criticism and correction nearly every poem he wrote from that time until Bierce's disappearance at the end of 1913. The manuscript of one poem indicates that of twenty-five suggestions noted by Bierce all but two were adopted. Nor was this instance exceptional. Association with Bierce was a major experience in Sterling's life and undeniably stimulating. Drawn throughout his life to characters stronger than his own, it is doubtful if he would ever have attained poetic maturity had it not been for Bierce. On Feb. 7, 1896, he married Caroline Rand of Oakland, Cal., daughter of David H. Rand of New Hampshire. They moved in 1908 from Oakland to Carmel, Cal., where Sterling became, in Bierce's phrase, "the High Panjandrum" of the artist colony then assembling in Carmel. Divorced by his wife on Feb. 5, 1915, he lived for a time in the East but returned to California in 1918 when informed of her death, a suicide. Between 1903 and 1926 he published ten volumes of verse, five separately published poems, a blank verse translation of Hugo von Hofmannsthal's *Everyman* (in collaboration with Richard Ordynski), four dramatic poems, much uncollected magazine prose and verse, and *Robinson Jeffers, the Man and the Artist* (1926). A volume of sonnets, *Sonnets to Craig* (1928), was posthumously published. His reputation was still local when, in 1907,

Bierce induced the *Cosmopolitan* to publish "A Wine of Wizardry." Extravagant praise by Bierce and much consequent publicity gave the poet and the poem an unenviable notoriety. A victim of an aroused "cismontane criticism," it was not until 1923 that he found an eastern publisher.

As much by his personal influence as by his poetry, Sterling revived the early literary traditions of California, which by 1892 verged on extinction. The remarkable range and the intimate quality of his acquaintance, coupled with his long residence in the West, gave a cultural significance to his career quite apart from his writing. He was an incurable romanticist and indefatigable Bohemian, and his poetry and character came in time to reveal the strain of an insupportable exertion after the elusive phrase, the delectable experience. The ambitious poems done in his grandiose early style will not be remembered as long as such charming lyrics as "Autumn in Carmel," "Willy Pitcher," "The Last Days," "Beyond the Breakers," "Spring in Carmel," which carry the unmistakable accent and quality of his personal manner, and a few magnificent sonnets. He left much unpublished manuscript. There has been no collected edition of his work, although *Selected Poems* (1923) contains most of his best work. "Saintly, whimsical, vagabondish," Sterling was a person of manifold contradictions; mild of manner but vehement of expression; riotously witty but momentarily morose and penitent; prodigal but capable of a painstaking practicality. A passion for action and an unbridled generosity were perhaps the only traits of his nature that were wholly free from contradiction. On Nov. 17, 1926, he committed suicide in his rooms at the Bohemian Club in San Francisco.

[The date of death is from the Dept. of Pub. Health, San Francisco. There is no biog. of Sterling. See A. M. Sterling, *The Sterling Geneal.* (1909), vol. II; Upton Sinclair, in *Sonnets to Craig* (1928) and *Bookman*, Sept. 1927; Mary Austin, in *Am. Mercury*, May 1927; *Overland Monthly*, Nov., Dec. 1926; *San Francisco Review*, Nov., Dec. 1926; H. S. R., in *Authors Today and Yesterday* (1933), ed. by S. J. Kunitz; *San Francisco Water*, July 1928, a pamphlet edited by E. F. O'Day, Spring Valley Water Company; Cecil Johnson, *A Bibliog. of the Writings of George Sterling* (1931); obituaries in *San Francisco Chronicle* and *San Francisco Examiner*, Nov. 18, 1926. See also the character of Russ Brissenden in Jack London's *Martin Eden* (copr. 1908) and, particularly, *The Letters of Ambrose Bierce* (1921), ed. by Bertha C. Pope, with a memoir by Sterling. There are colls. of Sterling's letters in the possession of the author, Mrs. Madeleine Diamond of Los Angeles (Sterling's sister), James Hart of San Francisco, James Hopper of Carmel, and others.]

C. McW.

STERLING, JAMES (1701?–Nov. 10, 1763), Anglican clergyman, author and colonial customs official, was born at Dowrass, Kings County, Ireland, the son of James Sterling, a half-pay captain of the British army. He was graduated (B.A.) from Trinity College, Dublin, in 1720, and much later, in 1733, proceeded to the M.A. degree in that institution. His literary career began with the publication in London in 1722 of the *Rival Generals,* a play with which the author claimed he "first awak'd the Irish Muse to Tragedy." The *Parricide* (1736) had a short run at Goodman's Fields, but neither this nor the earlier play sufficed to bring him the fame he sought as dramatist. He was not more fortunate as a lyric poet with his translation from Musaeus, *The Loves of Hero and Leander* (1728), and the *Poetical Works of the Rev. James Sterling* (1734). No trace remains of the political writing he is reputed to have done for the Opposition in these years, unless it be found in the favor with which certain proposals of his were met by eminent members of the party after they had come into office. About 1733 he entered Holy Orders and became a regimental chaplain, and it was probably just before this time that he lost his first wife, who had been a popular and accomplished Dublin actress.

A few years after ordination his attention was turned toward service in the colonies by his "near relation," Robert Auchmuty, d. 1750 [q.v.]. In 1737 he took the King's Bounty for Maryland, where he held successively the rectorships of All Hallows Parish, Anne Arundel County, of St. Ann's, Annapolis, and of St. Paul's, Kent County. Inducted to the last of these on Aug. 26, 1740, he remained its rector until his death in 1763. He was not content, however, with the limited duties and aspirations of a parish priest. He held a conviction that the future greatness of Britain was wrapped up in the development of her American colonies, and he gave expression to his imperialistic dream in a long poem of 1600 lines with the incongruous title, *An Epistle to the Hon. Arthur Dobbs,* which, written in Maryland in 1748, was published for him in London and Dublin in 1752, when he visited England. He published in 1755, in Annapolis and in London, an Assembly sermon, entitled in its English edition, *Zeal against the Enemies of our Country Pathetically Recommended,* a vigorous and well-informed piece of propaganda directed against the French aggression in America. Before returning to America in 1752, he obtained appointment as collector of customs at Chester, a customs district created by the treasury upon his unsupported recommendation that it was needed for the protection and development of the "Maryland Trade." This need was denied and

his appointment opposed by Governor Sharpe, the Maryland customs officials, and a strong group of London merchants trading with Maryland, but despite their continuous opposition his influence at the treasury remained strong enough to keep him in office as long as he lived. His literary efforts seem to have come to an end with the publication of a group of poems, not all clearly identified, in the *American Magazine,* established in 1757 by William Smith, 1727–1803 [q.v.]. On Sept. 19, 1743, he was married to Rebecca (Hynson) Holt, the widow of a fellow clergyman; their daughter, Rebecca, became the wife of William Carmichael [q.v.]. After his second wife's death he was married, on Sept. 7, 1749, to Mary Smith. Both of these wives were women of property and position. The poetical epitaph and the eulogy of Sterling published in the *Maryland Gazette* (Annapolis) for Nov. 17, 1763, indicate that he had gained the affection of his neighbors in the same degree that he had impressed them with his varied and exceptional abilities.

[L. C. Wroth, "James Sterling," *Am. Antiquarian Soc. Proc.,* Apr. 1931, with citations to sources in Md. and in England; *Dict. Nat. Biog.; Archives of Md.,* vols. VI (1888), pp. 8, 67, IX (1890), XLVI (1929); G. D. Burtchaell and T. U. Sadleir, *Alumni Dublinenses* (1924); *Md. Gazette, ante.*]
                                    L. C. W.

STERLING, JOHN WHALEN (July 17, 1816–Mar. 9, 1885), educator, was born in Blackwalnut, Wyoming County, Pa., a descendant of William Sterling who settled in Haverhill, Mass., in 1662. He was one of twenty children of Daniel Sterling, lumberman and government contractor, by the last two of three wives, his mother being the third wife, Rachel (Brooks) Sterling. Educated in the public school of his town and the academies of Hamilton and Homer, N. Y., he read law for two years in Wilkes-Barre, Pa., after which he entered the sophomore year of the College of New Jersey (later Princeton) and graduated there with honors in 1840. During the following year he was principal of Wilkes-Barre Academy. In 1841 he entered the Princeton Theological Seminary and during his three years there officiated as tutor in the College of New Jersey. He spent about a year as Presbyterian missionary in the Pennsylvania county in which he was born, taught in Carroll College, newly established under Presbyterian auspices at Waukesha, Wis., in 1846, and in 1847 opened a private school in Waukesha. Early in 1849 he became professor of mathematics, natural philosophy, and astronomy at the University of Wisconsin, and principal of the preparatory department. For about two years thereafter he and his preparatory school pupils, with the chancellor, formed the faculty and student body of the infant university.

After the resignation of the first chancellor, John Hiram Lathrop [*q.v.*], which took effect in January 1859, the internal administration of the university till the installation in July 1859 of the new chancellor, Henry Barnard [*q.v.*], was largely in the hands of Sterling, whom the regents made acting chancellor. Because of Barnard's ill health and frequent absence he continued to take much of the administrative responsibility until 1860, when Barnard's chancellorship came to an end, and during the next seven years, when the university was without a chancellor, he was the chief administrative officer, dean till 1865 and thereafter vice-chancellor. In the reorganization of the faculty under Paul Ansel Chadbourne [*q.v.*] in 1867, he was one of three retained from the old professional group, his title being professor of natural philosophy and astronomy. After Chadbourne resigned in 1870, the routine of administration was again placed in his capable hands, where it remained till the appointment of a new president a year later. The regents had conferred on him in 1869 the office and title of vice-president, which he held to the time of his death. In 1874 he became professor of mathematics; in 1883 professor emeritus. When his health weakened in 1874 under his double load of administration and teaching, he was given a six months' leave of absence, three months of which he spent in Europe. On Sept. 3, 1851, he had married Harriet Dean, daughter of Eliot Byram Dean of Raynham, Mass. He died in Madison, survived by his wife and three of their eight children. Characteristic of him were deep piety, unfailing kindliness, high standards of scholarship, great energy, and steadfast faith that, as he declared in a commencement address, his university would some day be "the chief pride of the state and its glory abroad." Because of this faith of his, which brought inspiration to others, and the thirty-six years of devoted service he rendered, he is regarded as the chief builder and the guiding spirit of the university in its early years. In 1921 the name Sterling Hall was bestowed by the regents of the university on a new building dedicated to the interests of physics and economics.

[A. M. Sterling, *The Sterling Geneal.* (1909), vol. I, with portrait; R. G. Thwaites, *The Univ. of Wis.* (1900); *Wis. State Jour.*, Mar. 9, 11, 14, 1885; *Univ. Press*, Mar. 14, 1885; *Wis. Alumni Mag.*, June–July 1904; information from Sterling's daughter, Susan Adelaide Sterling.]   W.J.C.

STERLING, JOHN WILLIAM (May 12, 1844–July 5, 1918), lawyer, philanthropist, was born at Stratford, Conn., the son of John William and Catharine Tomlinson (Plant) Sterling. His father was a sea captain, but retired from that calling before he was forty years old. He was a descendant of William Sterling who came to America before 1660, settling in Haverhill, Mass., and later moving to Lyme, Conn. Having prepared for college at Stratford Academy, John entered Yale in the fall of 1860. After graduation with the class of 1864, he remained at college for a year, reading under the guidance of Noah Porter [*q.v.*], chiefly in the fields of general literature and history. In October 1865 he went to New York to enter the Columbia Law School, then directed by Theodore W. Dwight [*q.v.*]. He was chosen valedictorian of his class (1867) and soon was engaged as a clerk (at first without pay) in the office of David Dudley Field [*q.v.*], who at that time probably had the largest law practice in New York. Within eighteen months Sterling was admitted to the new firm of Field & Shearman as junior partner.

All his life a man who hated and dreaded publicity, Sterling figured in sensational news that could not be kept out of the daily headlines, for his firm, as counsel for Jay Gould and James Fisk [*qq.v.*] in their control of the Erie Railway, was active for years in hard-fought litigation. Sterling himself obtained from Justice Barnard (later impeached) the mysterious order putting the Albany & Susquehanna Railroad into a receivership. After the famous "Black Friday" in Wall Street (Sept. 24, 1869), nearly a hundred suits were begun against Gould and Fisk as a result of their attempt to corner gold. A great part of the office drudgery in each case fell to the lot of the junior counsel. Sterling had not wished to be an "office lawyer," merely, but the logic of events made him that and the time came when he was fully reconciled to such an outcome; for the advance of "big business" demanded the kind of service that he was equipped to give—at the office desk rather than at the counsel table in court.

As early as 1873 the firm dissolved co-partnership, Thomas G. Shearman [*q.v.*] and Sterling setting up an office of their own. Their first important case was the defense of Henry Ward Beecher [*q.v.*] in the suit brought by Theodore Tilton. For this work, continuing for a year and a half, no compensation was received. Sterling's knowledge of business practice, not less than his mastery of the law, made his advice priceless to an increasing number of important clients. The National City Bank and Standard Oil groups, with many railroad corporations, availed themselves of his counsel. At Shearman's death in 1900 the firm name was retained, with Sterling as senior partner, others having from time to time been admitted to membership. His fees in the organization of combines and mergers, as well as in the settlement of estates, were very large, and the money so received was profitably invested. He toiled early and late, subjecting himself to a routine that for most men would have been painful. He had never married and only one or two of his friends knew that he had a definite objective in amassing a fortune. When he was about sixty years of age he said to at least one of those in his confidence that he had from the first cherished the ambition of making money which after his death should enrich Yale University. In hinting at the size of this prospective addition to Yale's resources he used the word "fabulous."

The only philanthropy in which he was known during his lifetime to be interested was the Miriam Osborn Memorial Home for old ladies at Harrison, N. Y., established by a friend of whose will he was executor. This also contributed to Yale indirectly, since tracts of land in Westchester County, N. Y., and in Connecticut, that he acquired while he was building the Osborn Home, were deeded by him to the University. While salmon fishing, as had long been his custom, at Lord Mount Stephen's lodge, Grand Metis, Que., he died suddenly from a heart attack. His will left his residuary estate to Yale University, under the direction of a board of trustees. Provision was made for the erection of buildings and the founding of professorships, fellowships, and scholarships. Yale has received from the trustees funds for the erection of the Sterling Memorial Library and other buildings, including a chemistry laboratory, a hall of medicine, law buildings, dormitories (Trumbull College), a hall of graduate studies, the Divinity School quadrangle, and a tower for the Sheffield Scientific School. The funds for buildings and maintenance and for endowments total many millions. This single benefaction doubled Yale's resources.

[A. M. Sterling, *The Sterling Genealogy* (2 vols., 1909); Samuel Orcutt, *A Hist. of the Old Town of Stratford and the City of Bridgeport, Conn.* (1886), vol. II; *Who's Who in America*, 1918–19; *N. Y. Times*, July 7, 1918; J. A. Garver, *John William Sterling . . . a Biog. Sketch* (1929); A. P. Stokes, unpublished reminiscences; A. R. Burr, *The Portrait of a Banker: James Stillman, 1850–1918* (1927); J. K. Winkler, *The First Billion: The Stillmans and the National City Bank* (1934), pp. 91–95; F. A. Vanderlip in *Sat. Eve. Post*, Jan. 5, 1935; *Yale Univ. Obit. Record . . . 1919* (1920); *Addresses at the Dedication of Sterling Memorial Library at Yale Univ.* (1931); *Charges of the Bar Asso. of N. Y. Against George G. Barnard and Albert Cardozo, Justices of the Supreme Court: Testimony before Judiciary Com. of Assembly* (1872), pp. 580–611.]   W. B. S.

STERN, JOSEPH WILLIAM (Jan. 11, 1870–Mar. 31, 1934), song-writer, music publisher, was born in New York City, the son of Charles and Theresa (Katz) Stern. His parents had both been born in Germany, his father in Cologne and his mother in Frankfort. After he had completed his elementary education Stern was put to work as a traveling salesman in his father's neckwear business (C. Stern & Mayer); his chief interest, however, was not in the selling of neckties but in music, which absorbed him. Since he had a gift for composing tunes, he decided to start a music-publishing business in partnership with a friend, Edward B. Marks. To Stern and Marks publishing songs meant writing them as well, and so together they produced their first song, "The Little Lost Child," with words by Marks and music by Stern. With this their sole product they opened offices as Joseph W. Stern & Company at 304 East Fourteenth St. in 1894. Partly because it was one of the sentimental narrative songs then in great vogue, and partly because Stern and Marks displayed great enterprise in promoting it, "The Little Lost Child" proved a tremendous success. It was one of the first songs to be sung with illustrated "song slides," which the authors themselves ordered made. The slides were used with stereopticons in hundreds of auditoriums, music halls, and theatres, and Stern and Marks became virtual pioneers in the art of "song plugging." Weekly they visited the principal resorts where music was performed, to persuade singers, pianists, and orchestra leaders to include Stern songs in their repertoires. In 1896 they wrote "My Mother Was a Lady, or, If Jack Were Only Here," a rather maudlin effort as successful as their first, suggested by an incident that occurred in a German restaurant when a waitress spoke indignantly in the words of the title to a patron who annoyed her by his attentions.

By ascertaining popular trends and observing public demand they secured from other writers compositions that achieved wide circulation, and they soon stood among the leading publishers of current successes. For many years Stern went abroad annually, bringing back with him the American rights to such foreign songs as the English popular song, "Elsie from Chelsea," which they published in 1896, Paul Lincke's "Glow Worm," and "The Parade of the Wooden Soldiers," which was published in 1911 but did not achieve popularity until it was used in the *Chauve-Souris* in 1922. Among the American popular songs issued by the firm were "A Hot Time in the Old Town" (later called "There'll Be a Hot Time in the Old Town Tonight"),

"Sweet Rosie O'Grady," "Under the Bamboo Tree," "Everybody Works But Father," and many others. When the craze for dancing swept America in the years just before the World War, Stern and Marks were quick to put their firm in the lead as publishers of dance music for the latest steps. In 1920 Stern retired from the business and devoted himself largely to raising prize flowers at his home in Brightwaters, Long Island. A few weeks before his death, which occurred at Brightwaters, he had decided to re-enter the song publishing business. He was survived by his wife, Leona Lewis, a singer, whom he had married in 1899.

[E. B. Marks, *They All Sang* (1934); Isaac Goldberg, *Tin Pan Alley* (1930); Sigmund Spaeth, *Read 'Em and Weep* (1926); obituaries in *Variety* and *N. Y. Herald Tribune*, Apr. 3, and *N. Y. Times*, Apr. 1, 3, 1934; information from Stern's widow.]   J. T. H.

STERNBERG, CONSTANTIN IVANO-VICH, Edler von (July 9, 1852–Mar. 31, 1924), pianist, composer, teacher, was born in St. Petersburg (later Leningrad), Russia. After the death of his father, Ivan von Sternberg, when Constantin was three, and the remarriage of his mother, he was reared by his grandmother and a French governess in somewhat pampered fashion. At six he spoke four languages and was beginning the study of music. After a few years in the St. Petersburg Lutheran School, which he left at eleven, and a year at school in Weimar, Germany, he was taken to Leipzig in 1865 upon the recommendation of Franz Liszt to become a pupil of Ignaz Moscheles, Coccius, and Ernst Friedrich Richter at the conservatory. In 1866, the cholera epidemic having sent the family to Dresden, he studied piano with Friedrich Wieck, father-in-law of Robert Schumann, who refused all payment for lessons. Upon returning to Leipzig, he directed an orchestra of forty and a chorus of twenty-four in *Martha, Stradella,* and *Fra Diavolo,* although he was not yet fifteen years old. His duties as conductor took him to Berlin, where in 1872 he formed a friendship with Moritz Moszkowski and, through Moszkowski, with Theodor Kullak. Under Kullak, who invited him to become his pupil and practically supported him for two years, he modernized his piano method and overcame the restrictions imposed by the more pedantic style of Moscheles. In February 1875 he made his début as a pianist in Berlin, and won the admiration and friendship of Anton Rubinstein. In the same year he was appointed court pianist at Schwerin, Mecklenburg-Schwerin, and head of the Academy Music School. At various times he acted as chorusmaster at the Stadt-Theater in Berlin, as summer conductor at Würzburg and Kissingen, and

as conductor at the court opera in Neustrelitz. In addition he found time for a number of lessons with Franz Liszt. In 1877 he was engaged for a tour as pianist with Madame Désirée Artôt, a celebrated singer, and spent the season of 1877–78 in concerts with her in Europe, Russia, Siberia, Asia Minor, and Egypt. A performance he gave on Mar. 22, 1880, before Kaiser Wilhelm I, led to engagements at embassies and palaces of the aristocracy, and to a tour of more than one hundred concerts in the United States, 1880–81. His first tour was followed by further engagements in successive years, some of them undertaken in conjunction with August Wilhelmj, the violinist, and others with Minnie Hauk, the singer. He was married in the year following his first American visit, and in 1886 settled in Atlanta, Ga., and became an American citizen. In 1890, moving to Philadelphia, Pa., he established the Sternberg School of Music, which he conducted until his death. He died in Philadelphia, survived by his wife, Tyl.

He had a position of importance in the musical life of America, principally as a teacher, although he was prominent also as a composer and pianist. His distinguished pupils included Olga Samaroff, Robert Armbruster, Gustave Becker, Robert Braun, and the modernistic composer, George Antheil. His compositions include a "Humoresque," five "Concert-Études," an "Impromptu," "Caprice Hippique," "Nuit Arabe," "En Bohème," and three "Preludes," all for piano; six trios for piano, violin, and violoncello; and many choral works and songs. Some of his music was played in concert by Josef Hofmann, Leopold Godowsky, Fannie Bloomfield Zeisler, and other pianists. His writings include *Ethics and Esthetics of Piano-Playing* (copyright 1917) and *Tempo Rubato and Other Essays* (copyright 1920). He wrote many articles for musical magazines; three autobiographical articles, "The Making of a Musician as Shown in the Reminiscences of Constantin von Sternberg," appeared in the *Musician,* December 1913, and January and February 1914.

[The most complete account of von Sternberg's life and career is given in his articles in the *Musician* in 1913 and 1914. See also *Grove's Dict. of Music and Musicians: Am. Supp.* (1926); *Baker's Biog. Dict. of Musicians* (3rd edition, 1919), ed. by Alfred Remy; W. R. Murphy, in *Musical America,* Apr. 5, 1924; obituary in *Pub. Ledger* (Phila.), Apr. 1, 1924.]
                                                    J. T. H.

STERNBERG, GEORGE MILLER (June 8, 1838–Nov. 3, 1915), bacteriologist, epidemiologist, and surgeon-general of the United States army, was born at Hartwick Seminary, Otsego County, N. Y., where he spent most of his childhood. His father, Levi Sternberg, a Lutheran clergyman who later became principal of Hartwick Seminary, was descended from a German family from the Palatinate, which had settled in the Schoharie valley in the early years of the eighteenth century. His mother, Margaret Levering (Miller) Sternberg, was the daughter of George B. Miller, also a Lutheran clergyman and professor of theology at the seminary, a Lutheran school. The eldest of a large family, George was early compelled to lighten his father's burden by gainful work. His studies at Hartwick Seminary were interrupted by a year of employment in a bookstore in Cooperstown and by three years of teaching in rural schools. During his last years at Hartwick he taught mathematics, chemistry, and natural philosophy, and devoted his leisure hours to the study of anatomy and physiology under Dr. Horace Lathrop of Cooperstown. After medical courses first in Buffalo and then at the College of Physicians and Surgeons (later part of Columbia University), where he received the degree of M.D. in the spring of 1860, he settled for practice in Elizabeth, N. J., and remained there until the outbreak of the Civil War. He was appointed assistant surgeon, United States Army, on May 28, 1861, and on July 21 of the same year he, was captured at Bull Run while serving with Gen. George Sykes's division in the Army of the Potomac. Escaping, he joined his command in front of Washington, and later participated in the battles of Gaines's Mill and Malvern Hill (Peninsular campaign). He contracted typhoid fever at Harrison's Landing and was sent north on a government transport. The remaider of his Civil War service he rendered mainly in military hospitals at Portsmouth Grove, R. I., and at Cleveland, Ohio. He received brevet commissions of captain and major for faithful and meritorious service during the war. From the close of the Civil War until 1879 he served at various army posts, first in Kansas, then on the Atlantic seaboard, and later in the Pacific northwest. In 1868–69 he took part in several expeditions against hostile Cheyennes along the upper Arkansas River in Indian Territory and western Kansas. During his service at Fort Barrancas, Fla., 1872–75, which was marked by frequent contact with yellow fever, he noted the efficacy of moving inhabitants out of an infected environment and successfully applied the method to the Barrancas garrison. About this time he published two articles in the *New Orleans Medical and Surgical Journal* ("An Inquiry into the Modus Operandi of the Yellow Fever Poison," July 1875, and "A Study of the Natural History

of Yellow Fever," March 1877) which gave him a definite status as an authority upon yellow fever. He was stricken with the disease himself in the summer of 1875, and recovered only after a critical illness and a long convalescence. Later, while serving at Fort Walla Walla, Wash., he participated in the Nez Percés campaign of 1877. In these days he was utilizing the time not taken up by his military duties in the studies and experiments which were the foundation for his later work. He perfected an anenometer and in 1870 patented an automatic heat regulator which has had wide use.

In April 1879 he was ordered to Washington, D. C., and detailed for duty with the Havana Yellow Fever Commission, his medical associates being Dr. Stanford Chaillé of New Orleans and Dr. Juan Guiteras [*q.v.*] of Havana. In the distribution of work, Sternberg was given the problems relating to the nature and natural history of the cause of the disease, which involved microscopical examination of blood and tissues of yellow fever patients. In these investigations he was one of the first to employ the newly discovered process of photomicrography, and he developed high efficiency in its use. During three months which he passed in Havana he was intimately associated with Dr. Carlos Juan Finlay [*q.v.*], the proponent of the theory of transmission of yellow fever by the mosquito. At the end of its year's work, however, the Commission came to the conclusion that the solution of the cause of the disease must wait upon further progress in the new science of bacteriology. Sternberg was next sent to New Orleans to investigate the conflicting discoveries of the *Plasmodium malariae* by Alphonse Laveran and of the *Bacillus malariae* by Arnold Carl Klebs and Corrado Tommasi-Crudeli. His report, made in 1881, stated that the so-called *Bacillus malariae* had no part in the causation of malaria. In this same year, simultaneously with Louis Pasteur, he announced his discovery of the pneumococcus, now recognized as the pathogenic agent in pneumonia, though it remained for Karl Frankel to show its relationship to the disease. In the United States he was the first to demonstrate the plasmodium of malaria (1885) and the bacilli of tuberculosis and typhoid fever (1886). His interest in bacteriology naturally led to an interest in disinfection, and with him and Koch scientific disinfection had its beginning. In 1878, using putrefactive bacteria, he had begun to experiment on disinfectants. He continued his experiments in Washington and in the laboratories of the Johns Hopkins Hospital at Baltimore under the auspices of the American Public Health Association. His essay, *Disinfection and Individual Prophylaxis against Infectious Diseases* (1886), received the Lomb prize and was translated into several foreign languages. During the Hamburg cholera epidemic of 1892 he was attached to the New York quarantine station as consultant upon disinfection as applied to ships and quarantine stations. Though the disease reached American shores, no case developed within the country.

In the meantime he was ascending in military grade. He was made captain in 1866, major in 1875, lieutenant-colonel in 1891, and on May 30, 1893, surgeon-general of the army with the rank of brigadier-general. His nine years' tenure of that office was marked by the establishment of the Army Medical School in 1893, the organization of the army nurse corps and the dental corps, the creation of the tuberculosis hospital at Fort Bayard and of many general hospitals during the Spanish-American War. His own early difficulties in acquiring the knowledge for which he thirsted led to a liberal-minded policy in the establishment of laboratories in the larger military hospitals where medical officers could engage in scientific research. In 1898, led by similar motives, he established the Typhoid Fever Board made up of Majors Walter Reed, Victor Clarence Vaughan [*qq.v.*], and Edward O. Shakespeare, which introduced new points of view for the prevention of this disease, and in 1900 he established the Yellow Fever Commission, headed by Reed, which fixed the transmission of yellow fever upon a particular species of mosquito. After his retirement from active duty in the army in 1902, he devoted his later years to social welfare activities in Washington, particularly to the sanitary improvement of habitations and to care of the tuberculous. He died at his home in Washington. His monument in Arlington Cemetery bears the inscription: "Pioneer American Bacteriologist, distinguished by his studies of the causation and prevention of infectious diseases, by his discovery of the microorganism causing pneumonia, and scientific investigation of yellow fever, which paved the way for the experimental demonstration of the mode of transmission of the disease." His name will survive as that of the American bacteriologist, contemporary of Pasteur and of Koch, who first brought the fundamental principles and technique of the new science within the reach of American physicians. From 1875, when he published his first articles on yellow fever, he was a frequent contributor to periodical literature of medicine. In 1892 he brought out his *A Manual of Bacteriology*, the first exhaustive treatise on the subject published in the United States. His books, reports, and articles number not less than one hundred and fifty.

He was a man of reverent piety and practical Christianity, modest and unassuming, gentle in manner and in speech, whose career was marked by devotion to duty and untiring industry. Faced in the Spanish-American War with great difficulties, he bore without reply the burden of much criticism, either unfounded or the result of conditions not of his making. He was short in stature, with a moderate stoutness in his later years. His portraits show how the smooth-faced youth of abundant dark hair changed to the middle-aged man of full beard, and finally to the retired officer with white mustache and fringe of white hair. Marked in them all are the high intelligent forehead and the keen speculative dark eyes. He was married on Oct. 19, 1865, to a daughter of Robert Russell of Cooperstown, N. Y., Louisa Russell, who died in 1867 from cholera at Fort Harker, Kan. On Sept. 1, 1869, he was married at Indianapolis, Ind., to Martha L. Pattison, daughter of Thomas T. N. Pattison of that city. There were no children.

[*Who's Who in America*, 1914–15; Martha L. Sternberg, *George Miller Sternberg* (1920), with portraits and bibliog.; *Addresses Delivered at the Complimentary Banquet to Gen. George M. Sternberg . . . on his Seventieth Birthday* (1908), ed. by G. M. Kober; A. C. Abbott, in *Trans. Coll. of Physicians of Phila.*, 3 ser., vol. XXXVIII (1916); H. A. Kelly and W. L. Burrage, *Am. Medic. Biogs.* (1920); obituary in *Evening Star* (Washington, D. C.), Nov. 3, 1915.]
                                                    J. M. P.

STERNE, SIMON (July 23, 1839–Sept. 22, 1901), lawyer and civic reformer, was a son of Henry and Regina Sterne. He was born in Philadelphia and attended the public schools there. Later, he traveled in Europe and for a short period studied at the University of Heidelberg. On his return he began preparation for the practice of law in the offices of George Sharswood and John H. Markland. In 1859 he was graduated from the University of Pennsylvania with the degree of LL.B., and the same year was admitted to the bar in Philadelphia.

Moving to New York in 1860, he was admitted to the bar there and began a successful practice and an active and varied career in promoting civic improvement. In 1863 he gave a series of lectures on economics at Cooper Institute. He wrote leading articles for the New York *Commercial Advertiser*, the property of one of his clients, and in 1865 he became editor of the *New York Social Science Review*. While in England in 1865 he obtained permission from Thomas Hare to adapt his ideas of representation to American conditions. The result was the founding of the Personal Representation Society, which advocated cumulative voting and induced the Illinois constitutional convention of 1870 to adopt it. He was the hard-working secretary of the Committee of Seventy which overthrew the "Tweed ring." In 1875 he assisted, as a member of Governor Tilden's commission, in devising a uniform plan of government for the cities of New York state. He served on a commission appointed by Governor Morton in 1895 to suggest improvements in the methods of legislation. In the interest of free trade he made numerous campaign speeches for the Democratic party from 1876 to 1888.

As his practice developed it tended to center in cases involving common carriers, and after 1875 his most important activities, both public and legal, were in this field. He believed that the common law of railroads, which had been adapted from the rules relating to highways and canals, was inadequate to guarantee proper service to the public and safety to investors. When the Hepburn committee of the New York Assembly met to inquire into alleged abuses (1879), he appeared as counsel for the board of trade and transportation and the chamber of commerce and practically conducted the investigation. The report of this committee was followed by the passage of the state railroad commission act of 1882, which he drafted. He later drafted essential provisions of the federal Interstate Commerce Act of 1887, incorporating the results of an extensive private investigation into the relations between railroads and the state in western Europe. He was employed as counsel by the Interstate Commerce Commission; by several large railway systems; by Northern friends of Jefferson Davis in 1865; by the bondholders of Louisiana in their suit in the Supreme Court against the state; and by Mark Twain and Joaquin Miller in copyright cases. In the course of his practice he secured important additions to the common law of New York—that elevated railroad companies are liable for damages for obstructing the passage of light and air; that the existence of a strike is no excuse for a common carrier to refuse to receive and forward freight; and that telephone service is analogous to that rendered by a common carrier.

He was the author of *On Representative Government and Personal Representation* (1871); *Constitutional History and Political Development of the United States* (copr. 1882); several articles for Lalor's *Cyclopædia of Political Science, Political Economy, and of the Political History of the United States* (3 vols., 1881–84); and many essays published in American and foreign periodicals, the best of which were republished in book form in 1912 under the title *Railways in the United States*. His writings, though marred by prolixity, show originality of thought and keen analysis of contemporary conditions. His most prominent personal traits were large sympathy, determination, intellectual enthusiasm, and mental agility. He died from an apoplectic stroke in his sixty-third year and was buried from Temple Emanu-El in New York City. His widow, the former Mathilde Elsberg, whom he married June 8, 1870, together with a daughter, survived him.

[John Foord, *The Life and Public Services of Simon Sterne* (1903); *Biog. Dir. of the State of N. Y.* (1900); *Who's Who in America*, 1899–1900; A. S. Gitterman, *Memorial Exercises at the Unveiling of a Small Fountain . . . 1902* (n.d.); introduction to *Railways in the U. S.* (1912); *N. Y. Times*, Sept. 23, 24 (editorial), 1901; *N. Y. Herald*, Sept. 23, 1901; *Jewish Messenger*, Oct. 6, 1901; *Hist. of the Bench and Bar of N. Y.* (1897), II, 360–62; *Asso. of the Bar of the City of N. Y.; Ann. Reports*, 1903.]   E. C. S.

STERNE, STUART [See Bloede, Gertrude, 1845–1905].

STERRETT, JAMES MACBRIDE (Jan. 13, 1847–May 31, 1923), Protestant Episcopal clergyman, philosopher, was born in Howard, Pa., the son of Robert and Sarah E. (MacBride) Sterrett. He graduated from the University of Rochester in 1867 and from the Episcopal Theological Seminary at Cambridge, Mass., in 1872. In the latter year he was ordained deacon and became assistant minister at Lawrence, Mass. Elevated to the priesthood in 1873, he served as rector of the church in Wellsville, N. Y., until 1877, marrying, Jan. 20, 1876, Adlumia Dent of Brookland, Pa. His next parish was in Bedford, Pa., where he ministered from 1879 to 1882. He was then called to the Seabury Divinity School, Faribault, Minn., as professor of philosophy, which position he held for the ensuing ten years, at the end of which time he assumed a similar professorship at Columbian (now George Washington) University, Washington, D. C. He was made professor emeritus in 1909. From 1892 to 1911 he served also as assistant minister of the Church of the Epiphany, Washington. Becoming rector of All Soul's Parish in 1911, he continued as such until 1917, and thereafter he was associate rector. During a period of ill health he committed suicide by shooting; he was survived by his wife and five sons.

As a philosopher, Sterrett's distinctive contribution to American thought was along the line of the development of idealistic philosophy, notably the idealism of Hegel. His close relation to William T. Harris [q.v.], the leading spirit of what is known as the "St. Louis School," would perhaps entitle him to be classed as an adherent of this school. He was especially interested in the field where philosophy and religion touch. Free from the implied pantheism of some idealists, and no slavish follower of Hegel, he turned his thought to the philosophical principles which underlie the intellectual aspect of religion. The titles of his several books indicate the line his interest followed: *Studies in Hegel's Philosophy of Religion* (1890), *Reason and Authority in Religion* (1891), *The Ethics of Hegel* (1893), *The Freedom of Authority* (1905), and *Modernism in Religion* (1922). His *Freedom of Authority* is a collection of essays, significant as showing his stanch defense of religion against attacks made by those of opposite mind. He was, however, never unfair to opponents nor did he criticize them for the mere sake of criticism.

His ethical viewpoint was the social one. It was his conviction that man finds his truest ethical life in conjunction with other men. The freedom of authority is the philosophical justification of authority in that under law one finds the best of one's own nature. Law is the expression of one's own moral self, whether this fact be consciously realized or not. Authority is real freedom; indeed, freedom is best actualized under and through authority. Thus freedom is given an ethical meaning. This was one of Sterrett's outstanding ideas and, applied to historical religion, became a plea for the episcopate, which seemed to him to be rationally justified and which he regarded as conducive to the best interests of the Church.

As a teacher he was enthusiastic in the presentation of his subject. He loved philosophy as men love an ideal and consistently followed the light that it yielded. He was eager to impress others with its knowledge and to make it a living force. As the leader of a church he was devoted to the spiritual welfare of those who looked to him for guidance, a fact especially evinced in the closing years of his life, when, after retirement from teaching, he assumed the active work of the ministry and wrought devotedly and effectively. His great work was in the field of philosophy, however, in which his clear, yet profound, thinking helped to give idealism a better standing as against the empirical pragmatic trend so pronounced in some quarters.

[Sterrett spelled his middle name with a small "b," though his mother's name was MacBride. Sources for this sketch include *Who's Who in America*, 1922–23; *Living Church*, June 9, 1923; *Washington Post*, June 1, 1923; personal acquaintance.]   E. E. R.

STERRETT, JOHN ROBERT SITLINGTON (Mar. 4, 1851–June 15, 1914), archaeologist, was born at Rockbridge Baths, Va., of Scotch-Irish ancestry, the son of Robert Dunlap and Nancy Snyder (Sitlington) Sterrett. From 1868 to 1871 he was a student in the University of Virginia, and then went abroad, where he studied at Leipzig, Berlin, and Munich, receiving the degree of Ph.D. from the University of Munich in 1880. He was a student at the American School of Classical Studies at Athens, from 1882 to 1883, and its secretary from 1883 to 1884.

Returning to the United States, he became professor of Greek at Miami University in 1886, retaining that position for two years and then holding a similar position at the University of Texas until 1892. Called to Amherst College, he was professor of Greek there until 1901, when he became head of the Greek department at Cornell University, remaining as such until his death. In 1896–97 he also served as professor in the American School of Classical Studies in Athens, Greece. On Mar. 1, 1892, he was married to Josephine Mosely Quarrier of Charleston, W. Va., by whom he had four children.

The ruling passion of Sterrett's life was exploration and archaeological research in Asia Minor and Babylonia, whither he led several expeditions, the fruits of which are contained in his publications. His unbounded enthusiasm for archaeology is evinced by the fact that he spent all his limited patrimony upon it. His main object was to explore the least known, and therefore the most dangerous, regions. On the Wolfe Expedition in 1885, for example, with a subsidy of only a thousand dollars, and with but two native servants, he was able—thanks to his economy, tact, personality, and knowledge of the Turkish language—safely to visit the unknown regions of Pisidia, Cilicia, Lycaonia, and Isauria and by his observations and measurements to reconstruct Heinrich Kiepert's maps of those countries. Sterrett's chorographic work is to be seen in the two subsequent maps made by Kiepert himself. In addition to the host of inscriptions which Sterrett published, he identified the sites of scores of important cities, among them the Lystra of St. Paul's travels. At the age of thirty-five he had made remarkable contributions to the fields of chorography and epigraphy.

His published works include: *Qua in re Hymni Homerici quinque maiores inter se differant* (1881); *Inscriptions of Assos, Inscriptions of Tralles* (1885); *An Epigraphical Journey in Asia Minor* (1888), containing 398 inscriptions; *The Wolfe Expedition to Asia Minor* (1888), containing 651 inscriptions;

Leaflets from the Notebook of an Archaeological Traveler (1889); *The Torch-Race at Athens* (1902); *Homer's Iliad: First Three Books and Selections* (copr. 1907), edited for school use; *The Outline of a Plan for the Exploration of Asia Minor, Syria, and the Cyrenaica* (1907); *A Plea for Research in Asia Minor and Syria* (1911).

Before his untimely death Sterrett had in mind the completion of three great tasks: an historical geography of the New Testament; a translation of Strabo's work on geography; and a two-year expedition to Asia Minor and Cyrenaica. He had collected material for the first task, had begun the second (see Preface to H. L. Jones, *The Geography of Strabo*, vol. I, 1917), and had started a campaign for $100,-000 to finance the third. He was a man of large physique and commanding personality, an inspiring teacher, and an indefatigable worker. Although uncompromising in his settled beliefs, he was modest and tolerant to a fault. He was intensely religious, caring only for the things of the spirit. When upon unearthing an inscribed stele at Tarsus it suddenly dawned upon him that the Apostle Paul had often beheld it, he burst into tears.

[Twenty-nine notebooks kept on the expeditions to Asia Minor, 1884–85, in Cornell Univ. Lib.; *Who's Who in America*, 1914–15; *Bull. of the Univ. of Tex.* (1889); *Boston Post*, May 8, 1888, *Independent*, May 10, 1888, *Nation* (N. Y.), May 10, 1888; *Classical Rev.*, July 1889; *Evening Post* (N. Y.), June 17, 1914.]

H. L. J.

STETEFELDT, CARL AUGUST (Sept. 28, 1838–Mar. 17, 1896), inventor and metallurgist, was born at Holzhausen, Gotha, Germany. He was the only son of August Heinrich Christian Stetefeldt and Friederika Christiane (Credner) Stetefeldt. His father was a Lutheran clergyman, who moved in 1847 to Hörselgau, where he kept a private school in addition to performing his clerical duties. Under his tutelage his son was prepared to enter the Gymnasium at Gotha at the age of fourteen. His career there was chiefly marked by a conflict that ended in his being permitted to give up the study of Hebrew, and by the founding of a natural history society among the students. After Gotha he spent two years at the university at Göttingen, entering the school of mines at Clausthal in 1860 and graduating in 1862. He received the highest rating in his class in all metallurgical and mining subjects and was immediately commissioned to make some investigations of metallurgical processes in the government works in the Harz. After a brief experience managing a small copper smelting

plant in Bohemia he came to the United States in 1863 and was immediately engaged as assistant to Charles A. Joy, professor of chemistry in Columbia College, New York City. The next year he became an assistant to the consulting firm of Adelberg & Raymond of which Rossiter W. Raymond [*q.v.*] was a member, and, in 1865, formed a partnership with John H. Boalt to operate an assay office and consulting business at Austin, Nev. He built the first lead blast furnace in the district at Eureka, Nev., but the enterprise failed because of the nature of the ore deposit.

Stetefeldt had taken out a patent on an improvement on the Gerstenhöfer roasting furnace soon after he came to America, and he followed it by developing the design known as the Stetefeldt furnace, the first successful one being built at Reno, Nev. It has since been superseded, but the advance it marked in the metallurgical processes for dealing with sulphide ores containing gold and silver by the chlorination process won for its inventor a high place in the history of metallurgy. Stetefeldt devoted most of his life thereafter to the construction and operation of his furnaces and to auxiliary processes, but he also did much to improve and recommend the Russell lixiviation process. He contributed more than a score of papers to the *Transactions of the American Institute of Mining Engineers* (see *Transactions*, vol. XXVI, pp. 542–43), and was twice vice-president of the Institute. He went to Europe in 1870 but returned to San Francisco in 1872, and was married there on Dec. 31, 1872. He had no children and his wife died before him. He resided in New York City from 1882 until 1889, and then returned to California, spending the rest of his life in Oakland studying general science. His book, *The Lixiviation of Silver-ores with Hyposulphite Solutions*, was published in 1888. He was a worthy representative of the group of German-trained metallurgists who contributed so much to the development of metallurgy in the United States in the latter half of the nineteenth century.

[Biographical article by R. W. Raymond, *Engineering and Mining Jour.*, Mar. 28, 1896; *Trans. of the Am. Institute of Mining Engineers*, vol. XXVI (1897); *San Francisco Chronicle*, Mar. 18, 1896.]

T. T. R.

STETSON, AUGUSTA EMMA SIMMONS (*c.* 1842–Oct. 12, 1928), Christian Science leader, daughter of Peabody and Salome (Sprague) Simmons, and a descendant of Moses Simmons, who came to Plymouth in 1621, was born in Waldoboro, Me. During her infancy the family moved to Damariscotta, Me., where her father was an architect. She early showed musical and elocutionary talent. Her education at the Damariscotta High School and in the Lincoln Academy, New Castle, Me., was adequate for the period. In 1864 she married Capt. Frederick J. Stetson, a ship-builder associated with Baring Brothers, London. Like his wife, he was of early New England ancestry, being a descendant of Robert Stetson who was living at Scituate, Mass., in 1634. His business took them to England, then to Bombay, and finally to Akyab, British Burma. His health, however, had been permanently injured by privations suffered in Libby Prison during the Civil War, and after a few years in the Orient it broke down completely. He and his wife returned to America and settled in Boston, where Mrs. Stetson undertook to support them as an elocutionist. Large and ample-bosomed, with a good voice and an ingratiating manner, she was well equipped for the rôle, and her elocutionary studies were of great assistance in her later career. While engaged in them she attracted the attention of Mary Baker Eddy [q.v.], who persuaded her to enter one of her classes. Immediately on completion of the three weeks' course she began to practise as a Christian Science healer. Her success in this and in preaching the new doctrine was so great that in November 1886 Mrs. Eddy sent her to New York City to open up the field there. The work at first moved slowly, but by February 1888 Mrs. Stetson was able to legally incorporate a church of seventeen members. The congregation met in a hall over Caswell and Massey's drug store at Fifth Avenue and Forty-seventh Street; the next year it moved to Crescent Hall at 123 Fifth Ave., and later to Hardman Hall at Fifth Avenue and Nineteenth Street. These changes of location were dictated by the increasing size of the congregation, which in 1894 made necessary a further move to Scottish Rite Hall, and in 1896 led to the purchase of the old Rutgers Presbyterian Church at 143 West Forty-eighth St. In 1899 property was secured at Ninety-sixth Street and Central Park West, where a magnificent building was erected which at its completion in 1903 was without mortgage although it had cost over a million dollars. Most of this sum was raised through the personal exertions of Mrs. Stetson. She herself lived on a lavish scale commensurate with her dwelling—a gift from her followers which cost about $100,000 and was adorned with a marble staircase, expensive rugs and tapestries, six grandfather's clocks, and other luxurious objects.

Her disciple's remarkably successful career

had now aroused the jealousy of Mrs. Eddy, and various by-laws were promulgated by her which aimed to limit the sphere of Mrs. Stetson's influence but still left her in actual control of her own church. In the summer of 1909, however, the Board of Directors of the Mother Church, at Mrs. Eddy's prompting, began to investigate certain charges against Mrs. Stetson, of which the chief were that she taught the sinfulness of physical procreation and endeavored by means of mental suggestion to bring illness and even death upon her enemies. These charges were found to be well grounded, and in November 1909 Mrs. Stetson was formally excommunicated. Refusing to admit that her leader had turned against her, Mrs. Stetson continued to proclaim Mrs. Eddy's semi-divinity and, after the latter's death in 1910, she prophesied her speedy resurrection. She published three volumes dealing largely with their mutual relations: *Reminiscences, Sermons and Correspondence* (1913), *Vital Issues in Christian Science* (1914), *Sermons and Other Writings* (1925). A fervent believer in the Anglo-Israelite theory, she became a violent Jingoist during the World War. Toward the close of her life she spent as much as $250,000 annually in self-advertising in the press or on the radio. She also formed a choral society which gave notable public performances during 1918–26, specializing in what she called "spiritual music." Shortly before her death, she announced that she would never die.

[L. A. Simmons, *Hist. of the Simmons Family* (1930), not altogether dependable; *Who's Who in America*, 1928–29; autobiog. passages in Mrs. Stetson's writings; E. F. Dakin, *Mrs. Eddy* (1928); Fleta C. Springer, *According to the Flesh* (1930); A. K. Swihart, *Since Mrs. Eddy* (1931); obituary in *N. Y. Times*, Oct. 13, 1928.]   E. S. B.

STETSON, CHARLES AUGUSTUS (Apr. 1, 1810–Mar. 28, 1888), hotel proprietor, the son of Prince and Hepzibeth or Hepzibah (Patch) Stetson, was born at Newburyport, Mass. He was a descendant of Robert Stetson, probably of England, who emigrated to America before 1634. His father was a tavern-keeper in that city, and in 1824, when he entertained Lafayette, young Charles acted as *valet de chambre* to the distinguished guest. In 1829 the famous Tremont House in Boston, then newly built, opened its doors with Charles Stetson, then nineteen years of age, as clerk and bell-boy. He was married to Lucy Ann Brown of Newburyport on Mar. 14, 1832. The Astor House in New York was completed in 1836, and Astor first leased it to the Boydens of Boston, owners of the Tremont House. His relations with them, however, were unsatisfactory, and in July 1838 Stetson took over the hotel, having at first as his partner, Robert B. Coleman, who presently retired. For nearly thirty years Stetson was the proprietor and literally the host of the Astor, probably the most famous host and hostelry in America at the time. In his first conversation with Astor, Stetson called himself a hotel-keeper, rather than a tavern landlord who merely "knows how to go to market, and how to feed so many people." "A hotel keeper," he declared, "is a gentleman who stands on a level with his guests" (Smith, *post*, p. 313).

Stetson was appointed a quartermaster-general of New York State on the staff of Governor Washington Hunt in 1851, and was known thereafter as "General" Stetson—a title which he used to best advantage as Mine Host. All celebrities who visited New York in the middle of the nineteenth century stopped at the Astor and were greeted by Stetson as if they had been guests in his own home. A sumptuous dinner to the Prince de Joinville at the Astor in 1840 was long considered a milestone in the city's history. Louis Kossuth addressed hordes of admirers from its windows in 1851. Room No. 11 was long the New York home of Thurlow Weed, and many a political deal, many a "slate" was arranged there. A certain suite of two rooms was always ready, even at a moment's notice, for Daniel Webster, a warm friend of Stetson's. "If I were shut out of the Astor," remarked Webster, "I would never go to New York again" (*New York Times*, Jan. 22, 1928). But notwithstanding Stetson's genius and hospitality, the Astor House was gradually outmoded by newer and larger hotels, and when he gave up its management in 1868 it was losing its fashionable preeminence. His son Charles operated it until 1875. During the last twenty-five years of his life, Stetson lived in quiet retirement. His home was at Swampscott, Mass., but he died at the home of one of his eight children in Reading, Pa.

[*Vital Records of Newburyport, Mass.* (2 vols., 1911); J. S. Barry, *A Geneal. and Biog. Sketch of the Name and Family of Stetson* (1847); N. M. Stetson, *Stetson Kindred of America* (1914); E. V. Smith, *Hist. of Newburyport* (1854); M. H. Smith, *Sunshine and Shadow in N. Y.* (1868); Jefferson Williamson, *The Am. Hotel* (1930); *Boston Daily Courier*, Oct. 19, 1829, on opening of Tremont House; *N. Y. Times*, Jan. 13, 1875, May 11, 1913, on history of Astor House; *N. Y. Times*, Mar. 30, 1888.]   A. F. H.

STETSON, CHARLES WALTER (Mar. 25, 1858–July 20, 1911), painter, born at Tiverton Four Corners, R. I., was the youngest of four children of the Rev. Joshua Augustus and Rebecca Louisa (Steere) Stetson. His father, a Free Will Baptist minister, was stationed suc-

cessively at Tiverton, Taunton, Mass., and Providence. Stetson had a high-school education in Providence and as a youth taught himself to draw and paint. Sending a picture to the Pennsylvania Academy of the Fine Arts, where it was well hung, he had encouragement from the critic, James Jackson Jarves, who visited Providence especially to meet the young artist, and from Benjamin Champney [*q.v.*]. He held a successful one-man show in 1884 at the Providence Art Club, of which he was one of the founders, and later an exhibition in Boston which was praised by John Boyle O'Reilly [*q.v.*]. He also made many etchings, exhibited at the Boston Museum of Fine Arts in 1913.

In 1884 he married Charlotte A. Perkins (later Charlotte Perkins Gilman), who won distinction as a lecturer and writer on social topics. They had one daughter, who became an artist. The marriage was unsuccessful, however, and in 1894 they were divorced. On June 11, 1894, Stetson married Grace Ellery Channing, a literary woman, grand-daughter of the Rev. William Ellery Channing [*q.v.*]. They lived for a time in southern California, whose landscape Stetson painted with keen appreciation of its beauty of line and romantic atmosphere. In 1897 they settled in Italy, where Mrs. Stetson studied and wrote much about the peasants while her husband painted them and their surroundings. John Elliott [*q.v.*] wrote of his pictures, which were exhibited in London and in Rome; "His chief charm is that he is American, pure and simple, with a sweet new-world sentiment and feeling for colour" (Maud H. Elliott, *John Elliott*, 1913, p. 78), and an Italian critic found in them "an artistic personality and the soul of a poet" (*American Art News*, May 6, 1905). Stetson, always a frail man, died at Rome, survived by his wife and his daughter by the first marriage. Shortly before his death he wrote, "I think I have learned my trade; now if I have even three years more, I will paint something" (*Stetson Kindred*, *post*, p. 14). In his early years he painted several official portraits; one of Henry Lippitt [*q.v.*], governor of Rhode Island; one of Judge George Moulton Carpenter of the United States district court; and one of Arthur Doyle, mayor of Providence. He became known, however, through his landscapes of California and Italy. He is best represented at the Rhode Island School of Design, Providence Museum of Art.

[See *Stetson Kindred of America*, no. 4 (1914), compiled by N. M. Stetson, with portrait; *Who's Who in America*, 1910–11; *A Catalogue of the Pictures . . . Exhibited by Charles Walter Stetson, at . . . the Providence Art Club . . .* (1884); obituaries in *Providence Daily Jour.*, July 21, and *Il Giornale d'Italia* (Rome),

July 23, 1911. An important coll. of Stetsoniana is owned (1933) by William A. Brown, Providence, R. I.]

F. W. C.

STETSON, FRANCIS LYNDE (Apr. 23, 1846–Dec. 5, 1920), lawyer, was born in Keeseville, N. Y., the son of Lemuel and Helen (Hascall) Stetson. His father, besides being a lawyer of distinction, was at one time in Congress (1843–45) and was an active member of the Democratic party of New York. After receiving his secondary education in the public schools of Plattsburg, Francis entered Williams College, graduating with honors in 1867. He then attended Columbia Law School, completing his course by 1869.

Following a short interval of practice with his uncle, William S. Hascall, he fell under the eye of William C. Whitney [q.v.] and was appointed assistant corporation counsel for the City of New York, remaining in this office until 1880. In this year he formed a partnership with Francis N., Francis S., and Charles W. Bangs under the name of Bangs & Stetson which was eventually succeeded by the firm of Stetson, Jennings & Russell. Although Stetson was a good trial lawyer, the importance of this phase of his work was overshadowed by the part he played in the organization and reorganization of corporate entities. It is of interest that he has been credited with first suggesting the use of the form of no par value stock (F. W. Wegenast, *The Law of Canadian Companies*, 1931, p. 452). Through Charles E. Tracy, at one time his partner, his firm acquired the business of J. Pierpont Morgan [q.v.], Tracy's brother-in-law, and ultimately Stetson became his personal counsel. "Morgan's attorney general," as he was jocularly known on Wall Street, was called upon to handle the legal details incident to the creation of the United States Steel Corporation, to play a large, if unostentatious rôle in the financier's efforts to reorganize the railroads of the continent, and to act as legal adviser to the many Morgan-controlled transportation and industrial concerns. As Morgan's counsel he appeared in the case of *Northern Securities Co.* vs. *United States* (193 U. S., 197), one of the most important cases under the Sherman Anti-Trust Act. Naturally this work brought him to the forefront of the New York bar both in prestige and in financial rewards. There was a rumor that he received $50,000 annually from Morgan merely to insure first call on his services (Ivy Lee, in *World's Work*, June 1904, p. 4880).

In the broader field of politics Stetson was likewise prominent, having been a member of the Young Men's Democratic Club (which did effective work in the overthrow of the "Tweed ring") and an ardent supporter of Samuel J. Tilden. As such he presented to the electoral commission the Democratic side of the Florida election returns in the Hayes-Tilden controversy. He was a friend and adviser of Cleveland, who sought his counsel both as governor and president and, had Stetson not wished otherwise, he would have been offered a cabinet position. This friendship was accentuated when Cleveland, between his presidential terms, was associated with Stetson's firm. To Stetson large credit must be given for Cleveland's policy of sound money. As Morgan's counsel, he attended the meeting at the White House at which the Morgan-Belmont syndicate offered to sell gold to the government to stem the drain on the waning gold reserves. In conjunction with Assistant Secretary Curtis he later framed the contract between the government and the syndicate. Although it is generally considered that a hard bargain was driven (and at the time scurrilous rumors pointed to the Cleveland-Stetson friendship as indicative of fraud), Stetson construed his action as high patriotism. To a Senate committee he stated: "I shall always consider it the most useful public service I could render" (*Senate Document 187, 54 Cong., 2 Sess.*, p. 281).

Stetson was "one of the most cultivated attorneys in the city, . . . a lifelong student, an omnivorous reader and man of exquisite courtesy and social grace" (Nevins, *post*, p. 451). It is not strange, in view of his affiliations with wealthy corporations and of his own ample means, that his economic views were of the most conservative nature. His article, "The Government and Corporations" (*Atlantic Monthly*, July 1912) is an amazing apologetic. (See also letter in *Outlook*, Feb. 16, 1907; *McClure's Magazine*, October 1908; and Stetson's article, "Control of Corporations Engaged in Interstate Commerce," *Case and Comment*, February 1912.) It is notable that he joined with Joseph H. Choate and others in opposing the sixteenth (income tax) amendment to the Constitution.

In private life he was friendly and generous. His marriage with Elizabeth Ruff, celebrated on June 26, 1873, having proved childless, he adopted his wife's secretary, Margery H. Lee, as daughter. Aside from law and politics his two great interests were the Episcopal Church and Williams College. He was credited with having framed the Episcopal canon on divorce, and as permanent trustee and benefactor of Williams his services were unflagging. So deep was his attachment to this institution that at his death he was interred in Williamstown beside the college campus.

[G. C. Holt, "Memorial of Francis Lynde Stetson," *The Asso. of the Bar of the City of N. Y., Year Book,* 1921; S. B. Griffin, "Francis Lynde Stetson," in *Obit. Record, Soc. of Alumni, Williams Coll.,* 1920–21; E. C. Hill (editor), *The Hist. Reg.* (1920), p. 231; *Who's Who in America,* 1920–21; *Who's Who in N. Y.,* 1918; *Who's Who in Finance* (1911); *Outlook,* Dec. 15, 1920; A.T. Clearwater, in *Proc. N. Y. State Bar Asso.,* 1920; Allan Nevins, *Grover Cleveland* (1933); *N. Y. Times,* Dec. 6, 1920.]   L. M. Su—s.

STETSON, JOHN BATTERSON (May 5, 1830–Feb. 18, 1906), hat manufacturer, philanthropist, was born at Orange, N. J., one of the twelve children of Stephen and Susan (Batterson) Stetson, who were both of New England descent. His father and several of his brothers were hatters, having acquired the trade in Connecticut, their native state. After the family's removal to New Jersey shortly before John's birth, the Stetsons helped build up a new center of the hat industry and the boy's school days were cut short that he might serve an early apprenticeship to the trade. John proved an apt worker, but after reaching his majority his business prospects as a junior partner in the family firm did not seem alluring and he decided to strike out for himself. Ill health, however, compelled him to quit work for a time and in an effort to recuperate he went to Illinois, Missouri, and later, during the gold-seeking period of the sixties, to Colorado. Outdoor life on the plains and in the foothills restored his health, and he returned to the East robust and energetic.

In 1865 he opened a one-man hat factory in Philadelphia. The hats, made by hand, he peddled among the local retailers. During the first six months he never sold as many as a dozen hats in a single order. Concluding that his product lacked distinction of style, he proceeded to make his own models instead of slavishly following the prescribed fashions of the period. Continuing as salesman-producer, he took and filled orders for larger and larger quantities until his fame as a hatter began to spread beyond the city. Besides renewing his health and strength, Stetson's journey to the Rocky Mountains had extended his knowledge of Americans and their ways. Having noted with interest the head gear then in vogue in the West, he was able to supply a type of hat that quickly became popular there. To build up his business he relied not on advertising, but wholly on the quality of his goods. The hats, he felt, must advertise themselves; in looks and wear they must appeal to buyers. With the increase in sales, Stetson never departed from the fixed-price policy with which he started.

As the demand for his product grew his manufacturing facilities kept pace; machinery was introduced, and gradually a great industrial plant was organized on the outskirts of Philadelphia, later to be surrounded by the growing city. By 1906 the Stetson works, equipped for every process involved in the making of high-grade fur-felt hats, employed 3500 hands and turned out 2,000,000 hats a year, which were distributed throughout the civilized world. An apprentice system with bonus was early established, to be followed in later years by annual gift distributions at Christmas, bonus awards for continuous services, stock allotments to employees, a home-building association, savings and benefit funds, and other welfare features. An auditorium was built primarily for Sunday-school purposes. A hospital with a capacity of 20,000 patients a year, served by a large permanent staff, was erected. The company was opposed to organized labor, and these paternalistic activities brought against it the charge of "benevolent feudalism" and the destruction of "the spirit of independence and liberty" (*American Federationist,* May 1916, pp. 383–85).

In 1888 Stetson, who had long been a generous giver to Baptist churches and benevolences, became interested in an academy at DeLand, Fla., where for many years he passed his winters. The name of the institution was changed to John B. Stetson University and Stetson gave liberally to it in money and buildings. He died of apoplexy at his DeLand home, leaving his entire estate, of approximately $5,000,000 to his family. He was twice married; by his first wife he had a daughter, and by his second, Sarah Elizabeth Shindler, two sons.

[Henry Whittemore, *The Founders and Builders of the Oranges* (1896); *Hat Review,* Mar. 1906; Elbert Hubbard, *A Little Journey to the Home of John B. Stetson* (1911); E. P. Oberholtzer, *Phil., a Hist. of the City and Its People* (n.d.), vol. IV; *Moody's Mag.,* Feb. 1914; A. T. Freeman, in *Annals Am. Acad. Pol. and Soc. Sci.,* Nov. 1903; *Profit-Sharing by Am. Employers* (1916), pub. by Welfare Dept., Nat. Civic Federation; *Who's Who in America,* 1906–07; *Pub. Ledger* (Phila.), Feb. 19, 1906.]   W. B. S.

STETSON, WILLIAM WALLACE (June 17, 1849–July 1, 1910), educator, was born in Greene, Me., the son of Reuben and Christiana (Thompson) Stetson, and a descendant of Robert Stetson who settled in Scituate, Mass., in 1634. The boy's early years were spent on his father's farm. He attended the local school and academy, and at the age of fifteen was appointed teacher in a district school. For some years he taught winters and worked for his father when not so engaged.

Deciding to use his savings in search of opportunities in the West, he left home in 1868, and in 1870 took a position as clerk in a combination drug and book store in Peoria, Ill. At the same time he enrolled in the preparatory department of Monmouth College and later entered the commercial department, withdrawing at the close of the academic year to accept an appointment as teacher in a local academy. Shortly before entering upon his new duties, he married, July 4, 1871, Rebecca Jane, daughter of William and Jane (Nicol) Killough, of Morning Sun, Iowa.

In 1880 he was appointed superintendent of schools in Rockford, Ill., a position which he held for four years. During this period he reorganized the city school system, and effected reforms in methods of instruction. His success and his popularity as a lecturer before teachers' meetings and institutes brought him recognition as a progressive administrator. He took an active part in the work of the Northern Illinois Teachers' Association, and was elected its president in 1883.

In 1884 he returned to Maine, to become principal of the Webster Grammar School in Auburn. A year later he was elected superintendent of schools. His unusual executive ability was immediately demonstrated; he regraded the schools, improved their equipment, established modern courses of study, and effected various reforms in methods of teaching. During the ten years of his administration his achievements, and his wise counsel on educational matters, made him widely known. He was president of the Maine Pedagogical Society, 1890–91, and president of the American Institute of Instruction, 1894–95. In 1895 he was elected state superintendent of public schools in Maine, which office he held until his retirement from active professional life in 1907. Among his accomplishments while in this position were the abolition of the district system, and the establishment of the present township system of school administration; the reclassification and consolidation of schools; the institution of free conveyance of pupils; the adoption of the free textbook system; the extension of free tuition privileges in secondary schools to all the pupils of the state; the improvement of courses of instruction in teacher-training institutions; the state certification of teachers; and the adoption of a plan of union supervision, designed to extend the advantages of expert guidance to the schools of all towns in the state. His reports from 1895 to 1907, widely recognized for their constructive suggestions, enhanced his reputation as a leader in educational reforms. In 1905, he was elected president of the department of superintendence of the National Education Association, an organization in which he had played an active rôle for

many years. He resigned as state superintendent in 1907 and spent the rest of his life in Auburn, Me. He was the author of *History and Civil Government of Maine* (copr. 1898), and of numerous articles and pamphlets in the field of educational administration. In 1911 *Ideals and Essentials of Education,* comprising selections from his publications and manuscripts, was issued by his wife.

[G. T. Little, *Genealogical and Family Hist. of the State of Maine* (1909), vol. I; *Reports of the State Superintendent of Pub. Schools of the State of Maine,* 1895–1906; Payson Smith, "William Wallace Stetson," in *Nat. Educ. Asso. of the U. S.: Jour. of Proceedings and Addresses,* 1911; *Who's Who in America,* 1910–11; *Lewiston Evening Jour.,* July 2, 1910; information from a brother, Dr. Herbert Lee Stetson, Kalamazoo, Mich.]   R. F. S.

STETTINIUS, EDWARD RILEY (Feb. 15, 1865–Sept. 3, 1925), industrialist, assistant secretary of war, was born at St. Louis, Mo., a son of Joseph and Isabel (Riley) Stettinius. The father had come of Maryland German stock and after a venture in river steam-boating had been employed for many years by a wholesale grocery firm at St. Louis. He died when Edward was only three years old. The boy was a student at St. Louis University, in the preparatory and collegiate departments, from 1874 through 1881. Then followed several years of employment by local business concerns and banks and after that one or two only partially successful personal ventures. His mother died in 1891 and in the following year he went to Chicago, becoming treasurer of Stirling & Company, manufacturers of machinery. Later he became vice-president and general manager and in a reorganization that occurred in 1905 he was made president; after a consolidation in 1906 with Babcock & Wilcox, he was made vice-president. Outside a small group of business associates, Stettinius was comparatively unknown when in 1909, at the age of forty-four, he was made president of the Diamond Match Company, of which in 1908 he had become treasurer. A single act of his administration brought him widespread prominence. On Jan. 28, 1911, his corporation freely dedicated to the public a patent (of Nov. 15, 1898) for a substitute for the poisonous white phosphorous used in the manufacture of matches. This generous action eventually removed the specter of slow poisoning from the employees of rival match factories the country over (*Scientific American,* Feb. 11, 1911).

After the Allies, in 1915, had retained the banking firm of J. P. Morgan & Company to handle their purchases of war supplies in the United States, the firm made a nation-wide canvass in search of a man able to control and bring to fruition so vast and unprecedented a business. The choice finally fell upon Stettinius, who after a few months resigned the Diamond Match presidency. His task was not merely to make contracts with persons and corporations offering products and materials desired by the Allies; he had to see that war munitions in enormous quantities should be produced in record time from remodeled and often improvised plants, whose owners were at first quite unversed in the munitions industry. Yet many such plants turned out within a stipulated period large consignments of shells that fully met the technical requirements set up by the Allied governments. This was accomplished so promptly and satisfactorily that Stettinius, almost over night, became an outstanding figure in the war. How his success impressed his immediate business associates is indicated by the announcement in January 1916 of his admission as a member of the Morgan firm. Within two years the total of Allied purchases through his agency reached $3,000,000,-000—truly a record for such transactions.

After the entry of the United States into the war, Stettinius was appointed surveyor-general of purchases, and, on Apr. 16, 1918, as second assistant secretary of war. Secretary Newton D. Baker saw him as "a man of great exactness and of an almost terrifying sense of responsibility" (quoted by Frederick Palmer, *Newton D. Baker*, 1931, vol. II, p. 396). In July 1918 he was sent to France as special representative of the Secretary of War in the matter of foreign orders for war materials placed by the American Expeditionary Force. Returning to New York after the Armistice, Stettinius left the government service in January 1919 and remained with the Morgan firm until his death at Locust Valley, L. I. On Oct. 18, 1894, he had married Judith Carrington of Richmond, Va.; she and their two sons and two daughters survived him.

[J. W. Ridings, "Edward R. Stettinius, Assistant Secretary of War," in *Mo. Hist. Rev.*, Oct. 1918; B. C. Forbes, "The Biggest Buyer in the World," *American Mag.*, Sept. 1917; Donald Wilhelm, "Stettinius, Master Buyer," *Am. Rev. of Reviews*, Mar. 1918; G. B. Clarkson, *Industrial America in the World War* (1923), pp. 53, 339; Benedict Crowell and R. F. Wilson, *Demobilization* (1921), pp. 297–98, 305–06; T. W. Lamont, *Henry P. Davison: The Record of a Useful Life* (1933), pp. 227–30; newspaper files and directories in St. Louis Pub. Lib.; *Who's Who in America*, 1924–25; obituary in *N. Y. Times*, Sept. 4, 1925.]
W. B. S.

STEUBEN, FRIEDRICH WILHELM LUDOLF GERHARD AUGUSTIN, Baron von (Sept. 17, 1730–Nov. 28, 1794), professional soldier, military expert, inspector general of the Continental Army, was given this name at his christening, seven days after his birth, in the German Reformed Church of Magdeburg. Later in life he changed it to Friedrich Wilhelm August Heinrich Ferdinand; and in America he was known as Frederick William Augustus von (or de) Steuben. His parents were Wilhelm Augustin von Steuben and Maria Dorothea von Jagow. His grandfather, Augustin Steube, a minister of the German Reformed Church, inserted the "von" in the family name about 1708. He was born in the fortress of Magdeburg, where his father was stationed as a lieutenant of engineers in the army of King Frederick William I of Prussia. He spent his early childhood in Russia, where his father served for several years in the army of the Czarina Anne. In his tenth year he returned to Germany with his father and received his education in the Jesuit schools in Breslau.

In his seventeenth year Steuben entered the officer corps of the Prussian army and served therein with credit throughout the Seven Years' War, first as a regimental officer of infantry and then as a staff officer. In 1761, after active service on the staffs of Generals von Mayer and von Hülsen he became a general staff officer and soon thereafter was promoted to the grade of captain. In January and February 1762, while serving at Königsberg, he received two personal letters from the King, Frederick the Great, thanking him for transmitting news of the death of the Czarina Elizabeth. These letters, an unusual compliment to a junior officer, are in the Prussian Archives. A few weeks later, Steuben went to St. Petersburg with Count von der Goltz, the new Prussian ambassador, and was engaged on confidential duties in connection with the peace negotiations between Prussia and Russia. Upon his return from St. Petersburg, in May 1762, and until the end of the war, he served at the Royal Headquarters as a general staff officer and as one of the aides-de-camp to the King. The significance of Steuben's general staff training and service has not been sufficiently appreciated. This is partly because the German word "Quartiermeister," signifying a general staff officer with troops, has been erroneously translated into English as "quartermaster." That Frederick the Great should select Steuben for general staff duty at the Royal Headquarters in time of war is the highest tribute to his professional standing. It was this specific training for and experience in the duties of the general staff, an agency then litttle known outside of Prussia, that so peculiarly equipped Steuben for his invaluable services to the cause of American independence. He brought to Washington's staff a technical training and equipment that was unknown in either the French or the British armies at that time.

Steuben was still a captain when he was discharged from the Prussian army shortly after the Peace of Hubertusburg in the spring of 1763. The circumstances attending his discharge at the early age of thirty-three, and so soon after gaining the royal favor, are obscure. His retirement left him without employment. In 1764, after unsuccessful negotiations to enter the Sardinian army, he was appointed chamberlain (*Hofmarschall*) at the Court of Hohenzollern-Hechingen upon the recommendation of Prince Henry of Prussia and his niece, the Princess Sophie Dorothea Fredericka of Württemberg. While at Hechingen he attained the rank of baron (*Freiherr*) and became a knight of the Margrave of Baden's Order of Fidelity. In 1771 the Prince of Hohenzollern-Hechingen, on account of financial embarrassment, decided to close his court and to reside abroad, incognito. Steuben was the only member of the court to accompany his patron and resided with him in France, principally at Montpellier. But the financial objects of the journey were not accomplished and in 1775 the Prince returned to Hechingen more embarrassed than ever. Steuben, who was always improvident, now found himself seriously in debt and sought employment elsewhere. Early in 1776 he entered into an unsuccessful negotiation to form a German regiment for the French army. Later he failed in an effort to enter the Austrian army and in April 1777 he visited Karlsruhe where he was again disappointed in an effort to enter the service of the Margrave of Baden. But while in Baden the Baron met a friend and correspondent of Benjamin Franklin who drew his attention to the American war as a field for his talents (Ebeling, *post*, p. 154). Accordingly, early in the summer of 1777, he set out for Paris with letters to Franklin and others.

Fortunately for Steuben, his high professional reputation as a trained Prussian staff officer had long been known to Count de St. Germain, the French minister of war. Just at that time St. Germain was making an unsuccessful effort to reform the French army by the introduction of Prussian methods of military efficiency and discipline. He recognized in Steuben an accomplished graduate from the school of Frederick the Great who was peculiarly qualified to give the American authorities much needed advice on military training, organization, and administration. He therefore commended Steuben to Beaumarchais, who was giving secret aid to the American colonies through the commercial corporation, Hortalez & Company, which he had formed with the connivance of the French government. Beaumarchais, Franklin, and Silas Deane recognized Steuben's merits and the importance of securing his services, but at first the negotiations failed because the American commissioners were not empowered to assure him adequate rank and pay or to make any contract with him in behalf of the Continental Congress. Later, however, it was decided that Hortalez & Company should advance the expenses of the journey and that the Baron should go purely as a distinguished volunteer and trust to fortune for a suitable opening for his recognized talents after his arrival in America. As his actual military rank of captain did not carry sufficient prestige to assure the success of this rôle, it was decided that he should assume the glamor of high rank. He was accordingly given letters from Franklin, Deane, and Beaumarchais to Washington, Henry Laurens, Robert Morris, and others in which he was introduced as a lieutenant-general. Indeed, in his letter to Washington, Franklin presented him as "a Lieutenant General in the King of Prussia's service" (Sept. 4, 1777, Kapp, *post*, p. 652). There could be no higher military prestige in the last quarter of the eighteenth century, and without this prestige Steuben could not have succeeded in his American mission.

The new "lieutenant-general," accompanied by a military secretary and an aide-de-camp, sailed from Marseilles on Sept. 26 and arrived at Portsmouth, N. H., on Dec. 1, 1777. After a sojourn of several weeks at Boston, where he was entertained as became his distinguished rank, he made the overland journey to York, Pa, the temporary seat of government, where he arrived on Feb. 5, 1778. He was received with high honors by the Continental Congress. When a special committee waited upon him to ascertain his aims, he waived all claim to rank or pay and asked only that his expenses should be paid while acting as a volunteer with the army. He proposed that if his services should contribute to the eventual success of the American cause, he would then expect compensation for his sacrifices in leaving Europe and such reward as Congress might be pleased to grant him, but that if the cause should fail, or if his services should not prove beneficial, he would make no claim whatever. This proposal to stake his fortunes upon the success of the cause made a deep impression upon the Congress. His services were accepted and he was directed to report to Washington at Valley Forge where he arrived on Feb. 23.

Steuben made a profound impression upon

the officers and men of the Continental Army. His professional reputation, so well advertised by his exalted rank, was supported by his martial bearing, his adaptability, and his picturesque personality. Washington was so favorably impressed by his practical knowledge and experience that he prevailed upon him to serve as acting inspector general and to undertake the training of the army. This involved serious difficulties as the Baron spoke no English and was required to act through interpreters. There was no time for the preparation and publication of a complete new drill manual. Steuben therefore prepared his drill instructions in brief installments. These were translated into English and issued to the regiments from time to time as the drills progressed. Fortunately, he had the tact to rely upon the power of example. He formed a model company of 100 selected men and undertook its drill in person. The rapid progress of this company under his skilled instruction made an immediate appeal to the imagination of the whole army. Drill became the fashion and within a few weeks the new gospel, imparted day by day to the model company, had spread throughout the army. This is perhaps the most remarkable achievement in rapid military training in the history of the world. The Baron's success was so speedy that on April 30 Washington recommended his appointment as inspector general with the rank of major-general. On May 5 the appointment was confirmed by the Continental Congress. The value of Steuben's instruction was soon manifested on the battlefield of Monmouth. There and thereafter throughout the war the Continental Army proved itself, battalion for battalion, the equal in discipline and skill of the best British regulars. Immediately before the battle Steuben served Washington as a general staff officer. He reconnoitered the enemy's position near Allentown and was first to report that his objective was Monmouth Courthouse. After the disastrous retreat of Charles Lee, in the ensuing battle, Steuben reformed Lee's disordered troops and led them back to the battlefield.

During the winter of 1778–79, Steuben prepared his *Regulations for the Order and Discipline of the Troops of the United States.* This manual of drill and field service regulations contained the essentials of military instruction and procedure adapted to the needs of the American citizen soldier. It was popularly known as the "blue book" and became the military bible of the Continental Army. No important book has ever been produced under greater difficulties. The Baron first wrote each passage in his practical but inelegant French. One of his staff officers then transposed it into literary French. Another translated it literally into English and a third then transposed it into correct and simple English. During most of 1779 and 1780 Steuben was busy with his duties as inspector general, perfecting the training and discipline of the army and developing his system of property accountability that went far to check the waste of public property which had formerly prevailed in the American army. During this period he grew steadily in popularity throughout the army and grew more and more in Washington's confidence. He was consulted upon all questions of strategic and administrative policy and performed all of the essential functions of a modern general staff. During the winter of 1779–80 he was Washington's representative with the Continental Congress in the efforts to reorganize the army.

In the autumn of 1780, when Greene was sent to the Carolinas to replace Gates after the disastrous defeat at Camden, Washington sent Steuben with the new commander to assist in reorganizing the southern army. Upon their arrival at Richmond, Greene realized that most of his replacements and supplies must come from Virginia. He therefore left Steuben in command in that state. Steuben immediately took comprehensive measures to make Virginia a base of supply for Greene's army. But his efforts were thwarted to a large extent by the invading forces under Benedict Arnold and Phillips which were effectively supported by British ships in James River. With his limited forces of ill-armed militia, Steuben could offer but limited resistance to the invaders. Many of his stores were captured and many more were dispersed and wasted by the successive drafts of ill-disciplined short-service militia. Greene, however, appreciated Steuben's difficulties and gratefully acknowledged that his support from Virginia, limited as it was, had been indispensable to the success of his campaign in the Carolinas. In April 1781 Lafayette took command in Virginia and Steuben served under his orders during Cornwallis' invasion. When Washington's army was assembled before Yorktown, Steuben was assigned to the command of one of the three divisions and served in that capacity until after the surrender. He also contributed materially to the success of the final campaign by virtue of the extensive experience in siege warfare which he had acquired during the Seven Years' War.

In the interval between the surrender of Cornwallis and the final conclusion of peace Steuben continued his duties as inspector general and as Washington's trusted adviser in all military affairs. In the spring of 1783 he assisted Washington in the preparation of a plan for the future defense of the United States and in the arrangements for demobilizing the Continental Army. This was published as *A Letter on the Subject of an Established Militia* (1784). At the same time he took a leading part in forming the Society of the Cincinnati. In August, Washington sent him to Canada to receive the frontier posts from the British, but his mission was unsuccessful as the British commander, General Haldimand, had not been authorized to treat with him. When Washington relinquished command of the army, Dec. 23, 1783, he deliberately made it his last official act to write a letter to the Baron commending his invaluable services to the United States throughout the war (Jared Sparks, *The Writings of George Washington*, VIII, 1833, pp. 503–04; W. C. Ford, *The Writings of George Washington*, X, 1891, p. 338). Steuben was honorably discharged from the army Mar. 24, 1784. He became an American citizen, by act of the Pennsylvania legislature in March 1783 and by act of the New York legislature in July 1786.

After Steuben's retirement from the army he made his residence in New York and became one of the most popular figures in the social life of the city and state. He was the president of the German Society and of the New York branch of the Cincinnati. In 1787 he was elected one of the regents of the University of the State of New York. Always careless in his business affairs and extravagant in his charities and hospitalities, he went heavily in debt in anticipation of the grant of about $60,000 for his military services which he claimed from Congress. In 1786 the State of New York granted him 16,000 acres of wild land near the present town of Remsen, north of Utica. In June 1790 the new federal government granted him a pension of $2500 per year instead of the lump sum which he had expected. Later in the year, through a friendly mortgage of his New York lands, Alexander Hamilton and other influential friends were able to settle the Baron's debts and to relieve him from bankruptcy. During the remaining years of his life he spent his winters in New York City and his summers on his estate in the Mohawk country. There he finally died of apoplexy on Nov. 28, 1794, and there his tomb now is. He was never married. In his will he left his estates in America to his former aides-de-camp, William North and Benjamin Walker (will in Kapp, p. 702).

Steuben's likeness is preserved in contemporary portraits by Charles Willson Peale, Ralph Earle, and Pierre Eugene du Simitiere and in the equestrian figure of him in John Trumbull's "The Surrender of Cornwallis," in the national capitol. He was of middle height. He had a fine soldierly bearing and his manners were graceful and courtly. His picturesque personality made a strong impression upon his contemporaries and the anecdotal history of the Revolution presents him as one of the most conspicuous figures in the esteem and affections of the rank and file of the Continental Army. Through his influence in converting the American army into an effective and highly disciplined military force he was an indispensable figure in the achievement of American independence. Here he performed an essential service that none of his contemporaries in America was qualified to perform.

[The generally accepted history of Steuben's early life in Europe is taken from Friedrich Kapp, *Leben des Amerikanischen Generals Friedrich Wilhelm Steuben* (Berlin, 1858), translated as *The Life of Frederick William von Steuben* (N. Y., 1859), and is largely apocryphal. Kapp did not have access to the documents in the Prussian Archives relating to Steuben's service in the Prussian army or to those in the Archives in Hechingen and Karlsruhe relating to his subsequent life in Hohenzollern-Hechingen, the south of France, and Baden, and was therefore unable to check the official records against certain questionable documents which he found in the "Steuben Papers" in the library of the N. Y. Hist. Soc. The contemporary German evidence is given by C. D. Ebeling in the "Nachrichten von den Lebensumständen des Baron von Steuben," in the *Amerikanisches Magazin* (Hamburg, 1796), Vol. I, pt. 3, pp. 148–63. Steuben's ancestry and family history are given by A. B. C. Kalkhorst in the *Neue Zeit*, New Ulm, Minn., Sept. 8–15, 1923, and by Hermann Stöbe, "General Steubens Herkunft," in *Jahrbuch der Historischen Kommission für die Provinz Sachsen und für Anhalt* (Magdeburg, 1931). An account of his Prussian military service is contained in A. B. C. Kalkhorst, "Steubens Dienstzeit in Preussischen Heere," *Erie Tageblatt*, Sept. 8, 1923. This article gives full references from the Prussian Archives. Kapp's history of Steuben after his arrival in America contains many excerpts from official documents and, in general, is reliable, but much of Steuben's voluminous personal correspondence and other valuable materials were not then accessible. There is much Steuben material in the Washington Papers and the Papers of the Continental Congress in the Lib. of Cong. and in the Old Records Division of the War Dept. His personal papers (16 vols.) are in the library of the N. Y. Hist. Soc. Letters from Steuben, both official and personal, are to be found in almost every public and private collection of manuscripts relating to the Revolutionary period. His correspondence with his aides-de-camp, William North and Benjamin Walker, now widely scattered, gives an intimate picture of his personality and of his financial indiscretions and difficulties after the Revolution. Much material relating to his New York estate is in the collection of the Oneida Hist. Soc., Utica, N. Y. J. B. Doyle, *Frederick William von Steuben and the American Revolution* (1913), is based on Kapp. J. McA. Palmer has chapters on Steuben in *Washington, Lincoln, Wilson* (1930), and is preparing a full biography.]

J. McA. P.

STEVENS, ABEL (Jan. 17, 1815–Sept. 11, 1897), Methodist Episcopal clergyman, editor, and historian, was the third child of Samuel and Mary (Hochenmeller) Stevens. He was born in Philadelphia, where his father, a native of Needham, Mass., had settled as a copperplate printer and engraver. Eight years after Abel's birth his father died, leaving the mother with five young children. The estate was mismanaged by the custodian and the family forced to undergo numerous hardships, but Abel was sent to Wesleyan Academy, Wilbraham, Mass., and later entered Wesleyan University, Middletown, Conn., though his stay at the latter institution was short, owing to his feeble health. The records of the University indicate, however, that he had completed the scientific course when he left college. Five years later (1839) Brown University conferred upon him the degree of M.A. While a very young man he displayed extraordinary ability as a speaker and at nineteen was financial agent of Wesleyan University. In 1834 he was admitted to the New England Conference on trial, was ordained deacon in 1836, and elder in 1838. From 1835 to 1837 he served the Church Street Church and the Bennet Street Church in Boston. He visited Europe in 1837 and his published letters from abroad attracted attention. Upon his return he became the minister of the Methodist church in Providence, R. I. At the age of twenty-five, on the recommendation of President Wilbur Fisk [q.v.] of Wesleyan University, he was made editor of *Zion's Herald*, an influential Methodist journal published in Boston. This position he held for twelve years.

In 1852 he became the editor of a new literary venture of the Methodists called the *National Magazine*, which position he held until June 1856. He again visited Europe in 1855 and on his return was chosen editor of the *Christian Advocate and Journal* in New York. Here he again displayed the highest degree of editorial ability. By this time the Methodist Episcopal Church had divided over the slavery issue, though there still remained in the Northern branch numerous slave-holding members. Stevens contended that nothing should be done to embarrass the border churches. He argued that the slave-holders had a constitutional right to church membership and protested against the attempt to expel them. He maintained, however, that he was an abolitionist. His position alienated the radicals and at the General Conference of 1860 he was not reëlected editor. To support the position of Stevens and other New York leaders on the slavery issue an independent journal was established in 1860 called *The Methodist*, which from the beginning had Stevens' substantial aid, and of which he was associate editor, 1871–74. From 1861 to 1865 he served two churches in the New York East Conference, to

which he had transferred on his removal to New York. For some years he was also constantly employed in writing and speaking in the interest of lay representation in the General Conference, and much of his writing in *The Methodist* was devoted to this subject.

Throughout his life Stevens was a tireless worker and a prolific writer. His first book, entitled *An Essay on Church Polity*, was published in 1847. This was followed in 1848 by the first volume of his *Memorials of the Introduction of Methodism into the Eastern States*, the second volume appearing in 1852. His most important works were the seven volumes dealing with the history of English and American Methodism. The *History of the Religious Movement of the Eighteenth Century, Called Methodism*, in three volumes, appeared between the years 1858 and 1861; the *History of the Methodist Episcopal Church in the United States*, in four volumes, between the years 1864 and 1867. These works, founded on extensive research and written with remarkable literary attractiveness, take high rank among denominational histories. He also published *Life and Times of Nathan Bangs* (2 vols., 1863). His last book was *Madame De Staël, A Study of her Life and Times* (2 vols., 1881). The books mentioned represent only his major publications.

At fifty years of age Stevens retired from active participation in the affairs of the Church, and after he had finished his histories took up his residence in Geneva, Switzerland, where he served as the minister of the Union Church and corresponded with several American newspapers. In 1888 he returned to the United States and made his home in San José, Cal., where he died suddenly of heart failure at the age of eighty-two. He had been married three times: in 1838, to Marguerite, daughter of the Rev. Bartholomew Otheman of Roxbury, Mass.; on Sept. 8, 1869, at Clinton, N. Y., to Amelia Dayton, who died within a year; and in 1871 to Frances C. Greenough, who, with three of the six children of his first marriage, survived him.

[Sources include *Christian Advocate* (N. Y.), Sept. 16, 23, 1897; *The New Schaff-Herzog Encyc. of Religious Knowledge*, vol. XI (1911); *Zion's Herald*, Sept. 15, 1897; *The Call* (San Francisco), Sept. 12, 1897. The date of birth sometimes appears as Jan. 19, but is given as Jan. 17 in the general catalogues of Brown and Wesleyan universities. Information regarding Stevens' family was obtained through the courtesy of Dr. James R. Joy.]   W. W. S.

STEVENS, ALEXANDER HODGDON (Sept. 4, 1789–Mar. 30, 1869), surgeon, was born in New York City, the third son of Ebenezer and Lucretia (Ledyard) Sands Stevens, and a brother of John Austin Stevens, 1795–1874 [*q.v.*]. His father, a descendant of John Stevens who came from Cornwall, England, to Boston about 1638, was a member of the group who took part in the Boston Tea Party. His mother was a native of Hartford, Conn., and a half-sister of William Ledyard [*q.v.*]. As a boy he studied at home until the age of twelve, when he entered the school of John Adams, 1772–1863 [*q.v.*], in Plainfield, Conn.; he graduated from Yale College in 1807. At eighteen he began the study of medicine in the office of Dr. Edward Miller [*q.v.*], professor of clinical medicine at the College of Physicians and Surgeons (later part of Columbia University), New York. He soon left, however, for the University of Pennsylvania, where he received the degree of M.D. in 1811. His thesis, *A Dissertation on the Proximate Cause of Inflammation, with an Attempt to Establish a Rational Plan of Cure* (1811), was highly commended by Benjamin Rush [*q.v.*]. After graduation he spent seven months in the surgical service of the New York Hospital. In 1812, on his way to Europe as a carrier of dispatches, he was captured and imprisoned in England. When he was released, he studied under John Abernethy and Sir Astley Cooper, and in Paris under Alexis Boyer, whose book on surgery he later translated as *A Treatise on Surgical Diseases and the Operations Suited to Them* (2 vols., 1815–16). His days in Paris brought him in close touch with such men as Félix Hyppolyte Larrey, Alfred Velpeau, and Guillaume Dupuytren. On his way home he once more became a prisoner of war, but was soon able to return home to act as army surgeon. From 1815 to 1826 he was professor of surgery at Queen's College (later Rutgers), where he was considered an excellent clinical teacher, following the methods of Hermann Boerhaave; in 1826 he became professor of surgery at the College of Physicians and Surgeons. His lectures were clear, comprehensive, familiar in style, quaint in expression, but emphatic and impressive. He began in 1817 his long career as surgeon to the New York Hospital, a post which he filled for the greater part of his life. A trustee of the College of Physicians and Surgeons, 1820–37, he served as president, 1843–55. In the meantime he had built up a large practice which, with his outside work, proved too much for his health, and in 1831 he was forced to go abroad for a rest. On his return he was plunged into the battle against the cholera epidemic of 1832, in which he played a notable part. Three years later, his health failing again, he took Dr. John Watson as a partner to relieve him of part of his practice and moved to Astoria, Long Island. He devoted

much of his time there to agriculture and in 1849 became president of the state agricultural society. Nevertheless he still maintained his interest and influence in medical matters. In 1842, when the Society for the Relief of Widows and Orphans was organized, he became a member; he was one of the leading spirits in the founding of the New York Academy of Medicine, of which he was president in 1851; and he served also as president of the American Medical Association, 1848, and of the Medical Society of the State of New York, 1849–51.

He was a stern, religious man with no sympathy for the ideas of Darwin, Spencer, or Huxley. Conservative, he cast aside the Brunonian theory under which he had been educated. He was a deliberate and cautious surgeon who preferred to treat surgical diseases rather than to resort to the knife. Accurate in diagnosis and prognosis, his therapeutics were rarely unsound, although he was often criticized for his lack of interest and persistence in following out details of protracted cases. He was unassuming and courteous, but firm in his decisions. His interest in medical education led him to institute in 1865 the Stevens Triennial Prize in the College of Physicians and Surgeons, for the best essay on a medical subject. His own writings were of no great value. His portrait was painted by Henry Inman, the original going to the New York Hospital and a facsimile to the College of Physicians and Surgeons. He was married three times: in 1813 to Mary Jane Bayard (d. 1817), daughter of John Murray Bayard of Millstone, N. J.; in April 1825 to Catherine Morris, daughter of James Morris of Morrisania, N. Y.; in 1841 to Phoebe Coles Lloyd, daughter of John Nelson Lloyd of Lloyd's Neck, Long Island. He had a son by his first wife, a daughter by his second, and two sons by his third.

[E. S. Barney, *The Stevens Geneal.* (1907); F. A. Virkus, *The Abridged Compendium of Am. Geneal.*, vol. II (1926); J. G. Adams, *Discourse Commemorative of the Life and Character of Alexander Hodgdon Stevens* (1871); S. W. Francis, *Biog. Sketches of Distinguished Living Surgeons* (1866); *The Coll. of Physicians and Surgeons, N. Y., A Hist.* (n.d.), vol. I, ed. by John Shrady; *N. Y. Medic. Gazette*, June 1853; *N. J. Medic. Reporter*, June 1854; *Obit. Record Grads. Yale Coll.* (1869); obituary in *Medic. Record* (N. Y.), May 1, and *N. Y. Tribune*, Apr. 1, 1869.] G. L. A.

STEVENS, BENJAMIN FRANKLIN (Feb. 19, 1833–Mar. 5, 1902), bookman and antiquary, was born in Barnet, Vt., brother of Henry Stevens [*q.v.*], and tenth of the eleven children born to Henry and Candace (Salter) Stevens. His father, a descendant of Cyprian Stevens who emigrated to New England before 1671, was not only a farmer, postmaster, innkeeper, and mill-owner, but a book-collector and antiquarian as well, founder and first president of the Vermont Historical Society. After attending Peacham Academy and Newbury Seminary, Benjamin in 1850 was assistant state librarian of Vermont, in 1852 deputy secretary of state, and in 1853–54 a student at the University of Vermont. In 1858–59 he worked in the Astor Library in New York City, where he acted also as an agent for Henry, then well established as a London bookseller. He sailed in 1860 to join Henry as partner, London being thereafter his home and bookselling his calling. In 1864 he left Henry to join another brother, Simon, but left him in 1866 to set up for himself, and so continued until 1899, when he took Henry J. Brown as partner. He came to know the Whittinghams of the Chiswick Press, and on Jan. 28, 1865, married Charlotte (d. July 22, 1903), daughter of Charles Whittingham (1795–1876). He was appointed United States dispatch agent, June 23, 1866, a post he filled until his death, which occurred at Surbiton, Surrey. This appointment brought him into contact with American diplomatic, consular, and naval officers passing through London and with many on the Continent. As bookseller, acting as agent for many American libraries and private buyers, he became one of the familiar personalities of the London trade. Though he took part in many business, social, and public activities, and was at his death recognized as one of the leading spirits in the American colony at London, he was first of all a bookman and antiquarian.

Early in life he had begun to help his father copy and index documents in American archives (he had been sent to Albany, N. Y., at fourteen to copy manuscripts), and this interest he carried to England. There it led him to make an index in 180 manuscript volumes (now in the Library of Congress, Washington, D. C.) to the manuscripts in foreign archives relating to America, 1763–83. (See Stevens' *Introduction to the Catalogue Index of Manuscripts in the Archives of England, France, Holland, and Spain Relating to America, 1763 to 1783,* 1902.) He made extensive transcripts for the Library of Congress, the New Hampshire, Pennsylvania, and New York Historical societies, and the New York Public Library. Between 1889 and 1895 he published twenty-four portfolios, *B. F. Stevens's Facsimiles of Manuscripts in European Archives Relating to America, 1773–1783,* with an index published in 1898. His other publications include *The Campaign in Virginia, 1781: An Exact Reprint of Six Rare Pamphlets on the Clinton-Cornwallis Controversy* (1888); *General Sir William Howe's Orderly Book . . . 1775*

(1890); *Christopher Columbus, His Own Book of Privileges, 1502: Photographic Facsimile of the Manuscript in the Archives of the Foreign Office in Paris* (1893); "Calendar of American Papers in the Earl of Dartmouth's Collection," in *Great Britain Historical Manuscripts Commission: Fourteenth Report: Appendix, Part X* (1895); *Facsimile of the Unpublished British Headquarters Coloured Manuscript Map of New York and Environs, 1782* (1900); and *Report on American Manuscripts in the Royal Institution of Great Britain* (4 vols., 1904–09, edited by H. J. Brown).

[F. P. Wells, *Hist. of Barnet, Vt.* (1923); G. M. Fenn, *Memoir of Benjamin Franklin Stevens* (priv. printed, 1903); S. S. Green, *Proc. Am. Antiquarian Soc.,* n.s., vol. XVI (1905); *Times* (London), Mar. 7 (death notice), Mar. 10 (obituary), and *Athenaeum,* Mar. 15, 1902.]   H. M. L.

STEVENS, CLEMENT HOFFMAN (Aug. 21, 1821–July 25, 1864), Confederate soldier, though born in Norwich, Conn., was of Southern parentage, his father being Lieut. Clement W. Stevens, United States Navy, and his mother, Sarah J. (Fayssoux) Stevens, a daughter of Dr. Peter Fayssoux [q.v.], Revolutionary surgeon-general of South Carolina. Leaving the navy, Lieutenant Stevens soon removed his family to Florida, and thence, in 1836, to Pendleton, S. C. Clement, after enjoying several years of travel and adventure as secretary to his kinsmen, Commodore William B. Shubrick [q.v.] and Commodore William Bee, in 1842 forsook the sea to enter the Planters' & Mechanics Bank, in Charleston, eventually becoming cashier. Enterprising and energetic, he also joined the firm of Hacker and Pickens, pioneer railroad contractors, and by 1861 was a successful business man. Meantime, through marriage with his cousin, Annie Bee, he had several children, of whom one son lived to maturity.

His invention and construction, early in 1861, of a land battery faced with iron and, later, of portable ovens for supplying his troops with fresh bread, justified an intimate associate in declaring, after the war, to one of Stevens' nieces: "Your Uncle Clem was a genius. Had he lived, the world would have heard of him." (Letter from Mrs. Helen Capers Stevens Du-Pré.) This battery, built on Morris Island, was shielded with railroad T-iron. It was perhaps the first armored fortification ever constructed, and was used successfully in the bombardment of Fort Sumter. As a volunteer aide to his brother-in-law, Gen. Barnard E. Bee [q.v.], Stevens was severely wounded at Manassas. Recovering, he commanded a militia regiment at Charleston, but was soon elected colonel of the 24th South Carolina Infantry, of which Ellison Capers [*q.v.*] was lieutenant-colonel. Stevens' skilful handling of flank detachments contributed greatly to the Confederate victory at Secessionville, June 16, 1862, and in 1863 he fought with Gist's brigade through the Vicksburg campaign. Transferred to Bragg's army, he led his regiment with reckless bravery at Chickamauga and was again badly wounded. Gen. S. R. Gist [*q.v.*] eulogized him as "the iron-nerved," while his division commander, Gen. W. H. T. Walker [*q.v.*], declared: "From what I know of his capacity, as an officer, from his gallantry in the field, and from his devotion to the cause, he would grace any position that might be conferred" (*War of the Rebellion: Official Records, Army,* 1 ser., vol. XXX, pt. 2, p. 242).

Although physically shattered, he was promoted brigadier-general Jan. 20, 1864, and commanded a Georgia brigade with distinguished ability through the Atlanta campaign, earning from his soldiers the affectionate nickname, "Rock" Stevens. Toward evening of July 20, 1864, in the headlong attack of his troops at Peach Tree Creek, he was mortally wounded. His horse, mangled by the same shot, hearing the call for battle formation, dragged himself to his accustomed place ahead of the line, and fell dead, mute witness to his master's habitual valor. Stevens died five days later. Of forceful but winning personality, he carried into his military career the earnestness and enthusiasm which had earned him success in civil life. These qualities enabled him to inspire in others his own devotion to principles and undeviating performance of duty.

[Ellison Capers, in C. A. Evans, *Confederate Mil. Hist.* (1899), V, 419–20; details regarding battery, *Ibid.*, pp. 16–17; *War of the Rebellion, Official Records (Army),* 1 ser., vols. XIV, XXX, XXXVIII; manuscript reminiscences of C. H. Steinmeyer; letters from Mrs. Helen Capers Stevens DuPré.]

J. M. H.

STEVENS, EDWIN AUGUSTUS (July 28, 1795–Aug. 7, 1868), engineer, financier, inventor, the sixth son of John [*q.v.*] and Rachel Cox Stevens, was born at "Castle Point," Hoboken, N. J. After receiving his education under private tutors, he engaged in the experiments and business enterprises of his father and older brothers until he was twenty-five, developing, meanwhile, a keen business sense and unusual organizing ability. He came to be regarded, in fact, as the family "fly-wheel," and in 1820, by family agreement, his father made him trustee of practically the whole of his estate. Although

the responsibility was great for so young a man, he succeeded admirably and, in addition, occasionally assisted both his father and his brother Robert L. Stevens [*q.v.*] in their engineering work. With the latter, he invented and patented, Aug. 23, 1821, a plow which was extensively used for years.

In 1825 he took charge of the Union Line, which operated freight and passenger stages between New York and Philadelphia. Two years later it became the property of himself and his brothers Robert and John Cox, Edwin continuing as business manager. When, in 1830, the Camden & Amboy Railroad & Transportation Company was chartered, he was made treasurer and manager. With his great business and organizing ability this first railroad project in New Jersey succeeded in an incredibly short time, and during the whole of his management, extending over thirty-five years, the stock of the company constantly appreciated in value and no dividend was passed. Occasionally, Stevens would try his hand at invention. For example, he designed a wagon body with removable sides, extensively used for many years in New York for hauling refuse and known as the "two horse dump wagon"; he also helped his brother Robert in designing the "closed fire-room" system of forced draft, patented Apr. 1, 1842, and first applied on Robert's steamboat *North America.*

As early as 1814 Stevens had become interested with his father and brother in armored naval vessels and had carried on experiments in which projectiles from a six-pounder cannon were fired against iron plating. Little public interest could be aroused at that time, however. The prospect of serious trouble with Great Britain in 1841 prompted Edwin to conduct a new series of experiments at Bordentown. He then applied to the United States Navy Department for permission to build an armored vessel, the design to be largely that of his brother Robert, and on Apr. 14, 1842, Congress authorized the Secretary of the Navy to enter into a contract with him. His struggle to build the *Stevens Battery,* as it was called, was of some years' duration, chiefly because of changes in Navy administration and improvements in ordnance. Not until 1854 were the ship's floor timbers actually laid, and two years later Robert, the leader in the undertaking, died. Edwin then assumed the whole burden, although he realized that the Navy Department had little belief that iron-clad vessels would ever come into general use. He met with small success in arousing any real interest until 1861, when, influenced by newspaper and periodical suggestions, the navy board condescended to make an examination of the Stevens plans. Its report to Congress was adverse, however. Undaunted, Stevens built, at his own expense, a small ironclad, twin-screw steamer, the *Naugatuck*, to demonstrate the practicality of his plans. Even though this vessel saw considerable service in and about Hampton Roads and proved the feasibility of the novel features it contained, the government's attitude remained unchanged. Stevens bequeathed it to the state of New Jersey together with one million dollars for its completion. The money was spent in 1869 and 1870 without finishing the vessel, and in 1881 it was dismantled and sold for junk.

Stevens' father had always hoped that some of his estate might be devoted to founding an "academy" for teaching fundamental subjects and science. Edwin kept this purpose always before him and particularly after he inherited much of his brother Robert's fortune. Accordingly, in his will he bequeathed both land and money sufficient to establish the Stevens Institute of Technology at Hoboken. He was twice married: first, in 1836, to Mary B. Picton of West Point, N. Y., who died in 1841; second, Aug. 22, 1854, to Martha Bayard Dod of Princeton, N. J., daughter of Prof. Albert Dod [*q.v.*]. By his first wife he had two children, and by the second, seven. His daughter Mary Picton Stevens became the wife of Muscoe Russell Hunter Garnett [*q.v.*]. Stevens' death occurred in Paris, France.

[A. D. Turnbull, *John Stevens, An Am. Record* (1928); R. H. Thurston, "The Messrs. Stevens of Hoboken," *Jour. Franklin Inst.*, Oct. 1874; J. E. Watkins, *Biog. Sketches of John Stevens, Robert L. Stevens, Edwin A. Stevens* (1892), and *The Camden and Amboy Railroad* (n.d.); *The Stevens Iron-clad Battery* (1874); *Jour. Franklin Inst.*, Sept. 1874; J. P. Baxter, Jr., *The Introduction of the Ironclad Warship* (1933); *N. Y. Geneal. and Biog. Record*, Jan. 1881, pp. 20, 28; *N. Y. Tribune*, Aug. 10, 1868; *N. Y. Times*, Aug. 11, 1868; Patent Office records.]
                                                    C. W. M—n.

STEVENS, EMILY (Feb. 27, 1882–Jan. 2, 1928), actress, was born in New York City, daughter of Robert E. Stevens and Emma (Maddern) Stevens. Her grandfather on her mother's side was Richard Maddern, an English musician who came to America in mid-nineteenth century with a large family, and organized a traveling concert company composed of his own children. She was educated at the Institute of the Holy Angels, Fort Lee, N. J., and at Saint Mary's Hall, Burlington, N. J., and when she was twenty played Miriam with her cousin, Minnie Maddern Fiske, in the latter's production of *Mary of Magdala*. She remained with Mrs.

Fiske for some years, playing Lady Blanche in a revival of *Becky Sharp,* and Berta in *Hedda Gabler* early in the century. Leaving her cousin's company, she acted with George Arliss in *The Devil* in 1908, and in *Septimus,* 1909. But it was not till the season of 1915–16 that she became a "featured" player. In 1914–15 she made an unsuccessful attempt in a fairy play called *The Garden of Paradise,* by Edward Brewster Sheldon, with scenery by Joseph Urban which rather over-topped the frail play. When she appeared in New York, Oct. 9, 1915, in *The Unchastened Woman,* by Louis Kaufman Anspacher, however, she was widely acclaimed. Her rôle was that of a witty, worldly, rather neurasthenic woman, restless and cruel, yet charming; and she made a minute and effective character study of the part. The play was very successful. An equally good new rôle was not forthcoming for some time, but she won attention with a revival of *Hedda Gabler.* On Mar. 3, 1924, at the Garrick Theatre, New York, she appeared as Mathilde Fay in the Theatre Guild's production of *Fata Morgana,* by Ernest Vajda, which enjoyed a long and prosperous run. Here again she was a woman of the world—restless, somewhat predatory, bored, subtle—and again she made of the rôle a fascinating character study. The next season she appeared in *The Makroupoulos Secret,* by Karel Čapek, based on the legend of the woman who has eternal youth. That was her last prominent rôle. She died in New York. She never married.

Strikingly fair in appearance, with a mass of gold hair, with brilliant eyes and coloring, she could assume the rôle of beautiful and alluring women without difficulty. She was herself witty, with an ironical twist of humor, which further fitted her for the parts in which she excelled. Her methods of acting had, quite naturally, been shaped by observation of her cousin when she was in Mrs. Fiske's company, and at times her voice and inflection echoed the older player's startlingly. But there the likeness ceased. Her playing was neither so brilliant nor so brittle as her cousin's; her stage personality was much less intellectual and much more alluringly feminine, though she was unable to suggest emotional depth. Her strength lay in depicting with minute understanding modern women of the world, witty, charming, and sexually restless.

[Emily Stevens' full name is said to have been Emily Mary Stevens. See *Who's Who in the Theatre* (1925); W. P. Eaton, *Plays and Players* (1916); George Arliss, *Up the Years from Bloomsbury* (1927); Burns Mantle and G. P. Sherwood, *The Best Plays of 1909–19* (1933); *N. Y. Times*, Jan. 3 (obituary), Jan. 4 (editorial), Jan. 15 (letter from Evelyn O'Connor in "The Dramatic Mail Bag," sec. 8), and obituary in *Herald*

Tribune (N. Y.), Jan. 3, 1928; theatre collections in the N. Y. Pub. Lib. and the Widener Lib., Harvard Univ.]   W. P. E.

STEVENS, GEORGE BARKER (July 13, 1854–June 22, 1906), theologian and educator, was born in Spencer, Tioga County, N. Y., the son of Thomas Jackson and Weltha (Barker) Stevens. Three years in Ithaca Academy prepared him to enter Cornell University in 1873. After two years he transferred, for pecuniary reasons, to the University of Rochester, graduating from that institution in 1877. For a year he studied in the Rochester Theological Seminary, then entered the middle class of Yale Divinity School, where he completed his course in 1880. He was ordained and installed over the First Congregational Church of Buffalo, N. Y., on Sept. 28, 1880, and on Nov. 23 of the same year was married to Kate A. Mattison of Oswego, N. Y. After two years of service in Buffalo he became pastor of the First Presbyterian Church of Watertown, N. Y., but continued his theological studies and received the degree of doctor of philosophy from Syracuse University in 1883. Two years later he was granted leave of absence by his parish to study in Germany. Here he displayed such marked proficiency that the faculty of the University of Jena encouraged him to submit a thesis ("The Rational Grounds of Theism") and stand an examination for the degree of doctor of divinity, which was granted him in 1886.

His brilliant record as a student led to his election, in the autumn of the same year, to the Buckingham Professorship of New Testament Criticism and Interpretation in Yale Divinity School, succeeding Timothy Dwight [q.v.], who was entering on his duties as president of Yale College. After some six years of intensive study in the field of exegesis, his vigorous mind produced in rapid succession works which attracted wide attention—*A Short Exposition of the Epistle to the Galatians* (1890, 1894), *The Pauline Theology* (1892, 1918), *The Johannine Theology* (1894), *Doctrine and Life* (1895). In 1895 he was appointed to the more congenial chair of systematic theology, succeeding Samuel Harris [q.v.], but his new duties and extensive preaching engagements did not abate his literary productivity. In 1896 appeared *The Life, Letters, and Journals of the Rev. and Hon. Peter Parker* (1896), followed by *The Epistles of Paul in Modern English* (1898), *The Theology of the New Testament* (1899), *The Messages of Paul* (1900), *The Messages of the Apostles* (1900), *The Teaching of Jesus* (1901), *The Christian Doctrine of Salvation* (1905). In what appeared

a slight illness he died suddenly on June **22,** 1906, in the fifty-second year of his age.

As a theologian Stevens was chiefly interested in the reinterpretation of religious truth in the light of the best scholarship of his day. His mind, eminently clear, balanced and energetic, neither clouded nor illumined by mysticism, made him a successful expounder of his substantial learning. His abounding vitality, his ability to kindle his own intellectual fires, **his** ready command of his acquisitions, enabled him almost at will to do his daily stint of writing and produce so many volumes of solid merit. A certain radiant healthfulness won him friends and strongly influenced his pupils.

[*Who's Who in America*, 1906–07; Williston Walker, *Professor George Barker Stevens, D.D., LL.D., An Address . . . Dec. 7, 1906* (n.d.); *Report of the President of Yale Univ.* (1907); *Obit. Record Grads. Yale Univ.*, 1907; *New Haven Evening Reg.*, June 23, 1906.]
                                                        C. A. D.

STEVENS, GEORGE WASHINGTON (Jan. 16, 1866–Oct. 29, 1926), educator, art museum director, author, was born at Utica, N. Y., the son of George and Elizabeth (Garripy) Stevens. Educated in the Utica schools and the Utica Academy, where he specialized in the natural sciences, he first became a reporter on the *Utica Press.* In 1889 he went to Ohio. A year later, after a short time on the Springfield *Republican-Times,* he went to Toledo, where he lived for the rest of his life. For five years he was on the staff of the *Toledo Bee.* From 1896 for a number of years he devoted his time to advertising, a field in which he was an early entrant. Later, while he was a member of the editorial staff, he conducted a column of original matter for the *Toledo Times,* 1900–03. At the same time he contributed to such popular magazines of the time as *Outing Magazine, Recreation, Smart Set, Success,* and *Ainslee's Magazine,* and wrote numerous poems, which were collected and published as *The King and the Harper Together with Other Poems* (1900) and *Things* (1903). One of his poems, "Be glad you're poor," was widely reprinted in newspapers in the years 1929–33.

Of unusual talent in both music and art, he had developed a great interest in painting as a pastime. He studied under the eminent landscapist, John Francis Murphy [q.v.], in 1896 in the Catskills and spent many summers painting in Holland, France, and Italy. He was a member of the Western Society of Artists, and exhibited in various museums and exhibitions in the country. In 1903 he became the first director of the Toledo Museum of Art, which had been founded two years before, and thereupon entered into close association with its great patron, Edward Drummond Libbey [q.v.]. Libbey had foreseen tremendous opportunities and possibilities in the field of art education, and it remained for Stevens, in company with his wife, Nina de Garmo Spalding of Port Huron, Mich., whom he had married, June 12, 1902, to develop a plan and policy for the future of the museum and to put it into effect. With a broad concept of art, which he defined as "that science whose laws applied to all things made by man make them most pleasing to the senses," and an ideal of a museum of usefulness and helpfulness, he was able to completely revolutionize museum practice in America and to influence it throughout the rest of the world. Under his guidance the Toledo Museum of Art became the first to admit freely children of all ages, the first to embark upon a policy of art education for all people, the first to maintain a free school of design, and among the first to accord to music equal rank with the other arts. As a result of his liberal policies, public interest in the Toledo Museum of Art attained such remarkable proportions that for many years it had the largest per capita attendance among art museums in American cities. His ideas for the building of museum collections are best exemplified in the George W. Stevens Gallery of Books and Manuscripts in the Toledo Museum. For it he acquired material which shows the development of writing and printing from the first crude beginnings of the alphabet through the early illuminated manuscripts and block books to the earliest printed books, the typographical masterpieces of later printers, and the art of the illustrator and the binder.

A man of broad civic interests, he served on the boards of the chamber of commerce and other civic institutions, and was a member of the city plan commission under which Toledo's zoning ordinances were perfected. He was an honorary secretary of the Egypt Exploration Fund; vice-president of the Faculty of Arts, London, England, 1908–10; president of the American Federation of Photographic Societies, 1909–10; and from 1919 until his death president of the Association of Art Museum Directors. He was also interested in astronomy and maintained a perfectly equipped observatory at his home.

[*Who's Who in America*, 1926–27; *Am. City*, Apr. 1916; *Outlook*, June 21, 1916; *Woman's Home Companion* (picture sec.), Sept. 1916; Nina S. Stevens, in *Am. Mag. of Art*, Dec. 1920; A. D. Albert, in *Collier's*, Jan. 8, 1921; Gardner Teall, in *Arts and Decoration*, Nov. 1921; Nell L. Jaffe, in *Fine Arts Rev.* (Cleveland, Ohio), May 1922; *Art News* (N. Y.), Nov. 6, 1926, and Feb. 12, 1927; *Art Digest*, Mar. 1, 1927; *Museum News* (Toledo Museum of Art), Feb., Mar., Dec. 1908, Jan. 1909, Oct. 1914, Dec. 1915, Feb., Dec. 1921, Jan. 1923, Apr. 1927; *Museum News* (Am. Asso.

of Museums), Nov. 15, 1926; *Bull. Minneapolis Inst. of Art*, Nov. 13, 1926; *Toledo News-Bee*, Dec. 7, 1922, Oct. 29–Nov. 2, 1926; *Toledo Blade* and *Toledo Times*, Oct. 29–Nov. 2, 1926; *Utica Press*, Oct. 30, 1926.]
B.–M. G.

STEVENS, HENRY (Aug. 24, 1819–Feb. 28, 1886), bookman, was born in Barnet, Vt., third child and second son of Henry and Candace (Salter) Stevens, and brother of Benjamin Franklin Stevens [q.v.]. On the title page of his *Recollections of Mr. James Lenox of New York and the Formation of His Library* (1886) he describes himself as "Bibliographer and Lover of Books," member of various historical and scientific societies, "Patriarch of Skull & Bones of Yale . . . as well as Citizen of Noviomagus et cetera." According to his own account he was at Middlebury College, 1839; in Washington as a clerk in the Treasury Department and the Senate, 1840; at Yale College, 1841–43, where he took the degree of B.A.; and at Harvard, 1844, where he studied law, "all the while dabbling in books and manuscripts by way of keeping the pot boiling." During his vacations he hunted through New England and the middle states for "historical nuggets" for Peter Force [q.v.] and his *American Archives*. "In July 1845," he relates, "I found myself in London, a self-appointed missionary, on an antiquarian and historical book-hunting expedition, at my own expense and on my own responsibility, with a few Yankee notions in head and an ample fortune of nearly forty sovereigns in pocket" (*Recollections of Mr. James Lenox*, pp. 15–16).

London was his home until his death and the world of books his life. He reached England just as Sir Anthony Panizzi began his development of the book stock of the British Museum, and had much to do with museum purchases of books relating to the New World. In America he helped build up the collections of John Carter Brown of Providence, R. I., James Lenox [qq.v.] of New York City, the Smithsonian Institution, and the Library of Congress, to mention but a few of his outstanding American customers. He came to hold high rank as an authority in the bibliographical history of the English Bible, and in the geographical and historical literature of the western world. As early as Nov. 14, 1846, in a letter to Lenox, he urged transcription of documents in European archives for the use of American scholars, and he was a pioneer in the use of photography to supplement bibliography (see his *Photo-bibliography*, 1878). His publications, which were for the most part annotated catalogues of items in his collections or reprints of rare documents, include *Historical Nuggets* (1862), a catalogue of the rarities in his library;

Bibliotheca Historica (1870); and *The Bibles in the Caxton Exhibition, MDCCCLXXVII* (1878). Though he agreed to make a catalogue of the Lenox library, he never fulfilled the promise. His conflicts with such men as Henry Harrisse and Justin Winsor were frequent. Characterized by Richard Garnett (*post*, pp. 65–69) as genial, expansive, sanguine, and as both crafty and candid, he was called "an enigma" by so restrained and careful a man as George Henry Moore (manuscript letter to John Russell Bartlett, Mar. 20, 1873, in the John Carter Brown Library). On Feb. 25, 1854, he married in London Mary (Newton) Kuczynski, a descendant of Sir Isaac Newton, widow of Vincent Kuczynski of H. M. State Paper Office. The bookselling business he founded was continued in London by his son and his grandson. He was buried in Hampstead Cemetery, London, where a monument, a block of Barre granite, cut at Montpelier, Vt., was erected to his memory by the Society of Noviomagus.

[Stevens' *Recollections of Mr. James Lenox* (1886) serves well for both author and subject. See also F. P. Wells, *Hist. of Barnet, Vt.* (1923); Richard Garnett, in *Lib. Chronicle* (London), May 1886; F. B. Dexter, *Obit. Record Grads. Yale Coll.* (1886); G. P. Winship, *The John Carter Brown Lib.; A Hist.* (1914); obituary in *New England Hist. and Geneal. Reg.*, July 1886; death notice and obituary in *Times* (London), Mar. 2, 5, 1886. There are manuscript letters from Stevens to Lenox and Brown in the N. Y. Pub. Lib. and the John Carter Brown Lib., Providence, R. I. Stevens' most important pubs. are listed in Joseph Sabin, *Bibliotheca Americana: A Dict. of Books Relating to America*, vol. XXIII (1923–33), continued under the editorship of R. W. G. Vail, and in M. D. Gilman, *The Bibliog. of Vt.* (1897).]   H. M. L.

STEVENS, HIRAM FAIRCHILD (Sept. 11, 1852–Mar. 9, 1904), lawyer, was born in St. Albans, Vt., the son of Dr. Hiram Fairchild and Louise I. (Johnson) Stevens. His father was an army surgeon during the Civil War and several times a member of the Vermont legislature; his career, however, was short, and his death in 1866 threw upon Hiram, the eldest son, the burden not only of his own support but, in part, that of the family. Nevertheless, the boy was able to work his way through Kimball Union Academy, Meriden, N. H., and to spend several terms at the University of Vermont. He then studied law with Judge John K. Porter of New York City, attended lectures at Columbia Law School with the class of 1874, and returned to practise his profession in St. Albans. He was one of the group which organized the American Bar Association at Saratoga in 1878.

In 1879 Stevens went to St. Paul, Minn., where he became a member of the law firm of Warner, Stevens & Lawrence. This connection he maintained until 1886, when he became counsel for the St. Paul Real Estate Title Insurance Company. Not long afterward, he was the head of a new firm, Stevens, O'Brien, Cole & Albrecht. In St. Paul he helped to organize the Ramsey County Bar Association and also the Minnesota State Bar Association, of which he was president in 1901. From 1892 to 1900 he lectured on real property at the law school of the University of Minnesota. This phase of law work especially engaged his interest and led him to take a leading part in launching the St. Paul College of Law in 1900; as its president he functioned until his death.

For a dozen years Stevens was especially active in politics. As a Republican he was elected in 1888 to the lower house of the state legislature from a strongly Democratic district, and in 1890 and 1894 he was elected to the state Senate. His leadership was recognized by his selection as chairman of the committee on the judiciary, a position from which he dominated the legislative body during the last half of his term of service. In 1901 he was made the chairman of a commission to revise the Minnesota statutes, but his death occurred before the task was completed.

A fluent speaker, he was much in demand for occasional addresses. He wrote frequently on law subjects. He edited and wrote portions of the *History of the Bench and Bar of Minnesota* (2 vols., 1904), an expansion of his chapter on "The Bench and Bar of St. Paul" in C. C. Andrews' *History of St. Paul* (1890). The range of his interests was wide; he was prominent in the St. Paul Chamber of Commerce, a member and president of the park commission, and a member of several fraternal orders—in short, he qualified as a "good mixer." On Jan. 26, 1876, he married Laura A. Clary of Massena, N. Y.; they had no children.

[E. V. Smalley, *A Hist. of the Republican Party . . . [and] a political Hist. of Minn.* (1896); C. C. Andrews, *Hist. of St. Paul, Minn.* (1890); *Proc. Minn. State Bar Asso.*, 1904; *Report . . . Am. Bar Asso.*, 1904; *Who's Who in America*, 1903–05; *Daily Pioneer-Press* (St. Paul), Mar. 10, 1904; *St. Paul Dispatch*, Mar. 10, 1904; *St. Paul Globe*, Mar. 10, 1904.]   L. B. S.

STEVENS, ISAAC INGALLS (Mar. 25, 1818–Sept. 1, 1862), soldier, governor of Washington Territory, was born at Andover, Mass., the son of Isaac and Hannah (Cummings) Stevens, and a descendant of John Stevens who was living in Andover as early as 1641. During his boyhood he helped on the farm and outstripped all his fellows in study. After a year and four months at Phillips Academy, where he excelled in mathematics, he entered the United States

Military Academy, graduating first in his class in 1839. Commissioned a second lieutenant of engineers, he was engaged for several years in the construction or repair of fortifications on the New England coast. While stationed at Newport, R. I., he met Margaret Hazard, whom he married Sept. 8, 1841. A son and four daughters were born to them.

During the Mexican War he was engineer adjutant on Scott's staff in Mexico, and at Contreras, Churubusco, and Chapultepec displayed a combination of judgment and cool daring for which he was brevetted captain and major. After the war, while recovering from wounds received in the capture of the city of Mexico, he was assigned once more to engineering duties in coastal fortifications until 1849, when Alexander D. Bache [q.v.] appointed him executive assistant in the United States Coast Survey at Washington. Here he demonstrated high talent for administration. He remained till 1853, meanwhile taking a deep interest in army reorganization and other questions calling for arguments before the departments, congressional committees, and the president. His clarity and breadth of thought, sound practical judgment, dignity, and power of statement made him an ideal worker for such ends. In 1851, partly as a critique of Major Roswell S. Ripley's *The War with Mexico* (1849), he published *Campaigns of the Rio Grande and of Mexico*. He desired to see historical justice done to Generals Scott and Taylor, who at the time were the victims of partisan prejudice. Yet, as a Democrat, in 1852 he campaigned for Pierce.

Early in Pierce's administration, upon the enactment of the law providing for Pacific Railway surveys, Stevens sought and secured appointment as director of exploration for the northern route. Just previously he had secured the governorship of Washington Territory, resigning from the army (Mar. 16, 1853) in order to accept it. Under the circumstances, precedent would have denied him assistants from the army; nevertheless, several young officers, including George B. McClellan [q.v.], volunteered for his survey and were permitted to serve under him. This survey, and the later effort to get the route he recommended accepted by government and people, constituted thereafter Stevens' most engrossing interest. Secretary Davis withheld the funds required for completing the work but Stevens used his meager resources as governor to bring it gradually to perfection, and in 1858 he dictated his final report, which is considered his masterpiece (*House Executive Document 56,* vol. XII, bks. I, II).

Meanwhile, the governorship of the Territory had proved a nightmare. Faced with the problem of opening 100,000 square miles of land to white settlement, Stevens began by making a series of Indian treaties. He was probably lacking in the requisite patience, and as usual, the negotiations caused restiveness among the tribes which eventuated in widespread and desolating Indian wars. Gen. John E. Wool [q.v.], commander of the army on the Pacific, refused to cooperate with the people of Washington and Oregon and even thwarted their military undertakings. The correspondence between Stevens and the General was long and bitterly controversial. A stormy episode resulting from the Indian troubles was the Governor's proclamation of martial law, the subsequent arrest of a federal judge, Edward Lander [q.v.], and the arrest of the Governor for contempt of court. In his great work, however, the endeavor to pacify the Indians, he succeeded partially.

Although subjected to a flood of criticism, from both within and without the Territory, Stevens was elected territorial delegate to Congress for the term beginning Mar. 4, 1857. Here he urged the ratification of his Indian treaties, winning against the bitter opposition of Wool's friends. He was returned to his delegate's seat for the following term. In 1860 he assumed the chairmanship of the Breckinridge and Lane national committee, Lane being a close personal friend. This action alienated the Douglas Democrats so that he failed of renomination as delegate to Congress, and when on the outbreak of the Civil War he proffered his services to the Federal government, the response was slow and grudging He finally accepted the colonelcy of the 79th Regiment of New York Volunteers ("The Highlanders"), was promoted to brigadier-general in September, and major-general as of July 4, 1862. He was gallantly leading a charge at Chantilly when a bullet in the temple instantaneously terminated his career.

In appearance Stevens was slight and undersized, but with a massive head, and great dignity both of bearing and speech. He was deeply serious and somewhat deficient in humor. Politically, he once called himself a "Democratic Abolitionist." He sincerely believed that Breckinridge's success in the election of 1860 would prevent a rupture of the Union. His loyalty was never questioned. In addition to the *Campaigns* and the report mentioned above, he published *A Circular Letter to Emigrants Desirous of Locating in Washington Territory* (1858) and *Address on the Northwest* (1858), delivered before the American Geographical and Statistical Society.

[Hazard Stevens, *The Life of Isaac Ingalls Stevens* (2 vols., 1900) is the best biography, though somewhat eulogistic; see also S. H. Paradise, "Isaac I. Stevens," *Phillips Bull.*, Oct. 1932; O. J. Victor, *Men of the Time* (3 vols., 1862–63); G. W. Cullum, *Biog. Reg. Officers and Grads., U. S. Mil. Acad.* (1891), vol. I; *Biog. Dir. Am. Cong.* (1928); *Harper's Weekly*, Sept. 20, 1862; *Daily Nat. Intelligencer*, Sept. 8, 1862; Ezra Meeker, *Pioneer Reminiscences of Puget Sound* (1905), contains a criticism of Stevens as a negotiator of Indian treaties.]   J. S.

STEVENS, JOHN (1749–Mar. 6, 1838), engineer, inventor, pioneer in the field of mechanical transportation, was born in New York City, the son of John Stevens, whose father, John, had come to America in 1699 at the age of sixteen as an indentured law clerk. The boy's mother was Elizabeth, daughter of James Alexander [q.v.] and sister of William [q.v.]. His father, a ship owner and master and a merchant, gradually acquired extensive land areas in New Jersey and in his later years entered politics. He served as treasurer of New Jersey, as president of various legislative meetings during the Revolution, and as president of the New Jersey convention which ratified the federal Constitution. His residence was at Perth Amboy, N. J., and here young John grew up, receiving his primary education from tutors and at Kenersley's College near Woodbridge. In 1760 his parents removed to New York, and after completing his school work in 1762 John joined the family there. Four years later he entered King's College (now Columbia), graduated in 1768, and during the next three years studied law. In 1771 he received his appointment as an attorney but did not practise his profession; instead he joined his father in his political activities in New Jersey, undertaking various commissions for the latter and an occasional service as special aide to Gov. William Franklin.

With the outbreak of the Revolutionary War he offered his services to General Washington and was immediately commissioned a captain and appointed loan commissioner for Hunterdon County, N. J., to collect money for the Continental Army. A few months later he was appointed treasurer of New Jersey, in which capacity he served for the duration of the war, advancing gradually in grade to colonel. In 1782–83 he held the office of surveyor-general for the eastern division of New Jersey, with headquarters in Trenton, and then returned to his home in New York, having married, Oct. 17, 1782, Rachel, daughter of Col. John Cox of Bloomsbury, N. J. In 1784 he bought at auction a large tract of land in New Jersey on the west side of

the Hudson River, which included most of what is now Hoboken, and for the succeeding three years he was busily engaged in developing the estate and building a home.

About 1788 his attention was drawn to the work of John Fitch and James Rumsey [qq.v.] in the development of the steamboat, and from that time until his death Stevens veritably gave himself, his family, and his fortune to the advancement of mechanical transport both on water and on land. Up to the moment he saw Fitch's steamboat on the Delaware River, he had given but little thought to engineering, though he had always been a great reader of science and natural philosophy. Now, thoroughly aroused, he concentrated his reading on steam. Soon he was working out on paper designs of boilers and engines unique for the time, and on Feb. 9, 1789, he petitioned the New York legislature for the exclusive privilege of building steamboats. Rumsey, however, had already submitted a similar petition to that body and received the grant. Stevens then turned to the federal government, which had not as yet formulated any patent laws. Through his friends in Congress and elsewhere he brought about the framing of the act establishing the first patent laws, which act was passed in April 1790, and in August 1791 he was among the first dozen citizens to receive United States patents. His inventions were an improved vertical steam boiler and an improved Savery-type steam engine, both intended for steamboats, and an application of steam to the working of bellows.

Upon the death of his father in 1792 it became Stevens' lot to administer the former's vast estate, and although an extremely busy man, he found time in the next five years to continue his steam-engine experiments. His greatest difficulty lay in his inability to get satisfactory work done. He had no skill of his own in this field and there were no mechanical shops nor competent workmen to be had. About 1797, however, he met Nicholas J. Roosevelt [q.v.], who was interested in a foundry at what is now Belleville, N. J., and had several workmen just "out" from England, and the prospects of actually building a steam engine and boat became brighter. Stevens now aroused the latent interest of his brother-in-law, Chancellor Robert R. Livingston [q.v.] of Clermont, N. Y., in the project, with the result that Stevens, Roosevelt, and Livingston became actively associated. Livingston succeeded in having the lapsed grant of Fitch for the exclusive privilege of steamboat operation on the waters of New York State transferred to him in 1798, and with this incentive the partners set to work with added vigor. An experimental boat, the

Polacca, was built and tried on the Passaic River, but proved unsuccessful. Experiments continued, however, during the succeeding two years, interpersed with alternate disagreements and compromises between the associates with respect to engine and boat design and methods of propulsion. In 1800 a definite twenty-year agreement of partnership between them was consummated. Shortly after, Livingston became American minister to France and his active part in the experiments ceased. About this time Stevens became consulting engineer for the Manhattan Company, organized to furnish an adequate water supply to New York City. He succeeded in convincing the directors that steam pumping engines should be used and installed such equipment of his own design, but it was not efficient and a Boulton & Watt type of engine was later substituted. He and Roosevelt went forward with their experiments, Stevens being determined to build a small steamboat to ferry him across the Hudson. He had also become greatly interested in promoting adequate transportation facilities generally, and devoted much time to educating the public on the subject. In 1802 he became president of the Bergen Turnpike Company, organized to construct suitable roads across Bergen County in New Jersey.

By Apr. 11, 1803, he had advanced sufficiently with his experiments to secure on that date a United States patent for a multitubular boiler, and the following year his small steamboat, operated by twin screw propellers and called *Little Juliana,* was taken back and forth across the Hudson by two of his sons. The steam engine and boiler of this boat are preserved in the National Museum at Washington. The successful performance of *Little Juliana* now spurred Stevens to greater effort. His goal was to inaugurate an adequate steam ferry system across the Hudson between Hoboken and New York and to operate a regular line of steamboats on the Hudson between New York and Albany and on other inland rivers. He gave what time he could during the next two or three years toward further experiment, and in 1806 began his plans for a 100-foot steamboat, the *Phoenix,* designed for passenger and freight service. Before this vessel was completed, however, Fulton's steamboat *Clermont* made in 1807 its successful voyage to Albany and return. The achievement was discouraging to Stevens in that the trip was made under a monopoly granted to Livingston and Fulton. He was later given the opportunity to join them but refused because of his agreement with Roosevelt and his firm belief that the monopoly was unconstitutional. Furthermore, he would have had to submerge his own accomplishments and inventions at the cost of partnership. Bitter debates ensued, and numerous proposals and counter proposals were made during the next seventeen years by Stevens and the monopolists, for each side had something the other could use to advantage; but the deadlock was never broken. Since he was restricted from using the Hudson River, he sent the *Phoenix,* completed in 1808, to Philadelphia in June 1809. It made the sea trip successfully and established for itself the record of being the first sea-going steamboat in the world. Thereafter, plying between Philadelphia and Trenton, it served as a unit in the cross-state transportation system controlled and managed by Stevens' sons. Still determined to develop a steam ferryboat system across the Hudson, he purchased a ferry license in New York in 1811 and built the *Juliana.* He then sublet the lease and a regular ferry system was soon inaugurated. Threats from Fulton and Livingston, however, compelled Stevens, who could not afford the expense of lawsuits, to remove the *Juliana* after a few months, whereupon it was sent to Connecticut and used in regular service on Long Island Sound.

Leaving steam navigation in the hands of his sons, about 1810 he began giving close attention to the adaptation of the steam engine as the motive power for railways. In letters to his political friends he urged the adoption of such means of conveyance rather than canals. His correspondence on this subject was voluminous but the results were far from satisfactory. Accordingly, in 1812, he published *Documents Tending to Prove the Superior Advantages of Rail-ways and Steam-carriages over Canal Navigation,* in which every conceivable phase of railway transportation was considered, engineering features explained, and construction costs worked out. All his friends conceded that his proposals were ingenious but, privately, they considered them the dreams of a visionary projector. He approached the state legislatures of New York, New Jersey, Virginia, North Carolina, and Pennsylvania with memorials asking them to open the way for railroads, and finally, on Feb. 6, 1815, the New Jersey Assembly created a company "to erect a rail road from the river Delaware near Trenton to the river Raritan at or near New Brunswick" (*Votes and Proceedings,* 1815, p. 193). This was the first American railroad act. After eight years' additional hammering at the Pennsylvania legislature, on Mar. 31, 1823, "on a memorial and representation of John Stevens," an iron railroad was authorized by that body. The bill allowed Stevens to form a company to erect a railroad from Philadelphia to Columbia, Pa., and upon the organization of the company Stevens was empowered to build it. The necessary funds could not be raised, however, and in 1826 the act was repealed, but another authorizing a railroad was passed. In 1828 the legislature appropriated $2,000,000 to construct the Philadelphia & Columbia Railroad, opened in 1834 and later acquired by the Pennsylvania Railroad. Since Stevens called his company of 1823 The Pennsylvania Railroad, he may be regarded as the founder of the Pennsylvania system (W. B. Wilson, *History of the Pennsylvania Railroad*, 1899, I, 10). Two years later the New Jersey legislature chartered the Camden & Amboy Railroad & Transportation Company and Stevens' sons Robert Livingston and Edwin Augustus [*qq.v.*] were elected president and treasurer, respectively. In neither of these legislative acts was the kind of motive power indicated, and Stevens, in an effort to convince the popular mind of the feasibility of the steam locomotive, designed and built in 1825, when seventy-six years old, an experimental locomotive and operated it on a circular track on his estate in Hoboken. This was the first American-built steam locomotive, although it was never used for actual service on a railroad, and on its completion Stevens brought his active engineering work to a close.

For the remaining years of his life he devoted his time to study, and wrote many essays on metaphysical subjects, political economy, and education, which, however, were not published. In addition to his pioneer work in the field of transportation, he and his sons put forward the idea of an armored navy as early as 1815. He developed plans for the protection of New York City; drew up the design of a bridge across the Hudson from New York to Hoboken; and proposed a vehicular tunnel under the Hudson as well as an elevated railroad system for New York. At the time of his death in Hoboken he was survived by his widow and seven children. His eldest son, John Cox Stevens, was a founder of the New York Yacht Club and head of the group which sent the *America* to England to compete for the international cup. Robert Livingston and Edwin Augustus, already mentioned, were engineers and inventors. One of his daughters, Mary, married Joshua R. Sands [*q.v.*] and after her death her sister Harriet married him.

[Collection of Stevens' papers and letters in the Lib. of the Stevens Institute of Technology, Hoboken, N. J.; A. D. Turnbull, *John Stevens, An American Record* (1928); J. K. Finch, *Early Columbia Engineers* (1929); R. H. Thurston, "The Messrs. Stevens of Hoboken," *Jour Franklin Institute*, Oct. 1874; J. E. Watkins,

Biog. Sketches of John Stevens, Robert L. Stevens, Edwin A. Stevens (1892), and *The Camden and Amboy Railroad* (n.d.); Charles King, *Progress of the City of N. Y.* (1852); *N. Y. Geneal. and Biog. Record*, Apr. 1881; *Morning Herald* (N. Y.), Mar. 8, 1838; Patent Office Records.]   C. W. M—n.

STEVENS, JOHN AUSTIN (Jan. 22, 1795–Oct. 19, 1874), banker, was born in New York City, the son of Lucretia (Ledyard) Sands Stevens and Ebenezer Stevens, of Boston, an officer of the Continental Army and later a prosperous importer in New York. Four of the sons graduated from Yale College, Alexander Hodgdon Stevens [*q.v.*] in 1807 and John Austin, the youngest, in 1813. Five years later John became a partner in his father's importing house, and he achieved business success. In 1824 he was married to Abby, the daughter of Benjamin Weld of Brunswick, Me., and Boston. One of their sons was John Austin Stevens, 1827–1910 [*q.v.*].

When, in the efforts to regain financial stability after the depression of 1837, a new state banking law was enacted, a group of New York capitalists and lawyers organized the Bank of Commerce in 1839. They installed Stevens as its first president and issued capital stock to the amount of $5,000,000, divided among 624 stockholders, and in 1856 increased the capital to $10,000,000. In the second year of its existence the bank took $1,000,000 of federal bonds at par and was made agent for government moneys collected in New York, and, having weathered the crisis of 1857, it was recognized at the outbreak of the Civil War as perhaps the strongest financial institution in the country. In the summer of 1861 he joined the other New York bankers in taking the federal government's loan of $50,000,000 and thereafter until the end of hostilities gave the Lincoln administration unwavering support. He was president of the Associated Banks of New York, Philadelphia, and Boston. He even led a group of bankers in advocating the Legal Tender Bill in 1861 (J. W. Schuckers, *Life and Public Services of Salmon P. Chase*, 1874, p. 243). His advice was more than once sought by the treasury department. In 1866 he resigned the bank presidency and passed the remaining eight years of his life in retirement. For half a century he had been an important figure in the life of the metropolis, as president of the Merchants' Exchange, as secretary of the Chamber of Commerce, and as excellent public speaker, devoted to literature. He died in New York City.

[F. B. Dexter, *Biog. Sketches of the Grads. of Yale College*, vol. VI (1912); *Appletons' Annual Cyc.*, 1874; *The N. Y. Geneal. and Biog. Record*, vol. VII (1876), p. 13; *Evening Post* (N. Y.), Oct. 19, 1874; information from the National Bank of Commerce.]   W. B. S.

STEVENS, JOHN AUSTIN (Jan. 21, 1827–
June 16, 1910), financier, author, was born in
New York City, the son of Abby (Weld) and
John Austin Stevens [*q.v.*]. He was educated in
the local schools and was graduated from Har-
vard College in 1846. He became cashier and
had charge of the entire correspondence of Spofford, Tileson & Co., a mercantile firm of New
York. In 1852 he went into partnership with
John Storey, of Cuba, and carried on an extensive Cuban importing business until the Civil
War. On June 5, 1855, he married Margaret
Antoinette Morris, the daughter of William
Lewis Morris and great-grand-daughter of Richard Morris [*q.v.*]. They had one son and two
daughters. During the panic of 1857 he was secretary of the exchange committee that was appointed by the banks to buy produce bills. He
was a stanch Republican and in 1860 helped to
organize a meeting at the Merchants' Exchange
to rally men of all parties to the support of Abraham Lincoln. In 1863 he was a leader in organizing the Loyal National League, which pledged
unconditional loyalty to the federal government
and support of its war efforts. He was active in
recruiting the 51st New York Volunteers and in
obtaining money to maintain it in the field. He
was manager and director of the Loyal Publication Society, secretary of the National War
Committee, and in 1862 secretary of the treasury
note committee that obtained the loan to the government of $150,000,000 in gold coin. He was
offered and declined the positions of commissioner of internal revenue and register of the treasury, as well as the post of consul-general at Paris.
He was secretary of the Chamber of Commerce,
1862–68, and began the collection of its gallery of
portraits. He resigned the secretaryship to visit
Europe, where he remained five years, mostly in
Paris. He was in London for a year, was Jay
Cooke's agent there for a Pacific railroad by the
northern route, and in 1872 went to Alsace and
Lorraine to try to arrange for extensive emigration to the United States.

He contributed to the *New York Times* in
September and October 1873 a series of articles
signed "Knickerbocker," afterward published as
Resumption of Specie Payment (1873). As a
delegate to the convention of the boards of trade
at Baltimore in 1874, he delivered an address on
the national finances. In 1876 he was elected
librarian of the New York Historical Society
and served for two years. He was one of the
founders of the Sons of the Revolution in 1876,
and in 1883 was chairman of the committee in
charge of the centenary celebration of the evacuation of New York. His portrait, owned by

the Sons of the Revolution, hangs (1935) in
Fraunces Tavern in New York City. In 1877 he
founded the *Magazine of American History,*
which he edited until 1881, and in which a number of his articles were printed. He wrote the
chapter on "The English in New York, 1664–
1689" for Justin Winsor's *Narrative and Critical History* (vol. III, 1885) and contributed several chapters to *The Memorial History of the
City of New York,* edited by James Grant Wilson (4 vols., 1892–93). Among his separate publications were *The Valley of the Rio Grande*
(1864), *Colonial Records of the New York
Chamber of Commerce . . . with . . . Historical
and Biographical Sketches* (1867); *Progress of
New York in a Century, 1776–1876* (1876); *The
Burgoyne Campaign* (1877); and *Albert Gallatin,* in the American Statesmen Series (1884).
He died at his home in Newport, R. I., where he
had lived since 1886.

[Notebooks, esp. on horse racing in America and
New York taverns, and typewritten historical addresses
in possession of N. Y. Hist. Soc.; manuscript biog. by
his daughter, Mary Morris Stevens, Newport, R. I.;
*Sons of the Revolution . . . of N. Y. Reports and Proc.
. . . 1909–10* (1911); *Who's Who in America,* 1910–11;
N. Y. Times, June 17, 1910.]   A. J. W.

STEVENS, JOHN HARRINGTON (June
13, 1820–May 28, 1900), pioneer and "first citizen" of Minneapolis, the son of Gardner Stevens
and Deborah (Harrington), was born at Bromp-
ton Falls, Quebec, a transplanted New England
community just over the Vermont border. At
the age of fifteen, after the family had gone back
to Vermont, Stevens joined an elder brother at
White Oak Springs, Wis. Pursuing lead-mining
ventures, the boy found himself at Galena where
he joined the militia called out to repress the
Winnebago Indians. It was then that he met
Governor Dodge who later was influential in securing for him a captain's commission in the
quartermaster's department of the army on the
outbreak of the Mexican War. He served
through the war, and resigned in 1848 to return
to Texas where he had preëmpted some land. He
was turned from this course by John Catlin, former secretary of Wisconsin Territory, who told
him of a new territory to be organized about the
Falls of St. Anthony. This region, said Catlin,
"was well known . . . to be the best climate in
the world for such invalids" as Stevens who had
come back from Mexico with "serious lung difficulties" (Stevens, *post,* pp. 2, 3). The following spring Stevens was in St. Paul where Franklin Steele, sutler at Fort Snelling, employed him
to help in his store.

Steele advised Stevens to squat on land on the
west bank of the Mississippi at the Falls where

the latter obtained 160 acres. He built a cottage, destined to be the first dwelling in the city of Minneapolis, in the autumn of 1849, and brought to it his bride, Frances Helen Miller, of Westmoreland, N. Y., to whom he had been married on May 1, 1850. They had six children. In the course of the next few years Stevens plotted his land and sold lots to newcomers, but as the settlement grew he turned over to Steele the remainder of his holdings, realizing but a very modest sum for what was to become the business district of Minneapolis. Ever a pioneer he obtained, in 1855, forty-five acres in Glencoe, McLeod County, which had just been opened to settlement. Here, among other enterprises, he edited the *Glencoe Register* from 1857 to 1863. As brigadier-general of militia he took an important part in the suppression of the Indian uprising during the last months of 1862, being for a time in charge of a long strip of the frontier. In September 1863 he was one of the commissioners to take the Minnesota soldier vote in the southern department, and, shortly afterward, he settled once more in Minneapolis where he lived for the remainder of his life. He engaged in various occupations, but his interest lay chiefly in the promotion of agriculture; he edited such papers as the *Farmers' Tribune, Farmer and Gardner,* and *Farm, Stock, and Home*; for many years was president of the Minnesota State Agricultural Society; and was keenly interested in the agricultural department of the University of Minnesota. In 1890 he published his *Personal Recollections of Minnesota and Its People,* a mine of information about early Minneapolis in which he "seems to have remembered everybody but himself" (Folwell, *post,* IV, 85n). He collaborated with Isaac Atwater in producing a *History of Minnesota* (1895), editing and writing portions of the part dealing with Hennepin County.

Stevens took no very active part in the politics of his day, although he was a member of the first state legislature, 1857–58, and that of 1876; he was state senator in 1859–60, but declined to contest a similar position in 1877 with Charles A. Pillsbury [*q.v.*]. While a good enough business man in a routine way, he apparently lacked that quality which many of his contemporaries utilized to build up a fortune through the exploitation of a new country, or else he was genuinely indifferent to the acquisition of great wealth, for he died a comparatively poor man.

[Stevens Papers, Steele Papers, Minnesota Historical Society; J. H. Stevens, *Personal Recollections of Minnesota and Its People* (1890); W. W. Folwell, *A Hist. of Minn.* (1921–30), vols. I, II, IV; C. E. Flandreau, *Encyc. of Biog. of Minn. and Hist. of Minn.*

(1900), vol. I; D. S. Hall and R. I. Holcombe, *Hist. of the Minn. State Agricultural Soc.* (1910); H. W. B., in *Farm Students' Rev.,* July 1899; D. B. Johnston, "Journalism in the Territorial Period," *Colls. Minn. Hist. Soc.,* vol. X (1905), pt. 1; *Minneapolis Times,* Dec. 28, 1898; *Minneapolis Tribune,* May 29, 1900.]
                                                    L. B. S.

STEVENS, JOHN LEAVITT (Aug. 1, 1820– Feb. 8, 1895), journalist and diplomat, was born at Mount Vernon, Me., where his father, John Stevens, a native of New Hampshire, settled in 1805. His mother was Charlotte (Lyford) Stevens. The son was educated at Maine Wesleyan Seminary and Waterville Classical Institute, entered the Universalist ministry in 1845, and for ten years held pastorates in Maine and New Hampshire. On May 10, 1845, he married Mary Lowell Smith, daughter of Daniel Smith of Hallowell, Me. Becoming interested in the antislavery cause and feeling that he could aid it best through newspaper writing, he joined with James Gillespie Blaine [*q.v.*] in acquiring the *Kennebec Journal,* of Augusta, Me., which he edited continuously from 1855 until 1869, and thereafter occasionally during intervals in his diplomatic service. He was minister to Paraguay and Uruguay from 1870 to 1874, to Norway and Sweden from 1877 to 1883, and to Hawaii from 1889 to 1893, at first as minister resident, later as envoy extraordinary and minister plenipotentiary.

The annexation of Hawaii by the United States, first seriously proposed in 1853 and again in 1854, when Kamehameha III negotiated for its admission as a state, became a live issue once more during the reign of Kalakaua. The extravagance and dishonesty of the government gradually led many men, genuinely attached to the monarchy, to the conviction that it must eventually be abolished; opinion was divided as to whether the establishment of a republic or annexation to the United States should follow. The death of Kalakaua in 1891 and the accession of his sister, Liliuokalani, gave a momentary hope of good government, which the new queen soon disappointed. The end came in January 1893, when the queen announced her intention of abrogating the constitution and proclaiming a new one which would increase her power. A committee of safety, composed of leading citizens, proclaimed a provisional government, of which Sanford Ballard Dole [*q.v.*] became head, and occupied the public buildings in Honolulu. On Feb. 1 Stevens recognized it, and upon his request the commander of the cruiser *Boston,* which was lying in the harbor at Honolulu, landed forces for the protection of life and property in case of riot. The queen, yielding, asserted that she had been dispossessed by force of American arms and appealed for redress to the president of the United States, to whom the provisional government also sent commissioners to negotiate for annexation. So much is history. As to Stevens' part in the proceedings there is dispute. Certainly he was always an open advocate of annexation, and it is claimed that he "overstepped the limits proper to a diplomatic representative in a friendly and peaceable country" (*The American Secretaries of State and Their Diplomacy*, vol. VIII, p. 244, S. F. Bemis, editor). But James Henderson Blount [*q.v.*], sent to Hawaii by President Cleveland as special commissioner, further alleged that Stevens had entered into a conspiracy with the revolutionists, that the use of American forces to overthrow the royal government had been promised in advance, and that otherwise the revolution would not have taken place. In reliance upon Blount's report, Cleveland endeavored by every means short of actual force to restore the queen to the throne, though without success. In passing upon the validity of the charges, not only Blount's temperament but the peculiarly one-sided character of his investigation must be considered. Most of those whose testimony he took were royalists, and of the small number of sympathizers with the revolution whom he examined few had taken prominent part in it. He interviewed only two of the thirteen members of the committee of safety, one of the four members of the executive committee, three of the fourteen members of the advisory committee; some of them offered him their testimony and were turned away. Nor did he seek information from Stevens himself, there present. An investigation conducted in 1894 by a Senate committee was more thorough. Stevens, who was questioned under oath at great length, denied all complicity. The sworn statements of nearly all persons concerned with the revolution—including all those who were alleged to be ringleaders—were obtained, and an ironclad oath taken by members of the committee of safety declared that "neither prior to nor after our appointment as such committee, did we or either of us, individually or collectively, have any agreement or understanding, directly or indirectly, with . . . Mr. Stevens . . . [to] assist in the overthrow of the monarchy or the establishment of the Provisional Government" (*Senate Report 227, post,* p. 590). No "plot" is necessary to explain the revolution. The endurance of men who wanted decent government had been strained too long. At last it snapped. After his return to the United States Stevens lived in Augusta, where he died, survived by one of his four children, a daughter.

Aside from his journalistic writings he was the author of a *History of Gustavus Adolphus* (1884) and *Picturesque Hawaii* (copyright 1894), republished as *Riches and Marvels of Hawaii* (copyright 1900).

[An authoritative account of Stevens' career is given in the *Daily Kennebec Jour.* (Augusta, Me.), Feb. 9, 1895, reprinted in part in *Representative Citizens of the State of Me.* (1903). See also W. D. Alexander, *Hist. of Later Years of the Hawaiian Monarchy* (copr. 1896), the best general account of the Hawaiian revolution; *Hawaii's Story by Hawaii's Queen* (1898), the standard royalist version, sponsored by Liliuokalani; Lucien Young, *The "Boston" at Hawaii* (1898), republished as *The Real Hawaii* (1899), the personal experiences of a naval officer; J. W. Pratt, "The Hawaiian Revolution: a Re-Interpretation," *Pacific Hist. Rev.*, Sept. 1932, an elaboration of the plot theory, which, however, the author discards in a later (unpublished) article; *Foreign Relations of the U. S., 1894; App. II, Affairs in Hawaii* (1895); *House Exec. Doc. 47, 53 Cong., 2 Sess.,* the Blount report; and *Sen. Report 227, 53 Cong., 2 Sess.,* the Senate Committee's investigation, which appeared as *Hawaiian Islands: Report of the Committee on Foreign Relations, U. S. Senate* (2 vols., 1894), with appendices containing all the diplomatic correspondence of the revolutionary period. The Univ. of Mich. has transcripts of unpublished material in both the Washington and Honolulu archives.]
T. M. S.

STEVENS, ROBERT LIVINGSTON (Oct. 18, 1787–Apr. 20, 1856), engineer, naval architect, inventor, the second son of John [*q.v.*] and Rachel (Cox) Stevens, was born on his father's estate, "Castle Point," Hoboken, N. J. He was educated under private tutors and at the same time assisted his father in his experimental engineering work, his first undertaking being the operation in 1804 of the steamboat *Little Juliana* on its journeys back and forth across the Hudson. In 1808 he helped in the design and construction of the *Phoenix,* introducing her concave water lines, and was master, under Capt. Moses Rogers [*q.v.*], on her pioneer sea voyage from New York to Philadelphia in 1809. For several years thereafter, with headquarters in Trenton, he managed the operation of the *Phoenix,* placed in service on the Delaware River and plying between Philadelphia and Trenton. While thus engaged, he helped his father build the ferryboat *Juliana,* which on Oct. 11, 1811, went into regular service between New York and Hoboken, thus establishing the world's first steam-ferry system.

By this time he had become wholly engrossed in naval architecture and for the succeeding twenty-five years was widely recognized as a leader of that profession. He designed and had built upwards of twenty steamboats and ferries, incorporating in them his successive inventions. Among these were the method of installing knees of wood and iron inside the ship's frame; a "cam-board" cut-off for steam engines; and balanced poppet valves. He replaced the old cast-iron walking beam with the wrought-iron skeleton type; shortened the length of the beam and added a wooden gallows frame; and introduced a forced-draft firing system under boilers, the split paddle wheel, "hog-framing" for boats, and the present type of ferry slip. He also increased the strength of steam boilers until pressures of fifty pounds per square inch could be safely carried, and was the first to perfect a marine tubular boiler. In addition to these activities he played an important part with his father and brothers in the cross-state transportation business, and upon the establishment, in 1830, of the Camden & Amboy Railroad & Transportation Company out of the Union Line (practically controlled by the Stevenses) Robert was elected president and chief engineer. That same year he went to England to study English locomotives then in service or under construction, with a view to purchasing one and ordering iron rails. On the way he designed the T-rail (the standard section on all American railroads), which, after much difficulty, he succeeded in having rolled in England. He designed at the same time the "hook-headed spike" (substantially the railroad spike of today), and the "iron tongue" (now the fish plate), as well as the bolts and nut to complete a rail joint. He purchased the locomotive *John Bull*, which on its trial trip at Bordentown, N. J., Nov. 12, 1831, with Stevens at the throttle, inaugurated the first steam railway service in New Jersey. He also designed the earliest locomotive pilot. During the succeeding fifteen years he divided his time between railroading and steam navigation. In the company's railroad shops in Hoboken he devised a double-slide cut-off for locomotives, designed and built several types of locomotives, improved boilers, and successfully burned anthracite coal under boilers.

Toward the close of the War of 1812, Stevens had perfected for naval use a bomb that could be fired from a cannon. He invented, too, an elongated percussion shell and sold large quantities to the federal government as well as the secret of its construction. This work led Stevens, his father, and brothers to give their attention to the introduction of armor on ships of war and brought into being plans for an unusual armored steamer for harbor defense, the design based upon extensive experiments which they had conducted. After submitting their plans to Congress they waited thirty years for authorization to construct a war steamer "shot and shell proof." Work was then started by Robert in a newly built drydock at Hoboken. Coincident with this undertaking began a great improvement in ordnance in all the principal navies of the world,

and as Stevens had contracted to build "shot and shell proof," he was compelled year after year to alter his plans, and before the vessel was finished he died. Besides constructing steamboats he designed and built a number of sailing vessels, the most famous of which was the yacht *Maria* (1850), the fastest sailing vessel of her day. It was this yacht that defeated the *America,* a few months before the latter won the memorable race in England. Stevens lived practically the whole of his life in Hoboken and New York, entering into the social activities of the metropolis and being prominent in musical circles. He never married, however, and died at Hoboken at the age of sixty-nine.

[A. D. Turnbull, *John Stevens, An American Record* (1928); R. H. Thurston, "The Messrs. Stevens of Hoboken," *Jour. Franklin Inst.,* Oct. 1874; J. E. Watkins, *Biog. Sketches of John Stevens, Robert L. Stevens, Edwin A. Stevens* (1892), and *The Camden and Amboy Railroad* (n.d.); Charles King, *Progress of the City of N. Y.* (1852); J. P. Baxter, 3rd, *The Introduction of the Ironclad Warship* (1933); *N. Y. Tribune,* Apr. 22, 1856; Patent Office records.]
C. W. M—n.

STEVENS, THADDEUS (Apr. 4, 1792–Aug. 11, 1868), lawyer, congressman, political leader, was born in Danville, Vt., of a family which had migrated from Massachusetts a few years earlier. His father, Joshua Stevens, an unthrifty shoemaker, died or disappeared at an undetermined date, leaving the mother, Sally (Morrill) Stevens, and four small sons in dire poverty. She was fortunately a woman of fine ideals and great industry, and made many sacrifices to educate Thaddeus, who as the youngest child, and lame and sickly from birth, required special care. The family soon removed to Peacham, Vt., to gain the advantages of the academy which had been established there in 1795. This village, just above the junction of the Connecticut and Passumpsic rivers in north central Vermont, was still part of a semi-frontier community, and the boy grew up in a ruggedly democratic society. He was early trained to hard work and an independent outlook, and though a chance visit to Boston at the age of twelve gave him an ambition some day "to become rich" (McCall, *post,* p. 7), he imbibed a strong feeling for the poor and an intense dislike of aristocracy and of caste lines.

Completing his course at Peacham Academy, Stevens entered Dartmouth College as a sophomore in 1811, and graduated in 1814. However, he spent one term and part of another at the University of Vermont. There are early evidences of his headstrong nature: at Peacham Academy he joined other students in presenting a tragedy in the evening, both the dramatic en tertainment and the hour being infractions of the rule, and at the University of Vermont he is said to have killed a cow. At the latter institution he also wrote a drama on "The Fall of Helvetic Liberty" and helped enact it. The instruction at Dartmouth and Vermont was limited and thorough, emphasizing Greek, Latin, higher mathematics, and ethics. From his classical training Stevens undoubtedly drew much of the clarity, exactness, and force which later characterized his public speaking, and which led Blaine to say that he rarely uttered a sentence that would not meet the severest tests of grammar and rhetoric (J. G. Blaine, *Twenty Years of Congress,* I, 1884, p. 325). He had determined to practise law, and began reading it in Vermont. On taking his degree he obtained a post as instructor in an academy at York, Pa., and continued his law studies under David Casset, leader of the local bar. Apparently to evade a time requirement in Pennsylvania, he took his bar examinations at Bel Air, Md., passing with ease when he proved that in addition to a little law he knew how to order Madeira for his examiners and to lose money at cards to them. He then removed to Gettysburg, Pa., in 1816 to practise.

For several years a struggling lawyer of narrow income, Stevens used his leisure to do much profitable reading in history and belles-lettres. But an important case in which he defended a man accused of murder on the then unusual plea of insanity gave him a large fee, said to have been $1500 (Hensel, *post,* p. 5), and a reputation. Thereafter from 1821 to 1830 he appeared in almost every important case at the county bar and won almost all of his numerous appeals to the state supreme court (Woodburn, *post,* p. 12). Since his county adjoined Maryland, Stevens saw much of the slavery system and of runaway negroes, and his instinctive New England dislike of slavery grew into a fierce hatred. It is said that he once spent $300 which he had saved to make additions to his law library in purchasing the freedom of a negro hotel-servant who was about to be sold away from his family (Hensel, pp. 7, 8). He defended numerous fugitive slaves without fee, and displayed great skill in gaining their freedom.

After practising law for ten years in Gettysburg, Stevens also entered the iron business by becoming in 1826 a partner in James D. Paxton & Company, which at once built Maria Furnace in Hamilton-ban Township, Adams County. The company, which became Stevens & Paxton in 1828, first tried to manufacture stoves and other light castings, but the metal was "cold-short" and the product frequently too brittle to

have a value. Stevens and Paxton therefore bought property near Chambersburg, where they built Caledonia Forge (probably named after Stevens' native county in Vermont), and mixed pig iron from Maria Furnace with other ores. In 1837 they also built Caledonia Furnace, and finding ample supplies of superior ore near it, the next year gave up their first furnace entirely. They confined themselves chiefly to the sale of blooms. The Caledonia establishment was never very profitable even in the earlier years. When it met the competition of more effective and economical iron works, Stevens kept it up primarily because he did not wish to deprive the surrounding community of its principal means of livelihood. From his manufacturing enterprise sprang Stevens' interest in protective tariff.

It was natural for a man who felt with his burning intensity on public questions to push into politics. In 1830 he was described as "a firm and undeviating Federalist" and "a violent opponent of General Jackson" (quoted, Woodburn, p. 13). But already the Anti-Masonic movement had attracted him, and he emerged into political prominence in 1831 at the Anti-Masonic Convention in Baltimore which nominated William Wirt for president, and at which he delivered a notable arraignment of secret orders. Two years later he was elected to the Pennsylvania House on the Anti-Masonic ticket, taking his seat in the last weeks of 1833. As a member of the legislature Stevens quickly became known as one of the most fiery, most aggressive, and most uncompromising leaders in Pennsylvania affairs. He served until 1841. For some years he introduced or supported much legislation striking at Masonic influences, and in 1835 was chairman of a committee which made abortive attempts to investigate the evils of Free-Masonry. But his range of interests was wide. He was a warm advocate of the act of 1834 extending the free school system of Philadelphia over the whole state. The next year, when in a reaction against the taxes that were required an effort was made to repeal this law, he sprang into statewide fame by a brilliant defense of free education,—a defense "which produced an effect second to no speech ever uttered in an American legislative assembly" (McCall, p. 38). His denunciation of class-hostility toward free public schools, his excoriation of the repeal as "an act for branding and marking the poor" (Woodburn, p. 45), and his panegyric of a democratic system of instruction, completely won the hostile House. What was more, it caused the Senate to reverse its position. Stevens also labored for larger appropriations for colleges, including Pennsylvania College (now Gettysburg College) at Gettysburg. He argued in behalf of the right of petition, appealed for a constitutional limit on the state debt, and defended the protective tariff and the United States Bank. In 1838 a disputed election in Philadelphia County brought on at Harrisburg the "Buckshot War," with the Whig and Anti-Masonic members of the House endeavoring to organize in opposition to the Democrats. Stevens was the chief leader in this attempt, showing the fierce fighting spirit and uncompromising disposition which marked him through life. At one time he escaped from a mob in the state capitol by leaping from a window. His faction was defeated, and the Democrats declared his seat vacated, but he was at once reëlected. In 1836–37 he offered a resolution in favor of abolishing slavery and the slave-trade in the District of Columbia. In the state constitutional convention of 1837 he displayed great bitterness in debate, opposing everything that smacked of privilege or class distinctions, and refusing to sign the constitution finally adopted because it limited suffrage to white citizens (McCall, p. 48). At his retirement from the legislature the Harrisburg *Pennsylvania Telegraph* pronounced him "a giant among pigmy opponents" (E. B. Callender, *Thaddeus Stevens, Commoner*, 1882, p. 51), and every one recognized him as one of the strongest men in the state.

His decision to quit politics was only temporary, for as the contest over slavery grew heated he was irresistibly drawn toward the arena. Pique over his failure to gain a place in the cabinet of Harrison, whom he had supported in 1836 and 1840, may have played a part in his retirement. His business had not prospered, and he had debts variously estimated at from $90,000 to $217,000 to pay off (Woodburn, p. 66). Removing in 1842 to Lancaster, he at once gained a place at its bar worth from $12,000 to $15,000 a year. As he repaired his fortunes he turned toward public life and in 1848 was elected on the Whig ticket to the Thirty-first Congress. Here he immediately took a leading place among the little band of free-soilers, surpassing such men as Joshua R. Giddings and G. W. Julian [*qq.v.*] in fieriness of temper as in general parliamentary versatility. He was willing to make no compromise whatever with slavery in the territories, and predicted that if ringed about by "a cordon of freemen," all slave states would within twenty-five years pass laws "for the gradual and final extinction of slavery" (Feb. 20, 1850, *Congressional Globe*, 31 Cong., 1 Sess., Appendix, p. 142). He denounced slavery as "a curse, a

shame, and a crime"; he compared it to the horrors of Dante's *Inferno* (June 10, 1850, *Ibid.*, Appendix, p. 767). He taunted men of the lower South as slave-drivers, and Virginians for devoting their lives "to selecting and grooming the most lusty sires and the most fruitful wenches to supply the slave barracoons" (Feb. 20, 1850, *Ibid.*, Appendix, p. 142). His invective was bestowed as harshly upon Northerners who condoned slavery as upon Southerners who practised it. He assailed the compromise measures of 1850, and did his utmost to defeat the Fugitive Slave Act. Southern members expressed horror at his gross language, which they declared too indecent for print, and at his reckless and incendiary sentiments. Reëlected in 1850, he renewed his assaults upon slavery and his warnings to the South against secession. He also spoke for increased tariffs. In March 1853, disgusted with the moderation of most Whigs, he quit Congress but not politics. For within a year Douglas had prepared his Kansas-Nebraska scheme, and the moment was ripe for a leader of Stevens' unsurpassed powers of agitation and denunciation.

In the formation of the Republican party in Pennsylvania, Stevens played a vigorous part. He helped organize Lancaster County in 1855, and in 1856 attended the National Convention at Philadelphia as a supporter of Justice McLean. His impassioned appeals at this gathering led Elihu B. Washburne to say that he had "never heard a man speak with more feeling or in more persuasive accents" (E. B. Washburne, ed., *The Edwards Papers*, 1884, p. 246, note). In 1858 he was reëlected to Congress and, with fire unabated at the age of sixty-eight, entered the last debates before the Civil War. His harshness of speech was as great as ever. An early colloquy with Crawford of Georgia almost provoked a riot on the floor (Woodburn, pp. 135–36). He also renewed his pleas for a protective tariff. In 1860 he again was a delegate to the Republican National Convention, and though he was constrained to support Cameron and preferred McLean, finally voted for Lincoln. Returning to Congress, he opposed any concessions to the Southerners as "the coward breath of servility and meanness"; he warned the South to secede at its peril, saying that if it tried to break up the Union "our next United States will contain no foot of ground on which a slave can tread, no breath of air which a slave can breathe" (Jan. 29, 1861, *Congressional Globe*, 36 Cong., 2 Sess., p. 624). He called upon Buchanan to exert the Federal authority sternly against those who were flouting the national government. In one memorable debate he denounced the plotters of "treason" so violently that the excitement, according to Henry L. Dawes, "beggared all description," and his friends formed a hollow square to protect him from the menaces of hostile members (McCall, pp. 127–28).

Stevens was again mentioned for a cabinet post, and when Lincoln chose Simon Cameron instead he criticized the cabinet as representing political expediency rather than efficiency. But he soon found himself in a position of greater power than if he had taken Cameron's place. He was made chairman of the ways and means committee, which gave him wide authority over all revenue bills and most other congressional measures dealing with the prosecution of the war; while as Blaine states, in everything he was "the natural leader, who assumed his place by common consent" (Blaine, *ante*, I, 325). Upon nearly all aspects of the war he had stern and positive views, and his ideas of policy diverged sharply from Lincoln's. In the field of finance he fortunately gave the administration loyal support. He was prompt in carrying through the House all necessary legislation authorizing Secretary Chase to float loans. He and his committee acted with expedition and nerve in devising new taxes and making them effective. He pressed the income tax against urban objection, the direct tax on real estate against rural objection. The internal revenue act of 1862 showed especial ingenuity in reaching almost every source of revenue, and for this he as well as Justin S. Morrill, chairman of the sub-committee on taxation, deserves credit. On the legal-tender legislation that became a matter of hard necessity following the suspension of specie payments he held doctrines possibly derived in large part from Eleazar Lord (McCall, p. 259; W. C. Mitchell, *A History of the Greenbacks*, 1903, pp. 47 ff.). He favored a uniform nation-wide paper currency issued directly by the United States without mediation of the banks, legal tender for all purposes, and interchangeable with six per cent. United States bonds (Woodburn, pp. 257–58). The act finally passed with numerous compromises, and the amendment which required the interest on government bonds to be paid in coin and not greenbacks was highly repugnant to Stevens. In his opinion it changed a "beneficent" measure into one "positively mischievous" by establishing one currency for the rich bondholder and another for the plowholder and fighter (Feb. 20, 1862, *Congressional Globe*, 37 Cong., 2 Sess., p. 900).

On the conduct of the war Stevens took a harsh and aggressive position. He was one of the two House members who in 1861 voted against the Crittenden resolution declaring that the war was not fought for conquest or subjugation, or to interfere with the established institutions of the South. From the early months he urged confiscation of all property used for insurrectionary purposes and the arming of slaves (Aug. 2, 1861, *Congressional Globe*, 37 Cong., 1 Sess., pp. 414–15). He bitterly criticized Lincoln for overruling Frémont and Hunter on military emancipation, and termed the President's proposal for compensated emancipation "diluted milk and water gruel" (*Ibid.*, 37 Cong., 2 Sess., p. 1154). In language often acrid and abusive he called upon Lincoln to turn out Seward, shake loose from the Blairs and other border-state politicians, and use every possible method of attack against the South. "Oh, for six months of stern old Jackson!" was one of his exclamations (Woodburn, p. 220). He helped make the committee on the conduct of the war, formed after Ball's Bluff, a thorn in the side of the administration. As the conflict progressed he asked ever-sterner measures. Believing the Constitution no longer applicable to the South, he had no difficulty in justifying demands for wholesale arrests, confiscations, and capital punishments. Early in 1862 he told the House that the war would not end till one party or the other had been reduced to "hopeless feebleness" and its power of further effort had been "utterly annihilated" (Jan. 22, 1862, *Congressional Globe*, 37 Cong., 2 Sess., p. 440). He went so far by 1864 as to speak of the necessity of seeing the "rebels" exterminated, and more than once spoke of desolating the section, erasing state lines, and colonizing it anew. It was charged that his shrill demands for vengeance after 1863 were prompted in part by the destruction of his iron works near Chambersburg in Lee's invasion of that year (Rhodes, *post*, V, 544). Confederate troops spent several days at the Caledonia iron works, where they removed all stores and supplies, then burning most of the settlement. In a letter Stevens describes the destruction in indignant terms. They "took all my horses, mules, and harness, even the crippled horses"; they seized two tons of his bacon, with molasses, other contents of the store, and $2,000 worth of grain; they burnt the furnace, rolling-mill, sawmill, two forges, bellows-houses, and other parts of the works; they "even hauled off my bar-iron, being as they said convenient for shoeing horses, and wagons about $4,000 worth"; and they destroyed fences and about eighty tons of hay (Stevens Papers, Library of Congress, vol. II). Stevens was forced to provide for the indigent families of the vicinity.

But his chief quarrel with Lincoln was upon reconstruction. He earnestly opposed Lincoln's ten per cent. plan, objected to the seating of congressmen from Louisiana under it, and in a notable speech on reconstruction laid down the rule that the South was outside the Constitution and that the law of nations alone would limit the victorious North in determining the conditions of restoration (Jan. 22, 1864, *Congressional Globe*, 38 Cong., 1 Sess., pp. 317–19). The Wade-Davis bill, embodying a rigorous scheme of reconstruction, did not go far enough for him, but when Lincoln gave this bill a pocket veto with an explanatory proclamation Stevens called the action "infamous" (Woodburn, p. 321). Though he supported Lincoln for reëlection in 1864 it was probably with secret hostility (G. W. Julian, *Political Recollections*, 1884, p. 243; Woodley, *post*, p. 405), and his sorrow over the President's assassination was not keen. Temporarily he hoped that Johnson would take the radical road. But within a month he saw that the new President was following Lincoln, and wrote Sumner in angry horror: "I fear before Congress meets he will have so be-devilled matters as to render them incurable" (Beale, *post*, p. 63). With Sumner, he at once prepared to give battle to Johnson for the purpose of reducing the South to a "territorial condition," making it choose between negro suffrage and reduced representation, imposing other harsh conditions, and fixing Republican supremacy—for which he appreciated economic as well as political arguments (Beale, pp. 73, 152, 206, 403–05). Like Sumner, he also set about promoting schism in Johnson's cabinet (Oberholtzer, *post*, I, 164).

As soon as Congress met, the two houses, on motion of Stevens, appointed a joint committee on reconstruction (Dec. 4, 1865, *Congressional Globe*, 39 Cong., 1 Sess., p. 6), of which he as chairman of the House group was the dominant member. A fortnight later (Dec. 18, 1865), he again asserted that rebellion had obliterated the Southern states and that the section was a "conquered province" with which Congress could do as it pleased. He also frankly avowed that one aim of representation was "to divide the representation, and thus continue the Republican ascendency" (*Ibid.*, pp. 73–74). The first open rupture with the President came in February 1866, on the Freedmen's Bureau Bill which Stevens belligerently pushed and Johnson vetoed. Beginning with Johnson's speech on Washington's birthday, the two men exchanged bitter attacks, and Stevens succeeded in passing both the Civil Rights Bill and a revised Freedmen's Bureau Bill over Johnson's veto. On Apr.

30, 1866, the joint committee reported the Fourteenth Amendment, which with a few changes Congress adopted, and a bill declaring that when the amendment became part of the Constitution any state lately in insurrection which ratified it and adopted a constitution and laws in conformity with its terms should be admitted to representation in Congress. But this bill never passed. It did not go as far as Stevens wished and on the last day of the session he tried to amend it to require full negro suffrage. Johnson opposed the congressional plan, the South with his apparent approval refused to accept the Fourteenth Amendment, and the whole issue went before the people in the congressional election of 1866. Economic factors strengthened Stevens' hands, for large elements feared loss of tariff advantages, railway grants, free homesteads, and gold bond-redemptions, with all of which the Republican party was identified (Beale, pp. 225–99). A sweeping victory that fall gave Stevens the whip-hand over Johnson and the South.

The first use which he made of his success was to impose military reconstruction and the Fifteenth Amendment upon the South. He had expected it to reject the Fourteenth Amendment and thus give him an opening, and he was prepared to make the most of a defiance which he had deliberately inspired and encouraged (Woodburn, pp. 436–37). His new measure, introduced Feb. 6, 1867, and passed in March, provided for temporary military rule while the states were remade in the South on the basis of negro suffrage and the exclusion of leading ex-Confederates. He pushed it through a reluctant House by invective, sarcasm, threats, taunts, and cracking of the party whip (Rhodes, VI, 17, 18). Having accomplished this, he turned to the chastisement of the President. He declared during the summer of 1867 that he would willingly help impeach Johnson but that he did not believe the measure would succeed (July 19, 1867, *Congressional Globe*, 40 Cong., 1 Sess., pp. 745–46). In December he did vote for an impeachment resolution which failed by nearly two to one. When Johnson summarily removed Stanton as secretary of war Stevens saw his chance, and the very next day reported an impeachment resolution based on the President's supposed disregard of the Tenure of Office Act (Feb. 22, 1868, *Ibid.*, 40 Cong., 2 Sess., p. 1336). He was made a member of the committee to draft articles of impeachment, and also one of the managers to conduct the case before the Senate. But his health had now hopelessly failed, and he took little part in the trial itself. Deeply disappointed by the President's acquittal, he sank so rapidly that when Congress recessed he could not be taken back to Lancaster, but died in Washington. He had never married, and only his nephew and colored housekeeper were at his bedside. By his own wish he was buried in a small graveyard in Lancaster. His tombstone bears an inscription prepared by himself: "I repose in this quiet and secluded spot, not from any natural preference for solitude, but, finding other cemeteries limited by charter rules as to race, I have chosen this, that I might illustrate in my death the principles which I advocated through a long life—Equality of Man before his Creator" (Woodburn, p. 609; Callender, p. 163).

Stevens was an intense partisan, and his career was marred throughout by a harsh and vindictive temper which in his last years made him frankly vengeful toward the South. Within a brief time after his death it was evident that he had fallen short of the measure of a statesman. His radical and bitter policy, offered as a means of obtaining equality and justice for the negro, aroused fierce resentment, accentuated racial antagonism, cemented the Solid South, and postponed for many decades any true solution of the race problem. He had rare parliamentary talents. Well-read, with a quick and lucid mind, of indomitable courage, a master of language and past master of invective, gifted with a sardonic humor and nimble wit, he was almost invincible on the floor. His private life was far from saintly, for gambling was but one of several habitual vices. But his leonine spirit, his terrible earnestness, his gay resourcefulness, and his fine intellectual equipment always inspired respect. Had tolerance and magnanimity been added to his character, he might have been a brilliant instead of sinister figure in American history.

[The best biography is J. A. Woodburn, *The Life of Thaddeus Stevens* (1913), though S. W. McCall, *Thaddeus Stevens* (1899) in the American Statesmen Series offers an incisive characterization, and there is material of value in T. F. Woodley, *Thaddeus Stevens* (1934). Much material on Stevens is also to be found in W. U. Hensel, *Thaddeus Stevens as a Country Lawyer* (1906), reprint from *Report . . . of the Pa. Bar Asso. . . . 1906* (1906); J. F. Rhodes, *Hist. of the U. S. from the Compromise of 1850*, vols. V, VI (1904–06); James Schouler, *Hist. of the U. S. of America under the Constitution*, vol. VII (1913); E. P. Oberholtzer, *A Hist. of the U. S. Since the Civil War*, vol. I (1917); H. K. Beale, *The Critical Year* (1930); G. F. Milton, *The Age of Hate: Andrew Johnson and the Radicals* (1930); C. G. Bowers, *The Tragic Era* (1929); and the reminiscences of many of Stevens' associates in public life. See also J. M. Swank, *Hist. of the Manufacture of Iron* (1884); E. B. Westling, "Old Iron Works of the Cumberland Valley," *Papers Read Before the Kittochtinny Hist. Soc.*, vol. X, no. 1 (1922); H. R. Mueller, *The Whig Party in Pa.* (1922); B. B. Kendrick, *The Journal of the Joint Committee of Fifteen on Reconstruction* (1934). No collection of his speeches exists, and they must be sought in the *Cong.*

Globe. Edward MacPherson made a collection of Stevens letters and papers which is in the Lib. of Cong.]
A. N.

STEVENS, THOMAS HOLDUP (Feb. 22, 1795–Jan. 21, 1841), naval officer, was born in Charleston, S. C. Left an orphan in early childhood, he was adopted by Col. Daniel Stevens of Charleston, and was also greatly befriended by Lieut. Ralph Izard, of the Charleston family of that name, the warm affection between the youth and these older officers being evident in letters still retained by the family. In place of his original surname Holdup, in 1815 by legislative enactment he took that of Stevens. He was warranted midshipman in the U.S.S. *Hornet* at Charleston in February 1809, and at the outbreak of the War of 1812 was in the *John Adams* at New York. Volunteering for lake service, he went to the Niagara frontier, and in a night assault on the enemy works opposite Black Rock, Nov. 27–28, 1812, was one of the leaders of a detachment which captured two enemy guns and dislodged an enemy force by firing their barracks. A canister shot through his right hand in this action inflicted permanent injury. Remaining after the retreat of his main party, he later with seven others recrossed the Niagara at great hazard in a leaky canoe. In recognition of his gallantry, Commodore Isaac Chauncey [q.v.] made him acting lieutenant (confirmed July 24, 1813). In April 1813 he joined Oliver Hazard Perry [q.v.] at Erie. In the battle of Lake Erie he commanded the sloop *Trippe* (one long 32-pounder), last in the line, which passed the *Tigress* and *Porcupine* to engage the *Queen Charlotte*, and after the action assisted the *Scorpion* in the pursuit and capture of two escaping enemy vessels. That he was not specifically mentioned in Perry's dispatches, Stevens attributed to differences with Jesse Duncan Elliott [q.v.], second in command, under whom he had served previously in the *Niagara*. He received the silver medal awarded by Congress to officers in the action, and a sword from his native city. In the summer of 1814 he was first lieutenant in the *Niagara* on Lake Huron, and in the autumn he was selected by Perry to join him in the *Java*, fitting for the Mediterranean. Her departure being delayed till after peace, however, he did not sail in her, but secured a furlough and was married in November or December 1815 to Elizabeth Read Sage (Andrews, *post*, p. 160), daughter of Ebenezer Sage, a prominent merchant of Middletown, Conn. His home in later years was in Middletown. In 1818–20 he had duty in the *Alert* and the *Constellation* at Norfolk, and from January 1823 to June 1824 he commanded successively the schooners *Jackal* and *Shark* of the West India Squadron under David Porter [*q.v.*] in energetic campaigns against the West Indies pirates. Made master commandant, Mar. 3, 1825, his next and last command afloat was the *Ontario,* Mediterranean Squadron, 1829–31. He had charge of the Boston naval rendezvous, 1832–36; was made captain, Jan. 27, 1836; and at the time of his sudden death had held command of the Washington navy yard for nearly a year. A miniature by Peale, owned by his descendants, pictures him as of strong and pleasing features, marked by a scar on the right cheek. Surgeon Usher Parsons [*q.v.*], a friend and fellow-officer of the lake campaign, speaks of him as "the very soul of chivalry, generous, high-minded," lively in conversation, being a "loud and free talker," and with "literary talent ... of a high order" (Parsons, *post*, p. 13). He had three daughters and three sons, but of the sons only one, Thomas Holdup, 1819–1896 [*q.v.*], lived to mature years. Buried first in the Congressional Cemetery, his body was later removed to Arlington.

[In addition to general naval sources, of which J. F. Cooper, *The Hist. of the Navy of the U. S. of America* (1839), is the fullest, see Usher Parsons, *Brief Sketches of Officers Who Were in the Battle of Lake Erie* (1862); H. F. Andrews, *Geneal. of Capt. Giles Hamlin of Middletown, Conn.* (1900); letters, etc., in the possession of Stevens' great-grand-daughter, Mrs. Frederick C. Hicks, Washington, D. C., and in the Navy Lib., where the Personnel Files contain detailed references; obituary in *Daily Nat. Intelligencer* (Washington, D. C.), Jan. 22, 1841.]   A. W.

STEVENS, THOMAS HOLDUP (May 27, 1819–May 15, 1896), naval officer, son of Commodore Thomas Holdup Stevens, 1795–1841 [*q.v.*], and Elizabeth Read (Sage) Stevens, was born in Middletown, Conn. As a youth he spent a year or more in the counting-house of his mother's cousin, Guerdon Hubbard, in Chicago, but then, following his early predilection, entered the navy as midshipman, Dec. 14, 1836. After a cruise in the Brazil Squadron he studied for several months at the Philadelphia naval school, ranking third in his class upon promotion to passed midshipman, July 1, 1842. Brief service as aide to President Tyler was followed by survey duty in the Gulf of Mexico and an assignment to the *Michigan,* Lake Erie, 1843–44. On Nov. 2, 1844, occurred his marriage at Erie, Pa., to Anna Maria Christie. He was afterwards naval storekeeper at Honolulu, 1845–48. Returning home with his wife and his daughter Ellen in the Chilean ship *Maria Helena,* he was wrecked, Jan. 4, 1848, on Christmas Island, the passengers and crew re-

maining there nearly three months before they were rescued. Stevens' account of this, *Narrative of the Wreck of the Chilean Ship Maria Helena* (1849), was reprinted in pamphlet form from the *Polynesian.* Subsequent service included duty at Sacketts Harbor, 1849; in the *Michigan,* Great Lakes, 1849–51; in west coast survey work, 1852–55; and in the *Colorado,* Home Squadron, 1858–60.

In the Civil War, commanding the gunboat *Ottawa,* he participated in the capture of Port Royal, Nov. 7, 1861, and in later operations on the southeast coast, commanding the first expedition up the St. John's River, March–April 1862, which resulted in the occupation of Jacksonville and other towns and fortified points, and the capture of the yacht *America,* then owned by the Confederacy. This vessel was turned over for naval use without claims for prize-money. Later in 1862 he engaged in numerous operations in Virginia waters, opening up the Pamunkey River in the *Maratanza,* May 12, in support of George Brinton McClellan [*q.v.*], capturing the gunboat *Teazer,* July 4, and commanding the *Monitor* in the James River in August during McClellan's withdrawal from the Peninsula. Transferred to the *Sonoma* in cruising operations, he chased the *Florida* thirty-four hours on the Bahama Banks, captured five prizes, and off Bermuda held up the steamer *Gladiator,* though convoyed by H. M. S. *Desperate,* until he was satisfied of her character, both naval vessels clearing for action. He commanded the monitor *Patapsco* in frequent actions around Charleston, August-September 1863, and, despite his unfavorable opinion of its success, was given charge of a desperate night boat attack, Sept. 8, on Fort Sumter, which was repulsed with 124 casualties in his force of about four hundred (see his account of "The Boat Attack on Sumter" in *Battles and Leaders of the Civil War,* vol. IV, 1888). In 1864 he commanded the *Oneida* of the Gulf Squadron, transferring temporarily to the monitor *Winnebago* in the battle of Mobile and later operating off Texas, where in July 1865 he was senior officer. From superiors, during this almost continuous active war service, he received uniformly high commendation for initiative and dependability (Hamersly, *post*). Made captain (1866), commodore (1872), and rear admiral (1879), he was assigned service as lighthouse inspector, 1867–70; command of the *Guerrière,* European Squadron, 1870–71; varied duties at Norfolk, 1873–80; and command of the Pacific Squadron, 1880–81. After retirement, May 27, 1881, he lived in Washington, D. C., occupying his leisure in part with writing on naval and other subjects. One of his articles, "Service under Du Pont," appeared in the *Times* (Philadelphia), Jan. 10, 1886. Of his family of three daughters and six sons, the eldest son became a rear admiral, and two others were officers respectively in the army and marine corps. He died at Rockville, Md., at the home of his daughter and was buried in Arlington Cemetery.

[*United Service* (Phila.), May 1891, with portrait; L. R. Hamersly, *Records of Living Officers U. S. Navy and Marine Corps* (4th edition, 1890); *War of the Rebellion: Official Records* (*Navy*); obituary in *Evening Star* (Washington, D. C.), May 15, 1896; papers in the possession of Stevens' granddaughter, Mrs. Frederick C. Hicks, Washington, D. C.]   A. W.

STEVENS, WALTER HUSTED (Aug. 24, 1827–Nov. 12, 1867), Confederate soldier, was born at Penn Yan, N. Y., the son of Samuel Stevens. He entered West Point as a cadet in 1844, graduated in 1848, fourth in his class, and was commissioned in the corps of engineers. Practically all of his service from then until the Civil War was in Louisiana and Texas, where he did some engineering work upon rivers and harbors, acted as lighthouse inspector for four years, and supervised the construction and repair of fortifications at Galveston and New Orleans. He was promoted first lieutenant in 1855. His life in the South and his marriage to a resident of Louisiana had made him entirely southern in sentiment, and after Texas passed the ordinance of secession he accordingly sent in his resignation from the army, Mar. 2, 1861. Without waiting for it to be forwarded to Washington, he offered his services to Texas and assisted in preparation for the war. The War Department accordingly withheld action on the resignation, and eventually he was dismissed, May 2, 1861, on the technical ground of failure to render his accounts. Meanwhile he had been appointed a captain of engineers in the Confederate army, accredited to the state of Texas. He served on the staff of Gen. Pierre Gustave Toutant Beauregard [*q.v.*] at the battle of Bull Run, and was then promoted major and assigned to duty as chief engineer of the Army of Northern Virginia, continuing in the field with it during the Peninsular campaign. When Lee succeeded Johnston in the command of the army, Stevens, now a colonel, was put in charge of the defenses of Richmond. These resembled field works rather than a fortress, being constructed on a much more modest scale than the contemporary fortifications of Washington, but they were of value in releasing troops for service at the front and proved of some direct use in checking the Kilpatrick-Dahlgren cavalry raid in 1864. Ste-

vens was appointed brigadier-general with rank from Aug. 28, 1864, and again became chief engineer of the Army of Northern Virginia, with which he served until the surrender. The defensive lines before Petersburg were constructed under his direction. It is said that on the evacuation of Richmond he turned back into the flames of the burning bridge over which the troops were marching in order that he might be the last soldier to leave the city he had defended so long. Paroled at Appomattox, he went to Mexico, apparently intending to make it his permanent home, and became superintendent and constructing engineer of a railroad between Vera Cruz and the city of Mexico. He died at Vera Cruz.

[*War of the Rebellion: Official Records* (*Army*); C. A. Evans, *Confederate Mil. Hist.* (1899), vol. III, pp. 664–65; G. W. Cullum, *Biog. Reg. Officers and Grads. U. S. Mil. Acad.* (1891), vol. II, p. 346; J. G. Barnard, *A Report on the Defenses of Washington* (1871), app. D. and F; *Confederate Veteran*, July 1922; unpublished records in the War Dept.]   T. M. S.

STEVENS, WILLIAM ARNOLD (Feb. 5, 1839–Jan. 2, 1910), New Testament scholar, was born at Granville, Ohio, son of the Rev. John and Mary (Arnold) Stevens. His father was for many years a professor at Denison University and an active factor in Baptist education in Ohio; his mother, the daughter of William Arnold of Charlestown, Mass., was a woman possessing to an unusual degree the gift of discernment and the grace of piety. William received his early education at Granville, spent three years of business experience at Cincinnati, where under the influence of Ezekiel Gilman Robinson [*q.v.*] he united with a Baptist church, and was graduated A.B. at Denison University in 1862. After a year in the short course at Rochester Theological Seminary, he returned to Denison as tutor in the classics, 1863–65, during which time he served for a while with the Christian Commission. Enrolling at Harvard in the fall of 1865 as a student of philology and theology, he studied under the eminent Greek, Professor E. A. Sophocles [*q.v.*], and, residing at the Newton Theological Institution, simultaneously pursued some studies there. In 1867–68 he was in Germany, at Leipzig and Berlin, and for the next nine years was professor of the Greek language and literature at Denison. In 1876 he published *Select Orations of Lysias.*

The most distinctive part of his career began with his call to Rochester Theological Seminary in 1877, where he was professor of New Testament interpretation for the rest of his life. An able and inspiring teacher, he helped equip more than a generation of Baptist ministers, whose preaching and pastoral work were partially shaped by his instruction. His greatest influence has been ascribed to the downright honesty and sincerity of his thinking. As a theological conservative but a truly scholarly student of the New Testament, he both worked harmoniously with his associates and encouraged methods of New Testament study which carried some of his students—notably Ernest DeWitt Burton and Walter Rauschenbusch [*qq.v.*]—to more liberal positions. Most of his published writings lay in the field of New Testament study. In 1887 he published *A Commentary on the Epistles to the Thessalonians,* in the American Commentary on the New Testament edited by Alvah Hovey, and in 1894 a *Life of the Apostle Paul.* He collaborated with E. D. Burton in an *Outline Handbook of the Life of Christ* (1892) and in *A Harmony of the Gospels for Historical Study* (1894), which years later remains the most widely used book of its kind. He was a man of broad culture, well read, especially in biography and poetry, with a wide range of classical and Biblical lore. In demeanor he was quiet and reserved. Especially appreciative of nature, he spent his vacations for many years on the Maine coast, particularly at Mount Desert, with its remarkable combination of wooded hills and ocean stretches. He was married, Apr. 5, 1876, to Caroline A. Clarke of Springfield, Ohio.

[*Who's Who in America,* 1908–09; *Memorial Volume of Denison Univ., 1831–1906* (1907); *The Record* (Rochester Theological Seminary), Feb. 1910; *Democrat and Chronicle* (Rochester), Jan. 3, 1910.]

W. H. A.

STEVENS, WILLIAM BACON (July 13, 1815–June 11, 1887), Episcopal bishop, historian, was born in Bath, Me., the youngest of three surviving children of William Stevens, a captain in the War of 1812, and his wife Rebecca, daughter of J. W. Bacon. The family soon moved to Boston where young Stevens received his first education in the city schools. At the age of fifteen he entered Phillips Academy, Andover, where he remained two years. Frail since birth, he now set out on a horseback trip through the Middle West in the hope of building up his strength, and upon his return took passage for Savannah, thence to the Sandwich Islands, and thence westward around the globe, visiting Java, China, and the Philippines. After his return to America he was called upon frequently to lecture on the missionary activities he had observed in China and the Sandwich Islands.

Though greatly improved in health, he determined as a precaution to settle in the South, and in the fall of 1836 entered the Medical College of the State of South Carolina in Charleston.

The following spring he returned to Savannah to continue his studies with Dr. Edward Coppée, whose daughter, Alethea, subsequently became his wife. In the summer he visited his home in Boston, and, deciding to finish his medical studies at Dartmouth, received the degree of M.D. from that institution in 1837. After visiting Florida, he returned to Savannah and entered a partnership with his father-in-law. His success was immediate; he was made physician and surgeon for the orphan asylum and for the Central of Georgia Railroad, and was appointed health officer for the port. He was also elected secretary of the Georgia Medical Society and in 1840 was sent as a delegate to the National Medical Convention in Washington. Upon settling in Savannah he had joined the Georgia Hussars in order to enlarge his social acquaintanceship and to secure release from militia and jury service.

Becoming interested in the history of the state, he was instrumental in founding the Georgia Historical Society in 1839, being elected its first recording secretary and later its librarian. He delivered the Georgia Day address before the Society in 1841, and set forth so eloquently the need for a history of the state that the Society commissioned him to write one. Accordingly, he published *A History of Georgia from Its First Discovery by Europeans to the Adoption of the Present Constitution in MDCCXCVIII,* the first volume appearing in 1847 and the second in 1859. Writing with precision and accuracy and using the documentary sources, he produced a history which has not yet been supplanted. Also he edited the first two volumes of the *Collections of the Georgia Historical Society* (1840, 1842).

Stevens, who was always of a religious bent, soon after he began his medical career found himself haunted by the feeling that he should enter the ministry. Though born into a Congregationalist family, he was early attracted by the Episcopal Church, and in Savannah he joined that communion. Under the dynamic influence of Bishop Stephen Elliott, he pursued a course of study, maintaining himself meanwhile by writing editorials for the *Georgian,* the principal newspaper in the city. On Feb. 26, 1843, he was ordered deacon and was appointed a missionary at Athens, Ga., the seat of the state university. Advanced to the priesthood, Jan. 7, 1844, he became rector of the Episcopal church in Athens. He had previously been appointed to the board of visitors of the university and elected (1843) to the new chair of oratory and belles-lettres, the duties of which he assumed, in addition to his rectorship, in January 1844. In 1847 he was appointed a delegate to the General Convention of his Church in New York, and the next year was persuaded to accept a call to St. Andrew's Church, Philadelphia. He visited the Holy Land and western Europe in 1857, and in the fall of 1861 was made professor of liturgics and homiletics in the Philadelphia Divinity School, established that year. In 1862 he became assistant bishop of the diocese of Pennsylvania, and three years later, on the death of Bishop Alonzo Potter [q.v.], he was made bishop. In 1868 he was given charge of the American churches in Europe, and for years thereafter he spent much time abroad, preaching in many of the churches and cathedrals of England and of other countries. He was chosen in 1876 to preach in St. Paul's Cathedral, London, the closing sermon of the Pan-Anglican Conference.

Stevens was instrumental in founding Lehigh University, of which his brother-in-law, Henry Coppée [q.v.], became president, and in 1869 he was made a trustee. He was also a trustee of the University of Pennsylvania from 1866 until his death. He was a member of nearly two dozen literary and historical societies. Besides his historical works, he wrote a great many books and pamphlets on religious subjects, the best known of which are: *The Bow in the Cloud; or, Covenant Mercy for the Afflicted* (1854); *The Parables of the New Testament Practically Unfolded* (1855); *Home Service: A Manual* (1856); *The Lord's Day* (1857); *The Past and Present of St. Andrew's* (1858); *Sabbaths of the Lord* (1872); *Early History of the Church in Georgia* (1873); *Sermons* (1879). Stevens was simple, modest, and unpretending, a forceful orator, tall and graceful in appearance. His first wife, Alethea Coppée, bore him three children. After her death he married, in 1869, Anna, daughter of J. N. Conyngham of Wilkes-Barre, Pa., and by her had a son and a daughter.

["Autobiog. of Bishop Stevens," *Church Magazine* (Phila.), Nov., Dec. 1887; A. L. Hull, *A Hist. Sketch of the Univ. of Ga.* (1894); A. D. Candler and C. A. Evans, *Georgia* (1906), III, 372; minutes of the trustees of the Univ. of Ga., 1835–57 (MS.); minutes of the vestry of Emmanuel Parish, 1843–93 (MS.); G. W. J. De Renne, *Observations on Doctor Stevens's Hist. of Ga.* (1849); *Hartford Courant,* May 9, 1840; *Galignani's Messenger* (Paris), June 13, 1887; *Evening City Item* (Phila.), June 12, 1871; S. F. Hotchkiss, *A Memoir of the Rt. Rev. William Bacon Stevens* (1899); M. A. De W. Howe, *A Discourse Commemorative . . . of the Rt. Rev. William Bacon Stevens* (1888); biog. sketch in *The Parables* (ed. of 1887); *Churchman,* June 18, 1887; *Pub. Ledger* (Phila.), June 13, 1887.]
E. M. C.

STEVENSON, ADLAI EWING (Oct. 23, 1835–June 14, 1914), congressman from Illinois, vice-president, was born in Christian County, Ky., the son of John Turner Stevenson and Eliza

(Ewing) Stevenson, both of whom were Scotch-Irish Presbyterians. His father was a small planter and slave-owner. In 1852 the Stevensons emigrated to Bloomington, Ill., where their conditions of life were not so primitive as to deny young Stevenson fair educational advantages. He taught country school, attended Illinois Wesleyan University as a preparatory student, and even spent two years at Centre College, Danville, Ky. There he met his future wife, to whom he was married on Dec. 20, 1866—Letitia, the daughter of Lewis W. Green [q.v.], the president of the college. Adlai left college before graduation because of the death of his father, read law, was admitted to the bar, and in 1858 opened an office at Metamora, Ill. A fortunate court appointment as master in chancery, and an even more fortunate election as state's attorney, gave him the needed start in his profession; and in 1868 he found it possible to return to Bloomington as the law partner of James S. Ewing. Like most country lawyers of the period, he never became a specialist along any particular line, but he did acquire a wide and varied practice. He was a successful advocate, prepared his cases carefully, and tried them well.

Always an ardent Democrat, he campaigned for Douglas against Lincoln in 1858 and 1860, and in 1864 he ran for elector on the McClellan ticket. He was unexpectedly swept into Congress on the Democratic tidal wave of 1874, was a candidate for reëlection in 1876 and lost, ran once more in 1878 with Greenback support and won. During his two rather undistinguished terms in Congress he made his low-tariff and soft-money views well known; but he was far from belligerent in pressing them, and he made hosts of friends, even among those who were opposed to his political principles. When Cleveland became president in 1885, it was well understood that thousands of fourth-class Republican postmasters would have to be removed to make way for deserving Democrats. The first assistant postmaster-general, to whom the duty of making these removals would fall, must therefore be a man of tact, who could serve his party's interests well and yet give as little offense as possible to the opposition. Stevenson was chosen for this place, and he made some forty thousand removals as painlessly as any one could have done it. Naturally his course provoked scathing denunciation, although very little of the criticism came from the men actually removed from office. In 1889 Cleveland would have rewarded him for his service by making him justice of the supreme court of the District of Columbia, but the Republican majority in the Senate, still smarting from the wounds his course in the post-office had inflicted on them, turned the nomination down. In 1892 he headed the Illinois delegation to the Democratic national convention and helped nominate Cleveland. Thereafter, when a man was sought on whom all factions of the party could unite for vice-presidential nomination, he was chosen for second place. Elected to preside over a Senate that only recently had refused to confirm him for a minor office, he displayed his usual good humor, won many friends, and made no enemies. On the money question he was known to be out of sympathy with the administration, but he was never guilty of embarrassing it. When he retired from office in 1897, President McKinley promptly appointed him a member of the monetary commission to Europe that sought unsuccessfully to pave the way for international bimetallism.

Twice after this his availability made him a candidate for office. In 1900 he was Bryan's running mate, with "Imperialism" as the paramount issue. In 1908 the Democrats of Illinois thought that in spite of his advanced age he was the best man to defeat Charles S. Deneen for the governorship, and he came within twenty-two thousand votes of election. During his declining years he put together a book of reminiscences and addresses, *Something of Men I Have Known* (1909). The book tells little of Stevenson's own career, but it reveals well his natural modesty, his capacity for friendship, and his great personal charm. He died in Chicago.

[J. W. Cook, "The Life and Labors of Hon. Adlai Ewing Stevenson," *Jour. of Ill. State Hist. Soc.*, July 1915; J. S. Ewing, "Mr. Stevenson, the Democratic Candidate for Vice-President," in *Review of Reviews* (N. Y.), Oct. 1900; F. E. Leupp, "Mr. Bryan's Running Mate," *Independent*, Sept. 6, 1900; *In Memoriam: Letitia Green Stevenson, Adlai Ewing Stevenson* (191–?); *Chicago Sunday Tribune*, June 14, 1914.]   J. D. H.

STEVENSON, ANDREW (Jan. 21, 1784–Jan. 25, 1857), congressman from Virginia, speaker of the House of Representatives, and minister to Great Britain, was the son of James and Frances (Littlepage) Stevenson and the nephew of Lewis Littlepage [q.v.]. He was born in Culpeper County, Va., where his father was rector of St. Mark's Parish, and was educated at the College of William and Mary. Later he studied law, was admitted to the bar, and began practice in Richmond. He was a member of the House of Delegates from 1809 to 1821, excepting the year 1817. He was speaker of this body from 1812 until 1815. In 1814 and again in 1816 he ran for Congress but was defeated. The next year he became a director of the Richmond branch of the Bank of the United States. He finally was successful in his campaign for Congress and served from 1821 to 1834, when he resigned. During this period his political influence became important on the federal theatre. Being an early supporter of Van Buren, he went over into the Jackson camp with his chief and became a member of the "Richmond Junto," which, beside himself, consisted of Spencer Roane, Thomas Ritchie, and William C. Rives. In 1827, with the support of Van Buren, he was elected speaker of the federal House of Representatives and served until 1834. Adams accused him of double dealing on the tariff question (Adams, *post*, VII, 369), and he immediately won the hatred of the opposition by appointing committees on a strictly partisan basis, thus breaking with the policy established by his immediate predecessors in office.

When the nullification controversy arose, he took the side of the Union and was one of the few congressmen of that persuasion who weathered the storm in Eastern Virginia. His stand was an important factor in preventing Virginia from following the lead of South Carolina in this matter. In 1832 he supported Van Buren for the vice-presidency and in 1835 was chairman of the Baltimore convention that nominated Van Buren for the presidency. In 1834 Stevenson was nominated by President Jackson as minister to Great Britain. The Senate refused to confirm his nomination at the time, but Jackson made no other appointment, and finally in 1836 Stevenson's appointment was confirmed. While serving in this capacity, he brought embarrassment upon himself by advising certain British investors that he believed the attack upon the Bank of the United States would fail. His service in England was terminated in 1841 by the Whig triumph of the previous year. Returning to Virginia, he made his home at "Blenheim" in Albemarle County, an estate that he had purchased in 1836. Ritchie tried to obtain his return to active political life when Polk was elected to the presidency, but the Polk administration did not accept the suggestion. In 1845 Stevenson was elected president of the Virginia Society of Agriculture and became a member of the board of visitors of the University of Virginia. In 1856 he was chosen rector of the university. He died at "Blenheim" and lies buried at "Enniscorthy," the estate of John Coles, his father-in-law, in Albemarle County.

He was married three times: first, to Mary Page White, the daughter of John White and the grand-daughter of Carter Braxton [q.v.], second, in 1816, to Sarah Coles, and third, to Mary Schaff, of Georgetown, D. C. His son was John White Stevenson [q.v.]. He is reputed to have been a courtly and talented man; but he was a machine politician, and his career lacks the stamp of a strong personality.

[47 vols. of his papers in Lib. of Cong.; *Memoirs of John Quincy Adams*, vols. VI–XII (1875–77); C. G. Bowers, *The Party Battles of the Jackson Period* (1922); J. S. Bassett, *The Life of Andrew Jackson* (1911), II; C. H. Ambler, *Sectionalism in Va.* (1910) and *Thomas Ritchie* (1913); J. B. McMaster, *A Hist. of the People of the U. S.*, vol. VI (1906); B. H. Wise, *The Life of Henry A. Wise* (1899); H. E. Hayden, *Va. Geneal.* (1891); Edgar Woods, *Albemarle County* (1901), p. 319.]   T. P. A.

STEVENSON, CARTER LITTLEPAGE (Sept. 21, 1817–Aug. 15, 1888), Confederate general, was born near Fredericksburg, Va., the son of Carter Littlepage and Jane (Herndon) Stevenson. He was the nephew of Andrew Stevenson [*q.v.*] and the grand-nephew of Lewis Littlepage [*q.v.*]. Entering West Point in 1834, he graduated in 1838, was commissioned second lieutenant in the 5th Infantry, and promoted to be first lieutenant in 1840. Before the Mexican War he served in Florida, Wisconsin, and Michigan. His wife, Martha P. Griswold, was a Michigan woman. He fought at Palo Alto and Resaca de la Palma, was promoted to the rank of captain in 1847, and, serving chiefly on the frontier until the Civil War, participated in several skirmishes with Indians and in the Utah expedition of 1858. On June 6, 1861, he presented his resignation to his commanding officer and departed on leave of absence, intending to offer his services to his native state; but his commanding officer left the same day for the same purpose, forgetting to forward the resignation. Finally it was found by the succeeding commanding officer, who sent it on to Washington, where it arrived a month after it had been written (Old Files Section, Adjutant-General's Office, War Department). Meanwhile, on June 25, an order for Stevenson's dismissal had been issued, "it having been ascertained . . . that he had entertained and expressed treasonable designs against the Government of the United States" (Cullum, *post*, pp. 727–28).

In July he was commissioned lieutenant-colonel of infantry in the Confederate Army and colonel of the 53rd Virginia Infantry. On Beauregard's recommendation he was appointed brigadier-general in February 1862 and sent to duty in the West, where he served in Tennessee and Kentucky. He was commissioned major-general in October 1862. In December his division was transferred from Bragg's command to Pemberton's and fought at Champion's Hill and Big Black Ridge in the Vicksburg campaign. He personally commanded the Confederate forces during their retreat into the city, while Pemberton hastened ahead to organize the defense. He

was in charge of the right of the Confederate lines during the siege and was paroled along with his division at the surrender in July 1863. The Confederate government declared the division exchanged and returned it to duty in September, an action the Union authorities insisted was a violation of the terms of the cartel. An acrimonious correspondence followed, but the division was not withdrawn from field service. Whether his government's action may be justified or not, Stevenson had no responsibility in the matter. He fought at Missionary Ridge in Hardee's corps and in Hood's through the Atlanta campaign, notably at Resaca and Kenesaw Mountain. When Hood was assigned to the command of the Army of Tennessee, Stevenson succeeded him temporarily as corps commander, until the assignment of S. D. Lee. His division was not engaged at Franklin but suffered heavily at the battle of Nashville and in covering the retreat. He again had temporary command of the corps when S. D. Lee was wounded. In 1865, with the remnant of his division, he was transferred to the east, where he served through the campaign of the Carolinas and at the battle of Bentonville. After the war he was a civil and mining engineer. He died in Caroline County, Va.

[G. W. Cullum, *Biog. Register of . . . Grads. of . . . West Point*, 3rd ed., vol. I (1891); *War of the Rebellion: Official Records (Army)*; R. U. Johnson and C. C. Buel, *Battles and Leaders of the Civil War*, vols. III, IV (1887–88); C. A. Evans, *Confederate Military Hist.* (1899), vol. III; H. E. Hayden, *Va. Geneal.* (1891); MS. in the War Department files.]   T. M. S.

STEVENSON, JAMES (Dec. 24, 1840–July 25, 1888), ethnologist, explorer, was born in Maysville, Ky., and educated in private schools. Coming into contact with the engineering corps of the government at sixteen, he engaged in explorations in the Northwest and afterwards became a member of the United States Geological Survey of the Territories under Dr. Ferdinand Vandiveer Hayden [*q.v.*]. With Dr. Hayden he explored the Missouri, Columbia, and Snake rivers to their sources. Inclination, training, and character made him an efficient aid in the conduct of the expeditions, and this meant much on the early wild frontiers. In 1871 he "took an active part in the survey of the Yellowstone region and was instrumental in having the heart of this 'wonderland' made a national park" (*American Anthropologist, post*, p. 558). In 1872 he was in charge of a division of Hayden's party that explored the Snake River in Idaho and Wyoming territories. During the surveys he came to know the Blackfeet and other Indians of Dakota, and grew interested in their languages, names, and customs, a preparation for his studies in the

Southwest. On the survey of 1872 he climbed the Great Teton, the first white man known to have reached the ancient Indian altar on its summit. Though he interrupted the work of exploration to join the Union army in 1861 and saw service in the 13th New York Volunteers, in 1866 he resumed the ethnological studies he had begun in previous years. He continued with these on the passing of the survey to the directorship of Major John Wesley Powell [q.v.], and at the inception of the Bureau of Ethnology in 1879 he engaged in research for it in the Southwest, where explorations were carried on among the Pueblo Indians and the remains of their former settlements. On Apr. 18, 1872, he married Matilda Coxe Evans of Washington [see Matilda Coxe Evans Stevenson], who became his associate in the Southwestern work. He outfitted and conducted expeditions of Frank Hamilton Cushing [q.v.], Mindeleff, and other explorers of the bureau investigating the ancient ruins and the living Navaho, Zuñi, Hopi, and other tribes. Gathering large collections of culture material, both ancient and modern, he prepared the first illustrated catalogues of specimens from the Southwest (*Second Annual Report of the Bureau of Ethnology . . . 1880–'81*, 1883, and *Third Annual Report . . . 1881–'82*, 1884), classified according to tribes, materials, and uses. These primer catalogues have a continuing use. He also made the first studies among the Navaho, "Ceremonial of Hasjelti Dailjis and Mythical Sand Painting of the Navajo Indians" (*Eighth Annual Report of the Bureau of Ethnology . . . 1886–'87*, 1891). He died in New York City as he was returning from Gloucester, Mass., to Washington, D. C. He was survived by his wife.

Although Stevenson amassed voluminous notes as the result of his observations, he was a man of action, irked by writing, and gladly turned over most of his material to his wife. He was wont to say that he was not a scientific man, little realizing that his great collection of material would remain a valuable and in most respects unique contribution to science. A pioneer making the ways straight for subsequent workers, he belonged to the type of American who prefers the freedom and adventure of the wilds to the life of cities, and he found his work in Washington on maps and field notes but a tedious prelude to his real life in the summer in the mesas and canyons of the West. Though he displayed the reserve and reticence of the frontiersman, his speech was as pointed as it was brief, and in action usually secured him what he wanted, a quality that made him invaluable to his department.

He was a man above medium height, meager of frame, with brown hair and beard.

[G. P. Merrill, *The First One Hundred Years of Am. Geology* (1924); *Tenth Ann. Report of the Bureau of Ethnology . . . 1888–89* (1893); *Sci.*, Aug. 10, 1888, pp. 63–64; *Am. Anthropologist*, Oct.–Dec. 1916; obituaries in *Evening Star* (Washington), July 26, and *Nat. Tribune* (Washington), Aug. 2, 1888; personal recollections.]
W. H.

STEVENSON, JOHN JAMES (Oct. 10, 1841–Aug. 10, 1924), geologist, was born in New York City. His father, the Rev. Andrew Stevenson, who was born in Ballylaw, Ireland, emigrated to America in 1831; his mother, Ann Mary (Willson) Stevenson, a native of Bedford, Pa., was a descendant of Zaccheus Willson who came to America in 1711. Educated in private schools in New York City and at the University of the City of New York (later New York University), from which he graduated in 1863, he first essayed teaching mathematics and natural science in the academy at Mexico, N. Y., but shortly resigned to take charge, in September 1864, of a school for boys at Astoria, N. Y. There he also edited the *American Educational Monthly*. In 1867, when he received the degree of Ph.D. from the University of the City of New York, he undertook professional work in western mining regions and contracted tuberculosis, from which he did not fully recover for several years. He was professor of chemistry and natural sciences in West Virginia University, 1869–71; assistant to Dr. John Strong Newberry [q.v.] on the geological survey of Ohio, 1871–72, and part-time professor of geology in the University of the City of New York, 1872. In 1873 he was appointed geologist on the surveys under Col. George Montague Wheeler west of the 100th meridian, and in 1875 was assistant geologist to Prof. Peter Lesley [qq.v.] in charge of the geological survey of Pennsylvania, where he was given charge of the work in Greene and Washington counties, and in 1876 and 1877 of Fayette and Westmoreland counties. In 1878 he rejoined the Wheeler survey in Colorado. In 1879, 1880, and 1881 he was engaged a part of the time in expert work in southwest Virginia and New Mexico, but returned to work on the Pennsylvania survey in 1881, and became professor of geology in New York University, holding the position until 1909 when he retired as professor emeritus.

As a teacher he was eminently successful. He had in a marked degree the ability to make his subject interesting, to hold the attention of his students, and to encourage and stimulate them. In addition to his scientific papers he contributed many articles on college problems and on the place of science in education to such magazines as *School and Society* and *Popular Science Monthly*. As a working geologist he covered a wide field, though he gave his greatest attention to stratigraphic problems and to those relating to coal. Apart from his publications in the reports of the Wheeler survey of 1875 and 1881 (*United States Geographical Surveys West of the 100th Meridian*, vol. III, 1875; supplement, 1881) and in reports of the Pennsylvania survey (*Second Geological Survey of Pennsylvania, 1875 ... Greene & Washington District*, vol. K, 1876; *Second Geological Survey of Pennsylvania, 1876 ... 1877 ... Fayette & Westmoreland District*, KK–KKK, 1877–78, and *Second Geological Survey of Pennsylvania ... The Geology of Bedford and Fulton Counties*, 1882), his best known studies are "Lower Carboniferous of the Appalachian Basin" (*Bulletin of the Geological Society of America*, vol. XIV, 1903) and "Carboniferous of the Appalachian Basin" (*Ibid.*, vols. XV, 2904, XVII, 1906, XVIII, 1907); "The Formation of Coal Beds" (*Proceedings of the American Philosophical Society*, vols. L–LII, 1911–13); and *Interrelation of the Fossil Fuels* (1921). Of particular interest were his conclusions that the New Mexican coal fields were cretaceous, and that the Laramie section of King and the Fort Union of Hayden were composite successions of the cretaceous age; he showed too that each coal bed of the Pennsylvania field had peculiarities of its own by which any particular bed could be recognized over wide areas.

Kindly and courteous, but incisive in expression, he was a man keenly and forcefully alert, capable of thoroughly enjoying a good fight when it was honorably conducted, whoever might be the victor. He was a good conversationalist and a delightful companion, being gifted with an unusual sense of humor. He was the first secretary of the Geological Society of America, which he had been active in establishing, and president in 1899; he was also president of the New York Academy, 1896–98; acting vice-president for the United States at the International Geological Congress in 1903, and a member of numerous scientific societies at home and abroad. He was twice married, first on Apr. 13, 1865, to Mary A. McGowan, who died in 1871, and second on Jan. 1, 1879, to Mary C. Ewing. There were three children by the first marriage and two by the second. Although his output of work was checked by failing eyesight during his last two years, he was mentally active until the last. He died of pneumonia in New Canaan, Conn., in his eighty-third year.

[*Who's Who in America*, 1922–23; I. C. White, in *Bull. Geological Soc. of America*, Mar. 1925, with bibliog.; Charles Keyes, in *Pan Am. Geologist*, Oct. 1924; *Gen. Alumni Cat. of N. Y. Univ., 1833–1905* (1906); obituary in *N. Y. Times*, Aug. 11, 1924; personal recollections.]

G. P. M.

STEVENSON, JOHN WHITE (May 4, 1812–Aug. 10, 1886), senator and representative in Congress and governor of Kentucky, was born in Richmond, Va., the only child of Andrew Stevenson [*q.v.*] and Mary Page (White) Stevenson. His mother dying at his birth, he was taken in charge and given his earliest training by his grandmother, Judith White. His first formal schooling was provided by private tutors in Virginia and also in Washington where he spent much time with his father. He attended Hampden-Sidney College, 1828–29, before entering the University of Virginia, where he graduated in 1832. He read law with Willoughby Newton, a prominent Virginia lawyer, and on the advice of James Madison decided to grow up in the West. He began the practice of law in Vicksburg, Miss., but in 1841 he settled in Covington, Ky., where he made his home throughout the rest of his life. His success as a lawyer was soon assured. In 1845 he was elected as a representative from Kenton County to the state legislature, and he was reëlected in 1846 and 1848. The next year he represented his county in the constitutional convention which met in Frankfort and remade the state constitution. With M. C. Johnson and James Harlan, he prepared for the state a *Code of Practise in Civil and Criminal Cases* (1854). He was a delegate to the National Democratic Conventions of 1848, 1852, and 1856, and was elected to the Thirty-fifth and Thirty-sixth congresses, serving from 1857 to 1861. He failed of reëlection to the following Congress.

On Jan. 30, 1861, he made his principal speech, regarding the perilous situation created by the secession movement. Imbued with a strong feeling for the Union, characteristic of Kentuckians, he called upon the Republicans to recede from the extreme policies of their platform and help to preserve the common country. Decrying the passions of the hour, he blamed the Republicans for the failure of the Crittenden propositions and all other compromises, and declared that "the slave states have a right to resist the execution of a policy at war with their interests, destructive of their peace, injurious to their rights, and subversive of the ends and objects for which the Union was formed" (*Congressional Globe*, 36 Cong., 2 Sess., Appendix, p. 144). Though strongly sympathizing with the Confederacy, he managed to keep out of war and free from Federal prisons, and not until 1865 did his name become prominent again. This year he attended as a delegate the Union Convention in Philadelphia called to indorse President Johnson's policy of reconstruction. In August 1867 he was elected lieutenant-governor of Kentucky and the next month succeeded to the governorship, on account of the death of Gov. John L. Helm [q.v.]. The next year he was elected to this position by a majority of more than four to one over his Republican opponent. He was a constructive and sane governor, using his influence and power to break up violent gangs of "Regulators," and aiding the development of a common-school system. He became entangled in a bitter controversy with Senator Thomas C. McCreery and Thomas L. Jones over charges and countercharges relative to a recommendation for the appointment to a federal office of Stephen G. Burkridge, a Union officer violently hated by Kentuckians. This controversy seems to have been preparatory to the contest between Stevenson and McCreery for the senatorship a few months later. Stevenson won and in February 1871 he resigned the governorship to serve a term in the United States Senate. For the next six years he tenaciously upheld a political faith from which he had never swerved —a faith which he had imbibed from Jefferson and Madison, both of whom he had known in their homes. He opposed the rivers and harbors appropriations bill of 1875 and in a speech against it declared that he clung to the "doctrines of close construction and rigid adherence to all the limitations of the Constitution upon congressional or executive power with greater tenacity now than ever, as the palladium of political safety" (*Congressional Record*, 44 Cong., 1 Sess., p. 4836). In the disputed election of 1876, he went to New Orleans as one of the visiting statesmen and became thoroughly convinced that the election had been fair in Louisiana.

On the expiration of his term he returned to Covington to resume the practice of law, and at the same time he accepted a position in the Cincinnati Law School to teach criminal law and contracts. In 1880 he was made chairman of the National Democratic Convention in Cincinnati, and four years later he was elected president of the American Bar Association. In 1842 Stevenson had married Sibella Winston, of Newport, Ky., and to them were born five children, three daughters and two sons. He was somewhat reserved in demeanor, was a great lover of the law, and was strongly religious. He was a member of the Episcopal Church and often attended its conventions. He died in Covington, Ky., and was buried in Spring Grove Cemetery, Cincinnati.

[*Biog. Directory of the Am. Congress, 1774–1927* (1928); *The Biog. Encyc. of Ky.* (1878); Lewis and R. H. Collins, *Hist. of Ky.* (2 vols., 1874); *Cincinnati Commercial Gazette*, Aug. 11, 1886; memoir in *Report of the Ninth Ann. Meeting of the Am. Bar Asso. . . . 1886* (1886), pp. 528–36. The principal speeches Stevenson made in Congress were reprinted as follows: *Speech of Hon. J. W. Stevenson, of Kentucky, on the State of the Union* (1875); *Tax and Tariff* (1875); *River and Harbor Appropriations* (1876); *The Electoral Vote* (1876). The Stevenson Papers, 1849–82 (9 vols.), are in the MS. Division, Lib. of Cong., and a few Stevenson letters are to be found in the Joseph Holt Papers in the same place.]   E. M. C.

STEVENSON, MATILDA COXE EVANS (*c.* 1850–June 24, 1915), ethnologist, was born in San Augustine, Tex., the daughter of Alexander H. and Maria Matilda (Coxe) Evans. Her parents moved in her infancy to Washington, D. C., and she was educated in Miss Anable's school in Philadelphia, Pa. Her marriage, Apr. 18, 1872, to James Stevenson [q.v.] of the United States Geological Survey, led to the beginning of her career as an ethnologist. She accompanied her husband on various expeditions into the Southwest and early became interested in the Zuñi Indians, who were more accessible, less modified, and more amenable to study than most. Her first work resulted in a paper almost unique in American studies, "The Religious Life of the Zuñi Child" (*Fifth Annual Report of the Bureau of Ethnology . . . 1883–84*, 1887). In 1888 she published an important paper on "Zuñi Religions" (*Science*, Mar. 23, 1888). Working among the Sia Pueblo Indians of the Rio Grande at an opportune time for ethnological studies, she produced some years later a paper, "The Sia" (*Eleventh Annual Report of the Bureau of Ethnology . . . 1889–'90*, 1894), the closest study of a Rio Grande Pueblo. One of her especially noteworthy discoveries was the existence of a Snake Society and ceremonial among the Sia. The Sia paper, full of social and material culture-elements, was a forerunner of her encyclopedic study of the Zuñi, "The Zuñi Indians: Their Mythology, Esoteric Fraternities, and Ceremonies" (*Twenty-third Annual Report of the Bureau of American Ethnology, 1901–1902*, 1904). Her fortitude in carrying out the work necessary for this study is almost unexampled among ethnologists, and her success in winning the confidence of the Indians was a triumph of character. The Zuñi, who loved her and called her "Mother," realized that a record of their civilization should be made, and expedited her work in every way, permitting her to observe the most secret ceremonies. As the result of later studies dealing with phases of Zuñi material culture she produced "Ethnobotany of the Zuñi Indians" (*Thirtieth Annual Report of the Bureau of American Ethnology . . . 1908–1909*, 1915), her last major work. She found time to write several less important articles, which appeared in the *American Anthropologist* at various dates, on more general aspects of the Pueblo Indian subject. Following her laborious work at Zuñi, she continued studies among the Rio Grande Pueblo Indians from 1904 to 1910, concentrating her attention especially on the Tewa and the difficult Taos Indians. In this her experience with the Zuñi and other tribes cleared away obstacles. Among her papers on these Indians were "Strange Rites of the Tewa Indians" (*Smithsonian Miscellaneous Collections,* vol. LXIII, 1914) and "The Sun and Ice People among the Tewa Indians of New Mexico" (*Ibid.,* vol. LXV, 1916). She made numerous collections of objects of material culture from the Pueblo Indians, being deputized to collect such objects for the Louisiana Purchase Exposition in 1903.

The scientific investigations carried on in anthropology at the time were not based on the more comprehensive and accurate methods of the modern school, but the necessity of careful observation and record was clearly recognized. Mrs. Stevenson's work rests on abundant and careful data, and, seen in perspective, it places her in a secure position in ethnological science. Since the Indians have changed greatly in the intervening years, her work has unique value. She was one of the founders of the Woman's Anthropological Society of Washington, and a member of a number of scientific societies.

[*Who's Who in America,* 1914–15; *Science,* July 9, 1915; W. H. Holmes, in *Am. Anthropologist,* Oct.–Dec., 1916; death notice in *Evening Star* (Washington, D. C.), July 24, 1915; personal acquaintance.]
W. H.

STEVENSON, SARA YORKE (Feb. 19, 1847–Nov. 14, 1921), archaeologist, was born in Paris, France. Through her father, Edward Yorke, a business man and banker, she was descended from Thomas Yorke who emigrated from England to what is now Berks County, Pa., about 1728. Her mother Sarah (Hanna) Yorke was the daughter of a planter in Louisiana. During her childhood she lived in Paris, where she was educated at the Cours Remy and the Institut Descauriet. She also spent a summer in Newport, a winter in New Orleans, and five years, 1862 to 1867, in Mexico. Her memories of the French intervention she later published in a book called *Maximilian in Mexico* (1899). Since her family had suffered severe financial losses, she went to Philadelphia to live in the quiet household of an aunt and two uncles. There she met Cornelius Stevenson to whom she was married on June 30, 1870. Their son William was born in 1878. Her dinners were notable, and she was a spirited and vivacious social leader. Rarely gifted, she possessed a magnetic personality, assured executive ability, and indomitable energy. The result was a record of unusual achievement.

She became interested in the Educational Home for Indian Boys and Girls, and then in the Depository and Philadelphia Exchange for Woman's Work, which afforded means of self-help to indigent gentlewomen. She helped found the Archaeological Association of the University of Pennsylvania, which became the University Museum, and was secretary for ten years and then president of the board of managers. It was she who started the museum building scheme. As early as 1894 she lectured at the University of Pennsylvania and at the Peabody Museum of Harvard University. At the World's Columbian Exposition in Chicago she was vice-president of the jury of awards for ethnology. In 1897 she made a trip to Rome for the department of archaeology and paleontology of the University of Pennsylvania and in 1898 to Egypt for the American Exploration Society and the city of Philadelphia. Besides a number of addresses and articles that she published on Egyptian archaeology and other subjects, one on *Insurance and Business Adventure in the Days of Shakespeare and in Those of William Penn* (1913) was republished and widely translated. She was president of the Pennsylvania branch of the Archaeological Institute of America from 1899 to 1903, had the honor of being elected a member of the American Philosophical Society, and was the first woman given an honorary degree by the University of Pennsylvania. Meanwhile she was enthusiastic in obtaining wider fields of opportunity for women and was the first president of the Equal Franchise Society of Pennsylvania. As first president of the Civic Club she helped inaugurate a movement that did much for the improvement of Philadelphia and soon became national. She was appointed to several important citizen's committees and from 1894 to 1901 was trustee of the Commercial Museum. She was a charter member and for twenty-five years president of the Acorn Club. The war brought her still more responsibility, for she was vice-chairman of the emergency aid and chairman of the French war relief committee, which raised $1,500,000. In recognition of her services the French government awarded her the academic palms as Officier d'Instruction Publique in 1916 and made her a Chevalier of the Legion of Honor in 1920. From 1908 until her death, she was literary editor of the *Public Led-*

ger as well as the contributor of "Peggy Shippen's Diary." Her keen wit, wide acquaintance,
and rich experience enabled her to wield extensive influence. She was as merciless in opposing
falsehood or dishonesty as she was courageous
in championing what she believed to be right.

[*Sara Yorke Stevenson, 1847–1921, A Tribute from
the Civic Club of Philadelphia* (1922); *Sara Yorke
Stevenson, 1847–1921. Addresses made at Meeting in
Her Memory Held in the Auditorium of the University
Museum . . . Apr. 29, 1922* (n.d.); *Who's Who in
America*, 1920–21; J. W. Jordan, *Colonial Families of
Philadelphia* (1911), vol. II; *Public Ledger*, Nov. 15,
1921.]
                                           A. L. L.

VOLUME IX, PART 2
STEWARD - TROWBRIDGE

(VOLUME XVIII OF THE ORIGINAL EDITION)

CROSS REFERENCES FROM THIS VOL-
UME ARE MADE TO THE VOLUME
NUMBERS OF THE ORIGINAL EDITION.

CONTRIBUTORS
VOLUME IX, PART 2

Charles David Abbott	C. D. A.
Thomas P. Abernethy	T. P. A.
Adeline Adams	A—e. A.
Arthur Adams	A—r. A.
Franklin P. Adams	F. P. A.
James Truslow Adams	J. T. A.
Randolph G. Adams	R. G. A—s.
Raymond William Adams	R. W. A.
Nelson F. Adkins	N. F. A.
Cyrus Adler	C. A.
Robert Greenhalgh Albion	R. G. A—n.
William F. Albright	W. F. A.
Arthur N. Alling	A. N. A.
William H. Allison	W. H. A.
John C. Almack	J. C. A—k.
Russell H. Anderson	R. H. A.
Gertrude L. Annan	G. L. A.
Katharine Anthony	K. A.
John Clark Archer	J. C. A—r.
Raymond Clare Archibald	R. C. A.
Frank Collins Baker	F. C. B.
Preston A. Barba	P. A. B.
Lewellys F. Barker	L. F. B.
Gilbert H. Barnes	G. H. B.
James Barnes	J. B.
Claribel R. Barnett	C. R. B.
John H. Barnhart	J. H. B—t.
Harold K. Barrows	H. K. B.
Clarence Bartlett	C. B—t.
Ernest Sutherland Bates	E. S. B—s.
H. Y. Benedict	H. Y. B.
Elbert J. Benton	E. J. B.
Percy W. Bidwell	P. W. B.
William C. Binkley	W. C. B.
Glen A. Blackburn	G. A. B.
Arthur A. Blanchard	A. A. B.
Edith R. Blanchard	E. R. B.
Wyndham B. Blanton	W. B. B.
Willard Grosvenor Bleyer	W. G. B.
Bruce Bliven	B. B.
Ernest Ludlow Bogart	E. L. B.
Louis H. Bolander	L. H. B.
Charles K. Bolton	C. K. B.
Ethel Stanwood Bolton	E. S. B—n.
Robert W. Bolwell	R. W. B.
Beverley W. Bond, Jr.	B. W. B., Jr.
Sarah G. Bowerman	S. G. B.
Julian P. Boyd	J. P. B.
William A. Braun	W. A. B.
Carl Bridenbaugh	C. B—h.
Jessica Hill Bridenbaugh	J. H. B—h.
Jean Lambert Brockway	J. L. B.
Alfred Mansfield Brooks	A. M. B.
C. A. Browne	C. A. B.
Robert Bruce	R. B.
Oscar MacMillan Buck	O. M. B.
Solon J. Buck	S. J. B.
F. Lauriston Bullard	F. L. B.
C. C. Burlingame	C. C. B.
Edmund C. Burnett	E. C. B.
C. Pauline Burt	C. P. B.
Henry J. Cadbury	H. J. C.
James M. Callahan	J. M. C.
Alfred Copeland Callen	A. C. C.
Henry Seidel Canby	H. S. C—y.
Zechariah Chafee, Jr.	Z. C., Jr.
Henry S. Chapman	H. S. C—n.
E. Clowes Chorley	E. C. C.
Robert C. Clark	R. C. C.
Robert Glass Cleland	R. G. C.
D. A. Clippinger	D. A. C.
Hugh McD. Clokie	H. M. C.
Frederick W. Coburn	F. W. C.
Hobart Coffey	H. C.
Esther Cole	E. Co.
Melvin E. Coleman	M. E. C.
E. Merton Coulter	E. M. C.
Isaac J. Cox	I. J. C.
Esther Crane	E. Cr.
Katharine Elizabeth Crane	K. E. C.
Avery O. Craven	A. O. C.
William J. Cunningham	W. J. C.
Edward E. Curtis	E. E. C.
Robert E. Cushman	R. E. C.
Stuart Daggett	S. D.
Arthur J. Daley	A. J. D.
Tenney L. Davis	T. L. D.
Edward H. Dewey	E. H. D.
Z. C. Dickinson	Z. C. D.
Irving Dilliard	I. D.
Charles A. Dinsmore	C. A. D—e.
Frank Haigh Dixon	F. H. D.
William E. Dodd	W. E. D.
Elizabeth Donnan	E. D.
Dorothy W. Douglas	D. W. D.
William Howe Downes	W. H. D.
Stella M. Drumm	S. M. D.
Edward A. Duddy	E. A. D.

Contributors

Clyde Augustus Duniway	C. A. D—y.	Joseph Mills Hanson	J. M. H.
William Frederick Durand	W. F. D.	Edward Rochie Hardy, Jr.	E. R. H., Jr.
Walter A. Dyer	W. A. D.	Alvin F. Harlow	A. F. H.
Edward Dwight Eaton	E. D. E.	Freeman H. Hart	F. H. H.
Walter Prichard Eaton	W. P. E.	Mary Bronson Hartt	M. B. H.
Everett E. Edwards	E. E. E.	Doremus A. Hayes	D. A. H.
Abram I. Elkus	A. I. E.	George H. Haynes	G. H. H.
Thompson C. Elliott	T. C. E.	Elizabeth Wiltbank Heilman	E. W. H.
Elizabeth Breckenridge Ellis	E. B. E.	Robert Herrick	R. H.
Elmer Ellis	E. E—s.	John Haynes Holmes	J. H. H.
Ephraim Emerton	E. E—n.	Roland Mather Hooker	R. M. H.
William M. Emery	W. M. E.	Walter Hough	W. H.
Margaret Sittler Ermarth	M. S. E.	John Tasker Howard	J. T. H.
John O. Evjen	J. O. E.	Archer B. Hulbert	A. B. H.
Hunter D. Farish	H. D. F.	Edward Hungerford	E. H.
Hallie Farmer	H. F.	William O. Inglis	W. O. I.
Ethel Webb Faulkner	E. W. F.	Ray W. Irwin	R. W. I.
Walter R. Fee	W. R. F.	Joseph Jackson	J. J.
Gustav Joseph Fiebeger	G. J. F.	Russell Leigh Jackson	R. L. J.
Mantle Fielding	M. F.	Edna L. Jacobsen	E. L. J—en.
James Kip Finch	J. K. F.	M. C. James	M. C. J.
Mary Elizabeth Fittro	M. E. F.	Theodore D. Jervey	T. D. J.
John C. Fitzpatrick	J. C. F—k.	W. L. G. Joerg	W. L. G. J.
Alexander Clarence Flick	A. C. F.	Edwin Lee Johnson	E. L. J—on.
John E. Flitcroft	J. E. F.	Joseph E. Johnson	J. E. J.
Jeremiah D. M. Ford	J. D. M. F.	Rufus M. Jones	R. M. J.
Douglas S. Freeman	D. S. F.	H. Donaldson Jordan	H. D. J.
John C. French	J. C. F—h.	George Morrow Kahrl	G. M. K.
Paul H. Furfey	P. H. F.	Katharine Amend Kellock	K. A. K.
Esson M. Gale	E. M. G.	Louise Phelps Kellogg	L. P. K.
William A. Ganoe	W. A. G.	Frederick P. Keppel	F. P. K.
Curtis W. Garrison	C. W. G.	John Kieran	J. K.
F. Lynwood Garrison	F. L. G.	Fiske Kimball	F. K.
Hazel Shields Garrison	H. S. G—n.	James Gore King, Jr.	J. G. K., Jr.
George Harvey Genzmer	G. H. G.	Richard R. Kirk	R. R. K.
John Lawrence Gerig	J. L. G.	Frank J. Klingberg	F. J. K.
W. J. Ghent	W. J. G.	Albert C. Knudson	A. C. K.
Edgar L. Gilcreest	E. L. G.	Ralph S. Kuykendall	R. S. K.
Leonidas Chalmers Glenn	L. C. G.	Leonard W. Labaree	L. W. L.
George W. Goble	G. W. G.	Robert La Follette	R. L-F.
Armistead Churchill Gordon, Jr.	A. C. G., Jr.	J. H. Landman	J. H. L.
Dorothy Grafly	D. G—y.	William Chauncy Langdon	W. C. L.
Charles Graves	C. G.	Conrad H. Lanza	C. H. L.
Henry S. Graves	H. S. G—s.	Kenneth S. Latourette	K. S. L.
Virginia Gearhart Gray	V. G. G.	William Lawrence	W. L.
Fletcher M. Green	F. M. G.	Anna Lane Lingelbach	A. L. L.
Dorothy Greenwald	D. G—d.	George W. Littlehales	G. W. L.
Anne King Gregorie	A. K. G.	Ella Lonn	E. L.
Martha Gruening	M. G.	Henry Noble MacCracken	H. N. M.
Gurney C. Gue	G. C. G.	Howard McClenahan	H. McC.
Sidney Gunn	S. G.	Roger P. McCutcheon	R. P. M.
Charles W. Hackett	C. W. H.	Joseph McFarland	J. McF.
Le Roy R. Hafen	L. R. H.	Walter M. McFarland	W. M. M.
Horace H. Hagan	H. H. H.	Alexius McGlannan	A. M.
Edwin H. Hall	E. H. H.	Reginald C. McGrane	R. C. M.
J. G. deR. Hamilton	J. G. deR. H.	Douglas C. McMurtrie	D. C. M.
Talbot Faulkner Hamlin	T. F. H.	T. F. McNeill	T. F. M.
		Helen Taft Manning	H. T. M.

Contributors

Asa Earl Martin	A. E. M.	J. Fred Rippy	J. F. R.
Karen Martin	K. M.	Frank H. Ristine	F. H. R.
William R. Maxon	W. R. M.	Donald A. Roberts	D. A. R.
Franklin J. Meine	F. J. M—e.	Burr Arthur Robinson	B. A. R.
Clarence W. Mendell	C. W. M—l.	Henry Morton Robinson	H. M. R.
A. Howard Meneely	A. H. M.	Herbert Spencer Robinson	H. S. R.
Newton D. Mereness	N. D. M.	William A. Robinson	W. A. R.
George P. Merrill	G. P. M.	James Grafton Rogers	J. G. R—s.
Frank J. Metcalf	F. J. M—f.	Eugene H. Roseboom	E. H. R.
Harvey C. Minnich	H. C. M.	Lois K. M. Rosenberry	L. K. M. R.
Broadus Mitchell	B. M.	Marvin B. Rosenberry	M. B. R.
Carl W. Mitman	C. W. M—n.	Henry Kalloch Rowe	H. K. R.
Harriet Monroe	H. M.	William Sener Rusk	W. S. R.
Robert E. Moody	R. E. M.	Verne Lockwood Samson	V. L. S.
John Hill Morgan	J. H. M.	M. G. Seelig	M. G. S.
Richard B. Morris	R. B. M.	Roy W. Sellars	R. W. S.
Jarvis M. Morse	J. M. M.	James Lee Sellers	J. L. S.
Sidney G. Morse	S. G. M.	Robert Francis Seybolt	R. F. S.
Harry W. Mountcastle	H. W. M.	George Dudley Seymour	G. D. S.
Kenneth B. Murdock	K. B. M.	Harry Shaw, Jr.	H. S., Jr.
I. William Nachlas	I. W. N.	William Bristol Shaw	W. B. S.
William Allan Neilson	W. A. N.	William E. Shea	W. E. S—a.
John Herbert Nelson	J. H. N.	Owen L. Shinn	O. L. S.
Lowry Nelson	L. N.	Lester B. Shippee	L. B. S.
H. Edward Nettles	H. E. N.	Richard H. Shryock	R. H. S.
Allan Nevins	A. N.	Wilbur H. Siebert	W. H. S—t.
A. R. Newsome	A. R. N.	Marian Silveus	M. S.
Franklin T. Nichols	F. T. N.	Francis Butler Simkins	F. B. S.
Jeannette P. Nichols	J. P. N.	Theodore Sizer	T. S—r.
Robert Hastings Nichols	R. H. N.	David Eugene Smith	D. E. S.
Roy F. Nichols	R. F. N.	Edward Conrad Smith	E. C. S.
Alexander D. Noyes	A. D. N.	Fred M. Smith	F. M. S.
Grace Lee Nute	G. L. N.	Warren Hunting Smith	W. H. S—h.
Robert B. Osgood	R. B. O.	William Roy Smith	W. R. S.
Victor H. Paltsits	V. H. P.	F. W. Sohon	F. W. S.
Scott H. Paradise	S. H. P.	Torald Sollmann	T. S—n.
Henry Bamford Parkes	H. B. P.	Herbert Solow	H. S.
Charles O. Paullin	C. O. P.	James P. C. Southall	J. P. C. S.
James H. Peeling	J. H. P.	E. Wilder Spaulding	E. W. S.
Henry F. Perkins	H. F. P—s.	Oliver L. Spaulding, Jr.	O. L. S., Jr.
Hobart S. Perry	H. S. P	Thomas M. Spaulding	T. M. S.
Frederick T. Persons	F. T. P.	Charles Worthen Spencer	C. W. S
James M. Phalen	J. M. P—n.	Robert E. Spiller	R. E. S.
Francis S. Philbrick	F. S. P.	Harris Elwood Starr	H. E. S.
Paul Chrisler Phillips	P. C. P.	Bertha Monica Stearns	B. M. S.
Ulrich B. Phillips	U. B. P.	George M. Stephenson	G. M. S.
David deSola Pool	D. deS. P.	Wendell H. Stephenson	W. H. S—n.
John M. Poor	J. M. P—r.	Wayne E. Stevens	W. E. S—s.
Alden L. Powell	A. L. P.	Helen R. Steward	H. R. S.
Julius W. Pratt	J. W. P.	George R. Stewart, Jr.	G. R. S., Jr.
Samuel C. Prescott	S. C. P.	Randall Stewart	R. S.
Henry F. Pringle	H. F. P—e.	Witmer Stone	W. S.
Charles McD. Puckette	C. M. P.	Carl G. Stroven	C. G. S.
Richard J. Purcell	R. J. P.	Edna Swenson Suber	E. S. S.
Arthur Hobson Quinn	A. H. Q.	Lionel M. Summers	L. M. S.
Charles Henry Rammelkamp	C. H. R.	William W. Sweet	W. W. S.
J. G. Randall	J. G. R—l.	Carl B. Swisher	C. B. S.
P. O. Ray	P. O. R.	Charles S. Sydnor	C. S. S.

Contributors

Thomas E. Tallmadge	T. E. T.	William H. Weston, Jr.	W. H. W., Jr.
Frank O. Taylor	F. O. T.	George F. Whicher	G. F. W.
William A. Taylor	W. A. T.	A. Curtis Wilgus	A. C. W.
Charles Hiram Thayer	C. H. T.	James F. Willard	J. F. W.
Charles M. Thomas	C. M. T.	Amelia Williams	A. W—s.
Irving L. Thomson	I. L. T.	Mary Wilhelmine Williams	M. W. W.
Willard Thorp	W. T.	Samuel C. Williams	S. C. W.
Edward Larocque Tinker	E. L. T.	Tyrrell Williams	T. W.
Charles C. Torrey	C. C. T.	H. Parker Willis	H. P. W.
Robert B. Tunstall	R. B. T.	Samuel Williston	S. W.
Alonzo H. Tuttle	A. H. T.	William H. Wilmer	W. H. W.
George B. Utley	G. B. U.	James Southall Wilson	J. S. W.
William T. Utter	W. T. U.	George B. Winton	G. B. W.
Robert W. G. Vail	R. W. G. V.	Clark Wissler	C. W.
John G. Van Deusen	J. G. V-D.	George Edward Woodbine	G. E. W.
Carl Van Doren	C. V-D.	Maude H. Woodfin	M. H. W.
Henry R. Viets	H. R. V.	Carl R. Woodward	C. R. W.
Harold G. Villard	H. G. V.	George Woolsey	G. W.
Eugene M. Violette	E. M. V.	C. P. Wright	C. P. W.
Albert T. Volwiler	A. T. V.	Walter L. Wright, Jr.	W. L. W., Jr.
Alexander J. Wall	A. J. W.	James Ingersoll Wyer	J. I. W.
Margaret F. Washburn	M. F. W.	Kimball Young	K. Y.
Francis P. Weisenburger	F. P. W.	Harold Zink	H. Z.
Allan Westcott	A. W—t.	Adolf Edward Zucker	A. E. Z.

DICTIONARY OF
AMERICAN BIOGRAPHY

Steward—Trowbridge

STEWARD, IRA (Mar. 10, 1831–Mar. 13, 1883), labor leader, was born in New London, Conn. At nineteen he went from Boston to Providence, R. I., and served an apprenticeship as a machinist under the twelve-hour system. Within a year he was agitating for shorter hours and was finally dismissed by the Draper Machine Company, for which he worked, because of "his peculiar views." In the fall of 1863, as a delegate to the convention of the International Union of Machinists and Blacksmiths in Boston, he secured the passage of a resolution that for the first time demanded an eight-hour labor law; he also secured large appropriations from his own union and the Boston Trades' Assembly for legislative lobbying. Henceforth, Steward and the eight-hour movement were one.

His insistence upon legislation in contrast to purely economic action by the unions sprang from his wish to reach the masses of the unskilled, whose low living standard constantly threatened the more advanced. He proposed to work through the existing political parties and to begin by endeavoring to secure an eight-hour day upon all government work. He labored indefatigably, appearing before every session of the Massachusetts legislature, contributing constantly to reform papers, making innumerable speeches, and organizing state and local eight-hour leagues. At the time of his death he was president of both the Boston Eight-Hour League and the National Ten-Hour League. Among Steward's influential co-laborers was Wendell Phillips [q.v.], who in 1869 helped establish the Massachusetts Bureau of Labor Statistics, the first in the country. Under Steward's friend, George E. McNeill [q.v.], as deputy chief, assisted by Steward's extremely able wife (Mary B.), the bureau published pioneer work on the condition of woman and child

wage-earners. Largely at its instance, Massachusetts in 1874 passed the first effective ten-hour law for women and children. Meanwhile, with the disbanding of the army after the Civil War, a number of eight-hour laws of the all-inclusive Steward type were pushed through various legislatures—six of them by 1867; but their opponents had so hedged them about with restrictions that they proved unenforceable. Steward opposed Greenbackism, as well as the formation of a separate labor party, but believed in the solidarity of labor and an ultimate socialistic state. In 1878 he and his followers, McNeill and young George Gunton [q.v.], joined with leading American members of the Marxian International Workingmen's Association to form the International Labor Union, the first large-scale attempt in America to organize the unskilled.

In 1878 Steward's wife died and he was "completely unnerved." For a number of years he had been planning a book to be entitled "The Political Economy of Eight Hours." Abandoning the post he had held since the early seventies as inspector at the Boston custom-house, he began to live upon the kindness of friends, ostensibly to write, but the book never materialized. In 1880 he moved to Plano, Ill., and married his cousin, Jane (Steward) Henning, a woman of considerable means. In March of 1883 he died there, aged only fifty-two. He left his unfinished notes to George Gunton who, finding them too fragmentary to put into shape for the press, published instead his own first book, *Wealth and Progress* (1887). For this action he was bitterly blamed by Steward's disciples. The original Steward manuscript is now in the library of the State Historical Society of Wisconsin. Like all Steward's writings, the fragments are keen and epigrammatic. Of published work, aside from articles in the *Daily Evening Voice* (Boston), the *Labor Standard,* and other papers, Steward left only one pamphlet, *A Reduction of Hours an Increase of Wages* (1865). It was republished together with the longest fragment from the manuscript collection, "The Power of the Cheaper over the Dearer," in *A Documentary History of American Industrial Society* (vol. IX, 1910), edited by J. R. Commons and others.

Steward's philosophy was strikingly novel for his day. He held that shorter hours develop leisure-time wants, hence a demand for higher wages; higher wages force the introduction of labor-saving machinery and better technique; these make possible mass production, which, to be stabilized, requires mass purchasing power. Mass purchasing power must be protected against the down drag of the unemployed by progressively shortening hours of labor in accordance with an index of unemployment. In the long run, effective regulation requires the cooperation of the leading industrial nations, which, in the 1860's, Steward considered ripe for an eight-hour limit. Ultimately, the working class would be able to buy the capitalist out—the abundance of its accumulations forcing down his interest rate—and thus inaugurate socialism. It was at this point that George Gunton broke away from his master and developed his own conclusion of a happy ending for capitalism, contending that higher wages would indeed result but also greater concentration of business and permanently increasing profits to present owners. Steward's influence in the labor movement suffered an eclipse when the body of American labor turned its back upon politics.

[*Chicago Daily Tribune,* Mar. 14, 1883; *Boston Commonwealth,* Mar. 24, 1883; *Comrade,* Dec. 1901; *American Federationist,* Apr., May 1902; J. R. Commons and others, *Hist. of Labour in the U. S.* (1918), vol. II; D. W. Douglas, "Ira Steward on Consumption and Unemployment," *Jour. of Pol. Econ.,* Aug. 1932.]

D. W. D.

STEWARDSON, JOHN (Mar. 21, 1858–Jan. 6, 1896), architect, was born in Philadelphia, the eldest child of Thomas and Margaret (Haines) Stewardson. His great-grandfather, Thomas, had emigrated from Westmoreland, England, to Philadelphia in 1789 and died in Newport, R. I., in 1841. The boy went first to private Philadelphia schools and, from 1873 to 1877, to Adams Academy at Quincy, Mass. He entered Harvard College with the class of 1881. At the end of two years he went to Paris and began his architectural study in the Atelier Pascal. He entered the École des Beaux Arts in 1881 and remained there but one year. During these three and a half years he spent all his leisure time in traveling over

France and sketching indefatigably. Upon his return to Philadelphia in 1882 he entered the office of T. P. Chandler. Working there and in other architects' offices until 1885, he rapidly became known for his ability and charm. In the meantime he had become acquainted with Walter Cope [*q.v.*], who like him was a pioneer in bringing into the garish and anarchic American architecture of the eighties a new taste, refinement, poise, and knowledge, and in 1886 they formed a partnership and entered on the career that was destined to be so important in improving the architecture of Philadelphia and the educational design of the whole country (see sketch of Cope). During this all-too-brief association of ten years, Stewardson found time for much additional travel, which undoubtedly vivified and stimulated the firm's output. He traveled in Italy and Belgium in 1888 and in England in 1894. It was on this later trip that he became so charmed with the brickwork of St. John's College in Cambridge that the University of Pennsylvania designs, then under way in the office, were changed from stone to brick stone-trimmed—the tower of the dormitory group there bears the date 1895.

He was one of those architects who are primarily artists. His many water colors, rich yet delicate, reveal the sensitiveness of his taste, which kept its basic romanticism from becoming sentimental or mawkish. Even his three years in Paris seem only to have deepened his love for the varied and fluid forms of Gothic, especially English Gothic, architecture, at a time when other Americans were being made over into good, bad, or mediocre classicists. The choir screen of St. Luke's Church in Philadelphia (erroneously attributed solely to Cope but chiefly the work of Stewardson) shows his sure Gothic sense; and the quietness of the Bryn Mawr College work and the directness of Blair Hall at Princeton University still set them off in contrast to the extravagances of much later work beside them. He had a love for people of all kinds that amounted to social genius and was attested by the many expressions of grief at his untimely death, alike from friends, office mates, and architects all over the country. In 1897 his friends collected a fund that was given to the University of Pennsylvania to endow a traveling fellowship under the auspices of the school of architecture, the Stewardson Fellowship. He was a fellow of the American Institute of Architects, one of the founders, and president, 1885–86 and 1891–92, of the T-Square Club. He was a member of the Episcopal Church. Tall and thin, he had always a passion for outdoor life of all kinds. He loved dogs and horses and rode a great deal, in the course of visits of inspection to works being carried on in the Philadelphia suburbs as well as for pleasure. He liked boating and skating. On a winter afternoon he went skating on the Schuylkill with some friends. In the late dusk he was separated from them; and there was heard the sound of breaking ice, and a cry, then silence. This accident seemed the more tragic because of his approaching marriage.

[Information from his brother, Emlyn Stewardson, his sister, M. M. Stewardson, and his former colleague, James P. Jamieson; manuscript of address of R. Clipston Sturgis, June 16, 1917, at the unveiling of a memorial tablet to Cope and Stewardson in Blair Hall, Princeton, in possession of Emlyn Stewardson and of author; *Third Report of . . . Class of 1881 of Harvard College* (1887); *Fifth Report . . . of 1881* (1898); *Brickbuilder*, Jan. 1896; *Am. Arch. and Building News*, Jan. 11, 1896.]　　　　　　　　　　T. F. H.

STEWART, ALEXANDER PETER (Oct. 2, 1821–Aug. 30, 1908), Confederate soldier, chancellor of the University of Mississippi, was born of Scotch-Irish ancestry in Rogersville, Tenn., the son of William and Elizabeth (Decherd) Stewart. At the age of seventeen he was appointed to the United States Military Academy, graduating in 1842. He was commissioned second lieutenant in the 3rd Artillery, but after being stationed a little over a year at Fort Macon on the coast of North Carolina, he was recalled to West Point to serve as assistant professor of mathematics. In May 1845 he resigned from the army, and on Aug. 7 of that year was married to Harriet Byron Chase, of Trumbull County, Ohio. From that time until the Civil War he was professor of mathematics and natural and experimental philosophy in Cumberland University at Lebanon, Tenn., and in Nashville University.

Although a Whig who had voted against secession, Stewart volunteered early and was made a major in the Confederate army. He soon distinguished himself, especially while in command of the heavy artillery at Columbus, Ky., and at the battle of Belmont. In consequence he was commissioned brigadier-general in Cheatham's division at the battle of Shiloh, and served with this division in the Kentucky campaign and the retreat toward Chattanooga. On June 2, 1863, he was advanced to the rank of major-general and was placed in command of a division of Hardee's corps. After participating in the fighting at Chattanooga and Chickamauga, his division took part in the campaign from Dalton to Atlanta, and he was made lieutenant-general on June 23, 1864, after Gen. Leonidas Polk was killed. Stewart was wounded in the battle of Mount Ezra Church near Atlanta. At the close of the war he was in North Carolina commanding the Army of the Tennessee.

After the war he turned for a second time from military to civil life and resumed his professorship in Cumberland University. Early in 1870 he made his only excursion into the field of business by going to St. Louis, Mo., to become secretary of the St. Louis Mutual Life Insurance Company. In 1874 he was elected chancellor of the University of Mississippi. His experience as a teacher, his prestige as a lieutenant-general, and his strong character were all needed, for the future of the university was not promising and attendance was decreasing. In private, the university students continued to refer to him as "Old Straight," the nickname first used by his soldiers during the war, both because of his military bearing and because of the impartial decisions which he strictly enforced during his twelve-year administration. Resigning in 1886, he spent the next four years partly in traveling and partly in the home of his son in St. Louis. When the Chickamauga and Chattanooga National Military Park was created in 1890, Stewart was appointed by President Harrison as the Confederate member of the controlling board of three commissioners. Taking his duties with characteristic seriousness, he moved to the reservation, supervised the laying out of roads and the placing of monuments, and had actual custody of the park for some years. In 1904 his health began to fail and two years later he moved to Biloxi, Miss., where he spent the last two years of his life. He performed his duties as park commissioner by correspondence. He was survived by his three sons, and is buried in Bellefontaine Cemetery in St. Louis.

[*Who's Who in America*, 1908–09; G. W. Cullum, *Biog. Reg. . . . Officers and Grads. U. S. Mil. Acad.* (1891); *War of the Rebellion: Official Records*, see Index; *Confed. Mil. Hist.* (1899), vol. I; *Confed. Veteran*, Sept. 1908, Jan. 1909; *Hist. Cat. of the Univ. of Miss., 1849–1909* (1910); New Orleans *Times-Democrat, St. Louis Globe-Democrat*, and *Chattanooga News*, Aug. 31, 1908.]　　　　　　　　　　C. S. S.

STEWART, ALEXANDER TURNEY (Oct. 12, 1803–Apr. 10, 1876), merchant, son of Alexander and Margaret (Turney) Stewart, was born in Lisburn, County Antrim, Ireland, of Scotch Protestant parents in modestly comfortable circumstances. His father died shortly after or before the birth of Alexander, and the latter at an early age was placed under the care of his maternal grandfather. The boy was bright, orderly, and careful, and the grandfather, intending to fit him for the ministry, placed him in an academy in Belfast. After his grandfather died, young Stewart, not predisposed toward clerical duties but with no definite notion as to a career, decided to visit America. He reached New York;

perhaps in 1820, bearing letters of introduction to several prominent persons, and for some months lived a quiet and rather studious life. For a short time he taught in a private school. He returned home to claim an inheritance, which amounted to $5,000 or more in American money. He had intended investing this in Ireland, but it is said that an American friend urged him to go into trade in New York, specifically advising him to import Irish laces. He knew little of business, but decided to follow the advice, and so invested about $3,000 in laces, returned to New York, and late in the summer of 1823 opened a small shop on lower Broadway in a room measuring twelve by thirty feet. Shortly he moved to a larger store, and soon afterward to another.

From the first he displayed not only a canniness in observing the market and the fashions, but an exactitude in method which was uncommon at the period. During the business depression of 1837 and thereafter, he bought at auction many stocks of merchants who had failed, and made good profits on them. In 1846 he built a marble-faced building at Broadway and Chambers Street, in which he installed both wholesale and retail dry-goods business (Stokes, *post*, vol. V). In 1850 he extended the building to Reade Street, and now had the largest establishment in the city. He had gained a large trade among wealthy and fashionable folk, and his business again rapidly outgrew its quarters. In 1862 he completed a new building of steel and stone, eight stories high, covering the entire block between Ninth and Tenth Streets, Broadway and Fourth Avenue, and costing nearly $2,750,000, and there opened what was then the largest retail store in the world. His wholesale department remained in the older building at Chambers Street. Stewart's enterprises had now become colossal for their day, and would have been remarkable at a much later date. In his new store some 2,000 persons were employed, and the current expenses were about $100,000 a year. The total sales of his wholesale and retail stores for the three years preceding his death were $203,000,000. During the Civil War, when he had large Army and Navy contracts, his annual income averaged nearly $2,000,000. In carrying on this huge business, he always paid cash for purchases, though he sold on credit, as did other merchants. He built or acquired a controlling interest in numerous mills in New England, New York, and New Jersey, manufacturing cotton, silk, and woolen goods, blankets, ribbons, thread, and carpets. For the buying of foreign merchandise, he installed offices and warehouses in several cities of England, in Ireland, Scotland, France, Germany, and

Switzerland. At his death he also owned the Grand Union Hotel and a retail store at Saratoga Springs, the Metropolitan Hotel, the Globe Theater, Niblo's Garden, and other enterprises in New York City. He was a shrewd trader and a strict disciplinarian. Some of his methods of dealing with employees, notably a system of money fines for lapses, were regarded as rigid and harsh, but he drove no one harder than he drove himself. There was much criticism of him during his life, the most justifiable being of a wage policy that was low even for his time, and acridity is seen in editorial comment after his death. However, he gave largely to charity at times; he sent a shipload of provisions to Ireland during the famine of 1847, and brought the vessel back loaded with immigrants, for many of whom he found work in America. During the Civil War he offered to give to the Sanitary Commission as much as Cornelius Vanderbilt did. Vanderbilt, piqued by this challenge, raised his subscription two or three times until at length he and Stewart each drew a check for $100,000. Stewart sent a shipload of flour to France after its war with Prussia in 1871, and in the same year gave $50,000 to the Chicago fire sufferers. In 1862 he gave $10,000 for the relief of English cotton mill operatives. At the time of his death he was erecting a building intended to supply working women and girls with board and lodging at cost; but the building later became the Park Avenue Hotel. Stewart's greatest semi-altruistic enterprise was the purchase of Hempstead Plains on Long Island, where he built the "model town" of Garden City for persons of modest means. He was appointed secretary of the treasury by President Grant in 1869 and confirmed, but was barred by the section of the law of Sept. 2, 1789, prohibiting the holding of the post by a man engaged in business (1 *Statutes at Large*, 67). A bill was introduced to repeal the section, and Stewart offered to turn his business over to trustees and donate its profits to charity during his incumbency, but action was indefinitely postponed. Meanwhile, George S. Boutwell was appointed to the post "to fill a vacancy."

Shortly after the Civil War Stewart erected a mansion on Fifth Avenue which was long regarded as the finest in America. There he gave sumptuous dinners and receptions, at which there were guests ranging from diplomats and millionaires to struggling artists and musicians. Stewart was a small, wiry, active man with sharp features, keen blue eyes, and reddish-sandy hair; he was always carefully dressed. He was survived for ten years by his wife, the former Cornelia Mitchell Clinch, whom he married on Oct.

16, 1823. On Nov. 7, 1878, the coffin containing his remains was stolen from the family vault in St. Mark's churchyard and held for reward, which was paid in 1880; the reinterment was at Garden City.

[Obituaries and editorials in *N. Y. Times*, Mar. 6–12, 1869, Apr. 11–14, 1876, Oct. 26, 1886; *Evening Post* (N. Y.), Apr. 10, 11, 13, 1876; *Sun* (N. Y.), Apr. 11–14, 1876; *Frank Leslie's Illustrated Newspaper*, Apr. 22, 1876; *Harper's Weekly*, Apr. 29, 1876; *Harper's New Monthly Magazine*, March 1867; A. T. Stewart Scrap Book, N. Y. Pub. Lib.; I. N. Phelps Stokes, *The Iconography of Manhattan Island*, vols. V, VI (1918–28); C. H. Haswell, *Reminiscences of an Octogenarian of the City of N. Y.* (1896); M. H. Smith, *Sunshine and Shadow in N. Y.* (1868); *The Posthumous Relatives of the Late Alex. T. Stewart. Procs. before the Surrogate. Extracts from Newspapers, etc.* (1876); New York City tax records; and Burial Certificate No. 234,380.]   A. F. H.

STEWART, ALVAN (Sept. 1, 1790–May 1, 1849), lawyer, abolitionist, was born in South Granville, N. Y., the son of Uriel Stewart, who five years after the boy's birth moved to Westford, Chittenden County, Vt. Alvan attended district school and in 1809 entered the University of Vermont, leaving there in 1812 to teach in Canada. After a visit home he was arrested as a spy in Schoharie County, N. Y., and upon his release went to Cherry Valley, Otsego County, N. Y., where he taught school and studied law. In 1815 he journeyed as far West as Paris, Ky., and there spent a year teaching and studying. He then traveled in the South for a time, finally returning to Cherry Valley, where he was admitted to the bar. About 1832 he moved to Utica. Here he acquired a considerable reputation as a lawyer and was regarded as a most formidable adversary before a jury (Proctor, *post*, p. 220). Originally a Democrat, he became an aggressive protectionist, and in 1828 published a pamphlet, *Common Sense*, opposing Jackson on the tariff question.

In 1834 he joined the newly organized American Anti-Slavery Society, and at once took the lead in establishing abolitionist organizations in New York. In 1835 he issued a call for a convention, which assembled at Utica on Oct. 21, and formed the New York State Anti-Slavery Society. During the next few years, as the society's president, he labored incessantly, collecting money, organizing auxiliaries, and making speeches. These speeches, characterized by a wildfire humor and a vivid, if somewhat exuberant, imagination, earned for him the title of humorist of the anti-slavery movement. He aspired to another title, however, that of constitutionalist to the cause. Basing his argument upon the due process clause of the Constitution, he contended that slaves were deprived of their freedom without due process of law, and that slavery itself was therefore in violation of the Constitution. This view he attempted to persuade the American Anti-Slavery Society at its 1838 meeting to adopt. It so outraged William Jay [*q.v.*], son of the great jurist, that he withdrew from the society; and though Stewart won over to his views a majority of the delegates, he was unable to convince the two-thirds necessary to amend the anti-slavery creed.

As president of the New York State Anti-Slavery Society, he took the position that the national society had no jurisdiction within the bounds of his organization. In the 1838 convention of the latter he proposed that agents of the national society be excluded from all the state auxiliaries, and the proposal was adopted. Furthermore, at the New York State Society headquarters, he opposed the pledging of contributions to the support of the national society. "A dollar spent at Utica," he told his constituents, "is worth three spent at New York." Erratic, independent, and intractable by nature, he placed himself at the head of the faction opposed to the operations of the American Anti-Slavery Society. More than any other abolitionist except William Lloyd Garrison [*q.v.*] he was responsible for the disruption of the national movement, which occurred in 1840.

At an early date Stewart had urged separate political anti-slavery organization. In 1840 he joined with Myron Holley [*q.v.*], the leading political abolitionist, in calling an anti-slavery political convention, which met in Albany, on Apr. 1, with Stewart as presiding officer. This convention organized the Liberty Party and nominated James G. Birney [*q.v.*] for president and Stewart for governor of New York; but in the subsequent campaign, Birney received only a few thousand votes and Stewart a few hundred. Disgusted with the outcome of political action, he returned to private life. He still served as president of the diminished New York society, and on occasion he donated his services as counsel for the slave. Before the supreme court of New Jersey, in a test case arranged by local abolitionists, he challenged the constitutionality of slavery with eloquence (*A Legal Argument before the Supreme Court of the State of New Jersey . . . for the Deliverance of Four Thousand Persons from Bondage*, 1845). In his early years he "was quite too much given to his cups," but later became an advocate of total abstinence and an effective temperance lecturer (Beardsley, *post*, pp. 159, 169). In 1835 he published *Prize Address for the New York City Temperance Society*. His wife was Keziah Holt of Cherry Valley, N. Y., by whom he had five children, three of them dying young. In 1860 *Writings and Speeches of Alvan Stewart on Slavery* was published by his son-in-law, Luther R. Marsh.

[*The Friend of Man* (Utica, N. Y.), 1835–42; *Emancipator* (N. Y. and Boston), 1833–42; Bayard Tuckerman, *William Jay and the Constitutional Movement for the Abolition of Slavery* (1893); Levi Beardsley, *Reminiscences* (1852); L. B. Proctor, *The Bench and Bar of N. Y.* (1870); G. H. Barnes, *The Anti-Slavery Impulse* (1933); D. S. Durrie, *A Geneal. Hist. of the Holt Family in the U. S.* (1864); *N. Y. Tribune*, May 3, 1849; *Oneida Morning Herald*, May 4, 1849.]

G. H. B.

STEWART, ANDREW (June 11, 1791–July 16, 1872), congressman from Pennsylvania, was born on his father's farm in German Township, Fayette County, Pa., the eldest son of Abraham and Mary (Oliphant) Stewart. Both parents were natives of Pennsylvania; the father had removed to Fayette County from York County, and the mother from Chester County before their marriage in 1789. Andrew attended the local schools, helping to defray expenses by working on a farm, teaching school, and working as a clerk in a store. He studied law in Uniontown, and on Jan. 9, 1815, he was admitted to the Fayette County bar. From 1815 to 1818 he was a member of the state House of Representatives. In 1818 he was appointed federal attorney for the western district of Pennsylvania, a position he held until his election to Congress in 1820. Believing the protective tariff and internal improvements to be the mainstays of the prosperity of the country as well as of Pennsylvania, he took up the cudgels in their behalf. He was returned to Congress continuously until 1828, when his support of Adams against Jackson led to his defeat. He was reëlected in 1830 and 1832 but was again defeated in 1834. In 1842 he was elected as a Whig, and after three terms he declined a renomination. In 1848 he was a candidate for the nomination for vice-president; and because of illness he was obliged to decline an appointment as secretary of the treasury in President Taylor's Cabinet. In 1870 he ran for Congress as a Republican but was defeated.

His speeches in Congress in defense of the protective tariff and advocating internal improvements received considerable attention; many of them were printed in full in Whig newspapers; and editions amounting to several hundred thousand copies were published in pamphlet form. Of these a collection, *The American System. Speeches on the Tariff Question, and on Internal Improvements, Principally Delivered in the House of Representatives of the United States* (1872), is perhaps the most important. He was so zealous an·advocate of protection that he was known to

his contemporaries as "Tariff Andy." Tall and of vigorous build his personality lent weight to his arguments, which, not devoid of humor, are set forth in plain and understandable terms and evidence an exhaustive knowledge of his subject. Among specific enterprises that he supported were the Cumberland road, the Chesapeake and Ohio Canal, and the Pittsburgh, Connellsville, and Baltimore railroad. He was a director in the Chesapeake and Ohio Canal Company. Besides his political interests he conducted an extensive private business in building and real estate; he erected and managed a blast furnace and numerous saw and flour mills; and he rebuilt a glass factory. He owned considerable property in Uniontown, on some of which he erected tenant houses; and the real estate that passed through his hands has been estimated at eighty thousand acres. In 1825 he married Elizabeth, the daughter of David Shriver of Cumberland, Md., superintendent of the eastern division of the National Road. They had six children. Stewart Township, in eastern Fayette County, was named for him.

[*Memoirs of John Quincy Adams*, vols. VII–XII (1875–77), ed. by C. F. Adams; *Biog. Dir. of the Am. Cong.* (1928); *History of Fayette County, Pennsylvania* (1882), ed. by Franklin Ellis, pp. 363, 595, 775; James Hadden, *A Hist. of Uniontown* (1913), pp. 775–778; *Biographical and Portrait Cyclopedia of Fayette County* (1889), ed. by J. M. Gresham; *Pittsburgh Commercial* and the *Pittsburgh Gazette*, July 17, 1872.]

S. J. B.

STEWART, CHARLES (July 28, 1778–Nov. 6, 1869), naval officer, was born in Philadelphia, Pa., and died at Bordentown, N, J. He was the son of Charles and Sarah (Ford) Stewart, who some years prior to the American Revolution emigrated from Belfast, Ireland, to Philadelphia. The elder Charles Stewart pursued a seafaring life, and at the time of his death, in 1780, appears to have been master of a merchant vessel. His widow, left with slender funds at her disposal, subsequently had great difficulty in providing for her eight children. Charles, the youngest, soon turned to the sea, securing, at the age of thirteen, employment as a cabin boy in the merchant service. During the next few years he rose through the successive grades until he became master of a merchantman.

When the dispute between the United States and France occurred, young Stewart entered the navy. On Mar. 9, 1798, he was commissioned lieutenant and began a cruise in West Indian waters aboard the frigate *United States*. On July 16, 1800, he received command of the schooner *Experiment*, which soon captured two armed French vessels, recaptured a number of American merchantmen, and, through an error in identity, badly crippled a Bermudian privateer. The

Experiment also provided convoy, and, near the end of the cruise, rescued a large number of women and children who had been shipwrecked after fleeing from the negro uprising in Santo Domingo. After returning to Norfolk in 1801, Stewart was for a time in charge of the frigate *Chesapeake,* but in 1802 went to the Mediterranean as first officer of the frigate *Constellation.* At the end of a year he was again in America. Receiving command of the brig *Siren,* he returned to the Mediterranean, where he participated in the destruction of the *Philadelphia* after its capture by the Tripolitans; engaged in maintaining a strict blockade of Tripoli; and distinguished himself in the numerous assaults upon the enemy during August and September 1804. At the close of the War with Tripoli he proceeded with the squadron under the command of Commodore John Rodgers, 1773–1838 [*q.v.*], to Tunis for the purpose of quieting that regency. The desired settlement was soon effected, and Stewart, commissioned captain, Apr. 22, 1806, returned to the United States. During a portion of the years 1806 and 1807 he was engaged in supervising the construction of gunboats at New York, and until the outbreak of the War of 1812 participated in commercial enterprises which took him to the East Indies, the Mediterranean, and the Adriatic.

At the outset of the struggle with Great Britain he urged a vigorous use of the navy. He soon received command of the brig *Argus* and the sloop-of-war *Hornet*; then, in December 1812, became commander of the *Constellation.* A superior British force kept the frigate confined at Norfolk, and during the summer of 1813 Stewart took charge of the *Constitution,* then being refitted at Boston. With her he subsequently made a brilliant record. On a cruise beginning in December 1813 he destroyed several British vessels, and in April of the following year returned to Boston after evading a strong blockading squadron. In December 1814 he again slipped out of the harbor. On this second cruise, while in the vicinity of the Madeira Islands, he separated and captured two British warships—the small frigate *Cyane* and the sloop-of-war *Levant.* A British squadron eventually recaptured the *Levant,* but Stewart succeeded in bringing the *Cyane* to the United States. In consequence of these achievements he received a great ovation from the people of New York, a sword of honor from the legislature of Pennsylvania, and a gold medal from Congress.

Stewart's service during the remainder of his life was varied. In 1816 ne was given command of the ship of the line *Franklin,* and during the following year sailed to the Mediterranean,

where he commanded a squadron until 1820. He subsequently served, until 1824, as commodore of a squadron in the Pacific; was a naval commissioner during the years 1830–32; and at various times (1838–41, 1846, 1854–61) had charge of the navy yard at Philadelphia. By act of Congress, Mar. 2, 1859, he was made "senior flag officer" (an office created for him in recognition of his distinguished and meritorious service). In 1862 he became rear-admiral on the retired list, and thereafter lived in his country house, "Old Ironsides," at Bordentown. On Nov. 25, 1813, while the *Constitution* was being refitted, he had married Delia Tudor, sister of Frederic Tudor [*q.v.*], and a member of an affluent and socially prominent Boston family. Two children from this union survived their father: Delia Tudor and Charles Tudor Stewart. The latter became a successful civil engineer and lawyer; the former married John Henry Parnell, and became the mother of Charles Stewart Parnell, eminent Home Rule advocate in the British Parliament.

With respect to person, Stewart has been described as about five feet nine inches in height, well proportioned, and prepossessing in appearance. He has been unstintedly praised for his coolness and courage in times of stress; for his broad and vigorous mentality, for his fund of information on a wide range of domestic and foreign subjects; and for his conversational abilities, which made him a favorite at social gatherings.

[*Stewart Clan Mag.,* Oct. 1930–31; *Biog. Sketch and Services of Commodore Charles Stewart* (1838); E. S. Ellis, "Old Ironsides," *Chautauquan,* July 1898; John Frost, *Am. Naval Biog.* (1844); Charles Morris, *Heroes of the Navy in America* (1907); C. J. Peterson, *The Am. Navy . . . and Biog Sketches of Am. Naval Heroes* (1858); Thomas Sherlock, *The Life of Chas. Stewart Parnell* (1881); William Tudor, *Deacon Tudor's Diary* (1896); *Pub. Ledger* (Phila.), Nov. 8, 1869.]

R. W. I.

STEWART, EDWIN (May 5, 1837–Feb. 28, 1933), naval officer, was born in New York City, son of John and Mary (Aikman) Stewart, and a younger brother of John Aikman Stewart [*q.v.*]. His father, a native of Lewis, in the Hebrides, had come to America from Stornoway, Scotland, when a boy. Edwin attended Phillips Academy, Andover, Mass., and later entered Williams College, preparatory to the study of law. His college work was interrupted by the Civil War, however, and though he received the degree of A.B. from Williams with the class of 1862, he joined the navy Sept. 9, 1861, as assistant paymaster.

He served first in the *Pembina* in the Port Royal campaign and, after promotion to paymaster Apr. 14, 1862, in the *Richmond.* West

Gulf Squadron, in operations on the Mississippi and at the battle of Mobile Bay. After the war, he was in the *Michigan* on the Great Lakes, 1865–68; fleet paymaster in the *Hartford*, Asiatic Squadron, 1872–75; and then for several years chiefly at New York, where in 1880–83 he was an inspector of provisions and clothing. Following duty in the *Lancaster*, European Squadron, he returned to New York as chief pay officer, and through his reports was largely instrumental in accomplishing the reform by which naval purchases, hitherto made by several bureaus, were centralized in a new bureau of supplies and accounts. He was appointed paymaster general, with the rank of commodore, and head of the bureau on May 16, 1890, and, with reappointments in 1894 and 1898, held this important post throughout the period of the Spanish-American War and up to his retirement for age May 5, 1899. He had been made pay director, then the highest rank of his corps, Sept. 12, 1891, and on May 5, 1899, he was made rear admiral. Secretary of the Navy John D. Long commended highly the work of Stewart's bureau, declaring that it was "performed with the most gratifying efficiency and promptness" (*Annual Reports of the Navy Department for the Year 1898*, I, 42). In his own report (*Ibid.*, pp. 665–670) Stewart remarked that his bureau had carried on the work of three army departments—pay corps, quartermaster general, and commissary—and that despite wartime expenditures amounting in 1898 to $11,422,640, the prices paid "were in most cases no higher, and in many cases lower, than before the commencement of hostilities." Notable in his handling of wartime supply problems was the use of refrigerator ships with both the Cuban and Philippine forces, and his pre-war memorandum anticipating the needs of Dewey's squadron. The latter prompted the departmental order of Apr. 6, 1898, enabling Dewey to purchase within forty-eight hours the collier *Nanshan* and supply ship *Zafiro* at Hongkong and load them with five months' stores.

After his retirement Stewart lived in Washington, D. C., until 1901, and later at South Orange, N. J., where he died in his ninety-sixth year, the oldest officer on the navy list. His burial was in Arlington Cemetery. He was commander of the District of Columbia Commandery, Military Order of the Loyal Legion, in 1900, and in 1913–17 was vice commander-in-chief of the Legion's national organization. He was twice married: first, Aug. 24, 1865, to Laura S. Tufts of Andover, Mass., who died Feb. 3, 1875, during his absence on the Asiatic station; and second, May 17, 1877, to Susan Maria, daughter of Ed-

ward Estabrook of Platteville, Wis. He had two sons by each marriage, three of whom survived him, one of them a naval officer.

[L. R. Hamersly, *The Records of Living Officers of the U. S. Navy and Marine Corps* (7th ed. 1902); *Fiftieth Anniv. Report of the Williams College Class of '62* (1913); *Who's Who in America*, 1920–21; *Army and Navy Reg.*, Mar. 4, 1933; *Army and Navy Jour.*, May 6, 1899; *Sun* (N. Y.), Feb. 28, 1933; *N. Y. Times*, Mar. 1, 1933.]   A. W—t.

STEWART, ELIZA DANIEL (Apr. 25, 1816–Aug. 6, 1908), humanitarian, advocate of temperance, was the daughter of James Daniel, a Southerner, and Rebecca (Guthery) Daniel. Her grandfather, Capt. John Guthery, an officer of the Revolution, founded Piketon, Ohio, where Eliza was born. She was orphaned at the age of twelve, and after being educated in Ohio seminaries, she earned her living by teaching school for many years. In 1848 she married Hiram Stewart, who died a few months later. During the Civil War she gathered and sent sanitary supplies to the Union armies and visited the sick soldiers, who gave her the name "Mother" Stewart, by which she was commonly known. She helped form the first woman's suffrage organization in 1869 in Springfield, Ohio, where she then lived, and was elected president. She was also active in charity work in Ohio, and was a member of the first national board of charities.

Her first and greatest interest, however, was in the fight against strong drink. In 1858 she became a charter member of the Good Templar Lodge founded in her home town, and until her death she campaigned with voice and pen against the use of liquor. Her most effective work began on Jan. 22, 1872, when she lectured on temperance in Springfield. Shortly afterwards she published in a city paper an appeal to women signed "A Drunkard's Wife." In 1872 and again in 1874, she made an eloquent and successful plea in court in a suit of a drunkard's wife against a saloon keeper, gaining wide publicity for her cause. She arranged temperance mass meetings in Springfield and other cities and in 1873 held prayer meetings in saloons, acting upon a suggestion of Dioclesian Lewis [*q.v.*], who had come West to investigate Mother Stewart's work. Under her leadership the praying "Crusade" against the drinksellers spread throughout the state and closed many drinking places—which soon opened, convincing her of the need for greater organization to secure outlawry of the liquor traffic. In December 1873 she had formed a Woman's League in Osborne, Ohio, the first organization in the Women's Christian Temperance Union movement. The next month she was made president of the new Springfield Union; then came

8

county organization; and soon afterwards she formed in Ohio the first state W. C. T. U. She was a leader in the rapid extension of the work into other Northern states, and in 1878 she traveled widely in the South, organizing both white and colored women. She spent five months in 1876 in Great Britain, lecturing and holding prayer meetings, which opened the "Whisky War," and resulted in the organization of the British Women's Temperance Association and the Scottish Christian Union.

In 1891 she represented the National W. C. T. U. at the World's Convention of Good Templars held in Edinburgh, and in 1895 she attended the World's W. C. T. U. Convention in London and made the opening speech. She spent the last five years of her life at Hicksville, Ohio, where she died. In addition to various articles on temperance, she wrote two books: *Memories of the Crusade* (1888), and *The Crusader in Great Britain* (1893). Mother Stewart had much personal charm, and was an original and forceful speaker. She was of medium height and ample figure, with a firm, kindly face set with piercing black eyes.

[Consult Mrs. Stewart's own works; *Who's Who in America*, 1903–05; C. C. Chapin, *Thumb Nail Sketches of White Ribbon Women* (1891); E. P. Gordon, *Women Torch-Bearers* (2nd ed., 1924); *Cyc. of Temperance and Prohibition* (1891); F. E. Willard and M. A. Livermore, *Portraits and Biographies of Prominent Am. Women* (copr. 1901); *Union Signal*, Aug. 13, 27, 1908; *Ohio State Jour.* (Columbus), Aug. 8, 1908.]   M. W. W.

STEWART, GEORGE NEIL (Apr. 18, 1860– May 28, 1930), physiologist, the son of James Innes and Catherine (Sutherland) Stewart, was born at London, Ontario, whither his parents, emigrants from Caithness, Scotland, had gone to engage in the fur trade with the Indians. After a few years, they returned to the towns of Wick and Lybster in Scotland on the North Sea, where his father engaged in the herring industry. The head-master of the village school became interested in the boy and prepared him for Edinburgh University. He matriculated in 1879, at the age of nineteen, and remained for seven years, receiving successively degrees in arts, M.A. in 1883, with honors in mathematics; in science, B.S. in 1886 and D.Sc. in 1887; in medicine, C.M. and M.B. in 1889, and M.D. in 1891; and finally, LL.D., *honoris causa,* in 1920. During his first year at Edinburgh, he served as assistant in physics to Tait, and it may be presumed that this contact with the brilliant and scholarly physicist fixed his taste for exact and experimental science and thus determined the cast of his life work. In Tait's laboratory he started his first research, and the application of physics to biology dominated his earlier and much of his later investigations.

In the winter of 1886 he went to Berlin to work on electro-physiology, under the renowned Emil Du Bois-Reymond, and from 1887 to 1889 he served an excellent apprenticeship in practical teaching as demonstrator of physiology, including histology and biochemistry, at Manchester, under William Stirling. He held the George Henry Lewes scholarship in physiology at Cambridge from 1889 to 1893, and was one of the group of brilliant young investigators who worked under the guidance of Sir Michael Foster and laid the foundations and established the traditions that are the glory of British physiology. He worked chiefly on the velocity of blood flow, on temperature regulation, and on the cardiac nerves. He also took the recently established course in public health, and secured the degree of D.P.H. at Cambridge in 1890. From 1891 to 1894 he served also as external examiner in physiology at the University of Aberdeen, and thus kept in contact with medical teaching.

He came to America in 1893 as an instructor at Harvard under Bowditch, and in 1894 was appointed to the chair of physiology at Western Reserve University, Cleveland, Ohio. To this, his first independent post, he gave nine of his best years. He supplemented his admirable didactic instructions with "practical exercises" by the students, to an extent which had not been deemed feasible before, especially with mammalian experiments, and which had a profound and lasting influence on the teaching of the subject in America. He incorporated his presentation of physiology in a textbook, *A Manual of Physiology* (1896), which was widely used and reached an eighth edition in 1918. Stewart continued his investigations, at first chiefly on circulation time, and then on the electric conductivity of the blood and hemolysis, as an approach to the problem of cell permeability. In 1903 he accepted the invitation to become the successor of Jacques Loeb [*q.v.*] as head of the department of physiology at the University of Chicago. He welcomed especially the new opportunity of teaching graduate students in physiology. His own investigations in this period were on cerebral anemia, resuscitation, and the respiratory center.

In 1907, friends of Western Reserve University established the H. K. Cushing Laboratory of Experimental Medicine, with the double purpose of promoting the experimental investigation of disease, and of attracting Stewart back to Cleveland. He accepted the invitation and headed this laboratory until his death. From 1910 to 1915 he devised and applied a calorimetric method of measuring the blood flow, suitable for clinical use. Between 1916 and 1923, he worked intensively on the epinephrine output of the adrenal glands, with the assistance of J. M. Rogoff. Their experiments led to the conclusion that the epinephrine output is not sufficient to perform the functions of a fight-and-fright hormone which had been attributed to it. From 1924 to 1927 they investigated the course of the removal of the adrenal glands, and proved that these effects are due entirely to deficiency of the adrenal cortex. They showed that life is prolonged by pregnancy, and in 1927 definitely established the efficiency of extracts of adrenal cortex. The results of these investigations were summarized in 1926 in the eleventh Mellon lecture (*Archives of Internal Medicine,* June 1929). Up to the time of his death, they were engaged in the purification of these extracts, to increase their safety for clinical use.

Although he lived in the United States for thirty-seven years Stewart remained a British citizen. He was a prodigious worker, with a brilliant intellect, keen penetration, sound judgment, and an infinite respect for facts. A rapid thinker, he had the power of vivid and lucid presentation, based upon broad culture and deep learning, a sense of human values and a quick and apt humor. During the later years of his life he was handicapped by the developments of pernicious anemia, to which he finally succumbed at Cleveland. He was survived by three sons, a daughter, and his widow, Louise Kate (Powell) Stewart, to whom he had been married on Sept. 20, 1906.

[J. J. R. Macleod, *Nature,* June 28, 1930; Torald Sollmann, *Bull. Acad. Med.* (Cleveland), July 1930; *Science,* Aug. 15, 1930; J. M. Rogoff, *Collected Papers H. K. Cushing Lab. Experimental Med.,* Western Reserve University, vol. IX (1927–31); *Cleveland Plain Dealer,* May 29, 1930.]   T. S—n.

STEWART, HUMPHREY JOHN (May 22, 1854–Dec. 28, 1932), organist, composer, was born in London, England, the son of Humphrey Stark of Reading, Berks County. At the age of eleven he began his career as chorister and organist, and until 1886 played the organ in various London churches. He matriculated in New College, Oxford, in 1873 and obtained the degree of B.Mus. in 1875. It is not known just when or why he changed his name to Stewart, but he did so some time between 1875 and 1886, when he came to the United States. He went immediately to San Francisco, Cal., where he became the organist at the Church of the Advent. During the following years he occupied similar positions at Trinity Church, and at the First Unitarian Church. In 1901 he was engaged for a number of organ recitals at the Pan-American Exposi-

tion, Buffalo, N. Y., and after this engagement went to Boston, where for two years he was organist of Trinity Church. He then returned to California, and from 1902 to 1914 was organist of St. Dominic's in San Francisco. In 1915 he was appointed official organist of the Panama-Pacific International Exposition in San Francisco, and from that time until his death he served as municipal organist of San Diego. In this position he gave almost daily recitals on the organ at Balboa Park, the first out-door organ in the world. Owing to the ideal climate, the recitals were seldom interrupted by rain, and the series offered from 250 to 300 concerts each year. In 1919 the programs presented 2270 selections by 385 composers.

As a composer Stewart achieved his greatest distinction for his choral work, "The Hound of Heaven." For the Bohemian Club of San Francisco he composed the music for four of the annual "Grove-Plays"—*Montezuma* (1903), *The Cremation of Care* (1906), *Gold* (1916), and *John of Nepomuk* (1921). Other important works are *The Nativity,* an oratorio (1888); *His Majesty,* a comic opera (1890); *The Conspirators,* an operetta (1900); two orchestral suites, *Montezuma* (1903), and *Scenes in California* (1906); a mass in D minor (1907); a mass in G (1911); a romantic opera, *Bluff King Hal* (1911); and *Requiem Mass* (1919), dedicated to the pope. In addition to these major works he composed songs, shorter choruses, pieces for violin, organ, and piano, and incidental music to several plays. He received many honors, and was awarded a number of prizes. He was a founder of the American Guild of Organists and in 1899 was awarded the gold medal of that organization for an anthem. In 1907 two of his choral works won prizes, one from the Chicago Madrigal Club and the other from the Pittsburgh Male Chorus. He was accorded the official flag of the City of New York "for distinguished ability as a recital organist" in 1921, and in 1930 received from Pope Pius XI the decoration of Commander of the Holy Sepulchre. He died in San Diego, and was survived by a daughter. Elson (*post,* p. 257) called him "the leading musical reviewer of the Pacific coast."

[*Who's Who in America,* 1932–33; *Alumni Oxonienses,* vol. IV (1888); J. T. Howard, *Our Am. Music* (1931); L. C. Elson, *The Hist. of Am. Music* (rev. ed., 1925); Rupert Hughes, *Am. Composers* (rev. ed., 1914); *Musical America,* Jan. 10, 1933; *Grove's Dict. of Music and Musicians, Am. Supp.* (1930); C. A. McGrew, *City of San Diego* (1922), vol. II; *San Francisco Chronicle,* Dec. 29, 1932.]   J. T. H.

STEWART, JOHN AIKMAN (Aug. 26, 1822–Dec. 17, 1926), banker, was born in New

York City. His father, John Stewart, was a native of the island of Lewis, in the Hebrides; his mother, Mary (Aikman) Stewart, was born in New York; Edwin Stewart [*q.v.*] was a younger brother. John attended the common schools and completed what was then called the "literary and scientific course" at Columbia College in 1840. He then took up civil engineering, being a member of the staff which surveyed the line of the New York, Lake Erie & Western Railroad in 1840–42. In 1842 he was appointed clerk of the board of education of New York City, and held the post for eight years. From 1850 to 1853 he was actuary of the United States Life Insurance Company, and is credited with having brought some new ideas into the insurance business.

Late in 1852, when he was only thirty years old, he laid before John Jacob Astor, Royal Phelps, Peter Cooper, and other prominent New York business men a plan for a novel banking institution which should serve largely in a fiduciary capacity. They saw merit in it and agreed to become stockholders; thus was born, early in 1853, the United States Trust Company. Stewart served as its secretary until the end of 1864. He was then elected president and held that office for thirty-eight years, retiring in 1902 to become chairman of the board of trustees, in which position he continued until his death. He had a personal acquaintance with all the Presidents of the United States from Lincoln to Coolidge. He was a trusted financial adviser to President Lincoln, and served as assistant treasurer of the United States under him in 1864–65. He again rendered valuable service to the country in 1894, during Cleveland's administration, when the gold reserve was dangerously depleted.

Stewart was a trustee of Princeton University from 1868 until his death, and, as senior trustee, served as president *pro tempore* of the University from October 1910, when Woodrow Wilson resigned to become governor of New Jersey, until the spring of 1912, when John Grier Hibben was chosen president. He did much for benevolence, education, and religion, was long a trustee of the John F. Slater Fund for the education of the freedmen of the South, and was one of the oldest and most zealous promoters of the American Bible Society. He was twice married: first, in 1847, to Sarah Yule Johnson of New York, who died in 1887; and second, Nov. 25, 1890, to Mary Olivia Capron of Baltimore, Md. His second wife, a son by his first marriage, and a daughter survived him. He gave up his daily attendance at his office in his latter years, but visited it frequently and kept in close touch with the business until shortly before his death in New York City, at the age of 104. He was slightly deaf, but read without spectacles and retained his mental faculties until the end.

[*Who's Who in America*, 1926–27; *Who's Who in New York*, 1907; *N. Y. Herald*, Aug. 26, 1921; *Trust Companies*, June 1921; *N. Y. Times* and *World* (N.Y.), Dec. 18, 1926; *N. Y. Herald Tribune* and *Wall Street Jour.*, Dec. 18, 21, 1926; records of the United States Trust Company; information concerning first marriage from John A. Stewart, Jr.]　　　A. F. H.

STEWART, PHILO PENFIELD (July 6, 1798–Dec. 13, 1868), missionary, college founder, inventor, was born in Sherman, Conn., the son of Philo and Sarah (Penfield) Stewart, and a descendant of Alexander Stewart who came to New London, Conn., from Ireland about 1719. At the age of ten, because of his father's death, Philo was sent to live with his grandfather Penfield in Pittsford, Vt., and when fourteen years old was apprenticed to an uncle in Pawlet, Vt., to learn harness making, serving for seven years, with the highly prized privilege of attending Pawlet Academy for three months each year. He early showed much mechanical aptitude.

Being attracted to Christian service, in 1821 he accepted appointment by the American Board of Commissioners for Foreign Missions as an assistant missionary among the Choctaws at Mayhew, Miss. He made the journey of nearly 2,000 miles on horseback, carrying his entire outfit in a pair of saddle-bags, preaching along the way, and completing the journey at an expense to the Board of ten dollars. At the mission he superintended its manual labor, taught the boys' school, and conducted services on Sunday in various Indian settlements. Ill health took him back to Vermont in 1825, but he returned in 1827, bringing several new workers. One of these, Eliza Capen from Pittsford, Vt., he married in 1828.

His wife's impaired health necessitated their leaving the mission in 1830 and Stewart in 1832 joined his fellow student of Pawlet Academy days, John J. Shipherd [*q.v.*], then pastor of a church in Elyria, Ohio. Both were ardently religious and born reformers. Together they evolved the plan of a community and school where their ideas could be realized. Stewart was especially attracted by the thought of a school combining study and labor with such economy that students might defray all their expenses. The result of their efforts was the founding of Oberlin. Together they selected a tract of forest land, about nine miles from Elyria, on which Oberlin now stands. During Shipherd's absence of several months in New England to acquire title to this land and seek funds and colonists, the Stewarts were with the Shipherd family in Elyria. Stewart occupied himself in perfecting a cookstove, undertaken originally to meet a need in Mrs. Shipherd's kitchen, the manufacture of which he hoped might yield substantial income to the projected school. At the same time he had general supervision of the work at Oberlin, meeting and encouraging the colonists as they came from the East. When the school was opened in 1833, the Stewarts took charge of the boarding hall. They had pledged themselves to the service of the "Institute" for five years, with no compensation beside their living expenses. For the first year Stewart was also treasurer and the general manager; but, disagreeing with his associates in his opposition to radical abolitionism and to the admission of negro students (R. S. Fletcher, "Oberlin, 1833–1866," MS.), he resigned in 1836 and returned to the East.

He now tried to perfect a planing mill which had been projected at Elyria, but the financial crash of 1837 ruined the undertaking and he came into financial straits. Making his home in Troy, he returned to the stove project, which proved so successful that in thirty years more than 90,000 stoves were sold. The patent for the "Oberlin stove," granted June 19, 1834, he had deeded to the Oberlin Collegiate Institute. Other patents were issued to him on Sept. 12, 1838, Apr. 12, 1859, and Apr. 28, 1863. His attempt to found a school in Troy was unsuccessful, as was also a water-cure establishment with an original system of gymnastics which he tried to establish. In their prosperous days the Stewarts adhered strictly to their former simplicity of living. They maintained great interest in Oberlin and made contributions to its work.

[Stewart Clan Mag., Dec. 1924; J. H. Fairchild, Oberlin, the Colony and the College (1883); D. L. Leonard, The Story of Oberlin (1898); A Worker and Worker's Friend: P. P. Stewart, as a Mechanic, Teacher, and Missionary (1873), apparently written by his wife; Troy Daily News, Dec. 14, 1868; information as to certain facts from Prof. R. S. Fletcher, Oberlin, Ohio.]   E. D. E.

STEWART, ROBERT (Jan. 31, 1839–Oct. 23, 1915), missionary, was born in Sidney, Ohio, the son of Dr. James Harris and Jane Abigail (Fuller) Stewart, and a descendant of George Stuart who settled in Pennsylvania at Marietta on the Susquehanna about 1717. Robert attended the public schools of Allegheny and the academies of Shirleysburg and Glade Run, Pa. In 1859 he graduated with first honors from Jefferson College, and in 1865 completed the course at the Allegheny United Presbyterian Theological Seminary. The following year, Nov. 9, he was ordained by the First Ohio Presbytery. For

some time he served churches of his denomination at Ashland, Savannah, and Dayton, Ohio, and at Davenport, N. Y.; from 1872 to 1878 he was professor of exegetics and homiletics in the Newburg (N. Y.) Theological Seminary; and from June 1879 until November 1880 he edited for his Church the Evangelical Repository and Sabbath School Helps.

As a member of the Board of Foreign Missions of the United Presbyterian Church he visited India and Egypt in 1880 as a special commissioner, and decided to join the India Mission. Returning to the United States, he was commissioned by the Board the following year and set sail for India on Nov. 5, 1881. In Cairo, Egypt, on Dec. 1, he was married to Eliza Frazier Johnston, of St. Clairsville, Ohio. From 1883 until 1892 he was in charge of the Christian Training Institute and principal of the Theological Seminary in Sialkot, Punjab, teaching in the latter institution Biblical languages, theology, and church history, and preparing translations for educational use. From 1892 until the latter part of 1900 he was in the United States engaged chiefly in writing. In November 1900 he returned to India, and at Jhelum, Punjab, where the Seminary was then located, he remained, except for a brief furlough in 1909–10, during the rest of his life, serving as senior professor and carrying forward the work of translation. In December 1901 he was a delegate to the Alliance of Reformed Churches in India, and in December 1902 a member of the India Decennial Missionary Conference (Madras).

By 1891 he had ready for the press translations into Urdu (Punjabi) of Philip Schaff's Ante-Nicene Christianity, W. D. Ralston's Talks on Psalmody, R. H. Pollock's The Saviour's Claim, and other works. During his extended furlough in America he published his Life and Work in India (1896), a comprehensive and authoritative account of missionary activities in India. During his latter term of service in India he issued a translation (Urdu) of the Psalms. Among his other numerous works were, in English, Filled with the Spirit (1896), Ancestors and Children of Colonel Daniel Fisher and His Wife Sybil Draper (1899), Apostolic and Indian Missions Compared (1903), Colonel George Steuart and His Wife Margaret Harris, Their Ancestors and Descendants (1907), Hinduism Historically Considered (n.d.); in Urdu, an introduction to the books of the New Testament (1909), a Protestant catechism, and a translation of W. D. Killen's work on the Apostolic Church. His death, in his seventy-seventh year, occurred at Sialkot.

[A sketch of Stewart appears in his *Colonel George Steuart* (1907); see also his *Life and Work in India* (1896); *Biog. and Hist. Cat. of Washington and Jefferson Coll.* (1902); *Reports of the Board of Foreign Missions of the United Presbyterian Church*, 1881–92, 1900–15; *Who's Who in America*, 1914–15; *United Presbyterian*, Oct. 28, 1915.]   J. C. A—r.

STEWART, ROBERT MARCELLUS (Mar. 12, 1815–Sept. 21, 1871), railroad president, governor of Missouri, was born at Truxton, Cortland County, N. Y., the son of Charles and Elisabeth (Severance) Stewart. At Truxton he obtained an academic education, and then taught school and studied law. The lure of the West drew him to Louisville, Ky., and finally to St. Joseph, Mo., where he settled in 1840. Here he soon developed a satisfactory law practice, and in 1845 was chosen a delegate to the Missouri constitutional convention. The following year he was elected to the state Senate, where he served until 1857. He inaugurated and financed the preliminary survey of the Hannibal & St. Joseph Railroad, became its attorney, and by lobbying at Washington obtained a grant of some 600,000 acres of choice federal land for his company. About 1854 he was chosen the first president of the corporation, and he saw the road practically completed before the opening of the Civil War, although it did not begin operation until 1867.

After Trusten Polk [*q.v.*] resigned the governorship of Missouri (in February 1857) Stewart was elected (in August) to that office as an anti-Benton Democrat. His opponents charged, and it was not denied, that he effectively used his position as head of the railroad company to gain votes in this campaign. As governor he stressed the material interests of the state, especially favoring a liberal policy toward railroad development. The problem of "bleeding Kansas" also absorbed much of his attention. In January 1859 the state assembly, at his request, voted him $30,000 with which to protect the western border of Missouri against a "band of thieves, robbers and midnight assassins" (*Messages and Proclamations, post*, III, 232) from Kansas. When the secession issue grew hot, Stewart took middle ground by upholding the Crittenden compromise proposals. He asserted, however, that Southerners had a right to take their slaves into Kansas territory. In an attempt to please the other camp he ridiculed "nullification, secession, disunion and all radical Southern fire-eating propositions" (Stevens, *post*, II, 398). In his final message to the legislature (Jan. 3, 1861) he straddled the issue by asserting that: "Missouri will . . . hold to the Union so long as it is worth an effort to preserve it. . . . She cannot be frightened . . .

by the past unfriendly legislation of the North, nor dragooned into secession by the restrictive legislation of the extreme South" (*Messages and Proclamations, post*, p. 144). After he retired from the governorship, he was elected a delegate to the state convention "to consider the . . . relations between the Government of the United States . . . and the Government and people of the State of Missouri" (*Journal and Proceedings of the Missouri State Convention, 1861*, p. 3), and veered round to his true convictions by taking a strong stand for the Union. He did not, however, favor coercing the seceding states.

Stewart edited the *St. Joseph Journal* until 1863 when Gov. Hamilton R. Gamble [*q.v.*] gave him a commission to recruit a brigade of Union men, but because of his excessive drinking General Halleck relieved him of his command (Rutt, *post*, p. 339). Except when his mind was clouded by alcohol, Stewart was an able executive. He was tall and handsome, with dark hair. He died unmarried, in St. Joseph, at the age of fifty-six.

[*The Am. Ann. Cyc. . . . 1871* (1872); W. B. Davis and D. S. Durrie, *An Illustrated Hist. of Mo.* (1876); Lucien Carr, *Missouri: A Bone of Contention* (1888); J. F. Severance, *The Severans Geneal. Hist.* (1893); H. L. Conard, *Encyc. of the Hist. of Mo.* (1901), vol. VI; W. B. Stevens, *Missouri: The Center State* (1915), vol. II; *The Messages and Proclamations of the Govs. of the State of Mo.*, vol. III (1922); files of the *St. Joseph Journal*; C. L. Rutt, *The Daily News' Hist. of Buchanan County and St. Joseph, Mo.* (1898); personal notes from Mrs. Mary L. Crane, a grandniece of Governor Stewart.]   H. E. N.

STEWART, WILLIAM MORRIS (Aug. 9, 1827–Apr. 23, 1909), lawyer, United States senator, was the eldest son of Frederick Augustus Stewart and his wife, Miranda Morris. From his birthplace, Galen, Wayne County, N. Y., his parents moved during his childhood to Trumbull County, Ohio. He spent three years in Farmington Academy (Ohio), and then returned to New York State, where he taught mathematics in the Lyons high school. Intending to study law, he entered Yale College in September 1848, but left early in 1850, lured by the discovery of gold in California. Reaching San Francisco in May, he engaged in mining in Nevada County, Cal. When he had accumulated about $8,000, he abandoned mining and began the study of law in the office of John R. McConnell, Nevada City, and was admitted to practice in 1852. The next year he was elected district attorney and wrote the first rules and regulations for quartz mining in Nevada County. In 1854 he served as acting attorney-general of the state, and formed a law-partnership in San Francisco with Henry S. Foote [*q.v.*], ex-governor of Mississippi, whose daughter, Annie Elizabeth, he married in the spring of the following year. Three daughters were born to them.

In 1856, Stewart moved to Downieville, Sierra County, Cal., but the discovery three years later of silver mines in Nevada drew him to Virginia City and Carson City, where his energy, resourcefulness, and knowledge of mining law and practice brought him to the front. During four years of complicated litigation he successfully defended the interests of the original claimants to the famous Comstock Lode, and received $500,000 in fees. He was president for a number of years of the Sutro Tunnel Company, founded by Adolph H. J. Sutro [q.v.]. Winning fame as a specialist in mining law, he was retained by some of the largest mining companies in the West.

With characteristic energy he threw himself into the turbulent politics of the nascent state of Nevada. In 1861 he was elected to the territorial council, and two years later to the constitutional convention, serving as chairman of the judiciary committee, but he led the forces that defeated the adoption of the proposed constitution because of a taxation provision obnoxious to the dominant mining interests. The following year, upon the admission of Nevada into the Union, Stewart was elected to the United States Senate as a Republican, remaining in that body until March 1875. During these years he was instrumental in securing the defeat of the proposed sale of mineral lands on the public domain to help pay the Civil War debt, and the passage of the mining laws of 1866 and 1872, which recognized and confirmed the rights of miners according to their rules and regulations. At first he supported President Johnson and his reconstruction measures, but eventually advocated Johnson's impeachment and voted for his conviction. In 1869 he was the author of the Fifteenth Amendment to the federal Constitution in the form in which it was finally adopted. Pacific railroad projects naturally received his hearty support. In 1871 he was offered, but declined, appointment to the Supreme Court (*Reminiscences*, p. 250). Returning to Nevada in 1875, he devoted the next dozen years to his mining interests and lucrative law practice.

In 1887 he was again elected to the Senate and served there continuously until 1905. He was perhaps the first member of either house to propose federal appropriations for the reclamation of Western arid lands. In 1891, with seven other Republican senators, he fought on the side of the Democrats to prevent the enactment of the Lodge Force Bill. His most distinguished efforts, however, were directed toward the re-

monetization of silver. In 1888 he was a delegate to the Republican National Convention and drafted the currency plank in the party platform. Incensed at what he regarded as Republican abandonment of this plank, he declined election as a delegate to the National Convention of 1892 and joined the Silver party; and, as a member of that party, was reëlected to the Senate in 1893 and 1899. He constantly denounced the "crime of 1873," and bitterly fought the repeal (1893) of the silver-purchase clause of the Sherman Silver Act of 1890. With the fervor of an apostle, he edited and published (in Washington, 1892–98) a weekly newspaper, first called the *Silver Knight* and later the *Silver Knight-Watchman* (see *Reminiscences*, p. 321). After the nomination of Bryan upon a free-silver platform in 1896, he counseled the Populist and Silver party leaders to indorse Bryan, which they did. Later, when the unexpected discoveries of new sources of gold had convinced him that the silver question was disposed of, he returned to the Republican party, indorsed McKinley in 1900, and vigorously attacked Bryan's silver speeches in that campaign. At the expiration of his term in 1905, he declined reëlection, returned to Nevada, and spent his last years at his newly established home in Bullfrog.

With John T. Boyle he was employed as counsel for the Roman Catholic prelates of California in the controversy with the Mexican government over the Pious Fund of the Californias, and as senior counsel for the claimants presented one of the winning arguments before the Permanent Court of Arbitration at The Hague in 1902 (W. L. Penfield, "The 'Pious Fund' Arbitration," *North American Review*, December 1902). He was a lifelong friend and adviser of Leland Stanford [q.v.], and was one of the first trustees of Stanford University. He accumulated several large fortunes which quickly disappeared, much going for charitable and educational purposes. Though no orator, he was a clear and impressive speaker. Possessed of unlimited self-confidence, colossal self-assertion, unflagging energy, and indomitable perseverance, he was a striking product of the mining frontier. Over six feet tall, of erect and massive figure, with long flowing beard and silvery hair, he was one of the most picturesque and rugged characters ever known in Washington. His first wife was killed in 1902 in an automobile accident at Alameda, Cal., and in the fall of 1903, at Atlanta, Ga., he married Mary Agnes (Atchison), widow of Theodore Cone. In 1908 *Reminiscences of Senator William Morris Stewart* was published under the editorship of George R. Brown,

[The *Reminiscences* and *Obit. Record Grads. Yale Univ.*, 1909, give the year of Stewart's birth as 1825, but the *Biog. Dir. Am. Cong.* (1928), *Who's Who in America*, 1908–09, and E. M. Mack, *post*, in both thesis and article, give 1827. The fullest account of his public life is Effie M. Mack, "Life and Letters of William Morris Stewart, 1827–1909" (unpublished dissertation, Univ. of Cal.); the author had access to Stewart's private papers and many letters are quoted at length. A shorter account by the same author appears in *Proc. of the Pacific Coast Branch of the Am. Hist. Asso.* (1930), pp. 185–92. See also Alonzo Phelps, *Contemporary Biog. of California's Representative Men* (1881); O. T. Shuck, *Representative and Leading Men of the Pacific* (1870); Eliot Lord, "Comstock Mining and Miners," *Monograph of the U. S. Geol. Survey*, vol. IV (1883); *The Call* (San Francisco), Apr. 24, 1909; and *San Francisco Chronicle*, Apr. 24, 1909.]

P. O. R.

STEWART, WILLIAM RHINELANDER (Dec. 3, 1852–Sept. 4, 1929), capitalist, philanthropist, was born in New York City. His parents, Lispenard and Mary Rogers (Rhinelander) Stewart, were descendants of some of New York's oldest families. Young Stewart was educated by tutors and in the private schools of Dr. Anthon and Dr. Charlier. He then entered the Columbia University Law School, where he was graduated in 1873. After several years' practice of law with the firm of Platt, Gerard & Buckley, he gave up the profession and devoted his time thereafter to the management of estates as executor and trustee, and to philanthropic work.

Appointed by Gov. Alonzo B. Cornell [*q.v.*] as commissioner for the first judicial district on the state board of charities, May 31, 1882, he served with that organization for forty-seven years; from 1894 to 1903 and from 1907 to 1923 he was president of the board. Upon his retirement in March 1929, Gov. Franklin D. Roosevelt wrote: "Your record is unique in the annals of the State's history, both in length of time and in the variety and scope of your activities" (*New York Times*, Sept. 5, 1929, p. 29). In regard to juvenile reformatories, he believed in "abandoning a system based upon punishment and retribution" and substituting "one which would provide for proper classification, open grounds for play and exercise, proper industrial and scholastic education, and care of the boys and the girls in separate institutions" (*Report of the State Board of Charities*, 1929, pp. 1–2). In 1898 he was elected president of the National Conference of Charities and Corrections, and received its gold medal in recognition of his services. In 1900 he organized the New York State Conference of Charities and Corrections, of which he was elected president in 1903. In 1910 he founded the New York City Conference of Charities and Corrections. He was for several years chairman of the state commission for the establishment of Letchworth Village, a farm colony for

the feeble-minded. During his presidency of the state board of charities, his public duties, which included much traveling among the state institutions, occupied at least half his time and sometimes more; those who knew him and his work testified that for much of his labor he received no emolument.

In 1889 he conceived the idea of building the Washington Arch in Washington Square at the end of Fifth Avenue, New York. He was treasurer of the committee appointed to further the project, did much towards raising funds, and in 1895 formally presented the Arch to Mayor Strong in a public ceremony. In 1894, after the Lexow Committee investigation of New York's city government, Stewart had been one of the Committee of Seventy who labored for the overthrow of Tammany Hall and the election of Mayor William L. Strong and a reform administration. The last task which he undertook was that of completing the tomb of General Grant on Riverside Drive, and at the time of his death he had collected $100,000 (including a substantial donation of his own) of the $400,000 needed. Meanwhile, on the business side, he was president of the Rhinelander Real Estate Company from 1908 until 1929 and a director in two banks and several corporations. He was also a member of many scientific and other learned societies. On Nov. 5, 1879, he married Annie M. Armstrong of Baltimore, by whom he had three children, one of whom died young. She divorced him, Aug. 24, 1906, and was afterward twice married. Besides a number of pamphlets and magazine articles, Stewart wrote two books, *The Philanthropic Work of Josephine Shaw Lowell* (1911), and *Grace Church and Old New York* (1924). He died in New York City.

[*Who's Who in America*, 1928–29; *N. Y. Times*, May 4, 5, 1895, on occasion of the dedication of the Washington Arch; *The Washington Arch: its Conception, Construction and Dedication* (1895); *N. Y. Times* and *N. Y. Herald Tribune*, Sept. 5, 6, 1929; annual reports of N. Y. State Board of Charities and Corrections, 1882–1929; *N. Y. Biog. and Geneal. Record*, July 1893.]

A. F. H.

STICKNEY, ALPHEUS BEEDE (June 27, 1840–Aug. 9, 1916), lawyer, railway builder, was born in Wilton, Me., the son of Daniel and Ursula Maria (Beede) Stickney, and a descendant of William Stickney who came to Boston in 1637 and two years later settled in Rowley, Mass. Educated in common schools and academies of Maine and New Hampshire until he was eighteen, he then began the study of law in the office of Josiah Crosby in Dexter, Me. His preparation was somewhat delayed by school-teaching which he was obliged to undertake in order to earn money, but in 1862 he was admitted to the bar, and moved to Minnesota, where he practised law until 1869.

Railroad building was just beginning in Minnesota and neighboring states, and in 1869 Stickney moved to St. Paul, gave up practice, and became connected with railroad enterprises. His first great undertaking, in 1871, was the St. Paul, Stillwater & Taylor's Falls Railroad—later a part of the Chicago, St. Paul, Minneapolis & Omaha system—which he served for several years as vice-president, general manager, and chief counsel. In 1879 he became superintendent of construction of the St. Paul, Minneapolis & Manitoba Railway, which subsequently became part of the Great Northern, and the following year was general superintendent of about 500 miles of the Canadian Pacific Railway. In 1881 he organized and built the first section of the Wisconsin, Minnesota & Pacific Railroad, and in 1881–82 he was vice-president of the Minneapolis & St. Louis Railway. In 1883 he organized and began the construction of the Minnesota & Northwestern Railroad, serving as president until its union with the Chicago, St. Paul & Kansas City in 1887, and then as president of the consolidated road. This office he held until 1892, when he was elected chairman of the board of directors. In that capacity he reorganized the road as the Chicago Great Western Railway, of which he was president from 1894 to 1900 and chairman of the board of directors from 1892 to 1908. When bankruptcy came in 1908 he was appointed receiver. In 1909 he retired from active work.

In his administration of the Chicago Great Western, Stickney endeavored to apply ideas both as to financing and operation which were novel in the United States. These he set forth in a book entitled *The Railway Problem* (1891). Following the English practice, he endeavored to raise the money for financing the road from the stockholders, and to reorganize it without a funded debt. In this way the stock would represent a real investment and would have first claim on surplus earnings, instead of being junior to a heavy mortgage. This scheme, admirable as it would be in periods of depression when fixed charges become insupportable, met two difficulties: in the first place, investors did not buy the railway stock offered, and in the second place, the earning power of the road did not increase as rapidly as had been estimated. The result was that the floating debt grew to unmanageable proportions, reaching $10,653,000 by January 1908, when the road was forced into the hands of a receiver. This experience seemed

to show that the Stickney plan of a bankruptcy-proof railroad was not proof against insufficient earnings, and that the general creditors could put a road in the hands of a receiver as effectively as could the owners of defaulted bonds.

In the actual operations of the Chicago Great Western Stickney applied methods that were in advance of his time. Assuming that carefully analyzed statistics of past records could be made the basis for the formulation of definite policies, he worked out methods of operation and maintenance and applied them ruthlessly. It is difficult to reach a definite conclusion as to the efficacy of these methods, for the road was exposed to the severest competition, and its officials, apparently, did not always carry out the Stickney plans wholeheartedly. Stickney himself charged in 1909 that many of the railroads had resumed the practice of rebating under such subterfuges as that of allowing large claims for overcharges and damages presented by favored shippers. The charges resulted in an investigation by the Interstate Commerce Commission, before which Stickney laid a plan for revising the rate laws so as to make such practices impossible. This was set forth in a pamphlet entitled *Railway Rates* (1909).

Stickney did much to develop the Northwest, encouraging settlers to come thither and persuading Eastern and European capitalists to make investments there. During his railroad career he acquired extensive outside interests, one of the chief of which was the St. Paul union stockyards and packing houses, which he built in 1882. He was twice married: first, in October 1864 to Kate W. H. Hall of Collinsville, Ill.; and second, in 1901, to May Crosby. By his first wife he had seven children. He died at his home in St. Paul.

[M. A. Stickney, *The Stickney Family* (1869); *Who's Who in America*, 1916–17; *Railway Age Gazette*, Aug. 18, 1916; *N. Y. Times*, Aug. 10, 1916; *St. Paul Dispatch*, Aug. 9, 1916.]   E. L. B.

STIEGEL, HENRY WILLIAM (May 13, 1729–Jan. 10, 1785), "Baron von Stiegel," ironmaster, glassmaker, townbuilder, about whose eccentricities and grandiose manner of living in Pennsylvania many stories, true and apocryphal, have been told, was born near Cologne, Germany, the son of John Frederick and Dorothea Elizabeth Stiegel, and the eldest of six children. His father died in 1741. Nine years later Heinrich Wilhelm, his mother, and his brother Anthony sailed from Rotterdam in the *Nancy* and arrived at Philadelphia on Aug. 31, 1750. After a year or two in Philadelphia, the mother and brother settled in Schaefferstown, and Heinrich apparently secured employment with Jacob Huber, ironmaster, near Brickerville, Lancaster County. On Nov. 7, 1752, he married Huber's daughter, Elizabeth, who died Feb. 13, 1758. Two daughters were born to them. About three months after his wife's death, in partnership with Charles and Alexander Stedman of Philadelphia, he bought his father-in-law's property, added to it, and named it Elizabeth Furnace. On Oct. 24 of the same year he married Elizabeth Hölz of Philadelphia, who bore him one son. On Apr. 10, 1760, he became a British citizen, taking the name of Henry William Stiegel. The soubriquet "Baron" was doubtless given him because of his lordly manner of living.

At Elizabeth Furnace he made six-plate and ten-plate stoves and all sorts of iron castings, including kettles for potash and soap works, and stoves, kettles, and other equipment for the West Indies sugar-makers. Thousands of acres of woodland were purchased, tenant houses were erected, and by 1760 Stiegel was one of the most prosperous ironmasters in the country. He built another residence there, as well as stores, a mill, and a malt house. In 1760 he purchased another forge, which he named Charming Forge, near Womelsdorf, Berks County, selling a half interest in it to the Stedmans in 1763. On Sept. 20, 1762, he acquired from the Stedman brothers a third interest in 729 acres of land in Lancaster County, laid out the town of Manheim, built and sold houses, and conducted a real estate boom. Here in 1763 he began to build himself a third large mansion, which had in it a chapel and on its roof a platform for performances by the band of musicians he had organized among his workmen.

In 1763–64 he went to England, visited London and Bristol, and is said to have brought back with him a number of skilled glass makers. Upon his return early in 1764 he began the erection of a glass manufactory at Manheim, meanwhile experimenting in the making of bottles and window glass at Elizabeth Furnace. The first glass-making at Manheim was begun in November 1765, and by 1767 the plant was in full operation. In 1769 he built a second factory there, known after 1772 as the American Flint Glass Manufactory, where glass was made until 1774. He had agents for the sale of his products in Philadelphia, Boston, New York, Baltimore, and numerous smaller towns in Pennsylvania and Maryland. At the Manheim works, in addition to window and sheet glass, was made the beautiful Stiegel glassware that is now eagerly sought by collectors . . . bottles, funnels, water lenses, retorts, flasks, measures, drinking glasses,

scent bottles, and toys . . . some of it engraved or enameled, in white, light green, deep emerald, olive, wine, amethyst, and the blue that was a favorite of the day. Thin and light in weight, with a brilliant surface and uniform color, it has great beauty of form and, as it was made largely by hand, an exquisite variety in proportion. The Metropolitan Museum of Art, New York, contains the large Hunter Collection, and there is a good one in the Pennsylvania Museum of Art, Philadelphia.

Though Stiegel was one of the wealthiest men in Pennsylvania, he was careless and happy-go-lucky, with a self-confidence so great that he could scarcely envisage the possibility of failure, and he wasted much of his substance both in extravagant living and in over-ambitious business ventures. A passionate lover of music and a connoisseur of beauty as well as mechanically skilful, he has been described as cursed with the "ironic gift of too great facility." Certainly his career was a meteoric one. Apparently prosperous enough in 1770–71, he began to suffer hard times in 1772, and in 1773 instituted a lottery in hope of recouping his fortunes. By 1774 he was obliged to sell his property (much of which he had mortgaged for the sake of his glass factories), became a bankrupt, and in the later months of the year spent some weeks in a debtor's prison. From that time his fortunes declined rapidly, and his hopes vanished. For a while he had a more or less self-assumed position as caretaker at Elizabeth Furnace and then was employed there by the new owner as foreman. In 1779, partially dependent on his brother, he turned country schoolmaster and music teacher at Brickerville and Schaefferstown, with an interval as clerk at the Reading Furnaces, Berks County. When his wife died in Philadelphia in 1782, she was buried there for lack of funds to bring her body to Schaefferstown. Three years later Stiegel himself died in poverty at Charming Forge, then in the hands of his nephew, and was buried in an unmarked grave.

[In the record of the ship Nancy, given in facsimile in R. B. Strassburger, Pa. German Pioneers (1934), vol. II, 155 C, Stiegel signed his name as Henderick Willem Stiegel. F. W. Hunter, Stiegel Glass (1914), contains by far the best biog. of Stiegel and includes a bibliog., geneal., lists of deeds, employees, purchasers of glass, etc. See also T. P. Ege, Hist. and Geneal. of the Ege Family . . . 1738–1911 (1911); W A. Dyer, Early Am. Craftsmen (1915); Rhea M. Knittle, Early Am. Glass (copr. 1927); Mrs. N. H. Moore, Old Glass, European and Am. (1924); F. W. Hunter, "Baron Stiegel and Am. Glass," Bull. Met. Museum of Art, Dec. 1913; Nat. Soc. Colonial Dames of America, Pa. Soc., Forges and Furnaces in the Province of Pa. (1914); A. S. Brendle, Henry William Stiegel (1912); and J. T. Faris, The Romance of Forgotten Men (1928), a popular account. Many of Stiegel's ledgers, daybooks, journals, etc., are in the colls. of the Hist. Soc. of Pa.]   W. A. D.

STILES, EZRA (Nov. 29, 1727 o.s.–May 12, 1795), scholar, Congregational clergyman, president of Yale College, was born in North Haven, Conn., then a part of New Haven, where his father, Isaac, was for more than thirty-five years pastor of the Congregational church. He was a descendant of John Stiles who emigrated from England and settled in Windsor, Conn., in 1635. Ezra's mother, Kezia, daughter of the Rev. Edward Taylor of Westfield, Mass., died five days after the child's birth, and the following year his father married Esther, daughter of Samuel Hooker, Jr., of Hartford. Prepared at home, Ezra was ready for college at the age of twelve, but did not enter until 1742, when he enrolled at Yale College. Here he distinguished himself in all branches of learning but showed special fondness for mathematics, astronomy, and Biblical history. After his graduation, in 1746, he remained in New Haven, devoting himself to intellectual pursuits, particularly to the study of theology, and on May 30, 1749, was licensed to preach by the New Haven Association of Ministers. The week before, he had been appointed tutor at Yale.

For six years he filled this position with more than ordinary acceptability, but his time and thought were by no means confined solely to its duties. His mental equipment and abilities as a speaker were such that he was the natural choice for orator on important public occasions. In 1750 he delivered the funeral oration in honor of Governor Jonathan Law [q.v.]; in 1753, an oration in memory of Bishop Berkeley; and in 1755, one in compliment of Benjamin Franklin during his visit to New Haven. All these were in Latin. Franklin, in 1749, had sent an electrical apparatus to Yale, and Stiles had engaged in some of the first electrical experiments carried on in New England. The two became friends and corresponded for the remainder of Franklin's lifetime. During his tutorship Stiles had doubts as to the advisability of his entering the active ministry. From childhood he had been of frail constitution, but an even more important reason for his hesitation was uncertainty of mind as to some of the dogmas of the Christian religion. Accordingly, he studied law and in November 1753 was admitted to the bar. His attitude toward religion at this time was not due to disbelief, but rather to an intellectual honesty which would not permit him to accept anything as true until thorough investigation had convinced him of its verity. A long and patient study of the Scriptures, carried on with every help available, at length brought him to a firm belief in the truth of revelation. His openness of mind is evinced by the fact that during visits to Newport, Boston, New York, and Philadelphia in 1754, he attended Quaker meetings and Episcopal, Reformed Dutch, and Roman Catholic services, in order to acquaint himself at first hand with the merits of different forms of worship. Several invitations to settle in the ministry came to him, and attempts were made to draw him into the Anglican communion, the Episcopalians of Stratford, Conn., urging him in January 1755 to succeed Dr. Samuel Johnson [q.v.] as their rector. He was disposed to continue the practice of law, but when in the early summer of 1755 the Second Congregational Church of Newport, R. I., called him to become its pastor, the attractiveness of that town with its foreign contacts—it was then a shipping center of importance—its Redwood Library, the prospect of leisure for study, his love of preaching, and the advice of his father and friends led him to accept. Resigning his tutorship, he was ordained and installed there on Oct. 22, 1755. On Feb. 10, 1757, he married Elizabeth, daughter of Col. John Hubbard of New Haven.

During the many years Stiles resided in Newport his interests and activities were amazingly varied. In 1756 he became librarian of the Redwood Library and continued as such as long as he remained in the town. He sought information on all manner of subjects, and his correspondence with prominent people at home and abroad was voluminous. Visitors to Newport of any importance inevitably found their way to his door. In 1765, upon the recommendation of Franklin, the University of Edinburgh conferred on him the degree of doctor of divinity. Although he was an ardent antiquarian, his interest in contemporary conditions was almost equally keen, and he gathered and recorded a great variety of statistics. His taste for scientific inquiry remained; he made observations of the comet of 1759 and of the transit of Venus ten years later, studied other natural phenomena, and carried on experiments in chemistry. Recognized as probably the most learned man in New England, he was made a member of the American Philosophical Society on Jan. 26, 1768, and in 1781 was elected a councilor. Having neglected Hebrew in college, in 1767, when forty years old, he set to work acquiring a thorough knowledge of that language; he also studied Arabic, Syriac, and Armenian, becoming for his day a very competent orientalist. Subsequently, he took a few lessons in French and was soon perusing works by French authors. When he began his diary,

January 1769, he was working on an ecclesiastical history of New England and British America, which he left incomplete. He was much interested in promoting the manufacture of silk and recorded in his diary, June 4, 1771: "I have now Three Thous^d Silkworms hatched." Based on his experiments and investigations in this field, he wrote "Observations on Silk Worms," a sizable manuscript which has been preserved. He found time, also, to supervise the early education of his children: "Ezra," he records in his diary, Jan. 9, 1769, "began to learn hebrew about this time, Æt. 10." He did not neglect the Bible or permit any of his family to do so. Reviewing his fidelity in this respect at a much later date, July 21, 1793, he wrote: "Besides read^g in course privately in my Study, I read thro' the Bible in my Fam^y at Morning Prayers from 1760 to 1791, Eight times, or once in 4 years. My Fam^y have had full opport^y of being acquainted with the sacred Contents of the Bible."

In spite of his varied intellectual pursuits and the hours spent in writing, he performed his ministerial duties with the utmost conscientiousness. In 1771 he made 926 pastoral calls and the following year, 1030. He gave much attention, also, to catechising the children. The spiritual welfare of the many slaves in Newport—Stiles himself owned one whom he later set free—was a matter of concern to him. On Feb. 24, 1772, he wrote: "In the Evening a very full and serious Meeting of Negroes at my House, perhaps 80 or 90: I discoursed to them on Luke xiv, 16, 17, 18, . . . They sang well. They appeared attentive and much affected." He was on intimate terms with the Jews of Newport, frequently attending their synagogue, and had friendly relations with Christian denominations other than his own. With Rev. Samuel Hopkins [q.v.], pastor of the First Congregational Church, he cooperated cordially, though he was not in sympathy with many of the views of that noted theologian. To President Clap of Yale he wrote protesting against the removal of deistical books from the college library, urging the vanity of trying to suppress such writings and the danger of suppressing truth. "The only way is," he maintained, "to come forth into the open field and dispute the matter on an even footing" (Holmes, post, p. 79). For the Church of England in America, however, he had no liking. "It is grievous to think," he complained, "that when our Pious Ancestors came over into this Land when an howling wilderness, to enjoy ye Gospel in ye purity & simplicity of it y^t the Chh of England should thrust it self in among us" (Diary, I, 125). Later, he declared that as he had observed it in New England, it was "inspired with a secular principle, unanimated with the Love of Jesus so much as with the Love of Dignities & Preeminence, making the Chh. an asylum for polite Vice & Irreligion" (Ibid., II, 113).

While in Newport he had an important part in the founding of Rhode Island College (Brown University). As early as January 1762 he had been considering the possibility of a third New England college, and when James Manning [q.v.] came to Rhode Island in the summer of 1763 with a project for establishing a Baptist institution of learning, Stiles gave it his support. It was agreed that the new college should be under Baptist control but that representatives of other denominations should have a share in its management. The work of drawing up a charter was committed to Stiles, since he was regarded by the Baptists as better fitted for that task than any of their own members. Accordingly, he prepared a document which provided for a board of thirty-five trustees, nineteen of whom were to be Baptists, seven Congregationalists, five Friends, and four Episcopalians; and a board of twelve Fellows, eight of whom were to be Congregationalists. The trustees were to elect the president, but practically all other control of the institution was left to the Fellows, subject to the sanction of the trustees. The charter was approved by the committee in charge of the project, but Providence Baptists in the Rhode Island Assembly objected to it on the ground that it provided for an essentially Congregational college, and Stiles was charged with playing a trick on the Baptists, though, as a matter of fact, they were given the final decision in all matters. Before the charter was granted by the Assembly, however, it was so changed as to insure a majority of Baptists on both the board of trustees and the board of Fellows. Stiles was named as one of the original Fellows but declined the office. In 1765 he was again elected and again he declined.

He was a stanch advocate of American rights and liberties, and prophesied that British oppression would force the colonies to declare their independence. Writing to Benjamin Franklin, Oct. 23 and Nov. 6, 1765, he said that he disapproved of the Stamp Act, but that after it was passed he remained loyal and had nothing to do with the mob violence that resulted in the resignation of the Newport stamp officer. Charges that he encouraged violence, he ascribed to the Episcopalians, who disliked him. When the Revolution broke out, however, he gave it wholehearted support. He followed its course with intense interest, and recorded in his diary much valuable information, including accounts of movements and battles, often illustrated by maps.

The Revolution brought to an end what was probably the happiest period of his life. Fearing that Newport would fall into the hands of the British, many of the inhabitants fled elsewhere for safety. On Oct. 10, 1775, Stiles wrote: "How does this Town sit solitary that was once full of People! I am not yet removed, altho' three quarters of my beloved Chh & Congregation are broken up and dispersed" (*Diary*, I, 624). In March 1776 he took his family and goods to Dighton, Mass., where he resided about fourteen months, supplying the church there and making occasional visits to Newport and other places. In the meantime, he was asked to take charge of churches in Taunton, Mass., and Providence, R. I.; Dr. Charles Chauncy, 1705–1787 [*q.v.*], also invited him to become his assistant in the work of the First Church, Boston. In May 1777, at the request of the First Church, Portsmouth, N. H., he removed to that town, but the following September was elected president of Yale College. It was some months before he made up his mind to accept. He had no illusions about the office: "At best," he wrote, "the Diadem of a President is a Crown of Thorns" (*Ibid.*, II, 209), and he was not disposed to occupy the seat of authority until he was sure of "sitting as easy in the Chair, as such a Cella Curulis would admit of" (*Ibid.*, II, 226). Finally, in March 1778 he signified his acceptance and on July 8 he was installed as president and as professor of ecclesiastical history. It is significant of the affection in which he was held by his Newport parishioners that they were unwilling to dismiss him and that he remained technically their pastor until May 18, 1786.

The unsettled state of the country during Stiles's presidency of Yale made his position an especially difficult one; furthermore, the funds of the college were practically exhausted. Stiles nevertheless carried the institution through the period with reasonable success. In addition to his administrative duties he bore a heavy burden of teaching, giving instruction in Hebrew, ecclesiastical history, philosophical and scientific subjects, and, for a time, in theology. He loved academic forms and ceremonies and introduced them whenever occasion permitted. An amusing incident of his New Haven career was occasioned by the support he gave to a dancing master. He permitted about seventy-five students to attend his classes and three of his own children as well. This, he says, produced "a great Combustion" and after "Violent Proceed^{gs}" the dancing master had to leave town (*Diary*, III,

10–11, 15). The most notable event of his administration was a change in the college charter, whereby several of the state officials were made *ex officio* members of the corporation with all the rights of the original Fellows, and certain financial aid from the state was secured. He preached often and took an active part in ecclesiastical matters; he was also the first president of the society for the abolition of slavery formed in Connecticut in 1790.

He died of "bilious fever," at his home in New Haven, in his sixty-eighth year, after a few days' illness. His first wife had died on May 29, 1775, having borne him two sons and six daughters, of whom one son, Isaac, and four daughters survived him; Isaac was lost at sea a few months after his father's death; a daughter, Ruth, was the mother of Ezra Stiles Gannett [*q.v.*]. On Oct. 17, 1782, Stiles married Mary (Cranston) Checkley, widow of William Checkley and daughter of Benjamin Cranston of Newport.

The almost incredible amount of work that Stiles accomplished was carried on in spite of physical handicaps. His son-in-law, Abiel Holmes [*q.v.*], describes him as "a man of low and small stature; of a very delicate structure; and of a well proportioned form. . . . The delicacy of his frame requiring a special care of his health, he was prudently attentive . . . to its preservation. . . . Having carefully studied his own constitution, he was generally his own physician. By regulating his diet, exercising daily in the open air, and using occasionally a few simple medicines, he was, by the divine blessing, enabled, with but very small interruptions, to apply himself assiduously to study, and to discharge the various duties of public and of domestic life" (*Life, post,* pp. 349, 350). Although he wrote much, he published little. A few of his sermons appeared in printed form, among them *The United States Elevated to Glory and Honor* (1783), an election sermon preached at Hartford, May 8, 1783; and his *History of Three of the Judges of King Charles I* was issued in 1794. Stiles bequeathed some of his manuscripts to Abiel Holmes, who in 1798 published, with many extracts from them, *The Life of Ezra Stiles, D.D., LL.D.* To his successor in the presidency of Yale College he also bequeathed a large number of manuscripts. From these have been printed *The Literary Diary of Ezra Stiles, D.D., LL.D.* (3 vols., 1901), and *Extracts from the Itineraries and Other Miscellanies of Ezra Stiles . . . with Selections from His Correspondence* (1916), both edited by Franklin B. Dexter [*q.v.*], and both of much historical value. Manuscripts more recently presented to Yale College are published in *Letters & Papers of Ezra Stiles* (1933), edited by Isabel M. Calder.

[Besides sources mentioned, see J. L. Kingsley, "Life of Ezra Stiles," in Jared Sparks, *The Lib. of Am. Biog.*, vol. XVI (1847); F. B. Dexter, *Biog. Sketches Grads. Yale Coll.*, vol. II (1896); W. B. Sprague, *Annals of the Am. Pulpit*, vol. I (1857); H. R. Stiles, *The Stiles Family in America* (1895); W. E. Channing, *A Discourse Delivered at the Dedication of the Unitarian Congregational Church in Newport, July 27, 1836* (1836); G. A. Kohut, *Ezra Stiles and the Jews* (1902); W. C. Bronson, *The Hist. of Brown Univ.* (1914); Ebenezer Baldwin, *Annals of Yale Coll.* (1831); T. D. Woolsey, *An Hist. Discourse* (1850); A. P. Stokes, *Memorials of Eminent Yale Men* (1914), vol. I; *Atlantic Mo.*, Aug. 1844. Constance Rourke, in *Trumpets of Jubilee* (1927), pp. 5–11, gives a gay and not too reverent appreciation; C. D. Ebeling, in *Amerikanisches Magazin* (Hamburg), I (1795), 172–73, publishes an obituary and tells of Stiles's kindness in sending him an account of early Connecticut history.]   H. E. S.

STILES, HENRY REED (Mar. 10, 1832–Jan. 7, 1909), physician, genealogist, historian, was born in New York City. His father, Samuel Stiles, head of a bank-note engraving company, was descended from John Stiles, one of four brothers who emigrated from Bedfordshire, England, to Windsor, Conn., in 1635. His mother was Charlotte Sophia (Reed), daughter of Abner Reed, to whom Samuel had been apprenticed to learn engraving.

Stiles studied for one year at the University of the City of New York and in 1849 entered Williams College as a sophomore. Ill health interrupted his studies and he did not graduate, but a quarter of a century later Williams granted him an honorary degree (1876). In 1855 he graduated from the Medical Department of the University of the City of New York, and also from the New York Ophthalmic Hospital. He practised medicine for a few months, first in New York City and then in Galena, Ill. During 1856, after his marriage (Jan. 31) to Sarah Woodward, he edited the *Toledo Blade*. For the next two years he was a partner in the firm of F. C. Brownell of Hartford and New York, publishers of educational books and the *American Journal of Education*. In 1857, when ill health made it inadvisable for him to apply himself closely to business, he began tracing the genealogy of his family among the early records of Windsor, Conn. The history of the ancient town soon engrossed him. From the records of town acts, tax lists, registers, old wills, petitions, letters, journals, newspapers, and church records, as well as from the memories of aged inhabitants, he collected a mass of historical and genealogical material which he published in a volume of a thousand pages, *The History of Ancient Windsor, Connecticut* (1859). Largely made up of extracts from old documents, this *History* is not a readable narrative, but as a source book of

genealogical and historical fact it is extremely valuable. A new edition, revised and greatly enlarged, *The History and Genealogies of Ancient Windsor, Connecticut* (2 vols.), appeared in 1891.

Stiles's interest in publishing the vital statistics, public documents, and personal papers of early New England and New York, begun thus casually, persisted throughout the remaining fifty years of his life and occupied fully half of his time. He compiled and published *A History of the City of Brooklyn* (3 vols., 1867–70), *The Stiles Family in America: Genealogies of the Connecticut Family* (1895), and *The History of Ancient Wethersfield, Connecticut* (2 vols., 1904) based on the collections of Sherman W. Adams; he assisted in compiling and edited *Letters from the Prisons and Prison-ships of the Revolution* and *Account of the Interment of the Remains of American Patriots Who Perished on the British Prison-ships,* both in the Wallabout Prison-Ship Series (1895); *The Civil, Political, Professional and Ecclesiastical History . . . of the County of Kings and the City of Brooklyn* (1884); *Joutel's Journal of La Salle's Last Voyage, 1686–7* (1906), and the genealogies of several families; and contributed articles to historical periodicals and biographical series. He was editor of the *Historical Magazine* from January to June 1866, and of the *New York Genealogical and Biographical Record* from 1900 to 1902. His genial, kindly manner, enthusiasm, and industry enabled him to interest others in the preservation of valuable historical material and made him a successful organizer and officer of historical and genealogical societies.

He carried on his professional career somewhat intermittently, practising medicine until 1863 and holding minor public medical offices from 1868 until 1877 when he took charge of the Dundee (Scotland) Homeopathic Dispensary and, for the first time, occupied himself solely with medical work. His health failed after four years here and he returned to New York City, where he maintained a consulting practice which gave him considerable time for historical compilation. From 1888 until his death he conducted a sanatorium at Hill View on Lake George, New York.

[Stiles's own publications: *The Stiles Family in America* (1895), Preface to *The Hist. of Ancient Windsor, Conn.* (1859), and *The Hist. and Geneals. of Ancient Windsor, Conn.* (1891), II, 712–14; T. A. Wright, "Henry Reed Stiles," *N. Y. Geneal. and Biog. Record*, Apr. 1909; *Brooklyn Daily Eagle*, Jan. 9, 1909.]
                                             V. L. C.

STILL, ANDREW TAYLOR (Aug. 6, 1828–Dec. 12, 1917), founder of osteopathy, was born ın Jonesville, Va., the son of Abram and Martha Poage (Moore) Still. His father, a Methodist preacher, removed his family in 1834 to Newmarket, Tenn., and then to Macon County, Mo., to Schuyler County, Mo., and in 1845 back to Macon County. Young Andrew during this period led a typical frontiersman's life, gaining what education he could from local schools. On Jan. 29, 1849, he married Mary M. Vaughn. Four years later, he removed with her to Wakarusa Mission, Kan., where she died in 1859. He devoted himself to farming, doctoring Indians, and studying anatomy on the bodies of dead Indians, obtained by grave snatching (*Autobiography, post*, p. 94). According to his own account, he took a course of medicine in the Kansas City School of Physicians and Surgeons, and fought with John Brown in the border warfare. In October 1857 he was elected as the Free-State candidate to the territorial legislature from Douglas and Johnson counties. On Nov. 15, 1860, he married Mary E. Turner. Enlisting in 1861, he obtained a captain's commission in 1862, and later in the same year, a major's commission in the Kansas militia.

On his return from the war, he was stimulated by a desire to aid alcoholic and drug addicts, who in their plight, appealed in vain to so-called regular doctors. He meditated over this and allied topics until, finally, the truth dawned on him "like a burst of sunshine" that he was "approaching a science by study, research, and observation" (*Autobiography, post*, p. 95). This great truth was reënforced by the personal tragedy of losing three children in an epidemic of cerebro-spinal meningitis in 1864, a tragedy that impelled him to the conclusion that "all the remedies necessary to health exist in the human body . . . they can be administered by adjusting the body in such condition that the remedies may naturally associate themselves together, hear the cries, and relieve the afflicted" (*Ibid.*, p. 100). On this doctrine he built and for twenty-five years sustained osteopathy, which, however, has been influenced also by other practitioners, by state laws, and by the development of general scientific knowledge and practice. He attempted to introduce the new system in Baker University of Baldwin, Kan., but met with so much opposition and ridicule that, in 1875, he removed to Kirksville, Mo., where he developed a considerable practice, in which he used both drugs and osteopathy. Up to 1892, he moved about a good deal, from Kirksville to Henry County, Mo., to Hannibal, to Macon, and finally back to Kirksville, all the while practising and spreading the teachings of osteopathy. As aids in this work,

he had three sons and a daughter, a quack pile doctor, and a lightning-rod peddler, all of whom he had indoctrinated in the new science and art (*Autobiography, post*, pp. 144–45). On May 10, 1892, he incorporated the American School of Osteopathy in Kirksville, Mo. One year after the founding of the school, he vigorously assaulted the doctrine of healing drugs with his assertions that he was "as much afraid of Dover's powders as a darkey is of a skeleton. If I should give calomel, I would do it with my eyes shut, and keep them shut for nine days, so uncertain would I be as to results" (*Autobiography, post*, p. 288). In 1894 he also established the *Journal of Osteopathy*. From this time up to his death, he busied himself with teaching at the school, writing for the journal, and treating patients who came in numbers to consult him. In 1897 he published privately his *Autobiography* (revised ed., 1908), dictated to Mrs. Annie Morgan, as amanuensis (p. 172). He also published *Philosophy of Osteopathy* (1899), *The Philosophy and Mechanical Principles of Osteopathy* (1902), *Osteopathy, Research, and Practice* (1910).

[*Autobiog., ante*, indispensable for understanding Still and the beginnings of osteopathy; C. P. McConnell, *Clinical Osteopathy* (1917), esp. for development and present status of osteopathy; D. W. Wilder, *The Annals of Kan.* (new ed., 1886), p. 193; articles on "A. T. Still" and "Osteopathy," in *Encyc. Am.* and *Encyc. Brit.* written by practitioners of osteopathy; Morris Fishbein, *The Medical Follies* (1925), destructively critical.]

M. G. S.

STILL, WILLIAM (Oct. 7, 1821–July 14, 1902), reformer, negro leader, was the son of Levin Steel, a former Maryland slave, who had gone North after purchasing his freedom. Subsequently, Levin was joined by his wife Sidney and their children, who had been recaptured by slave-hunters upon their first attempt to escape. To thwart further pursuit the family changed its name to Still—the mother also discarding the name Sidney for that of Charity—and settled among the sparsely inhabited pine lands at Shamong, Burlington County, N. J. Here William was born, the youngest of eighteen children. From an early age he worked on his father's farm, and his educational opportunities were few. In 1841 he left home and three years later moved to Philadelphia. In 1847 he married Letitia George by whom he had two sons and two daughters. The same year he became a clerk in the office of the Pennsylvania Society for the Abolition of Slavery.

Deeply impressed by his own family's experience, Still as clerk did all that lay in his power to help runaway slaves to freedom. Nineteen out of every twenty escaped slaves that passed through Philadelphia stopped at his house. In the decade 1851–61 he was the chairman and corresponding secretary of the Philadelphia branch of the Underground Railroad. The experiences of all those who had successfully fled from bondage he jotted down carefully, and in 1855 he made an extended tour through Canada to ascertain how the slaves that had made their way were faring. His *The Underground Railroad,* published in 1872, is one of the best accounts of how runaway slaves made their way to freedom. In 1859 he sheltered John Brown's widow and daughter when they passed through Philadelphia on their way to visit the leader of the Harpers Ferry raid before his execution. After the outbreak of the Civil War Still resigned as clerk and embarked first in the stove and then in the coal business. In February 1864 he was appointed post sutler at Camp William Penn for colored soldiers near Philadelphia. Methodical in his habits, he prospered in his business ventures.

Always intent on promoting the welfare of his race, in 1861 Still helped organize and finance a social, civil and statistical association to collect data about the colored people. Previous to this, in a remarkably well-expressed letter written on Aug. 30, 1859, to the *North American and United States Gazette,* he had begun a campaign against the regulation of the Philadelphia street car lines compelling all persons of color to ride on front platforms. This resulted in the Pennsylvania legislature ending this discrimination in 1867. Still's course during this controversy was bitterly assailed in colored circles so that he defended his attitude in a public address afterwards published in pamphlet form (*A Brief Narrative of the Struggle for the Rights of the Colored People of Philadelphia in the City Railway Cars,* 1867). The same procedure he followed in 1874 when he became unpopular among his own people by supporting the Democratic candidate for mayor of Philadelphia, publishing *An Address on Voting and Laboring.* In reporting against the establishment of a colored men's bank in Philadelphia he again displayed courage and independence. He served on the Freedmen's Aid Commission and was made a member of the Philadelphia board of trade. A devout Presbyterian he became superintendent of one of the denomination's Sunday schools in 1880 and the same year he founded the first colored Young Men's Christian Association. In welfare work he helped manage homes for aged colored persons and for destitute colored children; and also an orphan asylum for the children of negro soldiers and sailors.

[*Underground Railroad Records* (1886), a third edition of Still's book, contains a sketch of the author; see also *Appletons' Ann. Cyc. . . . 1902* (1903); W. J. Simmons, *Men of Mark* (1887); J. W. Gibson and W. H. Crogman, *The Colored American* (1902), pp. 490–98; *Pub. Ledger* (Phila.), July 15, 1902; A. S. Norwood, "Negro Welfare Work in Phila. as Illustrated by the Career of William Still," unpublished thesis, Univ. of Pa.]   H. G. V.

STILLÉ, ALFRED (Oct. 30, 1813–Sept. 24, 1900), physician, was born in Philadelphia, son of John and Maria (Wagner) Stillé and elder brother of Charles Janeway Stillé [*q.v.*]. He attended good preliminary schools and spent some time at Yale College, but left as the result of the "conic section rebellion" to transfer to the University of Pennsylvania, where he was graduated A.B. in 1832, A.M. in 1835, and M.D. in 1836. Fourteen years later he received the degree of M.A. from Yale, and was then enrolled as a member of the college class of 1832. Upon graduating in medicine he became house physician at "Blockley," now the Philadelphia General Hospital. Here he had the opportunity to study the typhus cases brought to the hospital during the epidemic of 1836 under Dr. William Wood Gerhard [*q.v.*], whose observations of these same cases led him to proclaim typhus as fundamentally different from typhoid fever. After a short service, however, Stillé resigned to spend two and a half years in study in Europe, a considerable part of the time in Paris, where he was profoundly influenced by Louis.

Returning to Philadelphia, he served as resident physician in the Pennsylvania Hospital, 1839–41, and then entered upon private practice. From 1849 to 1877 he was a visiting physician to St. Joseph's Hospital. In 1845 he began to lecture on pathology and the practice of medicine for the Philadelphia Association for Medical Instruction, and continued until 1851. In 1854 he was elected to the chair of practice of medicine in the Pennsylvania Medical College, continuing until 1859. In 1864 he succeeded the elder William Pepper [*q.v.*] as professor of the theory and practice of medicine in the University of Pennsylvania, holding this office until 1883, when he retired and was made professor emeritus. At this time he gave his valuable medical library to the University.

Stillé's first important writing, and the first American book on the subject, *Elements of General Pathology,* appeared in 1848. In 1860 he published *Therapeutics and Materia Medica* (1860). Probably his most striking literary production, written in collaboration with Professor John M. Maisch [*q.v.*], was the *National Dispensatory* (1879), an enormous work of 1628 pages. Of his numerous monographs and papers,

Epidemic Meningitis or Cerebro-Spinal Meningitis, published in 1867, is still looked upon as classic. He was president of the Philadelphia County Medical Society in 1862, one of the founders of the Philadelphia Pathological Society and its president from 1859 to 1862, one of the founders of the American Medical Association, its first secretary, and its president in 1871, a fellow of the College of Physicians of Philadelphia and its president in 1883.

Stillé was born and educated, lived, taught, and died in Philadelphia. He was always a proponent of higher standards of education. As a professor he was a perfect type of the old school —highly cultured and purely didactic. His high sense of morality and dignity can be divined from the closing sentence of his valedictory address: "Only two things are essential; to live uprightly, and to be wisely industrious." His lectures, scientifically correct, were polished literary essays, read to his classes year after year without addition or alteration. They were entirely lacking in inspiration, and since he had no connection with any hospital to which he could take his students, he could hold no clinics or ward classes by which to compensate for their deficiencies. In his later years he was a strikingly handsome old gentleman with delicate, sensitive, well-chiseled features, long white hair that curled about his collar, and a full white beard of considerable length. His appearance was venerable, benevolent, and patriarchal. He began to manifest the infirmities of age in his sixties and retired from his professorship and other activities at seventy, to live for seventeen years more, a recluse in his own home, where only a few friends visited him. He died in his eighty-seventh year, almost forgotten.

In 1841 he had married Caroline Barnett, who afforded him brief companionship and then acquired a mental disease from which she suffered for many years. After her death, he married, in June 1899, Katharine A. Blackiston of Chestertown, Md., who survived him, and according to instructions contained in his will published a small volume entitled *Fragments* (1901), composed of excerpts from his writings and letters. By his first marriage there were two sons and a daughter.

[C. W. Burr, "A Sketch of Alfred Stillé," *Univ. Medic. Mag.,* Jan. 1901; William Osler, "Memoir of Alfred Stillé," *Trans. Coll. of Phys. of Phila.,* 3 ser. XXIV (1902), pub. also in *Univ. of Pa. Medic. Bull.,* June 1902; E. E. Salisbury, *Biog. Memoranda Respecting . . . the Class of 1832 in Yale Coll.* (1880); *Obit. Record Grads. Yale Univ.,* 1901; J. W. Jordan, *Colonial Families of Phila.* (1911), vol. II; Katharine Blackiston Stillé, *Fragments* (1901); J. W. Croskey, *Hist. of Blockley* (1929); *Pub. Ledger* (Phila.), Sept. 25, 1900.]   J. McF.

STILLÉ, CHARLES JANEWAY (Sept. 23, 1819–Aug. 11, 1899), educator and historian, brother of Alfred Stillé [*q.v.*], was the son of John and Maria (Wagner) Stillé. His father was a descendent of Oloff Stillé, one of the Swedish settlers on the Delaware, who, arriving in 1641, established a home near Upland, now Chester, Pa., and later moved to Passyunk. His descendants were successful merchants in Philadelphia. Stillé's mother was descended from the Rev. Tobias Wagner of Reading, Pa., member of a Lutheran family in Württemberg, who emigrated to Pennsylvania in 1742.

Charles prepared for Yale College at a school conducted by the Rev. Dr. Steele at Abington, Pa., and the Edge Hill School near Princeton, N. J. He entered Yale in 1835, and upon graduation in 1839 delivered a valedictory oration, *The Social Spirit* (1839), which showed the ideals and ethical standards that were to characterize his life and writings. After studying in the office of Joseph Reed Ingersoll, he was admitted to the bar. His interests led him, however, rather to develop his taste for history and literature, in pursuance of which he visited Europe repeatedly.

During the Civil War he published a pamphlet entitled *How a Free People Conduct a Long War* (1862), drawing a comparison between the current conflict and the long struggle of Great Britain against the French Revolution and Napoleon; unusually free from harshness, it was pervaded with enlightened patriotism, and half a million copies of it were distributed. He was asked to serve as a member of the United States Sanitary Commission and as corresponding secretary of its Executive Committee, and had much to do with the success of the great "Sanitary Fair" held in Philadelphia in 1864, at which $1,-000,000 was raised for the work of the Commission. After the war he published *History of the United States Sanitary Commission* (1866). These activities taught him, he said, "to look upon important public questions in a large and liberal way" (*Reminiscences of a Provost,* p. 4) and thus prepared him for the responsibilities that soon came to him. Without having had previous experience in teaching, he was appointed in 1866 to the professorship of English literature and belles-lettres in the University of Pennsylvania. When he assumed his duties, the course of study in the college was substantially that of a century before, and the only gift of money the institution had received in over eighty years was one of $5,000. With characteristic zeal Stillé began at once to advocate the establishment of elective courses of study, which in

1867 were introduced into the upper classes of the college.

In 1868 he became the tenth provost of the University of Pennsylvania. His inaugural address, *The Claims of Liberal Culture in Philadelphia* (1868), presented the needs of the University as the center of the higher education of the community. The twelve years of his administration proved his unusual qualities as an educational leader and a practical executive. It was not easy to find support for his projects in the self-perpetuating Board of Trustees, long established in set grooves of action, yet he succeeded in obtaining their approval for marked changes. He aroused the interest of the community, enlisted the cordial cooperation of the faculty, and won the devoted affection of the students. New departments—of science (1872), music (1877), and dentistry (1878)—were created. Through the Provost's persistent efforts the city was induced in 1870 to sell on reasonable terms ten acres of land in West Philadelphia, where adequate facilities could be provided for the expansion of the University. There the cornerstone of College Hall, the first of the new buildings, was laid on June 15, 1871. The following year the city made a grant of five and a half acres for the erection of University Hospital, which was opened in 1874. Untiring in his efforts to put the University upon a sound financial basis, Stillé fell short of his high aim, but nevertheless he did obtain, among other gifts, the endowment of the Towne Scientific School, the John Welsh Chair, and the Bloomfield Moore scholarships for women, as well as a sum to found the Tobias Wagner Library. A notable means adopted for bringing the University into closer relationship with the city was the establishment of scholarships for graduates of the Philadelphia public schools. The extraordinary progress begun in his administration initiated the great expansion that was to continue under his immediate successors.

Stillé resigned the provostship in 1880 for reasons which he set forth in *Reminiscences of a Provost, 1866–1880* (n.d.); disagreeing with the board of trustees, he contended that the Provost should be a member of the board, that powers of discipline over students should be vested in the faculty, and that a great, united effort should be made to put the University finances on a stable basis. In 1881 he retired also from the John Welsh professorship, of which he was the first incumbent, and thereafter devoted himself to historical studies. In addition to a number of pamphlets, he published *Studies in Mediaeval History* (1882); *The Life and Times of John Dickinson* (1891); and *Major-General Anthony Wayne and the Pennsylvania Line in the Continental Army* (1893). On his second visit to Sweden, in 1888, he discovered the whereabouts of the records of the Swedish colonists on the Delaware. Abstracts of these, in translation, he afterwards presented to the Historical Society of Pennsylvania, of which he was president for eight years (*Pennsylvania Magazine of History and Biography*, January 1892). The Gloria Dei Church of Philadelphia, founded by Swedish Lutherans, deeply interested him and became the beneficiary of one-third of his residuary estate. On Apr. 21, 1846, he had married Anna Dulles, who survived him. They had no children but adopted Mrs. Stillé's niece as their daughter; she died in 1896. Stillé's death occurred at Atlantic City, N. J.

[Besides Stillé's *Reminiscences* mentioned above, see *Proc. Hist. Soc. of Pa. on the Death of Charles Janeway Stillé* (1900); *Obit. Record Grads. Yale Univ.*, 1900; J. W. Jordan, *Colonial Families of Phila.* (1911), vol. II; J. B. McMaster, *The Univ. of Pa. Illustrated* (1897); G. E. Nitzsche, *Univ. of Pa.* (1916); H. M. Lippincott, *The Univ. of Pa.* (1919); *Public Ledger* (Phila.), Aug. 12, 1899.]   A. L. L.

STILLMAN, JAMES (June 9, 1850–Mar. 15, 1918), banker and capitalist, was born at Brownsville, Tex. His parents, Charles and Elizabeth Pamela (Goodrich) Stillman, both came from families long settled at Wethersfield, Conn. Thither in 1703 had gone George Stillman, the first of the line in America, who had settled in Hadley, Mass., in 1690. Charles Stillman, as a young cotton merchant, had ventured into the Rio Grande valley before the Mexican War, settling at Matamoros, Mexico, and later at Brownsville on the Texas side of the river, where he acquired large tracts of land. About 1855 or 1856 the boy was brought to Connecticut and there he got his early schooling. Before the Civil War the family settled in New York City. During the war James continued his studies in private schools at Cornwall-on-Hudson and Sing Sing (now Ossining), N. Y. At sixteen he went to work with the mercantile firm, Smith, Woodward & Stillman, of which his father had long been a member and which had traded in cotton during the war. Young Stillman consorted with older men and in particular gained much from consultation with Moses Taylor [q.v.], the president of the National City Bank.

Charles Stillman having been forced by impaired health to retire from business, the son early assumed many responsibilities of the family's head. On June 14, 1871, he married Sarah Elizabeth Rumrill. She bore him three sons and two daughters, all of whom survived him; separated from him in 1894, she was not mentioned in his will. In 1872 Stillman received from his father a power of attorney. He became a member of the cotton firm, which enjoyed prosperity over a long period. As his surplus gradually increased and his outside investments were expanded, he naturally formed contacts with financiers and industrialists. In the directorate of the Chicago, Milwaukee & St. Paul Railway he met William Rockefeller [q.v.], then one of the magnates of the petroleum industry. The friendship between the two men, beginning in 1884, lasted throughout Stillman's lifetime. Both of Stillman's daughters married sons of Rockefeller.

Personally known to only a few of his business associates and not at all to the general public, Stillman reached and passed his fortieth year. One of his early ambitions he had achieved; he held a directorship in the National City Bank. On the death of Moses Taylor in 1882 his son-in-law, Percy R. Pyne, had succeeded to the presidency of that institution. In his final illness Pyne's choice for his own successor was Stillman, who was promptly elected by the directors in 1891. Everything Stillman did on assuming the office indicated adherence to the code and practice of Taylor, his first mentor in finance. The bank's reserves were increased far beyond the technical requirements. Gold accumulated in its vaults and the huge surplus caught the attention of conservative business men. Deposits grew with the surplus (in a few years they more than quadrupled) and the National City rose from the second to the first rank among Wall Street institutions. While it was being built up through the application of old and tried banking principles, it became a leader in a new field, as the foremost bank in the service of the great industrial and financial combines that marked the last decade of the nineteenth century and the first of the twentieth. Early in that era of consolidation Stillman allied himself with the Standard Oil group of financiers headed by H. H. Rogers [q.v.] and William Rockefeller. In 1899 the sales of stock of the Amalgamated Copper Company and the Consolidated Gas Company of New York were both conducted by the National City, although even Wall Street gasped when a national bank engaged in such promotions. The copper operation, designed to secure a monopoly, proved disastrous and became notorious (John Moody, The Truth about the Trusts, 1904, pp. 3-44). Stillman also developed close relations with E. H. Harriman [q.v.] in western railroad operations. There was considerable rivalry between the Harriman-Stillman-Rockefeller-Schiff group and the Morgan-Hill combination until

1907, when a greater "community of interest" developed.

In connection with the money panic of that year, Stillman, though overshadowed in the popular mind by J. P. Morgan [q.v.], was one of the more influential leaders, being particularly notable for his advocacy of the support of weaker New York banks by the stronger. (For an interesting contrast between Stillman and Morgan, see Corey, post, p. 260.) Two years later he retired from the presidency of the bank, retaining the chairmanship of the board of directors, and for several years passed most of his time in France, where he was able more fully to gratify his esthetic tastes. In the World War he identified himself fully with the Allied cause, giving generously from his private fortune in support of French effort. Late in 1917 he returned to America and for a few months devoted himself to the management of the bank while its president was busy in Washington. On Mar. 15, 1918, in New York City, he died of heart disease. His estate, valued at $50,000,000, went to his family (will in New York Times, Mar. 24, 1918). Much had been given to public causes during his lifetime; but in the main such gifts had been successfully concealed. The man's unusual reticence and hatred of publicity may have hidden even from associates his real character. There were those who thought they detected, beneath an affected hardness of manner, a vein of emotionalism, but he gave the general impression of coldness.

[Edgar Stillman, 1654-1903, Hist. and Genealogy of George Stillman, 1st, and His Descendants (1903), following another line, but giving information about original American ancestor; H. R. Stiles, The Hist. of Ancient Wethersfield, Conn. (1904), II, 667-84; Anna R. Burr, The Portrait of a Banker: James Stillman, 1850-1918 (1927), a highly uncritical biography, reviewed by Edwin Le Fevre, in Saturday Rev. of Literature, Nov. 26, 1927; John Moody, The Masters of Capital (1919); Lewis Corey, The House of Morgan (1930); J. K. Winkler, The First Billion. The Stillmans and the National City Bank (1934), undocumented, popular, and critical; F. A. Vanderlip, "From Farm Boy to Financier," Saturday Evening Post, Dec. 22, 1934, Jan. 19, Mar. 30, 1935; obituaries in N. Y. newspapers, Mar. 16, 1918.]   W. B. S.

STILLMAN, SAMUEL (Feb. 27, 1737, o.s.-Mar. 12, 1807), Baptist clergyman, was born in Philadelphia, Pa. The family moved to Charleston, S. C., where Samuel attended Rind's Academy and studied theology for one year under the Rev. Oliver Hart, pastor of the Baptist church with which he had united. He was ordained on Feb. 26, 1759, and preached for two years at James Island, in the vicinity of Charleston. In May 1759 he was married to Hannah Morgan, of Philadelphia, and they had fourteen children, only two of whom survived their father. Conditions of health led him northward and for two years he lived at Bordentown, N. J., where he supplied two churches. He received the honorary degree of Master of Arts from the College of Philadelphia in 1761, and the same degree, *ad eundem,* that same year from Harvard, and from Brown in 1769. The last-named University conferred on him the degree of Doctor of Divinity in 1788.

In 1763 Stillman visited Boston, where he was engaged by the Second Baptist Church as assistant pastor. After about a year he was called to the pastorate of the First Baptist Church, a position he retained for the rest of his life. He was installed on Jan. 9, 1765, by a council to which only "orthodox," *i.e.,* Congregational, churches were invited. At that time the First Baptist Church was not in very amicable relations with other Baptist churches; but, except with the Second Church, from which a number of members withdrew to follow Stillman, better relations were soon established. He brought his church into the Warren Association and became one of the outstanding leaders in that influential organization, in spite of the facts that the first half of his pastorate was very definitely handicapped by the strained relations with the Second Baptist Church. By the time he settled in Boston he was already interested in the movement to found Rhode Island College (Brown University), and was named among the original trustees in 1764. A year later, he became a fellow of the College, retaining the position for life. He was in constant association with James Manning and Hezekiah Smith [*qq.v.*], and his influence penetrated the religious and educational interests of the Baptists of New England for forty years.

He early acquired a reputation for intellectual ability. His preaching, prevailingly Calvinistic and evangelical, was not unmindful of the application of fundamental gospel principles to the public life of the day. One of his early sermons in Boston, *Good News from a Far Country* (1766), had its inception in the repeal of the Stamp Act. The General Court invited him to preach the annual election sermon in 1779 when the most vital public concern was the policy of the constitutional convention. Stillman frankly argued the necessity of inserting in the constitution of the state a Bill of Rights and provision for the separation of church and state, since only by this procedure could the sacred rights of conscience be secured. The citizens of Boston elected him as one of their twelve delegates to the convention for the ratification of the federal Constitution, and, on the first observance of Independence Day after the institution of the new

government, they requested him to preach the anniversary sermon. In 1808 his addresses were published under the title *Select Sermons on Doctrinal and Practical Subjects.* He was an active proponent of the Baptists and other dissenters in the famous Pittsfield case of 1779, but this was merely a continuation of his activities as chairman of the Baptist Committee on Grievances.

[In a funeral discourse preached by Dr. Thomas Baldwin, reference is made to Stillman's diary, but it does not seem to be extant. This discourse gives numerous biographical facts as does N. E. Wood, *The Hist. of the First Bapt. Ch. of Boston* (1899). There is a brief sketch in Stillman's *Select Sermons* (1808). David Benedict, in his *Gen. Hist. of the Bapt. Denomination* (2 vols., 1813), gives facts much used in the later sketches. See also *Hist. Cat. of Brown Univ., 1764-1914* (1914). Wm. Cathcart, ed., *The Bapt. Encyc.* (1881), adds little, but Wm. B. Sprague, *Annals Am. Pulpit,* vol. VI (1860), gives a detailed list of his published works, chiefly sermons, and personal recollections by two of his contemporaries.]   W. H. A.

STILLMAN, THOMAS BLISS (May 24, 1852–Aug. 10, 1915), chemist, educator, was born at Plainfield, N. J., the son of Dr. Charles Henry and Mary Elizabeth (Starr) Stillman. His early schooling at Plainfield was supplemented by studies at the grammar school of Madison University, Hamilton, N. Y., and at Alfred University, Alfred, N. Y. In 1870 he entered Rutgers College, from which he graduated in 1873 with the degree of B.S. He then pursued a special course in analytical chemistry at Rutgers, where he also assisted in teaching this subject.

In the spring of 1874 he was appointed chemistry assistant to Prof. A. R. Leeds of the Stevens Institute of Technology, Hoboken, and two years later went abroad to study analytical chemistry under the celebrated Dr. R. Fresenius at Wiesbaden, Germany. Here he remained two years, then, declining the offer of a position as instructor by Fresenius, returned to the United States and opened an analytical laboratory in New York City in 1879. He also became consulting chemist of the Sawyer-Mann Electric Light Company, associate editor in the science department of the *Scientific American,* and manager of the assay department of the *Mining Record.* In 1882 he resumed his connection as assistant to Professor Leeds at Stevens Institute, performing post-graduate studies for which he received the degree of Ph.D. in 1883. In 1886 he was appointed professor of analytical chemistry at Stevens and in 1902, upon the death of Professor Leeds, became head of the chemical department with the title of professor of engineering chemistry.

In addition to his work as a teacher, Stillman

conducted an outside consulting practice, serving as chemical expert to various municipalities in their water-supply problems, of which subject he had made a special study. He took also an active interest in the improvement of the milk supply of cities, and for a number of years was chemist to the Medical Milk Commission of Newark, N. J. In connection with his teaching and his consulting practice he published *Engineering Chemistry, a Manual of Quantitative Chemical Analysis for the Use of Students, Chemists and Engineers* (1897), a standard work which has gone through six editions and has long been used as a college textbook and practical treatise. In 1909 Stillman retired from his professorship at Stevens in order to devote all his time to consulting and chemical engineering practice. He became senior member of the firm of Stillman & Van Siclen, chemical experts, in New York. In 1911 he was appointed city chemist of Jersey City and Bayonne, a position which he continued to occupy until his death, four years later.

In addition to his *Engineering Chemistry*, Stillman published *Examination of Lubricating Oils* (1914) and was the author of more than thirty journal articles relating to chemical analysis and various chemical engineering subjects. He patented several processes, for manufacturing fertilizers, illuminating gas, *et cetera*, and attracted considerable attention by the "synthetic" dinner which he gave at the Hotel Astor, New York, on Feb. 21, 1906, at which he prepared many courses of the menu from synthetic products. He was a member of the American Chemical Society, American Electro-Chemical Society, American Institute of Mining Engineers, and chemical societies in Germany, Great Britain, and France. Though a man of genial disposition, he had a capacity for hard work. In 1881 he married Emma L. Pomplitz of Baltimore, Md., who survived him with three children.

[*Stevens Indicator,* Oct. 1915, with portrait and bibliog.; *Jour. Industrial and Engineering Chemistry,* Sept. 1915; B. P. Starr, *A Hist. of the Starr Family of New England* (1879); *N. Y. Times,* Aug. 11, 1915.]

C. A. B.

STILLMAN, THOMAS EDGAR (Mar. 23, 1837–Sept. 4, 1906), lawyer, was born in New York City, the son of Alfred and Elizabeth Ann (Greenough) Stillman. He successively attended public school No. 2, in New York City, the Free Academy of New York, and Alfred Academy (now Alfred University) at which latter institution he finished his secondary education and completed two years of college work. In 1857 he entered Madison College (now Colgate University), Hamilton, N. Y., where he attained a creditable scholastic record, graduating two years later. He remained in Hamilton for the next three years, studying law in the office of Joseph Mason, later county judge and member of Congress. Under the tutelage of Mason, his brother Charles Mason, who subsequently became a judge of the New York court of appeals and was then a justice of the New York supreme court, and David J. Mitchell, a prominent attorney, he received a thorough training for the profession. During this period he took part locally in Lincoln's campaign of 1860. Having been admitted to the bar in 1862, Stillman moved to New York, where, after a brief period of independent legal activity, he joined the firm of Barney, Butler & Parsons as managing clerk. Shortly afterwards he was admitted as junior partner, Barney and Parsons withdrew, and Thomas H. Hubbard [*q.v.*] joined the firm, which from 1874 until the date of Stillman's retirement in 1896, was known as Butler, Stillman & Hubbard.

Beginning his career in the field of commercial and general practice, Stillman soon began to give special attention to admiralty problems, gradually forging to the front of the admiralty bar by his able handling of important suits pertaining to this branch of jurisprudence. The first of these litigations was the case of the *Circassian* (*Fed. Cas.* No. 2723) in which he unraveled the tangled skein of legal troubles so successfully as to establish his reputation as an admiralty lawyer. Following that of the *Circassian* he took part in many maritime *causes célèbres,* some of which established new principles of American maritime law, such as those of the *Scotland* (105 *U. S.,* 24), the *Pennsylvania* (19 *Wallace,* 125), and the *Atlas* (93 *U. S.,* 302). From his admiralty practice Stillman passed into the field of corporation law, especially as it concerned railroads, and thus gravitated naturally into corporation management. This he first undertook in connection with the administration of the Mark Hopkins estate, valued in the neighborhood of $19,000,000, part of which represented substantially one-fourth ownership of the Southern Pacific Company. In fact, during his later years Stillman gradually withdrew from the practice of law to devote more time to corporate affairs, becoming president of the San Antonio & Aransas Pass Railway Company (1893–1900) and director of the Southern Pacific Company, of the United States National Bank, and of many minor companies.

From the personal standpoint Stillman appears to have led a well-rounded and active existence, passing an exceptionally happy family life with his wife, the former Charlotte Elizabeth Greenman, whom he had married on Jan. 10, 1865, and enjoying the society of a wide circle of friends. He was a man catholic in his tastes, with a wide interest in literature, art, and history,—public spirited, kindly, and charitable. Following his retirement from active business he devoted much of his time to travel, spending every summer in Europe. It was while traveling through France that he met his death as the result of injuries sustained in an automobile accident. He was survived by four daughters.

[T. H. Hubbard, "Memorial of Thomas Edgar Stillman," in *Asso. of the Bar of the City of N. Y.—1907* (1907), abridged in *Report . . . Am. Bar. Asso.*, 1908; *N. Y. Times, N. Y. Tribune*, and *World* (N.Y.), Sept. 5, 1906.]   L. M. S.

STILLMAN, WILLIAM JAMES (June 1, 1828–July 6, 1901), artist, journalist, and diplomat, was born in Schenectady, N. Y., the son of Joseph and Eliza Ward (Maxson) Stillman. After graduating from Union College in 1848, he studied landscape painting in New York during part of the next winter under Frederick Edwin Church [*q.v.*], and in December 1849 sailed for England, where, during his brief stay, he met J. M. W. Turner and began his long friendship with John Ruskin. In 1851 or 1852, after his return to America, he joined Kossuth and was sent to Hungary on a special mission, which, owing to Kossuth's incompetence in giving directions, failed. After a brief stay in France he opened a studio in New York and became art critic for the *Evening Post*. In January 1855 he founded the *Crayon: A Journal Devoted to the Graphic Arts, and the Literature Related to Them*. Although it was a literary success (numbering among its contributors James Russell Lowell), Stillman at the end of 1856 severed his connection with the paper because of financial difficulties and ill health. Through the *Crayon*, however, he had formed valuable acquaintances among the *literati* of Cambridge and Concord, and he now removed to Cambridge, where for a time he continued his landscape painting and was instrumental in forming the Adirondack Club, whose roster included the names of Emerson and Agassiz. In 1860 he was again in Europe pursuing his art and enjoying the company of Dante Gabriel Rossetti and Ruskin. Soon after the outbreak of the Civil War he became American consul at Rome (appointment confirmed, Feb. 19, 1862), where he and his wife, Laura Mack, whom he had married on Nov. 19, 1860, lived until 1865. At that time he received a consular appointment to Crete, and there soon found himself in the midst of the Cretan insurrection of 1866. He at once sided with the Cretans, but by his kindness to the natives he so incurred the enmity of the pasha that his own life and that of his family were much endangered. By 1868 the strain had become so great that he abandoned the consulate and removed to Athens, where his wife died the following year. He soon settled in London. For the next few years he engaged in literary pursuits. In 1871 he married Marie Spartali, daughter of the Greek consul-general in London. In 1875 he set out for Herzegovina, then on the point of insurrection, as a volunteer correspondent for the London *Times*, and he soon extended his activities into Montenegro and Albania. He spent much of his remaining life in the employ of the *Times* as a special correspondent, with his residence in Rome. In 1898 he retired on a pension and removed to Surrey, where three years later he died.

As a landscape painter, he had quite exhausted his enthusiasm by 1860, although during the ten preceding years he exhibited pictures at the National Academy and was elected an associate of that body in 1854. The critical influence of Ruskin, whom he regarded with utmost reverence, seems in a measure to have run counter to Stillman's native artistic bent and may have helped to silence his genius. But his ultimate abandonment of painting was probably due to the fact, as he himself hints, that his theoretic knowledge of his art surpassed his executive ability. His literary work reflects both his honesty and versatility. Of himself he once wrote that he had never published a book except from a desire to contribute to human knowledge. For *Old Italian Masters Engraved by Timothy Cole* (1892) he wrote the biographical and descriptive material; and for *Venus & Apollo in Painting and Sculpture* (1897), a series of handsome reproductions from photographs, he produced an introduction and notes. His interest in art and archaeology found further expression in *The Acropolis of Athens* (1870), a splendid group of illustrations from photographs taken by Stillman himself; in *On the Track of Ulysses* (1888); in the *Report of W. J. Stillman on the Cesnola Collection* (1885); and in letters appended to the first and second annual reports of the Archaeological Institute of America. Many autobiographical data went into the making of such historical works as *The Cretan Insurrection of 1866-7-8* (1874), *Herzegovina and the Late Uprising* (1877), *The Union of Italy, 1815–1895* (1898), and *Francesco Crispi: Insurgent, Exile, Revolutionist, and Statesman* (1899). As an essayist he is to be remembered as the author of *Poetic Localities of Cambridge* (1876) and

The Old Rome and the New and Other Studies
(1898). His love of animals, of whose immortality he was firmly convinced, was responsible
for two charming narratives, *Billy and Hans*
(1897) and *Little Bertha* (1898). In 1901 appeared *The Autobiography of a Journalist*.

An innate spirit of inquiry led him ever to seek
fresh fields of thought as well as endeavor. Hostile in early life to the teachings of evolution, he
ultimately accepted the scientific creed of Darwin. And he so far freed himself from the dogmas of Calvinism as fully to accept the tenets of
Spiritualism, although deprecating the professional medium. "Perhaps his material prosperity and success might have been more signal,"
wrote the London *Times* when he died, "had his
tastes and gifts been fewer. Certainly his life
would have been less full, and the man less engaging."

[W. J. Stillman, *The Autobiog. of a Journalist* (2
vols., 1901); *Who's Who in America,* 1899–1900;
Sophie S. Martin, *Mack Geneal.* (1903), vol. I; cats.
of the exhibitions of the Nat. Acad. of Design, 1851–
58; C. E. Norton, ed., *Letters of James Russell Lowell*
(2 vols., 1894), *passim*; H. E. Scudder, *James Russell
Lowell* (2 vols., 1901), *passim*; obituaries in *Evening
Post* (N. Y.), July 8, and *Times* (London), July 9,
1901.]   N. F. A.

STILWELL, SILAS MOORE (June 6,
1800–May 16, 1881), lawyer and writer on financial topics, was born in New York City, the
fifth of six children of Stephen and Nancy
(Moore) Stilwell. He was descended from
Nicholas Stillwell [*sic*], who was in Manhattan as early as 1645 and may have been in Virginia previously. Stephen Stilwell, a merchant
and veteran of the Revolution, moved his family
in 1804 to Glasco, Ulster County, N. Y., where
he bought a glass factory and iron foundry.
After investing heavily in Western lands, he
went bankrupt in 1810. Silas entered Woodstock Free Academy, but left at the age of
twelve to become a clerk in a New York hardware store. Two years later he went West to
work with land surveyors. At twenty-two he
was a member of the Tennessee legislature, soon
afterward moved to Virginia, and in 1824 was
admitted to the bar. He practised successfully
for several years and served as member of the
House of Burgesses. In 1828 he returned to
New York where he continued his political activities. Elected in 1829 to the Assembly on
the National Republican ticket, he served three
terms, 1830–33. The demands of the new Workingman's Party enlisted his sympathy, particularly the abolition of imprisonment for debt. On
this issue, says Thurlow Weed (*post*), Stilwell
staked his political future, and as a result of his
efforts the Stilwell Act, abolishing the penalty,

was passed in 1831. In 1834 he ran, unsuccessfully, for lieutenant-governor on the ticket headed by William H. Seward [*q.v.*]. Two years
later, as candidate for alderman in New York
City he was successful and as chairman of an
evenly divided board he exercised great authority in appointments.

Banking reform next attracted him. Disapproval of Jackson's withdrawal of government
deposits from the Bank of the United States
caused Stilwell to break with his party and join
the Whigs. On his interest in the revision of
banking laws in New York State has been based
the claim that he was the author of the Free
Banking Law of 1838. A pamphlet which he
published at this time, however, *A System of
Credit for a Republic, and the Plan of a Bank
for the State of New-York* (1838), shows that
what he had in mind was radically different from
the plan adopted. The election of Harrison to
the presidency brought Stilwell into touch with
national politics. He is said to have refused a
cabinet post because of his large losses in the
panic of 1837, but President Tyler appointed him
United States marshal for the southern district
of New York in 1841 and sent him on a special
mission to The Hague.

Stilwell's claim to authorship of the National
Banking Act is not recognized by historians of
American banking. During 1861 and 1862 he
was in Washington, where he was in close contact with Secretary Salmon P. Chase [*q.v.*] and
with Edward Jordan, solicitor of the treasury.
He prepared a pamphlet, published by the government, *A System of National Finance: Notes
Explanatory of Mr. Chase's Plan of National
Finance* (1861), and worked with Jordan on a
preliminary draft of the banking bill, but his
contribution to the Act as it finally emerged
seems to have been less important than that of
Elbridge Gerry Spaulding [*q.v.*] and Samuel
Hooper (Helderman, *post*, pp. 136–42). From
1861 to 1872 he wrote articles on financial topics for the *New York Herald* under the pseudonym Jonathan Oldbuck. He published in 1866
a lecture, *National Finances: A Philosophical
Examination of Credit,* and in 1879, *Private History of the Origin and Purpose of the National
Banking Law.* In later life he changed parties a
second time, becoming again a stanch Democrat.
A romantic episode in his career was his courtship of Caroline Norsworthy, the daughter of a
rich New York merchant and landowner, whom
he married in defiance of parental wishes. She
brought him a considerable fortune and with
what he had himself acquired he was regarded
at one time as a rich man. He had four children,

three of whom survived him. After his wife's death he became deeply interested in Spiritualism and prepared the manuscript of a book in its defense. He died in New York City.

[Dewitt and Lamont Stilwell, *Hist. and Geneal. Record of One Branch of the Stilwell Family* (1914); J. E. Stilwell, *The Hist. of Lieut. Nicholas Stillwell* (1929) and *The Hist. of Capt. Nicholas Stillwell and His Descendants* (1930); D. S. Alexander, *A Pol. Hist. of the State of N. Y.*, vol. I (1906); F. W. Seward, *Autobiog. of Wm. H. Seward . . . with a Memoir of His Life* (1877); *Autobiog. of Thurlow Weed* (1883), ed. by H. A. Weed; *A Report of Two Interviews with the Hon. Silas M. Stilwell* (1874); A. M. Davis, "The Origin of the National Banking System," in *Reports of the National Monetary Commission*, vol. XXXV (1910), being *Sen. Doc. 582*, 61 Cong., 2 Sess.; L. C. Helderman, *National and State Banks* (1931); *N. Y. Herald*, May 17, 1881.] P. W. B.

STILWELL, SIMPSON EVERETT (Aug. 25, 1849–Feb. 17, 1903), scout, peace officer, best known as "Jack" Stilwell, was born in Tennessee, the son of William and Clara Stilwell. While he was still a youth the family moved to Missouri and afterward to eastern Kansas. At the age of fourteen he left school and joined a wagontrain for Santa Fé, and for several years remained in New Mexico. On June 18, 1867, at Fort Dodge, Kan., he engaged for his first service as a scout, and on Aug. 28, 1868, he joined Maj. G. A. Forsyth's company of fifty scouts, operating from Fort Wallace in search of hostile Indians. On Sept. 17, on the Arikaree Fork of the Republican River, this company was suddenly surrounded by a force of 900 Cheyennes and Sioux, under Roman Nose, and a desperate battle followed, continuing until the arrival of a relief force eight days later. On the first night, Stilwell, with a companion, crept through the hostile cordon, and three days later reached Fort Wallace with the news. For this exploit he became famous. During the next thirteen years, enrolled under the names Simpson E. Stillwell, J. E. Stillwell, and Jack Stillwell, he was irregularly employed as a scout, serving under Custer, Miles, Mackenzie and others, and was often detailed to exceptionally hazardous ventures. His scouting service ended on Jan. 22, 1881. On hearing that his brother Frank, who had become an outlaw in Arizona, had been shot to death by Marshal Wyatt Earp at Tucson in March 1882, he started for the scene to avenge the killing, but it seems that on learning the facts of the case he quietly returned.

For a time he was a United States deputy marshal at the Cheyenne-Arapaho agency, in the present Oklahoma. On the opening of Indian territory to settlement, he made his home at El Reno, where he was elected a police judge. In 1894 he was appointed a United States commissioner, with station at Anadarko, and was re-appointed in 1897. In the meantime he had studied law and had been admitted to the bar. His health failing, he resigned his post on Nov. 10, 1898, and accepted an invitation from William F. Cody [*q.v.*] to move to the new town of Cody, Wyo. On Jan. 14, 1899, he was again appointed a United States commissioner. He was cared for in his last years on the ranch of "Buffalo Bill," and died at Cody. He had been married, at Braddock, Pa., on May 6, 1895, to Esther Hannah White, who survived him. In his scouting days he was slight and lithe, though later he became somewhat corpulent. His intelligence, daring, and resourcefulness are highly praised by all his commanders. He had an excellent command of Spanish and a workable knowledge of most of the languages of the plains Indians. He was modest in manner, and, as a rule, reticent of speech.

[J. E. Stillwell, *Hist. of Capt. Jeremiah Stillwell . . .* (1931), vol. IV of the *Stillwell Geneal.*; G. A. Custer, *My Life on the Plains* (1874); G. A. Forsyth, *Thrilling Days in Army Life* (1900); N. A. Miles, *Personal Recollections* (1896); R. G. Carter, *The Old Sergeant's Story* (1926); D. L. Spotts, *Campaigning with Custer* (1928); H. W. Wheeler, *Buffalo Days* (1925); service record from the Quartermaster-General's Office; information from his widow, Mrs. Carl Hammitt, Cody, Wyo., and from Dan W. Peery, Oklahoma City; *N. Y. Herald*, Sept. 21, 1902.] W. J. G.

STIMPSON, WILLIAM (Feb. 14, 1832–May 26, 1872), naturalist, was born in Roxbury, Mass., the son of Herbert H. and Mary Ann (Brewster) Stimpson. His early education was in the common schools of Boston, and in his sixteenth year he entered the upper class of the Boston High School, from which he was graduated in July 1848. At an early age William became interested in natural history. The possession of a copy of *Report on the Invertebrata of Massachusetts* (1841), presented to him by the author, Augustus A. Gould [*q.v.*], laid the foundation for a strong friendship between the distinguished conchologist and the young naturalist, and this connection brought him to the notice of Jean Louis Rodolphe Agassiz [*q.v.*], from whom he received great encouragement. His parents were desirous that he should go into business and his excursions to the seashore and other nature pursuits were looked upon as a waste of time. As a compromise he was permitted to study civil engineering, but his employer reported that he was more interested in hunting land snails than in surveying, and advised that the boy be permitted to enter upon a career more in accord with his inclinations. Accordingly, he was allowed to enter the Boston Latin School in 1848. The following summer he went on a fishing smack to Grand Manan, collecting and studying the marine animals of that region and later was associated with the workers in Agassiz's laboratory. Through the aid of friends he received an appointment as naturalist to the North Pacific Exploring Expedition in 1852, and all parental opposition to his career as a naturalist was finally removed. He spent four years with the expedition, and returned to the United States in 1856 to begin the classification of the immense amount of material gathered during these fruitful years. His headquarters were in the Smithsonian Institution, Washington, D. C. Nine years were thus occupied, in the course of which he visited Europe to collect comparative data, making many friends among European scientists. The results of his work were published in 1907 as volume XLIX of the *Smithsonian Miscellaneous Collections.*

Stimpson was called to the directorship of the Chicago Academy of Sciences in 1865 by his friend, Robert Kennicott [*q.v.*], while the latter was away upon the expedition to Alaska and the Yukon from which he never returned. Here, in a new building believed to be fire-proof, Stimpson assembled his great collection of manuscripts, drawings, and material loaned by institutions and collectors from many parts of the world. The Smithsonian collections, those of Louis François de Pourtalès [*q.v.*], and specimens from many eastern naturalists, were placed at his disposal. Priceless volumes in large number were loaned for his study, and manuscripts in preparation as well as some ready for publication were here assembled. It is probable that, previous to this time, no single depository contained as much valuable scientific material as did the Chicago Academy of Sciences in the latter part of 1871, when, in the great fire of October, the building and its treasures were destroyed. All that was left of William Stimpson's life work were some pieces of mound-builder pottery. From this tragic blow he never recovered. He had long been a sufferer from weakness of the lungs and his attempt to study the Gulf Stream with the Coast Survey in 1871–72 completely broke his health. He died at Ilchester, Md., scarcely eight months after his loss through the Chicago fire.

Stimpson's works were written in Latin, a noteworthy accomplishment in his day. He published many papers on mollusca and crustacea, among them being *A Revision and Synonymy of the Testaceous Mollusks of New England* (1851), *The Crustacea and Echinodermata of the Pacific Shores of North America* (1857); *Notes on North American Crustacea* (1859); *Prodromus Descriptionis Animalium Evertebratorum* (1857–60); *Researches upon the Hydro-*

biinæ and Allied Forms, Smithsonian Miscellaneous Collections, vol. VII (1865). He was honored by membership in the National Academy of Sciences in 1868, and in many other scientific societies, both at home and abroad. At his death he was survived by his wife, Annie Gordon, of Ilchester, Md., to whom he had been married on July 28, 1864, and several children.

[W. H. Dall, "Some American Conchologists," *Proc. of the Biological Soc. of Washington,* vol. IV (1888); *Proc. Chicago Acad. Sci.,* 1872; *Am. Naturalist,* vol. VI (1872); *Chicago Tribune,* June 12, 1872.]

F. C. B.

STIMSON, ALEXANDER LOVETT (Dec. 14, 1816–Jan. 2, 1906), expressman and author, was born in Boston, Mass., the son of Lovett and Sally (Fisher) Stimson. His father was a dancing master. Little is known of Stimson's early youth, but in 1840 he was in Georgia, working as a rodman on the survey of the Georgia Railroad under his elder brother, John K. Stimson, a civil engineer. During his stay in Georgia he studied law. Now and then in those earlier years he had a try at the newspaper business—in New York, in Boston, and in New Orleans—but did not remain in it for long periods. It gave him an itch for writing, however, and throughout life he produced articles and stories in large numbers for various periodicals. In 1846 he took a position as clerk in the New York office of Adams & Company, an express company, and this determined his future career. In 1850 he and his brother John launched an express line of their own, Stimson and Company's New Orleans and Mobile Express, operating by steamboat from New York to New Orleans and Mobile, but it was soon absorbed by Adams & Company.

In 1852 Stimson founded a magazine devoted to this youthful business, the *Express Messenger,* the first journal of its kind, and operated it as proprietor and editor for several years. It was during this period that he manifested his greatest literary activity. He wrote a history of the Mercantile Library Association of Boston and his two longest pieces of fiction, *Easy Nat; or The Three Apprentices* (1854), later republished as *New England Boys* (1856), and *Waifwood* (1864), a novel. In 1858 first appeared the work by which he is best known, his *History of the Express Companies: and the Origin of American Railroads.* It reappeared in 1881, largely rewritten, as *History of the Express Business, Including the Origin of the Railway System in America, and the Relation of Both to the Increase of New Settlements and the Prosperity of Cities in the United States.* His idea, originated in 1851, that express companies might act as purchasing agents, led to the development of order and commission departments in express companies. During the Civil War he served as representative of the Adams Express Company at various places in the South. Later he was with Wells Fargo & Company and the American Express Company. For several years in the latter part of his life he was attorney for the National Express Company. During this time he continued to write frequent articles for newspapers and express periodicals. His wife was Mary Jerome of Syracuse, N. Y., whom he married in New York City in 1844. She died in 1881. Stimson died in 1906 at Glens Falls, New York, where he had been living for six years. He was survived by one son.

[See *Express Gazette*, Jan. 1881, Jan. 15, 1906; Stimson's *Hist. of the Express Business* (1881), which contains a number of references to his own career; and obituary in *Glens Falls Morning Post*, Jan. 3, 1906. His death is recorded in the Vital Statistics Bureau, Albany, N. Y. Information has been supplied by the American Antiquarian Society.]   A.F.H.

STIMSON, LEWIS ATTERBURY (Aug. 24, 1844–Sept. 17, 1917), surgeon, was born in Paterson, N. J., the son of Henry Clark and Julia Maria (Atterbury) Stimson. On his father's side he was descended from John Stimson who emigrated from England and settled in Watertown, Mass., in 1635; on his mother's from Elias Boudinot, 1740–1821 [*q.v.*]. When he was barely fifteen he entered Yale College, the baby of his class. After graduation in 1863, he visited Europe. In 1864 he entered the Union army as a captain and rendered excellent service, but was invalided home near the end of the war with a severe typhoid fever that nearly ended his career. He soon entered his father's banking office, becoming a member of the New York stock exchange. On Nov. 9, 1866, in Paris, France, he married Candace T. Wheeler, daughter of Thomas M. Wheeler of New York. Having acquired a keen taste for a scientific life he began to study medicine in 1871, for the most part in Paris but with a year in the Bellevue Hospital Medical School, where he took the degree of M.D. in 1874. He then began practice in New York. In 1875 he won the James Wood prize with a paper entitled *Bacteria and Their Influence upon the Origin and Development of Septic Complications of Wounds* (1875), which showed the influence of his association with Louis Pasteur in Paris. In 1876, appointed visiting surgeon to the Presbyterian Hospital, he was one of the first in America to use antiseptics and to operate by the Lister spray method. He became visiting surgeon to Bellevue Hospital in 1879. He was professor of physiology (1883–85), professor of

anatomy (1885–89), and professor of surgery (1889–98) in the Medical College of the University of the City of New York (later New York University). In 1898 he became professor of surgery in the Cornell University Medical College, a position he held until his death. With Dr. William Mecklenburg Polk he was instrumental in founding this college and in securing an endowment and a building from Oliver Hazard Payne [*qq.v.*], his friend and classmate at Yale. In 1889 he resigned from the Presbyterian Hospital to become surgeon to the New York Hospital and its Chambers Street branch, where he gained much of his experience in traumatic surgery that formed the basis of his best-known book, *A Practical Treatise on Fractures and Dislocations* (1899), a classic in the subject. He also published *A Manual of Operative Surgery* (1878); *Clinical Lectures on Surgery* (1878), from the French of Léon Gosselin; *The Growth of a People, a Short Study in French History* (1883), from the French of Paul Lacombe; and edited *The Principles of Surgery and Surgical Pathology* (1894), from the German of Hermann Tillmanns. He was a much-admired and respected teacher. He was regent of the state of New York, 1893–1904, a member of the Société de Chirurgie of Paris, a founder of the New York Surgical Society, and a member of the New York Academy of Medicine.

The death of his wife, by whom he had a son and a daughter, occurred early in his surgical career (June 1876). Overwhelmed by this loss, he survived it "by years of constant grinding work." Sailing his 87-foot schooner yacht, *Fleur-de-Lys,* which he used for trips to Norway, Iceland, Labrador, and the Mediterranean, was his keenest pleasure. In *The Cruise of the Fleur-de-Lys in the Ocean Race* (1905) he describes the race for the Kaiser's Cup, in which he came in seventh at Falmouth. He was a man of fine presence and strong personality, and his reserve and self-restraint, once penetrated, showed a warm friendly nature. His convictions were clear and strongly held and expressed; he fought his opponents hard, but without venom or malice. On Sept. 17, 1917, he was out on the Shinnecock Hills, near his summer home, in full vigor, when death overtook him suddenly.

[L. E. and A. L. de Forrest, *The Descendants of Job Atterbury* (1933); F. A. Virkus and A. N. Marquis, *The Abridged Compendium of Am. Geneal.,* vol. I (1925); *Who's Who in America,* 1916–17; *Obit. Record Grads. Yale Univ.* (1918); E. L. Keyes, in *Civil War Memories of Lewis A. Stimson* (1918); D. B. Delavan, *Early Days of the Presbyterian Hospital, New York* (priv. printed, 1926); *Surgery, Gynecology, and Obstetrics,* Apr. 1927; and obituary in *N. Y. Times,* Sept. 18, 1917.]   G.W.

STINESS, JOHN HENRY (Aug. 9, 1840–Sept. 6, 1913), jurist, was born in Providence, R. I., the son of Philip Bessom and Mary (Marsh) Stiness. His grandfather, Samuel Stiness of Marblehead, is said to have fought in the Revolution and later to have taken part in the War of 1812. His father was a manufacturer of screws. He received his education in Providence at the old University Grammar School, and in Brown University, 1857–59. For two years he taught grammar school, intending to return to college, but when the Civil War began he enlisted in the Union army. Appointed second lieutenant in the 2nd New York Artillery, he served a year and a half, part of the time as adjutant, and also as judge advocate. He was discharged because of illness in November 1862. Since a boyhood experience as page in the Rhode Island General Assembly, he had made up his mind to become a lawyer. Without returning to the university to finish his course, in January 1863 he began the study of law in the office of a Providence firm. In 1865 he was admitted to the bar and made marked progress from the start. He was married on Nov. 19, 1868, to Maria Williams, and had a son and a daughter, both of whom survived him. In 1874 he became a Republican member of the state House of Representatives, and was chairman of the committee to appoint a successor to the retiring Senator William Sprague of Rhode Island. In the long-continued contest which resulted in the election of Gen. Ambrose E. Burnside he played an active part. On Apr. 13, 1875, he was elected a member of the supreme court of Rhode Island, an office which he occupied with distinction for twenty-nine years, twenty-five years as associate, and four as chief justice. His retirement from the bench occurred in 1904. That same year he became Republican nominee for representative in Congress, but was defeated in a close election.

Outside his legal activities, he had many interests. He was particularly devoted to the concerns of the Episcopal Church of Rhode Island and served it in various capacities. An authority on canon law, he acted as counsel for the church, notably so in the trial of Algernon Sidney Crapsey [q.v.] for heresy. In 1897 he was appointed by the governor on a commission to revise the state constitution, and, since that formidable task dragged on, was again appointed to a similar commission in 1912. He was awarded two honorary degrees by Brown University, and in 1897 he was elected a fellow. A lover of books and a keen student of history, he collected a fine library, and was the author of various articles and pamphlets on law and Rhode Island history. Among the better known are *Two Centuries of Liquor Legislation in Rhode Island* (1882), *A Century of Lotteries in Rhode Island* (1896), and *Civil Changes in the State* (1897). He was a ready, effective speaker and a genial raconteur. His outstanding characteristic was his extraordinary quickness and clarity of thought. His success on the bench was largely due to his ability to strip a case of its confusing features and to penetrate swiftly to the essential issues. The same clearness of expression was evident in his writing.

[See *Who's Who in America*, 1912–13; *Proc. R. I. Hist. Soc. 1913–14* (1914); *The Biog. Cyc. of Representative Men of R. I.* (1881), p. 566; *Providence Daily Jour.*, Oct. 11, 1904; obituary in *Providence Sunday Jour.*, Sept. 7, 1913. His opinions as judge are to be found in 11–26 *R. I. Reports.*]   E. R. B.

STIRLING, LORD WILLIAM [See ALEXANDER, WILLIAM, 1726–1783].

STITH, WILLIAM (1707–Sept. 19, 1755), historian, minister, and third president of the College of William and Mary, was born in Virginia, the son of Capt. John Stith of Charles City County and Mary (Randolph) Stith, the daughter of William Randolph of "Turkey Island," Henrico County, and the grand-daughter of William Randolph [q.v.]. After attending the grammar school attached to William and Mary, of which his mother had become matron following her husband's death, he matriculated at Queen's College, Oxford, on May 21, 1724. There he is entered on the register as seventeen years old and, by an error, the son of John Stith "of the Virgin Islands." On Feb. 27, 1727/28 he received his B.A. degree from the university, was ordained a minister of the established church, and on Apr. 12, 1731, having received the King's Bounty for clergymen to Virginia, returned to Williamsburg. "The Visitors and Governors of the College" elected him master of the grammar school, Oct. 25, 1731, and the next day he qualified for the office by assenting to the Thirty-nine Articles and by taking the customary oath *de fideli administratione*. Concomitantly with this position, he acted as chaplain to the House of Burgesses. Several of his sermons before that body were published at its request, *A Sermon Preached Before the General Assembly* (1745/46), *The Sinfulness and Pernicious Nature of Gaming* (1752), and *The Nature and Extent of Christ's Redemption* (1753). In July 1736, supported by indorsements from Governor Gooch and Commissary Blair, he was called to the charge of Henrico Parish, in Henrico County, where he remained for sixteen years, marrying meanwhile, on July 13, 1738, his first cousin Judith, the daughter of Thomas Randolph of "Tuckahoe," Henrico County, by whom he had three daughters.

In his leisure hours at the glebe near Varina he composed the only completed portion of his *History of the First Discovery and Settlement of Virginia* (Williamsburg, 1747; London, 1753), the earliest important secondary account of the colony from its beginnings through 1624 and one that has influenced most subsequent interpretations of the history of Virginia under the London Company. Although drawing upon John Smith's and Beverley's narratives for parts of his own—Smith's writings he considered "confused," but "of unquestionable Authority, for what is related, whilst he staid in the Country" (preface)—Stith, with systematic scholarship, likewise scrutinized the official records of the company, which were made accessible to him by William Byrd, and the public papers collected by his uncle, Sir John Randolph. His sympathies are strongly with the Sandys-Southampton faction in their defense of the company's chartered rights against the "arbitrary Proceedings and unjust Designs" (*Ibid.*) of James I; but as his case is built around the partisan and somewhat varnished Virginia court minutes his findings are necessarily one-sided. Significant and penetrating, nevertheless, is his consciousness of the importance of Virginia's early history and traditions, while his sturdy outspokenness against regal usurpations is an earnest of the developing spirit of American independence.

Late in 1751, having been chosen minister of St. Ann's, he resigned from his Henrico pastorate; but before his resignation became effective he succeeded his brother-in-law William Dawson as president of the College of William and Mary and qualified on Aug. 14, 1752. As a consequence of his having opposed Governor Dinwiddie's pistole levy for land grants, he was not appointed commissary to the Bishop of London and member of the governor's council as his predecessors had been. During his presidency, however, he served also as minister of York-Hampton parish, in York County. His brief administration was uneventful, save for the meeting of the clergy at the college in 1754, which resulted in providing a fund for the families of deceased clergymen.

[L. G. Tyler, *Williamsburg* (1907); W. F. Craven, *Dissolution of the Virginia Company* (1932); *William and Mary College Quart.*, esp. Apr. 1897, p. 244, Oct. 1898, pp. 99, 123, Jan. 1913, p. 185; L. W. Burton, *Annals of Henrico Parish* (1904), ed. by J. S. Moore; *Alumni Oxonienses* (1888), ed. by Joseph Foster, vol. IV.]

A. C. G., Jr.

STOBO, ROBERT (1727–c. 1772), soldier, was born and reared in Glasgow, the sole heir of William Stobo, a merchant. His mother was the daughter of James Mitchell of Balmore, descended from the family of the earls of Montrose. Stobo is said to have entered the University of Glasgow (*Memoirs, post,* p. 14), but after a brief time emigrated to Virginia where, as a merchant, he enjoyed the patronage of Governor Dinwiddie, and as a genial member of society gained considerable personal popularity. A captain in the Virginia militia, he fought with Washington at Fort Necessity, July 3, 1754, and was held as a hostage by the French under the terms of capitulation which were later violated by both parties. Convinced that he was no longer on parole, he dispatched secretly by Indians two letters to Washington containing a map and a description of Fort DuQuesne and urging immediate attack. The letters were carelessly circulated, and the French, hearing of their contents, refused to release Stobo and confined him in Quebec. One of his letters was captured by the French in Braddock's baggage, whereupon Stobo was tried for treason and on Nov. 8, 1755, sentenced to be executed. This sentence was never confirmed, however, and after several unsuccessful attempts he succeeded in escaping, with Lieut. Simon Stevens and others. After a hazardous thirty-eight days' flight down the Saint Lawrence River during April, May, and June 1759, he reached the British forces at Louisbourg. He immediately joined the expedition against Quebec, and from July 10 until Sept. 7, when he returned to General Amherst with dispatches, he ably assisted Wolfe, leading the attack on Pointe aux Trembles, and pointing out the Foulon where Wolfe later landed for the ascent to the Plains of Abraham.

In November he returned to Virginia, there to receive a vote of thanks of the House of Burgesses, a gift of £1,000, and his back pay as a major—a commission voted him while he was a prisoner in Canada (*Journals of the House of Burgesses of Virginia, 1758–1761*, 1908, pp. 150–52). After a brief visit to England, he returned to join Amherst, who on Pitt's recommendation commissioned him a captain in the 15th Regiment of Foot with which he served until 1770 in Canada, the West Indies, the Lake region, and England. On June 4, 1767, he purchased land on Lake Champlain apparently with the intention of settling there. He returned with his regiment to England, however, in July 1768, and before the end of August had made the acquaintance of Tobias Smollett, who wrote a very generous letter recommending him to David

Hume (E. S. Noyes, *The Letters of Tobias Smollett, M.D.*, 1926, pp. 103–04). After 1770 his name disappeared from the Army List. About this time, Washington made repeated efforts to find him, in order to purchase his claim to 9,000 acres of land on the Ohio River, due him as land bounty for military services. In the absence of records, it may be conjectured either that Stobo died in England or that he returned to America, settling on Lake Champlain or on the Little Kanawha River in what is now West Virginia.

Although Stobo played no large rôle in the events in which he participated, his adventurous career has formed a basis for romantic narrative. Some years after his death, *Memoirs of Major Robert Stobo of the Virginia Regiment* (1800) was published in London. In Sir Gilbert Parker's *The Seats of the Mighty* (1896), he appears as Robert Moray (Robert Stobo in the first version, a serial in the *Atlantic Monthly*, beginning March 1895); and he was probably the model for Tobias Smollett's great Scotch character Lismahago in *The Expedition of Humphry Clinker* (1771).

[*Memoirs of Major Robert Stobo* (1854), ed. by N. B. Craig, a reprint of the London edition of 1800, often incorrect; B. M. Nead, *Some Hidden Sources of Fiction* (1909); J. C. Fitzpatrick, *The Writings of George Washington*, vols. I, III (1931); S. M. Hamilton, *Letters to Washington and Accompanying Papers*, vols. I (1898), III (1901); E. B. O'Callaghan, *Docs. Rel. to the Colonial Hist. of the State of N. Y.*, vol. X (1858); *Rapport de l'Archiviste de la Province de Québec*, 1920–21, 1922–23, 1923–24, 1924–25, 1928–29; *Bulletin des Recherches Historiques* (Lévis), Oct. 1903, May–June 1908, Dec. 1925; *An Hist. Jour. of the Campaigns in North America for the Years 1757 . . . 1760 by Capt. John Knox* (3 vols., 1914–16), ed. by A. G. Doughty; *Journal du Marquis de Montcalm . . . de 1756 à 1759* (1895), ed. by H. R. Casgrain; *A Jour. of Lieut. Simon Stevens* (1760); J. M. Le Moine, *Maple Leaves* (Quebec), 4 ser. (1873), 6 ser. (1894), 7 ser. (1906); Stobo's letters describing Fort Duquesne in *Minutes of the Provincial Council of Pa.*, VI (1851), 141–43, 161–63; and his map in *Pa. Archives*, II (1853), 146.]   G. M. K.

STOCKBRIDGE, HENRY (Sept. 18, 1856– Mar. 22, 1924), jurist, the descendant of John Stockbridge who emigrated from England about 1635 and settled in Scituate, Mass., and son of Henry Smith Stockbridge [*q.v.*] and Fanny E. (Montague) Stockbridge, was born in Baltimore, Md., and was always identified with that city. He was the nephew of Levi Stockbridge and the cousin of Horace Edward Stockbridge [*qq.v.*]. He went to OverLea School near Catonsville, to Williston Seminary, Easthampton, Mass., and graduated from Amherst College in 1877. He received the LL.B. degree from the law school of the University of Maryland the following year. The succeeding January he was taken into partnership in his father's law office and remained in active practice until his eleva-

tion to the bench. In 1882 he received the appointment as examiner in equity in the Baltimore courts and served six years. He also found time for some political writing for the *Morning Herald* in 1882–83 and during 1887–88 for editorial articles for the *Baltimore American*. He was married on Jan. 5, 1882, to Helen M. Smith of Hadley, Mass. They had two sons. In 1888 he won the congressional seat from Isidor Rayner [*q.v.*] after a stubborn fight, in which, for the first time since the Civil War, the Republicans of Baltimore City elected a representative to Congress, and he served one term. He was a member of the state Republican committee for two years and gave his advice in the formulation of party strategy during the nineties. He accepted the position of commissioner of immigration for Baltimore from 1891 to 1893, a non-salaried position involving the organization of the service. In 1896 he became associate judge of the supreme bench of Baltimore. In April 1911 the Democratic governor, Austin Crothers, appointed him to the court of appeals, and the following fall he was elected with virtually no opposition. Failing health prevented the completion of his fifteen-year term, and he withdrew from active work in December 1923. His opinions from the bench (*Md. Reports*, 115–45) reveal the extent of his legal erudition, his perception of justice, his capacity for clarity of statement and for logical application of the rules of law and evidence —qualities that have made them a guide for other jurists. His associates recognized in him the sturdiness, energy, thrift, and conscientiousness characteristic of his New England strain, while his deep conservatism aroused the antagonisms of organized labor.

His judicial duties did not debar him from manifold other activities. He lectured at the University of Maryland from 1899 to 1914; he served as regent of the university from 1907 to 1920, as president of the board of trustees of the endowment fund from 1905 to his death, and as provost for a brief period in 1912. Trustee of Enoch Pratt Free Library for many years, member of innumerable learned societies, he was particularly active in patriotic organizations. He directed the efforts of the Society of the Sons of the American Revolution to the Americanization of immigrants, himself preparing an excellent handbook on the subject. Under congressional charter he became one of the incorporators and chairman of the Maryland branch of the Red Cross. He served with such distinction as a member from Maryland on the commission on uniform state laws that he was made president from 1920 to 1922. He had a long and useful connection with the Maryland Historical Society. For many years active in the Congregational Church, he withdrew his membership and became a member of the Presbyterian Church.

[Scrapbook in possession of his wife; M. P. Andrews, *Tercentenary Hist. of Md.* (1925), vol. III; E. F. Cordell, *Univ. of Md.* (2 vols., 1907); L. R. Meekins, *Men of Mark in Md.* (1910), vol. II; C. H. Forrest, *Official Hist. of the Fire Department of . . . Baltimore* (1898); *Md. Hist. Mag.*, June 1924; *Biog. Record of the Alumni . . . of Amherst College*, vol. II (1901), ed. by W. L. Montague; *Report of the Eighteenth Ann. Meeting of the Am. Bar Asso.* (1895); J. M. Smith, *Hist. of . . . Sunderland, Mass.* (1899); *Minute Man*, June 1924; *Baltimore American*, Mar. 23, 1924; *Sun* (Baltimore), Mar. 12, 1911, Mar. 23, 1924.]   E. L.

STOCKBRIDGE, HENRY SMITH (Aug. 31, 1822–Mar. 11, 1895), lawyer, was born in North Hadley, Mass., the brother of Levi Stockbridge [q.v.] and the son of Abigail (Montague) and Jason Stockbridge, a farmer of considerable wealth and a man of sufficient influence to serve in the state legislature in 1835 and 1836. He was the descendant of John Stockbridge who emigrated from England about 1635 and settled in Scituate, Mass. After spending his early years on the farm, the boy entered Amherst College, where he graduated in 1845. Instead of returning to his native environment, he went immediately to Baltimore and studied law in the office of Coleman Yellott. Admitted to the bar in 1848, he soon formed a partnership with Silas Morris Cochran, which was dissolved only when the latter was elected in 1861 to the court of appeals. On Aug. 31, 1852, he married Fanny E. Montague of Sunderland, Mass., by whom he had one son, Henry Stockbridge [q.v.]. His nephew was Horace Edward Stockbridge [q.v.]. In the twelve years before the Civil War, when the Murray Institute was a flourishing forum in Baltimore, he first attracted attention as a leader in its proceedings. Originally a member of the Whig party, after its dissolution he acted with those opposed to the Know-Nothing party. In 1859 he offered himself as a Reform candidate for the state legislature and led the ensuing contest for the seats of the city representatives. A certain degree of victory crowned his efforts, for in the closing days of the session the election was held a nullity. He also served as counsel for William G. Harrison in the latter's congressional contest for the seat of Henry Winter Davis. His earliest inclination toward the Republican party was manifested in his vote for Frémont in 1856. From the outbreak of the Civil War he proved a stanch Unionist. In 1862 he was appointed by Gov. Augustus W. Bradford one of the commissioners of the draft, and he served as a special district attorney for the war department. In 1864 he entered the Maryland legislature, where he became chairman of the committee on the judiciary. In this position he drafted the bill to summon the constitutional convention of that year. When that body convened, he was made chairman of its judiciary committee and thus obtained opportunity to contribute largely to the form of the constitution that abolished slavery in Maryland. He took the stump afterward to insure its adoption. He was made a vice-president of the Republican National Convention in 1868. Active participation in politics lapsed then until 1879, when he accepted the post of chairman of the Republican state committee, where he continued to serve until 1883.

During all these years of political activity he pursued an active private practice. In 1865 he served by appointment as judge of the Baltimore County court. In 1867 he failed to be elected to the court of appeals. For a time he was counsel for the Freedmen's Bureau of Maryland and fought the cause of colored children in the cases arising from apprentice laws that threatened to evade the emancipation clause. What might be termed his extra-professional activities were varied and important. For many years he was first vice-president of the Maryland Historical Society and chairman of its publication committee. From its beginning he served as president of the West Baltimore Improvement Association. He served on the board of trustees of Howard University, was the first governor of the Society of Colonial Wars, and helped to erect the Humphrey Moore Institute, which proved a life-long interest.

[*The Biog. Cyc. of Representative Men of Md. and the District of Columbia* (1879); C. H. Forrest, *Official Hist. of the Fire Department of Baltimore* (1898); *Report of the Eighteenth Ann. Meeting of the Am. Bar Asso.* (1895); *Biog. Record of the Alumni . . . of Amherst College*, vol. I (1883), ed. by W. L. Montague; Sylvester Judd, *Hist. of Hadley . . . Also Family Geneal.* by L. M. Boltwood (1905); L. E. Blauch, "Education and the Maryland Constitutional Convention, 1864," *Md. Hist. Mag.*, Sept. 1930; *Baltimore American, Sun, Morning Herald,* and *Baltimore News,* Mar. 12, 1895.]   E. L.

STOCKBRIDGE, HORACE EDWARD (May 19, 1857–Oct. 30, 1930), agricultural chemist, college president, and agricultural editor, son of Levi [q.v.] and Joanna (Smith) Stockbridge, was born and passed the first ten years of his life on his father's farm at Hadley, Mass., one of the largest in the Connecticut Valley. His father, the first professor of agriculture in the Massachusetts Agricultural College at Amherst and later its president, moved to Amherst in 1867. Horace prepared for college in the public schools and in 1874 entered the Massachusetts Agricultural College, graduating with the degree of B.S. in 1878. He then did graduate work at Boston University for two years, and, following in his father's footsteps, specialized in agricultural chemistry.

In the summer of 1880 he was employed for a short time in the United States Department of Agriculture under Dr. Harvey W. Wiley, chief of the division of chemistry. In 1881 he was appointed instructor in the Massachusetts Agricultural College. The following year he went to Germany to study at the University of Göttingen, where he received the degree of Ph.D. in 1884, being the first graduate of an American agricultural college to be awarded it. He then returned to the Massachusetts Agricultural College as associate professor of chemistry but almost immediately thereafter was selected by the Japanese government as one of the Americans to undertake the higher education of the Japanese students in that country. Accordingly, in the spring of 1885, having received an appointment as professor of chemistry and geology at the Imperial College of Agriculture and Engineering, he went to Sapporo, Japan. From 1887 to 1889 he was also chief chemist to the Japanese government. Along with other activities he began extensive agricultural experiments, some of which had important results. After four years' service he was given a six-month leave of absence at full pay, with the privilege of resigning at the end of that time. Before going to Japan he had married, on Mar. 30, 1885, Belle Lamar of Americus, Ga. On account of their children they decided that it was best to take up their residence again in the United States.

Soon after his return, Stockbridge accepted the appointment of director of the Indiana Agricultural Experiment Station at Lafayette. He organized the work but remained there only a few months, resigning in 1890 to accept the presidency of the North Dakota Agricultural College and directorship of the experiment station, both of which institutions were yet to be established. He selected the location, named the entire faculty and staff, and planned the buildings. Resigning in 1894, he moved to Americus, Ga., to give his personal attention to the old Sumter County plantation which he had purchased a few years earlier. He also became interested in a Florida orange grove, and in 1897 the trustees of the Florida Agricultural College and Experiment Station offered to create a department in that institution expressly for him. Thus persuaded to undertake work there, he remained as professor of agriculture and director of state farmers' institutes until 1902. He also served as secretary of the Florida state agricultural society and Florida state fair.

In the summer of 1906 he became agricultural editor of the *Southern Ruralist,* published in Atlanta, Ga. This position he held for sixteen years, meanwhile continuing to operate his plantation in Sumter County. During 1916–17 he served as president of the Farmers' National Congress. He refused to support the second Liberty Loan in 1917, because he objected to increased second-class postal rates, and Secretary of the Treasury William G. McAdoo published a letter of rebuke to him (*New York Times,* Oct. 8, 1917). In 1918 he was a trustee of the University of the South, Sewanee, Tenn. Resigning from the *Southern Ruralist* in 1922, he became editor of the *Southern Farm and Dairy,* which position he held until his retirement from work on account of failing health. He was the author of *Rocks and Soils* (1888, 1895, 1902), *Land Teaching, a Handbook of Soils, Gardens, and Grounds* (1910), and numerous reports and magazine articles. In politics he was a Republican and was treasurer of the Georgia Republican campaigns, 1920–24. For many years, until his health compelled him to withdraw, he was successively warden and vestryman of St. Philip's Cathedral, Atlanta, and served in many benevolent and religious activities connected with the Episcopal diocese. He died and was buried in Atlanta, survived by his wife, three sons, and a daughter.

[*Gen. Cat., Mass. Agriculture Coll.* (1886); *Who's Who in America,* 1930–31; *Am. Agriculturist,* July 1890; *Atlanta Constitution,* Oct. 31, 1930, and *Boston Transcript,* Oct. 30, 1930.]   C. R. B.

STOCKBRIDGE, LEVI (Mar. 13, 1820–May 2, 1904), agriculturist, educator, was born in Hadley, Mass., son of Deacon Jason and Abigail (Montague) Stockbridge and elder brother of Henry Smith Stockbridge [*q.v.*]. The responsibilities of the home farm early fell to him. After the district school he had attended Hopkins Academy, and his keen intellectual curiosity drove him to spend his evenings and rainy days in further study. For several winters he taught the district school and in the local Lyceum trained himself as a speaker and writer. Seeing clearly the need of improved farming methods and of greater knowledge of underlying scientific principles, he studied the works of Liebig, of Lawes and Gilbert, and of Johnson, and while still a young man, won for himself more than local repute as a pioneer in agricultural experiment.

His active interest in civic and political affairs brought about his election as a representative in the Massachusetts legislature in 1855,

1870, 1883, and as state senator in 1865–66. From 1869 to 1891 he served continuously as cattle commissioner, winning distinction by his vigorous and determined work in the control of contagious disease. For twelve years a member of the State Board of Agriculture, he was a powerful advocate of agricultural education and was associated from its earliest inception with the work of securing an agricultural college for the state.

When the Massachusetts Agricultural College took form at Amherst in 1867, he became its farm superintendent and instructor in agriculture. The public trials of plows and mowing machines which he conducted drew entries from manufacturers in all parts of the country, and did much for the improvement of farm implements. His years of experience as farmer and business man served him well in shaping for the students a course of instruction combining classroom lectures with practical work on the farm, a plan for which no pattern existed and few textbooks were available. Friend and counselor to "his boys," he won the respect and affection of all students. Tall, spare, bearded, with keen, compelling eye, he blended in his speech the English of the King James Bible with the forceful pungency of Yankee diction. Not only did many students receive from him aid in completing the college course, but even the College itself was at least once carried through a financial crisis by money raised on his personal notes.

As professor of agriculture from 1869 to 1880, and as president of the College, 1880–82, he carried out investigations on the origin of dew, on the value of the soil mulch, and, with the second lysimeter in the country, on the leaching of plant food from the soil. His most important publications, dealing with these investigations, were "Experiments in Feeding Plants," (*Thirteenth Annual Report of the Massachusetts Agricultural College*, 1876), and "Report to the Directors of the Massachusetts Experiment Station" (*Sixteenth Annual Report . . .*, 1879). His experiments with fertilizers led to the publication of the Stockbridge Formulas, the first effort by any agricultural investigator to compound for each crop a fertilizer which should contain nitrogen, phosphoric acid, and potash as well, in the required proportion. The first $1,000 received for the use of his name in the manufacture and sale of these fertilizers was used for the experimental work which laid the foundation for the later establishment of the Massachusetts Experiment Station.

Resigning from the College in 1882, Stockbridge was made honorary professor of agriculture. His activity in all town matters continued, however, until the end of his life. A firm believer in cooperative enterprise, he led in the organization of the Amherst Grange (1873), and of the Grange Store (1877). He was selectman during the years 1870, 1883–87, and 1889–90, was assessor for many years, and was many times moderator of town meeting. He married, first, Jan. 20, 1841, Syrena Lamson, who died in 1850; second, Nov. 4, 1853, Joanna Smith, who died in February 1882; and third, Oct. 23, 1883, Elizabeth (Ashcroft) Strong, who survived him. His son, Horace Edward Stockbridge [*q.v.*], also won distinction in agriculture, as investigator, writer, and editor.

[Private papers of Levi Stockbridge, in Mass. State College Hist. Collection; reports of the Mass. State Board of Agric., 1859–74; reports of the Mass. Agric. Coll., 1866–82; W. H. Bowker, *A Tribute to Levi Stockbridge* (1904), address at memorial exercises, Amherst, repr. in part in *Levi Stockbridge and the Stockbridge Principle of Plant Feeding* (1911); L. B. Caswell, *Brief Hist. of the Mass. Agric. Coll. . . . 1917* (n.d.); F. P. Rand, *Yesterdays at Mass. Agric. Coll.* (1933); J. M. Smith, *Hist. of the Town of Sunderland, Mass.* (1899), p. 461; *Springfield Republican* and *Greenfield Recorder*, May 4, 1904; *Amherst Record*, May 11, 1904.]   C. H. T.

STOCKDALE, THOMAS RINGLAND (Mar. 28, 1828–Jan. 8, 1899), congressman from Mississippi, the sixth child of William and Hannah (McQuaid) Stockdale and a grandson of James Stockdale who came to America at the close of the Revolution, was born on a farm near West Union Church, in Greene County, Pa. After overcoming economic obstacles in securing an education, he graduated from Jefferson (now Washington and Jefferson) College in 1856. In the same year he went to Mississippi, where he supported himself by teaching and devoted his spare time to reading law. This he did with such diligence that he was able to complete the two-year law course of the University of Mississippi in one year, graduating and being admitted to the bar in 1859. He began to practise at Holmesville, Pike County, in the southern part of the state. The young Pennsylvanian must have found a satisfactory place for himself in Mississippi before 1861, for upon the outbreak of the Civil War in April of that year he enlisted as a private in the Quitman guards. Before the close of the war, transferring from the infantry to the cavalry, he rose to the rank of lieutenant-colonel. Most of his service was in Mississippi. In May 1865, he was paroled from the army of Gen. N. B. Forrest [*q.v.*] and returned to his law practice at Holmesville. On Feb. 13, 1867, he married Fannie Wicker, the daughter of a planter of Amite County.

During the reconstruction period Stockdale

continued to ally himself with the native white people of Mississippi. In 1868 he represented Mississippi in the National Democratic Convention. The next year, now a resident of Lawrence County, he ran for the state Senate but with all the other Democrats of the county suffered defeat. During the campaign he spoke in opposition to Gov. J. L. Alcorn [*q.v.*], but most of his hearers were negroes and gave him scant attention. In 1872 and 1884 he was a presidential elector on the Democratic ticket. In 1886 he was elected to Congress, and served continuously for eight years (Mar. 4, 1887–Mar. 3, 1895). In the House he continued in his allegiance to the South, and used the fact of his Northern birth and education to drive home several telling blows in the course of sectional discussions. While not fluent, he spoke with rugged common sense and some humor. On May 5, 1888, he made a speech on the tariff, in which he pointed out that much of the burden of protection fell, in the form of increased cost of living, upon the negroes in agricultural work (*Congressional Record,* 50 Cong., 1 Sess., App., pp. 82–88). This argument was a unique weapon for a Southern representative to wield against Northern defense of the tariff. At the end of four terms in Congress he was defeated for renomination, but found some solace in being appointed, in 1896, an associate judge of the state supreme court, to complete a term which expired in May 1897. Two years later he died at his home in Summit, where he had resided for many years. A son and a daughter survived him.

[*Biog. Dir. Am. Cong.* (1928); *Pubs. Miss. Hist. Soc.*, vol. XI (1910); *Biog. and Hist. Memoirs of Miss.* (1891), vol. II; Dunbar Rowland, *Mississippi* (1907), vol. II; *Biog. and Hist. Cat. of Washington and Jefferson Coll.* (1902); *Hist. Cat. of the Univ. of Miss.* (1910); *Daily Democrat* (Natchez, Miss.), Jan. 10, 1899.]
C. S. S.

STÖCKHARDT, KARL GEORG (Feb. 17, 1842–Jan. 9, 1913), Lutheran clergyman, was born at Chemnitz, Saxony, the eldest of the four children of Julius Adolf and Rosalie (Liebster) Stöckhardt. His father, a distinguished chemist and teacher, was descended from five generations of Lutheran pastors, and in his only son the clerical instincts welled up with renewed force. He studied theology, 1862–66, at the universities of Erlangen and Leipzig, became an active member of the Christian (non-duelling) student corps, Wingolf, and, after taking his theological examinations, waited seven years for an appointment. Meanwhile, he taught till 1870 in a girls' school at Tharandt, studied for short terms at Berlin and Marburg, assisted for a few trying months of 1870 at the Église des Billettes in Paris, served as chaplain in the hospitals of Sedan, and latterly

became a teacher in the Gymnasium at Erlangen, at the same time holding a repetent's position in the University. Finally, in October 1873, he was made deacon of the State Church congregation at Planitz, near Zwickau, probably because it was thought that his zeal and orthodoxy would check the influence of Friedrich K. T. Ruhland, the Missouri-trained leader of the Saxon Free Church, who was pastor of St. John's in Niederplanitz. The easy-going ways of the State Church were utterly repugnant to Stöckhardt's nature, however; he was soon at loggerheads with his ecclesiastical superiors and with the greater part of his parish; and in 1876 he quit the State Church amid a blaze of polemics and joined Ruhland's party. He founded a paper, *Die Freikirche,* to continue the argument and, having charged the State Church with apostasy, was soon indicted for libel and blasphemy. At this juncture C. F. W. Walther [*q.v.*] came to his rescue, and in the early autumn of 1878 Stöckhardt left Germany to become pastor of Holy Cross Church, St. Louis, Mo. Some months later he was tried and convicted *in absentia* and sentenced to eight months in jail, but in 1891 and again in 1909 he revisited his old home and even preached from his old pulpit without molestation.

His thirty-four years in St. Louis, interrupted only by a severe illness in 1900–01 and by the two trips to Germany, were busy, happy, and rich in achievement. He was pastor of Holy Cross until 1887 and professor in Concordia Theological Seminary, in which he had given instruction in Biblical exegesis since 1879, from 1887 until his death. His literary productions included *Die Kirchliche Zustände Deutschlands* (1892); *Das Schlachtfeld von Sedan: Erinnerungen aus dem Kriegsjahr* (1914); three volumes of sermons—*Passionspredigten* (2 vols., 1884) and *Adventspredigten* (1887); and a series of exegetical works—*Kommentar über den Propheten Jesaia, Kap. I–XII* (1902), *Die Biblische Geschichte des Alten Testaments* (1896), *Die Biblische Geschichte des Neuen Testaments* (1898); *Kommentar über den Brief Pauli an die Römer* (1907); *Kommentar über den Brief Pauli an die Epheser* (1910); *Kommentar über den Ersten Brief Petri* (1912); *Ausgewählte Psalmen Ausgelegt* (1915); and numerous contributions to the periodicals and other publications of the Missouri Synod. He was editor, also, with E. W. Kähler, of Vol. X, *Die Catechetische Schriften* (1892), of the St. Louis edition of Luther's works. Within the limits set by his adherence to the old Lutheran doctrines of plenary inspiration and his consequently too simple view of the problems of date and authorship, Stöckhardt was a Biblical scholar of no mean stature, and his commentaries on Romans, Ephesians, and First Peter are masterpieces of their anachronistic kind. Frequent homiletic, devotional, and polemical passages enhance the interest and practical usefulness of his work, which still continues to shape the teaching and preaching of the Missouri Synod. Stöckhardt was twice married: in 1873 to Anna König of Tharandt, who died in 1898; and in 1901 to Mary Kohne of Pittsburgh, who survived him. He had two sons by adoption. His death came, without warning, of an apoplectic stroke.

[See Otto Willkomm, *D. Th. Georg Stöckhardt: Lebensbild eines deutsch-amerikanischen Theologen* (Zwickau, 1914); three articles by W. H. T. Dau, in *Theol. Quarterly* (St. Louis), Apr., July 1913, Jan. 1914; Franz Pieper, obituary and funeral address, *Der Lutheraner* (St. Louis), Jan. 21, 1913; *St. Louis Globe-Democrat*, Jan. 10, 1913. For Stöckhardt's father see the article by B. Lepsius, *Allgemeine Deutsche Biographie*, vol. XXXVI (Leipzig, 1893).]   G. H. G.

STOCKTON, CHARLES G. (Aug. 27, 1853–Jan. 5, 1931), physician, was born at Madison, Lake County, Ohio, the son of Charles Lewis and Sarah (Shaver) Stockton and a descendant of Richard Stockton who was in Flushing, L. I., in 1656, through his son Richard who settled at Princeton, N. J. His father, a practising physician, moved his family to Northampton County, Va., where the boy was educated in the local schools. Later, he attended Westfield Academy at Westfield, N. Y., and then took his medical courses at the University of Buffalo, graduating in 1878. He began practice in Buffalo, early specializing in diseases of the gastro-intestinal tract. In 1883 he was appointed professor of materia medica and therapeutics in the medical department of Niagara University, transferring in 1887 to the chair of medicine and clinical medicine at the University of Buffalo, which post he held until 1918, when he became professor emeritus. He attained an exceptional success as a practitioner of internal medicine and became one of the foremost consultants in the country. When in 1901 President McKinley was shot in Buffalo, Stockton was called in consultation and participated in the care of the dying President. During the greater part of his professional career he served on the medical staff of the Buffalo General Hospital and for years he was consultant physician at the Buffalo City Hospital and the state Hospital for Crippled and Deformed Children.

In addition to professional societies, he belonged to the American Society for the Advancement of Science, the Washington Academy of Sciences, the Buffalo Society of Natural Sciences, the Buffalo Society of Artists, and the Buffalo Historical Society. He contributed much to the literature of his specialty. In 1903 he published *Diseases of the Stomach,* a translation from the German of Franz Riegel, and was himself the author of *Diseases of the Stomach and Their Relation to Other Diseases* (1914). He was the editor of *Selected Papers, Surgical and Scientific, from the Writings of Roswell Park* (1914), containing "Roswell Park: A Memoir" written by Stockton and published in the *Buffalo Historical Society Publications* (vol. XXII) in 1918. The bulk of his writings appeared as journal literature and contributions to various systems of medicine. Among the latter were J. C. Wilson and A. A. Eshner, *An American Text-book of Applied Therapeutics* (1896); A. L. Loomis and W. G. Thompson, *A System of Practical Medicine* (4 vols., 1897–98); G. M. Gould, *A Cyclopedia of Practical Medicine and Surgery* (1900); and the *Oxford Medicine* (6 vols., 1920–21), edited by H. A. Christian and Sir James Mackenzie. A personal friend of Dr. William Osler [*q.v.*], he wrote the introduction to the section on diseases of the digestive apparatus for Osler's *Modern Medicine, Its Theory and Practice* (7 vols., 1907–10). He was also a contributor to *Nelson Loose-leaf Medicine.* He was a pioneer in his conception of social medicine, and his presidential address before the state medical society in 1910 was prophetic of the changes in medical practice which have taken place since that time. For years he was surgeon, with the grade of major, of the 74th Infantry, New York National Guard. During the World War he was chief of advisory boards of a district covering western New York. On Nov. 23, 1875, he married Mary L. Taylor of Westfield, N. Y. He died suddenly at his home in Buffalo from the rupture of an abdominal aortic aneurism.

[T. C. Stockton, *The Stockton Family* (1911), gives Stockton's middle name as Gleason, but a letter from Stockton himself in the Cat. Div., Lib. of Cong., states that "Charles G." was his baptismal name. For biog. data see *Jour. Am. Medic. Asso.*, Jan. 24, 1931; *N. Y. State Jour. of Medicine*, Feb. 15, 1931; *Who's Who in Am. Medicine* (1925); *Who's Who in America*, 1930–31; *Buffalo Evening News*, Jan. 6, 1931.]   J. M. P—n.

STOCKTON, CHARLES HERBERT (Oct. 13, 1845–May 31, 1924), naval officer, was a descendant of Richard Stockton who was in Flushing, Long Island, in 1656. Charles was born in Philadelphia, the son of Rev. William Rodgers Stockton, an Episcopalian clergyman, and Emma Trout (Gross) Stockton. After schooling at the Germantown Academy and the Freeland Academy (Collegeville, Pa.), he was appointed in November 1861 midshipman at the Naval Academy, then located at Newport, R. I.

In 1864 he saw his first active service, on board the *Macedonian* during her pursuit of the Confederate steamers *Florida* and *Tallahassee*. After his graduation in the following year he was ordered first to the *Dacotah,* then to the *Chattanooga,* and finally to the *Mohican,* in which he sailed for the Pacific, where he served three years. In the meantime he had been promoted ensign (1866), master (1868), and lieutenant (1869). In 1870 he joined the *Congress* and made an extensive cruise embracing the West Indies, the coast of Greenland, and the Mediterranean. In 1874–75, on board the *Swatara,* he made a voyage around the world, assisting on the Asiatic Station with the observations of the transit of Venus. After a year at the Hydrographic Office in Washington he was sent in 1876 to the *Plymouth* of the North Atlantic Squadron and served on board her until 1879, when he was ordered to the New York navy yard. The summer of 1880 he spent at the Torpedo Station, Newport, and in November was made a lieutenant commander.

From 1882 to 1885 he was again in the Pacific, this time serving as the executive officer of the *Iroquois* and taking part in the suppression of a riot on shore at Panama as commander of a battalion of seamen. A pamphlet entitled *Origin, History, Laws, and Regulations of the United States Naval Asylum,* which he compiled while attached to the Bureau of Yards and Docks, was published by the Navy Department in 1886. In the summer of 1887 and 1888 he lectured at the Naval War College, Newport, and in the latter year he served on the commission that located the Puget Sound navy yard, Bremerton, Wash. In 1889–91 he commanded the *Thetis* and made a cruise with the whaling fleet in Bering Sea and the Arctic Ocean. On his return home he was assigned to special duty at the Naval War College. While there he attained a proficiency in international law which led to his lecturing on that subject during several summers. In 1898–1900 he was president of the College. In 1898 he prepared and arranged for publication a book entitled *International Law: A Manual Based upon Lectures Delivered at the Naval War College by Freeman Snow,* and in 1904 his paper on the "United States Naval War Code" and his volume *International Law: Recent Supreme Court Decisions and Other Opinions and Precedents* were issued.

In the meantime he had been promoted commander (April 1892) and captain (July 1899) and had served on the Asiatic Station as commander of the *Yorktown* (1895–97). In 1901–03 he commanded on that station in the battleship *Kentucky,* and in 1903–06 he served as naval attaché in London, having a small part in the work of the Alaska Boundary Commission. On Jan. 7, 1906, he was promoted rear admiral. While holding that rank he was president of the board of inspection and survey and also of the naval examining and retiring boards and commander of a special service squadron sent to Bordeaux, France, for the Maritime Exposition. He was retired on Oct. 13, 1907.

Stockton's usefulness by no means came to an end with his retirement from the navy. In 1908–09 he was first delegate at the Declaration of London Conference. From 1910 to 1918 he served, without salary, as president of the George Washington University during a crucial period in the history of that institution. The university was reëstablished on a new site, its fiscal affairs were systematized, and the number of students was doubled. For more than a decade he lectured at the university on international law. In 1911 a new edition of the manual on international law was published, and in 1914 he brought out his standard work, *Outlines of International Law.* He also continued to add to his special studies in this field various articles contributed to periodicals.

A devout member of St. John's Episcopal Church in Washington, Stockton found time to act as vestryman and committeeman and in other administrative capacities. He was twice married: on June 23, 1875, to Cornelia A. Carter of New York, who died on July 1, 1876; and on Nov. 23, 1880, to Pauline Lentilhon King, also of New York. He had a daughter by his first wife and a son and daughter by his second. The Admiral was of robust constitution, stocky, a little below average stature—a friendly and genial man who throughout a long life was always adding to his attainments.

[Record of Officers, Bureau of Navigation, Washington, 1864–93; Navy Registers, 1862–1907; Marcus Benjamin, *Charles Herbert Stockton: An Eminent Churchman* (1925); *Who's Who in America,* 1924–25; T. C. Stockton, *The Stockton Family of N. J.* (1911); *Army and Navy Jour.,* June 14, 1924; *Evening Star* (Washington), June 1, 1924.]   C. O. P.

STOCKTON, FRANK RICHARD (Apr. 5, 1834–Apr. 20, 1902), novelist and story-writer, was born in Philadelphia, Pa., the third of nine children of William Smith and Emily (Drean) Stockton. The Stockton family, descended from Richard Stockton who came to Long Island before 1656, had been conspicuous and influential in New Jersey since the seventeenth century, and another Richard Stockton [*q.v.*] had been a signer of the Declaration of Independence. William Smith Stockton of the Burlington branch, though a layman, was eminent in Methodist affairs, a leader in the schism which resulted in the Methodist Protestant Church, and a voluminous writer on theological subjects. In secular matters he was a temperance advocate and an abolitionist. His son by an earlier marriage, Thomas Hewlings Stockton, was a clergyman of their denomination, chaplain in turn of both houses of Congress. The children of Emily Drean Stockton, who had been born in Leesburg, Loudoun County, Va., inclined less to theology than to literature. John Drean Stockton, at first a steel-engraver, was editor and later a proprietor of the *Philadelphia Post.* A sister, Louise Stockton (Aug. 12, 1839–June 12, 1914), a writer of children's stories, also was associated with the newspaper, as was, in some unidentified capacity, their brother Francis Richard, who seems always to have been called Frank R. Stockton.

The most talented of the three, unwilling to study medicine as his father desired him to, after his graduation at eighteen from the Central High School in Philadelphia Frank chose to learn wood-engraving, for which before the days of photo-engraving there was a large demand. He worked at his craft, in Philadelphia and New York, until 1866 and possibly later. On Feb. 20 of that year, Stockton, who then had an office in New York, patented an engraving tool of which he said: "The object of my invention is to furnish a graver by means of which both sides of a line is cut at the same time and by the same tool" (quoted from the original letters patent). He is said to have been an expert craftsman, but his wood-engravings for the *Poems* (1862) of his clerical half-brother are undistinguished. Stockton had won prizes for writing while still at school. Having married Marian Edwards Tuttle, of Amelia County, Va., in 1860, he published the same year a pamphlet called *A Northern Voice for the Dissolution of the United States of North America.* But while he remained a wood-engraver, what he wrote was, on the whole, hardly more than so much text for pictures. In 1867 he contributed to the *Riverside Magazine for Young People* the stories collected in 1870 as *Ting-a-Ling,* and he followed this with the abundantly illustrated *Round-About Rambles in Lands of Fact and Fancy* (copyright 1872).

He began to write for *Hearth and Home* in 1869, served for a few months on the staff, and became a frequent contributor to *Scribner's Monthly* (afterwards the *Century Magazine*). When in 1873 the *St. Nicholas Magazine* was founded, under the editorship of Mary Elizabeth Mapes Dodge [*q.v.*], Stockton was made assist-

ant editor. In this post he remained until 1881, when he retired from editing to live entirely by writing. As editor he had been primarily a writer. His experiences with *Hearth and Home* had led him to compile, in collaboration with his wife, a straightforward handbook on *The Home: Where It Should Be and What to Put in It* (1873). By his colleagues of *Scribner's* and *St. Nicholas* he had been, it appears, regarded as amusing, eccentric, and gifted, and encouraged to write for both magazines. During these years he published *What Might Have Been Expected* (1874), *Tales Out of School* (1875), *Rudder Grange* (1879), *A Jolly Fellowship* (1880), *The Floating Prince and Other Fairy Tales* (1881).

The quick success of *Rudder Grange,* of which an episode had appeared in *Scribner's* five years before, and others since, determined Stockton's subsequent career. At forty-five he was almost entirely unknown except for his stories for children, of which the *Ting-a-Ling* tales were as admirable as the later *Floating Prince* and *The Bee Man of Orn and Other Fanciful Tales* (1887) were to be. After 1880 he wrote largely for adults, out of the vein of absurd invention which he had discovered that he had and that the public liked in him. He followed *Rudder Grange* with two sequels, *The Rudder Grangers Abroad* (1891) and *Pomona's Travels* (copyright 1894), as he followed his masterpiece *The Casting Away of Mrs. Lecks and Mrs. Aleshine* (copyright 1886) with *The Dusantes* (copyright 1888), and *The Adventures of Captain Horn* (1895) with *Mrs. Cliff's Yacht* (1896). He said that he valued Defoe and Dickens most among "all who have created fiction" ("My Favorite Novelist and His Best Book," *Munsey's Magazine,* June 1897). But Stockton had the blunt verisimilitude of Defoe no more than he had the huge exuberance of Dickens or the moral earnestness of either of them. However circumstantial Stockton might be, his imagination worked in a world of cheerful impossibility, as easygoing as a fairy-tale or a Gilbert and Sullivan opera.

His novels are, in effect, loose-knit comic operas in prose without music. Even when the scenes are plausibly localized and the characters ostensibly actual, the stories have a farcical irresponsibility. In *Rudder Grange* the heroine, elaborated from a maid in Stockton's own household, marries a man who is shaking with ague, spends part of her honeymoon as a guest in a lunatic asylum and later has a child to which her mistress gives so much time that her master hires another child to occupy himself with. The Rudder Grangers live for a time in a canal boat.

They leave their house for a tent on their own estate, and then take refuge in the house, which has been deserted by the tenants, who have moved into the tent. In *The Casting Away of Mrs. Lecks and Mrs. Aleshine,* two middle-aged women, also studied from actual persons whom Stockton knew, are shipwrecked in the Pacific, paddle their way in life-preservers, using oars as if they were brooms, to a deserted island on which they find a comfortable house, and there live much as they would do at home, each week depositing in a ginger jar a sum for board and lodging from which they subtract a charge for doing the housework. When Stockton's invention is at its most fantastic his manner is at its gravest. He is Sindbad and Munchausen lying about domestic adventures as roundly as about events at the end of the earth. Though *Rudder Grange* established his reputation, and *Mrs. Lecks and Mrs. Aleshine* was without much doubt the top of his achievement, he made his chief stir in the world with the short story "The Lady or the Tiger?" which first appeared in the *Century* in November 1882 and furnished the title to a volume of stories in 1884. It owed its vogue to its posing of a dilemma which started insoluble arguments. Would a barbaric princess, forced to a decision by her father, give her lover up to another lady who must marry him or to a tiger which would certainly destroy him? Stockton ingeniously set the problem and stubbornly refused an answer. The chattering debate which the story roused became a nuisance and a handicap to Stockton, who could neither equal the invention nor live it down. Yet such other stories by him as "The Transferred Ghost" (1882), "The Remarkable Wreck of the 'Thomas Hyke'" (1884), "A Tale of Negative Gravity" (1884), and in general the stories in his own collection called *A Chosen Few* (1895) are almost equally ingenious. He survives by them, by one or two novels, and by some of his stories for children.

Stockton was the principal humorist of the genteel tradition during the 1880's. In the midst of all the crowding issues of the decade he remained gaily aloof, letting his lively fancy go its happy way in many books, some of them dictated while he lay at ease in a hammock. Though attached by his profession to New York, where his slight, limping figure and his swarthy face were always welcomed by his few close friends, he lived most of his later life in suburban New Jersey, at Nutley and at Convent Station. At the latter he was a neighbor of the congenial Arthur Burdett Frost [*q.v.*], Stockton's own favorite among his illustrators. His last three years he passed at a house which he had bought in West Virginia not far from Harpers Ferry. He was as sharp-eyed for Virginia singularities, for example in *The Late Mrs. Null* (1886), as for those he studied with greater variety in New Jersey. Always a traveler, he was one of the earliest Americans to write about the charms of Nassau in the Bahamas ("An Isle of June," in *Scribner's,* November 1877); his *Personally Conducted* (1889) was devoted to European travel. "The Lady or the Tiger?" was made into an operetta by Sydney Rosenfeld (Wallack's Theatre, May 7, 1888) and *The Squirrel Inn* (1891) into a play with the help of Eugene W. Presbrey, who produced it in 1893 (Theatre of Arts and Letters). Neither of them had notable success. Stockton's best book outside his fiction, *Buccaneers and Pirates of Our Coasts* (1898), handles a grim subject in a spirit both comic and romantic, as does *Kate Bonnet; The Romance of a Pirate's Daughter* (1902). A collected edition of his fiction, *The Novels and Stories of Frank R. Stockton,* was published in twenty-three volumes, 1899–1904. He died in Washington, D. C., survived by his wife. There were no children.

[Stockton lived reticently and has not been made the subject of the biography he deserves. A memorial sketch by his wife, prefixed to the posthumous volume, *The Captain's Toll-Gate* (1903), which also contains a bibliog., is the chief source of information but is lacking in detail. There are accounts of his editorial years in W. W. Ellsworth, *A Golden Age of Authors* (1919), R. U. Johnson, *Remembered Yesterdays* (1923), and L. F. Tooker, *The Joys and Tribulations of an Editor* (copr. 1924). See also T. C. Stockton, *The Stockton Family* (1911); C. C. Buel, in *Century,* July 1886; Julius Chambers, in *Author,* July 15, 1891; obituary in *N. Y. Times,* Apr. 21, 1902. The present account is based in part upon personal information, with particular indebtedness to Walter L. Pforzheimer.]

C. V–D.

STOCKTON, JOHN POTTER (Aug. 2, 1826–Jan. 22, 1900), senator, attorney-general of New Jersey, was born at Princeton, N. J. The son of Commodore Robert Field Stockton [*q.v.*] and Harriet Maria (Potter), he came of a distinguished line. After graduating from the College of New Jersey in 1843, he read law in the office of his cousin, Richard Stockton Field [*q.v.*], and was licensed as attorney in 1847 and admitted to the bar in 1850. His family connections brought him numerous opportunities for advancement. He was appointed one of the commissioners to revise and simplify legal procedure in New Jersey, and later he became reporter of the court of chancery, publishing *Reports of Cases . . . in the Court of Chancery, and on Appeal, in the Court of Errors and Appeals of . . . New Jersey* (3 vols., 1856–60). While his father's influence was at its height he secured from President Buchanan, June 15, 1858, appointment as minister resident to the Papal States. During the Civil War he conducted a law practice at Trenton and, as a Democrat, made his first serious attempt to enter politics. In 1862 he was sufficiently prominent to report at the state Democratic convention the resolutions extending to the Administration support in the "speedy suppression of the rebellion by all Constitutional means" but objecting to the suspension of the writ of *habeas corpus,* to the restriction of freedom of speech and of the press, and to the emancipation of slaves.

Three years later Stockton's election as United States senator gave rise to a celebrated contest. In the New Jersey legislature the Democrats and Union Republicans were so closely matched that the houses could organize only after a series of compromises. Stockton was elected on Mar. 15, 1865, but not until the legislature in joint session had substituted for the majority rule one making a plurality of votes sufficient to a choice. His right to his seat was promptly challenged, but the issue was not settled for a year. On Mar. 26, 1866, the judiciary committee of the United States Senate reported in his favor by a vote of 22 to 21, Stockton himself casting the decisive vote; but upon further protests, the next day he withdrew his vote and the committee unseated him, 23 to 21. The case attained great notoriety throughout the nation and led to a considerable pamphlet war. If Stockton, a Democrat, had retained his seat, the Senate might not have overridden President Johnson's veto of the Civil Rights Act. Indignant at the alleged flouting of New Jersey's sovereignty, the legislature—of which the Democrats had by now obtained control—attempted ineffectively to withdraw New Jersey's ratification of the Fourteenth Amendment, and the federal Congress was moved to regulate for the first time the election of senators (Act of July 25, 1866). In 1869 Stockton was again a candidate, and this time was elected without a question, but at the end of his term (1875), despite public respect for his name and family, he was superseded by another Democratic leader, Theodore Fitz Randolph [q.v.]. His hopes for the governorship were disappointed by the choice of Gen. G. B. McClellan [q.v.], and he had to be contented with the post of attorney-general, which from 1877 he held for twenty years.

Contemporaries describe Stockton as a convincing speaker, with a melodious voice and facile diction. His dignified manner does not seem to have been suited, however, to the increasingly urban Democracy of New Jersey, and he was further handicapped by residence in Mercer County whereas the party strength lay in the

northeastern counties. Thus, although he continued to take part in state politics, he was never a determining factor, and he held his place largely through family influence. After retiring from office in 1897, he practised law in Jersey City. He married Sarah Marks and had two sons and a daughter, all three of whom survived him.

[C. M. Knapp, *N. J. Politics during the Period of the Civil War and Reconstruction* (1924); W. E. Sackett, *Modern Battles of Trenton,* vol. I (1895); C. P. Smith, "Personal Reminiscences" (MS. in N. J. State Lib.); John Whitehead, *Judicial and Civil Hist. of N. J.* (1897); T. C. Stockton, *The Stockton Family of N. J.* (1911); *Biog. Dir. Am. Cong.* (1928); *N. Y. Times,* Jan. 23, 1900.]
H. M. C.

STOCKTON, RICHARD (Oct. 1, 1730–Feb. 28, 1781), lawyer, signer of the Declaration of Independence, son of John and Abigail (Phillips) Stockton, was born at Princeton, N. J., whither his grandfather, also Richard, had removed in 1696 and acquired a large tract of land. The first of his line in America was his great-grandfather, another Richard, who was in Flushing, L. I., as early as 1656. John Stockton was for many years presiding judge of the court of common pleas of Somerset County, N. J., and a liberal patron of the College of New Jersey, being largely instrumental in securing its removal from Newark to Princeton. Richard Stockton received his preparatory education at the academy conducted by the Rev. Samuel Finley [q.v.] in Nottingham, Md., and entered the College of New Jersey at Newark, from which he was graduated in 1748. He took up the study of the law in the office of David Ogden [q.v.] of Newark, was licensed in 1754 as an attorney, in 1758 as a counselor, and in 1764 as a serjeant. In the course of a decade he built up a large practice and became generally recognized as one of the most eloquent members of the bar in the middle colonies. Among his legal protégés who received their training in his busy office were Elias Boudinot, William Paterson, and Joseph Reed [qq.v.].

For some years Stockton had little time or inclination for politics. In a letter to Joseph Reed in 1764, he stated his position: "The publick is generally unthankful, and I never will become a Servant of it, till I am convinced that by neglecting my own affairs I am doing more acceptable Service to God and Man" (Reed, MSS., *post,* I, 47). Shortly afterward, however, he was drawn into public affairs. As a trustee of the College of New Jersey, he was requested by the board in 1766 to tender the presidency to John Witherspoon [q.v.], then residing at Paisley near Glasgow. Received in London by the King and the Marquis of Rockingham with every mark of respect and given the freedom of the city of Edinburgh at a public dinner (*New York Journal or General Advertiser*, June 4, 1767), he was yet unable at first to persuade Mrs. Witherspoon to consent to her husband's accepting the call. Undaunted, however, Stockton wrote his wife: "I have engaged all the eminent clergymen in Edinburgh and Glasgow to attack her in her intrenchments and they are determined to take her by storm, if nothing else will do" (Hageman, *post*, I, 80). Finally, after prolonged negotiations, in which the aid of young Benjamin Rush [*q.v.*] was enlisted, Mrs. Witherspoon yielded and Stockton's mission was successful (V. L. Collins, *President Witherspoon*, 1925, I, 72–81). Stockton always maintained a close attachment to his alma mater, was one of its chief financial advisers throughout his lifetime, and held the opinion that great changes would occur when the colleges had "thrown into the lower House of Assembly men of more foresight and understanding than they now can boast of" (Reed MSS., Oct. 8, 1764).

On his return home in 1767 he immediately took a prominent rôle in provincial politics. In 1768 he was appointed to the Council, which position he retained until the end of the royal government. A year later, during the rioting directed against lawyers because of the costs, abuses, and multiplicity of law suits, he took a vigorous stand and brought about the resumption of orderly judicial process in Monmouth County (Smith, *post*, p. 40). In 1774 he was commissioned one of the justices of the supreme court. Such leisure time as he enjoyed in this period was devoted to the improvement of his extensive landed estate, "Morven," at Princeton, where he bred choice horses and cattle and gathered art treasures and a considerable library.

His early position on the differences between the colonies and the mother country had been that of a moderate. In 1764 he suggested, as the readiest solution of the troubles, the election of some able Americans to Parliament (W. B. Reed, *Life and Correspondence of Joseph Reed*, 1847, I, 30), but a year later, during the controversy over the Stamp Act, he maintained positively that Parliament had no authority over the colonies (Keasbey, *post*, I, 308). Under date of Dec. 12, 1774, he drafted and sent to Lord Dartmouth "An Expedient for the Settlement of the American Disputes," in which he "suggested substantially a plan of self-government for America, independent of Parliament, without renouncing allegiance to the Crown" (Nelson, *post*, p. 429). Immediate measures would have to be taken, he averred, or else there would be an

"obstinate, awful and tremendous war" (T. B. Myers, *post*, pp. 176–77; *Historical Magazine*, November 1868, p. 228). This appeal is regarded as having been the basis, in part at least, of the petition of the Continental Congress to the King, July 8, 1775 (Justin Winsor, *Narrative and Critical History of America*, vol. VI, 1887, p. 108 n.). He was elected to the Continental Congress, June 22, 1776, and took his seat six days later in time to hear the closing debate on the Declaration of Independence. During his attendance at the subsequent sessions his name was brought forward by his friends at home as a candidate for governor, and on the first ballot in the legislature (Aug. 30, 1776) the votes were equally divided between Stockton and William Livingston [*q.v.*]. The next day Livingston was chosen governor and Stockton first chief justice of the new state, which position he declined, preferring for the time being the more active career in Congress.

During the summer and fall of 1776 Stockton served on numerous important committees of Congress. On Sept. 26 he was appointed with George Clymer [*q.v.*] to visit the northern army. Writing from Saratoga, Oct. 28, he reported that the New Jersey soldiers were "marching with cheerfulness, but great part of the men barefooted and barelegged. . . . There is not a single shoe or stocking to be had in this part of the world, or I would ride a hundred miles through the woods and purchase them with my own money" (Peter Force, *American Archives*, 5 ser. II, 1851, pp. 561, 1256, 1274). During his absence on this journey, Nov. 23, he was appointed as one of a committee "to devise . . . measures for effectually reinforcing General Washington, and obstructing the progress of General Howe's army" (*Journals of the Continental Congress*, vol. VI, 1906, p. 975). Before he could reach Princeton, however, the enemy had invaded New Jersey. He placed his family in the home of a friend, John Covenhoven, in Monmouth County, for safety, but while there was betrayed by Loyalists, dragged in bitterly cold weather to Perth Amboy, and confined in jail. Removed subsequently to New York, he was imprisoned and subjected to indignities which provoked a formal remonstrance from Congress (Jan. 3, 1777), and efforts to secure his exchange. His release found him in shattered health, his beautiful estate wantonly pillaged, and his fortune greatly depleted. He remained an invalid until his death at Princeton, Feb. 28, 1781, in his fifty-first year.

Stockton married Annis Boudinot, a talented poetess, the sister of Elias Boudinot who in 1762 married Stockton's sister, Hannah. Of Stockton's two sons, the elder, Richard [*q.v.*], became eminent at the bar, and of his four daughters, the eldest, Julia, married Dr. Benjamin Rush.

[Sources include: *New Jersey Gazette*, Mar. 7, 1781; Samuel Stanhope Smith, *A Funeral Sermon on the Death of the Hon. Richard Stockton* (1781); John Sanderson, *Biog. of the Signers to the Declaration of Independence*, vol. III (1823); R. S. Field, *The Provincial Courts of N. J.* (1849); W. A. Whitehead, "Sketch of the Life of Richard Stockton," *Proc. N. J. Hist. Soc.*, 2 ser. IV (1877); T. B. Myers, in *Orderly Book of Sir John Johnson during the Oriskany Campaign, 1776-77* (1882), pp. 173-78; William Nelson, in "Documents Relating to the Colonial History of the State of New Jersey," *Archives of the State of N. J.*, 1 ser. X (1886), 427-30 n.; E. Q. Keasby, *Courts and Lawyers of N. J.* (1912), I, 307-09; T. C. Stockton, *The Stockton Family of N. J.* (1911); J. F. Hageman, *Hist. of Princeton* (2 vols., 1879); letters of Stockton among the Reed MSS. in the N. Y. Hist. Soc. and the Green MSS. at Princeton Univ. Charges by William Gordon, *The Hist. of the Rise . . . of the U. S.* (1788), II, 300, that Stockton's defeat for the governorship was due to his refusal to furnish horses for public use are stoutly denied by other writers (see Hageman, *ante*, I, 118-19, and references there given).]   R. B. M.

STOCKTON, RICHARD (Apr. 17, 1764–Mar. 7, 1828), lawyer, politician, gentleman farmer, son of Richard [*q.v.*] and Annis (Boudinot) Stockton, was born at the family estate, "Morven," near Princeton, N. J. He was tutored privately and attended the College of New Jersey, where he graduated in 1779 and received a master's degree in 1783. At this time the young man expressed his determination to retire to "Morven" which he had inherited and there attend to his books, cultivate friendship, and be untroubled by the affairs of the world (Richard Stockton to Walter Stone, May 26, 1783). After studying law in Newark with his uncle, Elisha Boudinot, however, he was admitted to the bar in 1784 and by 1792 was able to write that he was "engaged in all the causes of importance to come on at the Supreme Court" (Stockton to Robert Watts, Aug. 17, 1792). In 1804 and 1805 he was arguing before the United States Supreme Court the case of *Graves and Barnewall* vs. *Boston Marine Insurance Company* (2 *Cranch*, 419). In the meantime he had served a short time in 1788 as treasurer of the College of New Jersey and in 1791 became one of its trustees, a position in which he was active until his death.

On Nov. 2, 1796, he was elected by the New Jersey legislature to fill the unexpired term of United States Senator Frederick Frelinghuysen [*q.v.*], who had resigned. In the Senate (Nov. 12, 1796–Mar. 3, 1799) he was an energetic supporter of Federalist principles. In January 1801 he was tendered by President Adams the position of circuit judge under the projected judiciary act (*The Works of John Adams*, vol. IX,

1854, p. 94), but declined the offer, probably because of his interest in the governorship of his state. Later the same year he became the Federalist candidate for that office, but was defeated by Joseph Bloomfield [*q.v.*], the candidate of the Democratic element. In 1802 he and Bloomfield received an equal number of votes; the tie was unbroken and there was no election. In 1803 and in 1804 he was the Federalist candidate and was again defeated.

In 1812 New Jersey Federalists temporarily improved their political position and Stockton was elected from the second district to the federal House of Representatives (1813–15). Strongly opposed to the second war with Great Britain, believing its declaration to have been an act of "political insanity," he was conspicuous in his opposition to the policies of the administration. He demonstrated his sympathy for the British point of view on impressment and urged that the "idle doctrine of free trade and sailors' rights" be dismissed. He prophesied that no treaty of peace would alter any of the maritime rights previously claimed by England; and when the treaty was negotiated, he considered it "a mere tub to the great whale" and "hardly worth a vote" (Stockton to David Daggett, Dec. 30, 1815).

Stockton was interested in the development of the steamboat, in the building and improvement of canals, and in undeveloped land investments. He owned large tracts in North Carolina and Oneida County, N. Y. Tall and stout, dignified to the level of haughtiness, he commanded respect by his appearance and ability; the younger members of the bar knew him as "the old duke" (Elmer, *post*, p. 414). He expressed his legal opinions and political views in logical, well phrased sentences. The federal Constitution he considered an ark of safety for personal liberty; and in his judgment it had not been improved by a single one of its amendments (Stockton to Rufus King, May 4, 1824). In 1820 he received eight votes from Massachusetts Federalists for the vice-presidency. In 1827 he was appointed a member of the New Jersey commission to settle the long-standing dispute with New York over the eastern boundary of the state. He died the following year at "Morven." Stockton was married to Mary Field of Burlington County, N. J., and Robert Field Stockton [*q.v.*] was one of their nine children.

[Letters scattered among the collections of the Lib. of Cong., Hist. Soc. of Pa., Princeton Univ., N. J. Hist. Soc., N. Y. Pub. Lib., N. Y. Hist. Soc., and Yale Univ.; L. Q. C. Elmer, *The Constitution and Govt. of the Province and State of N. J.* (1872); *Northern Monthly Mag.*, Sept. 1867; J. F. Hageman, *Hist. of Princeton and Its Institutions* (1879), vol. I; W. R.

Fee, *The Transition from Aristocracy to Democracy in N. J., 1789–1829* (1933); *Biog. Dir. Am. Cong.* (1928); *Gen. Cat. Princeton Univ.* (1908); T. C. Stockton, *The Stockton Family of N. J.* (1911); "Letters from Richard Stockton to John Rutherfurd ... in 1798," *Proc. N. J. Hist. Soc., 2 ser.* III (1874); *True American* (Trenton, N. J.), Mar. 8, 1828.]

W.R.F.

STOCKTON, ROBERT FIELD (Aug. 20, 1795–Oct. 7, 1866), naval officer, was born in Princeton, N. J., the fourth of the nine children of Richard, 1764–1828 [q.v.] and Mary (Field) Stockton. He was of the fifth generation from Richard Stockton, an English Quaker who came to Flushing, Long Island, before 1656 and whose son Richard moved to New Jersey in 1696. Robert's grandfather was Richard [q.v.], the Signer, and his father, "Richard the Duke," an eminent lawyer and United States senator and representative. At the age of thirteen Robert entered the College of New Jersey, where he excelled in mathematics, languages, and elocution. On Oct. 1, 1811, he was appointed midshipman and ordered to the *President*, the flagship of Commodore John Rodgers [q.v.], with whom he was closely associated throughout the War of 1812 —in the cruises of the flagship in the North Atlantic, in the construction of the *Guerrière* at Philadelphia, and in the military operations in defense of Washington and Baltimore. In these last-named operations, for his services as aide-de-camp, he was commended by Rodgers in official dispatches to the department. On Dec. 9, 1812, he was promoted to a lieutenancy, having previously served as master's mate.

In the war with Algiers, 1815, Stockton as first lieutenant of the *Spitfire* participated in the capture of two Algerine warships. In 1816 he began a tour of duty in the Mediterranean that lasted four years, during which he served first on board the *Washington*, 74, flagship of the squadron, and later on the *Erie*, of which vessel he was successively second lieutenant, executive officer, and commander. Always sensitive about points of honor, he enlivened his duties in the Mediterranean by fighting two duels, one with a British officer and the other with an American midshipman. Much interested in the American Colonization Society, Stockton in 1821 conveyed on board the *Alligator* to the west coast of Africa Dr. Eli Ayres, agent for the society, and obtained by means of a treaty with the native kings a new site for the agency, Cape Mesurado, later Liberia. On this cruise he captured several small French slavers and, after a sharp engagement, the Portuguese letter of marque *Mariana Flora*. The legality of this capture was sustained by the United States Supreme Court (11 *Wheaton*, 1–57), Justice Story delivering the opinion and

Daniel Webster representing the captor. In 1822, while employed in suppressing piracy in the West Indies, he made prize of or chased ashore several small vessels at Sugar Key. In 1823–24, when stationed with a surveying party on the Southern coast, he was married to Harriet Maria Potter of Charleston, S. C., who bore him nine children—three sons and six daughters; John Potter Stockton [q.v.] was his second son. In 1827–28 he was again employed with surveying duties.

Inheriting in the latter year the family homestead "Morven" at Princeton, N. J., he lived there, on leave of absence or furlough from the navy, for a decade, engaged in civilian pursuits. He invested his private fortune in the Delaware & Raritan Canal, serving as its first president, and in the Camden & Amboy Railroad. In behalf of these enterprises he visited Europe and furthered them in many other ways. He imported blooded horses from England and engaged in racing, one of his horses winning a stake of $10,000. He organized the New Jersey Colonization Society and became its first president. Taking an active part in New Jersey politics, he supported John Quincy Adams for a time, but later allied himself with Andrew Jackson and became one of the General's most intimate friends.

In 1830 Stockton was promoted master-commandant and in 1838, captain. Returning to active service in the latter year, he sailed for the Mediterranean in command of the *Ohio*, the flagship of the squadron. He made a study of the naval architecture and establishments of England and especially interested himself in a plan for a steamship for the American navy. In 1840, while on a furlough, he took part in the Presidential election of that year, speaking in most of the New Jersey counties in behalf of William H. Harrison. In 1841 he refused the offer of President Tyler to make him secretary of the navy. After assisting in the construction of the steamer *Princeton*, named for his home town, he became her first commander, 1843–45. He was in command of her when, during an excursion down the Potomac, one of her guns burst, killing among others Abel P. Upshur [q.v.], secretary of state, and Thomas W. Gilmer [q.v.], secretary of the navy. A court of inquiry exonerated him of blame for the accident. He was chosen by the President to convey to the Texan government the resolution of the American government providing for annexation.

War with Mexico now being imminent, in October 1845 he was ordered to proceed to the Pacific in the *Congress* and reinforce the American Squadron there, an assignment of duty which was destined to mark the climax of his naval career. Ambitious, self-confident, impulsive, eager to take the initiative, he was not likely to miss an opportunity for distinction. On July 15, 1846, he arrived at Monterey, Cal., the war having already begun, and on the 23rd he relieved Commodore J. D. Sloat [q.v.]. On the same day he issued a dashing proclamation to the Californians, now generally regarded as an unfortunate document. Assuming command of the land operations, he enrolled the Bear Flag battalion of John C. Frémont [q.v.] as volunteers of the American army and proceeded to conquer Southern California. After taking possession of Santa Barbara he sailed for San Pedro, where he arrived on Aug. 6. A week later, the combined forces of the navy and army entered Los Angeles and raised the American flag. On Aug. 17 he issued a proclamation declaring California a territory of the United States, and proceeded to organize a civil and military government, assuming for himself the title of governor and commander-in-chief. He placed the Mexican coast south of San Diego under blockade and planned for himself an expedition inland from Acapulco to the city of Mexico, but was forced to abandon this ambitious design on account of the recapture of Los Angeles by the Mexicans. Early in January 1847 the combined forces of Stockton and Gen. S. W. Kearney [q.v.], after fighting the battles of San Gabriel and Mesa, repossessed Los Angeles and ended the war on California soil. Soon thereafter Stockton was superseded. Returning overland, he arrived in Washington in October. On May 28, 1850, he resigned from the navy.

Elected to the United States Senate as a Democrat from New Jersey, Stockton served from Mar. 4, 1851, to Jan. 10, 1853. During his brief term he introduced a bill providing for the abolition of flogging in the navy and urged adequate harbor defenses, making speeches on both subjects. From 1853 until his death he was president of the Delaware & Raritan Canal Company. He espoused the American Party and was considered as a possible candidate for the presidency in 1856. He was delegate to the Peace Conference held in Washington early in 1861. Hopeful and buoyant, warm-hearted and generous, he possessed strong religious sentiments.

[Record of Officers, Bureau of Navigation, Washington, 1809–58; *Navy Reg.,* 1815–50; S. J. Bayard, *A Sketch of the Life of Com. Robert F. Stockton* (1856); T. C. Stockton, *The Stockton Family of N. J.* (1911); R. G. Cleland, *A Hist. of Cal.; The Am. Period* (1922); H. H. Bancroft, *Hist. of the Pacific States,* vol. XVII (1886); J. H. Smith, *The War with Mexico* (1919); *Sen. Exec. Doc. 31,* 30 Cong., 2 Sess.; R. W. Neeser, *Statistical and Chronological Hist. of the U. S. Navy* (1909); M. A. DeW. Howe, *Figures of the Past* (1926); J. E. Watkins, *The Camden and Amboy Railroad* (n.d.); *N. Y. Tribune,* Oct. 9, 1866.] C.O.P.

STOCKTON, THOMAS HEWLINGS (June 4, 1808–Oct. 9, 1868), Methodist Protestant clergyman, was one of the outstanding figures in the early history of his denomination. The son of William Smith Stockton and his first wife, Elizabeth Sophia (Hewlings), he was the eldest of a brilliant family of whom Frank R. Stockton [q.v.], his half-brother, was one of the younger members; he was born at Mount Holly, N. J., and his childhood was passed near Philadelphia. His career was determined by the religious interest of his father. The latter, an influential layman in the Methodist Episcopal Church, took a leading part in protesting against the arbitrary policy then prevailing among the bishops; and in 1828 he withdrew from the Methodist denomination with those reformers who later organized the Methodist Protestant Church.

This controversy, occurring during Thomas Stockton's formative years, not only turned him from the Methodist ministry, but provoked a hatred of sectarianism which influenced his entire career. At the age of nineteen he enrolled in Jefferson Medical College; but, disliking the profession of medicine, he cut short his training, and after an unproductive essay in literary work for periodicals, he entered the ministry of the newly organized Methodist Protestant Church. In 1830 he declined the editorship of the new denominational paper, the *Methodist Protestant,* recommending his friend Gamaliel Bailey [q.v.] instead. Two years previously he had married Anna Roe McCurdy, by whom he had eleven children (*Poems,* p. 300).

During the first years of his pastoral service, which were spent in northern Maryland, he discovered a capacity for pulpit oratory which was as unexpected as it was gratifying. His sermons were neither learned nor profound, but their style was graceful and literary, and they reflected the lovable spirit of the man himself. His reputation rapidly increased. When only twenty-five years of age, he was elected chaplain of the House of Representatives, an office which, except for one short interval, he filled until 1836.

Once more in the regular ministry, at Baltimore, Stockton became involved in the rising anti-slavery controversy. In 1838 he was again elected editor of the church paper, but when told that it should publish nothing on the subject of slavery, he resigned and removed to Philadelphia, where he preached to non-sectarian congregations for nine years, to the end that "professors of religion shall learn to live less for self and sect, and more for 'Christ and the Church' " (*Poems*, p. 306), but at the end of this time he returned to the Methodist Protestant denomination. During the remainder of his career, he alternately withdrew from his denomination and returned to it, meanwhile organizing independent, non-sectarian congregations. This he did in Cincinnati, in Baltimore, and again in Philadelphia. During these years, however, he attained a national reputation. In the capacity of chaplain of the Senate, in 1863, he conducted the religious services at the dedication of the Gettysburg national cemetery, when Lincoln made his immortal address. At the time of his death, in 1868, he was considered one of the greatest pulpit orators of his day.

Nothing that Thomas Stockton said or wrote long survived his death. His collected poems, *Floating Flowers from a Hidden Brook* (1844), and *Poems* (1862), are graceful and pleasing, but not inspired. His essays and controversial works, *The Bible Alliance* (1850), *Ecclesiastical Opposition to the Bible* (1853), and *The Book Above All* (1871), are without the charm and spirit that made his spoken words so memorable to his hearers. His one volume of collected addresses, *Sermons for the People* (1854), is, as Stockton himself said, not a learned book, "for the simple reason—which I greatly regret, though not without excuse—that there is no learning in the author himself" (*Sermons*, Preface, p. vii). It was only as minister to his congregations that in his day he touched greatness.

[Stockton's works, esp. autobiographical notes appended to his *Poems* (1862) ; T. C. Stockton, *The Stockton Family of N. J.* (1911) ; J. G. Wilson, *Life, Character, and Death of Rev. Thomas H. Stockton* (1869) ; Alexander Clark, *Memory's Tribute to the Life, Character and Work of Thomas H. Stockton* (1869) ; T. H. Colhouer, *Sketches of the Founders of the M. P. Church* (1880) ; A. H. Bassett, *A Concise Hist. of the M. P. Church* (1882) ; E. J. Drinkhouse, *Hist. of Meth. Reform . . . in the M. P. Church* (1899) ; *Public Ledger* (Phila.), Oct. 12, 1868.]

G. H. B.

STOCKWELL, JOHN NELSON (Apr. 10, 1832–May 18, 1920), mathematical astronomer, was born at West Farms, Northampton, Mass., the son of William Stockwell, a farmer, and his wife, Clarissa Whittemore. He was a descendant of William Stockwell, born at Thompson, Conn., about 1744, whose forebears had emigrated from England to New England at the beginning of the eighteenth century. After residing in West Farms for seven years the family moved to Ohio. John, the fifth of eight children, was sent to live on a farm with an uncle in Brecksville, Ohio, when he was eight years of age. In the kitchen of his uncle's house there hung the usual almanac,

in which it was stated that there would be a total eclipse of the moon on Nov. 24, 1844. This awesome event so thrilled the twelve-year-old lad that he then and there resolved to learn how to predict such phenomena. He had never heard of astronomy, and the opportunities for any formal education in that wilderness were limited, but during the winter months when the farm duties were few he studied all the almanacs he could find, solved many of the arithmetical problems proposed in a weekly periodical, the *Dollar Magazine,* and mastered an old arithmetic which fell into his hands. About this time he read of the discovery of the planet Neptune in 1846, and was inspired to begin alone to study algebra, geometry, and trigonometry, with the result that in an amazingly short time he seems to have mastered much of these subjects and even some of the calculus also. In Denison Olmsted's *Compendium of Astronomy* (1839), and also in the books of Thomas Dick, occasional references to Laplace and the *Traité de Mécanique Céleste* awakened the curiosity of the young scholar and he decided to order it through a book firm in Cleveland, Ohio. To his consternation he found not one but four stupendous tomes filled with the hieroglyphics of Laplace and, to add to his dilemma, a bill for forty dollars instead of five. He finally paid the bill by working on the farm, and then, by innate ability alone, mastered the great work. He was at the time twenty years of age.

In 1852 he published his first work, *The Western Reserve Almanac of the Year of our Lord, 1853.* For a short time, thanks to the offer of Benjamin A. Gould, 1824–1896 [*q.v.*], he worked as a computer in the longitude department of the United States Coast Survey and also in the United States Naval Observatory. A chance acquaintance with Leonard Case, 1820–1880 [*q.v.*], who had become interested in the Brecksville farmer-astronomer, led to Stockwell's appointment to the first chair of mathematics and astronomy at the Case School of Applied Science from 1881 to 1888. He was also chairman of the faculty. Both Mr. Case and Dr. Gould aided greatly in promoting his career, the former contributing considerable financial assistance toward his private researches after he resigned from his position at the Case School. He received honorary degrees from Western Reserve University, was a fellow of the American Association for the Advancement of Science, and a member of a number of scientific societies. His chief contributions, made over a period of seventy years, dealt with the theory of the moon's motion or with the computation of eclipses. One of his outstanding works was a *Memoir on the Secular Variations of the Elements of the Orbits of the Eight Principal Planets,* Smithsonian Contributions to Knowledge Series, volume XVIII (1873). In his last years he proposed, in *Ocean Tides* (1919), a theory of the tides in which he took issue with the accepted theory.

He was married on Dec. 6, 1855, to Sarah Healy, a foster-daughter of the Brecksville uncle. From this long and happy union there were born six children. Stockwell was a natural mathematician. His clear, analytical, and methodical mind enabled him to solve almost any mathematical problem in astronomy to which he turned his attention. Personally he was modest, genial, and gentle, and his life was one of extreme simplicity.

[Personal recollections of the writer; *Who's Who in America,* 1920–21; T. J. J. See, "Historical Notice of John Nelson Stockwell," *Popular Astronomy,* Dec. 1920; C. S. Howe, biographical sketch in *Science,* Jan. 14, 1921; *Cleveland Plain Dealer,* May 19, 1920.]

H. W. M.

STODDARD, AMOS (Oct. 26, 1762–May 11, 1813), lawyer, soldier, acting governor of Louisiana, was born in Woodbury, Conn., the eldest son of Anthony and Phebe (Reade) Stoddard, fourth in descent from the Rev. Solomon Stoddard [*q.v.*], and fifth in descent from Anthony Stoddard who arrived in Boston about 1639. When Amos was a few months old, his father moved to Lanesborough, Mass. In childhood the boy developed a retentive memory and was able to repeat prayers or sermons which he had just heard. Some of his Puritan ancestors had been clergymen of note, but Amos, as a frail boy less than seventeen, longed to join the Continental Army. Gathering the dirt under his heels to increase his height so that Baron Steuben would not reject him, he enlisted in the infantry in June 1779. Later he became a matross in the artillery and served until the close of the war. In spite of exposure and hard campaigns, his ʹealth improved so greatly that when mustered out, a six-foot youth, he could march forty miles a day without fatigue.

In 1784 he became assistant clerk of the supreme court of Massachusetts, living in the home of Charles Cushing in Boston, where he wrote, studied, and read 150 volumes in a year. He served as a commissioned officer in the suppression of Shays's Rebellion, returning late in 1787 to his clerkship and the study of law. In 1791 he went to England. To him has been attributed *The Political Crisis: or, A Dissertation on the Rights of Man,* published in London in that year (Willis, *post*). While in England he investigated his lineage, but failed to clear the title of his American relatives to the ancestral acres in Kent.

Returning to America, he was admitted to the Massachusetts bar in 1793, and opened an office at Hallowell in the District of Maine. He represented Hallowell in the Massachusetts legislature in 1797. He was in demand as an occasional speaker and several of his orations and addresses were published. After serving two years in the Massachusetts militia he returned to the United States Army in 1798, as a captain in the 2nd Regiment of Artillerists and Engineers, and in 1807 became a major.

When Louisiana was purchased, Stoddard was commissioned first civil and military commandant of Upper Louisiana, to serve until Congress enacted laws for its government. As the agent and commissioner of France, Mar. 9, 1804, in a ceremony at St. Louis, he received Upper Louisiana in the name of France from the Spanish governor, and raised the French flag. On the next day, with equal formality, he assumed the government in the name of the United States (*Missouri Historical Society Collections,* vol. VI, 1931, p. 320). Following Jefferson's instructions, he made practically no changes in the government and personnel. He kept the peace, was sparing in his gifts to the Indians but entertained others lavishly, and had marked success in destroying prejudice and in conciliating the inhabitants (*Governors Messages and Letters: Messages and Letters of William Henry Harrison,* vol. I, 1922, p. 170). He emphasized the importance of archives. He had previously exposed some fraudulent practices in regard to land grants. When he was relieved of civil authority, Sept. 30, 1804, the representatives of the several districts of Louisiana wrote of his "exemplary dispensation of justice" and of their "regret in parting" (*Missouri Historical Society Collections,* vol. III, 1908–11, p. 144). Assigned to duty in Lower Louisiana, he continued to gather all available information concerning the history and geography of the country, believing that if more were known concerning it, opposition to the purchase would cease. He incorporated this material in *Sketches, Historical and Descriptive, of Louisiana* (1812). During the War of 1812 he did notable work in preparing and subsequently defending Fort Meigs against attack. He was wounded during Procter's siege, and died of tetanus. He never married.

[Sources include Amos Stoddard MSS., Mo. Hist. Soc., also three letters, N. Y. Hist. Soc.; F. L. Billon, *Annals of St. Louis* (1886); Wm. Cothren, *Hist. of Ancient Woodbury, Conn.,* vol. I (1854); F. B. Heitman, *Hist. Reg. and Dict. U. S. Army* (1903), vol. I; *Mass. Soldiers and Sailors of the Rev. War,* vol. XV (1907); E. H. Nason, *Old Hallowell on the Kennebec*

(1909); J. W. North, *The Hist. of Augusta* (1870); C. and E. W. Stoddard, *Anthony Stoddard . . . a Geneal.* (1865); Wm. Willis, *A Hist. of the Law, the Courts, and the Lawyers of Me.* (1863); J. T. Scharf, *Hist. of St. Louis City and County* (1883), vol. I; Louis Houck, *A Hist. of Mo.* (1908), vol. II. A manuscript autobiography in private possession contains no additional facts of significance.]   H. R. S.

STODDARD, CHARLES WARREN (Aug. 7, 1843–Apr. 23, 1909), author, was born at Rochester, N. Y., the third of six children of Samuel Burr Stoddard and Harriet Abigail (Freeman) Stoddard of Lee, Mass. His father, a paper manufacturer and later a merchandise broker, was a descendant of the Rev. Solomon Stoddard [*q.v.*]. In 1855 the family moved to San Francisco. Returning to the East in the clipper ship *Flying Cloud,* which rounded Cape Horn, Charles attended an academy in western New York, 1857–59, and then rejoined his family in California, where he soon became a clerk in a book store. His first published poem appeared anonymously in 1861, and during the next two years his verse, under the pseudonymn of "Pip Pepperpod," was printed regularly in the *Golden Era,* to which Samuel Langhorne Clemens and Francis Brett Harte [*qq.v.*] were also contributors. Under the persuasion of Thomas Starr King [*q.v.*] he attended the preparatory division of the College of California (later merged with the University of California) at Oakland from 1863 until the fall of 1864, when, in poor health, he went to the Hawaiian Islands. Upon his return to San Francisco he contributed to the *Californian,* and in 1867 his *Poems* appeared, edited by Bret Harte. In the same year he ended his quest for religious satisfaction by becoming a Roman Catholic.

During the next twenty years he traveled widely. Between 1868 and 1873 he made two trips to Hawaii and one to Tahiti, which furnished material for his *South-Sea Idyls* (1873), reprinted in London as *Summer Cruising in the South Seas* (1874). In 1873 he went to Europe as traveling correspondent for the *San Francisco Chronicle,* and in London also served for a short time as secretary to Mark Twain. He lived in England and Italy for three years, made a year's tour of Egypt and the Holy Land in 1876–77 (recounted in *Mashallah!,* 1881, and *A Cruise under the Crescent,* copyright 1898), and then returned to the United States. After two years in San Francisco, he lived in Hawaii, 1881–84, where he wrote *A Troubled Heart* (1885), the story of his conversion. He was professor of English at the University of Notre Dame, February 1885 to June 1886, and lecturer on English literature at the Catholic University of America, Washington, D. C., 1889–1902.

When he was ordered to resign his position at the university in 1902, he tried to support himself in Washington for a year by writing. His health broke down, however, and he went to live with friends in Cambridge, Mass. In 1905, being in receipt of an annuity from Mrs. Bellamy Storer, and receiving a commission from the *Sunset Magazine* to write a series of articles on the California missions, he returned to San Francisco. Disappointed in the changed city of his youth, however, he soon removed to Monterey and there, accessible to only a few close friends, spent the remainder of his life.

He is remembered chiefly for his *South-Sea Idyls,* one of the few books that capture successfully the spirit of the South Seas. His other South Sea books, *The Lepers of Molokai* (copyright 1885), *Hawaiian Life* (1894), and *The Island of Tranquil Delights* (1904), though little known, contain some of his best writing. Among his other books are *The Wonder-Worker of Padua* (copyright 1896), *In the Footprints of the Padres* (1902), *For the Pleasure of His Company* (1903), his only novel, and *Exits and Entrances* (copyright 1903). His poems were collected by Ina Coolbrith as *Poems of Charles Warren Stoddard* (1917). In the charm and informality of his writing there is reflected the personal charm that won him innumerable friends and led Mark Twain to hire him less for his usefulness as a secretary than for his company. A man of great sweetness, kindliness, and gentleness, with a gift of whimsical humor, he is said to have had a wider friendship among literary folk than any one else in his day.

[See *Who's Who in America,* 1908–09; Charles and E. W. Stoddard, *Anthony Stoddard . . . a Geneal.* (1865); *Cath. Encyc.,* vol. XIV (copr. 1912); *Charles Warren Stoddard's Diary of a Visit to Molokai in 1884* (1933); G. W. James, in Stoddard's *Apostrophe to the Skylark* (copr. 1909), *Ave Maria,* May 22, 1909, and *Nat. Mag.,* Aug. 1911; Theodore Bentzon, in *Ave Maria,* May 15, 1909 (reprinted from *Revue des Deux Mondes*); Francis O'Neill, in *Cath. World,* July 1915; W. D. Howells, "The Editor's Easy Chair," *Harper's Monthly Mag.,* Dec. 1917; Thomas Walsh, in *Nation,* Oct. 4, 1922; Yone Noguchi, in *Nat. Mag.,* Dec. 1904; Joaquin Miller, in *Overland Monthly,* Oct. 1895; H. M. Bland, *Ibid.,* Apr. 1906; Charles Phillips, *Ibid.,* Feb. 1908; Barnett Franklin, *Ibid.,* June 1909; H. M. Bland, "Charles Warren Stoddard and His Place in Am. Literature," *Univ. of Cal. Chronicle,* Oct. 1909; obituary in *San Francisco Chronicle,* Apr. 25, 1909. Letters and other manuscript material are in the possession of *Ave Maria,* Notre Dame, Ind.; Mrs. J. Makee-Crawford, Berkeley, Cal.; Mrs. Finlay Cook, San Francisco; and the Bishop Museum, Honolulu, Hawaii. A biog. of Stoddard is being prepared by Carl G. Stroven, Univ. of Hawaii.]   C. G. S.

STODDARD, DAVID TAPPAN (Dec. 2, 1818–Jan. 22, 1857), missionary among the Nestorians in Persia, was born at Northampton, Mass., the son of Solomon and Sarah (Tappan)

Stoddard. His father, a lawyer and a member of the General Court, was a great-grandson of the Rev. Solomon Stoddard [*q.v.*] who was pastor of the church at Northampton for fifty-seven years and one of whose daughters was the mother of Jonathan Edwards. On his mother's side, David was a nephew of Arthur, Benjamin, and Lewis Tappan [*qq.v.*], and was related to Benjamin Franklin. He was named for a great-uncle who was professor of divinity at Harvard; his older brother, Solomon, won distinction as a Latinist. It is thus not surprising that David was a youth of promise and predisposed to both scholarship and religion. His mother hoped that he would enter the ministry and gave him careful religious instruction. As a boy he was active physically, although never robust, and was interested in mechanics. He studied at Round Hill School, Northampton, and in 1834, vivacious and attractive, entered Williams College as a sophomore. After a year there he transferred to Yale, where he graduated in 1838. As a student he developed a great interest in the natural sciences, making some of his own instruments, and in 1838–39 he was a tutor in Marshall College and in Middlebury College. During his first year at Yale, however, a profound religious experience had decided him to enter the ministry, and therefore, declining invitations to teach science in two Western colleges, he entered Andover Theological Seminary in 1839. Transferring after a year to Yale, he was a tutor there, 1840–42, meanwhile studying theology. He was licensed in 1842 in western Massachusetts, having some difficulty because of his adherence to the "New Haven theology," then regarded as heretical by the Calvinists of the older school, and was ordained in New Haven, Jan. 27, 1843.

At the time of his religious awakening in 1836, Stoddard had thought of becoming a missionary. That purpose, half forgotten, was reawakened in 1842 by contact with the Rev. Justin Perkins [*q.v.*], on furlough from Persia. Accordingly, in 1843, after his ordination and his marriage (Feb. 14) to Harriette Briggs, he went to Northwestern Persia under the American Board of Commissioners for Foreign Missions as a missionary among the Nestorians. In Oroomiah (Urmia), he was placed at the head of the chief school for boys conducted by his mission, and continued in charge after the school was moved to Seir. He also preached among the Nestorian churches. Persistently unwell, however, he returned in 1848 to the United States in an effort to regain his health. On the way, at Trebizond, his wife died. While in America he spoke extensively on missions, and for a time was in charge of two publications of his board, the *Dayspring* and the *Journal of Missions*. After the death of Mary Lyon [*q.v.*], in 1849, the trustees of Mount Holyoke Seminary approached him with a view to the possibility of his succeeding her as the head of that institution. His heart was in Persia, however, and in 1851 (after his marriage on Feb. 14 to Sophia Dana Hazen, who for several years had been a member of the staff of Mount Holyoke) he returned to resume his headship of the seminary at Seir. He was also in charge of a church ten miles away and did a great deal of preaching there and elsewhere.

Stoddard was a student of the Turkish and Persian languages and became something of an expert in Syriac. He aided Perkins in the translation of the New Testament into modern Syriac and prepared "A Grammar of the Modern Syriac Language, as Spoken in Oroomiah, Persia, and in Koordistan," published in the *Journal of the American Oriental Society* (vol. V, 1855–56). He was also the author of an arithmetic for the Nestorians, published by his mission. He continued his interest in the natural sciences, and through his knowledge of astronomy won the respect of some of the scholars of his district. He died at Seir, of typhus contracted while on a journey to Tabriz on business for his mission.

[J. P. Thompson, *Memoir of Rev. David Tappan Stoddard, Missionary to the Nestorians* (1858); F. B. Dexter, *Biog. Notices Grads. Yale Coll., Supp. to Obit. Record* (1913); C. and E. W. Stoddard, *Anthony Stoddard . . . a Geneal.* (1865); D. L. Tappan, *Tappan-Toppan Geneal.* (1915); ann. reports, Am. Board of Commissioners for Foreign Missions; *Missionary Herald*, vols. XL–LIII, *passim*, and obituary, June 1857.]

K. S. L.

STODDARD, ELIZABETH DREW BARSTOW (May 6, 1823–Aug. 1, 1902), novelist, poet, the wife of Richard Henry Stoddard [*q.v.*], was born in Mattapoisett, Mass., the second of nine children of Wilson and Betsey (Drew) Barstow. Her paternal ancestors came from Yorkshire, England, the first-known, William Barstow, having settled in Hanover, Mass., in 1649. He and his male descendants were shipbuilders, always prominent in their several localities, and frequently wealthy. Elizabeth attended school in Mattapoisett and was later sent to several educational institutions in New England, among them the Wheaton Female Seminary at Norton, Mass. From the first she showed a disinclination for prescribed study, although she read avidly. The works of Addison, Steele, Dr. Johnson, Fielding, Smollett, Sterne, and Sheridan she found in the library of her friend, the Rev. Thomas Robbins [*q.v.*] of Mattapoisett.

Through Rufus Wilmot Griswold [*q.v.*], indirectly, she met Stoddard, and after a short courtship she and the poet went to New York and were there married, probably in December 1851. They first lived in Brooklyn, then successively on East Thirteenth, East Tenth, and East Fifteenth streets, Manhattan. She and her husband were hospitable, and their home was ever a meeting-place for people of literary tastes. After her marriage, fostering a natural inclination and encouraged by her husband, she began to write. Short stories, poems, and sketches from her pen began to appear infrequently in the *Atlantic Monthly*, the *Knickerbocker*, *Harper's New Monthly Magazine*, *Appleton's Journal*, and other publications. In 1862 her first novel, *The Morgesons*, appeared. This was followed by *Two Men* (1865), *Temple House* (1867), both fiction; *Lolly Dinks's Doings* (1874), a book for children; and her collected *Poems* (1895). With her husband she edited several books of minor importance. As a writer Mrs. Stoddard was in advance of her time. Her novels, praised for their verisimilitude by Hawthorne and by Leslie Stephen, were realistic, even photographic, in detail in a day when the literature in vogue was either romantic or didactic and consciously ethical. The scene of each is laid in New England, and the characters are mainly the grim, determined folk of the author's girlhood. Although each of the works was twice reprinted, they were never really popular. In addition to the fact that they were out of the fashion and that they appeared when the Civil War and its consequences occupied the minds of everyone, they had many glaring faults. The humor was grim, the organization poor; a fertile imagination clogged the pages with plots and details. Mrs. Stoddard seemed never to feel the need for ordered expression and as a result her work is inchoate and without form. She had a certain narrative skill but an undisciplined technique. Her poetry, less popular with all and less important to her than her fiction, is a direct personal revelation. Uneven, careless in structure, it nevertheless burns with the intensity characteristic of the writer, and its morbidity of thought unfailingly reveals the frustration of her hopes and desires. Unsatisfied from childhood, she found little in her later life to lift her from morbidity: both her fiction and poetry were criticized severely; her husband was forced to poorly remunerated journeywork and subsequent ill-health; all three of her children met with an untimely death. A frail, nervous, highly imaginative woman, she was something of an angular individualist. Her tongue was sharp, and she frequently made enemies by its injudicious use. Nevertheless, those of her many acquaintances who understood her life knew her as a woman of kindliness and intelligence, with some literary talent, an apt critical judgment, and keen, tart, conversational power.

[*Who's Who in America*, 1901–02; R. H. Stoddard, *Recollections, Personal and Literary* (1903); *Mattapoisett and Old Rochester, Mass.* (copr. 1907); Mary Moss, in *Bookman*, Nov. 1902; obituary in *N. Y. Times*, Aug. 2, 1902.]   H.S., Jr.

STODDARD, JOHN FAIR (July 20, 1825–Aug. 6, 1873), educator and textbook writer, third of six children of Phineas and Marilda (Fair) Stoddard, traced his descent, through Solomon Stoddard [*q.v.*], from Anthony Stoddard of Boston, who emigrated to America from the west of England about 1639 and whose illustrious progeny included Jonathan Edwards and William Tecumseh Sherman [*qq.v*]. Born on a farm in Greenfield, N. Y., where he received his early education, he attended Montgomery Academy in Orange County, and the Nine Partners' School in Dutchess County, and by the time he was sixteen was teaching a district school. His major interest was mathematics, and the young teacher prepared and tried out in manuscript a textbook following the Pestalozzian trend made popular by Dana Pond Colburn [*q.v.*]. Encouraged by Prof. David Perkins Page [*q.v.*] of the State Normal College, Albany, N. Y., from which he was graduated in 1847, he published this as *The American Intellectual Arithmetic* in 1849. Its immediate success led to the preparation of a long series of mathematical works, some in collaboration with W. D. Henkle. Their popularity is shown by the fact that "up to 1860, 1,-500,000 copies had been issued, and the annual sales exceeded 200,000" (Greenwood and Martin, *post*, p. 852). Some of them were still in print in revised form in 1912. Stoddard's books gained from the ascendant theory of disciplinary values, which made arithmetic an "educational" as well as a practical subject. "That *Intellectual Arithmetic*," he said, "properly taught, is better calculated, than any other study, to *invigorate* and *develope* these [reasoning] faculties of the mind *cannot admit* of a doubt" (*The American Intellectual Arithmetic*, 1850, p. v). Sensible and helpful teaching suggestions were presented in these books, and in the *Report of the Commissioner of Education for the Year 1897–98, The American Intellectual Arithmetic* (revised edition, 1866) is rated as one of the very best mental arithmetics published.

Stoddard was an educator of eminence as well as a textbook writer. He headed Liberty Normal Institute (1847–51), the University of

Northern Pennsylvania (1851–54), and the Lancaster County Normal School (1855–57), all in Pennsylvania. He purchased the property of the closed University of Northern Pennsylvania and opened it as a teachers' college in April 1857. Within a month the buildings were destroyed by fire, but that fall he established the Susquehanna County Normal School at Montrose, which had an attendance of some three hundred, mostly teachers, for the next two years. In 1857 he was elected president of the Pennsylvania State Teachers' Association. He was a frequent speaker at teachers' institutes, fervently advocating higher standards in the profession.

With all his other activities, he continued his studies in higher mathematics. In 1853 he had received the degree of A.M. from the University of the City of New York (later New York University), and his removal to New York City in 1859 was partly due to his wish to make use of metropolitan facilities for advance study. He was principal of Grammar School No. 10 for several years. In 1864, in ill health, he retired to his birthplace, Greenfield, N. Y., where he continued writing and revising textbooks, and speaking at teachers' institutes. On Oct. 18, 1865, he married Eliza Ann, daughter of George W. and Eliza Platt. They had one daughter. In 1867 they moved to New Jersey, where they lived for the rest of Stoddard's life. He died at Kearny of what was called nervous consumption.

[Charles and E. W. Stoddard, *Anthony Stoddard of Boston, Mass., and His Descendants* (1865); Eliza P. Stoddard, *In Memoriam: Obituary and Addresses of the Late Prof. John F. Stoddard* (1874), with portrait; J. M. Greenwood and Artemas Martin, in *Report of the Commissioner of Educ. for the Year 1897–98* (1899); art. on Stoddard in "Pa. Educ. Biogs.," *Am. Jour. of Educ.*, Dec. 1865; W. S. Monroe, *Development of Arithmetic as a School Subject* (1917), p. 99; *The Am. Ann. Cyc.*, 1873; obituary in *Newark Daily Advertiser*, Aug. 6, 1873.]   E. W. F.

STODDARD, JOHN LAWSON (Apr. 24, 1850–June 5, 1931), lecturer and writer, was born at Brookline, Mass., the son of Lewis Tappan Stoddard and his second wife, Sarah H. (Lothrop) Stoddard, a nephew of David Tappan Stoddard [*q.v.*], and a descendant of the Rev. Solomon Stoddard [*q.v.*] of Northampton. After attending public school in Boston he entered Williams College, from which he graduated in 1871. He spent the next two years at the Yale Divinity School, but his increasing unorthodoxy led him to abandon the ministry and take up an instructorship in the classics in the Boston Latin School, 1873–74. After two years of foreign travel, chiefly in Greece, Palestine, and Egypt, and some further teaching, he entered in 1879 upon his highly successful career as a public lecturer. A pioneer in the use of the stereopticon, during the next eighteen years he traveled widely, visiting, as he said, "nearly every part of the habitable globe," and each winter delivered a series of illustrated lectures in the larger American cities, descriptive of European, Oriental, and American cities, life, and scenery. In this period he also published *Red-Letter Days Abroad* (1884); *Glimpses of the World* (1892), a volume of photographs with explanatory text; and a *Portfolio of Photographs* (copyright 1894), issued in sixteen weekly instalments. Broadly advertised by his speaking tours, which had made his name a household word, a series of ten volumes, *John L. Stoddard's Lectures,* first published in 1897–98, with five supplementary volumes in 1901, had an extensive and long-continued sale. His *Famous Parks and Buildings* (1899) and *Beautiful Scenes of America* (1902) catered similarly to the popular taste for pictures and light information. In April 1897 he retired and made his home in New York. He had been married, Dec. 24, 1877, to Mary Hammond Brown of Bangor, Me., and had a son, born in 1883, who also became a writer of distinction. Some five years later he became estranged from his wife, and on Aug. 15, 1901, after being divorced, he was married to Ida M. O'Donnell of Barnesville, Ohio. During subsequent years, spent chiefly in retirement abroad, he selected *The Stoddard Library; A Thousand Hours of Entertainment with the World's Great Writers* (12 vols., 1910), with an accompanying handbook published in 1915.

His European home was first in a villa at Meran in the Austrian Tyrol, then from about 1906 until 1914 on Lake Como, Italy, and afterwards until his death on a larger estate near Meran. Love for the Tyrol and its people, as well as his own strongly independent habits of thought, drew him during the World War into sympathy with the Central Powers, a feeling that finds expression in his pamphlet *Why Is It?*, published by the German-American Defense Committee in 1915, in *America and Germany* (1916), and in *La Decadence de l'Angleterre* (Berne, 1917). In religion he had been for many years a free thinker, but his harrowing wartime experiences in a frontier province and his suffering from typhus fever in 1917 inclined him toward Catholicism. In 1922, with his wife, he became a member of the Roman Catholic Church. Thereafter he gave his time almost wholly to religious study and writings, the latter including *Christ and the Critics* (2 vols., 1926–27), a translation of Dr. Hilarin Felder's *Jesus Christus; The Theology of Saint Paul* (2 vols., 1926–

27), from the French of Fernand Prat; *The Evening of Life* (1930), from the French of Louis Baunard; and *Yesterdays of an Artist-Monk* (copyright 1930), from Willibrord Verkade's *Die Unruhe zu Gott.* A volume of his verse, *Poems,* appeared in 1913, his *Rebuilding a Lost Faith* in 1921, and his *Twelve Years in the Catholic Church* (1930) just before his death in his Italian home. He is remembered far less for these later writings than for his extraordinary popularization, both on the platform and in published form, of the travel lecture which combined a wealth of pictures with entertaining accounts of strange people and scenes. Unlike the modern travelogue, however, which often degenerates into a mere running comment on the motion picture film, these lectures were prepared beforehand with the utmost care. Their success was even more a matter of delivery. By natural gifts and long training Stoddard was an excellent speaker, and from the moment his slender, erect figure appeared on the platform his audience was won by his eloquence and personal magnetism.

[Charles and E. W. Stoddard, *Anthony Stoddard . . . a Geneal.* (1865); *Who's Who in America,* 1930–31; *Obit. Record Soc. of Alumni Williams Coll.,* Apr. 1932; "Originator of the Modern Travel Lectures," *Hampton's Mag.,* Oct. 1910; G. E. Chase, in *Libraries,* May 1931; J. A. Walsh, in *Cath. World,* Oct. 1931; obituary in *Boston Transcript,* June 5, 1931.]
A. W—t.

STODDARD, JOHN TAPPAN (Oct. 20, 1852–Dec. 9, 1919), chemist and teacher, was a native of Northampton, Mass., the son of William Henry and Helen (Humphrey) Palmer Stoddard, a nephew of David Tappan Stoddard [*q.v.*]. He was of the seventh generation of Stoddards in America, a direct descendant of Anthony who emigrated from England to Boston in 1639, and of Anthony's son, Solomon [*q.v.*], who moved to Northampton to become the forebear of the large number of Stoddards prominent in its affairs from its settlement to the present (1932). The Northampton Stoddards were all well educated, some at Yale, some at Harvard, and those of later date at Amherst College. For the most part they were ministers and educators, men of loyalty and strength of purpose.

John Tappan Stoddard received the degree of A.B. from Amherst College in 1874, and the following year served as assistant principal of the Northampton high school. During the years 1876 to 1878 he studied in Germany, working under Hans Hübner at Göttingen and receiving the degree of Ph.D. in 1877. His dissertation, *Über Anhydrobenzamidotoluylsäure und über eine neue Ketonbase,* was published at Göttingen in the same year. In 1878 he returned to North-

ampton and became associated with Smith College, serving as professor of physics (1878–81) and as professor of physics and chemistry (1881–97). In 1897 he became the first chairman of the department of chemistry, and this post he held with distinction until the time of his death. He went to Smith College at a time when modern ideas of technical laboratory training were first being introduced into American colleges and universities. With the vision and imagination always characteristic of him, he soon introduced these at Smith and supervised the very considerable expansion of the department of chemistry. The chemistry building, renamed Stoddard Hall after his death, was erected two years after he assumed the headship of the department and was planned with so much foresight that a generation later it was still considered adequate in every way for scientific research.

He was the author of four textbooks, all of which went through several editions and were widely used: *An Outline of Qualitative Analysis* (1883), *Quantitative Experiments in General Chemistry* (1908), *Introduction to General Chemistry* (1910), and *Introduction to Organic Chemistry* (1914). In addition he contributed research articles to the *Journal of the American Chemical Society.* An enthusiastic billiards player, he was also the author of a unique book, *The Science of Billiards with Practical Applications* (1913); and as a result of experiments in photography, he published an article on "Composite Photography" in the *Century Magazine* (March 1887). His contributions to teaching and to science found less expression in his publications, however, than in his personal contacts with colleagues and students and in the practical projects committed to his direction. A man of foresight and of personal charm, he was a very considerable influence in the early history of Smith College. On June 26, 1879, he married Mary Grover Leavitt of Northampton; they had two sons and one daughter. He died at his home in Northampton.

[J. McK. Cattell, *Am. Men of Science* (2nd ed. 1910); *Bull. of Smith Coll., Ann. Report,* 1919–20; *Daily Hampshire Gazette* (Northampton), Dec. 9, 1919; *Celebration of the Quarter-Centenary of Smith Coll.* (1900); Solomon Clark, *Antiquities, Historicals, and Grads. of Northampton* (1882); H. J. Kneeland, *Some Old Northampton Homes* (pamphlet, 1909); Charles and E. W. Stoddard, *Anthony Stoddard . . . a Geneal.* (1865); Frederick Humphreys, *The Humphreys Family in America* (1883); *Who's Who in America,* 1918–19; *Boston Transcript,* Dec. 9, 1919.]
C. P. B.

STODDARD, JOSHUA C. (Aug. 26, 1814–Apr. 3, 1902), inventor, was born in Pawlet, Rutland County, Vt., the son of Nathan Ashbel and Ruth (Judson) Stoddard, and a descendant of the Rev. Solomon Stoddard [*q.v.*]. After obtaining a common-school education in his native town Joshua worked on his father's farm for many years, engaging in bee culture and the production of honey. This occupation he pursued with ordinary success throughout his life, particularly in Worcester, Mass., where he resided for well over half a century. He was something of a poet, lived in constant expectation of the end of the world according to the ingenious calculations of the "timists," and possessed considerable mechanical skill and ingenuity. In the course of his life he was granted sixteen patents, most of which were for improvements in horse-drawn hay rakes.

One invention, however, quite distinct from the rest, brought him much renown but no financial reward. This was a steam calliope, for which he received a patent on Oct. 9, 1855. It was based upon the conception that the bells of the whistle by the vibration of whose thin edges the sound of the steam whistle is produced, could be so arranged as to render accurately the diatonic scale in music. After experimenting for a number of years he succeeded in constructing a series of bells on which seven notes of the octave could be played by steam, and invented a delicate valve for the admission of steam to the whistles. His calliope consisted of a steam chest on top of which were a number of valve chambers (according to the number of whistles) having double poppet valves, and over each valve was a whistle of its own particular tone. A stem passed from each valve through the steam chamber to the outside, by which stem the valve could be opened and shut by the slightest pressure. A long cylinder with pins driven into it was so placed that when it was revolved the pins pressed on the valve stems and thus blew the whistles to play a tune. The ingenious part of the cylinder, however, was the use of pins of different shapes, whereby notes of varying lengths—whole, half, quarter, eighths, and even dotted notes—could be produced. Stoddard later made other improvements so that an organ or piano keyboard could be used in playing the instrument.

Late in 1855 he organized, in Worcester, the American Steam Music Company and began manufacturing instruments for use on steamboats, locomotives, and in circuses. The company held its first marine exhibit in August 1856 in the waters around New York, having fitted up an instrument on the side-wheel tugboat *Union.* This instrument was later placed permanently on the passenger boat *Glen Cove.* In 1858 the *Armenia,* in passenger service on the Hudson, was equipped with a 34-whistle, key-board calliope, which continued in use until 1870. Gradually instruments were installed on other vessels both in Eastern and mid-Western waters, and one or two were sold to circuses. Stoddard was an unworldly man with practically no business judgment and in less than five years was pushed out of the organization no better off than before making his invention.

Subsequently, he devised his hay-raking machines, for which he received patents, Aug. 6, 1861, Sept. 27, 1870, and Jan. 10, 1871. These were made under his name and widely used for many years. On Jan. 22 and Aug. 12, 1884, he received patents for improvements in fire escapes, and on Mar. 12, 1901, a patent for a fruit-paring machine; but nothing came of them. He was married on Jan. 23, 1845, at Canaan, N. Y., to Lucy Maria Hersey, and at the time of his death in Springfield, Mass., was survived by two sons.

[C. and E. W. Stoddard, *Anthony Stoddard . . . a Geneal.* (1865); *Springfield Republican,* Apr. 4, 1902; J. H. Morrison, *Hist. of Am. Steam Navigation* (1903); Patent Office records.]   C. W. M—n.

STODDARD, RICHARD HENRY (July 2, 1825–May 12, 1903), poet, critic, editor, was born at Hingham, Mass., the son of Reuben and Sophia (Gurney) Stoddard. On his paternal side he was a descendant of John Stodder who had emigrated to Hingham and received there a grant of land in 1638. His ancestors had followed the sea for several generations, and his father had risen, through hard work, from the rank of ordinary seaman to that of master and part-owner of the *Royal Arch,* on which he was lost when Stoddard was but a child of two or three. He seems to have been the one person who might have influenced the child's later literary pursuits, for in letters which he wrote his wife while he was away on voyages, signed interchangeably "Reuben Stodder" and "Reuben Stoddard," he exhibited a certain amount of untrained literary ability. The Gurneys were an uneducated and improvident family who, at the time Stoddard was a child, were principally employed as operatives in cotton mills throughout New England. After her husband's death Stoddard's mother made her home first with her husband's family and then with her own people, moving with them from one factory town to another. In the *Christian Parlor Book* (February, October 1851, and February 1852) and in *Recollections, Personal and Literary* (1903) Stoddard writes rather pathetically of his chaotic and squalid early life. His mother was a restless and lonely woman who, although she attempted to apply herself to her child's education, had neither the intelligence nor the emotional stability to give him much aid. After a few years in Hingham and in Abington, the ancestral home of the Gurneys, mother and son moved to Boston, where Stoddard ran about as a street urchin, while his mother was engaged in making rough clothes for the sailors who entered Boston harbor. She married again, another sailor, and with her husband and the ten-year-old child moved to New York in the autumn of 1835. Here Stoddard attended school for a few years, learning little, but reading cheap reprints of Burns, James Beattie, Cowper, and Shakespeare. At the age of fifteen he was compelled to begin to contribute to the support of the family. He thus became successively an errand boy, a shop boy, a legal copyist, "a sort of factotum" in the office of a short-lived journal, a bookkeeper, and at the age of eighteen an iron moulder.

It is difficult to understand how one with such a background could have entered upon literature as a profession. His mother and his step-father had been unsympathetic towards advanced learning and too poor even to provide their son with good books to read. But Stoddard, unschooled as he was, early began to cultivate his love for literature and literary figures. He assiduously studied the English masters and by 1845 had begun to write. He was the typical figure of the literary climber. He worked at his task of iron moulding uncomplainingly, buoyed up by the thought of friendly conversation with book-loving companions at night, and he sought out such men as Dr. Ralph Hoyt, Park Benjamin [q.v.] and Lewis Gaylord Clark [q.v.]. From them and the books he studied so earnestly he learned much of the history and forms of English poetry. His early verse appeared in such magazines as the Rover, the Home Journal, the Southern Literary Messenger, the Knickerbocker, the Union Magazine, and Godey's Lady's Book. In 1849 he brought out, at his own expense, his first volume, Foot-Prints, of which one copy (now in the Library of Congress, Washington, D. C.) was sold before Stoddard repented of his amateurish attempts and burned the whole edition. The poems are frankly imitative of Keats and Wordsworth. He was married, probably in December 1851, to Elizabeth Drew Barstcw of Mattapoisett, Mass. [see Elizabeth Drew Barstow Stoddard], a high-strung, temperamental woman who had a genius for conversation and some gift for writing. In the same year he brought out Poems, which was favorably reviewed, a much more finished work than Foot-Prints. In 1853 he received through the intervention of Nathaniel Hawthorne [q.v.], with

whom he had scraped up an acquaintance, an appointment as inspector of customs in the New York custom house, a position which he held until 1870. During his seventeen-year tenure of this office he wrote constantly. From 1860 to 1870 he was a literary reviewer for the World (New York). After his discharge from customs duty he became for some three years a confidential secretary to Gen. George Brinton McClellan [q.v.] in the docks department; in 1877 he was appointed city librarian, a political position involving the handling of municipal books, which he held for nearly two years. From 1880 until his death he was the literary editor of the Mail and Express. During this latter period of his life he was engaged in several editorial ventures, notably as editor of the Aldine, a short-lived journal, and the Bric-à-Brac and Sans-Souci Series. In 1880 appeared The Poems of Richard Henry Stoddard, a collected edition, and ten years later The Lion's Cub; with Other Verse. A fair sample of his editorial work is English Verse (1883), done in collaboration with W. J. Linton. In 1903 there appeared his Recollections, Personal and Literary, edited by Ripley Hitchcock, with an introduction by E. C. Stedman.

Stoddard was not in any sense a great poet. His ear was faulty, his powers of imagination were limited, but he often felt keenly and deeply the emotions which he expressed. Some of his poems have undoubted charm; still others are indisputably powerful, as, for example, his tribute to William Cullen Bryant, "The Dead Master," and his Abraham Lincoln: An Horatian Ode (1865). He was one of the first in America to deal with Oriental themes (Poems, 1852, and Songs of Summer, 1857). Nevertheless, he was clearly imitative in most of his verse; many of his poems echo trite sentiments and express feeble emotions. In the field of criticism, however, he did much able work. By constant study he made himself one of the most learned critics of his day, and though his critical work often shows mistaken judgment or even personal bias, as in the case of Poe, it is on the whole remarkably accurate and painstaking, considering that most of it was designed as mere hackwork. As an editor he was careful and comparatively sound in his judgment, although the appeal of much that he edited was distinctly popular (over 60,-000 copies of the Bric-à-Brac Series were sold in eighteen months).

When his reputation became assured, about 1870, his home assumed the aspects of a literary salon. He has been described as the "Nestor of American literature," and indeed for over thirty years his home was one of the most important centers of New York's cultural life. He served as a link between the older writers—Poe, Hawthorne, Lowell, Longfellow, Bryant, all of whom he had known—and the later writers of his own day—Bayard Taylor, Edmund Clarence Stedman, George Henry Boker, Thomas Buchanan Read, Paul Hamilton Hayne, and Herman Melville [*qq.v.*]. Widely popular, Stoddard received the poetic effusions of hundreds of poetasters from all over the land, but, although he was genial, he was none the less firm and unswerving in his literary judgment. He hated sham and vigorously condemned as he wholeheartedly praised; his remarks on Bohemianism, for example, were vitriolic. His conversation was vigorous and quite often profane. Withal he was a brave figure of a man, often railing at fate but going ahead methodically and painstakingly, dropping many caustic comments on life by the way. His friends understood and loved him, and the Authors Club dinner given him in 1897 was one of the most brilliant and sincere tributes ever offered a literary man.

In the later years of his life, as the result of rheumatism in childhood, two cataracts, and an attack of paralysis, he was an almost helpless invalid. A variety of other circumstances had combined as well to embitter him. His unfortunate early life, the poor royalties from his work and from his wife's novels, the early death of two children, a sorrow crowned by the death of his third son, Lorimer, the gifted playwright, followed within the year by Mrs. Stoddard's death—all served to drive him towards a madness from which only his beloved books and faithful friends saved him. Yet he remained unswerving in his devotion to literature and the literary life.

[The chief biog. source is Stoddard's *Recollections, Personal and Literary* (1903), with a rather full list of his works. See also *Who's Who in America*, 1901–02; A. R. Macdonough, in *Scribner's Monthly*, Sept. 1880, the best single article on Stoddard; S. A. Allibone, *A Crit. Dict. of Eng. Literature*, vol. II (1870), for a full bibliog. and references to reviews; obituary in *N. Y. Times*, May 13, 1903. Stoddard's lib. is in the possession of the Authors Club of N. Y. Many of his MSS. are in the possession of Mrs. Ripley Hitchcock of N. Y., and there are large colls. of his letters in the libraries of Cornell Univ. and the Am. Antiquarian Soc.]   H. S., Jr.

STODDARD, SOLOMON (September 1643– Feb. 11, 1728/29), Congregational clergyman, baptized in Boston, Mass., Oct. 1, 1643, when about four days old, was one of the fifteen sons of Anthony Stoddard, who settled in Boston in 1639, and of Mary, sister of Sir George Downing and niece of Gov. John Winthrop [*q.v.*]. He studied with Elijah Corlet of Cambridge, and graduated from Harvard in 1662. From 1667 to 1674 he was librarian of the college, being the first to hold that office. During this period, in 1667, for reasons of health, he went as chaplain to the Congregationalists in Barbados, on the invitation of ex-Governor Searle. In 1669 he returned to Boston and was about to sail for England when he was invited to preach at Northampton, Mass. He went thither in November, and in March 1670 the town called him to the pastorate of the church. He accepted in February 1672, was ordained on Sept. 11 of that year, and held the pastorate until his death. In March 1670 he married Esther Mather, widow of his predecessor, the Rev. Eleazar Mather and daughter of the Rev. John Warham of Windsor; they had twelve children, among whom were Col. John Stoddard (1681–1748), member of the governor's council and commander-in-chief of the western division of Massachusetts, and Esther, mother of Jonathan Edwards [*q.v.*], who in 1727 was ordained associate pastor of the Northampton church.

Stoddard accepted the Half-Way Covenant, proposed by the synod of 1662, by which persons not sufficiently advanced in grace to qualify for full membership in the church could secure baptism for their children; at some period, before 1677, he introduced into his church the practice, usually called "Stoddardeanism," of allowing professing Christians to take the communion and enjoy other privileges of full membership, even when they were not certain that they were in a state of grace. "My business," he said "was to answer a case of Conscience, and direct those that might have Scruples about Participation of the Lords-Supper, because they had not a work of Saving Conversion, not at all to direct the Churches, to admit any that were not to rational charity true Believers" (*An Appeal to the Learned*, pp. 2, 3). He advocated this practice in the Reforming Synod of 1679, persuading that body to make a mere profession of faith and repentance and not a relation of a personal experience of grace the requisite for church membership. Subsequently, he engaged in controversy with Increase Mather [*q.v.*], defending "Stoddardeanism" in *The Doctrine of Instituted Churches* (1700), *The Inexcusableness of Neglecting the Worship of God, under a Pretence of Being in an Unconverted Condition* (1708), and *An Appeal to the Learned* (1709). For a century most of the churches in western Massachusetts accepted Stoddard's view of church membership. Edwards, however, rejected it, and though this resulted in his dismissal from Northampton in 1750, his influence caused it to be gradually abandoned.

Stoddard published nineteen other sermons and pamphlets. He attacked the belief that "every particular Congregation is absolute and independant" (*The Doctrine of Instituted Churches,* quoted by Trumbull, *post,* II, 59), advocating a national church governed by a synod. He also argued that the clergy should have more power than had been customary in New England, believing that the laity should be allowed only the right of electing their ministers. He was sternly opposed to long hair, wigs, extravagance in dress, and excessive drinking, being partly responsible for the sumptuary laws of 1676, and attacking the aforementioned and other wicked practices in *An Answer to Some Cases of Conscience Respecting the Country* (1722). He urged ministers to speak frequently of hellfire, declaring that "if Sinners don't hear often of Judgement and Damnation, few will be converted." His views on this subject are developed in *The Efficacy of the Fear of Hell to Restrain Men from Sin* (1713), and in *A Guide to Christ* (1714). He took great interest in politics; for half a century he was the most influential person in western Massachusetts, and his letters to Boston, especially during the Indian wars, strongly affected the policy of the government. As minister he was very successful, promoting revivals of religion in Northampton in 1679, 1683, 1712, and 1718. He dominated his congregation, receiving from malcontents the nickname of "Pope." Personally, he was tall and dignified, and was an impressive conversationalist in any company. Not so learned as the Mathers, he was more forceful as a writer and more original as a thinker. As an ecclesiastical statesman he was unrivaled in his generation.

[*A Report of the Record Commissioners Containing Boston Births, Baptisms, Marriages and Deaths, 1630–1699* (1883), p. 16; Charles and E. W. Stoddard, *Anthony Stoddard of Boston, Mass., and His Descendants; a Geneal.* (1865); J. R. Trumbull, *Hist. of Northampton, Mass.* (2 vols., 1902); W. B. Sprague, *Annals Am. Pulpit,* vol. I (1857); J. L. Sibley, *Biog. Sketches Grads. Harvard Univ.,* vol. II (1881); Williston Walker, *The Creeds and Platforms of Congregationalism* (1893); "Stoddardeanism," *New Englander,* July 1846; "Diary of Samuel Sewall," *Mass. Hist. Soc. Colls.,* 5 ser. vols. V–VII (1878–83); *Boston Weekly News Letter,* Feb. 20, 1729.]   H. B. P.

STODDARD, WILLIAM OSBORN (Sept. 24, 1835–Aug. 29, 1925), author, inventor, secretary to President Lincoln, was born in Homer, N. Y., the son of Prentice Samuel Stoddard by his first wife, Sarah Ann (Osborn). He was a descendant of Ralph Stoddard, who was in Groton, Conn., as early as 1695. William received his early education in private schools and at Homer Academy. From 1849 until 1853 he worked in his father's book and publishing shop

at Syracuse. In 1858 he received the degree of A.B., *cum laude,* from the University of Rochester.

That same year he became affiliated with the *Central Illinois Gazette* at West Urbana, Ill., his name first appearing as joint editor of this weekly paper in August 1858. At West Urbana (now Champaign), Stoddard met Abraham Lincoln, and although reared in New York as a disciple of William H. Seward, he was instantly won by Lincoln's personality. The young editor worked ceaselessly for Lincoln's election in the Illinois senatorial campaign of 1858 and he was one of the first Illinois editors to suggest him for the presidency. In the *Atlantic Monthly* (February 1925), he recounts his efforts in the spring of 1859 to awaken interest in Lincoln as a candidate, saying: "In all the long list of possible presidential candidates, the name of Lincoln had not been spoken of in any newspaper publication that I knew anything about." He then quotes from two articles which appeared in the *Gazette* advocating Lincoln's candidacy, the implication being that both were published in the spring of 1859. The first article, a personal item, did appear in the *Gazette* on May 4, 1859, and in this appears the assertion: "No man in the West . . . stands a better chance [than Lincoln] for obtaining a high position among those to whose guidance our ship of state is to be entrusted." The second article, however, an editorial entitled "Who Shall Be President?" did not appear in the *Gazette* until Dec. 7, 1859. In spite of Stoddard's belief to the contrary, he was not the first editor to put Lincoln forward as a candidate. The *Olney Times* (Olney, Ill.) came out in his behalf on Nov. 19, 1858, and on Dec. 16, 1858, the Chicago *Press and Tribune* published an editorial reprint from the Reading, Pa., *Berks and Schuylkill Journal* in which Lincoln was suggested for the presidency.

Stoddard worked vigorously for Lincoln in the campaign of 1860, and in recognition of his services, Lincoln, in 1861, appointed him as a secretary to sign land patents. In April of the same year, with Lincoln's permission, he enlisted as a private for three months' service in the United States Volunteers. Upon his discharge, he was appointed an assistant private secretary to Lincoln, with the task of sorting out for the waste basket the scores of letters received from office seekers, "blackguards," and "lunatics." Except for occasional help from department clerks, John George Nicolay, John Hay [*qq.v.*], and Stoddard attended to all of the clerical work at the executive office during the early part of Lincoln's administration. Stoddard relates the "queer kind of tremor" that came over him as he copied from "Abraham Lincoln's own draft of the first Emancipation Proclamation" (*Atlantic Monthly*, March 1925, p. 337).

An ardent opponent of slavery, he was active in organizing in 1862 the Union League of America. In September 1864 he was appointed United States marshal of Arkansas, resigning this position in 1866 because of ill health. After 1866, he became engaged in journalistic activities and in telegraphic, manufacturing, and railway enterprises, obtaining nine patents for mechanical inventions. From 1873 to 1875 he served as a clerk in the department of docks, New York City. In all, Stoddart wrote over one hundred books, among which were: *Abraham Lincoln* (1884); *The Lives of the Presidents* (10 vols., 1886–89); *Inside the White House in War Times* (1890); and *The Table Talk of Lincoln* (1894). His books for boys, some seventy-six in number, were perhaps his greatest literary successes. On July 25, 1870, he married Susan Eagleson Cooper of New York, by whom he had five children. He spent the later years of his life at Madison, N. J., where he died.

[In addition to Stoddart's writings, see E. W. Stoddard, *Ralph Stoddard of New London and Groton, Conn., and His Descendants* (1872); *Gen. Cat., Univ. of Rochester* (1911); *Who's Who in America*, 1924–25; *N. Y. Times*, Aug. 30, 1925; *The Americana Annual* (1926); *The New International Year Book . . . 1925* (1926). Information as to certain facts was supplied by W. O. Stoddard, Jr.]   A.L.P.

STODDART, JAMES HENRY (Oct. 13, 1827–Dec. 9, 1907), actor, was born in Barnsley, Yorkshire, England, one of a family of ten. His father was James Henry Stoddart, a provincial actor fron. Scotland; his mother was Mary (Pierce) Stoddart of Yorkshire. In appearance, however, the son always suggested very strongly the Scotch side of his ancestry. The elder Stoddart had been for many years connected with the Theatre Royal, Glasgow, and all five of his sons became actors. James Henry began as a child of five and as a youth acted with the American star, Charlotte Cushman, in Glasgow, playing a gypsy boy in *Guy Mannering*. In 1854 he made a hazard of new fortunes and came to New York, where James William Wallack engaged him as a member of his company. He remained in Wallack's company for two years and then joined Laura Keene [*q.v.*]. In 1859 he was at the Winter Garden, where Dion Boucicault was the stage manager and Joseph Jefferson [*qq.v.*] the leading player. There he played Lafourche in the famous production of Boucicault's *The Octoroon*. From 1864 to 1866 he was at the Olympic, where he played Moneypenny in *The Long Strike*. In 1867 he went back again to Wallack's Theatre on Broadway at Thirteenth Street, and in 1875, after two unsuccessful seasons of touring as the star in *The Long Strike*, joined the company of Albert Marshman Palmer [*q.v.*] at the Union Square Theatre. He remained with this famous organization for two decades, moving with it to the Madison Square Theatre and playing in almost all the dramas to which it gave life. Consequently, he was identified at one time or another with most American actors of his period and with the works of many rising American playwrights, including Bronson Crocker Howard and Augustus Thomas [*qq.v.*]. One of his famous rôles was that of Pierre Michel in *Rose Michel*. Another, which illustrated his versatility and his sympathy with the newer drama of local color, was that of Colonel Preston in Augustus Thomas' play, *Alabama*. Here, in spite of his Scotch ancestry, he gave a convincing performance, carefully composed and natural in execution, of an old-school Southerner. The year 1896 found him playing in a melodrama, *The Sporting Duchess*, and on Jan. 30 the company held a celebration and gave him a loving cup in honor of his sixty-three years on the stage. Though, in all conscience, his career had been a long one, it was not till five years later that, for the second time, he became a star, and for the first time a successful one. During the season of 1901–02, at the Republic Theatre, New York, he played Lachlan Campbell in a dramatization of the then popular story by Ian Maclaren (John Watson), *Beside the Bonnie Briar Bush*. He had waited long, and worked hard, for his honors. As the proud, stern, self-contained father in this play, tender, true, and deeply religious, he not only created an authentic Scotch atmosphere but displayed a power and pathos that captured the public. He was still playing this rôle when he was stricken with paralysis in April 1905 in Galt, Ontario. He died in 1907 at his home in Sewaren, N. J. In 1902 he published his *Recollections of a Player*. His wife was Matilda (Phillips) Conover, whom he met and married, Oct. 28, 1855, when both were playing with Lester Wallack. They had two sons, one of whom died young, and a daughter.

Stoddart was so striking in appearance, especially in later life, that disguise was impossible, and he applied his skill to fitting his own personality to a part. Tall and slender, wiry of frame, with an extraordinarily wide mouth and wide-set, penetrating blue eyes, he had the face and figure of some old Scotchman carved out of rock and heather. But it was a face and figure oddly appealing, and Stoddart knew how to make the most of it, both for humor and pathos. He could play with a light touch, and he could strike deep. Till his final illness, he scarcely ever lacked employment in the best companies, and for fifty years was a valued and beloved figure on the American stage.

[*Who's Who in America*, 1906–07; J. H. Stoddart, *Recollections of a Player* (1902); *N. Y. Tribune*, Jan. 28, 31, 1896; G. C. D. Odell, *Annals of the N. Y. Stage*, vols. VI, VII (1931); obituaries in *N. Y. Times, Evening Post* (N. Y.), Dec. 10, 1907; Locke Coll., in N. Y. Pub. Lib., and Shaw Coll., Widener Lib., Harvard Univ.]
                                                    W. P. E.

STODDART, JOSEPH MARSHALL (Aug. 10, 1845–Feb. 25, 1921), editor and publisher, the son of Joseph M. and Elizabeth (Fahnestock) Stoddart, was born in Philadelphia, Pa., where his father was a dry-goods merchant. After a period in the public schools of his native city, he was sent to the Port Royal Academy, Frankford, also in Philadelphia. At the age of sixteen he was placed with the publishing firm of J. B. Lippincott & Company, Philadelphia, and remained there thirteen years, though in the last year of the Civil War he served two enlistments of three months each. In 1874 he left to become a publisher on his own account. In that year he published *Out of the Hurly Burly*, the first book of the humorist, Charles Heber Clark [*q.v.*], which became instantly popular and was a remarkable financial success. Stoddart is credited with "discovering" Clark; certainly he induced that author to continue with other laughable volumes, of which *Elbow Room* (1876), is best remembered. The first illustrations made by Arthur Burdett Frost [*q.v.*] appeared in *Out of the Hurly Burly*.

Stoddart was both keen and enterprising. Learning that a new edition of *The Encyclopædia Britannica* (the ninth) was on the eve of publication, he made an arrangement by which he received advance sheets that permitted him to begin reprinting the great work of reference in America simultaneously with its reprinting in Great Britain. This was continued from 1875 until the twenty-five volumes were completed in 1884. In the meantime he began the publication of *Stoddart's Encyclopædia Americana* (4 vols., 1883–89), a "companion" to the *Britannica*, written by American contributors and treating for the first time those American subjects neglected by the Edinburgh publication. When in 1878 Gilbert and Sullivan's comic opera, *H.M.S. Pinafore*, became a great success, he saw the value of publishing in the United States the words and scores of that and future productions by the gifted pair. On friendly terms with Richard D'Oyly

Carte, the London manager, he obtained the American rights and for some years remained the American representative of Gilbert and Sullivan. It was through his influence that the world première of *The Pirates of Penzance* took place in New York City on Dec. 31, 1879. The next year's opera was *Patience*. Through Stoddart's appreciation of novelty and publicity, Oscar Wilde, representative of the esthetic movement satirized in the opera, was brought to the United States to lecture in the cities where the opera was sung. Stoddart gave personal attention to Wilde's tour and published for him his reprint of Rennell Rodd's poems, under the title supplied by Wilde, *Rose Leaf and Apple Leaf* (1882), with an introduction and dedication by Wilde. It was the most sumptuous and artistically produced volume, as well as the daintiest, that had been produced in the United States up to that time. In 1877–79 he brought out a new three-volume edition of John Fanning Watson's *Annals of Philadelphia*, enlarged by Willis Pope Hazard. From 1880 to 1882 he issued *Stoddart's Review*, but in the latter year it was sold and consolidated with the *American* (Philadelphia).

About 1889 or 1890 he returned to the J. B. Lippincott Company to take over the management of *Lippincott's Monthly Magazine*, which immediately responded to his magic touch, improving in attractiveness and increasing in circulation. Amélie Rives's *The Quick or the Dead?*, her first novel, written at Stoddart's suggestion, appeared in that magazine, as did Rudyard Kipling's *The Light That Failed*, Conan Doyle's "The Sign of the Four," which resulted in the whole series of Sherlock Holmes stories, and Oscar Wilde's *The Picture of Dorian Gray*. Stoddart was also the first to encourage Sir Gilbert Parker. Subsequently he went to Collier's and became the editor of *Collier's Weekly*. He was editor of the *New Science Review*, 1894–95, and finally in 1900 edited the *Literary Era*, a monthly published by Henry T. Coates. Failing health in 1903 caused him to return to his home at Elkins Park, just outside of Philadelphia, where he died in 1921. He married in 1869 Isabella Herkness (d. 1900), daughter of Alfred Morris Herkness. He was survived by four children.

[*Who's Who in America*, 1903–05; obituary in *Evening Bull.* (Phila.), Feb. 26, 1921; other data from J. Alfred Stoddart, a son, and from personal knowledge.]
                                                    J. J.

STODDERT, BENJAMIN (1751–Dec. 17, 1813), first secretary of the navy, was born in Charles County, Md., the grandson of James Stoddert, a surveyor who emigrated from Scotland to La Plata, Md., about 1650. His father, Thomas Stoddert, was a lieutenant in the Maryland militia of the French and Indian War. His mother, Sarah (Marshall) Stoddert, was the daughter of Thomas Marshall of "Marshall Hall." The Revolutionary War began just as he was finishing his apprenticeship as a merchant, and he joined a Pennsylvania Regiment under Thomas Hartley [q.v.] in January 1777 with rank of captain. When his regiment was united to John Patton's in 1779 he found himself outranked by the new officers. In consequence he resigned on Apr. 16 (Letter of Apr. 16, 1779, in Papers of the Continental Congress, Library of Congress, no. 78, vol. XXI, folio 39). On Sept. 1, he was unanimously elected secretary to the board of war. He held this arduous post until Feb. 6, 1781, when he resigned (Ibid., folios 17, 21). On June 17, 1781, he married Rebecca Lowndes, the daughter of Christopher Lowndes, a merchant at Bladensburg, Md. She died about 1800 leaving eight children, one of whom became the mother of Richard Stoddert Ewell and Benjamin Stoddert Ewell [qq.v.]. With shrewd business instinct, he decided to begin his mercantile career in Georgetown, Md., at that time a small place with only one trifling retail shop. Because of its central location and shipping facilities Georgetown soon sprang into astonishing prominence as a port, and the firm that Stoddert had entered, Forrest, Stoddert, & Murdock, had a great share of the Potomac trade with branches established by Uriah Forrest at London and Bordeaux (Stoddert to John Templeman, undated, Library of Congress). Jointly or singly he purchased great tracts of land in what is now the District of Columbia and erected a charming dwelling in Georgetown overlooking the Potomac. Soon he came to know General Washington, first in a business way by furnishing supplies to his nephews. Stoddert's sagacity and business sense were later employed by the president in the first delicate and critical moves toward establishing the federal capital. With William Deakins, Jr., he was asked to purchase, privately, blocks on important sites at a price lower than the government could command. After the site of the federal city had been fixed the business was made public, and these lands were ceded to the government. Stoddert's signature is found on the deed from the original proprietors (Washington Papers, Library of Congress, Jan. 21, 1785, Oct. 24, 1792; Letter Book, Vol. XIII, pp. 48, 118, 121, 122, 124–26). In order to handle these extensive realty transactions, the Bank of Columbia was organized in January 1794 with Stoddert as an incorporator and, later, president.

In the well known crash through excessive speculation, several years later, he probably lost heavily.

It was his highly successful mercantile career and stanch Federalism that caused him to be made secretary of the navy. Following the declination of George Cabot [q.v.], President Adams appointed Stoddert on May 18, 1798, and three days later he was confirmed as the first secretary. The choice has been generally conceded as a most fortunate one in a critical time. The so-called naval war with France was imminent, and the navy was pitifully weak. By heroic measures some fifty ships were acquired in the next two years, and a fleet was built up under celebrated commanders with about six thousand men in service. After the "war," he recommended reduction and replacement by thirteen frigates and twelve 74-gun ships. With characteristic thoroughness and foresight he also drafted the bill for the government of the marine corps, began construction of the naval hospital at Newport, and began the work of locating docks and of establishing navy yards. The latter were not contemplated by Congress but maneuvered by a masterpiece of loose-construction on the ground that the yards already rented were too small for the 74-gun ships Congress had authorized. On the advice of Joshua Humphreys [q.v.] and of his captains, Stoddert purchased ground at Washington, Gosport, Va., Portsmouth, N. H., Charlestown, Mass., Philadelphia, and Brooklyn. This was virtually all carried out in 1800 and early in 1801, before the new administration could rescind it. He stayed on at the request of Jefferson until April 1801.

The remaining twelve years of his life were filled with pecuniary embarrassments that distracted and embittered him. Georgetown commerce was on the wane, owing, as he believed, to the European wars, which diverted to larger ports such a share of the carrying trade that it sucked in the local produce trade from smaller places (Stoddert to Templeman, ante). Jefferson's embargo, and finally the War of 1812, seemed to him to cap the climax of his suffering, and he died heavily in debt (Stoddert to James McHenry, eight letters, 1801–1812, Library of Congress; advertisements in Daily National Intelligencer of Washington, Jan. 31, Feb. 10, Feb. 21, 1814).

[Papers of the Continental Cong., Washington Papers and Letter Books, and Stoddert Coll. in Lib. of Cong.; H. S. Turner, "Memoirs of Benj. Stoddert," Columbia Hist. Soc. Records, vol. XX (1917); W. B. Bryan, A Hist. of the National Capital, vol. I (1914); C. O. Paullin, "Early Naval Admin. under the Constitution," U. S. Naval Institute Proc., vol. XXXII, no. 3 (1906); G. W. Allen, Our Naval War with France

(1909); *Jour. of the Continental Cong.*, vol. IX (1912) ed. by Gaillard Hunt, XIV (1909) ed. by W. C. Ford; *The Works of John Adams*, vol. X (1856), ed. by C. F. Adams; *National Intelligencer* (Washington), Dec. 24, 1813.]   C. W. G.

STOECKEL, CARL (Dec. 7, 1858–Nov. 1, 1925), philanthropist, patron of music, was born in New Haven, Conn., the son of Gustave Jacob Stoeckel and his wife, Matilda Bertha Wehner. The elder Stoeckel was a Bavarian musician who came to the United States in 1848, and became an instructor and professor of music at Yale University from 1855 to 1894. He was the first head of the Yale School of Music. Carl was educated at the Thomas School and the Hopkins Grammar School at New Haven, and with private tutors in America and in Europe. He was married on May 6, 1895, on the Isle of Wight, England, to Ellen Battell Terry, the daughter of Robbins Battell, jurist and philanthropist, of Norfolk, Conn. After their marriage Stoeckel and his wife made their home in Norfolk where they became patrons of art and music in a manner that exerted an influence on the development of musical life not only in their own community but throughout the country as well. Stoeckel founded the Litchfield County University Club in 1896, and in 1904 provided funds for the publication of books pertaining to Litchfield County to be written by members of the Club. Mrs. Stoeckel was instrumental in founding the Norfolk Glee Club, a chorus of mixed voices, in 1897, and two years later Stoeckel brought about the formation of the Litchfield County Choral Union, with a nucleus of the Norfolk Glee Club and the Winsted Choral Union. Three neighboring organizations were subsequently admitted to membership: the Salisbury Choir (1905), the Canaan Choral Society (1906), and the Torrington Musical Association (1906).

For the first seven years the concerts of the organization were devoted to choral works with orchestral accompaniment, but in 1907 concerts consisting exclusively of orchestral music were added to the festivals, held annually in June. The first festivals were held in the armory at Winsted, but from 1906 they were given in the "Music Shed," which Stoeckel erected for the purpose on his Norfolk estate. Until they were discontinued in 1923 the festivals represented an ideal in community expression, and in mutual cooperation and participation. Although guided and financed by the founders, the choral union and the festivals belonged to the members of the union. The concerts brought to Norfolk distinguished guests from America and Europe, and, commencing in 1908, eminent composers were commissioned to write works for perform-

ance at the festivals. By 1922 sixteen prominent composers had been commissioned for one or more works each. The Norfolk festivals inevitably reflected Stoeckel's personality, yet he constantly fought to keep them from exploiting either himself or any other individual. He resented particularly any reference to Norfolk as the "American Bayreuth," for he felt that Bayreuth had been founded for the glorification of one man, Richard Wagner. Before his death at his Norfolk home, Stoeckel edited and printed for free distribution two volumes of *The Correspondence of John Sedgwick* (1902–03). He also purchased the birthplace and farm of John Brown at Torrington, Conn., and presented it to the John Brown Association.

[*Who's Who in America*, 1924–25; J. H. Vaill, *Litchfield County Choral Union* (2 vols., 1912), and *The Litchfield County Club* (1931); *Waterbury American* (Waterbury, Conn.), Nov. 7, 1925; *N. Y. Times*, Nov. 15, 1925.]   J.T.H.

STOEK, HARRY HARKNESS (Jan. 16, 1866–Mar. 1, 1923), mining engineer, educator, was born in Washington, D. C., the son of Jacob F. and Susan (Lear) Stoek. He attended the public schools of Washington, graduating from the Central High School in 1883, and entered Lehigh University. During his college years he gave his summer vacations to practical work in geology and engineering. He graduated with the degree of B.S. in 1887, and with that of Engineer of Mines in 1888. He began his professional experience immediately as an assistant engineer for the Susquehanna Coal Company, Wilkes-Barre, Pa., doing mine surveying, engineering office work, and experimental work on the frictional resistance of mine-car wheels. In January 1890 he was called back to Lehigh as instructor in mining and geology, and at the close of the college year 1892–93 was appointed assistant professor of mining engineering and metallurgy at Pennsylvania State College. In this capacity he served until January 1898.

From teaching he now turned to technical journalism, becoming managing editor and later editor in chief of *Mines and Minerals* (Scranton, Pa.). His editorial work, his "Questions and Answers" department, his technical articles —for which he gathered material first-hand on visits to mining districts all over the country— made his name known throughout the mining world. He also wrote, or revised and edited, many of the mining instruction pamphlets of the International Correspondence Schools, Scranton. It is difficult to overestimate his influence on coal-mining education, for his writings were a veritable Bible for the men in the industry. In addition, he gave lectures on coal mining at

Yale, Pennsylvania State College, and Brooklyn Polytechnic Institute, prepared a chapter on the Pennsylvania anthracite coal field for the *Twenty-second Annual Report of the United States Geological Survey* (1902), and for the Carnegie Institution of Washington prepared an "Economic History of Anthracite" as a part of the "Economic History of the United States" which the Institution had projected.

In October 1909, Stoek relinquished the editorship of *Mines and Minerals* to accept a call from the University of Illinois to organize a department of mining engineering. Within three years he had drawn up a curriculum, built a laboratory, and initiated a large-scale program of research. His indefatigable labor and tireless energy resulted in a department which, while never large from the standpoint of student enrollment, was outstanding in the quality of its instruction and in the character and productivity of its research work. He served as its head until his death in 1923. One of his great interests was the vocational education of miners. In Pennsylvania he had seen the results of such education, offered both in the pages of his magazine and in night schools. Through his initiative the Illinois Miners' and Mechanics' Institutes were organized, under the department of mining engineering of the University, and began their work in January 1914. At this time he published a comprehensive bulletin, *Education of Mine Employees* (1914). During the summer of that year he visited England and the Continent, making a study of mining methods and of mining education, collegiate and vocational.

From 1910 until the reorganization of the state department of mines in 1917, he served as a member of the Mining Investigation Commission and as member and secretary of the Illinois Mine Rescue Commission. He was active in the affairs of the American Institute of Mining and Metallurgical Engineers, the American Mining Congress, the International Railway Fuel Association, and the Coal Mining Institute of America. He was a consulting engineer for the United States Bureau of Mines, and made many private reports and investigations on such subjects as the valuation of coal properties, coal storage, and mine safety. His numerous writings are found in the technical press, in the bulletins of the Engineering Experiment Station of the University of Illinois, and in the proceedings of engineering societies. They cover almost every phase of coal mining. It has been said that "To him, more than to any man of his generation, belongs the honor of changing coal mining from a rule-of-thumb trade to an engineering science"

(Dean E. A. Holbrook, in "Memorial Exercises," *post*).

Stoek was married to Miriam Ricketts of Wilkes-Barre, on Dec. 20, 1894. Death came to him suddenly, in Urbana, in his fifty-eighth year. His wife and son had died some years before; one daughter survived him. In 1926 a bronze tablet by Lorado Taft, commemorating Stoek's life and work, was unveiled in the College of Engineering Library at the University of Illinois.

[*Trans. Am. Inst. Mining & Metallurgical Engineers*, vol. XXIX (1923); *Coal Age*, Mar. 8, 1923; *Coal Mine Management*, Mar. 1923; *Jour. Western Soc. of Engineers*, Apr. 1923; *Who's Who in America*, 1922–23; "Memorial Exercises and Presentation of Tablet in Honor of Professor Harry Harkness Stoek, May 2, 1926," (MS. in Coll. of Engineering, Univ. of Ill.); personal acquaintance.]   A. C. C.

STOEVER, MARTIN LUTHER (Feb. 17, 1820–July 22, 1870), educator, author, was born in Germantown, Pa. After his graduation in 1838 from Pennsylvania (now Gettysburg) College, he became a teacher at Jefferson, Frederick County, Md., being deterred from entering the Lutheran ministry by a slight hesitancy in his speech. In the autumn of 1841 he was recalled to Gettysburg and spent the rest of his life there, as principal of the Academy, 1842–51, and as professor in the College after 1844, teaching history, 1844–56, and Latin, 1851–70. He was acting president in 1850 between the administrations of Charles Philip Krauth and Henry Louis Baugher [*qq.v.*]. On June 14, 1850, he married Elizabeth McConaughy of Gettysburg, who with their son, William Caspar, survived him. He was secretary for a number of years of the General Synod of the Evangelical Lutheran Church in the United States, was one of the editors, 1857–61, of the *Evangelical Review,* and was sole editor and proprietor, 1862–70. Articles from his pen appeared in every issue but two of its entire career, 1849–70. Though himself of the school of S. S. Schmucker [*q.v.*], he kept the pages of the *Review* open to contributors of every degree of orthodoxy and printed many literary essays, thereby making the journal both a theological and a cultural influence. In his travels in behalf of the College and the Church, he gathered information for a series of "Memoirs of Deceased Lutheran Clergymen," eighty-three in all, ranging from the shadowy figures of the early eighteenth-century pioneers to his own elder contemporaries. He supplied the bulk of the Lutheran material for W. B. Sprague's *Annals of the American Pulpit* and published separately a *Memoir of the Life and Times of Henry Melchior Muhlenberg* (1856) and a *Memorial of Rev. Philip F. Mayer* (1858), besides a few occasional addresses. He was accurate in his statement of facts and rescued not a few good men from oblivion, but his fondness for Latin quotations and his desire to improve every opportunity for edification sometimes interfered with the biographical intention. A daguerreotype shows him a stocky Pennsylvania German, with a broad, benign countenance rising moonlike above a thicket of beard. His kindness and hospitality were proverbial. He was a member of the United States Sanitary Commission. During the battle of Gettysburg he and his wife filled their house on the Square with wounded soldiers and turned their yard into a field kitchen with food and drink for every comer. After the Confederate retreat three Union officers emerged uncaptured from behind the cider barrels in the cellar. He declined calls to several educational institutions, the last offer of this kind—a tender of the presidency of the University of Nebraska —coming while his body awaited burial. He died in Philadelphia, while visiting relatives, after an illness of two days, and was buried in Germantown.

[J. G. Morris, *Fifty Years in the Luth. Ministry* (1878); E. S. Breidenbaugh, *The Pa. Coll. Book 1832– 82* (1882); C. B. Stover and C. W. Beachem, *The Alumni Record of Gettysburg Coll. 1832–1932* (1932); S. G. Hefelbower; *The Hist. of Gettysburg Coll. 1832– 1932* (1932); *The Press* (Phila.), July 25, 1870.]

G. H. G.

STOKES, ANSON PHELPS (Feb. 22, 1838– June 28, 1913), merchant, banker, publicist, son of James Boulter and Caroline (Phelps) Stokes and brother of William Earl Dodge Stokes [*q.v.*] and Olivia Egleston Phelps Stokes [*q.v.*], was born in New York City, where shortly before 1800 his grandfather, Thomas Stokes, coming from London, had settled as a merchant. On his mother's side, he was the grandson of Anson Greene Phelps [*q.v.*], and a descendant of George Phelps who emigrated from Gloucestershire, England, to Dorchester, Mass., about 1630. His immediate ancestors were noted, not only for their business ability, but also for their religious, civic, and philanthropic interests. Thomas Stokes had been one of the thirteen founders of the London Missionary Society, and after coming to the United States was an active supporter of the American Bible Society, the American Tract Society, and the American Peace Society. James Boulter Stokes was one of the founders of the Association for Improving the Condition of the Poor, and a trustee of other charitable institutions. Anson Phelps, also, was a man of pronounced piety and a promoter of benevolent enterprises.

When scarcely more than a boy, having received a good elementary schooling, Anson Phelps Stokes entered the employ of Phelps, Dodge & Company, a mercantile establishment founded by his grandfather. In 1861 he became a partner and also a member of the firm of Phelps, James & Company, Liverpool. On Oct. 17, 1865, he married Helen Louisa, daughter of Isaac Newton Phelps. Withdrawing from Phelps, Dodge & Company in 1879, with his father and his father-in-law he organized the firm of Phelps, Stokes & Company, bankers. Three years later, however, after the death of his father, he closed out the business. In 1895 he organized the Woodbridge Company, and in 1902, the Haynes Company, realty corporations, which constructed and operated office buildings in New York City. He was an official of the Ansonia Clock Company, Ansonia, Conn., a director of several banks and of the Liverpool and London and Globe Insurance Company.

Stokes continued the family tradition of public service, devoting much time and energy to problems of the day and to the work of benevolent institutions. A vigorous advocate of free trade and civil service reform, he was a founder and first president of the Reform Club, and the vice-president of the Nineteenth Century Club, a local organization for the consideration of social and political problems. In their early days he was one of the most active members of the Civil Service Reform Association and of the Free Trade League. A foe of Tammany Hall, he was chairman of a committee of seventy in 1887 which conducted a campaign in opposition to the election of Col. John R. Fellows, Tammany candidate for district attorney. Some years earlier he had refused the Democratic nomination as candidate for Congress, and in 1888 he declined President Cleveland's offer to name him minister to Austria. An ardent anti-imperialist, he was an incorporator and president of the National Association of Anti-Imperialist Clubs, and in 1900 he presided and spoke at the great Bryan anti-imperialist meeting at Madison Square Garden, New York. He made a study of the currency and trust problems and published *Joint-Metallism* (1894) and *Dangers of the Proposed Paper Money Trust* (1898). The former, which went through five editions, proposed a "plan by which gold and silver together, at ratios always based on their relative market values, may be made the metallic basis of a sound, honest, self-regulating and permanent currency, without frequent recoinings, and without danger of one metal driving out the other." His official connections with charitable organizations were numerous, and he was an early supporter of the first tuberculosis sanatorium in the United States, established by Dr. Edward L. Trudeau [*q.v.*] at Saranac, N. Y. He helped to found the Metropolitan Museum of Art, and was himself a collector of paintings and books, his library of Americana being especially notable.

Fond of outdoor activities, he made frequent trips to England to hunt with the Quorn and Pytchley hounds. As a youth he went abroad on the clipper ship *Dreadnought,* studying navigation under the captain, and ever after he was an enthusiastic sailor. He owned successively three schooner yachts, was a member of the New York Yacht Club, and in 1882–83 was its vice-commodore. His experiences and observations on two of his sailing trips are recorded in *Cruising in the West Indies* (1902, 1903) and *Cruising in the Caribbean with a Camera* (1903). He was a member of the Society of Naval Architects and Marine Engineers, New York, and of the Institution of Naval Architects, England, and was the inventor of a centerboard, patented Mar. 31, 1903, and of a globular floating battery for coast defense, patented Apr. 7 of the same year. He was also an enthusiastic promoter of fresh-water sailing in Upper Saint Regis Lake, where, on Birch Island, he had a camp. In 1898 an accident while he was riding near his country home at Lenox, Mass., resulted in the loss of one of his legs. At the time of his death in New York City, fifteen years later, he was survived by four sons and five daughters.

[*Stokes Records* (3 vols., 1910), prepared by Stokes and privately printed for the family; *Evening Post* (N. Y.), June 30, 1913; Patent Office records; *Who's Who in America,* 1912–13; O. S. Phelps and A. T. Servin, *The Phelps Family of America* (1899), vol. II; information from a son, Anson Phelps Stokes.] H. E. S.

STOKES, CAROLINE PHELPS (1854–1909). [See STOKES, OLIVIA EGLESTON PHELPS, 1847–1927.]

STOKES, MONTFORT (Mar. 12, 1762–Nov. 4, 1842), senator from North Carolina, governor, was born within the limits of what was then Lunenburg County, Va., the eleventh child of David Stokes, a planter and a member of the county court, and of Sarah (Montfort) Stokes. He was probably the descendant of Christopher Stokes who emigrated from England before 1624 and settled in Warwick County, Va., where he became a member of the House of Burgesses. Joseph Montfort Street [*q.v.*] was a nephew. Although the details of his service are in doubt, it is certain that Stokes served in the Revolutionary War. After the war he was a planter near Salisbury, N. C. From 1786 to 1791 he was a clerk of the state Senate, and for some years

thereafter clerk of the superior court of Rowan County. In 1804 he was elected to fill a vacancy in the federal Senate but declined the office. In the following year he was elected by the General Assembly a trustee of the University of North Carolina, an office he retained until 1838; and he was repeatedly chosen as a presidential elector on the Democratic ticket. About 1812 he removed to Wilkesboro and, during the War of 1812, served as a major-general of the state militia. Again elected a federal senator to fill a vacancy and reëlected for the full term, he served from Dec. 4, 1816, to Mar. 3, 1823. Active in the long struggle of the western counties to obtain more adequate representation, he was president of the convention that met at Raleigh in November 1823 to attempt constitutional reform. He sat in the state Senate in 1826 and in the House of Representatives in 1829 and 1830. In 1830 he was elected governor as the candidate of the western element in opposition to Richard Dobbs Spaight [*q.v.*]. He was married twice, first to Mary, the daughter of Henry Irwin. She died some years after their marriage. Later he married Rachel, the daughter of Hugh Montgomery of Salisbury, who survived him. A son, Montfort S. Stokes, served with distinction in the Mexican and Civil wars and was mortally wounded at Mechanicsville in 1862. On July 14, 1832, while still governor, Stokes was appointed by President Jackson one of the three commissioners to report on conditions in the present state of Oklahoma. When the legislature met, Nov. 19, following, he resigned and early in February 1833 was at Fort Gibson in the Indian Territory. On the conclusion of his two-year term he was appointed to another Indian commission, and in March 1836 became sub-agent for the Cherokees, Senecas and Shawnees. A year later, on the grant of a full agency to the Cherokees, he was placed in charge. Untiring in his labors, he strove to maintain at least a semblance of peace and order in what was then perhaps the most turbulent section of the Union. At the end of his term, in 1841, however, President Tyler refused him a reappointment. A post as register of the land office of Fayetteville, Ark., for which he did not qualify, was offered, and two months before his death the sub-agency for the Senecas, Shawnees, and Quapaws was given him, which he consented to fill. He died at Fort Gibson and was buried with military honors.

[L. C. Bell, *The Old Free State . . . Lunenburg County and Southside, Va.* (1927), vol. II; *Biog. Directory of the Am. Congress* (1928); J. H. Wheeler, *Hist. Sketches of N. C.* (1851), vol. II, and *Reminiscences and Memories of N. C.* (1884); Grant Foreman, *Pioneer Days in the Early Southwest* (1926); *Va. Mag. of Hist. and Biog.,* July 1898; W. K. Boyd, *Hist. of N. C.,* vol. II (1919); J. P. Arthur, *Western N. C.* (1914); *The State Records of N. C.,* vols. X, XVIII, XX–XI (1890–1903); *The Legislative Manual . . . of N. C. . . . 1874* (1874); K. P. Battle, *Sketches of the Hist. of the Univ. of N. C.* (1889); *Jour. of the Senate and House of Commons of . . . N. C. . . . 1832–33* (1833), pp. 143–46 for his resignation; *Jour. of the Exec. Proc. of the Senate of the U. S.,* vols. IV–VI (1887); *Ark. State Gazette* (Little Rock), Dec. 7, 1842.] W.J.G.

STOKES, OLIVIA EGLESTON PHELPS

(Jan. 11, 1847–Dec. 14, 1927) and Caroline Phelps Stokes (Dec. 4, 1854–Apr. 26, 1909), philanthropists, were born at Clifton Cottage, on the East River near 30th Street, New York, the sixth and the youngest of the ten children of James Boulter and Caroline (Phelps) Stokes. Their father was a wealthy banker, real estate owner, and philanthropist; their mother was a daughter of Anson Greene Phelps [*q.v.*]. Two of their brothers were Anson Phelps Stokes and William Earl Dodge Stokes [*qq.v.*]. The sisters were devoted to each other, were much alike in character and interests, cooperated on many philanthropic projects, and, since neither of them married, were seldom separated. They were educated at home, but Caroline also attended Miss Porter's School in Farmington, Conn., for several years. They were members of the Presbyterian Church but in later years felt drawn more and more to the liturgical worship and devotional life fostered by the Episcopal Church. After their father's death in 1881 they traveled extensively in the United States and Europe, visited Palestine, and in 1896 made a trip around the world. They both had a taste for writing, Caroline producing a novel, *Travels of a Lady's Maid* (1908), Olivia the *Letters and Memories of Susan and Anna Bartlett Warner* (1925), an unpublished memoir of her sister, and three small books of devotion. From both sides of their family they inherited strong religious feeling and many active philanthropic interests. Out of their ample fortune they made innumerable gifts to religious, educational, charitable, and other public enterprises. Among their principal benefactions were St. Paul's Chapel of Columbia University, Woodbridge Hall at Yale University, the chapel of Berea College, Dorothy Hall at Tuskegee Institute, the chapel at Yale in China, the gymnasium at the Constantinople Woman's College, Caroline Cottage at the New York Colored Orphan Asylum, the Haynes Memorial Gates at the First Church Cemetery in Hartford, Conn., the open-air pulpit at the Cathedral of St. John the Divine in New York, and the public library at Ansonia, Conn. They contributed with equal generosity to many other institutions. The welfare of the Indian, the negro, the poor whites of the South, and the slum-dwellers of New York were their most abiding concern, and with her residuary estate Caroline endowed the Phelps-Stokes Fund for their care. Olivia became the chief patron of the Fund. At the turn of the century Caroline's health began to decline, and she spent the rest of her life at Redlands, Cal., where she died in 1909 in her fifty-fifth year. Olivia survived her by more than eighteen years, dying at her winter residence in Washington, D. C., in her eighty-first year.

[T. J. Jones, *Educational Adaptations: Report of Ten Year's Work of the Phelps-Stokes Fund, 1910–1920* (1920); J. H. Dillard and others, *Twenty Year Report of the Phelps-Stokes Fund, 1911–1931* (1932); A. P. Stokes, *Stokes Records* (privately printed, 1910); O. S. Phelps and A. T. Servin, *The Phelps Family of America* (2 vols., 1899); Anna B. Warner, *Some Memories of James Stokes and Caroline Phelps Stokes: Arranged for Their Children and Grandchildren* (printed for the family, 1892); Olivia E. P. Stokes, "The Story of Caroline Phelps Stokes" (387-page typescript; copy in office of Phelps-Stokes Fund, 101 Park Ave., New York); obituaries in *N. Y. Times,* Apr. 28, 1909, and *N. Y. Herald Tribune,* Dec. 15, 1927.] G.H.G.

STOKES, ROSE HARRIET PASTOR

(July 18, 1879–June 20, 1933), American radical, was born in the small Jewish settlement of Augustowo, Suwalki, Russian Poland. She was the daughter of Jacob and Anna (Lewin) Wieslander but her father died when she was very young and her mother soon remarried, giving the child her step-father's name of Pastor. They were desperately poor. When Rose was three they moved to London, settling in the Whitechapel slums. There for a time she attended the Bell Lane Free School where Israel Zangwill was once a pupil and later a teacher. When she was eleven her people emigrated to America, settling in Cleveland, and for the next twelve years she helped support the increasing family—six other children were born—by her earnings in a cigar factory. Although her formal schooling ended, her mind was constantly active and rebellious. She read, wrote, and studied at night; some of her poems were published in the New York *Jewish Daily News*; and in 1903 she went to New York as a feature writer for this paper. Some five months after her arrival she interviewed the young millionaire James Graham Phelps Stokes—son of Anson Phelps Stokes [*q.v.*]—who was living at the University Settlement on the East Side and was interested in socialism. Out of this interview, which she wrote up with high praise for Mr. Stokes and his views, grew the romance which culminated in their marriage, July 18, 1905.

For some years both were active supporters of the Socialist Party, the Intercollegiate Socialist Study Society, and other radical movements, but in 1917 estrangement began between them over the World War. Both withdrew from the Socialist Party on July 9, 1917, after its adoption of the St. Louis Platform condemning American participation in the war, but after a few months Rose Pastor Stokes rejoined the party, and from that time was increasingly identified with its left wing and with those factions that eventually helped to found the American Communist Party. In 1918, she was sentenced to ten years in prison under the Espionage Act, for a letter written to the *Kansas City Star* denouncing the United States government as allied with the profiteers, but the sentence was reversed on appeal (*Stokes vs. U. S., 264 Fed. Reporter*, 18) and eventually the government dropped the case. In the course of this trial she made the *apologia* for her views which has since become famous: "For ten years I have worked and produced things necessary and useful for the people of this country and for all those years I was half starved. . . . I worked at doing useful work and never had enough. But the moment I left the useful producing class— the moment I became part of the capitalistic class which did not have to do any productive work in order to exist—I had all the vacations I wanted, all the clothes I wanted. I had all the leisure I wanted—everything I wanted was mine without my having to do any labor in return for all I had received." (*In the United States Court of Appeals, 8th Circuit, No. 5255: Rose Pastor Stokes, Plaintiff in Error vs. United States of America; Brief for Plaintiff in Error*, pp. 15, 16.)

The breach between wife and husband widened, and on Oct. 17, 1925, the latter was granted a divorce. Although Rose retained his name throughout her life, she never accepted any alimony from him, and lived from this time in poverty. She was several times arrested in the years that followed for picketing in strikes and taking part in radical demonstrations, and on one of these occasions it was revealed that some time in 1927 she had remarried. Her second husband was Isaac Romaine, a private language teacher and a Communist. In 1930 it was found that she was suffering from cancer, which Communists claimed had its inception when she was clubbed by police in a riot in December 1929, and she now became more than ever a symbol and a martyr. Liberal and radical friends raised funds to send her on a trip to Russia and also, on two occasions, to a German clinic for treatment, but she died in Frankfurt-am-Main in 1933.

Among her writings are a propaganda play, dealing with feminism and labor conditions, *The Woman Who Wouldn't* (1916); a translation with Helena Frank, *Songs of Labor* (1914), by the Yiddish poet, Morris Rosenfeld; and an autobiography, unpublished at the time of her death. Her contribution, however, was emotional rather than intellectual; she has been remembered not so much for anything she wrote or said, as for the ardor and sincerity with which she embraced the cause of rebel workers everywhere and acted in accordance with her convictions.

[The papers of Rose Pastor Stokes were turned over before her death to Samuel Ornitz, who plans to publish the autobiography. This sketch is based on *Who's Who in America*, 1918–19; *N. Y. Tribune*, Apr. 16, July 19, 1905; *Kansas City Star*, Mar. 17, 20, May 20–23, 1918; *N. Y. Times* (see Index) July 1917, Feb.-June 1918, May 1919, Oct. 1920, Sept., Nov., 1921, Oct. 1925, Apr., Nov. 1926, Feb. 1929, June 21, 1933; *Daily Worker* (N. Y.), June 21, 1933; reminiscences of personal friends.]

M. G.

STOKES, WILLIAM EARL DODGE (May 22, 1852–May 19, 1926), hotel owner and capitalist, was born in New York City, the son of James Boulter and Caroline (Phelps) Stokes. He was a brother of Anson Phelps Stokes, Caroline Phelps Stokes, and Olivia Egleston Phelps Stokes [*qq.v.*]. He graduated at Yale in 1874 and became a bank clerk, later entering his father's banking firm, Phelps, Stokes & Company. Inheriting a fortune said to have amounted to about $1,000,000 at his father's death, he retired from the banking business and for a number of years increased his fortune by shrewd real estate transactions in New York City. He was in those years one of the largest operators in realty in the district west of Central Park and did much to build up that quarter of the city. He was also one of the pioneers in the introduction of asphalt street paving into New York. Meanwhile he acquired mineral and timber lands in Rockingham County, Va., and built the Chesapeake Western Railway, a short railroad, from Elkton, Va., through Harrisonburg to these undeveloped lands. He had begun breeding racing horses on his Patchen Wilkes Farm, Lexington, Ky., and he gave thousands of dollars in prizes, mostly to boys and girls in Virginia, to encourage the breeding of the best poultry stocks. His enthusiasm for good blood later led him to write a book, *The Right to Be Well Born* (1917), in which he set forth his views on eugenics, based upon his experience in stock-breeding, and urged that the registration of the pedigrees of human beings be required by law. In 1906–07 he built the Hotel Ansonia, a huge, ornate, and highly successful structure at Broadway, 73rd and 74th Streets, New York City, and operated it until his death. Shortly after it was completed, the City Health Department summoned him to court for keeping hogs and geese, said to be fine blooded stock, on its roof, and forced him to remove them.

On Jan. 5, 1895, in New York City he married Rita Hernandez de Alba de Acosta, a beautiful Cuban heiress, who obtained a divorce in 1900, was re-married and divorced, and later became engaged to Percy Stickney Grant [*q.v.*]. There was one son by the marriage, who at first remained in his mother's care, but a few years later was returned to his father on the payment to his mother, it is said, of a million dollars. On Feb. 11, 1911, Stokes married Helen Elwood of Denver, Colo., by whom he had a son and a daughter. That same year, in a quarrel with two chorus girls, he was shot and painfully wounded. He grew more and more eccentric with age, and during his latter years his time was largely occupied in litigation. He brought suit against his second wife for divorce in 1919; she retorted with a counter-suit, and for the better part of four years their complicated actions were in the courts, the sensational charges and testimony furnishing much public entertainment through the newspapers. Because of certain testimony introduced in the case, Stokes was tried for conspiracy and subornation of perjury, but was acquitted. The wife finally obtained a legal separation and a large settlement. At the time of his death in New York City in 1926 there were damage suits pending against him, demanding in all about $8,000,000, practically the whole amount of his fortune, but most of these were subsequently dropped. He was survived by his three children.

[See O. S. Phelps and A. T. Servin, *The Phelps Family of America* (1899), vol. II; *Yale Univ. Obit. Record of Grads.* (1926); *World* (N. Y.), June 8, 1911, and May 20, 1926; obituaries in *Sun* (N. Y.), May 19, *N. Y. Times* and *N. Y. Herald-N. Y. Tribune*, May 20, 1926. New York newspapers and court records, 1919–24, supply many details as to his litigation with his wife, his attorneys, and others, and give sidelights on his character and career.]   A. F. H.

STONE, AMASA (Apr. 27, 1818–May 11, 1883), railroad builder, capitalist, philanthropist, was born on a farm in Charlton, Mass., the son of Amasa and Esther (Boyden) Stone, and a descendant of Simon Stone who settled in Watertown, Mass., in 1635. Amasa's education was confined to that afforded by the local town school. At seventeen he began to learn the carpenter's trade in Charlton, and three years later moved to Worcester. His was a non-technical non-scientific age and he progressed rapidly from carpentry into the fields of the contractor and the bridge-builder.

In 1840 with his brother-in-law, William Howe [*q.v.*], inventor of a wooden truss, he secured the contract to build the first railroad bridge over the Connecticut River at Springfield. Two years later, the firm of Boody, Stone & Company, contractors, acquired the patent rights to the Howe truss and entered upon a notable record of bridge building. On Jan. 13, 1842, Stone married Julia Ann Gleason of Springfield. In 1844 he became superintendent of the New Haven, Hartford & Springfield Railroad. Opportunities in Ohio, where dependence on canals and turnpikes was holding back development, lured him to the new West. In 1849, with Stillman Witt and Frederick Harbach, he contracted to build the Cleveland, Columbus & Cincinnati Railroad, first unit of the Big Four, and after its completion he became successively superintendent and president, with his home in Cleveland.

An industrial empire was in the making south of the Great Lakes; Cleveland was one of its centers; and Amasa Stone was one of the empire builders. He obtained the contract to build the Chicago & Milwaukee Railroad as well as the Cleveland, Painesville & Ashtabula Railroad. Of the latter he was president for thirteen years before it was merged in the Lake Shore & Michigan Southern, Jan. 1, 1869. For a time he was managing director of the new system. His interests expanded to include mines, iron and steel, banking and communications. As an officer of the Lake Shore Railroad, Stone recognized the South Improvement Company's system of rebates for a privileged list of oil refining companies, thereby saving the oil refining industry in Cleveland, but at the expense and embitterment of those producers less fortunate (Ida M. Tarbell, *The History of the Standard Oil Company*, 1904, I, 47, 277). The Lake Shore Railroad was his pride, but it was also his undoing. As president in 1863 he had insisted on using the Howe truss, with iron rather than wooden timbers, in designing the long bridge at Ashtabula, though warned by engineers that such a bridge would not be safe. After eleven years of service the bridge collapsed, carrying to destruction a train-load of people. He was blamed for an experiment "which ought never to have been tried" (verdict of coroner's jury, quoted in Dennett, *post*, p. 101). Under the weight of charges —many of them unfair—and the strain of sleepless nights, his health broke, and five and a half years later he ended his own life.

In business Stone was never able to endure a subordinate position. His friends saw a man of strong physique, courteous, kindly, unassuming, but when he passed beyond the fireside he became the dominant, even domineering, type of the business world. A life of struggle, achievement, and command made him so. Shortly before the end he made his greatest benefaction. He became interested in the project of moving Western Reserve College from Hudson to Cleveland and transforming it into an urban university, and for that purpose gave a half-million dollars. One of his daughters married John Hay [*q.v.*] and the other Samuel Mather [*q.v.*].

[The only satisfactory appraisal of Stone's place in history is in Tyler Dennett, *John Hay* (1933); in addition see John Hay, *Amasa Stone* (n.d.), which memoir appears also in *Mag. of Western Hist.*, Dec. 1885; *Report of the Joint Committee Concerning the Ashtabula Bridge Disaster, under Joint Resolution of the Gen. Assembly* (1877); *Cleveland Plain Dealer*, May 12, 1883; J. G. Bartlett, *Simon Stone Geneal.* (1926).]

E. J. B.

STONE, BARTON WARREN (Dec. 24, 1772–Nov. 9, 1844), frontier evangelist, who seceded from the Presbyterian denomination and was a leader in the establishment of churches designated by the name Christian, was the son of John and Mary (Warren) Stone. He was born near Port Tobacco, Md., reared in Pittsylvania County, Va., and in 1790, with the intention of becoming a barrister, he entered the academy at Guilford, N. C., conducted by Rev. David Caldwell [*q.v.*]. Converted under the influences created in that vicinity by the preaching of James McGready [*q.v.*], he became in 1793 a candidate for the ministry in the Orange Presbytery and put himself under the tutelage of Rev. William Hodge. Confused and depressed by the theology he encountered, he went to his brother's home in Oglethorpe County, Ga., and soon became teacher of languages at the seminary of the Methodist preacher, Hope Hull, in Washington, Ga. Returning to North Carolina in 1796, he was licensed by the Orange Presbytery. After itinerant preaching in Tennessee, he took charge of the churches at Cane Ridge and Concord, Bourbon County, Ky., and was ordained in 1798, accepting the Confession with the proviso "so far as I can see it consistent with the word of God" (*Biography, post,* p. 30), for some of the doctrines of Calvinism still troubled him. On July 2, 1801, he married Elizabeth, daughter of Col. William and Tabitha (Russell) Campbell.

The Great Revival, which had a notable manifestation at Cane Ridge, brought the conservative and "New Light" forces of the Presbyterian Church into sharp conflict. As a result, in September 1803, Stone and four others withdrew from the Synod of Kentucky and formed the Springfield Presbytery. They issued a three-fold "Apology," setting forth in detail their reasons for this act, the second section of which was written by Stone. The following year, convinced that there is no authority in the New Testament

for such an ecclesiastical organization, they dissolved the presbytery, signed its "Last Will and Testament," and agreed to acknowledge no name but Christian and no creed but the Bible. The remainder of Stone's life was spent chiefly in evangelical work and the establishment of churches. For the remarkable growth of the movement in Kentucky and Ohio he was largely responsible. His wife having died in 1810, he married, Oct. 31, 1811, her cousin, Celia Wilson Bowen, daughter of William and Mary Bowen. Some two years later they settled in Lexington, in which place and afterwards in Georgetown Stone taught school in connection with his religious activities. In 1826 he started a paper called the *Christian Messenger*. He had met Alexander Campbell [*q.v.*] in 1824 and formed a warm regard for him, although they were not in entire theological agreement. With the growth in Kentucky of the Disciples of Christ, as the Campbellites were called, Stone urged cooperation with them. At a conference held in his church at Lexington on Jan. 1, 1832, the Christians and Disciples agreed to act as one, and Rev. John T. Johnson, a Disciple, became coeditor of the *Christian Messenger*. A complete amalgamation never took place, however, and a religious body known as Christian persisted. Stone would never sanction the abandonment of that designation, but "This union, . . ." he declared, "I view as the noblest act of my life" (*Biography, post,* p. 79). In 1834 he moved to Jacksonville, Ill.; he continued, however, to edit the *Messenger* and to carry on evangelistic work. His tendency to theological speculation occasioned controversial pamphlets and led to his being denounced as a Unitarian. His own publications include: *Atonement* (1805), *A Reply to John P. Campbell's Strictures on Atonement* (1805), *An Address to the Christian Churches in Kentucky, Tennessee, and Ohio, on Several Important Doctrines of Religion* (1814; 2nd ed., corrected and enlarged, 1821), and *Letters to James Blythe, D.D., Designed as a Reply to the Arguments of Thomas Cleland, D.D., Against My Address, 2d ed., . . . on the Doctrine of the Trinity, the Son of God, Atonement . . .* (1824). The Rev. Thomas Cleland, Presbyterian, had attacked Stone in *The Socini-Arian Detected* (1815), and in *Letters to Barton W. Stone Containing a Vindication Principally of the Doctrines of the Trinity, the Divinity and Atonement of the Saviour* (1822); in 1825 he published *Unitarianism Unmasked; . . . A Reply to Mr. Barton W. Stone's Letters to the Rev. Dr. Blythe.* Stone died at the home of his son-in-law, Capt. S. A. Bowen, in Hannibal, Mo., and his remains were buried in the Cane Ridge, Ky., graveyard. By his first marriage he had had five children; by the second, six.

[*The Biog. of Eld. Barton Warren Stone, Written by Himself* (1847); C. C. Ware, *Barton Warren Stone* (1932); J. R. Rogers, *The Cane Ridge Meeting-house* (1910); C. C. Cleveland, *The Great Revival in the West* (1916); Lewis and R. H. Collins, *Hist. of Ky.* (2 vols., 1874); J. H. Garrison, *The Story of a Century* (1909); W. T. Moore, *A Comprehensive Hist. of the Disciples of Christ* (1919); N. S. Haynes, *Hist. of the Disciples of Christ in Ill.* (1915); A. W. Fortune, *The Disciples in Ky.* (1932); M. T. Morrill, *A Hist. of the Christian Denomination in America* (1912); W. E. Garrison, *Religion Follows the Frontier* (1931).]   H. E. S.

STONE, CHARLES POMEROY (Sept. 30, 1824–Jan. 24, 1887), soldier, was born at Greenfield, Mass., the son of Dr. Alpheus Fletcher Stone and Fanny (Cushing) Stone, widow of George Arms. He was a descendant of Gregory Stone who settled in Watertown, Mass., in 1635. Graduating at West Point in 1845, he served with the siege train throughout Scott's campaign in Mexico. Resigning in 1856, being then a first lieutenant, he was employed by a private association as chief of a commission for the exploration of the Mexican state of Sonora. His *Notes on the State of Sonora* was published in 1861.

On Apr. 16 of that year he was mustered into service as colonel, District of Columbia Volunteers; he was reappointed to the regular army as colonel, 14th Infantry, in July, and in August was appointed brigadier-general of volunteers, both commissions antedated to May. His reputation stood high, and he had every prospect of a brilliant career, until the disaster at Ball's Bluff, near Leesburg, Va., Oct. 21, 1861. With the recklessness common in brave but inexperienced officers, Col. Edward D. Baker [*q.v.*] involved a regiment of Stone's command in a skirmish with the Confederates under Gen. Nathan G. Evans [*q.v.*], which resulted in numerous casualties and Baker's death. The public was seized with a "victim-hunting mania" (Blaine, *post*, I, 382), and as Baker was a senator many of his colleagues were eager to avenge his death upon somebody. Their choice was Stone. Hints of incompetency were succeeded by whispers of treason. The display of credulity and cruelty which followed was hardly surpassed even in the World War. An investigator could solemnly set down, for example, the statement of a witness that he had heard the Confederate adjutant general say that General Evans said that Stone was a fine man and a gentleman. It is recorded that Stone "is too well spoken of in Leesburg to be all right" (War Department records). The Joint Committee on the Conduct of the War heard many witnesses, but refused their names to Stone, refused him their testimony, refused to

tell him what acts were charged against him. He was arrested at midnight, Feb. 8, 1862, and conveyed to Fort Lafayette, rising from the waters of New York harbor, where he was held in solitary confinement for fifty days. On the representations of his physician he was then transferred to Fort Hamilton, on land, where he was still kept in solitary confinement but was allowed to exercise under guard. His appeals to the War Department to know the charges against him were unanswered. Shame at last began to stir in Congress, though not in the War Department. He was released, Aug. 16, 1862, in reluctant compliance with an act of Congress, general in terms, but passed with this particular case in mind. The Joint Committee, the Secretary of War, and General McClellan have mutually blamed each other for the imprisonment. There is guilt enough for all.

Stone was left unemployed until May 1863, when he was sent to General Banks, at the latter's request, and served under him at Port Hudson and in the Red River campaign. On Apr. 4, 1864, for no cause stated or now known, he was mustered out of his volunteer commission and as a colonel of the regular army was again left unemployed. He was finally assigned to the Army of the Potomac; but, sick and despairing, he resigned from the army, Sept. 13, 1864. From 1865 to 1869 he was engineer and superintendent for the Dover Mining Company, Goochland County, Va. From 1870 to 1883 he served in the Egyptian army, becoming chief of staff and lieutenant-general. After his return home he was chief engineer for a year of the Florida Ship Canal Company. Later, he was constructing engineer for the foundations of the Statue of Liberty in New York harbor. He was twice married: first, to Maria Louisa Clary, daughter of Gen. Robert E. Clary; and, second, to Annie Jeannie Stone, daughter of John H. Stone of Louisiana. He died in New York City.

[J. G. Bartlett, *Gregory Stone Geneal.* (1918); *War of the Rebellion: Official Records (Army)*; *Battles and Leaders of the Civil War* (4 vols., 1887–88); J. G. Blaine, *Twenty Years of Congress*, vol. I (1884); *Report of the Joint Committee on the Conduct of the War*, pt. 2, 1863; *Speech of Hon. J. A. McDougall . . . on the Arrest of Gen. Stone, and the Rights of the Soldier and Citizen* (1862); *Eighteenth Ann. Reunion, Grads. U. S. Mil. Acad.* (1887); G. W. Cullum, *Biog. Reg., Officers and Grads. U. S. Military Acad.*, vol. II (1891); *N. Y. Tribune*, Jan. 25, 1887; unpublished records in the War Dept.; for a hostile view, J. D. Baltz, *Hon. Edward D. Baker* (1888).]   T. M. S.

STONE, DAVID (Feb. 17, 1770–Oct. 7, 1818), representative and senator from North Carolina, was born at "Hope," the family home, near Windsor, N. C. He was the son of Elizabeth (Williamson) Hobson Stone and Zedekiah Stone, who is said to have been a native of Massachusetts and a descendant of Gregory Stone, an English emigrant to Watertown, Mass., about 1635. Zedekiah Stone was a prosperous planter in Bertie County, N. C., and won distinction for his political activity during and after the Revolution. The boy was educated at the College of New Jersey (Princeton), where he was graduated in 1788. He studied law in Halifax under William Richardson Davie [q.v.] and was admitted to the bar in 1790. He was at once elected to the House of Commons from Bertie County and served four terms. On Mar. 13, 1793, he was married to Hannah Turner of Tennessee, who bore him five children. In 1794 he became a judge of the superior court but served only four years. Elected to the federal House of Representatives, he served from Mar. 4, 1799, to Mar. 3, 1801, and was a member of the first standing committee of ways and means. He was a brilliant man of great personal charm and magnetism, and of much independence of character. Generally he acted with the Republicans and voted to repeal the Sedition Act. In 1800 he supported Jefferson and voted for him in the House in 1801. Elected to the federal Senate in 1801, he continued to support Jeffersonian policies, and in the Chase impeachment he voted "guilty." He spoke seldom and, while regarded as able, was never a leader. He was defeated for reëlection by Jesse Franklin [q.v.] ; but the same legislature made him again a judge, and he resigned to accept. Two years later he was elected governor and served two terms from 1808 to 1810. In 1811 and 1812 he was again a member of the House of Commons and at the latter session defeated Jesse Franklin for the federal Senate. Taking his seat in 1813, he declined to vote for some of the important war measures of the administration, and thereby aroused so much feeling in North Carolina that he was censured by the legislature in December 1813. The newly elected legislature being also hostile, he resigned in 1814, filing with the governor an eloquent defense of his course, which met with the approval of the Federalists in the state. After his retirement he removed to Wake County, where the rest of his life was spent cultivating his plantation. In June 1817 he was married to his second wife, Sarah Dashiell, who survived him.

[S. A. Ashe, *Biog. Hist. of N. C.*, vol. IV (1906) ; *Biog. Directory Am. Cong.* (1928) ; J. G. Bartlett, *Gregory Stone Geneal.* (1918), footnote p. 132; *The Papers of Archibald D. Murphy* (2 vols., 1914), ed. by W. H. Hoyt ; *Raleigh Register*, Oct. 9, 1818.]

J. G. deR. H.

STONE, DAVID MARVIN (Dec. 23, 1817–Apr. 2, 1895), editor and publisher, was born in Oxford, Conn., the youngest of five children of a physician, Noah Stone, and his wife, Rosalind (Marvin) Stone. He was a descendant of John Stone who emigrated from England in 1639 and settled in what later became Guilford, Conn. He attended the village schools until he was fourteen, when he began earning his own living. After working hours he studied Latin and Greek by himself and at seventeen became a school teacher. In 1842 he found a place as clerk in a dry-goods house in Philadelphia and was employed there until the firm failed, seven years later. Meanwhile he had been writing correspondence for the *Dry Goods Reporter* of New York, and this led to his being offered the editorship of the magazine early in 1849. Though he was successful as an editor he could not agree with the owner of the paper and resigned later in the year. He then obtained a reporter's job on the New York *Journal of Commerce*, which, during the forty-four years that followed, became a veritable reflection of his own personality. During his earlier years with the *Journal* he was engaged in many other activities. For a time he edited the *Ladies' Wreath*, a popular magazine. At various times he contributed a weekly financial review to the *New York Observer* and conducted a similar department in *Hunt's Merchants' Magazine*. A Sunday-school novel from his pen entitled *Frank Forrest* was published in 1850 and ran through many editions. He also wrote many articles and stories for other publications. After the death of David Hale [q.v.], editor of the *Journal of Commerce*, much of his work fell upon Stone's shoulders. At the beginning of the Civil War, Gerard Hallock [q.v.], the principal owner of the paper, dictated a conciliatory policy towards the seceding states which became so offensive to the government that the *Journal* was forbidden the use of the mails and Hallock was forced to retire from its ownership. Stone and William Cowper Prime [q.v.] proposed taking it over, and learned that under their management it would be permitted to continue. In 1864 the *Journal*, together with other New York newspapers, was made the victim of a serious hoax, when a bogus "proclamation of the President" was delivered to it—supposedly from the New York Associated Press—and published. The editors of the *World* and the *Journal of Commerce* were ordered arrested and the papers suppressed; but it was quickly discovered that they had been the victims and not the perpetrators of the trick, and the papers were resumed. In 1866 Stone became editor-in-chief of the *Journal*, and in 1884 he bought out Prime's interest in the paper. In 1869 he was elected president of the New York Associated Press, the pioneer news-gathering agency of America. He held the latter position for almost twenty-five years, retiring only when the association was merged with the United Press.

As head of the *Journal of Commerce*, Stone became one of the best known editors in New York. Endowed by nature with a big, powerful body and perfect eyesight (he never wore spectacles), the amount of work he performed was prodigious. He remarked in 1889 that he had not had a whole day's absence from his office in twenty-nine years. During his latter years he had no editorial assistant and wrote with his own hand about three hundred editorial articles a month, covering a wide range of subjects. Frequently a lay sermon was found among the rest, for Stone was a prominent church and Sunday-school worker in Brooklyn, and delivered hundreds of lectures upon the life of Christ and other religious subjects. He retired from the *Journal of Commerce* in 1893 and died two years later in Brooklyn. His wife, the former Delia Charlotte Hall of Wallingford, Conn., whom he married on Sept. 7, 1841, died on Oct. 19, 1887. There were no children.

[W. L. Stone, *The Family of John Stone* (1888); *Jour. of Commerce*, Apr. 4, 1895, and Sept. 29, 1927; Victor Rosewater, *Hist. of Coöperative News-Gathering in the U. S.* (1930); obituaries in *N. Y. Herald, N. Y. Times,* and *World* (N. Y.), Apr. 3, 1895; information from friends and associates of Stone; burial records in Oxford, Conn., and Greenwood Cemetery, Brooklyn, N. Y.]

                           A. F. H.

STONE, ELLEN MARIA (July 24, 1846–Dec. 13, 1927), missionary and lecturer, was born in Roxbury, Mass., and died in Chelsea, Mass. She was a descendant of Gregory Stone who emigrated to Watertown, Mass., in 1635. Her father and her mother, Benjamin Franklin Stone and Lucy Waterman (Barker) Stone, were religiously minded, she was named for a missionary, and at her baptism her mother dedicated her to that calling. She graduated from the grammar and high schools of Chelsea and in 1866–67 taught there. From 1867 to 1878 she was on the editorial staff of the *Congregationalist*. Then, as the result of a deepening religious purpose, she offered herself to the American Board of Commissioners for Foreign Missions, was accepted, and was assigned to Samakov, Bulgaria. About 1883 she was transferred to Philippopolis, also in Bulgaria, and there for more than ten years she spent much of her time visiting women in their homes. Soon, too, she began a training class to prepare Bible-women

to do similar work. For a time she was in charge of the mission's school for girls, and in 1885, in the course of the uprising in which Eastern Rumelia was united to Bulgaria, she ministered to sick and wounded soldiers in Sofia. In 1898, after a furlough in the United States, she was assigned to Saloniki and placed in charge of the evangelistic work for women in that area. Her new duties involved a great deal of travel, most of it through rural and mountainous districts.

It was in connection with these journeys that there unexpectedly came upon her the great adventure of her life, which suddenly lifted her name from obscurity and for a time made it known throughout much of the civilized world. On Sept. 3, 1901, while on one of her regular tours, she and her party were attacked by brigands. She and Katerina Stephanova Tsilka, an American-educated Bulgarian who was attached to the mission, were held captive and a large ransom was demanded. The American Board felt that it could not pay the sum without encouraging the kidnapping of other missionaries, but with the indorsement of President Theodore Roosevelt and his secretary of state, a popular appeal for funds was made throughout the United States. A sum of about $66,000 was collected and after skilful negotiations paid to the brigands, and on Feb. 23, 1902, the two women were released. That spring Miss Stone returned to the United States. While her name was long retained on the staff of her mission, she never resumed her residence in the Near East. Instead, she traveled widely in America, telling the story of her captivity. Later, she became a lecturer of the Woman's Christian Temperance Union, for the most part speaking on missionary subjects. She also spent a great deal of time in Washington, attempting to obtain the passage by Congress of an appropriation which would reimburse those who had contributed to her ransom. Her account of her captivity, "Six Months Among the Brigands" (*McClure's Magazine,* May–July, September 1902), was her only published writing which obtained wide circulation.

[Manuscript files of the Am. Board of Commissioners for Foreign Missions; annual reports of the same, 1879–1908; *Missionary Herald,* Nov., Dec. 1901, Jan., Mar., Apr. 1902, Feb. 1928; *Who's Who in America,* 1916–17; "Repayment of Ransom of Ellen M. Stone," *House Report 807, 62* Cong., 1 Sess.; *Boston Transcript,* Dec. 14, 1927; J. G. Bartlett, *Gregory Stone Geneal.* (1918).]

                           K. S. L.

STONE, GEORGE WASHINGTON (Oct. 24, 1811–Mar. 11, 1894), Alabama jurist, was born in Bedford County, Va., the son of Micajah and Sarah (Leftwich) Stone. His grandfather, Micajah, had settled in Virginia before the Revolution. When George was seven years old the family migrated to Lincoln County, Tenn., where the father became a planter in comfortable circumstances. The boy was educated in the schools which were available in the local community and studied law in the office of James Fulton at Fayetteville, Tenn. Going to Alabama to take his bar examination, he was admitted to the bar in May 1834. He practised in Sylacauga and in Talladega until 1843, when he was appointed judge of the circuit court to fill out an unexpired term. In December of the same year he was elected by the legislature for the six-year term. In 1849 he resigned to resume his law practice, opening a new office in Hayneville, Ala.

In 1856 he was elected associate justice of the supreme court of Alabama and was reëlected in 1862. During the reconstruction period he was retired from the bench and practised in Montgomery. After the restoration of home rule in the state, he was appointed associate justice by Governor Houston. He held the office by appointment from 1876 to 1880, when he was elected to it for a term of six years. In 1884 he was appointed chief justice by Governor O'Neal. From 1886 until his death he held the office by election.

Stone served half a century on the bench of Alabama and twenty-five years of that time he sat on the supreme bench. He was not only learned in the law, but he had a judicial mind, and he was noted for the amount of labor he gave to preparing his decisions. His expression was clear and vigorous and his decisions were regarded as models of correct judicial style. When he came to the bench both the law and its administration were in a chaotic state in Alabama. The standards had not been high before the Civil War and the demoralization resulting from war and reconstruction had increased the confusion. Stone set himself to bring some sort of order into the judicial system of the state. He stood for a vigorous administration of criminal law and rigid honesty in the administration of civil law. He aided in the preparation of the Revised Penal Code in 1865 and was able to introduce some improvements into it. As chief justice for a quarter of a century he handed down more than two thousand decisions and through them materially improved the quality of judicial work. He was an earnest advocate of judicial reform. He opposed the separate courts of law and equity which existed in Alabama and the probate courts with their judges untrained in the law. He was not able, however, to win popular support for the reform of either of these conditions during his lifetime. Stone died in Montgomery in his eighty-third year. He had been three times married:

Dec. 16, 1834, to Mary Gillespie of Franklin, Tenn.; Sept. 4, 1849, to Emily Moore of Lowndes County, Ala.; Feb. 8, 1866, to Mary E. (Harrison) Wright of Lowndes County. He was survived by his third wife and several children.

[Stone's opinions may be found in 28–29 and 53–101 *Ala. Reports*; for general sources, see T. M. Owen, *Hist. of Ala. and Dict. of Ala. Biog.* (1921), vol. IV; Willis Brewer, *Ala., Her Hist., Resources, War Record and Public Men* (1872); *Memorial Record of Ala.* (1893), vol, II; William Garrett, *Reminiscences of Public Men in Ala., for Thirty Years* (1872); G. W. Stone, "Judicial Reform," *Proc. . . . Ala. State Bar Assoc.,* 1889; D. T. Blakey, "Hon. George W. Stone," *Ibid.,* 1895; "Half a Century on the Bench," *Ibid.,* 1893; "Memorial," 100 *Ala. Reports,* ix–xx; *Daily Reg.* (Mobile, Ala.), Mar. 13, 1894.]   H. F.

STONE, HORATIO (Dec. 25, 1808–Aug. 25, 1875), sculptor, the second child of Reuben and Nancy (Fairchild) Stone, was born at Jackson, Washington County, N. Y. When his father, who preferred work on the farm chores, failed to encourage his early interest in wood carving, the boy left home and did not communicate with his family until later years. Between 1841 and 1847 he practised as a physician in New York. Increasingly he turned to sculpture, however, especially after his removal in 1848 to Washington, where he had studios variously in the northwest section of the city, at the Navy Yard, and in the sub-basement of the Capitol building. During the Civil War, from Sept. 21, 1862, until his honorable discharge Sept. 20, 1865, he served as a contract surgeon with the Union forces. He was stationed at the Patent Office General Hospital and at the Columbian College Hospital, both in Washington, at West's Buildings General Hospital, Baltimore, and at Fort Delaware, Del. In 1864 he published *Freedom,* a small volume of poems containing besides the title piece, "Eleutheria," set to music by George Henry Curtis as a cantata, and "Day." The style is sonorous, if not turgid, and the sentiment inevitably seeks the point when America is sung as the climax of creation's travail. He was active in the organization of the Washington Art Association, which had among its objects the establishment of a national art gallery and the preservation of historic monuments, and in 1857 became its president. A year later there appeared his *Inaugural Address . . . and an Address on National Art.* It was as a result of the work of the Washington Art Association that the art commission of 1859 was appointed by President James Buchanan, and that in 1860 the National Gallery of Art was incorporated.

Four of Stone's works are preserved in the Capitol—his bust of Chief Justice Roger Brooke Taney, his statues of Alexander Hamilton (1864) and Senator Edward Dickinson Baker of Oregon (1874), and his masterpiece, a statue of John Hancock (1856), all in marble. The Hamilton (see Glenn Brown, *History of the United States Capitol*, vol. II, 1903, plate 291) shows the dramatic pose and careful details of the current style, but with a unity and simplicity that one likes to think also marked the doctor's efforts as surgeon if they did not his prose and poetry. His other works include busts of Hamilton and Jefferson, said to be copies of Jean Antoine Houdon's, a statue of Jefferson, and a bust and a statue of Thomas Hart Benton. He is said to have made a pair of bronze doors in New York and, more plausibly, to have executed the stone for his mother's grave (in the Jackson cemetery), carved in Italy and showing the three Marys at the tomb. Exhibitions of his works were held at the National Academy of Design in New York City in 1849 and in 1869. He never married. His personality is recalled as one of charm and versatility. At least twice during his career he visited Italy, and it was at Carrara that he died.

[*Art Jour.* (N. Y.), Nov. 1875; C. E. Fairman, *Art and Artists of the Capitol of the U. S. A.* (1927); obituary in *N. Y. Times*, Sept. 24, 1875; date of death and other information from H. E. Cole, Executive Department, Division of the Budget, Capitol, Albany, N. Y., and Adjutant-General C. H. Bridges, Washington, D. C.]
W. S. R.

STONE, JAMES KENT (Nov. 10, 1840–Oct. 14, 1921), educator and Roman Catholic priest, was born in Boston, Mass., the son of Dr. John Seely Stone [*q.v.*] and his second wife, Mary Kent (1807–1901). He was prepared for college at E. S. Dixwell's Latin School in Cambridge and entered Harvard in 1856 but did not graduate until 1861. At the conclusion of his freshman year he traveled in Europe for a time while perfecting himself in modern languages, and in 1860–61 studied at the University of Göttingen, where he became a good student, a skilled Alpine climber, and a disciple of German academic methods. After teaching for a while in Dixwell's Latin School, he enlisted as a private in the Union army, was advanced to a lieutenancy in the Second Massachusetts Volunteers, experienced hard fighting at Antietam, and was retired in January 1863. Appointed an assistant professor of Latin in Kenyon College, Gambier, Ohio, in January 1863, he studied theology, took orders in the Protestant Episcopal Church, and in 1867, after holding chairs in Latin and mathematics, became president of the college. In the meantime he had been married on Aug. 26, 1863, to Cornelia Fay, daughter of Harrison Fay, by whom he had three daughters.

His married life was happy, and his social relations with students and faculty were pleasant; but high church leanings in a low church atmosphere brought a conflict with the local bishop and the school of divinity that led him to resign. Called to the presidency of Hobart College at Geneva, N. Y., in 1868, he was happier as a "primitive Catholic" under Bishop Arthur Cleveland Coxe [*q.v.*], a high churchman. The death of his wife on Feb. 15, 1869, brought intense grief and months of solitude. After commencement, 1869, he resigned his presidency and on Dec. 8, 1869, apparently under no Catholic influences beyond an intimate knowledge of the Tractarian Movement, he was received into the Roman Catholic Church by Father Winand Michael Wigger [*q.v.*] of Madison, N. J. Though the Fays, who were concerned about the Stone children, took steps to have Stone committed to an asylum, his father stood in the way. Meanwhile Stone wrote his polemical volume, *The Invitation Heeded* (1870), which was compared by friendly critics to Newman's *Apologia* and went through several editions and into several foreign tongues. Desirous of becoming a priest, he declined a professorship at Georgetown College and joined the Paulists. On Dec. 21, 1872, he was ordained a priest by Archbishop John McCloskey [*q.v.*] and in 1874 became a master of novices. Finally, making a tragic sacrifice which he alone could gauge, he permitted the adoption of his two surviving daughters by Michael J. O'Connor (1820–90) and his wife, childless philanthropists of San Rafael, Cal.

He was now in a position to withdraw from the Paulists, and in 1876 he joined the more severe Congregation of the Passion at Pittsburgh, Pa. As Father Fidelis of the Cross, he took his final vows on Aug. 11, 1878, and found a welcome anonymity. In 1881, after some time in the Roman mother-house on Celian Hill, he was sent to establish his congregation in Argentina, where in his twelve years he founded several monasteries, was instrumental in building Holy Cross Church (Buenos Aires), and journeyed forbidding distances over the pampas giving missions. There were brief interims when he labored for his congregation in Paraguay, 1883; attended a general chapter in Rome, 1884; laid the foundation stone of the Passionist Church of San Luis in Valparaiso, Chile, 1886; visited the United States, 1885 and 1889, where he saw his children and preached at the opening of the Catholic University in Washington; and brought missionaries from Rome, 1891, to extend his work. After preaching throughout the United States, 1894–97, even in the Appleton Chapel at Harvard, he was elected consultor to the general and stationed at Rome. At the end of his term he became provincial consultor in the United States, 1899; master of novices, 1902; and provincial, 1905–08. Again he was sent to South America as provincial. Theodore Roosevelt [q.v.], impressed with the refined austerity and bearing of Father Fidelis, whom he met in Buenos Aires, said that at his entrance "you heard the clink of the saber" (Smith, post, p. 364). In 1911 Fidelis was commissioned to inaugurate the Passionist congregation in Brazil, where he erected foundations at São Paulo and Curitiba. In 1914 he was assigned to Mexico but was unable to enter the country under Carranza. Until 1917 he served in Cuba and in negro missionary work in Corpus Christi, Tex. At that time, upon the invitation of D. E. Hudson, C.S.C., he went to Notre Dame University to write an autobiographic sequel to his early volume under the title, *An Awakening and What Followed* (1920). Retired at the Passionist monastery in Chicago, he continued to work until shortly before his death, when he returned, in a sense, to the old family life with his two daughters at San Mateo, Cal.

[W. G. and Helen G. Smith, *Fidelis of the Cross, James Kent Stone* (1926) ; Felix Ward, C. P., *The Passionists, Sketches Hist. and Personal* (1923) ; G. F. Smythe, *Kenyon College, Its First Century* (1924) ; *The Am. Cath. Who's Who* (1911) ; review in *Cath. World*, Nov. 1870; "A Convert's Experiences of the Catholic Church," *Contemporary Rev.*, June 1900; *Fifth Report, Harvard Coll. Class of 1861* (1892) ; J. T. Morse, Jr., in *Harvard Graduates' Mag.*, Dec. 1921; death notice in *San Francisco Chronicle*, Oct. 15, 1921.]

R. J. P.

STONE, JOHN AUGUSTUS (Dec. 15, 1800– May 29, 1834), playwright and actor, was born in Concord, Mass., the youngest of four children of Joshua and Sarah (Avery) Stone. His father was a cabinet-maker, a descendant of Gregory Stone who came from England in 1635 and settled in Watertown, Mass. His early life is obscure, but he probably made his début at the Washington Garden Theatre, Boston, as Old Norval in *Douglas,* and he seems to have specialized in old men's parts, like Old Hardy in *The Belle's Stratagem,* in which he made his first appearance in New York, at the City Theatre in Warren Street, July 10, 1822. In the same year he married Mrs. Amelia (Greene) Legge, an actress in the same company, who is better known in the history of the stage as Mrs. Stone, and who later married Nathaniel Harrington Bannister [q.v.]. He appears at the new Chatham Garden Theatre in 1824, and there on Nov. 4 his first play, *Restoration; or, The Diamond Cross,* was performed, Stone playing Diego. It has disappeared, but it was evidently a romantic play, with Spanish characters. After he had filled engagements at the Bowery and the Chatham and at Niblo's Garden in 1828, his most important play, *Metamora; or, the Last of the Wampanoags,* was produced at the Park Theatre on Dec. 15, 1829, with Edwin Forrest [q.v.] as Metamora. Forrest had offered a prize of $500 and half the proceeds of the third night for the "best Tragedy, in five acts, of which the hero, or principal character shall be an aboriginal of this country" (*Critic,* Nov. 22, 1828). The committee of award, headed by William Cullen Bryant [q.v.], selected from among the fourteen plays submitted the Indian drama. It provided Forrest with one of his most popular parts and brought him thousands of dollars, none of which, however, were shared by the author. Forrest never permitted the publication of his successes, so that *Metamora* exists now only in a manuscript fragment, limited to the part of Metamora, in the Edwin Forrest Home for Aged and Infirm Actors in Philadelphia. From this and contemporary accounts, it is clear that the play provided Forrest with an appealing character, King Philip, the son of Massasoit, who defends his people against the English aggression and finally kills his wife, Nahmeokee, to save her from falling into the hands of the whites, dying himself from the bullets of his foes. While not the first Indian play, *Metamora* started the great vogue of the aboriginal drama and established the stage convention for the Indian dialect, a curious mixture of Ossian and the real Indian speech.

When Stone left New York for Philadelphia is not clear. His one extant play was published there in 1827, *Tancred; or, The Siege of Antioch,* a chronicle play, laid in the Christian camp before Antioch in 1097, in which Tancred triumphs over the wiles of the Grecian emperor and the sultana. But on Mar. 23, 1831, he acted at the Park Theatre in New York at his benefit, when his *Tancred, King of Sicily* was performed (evidently, judging from the cast, a totally different play from the earlier *Tancred*). Its first production had been on Mar. 16. And when *The Demoniac; or, The Prophet's Bride* was played at the Bowery on Apr. 12, 1831, he played Taher Ben Yhudah in what must have been an oriental drama. He next revised James Kirke Paulding's *The Lion of the West,* in which James Henry Hackett [qq.v.] had been acting since April 1831 the part of Nimrod Wildfire. Since both original and revision have disappeared, it is hard to assign Stone's share, but apparently he wrote a new play, a melodramatic comedy, in which Nimrod Wildfire from Kentucky straightened out all the complications. Beginning Nov. 14, 1831, at the Park, it became one of Hackett's famous parts. Stone wrote another play for Forrest, *The Ancient Briton,* produced first at the Arch Street Theatre, Philadelphia, Mar. 27, 1833. It was an historical tragedy, the action beginning about 60 A.D. in the mountains of Wales, during the reign of Nero, while Suetonius was general of the Roman forces. Boadicea defeats the Romans but afterwards commits suicide. The Britons were painted like the Indians in *Metamora.* Of other plays, like *Fauntleroy; or, The Fatal Forgery* and *La Roque, the Regicide,* attributed to Stone, little is known but the titles. A prize play for George Handel Hill [q.v.], *The Knight of the Golden Fleece, or, The Yankee in Spain,* was produced posthumously at the Park Theatre, Sept. 10, 1834. Charles Durang, who knew Stone, describes him as "a small man, slight in figure, but genteel." He was evidently of a despondent nature, or he may have been made so by the discouraging conditions of the stage. On May 29, 1834, he threw himself off the Spruce Street Wharf in Philadelphia into the Schuylkill River. He was survived by his widow and two sons. Forrest erected a handsome tombstone to his memory, in Machpelah Cemetery, with the inscription "Erected to the Memory of John Augustus Stone, Author of Metamora, By His Friend Edwin Forrest."

[Dates of birth and death are given on authority of the town clerk of Concord and the manuscript diary of William Wood, the Philadelphia manager, in the lib. of the Univ. of Pa. The *Pennsylvanian* (Phila.), May 31, 1834, however, gives the date of death as May 28. Stone's biog. must be gathered from Charles Durang, "The Phila. Stage," 3 ser., ch. 25, in *Sunday Despatch* (Phila.), beginning July 8, 1860; J. N. Ireland, *Records of the N. Y. Stage* (2 vols., 1866–67); James Rees, *The Life of Edwin Forrest* (1874); W. R. Alger, *Life of Edwin Forrest,* vol. I (1877); G. C. D. Odell, *Annals of the N. Y. Stage,* vols. III, IV (1928); R. D. James, *Old Drury of Phila.* (1932). See also J. G. Bartlett, *Gregory Stone Geneal.* (1918). For a portrait, see O. S. Coad and Edward Mims, Jr., *The Am. Stage* (1929). For dramatic criticism, see A. H. Quinn, *A Hist. of the Am. Drama from the Beginning to the Civil War,* vol I (1923).]
A. H. Q.

STONE, JOHN MARSHALL (Apr. 30, 1830–Mar. 26, 1900), governor of Mississippi, was born at Milan in west Tennessee, the son of Asher and Judith (Royall) Stone, both natives of south-side Virginia. He was the descendant of Joshua Stone who settled in Prince Edward County, Va., early in the eighteenth century. When John was eleven years old his father died leaving the mother with nine children to struggle against poverty. As a result, the boy's education was restricted to the common schools, but in spite of this he first earned his living as a school teacher. Then he was a clerk on a Tennessee River steamboat running from the Ohio to Eastport, Miss. After settling for a time at

Eastport, he became in 1855 station agent at the neighboring town of Iuka. With the opening of the Civil War, he became captain of the Iuka Rifles in the 2nd Mississippi Infantry, and in the spring of 1861 his company reached Virginia. He participated in most of the important battles in that state during the next four years and was wounded, though not severely. His ability and bravery obtained his advancement to the rank of colonel in the brigade commanded by Joseph R. Davis [q.v.]. At times, as during the Wilderness fighting, he was in charge of the brigade. Early in 1865 he was captured in North Carolina, while leading some Mississippi recruits to Virginia. Released from Johnson's Island in July 1865, he returned to his railroad agency at Iuka. There, on May 2, 1872, he married Mary Gilliam Coman. After their two children died in infancy, three of Stone's nieces were adopted.

After serving his political apprenticeship in several local offices, he was elected to the state Senate and, reëlected, he served from 1870 to 1876. Chosen by acclamation president *pro tempore* of that body, he became acting-governor of Mississippi on Mar. 29, 1876, after the forced resignation and removal of Gov. Adelbert Ames and Lieut.-Gov. A. K. Davis. The next year he was elected governor. The activities of his administration were chiefly devoted to reorganizing the government on the basis of control by the native white people of the state and to abolishing the extravagances of the recent Carpetbag government. In addition, the Mississippi Agricultural and Mechanical College (now Mississippi State College) was established, and a state board of health was created, which at once performed valiant service during the severe yellow-fever epidemic of 1878. He opposed the popular demand for the establishment of a railroad commission. Nevertheless, under his successor, Gov. Robert Lowry [q.v.], the commission was formed, and Stone was appointed a member in 1884. In 1889 he was again elected governor. Once more economy in state affairs was necessary owing to the panic of the early 'nineties. As his first administration marked the return of power to the white race, so his second gave a constitutional basis for the perpetuation of white control in the provisions of the constitution of 1890. Popular approval, which has sometimes approached reverence, for this document has brightened the halo about the name of Stone. Since the constitution of 1890 added two years to the terms of those holding state office, he served a six-year term, from 1890 to 1896. Nine months before his death he was made president of the Agricultural and Mechanical College.

He was an able administrator, and he was a man of substantial character who was above suspicion in all his public life. These facts, coupled with the length of his service, largely explain the great respect in which his administrations are held. Furthermore, his régime appeared in an excellent light in contrast with the corruptions of the Reconstruction period, and the fear of a return of those hardships kept the political leaders of Mississippi in a state of unusual harmony.

[Dunbar Rowland, *Mississippi* (1907), vol. II; *Biog. and Hist. Memoirs of Miss.* (1891), vol. II; Robert Lowry and W. H. McCardle, *A Hist. of Miss.* (1891); *Pubs. Miss. Hist. Soc.*, esp. vol. XII (1912); *Commercial Appeal* (Memphis), Mar. 27, 1900, Mar. 1, 1931.]

C. S. S.

STONE, JOHN SEELY (Oct. 7, 1795–Jan. 13, 1882), Protestant Episcopal clergyman, educator, was the ninth child of Ezekiel and Mary (Seely) Stone, and sixth in descent from William Stone—fourth son of the Rev. Samuel Stone of Hereford, England—who sailed from London to New England on May 20, 1639, and was one of the founders of Guilford, Conn. Born and brought up in West Stockbridge, Berkshire County, Mass., John shouldered his musket in 1814 and marched to the defense of Boston.

He graduated from Union College, Schenectady, N. Y., in 1823, and entered the General Theological Seminary, New York City. On Jan. 4, 1826, in St. Mark's Church, New York, he was ordered deacon by Bishop Hobart, and on Jan. 7, 1827, in Hartford, Conn., was ordained priest by Bishop Brownell. He was a tutor in Greek and Latin at Hobart College, 1825–27, and then became rector of St. Michael's Church, Litchfield, Conn. He was subsequently rector of All Saints Church, Frederick, Md., 1828–29; Trinity Church, New Haven, Conn., 1830–32; St. Paul's Church, Boston, 1832–41; Christ Church, Brooklyn, 1842–52; and St. Paul's Church, Brookline, Mass., 1852–62. In 1862 he was appointed professor of theology in the Philadelphia Divinity School, where he served until 1867. In that year he became the first dean and professor of systematic theology of the newly founded Episcopal Theological School, Cambridge, Mass. Retiring from that office and active service in 1876, he lived in Cambridge until his death, some six years later.

As a pastor, Stone was sympathetic, cheerful, and transparent as a child. As a dean he was more successful as a friend of the students than as an administrator. Young men felt and responded to his love of truth, his simplicity of nature, and his intellectual and moral courage. He was an eloquent preacher and a leader of thought in the Evangelical school of his Church. Hold-ing firmly to the standard of the Reformation, justification by faith, he sympathized with the orthodox rather than the advanced school of New England theology. Ecclesiastically, he was one of those who opposed the Tractarian Movement of Oxford and the teachings of Pusey and Newman in regard to the Sacraments, defining the visible Church of Christ as "a congregation of faithful men, in which the pure word of God is preached, and the Sacraments duly administered according to God's Ordinance."

Stone published *Memoir of the Life of the Rt. Rev. Alexander Viets Griswold* (1844); *The Mysteries Opened* (1844), republished as *The Christian Sacraments* (1866); *Lectures on the Institution of the Sabbath* (1844), republished as *The Divine Rest* (1867); *The Church Universal* (1846), republished as *The Living Temple* (1866); and *A Memoir of the Life of James Milnor, D.D.* (copr. 1848). On May 2, 1826, he married Sophie Morrison Adams, by whom he had five children, of whom only two were living when his wife died. On Sept. 5, 1839, he married Mary Kent, a daughter of Chancellor James Kent [*q.v.*] of New York. She was born in Albany, May 19, 1807, and died in Boston, Jan. 10, 1901. Of the children of this second marriage, the eldest, James Kent Stone [*q.v.*], after serving as president of Kenyon and Hobart colleges, was received by the Roman Catholic Church in 1869 and as a Passionist father, under the name Fidelis of the Cross, became a devoted missionary. Another son, Henry, died in service in the Civil War; a daughter, Elizabeth, was the wife of the Rev. Alexander V. G. Allen [*q.v.*], professor of ecclesiastical history in the Episcopal Theological School at Cambridge.

[G. Z. Gray, *John S. Stone, A Memorial Sermon* (1882); W. G. and H. G. Smith, *Fidelis of the Cross, James Kent Stone* (1926); C. L. Slattery, *Alexander Viets Griswold Allen* (1911); *Churchman*, Jan. 21, 1882; *Church Almanac*, 1883; *Boston Transcript*, Jan. 14, 1882; personal acquaintance.]

W. L.

STONE, JOHN WESLEY (July 18, 1838–Mar. 24, 1922), lawyer, jurist, and member of Congress from Michigan, was born at Wadsworth, Ohio, the son of Chauncey and Sarah (Bird) Stone. His father, a farmer, was a cooper by trade and a Methodist preacher; he was descended from Simon Stone, an emigrant from England, who was in Watertown, Mass., as early as 1635. John attended the district schools of Wadsworth, and a small academy at Spencer, Ohio. About 1856 the family moved to Allegan County, Mich., where Stone taught school in winter and in summer split rails and helped clear the new farm.

In 1859 he commenced the study of law with

Silas Stafford, an attorney in Plainwell, and the following year was elected clerk of Allegan County. Continuing the study of law, he was admitted to the bar in 1862. In the same year he was reëlected county clerk and served until 1864, when he was chosen prosecuting attorney. He was prosecutor for Allegan County until 1870. Meanwhile, in 1865 he formed a law partnership with Dan J. Arnold of Allegan, which continued until 1873, when Stone was elected circuit judge of the twentieth judicial district, comprising the counties of Allegan and Ottawa. He resigned this office on Nov. 1, 1874, and removed to Grand Rapids, where he became junior member in the firm of Norris, Blair & Stone.

From 1877 to 1881 Stone served as member of Congress from the fifth congressional district, then resumed the practice of law in Grand Rapids in partnership with Nathaniel A. Earle. Later these two formed a partnership with Edward Taggart. Early in the administration of President Harrison, Stone was offered but declined an appointment as governor of Washington Territory. In 1882 he was appointed United States attorney for the western district of Michigan, which office he held for four years, meantime forming a partnership with his assistant Wesley W. Hyde.

Stone's business had often taken him to the Upper Peninsula, and in 1887 he decided to move to Houghton, because of the financial opportunities offered by that rapidly developing country. He practised law in Houghton from 1887 to 1890 with the firm of Stone & Gray; in 1890 was elected circuit judge of the twenty-fifth judicial district, composed of the counties of Marquette, Delta, Menominee, Dickinson, and Iron, and the following year transferred his residence to Marquette. He held the office of circuit judge until Dec. 31, 1909, and the next day took his seat on the bench of the supreme court of the state, to which he had been elected in the preceding spring. He served on the supreme court until his death, twelve years later, at Lansing. Except for a few short breaks, his public service in the state of Michigan extended over a period of more than sixty years.

Tall, slender, with a ruddy complexion, Judge Stone was a distinguished figure. He was invariably even-tempered, and an indefatigable worker, even during his late years. His opinions as a member of the supreme court appeared in 159–217 *Michigan Reports*. They were, for the most part, excellently written, some of them models of brevity and conciseness, and all showing a keen analytical mind, wide learning, and a sound knowledge of the law. He was married,

May 2, 1861, to Delia M. Grover of Allegan, Mich., who died Jan. 25, 1902. To this marriage seven children were born.

[J. G. Bartlett, *Simon Stone Geneal.* (1926); *Who's Who in America*, 1922–23; *Biog. Dir. Am. Cong.* (1928); *Mich. Biogs.* (Mich. Hist. Com., 1924), vol. II; C. B. Howell, *Mich. Nisi Prius Cases . . . Biog. Sketches of the Judges of Mich.* (1884); G. I. Reed, *Bench and Bar of Mich.* (1897); *Detroit Free Press*, Mar. 25, 1922; personal letters from the family of Judge Stone.]
H.C.

STONE, LUCY (Aug. 13, 1818–Oct. 18, 1893), reformer and pioneer in the woman's rights movement, was born near West Brookfield, Mass. Her mother was Hannah (Matthews) Stone. Her father, Francis Stone, was a descendant of Gregory Stone who emigrated from England to Massachusetts Bay in 1635. Francis Stone was a well-to-do farmer and tanner who believed that men were divinely ordained to rule over women. Hannah, his wife, meek and docile, accepted this view; but Lucy, when still very young, became resentful of woman's lot. Upon discovering that the Bible seemed to uphold male domination she wanted to die. Soon, however, she began to suspect the man-made translations of the Scriptures and decided to study Greek and Hebrew to find out whether they were correct. Though her brothers were sent to college, her father was shocked when she expressed a wish to go, and he would give her no financial aid. Therefore, she determined to educate herself, and when sixteen began to teach district school at a dollar a week, "boarding around." For several years afterward she continued to teach, except for short periods at Quaboag Seminary in Warren, Mass., the Wesleyan Academy in Wilbraham, Mass., and at Mount Holyoke Female Seminary. During this time her hostility towards the existing status of women increased, for she learned that, because of her sex, she had no vote in the Congregational Church in West Brookfield of which she was a member. Finally, in 1843 she had enough money to start work at Oberlin College and registered there. For the first two years she helped eke out her expenses by teaching and by manual labor, but in her third year her father relented and came to her aid. At college she was looked upon as a dangerous radical, for she was an ardent abolitionist, was uncompromising on the question of woman's rights, and, under the influence of the brimstone sermons of Charles Grandison Finney [q.v.], became Unitarian in religion. In August 1847 she was graduated at Oberlin College.

A few weeks later she gave her first public address on woman's rights, from the pulpit of her brother, William Bowman Stone, at Gardner,

Mass. The following year she began to lecture regularly for the Anti-Slavery Society, but she urged the elevation of woman whenever pretext offered. After two or three years most of her time was given to free-lance lecturing on the rights and wrongs of her sex, and she traveled over much of the country delivering her message. Possessed of rare eloquence and a singularly beautiful voice, she was, as Elizabeth Cady Stanton said, "the first person by whom the heart of the American public was deeply stirred on the woman question" (Blackwell, *post,* p. 94). In 1850 she headed the call for the first national Woman's Rights convention, which was held at Worcester, Mass., and had much to do with arranging for the later conventions, which took place annually. She published the proceedings at her own expense. She had intended never to marry, in order that she might give all of her energies to the cause of woman's rights, but on May 1, 1855, she became the wife of Henry Brown Blackwell [*q.v.*], after he had offered to devote his life to the same cause. He kept his word. In connection with their marriage they drew up a joint protest against the legal disabilities of women that was given wide publicity. Lucy Stone felt that a woman's abandonment of her name upon taking a husband was symbolical of her loss of individuality, so she kept her own name after marriage, merely substituting the title Mrs. for Miss.

Following her marriage her labors for woman's rights continued and broadened. For a time the family lived in New Jersey, and there, in 1858, she let her household goods be sold for taxes and used the incident for a written protest against taxation without representation. When the Fourteenth Amendment to the federal Constitution was pending, she and her husband strove, in vain, to win suffrage for women through getting the word "male" struck from the bill. In 1866 when the American Equal Rights Association was formed she was made a member of the executive committee. In 1867, partly through her efforts, the New Jersey Woman Suffrage Association was organized, with her as president. For two months of the same year she and her husband campaigned in Kansas in behalf of amendments to the state constitution for extending suffrage to women and to negro men. In 1868, while still living in New Jersey, they helped organize the New England Woman Suffrage Association. Soon they removed to Boston to aid the woman movement in Massachusetts. Just at this time a split, over program and methods, occurred in the American Equal Rights Association, and in its place developed the National Woman Suffrage Association and the American Woman Suffrage Association. She helped form the latter, which concentrated on gaining suffrage by states. Twenty years later, upon the initiative of Alice Stone Blackwell, her daughter, the two organizations were united as the National American Woman Suffrage Association, and she was placed on the executive committee. She raised most of the money with which the *Woman's Journal* was founded in 1870. Two years later she and her husband assumed the editorship and were in charge of it for the remainder of their lives. Under their direction the publication became a tower of strength to the cause of woman's rights. Meanwhile she was the leading spirit in the Massachusetts Woman Suffrage Association, which she and her husband helped organize in 1870, and in the New England and the American associations; and she likewise gave much individual time to lecturing and drafting bills and to legislative hearings in the interest of a better status for women. She delivered her last lecture for the cause to which she devoted her life in connection with the World's Columbian Exposition at Chicago in 1893. Shortly afterward her health began to fail from an internal tumor. At her home in Boston she died, urging her daughter, Alice Stone Blackwell, to "make the world better" (Blackwell, *post,* p. 282). Her funeral, said a friend, was like a coronation (*Ibid.,* p. 285). She was short of stature but well built; her cheeks were rosy throughout life; her nose was broad and tip-tilted, adding to her expression of good nature and approachableness; her eyes were bright gray; her mouth, strong and kindly; and she had an abundance of dark brown hair, which had whitened very little when she died. She possessed unusual personal magnetism, but she had not much sense of humor. Ruggedly honest in acts and words, modest, unselfish, and fearless, she was kind in her human relationships, even to her opponents, and was very fond of children. She died at her home in Dorchester, Mass.

[Some letters in Lib. of Cong., but most of papers in possession of daughter, Alice Stone Blackwell; A. S. Blackwell, *Lucy Stone, Pioneer of Woman's Rights* (copr. 1930), "Lucy Stone, New Jersey Pioneer Suffragist," *The Civic Pilot,* Jan. 1923, and "Three Pioneer Women," in *Alpha Phi Quarterly,* Jan. 1927; *History of Woman Suffrage* (6 vols., 1881–1922), ed. by E. C. Stanton, S. B. Anthony, M. J. Gage, and I. H. Harper; J. G. Bartlett, *Gregory Stone Geneal.* (1918); *Boston Evening Transcript,* Oct. 19, 1893; *N. Y. Tribune,* Oct. 22, 28, 1893.]   M. W. W.

STONE, MELVILLE ELIJAH (Aug. 22, 1848–Feb. 15, 1929), journalist, was born at Hudson, Ill., second of the six sons of the Rev.

Elijah and Sophia Louisa (Creighton) Stone. His father was a Methodist Episcopal clergyman "on circuit," who supplemented his clerical income by manufacturing tools for saw mills; he was a descendant of Simon Stone who emigrated from England in 1635 and settled at Watertown, Mass. After attending the public schools in Chicago Stone became a newspaper reporter on the *Chicago Republican* but soon acquired an interest in an iron foundry. On Nov. 25, 1869, in Chicago, he married Martha Jameson McFarland, daughter of John Stuart McFarland, by whom he had two sons and a daughter. When the great Chicago fire of 1871 wiped out his foundry, he went back to newspaper work. In 1875, with two partners, he organized the first penny daily, the *Chicago Daily News,* launching an experimental issue on Christmas day. In 1881 with Victor Fremont Lawson [*q.v.*], whose partner he had become, he started a morning edition. Seven years later he sold out his interest in the papers to Lawson. After several years of European travel, he turned to banking and for a time was president of the Globe National Bank. He was also treasurer of the Chicago Drainage Canal, and president of the Citizens' Association and of the Civil Service Reform League.

In 1893 he was persuaded to become general manager of the Associated Press of Illinois, incorporated by the Western Associated Press when it refused a place in the merger of the New York Associated Press (founded 1848) and the United Press. He immediately contracted with the Reuter Telegram Company, Ltd., of Great Britain and its allied associations in other European countries for the exclusive right to use their news in the United States. When the United Press went into receivership in 1897, most of its papers joined the Associated Press; others formed the Publishers' Press, which later combined with the Scripps-McRae service to form the United Press Associations. In 1898 the supreme court of Illinois ruled that the Associated Press was bound to furnish its reports to any newspaper which applied for them (*Inter-Ocean Publishing Company* vs. *Associated Press,* 184 *Illinois Reports,* 438). This was fatal to the cooperative plan of the self-governing association, and in September 1900 the organization was dissolved in Illinois but simultaneously reorganized in New York under a statute permitting formation of corporations not for profit. This Stone headed as general manager and secretary until he retired in 1921, establishing in these years a number of important journalistic principles. He sedulously fostered the cooperative principle upon which the organization was

based, widely copied by such news agencies as the Canadian Press and the Shimbun Rengo Sha of Japan. He proved that news could be gathered and distributed free from partisanship and editorial bias, and without thought of monetary profit, a distinct departure from previously accepted practices, which had made press associations commercial in character. He also asserted that there was little true appeal to readers in episodic sensationalism and held that the news columns should mirror what he called the "substantial activities of the people," whether the actors in them were great or humble. Under his management there was fought through the federal courts to the Supreme Court of the United States a case which in 1918 established the legal principle that news is a commodity and that in it a property right exists (*International News Service* vs. *Associated Press,* 248 *United States Reports,* 215). On successive trips abroad he established Associated Press bureaus in the principal European capitals and persuaded chancelleries of the Old World to open their news sources to American correspondents.

His greatest personal triumph came in connection with the Russo-Japanese War of 1904–05. After going to Saint Petersburg (later Leningrad) and persuading Czar Nicholas II to remove the censorship from Russian press dispatches, he was influential in preventing the failure of the peace parley between the two countries at Portsmouth, N. H., in August 1905. Learning that the czar had instructed his plenipotentiaries to withdraw when the Japanese made demands for indemnity, he communicated with Pres. Theodore Roosevelt [*q.v.*] and with Emperor Wilhelm II of Germany, urging that pressure be brought to bear on both parties. The upshot was that Tokio withdrew its demand for a money payment, the czar authorized further negotiations, and peace followed. Stone's part in this was so confidential, however, that it was not known for some years. In 1921 his autobiography, *Fifty Years a Journalist,* appeared. He died in New York, survived by his wife and daughter, and was buried in the National Cathedral at Washington, D. C. He has been described as a man "of a constructive mind, remarkable executive powers, and a most frank, engaging, and delightful personality" (*Nation, post,* p. 274), and as "true and kindly, eminently interested in his work and his duty" (*Times,* London, quoted in *New York Times,* Feb. 18, 1929).

[J. G. Bartlett, *Simon Stone Geneal.* (1926); *Who's Who in America,* 1928–29; "*M.E.S.*" *His Book* (1918); Victor Rosewater, *Hist. of Coöperative News-Gathering in the U. S.* (1930); "'M.E.S.,'" *Nation,* Mar. 6,

1929; *N. Y. Times,* Feb. 16, Mar. 24, Mar. 31, 1929; records of the Associated Press.]   M. E. C.

STONE, RICHARD FRENCH (Apr. 1, 1844–Oct. 3, 1913), physician and editor, was born near Sharpsburg, Bath County, Ky., the son of Samuel and Sally (Lane) Stone. Samuel Stone, grandson of Josiah Stone, an English immigrant to Virginia, was a member of the Kentucky legislature and brigadier-general in the state militia. He moved his family to Putnam County, Indiana, in 1851, and there Richard received his early education in the public schools and in Bainbridge Academy. He taught school and studied medicine under Dr. J. B. Cross of Bainbridge for four years, and in 1863 entered Rush Medical College in Chicago. After one year he was appointed a medical cadet in the Union army and assigned to duty at Madison, Ind. He was shortly transferred to Philadelphia, Pa., where he served successively in three large military hospitals and attended the medical department of the University of Pennsylvania, from which he graduated in 1865. During the following year he served as acting assistant surgeon at camps at Key West and Cedar Keys, and in the post hospital at Monticello, Fla. He resigned from the military service in April 1866 and returned to Indiana, where he practised at New Albany, at Carpentersville, and finally at Bainbridge. In 1879 he participated in the founding of the Central College of Physicians and Surgeons, at Indianapolis, in which he held the chair of materia medica, therapeutics, and clinical medicine from 1880 until he resigned in 1886. After 1880 he lived in Indianapolis. At various times he was on the medical staffs of the Indianapolis City Hospital and City Dispensary (1882), the Marion County Asylum, and the Indiana Institute for the Education of the Blind. He took a lively interest in the activities of the Grand Army of the Republic and in local Democratic politics. He was a member of the pension bureau examining-board at Indianapolis, 1885–95, and in 1895 was appointed surgeon-general of the state militia with the grade of colonel. He contributed occasional papers to journal literature, perhaps the most notable being "Etiology of Specific Disease" (*Journal of the American Medical Association,* July 16, 1892), a discourse in opposition to the idea of the bacterial causation of disease. In 1885 he published *Elements of Modern Medicine,* and in 1894 his *Biography of Eminent American Physicians and Surgeons,* with a second and enlarged edition in 1898. This work required the labor of years. Though the sketches are often ill chosen, and in the case of living men largely autobiographical, it remains one of the best available sources of information for the biographer of American medical men.

In his earlier professional career Stone was a general practitioner who did some surgery and more obstetrics with creditable skill. His many outside activities, however, took toll of his clientele, and in his later years he added real estate promotion to a precarious practice, with scant success in either. He died in his office, probably a suicide, from asphyxiation by gas. An associate described him as being quiet and reserved, marked by a diffidence that interfered seriously with any activities involving public contacts. He was married on Nov. 24, 1869, to Matilda C. Long, daughter of Dr. William Long of New Maysville, Ind., by whom he had one son.

[R. F. Stone, *Eminent Am. Physicians and Surgeons* (1894), with portrait; H. A. Kelly and W. L. Burrage, *Am. Medic. Biogs.* (1920) ; Samuel Earp, in *Indianapolis Medic. Jour.,* Oct. 15, 1913; obituary in *Indianapolis Star,* Oct. 4, 1913, with portrait.]

J. M. P—n.

STONE, SAMUEL (July 1602–July 20, 1663), Puritan clergyman, the son of John Stone, a freeholder of Hertford, England, was baptized in Hertford on July 30, 1602. In 1620 he matriculated as a sizar from Emmanuel College in the University of Cambridge, where he received the B.A. degree in 1623. The year before, he took holy orders at Peterborough and resided in Aspen, Essex, at the home of Richard Blackerby. There he studied divinity, Bible exegesis, and Hebrew until his appointment as curate at Stisted, Essex. He held this curateship from June 13, 1627, to Sept. 13, 1630, when he was suspended for nonconformity. Through the influence of Thomas Shepard [*q.v.*] he then obtained the Puritan lectureship at Towcester in Northamptonshire. There he met Thomas Hooker [*q.v.*] and with him emigrated to Newtown (Cambridge) in New England as colleague minister in place of John Cotton [*q.v.*]. Eminently practical, he selected the site of Hartford, Conn., negotiated its purchase from the Indians and removed there in 1636. The town was probably named in honor of his birthplace. His first wife died in 1640. After Hooker's death, in 1647, he remained sole minister of the Hartford church until his own death. Although his godliness was especially revealed "in frequent *Fastings,* and exact *Sabbaths,*" he possessed "a certain Pleasancy" and a "most ready Wit" (*Magnalia, post,* III, 117). He represented his church at the New England synods of 1637, 1643, and 1646–48. As chaplain under John Mason [*q.v.*], he served through the Pequot War of 1637. On occasion he examined those accused and ministered to those convicted of witchcraft and even gave advisory opinions in civil cases. Apparently he was the "Rev. Mr. Stone" who accompanied Governor Winthrop of Connecticut to England in 1661 (*Haerlemse Saterdaeghse Courant* of Sept. 17, 1661, *New York Historical Society Collections*, 2 ser., I, 1841, 456). He found time to write a "Confutation of the Antinomians" and "A Body of Divinity," neither of which he published, and *A Congregational Church Is a Catholike Visible Church Or an Examination of Mr. Hudson* (1652).

The latter part of his life was embittered by a violent controversy with a party in his church led by William Goodwin, the ruling elder. Although its origin, as Cotton Mather tartly stated, "has been rendred almost as obscure as the Rise of *Connecticut* River" (*Magnalia, post,* III, 177), it is difficult to avoid the conclusion that personal friction between Stone and Goodwin both originated and prolonged the controversy. Qualifications for baptism, church membership, and the rights of the brethren were the main points at issue. Stone believed that the essence of Congregationalism was *"a speaking Aristocracy in the Face of a silent Democracy"* (*Ibid.,* 118). Although his ideas of church government approached Presbyterianism more than Independency, he was steadfastly supported by a majority. In this controversy, which deeply influenced religious life throughout New England, Stone's conduct was not above reproach; yet he consistently and conscientiously acted according to his own precepts. Upon his death at Hartford his inventory was £563. His will mentioned his second wife Elizabeth Allen, to whom he was married in 1641, and five of his children.

[Unpublished MSS. in possession of Mass. Hist. Soc.; Cotton Mather, *Magnalia Christi Americana* (1702), Book III, 62, 116–18; John and J. A. Venn, *Alumni Cantabrigienses*, pt. I, vol. IV (1927); Wm. Urwick, *Nonconformity in Herts* (1884), 518 ff.; John Winthrop, *The Hist. of New England* (1825), ed. by James Savage; *Conn. Hist. Soc. Colls.*, vol. II (1870); J. H. Trumbull, *The Memorial Hist. of Hartford County, Conn.* (1886), I, 262, 280; G. L. Walker, *Hist. of the First Church in Hartford* (1884), ch. vii; Sylvester Judd, *Hist. of Hadley* (new ed. 1905); Thomas Shepard, "Memoir of his own Life," in Alexander Young, *Chronicles of . . . Massachusetts* (1846); W. DeL. Love, *The Colonial Hist. of Hartford* (1914); James Savage, *A Geneal. Dict.*, vol. IV (1862), pp. 207–08; *Dict. Nat. Biog.*] F. T. N.

STONE, THOMAS (1743–Oct. 5, 1787), signer of the Declaration of Independence, was born on "Poynton Manor," Charles County, Md., the eldest son of David and Elizabeth (Jenifer) Stone and the great-great-grandson of William Stone, 1603–1660 [*q.v.*]. He received a classical education from a Scotch school-master and then went to Annapolis, where he studied law in the office of Thomas Johnson [*q.v.*]. After his ad-

mission to the bar in 1764, he went to Frederick to practise. He married Margaret Brown in 1768. Perhaps some of the £1,000 dowry was used to buy land near Port Tobacco, Charles County, where the family removed about 1771 and built "Habre-de-Venture," one of the most beautiful examples of colonial architecture in Maryland. In 1774, when the legality of the poll tax for the support of the clergy was tested, he was one of the sheriff's lawyers against Thomas Johnson, Samuel Chase, and William Paca [*qq.v.*], who were later to be his colleagues in Congress. Although his sympathies were entirely with the colonists when the break with England came, he always seems to have favored a milder course than many of his fellow representatives. He took his seat in the Continental Congress on May 13, 1775, and, except for a part of the year 1777 when he declined reëlection, he served until October 1778. His most important work was on the committee that framed the Articles of Confederation. Since, just a few days before the Declaration of Independence was voted upon, permission was given by Maryland to her delegates to vote as they thought best, he voted for the Declaration and signed it. He is the least known of the Maryland signers partly because he seldom spoke either in Congress or the Maryland Senate, and few of his letters have been preserved. He appeared, however, to have hated the thought of war and in September 1776 spoke in favor of treating with Lord Howe for peace (Burnett, *post,* II, 74, footnote).

Elected state senator for a five-year term in 1776 and reëlected twice he represented Charles County in the first three Senates, but he died before he completed his third term. He was one of the Maryland commissioners appointed to confer with those from Virginia over jurisdiction of the Chesapeake Bay. He opposed the movement for the issuance of paper currency and wrote to Washington for advice on the subject. Washington replied on Feb. 16, 1787, that if he were in the Maryland legislature, he would be decidedly against it and gave a number of reasons (*Writings of Washington,* IX, 1835, ed. by Jared Sparks, 231–32). This letter was reprinted frequently during the period of wildcat banking to show the opinion of the first president. Stone was also elected to the Congress of the Confederation in 1783 and took his seat on Mar. 26, 1784. He served as chairman of Congress for a few days toward the close of the session but declined reëlection and resumed his law practice. Although elected to the Constitutional Convention in Philadelphia, he declined to serve on account of the illness of his wife, who died in June

1787. Overcome with grief, he gave up his work and died four months later in Alexandria, Va., while waiting for a boat to take him to England. Three children survived him.

[Raphael Semmes Coll. in possession of Md. Hist. Soc., Baltimore; J. T. Scharf, *Hist. of Md.* (1879), II, 235–37; John Sanderson, *Biog. of the Signers to the Declaration of Independence* (1827), IX; H. E. Hayden, *Va. Geneal.* (1891); *Archives of Maryland*, vols. XI, XII (1892–93); E. C. Burnett, *Letters of Members of the Continental Cong.*, vol. II (1923).]
M. E. F.

STONE, WARREN (Feb. 3, 1808–Dec. 6, 1872), surgeon and physician, was born at Saint Albans, Vt., the youngest child of Peter and Jerusha (Snow) Stone, and a descendant of Simon Stone, who emigrated to New England in 1635 with his brother Gregory. His early education was limited, but he later studied assiduously under private tutors. He began his medical work at Keene, N. H., under Dr. Amos Twichell, and subsequently studied under Elisha Bartlett and Willard Parker [*qq.v.*] at Berkshire Medical Institution, Pittsfield, Mass., where he secured the degree of M.D. in December 1831. He settled in West Troy, N. Y., in 1832, but in October, as few opportunities for practice arose, he sailed from Boston for New Orleans on the brig *Amelia*. Storms and epidemic cholera caused the ship to be beached near Charleston, S. C., on Folly Island, where Stone labored among the sick until he himself contracted cholera. Arriving in December, sick, poor, friendless, he came to a New Orleans desolated by its first cholera epidemic. During his years in the city he was to serve through eighteen epidemics of cholera and yellow fever. After securing a supernumerary position in Charity Hospital, he served as assistant surgeon (1834–35), as resident surgeon (1835–39), and as visiting surgeon (1839–72). For many years he was consulting physician at Hôtel Dieu. In 1839, with Dr. William E. Kennedy, he founded the Maison de Santé, one of the earliest private hospitals in America. Here in 1841 he lost his eye from an infection following an operation. During his years on the staff of the Medical College of Louisiana (later Tulane University) from its opening in 1834 until his retirement in 1872, Stone rose from the position of acting demonstrator of anatomy (1834) to that of professor of surgery (1839–72). Though he lectured with earnest, long-remembered emphasis, he was a discursive, not a systematic, lecturer, often talking on unannounced subjects, and as a teacher of surgery he was too erratic to do full justice to his professorship. During the Civil War, Stone, who was an enthusiastic friend of Jefferson Davis [*q.v.*], in spite of his Northern birth accepted a Confederate commission and was appointed surgeon general of Louisiana. His incorrigible spirit brought him into conflict with the Federal military authorities in New Orleans, and at one time he was confined in Fort Jackson.

He has been called the "great commoner" of his profession in the South (Gross, *post*, p. 101), where his kind and winning, if somewhat blunt, manners won him great popularity and inspired unbounded confidence in his ability. Although he met emergencies with ingenuity and quickness, he was not what his contemporaries would have called a brilliant operator. He believed in the prompt opening and draining of suppurating joints, the frequent use of nourishment and stimulants, and the combination of codliver oil and phosphate of lime for use in diseases of the nutritive functions ("Phosphate of Lime in Scrofula and Other Depraved States of the System," *New Orleans Monthly Medical Register*, Oct. 1, 1851). Moreover, he was the first to resect part of a rib to secure permanent drainage in cases of empyema; he reported in 1850 the first successful cure for traumatic vertebral aneurism by open incision and packing ("A Case of Traumatic Aneurism," *New Orleans Medical and Surgical Journal*, Jan. 1850); he made the first cure of an aneurism of the second portion of the subclavian artery by digital compression upon the third portion; and he was the initial user of silver wire for the ligation of the external iliac ("Ligature of the Common Iliac Artery for Aneurism . . .," *Ibid.*, Sept. 1859). His fame was rather the result of his work than of his publications, though he published a number of articles, most of them in the *New Orleans Medical and Surgical Journal*, of which he was co-editor for a short time (1857–59). In 1868 appeared *Clinical Memoranda* and *Notes from the Lectures of Dr. Warren Stone*, edited by his son.

He was a man of unusual height and weight, with a large, rugged head and strong features. His pithy conversation was anecdotic and stimulating, and some of his sayings are still remembered. His quiet charity was not limited to professional services. He died in New Orleans of diabetes mellitus. In 1843 he had married Malvina Dunreith Johnson of Bayou Sara, who with a daughter and two sons survived him.

[J. G. Bartlett, *Simon Stone Geneal.* (1926); S. E. Chaillé, in *Medic. News* (N. Y.), Mar. 15, 1902; editorials in *New Orleans Medic. and Surgical Jour.*, July 1845, Mar. 1849, Jan. 1851; S. D. Gross, *Autobiog.* (1887), vol. II, pp. 100–01, 104–06; *A Century of Am. Medicine: 1776–1876* (1876), ed. by E. H. Clarke, etc.; A. B. Miles, in *Trans. Southern Surgical and Gynecological Asso.*, vol. VII (1895) and in *New Orleans Medic. and Surgical Jour.*, May 1895; F. B. J. Romer, in *New Orleans Medic. and Surgical Jour.*, Jan. 1875; R. F. Stone. *Biog. of Eminent Am. Physi-*

cians and Surgeons (1894); H. A. Kelly and W. L. Burrage, *Am. Medic. Biogs.* (1920); Edmond Souchon, in *Trans. Am. Surgical Asso.*, vol. XXXV (1917); F. W. Parham, in *Surgery, Gynecology, and Obstetrics*, Dec. 1923; obituary in *Nat. Republican*, Dec. 8, 1872.]

V. G. G.

STONE, WARREN SANFORD (Feb. 1, 1860–June 12, 1925), trade-union official, was born on a farm near Ainsworth, Iowa, the son of John and Sarah (Stewart) Stone. His paternal grandfather was an emigrant from Holland. At fifteen, after a farm boyhood with little schooling, he was able to enter Washington Academy nearby. He remained there for three years, an eager student, contributing to his own support by doing odd jobs, and then spent a year at Western College, Toledo, Iowa. In the fall of 1879 he went to work as a locomotive fireman on the Chicago, Rock Island & Pacific Railroad. At Agency, Iowa, on Oct. 15, 1884, he was married to Carrie E. Newell. Six months earlier, on becoming an engineer, he had joined the Brotherhood of Locomotive Engineers. He was soon afterward made secretary-treasurer of his local division and after a time was chosen as chairman of the Brotherhood's general committee of adjustments. His special talent as a negotiator won many decisions for the men, and he came to be well known throughout the organization. In August 1903, on the death of Peter M. Arthur [*q.v.*], he was chosen grand chief of the Brotherhood, a post he retained until his death. On taking office he faced a critical situation. Wages were low, living costs were rising, and the organization was losing membership. After a careful study of conditions, he formulated a plan for bettering wages and reducing hours by dealing with the railway managers through regional groups and carrying one contest to a finish before taking up another. The first struggle, with the Western group, was brought to a victorious conclusion in 1906; the second, with the Southeastern group, was settled in 1908. A bitter contest followed in 1912 with the Eastern group, the representatives of fifty-two powerful roads, who at first refused concessions. At a critical moment in the dispute the United States commissioner of labor and the presiding judge of the United States commerce court proposed mediation, and after hearings that lasted for five months a satisfactory compromise was reached. In the same year Stone succeeded in establishing a pension system in the Brotherhood, which was followed, nine years later, by a system of widows' pensions, the first in the history of American labor. In 1916 he led the railway unions in their successful fight for the passage of the Adamson Bill. In 1923, during the shopmen's strike, he intervened by drawing up a plan for settlement which brought the strike to an end. He was active in the movement which resulted in the founding, in October 1919, of *Labor,* the weekly organ of the railway unions. In the following year he brought the Brotherhood into the banking business, and at the time of his death the organization owned or controlled twelve banks and eight investment companies. In the spring of 1925 his health failed. He died at his home in Cleveland, survived by his wife. There were no children.

Stone's manner was genial, though bounded by a reserve that seemed to forbid a too close approach. By some he was thought to be domineering and obstinate. He differed from most trade-unionists in believing the compulsory closed shop unnecessary. He favored a greater degree of collectivization of industry and was a zealous advocate of the plan devised by Glenn Edward Plumb [*q.v.*] for the cooperative ownership of the railways. He also favored independent political action and was one of the leaders in the movement to bring labor to the support of LaFollette in the presidential campaign of 1924. He seems to have had no political ambitions and is said to have twice rejected a cabinet post. Much of the work he did for his organization is permanent. Under his control the Brotherhood increased in membership by 137 per cent. and greatly multiplied its resources. The vast financial structure he built up began to sag after his death, however, and suffered a series of disasters. His last days were troubled by a controversy which arose with the American Federation of Labor over the fact that a subsidiary corporation of the Brotherhood refused to pay union wages to its employees in the West Virginia mines. The matter had not been settled at the time of his death.

[*Who's Who in America,* 1924–25; *The New International Year Book,* 1925; *Locomotive Engineers Jour.,* July 1925; obituaries in *Cleveland Plain Dealer* and *N. Y. Times,* June 13, 1925.]

W. J. G.

STONE, WILBUR FISK (Dec. 28, 1833–Dec. 27, 1920), Colorado pioneer and jurist, the son of Homer Bishop and Lucy (Lindley) Stone, was born in Litchfield, Conn. He came of English stock, being a descendant of William Stone, one of the founders of Guilford, Conn. When he was six years old the family moved west, settling successively in New York, Michigan, Indiana, and Iowa. At eighteen he left the Iowa farm and went to Indiana where, after two years at the academy in Rushville, he attended Asbury University (later De Pauw) and Indiana University. He took the degree of A.B. at Indiana in 1857 and the degree of LL.B. in 1858.

During his college days he wrote essays and made contributions to various newspapers, and while studying law he acted as instructor in Greek and Latin at the university. For a year he served as editor of the *Daily Enquirer* at Evansville, Ind. He then began the practice of law. In the fall of 1859 he went to Omaha on legal business and was detained through the winter. There he served on the *Nebraskian* and, being able to write shorthand, reported the proceedings of the territorial legislature.

Meeting a number of returning "Pike's Peakers," he decided to go to the new gold country in the spring of 1860. He arrived in Denver after a six-weeks trip by ox team, followed the mining rush to South Park, and spent the winter at Cañon City, where he drafted the code for the first people's court of that section. He was elected a member of the legislature of Colorado in 1862 and 1864, and he served as assistant United States district attorney, 1862–66. In the winter of 1865–66 he returned to Indiana, and in February 1866 married Sarah Sadler of Bloomington, by whom he had two sons. Returning to Colorado, he and his wife settled at Pueblo, where Stone engaged in the practice of law, acted as an editor of the *Chieftain,* Pueblo's first newspaper, and in 1868 served as district attorney for the third (southern) judicial district. He was a promoter of the Denver & Rio Grande Railway, acting for some time as its attorney, and was instrumental in bringing the Atchison, Topeka, & Santa Fé Railroad to Pueblo. In 1875–76 he took a prominent part in drafting the constitution of the state of Colorado. He moved in 1877 to Denver, where he lived for the rest of his life. In October 1877, when a vacancy occurred in the state supreme court, he was nominated and elected without opposition. He served until January 1886 and then for nearly three years was judge of the criminal court at Denver. When Congress in 1891 created the court of private land claims to determine Spanish and Mexican land titles in the Southwest, he was appointed one of the five judges. His knowledge of Spanish and his association with Spanish-Americans of southern Colorado qualified him especially well for service on this unique court. He was sent by his colleagues to study the archives in Spain and to procure evidence in the famous Peralta case, involving a claim (later proved fraudulent) to over 12,000,000 acres of land in Arizona. When the work of the court was completed in 1904, he resumed private practice and spent much time in travel abroad. He was United States commissioner in the federal district court at Denver during the last five years of his life. During his twenty-six years of judicial service he won a name for clearness, impartiality, and integrity. He was an entertaining public speaker, his addresses being characterized by sparkling humor, and he wrote numerous articles for newspapers and magazines. The last work appearing under his name was a large *History of Colorado* (4 vols., 1918), of which he was consulting editor. He was an active member of the Episcopal Church.

[See J. M. Lindly, *The Hist. of the Lindley, Lindsley-Linsly Families,* vol. II (1924); *Who's Who in America,* 1916–17; W. F. Stone, ed., *Hist. of Colo.* (1918), vol. II, pp. 182 ff.; J. C. Smiley, *Semi-Centennial Hist. of the State of Colo.* (1913), vol. II, pp. 8–13; W. N. Byers, *Encyc of Biog. of Colo.* (1880); *Hist. of the City of Denver* (1901); T. F. Dawson, "Scrapbooks of Newspaper and Mag. Clippings," vol. LXV, pp. 21–31, in colls. of State Hist. Soc. of Colo.; H. D. Teetor, in *Mag. of Western Hist.,* Apr. 1889; *Report Colo. Bar Asso., 1921,* vol. XXIV, p. 166; obituary in *Rocky Mountain News,* Dec. 28, 1920. Information has been supplied by Stone's son. Stone's opinions as justice of the Colo. supreme court appear in 3–8 *Colo. Reports.* For the Peralta case see *Certificacion de ún Expediente, etc., etc., sobre los Bienes del difunto Don Miguel Nemecio Silva de Peralta de la Córdoba, etra.* (2 vols., 1892), in the Colls. of the State Hist. Soc. of Colo.]

L. R. H.

STONE, WILLIAM (*c.* 1603–*c.* 1660), third proprietary governor of Maryland, was born in Northamptonshire, England. He emigrated to Virginia sometime before 1628 and in 1633 served as justice of Accomac County, the name then applied to the entire eastern shore of Virginia. It was later called Northampton, possibly by Stone for his birthplace. He served as sheriff of Northampton for a term in the forties. He married Virlinda Cotton, the sister of William Cotton, a prominent minister. They had seven children. When Leonard Calvert [*q.v.*], governor of Maryland, died and designated a Roman Catholic, Thomas Greene, as his successor, Lord Baltimore soon removed Greene, placed him on the Council in August 1648, and appointed William Stone governor. Stone was a member of the Church of England but had non-conformist connections and sympathies. He brought thirty-three people with him to Maryland and received a grant of 5,000 acres "lying west of Nanjemi Creek on the Potomac."

He took a special oath when he came into office, in which he promised not to "trouble molest or discountenance any Person whatsoever in the said Province professing to believe in Jesus Christ and in particular no Roman Catholick for or in respect of his or her Religion" (*Archives, post,* III, 210). The Maryland Toleration Act, which is worded quite similarly, was passed by the Assembly on Apr. 21, 1649. The Governor's Council was reorganized with an equal number of Catholics and Protestants, and several Puritans were members of the Assembly. When Stone visited Virginia late in 1649 and left Greene in charge of the Maryland government, Greene at once proclaimed Charles II to be rightful heir to the English throne. Although Lord Baltimore and Stone both disavowed this act as soon as they heard of it, nevertheless, it aroused Puritan suspicion. In 1650 a commission was appointed by Parliament to reduce Virginia to Parliamentary authority. Construing its instructions to include Maryland, the members of the commission arrived at St. Mary's in 1652 and demanded that the Governor and Council be loyal to the Commonwealth of England and that all writs and warrants be issued in the name of the Keepers of England. When Stone agreed to the first but not the second, since according to his oath all writs had to be issued in the name of the Lord Proprietary, he was deprived of his commission. He was, however, reinstated a few months later when he decided to give in on the point (*Archives, post*, III, 275). The next year he found himself in trouble with the Puritans of Providence (now Annapolis) because he had imposed certain oaths upon them and had removed some Puritan officials. In vain they sent two petitions for aid to Virginia. However, at Lord Baltimore's command, Stone issued two proclamations, one that henceforth all writs would be issued in the name of the Lord Proprietary and another charging the commissioners with leading the people in rebellion against the proprietor. Then the commissioners returned, reinforced with Puritans from Providence and Patuxent, and again forced Stone to resign. When the news of this second surrender reached Lord Baltimore, he wrote Stone a letter demanding that he return to his duties. Stone gathered a small force and met the Puritans in the Battle of the Severn on Mar. 25, 1655. He was badly defeated, wounded, and captured. After the battle he was sentenced to death by a council of war but was saved by some of his friends among the Puritans. The Baltimore forces did not regain power until 1657 under Gov. Josias Fendall [*q.v.*]. Stone was a member of his Council. He died at his estate in Charles County.

[Raphael Semmes Colls. in possession of Md. Hist. Soc., Baltimore; *Archives of Maryland*, vols. I, III (1883, 1885); *Narratives of Early Maryland* (1910), ed. by C. C. Hall; J. H. Latane, "The Early Relations of Maryland and Virginia," *Johns Hopkins Univ. Studies in Hist. and Pol. Sci.*, 13 ser., vols. III, IV (1895); J. T. Scharf, *Hist. of Md.* (1879), vol. II; J. L. Bozman, *The Hist. of Md.* (1837), vol. II.]   M. E. F.

STONE, WILLIAM JOEL (May 7, 1848–Apr. 14, 1918), representative in Congress, governor of Missouri, United States senator, was born in Madison County, Ky. His father, William Stone, was a Virginian by birth, and his mother, Mildred Phelps, a Kentuckian. The boy worked on his father's farm and attended a rural school until he was fifteen years of age, then went to stay with a married sister at Columbia, Mo., where he attended the state university for three years and in 1867 entered the law office of his brother-in-law, Squire Turner.

He was admitted to the bar in 1869, and two years later settled at Nevada, Vernon County, Mo. From 1872 to 1874 he was prosecuting attorney of Vernon County. In 1884 he was elected to the lower house of Congress on the Democratic ticket, and served three terms. Going to Washington as a moderate reformer, he opposed corruption in big business and was instrumental in exposing several fraudulent railroad claims to lands in the Northwest. In 1892 he was elected governor of Missouri. Problems connected with the panic of 1893 absorbed the greater part of his attention as governor. He successfully managed the financial difficulties of the state and when strikes and other industrial disturbances occurred he was able to handle the situation without resort to military force. Upon retiring from the governorship in 1897 he practised law in St. Louis, but kept a dominant influence in political affairs, and in 1903 was chosen to succeed George G. Vest in the United States Senate. Now far more conservative, he served here continuously until his death.

Few equaled and probably none excelled Stone as a practical politician. When the state was rocked (1902–03) by the "boodling" exposures of Joseph W. Folk [*q.v.*], the name "Gum-Shoe Bill" was awarded to Stone by foes, and even accepted by friends, for his adroitness in avoiding charges of political corruption. Besides all but holding the state Democratic party in the hollow of his hand for twenty-five years, he was prominent in the national councils of the party, being a member of the National Committee from 1896 to 1904, and its vice-chairman during the last four years of that period. He was an ardent admirer and a follower of the principles of William Jennings Bryan.

In the United States Senate, Stone, as a faithful partisan, voted for the railroad rate regulation laws of 1906, filibustered against the Aldrich-Vreeland currency bill in 1908, and opposed the Payne-Aldrich tariff bill in 1909. During Wilson's administration he became the ranking member of the Finance Committee, and in the critical year of 1914 succeeded to the chairmanship of the important committee on Foreign

Relations. In this position he successfully steered to ratification the Bryan peace and arbitration treaties. He received a storm of criticism early in 1917 as one of the "little group of willful men" who blocked President Wilson's Armed Ship Bill (*New York Times,* Mar. 5, 1917).

In the crisis of March-April 1917 Senator James A. Reed warned Stone: "It is the decree of fate, war will be declared. A vote against it will mean your political ruin. You are old and you have no property." Stone, with deep feeling, replied: "I know what it means to me. I know this war is coming. I know the people are aflame with . . . battle. . . . But would you have me consider my personal welfare in a case that involves the lives of millions of men . . . ? I cannot vote to send our boys into this conflict" (*Memorial Addresses, post,* p. 74). Nevertheless, as the war went on he gave wholeheartedly his thought and energy to the success of the American forces. He became deeply depressed by the reverses of the Allies early in 1918, and this emotional strain no doubt hastened his end.

Stone was looked upon as being a man's man, and a good mixer. Although he was an able and successful lawyer, he failed to accumulate wealth. He was not a church member, but he stood high in several fraternal orders. On Apr. 2, 1874, he married Sarah Louise Winston, by whom he had three children.

[*The Messages and Proclamations of the Govs. of . . . Mo.,* vol. VIII (1926); *Hist. of Vernon County, Mo.* (1911), vol. II; A. J. D. Stewart, *The Hist. of the Bench and Bar of Mo.* (1898); H. L. Conard, *Encyc. of the Hist. of Mo.* (1901), vol. VI; *William Joel Stone: Memorial Addresses Delivered in the Senate* (1919); *Who's Who in America,* 1916–17; *Biog. Dir. Am. Cong.* (1928); Lincoln Steffens, "Enemies of the Republic," *McClure's Mag.,* Apr. 1904; "The Bourbon Democrat Who Holds the Senate Reins on Foreign Affairs," *Current Opinion,* Feb. 1916; "Mr. Stone Hears from the Country," *Lit. Digest,* Mar. 24, 1917; *Washington Post* and *St. Louis Globe-Democrat,* Apr. 15, 1918.]

H. E. N.

STONE, WILLIAM LEETE (Apr. 20, 1792–Aug. 15, 1844), journalist and historian, was a descendant of John Stone and of William Leete [*q.v.*], both among the first settlers of Guilford, Conn. The second of eleven children of Rev. William Stone, a Yale Congregationalist who served three years in the Revolution "with a Hebrew Bible and the whole works of Josephus in his knapsack" (W. L. Stone, Jr., "Life," *post,* p. 10), and of Tamson (Graves) Stone, he was born at New Paltz, N. Y. His father retired to a farm on the upper Susquehanna and young Stone grew up in a frontier atmosphere, but he had a good training in Latin, Greek, and Puritan theology from his strong-willed parent. This frontier-classical schooling was apparently all the formal education he secured. In 1809 he walked forty miles in a single night to offer himself as apprentice to the editor of the *Cooperstown Federalist;* he was accepted and remained for three years. In 1813 he purchased the Federalist *Herkimer American,* having for his journeyman Thurlow Weed [*q.v.*]. In 1814 Stone sold this paper and bought the *Northern Whig* at Hudson. By his marriage, Jan. 31, 1817, to Susannah Pritchard Wayland, daughter of Rev. Francis Wayland of Saratoga Springs and sister of Francis Wayland [*q.v.*], later president of Brown University, he acquired a literary adviser, and while at Hudson he edited two literary periodicals, the *Lounger* and the *Spirit of the Forum.* In 1816 he purchased the *Albany Daily Advertiser,* which was merged with the *Albany Gazette;* two years later his business failed and he became editor of the *Mirror,* Hartford, Conn., a journal formerly "vigilant and spicy" in its defense of Federalism, but under Stone's editorship harmlessly literary. Here he formed a literary club which edited a weekly magazine, *The Knights of the Round Table.*

His influence as an editor increased after 1821, when he became one of the proprietors of the *New York Commercial Advertiser.* He was one of the first to champion the cause of Greek independence; though a Federalist, he was a personal friend of DeWitt Clinton [*q.v.*] and zealously fought for the Erie Canal, writing on request *Narrative of the Festivities Observed in Honor of the Completion of the Grand Erie Canal* (1825); and as a "high Mason" he stepped forth as a mediator in the Anti-Masonic outburst following the disappearance of William Morgan [*q.v.*], writing *Letters on Masonry and Anti-Masonry* (1832), which evidently aimed at (but failed to obtain) wide circulation because of a strict impartiality designed to conciliate both sides. He ridiculed Frances Wright [*q.v.*] and women's rights, spoke sarcastically of extension of the suffrage, and advocated emancipation of slaves by Congress. An unwavering Federalist editor, he frankly admitted in 1829 that he had reached the top of his profession. He was director of the Institution for the Deaf and Dumb, for some time a school commissioner, and in 1843–44 superintendent of the common schools of New York City.

Throughout his life he was interested in the early history of his region. In *Tales and Sketches* (2 vols., 1834) he published an account of his own pioneer experiences and of Revolutionary traditions; "Uncle Tim and Deacon Pettibone" and "Dick Moon, the Peddlar," both of which appeared in *The Atlantic Club-Book* (2 vols.,

1834), were rather stereotyped reporting of New England rusticity and asceticism; "The Mysterious Bridal," in *Tales and Sketches,* reprinted in *The Mysterious Bridal and Other Tales* (3 vols., 1835), portrays a typical colonial New England Thanksgiving with such success that Chancellor Kent thought it deserved a place beside *Bracebridge Hall.* Another New England sketch, "Mercy Disborough; a Tale of the Witches" (in *Tales and Sketches*), deals with legends of the regicides, wherein Stone's ancestor, Governor Leete of Connecticut, appears to good advantage. In 1833 appeared *Matthias and His Impostures,* an account of remarkable deceptions occurring in New York, and in 1836, *Maria Monk and the Nunnery of the Hôtel Dieu,* after Stone had gone to Montreal to investigate charges made by a "silly and profligate woman." A social satire, *Ups and Downs in the Life of a Distressed Gentleman* (1836), and *Letter to Dr. A. Brigham, on Animal Magnetism* (1837) came next. Meanwhile, gathering great stores of manuscripts and books, Stone set out to write a history of the Iroquois, beginning with *Life of Joseph Brant—Thayendanegea* (1838). This was followed by *Life and Times of Red Jacket* (1841). Seven chapters of the life of Sir William Johnson had been completed at the time of the author's death; the work was finished by his son, William L. Stone, Jr. [*q.v.*]. Three volumes, *The Poetry and History of Wyoming* (1841), *Uncas and Miantonomoh* (1842), and *Border Wars of the American Revolution* (1843), were by-products of his chief interest. A result of still greater value was the creation in 1838 of the New York State Historical Agency for the transcribing of the documents in European archives later published by J. R. Brodhead [*q.v.*]. Stone's most lasting contribution was in awakening an interest in the state archives, though in his own day his greatest influence was exerted in the field of journalism. Stone had only the one son, but adopted his sister's son, William Henry, who changed his name to William Henry Stone.

[Stone's great mass of MSS. and books was scattered, a part going to the Fort Ticonderoga Museum. The best biographical sketch is that by his son, "Life and Writings of Col. William Leete Stone," in *The Life and Times of Sa-go-ye-wat-ha, or Red Jacket* (ed. of 1866), pp. 9–101. See also W. L. Stone, Jr., *The Family of John Stone* (1888); F. B. Dexter, *Biog. Sketches Grads. Yale Univ.,* vol. IV (1917), for sketch of the Rev. William Stone; journal of a trip from New York to Niagara, *Buffalo Hist. Soc. Pubs.,* vol. XIV (1910); J. D. Hammond, *The Hist. of Political Parties in the State of N. Y.* (1842), I, 452–53; *Autobiog. of Thurlow Weed* (1884), ed. by Harriet A. Weed; *Correspondence of James Fenimore Cooper* (2 vols., 1932); *N. Y. Tribune,* Aug. 17, 1844. Laughton Osborn, *The Vision of Rubeta* (1838), satirizing in verse Stone's exposé of the charges of Maria Monk, is an intelligent and valuable commentary and, portraying Stone as domineering and opinionated, provides a good corrective for the life by W. L. Stone, Jr.]   J.P.B.

STONE, WILLIAM LEETE (Apr. 4, 1835–June 11, 1908), journalist, historian, was the only child of William Leete Stone [*q.v.*], the well-known historian, and Susannah Pritchard (Wayland). He was born in New York City and received his early education there and in Saratoga Springs, his mother's home, to which she returned in 1844 after his father's death. Under his uncle, President Francis Wayland [*q.v.*], he entered Brown University in 1853 and received his degree five years later, John Hay being a classmate with whom he carried on a correspondence for years. The year 1856 he spent in Germany learning the language for the purpose of translating memoirs of German participants in the American Revolution. He took a course at the Albany Law School, was admitted to the bar, and practised his profession in 1860–63 at Saratoga Springs.

Literary work proved to be more inviting than the law, however, and he accepted the city editorship of the *New York Journal of Commerce,* 1864–67. As his father's literary executor, he completed in 1865 *The Life and Times of Sir William Johnson* for which his father had written the first seven chapters. The next year he wrote a guidebook, *Saratoga Springs,* and "Life and Writings of Col. William Leete Stone" in a reprint of his father's *Life . . . of Red Jacket.* In 1867 appeared his translation, *Letters and Journals Relating to the War of the American Revolution,* from the papers of the wife of General Riedesel, followed by *Memoirs and Letters and Journals of Major General Riedesel* (2 vols., 1868), and much later by *Journal of Capt. Pausch* (1886) and *Letters of Brunswick and Hessian Officers during the American Revolution* (1891). Meanwhile his printing shop in New York had succumbed to the panic of 1872 and the *College Review,* 1870–74, of which he was editor and proprietor, had proved to be unprofitable. He therefore obtained (1872) a position in the Customs House in New York which he held for many years. With an assured income, he devoted himself to historical projects. As one of the incorporators and secretary of the Saratoga Monument Association in 1871 he worked indefatigably. When the corner stone of the monument was laid on Oct. 17, 1877, he delivered an address and subsequently wrote *History of the Saratoga Monument Association* (pamphlet, 1879). During the Centennial of 1876, he was appointed historian for New York State. His interest in the Revolution resulted in the publication—in addition to the translations previously mentioned—

of *The Campaign of Lieutenant General John Burgoyne* (1877); *Memoir of the Centennial Celebration of Burgoyne's Surrender at Schuylerville* (1878); *The Orderly Book of Sir John Johnson* (1882); *Ballads and Poems Relating to the Burgoyne Campaign* (1893); and *Visits to the Saratoga Battle-Grounds 1780–1880* (1895). He found time also to write a *History of New York City* (1868); *Reminiscences of Saratoga and Ballston* (1875); the third supplement (1881) to Dowling's *History of Romanism*; a genealogy, *The Family of John Stone* (1888); *The Starin Family in America* (1892); several chapters in J. G. Wilson's *The Memorial History of the City of New York* (4 vols., 1891–93); and *Washington County, New York* (1901). He wrote articles for newspapers, historical journals, and genealogical and biographical encyclopedias, and left unfinished a history of the Six Nations and a life of George Clinton.

Although an editor and compiler rather than a creative historian, Stone won a creditable place among American literary men. Mayor Strong designated him one of a committee which supervised the publication of the *Records of New Amsterdam* (7 vols., 1897). He was an original trustee of the New York State Historical Association. Shortly before his death Governor Higgins appointed him a member of the commission for the Hudson-Fulton celebration in 1909. He was interested in reforms, education, sports, and public affairs, but was not ambitious for public honors. With a genial disposition and a ready wit, he was a welcome guest in a wide circle. He married, June 1, 1859, Harriet Douglas Gillette of Cleveland, Ohio, and they had six children, two of whom died in infancy. During the latter part of his life he lived at Jersey City Heights, N. J., and Mount Vernon, N. Y.

[A short autobiography to 1888 is included in *The Family of John Stone*, published that year. See also *Proc. N. Y. State Hist. Asso.*, vol. VIII (1909); *Publisher's Weekly*, June 20, 1908; *N. Y. Times*, June 12, 1908. Most of Stone's papers are in the possession of his wife at Mount Vernon, N. Y. His Brown University papers and correspondence with John Hay are at Providence, R. I. His historical library is in the Fort Ticonderoga Museum.]   A. C. F.

STONE, WILLIAM OLIVER (Sept. 26, 1830–Sept. 15, 1875), portrait painter, was born at Derby, Conn., the youngest of three children of Frederick William and Ellen (Stone) Stone. He was a descendant of William Stone who emigrated from England in the company of William Leete [q.v.] and settled in Guilford, Conn., in 1639. His grandfather, Leman Stone, was an important citizen of Derby, whose mansion house, the "Castle," in what is now East Derby,

near the confluence of the Housatonic and Naugatuck rivers, served both as residence and warehouse, the dock at the waterside enabling vessels from the West Indies to discharge their cargoes and store them in this building. William Oliver presumably received his early education in the Derby public schools. He became a pupil of Nathaniel Jocelyn [q.v.] of New Haven in the late forties, went to New York in 1854, and soon became a popular and successful portraitist. In 1859 he became an Academician and exhibited regularly at the National Academy of Design from then until the time of his death. Occasionally he sent portraits to the Royal Academy exhibitions in London, where they were well hung. Though his most successful portraits were those of women and children, "rich in color and graceful in treatment" (H. T. Tuckerman, *Book of Artists*, 1867, p. 399), he was always desirous of painting portraits of men and "expected to produce some notable masterpieces in this respect," an ambition that was fairly fulfilled. His best portrait of a man was generally considered to be that of the editor of the *New York Herald*, James Gordon Bennett, while one of his most charming portraits of women was that of Mrs. Hoey. His portrait of Miss Rawle has been shown at the Metropolitan Museum, New York. The New York Historical Society owns his portrait of Thomas Jefferson Bryan; the Union Club, New York, that of Howell L. Williams, and the National Academy of Design that of John Whetton Ehninger. Among his other subjects were Cyrus West Field, the Rev. Henry Anthon, William Wilson Corcoran, the founder of the Corcoran Gallery in Washington, Bishop Abram Newkirk Littlejohn of Long Island, and Bishop William Ingraham Kip of California. Though he was a prolific painter and in one year sent nine pictures to the Academy, his workmanship was of a distinctly superior order. In certain examples it reminds one not a little of the rugged style and admirable modeling of some of Sir Henry Raeburn's heads. Considering his popularity and the number of his works, it is surprising that he is among the least known of the portrait painters of his day. He died in Newport, R. I., at the age of forty-five. He was married early, before leaving his native place, and had one daughter, Louise, who married a man named Ingalls and lived with her father.

[W. L. Stone, *The Family of John Stone* (1888); Samuel Orcutt and Ambrose Beardsley, *The Hist. of the Old Town of Derby, Conn.* (1880); H. W. French, *Art and Artists in Conn.* (1879); *Boston Transcript*, Aug. 11, 1926; *Art Journal*, Nov. 1875; obituaries in *N. Y. Tribune*, Sept. 17, and *Derby Transcript*, Sept. 24, 1875; information from Emma E. Lassey, Derby Pub. Lib.]   W. H. D.

STONEMAN, GEORGE (Aug. 8, 1822–Sept. 5, 1894), soldier, governor of California, was born at Busti, Chautauqua County, N. Y., the eldest of ten children of George and Catherine (Cheney) Stoneman. He was a descendant of Richard Stoneman, who came to New Berlin, N. Y., after the Revolution. He received his preparatory education at an academy in the neighboring village of Jamestown and was appointed a cadet at the United States Military Academy where he was graduated in 1846. He was commissioned brevet second lieutenant in the 1st Dragoons (now the 1st Cavalry) and was detailed as quartermaster of the "Mormon Battalion," a volunteer unit which formed part of General Kearny's expedition to California. He served in the Southwest until 1855, having risen to the rank of captain in the newly organized 2nd (now 5th) Cavalry. At the opening of the Civil War he was in command at Fort Brown, Tex. Refusing to surrender to Gen. D. E. Twiggs, his immediate superior, who had cast in his lot with the Confederacy, he escaped with part of his command, and was assigned to temporary duty at the cavalry school at Carlisle, Pa. On May 9, 1861, he was promoted major in the 1st (now 4th) Cavalry, and later in the month was in command of the advance across the Long Bridge from Washington to Alexandria. He then served in West Virginia on the staff of General McClellan, who, when he took command of the armies, made him chief of cavalry of the Army of the Potomac with the rank of brigadier-general of volunteers. After the Peninsular campaign of 1862 he was assigned to command the 1st Division, III Corps, and in November of the same year took command of the corps as major-general of volunteers, serving with it through the Fredericksburg campaign. For gallantry in this battle he received the brevet rank of colonel in the regular army.

When Hooker took command of the Army of the Potomac he formed his cavalry into a separate corps of more than 10,000 men and gave the command to Stoneman. At the opening of the Chancellorsville campaign he sent him with most of this force to make a great raid toward Richmond and to operate against Lee's rear. This operation continued from Apr. 13 to May 2 and caused great alarm in Richmond; but since the main army was unsuccessful at Chancellorsville it had no influence upon the course of the campaign. In July 1863 Stoneman became chief of the Cavalry Bureau in Washington, but the next winter he joined the western armies, commanding the XXIII Corps. He was promoted lieutenant-colonel of the 3rd Cavalry in the regular army on Mar. 30, 1864. In April he was assigned to the cavalry corps of the Army of the Ohio, and with this command took part in the Atlanta campaign. Sherman sent him with his corps to break the railway at Jonesboro near Atlanta, and at Stoneman's request these orders were broadened to include also a raid by part of his force to release the prisoners of war at Macon and Andersonville. Early in August he was cut off at Clinton, Ga. He held the attention of the enemy, with one brigade, and was finally forced to surrender, but the rest cut their way back to the army with heavy loss. He remained a prisoner of war until he was exchanged and returned to duty in October. In December he made another raid, with considerable success, into southwestern Virginia, later operating in east Tennessee and the Carolinas in cooperation with Sherman. He received the brevet ranks of brigadier-general and major-general in the regular army in March 1865, and commanded in Petersburg and Richmond for the next four years. He became colonel of the 21st Infantry upon muster out of the volunteer service, joined that regiment in Arizona, and commanded it and the Department of Arizona until his retirement for disability in August 1871.

He then established himself near Los Angeles on his magnificent estate, "Los Robles" (see Archduke Ludwig Salvator, *Eine Blume aus dem Goldenen Lande*, 1878, pp. 214, 215). In 1883 he resigned his commission in the army to accept the Democratic nomination for governor of California. He was elected by a large majority and served until 1887. As a railway commissioner from 1879, he had opposed the increasing power of the Pacific railways in state affairs and in business, and had gained a strong popular following. He continued the same policies as governor, particularly in regard to railway taxation matters. He also favored legislation encouraging irrigation projects. These policies, involving highly controversial issues, made his administration a stormy one; the legislature was twice in extra session, and generally in deadlock over his recommendations. In 1891, by special act of Congress, he was restored to the army list as colonel, retired. At the end of the war he had married Mary Oliver Hardisty, of Baltimore, Md. She, with their four children, survived him when he died in Buffalo, N. Y. He was buried with military honors at Lakewood, on Chautauqua Lake, N. Y.

[Information from the family; G. E. Cullum, *Biog. Reg. . . . U. S. Mil. Acad.* (1891); D. N. Couch, obituary article, *Ann. Reunion, Asso. Grads., U. S. Mil. Acad., 1895* (1895); J. H. McClintock, *Arizona* (1916), vol. III; William Bushong, *The Last Great Stoneman*

Raid (1910); T. H. Hittell, *Hist. of Cal.*, vol. IV (1897); *Buffalo Courier*, Sept. 6, 1894.] O. L. S., Jr.

STORER, BELLAMY (Aug. 28, 1847–Nov. 12, 1922), congressman from Ohio, diplomat, was born at Cincinnati, Ohio, the son of Bellamy and Elizabeth (Drinker) Storer, and the descendant of William Storie, who with his father Augustine Storr, emigrated from England about 1636 and died in Dover, Me. Bellamy was the nephew of David Humphreys Storer and the cousin of Francis Humphreys Storer and Horatio Robinson Storer [*qq.v.*]. He was educated in the common schools of Cincinnati, in a private school at Boston, and in Harvard College, where he received the A.B. degree in 1867. In 1869 he graduated from the law school of Cincinnati College, commenced practising law in his native city, and was appointed assistant attorney for the southern federal district of Ohio, 1869–70. With Charles P. Taft [*q.v.*] he edited the first volume of the *Cincinnati Superior Court Reporter* (1872). His standing in Cincinnati was enhanced by his marriage on Mar. 20, 1886, with Maria (Longworth) Nichols, the widow of George Ward Nichols [*q.v.*] and aunt of Nicholas Longworth, 1869–1931 [*q.v.*]. A lifelong Republican, he was elected to the Fifty-second and Fifty-third congresses, Mar. 4, 1891–Mar. 3, 1895, serving on the committee on interstate and foreign commerce during both congresses and on the foreign affairs committee in the Fifty-third Congress. He took very little part in congressional debates and his only considerable utterance regarding foreign affairs was an attack upon the administration's policy in Hawaii (*Congressional Record*, 53 Cong., 2 Sess., pp. 1948–52).

An admirer of William McKinley, he helped both in the gubernatorial campaign in Ohio and later in the presidential campaign of 1896. His reward, an appointment on May 4, 1897, as minister to Belgium, seems to have been disappointing (*Selections from the Correspondence of Theodore Roosevelt and Henry Cabot Lodge*, 1925, I, p. 254), but in view of the fact that both he and his wife were Roman Catholics, the appointment was a logical one. He had been received into the Roman Catholic Church on Oct. 4, 1896. After two years of quiet usefulness at Brussels he was appointed on Apr. 12, 1899, to be minister to Spain. There he successfully handled such post-war problems as the return to Spain of Spanish prisoners of the Filipinos and the release of Cuban political prisoners in Spain. On Sept. 26, 1902, he was appointed by Theodore Roosevelt, a friend of himself and his wife, to be ambassador to Austria-Hungary. According to the Austrian foreign minister Storer became *"persona gratissima"* at the Austrian Court and the Emperor "spoke of him in terms of the highest consideration and personal esteem" (American chargé d'affaires *ad interim* at Vienna to the secretary of state, Mar. 22, 1906, Dispatches from Austria in the department of state). It was therefore a matter of some regret at Vienna when Storer was summarily removed from his position on Mar. 19, 1906. From Storer's *Letter . . . to the President and the Members of his Cabinet, November, 1906* (1906) it appears that the President, who had asked Storer to urge upon the Pope the claims of Archbishop Ireland to a cardinalate, had come to fear the political consequences of having his name involved in church controversies and had therefore rebuked both the Ambassador and Mrs. Storer for undue activity in ecclesiastical matters. The Storers failed to respond to the President's letter; the Ambassador's resignation was requested, and he was removed before his resignation had had sufficient time to reach Washington.

Storer returned to his practice in Cincinnati. During the World War he aided the Belgian relief work in Cincinnati, and during the winter of 1914 to 1915, which he spent at Rome, he organized a bureau of inquiry to handle the large correspondence addressed to the Pope regarding missing soldiers. The work of the bureau was continued at his expense until the end of the war. He died at Paris and was buried at Marvejols, France.

[M. L. Storer, *In Memoriam Bellamy Storer* (1923); *Who's Who in America*, 1922–23; *Harvard College Class of 1867. Secretary's Report*, no. 3 (1870), no. 8 (1887), no. 10 (1897); Malcolm Storer, *Annals of the Storer Family* (1927); *Papers Relating to the Foreign Affairs of the U. S.*, 1897–1906; some unprinted material in the department of state.] E. W. S.

STORER, DAVID HUMPHREYS (Mar. 26, 1804–Sept. 10, 1891), obstetrician and naturalist, was born in Portland, Me., the son of Woodbury and Margaret (Boyd) Storer. His father, a descendant of Augustine Storr, who emigrated from England to Boston in 1636, was chief justice of common pleas at Portland. After his graduation from Bowdoin College in 1822 and from the Harvard Medical School in 1825, he was apprenticed, as was the custom of the time, to the leading surgeon of Boston, John Collins Warren, 1776–1856 [*q.v.*]. In practice, he soon began to confine his work to obstetrics, and in this branch of medicine he became eminent both as a practitioner and as a teacher. Dissatisfied with the four months' winter term offered at the Harvard Medical School in 1839, Storer, Oliver Wendell Holmes [*q.v.*], and Edward Reynolds, under the leadership of Jacob

Bigelow, started the Tremont Street Medical School, Boston, which held courses throughout the year and flourished until the Harvard school was reorganized. At that time (1854) Storer became professor of obstetrics and medical jurisprudence, and carried on the work of his predecessor, Walter Channing [q.v.]. He served the school until 1868, acting as dean from 1854 to 1864. Popular as a teacher, he was much beloved as the dean. He did much to advance obstetrics in the United States, especially in relation to the work of the American Medical Association. His sound views on medical jurisprudence were clearly outlined in his discourse, *An Address on Medical Jurisprudence: Its Claims to Greater Regard from the Student and the Physician* (1851), before the Massachusetts Medical Society. He was, moreover, a lover of books, and it was through his efforts that over 10,000 volumes of medical works were collected for the Boston Public Library and later added to the Boston Medical Library after its founding in 1875.

It is as a naturalist and collector, however, that Storer is best remembered. He began collecting coins at an early age and is said to have made a bargain with all the toll gatherers of the Boston bridges and the keepers of sailors' boarding-houses in his efforts to obtain odd coins, shells, and rare fishes. He joined the Boston Society of Natural History in early manhood, immediately after it was founded in 1830, and contributed many papers to its proceedings. He collected and described the *Mollusca* of Massachusetts, and issued in 1837 a translation of L. C. Kiener's work on shells, *General Species and Iconography of Recent Shells, Comprising the Massena Museum, the Collection of Lamarck, the Collection of the Museum of Natural History, and the Recent Discoveries of Travelers*. His collection is now at Bowdoin College. When appointed on a committee for the natural history survey of Massachusetts, he reported on fishes and reptiles in *Ichthyology and Herpetology of Massachusetts* (1839), a work he later expanded as *A History of Fishes in Massachusetts* (1867), a "land-mark in the ichthyological literature of the country" (Scudder, *post*, p. 391). His *A Synopsis of the Fishes of North America* (1846), hurriedly written, is of less value. A conservative, faithful worker, he often spent the hours from five to breakfast-time in the museum of the Natural History Society, attended to a large obstetrical practice during the day, lectured at the Harvard Medical School, and sought the fish-wharves for strange specimens. For thirty-five years he is said never to have missed being at his desk, as medical examiner for an insurance company, when the clock struck noon. For many years he served on the staff of the Massachusetts General Hospital (1849–58) and the Lying-in Hospital (1854–68); he also acted as secretary to the Massachusetts Medical Society, founded the Obstetrical Society of Boston, and was a member of numerous scientific bodies. On Apr. 29, 1829, he married Abby Jane Brewer, sister of Thomas Mayo Brewer [q.v.]. Of their five children, Horatio Robinson Storer and Francis Humphreys Storer [qq.v.] became scientists of note. Storer's open, brilliant countenance and friendly eye have been finely shown in Frederick Porter Vinton's portrait in the Boston Medical Library.

[Malcolm Storer, *Annals of the Storer Family* (1927); H. A. Kelly and W. L. Burrage, *Am. Medic. Biogs.* (1920); G. C. Shattuck, O. W. Holmes, and others, in *Boston Medic. and Surgical Jour.*, Mar. 24, 1892; *Trans. Am. Gynecological Soc.*, vol. XVI (1891); *Jour. Am. Medic. Assoc.*, Oct. 3, 1891; T. F. Harrington, *The Harvard Medic. School* (1905), vol. II; S. H. Scudder, in *Proc. Am. Acad. Arts and Sci.*, vol. XXVII (1893); J. C. White, in *Proc. Boston Soc. Nat. Hist.*, vol. XXV (1892); "List of Pub. Writings of David Humphreys Storer," in Bowdoin Coll. Lib., *Bibliog. Contributions*, no. 2, Aug. 1892; obituaries in *Boston Transcript* and *Boston Herald*, Sept. 11, 1891.]

H. R. V.

STORER, FRANCIS HUMPHREYS (Mar. 27, 1832–July 30, 1914), chemist, was born at Boston, Mass., the second son of David Humphreys Storer [q.v.] and Abby Jane (Brewer) Storer. He was a brother of Horatio Robinson Storer and a first cousin of Bellamy Storer [qq.v]. He received his early education in the schools of Boston, and in 1850 entered the Lawrence Scientific School of Harvard University. His zeal and proficiency in chemistry attracted the attention of Prof. Josiah Parsons Cooke [q.v.], and for two years (1851–53) he was Cooke's assistant, at the same time teaching a private class in chemical analysis at the Harvard Medical School. In 1853 he accepted an appointment as chemist with the United States North Pacific exploring expedition, and visited the principal islands of the Atlantic and Pacific oceans. On his return he completed his chemical course, receiving the degree of B.S. from Harvard in 1855. After two years (1855–57) in Europe, where he studied with Robert W. Bunsen at Heidelberg, Theodor Richter in Freiberg, Julius Stöckhardt in Tharand, and Émile Kopp in Paris, he became chemist of the Boston Gas Light Company, a position which he retained until 1871. He made daily tests of the gas furnished by the company to consumers, conducted miscellaneous scientific researches upon the composition and illuminating power of coal and gas (see *American Journal of Science*, Nov. 1860, p. 420), and in addition (1857–65) maintained a private analytical and consulting laboratory.

With his fellow chemist, Charles William Eliot [*q.v.*], later president of Harvard, he began in 1860 a series of publications upon "The Impurities of Commercial Zinc" (*Memoirs of the American Association of Arts and Sciences*, vol. VIII, pt. 1, 1861) and other chemical subjects. These early chemical contributions, which included important research upon volatile hydrocarbons with Cyrus Moors Warren [*q.v.*], were published in the *Memoirs* and *Proceedings of the American Academy of Arts and Sciences*, in Silliman's *American Journal of Science* (for which Storer also wrote many abstracts and reviews upon technical chemistry) and in the *Répertoire de Chimie Pure et Appliquée*, of which he was American editor for a number of years. His interest in the field of pure chemistry during this period is exemplified by the publication of his first book, *First Outlines of a Dictionary of the Solubilities of Chemical Substances* (1864), a reference work of great value. In 1865 he gave up his consulting practice to accept the professorship of general and industrial chemistry at the newly organized Massachusetts Institute of Technology, where Eliot was professor of analytical chemistry and metallurgy. Having no books suitable for their work of instruction, Eliot and Storer together published *A Manual of Inorganic Chemistry* (1867) and *The Compendious Manual of Qualitative Chemical Analysis* (1868), both of which were extensively used for a long period. In 1867 Storer spent several months abroad in order to study the chemical exhibits at the Paris exposition and to investigate European processes of chemical industry.

The alliance with Eliot, which had been more closely cemented by Storer's marriage on June 21, 1871, to Eliot's sister, Catherine Atkins Eliot, continued to be of importance to his career. Among the first acts of Eliot's administration at Harvard was the organization of the Bussey Institution, a school of agriculture and horticulture, in which Storer was appointed professor of agricultural chemistry. In 1871 he became dean of the Institution as well and continued in these two offices until his retirement in 1907. It was during this period that he performed his most important work, chemical research upon soils, fertilizers, forage crops, cereals, fruits, vegetables, wood, and other products, most of the results being published in over fifty contributions to the *Bulletin of the Bussey Institution*, volumes I–III. This journal, founded and edited by Storer, was the forerunner of numerous later publications upon scientific agriculture. His vast knowledge of all phases of agricultural chemistry is best exemplified in the publication of his most important work, *Agriculture in Some of Its Relations with Chemistry* (1887), the two volumes of which were subsequently enlarged to three. This work, which ran through seven editions, "rendered special service because of its timeliness, appearing when the vast store of information it contained was very inaccessible" (*Experiment Station Record*, Nov. 1914, p. 698). His other publications include *A Cyclopaedia of Quantitative Chemical Analysis* (2 vols., 1870–73), *Elementary Manual of Chemistry* (1894), and *Manual of Qualitative Analysis* (1899), both of the latter with W. B. Lindsay. After his retirement at the age of seventy-five, he continued to maintain a deep interest in chemical instruction and research, though he no longer had a productive part in them. The genial nature of his personality and his friendly appreciation of the work of other contemporary American agricultural chemists, such as Samuel William Johnson and Eugene Woldemar Hilgard [*qq.v.*], are revealed in his books and letters.

[*Who's Who in America*, 1914–15; Benjamin Silliman, Jr., *Am. Contributions to Chemistry* (1874); *Harvard Grads.' Mag.*, Sept. 1914; L. W. Fetzer, in *Biochemical Bull.*, Mar. 1915, with bibliog.; C. W. Eliot, in *Proc. Am. Acad. Arts and Sciences*, vol. LIV (1919); *Industrial and Engineering Chemistry*, June 1924; *Jour. Chemical Educ.*, Jan. 1925; Storer's unpublished correspondence with H. W. Wiley; obituary in *Boston Transcript*, July 30, 1914.]   C. A. B.

STORER, HORATIO ROBINSON (Feb. 27, 1830–Sept. 18, 1922), gynecologist and medical numismatist, was born in Boston, Mass., the son of David Humphreys Storer [*q.v.*] and Abby Jane (Brewer) Storer, the latter a descendant of Governor Thomas Dudley [*q.v.*] of the Massachusetts Bay Colony. He was a brother of Francis Humphreys Storer and a first cousin of Bellamy Storer [*qq.v.*]. He graduated from Harvard College in 1850, having studied under Jean Louis Rodolphe Agassiz and Asa Gray [*qq.v.*], both close friends of his distinguished father. He went with Jeffries Wyman [*q.v.*] to Labrador in the summer of 1850 and furnished a report on the fishes of that region, *Observations on the Fishes of Nova Scotia and Labrador, with Descriptions of New Species* (1850), for the Boston Society of Natural History. After taking the degree of M.D. in 1853 at the Harvard Medical School, he studied abroad for two years in Paris, London, and Edinburgh. In Edinburgh he served as private assistant to Sir James Y. Simpson, who was then using chloroform as a general anesthetic. On his return to Boston he assisted W. O. Priestley in editing the *Obstetric Memoirs* of James Y. Simpson (2 vols., 1855–56) and introduced the use of chloroform in obstetrics to his father and Walter Channing [q.v.]. Moreover, he soon established a specialty, gynecology, not hitherto recognized as a distinct branch of medicine, and in 1869 was one of the founders of the *Journal of the Gynecological Society of Boston*, the first publication devoted exclusively to diseases of women. In 1865 he was appointed professor of obstetrics and medical jurisprudence in the Berkshire Medical College at Pittsfield, Mass., where he taught until the school closed two years later. He also attended the Harvard Law School, from which he obtained the degree of LL.B. in 1868, in order to equip himself with legal knowledge that would aid him in his crusade against criminal abortions, begun as early as 1857. In connection with this he published numerous papers and books. Among these were *Criminal Abortion in America* (1860), the best of them; *Criminal Abortion* (1868) written with F. F. Heard; and others of a more popular nature, such as *Why Not? A Book for Every Woman* (1866) and *Is It I? A Book for Every Man* (1867), which sold into many thousands of copies. Other less important books are *On Nurses and Nursing* (1868), *The Causation, Course and Treatment of Reflex Insanity in Women* (1871), and *Eutokia: A Word to Physicians and to Women upon the Employment of Anaesthetics in Childbirth* (1863). For many years he delivered a popular course of lectures on diseases of women to physicians from a large part of the United States. He also lectured in California in 1871. He was visiting physician to the Boston Lying-in Hospital and a founder of the Boston Gynecological Society.

In 1872, after an infection received in the course of an operation, from the effects of which he never fully recovered, he retired from practice. He spent five years in Italy, where he wrote *Southern Italy as a Health Station for Invalids* (1875), and then returned to live in Newport, R. I., until his death at the age of ninety-two. During this time he became the world authority on medical medals and devoted himself to adding to his collection, over three thousand in number, which he later gave to the Boston Medical Library. The catalogue of the Storer collection and all other known medals of medical interest, written by Storer and edited by his son, was published after his death as *Medicina in Nummis* (1931). On July 12, 1853, he married Emily Elvira Gilmore (d. 1872), by whom he had a daughter and three sons. On Sept. 20, 1872, he married her sister, Augusta Caroline Gilmore, who died two years later in Italy, leaving a

daughter. His third wife was Frances S. Mackenzie, a nurse and founder of the Saint Elizabeth's Hospital in Boston, whom he married on Sept. 15, 1876. It was after this marriage that Storer became an ardent Roman Catholic. Of his three sons, one became a physician in Boston. A plaque by R. Tait McKenzie (1913) is an excellent likeness of Storer.

[*Who's Who in America*, 1922–23; Malcolm Storer, *Annals of the Storer Family* (1927), art. in *Harvard Grads.' Mag.*, Mar. 1923, and note in *Medicina in Nummis* (1931); J. M. Toner, *A Sketch of the Life of Horatio R. Storer* (1878), with bibliog.; *Boston Medic. and Surgical Jour.*, Oct. 5, 1922, and Jan. 25, 1923; obituaries in *Boston Herald* and *Boston Transcript*, Sept. 19, 1922.]   H. R. V.

STOREY, MOORFIELD (Mar. 19, 1845– Oct. 24, 1929), lawyer, author, publicist, was born in Roxbury, Mass., the son of Charles William and Elizabeth (Moorfield) Storey. Both his parents were of colonial stock, his earliest paternal ancestor having come to Ipswich about 1635. About 1800 the spelling of the name was changed to agree with the spelling of an English branch of the family with which relationship was assumed. Storey attended the Boston Latin School and Harvard College, receiving the degree of A.B. from the latter institution in 1866, and proceeding to its law school. In October 1867, however, he was offered the position of clerk to the United States Senate committee on foreign relations, in effect the office of secretary to its chairman, Charles Sumner [q.v.], and, as the duties of this post were considered technically equivalent and superior as training to the methods usual at that time of preparing for the practice of law, he accepted it. As a result he was closely connected in an official capacity with the attempt to impeach President Andrew Johnson [q.v.]. In May 1869 he left Washington to study law in the office of Brooks and Ball in Boston, also securing an appointment as clerk in the office of the district attorney of Suffolk County. He qualified as a member of the bar on Aug. 28, 1869, and in October, when the position of assistant district attorney fell vacant, he was promoted to that office. From June 1871 until October 1873 he practised law with his father; he then returned to the office of Brooks and Ball as a partner. The firm he joined was regarded as the most active one in Boston in the practice of commercial law, and he quickly acquired a reputation that eventually grew to be international in range. Firms with which he was associated as a leading member were in the front rank for nearly fifty years. His own branch was the management of litigation, in which he was conspicuously successful, but his office also achieved high repute for the value of its opinions and the thoroughness with which its instruments were drafted. He once stated that he could remember only one instance in which an opinion given by his office as to the validity of bonds was overruled, and that was by a Texas decision that overruled nearly every lawyer in the country and had to be corrected by the legislature.

Though he was eminently successful as a lawyer, in politics he usually met with failure, indifference, or a success that earned him much dislike and suspicion and little in the way of gratitude or popularity. He was a crusader against political corruption, and because he attributed it to them, he attacked Benjamin Franklin Butler and James Gillespie Blaine [qq.v.], even opposing a memorial statute to Butler years after his death, and leading the Mugwumps in their desertion of Blaine for Cleveland in 1884. He was a leader in the Anti-Imperialist League that opposed United States ownership of the Philippines; he espoused the cause of the colored people (*Guinn* vs. *United States, 238 United States Reports,* 347; *Buchanan* vs. *Warley,* 245 *United States Reports,* 60; *Moore* vs. *Dempsey,* 261 *United States Reports,* 86), and defended the rights of the American Indian. He served many years (1877–88, 1892–1910) on the Board of Overseers of Harvard, and successfully opposed the granting of honorary degrees to Governor Butler and President McKinley. In 1900 he dallied with the possibility of running for president or vice-president on the third party ticket, and when that came to nothing, he was a candidate for Congress as an independent, but received only a few votes. He wrote something like eighty pamphlets or articles, and innumerable public letters, in addition to seven books, which include *Charles Sumner* (1900), *Ebenezer Rockwood Hoar* (1911) with E. W. Emerson, *The Reform of Legal Procedure* (1911), *Problems of Today* (1920), and *The Conquest of the Philippines* (1926). With the exception of some that were legal, historical, or biographical, most of his writings were on subjects on which feeling ran high or in which only a minority was interested. But not all his opinions, even when they were severely critical, were neglected or coldly received, for a speech before the American Bar Association in 1894 on the inefficiency and corruption of American legislatures made such a favorable impression that he was elected president of the organization the next year, and he was on the conservative side in the controversy over Nicola Sacco and Bartolomeo Vanzetti [*qq.v.*].

Though he was often called a Puritan, he did not deserve that designation if being a Puritan means, as some say it does, frantic striving to abolish everything the dour cannot trust themselves to indulge in moderately or to practise gracefully, for he lacked neither social nor intellectual accomplishments, and he had a sense of the ridiculous, which the true Puritan never has. He advocated unpopular causes effectively, being a good lawyer, and, though he may have attached more importance to the abstract than to the actual, he was honest and courageous in public affairs. He unquestionably exerted considerable influence on the development of commercial law in America. On Jan. 6, 1870, in Washington, D. C., he married Gertrude Cutts, who died in 1912. There were five children, four of whom, with grandchildren and great-grandchildren, survived him. He died in Lincoln, Mass., and was buried in Mount Auburn Cemetery.

[*Who's Who in America,* 1926–27; M. A. DeWolfe Howe, *Portrait of an Independent, Moorfield Storey, 1845–1929* (1932); J. T. Morse, in *Harvard Grads.' Mag.,* Mar. 1930; J. W. Allen, in *Am. Bar Asso. Jour.,* Feb. 1930; obituary in *Boston Transcript,* Oct. 25, 1929.]
                                              S.G.

STOREY, WILBUR FISK (Dec. 19, 1819–Oct. 27, 1884), newspaper editor, the son of Jesse and Elizabeth (Pierce) Storey, was born on a farm near Salisbury, Vt., where his grandfather, Solomon, a native of Norwich, Conn., had settled during the Revolution. After attending the local schools until he was twelve, Wilbur spent five years in the office of the Middlebury *Free Press* learning the printing trade. Then for a year and a half he was a compositor on the *New York Journal of Commerce,* and in 1838 he migrated to Indiana, where he published two short-lived newspapers, the *Herald* at La Porte, and the *Tocsin* at Mishawaka. Subsequently, after a brief experience as proprietor of a drug store, he moved to Jackson, Mich., where he read law for two years and established a new paper, the *Patriot,* which he sold upon his appointment as postmaster by President Polk. Removed from office by President Taylor, he again became a druggist. He attracted some attention in the Michigan constitutional convention of 1850 and his activities in politics led to his appointment as state prison inspector.

The significant part of his journalistic career began in 1853, when he bought an interest in the *Detroit Free Press* (established in 1831), of which he later became sole owner. He enlarged the paper and on Oct. 2, 1853, began the publication of a Sunday edition to take the place of the Monday issue. Under his direction the *Free Press* came to be regarded as one of the leading

Democratic newspapers in the West. In 1861, from Cyrus H. McCormick [q.v.], he purchased the *Daily Chicago Times* (established in 1854 in the interests of Stephen A. Douglas), bringing with him a large part of the staff of the *Free Press* when he took possession on June 8, 1861. Changing the title to *Chicago Times* (June 20), he continued the paper as a Democratic organ. After the Emancipation Proclamation, he ceased to favor the prosecution of the Civil War and bitterly assailed President Lincoln, with the result that the *Times* came to be regarded as a radical "copperhead" sheet. Finally General Ambrose E. Burnside [q.v.], commander of the Department of the Northwest, ordered its suppression because of its "repeated expression of disloyal and incendiary sentiments" (*War of the Rebellion: Official Records, Army,* 1 ser., XXIII, 381). On June 3, 1863, Union soldiers took possession of the plant; part of the issue of that day was destroyed, and the issue for the following day did not appear at all. This attempt to stifle the *Times* aroused vigorous protests from loyal citizens who regarded its suppression as an unwarranted interference with the freedom of the press. Lincoln promptly revoked Burnside's order, and the *Times* resumed publication on June 5. Its circulation and advertising increased after its brief suspension, and by the close of the Civil War it had become one of the most prosperous of the Chicago daily papers. After 1868 it was independent in politics.

When the great fire of 1871 destroyed the five-story plant erected in 1866, Storey was tempted to retire, but with improvised equipment the *Times* resumed publication on Oct. 18, 1871, and he decided to continue it, providing a new fireproof building which was completed in 1873. In 1877 he demonstrated his characteristic enterprise in gathering news by establishing a news bureau in London to get the latest reports of the progress of the Russo-Turkish War. In 1878 he went abroad, hoping to restore his failing health, but suffered a stroke and had to be brought home. His active career ended in that year, although he lived until 1884, being adjudged of unsound mind during the last year of his life. At the time of his death the *Times* was valued at a million dollars. He was married three times: in 1847 to Maria Isham of Jackson, Mich., whom he later divorced; about 1870 to Mrs. Harriet Dodge, who died in 1873; and on Dec. 2, 1874, to Eureka (Bissell) Pearson, who survived him.

Storey, unlike Greeley, Bowles, and Dana, was not primarily an editorial writer, but rather an executive who directed the news and editorial policies of his paper. In the emphasis which he constantly placed on the importance of news and in the vigor and fearlessness of the *Times's* editorial attacks, he seems to have been influenced by the elder James Gordon Bennett and the *New York Herald*. Like Bennett he kept aloof from his fellow citizens and engendered no little hostility on the part of the men whom his paper denounced.

[Nine-column obituary in *Chicago Times,* Oct. 28, 1884,written apparently by an associate of many years; A. T. Andreas, *Hist. of Chicago* (3 vols., 1884–86; F. W. Scott, "Newspapers and Periodicals of Ill., 1814–79," *Ill. Hist. Colls.,* vol. VI (1910); *The Biog. Encyc. of Ill.* (1875); *Encyc. of Biog. of Ill.,* vol. II (1894); H. P. Smith, *Hist. of Addison County, Vt.* (1886); *Chicago Tribune,* Oct. 28, 1884.]   W. G. B.

STORROW, CHARLES STORER (Mar. 25, 1809–Apr. 30, 1904), engineer, was a son of Thomas Wentworth and Sarah Phipps (Brown) Storrow. His mother was of old New England stock, as was his paternal grandmother, Ann (Appleton), who in 1777 married Capt. Thomas Storrow of the British army, then a prisoner of war. They subsequently lived in England, the West Indies, and Canada, but returned to Boston in 1795, where Thomas Wentworth Storrow became a successful merchant. Charles was born while his parents were temporarily residing in Montreal, Canada, but in his early childhood the family returned to Boston, where he began to go to school. Soon, however, his father removed the family to Paris, France, where the boy attended a private school. He returned to New England, however, to receive his college preparation at the Round Hill School, Northampton, Mass., and graduated from Harvard, first in his class, in 1829. In his senior year he began the study of civil engineering with Loammi Baldwin [q.v.], and some months after his graduation, entered the École Nationale des Ponts et Chaussées in Paris. After two years here he spent some time studying engineering works in France and Great Britain.

Upon his return to Boston in 1832 he became an engineer with the Boston & Lowell Railroad, then just beginning construction. He directed the running of the first train, drawn by the locomotive *Stephenson* from Boston to Lowell and return, May 27, 1835, and upon completion of the road the following year became its manager. In addition to his work in this capacity, he investigated the quantity of water utilized by the Lowell mills, and in 1835 he published a *Treatise on Water-Works*—something of a pioneer in its field. Ten years later he resigned his railroad position to become engineer, treasurer, and agent for the Essex Company at Lawrence, Mass. Showing broad appreciation of the work before him, he planned wisely for the long future. He laid out the city, designing the canals, designating the mill sites, and building several mills. From his own design he built the large masonry dam across the Merrimac River, a pioneer structure which is still in excellent condition and in use after nearly a century has elapsed. In 1853, when Lawrence was incorporated as a city, he was made its first mayor.

Storrow's work at Lawrence brought him into close association with Abbott Lawrence [q.v.], who was president of the Essex Company, and when the latter, in 1847, took steps toward the formation of the Lawrence Scientific School at Harvard, he tried to persuade Storrow to assume charge of the school as professor of engineering. Storrow declined this position, however, not desiring to leave his work at Lawrence. In 1860, though maintaining his connection with the Lawrence enterprise, he established his home in Boston. He served in 1861 as engineer member of the state commission on the drainage of the Sudbury and Concord meadows, and in 1862, as consulting engineer, went to Europe to study tunnels for the Hoosac Tunnel Commission, in his report, dated Nov. 28, 1862, advising the Commission upon plans and methods for the construction of the tunnel. At the age of eighty he retired, resigning his position with the Essex Company. His eminent services to engineering were recognized by his professional brethren in his election (1893) to honorary membership in the American Society of Civil Engineers. He was also a fellow of the American Academy of Arts and Sciences.

On Oct. 3, 1836, Storrow married Lydia Cabot Jackson, daughter of Dr. James Jackson [q.v.] of Boston. They had four daughters and three sons, one of whom was James Jackson Storrow [q.v.]. Storrow died in his ninety-sixth year, at Boston.

[*Proc. Am. Acad. Arts and Sci.*, vol. XL (1905); *Proc. Am. Soc. Civil Engineers*, vol. XXX (1904); *Engineering News*, Feb. 16, 1893, May 5, 1904; John Wentworth, *The Wentworth Geneal.* (1878), I, 513–14; M. B. Dorgan, *Hist. of Lawrence, Mass.* (1924); *Boston Transcript*, May 2, 1904.]   H. K. B.

STORROW, JAMES JACKSON (July 29, 1837–Apr. 15, 1897), lawyer, was born in Boston, Mass., the son of Charles Storer Storrow [q.v.], the engineer who planned and built the industrial city of Lawrence, Mass., and of Lydia Cabot (Jackson), daughter of the Boston physician, Dr. James Jackson [q.v.]. He attended Phillips Academy, Andover, for four years and entered Harvard in the fall of 1853. There he distinguished himself in literary and mathematical studies, was an editor of the *Harvard Maga-*

zine, and at graduation was chosen class orator. Though naturally quiet and studious, all his life he loved the outdoors. At Lawrence, where he lived until 1860, he rowed on the Merrimac; and at Cambridge he was on the Harvard crew. He graduated with the degree of A.B. in 1857, read law in the office of Elias Merwin, and spent a year in the Harvard Law School. He was admitted to the bar in February 1860, and soon made a reputation for ability, notably in the copyright case of 1869, *Lawrence* vs. *Dana et al.* (4 *Clifford,* 1; 15 *Federal Cases,* 26). For many years he had been in and about the shops at Lawrence. There his strong mechanical bent was stimulated which resulted in his devoting himself to patent law as his life work. On Aug. 28, 1861, he married Annie Maria Perry, a granddaughter of Commodore Oliver Hazard Perry [q.v.]. They had two sons and a daughter, all of whom survived him. James Jackson Storrow, Jr. (1864–1926), became a leader in civic and industrial life in Boston and New England. Mrs. Storrow died on Mar. 9, 1865, and on Sept. 12, 1873, he married Anne Amory Dexter of Brookline, who survived him. There were no children by the second marriage.

Beginning in 1878 Storrow was associated with Chauncey Smith [q.v.] as counsel for the Bell Telephone Company and its successors in the great litigation in the federal courts over the validity of the Bell telephone patents, which comprehended some 600 cases and lasted to 1896. Storrow's work in this litigation showed again and again his legal genius. He was masterly in his clear analysis of evidence, in his unerring discrimination of tangled issues, and in his cogent presentation of their merits. He frequently performed extraordinary feats of legal presentation, as in his oral argument before the United States Supreme Court in the Telephone Appeals (126 *U. S.,* 1 *The Telephone Cases*), published in 1887 as a bulky volume: *Supreme Court of the United States, October term, 1886; . . . Oral Argument on the Bell Patents . . . Jan. 24 to Feb. 8, 1887.* Another instance was his disposal of the claims of Antonio Meucci during an oral argument at New Orleans, Feb. 6, 1886; while he was still speaking the opposing attorneys interrupted him to withdraw that line of defense (*American Bell Telephone Company et al.* vs. *National Improved Telephone Company et al.;* 27 *Federal Reporter,* 663). Storrow allowed himself little diversion, even in the family circle, though he had a wide range of general interests. Even on mountain-climbing expeditions he often spent much time in thought. Such unremitting concentration demanded its penalty of him.

In 1895 Storrow took a purely personal interest in the Venezuela boundary question. In June his friend, Richard Olney [q.v.], became secretary of state. Knowing the thoroughness with which Storrow studied any question, Olney suggested to Señor Don José Andrade, the Venezuelan minister at Washington, that Venezuela retain Storrow in addition to its official adviser, William L. Scruggs [q.v.], to represent that goverment before the commission appointed by President Cleveland to determine the true boundary line. Storrow went to Caracas, Venezuela, and saw President Joaquin Crespo and his cabinet, who were so impressed that Secretary Olney's suggestion was forthwith adopted. Storrow's brief for Venezuela was published in the London *Times* on July 21, 1896. This was arranged unofficially by Olney through the able assistance of Henry White and had much to do with the change in attitude of the British government and its consent to submit the controversy to arbitration. Storrow went to Venezuela again in 1897 to submit to President Crespo and the Venezuelan legislature the protocol for an arbitration treaty agreed upon by Señor Andrade and Sir Julian Pauncefote and secured its approval. After his return Storrow went to Washington. On Apr. 15, 1897, while going through the new Library of Congress building, he suffered a heart attack from which he died. His body was brought back to Boston for a funeral in Trinity Church and then taken to Newport, R. I., for burial.

[J. J. Storrow Collection, Am. Telephone Hist. Lib., New York City; C. H. Swan, Narrative History of the Litigation on the Telephone Patents (MS., 1903); *Papers Relating to the Foreign Relations of the U. S.* . . . *1895* (1896), pt. II; Allan Nevins, *Henry White; Thirty Years of Am. Diplomacy* (1930); Henry James, *Richard Olney and His Public Service* (1923); Richard Olney, Address on James J. Storrow, Oct. 30, 1897 (Typed MS. in Lib. of Cong.); *Evening Star* (Washington, D. C.), and *Boston Evening Transcript*, Apr. 16, 1897; O. P. Dexter, *Dexter Genealogy, 1642–1904* (1904), p. 116; E. C. and J. J. Putnam, *The Hon. Jonathan Jackson and Hannah (Tracy) Jackson. Their Ancestors and Descendants* (1907); H. G. Pearson, *Son of New England, James Jackson Storrow, 1864–1926* (1932); information from the family, especially the grandson, James J. Storrow, III.]   W. C. L.

STORRS, RICHARD SALTER (Feb. 6, 1787–Aug. 11, 1873), Congregational clergyman, for sixty-two years pastor in Braintree, Mass., was the third in family descent of a distinguished line of Congregational ministers, whose combined service extended from 1763 to 1900. His grandfather was Rev. John Storrs (1735–1799), a graduate of Yale, a tutor there, and a chaplain in the Revolution; his father, Richard Salter Storrs (1763–1819), was for nearly thirty-four years pastor in Longmeadow,

Mass.; his son, also Richard Salter Storrs [q.v.], carried on the family tradition by a pastorate of more than fifty years at the Church of the Pilgrims, Brooklyn, N. Y. They were the descendants of Samuel, son of Thomas and Mary Storrs of Nottinghamshire, England, who emigrated to Barnstable, Mass., in 1663. On his mother's side, also, Richard 2nd was of ministerial stock. She was Sarah Williston, daughter of Rev. Noah Williston of West Haven, Conn.

Richard was born in Longmeadow, but when he was four years old, his grandfather Williston requested that the child be given to him and reared as his own. The parents consented and the boy's youth was spent in West Haven under a rigorous Puritanical tutelage. Prepared by his grandfather, he entered Yale in 1802; but after a year there he was compelled by ill health to withdraw. Returning now to his father's home, Longmeadow, he engaged in outdoor work, and later taught schools in West Suffield, Conn., Longmeadow, and West Haven, Conn. While in the last-named place he met Lyman Beecher [q.v.] of East Hampton, L. I., who persuaded him to go to that town and take charge of Clinton Academy. During his stay there he had the stimulating experience of living in Beecher's household. An interesting example of one phase of his work survives in *A Dialogue Exhibiting Some of the Principles and Practical Consequences of Modern Infidelity* (1806), which he prepared for a student exhibition; in 1932 it was reprinted in the *Magazine of History* (vol. XLV, Extra No. 180). He reëntered Yale in 1806 but soon transferred to Williams College, from which he graduated in 1807. He then studied theology with Rev. Aaron Woolworth of Bridgehampton, L. I., was licensed by the Suffolk Presbytery, supplied churches in Smithtown and Islip, and in May 1809 entered Andover Theological Seminary, graduating the following year. After six months' missionary work in Georgia as agent of the American Education Society, he was ordained and installed, July 3, 1811, as pastor of the First Congregational Church, Braintree, Mass.

Thenceforth, for considerably more than half a century, he was one of the conspicuous figures of New England Congregationalism. Stanchly orthodox, he energetically opposed the Unitarian movement and was one of the first Massachusetts preachers to refuse to exchange with any clergyman suspected of being unsound in the faith. Although not wholly in sympathy with political abolitionism, he boldly denounced slavery, and a discourse of his, *American Slavery and the Means of Its Removal*, was published in

1844. He was among the early promoters of Sunday schools and temperance societies, and served as secretary of the American Tract Society (1820–25) and director of the American Education Society (1821–30). He was especially interested in home missionary work, was for years an official of the Massachusetts Missionary Society, and during a five-year leave of absence from his church (1831–36) he went up and down New England as a missionary agent. In 1816 he became an editorial writer for the *Recorder* (later the *Boston Recorder*), established the year before, and served for eight years; from 1850 to 1856 he was an editor of the *Congregationalist*. As a director of the Doctrinal Tract Society (later the Congregational Board of Publication) he prepared many works for the press. His own contributions to periodicals were numerous, and in addition to sermons, he published *Memoir of the Rev. Samuel Green* (1836). A typical representative of the old-school New England clergy, severe but friendly, fearless in reproof and denunciation, burning with zeal to promote the spiritual welfare of the land, he was regarded with both awe and affection by his parishioners, and held in high esteem by leading men of his time. He was married first, Apr. 2, 1812, to Sarah Strong Woodhull, who died Apr. 4, 1818; second, Sept. 16, 1819, to Harriet Moore, who died July 10, 1834; and third, Oct. 18, 1835, to Anne Stebbins, who survived him.

[Charles Storrs, *The Storrs Family* (1886); Calvin Durfee, *Williams Biog. Annals* (1871); *Gen. Cat. of the Theological Seminary, Andover, Mass., 1808–1908*; W. S. Pattee, *A Hist. of Old Braintree and Quincy* (copr. 1879); E. A. Park, *A Sermon . . . at the Funeral of Rev. Richard Salter Storrs, D.D.* (1874); *Boston Transcript*, Aug. 12, 1873.]   H. E. S.

STORRS, RICHARD SALTER (Aug. 21, 1821–June 5, 1900), Congregational clergyman, for more than fifty years pastor of the Church of the Pilgrims, Brooklyn, N. Y., was the third of that name and the fourth in line of descent to gain distinction in the ministerial calling. His father was Rev. Richard Salter Storrs [*q.v.*] and his mother, Harriet (Moore) Storrs. Born in Braintree, Mass., he prepared for college at the academy in Monson, Mass., and graduated from Amherst in 1839. For the next two years he taught; first, at Monson, and later, at Williston Seminary, Easthampton, Mass. Abandoning an earlier intent to qualify for the bar after a year in the law office of Rufus Choate, he entered Andover Theological Seminary in 1842 and graduated in 1845. He was immediately called to the Harvard Congregational Church, Brookline, Mass., where, Oct. 22, he was ordained. On the first day of that month he had married Mary Elwell Jenks, daughter of Rev. Francis and Sarah (Phillips) Jenks, and a niece of Wendell Phillips. He had served hardly a year in his first parish when his abilities as a preacher led to his being called to the recently organized Church of the Pilgrims, Brooklyn, N. Y. Here, during a pastorate that covered the entire last half of the nineteenth century, he was a leading citizen, rivaling in influence and public esteem his contemporary, Henry Ward Beecher. When in 1869 he was called to the Central Church, Boston, more than a hundred of Brooklyn's most prominent men petitioned him to remain. On the fiftieth anniversary of his pastorate, at a gathering in the Academy of Music, he was presented with a medal in recognition of his civic services. A discourse, *The Church of the Pilgrims*, which he delivered and published in 1886, sets forth not only the growth of that organization but also the changes that had taken place about it during the past four decades. Many of those affecting the religious, educational, and philanthropic life of the city he had furthered. He was a corporate member of the Brooklyn Institute of Arts and Sciences, and one of its board of trustees; he was one of the foremost advocates of the movement that resulted in the establishment of Packer Collegiate Institute; he organized the great Sanitary Fair held in February 1864; he was president of the Long Island Historical Society; and in 1889 he served as park commissioner. For the city with whose growth and enrichment he was so long associated he had a jealous affection which made him a vigorous opponent of its consolidation with New York. As an orator he had a country-wide reputation, being popular as a lyceum lecturer, and acceptable at institutions of learning. While he cannot be credited with independent scholarship, his learning was comprehensive and his memory extraordinary. His appearance was "statuesque," and his discourses, enlivened with striking imagery, flowed forth in long, melodious sentences. The diversity of their content is suggested by such titles as "Libraries of Europe," "Climate and Civilization," "John Wycliffe and the First English Bible," "The Muscovite and the Ottoman." Many of his lectures appeared in pamphlet form and some are contained in *Orations and Addresses* (1901). Among his publications, also, are: *The Constitution of the Human Soul* (1857); *Conditions of Success in Preaching Without Notes* (1875); *The Divine Origin of Christianity Indicated by Its Historical Effects* (1884); *Bernard of Clairvaux, the Times, the Man and His Work* (1892). Theologically, "A more orthodox minister has not maintained the faith once delivered to the saints in our time than he" (Cuyler, *post*, p. 1416). From 1848 to 1861 he was one of the editors of the *Independent*; from 1888 to 1897 president of the American Board of Commissioners for Foreign Missions; and in 1895–96, president of the American Historical Association. He was also a trustee of Amherst College. His death occurred at his home in Brooklyn, and he was survived by three of four children.

[Charles Storrs, *The Storrs Family* (1886); *Obit. Record Grads. Amherst Coll. . . . 1900* (1900); *Gen. Cat. of the Theolog. Sem., Andover, Mass., 1808–1908*; *The Congregational Year-Book*, 1901; *Who's Who in America*, 1899–1900; T. L. Cuyler, in the *Independent*, June 14, 1900; *Congregationalist*, June 14, 1900; *Brooklyn Daily Eagle*, June 6, 7, 8, 1900; *Brooklyn Times*, June 6, 8, 1900.]   H. E. S.

STORY, ISAAC (Aug. 7, 1774–July 19, 1803), poet and miscellaneous writer, was the second son and second child in a family of eleven born to the Rev. Isaac and Rebecca (Bradstreet) Story of Marblehead, Mass. He was graduated from Harvard College in the class of 1793 and studied law. After a brief residence in Castine, Me., 1797–99, he settled in central Massachusetts, first in the town of Sterling, later in Rutland. He was hardly established in his profession, however, when he died, unmarried, in his twenty-ninth year, while visiting his parents at Marblehead. An obituary attributed to his cousin, the noted Joseph Story [*q.v.*], characterized him as: "In his manners bland, social and affectionate; in his disposition, sportive and convivial; in his morals, pure, generous, and unaffected; in his mind, vivacious, refined, and facetious" (*Salem Register*, July 25, 1803).

Isaac Story's literary career was closely patterned after that of Joseph Dennie, Royall Tyler, David Everett [*qq.v.*], and other young lawyers who wrote moral essays, political squibs, and light verse for the newspapers in the large leisure of waiting for professional employment. The current fashion of using pseudonyms makes the identification of his contributions difficult. Two of his juvenile poems, *Liberty* (1795) and *All the World's a Stage* (1796), both signed "The Stranger," were printed by William Barrett of Newburyport, Mass. For Barrett's *Political Gazette*, and later for the *Farmer's Museum* of Walpole, N. H., Story wrote a series of essays under the caption, "From the Desk of Beri Hesdin"; these were modeled on Dennie's "Lay Preacher" papers, but were more serious in tone and conventional in substance. He also contributed essays signed "The Traveler" to the *Columbian Centinel* of Boston and had some editorial connection with Daniel S. Waters' *Castine Gazette* (later the *Castine Journal and Eastern*

Advertiser), but what he wrote for the latter journal has not been determined. There survive in print *An Eulogy on the Glorious Virtues of the Illustrious Gen. George Washington* (Worcester, 1800), and *An Oration, on the Anniversary of the Independence of the United States of America* (Worcester, 1801). Three publications, *An Epistle from Yarico to Inkle* (Marblehead, 1792), which is in the main a reprint of a poem published in London in 1736, *The Barber's Shop: Kept by Sir David Razor* (Salem, n.d.), and *Original and Select Poems, By the Stranger* (Albany, 1827) have been erroneously ascribed to Story. Three manuscript books of his poems, with some letters and miscellaneous prose, are preserved in the library of Harvard University. He was best known for his verses signed "Peter Quince," in imitation of the burlesque odes of "Peter Pindar" (John Wolcot, 1738–1819). They were written originally for the Newburyport *Political Gazette*, but when that paper was discontinued in 1797, Story transferred the series to the *Farmer's Museum*. In 1801 a collection of them was published in Boston under the title, *A Parnassian Shop, Opened in the Pindaric Stile; By Peter Quince, Esq*. Besides many pieces of topical wit and political satire directed against Democrats of all descriptions, the volume contains some serious patriotic, moral, and sentimental poems. The verse is facile, but no longer sparkles.

[The date of birth, which is sometimes given as Aug. 25, is taken from *Vital Records of Marblehead, Mass.*, vol. I (1903). See also Perley Derby and F. A. Gardner, *Elisha Story of Boston* (1915); H. M. Ellis, "Joseph Dennie and His Circle," *Univ. of Tex. Bull., Studies in English, No. 4* (1915); G. A. Wheeler, *Hist. of Castine, . . . Me.* (1875); A. P. Peabody, "The Farmer's Weekly Museum," *Proc. Am. Antiquarian Soc.*, n.s., vol. VI (1890); E. A. and G. S. Duyckinck, *Cyc. of Am. Lit.* (1856), vol. I; obituary in *Salem Register*, July 25, 1803.]   G. F. W.

STORY, JOSEPH (Sept. 18, 1779–Sept. 10, 1845), jurist, eldest of the eleven children of Elisha and Mehitable (Pedrick) Story, was born in Marblehead, Mass. His father had seven children by an earlier marriage. Descended from another Elisha Story, who arrived in Boston from England about 1700, Joseph had forebears of some influence and position in colonial New England. Before the War of the Revolution his paternal grandfather, William Story, had held the office of registrar in the court of admiralty. His own father, who became a physician and surgeon of considerable reputation, had been associated with the Sons of Liberty and was one of the "Indians" who took part in the Boston Tea Party. His mother's father was a wealthy merchant of Marblehead and a Loyalist.

Story received the best education that the

times and the place afforded. He was one of the first pupils to attend the newly established academy at Marblehead. A misunderstanding with the master of the school caused him to leave the academy in the fall of 1794 with his preparation for college still incomplete. It was prophetic of the tremendous industry and power of concentration with which he was later to amaze the legal world by producing volume after volume of commentaries in rapid succession, that Story, just turned fifteen and almost alone and unaided, should not only have finished his preparatory studies, but further should have made himself sufficiently acquainted with the subjects covered by the college freshman class for the first six months, to pass the examinations and to become a regularly enrolled student in Harvard at the close of the January vacation in 1795. In his college career he was confessedly a grind: "I was most thoroughly devoted to all the college studies, and scarcely wasted a single moment in idleness. I trace back to this cause a serious injury to my health. When I entered College I was robust and muscular, but before I left I had become pale and feeble and was inclined to dyspepsia" (*Miscellaneous Writings*, p. 16). He was graduated from Harvard in 1798, being rated second to William Ellery Channing who led the class.

He returned to Marblehead and began the study of law in the office of Samuel Sewall, then a member of Congress and later chief justice of the supreme court of Massachusetts. Though by general acclaim he still ranks as the foremost of American legal writers, Story acquired the foundations of his legal knowledge by means and methods which would be anathema to the educators of today. As in the case of office students in all generations, he was left largely to his own devices and thrown back upon his own resources —perhaps not a handicap to one of his studious habits. For months at a time he not infrequently devoted fourteen hours a day to study. The scarcity of American reports—there were then only five or six volumes available—made it necessary for him to depend upon treatises, some of them already very old. He tells us that he read Blackstone with pleasurable comprehension, but that his next assignment, Coke on Littleton, proved so difficult that he wept bitterly over the failure of his first unsuccessful attempts to understand it. After mastering Littleton he turned to Saunders' *Reports* and the study of special pleading, developing such an interest in this branch of the law as to make it for several years his favorite subject. While still in Sewall's office he read through "that deep and admirable work

upon one of the most intricate titles of the law, Fearne on Contingent Remainders and Executory Devises" (*Ibid.*, p. 20). Apparently it was not until after he had begun the actual practice of law that he became acquainted with the *Year Books* and the early English reports that followed them.

On the appointment of Sewall to a judgeship, Story left his office and went to that of Samuel Putnam in Salem. This change probably accounts for the fact that on his admission to the bar, at the July term of the common pleas in Essex County, 1801, he opened his own office in that town. He began his career as a practising lawyer under circumstances that were neither auspicious nor pleasant. Story himself was an avowed Republican; the bench and bar of eastern Massachusetts were, practically without exception, Federalists. At first he was made to feel this political difference pointedly; was, as he says, "excluded from those intimacies which warm and cheer the intercourse of the profession" (*Ibid.*, p. 22). However, during his second year at the bar his practice began to grow. It increased, until at the time of his appointment to the Supreme Court of the United States some ten years later, it was, if we may believe his own statement, as extensive and lucrative as that of any lawyer in the county.

His participation in politics and public affairs began early in his career. He was chosen by Marblehead to deliver the eulogy on the death of Washington (published, 1800). In 1803 he was appointed to the station of naval officer for the port of Salem, but this appointment he declined. The next year he delivered the annual Fourth of July oration in Salem (published, 1804). He was Salem's representative in the legislature of Massachusetts in 1805 and again in 1806 and 1807. A memorial, relative to the infringements of the neutral trade of the United States, and addressed to the President and Congress in behalf of the inhabitants of Salem, was drawn up by him in January 1806 (*Ibid.*, p. 43). This same year, as chairman of the committee appointed to make a report on the matter, he was largely responsible for the act of the legislature raising the salaries of the judges of the supreme court of Massachusetts. In his time, as for a long time afterwards, there was no court of equity in Massachusetts. During the session of the legislature in 1808 he moved the appointment of a committee to take under consideration the establishment of a court of chancery. He was made chairman of the committee and drew up an exhaustive report in favor of the creation of such a court. The report was not accepted, but it is part of the history of Story and equity. Together with Chancellor Kent he will always be remembered as the founder of the system in the United States; in 1842 he drew up the rules of equity practice for the United States Supreme Court and the circuit courts; his *Commentaries on Equity Jurisprudence* (14th ed., 3 vols., 1918), and his *Commentaries on Equity Pleading* (10th ed., 1892), are still in use.

In the fall of 1808 he was elected a member of Congress to fill the vacancy caused by the death of Jacob Crowninshield. He remained in Congress for one session only, until Mar. 3, 1809, and declined to become a candidate for reëlection. The reasons for this refusal, as he later gave them, were that a continuance in public life would be incompatible with his complete success at the bar, and that obedience to party projects required too much sacrifice of opinion and feeling. That he was unwilling to sacrifice his own opinions for the sake of his party, during even his short stay in Congress, is shown by his attitude toward the Embargo, which, he had become convinced, had failed of its object and should be abandoned. Jefferson accused him of being responsible for the repeal of the Embargo—"I ascribe all this to one pseudo-Republican, Story" (P. L. Ford, *The Writings of Thomas Jefferson*, IX, 1898, p. 277). In another matter also he was openly in disagreement with his party. In January 1809 he offered a bill providing for a committee to inquire into the expediency of building up the United States navy. Such a plan was contrary to the principles of the Republican party, and the bill did not pass. On leaving Congress he was once more elected a member of the Massachusetts legislature; he was made speaker of the House of Representatives in January 1811, and again in May of the same year. After his elevation to the Supreme Court, though his interest in political affairs continued unabated, he made it a rule to take no active part in politics. The only recorded exception to this rule was his appearance at a town meeting in Salem, December 1819, where his animosity to slavery and the slave trade led him to speak strongly against the Missouri Compromise. It was this same feeling and subject which had inspired his sensational charge to the grand jury of the circuit court earlier in the year, for which he was taken to task by the newspapers of the day (*Life and Letters*, I, 336–48). The same hatred of slavery showed itself again some three years later (May term, 1822) in his opinion, much-discussed at the time, in the case of the alleged slave-runner *La Jeune Eugénie* (2 Mason, 409).

But even after he became a judge, Story was active in the field of public or semi-public usefulness. In August 1813, he delivered in Salem a eulogy at the burial of Captain James Lawrence who had been killed in the fight between the *Chesapeake* and the *Shannon*. He served as president of the Merchants' Bank of Salem from 1815 till 1835, and as vice-president of the Salem Savings Bank from 1818 till 1830. He was elected a member of the Board of Overseers of Harvard College in 1819, and in 1825 he became a fellow of the Corporation. In 1820 he drew up for the merchants of Salem a long memorial addressed to Congress asking that certain restrictions on commerce be removed (published, 1820); in this same year he was elected a delegate from Salem to the convention called to revise the constitution of Massachusetts. During the next year he found time to prepare and deliver a scholarly address before the members of the Suffolk bar on the progress of jurisprudence. Among his *Miscellaneous Writings* are to be found two other addresses which in the case of any one other than Story would be considered matters of major importance: a remarkable legal argument made in 1825 before the Board of Overseers of Harvard College (against the claims of the professors and tutors of the college that none but resident instructors could be chosen for fellows of the corporation), and the annual oration before the society of Phi Beta Kappa at Harvard in 1826. In this same busy period he drew up the Crimes Act of 1825, usually attributed to Daniel Webster, who carried it through Congress; in 1816 he had drawn up his bill to extend the jurisdiction of the circuit courts (*Life and Letters*, I, 293). He was one of the organizers of the Essex Historical Society, and a member of the board of trustees of Mount Auburn Cemetery from 1831 until his death.

On Nov. 18, 1811, shortly after he had passed his thirty-second birthday, Story was appointed an associate justice of the Supreme Court of the United States. By his panegyrists much has been made of the fact that he was the youngest person ever to be appointed to this position. It should be remembered, however, that Madison had already tried to honor with the position three other men in succession, all of them at that time more prominent than Story—Levi Lincoln, formerly in Jefferson's cabinet, who declined; Alexander Wolcott of Connecticut, whom the Senate refused to confirm; and John Quincy Adams, then minister at St. Petersburg, who preferred to remain there. Madison then turned to Story, at the suggestion, it is said, of Ezekiel Bacon, a congressman from Massachusetts. Though the salary of $3,500 was only slightly more than half of his professional income, Story at once accepted the office, motivated, he said, by the honor, the permanence of the tenure, and especially by "the opportunity it will allow me to pursue, what of all things I admire, juridical studies" (*Life and Letters*, I, 201). At this time the judges of the Supreme Court exercised also a circuit court jurisdiction. Story's circuit took in Maine, New Hampshire, Massachusetts, and Rhode Island. The illness and infirmities of his predecessor, William Cushing, had led to a vast accumulation of cases on the docket. By an early decision (*United States* vs. *Wonson*, 1 *Gallison*, 5) Story reversed the former practice of the circuit court of allowing appeals from the district court to the circuit court in jury cases at common law. By this ruling 130 cases were at once stricken from the docket. But the respite thus gained was of short duration. The War of 1812 gave the crippled shipping interests of Story's maritime circuit a chance to recoup their losses by turning to privateering. Soon his court was flooded with cases involving admiralty and prize law, subjects at that time but little understood, and depending on principles which were then neither well defined nor established. His decisions in these cases, the result of broad study on his part, first put the admiralty jurisdiction of the federal courts on a sound basis. What was perhaps the most famous of these cases, decided in 1815 (*De Lovio* vs. *Boit*, 2 *Gallison*, 398), was long afterwards referred to by a justice of the Supreme Court in these words, "The learned and exhaustive opinion of Justice Story, . . . affirming the admiralty jurisdiction over policies of marine insurance has never been answered, and will always stand as a monument of his great erudition" (*Insurance Company* vs. *Dunham*, 11 *Wallace*, 35). In 1816 William Pinkney [*q.v.*], who was considering the request of the government to go as minister to Russia, offered Story his law practice in Baltimore. Though this was estimated to be worth $20,000 a year, and though Congress had just refused to raise the salaries of the federal judges, Story, still far from the affluence which he later enjoyed, declined Pinkney's offer.

Many of the opinions written by Story as a justice of the Supreme Court impress us, even today, by their remarkable breadth of learning; some of them are elaborate to a degree; in some there is a marked tendency to range over the whole field in any way involved, and widely beyond the mere facts and law necessary for a judgment in the particular case. This tendency, natural to him, and unquestionably of great advantage in the writing of the commentaries, can hardly be said to enhance his reputation as a judge. Yet not a few of his opinions had important legal and constitutional results; many of them that no longer attract attention were of the most vital interest in their day. Among the latter class was (1815) his famous dissenting opinion in the case of the *Nereide* (9 *Cranch*, 388, 436), in which he, disagreeing with Marshall and the majority of the court, argued against the ruling that a neutral might lawfully put his goods on board a belligerent ship for conveyance. Unknown to the court until shortly thereafter, Lord Stowell had just decided a British case of similar nature on the basis of the very rule for which Story had contended. At about this same time Story was assigned the writing of the opinion in *Green* vs. *Liter* (8 *Cranch*, 229), presumably because no one of his colleagues had the necessary knowledge of the now almost obsolete old real actions adequately to discuss the principles of the writ of right on which the case was based. It has been called the "most prominent and elaborate opinion delivered by him at this time" (*Life and Letters*, I, 260), but it shows no great depth of historical legal learning, especially of the period when the writ of right was the supreme action in English law. One of the most important opinions in his whole career was delivered in 1816 in the case of *Martin* vs. *Hunter's Lessee* (1 *Wheaton*, 304), which decided that the appellate jurisdiction of the Supreme Court could rightfully be exercised over the state courts, "an opinion which has ever since been the keystone of the whole arch of Federal judicial power" (Charles Warren, *The Supreme Court in United States History*, 1922, vol. I, 449). Another opinion, extremely important in contemporaneous (1822) international politics, was that in the case of the *Santissima Trinidad* (7 *Wheaton*, 283); this held that a prize captured by a ship which had been guilty of a violation of American neutrality, and brought into a United States port, should be given back to the original owner. The constantly increasing extent of admiralty jurisdiction claimed by the federal courts, in the development of which claim Story had played a major part, had aroused a feeling of hostility among some of the inland states, which saw, or thought they saw, some phases of their common law jurisdiction menaced in inland waters. This feeling was allayed (1825) by Story's opinion in the case of the *Thomas Jefferson* (10 *Wheaton*, 428), which held that the admiralty jurisdiction of the federal courts did not extend beyond waters affected by the ebb and flow of the tide. A case which moved the country mightily at the time, 1841, was that of the *United States* vs. *Schooner*

Amistad (15 *Peters,* 518). A cargo of negroes on the *Amistad,* a slave-runner, had gotten control of the ship and murdered the officers; on being brought into port by a vessel of the United States navy they were claimed as slaves by certain Spaniards; the question before the court was whether or not the negroes were entitled to their freedom. Story's decision, for the court, held that they should be freed and sent back to Africa. Story's opinion in another case famous in its time (1844) because of its religious ramifications, *Vidal* vs. *Philadelphia* (2 *Howard,* 127), was so far approved by the court as a whole that he could later write to Kent that "not a single sentence was altered by my brothers, as I originally drew it" (*Life and Letters,* II, 469). It held valid the will of Stephen Girard who had bequeathed to Philadelphia several millions of dollars to found a college for poor white children, but on the condition that no ecclesiastic of any kind, or on any pretence or for any purpose, should ever be allowed to enter the institution. That opinion of Story which is today best known and most often read is doubtless his learned and powerful dissenting opinion in *Charles River Bridge* vs. *Warren Bridge* (11 *Peters,* 420, 583). It was one of three dissenting opinions, all on questions of constitutional law, which he wrote during the 1837 term. The opinion of the court as a whole seemed to Story to destroy the sanctity of contracts and to be immoral. His own opinion won the approval of many, if not most, of the best lawyers in the country; Webster called it his "ablest and best written opinion" (*Life and Letters,* II, 269).

It has been said that in the Supreme Court Story was dominated by John Marshall. In refutation of this statement one of the latest of Story's biographers has prepared the following succinct set of facts: Story wrote opinions in 286 cases in the Supreme Court; of these 269 are reported as the opinion of the court or of a majority; three were concurring opinions and fourteen dissenting opinions; he wrote four dissenting opinions on questions of constitutional law, one being in the lifetime of Marshall; in the only case (*Ogden* vs. *Saunders*) in which Marshall was in a minority upon a question of constitutional law, Story and Duval concurred with him in the question upon which he wrote the opinion; Story wrote the opinion of the majority of the court in five cases in which Marshall dissented; in four of the cases in which he dissented in Marshall's life, the latter wrote the opinion of the majority (W. D. Lewis, ed., *Great American Lawyers,* III, 1907, p. 150). Marshall died in 1835. Story was generally regarded as the logi-

cal successor to his position, and Marshall before his death is said to have favored that choice (*Life and Letters,* II, 210). Soon after Marshall's death, Story himself had protested as only a man alive to a probability would be likely to protest, that he had never for a moment imagined that he would be thought of, that he was "equally beyond hope or anxiety" (*Ibid.,* II, 201). Today we can see that there was no likelihood of his receiving the appointment. He was out of sympathy with Jackson, personally and politically. The President, on his part, could say no good word for what he called "the school of Story and Kent"; he had already referred to Story as "the most dangerous man in America" (*Ibid.,* II, 117). Within the year Roger B. Taney was appointed to fill Marshall's place.

In 1828 the Royall Professorship of Law at Harvard, then vacant, had been offered to Story. He declined it on the ground that he feared that an increase of duties at his age might seriously interfere with his health. But in the very next year Nathan Dane, after talking the matter over with Story, established a new professorship of law, with the understanding, and on the explicit condition, that the first occupant of the chair should be Story. He was elected to the position in June of that year, accepted it, and in September moved permanently from Salem to Cambridge. For the rest of his life the Law School was one of his chief interests. In a very real sense he may be regarded as its founder; along with his colleague J. H. Ashmun, who had accepted the Royall Professorship, and together with Tapping Reeve and James Gould [*qq.v.*] of the Litchfield Law School, he was one of the pioneers in law-school, as contrasted with office, instruction for those who are starting a legal education. His opening class at the law school numbered eighteen students; before he died his reputation and personality had brought the annual enrollment to almost 150. Through his efforts the permanent funds of the school were increased and the library was built up and expanded. His ability as a teacher seems to have been no less marked than his skill as an organizer, and this in spite of the fact that his own knowledge of the law had been acquired without benefit of teacher. But by far the most important fact in connection with Story's association with the Law School lies in another field. In establishing his professorship Dane had stipulated that a number of formal lectures in certain named branches of the law should be prepared, delivered, and revised for publication by the professor on his foundation. This did not fit into Story's scheme of teaching, for he wrote out no formal lectures, but taught by a method of informal discussion. So in place of publishing a series of lectures, he devised the plan which resulted in his well known *Commentaries*.

The continuing importance and reputation of these has almost obscured the fact that they were by no means Story's only legal treatises. Much writing of the same general nature had already come from his pen. As early as 1805 he had published, with valuable notes, *A Selection of Pleadings in Civil Actions*. At about the same time he undertook the task of making a digest of American law similar to, and supplementary to, Comyns' *Digest*. Though the project was finally abandoned, three large volumes in manuscript gave evidence of his endeavor. In 1809 he brought out a new edition of Chitty's *A Practical Treatise on Bills of Exchange and Promissory Notes,* and in the next year one of Charles Abbott's *A Treatise on the Law Relative to Merchant Ships and Seamen,* with annotations and references to American decisions. This work he reëdited in 1829. He was the editor of an annotated edition of Lawes's *A Practical Treatise on Pleading in Assumpsit* (1811). He was the writer of many of the elaborate notes in Wheaton's *Reports* (*Life and Letters,* I, 282–83). In 1828 he published in three volumes *Public and General Statutes Passed by the Congress of the United States, 1789–1827*.

The *Commentaries* themselves followed one another in quick order. *Bailments* appeared in 1832; *On the Constitution,* in three volumes, in 1833; *The Conflict of Laws* in 1834; *Equity Jurisprudence,* in two volumes, in 1836; *Equity Pleading* in 1838; *Agency* in 1839; *Partnership* in 1841; *Bills of Exchange* in 1843; *Promissory Notes* in 1845. That one man, with few precedents to depend upon, should have written these voluminous works on exact, technical legal subjects, within the space of a little more than twelve years, seems incredible—and even more incredible when it is considered that during the same period he performed in full his work as a law teacher and as a judge, the latter requiring attendance on the court at Washington and circuit-court duty as well. Add to all this the fact that within the same interval he published *The Constitutional Class Book* (1834), prepared and delivered a long discourse on Marshall (before the Suffolk bar, 1835), drafted the Bankruptcy Act of 1841, contributed nearly a score of articles on legal subjects to the *Encyclopedia Americana* (*Life and Letters,* II, 26–27), and we have an example of industry in legal scholarship that has yet to be equaled. The success of the *Commentaries* was widespread and immediate. Some

of them (*Bailments, Equity Jurisprudence*) went into third editions even during the short space of his remaining years. The financial returns from his books are said to have reached the then lofty figure of $10,000 per annum. Through his decisions, and his correspondence with some of the leading British jurists, Story was well known in England before his *Commentaries* appeared; with the translation of some of his works, notably *On the Constitution* and *The Conflict of Laws,* into French and German, he now acquired a truly international reputation. But, unlike more modern representatives of his type, he never went abroad, and never received any honorary degrees from foreign universities. At home he had already been honored with several.

Story's predominant personal characteristic was probably his unusual power of conversation. His son says that the father, a chronic dyspeptic at thirty-two, was practically unable to take physical exercise, apparently because of lack of time and interest, and that "his real exercise was in talking" (*Life and Letters,* II, 106). Poetry played a not inconsiderable part in his life. He read it habitually and wrote verse more or less throughout his life. The motto of the *Salem Register* was written by him and gives a good idea of his general style:

"Here shall the Press the People's right maintain,
Unawed by influence and unbribed by gain;
Here Patriot Truth her glorious precepts draw,
Pledged to Religion, Liberty, and Law."

Before 1804 he had the temerity to publish a long and youthful effusion, *The Power of Solitude* (1802?), written at a time when "his leisure moments were employed in writing love songs, full of rapturous exaggerations or sentimental laments" (*Life and Letters,* I, 100). Later on he repented of this act and bought up all the copies of the book that he could find. But there still remain a few copies to attest the wisdom of his efforts to destroy them. He was fond of music, drawing, and painting. His favorite novelist was Jane Austen. As a result, he tells us, of observing the intellectual attainments of the girls in the mixed classes which as a boy he attended at Marblehead Academy, he was an active champion for the higher education of women. Like many of the other leading men of eastern Massachusetts at that time he was a Unitarian. The picture of him given us by his son (*Life and Letters,* II, 552) is that of a man five feet eight inches tall, with a well-knit figure; active, restless, and nervous in his movements; with thick auburn hair in his youth, but bald in his later years save for a thick mass of silvery hair on the back of his head; his blue eyes were lively and his mouth was large and expressive.

Story died on Sept. 10, 1845. He had been married first to Mary Lynde Oliver on Dec. 9, 1804. She died in June of the next year. On Aug. 27, 1808, he married Sarah Waldo Wetmore, daughter of Judge William Wetmore. Of the seven children of this marriage only two survived him. One of these, Louisa, married George T. Curtis [*q.v.*]; the other was William Wetmore Story [*q.v.*], the sculptor.

[W. W. Story, ed., *Life and Letters of Joseph Story* (2 vols., 1851), is indispensable. Tinged with hero worship and pride of family, it is nevertheless reliable. Next in importance are *The Miscellaneous Writings of Joseph Story* (1852). Prefaced by a remarkable autobiographical letter written by Story in 1831, this book contains many of his addresses, and a number of book reviews of such substance as to be entitled to rank as essays. The best recent account of Story is that by William Schofield, in W. D. Lewis, ed., *Great American Lawyers*, III (1907). It is especially good for a discussion of the meaning and importance of some of Story's judicial opinions. On this matter the *Life and Letters*, and Charles Warren, *The Supreme Court in U. S. History* (3 vols., 1922), should also be consulted. For Story's connection with the Harvard Law School see, in addition to the *Life and Letters*, Charles Warren, *Hist. of the Harvard Law School* (1908), vols. I, II. Two funeral orations by men who were intimately acquainted with Story have been published: Simon Greenleaf, *A Discourse Commemorative of the Life and Character of the Hon. Joseph Story* (1845); Charles Sumner, *The Scholar, the Jurist, the Artist, the Philanthropist* (1846). See also *The Centennial Hist. of the Harvard Law School, 1817–1917* (1918); Perley Derby and F. A. Gardner, compilers, *Elisha Story of Boston and Some of His Descendants* (1915); and obituary in *Boston Daily Advertiser*, Sept. 12, 1845. Story's decisions in the Supreme Court will be found in Cranch's *Reports*, Wheaton's *Reports*, Peters' *Reports*, and Howard's *Reports*; his decisions upon his circuit are reported by Gallison, Mason, Charles Sumner, and W. W. Story, 13 vols. in all. The last editions of the *Commentaries* are as follows: *Bailments* (9th, 1878); *On the Constitution* (5th, 1891); *Conflict of Laws* (8th, 1883); *Equity Jurisprudence* (14th, 1918); *Equity Pleading* (10th, 1892); *Agency* (9th, 1882); *Partnership* (7th, 1881); *Bills of Exchange* (4th, 1860); *Promissory Notes* (7th, 1878).]   G. E. W.

STORY, JULIAN RUSSELL (Sept. 8, 1857–Feb. 23, 1919), portrait painter, was born at Walton-on-Thames, Surrey, England, youngest of the four children of William Wetmore Story [*q.v.*] and Emelyn (Eldredge) Story. He was educated at Eton and at Brasenose College, Oxford, where he received the degree of B.A. in 1879. A letter from William Wetmore Story to James Russell Lowell, written in 1864, mentions the younger Story's early determination to be an artist and the father's intention to let him reach his own decision in the matter (Henry James, *William Wetmore Story and his Friends*, 1903, vol. II, p. 147). Later Robert Browning writes the family of his admiration of an early exhibit by the young man at the Grosvenor Gallery in London (*Ibid.*, p. 279). Gifted with his parents' charm of manner, trained under Frank Duveneck [*q.v.*] in Florence and under Gustave Rodolphe

Boulanger and Jules Joseph Lefebvre in Paris, he became in later years a portrait painter of distinction, in whose work technical mastery was combined with charm of color and handling. In 1891 he married Emma Eames, a celebrated opera-singer, from whom he was divorced in 1907. In 1909 he married Elaine (Sartori) Bohlen of Philadelphia, Pa., who with three children survived him. For many years he centered his activities at Vallombrosa, Italy, travelling to Paris, London, and America as occasion required. Later he divided his time between Italy and Philadelphia, finally giving up the villa at Vallombrosa a few years before his death. He belonged to clubs in Florence, London, New York, and Philadelphia, and to the societies of portrait painters in Paris and London. In 1906 he became an associate of the National Academy. He received a third class medal and honorable mention at the Paris Salon of 1889, a gold medal at Berlin in 1891, and silver medals at expositions in Paris (1890), Buffalo (1901), and San Francisco (1915). In 1900 he became a chevalier of the Legion of Honor.

Story went through the usual transitions from Salon compositions ("The Entombment of Christ," Peabody Institute, Baltimore, Md.), historical compositions ("Mlle. Sembreuil," Pennsylvania Academy of the Fine Arts, Philadelphia), and realistic illustration ("Laboratory of Clinical Physiology at Saint Lazare") to portraiture à la mode in the larger cities of Europe and America. His masterpiece in this last field is probably his "Madame Emma Eames" in the Cincinnati Art Museum, Cincinnati, Ohio. Other portraits are to be seen in Philadelphia, where for a time Story was commissioned to portray many of the leaders of business and professional life and their wives. Story's style varies considerably with his subject. The observer notes his vigorous drawing, his conscientious modelling, his increasing boldness of handling and of lighting, and his ability to use color of the higher ranges without disintegration. His composition is invariably soberly satisfactory, his feeling for textures delightful. Less brilliant than his friend, John Singer Sargent [*q.v.*], he perhaps less frequently exploited the possibilities of mere technical virtuosity. He died in Philadelphia and was buried from the Church of St. Luke and the Epiphany.

[The date of birth has been supplied by the librarian of the National Academy of Design. See *Who's Who in America*, 1918–19; Mary E. Phillips, *Reminiscences of William Wetmore Story* (1897); *Am. Art Ann.*, vol. XVI (1919); obituaries in *Am. Art News*, Mar. 1, and *Pub. Ledger* (Phila.), Feb. 25, 1919. There are brief references in Samuel Isham, *The Hist. of Am. Painting* (1905); Henri Sylvestre, Jr., *The Marvels in Art of*

the Fin de Siècle (1893), vol. II ; G. W. Sheldon, *Recent Ideals of Am. Art* (1888). *Who's Who in Philadelphia,* 1925, inaccurate in details, contains a portrait.]
W. S. R.

STORY, WILLIAM EDWARD (Apr. 29, 1850–Apr. 10, 1930), mathematician, eldest son of Isaac and Elizabeth B. (Woodberry) Story, was born at Boston, Mass., and was descended from Elisha Story, who came from England to Boston about 1700. Joseph Story [*q.v.*], associate justice of the United States Supreme Court for many years, was a brother of his grandfather; and his great-grandfather, Dr. Elisha Story of Bunker Hill, was one of the "Indians" of the Boston Tea Party. After graduation from Harvard in 1871, Story spent three and a half years in European study, particularly with the mathematicians Weierstrass and Kummer at Berlin and with C. G. Neumann at Leipzig, where he received the degree of Ph.D. in 1875 with a dissertation entitled *On the Algebraic Relations Existing between the Polars of a Binary Quantic* (1875). After spending the year 1875–76 as tutor in mathematics at Harvard, he went to the Johns Hopkins University, where he was at first associate in mathematics and then associate professor until 1889. The first seven years of this period were the most notable in the history of American mathematics up to that time, because of the presence at Baltimore of J. J. Sylvester [*q.v.*], through whose influence the *American Journal of Mathematics* was founded, with Sylvester as editor-in-chief and Story as "associate editor in charge" (1878–82). In this journal he published most of his mathematical papers, but others appeared in *Proceedings of the London Mathematical Society* (vol. XXIII, 1892), *Mathematische Annalen* (vol. XLI, 1893), *Zeitschrift für Physikalische Chemie* (vol. LXXI, 1910), *Proceedings of the American Academy of Arts and Sciences* (vol. XL, 1904), *Transactions of the American Mathematical Society* (January 1907), *The London, Edinburgh and Dublin Philosophical Magazine* (July 1910), and the *Official Report . . . of the New England Association of Colleges and Preparatory Schools* for 1903. He founded, edited, and published the *Mathematical Review* at Worcester, Mass., between 1896 and 1899, but only 208 pages, in two numbers and part of a third, were actually issued. He was also joint editor (1899) of *Clark University, 1889–1899,* the decennial celebration volume.

From 1889 until 1921, when he became professor emeritus, Story was professor at Clark University. Twelve doctoral dissertations in the fields of geometry and algebra were completed under his direction. He was elected a fellow of the American Academy of Arts and Sciences (1876) and of the National Academy of Sciences (1908), and served as president of the Mathematical Congress at the World's Columbian Exposition, Chicago (1893), and of the Omar Khayyam Club of America (1924–27). His admirable address before this club in 1918, *Omar Khayyàm as a Mathematician,* was printed privately in book form, with Story's portrait, in 1919, and reprinted in *Twenty Years of the Omar Khayyàm Club of America* (1921). Among the eighty men listed as the chief research mathematicians of the United States in 1903, Story was ranked by his colleagues as fifteenth (*American Men of Science,* 5th ed., 1933, p. 1269). His interest in mathematical bibliography led him to accumulate a catalogue comprising tens of thousands of hand-written cards in 156 drawers and 35 boxes, now the property of the library of the American Mathematical Society (see its *Bulletin . . . Catalogue,* 1932). He was married June 20, 1878, to Mary Harrison of Baltimore, and they had one son.

[*Eleventh Report of the Class of 1871 of Harvard Coll.* (1921) ; *Vita* in Story's Leipzig dissertation, mentioned above; Perley Derby, *Elisha Story of Boston and Some of His Descendants* (1915) ; F. I. Virkus, *The Abridged Compendium of Am. Geneal.,* I (1925), 218–19; Florian Cajori, *The Teaching and Hist. of Mathematics in the U. S.* (1890) ; Story's own account of his research, in *Clark Univ., 1889–1899* (1899), pp. 71–73, 546–47; J. C. Poggendorff's *Biographisch-Literarisches Handwörterbuch . . . der exacten Wissenschaften,* vols. III (1898), IV (1904), V (1926) ; *Harvard Grads. Mag.,* June 1930 ; *Who's Who in America,* 1928–29 ; *Springfield Daily Republican,* Apr. 11, 1930.]
R. C. A.

STORY, WILLIAM WETMORE (Feb. 12, 1819–Oct. 7, 1895), sculptor, essayist, and poet, was born in Salem, Mass., the second son and sixth child of Joseph Story [*q.v.*] and Sarah Waldo (Wetmore) Story. When Story was ten years old, the family moved from Salem to Cambridge, where he was prepared for college by William Wells and had James Russell Lowell [*q.v.*] for constant companion, Charles Sumner [*q.v.*] for intimate family friend and boyhood hero, and Thomas Wentworth Higginson [*q.v.*] for youthful admirer. Higginson later recalled Story as "a sort of Steerforth" among his fellows. In Lowell's *Fireside Travels,* dedicated to Story in 1864, the opening essay, "Cambridge Thirty Years Ago," reminiscent of Washington Allston, Margaret Fuller Ossoli, and Harriet Martineau, describes the boy's environment. In 1838 he received the degree of A.B. and in 1840 the degree of LL.B. from Harvard. The genius for friendship and for concentrated work in varied lines which marked his entire life was exerting itself at this time as he began the practice of law, first with the firm of Hillard and Sumner, and later with his brother-in-law, George Ticknor Curtis [*q.v.*]. He was a leading member of the "Brothers and Sisters," and a little later of the group which met at the home of George Ripley [*q.v.*] for the discussion of literary and esthetic problems. Long an amateur of the various arts, he now combined the exacting duties of a law practice and the preparation of volumes in the field of jurisprudence with painting, modelling, and music, to which he devoted himself in his spare time. Moreover, he delivered the Phi Beta Kappa poem at Harvard in 1844, while the *Boston Miscellany* and Lowell's short-lived *Pioneer* carried poems and essays by him. Among his legal publications were two textbooks which long maintained their place as standards, *A Treatise on the Law of Contracts Not under Seal* (1844) and *A Treatise on the Law of Sales of Personal Property* (1847), and several volumes of reports. His *Poems* appeared in 1847, followed by a second volume with the same title, dedicated to Lowell, in 1856. He also served as commissioner in bankruptcy, and commissioner for the United States courts in Massachusetts, Maine, and Pennsylvania, and reporter for the United States circuit court for the district of Massachusetts. Due in part to such incessant labor, he suffered a severe attack of brain and typhoid fever, from which he had hardly recovered when his distinguished father died in 1845 and the turning point of his career occurred.

On the death of Judge Story the trustees of Mount Auburn Cemetery proposed the erection in the chapel of a marble statue of their late colleague, to be paid for by public subscriptions, and nominated young Story as sculptor. To equip himself for this commission he left for Italy in the fall of 1847, with his wife, Emelyn Eldredge of Boston, whom he had married on Oct. 31, 1843, and his two small children. On his return to America his sketch was accepted. During the eight months of his stay he prepared for the press the *Life and Letters of Joseph Story* (2 vols., 1851), followed later by an edition of *The Miscellaneous Writings of Joseph Story* (1852). Back in Italy, he completed the statue of his father. Another year in America followed, devoted to both his vocation and his avocation. But he finally gave in to the claims of sculpture and, settling in Rome (1856), devoted his chief efforts to that art. "My mother," he later recalled, "thought me mad and urged me to pursue my legal career, in which everything was open to me, rather than take such a leap in the dark. But I had chosen, and I came back to Italy, where I

have lived nearly ever since" (James, *post*, vol. I, p. 32). The choice of Washington Allston under analogous stress, leading to stagnation in Cambridge, that of Lowell, leading to the Court of St. James's as ambassador, and that of the younger Henry James, Story's sensitive biographer, leading eventually to British citizenship, provide alluring contrasts and, along with Story's nostalgia for European culture, help to clarify a significant phase of American adolescence. The winter he spent listening to law lectures in Germany during his years of wavering, subsequent seasons in England and visits to France, and, much later, life in the Engadine, varied by occasional visits to America, suggest the breadth of background against which the sculptor moved. But in 1856 the burden of proof was still on Story. Indeed, the corner was not turned until the International Exhibition in London in 1862, when the "Cleopatra" (a replica of which is in the Metropolitan Museum, New York City) and the "Libyan Sibyl" (in the National Gallery of Art, Washington, D. C.) placed Story, at least in English eyes, in the forefront of Anglo-American sculpture. The considerations that Story won this position without the rigor of the usual technical training, that the reputation he achieved in his own day has not been maintained in the following century, and that he might have gone farther in law or in poetry if he had stayed in America are all beside the point. The main significance of his career is that of one whose versatility and charm enabled him to cross cultural boundaries to the advantage of the peoples concerned.

An apartment in the Palazzo Barberini in Rome became the center from which radiated the influence of the Storys. Their most celebrated contact was with the Brownings, with whom they were in almost daily intimacy until the death of Elizabeth Barrett Browning. Nathaniel Hawthorne [*q.v.*] rewarded Story for permitting his shy presence in his studio by describing the "Cleopatra" in *The Marble Faun* with such power that the public ever since has seen the fire of the novelist rather than the cool accuracy of the sculptor. During a childhood illness of Story's daughter, we read of Thackeray's and Hans Christian Andersen's being drafted for the amusement of the little convalescent. Charles Eliot Norton [*q.v.*], Mrs. Gaskell, Walter Savage Landor, Lady William Russell, Richard Monkton Milnes, Russell Sturgis [*q.v.*], and John Lothrop Motley [*q.v.*] add further distinction to the list of the close friends of the Storys. Only in the unforgotten death of their six-year-old son, Joseph Story, do they seem to have suffered a major grief. Without being in any direction a genius, Story learned the secret of happiness by the wise development of his many talents.

As a sculptor Story sought to give internal validity to his figures. He chose subjects of dramatic interest and, in so far as his smooth surfaces and careful accessories permitted, he expressed their inherent passion. Yet his approach to his conceptions was fundamentally an intellectual one, and he perhaps never learned to sacrifice what he knew about the subject to the demands of plastic creation. "Saul" (1863), reminiscent of Michelangelo's "Moses," "Medea" (1864), a center of interest at the Centennial Exposition in Philadelphia, and now in the Metropolitan Museum, "Salome" (1870), "Jerusalem in her Desolation" (1873), now in the Pennsylvania Academy of the Fine Arts, Philadelphia, and "Alcestis" (1874) represent, with the "Sibyl" and "Cleopatra," the most successful of the ideal figures. The fact that now and then he treated the same subject in both sculpture and poetry, and that in the case of "Cleopatra" at least he succeeded better in verse indicates the weakness of his plastic expression. Of his portrait figures, the seated "George Peabody" in London, in bronze, of which a replica was erected in Baltimore, and the dignified statues of John Marshall and Joseph Henry in Washington are the most adequate, while his last work, the stone for the grave of his wife in Rome, provides one of the few instances of that intensity, the lack of which in many other works causes them to miss immortality. Sumner, near the close of the Civil War, urged Story to become the sculptor of free America. When one recalls the Farragut and Sherman and Shaw and Lincoln of Augustus Saint-Gaudens, one realizes how fruitless was the request. Story's interest in sculpture, rather than his sculpture, is of importance.

A collection of essays gathered from the *Atlantic Monthly* and elsewhere, *Roba di Roma,* appeared in 1862 and long remained the outstanding appreciation of the spirit of contemporary Italy. Later came *Vallombrosa* (1881), *Fiammetta; a Summer Idyl* (1886), and *Excursions in Art and Letters* (1891). The *Graffiti d'Italia* (1868), containing "Ginevra da Siena," "Cleopatra," and "Giannone," despite the echoes of the forms of Browning and the felicities of Lowell, represents Story's most sustained poetry. Mention should also be made of his widely influential letters to the London *Daily News* (Dec. 25, 26, 27, 1861), reprinted as *The American Question* (1862), in which he debated and upheld the validity of the Federal position on union and emancipation. Several of his plays, usually prepared for private theatricals, reached the public in printed form, and a treatise on *The Proportions of the Human Figure* was published in 1866. Honors included doctorates from Oxford and from Bologna, and decorations from the governments of Italy and France. When he visited America in 1877 he was widely entertained in Boston and New York as America's outstanding representative of the arts. Mrs. Story's death in 1894 marked the end of his active career. He lived only until the following year, dying at the home of his daughter, Madame Edith Story Peruzzi, wife of the Marquis Simone Peruzzi di Medici, at Vallombrosa, Italy. He was buried beside his wife and son in the Protestant Cemetery at Rome, "il simpatico Americano." The two surviving sons continued their father's devotion to the arts, Thomas Waldo in sculpture and Julian Russell [*q.v.*] in painting.

[Henry James, *William Wetmore Story and His Friends* (2 vols., 1903); Mary E. Phillips, *Reminiscences of William Wetmore Story* (1897); Lorado Taft, *The Hist. of Am. Sculpture* (1903); W. J. Clark, *Great Am. Sculptures* (1903); *Passages from the French and Italian Note-Books of Nathaniel Hawthorne* (2 vols., 1872); *The Letters of Elizabeth Barrett Browning* (2 vols., 1897); C. R. Post, *A Hist. of European and Am. Sculpture* (1921), vol. II; obituary in *Evening Post* (N. Y.), Oct. 8, 1895.]   W. S. R.

STOTT, HENRY GORDON (May 13, 1866–Jan. 15, 1917), electrical engineer, was born in the Orkney Islands, the son of the Rev. David Stott and Elizabeth Jane Dibblee. Prepared in part by his father, he attended Watson Collegiate School, Edinburgh, proceeding thence to the College of Arts and Sciences at Glasgow, where he completed the course in mechanical engineering and electricity in 1885. During the previous year he had been employed by the Electric Illuminating Company of Glasgow, and upon graduation he became assistant electrician on board the steamship *Minia* of the Anglo-American Telegraph Company, principally engaged in repairs to cable lines. During his four and a half years with this organization he conducted experiments resulting in improved methods of cable repair and "was identified with the 'duplexing' of the United States Cable Company's main cable (2,750 knots), the longest duplex cable in the world" (*Transactions, post,* LXXXI, 1776).

After about a year as assistant engineer of the Brush Electric Engineering Company, Bournemouth, England, and another in a similar capacity with Hammond & Company, engaged in the construction of a power plant and an underground cable line at Madrid, Spain, he came to the United States in 1891 to construct the underground cable and conduit system for the Buffalo Light & Power Company. His performance of this task led to his appointment as engineer of the company, in which connection, during the ensuing decade, he had an active part in the industrial development of Buffalo. Among the notable projects for which he was responsible was the Wilkerson Street power plant, which he designed and executed. In 1901 he removed to New York City to become superintendent of motive power for the Manhattan Railway Company, assuming charge of the organization of the operating force, the construction of the power plant in Seventy-fourth Street, substations, and transmission lines. Retained in the same position after the amalgamation of the Manhattan system with the Interboro Rapid Transit Company, he supervised the construction of the Fifty-ninth Street power plant and the design, construction, and operation of the power-generating stations of the distributing system of the gigantic Interboro company, which controlled subway, elevated, and surface lines of New York City.

Stott was an active participant in the affairs of numerous professional societies; he was president of the American Institute of Electrical Engineers (1907–08), vice-president of the American Society of Mechanical Engineers (1912–14), a director of the American Society of Civil Engineers (1911), and vice-president and trustee of the United Engineering Society (1911). To the *Transactions* of a number of these bodies he contributed papers revealing an unusual capacity for minute analysis of engineering problems. Among them were "Locating Faults in Underground Distribution Systems" and "The Distribution and Conversion of Received Currents" (*Transactions of the American Institute of Electrical Engineers,* vol. XVIII, 1902); "Power Plant Economics" (*Ibid.,* vol. XXV, 1907); "Notes on the Cost of Power" (*Ibid.,* vol. XXVIII, pt. 2, 1910); "Test of a 15,000 Kilowatt Steam-Engine Turbine Unit," with R. J. S. Pigott (*Ibid.,* vol. XIX, pt. 1, 1911). He was in the front rank of both electrical and mechanical engineers and with his technical qualifications combined an extraordinary executive ability—a power of inspiring the confidence of his employees and of bringing out their best efforts. He early became a United States citizen. On July 22, 1894, he married Anna Mitchell, who with a son and a daughter survived him. He was an active member of the Protestant Episcopal Church of New Rochelle.

[*Who's Who in America,* 1916–17; *Proc. Am. Inst. Elec. Engineers,* Feb. 1917; *Jour. Am. Soc. Mech. Engineers,* Feb. 1917, with portr.; *Trans. Am. Soc. Civil Engineers,* vol. LXXXI (1917); *Power,* Jan. 23, 1917, pp. 121, 132; *Cassier's Mag.,* Apr. 1906; *N. Y. Times,* Jan. 17, 1917.]   B. A. R.

STOUGHTON, EDWIN WALLACE (May 1, 1818–Jan. 7, 1882), lawyer, was born in Springfield, Windsor County, Vt., the son of Thomas P. Stoughton by his first wife, Susan (Bradley) of Windsor, Vt. He was descended from Thomas Stoughton who came with his brother Israel to Dorchester, Mass., about 1630 and some ten years later settled in Windsor, Conn. What formal academic training Edwin had he received at local schools and at a neighboring academy. At eighteen he forsook his father's homestead and went to New York City to seek his fortune at the bar so that he might capitalize his eloquence and his analytical thinking. In May 1837 he commenced the study of the law in the office of Philo T. Ruggles, but soon became a clerk in the offices of Seeley & Glover, with the privilege of using the firm's library for reading and study. He eked out his meager salary by contributing to magazines, writing for *Hunt's Merchants' Magazine* in 1839 and later for the *New World.* His literary efforts displayed an understanding of current events, history, and economics, together with a fairly lucid literary style. In 1840 he was admitted to the bar.

Stoughton constituted his own law firm. His practice was confined largely to court-room work, and his legal renown was won chiefly in a series of patent suits. Notable among these were the Charles Goodyear patent cases (76 *U. S.,* 788), the Woodworth planing-machine cases, the Ross Winans eight-wheel car patent cases, the Wheeler & Wilson sewing machine cases, and the Corliss steam-engine patent case. He appeared for the United States and New Jersey in *U. S. vs. Callicott* (14,710 *Federal Cases*), when the defendant was convicted of malfeasance in the Internal Revenue office; and was retained by William M. Tweed as an adviser, but took no active part in Tweed's defense.

In early life Stoughton was a War Democrat, but when his party publicized complaints respecting the use of the federal troops made by President Grant in Louisiana he defended the President, and thenceforth his sympathies were with the Republican party. He became a personal friend of President Grant and accepted his request to become a member of a commission of leading Republicans and Democrats which was to report on the controversial Hayes-Tilden election of 1876 in the state of Louisiana. He went to New Orleans and personally observed the canvassing of votes by the Returning Board. Subsequently he was one of those who represented the Republican cause before the Electoral Commission, arguing, in two addresses, that Congress could not go behind the decision of a state and that the election certificate must be accepted if the proper state authorities signed it. The commission accepted this legal reasoning and honored all the disputed Republican electoral votes. He contributed an article entitled "The 'Electoral Commission' Bubble Exploded" to the *North American Review*, September-October 1877.

As a reward for his services, President Hayes appointed Stoughton envoy extraordinary and minister plenipotentiary to Russia, Oct. 30, 1877. Because of ill health, he left St. Petersburg on leave of absence early in 1879, but failed to recover his strength in southern Europe and returned to New York, resigning his post in July of that year. Less than three years later he died, in New York, of Bright's disease and dropsy. He was married, Mar. 3, 1855, to Mary Fiske, a widow, but left no children

[H. R. Stiles, *The Hist. and Geneals. of Ancient Windsor, Conn.*, II (1892), 736; *N. Y. Tribune, N. Y. Times, N. Y. Herald*, Jan. 8, 1882; *Papers Relating to the Foreign Relations of the U. S.*, 1878, 1879; *Medico-Legal Journal* (N. Y.), Dec. 1883; *Encyc. of Contemporary Biog. of N. Y.*, vol. I (1878); G. W. Fuller, *Descendants of Thomas Stoughton* (1929); *In Memory of Edwin Wallace Stoughton: Report of a Meeting of the Bar of the Courts of the State of N. Y., and of the U. S. for the Second Circuit . . . Jan. 13, 1882*; *Letter of Judge Black to Mr. Stoughton, Reply to Stoughton's Defence (?) of the Great Fraud* (1877).]

J. H. L.

STOUGHTON, WILLIAM (Sept. 30, 1631–July 7, 1701), colonial magistrate, was the second son of Israel Stoughton, who came to New England about 1630, was one of the founders of Dorchester, and became one of the largest landowners in the Massachusetts Bay Colony. Israel was a brother of John Stoughton, rector of Aller, Somerset, and step-father of Ralph Cudworth, the Cambridge neo-platonist. It is probable that William was born in England. After graduating from Harvard College in 1650, he went to England to continue his studies at Oxford, where he became a fellow of New College and received the degree of M.A. on June 30, 1653. He was curate at Rumboldswyke, Sussex, in 1659. Ejected from his fellowship at the Restoration (1660), he returned to Massachusetts in the summer of 1662. He preached for several years in the Dorchester church and was paid for his services, but repeatedly declined to become pastor there or at Cambridge. In 1668 he preached an election sermon in which he asserted that "God sifted a whole Nation that he might send Choice Grain

over into this Wilderness" (*New Englands True Interest; . . . A Sermon*, 1670, p. 19).

Stoughton served as an assistant of Massachusetts Bay, 1671–86; as a commissioner of the United Colonies, 1674–76, 1680–86; and as judge of various courts. With Peter Bulkeley he represented Massachusetts before the King in the controversy over the Mason claims, 1676–79, and by adopting the conciliatory attitude he deemed necessary in these negotiations greatly displeased the radical element in Massachusetts. In 1681 Stoughton and Joseph Dudley [*q.v.*] were appointed, at their own suggestion, to examine land titles in the Nipmuck country—a profitable service, since each agent received a liberal portion of the land ceded by the Indians as the result of the investigation. As a stanch political friend of Dudley, Stoughton declined office in 1684 and 1686, when the former failed of reëlection to the office of assistant.

When Dudley became president of the temporary government established in 1686 after the revocation of the charter, he appointed his adherent deputy president. Apparently a loyal servant of the King—except when the interests of the Crown conflicted with his own interests as a landholder or the interests of Harvard College, of which he was one of the most generous native benefactors (Sibley, *post*, p. 319)—Stoughton was on the council of Gov. Edmund Andros [*q.v.*]; but when rebellion came he signed an address of the magistrates advising the Governor to deliver the fort to the revolutionists, and in 1690 he signed a paper drawn up by members of the former council denouncing Andros' acts while governor. Named lieutenant-governor May 1692 under Sir William Phips [*q.v.*], he became acting governor on the latter's departure for England in 1694, and was the active head of the government thereafter until his death, except from May 1699 to July 1700, when Governor Bellomont was in Boston.

Stoughton was chief justice of the court of oyer and terminer which tried the Salem witchcraft cases in 1692, and by his insistence on the admission of "spectral evidence," as well as by his overbearing attitude toward the accused, the witnesses, and the jury, was largely responsible for the tragic aspect they assumed (Phips to the Earl of Nottingham, *Calendar of State Papers, Colonial Series, America and West Indies, January 1693–14 May 1696*, 1903, p. 30; Robert Calef, *More Wonders of the Invisible World*, 1700). He seems never to have repented (Calef, *op. cit.*; Hutchinson, *post*, II, 61), and his refusal to yield to feelings of compassion after most others had become enlightened indicates his essentially cold, proud, and obstinate nature. It is notable, however, that his part in the witchcraft delusion did not damage him in the eyes of his contemporaries, and that he died respected as one of the most eminent citizens of the colony.

[Sources include: *Records of the First Church at Dorchester . . . 1636–1734* (1891); *A Report of the Record Commissioners of . . . Boston,* no. 21 (1890); Joseph Foster, *Alumni Oxonienses,* vol. IV (1892); Edward Calamy, *An Abridgment of Mr. Baxter's Hist. of His Life and Times* (2nd ed., 1713), vol. II; A. G. Matthews, *Calamy Revised* (1934); "The Diaries of John Hull," *Trans. and Colls. Am. Antiq. Soc.,* vol. III (1857); N. B. Shurtleff, *Records of the Gov. and Company of the Mass. Bay,* vols. IV–V (1854); Thomas Hutchinson, *The Hist. of the Colony of Massachuset's Bay,* vol. I (1765), the most favorable treatment; R. N. Toppan, *Edward Randolph; Including His Letters and Official Papers,* vols. III–VI (1899–1909); W. H. Whitmore, *The Andros Tracts,* vol. I (1868); *Calendar of State Papers, Colonial Series, America and West Indies, 1701* (1910), p. 164; *Proc. Mass. Hist. Soc.,* 2 ser. I (1885); J. L. Sibley, *Biog. Sketches Grads. Harvard Univ.,* vol. I (1873); J. W. Dean, "William Stoughton," *New Eng. Hist. and Geneal. Reg.,* Jan. 1896; J. G. Palfrey, *Hist. of New England,* vol. III (1864), a severe judgment; C. W. Upham, *Salem Witchcraft* (1867), vol. II, and Emory Washburn, *Sketches of the Judicial Hist. of Mass.* (1840), the last two being more severe than Palfrey in their judgments of Stoughton. A writer in *Putnam's Mag.,* Sept. 1853, attributing to the Chief Justice an act of repentance resembling that of Samuel Sewall [*q.v.*], has apparently confused the two men.]   S. G. M.

STOW, BARON (June 16, 1801–Dec. 27, 1869), Baptist minister, was named in honor of Baron Steuben, but the middle name was early dropped from use. The first of five children of Peter Stow, a native of Grafton, Mass., and Deborah (Nettleton) Stow of Killingworth, Conn., he was born at Croydon, N. H. About 1809 the family moved to a farm in the adjacent town, Newport, where the boy attended district school, read avidly, and was marked as a student of promise. When he was sixteen, the death of his father threatened to hold him to the farm, but his interest lay elsewhere. He united with the Baptist church at Newport, being baptized Dec. 31, 1818, and immediately turned toward the ministry. After preparation in the academy at Newport, in September 1822 he was admitted to Columbian College, Washington, D. C. Here he made contacts with teachers and fellow students which became important for his later career. Although his health was not robust, he completed his course in a little over three years, being appointed valedictorian at his graduation, December 1825.

He had already devoted considerable time to editorial work on the *Columbian Star,* the weekly journal of the Triennial Convention, and from Jan. 28, 1826, until the summer of 1827 he was the editor of that periodical. An unfortunate episode of this editorial experience was his publication of insinuations against Luther Rice [*q.v.*].

Rice's counter-blast in a local Washington newspaper, the *Daily National Journal,* Nov. 9, 1826, led to immediate action by the First Baptist Church (manuscript records, Nov. 10, 1826), but the matter was cleared up commendably by a statement of regret in an agreement which both men signed.

On Sept. 7, 1826, Stow had married Elizabeth L. Skinner of Windsor, Vt. In the summer of 1827 he went to Portsmouth, N. H., where he was ordained on Oct. 24. Here he developed the methods of religious work which characterized his entire ministry. His preaching was distinctly evangelistic, with very direct appeal to the individual. He was constant in pastoral visitation even when increasingly tasks for the larger religious community were placed upon him. With John Newton Brown [*q.v.*] he had an indeterminable part in the production of the New Hampshire confession of faith. The most distinguished period of his career was his pastorate of the Second or Baldwin Place Church in Boston, where he succeeded his college roommate, Dr. James D. Knowles. Installed there in November 1832, he entered upon a pastoral and preaching ministry of marked power. Changes in the northern part of the city, where the church was located, and dissatisfaction with results, felt more by Stow himself than by his parishioners, led to his resignation in May 1848. In October of that year, he began an almost equally significant pastorate at the Rowe Street Baptist Church which continued until early in 1867.

Of an especially sensitive temperament, he was frequently physically incapacitated; trips to Europe in 1840–41 and in 1859 brought physical recuperation and enrichment of his mental powers. He refused many calls to other pastorates, to secretarial positions, and to the presidencies of at least three colleges. He was actively associated with the foreign missions enterprise and was one of the leaders in its reorganization by the Northern Baptists in 1845. Although of irenic disposition—well illustrated in his *Christian Brotherhood* (1859), a forceful plea for Christian union—he possessed strong feelings which occasionally dominated him and led to some trying experiences. He wrote prolifically for the religious press, including two brief works on missionary history prepared especially for the Sunday School library and a devotional book, *Daily Manna for Christians* (1843), which was much read. With Samuel F. Smith [*q.v.*] he edited *The Psalmist* (1843), which was for several decades the hymnal most widely used by American Baptists.

[J. C. Stockbridge, *A Model Pastor: A Memoir of the Life and Correspondence of Rev. Baron Stow, D.D.* (1871) ; memorial discourses in R. H. Neale, *The Pastor and Preacher* (1870) ; *The Bapt. Encyc.* (1883) ; records of the First Baptist Church, Washington, D. C. ; *Boston Transcript*, Dec. 28, 1869.]   W. H. A.

STOWE, CALVIN ELLIS (Apr. 26, 1802–Aug. 22, 1886), educator, was born in Natick, Mass., the son of Samuel and Hepzibah (Biglow) Stow. He added the final "e" to the family name after his graduation from college. He was a descendant of John Stowe who settled in Roxbury, Mass., and took the freeman's oath in 1634. When he was six years old, his father, the jovial village baker, died, leaving his widow in poverty. At twelve, the boy was apprenticed to a paper maker. He prepared for college at Gorham Academy, Gorham, Me., and entered the class of 1824 at Bowdoin College. Franklin Pierce [*q.v.*] was a classmate and William Pitt Fessenden [*q.v.*] was in the class above them. Graduating with valedictory honors, Stowe remained for a year as librarian and instructor. In 1825 he entered Andover Theological Seminary. During his senior year he made a translation from the German of Johann Jahn which was subsequently published as *Jahn's History of the Hebrew Commonwealth* (Andover 1828, London 1829) ; the following year he was editor of the *Boston Recorder*. In 1829 he revised and edited with notes *Lectures on the Sacred Poetry of the Hebrews*, a translation by G. Gregory from the Latin of Robert Lowth.

In 1831 he became professor of Greek in Dartmouth College. The following year he married Eliza, daughter of Rev. Bennet Tyler [*q.v.*] of Portland, Me., and in 1833 was called to the chair of Biblical literature in Lane Theological Seminary, Cincinnati, Ohio. His wife died in 1834, and on Jan. 6, 1836, he married Harriet Elizabeth (see Harriet Elizabeth Beecher Stowe), daughter of Lyman Beecher [*q.v.*], president of the Seminary. While in Cincinnati Stowe was actively interested in the improvement of the common schools, regarding such improvement as the great need of the West. The College of Teachers in Cincinnati was founded in 1833 largely through his influence. He published in 1835 *Introduction to the Criticism and Interpretation of the Bible.* In 1836 the state of Ohio appointed him commissioner to investigate the public school systems of Europe, especially of Prussia. For this congenial task he was given every facility in England and on the Continent. Returning in 1837, he published his famous *Report on Elementary Instruction in Europe*, a copy of which the legislature put into every school district of the state. It was reprinted by the legislatures of Massachusetts, Pennsylvania, Michigan, and other states, in *Common Schools and Teachers' Seminaries* (1839), and in E. W. Knight, *Reports on European Education by John Griscom, Victor Cousin, Calvin E. Stowe* (1930).

In 1850 Stowe accepted a call to the chair of natural and revealed religion at Bowdoin. Two years later he went to Andover Theological Seminary as professor of sacred literature. In 1853, 1856, and 1859, he visited Europe with his wife, whose *Uncle Tom's Cabin*, published in 1852, occasioned the enthusiastic reception which was accorded them, especially in England. Failing health caused him to resign the Andover professorship in 1864, and Hartford, Conn., became the family home. In 1866 the Stowes began spending their winters at Mandarin, Fla., on the St. John's River, where they took oversight of the religious welfare of the neighborhood. In 1867 he published *Origin and History of the Books of the Bible.* He was at home in many languages, ancient and modern. A man of large frame and wearing a patriarchal beard, he was a child in financial and practical matters. He was a born story-teller and his tales of the characters he knew in his boyhood furnished much of the local coloring for his wife's *Old Town Folks.* Early in their married life, he urged his wife to enter upon a literary career, and his enthusiasm was her constant encouragement. He always carried with him pocket editions of the Greek New Testament and Dante's *Divina Commedia;* they were under his pillow throughout his last illness.

[*New England Hist. and Geneal. Reg.*, Apr. 1856; *Vital Records of Natick* (1910) ; *Gen. Cat. of Bowdoin Coll.* (1912) ; Nehemiah Cleaveland, *Hist. of Bowdoin Coll.* (1882), ed. by A. S. Packard ; *Congregationalist*, Aug. 26, Sept. 2, 1886; C. E. Stowe, *Life of Harriet Beecher Stowe* (1889) ; C. M. Rourke, *Trumpets of Jubilee* (1927) ; *Boston Transcript*, Aug. 23, 1886.]   E. D. E.

STOWE, HARRIET ELIZABETH BEECHER (June 14, 1811–July 1, 1896), author and humanitarian, was born in the town of Litchfield, Conn. Her father, Lyman Beecher [*q.v.*], was the pastor of the Congregational Church and a stern Calvinist. A vigorous, enthusiastic man, he was accustomed to work off his surplus energies by shoveling sand from one pile to another in the cellar of his house. He was fond of music and played the violin. An upright piano, which he had brought from New Haven, was borne into the house with as much reverence, said his daughter, as if it had been "the ark of the covenant."

Roxana Foote, the minister's first wife and the mother of eight children, died when her daughter Harriet was only four. She had been a mill girl of the type made famous by Lucy Larcom and her friends. She had read Samuel Richardson's *History of Sir Charles Grandison* in her girlhood days and a copy of it lay on the parlor table of the Beecher home. Shy and diffident, she could never lead the services in the weekly women's prayer meetings. "She never spoke in company or before strangers without blushing," said Harriet (Fields, *Life and Letters, post,* p. 13). Her wish was that all of her sons should become ministers—a wish that was fulfilled with one exception by Harriet's six brothers.

The future author of *Uncle Tom's Cabin,* although brought up in New England, numbered among her childhood friends members of the negro race. Candace, her mother's washerwoman, and Dinah, the servant at Aunt Harriet Foote's were destined to appear again and again among the author's favorite characters. The motherly colored woman, Candace, who was so devoted to the memory of her dead mistress, left a strong impression on the mind of little Harriet. The children turned to her for comfort in their sorrow and bereavement. They stood somewhat in awe of their new stepmother, Harriet Porter, who soon came from Portland, Me., and seemed to them extremely fine and elegant.

Harriet's education, like that of most Puritan children, was two-thirds religious. At the age of eleven she wrote a composition on the subject: "Can the Immortality of the Soul be Proved by the Light of Nature?," and chose to defend the negative. When her paper was read aloud at the school exhibition, her father praised it without knowing it was hers. "It was the proudest moment of my life," she said in after years. A contrast to her father's orthodox theology was furnished by her uncle, Samuel Foote, a seafaring man and a frequent visitor at the Beecher home. Uncle Sam, as he was called, had been to the ends of the earth and was a romantic figure in the eyes of his niece. He sometimes insisted that Turks were as good as Christians, and Catholics as good as Protestants, and he could argue so skilfully that the minister was hard put to it to defend his own view. The poetry of Byron, which Harriet read before her teens, likewise made a strong impression on her. Her father talked a great deal about the English poet, whom he admired while he also condemned him. On Byron's death, he preached a sermon which Harriet long remembered.

Like her elder sister Catherine, Harriet was unable to accept her father's Deity unquestioningly. A great deal of doubt and conflict accompanied her conversion at the age of fourteen. Years of morbid introspection darkened her girl-

hood and left their traces on her maturity. All her writings testify to a life-long preoccupation with the problem of religion. Even in her fiction the conflict between faith and doubt forms an ever-present theme. Somewhat late in life she attended the Episcopal Church with her daughters who were Episcopalians. The loss of a beloved son caused her to become interested in spiritualism, and she corresponded on the subject with Elizabeth Barrett Browning.

Up to the age of thirteen, when she was sent to Hartford to attend a school for girls, her most intimate companion had been her brother Henry Ward [*q.v.*]. "Harriet and Henry come next," wrote the second Mrs. Beecher, describing her step-children, "and they are always hand in hand." Hand in hand, they went to the dame school where they learned to read. The sympathy thus founded lasted all their lives. Hand in hand they waged their great battle against slavery. When Beecher was in England speaking for the cause, he awoke one morning so hoarse that he could scarcely use his voice. "I will speak to my sister three thousand miles away," he said, and called out, "Harriet." With this his voice returned and he made that day one of his most famous speeches (Annie A. Fields, *Memories of a Hostess,* 1922, p. 268). His sister adored him. "He is myself," she wrote to George Eliot during the Beecher trial. "I know you are the kind of woman to understand me when I say that I felt a blow at him more than at myself" (C. E. and L. B. Stowe, *post,* p. 291).

In October 1832 the family moved to Cincinnati, where Dr. Beecher had been called to be the head of the Lane Theological Seminary and where his daughter Catherine [*q.v.*] established the Western Female Institute. Her uncle Samuel Foote also joined the colony. Harriet liked her new environment and wrote cheerful letters home. Employed as a teacher in her sister's school, she still found time to try her hand at divers kinds of writing. For the first time she began to unfold the more playful and imaginative side of her nature. She wrote sketches for the *Western Monthly Magazine* and received a prize of fifty dollars for a story—"Prize Tale, a New England Sketch"—which appeared in the issue of April 1834, and was separately printed under that title. It was subsequently reprinted in *The Mayflower* (1843) as "Uncle Tim" and again reprinted in *The Mayflower* (1855) with the name of the leading character and the title changed to "Uncle Lot." Her marriage, Jan. 6, 1836, to Calvin Ellis Stowe [*q.v.*], professor of Biblical literature in her father's seminary, put an end for the time being to her career of authorship. Except for a few tales and sketches, published in *The Mayflower,* she produced almost nothing until 1852. These, however, convinced her husband that she must be "a literary woman" and he urged her strongly to write, and also to drop the E from her signature.

Altogether, she spent eighteen years in Cincinnati. It was a period of much poverty and hardship but rich in observation and experience which she afterwards turned to good account in her tales and novels. There six of her seven children were born and one of them was buried. She lived through the cholera epidemic of 1849, to which her baby was a sacrifice. She visited a Kentucky plantation and saw the life of the slaves in their cabins. To the impressions thus gained were added, however, those of her brother who had seen New Orleans and ascended the Red River. Her father's seminary was a hotbed of anti-slavery sentiment; one of the most extreme advocates of Abolitionism, Theodore D. Weld [*q.v.*], was an early student there. Mrs. Stowe and her brother Henry, then editor of a newspaper, became deeply interested in the cause. Her letters confirm her son's statement that she "was anti-slavery in her sympathies, but she was not a declared abolitionist" (C. E. Stowe, *post,* p. 87). When the press of J. G. Birney [*q.v.*] was destroyed by a mob she was more concerned about the violation of private rights and mob violence than defense of abolitionism. It was not until her return to New England in 1850 during the discussion over the Fugitive Slave Law, that her anti-slavery feeling became intense.

In 1850 Stowe was called to a professorship in Bowdoin College, Brunswick, Me. On her way thither Mrs. Stowe stopped in Brooklyn for a visit with her brother who had become the popular pastor of Plymouth Church. "Henry's people," she wrote her husband, "are more than ever in love with him, and have raised his salary to $3,300 and given him a beautiful horse and carriage worth $600." To the Stowes, who were extremely poor at this time, more so in fact than they were ever to be again, this seemed like unexampled prosperity. By all accounts the family arrived in Brunswick at the nadir of their fortunes. A visit to her brother, Edward Beecher [*q.v.*], fanned her sentiments on slavery to white heat. Edward thundered from his Boston pulpit against the Fugitive Slave Law and his wife wrote to Mrs. Stowe, who had just borne her seventh child, "Now, Hattie, if I could just use the pen as you can, I would write something that would make this whole nation feel what an accursed thing slavery is." To this Mrs. Stowe

replied, "As long as the baby sleeps with me nights, I can't do much at anything; but I will do it at last. I will write that thing if I live" (Fields, *Life and Letters, post,* p. 130). When she told her brother Henry that she had begun her story, he answered heartily, "That's right, Hattie! Finish it, and I will scatter it thicker than the leaves of Vallombrosa" (C. E. and L. B. Stowe, *post,* p. 288).

The outcome of her endeavor was *Uncle Tom's Cabin, or Life Among the Lowly,* first published as a serial (June 5, 1851–Apr. 1, 1852) in the *National Era,* an anti-slavery paper of Washington, D. C. She gives two accounts of the origin of this book (see Fields, *Life and Letters, post,* pp. 130 ff., 147, 164–65). In one instance, she states that she wrote the pages which describe the death of Uncle Tom in Brunswick and read them to her little boys. In the other, she says that she wrote the passage in Andover and read it to her husband. Both accounts agree in stating that the first part of the book ever committed to writing was the death of Uncle Tom. She wrote this at one sitting and when her supply of writing paper gave out, finished it on some scraps of brown paper taken from a grocer's parcel. She then composed the earlier chapters and sent them to the *National Era,* which paid her $300 for the serial. The Boston publisher who had contracted for the book rights protested that she was making the story too long, but she replied that she did not write the book; it wrote itself. It was finally brought out by John P. Jewett [*q.v.*] on Mar. 20, 1852, in two volumes, with a woodcut of a negro cabin as the frontispiece.

Although no one had expected the work to be popular or successful, ten thousand copies were sold in less than a week. Within a year the sales amounted to three-hundred thousand. It was generally supposed that Mrs. Stowe had made a fortune out of it, but her returns were far below what they should have been. She received a royalty of ten per cent. on the American sales but not a penny for the dramatic rights, although *Uncle Tom's Cabin* was one of the most popular plays ever produced on the American stage. The English circulation, which reached a million and a half, was a triumph of pirated editions. The young man who worked at Putnam's and sent the book to England received five pounds for his trouble (*The Times Literary Supplement,* London, July 8, 1926, p. 468).

The hero of *Uncle Tom's Cabin* is a colored man, a slave, who passed from the ownership of a Kentucky planter to that of a New Orleans gentleman and thence to that of a cotton planter on the Red River. In Colonel Shelby, St. Clare, and Simon Legree, the author depicted three types of Southern slave-owners. Uncle Tom's first master was drawn from a benevolent planter of the same name, whom Mrs. Stowe had known in Kentucky. St. Clare was an idealized portrait and still lives in fiction as the type of a gracious, high-bred gentleman. Simon Legree, who caused the death of Uncle Tom, was likewise destined to survive as a historic villain. The patience and piety of the humble hero and the spiritual beauty of the child Eva were drawn from cherished ideals peculiar to the author. In the death of little Eva and the martyrdom of Uncle Tom, the author reached the high notes of her pathos; but the struggle of George and Eliza for freedom and their final achievement of it through flight to Canada was probably the most popular feature of the book. In the description of George Harris as a freeman, the style rises to eloquence.

Mrs. Stowe had not foreseen the storm of wrath which *Uncle Tom* was to evoke. In the South her name was hated. A cousin living in Georgia told her that she did not dare to receive letters from her with her name on the outside of the envelope, and the *Southern Literary Messenger* declared the book a "criminal prostitution of the high functions of the imagination," saying that the author had "placed herself without the pale of kindly treatment at the hands of Southern criticism" (December 1852, pp. 721–31; October 1852, pp. 630–38). While Mrs. Stowe had feared the abolitionists would find the work too mild, they proved at last to be its only partisans. From all sides she was attacked and the accuracy of her facts questioned. Her reply to this criticism was *A Key to Uncle Tom's Cabin* (1853). Much of the material was collected after *Uncle Tom's Cabin* was written, though the defense was announced as containing the facts on which the story was based (Rourke, *post,* p. 100). From the popular point of view, this book was a complete failure. As a defense, it was hardly more successful. It failed to disprove the charge that there were errors of fact in her earlier work, and its indictment of slavery was far less powerful. Its polemics added nothing to the pathos of her novel.

From the first there was some discussion of the literary value of *Uncle Tom's Cabin.* Her critics thought she owed a great deal to her subject. As a romance and a picture of American manners, however, it undoubtedly deserves high rank. Mrs. Stowe apparently had a fondness for the South. While she hated it for being on the side of slavery, she portrayed its atmosphere with fire and sympathy. She was the first American writer to take the negro seriously and to con-

ceive a novel with a black man as the hero. Although it was written with a moral purpose, the author forgot the purpose sometimes in the joy of telling her tale. The influence of Sir Walter Scott, whom she had read in girlhood, and of Charles Dickens, her great contemporary, is clearly visible.

Mrs. Stowe had her first inkling of the fame she had acquired when she went to buy a seat for Jenny Lind's concert and found there were no more. Otto Goldschmidt, the singer's husband, hearing that the author of *Uncle Tom's Cabin* had been turned away, immediately sent tickets with the compliments of his wife. The English abolitionists paid her every honor. When she went to visit England soon after the appearance of the book, people thronged the docks to have a glimpse of her. Lord Shaftesbury composed an address of welcome on behalf of the women of England, a great demonstration was held at Stafford House in her honor, and the Duchess of Sutherland presented her with a gold bracelet in the form of a slave's shackle. One hundred thousand copies of her second antislavery novel, *Dred, A Tale of the Great Dismal Swamp* (1856), were sold in England in less than a month. She met Lord Palmerston, Charles Dickens, and other celebrities of the English world. A considerable sum was collected for her anti-slavery work in America. On the proceeds of her literary ventures, she made two subsequent visits to England and toured the Continent with her family. Among her friends were Lady Byron, George Eliot, and the Ruskins. Her friendship with Lady Byron led to Mrs. Stowe's spectacular contribution to the Byron controversy several years later, when she published in the *Atlantic Monthly* (September 1869) "The True Story of Lady Byron's Life." In this article she charged Lord Byron, on the alleged authority of Lady Byron, with having had a guilty love for his sister, Mrs. Leigh. For the second time, Mrs. Stowe became the focus of a public storm, and for the second time she appeared in print with a detailed argument in her own defense, renewing and elaborating in *Lady Byron Vindicated* (1870) the charge of incest against Byron and adding that a child had been born of the union. The feeling aroused against her in England was intense. Charles Dickens wrote to James T. Fields: "Wish Mrs. Stowe was in the pillory" (Annie A. Fields, *Memories of a Hostess,* p. 191). She had precipitated a bitter controversy which was to last for years. Even those who believed the story could not understand her action. She was accused of scandalmongering and a desire for notoriety (see *American Mer-*

cury, April 1927). Mrs. Stowe could not be judged by ordinary standards, however. Her interest in the case was sincere and conscientious. The life of Byron had always had a strong fascination for her. Like her father, she admired his genius while she mourned his faults. Since Lyman Beecher had once preached a sermon on Byron's life and character, his daughter saw no harm in writing a book on the same subject. It was to her a public question, like that of slavery, and she handled it in the same indomitable spirit.

As a writer, Mrs. Stowe was exceedingly industrious. Already past forty when she published her first book, she continued to pour forth a steady stream of fiction. Throughout the high excitement that followed *Uncle Tom,* the distraction of her trips to Europe, the removals of her family from one home to the other, she kept up her literary industry. The *Atlantic Monthly,* the New York *Independent,* and the *Christian Union,* of which her brother Henry was the editor, contained regular contributions from her pen. For nearly thirty years, she wrote on the average almost a book a year. Following *Uncle Tom's Cabin* and *Dred,* she turned to her New England background. In *The Minister's Wooing* (1859), *The Pearl of Orr's Island* (1862), and *Oldtown Folks* (1869), she pictured types and scenes familiar in her girlhood. For the last named, perhaps "the richest and raciest" of her novels, she drew largely on her husband's reminiscences, as she did also in writing *Sam Lawson's Oldtown Fireside Stories* (1872). In *Poganuc People* (1878) she described her early childhood. The originals of most of her characters were close at hand and can often be identified. Sometimes she did not even disguise the names. A comparatively recent critic declares that "the autobiographical material that fills her later work . . . is much more than autobiography; it is intimate history of New England. . . . As the historian of the human side of Calvinism she tempered dogma with affection." He adds, "She could bring her soul under discipline but not her art. . . . The creative instinct was strong in her but the critical was wholly lacking" (Parrington, *post,* II, 372, 375, 376). In addition to her numerous novels, she published with her sister Catherine *Principles of Domestic Science* (1870) and *The New Housekeeper's Manual* (1873); she also issued a volume entitled *Religious Poems* (1867), containing "Still, still with Thee, when purple morning breaketh," which became a popular hymn. An edition of her works in sixteen volumes, *The Writings of Harriet Beecher Stowe,* appeared in 1896.

After the Civil War she bought a home in Florida, where she spent most of the years that remained to her. Her old age was not prosperous, for she was not a good business woman, and her husband was, if possible, more impractical than she. Her son and grandson tell us that she invested ten thousand dollars in a scheme for raising cotton on a Florida plantation and that all of this was lost. She had previously spent large sums on a house in Hartford which, when built, proved unsuitable for use. While writing *Oldtown Folks,* she was obliged to live on advances from her publishers, because her investments, amounting to thirty-four thousand dollars, were entirely unremunerative. The *Christian Union,* her brother's paper, cost her considerable sums. Even at the height of her prosperity, she was never free from money worries. The modest place at Mandarin where she spent her declining years was at last sold for a song.

The life-time of Mrs. Stowe almost spanned the nineteenth century. Born and bred to womanhood in Puritan New England, she spent her first maturity at a Western outpost. When her family went to Cincinnati in 1832 they traveled by stage-coach and steamboat, and hogs still ran about the dusty city streets. She lived to speed by railway through the Middle West and give readings from her stories on Lyceum platforms. On her wedding journey she had traveled through Ohio in a stage-coach. On her lecture trips she went over the same ground by express train. The World's Fair at Chicago found her, as she would have said, "still this side of spiritland"; but that great blast of progress could no longer rouse her. She had the rare experience of waking up one morning and finding herself famous. Her brother Edward wrote to her and warned her against pride. It was not necessary. The daughter of Lyman Beecher could not be corrupted by success. She remained herself through all vicissitudes—earnest, whimsical, devoted. From her childhood, she was preoccupied and absent-minded, not hearing what was said to her and making funny blunders. This tendency increased with her advancing years. A full decade before her death, she lapsed into a dreamy state which lasted to the end. When they brought her a gold medal, she thought it was a toy.

[The standard biogs. are C. E. Stowe, *Life of Harriet Beecher Stowe, Compiled from Her Journals and Letters* (1889); A. A. Fields, *Life and Letters of Harriet Beecher Stowe* (1897); and C. E. and L. B. Stowe, *Harriet Beecher Stowe, the Story of Her Life* (1911). Joseph Sabin and others, *Bibliotheca Americana,* vol. XXIV (1933–34) lists her writings before 1860, including translations, and contemporary works on *Uncle Tom's Cabin.* J. F. Rhodes, *Hist. of the U. S. from the Compromise of 1850,* vol. I (1893), describes the reception of *Uncle Tom's Cabin* at home and abroad.

See also A. A. Fields, *Authors and Friends* (1896); V. L. Parrington, "The Romantic Revolution in America, 1850–1860," *Main Currents in Am. Thought*, vol. II (1927); C. M. Rourke, *Trumpets of Jubilee* (1927); L. B. Stowe, *Saints, Sinners, and Beechers* (1934); *Boston Transcript*, July 1, 1896.]   K. A.

STRACHEY, WILLIAM (fl. 1606–1618), historian and first secretary of the Virginia colony, was descended from the honorable and ancient Strachey family of Essex. He appears not to have been the son of William who married Mary Cook (as is sometimes stated), but of John Strachey, whose son William was baptized in Saffron Walden church, Mar. 16, 1567/8. There are other conjectures which point towards him as the William Strachey who matriculated at Emmanuel College, Cambridge, in 1588 (John and J. A. Venn, *Alumni Cantabrigienses*, pt. 1, vol. IV, 1927, p. 172); who married Frances Foster, 1588, and had a son William; and who died in 1634. It is known that he wrote verse, little of which was published, that he was a friend of the poet Donne, and that Thomas Campion praised—overgenerously, to judge from surviving specimens—his poetic gifts in an epigram wherein he termed Strachey "my old boon companion" (*sodalis*). His writings attest that he was a pious anti-papist, a man of considerable culture and learning, a keen, scientific, and dependable observer, as well as the master of a prose style which, if at times pedantic, possesses dignity and power and occasionally eloquence; while it may be assumed from knowledge of the other incumbents of the Virginia secretaryship that he was considered one of the most prominent citizens of the colony, of competent fortune, superior talents, and experience in public affairs. In the dedication to Bacon (some time after July 11, 1618) of his *Historie of Travaile*, Strachey designates himself "one of the Graies-Inne Societe," but his name does not appear in the index to Joseph Foster's *Register of Admissions to Gray's Inn* (1889). Save that he contributed a second-rate sonnet to the commendatory verses of Ben Jonson's *Sejanus* (1604), there is little specific fact bearing on his career prior to the summer of 1606, when he accompanied Sir Thomas Glover to Constantinople as secretary (*Times Literary Supplement*, London, July 3 and 24, Aug. 7, 1930). His friendly intercourse with Sir Henry Lello, whom Glover had gone to supplant as ambassador, so enraged his employer that Strachey was soon dismissed, returning considerably aggrieved to England.

His name next appears among the grantees under King James's second charter to the London Company of Virginia, to which he paid a £25 subscription. On June 2, 1609, he sailed for Virginia; but his ship, the *Sea Adventure* (having aboard both the new governor, Sir Thomas Gates [*q.v.*], and Sir George Somers, admiral of the little fleet), became separated from the others in a severe storm late in July and was wrecked on the Bermudas. There the party wintered, constructing two small vessels, and on May 23, 1610, reached Jamestown, to find matters so desperate that only the opportune arrival of Lord De La Warr [*q.v.*] prevented the abandoning of the colony.

De La Warr appointed Strachey to his council, as secretary and recorder, and when Gates left for England in July he carried with him two interesting papers from the secretary's pen. One was De La Warr's dispatch (obviously drawn up by Strachey) to the patentees in England, announcing his arrival, the safety of the shipwrecked party, and the state of the colony (Major, *post*); the other was Strachey's more detailed letter to an "excellent lady," which was repressed by the Company in consequence of its outspoken account of the settlement and was first printed by Samuel Purchas in 1625 as "A True Reportory of the Wracke, and Redemption of Sir Thomas Gates . . ." (*Purchas His Pilgrimes*, vol. IV; reprinted in *Hakluytus Posthumous or Purchas His Pilgrimes*, vol. XIX, 1906). In manuscript, however, it furnished material both for *A True Declaration of the Estate of the Colonie in Virginia* published by the patentees in 1610 (reprinted in Peter Force, *Tracts*, vol. III, 1844) and for Shakespeare's play *The Tempest* (C. M. Gayley, *Shakespeare and the Founders of Liberty in America*, 1917, pp. 40–76; R. R. Cawley, "Shakespeare's Use of the Voyagers in *The Tempest*," *Publications of the Modern Language Association of America*, vol. XLI, 1926).

Late in 1611 Strachey returned to London, where at his "lodging in the blacke Friers" he edited the first written code of laws for the Virginia settlement, *For the Colony in Virginea Brittania: Lavves Diuine, Morall, and Martiall* (1612; reprinted in Force, *Tracts*, vol. III), the military part based on Dale's enlargement of the *Lawes for governing the Armye in the Lowe Countreyes* and the civil code being his own compilation. The tract entitled *The Proceedings of the English Colonie in Virginia*, by "W. S.," printed at Oxford the same year and long attributed to Strachey, even to the point of confusing it with his *True Reportory*, is now recognized as the work of the Rev. Dr. William Symonds, who had delivered the sermon *Virginea Britannia* to the prospective colonists in April 1609 at Whitechapel (Gayley, *ante*, p. 74). Before the close of 1613 (Major, *post*, pp. 5, 140) Strachey completed the first two books of his most ambitious literary undertaking, *The Historie of Travaile into Virginia Britannia, Expressing the Cosmographie and Comodities of the Country, Togither with the Manners and Customes of the People,* and inscribed the manuscript to Sir Allen Apsley. Neither Apsley nor the Virginia Committee encouraged him to publish (although it has been said that the *Historie* induced Apsley to advise the Pilgrim emigration to America), nor did he meet with better success five or six years later when he inscribed it afresh to Francis Bacon. In consequence, the work remained unfinished and, until its publication by the Hakluyt Society in 1849 (R. H. Major, editor), was overlooked by writers on Virginia; yet it is a highly authoritative work and probably the most ably written of the contemporary histories of the region, valuable alike for its ethnological account of the Virginia Indians and—so far as it goes—for its commentary on early American discoveries and settlements. Of the author's subsequent career, nothing is known.

[Major's comments in Strachey's *Historie* (1849); P. A. Bruce, *Institutional Hist. of Va. in the Seventeenth Century* (1910), vol. II; H. L. Osgood, *The Am. Colonies in the Seventeenth Century,* vol. I (1904); *Mass. Hist. Soc. Colls.,* 4 ser. I (1852), reprinting accounts of the Roanoke and Sagadahoc colonies from Strachey's *Historie* ; *Wm. and Mary Coll. Quart. Hist. Mag.,* Jan., July 1896, Jan. 1902; Alexander Brown, *The Genesis of the U. S.* (2 vols., 1890).]

A. C. G., Jr.

STRAIGHT, WILLARD DICKERMAN
(Jan. 31, 1880–Dec. 1, 1918), diplomat, financier, and publicist, was born at Oswego, N. Y., the son of Henry H. and Emma May (Dickerman) Straight, both of English stock. Henry Straight, an instructor in natural science at Oswego Normal School, and after 1883 in the Cook County Normal School at Normal Park, Ill., died in 1886 of tuberculosis. From 1887 to 1889 his widow taught in the Girls' Normal School in Tokyo, Japan. She returned to the United States in 1889 and died in 1890, also of tuberculosis. Willard and his sister Hazel were then adopted jointly by Dr. Elvire Rainier and Miss Laura Newkirk, of Oswego. Willard was educated in the Oswego public schools, the Bordentown (N. J.) Military Institute, and Cornell University, where he studied architecture and was graduated in 1901, with the degree of B. Arch.

In November of that year, he went to China to take a post in the Imperial Maritime Customs Service. He remained in this service until the Russo-Japanese War, when he went to Korea (Chosen) as a correspondent for Reuter's News Service. There he was soon made vice-consul and secretary to the American minister to Seoul (Keijo). In 1906, he served for a few months as secretary to the American Legation in Cuba but in the same year he returned to the Orient as consul-general at Mukden (Moukden). From November 1908 to June 1909 he was acting chief of the Division of Far Eastern Affairs in the Department of State. In 1909 he returned to the Orient as a representative, first of a group of American bankers, and then of a similar international group, interested in developing railways in Manchuria and the northern part of China proper. Through the political opposition of Russia and Japan, this scheme failed.

Straight thereupon played an important part in the attempt at an international loan to the Chinese government by a consortium of bankers (see sketch of Jacob Henry Schiff). Shortly thereafter, the Chinese Revolution took place and, in 1912, Straight left the Orient forever. On Sept. 7, 1911, he had married Dorothy Whitney, daughter of William C. Whitney [*q.v.*], the well-known Wall Street capitalist. On his return to New York, he planned to study law with the purpose of ultimately practising in the field of international law; but, in the meantime, he continued the association, as Far-Eastern expert, with J. P. Morgan & Company which had grown out of his work for the bankers in the Orient. In 1915 he was persuaded to accept a post as third vice-president of the American International Corporation, formed to facilitate American participation in foreign developments in engineering, railroads, and industrial projects, and in public finance. In the previous year, he had signalized his interest in public affairs by making possible, in cooperation with his wife, the publication of a weekly journal, *The New Republic.* He had previously been greatly attracted by the book, *The Promise of American Life* (1909), by Herbert D. Croly and had sought the acquaintance of the author. The idea of establishing the paper grew spontaneously out of one of their conversations, and Croly became its chief editor. In 1915, Straight's keen interest in the Orient found a definite outlet in the creation of the monthly magazine first called the *Journal of the American Asiatic Association* and later, radically changed in form, called *Asia.* During these years he was also a guiding spirit in the American Asiatic Association, the American Manufacturers' Export Association, and India House, a club in New York started to encourage foreign trade.

With the entrance of the United States into the World War, Straight promptly volunteered for service and was commissioned as major attached to the Adjutant General's office. On Oct. 29, 1917, he was put in charge of organizing the overseas administration of the War Risk Insurance Bureau. In one month and sixteen days, he and his handful of assistants arranged a canvass of 250,000 American soldiers and persuaded them to sign up for insurance to the value of more than $1,000,000,000. Thereafter, he became a student in the staff college at Langres, France. At the beginning of June, he was placed in charge of liaison for the III Corps. He distinguished himself by preparing a liaison manual which was adopted almost *in toto* for the American Expeditionary Force. He died in Paris on Dec. 1, 1918, of influenza and pneumonia.

Willard Straight was a man of varied talents. His many published drawings and sketches show his decided artistic ability. He also had unusual native gifts as a writer. He made remarkable progress in a short time in studies of Oriental languages, history, and politics. That he had noteworthy capacity as an executive and leader of men is shown by the series of responsible posts he held while still in his late twenties and early thirties.

[H. D. Croly, *Willard Straight* (1924); Louis Graves, *Willard Straight in the Orient* (1922), reprinted from "An American in Asia," *Asia*, Sept. 1920–May 1921; "Willard Straight," in *New Republic*, Dec. 7, 1918, pp. 163–64; obituary in *N. Y. Times*, Dec. 2, 1918; *Who's Who in America*, 1918–19; E. D. and G. S. Dickerman, *Dickerman Genealogy. Descendants of Thomas Dickerman . . .* (1922).]   B. B.

STRAIN, ISAAC G. (Mar. 4, 1821–May 14, 1857), naval officer and explorer, son of Robert Strain and Eliza (Geddes) Strain, was born in Roxbury, Pa. He entered the navy as a midshipman, Dec. 15, 1837, and first saw service in the West Indies and on the Brazilian coast. In 1842 he was ordered to the naval school at Philadelphia, which he attended for nearly a year. He then secured leave of absence from the navy for the purpose of conducting an exploring expedition into Brazil. This expedition, partly financed by members of the Academy of Natural Sciences of Philadelphia, was not entirely successful, and in 1844 Strain joined the *Constitution* at Rio de Janeiro and served on her in the East Indies. In 1848 he served on the west coast of Mexico in the *Ohio* in the vicinity of Mazatlán and Guaymas. That summer, following the close of the war with Mexico, while the *Ohio* lay anchored at La Paz, Lower California, Strain landed and explored the peninsula as far as the time allotted him would allow. Early in the winter of 1848–49 he took passage in the *Lexington* for New York but obtained permission to leave his ship at Valparaiso. From there he crossed the continent to Buenos Aires, embodying his observations in a book, *Cordillera and Pampa, Mountain and Plain: Sketches of a Journey in Chili and the Argentine Provinces in 1849* (1853). He was lent to the Interior Department (Jan. 23, 1850) to serve on the Mexican Boundary Commission, and in 1853 volunteered to conduct an exploration of the Isthmus of Darien between Caledonia Bay on the Caribbean and the Gulf of San Miguel on the Pacific, to determine the possibility of a ship-canal across the isthmus by that route. The privations and sufferings endured by his party, as well as his own energy and fortitude, brought him into public notice. In his report to the Department he declared this route to be "utterly impracticable" (*Report of the Secretary of the Navy, 1854*, n.d., p. 426). In the summer of 1856 he joined the expedition in the steamer *Arctic* under Lieut. Otway H. Berryman to ascertain by soundings the possibility of a submarine telegraph cable between the United States and Great Britain. Never recovering from the effects of the hardships of the Darien expedition, he died at Aspinwall (later Colón), Panama.

Though he never attained a higher rank than lieutenant, nor ever commanded a ship, his restless ambition led him to seek occasion to explore unknown lands and won him the recognition of his superiors. By the secretary of the navy, James Cochran Dobbin, he was called "an accomplished and enterprising officer" (*Ibid.*, p. 384). Though nine lives were lost in the Darien expedition, he met disaster with unflinching courage; English naval officers at Panama considered the conduct of his command the "perfection of military discipline." He was a corresponding member of the Historical and Geographical Institute of Brazil, the American Ethnological Society of New York, and the Academy of Natural Sciences of Philadelphia. Besides his *Cordillera and Pampa* he wrote *A Paper on the History and Prospects of Interoceanic Communication by the American Isthmus* (1856).

[Extensive search has failed to reveal Strain's middle name. See *Proc. Acad. of Nat. Science of Phila.*, vol. II (1846); J. T. Headley, *Darien Exploring Expedition under the Command of Lieut. Isaac G. Strain* (1885); U. S. Navy Dept. Registers, 1837–57; manuscript log of U.S.S. *Ohio*, 1847–48; *Exec. Doc. 34*, 31 Cong., 1 Sess., for report of Mexican Boundary Commission; *Report of the Secretary of the Navy, 1856* (n.d.), pp. 466–68; U. S. Navy Dept. Archives; Nathan Crosby, *Ann. Obit. Notices of Eminent Persons . . . 1857* (1858); *Springfield Pioneer* (Springfield, Ohio), Dec. 25, 1835; *Springfield Weekly Republic*, Dec. 24, 1841, and June 12, 1857.]   L. H. B.

STRANAHAN, JAMES SAMUEL THOMAS (Apr. 25, 1808–Sept. 3, 1898), capitalist, civic leader, was born at Peterboro, Madison County, N. Y., a son of Samuel and Lynda (Josselyn) Stranahan, and a descendant of James Stranahan who emigrated to Scituate, R. I., probably in 1725. His parents (both of Scotch-Irish stock) had come from Connecticut to the Mohawk Valley as pioneers. When James was eight years old his father died; his mother remarried, and he spent the remainder of his boyhood on the farm of his step-father, John Downer. So well did he avail himself of the country schools in the neighborhood that long before he was twenty-one he was a schoolmaster himself. A year at Cazenovia Seminary completed his formal education, but he had mastered enough of the elements of land surveying to enable him to set up in that calling, then fairly remunerative in a new country. During the thirties, while Stranahan was a wool merchant at Albany, Gerrit Smith [q.v.], the wealthy abolitionist, who had known him at Peterboro, interested him in the development of some of his Oneida County properties, and particularly in the promotion of the village of Florence as a manufacturing center. A term as assemblyman at Albany in 1838 gave Stranahan an insight into legislative methods that was to serve him well forty years later.

In 1840 he went to Newark, N. J., and became a successful railroad contractor. He was one of the earliest operators on a large scale to take railroad stock in payment for construction work. After four years he transferred his activities to Brooklyn, N. Y., then a city of less than 100,000, where harbor improvements known as the Atlantic Basin and Docks had been projected. He entered into this enterprise with great energy and enthusiasm, bringing it to ultimate success, although it was twenty-six years before a dividend could be paid on the corporation stock. Meanwhile he invested in East River ferries and came to be known as one of Brooklyn's public-spirited and substantial citizens. His election to Congress as a Whig in 1854 came after a defeat as candidate for mayor. Yet his lasting reputation was to be won as a servant of the city rather than of the nation. As president of the Brooklyn park board (1860–82) he was largely responsible for the creation of Prospect Park at a time when few American public men saw the importance of public parks in municipal development. Much of the time he worked almost single-handed. His services were recognized in an unusual way during his lifetime by the dedication on June 6, 1891, of a statue of him by Frederick William MacMonnies, erected through public subscription. Hardly less significant was his early and persistent espousal of the plans for the original East River Bridge. In 1883, the year in which

he presided at the formal opening of the bridge, he pledged support of the Greater New York consolidation plan, which involved the loss of Brooklyn's identity as a city and ran counter to the cherished ideas of some of his co-workers and friends. He was seventy-five when he set out to win over Brooklyn for consolidation; he was ninety when the goal was finally reached, and he was hailed as one of the fathers of the greater city. He was twice married: first, on May 4, 1837, to Mariamne Fitch (d. 1866) of Oneida County, N. Y., and second to Clara Cornelia Harrison, author of *A History of French Painting* (1888). He died at Saratoga, N. Y., survived by his wife and one of the three children of his first marriage.

[H. R. Stiles, *Geneals. of the Stranahan, Josselyn, Fitch, and Dow Families in N. Am.* (privately printed, 1868), and *A Hist. of the City of Brooklyn*, vol. III (1870); *Biog. Directory of the Am. Cong., 1774–1927* (1928); *An Account of the Dinner by the Hamilton Club to Hon. James S. T. Stranahan, . . . Dec. 13, 1888* (1889); ann. reports of the Commissioners of Prospect Park, 1861–67, Brooklyn Park Commissioners, 1868–82; obituary in *Brooklyn Daily Eagle*, Sept. 3, 1898.]
W. B. S.

STRANG, JAMES JESSE (Mar. 21, 1813–July 9, 1856), leader of the Mormon sect known by his name, was born in Scipio, N. Y., the son of Clement and Abigail (James) Strang. He seems to have been named Jesse James for his mother's father, but in 1831–32 reversed the order (Quaife, *post*, p. 2). In February 1816, the family settled near Hanover, Chautauqua County, N. Y. After a period of bad health, Strang in his early youth began to show precocious intellectual interests, though, aside from a period at the Fredonia Male Academy, his formal education was spasmodic. For the most part he was a moody, introspective lad, although his membership in the church of his parents and his attendance at the popular debating societies did something to socialize him. In spite of a strict religious background in his Baptist home, his reading of the works of Volney, Paine, and Shelley led to a lively skepticism. After a season or two of teaching he studied law and was admitted to the bar in October 1836. In the same year he married Mary Perce. Besides practising law he served as postmaster at Ellington, N. Y., from 1838 to 1843. For two years he also owned and edited the Randolph *Herald*.

It was not until 1843, after the family had moved to Burlington, Wis., to settle near his wife's people, that Moses Smith, husband of the sister of Strang's wife and an ardent Mormon, interested him mildly in the new sect. Stimulated by Aaron and Moses Smith, in February 1844 he made a trip with the former to Nauvoo,

Ill., more out of curiosity than enthusiasm for the new gospel. Yet under the influence of Joseph and Hyrum Smith the erstwhile "cool Philosopher" (Quaife, p. 201), as Strang had often dubbed himself, became an ardent convert. Learning that the Prophet was laying plans to move out of Illinois, Strang enthusiastically suggested the advantages of Wisconsin. On June 27, the day when Joseph Smith was killed by a mob at Carthage, Ill., Strang claims to have had a visitation from the angels of God, who ordained him to be ruler of the Mormons in the Prophet's place. To bolster this claim, Strang exhibited a letter alleged to have been written by Smith in which he instructed Strang to found an ecclesiastical unit of the Mormon church in Wisconsin and further gave a premonition of his own death and named Strang as his prophetic successor. In the struggle of various factions for control of the church after Smith's death this vision and the letter were the subject of heated dispute. In spite of the power of opposing factions, Strang drew around him at Voree, Wis. (near Burlington), a group of followers including Apostle John E. Page and Patriarch William Smith, the Prophet's brother.

Strang made an unsuccessful attempt to win the support of converts in the eastern states and especially in Great Britain, and for some years the little colony at Voree barely kept going in the face of internal dissension and economic hardship. In this period, 1844–47, Strang poured out a number of revelations, reported finding sacred plates, which he translated, and gave out creedal pronunciamientos including instructions to found a communistic order, to build a temple, and to erect a home for him at the expense of the Saints. Under the influence of one of his followers, John C. Bennett, he also established the Order of the Illuminati, in effect a secret society sworn to support him and his organization even though they ran counter to the laws of the civil government. Strang decided in 1847 to remove his followers to the Beaver Islands, in the northern waters of Lake Michigan. But it was not until 1849, when the city of St. James was established on Big Beaver Island, that the success of the new venture was assured. In the face of Gentile opposition and the rigors of the wilderness he established his new Zion, and on July 8, 1850, with proper divine revelations to support the project, he was crowned King. His religious "kingdom" was patterned on *The Book of the Law of the Lord*, which he alleged was an ancient Mosaic document given him by divine powers for translation.

Strang held or controlled the principal local offices, and he was twice (1852, 1854) elected member of the Michigan state legislature. Through measures sponsored by him the civil government of the northern Michigan counties was thoroughly organized for the first time. When recourse to mob action failed, his enemies resorted to lawsuits in their efforts to drive him out. The most famous of these court actions was brought in Detroit in May and June 1851, by George C. Bates, then United States district attorney, who charged Strang and his chief henchmen with counterfeiting, robbing the mails, and trespassing on federal lands. The Whig press, because of his political affiliation with the Democrats, flayed him unmercifully, but in spite of public agitation against him he was acquitted. Although at the outset of his sectarian venture Strang had been violent in his opposition to the polygyny or spiritual wifery practised among the Nauvoo Mormons, in 1850 he announced a revelation proclaiming plural marriage to be a divinely appointed institution. His followers, for the most part, accepted this *volte-face,* but poverty and the lack of available unmarried women prevented its extensive practice. Strang himself had four polygynous wives. While the growing economic strength of the Mormon colony in competition with the Gentile communities was a factor, it was dissension within his own ranks which brought about his assassination and the brutal dispersal of his people at the hands of a mob stimulated by various apostates. Dr. Hezekiah McCulloch, a trusted adviser of Strang who had broken with him, appears to have planned his death. On June 16, 1856, Strang was shot down by Alexander Wentworth and Thomas Bedford as he was about to board the armored steamer *Michigan.* He was removed to Voree, where he died on July 9. "With Strang's death died his Church" (Quaife, p. 179), for he steadfastly refused to name a successor, although he knew he would never recover.

Strang was intellectually one of the most able of the early Mormon leaders. He was fearless and capable in debate, an effective orator, and a lucid journalist. In dealing with his followers, although an absolute dictator, he was goodnatured, kind, and self-confident. In fact, because of his success in vanquishing opposition both from within his Church and from his enemies without, his sense of power at the end of his life amounted almost to a megalomania. His own works, especially *The Book of the Law of the Lord* (1856), and *Ancient and Modern Michilimackinac, . . .* (1854), give an excellent picture of his kingdom and his struggle with the Gentiles. Other writings were *The Diamond* (1848), and *The Prophetic Controversy* (1854).

[M. M. Quaife. *The Kingdom of Saint James* (1930); H. E. Legler, "A Moses of the Mormons," *Publications Parkman Club* (Milwaukee), nos. 15–16 (1897); Orrin Poppleton, "The Murder of King Strang," *Hist. Collections . . . Made by the Mich. Pioneer and Hist. Soc.*, vol. XVIII (1892); C. J. Strang, "A Michigan Monarchy," *Ibid.*; *Detroit Free Press*, July 13, 1856; O. W. Riegel, *Crown of Glory: The Life of James Jesse Strang*, was announced for publication in the fall of 1935.]   K. Y.

STRATEMEYER, EDWARD (Oct. 4, 1862–May 10, 1930), writer of juvenile fiction, was born in Elizabeth, N. J. His father, Henry Julius Stratemeyer, who came from Germany in 1848 and in 1849 joined the California gold rush, returned to New Jersey to settle the affairs of a brother who had died. Later he married his brother's widow, Anna (Seigel) Stratemeyer, by whom he had two sons and a daughter, and established himself as a tobacconist in Elizabeth. Stratemeyer attended the public schools of Elizabeth and after his graduation from high school had private tutoring in rhetoric, composition, and literature. For several years, while he worked as a clerk in a tobacco store owned by his step-brother, he tried to write stories modeled on those of William Taylor Adams ("Oliver Optic") and Horatio Alger [*qq.v.*]. In 1888 he sold his first story, "Victor Horton's Idea," to *Golden Days for Boys and Girls,* a weekly published in Philadelphia, for seventy-five dollars, and definitely decided upon a career as a writer of books for boys. After 1890 he lived in Newark, N. J., where until about 1896 he owned and managed a stationery store. In March 1891 he was married to Magdalene Baker Van Camp of Newark.

From 1891 to 1893 he wrote six serial stories for Frank A. Munsey's *Argosy.* In 1893 he became editor of *Good News,* a weekly magazine for boys, to which he contributed many stories during the years 1893–95; in 1895 he edited *Young People of America,* and in 1896 ran a periodical of his own called *Bright Days,* at first a monthly, later a weekly. By this time he had adopted the pen name of Arthur M. Winfield. His first book, *Richard Dare's Venture; or, Striking Out for Himself,* appeared in 1894 as the first volume of the Bound to Win Series, and about 1896 he began to give all his time to the writing of full-length stories in series. The first of these to gain him popularity was the Old Glory Series, which began with the success of *Under Dewey at Manila* (1898). In 1899 he started the Rover Boys' Series for Young Americans, most popular of all his work, of which the thirtieth volume was published in 1926. Under

the name of Captain Ralph Bonehill he wrote the Flag of Freedom Series (1899–1902), the Mexican War Series (1900–02), the Frontier Series (1903–07), and the Boy Hunters Series (1906–10), and others, as well as numerous separate volumes. In 1906 he founded the Stratemeyer Literary Syndicate in New York City and employed many writers of juvenile fiction to elaborate plots which he supplied into book-length stories. Under this plan were produced the Tom Swift and Motor Boys Series for boys and the Bobbsey Twins for young children, which rivalled some of his own series in popularity. Stratemeyer, who was a very methodical and industrious man, spent a great deal of time studying and collecting data for his books and wrote steadily throughout his life, amply realizing his early ambition to sell a million copies of his books. His total output was over one hundred and fifty books, and he was the originator of over six hundred others. His stories, which frequently depict preparatory school and college life, are full of action and none-too-plausible adventure; there is little attempt at character-drawing. Stratemeyer died in Newark of pneumonia. He was survived by his wife and his two daughters.

[*Who's Who in America,* 1928–29; G. W. Browne, in *Writer,* Mar. 1902; *Proc. N. J. Hist. Soc. . . . 1930,* vol. XV (n.d.); *Fortune,* Apr. 1934; *N. Y. Times,* May 13, 1930 (editorial); *Newark Evening News,* June 4, 1927, and May 12, 1930 (obituary); information from a daughter, Edna C. Stratemeyer, 171 North Seventh St., Newark, N. J..]   E. S. S.
                                    R. W. B.

STRATON, JOHN ROACH (Apr. 6, 1875–Oct. 29, 1929), clergyman and reformer, was born in Evansville, Ind., the son of Julia Rebecca (Carter) and Henry Dundas Straton, a Baptist preacher of rigorous orthodox faith. He was a student at Mercer University, from 1895 to 1898 and was professor of oratory and interpretation of literature there in 1899. He attended the Southern Baptist Theological Seminary, in Louisville, Ky., where he was ordained in 1900 and graduated in 1902. After teaching two years, 1903–05, in Baylor University at Waco, Tex., he became pastor of the Second Baptist Church in Chicago. In 1908 he went to the Seventh Immanuel Church in Baltimore, Md. From 1913 to 1917 he was minister of the First Baptist Church in Norfolk, Va. In 1918 he accepted the pastorate of the Calvary Baptist Church in New York City.

The frankness with which he assailed the excesses of the years after the World War was in itself enough to attract immense public attention; but this was accentuated by sensational methods of public appeal that precipitated feverish controversy. He preached on cabaret orgies, the ouija board, and the Elwell murder mystery. He made a tour of the tenderloin district, and on an Easter Sunday, in 1920, denounced the whiskey drinking, soliciting, and dancing he had seen. He attended the Dempsey-Carpentier prizefight and used his experience as the basis of a furious pulpit denunciation of the sport. He attacked the atheists and forced trial of a suit against Charles L. Smith, president of the American Association for the Advancement of Atheism, for sending annoying literature through the mails. Repeatedly he conducted exciting revival services. These activities, sustained with immense vitality and resource, made him a figure of first-class local importance. In his later years, he became a national figure as well. His evolution debates with Charles Francis Potter carried his name and word to all parts of the land (see his *The Famous New York Fundamentalist—Modernist Debates, the Orthodox Side,* 1925). On the death of William Jennings Bryan, he assumed undisputed leadership of the Fundamentalist forces. Bitter controversy with Gov. Alfred E. Smith led him into the presidential campaign of 1928, and for weeks, in the blasting heat of summer, he toured the Southern states in opposition to the "wet," Catholic, Tammany standard-bearer of Democracy. Among the books he published were, *The Menace of Immorality in Church and State* (1920), *The Gardens of Life* (1921), and *The Old Gospel at the Heart of the Metropolis* (1925).

He was in appearance and temper the typical Protestant zealot. His lean, handsome face had a granite-like quality of grim and terrible resolution. His tall, spare, and powerful figure quivered with nervous energy, yet was held taut in masterful control. A fine voice gave wings to a natural eloquence, carefully trained to full effectiveness. His mind, set like hardened cement by early domestic and educational influences, became impervious to later impressions of thought and life. He read widely and more than once confounded his opponents by unexpected knowledge of facts; but these facts were held at arm's length like stones to be broken by the hammers of controversy, never received into his mind like food to be digested and absorbed. He was less intolerant and more tender than his critics imagined; if he appeared stern and unrelenting, it was because of his dogmatic assurance of the rightness of his position. His superb showmanship, which included early use of the radio and constant resort to newspaper publicity, was as sincere as it was ingenious and occasionally vulgar: it was motivated not by self-seeking but by shrewd understanding of the popular mind and determination to capture that mind at any cost for the causes he had at heart. An ironic humor, a genuine courage, a fierce scorn of consequences armored him against storms of public ridicule. There was comfort, also, in the unshakable loyalty of hosts of followers. It is doubtful, however, if he ever suspected the vicarious enjoyment of wickedness he supplied in sermons that gave his hearers the nearest thing to indulgence in what he denounced. The severity of his campaign exertions, following upon the strain of his New York ministry, led to a paralytic stroke. He died at a sanitarium in Clifton Springs, N. Y., survived by his wife, formerly Georgia Hillyer of Atlanta, Ga., to whom he was married on Nov. 2, 1903, and by four sons.

[*Who's Who in America,* 1928–29; *New Republic,* Nov. 13, 1929; *N. Y. Times,* esp. Oct. 30, Nov. 7, 1929.]   J.H.H.

STRATTON, CHARLES SHERWOOD (Jan. 4, 1838–July 15, 1883), midget, better known as General Tom Thumb, was born at Bridgeport, Conn., of English colonial stock, the third of the four children of Sherwood Edwards Stratton, a carpenter, and his wife, Cynthia (Thompson). The other members of the family were of normal stature, but Charles stopped growing when six months old, and until he entered his teens he remained two feet one inch tall and weighed only fifteen pounds. Later he grew to a height of three feet four inches, and good living ultimately increased his weight to seventy pounds. In the fall of 1842 P. T. Barnum [*q.v.*], staying overnight in a Bridgeport hotel, heard of the local dwarf, drove a quick bargain with the parents, taught the boy to dance, sing, tell stories, and strut the stage in various guises, advertised him as "General Tom Thumb, a dwarf eleven years of age, just arrived from England," and put him on exhibition in his New York museum. Under Barnum's tutelage the bashful boy was turned into a pert, graceful entertainer. He had a ready wit and a good sense of showmanship, was healthy and symmetrically formed, cheerful, lively, and winning. He became at once a celebrity; money flowed into Barnum's coffers; and when the two departed for England Jan. 18, 1844, accompanied by a tutor and the General's parents, the New York municipal brass band and some 10,000 people thronged to the wharf to see them leave.

In England Barnum achieved even greater success with his protégé than in the United States. Starting with a letter of introduction from Horace Greeley to the American minister, Edward Everett, he conducted his publicity campaign until it attained its climax in an invitation to Buckingham Palace. Queen Victoria, then twenty-five years old, was amused and charmed by the General, and thereafter his tour of England and of the Continent was a triumphal progress. One of his performances was an impersonation of Napoleon, which was much admired by the Duke of Wellington and which Louis Philippe, at his own request, was also privileged to see. When Stratton returned to the United States in 1847 his European acclaim had increased his popularity. He toured the country and visited Cuba, but in 1852 or thereabouts he retired to his native town. Subsequently he made several visits to Europe and in 1872 a trip around the world. Sometimes he traveled under Barnum's management, sometimes under his own. Barnum appears to have been his one intimate friend.

In 1862 he met another one of Barnum's dwarfs, Lavinia Warren (Oct. 31, 1841–Nov. 25, 1919) of Middleboro, Mass., whose full name was Mercy Lavinia Warren Bumpus. While they were Barnum's week-end guests at Bridgeport, he proposed marriage to her and was accepted. The wedding was celebrated in Grace Episcopal Church, New York, Feb. 10, 1863; and the New York newspapers in their efforts to report the event adequately almost forgot the Civil War. The Strattons' one child, a daughter, died in early childhood. In his youth Stratton had evinced more than his share of Yankee thrift and acquisitiveness. He had a sharp eye for a first mortgage and owned considerable real property in Bridgeport. Later he joined the Masons and cultivated a taste for expensive cigars and rather more expensive horses and yachts. He died unexpectedly, on his estate in Middleboro, Mass., of an apoplectic stroke. When his affairs were settled, it was found that his wealth had been all but completely squandered. He was buried at Bridgeport, where there is a monument to his memory. His widow married an Italian dwarf with a Papal title, Count Primo Magri.

[H. R. Stratton, *A Book of Strattons* (2 vols., 1908–18), is authority for day of birth, given by Barnum as Jan. 11. See also *An Account of the Life, Personal Appearance, Character, and Manners of Charles S. Stratton, the American Man in Miniature* (London, 1844); *Life and Travels of Thomas Thumb, in the U. S., England, France, and Belgium* (copr. 1849); *Adventures of Mr. and Mrs. Tom Thumb, at Home and Abroad* (1863); *Sketch of the Lives . . . of Charles S. Stratton . . . and His Wife Lavinia Warren* (London, 1865); Sylvester Bleeker, *Gen. Tom Thumb's Three Years' Tour around the World* (1872); M. R. Werner, *Barnum* (1923); P. T. Barnum, *Struggles and Triumphs: or, The Life of P. T. Barnum* (2 vols., 1927), ed. by G. S. Bryan; *N. Y. Tribune*, July 16, 1883.] 　G. H. G.

STRATTON, SAMUEL WESLEY (July 18, 1861–Oct. 18, 1931), creator of the Bureau of Standards, was born on his father's farm at Litchfield, Ill., the son of Samuel and Mary B. (Webster) Stratton. From early youth the son shared in the farm labor, and from boyhood he showed the keenest interest in mechanics. He attended the schools of his native township, and, after working for two years to earn money for further education, he entered the University of Illinois in 1880 as a special student. He quickly decided to undertake the four-year course in Mechanical Engineering. Earning his way from year to year, he received the degree of Bachelor of Science in 1884 and engaged in special research problems. In 1885 he was appointed instructor in mathematics in the university; but his work was soon confined to physics alone, and he became professor of physics in 1891. In 1891 he was asked to establish and take charge of a new course in electrical engineering. In 1892 he became assistant professor of physics at the newly organized University of Chicago, where he remained until 1901. While there he became associated with Michelson on his investigation on the speed of light, planned and supervised construction of the Ryerson laboratories, and gave much attention to the application of physics to engineering. From college days he had always maintained a deep interest in military affairs and on taking up his work in Chicago joined the naval militia and rose to the rank of lieutenant-commander. As head of this organization, he entered the naval service during the Spanish-American War in 1898, with the rank of lieutenant. His unit was assigned to the *Texas*.

Two years later, in 1900, through the instrumentality of the assistant secretary of the treasury, Frank A. Vanderlip, who had been one of his close college friends at Illinois, he was asked by the secretary of the treasury, Lyman J. Gage, to prepare a report for a proposed bureau of standards. The bill authorizing the establishment of the bureau was drawn by him, with the existing office of weights and measures as a nucleus, and the many hearings and demonstrations before the congressional committee were skilfully handled by him and won acceptance and generous support. The bill was passed in 1901 and the bureau of standards became an actuality. On the insistence of Gage, he became its first director. His vision of the usefulness of such a bureau was so clear that he was never seriously handicapped by the limitations of function expressed in the organic act, and from the beginning the work of the bureau expanded greatly in scope and usefulness. In 1903 the bureau was transferred to the department of commerce, thereby making possible a greater opportunity for emphasizing and assisting in the prosecution of research as an aid to commerce and industry. He and the bureau became important factors in the international conference on weights and measures, as well as in manifold advisory committees for the better development and standardization of basic industries. He had the gift of obtaining first the confidence and then the co-operation of industrial leaders and men of vision and high character in many technical fields. Under his direction the bureau grew to be a great research center. With the advent of the World War the service he rendered the government, both personally and through the bureau, was invaluable. The reputation attained by the bureau of standards, not only in American industry but also in the world, is in reality largely due to this man, who picked his lieutenants with rare judgment and gave them the credit for work that was often to a great degree the product of his own logical thinking and carefully organized experimentation. He made it a rule to give the credit to the younger men who collaborated with him on problems which greatly interested him. This policy dated from his university experience, where he was the junior worker and received too little consideration for the part he took in the research work. Largely on account of this generosity only a small number of scientific papers appeared under his name, aside from his annual bureau reports and such official reports as "Metric System in Export Trade" (*Sen. Doc. 241, 64th Cong., 1 Sess.,* 1916). Notable among his scientific papers are "A New Harmonic Analyser" published with Michelson in the *Philosophical Magazine* (Jan. 1898) and "Metrology in Relation to Industrial Progress" in the *Journal of the Franklin Institute* (Oct. 1912).

While at the bureau, he never lost interest in technical education, and when he was invited to become the president of the Massachusetts Institute of Technology in 1923 he accepted, in the belief that he could render a special service both to the Institute because of his knowledge of the needs of industry, and to American industry by participating actively in the training of men of the type who would become the leaders in the industrial fields. He felt strongly that technical schools should render an increasing service to industry and to the public through basic instruction and through emphasis on research in both pure and applied science, and during his presidency worked with these ends in view. For many years the position of president of the Institute had made exacting and almost impossible demands on the energies of its incumbent. In 1930 a reorganization of administrative policy was

effected, whereby he became chairman of the corporation, and Karl T. Compton was elected to the office of president. Thus two men shared the many and varied responsibilities that one had always borne hitherto. This arrangement was of brief duration, however, for Stratton died suddenly, while in the act of dictating a eulogy of his friend Edison, who had died earlier that same day. He had never married.

Unusually modest and often unassertive to the point of shyness, he had qualities that greatly endeared him to a very wide circle of devoted friends. He was a man of strong personality, of forceful character, and of unswerving loyalty. His mind was a storehouse of specialized knowledge in many fields, textiles, china and glass, antique furniture, and mechanical devices of every sort, as well as the latest technical advances in physics and engineering. Throughout his life he found particular enjoyment in constructing with his own hands pieces of scientific apparatus, or cabinets and articles of furniture, and whether working with wood or metal his technique and attention to detail were complete and faultless. In this avocation he not only found relief from the greater problems and cares incident to his office, but his work expressed that striving for exactness and high quality, even to perfection, which characterized his life. He was a member of several of the learned societies, chairman of the international conference on weights and measures, and a chevalier and an officer of the French Legion of Honor. Many honors came to him from universities at home and abroad. He was awarded the Cresson Medal of the Franklin Institute and the Public Service Medal of the National Academy. With A. Lawrence Lowell, president of Harvard University, and Judge Robert Grant he was appointed on a commission to advise the governor of Massachusetts in the case of Bartolomeo Vanzetti and Nicola Sacco [*qq.v.*] and signed the report of the committee in the *Decision of Gov. Alvan T. Fuller in the . . . appeal of Bartolomeo Vanzetti and Nicola Sacco* (1927).

[*Technology Rev.*, Nov. 1931; *Science*, Oct. 30, 1931; *Record and Index of the Am. Soc. of Mechanical Engineers*, 1931; *Who's Who in America*, 1930–31; *Boston Evening Transcript*, Oct. 18, 1931; personal acquaintance.]   S. C. P.

STRAUS, ISIDOR (Feb. 6, 1845–Apr. 15, 1912), merchant, was born at Otterberg, Rhenish Bavaria. His parents, who were first cousins, were Lazarus and Sara (Straus) Straus. His father came to the United States in 1852 and settled at Talbotton, Ga., where in the fall of 1854 he was joined by his wife and four children, Isidor, Hermina, Nathan [*q.v.*], and Oscar Solomon [*q.v.*]. Isidor was educated at the Collinsworth Institute in Talbotton. In 1871 he married Ida Blun of New York, who bore him four sons and three daughters. Since the outbreak of the Civil War frustrated his ambition to prepare for the United States Military Academy at West Point, he became a clerk in his father's store. In 1863 he went to Europe as secretary to John E. Ward of Savannah, Ga., on a commission to purchase supplies for the Confederacy; as the blockade of Southern ports rendered this futile, however, he worked in a shipping office at Liverpool, England, in 1864. He also dealt in Confederate bonds and sold cotton acceptances, and returned to New York in 1865 with some $12,000. With the help of this capital his father and he formed the crockery firm of L. Straus & Son (later L. Straus & Sons) in New York, which in 1874 took over the crockery and glassware department of R. H. Macy and Company. In 1888 Isidor and his brother Nathan were admitted to partnership in Macy's, and in 1896 they became its sole owners, developing it into the biggest department store in the world. They also built up the Brooklyn department store of Abraham & Straus. Straus was a vice-president of the chamber of commerce of the state of New York, director of several banks, the first president of the New York Crockery Board of Trade, president of the New York Retail Dry Goods Association, and a member of the World's Fair Commission in New York.

He was a warm friend of President Cleveland and took an active part in the campaign which resulted in Cleveland's reëlection in 1892. It is said that he was invited to become postmaster general, but declined the honor. It was due to his influence that Cleveland set himself squarely behind the gold standard and called Congress in extra session (Aug. 7, 1893) for the repeal of that clause of the Sherman Act of 1890 which compelled the Treasury to make monthly purchases of silver bullion for monetary purposes. Straus remained a Gold Democrat, losing his party enthusiasm when his party adopted the Free Silver platform under Bryan's leadership. He was strongly opposed to the protective tariff. At a special election in 1893, he ran for Congress on the issue of the Wilson Tariff Bill and was elected by a large plurality. He served from Jan. 30, 1894, to Mar. 3, 1895, declining renomination. He also declined to be considered for the Democratic nomination for mayor of New York in 1901 and 1909. His philanthropic activities were many. He was president of the Educational Alliance, "the people's palace" of New York's congested East Side, from its organization

(1893) until his death, a vice-president of the J. Hood Wright Memorial Hospital, a trustee and treasurer of the Montefiore Home from its establishment in 1884, a trustee of the Birkbeck Company, and a member of the American Jewish Committee from its inception. He was keenly interested in the Jewish people.

He and his wife, a woman of sweetness and strength, were passengers on the S.S. *Titanic* on its ill-fated maiden voyage across the Atlantic. When the order was given for women and children to take to the life-boats, Mrs. Straus would not leave her husband. Straus was strongly urged to take a place in the boats with her, but refused to do so as long as any women remained on board. Mrs. Straus declined to be separated from her companion of forty years, so the aged couple went down with the ship. Straus's was a strong individuality, compounded of keen insight, sound judgment, high integrity, candid statement, and high executive powers. He was a man of simple tastes, democratic accessibility, and cordial large-heartedness.

[*Who's Who in America*, 1912–13; *Biog. Directory of the Am. Cong., 1774–1927* (1928); *Nineteenth Ann. Report, 1911: The Educ. Alliance . . . N. Y.* (1912); Edward Hungerford, *The Romance of a Great Store* (1922); O. S. Straus, *Under Four Administrations: From Cleveland to Taft* (1922); *Am. Hebrew and Jewish Messenger*, Apr. 26, 1912; *N. Y. Herald*, Apr. 16–21, 1912; *N. Y. Times*, *N. Y. Tribune*, *World* (N. Y.), *Evening Post* (N. Y.), Apr. 15–21, 1912.]

D. deS. P.

STRAUS, NATHAN (Jan. 31, 1848–Jan. 11, 1931), philanthropist, was born in Otterberg, Rhenish Bavaria, son of Lazarus and Sara (Straus) Straus, and brother of Isidor and Oscar Solomon Straus [*qq.v.*]. In 1852 his father emigrated to the United States, where two years later he was joined by his wife and their four children. Nathan was educated in Talbotton, Ga., in a log cabin school and the Collinsworth Institute. After the Civil War the family moved to New York, where in 1866 Nathan joined his father's firm of L. Straus & Son. By 1888 he had become one of the owners of R. H. Macy and Company. It was he who originated, among other things, the depositors' account system, rest rooms, medical care, and a cost-price lunchroom for the employees of the store. He retired from active concern with business in 1914. On Apr. 28, 1875, he married Lina Gutherz, a woman of cultured mind, who shared unwearyingly in all his philanthropies. He was park commissioner in New York City (1889–93) and president of the board of health (1898). In 1894 he refused the Democratic nomination for mayor.

His philanthropies were numerous and of wide scope. In the panic winter of 1892–93 he distributed food and 1,500,000 buckets of coal for five cents each. In the following winter he issued over two million five-cent tickets for coal or food or lodging, and established lodging houses providing bed and breakfast for five cents. In 1892 he began a campaign for pasteurization of milk, in which he had to combat public ignorance and indifference, professional prejudice, commercial greed and political corruption, but which led ultimately to the compulsory pasteurization of milk in most cities. In 1891, 241 of every thousand babies born in New York City died before their first birthday, but of 20,111 babies who received his pasteurized milk during four years only six died. By 1909 the death rate of children under five had been halved, largely as a result of milk pasteurization. Straus continued to open milk depots at his personal cost, until in 1920 he had 297 milk stations in thirty-six cities in the United States and abroad. In 1909 he established in his cottage in Lakewood, N. J., the pioneer tuberculosis preventorium for children. In 1911 President William Howard Taft appointed Straus sole delegate from the United States to the Third International Congress for the Protection of Infants, held in Berlin. The first International Child's Congress under the auspices of the League of Nations (August 1925) officially recognized his work. Layman though he was, without pretensions to medical knowledge, he lives in the annals of medicine as a pioneer in public health.

As the years went on philanthropy became his ruling passion. Never a man of great wealth, he deliberately reduced his fortune through his gifts, and responded munificently to every campaign for relieving primary needs. In his devotion to Palestine his Jewish soul found its most complete expression. For the last fifteen years of their lives he and his wife lived with this as the dominant interest in their lives, and in the last two decades of his life he gave nearly two-thirds of his fortune to Palestine. In 1912 he established there a domestic science school for girls, a factory for men, a health bureau to fight malaria and trachoma, and a free public kitchen, which he made into a permanent foundation. Later he opened a Pasteur Institute, child-health welfare stations (through the Women's Zionist Organization, Hadassah), and the monumental Nathan and Lina Straus Health Centers in Jerusalem and Tel Aviv. In 1927, when almost an octogenarian, he journeyed to Jerusalem for the fourth time and laid the cornerstone of its health center, at the entrance to which his inscription in English, Arabic, and Hebrew proclaims that it is for all inhabitants of the land, Christian, Moslem, and Jew. The bloody rioting of the Arabs of Palestine in August 1929 robbed both him and his wife of the joy of life, and hastened the death of Lina Gutherz Straus (May 4, 1930). Less than a year later, shortly before his eighty-third birthday, Straus died in New York City, survived by two sons and one daughter.

In 1923 he was chosen by popular vote as the citizen who had done most for public welfare during the quarter of a century in which Greater New York had existed. In 1930 the National Institute of Social Sciences awarded him a gold medal in recognition of his distinguished and wide-spread social service rendered in behalf of humanity. The distinctiveness and originality of his character lay in the fact that he responded equally to the keen, sound judgments of his vigorous mind, and to the undisciplined spontaneity and impulsiveness of his tender heart. A deeply feeling Jew whose humanity transcended creed and race, he has been described as "a man of exalted spirituality, and firm convictions of righteousness in public and private affairs, ... with a heart overflowing with human sympathy and understanding" (*The American Jewish Year Book, post,* p. 154). Taft summed up the popular judgment when he said, "Dear old Nathan Straus is a great Jew and the greatest Christian of us all" (*Ibid.,* p. 152). Foreign born, he was a passionate lover and servant both of America and of Palestine. He was a practical visionary, a fighting philanthropist, a belligerent pacifist, a lover of all men, yet capable of strong dislikes, an idealist, yet a hearty lover of the good things of life.

[*Who's Who in America,* 1930–31; Lina G. Straus, *Disease in Milk* (2nd ed., 1917); *Jewish Tribune,* Feb. 2, 1923; *New Palestine,* Feb. 3, 1928; D. deSola Pool, in *The Am. Jewish Year Book,* vol. XXXIII (1931), pp. 135–154; Edward Hungerford, *The Romance of a Great Store* (1922); J. W. Wise, *Jews Are Like That!* (1928); obituary in *N. Y. Times,* Jan. 12, 1931.]   D. deS. P.

STRAUS, OSCAR SOLOMON (Dec. 23, 1850–May 3, 1926), lawyer, diplomat, and author, was born in Otterberg, Rhenish Bavaria, the third son of Lazarus and Sara (Straus) Straus, whose other two sons, Isidor and Nathan [*qq.v.*], achieved fame as merchants and philanthropists. After emigrating to the United States in 1854, the family settled first in Talbotton and Columbus, Ga., and later in New York City. Oscar studied at private schools, at Columbia College, from which he was graduated in 1871, and at the Columbia law school, where he obtained his degree in 1873. After being associated for a short time with the law firm of Ward, Jones & Whitehead, he established a law partnership with James A. Hudson and Simon Sterne. In 1881, however, he gave up law and became a partner in L. Straus & Sons, merchants in china and glassware.

It is as a diplomat that he makes his chief claim to historical fame. A progressive Democrat in politics, he first drew the attention of President Cleveland, who, at the instance of Henry Ward Beecher [*q.v.*], named him minister to Turkey (appointment confirmed, Dec. 21, 1887), a post that he held until 1889. Here his diplomatic tact and zeal enabled him to obtain concessions for American interests in Turkey, chiefly of an educational and religious nature. At the same time he won the admiration of the sultan to such a degree that he was invited to arbitrate between the Turkish government and Baron Maurice de Hirsch in a matter concerning the building of railroads. In 1898 he was again appointed to the post at Constantinople (appointment confirmed June 3, 1898) by President McKinley, whom he had supported because of McKinley's opposition to the Free Silver pledge of the Bryan Democrats. His tactful and successful work at the Sublime Porte again won him the commendation of the State Department. He resigned at the close of 1900. During the presidency of Theodore Roosevelt, he was frequently called upon to give his advice on matters of national and international importance. In 1902 he was appointed a member of the Permanent Court of Arbitration at The Hague, and was subsequently reappointed in 1908, 1912, and 1920. In December 1906 (appointment confirmed, Dec. 12) Roosevelt named him secretary of commerce and labor, a post he held until Mar. 4, 1909. As secretary his chief problems were those of Japanese immigration and naturalization. In 1909, under William Howard Taft, he went once more to Turkey, this time as the first American ambassador to the Ottoman Empire (appointment confirmed, May 17, 1909). Again he distinguished himself by obtaining special securities for American interests in Turkey, notably in the exemption of foreign religious, educational, and benevolent institutions from supervision by the Turkish authorities; and in the special sanction to American colleges to own property in their own names. It is worthy of note that his service under both Democratic and Republican administrations made him one of the earliest American career diplomats.

When he resigned his mission to Turkey in December 1910, it was only to throw himself more actively into the arena of national politics, which was at that time agitated by the Taft-Roosevelt split and the emergence of the Progressive party. As nominee for governor he headed the Progressive ticket in New York State, and, while the party went down generally to defeat at the polls, his own popularity was so great that he ran ahead not only of his ticket but even of Roosevelt himself. In 1913 he travelled through North Africa and Europe, the better to acquaint himself with foreign affairs. In 1915 he was appointed chairman of the New York Public Service Commission by Gov. Charles S. Whitman. He was a member of the League to Enforce Peace, and by interviewing many influential persons in London and Paris he actively assisted Wilson in his successful attempt to incorporate a League of Nations in the Versailles treaty. He was a persuasive and eloquent speaker not only by virtue of the enthusiasms that animated him but by the possession of a literary skill that he showed at an early age. Throughout his career he made many polished addresses. His published writings include *The Origin of Republican Form of Government in the United States* (1885), *Reform in the Consular Service* (1894), *The American Spirit* (1913), *Roger Williams, The Pioneer of Religious Liberty* (1894), and his autobiographical memoirs, *Under Four Administrations: From Cleveland to Taft* (1922).

Both the tradition of his family and his own inclinations led him to make many efforts in behalf of his co-religionists. When he met Baron Maurice de Hirsch he discussed with him plans for the amelioration of the lot of the Russian Jews. As one of a committee, he presented to President Harrison a description of their sad circumstances. In 1903, when the Kishinev pogroms outraged the civilized world, he discussed with President Roosevelt the note that was later sent to the Russian government, and aided in the collection of funds for the relief of the destitute. During the Russo-Japanese Treaty of 1905, he met with Count Sergius Witte to discuss the question of the Jews in Russia. When in Turkey he conferred with Dr. Theodor Herzl and took up with him the Zionist movement, of which Dr. Herzl was founder. At the Peace Conference in Paris he assisted in providing for the safeguarding of the Jewish minorities in Europe. He was active during and after the World War in the American Jewish Committee, the Jewish Welfare Board, and the Joint Distribution Committee. He was founder (1892) and first president of the American Jewish Historical Society, and a patron and friend of numerous other Jewish organizations. In private and in public life he was singularly charming. On Apr. 19, 1882, he was married to Sarah Lavanburg, who with two daughters and a son survived him. Towards the latter part of his life he was frequently ill, but he always remained a dynamo of energy. When he died in New York City he was mourned as an outstanding public citizen.

[O. S. Straus, *Under Four Administrations: From Cleveland to Taft* (1922); *Who's Who in America,* 1924–25; James Creelman, *Israel Unbound* (1907); W. W. Howard, *Oscar S. Straus in Turkey* (1912); Cyrus Adler, in *The Am. Jewish Year Book,* vol. XXIX (1927); Peter Wiernik, *Hist. of the Jews in America* (1912); Paul Masserman and Max Baker, *The Jews Come to America* (1932); obituary in *N. Y. Times,* May 4, 1926.]   A. I. E.

STRAUS, SIMON WILLIAM (Dec. 23, 1866–Sept. 7, 1930), banker, realty financier, was born at Ligonier, Ind., the son of Frederick William and Madlon (Goldsmith) Straus. His father, a native of Rhenish Prussia, was the founder and head of the Citizens' Bank of Ligonier; later he went to Chicago and started a mortgage and loan business. Young Simon attended the public schools of Chicago and Hughes High School in Cincinnati, Ohio, and in 1884 entered his father's business in Chicago, which was then known as F. W. Straus & Company. On Apr. 25, 1893, he married Hattie Klee of Pittsburgh, Pa. In 1898, his father having retired, he assumed the presidency of the business, the name of which had been changed to S. W. Straus & Company. He continued as president until two years before his death, when he became chairman of the board. As the business grew, branches began to be established in other cities, and in 1915 Straus removed his office and home to New York, the branch there having become the most important of the chain. He was a pioneer in promoting the building of skyscrapers and originated the idea of real estate bonds used to finance a building project, his company floating the first issue of that sort of paper in 1909. Between that time and his death his company financed building by that method to the extent of more than a billion dollars, and did a huge business in the sale of mortgages and securities. The Straus Company supplied money for some of the greatest office buildings, apartment buildings, and hotels in New York and Chicago, among them the Chrysler Building, New York, the tallest building in the world at the time of its completion, and the Chanin Building. At the time of Straus's death, the company had branches in fifty cities. Its $4,000,000 building in New York boasted one of the handsomest banking rooms in America, while the Chicago office of the company was a thirty-two story building costing $12,000,000.

In 1911 Straus founded the Franklin Trust and Savings Bank of Chicago, and in 1928 the Straus National Bank and Trust Company of Chicago, acting as president of both until his death. He took over and became the first president of the Ambassador hotels in New York and elsewhere. As early as 1927 he became aware that the saturation point in building in New York was near and urged caution, but was not heeded. He encouraged thrift among his employees by adding bonuses to their savings accounts. He founded the American Society for Thrift in 1914, was its president for several years, and was active in the International Congress for Thrift, 1915, at the San Francisco Exposition. He also wrote many articles for newspapers and magazines on thrift, and gave advice as to lending and borrowing on mortgages. In 1920 he published *History of the Thrift Movement in America.* He became noted as a bitter opponent of tipping, but found after some years of effort that opposition was useless. Always eager to help the laborer and the middle-class employee, in 1928 he worked out and arranged to finance an employee-management plan for a large plumbing-fixture corporation in Chicago in the hope of bringing the idea of employee-management into the building industry. He gave liberally of his time and money to philanthropy in both America and Europe. In recognition of his charitable work in France, the French government in 1927 conferred on him the Cross of the Legion of Honor. He died in New York City, survived by his wife and three daughters.

[*Who's Who in America,* 1930–31; obituaries in *N. Y. Times, World* (N.Y.), and *N. Y. Herald Tribune,* Sept. 8, 1930.]   A. F. H.

STRAWBRIDGE, ROBERT (d. August 1781), one of the earliest apostles of Methodism in America, was born in Drummersnave (now Drumsna), near Carrick-on-Shannon, County Leitrim, Ireland. His father, a farmer in comfortable circumstances apparently, was also named Robert, and there was at least one other son, Gilbert. The younger Robert came under Methodist influences and was converted. His championship of the doctrines and ways of Methodism aroused violent opposition from his neighbors, and he removed to Sligo, where he joined a Methodist society. During the next few years he seems to have lived in several different places, preaching and working as a house-builder. Meanwhile, he married a woman whose maiden name was Piper.

Sometime between 1759 and 1766, he emigrated to Maryland and settled on Sam's Creek, Frederick County. Upon the year of his arrival depends the answer to the long-debated question whether to him or to Philip Embury [*q.v.*] belongs the honor of having formed the first Methodist Society and built the first Methodist meeting house in America. The dates of Embury's achievements are not disputed, and the burden of proof rests upon Strawbridge's supporters. A review of the evidence leaves a disinterested person convinced that unless new facts are discovered, while there is a reasonable doubt of Embury's priority, that of Strawbridge cannot be established. It is certain, however, that he was the earliest apostle of Methodism in Maryland, and that his influence was a considerable factor in its establishment in America. Soon after his arrival he began to preach, meetings were held in his house, a small society was formed, and a log meeting house erected about a mile from his home. He lived on Sam's Creek for about sixteen years, ministering there and making preaching tours in eastern Maryland and across the borders into Virginia, Delaware, and Pennsylvania, his farm and family being cared for in the meantime by neighbors. As a result of his activities, many were converted, some of whom later became preachers, and a number of societies were formed. During the later years of his life his home was in the upper part of Long Green, Baltimore County, on a farm the use of which had been given him by Capt. Charles Ridgely.

Henry Boehm [*q.v.*], in his *Reminiscences* (*post*, p. 19) writes: "I heard Strawbridge preach at my house in 1781. . . . He was a stout, heavy man, and looked as if he was built for service. My father was much pleased with him and his preaching. He was agreeable company, full of interesting anecdotes." He is traditionally regarded as having been "generous, energetic, fiery, versatile, somewhat intractable to authority, and probably improvident" (Stevens, *post*, p. 42). When Wesley's missionaries came to America in the fall of 1769, Strawbridge was at first inclined to cooperate with them and to conform to the English forms of Methodist procedure. He visited Joseph Pilmore [*q.v.*] in Philadelphia not long after his arrival, and was there again the following year, when he preached in St. George's Chapel. In 1773 he and his Maryland associates deeded at least six meeting houses to trustees to hold for John and Charles Wesley and such persons as should be "appointed at the yearly conference of the people called Methodists in England." Although he was not present at the first American Methodist Conference, held in Philadelphia, July 11, 1773, he was appointed to the Baltimore circuit along with Francis Asbury and two others, but his name does not appear on the Conference minutes after 1775. Probably the reason for this fact is to be found in his unyielding attitude on the question of administering the Sacraments. Strawbridge was a lay preacher, but no doubt because of the limited opportunities for receiving the Sacraments in the sections where he labored, he had himself administered them before Wesley's missionaries had arrived. The first American Conference, however, decreed that the lay preachers must strictly avoid "administering the ordinances of baptism and the Lord's Supper." The Conference probably knew that Strawbridge would be obdurate, for, according to Asbury, it made an exception in his favor, but with the proviso that he should do so only "under the particular direction of the assistant" (*Journal of Rev. Francis Asbury*, 1852, I, 80). Strawbridge would not be bound by any such condition. He "appeared to be inflexible," Asbury wrote, "He would not administer the ordinances under our directions at all" (*Ibid.*, pp. 82–83). The last years of his life, therefore, he continued his circuit work independently, preaching around Baltimore, at Sam's Creek, and at Bush Chapel, Harford County. While on one of his itineraries in 1781 he became ill and died at the house of Joseph Wheeler, near Towson. He was buried not far from his own home and later his remains were removed to Mount Olivet Cemetery, Baltimore. He had six children, three of whom died early. So great was Asbury's resentment of Strawbridge's behavior that his reference to the latter's death (*Ibid.*, I, 431) was neither fair nor kind: "He is now no more: upon the whole, I am inclined to think that the Lord took him away in judgment, because he was in a way to do hurt to his cause; and that he saved him in mercy, because from his deathbed conversation he appears to have had hope in his end."

[For the Embury-Strawbridge controversy consult *Meth. Quart. Rev.*, July 1856; John Atkinson, *The Beginnings of the Wesleyan Movement in America* (1896); report of the Joint Commission on the Origin of Am. Methodism in *Jour. of the Twenty-Seventh Delegated Gen. Conf. of the M. E. Church*, 1916; *Meth. Rev.*, Jan., May 1928. See also William Crook, *Ireland and the Centenary of Am. Methodism* (1866); Nathan Bangs, *A Hist. of the M. E. Church* (3rd ed., vol. I, 1844); Henry Boehm, *Reminiscences, Hist. and Biog. of Sixty-four Years in the Ministry* (1865); Abel Stevens, *A Compendious Hist. of Am. Methodism* (1867); W. B. Sprague, *Annals of the Am. Pulpit*, vol. VII (1859); W. J. Townsend, H. B. Workman, and George Eayrs, *A New Hist. of Methodism* (2 vols., 1909); P. N. Garber, *The Romance of Am. Methodism* (1931); W. W. Sweet, *Methodism in Am. Hist.* (copr. 1933).]   H. E. S.

STRAWN, JACOB (May 30, 1800–Aug. 23, 1865), cattleman and farmer, was of English-

Welsh descent, the sixth and youngest child of Isaiah and Rachel (Reed) Strawn, who were Quakers. His great-grandfather, Lancelot Straughan, had settled in Pennsylvania in the first decade of the eighteenth century. Jacob was born and spent his first seventeen years on his father's farm in Somerset County, Pa. Attending the district school for a few months each winter, he received a meager education. In 1817 he moved with his parents to central Ohio. After working for his father until 1819, he settled on a nearby farm and began farming and dealing in live stock for himself. In 1828 he bought 395 acres of land about four miles southwest of Jacksonville, Ill. Moving to this farm in May 1831, he began the operations which earned for him the title of "cattle king," extending his holdings in Morgan, Sangamon, and LaSalle counties until he held over twenty thousand acres, chiefly in two tracts.

Except for the first few years, when he raised wheat and engaged in milling and butchering, he devoted his Illinois land to timber, pasture, and corn. In 1854 he raised 2,900 acres of corn, all of which was fed to stock, and owned 2,000 cattle, 700 hogs, and more than a hundred horses and mules. Later he was reputed to have fattened more than five thousand cattle in one year. He introduced into Illinois the practice of feeding shock corn to cattle. He bred few cattle, preferring to buy, fatten, and sell. On horseback he scoured central and southern Illinois, Missouri, and the settled parts of Iowa for feeder cattle which he drove to his Illinois farms. Here they were fattened for the markets in the East, New Orleans, and St. Louis. For several years he largely controlled the cattle market at St. Louis. On one occasion, to thwart a conspiracy of buyers to break his hold on that market, he sent agents out on all the roads leading into the city and bought all incoming herds. He broke the combination in two days and had no more difficulty of that kind. After 1850 he began to confine himself largely to grazing and feeding and to market more of his cattle at home.

In the last few years of his life he curtailed his operations. Possessed of a powerful physique and a strong constitution, he was an active man, spending most of his time outdoors, much of it in the saddle. He believed in hard work and in frugal, simple living, despised show, was plain in dress and rough in speech. He was scrupulously honest, prompt in his dealings, sympathetic toward those in distress, had a strong sense of honor, and commanded universal respect. Although he made no profession of religion, he was sympathetic toward it. He ab-stained from the use of tobacco and liquor, and declined to serve the latter to his harvest workers. He was a Whig and a Republican, but sought no office. During the Civil War he actively supported the Union and aided in relief work among Union troops. In 1819 he married Matilda Green, daughter of John Green, a Baptist minister of Licking County, Ohio. She died in 1831 after having borne seven children. The following year he married Phoebe Gates, daughter of Samuel Gates of Greene County, Ill. By this marriage he had five sons and a daughter. He was buried in the Diamond Grove Cemetery, Jacksonville, Ill.

[*Prairie Farmer*, Nov. 1854, Oct. 4, 1860, Sept. 2, 1865; *Valley Farmer*, May 1859; *Quincy Whig*, July 3, 1854; *The Biog. Encyc. of Ill.* (1875); *History of Morgan County, Ill.: Its Past and Present* (1878); C. M. Eames, *Historic Morgan and Classic Jacksonville* (1885); *Encyc. of Biog. of Ill.*, vol. I (1892); Newton Bateman and Paul Selby, *Biog. and Memorial Ed. of the Hist. Encyc. of Ill.* (1915), vol. II; *Jour. Ill. State Hist. Soc.*, Apr. 1925; L. M. Glover, *Discourse Occasioned by the Death of Jacob Strawn, the Great Am. Farmer* (1865); Ellwood Roberts, *Old Richland Families* (1898); C. V. Roberts, *Early Friends Families of Upper Bucks* (1925); information from Samuel Clark, Princeton, Ill.]   R. H. A.

STREET, ALFRED BILLINGS (Dec. 18, 1811–June 2, 1881), lawyer, poet, librarian, was born in Poughkeepsie, N. Y., the son of Randall Sanford Street and Cornelia (Billings) Street. His immigrant ancestor, the Rev. Nicholas Street, came to Massachusetts between 1630 and 1638 and settled at Taunton, whence his progeny went via Connecticut to New York just before the Revolution. His father, a general in the state militia, served in the War of 1812, was twice district attorney of the second judicial district of New York, and, 1819–21, served as Democratic congressman for the fourth New York district. Alfred attended the Dutchess County Academy until the family's removal in 1825 to Monticello, N. Y., where after finishing his schooling he read law in his father's office. He was admitted to the bar and, although the law had little attraction for him, he practised at Monticello until his removal to Albany in 1839. There he set up a law office and for years maintained a sort of connection with the law, but literature, and particularly poetry, soon claimed him. He had indeed written poetry much earlier. His "A Winter Scene" and "A Day in March" were printed in the *Evening Post* (New York) during his fifteenth year (Griswold, *post*, p. 395). In Albany, where he had social standing, congenial companions, and access to books, his literary talents were encouraged and enlarged. On Nov. 3, 1841, he married Elizabeth, daughter of Smith Weed of Albany, by whom he had one son. From 1843 to 1844 he was editor of the *Northern Light,* a pretentious literary journal sponsored by a group of prominent citizens of Albany headed by John Adams Dix [*q.v.*]. To it Street contributed twelve poems, and eight articles of some length. He was director of the New York State Library from 1848 to 1862, and continued as law librarian until June 1868. While these posts may have been procured by his friends more in recognition of his renown as a poet than for competence as a librarian, yet he took his directorship seriously, was diligent and attentive, and produced less work of his own while he was librarian than before or after. During these years he wrote *The Council of Revision of the State of New York: Its History* (1859) and compiled *A Digest of Taxation in the States* (1863).

His best known books are *The Burning of Schenectady* (1842), and *Frontenac* (1849), a vigorous historical poem of seven thousand lines, of which a London edition was also issued in 1849. Two books, "Lake and Mountain or Autumn in the Adirondacks" and "Eagle Pine, or Sketches of a New York Frontier Village," said to have been prepared for the press (Allibone, *post*), seem never to have been published. In 1845 *The Poems of Alfred B. Street* appeared. Separately printed occasional poems are *Our State* (1849), *Burgoyne* (1877), *Knowledge and Liberty* (1849), *In Memoriam: President Lincoln Dead* (1870). The poems usually found in anthologies are "The Gray Forest Eagle," which is a spirited patriotic lyric, "Lost Hunter," "The Settler," and the more pretentious "The Burning of Schenectady" and "Frontenac." Street's literary place among American poets has been described as "the same as that generally assigned to Dryden among English poets,—one of the first of the second class" (Allibone, *post*). Primarily a poet of nature, he found his themes in the forests, mountains, and lakes of New York state. His work was marked by close and accurate observation, fidelity of description, directness, and occasionally by animation and vigor. Though he was diffuse, repetitious, sometimes over-minute, his verse scarcely deserves the neglect into which it has fallen. Some of his poems were translated into German, and they were well received in England. Disraeli paid tribute to his "originality and poetic fire"; Poe praised him as a descriptive poet (Allibone, *post*). But critics never noted in him imagination, inspiration, fancy, or high artistry. He was plain in person, taste, and attire; small, mild-mannered, a recluse to the borders of eccentricity.

[H. A. and M. A. Street, *The Street Geneal.* (1895); R. W. Griswold, *The Poets and Poetry of America* (1843); William Hunt, *The Am. Biog. Sketch Book* (1848), pp. 97–101; S. A. Allibone, *A Critical Dict. of Eng. Lit.,* vol. II (1870), with a full list of titles, and references to reviews and critical comments; E. A. and G. L. Duyckinck, *Cyc. of Am. Lit.* (1875), vol. II, p. 434; F. L. Mott, *A Hist. of Am. Mags.* (1930); reviews of Street's poems in *U. S. Mag. and Democratic Rev.,* Jan. 1846, pp. 76–77, and *Am. Rev.,* Apr. 1846, pp. 425–41; memoir in *Bentley's Miscellany,* vol. XXV (1849), pp. 563–66; obituaries in *Albany Argus* and *Albany Evening Jour.,* June 3, 1881.]   J. I. W.

STREET, AUGUSTUS RUSSELL (Nov. 5, 1791–June 12, 1866), leader in art education and in the study of modern languages, and, at the time of his death, "the most munificent benefactor of Yale College since its foundation," was born and bred in New Haven, Conn. He was the eldest of the five children of Titus Street (1758–1842), a prosperous New Haven merchant, and Amaryllis (Atwater) Street, and a descendant of the Rev. Nicholas Street, who came from England to Taunton, Mass., between 1630 and 1638, and later removed to New Haven. He was graduated from Yale in 1812. As he became a confirmed invalid during his student days his college life was singularly uneventful. He was, however, one of the eighteen members of the Phi Beta Kappa Society and one of the twenty-six of the Linonian Society. After graduation he studied law with Judge Charles Chauncey of New Haven but never practised that profession. For a number of years he was a silent partner in the bookselling and publishing firm of Hezekiah Howe & Company of New Haven, and in 1827 he was treasurer of the New Haven Tontine Company, which maintained a hotel facing the Green. He was later the builder and owner of the famous New Haven House and the adjoining property. On Oct. 29, 1815, he married Caroline Mary (b. 1790), the elder daughter of William Leffingwell (1765–1834), a wealthy resident of New Haven. The young couple settled quietly in New Haven and reared a family of girls, whose education their father carefully guided. After the death of Titus Street, the whole family resided in Europe for five years, their travels extending to Greece and Egypt. This gave Street "ample time for study and close observation . . . leading to [the] reflection upon the advantages of a thorough European culture, and the need of rounding out our ordinary American education by the study of the modern languages and the cultivation of the aesthetic arts" (Hoppin, *post,* vol. II, p. 146).

A number of years after his return to New Haven he began a series of notable gifts to Yale in the fields of modern languages and the arts.

These benefactions, which included the establishment of the Titus Street Professorship of Ecclesiastical History and a scholarship in the theological department, began in 1855 with a partial endowment of a professorship of modern languages, which he completed in 1863. During the first century and a quarter, though there had been some instruction, there was no official recognition of modern languages by the college. The first Street Professor of Modern Languages was appointed in 1864. In the same year Street made another important gift. The Trumbull Gallery, the earliest art museum connected with a college or university in America, had been maintained at Yale since 1832. Street now came forward with an offer to erect at his expense a building for a school of the fine arts. The building, designed by Peter Bonnett Wight [q.v.] in the Venetian Gothic style made popular by Ruskin's *The Stones of Venice*, was completed in 1866 shortly after the donor's death, his will having provided for its completion and partial endowment. It was in Street Hall, as it was known, that the important collection of paintings made by James Jackson Jarves [q.v.] was deposited, later to become the possession of the college. After her husband's death Mrs. Street endowed a professorship of painting in fulfillment of his plans, and later one of drawing. In the autumn of 1866 the college corporation created the Yale School of the Fine Arts, founded and partially endowed by the Streets, one of the earliest art schools in the country connected with an institution of higher learning. The "admission of pupils of both sexes" was specified by the donor, thus opening the doors of Yale to women for the first time.

The Streets lived for a dozen or more years in a fine house at the corner of Chapel and Temple Streets but in 1855 lent it to their eldest daughter, who had become the second wife of Rear Admiral Andrew Hull Foote [q.v.]. Later the lonely couple, who survived all seven of their daughters, lived in rooms in the New Haven House. Mrs. Street, who was very popular among Yale undergraduates, continued to live in the New Haven House until her death, at the age of eighty-seven, on Aug. 24, 1877. She built the Street Home for poor girls in Middletown, Conn., and in her will left a considerable sum for a variety of charitable purposes, among them funds for promoting the cause of Protestantism in Mexico. She was buried beside her husband in the Grove Street Cemetery.

[See records of the United Church and First Congregational (Center) Church, New Haven Conn.; H. A. and M. A. Street, *The Street Geneal.* (1895), where, however, birth and marriage dates are given incorrectly; *Yale Coll. in 1868* (n.d.); F. B. Dexter, *Biog. Sketches Grads. Yale Coll.*, vol. VI (1912), *A Cat. . . . of the Portraits, Busts, etc. Belonging to Yale Univ.* (1892), and *A Selection of the Miscellaneous Hist. Papers of Fifty Years* (1918); *Obit. Record Grads. Yale Coll. . . . 1866* (1866); J. F. Weir, "Yale School of the Fine Arts," and J. M. Hoppin, "Augustus Russell Street," in *Yale Coll.* (2 vols., 1879), ed. by W. L. Kingsley; E. V. Meeks, in *Yale Alumni Weekly*, Nov. 4, 1932; N. P., in *Yale Courant*, June 27, 1866; obituaries in *Daily Register* (New Haven), June 12, *New Haven Daily Morning Jour. and Courier*, June 13, and *Columbia Weekly Register* (New Haven), June 16, 1866; minutes of the Yale Corporation, copies of the wills of Street and his wife, letters, inventories, deeds of property, etc. in the office of the treasurer at Yale. Portraits of Street, his wife, and his father-in-law are at Yale.]   T.S—r.

STREET, JOSEPH MONTFORT (Dec. 18, 1782–May 5, 1840), editor and Indian agent, was born in Lunenburg County, Va., the son of Anthony Waddy and Mary (Stokes) Street and the grandson of John Street of Bristol, England, who settled in New Kent County, Va., early in the eighteenth century. His father was a prosperous planter, a member of the county court, and vestryman of Cumberland Parish, and his mother was the sister of Montfort Stokes [q.v.]. In Richmond he met John Wood, a newspaper man of doubtful reputation from New York, with whom he entered into what Wood later described to Henry Clay as an "ardent friendship" such as "frequently entails misery on those who are the slaves of such a strong passion" (letter of Oct. 9, 1806, Clay Papers, vol. I, no. 75). On July 7, 1806, they began to publish the *Western World* in Frankfort, Ky. A Federalist sheet, it was active in instigating the investigations that proved Benjamin Sebastian [q.v.] guilty of taking a Spanish pension, retired John Brown [q.v.] to private life, and forced Aaron Burr [q.v.] to appear before a grand jury in Kentucky twice in 1806. It also accused Harry Innes [q.v.] of corrupt intrigue, and Innes sued Street for libel. Another libel suit, begun by Christopher Greenup [q.v.], was discontinued upon Street's public retraction. Street was everywhere the object of vituperation and revenge. Challenged to a succession of duels, after demonstrating beyond doubt both his courage and his skill, he refused to fight again and announced that he would merely file further challenges and publish them in proper order. As he grew more intimate, personally and politically, with Humphrey Marshall and Joseph H. Daviess he became estranged from Wood, who accused him of swindling him out of the money invested in the paper and in 1807 withdrew. Street continued to publish the *Western World* for a time but then lost control. The paper declined in popularity, partly through the bitterness of its criticism of the federal government and of the administration of foreign affairs and partly through the changes that came over Kentucky with growing prosperity. He was married, on Oct. 9, 1809, to Eliza Maria (Posey) Thornton, the daughter of Thomas Posey [q.v.]. On May 9, 1811, he executed a deed of trust to John Posey conveying more than 6,000 acres of land, six negroes, four horses, two cows, and household furniture in trust for her (Innes Papers, vol. XVIII, no. 40, 2/3 way through vol.). When, a little more than a year later, he lost the suit for libel brought by Innes and was ordered to pay heavy damages, he made the plea that the amount ordered was entirely beyond his means and sought an accommodation (see Innes sketch).

In these circumstances he took his wife and baby son, the first of fourteen children, to the western frontier. During the summer of 1812 he built a log house at Shawneetown, Ill., where he was active in local politics and became a brigadier-general of militia. In 1827 he was appointed Indian agent to the Winnebago at Prairie du Chien. He was later at Rock Island, again at Prairie du Chien, and the last months of his life near the present Agency City, Iowa. Without comprehending the essential difficulties or possibilities of the Indian problem he maintained cordial relations with his wards and was active in defending them. He sought, unsuccessfully, in 1827 to remove Henry Dodge [q.v.] and the other squatters at the lead mines reserved by treaty to the Winnebago. He caused the arrest of Jean Brunett in 1829 for cutting timber on Indian lands and was himself forced to pay a fine for exceeding his authority. In 1838 he undertook, again unsuccessfully, to prevent fraud in disbursing monies to the Winnebago under a commission composed of Simon Cameron [q.v.] and James Murray. He was hopeful that westward removal would help the Indians and advocated mission schools, training in agriculture and industrial crafts, division of land in severalty, and the curtailment of the influence of the fur traders. He rendered valuable service to the government in the Black Hawk War, keeping the Winnebago neutral and, after the capture of Black Hawk [q.v.], persuading them to deliver the prisoner to the federal army. He died near the present Agency City, Iowa.

[Issues of the *Western World* in Harper Library, Univ. of Chicago, through the courtesy of Winifred Ver Nooy, Chicago; Street letters and papers in Hist., Memorial and Art Department of Iowa, Des Moines, in Wis. State Hist. Lib., Madison, and in files of the Indian office, Washington, D. C.; Clay Papers and Harry Innes Papers, esp. vols. XVIII, XXII, in Lib. of Cong.; *Annals of Iowa*, Apr. 1901, Jan. 1921, Apr. 1927; "The Edwards Papers," *Chicago Hist. Soc. Colls.*, vol. III (1884), ed. by E. B. Washburne; W. B. Street, "General Joseph M. Street," *Annals of Iowa*,

July–Oct. 1895; I. M. Street, "Joseph M. Street's Last Fight with the Fur Traders," *Ibid.*, Oct. 1929; George Wilson, "A Neglected Kentucky Hero," *Register of the Ky. Hist. Soc.*, Sept. 1906; R. G. Thwaites, "The Ohio Valley Press," *Proc. Am. Antiquarian Soc.*, n.s., XIX (1909); L. C. Bell, *The Old Free State . . . Hist. of Lunenburg County* (1927), vol. II, p. 338; Wm. Meade, *Old Churches* (1857), vol. I; H. A. and M. A. Street, *The Street Geneal.* (1895); *Wm. and Mary College Quart.*, Apr. 1928; *Va. Mag. of Hist. and Biog.*, Apr. 1904, p. 422.]
K. E. C.

STRICKLAND, WILLIAM (c. 1787–Apr. 6, 1854), architect, engineer, engraver, was born of humble parents in Philadelphia. His father, John, was a carpenter who during William's boyhood worked for Benjamin H. Latrobe [q.v.], and through this connection the son came to the notice of Latrobe, from whom he received his professional training. In 1807 he accompanied his father to New York, where the latter was engaged in the remodeling of the Park Theatre, and here learned something of scene painting. Upon his return to Philadelphia, finding at the moment little demand for his services as an architect, he set himself up "as a sort of artist in general" (Kane, *post*, p. 29), selling landscapes when he could, painting scenery, making designs for carpenters and plasterers. He became a competent engraver and aquatinter, executed a number of plates for the *Port Folio* and the *Analectic Magazine*—chiefly dealing with scenes and episodes of the War of 1812— and made fourteen engravings from the drawings of David Porter [q.v.] to illustrate Porter's *Journal of a Cruise Made to the Pacific Ocean . . . 1812, 1813, and 1814* (2 vols., 1815). He was not an educated man in any formal sense, but by nature he was endowed with a remarkable visual memory, good reasoning powers, and a skilful hand. That he was one of those men who can undertake successfully almost any kind of work is evidenced by his varied achievements in the fields of architecture and engineering.

In the former field, he is remembered as an outstanding exponent of the Greek Revival in America, which had its first monument in the Bank of Pennsylvania, designed by his preceptor, Latrobe. Judge John Kintzing Kane [q.v.], who delivered an obituary oration on Strickland before the American Philosophical Society, which had elected him to membership in 1820, characterized his taste as disciplined in the severe harmonies of Grecian architecture, adding that he became a purist in art as he grew older, caring less and less for decoration. This fact is illustrated by the contrast between his first building, the Masonic Temple, Philadelphia (so-called Gothic, 1810), and his later, coldly severe, Custom House, still standing. The latter, built for the Bank of the United States and completed in 1824, was modeled on the Parthenon. Strickland had a more graceful side, however, which appears in his Merchants' Exchange (1834), likewise in Philadelphia. This delightful building is unique because of its colonnade curved on plan, and because it is crowned with a copy of the Choragic Monument of Lysicrates. Colonial and early Federal architecture, harking back to Rome by way of England, France, and the Italian Renaissance, was committed to domes, but the Greek Revivalists could not use the dome, that most precious property of their predecessors, because there was no precedent for it in Greek architecture. Strickland substituted the Monument of Lysicrates, and has been called the inventor of this happy expedient (Tallmadge, *post*). Among his other Philadelphia buildings were the first United States Custom House (1819), the New Chestnut Street Theatre (1822), St. Stephen's Church, a Jewish synagogue, the Friends' Lunatic Asylum, the United States Naval Asylum (1827), and the United States Mint (1829). In 1828 he designed a restoration, in wood, of the original steeple of the State House (Independence Hall); he designed the marble sarcophagus of Washington at Mount Vernon and certain alterations in Washington's tomb (1837), and at the time of his death was engaged on the Tennessee capitol, Nashville, beneath which distinguished work of the period he was buried.

Concurrently with his architectural work, he was engaged in numerous significant engineering enterprises. In 1824 he made a reconnaissance for the Chesapeake and Delaware Canal. In 1825, taking with him his young assistant, Samuel Honeyman Kneass [*q.v.*], he went to Great Britain for the Pennsylvania Society for the Promotion of Internal Improvement, to investigate canals, roads, railways, and bridges, and upon his return made a report asserting that railroads were bound in time to supersede the canals then being built so extensively. This view was considered altogether too impracticable for the Society to accept, and accordingly Judge Kane rewrote the last paragraphs of Strickland's report before publication (Kane, *post*, p. 30). Upon his return to the United States, Strickland became engineer for the Pennsylvania State Canal. He designed and built the Delaware Breakwater, begun in 1829, for the United States government, and in 1835 he made the survey for a railroad between Wilmington, Del., and the Susquehanna River. He was subsequently one of the editors of *Public Works of the United States of America* (London, 1841), a folio atlas of plates, and its accompanying vol-

ume, *Reports, Specifications and Estimates of Public Works in the United States of America* (1841). Other publications of his include the important *Reports on Canals, Railways, Roads, and Other Subjects Made to "The Pennsylvania Society for the Promotion of Internal Improvement"* (1826); *Address upon a Proposed Railroad from Wilmington to the Susquehanna* (1835); and *Tomb of Washington at Mount Vernon* (1840).

[Memorial address by J. K. Kane, *Proc. Am. Philosophical Soc.*, vol. VI (1859); Joseph Jackson, *Early Phila. Architects and Engineers* (1923), and *Encyc. of Phila.*, vol. IV (1933); J. T. Scharf and Thompson Westcott, *Hist. of Phila.* (3 vols., 1884); Wm. Dunlap, *A Hist. of the Rise and Progress of the Arts and Design in the U. S.* (3 vols., 1918), ed. by F. W. Bayley and C. E. Goodspeed; T. E. Tallmadge, *The Story of Architecture in America* (copr. 1927); A. F. Harlow, *Old Towpaths* (1926); F. A. Cleveland and F. W. Powell, *Railroad Promotion and Capitalization in the U. S.* (1909); *Republican Daily Banner and Nashville Whig*, Apr. 8, 1854.]

A. M. B.

STRINGFELLOW, FRANKLIN (June 18, 1840–June 8, 1913), Confederate Scout, was born at "The Retreat" near Raccoon Ford, Culpeper County, Va., where his father, Rittenhouse, and grandfather, Robert, had lived and played the rôle of planter for many years. His mother was Anne (Slaughter) Stringfellow, a member of another family of local distinction. He was named Benjamin Franklin Stringfellow but was usually known as Frank. He was sent to school first in Albemarle County and then at the Episcopal High School of Alexandria. From Alexandria he went to Shuqualak, Noxubee County, Miss., where he became teacher of Latin and Greek in the Stanton School. Drawn back to Virginia by the intense excitements of the spring of 1861, he sought to enter the Confederate army. Delicate in health and weighing only ninety-four pounds, his applications were several times rejected. However, on May 28, 1861, he attained the status of a private in the Powatan troop, 4th Virginia Cavalry, and rendered distinguished service as a courier in the battle of Bull Run, which led to his assignment to the staff of Gen. J. E. B. Stuart, who asked his appointment to a captaincy the next year. After the battle of Gettysburg he was attached to the staff of Gen. Robert E. Lee for secret scout service, whence he rose to the rank of chief of scouts in the Army of Northern Virginia. Small and wiry of stature, he sometimes entered the lines of the enemy as a woman, moved about under different disguises, hid himself under brush heaps at night near Union headquarters and managed to read army orders before they were issued and to forward the information to General Lee. His services were many and extraordinary and all but caused the defeat of General Grant in the battle of the Wilderness in 1864. He was many times a prisoner within the Union lines, from which he escaped again and again with valuable information. Detained as a spy in the Old Capitol prison in 1865, he managed to escape just before the assassination of Lincoln and, having stopped on his way home at the house of Mrs. Mary E. Surratt, he was naturally in some danger and hurried away to Canada, where he remained some years. When the excitements of 1865 and 1866 calmed he returned to Fairfax County, Va., where he married Emma Frances Greene, the daughter of James Greene, and took up his residence at "Wakefield," in the vain hope that the old planter life of his boyhood might be renewed. They had six children.

Being of a most religious nature, he studied theology at the Episcopal Seminary in Virginia and was graduated in 1876. For thirty years he served different parishes as a clergyman in the Episcopal church; and toward the end of the century he became one of the most popular public lecturers in the South, using the amazing experiences of his scout life for his themes. He held audiences spellbound for two hours at a time rehearsing the hairbreadth escapes from enemy headquarters, his services as a spy in Washington City, and his inventiveness when the enemy seemed about to make an end of him. His closing years were spent as rector of Saint John's Church, Mechanicsville, in Louisa County, not far from the scenes of his wartime exploits.

[Personal letters from Jefferson Davis, Robert E. Lee, and J. E. B. Stuart, published in an undated pamphlet *War Reminiscences*; *War of the Rebellion: Official Records (Army)*, 1 ser., XI, pt. 2, XXIX, pt. 1; XXXIII, XXXVI, pt. 3; P. A. Bruce, *Brave Deeds of Confederate Soldiers* (copr. 1916); W. A. R. Goodwin, *Hist. of the Theological Seminary in Va.* (1924), II, 154; L. S. Watkins, *The Life of Horace Stringfellow* (1931), esp. pp. 104–06, 125–28, 148–51; *Geneal. and Hist. Notes on Culpeper County, Va.* (1900), comp. by R. T. Green; information from his grandson, Frank Stringfellow Barr, University of Virginia; the author heard him deliver some of his lectures.]   W. E. D.

STRINGHAM, SILAS HORTON (Nov. 7, 1797–Feb. 7, 1876), naval officer, son of Capt. Daniel Stringham and Abigail (Horton) Stringham, was born in Middletown, N. Y. He entered the navy as a midshipman, Nov. 15, 1809, serving first in the frigate *President* under Commodore John Rodgers, 1773–1838 [*q.v.*]. In this ship he participated in the *Little Belt* affair, and during the War of 1812 took part in the engagement with the *Belvidera*. During the second war with Algiers he served in the brig *Spark* in Commodore Isaac Chauncey's squadron, returning

to the United States in 1818. While on this station he distinguished himself during a storm near Gibraltar by going to the rescue of a capsized French brig. Though he and his men rescued the crew, he was unable to return to port and was blown off Algeciras, where his boat capsized, and one of his own men and two Frenchmen were drowned. He was an officer in the *Cyane* when in 1820 she convoyed the *Elizabeth,* the vessel that carried the first settlers to Liberia. For the next two years he served on the African coast, assisting in the suppression of the slave trade. Two slavers were captured, one American from Baltimore and one Spaniard. With these two ships under his command he captured two more slavers, all of which he brought to New York, where they were condemned as prizes. He spent the next two years as executive officer of the *Hornet* in the West Indies in operations against the pirates. There the pirate schooner *Moscow* and other vessels were captured. From 1823 until the opening of the Mexican War his naval career was quite uneventful, but in 1847 he was given command of the ship-of-the-line *Ohio,* and in her took part in the bombardment of Vera Cruz, being present at the capitulation of the city. For a short time he commanded the Brazilian squadron and from 1853 to 1855 was in command of the Mediterranean squadron with the ill-fated *Cumberland* as his flagship.

In March 1861 he was summoned to Washington to confer with Gideon Welles, secretary of the navy, regarding the relief of Fort Sumter. Welles wrote, "Whilst there were doubts and uncertainty on every hand as to who could be trusted, I knew Commodore Stringham to be faithful, and . . . selected him to assist me in matters of detail. With him I communicated freely and fully in regard to the condition of Sumter . . ." (*Diary of Gideon Welles, post,* p. 5). Stringham made definite plans for the relief of the beleaguered garrison but was forced to give them over. He took command of the Atlantic blockading fleet, May 13, 1861, and planned a combined naval and military expedition against the forts at Hatteras Inlet, N. C., guarding Pamlico Sound. Stringham himself took command of the attacking fleet, supported by Gen. Benjamin F. Butler in command of the land forces. The bombardment began on Aug. 28, 1861, and the two forts capitulated the following day. It was the first great naval victory of the war. In compliance with orders, Stringham returned with his fleet to Hampton Roads. Though the Northern press criticized him severely for not advancing with his fleet into Pamlico Sound, it was proved that his vessels drew too much water to advance further, and that, moreover, his orders were to return to Hampton Roads. Wounded by this criticism, however, and irritated by a rebuke from the Navy Department for allowing vessels to slip through the blockade, he asked on Sept. 16, 1861, to be relieved of his command. He was made rear-admiral on the retired list the following year, and for the last two years of the war served as commandant of the Boston navy yard. His expedition against the Hatteras forts was ably planned and admirably conducted, not a single Union man being lost. In relieving him of his command Welles expressed high appreciation of his patriotism and zeal. After his retirement from the service he spent his declining years in Brooklyn, N. Y. In 1819 he married Henrietta Hicks, by whom he had four daughters.

[The date of birth is from G. F. Horton, *The Hortons in America* (1929), ed. by A. H. White. See also L. R. Hamersly, *The Records of Living Officers of the U. S. Navy* (4th ed., 1890); U. S. Navy Dept. Registers; *War of the Rebellion: Official Records (Navy)*; manuscript Log of U. S. S. *Ohio*, 1847–48; *Diary of Gideon Welles* (1911), vol. I, pp. 5–12; *Private and Official Correspondence of Gen. Benjamin F. Butler* (5 vols., 1917); J. T. Headley, *Farragut and Our Naval Commanders* (1867); *Army and Navy Jour.*, Feb. 12, 19, 1876; and obituary in *N. Y. Times*, Feb. 8, 1876. Information has been supplied by Stringham's grand-daughter.]   L. H. B.

STRINGHAM, WASHINGTON IRVING (Dec. 10, 1847–Oct. 5, 1909), mathematician, was born in Yorkshire Center (later Delevan), N. Y., the youngest of nine children of Henry and Eliza (Tomlinson) Stringham. He was a descendant in the fourth generation of Jacob Stringham, of Huguenot ancestry. In 1865 he went to Topeka, Kan., where he studied in the preparatory department of Lincoln (later Washburn) College, and between 1867 and 1873 spent three years in the college itself, interrupting his college course at intervals to work at sign-painting and bookkeeping. In 1873 he entered Harvard College, and in 1877, at the age of thirty, he graduated with the degree of A.B. At Harvard he came under the influence of Benjamin Peirce [*q.v.*] and was initiated by him into the mysteries of the relatively new branch of quaternions. Upon his graduation from Harvard he was appointed to a fellowship in the Johns Hopkins University, where he studied for three years under James Joseph Sylvester [*q.v.*], taking the degree of Ph.D. in 1880. It was during this period that he contributed to the *Proceedings of the American Academy of Arts and Sciences* (vol. XIII, 1878) his first piece of original work, "Investigations on Quaternions." While he was working at Johns Hopkins he also contributed to the *American Journal of Mathematics,* then almost the sole medium in the United States for mathematical papers of distinctly high quality, three important memoirs: "Some General Formulæ for Integrals of Irrational Functions" (June 1879), "The Quaternion Formulæ for Quantification of Curves, Surfaces, and Solids and for Barycentres" (September 1879), and "Regular Figures in n-dimensional Space" (March 1880). After leaving Johns Hopkins he spent two years, 1880–82, at Leipzig, which Felix Klein was then making one of the mathematical foci of Europe, on the Parker fellowship of Harvard. He was thus among the early pupils of two men, Peirce and Klein, whose influence upon American mathematics was destined to be so marked in the quarter of a century which followed. Leaving Germany, he became professor of mathematics in the University of California (1882), where he remained until his death, and where he was active in setting a high standard of scholarship. He married on June 28, 1888, Martha Sherman Day, great-grand-daughter of Jeremiah Day [*q.v.*].

He was a frequent contributor to the *American Journal of Mathematics,* the *Transactions of the American Mathematical Society,* the *Proceedings of the American Association for the Advancement of Science,* and the publications of various other learned bodies. He was vice-president of the American Mathematical Society (1906) and a member of its council (1902–05). His books were not so important as his contributions to mathematical periodicals. He revised the English algebra of Charles Smith, *Elementary Algebra for the Use of Preparatory Schools* (New York, 1894), but the work was too scholarly for general use in the United States at that time. In 1893 there appeared his *Uniplanar Algebra: Being Pt. 1 of a Propaedeutic to the Higher Mathematical Analysis,* a part of which had already been published (1891) as a synopsis of a course of university extension lectures given in San Francisco during the winter of 1891–92. The work, however, was not well adapted to the classroom. He died at Berkeley at the age of sixty-two years, survived by his wife, two daughters and a son.

[*Who's Who in America,* 1908–09; *Harvard Coll. Class of 1877: Seventh Report, June 1917* (n.d.), with bibliog.; W. T. Reid, in *Univ. of Cal. Chronicle,* Jan. 1910; M. W. Haskell, *Ibid.*; W. C. Jones, *Illus. Hist. of the Univ. of Cal.* (1895); obituary in *Los Angeles Times,* Oct. 6, 1909.]   D. E. S.

STROBEL, EDWARD HENRY (Dec. 7, 1855–Jan. 15, 1908), diplomatist, was the son of Caroline Lydia (Bullock) and Maynard Davis Strobel. He was born in Charleston, S. C., where his great-grandfather had settled about a century earlier. His father, a bank cashier, died in 1868, after losing all his money in Confederate bonds. In spite of such discouraging circumstances, Strobel entered Harvard College and graduated in 1877. Graduating from the Harvard Law School in 1882, he was admitted to the New York bar in 1883 and for a time practised law in New York City. He decided, however, that the legal profession was overcrowded and turned to the field of international affairs. He wrote for the Cleveland campaign *Mr. Blaine and His Foreign Policy: An Examination of His Most Important Dispatches While Secretary of State* (1884), and in August 1885 Cleveland appointed him secretary of the legation at Madrid. He served until March 1890, acting as chargé d'affaires about one-third of the time. He made two important visits to Morocco, in which his diplomatic ability was strikingly demonstrated. He was third assistant secretary of state, 1893 to 1894, when he was appointed minister to Ecuador. In December of the same year he became minister to Chile. His comprehensive report on *Resumption of Specie Payments in Chile* (1896) was regarded as a timely and authoritative document on the currency question. Before leaving Santiago in 1897, at the request of France and Chile he acted as arbitrator of the Fréraut claim, with such satisfactory results that the French government made him an officer in the Legion of Honor in 1898, and in 1899 he was appointed counsel for Chile before the United States and Chilean claims commission at Washington. Returning to the United States he published *The Spanish Revolution, 1868–1875* (1898), for which he had gathered material at Madrid. The same year he was appointed Bemis Professor of International Law in the Harvard Law School.

In 1903 he became general adviser to the government of Siam, with the rank of minister plenipotentiary. He sailed in October 1903 for Paris, where the French foreign office and the Siamese minister were negotiating a treaty. The treaty was signed on Feb. 13, 1904, and he carried it with him to Bangkok. Almost immediately he gained the confidence and affection of the Siamese people to a remarkable degree. He accomplished the abolition of licensed gambling, which not only had a tremendous hold upon the people but furnished the government with a substántial revenue, and worked out a compensating system of land-tax laws and import duties. He effected a revision of the harbor regulations, a task necessitating skilful negotiations with the treaty powers, reorganization of the telegraph and pos-

tal services, extension of the government railways, the abolition of debt slavery, revision of the penal code, and improvement of the courts. New treaties favorable to Siam were concluded with Italy and Denmark. Siam's first foreign loan was negotiated in Paris and London, establishing her international financial standing. In November 1905 the King bestowed upon him the highest honor in Siam, the Grand Cross of the Order of the White Elephant. A month later he left Siam for a year's leave of absence in America. While visiting Egypt on the way, he was stricken with a grave illness, a streptococcic infection, apparently resulting from an insect's sting. He was removed to Paris and then to the United States. On Jan. 2, 1907, making light of his illness, he sailed again for Siam. He reached Bangkok the first of March, and although confined to his bed and suffering much pain he mustered all his energies to the task of negotiating a new treaty with France, which was signed on Mar. 23. This settled issues that had been a source of irritation between Siam and France for decades, and for the first time relations between the two nations were on a stable and friendly basis. The French government made him a grand officer of the Legion of Honor. He died in Bangkok at the beginning of the next year. He had never married.

[Letters in Lindsay Swift Correspondence, in Widener Lib., Harvard Univ.; official correspondence in archives of the state department; sketch by Lindsay Swift, *Harvard Graduates' Mag.*, March 1908 and briefer note in *Harvard College Class of 1877, Seventh Report* (1917); *Harper's Weekly*, Mar. 21, 1908; *American Jour. of International Law*, Jan. 1908; *Who's Who in America*, 1906–07; *Proc. Mass. Hist. Soc.*, vol. XLIX (1916); *Boston Evening Transcript*, Jan. 16, 18, 1908; *Boston Globe*, Jan. 16, 1908.]   I.L.T.

STROMME, PEER OLSEN (Sept. 15, 1856– Sept. 15, 1921), journalist and author, the third of the thirteen children of Ole and Eli (Haugen) Olsen, was born in Winchester, Wis. His grandparents had emigrated to America from Norway. At the age of thirteen he was sent to Luther College, Decorah, Iowa, and was graduated with the A.B. degree in 1876. He studied theology at Concordia Seminary in St. Louis, Mo., from 1876 to 1879, and was ordained to the Lutheran ministry. He served Norwegian congregations near Hendrum, Minn., and on the Dakota side of Red River from 1879 to 1881, in Ada, Minn., 1881 to 1886, and near Nelson, Wis., 1886 to 1887. While at Ada, he was also superintendent of schools of Norman County. He taught for one year at St. Olaf College, Northfield, Minn., and then he turned to journalism. He edited *Norden*, a Norwegian weekly, published in Chicago, from 1888 to 1890, and again in 1892. In the interval he made his initial visit to Norway, followed from time to time by ten other visits to Europe, including two journeys around the world as press correspondent in 1906 and 1910. In 1892 he bought and edited the *Superior Posten,* Superior, Wis., but soon gave it up to accept the headship of an academy at Mount Horeb, Wis. In 1894 he did journalistic work for the *Milwaukee Journal,* and from 1895 to 1898 edited the *Amerika,* a Norwegian weekly published in Chicago. From 1898 to 1900 he was on the editorial staff of the *Minneapolis Times,* covering especially the Minnesota state legislature. He did editorial work on the *Politikken* and the *Vor Tid,* Minneapolis periodicals, in 1904–05. In 1909 he was editor of the *Eidsvold,* a Norwegian magazine issued at Grand Forks, N. D., and, from 1911 to 1918, of the *Nordmanden,* published in the same city. He also wrote for the *Decorah Posten,* Decorah, Iowa, the *Daily News* and the *Skandinaven,* of Chicago.

Stromme was a Democrat and from time to time published campaign literature, organized democratic societies, and delivered political addresses for his party. In 1898 he ran on the Democratic ticket in Wisconsin for the office of state treasurer, but failed to be elected. He was a popular lecturer on Norwegian culture and literature, subjects to which he was deeply devoted. He was an unusually effective platform speaker, of fluent speech and ready wit, tall, and Vikinglike, with a rugged, jovial face. His memory for poetry was phenomenal and he possessed a museum of telling mimicry. He was known as the Mark Twain among Norwegian Americans. His best contribution to fiction was *Hvorledes Halvor blev Prest* (1893), an excellent description of the early period of the Norwegian-Americans immigration. *Unge Helgesen* (1906) does not match it in literary value. He compiled a *Compend of Church History* (1902), and wrote discriminatingly about Mark Twain and Waldemar Ager, journalist and novelist, for *Symra,* a literary magazine. A volume of his poems, *Digte,* was published in 1921.

Stromme was a translator of ability. He received a prize for his translation of Aasmund Vinje's "Fedraminne." In 1909 he translated Gustav Frenssen's *Jörn Uhl* (1901) into English and stories by Byron A. Dunn and Stanley Waterloo into Norwegian. His most careful work was the translation into English of *Laaches Husandagtsbog,* a Norwegian devotional classic, under the title *Laache's Book of Family Prayer* (1902). In 1918 he translated J. W. Gerard's *My Four Years in Germany* (1917) into Norwegian. His memoirs, *Erindringer,* published in

book form in 1923, first appeared in the *Nordmanden,* and contain descriptions of hundreds of contemporaries whom the author learned to know in his busy, colorful career, as a student, minister, schoolman, author, lecturer, campaigner, newspaper man, and traveler, and is a highly creditable contribution to cultural history. Stromme was married to Laura Marie Eriksen, of Lansing, Iowa, on Nov. 12, 1879. She and six children survived him.

[*Who's Who in America,* 1920–21; *Who's Who Among Pastors in all the Norwegian Luth. Synods of America* (rev. ed. 1928); Stromme's memoirs, *Erindringer* (1923); *Luther Coll. Through Sixty Years* (1922); *Wis. State Jour.,* Sept. 15, 1921.] J. O. E.

STRONG, AUGUSTUS HOPKINS (Aug. 3, 1836–Nov. 29, 1921), theologian, born at Rochester, N. Y., was the son of Alvah and Catharine (Hopkins) Strong and a descendant of John Strong who came to Massachusetts in 1630 and was subsequently one of the founders of Northampton. Alvah Strong was for years publisher of the *Rochester Democrat,* and Augustus, after preparatory studies at Rochester Collegiate Institute, had one year of business experience in that newspaper's office. He graduated from Yale College in 1857 and from Rochester Theological Seminary in 1859, then spent a year at the University of Berlin and in travel.

Returning to America, he was ordained to the Baptist ministry at Haverhill, Mass., Aug. 3, 1861. He served as pastor of the First Baptist Church of Haverhill, 1861–65, and of the First Baptist Church of Cleveland, Ohio, 1865–72. Here he acquired a reputation as a scholarly preacher, possessing keen theological discernment. Among his parishioners was Mr. John D. Rockefeller, whose daughter later married Strong's eldest son. In 1872 Strong was chosen president of Rochester Theological Seminary and professor of Biblical theology, succeeding Ezekiel Gilman Robinson [q.v.] in both positions. He served actively in his double rôle until 1912, when he retired with the title of president emeritus. Vigorous minded, affable, yet somewhat awe-inspiring, Strong has been ranked with William Newton Clarke, Alvah Hovey [qq.v.], and George W. Northrup as one of the four most influential Baptist theological teachers of his period. He represented the dogmatic tradition but, like the others, encouraged his students to pursue their own researches in the entire realm of truth. His method provided a large place for historical theology, but he was probably less influential than Clarke in promoting historical research in the Biblical field. The most liberal period of his career was probably the decade centering about the turn of the century.

Aside from his classroom teaching, he had wide influence through his theological writings. His *Systematic Theology* (1886), much enlarged in the three-volume edition of 1907–09, found its way into many a minister's library, as did his *Philosophy and Religion* (1888) and *Christ in Creation and Ethical Monism* (1899). Two volumes entitled *Miscellanies* (vols. I and II, 1912) gathered up various papers and addresses, historical and theological; of more popular interest were six other published works: *The Great Poets and Their Theology* (1897); *One Hundred Chapel-Talks to Theological Students* (1913); *Union with Christ* (1913); *Popular Lectures on the Books of the New Testament* (1914); *American Poets and Their Theology* (1916); and *A Tour of the Missions, Observations and Conclusions* (1918). This last book, the result of a world tour of Baptist mission fields made by Strong and his wife in 1916–17, is an evidence of his lifelong interest in the foreign mission movement. Considerably more than a hundred of his students went to the foreign fields; he served as president of the American Baptist Missionary Union from 1892 till 1895; on many occasions his counsel was sought, and he was often called upon for missionary sermons and addresses.

His educational influence was not limited to the administration of his own seminary. From 1884 to 1918 he served as trustee of Vassar College, from 1906 to 1911 being chairman of the board. Perhaps his greatest contribution to the cause of education was his share in starting the movement which resulted in the establishment of the new University of Chicago. Having long felt the inadequacy of opportunity for higher education under Baptist auspices, he conceived of the organization of a true university in New York City, with opportunities for research such as did not exist at that time, although Columbia University was soon to provide them. He tried to interest Mr. John D. Rockefeller in the plan and printed a pamphlet setting forth the importance of university education and pointing out the tendency in Europe and in America toward the great centers of population as the foci of educational enterprise. He received many responses, and these, with the pamphlet, he laid before Mr. Rockefeller, with whom he also discussed the matter during a trip to Europe. Furthermore, it was Strong who introduced William Rainey Harper [*q.v.*] to Mr. Rockefeller, having previously characterized Harper as the greatest organizer among American Baptists. Thus, while his own project was not adopted and Thomas W. Goodspeed and Frederick T. Gates [*qq.v.*] were undoubtedly chiefly responsible for securing Mr.

Rockefeller's support for the refounding of the University of Chicago, Strong seems to have been the man who first inculcated the university idea in Mr. Rockefeller's mind (F. T. Gates, in *Fourth Annual Meeting of the American Baptist Education Society,* 1892). Strong was a founder of the Rochester Historical Society and its president in 1890. He was married on Nov. 6, 1861, to Harriet Louise, daughter of Eleazer Savage; she died in 1914, and on Jan. 1, 1915, he married Marguerite Geraldine, daughter of Gerrit van Ingen and widow of John Jay Jones. She, with four daughters and two sons of his first marriage, survived him.

[*The Record* (Rochester Theological Seminary), May 1912, and supplement to issue of May 1922; unpublished autobiographic account of the effort to establish a Baptist university in New York; J. H. Strong, "Augustus Hopkins Strong," *Rochester Hist. Soc. Pubs.,* vol. I (1922); *Yale Univ. Obit. Record,* 1922; T. W. Goodspeed, *A Hist. of the Univ. of Chicago* (1916); *Who's Who in America,* 1920–21; B. W. Dwight, *The Hist. of the Descendants of Elder John Strong* (2 vols., 1871); *Democrat and Chronicle* (Rochester, N. Y.), Nov. 30, 1921.]   W. H. A.

STRONG, BENJAMIN (Dec. 22, 1872–Oct. 16, 1928), banker, was born at Fishkill on Hudson, N. Y., the son of Benjamin and Adeline Torrey (Schenck) Strong, and a descendant of John Strong who emigrated to Massachusetts in 1630 and in 1659 settled in Northampton. His grandfather, Oliver Smith Strong, had been a merchant in New York, while his father had experience in the management of railroad properties and in financial administration. Graduating from the high school of Montclair, N. J., at eighteen, he entered upon duty with the firm of Jesup, Paton & Company (later Cuyler, Morgan & Company), private bankers of New York. In 1901 he became assistant secretary in the Atlantic Trust Company, and in 1903 secretary of the newly organized Bankers' Trust Company. He married in 1895 Margaret Guitton Le Boutillier (d. 1905), daughter of John Le Boutillier of New York. On Apr. 10, 1907, he married Katherine Converse, a daughter of E. C. Converse, from whom he was divorced in 1920. After serving as vice-president, on Jan. 1, 1914, he became president of the Bankers' Trust Company, but soon he was appointed governor of the Federal Reserve Bank of New York, organized in 1914.

This selection was unexpected, for Strong had been active in the movement which aimed to secure the adoption of what was known as the Aldrich Bill (the banking reform plan proposed under the authority of the National Monetary Commission) and had supported the congressional campaign against the Federal Reserve

Act. Assuming office, he found the country convulsed by the early financial difficulties attendant upon the World War and the government desirous of hastening the organization of the Reserve institutions. Though he sharply opposed the hasty opening of the Federal Reserve banks, a peremptory order issued by the secretary of the treasury, W. G. McAdoo, compelled their opening on Nov. 16, 1914. The Federal Reserve Bank of New York took root slowly, most of the local institutions being opposed to it. Following the entrance of the United States into the war, however, it grew rapidly and was for years largely occupied with the financing of the successive issues of Liberty Bonds, in harmony with policies formulated in Washington. After the close of the World War there was an active movement in New York financial circles for the broadened use, in securities operations and in foreign trade, of the new funds growing out of the war profits of American industry and the inflowing tide of gold. Although Strong had from the first opposed the introduction and development of the "open-market powers" of the Federal Reserve system, he now perceived their great possibilities and began to use them. His object, explained in a memorandum written at the end of 1924, was to produce in that year of recession a condition of "easy money," designed to foster business activity and to raise commodity and security prices (Burgess, *post*, p. 256). Later, the Federal Reserve system was unable to cope with the outburst of speculation which reached a climax in 1929, though Strong had advocated a credit pressure which might have averted the ultimate collapse (*Ibid.*, pp. xxii–xxiii). During its earlier stages his policy probably assisted some of the European countries to facilitate, by international credit expansion, a premature movement toward the restoration of the gold standard. Its ultimate fruits, however, were slow in maturing. Strong paid frequent visits abroad and came to be regarded by many foreigners as the real head of the Federal Reserve system. Meanwhile he had drawn nearer to his end, partly owing to tuberculosis, a disease which he had contracted in 1916. During the post-war period frequent leaves of long duration necessitated his entrusting the management of the bank to others, though he had never been willing to give up control, and at the time of his death in October 1928 he had been absent from active work several months. A man of positive and dominant personality, he died in New York City, survived by his two sons and three daughters.

[B. W. Dwight, *The Hist. of the Descendants of Elder John Strong, of Northampton, Mass.* (1871), vol. I; *Who's Who in America*, 1928–29; W. R. Burgess, ed., *Interpretations of Federal Reserve Policy in the Speeches and Writings of Benjamin Strong* (1930), with biog. sketch and reports of Strong's testimony before committees of the Senate and the House of Representatives, 1922–28; unpublished minutes and docs. of the Federal Reserve Board, 1914–28; obituaries in *N. Y. Evening Post,* Oct. 16, and *N. Y. Times,* Oct. 17, 1928; information from family in regard to certain dates.]   H. P. W.

STRONG, CALEB (Jan. 9, 1745–Nov. 7, 1819), lawyer and Federalist statesman, was born in Northampton, Mass., the son of Caleb Strong, a tanner, and Phebe (Lyman). He was fifth in descent from John Strong, who emigrated to Massachusetts in 1630, settling ultimately in Northampton. Prepared by Rev. Samuel Moody of York, he entered Harvard College, graduating in 1764 with highest honors. On his way home he contracted smallpox, which permanently impaired his sight, but after family help in reading law, and study under Joseph Hawley [*q.v.*], he was admitted to the bar in 1772. Chosen a selectman of Northampton the same year, he served from 1774 throughout the Revolution on the town's committee of safety. He sat in the General Court of 1776 and thenceforward for twenty-four years he served as county attorney. A delegate to the Massachusetts constitutional convention of 1779, he was a member of its drafting committee. He sat in 1780 on the last Massachusetts Council to wield the executive power. The same year he declined a seat in the Continental Congress, becoming a state senator and serving until 1789. In 1783 he declined, for pecuniary reasons, an appointment to the supreme judicial court.

Strong represented Massachusetts in the Federal Convention of 1787, sharing modestly in its work till August, when he was called home by illness in his family. Although favoring a stronger Union, he upheld democratic town-meeting principles, advocating low salaries and annual elections of representatives. He desired one rank and mode of election for the houses of Congress; yet, to conciliate the small states, he voted for the vital compromise which accorded them equal representation in the Senate. He opposed a council of revision; preferred a choice of the president by Congress to the institution of the electoral college; and moved successfully that the House alone should originate money bills, though the Senate might amend them. A leading Federalist in the Massachusetts ratifying convention, he was active and persuasive. Chosen senator from Massachusetts in 1789, he drew a four-year term. He was active in framing the Judiciary Act and served on numerous committees which drafted other formative laws—legal, financial, and miscellaneous. Forming, with

Oliver Ellsworth and Rufus King [*qq.v.*], an Administration bulwark in the Senate, he was chosen in 1791 to report Hamilton's plan for a national bank. After his reëlection in 1793, he actively urged a mission to England and supported Jay's Treaty. In 1796 he resigned and resumed private law practice.

Four years later, on the eve of Jeffersonian victory in the nation, the Massachusetts Federalists chose Strong as their candidate for governor. He consistently shared his party's views, but without its domineering temper and asperities. Of simple, engaging manner, he was conciliatory toward friend and opponent. He was a sober Calvinist withal, guided by duty, deliberate and firm in judgment, and the Massachusetts electorate found him transparently responsible, fair-minded, true to trust. Far more popular than his party, he defeated Elbridge Gerry [*q.v.*] in 1800, and continued governor by annual election throughout the prosperous, politically quiet years of Jefferson's first term. His popularity withstood the steady Democratic trend even after 1804, when Massachusetts chose Jeffersonian electors. Narrowly elected a seventh successive time in 1806, though with a Democratic legislature, he was finally defeated in 1807 by James Sullivan [*q.v.*]. Strong refused nomination in 1808, but in 1812, when war was near and Gerry governor, he consented again to run. Barely winning, despite the "gerrymander" which redistricted the state in Democratic interests, he was moderate in countering Gerry's proscription of Federalist officials.

Congress declared war against Great Britain, June 18, 1812. New England, fearing commercial ruin, opposed hostilities from the start. On June 26, Strong proclaimed a public fast because of war "against the nation from which we are descended" (Niles' *Weekly Register*, Aug. 1, 1812, p. 355), and the Massachusetts House asked public disapproval of the war in town and county meetings. Secretary of War Eustis requested Strong to order part of the militia into federal service, and General Dearborn twice made requisition for these troops. Strong, however, believed that he, as governor, should decide whether the Constitutional exigency existed which empowered the president to call out state militia, and that the militia must remain under state officers. The supreme judicial court, acting through Chief Justice Parsons, and Justices Sewall and Parker, sanctioned these views. Supported by his Council, Strong decided no exigency existed, and refused to furnish the troops.

His general order of July 3, 1812, required the militia to keep in instant readiness for state defense. On Aug. 5, believing the exigency of "foreign invasion" now existed, he ordered a small force into federal service for the defense of eastern Maine, to Chief Justice Parsons' disgust (W. H. Sumner, *A History of East Boston*, 1858, p. 738). The war dragged on and Massachusetts, led by Strong and the legislature, steadily hung back. Federal troops were sent elsewhere. In 1814 the British occupied eastern Maine, threatening coastal Massachusetts, and on Sept. 6, Strong called out the militia, independently of the national government. On his query, Secretary of War Monroe stated that its expenses would not be reimbursed. Addressing a special session of the legislature he had called, Oct. 5, Strong now held that the people of Massachusetts had been deserted by the United States and must take measures for self-preservation (*Niles' Weekly Register*, Oct. 29, 1814, p. 113). The legislature, controlled by extreme Federalists, promptly provided for a state army, apart from the militia; and for the calling of a New England convention to further mutual defense and eventual reshaping of the Federal compact. On Oct. 17 it invited the other New England states to this conference, and two days later chose delegates, Connecticut and Rhode Island quickly following suit. Strong approved the calling of the Hartford Convention, which met Dec. 15, and, with the legislature, approved its report; but the Massachusetts commissioners appointed pursuant to this report reached Washington along with the news of peace.

Strong had thought the first British peace conditions reasonable, including concessions by Massachusetts of territory and fisheries, and he blamed the American negotiators for rejecting them (Henry Adams, *History of the United States*, vol. VIII, 1891, p. 288). The winter of peace found Massachusetts' independent defense crippled, the Boston banks now refusing credit to the state as they had to the nation. Throughout the war Massachusetts, openly yearning for peace, had failed to cooperate with the Union, though remaining within it. Proceeding with measured care, Strong represented the attitude of his state, preventing overt disunionist acts but obeying the letter, not the spirit, of federal obligation.

Annually elected governor from 1812, he refused renomination in 1816, and retired. A humane, religious man, even-tempered, conscientious, moderate, he adhered through life to carefully thought out views. Some of these are set forth in his published speeches: *Patriotism and Piety: The Speeches of His Excellency*

Caleb Strong, Esq., to the Senate and House of Representatives . . . and Other . . . Papers from 1800 to 1807 (1808), and *The Speech of His Excellency Governor Strong, Delivered before the Legislature . . . October 16, 1812; with the Documents . . .* (1812). His wife, Sarah Hooker, whom he had married Nov. 20, 1777, died in 1817. Strong himself died in Northampton suddenly, of angina pectoris, survived by four of his nine children.

[H. C. Lodge, *A Memoir of Caleb Strong* (1879), also printed in *Proc. Mass. Hist. Soc.*, vol. I (1879), supersedes Alden Bradford's *Biog. of the Hon. Caleb Strong* (1820). See also Appendix to Joseph Lyman, *Sermon . . . at the Interment of Hon. Caleb Strong* (1819); B. W. Dwight, *The Hist. of the Descendants of Elder John Strong of Northampton, Mass.* (2 vols., 1871); *The Records of the Federal Convention of 1787* (3 vols., 1911), ed. by Max Farrand; H. V. Ames, *State Documents on Federal Relations Number 2: State Rights and the War of 1812* (1900); S. E. Morison, *The Life and Letters of Harrison Gray Otis* (2 vols., 1913); *Biog. Dir. Am. Cong.* (1928); *Boston Daily Advertiser*, Nov. 11, 1819. Some letters are in the Pickering Papers, Mass. Hist. Soc., Boston (see "Historical Index to the Pickering Papers," *Mass. Hist. Soc. Colls.*, 6 ser., vol. VIII, 1896).]

J. G. K., Jr.

STRONG, CHARLES LYMAN (Aug. 15, 1826–Feb. 9, 1883), mining engineer, was born at Stockbridge, Vt., the eldest child of David Ellsworth and Harriet (Fay) Strong and a descendant of Elder John Strong, who came from England in 1630, was an early settler of Windsor, Conn., and in 1659 removed to Northampton, Mass. David Strong was a merchant and farmer. Charles attended public schools in Stockbridge and Williston Academy, but his father's death defeated his plans for a college education. In 1842 he went to New York City, where he obtained employment as a book-keeper and remained some eight years.

About 1850 he went to San Francisco, as confidential clerk of Wells & Company of New York, to establish a bank for that firm. Most of his records were destroyed in the great fire of 1851, and he himself suffered severe injuries in attempting to save them; but after his recovery he settled all the institution's accounts from memory, and his settlements were subsequently upheld by the courts. In 1852 he became a partner in the firm of LeCount & Strong, booksellers and publishers (1854–55) of *The Pioneer*, edited by Ferdinand Cartwright Ewer [*q.v.*], the first literary periodical in California. To house the enterprise Strong built the first four-story brick building on the Pacific Coast, and for its use manufactured the first gas. He subsequently spent a small fortune in hunting for codfish as well as salmon in Puget Sound, but in 1860 abandoned the fisheries to become the first superintendent of the Gould & Curry mine at Virginia

City, Nev., one of the great bonanzas of the Comstock Lode. The owners, possessed of a source of seemingly inexhaustible wealth, desired a reduction works that would outrival anything of the kind ever before constructed anywhere. Giving free reign to his ideas, Strong built and equipped a magnificent structure, surrounded by beautifully landscaped grounds, at a cost of nearly a million dollars. This mill was used for a few years, but was then superseded by one more economical and efficient to maintain and operate. Little thought was given to economy in those early prosperous days on the Comstock, because the stockholders' demands for large dividends could be met by increasing ore production, despite the high cost and excessive waste of over-rapid and careless reduction. While superintendent of the Gould & Curry mine, Strong had seven or eight mills at times and as many as 1,000 men under him. He made daily visits to the widely scattered company works, on horseback or driving a rapid four-in-hand, and at night attended to his records and correspondence. Possessed of strong will and a keen sense of justice, he was an able director of men. Foremen said that they received more help from the few instructions he gave without alighting from his carriage than from other superintendents in half a day. Instead of bringing suit against those who attempted to secure part of the great wealth of the company's property by working spurs on their lode, he advocated pushing the mining work from the main ore-body out to the opponents' ground, thus proving the company's property rights. This policy often prevented litigation, or if not, facilitated successful defense.

Strong's strenuous program was too much for him, and early in 1864, his health broken from overwork, he retired, to spend several years in travel. About 1867 he purchased a ranch in the San Gabriel Valley, near the present Whittier, Cal., where he gave some attention to orange growing. About 1874, however, he returned to mining, developing mines and erecting mills in California, Arizona, and Nevada, but the strain of work and worry, in futile efforts to save a gold-mining venture at Auburn, Cal., in which he and his friends were interested, proved too great for him to stand, and in 1883 he committed suicide. He was survived by his wife, Harriett Williams (Russell) Strong [*q.v.*], whom he married Feb. 26, 1863, and by four daughters. It is said that when Nevada was first admitted as a state he was offered but declined a nomination as governor and that he later declined to become a candidate for the United States Senate. He has sometimes been credited with a share in the development of the cyanide process for extracting the precious metals from low-grade ores, but that he had any significant share in it is very unlikely, since the process was not successfully applied commercially until several years after his death.

[B. W. Dwight, *The Hist. of the Descendants of Elder John Strong* (2 vols., 1871); E. E. Olcott, "Charles L. Strong," in *Engineering and Mining Jour.*, Feb. 16, 1884; J. S. McGroarty, *Hist. of Los Angeles County* (1923), vol. III; Eliot Lord, "Comstock Mining and Miners," *Monographs of the U. S. Geol. Survey*, vol. IV (1883); *Mining and Scientific Press*, Feb. 24, 1877; *Daily Examiner* (San Francisco), Feb. 10, 1883; *Evening Bulletin* (San Francisco), Feb. 10, 1883.]
B. A. R.

STRONG, HARRIET WILLIAMS RUSSELL (July 23, 1844–Sept. 16, 1926), horticulturist, engineer, civic leader, the fourth daughter of Henry Pierrepont and Mary Guest (Musier) Russell, was born at Buffalo, N. Y. In 1852, in the hope of improving the health of their mother, who was threatened with invalidism, the family crossed the plains to California, but after living for a time in that state moved to Nevada, where the father served for a time as state adjutant-general.

Harriet was educated by private teachers and in Miss Mary Atkins' Young Ladies Seminary in Benicia, Cal. On Feb. 26, 1863, at Virginia City, Nev., she married Charles Lyman Strong [*q.v.*], then engaged as superintendent of the Gould & Curry Mining Company in exploiting the Comstock Lode. Four daughters were born of this union. In 1883 Strong committed suicide, leaving to his widow a considerable estate, but for eight years she was obliged to defend her claims to it in the courts against her husband's former partners. During the progress of this litigation she began a long and active career as horticulturist, engineer, and public citizen. From her ranch near Whittier came the white pampas plumes which so prominently figured in the presidential campaign of the "Plumed Knight," James G. Blaine, in 1884. On the same ranch she planted 150 acres to walnut trees, being a pioneer in the walnut industry in California. Her walnuts received numerous awards, including a silver medal at the Paris exposition of 1900, and brought her another fortune. Her name is intimately connected with the development of irrigation, and she was among the first, if not the first, to advocate the conservation of water by building storage dams near the source of mountain streams. On Dec. 6, 1887, she patented a design for a series of dams in river channels for the storage of water for irrigation and flood control and later, Nov. 6, 1893, she secured a patent for impounding debris and water in hydraulic mining. For this invention she received two medals at the World's Columbian Exposition, Chicago, in 1893. She was also one of the early advocates of the conservation of the flood waters of the Colorado River for irrigation, the safety of the Imperial Valley, and the development of hydro-electric power. With her daughters she organized a water company and sank a number of artesian wells, but sold the enterprise after a few years. She subsequently sank several successful oil wells.

In addition to her business activities, she played an important part in the political, civic, and cultural life of California. She was a founder of the Ebell Club and the Hamilton Club of Los Angeles, and for many years was first vice-president of the Los Angeles Symphony Orchestra. She was vitally interested in the education of women, especially in that type of education which would enable them to care for their own economic interests and to meet the problems of the business world. She was a member of the Republican party and took an active part in its affairs, national as well as local. The editor of *Southern California Business* wrote of her: "For many years she was probably the most active figure among women in the entire Southland in civic work of every description" (*post*, p. 26). She met her death in an automobile accident on the way from Los Angeles to her ranch near Whittier. Three of her four daughters survived her.

[J. S. McGroarty, *Hist. of Los Angeles County* (1923), vol. III; *Southern California Business* (official organ of the Los Angeles Chamber of Commerce), Nov. 1926; Bertha H. Smith, "Harriet W. R. Strong: Walnut Grower," *Sunset*, Apr. 1911; *Los Angeles Times*, Sept. 17, 1926.]
R. G. C.

STRONG, JAMES (Aug. 14, 1822–Aug. 7, 1894), Biblical scholar, born in New York City, was the son of Thomas Strong, an emigrant from England, and his wife, Maria (Peers), member of a Dutch family of New York State. His parents died when he was very young, and with his only brother he was brought up in the Episcopal Church by an aunt and his maternal grandmother. Abandoning his plan to study medicine because of uncertain health, he prepared for college at Lowville Academy and, having been converted under Methodist influences, entered Wesleyan University, Middletown, Conn., where he graduated in 1844 as valedictorian of his class. For the next two years he taught ancient languages in Troy Conference Academy, Poultney, Vt., and here met Marcia Ann Dustin of Middlebury, whom he married July 18, 1845.

The year after his marriage, Strong withdrew for a time from teaching, though he continued his studies in the ancient languages. Buying property and establishing a home in Flushing, he became interested in the building of railroads on Long Island and served as president of the Flushing Railroad Company for some two years prior to the opening of its road in 1854. He was also active in civic affairs, being a justice of the peace for several years and president of the corporation of the village of Flushing in 1855. Meanwhile, in addition to his business activities he published *A New Harmony and Exposition of the Gospels* (1852), epitomes of Hebrew and Greek grammar, Sunday School question books, and several other works. In 1858 he became professor of Biblical literature in Troy University, serving until his return to Flushing in 1863, part of the time as acting president. During this period he published *Theological Compend* (1859).

In 1867 Drew Theological Seminary was established at Madison, N. J., and the following year Strong was elected to its chair of exegetical theology, from which he retired as professor emeritus only a year before his death. It was during his twenty-seven years in this professorship that he accomplished most of his enormous amount of literary work. Before going to Troy University he had begun work with Dr. John M'Clintock [*q.v.*] on the monumental *Cyclopædia of Biblical, Theological, and Ecclesiastical Literature* (10 vols., 1867–81), of which only three volumes were published before his colleague's death. Strong completed this work and edited the Supplement, in two volumes (1885–86). To *The Exhaustive Concordance of the Bible* (copyright 1890), he gave long years, and it still stands as a monument of labor and painstaking accuracy. He edited the sections on Daniel (vol. XIII, 1876) and Esther (vol. VII, 1877) in the Schaff edition of J. P. Lange's *Commentary on the Holy Scriptures*; was the author of *Irenics* (1883), *The Tabernacle of Israel in the Desert* (1888), *The Doctrine of a Future Life* (1891), *Sketches of Jewish life in the First Century* (1891), *The Student's Commentary . . . on . . . Ecclesiastes* (1893), *The Students' Commentary . . . The Book of Psalms* (published posthumously, 1896), and many lesser works; and contributed frequently to religious periodicals.

Strong's great enthusiasm was the interpretation of the Bible, to which he brought independence of judgment and immense learning, including a profound knowledge of Greek, Hebrew, and the other Semitic languages. He traveled extensively in the Orient and acquainted himself with the latest developments in archeological research. He was also at home in the French and German literature pertaining to this field. His position was conservative: he stoutly defended the Mosaic authorship of the Pentateuch and the accuracy of the Mosaic account of creation, contended that there was but one Isaiah, and supported the Pauline authorship of the Epistle to the Hebrews; in all this, however, he was actuated not by blind obedience to the traditional, but by conviction based on his own studies. He was a member of the Old Testament Company of the American Committee for the Revision of the Bible, and a member of the Palestine Exploration Society. As a teacher, he was at his best; he could treat the Bible in its broad outlines, or turn to the most exhaustive and microscopic examination of particular words and phrases. His manner in the classroom was vigorous and dogmatic, yet often revealed tenderness and wit. Although a trainer of ministers, he insisted on remaining a layman and as such had great influence in bringing about lay representation in the General Conference of the Methodist Episcopal Church. He himself was lay delegate to the General Conference of 1872. For several years he lectured at the Chautauqua Assembly, and he was attending a summer institute for ministers at Round Lake, N. Y., as instructor in Greek and lecturer on the Holy Land, at the time of his death. His funeral was held at Round Lake and he was buried at Flushing. His wife and four of their six children survived him.

[H. A. Buttz, "Prefatory Memoir," in Strong's *Student's Commentary . . . The Book of Psalms* (1896); *Alumni Record of Drew Theol. Sem.* (1926); *Appletons' Ann. Cyc. . . . 1894* (1895); E. S. Tipple, *Drew Theol. Sem. 1867–1917* (copr. 1917); *N. Y. Tribune*, Aug. 8, 1894; manuscript sketch by a daughter, Miss Emma Strong, Oxford, Md.]   O. M. B.

STRONG, JAMES HOOKER (Apr. 26, 1814–Nov. 28, 1882), naval officer, was born in Canandaigua, N. Y. His father, Elisha Beebe Strong, first judge of common pleas of Monroe County, N. Y., was descended from John Strong who came to New England with his father, John, in 1630, and died in Windsor, Conn., in 1698; his mother was Dolly Goodwin, daughter of Capt. James Hooker, of Windsor, Conn. In 1827 Strong entered the seminary at Chittenango, N. Y., the "Polytechny," and on Feb. 2, 1829, was appointed a midshipman in the navy. No berth being available for him, he continued his studies in the "Polytechny," but on Mar. 18, 1831, joined the U.S.S. *Lexington*, Commander Silas Duncan. The following winter he participated in an expedition which broke up an establishment on the Falkland Islands maintained by one Louis Vernet, who had confiscated three American ships and held their crews. Since Vernet acted under Argentinian authority, the affair caused an international imbroglio. Strong's service from that time until the Civil War was uneventful. On Mar. 1, 1861, he was given command of the *Mohawk* and was ordered to the Gulf of Mexico, where he was stationed for a year. In 1862 he commanded the steamer *Flag* in the South Atlantic Blockading Squadron, and the following year the *Monongahela*. In October 1863, with the *Monongahela, Owasco,* and *Virginia* under his command, he convoyed an expedition of nine thousand men under Gen. Nathaniel P. Banks [*q.v.*] to the mouth of the Rio Grande. Brownsville, Corpus Christi, Aransas Pass, and Fort Esperanza at Pass Cavallo were captured. On Nov. 17 he landed troops at Mustang Island, and shelled a shore battery which quickly surrendered.

The *Monongahela* under Strong was in the attacking column at Mobile Bay, Aug. 5, 1864, and after the passage of Fort Morgan, Commander Strong sheered out of line without orders and ordered full speed ahead for the Confederate ram *Tennessee,* striking her a glancing blow and pouring a full broadside of 11-inch shot into her, which had but little effect. On signal from Farragut he rammed her a second time and was about to strike her again when the *Tennessee* surrendered. The iron prow and cutwater of the *Monongahela* were carried away by the force of the collisions, and she was pierced twice by shells from the *Tennessee.* Strong's Civil War record was admirable, his conduct of the Banks expedition eliciting high praise from Banks himself, and from Major-General Dana. His plucky attack on the *Tennessee* kept her from destroying the weaker vessels of the Union fleet, and materially aided in compelling her surrender. He was mentioned favorably in Admiral Farragut's report of the battle.

After the war Strong served for two years as inspector of the Brooklyn Navy Yard, and in 1868–69 commanded the steam-sloop *Canandaigua* in the European Squadron. He was lighthouse inspector from 1871 to 1873, and the following year was in command of the South Atlantic Station. He was commissioned rear admiral on Sept. 25, 1873, and was retired on Apr. 25, 1876. He married Maria Louisa Von Cowenhoven of Long Island in 1844, by whom he had a daughter and a son who became a naval officer. He died in Columbia, S. C.

[For biog. data see B. W. Dwight, *The Hist. of the Descendants of Elder John Strong* (2 vols., 1871); L. R. Hamersly, *The Records of Living Officers of the U. S. Navy and Marine Corps* (4th ed., 1890); *Army and Navy Jour.,* Dec. 2, 9, 1882; *N. Y. Tribune,* Nov. 29, 1882; *News and Courier* (Charleston, S. C.), Nov. 29, 1882. For the Falkland Islands affair, see Julius Goebel, *The Struggle for the Falkland Islands* (1927); *Niles' Weekly Reg.,* Apr. 28, May 12, 1832; log of the *Lexington,* 1831–32, and letters of Commander Silas Duncan (MSS. in Navy Dept.). For Strong's Civil War Service, see *Battles and Leaders of the Civil War* (1887–88), vols. III, IV; A. T. Mahan, *The Gulf and Inland Waters* (1883); F. A. Parker, *The Battle of Mobile Bay* (1878); log of the *Monongahela,* 1863–64 (MS., Navy Dept.); *Official Records of the Union and Confed. Navies,* 1 ser. IV, XIII, XIV, XVI, XVII, XX–XXII.]   L. H. B.

STRONG, JAMES WOODWARD (Sept. 29, 1833–Feb. 24, 1913), Congregational clergyman, college president, son of Elijah Gridley and Sarah Ashley (Partridge) Strong and brother of William Barstow Strong [*q.v.*], was born in Brownington, Vt. A descendant of John Strong of Plymouth, England, who came to Massachusetts in 1630 on the ship *Mary and John* and was later one of the founders of Northampton, he inherited much of the piety and austerity of his Puritan ancestors. Since the family patrimony had been lost as a result of the panic of 1837, James was subjected to the discipline of labor for his education and support. After attending the common schools, he found work in a printing office, was subsequently employed in a Burlington book store, and then taught a country school. His family joined the stream of migration to the West in 1851, settling in Beloit, Wis., to have the advantages of life in a college town. Three years in the preparatory department, varied with intervals of teaching school, enabled him to enter the freshman year of Beloit College in 1854. In spite of ill health, the necessity of earning his expenses by divers means, and weakness of vision which made him dependent upon the help of a reader for studying, the ambitious youth was valedictorian of his class in 1858.

He had always expected to enter the ministry, having been imbued with this purpose by his mother. Friends and classmates enabled him to go to Union Theological Seminary, taking notes of lectures and reading for him until his marriage to Mary Davenport in 1861, when she became his reader. After graduation in 1862 he was for two years pastor in Brodhead, Wis., and then became pastor of Plymouth Congregational Church in Faribault, Minn.

Here he came into contact with other Congregationalists who were seeking to establish in Minnesota "a second Oberlin or Beloit." He served as a trustee of Northfield College, in the village of Northfield, from its organization in 1866 until he was persuaded to become its first president in 1870, undertaking to develop it from a feeble preparatory school into a standard college. Encouraged by many gifts from Minnesota friends of the project, he resorted to New England—prolific source of educational benefactions from Eastern kinsmen to Western pioneer institutions. Philanthropic purses were promptly opened to him, one donor (William Carleton) attaching his name to the college by a single gift of $50,000. For thirty-three years President Strong—"in person," said the *Hartford Courant* in 1875, "slightly built, sinewy, energetic, and a very clear and interesting speaker"—labored to win suport for his non-sectarian Christian college, and led devoted teachers and trustees to the realization of collegiate visions after patterns set by their forebears. Never discouraged, even by periods of financial stringency and depression or by his own ill health and impaired vision, he persisted until he built Carleton into a standard college of liberal arts, with a foundation in the way of equipment and endowments upon which his successors could build still more adequately. He retired in 1903, living in Northfield as president emeritus until his death there ten years later.

[D. L. Leonard, *The Hist. of Carleton Coll.* (1904), esp. pp. 166–73; M. M. Dana, *The Hist. of the Origin and Growth of Carleton Coll.* (1879); Warren Upham, *Congreg. Work of Minn., 1832–1920* (1921); Warren Upham and Rose B. Dunlap, *Minn. Biogs.* (1912); B. W. Dwight, *The Hist. of the Descendants of Elder John Strong* (2 vols., 1871); *Addresses Delivered at the Quarter Centennial Anniv. of Carleton Coll.* (1895); *Alumni Cat. of the Union Theol. Sem. in the City of N. Y.* (1926); *Who's Who in America,* 1912–13; *Minneapolis Journal,* Feb. 24, 1913; MSS. and papers at Carleton College.]   C. A. D—y.

STRONG, JOSIAH (Jan. 19, 1847–Apr. 28, 1916), clergyman, social reformer, author, was born in Naperville, Ill., the son of Josiah and Elizabeth C. (Webster) Strong, and a descendant of Elder John Strong who came to Massachusetts in 1630, settling first in Dorchester and ultimately in Northampton. In 1852 his parents moved to Hudson, Ohio, then the site of Western Reserve College. From this institution Josiah was graduated in 1869 and at once entered Lane Theological Seminary in Cincinnati.

He began his professional career in 1871 at Cheyenne, Wyo., where he was ordained (Sept. 8) and installed as pastor of a Congregational church. Ten days before (Aug. 29), at Chardon, Ohio, he had married Alice Bisbee, daughter of Charles and Cordelia (Packard) Bisbee. The next eighteen years were a restless period in which a man of fine efficiency, ardent spirit, and ever-widening social interest and vision sought with feverish intensity the field appointed for his labors. He was everywhere successful, but nowhere satisfied. Thus after only two years in Cheyenne he returned to Western Reserve College to serve as chaplain and instructor in theol-

ogy. Three years later he accepted a call to a pastorate in Sandusky, Ohio. In 1881 he became a secretary of the Congregational Home Missionary Society, for the work in Ohio, Kentucky, West Virginia, and western Pennsylvania. In 1884 he returned again to the parish ministry as head of the Central Congregational Church in Cincinnati.

With the publication of his book, *Our Country,* in 1885, came the turning-point of Strong's career. This work had its origin in a small manual of the same title, issued years before by the Congregational Home Missionary Society, which he had been asked to revise and bring up to date; but in performing the task, Strong made the book his own through his clear and forceful style, his ample collection of new material, his first-hand Biblical knowledge, and his ardent social and spiritual idealism. As it came afresh from his hands, *Our Country* was a pioneer sociological treatise, already radical in its emphasis on the dangers of over-accumulation and concentration of capital, its sympathy with the discontents of labor, and its challenge to the church for concern with social problems. The book created a sensation. It was translated into foreign languages, Oriental as well as European, and reissued in new and revised editions in America. It made Strong a national figure, brought him repeated requests for lectures and speeches, and was the occasion of his appointment as secretary of the American Evangelical Alliance.

Josiah Strong had now found himself. He understood his message and his mission, both of which he stated in his second book, *The New Era,* which was published simultaneously in the United States and England in 1893, and, like its famous predecessor, had instant circulation of wide dimensions. In this volume the author laid down the principle that the teachings of Jesus center in the concept of "the Kingdom" as an ideal society here and now upon the earth. Jesus came to found this "Kingdom." The Christian church exists to extend it, to purify and perpetuate it. This purpose requires an organization commensurate with the task—a federation which shall overleap or absorb competing denominations, and direct their power to the solution of civic and industrial problems by generating a primary enthusiasm for human welfare.

Strong hoped to find or make such an organization in the Evangelical Alliance, but that society proved to be too conservative in its ideas, too pietistic in its practices. In 1898, therefore, he resigned his office and founded his own organization, the League for Social Service, which was reorganized in 1902 as the American Institute for Social Service. The history of the Institute is the record of his life work. He was tireless as a writer and lecturer. Active in the service of every constructive and beneficent public cause, he labored unceasingly to awaken the churches to a recognition of their social responsibility and to unite them in common labors for the common good. Passionate in his prophetic zeal, he was statesmanlike in his ingenious devising of practical methods of action. The "Safety First" movement, for example, was his original conception, and the American Museum of Safety one of the chief developments of the Institute. The Federal Council of the Churches of Christ in America, in the establishment of which he was an active participant, was to no small extent the fruit of his example. A born missionary, he went to England in 1904 and organized the British Institute of Social Service. Five years later (in 1909–10) he visited South American countries in the interest of the Institute idea and of the "Safety First" movement. His books written during this period include *The Twentieth Century City* (1898), *Religious Movements for Social Betterment* (1900), *Expansion under New World Conditions* (1900), *The Times and Young Men* (1901), *The Next Great Awakening* (1902), *Social Progress: A Yearbook* (1904–06), *The Challenge of the City* (1907), *My Religion in Every-Day Life* (1910), *Our World: The New World Life* (1913) and *Our World: The New World Religion* (1915), the first two of four projected volumes. He also edited *The Gospel of the Kingdom,* a monthly begun in October 1908, and published numerous sermons, addresses, and pamphlets.

Josiah Strong was tall and vigorous—a handsome man, with shining eyes. Passionate in his idealistic zeal and consecration, he was saved from fanaticism by abundant sanity, ripe scholarship, unfailing good nature, and unshakable confidence in his fellow men. With Francis G. Peabody, Washington Gladden, John Graham Brooks, and Walter Rauschenbusch, he was a pioneer and prophet of that social Christianity whose advent marks the most important chapter of recent religious history. He died in his seventieth year, after a prolonged and painful illness.

[B. W. Dwight, *The Hist. of the Descendants of Elder John Strong* (1871), vol. I; *Who's Who in America,* 1916–17; *New Church Rev.,* Jan. 1922; *Outlook,* May 10, 1916; *N. Y. Times,* Apr. 29, May 8, 1916; personal acquaintance.]   J. H. H.

STRONG, MOSES McCURE (May 20, 1810–July 20, 1894), surveyor, lawyer, legislator, was born at Rutland, Vt., son of Moses and Lucy Maria (Smith) Strong and a descendant of Elder John Strong, who emigrated to America in 1630 and settled first at Dorchester, Mass., later at Northampton. His father was a lawyer and land-holder. After attending grammar school in Castleton, Vt., Strong went first to Middlebury College (1825–28) and then to Dartmouth, from which he graduated in 1829. He studied law in an office and at the law school at Litchfield, Conn., and was admitted to the bar in 1831. On July 31, 1832, he was married to Caroline Frances Green, daughter of Dr. Isaac Green of Windsor, Vt., by whom he had four children. After practising law in Rutland, Vt. (1831–36), and serving as deputy surveyor general of Vermont for one or two years, Strong went to Wisconsin in 1836, opened a law and land office at Mineral Point, and in 1837 became United States surveyor, assigned to the survey west of the Mississippi River. His native ability and thorough training made him prominent in territorial affairs. He was United States attorney for the territory of Wisconsin (1838–41), was instrumental in establishing the capital at Madison, and was elected a member of the territorial council to fill a vacancy in 1842 and for a full term of four years in 1843. While he never entirely gave up the practice of law, it was for many years subordinated to his other interests. He was a member of the constitutional convention of 1846 and became a member of the Assembly in 1850, when he served as speaker, and again in 1857. In the early fifties he became interested in the promotion of railway construction in Wisconsin, as a result, it is said, of a very long and uncomfortable coach journey from Milwaukee to Mineral Point. For six or seven years he was active in promoting and organizing railway and associated enterprises, but he also gave much time to mining, lumbering, and real estate development.

He was a man of heavy, stocky frame and strong features, quick and energetic in his movements. In disposition he was quiet, reserved, and somewhat withdrawn, but generous almost to a fault. Much given to thinking things out for himself, both in the practice of law and in connection with his other interests, he looked more to the rationale than to the language of opinions and dissertations, and he devoted himself assiduously to any matter that won his attention. He had a hasty temper which he controlled admirably, but that and his inability to surrender his convictions and adapt himself to the moods of the populace prevented him from winning public favor. He was active in establishing the Protestant Episcopal Church in Mineral Point, and at the time of his death was chancellor of the diocese of Milwaukee. He has been described as reasonable, fair-minded and unfailingly constant in his opinions and attachments (*Wisconsin Reports, post*). He died at Mineral Point, where he had lived since 1837.

[B. W. Dwight, *The Hist. of the Descendants of Elder John Strong* (1871), vol. II; H. P. Smith and W. S. Rann, *Hist. of Rutland County, Vt.* (1886), p. 911; A. M. Hemenway, *The Vt. Hist. Gazetteer*, vol. I (1868), pp. 1–10; J. R. Berryman, *Hist. of the Bench and Bar of Wis.* (2 vols., 1898); M. M. Strong, *Hist. of the Territory of Wis.* (1885), pp. 356, 387–88, 512; "Strong and Woodman Manuscript Colls. in Wis. State Hist. Lib.," *State Hist. Soc. of Wis. Bull.* . . . No. 78, Nov. 1915; 90 *Wis. Reports*, lix; obituary in *Milwaukee Jour.*, July 20, 1894; information from Strong's grand-daughter, Anna Strong Parkinson.]
M. B. R.

STRONG, THEODORE (July 26, 1790–Feb. 1, 1869), mathematician, descended from Elder John Strong who in 1630 emigrated from England to Massachusetts, was born at South Hadley, Mass., the second son of a Congregational minister, Joseph Strong, and his wife Sophia, daughter of the Rev. John Woodbridge. Prepared for college by his uncle, Col. Benjamin R. Woodbridge, Theodore graduated in 1812 at Yale, where his father and both grandfathers had graduated before him. He was immediately appointed tutor in mathematics at Hamilton College, then just organized, and in 1816 he was there made professor of mathematics and natural philosophy, a post which he held until he accepted a similar position at Rutgers College, New Brunswick, N. J., in 1827. Here he remained until he became professor emeritus in 1861. From 1839 to 1863 he was vice-president of Rutgers.

Strong was the author of scores of brief mathematical communications. His first paper, "Demonstrations of Stewart's Properties of the Circle," was published while he was still an undergraduate, in *Memoirs of the Connecticut Academy of Arts and Sciences* (vol. I, pt. 4, 1816). Other communications appeared in Gill's *Mathematical Miscellany*, Silliman's *American Journal of Science*, Runkle's *Mathematical Monthly*, *Proceedings of the American Academy of Arts and Sciences*, and *Proceedings of the American Philosophical Society*. Of his two books, *A Treatise on Elementary and Higher Algebra* (1859) and *A Treatise on Differential and Integral Calculus* (1869), the latter was in the press at the time of his death. Both works possessed many original features, but since these were not always improvements, and the arrangements were defective, the texts were unsuited for the classroom.

Strong became a fellow of the American Academy of Arts and Sciences in 1832 and of the American Philosophical Society in 1844; in 1863 he was one of the fifty incorporators of the National Academy of Sciences, to which he communicated five papers (1864–67). From the world point of view he made to mathematics no contribution of moment, and he was not in the same class with certain other Americans, such as Nathaniel Bowditch and Benjamin Peirce [*qq.v.*], but he was a vitalizing force in academic councils and a successful teacher, endowed with "remarkable geniality and unfailing kindness . . . childlike faith and simplicity, and tender bearing" (resolution of the Rutgers Faculty, 1869). On Sept. 23, 1818, he married Lucy Dix, daughter of Capt. John Dix of Boston, Mass., and by her had two sons and five daughters. One of the daughters became the wife of John W. Ferdon, Congressman from New York, and another became the mother of John C. Van Dyke [*q.v.*], long professor of the history of art at Rutgers College.

[B. W. Dwight, *The Hist. of the Descendants of Elder John Strong* (2 vols., 1871), portr.; *Memorial of Theodore Strong* (1869); J. P. Bradley, *Memoir of Theodore Strong* (1879), printed also in *Nat. Acad. Sci. Biog. Memoirs*, vol. II (1886); *A Hist. of the First Half-Century of the Nat. Acad. of Sci.* (1913); *Proc. Am. Acad. Arts and Sci.*, vol. VIII (1873), with bibliog.; *Am. Portrait Gallery with Biog. Sketches*, vol. III (1877); J. C. Poggendorff, *Biographisch-Literarisches Handwörterbuch*, vol. III (1898); *Cat. of the Officers and Alumni of Rutgers Coll.* (1916); Florian Cajori, *The Teaching and Hist. of Mathematics in the U. S.* (1890), p. 398; *Obit. Record Grads. Yale Coll.*, 1869; death notice in *N. Y. Tribune*, Feb. 3, 1869.]
R. C. A.

STRONG, WALTER ANSEL (Aug. 13, 1883–May 10, 1931), journalist and publisher, was born in Chicago and identified with its interests all his life. His parents were Dr. Albert Bliss Strong, a skilful Chicago physician, and Idea (Cook) Strong; he was descended from Elder John Strong who came to Massachusetts on the *Mary and John* in 1630. When Walter was fifteen years old his father died, leaving the family without financial resources, but, with assistance from a relative supplementing his own earnings, the boy succeeded in putting himself through high school and an engineering course at Lewis Institute. Later he took a law course at John Marshall Law School, Chicago. Entering Beloit College, supporting himself in part by working on a Beloit newspaper, he graduated in 1905 with the degree of B.A.

Returning to Chicago, Strong established connection with the *Chicago Daily News* as an audit clerk, soon becoming auditor and later business manager, which post he held at the time of the death, in August 1925, of Victor F. Lawson [*q.v.*], editor and publisher. Disposition of the paper was, under Lawson's will, left in the hands of his executor, John J. Mitchell, president of the Illinois Merchants Trust Company, and in December 1925 the *Daily News* was bought for $13,500,000 by a group headed by Strong, who had bent every effort to insure its continued control by those who would maintain the previous owner's high ideals and carry on his policies. Even before Lawson's death Strong had recognized the need of a new plant, and as soon as he became head of the *Daily News* he began plans for a new building. The site selected utilized for the first time in Chicago's history air rights over a railroad, the building being constructed, in part, over tracks of the Chicago & Northwestern, and on June 8, 1929, the *Daily News* moved to its imposing new quarters. In the reorganization a stock company was formed, Strong acquiring a majority of the stock and continuing to be the controlling stockholder until his death.

He was early interested in radio broadcasting and in 1922 the *Daily News,* largely through his influence, purchased half interest in a local station and became the first newspaper in Chicago, and one of the first in the country, to operate a radio station. In 1930 the station (WMAQ) was organized as a separate corporation, Strong becoming chairman of the board of directors. As a result of his efforts, a plan for pensioning *Daily News* employees after a certain number of years, and for protecting them with insurance during their lifetime, was evolved and put into operation. His interests extended widely into national organizations connected with newspaper publishing. He either had been or at the time of his death was a director of the Audit Bureau of Circulations, the American Newspaper Publishers Association, and the Associated Press. He was chairman of the board of the Advertising Federation of America—to which organization he gave much time hoping through it to improve standards of advertising throughout the country. He was an ardent supporter of the Boy Scout movement, a member of the Episcopal Church, serving for years as vestryman, and active in the community interests of Winnetka, the Chicago suburb of which he was a resident. For years he was a trustee of Beloit College. He had an essentially constructive mind; combined vision, business sagacity, and creative energy; possessed tremendous vitality and moral courage, and although only forty-seven at the time of his sudden death, had reached the front rank of the newspaper world through sheer force of personality, ability, and character. On Apr. 14, 1913, he married Josephine Haviland Webster, daughter of Towner Keeney Webster

of Evanston, Ill. Five children were born to them.

[*Chicago Daily News,* May 11, 1931, and succeeding days; nearly all metropolitan papers of the country, May 11, 1931; *Who's Who in America,* 1930–31; B. W. Dwight, *The Hist. of the Descendants of Elder John Strong, of Northampton, Mass.* (2 vols., 1871).]

G. B. U.

STRONG, WILLIAM (May 6, 1808–Aug. 19, 1895), justice of the Supreme Court, was born in Somers, Conn., the eldest of eleven children of William Lighthouse Strong and Harriet (Deming) Strong. He was descended from John Strong, who came from England to Dorchester, Mass., in 1630 and settled finally in Northampton. He attended schools in Monson and Plainfield, Mass., and then entered Yale College, from which he received the B.A. degree in 1828 and that of M.A. three years later. While teaching in various Connecticut towns, and in an academy in Burlington, N. J., he read law, and he studied for some months in the Yale Law School. He was admitted to the Philadelphia bar in October 1832 (J. H. Martin, *Martin's Bench and Bar of Philadelphia,* 1883, p. 315), but almost immediately entered practice in Reading. Everybody there spoke German; he mastered that language, gained universal respect, and as a lawyer attained an acknowledged preëminence. Also active in civic affairs, he was twice elected as a Democrat a representative in Congress, serving from 1847 to 1851. In 1857 he was elected for a fifteen-year term on the supreme court of Pennsylvania, and served with great distinction until he resigned in 1868, apparently because of the inadequacy of his income. He then practised in Philadelphia.

His nomination by President Grant as an associate justice of the Supreme Court of the United States was transmitted to the Senate on Feb. 7, 1870, and was confirmed, after strong opposition, on the 18th (*Journal of the Executive Proceedings of the Senate of the United States of America,* vol. XVII, 1901, pp. 359, 369; Warren, *post,* II, 518). He was precipitated into the critical controversy over the Legal Tender Act of Feb. 25, 1862. Among the supreme courts of fifteen states that had held the act constitutional was that of Pennsylvania (1866, *Shollenberger* vs. *Brinton,* 52 *Pennsylvania State Reports,* 9), with the concurrence of Strong, who was a stanch Unionist and acted with the majority of his court during the war years in sustaining the national government. In *Hepburn* vs. *Griswold* (8 *Wallace,* 603) the question of its constitutionality was directly raised before the United States Supreme Court. This case was argued, the Court's decision agreed upon, and the form of the opinion settled before the nominations of Strong and Joseph P. Bradley [*q.v.*] on Feb. 7. The decision, however, was announced on that day, Chase and three Democratic colleagues holding the act unconstitutional and three Republicans dissenting. Immediate steps were taken to insure a reargument, and this resulted in an outright reversal on May 1, 1871 (*Knox* vs. *Lee*, 12 *Wallace*, 457), Strong writing the majority opinion. There had been procedural steps without precedent; the new justices perhaps had been indiscreetly active; and there had been an undignified dispute among the justices in open court, on a motion for reargument, as to alleged agreements regarding the Hepburn decision. Whether the reversal, at least so promptly and by a vote of 5 to 4, was itself a mistake, is a question upon which lawyers greatly differ. The charge was promptly made, and has often been repeated, that the President "packed" the Court to insure a reversal. When the chief justiceship was vacated by Taney's death, Lincoln had frankly declared that he wanted a successor, who would "sustain what has been done in regard to emancipation and the legal tenders," and that necessarily a man of known opinions must be chosen (G. S. Boutwell, *Reminiscences of Sixty Years in Public Affairs*, 1902, vol. II, 29). Strong was considered by him as Taney's successor, and Chase, who was appointed, as secretary of the treasury had been responsible for the passage of the Legal Tender Act by Congress and might have been expected to uphold it. How Grant felt is shown by his later statement to Hamilton Fish (*Political Science Quarterly*, Sept. 1935, p. 351). He knew Strong's attitude and thought he knew Bradley's, and, while requiring no declaration of them, desired that the Legal Tender Act be upheld. Strong and Bradley were certainly the leading lawyers of their circuit, from which precedent required that at least one new justice be drawn; and weeks before the Hepburn decision was pronounced Strong was Grant's first choice for the vacancy created by the resignation (effective Feb. 1, 1870) of Justice Robert C. Grier [*q.v.*]. The Secretary of the Treasury revealed years later that he knew of the decision in advance (Boutwell, *Reminiscences*, II, 209), but there is no certain evidence that anybody else did. For a time at least, the case greatly impaired the Court's prestige, but Strong's position was wholly consistent with his record.

Strong remained a power in the counsels of the Court. Among many important cases on which he wrote the opinion of the Court were one on the Confiscation Act (*Bigelow* vs. *Forrest*, 9

Wallace, 339); the case of the state freight tax (15 *Wallace*, 232); *Tennessee* vs. *Davis* (100 *United States*, 257), concerning the powers of the federal courts within the states; and several of the leading cases on civil rights—(*Blyew* vs. *United States*, 13 *Wallace*, 581; *Strauder* vs. *West Virginia*, 100 *United States*, 303; *Ex Parte Virginia*, *Ibid.*, 339). Possessed of remarkable powers of analysis and exposition, and unusually sound judgment, he is generally regarded as one of the truly great judges of the Court in its long history. Upon his resignation (Dec. 14, 1880) the members of the bar of the Court expressed their appreciation of "the large and varied learning, the wide experience, the strong intellectual force, the rigid impartiality" that had characterized his service (102 *United States*, ix-x). He enjoyed in remarkable degree the affection and reverence of the people of Pennsylvania; and Senator George F. Hoar, intimately acquainted through three decades with most members of the Supreme Court, believed that in purity and integrity of character he was comparable perhaps to John Jay alone among his predecessors (Bradley, *post*, p. 58).

Strong was a member of the Electoral Commission of 1877. After his retirement he lived in Washington. An offer by President Hayes of the secretaryship of the navy was declined (*New York Tribune*, Aug. 20, 1895). He taught law in the Columbian (later George Washington) University in that city, and gave in the Union Theological Seminary of New York *Two Lectures upon the Relations of Civil Law to Church Polity, Discipline, and Property* (1875?). An ardent Presbyterian, and for many years probably the most prominent lay member of that church, he was long president (1883-95) of the American Sunday School Union, vice-president (1871-95) of the American Bible Society, and president (1873-95) of the American Tract Society. Of many public addresses there survive *An Eulogium on the Life and Character of Horace Binney* (1876); and a paper on *The Growth and Modifications of Private Civil Law* (1879). After his retirement he published his views on "The Needs of the Supreme Court" (*North American Review*, May 1881).

Strong was married on Nov. 28, 1836, to Priscilla Lee Mallery of Easton, Pa., who before her death in 1844 bore him two daughters and a son. On Nov. 22, 1849, he married Rachel (Davies) Bull of Churchtown, Pa., widow of Levi Bull; by her he had two daughters and two sons. Three daughters survived him. He was athletic, fond of outdoor sports and hunting, and sociable in his tastes.

[Strong's opinions are in *Pa. State Reports,* vols. XXX–LIX, and *U. S. Reports,* vols. LXXVI–CII. For the Legal Tender Cases, see H. L. Carson, *The Supreme Court of the U. S. Its History* (1892), II, 441–57; Moorfield Storey and E. W. Emerson, *Ebenezer Rockwood Hoar* (1911), pp. 198–202; Charles Warren, *The Supreme Court in U. S. History* (1926 ed.), II, ch. xxxi; G. F. Hoar, *Autobiography of Seventy Years* (1903), I, 284–88; Charles Bradley, ed., *Miscellaneous Writings of the Late Joseph P. Bradley* (1902), pp. 45–74, with the contemporary statement of the five justices who reversed *Hepburn vs. Griswold*; C. B. Swisher, *Stephen J. Field* (1930), pp. 174–97; P. G. Clifford, *Nathan Clifford* (1922), pp. 281–85; A. B. Hart, *Salmon Portland Chase* (1899), pp. 389–412; Sidney Ratner, "Was the Supreme Court Packed by General Grant?" *Pol. Science Quart.,* Sept. 1935. More personal materials are in Carson, *supra,* II, 461–63; B. W. Dwight, *The History of the Descendants of Elder John Strong* (1871), II, 1047–48; *Obit. Record of Grads. of Yale Univ. Deceased During . . . Year Ending . . . June, 1896,* pp. 353–54; obituaries in *N. Y. Tribune* and *N. Y. Times,* Aug. 20, 1895.]   F. S. P.

STRONG, WILLIAM BARSTOW (May 16, 1837–Aug. 3, 1914), railroad official, was born at Brownington, Orleans County, Vt., the son of Elijah Gridley Strong and Sarah Ashley (Partridge) Strong, and a brother of James Woodward Strong [*q.v.*]. He was a descendant of John Strong who was in Massachusetts in 1630 and settled first at Dorchester, later at Northampton. He attended public schools at Beloit, Wis., and graduated in 1855 from Bell's Business College of Chicago, Ill. He began railroad work as a station agent and telegraph operator at Milton, Wis., in March 1855. During the next twelve years he was employed by the Milwaukee & St. Paul Railroad (later the Chicago, Milwaukee & St. Paul) or by roads which became part of the St. Paul system. In 1867 he left the St. Paul to serve as general western agent of the Chicago & Northwestern Railway with headquarters at Council Bluffs, Iowa. He served as assistant general superintendent of the Chicago, Burlington & Quincy Railroad at Burlington, Iowa (1870–72), was assistant general superintendent of the enlarged Burlington system, which later included the Burlington & Missouri River Railroad in Iowa (1872), and became general superintendent of the Michigan Central Railroad (1874). In 1875 he returned to the Burlington as general superintendent.

In 1877 he was invited to take active direction of the extension program of the Atchison, Topeka & Santa Fé Railroad as vice-president and general manager, and his reputation depends, in the main, upon his success in transforming this small western railroad into a system of importance. The Santa Fé, when he took charge of the property, operated 786 miles of line, nearly all in Kansas; in 1889 when he resigned the presidency, which he had held since 1881, the mileage of the system was about 6,960

miles, and the Santa Fé ranked as one of the country's largest lines. The systematic expansion which he directed consisted of construction through Kansas to Colorado, connection with the Pacific coast by construction, lease, or traffic agreements, connection with the Gulf coast, and connection with Chicago. The Santa Fé was unsuccessful, however, in an attempted development in Colorado, and built competitive lines in Kansas which were probably ill-advised. Public opinion was tremendously impressed by the resources that Strong commanded during the period of his presidency, and by the energy and skill with which he directed Santa Fé affairs. This high regard for his capacity is shared by later students of Western railroad history, although the heavy cost of the new construction which he carried through, joined with the recession in general business that occurred in 1887 and 1888, compelled his company to reorganize in 1889. At that time, although he was reëlected president, the arrangements did not prove satisfactory, and he presently resigned. Comment at the time characterized him as an "honest, honorable, large hearted man, a born leader, an executive whose field is large affairs, and a practical railway manager of the highest ability" (*Railway Age, post,* p. 568). After he left the Santa Fé he took up his residence on a farm near Beloit and did not again return to railroad work, although at Beloit he was for a time president of a local bank and took some part in other business enterprises. He married Abby Jane Moore of Beloit on Oct. 2, 1859. At the time of his death, which occurred at Los Angeles, Cal., where he spent his last seven years, he was survived by one daughter and two sons.

[B. W. Dwight, *The Hist. of the Descendants of Elder John Strong, of Northampton, Mass.* (2 vols., 1871); *Who's Who in America,* 1914–15; R. E. Riegel, *The Story of the Western Railroads* (1926); G. D. Bradley, *The Story of the Santa Fe* (1920); Stuart Daggett, *Railroad Reorganization* (1908); *Railway Age,* Aug. 30, 1889; *Railway Age Gazette,* Aug. 7, 21, 1914; obituary in *Times* (Los Angeles), Aug. 4, 1914.]   S. D.

STRONG, WILLIAM LAFAYETTE (Mar. 22, 1827–Nov. 2, 1900), merchant, mayor of New York City, was born in Richland County, Ohio. His father, Abel Strong, was of New England descent; his mother, Hannah (Burdine) Strong, a native of Pennsylvania. His father died when William was thirteen, and soon afterward he began work as a clerk in a country store to aid in the support of his mother and four other children. After working in a store in Mansfield, Ohio, in 1853 he went to New York with the fixed determination of making a fortune, an ambition in which he succeeded so well that at his death he was a millionaire. His first position in New York was that of clerk in the wholesale dry-goods house of L. O. Wilson & Company, the business which he followed throughout his adult life. After sixteen years as an employee he considered himself financially ready to launch his own business, and at forty-two established the firm of W. L. Strong & Company, which from the first was greatly successful. He was also president of the Central National Bank and of the Homer Lee Bank Note Company, vice-president of the New York Security and Trust Company, and a director in other banks, insurance, and railroad companies.

An ardent Republican, he served for long periods as president of the Union League and the Business Men's Republican Association, but sought public office only twice. In 1882 he ran for Congress unsuccessfully. In 1894, following exposures by the Lexow Committee of corruption in New York's city government, the "Committee of Seventy" (representing clubs and other organizations standing for civic betterment) selected Strong as its non-partisan candidate for mayor, and he was elected by a large majority over the Tammany Hall candidate. He had scarcely been inaugurated, however, when he began to be troubled by dissensions among his supporters, and his whole incumbency was beset by difficulties such as few mayors have encountered. His sole idea was to conduct his office in behalf of good government and without regard to political considerations. But the various elements which had brought about his election fought for precedence and for the appointment of their candidates to office, and Strong's political inexperience, his unwillingness to bargain in matters of right and wrong, kept him in stormy weather all through his single term. So unpleasant were his experiences that he positively refused to consider a renomination in 1897, and said that he would never again offer himself for public office. Nevertheless, under him the city was honestly governed for the first time in many years, and in some departments there was great improvement in efficiency. Two of his memorable appointments were those of Theodore Roosevelt [q.v.] as police commissioner and Col. George E. Waring as street commissioner, under whose régime the city had the cleanest streets yet known in its history. The New York and East River Bridge, the consolidation of the New York Public Library, and other large projects were begun during his administration. As a result of Strong's independent attitude, he and Thomas Collier Platt, the Republican boss, became enemies, and after his own term expired

Strong supported Seth Low [qq.v.], the Independent candidate for mayor, as against the Republican nominee, though he still considered himself a Republican. At his death in 1900 he was survived by his wife, the former Mary Aborn of Orange, N. J., a son, and a daughter.

[See *Who's Who in America*, 1899–1900; *Nat. Mag.*, Nov. 1891; T. C. Quinn, in *Munsey's Mag.*, Jan. 1895; *N. Y. Tribune*, Oct. 6, 1894, Dec. 31, 1897, and Nov. 3, 1900; obituaries in *Evening Post* (N. Y.), Nov. 2, and *N. Y. Herald, N. Y. Times, World* (N. Y.), Nov. 3, 1900. Much material is to be found in N. Y. newspapers during the municipal campaign of 1894, and during Strong's administration, 1895–97.] A. F. H.

STROTHER, DAVID HUNTER (Sept. 26, 1816–Mar. 8, 1888), soldier, writer, illustrator, son of Col. John and Elizabeth Pendleton (Hunter) Strother, was born at Martinsburg in what is now West Virginia. The Strothers, since their arrival in Virginia from Northumberland, England, about 1650, had been a family of soldiers. David's grandfather fought in the Revolutionary War, his father in the War of 1812, David himself in the Civil War, and one of his sons in the Spanish-American War. He was educated at the Old Stone Schoolhouse in Martinsburg, and at Jefferson College, Canonsburg, Pa., studied art in Philadelphia, and continued his studies in France and Italy during the years 1840–43.

On his return to America in 1844 he began making drawings for magazines. He illustrated the 1851 edition of *Swallow Barn*, by his cousin John P. Kennedy [q.v.], who had assisted him in his artistic endeavors. Next he made the drawings for *The Blackwater Chronicle* (1853), by Pendleton Kennedy, a brother of John P. Kennedy; this book has sometimes been attributed to Strother himself. In December 1853 he contributed to *Harper's New Monthly Magazine* an article called "The Virginian Canaan," in which he gave an account of a visit to the Blackwater region of Randolph County. This was the first of a series of sketches dealing with life in the South which, with numerous pen drawings, appeared from time to time in *Harper's* under his pseudonym, "Porte Crayon." In 1857 some of these sketches were gathered into a volume, *Virginia Illustrated, by Porte Crayon*, containing 138 pen drawings. At this time Strother was one of the highest-paid contributors to *Harper's*, having a roving commission to travel and write for the magazine. Three characteristic series of articles, appearing at irregular intervals, were "North Carolina Illustrated" (1857), "A Winter in the South" (1857–58), "A Summer in New England" (1860–61).

At the outbreak of the Civil War, Strother, a

Unionist, offered his services to the North, and because of his knowledge of the Shenandoah Valley and his skill with the pen was assigned to the topographical corps. He served at different times on the staffs of Generals McClellan, Banks, Pope, and Hunter, went through thirty battles unwounded, and received one promotion after another until his resignation in September 1864. After the close of the war, he was brevetted brigadier-general. He now made his home at Berkeley Springs, W. Va., devoting his time to literature and art. During the years 1866–68 he contributed to *Harper's* a series of articles entitled "Personal Recollections of the War, by a Virginian," based on his diary and pen sketches made on the battlefields. Between 1872 and 1875 he contributed to the same magazine a series on "The Mountains," but by this time a change in the literary taste of the reading public had reduced the demand for writings of the sketchbook and diary type. He was appointed United States consul-general in the city of Mexico in 1879, returned to West Virginia in 1885—making his home at Charles Town—and at the time of his death was writing a book on the Mexicans. In 1849 he married Anne Wolfe, by whom he had a daughter, Emily, who married John Brisben Walker [*q.v.*]; in 1861 he married Mary Hunter, by whom he had two sons.

Strother's writings are in the Irving tradition —slow-moving, humorous, picturesque accounts of people and places, with numerous quotations from other writers. Illustrated with copious pen drawings, they preserve a record of the old South, portraying such places as Hot Springs, White Sulphur Springs, and the University of Virginia as they appeared in the fifties and sixties of the nineteenth century.

[H. T. Tuckerman, *The Life of John Pendleton Kennedy* (1871); *Library of Southern Literature*, vol. XI (1909); T. C. Miller and Hu Maxwell, *W. Va. and Its People* (1913), III, 1098–99; F. B. Heitman, *Hist. Reg. and Dict. U. S. Army* (1903), vol. I; *N. Y. Times* and *N. Y. Tribune*, Mar. 9, 1888.]   F. M. S.

STRUBBERG, FRIEDRICH ARMAND (Mar. 18, 1806–Apr. 3, 1889), novelist, was born in Cassel, Germany, the son of Heinrich Friedrich and Frederique Elise (Marville) Strubberg. The father was one of the foremost tobacco merchants in Germany. Although his vast business was greatly hampered by the Napoleonic embargo, his son was given the best instruction that wealth could afford. Nor was his physical education neglected. Especially was he trained to ride and shoot—accomplishments which later proved to be of great advantage. In 1822 Fritz Strubberg entered one of the large mercantile houses in Bremen as an unsalaried clerk, to fit himself for a business career, but after four years he became involved in a duel in which he wounded his adversary and found it wisest to flee. To the German youth of that day there could be only one destination: America, where he remained for the next three years, making extensive journeys for various mercantile houses. A financial crisis in his father's affairs led him to return to Germany late in the autumn of 1829, and when the business passed finally into other hands at the end of the thirties he once more set out for America. He studied for two years in the medical school at Louisville, Ky., receiving the M.D. degree, then journeyed down the Mississippi River to Memphis, and finally made his way to the extreme frontier of Texas where he settled on the Leona River, eighty hours from the nearest settlement. As Dr. Schubbert, a name he assumed when he fled for the frontier after having killed his adversary in a second duel in New York, he spent a few happy years at his fortress on the Leona, but in time other pioneers settled there and he sought new fields.

He spent one of the most interesting years of his adventurous career as physician and colonial director of the *Mainzer Adelsverein,* organized in 1843 by a group of German noblemen to aid and conduct German emigrants to Texas. Of these activities he writes at length in the two volumes of *Friedrichsburg, die Colonie des deutschen Fürsten-Vereins in Texas* (1867). Later he responded to the urgent appeal for physicians in Arkansas which was being devastated by smallpox, cholera, and fevers. Here he was stung in the eye by a poisonous insect and his sight endangered. He sailed for France in 1854 to consult eye specialists and the eye was eventually saved but his vision was impaired. Strubberg henceforth remained in Germany, his only sister having attracted the wanderer to his native Cassel. He was married on June 5, 1866, to Antoinette Rosine Henrietta Sattler, the love of his early days in Bremen. Shortly afterwards his wife suffered a relapse into a mental disability which caused her death in an asylum. Strubberg suffered this experience silently, and later seems to have tried to conceal the fact of his marriage.

His fascinating personality and his abilities as a raconteur made him a welcome figure among the friends of his youth. Urged to put his adventures into literary form, Strubberg, now more than fifty years old, entered upon that career which made him one of the most widely read novelists of the day. His first work, *Amerikanische Jagd-und Reiseabenteuer aus meinem*

Leben in den westlichen Indianergebieten (1858), was well received and reached seventeen editions, the last in 1933. He centered his entire interest and energy upon his literary work and let his lively imagination draw upon his long career in America as an inexhaustible source of literary material. Under the pen name of Armand there followed in rapid succession more than fifty volumes of fiction. Among the most important of his works must be mentioned *An der Indianer-Grenze* (4 vols., 1859), in which American border life is graphically depicted; *Alte und neue Heimath* (1859), an important contribution to the cultural history of the Germans in America; *Scenen aus den Kämpfen der Mexicaner und Nordamerikaner* (1859); *Sklaverei in Amerika* (3 vols., 1862), an epic of the negro; and *Carl Scharnhorst* (1863), a tale of the adventures of a German boy, a youthful Leatherstocking, on the Western frontier. *Carl Scharnhorst* passed through twelve editions and still occupies a prominent place among the juvenile books in German literature. In 1885 the novelist moved from Cassel to the little Hessian town of Gelnhausen where he died and lies buried.

[Otfrid Mylius, "F. A. Strubberg," *Kölnische Zeitung*, Aug. 18, 1889; W. Bennecke, "Aus Armands Leben," *Hessenland*, May 2, 1889; Ludwig Fränkel, biographical article in *Allgemeine Deutsche Biographie*, vol. XXXVI (1893); P. A. Barba, *The Life and Works of Friedrich Armand Strubberg* (1913), in the Americana Germanica Series.]   P. A. B.

STRUDWICK, EDMUND CHARLES FOX (Mar. 25, 1802–Nov. 30, 1879), physician, was born near Hillsboro, N. C., the son of William Francis Strudwick, who had served as a member of Congress in 1796–97, and of Martha (Shepperd) Strudwick. He began the study of medicine under a local physician, James Webb, and received the M.D. degree at the University of Pennsylvania in 1824. He remained in Philadelphia two years, practising in the alms house, and then returned to take up practice at Hillsboro in 1826. In the next year he was married to Ann E. Nash, the daughter of Frederick Nash [*q.v.*]. They had five children. While engaging in a general practice, he became particularly interested in surgery and proved to be unusually skilful in this field. He performed scores of operations for cataract, by the old needle method, without the loss of an eye, and he was also noted as the leading lithotomist in his state. This did not mean, however, that he became a specialist in the modern sense; indeed in courage, skill, and devotion to his patients he represented the best type of the heroic "country doctor."

Like many physicians of his time, he took an active interest in public affairs, was one of the first directors of the North Carolina Railroad, and was an active Whig in politics. He remained a "Union man" until 1860, when a visit to Alabama convinced him that, regardless of right or wrong, North Carolina must inevitably side with her sister states "in resisting the coercion of the North." He presided over the first war meeting held at Hillsboro on Apr. 14, 1861, supported the Confederacy most loyally thereafter, and was financially ruined as a result. Refusing to take advantage of bankruptcy proceedings, he surrendered everything to his creditors and took up life anew in a two-room cottage. In his later years he was made the first president of the revived Medical Society of the State of North Carolina. He continued his practice until the day of his death, which was occasioned by accidental poisoning with atropine.

[*Biog. Sketch of Dr. Edmund Strudwick* (1879?); Frank Nash, *Edmund Strudwick: Man and Country Doctor* (1927); *Fourteen Distinguished Physicians and Surgeons: Brief Sketches of Eminent Men for whom Duke Hospital Wards are Named* (1931); *The Papers of Thomas Ruffin*, vols. I–III (1918–20), ed. by J. G. deR. Hamilton; *Daily Charlotte Observer*, Dec. 2, 1879; personal information from Mrs. Ann Strudwick Nash, a grand-daughter, of Raleigh, N. C.]
       R. H. S.

STRUVE, GUSTAV (Oct. 11, 1805–Aug. 21, 1870), German-American publicist, political agitator, and soldier, was born in Munich, the son of the Russian diplomat Johann Gustav von Struve and Friederike Christine Sibille, *née* von Hockstetter, of a Swabian noble family. He attended preparatory schools in Munich and Karlsruhe, and from 1824 to 1826 studied law in Göttingen and Heidelberg. He accepted a post as secretary of the Oldenburg legation at Frankfurt, but soon found himself at odds with the stuffy diplomacy of the Metternich period. For a while he became a judge in Jever and afterwards settled as lawyer in Mannheim. He published a work on constitutional law, *Ueber das positive Rechtsgesetz* (1834), and one on current politics, *Briefwechsel zwischen einem ehemaligen und einem jetzigen Diplomaten* (1845), which earned him a short jail sentence because he accused Metternich of treason. The same thing happened shortly afterward because of another of the many pamphlets which he issued during the forties. In 1843 he founded the *Zeitschrift für Phrenologie* and published *Phrenologie in und ausserhalb Deutschland*, at the same time lecturing on the subject at Heidelberg and Mannheim. He agitated against capital punishment and advocated that phrenologists be put in charge of prisons.

In 1845 he became editor of a political journal,

Das Mannheimer Tageblatt, and when he proved too radical for the owners he founded his own, the *Deutscher Zuschauer,* and began the agitation for a German republic culminating in the Revolution of 1848. He was instrumental in calling the popular mass meeting at Offenburg in Baden, on Mar. 19, 1848, in which the revolutionary demands were formulated. He was elected a member of the *Vorparlament* but left this body when it proved too meek and impatiently organized an armed band of 300 men to cooperate with Friedrich K. F. Hecker [*q.v.*] for the establishment of a republic. After a clash with government troops he was arrested at Säckingen, and released on condition that he emigrate to Switzerland. After a short time he returned with 200 men to support Franz Sigel [*q.v.*], but they were again defeated at Freiburg, and Struve fled to Switzerland where he made preparations for renewed fighting. In September 1848 he appeared at Lörrach, proclaimed the republic of Baden, seized public treasuries, and took the field with 4000 men. He was again defeated by regular troops and condemned to five years of penal servitude for treason but was freed from prison by a mob. When the ephemeral republic under Brentano collapsed he fled again to Switzerland, was expelled to England, and finally emigrated to America in 1851.

He settled on Staten Island, but his efforts at journalism and play-writing did not prove successful. A wealthy German brewer by the name of Biegel invited him to live on his estate at Dobbs Ferry on the Hudson for the purpose of writing a history of the world from a democratic point of view; Struve considered this *Weltgeschichte* (1852–60), in nine volumes, his *magnum opus.* His main thesis was that tyranny and repression are detrimental to economic and cultural progress—America's progress in the nineteenth century he considered due to freedom from restrictions as much as to natural resources. Greatly interested in education, Struve was very active in promoting the German public schools of New York City. He edited the socialist periodical *Die Sociale Republik* in 1858 and 1859, and worked for the cooperation of labor groups in New York and Philadelphia. In 1856 he supported Frémont against Buchanan and in 1860 ardently worked for the election of Lincoln, for, like all the "Forty-eighters," he was a strong opponent of slavery. In 1861, at the age of fifty-six years, he entered the Union army as a private in the 8th German Volunteer Regiment under Louis Blenker, soon advancing to the rank of captain. He was discharged, however, in November 1862, because he protested against the appointment of Prince von Salm-Salm as Blenker's successor against the wishes of the entire regiment.

In 1863, his wife, Amalie Düsar, to whom he had been married in 1845, died, and he returned to Germany. He settled in Coburg where he was married to a Frau von Centener. He continued to publish various works, chiefly on America and on the Revolution. An autobiographical work, *Diesseits und Jenseits des Oceans,* appeared in 1863. Lincoln appointed him consul to the Thuringian states, but that government declined his appointment because his radical writings had involved him in renewed difficulties. In 1869 he settled in Vienna, where he died. He was survived by his second wife, and two of his three daughters by his first wife. Descriptions of Struve's character and even personal appearance differ from adulation to sarcastic belittlement. As a nineteenth century disciple of Rousseau and Robespierre he combined the noblest humanitarian intentions with opinionated impracticability. There seems to be general agreement that he utterly lacked qualities of leadership, but that he possessed idealism and tenacious courage.

[Information from Dr. Heinz Struve, Leipzig; *Allgemeine deutsche Biographie,* vol. XXXVI (1893); Friedrich von Weech, *Badische Biographieen* (rev. ed., part II, 1881); Gustav Struve, *Diesseits und Jenseits des Oceans* (1863); Karl Heinzen, *Erlebtes* (1864); *Allgemeine Zeitung* (Munich), Aug. 27, 1870.]

A. E. Z.

STRYKER, MELANCTHON WOOLSEY (Jan. 7, 1851–Dec. 6, 1929), Presbyterian clergyman and college president, descended from Jan Strÿcker who came to New Amsterdam in 1652, was the son of the Rev. Isaac Pierson Stryker, a presbyterian clergyman, and his wife, Alida Livingston Woolsey. Born in Vernon, N. Y., he had his schooling near by, at Rome. He spent three years in Hamilton College, and after a year's work in the New York City Y.M.C.A., returned to college and graduated in 1872. He studied for a year in Auburn Theological Seminary, preached the next year in Bergen, N. Y., then returned to Auburn, where he graduated in 1876. On May 30 of this year he was ordained and installed as pastor of Calvary Presbyterian Church, Auburn. Thence two years later he went to the First Presbyterian Church of Ithaca, N. Y., where he ministered until 1883. After two years in the Second Congregational Church of Holyoke, Mass., in 1885 he became pastor of the Fourth Presbyterian Church, Chicago. In his seven years there he attracted attention by his eloquent preaching.

Called to the presidency of Hamilton College

in 1892, he held that office for twenty-five years. In addition to performing his administrative work, he was pastor of the college church and taught classes in Biblical subjects and ethics. The college was in a precarious position when Stryker became its head, but his inspiring personality provided the needed leadership. He won influential friends for the institution and procured large additions to its funds. During his presidency important buildings were erected, so that the college was better equipped for instruction and living. The faculty was enlarged and strengthened. While intellectually progressive, Stryker stood for college education of the traditional type, aiming at general culture, in a time when different tendencies were strong. With his energetic nature, his broad culture, and his telling speech he affected all parts of the life of the college, leaving it better in every way than he found it, and relatively secure for the future.

Stryker was much interested in hymnology and church music. In his pastorates he strove to improve congregational singing, and in Hamilton College he trained the choir. He wrote and translated many hymns, none of which, however, have come into general use. He edited several hymnals: *Christian Chorals* (1885), *Church Song* (1889), *Choral Song* (1891), *College Hymnal* (1897, 1913), *Christian Praise* (1920). His own hymns are included in these collections. All his life he wrote verse, which was uneven and often labored and obscure, but contained passages of real beauty. Eight volumes were issued, among them *Hymns and Verses* (1883), *The Song of Miriam* (1888), *Lattermath* (1895), *Vesper Bells* (1919), *Embers* (1926). He published also *Psalms of Israel in Rhymed English Meter* (1915) and an edition of *Dies Irae* containing the Latin text and five metrical translations (1892). He was much in demand as a preacher and public speaker. A strong Republican, he frequently made campaign speeches. Some of his public utterances appeared in *The Well by the Gate* (sermons, 1903), *Baccalaureate Sermons, 1893–1905* (1905), and *Hamilton, Lincoln and Other Addresses* (1896). Out of his teaching came *Ethics in Outline* (1923) and textbooks in Biblical introduction.

After his retirement from the presidency of Hamilton in 1917, he lived at Rome, N. Y., until his death, serving as trustee of the college. He was married on Sept. 27, 1876, to Clara Elizabeth Goss of Auburn, N. Y., who survived him with two sons and three daughters. Stryker's adventurous, warm-hearted character and handsome appearance made him an impressive presence everywhere, and an enduring memory.

[*Hamilton College Bulletin*, Apr. 1930; W. S. Stryker, *Geneal. Record of the Strÿcker Family* (1887); *Gen. Biog. Cat. Auburn Theological Seminary* (1918); John Julian, *A Dict. of Hymnology* (1891); *Who's Who in America*, 1928–29; *N. Y. Times*, Dec. 7, 1929.]   R. H. N.

STUART, ALEXANDER HUGH HOLMES (Apr. 2, 1807–Feb. 13, 1891), congressman, secretary of the interior, was born at Staunton, Va., the son of Archibald Stuart [*q.v.*] and Eleanor (Briscoe) Stuart and the great-grandson of Archibald Stuart, a Scotch-Irish emigrant to Pennsylvania about 1727. He was educated at the academy in Staunton, at the college of William and Mary, and later at the University of Virginia, where he was graduated in 1828. During the same year he was licensed to practise law and began his professional career in Staunton. The Whig party soon claimed his support. As a champion of Henry Clay, he took a leading part in the Young Men's National Convention, which assembled at Washington in 1832. In 1836 he began a service of three years in the Virginia House of Delegates and made himself conspicuous as a champion of internal improvements. In a report of 1838 he proposed a comprehensive system of communications that would have linked the different parts of the state commercially (*Substance of the Remarks of Mr. Stuart of Augusta on the . . . General System of Improvement,* 1838). Though the plan as a whole was defeated, some of his proposals were carried into effect. In 1841 he became a member of the federal House of Representatives. There he was one of the few Southerners who supported Adams in his opposition to the "gag rule," and, when Clay broke with President Tyler, Stuart took the side of the former. Retiring from Congress in 1843, he did not again hold office until President Fillmore appointed him secretary of the interior in 1850. He was largely responsible for organizing the department as it had not been done by his predecessor (Robertson, p. 55). In 1853 he again retired to private life, but continued to take an active interest in politics. When the Whig party disintegrated and the American party was formed upon its ruins, he espoused the new cause and in 1856 published a series of letters, the "Madison" letters (Robertson, *post*, pp. 59–162), which came to be looked upon as an authoritative exposition of the doctrines of the party. The next year he was elected to the state Senate and served until the outbreak of the Civil War. He was chairman of a legislative committee which drew up a report on John Brown's raid (*Ibid.,* App. 1, pp. 383–405). In the document, New England abolitionism was roundly denounced, and the righteousness of the

Northern attitude in regard to slavery was questioned.

He was a member of the Virginia convention of 1861, and, while not denying the right of secession, he condemned the move as inexpedient, accurately foretold its dire consequence, and opposed it as long as opposition was practicable. During the war, his sympathy was with his section, but his age obviated his taking an active part in the struggle. Immediately after the surrender, he took the leading part in assembling a popular meeting in Augusta County looking toward the reëstablishment of peaceful relations with the Union. In 1866 he published a pamphlet, *The Recent Revolution, It's Causes and It's Consequences.* In 1870 he was instrumental in the creation and active in the work of the "committee of nine" that went to Washington and persuaded Congress and the President to permit Virginia to exclude clauses from the "Underwood constitution," which would have disfranchised the leading elements in the white population of the state and perpetuated "carpetbag" ascendency. The restoration of home rule to Virginia was, therefore, largely his work (C. G. Bowers, *The Tragic Era,* 1929, p. 277). In 1865 he was elected to Congress but was not permitted to take his seat. In 1873 he consented to serve once again in the House of Delegates but retired on account of his health at the end of three years. Throughout the period he advocated the payment of Virginia's pre-war debt. In 1876 he became rector of the University of Virginia, served until 1882, and again from 1884 to 1886. From 1871 to 1889 he served as a trustee of the Peabody education fund. In this capacity he urged upon the federal government the desirability of its contributing to the education of the negroes (Robertson, *post,* App. 3, pp. 462–78). In 1888 he published *A Narrative of the Leading Incidents of the Organization of the First Popular Movement in Virginia in 1865 to Reëstablish Peaceful Relations . . . and of the Subsequent Efforts of the "Committee of Nine"* . . . (also, Robertson, *post,* App. 2, pp. 406–61).

In person, Stuart was over six feet tall, handsome and dignified, serious but affable. On Aug. 1, 1833, he married his cousin, Frances Cornelia Baldwin, the daughter of Briscoe G. Baldwin of Staunton. They had nine children.

[A. F. Robertson, *Alexander Hugh Holmes Stuart* (1925) ; H. H. Simms, *The Rise of the Whigs in Va.* (1929) ; A. C. Cole, *The Whig Party in the South* (1912).]   T. P. A.

STUART, ARCHIBALD (Mar. 19, 1757–July 11, 1832), Revolutionary soldier, legislator, jurist, was for many years a prominent leader of the conservative wing of the Jeffersonian Democrats in his state. He was the son of Alexander and Mary (Patterson) Stuart and the grandson of Archibald Stuart, an Ulster Scotsman, who emigrated to Pennsylvania about 1727. Archibald was born near Staunton in the Valley of Virginia, which was then a frontier area. His preliminary education was received in the Augusta Academy. For some time during the Revolution he was a student at the College of William and Mary, where he played a prominent part in Phi Beta Kappa and was offered the chair of mathematics. He fought under his father at Guilford Court House and served in the Yorktown campaign. After the Revolution he studied law with Thomas Jefferson and then began the extensive practice that carried him to nearly every county in the Valley as well as to many outside of that section.

His political career began in 1783 with his election to the Virginia House of Delegates from Botetourt County. Very soon he stood out as one of the leaders in that body in the formative period between the Revolution and the organization of the new government in 1789. He aligned himself with Madison in the championing of such measures as the reform of the state court system, the payment of British debts, the various measures that made for religious liberty, the opening of the James River for navigation, the repudiation of paper money, and the reorganization of the federal and state governments. It is significant that he championed most ardently the two of these movements that were the most difficult to accomplish, that is, the reform in the state court system and the reorganization of state government. Both were eventually realized. After playing a prominent part in the ratification of the new federal Constitution in 1788, he was inactive in politics for nearly a decade, except for membership on the Virginia-Kentucky Boundary Commission in 1795. At the turn of the century he was a member of the state Senate, a leader in the passage of the Virginia Resolutions. From 1800 until just before his death he was a judge of the general court of Virginia. He was a presidential elector for the Jefferson Democrats from 1800 to 1824. In 1828 he supported Adams and thus indicated his strong inclination toward the conservative wing of his old party. From the earliest days of his political career he was an aristocrat who wanted to be a democrat but was uncertain whether the populace could be trusted. To both Madison and Jefferson he was an able lieutenant, and in each he found a warm personal friend. Jefferson designed the substantial home he built in Staunton,

Va., in the later years of the eighteenth century and in which Stuart's grand-daughter still (1935) lives. In May 1791 he married Eleanor Briscoe, the daughter of Gerard Briscoe of Frederick County, Va. Alexander Hugh Holmes Stuart [*q.v.*] was their son.

[H. G. Grigsby, "The Hist. of the Va. Federal Convention of 1788," *Va. Hist. Colls.*, new series, vol. X (1901); *Washington and Lee Univ. Hist. Papers*, vol. II (1890); A. F. Robertson, *Alexander Hugh Holmes Stuart* (1925); collections of correspondence, particularly the Breckenridge Papers in Lib. of Cong.]

F. H. H.

STUART, CHARLES (1783–1865), abolitionist, was born in Jamaica, the son of a British army officer, and spent his boyhood in various military posts. He was given his elementary education by his mother, a Scotch Presbyterian of the strictest Calvinistic stamp, and was sent to Belfast, Ireland, for his academic training. At the age of eighteen he secured a lieutenant's commission in the British East India Company's forces, with which he served for thirteen years, resigning with the rank of captain on a pension of $800 a year. He then migrated to America, received a grant of land on Lake Simcoe in upper Canada where he lived intermittently for some years, served as justice of the peace, and published *The Emigrant's Guide to Upper Canada* (1820). For part of the time he taught school during the winters and distributed Bibles and religious tracts at his own expense during his vacations. In 1824, when he was principal of a boys' academy in Utica, N. Y., he met Theodore D. Weld [*q.v.*], then a youth of fifteen, and conceived for him a regard "more than a father's affection for his first born" (Weld-Grimké *Letters, post,* II, 557). The next year both Stuart and Weld were converted as a result of the preaching of Charles G. Finney [*q.v.*], joined the "holy band" of Finney's assistant revivalists, and accompanied him for much of the next two years in the mighty revivals which he conducted in western New York.

Stuart sent Weld to Oneida Institute in 1827 to prepare for the ministry, and, after another year in Finney's "holy band," sailed to England in order to take part in the movement to abolish slavery in the British West Indies. At his own expense he traveled through the provinces as lecturing agent, and wrote pamphlets for the anti-slavery press. His tract, *The West India Question: Immediate Emancipation Safe and Practical* (1832, often reprinted), was one of the most famous pamphlets in the British propaganda. His most distinguished service, however, was in connection with the campaign of the American Colonization Society which was begun in 1830 to secure British support for their cause.

Against the "malignant jesuitry" of the colonization program Stuart penned a succession of pamphlet philippics, of which *Prejudice Vincible* (subsequently published with James Cropper's *A Letter to Thomas Clarkson*, 1832) was the most devastating. By the winter of 1831 he had turned not only the leading abolitionists but also the British public against the colonization cause.

Meanwhile Stuart had rendered invaluable service to anti-slavery beginnings in America. From the first he had imbued his disciple, Theodore Weld, with anti-slavery principles; and in the spring of 1831, when Arthur and Lewis Tappan [*qq.v.*], the New York philanthropists, called a council of reformers to plan an "American National Anti-Slavery Society" on the British model, it was Stuart's abolition doctrine which Weld expounded to the council. Indeed, for several years after the American Anti-Slavery Society had been organized, his pamphlet, *The West India Question*, was the approved statement of its abolition creed. Other notable anti-slavery tracts, among the scores he wrote, were *Is Slavery Defensible from Scripture?* (1831) and *A Memoir of Granville Sharp* (1836). More than any other man, Stuart brought the impulse of the British anti-slavery movement to the rising agitation in America.

In 1834 Stuart returned to the United States and, as the American Anti-Slavery Society's agent but at his own expense, lectured in Ohio, Vermont, and New York, suffering considerable mob violence at times, but courageously maintaining his course. In 1838 he visited the West Indies, where he studied the workings of emancipation, reporting his findings both to the American and to the British anti-slavery press. He returned from this mission in 1840, in time to attend the world anti-slavery convention at London. During the next two years he spoke and collected funds in England for those American abolitionists who had separated from the faction of William Lloyd Garrison [*q.v.*]. At the world anti-slavery convention of 1842, the British philanthropists with whom he had so long been associated united to do him honor. Stuart had also done pioneer work in England and Scotland in behalf of the American temperance movement, and he was subsequently instrumental in America in organizing relief for the sufferers in the Irish potato famine. In the main, however, his work was done, and he retired about 1842 to his property on Lake Simcoe, where he lived until his death.

[An autobiog. sketch and numerous letters in the Weld MSS., in private hands; notices of his labors in the anti-slavery reports and periodicals of England

and America *Letters of Theodore Dwight Weld, Angelina Grimké Weld, and Sarah Grimké* (2 vols., 1934), ed. by G. H. Barnes and D. L. Dumond; G. H. Barnes, *The Anti-Slavery Impulse, 1830–1844* (1933); W. P. and F. J. Garrison, *William Lloyd Garrison* (4 vols., 1885–98).]

G. H. B.

STUART, CHARLES BEEBE (June 4, 1814–Jan. 4, 1881), engineer and author, was born at Chittenango Springs, Madison County, N. Y., the son of Henry Y. and Deborah Stuart. He began his professional career at the age of eighteen, under Jonathan Knight [q.v.] on the Baltimore & Ohio Railroad. Between 1833 and 1840 he was engaged on various lines under construction in northern New York; in 1840 he was chief engineer of the New York & Erie, and in 1842 became chief engineer of the line between Batavia and Rochester, now part of the New York Central. During six years' residence in Rochester he served twice as city surveyor, laying out Mount Hope Cemetery; he also located what became the Rochester and Niagara Falls branch of the New York Central, and a part of the line of the Great Western Railway of Canada, proposing to connect the two roads by a railway suspension bridge over the Niagara River two miles below the Falls. His scheme was generally considered impractical until the bridge was nearly ready for the passage of trains; among engineers only Charles Ellet, Jr., John A. Roebling, Edward W. Serrell [qq.v.], and Samuel Keefer believed that it could be accomplished. In November 1847, however, Stuart, as director of the American and Canadian bridge companies, contracted with Ellet for the construction of such a railroad and carriage bridge over the Niagara; work was commenced in the spring of 1848, and, after Ellet's resignation, was completed by Roebling in 1855.

In 1849 Stuart was state engineer and surveyor of New York, and in October of that year entered the service of the United States government as engineer in charge of the Brooklyn dry docks, which had been under construction since 1842 under the supervision of many different distinguished engineers. This task he completed in August 1851. Meanwhile, Dec. 1, 1850, he had been appointed engineer-in-chief of the United States Navy, a position he held until his resignation on June 30, 1853. In this capacity he wrote the specifications for the California floating sectional dry dock, which was constructed in New York under his supervision and shipped to San Francisco early in 1852. He was subsequently associated with Edward W. Serrell in the engineering firm of Stuart, Serrell & Company. In the middle fifties he became interested in Iowa railroads and as president of the

Iowa Land Company was concerned with the laying out of Clinton, Iowa. He was also financially interested in a railroad in Georgia, and in 1860 was consulting engineer for a projected railroad in Texas.

Upon the outbreak of the Civil War, he raised a regiment of engineers which was mustered into service at Elmira, Aug. 15, 1861, as Colonel Stuart's Independent Regiment, New York Infantry, subsequently the 50th New York Engineers. This regiment served with the Army of the Potomac in the construction of fortifications and bridges, participating in many engagements from the siege of Yorktown, Apr. 5–May 4, 1862, to the end of the war; Stuart, however, resigned his commission in June 1863 because of impaired health, and was honorably discharged.

Besides being an accomplished engineer, he was an effective writer. "Few makers of books have done so much themselves worthy of an enduring record; and still fewer have written a narrative, in which their own deeds figure largely, with so much modesty and good taste" (*New York Tribune*, quoted in "Press Notices," p. 15, *Naval and Mail Steamers*). Among his published works, besides numerous engineer's reports, were *The Naval Dry Docks of the United States* (1852); *The Naval and Mail Steamers of the United States* (1853); and *Lives and Works of Civil and Military Engineers of America* (1871), a valuable source of information concerning his eminent predecessors and contemporaries.

Stuart was married twice: first, at Glens Falls, N. Y., July 2, 1836, to Sarah Maria Breese, who died at Schenectady, Sept. 28, 1838; and second, at Tioga Point, Pa., Apr. 17, 1841, to Frances Maria Welles, who with two daughters and a son survived him. Two sons born of the first marriage and one born of the second died in infancy. At the time of his death Stuart was chief engineer of the Conotton Valley Railroad, then being built from the coal-fields in Carroll County to Cleveland, Ohio. He died at Cleveland of senile gangrene following a sprained ankle.

[*N. Y. Times*, Jan. 5, 1881; *Frank Leslie's Chimney Corner*, Feb. 8, 1873; F. M. Bennett, *The Steam Navy of the U. S.* (1896); *Trans. Am. Soc. Civil Engineers*, X (1881), 195 ff.; autobiog. material in Stuart's own writings; copy of record from family Bible, through the courtesy of the Veteran's Administration.]

B. A. R.

STUART, CHARLES MACAULAY (Aug. 20, 1853–Jan. 26, 1932), Methodist clergyman, educator, editor, was born in Glasgow, Scotland, the son of Lewis and Mary (Home) Stuart. Coming to the United States in youth, he spent a few years in business and then entered Kalamazoo College. Here, under the influence of two

Methodist ministers, Lewis R. Fiske and William X. Ninde, he decided to enter the ministry, and upon his graduation in 1880 he became a student in Garrett Biblical Institute. During his theological course he served as student pastor of the church at River Forest, Ill. In 1883 he graduated from Garrett, was received into the Detroit Conference of the Methodist Episcopal Church, and became pastor of the Fort Street Church in that city. On Oct. 10 of the same year he married Emma Rachel Littlefield, daughter of a fellow minister. To their great sorrow they had no children.

In 1885 Stuart became associate editor of the *Michigan Christian Advocate,* an independent Methodist journal under the control of the Detroit Conference. His gifts as a writer attracted the attention of Dr. Arthur Edwards, editor of the *Northwestern Christian Advocate,* Chicago, and in 1886 Stuart was called to become assistant editor of that important weekly. Here he served for ten years with ability and distinction. From 1896 to 1909 he was professor of sacred rhetoric in Garrett Biblical Institute, but in 1909, upon the sudden death of David D. Thompson, was recalled to the *Northwestern Christian Advocate* as its editor. After some three years in this post, he was elected to a professorship of Christian ethics and the philosophy of religion at Wesleyan University, Middletown, Conn., and almost at the same time was chosen president of Garrett Biblical Institute, to succeed Charles J. Little [*q.v.*]. After some hesitation Stuart chose the latter position, and from 1911 to 1924, when he became president emeritus, performed a notable work in the development of Garrett.

During his administration many changes were made both in the educational program and in the physical equipment of the institution. The burning of the principal dormitory in 1914 and the large increase in the number of students made a building program a necessity. With energy and foresight Stuart entered upon a plan of expansion which eventually resulted in the erection of a notable group of buildings, the center of the group being the Charles Macaulay Stuart Chapel. As an administrator Stuart was always kind and considerate, laying no claim to unusual executive ability, but nevertheless succeeding in maintaining a spirit of confidence and cooperation within the faculty and student body.

Among his other activities, he served his church as secretary of the joint hymnal commission which produced the *Methodist Hymnal* (1905), now in use in both branches of Episcopal Methodism. He was also three times the representative of the Rock River Conference in the General Conference of the Methodist Episcopal Church. His output of books was not large, but they all possess literary distinction and grace of expression. The most notable of his works are perhaps *The Vision of Christ in the Poets* (1896) ; *The Story of the Masterpieces* (1897) ; *In Memoriam: Charles Joseph Little* (1912) ; and *The Manifold Message of the Gospel* (1913). As a speaker he had grace and charm and was in considerable demand. He died at La Jolla, Cal.

[“Charles Macaulay Stuart: A Memorial,” *Garrett Biblical Inst. Bull.*, June 1932 ; *Who's Who in America,* 1930–31 ; *Minutes of the Rock River Conference,* 1932 ; *Hist. Cat. . . . Kalamazoo Coll. and Kalamazoo Theol. Sem.* (1903) ; *Northwestern Christian Advocate* (Chicago), Feb. 4, 1932 ; *Chicago Daily News,* Jan. 27, 1932.]

W. W. S.

STUART, GILBERT (Dec. 3, 1755–July 9, 1828), painter, was born in the township of North Kingstown, Kings (later Washington) County, in His Majesty's Colony of Rhode Island and Providence Plantations. The often repeated statement that he was born in Narragansett is incorrect without the explanation that “Narragansett” at that time was merely a popular name for “the Narragansett Country,” the vague territory west of Narragansett Bay and, after 1677, south of East Greenwich. (See S. G. Arnold, *History of the State of Rhode Island and Providence Plantations,* 2 vols., 1859–60.) His father, Gilbert Stuart, a millwright and a native of Perth, Scotland, emigrated to Rhode Island to engage in the manufacture of snuff and was married in Newport on May 23, 1751, to Elizabeth, a daughter of Albro Anthony, a substantial land owner of Middletown, R. I. In partnership with Edward Cole and Dr. Thomas Moffatt, both of Newport, Stuart erected at the junction of the Mattatoxet stream and the Pattaquamscott tidal river a two-story building with gambrel roof, the snuff mill occupying the lower and the dwelling the two upper stories. In the northeast bedroom of the building, which is still (1935) standing, Gilbert Stuart was born. He was baptized by the Rev. James MacSparran in St. Paul's, “the Old Narragansett Church,” on Palm Sunday, Apr. 11, 1756. The manufacturing venture failing, the elder Stuart in 1761 sold his interest in the mill, and the family moved to Newport, where they lived “next to Mr. Abraham Redwood” in a house satirically referred to by Stuart in later life as “a hovel on Bannister's Wharf,” evidently in the rear of what is now 341–45 Thames St. There Stuart attended the school founded by Nathaniel Kay, collector of customs under Queen Anne, who bequeathed to Trinity Church in 1734 a fund “to teach ten poor boys their grammar and the mathematics gratis” (G. C. Mason, *An-*

nals of Trinity Church, Newport, R. I., 1698–1821, 1890, p. 28). According to Benjamin Waterhouse [*q.v.*], who was also at this school (*Monthly Anthology,* November 1805), Stuart early evidenced a talent for drawing. Waterhouse says that he copied pictures when he was but thirteen years old and a little later attempted to draw portraits in black lead (Dunlap, *post,* vol. I, p. 197). About 1769 a mediocre Scotch artist, Cosmo Alexander, came to Newport and painted portraits of some of its residents, among others Dr. William Hunter, a friend of the Stuart family. Stuart became his pupil and received what has been described as training in drawing and in the "groundwork of the palette" (*Ibid.,* p. 198). After going to Edinburgh with Alexander, who died there on Aug. 25, 1772 (Whitley, *post,* p. 8), he attempted to support himself by his art and, failing, is said to have worked his way home in 1773 or 1774 on a collier bound for Nova Scotia. We know little concerning the two years following Alexander's death except that he busied himself in painting, some of his clients coming from a colony of cultivated Jews settled in Newport, and in studying music, in which he was also talented. In this period shortly before the Revolution it was apparent that the American colonies, for the time being, were no place in which to practise the painter's art, and in June 1775 Stuart, alone, with little money and but one letter of introduction, sailed for London, determined to enter upon a painter's career. It is possible that he stopped in Philadelphia on the way, for an entry in the account books of Joseph Anthony, his uncle, shows a loan to Stuart in July 1775.

He reached London probably in November 1775 and, according to his daughter Jane, "went into cheap lodgings," sought clients, and occasionally painted portraits "at prices so low as scarcely to give him bread" ("The Youth of Gilbert Stuart," *Scribner's Monthly,* Mar. 1877, p, 642). There is a well authenticated story that he obtained employment as organist in a church in Foster Lane, probably Saint Vedast's. Although the church records rarely mention the names of the deputy organists, William Duncombe, who gave Saint Vedast's its organ in 1774, undertook either to "play himself or to find an able performer in his place" (letter to the author from the Rev. Andrew Freeman, Standish Vicarage, Stonehouse, Gloucester), and it is probable that Stuart eked out the slender earnings from his profession in this way. Stuart's classmate, Waterhouse, had spent a year in Scotland studying medicine and in the summer of 1776 removed to London to attend Saint Thomas' and Guy's hospitals. There he found Stuart lodging in York Buildings (Buckingham Street, Strand) with one picture on his easel, a family group painted for Alexander Grant. Stuart moved to Gracechurch Street to be near Waterhouse, and the two youths devoted one day a week to rambling about London and visiting its sights and picture galleries. Even at this early period, Stuart neglected his work and was in constant money difficulties. Finally, unable to support himself, he wrote Benjamin West, 1738–1820 [*q.v.*], a letter in which he described himself as "just arriv'd att the age of 21," "without the necessarys of life," his "hopes from home Blasted & incapable of returning thither," and asked West's help (facsimile in J. H. Morgan's life in Park, *post,* vol. I, p. 29). Upon the immediate response of West, at this time the leading figure in historical painting in England, with a studio that was a meeting place for the fashion of the day, Stuart moved to 27 Villiers St., not far from West's house in Newman Street, and became his pupil; later, probably in the summer of 1777, he became a member of West's household and remained with him for nearly five years.

He contributed one portrait to the Royal Academy exhibition in 1777, three in 1779, two in 1781, and four in 1782. By 1781 his work was attracting the favorable attention of the London critics, but in 1782 his famous "Portrait of a Gentleman Skating" (a full length of his friend William Grant of Congalton) brought him prominently to the attention of the public, and some time after the close of the exhibition he took rooms at No. 7 Newman St. It is probable that he continued to assist West for a time thereafter, but he seems to have received many commissions at once and in 1783 sent nine portraits to the Exhibition of the Incorporated Society of Artists, of which he became a member in December 1783. A list of his patrons for the next five years makes it clear that he had a large share of fashionable patronage at prices, Dunlap says, "equal to any, except Sir Joshua Reynolds and Gainsborough." John Boydell, the leading print seller of London, engaged him to paint fifteen portraits of contemporary painters and engravers, including Reynolds and West, from which plates were engraved and the prints sold by Boydell to the public. He exhibited for the last time in the Royal Academy of 1785. His address at this time is given as New Burlington Street, where he occupied a house at a rent of a hundred guineas (Whitley, *post,* p. 51). Here, according to tradition, he entertained lavishly, hiring a French chef, engaging professional musicians, and often performing himself, and it was here that he brought his bride, Charlotte Coates, daughter of a physician of Reading, Berkshire, after their marriage on May 10, 1786. The match had been opposed by the Coates family, but it seems to have been a happy one. Of the twelve children born of the union, the second son, Charles Gilbert, who died at twenty-six, and Jane, the youngest daughter, inherited some of their father's ability. Jane Stuart excuses the extravagances of her father's London life on the ground that his fine clothes, his costly establishment, and his many entertainments were required by a fashionable clientèle—a conclusion which does not necessarily follow.

Stuart's rise during these twelve years in London can be fully measured only when it is remembered that he spent most of the first twenty years of his life under unfavorable conditions, that he had had no teacher but Alexander and few, if any, great paintings to copy, that his environment provided very little stimulus, and that he had only a small circle to appreciate his gifts. Yet at nineteen, alone, inexperienced, without resources or friends, he had courage enough to travel from the Colonies to London, seeking his fortune in a calling where influence and favor were half the battle. Within five years after becoming West's pupil he was able to begin an independent career; within five years more he had become one of the leading portrait painters of London—and this in the London of Ramsay, Reynolds, Romney, and Gainsborough, at a time when portrait painting had reached the highest point attained by British art. Such distinction would have been sufficient to crown the work of a lifetime, yet it was achieved by Stuart before he reached the age of thirty-two.

In 1787, however, he had left England for Ireland. According to Jane Stuart, he went at the request of the Duke of Rutland, then lord lieutenant of Ireland, to paint his portrait, and entered Dublin on the day of the funeral of the duke (*Scribner's Monthly*, Mar. 1877, p. 645), who died on October 24. What really formed his determination to leave London when the full tide of success apparently had set in, may never be known; but it seems most probable that his improvidence and utter lack of business sense forced the change, since at the time imprisonment for debt was usually the end of reckless living. Mention of Stuart's name disappears from contemporary newsprints and periodicals in the summer of 1787, and his new-found prosperity apparently had utterly collapsed. Yet, whatever may have been the conditions determining his move, in Dublin again he was most successful. He painted the portraits of many of those prominent

in political, social, and professional life, and was without a competitor worthy the name. He resided for a time in Pill Lane, Dublin, and later moved to Stillorgan, a suburb. Inordinately fond of social pleasures and delighted with the polished manners and the hospitality of Irish society which suited his genial temperament so well, he repeated his London life. His daughter says that Stuart "entered too much into these convivialities" and that her mother could never be induced to talk upon these Irish experiences, as it gave her "pain to remember anything associated with reckless extravagances, or what she called his folly" (*Ibid.*).

Stuart sailed for New York late in 1792 or early in 1793, and painted the portrait of the owner of the ship, one John Shaw, in payment for his passage. He is quoted as saying that he returned to his native land hoping to make a fortune by painting portraits of Washington: "I calculate upon making a plurality of his portraits, whole lengths, that will enable me to realize; and if I should be fortunate, I will repay my English and Irish creditors" (Herbert, *post*, p. 248). He also expected to profit through the sale of prints from a plate made from a portrait of Washington. He leased a studio on Stone, near William Street, and Dunlap, who was then living in New York, wrote that all who were distinguished by office, rank, or attainment availed themselves of his talents. Late in November 1794 he moved to Philadelphia, then the seat of the federal government, and opened a painting room on the south-west corner of Fifth and Chestnut Streets. As he had great social gifts and made it his practice to associate with the leaders of intellect and fashion in each land in which he resided, it was natural that he should choose to go to Philadelphia, then the largest city in America, but from a letter to his uncle, Joseph Anthony, it is plain that his immediate motive was to finish his uncle's portrait and to paint one of the President. The Philadelphia period is important by reason of the brilliant series of women's portraits which Stuart there completed; though it has always been conceded that he was a notable painter of old men, this group entitles him to high rank as a portrayer of women. His stay in Philadelphia will also be memorable because there he painted his first two life portraits of Washington. The first, a bust portrait, showing the right side of the face, known as the Vaughan Type, was painted in the late winter of 1795. "A list of the gentlemen who are to have copies of the portrait of the President of the United States" in Stuart's handwriting, dated Apr. 20, 1795, names thirty-two subscribers calling for thirty-nine "copies." Stuart received sittings, beginning Apr. 12, 1796, from Washington for his second life portrait, a life-size standing portrait, showing the left side of the face, eyes gazing right (left of spectator), right hand outstretched as if addressing an audience, which is known as the Lansdowne Type. His painting room was so thronged with visitors and patrons, however, that he was unable to finish his commissions, and in the summer of 1796 he moved to Germantown and fitted up the stone barn of the Wister mansion (now 5140 Main St.) as a studio. Here in the early fall of 1796, at the request of Mrs. Washington, the President sat for the third life portrait, bust size, showing the left side of the face, eyes front. This is the familiar "Athenaeum Head," unfinished as to the stock and coat, now in the Boston Museum of Fine Arts, which Stuart kept with him until his death. It is a highly idealized representation of Washington in his old age, when the loss of his teeth had changed not only the shape of his face but the expression as well. Following the seat of government to Washington in 1803, Stuart opened a studio at the corner of F and Seventh Streets, and for two years was fully occupied. He painted Jefferson, Madison, Monroe, William Branch Giles, and many others among the leaders, one contemporary writing that he was "all the rage" and "worked to death."

Sometime in the summer of 1805 he moved to Boston, where he lived for the remainder of his life. Here again he met with instant success. Charles Fraser [q.v.], the miniature painter, at the beginning of this period wrote that Stuart "had all the beauty and talents of Boston under his pencil" (A. R. and D. E. Huger Smith, *Charles Fraser,* 1924, p. 18). The remaining twenty-three years of his life in Boston ran true to form. He was overrun with commissions but, as he kept no books, "he did not know, at times, whether a picture he had finished had been paid for; so indifferent was he to all business matters" (Mason, *post,* p. 45). His health began to fail in 1825, and somewhat later symptoms of paralysis in his left arm depressed him greatly. He still continued to paint but with great difficulty. In the spring of 1828 he was attacked by gout, and on July 9, 1828, he died in his home on Essex Street. He was buried in Tomb 61 in the Central Burying Grounds on Boston Common, situated under the Mall which leads from Park Square to the Park Street Church. He died without a will. The inventory of his estate, which included an organ, eight "unfinished Sketches of Heads," household furniture, glass, china, etc., was valued at $375; his debts, which

were largely for household supplies, showed a deficit of $1,778 after the payment of five preferred claims, two of which were: "Paid for coffin and undertaker's bill . . . $36," and "Dr. Warren's bill for the last illness of deceased . . . $132" (probate records in Old Court House, Boston). He was survived by his wife and four of his daughters, Anne (Mrs. Stebbens), Agnes, Emma, and Jane Stuart, and as he left little but unfinished canvases, including the portraits of the President and Mrs. Washington, an exhibition of his work was held for their benefit at the Boston Athenaeum, which brought together 211 of his portraits.

There are several portraits of Stuart. The self-portrait of 1778 and the bust modeled by John Henri Isaac Browere [q.v.] from a life mask, which Jane Stuart called, "a most living and beautiful thing," best represent him in youth and old age. Of his most familiar likeness— the portrait by John Neagle [q.v.]— his daughter wrote that it was "utterly devoid of intellectual expression," and was considered "a positive caricature by his family and his intimate friends" ("Anecdotes of Gilbert Stuart," *Scribner's Monthly,* July 1877, p. 379). A contemporary writes of him: "In his person, Stuart was rather large, and his movements, in the latter part of his life, were slow and heavy, but not ungraceful. His manners had something of the formality of the old school. . . . He was sometimes a little fastidious and eccentrick; but never lost the manners of a gentleman on any occasion. . . . The lives and works of the great artists of all ages were familiar to him as his palett. He discoursed upon their excellences, defects, and peculiarities, as one who had read and examined them all most thoroughly. His eloquence was peculiar and attractive; his voice was strong and deep; his enunciation clear and distinct; and his countenance came in aid of his voice, for his features were bold and lion-like . . ." (Knapp, *post,* p. 196). In addition to Stuart's talents as a painter and musician, there are innumerable references to his gifts as a conversationalist. John Quincy Adams, whose character, education, and wide experience of the world rendered him no mean judge of men, wrote in his diary on Sept. 19, 1818, "I sat to Stuart before and after breakfast, and found his conversation . . . very entertaining. His own figure is highly picturesque, with his dress always disordered and taking snuff from a large, round tin wafer-box, holding, perhaps, half a pound, which he must use up in a day." Jane Stuart alludes to his irony and his keen sense of the ridiculous, but she and others stress his kindliness and benevolence. "Anything," she wrote, "like adverse fortune or neglected merit was sure to find a place in his regard" (*Ibid.*, p. 376). He was procrastinating and would only paint when in the mood, sometimes refusing a commission from distaste for the subject, sometimes for no apparent reason whatsoever. He failed even to answer the letter of the Pennsylvania Academy of the Fine Arts offering $1,500 for a replica of his Washington portrait of the Lansdowne Type, two and one-half times what he had been paid for the original, and he neglected the request of the authorities of the Pitti Palace, Florence, for his own portrait to add to its gallery of eminent artists. He was quick to take offense and impatient of any criticism of his work, often refusing to finish a portrait (for example, that of Prince Jerome Bonaparte) because of some fancied slight. If one of his portraits pleased him he often neglected to finish it, and had to be begged and cajoled into completing the canvas. While the artistic temperament is proverbially improvident and the mere pursuit of money rarely interests those gifted with unusual talents, still, in view of Stuart's ancestry, the poverty of his youth, his bitter experience in London, and his inability to order his early success there, it is difficult to understand why he never learned the lesson of prudence.

Stuart's palette, set in high key, often has been described, but West is quoted as having said, "It is of no use to steal Stuart's colors: if you want to paint as he does you must steal his eyes" (Mason, *post*, p. 39). It was Stuart's mastery of the use of what may be called transparent color which gave his portraits their lifelike and luminous effect, and it is in this quality that they stand supreme among American paintings. His chief object was always to paint his sitter so as to preserve the character and likeness of the individual. He had what Washington Allston [*q.v.*] described as "the faculty of distinguishing between the accidental and the permanent, in other words, between the conversational expression which arises from *manners* and the more subtle indication of the individual mind" (*Boston Daily Advertiser*, July 22, 1828). William Temple Franklin wrote Benjamin Franklin in 1784 that he had heard West say that Stuart " '*nails* the face to the canvas.' " Stuart's heads are well placed, powerfully and subtly modeled, and (when not on a panel) often so thinly painted as to show the web of the coarse English canvas, which he preferred, through the pigment. After completing the head he lost interest, and careless drawing will be found sometimes in the accessories. When criticized for this and for not paying more attention to the decorative side of portrait painting, his reply was, "I copy the works of God and leave clothes to tailors and mantua-makers" (Mason, *post*, p. 38); yet when the whim took him he would with a few bold strokes paint a piece of lace to perfection, as if to show how simple it was to produce such an effect. While many of his portraits as compositions lack the decorative qualities of those of his British contemporaries, Stuart's heads, in their absence of flattery and in their scrupulous fidelity to nature, bring to mind those of the seventeenth-century Dutch painters. Early in his career Stuart said: "For my part, I will not follow any master. I wish to find out what nature is for myself and see her with *my own eyes*" (Dunlap, *post*, vol. I, p. 216). In this is the key to a full appreciation of his work. He left a reputation without rival in the United States, and the passing of the century since his death still finds his name first in the list of American portrait painters.

[Stuart's name sometimes appears as Gilbert Charles. For biog. material see, William Dunlap, *A Hist. of the Rise and Progress of the Arts of Design in the U. S.* (3 vols., 1918), ed. by F. W. Bayley and C. E. Goodspeed; G. C. Mason, *The Life and Works of Gilbert Stuart* (1879); Lawrence Park, *Gilbert Stuart, An Illustrated Descriptive List of His Works* (4 vols., 1926), with an account of his life by J. H. Morgan; W. T. Whitley, *Gilbert Stuart* (1932); J. H. Morgan and Mantle Fielding, *The Life Portraits of Washington and Their Replicas* (1931); J. D. Herbert, *Irish Varieties, for the Last Fifty Years* (1836); S. L. Knapp, *Lectures on Am. Lit.* (1829); J. H. Morgan, "Gilbert Stuart; Miniature Painter," *Antiques*, Oct. 1929, and "The Date of Stuart's Death, the Place of his Burial, and the Inventory of his Estate," *Ibid.*, Mar. 1934; W. G. Strickland, *A Dict. of Irish Artists* (2 vols., 1913); H. E. T., in *Bull. of the R. I. School of Design*, Oct. 1914, Jan. 1915; obituary notice in *Columbian Centinel*, July 12, 1828; probate records in Old Court House, Boston, Mass.]   J. H. M.

STUART, GRANVILLE (Aug. 27, 1834–Oct. 2, 1918), Montana pioneer, was of Scotch descent, the son of Robert and Nancy Currence (Hall) Stuart, and was born at Clarksburg, Va. (now W. Va.). In 1837 the family moved to Princeton, Ill., and a year later to the newly opened lands of the Black Hawk Purchase, in what is now Muscatine County, Iowa. With his brother James, young Stuart worked about the farm, hunted for game, and at times attended school. In the spring of 1852, the father, a returned Argonaut of '49, taking Granville and James with him, again set out for California, reaching the gold regions in September. All three became prospectors. The father went back to Iowa in 1853, and in June 1857 the sons, with nine companions, also set out for the East. On approaching Great Salt Lake they became alarmed at the hostility of the Mormons and turned north. In October they crossed the Continental Divide and entered Beaverhead Valley, in the present state of Montana. Proceeding to Deer Lodge Valley in April 1858, Granville and James, with two others, found gold and were thus among the early discoverers of the metal in that state. A journey to Fort Bridger followed, but in May 1861 the brothers were again in the valley, where they found more gold. A letter to a third Stuart brother, Thomas, then in Colorado, brought to the territory its first party of avowed prospectors in June 1862. On May 2 of that year Granville was married to Aubony (or Ellen), a Shoshone girl, who was to bear him nine children.

For some years Stuart followed the rush to the various new mining camps, engaging in many activities, but in 1867 he settled in Deer Lodge. With the growth of settlement he took a leading part in community affairs, and in 1871 was elected to the territorial council. In 1876 and in 1879 he was elected to the lower house, and in 1883 again to the council, being chosen president. Impressed with the practicability of cattle-raising on the open range, he organized, in 1879, the Davis, Hauser, and Stuart Company, of which he was made general manager. In the following year he placed a large herd in the Judith Basin. The experiment was for a time successful, but, by reason of overstocking the range and of losses suffered during the terrible winter of 1886–87, it ended in disaster. His Indian wife died in 1887, and in 1891 he was married to Isabel Allis Brown, a school-teacher. In the same year he was appointed state land agent. In 1894 President Cleveland appointed him minister to Uruguay and Paraguay, a post he retained for more than four years. In 1904 he became librarian of the Butte city library. His later years were spent in or near Missoula. In 1916 he was commissioned by the legislature to write a history of Montana, but it was not completed. He died at Missoula, and the body was interred at Deer Lodge. His wife and several children by his first marriage survived him.

Stuart was more than six feet tall, and somewhat gaunt of frame. His portrait reveals a finely formed head and a kindly, intellectual face. His manner was suave and courtly. He was a student, an observer, and an experimenter, and to the end his mind was alert and keen. Perhaps no one in the state more fully enjoyed the confidence and respect of his fellows. He was the first secretary of the Montana Historical Society, organized in Virginia City in 1864, and president from 1890 to 1895; in 1886–87 he was president of the Society of Montana Pioneers, for seven years president of the board of stock

commissioners, and for sixteen years a school trustee. In 1865 he published *Montana As It Is,* a book important for its historical information and now exceptionally valuable by reasons of its rarity. His invaluable journals, with those of his brother James, were published in part, under the title *Forty Years on the Frontier,* in 1925.

[P. C. Phillips, ed., *Forty Years on the Frontier* (2 vols., 1925); articles and references throughout the *Contributions to the Hist. Soc. of Mont.*; *Montana Record-Herald* (Helena), and *Anaconda Standard,* Oct. 4, 1918; information from David Hilger, Helena.]
W. J. G.

STUART, HENRY ROBSON [See Robson, Stuart, 1836–1903].

STUART, ISAAC WILLIAM (June 13, 1809–Oct. 2, 1861), historian and orator, was born in New Haven, Conn., one of nine children of Abigail (Clark) Stuart and the Rev. Moses Stuart [*q.v.*], who was then pastor of the First Church of Christ (Congregational) in New Haven. He was graduated from Yale in 1828. After teaching for a short period in the historic Hopkins Grammar School in Hartford, he became professor of Greek and Latin in South Carolina College, Columbia, S. C. Returning to Hartford in 1840, he made that city his home for the rest of his life, devoting himself to historical and antiquarian pursuits. He was for some years much interested in politics, being an admirer of Henry Clay and a believer in a protective tariff, and holding moderate views on the slavery question. He was a member of the Connecticut House of Representatives in 1844 and of the Connecticut Senate in 1845 and 1846. He achieved local fame as an orator and as a lecturer on historical subjects, and was much in demand as a speaker. In November 1834 in New York he married Caroline Bulkeley, by whom he had three daughters. From her father, Stephen Bulkeley, a wealthy merchant of Hartford, Mrs. Stuart inherited the ancient Wyllys estate in Hartford, on which stood the Charter Oak. Stuart died in Hartford. At his funeral, held in St. John's Church, Oct. 5, 1861, the Putnam Phalanx, of which he was a founder and first judge advocate, acted as a military escort.

He published a translation of an essay by J. G. Honoré Greppo, *Essay on the Hieroglyphic System of M. Champollion, jun.* (Boston, 1830), edited *The Oedipus Tyrannus of Sophocles* (New York, 1837), and wrote *Hartford in the Olden Time* (Hartford, 1853), originally contributed as a series of articles to the *Hartford Daily Courant* under the pen name of "Scaeva" and published under that name, *Life of Captain Nathan Hale, the Martyr-Spy of the American*

Revolution (Hartford, 1856), *Excursion of the Putnam Phalanx to Boston, Charlestown, and Providence, Oct. 4, 5, 6, and 7, 1859* (Hartford, 1859), and a *Life of Jonathan Trumbull, Sen., Governor of Connecticut* (Boston, 1859).

[*Obit. Record Grads. Yale Coll.* (1862); obituary in *Hartford Daily Courant*, Oct. 4, 1861; and gravestone in Cedar Hill Cemetery, Hartford.]   A—r A.

STUART, JAMES EWELL BROWN (Feb. 6, 1833–May 12, 1864), soldier, born on "Laurel Hill" plantation, Patrick County, Va., was of Scotch-Irish stock on the side of his father, Archibald Stuart, and on that of his mother, Elizabeth Letcher (Pannill), was of blood predominantly Welsh. Like his distant cousins, Archibald (1757–1832) and Alexander H. H. Stuart [*qq.v.*], he was descended from an earlier Archibald Stuart who settled in Pennsylvania in 1726 and moved to Virginia in 1738. His father was a member of the two Virginia constitutional conventions and served a term in the federal House of Representatives. The seventh of ten children, he received his early schooling at home and in Wytheville, Va., and attended Emory and Henry College, 1848–50. On July 1, 1850, he entered the United States Military Academy; he graduated No. 13 in a class of forty-six. He was a popular cadet, and was distinguished for his quiet, wholesome religion and, paradoxically, for his "almost thankful acceptance" of every challenge to a fight, even though he was often beaten.

Commissioned brevet second lieutenant in the Mounted Rifles in July 1854, he received regular commission Oct. 31, 1854, and in December joined his command in Texas. On March 3, 1855, he was transferred to the 1st United States Cavalry, and spent most of the subsequent six years in Kansas, where, on Nov. 14, 1855, after a whirlwind courtship, he married Flora, daughter of Col. Philip St. George Cooke. Three children were born of this marriage, a son and a daughter surviving him. Promoted first lieutenant Dec. 20, 1855, Stuart soon disclosed definite aptitude for outpost duty. During the summer of 1859 he came East, chiefly in the hope of selling to the war department the rights to a device he had invented for attaching the cavalry sabre to the belt (Patent No. 25,684; Oct. 24, 1859). While in Washington, in October, he was asked to ride in haste to "Arlington" with a sealed message for Col. R. E. Lee, who had been superintendent of the military academy for the last two years of his cadetship. Being accepted as Lee's aide, Stuart went with him to Harpers Ferry and there recognized "Osawatomie" (John) Brown, whom he had met in Kansas. Back on the frontier, Stuart on

Jan. 15, 1861, wrote Jefferson Davis asking that Davis procure for him "a position" in the "Army of the South." In March Stuart got leave for two months and, learning of the secession of Virginia, started for his native state. En route he mailed his resignation (dated May 3, accepted May 14) from the United States Army in which, Apr. 22, 1861, he had been promoted captain.

Because of the diarchy then prevailing, he was commissioned lieutenant-colonel of Virginia infantry, May 10, 1861, and captain of Confederate cavalry May 24, 1861. At Harpers Ferry, with about 300 horsemen, soon regimented as the 1st Virginia Cavalry, he successfully screened a wide front. At First Manassas he protected the Confederate left and, with a well-timed charge, contributed to the victory of July 21. He was made brigadier-general Sept. 21, 1861, and, though roughly handled in an unequal engagement at Dranesville, Va., Dec. 20, 1861, he organized an admirable outpost system and brought to high efficiency his cavalry, who, by the end of the year, numbered about 2,400 officers and men. Accompanying Joseph E. Johnston to the Peninsula, he did what seemed possible to cover the withdrawal of the army to the Chickahominy. From Lee, who had taken command June 1, 1862, he received on June 11 written orders to "make a secret movement to the rear of the enemy, now posted on the Chickahominy." In particular Lee wished to know whether the Federals occupied the watershed between the Chickahominy and the Totopotomoy, down which he intended to bring Jackson's Army of the Valley in a turning movement. The next day with 1,200 selected cavalry and a section of artillery, Stuart set out. He soon ascertained that McClellan's right did not extend across the watershed. He might then have turned back, but it was in his opinion the soundest prudence, as well as the more soldierly course, to make a complete circuit of the Federal army. When he reported to Lee on the 15th he brought with him 165 prisoners and 260 horses and mules. This operation was a model of its kind and involved the loss of one man only. Some critics have regarded it as a mistake because it warned McClellan of what was impending; but McClellan minimized its significance and did little to strengthen his exposed flank.

During the Seven Days' campaign, when he had under his command seven mounted regiments and the equivalent of four additional battalions, Stuart kept to the left of the attacking Confederate force, struck McClellan's base as it was being abandoned and, on the night of July 1, reached the vicinity of Malvern Hill after the battle of that day. On the 3rd, he seized Evelington Heights, which dominated the Federal camps at Harrison's Landing. Stuart's impetuosity led him to open fire with his solitary howitzer. General Franklin then moved out troops to occupy and to fortify the heights. Thus was thrown away the one chance of following up successfully the indecisive action of July 1. This, however, was not realized at the time and did not impair Stuart's reputation. On July 25 he was made major-general and in that grade was confirmed Sept. 27, 1862.

During the preliminaries of Second Manassas, all the cavalry of the army was placed under Stuart's orders. On the morning of Aug. 18 at Verdierville, he barely escaped capture but got personal revenge by raiding Pope's headquarters at Catlett's Station on the night of Aug. 22. Stuart next covered Jackson's movement to Bristoe Station and to Manassas Junction, and supported him most efficiently at Groveton. In the final fighting at Manassas and during the Maryland operations Stuart's conduct repeatedly won the praise of Lee. Following Lee's return to Virginia, Stuart on Oct. 9, 1862, set out across the Potomac with 1800 men and four guns to make a raid into Pennsylvania. He reached his objective, the bridge over the Conococheague at Chambersburg, but could not destroy the iron structure and had to turn back. Riding around the Federal army, he returned to Virginia via White's Ford on the morning of Oct. 12 and brought with him 1,200 Federal horses.

Stuart made the most of the popularity he gained by these spectacular achievements. For while his patriotism was above challenge, and his private life clean and beautiful, he had a lingering adolescent love of being dramatically conspicuous. He always rode a splendid horse—and rode so hard that no animal could long survive his galloping. His gray cloak was lined with red; in the lapel of his jacket was a red flower or ribbon love-knot; his hat was cocked on one side with a star of gilt that held a peacock's plume. In his camp there was music and dancing and much jollity, but never any drinking under Stuart's eye, any swearing in his presence, or any discoverable loose living. His tactical skill, though marked, was not startling or original and his strategic sense was not outstanding, but by the winter of 1862 his early aptitude for outpost service had developed into most extraordinary skill as an intelligence officer. Lee regarded Stuart as the "eyes of the army" and when he heard of Stuart's death said in a broken voice: "He never brought me a piece of false in-

formation" (R. E. Lee, Jr., *Recollections and Letters of General Robert E. Lee*, 1904, p. 125). Stuart had the good will of men as dissimilar as Jackson and Longstreet, and most of the younger men in the cavalry corps idolized him. Lee regarded him almost as a son and remarked after the war that Stuart was his ideal of a soldier. Stuart had, however, his bitter enemies, some of them in his own corps. They accused him of selfish disregard of the feats of his subordinates, of parading himself for admiration, and of claiming credit that belonged to others.

At Fredericksburg Stuart confounded his critics and vindicated all good opinions by his admirable employment of his artillery on the Confederate right; during the winter of 1862–63 he held the line of the Rappahannock with much skill, though the lack of forage already gave warning of later disaster. He gave Lee prompt notice of Hooker's movement across the Rappahannock at the beginning of the Chancellorsville operations, and then, under Lee's orders, he kept most of his troops concentrated, in complete disregard of Stoneman's raid against Lee's communications. He helped to find and to protect the roads of Jackson's march. After Jackson was wounded and A. P. Hill was temporarily incapacitated, Stuart was summoned to take command of the II Corps, and he handled it with skill, if perhaps without regard to losses, on May 3. The absence of even a hint that Lee considered him as Jackson's successor is indirect evidence, if negative, that Lee regarded him as indispensable at the head of the cavalry corps, which had been reorganized in brigades Nov. 10, 1862.

The Gettysburg campaign represents the most disputable chapter in the career of Stuart. He directed on June 9 the large, indecisive action of Brandy Station; and, as the advance continued, he was frequently engaged and with larger resources than he had at any time commanded. The general plan was that he was to hold the mountains till the Confederate infantry passed; then he was to cross the Potomac, make contact with Ewell's advanced column, and play his usual rôle in screening the army's movements and in collecting information and provisions. Stuart may have been spurred by recent criticisms in the press for failing to display initiative, not less than by his adventurous nature, to seek opportunity for some brilliant exploit. He proposed that he attempt to interpose the cavalry corps between the Federal army and Washington and then perform his mission in Pennsylvania. Lee assented but under conditions that he thought would give ample guarantee of Stuart's early presence on Ewell's flank in any event. Stuart was delayed by the presence of heavy Federal columns and did not pass the Potomac until the night of June 27–28. Inflicting such damage as he could on supply-trains and communications, he struck for Dover, Pa. Finding no Confederates there, he marched to Carlisle where, on the night of July 1, he received Lee's orders to report at Gettysburg. The next afternoon he rejoined the main army and, for the rest of the campaign, was ceaselessly active. In his report he claimed that he had performed a larger service than he could have rendered had he remained with the main army, which, he said, had Jenkins' large brigade available for outpost duty. Lee and all his senior lieutenants had, however, been groping in the dark because of Stuart's absence, and many asserted that Stuart had deprived his chief of victory by riding off on a bootless raid. There developed a heated controversy that has been revived at intervals ever since. The evidence probably permits of no more definite conclusion than that Lee's orders to Stuart, though somewhat vague, imposed an obligation to abandon the attempt to cross the Potomac east of Hooker's army should Stuart, in the attempt, meet with hindrance that would delay him. Stuart encountered such hindrance but impetuously determined to press on his adventure, doubtless in the belief that he could make up for the time he lost.

Never thereafter could Stuart be accused of failing to keep the commanding general informed of hostile movements. Except during the heaviest weather of winter, scouting was constant. Stuart himself preferred to live at an outpost and he perhaps found his highest excitement in lesser engagements. Among the most interesting of these were that of June 1863, in northern Virginia, the Auburn affair of Oct. 13–14, and the so-called "Buckland Races" of Oct. 19, 1863. The hard riding of the battles of 1863 almost destroyed the cavalry corps of the Army of Northern Virginia. Moreover, as the infantry was weakened, the cavalrymen often had to be called upon to dismount and to perform the same duty as infantry. Despite extravagant claims made concerning Stuart's contribution to the tactical employment of dismounted cavalry, it cannot be demonstrated that he initiated anything that had not previously been done in this respect.

With the approach of spring in 1864, it was plain that the cavalry could not undertake long operations on such forage as the quartermasters could provide. After Grant crossed the Rapidan May 4, 1864, Stuart, for a few days, by the full display of his skill was able to cover Lee's opera-

tions and to supply indispensable information concerning Federal movements. On May 9, however, Sheridan, with 12,000 sabres, made a wide detour and headed South from Spotsylvania for Richmond. Summoning all the men he could muster—approximately 4,500—Stuart demanded of the weak horses their last mile of endurance and contrived to get between Sheridan and Richmond at a place called Yellow Tavern. There, in a cruel clash, he turned off Sheridan's columns from the straight road to Richmond. In the action, however, Stuart himself, who had never been touched by a bullet or a sabre in all his combats of the war, was wounded (May 11, 1864) at close range by a dismounted Federal cavalryman. He died the next day in Richmond. He was buried in Hollywood Cemetery, Richmond, in which city an equestrian statue to him was erected in 1907.

[The records of Stuart's cadetship are among the MSS. of the Military Academy; his MS. reports and a fragmentary MS. diary of the cavalry corps are in the Confederate Museum, Richmond, Va. Virtually the whole of these is printed in *War of the Rebellion: Official Records (Army)*. The standard early biography is H. B. McClellan, *The Life and Campaigns of Major-General J. E. B. Stuart* (1885). This and some previously unpublished letters and family papers were made the basis of the very readable biography by J. W. Thomason, Jr., *Jeb Stuart* (1930). Of the books by Stuart's subordinates, among the most useful are: Heros von Borcke, *Memoirs of the Confederate War for Independence* (2 vols., 1866); Heros von Borcke and Justus Scheibert, *Die grosse Reiterschlacht bei Brandy Station* (1893); R. L. T. Beale, *History of the Ninth Virginia Cavalry* (1899); G. W. Beale, *A Lieutenant of Cavalry in Lee's Army* (1918); G. C. Eggleston, *A Rebel's Recollections* (1875); T. S. Garnett, *J. E. B. Stuart* (1907); J. E. Cooke, *Wearing of the Gray* (1867). The controversy over Stuart's conduct during the Gettysburg campaign has provoked numerous publications. These are listed, and the main outlines of the controversy are traced in App. III–1 of D. S. Freeman, *R. E. Lee* (4 vols., 1934–35), in which also, the relations of Lee to Stuart are set forth at length. A recent MS. memorandum by the historical section of Army War College admirably relates Stuart to the development of American cavalry tactics.]   D. S. F.

STUART, JOHN (c. 1700–Mar. 25, 1779), superintendent of Indian affairs for the southern district, was a native of Scotland who emigrated to America about 1748. He is said to have campaigned with his brother Francis against the Spaniards in Florida. In 1757 he was commissioned captain in the South Carolina provincials by Gov. William Henry Lyttleton [q.v.]. He married Miss Fenwick, of a prominent Carolinian family, and in 1759 a son was born who was to win fame in the Peninsular War and become Lieut.-Gen. Sir John Stuart. After the capture of Fort Loudon by the Cherokee under Oconostota [q.v.], Stuart was spirited away by Attakullaculla (Little Carpenter) whom he sent back to promote peace. In 1762 he was appointed superintendent of Indian affairs for the southern district, with a salary of £1,000 and £3,000 for Indian presents and other expenses. In 1772 he built a beautiful house in Charlestown, now Charleston, which is still (1935) standing, and he acquired a plantation on Lady's Island. At first he was without definite powers and a staff, and he was subservient to the governors, who had largely handled Indian affairs themselves. Following the proclamation of 1763, he became responsible to the secretaries of state in England, though still cooperating with the governors and commander-in-chief. During the summer and autumn of 1764 he was in the Floridas, and in October he was included in East Florida's Council by Gov. James Grant. In 1765 he utilized the "Plan for the Future Management of Indian Affairs," emanating from the Lords of Trade, to obtain full imperial status for his department. In November 1765 he and Governor Grant met the Creeks at Fort Picolata, East Florida, where peace was assured and boundaries were defined. In December 1766 Stuart was informed by Lord Shelburne that he had adopted the new plan too quickly in West Florida, and that his expenses were running above all expectation and proportion (*The New Régime*, 1916, ed. by C. W. Alvord and C. E. Carter, p. 451). In order to strengthen his authority Stuart suggested to Lord Hillsborough his appointment on the councils of all colonies within his district, and in April 1770 *mandamuses* were received by the governors of Virginia and of the provinces southward naming Stuart "councillor extraordinary" to advise them and their boards on Indian affairs. Thus the superintendent was able during the next five years to extend his influence widely. His predecessor's expenditures seem not to have exceeded £1,500 sterling a year, but his had increased steadily on account of numerous congresses and the lavish distribution of Indian presents. In 1768 they had been fixed at £4,000. By 1776 they had reached the "imperial" figure of £19,000, and they continued to mount until his death. During the rest of the British régime they were kept down to about £3,900.

Early in June 1775 his arrest was ordered by the assembly of South Carolina on the charge of attempting to incite the Catawba and Cherokee in the British interest. Fleeing from Lady's Island to Savannah and thence to St. Augustine, he remained until his death a refugee in the Floridas. His management of the southern tribes was much hampered by Revolutionary developments to the northward and was subject to the plans of British commanders operating in the south. Early in 1776 his wife and her daughter were restricted to their Charlestown home and

allowed £100 a month in currency from his estate, which had been sequestered. Later Mrs. Stuart managed to escape. To carry into effect Sir William Howe's directions about the management of the Indians, Stuart removed to Pensacola in July 1776. In February 1778 he sent two of his deputies to prepare the Cherokee and Seminole for action when summoned. He also organized three companies of refugees, one of which he dispatched to stop the rum traffic at Mobile. In March he posted two parties of whites and Indians on the Mississippi in compliance with Lord George Germain's warning of a possible invasion by that route. Nevertheless, James Willing's expedition surprised Natchez on Mar. 20 and compelled its neutrality. Another mischance, despite instructions, was the failure of the Indians to cooperate on the frontiers with Col. Archibald Campbell's expedition to Georgia in the winter of 1778. While under the severe censure of the British government for these reasons and the prodigious increase of his expenses, Stuart died at Pensacola.

[W. H. Siebert, "Loyalists in East Fla.," *Pubs. Fla. State Hist. Soc.*, no. 9 (2 vols., 1929) with citations esp. to Public Record office, London; Helen L. Shaw, *British Admin. of the Southern Indians, 1756–1783* (1931); P. M. Hamer, "John Stuart's Indian Policy during the Early Months of the Am. Rev.," *Miss. Valley Hist. Rev.*, Dec. 1930; G. B. Jackson, "John Stuart," *Tenn. Hist. Mag.*, Sept. 1917; Edward McCrady, *The Hist. of S. C. under the Royal Government* (1899); *Ga. Hist. Soc. Colls.*, vol. III (1873), pp. 189, 251; *The Correspondence of Gen. Thomas Gage*, vols. I, II (1931–33), ed. by C. E. Carter; "Observations of Supt. John Stuart and Gov. James Grant of E. Fla. on the Proposed Plan of 1764 for the Future Management of Indian Affairs," *Am. Hist. Rev.*, July 1915; W. H. Mohr, *Federal Indian Relations* (1933).]   W. H. S—t.

STUART, JOHN TODD (Nov. 10, 1807–Nov. 28, 1885), Illinois lawyer and congressman, though prominent in his own right is chiefly remembered as the friend, first partner, and political mentor of Abraham Lincoln [*q.v.*]. Among the prime factors of his life were his Scotch-Irish ancestry, his Kentucky background, and his Southern traditions. Born near Lexington, Ky., he came of substantial family, his father, Robert Stuart, being a Presbyterian minister, formerly of Virginia, who became the first professor of languages in Transylvania University. His mother, Hannah Todd, was the daughter of Gen. Levi Todd; he was thus a cousin of Mary Todd Lincoln [*q.v.*]. He graduated from Centre College, Danville, Ky., in 1826, was licensed as an attorney in 1827, and in 1828 made the rough journey on horseback to Springfield, Ill., then a small frontier village, where he opened a law office. He enlisted as a private in the Black Hawk War, was elected major, served in the same battalion as Lincoln, and, like Lincoln, reënlisted after discharge. Follower and admirer of Henry Clay, he soon became the leading spirit among the Whigs of the Sangamon region. After serving in the state legislature (1832–36), he sought election to Congress. He was defeated in the congressional election of 1836; but in 1838 he defeated Stephen A. Douglas in a contest which was spectacular and wholly remarkable. It was a rough frontier election in which the candidates used "veritable stumps, ox carts, . . . barrels, [or] the canal dump . . ." for platforms (Stevens, *post*, p. 317); and so close was the race that Stuart won by a majority of 36 in a total vote of over 36,000. Reëlected in 1840, he served four years in Congress (1839–43), being a member of the important committee on territories. On Oct. 25, 1837, he married Mary Virginia Nash of Jacksonville, Ill. There were six children of this union.

As a lawyer Stuart first practised independently, then (1833–37) in partnership with Henry E. Dummer. He had notably befriended Lincoln, with whom he had served in the legislature, the two men being described as "congenial spirits" who "seemed inseparable" (Angle, *post*, p. 17); and in April 1837 the *Sangamo Journal* announced the firm of Stuart and Lincoln at "Office No. 4, Hoffman's Row, up stairs." This partnership, which was most influential in Lincoln's life, lasted until 1841; in 1843 Benjamin S. Edwards and in 1860 C. C. Brown were added to the firm. Meanwhile, Stuart was again elected to public office, serving in the state Senate, 1848–52. He was typical of that group of old-line Whigs who opposed the Republican party: he supported Bell in 1860 and, while steadfastly loyal to the Union, became during the war an active opponent of the Lincoln administration, whose emancipation policy he abominated. This circumstance led to a striking result in 1862 when as Democratic candidate for Congress he defeated the administration candidate, Leonard Swett, in the President's own district. Seeking reëlection in 1864, however, he was defeated by Shelby M. Cullom. He continued his law work long after the war and found time for active connection with such enterprises as the Springfield City Railway Company, the Bettie Stuart Institute (a school for girls), the Illinois Watch Company, the building of the state house, and the Lincoln monument association, of which he was president.

Stuart was tall, sturdy, and strikingly handsome. The law was his life work: entering the profession as a mere youth he practised with distinction for over fifty years. He discouraged frivolous litigation, putting soundness of argu-

ment, clarity of statement, and honesty, above cleverness. His personal relationships were of the finest. When opposing Lincoln during the war he was careful to say: "Difference in political opinion since 1856 has in no wise diminished my respect for the man or the . . . confidence I have ever had in his . . . integrity" (Angle, 39). Vigorous in old age, he was steadily at work until a week before his death.

[Paul M. Angle, *One Hundred Years of Law: An Account of the Law Office Which John T. Stuart Founded . . .* (1928); A. J. Beveridge, *Abraham Lincoln: 1809–1858* (2 vols., 1928); *Biog. Dir. Am. Cong.* (1928); J. M. Palmer, *The Bench and Bar of Ill.* (1899), I, 187–90; C. C. Brown, "Major John T. Stuart," *Trans. Ill. State Hist. Soc.*, 1902, pp. 109–14; H. E. Pratt, "The Repudiation of Lincoln's War Policy in 1862," *Jour. Ill. State Hist. Soc.*, Apr. 1931; F. E. Stevens, "Life of Stephen A. Douglas," *Ibid.*, Oct. 1923–Jan. 1924; Joseph Wallace, *Past and Present of . . . Springfield* (2 vols., 1904), I, 44–45; *Chicago Legal News*, Dec. 5, 1885; *Chicago Daily Tribune*, Dec. 1, 1885.]
J. G. R—l.

STUART, MOSES (Mar. 26, 1780–Jan. 4, 1852), clergyman and Biblical scholar, was born at Wilton, Conn. His father, Isaac Stuart, a descendant of Robert Stewart, who was in Norwalk, Conn., about 1660, was a farmer; his mother, Olive (Morehouse) Stuart, who possessed somewhat more education than her husband, exercised a decisive influence in interesting her son in books. He learned to read at the age of four and exhibited unusual intelligence in childhood. In his fifteenth year he was sent to an academy at Norwalk, Conn., where he made a brilliant record. He entered the sophomore class at Yale in May 1797, and two years later was graduated at the head of his class, having done particularly well in mathematics. For the first year after his graduation he taught in an academy at North Fairfield (later Easton), Conn. During part of the following year he was principal of a high school at Danbury, which he left in order to continue his study of law in Newtown. He was admitted to the bar at Danbury in 1802, but, having received an appointment for two years as tutor at Yale, he never practised law. At Yale he became interested in religion, owing to the influence of President Timothy Dwight, 1752–1817 [*q.v.*], and in 1803 he was licensed to preach. Ordained to the ministry on Mar. 5, 1806, he became pastor of the First Church of Christ (Congregational) in New Haven, where he rapidly achieved a considerable reputation as a preacher. Less than four years later, though he knew no Hebrew, he was called to the professorship of sacred literature at Andover Theological Seminary, Andover, Mass., and was inaugurated on Feb. 28, 1810.

At that time there was probably no native-born

American who knew enough Hebrew to teach it properly. Biblical studies were entirely neglected, and the minister who showed too much interest in European Biblical scholarship was suspected of heterodoxy. (See Stuart's "Letter to the Editor, on the Study of the German Language," *Christian Review*, September 1841, p, 448.) He began at once to study Hebrew seriously and wrote a short Hebrew grammar which he circulated among his students in manuscript. In 1821 he imported a font of Hebrew type and printed a larger Hebrew grammar, the first to appear in America. Since no compositor was able to handle it, he had to set most of the type himself. In eight years he was able to add fonts of type for eleven oriental scripts. Having mastered Hebrew, he attacked the study of German. While it was hard to convince theologians and clergymen of the value of Hebrew, it was much more difficult to induce them to study German scholarly literature. Indeed, it was twenty years before Stuart's fight for the recognition of the importance of German scholarly work can be said to have triumphed. His translations include *A Greek Grammar of the New Testament* (1825), from the German of Georg Benedikt Winer, done with Edward Robinson, 1794–1863 [*q.v.*], and *Hebrew Grammar of Gesenius as Edited by Roediger* (1846), also from the German. In a series of elaborate commentaries (published 1827–52) on *Hebrews, Romans, Revelation, Daniel, Ecclesiastes,* and *Proverbs,* he showed in detail how German scholarship had revolutionized the field of Biblical studies. Among his most important other books are his *Letters to the Rev. Wm. E. Channing Containing Remarks on His Sermon Recently Preached and Published at Baltimore* (1819), *Letters on the Eternal Generation of the Son of God, Addressed to the Rev. Samuel Miller, D.D.* (1822); *Elements of Interpretation; Translated from the Latin of J. A. Ernesti* (1822), and *Critical History and Defence of the Old Testament Canon* (1845). Altogether he published almost forty books and brochures, a remarkable achievement when it is realized that he was the first American theologian to become favorably known abroad, and that the quality of his work was sufficiently good to deserve an encomium from Friedrich A. G. Tholuck.

His mental energy was enormous. Indeed, it was so far ahead of his physical stamina that he was obliged to restrict himself to four hours of study and writing a day, during which he refused to permit any interruption. He was extremely gifted as a teacher and lecturer, and exerted a remarkable influence through his students. He taught more than 1,500 ministers, and some seventy men who later became professors or presidents of colleges. In 1848 he resigned his chair, but he continued his studies and wrote several more books. Four years later he died of an illness which was said to be influenza accompanied by typhoid fever. In 1806 he had married Abigail, daughter of James Clark of Danbury, by whom he had four sons and five daughters. One of his sons was Isaac William Stuart; Austin Phelps [*qq.v.*] was twice his son-in-law. Calvin Ellis Stowe [*q.v.*] of Andover, who knew him well, describes him as "tall, muscular, and lean; with a sharp and eager face and with rapid, nervous movements" (Sprague, *post*).

[E. A. Park, *A Discourse Delivered at the Funeral of Professor Moses Stuart* (Boston, 1852); William Adams, *A Discourse on the Life and Services of Professor Moses Stuart* (New York, 1852); W. B. Sprague, *Annals of the Am. Pulpit*, vol. II (1857), pp. 475–81; F. B. Dexter, *Biog. Sketches Grads. Yale Coll.*, vol. V (1911); A. P. Stokes, *Memorials of Eminent Yale Men* (1914), vol. I; J. G. Davenport, and Sarah Stuart Robbins, in *Conn. Mag.*, 1907, no. 1; S. A. Allibone, *A Critical Dict. of Eng. Lit.*, vol. II (1870), for bibliog. and list of reviews; Leonard Woods, *Hist. of the Andover Theological Sem.* (1885); *Gen. Cat. of the Theological Seminary, Andover, Mass., 1808–1908* (1909), with portrait; death notice in *Daily Evening Transcript* (Boston), Jan. 5, 1852.]

W. F. A.

STUART, ROBERT (Feb. 19, 1785–Oct. 29, 1848), fur trader, was the son of John and Mary (Buchanan) Stuart, and was born in Callander, Perthshire, Scotland. Except that he received a good common-school education, little is known of his youth. In 1807 he arrived in Montreal to join his uncle, David Stuart, then an agent of the North West Fur Company, and sometime later entered the fur company's service. In the spring of 1810 he met Wilson Price Hunt [*q.v.*], who had gone to Montreal to complete the organization of John Jacob Astor's Pacific Fur Company, and following the example of his uncle he became a partner in the new organization. Arriving in New York, he took lodgings in Brooklyn, where he met Elizabeth Emma Sullivan, to whom three years later, on July 21, 1813, he was married. On Sept. 6 of that year he took passage on the *Tonquin* with the expedition for the Columbia. From the time of the arrival on Mar. 25, 1811, Stuart was active and efficient in the affairs of the colony. In the summer of 1812 he was chosen by the partners as a courier to carry dispatches overland to Astor, and on June 29, with six companions, one of whom was Ramsay Crooks [*q.v.*], he left Astoria. After a perilous journey, attended by extreme privation and suffering, over a route which in considerable part had never before been seen by white men, the little party arrived in St. Louis on Apr. 30, 1813.

From St. Louis Stuart hurried on to New

York, where the dispatches were delivered. Astor employed both men, Stuart for several years serving as a traveling agent in the East, and later as Crooks's assistant at Mackinac. About 1820, on the transfer of Crooks to New York, Stuart succeeded him, and for the next fourteen years he remained as the head of the American Fur Company for the upper lakes region. A man of great executive ability, energetic, politic, and shrewd, he managed the organization's affairs with signal success, being particularly interested in 1824 in lobbying for high duties for blankets and guns for trading purposes. For a short time after Astor's retirement and Crooks's assumption of the presidency of the reorganized company in 1834, he appears to have remained at Mackinac, but in 1835 he established a home in Detroit. Here he invested heavily in real estate, and with ample time on his hands busied himself in civic, educational, and church affairs. In 1837 and again in 1839 he was director of the Detroit poor. In 1840 he was appointed by the governor to fill a vacancy as state treasurer—an office which he held for more than a year, and, from early in 1841 to Apr. 14, 1845, he was superintendent of Indian affairs for Michigan. Business in connection with the project of constructing a canal from Lake Michigan to the Illinois River took him, in the fall of 1845, to Chicago, where he became the secretary of the Canal Company's trustees. Here, three years later, he was seized with a sudden illness, from which he died. The body was returned to Detroit for burial. His widow, two daughters, and three sons survived him. His son David became a prominent attorney in Detroit, a representative in Congress, and, as a soldier in the Civil War, attained the rank of brigadier-general.

Stuart is described by a contemporary as "a severe man in all things," including family discipline and religious observance (Palmer, *post*, p. 537). At Mackinac he had come under the influence of the Presbyterian missionary, the Rev. William M. Ferry, who seems to have converted him from a state of complete indifference to religion to one of zealotry, and tamed considerably the hot-headedness which, on one occasion, led him to fracture the skull of a worker who became unruly. He became deeply concerned about many of the questions of his time. Though opposed to outright abolition of slavery, he was a friend and helper of runaway slaves; he was an advocate of justice to the Indian, of temperance, of better educational facilities, of adequate relief for the poor. The characterization made of him as a "severe man," however, is not borne out by his letters, especially those to Crooks, which re-

veal in him a warm-hearted friendliness and an engaging playfulness of mood.

[*Michigan Pioneer Colls.*, vol. III (188:), pp. 52–56; Friend Palmer, *Early Days in Detroit* (1906); Leo C. Lillie, *Historic Grand Haven and Ottawa County* (1931); Silas Farmer, *The Hist. of Detroit* (2nd ed., 1889), vol. I; E. O. Wood, *Historic Mackinac*, 2 vols. (1918); *Wis. Hist. Soc. Colls.*, vols. XIX, XX (1910–11); Kenneth W. Porter, *John Jacob Astor, Business Man*, 2 vols. (1931); *Daily Free Press* (Detroit), Nov. 1, 1848. The account of the journey from Astoria is given in Stuart's journal and traveling memoranda as printed in Philip A. Rollins' *The Discovery of the Oregon Trail* (1935), and is summarized in Washington Irving, *Astoria* (1836), and in H. M. Chittenden, *The Am. Fur Trade of the Far West*, 2 vols. (rev. ed., 1935).]
W. J. G.

STUART, ROBERT LEIGHTON (July 21, 1806–Dec. 12, 1882), sugar refiner, philanthropist, was born in New York City, one of the two sons of Kinloch and Agnes Stuart, who had arrived in America the year before from Edinburgh, Scotland. The father was a confectioner in a small way on the lower West Side of the city. He prospered moderately and at his death in 1826 he left to his wife and sons a profitable business, which seems to have been conducted in the widow's name until Robert reached his majority.

In 1828 Robert and his younger brother, Alexander, formed a partnership under the name of R. L. and A. Stuart, which lasted for half a century. They continued the candy business until 1856 but for the greater part of the time the chief activity of the firm was the refining and marketing of sugar. In 1832 they began the use of steam, then a new agency in sugar-refining processes. At first the capacity of their plant did not exceed 3,000 pounds a day, but a new building opened in 1835 enabled them to quadruple their product; fifteen years later the output was raised to over 40,000,000 pounds annually, valued at $3,000,000. During the succeeding twenty years the industry yielded good profits, but in the early seventies the Stuarts faced the necessity of introducing much new and costly machinery and of building refineries on the water front if they were to withstand competition. Rather than take such risks with their capital, they preferred to retire from the field.

With the beginning of their business prosperity the brothers had entered on a program of systematic giving to Presbyterian benevolences. From 1852 to 1879 (the year of Alexander's death) they gave in this way well over $1,000,-000, including large sums to the Presbyterian Hospital, Princeton Theological Seminary, and Princeton College. Robert was married in 1835 to Mary, daughter of Robert McCrea, one of the leading dry-goods importers and merchants of New York. She, too, was of Scotch Presbyterian ancestry and fully sympathized with her husband in all his religious and philanthropic activities. She also helped him to acquire an art collection of some distinction in its day. In the nine years of her widowhood she consistently carried on the Stuart tradition of generous giving. The outcome of the agitation for Sunday opening of museums, to which her husband had been opposed, constrained her, however, to withhold the funds over which she had stewardship from every institution adopting Sunday opening as a policy. Consequently, she revoked large bequests already made in her will to the American Museum of Natural History, of which her husband had been president (1872–81), and the Metropolitan Museum of Art. She had no children, and after her death more than $4,000,000 was distributed to various societies and institutions. The Stuart pictures and books went to the Lenox Library, later incorporated with the New York Public Library. By perpetual inhibition the room containing those collections is closed to the public on Sundays.

[*Evening Post* (N. Y.), Dec. 13, 1882; W. M. MacBean, *Biog. Reg. of St. Andrew's Soc. of the State of N. Y.*, vol. II (1925); George Wilson, *Portrait Gallery of the Chamber of Commerce of the State of N. Y.* (1890); H. F. Osborn, *The Am. Museum of Natural Hist.* (1910); P. L. Vogt, *The Sugar Refining Industry in the U. S.* (1908); J. L. Bishop, *A Hist. of Am. Manufactures*, II (1864), 593–94; H. M. Lydenberg, *Hist. of the N. Y. Pub. Lib.* (1923); *N. Y. Times*, Dec. 13, 1882; *N. Y. Tribune*, Jan. 1, 6, 1892.]   W. B. S.

STUART, RUTH McENERY (May 21, 1849– May 6, 1917), author, was the eldest of the eight children of James and Mary Routh (Stirling) McEnery of Marksville, Avoyelles Parish, La. Her father was born in Limerick, Ireland; her mother, of St. Francisville, La., was the daughter of Sir John Stirling, a Scotchman from Edinburgh. Plantation owners and professional and business men, the Stirlings and McEnerys and their kinsfolk were also active in affairs of state. From the age of three Ruth McEnery lived in New Orleans, where she attended both public and private schools and for several years taught in the primary grades. On Aug. 6, 1879, she married Alfred Oden Stuart, a cotton planter of Washington, Ark. She had one child, a son, who died in 1904. In 1883 her husband died, and she returned to New Orleans. She now began to turn to account a remarkably full and accurate knowledge of Southern "characters"—Louisiana Creoles, New Orleans trades- and market-people, plantation negroes, Arkansas "poor whites." Her first story appeared in the *New Princeton Review* in January 1888; her second, the characteristic "Lamentations of Jeremiah Johnson," in *Harper's New Monthly Magazine*, May 1888.

In the early nineties she moved to New York City. Between 1891 and 1917 she published more than twenty books, most of them collections of humorous short stories, sketches, and verses reprinted from *Harper's*, the *Century Illustrated Monthly Magazine*, and other magazines. These include *A Golden Wedding and Other Tales* (1893), *Carlotta's Intended and Other Tales* (1894); *Solomon Crow's Christmas Pockets and Other Tales* (copyright 1896); *In Simpkinsville; Character Tales* (1897); *Napoleon Jackson, the Gentleman of the Plush Rocker* (1902); *The Second Wooing of Salina Sue, and Other Stories* (copyright 1898); *Aunt Amity's Silver Wedding, and Other Stories* (1909); *The Unlived Life of Little Mary Ellen* (copyright 1910); and *Daddy Do-Funny's Wisdom Jingles* (1913). She also became well and favorably known as a public reader of her own compositions. Occasionally, for brief periods, she served as substitute editor of *Harper's Bazar* and other publications. Though always an industrious writer, she made many friends, for she possessed charm and sympathy, and her vivacious and witty conversation made her a delightful companion.

Her fiction was well received, not wholly, it may be thought, because the South had recently become an interesting literary subject, or because she wrote with a sometimes extravagant humor and with sentiment and optimism—rewarding the deserving, finding the long lost, and uniting the long separated. She was the first to describe the after-the-War plantation negro in his own social environment; she had a genuine affectionate sympathy for the originals of her characters; and she had an extraordinary skill in the use of the habitual locutions of her illiterate whites and blacks, a manner of speaking manifestly no one's invention, accurate in spirit and letter. While her plantation negroes are probably her most notable creations, her "Simpkinsville" people have contributed greatly to the gaiety of her books, and an Arkansas "poor white" story, *Sonny* (1896), has been her most popular work, and is very characteristic. Its chapters are monologues in dialect; its humor is of the laughter-provoking kind; and its people, if not lovable, are at least made likable by their author's affection for them.

[See *Who's Who in America*, 1916–17; E. L. Stevens, in *Lib. of Southern Lit.*, vol. XI (1909), ed. by E. A. Alderman, etc.; *The South in the Building of the Nation* (copr. 1909), vol. XII, ed. by J. A. C. Chandler, etc.; *Lib. of the World's Best Lit.*, vol. XXIV (1897), ed. by C. D. Warner; Candace Wheeler, in *Harper's Bazar*, Dec. 16, 1899, with portrait; Julia R. Tutwiler, in *Bookman*, Feb. 1904, with portrait; *La. Hist. Soc. Pubs.*, vol. X (1918); G. W. Nott, in *New Orleans Item*, July 10, 1927; H. B. McKenzie, in *Arkansas Gazette*, Aug. 27, 1924; article by Kate Chopin reprinted in D. S. Rankin, *Kate Chopin and Her Creole Stories* (1932); editorial in *N. Y. Times* Bk. Rev., May 13, 1917; obituary in *Times-Picayune* (New Orleans), May 8, 1917. Biog. information has been supplied by a member of the McEnery family.]   R. R. K.

STUB, HANS GERHARD (Feb. 23, 1849–Aug. 1, 1931), Norwegian Lutheran clergyman, the son of Hans Andreas and Ingeborg Margrethe (Arentz) Stub, was born at Muskego, Wis., where his father, an emigrant from Norway in 1848, and one of the founders of the Norwegian Synod, was pastor. At the age of twelve Stub accompanied his father to Bergen, Norway, where he attended the Cathedral School from 1861 to 1865. Upon their return he attended Luther College, Decorah, Iowa, for one year and received the A.B. degree in 1866. From 1866 to 1869 he attended Concordia College, Fort Wayne, Ind., and then for three years the Concordia Theological Seminary, St. Louis, Mo. He was ordained in 1872 and for the next five years was a pastor in Minneapolis, Minn. He was professor in Luther Seminary at Madison, Wis., and later at Robinsdale, Minn., from 1878 to 1896, with the exception of one year of study at the University of Leipzig (1881–82). He served as pastor in Decorah, Iowa, from 1896 to 1900, doing part-time teaching in Luther College, and from 1900 to 1916 was again professor in Luther College. He was vice-president of the Norwegian Synod, 1905–11, and president, 1911–17. In 1906 he was a member of a group of Norwegian-Americans who made a voyage to Norway to attend the coronation of King Haakon VII and while there was decorated Knight of the Order of St. Olav.

Stub's name is linked with two achievements especially notable in the eyes of his constituents: the raising of an endowment fund of $250,000 for Luther College, and the merging of the Norwegian Synod, the Hauges Synod, and the United Norwegian Lutheran Church into the Norwegian Lutheran Church of America in 1917. He was president of the new body until 1925, when he resigned to become president emeritus. He, more than any other, was the effecter of this union, negotiations for which had been going on for eleven years. In 1914 he made another visit to Norway, this time bringing along a "memorial gift" gathered among Norwegians in America for presentation at the Centennial. Royalty again favored him in 1914 when he became Commander of the Order of St. Olav, and, in 1922, wearer of the Grand Cross, a decoration which he was wont to display. From 1918 to 1920 he was president of the National Lutheran Council, a temporary concession of ecclesiastical sectionalism in the East to the West. He preached the opening ser-

mon at the Lutheran World Convention held in 1923 at Eisenach. He was joint or sole editor of *Evangelisk Luthersk Kirketidende*, 1889–1902, and of *Theologisk Tidsskrift*, 1899–1908, both uncompromisingly confessional-orthodox periodicals. He was the author of *Naadevalget* (1881); *Udvälgelsen* (1882), a defense of the Missourian doctrine of predestination and election; *Mod Frimureriet* (1882), an attack on Freemasonry; and *Kristofer Jansen og Ludvig Helger* (1894). He wrote on pioneer days, "Fra Fars og Mors Tid," for the periodical *Symra* in 1907. The surveys, *Hvad staar iveien?* (1911) and "Lidt af den nyere kirkehistorie iblandt os," in *Lutheraneren*, 1920–22, summarize local doctrinal conquests hoped for and achieved through ecclesiastical union. Numerous American institutions conferred honorary degrees on him.

Stub was married three times. His first wife, Diderikke Aall Ottesen, to whom he was married on Aug. 11, 1876, bore him two sons and died in 1879. He was married to Valborg Hovind, of Christiania, Norway, on July 31, 1884, and they had one son. She died in 1901, and, on Aug. 8, 1906, he was married to Anna Skabo, also of Christiania, who, with the three sons by former marriages, survived him when he died in St. Paul. Stub was the image of the aristocratic clergyman of Norway a century ago. His ways were gently condescending, his actions studied. He moved with ease and dignity in admiring circles who yearned for the authority and splendor of an ecclesiastical age gone by. He was a pulpit orator of ability, a theological professor reproductive but not creative, an organizer too prone to identify his doings with those of the Lord, as in the case of the merging of 1917, in which he saw a partial fulfilment of John 17:21.

[*Who's Who in America*, 1930–31; J. A. Bergh, *Den Norsk Lutherske Kirkes Historie i Amerika* (1914); *Luther Coll. Through Sixty Years* (1922); *Who's Who Among Pastors in all the Norwegian Luth. Synods of America* (rev. ed., 1928); *Lutheraneren*, Oct. 14, 1931; *Minneapolis Sunday Tribune*, Aug. 2, 1931.]
                                         J. O. E.

STUCK, HUDSON (Nov. 11, 1863–Oct. 10, 1920), Protestant Episcopal clergyman, archdeacon of the Yukon, was born in Paddington, London, England, the son of James and Jane (Hudson) Stuck. He attended Westbourne Park Public School and King's College, London. In 1885 he came to America and within three years was acting principal in the public schools of San Angelo, Tex. While in San Angelo he served as a lay reader in the Episcopal Church, and in 1889 he entered the Theological Department of the University of the South, Sewanee, Tenn. He was ordained priest in 1892 and became rector of

Grace Church, Cuero, Tex. In 1894 he was made dean of St. Matthew's Cathedral at Dallas, Tex., where he remained ten years, during this period establishing St. Matthew's Grammar School and a home for old people. He was a deputy to the General Conventions of the Protestant Episcopal Church in 1898, 1901, and 1913. Resigning from St. Matthew's in 1904, he became archdeacon of the Yukon under Bishop Peter Trimble Rowe, first missionary bishop of Alaska, and in this capacity served until the end of his life. He apparently never relinquished his British nationality.

Stuck's articles published in the *Spirit of Missions* in 1909 are interesting but conventional accounts of his work as a missionary; in 1920 he published *The Alaskan Missions of the Episcopal Church*. More noteworthy are his descriptions of the Yukon country. His *Ten Thousand Miles With a Dog Sled* (1914) and *Voyages on the Yukon and Its Tributaries* (1917) describe his travels at different seasons; the latter book was characterized by Cyrus C. Adams (*Geographical Review*, August 1920, p. 118) as "a fairly complete summary of Alaska, in most of its aspects." In 1913, with Harry P. Karstens, R. G. Tatum, and Walter Harper, he made the first complete ascent of Mount McKinley. In his descriptions of the achievement—an article in *Scribner's Magazine* (November 1913) and a book, *The Ascent of Denali* (1914), he urged that the native names of Denali, "the great one," and Denali's Wife be returned to Mount McKinley and Mount Foraker. In March 1919 the Royal Geographical Society bestowed the Back Grant upon him in recognition of his travels in Alaska and his ascent of Mount McKinley. He always regretted his lack of scientific training for exploration, but his careful observation was highly regarded by the scientific bodies before which he lectured and he was a fellow of both the Royal Geographical Society and the American Geographical Society. His last book, *A Winter Circuit of Our Arctic Coast* (1920), is the record of a journey—considered a greater *tour de force* than his ascent of Mount McKinley—made in the winter of 1917–18 when temperatures in the interior went down to —60°.

Stuck's writings reveal him as a warm and forceful character. The breadth of his culture is shown especially in *A Winter Circuit,* which deserves a place among belles-lettres. In all his books he stressed the peaceable and tractable nature of the Eskimos and Indians and stated his conviction that they are capable of considerable development. On the ground that the frontier of civilization always attracts the least desirable element of society, he pleaded for mission work

in Alaska as a means of protecting the natives against unscrupulous adventurers and counteracting their detrimental influence by the influence of men of a higher type. Convinced of the civilizing power of books, he established a library in Fairbanks.

Stuck never married. He died at the home of Dr. Grafton Burke, Fort Yukon, Alaska, where St. Stephen's Hospital (since 1921 the Archdeacon Stuck Memorial Hospital) had been built largely through his influence. Two funds have been established in his memory: one of $25,000, given in part by Indians and other people in Alaska, to be used for medical work at Fort Yukon; the other, of $18,000, given to the University of the South.

[*Who's Who in America*, 1920–21; *Who's Who* (British), 1920; *Spirit of Missions*, Jan., July, Aug. 1921; *Churchman*, Oct. 23, 1920; *Geog. Rev.* (N. Y.), Apr. 1921; *Geog. Jour.* (London), Jan., Sept. 1914, Oct. 1918, Mar., Apr., July 1919, Jan. 1921; *Evening Star* (Washington, D. C.), Oct. 13, 1920; *Alaska Daily Empire* (Juneau), Oct. 12, 1920; information from the bishops of N. Y., La., and Tenn., from officials of the University of the South, from Dr. John W. Wood, Exec. Sec., Nat. Council, P. E. Church, and from other personal acquaintances; letters from a sister, Miss Caroline Stuck, Heathfield, Sussex, England.]

E. W. H.

STUCKENBERG, JOHN HENRY WILBRANDT (Jan. 6, 1835–May 28, 1903), theologian, sociologist, the son of Herman Rudolph and Anna Maria (Biest) Stuckenberg, was born at Bramsche, Hanover, Germany. His name before it was anglicized was Johann Heinrich Willbrand Stuckenberg. With his mother, three sisters, and one brother, he came to Pittsburgh, Pa., in 1839 to join his father and eldest sister, who had emigrated two years before. The family finally settled in Cincinnati, Ohio, where young Stuckenberg received most of his early schooling. He received his college and theological education at Wittenberg College, Springfield, Ohio, and was graduated with the A.B. degree in 1857 and the theological degree in 1858. He was pastor of a Lutheran congregation in Davenport, Iowa, for a year and then studied in the University of Halle, Germany, from 1859 to 1861. He was chaplain in the 145th Pennsylvania Volunteers from September 1862 to October 1863, served another congregation of the General Synod from 1863 to 1865 in Erie, Pa., and again went to Germany, where he studied from 1865 to 1867 in the universities of Göttingen, Tübingen, and Berlin. Pastorates in Indianapolis, Ind., and in Pittsburgh occupied him from 1867 to 1873, when he was made professor of exegesis in Wittenberg College. In 1880, for the third time, he went to Germany, this time to stay for fourteen years as pastor of the American Church in Berlin.

Stuckenberg derived unusual intellectual and social benefits from his Berlin pastorate, combining with extraordinary fruitfulness the duties of pastor, student adviser, lecturer, and author. He also enjoyed contacts with many of the faculty members of the university in Berlin, and was a member of the Philosophical Society of Berlin. He was a regular visitor to the large libraries, had access to all kinds of source material and professional periodicals, and was an indefatigable writer. Many of his articles are to be found in the *Evangelical Quarterly Review* (see particularly, January 1865, April 1867, July 1869), and the *Quarterly Review of The Evangelical Lutheran Church* (see January 1871, July 1876, April 1880, July 1886). He was for some time editor of the *Lutheran Quarterly* and of the *Evangelist*, and wrote for the *Andover Review* and the *American Journal of Theology*. His weightiest contributions appeared in a series of 200 articles in the *Homiletic Review* from 1884 to 1902, and for many years was in charge of its department of Christian sociology.

Among American writers, Stuckenberg's work in sociology places him beside Lester F. Ward [*q.v.*] as a pioneer in that field, although his treatment was largely philosophic while Ward was more concerned with natural scientific treatment. The problem of the state particularly attracted Stuckenberg. He made a particular study of international law, and was an ardent collector of maps, one of which was reproduced in 1895 in a New York paper as containing the key to the Venezuela territorial dispute. He was a champion of labor and in his later years lectured before many labor groups throughout the country. His most important books are: *Ninety-five Theses* (1868); *History of the Augsburg Confession* (1869); *Christian Sociology* (1880); *The Life of Immanuel Kant* (1882), the first biography of Kant in English; *Grundprobleme in Hume* (1885, pamphlet No. 13 of the 3rd Series issued by the Philosophical Society of Berlin); *The Final Science* (1885); *Introduction to the Study of Philosophy* (1888); *The Age and the Church* (1893); *Tendencies in German Thought* (1896); *The Social Problem* (1897); and *Introduction to the Study of Sociology* (1898). His *magnum opus* was *Sociology, The Science of Human Society* (2 vols., 1903).

Stuckenberg was a straight, tall, broad-shouldered man of commanding presence, quick of movement, fluent in speech, thoroughly at ease before his audiences. He was almost as well known in British circles as in American, his books receiving many elaborate and sympathetic reviews in leading English literary periodicals. He possessed a large library on theology, sociology, economics, political science, and philosophy, now in the library of Gettysburg College. He died in London, where he had gone to gather material for a new book. He was survived by his wife, Mary Gingrich, of Erie, Pa.; to whom he was married on Oct. 27, 1869. She was a leader in the Woman's Christian Temperance Union movement.

[A great amount of biographical material pertaining to Stuckenberg is now in the hands of the author of this sketch, by whom a biography is being prepared. Gettysburg College is in possession of his map collection. Besides the literature mentioned above, see *Who's Who in America*, 1901–02; *The New Schaff-Herzog Encyc. of Religious Knowledge*, vol. XI (1911); articles by S. G. Hefelbower in the *Luth. Observer*, Nov. 29, 1912; Harry E. Barnes in the *Luth. Quart.*, Oct. 1921, and C. T. Pihlblad in the *Ohio Sociologist*, Sept. 1928.]

J.O.E.

STUDEBAKER, CLEMENT (Mar. 12, 1831–Nov. 27, 1901), manufacturer of wagons and carriages, was of the fourth generation after Clement and Anna Catherine Studebecker, who arrived at Philadelphia in the ship *Harle* from Rotterdam on Sept. 1, 1736. They settled among their German brethren in what is now Adams County, Pa. John Studebaker, grandson of the immigrant, married Rebecca Mohler, a woman of exceptional character. Their fifth child and second son, Clement, better known throughout his life as Clem, was born on his father's farm at Pinetown, a few miles from Gettysburg, Pa. His father, having met with financial difficulties, moved his family and possessions, in wagons of his own manufacture, to Ashland County, Ohio, in 1836. Two years later his creditors dispossessed him of the one hundred and sixty acre farm he had bought, and he purchased a small tract where he was unsuccessful in a milling venture. He then rented a smaller patch and engaged in blacksmithing and wagon making.

Clem worked in his father's shop and on nearby farms and attended the district school. In 1850 he moved to the vicinity of South Bend, Ind., where he was engaged to teach the district school at fifteen dollars a month. Studying to make up the deficiencies in his own education, he successfully taught a winter and a spring term. In his free time he worked in a blacksmith shop for fifty cents a day. In the spring of 1852 he established, with his older brother Henry, the firm of H. & C. Studebaker. Their capital consisted of sixty-eight dollars and some blacksmith tools. In addition to doing ordinary blacksmith work, they made two wagons, the first of over three quarters of a million. The introduction of the railroad and the consequent development of agriculture in the Middle West increased the demand for wagons, and they supplied this demand with an excellent product. Quality was almost a fetish with them. The Studebakers' first notable advance came when they received a sub-contract for government wagons through George Milburn, Clem's future father-in-law. They sagaciously put the name of Studebaker on these and thus came to the notice of the government, which gave them many contracts. About 1857 Henry withdrew from the partnership. He was succeeded by another brother, John M., who had lately returned from California. In 1868 they organized the Studebaker Brothers Manufacturing Company with Clem Studebaker as its first president. Peter E. Studebaker joined his brothers at this time and, in 1870, established the company's first branch house at St. Joseph, Mo., to outfit emigrants crossing the plains. The youngest brother, Jacob F., joined them in 1870. The company thus formed became the largest manufacturer of horse-drawn vehicles in the world. Clem Studebaker was alive to the possibilities of self-propelled vehicles and began experiments with them in 1897. The manufacture of both electric and gasoline automobiles was begun by the company soon after his death.

Studebaker was in all respects an admirable character. He was a man of good judgment and high moral standards. Despite his limited formal education he maintained a home and social life of culture and refinement. Men of distinction, including Presidents Grant, Harrison, and McKinley, and leaders in industry, literature, and science were entertained in his home. His parents were German Baptists or Dunkers but he became a Methodist and an influence in the Church. He presented the congregation at South Bend with a church edifice. A strong Republican, he became prominent in party councils. As a delegate to the presidential convention of 1880 he was a member of the old-guard contingent that held out in vain for Grant. In 1888 he was again a delegate to the Republican National Convention. He represented Indiana at the Paris Exposition in 1878, the Centennial Exposition in Cincinnati in 1888, and the World's Columbian Exposition in Chicago in 1893. President Harrison appointed him a delegate to the Pan-American Congress in Washington in 1889. He was active in the educational activities of the Methodist Church, being for many years a trustee and for a time president of the Chautauqua Association, a member of the book committee which supervised the publications of the church, and a trustee and benefactor of De Pauw University. His first wife was Charity M. Bratt, by whom he had two children

who died in infancy. She died in 1863, and in 1864 he married Ann Milburn Harper, daughter of George Milburn of Mishawaka, Ind. To this union were born three children.

[Information furnished by C. A. Carlisle, including a manuscript life of Studebaker approved by the subject; *Ashland Times*, Oct. 13, 1897, containing autobiog. account read by Studebaker at a reunion at Ashland, Ohio, in 1897; *South Bend Daily Times*, Nov. 27, 1901; *Who's Who in America*, 1901–02; *Hist. of St. Joseph County, Ind.* (1880); *A Biog. Hist. of Eminent and Self-Made Men of the State of Ind.* (1880), vol. II; *Pictorial and Biog. Memoirs of Elkhart and St. Joseph Counties, Ind.* (1893); T. E. Howard, *Hist. of St. Joseph County, Ind.* (2 vols., 1907); I. H. Betz, "The Studebaker Brothers, the Wagon Builders of South Bend, Ind.," *Pennsylvania-German*, Apr. 1910; A. R. Erskine, *Hist. of the Studebaker Corporation* (1924); *Chicago Tribune*, Nov. 28, 1901; St. Joseph County, Ind., Marriage Record, V, 227.] R. H. A.

STURGIS, RUSSELL (Oct. 16, 1836–Feb. 11, 1909), architect, critic, writer, was born in Baltimore, Md., the son of Russell and Margaret D. (Appleton) Sturgis. His father, then living temporarily in Baltimore, was a shipping merchant and a commissioner of pilots in New York City; he was a descendant of Edward Sturgis who was in Charlestown, Mass., in 1634 and was one of the first settlers of Yarmouth. Sturgis was educated in the public schools of New York and in the Free Academy of the City of New York (later the College of the City of New York), from which he was graduated with the degree of A.B. in 1856. After a year as a student in the office of Leopold Eidlitz [q.v.], he went to Munich for a year and a half of study. He was associated with Peter Bonnett Wight [q.v.] from 1863 to 1868, and then practised alone until about 1880. His architectural practice included several New York town houses, the Flower Hospital (New York), and three interesting "model tenements" in West Nineteenth Street, New York, besides many country houses throughout the East. These are usually in current versions of the popular Néo-Grec or Victorian Gothic styles. He designed four buildings—Farnam, Durfee, and Lawrance halls, and Battell Chapel—for Yale University between 1870 and 1885. By far the most interesting example of his work is the Farmers' & Mechanics' Bank, Albany, N. Y., unusually delicate in scale, its style based on French work of the period of Louis XII. But it was not Sturgis' architecture that made him famous.

Soon after leaving college, Sturgis and a few friends, founders of the Society for the Advancement of Truth in Art, published a serious little art magazine (1863–64) called the *New Path*. The articles by Sturgis were its backbone, and they already revealed his deep critical interest in his profession. In 1868 he wrote a *Manual* of the Jarves Collection of Early Italian Pictures in the Yale School of Fine Arts . . . A Brief Guide to the Study of Early Christian Art (New Haven), and he soon began to contribute to such magazines as the Nation frequent articles interpreting not only architecture but the whole field of art to the layman. From 1878 to 1880 he held a chair in architecture and the arts of design at the College of the City of New York. After four years abroad with his family, chiefly in Florence and Paris, he was for a brief period secretary to the municipal civil service board of New York, but the political complications of the position were not to his taste, and he soon resigned to devote himself almost exclusively to writing. In addition to serving as art editor for various encyclopaedias and dictionaries, he edited "The Field of Art" in Scribner's Magazine from 1897 until his death. He was co-author with Charles Eliot Norton [q.v.] of a Catalogue of . . . Ancient and Modern Engravings, Woodcuts and Illustrated Books, Parts of the Collections of C. E. Norton and R. Sturgis (1879), editor-in-chief of A Dictionary of Architecture and Building (3 vols., 1901–02), editor of Outlines of the History of Art (2 vols., 1904), and author of a series of books (1903–08) on the appreciation of architecture, sculpture, and painting. In 1904 he gave the Scammon lectures at the Art Institute of Chicago, which were published as The Interdependence of the Arts of Design (1905). Of his shorter brochures, The Etchings of Piranesi (1900) and Ruskin on Architecture (1906) deserve notice. The climax of his writing career was the ambitious A History of Architecture (4 vols., 1906–15), on which he was working at the time of his death and of which he completed only two volumes. In his articles on contemporary architects published by the Architectural Record in the Great American Architects Series he gave vivid expression to the architectural ideals of his day, and pointed out with a canny discrimination both its shortcomings and its achievements.

As a critic he was less profound than provocative and persuasive. He was animated by a sincere passion for beauty in the largest sense, and he had as background an unusually wide knowledge of the history and technique of the arts. He wrote well, in an easy, sometimes over-facile style that caught the public ear. Though his history is seldom original in point of view, it is the work of a true connoisseur, alert, sensitive, discriminating, a man of trained and generally sound taste. He was not without prejudices, for the precepts of Ruskin colored his views for his entire life. Thus he could only view with disgust the overwhelming swing of popular taste towards

Renaissance and classic eclecticism which characterized the end of the nineteenth century. Perhaps it was this hatred of the classic phase which made him so prophetically alert to rebellions against it. To him Louis Henri Sullivan [q.v.] seemed the bearer of a new light, and again and again he pointed to Sullivan's work, revolutionary as it was, as the most significant that was being done in America. His writing was perhaps the most important single factor in the artistic reawakening of the American people that characterized the early years of the twentieth century.

"Curious in viands and vintages," he was as much a connoisseur in living as in the field of art. And he looked the part, with his white hair and his distinguished beard and thin, sensitive nose. A student to the end of his life, he went out but little; he had, however, to compensate, a small circle of close friends—Robert Underwood Johnson, Montgomery Schuyler, Richard Watson Gilder [q.v.], William Crary Brownell [q.v.], and especially John La Farge [q.v.], his most sympathetic companion. He lived for many years at 307 East Seventeenth St., which was his office and study, and housed his magnificent library and collection of prints, and it was there he died. He had married, May 26, 1864, Sarah Maria, daughter of Danford Newton Barney. They had three daughters and four sons, of whom one son died in infancy. Sturgis was a fellow of the American Institute of Architects, a member of the Architectural League of New York and its president, 1898–1902; a member and first president of the Fine Arts Federation of New York; and a trustee (1873–76) and corresponding secretary (1870–73) of the Metropolitan Museum of Art.

[R. E. Sturgis, Edward Sturgis of Yarmouth, Mass., 1613–1695, and His Descendants (1914); Who's Who in America, 1908–09; Who's Who in N. Y., 1907; E. P. Wheeler, in City Coll. Quart., Mar. 1909, with portraits; Montgomery Schuyler, in "The Field of Art," Scribner's Mag., May 1909; "Russell Sturgis's Architecture," in Architectural Record, June 1909; P. B. Wight, Ibid., Aug. 1909; obituaries in N. Y. Times and N. Y. Tribune, Feb. 12, 1909; information from Edward B. Sturgis, Sturgis' son.]   T.F.H.

STURGIS, SAMUEL DAVIS (June 11, 1822–Sept. 28, 1889), soldier, was born at Shippensburg, Pa., the son of James and Mary (Brandenburg) Sturgis, and a descendant of William Sturgis who came to Pennsylvania from Ireland about 1745. Samuel entered West Point, July 1, 1842, graduated July 1, 1846, and joined the 2nd Dragoons, with which he fought at Palo Alto and Resaca de la Palma. Before the battle of Buena Vista he volunteered for a reconnaissance which resulted in his capture but also in gaining essential information about the enemy. He remained a prisoner eight days. After the Mexican War he served in the West with the 1st Dragoons, in which he was promoted first lieutenant, July 15, 1853, and the 1st (now 4th) Cavalry, in which he was appointed captain, Mar. 3, 1855. At West Ely, Mo., July 5, 1851, he married Jerusha Wilcox, daughter of Jeremiah Wilcox of Akron, Ohio. He took part in an Indian campaign in New Mexico in 1855, the Utah expedition of 1858, and a campaign against the Kiowas and Comanches in 1860, after which he was charged with settling difficulties between white settlers and Indians on the "neutral lands" of the Cherokee border.

In 1861 he was in command at Fort Smith, Ark. All his officers resigned to join the Confederate army and the post was surrounded by hostile militia. Sturgis brought off his troops, however, with most of the government property under his care. He was promoted major, May 3, 1861. He fought at Wilson's Creek, succeeding to the command when Gen. Nathaniel Lyon [q.v.] was killed, and was appointed brigadier-general of volunteers with rank from Aug. 10, 1861, the date of the battle. He was in charge of the district of Kansas for a time and then commanded the defenses of the city of Washington until sent into the field for the second battle of Bull Run. He commanded a division of the IX Corps at South Mountain, Antietam, and Fredericksburg. At Antietam it was his division that carried the famous bridge, Sturgis himself leading the charge. He was transferred to the West with the IX Corps, and later had small commands in Tennessee and Mississippi, suffering a severe defeat by Gen. N. B. Forrest [q.v.] at Brice's Cross Roads (Guntown) in June 1864. Grant wrote to Stanton (Oct. 14, 1865): "Notwithstanding his failure at Guntown, Miss., I know him to be a good and efficient officer, far above the average of our cavalry colonels. From the beginning of the war he has suffered from having served in Kansas, and coming in contact with, and in opposition to, civilians, Senator Lane probably in the lead" (War Department records). He was mustered out of the volunteer army, Aug. 24, 1865, and went to duty as lieutenant-colonel of the 6th Cavalry, having been promoted Oct. 27, 1863. He became colonel of the 7th Cavalry, May 6, 1869, saw considerable service in Indian campaigns, was governor of the Soldiers' Home from 1881 to 1885, and retired in 1886. Criticism of his conduct at Brice's Cross Roads having been revived in 1882 he published *The Other Side as Viewed by Generals Grant, Sherman, and Other Distinguished Offi-*cers, Being a Defence of his Campaign into N. E. Mississippi in the Year 1864. He died at St. Paul, Minn. His son, Samuel Davis Sturgis, Jr., became a major-general in the regular army in 1921.

[*War of the Rebellion: Official Records (Army)*; *Battles and Leaders of the Civil War* (4 vols., 1887–88); *Twenty-first Ann. Reunion Asso. Grads. U. S. Mil. Acad.* (1890); G. W. Cullum, *Biog. Reg. Officers and Grads. U. S. Mil. Acad.* (3rd ed., 1891), vol. II; *Army and Navy Jour.*, Oct. 5, 1889; *Pioneer Press* (St. Paul, Minn.), Sept. 29, 1889; unpublished records in the War dept.; information from son.]   T. M. S.

STURGIS, WILLIAM (Feb. 25, 1782–Oct. 21, 1863), merchant, only son of William and Hannah (Mills) Sturgis, was born in Barnstable, Mass. His father, a Revolutionary soldier, was a Cape Cod shipmaster of repute; his mother was a daughter of the Rev. Jonathan Mills of Harwich, Mass. Sturgis was a descendant of Edward Sturgis, who settled in Charlestown in 1634 and in Yarmouth, Mass., in 1638. He had but little schooling, and when only fourteen was employed in counting houses in Boston. On the death of his father in 1797 he shipped as a sailor before the mast. The boy studied navigation and used every means to advance himself in his calling. His voyages took him to the Northwest coast, where the ships bartered goods with the Indians for furs. Sturgis made a study of the Indian languages, became an adept trader, and cultivated friendly relations with the natives, among whom he was popular. At the age of nineteen, with less than four years' experience, he became master of the ship *Caroline*. His cruises sometimes led him into perilous situations, as when his ship *Atahualpa* battled with pirates off the Chinese coast in August 1809. In 1810 he formed a partnership with John Bryant as resident Boston merchants and in the fifty-three years of their association created an ample fortune. It has been said that more than half of the trade carried on from the United States with China and other countries of the Pacific coast from 1810 to 1840 was under their direction (Loring, *post*, p. 433). They also had dealings in nearly every quarter of the globe. Sturgis married in 1810 Elizabeth Marston Davis, daughter of John Davis, 1761–1847 [q.v.], judge of the United States district court. There were six children of this marriage, one son and five daughters.

For twelve years between 1814 and 1846 Sturgis was a member of the Massachusetts House of Representatives; he was a state senator in 1827 and 1836, and a member of the convention for revising the constitution of Massachusetts in 1820. He was president of the Boston Marine Society and a member of the Massachusetts Historical Society, to whose activities he made important contributions and to whose funds he was a liberal benefactor. He contributed $10,000 to the observatory in Cambridge, and erected in Mount Auburn Cemetery, Cambridge, a monument to Dr. Johann Gaspar Spurzheim, the phrenologist, who died in Boston in 1832. Distinguished for a highly cultivated intellect and a remarkably extensive knowledge, he was of almost Spartan simplicity in his personal habits. He was conspicuous for his firm yet liberal principles, and a high sense of honor. In October 1822 he contributed an article to the *North American Review,* "Examination of the Russian Claims to the Northwest Coast of America," and on Aug. 4 and 5, 1843, two articles on the *Somers* naval mutiny to the *Boston Courier.* During the controversy between the United States and Great Britain over the Oregon boundary, his personal acquaintance with the region and his familiarity with its history were of highest importance to the American government. His pamphlet, *The Oregon Question* (1845), presented a valuable discussion of the question, while his private correspondence with distinguished statesmen, both at home and abroad, is said to have had no small influence in bringing the controversy to an amicable and satisfactory issue (*Ibid.,* p. 458). He died in Boston, survived by his wife and three daughters.

[R. F. Sturgis, *Edward Sturgis of Yarmouth, Mass., 1613–1695, and His Descendants* (priv. printed, 1914) ; C. G. Loring, in *Proc. Mass. Hist. Soc.,* 1 ser., vol. VII (1864), pp. 420–73; card index of members of Mass. legislature, State Lib., Boston; obituaries in *New Eng. Hist. and Geneal. Reg.,* Apr. 1864, and *Boston Transcript,* Oct. 22, 1863.]   W. M. E.

STURTEVANT, BENJAMIN FRANKLIN (Jan. 18, 1833–Apr. 17, 1890), inventor, manufacturer, was born at Martin's Stream, Norridgewock, Me. He was the son of Seth and Hulda (Besse) Sturtevant and a lineal descendant of Samuel Sturtevant who emigrated to Plymouth in 1642 from Rochester, Kent, England. Sturtevant's parents were poor and his father was in ill health so that the boy had little opportunity for an education, being compelled to help in supporting the family by laboring on a farm. Desiring something better, he left home when he was fifteen and worked his way to Northbridge, Mass., and then back to Skowhegan, Me., where he entered a cobbler's shop and during the next eight years became a skilled shoemaker.

This confining employment injured his health, however, and in the hope of bettering his condition he turned his attention to the possibility of devising a machine to peg boots and shoes. Although he possessed no knowledge of mechanics and had had no experience with machinery, he devised a crude model of a shoe-pegging machine in a few months. Proceeding immediately to Boston with the model but no money, he assigned one-half of his invention absolutely and the entire control of the remaining half to a local business man in return for a meager living wage. From 1857 to 1859 he was engaged in making improvements on the original machine, for which he secured five patents. Meanwhile, another patentee of a shoe-pegging machine, wholly worthless, met Sturtevant's backer and skilfully frightened him into believing that Sturtevant's ideas were infringements and open to possible lawsuits. As a result, Sturtevant lost his only financial support in addition to all rights in his patents, and was again penniless. He had not, however, divulged all of his ideas to his guarantor, and immediately turned his attention to peg-making machinery, realizing that any shoe-pegging machine was worthless without pegs. By December 1859 he had devised and patented (No. 26,627) a pegwood lathe which cut a spiral veneer from around a log, and by July 1862 (No. 35,902) the process and machinery for converting such veneer ribbons into pegs. This process involved drying the veneer, beveling one edge, which edge was then compressed and toughened (all by machinery of his invention) and the whole ribbon, usually 100 feet long, made into a roll ready for use in the shoe-pegging machines. Unfortunately, to obtain money for this work which consumed all of his time from 1860 to 1863, Sturtevant had to sell, bit by bit, most of the rights and other possible applications of these inventions, being able to retain for himself only such parts as applied to the production of shoe-pegs. One of the applications of his patents which he thus lost was for the manufacture of wooden toothpicks. Nevertheless, he secured enough capital to establish a ribbon pegwood manufactory at Conway, N. H., which was highly successful, having markets throughout the world.

The dust created by the buffing wheels in the early shoe factories was very annoying and about 1864 Sturtevant began considering ways and means of eliminating it. His solution of the problem was the invention of a rotary exhaust fan (patented Oct. 29, 1867) which within a comparatively short period he was supplying to the local trade in Boston. By applying the same mechanical features to the crude air blowers then existing he produced a greatly improved machine and developed so many new applications for it, such as pressure blowers, ventilating fans, and pneumatic conveyors, that he literally created a new industry. His business was at once successful and grew to such proportions that in 1878 he built a new plant at Jamaica Plain, Mass., which was the largest of its kind in the world. At the time of his death his manufactory produced over 5,000 blowers yearly and employed about 400 men. He gave liberally of the fortune he acquired to educational and religious institutions, contributing largely to Colby University, Vermont Academy, and Newton Theological Seminary. He was married at Norridgewock, Me., in 1852, to Phoebe R. Chamberlain and at the time of his death in Jamaica Plain was survived by his widow and two daughters.

[J. D. Van Slyck, *New England Manufacturers and Manufactories* (1879); W. B. Kaempffert, *A Popular Hist. of Am. Invention* (1924), vol. II; *Boston Daily Advertiser*, Apr. 18, 1890; *Boston Post*, Apr. 18, 1890; *Boston Transcript*, Apr. 17, 1890; Patent Office records; information from a son-in-law, W. V. Kellen, Esq.]
C. W. M—n.

STURTEVANT, EDWARD LEWIS (Jan. 23, 1842–July 30, 1898), agricultural scientist, the second of three sons of Lewis W. and Mary Haight (Leggett) Sturtevant, was born in Boston, Mass. The father traced his lineage to Samuel Sturtevant who landed at Plymouth in 1642, and the mother's family were Quakers who settled at West Farms, N. Y., about 1700. In Edward's childhood his parents died, leaving their sons to be reared by an aunt at Winthrop, Me., the father's birthplace. Having prepared for college at Blue Hill, Me., Sturtevant entered Bowdoin in 1859. To its classical course he was largely indebted for his ability as a writer and linguist. In 1861 he joined Company G, 24th Maine Volunteers, serving as lieutenant and captain until typhoid malaria contracted at Port Hudson compelled his return to Winthrop in 1863. He graduated from Bowdoin in that year and from the Harvard Medical School in 1866. He never practised medicine, but its training developed his interest in scientific research.

In 1867 the Sturtevant brothers purchased and began the development of "Waushakum Farm," near South Framingham, Mass., notable as the scene of "a series of brilliant experiments in agriculture which are still models in experimental acumen and conscientious execution" (Hedrick, in *Sturtevant's Notes, post,* p. 2). Their initial interest was a model dairy of Ayrshire cattle, based on stock which Sturtevant personally selected in Scotland. With his brother Joseph he prepared *The Dairy Cow: A Monograph on the Ayrshire Breed* (1875), long a standard work, and four volumes of the *North American Ayrshire Register* (South Framingham, 1875–80). His study of the physiology of milk and milk secretion was instrumental in gaining a general

audience for his research. For several years (1876–79) he was editor or coeditor of the *Scientific Farmer*. A lysimeter, the first in America, was erected at "Waushakum Farm" in 1875, and its records covering four years were presented at scientific meetings. His lifelong study of the history of edible plants resulted in many articles and books on the subject. To further this work he collected hundreds of books, including a valuable pre-Linnean library which, together with his herbarium and numerous notes, he presented to the Missouri Botanical Garden (catalogue in its *Seventh Annual Report,* 1896). His "Varieties of Corn" (*United States Experiment Station Bulletin,* no. 57, 1899) is an epitome of his twenty years' investigations of the maize plant. Among his practical achievements were the development of the Waushakum variety of yellow flint corn and the New Christiana muskmelon.

Sturtevant's eminence in agricultural research led to his being chosen the first director of the New York Agricultural Experiment Station at Geneva in 1882. During his administration he outlined the broad plans on which the work of the station has been developed, and assembled a small but notable corps of assistants. He was a leader in the movement for experiment stations and his objectives at Geneva were largely followed by the stations established under the Hatch Act of 1887.

In that year, having ample means, Sturtevant retired to his home at South Framingham to complete his historical study of edible plants. Beginning in 1893, he spent three winters in California in an unsuccessful attempt to secure relief from tuberculosis. His home life was singularly close and happy. He was married twice: on Mar. 9, 1864, to Mary Elizabeth Mann, who died in 1875, and on Oct. 22, 1883, to Hattie Mann, a sister of his first wife. By the first marriage he had two sons and two daughters, and by the second, one son. His eldest daughter, Grace, and his second wife supplied drawings for a number of his writings.

A man of small stature and nervous temperament, Sturtevant had an intensely active mind. He enjoyed analytical discussion and was always propounding new problems for solution. He was liberal with helpful suggestions to associates and to the scientific societies of which he was an active member. "He was not a great mingler with men, but he had a wide circle of friends and prized their friendship. Quiet by nature, a lover of his home and home life, he sought his greatest pleasures in his family, among his books or at his work" (Plumb, in *Proceedings, post,* p. 218). In 1919, more than two decades after his death

Sturtevant's Notes on Edible Plants was published under the editorship of U. P. Hedrick.

[Biog. sketch by U. P. Hedrick, and bibliog., in *Sturtevant's Notes on Edible Plants* (1919); U. P. Hedrick, *A Hist. of Agric. in the State of N. Y.* (1933); C. S. Plumb, in *Proc. of the Nineteenth Ann. Meeting of the Soc. for the Promotion of Agric. Sci.* (1898), in *Tenth Ann. Report Mo. Bot. Garden* (1899), with bibliog. and portrait, and in *Experiment Station Record*, vol. X (1898–99); W. C. Strong and B. P. Ware, in *Trans. Mass. Hort. Soc. for 1898* (1899); E. L. Sturtevant, "Joseph N. Sturtevant," *Scientific Farmer*, Feb. 1879; H. H. Wing, in L. H. Bailey, *Cyc. of Am. Agric.*, vol. IV (1909); L. H. Bailey, *Standard Cyc. of Hort.*, vol. III (1915); *Country Gentleman*, Aug. 4, 1898; *Bot. Gazette*, Sept. 1898; *Boston Transcript*, Aug. 1, 1898; G. N. Mackenzie, *Colonial Families in the U. S. A.*, vol. III (1912); correspondence with Miss Grace Sturtevant, Wellesley Farms, Mass.]   E. E. E.

STURTEVANT, JULIAN MONSON (July 26, 1805–Feb. 11, 1886), educator, Congregational clergyman, was born in Warren, Conn., second of the four children of Warren and Lucy (Tanner) Sturtevant. He was a descendant of Samuel Sturtevant who was in Plymouth as early as 1642. When Julian was eleven years old his father, financially distressed like so many other New England farmers by the economic consequences of the War of 1812, emigrated with his family to the Western Reserve, settling in what is now Tallmadge, Ohio. Here the boy attended an academy and in June 1822, with several companions, set out in a one-horse wagon for New Haven, Conn., to enroll at Yale College. Four years later he was graduated. He taught school in New Canaan, Conn., during the winter of 1826–27, and subsequently returned to Yale to study theology.

While a Divinity student he became one of the "Illinois Association" or "Yale Band," the members of which pledged themselves to devote their lives to the furtherance of religion and education in the West. On Aug. 27, 1829, he was ordained to the Congregational ministry at Woodbury, Conn., by the Association of Litchfield South, and four days later was married to Elizabeth Maria Fayerweather of New Canaan. She died on Feb. 12, 1840, and on Mar. 3 of the following year he married her sister, Hannah. By each he had five children. Shortly after his first marriage, with his friend and fellow member of the "Band," Theron Baldwin [q.v.], he left for the West. Settling at Jacksonville, Ill., he became the first instructor in Illinois College, which opened with an enrollment of nine on Jan. 4, 1830. With this institution he was connected for more than fifty-five years. From 1831 to 1844 he was professor of mathematics, natural philosophy, and astronomy. In the latter year he succeeded Edward Beecher [q.v.] as president and became also professor of mental science and sci-

ence of government. He served the college as president until 1876 and remained a member of the faculty until 1885.

For many years Sturtevant was one of the leaders in the religious and educational movements of the Middle West; in addition he took an influential part in the discussion of many important public questions. In religion, while by no means a radical, he represented a refreshingly independent and liberal point of view. In spite of many discouragements, he fought manfully to keep Illinois College free from narrow sectarian control and while president insisted upon a reasonable freedom in the discussion of theological matters. At the first National Council of Congregational Churches, held in Boston in 1865, he delivered the opening sermon. When the slavery question became an important issue in the West, while refraining from identifying himself with the radical abolitionists, he became a strong advocate of freedom. He was a friend of Abraham Lincoln, conferring and corresponding with him on the important issues of the day. When Richard Yates [q.v.], the war governor of Illinois, was about to depart for Altoona to attend the convention of loyal governors, he wrote to Sturtevant for advice; assuring him that such advice would have weight in determining his course (*Autobiography, post*, p. 299). During the Civil War, when attendance in the college had dropped to a low point, Sturtevant was sent to England, with the encouragement of Lincoln and armed with letters to prominent Englishmen, to win a more sympathetic support for the Northern cause.

Although not a prolific writer, he was in later life an occasional contributor to such periodicals as the *New Englander*, the *Congregational Review*, and the *Princeton Review*. Many of his addresses were published and he was the author of three books: a small but stimulating volume entitled *Economics, or the Science of Wealth* (1877); *The Keys of Sect* (1880), a discussion of sectarianism; and an autobiography, published ten years after his death. He died in Jacksonville, Ill.

[In addition to *Julian M. Sturtevant: An Autobiog.* (copr. 1896), ed. by his son, see *Quarter Century Celebration of Ill. Coll.: Hist. Discourse* (1855), by Sturtevant, and his "Address at the Semi-Centennial Anniversary of the Founding of Ill. Coll.," in the *College Rambler*, June 1879; also, *Obit. Record Grads. Yale Coll.*, 1886; C. H. Rammelkamp, *Ill. Coll.: A Centennial Hist.* (1928); G. F. Magoun, *Asa Turner, a Home Missionary Patriarch and His Times* (1889); *Daily Inter Ocean* (Chicago), Feb. 12, 1886.]   C. H. R.

STUTZ, HARRY CLAYTON (Sept. 12, 1876–June 25, 1930), automobile manufacturer, son of Henry J. and Elizabeth (Snyder) Stutz, was born on his father's farm at Ansonia, Ohio.

After receiving a public-school education he learned the machinist trade and upon finishing his apprenticeship at the age of twenty-one opened a small machine shop in Dayton, Ohio. The automobile, which was then beginning to appear on city streets, appealed to him strongly and he was one of the first residents of Dayton to secure and drive one. He kept himself informed as to its development while continuing to repair and manufacture farm pumping engines. In 1903 he made his first step into the automobile industry by accepting the management of the Lindsey-Russell Axle Company at Indianapolis, Ind. To enlarge his experience he subsequently worked for the G. & J. Tire Company and the Schebler Carburetor Company of Indianapolis. From 1906 to 1910 he was engineer and factory manager of the Marion Motor Car Company, and designed the first "underslung" pleasure car, which was manufactured by that company.

Toward the close of this period Stutz became associated with Henry Campbell, and the two organized the Stutz Auto Parts Company. The following year the partners organized the Ideal Motor Car Company to manufacture an automobile designed by Stutz. The completed car competed in the first five-hundred-mile Indianapolis Speedway race and finished in eleventh place. After continuing with his designing work for the succeeding two years, Stutz combined the Auto Parts Company and the Ideal Motor Car Company into the Stutz Motor Car Company, and served as president until 1919, when he disposed of his interests and joined with Campbell in the organization of the H. C. S. Motor Car Company of Indianapolis for the manufacture of inexpensive automobiles and taxicabs. It was during the six-year period from 1913 to 1919 that the Stutz automobile gained its greatest reputation, and between 1913 and 1915 Stutz cars were the leaders in most of the important automobile races. In 1924 Stutz abandoned the automobile field temporarily and devoted his attention to airplane engines; at the time of his death he was negotiating with airplane manufacturers for the use of a four-cylinder airplane engine of this design.

Stutz was greatly interested in sports, particularly in trap shooting, and was reputed to be one of the best shots in his section of the country. He was also a collector of sporting firearms and had one of the foremost collections in the United States. After disposing of his automobile interests he made his home in Orlando, Fla. He died in the night of June 25, 1930, in a hospital in Indianapolis, following an operation for appendicitis. He was twice married: on Oct. 25, 1898, to Clara M. Dietz of Dayton, from whom he was divorced; and in 1925 to Blanche Clark of Indianapolis, who with a daughter by his former marriage survived him.

[*Soc. of Automotive Engineers Jour.*, Sept. 1930; *Automobile Topics*, June 28, 1930; *Automotive Industries*, July 5, 1930; *Who's Who in America*, 1926–27; *N. Y. Herald Tribune*, *N. Y. Times*, and *Indianapolis Star*, June 27, 1930; information as to certain facts from daughter, Mrs. Emma Belle Horn.]

C. W. M—n.

STUYVESANT, PETRUS (1592–Feb. 1672), called Peter by the English, director-general of New Netherland, was a grandson of Johannes of Dokkum, in West Friesland, Netherlands, and a son of the Rev. Balthazar Johannes Stuyvesant, graduate of the University of Franeker, and his wife Margaretta (Hardenstein) Stuyvesant. His father was before 1619 the pastor of the Dutch Reformed Church at Scherpenzeel (now in West Stellingwerf), but in 1622 removed to Berlicum, in the classis of Franeker. The mother of Petrus having died in 1625, his father remarried in 1627, and was in a third pastorate at Delfzyl in Groningen from April 1634 until his death on May 26, 1637. Petrus had a sister Anna, who was married to Samuel Bayard, and he had two half-brothers and two half-sisters. He early entered a military career, serving his country at home and abroad and thus supplying the desires of his adventurous spirit. He was in the service of the Dutch West India Company in 1635 as a supercargo in Brazil. In 1643 he went to the Leeward Islands as governor of the Dutch possessions of Curaçao and adjacent islands, and in 1644 led an expedition against the island of St. Martin, making an attack in March and raising the siege on April 16. It was in this affair that Stuyvesant was shot in the right leg, which was afterward amputated and buried at Curaçao and not in Holland, as hitherto claimed (Stokes, *post*, VI, 64, under 1645). He returned to the Fatherland for recuperation and to have an artificial limb supplied, referred to afterwards as his "silver leg" on account of its adornments. He married on Aug. 13, 1645, Judith Bayard (1608–1687), in the Walloon Church of Breda, where her father, the Rev. Lazare Bayard, deceased, had been for years minister of that French Protestant congregation. She was a sister of Samuel Bayard of Amsterdam who had married Stuyvesant's sister Anna. Two sons were born in New Netherland of his marriage, Balthazar Lazarus (baptized May 27, 1647) and Nicholas William (1648–1698).

On Oct. 5, 1645, Stuyvesant appeared in person before the Zealand Chamber of the Dutch West India Company, "offering his services" and requesting speedy aid in his equipment to go to New Netherland (Stokes, IV, 105). On July 28, 1646, he was commissioned by the States-General as director-general of "New Netherland and the places situated thereabout, as well as the aforementioned islands of Curaçao, Buenaire, Aruba and the dependencies and appurtenances thereof" (*New York Historical Society Quarterly Bulletin*, Apr. 1926, p. 9), and on Christmas of 1646 his expedition of four vessels sailed out of the Texel to sea. Besides the soldiery, servants, traders, and adventurers there were on board a new body of officials for New Netherland, Stuyvesant's wife and his widowed sister Anna, with her three sons. Stuyvesant ordered the ships to stop first at Curaçao, whence, after a few weeks, they sailed to New Amsterdam; there the fleet anchored on May 11, 1647, amid great rejoicing of the commonalty. A few years later Stuyvesant's critics said his bearing on this occasion was "like a peacock, with great state and pomp" (Jameson, *post*, p. 342), and as thoughtless of others as if he were the Czar of Muscovy. But such charges need to be judged in the maze of political controversy and in comparison with other events. On May 27 he appointed a naval commander and a superintendent of naval equipments, and on June 6 provided to fit out a naval expedition against the Spaniards who were operating within the limits of the West India Company's charter. The first ordinance promulgated after his arrival at New Amsterdam for internal good order was on May 31 on the sale of intoxicants and on Sunday observance. He became a church-warden on July 22 and took up the reconstruction of the church in Fort Amsterdam. Son of a minister and son-in-law of another, he was himself a strict adherent of the Reformed Church and not liberal to other ideas in religion. This inclination, egged on by the clergy and the provincial council, led to the enactment of an ordinance on Feb. 1, 1656, forbidding "Conventicles and Meetings, whether in public or private" (Stokes, IV, 164) that were not according to the synod of Dort, principally directed against the Lutherans, but operative as well against Quakers and others. In June, the secular directors of the company at Amsterdam reproved Stuyvesant and urged leniency, but the general attitude against dissent in New Netherland remained throughout the Dutch régime.

In 1650 Stuyvesant's salary was 250 guilders monthly and a subsistence of 900 guilders per annum. On Mar. 12, 1650, the directors of the company conveyed to him their "Great Bouwery," or Farm No. 1, for 6,400 guilders, located at "about the present 5th to 17th Streets and

from the East River to an irregular line coinciding approximately with Fourth Avenue," New York City, known thereafter as "Stuyvesant's Bouwery" (Stokes, I, 34). In 1658 there was conveyed to him a town site on the East River (now State Street), then at the foot of the present Whitehall Street, upon which he erected a substantial mansion with gardens, owned in 1686 by Governor Dongan and named by him "The Whitehall." This was perhaps the finest residence in New Amsterdam.

Stuyvesant's career as director-general was marked by many progressive measures. He promoted intercolonial relations with the English, drove the Swedes from the Delaware, increased commerce, and by a variety of edicts sought to regulate internal affairs. His acts were often harsh and dictatorial. He was jealous of his official prerogatives. His idea of government was submission of the people to the official will. On Sept. 25, 1647, he instituted a Board of Nine Men to aid in promoting the general welfare and many good things were done for a time by this cooperation. But in 1649 the scenes were stormy. The commonalty sought and Stuyvesant opposed an independent municipal control at New Amsterdam. The people's representatives drew up a "Remonstrance" (*Vertoogh*) on July 28 to the States-General for redress of their grievances of many years (O'Callaghan, *post*, I, 271–318; Jameson, pp. 293–354). The people won their municipal government by proclamation of Feb. 3, 1653. But the inhabitants were as lax in public obligations to their city officials as they had been and continued to be toward the provincial authority.

After Stuyvesant's surrender of New Netherland to the English at his farm house on Aug. 27/ Sept. 6, 1664, he withdrew from all public affairs. In 1665 he went to the Netherlands to defend his official conduct and upon his return to New York lived on his farm until his death at the age of eighty years. He was buried beneath the chapel he had erected on his farm in 1660. The site is now (1935) St. Mark's Episcopal Church, where a stone tablet in the eastern wall records his interment. In 1922 St. Mark's commemorated the two hundred and fiftieth anniversary of his death.

[Not much exists for a personal biography of Stuyvesant, though there is much on his official career in New Netherland. Bayard Tuckerman, *Peter Stuyvesant* (1893), has some interest, but is far from satisfactory. The genealogy is best in Mrs. Alma R. Van Hoevenberg's article, "The Stuyvesants in the Netherlands and New Netherland," in *N. Y. Hist. Soc. Quart. Bulletin*, Apr. 1926; it is based on new researches. For his career in New Netherland the best body of materials, drawn anew from original sources, is found in I. N. Phelps Stokes, *The Iconography of Manhattan Island*

(6 vols., 1915–28), and see vol. I, 25–113 for a summary of the acts of his official régime, contributed by the present writer to that work. See also *Collections of the N. Y. Hist. Soc.*, 2 ser., II (1849); E. B. O'Callaghan, *Documents Relative to the Colonial History of the State of N. Y.*, vols. I–III (1855–56); J. F. Jameson, *Narratives of New Netherland* (1909); Berthold Fernow, *The Records of New Amsterdam* (7 vols., 1907); E. T. Corwin, ed., *Ecclesiastical Records. State of N. Y.* (7 vols., 1901–16).]   V. H. P.

SUBLETTE, WILLIAM LEWIS (1799?–July 23, 1845), fur trader, merchant, the son of Philip and Isabel (Whitley) Sublette, was born in Lincoln County, Ky. The Sublettes were Huguenots who settled in Manakin-Town, Va. Col. William C. Whitley, the grandfather of William Sublette, was likewise a Virginian. With his family and friends Whitley accompanied his kinsman, George Rogers Clark, to Kentucky in 1772, and was engaged in close combat with Chief Tecumseh [q.v.] in the battle of the Thames, where both were killed. The Sublette name was conspicuous in the fur trade, five brothers being thus engaged. Milton, long known as one of the most enterprising and daring Indian traders, was second in prominence to William. The family moved to St. Charles, Mo., about 1818, where William served as constable. Lured by the advertisements of William Henry Ashley [q.v.] for "enterprising young men," William Sublette joined Ashley's expedition to the Rocky Mountains (Chittenden, *post*, I, 252). Citizens of St. Charles fitted him out with a rifle and buckskin suit, his sole possessions. He was with Ashley in the Arikara fight on June 2, 1823, and served as sergeant-major under Colonel Leavenworth in the attack upon the Arikara villages in August. Ashley formed a strong friendship for him, and after five years outfitted him for an expedition of his own. Sublette made a fortune, and with two former companions, Jedediah S. Smith [q.v.] and David E. Jackson, finally bought out Ashley. Part of the Oregon Trail was first known as Sublette's cut-off, and Sublette's trace.

The firm of Smith, Jackson, and Sublette took the first wagons over the difficult trail to the Rockies, a feat previously deemed impossible. The last rendezvous of this firm was held in the summer of 1830. They sold out their joint interests but retained their furs, cattle, and wagons. This wagon train and collection of furs was so large as to create a sensation on arrival at St. Louis in the fall. The same men ventured on an expedition to Santa Fé in 1831, when Smith was killed by Indians. In the summer of 1832 William Sublette went again to the Rocky Mountains, and was wounded in the famous fight at Pierre's Hole. In December 1832 he formed a

partnership with another of Ashley's men, Robert Campbell [q.v.]. This firm continued in business for ten years and was a serious competitor of the American Fur Company. Their principal trading posts were on the Platte River at the mouth of the Laramie, and on the Missouri near Fort Union. They had a large store in St. Louis. Sublette had a wigwam built in the rear of this store, where he maintained a family of Indians during his lifetime. He died in Pittsburgh, Pa., while on his way to Cape May in search of health. William Sublette was a bold, shrewd, character. He was appointed in 1841 to the staff of Gov. Thomas Reynolds of Missouri, with the rank of colonel, the title by which he was generally known. He was married on Mar. 21, 1844, to Frances Hereford of Tuscumbia, Ala. He filled several public stations, was a presidential elector for his district in 1844, and was a candidate for Congress. He is buried in St. Louis.

[Sublette Manuscripts in the Mo. Hist. Soc.; H. M. Chittenden, *Am. Fur Trade of the Far West*, 2 vols. (2nd ed. 1935); Ednah W. McAdams, *Ky. Pioneer and Court Records* (1929), p. 120; Census of Lincoln County, Ky., 1810; W. S. Bryan, and Robert Rose, *Hist. of the Pioneer Families of Mo.* (1876), p. 187; *Mo. Republican* (St. Louis), Oct. 19, 1830, Oct. 16, 1832, June 16, 1837; *Daily Mo. Republican*, Aug. 1, 1845.]
                                        S. M. D.

SULLIVAN, GEORGE (Aug. 29, 1771–June 14, 1838), lawyer, congressman, was born at Durham, N. H. His parents were Gen. John Sullivan [q.v.] and Lydia (Worcester) Sullivan and he inherited the advantages of his father's prestige. He received a good education at Phillips Exeter Academy and Harvard College, graduating from the latter institution in 1790. He studied law in his father's office, was admitted to the bar, and began practice in Exeter, where he was henceforth a member of that remarkable local group of lawyers and politicians who exercised such an influence on the affairs of the state. A Federalist, he represented Exeter in the legislature (1805) and seemed to have a promising political career before him when the decline of Federalist strength began. He served one year as state attorney-general (1805–06), and in the reaction against the Jeffersonian policies which followed the Embargo, he was elected to the Twelfth Congress (1811–13). A single term in Washington offered no particular opportunity for distinction but he returned to New Hampshire well known as a stubborn opponent of Madison's foreign policies in general and of the War of 1812 in particular. His name appears at the head of a list of thirty-four congressmen who signed *An Address of Members of the House of Representatives . . . to Their Constituents, on the Subject of the War with Great Britain*

(1812), denouncing the war as contrary to all moral and prudential considerations. His speech delivered early in August 1812 at a convention of the Friends of Peace of Rockingham County was a scathing attack on President Madison, who according to the orator was responsible for American subserviency to French influence— "the greatest of all possible calamaties." This speech was printed and widely circulated by the Federalists and later proved embarrassing both to Sullivan and to Daniel Webster, who had headed the resolutions committee on that occasion.

During the war Sullivan served in the New Hampshire legislature (House, 1813–14; Senate, 1814–16). With the era of good feeling which followed, like many contemporaries he forgot the animosities of the earlier period. On Dec. 19, 1815, he began a period of almost twenty years of service as attorney-general, combining an extensive private practice with his public functions and retiring in 1835 when a statute required the incumbent of his office to give his entire service to the state. In 1817 he represented New Hampshire in the Dartmouth College Case, arguing with great eloquence and an imposing array of authority that the General Court had the right to alter and amend the college charter (Timothy Farrar, *Report of the Case of the Trustees of Dartmouth College against William H. Woodward*, n.d., pp. 70–104). While often grouped with Daniel Webster, Jeremiah Smith, Ichabod Bartlett, Jeremiah Mason, and other eminent New Hampshire lawyers of his time, Sullivan was probably inferior to these men in scope of legal attainments. "He relied too little on his preparation and too much upon his oratory, his power of illustration and argument" (J. M. Shirley, *The Dartmouth College Causes*, 1877, p. 29). He was, however, an extremely able leader of the bar, a most effective jury lawyer, and a man of integrity who exercised a salutary influence in the New Hampshire courts. He was twice married: on Aug. 6, 1799, at Exeter, to Clarissa Lamson, who died in 1824, having borne ten children; and on Jan. 14, 1838, to Philippa Call. He died in Exeter.

[C. H. Bell, *The Bench and Bar of N. H.* (1894) and *Hist. of the Town of Exeter, N. H.* (1888); E. S. Stackpole and Lucien Thompson, *Hist. of the Town of Durham* (2 vols., n.d.); W. J. Lamson, *Descendants of Wm. Lamson of Ipswich, Mass.* (1917), p. 87; *Biog. Dir. Am. Cong.* (1928); *Portsmouth Journal*, June 23, 1838.]
                                                    W. A. R.

SULLIVAN, JAMES (Apr. 22, 1744–Dec. 10, 1808), statesman, fourth son of John and Margery (Browne) Sullivan, was born at Berwick, in the District of Maine, where his father taught school. After studying under his father, James became a student in the law office of his brother John [*q.v.*] at Durham and there met Mehitable Odiorne, whom he married Feb. 22, 1768. The couple settled in a two-room house at Biddeford, but Sullivan soon prospered and moved to the new town of Limerick. Here he became king's counsel for York County and one of the most influential men in the District of Maine. He took a prominent local part in the early movement toward revolution and was a member of the Provincial Congress of Massachusetts and of numerous committees, including the Committee of Safety. In 1776 he was appointed a justice of the supreme court of Massachusetts and throughout the war continued to be returned as a member of the legislature.

In 1778 he moved to Groton, Mass. When the new state was organized in 1780 he was one of the committee to reorganize the laws. Two years later he resigned from the bench and in 1783 moved to Boston and was elected to Congress. On Jan. 26, 1786, his wife died, leaving six young children—among them William Sullivan [*q.v.*] —and on Dec. 31 he married Martha Langdon, sister of John and Woodbury Langdon [*qq.v.*]. During these years he was occupied largely with politics: holding public office, writing for the press, and active in the inner councils of his party. He advocated the adoption of the federal Constitution in letters signed Cassius, printed in the *Massachusetts Gazette*, Sept. 18–Dec. 25, 1787 (P. L. Ford, *Essays on the Constitution*, 1892). Toward the end of 1788 or in the beginning of 1789 he made a trip through the South, probably in the interest of Hancock, with a view to securing him the vice-presidency. In 1790 he resigned the position of probate judge, which he had held for a short time, and was made attorney-general of Massachusetts. In 1796 he was appointed agent to maintain the interests of the United States before the commissioners at Halifax who were to determine the disputed boundary line of Maine.

By this time Sullivan had become one of the most prominent lawyers in Massachusetts, with a large and very lucrative practice. In 1797 he ran for governor, but was defeated by the Federalist candidate. Ten years later, however, in June 1807, he was elected to the office. At this time occurred his controversy with Timothy Pickering [*q.v.*] in the course of which he refused to communicate Pickering's letter on the Embargo to the state legislature. A war of letters and pamphlets followed, on the eve of the election of 1808, and although Sullivan was re-elected governor by a small majority, the election generally was a pronounced Federalist victory.

Sullivan was never a national leader, but he was throughout his career a man to be reckoned with as perhaps the richest, ablest, and most powerful of the Democrats, or Republicans as they were then called, in what was, for most of his life, Federalist territory. His writings for the press on contemporary issues, published under several pen names, were innumerable and carried great weight. Although he died in the governorship it is unlikely that if he had lived he would have risen to higher office. He was more than a mere politician, however, and was keenly interested in several fields of thought outside of politics. In 1801 he published *The History of Land Titles in Massachusetts,* a valuable work, and at that time was planning a history of Massachusetts criminal law. His interest in the history in America of his profession is, perhaps, his chief claim to intellectual distinction. He was one of the first members of the American Academy of Arts and Sciences, and one of the founders, for some years president, and a contributor to the early *Collections* of the Massachusetts Historical Society. In 1795 he published *The History of the District of Maine,* still valuable. He was also the author of *Observations upon the Government of the United States* (1791), a treatise on the suability of states, and is credited with having been influential in securing the adoption of the Eleventh Amendment to the Constitution. In 1792 he published *The Path of Riches: An Inquiry into the Origin and Use of Money; and into the Principles of Stocks and Banks,* and in 1801, *A Dissertation upon the Constitutional Freedom of the Press in the United States of America.* Both as citizen and capitalist he was interested in "public improvements" as then understood and he was the projector and for long president of the Middlesex Canal.

[T. C. Amory, *Life of James Sullivan* (2 vols., 1859); Henry Adams, *Hist. of the U. S.,* vol. IV (1890); Octavius Pickering and C. W. Upham, *The Life of Timothy Pickering* (4 vols., 1867–73), esp. vols. III, IV; *Interesting Correspondence between His Excellency Gov. Sullivan and Col. Pickering* (1808); T. C. Amory and G. E. Meredith, *Materials for a Hist. of the Family of John Sullivan of Berwick, New England* (1893); *New Eng. Hist. and Geneal. Reg.,* Oct. 1865; Geo. Folsom, *Hist. of Saco and Biddeford* (1830); *Columbian Centinel* (Boston), Dec. 14, 17, 1808.]

J. T. A.

SULLIVAN, JAMES EDWARD (Nov. 18, 1860–Sept. 16, 1914), promoter of amateur sports, was born in New York City, the son of Daniel and Julia (Halpin) Sullivan of County Kerry, Ireland. Springing from solid Irish stock not far removed from the soil, he grew up with a love for outdoor life and sports of every kind. His father was a foreman in the construction work of the New York Central Railroad, a man of little money and no pretensions. Sullivan's education was limited entirely to New York's public schools. He was determined to succeed, however, and was unwilling to drift into manual labor. Night study and voracious reading sharpened his quick mind. In 1878 he entered the publishing house of Frank Leslie [*q.v.*] and publishing and editing became his life work. The year before he had joined the Pastime Athletic Club, and thereafter athletics were his hobby.

He might have become a national champion in any one of a half dozen different sports but he preferred to compete in as many as he could. Even in track and field events, which he most enjoyed, the powerfully built Sullivan was an all-around man with a versatility quite comparable to the decathlon men of the present day. His best individual performance was winning second place in the Canadian half-mile championship of 1884. As a competing athlete he saw through the sham and hypocrisy of "amateurism" as it was exploited by the National Association of Amateur Athletes of America, which then ruled most amateur sports. Fired with the resolution to stamp out these athletic malpractices, in 1888 he and several others formed the Amateur Athletic Union of the United States. For one year there was a terrific sports war between the two organizations for control; but Sullivan, unswerving in purpose, had founded the Union on the rock of honesty. It survived and the National Association capitulated and disbanded. During the early days of the Union Sullivan paid most of the expenses himself, and until he died he was always an officer, serving as its secretary (1889–96), as president (1906–09), as secretary-treasurer (1909–14). In reality he was the first sports czar. He ruled with an iron hand. Technically there could be appeals from his decisions; actually there were none. Athletes, used to the slip-shod methods of the older organization, at first resented Sullivan's rigid discipline, but once they realized the deep sincerity of the man they swung to his side with enthusiasm.

He had a genius for organization and an almost prophetic vision of the recreational needs of the thousands of children and youths in large cities. It was he who suggested the founding of New York's Public School Athletic League, now the largest of its kind, and he was one of its incorporators. He also opened the first public playground and gymnasium in New York City in 1898. His fame was international and he was always appointed the American director of the various Olympic Games. President Theodore Roosevelt and President Taft named him as their personal representative at the Olympic

Games from 1906 to 1912. No other man had received such a distinction, and none has since. At each Olympic Games kings and princes decorated him. When the American Olympic team of 1906 returned from Athens the banners of greeting read, "Welcome home J. E. Sullivan and the American team." So zealous was he in his espousal of the amateur cause that he hesitated not a second in barring Jim Thorpe when the Indian was at the height of his Olympic glory; he was equally quick to bar Arthur Duffey, another hero. Even his own nephew, Timothy J. Sullivan, felt the force of his wrath and was declared a professional because of his participation in one basketball game that his uncle thought was not as strictly amateur as it might have been.

While he was fostering amateur sports, he continued his connection with Leslie's publishing house until 1889, when he resigned to become business manager and editor of the *New York Sporting Times*, which he bought in 1891. The following year he assumed the presidency of the American Sports Publishing Company. He held this position until his death, editing the hundreds of books known as "Spalding's Athletic Library." In 1882 he married Margaret Eugenie Byrne, who with two children, a son and a daughter, survived him.

[*Official . . . Handbook of the Amateur Athletic Union,* 1914; files and records of the Amateur Athletic Union of the United States; *N. Y. Times,* Sept. 17, 1914; *Who's Who in America,* 1914–15; information from associates and relatives.]   A. J. D.

SULLIVAN, JOHN (Feb. 17, 1740–Jan. 23, 1795), Revolutionary general and statesman, brother of James Sullivan [*q.v.*], was born at Somersworth, N. H., across the Salmon Falls River from Berwick, Me. His father, John Sullivan of Limerick, Ireland, and his mother, Margery Browne of Cork, had emigrated as redemptioners to Maine, about 1723; John is said to have bought Margery's freedom.

The younger John Sullivan studied law at Portsmouth under Samuel Livermore. In 1760, he married Lydia Worcester. An able, if somewhat litigious, lawyer, he was successful enough to maintain his family, which included two daughters who died in infancy and a daughter and three sons—one of them George Sullivan [*q.v.*]—who survived. In 1772 he was appointed major of the New Hampshire militia. He seems to have inherited an antipathy for England which led him to the patriot side in the American Revolution. Sent as delegate to the First Continental Congress in Philadelphia, he took his seat Sept. 5, 1774. By December he was back in New Hampshire, in time to receive Paul Revere's warning of a British threat, whereupon he rallied a band that captured Fort William and Mary at the entrance of Portsmouth harbor, and appropriated above one hundred barrels of gunpowder. On May 10, 1775, he took his seat in the Second Continental Congress, by which body he was (June 22) appointed brigadier-general.

In July Sullivan joined Washington's army outside of Boston and was stationed with his brigade at Winter Hill. With the exception of trips to organize the defenses of Portsmouth in October 1775, he served through the siege of Boston, until the evacuation, Mar. 17, 1776. Then ordered to the Northern army, which was retreating from Canada after Montgomery's defeat at Quebec, he reached Chambly early in June, and upon the death of Gen. John Thomas [*q.v.*] succeeded to the command. Superseded by Horatio Gates [*q.v.*] in July, he went to Philadelphia and offered his resignation, but a personal conference with President John Hancock led him to withdraw it.

On Aug. 9, 1776, Sullivan was promoted to be major-general. He joined the main army and was stationed with his command on Long Island. In the battle of Aug. 27, he was captured by the British and taken before Lord Howe, who wished to send him with overtures of peace to the Americans. Having obtained Washington's permission, Sullivan went to Philadelphia. During the negotiations between Congress and Howe, Sullivan was exchanged for the British general, Richard Prescott. He then rejoined the American army in Westchester County, N. Y., shared in the retreat across the Jerseys, led the right column at Trenton, and pursued the British at Princeton. The winter of 1777 he spent in northern New Jersey, conducting various skirmishes against the British outposts.

In March 1777, Sullivan returned to New Hampshire to expedite the preparations for the ensuing campaign. On July 1 he joined Generals Nathanael Greene and Henry Knox [*qq.v.*] in threatening to resign if Congress persisted in elevating the newly arrived French officer, Du Coudray, over their heads. Congress demanded an apology, and suggested that otherwise they might be asked to resign. Neither apologies nor resignations were forthcoming, but Du Coudray was accidentally drowned Sept. 15. On Aug. 21 and 22, Sullivan led an expedition against the British posts on Staten Island, which, although conducted with spirit, failed of its objective. This failure coupled with the Du Coudray affair made him enemies in Congress who began to question his capacity. Meantime, he hurried his division to the south to join Washington in defending Philadelphia against Howe.

In September a proposition was made in Congress to suspend Sullivan from command, pending a court of inquiry into his conduct of the Staten Island affair. This matter was now complicated by violent criticism, on the part of delegate Thomas Burke [q.v.] of North Carolina, of Sullivan's conduct at Brandywine. Washington, however, refused to recall Sullivan, and the investigations exonerated him from blame. At the battle of Germantown he executed the movements assigned to him, and the American discomfiture on that occasion was due to the progress of the action elsewhere.

Sullivan spent the winter of 1777–78 at Valley Forge, and in the spring was directed to take the command in Rhode Island, with a view to driving the British from Newport. Everything depended on the active cooperation of the French army and fleet under D'Estaing. In August Sullivan threw his armies around Newport and began the siege. Lord Howe's British fleet appeared, and D'Estaing stood out to meet him. A storm scattered and injured both squadrons before any action was possible. D'Estaing's captains then counseled him to withdraw his fleet and army to Boston, which left Sullivan in an awkward position, with inferior forces. He withdrew to the north end of the island on which Newport stands, where the British attacked him on Aug. 29, 1778. In the following battle the British were severely repulsed, but since Lord Howe now reappeared, Sullivan's position was very dangerous, and during the night he withdrew his entire force, with baggage and artillery, to the mainland. It required all of Washington's tact and Lafayette's loyalty to smooth down the anger which Sullivan and his men exhibited at what they regarded as D'Estaing's desertion.

Sullivan remained at Providence until March 1779, when he was ordered to take an expedition into western Pennsylvania and New York to lay waste the Iroquois country. While a force, under Col. Daniel Brodhead [q.v.] made an independent raid up the Allegheny, another, under Gen. James Clinton [q.v.], marched from Canajoharie to join Sullivan near the New York-Pennsylvania line. On Aug. 29, thus reinforced, Sullivan completely routed the combined Indian and Loyalist forces, near modern Elmira, N. Y. After pursuing them through the length of the Finger Lake country, burning and harrying the countryside as far west as modern Livingston County, he returned with health so impaired that he was compelled to resign from the army (Nov. 30, 1779).

In 1780–81 he reappeared in Congress. At this time his brother Daniel, who was dying as a result of ill treatment received aboard one of the British prison hulks, brought to him a further overture of peace from the British. Sullivan himself flatly refused to have anything to do with the matter, but brought it to the attention of Luzerne, the French minister. Since Luzerne had loaned Sullivan money, this episode was dragged out after the latter's death to insinuate that he was a pensioner of the French, but the charge has been thoroughly refuted. In 1782 Sullivan was a member of the New Hampshire constitutional convention. From 1782 to 1786 he was attorney-general of New Hampshire, and during this period served also in the state Assembly, as speaker (1785). In 1786 he was elected president (governor) of the state, and during his tenure put down the paper-money riots with great firmness and moderation. He was reëlected president in 1787, acted as chairman of the New Hampshire convention of 1788 which ratified the federal Constitution, in the same year was again speaker of the Assembly, and in 1789 was made president for the third time. In September 1789 he was also appointed United States district judge of New Hampshire, a position which he held until his death at Durham in 1795. Descriptions of Sullivan's character reveal traits typical of his Irish ancestry: he was brave, hot-headed, oversensitive, fond of display, generous to a fault, usually out of money, and a born political organizer.

[T. C. Amory, The Mil. Services and Pub. Life of Maj.-Gen. John Sullivan (1868), supersedes sketch by O. W. B. Peabody in Jared Sparks, The Lib. of Am. Biog., 2 ser. III (1844), but must be used in connection with O. G. Hammond, Letters and Papers of Maj.-Gen. John Sullivan (2 vols., 1930–31), being N. H. Hist. Soc. Colls., vols., XIII and XIV. See also New Eng. Hist. and Geneal. Reg., Oct. 1865; T. C. Amory and G. E. Meredith, Materials for a Hist. of the Family of John Sullivan (1893); Provincial Papers . . . of N. H., vol. VII (1873); State Papers . . . of N. H., vols. VIII (1874), X–XVII (1877–89); Early State Papers of N. H., vols. XX–XXII (1891–93); E. C. Burnett, Letters of Members of the Continental Congress, vols. I–VII (1921–33); Journals of the Continental Congress; the various editions of Washington's writings; Proc. Mass. Hist. Soc., 1 ser. IX (1867), XX (1884), 2 ser. I (1885). A. T. Norton, Hist. of Sullivan's Campaign against the Iroquois (1879), is superseded by Jours. of the Mil. Exped. of Maj. Gen. John Sullivan against the Six Nations (1887), ed. by G. S. Conover. See also The Sullivan-Clinton Campaign in 1779: Chronology and Selected Docs. (1929), and Louise W. Murray, Notes from the Craft Coll. in Tioga Point Museum on the Sullivan Exped. (1929). The various refutations of George Bancroft's ill-natured comments on Sullivan (Hist. of the U.S., vols. IX, 1866, X, 1874) are gathered in Gen. Sullivan not a Pensioner of Luzerne . . . with the Report of the N. H. Hist. Soc. (1875).]
R. G. A—s.

SULLIVAN, JOHN LAWRENCE (Oct. 15, 1858–Feb. 2, 1918), pugilist, was born in Boston, Mass. He inherited pugnacity from his father, Michael Sullivan of Tralee, Ireland, a fiery little laborer, small in stature. From his mother, whom he greatly resembled, a kindly giantess weighing 180 pounds, he derived his marvelous body and good nature. Even as a youth he displayed prodigious strength. Graduating from grammar school when he was sixteen, he found work as a plumber's assistant and later as a tinsmith. He was fond of sports and received several offers to engage in professional baseball.

A casual invitation to box in a Boston theatre when he was nineteen started him on his pugilistic career. His first blow knocked an opponent into the orchestra. For a year (1877–78) he gave boxing exhibitions in a variety show conducted by William Muldoon; twenty-five dollars was promised anyone who could last one round against him. Subsequent engagements gave him the reputation of being able to hit "hard enough to knock a horse down," and late in 1880 he issued a challenge, offering "to fight any man breathing, for any sum from $1000 to $10,000 at catch weights," adding, "This challenge is especially directed to Paddy Ryan." Ryan was the American champion and Sullivan had to show his powers in other contests before Paddy would meet him. A match was finally fought at Mississippi City, Miss., Feb. 7, 1882, with bare knuckles and on the turf, in which Sullivan knocked out the champion in the ninth round.

This victory made him a popular idol. Crowds flocked to see him on his journey North, and Boston, his home town, welcomed him with great acclaim, tendering him a reception in the Dudley Street Opera House. For the next ten years "The Boston Strong Boy" dominated the American prize ring and was one of the spectacular figures of the country. He was 5 feet 10½ inches tall, and when in condition weighed 180 pounds. His method of fighting was simply to hammer his opponent into unconsciousness. His hazel eyes, burning black with fury, and his blatant confidence seemed to paralyze his opponents. An habitué of saloons, he lived a riotous life, but even when not in condition was able to knock out his antagonists. He was ready to meet all comers, though his manager, Jimmy Wakely, barred the negro Peter Jackson. Flamboyantly patriotic, he had a fierce animosity for "foreign fighters." Among his engagements was one fought in Madison Square Garden, New York, Aug. 6, 1882, with the New Zealander Herbert Slade, "The Maori," whom he terrified and knocked out in three rounds. The Englishman Charlie Mitchell gave him the most trouble. In a fight in New York, May 14, 1883, Mitchell,

to the consternation of everyone including Sullivan, actually knocked the champion down. In the third round, however, the police interfered to save Mitchell's life. On Aug. 8, 1887, at the Boston Theatre, with high municipal officials present, Sullivan's admirers presented him with a $10,000 diamond-studded belt. In October of that year he went abroad, visiting England and Ireland, where he received frenzied ovations. He met the Prince of Wales at the Prince's request and treated him with the easy condescension he displayed toward American presidents and prelates with whom he became acquainted. A match between Sullivan and Mitchell took place, Mar. 10, 1888, on the estate of Baron Rothschild, at Chantilly, France. A fierce battle of some three hours was waged, at the end of which, much to Sullivan's chagrin, the fight was declared a draw. Both contestants were arrested. After a night in jail Sullivan posted bail of $1600 and fled the country. By 1889 he was a flabby wreck from dissipation, but William Muldoon trained him into condition, and on July 8, 1889, after seventy-five rounds under a glaring sun at Richburg, Miss., against Jake Kilrain, Sullivan was given the decision. This was the last bare-knuckle championship contest. A little more than three years later, Sept. 7, 1892, the clever, agile, hard-hitting James Corbett, in the twenty-first round, ended Sulivan's pugilistic career.

He had wasted a fortune; his diamond belt had gone for his debts. For several years he acted in various plays, touring the United States and visiting Canada and Australia; later he appeared in vaudeville. He opened a bar in New York and acquired an interest in a saloon in Boston. There was some talk of nominating him for Congress. Finally, in 1905, he reformed and became a temperance lecturer. He had married a chorus girl, Annie Bates, in 1883, but they soon separated. In 1908 he divorced her and married Kate Harkins of Roxbury (part of Boston), Mass., a boyhood sweetheart who had opposed his drinking and fighting. In 1912 they acquired a farm in West Abington, Mass. Five years later his wife died, and his last days were spent in poverty with an old sparring partner, George Bush, as a companion.

[In 1892 there appeared under Sullivan's name *Life and Reminiscences of a 19th Century Gladiator*. See also R. F. Dibble, *John L. Sullivan* (1925); William Inglis, *Champions off Guard* (1932); *Literary Digest*, Feb. 23, 1918; *N. Y. Tribune*, Feb. 8, 1882, July 9, 1889, Sept. 8, 1892; *N. Y. Times*, Feb. 3, 1918.]

W.O.I.

SULLIVAN, LOUIS HENRI (Sept. 3, 1856–April 14, 1924), architect, was born in Boston, Mass., the son of Patrick and Andrienne (List)

Sullivan. In looks, manner, and name he was an Irishman, but he referred to himself as of "mongrel origin." He placed great store on his genealogy, however, as a partial clue to his own personality. His father was a pure-blooded Celt, who from a waif became a wandering musician, and by grim pride and ambition advanced himself to the proprietorship of an academy of dancing in London, traveled, studied dancing in Paris, and visited Geneva. He sailed to Boston in 1847, opened a music and dancing academy there, and again prospered. According to his son, grace, rhythm, symmetry were his watchwords, and their consideration and practice obsessed his existence. In 1852 in Boston he married Andrienne List, a beautiful, highly emotional girl, of a strong personality, who had emigrated from Geneva with her parents in 1850. Her mother was French, but her father, Henri List, was pure German—an intellectual, said to have been educated for the priesthood but to have fled the convent for Geneva, where he taught school. Louis, the child of this Irish-French-German union, was self-willed, emotional, courageous, energetic. During his childhood, after a year or two with his grandparents, he spent winters with his father and mother at Boston, Newburyport, and Halifax, and summers with his grandparents at Wakefield, Mass., then called South Reading. In Boston he attended the public schools—the Brimmer school, the Rice school, and the English High School—and in his autobiography he gives great praise to a certain Moses Woolson, teacher in the English High School, who, he says, inculcated methods of thought, study, and work on which he relied through life. When in 1869 his father moved to Chicago in an effort to find a climate more lenient to the health of the mother, Louis was left with his grandparents. In this same year, at the age of thirteen, he determined to become an architect.

Two years later, owing to the death of his grandmother and the removal to Philadelphia of old Henri List, who had been his beloved counselor and companion, his home was once more broken up, and he moved to the house of a neighbor. At the end of the school year he passed the entrance examinations for the Massachusetts Institute of Technology, where in 1872 he entered the course in architecture under the tutelage of William Robert Ware [q.v.] and his romantic assistant, Eugène Létang, who was a graduate of the famous, almost mythical, École des Beaux Arts in Paris, regarded by Americans, chiefly because of deeds of its distinguished sons, Henry Hobson Richardson and Richard Morris Hunt

[qq.v.], as the miraculous fountain-head of all architectural knowledge, and the open sesame to success and renown in the practice of architecture. The study of academic architecture irked Sullivan, however, and he would desert the Greek and Roman orders to contemplate the recently completed Brattle Street Church tower in the virile and stimulating Romanesque as revived by Richardson. After a year there (1872–73) he decided that the Institute was no place for him, and his thoughts turned to Paris. Going to New York in the spring, he went to see Richard M. Hunt, bluff old autocrat, America's first and most distinguished eclectic, who was very kind to the boy, slapped him on the back, and told him to go to Paris. He did finally, but via Philadelphia and Chicago. In Philadelphia he tarried, working in the office of Furness and Hewitt. Here, as in all offices except Richardson's, the architectural vernacular was largely Victorian Gothic, which Sullivan aptly describes as "Gothic in its pantalettes." But the panic of 1873 left him without a job, and he betook himself to Chicago. The raw and unfinished city, rising from the ruins of the great fire, immediately captivated him. Here he stayed for a year, working principally in the office of Major William Le Baron Jenney [q.v.], afterwards to become famous as the first architect to utilize in a tall building a skeleton of metal as the basic element of its construction. At this time Sullivan's principal interest was engineering, and the Eads bridge, about to leap across the Mississippi, fired his imagination far more than any building he had seen. Still searching for the Holy Grail of his imagination, an underlying law for architecture, he set out for Paris in July 1874. Only six weeks intervened between his arrival and the examinations for entrance to the Beaux Arts. Sullivan laid out a schedule that demanded eighteen hours of study a day; at the end of a month, threatened with a collapse, he took a day off and recovered. He wore out three tutors, but passed his examination with éclat and then took a flying trip to Rome to verify, he says, Taine's description of Michelangelo's ceiling. A statement of his professor of mathematics kept ringing in his head, "—here our demonstrations shall be so broad as to admit of *no exception!*" That was what he must find for architecture—a rule that admits of no exceptions. His work at the Beaux Arts, most unfortunately, gave him no answer to his riddle, though his year in the atelier Vaudremer was filled with interesting experiences and youthful delight.

In a year he had returned to Chicago. After work in various offices, where he acquired a reputation as a remarkably skilful and rapid draftsman, in 1879 he entered the office of Dankmar Adler as a "probationary" partner; on May 1, 1881, the firm became Adler and Sullivan. The rise of the new firm was extremely rapid; in but a year or so its practice was exceeded by that of only one other in the city. The chief problem confronting the designer of large buildings in those days was to obtain more light for offices and to devise means for building ever higher, a problem essentially structural and economic which to Sullivan was of absorbing interest. Although he asserts that such buildings as the Borden Block, built in these early days, were a radical departure from their contemporaries, there is little to be seen in them that substantiates him. He designed in the vernacular, which was bad, a strange combination of Victorian Gothic, English "Eastlake," and French Néo-Grec. In the early eighties Chicago rushed headlong into Richardson's Romanesque revival, Sullivan along with John Wellborn Root [q.v.] and the rest, although he denies it. When the Auditorium Building, Chicago, was projected, Adler and Sullivan built a trial audience room, seating over six thousand, in the old Exposition Building, demonstrated their mastery of the problem of acoustics, and thereby won the contract for designing the new building. At the time of its building (1886–90), it was the city's greatest architectural monument, and the auditorium proper, only a part of a huge building devoted to the purposes of hotel and office building in addition, remains (1935) the greatest room ever built for the purpose of opera. It not only won the firm international recognition but also marked the critical crossing of the ways in the career of Louis Sullivan. Though the exterior was in the vernacular of the Romanesque revival, the fashionable style, the interior—designed, or at least detailed, after the exterior was completed—shows clearly the architect's break with the past and his embarkation on the unknown path of original design. In the meantime the practicability of skeleton construction had been demonstrated by Holobird and Roche in the Tacoma Building, Chicago. After a nervous breakdown that compelled a prolonged stay (1889–1900) in Ocean Springs, Miss., there followed a series of important buildings, designed by Sullivan in consistent adherence to the principles and peculiar forms set forth in the interior of the Auditorium, and accepting with enthusiasm the revolutionary principle of skeleton construction. Notable among these are the Wainwright Building, St. Louis, Mo., the first complete expression of his principles of construction combined with

his original decorative treatment; the Transportation Building with its "Golden Arch," the sensation of the World's Columbian Exposition of 1893 and the formal introduction of Sullivan's new conception of architecture to the world; the Gage Building, Chicago, an almost perfect solution—structurally and architecturally—of the steel-constructed skyscraper; and the Getty Tomb, Graceland Cemetery, Chicago, a singularly beautiful and original architectural tour de force. Others are the Stock Exchange Building, the Schiller Theatre (later the Garrick), the Schlesinger and Mayer Building (later the Carson, Pirie, Scott & Company Building), all in Chicago; the Union Trust Building and the St. Nicholas Hotel, St. Louis; the Condict Building, New York, and the Guaranty Building, Buffalo, N. Y.

On July 1, 1899, Sullivan married Margaret Hattabough of Chicago, from whom he was divorced in 1917. There were no children. In 1900 he returned to Chicago, but with the death of Dankmar Adler in that same year his opportunity to do work on a large scale ceased. In addition to the fact that the clients of the firm were for the most part Adler's clients, Sullivan's haughty and uncompromising attitude turned away commissions, and his irregular and nonconforming mode of life did little to inspire confidence. The last years of his life, although beset by privations and harried by the triumph of eclecticism and the apparent defeat of his principles, were yet fruitful in many ways. He produced a series of small banks brilliant in design and rich in practical innovations, beginning with the National Farmers' Bank, Owatanna, Minn., and including the Merchants' National Bank, Grinnell, Iowa, and banks at Columbus, Wis., Cedar Rapids, Iowa, Lafayette, Ind., and Sidney, Ohio; a church, St. Paul's Methodist, at Cedar Rapids, and a residence or two. He also produced the twenty original drawings, unique in their beauty and importance, illustrating his philosophy of ornament (now in the possession of the Art Institute of Chicago), which were published as *A System of Architectural Ornament According with a Philosophy of Man's Powers* (1924), and he wrote in his last days his extraordinary *The Autobiography of an Idea* (1924).

The rule that would admit of no exception, the voice that cried "*Yea*" in thunder tones in the stillness of the Sistine Chapel, the Idea of which he wrote the autobiography was that "form follows function." The most grievous violation of this principle was the treatment of the skyscraper in Roman mode between the World's Columbian

Exposition and the World War. Most of Sullivan's energy was expended in pointing out the essentially modern function of the skyscraper, its peculiarly American character and unprecedented construction, and the proper form for its expression. The novelty of its steel skeleton construction, the vast opportunity that lay in truthfully expressing it, and the falsity inherent in the popular garment of Roman architecture with which it was clothed and concealed he dinned into the deaf ears of American architects until he became almost a nuisance. (See his *Kindergarten Chats on Architecture, Education and Democracy*, 1934, first published in the *International Architect and Builder* in 1901; "The Tall Office Building Artistically Considered," reprinted in *Western Architect*, January 1922; "The Young Man in Architecture," *Ibid.*, January 1925; and "The Chicago Tribune Competition," *Architectural Review*, February 1923.) The rise of Classicism or Eclecticism which followed the Chicago Exposition of 1893 was too strong, however, for Sullivan and his followers, the "Chicago School," to combat successfully at the time. But Sullivan, whose confidence in the ultimate outcome never failed, saw the turn of the tide in the overwhelming acclaim that greeted the second-prize design of Eliel Saarinen in the *Chicago Daily Tribune* competition of 1924.

Sullivan's permanent place in the roster of great architects is assured. Chronologically, at least, he is the father of Modernism in architecture—the Transportation Building at the World's Columbian Exposition anticipated by five years the Art Nouveau movement in Europe. He founded a school of architectural philosophy which has become almost universally accepted. He, more than any man, helped to make of the skyscraper America's greatest contribution to architecture. His original "Sullivanesque" style of architectural ornament, while too personal and complicated for popular acceptance, was yet a distinct and valuable contribution to the thesaurus of architecture, and his book, *The Autobiography of an Idea*, an intensely personal revelation, is a notable addition to American literature. On the back of the monolith in Graceland Cemetery erected to him by the architects and builders of Chicago is the following inscription: "By his buildings great in influence and power; his drawings unsurpassed in originality and beauty; his writings rich in poetry and prophecy; his teachings persuasive and eloquent; his philosophy where, in 'Form Follows Function,' he summed up all truth in Art, Sullivan has earned his place as one of the greatest architectural forces in America."

[The spelling of Sullivan's middle name is from *The Autobiog. of an Idea*, which contains a detailed account of his early life. See also *Who's Who in America,* 1922–23; memorial issue of *Western Architect*, June 1924; L. P. Smith and H. W. Desmond, in *Architectural Record*, July 1904; L. J. Millett, *Ibid.*, Oct. 1908; Montgomery Schuyler, *Ibid.*, Jan. 1912; A. N. Rebori, *Ibid.*, May 1916; F. L. Wright, *Ibid.*, July 1924; Fiske Kimball, *Ibid.*, Apr. 1925; Robertson Howard, in *Architectural Jour.*, June 18, 1924; *Am. Architect*, May 7, 1924; T. E. Tallmadge, *Ibid.*, Oct. 23, 1918, in *Building for the Future*, Oct. 1930, and *The Story of Architecture in America* (1927); G. H. Edgell, *The Am. Architecture of Today* (1928); and obituary in *Chicago Daily Tribune*, Apr. 15, 1924.]   T. E. T.

SULLIVAN, LOUIS ROBERT (May 21, 1892–Apr. 23, 1925), physical anthropologist, was born in Houlton, Me., the son of James and Mary (Mitchell) Sullivan. He was graduated from Bates College, Lewiston, Me., in 1914, taught biology for a year in Tilton Seminary, Tilton, N. H., and then went to Brown University as assistant in biology under Prof. H. E. Walter. He was married on Nov. 24, 1915, to Bessie Pearl Pathers, of Lewiston, Me. In 1917 he was appointed assistant curator in physical anthropology at the American Museum of Natural History in New York City and associate curator in 1924. He received the Ph.D. degree from Columbia University in 1922. His first important scientific contribution was a study of race differences in the articulation of the lower jaw, but the World War soon called him from the laboratory. He was assigned to duty as first lieutenant in the anthropological division of the surgeon-general's office to assist in compiling data on drafted men. His special contribution to the study of these data was the determination of standard population areas in the United States, according to homogeneity in national and racial origins. The subsequent publication of studies has shown them to be fundamentally basic in relation to the geographical distribution of anthropological types. Later Sullivan was assigned to Camp Grant where he made a systematic anthropometric survey of all recruits, but unfortunately a fire in his quarters destroyed these records.

At this cantonment he suffered a severe attack of influenza which permanently impaired his health, but upon his return to the Museum in New York he began to plan new programs of research. He accepted with enthusiasm an opportunity to work at the Bernice P. Bishop Museum in Hawaii on an intensive study of native races in the island countries of the Pacific. His objective here was not only to study native adults but also to observe the growth of children, especially in Hawaii where race crossing was operating on a large scale. Unfortunately, steadily declining health made a change of climate necessary, so, after two years, he went to Tucson, Ariz. In this new environment he planned a study of race characters as observed among the Indians, Mexicans, and other types to be found in Arizona and neighboring states. He visited most of the United States Indian and public schools in the area, but, finally, when these data had been gathered, his vitality failed and he died at the age of thirty-three.

Notwithstanding the difficulties under which he labored, Sullivan published during his brief career twenty-five papers in anthropology, at least nine of which are considered contributions of importance. Though the bulk of the data gathered in Hawaii and the United States was left incomplete, his records were so clear and definite, his outlines for treatment so complete, that two major papers were subsequently issued, one covering the growth of children in Hawaii, the other the distinguishing face characters of North American Indians. A bibliography of his works appeared in the *American Journal of Physical Anthropology*, October–December 1925. In addition to these achievements Sullivan gave evidence of real genius in museum work particularly in dealing with the details of any exhibit demonstrating anatomical and race characteristics.

His scientific work was characterized throughout by originality and accuracy of observation. Almost from the start he set as his ultimate research objective the discovery of genetic relations among the known divisions of mankind, a problem that still remains peculiarly baffling. His scientific faith was in precise observation and originality in classification, believing that the consistent analysis of human qualitative characters such as particular forms of eye, ear, nose, lips, etc., rather than differences in measurement would point the way to genetic relations. Perhaps no other physical anthropologists possessed equal genius in setting up rating scales so that fruitful comparisons could be made, not only in the study of growth in size, but also in the establishment of race criteria. It is little short of a tragedy that Sullivan's early death barred the possible realization of the main objective in his life plan. Certainly his published work gave promise of at least a suggestive clarification of the race origin problem.

[J. M. Cattell, D. R. Brimhall, *Am. Men of Sci.* (3rd ed., 1921); *Gen. Cat. of Bates Coll.* (1915); *Anthropological Papers, Am. Museum of Natural Hist.*, vol. XXIII (1925); *Am. Anthropologist*, Apr.–June 1925; *Am. Jour. of Physical Anthropology*, Oct.–Dec. 1925.]
C. W.

SULLIVAN, TIMOTHY DANIEL (July 23, 1862–Aug. 31, 1913), politician, the son of Daniel and Catherine (Connelly) Sullivan, was born in a New York City tenement. His father, a laborer, died when the boy was four years old, leaving the mother with half a dozen young children, and almost penniless. At seven or eight years of age Tim was on the street selling papers. He had only a few bits of primary schooling. Before he was fifteen he was making himself useful to the Tammany politicians in the Sixth Ward, the turbulent Five Points district, and thus he got his start in politics. He was scarcely twenty-one when he found a backer who set him up as a saloon keeper. A few years later he was either sole or part proprietor of six saloons. In 1886, at the age of twenty-three, he was elected to the state Assembly, and in the following year he married Helen Fitzgerald. In 1893 he was elected to the state Senate and served there until 1902. In 1892 he succeeded to the Democratic leadership of the Third Assembly District—the Bowery region—and before 1900 he was the uncrowned king of the lower East Side.

Besides his activities in the liquor business, he had interests in several successful theatres and as half owner of the Sullivan & Considine vaudeville circuit in the Western states. By 1898, outside of Brooklyn, no one could put on a boxing match in the State of New York save in clubs licensed by and paying tribute to Sullivan. He was likewise a leading member of a syndicate which levied tribute on gambling in New York City. The *New York Times* in articles beginning Mar. 9, 1900, charged that the annual takings of this ring were $3,095,000. Between 1900 and 1910 Sullivan was admittedly the most powerful politician in New York. He could have become dictator of Tammany Hall upon the retirement of Richard Croker [q.v.] in 1902 had he so desired, but his own position was more lucrative and more to his taste, so he worked for the appointment of his friend Charles W. Murphy [q.v.]. Known most commonly and affectionately to constituents as "Big Tim" or "The Big Feller," he was a handsome, jovial giant who distributed with a lavish hand a goodly percentage of the money which he was so shrewd in collecting through various channels. Vice and crime were carefully organized in his territory and paid graft to his machine, as did many lines of legitimate business, even to the pushcart peddlers. Nevertheless, there was probably never a leader so idolized by his constituents. It was said of him that he made millions and gave away millions. He gave a Christmas turkey dinner every year to from 5,000 to 7,000 poor men and derelicts, and presented each with a pair of stout shoes and socks. He was one of the most magnetic personalities ever known in American politics. An observer once remarked that his smile could adequately be described only by the word beautiful. When charged with grafting or partnership with crime and vice, he could arise in the Assembly or on a campaign rostrum, and by telling the story of his tenement boyhood and the sacrifices of his mother, reduce even hardened political opponents to tears.

He was elected to Congress in 1902, and re-elected in 1904, but he did not care for national politics, and retired in 1906. In 1908 he was again elected to the state Senate. His health was slowly failing, however, and in 1912, following the death of his wife and of his two favorite cousins and lieutenants, "Florrie" and "Little Tim" Sullivan, his mind began to give way. Nevertheless, he was elected to Congress that fall, though he made no campaign and did not even go to Washington to be sworn in. For a time he was confined in a sanitarium and later lived in a house belonging to his brother. On the night of Aug. 30, 1913, eluding observation, he wandered away. A train early next morning, a few miles from Eastchester, ran over the body of a man who, as the crew believed, was already dead. Strangely enough, the search for Sullivan continued while the body lay unidentified in a morgue for two weeks. Just as it was about to be sent to the potter's field it was identified by a policeman. The funeral was one of the most imposing ever seen in New York; it was estimated that 25,000 sincere mourners followed "Big Tim" to the grave. It was Sullivan who was responsible for Columbus Day becoming a legal holiday in New York, and for the law making the carrying of concealed weapons a felony.

[Newspaper literature on Sullivan is voluminous; see *N. Y. Herald*, Apr. 28, 1901, May 19, 1907, and Nov. 1, 1909; *World* (N. Y.), Oct. 27, 1901, June 14, 1903, and Feb. 16, 1913; *N. Y. Press*, Dec. 3, 1905, Sept. 29, 1912, and Nov. 17, 1912; *N. Y. Tribune*, Sept. 19, 1901; and all New York newspapers of Sept. 14, 15, 1913. Other sources include *Biog. Dir. Am. Cong.* (1928); G. K. Turner, "Tammany's Control of N. Y. by Professional Criminals," *McClure's Mag.*, June 1909; *Ten Months of Tammany* (1901), pub. by City Club of N. Y.; *Report of the Special Committee of the Assembly . . . to Investigate the Pub. Offices . . . of N. Y.* (5 vols., 1900); A. F. Harlow, *Old Bowery Days* (1931); M. R. Werner, *Tammany Hall* (1928); Harold Zink, *City Bosses in the U. S.* (1930); memorial addresses, *House Doc.* 1177, 63 Cong., 2 Sess.; *Proc. of the Legislature of the State of N. Y. on the Life . . . of Timothy D. Sullivan* (1914); *Current Lit.*, Dec. 1909; *Munsey's Mag.*, Dec. 1913.]
A. F. H.

SULLIVAN, WILLIAM (November 1774–Sept. 3, 1839), lawyer and writer, was born at Biddeford, Me., on the Saco River, son of James Sullivan [*q.v.*], later governor of Massachu-

setts, and Mehitable (Odiorne) Sullivan. Prepared for college by the Rev. Phillips Payson of Chelsea, Mass., he was graduated from Harvard with honors in 1792, studied law in his father's Boston office, and was admitted to the bar in 1795. On May 19, 1802 he married Sarah Webb Swan, daughter of Col. James Swan [*q.v.*]; to them ten children were born.

In Boston Sullivan proved himself an able lawyer and shared in the increasing fortunes of the growing city. During the early years of his practice he was frequently called upon to give legal advice to the selectmen (Boston Town Records, *passim*); in 1814 he served as fire ward, in 1821 he aided in drafting a charter for the city (Morison, *post*, II, 237). As chief marshal of the Boston Centennial Celebration in 1830, he left behind a characteristic letter addressed to the Chief Marshal of the Celebration of Sept. 17, 1930 (*Boston Transcript*, Jan. 23, 1926, pt. III).

He also played a prominent rôle in politics, despite his Democratic parentage allying himself with the Federalists. In 1804 he was elected to the Massachusetts General Court and thenceforth until 1830 was in almost continuous service as representative, senator, or member of the executive council of the state. In 1812 he was a member of the Federalist Convention in New York and of the Central Committee of Federalists in Massachusetts. Though not a delegate to the Hartford Convention, he was in sympathy with its actions and was sent with Harrison Gray Otis and Thomas H. Perkins [*qq.v.*] to carry to Washington the protest of the Massachusetts legislature which grew out of the report of that convention. Fourteen years later he joined with others to defend the convention against the charge brought by John Quincy Adams that the Federalists there present had advocated disunion (Henry Adams, *Documents Relating to New-England Federalism*, 1877, pp. 43–45, 63–91).

In 1829 his wife inherited a competence sufficient for the future needs of the family, making it possible for him to abandon the practice of law for the writing which had already become his greatest pleasure. His conviction that the permanence of the institutions of his country depended upon the spread of popular education induced him to prepare a series of "class books": *The Political Class Book* (1831); *The Moral Class Book* (1831); *Historical Class Book; (Part First) Containing Sketches of History . . . to . . . A.D. 476* (1833); *Historical Causes and Effects, from the Fall of the Roman Empire, 476, to the Reformation, 1517* (1838). In 1835 and 1836 he gave a series of historical lectures in Boston; these are preserved in manuscript in the Boston Public Library. In 1837 he brought out *Sea Life*. His most considerable work, *Familiar Letters on Public Characters and Public Events from the Peace of 1783 to the Peace of 1815* (1834), was republished in 1847 with notes and a sketch of the author by his son, under the title, *The Public Men of the Revolution*. He was in constant demand as a public speaker and a number of his occasional addresses were published. At his death he was described as a man of "most amiable and benevolent disposition, varied and extensive accomplishments" (*Boston Daily Advertiser*, Sept. 4, 1839). He was by all agreed to be hospitable, cheerful, of lively wit, sound sense, and great intelligence. His writing was simple and lucid—as he himself said, "not in the fashion of his day."

[Biog. sketch by J. T. S. Sullivan, in *The Pub. Men of the Revolution* (1847); MSS., Mass. Hist. Soc.; *New Eng. Hist. and Geneal. Reg.*, Oct. 1865, Oct. 1892; T. C. Amory, *Memoir of Hon. William Sullivan* (1879), pub. also in *Proc. Mass. Hist. Soc.*, vol. II (1880); *Col. Soc. of Mass. Pubs.*, vols. VII (1905), XVII (1915), XXVI (1927); J. T. Sargent, *A Discourse on the Death of William Sullivan* (1839); G. W. Warren, *The Hist. of the Bunker Hill Monument Asso.* (1877); T. C. Amory, *Life of James Sullivan* (2 vols., 1859); S. E. Morison, *The Life and Letters of Harrison Gray Otis* (2 vols., 1913).]   E. D.

SULLIVAN, WILLIAM HENRY (Aug. 9, 1864–Jan. 26, 1929), lumberman and civic leader, was born in Port Dalhousie, Ontario, Canada, the son of Timothy and Margaret (Sinnett) Sullivan; both parents were of Irish descent. The boy was educated in the public schools of St. Catharines, Ontario. While yet in his teens he went to Buffalo, N. Y., and followed there for a time the trade of a carpenter, which he had learned in Canada. Subsequently, he obtained employment in the Garretson furniture plant and soon became manager. In 1886 he was intrusted with the responsibility of building a sawmill for his employer, L. L. Garretson, who had bought a hardwood tract of 14,000 acres near Austin, Pa., and on the completion of this mill he was put in charge of its operation. Meanwhile, he had become acquainted with the Goodyears of Buffalo and for a while conducted some lumber mills for them at Galeton, Pa.

In 1902 the Goodyears decided to turn their attention to lumbering in the South and began acquiring extensive tracts of land in Washington and St. Tammany parishes in southeastern Louisiana and the adjoining counties of Pike and Marion in southern Mississippi. In 1906, having organized the Great Southern Lumber Company, they sent some representatives, including Sullivan, to select a site for a lumber mill. Largely at his suggestion, they finally decided upon a tract of land in Washington Parish,

La., along a stream called Bogue Lusa, which empties into the Pearl River. On this tract Sullivan directed the building of the largest sawmill in the world, with a capacity of 1,000,000 feet per day, and laid out a town which he named Bogalusa. He soon became vice-president and general manager of the company and organized other industries, such as a paper mill, a box and crate factory, and a turpentine and creosote plant, which were operated along with the lumber mill. His last project was the manufacture of California redwood lumber, an enterprise which was inaugurated at a cost of $1,000,000 and put into successful operation only a few days before his death. With the growth of the varied interests of the company, the town of Bogalusa developed rapidly into a thriving industrial community of about 14,000 people. As an executive, Sullivan planned on a large scale and with a view to permanence, mixing sentiment and good busines sense. He worked hard to make Bogalusa a beautiful and comfortable place in which to live and to preserve it from extinction through the exhaustion of the timber resources of the vicinity. He induced the company to reforest large tracts of its cut-over lands and encouraged other land owners in that region to do the same thing. His contribution to the development of the lumber industry of Louisiana into one of the leading industrial activities of the state was greater perhaps than that of any other single individual. He was also active in the development of farming interests and offered special inducements to farmers settling on the company's cut-over lands that were not reforested.

When the town was incorporated in 1914, Sullivan was elected mayor under the commission form of government and was continued in that office without opposition until his death. In all its civic and business activities he took a leading part. During the flood of 1927 he was one of the three principal advisers of Secretary of Commerce Hoover in the relief work of the Mississippi Valley and at Hoover's suggestion became the director of that work in Louisiana. He was of striking physical appearance—tall, large of frame, and well proportioned; he had a forceful personality, engaging manners, and inexhaustible energy. He was married twice: first, on Oct. 4, 1886, at Buffalo, N. Y., to Elizabeth Calkins, who died on July 11, 1918; and second, on Jan. 27, 1922, at Slidell, La., to Ella Rose Salmen, who died less than two months before his own death. Three children were born to the first of these unions and two to the second. In 1927 he was made a member of the military staff of Governor Simpson of Louisiana and from that time was popularly known by the title of colonel.

[*Times-Picayune* (New Orleans), the *New Orleans Item-Tribune*, and the *Bogalusa Sunday Times*, Jan. 27, 1929; *Lumber Trade Jour.*, Feb. 1, 1929; *Southern Lumberman*, Feb. 2, 1929; *Who's Who in La. and Miss.* (1918); Alcée Fortier, *Louisiana* (1909), vol. I; P. B. Carter, "Hist. of Washington Parish," *La. Hist. Quart.*, Jan. 1931; information from D. T. Cushing, general manager of the Great Southern Lumber Company.]   E. M. V.

SULLIVANT, WILLIAM STARLING (Jan. 15, 1803–Apr. 30, 1873), botanist, distinguished as America's foremost bryologist, was born at Franklinton, a frontier settlement near the present site of Columbus, Ohio, the eldest of four children of Lucas Sullivant, a Virginian, and Sarah (Starling) Sullivant. His father, having been commissioned by the federal government to survey this virgin region, had purchased a large tract along the Scioto River. Here young Sullivant grew up, self-reliant and notably sturdy of physique. He attended school in Kentucky, entered Ohio University at Athens, and was graduated from Yale College in 1823. His father's death in the same year obliged him immediately to assume management of the family properties in Ohio, so that he became at once a surveyor and engineer. Until late in life he engaged successfully in business affairs.

When about thirty Sullivant first became interested in botany. He studied the flowering plants and in 1840 published *A Catalogue of Plants, Native and Naturalized, in the Vicinity of Columbus, Ohio*. Shortly, however, he turned to the mosses, a difficult group requiring microscopic examination and thus well suited to his bent for scrupulously accurate and detailed study. His *Musci Alleghanienses* (2 vols., 1845–46) was accompanied by beautifully prepared specimens of the mosses and hepatics discussed, mostly of his own collecting in the southern Alleghanies. Next came two papers entitled "Contributions to the Bryology and Hepaticology of North America" (*Memoirs of the American Academy*, new ser., vols. III, 1848, and IV, 1849), illustrated by engravings. Far more important was his contribution to the second edition (1856) of Gray's *Manual* of a synoptical illustrated treatise upon the bryophytes. This was republished separately as *The Musci and Hepaticae of the United States East of the Mississippi River* (1856), and it laid the foundation for subsequent bryological studies in the United States. With the assistance of Leo Lesquereux [*q.v.*], Sullivant issued also in the same year the well-known exsiccati *Musci Boreali-Americani* in fifty uniform sets of about 360 specimens each. In 1865 he prepared a similar but larger

series of exsiccati which included many recent species from California, and he assisted C. F. Austin in publishing the classic *Musci Appalachiani* (1870) also. In the meantime he had published upon part of Charles Wright's Cuban mosses and upon important collections obtained by several governmental surveys, the most noteworthy result being an elaborately illustrated folio (1859) describing the mosses collected by the United States Exploring Expedition under Lieut. Charles Wilkes [*q.v.*]. Sullivant's greatest work, however, is the *Icones Muscorum* (1864), a thick imperial octavo volume with 129 illustrations in copperplate, being "figures and descriptions of most of those mosses peculiar to eastern North America which have not been heretofore figured." This publication placed him in the front rank of bryologists. A *Supplement* to it appeared the year after his death, which resulted from pneumonia. His bryological collections and books were bequeathed to Harvard University.

Sullivant was married, Apr. 7, 1824, to Jane Marshall, of Kentucky (a niece of Chief Justice Marshall), who died within a year. His second wife, Eliza Griscom Wheeler of New York, whom he married Nov. 29, 1834, was an acute bryologist who assisted in all his scientific work up to her death, Aug. 23, 1850. On Sept. 1, 1851, he married Caroline Eudora Sutton, who survived him. By the three marriages there were thirteen children. He is commemorated by the genus *Sullivantia*, a unique plant of the saxifrage family, which he himself discovered in Ohio.

[Data are mainly from a biog. memoir by his longtime friend Asa Gray, in Sullivant's *Icon. Musc. Suppl.* (1874), pp. 1–8, repub. in *Am. Jour. Sci.*, 3 ser., vol. VI (1873); *Proc. Am Acad. Arts and Sci.*, vol. IX (1874); *Biog. Memoirs Nat. Acad. Sci.*, vol. I (1877). See also W. J. Youmans, *Pioneers of Science in America* (1896), pp. 394–401, esp. the concluding portion, as to admirable personal traits; and Joseph Sullivant, *A Geneal. and Family Memorial* (1874). For list of plant species named in Sullivant's honor, see article by Clara Armstrong in *Ohio Naturalist*, vol. I, pp. 33–35, Jan. 1901.]   W. R. M.

SULLY, DANIEL JOHN (Mar. 9, 1861–Sept. 19, 1930), cotton speculator, son of Abraham (or Abram) Charles and Jane Sully, was born in Providence, R. I. He attended the Norwich Free Academy and in his teens found his first employment as clerk in a coal merchant's office. On Oct. 1, 1885, he married Emma Frances Thompson, daughter of the manager of the great Knight cotton mills at Providence. Sully entered the employ of the Knight organization and became deeply interested in the production of raw cotton. Realizing the value of an intimate knowledge of the subject, he persuaded his employers to let him spend the better part of two years in the South in the study of the growing and marketing of cotton. He served with the Knight mills for some time longer, but his interest in manufacture was waning, and he was becoming more and more absorbed in the speculative feature of the cotton trade. He finally resigned and entered a brokerage office in Boston, where he spent four years, returning to Providence in 1891 to become a member of the brokerage firm of F. W. Reynolds & Company. Here he specialized in Egyptian cotton. American cotton production appeared to him to be a waning industry, and therefore, when he went to New York in 1902 and opened a brokerage office of his own, he was a pronounced "bull" in the market. Theodore Price, the dominant "bull" up to that time, had pushed the price of cotton up to nine cents but feared to attempt going further. At this point Sully practically took charge of the market. Steadily he bought and pushed the price upward. By May 1903 he was believed to have made a million dollars profit. He sold out most of his holdings and took his family for a brief trip to Europe. During his absence prices continued strong, and on his return he plunged into buying again. For the next few months he dictated the price of cotton. His operations not only covered the cotton markets of the South but extended to the exchanges of Liverpool and Alexandria, Egypt. As he completed his "corner" and prices climbed steadily upward, the public entered into the speculation on an unprecedented scale. Cotton finally rose to a few points above seventeen cents. Sully meanwhile was speculating in stocks, grain, and other commodities, and his credit was greatly extended. On Mar. 18, 1904, a panic seized the cotton market, and a drop of twelve to thirteen dollars per bale occurred, throwing Sully into bankruptcy. His liabilities were $3,000,000, and he could pay only fifty cents on the dollar. Next he took over a soap company and endeavored to establish an international organization, but this failed in 1908. His noted art collection was sold, and he was forced to turn his handsome seaside home at Watch Hill, R. I., into a summer boarding-house. This, too, was sold to pay debts in 1914, and he spent his later years in rather reduced circumstances. He died in Beverly Hills, Cal. He was survived by his wife, a son, and two daughters, one of whom was the first wife of Douglas Fairbanks, the actor.

[See *Who's Who in America*, 1920–21; *N. Y. Tribune*, Mar. 19, 1904; obituaries in *N. Y. Times*, *World* (N.Y.), and *N. Y. Herald Tribune* and in *Providence Journal*, Sept. 20, 1930; city records of Providence, R. I. The New York newspapers—especially *Commercial Advertiser*, and *Wall Street Journal*—during 1903

and 1904 are full of references to Sully's "corner" in cotton and to his failure.]   A. F. H.

SULLY, THOMAS (1783–Nov. 5, 1872), painter, was born at Horncastle, Lincolnshire, England, the fourth child of Matthew and Sarah (Chester) Sully, who were actors. In 1792 the Sullys came to America with their family of four sons and five daughters, and settled in Charleston, S. C. Influenced largely by prudential motives they decided upon a business career for Thomas, and at the age of twelve he was placed with an insurance broker, who soon discovered that the boy's heart lay elsewhere and advised his father that he should be a painter. His artistic tastes were first stimulated by the influence of a schoolmate, Charles Fraser [q.v.], who instructed him in the "rudiments of the art," and later by his elder brother Lawrence (1769–1803), a miniature and device painter. For a time he was under the instruction of a Monsieur Belzons, the husband of one of his sisters, but as the two were temperamentally far apart Sully soon broke away from his French brother-in-law (c. 1799). Upon the invitation of his favorite brother, Lawrence, who had moved to Richmond, Va., he went to live with him and his wife, the former Sarah Annis of Annapolis, Md., and became his brother's pupil. The two brothers later decided to remove to Norfolk, and it was there on May 10, 1801, that Sully painted his first miniature from life, a likeness of his brother Chester. In this same year he painted "ten pieces valued at one hundred eighty dollars," and in the following year he achieved his "first attempt in oil colors," a small portrait of William Armistead. He began, early in his painting career, his methodical "Account of Pictures" (oftener spoken of as his "Register"), which suggests that he thought he had entered upon his rightful vocation and that he looked forward to a steady and increasing employment. On the pages of the "Register," ruled in columns, he entered the date on which a likeness was begun, the size of the picture, the sitter's name, with an occasional explanatory note, the price received, and the date of the completion of the picture. This record he continued until the end of his career.

The Sullys lived and worked together in both Richmond and Norfolk until the death of Lawrence Sully in Richmond in 1803. On June 27, 1805 (Hart, *post*, p. 13), Thomas married his widowed sister-in-law, whom with her three children he had supported for two years. She bore him six daughters and three sons. Of the sons one became an artist; another, Alfred Sully, a soldier and Indian fighter. The marriage was a happy one and the family life unusually har-

monious. In November 1806, after several years
of hard work and little remuneration, on the
advice of Thomas Abthorpe Cooper [*q.v*], the
distinguished actor, Sully removed to New York
City. This proved a turning-point in his career,
for he was introduced there to his patron's wide
circle of friends, many of whom he painted.
There are records of his having painted during
this period John E. Harwood, Mr. Twaits, Mr.
and Mrs. John Darley, all on Cooper's order,
and later Mrs. Villars as "Lady Macbeth," and
Mrs. Ann Brunton Warren of the Philadelphia
Theatre. At the end of 1807 he had produced
"pieces" to the number of seventy and listed his
receipts at $3,203. The Embargo at the end of
this year greatly injured his prospects, so that
he was forced to paint a series of "thrift" portraits for thirty dollars each. He was fortunate,
however, in meeting Gilbert Stuart [*q.v.*], then
at the height of his fame (1807) and living in
Boston. Allowed to stand by the great artist's
chair while he painted, Sully relates that it was
"a situation I valued more at that moment than
I shall ever again appreciate any station on
earth" (Dunlap, *post,* vol. II, p. 250). Stuart
consented to criticize a portrait of Isaac P. Davis
which Sully was engaged to paint, and the few
words of praise from the great painter, "Keep
what you have got, and get as much as you can"
(*Ibid.,* p. 251), came like a benediction to the
younger man. Following his Boston visit, Sully
determined to go to Philadelphia to live. He
made a preliminary visit in 1807, when he painted
a portrait of Miss Wilcocks, sister of his friend
Benjamin Chew Wilcocks, and in 1808 settled
in the city, which remained his home for the rest
of his life. One of his letters of introduction was
written by Washington Irving to Rebecca Gratz
[*qq.v.*], whom he later painted. At this time he
was receiving an almost ludicrously small sum
for his work, fifty dollars being his regular price
for a bust portrait, though a half-length sometimes brought him eighty dollars. Yet these likenesses from the hand of the still young painter
had the quality of enduring art, and many of
them will remain among the loveliest portraits
of all time.

A great longing for improvement in his art
and a desire for wider opportunities made Sully
again contemplate a trip abroad which he had
given up at the time of his brother's death. Wilcocks and six of his friends each promised to
give two hundred dollars towards a proposed
journey to England. In return Sully offered to
make a copy of some one of the great masters for
each of his six benefactors while he was abroad,
a promise which, though it meant nine months

of incessant application and more than rigid
economy, he scrupulously fulfilled. On May 17,
1809, he was admitted to American citizenship
and on June 10 he set sail for England, landing
five weeks later, July 13, 1809, in Liverpool. In
two weeks' time he was painting in London.
Among his letters of introduction was one from
William Rawle to Benjamin West, 1738–1820
[*qq.v.*], who received him kindly and asked to
see a sample of his work. Though West appeared
to be impressed with the portrait of Charles King
which Sully painted to show him, he questioned
Sully's knowledge of the anatomy and structure
of the head, and recommended the serious study
of osteology and anatomy. Sully followed his advice with profit, and at the further suggestion of
West, who had almost given up portrait painting
in favor of historical pieces, he sought out and
observed the work of the best portrait artists of
the day. Particularly attracted by the portraits
of Sir Thomas Lawrence, he made the painter's
acquaintance and was introduced by him to many
important people, some of whom became his
sitters. Among these was the Kemble family.
He painted the lovely Frances Anne Kemble
[*q.v.*] at various times later on, sometimes as her
natural self and sometimes in her acting rôles.

On Mar. 10, 1810, he set sail for home and on
Apr. 24 once more resumed his brush in Philadelphia at 56 South Eleventh St. There he
finished many head and bust portraits, and attempted some whole-length figures, the first being a composition piece after Schiller's play,
The Robbers, which featured the portrait of William B. Wood as Charles de Moor. This picture
was soon followed by another that attracted even
greater attention, that of George Frederick
Cooke in the rôle of Richard III. During the
next succeeding years Sully painted portraits
that showed him at his very best, and his reputation was soon firmly established as a "History
and Portrait Painter." His income, while not
large, was steadily increasing, and he was free
from pecuniary anxieties. He joined the Pennsylvania Academicians, a body of artists looking
to the then recently established Academy of the
Fine Arts, and served on a committee for the
management of the schools of the academy. In
1818, when the legislature of North Carolina
asked him for two full-length portraits of Washington, he proposed instead that he paint an historical picture showing Washington crossing the
Delaware to attack Trenton. When the picture
was completed, however, it was so large (17'4"
x 12'5") that it was not accepted, and Sully finally disposed of it for $500 to a frame-maker.
It now hangs in the Boston Museum of Art. An-

other important composition was "The Capture of Major André." Sully left South Eleventh Street in 1812 for the Philosophical Hall, where he painted for the next ten years and opened a gallery of pictures to the public for twenty-five cents admission. Later he changed his address many times, finally settling about 1830 in a house near the corner of Fifth and Chestnut streets which belonged to Stephen Girard [q.v.]. There he made his home for the remainder of his life, about forty-four years. When in 1824–25 the Marquis de Lafayette paid his farewell visit to the United States, he was invited by six prominent gentlemen of Philadelphia to sit to Sully for his portrait. The picture, done in Washington (Sully, "Recollections of an Old Painter," *Hours at Home,* November 1869, p. 74), was apparently painted by subscription and was valued by the artist at six hundred dollars, but as the money was not immediately forthcoming Sully held the picture for some time, finally handing it over to the subscribers for about two hundred and fifty dollars. The finished picture now hangs in Independence Hall, Philadelphia. After Charles Willson Peale's death in 1827 and Gilbert Stuart's in 1828, Sully had no formidable rivals in his art, and in 1837 when he made his second visit to England and painted the young Queen Victoria from life he reached the summit of his fame.

It was in the high tide of his power that Sully determined upon his second visit to England. Several of the great painters who were alive at the time of his first visit had died, and it seemed a propitious time for an American artist with an established reputation to try his fortune in the English capital. Just on the eve of his departure he was commissioned by the Society of the Sons of Saint George in Philadelphia to "memorialize" Queen Victoria by a portrait to be owned by the society. When the queen's permission had been obtained, a painting-room was established in Buckingham Palace, and the first sitting for the head took place on Mar. 22, 1838. Blanche Sully, who had accompanied her father to England, usually sat for the queen's regalia, which weighed thirty or forty pounds. The original sketch for the head is owned by the Metropolitan Museum in New York; the finished picture, full length, belongs to the Society of the Sons of Saint George in Philadelphia. The visit was altogether a success. While awaiting the queen's pleasure Sully painted portraits of many distinguished people; he was elected to honorary membership in the Garrick Club for three months; and he and his daughter, who had established themselves at 46 Great Marlborough St., were

the recipients of many delightful invitations. At the end of September 1838 he was in his Philadelphia studio once more. His prestige was even greater than before, and as he grew older he continued to command his field. At the age of seventy-five and even eighty years he was singled out by people of culture and discrimination who wished to have portraits painted. In his career he produced upwards of twenty-six hundred works, an average of thirty-seven for each year in which he painted, a notable example of industry. Many of the portraits, which include the most distinguished men and women of the day, are in the possession of the Pennsylvania Historical Society, the Pennsylvania Academy of the Fine Arts, the Metropolitan Museum, and the United States Military Academy at West Point. Mrs. Sully died on July 25, 1867 (Hart, *post,* p. 13), and it was his daughter Blanche who ministered to Sully during his last years. He died on Nov. 5, 1872, and was buried on Nov. 9 in Laurel Hill Cemetery, Philadelphia, where lie many of the Sully name. He is described by his contemporary, William Dunlap, as walking with the stride of a man of six feet, though he was not over five feet eight inches in height, and as having a face "marked with the wish to make others happy" (Dunlap, *post,* vol. II, p. 276). His whole life, indeed, was characterized not only by great consideration for others but by the utmost fairness and honesty. In 1873 *Hints to Young Painters and the Process of Portrait-Painting as Practiced by the Late Thomas Sully* was published. Sometimes called "the Sir Thomas Lawrence of America," he was undoubtedly influenced by the work of the older artist, especially in his delineation of women and of children, who are the embodiment of innocence and happiness, depicted with grace and charm. He was at his best when portraying the lovely women who flocked to his studio at the height of his success, but some of his portraits of men, such as his "Dr. Samuel Coates," are marked by an admirable firmness. Although occasionally his draftsmanship leaves something to be desired, he was always a master of color, and his paintings have a warmth and beauty seldom if ever surpassed.

[The date of Sully's birth is given variously as June 8 and June 19, 1783. See Edward Biddle and Mantle Fielding, *The Life and Works of Thomas Sully* (1921), with a complete list of Sully's paintings; C. H. Hart, *A Register of Portraits Painted by Thomas Sully 1801–1871* (1908); *Memorial Exhibition of Portraits by Thomas Sully* (1922), Pa. Acad. of the Fine Arts; William Dunlap, *A Hist. of the Rise and Progress of the Arts of Design in the U. S.* (3 vols., 1918), ed. by F. W. Bayley and C. E. Goodspeed, with many contemporary anecdotes; Henry Budd, "Thomas Sully," *Pa. Mag. of Hist. and Biog.,* vol. XLII (1918), p.

97; H. T. Tuckerman, *Book of the Artists* (1867); Samuel Isham, *The Hist. of Am. Painting* (1905); Suzanne La Follette, *Art in America* (1929), brief comment; J. D. Champlin and C. C. Perkins, *Cyc. of Painters and Painting*, vol. IV (1887); and obituary in *Press* (Phila.), Nov. 6, 1872. There are occasional references to Sully in Frances Anne Kemble, *Records of Later Life* (1882).]   M. F.

SULZBERGER, CYRUS LINDAUER (July 11, 1858–Apr. 30, 1932), merchant, leader in Jewish affairs, civics, and philanthropy, was the son of Leopold and Sophia (Lindauer) Sulzberger and a first cousin of Mayer Sulzberger [*q.v.*]. Born in Philadelphia, he received his education at Central High School there. At the age of sixteen he was one of the founders of the Young Men's Hebrew Association of Philadelphia. In 1877 he removed to New York to become bookkeeper of the textile importing firm of N. Erlanger, Blumgart & Company, of which he became a member in 1891, president in 1902, and chairman of the board in 1929.

Although he won marked success in the business world, Sulzberger was best known for his constructive work in dealing with Jewish immigration when the great inrush of foreign peoples was a national problem, and for his activities in Jewish philanthropic endeavor. He was one of the organizers in 1900 and chairman from 1904 to 1909 of the Industrial Removal Office, an organization with branches in 108 cities in the United States, which endeavored to relieve the congestion of Jewish immigrants in New York City by aiding them to settle in other localities. His work in this field coincided with the peak years of immigration; in his statement and testimony before the Congressional Immigration Commission, Mar. 11, 1910, he was able to show that the Industrial Removal Office, in the period 1902–09, had sent 45,711 immigrants from New York City into 1,278 towns and cities ("Reports of the Immigration Commission," *Senate Document 764,* 61 Cong., 3 Sess., XLI, 194). A deep student of immigration problems, he was also an able spokesman for the continued liberalization of the laws governing entry into the United States, recognizing, while laboring to this end, the necessity of providing for the distribution and Americanization of immigrants. Besides his chairmanship of the Industrial Removal Office he was president (1903–09 and 1919–21) of the Jewish Agricultural and Industrial Aid Society, which helped in placing some 80,000 Jews on farms in the United States. In October 1910 Gov. Charles E. Hughes appointed him a member of the New York state commission on congestion of population, which presented a report in February 1911 recommending legislation to create a permanent commission on distribution of population; to provide for an inquiry into manufacturing in tenement homes; to inaugurate the annual publication of a directory of industrial opportunities to promote the spread of factories to a greater number of towns, and to furnish additional facilities whereby the state labor department might permanently spread the supply of laboring population to avoid excessive unemployment in congested communities. The commission also recommended the placing of public institutions outside city limits and definite measures to remove city dwellers to small land holdings and farms (*Documents of the Assembly of the State of New York . . . 1911,* vol. XXV, no. 34).

Sulzberger's activity in organized philanthropy included service as president of the United Hebrew Charities of New York (1908) and of the National Conference of Jewish Charities (1912–14), as member of the executive committee of the American Jewish Committee in 1907 and its secretary in 1914–15 when that organization collected vast sums for the relief of Jews overseas, and as trustee of the Federation for the Support of Jewish Philanthropic Societies of New York City (1919). He was a founder of the *American Hebrew* in 1879, and aided in the publication of *The Jewish Encyclopedia.* Despite his high responsibilities, he was a self-effacing man who preferred labor to the honor of office. With vigor and intelligence he applied a broadly social mind to philanthropy, and his constructive ideas supplied the motivation of many activities carried on in the names of others. A leader in civic reform, he ran for public office only once, as candidate for president of the Borough of Manhattan, New York City: on the unsuccessful Fusion ticket of 1903.

He married, May 13, 1884, Rachel Peixotto Hays, by whom he had five children. Two sons, with his wife, survived him. He died in New York City.

[*Am. Hebrew and Jewish Tribune,* May 6, 1932; *Who's Who in Am. Jewry,* 1928; *Who's Who in America,* 1932–33; *Jewish Encyc.,* vol. XI; *Am. Hebrew,* July 13, 1928; *Jewish Tribune,* July 13, 1928; *Am. Jewish Year Book, 1933–34* (1933); *N. Y. Times,* May 1, 1932; information from Dr. Cyrus Adler.]   C. M. P.

SULZBERGER, MAYER (June 22, 1843–Apr. 20, 1923), jurist, scholar, was born in Heidelsheim, Baden, Germany, the son of Abraham and Sophia (Einstein) Sulzberger. He came of a family which had included a number of rabbinical scholars. His father, a minister and teacher in Heidelsheim, came to America as a result of the Revolution of 1848, settling in Philadelphia where a brother, Leopold, father of Cyrus L. Sulzberger [*q.v.*], had settled some ten years before. Mayer Sulzberger received the degree of A.B. from the Central High School of Philadelphia in 1859, attended a business college, worked as bookkeeper for a business concern, studied law in the office of Moses A. Dropsie [q.v.], and in 1865 was admitted to the bar. After thirty years of successful practice he was elected in 1895 a judge of the court of common pleas and served by reëlection until his retirement, Jan. 3, 1916, being president judge from 1902.

As a judge Sulzberger was penetrating, impartial, and witty. A few of his papers and addresses were printed: "Nominations for Public Office" (*Penn Monthly,* March 1881), presented at a meeting of the Philadelphia Social Science Association; "The Practice of Criminal Law" (*American Law Register,* June 1903); *Politics in a Democracy* (1910), address delivered at the Silver Jubilee of Temple University; two lectures on "Medical Jurisprudence" (*The Jeffersonian,* January and February 1915). He gave his law library to the court upon his retirement from the bench. He was subsequently a member of the committee to revise the constitution of Pennsylvania and of the Philadelphia Board of City Trusts.

Sulzberger as a young man was greatly influenced by the Rev. Isaac Leeser [q.v.] of Philadelphia, one of the prominent Jewish leaders of the day, and throughout his life he was active in Jewish welfare work and in the promotion of Jewish education and higher Jewish learning in America. He was a trustee of the Baron de Hirsch Fund (1884) and of the Mikveh Israel Congregation of Philadelphia; first president of the Young Men's Hebrew Association of Philadelphia in 1875, and president again in 1885. From 1865 he served actively on the board of the Jewish Hospital of Philadelphia, founded by his father, and he was also a trustee of the Jefferson Medical College. As president of the American Jewish Committee from 1906 to 1912 he took an active part in the movement that brought about the abrogation of the treaty of commerce with Russia in the latter year. He was offered appointment as minister to Turkey by President Harrison and as ambassador to Turkey by President Taft, but declined in both cases. He was secretary of the board of trustees of the short-lived Maimonides College, Philadelphia (1867–73); trustee of Gratz College, Philadelphia, from its foundation in 1897; a director of the Jewish Theological Seminary from 1901; an original governor of the Dropsie College for Hebrew and Cognate Learning; one of the founders of the Jewish Publication So-

ciety of America and chairman of its publication committee, 1888–1923; and a founder of the Oriental Club of Philadelphia. At a time when there was no important collection of Hebraica and Judaica in the United States he expended a considerable part of his income for the purchase of Hebrew manuscripts and incunabula and the assembling of a general Jewish library, which in 1902 he turned over to the Jewish Theological Seminary of America. He also collected Arabic, Ethiopic, and Samaritan manuscripts, which together with a small collection of Egyptian objects and Assyrian and Phoenician seals were presented to the Dropsie College.

In his youth, Sulzberger translated into English the dictionary of Hebrew authors of Azariah de Rossi and part of Maimonides' "Guide of the Perplexed," both translations being published serially in the *Occident,* and for a year after the death of Isaac Leeser he edited that periodical. The latter years of his life he devoted to a series of Biblical studies which resulted in the publication of four books: *The Am Ha-Aretz, the Ancient Hebrew Parliament* (1910); *The Polity of the Ancient Hebrews* (1912); *The Ancient Hebrew Law of Homicide* (1915); *The Status of Labor in Ancient Israel* (1923). After his retirement from the bench he became an honorary lecturer on Jewish jurisprudence and institutes of government in the Dropsie College. He died, unmarried, in his eightieth year.

[*Address of Hon. Norris S. Barratt . . . upon the Presentation . . . of the Portrait . . . of Hon. Mayer Sulzberger . . . also Proc. of the Law Asso. of Phila.* (1916); *Addresses Delivered in Memory of Mayer Sulzberger . . . May 30, 1923* (1924); *Am. Jewish Hist. Soc. Pubs.,* no. 29 (1925); L. E. Levinthal, *Mayer Sulzberger* (1927), with intro. by Robert von Moschitzker; S. W. Pennypacker, *Autobiog. of a Pennsylvanian* (1918), pp. 241–42; H. S. Morais, *The Jews of Phila.* (1894); *Who's Who in America,* 1922–23; *Jewish Encyc.,* vol. XI; *The Am. Jewish Year Book,* vol. XXVI (1924); *Jewish Chronicle* (London), Apr. 27, 1923; *Jewish Exponent,* Apr. 27, May 4, 25, June 1, 1923; *Jewish Tribune,* Apr. 27, 1923; *Pub. Ledger* (Phila.), Apr. 21, 1923.]
                                          C.A.

SUMMERS, GEORGE WILLIAM (Mar. 4, 1804–Sept. 19, 1868), congressman from western Virginia, was a prominent representative of his section in the struggle which resulted in the division of the state at the outbreak of the Civil War. He was born in Fairfax County, the youngest of ten children of Col. George and Ann Smith (Radcliffe) Summers and a great-grandson of John Summers who built the first cabin on the site of Alexandria. In 1813, however, his family moved to Kanawha County in the western part of the state (now W. Va.) and after the death of the father, in 1818, George William lived in Charleston with his mother and elder brother Lewis. After attending school here and

Washington College, Lexington, Va., he matriculated at Ohio University (Athens), where he graduated in 1826. He then began the study of law under his brother, and in 1827 was admitted to the bar.

Becoming active in politics, he was elected from Kanawha to the House of Delegates in 1830 and was reëlected in 1831, 1834, and 1835. During his first term, favoring the interest of the West against Tidewater policy, he tried to get an extension of the proposed Staunton and Potomac railroad to the Kanawha, but was defeated. In the legislative debates of 1831–32 he opposed slavery and suggested that the proceeds of public lands be used to effect emancipation. He was elected to the federal House of Representatives in 1841 and reëlected in 1843. In a speech of 1842 favoring a protective tariff he stated that diversities of soil, climate, products, and population within the United States were the true elements of strength and perpetual union rather than of opposing interests and conflicting policies. He was a thorough Unionist, holding that the Constitution and laws of the United States, and its treaties, are the supreme law of the land. In the state constitutional convention of 1850 he won distinction by a speech on the basis of representation, presenting the views of transmontane against tidewater Virginia. He was Whig candidate for governor in 1851 under the new constitution and in his campaign not only denied the right of secession but maintained the duty of the president to enforce federal laws in South Carolina should that state attempt to secede. His defeat by Joseph Johnson, the Democratic nominee, was due in part to charges that he was affiliated with abolitionists, or at least was too friendly toward the Methodists who were preaching abolition. In May 1852 he was elected judge of the 18th judicial circuit of Virginia, serving until his resignation, July 1, 1858, two years before the expiration of his term.

He was a member of the Peace Conference at Washington in the spring of 1861, and throughout the critical period before the war was an active Union man. As a delegate to the Richmond convention which passed the Virginia ordinance of secession he made a vigorous speech in support of the Union (*Speech of Honorable George W. Summers on Federal Relations . . . March 11, 1861*, 1861). He took no part in the organization of the "restored" state of Virginia, however, preferring to remain neutral, and thereafter he refused to accept any office, although he continued the practice of law until his death.

He died in Charleston and was buried on his Kanawha River farm.

On Feb. 14, 1833, he married Amacetta Laidley, daughter of John Laidley of Cabell County. Only one of his five children survived him.

[W. S. Laidley, *Hist. of Charleston and Kanawha County* (1911); *W. Va. Hist. Mag. Quart.*, July 1903; T. C. Miller and Hu Maxwell, *W. Va. and Its People* (1913), vol. III; *Bench and Bar of W. Va.* (1919), ed. by G. W. Atkinson; *The W. Va. Encyc.* (1929); D. L. Pulliam, *The Constitutional Conventions of Va. from the Foundation of the Commonwealth to the Present Time* (1901); *Biog. Dir. Am. Cong.* (1928); C. H. Ambler, *Sectionalism in Va. from 1776 to 1861* (1910) and *A Hist. of W. Va.* (1933); H. T. Shanks, *The Secession Movement in Va.* (1934); *Daily Nat. Intelligencer* (Washington, D. C.), Sept. 30, 1868.]

J. M. C.

SUMMERS, THOMAS OSMOND (Oct. 11, 1812–May 6, 1882), Methodist clergyman and editor, was born near Corfe Castle, Isle of Purbeck, Dorsetshire, England, the son of James and Sarah Summers. Left an orphan at the age of six, he was reared by his maternal grandmother and, later, by an aunt. The latter died when Thomas was sixteen, leaving him a small patrimony. About two years thereafter he decided to emigrate to the United States and in 1830 arrived in New York City.

His parents were rigid Calvinists and he had had a careful religious training but had received only the rudiments of a secular education. He was a good penman and accountant, however, and easily found employment. Pursuing theological studies because of an inherent interest in them, he finally discarded Calvinism and became a devout follower of John Wesley. Soon, both by inclination and the advice of friends, he was led to enter the ministry of the Methodist Episcopal Church. In 1835 he was admitted on trial to the Baltimore Conference; the following year he was ordained deacon, and in 1839, elder. From 1836 to 1839 he was stationed in Baltimore, and in the latter year was sent to West River, Md. Conscious of his meager education, he applied himself industriously to study. In spite of defective vision and the exacting demands of his ministry, he made rapid progress and in time his knowledge became cyclopedic.

In 1840 he went to Texas, where he undertook missionary work in Houston and Galveston, and was one of the founders of the Texas Conference. He became a member of the Alabama Conference in 1844 and the following year was one of its delegates to the General Convention at Louisville, Ky., which organized the Methodist Episcopal Church, South. Of this Convention he was secretary and he also served as assistant secretary of the first General Conference of the Church, which was held the succeeding year.

Thereafter until his death he was secretary of all its sessions. In 1846 he was made assistant editor of the *Southern Christian Advocate,* which position he held until 1850, when he was elected book editor of the Church. Its publication house was established in Nashville, Tenn., and from then on, except for a period during the Civil War which he spent at Tuscaloosa, Ala., that city was his home. In addition to performing the routine duties of his office, from 1851 to 1856 he was editor of the *Sunday School Visitor.* In July 1858 he assumed editorship of the *Quarterly Review of the Methodist Episcopal Church, South.* This suspended publication in 1861 and was revived in 1879, Summers being elected editor in October of that year. From 1868 to 1878 he was editor of the *Christian Advocate,* Nashville. He had little capacity for original writing and left few works of his own; but he revised, corrected, and compiled, with an industry that never flagged, a minute attention to details, and a memory that was well-nigh infallible. Among his publications were *Biographical Sketches of Eminent Itinerant Ministers* (1858) and *Commentary on the Gospels* (4 vols., 1869–72). He devoted much attention to hymnology and ritual, for which he had a natural fondness.

In 1875 Vanderbilt University opened its doors, and the following year Summers consented to add to his editorial responsibilities those of dean and professor of systematic theology. By the time of the meeting of the General Conference held at Nashville in May of 1882, his health had become much impaired. He was gratified by being made secretary once more, but a few days later he died. His lectures at Vanderbilt were edited by J. J. Tigert and published in 1888 under the title *Systematic Theology.* He had married in 1844 N. B. Sexton of Tuscaloosa, Ala., who with a son survived him.

[O. P. Fitzgerald, *Dr. Summers: A Life-Study* (copr. 1884), reviewed in *Meth. Rev.* (N. Y.), May 1885; Gross Alexander, *A Hist. of the Methodist Episcopal Church South* (1894); J. T. Acklen, *Tenn. Records: Tombstone Inscriptions and Manuscripts* (1933); John Wooldridge, *Hist. of Nashville, Tenn.* (1890); *Methodist* (N. Y.), May 20, 1882; *Daily American* (Nashville), May 6, 8, 1882; personal acquaintance.]
G. B. W.

SUMNER, CHARLES (Jan. 6, 1811–Mar. 11, 1874), United States senator, notable advocate of the emancipation of the slave and the outlawry of war, son of Charles Pinckney Sumner and Relief (Jacob) Sumner, was born in Boston, Mass. His father—a descendant of William Sumner, who had come to Dorchester from England about 1635—was graduated from Harvard College in 1796 and read law in the office of Josiah Quincy. For many years he served as

sheriff of Suffolk County. He was a man of sound learning, independent in thought and action, outspoken in condemnation of slavery, and so earnest an advocate of "equal rights" that he opposed the exclusion of negro children from the schools and the law prohibiting intermarriage of blacks and whites. At the Boston Latin School (1821–26), the intimates of Charles Sumner were Robert C. Winthrop, James Freeman Clarke, Samuel F. Smith, and Wendell Phillips. Disappointed in his ambition to secure an appointment to West Point, at the age of fifteen he entered Harvard College where he showed (1826–30) great aptitude for history, literature, and forensics.

In the Harvard Law School (1831–33) Sumner became the devoted pupil and friend of its most eminent professor, Joseph Story, and at the end of his studies was urged to join the staff as an instructor, but he preferred to try his powers in active practice. Before entering upon its routine he took an orientation journey to Washington, especially to attend sessions of the Supreme Court, upon which Story was then sitting. For weeks young Sumner enjoyed the privilege of sitting at table in friendly intercourse with Chief Justice Marshall and his colleagues. He heard Webster and Francis Scott Key clash as opposing counsel before the Supreme Court, and in the Senate listened to the "splendid and thrilling" eloquence of Clay. Nevertheless, he left Washington declaring that nothing he had seen had made him look upon politics "with any feeling other than loathing" (*Memoir,* I, 142). Upon return to his office the drab routine of practice proved little to his liking. He became a lecturer in the Harvard Law School, a frequent contributor to the *American Jurist,* and devoted much time to reviewing and revising legal textbooks. He came into close intimacy with Francis Lieber and with William Ellery Channing, who exercised a profound influence upon him, and he formed a deep and lifelong affection for Whittier, Longfellow, and Emerson.

At twenty-six, though he had made no assured start in his profession, to the dismay of his friends he borrowed money and broke away from the law office for an indefinite sojourn in Europe. He remained abroad more than two years. It was no holiday trip. In every land which he visited he was an eager student and close observer. This experience gave him facile command of French, German, and Italian, an understanding of European governments and jurisprudence, and an intimate acquaintance with many of the leaders in public life and in letters in England, France, and Germany. Upon his return to Boston he had the entrée to the city's most cultivated social and intellectual circles. But he found the work of the law office weary, stale, and unprofitable. "Though I earn my daily bread, I lay up none of the bread of life" (*Memoir*, II, 167). The one position which would then have satisfied his ambition was that of reporter of the Supreme Court. That appointment went to another, and Sumner brought himself to the verge of collapse by undergoing the heartbreaking drudgery of annotating Francis Vesey's *Reports of Cases . . . in the High Court of Chancery* (20 vols., 1844–45).

In 1845 Sumner was chosen as the orator for Boston's Independence Day celebration. The delivery of that oration proved a turning-point in his career. For the first time he faced a great assembly gathered to hear him. He now stood six feet four inches in height, and his strong face kindled with animation as he spoke. His voice was of great power, and he used it with skill. Of that brilliant audience not less than one hundred were in full military or naval dress uniform. With terse introduction, Sumner announced the theme of his oration: "What is the true grandeur of nations?" He then proceeded to lay down his thesis, putting it interrogatively: "Can there be in our age any peace that is not honorable, any war that is not dishonorable?" (*Works*, I, 9). The city's military and naval guests felt themselves "officially assailed by the speaker as well as personally insulted" (*Memoir*, II, 346) and were with difficulty restrained from leaving the hall while he was still speaking. Ex-Mayor Eliot, whom Webster called "the impersonation of Boston," commented: "The young man has cut his throat!" (Quoted by Wendell Phillips, in *Boston Daily Advertiser*, Mar. 13, 1877). That oration revealed to Sumner not less than to his friends that he could thrill and sway great audiences. It brought him into closer cooperation with leaders like Theodore Parker and John A. Andrew. For years thereafter no lecturer on the Lyceum platform was more welcome than Sumner.

In the annual address before the American Peace Society (1849) he made a strong plea for "a Congress of Nations, with a High Court of Judicature," or for arbitration established by treaties between nations (*Works*, pp. 262–67). When his boyhood friend, Congressman Robert C. Winthrop, voted for the Mexican War bill, Sumner wrote a succession of letters publicly accusing him of sanctioning "the most wicked [act] in our history" (*Works*, I, 322). Such imputations brought upon Sumner a storm of criticism. Winthrop declined further social relations

with him, and Boston's social autocrat, Ticknor, declared that Sumner was "outside the pale of society" (Haynes, *post,* p. 4).

From Sumner's office was issued the call for a convention of all citizens of the Commonwealth opposed to the nomination of Cass and of Taylor. In that convention, at Worcester on June 28, 1848, Sumner made the principal speech, and his denunciation of the conspiracy "between the lords of the lash and the lords of the loom" (*Works*, II, 81) increased the antipathy of the rich and conservative Whigs of Boston for him. He was put forward as a candidate for the United States Senate by a coalition of Free Soilers and Democrats, but his election was blocked for more than three months by the impossibility of securing a two-thirds majority in the House. Finally the deadlock was broken when in several towns the voters met in special meetings, legally called for that one purpose, and by formal vote instructed their representatives to support Sumner.

He entered the Senate on Dec. 1, 1851. By the great majority the compromise measures of 1850 were accepted as a finality. Only five days before the end of the nine months' session, Sumner gained the floor as a matter of right, to speak to an amendment which he had moved, that no allowance under the pending appropriation bill should be authorized for expenses incurred in executing the law "for the surrender of fugitives from service or labor; which said Act is hereby repealed" (*Works*, III, 94). For more than three hours he presented a tremendous arraignment of the Fugitive-slave Law. The galleries filled. For an hour Webster himself was an attentive listener, this being his last visit to the Senate chamber. Near Webster, while Sumner was speaking, sat Horace Mann, who wrote in his journal: "the 26th of August, 1852, redeemed the 7th of March, 1850" (Mary T. P. Mann, *Life of Horace Mann*, 1865, p. 381). In the debate Southern senators heaped angry derision upon Sumner's amendment. Only Chase and Hale took the floor in its support, and but four votes were given in its favor. Nevertheless, Chase declared that in American history Sumner's speech would mark the day when the advocates of the restriction of slavery "no longer content to stand on the defensive in the contest with slavery, boldly attacked the very citadel of its power in that doctrine of finality" which both political parties were endeavoring "to establish as the impregnable defense of its usurpations" (*Congressional Globe*, 32 Cong., 1 Sess., App., p. 1121).

Sumner was outspoken, both in the Senate and

in the Massachusetts convention, in opposition to the Kansas-Nebraska Bill. This brought him into greater disfavor with the Boston press and society, both dominated by conservative Whigs, whom he still further offended by presenting in the Senate "with pleasure and pride" petitions from New England clergymen protesting against the passage of that bill. In the debate upon the right of petition Southern senators who had hitherto been on friendly terms with Sumner poured contempt upon his "vapid rhetoric," charged him with repudiating his oath of office and with declaring his intention to disobey the Constitution, and denounced him as a "miscreant," a "sneaking, sinuous, snake-like poltroon." They urged his expulsion, but an informal poll showed that the requisite two-thirds vote could not be secured. Sumner declared that he had sworn to support the Constitution as he understood it. "Does he recognize the obligation to return a fugitive slave?" demanded Toucey. Sumner's reply was: "To that I answer distinctly, 'No.'" (June 28, 1854, *Congressional Globe,* 33 Cong., 3 Sess., p. 1559). Sumner's vindication of Massachusetts against attack and his courage in maintaining his own opinion won admirers in quarters where he had been held in slight regard.

Sumner had a large part in the organization of the Republican party. Resistance of influential Whigs to the formation of a new party with the main object of opposing the extension of slavery gave opportunity for the rapid growth of the Know-Nothing party, by the votes of whose oath-bound members some Massachusetts politicians, notably Henry Wilson and Nathaniel P. Banks, were enabled to climb to high office. Sumner scorned such association, and boldly denounced "a party which, beginning in secrecy, interferes with religious belief, and founds a discrimination on the accident of birth" (*Works,* IV, 80). Such defiant language led to some futile intriguing to prevent his reëlection.

At the opening of the new Congress, Dec. 5, 1855, hot debate began at once with the Senate's demand for documents relating to the struggle in Kansas. With sure prescience Sumner declared: "This session will not pass without the Senate Chamber's becoming the scene of some unparalleled outrage" (T. W. Higginson, *Contemporaries,* p. 283). Two days before he was to speak, he wrote to Theodore Parker: "I shall pronounce the most thorough philippic ever uttered in a legislative body" (*Memoir,* III, 439). When he began his speech, "The Crime against Kansas" (*Works,* IV, 137-256), the air was tense in the Senate chamber, for none of his hearers could doubt that blood would soon be

shed in the territory. Sumner denounced the Kansas-Nebraska Act as "in every respect a swindle . . . —no other word will adequately express the mingled meanness and wickedness of the cheat" (*Works,* IV, 155). Turning his attention to the senators who "had raised themselves to eminence on this floor by the championship of human wrongs," he characterized Butler as Don Quixote, paying his vows to a mistress who, "though polluted in the sight of the world, is chaste in his sight. I mean the harlot, Slavery." Douglas he described as "the squire of Slavery, its very Sancho Panza, ready to do its humiliating offices" (May 20, 1856, *Congressional Globe,* 34 Cong., 1 Sess., App. pp. 530-31). Of Mason, the author of the Fugitive-slave Law, he said: "He holds the commission of Virginia . . . of that other Virginia from which Washington and Jefferson avert their faces, where human beings are bred as cattle for the shambles" (*Ibid.,* p. 543). Writhing under Sumner's denunciation of the Kansas-Nebraska Bill as a "swindle," Douglas shouted: "Is it his object to provoke some of us to kick him as we would a dog in the street, that he may get sympathy upon the just chastisement?" (*Ibid.,* p. 545). Mason deplored the political necessity of tolerating in the Senate a man whose very presence elsewhere would be "dishonor," and "the touch of whose hand would be a disgrace" (*Ibid.,* p. 546). Sumner branded some of Douglas' statements as false, and rejoined: "No person with the upright form of man can be allowed, without violation of all decency, to switch out from his tongue the perpetual stench of personality. . . . The noisome, squat and nameless animal, to which I refer, is not the proper model for an American Senator" (*Ibid.,* p. 547). Sumner's brutal frankness may find some palliation in the fact that heretofore he and other anti-slavery leaders had been subjected to the most galling epithets. His speech gave great satisfaction to anti-slavery men throughout the North. Within a few weeks a million copies of it had been distributed.

Two days after his speech was delivered, at the end of the day's session Sumner, who had remained at his desk, heard his name called. Looking up he saw a tall stranger who said: "I have read your speech twice over carefully; it is a libel on South Carolina, and Mr. Butler, who is a relative of mine" (Sumner's testimony, *Works,* IV, 261)—and down upon the head of the defenseless man crashed a blow from a heavy walking stick. Pinioned by his desk, Sumner could not rise till he had wrenched it from its fastenings. Blow followed blow, till he fell bleeding and unconscious to the floor. The man guilty of this brutal assault was Representative Preston S. Brooks [q.v.] of South Carolina. From the North came an outburst of universal condemnation of the attack and expressions of deepest sympathy for its victim. Sumner's injury was far more serious than at first appeared. Twice he tried to resume his duties, only to find that he could not undertake even the lightest tasks. Haunted by "the ghost of two years already dead," he went to Europe in quest of health a second time, and subjected himself many times without anesthetic to the moxa, which his physician described as "the greatest suffering that can be inflicted on mortal man" (Dr. Brown-Séquard, quoted in *Memoir,* III, 564–65). Three and a half years had passed before he was sufficiently recovered to return to the Senate. Meantime he had been reëlected by the almost unanimous vote of the Massachusetts legislature.

Sumner found a new Senate in which Southern leaders were taking more aggressive ground than ever before. Jefferson Davis' resolutions, affirming the sanctity of slave property in the territories, were passed by a vote of two to one. Under these circumstances Sumner determined to attempt an "assault on American slavery all along the line" (*Memoir,* III, 606). In the debate on the bill for the admission of Kansas as a free state, in an impassioned speech, "The Barbarism of Slavery" (*Works,* V, 1–174), he proceeded to set forth his indictment of slavery in its social, moral, and economic as well as political aspects. Many of his friends doubted the wisdom and timeliness of such an utterance on the eve of a presidential election; but it proved of immense influence and was distributed broadcast by the Republican national committee.

In the months following the Republican victory in 1860, alone among the Massachusetts delegation in Congress Sumner opposed the state's being represented in the peace conference (February 1861) and he was unyielding to petitions signed by tens of thousands of Massachusetts citizens urging his support of the Crittenden Compromise. In October 1861, at the Massachusetts Republican convention, he was the first statesman of prominence to urge emancipation, insisting that the overthrow of slavery would make an end of the war. Throughout the following year in the Senate, in public addresses, and in conferences with the President he never ceased to press for emancipation. When the Proclamation was finally issued, no man had done more than Sumner to prepare public sentiment for its approval.

When the Republicans got control of the Senate in 1861, for the first time Sumner received a committee assignment worthy of his abilities: he was made chairman of the committee on foreign relations, a position for which he was preëminently fitted and in which he was destined to render invaluable service. Although Captain Wilkes's seizure of Mason and Slidell was hailed with wild enthusiasm and at first seemed to have official approval, Sumner at once declared: "They will have to be given up" (G. H. Monroe, in *Hartford Courant,* Nov. 22, 1873). By the President's invitation he came into conference with the cabinet, set forth the principles of international law involved in the case, and read letters which he had just received from Cobden and Bright. The next day, with suitable apologies, Seward informed the British minister that the envoys would be given up. Sumner's influence was undoubtedly potent both in effecting a peaceful solution and in reconciling the American people to the inevitable surrender. In his chairmanship of the committee on foreign relations he aided the Union cause by defeating or suppressing resolutions which would almost inevitably have involved the United States in war with France and with Great Britain.

Already in the second year of the war he began the struggle to secure for all citizens of the United States, regardless of race or color, absolute equality of civil rights. As early as February 1862, he announced his extravagant doctrine that the seceded states had abdicated all rights under the Constitution; as he later phrased it, they had committed suicide (*Congressional Globe,* 37 Cong., 2 Sess., pp. 736–37, 2189). He was insistent that the initiation and the control of reconstruction should be by Congress, not by the President. It was Sumner's influence more than that of any other, as Lincoln declared in a cabinet meeting on the last day of his life, that blocked the recognition of Louisiana which was the most vital point for reconstruction in accordance with the Lincoln plan. Despite Sumner's opposition to policies nearest to the President's heart, he treated him with the greatest personal consideration.

During the Johnson administration Sumner and Thaddeus Stevens [q.v.] were brought into a strange cooperation as the Senate and House leaders, respectively, of the opposition to the President's reconstruction policy. Sumner was intent upon securing equality of civil rights for the freedmen, while Stevens' main concern was to prevent the defeat of the Republican party by Democratic reënforcements from the Southern states. It was Sumner's persistence which led the Senate to add to the requirements for "re-admission" of the seceded states the insertion in their constitutions of a provision for equal suffrage rights for whites and blacks. In effect this act of Congress, passed over the President's veto, abolished all the Johnson governments in the South. Sumner has been justly criticized for insisting upon the immediate grant of the ballot to the freedmen. It should be remembered, however, that in his own plan federal law was to guarantee to the blacks not only the ballot but also free schools and free farmsteads. In the movement for the impeachment of Johnson, Sumner took a prominent part. His first impressions favorable to the President soon gave way to a settled conviction that he was the chief menace to the country. Sumner regarded impeachment as a political rather than a judicial proceeding; hence neither in the Senate nor elsewhere did he put any curb upon his denunciations of Johnson's "misdeeds," and his opinion, filed with those of eighteen of the thirty-five who voted for conviction, was the longest and most bitter of them all (*Works*, XII, 318–410). He declared he would vote, if he could, "Guilty, of all [the charges] and infinitely more" (*Ibid.*, XII, 401). In this document Sumner is seen at his worst. Lurid and furious invective largely took the place of argument. In his view, Johnson was the "enormous criminal" of the century.

By temperament, training, and experience President Grant and Sumner were antipathetic, and they soon came into antagonism. Sumner's opposition on constitutional grounds was largely responsible for the rejection of the nomination of Stewart for secretary of the treasury. Though Motley was named minister to England upon Sumner's recommendation, he was later removed. The President seemed to take no serious exception to Sumner's influence in preventing the ratification of the Johnson-Clarendon Convention, nor to his startling assertion of the United States' "national claims," amounting to billions of dollars, against Great Britain, owing to her concession of ocean belligerency to the Confederate States. The most violent clash developed over the President's pet project, the acquisition of Santo Domingo. Sumner's committee brought in an adverse report upon the treaties that had been negotiated by Grant's personal envoy. Motley's removal at this juncture seemed like retaliation. Grant persisted in urging annexation. Finally, in a scathing speech—made more exasperating by his entitling it "Naboth's Vineyard"—Sumner denounced the whole Santo Domingo project (*Works*, XIV, 89–130; see also, pp. 168–249).

While these controversies were in progress there came to Sumner one of the greatest griefs of his life, his demotion from the chairmanship of the committee on foreign relations. In distinguished qualifications for this position he was without a peer in public life. But the tension had become so great that Sumner was not on speaking terms with the President and the Secretary of State. His champions asserted that this was but "a flimsy pretext" and that "the San Domingo scheme was at the bottom of the whole difficulty" (Haynes, p. 366). A more reasonable explanation of the administration's pressure may have been a fear that his extraordinary views as to "national claims" against Great Britain would prove an obstacle to the adjustment which was then under negotiation. Though thus shut out from any official relations with the joint commission, Sumner was frequently consulted by its members, and was shown great consideration by the British commissioners, whose head told Sumner that without his speech "the treaty could not have been made and that he worked by it as a chart" (*Memoir*, IV, 491). Despite his demotion, Sumner not only gave his vote for the Treaty of Washington but made the principal speech in exposition and support of it (*Memoir*, IV, 489–90). It is clear that Sumner himself did not expect that the enormous sums suggested by him would actually be paid by Great Britain. He was reasonably satisfied with the result—that the new treaty, at least as construed by the United States, would secure an arbitral adjustment of all claims, whether individual or national, growing out of the cruisers' depredations. He considered this a most important advance in establishing the principle of arbitration, and predicted: "Great Britain will never, in any future wars, place herself in the predicament in which my speech demonstrated she was placed in the matter of the rebel cruisers" (Whipple, *post*, p. 209).

At the opening of the regular session of Congress in December 1872, Sumner introduced a bill which provided that, inasmuch as "national unity and good will among fellow-citizens can be assured only through oblivion of past difference, and it is contrary to the usage of civilized nations to perpetuate the memory of civil war," the names of battles with fellow-citizens should not be continued in the Army Register, or placed on the regimental colors of the United States (*Works*, XV, 255). Apparently as a penalty for his opposition to Grant in the preceding campaign a bill of precisely opposite intent was introduced in the House, passed and sent to the Senate, where both bills were temporarily laid on the table because of Sumner's illness. Meantime, in the Massachusetts legislature a report denouncing Sumner's bill as "an insult to the loyal soldiers of the nation" and as "meeting the unqualified condemnation of the people of the Commonwealth" was adopted (*Journal of the Extra Session of the House of Representatives of Massachusetts, 1872,* 1873, p. 54). Sumner was deeply grieved by this injustice. Forthwith Whittier took the lead in a movement to rescind this resolution of censure, and two years later by large majorities in both houses of a new legislature it was annulled (*Journal of the House of Representatives of Massachusetts, 1874,* 1874, pp. 131–35).

On Mar. 10, 1874, against his physician's advice, Sumner went to the Senate, for on that day his colleague was to report the rescinding resolution. His fellow Senators were generous in their expressions of congratulation and goodwill. That evening he was prostrated by a heart attack and the next day he died. His body lay in state in the rotunda of the Capitol, and the funeral services were held in Cambridge. On Oct. 17, 1866, at the age of fifty-five, he had married Mrs. Alice (Mason) Hooper, a young widow; but they separated within a year and later were divorced (Shotwell, *post,* pp. 557–58, 584–85).

At the end of the Civil War, it has been said that the two most influential men in public life were Abraham Lincoln and Charles Sumner (Rhodes, *post,* V, 55). Time has dealt very differently with them, for Sumner's figure has been crowded into the background. Unlike Lincoln, he outlived his best days. His most characteristic and beneficent labors belonged to the epoch closed by the war; their fruits were merged in its triumphs. His later years brought misfortunes in full train: domestic sorrow, racking illness, the loss of friends, and ceaseless struggle over the problems of reconstruction, with some of which he was little fitted to cope. In contrast with most other American leaders of comparable political influence, Sumner entered public life "at the top": when he took his seat in the Senate he had never held public office of any kind. By no effort, he found himself thrust forward as the champion of an unpopular cause. Throughout his many years in the Senate, the goal of his constant striving was "absolute human equality, secured, assured, and invulnerable." He judged every man and every measure by reference to that goal. That any slave could be happy or that any slave-owner could be humane seemed to him impossible. As years passed, he became more intolerant not only of opposition but also of dis-

sent. His arraignments of Johnson and of Grant were extravagant beyond all reason. When George William Curtis, discussing with him some public question, suggested: "But you forget the other side!" Sumner's voice "shook the room, as he thundered in reply: 'There is no other side!'" (C. E. Norton, ed., *Orations and Addresses of George William Curtis,* 1894, vol. I, 256). To a senator's argument that the Constitution gave no authority for action which Sumner was urging, his reply was: "Nothing against slavery can be unconstitutional!" (Haynes, p. 279).

At the end of the war, the senator who for many years had been most vehement in denouncing all owners of slaves as "slave-mongers" was not the man to deal most tactfully and discriminatingly with the reconstruction problems. There is a measure of justice in the comment: "He would shed tears at the bare thought of refusing to freedmen rights of which they had no comprehension, but would filibuster to the end of the session to prevent the restoration to the southern whites of rights which were essential to their whole concept of life" (W. A. Dunning, *Reconstruction, Political and Economic,* p. 87). Yet in his later years Sumner displayed a kindness of sympathy toward the impoverished and suffering people of the South, and a magnanimity (as in his battle-flag resolution) which Congress did not reach till a full generation had passed.

Despite Sumner's intense devotion to the one "cause" which he championed with a crusader's zeal, he was diligent in the routine work of a senator, and commanded respect in his discussion of such topics as money and finance, the tariff, postal regulations, and copyright. He was much concerned over the abuses of patronage, through presidential favoritism or "senatorial courtesy," and introduced a well-thought-out bill for civil service reform. But his great work was not in the framing of laws. His was, rather, the rôle of an ancient Hebrew prophet—the kindling of moral enthusiasm, the inspiring of courage and hope, the assailing of injustice. His fearlessness in denouncing compromise, in demanding the repeal of the Fugitive-slave Law, and in insisting upon emancipation made him a major force in the struggle that put an end to slavery. It was his magnanimity and pertinacity that held in check barbarous attempts at retaliation, whether in the grant of letters of marque and reprisal, in the treatment of Confederate prisoners, or in the seizure of unoffending citizens of foreign countries in return for wrongs inflicted upon Americans abroad. Throughout the great national crisis his service was of inestimable value in keeping the United States at peace with Great Britain and with France, when war with either of them would have meant the disruption of the Union.

[*The Works of Charles Sumner* (15 vols., 1870–83), mostly edited by him, were considered by him a faithful record of his career. The references in the text are to this edition. Another edition, with introduction by G. F. Hoar, is *Charles Sumner, His Complete Works* (20 vols., 1900). The Sumner collection in the library of Harvard Univ. contains 40,000 letters received by him. E. L. Pierce, *Memoir and Letters of Charles Sumner* (4 vols., 1877–93), contains whatever seemed significant to an intimate of thirty years but lacks sense of proportion. Shorter biographies are those by A. M. Grimké (1892), a negro lawyer of Boston, which is mainly a tribute of gratitude to a champion of the author's race; by Moorfield Storey (1900), an excellent summary by an eminent lawyer who was for several years Sumner's private secretary; by W. G. Shotwell (1910), eulogistic and discursive; and by G. H. Haynes (1909). Storey's biography may be supplemented by M. A. DeW. Howe, *Portrait of an Independent: Moorfield Storey, 1845–1929* (1932). Sumner's personality was set forth in eloquent orations by G. W. Curtis and Carl Schurz, published separately and in *A Memorial of Charles Sumner* (1874), and in essays by intimate friends: E. P. Whipple, *Recollections of Eminent Men* (1887); and T. W. Higginson, *Contemporaries* (1899). *Memorial Addresses on the Life and Character of Charles Sumner . . . Forty-Third Congress, First Session, Apr. 27, 1874* (1874) include the notable tribute by L. Q. C. Lamar, which made a profound impression in both North and South, and the discriminating appraisal by G. F. Hoar. There is an obituary in *Boston Evening Transcript*, Mar. 12, 1874. J. F. Rhodes, *Hist. of the U. S.* (7 vols., 1893–1906), contains many references. W. A. Dunning, in *Reconstruction, Political and Economic* (1907), and *Essays on the Civil War and Reconstruction* (1898), is severely critical of Sumner. More recent writers on Reconstruction, such as H. K. Beale, *The Critical Year* (1930), and G. F. Milton, *The Age of Hate* (1930) are even more severe. For Sumner's relation to the *Alabama* claims, see C. F. Adams, Jr., *Charles Francis Adams* (1900), and "The Treaty of Washington," in *Lee at Appomattox and Other Papers* (1902); J. B. Moore, *Hist. and Digest of the International Arbitrations to Which the United States Has Been a Party*, vol. I (1898), ch. XIV; D. H. Chamberlain, *Charles Sumner and the Treaty of Washington* (1902); J. C. B. Davis, *Mr. Sumner, the Alabama Claims, and Their Settlement* (1878). Sumner's own statement of the controversies with Grant and Fish is in his *Works*, IV, 254–76.]
G. H. H.

SUMNER, EDWIN VOSE (Jan. 30, 1797–Mar. 21, 1863), soldier, was born at Boston, Mass., the son of Elisha and Nancy (Vose) Sumner, and a descendant of William Sumner who came to Massachusetts about 1635 and settled at Dorchester. He was commissioned second lieutenant in the 2nd Infantry, Mar. 3, 1819, promoted first lieutenant, Jan. 25, 1823, and served in that regiment until he was appointed captain, Mar. 4, 1833, in the newly organized 1st Dragoons (now the 1st Cavalry). His service was chiefly on the frontier until the outbreak of the Mexican War, when he was appointed major of the 2nd Dragoons, June 30, 1846, and joined Gen. Winfield Scott's army in Mexico. Scott's

faith in Sumner was such that he wished to relegate the latter's senior, Col. William S. Harney [*q.v.*], for whom he had no liking, to an unimportant command in Taylor's army. In the end, both Harney and Sumner remained, but the relations between them were permanently strained. The regiment of Mounted Riflemen (now 3rd Cavalry) had just been organized, most of its officers being wholly without military training. It needed an exceptionally strong man to command it, and Sumner was detached from the dragoons for that purpose. His service throughout the campaign was distinguished, at first in command of the Mounted Riflemen and later of his own regiment. He was wounded at Cerro Gordo and received brevets for his conduct there and at Molino del Rey. He was promoted lieutenant-colonel of the 1st Dragoons, July 13, 1848, and colonel of the 1st (now 4th) Cavalry, Mar. 3, 1855. Meanwhile, in the summer of 1852, after the death of the civil governor, J. S. Calhoun, Sumner as military commandant of the region was acting governor of New Mexico.

In September 1855, under orders from General Harney, Sumner's regiment left Fort Leavenworth for Fort Laramie, to arrive there ready for a spring campaign, but after marching west four hundred miles he turned back to Leavenworth, declaring that to continue would sacrifice most of the horses. Harney preferred charges for disobedience of orders, but Sumner was supported by the War Department. As commander of the post at Fort Leavenworth in 1856 during the struggle between Free-Soilers and proslavery men for the control of Kansas, he attempted to preserve order, dispersing armed bands of partisans of both sides, and under the direction of Gov. Wilson Shannon [*q.v.*], the "pretended" Topeka legislature. In 1857 he was engaged in a campaign against the Cheyennes in Kansas and the following year he assumed command of the Department of the West, with headquarters at St. Louis.

Sumner was of Northern birth; his wife also was a Northerner: Hannah W. Forster, daughter of Thomas Forster of Erie, Pa., whom he married Mar. 31, 1822. There is no apparent reason why any one should suspect him of sympathy with secession—except, possibly, the marriage of his daughter to a Southerner, Armistead Lindsay Long [*q.v.*]—but such sentiment was strong in St. Louis, and it is suggestive that on Jan. 5, 1861, he wrote, in a personal letter to General Scott: "I have belonged to the general government over forty years, and I consider it my government, and so long as it lasts, the only government to which I owe fealty. As I view this obligation, I feel bound in honor to devote myself to the preservation of the Union." (Unpublished letter.) Scott's opinion is indicated by his selection of Sumner to accompany the president-elect to Washington. Sumner was appointed brigadier-general, Mar. 16, 1861. He commanded the II Corps in the Peninsular campaign, at South Mountain, and at Antietam. McClellan recommended his promotion, writing to the War Department of his "extreme gallantry" and of "the judgment and energy he displayed in saving the day at the battle of Fair Oaks," and he was accordingly appointed major-general of volunteers with rank from July 4, 1862. He commanded the right grand division at the battle of Fredericksburg, and was then relieved from duty with the Army of the Potomac at his own request. He died at Syracuse, N. Y., while on the way to his new command in Missouri. One son, Edwin Vose Sumner, Jr., became a brigadier-general in the regular army; and another, Samuel Storrow Sumner, a major-general.

[*War of the Rebellion: Official Records (Army);* *Battles and Leaders of the Civil War* (4 vols., 1887–88); J. H. Smith, *The War with Mexico* (2 vols., 1919); W. S. Appleton, *Record of the Descendants of William Sumner* (1879); *Kan. Hist. Colls.,* vols. VIII (1904), XVI (1923–25); G. B. Grinnell, *The Fighting Cheyennes* (1915); P. G. Lowe, *Five Years A Dragoon* (1906); H. H. Bancroft, *Hist. of the Pacific States,* vol. XII (1888); F. A. Walker, *Hist. of the Second Army Corps in the Army of the Potomac* (1887); *Sen. Ex. Doc. No. 5, and No. 10* and *House Ex. Doc. No. 4* (pt. 2), 34 Cong., 3 Sess. (1856); *N. Y. Herald,* Mar. 22, 1863; unpublished records in the War Dept.]
T. M. S.

SUMNER, INCREASE (Nov. 27, 1746–June 7, 1799), jurist, governor of Massachusetts, was born in Roxbury, Mass., son of Increase Sumner, a well-to-do farmer of colossal size and strength, and Sarah (Sharp) Sumner, daughter of Robert Sharp of Brookline and first cousin of John Adams' mother. He was descended from William Sumner who came to Massachusetts about 1635 and settled in Dorchester. Having prepared for college in the Roxbury grammar school (now Roxbury Latin school), he entered Harvard, where he was graduated with distinction in 1767. He then taught in the Roxbury school for two years, studying law meanwhile under Samuel Quincy, solicitor general of the province and loyalist brother of Josiah Quincy [*q.v.*] the patriot. After admission to the bar in 1770, Sumner opened an office in his Roxbury home. His practice soon became important and lucrative. He married, Sept. 30, 1779, Elizabeth, daughter of William Hyslop, a prosperous Boston merchant. She survived Sumner, leaving a son and two daughters.

Early in life he took from the arms of the Kentish Sumners the motto, *In medio tutissimus ibis,* and shaped his whole political career accordingly. Though he was mildly opposed to the British contentions, his only part in the Revolution was to serve as representative in the General Court, 1776–79; and as senator, 1780–82. He was a member of the constitutional convention whose work was rejected by the voters in 1778, and of the convention of 1779–80 that framed the Massachusetts constitution. In June 1782 the legislature elected him to Congress to fill a vacancy, but he never sat because in August he was appointed associate justice of the supreme judicial court of Massachusetts. The work of the judges needed much courage during the turbulent times when the new state government had just been set up and there was much hostility to the comomn law and those who enforced it. The judges, as Sumner's portrait shows, still wore their pre-Revolutionary black silk gowns with white bands, but despite Sumner's vigorous protest Chief Justice Dana, followed by the other justices, soon abandoned them, and they were not resumed until 1901. Sumner acquired a reputation as "a dispassionate, impartial, discerning, able and accomplished judge" (W. H. Sumner, *post,* p. 12). Since the judges did not habitually write out their decisions until 1804, no printed reports of his legal views exist, but the Massachusetts Historical Society possesses his manuscript notes of his cases. As a member of the Massachusetts convention of 1788 which ratified the federal Constitution, Sumner delivered several speeches, especially in support of biennial rather than annual elections of Congress. He remained a warm supporter of the new national government, replying to Fisher Ames's "I say it won't last" with, "Let us see how it works. Let us give it a fair trial" (*Ibid.,* p. 16).

Almost against his will, Sumner was put forward by the Federalists in 1796 as their gubernatorial candidate against Samuel Adams. There was little to recommend him in comparison with Adams, who was triumphantly reëlected. In 1797, Adams having retired, Sumner swept the state against the divided Democratic-Republican opposition of James Sullivan and Moses Gill, and was sworn in as governor on June 2, 1797, his tall and commanding figure a striking contrast to the gouty infirmity of Hancock, who had to be carried to the Council chamber in a chair, and to the bent old frame of Adams. Having inherited considerable property from his father-in-law, he entertained lavishly and drove a coach and four on all public occasions. His middle-of-the-road policy was just what Massachusetts needed to calm the dissensions aroused by the proposed French war and the Alien and Sedition Acts. "He had indeed 'united all hearts,' and his freedom from political bias made of him a refreshing and admirable contrast to the bitter actions and animosities of the politicians of that period" (Morse, *post*, p. 178). He was reëlected in 1798 and 1799 by overwhelming majorities, getting the unanimous vote of many towns. During his administration, Jan. 11, 1798, the government was removed to the new State House on Beacon Hill. His chief activities were in military affairs. He worked to increase munitions, obtain additional arsenals for the artillery, and fortify the sea coast of the state. He wore a uniform at all military ceremonies, despite the efforts of the bench and bar to dissuade him. At his third election in 1799 he was ill with angina, and he was sworn in on his death bed in Roxbury.

Sumner was a practical farmer, attending personally to his estates and much interested in advancing agriculture. His personality was impressive but kind. "He never . . . forgot his dignity in any place or circle, even in the moments of his greatest familiarity" (W. H. Sumner, *post*, p. 32). He was solid and judicious rather than brilliant. "In the analysis of his mind there is not to be found one extraordinary power, nor one mean quality" (Knapp, *post*, p. 94). He was given a public funeral and buried in the Granary Burial Ground in Boston.

[S. L. Knapp, *Biog. Sketches of Eminent Lawyers* (1821); W. H. Sumner, *Memoir of Increase Sumner . . . together with a Geneal. of the Sumner Family* (1854), reprinted from *New England Hist. and Geneal. Reg.*, April 1854; Eliphalet Porter, *A Sermon . . . Occasioned by the Death of . . . Increase Sumner* (1799); Abiel Holmes, *A Sermon Preached . . . After the Interment of . . . Increase Sumner* (n.d.); Peter Thacher, *A Sermon . . . at the Interment of . . . Increase Sumner* (n.d.); W. S. Appleton, *Record of the Descendants of William Sumner* (1879); A. E. Morse, *The Federalist Party in Mass.* (1909); Alden Bradford, *Hist. of Mass.*, vol. III (1829); J. S. Barry, *The Hist. of Mass.*, vol. III (1857); A. B. Hart, ed., *Commonwealth Hist. of Mass.*, vol. IV (1930); T. C. Amory, *Life of James Sullivan* (1859).]   Z. C., Jr.

SUMNER, JETHRO (*c.* 1733–March 1785), Revolutionary soldier, the son of Jethro and Margaret (Sullivan) Sumner, was born in Nansemond County, Va., where his grandfather, William Sumner, had become a freeholder about 1691. He served from 1755 to 1761 in the Virginia militia during the French and Indian War, rising to a lieutenancy and to the command of Fort Bedford in 1760. Prior to the autumn of 1764 he emigrated to North Carolina and was married to Mary, the daughter of William and Christian McKinnie Hurst, of Granville County.

She brought him a large inheritance and he established himself as a tavern-owner and planter at the seat of Bute (later Warren) County. With a fair education, military experience, business acumen, handsome physique, native ability, and attractive personality, Sumner rose to local prominence as justice of the peace in 1768 and as sheriff, 1772–77. He represented Bute County in the revolutionary provincial congress of August–September 1775, which elected him major of the minute-men of Halifax district. In November he went to the aid of the Virginia patriots near Norfolk; and, following his election on Apr. 15, 1776 by the fourth provincial congress as colonel of the third battalion of North Carolina continentals, he marched first to the lower Cape Fear, thence to aid in the successful defense of Charlestown in June. Later he joined Charles Lee, 1731–1782 [*q.v.*], on the projected expedition against Florida, but left it at Savannah in September to return to North Carolina for supplies. He led his battalion northward in the following spring and served in Washington's army through Brandywine, Germantown, and Valley Forge, until illness in the spring of 1778 compelled his return to North Carolina. During the summer he recruited for the continental battalions.

Elected brigadier-general by the Continental Congress on Jan. 9, 1779, Sumner led a brigade of newly recruited continentals to South Carolina and participated in the battle of Stono Ferry on June 20. For more than a year from July he was recruiting the North Carolina battalions. As commander of a brigade of militia in the southern piedmont region he assisted in the gallant defense of North Carolina against Cornwallis' invasion in the fall of 1780 until, in October, piqued by the elevation of General Smallwood to the command of the state forces, he declined further militia service. However, at General Greene's request, he offered his services again in February 1781; but General Caswell did not give him a militia command. Again he endeavored to raise troops until July, when he reinforced Greene with a brigade of three small battalions of raw continentals, who fought like veterans at Eutaw Springs on Sept. 8. During the remainder of the war, he was in charge of military forces in North Carolina. In 1783 he retired to the supervision of his tavern, his plantations, and his three minor orphan children. On Apr. 18, 1784, he presided at the meeting of the North Carolina Society of the Cincinnati in Hillsboro. With his strong constitution undermined by the exposures of war, he died at his home in Warren County between

Mar. 15 and 19, 1785. His possessions included approximately 20,000 acres and thirty-four slaves. Sumner was a brave and reliable officer, considerate of his soldiers, and a good disciplinarian. His creditable, varied, and continuous service throughout the war ranks him among the foremost of North Carolina patriots in the Revolution. His daughter, Jacky Sullivan Sumner, became the wife of Thomas Blount [*q.v.*].

[*Colonial Records of N. C.* (10 vols., 1886–90); *State Records of N. C.* (16 vols., 1895–1905); Jethro Sumner Papers, 1760–1784, in N. C. Historical Commission; Bute and Warren County Records; J. F. D. Smyth, *A Tour in the U. S. A.* (2 vols., 1784); *Jours. of the House of Burgesses of Va.*; S. A. Ashe, "Jethro Sumner," in S. A. Ashe, *Biog. Hist. of N. C.*, vol. V (1906); K. P. Battle, "The Life and Services of Brigadier General Jethro Sumner," in *The N. C. Booklet*, Oct. 1908.]   A. R. N.

SUMNER, WILLIAM GRAHAM (Oct. 30, 1840–Apr. 12, 1910), educator, economist, publicist, and social scientist, was born in Paterson, N. J. His father, a Lancashire artisan, had emigrated from England to Paterson in 1836, and there married Sarah Graham, whose parents were also from Lancashire. Soon after his son's birth, Thomas Sumner, in the hope of bettering his condition, moved with his family westward, but after a period of wandering returned to the East and finally settled in Hartford, Conn., where for many years he was employed in the repair shop of the Hartford and New Haven Railroad Company. An uneducated workman, but a reader and thinker with intelligent views on social and economic questions, he exerted a lasting influence upon his son. Prepared in the public schools of Hartford, young Sumner entered Yale in 1859. Here he took high rank as a scholar and was known as a reserved, soberminded, self-reliant youth, independent in his thinking, who spent his spare time in general reading rather than in athletic or social activities. His sterling qualities, however, won him the lasting friendship of associates who were later prominent in the industrial and political affairs of the country. Through the aid of these, he went abroad after his graduation in 1863 for further study. From boyhood he had looked forward to entering the ministry, and he now prepared for that calling at Geneva, Göttingen, and Oxford. Returning to the United States, he was tutor at Yale from 1866 to 1869. During this period, Dec. 28, 1867, he was admitted to the diaconate of the Protestant Episcopal Church, and in 1869 he became assistant to Dr. E. A. Washburn, rector of Calvary Church, New York, where he was ordained priest, July 15, 1869. In addition to his clerical duties he helped to establish, and edited, *The Living Church*, an

able monthly published in the interests of the Broad Church party, which, however, survived but a year. He was also engaged at this time in translating and editing the second book of K. C. W. F. Bähr's "The Books of the Kings" in J. P. Lange's *Commentary on the Holy Scriptures*, the translation being published in 1872. In September 1870 he became rector of the Church of the Redeemer, Morristown, N. J., and on Apr. 17 of the following year he married Jeannie Whittemore Elliott, daughter of Henry Hill Elliott, a New York merchant, and Elmira (Whittemore) Elliott.

Sumner was an able preacher and performed scrupulously the other duties of his office, but his interest turned increasingly to public questions and matters of social and economic import, upon which he could not express himself freely in the pulpit. Accordingly, in 1872 he accepted a call to the newly created chair of political and social science at Yale University. In the service of this institution he spent the remainder of his life, though his fame and influence rapidly extended beyond its borders. His activities were varied. For three years (1873–76) he was one of New Haven's board of aldermen; for twenty-eight years (1882–1910) he was an active member of the Connecticut State Board of Education and contributed much to the improvement of the common school system; his utterances on public questions attracted wide attention and he was constantly importuned for addresses and magazine articles; he was the author of numerous books still regarded as authoritative; he carried on extended research into the origin of social institutions which give him rank among the foremost students in this particular field. His industry was prodigious. He worked long hours and seldom took a holiday. Not only did he cultivate all the social sciences, but as aids in his work he informed himself on such subjects as anatomy, biology, and even calculus. He had a good working knowledge of at least a dozen languages, familiarity with the most of them having been acquired after he was forty-five years old.

Outside activities, however, were never permitted to interfere with his college duties. He considered teaching his first business. Of large frame—always fastidiously dressed—fine head "magnificently bald," somewhat stern countenance, keen eye and "iron voice," thoroughly conversant with his subject and boldly independent in his treatment of it, he commanded the respect and confidence of his classes. He made everyday affairs his textbook, and beginning with these, set forth the underlying economic and social facts and principles with a freshness and vigor then and always rare in college teaching. Going straight to the heart of his subject, he stated the facts in plain and often epigrammatic language. Honest and fearless, despising gush and sentimentality, indifferent to tradition, he struck hard blows, never glossed over anything, and never spared anybody's feelings. Contemptuous of pedagogical methods, he was, nevertheless, one of the most effective teachers of his generation. His lecture room was crowded and no one at Yale was considered by the students really to have qualified for a degree if he had not been under Sumner. Instructors in other colleges visited his classroom, or wrote to him, seeking the secret of his success. In addition to teaching he did his full share of administrative work. He rebelled against the conservatism strongly entrenched at Yale when he went there, deplored the prominence given to the classics, and labored, against much opposition, to broaden the curriculum, especially by introducing scientific studies into the academic department. When President Noah Porter [q.v.] objected to Sumner's use of Herbert Spencer's *The Study of Sociology* as a textbook, he waged and won a vigorous fight for academic freedom, which through newspaper reports attracted wide attention.

As soon as he was free from the restrictions his clerical position imposed, Sumner at once proceeded to take up the cudgel against economic and political evils and in behalf of what he deemed sound governmental principles. This warfare he carried on through public addresses, but more particularly through essays published in various periodicals, so keen in analysis, flawless in logic, and full of fire that they attracted country-wide attention. Their very titles were such as to arrest attention—"The Absurd Attempt to Make the World Over," "That It Is Not Wicked to Be Rich; Nay, Even, That It Is Not Wicked to Be Richer Than One's Neighbor," "Protectionism, the —Ism Which Teaches that Waste Makes Wealth," "Prosperity Strangled by Gold," "The Delusion of the Debtors," "The Conquest of the United States by Spain." Practically every social question of the day is treated, and such underlying subjects as equality, rights, duty, and liberty are stripped of all their traditional and sentimental trappings and critically examined. Throughout his career he was an outstanding advocate of a sound monetary system, opposing free silver, bimetalism, and all inflationary expedients. For years, often almost single-handed, he fought protectionism, maintaining that as a prosperity measure it was economic quackery, and from a moral point of view,

pernicious. He deplored the agitation against "big business," regarding the evolution of trusts as a natural and expedient phenomenon, and vigorously opposed any infringement of the government upon the industrial field, maintaining that state interference could not be scientific, or even intelligent, and that the remedies would be worse than the disease. His arguments against socialism have been considered the most difficult to answer that have been put forth. He was long prominent among the leaders in civil service reform; in the days of the Spanish-American War he was one of the small and unpopular group of anti-imperialists. Though he is usually classed as an advocate of *laissez-faire,* it was only to what he called "empiricism," unintelligent experimentation and social panaceas, that he was opposed. That social conditions can be improved he firmly believed, but such improvement can come, he was convinced, only by scientific procedure carried on by thoroughly informed individuals. In a democracy, therefore, the right kind of education is of supreme importance. In all his aggressive presentation of these subjects, he was inspired by strong moral convictions, and with hatred of shams, loose thinking, sentimental motive, and especially of jobbery and injustice. He was especially solicitous for the "Forgotten Man," a term which he chose as the title for one of his public lectures (1883). By the "Forgotten Man," he meant the self-supporting and self-respecting person who has to bear the cost of all the political bungling and the social quackery. "I affirm that there is always somebody who pays, and that it is always the sober, honest, industrious, economical men or women, who attend no meetings, pass no resolutions, never go to the lobby, are never mentioned in the newspapers, but just work and save and pay" (*William Graham Sumner, post,* p. 287).

The most significant of Sumner's essays have been edited by Albert G. Keller and published under the titles: *War and Other Essays* (1911), *Earth Hunger and Other Essays* (1913), *The Challenge of Facts and Other Essays* (1914), and *The Forgotten Man and Other Essays* (copr. 1919). In 1924 *Selected Essays of William Graham Sumner,* edited by Keller and M. R. Davie, was issued. Among Sumner's more ambitious publications in the economic field were *A History of American Currency* (1874); *American Finance* (1875); *The Financier and Finances of the American Revolution* (2 vols., 1891); "Monetary Development," in *The First Century of the Republic* (1876), edited by T. D. Woolsey and others; "A History of Banking in the United States" (1896), being the first volume of *A His·*

tory of Banking in All the Leading Nations, edited by A. W. Dodsworth. He also wrote three biographies, aside from *The Financier,* which, within the limits set by the author, rank among the best that have appeared—*Andrew Jackson as a Public Man* (1882), *Alexander Hamilton* (1890), and *Robert Morris* (1892). One of his most widely read publications, *What Social Classes Owe to Each Other,* notable for its cold, keen logic and pungency, appeared in 1883, and has since been several times republished.

Having, as a young man, stormed his way with incredible industry and vigor into the political economy and political science which he was called to Yale to develop, he found himself less and less satisfied, as the years passed and he came more and more under the influence of Herbert Spencer, to stay within the traditional boundaries of these subjects. Economics and politics were only a part of the picture; there were also religion and marriage, alongside and intricately interconnected with the economic and political organizations. To see society truly, one must view all of its institutions, not some of them—and all of them in their interrelations. Sumner's interest broadened into preoccupation with a general science of society, so that in middle life he began to recede from economics, eventually withdrawing his long-popular courses in that subject and turning with eagerness and vigor, despite broken health, toward anthropology and what he called "societology."

This venture involved the study of all the institutions of society in their evolution from the simplest, primitive forms. Accordingly, he submerged himself in the literature relating to these and within ten to fifteen years had assembled a large amount of classified material from the best sources in a number of languages. Eventually he started upon a treatise on the science of society; but, as he reduced his materials to order and his conclusions to writing, he found himself forced to generalize, beyond and beneath institutions of all kinds, to the underlying stratum, custom, out of which they all have developed. When he was about two-thirds through a first draft of his treatise, he arrived reluctantly at the conviction that he had omitted an absolute essential, namely, the analysis of custom. He set aside the manuscript and devoted several years to work on this essential, emerging with that classic of the science, *Folkways* (1907). He remarked at the time of its publication that what he had done on the science of society must now be rewritten in the light of the mores; his age and illness made that task impossible.

The logical necessity felt by Sumner and met by his conception and analysis of the folkways and mores confronts any serious student of society's evolution. His *Folkways,* as is becoming more evident every year, is a fundamental contribution to one and all of the social sciences. Relatively minor, though exceedingly important contributions, such as that of the aleatory element as the basis of religion, occur throughout Sumner's studies in society's evolution. Furthermore, he is one of the very few "sociologists" who have had the disposition and the industry to eschew *a priori* reasoning and sentimentality in favor of induction from arduously gathered facts.

Seventeen years after Sumner's death, his *Science of Society* (1927), with the mass of data he had accumulated entirely sifted, and reclassified, with much important evidence added, and with the system he had outlined considerably revised, was published in four volumes by his successor at Yale, Professor Albert G. Keller. This joint work is to be classed with *Folkways* as one of the most important contributions yet made in the field of social science. While it is impossible to apportion the parts supplied by the two authors, it is certain that the volumes preserve the spirit of Sumner and contain his corrected and recorrected conclusions as to the nature and life of human society. A popular abridgment by Keller, *Man's Rough Road,* appeared in 1932. In 1934 a two-volume edition of the essays, entitled *Essays of William Graham Sumner,* edited by A. G. Keller and M. R. Davie, was issued. It includes a number of hitherto unpublished essays and a bibliography of writings and of leading biographical articles.

In spite of physical handicaps Sumner kept at his work with indomitable will until the end. On Dec. 26, 1909, he went to New York to deliver an address as president of the American Sociological Society. At the Murray Hill Hotel he collapsed, and on Apr. 12 following he died in the Englewood (N. J.) Hospital, survived by his wife and two sons. His funeral was held in Battell Chapel, New Haven, and he was buried in Guilford, Conn.

[A bibliog. of his writings, prepared by M. R. Davie, is in *The Forgotten Man and Other Essays* (copr. 1919); a sketch of his life, largely autobiographical, appeared in *Popular Science Mo.,* June 1889, and is reprinted in *The Challenge of Facts and Other Essays* (1913); the most complete portrayal of his career, based partly on family and other unprinted sources, is H. E. Starr, *William Graham Sumner* (1925). See also introduction to *War and Other Essays* (1919); A. G. Keller, *Reminiscences (Mainly Personal) of William Graham Sumner* (1933) and "The Discoverer of the Forgotten Man," *Am. Mercury,* Nov. 1932; *N. Y. Times,* Apr. 13, 14 (editorial), 1910; *New Haven Evening Register,* Apr. 13, 1910.]   H. E. S.

SUMTER, THOMAS (Aug. 14, 1734–June 1, 1832), Continental officer, guerrilla, senator, and representative, was born near Charlottesville, Va. It is said that his father, William Sumter, was an English redemptioner of Welsh extraction who died when Thomas was very young, and that his mother, Patience, was a midwife, who lived to a great age. With little schooling, the boy worked in his father's mill, tended his mother's sheep, and went with wild youths on the campaigns of Braddock and Forbes. His most enlightening experience, perhaps, was in 1762, when, after serving as sergeant of Virginia troops against the Cherokees, he accompanied Henry Timberlake [q.v.] on a mission to the head men and visited England with Chief Outacity [q.v.]. He was lodged for debt in the Staunton jail, escaped, and in 1765 acquired lands near Eutaw Springs, S. C. Here he opened a crossroads store near Nelson's Ferry, became a justice of the peace, and in 1767 married Mrs. Mary (Cantey) Jameson, of an old and prominent South Carolina family; she was the widow of William Jameson.

Elected to the first and second provincial congresses, he served as captain with the mounted rangers under William Thomson [q.v.]; and during an arduous Cherokee campaign he was placed in the Continental service as lieutenant-colonel of the 2nd Regiment of riflemen (later the 6th). After campaigns in Georgia and Florida he resigned, on Sept. 19, 1778, a full colonel, and was in retirement when the British conquered South Carolina in 1780. Unlike most South Carolina leaders, he did not take protection, and when Tarleton raided and destroyed his home, he joined Whig refugees near Charlotte, N. C. Informally elected general, he established headquarters on Sugar Creek, and revived resistance so successfully that Lord Rawdon offered 500 guineas for his betrayal. Repulsed at Rocky Mount on July 30, 1780, he was successful at Hanging Rock on Aug. 6, but in cooperating with Gates he was overtaken by Tarleton at Fishing Creek on Aug. 18 and completely routed. Within a short time, however, he resumed operations, and on Oct. 6, 1780, was commissioned brigadier in command of South Carolina militia. At Fishdam Ford on Nov. 9 he escaped Wemyss' attempt to kidnap him, and on Tyger River on Nov. 20 he repulsed Tarleton in the well-fought battle of Blackstock's Hill, where he was severely wounded. For these achievements he received the thanks of Congress on Jan. 13, 1781. Declining activity until Feb. 16, 1781, he marched then for Granby, but finding the post had been warned, he went on a daring raid against Thomson's, Fort Watson, and Nelson's Ferry, and successfully returned to Sugar Creek.

In spite of the non-existence of the state government, Sumter now undertook to raise a dependable force of mounted state troops. With the sanction of Governor Rutledge and General Greene, he enlisted regulars for ten months' service, to be paid in negroes and plunder from Loyalists. The scheme, known as "Sumter's law," was successful in procuring a force, but it augmented civil war between Whig and Tory, and gave Sumter the name of plunderer. Without an open break with Greene, Sumter maneuvered to maintain his command as a separate unit until July 1781, when, having finally joined Greene, he led the "raid of the dog days" into the low country. Though causing Dorchester and Biggin to be evacuated, he was repulsed at Quinby, and then to Greene's consternation he disbanded for the summer and retired to North Carolina. In the ensuing campaign, therefore, Greene dismounted and diverted Sumter's force and stationed him at Orangeburg for police duty. Disgusted, Sumter resigned before March 1782, after serving as senator in the Jacksonboro Assembly. In 1783, he received the thanks of the South Carolina Senate, was voted a gold medal, and declined his election to the Continental Congress. He served many terms in the South Carolina House, and after legislative investigation at his own request of "Sumter's law" he was exonerated and asked to wind up accounts with the state troops. The legislatures of both North and South Carolina by enactment forbade state courts to entertain suits for losses under his scheme.

After the war, he founded the village of Stateburg, S. C., bred race-horses, was a charter member of the Santee canal company, and of the Catawba company, took out grants for more than 150,000 acres of land, and experimented with tobacco and cotton in an effort to find a staple to replace indigo. In the South Carolina convention to consider the federal constitution, he opposed ratification before Virginia could be heard from. As a member of the First Congress, his speeches voiced antifederalist fears, and he was among the last to be won to assumption. He was defeated in 1793 because of supposed speculation in government paper, but was reelected in 1796 and remained in the House until sent to the Senate in December 1801. A devoted Jeffersonian, yet among the few senators to oppose Jefferson, he was gratified by the appointment of his only son Thomas as secretary of legation to France, and later as minister to Portugal in Brazil. In December 1810 he resigned from the Senate, and for the next twenty-two years was harried by litigation and creditors, until the South Carolina legislature in 1827 granted him a moratorium for life from his debt to the bank of the state of South Carolina. Although a small man, Sumter's strength and agility were as remarkable as his longevity, and he rode horseback until the day of his death on his estate near Stateburg in his ninety-eighth year.

The most significant phase of Sumter's career was in the Revolution; his importance was out of all proportion to the small numbers he commanded. The popular uprising of which he was part was an essential factor in the climax at Yorktown. Known as the "Gamecock of the Revolution," and the most feared of the partisans, he kept the largest body of militia in the field and was the first to make them stand against British regulars. But with all his imagination for daring schemes, he seems to have lacked the capacity for attention to detail that would insure success. In war he was a politician, and in politics he was an old soldier. Adaptable and progressive, he acquired dignity as he advanced and might well be called a typical American of the frontier school. Fort Sumter, S. C., was named in his honor.

[Manuscript materials on Sumter are in the Library of Congress, the William L. Clements Library, the Wisconsin State Historical Library, and the New York Historical Library. A comprehensive bibliography is included in A. K. Gregorie, *Thomas Sumter* (1931). See also letters published in *Year Book City of Charleston, 1899, Pubs. South. Hist. Asso.*, Mar. 1907; Kate Furman's article, *Ibid.*, Sept., Nov. 1902; and the account of his funeral in the *Camden Jour.*, June 9, 1832.]   A. K. G.

SUNDERLAND, ELIZA JANE READ (Apr. 19, 1839–Mar. 3, 1910), lecturer, writer, reformer, and educator, was born on a farm near Huntsville, Ill., under pioneer conditions. Her Quaker father, Amasa Read of Uxbridge, Mass., died when Eliza was very young; her mother, Jane Henderson, an Ohioan of Scotch descent, was a woman of strong mind and character. After a short time at an Abingdon (Ill.) seminary, Eliza, then aged fifteen, began teaching a district school which had driven out a succession of men teachers, and she quickly tamed the rebellious pupils. Having earned enough money for further study, she entered Mount Holyoke Seminary in 1863, and was graduated two years later. Conditions at home prevented her from accepting an invitation to join the seminary faculty, and she took a position in the Aurora (Ill.) high school. In 1867 she was made principal, thus becoming one of the first women in the United States to head a public secondary school. Her gifts as an educator were quickly apparent. The institution became known as the "model school" of Illinois, and helped raise educational standards in the Middle West. In 1871 she gave up her position

to marry, Dec. 7, Jabez Thomas Sunderland, an Englishman who was pastor of a church in Milwaukee, Wis., and later was prominent in the Unitarian denomination. Subsequently, she taught in high school at Chicago and Ann Arbor, Mich., where her husband had charges. The family lived in the latter place for twenty years (1878–98) and she seized the opportunity to study at the University of Michigan, from which she received the degree of Ph.B. in 1889, and that of Ph.D. in 1892, specializing in philosophy. Her education was also widened by extensive travel in Europe, Palestine, and Egypt.

Her interests included all matters concerned with human betterment, especially temperance, the advancement of women, the improvement of education, and the elevation of religion. For many years she was probably the leading woman of Michigan in such activities. For a short time, while living in Chicago, she was associate editor of the *Illinois Social Science Journal* (1878); during residence in Hartford, Conn., she was a member of the city school board (1907–10), and several times addressed the state legislature in behalf of educational and other reforms. She was also chief organizer and first president of the Women's Western Unitarian Conference, and from 1886 to 1891 was a vice-president of the Association for the Advancement of Women. She was a speaker of force and eloquence, lecturing extensively and often preaching in Unitarian and Universalist churches. In 1893 she spoke in Chicago at the Congress of Women of the World's Columbian Exposition, and at the World's Parliament of Religions, her paper before the latter being considered one of the best on the program. Her chief interest was religion, which she regarded not as a matter of creed but of conscience and heart. She constantly worked for a broader and finer religious faith. Her wide, sympathetic spiritual insight was remarkable: she mothered University of Michigan students perplexed with religious problems; and she regarded with kindly understanding the monuments of ancient polytheism on the banks of the Nile.

Besides articles—mostly religious—in newspapers and magazines, she published a number of pamphlets, contributed "Importance of the Study of Comparative Religions" to *The World's Congress of Religions* (1894), and, in collaboration with her husband, wrote *James Martineau and His Greatest Book* (1905). She died in Hartford, Conn., where her husband had been minister of the Unity Church since 1907, survived by him and by two daughters and a son.

[*Who's Who in America*, 1910–11; *Eliza Read Sunderland; a Brief Sketch of Her Life: Memorial Ad-*

dresses (n.d.); F. E. Willard and M. A. Livermore, *Am. Women* (1897); M. K. Eagle, *The Cong. of Women . . . World's Columbian Exposition* (1894), vol. I; *Christian Reg.*, Mar. 10, 1910; *Chicago Tribune*, Sept. 16, 1893; *Hartford Courant*, Mar. 4, 1910.]

M. W. W.

SUNDERLAND, LA ROY (Apr. 22, 1804–May 15, 1885), abolitionist, was born in Exeter, R. I. He received a common-school education, was a student for a time at Day's Academy, Wrentham, Mass., and in 1826 was admitted into full connection by the New England Conference of the Methodist Episcopal Church. Though he was little more than five feet tall, the emotional intensity of his preaching style was such that his colleagues prophesied that he would become the greatest revivalist of his time; but Sunderland himself became increasingly doubtful as to the divine origin of his powers and in 1833 withdrew from the active ministry. Meanwhile, however, he had begun to further the anti-slavery cause among the Methodist ministers of New England. The initial document of this agitation, "An Appeal on the Subject of Slavery" (*Zion's Herald*, Extra, Dec. 5, 1834), was from his hand, and the first anti-slavery society in the Methodist Church was organized through his efforts. In 1836, when despite the active hostility of the church press, the board of bishops, and even the General Conference, the anti-slavery faction founded *Zion's Watchman* in New York City, he became its editor, to lead the van of Methodist abolitionism.

He continued to meet with opposition within the church. In six successive sessions of the New England Conference, of which he was still a member, presiding bishops and dignitaries from New York brought charges against him, ranging from slander to immorality. The General Conference went so far as to change its rules in order to make him amenable to ecclesiastical discipline, and he was unsuccessfully sued for libel in the courts. Finally, in 1842, he withdrew with other radicals from the Methodist Episcopal Church and signed their call for a new church, the Wesleyan Connection of America, without an episcopacy and on an anti-slavery basis.

Sunderland, however, did not join the new denomination. The bitterness of his persecution and the acerbity of his resistance had left their mark upon his loyalties. Moreover, he had long been convinced that his early success as a revivalist had been due solely to hypnotic powers. Conversion, he concluded, was a "natural," not a miraculous, phenomenon, and religion itself was a fraud. Caught up in the restless reformism of the forties, he supported successively Mesmerism, Grahamism, and faith-healing, and

invented a faith of his own, which he called Panthetism. During his last years he became a leading exponent of "infidelity." To the confusion of the orthodox, who had hoped for a death-bed scene of despair if not of repentance, he died cheerfully and courageously facing an end which to him had no hereafter. He had been married, but his wife left him some time before his death; an obituary mentions several grandchildren (*Christian Advocate*, June 4, 1885).

Sunderland was a prolific writer in many fields, but only his editorial writings and a few of his tracts had any significance: one published sermon, "This Life a Time of Probation" (first printed in the *Methodist Preacher*, September 1830); an early plea for theological education (*Methodist Magazine and Quarterly Review*, October 1834); and the famous "Appeal on the Subject of Slavery." His *Panthetism . . . An Essay Toward a Correct Theory of Mind* (1847), *Book of Psychology* (1853), *Book of Human Nature* (1853), and *Ideology* (1885), contain some autobiographical information and reveal the trend of his thought.

[Sources include *Zion's Herald*, 1823–42, and issues of Apr. 22, June 3, 1885; *Christian Advocate*, 1837–42, and issues of May 28, June 4, June 11, 1885; *Zion's Watchman*, 1836–43; James Mudge, *Hist. of the New England Conference* (1910); Sunderland's tracts and books. His *Book of Human Nature*, p. x, is authority for date of birth given above; *Christian Advocate*, May 28, 1885, gives May 18, 1802.]

G. H. B.

SURRATT, JOHN H. (b. 1844) [See BOOTH, JOHN WILKES, 1838–1865].

SURRATT, MARY E. (1820–1865) [See BOOTH, JOHN WILKES, 1838–1865].

SUTHERLAND, JOEL BARLOW (Feb. 26, 1792–Nov. 15, 1861), congressman, was born at Clonmel, Gloucester County, N. J., the son of Daniel and Jane Sutherland, Scotch immigrants. He attended common schools and graduated (1812) from the University of Pennsylvania Medical School, enlisted in the War of 1812 as assistant surgeon in the "Junior Artillerists of Philadelphia," and before the end of the war became a lieutenant-colonel of rifles in the state militia. While the conflict was still in progress he entered politics and was elected to the Pennsylvania Assembly as an insurgent Democratic-Republican three successive times, 1813–15. When war ardors had somewhat cooled, the voters forced him to return to medical practice and the none too pleasant duties of lazaretto physician at the port of Philadelphia. On Apr. 13, 1815, he married Mary Read.

He still thirsted for politics, however, and, concluding that law would aid him more than medicine in his striving, he studied law and was admitted to the bar, Mar. 30, 1819. In two years he was back in the legislature, serving in the lower house until 1825; during the last year of his service he was speaker. In 1822 and 1824 he had been defeated for Congress but in 1826 he was elected both to that body and to the state Senate. He sat in the Senate through one session and then resigned to enter Congress in December 1827. He retained his seat for five terms, interspersing periods in Washington with legal work in Philadelphia as deputy prosecuting attorney for the county, 1830, 1832, 1833, and as associate judge of the court of common pleas, 1833–34. In 1835 he sent his resignation from Congress to the governor, to enter upon a longer term as judge of the common pleas, but for some reason the resignation did not take effect and he remained in the House. There as in the legislature he proved himself specially adept at persuading his fellow members in private conversation to vote for his measures, but he was also a good debater and skilful in parliamentary procedure. He wrote a *Manual of Legislative Practice and Order of Business in Deliberative Bodies* (1827), to be used in state legislatures, which went into a fifth edition as late as 1853, and a *Congressional Manual* (1839). In 1831 he received fifty-four votes in opposition to Andrew W. Stevenson, the successful candidate for speaker. As member and chairman of the committee on commerce he devoted himself to river and harbor development and to the promotion of Philadelphia projects, especially the navy yard and the Delaware Breakwater. Though he considered himself an enthusiastic Jacksonian, he was so loyal to Pennsylvania interests that he became an ardent protectionist and opposed Jackson on the Maysville road veto and the veto of the bill rechartering the United States Bank. Because of these heresies he was defeated in 1836 by another Democrat and when he ran again in 1838, on the Whig ticket, he was once more defeated.

No preferment came his way thereafter except indirectly, by the appointment of two of his sons to the army and marine corps and one to the civil service. He maintained a law practice, served on the board of trustees of Jefferson Medical College (latterly as its president), and was first president of the Society of the War of 1812. He seems to have been dynamic, brilliant, and impulsive without possessing much depth or a great amount of tact or good judgment.

[A son, Charles Sutherland, prepared *Memoir of Joel Barlow Sutherland* (n.d, n.p.). See also J. T. Scharf and Thompson Westcott, *Hist. of Phila.* (1884), vols. I, II; *Phila. Inquirer*, Nov. 18, 1861; *Biog. Dir. Am. Cong.* (1928). A number of his letters are in the Buchanan MSS. and the George Wolf MSS. in the Hist. Soc. of Pa.]   R. F. N.

SUTRO, ADOLPH HEINRICH JOSEPH (Apr. 29, 1830–Aug. 8, 1898), mining engineer, bibliophile, mayor of San Francisco, was born in Aix-la-Chapelle, Prussia, of Jewish parentage. His father, a cloth manufacturer, died in 1847, and the Prussian revolution of the following year ruined the business. Consequently his mother with her seven sons and four daughters emigrated to America in 1850, settling in Baltimore. Fired by the gold discoveries in California, Adolph set out for the Pacific Coast via Panama, and arrived in San Francisco in November 1851. For the next nine years he was engaged in mercantile pursuits in that city and in Stockton.

In 1860 he was drawn to Nevada by interest in the great bonanza strike. He established a quartz-reducing mill at East Dayton, where he worked over the tailings of other mills by a new process of amalgamation and thus laid the foundation of his later fortune. Impressed by the old-fashioned and inefficient mining methods then employed in the region of the Comstock lode, he conceived the idea of driving a tunnel ten feet high, twelve feet wide, and some three miles long, with lateral branches bringing the total length to over five miles, into Mount Davidson from Carson River to the Comstock lode, to provide ventilation, drainage, and an easy means of transporting men and materials to and from the mines. "He employed journalists to explain the advantage of the tunnel, civil engineers to examine the country and locate the line, and geologists to report on the mineral character of the Comstock lode and the country rock" (Hittell, *post*, p. 413). He then formed the Sutro Tunnel Company; obtained, on Apr. 4, 1865, a charter from the Nevada legislature; and persuaded mine owners to sign contracts to pay the company two dollars per ton for all ore mined after the opening of the tunnel for their use. A coterie connected with the Bank of California in San Francisco gave him their support and helped to get through Congress (July 25, 1866) an act which granted Sutro and his associates the right of way through the public lands crossed by the tunnel, and several incidental franchises.

Shortly thereafter Sutro's California supporters turned against him, their object being to get control of the tunnel and thereby reap the immense profits which were anticipated. With indomitable perseverance he first sought, in vain, the aid of New York capitalists; then, in 1867, he went to Europe and visited a dozen countries and their mines, studying their tunnels, consulting their engineers, and obtaining indorsement for his own plans. In 1868 he published *The Mineral Resources of the United States and the Importance and Necessity of Inaugurating a Rational System of Mining with Special Reference to the Comstock Lode and the Sutro Tunnel in Nevada.* In Europe and from subscriptions by enthusiastic Nevada miners, he secured the initial funds with which to begin work in October 1869. Nine years later, at a cost of about $6,500,000, including interest, the tunnel was completed to the Comstock lode, and its opening marked the beginning of a new era in western mining.

The project proved immediately and immensely profitable. In 1879 Sutro sold his interest and returned to San Francisco, where he invested his tunnel profits in real estate, at one time owning one-twelfth of the acreage in San Francisco city and county. In the early eighties he bought the Cliff House and a thousand acres of land in the vicinity fronting on the ocean—Sutro Heights. In 1892 he began construction of the enormous Sutro salt-water baths, costing nearly a million dollars, and forming, when completed, the finest bathing pavilion then in existence. In 1894 he was elected mayor of San Francisco on the Populist ticket, and during his two-year term was constantly in strife with the board of supervisors and the railways operating within the city.

Sutro was deeply interested in the beginnings of science and of the art of printing, and ransacked Europe for *incunabula* of printing and block engraving. He collected a library of over 200,000 rare volumes, mainly of scientific and technical works, about half of which were destroyed in the fire of 1906. The balance now forms a part of the San Francisco Public Library. Although giving away much in unostentatious charity, he left an estate valued at about $3,000,000, which was divided among the four daughters and two sons who survived him. His wife, Leah Harris, whom he married in 1856, had died in 1893.

[*San Francisco Chronicle,* Aug. 9, 1898, Apr. 4, 1933; *San Francisco Call,* Aug. 9, 1898; H. H. Bancroft, *Chronicles of the Builders,* IV (1892), 195–97; G. W. James, *Heroes of Cal.* (1910); E. K. Holmes, *Adolph Sutro* (1895); *San Francisco: Its Builders, Past and Present* (1913), I, 53–62; S. P. Davis, *The Hist. of Nev.* (1913), I, 399–405; J. P. Young, *San Francisco* (1912), I, 385–86, II, 570, 805; J. S. Hittell, *The Commerce and Industries of the Pacific Coast* (2nd ed., 1882), pp. 413–14; "Report of the Commission to Examine and Report Upon the Sutro Tunnel, in Nevada," *Sen. Ex. Doc. No. 15,* 42 Cong., 2 Sess. (1872).]

P. O. R.

SUTTER, JOHN AUGUSTUS (February 1803–June 18, 1880), adventurer and colonist, originally named Johann August Suter, was born in Kandern, Baden. The facts regarding

his ancestry and early life are obscure; his own statements were untruthful and contradictory. His parents are said to have been Johann Jakob Suter, a paper manufacturer, and Christine Wilhelmine (Stoberin), daughter of a clergyman (Dana, *post,* pp. 1–2). A part of his youth was spent in the village of Rünenberg, Basel Canton, Switzerland; he is said to have attended the military academy at Neuchâtel (*Ibid.,* p. 3); it is certain that he was officially recognized as a Swiss citizen and that he served his time in the Swiss army, possibly attaining the rank of captain. In 1826 he married Anna (or Annette) Dübeld (or Dubelt), by whom he had three sons and a daughter. After a number of escapades, he decamped from Berne in the spring of 1834, made his way to Havre, and sailed for America. He landed in New York, journeyed to St. Louis, Mo., and may have settled for a time at St. Charles. In 1835 and again in 1836 he accompanied a trading party to Santa Fé. In 1838 he accompanied the Eells-Walker missionary party to Oregon, arriving at Fort Vancouver in October. Eager to reach California, and finding the land journey impossible at that season, he sailed for Honolulu and then for Sitka, whence he was enabled to reach San Francisco Bay on July 1, 1839. Four days later, at Monterey, he presented to Governor Alvarado a project for establishing a colony on the unknown frontier to the north. Alvarado empowered him to select a tract, with the promise that in a year's time a grant would be made. On the south bank of the American River, at its junction with the Sacramento, Sutter landed a small party about Aug. 16. Indians from the former missions were employed; land was cleared; irrigating ditches were dug; grain was sown, orchards and vineyards were planted, and in time a fortified post was erected. To his colony he gave the name of Nueva Helvetia. In June 1841, on a second visit to Alvarado, he was made a Mexican citizen, and a grant of eleven square leagues of land was given to him.

His success was phenomenal. He rapidly built up a vast baronial estate, and though nominally a Mexican subject was virtually the independent ruler of his domain. For military aid given to Governor Micheltorena an additional grant of twenty-two square leagues of land was given him (Feb. 5, 1845). About this time he began to be hailed as "General" Sutter. He befriended the early American settlers drifting into the country, and his settlement became the rallying place for those who favored an uprising against the Mexican government; but on June 14, 1846, Frémont, suspicious of his attitude, seized his fort. Later it was restored to him, and with the conquest of

California his fortunes seemed secure. In 1849 he was a delegate to the convention which drafted the state constitution; he presided at its last session, and was a candidate for the governorship at the first election. His son, John A. Sutter, Jr., had joined him at the end of 1844 and in 1851 his wife and the remaining children followed.

Meanwhile, however, the discovery of gold on his estate, Jan. 24, 1848, had marked the beginning of his ruin. His workmen deserted him; his flocks and herds disappeared, and squatters settled upon his lands. By 1852 he was bankrupt. Later the United States Supreme Court, while invalidating his claim to the Micheltorena tract, confirmed the earlier grant, but he could not afford the litigation necessary to recover his property. In 1864, the California legislature voted him a pension of $250 a month, which was continued until 1878. In 1865 his homestead on the Feather River was destroyed by fire. Late in that year he went to Washington, where he submitted a petition to Congress. By 1871 he had established a home in the Moravian village of Lititz, Lancaster County, Pa., though he spent his winters in Washington. In 1876 and again in 1880 bills for his relief were favorably reported in the House of Representatives, and on June 11 of the latter year a joint resolution in his behalf was introduced in the Senate, but immediately ordered to lie on the table. A week later, at Mades' Hotel, he died. His widow survived him by seven months, dying on Jan. 19, 1881.

Sutter was short and fat, with a broad head, and, in his maturity, a bald crown fringed with flaxen, graying hair. His manner was genial and at times expansive. His character and attainments have been variously estimated. Bancroft, whose personal judgments were often extreme, concedes him no merit but kindliness, and says that he was without ability, honor, truthfulness, or respect for the rights of others. A recent biography of him, by Julian Dana, is fervently eulogistic. By reason of his unique career, his vicissitudes of fortune, and his long and futile struggle for justice, he remains one of the most appealing figures in American history.

[See the summary in H. H. Bancroft, *Hist. of Cal.* (1886), V, 738–40, and bibliog. data, *Ibid.*, IV, 122–39; T. J. Schoonover, *The Life and Times of Gen. John A. Sutter* (1895); *The Diary of Johann August Sutter* (1932), with Intro. by D. S. Watson; *A Nation's Benefactor: Gen'l John A. Sutter . . . An Appeal* (1880); "Petition of John A. Sutter," *Sen. Misc. Doc. 38*, 39 Cong., 1 Sess. (1866); *Memorial of John A. Sutter to the Senate and House of Representatives of the U. S.* (1876); J. B. Landis, "The Life and Work of Gen. John A. Sutter," *Papers Read before the Lancaster County Hist. Soc.*, vol. XVII, no. 10 (1913); W. H. Davis, *Seventy-five Years in Cal.* (1929); Julian Dana, *Sutter of Cal.* (1934); *Evening Star* (Washington, D. C.), June 19, 1880. Blaise Cendrars, *L'Or* (trans. as *Sutter's Gold,* 1926) is a highly romantic treatment. The day of Sutter's birth is given variously as Feb. 8, 15, 23, and 28, 1803.]
             W. J. G.

SUTTON, WILLIAM SENECA (Aug. 12, 1860–Nov. 26, 1928), educator, was born in Fayetteville, Ark., the son of James Tillton and Francena Lavinia (Martin) Sutton. His father was a merchant; his mother, for many years, was a teacher in the preparatory department of the Arkansas Industrial University (now the University of Arkansas). From this young and struggling institution, Sutton received the bachelor of arts' degree at the early age of eighteen.

Intending to study law, he taught a country school for a year and discovered the vocation that had much the strongest appeal for him. For a year he was a school principal at Fayetteville, at the end of which time he became superintendent. In 1883 he went to Ennis, Tex., as principal; on June 12, 1884, he married Annie Blackman Erwin, by whom he had two children. He was made principal of the Houston high school in 1886 and in the following year succeeded to the superintendency of the Houston schools. In this office he served with conspicuous success until 1897, when he was called to the headship of the school of education in the University of Texas. Here he was dean and founder of the Summer School, 1898–1918, dean of education, 1909–28; and acting president, 1923–24. He was a skilful teacher and administrator and a leader in the broadening of the curriculum and degree requirements and in establishing intimate relations with the high schools through a system of affiliation.

His influence was felt throughout Texas. In connection with the State Teachers' Association, of which he was president in 1896, he worked for higher personal and professional qualifications in teachers, and for better support for all schools. He was effective in securing better school laws, and was the founder of a Conference on Education that for a series of years caused many leading citizens to take much greater and more informed interest in education. He was honest, constructive, far-seeing, tolerant, good-humored in debate. Hating class spirit and sectarianism, animated by a genuinely democratic sympathy, he could speak with a homely and friendly effectiveness. In collaboration with W. H. Kimbrough and W. H. Bruce, he prepared a series of arithmetics; with P. W. Horn, he wrote *Schoolroom Essentials* (copyright 1911). In 1913 he published *Problems in Modern Education,* and, between 1891 and 1924, about forty articles on a wide variety of topics. A prolonged and emaciating sickness clouded his last years. He is buried in the State Cemetery at Austin.

[F. Eby and others, *In Memory of William Seneca Sutton* (1930), a record of exercises dedicating Sutton Hall at the Univ. of Tex.; *Who's Who in America,* 1926–27; records of Texas Teachers' Asso. and the Univ. of Tex.; *Dallas Morning News,* Nov. 27, 1928.]

H. Y. B.

SUZZALLO, HENRY (Aug. 22, 1875–Sept. 25, 1933), teacher and educational leader, began an address on the Anglo-Saxon tradition at a luncheon of the Pilgrims in London on May 29, 1931, with the statement that there was not a drop of Anglo-Saxon blood in his veins. Yet there was not a thought in his mind, he said, nor an aspiration in his heart, which was not a part of this same tradition, a tradition which was brought to him, the son of immigrants from the Adriatic, through the American system of public education. His paternal grandfather was a native of Herzegovina. His father, Peter, who was born in the Adriatic port town of Ragusa (now Dubrovnick), followed a family tradition by taking to the sea as a boy. Later he spent some years in the California gold fields. At forty he returned to Ragusa to marry a distant cousin, Anne Zucalo (another form of the family name) and took his bride back to California. After various vicissitudes, the family settled in San José, where Anthony Henry was born, the eighth of nine children, only four of whom lived to maturity.

The family had small means, and the boy had to work after school hours. His opportunity for a higher education was due in large measure to the kindly interest of two local business men, Emil and Jesse Levy, who gave him employment, encouraged him in his ambitions, and advanced money when necessary. His school record was not remarkable, partly owing to rather delicate health, partly to calls of outside work, and partly to lack of interest. At any rate, he was not admitted directly to Stanford University, newly established in the neighboring town of Palo Alto, but had first to complete the program of the local normal school, earning his way there and throughout the long period of his professional preparation by teaching. At Stanford, where he entered in the fall of 1895, Suzzallo found himself. The faculty was young and enthusiastic, and a high proportion of his fellow-students were destined to make their mark in later life. Despite the outside calls upon him, which included a year's leave of absence as principal of a rural school, his academic record was brilliant and he took an active part in student affairs. Although he had earlier wavered between medicine and the law, he was now in no doubt as to the future.

Practical success as a teacher and principal, and, it is said, conflict with unenlightened school authorities, had turned him definitely toward education as a profession.

Following his graduation in 1899 came full-packed years of combined teaching, educational administration, and further study. In the San Francisco public-school system, Henry Suzzallo (he had dropped the Anthony) rose rapidly to the deputy superintendency, serving in that capacity for five months of each year. This arrangement made it possible for him to rise meanwhile (1902) to an assistant professorship in education at Stanford, and to complete the requirements at Columbia University for the master's degree in 1902 and the doctor's degree in 1905. In 1907 he went to New York as adjunct professor of education at Teachers College, Columbia University, and two years later was promoted to the professorship of educational sociology. While holding this professorship he served for a time as acting dean of Teachers College. In addition to his regular teaching duties at Stanford and Columbia, he taught for shorter periods at other universities, including Chicago, California, and Yale.

In 1915 he was elected to the presidency of the University of Washington, at Seattle. The period of his tenure was one of rapid development for American state universities, and in this development Washington had its full share. Though standards of admission and graduation were steadily advanced, the enrollment was more than doubled during these years, and the number of degrees granted annually was nearly trebled. A general plan for campus development was adopted and ten academic buildings were erected, four of them by private gift. State support for general maintenance was more than trebled and the salary scale for professors doubled. Perhaps Suzzallo's outstanding contribution was his success in coordinating the services of the university with the needs of the state. He entered promptly into the life of the community. He became a member of the state Board of Education and served in many other capacities. With the entry of the United States into the World War, he was plunged in a new set of responsibilities. In June 1917 he became chairman of the state Council of Defense, later a representative of the Shipping Board in the Northwest, adviser to the War Labor Policy Board, and a wage umpire for the National War Labor Board at Washington. He was mediator and conciliator in more than fifty strikes affecting war efficiency. During an extended illness of the Governor, he was in fact, if not in title, the governor of the state.

The steps leading to his removal from the presidency of the University in 1926 are too complicated for recital here. The issues were personal and political rather than educational. Though both the state legislature and the University regents were involved in the controversy, the real issue lay between the recently elected governor, Roland H. Hartley, and Suzzallo. The two men had come into sharp conflict some years before, during the latter's war service and when the former was active in the lumber industry, over the question of the eight-hour day, and it is generally believed that this had much to do with the later difficulties. Suffice it to say that the Governor's action in removing him from office, after he had declined to resign without the filing of specific charges, aroused nationwide discussion, but never even threatened Suzzallo's standing as an educator or as a citizen. Certainly there was no lack of opportunity for him to serve elsewhere. On leaving Washington he was in constant demand. Though he could have chosen from a number of college and university presidencies, he preferred to return to his old chair at Teachers College. He also organized a study of graduate instruction throughout the United States. In 1927 he served as visiting professor of the Carnegie Endowment for International Peace at Vienna and Budapest, and spent some time in the land of his forefathers, Dalmatia. In 1929 he was called to Washington to act as director of the National Advisory Committee on Education, in charge of the preparation of a report to the president of the United States, financed by a grant of $100,000 from the Rosenwald Fund.

Suzzallo had, in 1919, become a trustee of the Carnegie Foundation for the Advancement of Teaching, and during 1926–27 had served as chairman of the board. Upon the retirement of Dr. Henry S. Pritchett in 1930, he was elected to the presidency of the Foundation. His position made him, *ex officio,* a trustee of the Carnegie Corporation, and in the three years which remained to him he became one of the most influential trustees of the larger foundation. The work of preparing the report of the National Advisory Committee carried on into the first months of his presidency (*Federal Relations to Education. Report of the National Advisory Committee on Education,* 2 parts, 1931). His next important task was the personal direction of a study of higher education in the state of California, which the state government had invited the Carnegie Foundation to make (*State Higher Education in California. Report of the Carnegie Foundation for the Advancement of Teaching,* 1932). The economic depression having meanwhile created a critical situation, he was called to make a study in several regions of the possibilities of drastic economies without loss of essential efficiency in the conduct of systems of higher education.

To follow the central thread of his career is not to tell the whole story. He was a man of wide-ranging interests, with quick enthusiasms and an instinctive readiness to do his full share of any work to be done. His boyhood days, spent in the beautiful Santa Clara Valley, with summer holidays by the sea at Monterey, bred in him a lifelong appreciation of beauty in all its forms. It is characteristic that his first graduate work was done in the field of esthetics, and that years later he was responsible for building up a department of fine arts at the University of Washington, and for stimulating a community interest in the arts in Seattle. After returning to New York in 1930, he played an active part in developing the art program of the Carnegie Corporation. He was always interested in political affairs, and unusually well-informed as to political conditions. If he could have satisfied the technical requirements as to residence, it is said that he would have been nominated and elected "reform" mayor of San Francisco in 1906. Later on he served as a member of the committee on plans and platforms of the Republican National Committee. His services in the Northwest were perforce largely political, though never partisan. He was deeply concerned with ethical and religious questions, but his interest was not of the type to fit any denominational pattern. Reared in the faith of his fathers, Roman Catholicism, he early found himself more in sympathy with Protestantism, but though he attended the services of the Episcopal Church, he never joined its membership. His marriage, Feb. 8, 1912, to Edith Moore, a graduate of the University of Chicago, inaugurated an unusually close companionship. Since there were no children Mrs. Suzzallo could accompany him on his journeys, and wherever his duties might temporarily call him she established a home.

Even an incomplete list of the organizations in which he played an active part will indicate something of the calls upon his time in addition to his regular professional responsibilities. In the field of education the institutions which he served, either as officer or member of the governing or advisory board, include the National Education Association, the American Council on Education, the Association of State Universities, the Institute of International Education, the American Association for Adult Education, the Educational Research Committee of the Commonwealth Fund, the Cleveland Conference. At different times he served as trustee of Stevens Institute of Technology, as visitor to the United States Naval Academy, as editor of the *Journal of Educational Sociology,* and was active in nursing, pharmaceutical, religious, and other vocational studies. He also rendered special advisory services to the Universities of Wyoming, Denver, and Omaha, to Colorado College, and to the systems of higher education in Georgia and Oregon. In 1900 he became editor of the Riverside Educational Monographs which now include more than seventy titles, and a little later, the editor of the Houghton-Mifflin Educational Classics (6 vols.). After leaving the University of Washington, he undertook the editorship-in-chief of Collier's *The National Encyclopaedia* (10 vols., 1932). Besides several textbooks and numerous articles of a professional and general character, he is the author of *Our Faith in Education* (1924).

While all these interests and activities took their toll, perhaps the heaviest inroads upon what should have been his leisure came from incessant invitations to lecture both on educational and upon more general subjects. His lectures took him all over the country, enlarged the circle of his friends, extended his influence, and contributed to his unusual knowledge of social and political conditions throughout the United States. But these excursions meant a steady depletion of his reserves of strength. It was not until after the successive and heavy demands of the National Advisory Committee on Education and the California study that he realized that his health had become seriously impaired. He was persuaded to devote the summer of 1933 to rest and relaxation in California. The lightening of the load had come too late, however; he and Mrs. Suzzallo started to make their return trip by way of Canada, but on the voyage to Seattle his heart showed disquieting symptoms. He was taken directly to the Seattle General Hospital upon landing, and six days later, on Sept. 25, 1933, he died in the city where he had achieved some of his signal successes and had suffered his greatest disappointment. Had he lived a few days longer, he would have heard of the adoption by the regents of the University of a resolution designating the central building of the campus as the Henry Suzzallo Library. Since the death of Charles W. Eliot, probably the closing of no educational career attracted such widespread attention or evoked such appreciative editorial comment.

The first results of the two major surveys to which he devoted himself so unreservedly were disappointing. He failed to obtain the unanimous support of the National Advisory Committee on Education, minority reports being filed by the heads of negro institutions and by Roman Catholic educators; and public and political attention was directed almost wholly to a reference in the majority report to the ultimate desirability of giving education a place in the president's cabinet, to the neglect of recommendations of more immediate significance. The influence of the report grew steadily, however, and has been shown in great improvements in the educational service for the Indians and in the merger of the hitherto independent Board of Vocational Education with the federal Office of Education. The immediate effect of the publication of the California study seemed to be to accentuate the conflict of authority and influence between the state Board of Education and the regents of the University, but since Suzzallo's death the legislature has followed one of its chief recommendations in the creation of the state Council for Educational Planning and Coordination. The recommendations of the Commission (Part Two of the California report), written by Suzzallo himself, provide what might be called a charter of higher education for the country as a whole; and both reports set forth basic principles and make suggestions as to the elimination of duplication and other desirable and practicable economies.

In the judgment of those who knew him best, Henry Suzzallo will be remembered as an outstanding figure in his generation, not as a scholar, though his scholarship was sound and he made important contributions to educational sociology—a new field in which his alert and agile mind played over a wide range; not as a teacher in the ordinary sense of the term, though his classrooms were always overcrowded; not as an administrator, though his accomplishments at Seattle and elsewhere were distinguished. It will be rather as a man of many talents, of broad sympathies and interests who retained to the end of his life the curiosities and enthusiasms of his youth. His ability to enter immediately into an understanding with those with whom he came into contact and to share with them his own interests and sympathies had much to do with the influence he exerted. It was said of him that he never taught a subject, but always a student, and that what he taught, not only in the classroom but also on the lecture platform and through his writings, was a broad social and intellectual tolerance and a realizing sense of the place of education in a modern democracy.

[*The Carnegie Foundation for the Advancement of Teaching.* .... *Ann. Reports of the President and the Treasurer,* 1931–33; *Henry Suzzallo, 1875–1933* (1934).

report of memorial meeting at Teachers College, Dec. 18, 1933; for the Hartley controversy, *N. Y. Times*, Oct. 6, 7, 1926, and *Seattle Daily Times*, beginning Oct. 5, 1926; obituaries in *Seattle Daily Times*, Sept. 25, 1933; *Seattle Post Intelligencer* and *N. Y. Times*, Sept. 26, 1933; *School and Society*, Sept. 30, 1933; family papers and personal acquaintance.]   F. P. K.

SVERDRUP, GEORG (Dec. 16, 1848–May 3, 1907), theologian, educator, the son of Harald Ulrik and Karoline Metella (Suur) Sverdrup, was born at Balestrand near Bergen, Norway. His father was a clergyman and for many years a member of the Storthing; his uncle Johan was for a generation the leader of the political liberals in the Storthing and prime minister of Norway from 1884 to 1889. One of his brothers likewise was a member of the Storthing. He received a classical education in the Nissen Cathedral School in Christiania and was graduated in theology from Christiania University in 1871. He then studied Semitics in the University of Paris, where he came to know Sven Oftedal [*q.v.*], and visited several German universities. In 1874 he left Norway to become professor of theology in Augsburg Seminary, in Minneapolis, Minn., where he taught for thirty-three years. From 1876 he was president of the institution.

A conservative eclectic Lutheran, with wholesome liberal leanings, Sverdrup's special fields were the Old Testament and dogmatics. As a practical churchman—he had no desire to be ordained—he stressed "Spirit and Life" over against dead orthodoxy and congregational inactivity. His peculiar view in the field of church polity that the local church is the right form of the Kingdom of God was followed by the Norwegian Lutheran Conference, 1869–90, and specifically adopted by its heir, the Norwegian Lutheran Free Church, whose moderator he was for several years. These bodies thus deviated from the well-grounded doctrine of the Lutheran Church that church polity is an adiaphoron. To Sverdrup the state church conception of church, of ministry, and of ministerial education was highly objectionable. Through Augsburg Seminary he wished to resurrect what he claimed to be the New Testament idea of *ekklesia* and to educate a democratic ministry. He regarded the organized local congregation of believers as the only quantity entitled to the name of church. All other so-called ecclesiastical organizations such as council, synod, state church, were purely human. He stressed lay preaching as the chief charism, a complement to the public ministry, which he regarded as highly necessary, but not as a *jure divino* institution. In liturgy, he was a low churchman.

Sverdrup championed congregationalistic ideas, which he called "free church ideas," in the lecture room, on the floor of synod, and in the press. He was a brilliant lecturer, a keen dialectician, schooled in Plato and Hegel, a resourceful parliamentarian, and a writer of clear and forceful Norwegian, the preferred language of his church body. He was an able linguist of extraordinary training, and a scholar of the first water. He was joint editor of *Theologisk Kvartalskrift* from 1875 to 1881, and sole editor, 1877–81; joint editor of *Lutheraneren,* a church weekly, 1885–90; joint editor of its successor, *Luthersk Kirkeblad,* 1890–94; and editor of *Gasseren,* a monthly on foreign missions in Madagascar, 1900–07. His ecclesiastico-political organ was *Folkebladet,* a weekly newspaper to which he was a continuous contributor for a generation, being for some time part owner and editor. A considerable amount of the material contributed by Sverdrup to these periodicals and his introduction to the Old and New Testament are published in Sverdrup's *Samlede Skrifter i Udvalg,* edited by Andreas Helland, (1909–12). Some of his sermons were published under the title *Aand og Liv* in 1897. He was active on many church boards, especially those handling foreign missions and deaconess work sponsored by Norwegian-Americans. Due to his influence they entered upon deaconess work in the West and missions in Madagascar.

Sverdrup was twice married: to Kathrine Elisabet Heiberg in 1874, and, three years after her death in 1887, to her sister Elise Susanna Heiberg. He was survived by his widow, five children of his first wife, and two of his second.

[*Who's Who in America,* 1906–07; Andreas Helland, *Augsburg Seminar gjennem femti aar 1869–1909* (1920); J. O. Evjen, *Veiledning i den lutherske Frikirkes Principer* (1914), an article on Sverdrup in Herzog-Hauck, *Realencyklopaedie für protestantische Theologie und Kirche,* vol. XXIV (3rd ed., 1913), and one on the Lutheran Free Church in *Distinctive Doctrines and Usages of the General Bodies of the Evangelical Luth. Ch. in the U. S.* (4th ed., 1914); discussions in the papers: *Indremissionsvennen,* 1930–32, *Reform,* 1932–33, and *Skandinaven,* 1932–33. Consult also articles on Erik K. Johnsen, Friedrich A. Schmidt, and Hans G. Stub in the *Dict. of Am. Biog.*; *Minneapolis Tribune,* May 4, 1907.]   J. O. E.

SWAIN, CLARA A. (July 18, 1834–Dec. 25, 1910), pioneer woman medical missionary in India, was born in Elmira, N. Y., the youngest of the ten children of John and Clarissa (Seavey) Swain. When she was two years old her parents returned to their former home in Castile, N. Y., where she spent her early life. Her education, received chiefly in schools of the neighborhood, was broken by periods of teaching. Finally, when she was twenty-two or more, she secured a position in the public schools of Canandaigua, in the seminary of which town she had just finished a year's course. As a young girl she had shown aptitude for nursing, and though she continued to teach for some time, she all the while harbored the desire of becoming a physician. At length she began a three-year course of training in the Castile Sanitarium, under Dr. Cordelia A. Greene. Upon its completion she entered the Woman's Medical College in Philadelphia, from which she graduated in 1869.

Just at this time there was a call for a trained person who could inaugurate medical instruction and care for women in India. Appeal was made to the Woman's Medical College, and Clara Swain was recommended. Interested in religious work and an active member of the Methodist Episcopal Church, she consented to undertake the mission, and, sponsored by the Woman's Foreign Missionary Society of her denomination, she sailed from New York, with Isabella Thoburn [q.v.], on Nov. 3, 1869. On Jan. 20, 1870, she arrived in Bareilly, which was the seat of her labors for more than fourteen years, though from 1876 to 1879 she was in the United States because of ill health. She is said to have been the first fully accredited woman physician to be sent by any missionary society to the non-Christian world. She became associated with the girls' orphanage at Bareilly, and at once started a medical class of fourteen native girls, thirteen of whom in April 1873 passed examinations before two civil surgeons and a missionary and were granted certificates authorizing them to practise "in all ordinary diseases." She also carried on a large practice among the women and children of the city, treating them both at the mission and in their homes. In 1871 the Nawab of Rampore gave an estate adjoining the mission property as a site for a hospital for women. A dispensary building was completed in May 1873, and in January 1874 the first woman's hospital in India was opened. Miss Swain continued her work at Bareilly until March 1885, when at the request of the Rajah of Khetri, Rajputana, she became physician to the Rani and the ladies of the palace. She served in this capacity for more than ten years, spending an eighteen-month furlough in the United States (1888–89). In 1896 she returned to Castile, which was her home until her death. In 1906–08 she revisited India, primarily to attend the jubilee of the founding of the Methodist mission there in 1856. A collection of her letters entitled *A Glimpse of India* was published in 1909; it tells the story of her work and gives an interesting picture of various aspects of Indian life.

[In addition to the above, see Mrs. Robert (Charlotte L. R.) Hoskins, *Clara A. Swain, M.D.* (1912); Mrs. J. T. Gracey, *Medical Work of the Woman's Foreign Missionary Soc., M. E. Church* (1881); and *Eminent Missionary Women* (1898); J. S. Dennis, *Christian Missions and Social Progress*, vols. I, II (1897); *Christian Advocate* (N. Y.), Jan. 5, 1911. Exact date of birth was furnished by the Rev. D. F. Eggleston, Castile, N. Y.]
H. E. S.

SWAIN, DAVID LOWRY (Jan. 4, 1801–Aug. 27, 1868), governor of North Carolina, college president, was born in Buncombe County, N. C. His father, George Swain, a native of Massachusetts and a man of some learning and much intelligence, had gone South in 1785, and, after service in the legislature and a constitutional convention of Georgia, had moved to North Carolina. He was a hatter by trade, ran a small farm, and for many years was postmaster of Asheville. There he married a widow, Caroline (Lane) Lowry. David, the second child, was taught at home until he was fifteen, and was then sent to school in Asheville. He entered the University of North Carolina in 1821 but remained only four months, leaving to begin the study of law in Raleigh. He was admitted to the bar late in 1822 and on Jan. 12, 1823 (Ashe, *post*) married Eleanor H. White of Raleigh.

He represented Buncombe in the House of Commons from 1824 to 1827, and from 1828 to 1829, when he became solicitor of an eastern district. Within a year he was a superior court judge, and, after two years, was elected governor, the youngest in the history of the state. Re-elected twice, he served from 1832 until 1835. In the latter year he was a member of the constitutional convention and was elected president of the University of North Carolina. In 1857 he was made a commissioner of the sinking fund and in 1861 was sent by the legislature to Montgomery, Ala., as one of a commission to represent the state near the Confederate government. A Union Whig, he did not believe in secession, but, after the call for troops, accepted it as a necessity. In 1863 Gov. Zebulon Vance [q.v.] wished to appoint him to the Confederate Senate that he might "modify and soften the present violent and desperate temper of Congress," but he declined. Throughout the war he was the constant and invaluable adviser of the governor. In April 1865 he went as a special commissioner to meet General Sherman on his approach to Raleigh and arrange favorable terms for the surrender of the state, and on Apr. 13, he surrendered the keys of the capitol to Sherman when he entered the town. The next month he was summoned by President Johnson to advise him as to reconstruction, and during the three years following he was consulted constantly by the

President and by Gov. Jonathan Worth [*q.v.*]. Johnson appointed him to the board of visitors of West Point and secured for the University of North Carolina its share of the public land allotted under the Morrill Act, but Congressional reconstruction resulted in the displacement of the trustees and faculty of the University and in virtual heartbreak for Swain; soon afterwards he was injured in a runaway accident and died within ten days.

In North Carolina history Swain was a constructive figure of first rank. An excellent lawyer and judge, he performed his greatest service as legislator and governor, effectively pressing forward the cause of tax reform, public education, internal improvements, and amendment of the constitution to put an end to the dangerous sectional controversy then existing. He had acquired by 1832 remarkable personal influence, and his messages—dynamic, and charged with telling facts presented in vigorous style—aroused the state. He induced the legislature to call the constitutional convention of 1835, and in it he led the western forces, which were bent on reform. A skilful politician, he was fair, patient, tactful, and yet perfectly frank; to him more than to anyone else belongs the credit of what the convention accomplished. He desired that the constitution be entirely rewritten, but, that being impossible, he favored every liberal reform proposed, advocating complete religious toleration, the reform of the system of representation, and popular election of the governor. He opposed the disfranchisement of free negroes. He spoke but seldom, doing his chief work off the floor, but when he raised his voice the convention listened. Occasionally he was fiery in speech, as when he warned the convention, "Unless our demands are granted, unless our wrongs are righted, we will rise like the strong man in his unshorn might and pull down the pillars of the political temple" (Ashe, *post*, p. 450).

Swain was also a constructive figure in a quite different sphere of activity. His choice as president of the University aroused much feeling in the faculty, one professor acidly remarking that the people of the state, having elected Swain to every office in their gift, were now sending him to the University to be educated. The trustees were wise in their choice, however, for he proved an excellent executive. He was a shrewd and able business man and the funds of the institution under his management increased largely. The student body was multiplied more than fourfold, and by 1860 included representatives from every Southern state and many Northern ones. The faculty was strengthened and enlarged. He pop-

ularized the institution until the state for the first time felt a consciousness of ownership. Teaching constitutional and international law, history, and moral science, he proved a rare teacher; though unconventional he had a dynamic personality and inspired his students with passion for public service. He established the North Carolina Historical Society with headquarters at the University and began there a notable collection of historical material. He founded the *University of North Carolina Magazine* and by his own contributions and those which he secured made it unique among college publications. In 1854 he was appointed the state's agent for the collection of historical material and began the work which resulted years later in the publication of the *Colonial and State Records*. With Francis L. Hawks [*q.v.*] he projected a documentary history of the state, which project was stopped by the war. He published several valuable historical monographs, the best known being "The British Invasion of North Carolina in 1776" (*University of North Carolina Magazine*, May 1853). During the Civil War by heroic efforts he kept the University open, delaying the conscription of students and carefully husbanding its diminishing resources. The war swept away the endowment, however, and only Swain's resourcefulness made it possible for the institution to continue in operation until 1868.

He was tall and heavy with a grotesquely ugly figure and ungraceful carriage. His voice was harsh, hollow, and high-keyed, but these defects were soon forgotten in the charm of his conversation. In temperament he was cautious and politic; in manner, suave and mild; but, as his political career showed, he had an abundance of fighting spirit. He was a genuine liberal, and so wise in counsel that he was kept in close touch with public life by those who sought his advice.

[Z. B. Vance, *Life and Character of Hon. David Lowry Swain* (1878); R. D. W. Connor, *Ante-Bellum Builders of N. C.* (1914); S. A. Ashe, *Biog. Hist. of N. C.*, vol. I (1905); *Proc. and Debates of the Convention of N. C. . . . . 1835* (1836); *N. C. Legislative Jours.*; K. P. Battle, *Hist. of the Univ. of N. C.* (1907); W. J. Peele, *Lives of Distinguished North Carolinians* (1898); *Daily North Carolina Standard* (Raleigh), Aug. 28, 1868; *New-England Hist. and Geneal. Register*, Oct. 1870; Swain Papers in possession of the Univ. of N. C.]   J. G. deR. H.

SWAIN, JAMES BARRETT (July 30, 1820–May 27, 1895), journalist, was the son of Joseph and Jerusha (Everts) Swain of New York City and a descendant of Jeremiah Swain who was living in Charlestown, Mass., as early as 1638. After the usual schooling and apprenticeship, his newspaper work was begun on the ephemeral Harrison organ, *The Log Cabin*, published by

Horace Greeley in 1840. While running a private printing establishment in the succeeding years, he found time to publish *The Life and Speeches of Henry Clay* (Greeley & McElrath, 1843), the "Life" consisting of an unimportant memoir in the first volume. After this he was successively owner of the *Hudson River Chronicle* (1844–49), a small sheet published at Sing Sing; assistant on Greeley's *New York Tribune*; independent printer; city editor on the fledgling *New York Times* (1852); then the *Times* correspondent at Albany, writing under the name of Leo. From 1855 to 1857 he turned for the moment to the very different occupation of state railroad commissioner—one of three—but meanwhile found time to establish the *Free State Advocate* (1856) and the *Albany Statesman* (1857) in the interests of Frémont, both short-lived publications. In 1860 he was again representing the *Times*, in Washington. One of his real accomplishments in the newspaper field was the introduction of the correspondent system, extensively used before the day of the great newsgathering agencies.

Caught in the tide of war, he received an appointment as second lieutenant, and later as first, with authority to raise a regiment of cavalry. By May 1862, the ranks of "Scotts 900," as he called it, officially known as the 11th New York, were filled, and, newly commissioned colonel (Apr. 30), he conducted it to Camp Relief at Meridian Hill, Washington, named in honor of his wife, Relief Davis Swain, whom he had married in 1842. One of his sons, Chellis, was a lieutenant under him. Odd jobs, such as guard duty and reconnoitering were about all the regiment or its detachments were permitted, and on Feb. 12, 1864, for obscure reasons, Swain was dismissed, the regiment moving to the Gulf under another command. In 1866 this dismissal was revoked, and he was given honorable discharge (Frederick Phisterer, *New York in the War of the Rebellion*, 1st ed., 1890, pp. 73 and 311; 3rd ed., 1912, II, 958).

On his return home, he was appointed in 1865 engineer-in-chief on the staff of Gov. Reuben S. Fenton [*q.v.*]. This appointment led to a rather bizarre adventure in rapid transit development. A welter of visionary suggestions were in the air, and after unsuccessful projects, first in 1866, and then with the Tweed group in 1871, Swain applied in 1872 for a charter for the Metropolitan Transit Company, which, after a struggle, he secured, with a stock authorization of five million dollars. His scheme provided for "a three deck highway. . . . The lowest level . . . to be a subway for freight, the next a slightly depressed

road for passenger traffic, and the third . . . an elevated structure from which passenger cars would hang suspended and be drawn by horses driven on the road below" (Walker, *post,* p. 103). The service was to extend from the Battery to Harlem River, with side lines. Though he was unsuccessful in soliciting capital with which to realize this dream, his wants were nevertheless supplied by the prosaic positions of weigher in the New York Custom House, 1867–71; Senate reporter for the *New York Tribune* and clerk of one of the Assembly committees in 1872. His fluctuating and varied life was rounded out by a return to his comfortable, four-page, Republican sheet, the *Hudson River Chronicle,* which he revived in 1876 and which ceased publication with his death.

[Obituary notices in the *N. Y. Tribune* and *N. Y. Times,* May 28, 1895; W. C. Swain, *Swain and Allied Families* (1896); T. W. Smith, *The Story of a Cavalry Regiment, "Scotts 900"* (1897); J. B. Walker, *Fifty Years of Rapid Transit* (1918); *U. S. Official Reg.,* 1871; N. Y. Senate and Assembly journals, 1872; J. T. Scharf, *Hist. of Westchester County, N. Y.* (1886), vol. II.]   C. W. G.

SWALLOW, GEORGE CLINTON (Nov. 17, 1817–Apr. 20, 1899), geologist, was born in Buckfield, Oxford County, Me., the son of Larned and Olive Fletcher (Proctor) Swallow, and a descendant of Ambrose Swallow, who emigrated from England to Chelmsford, Mass., about 1666. Though he was largely self-taught as a boy, he completed his preparatory studies at the New Yarmouth Academy and graduated in 1843 from Bowdoin College, Brunswick, Me., where he studied the sciences under Parker Cleaveland [*q.v.*]. Immediately after graduation he gave a course of lectures to the senior class of his college on botany as applied to agriculture and the mechanic arts. From 1843 to 1849 he was principal of Brunswick Female Seminary. In 1849 he was elected principal of Hampden Academy, Hampden, Me., and became a member of the state board of education. During this time he was also active as a public lecturer throughout many of the counties of the state, and in 1851 was elected to the professorship of geology, chemistry, and mineralogy in the University of Missouri at Columbia. Soon after going to Missouri he was influential in establishing state wide agricultural and mechanical associations. When the Missouri geological survey was established in 1853 he became state geologist and held the position until the survey was abolished in 1861. In 1865, as state geologist of Kansas, he surveyed the coal fields and showed the positions of the various geological formations of the state. His demonstration in 1858 of the existence of Permian rocks on the American continent led to a personal controversy of some bitterness with Fielding Bradford Meek [*q.v.*]. (For an account see Merrill, *The First One Hundred Years of American Geology, post,* pp. 368–70.) During 1867–70 he was engaged in mining operations in Montana. At the end of that time he was appointed professor of agriculture in the agricultural and mechanical college of the University of Missouri. He became dean in 1872 and professor of botany, comparative anatomy, and physiology in the medical school of the university. In 1882 he removed to Helena, Mont., to edit the *Daily Independent,* and later became state inspector of mines, 1888–90. Swallow was a handsome man of over six feet. He married on Mar. 17, 1844, Martha Ann Hill of Columbia, Mo. (d. 1898). They had a son, who died in childhood, and a daughter. Swallow died at the home of his daughter in Evanston, Ill.

An all-round scientist and a very close observer, Swallow succeeded in producing work up to the highest standard of the time in spite of the fact that he labored under unfavorable conditions. In his Kansas work he erred, perhaps, in making exact statements where only approximations were possible and in attempting too rapid explorations in obedience to an unreasonable public demand for immediate results, but in his Missouri work it is recognized that he made a remarkably able classification of the rocks involved and defined with general accuracy the distribution of the formations. Of the five reports published, the second (1854) is the one commonly accepted as his principal work.

[A. G. Baker, *Geneal. of the Swallow Family* (1910); *Obit. Record Grads. Bowdoin Coll. . . . 1899* (n.d.); G. P. Merrill, *The First One Hundred Years of Am. Geology* (1924), *Contributions to a Hist. of Am. State Geological and Nat. Hist. Surveys* (1920), and "Contributions to the Hist. of Am. Geology," in *Ann. Report of the Board of Regents of the Smithsonian Institution . . . 1904* (1906); Frederick Starr, in *Popular Sci. Monthly,* Mar. 1898; C. R. Keyes, in *Am. Geologist,* June 1900; biog. sketch and bibliog., *Ibid.,* July 1899.]
G. P. M.

SWALLOW, SILAS COMFORT (Mar. 5, 1839–Aug. 13, 1930), Methodist Episcopal clergyman, reformer, Prohibition candidate for president, was born near Wilkes-Barre, Pa., the son of George and Sarah Swallow. Because of the illness of his father, he assumed the management of the farm at the age of fourteen. By diligent labor and the practice of economy he obtained sufficient money to enter Wyoming Seminary at Kingston, Pa. After his graduation he taught a country school for five years, and then began the study of law in the office of Volney B. Maxwell of Wilkes-Barre. Before his admis-

sion to the bar, however, he decided to enter the ministry of the Methodist Episcopal Church, and after pursuing theological studies in the Susquehanna Seminary, Binghamton, N. Y., was admitted on trial by the East Baltimore Conference of his church in 1863. He began preaching on a circuit in central Pennsylvania at a salary of $100 a year. Twice during the Civil War, in 1862 and 1863, he served for brief periods in the Pennsylvania Emergency Volunteers. Throughout the war his religious work was seriously handicapped by his outspoken anti-slavery pronouncements and his support of the Union cause in a region where a considerable pro-slavery and anti-war sentiment prevailed. On one occasion his church was padlocked by disgruntled members. He married Rebecca Louisa Robins of Elysburg, Pa., Jan. 20, 1866, was ordained elder the following year, and during the next two decades served many pastoral charges in central Pennsylvania. Between 1892 and 1905 he was superintendent of the Methodist Book Rooms in Harrisburg and editor of the *Pennsylvania Methodist* and of the short-lived *Church Forum.*

From early manhood Swallow was an earnest advocate of moral and spiritual discipline which rivaled that of the Puritans of the seventeenth century. From the time when in 1864 he threw his tobacco box "over the house" and took a solemn vow that tobacco should never again enter his lips unless to save his life, "and then only on the written prescription of two full-fledged physicians," and when, two years later, on his honeymoon trip to Philadelphia he walked out of the only theatre which he had ever entered because John S. Clark in *She Stoops to Conquer* said "I'll be d—d," he was an uncompromising enemy in both word and action of the use of tobacco and liquor in all forms, of dancing, of roller-skating, and of secular amusements in general. The militant attitude which he assumed in his condemnation of these diversions made him many bitter enemies and involved him in a large number of personal controversies. During the late nineties he made the Republican machine in Pennsylvania a target for his thrusts. His persistent attacks upon prominent politicians resulted in the filing of charges of libel against him on several occasions and the divided allegiance of many Methodist ministers, who sought to divorce religion and politics. The controversy in the church reached an acute stage in the fall of 1901, when he was suspended from all ministerial duties and church privileges until the next annual meeting of the Central Pennsylvania Conference at Bellefonte, in March 1902. Although this body failed to sustain the charges of "lying and insubordination," it declared him "to be guilty of highly imprudent and unministerial conduct" and authorized the Bishop to administer a "public reproof" (*The Minutes of the Central Pennsylvania Annual Conference*, 1902, p. 60).

Meanwhile the "fighting Parson," as he was termed, was waging a valiant campaign against the firmly entrenched liquor interests of the state and nation. In 1896 he was elected a delegate to the Prohibition National Convention, and the next year he carried eleven counties in his candidacy for state treasurer, while in 1898 as the Prohibition candidate for governor he received some 130,000 votes. Six years later he became the nominee of his party for the presidency and polled 258,847 votes. (See his article, "The Prohibition Party's Appeal," *Independent,* New York, Oct. 13, 1904.) During the remainder of his life he devoted his whole time to preaching, writing, and lecturing. In 1909 he published a volume of reminiscences entitled *III Score & X or Selections, Collections, Recollections of Seventy Busy Years*; in 1920, a pamphlet, *Then and Now or Some Reminiscences of an Octogenarian*; and in 1922, a supplementary pamphlet, *Fourscore and More.* He died in 1930 at the age of ninety-one.

[Swallow's autobiog. writings; *Minutes of Conferences of the M. E. Church,* 1863 ff.; *Who's Who in America,* 1920–21; *Who's Who in Pa.,* 1904; *Phila. Inquirer,* Aug. 14, 1930; *N. Y. Times,* Aug. 14, 1930.]
A. E. M.

SWAN, JAMES (1754–July 31, 1830), financier, agent of the French Republic, was born in Fifeshire, Scotland. Emigrating to Boston in 1765, he became a clerk in a counting-house near Faneuil Hall. He early found his place among the radically patriotic youth of the city and became a member of the Sons of Liberty. He was a participant in the Boston Tea Party and was wounded twice at the battle of Bunker Hill. He attained the rank of major by the close of the Revolution and was later made a colonel. Married to Hepzibah Clarke of Boston (intention signified, Oct. 3, 1776), Swan abandoned active service and became a placeman, serving as secretary to the Massachusetts Board of War in 1777, as a member of the Massachusetts legislature in 1778, and then as adjutant-general of the commonwealth. He used an inheritance of his wife to live lavishly, to invest in Loyalist properties confiscated by the commonwealth, and to speculate in lands in Pennsylvania, Virginia, and Kentucky. In 1786 he purchased the Burnt Coat group of islands lying off the east coast of Maine, the largest of which bears his name.

Heavily in debt by 1787, Swan went to France to recuperate his fortunes. Assisted by his constant friend, Lafayette, he obtained remunerative contracts to furnish the French marine with naval stores and salt meat provisions, and in 1795 was able to make another profitable deal by which he gained control of the remainder of the United States debt to France, amounting to $2,024,899.93. Successful in gaining the appointment as agent of the French Republic, he outwitted his banking competitors, among whom were the American speculators, Gouverneur Morris and Robert Morris [*qq.v.*], the Boston banker, Daniel Parker, and the powerful bankers of the United States government at Amsterdam, Willink, Van Staphorst, and Hubbard, by his scheme for commuting the debt. By the congressional act of Mar. 3, 1795, it was made possible for American debt obligations to France to be exchanged for 4½ and 5½ per cent. United States domestic stock issued under authority of this act. Acting both as agent of the French Republic and as broker, Swan accepted American debt obligations from France in payment for supplies furnished or to be furnished the French marine, and in turn exchanged these for American domestic stock on which the interest rate was one-half per cent. higher. On June 15, 1795, the arrangement was closed, and the American foreign debt to France was transformed into a domestic one. Swan returned to the United States the better to direct these transactions and remained until 1798. Going back to France he engaged in further mercantile ventures which met with only varying success, and in 1808 he was cast into a debtor's prison in Paris where he died on July 31, 1830. Though he lived in some comfort on a stipend from his wife, he refused to have what he considered an unjust debt paid by her. His wife, son, and three daughters—one of them the wife of William Sullivan [*q.v.*]—remained in the United States during his twenty-two years of imprisonment. Swan published *A Dissuasion to Great-Britain and the Colonies, from the Slave-Trade to Africa* (1773), *National Arithmetick: or, Observations on the Finances of the Commonwealth of Massachusetts* (1786), and *Causes Qui Se Sont Apposées aux Progrès du Commerce entre la France et les États-Unis de l'Amérique* (Paris, 1790).

[*Proc. Mass. Hist. Soc.,* 1 ser., vol. XIII (1875), pp. 209–10, 2 ser., vol. IV (1889), pp. 46 ff.; Dispatches, France, vols. I–III, IIIa, and Miscellaneous Letters (1789–1800), MSS. in State Dept. Archives; French Archives Photostats, *Affaires Étrangères, Correspondance Politique États-Unis,* vols. XVIII–XXII, and the William Short Papers, Lib. of Congress; S. F. Bemis, in *Current Hist.,* Mar. 1926; H. W. Small, *A Hist. of Swan's Island, Me.* (1898).]
R. L–F.

SWAN, JOSEPH ROCKWELL (Dec. 28, 1802–Dec. 18, 1884), jurist, legal writer, was born at Westernville, Oneida County, N. Y., a descendant of John Swan, who resided successively in Stow and Lunenburg, Mass., and Peterborough, N. H., where he died about the time of the American Revolution. Joseph's parents, Jonathan and Sarah (Rockwell) Swan, were Quakers, the former a merchant. About 1813 the family moved to Aurora, N. Y., where the youth received his academic training and began the study of law. In 1824 he entered the law office of his uncle, Gustavus Swan, at Columbus, Ohio. Soon afterward he was admitted to the bar. From 1830 to 1835 he was prosecuting attorney of Franklin County, and in 1834 he was elected by the General Assembly a judge of the common pleas court; in 1841 he was reëlected. At the end of his term he returned to the practice of law in Columbus in partnership with John W. Andrews. In 1854 he was elected a judge of the supreme court of Ohio. He was an ardent abolitionist and his election by an unprecedented majority was due to a coalition of the anti-slavery element of all parties. He served on this court but one term (to November 1859) and, though he lived twenty-five years longer, he never again accepted a judicial office or engaged in active practice, but devoted his time to wide reading, particularly in the field of seventeenth-century English history, to extensive writing, and to civic and business enterprises. He also rendered much aid to legislative committees, which habitually called on him for help in drafting important legislation.

For one whose tenure on the supreme court bench had been so brief he enjoyed a high reputation as a judge. "He probably held as high a place in the estimation of the Bench, the Bar and the Public as has ever been reached by any one of the many distinguished men who have adorned our judicial history" ("In Memoriam," *post,* p. vi). The explanation for this great reputation is found in his opinion in a single case, *Ex parte Bushnell* (9 *Ohio State,* 78). It was sought in this case under a writ of *habeas corpus* issued from the supreme court of Ohio to override a judgment of the district court of the United States and to discharge from jail a prisoner who had been convicted and sentenced by that court for a violation of one of the sections of the Fugitive Slave Law. Gov. Salmon P. Chase declared that if the prisoner were discharged the armed forces of the state would be used to prevent his reimprisonment by the federal government. Swan as chief justice cast the deciding vote in the court, which held that the state could not interfere with the actions of the federal courts within the limits of their constitutional power and that the application for the prisoner's dis-

charge should be denied. Swan wrote the opinion, which has become a classic and given him a reputation for great judicial and moral courage. As a result of this opinion the Republican party then in state convention refused to renominate him. Nevertheless, he was later three times offered appointment to the supreme court to fill vacancies, and once, a nomination by the Republican party.

It is upon his work as a legal writer, however, that his fame most depends. He was author of *The Practice in Civil Actions and Proceedings at Law in Ohio, and Precedents in Pleading* (2 vols., 1845, 1850), and *Commentaries on Pleading under the Ohio Code, with Precedents of Petitions* (1861). The latter work was largely responsible for the acceptance of a broad interpretation of the civil code, in the spirit of the code itself and not in the technical spirit of the common law. He made four general revisions of Ohio statutes (1841, 1854, 1860, 1868). The book which gave him his greatest renown, however, was published as early as 1837. It was entitled *A Treatise on the Law Relating to the Powers and Duties of Justices of the Peace ... in the State of Ohio,* and has been called "probably the most useful book ever published in Ohio" (Andrews, *post,* p. ix). Swan himself prepared twelve editions and up to 1930 twenty-seven editions had appeared.

Swan held many important positions other than judicial. In 1850 he was elected a member of the constitutional convention, at which he was recognized as one of its most influential members. He also served as general solicitor of the Pittsburg, Cincinnati, St. Louis Railroad Company (1869–79) and president of the Columbus & Xenia Railway. He was married in 1833 to Hannah R. Andrews of Rochester, N. Y., who died in 1876. His own death occurred in Columbus, Ohio. He was survived by three sons and two daughters.

[A. L. Priest, "John Swan . . . and Descendants" (typescript, Lib. of Cong., 1934); J. W. Andrews, "Joseph Rockwell Swan—An American," *Columbus Dispatch,* Dec. 19, 1884, repr. in later editions of Swan's *Treatise;* "In Memoriam," 42 *Ohio State Reports;* G. I. Reed, *Bench and Bar of Ohio* (1897); *Ohio State Bar Asso. Reports,* vol. V (1885); *Ohio Law Jour.,* Dec. 27, 1884; *Ohio State Jour.* (Columbus), Dec. 20, 1884; *Cincinnati Enquirer,* Dec. 19, 1884.]

A. H. T.

SWAN, TIMOTHY (July 23, 1758–July 23, 1842), composer and compiler of psalm-tunes, was born in Worcester, Mass., the eighth of the thirteen children of William and Lavina (Keyes) Swan. He was a descendant of Thomas Swan, who settled in Roxbury, Mass., before 1681. After the death of his father he spent a few years as an apprentice in the family of a Mr. Barnes, a loyalist in Marlboro, but in 1775 he went to Groton, Mass., to live with a brother, a merchant. Later he went to Northfield, where he learned the trade of hatter. His musical education was limited to three weeks in a singing school, although he received some instruction upon the fife from a British musician. In 1782 he moved to Suffield, Conn., where he lived for nearly thirty years. On Apr. 10, 1784, he married Mary Gay, daughter of the Rev. Ebenezer Gay of Suffield. There were fourteen children, four of whom died while young.

During his apprenticeship Swan composed the tune "Poland," and this was followed by many other tunes for church hymns, which were used in manuscript in many parts of New England. It was his habit to compose his tunes while at work—first the melody, then the harmonic parts, a few notes at a time, until the composition was complete. Swan's music was very popular in its day. Oliver Brownson printed half a dozen tunes in his *Select Harmony* (1783), including "Poland," "Lisbon," and "Majesty"; Simeon Jocelin wrote for permission to use some of the tunes; in 1810 Daniel Read [*q.v.*] offered to purchase "China" and "London" for three dollars, and one correspondent wrote, "I must publish 'Flanders,' unless you absolutely forbid me." "China" was composed in 1790 and first sung in public in 1794 (notation in Swan's *New England Harmony*, 1801, in the Collections of the American Antiquarian Society, Worcester, Mass.). This Swan considered his best tune, and later bookmakers have concurred in this opinion, for it is the only one of his tunes that has retained a place in modern hymnals; it is usually set to the words of Watts' "Why do we mourn for dying friends?" He loved poetry, Burns being his favorite author, and he wrote considerable verse for the local paper, much of it in the Scottish dialect. About 1800 he published *The Songster's Assistant,* a thirty-six page pamphlet of songs in two parts, most of the music never before published. The following year, 1801, *New England Harmony,* a volume of 103 pages, was published at Northampton, and in 1803 *The Songster's Museum.* The latter was published anonymously, but much of its music, 204 pages of secular music, was furnished by Swan. The authorship of *The Federal Harmony* (not to be confused with another book of the same title issued the same year by Asahel Benham) is questionable, but it has been attributed to Swan (Charles Evans, *American Bibliography,* vol. VI, 1910, p. 384, and vol. VII, 1912, p. 268; H. P. Main, in *The Music of the Modern World,* 1895, edited by Anton Seidl), and it may have been the first of his publications.

Four editions of the book appeared between 1785 and 1792, all printed in Boston. It contains only two tunes known to be Swan's, "China" and "Lisbon." He died in Northfield, Mass.

[A sketch of Swan, said to have been revised by his daughter, appeared in *The Christian Parlor Book* (1855), pp. 137–38. A small book of original music, some correspondence, and other papers relating to Swan are in the Lib. of the Am. Antiquarian Soc., Worcester, Mass. See also Joseph Sabin, *Bibliotheca Americana,* vol. XXIV (1933–34), cont. by Wilberforce Eames and R. W. G. Vail; F. J. Metcalf, *Am. Writers and Compilers of Sacred Music* (1925); *Celebration of the Two Hundred and Fiftieth Anniversary of the Settlement of Suffield, Conn.* (1921), p. 172; J. H. Temple and George Sheldon, *Hist. of the Town of Northfield, Mass.* (1875); Joel Munsell, *Reminiscences of Men and Things in Northfield* (n.d.); *Am. Musical Rev.,* May 1852; *Musical Herald,* Oct. 1882; obituary in *Boston Daily Advertiser,* Aug. 5, 1842.]   F. J. M—f.

SWANK, JAMES MOORE (July 12, 1832–June 21, 1914), statistician, historian, executive secretary of the American Iron and Steel Association, was born in Westmoreland County, Pa., the son of George W. and Nancy (Moore) Swank. His ancestors, rigid Scotch-Irish Presbyterians on his mother's side and German Lutherans on his father's, had lived in Pennsylvania since early colonial days. In 1838 his parents moved to Johnstown. After attending Jefferson College in Canonsburg, Pa., for one year, he clerked in his father's store, taught school, read law, and edited a Whig newspaper. In 1869 he went to Washington to serve as clerk of the House committee on manufactures, of which his friend Daniel J. Morrell, afterwards president of the American Iron and Steel Association, was chairman. Two years later he became a clerk in the Department of Agriculture and specialized in statistics; within six months he became chief clerk. During this time he wrote *The Department of Agriculture: Its History and Objects* (1872), the first history of the department. In 1873 he was chosen secretary of the American Iron and Steel Association, with headquarters in Philadelphia, and from 1885 until 1912, when he retired, he was vice-president and general manager. During much of this time he also served as secretary of the Industrial League of America, an organization which used the same headquarters as the Association and had similar political aims. Swank's previous training and mental traits fitted him well for this work. During his first year he compiled a *Directory to the Iron and Steel Works of the United States,* of which seventeen editions were published. He was a pioneer in collecting and publishing data for the iron and steel industry, and gained an international reputation as a statistician. Under his editorship the bulletin of the Association became an informing and influential periodical, particularly in relation to tariff legislation.

It was fortunate for the iron and steel interests that they secured Swank's services in 1873, for the strength of the Republican party in Congress was waning and the enemies of the protective tariff were pointing to it as one of the major causes of the panic of 1873. To counteract such influences, protectionists turned to the newspapers, only to find that in the very sections they needed most to reach—the South and West—the newspapers were hostile. To reach the voters, therefore, well edited pamphlets were printed, and widely and methodically distributed under Swank's leadership. Not one contained a special plea for iron and steel. As bill after bill for the reduction of duties was introduced into Congress, Swank redoubled his energy. Between 1880 and 1882, over 1,000,000 tracts were distributed. After Cleveland's famous tariff message in 1887, Swank distributed in nine months 1,387,864 tracts, principally in the Northwest (Bulletin of the American Iron and Steel Association, Nov. 7 and 14, 1888, p. 333). He also played a prominent rôle in bringing about and maintaining close cooperation between eastern business men and the leaders of the Republican party. Now and then he saw to it that a friendly, hard-pressed member of Congress had sufficient campaign funds. When the representatives of the iron and steel interests appeared before committees of Congress, Swank often accompanied them, and ably and adroitly supplied facts, figures, and suggestions, which usually resulted in favorable tariff legislation. He did this so fairly and courteously that, although he went through innumerable bitter tariff contests, no aspersions were ever cast on his character. Andrew Carnegie once declared that iron and steel owed "an unpayable debt" to Swank (quoted in McPherson, post, p. 265). During the period in which he served the Association, he saw pig iron production in the United States increase from 2,560,-963 to 29,726,937 gross tons and steel production from 198,796 to 31,251,303 tons; he also saw the fear of European competition pass away in this field and the protective principle become established.

In 1880, as special agent for the census office, he collected statistics for iron and steel manufacturing and wrote an historical sketch to accompany them (Report on the Manufactures of the United States at the Tenth Census, 1883, pp. 729–901). This led to his well-known work on The History of the Manufacture of Iron in All Ages (1884). He also published The Industrial Policies of Great Britain and the United States

(1876), an historical account with a spirited defense of the protective tariff principle as developed in the United States, Introduction to a History of Ironmaking and Coal Mining in Pennsylvania (1878), Notes and Comments on Industrial, Economic, Political, and Historical Subjects (1897), Progressive Pennsylvania (1908), and Cambria County Pioneers (1910). He died in Philadelphia, survived by his second wife, Anna Park (Linton) Swank.

[Who's Who in America, 1914–15; H. W. Storey, Hist. of Cambria County, Pa. (1907), vol. II, pp. 481–85; J. B. McPherson, in Bull. Nat. Asso. of Wool Manufacturers, Sept. 1913; Monthly Bull. Am. Iron and Steel Institute, Jan. 1913, p. 20; A. T. Volwiler, in Am. Hist. Rev., Oct. 1930; Swank Papers, Cambria Free Lib., Johnstown, Pa., and obituary in Pub. Ledger (Phila.), June 22, 1914.]   A. T. V.

SWANN, THOMAS (c. 1806–July 24, 1883), mayor of Baltimore, governor, and congressman, was born in Alexandria, then a part of the District of Columbia, the son of Thomas Swann, a prominent lawyer of Washington, and Jane Byrd (Page). After attending the preparatory school of Columbian College in the national capital and subsequently the University of Virginia (1826–27), he studied law in his father's office. On Mar. 2, 1833, he was named by President Jackson as secretary of the commission to Naples to negotiate a settlement of spoliation claims.

Shortly after his return from this mission he married, in 1834, Elizabeth Gilmor Sherlock of Baltimore, and moved to that city to engage in business. Here, as the energetic and indomitable president of the Baltimore & Ohio Railroad Company, he first rose to prominence. Acquisition of a considerable amount of stock of the struggling railroad brought him to a director's seat in 1847, and in October 1848 to the presidency. By 1853, despite almost insuperable obstacles—the credit of the company was practically nil, the city of Baltimore and the state at large were extremely skeptical—he had succeeded in extending the railroad through some two hundred miles of thinly settled, mountainous country to reach the Ohio River. This object accomplished he felt free to resign, but almost immediately undertook the presidency of the Northwestern Virginia Railroad (now the Grafton-Parkersburg line of the Baltimore & Ohio), which had obtained its charter through his efforts. Had he chosen, he might have acquired a reputation as a master railroad builder; instead he preferred to pour his energies into political channels.

He first appeared as a candidate for mayor of Baltimore on the ticket of the Native American party in 1856. The election was attended with great disorder and terrorism, as was the next election in 1858, but on each occasion Swann was declared elected. Whatever the tactics by which he secured office, as mayor he employed his high order of executive ability and broad comprehension of the material interests of the city to render it a signal service. Among other improvements, he replaced the inefficient volunteer fire companies by a municipal department equipped with modern apparatus, installed the police and fire alarm telegraph system, introduced a street railway and by imposing a park tax as compensation for the franchise made it possible to beautify the city.

When the Civil War began, Swann, who had already emancipated his large group of slaves, took decided ground against secession and remained throughout the struggle an unwavering Unionist. In 1864 he was elected governor of Maryland by the Union party under the constitution of that year, though he did not take office until the expiration of his predecessor's term in January 1866, and served only three years. He supported the Lincoln and Johnson plans for reconstruction, but as the Radicals developed their plans he joined forces with Maryland Democrats to secure removal of disfranchisement. He made possible the overthrow of the Radical Republican machine at the election of 1866 when he replaced the Republican police commissioners against whom certain charges had been preferred by men of less radical stamp. As a result of this move the registration books were opened, oaths were not exacted, the franchise was effectively restored to many former Southern sympathizers, and the conservatives won the election. The Democratic legislature rewarded Swann in 1867 by electing him to the United States Senate, but after consultation with political leaders he declined the post because he feared that the radical lieutenant-governor, Christopher C. Cox, might undo what he had accomplished. He also thought he discerned a plot on the part of the radical senators in Washington to reject his credentials. With this decision he sacrificed his most cherished ambition. He was not denied service in Congress, however, for in 1868, though the angry Republicans made a special effort to defeat him, he was elected a representative on the Democratic ticket. Reëlected for four successive terms, he remained in the House for ten years, rising to the chairmanship of the committee on foreign relations and enjoying contacts which probably made these the most satisfying years of his life. At the close of his congressional career in 1879 he retired to his estate, "Morven Park," near Leesburg, Va. In June 1878, two years after the death of his first wife, he married Josephine (Ward) Thom-

son, daughter of Gen. Aaron Ward and widow of John Renshaw Thomson, a former senator from New Jersey. This marriage brought little joy to the aged statesman, however, for a separation soon occurred. A daughter of the first marriage became the wife of Mayor Ferdinand C. Latrobe of Baltimore.

[*Tercentenary Hist. of Md.* (1925), vol. IV; H. E. Buchholz, *Govs. of Md.* (1908); W. F. Coyle, *The Mayors of Baltimore* (1910); *Baltimore Past and Present* (1871), ed. by F. A. Richardson and W. A. Bennett; J. T. Scharf, *The Chronicles of Baltimore* (1874); F. R. Kent, *The Story of Md. Politics* (1911); Edward Hungerford, *The Story of the Baltimore & Ohio Railroad* (1928); *Biog. Dir. Am. Cong.* (1928); M. P. Andrews, *Hist. of Md.* (1929); *Baltimore American and Commercial Advertiser* and *The Sun* (Baltimore), July 24, 25, 1883.]　　　　　　　　　　　E. L.

SWARTWOUT, SAMUEL (Nov. 17, 1783–Nov. 21, 1856), soldier, merchant, speculator, and politician, was born in Poughkeepsie, N. Y., a descendant of Tomys Swartwout, who emigrated from Amsterdam to New Netherland in 1652. He was the son of Abraham and Maria (North) Swartwout. From 1804 onwards he was closely connected with Aaron Burr, 1756–1836 [*q.v.*]. It was Swartwout who on Oct. 8, 1806, delivered to Gen. James Wilkinson [*q.v.*] the famous cipher letter from Burr which was to produce such a strong impression of Burr's treason. Swartwout was afterwards arrested in New Orleans on Wilkinson's order and sent to Washington for trial as an accomplice in Burr's schemes. The proceedings attracted wide attention, for on their outcome rested the fate of Burr (4 *Cranch*, 75, *Ex parte Bollman*, and Appendix). After his own trial and acquittal, Swartwout served as an important witness against Burr (*Annals of Congress*, 10 Cong., 1 Sess., Appendix, pp. 633, 678), but he steadfastly refused to acknowledge any treasonable purpose in the other's designs or in his own agency. After the trial he sought to provoke a duel with General Wilkinson and, when he failed, posted the general as a coward. He accompanied Burr from Richmond to Baltimore, helped him in his arrangements to sail to England, and preceded him to that country to prepare for his favorable reception. He also, it seems, proposed to open up trade with the Mississippi Valley through Mobile and Pensacola in contravention to Jefferson's embargo. Apparently he did not succeed in either policy, although he remained in England for some time after Burr's arrival (Williamson Papers, *post*, Feb.–May 1808, and *Swartwout Chronicles*, *post*, pp. 341–42). After serving in the War of 1812 as captain in the "Iron Grays," he was connected with his brothers, Robert and John, as a merchant. In 1814 he married Alice Ann Cooper, by whom he had a son who died young and a daughter.

From this time on his fortunes were bound up with those of Andrew Jackson. Commended to the general by his audacious challenge to Wilkinson, he worked hard, doubtless spurred on by Burr, to make Jackson a presidential possibility. His personal charm, his energetic efforts, and his unswerving loyalty brought him the appointment (Apr. 25, 1829) of collector of the port of New York, the most lucrative public office in Jackson's gift. Despite the warnings of Van Buren, who distrusted Swartwout's reputation for speculation (H. F. De Puy, *post*, pp. 25–27; J. C. Fitzpatrick, *post*, pp. 262, 263, 266), Jackson continued him in office, and Van Buren as president followed suit. Notwithstanding the demands of the position, Swartwout found time for extensive speculations in lands, canals, and railways. At the expiration of his term (Mar. 29, 1838) his accounts with the government remained unsettled, and the inevitable investigation of his office reached a climax in January 1839, when it was found that, beginning within a few months of his appointment, he had appropriated more than a million dollars of public funds (*Congressional Globe*, 25 Cong., 3 Sess., pp. 19, 20–21, and Appendix, pp. 31–35, 89–111). Swartwout had already attempted to meet his shortage by sailing to England (August 1838), where he hoped to dispose of certain valuable coal and iron lands. Failing, he remained abroad until 1841. Then, assured that he would not be prosecuted—his property had been surrendered to meet claims—, he returned to the United States and lived in retirement until his death in New York, Nov. 21, 1856.

[In addition to the sources for Aaron Burr, which are useful for Swartwout, see A. J. Weise, *The Swartwout Chronicles, 1338–1899* (1899); Williamson Papers, MSS. in Newberry Lib., Chicago, Ill.; R. C. McGrane, *The Correspondence of Nicholas Biddle* (1919); H. F. De Puy, "Some Letters of Andrew Jackson," *Proc. Am. Antiquarian Soc.*, n.s., vol. XXXI (1922); J. C. Fitzpatrick, "The Autobiog. of Martin Van Buren," *Ann. Report Am. Hist. Asso. . . . 1918*, vol. II (1920); *House Doc. 111*, 25 Cong., 2 Sess., vol. V, and *House Doc.*, 13, 25 Cong., 3 Sess., vol. II; J. S. Bassett, *Correspondence of Andrew Jackson*, vols. III–IV (1928–31), vol. VI (1933); A. J. Beveridge, *The Life of John Marshall* (1919), vol. III; B. J. Poore, *Perley's Reminiscences* (2 vols., 1886); obituary in *N. Y. Tribune*, Nov. 24, 1856.]   I. J. C.

SWAYNE, NOAH HAYNES (Dec. 7, 1804–June 8, 1884), jurist, was born in Frederick County, Va. He was of Quaker ancestry, being a descendant of Francis Swayne who came with his family to America in 1710 and settled near Philadelphia. Noah was the youngest of nine children of Joshua Swayne, who died in 1808;

his mother was Rebecca, daughter of John and Ann Smith of Chester County, Pa. At the age of thirteen he was sent to the Quaker academy of Jacob Mendenhall at Waterford, Va. Two years later he began the study of medicine with an apothecary and physician at Alexandria, but abandoned it upon the death of his teacher. Turning next to the law, he entered the office of John Scott and Francis Brooks at Warrenton, Va. Admitted to the bar in 1823, he immediately moved to Ohio on account of his opposition to slavery. Here he located for one year at Zanesville and then moved to Coshocton, where he began practice. His success was immediate. In 1826 he was appointed prosecuting attorney for Coshocton County and in 1829 was elected as a Jeffersonian Democrat to the state legislature. In 1830 he was appointed by President Jackson United States attorney for the district of Ohio, which position he held for nine years, making his home in Columbus, where he remained until his appointment to the United States Supreme Court. In 1832 he married Sarah Ann Wager of Harpers Ferry, Va. (now W. Va.). His wife owned slaves, but, sharing his views as to the evils of slavery, she emancipated them.

During the more than thirty years he practised in Columbus he took high rank at the Ohio bar and was employed in many important cases in both the state and federal courts. One of his noted efforts was his defense, in 1853, before the United States circuit court in Columbus, of William Rossane and others who were accused of the burning of the steamboat *Martha Washington* for the fraudulent purpose of procuring insurance. Aside from his practice during this period he was a member of a state fund commission charged at a critical period in the finances of the state with the management of the state debt; a member of a commission to settle a dispute between Ohio and Michigan over the state boundary; and a member of still another commission to study the need of a state institution for the care of the blind.

On Jan. 21, 1862, President Lincoln appointed him a justice of the United States Supreme Court, and the appointment was confirmed on Jan. 24. The reason for his appointment is a little difficult to determine. He had had no judicial experience and though prominent as a lawyer in central Ohio was not a national figure. Justice McLean, whom he was to succeed, was a close friend and had expressed the hope that Swayne would be his successor. His appointment was strongly urged by Governor Dennison of Ohio and by the entire Ohio delegation in Congress, including Senators B. F. Wade and John Sherman. There seems to be no basis for the persistent tradition that President Lincoln got the names of J. R. Swan [*q.v.*] and Swayne confused and really meant to appoint the former, who had become a national figure on account of his great opinion in the *Ex parte Bushnell* case (9 *Ohio*, 77).

His career of nineteen years was altogether satisfactory, though not brilliant. Two other appointees of Lincoln, Samuel F. Miller and Stephen J. Field [*qq.v.*], surpassed him in influence and reputation. His most noteworthy opinions were those given in the cases of *Gelpcke* vs. *City of Dubuque* (68 *U. S.*, 175) and *Springer* vs. *U. S.* (102 *U. S.*, 586). In the former case he took issue with Miller, arguing that though it was the general practice of the Supreme Court to follow the latest adjudications of state courts in construing the laws and constitutions of the states, this practice could not be followed when it would result in a sacrifice of justice. This decision had much to do in establishing the doctrine set forth in *Swift* vs. *Tyson* to the effect that in the interpretation of contracts and other instruments of a commercial nature, the true interpretation is to be sought not in the discussions of the local tribunals, but in the general principles and doctrines of commercial jurisprudence (41 *U. S.*, 2). In *Springer* vs. *U. S.* (102 *U. S.*, 586), he wrote an able opinion upholding the constitutionality of a federal income tax, an opinion overruled in the later "Income Tax Cases," but still believed by many able lawyers to be the correct interpretation of the Constitution. During the time he sat on the bench he was the most nationalistic-minded member of the court. In his dissents in the famous cases of *Texas* vs. *White* (74 *U. S.*, 700) and *Hepburn* vs. *Griswold* (75 *U. S.*, 603) and in the Slaughter House Cases (83 *U. S.*, 36), he stood for a more nationalistic position than even the Supreme Court as then constituted was willing to sustain. Possessed of a robust health, during his entire service he was present at practically every session and conference of the court. "He came," said Chief Justice Waite, "from a large . . . practice at the Bar, and brought with him an unusual familiarity with adjudged cases, and settled habits of labor and research. As might be expected, he soon became one of the most useful members of the Court, and took an active and leading part in all its work" (103 *U. S. Reports*, xii).

On Jan. 25, 1881, at the age of seventy-six, he retired from the bench under the authority of the federal statute. For a year he lived in Washington but after the death of his wife moved to New York City, where a son, Wager Swayne

[*q.v.*], was engaged in the practice of law. Here he died, survived by four sons and one daughter. He was buried in Oak Hill Cemetery, Washington, D. C.

[N. W. Swayne, *The Descendants of Francis Swayne* (1921); *Am. Law Rev.*, July–Aug. 1884; *Ohio State Bar Asso. Reports*, vol. V (1885); 103 *U. S. Reports*, ix–xii; 118 *U. S. Reports*, 699–700; H. L. Carson, *The Supreme Court of the U. S.: Its Hist.* (1892), vol. II; *The Biog. Cyc. . . . of the State of Ohio*, vol. V (n.d.); *Mr. Justice Swayne* (n.d.), pamphlet prepared by his sons; *N. Y. Tribune* and *Evening Star* (Washington), June 10, 1884.]   A. H. T.

SWAYNE, WAGER (Nov. 10, 1834–Dec. 18, 1902), soldier and lawyer, was born in Columbus, Ohio, the son of Noah Haynes Swayne [*q.v.*] and Sarah Ann (Wager). He was graduated at Yale in 1856, after losing a year on account of serious illness, and at the Cincinnati Law School in 1859. Having been admitted to the Ohio bar he commenced the practice of law in partnership with his father, then a leading attorney in Columbus and later as associate justice of the United States Supreme Court.

On Aug. 31, 1861, he entered the army as major, 43rd Ohio Infantry, and was promoted lieutenant-colonel, Dec. 14, 1861. Until February 1862 the regiment was in training in Ohio. It then joined the army under Pope and took part in the actions at New Madrid and Island No. 10 which opened the upper Mississippi. Later it was present at the siege of Corinth; in the battle of Corinth, Oct. 4, 1862, Swayne, already known as an efficient regimental commander, displayed such distinguished courage in the face of threatened panic among the troops, that upon Gen. D. S. Stanley's urgent recommendation he received the award of the medal of honor, the highest American decoration for heroism in action. On Oct. 18, 1862, he was promoted colonel. He commanded a brigade of the XVI Corps, Army of the Tennessee, in the Atlanta campaign, the march to the sea, and the campaign of the Carolinas, attracting favorable notice from Gen. O. O. Howard [*q.v.*], a circumstance which had important consequences later. He was in action at Resaca, Dallas, Kenesaw, and Atlanta. At Rivers Bridge, S. C., he received a shell wound, Feb. 2, 1865, which caused the amputation of his right leg. He was appointed brigadier-general of volunteers in April, with rank from Mar. 8, 1865.

Later in that year he was selected by General Howard, then organizing the Freedmen's Bureau, as an assistant commissioner in charge of the bureau's operations in Alabama; he was also in military command, and in order that he might have appropriate rank was appointed, in May 1866, major-general of volunteers, with commission dated back to June 20, 1865. He was not finally mustered out of the volunteer army until Sept. 1, 1867. Meanwhile, he had been appointed, July 28, 1866, colonel in the regular army, for the newly organized 45th Infantry. His service in Alabama with the Freedmen's Bureau continued until January 1868, and was especially marked by the establishment of numerous schools, some of which are still in existence. He married Ellen, daughter of Alfred Harris of Louisville, Dec. 22, 1868. The drastic reduction of the regular army in 1870 required the removal of all officers suffering from any form of physical disability, and Swayne was accordingly placed on the retired list in July.

He took up the practice of law in Toledo, in partnership with John R. Osborn, also serving for some years as a member of the board of education. In 1881 he removed to New York, where, in partnership with John F. Dillon [q.v.] and others, he continued to practise law until shortly before his death. His firm acted as counsel for the Associated Press, the Western Union Telegraph Company, the Wabash Railway, and other important corporations. A distinguished lawyer and a successful commander of troops, Swayne was also a most public-spirited citizen, always interested in philanthropic activities, particularly church and educational work.

[N. W. Swayne, *The Descendants of Francis Swayne and Others* (1921); *War of the Rebellion: Official Records (Army)*; F. B. Heitman, *Hist. Reg. and Dict. U. S. Army* (1903), vol. I; G. M. Dodge, in *Loyal Legion, Commandery of N. Y., Circular No. 10* (1903); *Obit. Record Grads. Yale Univ.*, 1903; O. O. Howard, *Autobiography* (1907), vol. II; *Bureau of Refugees and Freedmen: Report of the Assistant Commissioner for Ala.* (1866, 1867); *The Biog. Encyc. of Ohio of the Nineteenth Century* (1876); *Who's Who in America*, 1899–1900; *N. Y. Times*, Dec. 19, 1902.]   T. M. S.

SWEENY, PETER BARR (Oct. 9, 1825– Aug. 30, 1911), politician, son of James and Mary (Barr) Sweeny, was born in New York City. His father was a saloonkeeper there and later engaged in the same business in Jersey City. In the latter place young Peter served as a waiter. He received some education at a parochial school and at Columbia College. Having studied law in the office of James T. Brady [q.v.], he was admitted to the bar and practised successfully. He soon became interested in politics, and was active on the Tammany General Committee in 1852. In 1854 he was in Albany with his uncle, Thomas J. Barr, a state senator, lobbying in the interest of city stage-coach franchises as against street railroads. Silent and reticent by nature, Sweeny could not speak in public, his preference being for secret or "gumshoe" methods. He was elected district attorney in 1857, but broke down in his first speech before

a jury and was so humiliated that he resigned his position.

By the early sixties Tammany Hall was coming under the control of a small group of men, of whom Sweeny and William M. Tweed [q.v.] were the most important. It has always been asserted, and apparently upon good authority, that Sweeny was the real guiding intelligence of the "Tweed ring"; hence his initial B. was humorously supposed to stand for "Brains" or "Bismarck." In 1863 Tweed became grand sachem of the Tammany Society, but Sweeny was behind the throne, working secretly as always. They now began filling important city offices with their henchmen, and the members of the "ring" were soon absolute masters of the city. Tweed is said to have feared Sweeny. "Sweeny is a hard, over-bearing, revengeful man . . .," Tweed testified when a witness before a special committee of the board of aldermen in 1877. "We were so opposite and unalike that we never got along very well" (Lynch, *post*, p. 278). Of himself Sweeny said modestly, "I am not and never claimed to be a leader. . . . I am a sort of adviser. I try to harmonize the interests of the party" (*North American Review*, October 1874). Sweeny acquired the position of city chamberlain in 1866, and Tweed testified later that he "heard" that Sweeny paid $60,000 for the job (*Report of Special Committee, post*, pp. 105, 112). In 1867 he astonished the public by turning over to the city treasury $200,000 in interest on public funds which his predecessors in the office had considered their personal perquisite. By this shrewd move he set up a specious reputation for honesty. In 1869 he was appointed park commissioner by Mayor A. Oakey Hall [q.v.]. He was associated with James Fisk [q.v.], in the manipulation of Erie Railroad stock, he and Tweed being elected directors of the company and helping to force out Daniel Drew and Cornelius Vanderbilt [qq.v.]. He also dealt largely in street railroad franchises. In 1869, at a meeting in Sweeny's hotel room in Albany, it was decided that fifty per cent. for graft should be added to all bills rendered against the city and county (*Ibid.*, pp. 75–78). Later this percentage was greatly increased. The loot thus secured was to be divided into five parts, Tweed, Sweeny, Comptroller Richard B. Connolly, and Mayor Hall receiving one share each, while the fifth share was to be used for the bribery of smaller politicians. Sweeny's devious nature is seen in the fact that his share was always paid to him through his brother James, a city employee. When the "ring" was overthrown in 1871 Sweeny resigned his city offices and fled to

Canada and from there to France. As the trial of Tweed drew on, Sweeny offered, if guaranteed immunity from prosecution, to refund $400,-000 which "his brother James" had gotten from New York City. This deal was consummated, and after several years' residence in Paris, Sweeny, still comfortably wealthy, returned to the United States and died in 1911 at Lake Mahopac, N. Y. He married Sara Augusta Dotherty and was survived by a son.

[*Evening Post* (N. Y.), Aug. 31, 1911; *N. Y. Times, World, N. Y. Herald, Sun,* Sept. 1, 1911; *Report of the Special Committee of the Board of Aldermen Appointed to Investigate the "Ring" Frauds, Together with the Testimony Elicited during the Investigation* (Board of Aldermen, Jan. 4, 1878, Doc. No. 8); *N. Y. Times* and *Harper's Weekly,* 1869–72; C. F. Wingate, "An Episode in Municipal Govt.," *North Am. Rev.,* Oct. 1874, Jan. 1875, July 1875, Oct. 1876; W. C. Gover, *The Tammany Hall Democracy of the City of N. Y. and the General Committee for 1875* (1875); Rufus Home, "The Story of Tammany," *Harper's Mag.,* Apr.–May 1872; A. P. Genung, *The Frauds of the New York City Govt. Exposed* (1871); M. R. Werner, *Tammany Hall* (1928); D. T. Lynch, *"Boss" Tweed* (1927); R. H. Fuller, *Jubilee Jim* (1930); A. B. Paine, *Thomas Nast: His Period and His Pictures* (1904); scrapbooks of newspaper clippings relating to N. Y. City politics, N. Y. Pub. Lib.; names of parents and date of birth from N. K. Averill, Esq., Lake Mahopac, N. Y., at whose home Sweeny died; name of wife from Mrs. Arthur Sweeny.]   A. F. H.

SWEENY, THOMAS WILLIAM (Dec. 25, 1820–Apr. 10, 1892), soldier, Fenian leader, was born in County Cork, Ireland, the son of William and Honora (Sweeny) Sweeny. He emigrated to the United States in 1832. About 1843 he joined the "Baxter Blues" of New York City, and in 1846 became second lieutenant of New York volunteers in the Mexican War. He was with General Scott from Vera Cruz to the capture of Churubusco, where he received a wound that necessitated the amputation of his right arm. Following the war, as lieutenant in the 2nd United States Infantry, Sweeny was engaged almost continuously in operations against the Yuma Indians of the Southwest or the Sioux of the Nebraska region until January 1861, when he was promoted captain and ordered to the federal arsenal at St. Louis.

After serving under Gen. Nathaniel Lyon [*q.v.*] in the capture of Camp Jackson, Sweeny was commissioned brigadier-general of the three months' Missouri volunteers, May 20, 1861, and sent with Franz Sigel [*q.v.*] into Southwest Missouri to prevent the junction of the state troops under Gen. Sterling Price and Gov. C. F. Jackson [*qq.v.*] with the Confederate army under Gen. Ben McCulloch [*q.v.*]. Sigel's rash attempt with 1,100 men to stop Jackson's 4,000 at Carthage resulted in a rout, and the expedition failed of its objective. On Aug. 14, 1861, four days after receiving a severe wound in the battle

of Wilson's Creek (McElroy, *post,* p. 183), Sweeny was mustered out of the Missouri volunteers, but he returned to the volunteer service as colonel of the 52nd Illinois on Jan. 21, 1862, and under Grant aided in the capture of Fort Donelson. He was given outstanding credit by Sherman for helping save the day at Shiloh, Apr. 6 (*Battles and Leaders, post,* I, 511), and rendered praiseworthy service in the battles of Corinth, Oct. 3–4, 1862, Kenesaw Mountain, June 27, 1864, and Atlanta, July 20–22, 1864. He was commissioned brigadier-general of volunteers Nov. 29, 1862, and was honorably discharged from the volunteer service in August 1865. As the result of a quarrel with his superior officer, Gen. G. M. Dodge, after the battle of Atlanta, Sweeny was arrested and court-martialed, but acquitted. On Dec. 29, 1865, he was dismissed from the army for absence without leave, but on Nov. 8, 1866, was reinstated. Although a quick thinker and an aggressive fighter, he apparently lacked coolness and sound judgment.

While out of the service he received much notoriety as the leader of the ill-starred Fenian raid on Canada in 1866. An ardent Irish partisan, he was made secretary of war of the "Irish Republic" when William R. Roberts [*q.v.*] was elected president by the Fenian Congress in 1865. With Roberts he urged that Canada be conquered as a step toward freeing Ireland, and in 1866, superintended the details of the invasion of June 1–2 at Niagara and the simultaneous attempts to cross the border at Potsdam, N. Y., and St. Albans, Vt. The "invasion" was a fiasco. Sweeny, with some others, was arrested by United States authorities but was soon released without trial, and thereafter his interest and influence in the Fenian movement declined. Following this interlude he returned to the regular army until his retirement in 1870 with the rank of brigadier-general. Sweeny was married twice: first, to Eleanor Swain Clark of Brooklyn, and second, to Eugenia Octavia Reagan of Augusta, Ga. He died at his home in Astoria, L. I., survived by his second wife, three sons, and a daughter.

[Sketch by a son, W. M. Sweeny, in *Am.-Irish Hist. Soc. Jour.,* vol. II (1899); Sweeny's report of the Fenian raid, *Ibid.,* vol. XXIII (1924); F. B. Heitman, *Hist. Reg. and Dict. U. S. Army* (1903), vol. I; *War of the Rebellion: Official Records (Army),* 1 ser. III, XXXVIII (pts. 1–5); *Battles and Leaders of the Civil War* (4 vols., 1887–88); R. J. Rombauer, *The Union Cause in St. Louis in 1861* (1909); J. Fairbanks and Edwin Tuck, *Hist. of Greene County, Mo.* (1915), vol. I; T. L. Snead, *The Fight for Missouri* (1886); John McElroy, *The Struggle for Missouri* (1909); J. A. Macdonald, *Troublous Times in Canada: A Hist. of the Fenian Raids* (1910); C. P. Stacey, "Fenianism and the Rise of National Feeling in Canada," *Canadian*

Hist. Rev., Sept. 1931; *Army and Navy Jour.*, Apr. 16, 1892; *N. Y. Times*, Apr. 12, 1892; name of Sweeny's mother from his son, W. M. Sweeny.]   H. E. N.

SWEET, JOHN EDSON (Oct. 21, 1832–May 8, 1916), mechanical engineer, manufacturer, was the son of Horace and Candace (Avery) Sweet, and was born on his father's farm at Pompey, Onondaga County, N. Y. He was a descendant of John Sweet who settled in Salem, Mass., in 1631 (Smith, *post,* p. 19). Educated in the district school, he developed a mechanical turn, decided to learn a trade, and in 1850 went to Syracuse, N. Y., and apprenticed himself to a carpenter and joiner. In the winter of 1850–51 he found the opportunity to work in an architect's office and learned something of drawing and architecture; during another lull in carpentry he worked for an artist. He then engaged in designing and building until the Civil War, when he had charge of the construction of a hotel in Selma, Ala. Until 1867 he worked as a draftsman, pattern-maker, and designer in Syracuse, with the exception of a period (1862–64) when he worked for the Patent Bolt and Nut Company, Birmingham, England, which was engaged in building a nail-making machine he and his brother had invented. In 1867 he personally exhibited at the Paris Exposition a typesetting machine which he had designed. From 1868 to 1871 he was superintendent in a manufacturing plant, and then for two years engaged in bridge building in New York state. In 1873 he was appointed master mechanic and director of the machine shop of Sibley College, Cornell University, where he remained for six years. His method of instructing students in shop practice was to have them develop and construct tools and equipment for which there was need. Thus were made standard gauges, straight edges, squares, and angles, the gauges being made by the use of a measuring machine (the first of its kind in the United States), devised by Sweet and built by the students, which read to the 10/100th of an inch. Under Sweet's direction the students built, too, one of the earliest American-made Gramme dynamos and a straight line reciprocating steam engine designed by Sweet. In 1879 he resigned and returned to Syracuse, where in 1880 he organized the Straight Line Engine Company. From that time until his death he was the active head of the company, which enjoyed a worldwide reputation.

He was much respected by his students, his employees, and all others who knew him. He played a leading part in the formation of the American Society of Mechanical Engineers, of which he was president, 1883–84, and in 1914

received the John Fritz Medal—the highest award of the four national engineering societies —"for his achievement in machine design and for his pioneer work in applying sound engineering principles to the construction and development of the high-speed steam engine." He wrote *Things That Are Usually Wrong* (1906) and contributed many articles to technical journals and newspapers, beginning in the 1850's with a series of articles on architecture which ran for twelve years. He traveled extensively and carefully recorded his experiences. On Nov. 24, 1870, he married Caroline V. Hawthorne (d. 1887) of Fulton, N. Y.; on May 9, 1889, he married Irene A. Clark of Syracuse. He died in Syracuse and was buried there.

[*Who's Who in America,* 1916–17; A. W. Smith, *John Edson Sweet* (1925); *Am. Machinist,* May 18, 1916, pp. 871–72; *Trans. Am. Soc. Mech. Engineers,* vol. XXXVIII (1916), pp. 1321–28; *Mech. Engineering,* May 1927, p. 477; obituary in *N. Y. Times,* May 9, 1916.]   C. W. M—n.

SWENSSON, CARL AARON (June 25, 1857–Feb. 16, 1904), Swedish Lutheran clergyman, educator, author, politician, was born in Sugargrove, Pa., the son of Jonas and Maria (Blixt) Swensson. His father was a pastor in the Church of Sweden and came to the United States in 1856 to minister to his countrymen. He was one of the founders of the Augustana Synod, a branch of the American Lutheran Church. Under his father's influence Carl acquired such a profound love for his Swedish heritage that when he matriculated at Augustana College and Theological Seminary at Paxton, Ill., he had contempt for the English language and things American, but at the time of his graduation from college in 1877 and his ordination to the ministry two years later, he had obtained a better perspective and had become intensely American. After his ordination he served the Swedish Lutheran congregation at Lindsborg, Kan. He won the admiration of the Swedish pioneers in the Smoky Hill Valley, and became so attached to them that he retained his residence in Lindsborg until his death. Through his magnetic personality and unbounded energy and ambition he became an invaluable advertising agent for the community. He was instrumental in founding Bethany College there in 1881 and made Lindsborg the cultural center of the Swedish population in the Southwest. He became a power not only in the Augustana Synod but also in the General Council of the Evangelical Lutheran Church. He was the first of the American-born Swedish clergymen to rise to eminence and, unlike most of his brother pastors, won popularity in both Sweden and America.

The beginnings of Bethany College were not auspicious, and in the earliest years Swensson assumed the entire financial risk. In 1884, however, he succeeded in having the Kansas Conference of the Augustana Synod adopt the school, and it speedily rose to collegiate rank and added departments of commerce and music. The annual rendition of Handel's "Messiah" attracted thousands of music lovers and artists to Lindsborg every year, and the chorus organized by Swensson in 1881 has made the name of the town well-known. While he served as pastor and college president, 1889–1904, Swensson wrote four books: *I Sverige* (1891), *Åter i Sverige* (1898), *Vid hemmets härd* (1890), and *I morgonstund* (1903). He was editor of *Förgät-mig-ej* in 1902, a publication setting forth the progress of Bethany College, and joint editor of *Korsbaneret*, 1880–85, *Ungdomsvännen*, 1880–87, and *Jubel-album*, 1893, a work commemorating the activity of the Augustana Synod. He was successively editor and publisher of the *Lindsborgs-Posten*, the *Lindsborg Record*, and *Pedagogen* and contributing editor of *Fosterlandet*. He was politically ambitious and was elected to the Kansas legislature in 1889. As a campaign spellbinder he was in great demand, being almost equally effective in both Swedish and English in presenting the cause of old-line Republicanism against the onslaughts of Democrats and Populists. He was delegate-at-large to the Republican National Convention in 1896. On Sept. 15, 1880, he was married to Alma Christina Lind, of Moline, Ill., who, with two daughters, survived him when he died suddenly in Los Angeles, Cal., where he was to participate in the dedication of a church.

[*Who's Who in America*, 1903–05; G. M. Stephenson, *The Religious Aspects of Swedish Immigration* (1932); Alfred Bergin, *Lindsborg efter femtio år* (1919); Ernst Skarstedt, "Läroverkspresidenten Carl Swensson," in *Prärieblomman: Kalender för 1905*, pp. 77–93; J. E. Floren, "Dr. Carl Aaron Swensson," in *Korsbaneret: Kristlig kalender för 1905*, pp. 175–193; *Trans. Kan. State Hist. Soc.*, vol. VIII (1904); *Topeka Daily Capital*, Feb. 17, 1904.]   G. M. S.

SWETT, JOHN (July 31, 1830–Aug. 22, 1913), educator, was born on a farm near Pittsfield, N. H., the son of Eben and Lucretia (French) Swett, and a descendant of John Swett who emigrated from Devonshire, England, to Massachusetts in 1642. He attended the district school (1837–43) and Pittsfield Academy (1844–47). After a few weeks of attendance at Pembroke Academy, he was granted a teacher's certificate by the Pembroke school board and put in charge of the Buckstreet school, where he taught during 1847 and 1848, paid at the rate of ten dollars a month by subscriptions. His second school was at West Randolph, Mass., 1849 and 1850. He was given a tempting offer for the next year, but "debarred from the college course by delicate health and chronic weakness" of one of his eyes, he resolved to go west to the gold mines. He arrived in San Francisco in a sailing vessel by way of Cape Horn, Jan. 31, 1853. After five months in the mining country near Marysville and several more on a ranch near San José, he returned to San Francisco and began teaching in the Rincon school, where he remained until 1862. On May 8, 1862, he was married to Mary Tracy, daughter of Judge Frederick P. Tracy, by whom he had two daughters and four sons. Elected state superintendent of public instruction in 1862, he entered upon his duties at a time when little had been done to establish educational standards in the state. During the five years in which he held office, he labored with marked success for an allocated state school tax, for a system of state teaching certificates, for the use of uniform textbooks throughout the state, and for the provision of adequate buildings and good teaching. He helped to establish a state teachers' organization, held teachers' institutes, and was active in the founding of the *California Teacher*, which was first issued in August 1863. In 1868 he became principal of the Denman grammar school for girls in San Francisco and remained in that position, with exception of the years 1870–73 when he was deputy superintendent of the city schools, until 1876. At that time he became principal of the Girls' High School, where he was very successful. In 1889, after having been forced to resign his principalship as a result of his sturdy opposition to political influences in the schools, he was elected city superintendent of schools by popular vote. He continued to be an active opponent of the spoils system of appointing teachers, and an advocate of professional training for teachers and permanent certification. In 1895 he retired to his farm near Martinez, Cal., but held a number of advisory educational positions during the next thirteen years. He died at his farm. He numbered among his intimate friends John Muir, William Keith, Henry George, and Joaquin Miller [*qq.v.*].

He published a few poems, and many addresses and magazine articles, among them three of an autobiographical nature—"My Grandmother's Kitchen" (*Pioneer Magazine*, January 1855), "The Old Schoolhouse" (*Ibid.*, June 1855), and "My Schools and Schoolmasters" (*Educational Review*, December 1901). Among his books are *Common School Readings* (1867), *A History of the Public School System of Cali-*

fornia (1876), *Methods of Teaching* (1880), *A Normal Word Book* (1879), *School Elocution* (1884), *American Public Schools* (1900), and *Public Education in California* (1911), which was partly autobiographical. His state reports were published in 1864–65, and 1866–67; his city reports annually from 1891 to 1894. He collaborated with William Swinton [*q.v.*] in a number of elementary school textbooks in English composition, grammar, and geography, and prepared several readers.

[In addition to *Pub. Educ. in Cal.* and the autobiog. articles referred to, see W. G. Carr, *John Swett, the Biog. of an Educ. Pioneer* (1933), and obituary in *San Francisco Examiner*, Aug. 23, 1913. Family papers are in the possession of Frank Swett, Hill-Girt Farm, Martinez, Cal.]   J. C. A—k.

SWIFT, GUSTAVUS FRANKLIN (June 24, 1839–Mar. 29, 1903), meat packer, was born on his father's farm near Sandwich, Mass., the ninth of twelve children, and the fifth son, of William and Sally Sears (Crowell) Swift. Through his father he was descended from William Swift (or Swyft) who settled at Sandwich on Cape Cod in 1637, and through his mother, from Elder William Brewster of the *Mayflower*. He attended the common school and at fourteen went to work for his brother, the village butcher. At sixteen, he made his first independent venture, buying a heifer which he slaughtered himself, and peddling the dressed meat from door to door. Before he was twenty he had begun to journey once a week to the cattle market at Brighton, where each time he bought and killed a steer, returning to Cape Cod and peddling his meat before the next market day. In 1859–60 he opened his first butcher shop, at Eastham, Mass.; this shop he soon turned over to a brother, establishing another in Barnstable. Energetic and ambitious, he subsequently opened meat markets in Clinton and Freetown, and from these centers sent meat wagons out daily over regular routes, thus serving a considerable territory. Meanwhile he had acquired a reputation as a shrewd judge of beef cattle and had built up a thriving business as a cattle dealer. In 1872 James A. Hathaway, a Boston meat dealer, took him into partnership to do the buying for the firm, and Swift, following the cattle market westward toward the source of supply, established his headquarters successively at Albany, at Buffalo, and in 1875 at Chicago.

At that time, beef consumed in the East was still shipped in the form of live cattle and slaughtered locally. The cost of feeding stock in transit, loss of condition from overcrowding, and the fact that freight was paid on the entire animal whereas some parts were considered unsalable made the process unduly wasteful, in Swift's estimation, and he determined to ship dressed beef. He sent his first carload to Boston in the late fall of 1877. Hathaway, afraid of the new project, dissolved the partnership, but Swift persisted in his efforts. Successful winter shipments of dressed beef had been made previously, but attempts at refrigeration for warm-weather shipment had not met with great success, and to Swift is largely due credit for the practical development of the refrigerator car. The engineer he employed designed a car in which there was a circulation of fresh air, chilled by passing over ice. This arrangement proved satisfactory, and an essential step toward a revolution in the meat industry of the world had been accomplished. The problem of refrigeration was only one of those confronting the Western packers, however. The Eastern consumers had to be convinced of the quality of Chicago beef; the railroads, enjoying revenue derived from carrying livestock, fought the change by excessive charges on shipments of dressed meat; the Eastern butchers resented the competition. Swift, with his intimate knowledge of the meat trade in New England, introduced his product and won cooperation by forming a series of partnerships with local butchers. For the transportation of his beef he negotiated with the Grand Trunk Railway, which, having carried few cattle, had no stockyards to be maintained along its route. His refrigerator cars, however, he was forced to build at his own expense.

When Swift went to Chicago, Nelson Morris and Philip D. Armour [*qq.v.*] were both established packers, and competition was keen. In the effort to cut costs, waste was eliminated wherever possible. Because cleanliness reduced loss through spoilage, Swift insisted on scrupulous cleanliness in his plant. He was a pioneer in the development of by-products from parts of the animal formerly thrown away—oleomargarine, glue, soap, fertilizer, and eventually pharmaceutical preparations. He put all his profits and all the money he could borrow into the expansion of his business, which in 1885 was incorporated as Swift & Company with a capital of $300,000, twenty months later was capitalized at $3,000,-000, and before his death, at $25,000,000. In his endeavor to secure a place for American beef in the British market, he himself made a number of trips across the Atlantic, and his hard-won success in Great Britain was followed by the establishment of distributing houses in Tokyo, Osaka, Shanghai, Hongkong, Manila, Singapore, and Honolulu. Additional packing plants were established in the newer cattle centers—St.

Louis, Kansas City, St. Joseph, Omaha, St. Paul, and Fort Worth. In 1902, with J. O. Armour and Edward Morris he formed the National Packing Company, a combination subsequently dissolved by court order.

Thrifty, industrious, rigidly honest, Swift was rigorous in his requirements both of himself and of his employees. He was unsparing in criticism, rarely gave praise, but was quick to recognize merit by promotion. He had a gift for training men; most of his executives, including his own sons, were brought up from the ranks. About 1900 he began to encourage his employees to buy stock in the concern. His attention was devoted almost entirely to his business until the last decade of his life, when his philanthropies began. He was one of the founders and chief supporters of St. James Methodist Episcopal Church, Chicago, and a liberal donor to the University of Chicago, Northwestern University, the Y. M. C. A., and other causes.

On Jan. 3, 1861, he married Annie Maria Higgins, who with nine of their eleven children survived him. He died in his sixty-fourth year, of an internal hemorrhage following an operation.

[G. H. Swift, *William Swyft of Sandwitch and Some of His Descendants* (1900); T. W. Goodspeed, *The University of Chicago Biog. Sketches*, vol. I (1924); L. F. Swift and Arthur Van Vlissingen, Jr., *The Yankee of the Yards: The Biog. of Gustavus Franklin Swift* (1927); E. N. Wentworth, *A Biog. Cat. of the Portrait Gallery of the Saddle and Sirloin Club* (1920); R. A. Clemen, *The Am. Livestock and Meat Industry* (1923); Charles Winans, "The Evolution of a Vast Industry," *Harper's Weekly*, Nov. 11, 1905–Jan. 13, 1906; H. C. Hill, "The Development of Chicago as a Center of the Meat-Packing Industry," *Miss. Valley Hist. Rev.*, Dec. 1923; *Report of the Federal Trade Commission on the Meat Packing Industry: Summary and Part I* (1919); *Cosmopolitan*, May 1903; *Northwestern Christian Advocate*, Apr. 1, 1903; *National Provisioner*, Apr. 4, 1903; *Butchers' Advocate* (Chicago), Apr. 1, 1903; *Chicago Daily Tribune*, Mar. 30, 1903.]
E. Co.

SWIFT, JOHN FRANKLIN (Feb. 28, 1829–Mar. 10, 1891), lawyer, diplomat, was born of poor parents in Bowling Green, Mo. When he was six or seven years of age, his family moved to Illinois, where they resided eight years before returning to Missouri. He received a very limtied education in the country schools, and at the age of eighteen went to St. Louis to learn the trade of tinsmith. In 1852 he started overland for San Francisco and became a produce merchant in that rapidly rising city. During his spare time he studied law and was admitted to the bar in 1857. In a short time he became a prominent lawyer and acquired considerable wealth. He was elected to the lower branch of the legislature in 1863, and became a leader of the anti-monopoly movement. In 1865 he was appointed register of the land office in San Fran-

cisco by President Lincoln, but resigned in 1866 to take an extended trip to Europe and the East. He returned in time to participate in the Grant presidential campaign of 1868. In 1873 he served again in the legislature, and the following year he ran unsuccessfully for Congress on the anti-monopoly ticket. He was an independent candidate for the assembly in 1877 and was elected with the indorsement of many Republicans although he failed to get the regular nomination of the party. About this time he gained considerable fame in the prosecution of J. J. Marks, state harbor commissioner, and in winning for the city of San Francisco the suits brought against it by the Spring Valley Water Company.

Throughout his career Swift was an outstanding opponent of the monopolistic corporations which figured so largely in California politics. He was author of the provisions in the California constitution which vested in county boards of supervisors authority to control and annually revise water-rates. In 1880 he was appointed member of a commission, with James B. Angell and William H. Trescot [*qq.v.*], to negotiate modifications of the Burlingame Treaty with China. As chairman of a committee appointed by an anti-Chinese convention of citizens at Sacramento, he drew up a very able anti-Chinese memorial to Congress. The same year he was nominated for governor by both the Republicans and the American (anti-Catholic) party, but he rejected the latter as an "unsolicited and undesired honor," emphatically repudiating the peculiar views of the American party (Davis, *post*, p. 530). This action may have cost him the election, as he was defeated by a few hundred votes.

In 1888, with Stephen Mallory White [*q.v.*], he was employed by the California legislature to assist the United States attorney-general in winning a decision before the United States Supreme Court sustaining the constitutionality of the Chinese Exclusion Act (*Chae Chan Ping* vs. *United States*, 130 *U. S.* 581). The same year he was a delegate-at-large to the Republican National Convention. Swift seems to have been prominently considered for a position in President Harrison's cabinet, but in March 1889, he was finally appointed United States minister to Japan where he died two years later. His remains were brought to San Francisco and buried with military honors in Lone Mountain Cemetery. His wife, the daughter of Col. W. G. Wood, of San Francisco, survived him. A fluent speaker and a ready debater, Swift was an exceptionally popular after-dinner speaker. He contributed to magazines and reviews and published two books: *Going to Jericho* (1868), an entertaining narrative of the author's trip to Palestine, and *Robert Greathouse* (1870), a novel depicting frontier life in Nevada during the bonanza era. From 1872 to 1888 he was a regent of the University of California.

[W. J. Davis, *Hist. of Pol. Conventions in Cal.* (1893); T. H. Hittell, *Hist. of Cal.*, vol. IV (1897); San Francisco *Evening Bull.*, Mar. 10, *San Francisco Chronicle*, and *Morning Call*, Mar. 11, 1891.]

P. O. R.

SWIFT, JOSEPH GARDNER (Dec. 31, 1783–July 23, 1865), soldier and engineer, a descendant of Thomas Swift who was in Dorchester, Mass., as early as 1634, and a brother of William Henry Swift [*q.v.*], was born on the island of Nantucket. His father, Foster Swift, a physician in private practice, had recently been surgeon on a naval vessel and from 1814 until his death in 1835 was an army surgeon; his mother was Deborah, daughter of Thomas Delano of Nantucket, of Huguenot ancestry. Swift was appointed on May 12, 1800, a cadet (apprentice officer) in the corps of artillerists and engineers and served at Newport, R. I., until transferred to West Point, N. Y., in October 1801. On Mar. 16, 1802, the United States Military Academy was formally established to provide for the training of cadets at that place instead of with their several organizations as formerly. At first there was no definite period of residence or course of study. Swift and one other, commissioned second lieutenants on Oct. 12, 1802, are regarded as the first graduating class.

The rapid expansion of the tiny American army gave Swift correspondingly rapid promotion. He was promoted first lieutenant of engineers, June 11, 1805, immediately after his marriage (June 6) to Louisa Margaret, daughter of James Walker of Wilmington, N. C. He became captain, Oct. 30, 1806; major, Feb. 23, 1808; lieutenant-colonel, July 6, 1812; and on July 31, 1812, at the age of twenty-eight, he was appointed colonel and chief engineer of the army. He was in the field with Gen. James Wilkinson's army in 1813 during the abortive invasion of Canada which is chiefly remembered for the battle of Chrystler's Fields, and received for his services the brevet rank of brigadier-general in February 1814. Later in that year he was in charge of the construction of the fortifications of the city of New York, undertaken as a result of the British raids in Chesapeake Bay and completed in great haste following the capture of Washington. The work was prosecuted by the voluntary labor of thousands of citizens. The grateful city presented a barge, a silver service, and a set of silver drawing instruments to Swift

and had his portrait painted for the City Hall.

In 1816 the government brought the French military engineer, Simon Bernard [*q.v.*], to the United States and placed him in practical charge of all fortification work, though without actual rank. Swift remained chief engineer of the army, but his activities did not extend much beyond the administration of the Military Academy, of which the chief engineer was then *ex officio* superintendent. Finding the situation intolerable, he resigned from the army, Nov. 12, 1818. He was surveyor of the port of New York until 1826, and then chief engineer of several railroads, including the Baltimore & Susquehanna, the New Orleans & Lake Pontchartrain, and the New York & Harlem. From 1829 to 1845 he was a civil engineer in government service, in charge of harbor improvement on the Great Lakes. He spent the latter part of his life at Geneva, N. Y. He was almost—perhaps quite—the first American engineer of distinction whose training was acquired wholly in the United States. On account of his influence over younger engineers, such as his brother-in-law, George W. Whistler, and William Gibbs McNeill [*qq.v.*], who looked up to him as their leader and model, he is an important figure in the history of his profession. Personally, he was "a pink-cheeked, chubby optimist, a handsome man, a hard and methodical worker" (personal letter from William Patten).

[See *The Memoirs of Gen. Joseph Gardner Swift* (1890), ed. by Harrison Ellery, being diaries from 1807 to 1865; C. B. Stuart, *Lives and Works of Civil and Military Engineers of America* (1871); G. W. Cullum, *Biog. Reg. . . . U. S. Mil. Acad.* (3rd ed., 1891), and *Campaigns of the War of 1812–15* (1879); B. J. Lossing, *The Pictorial Field Book of the War of 1812* (1868), for a good brief description of the New York fortifications, of which the N. Y. Hist. Soc. has the drawings; *N. Y. Herald*, July 27, 1865. Swift's military papers are at West Point. There are collections of his letters in the N. Y. Pub. Lib. and in the possession of his descendant, William Patten of Rhinebeck, N. Y.]

T. M. S.

SWIFT, LEWIS (Feb. 29, 1820–Jan. 4, 1913), astronomer, sixth of the nine children of Gen. Lewis and Anna (Forbes) Swift, was born at Clarkson, Monroe County, N. Y. He was descended from William Swift, who settled at Watertown, Mass., before 1634 and later moved to Sandwich, Mass. Because of an accident in his thirteenth year that permanently lamed him and incapacitated him for farm work, Swift attended Clarkson Academy for three years, walking two miles each day on crutches in order to do so. From 1838 to 1846 he helped to make horse rakes, an invention of his father's. He then became a lecturer on scientific subjects and in 1851 entered business at Hunt's Corners, Cortland

County, N. Y. Becoming interested in astronomy, he began about 1855 a survey of the heavens with a somewhat damaged 3-inch lens purchased for five dollars, for which he made an eyepiece and mounting. This lens being accidentally broken, about 1860 he purchased a 4½-inch lens made by Henry Fitz [q.v.]. With this telescope, mounted on a platform attached to his barn in Marathon, N. Y., where he was then living, he discovered his first comet (1862 III). In 1872 he entered the hardware business at Rochester, N. Y., and there, with his telescope stationed on the roof of a cider mill, he continued to search for comets. The necessity of removing optical parts when the telescope was not in use finally resulted in the breaking of the flint disk, which was replaced by one from Alvan Clark [q.v.] and his sons. Between 1884 and 1893 he appears in Rochester directories as astronomer at the Warner Observatory, built and supported by H. H. Warner of Rochester, manufacturer of proprietary medicines. Upon the failure of Warner's business in 1893, the instrumental equipment was moved to the observatory built by the inventor Thaddeus S. C. Lowe [q.v.] on Echo Mountain, Cal. Swift continued his work there until about 1901, when his failing health compelled his retirement to his earlier home at Marathon, N. Y., for the remainder of his life. He lived a simple, frugal life and was capable of great physical endurance. In exposition he was clear and direct, and to those seeking his counsel he was kindly and helpful. He was twice married, first to Lucretia Hannah Hunt on June 26, 1850, and second to Caroline Doane Topping on Aug. 24, 1864. He had two children by his first marriage and three by his second, the youngest of whom, Edward D. T. Swift, discovered comet 1894 IV.

Swift discovered twelve comets and over twelve hundred nebulae, and observed three total eclipses of the sun, those of 1869, 1878, and 1889. During the eclipse of 1878 he observed two objects at first thought to be intramercurial planets, about which a similar observation was made by James Craig Watson [q.v.]. Though Swift continued to maintain his conviction of the reality of his discovery, the observation was never confirmed. Among his publications are "Appearance of the Great Comet of 1858" (Astronomical Journal, Nov. 2, 1858), "Entdeckung eines neuen Cometen" (Astronomische Nachrichten, Nov. 19, 1889), "The Merope Nebula" (Monthly Notices of the Royal Astronomical Society, January 1882), "Double Meteors," (The Sidereal Messenger, August 1882), and "Observations on the Secondary Tail of the Pons-Brooks Comet" (Ibid., February 1884). Besides cash prizes to-

taling over eleven hundred dollars he received for the discovery of comets three gold medals from the Vienna Academy of Sciences, a silver medal as part of the Lalande prize (1881), four bronze medals of the Astronomical Society of the Pacific, and the Jackson-Gwilt bronze medal of the Royal Astronomical Society (1897), of which he was the first recipient. He was a member of the British Astronomical Association, a Fellow of the American Association for the Advancement of Science, and a Fellow of the Royal Astronomical Society.

[G. H. Swift, William Swyft of Sandwitch and Some of His Descendants (1900); Who's Who in America, 1912–13; Gen. Cat. Univ. of Rochester (1911); Lewis Swift, in Popular Astronomy, Nov. 1901; bibliog. in Cat. of Sci. Papers, 4 ser., vol. XVIII (1923), comp. by Royal Soc. of London; E. E. Barnard, in Astronomische Nachrichten, Band 194, Seite 133; E. B. K., in Monthly Notices of the Royal Astronomical Soc., vol. LXXIII, p. 219; obituaries in Pubs. Astronomical Soc. of the Pacific, Feb. 1913, and in N. Y. Times, Jan. 6, 1913.]
J. M. P—r.

SWIFT, LUCIUS BURRIE (July 31, 1844–July 3, 1929), civil service reformer, writer, lawyer, the seventh child of Stephen Swift and Content (Aber) Swift, was a descendant of William Swyft, of Essex County, England, who came to America about 1630. He inherited a Puritan training and grew up on a farm in Orleans County, N. Y., where a typical district school, Yates Academy, and a home with sufficient books and newspapers helped to develop his intellectual interests. After two years of service with the 28th N. Y. Infantry in the Civil War, he entered the University of Michigan and was graduated in 1870. Returning to Medina, N. Y., he studied law and came under the liberal influences of George Kennan [q.v.] and of Godkin's Nation. From 1872 to 1879 he served as principal and superintendent of schools at La Porte, Ind. Here he was married to Mary Ella Lyon, a teacher who had been graduated from Elmira College, Elmira, N. Y. No children were born to them.

Swift moved to Indianapolis to practise law in 1879 and became nationally known during the eighties and nineties for his untiring labors in behalf of civil service reform. As chairman of the Indiana Independent Committee of One Hundred he canvassed his state for Cleveland in 1880, and the next year, with Wm. D. Foulke, and others, organized the Indiana Civil Service Reform Association. In 1886 he conducted an exhaustive inquiry and published the results in A Report Relating to the Federal Civil Service in Indiana (1886). He exposed gross violations of the Pendleton Civil Service Act and the evils of the patronage system. He was subsequently invited to the White House for a conference, appeared also before a Senate committee, and participated in a national conference of civil service reformers in New York. His influence was in part responsible for the unfavorable attitude taken by the reformers towards Cleveland's earlier policies. Meanwhile, he was fearlessly fighting for civil service reform in his state. Without compensation, he took charge of a legislative inquiry into the Indiana Hospital for the Insane, and in his report revealed wholesale corruption and revolting treatment of patients. This report was an important factor in causing the defeat of the Democrats in 1886 and 1888, in the establishment by law of non-partisan boards of control, and in the introduction of the merit system for employees. In 1888 he and most of his fellow reformers supported Harrison for the presidency, but, disappointed again, they returned to support Cleveland in 1892.

Swift rejected fealty to party organization as a means of accomplishing desired results, and in fidelity to principle few men were more unswerving. True to his Puritan inheritance he was little influenced by abuse or ridicule, material rewards, or popularity. Assisted only by his wife, he began to edit and publish the *Civil Service Chronicle* in 1889. For eight years the *Chronicle* was one of the most influential periodicals devoted to civil service reform in the United States. By 1896, after Cleveland had added 42,511 positions to the classified civil service list, Swift felt that the *Chronicle* had served its purpose and he discontinued it. Throughout this struggle for good government he enjoyed the intimate friendship and encouragement of Theodore Roosevelt. During the World War, like most Americans, he firmly supported the Allied cause by making addresses and writing pamphlets, but without giving due weight to its shortcomings or the merits of Germany's case. In 1928 he published a booklet, *How We Got Our Liberties,* wherein he traced the long struggle of the Anglo-Saxon peoples for freedom and liberty and sought to increase appreciation of this heritage.

[Meredith Nicholson, "An American Citizen," *Scribner's Mag.,* Dec. 1922; W. D. Foulke, *Lucius B. Swift, A Biography, Ind. Hist. Pubs.,* vol. IX (1930); G. H. Swift, *William Swyft of Sandwitch and Some of His Descendants* (1900); *The Mich. Alumnus,* Sept. 14, 1929; *Indianapolis Star* and *Indianapolis News,* July 4, 1929.]
A. T. V.

SWIFT, WILLIAM HENRY (Nov. 6, 1800–Apr. 7, 1879), soldier and engineer, was born in Taunton, Mass. He was the son of Dr. Foster Swift and Deborah (Delano) Swift, and brother of Joseph Gardner Swift [*q.v.*]. Entering the United States Military Academy as a cadet in

August 1813, when he was not yet thirteen years old, he remained at West Point until December 1818, when he left to accompany the expedition of Maj. Stephen H. Long [*q.v.*] to the Rocky Mountains, being allowed, however, to retain his cadetship. He was commissioned second lieutenant of artillery, July 1, 1819, being ranked at the foot of his class because his academic course was incomplete; and promoted first lieutenant, Aug. 5, 1824. Although nominally an artilleryman he was employed constantly on engineering duties, working not only on defensive projects but also on river and harbor improvement along the Atlantic and Gulf coasts, on surveys for the Chesapeake & Ohio Canal, for a projected canal across the Florida peninsula, and for several railroads. The extensive internal improvements then being undertaken—railroads and canals—caused a greater demand for civil engineers than the profession could supply, and Swift's services, like those of some other military engineers, were lent by the government to private corporations for some time.

In August 1832 he was given the brevet rank of captain as an assistant topographical engineer and in July 1838 the actual rank, upon the creation of an independent corps of topographical engineers. The elaborate post route map constructed in 1830–32 was almost entirely his work. From 1833 to 1843 he was on duty with the Coast and Geodetic Survey, and from then until 1849 he was the principal assistant in the topographical bureau in Washington. He was responsible for the construction, at Black Rock Harbor, Conn., of the first skeleton iron tower lighthouse in the United States, having studied this design while in Europe on government business in 1840–41. He built a similar lighthouse on Minot's Ledge, near Cohasset, Mass., in 1847–48, which was carried away during the great storm of Apr. 16, 1851, probably on account of unauthorized loading beyond the limit for which it was designed. He resigned from the army, July 31, 1849, and became successively president of the Philadelphia, Wilmington & Baltimore Railroad, now a part of the Pennsylvania system, and of the Massachusetts Western Railroad, now the Boston & Albany. In 1845, while still in the army, he had been chosen president of the board of trustees of the Illinois & Michigan canal, an office which he continued to hold until 1871. He was a director of many corporations and the trusted financial adviser of Baring Brothers, of his brother-in-law, George W. Whistler [*q.v.*], and others. Of the occasional professional papers which he wrote, a report on the Chesapeake & Ohio Canal was published in

1846 and one on the railroads of Massachusetts in 1856. "He was a broad minded, shrewd, business-like individual, wise, helpful, always fair and scrupulously honest" (personal letter from William Patten). He was appreciative of books and art, visited and encouraged young James McNeill Whistler while yet an obscure artist in Paris, and advised the young man's mother to let him go on painting. He was twice married: first, in 1825, to Mary, daughter of Charles Stuart, British consul in New London, who died in November 1837; and second, in 1844, to Hannah, daughter of John Howard of Springfield, Mass. He died in New York.

[See *The Memoirs of Gen. Joseph Gardner Swift* (1890), ed. by Harrison Ellery; G. W. Cullum, *Biog. Reg. . . . U. S. Mil. Acad.* (3rd ed., 1891); *N. Y. Tribune*, Apr. 9, 1879. Some of Swift's professional papers were left to the Chicago Hist. Soc., and many of his letters are in the possession of William Patten of Rhinebeck, N. Y.]
T. M. S.

SWIFT, ZEPHANIAH (Feb. 27, 1759–Sept. 27, 1823), Connecticut jurist, was born in Wareham, Mass., the son of Roland, a descendant of William Swyft, who emigrated from England to America before 1638 and settled in Sandwich, Mass., and his wife, Mary Dexter. In childhood, he moved with his parents to Lebanon, Conn., where he was reared and schooled, partly by the famed Master Tisdale. Enrolling in a remarkable class which included Joel Barlow, Uriah Tracy, and Oliver Wolcott [qq.v.], he was graduated from Yale College with both the baccalaureate and master's degrees (1778, 1781). Thereupon, he read and actually studied law, and on admission to the bar established a practice in the town of Windham, Conn. Despite his lack of a military record, he was elected a representative to the general assembly, 1787–93, serving as clerk of the lower house for four sessions, and as speaker in 1792. As a Federalist, he sat for two terms in the lower house of Congress, 1793–97, and then returned to his practice and to the study of law. In 1800, as secretary to Oliver Ellsworth [q.v.] on his mission to France, his provincial outlook was greatly broadened and yet his national patriotism was intensified. On his return he was elected to the state council of the general assembly.

In the meantime, Swift stood forth as a stout opponent of slavery with the publication of *An Oration on Domestic Slavery, Delivered at the North Meeting-House in Hartford* (1791) in which America is described as "the only christian country where domestic slavery is tolerated in any considerable degree . . ." (p. 11). Two years later he published *The Correspondent; Containing the Publications in the Windham*

Herald Relative to the Result of the Ecclesiastical Council, Holden 1792, Respecting the Rev. Oliver Dodge which resulted in a war of pamphlets with the Rev. Moses C. Welch. This was followed by *A System of the Laws of the State of Connecticut* in two volumes (1795, 1796), the first American law text. It displayed a thoughtful philosophy of government as well as a thorough presentation of the constitutional and working government of the state. Elected by the general assembly, he commenced in 1801 a long term on the superior court. A moderate Federalist and a free-thinker in a Christian community, Swift escaped the usual Republican abuse although he was a supporter of the standing order and a firm upholder of the independence of the judiciary. He became chief justice of the court but after he sponsored the Hartford Convention and became a party to its deliberations, he was bracketed with the state rulers who must be dethroned, and, in 1819, after the completion of the Republican-Tolerationist revolution he ceased to be chief justice.

Honored for his service and political orthodoxy by Yale and Middlebury colleges, Swift retired to his legal researches. As far as Connecticut was concerned, a eulogist was quite correct in the appraisal: "No other individual has done so much towards reducing the laws to an intelligible system adapted to our habits and condition" (see Dexter, *post*). In 1810 he published a *Digest of the Law of Evidence, in Civil and Criminal Cases; And a Treatise on Bills of Exchange, and Promissory Notes,* and in 1816 he printed *A Vindication of the Calling of the Special Superior Court, at Middletown . . . for the Trial of Peter Lung* which arraigned legislative interference with the judiciary and defended his own conduct as chief justice. In his retirement, broken only by two years in the general assembly, 1820–22, he published a *Digest of the Laws of the State of Connecticut* (1822–23), of which the second volume came out posthumously. As this work was used rather generally throughout the country in legal instruction and as a guide for courts, it further increased the indebtedness of bench and bar to Connecticut's leading judicial scholar.

After the death of his first wife, Jerusha Watrous, of Colchester, in 1792, he was married on Mar. 14, 1795, to Lucretia Webb, the daughter of Capt. Nathaniel Webb, of Windham. A son by his first wife died in infancy. Of the seven children of the second the most distinguished was Mary A. Swift, author of *First Lessons on Natural Philosophy for Children* (2 volumes, 1833–1836). Swift died while visiting a son in Warren, Ohio, and was buried there.

[G. H. Swift, *Wm. Swyft of Sandwitch and Some of His Descendants* (1900); S. E. Baldwin, "Zephaniah Swift," *Great Am. Lawyers*, vol. II (1907); F. B. Dexter, *Biog. Sketches of the Grads. of Yale Coll.*, vol. IV (1907); E. D. Larned, *Hist. of Windham County, Conn.*, vol. II (1880); *Proc. Am. Antiquarian Soc.*, Apr. 1887; memoir in Swift's *Digest of the Laws of the State of Conn.*, vol. II (1823); R. J. Purcell, *Conn. in Transition* (1918); *Encyc. of Conn. Biog.* (1917), vol. I; *Biog. Directory of the Am. Cong.* (1928); *Amer. Hist. Rev.*, July 1934; *Am. Mercury* (Hartford), *Conn. Courant*, Oct. 14, 1823.]   R. J. P.

SWING, DAVID (Aug. 23, 1830–Oct. 3, 1894), preacher, was the second of the two sons of David and Kerenda (Gazley) Swing. His father, who died of the cholera in 1832, was an Ohio River pilot, and David was born over a store kept by his uncle, on the Cincinnati riverfront. He was a descendant of Samuel Schwing who emigrated to America in 1752, settling finally in New Jersey; and, on his mother's side, of John Gazley who emigrated from England in 1715 and established himself in Dutchess County, N. Y. When the boy was about five years old his mother married James Hageman, a blacksmith of Reading, Ohio, who also had two children, and in 1840 the Hagemans and Swings made a home for themselves on a farm near Williamsburg, Clermont County, Ohio. Here, not unacquainted with hardships, a shy, homely, tender-hearted boy, quick of mind and sensitive to beauty, David grew up. Converted at a Methodist revival when he was fifteen, he joined the Presbyterian church. He graduated from Miami University, Oxford, Ohio, in 1852, and after studying Old School theology, and being repelled by it, under Dr. Nathan L. Rice [*q.v.*] of Cincinnati, he became in 1853 professor of Latin and Greek and principal of the preparatory department at Miami. He married Elizabeth Porter, daughter of an Oxford physician, who bore him two daughters and died of tuberculosis on Aug. 2, 1879.

Swing finished his theological training under a local pastor, but during the twelve or more years he was in Oxford his chief intellectual interest was in literature and history. He also supplied neighboring churches. In 1866 he was persuaded by a former pupil to accept a call to the Westminster Presbyterian Church, Chicago, which in 1868 united with the North Church under the name of the Fourth Church. In the fire of 1871, its place of worship, Swing's dwelling, and all his books and papers were destroyed. He conducted services in a hall and later in Mc-Vicker's Theatre until a new edifice, for which he raised funds in the East, was completed. The originality, liberal spirit, and practical helpful-

ness of his sermons were now attracting attention not only in Chicago but elsewhere; *The Alliance* (1873–82), of which Swing was an editor, printed one of his sermons each week, as did also the *Inter-Ocean* and the *Chicago Tribune*. In 1874 he published *Truths for Today*, a volume containing fifteen sermons. He had already been attacked on the ground of heterodoxy by Francis L. Patton [*q.v.*], professor in the Presbyterian Theological Seminary of the Northwest and editor of *The Interior*; his book involved him in a trial for heresy. In April 1874 charges against him were filed with the Chicago Presbytery. The trial, which aroused widespread interest, resulted in the verdict "not proved." Patton asked for an appeal to the Synod of Illinois, North. Averse to controversy and extended litigation, Swing withdrew from the presbytery, although he did not resign his pulpit until October 1875.

Leading citizens of Chicago at once took measures to establish a new down-town church, and in December 1875 Central Church was organized with about 500 members. It first occupied Mc-Vicker's Theatre, but in 1880 Central Music Hall, built primarily to provide a platform for Swing, was dedicated. Here until his death he preached to two or three thousand each week and through his published sermons spoke to countless more. Although he was homely and awkward, without oratorical gifts, an essayist rather than a preacher, his personal charm, his ethical enthusiasm, and his substitution of the truths revealed by human experience as a basis of faith and conduct had great effect. He was a devotee of beauty and had the mind of a poet rather than that of a logician, yet he was strongly pragmatic in method. His sermons and lectures had literary excellence and came from a richly furnished mind; his comprehension was sufficiently limited, however, to permit him to say that the studies of Darwin were "so unimportant that few care whether they are true or false" (*David Swing: A Memorial Volume, post,* p. 102). For years he was one of the institutions of Chicago, beloved by its inhabitants and sought out by visitors from near and far. Among the several volumes of his utterances published during his lifetime are a second series of *Truths for Today* (1876); *Motives of Life* (1879); *Club Essays* (1881, 1889; 4th ed., 1898), read before the Chicago Literary Club; *Sermons* (1874, 1884, 1895). After his death, which occurred in his sixty-fourth year, numerous selections from his sermons and addresses appeared.

[G. S. Swing, *Events in the Life and History of the Swing Family* (1889); J. F. Newton, *David Swing, Poet-Preacher* (1909), containing bibliog.; *David Swing: A Memorial Volume* (1894), ed. by Helen Swing Starring, a daughter, including biog. sketch, sermons, and tributes; *The Message of David Swing to His Generation* (1913), with introduction by N. D. Hillis; *Chicago Tribune, Chicago Herald,* Oct. 4, 8, 1894.]   H. E. S.

SWINTON, JOHN (Dec. 12, 1829–Dec. 15, 1901), journalist, social reformer, was born in Salton, near Edinburgh, Scotland, the son of William and Jane (Currie) Swinton, and the brother of William Swinton [*q.v.*]. In 1843 the family moved to Canada, settling in Montreal, and young Swinton shortly afterward began work as a printer's apprentice in the office of the Montreal *Witness*. Later the family moved to New York City. Swinton entered Williston Seminary, at Easthampton, Mass., in 1853, but after a time returned to typesetting. As a journeyman printer he traveled in the South and the Middle West. In 1856 he went to Kansas to take part in the free-state movement and became manager of the Lawrence *Republican*. The next year he was back in New York City, where for a time he studied both law and medicine. A casual contribution to the *Times* brought him to the attention of Henry J. Raymond [*q.v.*], who gave him employment. In 1860 he was made chief of the editorial staff of the paper, a place he retained for ten years. For the next five years he was variously employed. He had become deeply interested in the cause of the wage-workers and in the spring of 1874 took a conspicuous and daring part in the great labor demonstration at Tompkins Square which was broken up by the police. In the same year he was the candidate of the Industrial Political Party for mayor.

Despite his radicalism, Charles A. Dana [*q.v.*], who greatly admired his talent, gave him a place on the editorial staff of the *Sun*. Here he remained for the years 1875–83, becoming the chief of the editorial staff. In the meantime, in 1877, he had been married and had established a home in Brooklyn. His wife was Orsena (Fowler) Smith, the widowed daughter of Prof. Orson Squire Fowler [*q.v.*]. On Oct. 14, 1883, having retired from the *Sun*, he started *John Swinton's Paper*, a four-page weekly labor journal. It was a brilliantly written paper and attracted wide attention, but it was poorly supported by the wage-earners, and was even boycotted by the powerful Knights of Labor. On Aug. 21, 1887, broken in health and with all his savings exhausted, he published the last number. For a time he seems to have been idle and in distress, but Dana soon reëmployed him and he remained

with the *Sun* until the editor's death. In his later years he wrote for various publications and was the correspondent for five or six European newspapers. He died after an illness of ten days at his Brooklyn home. His wife survived him. They had no children.

In his later days, usually accompanied by his wife, Swinton was a familiar sight at labor and social reform gatherings; his large head, with its bushy shock of white hair flowing out from under a skull cap, his strong, expressive face, and dark, piercing eyes surmounted by great shaggy eyebrows, and his luxuriant iron-gray mustache made an unforgettable picture. He was an omnivorous reader and nothing escaped his interest. He was the author of several pamphlets. In 1880 he published a booklet, *John Swinton's Travels,* the record of a brief European trip with his wife, and fourteen years later he published *Striking for Life,* a work on the labor movement. He had no ordered philosophy. Though a friend and great admirer of Karl Marx, he was not a Socialist. An advocate of the utmost degree of organization for others, he played a lone hand. As a writer he was distinguished; he had a rare sense of word values, and both in vehement invective and in biting sarcasm he was a master of the language of opprobrium. With all his radicalism, he remained a fervently religious Scotch Calvinist. Raymond spoke of him as "the only man I ever knew who had no axes of his own to grind" (*New York Times, post*). He was a man of unblemished integrity.

[*Who's Who in America,* 1901–02; John H. Brown, *Cyc. of Am. Biog.* (vol. VII, 1903); Robert Waters, *Career and Conversation of John Swinton* (1902); *N. Y. Times, N. Y. Tribune,* the *Sun* (N. Y.), Dec. 16, 1901; recollections of the writer.]   W. J. G.

SWINTON, WILLIAM (Apr. 23, 1833–Oct. 24, 1892), war correspondent, author, was born at Salton, near Edinburgh, Scotland, the son of William and Jane (Currie) Swinton, and a brother of John Swinton [*q.v.*]. The family emigrated to Canada in 1843. Swinton received his preparatory education at Knox College, a Presbyterian school which later became one of the colleges of the University of Toronto. He entered Amherst College with the class of 1856 but remained for only part of his freshman year. In 1853 he married Catherine Linton of Canada and secured a position as teacher of languages in the Edgeworth Female Seminary at Greensboro, N. C. From 1855 to 1858 he taught in the Mount Washington Collegiate Institute in New York City, meanwhile preparing for the Presbyterian ministry. He had already done some successful magazine writing, and soon after securing a position with the *New York Times* in 1858, he definitely abandoned plans for a ministerial career. Early in the Civil War he was sent to the front as the *Times* special correspondent with the armies in the field, where his savage criticisms of leading generals kept him in bad grace with the authorities. In this matter he can hardly be said to have transgressed the ethical code of the newspapers of the time, but in some respects his conduct would not bear scrutiny at any time or under any circumstances. He sought to secure privileges by methods savoring of blackmail and to get information by means that may very gently be called undignified. Early in the Virginia campaign of 1864 one of Gen. U. S. Grant's staff officers unceremoniously pulled him out of the hiding place where he was listening to a conference between Grant and Gen. George G. Meade. The patience of the War Department was finally exhausted, and on July 1, 1864, an order was issued depriving him of privileges as a correspondent and forbidding him to remain with the army. During the next few years he published several books dealing with the war: *The Times Review of McClellan; His Military Career Reviewed and Exposed* (1864), *Campaigns of the Army of the Potomac* (1866), *The Twelve Decisive Battles of the War* (1867), *History of the New York Seventh Regiment During the War of the Rebellion* (1870).

In 1869 he became professor of English at the University of California, then just established on its new (but temporary) site at Oakland. President Daniel Coit Gilman's policies were so strongly opposed by Swinton that the latter's resignation in 1874—with that of one other professor—was necessary to the restoration of harmony in the faculty. Swinton then turned to writing school textbooks, with such success that a gold medal was awarded to him at the Paris exposition of 1878 and his royalties sometimes reached $25,000 a year. He produced geographies, spelling books, readers, grammars, histories of the United States and of the world—in short, he covered almost the whole field of juvenile human knowledge. He was a hard but highly erratic worker, and so careless in his financial habits that he was frequently pressed for money. At such times he was ready to dispose of valuable copyrights for a comparatively small sum in cash. He spent this period of his life in Brooklyn, N. Y., and there he died, survived by three sons and two daughters.

[See H. C. Graves, *Hist. of the Class of 1856, Amherst Coll.* (n.d.); R. S. Fletcher and M. O. Young, *Amherst Coll. Biog. Record* (1927); W. C. Jones, *Illus. Hist. of the Univ. of Cal.* (1901); W. W. Ferrier, *Origin and Development of the Univ. of Cal.*

(1930); *Hist. Mag.,* Nov. 1869, pp. 295–98; obituary in *N. Y. Times,* Oct. 26, 1892. For Swinton's methods as war correspondent, see J. D. Cox, *Mil. Reminiscences of the Civil War* (1900), vol. I, pp. 76–78, and *Personal Memoirs of U. S. Grant,* vol. II (1886), pp. 143–45.]   T. M. S.

SWISSHELM, JANE GREY CANNON (Dec. 6, 1815–July 22, 1884), reformer and editor, was the daughter of Thomas and Mary (Scott) Cannon, Scotch-Irish Covenanters of Pittsburgh, Pa. She spent her youth in the new settlement of Wilkinsburg, to which her parents removed soon after she was born. At the age of three she began attending school; by the time she was ten she was aiding her widowed mother in earning a living; at fourteen she became active in the anti-slavery cause; before her fifteenth birthday she took charge of the only school in the village. After six years of teaching she married, Nov. 18, 1836, James Swisshelm, a young farmer of the neighborhood. In 1838 she accompanied him to Louisville, Ky., where he attempted, unsuccessfully, to establish a business, and she earned what she could as seamstress and teacher. Her hatred of slavery became an absorbing passion during this sojourn. Returning to Pennsylvania, she took charge of a seminary at Butler in 1840, and began to use her pen in defense of the rights of married women. Two years later she rejoined her husband on a farm, which she named Swissvale, near Pittsburgh. In the midst of domestic duties she continued to write, supplying stories and verses to the *Dollar Newspaper* and to *Neal's Saturday Gazette.* At the same time she contributed to the *Spirit of Liberty,* the *Pittsburgh Gazette,* and to the *Daily Commercial Journal* racy, vehemently written articles on abolition and the property rights of women.

In 1847 she used a legacy from her mother to establish the *Pittsburgh Saturday Visiter* (*sic*), a political and literary weekly, advocating abolition, temperance, and woman's suffrage, the first number of which appeared on Dec. 20. She edited this paper with such spirited audacity that she became widely known for her powers of denunciation. "Beware of sister Jane," contemporary editors said to each other. Most notable among her attacks was one that she published in 1850 upon Daniel Webster's private life. This, she loved to believe, ruined his chances for becoming president. In 1853 she published a volume called *Letters to Country Girls,* compiled from articles in the *Visiter.* In 1857 she sold her paper, separated permanently from her husband—who secured a divorce from her on the ground of desertion a few years later—and, accompanied by her only child, took up her residence in Minnesota. The following year she began the *St. Cloud Visiter*. A libel suit ended this publication in a few months. She at once established the *St. Cloud Democrat,* a Republican paper, which she conducted in her usual intrepid, intensely personal manner until 1863. During this time she lectured frequently throughout the state on political subjects.

In the midst of the Civil War she went to Washington, D. C., and while doing clerical work in a government office and assisting in a war hospital contributed to the *New York Tribune* and to the *St. Cloud Democrat.* During this period she became a warm personal friend of Mrs. Lincoln. In the course of Andrew Johnson's administration she started a radical paper called the *Reconstructionist.* In this she attacked the President with such violence that in 1866 he dismissed her from the government service. Returning to Swissvale, she made that place her home for the rest of her life. In 1880 she published *Half a Century,* an entertaining account of her life to the year 1865. Her extreme individualism made her a free lance in all her undertakings. She never worked happily in reform organizations, preferring always to forge her own thunderbolts. Her firm convictions, her powers of sarcasm, her stinging yet often humorous invective, and her homely, vigorous style made her a trenchant journalist.

[In addition to *Half a Century,* see L. B. Shippee, "Jane Grey Swisshelm: Agitator," *Miss. Valley Hist. Rev.,* Dec. 1920; *Minn. Hist. Soc. Colls.,* vol. XII (1908); S. J. Fisher, "Reminiscences of Jane Grey Swisshelm," *Western Pa. Hist. Mag.,* July 1921; B. M. Stearns, "Reform Periodicals and Female Reformers," *Am. Hist. Rev.,* July 1932; A. J. Larsen, *Crusader and Feminist: Letters of Jane Grey Swisshelm, 1858–1865* (1934); *N. Y. Times,* July 23, 1884.]   B. M. S.

SWITZLER, WILLIAM FRANKLIN (Mar. 16, 1819–May 24, 1906), journalist, historian, and politician, first of two sons of Simeon and Elizabeth (Cornelius) Switzler, was born on a farm in Fayette County, Ky. His father was a native of Virginia, his mother of Kentucky, and his paternal grandparents of Switzerland. His family moved to Fayette, Mo., in 1826, and William began his schooling in a log house. Later his father bought a farm near Franklin, Mo., on which the boy grew up. He supplemented his training at Mount Forest Academy by omnivorous reading, including law, which he practised three years. In 1841 he became editor of the oldest Missouri newspaper outside of St. Louis, the *Columbia Patriot,* then a Whig weekly (founded at Franklin in 1819 as the *Missouri Intelligencer*); this he purchased in December 1842 and renamed the *Missouri Statesman.* An ardent Whig editorially, he nevertheless saw

that Democratic news was faithfully reported. So well known were his remarkable memory and his insistence on accuracy that citation of the *Statesman* was freely accepted as proof. He served three terms in the Missouri legislature, being elected in 1846, 1848, and 1856, and supported progressive and anti-slavery measures. During the Civil War he was so strong a Unionist that a guerrilla band threatened his life. Although he served as delegate to the National Constitutional Union Convention (Democratic) in Baltimore in 1860, Lincoln appointed him secretary of state in the provisional government in Arkansas two years later. But the appointment did not alter his politics, and in 1864 he supported George Brinton McClellan [*q.v.*]. Democratic candidate for national representative in 1866 and 1868, he each time unsuccessfully contested the election of his opponent. He contended that Democratic voters had been disfranchised by the Missouri constitution of 1865, which he was chosen to help frame and whose adoption he vigorously opposed. He was also a delegate to the state constitutional convention of 1875 and drafted the section on education. He edited the *Statesman* until 1885, when President Cleveland appointed him chief of the bureau of statistics in the Treasury Department. For short periods he also edited newspapers in St. Joseph and Chillicothe, Mo., and from 1893 to 1898, the *Missouri Democrat* at Boonville.

Switzler was one of the best informed men of his time on the history of his state. His publications include the *Early History of Missouri* (1872), the section on history in C. R. Barns's *The Commonwealth of Missouri* (1877), *Switzler's Illustrated History of Missouri* (1879), *History of Boone County, Missouri* (1882), and *History of Statistics and Their Value* (1888). He also contributed to H. L. Conard's *Encyclopedia of the History of Missouri* (1906). His last years he spent writing a history of the University of Missouri. A founder of the first circulating library in Columbia, head of the lyceum there in the 1840's, and sponsor of its first brass band, he was in his last decade still working for local improvements. In 1849 he helped lead a movement opening the way for the founding of Christian College (1851), of which he was a trustee for many years, and the Baptist (later Stephens) College (1856). He was a good public speaker, and his bearded face was a familiar sight at fairs, dedications of covered bridges, and Fourth of July celebrations. He was a Presbyterian and a vigorous temperance leader. In his latter years he enjoyed the editorial rivalry of Edwin William Stephens [*q.v.*]. Survived by two sons and a daughter, Switzler died of the infirmities of age in his eighty-seventh year in Columbia. His wife, Mary Jane Royall, of Columbia, whom he married Aug. 31, 1843, died in 1879. He left his mark as the dean of Missouri journalists, and three years after his death the first building of the School of Journalism of the University of Missouri was named in his honor.

[N. T. Gentry, in *Mo. Hist. Rev.*, Jan. 1930; H. L. Conard, *Encyc. of the Hist. of Mo.* (1906); *Kansas City Star*, Feb 4, 1900; obituaries in *St. Louis Post-Dispatch* and *Columbia Daily Tribune*, May 24, and in *Kansas City Jour.*, May 25, 1906; *House Miscellaneous Doc. 14*, 41 Cong., 2 Sess.; information from Switzler's daughter, Mrs. J. S. Branham, and F. C. Shoemaker, both of Columbia, Mo.]   I. D.

SYKES, GEORGE (Oct. 9, 1822–Feb. 8, 1880), soldier, was born at Dover, Del., the son of William Sykes and the grandson of James Sykes, noted physician and governor of Delaware, 1801–02. Sykes received his early education in Dover and was sent to the United States Military Academy at West Point, N. Y., in 1838. He was graduated in 1842 as a second lieutenant, 3rd Infantry, and went immediately to Florida where he took part in the Seminole War. He was promoted to the rank of first lieutenant in 1846, served in the war with Mexico during the entire campaign from Vera Cruz to Mexico city, and was brevetted captain for gallant conduct at Cerro Gordo. After the war he served mostly in the Southwest.

At the outbreak of the Civil War Sykes became a major, and, at the first battle of Bull Run, he commanded a battalion of regulars which particularly distinguished itself by protecting the disordered retreat of the Federal troops. For this service he was appointed a brigadier-general of volunteers. In the spring of 1862, Sykes commanded a brigade, subsequently the 2nd Division, V Corps, composed mostly of regulars, in the Peninsular campaign in Virginia. He valiantly defended his position at the battle of Gaines's Mill, checking the Confederate attack until darkness enabled the Union army to be withdrawn. At Malvern Hill on July 1, 1862, he again assisted in repulsing the enemy. In the second Manassas campaign, Sykes's division, part of Porter's V Corps, experienced heavy fighting, especially on Aug. 30, but held its ground until ordered back. Sykes was only lightly engaged at Antietam and at Fredericksburg. Late in the year he was promoted to the rank of major-general. At Chancellorsville, while Stonewall Jackson was fighting the main Federal forces, Sykes operated towards Fredericksburg against Lee's army.

In the Gettysburg campaign Sykes commanded the V Corps. It did not arrive on the battle-field until July 2, when it was ordered to hold the Round Tops, threatened by an enemy attack. Severe fighting occurred in which Sykes bravely led his men to hold these hills for the Federal army. At a council of war that night, he advised remaining on the defensive for one more day. This plan was adopted by Meade. When the Confederates made their famous charge on July 3, he was not directly engaged, although his troops suffered from artillery fire. An opportunity existed after the repulse of the enemy for a counter-attack by the V Corps and there seems to have been some controversy between Sykes and Meade as to whether Sykes had been ordered to do this. Sykes denied that he had been so directed, but, in any case, the chance passed without being utilized. He was brevetted brigadier-general in the regular army for his conduct in this battle.

Upon the reorganization of the Army of the Potomac early in 1864, Sykes was relieved from the V Corps, and sent to Kansas, where he remained on unimportant duties until the end of the war. In 1866 he was mustered out of the volunteer service as a major-general and reverted to the rank of lieutenant-colonel, 5th Infantry, in the regular army. The rest of his service was mainly in the West. He became colonel of the 20th Infantry in 1868, and died at Fort Brown, Texas, while commanding that regiment. Serious illness and great suffering marred the last years of his life. His wife, Elizabeth, was the daughter of Robert Goldsborough of Cambridge, Md. Sykes as a general was excellent on the defensive, but he lacked initiative. He was nicknamed "Tardy George," but his tardiness was mental, not physical.

[*War of the Rebellion: Official Records (Army)*, 1 ser., vols. X, part 2, XI, parts 1, 2, XXVII, part 1 (1884–89); *Battles and Leaders of the Civil War*, 4 vols. (1887–88); G. W. Cullum, *Biog. Reg. . . . Officers and Grads., U. S. Mil. Acad.* (1891); article by Henry Coppee in *Ann. Reunion, Asso. Grads., U. S. Mil. Acad.* (1880); G. J. Cross, *The Battle-field of Gettysburg* (1866); J. T. Scharf, *Hist. of Del.* (1881), vol. I; *Galveston Daily News*, Feb. 10, 1880.]   C. H. L.

SYLVESTER, FREDERICK OAKES (Oct. 8, 1869–Mar. 2, 1915), painter, poet, was born in Brockton, Mass., only son and second child of Charles Fred and Mary Louise (Kilburn) Sylvester. His father, a fashioner of shoemaking tools and later a hardware merchant, belonged to a Plymouth family, while his mother was a descendant of a line of Provincetown seafarers. After graduating from high school in Fall River in 1888, Sylvester went to the Massachusetts Normal Art School. Completing his course in 1891, he was appointed assistant professor of drawing and painting in Newcomb College, Tulane University, New Orleans, La. On Christmas of that year he married Florence Isabel Gerry of Fall River. In September 1892 he became head of the drawing department in the Normal and High School, St. Louis, Mo., and he taught in the St. Louis school system until 1913, when long illness finally forced him to take a leave of absence. He resigned the next year. An early convert to Christian Science, he had become meanwhile (1901) one of the first teachers at the Principia, with whose development he was closely associated until his death.

The Mississippi River, which became his favorite subject for painting, first aroused Sylvester at New Orleans, where he painted waterfront objects. On removing to St. Louis he continued in this vein, and at the Louisiana Purchase and Portland expositions he received medals for studies of the Eads bridge. Later, omitting all signs of man and commerce, he began to record the simple majesty of the river's various moods, especially as revealed in the region of its towering palisades above Alton, Ill. His "unquestioned . . . place in the art of the Middle West" (*Christian Science Monitor*, Sept. 17, 1915) rests on the many canvases produced in his bluff-crest studio near Elsah, Ill., which afforded a particularly fine view of the broad river. He preferred quiet tones—pale greens, mild blues, gray and rose—but also employed the bolder hues of sunset and autumn foliage. Typical of his work is "The River's Golden Dream," which hangs in the City Art Museum, St. Louis. A collection has been assembled at the Principia, while there are other examples in the St. Louis public library, at the University of Missouri, Christian College, and in private hands. When not teaching or painting, Sylvester devoted himself to writing. Like his canvases, his books, *Verses* (1903) and *The Great River: Poems and Pictures* (1911), reveal the solace he found in the contemplation of nature. He took a leading part in the development of the art colony of St. Louis and was head of its Artists' Guild, 1907–08. Always frail, he died of tuberculosis in his forty-sixth year, survived by his widow, a daughter, and a son. As he requested, his body was cremated, and the ashes were scattered in the river which was his joy in art and life.

[See *Who's Who in America*, 1914–15; F. W. Ruckstull, *Great Works of Art and What Makes them Great* (1925); Clarence Stratton, in *Art and Progress*, Sept. 1913; Laura R. Way, in *School Arts Mag.*, Nov. 1912; John Finley, in *Scribner's Mag.*, Oct. 1912; *Bull. of the St. Louis Art League*, July 1915; *N. Y. Times*, Mar. 3, 1915; obituaries and editorial in *St. Louis Post-Dispatch*, Mar. 3 and 4, 1915. A thesis on Sylvester's life and work by Mrs. Lulu Guthrie Emberson is in the Univ. of Mo. lib. Clippings, notebooks, and MSS. are in the possession of Mrs. Sylvester and Warren Sprague, both of St. Louis, and the Principia.] I. D.

SYLVESTER, JAMES JOSEPH (Sept. 3, 1814–Mar. 15, 1897), mathematician, was born in London, the youngest of six sons of Abraham Joseph. In later years his eldest brother adopted the surname Sylvester, and the rest of the brothers followed suit. James attended a school for Jewish boys in London and finished with honor his preparation for the university at the Royal Institution, Liverpool. In 1831 he matriculated at St. John's College, Cambridge, but after 1833 "degraded" for two years, returning in 1836. He was second wrangler in the mathematical tripos of 1837, but because of his Jewish faith was barred from a degree, as well as from prizes and a fellowship. After the Test Act of 1872, he was awarded both bachelor's and master's degrees. In 1837 he succeeded William Ritchie as professor of natural philosophy at University College, London, where he taught for four years. In 1841 he was granted the degrees of B.A. and M.A. by the University of Dublin, and in the same year accepted a call to the chair of mathematics in the University of Virginia.

Sensitive, race-conscious, and unable to control his temper, he was ill-fitted to meet the provincial prejudice of some of his students and to handle disciplinary problems. On Feb. 24, 1842, after about three months of service, he resigned his professorship because of the refusal of the faculty to expel a student with whom he had had difficulty (Bruce, *post*, III, 73–76). Going first to Washington and then to New York, where he lived with his eldest brother, he endeavored unsuccessfully to get appointments at Columbia and at Harvard.

Returning to London, he was engaged in actuarial work from December 1844 until 1856; at the same time he studied law in the Inner Temple and on Nov. 22, 1850, was called to the bar. During this period he was closely associated with Arthur Cayley (see *Dictionary of National Biography*), seven years his junior, a gifted mathematician who had also been called to the bar. In 1855 Sylvester was appointed professor of mathematics in the Royal Military Academy at Woolwich, where he taught until he was retired in July 1870. He had been president of the London Mathematical Society in 1866, and in 1869 presided over the meeting of the mathematical and physical science section of the British Association. In 1876, upon the recommendation of Joseph Henry and Benjamin Peirce [*qq.v.*], he was called to the newly opened Johns Hopkins University in Baltimore. Here he rendered memorable service. "As a source of intellectual enthusiasm, Sylvester stood out above all his colleagues," wrote one of his associates (Franklin, *Gilman, post,* p. 213). The oldest member of the faculty, he brought to the new institution not only his reputation and ability as one of the greatest mathematicians of his time, but an infectious eagerness for intellectual endeavor which had a stimulating effect upon the whole university. Setting new standards for mathematical research in America, inspiring scores of future teachers and investigators, he gave a marked impetus to the development of his science in the United States. From the foundation of the *American Journal of Mathematics* by the University in 1878 until May 1884 he was its editor, giving it at once a distinguished place among the learned journals of the world. In December 1883 he resigned his chair to accept election as Savilian Professor of Geometry at Oxford, in which position he continued for the remainder of his life, although failing health caused him to retire from teaching in 1894. His death three years later followed an apoplectic stroke.

Sylvester has been characterized as "perhaps the mind most exuberant in original ideas of pure mathematics of any since Gauss" (*Collected Papers of Charles Sanders Peirce,* vol. IV, 1933, p. 506). His work was chiefly in the domain of analysis rather than in that of geometry. In particular he devoted his attention to the theory of numbers—including the partitions of numbers and the distribution of primes; to higher algebra, as in the completion of Newton's work on the number of imaginary roots in an algebraic equation; and—building upon the foundations laid by Boole and Cayley—to the theory of invariants, a subject in which he was recognized as preëminent. He was the recipient of many honors while he lived, and after his death the Royal Society of London gave his name to a triennial award—the Sylvester Medal —for the encouragement of research in pure mathematics, while the Johns Hopkins University in 1901, wishing to do signal honor to two of the greatest living scientists, Lord Kelvin and Simon Newcomb, awarded them each a medallion bearing Sylvester's portrait.

Many of his papers, which during his lifetime appeared in various learned journals, were gathered into *The Collected Mathematical Papers of James Joseph Sylvester* (4 vols., 1904–12), edited by H. F. Baker. In 1870 he published *The Laws of Verse,* in which from his own polished translations of certain odes of Horace and several German poems he illustrated the principle of "phonetic syzygy"—"the apt juncture of syllables." "The most interesting thing about it," says Prof. George Saintsbury, speaking of this little volume, "is the author's agreement, from almost the most opposite preparation and point of view conceivable, with Poe—an agreement which extends to the doctrine that accent *creates quantity*" (*A History of English Prosody,* 1910, III, 444–45). Most of Sylvester's original verse showed more ingenuity than poetic feeling. He was completely at home in English, French, German, Italian, Latin, and Greek; was very fond of music; though eccentric and often irritable had considerable humor; was vivacious in conversation, and greatly enjoyed society. He never married.

[H. F. Baker, "Biographical Notice," in *The Collected Mathematical Papers of James Joseph Sylvester,* vol. IV; *Who's Who* (British), 1897; Arthur Cayley, "James Joseph Sylvester," *Nature* (London), Jan. 3, 1889; G. B. Halsted, "Sylvester at Hopkins," *The Johns Hopkins Alumni Mag.,* Mar. 1916; D. S. Blondheim, "A Brilliant and Eccentric Mathematician," *Ibid.,* Jan. 1921; *Johns Hopkins Univ. Circulars,* vol. I (Apr. 1880), p. 38, vol. III (Jan. 1884), p. 31; P. E. Matheson and E. B. Elliott in *Dict. Nat. Biog.,* first Supp.; Alexander MacFarlane, *Lectures on Ten British Mathematicians of the Nineteenth Century* (1916); P. A. Bruce, *Hist. of the Univ. of Va.,* vol. III (1921); D. C. Gilman, *The Launching of a University* (1906), pp. 65–70; Fabian Franklin, *The Life of Daniel Coit Gilman* (1901), and memorial address on Sylvester (1897), repub. in *People and Problems* (1908); P. A. MacMahon, in *Nature* (London), Mar. 25, 1897; *Science,* Apr. 16, 1897; M. Noether in *Mathematische Annalen,* vol. L (1898); D. E. Smith and Jekuthiel Ginsburg, *A Hist. of Mathematics in America before 1900* (1934); *N. Y. Times,* Mar. 16, 1897; R. C. Archibald, "Unpublished Letters of James Joseph Sylvester and Other New Information Concerning His Life and Work," *David Eugene Smith Presentation Volume* (*Osiris,* vol. I, 1936).]   D. E. S.

SYLVIS, WILLIAM H. (Nov. 26, 1828–July 27, 1869), reformer and labor leader, was born in the village of Armagh, Indiana County, Pa., the second son of Maria (Mott) and Nicholas Sylvis. His father, a wagon-maker and a Democrat, was very poor. The panic of 1837 scattered the family for a while, William going by contract to a neighbor through whom he gained a slight education, an interest in Whig politics, and an admiration for Henry Clay. In the Forest Iron Works, Union County, he learned the trade of iron moulding. After a period of wandering as a journeyman, he married Amelia A. Thomas, Apr. 11, 1852, and settled in Philadelphia. By this, and a second marriage in 1866 to Florrie Hunter of Hollidaysburg, Pa., he had five sons.

As a result of a strike in 1857, during which

he was elected shop secretary, he joined and was made recording secretary of an iron-moulders' union which had been organized in Philadelphia in 1855. Shortly afterward he initiated a resolution in the union advocating a national convention of iron moulders, and with the president of the local union signed a call for the first convention of the Iron-Moulders International Union, which was held in Philadelphia in July 1859. Sylvis' address to the iron moulders of America became the preamble to the constitution of the new union, and at its second convention, Jan. 10, 1860, in Albany, he was elected treasurer. When the Whig party ceased to exist, he became a Union Democrat and in 1860 supported Douglas. On Feb. 22, 1861, in Philadelphia, he called to order the national convention of workingmen opposed to war. After the Civil War had begun he helped recruit a company for the Union army, but declined the lieutenancy offered him and worked as a teamster in Washington for nine months.

In 1863, at Sylvis' instigation the moulders' organization reconvened in Pittsburgh with half the original number of delegates, and elected him president. Single-handed, he reorganized the war-shattered union. In his report to the Pittsburgh convention in 1864 he recommended the establishment of cooperative foundries and, borrowing an idea from the Machinists' and Blacksmiths' International, the formation of a national trades assembly. He was intimately associated with the activities resulting in the "Labor Congress" at Baltimore in 1866, the first meeting of the National Labor Union, and in 1868 was elected president of that body, thus becoming the representative of 600,000 organized workers. Shortly after his election he appointed a permanent lobbying committee of five to remain in Washington during the sessions of Congress.

With most of the purposes of the National Labor Union Sylvis was in complete accord: he favored the Labor Reform Party, cooperation, the monetary reforms of Edward Kellogg [q.v.], Greenbackism, the eight-hour day, arbitration of labor conflicts, support of "the sewing-women and daughters of toil in this land," tenement-house reform, more rigid enforcement of the apprentice system, the establishment of working-men's lyceums, institutes, and reading rooms, and the reservation of public lands for bona fide settlers. In theory he opposed strikes, but in practice he led some of the first great struggles of American trade unions. He strongly urged affiliation with the First International and maintained a regular correspondence with its leaders.

He was, however, influenced more by the English cooperative movement.

For a year just after the Civil War Sylvis edited the *Iron-Moulders International Journal,* and about 1869 he became joint proprietor of the *Workingman's Advocate,* the official organ of the National Labor Union, published simultaneously in Chicago and Philadelphia. His writings, scattered but prolific, touched all the political and labor questions of the day. He was a competent orator and the best known labor leader of his time. Throughout his life he remained a Methodist and was active in the temperance movement. He was often prominently mentioned by the labor press for the vice-presidency on a Labor or Democratic ticket. He died at the height of his career, before he was forty-one.

[J. C. Sylvis, *The Life, Speeches, Labors, and Essays of William H. Sylvis* (1872); T. V. Powderly, *Thirty Years of Labor, 1859–1889* (1889); J. R. Commons and associates, *Hist. of Labour in the U. S.* (1918), vol. II; N. J. Ware, *The Labor Movement in the U. S. 1860–1895* (1929); *Public Ledger* (Phila.), July 29, 1869.]
                                                    H. S.

SYMMES, JOHN CLEVES (July 21, 1742– Feb. 26, 1814), pioneer, was born at Southold, Long Island, the son of the Rev. Timothy and Mary (Cleves) Symmes and the descendant of Zechariah Symmes who emigrated from England to Charlestown, Mass., in 1634. His education was fairly adequate, and for a time he taught school. In 1770 he settled in Sussex County, N. J., and in 1780 he removed to Morristown. Taking a leading part in Revolutionary activities in New Jersey, he became chairman of the committee of correspondence for Sussex County in 1774, and in 1775 he was appointed a colonel in the militia. He helped cover Washington's retreat through New Jersey in 1776, and from 1776 to 1779 he fought in a number of battles, notably at Monmouth and at Short Hills. As a member of the New Jersey convention in 1776, he was on the committee that drew up the new state constitution, and in 1776, 1780, and 1785 he was elected to the New Jersey legislative council. Also in 1776 he was on a commission to investigate the dissatisfaction among the New Jersey state troops at Ticonderoga. A year later he was elected an associate justice of the supreme court of New Jersey, a commission that was renewed in 1783. In 1778 he represented New Jersey at the New Haven convention to regulate prices.

He was elected a member of the Continental Congress from New Jersey in 1785 and was re-elected in 1786. As a member of Congress he speedily became interested in western colonization. The immediate impetus to action probably came from Benjamin Stites who, while trading along the Ohio, had been greatly impressed with the possibilities of the fertile region that stretched northward from that river, between the Miami and the Little Miami rivers. Stites pointed out the many possibilities of these lands, and Symmes made a trip down the Ohio in the spring of 1787, certainly as far as the falls (Louisville). With characteristic impulsiveness he proposed at first to found a settlement on the Wabash above Vincennes; but after due reflection he applied to Congress for 2,000,000 acres in the more accessible region between the two Miamis. On Oct. 3, 1787, Congress authorized a formal contract with him, but before it was signed he issued his "Trenton Circular," which outlined his terms for granting land and called attention to the resources and the favorable location of the proposed colony. On Feb. 19, 1788, Congress appointed him a judge of the newly erected Northwest Territory, and, after making the first payment for his land, he left in July for the western country, although not until Oct. 15, 1788, was he given a definite contract for 1,000,000 acres, the Miami Purchase. About four and a half months later, he founded a settlement at North Bend, the third one on his lands. Soon he was selling many warrants for lands; but collections were poor, and he could not meet the payments due under his contract. Jonathan Dayton and Elias Boudinot [qq.v.], both of whom were personally interested in the new colony, came to his aid, and the president issued a patent, on Sept. 30, 1794, for the 311,682 acres Symmes had actually paid for.

As a colonizer, he had the perseverance and qualities of leadership that eventually won success. Yet he was quarrelsome and exceedingly careless, issuing conflicting warrants and even selling lands outside his patent. As a result he was made a defendant in many lawsuits, and, when he died in Cincinnati, the bulk of his property had been dissipated. Nevertheless, he had planted an important colony, with its chief settlement, Cincinnati, perhaps the most important military and commercial outpost in the early West. As a jurist, he was not at all noteworthy, holding his appointments from influence, rather than from any reputation for profound legal knowledge. In his capacity of territorial judge he did not cooperate wholeheartedly with Gov. Arthur St. Clair [q.v.], and differences between the two were common. His first wife, Anna Tuttle of Southold, Long Island, left two daughters, one of whom became the wife of William Henry Harrison [q.v.]. Mrs. Mary Halsey of New Jersey was his second wife, and his third

wife was Susanna Livingston, the daughter of William Livingston [q.v.], of New Jersey.

[C. T. Greve, *Centennial Hist. of Cincinnati* (1904), vol. I; C. H. Winfield, *Life and Public Services of John Cleves Symmes* (1877), also in *N. J. Hist. Soc. Proc.*, ser. 2, vol. V, pp. 22–43 (1879); *The Correspondence of John Cleves Symmes* (1926), ed. by B. W. Bond, Jr.; *Western Spy* (Cincinnati), Mar. 12, 1814; *New-England Hist. and Gen. Register*, Apr. 1859; Memo. of Record of John Cleves Symmes during the Revolutionary War (in Symmes's handwriting), Clarke MSS. II fo. 3, Hist. and Phil. Soc. of Ohio, Cincinnati.]
B. W. B., Jr.

SYMONS, GEORGE GARDNER (1865–Jan. 12, 1930), landscape painter, better known as Gardner Symons, was born in Chicago, Ill., of Jewish descent. After studying at the Art Institute of Chicago, he was a student in Munich, London, and Paris. He returned to the United States in 1909 and took up his residence in Brooklyn, N. Y. He spent most of his life in New York but made frequent sketching trips to the Berkshire hills, the valley of the Deerfield River, Gloucester, Mass., Cornwall, England, to various parts of Europe, whither he went almost every year to paint, and to southern California. In the latter part of his life he did much of his work at his country home in Colrain, Mass. He specialized in winter landscapes. He won the Carnegie prize of the National Academy of Design in 1909 for his "Opalescent River" and in 1911 became an Academician. In 1912 the National Arts Club conferred on him a gold medal and a prize of $1000 for his painting of "The Sun's Glow and Rising Moon." He was awarded a bronze medal at the International Exposition, Buenos Aires, 1910; the third W. A. Clarke prize and Corcoran bronze medal, Corcoran Gallery of Art, Washington, D. C., 1912; and the Saltus medal for merit, National Academy of Design, 1913. At the inaugural exibition of the Toledo Museum of Art, 1912, he exhibited "Rock-ribbed Hills of New England" and "Snow-clad Fields in Morning Light"; at the Carnegie Institute, Pittsburgh, 1913, "Breaking of the Winter Ice" and "November, Dachau, Germany"; and at the sixth annual exhibition of the Concord Art Association, Concord, Mass., "Morning Light." He died in Hillside, N. J., at the home of a brother-in-law. He was a member of numerous clubs and societies of artists both in the United States and abroad.

His "Snow Clouds" is in the Corcoran Gallery of Art, "The Winter Sun" in the Art Institute of Chicago. There are other examples of his work in art museums in Los Angeles, St. Louis, Toledo, Brooklyn, Pittsburgh, and in numerous other cities throughout the country. "Opalescent River," in the Metropolitan Museum of

Art, New York, a typical Symons painting, shows bright sunlight shining on the snow and floating ice in the river, with groups of trees and farm buildings beyond, and hills in the distance. His pictures, which have been praised for their strength and originality, are characterized as well by great sincerity and truth, and by a warm sympathy of imagination.

[*Who's Who in America*, 1928–29; Eugen Neuhaus, *The Hist. and Ideals of Am. Art* (1931); L. M. Bryant, *Am. Pictures and Their Painters* (1917); Mantle Fielding, *Dict. of Am. Painters, Sculptors, and Engravers* (1926); *America*, Feb. 26, 1910, pp. 526–28; *Art News*, June 20, 1925, and Jan. 25, 1930; *Century*, Mar. 1920; *Am. Art Ann.*, 1923; *Boston Transcript*, Feb. 1, 6, 1912, May 15, 1922, and Jan. 14, 1930.] W. H. D.

SYMONS, THOMAS WILLIAM (Feb. 7, 1849–Nov. 23, 1920), military engineer, was born at Keeseville, Essex County, N. Y., the son of Thomas and Syrena (Eaton) Symons. After a year spent at the Michigan Agricultural College, Lansing, he secured an appointment to the United States Military Academy at West Point. Graduating at the head of his class in 1874, he was commissioned second lieutenant in the corps of engineers. After service at Willet's Point, N. Y., 1874–76, and with the survey expedition under Lieut. George M. Wheeler [*q.v.*], 1876–79, during which time, May 2, 1878, he was promoted first lieutenant, he was made engineer officer of the Department of the Columbia.

In the course of his varied duties in this position he made a survey of the Columbia River, the results of which were published (*Senate Executive Document 186*, 47 Cong., 1 Sess.). From Dec. 28, 1882, until June 7, 1883, he was on duty with the Mississippi River Commission, and from June 18 to Dec. 15, 1883, with the Mexican boundary survey. For the next few years, except for a very brief tour of duty in March 1885 at Hot Springs, Ark., he was in Washington, D. C., aiding in the construction of the Washington aqueduct and serving as assistant to the engineer commissioner of the District of Columbia. On June 2, 1884, he was promoted captain. From November 1889 to October 1895 he was stationed in Portland, Ore., in charge of important river and harbor works in the Portland district.

Transferred to Buffalo, he now began notable engineering projects on the Great Lakes. He had charge of the construction of the Buffalo breakwater, which, when completed, was the largest in the world. He was promoted major Mar. 31, 1896. During the following year he made a study of the problems involved in a project for a ship canal to open the Great Lakes to ocean shipping and published several reports.

From July 1898 to April 1903 he was engineer of the 10th Lighthouse District, which included the Great Lakes system (within United States territory) up to the outlet of Lake Huron. In 1899 Gov. Theodore Roosevelt of New York appointed him a member of the state canal commission, in which capacity he was a strong advocate of the construction of the New York State Barge Canal. In 1903 he was appointed to succeed Col. Theodore Bingham as superintendent of public buildings and grounds in Washington, D. C., and as military aide to President Theodore Roosevelt. By special act of Congress, Apr. 20, 1904, he was granted leave of absence from June 2 of that year to July 1908, during which time he served on the advisory board of consulting engineers which supervised the construction of the New York State Barge Canal of which he came to be known as the "Father." Unfortunately, this great project, although technically a fine example of engineering skill, proved to be of little economic value and a complete financial failure. Symons was appointed colonel on May 8, 1908, and was retired at his own request on July 28 of that year. Thereafter his residence was in Washington, where he died. On Oct. 12, 1884, he married Letitia V., daughter of Alexander Robinson of Philadelphia, by whom he had two sons and a daughter.

[G. W. Cullum, *Biog. Reg., Officers and Grads. U. S. Mil. Acad.* (3rd ed., 1891) and supplements; *The Centennial of the U. S. Mil. Acad.* (1904), vol. II; *Army and Navy Jour.*, Dec. 4, 1920; *The Military Engineer*, Jan.–Feb. 1921; N. E. Whitford, *Hist. of the Barge Canal of N. Y. State* (1921); "N. Y. State's White Elephant," *Independent*, Feb. 7, 1925; *Who's Who in America*, 1920–21; *Evening Star* (Washington), Nov. 23, 1920.] J. K. F.

SYMS, BENJAMIN (1591?–1642?), planter and philanthropist, was probably born in England. His name was spelled variously, as Sim's, Simes, Sym, Symms, Syms, and Symes. He was reported in the census of Virginia in 1624/25 as thirty-three years old and living at Basse's Choice in what was later known as Isle of Wight County. Although he had paid for the passage of Joan Meatheart to America, intending to make her his wife, they quarrelled in May 1626, and he appeared against her at a court session held in James City on Oct. 11, 1627. The court decided that Joan should serve a certain John Gill for two years, in return for which service Syms should be paid 100 weight of tobacco and three years' service from the first man servant to arrive in the colony on any vessel. There is no indication that he ever married. In 1629/30 he was living in Jamestown.

Notwithstanding the meagerness of this account of his life, it is nevertheless true that he left a clear record to show that he was one of the earliest and probably the earliest inhabitant of any North American colony to bequeath property for the establishment of a free school. On Feb. 12, 1634/35, two years before the first possible date for the gift of John Harvard [*q.v.*] to the college that bears his name, he wrote a will leaving a farm of two hundred acres situated on the Poquoson River in Elizabeth City County, together with the milk and the increase of eight cows to provide a free school for the children of the parishes of Elizabeth City and Kiquotan (Hening, *post*, VI, 389–90). This will was confirmed by the General Assembly held at James City in 1642/43. A fund was established that provided for the Syms School until 1805 and then formed part of the endowment of Hampton Academy, often referred to as the Syms-Eaton Free School, until 1852, when a public school system was established. In 1933 it was reported as a fund of $10,100 and is still used by the public school commissioners to educate the children of the county. In a pamphlet of unknown authorship published in London in 1649, *A Perfect Description of Virginia* (*The Virginia Historical Register and Literary Advertiser*, Apr. 1849, p. 75), the author mentioned "a free school, with two hundred acres of land, a fine house upon it, forty milch kine" and wrote that "the benefactor deserveth perpetual memory; his name, Mr. Benjamin Symes, worthy to be chronicled."

[J. C. Hotten, *The Original Lists of . . . Emigrants* (1874); W. W. Hening, *Statutes at Large*, vol. I (1810), p. 252, vol. VI (1819), pp. 389–92; E. D. Neill, *Virginia Carolorum* (1886); *The Virginia Mag. of Hist. and Biog.*, Oct. 1893, Jan. 1894, July 1916, July 1920; *William and Mary College Quart.*, Oct. 1897; *The Syms-Eaton Free School* (n.d.), comp. by Mrs. F. M. Armstrong, lent through the courtesy of Robert M. Newton, Hampton, Virginia who also supplied information concerning the present fund; Esther Crane, "The Tercentenary of an Educational Bequest," *Elementary School Journ.*, Nov. 1934.]

E. Cr.

SYNG, PHILIP (Sept. 29, 1703–May 8, 1789), silversmith, son of Philip and Abigail (Murdock) Syng, was born in Cork, Ireland, where Philip Syng the elder, "Goldsmith and Gentleman," practised his craft. Setting out for America the family landed at Annapolis, Md., on Sept. 29, 1714. Whether they went at once to Philadelphia is not clear; they were established there by 1720. About 1723 the father, who had trained three of his sons in his work, left his family and business and returned to Annapolis to live and work to the end of his life. At the time of his father's departure Syng took over the shop that had been established on Market Street and began to build for himself the reputation of being the finest craftsman of the family and one of the two finest that Philadelphia produced. The most noted example of his silverwork is the inkstand which he made for the Assembly of Pennsylvania in 1752 at a cost of £25 16s. This inkstand was used at the signing of the Declaration of Independence and of the Constitution, but its historical interest is not greater than its artistic merit. Besides the many pieces of Syng's plate that have come to light, there are a number of pieces of jewelry, simple in style but well designed. It is probable that Syng's mark, as distinguished from that of his father, consisted of his initials in Roman capitals enclosed in a rectangle, with a leaf below, or before and after (Maurice Brix, *List of Philadelphia Silversmiths . . . 1762 to 1850*, 1920, frontispiece).

He was early a member of Benjamin Franklin's Junto, and when popular interest turned to the "electrical rod" he was one of the two or three serious experimenters with Franklin, who wrote in 1747 to Peter Collinson in London that Syng had invented a machine that aided in the generation of electricity (A. H. Smyth, *The Writings of Benjamin Franklin*, vol. III, 1905, pp. 306, 310 n.). He was also an early member of the American Philosophical Society, of which he was treasurer, 1769–71; one of the grantees of the charter for the Philadelphia Library Company, which was established in a room on Pewter Platter Alley; and one of the twenty-four trustees who met in Roberts' Coffee-shop in 1750 to organize the College and Academy of Philadelphia, which eventually became part of the University of Pennsylvania. He was a warden of Philadelphia (1753) and for ten years its treasurer (1759–69), a member of the Provincial Commission of Appeals (1765), and a signer of the Non-importation Agreement (1765). He was also Junior Warden of the first Masonic Lodge in America and from 1747 to 1749 a vestryman of Christ Church. He and his wife, Elizabeth Warner, whom he married on Feb. 5, 1729/30, are said to have had twenty-one children (Conner, *post*, p. 3), most of them girls, and only one son, Philip, who died in his twenty-seventh year, learned his father's art. One of his grandsons was Philip Syng Physick [*q.v.*], the surgeon. At his death Syng left a property of some size, including several houses and a country place called Prince of Wales Farm.

[See P. S. P. Conner, *Syng, of Phila.* (1891); J. W. Jordan, *Colonial Families of Phila.* (1911), vol. I; Louise Manly, *The Manly Family* (1930); H. F. Jayne and S. W. Woodhouse, Jr., in *Art in America*, Oct. 1921; Clara L. Avery, *Early Am. Silver* (1930). For an account of the elder Syng, see J. H. Pleasants and Howard Sill, *Maryland Silversmiths* (1930), pp. 72–74.]

K. A. K.

SZOLD, BENJAMIN (Nov. 15, 1829–July 31, 1902), rabbi, was born at Nemiskert, County of Neutra, Hungary, the son of Baruch Szold, a farmer, and Chaile (Endler). His was the only Jewish family in the village. Early left an orphan, he was brought up by his uncles. He received his training in Hebrew and rabbinics from private tutors (becoming *Morenu* at the early age of fourteen), and later, at the Presburg Talmudical College. His studies in Vienna were cut short by the revolution. For the next five years he acted as tutor in private families. He gained his academic knowledge at Frankel's Rabbinical Seminary and the University at Breslau, Silesia. On Aug. 10, 1859, at Cziffer, near Tirnova, he married Sophie Schaar, who survived him, together with four of the eight children that were born to them. The last eight years of his life were beclouded by a painful ailment, but he retained his mental vigor to the end. He died at Berkeley Springs, W. Va.

While a student, he officiated in synagogues at Brieg, Silesia (1857), and at Stockholm, Sweden (1858). The latter position he surrendered to Dr. Lewisohn who had received a call from the Congregation Oheb Shalom of Baltimore, Md., and he went to Baltimore in Lewisohn's stead. Arriving in the United States on Sept. 21, 1859, he served that congregation until 1892, when he was elected rabbi emeritus. He steered it away from extreme reform tendencies, and prepared for it the more traditional prayer book *Abodat Yisrael* (1863), with a German translation. New editions appeared in 1864, 1865 (with an English translation), and, revised jointly by himself, Marcus Jastrow [*q.v.*], and Henry Hochheimer, in 1871 and subsequently. Under his saintly influence his congregation soon became known for its strict observance of the Sabbath. He aided in establishing charitable institutions of Baltimore, and devoted himself to helping Russian Jewish refugees. He was a convinced Zionist long before Herzl organized the Zionist movement. During the Civil War he stood out boldly against slavery in the face of excited popular opinion in Maryland. On one occasion, having been unable to induce either General Meade or President Lincoln to pardon a deserter, in reckless protest he held the hand of the condemned soldier while the firing squad of twelve muskets fired the volley which ended the man's life.

Besides writing a number of unpublished studies in the Bible and the Talmud, Szold published *The Book of Job with a New Commentary* (1886), which shows marked originality, especially in the attention paid to the exegetic value of the masoretic accents. He was the author of some textbooks, minor publications, and a commentary on the eleventh chapter of Daniel for G. A. Kohut's *Semitic Studies in Memory of Rev. Dr. Alexander Kohut* (1897); he also edited Michael Heilprin's *Bibelkritische Notizen* (1893). He was outstanding in scholarship, forceful in his natural eloquence, moderate in his religious views, sharing neither orthodox rigidity nor reform's radicalism. His sweet and sincere humanity made him a champion of the unfortunate, and won for him the esteem of Jew and Gentile alike.

[*Jewish Comment* (Balto.), Nov. 17, 1899, Aug. 1, 8, Oct. 3, 1902; *Jewish Exponent* (Phila.) and *Am. Hebrew* (N. Y.), Aug. 8, 1902; *The Jewish Encyc.* (ed. 1925), vol. XI; *Year Book of the Central Conference of Am. Rabbis*, vol. XIII (copr. 1904); *Deborah* (Cincinnati), vol. II (1902); Peter Wiernik, *Hist. of the Jews in America* (1931); Emanuel Hertz, *Abraham Lincoln: The Tribute of the Synagogue* (1927); *Allgemeine Zeitung des Judenthums*, vol. XXXIII (1869); *Sun* (Balto.), Aug. 1, 1902.]   D. deS. P.

TABB, JOHN BANISTER (Mar. 22, 1845–Nov. 19, 1909), poet and priest, was born at "The Forest," Amelia County, Va., the son of Thomas Yelverton and Marianna Bertrand (Archer) Tabb. His father was seventh in direct line from Humphrey Tabb who settled in Elizabeth City County, Va., in 1637. The family had reason to be proud of its fame in the colonial and Revolutionary history of the state. Tabb's boyhood was spent under the influence of the ante-bellum régime, his mother and a tutor giving him his first lessons. For poetry and music he showed an early aptitude and passion. Though his weak eyesight prevented his enlistment in 1861, in the second year of the Civil War he was allowed to go to England with an expedition dispatched to transport supplies for the Confederacy, and in London and Paris he touched briefly the world of letters and the arts. On his return to Charleston he was transferred to the *Robert E. Lee,* most daringly successful of the blockade runners, but because of illness was not on the ship when it later fell into Union hands in November 1863. In the spring of 1864 he carried dispatches on the *Siren* until its capture on June 4. Tabb sank his papers but was taken, court-martialed, and sentenced to prison at Point Lookout, Md. One circumstance brought him comfort in prison: he met there Sidney Lanier, whose flute he heard one day as he lay prostrated with fever. When release came in February 1865, Tabb found Richmond a capitulated city. Until support was unavoidably withdrawn, he studied music in Baltimore. He then taught at Saint Paul's School, Baltimore, and in 1870 for a few months at Racine College, Racine,

Tabb

Wis. Though he was preparing for the Episcopal ministry, Catholicism had since 1862 increasingly attracted him. The conversion of his friend, Father Alfred Allen Curtis [q.v.], later bishop of Wilmington, hastened his turning, and on Sept. 8, 1872, he was baptized in the communion. Deciding to take priest's orders, he attended Saint Charles' College, Ellicott City, Md. (1872–75). It was not until 1881, however, that he entered Saint Mary's Seminary in Baltimore to complete his theological studies. He was ordained on Dec. 20, 1884. Meanwhile he taught at Saint Peter's Boys' School in Richmond, Va., and at Saint Charles', where, after his ordination, he conducted classes in English for the rest of his active life.

Father Tabb commenced poet when he was in the Confederate service. His first volume, issued privately in 1882 (Litz, *post*, p. 97), was experimental. His first widely known volume, *Poems* (1894), preceded by *An Octave to Mary* (1893), reached a seventeenth edition. By the time of publication of *Lyrics* (1897), the periodicals bought his poems eagerly. His reputation was further augmented, particularly in England, by *Later Lyrics* (1902), *The Rosary in Rhyme* (1904), and *A Selection from the Verses of John B. Tabb,* compiled by Alice Meynell in 1907. After his death appeared *Later Poems* (1910) and *The Poetry of Father Tabb* (1928), edited by F. A. Litz, which printed selections from manuscript volumes privately owned. The poems in *Child Verse* (1899) and *Quips and Quiddits* (1907) are trivialized by Tabb's love of punning and elfish humor. In spite of his admiration for the romantic poets, his verse bears little resemblance to theirs in form. His most intense lyric utterance suggests the epigrammatic crypticism of Emily Dickinson. His nature poetry is often merely fanciful, but his religious lyrics for their intensity invite comparison with those of the seventeenth-century metaphysical poets.

As a priest Father Tabb never aspired beyond his dear duty at the college. He mingled little with the world beyond the college and the city of Baltimore. To the last he called himself an "unreconstructed rebel" (*Ave Maria, Aug. 2, 1930, p. 132*). His pupils loved him devotedly, and were molded by his rich and paradoxical nature. Blindness shadowed the last years of his life, and general paralysis preceded his death.

[See *Who's Who in America*, 1908–09; F. A. Litz, *Father Tabb: A Study of His Life and Works* (1923); Jennie M. Tabb, *Father Tabb* (1922); Alice Meynell, "Father Tabb as a Poet," *Cath. World*, Feb. 1910; J. M. Cooney, in *Ave Maria*, Aug. 2, 9, 16, 1930; obituary in Baltimore *Sun*, Nov. 20, 1909. For the spelling of Tabb's middle name, see Litz, *op. cit.*, p. 273, n. 1.]
W.T.

Tabor

TABOR, HORACE AUSTIN WARNER (Nov. 26, 1830–Apr. 10, 1899), bonanza king, was born at Holland, Vt., the son of Cornelius Dunham and Sarah (Farrin) Tabor. His early years were spent on the farm and at the village school. He was a stonecutter for eight years. In 1855 he joined a company of Free-Soil emigrants to Kansas and in 1856 and 1857 was a member of the Topeka legislature, returning to Vermont to marry on Jan. 31, 1857, Augusta Pierce, daughter of his former employer.

Unsuccessful as a farmer in Kansas, in 1859 he took wife and baby and joined the Pike's Peak gold rush. His first season of prospecting was barren of results, and his wife took in boarders to pay expenses through the winter. The next spring Tabor went to the headwaters of the Arkansas, where rich placers were found. Here he prospered, first as a miner, then as a merchant, until the diggings played out and his business dwindled. Soon, however, the black sand that had cluttered the sluice boxes was found to contain silver, and a new rush to the district set in. Tabor, continuing with his store, grubstaked needy prospectors, among them August Rische and George F. Hook, who in May 1878 discovered the body of silver ore which became the famous Little Pittsburgh Mine. On account of the grubstake, one third of the find came to Tabor. He bought up near-by prospects and they turned into rich mines. In that same year he became the first mayor of Leadville.

The silver stream that poured into his lap he spent with lavish hand. In the saloon he was prodigal; at gambling his stakes were high; no beggar went from him empty-handed. An opera house and gifts for civic and fraternal purposes were bestowed on Leadville. His bounty extended to Denver and was reflected in the Tabor Block and the magnificent Tabor Grand Opera House. His investments were important in transforming Denver from a town into a city and in determining the direction of its growth. His popularity made him lieutenant-governor of Colorado in 1879–83, and his money procured him a seat in the United States Senate (Jan. 27–Mar. 3, 1883), to complete an unexpired term. The conservative wife who had endured his poverty was put aside for a dashing young divorcée, Elizabeth (McCourt) Doe, to whom he was married secretly Sept. 30, 1882, and remarried publicly Mar. 1, 1883, with President Arthur as a guest of honor.

By now, however, as the money he put into

banks, real estate, and business buildings showed good returns, Tabor had turned to less conservative buying. Promoters were able to sell him worthless mines in Mexico and South America, timber lands in Central America, and railroads built on paper. Then the production of his mines decreased and the price of silver declined; to bolster weak holdings he mortgaged sound ones; and the crash of 1893 and the repeal of the Sherman Act left him bankrupt. Heroically but vainly he tried to recoup his losses. He was old and broken in 1898 when friends secured him appointment as postmaster of Denver, and the following year he died. One son of his first marriage and two daughters of his second survived him. His first wife had died in 1895; the second returned to Leadville and spent her last years in destitution in a shack beside the Matchless Mine; here on Mar. 7, 1935, she was found frozen to death.

[Interviews with Tabor and Mrs. Tabor (1884) and with their son Maxcy (1922), and the Dawson Scrapbooks, in the possession of the State Hist. Soc. of Colo.; *Hist. of the City of Denver* (1880); L. A. Kent, *Leadville* (1880); *Portr. and Biog. Record of the State of Colo.* (1899); W. N. Byers, *Encyc. of Biog. of Colo.* (1901); J. C. Smiley, *Semi-Centennial Hist. of the State of Colo.* (1913), vol. II, and *Hist. of Denver* (1901); *Biog. Dir. Am. Cong.* (1928); David Karsner, *Silver Dollar, the Story of the Tabors* (1932), containing much fictionized detail; H. D. Teetor, in *Mag. of Western Hist.*, Jan. 1889, pp. 268–73; G. F. Willison, *Here They Dug the Gold* (1931); L. C. Gandy, *The Tabors: A Footnote of Western Hist.* (1934); *Rocky Mountain News* (Denver), *Denver Republican, N. Y. Times,* and *Washington Post,* Apr. 11, 1899; *N. Y. Times,* Mar. 8, 1935.]   L.R.H.

TAFT, ALPHONSO (Nov. 5, 1810–May 21, 1891), judge, secretary of war, attorney-general, diplomat, was the first member of his family to achieve national prominence. Born on a farm in Townshend, Vt., he was the only child of Peter Rawson Taft and Sylvia Howard. The first American Taft was Robert, who was born prior to 1640, came from England, and was one of the Braintree men who formed Mendon, Mass., in 1667; the name may originally have been either Toft or Taffe. Efforts to trace the birthplace of Robert Taft have been unavailing, however. It has been assumed by genealogists that his forebears were Scotch or Irish. Sylvia Howard, Alphonso's mother, was also Scotch or Irish. The first of her line (then probably Hayward) settled near Braintree, Mass., in 1642. Robert Taft of Mendon was a carpenter and farmer. Alphonso was descended from his son Joseph, who was a captain in the militia. The descent continues through Peter, also in the militia, and Aaron Taft, Alphonso's grandfather, who moved from Massachusetts into Vermont and settled at Townshend in 1799. The Tafts were people of substance and education, but were not wealthy. Aaron Taft studied at Princeton. Peter Rawson Taft, although largely self-educated, was a member of the Vermont legislature and judge of the probate and county courts of Windham County.

Until he was sixteen Alphonso Taft attended local schools. Then he taught school in order to have funds to study at Amherst Academy. In 1829 he entered Yale College and was graduated with honors four years later. He had decided to study law. He taught school, again for funds, at Ellington, Conn., for two years. While studying law he held a tutorship at Yale. He was admitted to the bar of Connecticut in 1838, but did not intend to remain in New England. Vermont, he wrote his father (July 22, 1837), "is a noble state to emigrate from"; and he joined the march westward. He rejected New York as a place to practise because of its "selfishness and dishonesty," because "money is the all in all" (Alphonso Taft to Fanny Phelps, Oct. 9, 1838). Instead, he selected Cincinnati where he thought an income of from $3,000 to $5,000 was possible, while the competition was less severe.

His success at the bar was prompt; by 1854 he had more business than he could handle. Among his important cases was a suit to set aside the will of Charles McMicken whereby $500,000 had been left to the City of Cincinnati for a free university. Taft defended the will and won (165 *United States*, 465). He also successfully upheld the constitutionality of a law by which the city issued $2,000,000 in bonds to complete the Cincinnati Southern Railroad (1 *Cincinnati Superior Court Reporter,* 121; 21 *Ohio State Reports,* 14). He was greatly interested in railroad development in Ohio and the Middle West, and was connected with traction line projects in Cincinnati. In 1865 he was appointed to the superior court of Cincinnati to fill a vacancy and was elected to that bench for two terms. He resigned to resume his law practice on Jan. 1, 1872, and in March 1876 was called to Washington by President Grant to become secretary of war; after less than three months he became attorney-general. These posts did not offer great opportunities; Grant went out of office in 1877. But Taft assisted, as attorney-general, in drafting a bill which created the commission to settle the Hayes-Tilden election.

Politically Taft was a conservative. "I know not," he wrote to Fanny Phelps (Apr. 3, 1841), "what could lead you to suppose me anything else than a Whig." But he attended, in 1856, a conference at Pittsburgh which preceded the birth of the Republican party. On two occasions, in 1875 and 1879, he was an unsuccessful candidate for the Republican nomination for governor of Ohio. In 1882 he was appointed minister to Austria-Hungary by President Arthur. On July 4, 1884, he was transferred to St. Petersburg, where he remained until August 1885. His diplomatic career, which typified in the main his whole career, was not distinguished. No major questions arose for settlement. Alphonso Taft's life was marked by integrity rather than daring. He had character rather than genius.

On Aug. 29, 1841, he was married to Fanny Phelps of West Townshend, Vt. Of this marriage there were five children, of whom three died in infancy. Charles Phelps [q.v.] and Peter Rawson survived. She died on June 2, 1852. On Dec. 26, 1853, he was married to Louisa (usually called Louise) Torrey of Millbury, Mass. They had five children, of whom four survived: William Howard [q.v.], Henry Waters, Horace Dutton, and Fanny Louise. Alphonso Taft died in California on May 21, 1891.

[The sketch is based almost wholly on the Alphonso Taft and William Howard Taft papers in the Lib. of Cong. They are very extensive. L. A. Leonard, *Life of Alphonso Taft* (1920), was obviously written at the behest of the family. In the Taft papers is a sketch of Alphonso Taft in manuscript form by Adolph Richter, an old law associate. For genealogical material see *Genealogy, a Weekly Journal of American Ancestry,* Apr. 13, 1912; Mabel T. R. Washburn, *Ancestry of William Howard Taft* (1908); *Taft Family Gathering Proceedings . . . August 13, 1874* (1874). See also *Obituary Record of Grads. of Yale Univ. Deceased from June 1890 to June 1900* (1900); obituary in *Times-Star* (Cincinnati), May 22, 1891.]   H. F. P—e.

TAFT, CHARLES PHELPS (Dec. 21, 1843–Dec. 31, 1929), lawyer, publisher, philanthropist, born in Cincinnati, Ohio, was the eldest son of Alphonso Taft [q.v.] and the latter's first wife, Fanny Phelps, and a half-brother of William Howard Taft [q.v.]. He went to the Cincinnati public schools, prepared for college at Phillips Academy, Andover, and was graduated from Yale in 1864, receiving the M.A. degree from that institution in 1867. Meanwhile, he studied law at Columbia University, received the LL.B. degree in 1866, and was admitted to the bar that year. He practised for a few months with his father in Cincinnati and then went abroad for further study at Heidelberg, where he was awarded the degree of J.U.D., and at the Sorbonne. He traveled extensively through Europe; an interest in painting and sculpture, there aroused, never left him.

From 1869 to 1879 he practised law in Cincinnati. On Dec. 4, 1873, he was married to Annie Sinton, daughter of David Sinton of Cincinnati. They had two sons and two daughters. In 1879 he and his father-in-law acquired a controlling interest in the Cincinnati *Times,* which was consolidated the next year with the *Star,* another afternoon paper, as the *Times-Star.* Taft, as editor and ultimately as sole proprietor, built it into a profitable newspaper property. This, with the management of a very large estate left by his father-in-law, consumed most of his time. He was also identified with Ohio utility companies and with Cincinnati real estate, and for several years was part owner of the Chicago and Philadelphia National League baseball clubs.

During his early years as a lawyer, he codified the school laws of his state and he was joint editor of *The Cincinnati Superior Court Reporter* for the years 1870–71 and 1872–73 (vols. I, II, 1872, 1873). A lifelong Republican, he sought public office on several occasions. In 1872 he was defeated for Congress. He served one term in Congress (1895–97), without special distinction. In 1909 he became a candidate for the senatorial nomination, but withdrew in order to avoid possible embarrassment to his half-brother, who was then president-elect. Though well-known in Cincinnati and Ohio, he was usually identified to the rest of the country as the brother of William Howard Taft, whose career, indeed, he played a large part in shaping. But for his advice and financial assistance, it is virtually certain that William Howard Taft would never have become president. Unwittingly, he was a factor in the break between his brother and Theodore Roosevelt. After his election in 1908, Taft wrote Roosevelt, "you and my brother Charley made that possible." In due time, as the breach widened, friends of Roosevelt twisted this to mean that greater credit had been given Charles P. Taft, and Roosevelt resented it. The truth is that the President was very grateful for all that his brother had done, but was careful to insist that without Roosevelt's aid it would not have been possible for Charles to help.

Charles P. Taft, the most cultured member of his distinguished family, made notable contributions to the esthetic life of his native community. In May 1927 he and his wife gave to the Cincinnati Institute of Fine Arts their private art collection, their homestead, and an endowment of one million dollars for the Cincinnati Symphony Orchestra. He also made substantial gifts to the Cincinnati Law School. He died on Dec. 31, 1929.

[This sketch is based on the private papers of C. P. Taft and W. H. Taft in the Lib. of Cong. See also Cincinnati *Times-Star,* Jan. 1, 1930, for an authorized obituary; *Bulletin of Yale Univ. Obituary Record of Graduates Deceased During the Year Ending July 1, 1930* (1930); L. A. Leonard, *Life of Alphonso Taft* (1920).]   H. F. P—e.

TAFT, WILLIAM HOWARD (Sept. 15, 1857–Mar. 8, 1930), president and chief justice of the United States, was of the third generation in his family to follow the law. His grandfather, Peter Rawson Taft, was a judge of the probate and county courts of Windham County, Vt.; and his father, Alphonso Taft [q.v.], served two terms on the superior court in Cincinnati, Ohio. Though born and brought up in Cincinnati, William Howard Taft belonged to New England rather than the Middle West. Beginning with Robert Taft, his ancestors on his father's side had dwelt in Massachusetts and Vermont since the seventeenth century. His mother was Louisa Maria Torrey (she signed herself Louise), the second wife of Alphonso Taft. Her ancestor, William Torrey of Combe St. Nicholas, Somersetshire, England, emigrated to America in 1640, settled at Weymouth, Mass., and served as a clerk of the Massachusetts House of Deputies, a magistrate, and a captain of the militia. His descendant, Samuel Davenport Torrey, born at Mendon, Mass., on Apr. 14, 1779, married as his second wife Susan Holman, who was the mother of Louisa Maria Torrey (born Sept. 11, 1827).

William Howard had two half-brothers, Charles Phelps [q.v.] and Peter Rawson; there were two younger brothers, Henry Waters and Horace Dutton, and a sister, Fanny Louise. At twelve he was at the head of his class, at thirteen he entered the Woodward High School in Cincinnati, and at seventeen he was ready for Yale, where he matriculated in the fall of 1874. Taft did well at Yale. He delivered the class oration on his graduation in 1878, and was second in a class of 121. Then turning his face westward, he went back to Cincinnati where, in 1880, he received his law degree from the Cincinnati Law School and was admitted to the Ohio bar. He was a large, too good-natured young man with a tendency toward sloth which worried his father and his youngest brother, Horace. Thus he was rebuked by the former in the summer of 1879 for being at a boat race when he might have been handling a minor law suit. "As usual," wrote Horace to his mother, "he put the thing off until he had only two or three days to prepare in" (Apr. 19, 1885). This weakness for procrastination never really left Taft. He was constantly complaining, when in the White House, that he had not yet had time to prepare some speech and would have to get it in shape in too brief a time. On the other hand, the law was a rather casual mistress in the eighties. While studying, he also had time to serve as a court reporter for the *Cincinnati Commercial*.

Taft's first participation in politics also oc-

curred in 1880 when, encouraged by his father to develop himself as a speaker, he did some spell-binding for the Republican state committee. That he was to follow his father into that party was, of course, foreordained. The next year he campaigned for Miller Outcault, candidate for prosecuting attorney of Hamilton County; his reward, when Outcault was elected, was a post as assistant. This was his first public office. In 1882 he learned that politics had an unsavory side. Appointed collector of internal revenue for Cincinnati in March, he was promptly subjected to demands that he oust four or five office holders, "the best men in the service." Their removal, he wrote his father, "will cause a very big stink" and he declined to do such "dirty work" (July 24, 1882). He resigned several months later, resumed the practice of law, and toured Europe. He took an active part in the campaigns of 1884, although he shared his father's disappointment in the nomination of James G. Blaine. By now he was a partisan, although not a machine, Republican. The Mugwump movement did not penetrate Ohio to any extent. So William and Charles Taft, possibly because they knew that their father's diplomatic career would terminate unless Blaine won, did their best for the Republican nominee. In addition, William was chief supervisor of the election in Cincinnati. "You must have had a hard struggle to keep . . . the Kentuckians from voting at our polls," wrote his father from St. Petersburg (Nov. 3, 1884). Taft had an interest greater than the campaign. This was a disbarment case against Tom Campbell, a local politician-lawyer (Duffy, *post,* pp. 9–12). Taft was appointed to the staff which conducted the case against Campbell in the summer of 1884. In January 1885 he made the opening address and spoke, according to his admiring young brother, for over four hours during which "the life, the interest, the logic, the facts and the eloquence did not fail for one minute" (Horace to Alphonso Taft, Jan. 11, 1885). In May he became engaged to Helen Herron, the daughter of John W. Herron of Cincinnati, "a woman who is willing to take me as I am, for better or for worse." They were married on June 19, 1886, and in the course of time had three children, Robert Alphonso, Helen, and Charles Phelps.

Taft ascended the bench, the place beyond all others where he was happy, for the first time in March 1887. Gov. Joseph B. Foraker appointed him to the superior court of Ohio for the unfinished term of Judge Judson Harmon, who had resigned. In April 1888 he was elected for a five-year term; this was the only office save the presidency which he achieved by popular vote. Few of the youthful judge's opinions were of legal importance. Then, as later, he had a weakness for verbosity in writing. His most important case, perhaps, was *Moores & Company* vs. *The Bricklayers' Union, No. 1, W. H. Stephenson, et al.* Moores & Company, building supply dealers, boycotted by the union, had been awarded $2,250 damages by a jury in the lower court. Taft wrote an exhaustive opinion in which he declared the boycott illegal and confirmed the damage award (*Weekly Law Bulletin and Ohio Law Journal*, Jan. 20, 1890). The ruling attracted wide attention and was one of the factors which caused labor so bitterly to oppose him in later years.

The star of Taft was rising. It was a placid star, not a comet, against the judicial and political sky. In 1889, although but thirty-two, he was discussed for associate justice of the Supreme Court, but refused to share "the very roseate view" of those who thought he might be appointed. "My chances of going to the moon and of donning a silk gown at the hands of President Harrison," he wrote his father, "are about equal" (Aug. 24, 1889). He received, instead, a post as solicitor-general at Harrison's hands and the stage of his activity was enlarged to include Washington, D. C., where he assumed office on Feb. 4, 1890. Apprehensive about his ability, he wrote his father that he had had no experience in the federal statutes, and that the prospect was "rather overwhelming." But he did well. Within a year he could report that he had argued eighteen cases in the Supreme Court and won fifteen (to Alphonso Taft, Feb. 9, 1891). In March 1891 Congress created a new judgeship for each circuit of the federal circuit court and Taft was mentioned for an appointment to the sixth, which covered Kentucky, Ohio, Michigan, and Tennessee. Mrs. Taft was opposed. "If you get your heart's desire," she wrote him that summer, "it will put an end to all your opportunities ... of being thrown with big-wigs" (July 18, 1891). But Taft had small taste for big-wigs. Clearly, he was less ambitious than other members of the family. He did not mind being poor, he said, for people with small incomes were as happy as those with fortunes. For eight years, from Mar. 17, 1892, he served on the circuit court.

For a man of judicial tastes, who was also becoming a profound legal scholar, the appointment was ideal. Noting that there was "only one higher judicial position in the country," Taft continued to keep an eye on the Supreme Court. Meanwhile, the work was absorbing.

Many decisions related to labor, and Taft was to be damned for these in 1908 and 1912. The man and the jurist must be kept distinct in any attempt accurately to portray Taft's views on labor. A large element of conservative public opinion was exceedingly alarmed over the state of the nation in 1892. The Haymarket bombing of 1886 was still all too vivid. The Homestead riots were in a few months to make crimson the muddy Ohio River. Financial panic and breadlines were to follow in a year. That Taft, as a private citizen, shared the alarm of the respectable people is clear. In July 1894 the Pullman strike was raging in Chicago. "It will be necessary for the military to kill some of the mob before the trouble can be stayed," he wrote his wife. "They have only killed six ... as yet. This is hardly enough to make an impression" (July 8, 1894).

His first major labor case as circuit judge was when P. M. Arthur, grand chief of the Brotherhood of Locomotive Engineers, ruled that the members of the organization would refuse to handle freight of the Toledo, Ann Arbor & North Michigan Railway, which had declined to raise wages. They were to refuse, that is, even if they worked only on connecting lines. Taft upheld a temporary injunction previously issued by himself against this order and was criticized, unjustly, on the mistaken theory that he had ruled against strikes (54 *Federal Reporter*, 730; Duffy, pp. 35–36). In the case of Frank M. Phelan, a lieutenant of Eugene Debs, he made his viewpoint clear. Phelan, during the Pullman strike, urged the employees of the Cincinnati Southern Railroad, in receivership and therefore under the jurisdiction of the federal court, to cease work. He was enjoined. When he violated the injunction he was sentenced by Taft to six months' imprisonment (62 *Federal Reporter*, 803). "I shall find him ... guilty on [*sic*] conspiring unlawfully to tie up the road by a boycott" (W. H. Taft to Helen Herron Taft, July 11, 1894). The decision was handed down on July 13, 1894. At the same moment when, as a private citizen, Taft was voicing approval of Chicago bloodshed he declared, as a judge, that the employees of the Cincinnati Southern had a right to organize, join a union, conspire to strike, and conduct a strike. "They have labor to sell," he said. "If they stand together, they are often able ... to command better prices ... than when dealing singly with rich employers" (62 *Federal Reporter*, 817). But he felt that the employees of the Cincinnati Southern had, in this instance, no grievance. Phelan was part of a combination which was illegal. The boycott he sought was illegal (Duffy, pp. 39–45). Actually, Taft's position on the right of labor to organize was definitely in advance of the existing legal opinion of the day. He gave further evidence of his sympathy for the workingman in his decision (on which he was reversed by the Supreme Court) that an employer could not relieve himself from negligence in accident cases by requiring employees to agree to non-liability (79 *Federal Reporter*, 561; see also 176 *United States*, 498). In another case (96 *Federal Reporter*, 298) he ruled that employers could not plead contributory negligence on the part of employees where statutory safety provisions had been violated. While on the circuit bench, Taft also strengthened the Sherman anti-trust law. In 1898 he decided, in the Addyston Pipe Case, that a combination of manufacturers of cast-iron pipe was in restraint of trade and issued an injunction (85 *Federal Reporter*, 271; Duffy, pp. 49–51).

In 1899 Taft was asked by the "liberal element" of the Yale Corporation to consider election to the presidency of the university (H. W. Taft to W. H. Taft, Jan. 14, 1899). He answered that "two insuperable objections" made this impossible. The first was that he was a Unitarian and this would "shock the conservative element" of the alumni. The second was that he did not feel qualified for the post (W. H. Taft to H. W. Taft, Jan. 21, 1899). A far different assignment lay ahead. On Mar. 15, 1900, he resigned from the bench, at the instance of President McKinley, to become president of the Philippine Commission. For the first time he was to be an executive and administrator. The reputation he earned did much to advance him toward the presidency. Emotionally, he grew very much attached to the little brown inhabitants of the Philippine Islands and their welfare always remained close to his heart.

On his arrival early in June 1900, Taft concluded that "the back of the rebellion" was broken and that the first immediate necessity was to end military rule in the islands. He was not a sentimentalist; the Filipinos who persisted in lawlessness were, when caught, to be "either hung or banished in Guam" (W. H. Taft to B. I. Wheeler, Oct. 17, 1900). Executions were not necessary. Education, pacification of still rebellious natives, and settlement of the perplexing issue of the friars' lands were the immediate objectives of the Philippine Commission. Taft directed his efforts to these as soon as he had relegated the military command of the islands to a secondary position. The Philippines, under Spain, had to a large extent been ruled by friars.

That they had abused their authority was, when Taft arrived, a firm conviction of the Filipinos. Many of the friars had been slain in the insurrections prior to the war with Spain. Their lands had been confiscated by the Philippine Congress. Taft concluded that this was "a political and not a religious question" (W. H. Taft to J. J. Hooker, Jan. 7, 1901). Most of the surviving friars had fled the islands and Taft's conviction was that the Roman Catholic hierarchy must not insist on their return. A specific part of the problem was settlement for the 400,000 acres of land owned by the friars and, until the insurrection, rented to the natives. Taft desired to purchase these lands and sell them to the natives at fair prices (Duffy, p. 109). After prolonged negotiations, which included a journey to Rome and conferences, in June 1902, with Pope Leo XIII, an agreement was reached. Ultimately, the United States paid $7,200,000 for the friars' lands. Meanwhile, in July 1901, Taft had been made civil governor of the islands. Until January 1904, when President Roosevelt called him back to become secretary of war, he devoted himself with great energy to improving the economic status of the Philippines, to the building of roads and harbors, toward establishing limited self-government.

On two occasions while Taft was in the Philippines he was offered an appointment to the Supreme Court by President Roosevelt. He declined because he felt that his task had not been completed. He accepted the post of secretary of war on the ground that he could continue his supervision of the affairs of the islands. But this was only part of his work. Taking office on Feb. 1, 1904, he soon became a close adviser to the President. Roosevelt and Taft made an excellent team; the latter's easy-going conservatism counteracted the President's impulsive qualities. Taft became, in effect, the "trouble shooter" of the administration. He took on his too-broad shoulders the task of starting actual construction of the Panama Canal and hurried to the Canal Zone for that purpose. When Roosevelt left Washington for a vacation he made his secretary of war, to all purposes, secretary of state as well. Everything was all right, the President said, with Taft "sitting on the lid." In September 1906, Taft was rushed to Cuba to effect peace when a revolution threatened. Clearly, Taft had been revealing unusual talents as an administrator and even more as a conciliator. Soon after Roosevelt's declaration in 1904 that he would not run again, the name of Taft as a successor came to the front. His private letters show that he had no taste for the office, that he believed himself disqualified because of his labor decisions when on the bench. But Mrs. Taft and his brothers desired that he stand for the nomination (Pringle, p. 498). His private letters of protest grew weaker as 1905 advanced. Late in 1907 he received definite word that he was the chosen candidate of the President. He ran as Roosevelt's man. He was elected in November 1908 over Bryan by an electoral vote of 321 to 162 and a popular plurality of more than a million. He took office in March 1909. He was troubled, bothered, and harassed almost from the start.

With Roosevelt's cordial assent, Taft chose his own cabinet. Secretary of State Philander C. Knox, Attorney-General George W. Wickersham, and, to a degree, Charles Nagel, secretary of commerce and labor, were the members on whom Taft was to lean most. His advisory board was not distinguished for its strength. Like most such bodies, it represented compromise. It included no member of the insurgent wing of the Republican party and to that degree was reactionary. But it was not a "Wall Street" cabinet, either. Wickersham was to annoy the financial interests in New York by his trust prosecutions. Taft began his presidency with a divided party, although technically he had both houses of Congress behind him. His fatal error of political thought, as distinct from specific mistakes, was his belief that the Republican party could be continued in power without giving ground to its more liberal wing. At the start and on the specific advice of Roosevelt, he declined to join in the fight of the House insurgents on the autocratic powers of Speaker Joseph G. Cannon (W. H. Taft to W. A. White, Mar. 12, 1909). His real difficulty, of course, was that he did not possess his predecessor's great genius for guiding, sometimes confusing, public opinion. His honesty of purpose was stolid and plodding. He could not magnify minor issues. "There is no use trying to be William Howard Taft with Roosevelt's ways," he said, ". . . our ways are different" (Butt, *post*, I, 236). Roosevelt had zealously refrained from attempting tariff revision, thus avoiding an issue fraught with death to presidents. Taft promptly plunged into it.

Tariff revision was part of the general demand, more vocal in the Middle West and the West than in the East, for a more equal distribution of wealth. Roosevelt had stilled the outcry only partially. Now, in 1909, a wide segment of public opinion insisted that tariff revision downward would further control the trusts. So Taft called a special session of Congress. The House schedules, while not revolutionary, marked real reductions. But the Senate, with Nelson W. Aldrich as the extreme high-tariff advocate, amended the bill almost beyond recognition. Taft effected many compromises and said, in a detailed explanatory letter of June 27, 1909, to his brother Horace, that "the Payne bill was a genuine effort in the right direction." "I am not a high-tariff man; I am a low-tariff man," he insisted (W. H. Taft to W. D. Foulke, July 15, 1909). Shortly afterward he wrote his wife that he would either beat the bill or get what he wanted. After the Payne-Aldrich bill was passed, the President felt that it was a distinct step forward, "the best bill that the party has ever passed" (W. H. Taft to R. M. Wanamaker, Nov. 24, 1909). This was not wholly untrue; the Payne-Aldrich act was of slight economic importance, but it did mark a recession of the Republican urge toward higher and higher duties. Taft agreed that he "could make a lot of cheap popularity by vetoing the bill" (W. H. Taft to Horace Taft, June 27, 1910). Instead, he made himself its defender, praised it too lavishly, and so reaped the unpopularity which the act itself received.

"I have had a hard time . . . I have been conscientiously trying to carry out your policies but my method of doing so has not worked smoothly," wrote Taft to Roosevelt as the latter prepared to return from his African jaunt (May 26, 1910). Taft's cup of woe was brimming. On the one hand, in his own party, he faced such insurgents as Senators LaFollette, Cummins, Dolliver, Bristow, Borah, Clapp, and Beveridge. On the other, he was threatened by the growing strength of the Democratic party, which was to take over the House in November 1910, and the imponderable strength of Woodrow Wilson as a possible Democratic nominee. Worse than all was the friction with Roosevelt, to whom the insurgents were appealing and who disapproved of Taft's action in dismissing Gifford Pinchot because of his charges against the secretary of the interior, Richard A. Ballinger [q.v.]. Yet there were many accomplishments to which Taft might have pointed with pride had he been more of a political leader and less judicial. By means of the Tariff Board he started the first scientific investigation of rates. He created the postal savings system. He was a sincere friend of conservation, despite subsequent accusations from the Progressives. He negotiated an agreement with Canada which meant relatively free trade between that country and the United States. He then secured ratification by Congress only to have Canada, at first enthusiastic for the measure, ultimately reject it. Deeply interested in international peace, he attempted to arrange treaties of arbitration with Great Britain and France. They were so amended by the Senate that Taft discontinued the effort to secure senatorial concurrence. Under Attorney-General Wickersham a series of vigorous prosecutions against trusts were started; as a "trust-buster" President Taft was, in fact, more active than Roosevelt. Among his other accomplishments were efforts toward economy and efficiency in government, the first step toward a federal budget; the appointment of a commission to investigate the question of additional safety and workmen's compensation legislation; the admission of New Mexico and Arizona as states.

The Roosevelt-Taft "break," so-called, was inevitable from the time that Taft's predecessor returned from Europe in the summer of 1910. But there is no specific incident from which it can be dated. In general, it was due to the complete antithesis between the two men. Taft believed in a government of laws, not of men. Roosevelt held the law lightly; he believed in a government of men or, more accurately, of a single man—himself. Roosevelt was a consummate politician, in contrast to Taft. He enjoyed the presidency. Taft's four years in the White House were probably the unhappiest of his life. He was not such a misfit as Roosevelt came to believe, but he had no taste for politics. His private letters reveal that he was discouraged early in his administration and did not believe he would be reëlected. On Sept. 6, 1911, he confessed to his brother Charles: "I am not very happy in this renomination and reelection business. I have to set my teeth and go through with it. . . . But I shall be willing to retire and let another take the burden." He grew more conservative as the years passed, leaning more and more on such men as Aldrich. Roosevelt, in evolving his New Nationalism, grew more radical. Finally, he called for the initiative and referendum and for the recall of judicial decisions. The last, in particular, made Taft recoil. The two men drifted; Taft toward the nomination which he had to accept from his party whether he wanted it or not, and Roosevelt toward a contest for that nomination. At the Republican National Convention in Chicago in June 1912, Taft was renominated by routine steam-roller methods and was accused by Roosevelt of having "stolen" the convention. Roosevelt organized the Bull Moose Party and the campaign, the most bitter since that of 1876, began. Taft's defeat was inevitable. "As a leader, I had to have confidence and hope, but in my heart I have long been making plans for my future," he wrote when it was over (W. H. Taft to C. H. Clark, Nov. 9, 1912). He received only 8 electoral votes against 88 for Roosevelt and 435 for Wilson. He was condemned by contemporary historians as one of the most lamentable of White House failures, a greater failure even than Grant. The appraisal was not sound. Taft would under no conditions have been a great president, but the political situation between 1909 and 1913 was such that no Republican, even Roosevelt, could have been successful. Taft was unique in that he did not want the office and surrendered it gladly. "Politics makes me sick" is a phrase which beats like a minor refrain through his private letters when he was president. The office brought out all his worst traits: vacillation, irritability, a complete inability to lead. It obscured very real gifts: an excellent judicial mind, an integrity which was never clouded, great talent as an administrator, a wide and broad sympathy for human problems.

He retired in March 1913 to the campus of his beloved Yale as Kent Professor of Constitutional Law. During the World War he served as joint-chairman of the National War Labor Board. Then, on June 30, 1921, President Harding gratified his heart's desire by naming him chief justice of the United States. It is not impossible that his work as administrator of the nation's highest court was more important than his decisions. He found himself, in 1921, on a bench which was badly divided; out of 180 opinions handed down in 1921–22, dissents were expressed in forty-five cases—exactly one-fourth of the total. Moreover, the Court was behind in its work. Taft's private letters disclose his concern, in the matter of new appointments to the Supreme Court, that the number of dissents be cut down. Regarding one candidate he wrote that the jurist "is rather an off horse and dissents a good deal" (W. H. Taft to C. D. Hilles, Dec. 1, 1922). "It would be too bad," he continued, "if we had another on the bench who would herd with Brandeis . . . as Brandeis is usually against the Court." The Chief Justice, in this instance, was not objecting to the liberal views of Associate Justice Brandeis, but to the frequency of his dissents, whether liberal or conservative. This is not an implication, on the other hand, that Taft was not, on the whole, conservative in his interpretation of the law.

As president he had been "to a unique degree . . . interested in the effective working of the judicial machinery and conversant with the details of judicial administration" (see Frankfurter and Landis, *post,* pp. 156–58). As chief justice he immediately interested himself in finding some relief from the mass of litigation which was swamping the Supreme Court and the lower federal courts. His first accomplishment was authorization by Congress in 1922 for the creation of a conference of senior circuit judges, with the chief justice as its head. This introduced the first degree of coordination into the federal judicial system (*Ibid.*, pp. 241–54). Even more important was his part in effecting the passage of the act of Feb. 13, 1925. This was known as the Judges' Bill and, stripped of technicalities, it gave the Supreme Court a greatly increased discretion over the cases which came before it. It terminated certain classes of appeals as matters of right and made them reviewable only through the discretionary writ of certiorari. The Supreme Court now had time to give prompt action on questions of constitutionality and other cases of national significance (*Ibid.*, pp. 261–86). When he retired in February 1930, the business of the court was practically current.

The reputation of Taft for conservatism came, in part, from the so-called Child Labor Case and the Coronado Coal Company Case. The former (*Bailey* vs. *Drexel Furniture Co.*; 259 *United States*, 20) resulted from an attempt of Congress to control child labor by the imposition of a tax imposed on interstate products manufactured through its aid. This, Taft wrote, was an infringement on the rights of the states and not a proper use of the power to tax; "to give such magic to the word 'tax,'" he held, "would be to break down all constitutional limitation of the powers of Congress and completely wipe out the sovereignty of the States." The Coronado case (*United Mine Workers of America* vs. *Coronado Coal Co.*; 259 *United States*, 344) grew out of a strike in the Prairie Creek field in Arkansas in 1914. Property of the Coronado Coal Company was destroyed and action for damages against the United Mine Workers had resulted in a verdict for the company in a lower court. Taft wrote the opinion, denying federal jurisdiction since coal-mining was not interstate commerce, but holding that the union, even though unincorporated, could be sued under the antitrust laws; its funds, accumulated for conducting strikes, were subject to execution for unlawful acts committed during a strike. "The circumstances are such," said he, "as to awaken regret that, in our view of the federal jurisdiction, we can not affirm the judgment" (259 *United States*, 413).

The most important dissent by Taft was against the majority opinion of Justice Sutherland invalidating the law of 1918 which fixed a minimum wage for women in the District of Columbia (*Adkins* vs. *Children's Hospital*; 261 *United States*, 525). The majority of the Court held that the act did not deal with any business charged with the public interest or with any temporary emergency. But the Chief Justice held that a minimum wage law for women was constitutional because sweatshop wages did just as much to impair their health and morals as did long hours (see C. E. Hughes, *The Supreme Court of the United States*, 1928, pp. 209–10). Taft did not fulfill, however, this promise of leading the Court toward an increasingly liberal view in social and labor questions. It is clear that his duties as administrative officer of the Court gave him, as a general thing, no desire to dissent.

In so far as Taft sanctioned the control of commerce and industry he believed, his decisions show, that supervision by the federal government was superior to that by the states. He agreed with the Court in nullifying the Kansas law creating a court of industrial relations, on the ground that the industries it proposed to control —and the act gave extraordinary powers to the court of industrial relations—were not affected with the public interest. It had never been supposed, he said "that the business of the butcher or the baker, the tailor, the woodchopper . . . was clothed with such a public interest that the price of his product or his wages could be fixed by State regulation" (Hughes, pp. 211, 221–22). But he was, in contrast, an advocate of broad federal powers under the commerce clause of the Constitution. The Supreme Court had already refused to limit the power of Congress; in 1905 Associate Justice Holmes had held that the packers were engaged in interstate commerce even though their actual business might be limited to the stockyards of Chicago. Taft extended this doctrine when he wrote the opinion upholding the stockyards act (*Stafford* vs. *Wallace*; 258 *United States*, 495). The packing and stockyards industry, he said, was national in scope and susceptible to federal regulation even to the point of letting the secretary of agriculture fix brokers' prices. Several other cases might be cited in which he further amplified this view. In the case of *Myers* vs. *United States* (272 *United States*, 52), the Supreme Court settled an ancient controversy by sustaining the presidential power to remove executive officers. Taft's opinion, it has been said, "will probably rank as one of his most important contributions to constitutional law" (*Proceedings of the Bar and Officers of the Supreme Court of the United States in Memory of William Howard Taft*, 1931, p. 37).

Yet Taft, a coordinator and conciliator all of his life rather than an advocate, was not a leader of judicial thought in the sense that Justice Holmes was a leader—or Justice Brandeis or Cardozo. The new Supreme Court building will remain as a permanent monument to his constructive talents; he was largely responsible for the congressional act under which it was built. On Feb. 3, 1930, bad health, due chiefly to heart disease, forced his retirement from the bench. He died in Washington on Mar. 8, 1930, and was buried in the Arlington National Cemetery.

Taft's published writings, outside of his legal opinions, were not important. Most of them were revised from public lectures. Among them might be mentioned: *Popular Government* (1913); *The Anti-Trust Act and the Supreme Court* (1914); *Ethics in Service* (1915); *Our Chief Magistrate and His Powers* (1916). Taft was not the type who would contribute very much to contemporary thought by his pen. He blazed few new trails, even in the law. He was thorough rather than original in his mental processes. The final decade of his life, as chief justice, was beyond any doubt the happiest. During it he was doing the work he loved. He was filling the post to which he had always aspired. Before he died, it is a safe assumption, his quadrennium in the presidency had faded like an evil dream into those mists which memory no longer penetrates.

[This sketch is based very largely on the William Howard Taft papers at the Lib. of Cong., which are open to students under certain restrictions. A critical biography is under preparation by Henry F. Pringle who has had free access to them. For Taft's decisions as superior court judge of Ohio see the files of *The Weekly Law Bulletin and Ohio Law Journal* (1887–1890). An adequate analysis of his services on the U. S. Circuit is in H. S. Duffy, *William Howard Taft* (1930); the cases can be found in *Federal Reporter*, vols. LI–CI. The Taft papers are voluminous for his periods as governor of the Philippine Islands, secretary of war, and president. They contain much source material on the campaign of 1912. His services in the reorganization of the Supreme Court are described in Felix Frankfurter and J. M. Landis, *The Business of the Supreme Court* (1928). His labor decisions are discussed by A. T. Mason, in *Univ. of Pa. Law Review*, March 1930. Secondary sources of value include: A. W. Butt, *Taft and Roosevelt: The Intimate Letters of Archie Butt* (2 vols., 1930); H. H. Kohlsaat, *From McKinley to Harding* (1923); Mrs. W. H. Taft, *Recollections of Full Years* (1914); C. W. Thompson, *Presidents I've Known and Two Near Presidents* (1929); W. A. White, *Masks in a Pageant* (1928); N. W. Stephenson, *Nelson W. Aldrich, A Leader in American Politics* (1930); H. L. Stoddard, *As I Knew Them* (1927); Samuel Gompers, *Seventy Years of Life and Labor* (2 vols., 1925); L. White Busbey, *Uncle Joe Cannon* (1927); C. M. Depew, *My Memories of Eighty Years* (1922); J. B. Foraker, *Notes of a Busy Life* (2 vols., 1916); *La Follette's Autobiography* (1913); T. B. Mott, *Myron T. Herrick, Friend of France* (1929); *Harvey W. Wiley, An Autobiography* (1930); H. F. Pringle, *Theodore Roosevelt, A Biography* (1931). For genealogy and other personal details, see Mabel T. R. Washburn, *Ancestry of William Howard*

Taft (1908); "The Ancestry of William Howard Taft," in *Genealogy*, Apr. 13, 1912; *Quarter-Centenary Record of the Class of 1878, Yale Univ.* (1905); *Bulletin of Yale Univ. Obituary Record* (1930), pp. 69–72.]
H. F. P—e.

TAGGART, THOMAS (Nov. 17, 1856–Mar. 6, 1929), politician, hotel proprietor, banker, the son of Thomas and Martha (Kingsbury) Taggart, was born in County Monaghan, Ireland, emigrated with his parents to the United States in 1861, and spent his childhood in Xenia, Ohio, where his father worked on a railroad. Forced by poverty at the age of twelve to find employment in a railroad restaurant, he studied at night and finally reached high school. Cleanliness, cordiality, and memory for names and tastes earned him a transfer to a restaurant in Garrett, Ind., in 1874 and in 1877 to one in Indianapolis.

Here he shortly became active in politics, starting as a precinct committeeman and later becoming a ward leader. From 1886 to 1894 he filled the lucrative office of auditor in Marion County. As chairman of the Democratic county committee he managed, in 1888, a highly successful campaign that brought him in 1892 the chairmanship of the state committee. During the years 1895–1901 he ably served three terms as mayor of Indianapolis, stressing governmental economy and reasonable enforcement of liquor laws and adding notably to the park system. In 1904 he supported the presidential candidacy of Alton B. Parker [*q.v.*] and as chairman of the Democratic National Committee directed the campaign. He remained a national committeeman until 1916. In 1908 he failed to control the Democratic state convention but at the national convention secured the nomination of John Worth Kern [*q.v.*] for the vice-presidency. Two years later, when the state convention was considering whom to select as candidate for the United States Senate nomination, Taggart withdrew in Kern's favor. In 1912 he placed Samuel M. Ralston [*q.v.*] in the governor's chair and, according to Chairman McCombs, played a vital part in nominating Woodrow Wilson.

During the years following 1912 Taggart exerted great political influence in Indiana, conferring frequently with the governor and Democratic members of the legislature and of Congress. At the death of Senator Benjamin F. Shively, in 1916, Governor Ralston appointed Taggart United States senator, in which capacity he served from Mar. 20 to Nov. 7. Despite newspaper ridicule, he displayed serious interest in Senate business and dealt some telling blows at "pork-barrel" legislation, but was defeated at the election to fill the unexpired term. In 1920 he again encountered defeat but in 1922 brought about the election of his friend Ralston. Taggart's greatest political disappointment occurred at the Democratic National Convention of 1924 when, after months of labor on his part and with what he considered victory within grasp Ralston withdrew as a candidate for the presidential nomination.

Taggart showed exceptional ability in the operation of the Grand and the Denison hotels in Indianapolis and in the management of the large resort hotel at French Lick. He also interested himself in mining and banking, serving as vice-president of the Fletcher-American Company and as chairman of the board of directors of the Fletcher-American National Bank—at the time one of the largest banks in Indiana. Endowed with remarkable vitality, unusually attractive personal characteristics, great capacity as an organizer, a keen sense of humor, genuine fondness for people, and contempt for vindictiveness, he attained more than average success in both political and business affairs. Inclined to be silent himself, he had little regard for oratory. He emphasized practical results, at times perhaps, with ruthlessness. His deep blue eyes, blonde complexion, conservative dress, and erect carriage made him physically distinctive. He was a crack shot, a good horseman, and a race-track enthusiast, with his own stables. On June 17, 1877, he married Eva D. Bryant of Garrett, Ind., and he was the father of six children, five of whom survived him. He died in Indianapolis.

[J. B. Stoll, *Hist. of the Ind. Democracy, 1816–1916* (1917); *Biog. Dir. Am. Cong.* (1928); *Who's Who in America*, 1928–29; *Outlook*, Mar. 29, 1916; files of the *Indianapolis News*; obituary in *Indianapolis Star*, Mar. 7, 1929; information as to certain facts from Miss Lucy Taggart.]   H. Z.

TAGLIABUE, GIUSEPPE (Aug. 10, 1812–May 7, 1878), inventor, instrument maker, was born in Como, Italy, the son of Caesar Tagliabue, founder of the great scientific instrument business of London, and grandson of Caesar Tagliabue of Como, Italy, who was one of the first persons in the world to make thermometers in quantity. Caesar Tagliabue, the second, was well established in London when his son Giuseppe was born and the latter, after obtaining an ordinary education and learning cabinet making in Italy, entered his father's establishment and there acquired the trade of thermometer maker. Upon completing his apprenticeship in 1829, Tagliabue, although only seventeen years old, left London and went to Rio de Janeiro to ply his trade. After spending two years there without experiencing any material benefit, he emigrated to New York with all his worldly possessions, which consisted of a bellows, a bundle of glass tubing, a pan of tallow, and less than five dollars.

Renting a single room on Water Street directly back of 298 Pearl Street, he began making and selling thermometers. His business soon outgrew these limited quarters and he acquired a four-story house at 298 Pearl Street, which not only served as his store and workshop but for a time was his residence as well. For upwards of forty-seven years he carried on his trade, becoming one of the most prominent and successful instrument makers of the United States. To him came Kane and Hall, the Arctic explorers; Bache and Hilgard of the United States Coast and Geodetic Survey; Borden, the inventor of the process of condensing milk; and Havemeyer, the sugar refiner—all to secure the delicate instruments so necessary to their several undertakings. Besides his thermometers he made a great variety of hydrometers, including original forms and new adaptations to meet the changing manufacturing requirements. Many of the instruments used by the Geodetic Survey were constructed by Tagliabue and his hydrometer for the proving of whiskey was officially adopted by the United States revenue bureau. He was always enthusiastic about his work and gave considerably more attention to the excellence of his instruments than to the money he received. Between 1859 and 1871 he found time to perfect a few instruments of original design, which he had patented. These included a mercurial barometer; an apparatus for testing iron and coal; an instrument to determine the amount of water in a barrel of oil; a number of hydrometers; and an apparatus for determining the proof spirits in fermented mash. These inventions were ever a source of loving pride to him and were profitable as well. He was married twice; his second wife was Adelaide Arniboldi of New York City, who with their six children survived him. He died at his home in Mount Vernon, N. Y.

[Correspondence with C. J. Tagliabue Manufacturing Company; *N. Y. Daily Tribune*, May 8, 1878; Patent Office records.]   C. W. M—n.

TAIT, ARTHUR FITZWILLIAM (Aug. 5, 1819–Apr. 28, 1905), landscape and animal painter, was born at Livesey Hall, near Liverpool, England. After attending a country school at Lancaster, at the age of twelve he went to work in Agnew's picture store, Manchester. There he devoted himself to studying from casts at the Royal Manchester Institution and had an opportunity to see many of the best English pictures of the period. In art he was almost entirely self-taught. In 1850 he emigrated to the United States and settled in New York. He was made a member of the National Academy of Design in 1858, and was a member of the Artists' Fund Society and the Lotos Club. He made most of his studies from nature in the Adirondacks and elsewhere during the summer months, and in 1874 spent four months in Europe. He contributed numerous paintings to the exhibitions of the National Academy, among other things "A Duck and her Young" (1868), "Ruffed Grouse" (1869), "Woodcock Shooting" and "The Halt on the Carry" (1871), "Racquette Lake" (1873), and "Lake Trout" (1878). He was represented at the Centennial Exhibition, Philadelphia (1876), by "The Portage—Waiting for the Boats," painted in conjunction with James MacDougal Hart [q.v.] His "Quail and Young," painted in 1856, is in the permanent collection of the Corcoran Gallery of Art, Washington, D. C. His "The Happy Family," dated 1855, was in the S. B. Fales collection, which was sold at auction in New York, 1881. His picture of a Gordon setter belongs to the Charles Stewart Smith collection. Many of his pictures of animals and birds were lithographed and widely circulated. He was a skilful academic painter who had a high reputation in his day in a community which had no very close acquaintance with the best of art at home or abroad, but his work shows little trace either of genius or of imagination. He died at his home in Yonkers, N. Y., survived by his wife and two sons.

[*Who's Who in America*, 1903–05; J. D. Champlin and C. C. Perkins, *Cyc. of Painters and Paintings* (4 vols., 1886–87); Clara E. Clement and Laurence Hutton, *Artists of the Nineteenth Century* (1879); cats. of the S. B. Fales coll. (1881), of the Corcoran Gallery of Art, Washington, D. C., of the Nat. Acad. Exhibition, N. Y., 1894; obituaries in *Am. Art. Ann.*, 1905–06, and *N. Y. Times*, Apr. 29, 1905.] W. H. D.

TAIT, CHARLES (Feb. 1, 1768–Oct. 7, 1835), jurist, United States senator, and scholar, the son of James and Rebecca (Hudson) Tait and cousin of Henry Clay, was born in Louisa County, Va. The Taits, who were of Scotch ancestry, had emigrated to Virginia during the seventeenth century. James, a planter of some means, settled in Elbert County, Ga., in 1783. Charles received some schooling in Virginia and in 1786–87 attended Wilkes Academy, Washington, Ga. About this time he was thrown from a horse, receiving an injury to his leg which necessitated its amputation. Early in 1788 he entered Cokesbury College, Abingdon, Md., where in September he was made an instructor. He left Cokesbury in 1794, and, having read law while teaching, was admitted to the bar at Elberton, Ga., in February 1795. A few weeks later he was made rector of Richmond Academy, Au-

gusta, Ga., where William H. Crawford [q.v.] became his associate.

He began the practice of law at Lexington, Ga., in 1798, Crawford joining him as partner the following year. Both were soon drawn into the political feud which grew out of the Yazoo land frauds. Tait became a prominent figure in the faction known successively as the Jackson, Crawford, and Troup party, the leaders of which had opposed the Yazoo sales, and which embraced the planter, professional, and Virginian elements in the state. The opposing faction was led by John Clark [q.v.]. Tait's friendship for Crawford and his somewhat moody and sensitive nature involved him in a number of controversies with Clark men. In 1802, after considerable provocation, he challenged Peter Lawrence Van Allen. In the meantime, however, Van Allen insulted Crawford, Tait's second, who killed him in a duel. A challenge to John M. Dooly the next year did not result in a duel. From 1803 to 1809 Tait served as judge of the superior court for the western district of Georgia. He incurred the special enmity of Clark through the performance of official duties and in 1806 Clark memorialized the Georgia legislature, asking that Tait be impeached for official misconduct. Although Tait was exonerated, Clark later attacked him in pamphlets and in 1807 assaulted him with a horsewhip.

In 1809 he was elected to the United States Senate to fill the vacancy resulting from the resignation of John Milledge [q.v.], a position which he held by reëlection until Mar. 3, 1819. His most conspicuous public service was rendered through untiring efforts in behalf of the navy during that critical period. Made a member of the Senate committee on naval affairs in 1812, he served as chairman from 1814 to 1818, in which capacity he secured an appropriation of $1,000,000 for the Navy. He aided in the formation of Alabama as a separate territory and in securing its admission to the Union. His Admission Bill (3 *U. S. Statutes at Large*, 489–92) made provision for a state university comparable with the best institutions of the country. Having offended his constituents by contending that he should be allowed a salary as representative, and having acquired a fortune through planting, he removed in 1819 to Claiborne, Monroe County, Ala. In May 1820 President Monroe appointed him first federal judge of the District of Alabama. Retiring in 1826, he devoted himself to planting on land he owned in Wilcox County and to scientific study. In 1828 he declined a mission to Great Britain (Tompkins, *post*, p. 29). Soon after settling in Alabama

Tait made known to the scientific world the "Claiborne beds," one of the notable Eocene deposits of the country (Lea, *post*, pp. 27–28). His scientific acquirements won for him membership in the American Philosophical Society in 1827 and in 1832 he was elected a corresponding member of the Academy of Natural Sciences of Philadelphia. He was twice married: first, Jan. 3, 1790, to Mrs. Anne (Lucas) Simpson, of Baltimore; second, in 1822, to Mrs. Sarah (Williamson) Griffin of Georgia. He was survived by one son.

[The Tait Papers, comprising letters and plantation jottings, are in the Ala. department of archives at Montgomery; for published sources, see Alma Cole Tompkins, *Charles Tait* (1910), in the Ala. Polytechnic Inst. Hist. Series, short but reliable; J. E. D. Shipp, *Giant Days, or the Life and Times of Wm. H. Crawford* (1909); U. B. Phillips, *Life and Labor in the Old South* (1929); Willis Brewer, *Ala.: Her Hist., Resources, War Record, and Pub. Men* (1872); Isaac Lea, *Contributions to Geology* (1833); T. M. Owen, *Hist. of Ala. and Dict. of Ala. Biog.* (1921); *Biog. Dir. Am. Cong.* (1928); P. A. Brannon, "Jour. of James A. Tait for the Year 1813," *Ga. Hist. Quart.*, Sept. 1924; John Clark, *Considerations on the Purity of the Principles of William H. Crawford . . . in Connexion with that of Charles Tait* (1823); *Mobile Daily Commercial Register and Patriot*, Oct. 16, 1835.] H. D. F.

TAKAMINE, JOKICHI (Nov. 3, 1854–July 22, 1922), chemist, industrial leader, was born in Takaoka, Japan, the son of Seichi and Yukiko Takamine. His father was a physician, as were many of his ancestors, and his early years were spent in an environment of scientific culture and the tradition of the Samurai. His father, with admirable foresight, sent him, at the age of twelve, to Osaka that his studies might there include the English language. Later he pursued his studies in Kyoto and Tokio and was graduated at government expense from the college of science and engineering of the University of Tokio in 1879. His high scholarship caused him to be selected as one of twelve to be sent by the Japanese government for post-graduate study at Glasgow University and Anderson's College, 1879–81. During his summer vacations he visited various industrial plants to observe the manufacturing of soda and fertilizers. Returning to Japan in 1883, he entered the department of agriculture and commerce where his work was guided by his belief that chemical industries should first be developed not to compete with other nations but to foster agriculture and industry indigenous to Japan.

Takamine first visited the United States in 1884 as one of the Japanese commissioners to the international Cotton Centennial Exposition in New Orleans. Here he met and, in 1885, was married to Caroline Field Hitch, the daughter of Col. Eben Hitch. This event brought him finally to make the United States his adopted country. He then returned to Japan and was made chief of the division of chemistry in the department of agriculture and commerce, and, later, acting chief of the patent bureau. In 1887 he left the government service to develop the first superphosphate works in Japan, the Tokyo Artificial Fertilizer Company. Meanwhile in his private laboratory he had developed from a special type of fungus the potent starch-digesting enzyme, Takadiastase. In 1890 he was suddenly called to Chicago and Peoria, Ill., to apply this substance practically to the distilling industry. Fire, commercial opposition, and serious illness harassed him until, in 1894, the Takamine Ferment Company, which he had founded, was little more than a name. He moved to the vicinity of New York City to further the industrial development of Takadiastase. The production of the enzyme for medicinal use was taken over by Parke, Davis & Company, of Detroit, Mich., with whom, from that time on, Takamine was closely associated. The crowning achievement of his life was the isolation of adrenalin from the suprarenal gland in 1901. This was the first of all gland hormones to be discovered in pure form, and the value of the substance to medicine and surgery can scarcely be overestimated. It was discovered almost simultaneously by another scientist, whose work Takamine was quick to recognize.

Takamine's commercial and scientific interests broadened. Among other industries he aided in the development in Japan of dyes, aluminum fabrication, Bakelite, the electric furnace, and nitrogen fixation. Through his influence the Imperial Research Institute was established in Japan in 1913. Prosperity and honors came to him in abundance. He continued his private research in his laboratory at Clifton, N. J., and strove continually for better understanding between his native land and his adopted land. Remembering his own struggles, he delighted in aiding young men; young chemists were encouraged and employed by him; young artists studied painting and music in France and Italy with his financial and moral assistance. His advice was sought not only by the humble and poor but also by captains of industry, diplomats, ambassadors, and princes. His home on Riverside Drive in New York City presented an historical development of Japanese art, and his country home at Merriewold Park furnished an example of the best in Japanese landscape gardening. Both were centers of culture and offered gracious hospitality to a wide circle of friends.

Takamine was co-founder and president of the Japanese Association of New York and of the Nippon Club, and a member of the Lotos, Chemists, Bankers, Drug and Chemical, and New York Athletic clubs. He was honored by the Imperial University of Japan in 1899, 1906, and 1912, became a member of the Royal Academy of Science of Japan in 1913; he received the Fourth Order of the Rising Sun in 1915, and the Senior Degree of the Fourth Rank (Sho Shii) and the Third Merit (Kum Santo) in 1922. His wife and their two sons survived him at his death.

[Information from the family and Takamine's secretary; *Who's Who in America*, 1922–23; K. K. Kawakami, *Jokichi Takamine; A Record of his Am. Achievements* (1928); *Am. Jour. of Pharmacy*, Nov. 1901; *N. Y. Times*, July 23, 1922.]   F. O. T.

TALBOT, EMILY FAIRBANKS (Feb. 22, 1834–Oct. 29, 1900), philanthropist, was born in Winthrop, Me., the descendant of Jonathan Fayerbanke (variously spelled) who emigrated from England in 1633 and later settled in Dedham, Mass. Her parents, Columbus and Lydia (Tinkham) Fairbanks, were farming people in very moderate circumstances. The daughter's formal education was limited to that provided by the local schools, but her mother's strong character, unusual native intelligence and social interests had perhaps as great an influence in the daughter's education as any formal schooling. When Emily was sixteen years old she taught an unruly school in Augusta, Me., with great success, a success especially notable because her predecessors had not been able to finish out their terms. In 1854, while teaching in Baltimore, Md., she met Israel Tisdale Talbot [*q.v.*]. They were married on Oct. 29, 1856. In 1857 they went to Europe for a prolonged tour and on their return took up what was to be their permanent residence in Boston. They had six children, four of whom reached adult life. A fair was held in Boston in 1859 to assist the Homeopathic Medical Dispensary, and it was there that Mrs. Talbot's first public work took place. From that moment she cooperated with her husband. She had a large part in obtaining funds for the support of the Massachusetts Homeopathic Hospital and was appointed by the governor of Massachusetts a member of the first board of trustees of the state insane hospital at Westboro. In 1887 honorary associate membership in the American Institute of Homeopathy was conferred upon her. As secretary of the education department of the American Social Science Association she personally consulted with Charles Darwin, and together with Dr. William T. Harris gave real impetus to child study in the United

States. The education of her two daughters was a matter of absorbing interest to her, and in 1877, largely through her leadership and organizing power, the public Latin school for girls was established in Boston in order to give the facilities for college preparation to girls such as were open to boys. When her daughters were students in the college of liberal arts of Boston University, she became deeply interested in the efforts made by young women to obtain a college education in spite of lack of money. The practical result of this interest was the aid she gave in organizing the Massachusetts Society for the University Education of Women, of which she was a director for several years.

Her most important contribution in education was, however, her plan for the cooperation of the college women of the country in opening educational opportunities for women, in enabling women graduates to make the best use of their training through mutual deliberation and counsel, and in stimulating young women to attend colleges and universities and to undertake graduate work. It was from her suggestion made in October 1881 that the Association of Collegiate Alumnae was organized, an association which was one of the three charter members of the International Federation of University Women formed in 1919, and which in 1921, together with the Southern Association of College Women, became the American Association of University Women. She died at her summer home in Holderness, N. H., on the anniversary of her wedding day and of the birthday of her husband.

[Manuscript sketch by her daughter, Marion Talbot; Marion Talbot and L. K. M. Rosenberry, *The Hist. of the American Asso. of Univ. Women* (1931); L. S. Fairbanks, *Geneal. of the Fairbanks Family in America* (1897); *Boston Evening Transcript*, Oct. 31, 1900.]
          L. K. M. R.

TALBOT, ETHELBERT (Oct. 9, 1848–Feb. 27, 1928), bishop of the Protestant Episcopal Church, was born in Fayette, Mo., the son of John Alnut and Alice (Daly) Talbot. He was graduated from Dartmouth College in 1870, and from the General Theological Seminary, New York, in 1873. In that same year he was ordained deacon (June 29) and priest (Nov. 4), and became rector of St. James Church, Macon, Mo. Here, in addition to the work of the parish and neighboring missions, he founded a school, which grew into St. James' Military Academy. New buildings had recently been erected, and a separate girls' school established, when the General Convention of 1886 elected Talbot missionary bishop of Wyoming and Idaho. After some hesitation he left his work in Macon, and was consecrated on May 27, 1887.

Upon arrival in his diocese, he found only four clergy in each of the states it comprised. Within ten years he had built a cathedral at Laramie and thirty-eight churches, and had founded three schools, including a school for Indian girls, and a hospital. His summers were largely spent in preaching in mining camps and towns, and he traveled extensively in the East and even in the British Isles in behalf of his work. His experiences in the West are the basis of *My People of the Plains* (1906), a book which, without the loss of its serious character, is filled with anecdotes which support his reputation as a raconteur. In 1891 he was elected bishop of Georgia but declined; six years later, however, he was elected bishop of Central Pennsylvania and accepted. The people of his Western diocese saw him go with regret, non-churchmen as well as churchmen. He had been offered nominations for governor and senator and was regarded by all as "our bishop."

On Feb. 2, 1898, Talbot was enthroned in the pro-cathedral, the Church of the Nativity, South Bethlehem. He at once began to work towards the division of his unwieldy diocese, which project was accomplished by the erection of the Diocese of Harrisburg in 1904. Talbot continued in charge of the remaining area, which in 1909 took the name Diocese of Bethlehem. The number of communicants having doubled since his coming, each diocese was by now almost as strong as the original one had been. The project of an associate mission led to the opening of Leonard Hall, South Bethlehem, in 1908. This developed mainly, in accordance with a minor purpose in its foundation, as a residence for postulants for holy orders taking their college work at Lehigh University. In his later years, Bishop Talbot's attention was given increasingly to the growing industrial and foreign population of his diocese, social problems, and church unity. He served for some time as chairman of the General Convention commission on Christian unity. A contribution by him to a symposium, *The Problem of Christian Unity* (1921), recommends as "The Next Step" immediate organic unions between American Protestant bodies. Meanwhile, he had summed up his teaching in two books—*A Bishop among his Flock* (1914), addressed to the laity of his diocese; and *A Bishop's Message* (1917), addressed to the clergy. In 1914 he published *Tim; the Autobiography of a Dog,* a sentimental and humorous account of his daughter's bulldog.

In 1923 he obtained the assistance of a coadjutor, Bishop Frank W. Sterrett. By the death of Bishop Alexander C. Garrett of Dallas on Feb. 18, 1924, Talbot became senior diocesan, and presiding bishop of the Protestant Episcopal Church. He was the last to hold the office by seniority, since it was about to be changed from a formal and representative to an administrative post. In 1925 he presided at the General Convention, and Jan. 1, 1926, handed over the office to the first elected presiding bishop, John Gardner Murray [*q.v.*]. Rapidly aging, on Sept. 15, 1927, he resigned the administration of his diocese to Bishop Sterrett, and a few months later died. Successful as administrator, Talbot was loved as pastor and friend by both clergy and laity. In thought his position was a moderate, but definite, Anglicanism aiming at charity both within and without the Church. He had learned to combine breadth of sympathy with firmness of conviction in the days when he preached to "wild westerners" on "temperance, righteousness, and judgment to come." On Nov. 5, 1873, he married Dora Frances Harvey, of Roanoke, Mo., and he was survived by one daughter, at whose home at Tuckahoe, N. Y., he died.

[*My People of the Plains*; autobiog. address to Bethlehem Convention, pub. in its *Journal*, 1912; official reports in convention journals of Mo., Central Pa., and Bethlehem dioceses; *Living Church*, Mar. 1, 1924, Mar. 3, 1928; *Bethlehem Churchman*, Mar. 1928; *The Living Church Annual . . . 1929*; J. W. Miller, *Hist. of the Diocese of Central Pa.* (1909); *Who's Who in America*, 1926–27; *N. Y. Times*, Feb. 28, 1928.]   E. R. H., Jr.

TALBOT, HENRY PAUL (May 15, 1864– June 18, 1927), chemist, was born in Boston, Mass., the son of Zephaniah and Eliza Frances (Paul) Talbot. The Talbot family was one of the earliest to settle in Massachusetts. William Cushing and Silas Talbot [*qq.v.*] are among the distinguished ancestors. Henry Talbot's boyhood was spent in Holliston and Boston. He was graduated from the Holliston High School in 1881 and attended the Massachusetts Institute of Technology, receiving the degree of S.B. in 1885. For three years he served as assistant and instructor at the Institute, and then he spent two years at the University of Leipzig, majoring in organic chemistry under Wislecenus and taking courses in the new field of physical chemistry under Ostwald. He received the Ph.D. degree, *summa cum laude,* in 1890, and returned to the Institute of Technology, which he served continuously until his death, rising from the rank of an instructor to the headship of the departments of chemistry and chemical engineering, 1902–20, and of the department of chemistry, 1920–22. He was chairman of the faculty from 1919 to 1921, chairman of the administrative committee which conducted the affairs of the Institute following the death of Richard C. Maclaurin [*q.v.*], and dean of students from 1921 until his death.

He served as a member of the Advisory Board of the United States Bureau of Mines, Department of Gas Defence, in 1917. He published two textbooks of chemistry and numerous papers upon scientific and educational subjects. Talbot served, both as an officer and constant counselor, many professional organizations, the American Chemical Society, the Society for the Promotion of Engineering Education, the New England Society of Chemistry Teachers, and the American Academy of Arts and Sciences, with the same devotion that he served the Institute of Technology. As a teacher his presentation of his subject of analytical and inorganic chemistry was clear, logical, and inspiring. In the earlier days he conducted one of the first courses in physical chemistry given in an American institution. His personal interest in the students under his influence bore fruit in many of the careers of later leaders in education, research, and chemical industry. Talbot was always a friend to the furtherance of scientific research, but he was so absorbed in his main objective that he had little leisure to spend in research. As an administrator he went far in encouraging research, but always the education of students was the goal, and the research among members of the instructing staff was encouraged in so far as it contributed to their efficiency as educators. His greatest concern was with the traits which make the real teacher.

His comparatively early death, three weeks after undergoing a major operation, was a heavy loss to his associates and to the institution which he had so faithfully and ably served. On June 17, 1891, he married Frances E. Dukehart, of Baltimore, Md., who survived him. They had one son who died as a child.

[Personal acquaintance; correspondence with Mrs. Talbot; *Who's Who in America,* 1926–27; J. M. Cattell, D. R. Brimhall, ed., *Am. Men of Sci.* (3rd ed., 1921); articles by J. F. Norris in *Technology Rev.,* July 1927, and A. D. Little, *Industrial and Engineering Chemistry,* Aug. 1927; *Technology's War Record* (1920); *Boston Evening Transcript,* June 18, 1927.]

A. A. B.

TALBOT, ISRAEL TISDALE (Oct. 29, 1829–July 2, 1899), physician, was born at Sharon, Mass., the son of Josiah and Mary (Richards) Talbot, and a descendant of Peter Talbot who was in Dorchester, Mass., before 1677. He received a common-school education and at the age of eighteen went to Baltimore, Md., where he established a private school. Although the venture proved successful, Talbot soon returned to New England and continued his studies at South Woodstock, Conn., and later at Worcester Academy, Worcester, Mass. In

March 1851 he became a medical student in the office of Dr. Samuel Gregg of Boston, and subsequently pursued courses in the Tremont Street Medical School (which in 1858 was united with the Harvard Medical School) and at the Homœopathic Medical College of Pennsylvania (later the Hahnemann Medical College), from which he was graduated in 1853. Returning to Boston, he took additional courses at the Harvard Medical School and in 1854 received the degree of M.D. from that institution. The following fifteen months were spent in hospitals and medical schools of Europe.

From the early days of his practice in Boston he took a leading part in the organization activities of the homœopaths. In this work his wife, Emily (Fairbanks) Talbot [*q.v.*], whom he married Oct. 29, 1856, gave him able assistance. Largely through his efforts a charter was secured for the Massachusetts Homœopathic Medical Society and for a medical dispensary. Of the society Talbot was recording secretary from 1861 to 1866; vice-president in 1866; and president in 1867. He was also one of those instrumental in the opening in 1870 of a small hospital, which was the nucleus of the Massachusetts Homœopathic Hospital. Upon the establishment of the Boston University School of Medicine in 1873, he was appointed dean and professor of surgery. The establishment of the state hospital for the insane at Westboro, Mass., was in no small measure the result of his endeavors. He took a prominent part in the proceedings of the American Institute of Homœopathy, serving as its general secretary from 1866 to 1869, and its president in 1872. Its *Transactions* list approximately a hundred papers read by him at meetings of the Institute. From 1867 to 1873 he was an editor of the *New England Medical Gazette.* In his younger years he was fond of mountain climbing and in 1854 made an ascent of Mont Blanc, which is said to have been the second complete ascent of that mountain made by an American. He died in Hingham, Mass.

[T. L. Bradford, *Biog. Index of the Grads. of the Homœopathic Medic. Coll. of Pa.* (1918); T. C. Bradford, "Biogs. of Homœopathic Physicians," vol. XXXI (MS. Hahnemann Medic. Coll., Phila.); *Proc. Mass. Homœopathic Medic. Soc.,* vol. XIII (1900); *Trans. Thirty-fifth Session, Homœopathic Medic. Soc. of the State of Pa.* (1900); *Trans. Fifty-sixth Session Am. Inst. Homœopathy* (1901); *Medic. Student,* Jan. 1900; *Am. Alpine Jour.,* May 1935; *Boston Transcript,* July 3, 1899.]

C. B—t.

TALBOT, JOHN (1645–Nov. 29, 1727), Anglican clergyman, missionary, was born in Wymondham, Norfolk, England, the son of Thomas Talbot and Jane, daughter of Sir John Mede of Lofts, Essex. He was admitted sizar at

Christ's College, Cambridge, graduated B.A. in 1663/4 and M.A. in 1671, and was a fellow of Peterhouse from 1664 to 1668 when he admitted marriage and forfeited his fellowship. His wife was a daughter of Sir Arthur Jenney of Knotshall, Suffolk. Talbot was rector of a church in Icklingham, Suffolk, 1673–89; he seems to have visited Virginia about 1693 (Hills, *History of the Church in Burlington, post,* p. 35) ; and from 1695 to 1701 he was rector of the church at Fretherne, Gloucestershire.

On Apr. 28, 1702, he sailed from Cowes for the port of Boston as chaplain of the *Centurion.* With him were George Keith [*q.v.*] and Patrick Gordon, the first missionaries sent to the colonies by the Society for the Propagation of the Gospel in Foreign Parts. In Boston he preached a sermon at Queen's Chapel, June 28, and soon afterward was chosen by Keith as assistant in his missionary travels. On Sept. 18, 1702, he was appointed a missionary of the Society. Setting off with Keith on an intercolonial journey for the purpose of consolidating the Church of England forces on the northeastern seaboard, he preached at Philadelphia to assemblies so large that no church could be found to hold them, and had similar successes in New York and New Jersey. "We find," he wrote, "a great ripeness and inclination amongst all sorts of people to embrace the Gospel" (Hills, *Church in Burlington,* p. 27). With him he carried a "wallet full" of books explanatory of the doctrine and liturgy of the Church of England. He soon became convinced that America needed a bishop, "to visit all the churches, to ordain some, to confirm others, and bless all" (*Ibid.*), and thenceforward was untiring in his effort to secure an ecclesiastic qualified to perform these functions. There was strong objection in the Colonies to the project of an episcopate, however, as much political as ecclesiastical, and Talbot's continued efforts to set up the mitre were opposed on every side.

In 1704, upon the petition of the churchmen of Burlington in the Jerseys, he became rector of the newly built St. Mary's Church there, but in the same year when certain members of the clergy began to agitate for a suffragan bishop, he went to England to plead the cause before the Society, and again took up his residence in Fretherne until 1708, when he returned to America. Four years later the Society for the Propagation of the Gospel empowered Gov. Robert Hunter [*q.v.*] to prepare a residence for Talbot in Burlington, and an established bishopric loomed as a certainty. With the accession of George I, however, the old Jacobite-Hanoverian quarrels were reopened, and Talbot, asked to renew the oath of allegiance, refused. Governor Hunter immediately charged him with incorporating the Jacobites in the Jerseys, refused to grant him residence, and in 1716 accused him of omitting certain prayers from the liturgy. In 1720–23 Talbot visited England, where he presented another petition to the Society for the Propagation of the Gospel. He was now granted the interest from the legacy left by Archbishop Tenison for the support of a bishop in America or, until the appointment of such a bishop, the support of a deserving missionary (Hills, *op. cit.,* pp. 161–62; Perry, *post,* I, 550). The tradition that while in England Talbot received episcopal consecration clandestinely at the hands of a nonjuror (Hills, "John Talbot," *post*), rests upon very questionable evidence (Fulton, *post*). Returning to America in 1723, he reopened negotiations with Governor Hunter, and the two became reconciled. The following year, presiding at a convocation of clergy who upheld the action of the vestry of Christ Church, Philadelphia, in dismissing the Rev. John Urmiston, and later supplying the vacant pulpit himself, Talbot gained an enemy in Urmiston, who made complaint, insinuating that Talbot had assumed the rôle of bishop, and recalled the old accusation of Jacobite sympathies. Urmiston's charges were reported to the Society for the Propagation of the Gospel, and in October 1724 Talbot was removed for disaffection toward the government. In July 1725 he wrote the Society that he had learned indirectly that he had been dismissed for "exercising acts of jurisdiction" over his fellow missionaries, which charge he emphatically denied. He was not reinstated, however, although shortly afterward the visiting commissary of the Bishop of London wrote to England in his behalf, characterizing him as "a man universally beloved, even by the dissenters" (Tiffany, *post,* p. 198). About this time he married Mrs. Anne Herbert, who survived him. He died at the age of eighty-two and was buried in St. Mary's Church, Burlington.

[G. M. Hills, "John Talbot, the First Bishop in North America," *Pa. Mag. of Hist. and Biog.,* vol. III, no. 1 (1879), and *Hist. of the Church in Burlington, N. J.* (2nd ed., 1885) ; John and J. A. Venn, *Alumni Cantabrigienses,* pt. 1, vol. IV (1927) ; Francis Blomefield, *An Essay towards a Topographical Hist. of the County of Norfolk,* I (1739), 722 ; George Keith, *A Jour. of Travels ... on the Continent of North America* (1706) ; A. L. Cross, *The Anglican Episcopate and the American Colonies* (1902) ; H. D. Evans, *An Essay on the Episcopate of the Protestant Episcopal Church in the U. S. A.* (1855) ; E. P. Tanner, *The Province of New Jersey, 1664–1738* (1908) ; W. A. Whitehead, *Docs. Rel. to the Col. Hist. of ... N. J.,* 1 ser. IV (1882) ; Ernest Hawkins, *Hist. Notices of the Missions of the Church of England in the North American Colonies* (1845) ; John Fulton, "The Non-Juring Bishops in America," in W. S. Perry, *The Hist. of the Am. Episcopal Church*

(1885), vol. I ; C. C. Tiffany, *A Hist. of the Protestant Episcopal Church in the U. S. A.* (1895).]   E. H. D.

TALBOT, SILAS (Jan. 11, 1751–June 30, 1813), naval officer, was born at Dighton, Bristol County, Mass., the ninth of fourteen children of Benjamin and Rebecca (Allen) Talbot. At the age of twelve he lost his father, a farmer. Learning the trade of a stone-mason, he soon abandoned it for sea-going and mercantile pursuits. In 1772 he was married to a Miss Richmond and settled in Providence, R. I., where he had purchased a house out of his own earnings. Some preliminary drilling with a band of volunteers recommended him as a military man to the Rhode Island government, and, on June 28, 1775, he was appointed captain in one of its regiments. Three days later he received a commission as captain in the Continental Army. After participating in the siege of Boston and aiding in the transporting of troops to New York, he obtained command of a fireship and made a spirited attempt to burn the warship *Asia*. This enterprise, though unsuccessful, brought him to the attention of Congress, which on Oct. 10, 1777, promoted him to the rank of major.

In the defense of Hog Island, in the Delaware River, Talbot was so severely wounded that he retired to Rhode Island on leave of absence, but in the summer of 1778 he again saw active service in the Rhode Island campaign of Gen. John Sullivan [*q.v.*]. Fitting out the *Hawke* he captured the *Pigot* in October, again exhibiting initiative and gallantry. On Nov. 14, Congress rewarded him with a promotion to a lieutenant-colonelcy and Rhode Island about the same time recognized his services with the gift of a sword. As commander of the *Pigot* and later of the *Argo*, both under the army, he cruised against the small enemy vessels that interrupted the American trade between Long Island and Nantucket and captured more than a dozen of them. In recognition of these exploits Congress made him a captain in the Continental Navy, on Sept. 17, 1779, but when he failed to obtain a ship commensurate with his rank he put to sea as commander of the privateer *General Washington*. He had taken but a single prize when he ran into the British fleet off New York and after a chase surrendered to the *Culloden*, 74 guns. For a time he was confined on board the famous *Jersey* prison ship at New York, but later was transported to England and confined in a prison. After undergoing many hardships and making several futile attempts to escape he was exchanged for a British officer and landed at Cherbourg, France, in December 1781. Obtaining pecuniary aid from Franklin, he sailed for America, but before reaching his destination the vessel on which he had taken passage was captured by a British privateer. The British captain, however, considerately put him aboard an English brig bound for New York.

The settlement of his claims against the government and a prize case before the Pennsylvania Admiralty led Talbot to spend much time in Philadelphia, where, after the death of his first wife, he was married to a Miss Morris, grand-daughter of Gen. Thomas Mifflin [*q.v.*]. Soon after his marriage he established himself as a farmer in Fulton County, N. Y., on a section of the forfeited estates of Sir John Johnson [*q.v.*]. In 1792–93 he was a member of the New York Assembly, and, in 1793–95, of the federal House of Representatives. On June 5, 1794, President Washington chose him third in a list of six captains of the new navy then under organization. Before the end of his term in Congress he entered upon the superintendency of the construction of the frigate *President* at New York. From 1796, when work on this vessel was suspended, until the outbreak of the naval war with France in 1798, he was without naval duties. On May 11, 1798, President Adams reappointed him captain, an unnecessary act that led to a long and bitter controversy between Talbot and Thomas Truxtun [*q.v.*] over their rank; the President supported Talbot.

As commander of the Santo Domingo station, 1799–1800, he made a rather uneventful cruise in the West Indies on board the *Constitution*. One exploit that he conceived led to the capture of the *Sandwich* in the Spanish harbor of Puerto Plata, Santo Domingo. This capture, being illegal, cost the captors dearly. At the end of the cruise Talbot was commended by the secretary of the navy for his services in protecting American commerce and for laying the foundation of a permanent trade with Santo Domingo. He resigned from the navy on Sept. 23, 1801, and died twelve years later in New York City. From his third wife, a Mrs. Pintard of New York, he was separated. From his first two marriages he had at least four children. He is described as tall, with attractive features, impulsive, and fearless.

[Bureau of Navigation, Records of Officers, 1798–1801 ; *An Hist. Sketch to the End of the Revolutionary War of the Life of Silas Talbot* (1803) ; H. T. Tuckerman, *Life of Silas Talbot* (1850), also published in *Mag. of Hist.*, Extra Nos. vol. XXX (1926), no. 120 ; G. W. Allen, *Naval Hist. of Am. Rev.* (2 vols., 1913), and *Our Naval War with France* (1909) ; *Proc. of U. S. Naval Institute* (1906) ; C. W. Goldsborough, *U. S. Naval Chronicle* (1824) ; *Jour. of Continental Cong.*, vol. IX (1907), XII (1908), XV (1909) ; *Judgements in the Admiralty of Pa.* (1789) ; New York *Evening Post*, June 30, 1813.]   C. O. P.

TALCOTT, ANDREW (Apr. 20, 1797–Apr. 22, 1883), soldier, engineer, son of George and Abigail (Goodrich) Talcott, was born in Glastonbury, Conn. He was a lineal descendant of John Talcott, one of the first settlers of Hartford. Entering the United States Military Academy in March 1815, he was graduated, second in his class, in July 1818, and made a brevet second lieutenant in the corps of engineers. Having been advanced through the intervening grades, he became captain on Dec. 22, 1830.

After serving as assistant engineer in connection with the construction of fortifications at Rouse's Point, N. Y., 1818–19, he was engineer and aide-de-camp to Gen. Henry Atkinson in the establishment of posts on the upper Missouri and Yellowstone rivers, 1820–21. For the next five years he was engaged in engineering work on fortifications in Virginia, Rhode Island, New York, and Delaware. From 1826 to 1828 he superintended the construction of the canal through the Dismal Swamp in Virginia, and from 1828 to 1834, the construction of Fort Monroe and Fort Calhoun, Hampton Roads, Va. He also served as astronomer in determining the boundary line between Ohio and Michigan, 1832–36; and as superintending engineer of improvements on the Hudson River, 1834–36.

In 1836 he resigned his commission in the army to engage in work as a civil engineer. The varied tasks he was now called upon to execute bear evidence of his complete mastery of his profession. He was chief engineer in charge of the western division of the New York & Erie Railroad, 1836–37; superintendent of the improvement of the delta of the Mississippi River, 1837–39; member of the commission for the exploration and survey of the northeast boundary of the United States, 1840–43; member of a board of naval officers and engineers for examining Portsmouth and Pensacola navy yards and projecting stone and floating docks, 1844–45; chief engineer of the Richmond & Danville Railroad, 1848–55; astronomer and surveyor for marking the northern boundary of Iowa, 1852–53; superintendent of repairs of the United States Mint in Philadelphia, 1855–56; chief engineer of the Ohio & Mississippi Railroad from Cincinnati to St. Louis, 1856–57. In December 1857 he began his last and most important work, the location and construction of the railroad from Vera Cruz to the city of Mexico. On this project he was engaged until March 1867, with the exception of a period in 1860–61 when work was suspended because of a reorganization of the company. During this period of suspension he was manager of the Sonora Exploring & Mining Company and chief engineer of the state of Virginia. When he retired from the Mexican undertaking in 1867 on account of political changes, the difficult feat of engineering involved was nearing completion. After his retirement he traveled abroad and upon his return settled in Baltimore, moving later to Richmond, where he died.

Talcott was always interested in practical astronomy, and while working on the Michigan-Ohio boundary line devised a method of determining terrestrial latitudes through the observation of stars near the zenith, adapting the zenith telescope to the purpose. "Talcott's method" was first described in the *Journal of the Franklin Institute* (October 1838), and its adoption by the Coast Survey led to great improvements in the zenith telescope and to the utilization of the method in all the great United States government surveys. Talcott never claimed any credit for originality in his method; he simply considered it the best means of determining latitude from his knowledge of practical astronomy and with the instruments then available. Credit was given him by others, however, and he was elected a member of the American Philosophical Society and an honorary member of the Connecticut Association of Arts and Sciences. He was twice married: first, in April 1826, to Catherine Thompson of Philadelphia, who died in 1828 leaving no child; second, Apr. 11, 1832, at Norfolk, Va., to Harriet Randolph Hackley, by whom he had six sons and five daughters. Seven of these children survived him.

[S. V. Talcott, *Talcott Pedigree in England and America* (1876); G. W. Cullum, *Biog. Reg. Officers and Grads., U. S. Mil. Acad.*, vol. I (1891); Alfred Mordecai, in *Fourteenth Ann. Reunion, Asso. Grads., U. S. Mil. Acad.* (1883); W. L. Marshall, *Notes on Talcott's Method* (1893); *Daily Dispatch* (Richmond, Va.), Apr. 24, 1883.]   G. J. F.

TALCOTT, ELIZA (May 23, 1836–Nov. 1, 1911), missionary to Japan, was born in Vernon, Conn., the daughter of Ralph and Susan (Bell) Talcott. Her father was a pioneer manufacturer of Rockville, in the town of Vernon, and a descendant of John Talcott, one of the first settlers of Hartford; her mother's ancestry went back to Thomas Hooker, founder of Hartford Colony. Eliza studied in the school of Sarah Porter [q.v.] at Farmington, Conn., and also taught there. Later, she attended the Connecticut Normal School at New Britain and for several years was a teacher in both public and private schools.

In 1873 she sailed for Japan under appointment of the American Board of Commissioners for Foreign Missions, being one of its first woman missionaries to that country. She acquired the language quickly and was soon engaged in various activities. In 1875 she helped to found and became the first principal of Kobe House, a boarding school for girls which developed into Kobe College. In 1880 she became a touring missionary from Okayama as a center, enduring the hardships of primitive travel and difficult living conditions, mingling with the people both as nurse and as religious teacher. This work was interrupted in 1884 by her first furlough. Returning to Japan the following year, she became the evangelistic head and house mother of the Doshisha Nurses Training School at Kyoto. During the Chino-Japanese War of 1894 she was at Hiroshima, an unofficial visitor to the sick and wounded in the six military hospitals there, bringing such sympathy and encouragement that soldiers testified: "Her visits do us more good than the visits of the doctors." After an attack of cholera, she returned to the United States in 1900 on a furlough which was prolonged for a number of years because of the condition of her health. Sailing again for her field in 1900, she was detained for two and a half years in the Hawaiian Islands to assist in work among the Japanese who were settled there. When at length she reached Japan she took up the training of evangelistic workers at the Woman's Bible School at Kobe, where she remained until her death.

She was gentle and unassuming, yet she gave the impression of great strength. Her parish was the entire Empire and she probably exerted a greater Christian influence than any other foreigner of her time. She recognized good in religions other than her own and she had unbounded faith in human nature and charity toward the erring. Her command of the Japanese language was perfect and she had so mastered the intricacies of Japanese etiquette that she commanded the confidence and respect of all classes of people. One of the Chinese prisoners to whom she had ministered said: "She had within her a mysterious happiness which we could not understand. No amount of preaching could have made such an impression as her work and example."

[S. V. Talcott, *Talcott Pedigree in England and America* (1876); *Missionary Herald*, Jan. 1912; *Mission News*, Dec. 1911; *Life and Light for Women*, Jan. 1911, Jan., Apr. 1912; L. E. Learned, *Eliza Talcott, the Florence Nightingale of Japan* (Woman's Board of Missions, 1917); *Japan Weekly Mail* (Yokohama), Nov. 11, 1911.]   F. T. P.

TALCOTT, JOSEPH (November 1669–Nov. 11, 1741), colonial governor, was born in Hartford, Conn., the fourth son of Lieutenant-Colonel John Talcott and his first wife Helena (Wakeman) Talcott. His grandfather, John Talcott, who emigrated to Boston in 1632, was one of the founders of Hartford and was descended from the Talcotts of Colchester and Braintree, Essex, England. Both his father and grandfather were influential men in the Connecticut colony and inculcated in him a tradition of public service. At the age of twenty-three he was chosen selectman of Hartford, a unique honor for one of his age. In 1697 he began his military career as ensign of the Hartford train-band; he soon rose to the position of lieutenant and then to that of captain. He was commissioned major of the 1st Regiment of Connecticut troops in 1710 and retained that rank until he became governor. In 1723–24 he campaigned successfully against the Indians; for this service he was rewarded by the Connecticut General Assembly with a special grant of £15. Although he had not received a college education, he became prominent as a judge. In May 1705 he was appointed justice of the peace for Hartford County. Later he became judge of the county court, and court of probate in Hartford County, and in 1721 was made judge of the superior court of the colony.

He entered colonial political life in October 1708 when he was elected deputy from Hartford to the General Assembly. In 1710 he was elected speaker of the House, and in the following year was elected to the upper chamber of the Assembly, becoming one of the assistants or magistrates of the colony. He served in this capacity until 1723, when he was elected deputy-governor. A year later Gov. Gurdon Saltonstall [q.v.] died, and Talcott was chosen by the Assembly to complete Saltonstall's unexpired term. From that time until his death he was annually elected governor of Connecticut by the freemen of that colony. He was the first governor of Connecticut who had been born in the colony, most previous governors having been born in England. His term of office, seventeen years, was the second longest in the entire history of Connecticut, being exceeded only by that of Gov. John Winthrop. From his early youth he devoted himself so faithfully to the service of Connecticut that he became one of the outstanding men of his generation in the colony. He subordinated his personal life to the interests of the colony, as is shown by the fact that at the time of his second wife's death, in order to avoid the suspension of a session of the Assembly, he remained at his post as presiding officer of the Assembly until all necessary legislation had been completed.

Talcott's first wife was Abigail Clark of Milford, Conn., whom he married in 1693. She died in 1705. On June 26, 1706, he married a widow, Eunice (Howell) Wakeman of Southampton, Long Island, who died May 25, 1738. He had three sons by his first wife, two sons and four daughters by his second. While not a brilliant man, Talcott was an able executive and had the power of making others carry out his orders. He had an abundance of good judgment and performed his duties as statesman and soldier to the entire satisfaction of the freemen of Connecticut. He was not a radical, nor even a liberal, being possessed of a profound distrust for any new or untried policies, a conservatism that was characteristic of the colonial Connecticut of his time.

[The date of Talcott's birth is given variously as Nov. 11 and Nov. 16. See *Conn. Hist. Soc. Colls.*, vols. IV–V (1892–96), "The Talcott Papers," ed. by Mary K. Talcott; S. V. Talcott, *Talcott Pedigree in England and America* (1876); C. J. Hoadly, *The Pub. Records of the Colony of Conn.* (15 vols., 1850–90), vols. IV–VIII.]   R. M. H.

TALIAFERRO, LAWRENCE (Feb. 28, 1794–Jan. 22, 1871), Indian agent, came of a prominent Virginia family. He was born at "Whitehall," King George County, Va., the fourth son in the large family of James Garnett and Wilhelmina (Wishart) Taliaferro of "Oakland," King George County. After an education under tutors he enlisted, on Aug. 5, 1812, in a volunteer company of light infantry. He served on several fronts and was promoted to a first lieutenancy. At the end of the War of 1812 he retained his rank and served with the 3rd Regiment at many frontier posts. In 1819 he was appointed by President Monroe to be Indian agent at the fort, now called Fort Snelling, that was about to be constructed at the mouth of the St. Peter's (now the Minnesota) River. At first he had charge of both Sioux and Chippewa Indians, but in 1827 the Chippewa of the Upper Mississippi were ordered by the war department to place themselves under the Sault Sainte Marie agency. The age-long feud between the Sioux and the Chippewa, and the enmity of the Sioux and the Sauk, Foxes, and Winnebago, made his position anything but a sinecure. His endeavors to keep peace between the tribes were earnest and often successful, for the Indians came to believe that the "Iron Cutter," as the agent was called, was their friend and protector. His efforts in the Indians' behalf produced almost constant strife between himself and the traders, all of whose efforts to bribe or oust him failed. The American Fur Company contracted against him an especial dislike and distrust, but even this great monopoly's efforts to have him removed

from office were unsuccessful, and in 1839 he was appointed for the sixth time.

In 1839 he resigned his post and left the Indian country, leaving a quarter-breed daughter Mary L., who had been born on Aug. 17, 1828, and was educated by him at a local mission school. She later married a former soldier at Fort Snelling named Warren Woodbury and lived in West St. Paul, Minn. In 1862 she was captured with many others by the Sioux in their uprising of that year and rescued after six weeks' captivity. An orphan niece was reared in the Taliaferro home almost as a daughter. By his wife, Eliza Dillon, who was the daughter of a hotel-keeper of Bedford, Pa., and who accompanied him to the St. Peter's agency after their marriage in the summer of 1828, he had no issue. Most of his time after 1840 was spent at Bedford, where mineral waters had attracted him early in life. On Mar. 14, 1857, he reëntered military service in the quartermaster department and served at San Antonio, Fort Leavenworth, Pittsburgh, and Bedford. In 1863 his name was put on the retired list. He was a member of the Masonic Order and a deacon in the Presbyterian Church at Bedford. In the Civil War he was an ardent Unionist, though earlier in life he had been a slaveholder. He died at Bedford, where his widow remained for some years.

[Autobiography in *Minn. Hist. Soc. Colls.*, vol. VI (1894); a large collection of his diaries, correspondence, and accounts, an affidavit by his daughter, and a letter by a Bedford neighbor, Maria L. Rupp, all in the possession of the Minn. Hist. Soc.; W. M. Babcock, "Major Lawrence Taliaferro, Indian Agent," in *Miss. Val. Hist. Rev.*, Dec. 1924; L. P. du Bellet, *Some Prominent Va. Families*, vol. II (1907).]   G. L. N.

TALIAFERRO, WILLIAM BOOTH (Dec. 28, 1822–Feb. 27, 1898), Confederate soldier, only child of Warner and Frances (Booth) Taliaferro, was born at "Belleville," his mother's family estate, in Gloucester County. Through his father he was descended from Robert Taliaferro, gentleman, an immigrant to Virginia as early as 1647. He graduated in 1841 at the College of William and Mary and studied law at Harvard. As a captain in the 11th United States Infantry, he distinguished himself in Mexico, being discharged in August 1848 with the rank of major. On Feb. 17, 1853, he married Sally N. Lyons, of Richmond, by whom he had eight children. He represented Gloucester County in the House of Delegates, 1850–53, was a Buchanan presidential elector in 1856, and took command of the militia at Harpers Ferry in November 1859 after the capture of John Brown.

Early in the Civil War, as colonel, Confederate States Army, he served brilliantly under

Jackson in western Virginia, but in January 1862, with the commanders of other regiments stationed in a bleak encampment at Romney, he signed a petition which ultimately reached the Secretary of War, asking that the troops be moved to a more favorable locality (*War of the Rebellion: Official Records, Army*, 1 ser., V, 1046 ff.). This action greatly incensed Jackson, but thanks to proved capacity, Taliaferro retained his chief's confidence. Appointed brigadier-general on Mar. 4, 1862, he led a brigade throughout the Valley campaign, contributing notably to the victories of McDowell, Winchester, and Port Republic. At Cedar Mountain, Aug. 9, after the death of General Winder, he was called to command Jackson's old division when it had been almost routed. Under "Stonewall's" eye he extricated his troops skilfully, earning the permanent command of this redoubtable division. Three weeks later, at Groveton, he was severely wounded and incapacitated, but at Fredericksburg again directed his troops in repulsing Meade's attack on Jackson's corps.

In February 1863 he was ordered to Savannah, but General Beauregard soon called him to Charleston, and he defended Battery Wagner, on Morris Island, during the memorable assault of July 18, when with fewer than twelve hundred men he repulsed 5,000 assailants (*Official Records*, 1 ser., XXVIII, pt. 1, pp. 415–21). Later, commanding on James Island for over a year, he baffled all efforts of the Federals to reach Charleston. Because he was a near relative, the Secretary of War, James A. Seddon [*q.v.*], hesitated to urge his promotion (*Ibid.*, XXXV, pt. 1, pp. 622–23), and he was not commissioned major-general until Jan. 1, 1865. In the meantime he commanded briefly in eastern Florida, and in December 1864 safeguarded the garrison of Savannah in escaping from Sherman. After evacuating James Island in February 1865, with Rhett's and Elliott's brigades he fought stubbornly at Bentonville, but surrendered with Johnston's army in April.

Following the war, he served again in the legislature, 1874–79, distinguishing himself in opposition to repudiation of the state debt. He was Grand Master of Masons in Virginia, 1876–77; judge of the Gloucester County court, 1891–97, and long a member of the boards of visitors of the Virginia Military Institute, the College of William and Mary, and other institutions of the state.

Six feet tall and full-bearded, Taliaferro was by tradition and character a Virginia gentleman and a leader, temperamentally akin to Washington and Lee. Like them, he fulfilled his obligations punctiliously. As a soldier, though denied opportunities for independent command, he frequently displayed high tactical abilities. In peace time a farmer-lawyer, he could not be tempted to abandon the rural life. The foremost men of the Old Dominion frequented his hospitable manor house, "Dunham Massie," where in the hallway hung a Confederate flag beneath which every visitor passed. Here he ended his days, and his body was buried in the cemetery of Ware Church, built by his ancestors in the seventeenth century.

[Besides the volumes of *Official Records* cited above, see 1 ser. II, XII, XXI, XLIV, XLVII; C. A. Evans, *Confed. Mil. Hist.* (1899), vol. III; "A Soldier Sleeps," *Richmond Dispatch*, Mar. 1, 1898; G. F. R. Henderson, *Stonewall Jackson* (1898); G. T. Beauregard, "The Defense of Charleston," *Battles and Leaders of the Civil War* (1887–88), IV, 1–23; and Taliaferro's article, "Jackson's Raid Around Pope," *Ibid.*, II, 501–11; W. B. McGroarty, *Geneal. Chart of the Taliaferro Family* (1926). Information as to certain facts has been supplied by W. T. L. Taliaferro of College Park, Md., a son, and T. S. Taliaferro, Rock Springs, Wyo., a nephew of W. B. Taliaferro.]   J. M. H.

TALLMADGE, BENJAMIN (Feb. 25, 1754–Mar. 7, 1835), soldier and congressman, was born at Brookhaven, N. Y., second of five surviving children of the Rev. Benjamin and Susannah (Smith) Tallmadge. He was descended from Thomas Talmadge who was an early settler of Southampton, Long Island. Tutored by his father, Benjamin entered Yale in 1769, although the authorities there would have permitted him to matriculate at an earlier date. He states in his autobiography that idleness and an attack of measles prevented his making a particularly brilliant record in college, but he also mentions the fact that when he received his degree in 1773 he spoke publicly at the commencement exercises (*Memoir, post*, pp. 1–6).

Soon after his graduation he became superintendent of the high school in Wethersfield, Conn., a position which he held until the outbreak of the Revolution. On June 20, 1776, he was appointed lieutenant and adjutant in Chester's Connecticut State Regiment; he displayed superior military abilities and rose rapidly in rank, becoming captain Dec. 14, 1776, major Apr. 7, 1777, and brevet lieutenant-colonel Sept. 30, 1783. He participated in the battles of Long Island (Aug. 27, 1776), White Plains (Oct. 28), Brandywine (Sept. 11, 1777), Germantown (Oct. 4), and Monmouth (June 28, 1778), besides many smaller engagements. One of the most notable of his military achievements was the capture and destruction of Fort St. George, Long Island, Nov. 22, 1780. For this service he received the thanks of Washington, and of Congress. During the years 1778–83 he was occupied largely with important secret service, carrying on a confidential correspondence with Washington. He had charge of Major André during the latter's imprisonment in 1780, and became deeply attached to the young English officer. "When I saw him swinging under the gibbet," he wrote, "it seemed for a time as if I could not support it" (*Memoir*, p. 57).

After the close of the Revolution, Tallmadge engaged successfully in commercial pursuits in Litchfield, Conn. In 1800 he was elected as a Federalist to the United States House of Representatives, and was continued in that office for eight terms (1801–17), declining in 1816 to stand for reëlection. As a member of Congress he served on numerous committees, and was for a time chairman of the committee on military affairs. Since he was widely recognized as a devout Christian, many petitions involving religious interests were submitted to him to be presented to the House (Hickok, *post*, pp. 18–19).

Tallmadge married first, Mar. 18, 1784, Mary Floyd of Mastic, L. I., daughter of William Floyd [*q.v.*], a signer of the Declaration of Independence; she died June 3, 1805, leaving five sons and two daughters, and on May 3, 1808, he married Maria Hallett of New York City, who survived him. In person he was of more than average height, was well-proportioned, and retained his military bearing throughout his later life. His manners were those of the polished gentleman; in his charities he was noted for liberality. He died in Litchfield.

[A. W. Talmadge, *The Talmadge, Tallmadge, and Talmage Geneal.* (1909); P. Hickok, *A Sermon Preached at the Funeral of Col. Benj. Tallmadge* (1835); *Memoir of Col. B. Tallmadge, Prepared by Himself, at the Request of His Children* (1858), repr. in 1904; F. B. Dexter, *Biog. Sketches Grads. Yale Coll.*, vol. III (1903); *Biog. Dir. Am. Cong.* (1928); F. B. Heitman, *Hist. Reg. of Officers of the Continental Army* (1914); H. P. Johnston, *The Record of Conn. Men in the Military and Naval Service during the War of the Revolution* (1889), and "The Secret Service of the Revolution," *Mag. of Am. Hist.*, Feb. 1882; P. K. Kilbourne, *Sketches and Chronicles of the Town of Litchfield, Conn.* (1859).]

R. W. I.

TALLMADGE, JAMES (Jan. 28, 1778–Sept. 29, 1853), lawyer and statesman, descended from Thomas Talmadge who emigrated to New England some time after 1630 and settled at Southampton, Long Island, about 1642, was born at Stanford, Dutchess County, N. Y., the son of Colonel James and Ann (Southerland) Tallmadge. During the Revolution the father was an ardent patriot and commanded a company of Dutchess County volunteers at Saratoga. James graduated from Rhode Island College (now Brown University) in 1798 and practised law at Poughkeepsie, becoming one of the leading law-

yers in the state. He was also interested in agriculture, and owned a large farm in Dutchess County. A Democrat in politics, he attached himself to the group headed by Gov. George Clinton [*q.v.*], and for a time served as Clinton's private secretary. In 1813 he was appointed brigadier-general of the New York militia, but while on his way to take command of troops on the northern frontier became ill and was unable to proceed. Before the close of the war, however, he took command of troops for the defense of New York City.

From 1817 to 1819 Tallmadge served as a member of Congress, soon distinguishing himself in debate. On Feb. 15, 1819, he introduced a notable amendment to a bill regarding the admission of Missouri to statehood (*Annals of Congress*, 15 Cong., 2 Sess., I, 1170, 1203–14). His amendment was designed to prohibit the further introduction of slaves into Missouri and to provide for the gradual emancipation of those born there after the admission of the state. Approved by the House but defeated by the Senate, it precipitated a controversy which became nation wide. In the argument over Andrew Jackson's dramatic Seminole campaign of 1819, Tallmadge eloquently defended Jackson's conduct. With respect to American industry he urged more adequate protection against foreign competition. Refusing to accept renomination, he retired to private life until 1821, when he became a delegate to the New York constitutional convention. Three years later, as a member of the state legislature, he advocated a more popular method of choosing presidential electors, and, during the same session, successfully opposed the collection of tonnage duties on the Erie Canal. In 1825 he became lieutenant-governor, in which capacity he served creditably for two years.

The remainder of his life was crowded with non-political activities. From 1828 until his death he spent the summer months at his country seat in Dutchess County and the winters in New York City. He was one of the founders of the University of the City of New York (now New York University) and president of its council, 1834–46; he was also a founder of the American Institute of the City of New York, for the promotion of useful arts, and from 1832 until his death served almost continuously as its president. In 1838 he went to Europe, where he was received with marked distinction. While there he collected information for the Institute; secured the removal of certain useless quarantine restrictions which handicapped American trade in Northern Europe; and took steps to aid Russia in obtaining machinery for the manufacture of cotton products. In 1846 he again served as delegate to a New York constitutional convention. A number of his speeches, both political and non-political, were published in pamphlet form.

Tallmadge was a man of fine presence, polished manners, and broad sympathies. On Jan. 21, 1810, he married his second cousin, Laura Tallmadge, who died in 1834. Of several children born to this union, only one, Mary, survived. She married Philip Van Rensselaer, proprietor of the Metropolitan Hotel, New York, at which her father died.

[A. W. Talmadge, *The Talmadge, Tallmadge, and Talmage Geneal.* (1909); G. B. Andrews, *A Sermon Occasioned by the Death of the Honorable James Tallmadge* (1853); *Hist. Cat. Brown Univ.* (1914); *Biog. Dir. Am. Cong.* (1928); Isaac Huntting, *Hist. of Little Nine Partners . . . and Pine Plains, N. Y.* (1897); *N. Y. Daily Times,* Oct. 1, 1853; and *Poughkeepsie Eagle,* Oct. 8, 1853.]   R. W. I.

TALMAGE, JAMES EDWARD (Sept. 21, 1862–July 27, 1933), geologist, theologian, was born in Hungerford, Berkshire, England, the first son and second child of eight in the family of James Joyce Talmage and Susannah (Preater) Talmage. He attended the schools of the local district and in 1874 was the Oxford diocesan prize scholar. Two years later the family emigrated to the United States and settled in Provo, Utah, where James was a student of Brigham Young Academy (later University) from 1876 to 1882. He afterwards attended Lehigh University (1882–83), the Johns Hopkins University (1884), and Illinois Wesleyan University (1896). Until 1911, when he was ordained an apostle in the Church of Jesus Christ of Latter-day Saints, he devoted himself to teaching. He was successively professor of chemistry and geology in Brigham Young Academy (1884–88), president of the Latter-day Saints College, Salt Lake City (1888–93), and president of the University of Utah (1894–97), resigning in 1897 to devote his full time to the chair of geology, which he held until his resignation in 1907. After 1907 he carried on a private practice as consulting mining geologist. In 1897 he was a delegate from the Royal Society of Edinburgh to the International Geological Congress at Saint Petersburg (later Leningrad), Russia. He was a fellow of numerous scientific societies in Great Britain and the United States, a life associate of the Philosophical Society of Great Britain, and a life member of the National Geographic Society. On Dec. 7, 1911, he was appointed to the Council of the Twelve Apostles, and from that time until his death gave himself to the service of the church. On June 14, 1888, he married Mary May Booth, daughter of Richard Thornton and Elsie (Edge) Booth, by whom he had four sons and four daughters. He was the author of numerous articles, sermons, addresses, and books on scientific and religious themes. Among the more important of his scientific books are *First Book of Nature* (1888), *Domestic Science: A Book for Use in Schools and for General Reading* (1891), *Tables for Blowpipe Determination of Minerals* (1899), and *The Great Salt Lake, Present and Past* (1900). Among his religious books are *The Articles of Faith* (1899), *The Story of "Mormonism"* (1907), *The Great Apostasy* (1909), *The House of the Lord* (1912), *Jesus the Christ* (1915), *The Vitality of "Mormonism"* (1919), and *Sunday Night Talks* (1931), first given an radio speeches.

He had unusual ability in expository writing and speaking, being skilful in verbal definition and in conveying delicate shades of meaning. His remarkable and capacious memory added greatly to his efficiency as a writer and speaker. His scholarly manner, his connections with learned societies, and his unusual ability as a teacher and expounder secured for him a prestige among his own people which has probably never been equaled by any other leader of this Church. He became their leading authority on technical theological questions, while his opinion on the relation of Church dogma to science probably outweighed that of all his compeers. Using his talents to justify and defend Mormonism, Talmadge expounded with great force his rationalisation of the creed, and skilfully arrayed and supported the *raison d'être* of the faith he and his family had embraced.

[*Who's Who in America,* 1930–31; J. M. Cattell and D. R. Brimhall, *Am. Men of Sci.* (3rd ed., 1921); Andrew Jenson, *Latter-Day Saint Biog. Encyc.,* vol. III (1920), pp. 787–89; M. J. Ballard, in *Improvement Era,* Sept. 1933; B. S. Hinckley, *Ibid.,* July 1932; R. S. Bennett, in *Latter-Day Saints Millenial Star,* July 28, 1932, Aug. 1933; J. F. Merrill, *Relief Soc. Mag.,* Sept. 1933; *Deseret News* (Salt Lake City), July 27–29, and *Salt Lake Tribune,* July 28, 1933.]   L. N.

TALMAGE, JOHN VAN NEST (Aug. 18, 1819–Aug. 19, 1892), missionary to China, was born on a farm in Somerville, N. J., the son of David and Catharine (Van Nest) Talmage, and a descendant of Thomas Talmadge who emigrated from England to Massachusetts some time after 1630 and settled at Southampton, Long Island, about 1642. John's father was a man of sterling character; he served several terms in the state legislature and for a time was high sheriff of Somerset County. His home was a deeply religious one, but its religion was of a happy and cheerful type; of the seven sons four entered the ministry, one of them being Thomas De Witt Talmage [*q.v.*]. John spent most of his boyhood at Gatesville, N. J., where his father kept a tollgate, and attended a private school at Boundbrook. He was active physically and something of a leader among his mates. Having prepared for college in the home of an elder brother, a pastor at Blawenburgh, N. J., he entered Rutgers as a sophomore, was graduated in 1842, and then went to the New Brunswick Theological Seminary, where he was graduated in 1845.

As a lad he had read the biographies of missionaries and while in college had continued to keep in touch with missionary literature. It was not surprising, therefore, that an address by a missionary, the Rev. Elihu Doty [*q.v.*], which Talmage heard while a student, should have led him to decide to give his life to that calling. On leaving the seminary he offered himself to the American Board of Commissioners for Foreign Missions, with which his denomination, the Dutch Reformed, then cooperated. The Board's financial condition precluded sending him immediately, and for two years he served as assistant pastor in the Central Reformed Church of Brooklyn, being ordained at Millstone, N. J., on Aug. 26, 1846. In 1847 he sailed for Amoy, China, and arrived only a few years after the first Chinese treaties with Western powers had opened it to foreign residence. There he spent the major part of the remainder of his life, most of the time making his home on the island of Kulangsu, on the opposite side of the harbor from the city. The first of his infrequent trips to America was in 1849, barely two years after his arrival in China, to escort a member of his mission who was being invalided home. Before returning he married, Jan. 15, 1850, Abby F. Woodruff. His second voyage home was in 1862, when, after the death of his wife, he felt that he must take his four children to the United States. While in America he pleaded with the General Synod of his church to permit the cooperation of its missionaries with those of the English Presbyterians in the formation of an independent Chinese church in Amoy and the adjoining territory, and published in 1863 *History and Ecclesiastical Relations of the Churches of the Presbyterian Order at Amoy, China.* At first defeated, he later won his point. In November 1864 he married Mary E. Van Deventer and soon afterward returned to Amoy.

Here he continued to contribute to the building of a growing Chinese church. He shared both in preaching and in teaching. He was noted, too, for his literary achievements. In his student days he had shown himself so proficient in Hebrew and Greek that on graduating from the theological seminary he was urged to allow his name to be considered for a professorship of languages in that institution. In Amoy he gave much attention to developing a romanized form of writing the vernacular, to enable illiterate Christians quickly to read the Bible and other religious literature, and prepared a good deal of printed material in that medium. Included in this material are a primer (1852), a reader (1853), a version of *Pilgrim's Progress,* the Book of Ruth, and portions of the New Testament. In the closing years of his life he finished a dictionary of the Amoy dialect. Able, cheerful, hopeful, hard-working, persistent, in the course of nearly half a century in Amoy he made a profound impression upon the missionaries and the rising churches of that region. Ill, he returned to America in 1889 and spent his remaining years at Boundbrook, near his boyhood home.

[A. W. Talmadge, *The Talmadge, Tallmadge, and Talmage Geneal.* (1909) ; *Biog. Notices of Officers and Grads. of Rutgers Coll. Deceased during the Academical Year Ending in June, 1893* (1893) ; *Biog. Record, Theological Sem. of New Brunswick* (1912) ; J. G. Fagg, *Forty Years in South China: The Life of Rev. John Van Nest Talmage, D.D.* (1894) ; J. I. Good, *Famous Missionaries of the Reformed Church* (1903) ; Ann. reports of the Am. Board of Commissioners for Foreign Missions, 1848–58, and of the Board of Foreign Missions of the Reformed Church in America, 1857 ; E. T. Corwin, *A Manual of the Reformed Church in America* (1902) ; *Christian Intelligencer,* Aug. 24, 1892 ; *Christian Herald,* Sept. 7, 1892 ; *Brooklyn Daily Eagle,* Aug. 20, 1892.]   K. S. L.

TALMAGE, THOMAS DE WITT (Jan. 7, 1832–Apr. 12, 1902), clergyman, editor, and lecturer, was born near Boundbrook, N. J., the son of David and Catharine (Van Nest) Talmage, and a younger brother of John Van Nest Talmage [*q.v.*]. His father was a farmer and a tollgate keeper. Thomas De Witt attended a school in New Brunswick, and at nineteen entered the University of the City of New York, where he studied law. He did not graduate, for before he had completed his course he turned to the ministry, in which profession three brothers, a brother-in-law, and two uncles were already engaged. In 1862, however, the University awarded him the degree of A.M. He graduated from the New Brunswick Theological Seminary in 1856, and in the same year was ordained (July 26), a minister of the Dutch Reformed Church, installed in his first charge at Belleville, N. J., and married to Mary R. Avery of Brooklyn, N. Y. Called to Syracuse, N. Y., in 1859, he served there until 1862, when he went to the Second Dutch Reformed Church of Philadelphia. Shortly after settling there, his wife, by whom he had had two children, was drowned in the Schuylkill River, June 9, 1862, and the following year he married Sarah Whittemore of Greenpoint, Long Island, a young woman of considerable means.

When he took charge of the church in Philadelphia it was quiet and old-fashioned, and had no great influence; but Talmage's magnetic and rather sensational style of preaching soon began to draw large audiences, and the church prospered. He had a fine, erect figure, strong, clear-cut features and a winning manner, and he used many startling gestures and illustrations to rivet attention. His critics called him a pulpit clown and a mountebank, but there were thousands who admired and reverenced him. His reputation increased so rapidly that he had several calls to other churches, and in 1869 accepted an invitation to the Central Presbyterian Church of Brooklyn, N. Y., a church then torn by dissension. His success there, notwithstanding some caustic criticism in the metropolitan newspapers, was immediate and impressive, and he was soon drawing the largest audiences which assembled to hear any minister in America. To take care of the throngs which came to hear him, a new church called the Tabernacle was hastily built. The burning of this edifice on Sunday morning, Dec. 22, 1872, just before the hour for service, was one of the memorable fire disasters in Brooklyn's history. A new and greater Tabernacle was completed by January 1874, the congregation meanwhile occupying the Academy of Music. At the height of his fame, Talmage's sermons were published weekly in about 3,500 newspapers. He was one of the most successful lecturers of modern times, for many years delivering an average of fifty lectures annually. In 1879 he was accused before the Brooklyn Presbytery of "falsehood and deceit, and . . . using improper methods of preaching, which tend to bring religion into contempt." He was acquitted, though the vote of the court on some of the counts was close. He was keenly alive to the value of publicity and while on a tour of Palestine in 1889 arranged to baptize a man in the River Jordan. His second Tabernacle was destroyed by fire in 1889; a third was erected, and this also was burned, in May 1894. Momentarily discouraged, he announced that he would give up his pastorate and devote his time to evangelism. He changed his mind, however, and accepted a call to the First Presbyterian Church of Washington, D. C.

He had long been more or less interested in religious journalism, having edited the *Christian at Work* (1874–76) and *Frank Leslie's Sunday*

Magazine (1881–89), and in 1899 he resigned his Washington pastorate and devoted himself to conducting the *Christian Herald,* of which he had been editor since 1890. His second wife, who bore him five children, died Aug. 5, 1895, leaving him $200,000, and on Jan. 22, 1898, he married Eleanor (McCutcheon) Collier, the well-to-do widow of Charles W. Collier of Allegheny City, Pa., who survived him. Among his numerous published works were *Crumbs Swept Up* (1870); *The Abominations of Modern Society* (1872); *Sermons* (1872); *Points* (1873); *Old Wells Dug Out* (1874); *Around the Tea-Table* (1874); *Every-Day Religion* (1875); *The Night Sides of City Life* (1878); *The Masque Torn Off* (1880); *Mormonism* (1880); *High License* (1884); *Rum, the Worst Enemy of the Working Classes* (1886); *The Marriage Ring* (1886); *Social Dynamite* (1887); *The Key-Note of the Temperance Reform* (1890); *Twenty-five Sermons on the Holy Land* (1890); *The Marriage Tie* (1890); *From Manger to Throne* (1890). An autobiography, *T. De Witt Talmage as I Knew Him,* with concluding chapters by his widow, appeared in 1912, and in 1923 a compilation entitled *Fifty Short Sermons by T. De Witt Talmage* was published by his daughter, May Talmage.

[*Who's Who in America,* 1901–02; *North American and U. S. Gazette* (Phila.), and *Press* (Phila.), June 10, 1862; *World* (N. Y.), Jan. 28, 1894, Apr. 13, 1902; *N. Y. Times, N. Y. Herald, Sun* (N. Y.), *Brooklyn Eagle,* and *Washington Post,* Apr. 13, 1902; A. W. Talmage, *The Talmadge, Tallmadge, and Talmage Geneal.* (1909); *Record of Proc. in the Talmage Case Before the Presbytery of Brooklyn* (1879); John Rusk, *The Authentic Life of T. De Witt Talmage* (1902); C. F. Adams, *The Life and Sermons of Rev. T. De Witt Talmage* (1902); *Life and Teachings of Rev. T. De Witt Talmadge, D.D.* (1902), memorial vol.; C. E. Banks, *Authorized and Authentic Life and Works of T. De Witt Talmadge* (1902).]   A. F. H.

TALVJ [See Robinson, Therese Albertine Louise von Jakob, 1797–1870].

TAMARÓN, PEDRO (d. Dec. 21, 1768), bishop of Durango, was a native of La Guardia in the archbishopric of Toledo, Spain. He was the domestic chaplain of Bishop Juan Joseph de Escalona y Calatayud of Carácas, Venezuela, with whom he came to America when very young. He studied at the University of Santa Rosa, Carácas, and there he received the doctor's degree and served as professor of canonical law. He obtained the curacy of the cathedral there and the ranks of teacher of divinity (*maestrescuela*) and precentor. In 1758 the king nominated him as bishop of Durango, and in the same year he took charge of the bishopric. Between 1759 and 1763 he personally visited the most remote provinces of his diocese, even proceeding to the north as far as the last pueblo of New Mexico before he returned to his capital, Durango. In New Mexico in 1760 Tamarón "had occasion at many points to administer severe reproof; and the friars, while making various excuses for their remissness, denying some of its worst results, and even promising reforms, did not claim the ability to communicate with their neophytes, except through interpreters. Charges of neglect in other matters, of oppressing the natives, of being frequently absent from their posts, and of undue fondness for trade are not supported by any evidence of this period . . ." (H. H. Bancroft, *History of Arizona and New Mexico, 1530–1888*, 1889, pp. 269–70). The bishop offered to print *confesionarios* in native languages, if the friars would write them. Some promises were secured and some correspondence was carried on concerning the matter, but nothing was effected down to 1763.

The diary which Tamarón kept of his episcopal tour is his most notable writing. It is entitled "Descripción del Obispado de Durango; ó Diario de la Santa Visita de toda aquella Diócesis, dedicado al Rey Ntro. Sr. D. Carlos III." A copy of the diary was sent to the king and the original was deposited in the ecclesiastical archives at Durango, where it was as late as 1883. The diary is a most detailed description of the bishopric, having been written with such thoroughness that there is no pueblo, hacienda, or ranch which is not described; in addition, distances and directions are recorded. Tamarón governed with ability and zeal until Dec. 21, 1768, when he died at the pueblo of Bamoa, Sinaloa.

[Brief sketches of Tamarón's life and work are to be found in Antonio de Alcedo, *Diccionario Geográfico-Histórico de las Indias Occidentales ó América*, vol. II (Madrid, 1787), p. 56; H. H. Bancroft, *Hist. of the North Mexican States and Texas*, vol. I (1884), pp. 594–95; J. M. Beristain de Souza, *Biblioteca Hispano Americana Septentrional*, vol. III (Mexico, 1821), pp. 169–70; and *Diccionario Universal de Historia y de Geografía*, vol. III (Mexico, 1853), p. 144, and vol. VII (Mexico, 1855), pp. 207–08.]   C. W. H.

TAMMANY (fl. 1685), was a chief of the Lenni-Lenape, or Delaware, Indians, whose name—sometimes appearing as Tamanend—may mean "affable" or "deserving." The known facts regarding his life are meager, and much that has been written about him is purely fanciful. It seems probable that his home was somewhere along the Delaware River, in the present Bucks County, Pa., but even the approximate time of his death is unknown. Tradition places him among those who welcomed William Penn on his arrival in America, Oct. 27, 1682. His name first appears in writing on a deed of June 23, 1683 (*Pennsylvania Archives*, 1 ser., vol. I, 1852, pp. 62–65), and later is found on several other documents. The most important record concerning him is in the minutes of a conference held on July 6, 1694, between the Provincial Council of Pennsylvania and a delegation of Indians (*Minutes of the Provincial Council of Pennsylvania*, vol. I, 1852, p. 447). At this conference Tammany made a speech in which he professed strong friendship for the whites. He seems, however, not to have been the principal chief, and there is no authentic contemporary mention of him during his fifteen years' contact with the whites which gives him exceptional standing for character or capacity.

The last contemporary mention of him is in 1698 (Gabriel Thomas, *An Historical and Geographical Account of the Province and Country of Pensilvania and of West-New-Jersey in America*, 1698). For more than seventy years following the records are blank. It is evident, however, that oral tradition kept his name in remembrance and gradually invested him with the noblest attributes. By 1771 he begins to emerge as a chieftain devotedly attached to the whites and endowed with every virtue and ability. His name appeared on calendars, and for a time, at several places in the central colonies, informal gatherings were held in his honor on May 1. The seething ferment that preceded the Revolution brought forth a number of organizations to oppose the St. George, St. Andrew, and St. David societies, and by many of the insurgent groups Tammany was adopted as the tutelary saint. He soon came to be regarded as a symbol of American resistance to British aggression. A predominantly Loyalist society, organized in Philadelphia on May 1, 1772, as the Sons of King Tammany, shifted its political attitude by Apr. 28 following and thereupon altered its name to Sons of Saint Tammany. In the days immediately following the Revolution the chieftain underwent another transformation and became the patron saint of those who stood for democracy and opposed aristrocracy and privilege. During the period a number of new Tammany societies were founded. Only one of these, the famous and powerful Society of Tammany, of New York City, founded in 1786 by William Mooney [*q.v.*], a Revolutionary veteran, and reorganized in 1789, was fated to endure.

[E. P. Kilroe, *Saint Tammany and the Origin of the Society of Tammany* (1913) is a careful inquiry into all the legends and historical sources.]   W. J. G.

TANEY, ROGER BROOKE (Mar. 17, 1777– Oct. 12, 1864), attorney general, secretary of the treasury, chief justice of the United States, was born on a tobacco plantation in Calvert County, in southern Maryland. His father, Michael Taney, was a member of a family of planters; the founder of this was another Michael Taney, who about 1660 had come to Maryland as an indentured servant but had died the possessor of considerable property in land and slaves. His mother, Monica (Brooke) Taney, was descended from another family of the landed aristocracy; her first American ancestor had come to Maryland in 1650 with fox hounds and other trappings indicative of gentlemanly status. During the years of his boyhood Roger Taney imbibed the culture and the accepted ideas of his class. After studying in local rural schools and with a family tutor he went to Dickinson College in 1792 and graduated in 1795. The production of tobacco being less profitable than formerly, and there being no land in the family holdings for Roger Taney, who was a second son, he was trained for a career at the bar and in politics. He read law in the office of Judge Jeremiah Townley Chase, of the Maryland general court, at Annapolis, and was admitted to practice in 1799. With the aid of his father and other gentlemen of Calvert County he was elected to the state legislature for the term of 1799–1800. His political career was checked in 1800, however, when national issues caused the defeat of many Maryland Federalists in state politics. He moved to Frederick in 1801, his enemies declaring that he had been laughed out of Calvert County for being an aristocrat. He lived in Frederick until 1823, achieving a position of prominence in the community, and conducting a growing and increasingly profitable law practice.

On Jan. 7, 1806, he married Anne P. C. Key, daughter of a well-to-do farmer, John Ross Key, and the sister of Francis Scott Key [q.v.]. Six daughters, and a son who died in infancy, were born to them. One daughter and his wife died in 1855; the others survived him. Despite his constantly poor health, and the necessity of diligent labor to support his growing family, and despite his lack of success as a candidate, Taney continued active in politics, and became prominent among the leaders of the Federalists of the state. He broke with the more prominent and wealthy Federalists in 1812, however, when they refused or granted reluctantly their support to the government in the conduct of the war with Great Britain, and became a leader of the dissenting faction who were derisively called "Coodies." Taney's position was indicated by the title "King Coody." The "Coodies" were in the minority in the party during the war, but ultimately the disloyalty of the extreme Federalists brought them into disrepute, and in order to maintain their control of the state legislature they had to make concessions to Taney's faction. As a result he was chosen in 1816 for a five-year term in the state Senate, where he ousted the opposing faction from control and dominated the Federalist party during the few years in which it continued to survive. His major interest, apart from the issues of party politics, seems to have been in laws to prevent the evils due to unsound currency and bad banking, and in laws to protect the rights of negroes in the state, whether freemen or slaves.

He moved in 1823 to Baltimore, where professional opportunities were greater, and where he was recognized as one of the most eminent members of the bar. He was a master of the technicalities of procedure, on which turned the disposition of many cases of the period, although he never resorted to cheap trickery and was noted for complete fairness to his opponents. He was tall and flat-chested, with broad and stooping shoulders. His face was long and his features were uneven. His voice was low and hollow. His style of delivery was one of simple and direct earnestness, however, and was highly effective in spite of the absence of the florid eloquence which was characteristic of the time. It provided the basis for the clarity and persuasiveness of many of his judicial opinions in later years. He seems to have taken cases whenever they were offered, and there is no evidence that he hesitated to serve clients whom he believed to be in the wrong.

The Federalist party having been virtually dissolved, Taney in 1824 gave his support to Andrew Jackson. When, after Jackson's defeat in that year, a party was organized to bring about his election in 1828 Taney was made chairman of the state central committee. He seems not to have desired appointment to federal office at this time. He had to keep up his extensive practice in order to maintain the income to which he had become accustomed, his health was too poor to justify added exertions, and he was already in a position of some honor, having been appointed attorney general of Maryland in 1827. In 1831, however, when President Jackson found it necessary to reorganize his cabinet, Taney accepted a recess appointment as attorney general of the United States. He took the oath of office on July 20, assuming also for a short time the duties of acting secretary of war, and was duly confirmed as attorney general in December.

Taney's most significant activities as a member of the Jackson cabinet had to do with the second Bank of the United States, now seeking from Congress the renewal of its charter. Taney had long been interested in banking and currency problems. He had been a director of a branch of a state bank in Frederick from 1810 to 1815; in 1818 he had successfully sponsored a bill to charter the Frederick County Bank, and he had been a director from 1818 to 1823. While a member of the state Senate he sponsored legislation to prevent the circulation of bank notes at less than their face value, and to prevent the deliberate depreciation of the value of the notes of rural banks for which Baltimore bankers and brokers were said to be in part responsible. At first he evidently regarded a national bank as a desirable instrument for regulating the currency, and perhaps for restraining the predatory activities of the more powerful banks chartered by the states. He voted with the minority against the bill to tax the notes of the Baltimore branch, which in 1819 was declared unconstitutional by the Supreme Court of the United States, speaking through Chief Justice Marshall in *McCulloch* vs. *Maryland*. The subsequent conduct of the Bank of the United States, however, was not such as he could approve. He was for several years counsel in opposition to it in a case in which he felt that the officers of the bank had been guilty of sharp and unethical practice. After he moved to Baltimore, as counsel for the Union Bank of Maryland he observed both the power and the tendency toward ruthlessness of the Bank of the United States. When he entered the Jackson cabinet he held the conviction that if the institution was to be rechartered it must be with definite limitations on its powers. He so advised the President, and when the friends of the bank attempted at the session of Congress of 1831–32 to force the enactment of a law granting a new charter, believing that Jackson would not dare oppose it just before a presidential election, Taney advised him to veto it. Jackson was persuaded, and when other members of his cabinet refused to aid him in the preparation of a veto message on the merits of the case he called Taney to aid in redrafting the document which had been begun by Amos Kendall [*q.v.*].

The message, containing a compact legal argument which was evidently prepared by Taney, embedded in dynamic political materials presumably arranged by Kendall and others, was reprinted in the Jackson papers all over the country, and became one of the outstanding documents in the ensuing campaign. The officers of the bank, in spite of the fact that the government itself held one-fifth of the stock, spent thousands of dollars of bank money in circulating speeches

of Daniel Webster and others in the attempt to block Jackson's reëlection on the bank issue. Jackson succeeded in spite of the opposition, and in the months which followed he and other enemies of the bank learned more fully how it had participated in the presidential campaign, and also how its president, Nicholas Biddle, had schemed to block the government program of paying off the national debt with funds deposited in the bank. Taney and others thereupon advised Jackson immediately to withdraw the government deposits from the Bank of the United States and place them in selected state banks.

Jackson considered the measure at length, and secured Taney's promise to accept the post of secretary of the treasury if William J. Duane [*q.v.*], who then held that position, should refuse to remove the deposits. Although admitting the strength of the argument in the "Paper read to the Cabinet," which had been largely redrafted by Taney and presented to the cabinet to justify the removal of the deposits, Duane refused to take the step. Jackson dismissed him, and on Sept. 23, 1833, by recess appointment, Taney became secretary of the treasury. Three days later he announced that on and after Oct. 1 government deposits would no longer be made in the Bank of the United States and its branches but in certain specified state banks.

During the ensuing nine months he set up a system of government depositories which continued to function in spite of the concentrated opposition of all the forces back of the Bank of the United States. For the part which he played Taney was labeled by Webster, Clay, and other friends of the bank as the "pliant instrument" of Andrew Jackson. Early historians accepted this political indictment as true. Further examination of the facts, however, reveals that Taney was fundamentally anything but pliant. He was tactful in his methods, it is true, as one who succeeded in influencing the conduct of Andrew Jackson had to be, but it is evident that from the beginning he labored persistently to curtail the power of an institution which he had come to regard as a menace to the country. He had a program for improving the currency which included doing away with small denomination notes altogether. Unfortunately for the program it required the cooperation of Congress and of the states, and it required also that he should remain in office. This he was unable to do. The enemy was so strong in the Senate that when, toward the end of the session, his appointment was presented for confirmation, it was rejected (June 24, 1834), and he was retired to private life. His attack upon the bank, however, had been decisive, and the institution was not rechartered.

On Jan. 15, 1835, doubtless as much as a political reward as in recognition of merit, Jackson nominated Taney for the position of associate justice of the Supreme Court. His enemies defeated the nomination by postponing it indefinitely (Mar. 3, 1835). On Dec. 28, Jackson nominated him for the position left vacant by the death of Chief Justice Marshall. Many changes had taken place in the Senate since the preceding session, and on Mar. 15, 1836, the appointment was confirmed in spite of Whig opposition. His accession to the chief justiceship did not bring into the decisions of the Supreme Court the petty politics which his enemies had feared. It did, however, result in the reversal of certain trends which characterized the work of his predecessor. During the Marshall régime the Supreme Court had curbed at various points the legislative activities of the states, and had exercised a jealous guardianship over contract rights, including those conferred by corporation charters. One of the first important questions with which Chief Justice Taney was faced was whether rights not specifically conferred by a charter could be inferred from the language of the document. Speaking for a majority of the court in *Charles River Bridge* vs. *Warren Bridge* (36 *United States,* 420), and against a powerful dissent by Justice Story, the spokesman of the Marshall group, he held that rights could not be so inferred, and that rights granted by charters were to be construed narrowly. "While the rights of private property are sacredly guarded," he declared, "we must not forget that the community also have rights, and that the happiness and well being of every citizen depends on their faithful preservation" (36 *United States,* 548). The decision reflected his experience with the predatory activities of corporations, and particularly of the Bank of the United States. The legal principle which he asserted became a permanent and valued fixture in American constitutional law.

The decision did not mean, however, that Taney planned, by interpretation, to devitalize the obligation of contract clause of the Constitution, as was shown by his opinion in *Bronson* vs. *Kinzie* (42 *United States,* 311), in which he held unconstitutional a state law interfering with the execution of mortgages. Neither did it mean that his decisions would always be uncompromisingly against corporations. In *Bank of Augusta* vs. *Earle* (38 *United States,* 519), he asserted the important principle that although a state might exclude from its borders the cor-

porations of other states, the courts, in the absence of specific legislation to that effect, would observe the rule of comity and hold that it had not done so. The change from the old régime represented merely a modification of the assumption that unchecked centralization of power in the federal government and unqualified judicial benevolence toward private aggregations of wealth and power worked always for the good of the country.

Taney always felt that the commerce clause of the Constitution should be interpreted narrowly when the issue was whether it should be used to defeat state laws (see for example *License Cases,* 46 *United States,* 504; and his dissent in *Passenger Cases,* 48 *United States,* 283). His opinions on the subject rarely suggested a denial of federal power to regulate, but tended rather to oppose the use of the Constitution to prevent state regulation where regulation otherwise would not exist. In other words, he apparently had little sympathy for the régime of *laissez-faire* which the Constitution was being used to enforce upon the states. He concurred in some opinions of his brethren upholding state laws as police regulations, but he seems to have felt that the rights of the state ought to be protected without resort to a special doctrine of police powers, which was then in evolution. The states were sovereign within their sphere. That ought to be enough, in cases where they had not by the Constitution specifically surrendered their power to act. In dealing, on the other hand, with the related subject of the extension of admiralty laws to inland waters, and the jurisdiction of federal courts over cases arising there, he asserted a breadth of federal power which had not been claimed even by Marshall (see *The Propeller Genesee Chief* vs. *Fitzhugh,* 53 *United States,* 443).

In many ways Taney showed great restraint in the exercise of power. He abandoned the custom of delivering political charges to grand juries summoned before the circuit court of the United States. In his dissenting opinion in *State of Rhode Island* vs. *State of Massachusetts* (37 *United States,* 657) he went to the extreme of denying the jurisdiction of the Supreme Court in suits between states to determine boundary lines when acting in their sovereign capacity. In *Luther* vs. *Borden* (48 *United States,* 1) he used the doctrine of political questions to justify a denial of jurisdiction in a case involving the question as to which of two organizations was the legitimate government of a state. Despite this typical restraint, he went to the verge of impropriety in publishing a dissenting opinion in a case involving the Bank of the United States in which he had not heard the arguments and turning in part upon his activities as attorney general (*Bank of the United States* vs. *United States, 43 United States, 710*; see the appendix, p. 745). Nor should the fact be obscured that during the Civil War he was a number of times at the point of defying the military and civil officers of the Federal government.

While slavery issues are usually overemphasized in brief accounts of Taney, his life is not to be understood without reference to these issues and to the broader ones of economic and cultural conflict between the North and the South. Taney had been brought up in an undiluted Southern agrarian atmosphere, and his life was permanently conditioned by it. Like many of his Southern neighbors he cooperated in projects for colonizing free negroes in Africa; he manumitted his own slaves and even purchased others to enable them to work out their freedom. But he concluded from observation that white and colored people, being what they were, could not satisfactorily live together in large numbers as equals, and that slavery was probably necessary as long as negroes remained in the country. He was convinced that the solution of the problem, at any rate, was to be arrived at only by the people who were in immediate contact with it, and not by Northern abolitionists who had no comprehension of its complexity. This attitude doubtless added strength to his belief that in general the courts ought scrupulously to guard the sovereignty of the states from federal encroachment—for the population dominated by Northern culture and interests was gaining rapidly over the population of the South, and must in time control the federal government.

In 1856 Taney expressed privately the belief that the South was doomed to sink to a state of inferiority, and that power would be exercised to gratify Northern cupidity and evil passions without reference to the principles of the Constitution. His feelings being what they were, it is not surprising that when, a few months later, one of his colleagues prepared to present in *Dred Scott* vs. *Sandford* (60 *United States*, 393) an unnecessary argument in favor of the constitutionality of the Missouri Compromise, he consented to discuss for the court from the opposing point of view this and other sectional issues which might easily have been avoided. He argued that negro could not possess the rights of citizenship which entitled him to sue in a federal court, and that therefore the lower court, in the case at hand, had erred in taking jurisdiction. Since doubt had been expressed, however, as to

whether this phase of the question of jurisdiction could now legitimately be determined by the Supreme Court, he sought to strengthen his position by another argument demonstrating that the lower court had been in error in taking jurisdiction. This argument was based on the fact that a slave could not possess rights of citizenship permitting him to sue in a federal court. It was admitted that Dred Scott had been born a slave. Taney sought to demonstrate that he was still a slave, and that he had not, as contended, become free because of residence in territory made free by act of Congress, because Congress had never had the constitutional power to exclude slavery from the territories.

Thus under cover of a discussion of jurisdiction Taney passed upon questions which lay at the base of the heated controversy between the North and the South. That the case could have been decided on narrower grounds was made apparent at the time both by the dissenting opinions and by the diversity of the opinions of the judges who concurred in the judgment. With unprecedented bitterness Republican and abolitionist leaders attacked Taney and the majority of the court for deciding unnecessarily that Congress had no power to exclude slavery from the territories, and for comments made on the rights of negroes. They misrepresented Taney's opinion to make him say that the negro now had no rights which the white man was bound to respect. So effective was the use to which the decision was put that it played an important part in ensuing elections, and has commonly been regarded as one of the major causes of the Civil War. Taney's opinion was sharply criticized by Northern lawyers on the ground that many of his arguments were *obiter dicta*. They were such, however, only by a narrow definition of the term, and, it might be added, only in the sense that many of the much-lauded doctrines of Chief Justice Marshall, announced in the foundation cases of American constitutional law, were *obiter dicta*. Fundamentally it was their content, and not their status as *obiter dicta*, which provoked Northern hostility. As his predecessor had taken advantage of his position to promulgate doctrines to justify the establishment of the strong central government which he thought desirable, so Taney, by the use of different doctrines, had attempted to protect the weaker of two diverse cultures from being smothered by the stronger. It is true that he had wholly miscalculated the effects of the decision, and that it hastened rather than retarded the ultimate subjugation of the South. Nevertheless, his opinion is to be accurately explained only in terms of what he attempted to do.

He wrote two other opinions of major importance in connection with sectional issues. In discussing the constitutionality of the Fugitive-slave Law, in *Ableman* vs. *Booth* (62 *United States,* 506), he presented a penetrating analysis of the relations between the state and national governments which was to be accepted as a masterpiece and quoted time and again by his colleagues and successors in future years. Unhappily the crisis was too close at hand for a general calm appraisal of the opinion at the time when it was delivered. In *Ex parte Merryman* (*Federal Cases* No. 9,487) he delivered a brilliant defense of the rights of civilians in war time, only to make himself again the object of bitter denunciation. The private records of the period reveal on his part a complete lack of sympathy with the national government in the conduct of the war, and the belief that force should not have been used to prevent the South from leaving the Union. Hence it was that when he died in Washington, on Oct. 12, 1864, he was scorned by the war-frenzied masses.

Taney's personality and his private life were such as to lend an air of incongruity to the hatred he aroused. He was considerate of others, gracious, dependable. Owing to his low salary, his open-handed charity, and the heavy expenditures arising from the fact that he and other members of his family were semi-invalids, he was always near to a state of financial embarrassment. Yet he paid all debts with scrupulous care, and refused aid, even from his best friends. He long hoped to make a contribution to history by writing at length the story of the battles of the Jackson period, but although rough drafts of certain segments were left for posterity his poor health prevented the completion of his dramatic account. Like his ancestors for a number of generations, he was a Roman Catholic. He was devoted to his church, and was sincere, humble, and devout in participation in its forms of worship. He carried his religion into the performance of his professional tasks to the extent of beginning each day's work in court only after having privately spent a few moments in prayer. He was broadly tolerant, however, and not much concerned with matters of creed. His wife was a Protestant, and he refused to permit members of his church to press the claims of Catholicism upon her or his daughters. He deeply resented the Know-Nothing movement, in so far as it represented an attack upon members of his faith, but his wrathful private protests were for the most part defensive in character, and he never attempted to carry war into opposing camps. Only on rare occasions, such as in some instances during the bank war, in two or three letters written after the Dred Scott decision, and certain letters dealing with the mistreatment of one of his daughters by her husband, do the records show that beneath his calm and courteous exterior was a fiery temper resembling that which had made it necessary for his father (1819) to flee from a charge of manslaughter.

With the passing of the years resentment against him has died down, and his character and his motives have come more and more to be understood. He has won the respect of thoughtful students even though they may not accept his point of view, and Charles Sumner's vindictive prophecy that his name should be "hooted down the page of history" seems certain to go unfulfilled. More and more, sentiment concerning him can be accurately embodied in the declaration of his successor, Charles E. Hughes, that "he was a great Chief Justice."

[Available sources include: Samuel Tyler, *Memoir of Roger Brooke Taney, LL.D.* (1872); B. C. Steiner, *Life of Roger Brooke Taney* (1922); C. B. Swisher, *Roger B. Taney* (1935); *The Unjust Judge. A Memorial of Roger Brooke Taney, Late Chief Justice of the United States* (1865); E. S. Corwin, "The Dred Scott Decision, in the Light of Contemporary Legal Doctrines," *Am. Hist. Review,* Oct. 1911, pp. 52–69; H. H. Hagen, "The Dred Scott Decision," in *Georgetown Law Journal,* Jan. 1927; and "Ableman vs. Booth," in *Am. Bar Asso. Journal,* Jan. 1931; a longhand manuscript in the Lib. of Cong. by Taney giving an account of the struggle with the Bank of the United States; J. M. Campbell, ed., *Reports of the Cases at Law and Equity and in the Admiralty Determined in the Circuit Court of the United States for the District of Maryland by R. B. Taney* (1871); Charles Warren, *The Supreme Court in United States History* (2 vols., rev. ed., 1926); Mrs. J. C. Lane, *Key and Allied Families* (1931); death notice and obituary, *Daily National Intelligencer* (Washington, D. C.), Oct. 13, 14, 1864. Taney's home in Frederick, Md., preserved as a museum, contains some of his furniture, pictures, clothing, and other items.]   C. B. S.

TANNEBERGER, DAVID (Mar. 21, 1728–May 19, 1804), organ builder, also known as Tannenberg and Tanneberg, was born on Count Nicholas von Zinzendorf's estate, Berthelsdorf, in Upper (Saxon) Lusatia, the son of Johann and Judith (Nitschmann) Tanneberger. His family belonged on both sides to the Unitas Fratrum, his parents emigrating to Berthelsdorf in 1726 from Zauchtenthal in Moravia. As one of John Nitschmann's colonists, Tanneberger landed at New York from the Moravian missionary snow, *Irene,* on May 12, 1749, and proceeded to Bethlehem, Pa., where he was married on July 15 to Anna Rosina Kerner (or Kern) of Ebersdorf, Upper Lusatia, who had come to America in the same company. Thirty other couples were married that day, which was long celebrated at Bethlehem as the anniversary of the "Great Wedding." He was a skilful joiner, had a notably good tenor voice, and played the violin. In 1757 John Gottlob Klemm of Dresden, Saxony, who had learned organ building in Germany, took him as helper to repair the Bethlehem church organ. This, the first American-built organ, had been constructed by Gustavus Hesselius [q.v.] in 1746 and installed by Klemm at Bethlehem, where it was overhauled in 1751 by Robert Harttafel, whose later life was spent at Lancaster, Pa. These men were the first American organ builders; Tanneberger became the most expert and renowned of them all and contributed substantially to the musical culture of his time. He and Klemm set up a shop at Nazareth but relocated it at Bethlehem in 1760. Records exist of Tanneberger's trips to various points in quest of suitable timber for their work. Two of their instruments have been identified, one built (1758) for the chapel of the Manor House (Nazareth Hall), the other (1759) for the Bethlehem church. In 1761 Tanneberger transported Hesselius' old organ to Lititz in Lancaster County and installed it there. Klemm died May 5, 1762, and in 1765 Tanneberger removed to Lititz and bought the "Pilgerhaus" for a home and workshop. Organs of his manufacture were in high repute and were shipped all over eastern Pennsylvania from his Lititz shop and even to such distant points as Albany, N. Y. (1767), Salem, N. C. (1798), Baltimore (1798), and Madison, Va. (1801). He made organs not only for Moravian but also for Reformed, Lutheran, and Roman Catholic churches. He also built pianos, which he sold for twenty-two pounds ten shillings. His wife, who had borne him three daughters and two sons, died in 1792; and in 1800 he married Anna Maria (Fischer) Hall Lange of Heidelberg, Pa., who had been twice a widow. His last organ was built in 1804 for Christ Lutheran Church at York. While installing it, Tanneberger suffered a paralytic stroke, fell from a bench or scaffold, and died a few days later. He was buried at York, the organ playing for the first time at his funeral. He was survived by his three daughters. John Philip Bachmann, his son-in-law, continued the business at Lititz for more than twenty years.

[J. W. Jordan, "Early Colonial Organ-Builders of Pa.," *Pa. Mag. Hist. and Biog.*, July 1898, and "Moravian Immigration to Pa., 1734–67," *Trans. Moravian Hist. Soc.*, vol. V (Nazareth, Pa., 1899); P. E. Beck, "David Tanneberger, Organ Builder," *Papers Read before the Lancaster County Hist. Soc.*, Jan. 8, 1926; A. R. Beck, "David Tannenberg," *Pa.-German*, July 1909, and "The Moravian Graveyards of Lititz, Pa., 1744–1905," *Trans. Moravian Hist. Soc.*, vol. VII (1906); J. M. Levering, *A Hist. of Bethlehem, Pa., 1741–1892* (Bethlehem, 1903); A. G. Rau, "A List of the Bohemian and Moravian Emigrants to Saxony," *Trans. Moravian Hist. Soc.*, vol. IX (1913); *Church Music and Musical Life in Pa. in the Eighteenth Cent.*, vol. II (1927), Pubs. Pa. Soc. Colonial Dames of America, no. 4.]   G. H. G.

TANNER, BENJAMIN (Mar. 27, 1775–Nov. 14, 1848), engraver, was born in New York City. Having early displayed a talent for drawing and designing, he was placed with Peter C. Verger, a French engraver in that city, to learn the art. Though he remained with Verger until he was of age, engravings signed by him as early as 1792 are known, and in 1795 he engraved six of the small folio plates that illustrate Paul Wright's *The New and Complete Life of Our Blessed Lord and Saviour Jesus Christ*. Upon the completion of his apprenticeship he set up for himself in his native city, but in 1799 he went to Philadelphia, where he lived for the rest of his life. Between the years 1800 and 1805, however, his name does not appear in the directories of that city. In 1800 he engraved a portrait of Washington for Mason L. Weems's *A History of the Life and Death, Virtues and Exploits of General George Washington* (1800), which was published by John Bioren, Philadelphia. On Sept. 6, 1806, he was married in Philadelphia to Mary Bioren, probably a daughter of the publisher (notice in *Poulson's American Daily Advertiser*, Sept. 10, 1806). To his younger brother, Henry Schenck Tanner [q.v.], he taught the art of engraving, and, since the latter was interested in geography, the two began in 1811 the business of map engraving and publishing in Philadelphia. In 1817 Tanner joined Francis Kearny and Cornelius Tiebout [qq.v.] in banknote engraving under the firm name of Tanner, Kearny & Tiebout. By 1818 he had organized a second firm —Tanner, Vallance, Kearny & Company— which occupied the same premises and engaged in general engraving. Of this firm, which existed until 1824, Tanner's brother was a member. About 1828 Tanner or his young brother —the credit is variously assigned—devised a check blank engraved in such a way as to prevent alteration without detection. In 1835 Tanner abandoned general engraving, and made the production of check and note blanks his business, printing his product under the trade name "stereograph." He retired in 1845 because of failing eyesight and carried on his business through an agency. Shortly afterward he was found to be suffering from an abcess of the brain. He went to Baltimore for treatment and died there at the house of his son on Nov. 14, 1848.

His early engraved work which was in the

line manner, was somewhat crude. Later he improved immeasurably, and engraved many fine plates in line and in stipple. Among his best plates were both portraits and historical subjects connected with the Revolution and the War of 1812, such as "Perry's Victory," "Capture of the *Macedonian*," and "Surrender of Cornwallis." He engraved many designs by John James Barralet, including an imperial folio plate in stipple of "Apotheosis of Washington" (1802), and "America Guided by Wisdom." His portraits were usually in stipple and his subject plates in line. In conjunction with William Satchwell Leney [*q.v.*] he engraved a royal folio portrait (1812) of Archbishop John Carroll of Baltimore. He also engraved maps and charts, among them one for a volume of maps supplementing John Marshall's *The Life of George Washington* (5 vols., 1804–07), and plates for some annuals. Among the plates for the 1802–03 edition of W. F. Mavor's *Historical Account of the Most Celebrated Voyages* were many engraved by Tanner. In the exhibition of the works of American engravers in the New York Public Library in 1928, he was represented by several plates.

[Frank Weitenkampf, *Am. Graphic Art* (1912); W. S. Baker, *Am. Engravers and Their Works* (1875); D. M. Stauffer, *Am. Engravers upon Copper and Steel* (2 vols., 1907), with supplementary vol. (1917) by Mantle Fielding; *One Hundred Notable Am. Engravers, 1683–1850* (1928), cat. of exhibition at N. Y. Pub. Lib.; death notices in *Pub. Ledger* (Phila.) and *Sun* (Baltimore), Nov. 16, 1848.]   J. J.

TANNER, BENJAMIN TUCKER (Dec. 25, 1835–Jan. 15, 1923), bishop of the African Methodist Episcopal Church, was born in Pittsburgh, Pa., the son of Hugh S. and Isabel H. Tanner. His father died before the boy had finished his schooling and he was compelled to meet his expenses at Avery College, Allegheny City, from 1852 until 1857, by working as a barber in his spare time. In 1856 he was converted and became a licensed preacher of the African Methodist Episcopal Church. The year following he entered Western Theological Seminary, where he remained until 1860 and was then ordained as deacon and elder. Obliged to decline an appointment to the Sacramento station in California on account of a lack of means, he served as a substitute preacher for a year or more for a Presbyterian church in the District of Columbia. After the outbreak of the Civil War he organized a Sunday school for the freedmen newly enlisted in the navy, and in April 1862 was installed as head of the Alexander mission in E Street, the first of its kind to be established in Washington by the

African Methodist Episcopal Church. Having become a member of the Baltimore Conference in 1862, he was appointed the following year pastor of a Georgetown church, and in 1866 was promoted to a pastorate in Baltimore. He resigned from this position to become the principal of the Conference school at Frederick, Md. At the General Conference of his Church held in Washington in 1868 he was made its chief secretary and at the same time editor of the *Christian Recorder*. In 1881 he attended the Ecumenical Conference in London and in 1884 left the *Christian Recorder* to become the editor of the *A. M. E. Church Review*, which periodical he had helped to found. In 1888 he was elected bishop and assumed charge of the first district of the denomination with headquarters in Philadelphia. In September 1901 he was a delegate to the Third Ecumenical Conference on Methodism. At the General Conference held in May 1908 he was relieved of his duties at his own request and retired on half pay, being the first African Methodist Episcopal bishop to be given a pension.

His published writings include *An Apology for African Methodism* (1867); *The Negro's Origin; and Is He Cursed of God* (1869); *An Outline of Our History and Government for African Methodist Churchmen* (1884); and *Theological Lectures* (1894). On Aug. 19, 1858, he married Sarah Elizabeth Miller by whom he had two sons and five daughters.

[W. J. Simmons, *Men of Mark* (1887); B. W. Arnett, *The Budget . . . of the African Methodist Episcopal Church* (1884); *Who's Who of the Colored Race* (1915); R. R. Wright, *Centennial Encyc. of the African Methodist Episcopal Church* (copr. 1916); *Who's Who in America,* 1920–21; *Public Ledger* (Phila.), Jan. 16, 1923; *N. Y. Times,* Jan. 16, 1923.]   H. G. V.

TANNER, HENRY SCHENCK (1786–1858), cartographer and statistical geographer, was born in New York City but removed in early life to Philadelphia, Pa., where he was first associated with his brother Benjamin [*q.v.*], an engraver, and later with his brother's firm of Tanner, Vallance, Kearny & Company. Although trained as an engraver he was endowed with that combination of scientific and artistic sense that spells the true cartographer and that led him ultimately to produce for his time the outstanding map representations of the territory of the United States, based on a critical study of the source material. He engraved the thirty-one maps in *A New and Elegant General Atlas Containing Maps of Each of the United States* (*c.* 1812), the frontispiece map in *Travels in the United States* (1912) by John Melish [*q.v.*], two-thirds of the maps in Melish's *A Military and Topographical Atlas of the United States* (eds. of 1813, 1815), and, with J. Vallance, Melish's fundamental *Map of the United States . . . With the Contiguous British & Spanish Possessions* (1816), of 60 miles to the inch. Accompanying the last of these was a text—*A Geographical Description of the United States* (1816)—that included a brief discussion of the source maps on which the compilation was based. This text, as well as the work on the map itself, cannot but have exerted a shaping influence on Tanner's thought.

But all these undertakings were merely a prelude to Tanner's greatest work. The underlying principles of uniformity of scale and foundation on primary source material are expressed in its title: *A New American Atlas; Containing Maps of the Several States of the North American Union, Projected and Drawn on a Uniform Scale from Documents Found in the Public Offices of the United States . . . and Other Original and Authentic Information* (5 pts., 1818–23). It consisted primarily of maps of the individual states or of state groups, all on the scale of 15 geographical (or 17⅓ statute) miles to the inch, which would be large for many states even in a modern atlas. It ran through numerous editions until at least 1839. No modern atlas of relatively equal merit is available to the American public today, and the first paragraph of Tanner's announcement in the first instalment, dated Philadelphia, July 10, 1818, might still well serve as a charter for American cartography after a lapse of considerably more than a century. After criticizing previous American maps of the United States for their failure both "to convey an adequate idea of the subject" and "to do justice to the improved state of Geographical Science in the United States," and those published in Europe for their defectiveness and incorrectness, he expresses the view that "the subject must be brought to maturity" in America, where "we possess the materials and skill sufficient to exhibit a topographical representation of the United States, infinitely superior, as it regards correctness and detail, and every way equal in style, to any European publication of the kind."

The compilation of the maps in the *New American Atlas* gave Tanner a mastery of the cartographic sources relating to the United States. This, together with the rapid appearance of new material, led him to plan a synoptic view of the whole country, and in 1829 he published a map entitled simply *United States of America*, 64 by 50 inches in size, on the scale of exactly 1:2,000,000, or about 32 miles to the inch—practically twice as detailed as Melish's map of 1816. The selection of a so-called natural scale for the construction of the map—*i.e.*, an absolute scale expressing ratio in terms of size of the earth as against the universal practice of the time of utilizing relative scales expressing ratio in terms of conventional units of measure on the map itself, such as miles to the inch—throws an interesting sidelight on the scientific bent of Tanner's mind. Characteristically, also, during the compilation he addressed a circular letter inviting information as to recent surveys in the recipient's local region. He accompanied the map with a *Memoir on the Recent Surveys, Observations, and Internal Improvements, in the United States, With Brief Notices of the New Counties, Towns, Villages, Canals, and Rail Roads . . .* (Philadelphia, 1829), which is a model of a scientist's rendering of account. Tanner published many other maps, atlases, and guide books, and geographical compendia; the price list at the end of the 1829 *Memoir* enumerates no less than eighty items. Among these are his *A Map of the United States of Mexico, Constructed from a Great Variety of Printed and Manuscript Documents* (1825), on the scale of 85 miles to the inch; Robert Mills's *Atlas of the State of South Carolina* (Philadelphia, 1825), consisting of county maps engraved by Tanner on the relatively large scale of 2 miles to the inch; *A Description of the Canals and Rail Roads of the United States* (New York, 1840), *The American Traveller* (1834), and *The Central Traveller* (1840). In 1850 he returned to New York, where he died eight years later.

[Bibliog. data are to be found in P. L. Phillips, *A List of Geographical Atlases in the Lib. of Cong.* (4 vols., 1909–20) and *A List of Maps of America in the Lib. of Cong.* (1901); Joseph Sabin, *A Dict. of Books Relating to America*, vol. XXIV (1933–34); and the maps, atlases, and other pubs. of Tanner in the Lib. of Cong. and the Am. Geographical Soc. of N. Y. There is a critical appraisal in W. L. G. Joerg, "Henry S. Tanner of Phila.," *Annals Asso. Am. Geographers*, vol. XXV (1935).]   W. L. G. J.

TANNER, JAMES (Apr. 4, 1844–Oct. 2, 1927), lobbyist, United States pension commissioner, better known as "Corporal Tanner," was born at Richmondville, Schoharie County, N. Y., the son of Josiah and Elizabeth (Earle) Tanner and a descendant of William Tanner who settled in Rhode Island about 1679. He attended the district schools and became a teacher at the age of seventeen. In September 1861 he ran away from his father's farm to enlist in the 87th New York Volunteer Infantry. Promoted to be corporal, he took part in the Peninsular campaign in the spring of 1862 and in the battles of Warrenton, Bristoe Station, and Second Manassas (Bull Run). At Bull Run (Aug. 29–30, 1862) he received a wound necessitating amputation of both legs four inches below the knees. He recovered, learned to walk with artificial limbs, and studied stenography. Friends procured for him the post of under-doorkeeper of the New York Assembly and late in 1864 a clerkship in the War Department at Washington. He was summoned from his room next door to the house where Lincoln lay dying to take stenographic notes on the first examination of witnesses of the assassination.

After the close of the war he returned home, studied law in the office of Judge W. C. Lamont, and was admitted to the bar in 1869. He held various positions in the custom house at New York, 1869–77, and was tax collector of Brooklyn, 1877–85. In his spare time he was a candidate for political offices, appeared often on the lecture platform, and was active in the Grand Army of the Republic. While commander of the Department of New York in 1876, he caused the legislature to be deluged with petitions for the establishment of a soldiers' home. The successful outcome of this agitation gained him a place on the pension committee of the Grand Army, with the duty of lobbying before congressional committees. Republican campaign managers sent him on speechmaking tours of California and Oregon in 1886 and 1887, and of Indiana in 1888. His friends claimed that his efforts won for Benjamin Harrison the small margin of votes by which he carried Indiana.

Tanner's reward for this service was the post of commissioner of pensions in the new administration. Thankful that "at these finger tips there rests some power," he declared his intention of raising all pensions to at least four dollars a month, "though I may wring from the hearts of some the prayer, 'God help the surplus!'" (speech at Columbia, Tenn., May 10, as quoted in *New York Tribune*, May 11, 1889). He raised the disability ratings of many pensioners, in some cases without application on their part, and ordered the payment in lump sums of thousands of dollars accrued before the original application. Many of the beneficiaries were persons with political influence. The employees of the Pension Office, taking advantage of Tanner's administrative ineptitude, proceeded to give each other higher ratings. The number of new names on the pension rolls was also increased on the principle of giving "an appropriation to every old comrade that needs it" (quotation in the *Nation,* Aug. 1, 1889). After a few

months the secretary of the interior interfered for reasons of economy. Tanner insubordinately informed him that he alone was responsible for the Pension Office; but, receiving no official encouragement, he sent a letter of resignation to the president in September 1889, and retired to private life as a pension attorney.

President Harrison, in accepting the resignation, affirmed his belief in Tanner's personal honesty, and public opinion concurred. It is fairly obvious that Tanner's failure was due to his limited education and his lack of good administrative standards. In 1904 President Theodore Roosevelt appointed him register of wills of the District of Columbia; and the Grand Army of the Republic made him its commander-in-chief for the year 1905–06. He was married in November 1866 to Mero L. White of Jefferson, N. Y., and was survived by two sons and two daughters. He died in Washington, D. C.

[J. E. Smith, *A Famous Battery and Its Campaigns* (1892); H. R. Stiles, *The Civil . . . Hist. . . . . of the County of Kings* (1884); W. E. Roscoe, *Hist. of Schoharie County, N. Y.* (1882); *Who's Who in America,* 1918–19; G. C. Tanner, *William Tanner, Sr., of South Kingstown, R. I., and His Descendants* (1910); W. H. Glasson, *Federal Military Pensions in the U. S.* (1918); Report of the Secretary of the Interior for 1889, *House Ex. Doc. 1* (pt. 5), 51 Cong., 1 Sess.; articles by D. L. McMurry, in *Miss. Valley Hist. Rev.,* June 1922 and Dec. 1926; *N. Y. Times, N. Y. Herald Tribune, Washington Post,* Oct. 3, 1927.]   E. C. S.

TAPPAN, ARTHUR (May 22, 1786–July 23, 1865), philanthropist, abolitionist, was born at Northampton, Mass., the eighth of eleven children of Benjamin and Sarah (Homes) Tappan. Benjamin and Lewis Tappan [*qq.v.*] were his brothers. Reared in a serious, pious household, he attended the town school until the age of fifteen, when he was given a clerkship with Sewall & Salisbury, hardware and dry-goods dealers in Boston. Here for a time he sat under the preaching of William Ellery Channing. He entered business for himself as a dry-goods importer at the age of twenty-one, establishing the firm of Tappan & Sewall in Portland, Me., with a nephew of one of his former employers. Some two years later he moved his business to Montreal, where he married Frances Antill, Sept. 18, 1810. To them were born two sons, one of whom died in infancy, and six daughters.

Returning to the United States after the outbreak of the War of 1812, Tappan struggled against difficulties for several years before, in 1826, he started his most successful enterprise—a silk jobbing firm in New York in which he was joined two years later by his brother Lewis. Although he met with various reverses, he came to be esteemed a wealthy man. He attributed his success to the fact that he charged a fixed uniform price for articles, a practice not then customary. "I had but *one price*," he said, "and sold for cash or short credit" (L. Tappan, *Life, post,* p. 70). Heavily overstocked in a period of falling prices, the firm of Arthur Tappan & Company was forced to close its doors during the panic of 1837, but in eighteen months its creditors had all been paid.

As soon as he began to accumulate wealth Tappan began "to reflect seriously upon his obligations as a STEWARD of the Lord" (*Life,* p. 62). He gave generously of his substance and of his time, strength, and executive ability, to a multitude of religious and humanitarian causes. He was a supporter of the American Sunday School Union, the American Bible Society, the American Tract Society, the American Education Society, and the American Home Missionary Society, and held office in most of these organizations. He was concerned in the movement for stricter Sabbath observance, the temperance crusade, and the fight against tobacco. In 1827 he founded the *New York Journal of Commerce* to provide the city with a daily newspaper free from "immoral advertisements" and regardful of the Sabbath, but it did not prove the moral force he had desired, and after a year he turned it over to his brother Lewis. He supported the effort made to suppress licentiousness and vice in New York and in 1831 was president of the New York Magdalen Society, which sponsored a sensational report exposing conditions in that city. Though for some years a member successively of the Presbyterian congregations of John Mitchell Mason and Samuel Hanson Cox [*qq.v.*], he was an active promoter of the free church movement in New York, and with his brother was instrumental in leasing the Chatham Street Theatre and subsequently building the Broadway Tabernacle for Charles Grandison Finney [*q.v.*]. He gave a scholarship to Andover Theological Seminary and paid the tuition of a large number of divinity students at Yale. He contributed toward the establishment of Kenyon College, Gambier, Ohio, of Auburn Theological Seminary, of Lane Theological Seminary, Cincinnati; and in 1835, after the withdrawal of most of the Lane students because of restrictions upon the discussion of slavery, gave $10,000 and made a private pledge of his entire income in order to secure the establishment of Oberlin College.

Moved by concern for the welfare of the negroes, he joined the American Colonization Society, but becoming convinced that its policy was wrong withdrew and united with those who were agitating for the abolition of slavery. He first became associated with William Lloyd Garrison [*q.v.*] in 1830 by paying a fine to free Garrison from prison in Baltimore, and subsequently helped support the publication of the *Liberator.* About 1831 he promoted an unsuccessful project to establish a college for negroes in New Haven. In March 1833 he took an active part in launching the *Emancipator* in New York; in October of the same year he helped form the New York City Anti-Slavery Society, and in December, the American Anti-Slavery Society, being chosen the first president of each. In 1835 he volunteered assistance to Prudence Crandall [*q.v.*], arrested for opening a school for negro girls at Canterbury, Conn., and in this connection financed the establishment in Windham County of the anti-slavery *Unionist,* under the editorship of C. C. Burleigh [*q.v.*].

In 1840, believing that Garrison would weaken the cause of abolition by his action in associating with it other movements, such as that for women's rights, Tappan with others withdrew from the American Anti-Slavery Society, formed a new organization—the American and Foreign Anti-Slavery Society, of which he was elected president—and founded a new journal, the *American and Foreign Anti-Slavery Reporter.* Convinced that slavery could be destroyed under the Constitution by political action, he supported the Liberty Party and its presidential candidate, James G. Birney [*q.v.*], and was instrumental in establishing in Washington the anti-slavery weekly, the *National Era.* Meanwhile, in 1846, distressed by the refusal of several of the missionary organizations he had aided to espouse the cause of abolition, he took part in founding the American Missionary Association, and remained a member of its executive committee until his death. After the passage of the Fugitive Slave Law of 1850 he declared his determination "in the fear of God" to disobey it, and continued to give all the aid within his power to escaping fugitives.

Tappan was never of strong constitution and throughout his mature years suffered from constant headache. He had no humor and was stern and severe, with himself as well as others. As a champion of unpopular movements, through most of his career he was subjected to violent criticism; his business was endangered; and he himself was threatened with kidnapping, assault, and assassination. Abuse and threats, however, for the most part he heard calmly and ignored. He had a certain rigidity in maintaining his principles, owing partly to his natural austerity of thought and partly to the position of eminence he attained as the financial backer of many reform movements. Though his money gifts were somewhat curtailed—to his great distress—by his failure about 1842 through ill-advised speculation in real estate, he kept up his active interest in reform until his death. In 1849 he purchased an interest in "The Mercantile Agency" established by his brother, but retired from all business some five or six years later and took up his residence in New Haven, where he died.

[D. L. Tappan, *Tappan-Toppan Geneal.* (1915); Lewis Tappan, *The Life of Arthur Tappan* (1870); C. W. Bowen, *Arthur and Lewis Tappan* (1883); J. A. Scoville ("Walter Barrett"), *The Old Merchants of N. Y. City,* vol. I (1863); G. H. Barnes, *The Anti-Slavery Impulse* (1933); W. P. and F. J. Garrison, *William Lloyd Garrison* (4 vols., 1885–89); Annie H. Abel and F. J. Klingberg, *A Side-Light on Anglo-American Relations . . . Correspondence of Lewis Tappan* (1927); D. L. Leonard, *The Story of Oberlin* (copr. 1898); Joseph Sturge, *A Visit to the U. S. in 1841* (1842); *N. Y. Herald,* July 25, 1865.]   F. J. K.

TAPPAN, BENJAMIN (May 25, 1773–Apr. 20, 1857), senator, jurist, anti-slavery leader, was born in Northampton, Mass., eldest of the seven sons of Benjamin and Sarah (Homes) Tappan. Among the other children of the family were the eldest sister, Sarah, who became the mother of David Tappan Stoddard [*q.v.*] and the much younger brothers Arthur and Lewis Tappan [*qq.v.*]. Their father, a goldsmith, later a dry-goods merchant, was descended from Abraham Toppan, who came from Yarmouth, England, to settle in Newbury, Mass., in 1637; their mother, of Irish Presbyterian stock through the paternal line, was also a grandniece of Benjamin Franklin. A public-school education for the younger Benjamin was followed by an apprenticeship to a copperplate printer and engraver, a voyage to the West Indies, brief study of portrait painting under the famous Gilbert Stuart, and then a thorough legal education under Gideon Granger [*q.v.*].

Admitted to the bar at Hartford, Conn., in his twenties, he became a first settler (1799) of what is now Portage County, Ohio. On Mar. 20, 1801, he was married in Wethersfield, Conn., to Nancy Wright (d. 1822), sister of John Crafts Wright, later a congressman from Ohio. Accompanied by his bride he returned to Ravenna, Ohio, where he became an aggressive force in local politics. Having served as a member of the state Senate, 1803–05, he moved in 1809 to Steubenville, where he continued the practice of law. He served as an aide to Major-General Elijah Wadsworth during the War of 1812 and as president judge of the 5th circuit of the court of common pleas, 1816–23. His decisions for 1816–19, published as *Cases Decided in the Courts of Common Pleas, in the Fifth Circuit of . . . Ohio* (1818–19), referred to as *Tappan's Reports,*

were the first law reports in the state. Failing to be reëlected (Tappan to E. A. Brown, Steubenville, Jan. 29, 1823; MS. in Ohio State Library), he returned to private practice. He then served as an Ohio canal commissioner.

An ardent Jacksonian, he was a presidential elector in 1832, and served as a federal district judge until his appointment, together with those of other Democrats, was rejected by the Senate in May 1834. In 1838, Thomas Morris [*q.v.*] having assumed a position as "the first abolition senator" (Smith, *post,* p. 24) that made him unacceptable to the Ohio Democracy, Tappan was chosen as his successor. The latter had long been known as an opponent of slavery "in all shapes except that of abolitionism" (*Cincinnati Gazette,* Dec. 27, 1838); hence his selection satisfied the anti-slavery Democrats. His law office was then intrusted to his partner, Edwin M. Stanton [*q.v.*].

In the Senate, Tappan refused to present abolition petitions from his constituents, asserting that Ohioans should not attempt to interfere with local institutions elsewhere and chiding women petitioners for leaving the home "to mix with the strife of ambition or the cares of Government" (*Ohio Statesman,* Feb. 10, 1840). He was an anti-bank Democrat and "as uncompromising upon hard money as the Rock of Gibraltar" (Matthias Martin to William Allen, quoted by Holt, *post,* p. 576). His agency in the publication in the New York *Evening Post* (Apr. 27, 1844) of Calhoun's proposed treaty for the annexation of Texas, which was being secretly considered, led to a severe censure by the Senate (*Senate Journal,* 28 Cong., 1 Sess., pp. 439ff.). Like his colleague Allen, in 1845 he refused to follow the instructions of the Whig legislature in opposition to Texas annexation. Remaining an anti-slavery man, on July 12, 1849, he presided at a Northwest Ordinance (Free Soil) political celebration at Cleveland, and in 1856 he cast his last presidential vote for Frémont.

A lawyer of eminent talents and consistently a man of democratic principles, "of an intractable disposition" (*American Union,* Apr. 22, 1857), and with a gift of sarcasm which he used on friend and foe, he held firmly to his independent convictions. His views on slavery and corporate privileges were deemed radical by many of his contemporaries and he was referred to as "the hoary-headed skeptic" (McLean MSS., Library of Congress) because of his blunt professions of religious heterodoxy. Exemplary in private life and scholarly in tastes, he devoted his last years to an interest in mineralogy and conchology. At his death in Steubenville he was survived by two sons, Benjamin and Eli Todd Tappan [*q.v.*], the latter born to his second wife, Betsy (Lord) Frazer (d. 1840), whom he had married in 1823.

[MSS., including an autobiography to 1823, are owned by J. K. Wright of New York; other Tappan MSS. are in the Lib. of Cong. Sketches are found in D. L. Tappan, *Tappan-Toppan Geneal.* (1915); *U. S. Mag. and Democratic Rev.,* June–July 1840; J. B. Doyle, *20th Century Hist. of Steubenville and Jefferson County, Ohio* (1910); *Biog. Dir. Am. Cong.* (1928). See also F. P. Weisenburger, "Ohio Politics during the Jacksonian Period" (unpublished dissertation, Univ. of Mich.); T. C. Smith, *The Liberty and Free Soil Parties in the Northwest* (1897); E. A. Holt, "Party Politics in Ohio, 1840–1850," *Ohio Arch. and Hist. Soc. Quart.,* July 1928, Jan.–Apr. 1929. The best obituary is in the *Evening Post* (N. Y.), Apr. 24, 1857. The Tappan family Bible, owned by Mr. Wright, and the *American Union* (Steubenville), Apr. 22, 1857, give Apr. 20, 1857, as the date of Tappan's death.]

F. P. W.

TAPPAN, ELI TODD (Apr. 30, 1824–Oct. 23, 1888), educator and author, was born in Steubenville, Ohio, the only child of Benjamin Tappan [*q.v.*] by his second wife, Betsy (Lord) Frazer. The boy was educated in the public schools of Steubenville, under private tutors, and in St. Mary's College, Baltimore, Md. Leaving without taking a degree, he began the study of law in 1842 under his father and his father's partner, Edwin M. Stanton [*q.v.*], and was admitted to the bar in 1846. He founded the weekly *Ohio Press,* Columbus, that same year, and was its editor for two years. He then practised law in Steubenville for seven or eight years. In 1852 he served as mayor. He began teaching in the public schools in 1857, and from March 1858 to June 1859 was superintendent.

This last experience fixed his life career, and he was thereafter engaged in educational work. He was professor of mathematics in Ohio University, 1859–60, and again 1865–68, and teacher of mathematics in Mount Auburn Young Ladies' Institute in the interval, 1860–65. He became president of Kenyon College, Gambier, Ohio, in 1869, serving until 1875 when he was made professor of mathematics and political economy in the same institution. As president he completed the chapel known as "Church of the Holy Spirit" and completely revised the curricula of the college. He was also a champion of common schools. As early as 1854, in lectures to teachers, he revealed an insight into school organization and methods of instruction which was in advance of his time. While he was professor in Mount Auburn Young Ladies' Institute he published *Treatise on Plane and Solid Geometry* (1864), based in large measure upon well known French and German textbooks, to supplement the widely used series of arithmetics and algebras by Joseph

Ray. He was the author of the history of school legislation in Ohio from the beginning to the Codification Act of 1873 which formed part of the state's exhibit at the Centennial Exhibition in Philadelphia, and he contributed many articles to educational journals. He was a member of the first Ohio state board of school examiners in 1864, was elected president of the Ohio State Teachers Association in 1866; became a charter member of the council of the National Educational Association in 1880, its treasurer in 1880–81, and its president in 1883. In 1887 he was elected commissioner of common schools of Ohio, in which office he died. He was a member of the Episcopal Church for many years.

Tappan married Lydia McDowell of Steubenville, Feb. 4, 1851. Two children were born to this union: a son, and a daughter, Mary, who married John Henry Wright [*q.v.*], later a professor at Harvard, and became a writer of some repute.

[D. L. Tappan, *Tappan-Toppan Geneal.* (1915); *Thirty-fifth Ann. Report of the State Commissioner of Common Schools . . . of Ohio . . . 1888* (1889); J. J. Burns, *Educ. Hist. of Ohio* (1905); *Ohio Educ. Monthly,* Dec. 1888; *Ohio State Journal* (Columbus), Oct. 24, 1888; J. B. Doyle, *20th Century Hist. of Steubenville and Jefferson County, Ohio* (1910); *The Biog. Cyc. and Portrait Gallery . . . State of Ohio* (1895); *Nat. Educ. Asso. Jour. of Proc. and Addresses,* 1889.]

H. C. M.

TAPPAN, EVA MARCH (Dec. 26, 1854– Jan. 29, 1930), author of anthologies, textbooks, and stories for children, was born in Blackstone, Mass., the daughter of Edmund March and Lucretia (Logée) Tappan. Her father, a graduate of Dartmouth College and pastor of the Free Baptist Church, was the descendant of Abraham Toppan, who emigrated with his family from Yarmouth, England, and was admitted a freeman of Newbury, Mass., in 1637. When she was six her father died, and for the remainder of her childhood she lived at various seminaries, where her mother taught. She received an A.B. degree at Vassar College in 1875. For the next twenty years she taught school, first at Wheaton Seminary, Norton, Mass., from 1875 to 1880, and later at Raymond Academy, Camden, N. J., where she was associate principal from 1884 to 1894. In 1895 she received an A.M. degree and a Ph.D. in 1896 from the University of Pennsylvania. The next year she became head of the English department of the English High School at Worcester, Mass. Seven years later, when she was the author of several school books of recognized merit, she gave up teaching to devote all of her time to writing.

She published her first book, *Charles Lamb, the Man and the Author,* in 1896. In 1900 she published her second, *In the Days of Alfred the Great,* and the next year three others: *In the Days of William the Conqueror, Old Ballads in Prose,* and *England's Story.* By using an informal, lucid style, picturesque details, and well planned, compact organization she realized an ambition, cherished since childhood, of writing books that children would love to read. For the remainder of her life, except for an occasional year that she devoted to the care of her aged mother, she continued to write reference and textbooks for use in grade and high schools. Many of these are histories: *Our Country's Story* (1902), *The Story of the Greek People* (1908), *Our European Ancestors* (1918), *The Story of Our Constitution* (1922). In some she tried to acquaint children with the social and political background of historical periods: *In the Days of Queen Elizabeth* (1902) and *In the Days of Queen Victoria* (1903). In others, such as *American Hero Stories* (1906) and *Old World Hero Stories* (1911), she sought to lay a foundation for the future study of biography. In a series of supplementary readers she provided interesting facts about agriculture and industry: *The Farmer and His Friends, Diggers in the Earth, Makers of Many Things,* and *Travelers and Traveling,* all in 1916. In *Ella, a Little Schoolgirl of the Sixties* (1923) she recounted her own childhood experiences. Her writing gave her the means of realizing a second long-cherished desire: to provide a home for her mother. She never traveled abroad and but rarely in America, preferring to remain with her mother, who was unable to travel. After her mother's death in 1911, her own established habits kept her at home reading and writing. She died at Worcester, Mass.

[Foreword by Eva March Tappan in Edward March Tappan, *The Words of a Man* (1914) ; D. L. Tappan, *Tappan-Toppan Genealogy* (1915) ; *Boston Transcript,* Jan. 30, 1930 ; *Who's Who in America,* 1928–29 ; correspondence with Miss Lillian E. Prudden, New Haven, Conn.]   V. L. S.

TAPPAN, HENRY PHILIP (Apr. 18, 1805–Nov. 15, 1881), clergyman, philosopher, first president of the University of Michigan, was born at Rhinebeck on the Hudson, N. Y., of mixed Dutch and Huguenot ancestry. His father, Peter Tappan, an officer in the Revolutionary army, was a descendant of Jurian Teunnisse Tappan, who emigrated from Holland to Manhattan in 1625. The Tappan family had intermarried with the Clintons, and Tappan's mother, Ann DeWitt, could trace her family back to a connection with the famous DeWitts, the rivals of the House of Orange. Henry Philip was the youngest of seven children. From the district

school he was sent to Greenville Academy, but in 1819 he was forced to leave because of family financial troubles. He resorted to teaching to earn money and two years afterward entered Union College, Schenectady, whence he graduated in 1825 with the degree of B.A. Deciding for the ministry, he next entered Auburn Theological Seminary and was graduated in 1827. On Apr. 17, 1828, he married Julia Livingston, daughter of Col. John Livingston of New York City, by whom he had a son and four daughters. He was ordained at Pittsfield, Mass., in September 1828 as minister of the Congregational Church. His ministerial career was cut short, however, by an infection of the throat which forced him to travel to the West Indies for his health. In 1832 he became professor of moral and intellectual philosophy in the newly established University of the City of New York (later New York University), and from that time devoted his energies to philosophy and the theory of education. Unfortunately, the new university was not well managed, financially or otherwise, and in 1837 Tappan was dismissed along with seven others who had signed a statement expressing lack of confidence in the administration. For a brief interval thereafter he was the head of a private seminary, a young ladies' school in Leroy Place, Bleecker Street, N. Y.

Meanwhile he had written and published several books on philosophy, which in those days was scarcely separable from theology. Jonathan Edwards, 1703–1758 [*q.v.*], had set the stage by his famous treatise on the freedom of the will, and it was this problem which Tappan essayed to reanalyze. He began his publications in 1839 with his *Review of Edwards's "Inquiry into the Freedom of the Will."* This was followed in 1840 by his *Doctrine of the Will Determined by an Appeal to Consciousness* and in 1841 by his *Doctrine of the Will Applied to Moral Agency and Responsibility.* Though he shows the influence of Victor Cousin, the famous eclectic French philosopher of the time, yet there are touches of genuine originality in his handling of the problems. Tappan argued for a generic principle of contingency of which the free will is an expression. This thesis was supported by an appeal to consciousness, because "the causes first and best known to us are ourselves." He also published *Elements of Logic* (1844). In 1852, when he had received recognition both at home and abroad, he was offered his former chair, but declined it for the presidency of the University of Michigan. Although Michigan was still a pioneer state, he saw there an opportunity to integrate the university with the whole educational system and to make of it something more than the college which had served up to this time to complete American education. In his views on education—expressed in *University Education* (1851)—he was influenced by the Prussian system, which he had been able to examine during a visit abroad. Being convinced that much more than the college was needed to lift American thought to a creative level, he was careful in his selection of professors and gathered around him several brilliant men. To his credit, also, goes the founding of the Detroit astronomical observatory. Unfortunately, minor conflicts arose over such a matter as the serving of wine in his home, for the temperance movement was strong and already fanatical. But the university continued to grow and to make innovations under his leadership. A new board of regents which came into office in 1858 was unsympathetic, and in June 1863, after about five years of increasing friction, Tappan was suddenly asked to resign. There were protests throughout the state, but the action was not reconsidered. It remains to be noted that within a few years the regents expressed regret, and that in June 1875 they passed resolutions recognizing Tappan's distinguished ability and services.

Tappan spent the remaining years of his life in Europe, chiefly in Germany and Switzerland, often visiting his daughter and his son-in-law, the famous astronomer, Francis Brünnow, in Ireland. He died abroad, survived by his wife and one daughter, and was buried on the slopes of Vevey facing Lake Geneva. Tappan was a man of striking personal appearance, fully six feet in height, with massive head and shoulders. While he was a very capable thinker in the field of philosophy, he seems to have been at his best as an educator; in this field he was a genuine pioneer whose work was characterized by foresight and by imagination.

[See W. R. Cutter, *Geneal. and Family Hist. of Southern N. Y. and the Hudson River Valley*, vol. I (1910); B. A. Hinsdale, *Hist. of the Univ. of Mich.* (1906); C. M. Perry, *Henry Philip Tappan* (1933); A. D. White, in *Mich. Alumnus*, Mar. 1903; H. S. Frieze, *A Memorial Discourse, on the Life . . . of Rev. Henry Philip Tappan* (1882); and obituary in *N. Y. Tribune*, Nov. 18, 1881. There is a coll. of Tappan's MSS. in the lib. of the Univ. of Mich.]   R. W. S.

TAPPAN, LEWIS (May 23, 1788–June 21, 1873), merchant, abolitionist, brother of Benjamin and Arthur Tappan [*qq.v.*], was born in Northampton, Mass., and grew up in the devout household presided over by his father, Benjamin, and his mother, Sarah (Homes) Tappan. He was educated in the town school and at the age of sixteen became an apprenticed clerk to a dry-goods importing firm in Boston. Here he sat for

a time under the preaching of William Ellery Channing, and in 1825, to the distress of his Calvinistic family, served as treasurer of the American Unitarian Association. Soon, however, he returned to Orthodox views, and by 1828 was writing pamphlets upholding Evangelical convictions against Unitarianism. The family Calvinism also appears in his *Memoir of Mrs. Sarah Tappan* (1834). Meanwhile, assisted by his employers, he had endeavored to set up a business of his own, but in 1828 he entered into partnership with his brother Arthur as a silk jobber in New York. In the same year he took over from Arthur the *New York Journal of Commerce,* but in 1831 sold it to David Hale and Gerard Hallock [*qq.v.*]. As credit manager of Arthur Tappan & Company he was an important factor in the prosperity of the firm in the years preceding the panic of 1837. Shortly thereafter he withdrew from the partnership, and in 1841, under the firm name of Lewis Tappan & Company, established "The Mercantile Agency," the first commercial-credit rating agency in the country. He conducted this enterprise with great success until 1849, when he retired to devote himself to the humanitarian labors which had become his chief concern. In deliberately planning to draw upon his accumulated capital for his support for the rest of his life he was acting upon theories regarding the use of wealth which he later set forth in a pamphlet entitled *Is It Right to Be Rich?* (1869).

Like his brother Arthur, Lewis Tappan from the time of his first business success was a supporter of the American Board of Commissioners for Foreign Missions and the American Bible Society. He was a promoter of the free church movement in New York, and with Arthur was instrumental in leasing the Chatham Street Theatre and building the Broadway Tabernacle for the revivalist Charles Grandison Finney [*q.v.*], and subsequently in sending Finney as professor of theology to Oberlin College. He was one of the founders of the New York Anti-Slavery Society and the American Anti-Slavery Society in 1833, and by his activities in behalf of abolition drew upon himself hate and obloquy; in July 1834 his house was wrecked by a mob, and his furniture burned. In 1839–41 he was the outstanding member of the committee which undertook to secure the freedom of the *Amistad* captives, successfully defended before the Supreme Court by John Quincy Adams [*q.v.*]. Although at first both Tappans worked with William Lloyd Garrison [*q.v.*], Lewis, like Arthur, repudiated Garrison when the latter proposed to attach other reforms to the cause of abolition, and with the resulting schism in the American Anti-Slavery Society in 1840, he took a leading part in forming the American and Foreign Anti-Slavery Society, of which he was the first treasurer. He was especially conscious of the international aspect of the American struggle and for this reason maintained a wide and frequent correspondence with sympathetic interests in England, especially with the British and Foreign Anti-Slavery Society. At the suggestion of John Quincy Adams, he attended the international anti-slavery convention in London in 1843 (*Memoirs of John Quincy Adams*, vol. XI, 1876, pp. 380, 405). Realizing that the attitude of Great Britain could have an almost decisive bearing on the outcome of the struggle in the United States, he discussed with his English friends such matters as the annexation of Texas, the position of the negro in the United States, Canada, and Liberia, the coastwise slave trade, and the attitude of the churches. Believing that slavery could be abolished within the Union, he worked to win the cooperation of churches and missionary societies. When the older foundations which he had supported, notably the American Board, declined to enlist in the fight for abolition, he helped to found and became treasurer of the American Missionary Association (1846), explicitly committed to the cause of the negro. After the passage of the Fugitive Slave Act in 1850, he became a supporter of the work of Alexander M. Ross, who traveled through the South helping slaves to escape by the Underground Railroad (W. H. Siebert, *The Underground Railroad*, 1898, p. 180; A. M. Ross, *Recollections of an Abolitionist*, 1867).

As the struggle in America reached its crisis, Tappan gradually adopted the view that slavery was illegal everywhere and could be abolished by the federal government in all the slave states under the terms of the Constitution. He thus came to favor a more radical method of action than that sponsored by the American and Foreign Anti-Slavery Society, and in 1855 resigned as corresponding secretary of that body to accept office in a new organization known as the Abolition Society. By now, however, age was beginning to limit his activity. As the need for anti-slavery agitation lessened, he gave more attention to the constructive work for negroes being undertaken by the American Missionary Association. In 1870 he published *The Life of Arthur Tappan*, and suffered a paralytic stroke just as the book went to press. Three years later he died, as the result of another stroke, at the age of eighty-five. He was married twice: first, Sept. 7, 1813, to Susanna Aspinwall, by whom

he had six children, and second, in 1854, to Mrs. Sarah J. Davis. The youngest of his five daughters married Henry Chandler Bowen [*q.v.*]. From 1856 Tappan was a member of Plymouth Church, Brooklyn, and his funeral sermon was preached by his pastor, Henry Ward Beecher.

[D. L. Tappan, *Tappan-Toppan Geneal.* (1915); C. W. Bowen, *Arthur and Lewis Tappan* (1883); J. A. Scoville ("Walter Barrett"), *The Old Merchants of N. Y.*, vol. I (1863); E. N. Vose, *Seventy-five Years of The Mercantile Agency, R. G. Dun & Co., 1841-1916* (1916); G. H. Barnes, *The Anti-Slavery Impulse* (1933); G. H. Barnes and D. L. Dumond, *Letters of Theodore Dwight Weld, Angelina Grimké Weld, and Sarah Grimké* (2 vols., 1934); A. H. Abel and F. J. Klingberg, *A Side-Light on Anglo-American Relations, 1839-1858, Furnished by the Correspondence of Lewis Tappan and Others with the British and Foreign Anti-Slavery Society* (1927); W. P. and F. J. Garrison, *William Lloyd Garrison* (4 vols., 1885–89); Joseph Sturge, *A Visit to the U. S. in 1841* (1842); *Am. Missionary*, Aug. 1873; *Harper's Weekly*, July 12, 1873; *N. Y. Times*, June 23, 1873.]   F. J. K.

TAPPEN, FREDERICK DOBBS (Jan. 29, 1829–Feb. 28, 1902), banker, was born in New York City, one of eleven children of Charles Barclay and Elizabeth (Dobbs) Tappen. His father was a veteran of the War of 1812 and a colonel of the New York state militia. Tappen received his early education at the Columbia College Grammar School. For a year he was engaged as civil engineer on the Erie Railroad. In 1850 he became "specie clerk" at the National Bank of New York, whose title was subsequently changed to that of Gallatin National Bank. With this institution he was identified during the rest of his life, being chosen as its cashier in 1857 and serving as its president, 1868–1902. His part in the American finance of his day was of distinctive and notable character. He became known as the "banking dictator" who, in days before the creation of the Federal Reserve system and in the absence of any central banking institution in America, was invariably chosen by the New York banks, at times of financial panic, to prescribe and direct their united policy.

Tappen's view of the manner in which a formidable financial crisis should be met was based on close-range personal observation of the panic of 1857 and the Wall Street gold-market crisis of "Black Friday" 1869. The New York Clearing House Association, otherwise known as the New York Associated Banks, an organization originally formed merely to facilitate exchange of checks, had already come to exercise partial supervision over credit policies. On the outbreak of panic in 1873, Tappen was chairman of the clearing-house committee, and was at once made chairman of its special "loan committee." His first expedient was the adoption of "clearing-house certificates," a device whereby hard-pressed banks in the clearing house, instead of being required to pay their mutual debit balances in cash at a moment of panicky money-hoarding, were authorized to make such inter-bank payments in bills of credit bearing high interest rates, secured by banking collateral approved and accepted by the loan committee. This machinery was not wholly new, but 1873 was the first occasion on which it was applied in a financial panic of the traditional character. The powers exercised by Tappen in 1873 and afterward were, however, much larger than this. The emergency of that year was so critical, and general insolvency seemed so imminent, that virtual dictatorship was granted him. The principles on which he based his program, as afterward enunciated by him, were that the banks act together under dictatorial powers of the central committee; that no solvent bank be allowed to fail because of depletion of its cash reserve; that the money market be relieved, but in such a way and on such terms that the genuineness of an applicant's need for credit would be proved by his readiness to accept them. Exercising his special powers, Tappen met the panic emergency of 1873, when $26,265,000 clearing-house certificates were issued, and general suspension by banks and banking houses was averted; of 1884, when the issue was $24,915,000; of 1890, when it was $16,645,000, and of 1893, when it reached $41,490,000. On some of these occasions he was not even on the managing committee, yet was at once appointed head of a special loan committee which superseded all others. In each of these formidable crises, he determined personally the manner in which the "pooled" credit resources should be applied.

This remarkable uniformity of recourse to Tappen as dictator in a panic emergency was partly ascribed to his presidency of a relatively small New York bank, whereby he escaped professional jealousies. But it was far more directly a tribute to his promptness of decision, financial insight, courage, and unquestioned fairness and integrity. His banking associates, at the memorial meeting in 1902, described him as possessing "the rare gift of knowing when to act, how to act, and of persuading others to act with him"; of being able to "detect bad banking almost through the leather of a portfolio," and of being ready, if circumstances required, to "close a bank, under his power from this body, with less concern than he would show to give help where it is deserved." He was a man of great individual popularity, of frank and winning personality, so readily accessible that the office in which he did his work was visible at once to any

one entering the front door of the bank. He spoke French fluently, was fond of literature and music, and was an expert fisherman. He was director in several hospitals and charities, and an active churchman. He died in Lakewood, N. J. He was survived by his wife, Sarah A. B. Littell, whom he had married about 1859, and one daughter.

[*Who's Who in America*, 1901–02; obituary of Charles Barclay Tappen, in *N. Y. Tribune*, Apr. 21, 1893; *Year Book of the Holland Society of New York*, 1902, pp. 125–32; *Proc. of a Meeting . . . in Memory of Frederick D. Tappen at the Clearing House*, Mar. 10, 1902 (n.d.); W. J. Gilpin and H. E. Wallace, *N. Y. Clearing House Asso., 1854–1905* (1905); editorial in *Commercial and Financial Chronicle* (N. Y.), Mar. 8, 1902; obituaries in *N. Y. Tribune* and *N. Y. Herald*, Mar. 1, 1902.]   A. D. N.

TAPPER, BERTHA FEIRING (Jan. 25, 1859–Sept. 2, 1915), pianist, teacher, was born at Christiania, Norway, the daughter of Lars Olsen Feiring and Berthe (Iversen) Feiring. She was musically inclined from childhood and commenced her first studies in her native town with Johann Svendsen and Agathe Backer-Gröndahl. Later she went to Leipzig, Germany, where she was graduated from the conservatory of music in 1878. Three years later she came to the United States and became active as a teacher of piano and as a pianist, playing principally with chamber music groups, notably with Franz Kneisel [*q.v.*] and the Kneisel Quartet. From 1889 to 1895 she was a graduate teacher at the New England Conservatory of Music in Boston, Mass. In October 1895 she went to Vienna to study with Theodor Leschetizky and remained there until 1896 when she returned to the United States. She continued her career as a teacher and from 1905 to 1910 was an instructor of advanced piano pupils at the Institute of Musical Art in New York City. A number of her pupils, among them, Leo Ornstein, Newton Swift, and Abram Chasins, achieved distinction on the concert platform and as composers and teachers. As a teacher she possessed a keen perception of how much could be made of embryonic talent, and she always had an accurate idea of the technical equipment necessary for each pupil to achieve the goal she had set for him. Moreover, she was quick to realize how long she herself should teach each student and when he should go abroad for study to broaden his training and his imagination under new tutorship and in a new environment. She befriended and inspired her pupils; often she would take one of them to the Tapper summer home at Blue Hill, Me., for an entire season. She composed a number of piano pieces and songs and contributed articles to musical journals. Her most important published work was *Grieg's Piano Works* which she edited for the *Musician's Library* (2 volumes, 1908, 1909).

Bertha Feiring was married twice; first, to her piano instructor at the Leipzig conservatory, Louis Mass, and, second, on Sept. 22, 1895, to Thomas Tapper, musician, editor, and author of books on musical subjects. She died in Boston, where she had been taken following an illness at Blue Hill, and was buried at Canton, Mass. Her husband, a daughter, and a son by her previous marriage survived her.

[Information from the family; *Who's Who in America*, 1914–15; *Grove's Dict. of Music and Musicians, Am. Supp.* (1930); A. W. Kramer, "Bertha Feiring Tapper: Altruist," *Musical America*, Sept. 25, 1915; *Boston Evening Transcript*, Sept. 4, 1915.]

J. T. H.

TARBELL, FRANK BIGELOW (Jan. 1, 1853–Dec. 4, 1920), archaeologist, was born in West Groton, Mass., the son of John and Sarah (Fosdick) Tarbell. His father, a jeweler and watchmaker, traced his ancestry to Thomas Tarbell, who emigrated to America in 1647, lived for a time in Watertown, Mass., and later established a more permanent home in Groton. Tarbell first attended the district school of West Groton, and then studied at Lawrence Academy in Groton, 1865–68. After waiting a year he entered Yale College, where he received the degree of A.B. in 1873. He won many scholarships and prizes, and was valedictorian of his class, a member of Phi Beta Kappa, and an editor of the *Yale Literary Magazine*. Following his graduation he spent two years in Europe with a New York family and then returned to Yale as teacher and student. He received the degree of Ph.D. at Yale in 1879. He was tutor in Greek, 1876–82, and assistant professor of Greek and instructor in logic at Yale, 1882–87. During 1888–89 he served as annual director of the American School of Classical Studies at Athens; from 1889 to 1892 he was instructor in Greek at Harvard College and in 1892–93 went back to Athens as secretary of the American School. He returned to America to become a member of the faculty of the new University of Chicago. There he served as associate professor of Greek, 1892–93, and then as professor of archaeology from 1893 until 1918, when he retired from teaching and made his home in Pomfret, Conn. He died following an operation at New Haven on Dec. 4, 1920. He never married. He contributed many articles and reviews to journals, edited *The Philippics of Demosthenes* (1880), wrote *A History of Greek Art* (1896) and the descriptive matter for an *Illustrated Catalogue of Carbon Prints on the Rise and Progress of Greek and Roman Art* (1897), and in 1909 made a catalogue of the

bronzes in the Field Museum, Chicago. He was a member of the Society for the Promotion of Hellenic Studies and the Archaeological Institute of America, and served on the advisory council of the Simplified Spelling Board. At the time of his death he left a bequest to Yale College which is used for the support of instruction in classical archaeology.

Although he was one of the first among Americans to enter the field of classical archaeology and achieve distinction there, it is rather as a personality influencing students and colleagues that he will be remembered. He is described by one of his students at Yale as somewhat severe, formal, and distant in manner, yet able "'by sheer intellectual distinction and force of character" to exert the greatest personal influence upon those who studied under him, giving quite unconsciously an example of intellectual honesty and candor (William Lyon Phelps, quoted in Herrick, *post,* p. 59). Frail, shy, and reserved, with a New England frugality of speech that sometimes broke into brusqueness, he was incapable of even the casual insincerities of social intercourse, as he was incapable of any pretension. His love of beauty and his devotion to truth were seldom given expression in words. They made him, nevertheless, a fastidious and accurate scholar, marked him with an austere serenity of spirit and of bearing, and led him to follow consistently and unaffectedly, without defiance or compromise or harsh judgments, the path of his own ideals.

[C. H. Wight, *Thomas Tarbell and Some of His Descendants* (1907); *Who's Who in America*, 1920–21; *Hist. of the Yale Class of 1873* (n.d.); *Fifth Supp. to the Hist. of the Yale Class of 1873 . . . 1926;* Robert Herrick, in *Univ. Record* (Univ. of Chicago), Jan. 1921; *Yale Univ. Obit. Record of Grads.* (1921), pp. 86–88; obituaries in *Am. Jour. of Archaeology*, Jan.–Mar. 1921, p. 85, and *Chicago Daily Tribune*, Dec. 6, 1920.]

R. H.

TARBELL, JOSEPH (*c.* 1780–Nov. 25, 1815), naval officer, was probably a native of Massachusetts. In December 1798 he was appointed a midshipman on the *Constitution* and served on board her during the naval war with France. He was with that ship when she captured the *Sandwich* and for a time was the prize-master of the prize. On Aug. 25, 1800, he was promoted lieutenant. Retained under the peace establishment of 1801, he was ordered to the *Essex*. In 1803 he sailed for the Mediterranean as a lieutenant of the *Constitution* and two years later returned home in the *President*. As one of the officers of Commodore Edward Preble [*q.v.*], he was included in the resolution of Congress of Mar. 3, 1805, expressing the thanks of that body for the gallantry and good conduct displayed in the attacks on Tripoli in 1804 (2 *U. S. Statutes at Large,* 346). After service at Havre de Grace, Md., on ordnance duty, he was made master of the Washington navy yard in 1806. In 1807 he joined the gunboat flotilla of Capt. Stephen Decatur [*q.v.*] and in the following year was a member of the court that tried Capt. James Barron [*q.v.*] after the *Chesapeake-Leopard* affair. On Apr. 25, 1808, he was commissioned master commandant. In 1810–11, as commander of the *Siren,* he helped to enforce the embargo at Charleston, S. C., and the suppression of the slave trade at New Orleans. In 1811 after preparing the *Hornet* for sea at Washington, he was ordered to take command of the *John Adams* at Boston. His principal service during the War of 1812 was performed at Norfolk where he commanded first the *Constellation* and later the gunboat flotilla. On June 20, 1813, fifteen gunboats under his command engaged the *Junon,* 38, and two other small frigates, becalmed at Hampton Roads, with a slight loss on each side. This was the chief event in his naval career. He remained with the flotilla until the end of the war, being promoted captain in July 1813. In 1808 he married Eliza Cassin, the daughter of a naval officer; he died in Washington, D. C., survived by his wife and their two daughters. In 1918 a torpedo-boat destroyer was named for him.

[Bureau of Navigation, Record of Officers, 1798–1817; Naval Archives, 1798–1815: Letters to Officers, Sps. of War, Appointments and Resignations, Nominations and Appointments, Officers' Letters and Captains' Letters; Niles' *Weekly Register,* July 3, 1813; Abel Bowen, *The Naval Monument* (1840); Theodore Roosevelt, *The Naval War of 1812* (1882); *Sen. Doc. 92, 26 Cong., 1 Sess.*; *Norfolk and Portsmouth Herald,* Dec. 1, 1815; *Daily National Intelligencer,* Nov. 27, 1815; Veterans' Administration, Pension Files, War of 1812; Probate Court Files, Washington, D. C.]   C. O. P.

TARBOX, INCREASE NILES (Feb. 11, 1815–May 3, 1888), author, clergyman, was born in East (later South) Windsor, Conn., the son of Thomas and Lucy (Porter) Tarbox, and a descendant of John Tarbox who was in Lynn, Mass., in 1639. Orphaned at nine, he lived with an uncle from 1825 to 1829, worked on a farm in East Windsor, and attended the common schools. At eighteen he began teaching in a district school. He attended the academy at East Hartford for a time in order to prepare for college and in 1839 received the degree of A.B. from Yale. After teaching for two years in the East Hartford academy, he served at Yale as tutor in Latin (1842–44) and studied in the Divinity School. He was graduated in 1844 and ordained in November of the same year at the Hollis Evangelical (later the Plymouth Con-

gregational) Church in Framingham, Mass., where he served until 1851. On June 4, 1845, he was married to Delia (or Adelia) Augusta Waters of Millbury, Mass., by whom he had a son and three daughters. He was a founder and one of the original editors (1849–51) of the *Congregationalist.* In 1851 he gave up his church in Framingham to become secretary of the American Education Society (reorganized in 1874 as the American College and Education Society), and from that time until 1884, when he retired, he devoted himself to the work of providing help to students preparing for the ministry. Possessed of a balanced judgment, and being by nature sympathetic and kindly, he was markedly successful in the work.

His literary interests, which were strong, manifested themselves in various ways. He wrote juveniles for Sunday schools, poems—sometimes devotional, sometimes mildly satirical—and numerous articles on historical, religious, and literary subjects, which appeared in the *Congregational Quarterly,* the *New Englander,* and other magazines. Among his books are *Missionary Patriots: Memoirs of James H. Schneider and Edward M. Schneider* (1867), *Life of Israel Putnam ... Major-General in the Continental Army* (1876), and *Songs and Hymns for Common Life* (1885). He edited *Sir Walter Ralegh and His Colony in America* (1884), with a memoir, for the Prince Society, and the *Diary of Thomas Robbins, D.D., 1796–1854* (2 vols., 1886–87). From 1881 to 1888, as historiographer of the New England Historic Genealogical Society, he wrote numerous brief, careful memoirs of members of the society, as well as seven more extensive biographies, which appeared in the *New England Historical and Genealogical Register.* It is for such articles as these that he is best remembered. Without great importance individually, these notes and memoirs form when taken together an interesting and valuable record. What Tarbox said of another writer on genealogical subjects might be said with equal truth of him: "It is a most fortunate thing for the world at large, that a few men have such natural or acquired tastes for certain kinds of literary work, that they will do it, regardless of trouble or expense . . ." (*New Englander,* April 1876, p. 280). He himself may be credited with the "large share of 'love to being in general' " which he attributes to such writers. The benignity of his appearance was, it is said, "the true index of a real benignity of character" (Stiles, *post,* p. 749). He was gentle and sensitive, perhaps even over-sensitive, yet in matters of conviction firm and independent. He died in

West Newton, Mass., where he had lived since 1860, survived by two of his daughters. He was buried in Framingham.

[H. M. Dexter, in *New England Hist. and Geneal. Reg.*, Jan. 1890; H. R. Stiles, *The Hist. and Geneals. of Ancient Windsor, Conn.*, vol. II (1892); *Vital Records of Millbury, Mass.* (1903); *Obit. Records Grads. Yale Univ.... 1880–90* (1890); *Fourteenth Ann. Report ... Am. Coll. and Educ. Soc. ... May 21, 1888*; *Congregationalist*, May 10, 1888; death notice and obituary in *Boston Evening Transcript*, May 4, 1888.]

D. G—d.

TARR, RALPH STOCKMAN (Jan. 15, 1864–Mar. 21, 1912), geologist, geographer, teacher, was born in Gloucester, Mass. He was the son of Silas Stockman Tarr, a contractor, and Abigail (Saunders) Tarr, and a descendant of Richard Tarr, first settler of Rockport, Mass. After his graduation from high school in 1881, he attended the summer school of zoölogy at Salem and in the autumn entered Harvard as a special student at Lawrence Scientific School. His course was interrupted several times and he did not take his degree for ten years. In the meantime, however, he had done summer work under the zoölogists Alpheus Hyatt and Spencer F. Baird [*qq.v.*], had spent a winter in the Smithsonian Institution, and in the employ of the United States Geological Survey had carried on intensive investigations on Cape Ann, the results of which were used by Professor Nathaniel Southgate Shaler [*q.v.*] in his monograph *The Geology of Cape Ann* (1890), with the wholehearted acknowledgment that "the larger part of the field observations" had been made by his assistant. Tarr had also mapped glacial moraines in Massachusetts for the Survey, and had done geological field work in New Mexico, Montana, and Texas. In 1890 he returned to Cambridge as an assistant to Shaler, and completed his work for the degree of B.S. in 1891.

On Mar. 28, 1892, he married Kate Story of Gloucester, and later the same year was appointed assistant professor of geology at Cornell University. In 1906 he was made full professor and head of the department of physical geography. He organized the Cornell Greenland Expedition which went north on Peary's ship in 1896, and in 1909 and 1911 conducted the National Geographic Society's expeditions to Alaska. He also took advantage of the opportunities which the country near Ithaca offered him to study physiographic and glacial problems and drainage, and investigated the geological history of the Finger Lake region, making surveys and a complete areal study under the auspices of the United States Geological Survey. The year before his death he was given charge of the Cornell seismographic station. He died in Ithaca, survived by his wife, a son, and a daughter.

Tarr was president of the Association of American Geographers (1911–12), foreign correspondent of the Geological Society of London, and a member of several other professional societies. He served on the International Committee on Glaciers, and was elected corresponding member of the Royal Geographical Society of Vienna shortly before his death. He was an associate editor of the *Bulletin of the American Geographical Society* from 1899 to 1911 and of the *Journal of Geography* from 1902 to 1912. He was the author of widely used textbooks, including *The Economic Geology of the United States* (1893), *Elementary Physical Geography* (1895), *First Book of Physical Geography* (1897), *Elementary Geology* (1897), the school geographies (1900) prepared in collaboration with Frank Morton McMurry, *New Physical Geography* (1904), and *College Physiography* (published posthumously in 1914). His professional publications include *The Physical Geography of New York State* (1902) and contributions to the Geological Survey dealing with the Yakutat Bay region in Alaska and the Watkins Glen region of New York. With Lawrence Martin he wrote *Alaskan Glacier Studies* (1914), awarded the gold medal of the Société de Géographie de Paris. Tarr also wrote scores of short scientific papers and geographical reviews and contributed a number of articles to *Johnson's Encyclopedia*, the *International Encyclopedia*, and the tenth edition of the *Encyclopedia Britannica*. His contributions to glaciology included studies of the relation of eskers, kames, and kettle holes to the ice sheet, the significance of hanging valleys and other features of glacial erosion, the nature of ablation moraine and of the through glacier, the rôle of earthquakes in glacial advance, and the cause of flowage in ice. He also verified, through his researches near the living glaciers in Greenland, Alaska, Norway, Spitzbergen, and the Alps, the deductions drawn from similar phenomena in far-removed regions of former glaciation. A contemporary authority said that Tarr's studies of the dislocation giving rise to the Alaskan earthquake of 1899 were "a most important addition to our knowledge of the relation of earthquakes and faults, with accompanying changes of level of the land in relation to the sea" (Woodworth, *post*, p. 37). His work on the peneplain, on extended rivers, and on rifting in granite, was also important.

[A. P. Brigham, in *Annals of the Asso. of Am. Geographers*, vol. III (1913); J. B. Woodworth, in *Bull. Geol. Soc. of America*, vol. XXIV (1913), with bibliog.; Lawrence Martin, in *Zeitschrift für Gletsch-erkunde*, vol. IX (1914), with bibliog. of Tarr's writings on glaciers and glaciation by E. F. Bean; W. T. Hewett, *Cornell Univ., A Hist.* (1905), vol. II; *Cornell Alumni News*, Mar. 26, 1913; *Harvard Coll. Class of 1891, Secretary's Report*, No. 4 (1906), No. 5 (1911); *Who's Who in America*, 1912–13; *Am. Men of Science*, 1910; *N. Y. Times*, Mar. 22, 1912.]

K. M.

TASHUNCA-UITCO [See CRAZY HORSE, *c.* 1849–1877].

TASHRAK [See Zevin, Israel Joseph, 1872–1926].

TATHAM, WILLIAM (Apr. 13, 1752–Feb. 22, 1819), civil engineer and geographer, was born at Hutton-in-the-Forest, Cumberland, England, eldest son of the Rev. Sandford Tatham and his wife, a daughter of Henry Marsden of Gisborne Hall, Yorkshire (John and J. A. Venn, *Alumni Cantabrigienses*, pt. 1, vol. IV, 1927). Sent to Virginia in 1769 to seek his fortune, he became a clerk in the trading house of Carter & Trent, on James River. Early in 1776 he removed to the Watauga settlement in the Tennessee country, where he was employed in the mercantile establishment of John Carter. For a time he was clerk of the celebrated Watauga Association. He drafted the petition (July 5, 1776) of the inhabitants on the western waters praying for incorporation into the government of North Carolina (J. G. M. Ramsay, *The Annals of Tennessee*, 1853, pp. 134–38). Throughout the Revolution he served the American cause intermittently, taking part first in the defense of Fort Caswell-on-Watauga in July 1776, and last in the operations at Yorktown, October 1781.

In 1780, in collaboration with Col. John Todd of Kentucky, Tatham prepared a "History of the Western Country," which is said to have received the approbation of Jefferson. This work was never printed and the manuscript has been lost. After a brief mercantile venture in Philadelphia and a visit to Havana in 1783, Tatham returned to Virginia where he became clerk of the council of state. He studied law under Samuel Hardy, a member of the council, and subsequently under William R. Davie [*q.v.*] of North Carolina, and was admitted to the bar Mar. 24, 1784. He was a delegate from Robeson County in the general assembly of North Carolina in 1787, and was elected by that body a lieutenant-colonel of militia. After a visit to England, he was prevailed upon to organize a geographical department for Virginia, and in 1791 published *A Topographical Analysis of the Commonwealth of Virginia for 1790–91.*

Tatham returned in 1792 to the Tennessee country, where he practised law, mapped the region, and gathered considerable materials for its history. Visiting Spain in 1796 on a mysterious mission connected with affairs in the West, he was ordered to leave the country. Removing to London, he devoted much time to literary pursuits, contributing to magazines and publishing works on engineering and agricultural subjects: *A Plan for Insulating the Metropolis by a Canal* (1797); *Remarks on Inland Canals* (1798); *The Political Economy of the Inland Navigation* (1799); *An Historical and Practical Essay on the Culture and Commerce of Tobacco* (1800); *Auxiliary Remarks on an Essay on the Comparative Advantages of Oxen in Tillage* (1801); *National Irrigation* (1801); *Report on a View of Certain Impediments and Obstructions, in the Navigation of the River Thames* (1803); and *Navigation and Conservancy of the River Thames* (1803). In 1801 he was appointed superintendent of construction of the elaborate Wapping Docks in the Thames at London.

Returning to America in 1805, Tatham was engaged for some years in a survey of the coast from Cape Fear to Cape Hatteras. In that field he was a pioneer. He was an assiduous collector of manuscript maps and historical data, and his invaluable collection was offered for sale, without success, to Congress in 1806 and again in 1817. In his proposal of 1806 (*American State Papers, Miscellaneous*, I, 1834, pp. 457 ff.), Tatham was probably the first to define the functions of a national library for the United States (W. D. Johnston, *History of the Library of Congress*, 1904, I, 50). He spent about five years as draftsman and geographer in the Department of State at Washington, and in 1817 President Monroe gave him a comfortable position in the government arsenal on James River.

Tatham was the friend and correspondent of Jefferson and other statesmen of his times, and collaborated with Robert Fulton in the field of canalization. He was a man of brilliant parts and great versatility, but was eccentric and lacking in mental poise. He had become addicted to the use of intoxicants and in a moment of intemperance stepped in front of a gun about to be fired in a salute and was killed instantly. Papers he left and his conversation previously indicated that the act was deliberate. He was unmarried.

[S. C. Williams, "William Tatham, Wataugan," in *Tenn. Hist. Mag.* for Oct. 1921, also printed separately (1923) under same title; *Public Characters of 1801–1802* (1804); *The Ann. Biog. and Obituary for the Year 1820* (1820), pp. 149–68, an excellent sketch, with autobiog. material and a list of Tatham's publications; G. W. Munford, *The Two Parsons* (1884);

Calendar of Va. State Papers, vols. V, VI (1885–86); The State Records of N. C., vols. XX (1902), XXIV (1905); Schedule of Vouchers, Tending to Prove that William Tatham Has Served the U. S. Near Forty Years (1815); Gentleman's Mag. (London), Apr. 1819; Richmond Enquirer, Feb. 23, 25, and autobiog. sketch, Mar. 2, 1819.]   S. C. W.

TATTNALL, JOSIAH (Nov. 9, 1795–June 14, 1871), naval officer, was born at the family estate "Bonaventure," a few miles below Savannah, Ga., the son of Josiah and Harriet (Fenwick) Tattnall. His paternal great-grandfather, who came to South Carolina in 1700, was of English and French stock; his mother was of English stock. He was left an orphan when he was nine years of age and in his tenth year was sent to London to be educated under the supervision of his maternal grandfather. He remained abroad six years. A few months after his return home he was, on Mar. 10, 1812, appointed midshipman. After a few weeks of instruction in the naval school of Andrew Hunter [q.v.] at the Washington navy yard he was ordered to the *Constellation,* which, because of the blockade, remained at Hampton Roads throughout the war. In the engagement of Craney Island, Va., on June 22, 1813, he received his first baptism of fire and was one of a party that waded out from shore to take possession of the barges of the enemy.

The following year, after assisting in conveying reinforcements to Lake Erie, he was sent to the *Epervier* at Savannah where he was stationed when the war ended. Continuing with this vessel when she was attached to the squadron of Stephen Decatur, 1779–1820 [q.v.], he participated in 1815 in the war with Algiers. He was promoted to the rank of lieutenant on Apr. 1, 1818, and soon afterwards joined the *Macedonian* at Baltimore and made an extensive cruise in the Pacific. At Valparaiso, offended by the remarks of an English naval officer depreciating the part of the United States in the late war, he challenged him and wounded him in a duel. A period of professional study at Partridge's military school at Norwich, Vt., was followed in 1823 by an uneventful cruise in the West Indies as first lieutenant of the *Jackal,* one of Commodore David Porter's vessels engaged in suppressing piracy in the West Indies. After a tour of duty in the Mediterranean, 1825–26, he was again in the West Indies, this time on board the *Erie.* At St. Bartholomew he commanded a boat expedition that captured the piratical privateer *Federal.* In 1829 he was in charge of a survey of the Tortugas reefs and keys off the Florida coast. In 1831–32 he commanded the *Grampus* during a cruise off the

Mexican and Texas coast for the protection of American commerce, a service marked by the capture of the Mexican schooner *Montezuma.* In 1837 he conveyed to Vera Cruz on board the *Pioneer* the Mexican general, Santa Anna, captured by the Texans at San Jacinto.

He was promoted commander in 1838 and soon was made commandant of the Boston navy yard. In 1840 he was associated with Matthew C. Perry [q.v.] in ordnance experiments. Service in the Mediterranean as commander of the *Fairfield* was shortly brought to an end by reason of differences with his commodore, and he subsequently commanded the *Saratoga* of the African Squadron, 1843–44. In the Mexican War he had a conspicuous part in the navy's operations on the east coast of Mexico. In charge of the mosquito division with the *Spitfire* as his flagship, he bombarded the city of Vera Cruz and the Castle of St. Juan d'Ulloa and exhibited great daring. In the capture of Túxpan the *Spitfire* was in the lead and began the action, her commander receiving a wound in the arm. Tattnall returned to the United States with his health impaired. His native state recognized his services in the war with a vote of thanks and the gift of a sword.

After two years at the Boston navy yard he was ordered to the *Saranac* and sent to Cuba to maintain American rights imperiled by a revolution. He next took command of the naval station at Pensacola. In the meantime he had been promoted captain from Feb. 6, 1850. Ordered to the *Independence,* he cruised in the Pacific during 1854–55, until a difference with his commodore over questions of discipline led to his return to the United States. Dismissing the charges against him, the department ordered him to the naval station at Sacketts Harbor, N. Y. On Sept. 17, 1857, he was detached from this duty and appointed to the command of the squadron on the East India station. His most important work there was in connection with the negotiation of new treaties with China by the Occidental powers. He placed every facility of the fleet at the disposal of the American envoy. When the British fleet was defeated in 1859 at the mouth of the Pei-ho River he gave aid to the British that under the circumstances violated the neutrality of the United States. In explanation of his conduct he quoted the adage "Blood is thicker than water." The American government upheld his acts and the British government expressed its thanks to President Buchanan. When late in life he was in need of funds some British officers subscribed a sum of money for his relief. In 1860 he returned to

San Francisco on the *Powhatan,* giving passage to a numerous embassy of Japanese officials. Soon afterwards he was again assigned to the command of the Sacketts Harbor naval station, his last duty as an officer of the American navy.

Although opposed to secession, Tattnall was loyal to his native state and resigned from the navy on Feb. 20, 1861, to accept the appointment of senior flag officer of the Georgia navy in the Civil War. In March he was made a captain in the Confederate States Navy and shortly took command of the naval defenses of Georgia and South Carolina, improvising a small fleet with the *Savannah* as flagship. In November in Port Royal Sound, he ineffectually opposed the superior Union fleet, and early in the following year cooperated with the Confederate army in the defense of Fort Pulaski. On Mar. 29, 1862, he succeeded Franklin Buchanan [*q.v.*] in command of the naval defenses in the waters of Virginia with the ironclad *Merrimac,* renamed the *Virginia,* as his flagship. Several times he attempted to effect an engagement with the *Monitor* but the latter declined the challenge. In May when Norfolk was abandoned, he burned the *Merrimac* to prevent her capture. Tattnall was severely criticized, but a court martial upheld his action. Returning to Savannah in April he again took command of the Georgia naval defenses until March 1863. After that his activities were confined to Savannah, where he remained until December 1864 when the city was occupied by Sherman. Destroying the public property in his charge, he retreated to Augusta and was captured with the army of General Johnston. He was paroled in May 1865.

In 1866 he took up his residence with his family near Halifax, Nova Scotia, where he lived for four years. In January 1870 he was appointed to the office of inspector of the port of Savannah, holding it until his death. On Sept. 6, 1821, he had been married to Harriette Fenwick Jackson, who, with several daughters and a son, survived him.

[Bureau of Navigation, Record of Officers, 1809–63; D. E. Huger Smith, "An Account of the Tattnall and Fenwick Families in South Carolina," *S. C. Hist. and Geneal. Mag.,* Jan. 1913; F. F. Starr, *The Edward Jackson Family* (1895); C. C. Jones, *The Life and Services of Comm. Josiah Tattnall* (1878); *War of the Rebellion: Official Records* (Navy), vol. VII (1898), XII (1901), XVI (1903); J. T. Scharf, *Hist. of the Confed. States Navy* (1887); R. W. Neeser, *Statistical and Chronological Hist. of the U. S. Navy* (1909); Tyler Dennett, *Americans in Eastern Asia* (1922); Horatio Bridge, *Jour. of an African Cruiser* (1845); articles by W. H. Shock, *United States,* May 1892; C. O. Paullin, *Proc. U. S. Naval Institute,* June 1911; E. S. Maclay, *Ibid.,* July–Aug. 1914; *Savannah Daily Republican,* June 15, 16, 17, 1871.]   C. O. P.

TAUSSIG, WILLIAM (Feb. 28, 1826–July 10, 1913), physician, business man, civic leader, was born in Prague, Bohemia, fourth among some fifteen children of John L. Taussig and Charlotte (Bondy), his wife. Hebrew blood ran in the veins of his father, a native of Prague who manufactured cotton goods on a small scale. Completing the classical course in the University of Prague at eighteen, William turned to the study of chemistry and three years later emigrated to New York. The next year found him in St. Louis, Mo., chemist for Charless, Blow & Company, frontier druggists. During the cholera scourge which swept the city in 1849 he distinguished himself by his fearlessness as apothecary at quarantine. A year later he received the degree of M.D. from the St. Louis Medical College and established himself for practice in nearby Carondelet, of which town he was elected mayor in 1852. On May 3, 1857, he married Adele Wuerpel of St. Louis, daughter of a German teacher who had quit the Rhineland in 1848.

On the reorganization, in 1859, of the St. Louis county court, an executive body, Taussig was elected one of the five reform members. Among his first official acts was a report on the application of U. S. Grant to be superintendent of county roads—unfavorable, because he was not sure of Grant's loyalty to the Union. In general, however, he administered so wisely the affairs of the county, torn as it was between two camps during the forepart of the Civil War, that he was reëlected in 1863 and designated presiding judge. Following the destruction of an insane asylum in Fulton, Mo., by marauders and the failure of the state to provide relief for the homeless unfortunates, he at personal risk took them to St. Louis where they were lodged first in St. Vincent Asylum and later in the city insane asylum, the cornerstone of which he laid in 1864. During the war he held the post of examining surgeon for drafted soldiers.

Compelled, through long illness, to give up the medical profession, he was appointed collector of internal revenue by Lincoln in January 1865, and was thereby led to a complete change of career. After resigning the collectorship (1866) he turned to banking, and was president of the Traders' Bank from 1866 to 1869. Following the liquidation of the bank, he became associated with the project to bridge the Mississippi at St. Louis, and soon became the manager, later president, of the bridge company. In this capacity he faced business problems almost as great as the structural problems which confronted the bridge's engineer, James Buchanan Eads [*q.v.*].

The bridge company and others growing out of it were merged in 1889 in the Terminal Railroad Association, of which Taussig remained president until his retirement in 1896. Through his judgment and foresight, and because of the confidence of railway executives in his integrity and impartiality, all railroads entering the city joined in the establishment of a single union station—a traffic reform of the first importance. The station built under his administration was the finest of its time.

When he died of pneumonia in his eighty-seventh year, he was still head of the bridge company, a director in the St. Louis Union Trust Company, a director of Washington University, president of the Self-Culture Hall and Tenement House associations, and active in the Ethical Society. In memory of his service as president of the St. Louis board of education a public school was named for him. He was survived by his widow, a daughter, and two sons. His body was cremated and the ashes placed in Bellefontaine Cemetery. In politics he was associated with Carl Schurz, B. Gratz Brown, William M. Grosvenor, Henry T. Blow, and Emil Preetorius [qq.v.] in promoting the Liberal Republican movement. A model citizen, a cultured gentleman, practical yet imaginative, industrious and generous—he long gave shoes and clothing to needy school children anonymously—he was unusually well fitted for meeting the problems that came with the rise of the city.

[*Who's Who in America*, 1912–13; Wm. Hyde and H. L. Conard, *Encyc. of the Hist. of St. Louis* (1899), vol. IV; C. M. Woodward, *A Hist. of the St. Louis Bridge* (1881); Taussig's own "Personal Recollections of General Grant," in *Mo. Hist. Soc. Pubs.*, vol. II, no. 3 (1903), and his "Development of St. Louis Terminals" in "Addresses of the St. Louis Commercial Club" (St. Louis Public Library); *St. Louis Globe-Democrat*, July 11, 1913 and July 23, 1922; information from a son, Prof. F. W. Taussig.]   I. D.

TAWNEY, JAMES ALBERTUS (Jan. 3, 1855–June 12, 1919), representative in Congress from Minnesota, son of John E. and Sarah (Boblitz) Tawney, was born in Mount Pleasant Township, near Gettysburg, Pa. He is said to have been a descendant of John Tawney, who emigrated from England and landed at Baltimore about 1650. Leaving school at fourteen, he was trained by his father, a farmer and blacksmith, to follow in his footsteps; later he also learned the machinist's trade. After working in a machine shop in western Pennsylvania he went west and in 1877 established himself in Winona, Minn., where he worked at his trade, studied law by himself and in the office of Bentley and Vance, and was admitted to the bar (1882). He finished his legal training with a

term in the law school of the University of Wisconsin (1882–83). At Winona he was married on Dec. 19, 1883, to Emma B. Newell. As in the case of many young lawyers, his legal work was a stepping-stone to politics. In 1890 he was elected to the state Senate; in 1892 he was chosen to represent the first district of Minnesota in Congress and continued to be reëlected until his defeat in 1910. From the beginning he was an old-line Republican. Unquestioned ability, regularity, and length of service secured for him a position on the committee on ways and means from 1895 to 1905, on the committee on insular affairs from December 1899, and, in 1905, the chairmanship of the committee on appropriations. He was one of the quintet, along with Joseph Gurney Cannon [q.v.], S. E. Payne, John Dalzell [q.v.], and J. S. Sherman, which dominated the House until the smash of 1910.

In his first session Tawney demonstrated his Republicanism by making an attack on the proposal to repeal the Federal Election Law, by advocating increased duties on barley (which gained for him the sobriquet of "Barley Jim"), and by bringing forward pension bills on every possible occasion. In 1897 he took a leading part in framing the Dingley Tariff, having especial care for the lumber interests of his state (Tawney Papers, *post*). He was, indeed, always considered especially tender toward lumber interests (Folwell, *post*, p. 250). A consistent protectionist, he was opposed to special favors for Cuban sugar, but he believed in free trade between the United States and Puerto Rico as a "permanent policy" (letter to A. T. Stebbins, Mar. 1, 1900, Tawney Papers, *post*), although he supported the Foraker Bill as a temporary expedient. He had a voice in dissuading Roosevelt from pressing revision of the tariff when the latter was inclined to urge a special session for the purpose (Theodore Roosevelt to Tawney, Nov. 10, 17, 1904, *Ibid.*). Tawney was more or less a national figure from his position in the House, and his notoriety, if not fame, was enhanced by a clash with Roosevelt over appropriations for the secret service division of the Treasury Department in 1908. Following Roosevelt's caustic reference to the matter in his annual message of 1908, the House, wounded in its *amour propre*, tabled that portion of the message as well as a special message explanatory of the passage, thus upholding Tawney, who had been mentioned by name and who defended himself and the committee from what were considered personal aspersions (*Congressional Record*, 60 Cong., 2 Sess., pp. 660–64). This episode brought almost immediate repercussions. A defender of the Payne-

Aldrich Tariff, Tawney further weakened his position with his constituents, already shaken by the brush with the President. William Howard Taft's defense of Tawney, along with the tariff act, in the famous Winona speech and Roosevelt's speech attacking him contributed to his defeat in the election of 1910. An appointment to the international joint commission on the United States–Canadian boundary provided him with a lame duck's refuge and the only political position he held until his death at Excelsior Springs, Mo., in 1919. He was survived by his wife and five of his six children.

[*Who's Who in America*, 1918–19; *Biog. Dir. Am. Cong.* (1928); Tawney Papers, in the Minn. Hist. Soc. colls.; W. W. Folwell, *A Hist. of Minn.*, vol. IV (1930); *Current Lit.*, Nov. 1909, pp. 477–78, 481; *Independent*, May 28, 1908, pp. 1185–90; *Am. Rev. of Revs.*, Jan. 1909, pp. 39–41; E. V. Smalley, *A Hist. of the Republican Party* (1896); H. F. Stevens, *Hist. of the Bench and Bar of Minn.* (2 vols., 1904); Theodore Christianson, *Minn.*, vol. III (1935), pp. 27–30; obituary in *Minneapolis Jour.*, June 12, 1919.] L. B. S.

TAYLOR, ALFRED ALEXANDER (Aug. 6, 1848–Nov. 24, 1931), congressman, governor of Tennessee, the third of the nine children of Nathaniel Green and Emmeline (Haynes) Taylor, was born in Happy Valley, Carter County, Tenn. His ancestors on his mother's side were among the founders of the Watauga settlement in 1769, and were leaders in the establishment of the Watauga Association and in the government of the state of Franklin. His father, a graduate of the College of New Jersey (later Princeton), was a prominent lawyer, preacher, and Whig politician, who served both before and after the Civil War as representative in Congress from Tennessee. Educated at Duffield Academy, Elizabethton, Tenn., at Pennington Seminary, Pennington, N. J., and at Buffalo Institute (later Milligan College), Milligan, Tenn., Taylor served briefly under his father in Washington, studied law, and, following his admission to the bar in 1870, established himself in Jonesboro, Tenn. Turning to politics almost immediately, he served as a member of the lower House of the Tennessee legislature in 1875–76. Because of his ready wit and his ability as a speaker he made such a strong popular appeal as a Republican campaigner in the state election of 1882 that he was selected by his party as its candidate for governor in 1886 in a futile effort to prevent the nomination of his brother, Robert Love Taylor [*q.v.*] by the Democrats. The result was a unique and picturesque political campaign in which the two brothers canvassed the state in joint debate, attracting widespread attention more because of their ability as entertainers than because of the issues involved in the campaign.

Soon labelled "Alf" and "Bob" by popular fancy, they waged a bloodless "War of the Roses" in which the weapons were droll anecdotes, scintillating repartee, and a matching of their skill as fiddlers.

When "Bob" won the election, "Alf" returned to his law practice, and in 1888 was elected representative in Congress from the first Tennessee district, serving in this capacity from March 1889 to March 1895. Upon his retirement from Congress, he joined his brother in a lyceum lecture tour of the United States, and later divided his time between his law practice and frequent lecture engagements until the Republican landslide of 1920 brought his election to the governorship. After serving one term (1921–23) as governor, he was defeated for reëlection and retired to his home near Johnson City, Tenn., where he spent the remainder of his life. He was married on June 22, 1881, to Jennie Anderson of Buffalo Valley, Tenn., by whom he had ten children. He was survived by six sons and two daughters. On the whole his direct influence upon the political affairs of Tennessee was perhaps slight; but indirectly, through his close association with his more famous brother, he contributed much toward encouraging the rural voters of the state to assert themselves. In his old age he attributed the success with which he and his brother met to the fact that, "We played the fiddle, were fond of dogs, and loved our fellow men."

[*Who's Who in America*, 1930–31; *Biog. Directory of the Am. Cong.* (1928); D. M. Robison, *Bob Taylor and the Agrarian Revolt in Tenn.* (1935); DeLong Rice, *"Old Limber," or the Tale of the Taylors* (copr. 1921); P. D. Augsburg, *Bob and Alf Taylor* (1925); *Notable Men of Tenn.* (1905), ed. by John Allison; obituary in *Nashville Banner*, Nov. 25, 1931.] W. C. B.

TAYLOR, ARCHIBALD ALEXANDER EDWARD (Aug. 27, 1834–Apr. 23, 1903), Presbyterian clergyman and educator, was born in Springfield, Ohio, the son of Edward Taylor, a physician, and Penelope Virginia (Gordon) Taylor. After attending the school of E. S. Brooks in Cincinnati, he studied seven years in Princeton, graduating from the College of New Jersey in 1854 and from the Theological Seminary in 1857. He then entered the ministry of the Old School Presbyterian Church, being licensed by the Presbytery of Cincinnati on June 17, 1857, and ordained by the Presbytery of Louisville on May 6, 1858. At ordination he was installed as pastor of the church at Portland, Ky., which he had been serving since September 1857. Subsequently, he was pastor of the First Church of Dubuque, Iowa (1859–65), the Bridge

Street Church of Georgetown, D. C. (1865–69), and the Mount Auburn Church of Cincinnati (1869–73). In 1870–71 he was editor of *Our Monthly*.

He was elected president of the University of Wooster, Ohio, in 1873, being the second to occupy that office. During the ten years of his incumbency he did his principal work, ably and successfully managing the affairs of the institution and holding influential relations with the students. His contribution to its development was acknowledged in 1902 by the naming of a new building Taylor Hall. While president he was also professor of Biblical instruction and apologetics. After his resignation of the presidency in 1883, he was absent from Wooster for two years, but returned in 1885 to serve for three years as professor of logic and political science. He was a trustee of the university from 1873 to 1902, and president of the board of trustees during the last seven of these years. In 1888 he became editor of *The Mid-Continent,* a Presbyterian weekly published in St. Louis, which position he held until 1891. For part of this time he was in charge of the Presbyterian church in Ferguson, Mo. From 1892 to 1899 he was pastor of Westminister Presbyterian Church of Columbus, Ohio. Thereafter he lived in Columbus in declining strength until his death. He had the unusual distinction of being five times moderator of his Synod, and he was four times a commissioner to the General Assembly, a member of the Presbyterian boards of education and church erection, and a director of Western and McCormick theological seminaries. He wrote numerous articles for religious periodicals, and published sermons and addresses and a volume of verse entitled *Claudia Procula and Other Verses* (1899).

Taylor was an unusually interesting and attractive personality. He had a fertile mind, with a good deal of poetic imagination. He was long remembered for his kindliness, cheerfulness, and good conversation. As pastor and teacher he showed a gift for winning the confidence of all sorts of people. His humor was abundant and lively—in the view of some, to a degree beyond what befitted a minister. He had a large library and read in many fields with fine appreciation. He was a hunter and fisherman and lover of the woods. On Aug. 2, 1858, at Freehold, N. J., he was married to Annie Vanderveer, who died in 1867; and on May 21, 1868, at Munson Hill, Va., to Lucy Eleanor Munson, who survived him as did also a son by his first wife and a daughter by the second.

[*Princeton Theological Sem., Necrological Report* (1904); *Who's Who in America,* 1901–02; *The Presbyterian* (Phila.), Apr. 29, 1903; *Ohio State Jour.* (Columbus), Apr. 24, 1903; report of board of trustees of University of Wooster, in minutes of the Ohio Synod, 1903; information from College of Wooster (formerly University) and from Edward Taylor of Xenia, Ohio, a grandson.]
R. H. N.

TAYLOR, BAYARD (Jan. 11, 1825–Dec. 19, 1878), traveler, translator, man of letters, was born at Kennett Square, Chester County, Pa. His earliest American ancestor, Robert Taylor, had come from England with William Penn and had settled near Brandywine Creek. There the Taylors had remained purely English and strictly Quaker until John Taylor, grandfather of Bayard, married Ann Bucher, of a Swiss Mennonite family, and was expelled from meeting. John Taylor's son Joseph married Rebecca Bauer Way, of English and German stock. The Swiss and German strains, however, did not disturb the Quaker discipline of the household in which Bayard Taylor was brought up. The village of Kennett Square and the Taylor homestead, a mile away, were quiet, orderly, and—for him—dull. At fourteen he was told by a lecturing phrenologist, Thomas Dunn English [*q.v.*], that he would be a traveler and a poet. His poems, which he began to write as early as seven, were symptoms of his restlessness. Neither they nor his studies at Bolmar's Academy in West Chester and at the Unionville academy could satisfy his intense hunger for the world beyond his Quaker horizon. He wrote to John Sartain [*q.v.*] asking to be apprenticed as engraver. He was apprenticed instead to the printer of the West Chester *Village Record* at seventeen. Poetry helped him to escape. Having attracted the attention of Rufus Wilmot Griswold [*q.v.*], editor of *Graham's Magazine* and anthologist of the American ephemerides, Taylor was encouraged to publish his first volume of verse, *Ximena* (1844), and was enabled to get free of his apprenticeship. With money advanced by the *Saturday Evening Post* and the *United States Gazette* of Philadelphia for letters which he was to send back from his travels, he walked to Washington for a passport. In New York he was generously received by Nathaniel Parker Willis, and he made a conditional agreement with Horace Greeley [*qq.v.*] for letters on Germany to the *Tribune.* He sailed for Liverpool in July 1844 with his cousin Franklin Taylor and his friend Barclay Pennock.

Only nineteen, Bayard Taylor had already shown the energy, eagerness, and charm which were to clear every path before him and make him his age's young hero among travelers. With one or both of his companions he spent two years in Europe. After a turn in Scotland, he visited London, hurried to the Rhine and Heidelberg, and then settled down for six months in Frankfurt. By Leipzig, Dresden, Prague, he went on foot to Vienna, and later journeyed in the same way to Italy, where he stayed longest in Florence. He shipped to Marseilles, tramped to Paris, returned to London. Once more back in New York, he published his *Views Afoot* (1846), which had an introduction by Willis and which ran to six editions within the year and to twenty in nine years. Taylor had traveled like a penniless, well-behaved undergraduate, excitedly alive to all he saw. He wrote ingenuously and engagingly.

Editors and publishers hastened to work the vein he had revealed in himself. After a year in Phoenixville, Pa., where he bought, ran, and soon sold the *Gazette* (re-named the *Pioneer*), he left to try his luck in New York in December 1847. First the contributor of a weekly article to the *Literary World*, after January 1848 he was manager of the miscellaneous and literary department of the *New York Tribune*. He made friends with writers in both New York and Boston, and moved in mildly Bohemian circles, a poet in private, a journalist in public. The California gold rush took him, on a commission for the *Tribune*, to the Pacific. He sailed June 1849 by way of Panama, spent five months in California, enjoyed the high spirits and variety of the gold regions without minding the hardships or violence, crossed Mexico from Mazatlán to Vera Cruz, and was in New York again by March 1850. His *Eldorado* (1850) doubled his fame as a traveler. As poet he was that year invited to deliver the Phi Beta Kappa poem at Harvard, and he won a prize offered by P. T. Barnum for the best lyric to be sung by Jenny Lind on her appearance at Castle Garden.

Long in love with Mary Agnew of Kennett Square, Taylor was married to her on Oct. 24, 1850, that they might be together during the few months she had still to live. She died in December. Profoundly grieved, and exhausted from overwork, he left New York in August 1851 for more than two years of travel in Egypt, Abyssinia, Syria, Palestine, Turkey, India, China. At Shanghai he joined Commodore Matthew Calbraith Perry's squadron and spent the summer of 1853 as master's mate, writing an account of the Japanese expedition which by the rules of the service he was never allowed to publish. Returning to New York around the Cape of Good Hope, he told about his travels in *A Journey to Central Africa* (1854), *The Lands of the Saracen* (1855), and *A Visit to India, China, and Japan, in the Year 1853* (1855), and gave countless lectures to lyceum audiences. He never outlived these journeys. For the home-keeping Americans of that generation he remained a Marco Polo, masterfully familiar with incredible lands. In Whittier's "The Tent on the Beach" Taylor appears as the Traveler.

He himself, if not tired of travel, at least desired increasingly to be known as a man of letters. Habit, facility, and need of funds sent him again to Europe during 1856–58 and made him write *Northern Travel* (1858), *Travels in Greece and Russia* (1859), and *At Home and Abroad* (1860). But having married Marie Hansen, daughter of the Danish astronomer Peter Andreas Hansen, at Gotha in Oct. 27, 1857, Taylor gradually withdrew to a farm which he had bought near his native village and on which he built a house called Cedarcroft. It was a delusive retirement. When he established himself, with his wife and daughter, there in May 1860 he was still only thirty-five, full of vivacious impulses and cosmopolitan tastes. The neighborhood which he had come to remember as pastoral turned out to be as dull as ever. It bored him with its primness and disapproved of him, especially for his robust use and praise of alcohol. His chief country friends were the family of Horace Howard Furness, the elder [*q.v.*], at Wallingford twenty miles away. In spite of Taylor's pleasure in Cedarcroft it was a burden for him to maintain it and its open-handed hospitality. To the end of his life he was strained with anxiety and hackwork. During the Civil War he served for a time as correspondent of the *Tribune* at Washington. In May 1862 he went to Saint Petersburg (Leningrad) as secretary of legation under Simon Cameron, the new minister to Russia. Left in charge in September, Taylor had a hand in keeping Russia friendly to the Union, but he was not, as he hoped, chosen to succeed his chief. Once again at Cedarcroft in September 1863 he published a novel he had completed in Russia, *Hannah Thurston* (1863), and followed it with two others, *John Godfrey's Fortunes* (1864) and *The Story of Kennett* (1866). His novels were vigorously crowded with things he had experienced or observed in America, but they were without distinction. So were the poems with which, earlier and later, he filled more than a dozen volumes, among them: *Rhymes of Travel, Ballads and Poems* (1849), *A Book of Romances, Lyrics, and Songs* (1852), *Poems of the Orient* (1855), *The Poet's Journal* (1862), *The Picture of St. John* (1866), *The Masque of the Gods* (1872), *Lars: A Pastoral of Norway* (1873), *The Prophet* (1874), *Home Pastorals, Ballads and Lyrics* (1875), *The Echo Club and Other Literary Diversions* (1876),

Prince Deukalion (1878). Except in a song and a ballad or two, and the agile, amusing parodies of the *Echo Club,* he was diffuse and commonplace. Between 1863 and 1870 he gave himself up, with intervals of travel and necessary odd jobs, to his translation, in the original meters, of *Faust* (2 vols., 1870–71). He knew all of the first and most of the second part so well that he could often translate without consulting the text. This translation was to be the English *Faust.* Instantly applauded, it has ever since been looked upon as the best version, and has been extravagantly praised. But its fidelity and sonorousness should not be allowed to hide the fact that Taylor rendered *Faust* in the second-rate English poetry which was all he knew how to write.

His last years were full of honors. He held the position of non-resident professor of German literature at Cornell from 1870 to 1877 and gave occasional lectures at the university. He was chosen to write the Gettysburg Ode in 1869 and the Centennial Ode in 1876. His renown in Germany was immense. He planned to crown his life with a great biography of Goethe. Sent as minister to Germany in April 1878, he saw himself at last free to live and write as he desired. But he had worn himself out doing what he thought he did not want to do, and he died in December of the same year. His body, brought home, lay in state in the New York city hall and was buried in the Hicksite Cemetery in Longwood, Pa. There was hardly a poet in America who did not celebrate Taylor's death in generous verse. The brilliance of his life for years blinded men to the mediocrity of his actual achievement.

[Taylor's name is sometimes given as James Bayard Taylor, but he himself says that it was simply Bayard. In addition to his own travel books, which are full of autobiog., see Marie Hansen Taylor and H. E. Scudder, *The Life and Letters of Bayard Taylor* (2 vols., 1884) ; Marie Hansen Taylor and Lilian Bayard Taylor Kiliani, *On Two Continents* (1905) ; A. H. Smyth, *Bayard Taylor* (1896), an excellent biog., with thorough bibliog.; *The Cambridge Hist. of Am. Lit.,* vol. III (1921), pp. 38–43; A. R. Justice, *Descendants of Robert Taylor* (1925) ; obituary in *N. Y. Times,* Dec. 20, 1878. R. H. Conwell, *The Life, Travels, and Lit. Career of Bayard Taylor* (1881), is inadequate. Numerous references to Taylor are to be found in the memoirs and biogs. of almost all his contemporaries. Juliana Haskell, *Bayard Taylor's Translation of Goethe's Faust* (1908) exactingly studies the reputation and merits of the work for which he is best known.]

C. V–D.

TAYLOR, BENJAMIN FRANKLIN (July 19, 1819–Feb. 24, 1887), poet, journalist, lecturer, was born in Lowville, N. Y., the son of Stephen William and Eunice (Scranton) Taylor. His father in the last five years of his life was president of Madison (later Colgate) University, Hamilton, New York. Graduating from Hamilton Literary and Theological Institute (later Madison University) in 1838, young Taylor went to Michigan seeking employment. After three years of hardship, fighting poverty and malaria, because of ill health unable to gain a foothold in that pioneer environment, he returned to New York and for several years taught school in Springville, Norwich, and other places. In 1845 he went to Chicago, where he soon became literary editor of the recently established *Chicago Daily Journal.* During the last two years of the Civil War he served as war correspondent for the *Journal,* and his realistic reports of the battles of Missionary Ridge, Lookout Mountain, and other engagements, widely copied by other papers, gave him a national reputation. These accounts were published under the title *Mission Ridge and Lookout Mountain, with Pictures of Life in Camp and Field* (1872). Severing his connection with the *Journal* in 1865, Taylor left Wheaton, Ill., where he had been living, and became a free-lance writer and lecturer, making his home at Laporte, Ind., Dunkirk and Syracuse, N. Y., and, for the last six years of his life, in Cleveland, Ohio. He wrote three travel books, *The World on Wheels* (1874), *Summer-Savory* (1879), and *Between the Gates* (1878), the latter describing a transcontinental trip by rail, *Attractions of Language* (1842), *January and June* (1854), and a novel, *Theophilus Trent* (1887), based on his early school-teaching experiences in Michigan, which was published shortly after his death. He was, however, best known and admired as a poet. His volumes of verse—*Old-Time Pictures and Sheaves of Rhyme* (1874), *Songs of Yesterday* (1875) and *Dulce Domum* (1884), all included in *Complete Poetical Works* (1886)—touched the popular fancy and taste, were widely quoted, and brought their author wide recognition. His themes, chiefly drawn from farm life, the rural home, the days of the spinning wheel and the singing school, expressed the sentiment of the common people. Although painfully diffident and shy and utterly lacking in oratorical graces, he was for years in demand as a lecturer and from early life to the end of his career was one of the most familiar platform figures in America. He contributed both prose and verse to the *Atlantic Monthly, Harper's Monthly Magazine, Scribner's Monthly,* and other magazines. He had the friendship of many prominent men of his day, and his writings were widely reviewed at home and abroad. Whittier especially praised his ability to reproduce the scenes of long ago.

Taylor was of medium height, thick-set, smooth-shaven in a bewhiskered era. He was a brilliant conversationalist, and had a cordial, sympathetic nature that won him friends. He was married at Brooklyn, Mich., on Sept. 2, 1839, to Mary Elizabeth Bromley (d. July 2, 1848), seventeen-year-old daughter of Isaac Bromley of Norwich, Conn. On June 7, 1852, he married Lucy E. Leaming, daughter of Daniel M. Leaming of Laporte, Ind. He died in Cleveland, Ohio, survived by his wife and two sons by his first marriage. He was buried beside his father in the University Cemetery at Hamilton, N. Y.

[See Erastus Scranton, *A Geneal. Reg. of the Descendants of John Scranton of Guilford, Conn.* (1855); V. A. Bromley, *The Bromley Geneal.* (1911); *Am. Biog., A New Cyc.*, vol. XI (1922), pub. by Am. Hist. Soc.; obituaries in *Chicago Evening Jour., Chicago Tribune*, and *Cleveland Plain Dealer*, Feb. 25, 1887. Some of Taylor's letters are in the possession of Mrs. Eleanor Gridley, Chicago, and much miscellaneous material has been collected by the pub. lib., Lowville, N. Y.]

G. B. U.

TAYLOR, BERT LESTON (Nov. 13, 1866–Mar. 19, 1921), author and newspaper columnist, was born at Goshen, Mass., the son of A. O. and Katherine (White) Taylor. He attended New York public schools and in 1881–82 was a student in the sub-freshman class of the College of the City of New York. His first newspaper affiliation was with a weekly in Plainfield, N. H., and the *Argus and Patriot*, Montpelier, Vt. In 1896 he went to Duluth, Minn., where he became editorial writer for the *News-Tribune*. He used to say that his editorials generally were of the "What-does-the-New-York-Sun-mean-by-the-following?" variety. From 1899 to 1901 he was on the staff of the *Chicago Journal*, editing a column of comments upon the day's news, miscellaneous verse, and editorial paragraphs, called "A Little About Everything." From that he went to the *Chicago Daily Tribune*, where he established the "A Line o' Type or Two" column. In 1903 he wrote a column called "The Way of the World" for the New York *Morning Telegraph*, and in 1904 joined the staff of *Puck*, of which he was assistant editor until 1909. Then, recalled by the *Chicago Tribune*, he revived, with tremendous success, his "A Line o' Type or Two," which he conducted uninterruptedly until a few days before his death. On Nov. 16, 1895, he married Emma Bonner of Providence, R. I., who with their two daughters survived him. He died in Chicago.

Taylor became widely known as B. L. T., which was his signature at the bottom of his daily columns. "A Line o' Type or Two" achieved the widest fame and the greatest literary distinction of all newspaper departments in any way similar—and that in Chicago, where

Eugene Field's "Sharps and Flats" and George Ade's "Stories of the Streets and of the Town" had preceded it and set standards for originality and literary excellence. A complete newspaper column in length, appearing six days a week, it contained editorial comment (not necessarily in harmony with the editorial policy of the paper), excerpts from the rural press, and Taylor's own highly polished satirical verse, which was more in the manner of Calverley and Gilbert than in the homely style of Eugene Field [*q.v.*]. The column surpassed Field's in the variety of topics treated, but it followed the day's news so closely, and its general content was so timely, that most of it was as perishable as the day's news itself. Taylor printed also the signed contributions of hundreds of persons who sent to his column clippings, verses, and paragraphs of every conceivable sort. His requirements were high, and it was considered a distinction to "make the Line," a goal that was achieved by some of the best known writers in the country, whose habit it was to sign merely their initials or pseudonyms. Taylor set a standard for newspaper columning in the United States that has been the inspiration and despair of dozens of newspaper writers.

In addition to many short stories he wrote *The Well in the Wood* (1904), a juvenile; *The Charlatans* (1906), a novel of musical life; and the libretto for a musical comedy, *The Explorers*, with music by Walter H. Lewis, produced in Chicago in 1902. His other books—*Line-o'-Type Lyrics* (1902), *A Line-o'-Verse or Two* (1911), *The Pipesmoke Carry* (1912), *A Line o' Gowf or Two* (1923), *Motley Measures* (1913), *The East Window, and the Car Window* (1924), *A Penny Whistle* (1921), and *The So-Called Human Race* (1922)—all were reprints from his column, as were two pamphlets, *The Biloustine* (1901), a burlesque of Elbert Hubbard's the *Philistine*, and *The Book Booster* (1901), a satire on the *Bookman* and various aspects of book publishing.

[*Who's Who in America*, 1920–21; "'B. L. T.' by Himself," *Everybody's Mag.*, Oct. 1920; introductions to Taylor's posthumous books by F. P. Adams, in *A Penny Whistle*, Ring Lardner, in *Motley Measures* (1927 ed.), J. R. Angell, in *The East Window, and the Car Window*, H. B. Fuller, in *The So-Called Human Race*, and Charles Evans, Jr., in *A Line o' Gowf or Two; In Memory of Bert Leston Taylor* (1921), program of a pub. meeting, Blackstone Theatre, Chicago, Mar. 27, 1921; "The Lost 'Colyumnist,'" *Lit. Digest*, Apr. 9, 1921; *Poetry*, May 1921; obituary *Chicago Sunday Tribune*, Mar. 20, 1921; personal acquaintance.]

F. P. A.

TAYLOR, CHARLES FAYETTE (Apr. 25, 1827–Jan. 25, 1899), orthopedic surgeon, was born in Williston, Vt., the son of Brimage and Miriam (Taplin) Taylor, and was brought up on a farm. His early educational opportunities were few, and, though his decision to study medicine was made in his young manhood, it was not until he was twenty-eight years old that he was able to attend a course of lectures at New York Medical College during the summer and winter of 1855. He was married on Mar. 7, 1854, to Mary Salina Skinner. In 1856, when he was serving as apprentice to a physician in Burlington, Vt., he was invited by the professors of the University of Vermont, because of his proficiency, to stand for public examination and as a result was awarded the degree of M.D. Almost immediately he sailed for England to study curative exercises and the Swedish system of Per Henrik Ling. In 1857 he began practice in New York, where for a time he was associated with his older brother, Dr. George H. Taylor. In 1861 he published *The Theory and Practice of the Movement Cure,* an effort to express ideas he had absorbed in London, but he later said that he "soon got over that infliction" and afterwards began to think his own thoughts. He never lost his interest in the "movement cure," however, and always practised it on suitable cases, inventing many machines which increased the efficiency of this form of physical therapy.

Taylor's great achievement lay in devising, and then applying, a method to relieve and eventually to cure a previously incurable disease, a spinal lesion known as Pott's disease (later discovered to be due to an infection of the bone by the bacillus of tuberculosis). His interest in spinal disease had been excited by Dr. John Murray Carnochan [*q.v.*], but he had no remembrance of having observed a case before 1857. At that time, from the attitude of a patient, he made a correct diagnosis of spinal disease. His failure to relieve this and other cases made a tremendous impression upon him and led to his invention of "the spinal assistant," designed to give protection to the diseased vertebrae through the principle of fixed points for adequate support. Relief and eventual cures followed. Patients multiplied. Sound mechanical principle was served by accurate mechanical detail, and Taylor became the first great American surgeon-mechanic, planning and accurately fitting back braces and later many other types of orthopedic appliances for chronic bone, joint, and muscle lesions. But he was much more than a brace-maker. Early in his life he recognized the influence of mental states upon physical conditions, and he constantly practised what has been described as "a common sense psychotherapy" with the happiest results. He also established a dispensary, and gave his services and his goods to the needy until his strength and his resources were threatened. Then with the help of rich friends and grateful patients he was instrumental in establishing the New York Orthopaedic Dispensary, from which developed the great New York Orthopaedic Dispensary and Hospital.

Possessed of great energy and an alert, inquiring mind, he was very modest at heart and felt throughout his life his lack of early education. He published significant articles as important in their time as their titles suggest: *Mechanical Treatment of Angular Curvature or Pott's Disease of the Spine* (1863), *Spinal Irritation or the Causes of Backache among American Women* (1864), *Infantile Paralysis* (1867), *Mechanical Treatment of Diseases of the Hip* (1873), and "Emotional Prodigality" (*Dental Cosmos,* July 1879). Tempted more than once to concentrate his practice on gynecology because of his success in handling gynecological cases and because of their large financial return, he chose the less lucrative field of orthopedic surgery, convinced of his ability to serve his fellows more completely in this branch of medicine. About 1882 his health weakened, and after traveling widely abroad he settled in southern California. He died in Los Angeles, survived by his wife and four children, one of whom, Henry Ling Taylor, became a well-known surgeon. He was a member of numerous medical and scientific societies, and received several medals in honor of his work.

[Taylor's personal reminiscences, written for his family in 1887; H. L. Taylor, in *Am. Medic. Biogs.* (1920), ed. by H. A. Kelly and W. L. Burrage, and in *Am. Physical Educ. Rev.,* Sept. 1899, with bibliog.; E. H. Bradford, in *Trans. Am. Orthopedic Asso., 1899,* vol. XII (1899); *Pediatrics,* Mar. 1, 1899; J. G. Kuhns and R. B. Osgood, "Am. Explorers in Orthopaedic Surgery," *Crippled Child,* Dec. 1931; obituary in *N. Y. Tribune,* Jan. 26, 1899.]   R.B.O.

TAYLOR, CHARLES HENRY (July 14, 1846–June 22, 1921), journalist, of Colonial ancestry, the son of John Ingalls and Abigail Russell (Hapgood) Taylor, was born near the Navy Yard in which his father was employed and almost under the shadow of the Bunker Hill monument, in Charlestown, then a separate municipality, later a part of Boston, Mass. The eldest of seven children, he left high school at fifteen to become a wage earner in a Boston printing office; during the Civil War at the age of sixteen, he managed to enlist in a volunteer regiment in spite of one rejection due to defective vision, and when nearly seventeen he was wounded in the assault on Port Hudson, La. At eighteen he was setting type for the *Daily Evening Traveller* (Boston), and at nineteen he became a reporter for that paper and correspondent for the *New*

York Tribune, earning the latter appointment by his recognition of the news value of William Lloyd Garrison's anti-slavery valedictory. In 1869 Taylor became private secretary to Gov. William Claflin [*q.v.*], in 1872 a member of the legislature, and in 1873 clerk of the House and publisher of the *Boston Daily Globe.* The remainder of his life was completely invested in the newspaper which represented his character and became his monument.

The great fire of 1872 had destroyed his hopes for a ten-cent magazine, *American Homes,* which had attained a circulation of 40,000, when he accepted the renewed invitation to manage the *Globe,* just in time to be caught in the panic of 1873. The paper, founded in 1872, already had lost $100,000, and every week added a $1200 deficit. For grim determination and enormous industry Taylor's next four years can hardly be surpassed in American journalism. He often said he never was more than one jump ahead of the sheriff. His work day covered sixteen hours. His assets were such intangibles as intelligence, energy, and integrity. He scorned to pay any debts by bankruptcy. A sense of humor and his unfailing optimism sustained him. He mastered every phase of newspaper work, "Upstairs" and "Downstairs," in both newsroom and counting room. In 1877 he made the great change which brought success. The *Globe* came out as an independent Democratic daily, the price (originally four cents) was reduced, and special appeal was made for women readers. In three weeks the circulation leaped from 8,000 to 30,000. In October the *Sunday Globe* was started, followed five months later by a daily evening edition. Thereafter Taylor developed the paper as "a reflection of New England life and thought." He eschewed many popular metropolitan features, clung to numerous old-fashioned ways, specialized in neighborhood news. Intolerant of orthodox practices, he did some unusual stunts, as when on the day of Garfield's funeral, Sept. 27, 1881, he filled the entire front page with original poems written for the occasion by such writers as Oliver Wendell Holmes and Julia Ward Howe. That edition sold 40,000 extra copies. The remainder of Taylor's life is the record of the growth of a prosperous newspaper. He strove throughout to earn for it an established position as a family friend. Such sayings as "When you make a caricature of a public man make one that even his wife can laugh at" expressed his temper and policies. At the time of his death he was the dean of American journalists.

"General" Taylor, as he was called from his rank as a member of the staff of Gov. William Eustis Russell [*q.v.*], was a man of simple habits, with a genius for friendship. His love of the "newspaper game" continued to the end. He kept in rare degree the loyalty of his employees. He married on Feb. 7, 1866, Georgiana Olivia Davis, who died in 1919. Three sons and two daughters survived him.

[*Who's Who in America,* 1920–21 ; Warren Hapgood, *The Hapgood Family* (1898) ; James Morgan, *Charles H. Taylor : Builder of the Boston Globe* (1923) ; obituaries in *Boston Transcript,* June 22, and in *Boston Daily Globe* and *N. Y. Times,* June 23, 1921 ; personal interviews with friends and relatives.]   F. L. B.

TAYLOR, CHARLOTTE DE BERNIER (1806–Nov. 26, 1861), entomologist, the daughter of William Scarbrough [*q.v.*] and of Julia (Bernard) Scarbrough, was born in Savannah, Ga. She attended Madam Binze's School in New York City and toured Europe after she was graduated. Upon her return to Savannah she was married to James Taylor, of the mercantile firm of Low, Taylor & Company, on Apr. 27, 1829. They had two daughters and one son. Possessed of leisure and means, Mrs. Taylor began, in the thirties, seriously to cultivate an interest which she had early acquired in entomological studies. There were few formal opportunities for study in this field in the United States, and undoubtedly she was largely self-trained. Her writings indicate that she was widely read and possessed contemporary agricultural and zoölogical works but was not familiar with the progress of research in agricultural chemistry. In a word, she was a naturalist rather than a laboratory scientist. Living in a society dominated by plantations she became especially interested in the insect life associated with the staple crops of the southern seaboard. She conducted patient and exact observations of the insect parasites of the cotton plant for over fifteen years before attempting to write on the subject. She employed magnifying glasses of some power but probably did not use the compound microscope. She made excellent drawings of the various parasites, though her accompanying sketches of plant forms were not so reliable.

During the fifties, she began publishing her findings in a number of American periodicals, her most important articles appearing in *Harper's New Monthly Magazine.* She imparted to her articles a literary charm somewhat unusual in the zoölogical literature of the period. Her understanding of the agricultural significance of entomological studies was also extraordinary in a day when agricultural writers were largely preoccupied with problems of soil exhaustion (see "Insects Belonging to the Cotton Plant," *Harper's New Monthly Magazine,* June 1860).

From the observation of the parasites of the cotton plant, her interests extended to the wheat parasites, and she called attention to the economic necessity for their systematic destruction (*Ibid.,* December 1859). A detailed study of the anatomy and natural history of the silk worm led her to predict a revival of the silk-raising industry in the United States (*Ibid.,* May 1860). Perhaps her most ambitious zoölogical study was that on the anatomy and natural history of spiders (*Ibid.,* September 1860). She revealed a remarkable skill of observation and knowledge of the general literature on the subject. Despite its literary quality and its emphasis upon the utilitarian there is little evidence that her work modified contemporary agricultural practice or later scientific investigations. It may be that the appearance of her articles in general literary journals rather than in scientific publications caused them to be neglected by subsequent investigators.

Mrs. Taylor was a woman of great personal charm. On the approach of the Civil War, she left Savannah for England and was thereafter cut off not only from friends but from her income as well. While on the Isle of Man in 1861, she began to write, but never completed, a work picturing life on a plantation. She is said to have suffered from pulmonary tuberculosis and died on the Isle of Man.

[S. A. Allibone, *A Critical Dict. of Eng. Literature and British and Am. Authors,* vol. III (1871); information from Mr. William Harden, of the Georgia Historical Society of Savannah.]   R. H. S.

TAYLOR, CREED (1766–Jan. 17, 1836), judge, law teacher, born apparently in Cumberland County, Va., was the son of Samuel and Sophia Taylor. As a lad he supplemented meager educational opportunities by service in the clerk's office of Cumberland County, first under Col. George Carrington, Jr., a well-informed lawyer, and later under Miller Woodson, a man of local prominence, allied by marriage to the large body of descendants of Baron Christopher de Graffenried, landgrave of North Carolina. Taylor, probably about 1797, married Woodson's daughter, Sally, who has come down in Virginia annals as a *grande dame* of her day. They had no children but adopted five, three of them the children of Taylor's nephew. Leaving the clerk's office, Taylor entered upon the practice of law and soon attained a position of importance, with a high reputation as an advocate. From "Needham," his estate in Cumberland County, named for his wife's English ancestors, he conducted an extensive correspondence, some of which survives. With the Randolphs of "Bizarre," especially, he

maintained a lifelong intimacy, and he sponsored the entrance into public life of John Randolph of Roanoke [*q.v.*].

In 1788 Taylor served in the House of Delegates, and from 1798 to 1805 in the state Senate, being speaker of that body in his last two terms. He represented Virginia on commissions to settle the Kentucky and Tennessee boundaries. On Nov. 2, 1805, he was named a judge of the general court, and on June 14, 1806, was appointed chancellor of the superior court of chancery for the Richmond district to succeed Chancellor Wythe. The appointment was unanimously confirmed by the General Assembly at its next session. In 1813 the Lynchburg district was added to his jurisdiction. He continued to reside at "Needham," notwithstanding some controversy on that subject, and retained his chancellorship until the abolition of the separate courts of chancery in 1831. Many of his decisions on points of practice were included with the official reports of decisions by the supreme court of appeals (*Hening and Munford's Reports,* vols. I, II, IV).

He participated in the establishment of the town of Farmville, and in plans for a canal connecting the waters of the Roanoke and Appomattox rivers, and was one of the commissioners to choose a site for the University of Virginia. His principal avocation, however, consisted in the conduct, at "Needham," of a law school at which many Virginia lawyers received their training. His correspondence shows that he had considered a similar project in 1810, but it was not until 1821 that the school was opened, with Taylor as "patron." He contemplated publishing in four volumes a journal of the school and of the moot-court attached to it, which with its appendices would constitute a complete form-book for the Virginia lawyer. This purpose was in large part frustrated by the discontinuance of the publication after the appearance of the first volume; but from that volume we may draw a favorable impression of the school, which was commended to the public by Jefferson, Madison, and Marshall. In methods, the school was characteristic of its day. The influence of the apprentice training system was not spent, procedural questions were emphasized, and the aim was to produce practitioners rather than legal scholars.

A leading figure in the Anti-Federalist movement of 1800, Taylor was nominated as a presidential elector; and on the adoption of the statewide system for choosing electors he presided over the election held in Richmond for the purpose of organizing the state. An old Republican of the school of Randolph and John Taylor of

Caroline, he favored Monroe for president over Madison in 1808. But gradually, doubtless influenced by the demands of his judicial position, he seems to have withdrawn from the political scene. His latter years were troubled by financial cares and declining health. A discriminating obituary at the time of his death (*Richmond Enquirer,* Jan. 28, 1836) described Taylor's public services as "less splendid than useful," but spoke of his private character in terms of eulogy.

[For source material consult E. G. Swem, *Va. Hist. Index,* vol. II (in preparation); MS. copies of Taylor's correspondence in Va. State Lib. (Archives Division); *Journal of the Law School and of the Moot Court Attached to It,* vol. I (1822), by Creed Taylor; E. G. Swem and J. W. Williams, *A Register of the Gen. Assembly of Va.,* *1776–1918* (1918); J. J. Casey, *Personal Names in Hening's Statutes at Large* (1896); *The Enquirer* (Richmond), June 17, 24, 1806; *Richmond Enquirer,* June 27, 1823, Jan. 28, 1836; *Constitutional Whig,* Mar. 5, 1824; Richmond *Whig and Public Advertiser,* Jan. 26, 1836. As to the controversy concerning his residence when chancellor, see *Journal of House of Delegates* (1817), p. 86, and *Journal of the Senate* (1817), p. 114. For thumb-nail sketches see *Sketches and Recollections of Lynchburg* (1858), by the Oldest Inhabitant (Mrs. Margaret C. A. Cabell); R. H. Early, *Campbell Chronicles and Family Sketches* (1927); H. M. Woodson, *Hist. Genealogy of the Woodsons and Their Connections* (1915); T. P. de Graffenried, *Hist. of the de Graffenried Family* (1925). Striking portraits of Taylor and his wife by C. B. J. Fevret de Saint-Memin are in the possession of his great-grandniece, Ellen Glasgow, of Richmond, Va. For the law school, see A. M. Dobie, "A Private Law School in Old Virginia," *Va. Law Review,* June 1930.]

R. B. T.

TAYLOR, EDWARD THOMPSON (Dec. 25, 1793–Apr. 5, 1871), chaplain of seamen making port in Boston, was born at Richmond, Va. Left an orphan so young that he had but the dimmest recollections of his parents, he was given a home by a woman about whom he seems to have remembered hardly more, for at the age of seven he left her and went to sea as a cabin boy. After ten years spent chiefly on shipboard, being ashore in Boston, he experienced an old-fashioned conversion in a Methodist chapel of which the Rev. Elijah Hedding [*q.v.*] was in charge. In 1812 he went to sea again, on the privateer *Black Hawk,* which was captured by a British man-of-war, and Taylor presently found himself in a prison at Halifax. Not relishing the prayers for the King read by the prison chaplain, the American captives successfully petitioned the commandant to let them provide their own chaplain, and Taylor was requisitioned to pray for them and to preach.

Upon his release, he returned to Boston and became a peddler for an Ann Street junk-dealer. Although he was illiterate, his religious fervor and unusual natural gifts led the quarterly conference of the Bromfield Street Methodist Church to license him to preach, and as he traveled about

the country he combined exhorting with the collecting of rags and the selling of tin ware. A widow in Saugus, Mass., offered him a home if he would care for her farm. He accepted the proposition, and the widow taught him to read. Holding meetings regularly in a schoolhouse of the town, and preaching occasionally elsewhere, he exerted a powerful influence upon people by his blunt, fearless honesty, his quickness of wit, his lively imagination, and his picturesque language. Impressed with his capabilities, a merchant, Amos Binney, sent him to Wesleyan Academy, Newmarket, N. H., but he was badly out of place there and remained only six weeks. In 1819 he was admitted to the New England Conference of the Methodist Episcopal Church on trial and later into full connection. On Oct. 12 of that year, he married Deborah D. Millett of Marblehead, Mass.

The first ten years of his ministry were chiefly in towns lying along the coast. Nowhere was he so much at home as among seamen. Late in 1829 some Methodists formed the Port Society of Boston to further the moral and religious welfare of sailors, and the following year established the Seamen's Bethel. Taylor was immediately chosen as the one uniquely fitted to be its minister. He soon won the admiration and affection of all classes, and in 1833 a building costing $24,000 was erected for him, largely through the activities of Unitarian merchants and ministers. Here for more than forty years Father Taylor, as he came to be affectionately called, walked "the quarter deck," more like a sea captain in appearance than a parson, but admittedly one of the greatest American preachers of his generation. Harriet Martineau, Charles Dickens, Emerson, and Walt Whitman have all left tributes to his uniqueness and power, and the sermon of Father Mapple in Herman Melville's *Moby Dick* is obviously a portrayal of Taylor's manner of preaching. Emerson said of him: "He is the work of the same hand that made Demosthenes, Shakespeare, and Burns, and is guided by instincts diviner than rules" (*Journals, post,* III, 431). His sermons were full of the imagery and language of the sea, of pathos and sarcasm, of humor and striking similes, of hope and denunciation—all unpremeditated and delivered with unstudied dramatic effect. "I am . . . no man's copyist," he declared; "I go on my own hook,—shall say what I please" (Haven and Russell, *post,* 1904, p. 260); but his utterances were seldom resented. Sailors knew he was their stanch friend; others, of whatever rank, had to give place to them in the Bethel, which was commonly crowded to the "hatches"; they trusted him implicitly and firmly believed that his prayers for them must be answered, so full of impassioned pleading were they. A Methodist always, he was affectionately tolerant toward all, and radiated a wholesome joyousness and faith. He was noted for his epigrammatic sayings, and his blunt honesty. Daniel Webster, for whom he had great admiration, he characterized as the best bad man he ever knew. Of his friend Emerson he declared: "[He] is the sweetest soul God ever made; but he knows no more of theology than Balaam's ass did of Hebrew grammar" (*Ibid.*, p. 337). In his labors he was loyally helped by Mother Taylor, who cared for his secular affairs and saved him from giving away quite all his money to those in need. He made three trips to Europe, the last as chaplain on the *Macedonia*, laden with supplies for starving Ireland. Survived by four of his six children, he died at his home in Boston.

[*Minutes of the Ann. Conferences of the M. E. Ch.* (1871); James Mudge, *Hist. of the New England Conference of the M. E. Ch., 1796–1910* (1910); Gilbert Haven and Thomas Russell, *Father Taylor, the Sailor Preacher* (1871); reprinted with much supplementary material in *Life of Father Taylor* (1904); Harriet Martineau, *A Retrospect of Western Travel* (1838), vol. II; Charles Dickens, *Am. Notes for General Circulation* (1842); Walt Whitman, in *Century*, Feb. 1887; J. R. Dix, *Pulpit Portraits of Distinguished Am. Divines* (1854); E. W. Emerson and W. E. Forbes, *Journals of Ralph Waldo Emerson* (10 vols., 1909–14), *passim*; *New Eng. Quart.*, Oct. 1935; *Boston Transcript*, Apr. 5, 1871.]   H. E. S.

TAYLOR, FRANK WALTER (Mar. 8, 1874–July 27, 1921), illustrator, painter, was born in Philadelphia, Pa., the son of Frank Hamilton and Margaret (Johnston) Taylor. His father was an artist well known for drawings of old Philadelphia. Taylor attended Friends' School and studied at the Pennsylvania Academy of the Fine Arts, where he won a traveling scholarship in 1896 that enabled him to visit the principal art centers of Europe and, for a time, to settle in Paris, where he studied independently. In 1898 he opened his own studio in Philadelphia. Desiring to paint, he was, nevertheless, thrown into illustration as a ready means to earn a livelihood. During a long association with Charles Scribner's Sons, 1904–08, he illustrated Scribner books, and articles, stories, and poems for *Scribner's Magazine*. Especially noteworthy were his pictures for a special edition (1905) of Henry Van Dyke's *Fisherman's Luck*, Mary R. S. Andrews' *The Perfect Tribute* (1906), F. Hopkinson Smith's *The Veiled Lady* (1907), and Mary A. K. Waddington's *Château and Country Life in France* (1908). He also contributed illustrations to numerous popular magazines. For a time he was instructor in illustration at the Art Students' League, New York, and at the School of Design for Women, Philadelphia. In 1921 he was appointed instructor in illustration at the Pennsylvania Academy of the Fine Arts. He contributed to international exhibitions in Rome, London, and Paris as well as in America, and in 1915 he won the special gold medal of honor for illustration at the Panama-Pacific Exposition, where he exhibited illustrations and charcoal portraits. His draftsmanship was distinguished, and his drawings had a velvety richness that was the result of his mastery of the charcoal medium. Whether he used black and white or color, he pitched his work in rather a low key. His friend Joseph Pennell [*q.v.*] described him as "the last of the American illustrators."

His other work includes many sketches of out-of-the-way places, the result of his anual trips abroad, as well as a series of sketches of the Thames. He was especially fond of France, and an admirer of Gaston La Touche and Pierre Auguste Renoir. He also produced portraits in oil and in charcoal, chiefly of artists, whom he preferred as subjects. Among his sitters were Joseph Pennell; John McLure Hamilton, the painter; George Arliss and Otis Skinner, actors; and R. Tait McKenzie, the sculptor. During the World War he was one of a group of Philadelphia artists who gave their services to aid government loan campaigns. Shortly before his death he contemplated a different type of illustrating, and was engaged on preliminary sketches for new editions of Oscar Wilde's *Ballad of Reading Gaol* and Whitman's *Leaves of Grass*. He also devoted more time to portraiture and to pictorial rendering of constructive drawings for architects. Among his last works was a series of nudes in chalk and charcoal.

He is represented in the Pennsylvania Museum and School of Industrial Art, the Free Library of Philadelphia, the Pennsylvania Academy of the Fine Arts, the University of Nebraska, the Rhode Island School of Design, the New York Public Library, the Society of Illustrators, New York, the Metropolitan Museum of Art, and the Library of Congress, Washington, D. C. He died in Ogdensburg, N. Y. He was survived by his wife, Elsie Carleton Megary, whom he had married on Apr. 19, 1917. There were no children.

[*Who's Who in America, 1920–21*; Joseph Pennell, in Cat. of Memorial Exhibition, M. Knoedler and Company, Jan. 1922; *Arts and Decoration*, Mar. 1922; *Pub. Ledger* (Phila.), July 28 (obituary), Aug. 28, Nov. 13, 1921; information from Taylor's wife, J. H. Chapman, and Albert Rosenthal.]   D. G—y.

TAYLOR, FRED MANVILLE (July 11, 1855–Aug. 7, 1932), economist, was born at Northville, Mich., the son of the Rev. Barton S. and Marietta (Rowland) Taylor. After his collegiate training in Northwestern University (A.B. 1876, A.M., 1879) he was teacher and principal in the Winnetka High School, Winnetka, Ill. (1876–78), and then became professor of history and politics at Albion College, Albion, Mich., where he taught from 1879 to 1892. On July 15, 1880, he married Mary Sandford Brown of Ann Arbor, Mich., by whom he had two sons and two daughters. In 1888 he received the degree of Ph.D. from the University of Michigan. Here his talents were recognized by such men as the professor of political economy, Henry Carter Adams [q.v.], and in 1892 Taylor began the teaching of economics at Michigan which occupied him until his retirement in 1929. He was assistant professor of political economy, 1892–93; junior professor, 1893–1904; professor, 1904–20; and professor of economics, 1920–29. After 1906, when he published *Some Chapters on Money*, and began to print the leaflets which grew into his *Principles of Economics* (1911), he devoted himself chiefly to studies in general economic theory. The earlier phase of his development had promised a goodly volume of publications of high quality, in spite of his frail health and heavy teaching load. His thesis, *The Right of the State to Be* (1891), together with several articles of that period, was very favorably received by leading critics, and by 1898 he had also earned an enviable reputation as an authority on currency and banking. His writings in this field refined Gresham's Law, and subjected the topics of circulation and qualities of monetary standards to penetrating analysis. He also did pioneer work on some relations between money and prices—for example, on the contrast in effects between changes in quantity of money, and changes in costs and demands of goods. His output of writings was restricted, however, and withheld from the wider public, by his too severe self-criticism.

His studies in money, moreover, were crowded into the background as he became preoccupied with general economic theory and with incessant revisions of his *Principles,* which reached its ninth edition in 1925. In form this book is a college text, entirely undocumented, containing some pedagogical novelties modeled upon natural science texts, and deliberately excluding "literary" style. It became, however, much more than an elementary text. During many years Taylor conducted his quizmasters and other advanced students through most of the subtleties

of theoretical literature, firing their enthusiasm for his handling of these points, so that they carried his reputation abroad, and all this took effect upon the book. It far surpassed his modest hope "to restate the generally accepted doctrine, in a manner more organic and self-consistent than is usual" (Taylor to F. A. Hayek, Feb. 18, 1930). He integrated, perhaps more successfully than any predecessor, the influences of cost and demand (under all their aspects) in economic functioning. Other important contributions include his exposition and critique of "the present economic order of individual exchange-cooperation," and his overhauling of the theories of imputation, rent, capital, profit, and outputs in relation to variable inputs. Though he argued against most of the practical proposals inspired by socialists, his lifelong study of their literature left many imprints upon his *Principles*, and his last essay, the presidential address to the American Economic Association, 1928, dealt with some abstract features of "The Guidance of Production in a Socialist State" (*American Economic Review*, March 1929). He died in Pasadena, Cal., where he had lived since his retirement.

[Sources include *Who's Who in America*, 1930–31; *Northwestern Univ. . . . Alumni Record of the Coll. of Liberal Arts* (1903), ed. by C. B. Atwell; *Mich. Alumnus*, Apr. 22, 1933; obituary in *N. Y. Times*, Aug. 9, 1932; personal acquaintance. A bibliog. of Taylor's writings is being prepared for publication. Fragments of his letters and other unpub. papers are in the lib. of the Univ. of Mich.]   Z. C. D.

TAYLOR, FREDERICK WINSLOW (Mar. 20, 1856–Mar. 21, 1915), efficiency engineer, inventor, was born in Germantown, Philadelphia, Pa., the youngest child of Franklin and Emily Annette (Winslow) Taylor. He was a descendant of Samuel Taylor, who settled in Burlington, N. J., in 1677. His father was a lawyer, more interested, however, in literature than law; his mother was an ardent abolitionist and a co-worker with Lucretia Mott [q.v.] in this cause. Taylor received his early education from his mother. In 1872, after two years of schooling in France and Germany, followed by eighteen months of travel in Europe, he entered Phillips Exeter Academy at Exeter, N. H., to prepare for the Harvard Law School. Though he graduated with his class two years later, his eyesight had become in the meantime so impaired that he had to abandon further study, and between 1874 and 1878 he worked in the shops of the Enterprise Hydraulic Works, a pump-manufacturing company in Philadelphia, learning the trades of pattern-maker and machinist. In the latter year he joined the Midvale Steel Company, Philadelphia, as a common laborer. In the succeeding twelve years he not only rose to be chief engineer (1884), but in 1883, by studying at night, obtained the degree of M.E. from Stevens Institute of Technology, Hoboken, N. J. On May 3, 1884, he married Louise M. Spooner of Philadelphia. His inventions during these years effecting improvements in machinery and manufacturing methods were many, the outstanding one being the design and construction of the largest successful steam hammer ever built in the United States (patent No. 424,939, Apr. 1, 1890). After three years (1890–93) as general manager of the Manufacturing Investment Company, Philadelphia, operators of large paper mills in Maine and Wisconsin, he began a consulting practice in Philadelphia—his business card read "Systematizing Shop Management and Manufacturing Costs a Specialty"—which led to the development of a new profession.

Behind this lay Taylor's years of observation and study of manufacturing conditions and methods. From these he had evolved a theory that, by scientific study of every minute step and operation in a manufacturing plant, data could be obtained as to the fair and reasonable production capacities of both man and machine, and that the application of such data would, in turn, abolish the antagonism between employer and employee, and bring about increased efficiencies in all directions. He had in addition worked out a comprehensive system of analysis, classification, and symbolization to be used in the study of every type of manufacturing organization. For five years he successfully applied his theory in a variety of establishments, administrative and sales departments as well as shops. In 1898 he was retained exclusively for that purpose by the Bethlehem Steel Company, Bethlehem, Pa. In the course of his work there he undertook, with J. Maunsel White, a study of the treatment of tool steel which led to the discovery of the Taylor-White process of heat treatment of tool steel, yielding increased cutting capacities of 200 to 300 per cent. This process and the tools treated by it are now used in practically every machine shop of the world. While he was at Bethlehem, too, Taylor's ideas regarding scientific management took more concrete form. Being convinced of the results that would be attained if these principles should be generally adopted throughout the industrial world, he resigned from the Bethlehem Steel Company in 1901, returned to Philadelphia, and devoted the remainder of his life to expounding these principles, giving his services free to anybody who was sincerely desirous of carrying out his methods. While he met with many unbelievers among both employers and

employees, he lived to see his system widely applied. In 1911 the Society to Promote the Science of Management (after his death renamed the Taylor Society) was established by enthusiastic engineers and industrialists throughout the world to carry on his work.

Among Taylor's contributions to the technical journals were "A Piece-Rate System" (*Transactions of the American Society of Mechanical Engineers*, vol. XVI, 1895), an exposition of the principles on which his system of management was subsequently based, and "Shop Management" (*Ibid.*, vol. XXIV, 1903), which was translated and published in almost every country of Europe. An active member of the American Society of Mechanical Engineers, he served as vice-president in 1904–05 and as president in 1906, when he delivered as his presidential address his exhaustive monograph "On the Art of Cutting Metals" (*Ibid.*, vol. XXVIII, 1907). In 1911 he published *The Principles of Scientific Management*, and submitted to Congress a report entitled " 'Taylor System' of Shop Management" (*House Report 52*, 62 Cong., 1 Sess.). In addition to these publications he was joint author with Sanford E. Thompson of two works on concrete, *A Treatise on Concrete, Plain and Reinforced* (1905) and *Concrete Costs* (1912). He received about one hundred patents for various inventions during his lifetime. For his process of treating high speed tool steels he received a personal gold medal at the Paris exposition in 1900, and was awarded the Elliott Cresson gold medal that same year by the Franklin Institute, Philadelphia. He was much interested in amateur sports, particularly tennis, and with Clarence M. Clark won the doubles championship of the United States at Newport, R. I., in 1881. He died in Philadelphia of pneumonia, survived by his widow and three adopted children.

[Kenelm Winslow, *Winslow Memorial*, vol. II (1888); *Who's Who in America*, 1914–15; F. B. Copley, *Frederick W. Taylor, Father of Scientific Management* (2 vols., 1923); *Trans. Am. Soc. Mech. Engineers*, vol. XXXVII (1916); *Frederick Winslow Taylor, A Memorial Vol.* (1920); obituary in *Pub. Ledger* (Phila.), Mar. 22, 1915; Patent Office records.]
C. W. M—n.

TAYLOR, GEORGE (1716–Feb. 23, 1781), ironmaster, signer of the Declaration of Independence, was born probably in northern Ireland of a good family. He had some education, for when he arrived in Pennsylvania, about 1736, he became a clerk in the Warwick Furnace and Coventry Forge in Chester County, and later manager. He was married in 1742 to Mrs. Anne Taylor Savage, who died in 1768. About 1754 he moved to Durham, in Bucks County, where he and a partner had leased a furnace, and during the remainder of his life his business interests lay largely there. After 1763 he lived much of the time at Easton, in Northampton County, which became the scene of his political activities. In October 1764, he was elected to the provincial assembly, and was returned annually for the next five years (*Pennsylvania Gazette*, Oct. 4, 1764, *et passim*). He was a member of the minority proprietary party and bitterly opposed a royal government and its chief advocate, Franklin (*Votes and Proceedings of the House of Representatives of the Province of Pennsylvania*, volume V, 1775, pp. 379 ff.). Unlike John Dickinson [*q.v.*], Taylor's opposition arose from his western radicalism. His attitude toward imperial affairs at this time was evinced by his membership on the committeee that drew up instructions for delegates to the Stamp Act congress.

After a politically inactive or unsuccessful interval of four years, he reappeared as chairman of a meeting of the principal inhabitants of the county protesting against closing the Boston harbor and favoring an intercolonial congress; six men, including Taylor, were named a Committee of Correspondence. He did not attend the conference of deputies in Philadelphia in July, but his absence was probably not due to lack of sympathy, for he went to the similar convention in January 1775. The following July he was elected to a colonelcy in the Bucks County militia and although he never saw active service he retained the title. Sent again to the assembly by Northampton in October 1775, he served with distinction on many important committees and helped draft instructions for delegates to Congress in November. Although a member of the second Committee of Safety from October 1775 to July 1776, he rarely attended. His membership in the too conservative assembly doubtless explains his absence from the radical conference of committees of June 1776, and from the usurping convention which grew out of it. His views, however, are indicated by his appointment by the latter body as delegate to the Continental Congress on July 20, in the place of one of several Pennsylvanians who had refused to approve the Declaration of Independence. He signed the engrossed copy of that document on Aug. 2, or thereafter, but took no other part in the activities of Congress, except to represent it, with George Walton [*q.v.*], at a conference with Indians at Easton in January 1777. He evidently quit Congress soon afterward. In March he was elected from Northampton to the new Supreme Executive Council of Pennsylvania, but because of illness he served only six weeks and then retired from active public affairs. He had been a moderate radical, whose attitude was largely provincial, and whose interest in politics was never absorbing.

Taylor had two legitimate children, and five natural children by his housekeeper, Naomi Smith. Of the former, the daughter died in childhood and the son predeceased his father, leaving a large family.

[Source material for Taylor's life is scarce, and there is no complete, accurate, secondary account. The sketch in John Sanderson, *Biog. of the Signers of the Declaration of Independence*, vol. IX (1827), is not trustworthy. A substantially accurate article, with much new material, by Warren S. Ely is published in *Bucks County (Pa.) Hist. Soc. Pubs.*, vol. V. See also J. B. Laux, "The Lost Will of George Taylor, the Signer," *Pa. Mag. of Hist. and Biog.*, Jan. 1920; E. C. Burnett, *Letters of Members of the Continental Cong.*, vol. II (1923); W. C. Ford, ed., *Jour. of the Continental Cong.*, vol. VII (1907), see index volume.]   J. E. J.

TAYLOR, GEORGE BOARDMAN (Dec. 27, 1832–Sept. 28, 1907), Baptist clergyman, missionary, author, was born in Richmond, Va., the son of the Rev. James Barnett Taylor [*q.v.*] and Mary (Williams), and was named in honor of the early missionary to Burma, George Boardman. He was graduated from Richmond College in 1851, taught a year in an old-field school in Fluvanna County, and then went to the University of Virginia for three years. He had early joined the Baptist Church and while at the University preached regularly to a rural congregation. He was ordained to the ministry in Charlottesville and in 1855 became pastor of the Franklin Square Baptist Church in Baltimore. Here in 1857–58 he assisted Dr. Franklin Wilson in editing the *Christian Review*. Leaving Baltimore in November 1857 to become pastor of the Baptist Church in Staunton, Va., he was married on May 13, 1858, to Susan Spotswood Braxton, of Fredericksburg, daughter of Carter Braxton and Elizabeth Teackle Mayo. She was a bright, devout, tender woman with the heritage of the Virginia aristocracy, and gave her husband heartening companionship and help until her death in Rome, Mar. 7, 1884. Of their eight children, two sons and two daughters survived their parents. Through the years of his ministry in Staunton Taylor taught in several schools in the city and wrote a number of books for Sunday school libraries—notably a series called the Oakland Stories—to supplement a dwindling salary in the support of a growing family. With the outbreak of the Civil War he was elected captain of a company of home guards in Staunton and for a time was chaplain of the 25th Virginia Regiment in Stonewall Jackson's command.

For two years (1869–71) he was chaplain at the University of Virginia and in the summer of

1870 he went with his brother Charles on a tour through England, France, and Italy. In this same year he published a historical novel, *Walter Ennis,* depicting the struggles of the Baptists for religious liberty in eighteenth-century Virginia. From the University he returned to his pastorate in Staunton, and here, in 1872, at a meeting of the Baptist General Association of Virginia there was launched the Memorial Movement to raise $300,000 for the endowment of Richmond College, which his father had helped to found. Taylor bore a large share in this campaign and on release from his church traveled in the North collecting funds.

While engaged in this effort he was appointed by the Foreign Mission Board of the Southern Baptist Convention as missionary to Rome, to continue the work recently undertaken in that city. Reaching his post in the summer of 1873 he found that the mission consisted of a day and night school among the poor, a discharged evangelist, and a missionary who was released the week after his arrival. The rest of his life was given to an unremitting effort to spread the Baptist faith in Roman Catholic Italy. In 1878 he dedicated a chapel in Rome and returned to the United States to raise the money to pay for it. Occasional furloughs home, the longest in 1885–87 when he again served for two years as chaplain of the University of Virginia, were the only interruptions in his thirty-four years of missionary work. He saw Baptist congregations grow up in many of the cities of Italy and numerous native preachers go out from the theological school he had helped establish in Rome. At this school he continued to teach systematic theology, in spite of frail health and increasing deafness. In 1906 he had a fall, breaking a small bone in his hip; he remained cheerful in spirit, but after this accident his strength declined, and the following year he died. He was buried beside his wife, in Rome, in the Protestant Cemetery.

In 1872 Taylor published *Life and Times of James B. Taylor.* His most notable book, designed to promote the cause of Protestant missions, was *Italy and the Italians* (1898), a friendly and well-informed survey of the land, its history, its art, its religion and its people. During his last two years he was a member of the commission for the revision of the Italian New Testament (for the British and Foreign Bible Society), and shortly before his death he published in Italian a textbook of systematic theology.

[Files of the Foreign Mission Board, Southern Baptist Convention, Richmond; works by Taylor's son, George Braxton Taylor: *Life and Letters of Rev. George Boardman Taylor, D.D.* (1908); *Southern Baptists in Sunny Italy* (1929), and *Va. Baptist Ministers: Fifth Ser.* (1915); W. S. Stewart, *Later Baptist Missionaries and Pioneers,* vol. I (1928); *Who's Who in America,* 1906–07; *Religious Herald* (Richmond), Oct. 3, 1907).]   M. H. W.

TAYLOR, HANNIS (Sept. 12, 1851–Dec. 26, 1922), lawyer, scholar, and diplomat, was born in New Bern, N. C., the son of Susan (Stevenson) and Richard Nixon Taylor, merchant. He was the grandson of Mary (Hannis) and William Taylor, who had emigrated before the Revolution from Paisley, Scotland to North Carolina. He attended Lovejoy's school at Raleigh, Dr. Wilson's school in Alamance County, and in 1867 entered the University of North Carolina, from which he withdrew at the end of a year because of his father's financial reverses. He began the study of law in an office at New Bern and after the removal of his family in 1869 to Mobile, Ala., continued the study in that city in the offices of Anderson and Bond. Admitted to the bar in 1870 he practised at Mobile until 1892, achieving prominence in his profession as solicitor for Baldwin County, as counsel in certain well-known cases (such as the Louisiana Lottery Case, *Ex parte Rapier,* 143 *United States,* 110, which was argued before the United States Supreme Court), and as president of the Alabama Bar Association (1890–91). On May 8, 1878, he married Leonora, daughter of William A. LeBaron of Mobile, Ala. There were three sons and two daughters, all of whom survived him.

He was appointed by President Grover Cleveland on Apr. 8, 1893, American minister to Spain. His four years at Madrid were critical ones for Spanish-American relations, and he seems to have conducted the many difficult negotiations entrusted to him with credit. He inherited such troublesome controversies as the settlement following the exclusion of missionaries from the Caroline Islands, and the Mora claim for indemnity for confiscations by the Cuban government which dated from early seventies and which was settled in 1895 largely through Taylor's efforts. After the termination of the commercial reciprocity agreement with Spain by the passage of the tariff act of 1894, he obtained preferential treatment for certain American exports to Cuba and Puerto Rico. The outbreak of further disorders in Cuba in 1895 led to friction between the two governments. Taylor protested the arrests of numerous American citizens or the confiscation of their property by Cuban authorities. His negotiations were often successful, as when in 1895 the Spanish government expressed regret that a gunboat off the Cuban coast had fired on the American ship *Alliança;* and when Americans on the *Competitor,* condemned to be executed for landing arms in Cuba, were granted a new trial.

After his return from Madrid Taylor turned to the practice of his profession, with headquarters in Washington, and to scholarship. In 1902 he served as special counsel for the United States before the Spanish Treaty Claims Commission, and in 1903 was junior American counsel before the Alaska Boundary Tribunal. He lectured on legal subjects in several Washington institutions, George Washington University, Georgetown University, and National University, served in 1906–07 as associate editor of the *United States Law Review*, and wrote prolifically. His first important work, *The Origin and Growth of the English Constitution* (2 vols., 1889–98), brought him wide recognition as a student of legal institutions. The book was, however, marred by certain defects, such as a tendency to digress, reliance upon questionable authorities, and consequent inaccuracies. He occasionally invited criticism by defending a thesis generally recognized as untenable, as when, in *The Science of Jurisprudence* (1908) and in *The Origin and Growth of the American Constitution* (1911), he credited Pelatiah Webster with virtual joint authorship of the federal Constitution; this thesis he had already stated in his *To The Congress of the United States: A Memorial in Behalf of the Architect of Our Federal Constitution, Pelatiah Webster* (n.d.). His other writings included: *A Treatise on International Public Law* (1901); *Jurisdiction and Procedure of the Supreme Court* (1905); *The Constitutional Crisis in Great Britain* (1910); *Why the Pending Treaty with Colombia Should be Ratified* (1914); *Due Process of Law and the Equal Protection of the Laws* (1917); and *Cicero . . . A Commentary on the Roman Constitution* (1916). In his vitriolic pamphlet, *A Review of President Wilson's Administration* (n.d.), he announced that although he had supported Wilson in 1912 he would vote for Hughes in 1916.

[T. M. Owen, *Hist. of Ala.* (1921), IV, 1649; Erwin Craighead, *Mobile: Fact and Tradition* (1930); *Register of the Dept. of State*, esp. for the years 1893, 1897; *Papers Relating to the Foreign Relations of the U. S.*, vols. for 1893–97 (1894–98); State Dept. records; critical reviews of three of his books in *Am. Hist. Review*, Jan. 1899, pp. 348–51; Jan. 1909, pp. 329–31; Oct. 1911, pp. 162–64; *Who's Who in America*, 1922–23; obituary in *Evening Star* (Washington, D. C.), Dec. 27, 1922; data concerning ancestry from his daughter, Mrs. Reid Hunt of Boston.]　　E. W. S.

TAYLOR, HARRY (June 26, 1862–Jan. 28, 1930), soldier, was born at Sanbornton Bridge, now Tilton, N. H., the son of John Franklin and Lydia J. (Proctor) Taylor, and a descendant of Nathan Taylor who was in Massachusetts about 1690. He attended public schools, the New Hampshire Conference Seminary, and the United States Military Academy from which he was graduated in 1884 as a second lieutenant of engineers. His early career in the army was concerned with river and harbor developments on both the Atlantic and Pacific coasts, except for one year, 1888–89, during which he was assistant professor of mathematics at the Academy. His long service in civil engineering did not change until 1903, when he was sent to the Philippines to command a battalion of engineer troops. Two years later he returned to the United States to construct defenses and to improve navigation at the east entrance of Long Island Sound. In 1911 he was called to Washington as assistant to the chief of engineers of the United States army. He was promoted to the rank of colonel in 1915 and was placed in charge of the harbor work about New York City and along the Hudson River.

In May 1917 he was selected to be chief engineer of the American Expeditionary Force in France. He sailed the same month as a member of General Pershing's staff, with only two captains and three clerks to assist him in organizing abroad the extensive engineering forces which would be needed. He selected and prepared plans for ports for the debarkation of American armies. He inspected, planned, and constructed bases and training camps for the two million American soldiers in France. He assumed the management of certain French railroads, built connecting lines, and improved equipment—a task which he completed with remarkable efficiency and speed. In addition to construction, his duties as chief engineer required the procurement and placement of an enormous mass of engineering supplies for troops in modern warfare. This included equipment for offensive and defensive gas warfare, searchlights, trench tools, material for wire entanglements and for mining, explosives for destroying similar works of the enemy, and the training of troops to use them. An elaborate forestry service was organized to obtain the immense quantity of lumber needed. As American troops took over parts of the front the engineering department, under Taylor, built water systems for them, provided electricity, constructed roads, and performed many miscellaneous duties. Schools were opened for training recently appointed engineer officers in their duties. When the spring campaigns of 1918 started the original force of five assistants had been increased to 31,-000 officers and men, and Taylor had become a brigadier-general.

In September 1918 Taylor returned to the United States to be once more assistant chief of engineers at the War Department. In June 1924 he succeeded to the office of major-general and became chief of engineers. In the two years during which he occupied this position, the engineering project at Muscle Shoals, Ala., was practically completed, and under his supervision, large and important improvements were made on the Ohio, Missouri, and Mississippi rivers. He was retired in 1926 and died at his home in Washington, D. C. On Oct. 30, 1901, he had been married to Adele Austin Yates, who, with their two children, survived him. For his work during the war he received the Distinguished Service Medal.

[War diary of General Taylor, manuscript in War Department files; *Who's Who in America*, 1928–29; W. L. Proctor, *A Geneal. of Descendants of Robert Proctor* (1898); M. T. Runnels, *Hist. of Sanbornton, N. H.*, vol. II (1881); G. W. Cullum, *Biog. Reg.* . . . ; *U. S. Mil. Acad.* (1891); *Hist. Report of the Chief Engineer, 1917–1919* (1919); *Evening Star* (Washington, D. C.), Jan. 28, *N. Y. Times*, Jan. 29, 1930.]

C. H. L.

TAYLOR, JAMES BARNETT (Mar. 19, 1804–Dec. 22, 1871), Baptist clergyman, administrator, son of George and Chrisanna (Barnett) Taylor, was born in the village of Barton-upon-Humber, Lincolnshire, England, and baptized in the Church of England. His father, a cabinet maker, brought his wife and infant son to the United States in 1805, and settled in New York. Following an illness, George Taylor joined a Baptist church and with his wife was baptized in 1807. Their only son in his thirteenth year was again baptized, becoming a member of the First Baptist Church, New York.

The family moved to Virginia in 1817, living first in Petersburg and then in Mecklenburg County, where James worked in his father's cabinet shop, meanwhile studying with Dr. Bartholomew Egan, principal of an academy at Christiansville near by. Devout and studious, he began speaking in religious meetings when but sixteen years old. When his family moved to Clarksville, across the Roanoke River, he continued his studies through his own reading. At the age of twenty he was licensed to preach and in 1826 was sent as a missionary to the counties of Dinwiddie, Brunswick, Nottoway, and Lunenburg. After several months he resigned this appointment but continued to live in Dinwiddie, studying, preaching, and writing for the *Columbian Star*, a Baptist weekly. Ordained May 2, 1826, at Sandy Creek, he became pastor of the Second Baptist Church in Richmond, a church group of some eighteen white and about as many colored members that had persisted as an organized band for seven years. On Oct. 30, 1828, he married, in Richmond, Mary, daughter of

Rev. Elisha Scott Williams of Beverly, Mass. They had three daughters and three sons, all of whom lived to maturity; one of the sons was George Boardman Taylor [*q.v.*].

Success came to the young minister in his pastorate and he saw his flock grow in numbers and strength. He did editorial work for the *Religious Herald* and in 1836 was elected moderator of the General Association of the state, which office he held for some twenty years. He also found time to publish *Biography of Elder Lott Cary* (1837) and *Lives of Virginia Baptist Ministers* (1837; revised and enlarged, 1838; augmented and issued in 2 vols., 1860).

In 1839 he became chaplain of the University of Virginia, where he attended lectures in Latin, Greek, and Anglo-Saxon and found time to write *Memoir of Luther Rice* (1840) at the request of the trustees of Columbian College. Upon returning to Richmond in 1840, he became pastor of Third Church, subsequently known as Grace Street Church. He deplored the separation of Northern and Southern Baptists, though in 1845 he attended the convention at Charleston that formed the Southern Baptist Convention. Chosen as corresponding secretary of the Foreign Mission Board of the new body, he at first declined the office, but volunteered to give two days a week to its services and in 1846 relinquished his pastorate to assume the secretaryship and devote the major part of his time to missions. For fourteen years, however, he continued to preach twice a month at Taylorsville, near Richmond. He was hopeful in spirit, modest in his estimate of himself, careful in business arrangements, friendly in his counsel to the missionaries, and zealous in traveling, preaching, and writing to enlist interest and aid for the missionary program of his denomination.

At a meeting of the General Association at his church in 1830, with his close friend, J. B. Jeter [*q.v.*], Taylor helped form the Virginia Baptist Education Society to promote the education of ministers. This movement resulted in the establishment of Richmond College. He sought funds for that institution in its early years and was its persistent friend and a vital force in its upbuilding. He also aided in the establishment of a Baptist school for girls which in 1853 was chartered as Richmond Female Institute. During the Civil War his activities in behalf of missions were necessarily curtailed, and resigning his Taylorsville pastorate he became a colporteur for the Virginia Sunday School and Publication Board laboring in camps and hospitals and later became a Confederate post chaplain. After the war his business sense and able leadership were instrumental in reviving Richmond College. He resigned his mission secretaryship only a short time before his death, which occurred in Richmond in his sixty-eighth year.

[George Boardman Taylor, *Life and Times of James B. Taylor* (1872); George Braxton Taylor, *Virginia Baptist Ministers: Third Ser.* (1912); *Religious Herald* (Richmond), Jan. 4, 1872; *Richmond Dispatch*, Dec. 23, 1871; Taylor's diary and letters in archives of the Foreign Mission Board of the Southern Baptist Convention, Richmond.]
                                                    M. H. W.

TAYLOR, JAMES BAYARD [See TAYLOR, BAYARD, 1825–1878].

TAYLOR, JAMES MONROE (Aug. 5, 1848–Dec. 19, 1916), Baptist clergyman, college president, was born in Brooklyn, N. Y., the son of the Rev. Elisha E. L. and Mary Jane (Perkins) Taylor and the descendant of Edward Taylor who emigrated from England to New Jersey at the end of the seventeenth century. After five years schooling in the seminary at Essex, Conn., he entered the University of Rochester and graduated in 1868. In 1871 he was graduated at Rochester Theological Seminary. A year's study in Europe in 1872 had much influence on him. On Sept. 10, 1873, he married Kate Huntington of Rochester. Three sons and a daughter were born of this union. For fourteen years he preached, filling Baptist pastorates at South Norwalk, Conn., and Providence, R. I.; and, in 1886, he was elected president of Vassar College, the third Baptist clergyman to hold this post. The college was in sound condition, though suffering from ineffective administration and a certain complacency of attitude.

He obtained ample powers from the trustees at the start, and with great energy, which fully made up for his own deficiency of experience in higher education, he flung himself into his task. Critical alumnae were reconciled and organized into effective battalions, and provision was made for their election as trustees. Incessant travel and public speaking made the college better known and made friends of the school world. Money was solicited under Taylor's watchword "Endow the college." The will of John G. Vassar, Jr. (died 1889) brought several hundred thousand dollars to the college, and Taylor pleaded for the endowment of professorships. The trustees preferred to purchase land and to erect buildings. He succeeded, however, in raising $100,000 before the panic of 1893, and over half-a-million dollars were raised after the panic of 1903, the total endowment due to Taylor's efforts being about one million dollars. This was a tremendous effort for one man, who at the same time was conducting daily chapel, teaching psychology, ethics, and philosophy, and ad-

ministering the whole official college correspondence and registry with but slight assistance. Moreover, he found time for some writing: *Elements of Psychology* (1892), *A New World and Old Gospel* (1901), and *Practical or Ideal?* (1901), as well as *Before Vassar Opened* (1914) and, with E. H. Haight, *Vassar* (1915). It told heavily upon his health, and twice, in 1895 and 1905, he went to Europe for a year's rest. He was one of the first to object to the current conception of the college president's duties as those of a promoter rather than those of an intellectual leader. During this whole period, the trustees maintained their interest in buildings. Taylor's greatest service to Vassar, however, was the high standard he set for its academic work, a standard never relaxed. The college was freed from special and preparatory students, and became a compact, unified faculty of liberal arts. He gathered about him a strong group of teachers, highly individual and often of views on education opposed to his own, with whom he remained on the friendliest terms. Few presidents have held unwavering support for nearly thirty years, as he did.

His early training had been strongly conservative, but his sympathies were with youth, and he steadily broadened the curriculum, especially in the social sciences, in history, economics, political science, sociology, and religion. He obtained the recognition of art and music as academic subjects, and the teaching of science on strictly experimental bases. He created an intense personal devotion to himself and to his college, which for years distinguished Vassar graduates. His refusal of the presidency of Brown University in 1899 elicited marked evidence of this. He was for four years a member of the Carnegie Foundation, 1910–14, and his advice on educational policy was widely sought. His later years in office were somewhat hampered by physical causes, and in 1914 he resigned. His death followed after only two years. Memorials to him exist at Vassar in a gate, a stained-glass window, a professorship of philosophy, an endowment fund, a library fund, and Taylor Hall of Art. A portrait by William Chase was presented by the alumnae. All these are less significant than the innumerable memories of his idealism and genial humor in the unrecorded history of the college, and the loyalty that he guided to fruition in the college of today.

[MSS. in Vassar College archives; *Vassar*, ante; E. H. Haight, *Life and Letters of James Monroe Taylor* (1919); Elisha Taylor, *Geneal. of Judge John Taylor and His Descendants* (1886); *N. Y. Times*, Dec. 20, 1916.]
                                                    H. N. M.

TAYLOR, JAMES WICKES (Nov. 6, 1819–Apr. 28, 1893), consular officer, author, journalist, was born at Starkey, Yates County, N. Y., the eldest of five children of James and Maria (Wickes) Taylor. His father was a lawyer, the son of an Englishman who had served in Burgoyne's army. Taylor was graduated from Hamilton College in 1838 and soon settled in Cincinnati, where he combined the study of law with journalism. He established the *Cincinnati Morning Signal* in 1846 and later edited a newspaper at Sandusky. He was a representative at the second Ohio constitutional convention, 1850–51; secretary of a commission to revise the judicial code of the state, 1851–52; and head of the Ohio state library, 1854–56 (see D. J. Ryan, "The State Library and Its Founder," *Ohio Archaeological and Historical Quarterly,* January 1919). In 1856 he established a law office in Saint Paul, Minnesota Territory. Already the author of *The Victim of Intrigue* (1847), a defense of Senator John Smith [*q.v.*] of Ohio in relation to the Burr conspiracy; a competently done *History of the State of Ohio* (1854), covering the period to 1787; and a *Manual of the Ohio School System* (1857), he took an active part in discussions preceding the first constitutional convention of Minnesota. As secretary of the Minnesota and Pacific Railroad he urged upon the state legislature the passage of a "Five Million Loan" to railroads distressed by the panic of 1857.

Sensing the growing importance of the Canadian Northwest, he made a report to the Minnesota legislature on *Northwest British America and Its Relations to the State of Minnesota* (1860). In 1859 he had been appointed a special agent of the Treasury Department, charged with investigating trade and transportation between the United States and Canada, and in 1860 with I. T. Hatch of New York state he reported on the reciprocity treaty of 1854 (*House Exec. Doc. 96, 36 Cong., 1 Sess.*). In 1862 he reported on relations between the United States and Northwest British America (*House Exec. Doc. 146, 37 Cong., 2 Sess.*), and in a later study (*House Exec. Doc. 128, 39 Cong., 1 Sess.*) proposed a union of the United States and British America. With J. Ross Browne he published *Reports upon the Mineral Resources of the United States* (1867). After leaving the service of the Treasury Department (1869) he became an agent for the Lake Superior and Mississippi Railroad and for the Saint Paul and Pacific Railroad, composing newspaper articles and helping with congressional legislation. The outbreak of discontent in Canada in the Red River Rebellion of

1869–70 brought him an appointment as special agent for the State Department. (For some of Taylor's reports, see *Sen. Exec. Doc. 33, 41 Cong., 2 Sess.*) In 1870 he became American consul at Winnipeg (appointment confirmed, Dec. 9, 1870). Through his discovery of plans for a Fenian attack from the United States upon Manitoba (1871), the authorities were enabled to check the movement immediately. Later, in 1885, when Saskatchewan half-breeds rose against the Dominion government, he prevented assistance to them from Indians in the United States. His valuable service and loose political attachments secured his retention under both Republican and Democratic administrations until his death at Winnipeg from paralysis. Scholarly rather than political in his inclinations, a gentleman of charming personality, he endeared himself not only to Americans but to Canadians, who placed a large portrait of him in the city hall at Winnipeg. His wife, Chloe Sweeting Langford, whom he married in 1845 (Blegen, *post,* p. 156), bore him four daughters, two of whom survived him. He was buried at Utica, N. Y.

[See T. C. Blegen, "James Wickes Taylor: A Biog. Sketch," *Minn. Hist. Bull.,* Nov. 1915, based on extensive colls. of Taylor MSS., with bibliog.; W. W. Folwell, *A Hist. of Minn.,* vol. II (1924), pp. 102 n., 257, vol. III (1926), pp. 377, 379; H. M. Wriston, *Executive Agents in Am. Foreign Relations* (1929), pp. 738–42; obituaries in *Appletons' Ann. Cyc.,* 1893, and *Daily Pioneer Press* (St. Paul), Apr. 29, 1893. Examples of Taylor's consular reports are in *Ann. Report on the Commercial Relations between the U. S. and Foreign Nations . . . 1871* (1872), and *Commercial Relations of the U. S. with Foreign Countries, 1893* (1894).]

F. P. W.

TAYLOR, JOHN (1752–Apr. 12, 1835), frontier Baptist preacher, was the son of Lazarus and Anna (Bradford) Taylor of Fauquier County, Va., and the great-grandson of John Taylor, who with two brothers, Argyle and William, emigrated from England to Virginia in 1650. His maternal grandfather was a native of Scotland; his maternal grandmother, of France. During John's early boyhood his father moved to Frederick County, on the Shenandoah River. Because of the intemperate habits of the father, the burden of supporting the family came to rest chiefly on the son, and as a result he grew up with little education. At about the age of seventeen, he fell under the influence of William Marshall, a Baptist minister, uncle of the future Chief Justice of the United States, and professed conversion. Three years later he was baptized by John Ireland, one of the famous Virginia Baptist preachers. Soon afterward he was licensed to preach and for a number of years, he, with Joseph Redding, another Baptist minister, ranged through the mountains preaching and organizing churches among the scattered settlements on the Shenandoah, Potomac, Monongahela, and Green Brier rivers, occasionally crossing into Kentucky.

In 1782 he was married to Elizabeth, the daughter of Philemon and Nancy (Cave) Kavanaugh, "a young lady of a respectable family, and a member of the Baptist Church" (Sprague, *post*, p. 154). Soon after his marriage he fell heir to the estate of a bachelor uncle in Virginia, amounting to about $3,000. In 1783, he moved with his wife to Kentucky, sojourning for a time on Gilbert's Creek, south of the Kentucky River, and in 1784 settling in Woodford County, where he acquired about 1,500 acres of land, which, with the exception of some 400 acres, he gradually disposed of to friends. Here he lived until 1795, in which year he moved with his family to Boone County, across from the mouth of the Great Miami, where he had acquired 3,000 acres of land in different tracts. In 1802 he transferred his abode some sixty miles down the Ohio to Corn Creek, across from the present site of Madison, Ind. Here again he soon had a large farm under cultivation. Thirteen years later he moved to Big Spring in Woodford County. Altogether, Taylor cleared more than four hundred acres of heavily timbered land in Kentucky besides making other improvements.

Throughout his life he was active in the work of frontier Baptist churches, and is one of the best examples of the farmer-preachers who were so largely responsible for the founding of Baptist churches in Western Virginia, North Carolina, Kentucky, and Tennessee. He was connected with ten different churches, two in Virginia and eight in Kentucky; the story of his pastoral activities he related in *A History of Ten Baptist Churches* (1823), which presents an excellent picture of frontier religion. It was Taylor's custom to visit eight or ten Baptist associations each year, and in these his counsel was always highly valued. In 1820, he published a pamphlet called *Thoughts on Missions,* in which he bitterly attacked the missionary movement just then getting under way in the West. He contended that the missionary system was opposed to the Baptist scheme of church government and that the chief object of the missionary societies was to get money. During the latter years of his life he seems to have repented of his opposition, but his pamphlet was one of the principal influences which started the anti-mission movement among Western Baptists. He was also the author of *History of Clear Creek Church: and Campbellism Exposed* (1830). He was strong of body, bold and fearless, always cheerful, judicious, and zealous. Probably he exercised a larger influence among Baptists in Kentucky during his generation than any other single individual.

[Besides the books mentioned above, see W. B. Sprague, *Annals of the Am. Baptist Pulpit* (1860); W. W. Sweet, *Religion on the Am. Frontier: The Baptists* (1931); J. H. Spencer, *A Hist. of Ky. Baptists* (copr., 1885), vol. I; J. B. Taylor, *Va. Baptist Ministers,* 1 ser. (1860); *Frankfort Argus,* Apr. 22, 1835, which gives date of death.]　　　　W. W. S.

TAYLOR, JOHN (Dec. 19 (?), 1753–Aug. 21, 1824), political writer and agriculturist, generally known as "John Taylor of Caroline," was the son of James and Ann (Pollard) Taylor. The exact place of his birth has not been established, both Orange and Caroline Counties in Virginia claiming the honor, with inconclusive evidence in favor of the latter. His father died when John was three years of age and his mother a few years later, leaving his rearing to Edmund Pendleton [*q.v.*], who was the double first cousin of James Taylor and had married Ann Pollard's sister. The boy received his early education from private tutors and in a private school conducted in King and Queen County by Donald Robertson, also the teacher of President James Madison, whose grandmother, Frances Taylor, was a first cousin of John's father. Here he studied Greek and Latin and acquired the rudiments of both French and Spanish. In 1770 he entered the College of William and Mary, continuing for at least two years, and then turned his efforts to the reading of law in the office of his patron. He received a license to practise in 1774.

With the outbreak of the American Revolution Taylor entered the army. He served first in his native state, then around New York and Philadelphia. He had reached the rank of major when the reduction of the Continental Army in 1779 left more officers than were needed, causing him to resign and return home. Two years later he was appointed lieutenant-colonel in the Virginia militia and ended his military career fighting with Lafayette against the invading Hessians. In 1783 he was married to a cousin, Lucy Penn, daughter of John Penn [*q.v.*], the signer, a prosperous lawyer and planter of North Carolina, who was to contribute generously to his economic establishment. To them were born six sons and two daughters. They made their home at "Hazlewood," one of several plantations purchased by Taylor in Caroline County.

On his return from the army in 1779 he was elected to the Virginia House of Delegates, where he remained, with the exception of the year 1782, until 1785. He returned again for a four-year period in 1796. At three different times he was a member of the United States Senate. In 1792 he was chosen to fill the post vacated by the illness of Richard Henry Lee, and served until 1794. The death of Senator Stevens Thomson Mason in 1803 brought him back for a second period of service and the resignation of James Pleasants, Jr., in 1822 led to his appointment for a third time. Taylor early cast his lot with the rising democratic group led by Thomas Jefferson. In the Virginia House he took part in the final steps toward religious freedom and was prominent in forwarding land legislation and extending the North Carolina boundary line to the advantage of actual settlers. He favored a wider franchise and supported the moves for a more equal system of representation. Though not a member of the Virginia convention which ratified the federal Constitution, he joined with Patrick Henry and George Mason in opposition on the grounds that the rights of the individual and of the states were not sufficiently protected. When the new central government was established and showed signs of making the most of its powers, he quickly saw the dangers in "consolidation" and the desirability of a strict construction of the Constitution. His first political pamphlets, *A Definition of Parties* (1794) and *An Enquiry into the Principles and Tendencies of Certain Public Measures* (1794), were a condemnation of Hamilton's funding and banking measures. These he viewed as "usurpations upon constitutional principles" which, "if suffered to acquire maturity" would "only yield to the dreadful remedy of a civil war." They aimed, he thought, at the creation of an aristocratic "paper" junto and the subversion of democratic government. In 1795 he published *An Argument Respecting the Constitutionality of the Carriage Tax*. He held the Alien and Sedition Acts null and void and in December 1798 introduced into the Virginia legislature the famous resolutions in support of the doctrine of delegated powers and the right of the states to interpose in cases of "deliberate, palpable and dangerous exercise of other powers."

Taylor was a stanch supporter of Jefferson in the presidential election of 1800 and played an important part in the passage of the Twelfth Amendment in order to protect the popular choice of the president. In *A Defence of the Measures of the Administration of Thomas Jefferson* (1805) he upheld even the purchase of Louisiana, but drifted gradually over to the Tertium Quid group and supported Monroe against Madison in 1808. Always consistent, he

opposed the War of 1812 as tending to increase the activity and powers of the Central government and endangering "the pursuit of happiness."

Taylor's greatest influence came from his larger political writings. In 1814 he published *An Inquiry into the Principles and Policy of the Government of the United States*—a volume first conceived in 1794 as an answer to John Adams' *A Defence of the Constitutions of Government of the United States of America*. Of this work it has been said: "Whatever its shortcomings in prolixity of style, it deserves to rank among the two or three really historic contributions to political science which have been produced in the United States" (Beard, *post*, p. 323). In it he denied the existence of "a natural aristocracy" and condemned a permanent debt with taxes and a banking system to support it. He thought the executive too powerful. He would shorten the terms of both the president and the senators and check their patronage. The American government, he explained, was one of divided powers, not classes, and its agents were responsible to the sovereign people alone. The great danger to democracy lay in consolidation and in the creation of an aristocracy of "paper and patronage." In 1820 his *Construction Construed and Constitutions Vindicated* appeared. John Marshall's decisions, especially in the case of McCulloch vs. Maryland, had aroused him and the Missouri Compromise excited his fears. He sharply denied the validity of appeals from state courts to the United States Supreme Court and insisted that the jurisdiction of the latter, except in specified cases, was confined to appeals from courts established by Congress. The states, he thought, had the right to unlimited taxation, except on imports and exports. Marshall's bank decision was a continuation of the old effort to create private property beyond the reach of the state and to upset the balance created by the Constitution in which neither state nor federal government was supreme or subordinate. The whole question of a federal negative on state action, he later declared, had been discussed and rejected in the Constitutional Convention. To Taylor the Missouri question was also the product of the same self-seeking group who had brought forward the bank and the bounties to manufactories. Slavery was but an excuse for securing a balance of sectional powers in order to "beget new usurpations of internal powers over persons and property" (*Construction Construed*, p. 298). He denied the right of Congress to dictate to Missouri, since the presence or absence of slavery had nothing to do with a republican form of government. A third pamphlet, *Tyranny Unmasked* (1822), was a direct and powerful attack on the protective tariff system. He viewed this as unconstitutional and as creating privilege and diminishing revenue. The home-market argument was false, the idea of a favorable balance of trade foolish. Tariffs interfered with the sound and natural development of the nation's economic life. Government was becoming superior to the governed. Another work was *New Views of the Constitution of the United States* (1823).

As implied in these writings, Taylor's fundamental purpose was to preserve the old agricultural order and the security of the freeholder on which it rested. His practical efforts were aimed in the same direction. A farmer himself, he strove to improve agricultural methods on his own estate and in 1803 published a series of essays in a Georgetown newspaper to explain his methods and his ideas. These were later reprinted (1813) in book form under the title *The Arator*. The central idea in this work was the restoration of lost fertility to the soils by what he called "enclosing." He believed that plants drew on the atmosphere for life and that as a result of plowing under crops and applying manure soils would regain lost fertility. He would exclude all stock from arable and grass lands and produce only those crops which afforded the largest quantity of offal for feeding and plowing under. His favorite crop was corn but he advocated the growing of clover and field peas in rotation, and the employment of deeper plowing for all crops. He rejected tobacco, the overseer system, and the use of unprofitable slaves. He would make the farmer a power capable of protecting his interests against the encroachments of central government.

John Taylor was one of America's greatest disciples and philosophers of agrarian liberalism. He was the champion of local democracy and one of the first and clearest spokesmen of state rights. The laborious style of his writings has probably prevented his receiving recognition equal to that given other champions of these ideas.

[H. H. Simms, *Life of John Taylor* (1932); W. E. Dodd, "John Taylor, of Caroline, Prophet of Secession," in *The John P. Branch Hist. Papers of Randolph-Macon College*, vol. II (1908); Gaillard Hunt, ed., *Disunion Sentiment in Congress in 1794. A Confidential Memorandum . . . by John Taylor of Caroline* (1905), with a useful introduction; J. T. Carpenter, *The South as a Conscious Minority* (1930); C. A. Beard, *Economic Origins of Jeffersonian Democracy* (1915), ch. XI; B. F. Wright, Jr., "The Philosopher of Jeffersonian Democracy," in *Am. Pol. Science Review*, Nov. 1928; A. O. Craven, *Soil Exhaustion as a Factor in the Agricultural Hist. of Va. and Md., 1606–1860* (1925); L. C. Gray, *Hist. of Agriculture in the Southern U. S. to 1860* (2 vols., 1933).] A. O. C.

TAYLOR, JOHN (Nov. 1, 1808–July 25, 1887), third president of the Utah branch of the Mormon Church, was born in Milnthorpe, Westmoreland County, England, the son of James and Agnes (Taylor) Taylor. He received only the rudiments of an elementary education, being apprenticed at fourteen to learn the trades of cooper and turner. Although his family was nominally Anglican, in his sixteenth year he became interested in Methodism and during the following year was appointed exhorter, or local preacher. In 1832 he followed his parents to Toronto, Canada. The next year he married Leonora Cannon. In Canada he at once became active in the local Methodist organization, but, possessed of somewhat mystical tendencies, he was not entirely satisfied with Methodism, and turned to Irvingism, which, also, in a short time he abandoned. Not long afterward he was introduced to Mormonism by Parley P. Pratt [q.v.] and in 1836 was baptized in the Mormon church. Presently he was ordained an elder and put in charge of missionary work in upper Canada.

He made several visits to Kirtland, Ohio, participated in the Mormon migration to Missouri in 1838, and on July 8 of that year was chosen by Joseph Smith [q.v.] an apostle "by revelation." He did not assume his official responsibilities until December, however, when he was "ordained to the office" by Brigham Young and Heber C. Kimball [qq.v.]. During the conflicts between Mormons and non-Mormons in Missouri and Illinois he played a prominent rôle in defending the Mormon cause and in keeping up morale. At Nauvoo, Ill., he served from 1842 to 1846 as editor for the *Times and Seasons,* the official Mormon periodical, and also owned and published the *Nauvoo Neighbor,* a strong pro-Mormon newspaper. He was city councilman, a regent of "Nauvoo University," and judge advocate of the Nauvoo Legion. When in June 1844 Joseph and Hyrum Smith were imprisoned in the jail at Carthage, Ill., Taylor and Willard Richards, another apostle, accompanied them "as friends." In the attack on the jail by the lynching mob seeking the Prophet, Taylor was seriously wounded, but recovered.

In the controversy over the successorship to Smith, Taylor, like most of the Twelve Apostles, threw in his lot with the Brigham Young faction. He trekked across the plains to Utah, assisted in colonizing there, and was always ready to defend his Church against all critics. He was a member of the territorial legislature from 1857 to 1876 and served as speaker of the lower house for five successive sessions, beginning in 1857. From 1868 to 1870 he was probate judge of Utah County, and in 1877 he was elected territorial superintendent of schools. After Brigham Young's death in 1877, Taylor, who was head of the quorum of Twelve Apostles, directed the affairs of the Church for three years in the capacity of acting president. It was not until October 1880 that he was officially sustained by the semi-annual conference as "President of the Church of Jesus Christ of Latter-day Saints and Prophet, Seer, and Revelator to the Church in all the world" (Jenson, *post*, p. 18).

A man of great spiritual gifts, Taylor had a strong faith in divine revelation. He did not add materially to church dogma or organization, but ably carried on the traditions established by his two predecessors. He was a very effective speaker, and his most noteworthy contribution was his active proselyting. His first extensive missionary work was done in 1840 and 1841 in England; he introduced Mormonism to the Isle of Man, to Ireland, and to Scotland, and managed the migration of many of the new converts from England to the United States. After Brigham Young assumed control over the main body of the Mormons and had managed their exodus from Illinois to the Missouri River, Taylor, with Orson Hyde and Parley P. Pratt, returned to England in 1846 to insure the support of the British converts. He and his colleagues successfully counteracted the claims of Sidney Rigdon [*q.v.*] to be successor to Joseph Smith, and the similar claims of James J. Strang [*q.v.*], thus saving the British mission to the Utah Mormons. After a short period in Utah, Taylor was dispatched to France in 1849 and later to Germany to carry the Mormon gospel to these countries. He arranged for both the German and the French translations of *The Book of Mormon*. During the fifties, when the conflict between the Mormons and non-Mormons in the United States took on national interest, he was put in charge of missionary work in the Eastern states. In 1854 he established a newspaper in New York City called *The Mormon*, designed to answer the attack of anti-Mormon agitators, most notable among whom was James Gordon Bennett [*q.v.*]. In 1857, because of the impending invasion of Utah by federal troops, he gave up his newspaper campaign and returned to Salt Lake City, but in the years that followed continued to answer the accusations of the critics of his faith both in the local and in the Eastern metropolitan press. His replies to the charges of Vice-President Schuyler Colfax [*q.v.*], who had taken a hand in the public clamor, furnish

an excellent picture of the pro-Mormon view of the so-called Mormon "menace."

Taylor accepted the doctrine and practice of plural marriage in Nauvoo. He had seven wives, four of whom outlived him. These women bore him thirty-four children. After the passage of the Edmunds-Tucker act in 1882, Taylor tried to assuage the federal prosecution by maintaining his official residence in the Gardo House in Salt Lake City with his sister as his housekeeper, while his wives and children remained in semi-seclusion in their respective households. In spite of this public gesture of compliance, and in spite of his public admonition to his followers to "be quiet" in the face of federal prosecution, Taylor himself was forced in 1884 to go into voluntary exile to escape arrest. His health became rapidly enfeebled and he died in 1887 at Kaysville, Utah. For nearly three years he had directed the Church while in effect a fugitive from justice. He published a theological work entitled, *An Examination into and an Elucidation of the Great Principles of the Mediation and Atonement of Our Lord and Savior Jesus Christ* (1882), and was the author of numerous pamphlets, editorials, and letters.

[Andrew Jenson, *Latter-day Saint Biog. Encyc.* (1901), I, 14–19; B. H. Roberts, *The Life of John Taylor* (1892) and *A Comprehensive Hist. of the Church of Jesus Christ of Latter-Day Saints: Century I* (1930); *Deseret Evening News,* July 26, 1887.]

K. Y.

TAYLOR, JOHN LOUIS (Mar. 1, 1769–Jan. 29, 1829), jurist, was born in London, England, of Irish parentage. At the age of twelve he came to America, an orphan, with his elder brother James, by whose assistance he was able to pursue classical studies at William and Mary College. Compelled to leave college before graduation, he went to North Carolina, studied law, was licensed to practise in 1788, and settled at Fayetteville. His handsome physique, native talent, genial nature, ingenuity in argument, power of oratory, and Federalism in politics, quickly brought him legal, social, and political distinction. As borough representative of Fayetteville in the House of Commons (1792, 1794–95), he supported measures to encourage trade, prohibit the importation of slaves, permit manumission, and improve the administration of justice. He was a presidential elector in 1792 and an unsuccessful candidate before the General Assembly for solicitor general in 1790 and for attorney general in 1795. His first wife was Julia Rowan, by whom he had a daughter. About 1797 he moved to New Bern and in that year married Jane, the sister of William Gaston [*q.v.*], by whom he had a son and a daughter.

In 1798 he was elected by the General Assembly as a judge of the superior court and began a distinguished judicial career of thirty years. In the absence of a state court of appeals, the superior court judges were required from 1799 to meet twice each year in Raleigh as a court, called the court of conference from 1801 and the supreme court from 1805, for the determination of questions of law and equity arising on the circuits. In pursuance of a law of 1810, the judges selected Taylor in July 1811 as presiding officer with the title of chief justice. From about this time he resided in Raleigh. In 1818 the General Assembly established a distinct supreme court and chose Taylor one of the three judges. At the first term of this court, in January 1819, his associates elected him chief justice—a position which he held until his death in 1829. As the first chief justice, Taylor brought learning, respectability, and prestige to the supreme court. "Preëminently a safe judge" who followed precedent with religious zeal, he made no distinctive contributions to jurisprudence; but broad information, exemplary patience, unfailing courtesy, high feelings, good judgment, and love of justice won esteem for him and respect for the law. His opinions, as found in 1–12 *North Carolina Reports* are marked in many instances by thoroughness of legal investigation and clarity of composition.

Early in his career he began to make notes on cases which came before him and in 1802 issued *Cases Determined in the Superior Courts . . .*, reprinted in the first volume of *North Carolina Reports*. He subsequently published *Carolina Law Repository* (2 vols., 1814–16), and *Cases Adjudged in the Supreme Court of North Carolina from July Term 1816, to January Term, 1818, Inclusive* (1818), known as "North Carolina Term Reports," both reprinted in part in 4 *North Carolina Reports*. Under legislative appointment of 1817 to revise the statute law, Taylor, Henry Potter, and Bartlett Yancey issued *Laws of the State of North Carolina* (2 vols., 1821), known as "Potter's Revisal"; Taylor continued the work through 1825 in *A Revisal of the Laws . . .* (1827), known as "Taylor's Revisal." He also published *A Charge Delivered to the Grand Jury of Edgecombe Superior Court . . .* (1817) and *A Digest of the Statute Law of North Carolina Relative to Wills, Executors and Administrators, the Provision for Widows, and the Distribution of Intestates Estates* (1824). He was grand master of the Masonic fraternity in North Carolina (1802–05, 1814–17), a benefactor of the University of North Carolina, and a trustee (1793–

1818). His death occurred at his home in Raleigh.

[*Laws of N. C.*, 1799–1818; *Jours. of the House of Commons*, 1790–1818; Craven County Marriage Bonds, in N. C. Hist. Commission; *Fayetteville Gazette*, Dec. 11, 1792; *Raleigh Reg. and North-Carolina State Gazette*, July 5, 1811; *Raleigh Reg. and North-Carolina Gazette*, Jan. 8, 1819, Feb. 3, 1829; W. H. Hoyt, *The Papers of Archibald D. Murphey* (1914), vol. I; 16 *N. C. Reports*, 308; 107 *N. C. Reports*, App. following p. 985; W. H. Battle, "Memoir of John Louis Taylor," in *N. C. Univ. Mag.*, Mar. 1860; S. A. Ashe, *Biog. Hist. of N. C.*, vol. V (1906); K. P. Battle, *Hist. of the Univ. of N. C.*, vol. I (1907); Walter Clark, "Hist. of the Superior and Supreme Courts of N. C.," in *The N. C. Booklet*, Oct. 1918.]

A. R. N.

TAYLOR, JOHN W. (Mar. 26, 1784–Sept. 18, 1854), anti-slavery leader, was born at Charlton, N. Y., the son of Judge John Taylor and Chloe (Cox) Taylor, and a descendant of Edward Taylor who settled in Monmouth County, N. J., in 1692. After graduating from Union College, Schenectady, he began the study of law with Samuel Cook. Admitted to the bar in 1807, he formed a partnership with Cook and began to practise at Ballston Spa. On July 10, 1806, he married Jane Hodge, who died in 1838, having borne him three daughters and five sons. After two years in the New York Assembly (1811–12), he represented Saratoga County for twenty consecutive years in the federal House of Representatives (Mar. 4, 1813–Mar. 3, 1833). He favored a national bank and a protective tariff, although he regarded federal appropriations for roads and canals as unconstitutional. During the presidency of the second Adams he was a leader of administration policies and later a member of the Whig party.

The slavery question brought him into national prominence. He seconded the amendment of James Tallmadge [*q.v.*] to the Missouri bill, prohibiting the further introduction of slavery in the proposed state and liberating at the age of twenty-five all children born of slave parents. To the bill organizing Arkansas Territory, he moved a similar amendment. When his motion was lost he submitted a proposal prohibiting the introduction of slavery into the territories north of 36° 30′, in support of his restrictive policy delivering some of the first anti-slavery speeches heard in Congress (*Annals of Congress*, 15 Cong., 2 Sess., pp. 1170–93; 16 Cong., 1 Sess., pp. 958–66). He argued that the power of Congress to admit new states implied a power to refuse to admit, and hence a power to prescribe conditions on which it would admit. As precedents he pointed to Ohio, Indiana, and Illinois, which had been compelled to frame constitutions excluding slavery, and to Louisiana, where Congress had insisted on English as the official language and the guarantee of *habeas corpus*, jury trial, and religious liberty. He also held that the provision vesting in Congress power to prohibit the "importation or migration" of slaves after 1808 was applicable in this connection, since the word "migration" meant the passage from one commonwealth to another. As to the expediency of restriction, he contended that slavery was ruinous to the economy of the country. He declared, also, that Congress was obligated to restrict slavery since slavery was incompatible with the "republican form of government" which it was the constitutional duty of the United States to guarantee to every state.

Taylor served two terms as speaker of the House of Representatives (Nov. 15, 1820–Mar. 3, 1821, Dec. 5, 1825–Mar. 3, 1827), in each case being defeated for reëlection. In a letter to his son, he said: "I lost my third election as Speaker through my direct opposition to slavery" (MS., in the possession of Taylor's granddaughter, Mrs. Clarissa Taylor Bass, Freeport, Ill.). While the South never forgave the part he played in the Missouri controversy, the chief opposition came from his own state The anti-Clintonian faction in New York encompassed his defeat in 1821, and the Van Buren Democrats were largely responsible for it in 1827. In November 1832 they thwarted his reëlection to Congress. From 1840 to 1842 he was a member of the New York Senate, from which ill health compelled his retirement. In 1843 he removed to Cleveland, Ohio, where he spent the remainder of his life at his daughter's home.

[Elisha Taylor, *Geneal. of Judge John Taylor and His Descendants* (1886); *Biog. Dir. Am. Cong.* (1928); *Memoirs of John Quincy Adams*, vols. IV–VII (1875); S. B. Dixon, *The True Hist. of the Mo. Compromise and Its Repeal* (1899); D. S. Alexander, *A Pol. Hist. of the State of N. Y.*, vols. I, II (1906); E. F. Grose, *Centennial Hist. of the Village of Ballston Spa* (1907); *N. Y. Tribune*, Sept. 22, 1854.]   J. G. V—D.

TAYLOR, JOSEPH WRIGHT (Mar. 1, 1810–Jan. 18, 1880), philanthropist, physician, merchant, founder of Bryn Mawr College, was born in a farmhouse in Upper Freehold Township, Monmouth County, N. J., the youngest of a family of seven. His father, Edward, descended from Edward Taylor who settled in Monmouth County in 1692, was a country physician, a graduate of the College of New Jersey. The Taylors were Baptists, but Edward joined the Society of Friends after his marriage to Sarah Merritt, whose family had been among the early Quaker settlers of New Jersey. Sarah Taylor "had a concern" (in the Quaker phrase) for the insane, and in 1823 she and her husband became respectively matron and physician of the Friends' Asylum near Frankford, a suburb of Philadelphia. Joseph was educated at a boarding school near Frankford, and later studied medicine at the University of Pennsylvania, where he received the degree of M.D. at the early age of twenty. That same year, 1830, he sailed for India as surgeon and supercargo on a merchant vessel. Three years after his return he set off to join his brother Abraham, who had successfully established himself ten years earlier in Cincinnati as a tanner and dealer in leather. Joseph became purchasing agent for the firm and traveled widely in Ohio, Kentucky, and Indiana.

After fifteen prosperous years Taylor, an ardent traveler, started on his first European tour, and two years later settled in Burlington, N. J., where he purchased an estate and lived the life of a country gentleman. He was unmarried, but was devoted to his sister Hannah who kept house for him and had several warm friendships with other cultivated women. Descriptions in this period picture him as of medium height, unusually handsome in feature, exquisitely neat in dress, and distinguished in carriage. In 1861 he took another trip to England and the Continent, and in his later life traveled much in the United States. He was able to increase his fortune very materially by judicious investments after retiring from his brother's business.

Taylor was interested in most of the causes supported by the Society of Friends, such as abolition of slavery and promotion of international peace, temperance, and education. His determination to found a woman's college, which appears to have been fixed by the year 1875, probably had its origin in his perception of the real need for such an institution for the education of Quaker girls and his feeling that it was consistent with Quaker principles to provide the same facilities for the higher education of women in the neighborhood of Philadelphia as was provided for the education of men at Haverford College, of which he had been one of the managers since 1854.

His first plan was to open the college at Burlington near his own house in order to direct its growth himself. He was persuaded by his advisers, of whom Francis King, the president of the trustees of the Johns Hopkins Hospital, was the most trusted, that it would be wise to find a location more convenient to Philadelphia. President Gilman of Johns Hopkins, President Seelye of Smith, and other experienced educators were consulted, and two trips were made to New England to visit Mount Holyoke, Smith, and Wellesley. Land was purchased at Bryn Mawr, eleven miles from Philadelphia, in 1878, and the building begun in 1879. Taylor directed the architect to use the administration building at Smith College as the model for the main building, later named Taylor Hall. He superintended the work of construction himself, making almost daily trips to Bryn Mawr. These activities were apparently too strenuous for his health and hastened his death, which resulted from heart disease. He bequeathed practically his entire fortune of about eight hundred thousand dollars, in addition to the land and buildings, to Bryn Mawr College, appointing a board of trustees of eminent Quakers, among them Dr. James E. Rhoads [q.v.], later president of the College. While unquestionably Taylor's purpose in founding Bryn Mawr was in part religious and even sectarian, it is clear from his choice of advisers and careful consideration of the need for educational facilities in the broadest sense that he wished to found a college which would be preëminent in cultivating the intellectual as well as the spiritual interests of the rising generation of women.

[*Memoir of Joseph W. Taylor, M.D.* (privately printed, 1884), written by President Rhoads in consultation with members of the Taylor family; Joseph Parrish, "Memorial Notice of Dr. Joseph W. Taylor," *Trans. Medic. Soc. of N. J.*, 1880; *Addresses at the Inauguration of Bryn Mawr College* (1886); Elisha Taylor, *Geneal. of Judge John Taylor and His Descendants* (1886); *Phila. Inquirer*, Jan. 20, 1880; unprinted letters and diaries in the possession of the Taylor family.]

H. T. M.

TAYLOR, MARSHALL WILLIAM (July 1, 1846–Sept. 11, 1887), Methodist Episcopal clergyman and editor, was born in Lexington, Ky. Both his parents were, or had been, slaves; ultimately both acquired freedom. Marshall, according to one authority, adopted the name of Taylor, that of his father being Samuel Boyd and that of his mother Nancy Ann (Williams, *post*, p. 469). The former was of Scotch-Irish and Indian descent; the latter, of African and Arabian, her mother having been brought from Madagascar when a child. Marshall's opportunities for education were few. He attended schools for free negro children in Lexington and at Louisville, to which place the family moved after his father's death. In the latter city he became a messenger for a law firm. In 1866 he taught school in Breckenridge County, Ky., and two years later presided at an educational convention held at Owensboro, Ky.

At a quarterly conference of the Hardinsburg Circuit, Ky., in 1869 he was licensed as a Methodist Episcopal preacher. He then did missionary work in Arkansas and other parts of the Southwest. In 1872 he was admitted on trial to the Lexington Conference, and that same year was sent to the General Conference as a lay delegate. For five consecutive years he was corresponding secretary of the Annual Conference to which he belonged. He was ordained deacon in February 1874, and elder in March 1876. From 1872 to 1875, in addition to his pastoral work, he issued the *Kentucky Methodist*. He served first as pastor of the Litchfield Circuit and then of the Coke Chapel Circuit at Louisville. In 1875 he was placed in charge of Coke Chapel at Indianapolis, and two years later was sent to the Union Methodist Episcopal Church in Cincinnati. In 1878 he became presiding elder of the Ohio District. He was a fraternal delegate from his Church to a conference of the African Methodist Episcopal Church, in 1880, and the following year a delegate to the Ecumenical Conference in London. Made presiding elder of the Louisville District in 1883, he was the senior ministerial delegate to the General Conference of 1884. At this gathering he was chosen at a caucus of the negro delegates as their nominee for the bishopric of West Africa. His health was poor, however, and, fearing the effect of the African climate, he declined to be a candidate. He was thereupon elected editor of the *Southwestern Christian Advocate*, published in New Orleans, which position he filled until the time of his death.

The acceptance of this editorship proved to be an unfortunate move for Taylor. Desk work was unfavorable to his health and he disliked it. Furthermore, although in private intercourse and in his public addresses he spoke fluently, he could not express himself as easily and forcibly in print. A zealous adherent of his Church, he upheld the action of the Methodist authorities in refusing to admit negroes to the Chattanooga denominational school established for white pupils. In his editorials he urged the colored people to work out their own destiny apart from the whites if necessary and not to strive for educational, social, and religious equality with them. The negro press took exception to his views, which differed widely from those held by many leaders of his race, so that in his later years he lost in popularity. In his own Church he attained a high reputation. He contributed to Methodist periodicals, wrote *The Life . . . of Mrs. Amanda Smith: The Famous Negro Missionary Evangelist* (1886) and published *A Collection of Revival Hymns and Plantation Melodies* (1882). His voice was sonorous and musical and his manners were ingratiating. He married Kate Heston, by whom he had two children.

[W. J. Simmons, *Men of Mark* (1887); G. W. Williams, *Hist. of the Negro Race in America* (1883), II,

337

469–74; *Minutes of the Annual Conferences of the Methodist Episcopal Church*, 1888; *Christian Recorder*, *Christian Advocate* (N. Y.), and *Southwestern Christian Advocate*, Sept. 22, 1887; *Indianapolis Jour.*, Sept. 14, 1887.]   H. G. V.

TAYLOR, MOSES (Jan. 11, 1806–May 23, 1882), banker and capitalist, was born in New York City, a son of Jacob B. and Mary (Cooper) Taylor and great-grandson and namesake of the founder of the family in America, who came from England in 1736. Moses' father was a New York business man, a confidential agent of John Jacob Astor. He lived on lower Broadway and the boy attended at least three private schools in the vicinity of his home. At fifteen, however, his school days were over and he became a clerk with the importing house of G. G. & S. Howland on South Street. That clerkship marked the beginning of a business career filling six decades, in which nothing was permitted to interrupt his continuous accumulation of wealth.

By 1832 he had amassed a capital of $15,000 and was in a position to set up in trade for himself. He began by handling the output of Cuban sugar planters and in his hands this business became a profitable enterprise. The great fire of December 1835 destroyed his South Street store and practically all his possessions, but hardly halted his advance to business success. At forty he was a capitalist and before he was fifty, he could well afford to leave the importing trade to become president, in 1855, of the City Bank. The panic of 1857, causing distress to more than one bank president, was for Taylor an ill wind that brought economic good. When the Delaware, Lackawanna & Western Railroad stock had fallen to five dollars a share he was able to buy outright in the open market a controlling interest in the road, which he retained until his death. Within seven years after the purchase the stock was selling at $240 a share.

Taylor was induced by Cyrus W. Field [*q.v.*] to join him in the first Atlantic Cable venture and he acted as treasurer of the company throughout its period of failure and near-collapse until success was won. After the discouraging break in the first cable the country was involved in civil war, with the Lincoln administration looking to New York for financial backing and leadership. Taylor, who was known as a "hardmoney" Democrat but a supporter of the Washington government, acted as chairman of the bankers' committee which took the first federal loan in 1861. After the war he made heavy investments in public utilities, but the Delaware, Lackawanna & Western Railroad, in which he was closely associated with Samuel Sloan [*q.v.*], and the allied Lackawanna Coal & Iron Company remained his chief interests. He was noted for his complete mastery of the complicated details of his business and as late as 1870 kept his own set of books at his Fifth Avenue home (Smith, *post*, p. 376). His most distinctive banking policy was the holding of large cash reserves. In 1832 he married Catherine A. Wilson, who with three daughters and two sons inherited his estate, estimated at $40,000,000.

[*N. Y. Tribune*, May 24, 1882; *Merchants' Mag. and Commercial Rev.*, June 1864; *Railway World*, May 27, 1882; *Geneal. Record: St. Nicholas Soc. of the City of N. Y.*, vol. II (1916); George Wilson, *Portrait Gallery of the Chamber of Commerce of the State of N. Y.* (1890); H. M. Field, *Hist. of the Atlantic Telegraph* (1866); M. H. Smith, *Twenty Years among the Bulls and Bears of Wall Street* (1870); J. I. Bogen, *The Anthracite Railroads* (1927); Henry Clews, *Twenty-eight Years in Wall Street* (1886).]   W. B. S.

TAYLOR, NATHANIEL WILLIAM (June 23, 1786–Mar. 10, 1858), theologian and educator, born in New Milford, Conn., was the second son of Nathaniel and Anne (Northrop) Taylor, and grandson of the Rev. Nathanael Taylor for some fifty years the pastor of the church in that town. His first American ancestor was John Taylor who came to Windsor, Conn., probably about 1639. Prepared for college by the Rev. Azel Backus [*q.v.*] of Bethlehem, Nathaniel entered Yale in 1800, one of his classmates being Bennet Tyler [*q.v.*]. An affection of the eyes twice interfered with his studies, deferring his graduation until 1807. For a year he served as tutor in the family of Gen. Stephen Van Rensselaer of Albany, then he returned to New Haven to study theology with President Timothy Dwight [*q.v.*]. He was taken into the family of the president and became his amanuensis. This intimate association stimulated his interest in theological doctrines and profoundly influenced his thought and career. On Oct. 15, 1810, he was married to Rebecca Maria Hine of New Milford, and on Apr. 8, 1812, was ordained and installed minister of the First Church of Christ, New Haven. This pulpit he filled with conspicuous success for ten years. His personal dignity and uncommon beauty, reinforcing an eloquence expressive of weighty and well-ordered thought, made him one of the most powerful preachers of his day. In September 1822, upon the formation of a theological department in the college known as the Yale Divinity School, he was appointed Dwight Professor of Didactic Theology, a professorship established by the eldest son of President Dwight with the understanding that it be filled by Taylor.

The creedal faith of the Congregational and Presbyterian churches in America in those years was a type of thought associated with Augustine, systematized by Calvin, and adapted to the conditions of this country by Jonathan Edwards [*q.v.*]. In order to guard against the idea that man is saved by any merit of his own, Calvinism seemed to exclude any real freedom of choice. Edwards in his treatise on the will in grappling with this difficulty had declared that man has a natural ability to repent but is inhibited by his moral disinclinations; his only freedom is liberty to obey the strongest motive. The Edwardean system of thought, modified by Hopkins, Bellamy, and Dwight, was the orthodox belief commonly held in the New England churches and was largely influential in the West and South when Taylor assumed his duties at Yale. Being of a bold and original mind, endowed with speculative talents of a high order, and having for a motto, oft repeated, "Follow truth if it carries you over Niagara," he broke through the narrow confines of the accepted theology. Moreover, he was a revival preacher deeply concerned with relating religious truth to the facts of human consciousness. His point of divergence was the reality of the freedom of choice. He denied that our consciousness of freedom is an illusion and asserted that the will is not another name for the strongest motive, but is a power to chose between motives. Man, he affirmed, is not born totally depraved, but with certain sinful inclinations, and his "sin consists in sinning." To induce men to turn from their evil ways and choose the highest good, appeal must be made to man's natural desire for happiness, which Taylor unfortunately called "self-love." This self-love will finally become, in a regenerated mind, identical with an unselfish love for God. Such an interpretation of the freedom of the will and the modifications of Calvinism attendant upon it aroused a storm of controversy and divided the churches of New England into "Taylorites and Tylerites" the adherents of Taylor and of his principal opponent, Bennet Tyler. The debate, passing beyond the borders of New England, became the chief theological reason for the disruption of the Presbyterian Church in 1838. Taylor's controversial articles were contributed chiefly to the *Christian Spectator* (later the *Quarterly Christian Spectator*) and to the *Spirit of the Pilgrims*. Other writings of his appeared posthumously and include *Practical Sermons* (1858), *Lectures on the Moral Government of God* (1859), *Essays . . . upon Selected Topics in Revealed Theology* (1859).

Taylor continued in his professorship until within a few weeks of his death. He was beloved by his pupils for his intellectual independence, the stimulating power of his thought, and his personal kindness. In 1902 the Nathaniel W. Taylor Lectureship was established in the Yale Divinity School by his daughter.

[W. O. Taylor, *Descendants of John Taylor of Windsor* (4 vols., 1931); Samuel Orcutt, *Hist. of the Towns of New Milford and Bridgewater, Conn.* (1882); F. B. Dexter, *Biog. Sketches Grads. Yale Coll.*, vol. VI (1912); Timothy Dwight, *Memories of Yale Life and Men* (1903); *Semi-Centennial Anniversary of the Divinity School of Yale Coll.* (1872); Leonard Bacon and others, *Memorial of Nathaniel W. Taylor, D.D., Three Sermons* (1858); F. H. Foster, *A Genetic Hist. of the New England Theology* (1907); T. D. Bacon, *Leonard Bacon: A Statesman in the Church* (1931).]

C. A. D—e.

TAYLOR, RAYNOR (c. 1747–Aug. 17, 1825), musician, composer, was born in England. Data concerning his early life are meager, and the year of his birth must be conjectured from the fact that he was twelve years old when he attended Handel's funeral as a choir boy of the Chapel Royal in 1759, and from his tombstone at St. Peter's Church, Philadelphia, Pa., which states that he died in his seventy-eighth year. He was educated at the King's Singing School in London and in 1765 became organist of a church at Chelmsford. In 1765 he became music director at Sadler's Wells Theatre in London and achieved some success as a composer of ballads. Some of his time was spent in teaching, and among his pupils was Alexander Reinagle [*q.v.*]. Taylor followed Reinagle to America in 1792, making his first appearance in Baltimore, Md., at a musical entertainment in October. He then settled in Annapolis where he had been appointed organist of St. Anne's Church, but left after a few months to become organist at St. Peter's Church in Philadelphia. He held this position until the closing years of his life. In 1820 he was one of the group that founded the Musical Fund Society in Philadelphia.

Taylor is most interesting for the type of entertainment he offered. His "olios," as he called them, were burlesques and parodies. In January 1793 he presented a "Dramatic proverb being a burletta, in one act, called *The Gray Mare's The Best Horse*"; this consisted of such episodes as "A Breakfast scene a month after marriage," "Mock wife in a violent passion," "A Father's advice to his son in law," "Dame Pliant's obedience to her husband," etc. (*Maryland Gazette*, Jan. 24, 1793). In Philadelphia Taylor gave more of his entertainments, one of them an "olio," "The Poor female ballad singer, a pathetic song; . . . Ding, Dong Bell, or the Honeymoon expired; . . . Character of smart Dolly, a laughing song; Rustic courtship, or the unsuccessful love of poor Thomas, a crying song with duet," etc. (*Dunlap and Claypoole's American Daily Advertiser*, Jan. 11, 1794). In April 1796 he gave an orchestral concert at Oeller's Hotel in Philadelphia; his own works on the program were "New Overture," "Divertimento" for orchestra, and a violin concerto.

Of Taylor's compositions published before he came to America, three may be found in the *Cathedral Magazine of London:* "Hear my Crying O God" (volume I, pp. 146–160); "Hear, O Lord, and Consider my Complaint" (volume II, pp. 85–96); "I Will Give Thanks unto the Lord" (volume III, pp. 85–96). A number of his works composed in America are still extant. Several songs and the libretto of a melodrama, *The Rose of Arragon* (1822), are in the New York Public Library; a manuscript piece for piano, "The Bells" (included in J. T. Howard, *A Program of Early American Piano Music,* 1931), and printed copies of "The Wounded Sailor" and "The Philadelphia Hymn" are in the Hopkinson collection at Philadelphia; two songs, *The Merry piping lad,* and *The Wand'ring village maid,* are in the Yale library. Taylor also composed music for the ballad-operas, *La Petite Piedmontesse* (1795); *The Iron Chest* (1797), *The Shipwrecked Mariner Preserved* (1797), and, with Alexander Reinagle, *Pizarro, or The Spaniards in Peru* (1800).

[In the Philadelphia city directories for the years 1810 and 1817, Taylor's first name appears as René; on his tombstone, see *Inscriptions in St. Peter's Churchyard, Philadelphia* (1879), p. 375, it appears as Rayner. For further biographical data, see *Grove's Dict. of Music and Musicians, Am. Supp.* (1930); O. G. Sonneck, *Bibliography of Early Secular Music* (1905), *Early Concert-Life in America* (1907); L. C. Madeira, *Annals of Music in Phila.* (1896); J. T. Howard, *Our Am. Music* (1931); *Poulson's Am. Daily Advertiser,* Aug. 18, 1825.]　　　　J. T. H.

TAYLOR, RICHARD (Jan. 27, 1826–Apr. 12, 1879), Confederate soldier, the only son of Zachary [*q.v.*] and Margaret Mackall (Smith) Taylor, was born at "Springfields," the family estate near Louisville, Ky. After spending much of his boyhood at frontier camps, he was tutored by a certain Brooks at Lancaster, Mass. He was sent to Europe, probably in 1841, and studied at Edinburgh and in France. In 1843 he entered Harvard College but soon transferred to Yale, where he graduated in 1845. In July of the following year he visited General Taylor's camp at Matamoras, but rheumatism forced him to seek relief at Arkansas and Virginia springs. After managing his father's Mississippi cotton plantation, 1848–49, he established "Fashion," a sugar plantation in Saint Charles Parish, La. There he collected a valuable library, studied the works of great military masters, and read widely in English and French literature. In February 1851 he was married to Louise Marie Myrthé

Bringier (d. 1875); of their five children, two died of scarlet fever during the Civil War. Originally a Whig, Taylor became a Democrat in the fifties, attended the Charleston convention in 1860, and sought to prevent a disruption of his party. As chairman of the committee on federal relations in the state Senate, where he served from 1856 to 1861, he reported the bill to call a convention which assembled in 1861. He was elected a delegate to that body, voted for secession, and as chairman of the committee on military and naval affairs urged preparation for war. Appointed colonel of the 9th Louisiana Infantry, mustered into service July 6, he hastened to Virginia but arrived too late to participate in the Confederate victory at Bull Run. On Oct. 21, 1861, he was appointed brigadier-general by President Jefferson Davis, and served in the Valley campaign under "Stonewall" Jackson. As part of Jackson's command he joined Lee at Richmond, and, although prostrated by illness during the Seven Days' battles, he directed his troops from an ambulance. In July 1862 Taylor was promoted major-general and assigned command of the District of West Louisiana. Avoiding drawn battles, as his men were greatly outnumbered, he made numerous surprise attacks, captured arms, ammunition, and medical stores, and destroyed Federal gunboats. On Apr. 8–9, 1864, he stopped Nathaniel P. Banks's Red River campaign by decisive battles against great odds at Pleasant Hill and Mansfield (Sabine Crossroads), but was prevented from following up his victory by what he regarded as the stupid policy of the departmental commander, Edmund Kirby-Smith. In spirited letters to his superior officer he asked to be relieved of his command. After brief residence with his family at Natchitoches, he was promoted lieutenant-general on Aug. 15, 1864, and assigned to the Department of East Louisiana, Mississippi, and Alabama; three months later the command of Gen. John Bell Hood's defeated army also devolved upon him. Prompt and vigorous action was insufficient to overcome demoralization, desertion, and fraudulent practice, and on May 4, 1865, he surrendered the last Confederate army east of the Mississippi to Gen. Edward R. S. Canby at Citronelle, Ala.

Taylor's estate had been confiscated during the war, and after its close he divided his time between New Orleans and New York. He visited Washington frequently, labored to secure release of imprisoned Confederates, and exerted some influence upon President Johnson's Louisiana policy, though he failed to persuade Grant to withdraw Federal support from the Kellogg-Packard régime. In May 1873 he sailed for

Europe and was cordially received in England, France, and Germany. In his later years he served as trustee of the Peabody Education Fund for promotion of education in the South. He died of dropsy in 1879 at the home of a New York friend, Col. S. L. M. Barlow. His reminiscences, *Destruction and Reconstruction* (1879), parts of which appeared in the *North American Review,* January–April 1878, reveal literary ability of a high order. His pen portraits of Civil War characters, whether Union or Confederate, are unusually fair; his discussion of the Reconstruction period is less bitter than one might expect.

[In addition to Taylor's reminiscences, see *Official Jour. Senate of La. . . . 1856–61;* *Official Jour. of Proc. Convention of the State of La.* (1861); *War of the Rebellion: Official Records (Army)*; *Lib. of Southern Lit.,* vol. XII (1910), ed. by E. A. Alderman, etc.; *Letters of Zachary Taylor* (1908); *Obit. Record Grads. Yale Coll. . . . 1879* (1879); *Times-Picayune* (New Orleans), Apr. 5, 1925; obituary in *N. Y. Times,* Apr. 13, 1879, and the Richard Taylor Scrapbook, in the possession of his daughter, Mrs. Betty Taylor Stauffer.]

W. H. S—n.

TAYLOR, RICHARD COWLING (Jan. 18, 1789–Oct. 27, 1851), geologist and antiquarian, was born in England at Hinton, Suffolk, or at Banham, Norfolk, the third son of Samuel Taylor, a weathy farmer. His early education at Halesworth, Suffolk, was extensive in higher mathematics and mapping, and about 1805 he was articled to a land surveyor in Gloucestershire, with whom he remained until about 1811. His first instructor, William Smith, the "Father of British Geology," later became his close friend. A Norman ruin on his father's estate interested Taylor in antiquities, and in 1821 he published his first volume, *Index Monasticus, or the Abbeys and Other Monasteries . . . Formerly Established in the Diocese of Norwich and the Ancient Kingdom of East Anglia.* Later (1830) he brought out an index to the new edition of Sir William Dugdale's *Monasticon Anglicanum; A History of the Abbies and Other Monasteries . . . in England and Wales.* These works brought him high commendation from such men as Sir Walter Scott, who expressed his admiration of the book in a letter to Taylor (Taylor, *post,* p. 39). In the meantime his interest in geology had been growing. Between 1811 and 1813 he surveyed in various parts of the country, and at one time had charge of a department of the ordnance for Buckingham and Bedford. In the fall of 1826 he removed to London, where he was engaged on the ordnance survey of England. A year later he published *On the Geology of East Norfolk* (1827), which emphasized facts relating to successive stratification. Among his reports on

mining properties was one on the British Iron Company of South Wales, and his plaster model of its mines, said to be the first ever made, earned the Isis Medal of the Society of Arts.

In July 1830 Taylor sailed with his wife, Emily Errington, whom he had married in 1820, and four daughters for the United States. British geologists and engineers later believed that, had he remained a little longer in England, he would have taken a leading part in railway development. In Pennsylvania he became engaged in a survey of the Blossburg coal region, and in the exploration of the coal and iron veins of the Dauphin & Susquehanna Coal Company. He was able, because of his intimate knowledge of theoretical geology, for the first time to relate the Old Red Sandstone underlying the coal fields of Pennsylvania to its true place, corresponding with its place in the series of European rocks. He later explored many mineral districts containing gold, silver, lead, copper, coal, asphaltum, and other materials, and ranged as far as the copper mines of Cuba, the gold fields of Panama, and the asphaltum of New Brunswick. His chief and monumental work, *Statistics of Coal* (1848), published in Philadelphia, drew extravagant praise from scientific journals of the day all over the world. He himself felt the results to be extremely uncertain because "this species of investigation savours too much of scrutiny into the private concerns of men" (*Statistics of Coal,* p. xi). While some of his conclusions were disproved in later years in the light of subsequent investigations (Lesley, *post,* p. 20), his careful and intricately detailed work in geology placed him in the first ranks of his day. He died in Philadelphia.

[P. M. Taylor, *A Memoir of the Family of Taylor of Norwich* (privately printed, 1886); *Dict. of Nat. Biog.;* Isaac Lea, in *Proc. Acad. Natural Sciences of Phila.,* vol. V (1852); G. P. Merrill, *The First One Hundred Years of Am. Geology* (1924), pp. 211–12, 667; J. P. Lesley, *Hist. Sketch of Geological Explorations in Pa. and Other States* (1876); obituary in *Gentleman's Mag.* (London), Feb. 1852; death notice in *North Am. and U. S. Gazette* (Phila.), Oct. 28, 1851.] H. S. G—n.

TAYLOR, ROBERT LOVE (July 31, 1850– Mar. 31, 1912), governor of Tennessee, United States senator, lecturer, the fourth of the nine children of Nathaniel Green and Emmeline (Haynes) Taylor, was born in Happy Valley, Carter County, Tenn. He apparently absorbed more politics from his mother's brother than from his father, with the result that from early boyhood he and his elder brother, Alfred Alexander Taylor [*q.v.*], consistently took opposite sides on political questions. He was educated at Pennington Seminary in New Jersey and at Buffalo Institute (later Milligan College), Milligan,

Tenn., and later studied law. Immediately following his admission to the bar in 1878, he became a successful candidate for representative in Congress. He served in Congress (1879–81) as a Democrat from the same district that his father had represented as a Whig and that his brother was later to represent as a Republican. He was defeated for reëlection in 1880 and in 1882. Following his retirement from Congress he engaged in the practice of law and became publisher of the *Johnson City Comet,* but met with little financial success in either undertaking. In December 1885 he was appointed federal pension agent at Knoxville (appointment confirmed, Apr. 16, 1886), a position which he held until 1887.

In 1886, as the result of factional strife between the old state-rights group and the new Whig-industrialist group within the Democratic party, the rural element, which had little sympathy with either faction and which had been leaderless since the death of Andrew Johnson [*q.v.*], joined the young men of the party to force the nomination of Taylor, who was recognized to be a rising young leader, as the Democratic candidate for governor. He was accepted by the party leaders only when it became evident that any other course would bring a victory for the Republicans, who had already named his brother, Alfred, as their standard bearer. The result was the picturesque "War of the Roses," in which "Bob" and "Alf" canvassed the entire state in joint debate and through their inimitable skill as entertainers kept the campaign from becoming centered around issues which might arouse strife. "Bob" won the election, but as governor soon faced the opposition of the party leaders, who sought to prevent his renomination. In 1888, however, the same forces which had brought about his success in 1886 staged a determined fight in the party convention, and he again led his party to victory in the election. During his two terms as governor (1887–91) he applied his political philosophy that more could be gained by cooperation and conciliation than by antagonism, and succeeded in securing a more equitable distribution of the burden of taxation, in providing for improvement of the state educational system, in starting a movement for reform of the state prison system, and in encouraging the development of the natural resources of the state.

At the end of his second term, turning to the lecture platform as a means of making a living, he established a reputation through his ability to combine humor and pathos in describing the life and thoughts of the common man in such lectures as "The Fiddle and the Bow," "Visions and Dreams," and "Castles in the Air." When in 1895 his brother joined him in a lyceum lecture tour, the two are said to have taken in $40,000 in seven months with a joint lecture on "Yankee Doodle" and "Dixie." In the meantime the condition of the Democratic party in Tennessee was once more becoming precarious because of the development of the agrarian movement and the extreme conservatism of the controlling faction. As a result Taylor was again drafted in 1896 as his party's nominee for the governorship and after a strenuous campaign succeeded in defeating his Republican opponent by a small margin. The opposition of the party machine had repeatedly frustrated his ambition to become a United States senator, but in 1906, when he opposed the popular Senator Edward Ward Carmack [*q.v.*] for the Democratic nomination in the first senatorial primary election held in Tennessee, he received a majority of the votes and took the seat in 1907 which he held until his death. In 1910, however, he was again drafted by his party to become a candidate for governor in an attempt to close a break that had occurred in the party ranks. Again the young men in the party were in revolt, and for the first time in his life he was the favorite of the party leaders and organization. But he was now an old man, the people failed to respond to his appeals, and the Republican candidate was elected by a large majority. For a time, between his last term as governor and his first term as senator, he lectured and published *Bob Taylor's Magazine,* which in 1907 became the *Taylor-Trotwood Magazine.* He was married three times, first in 1878 to Sarah L. Baird of Asheville, N. C., second to Mrs. Alice Hill of Tuscaloosa, Ala., and third in 1904 to Mamie L. St. John of Chilhowie, Va. He was survived by five children of his first marriage. In 1912 the *Lectures and Best Literary Productions of Bob Taylor* was published.

Immensely popular with the common people because of his genial personality and his ability to entertain them through lectures which Champ Clark once called "a strange commingling of wit, humor, philosophy, pathos, eloquence, common sense, and good morals," Taylor was unpopular with the party leaders, who could not control him, and who sought to discredit him by branding him as "a shallow fiddler." Yet, because he could not be ignored, he secured his opportunity to play the rôle of conciliator, and thus to make his greatest contribution to the political history of his state. He was preëminently a Democrat to whom party interest was above faction and above the individual. He probably saved his state from the excesses of the agrarian revolt, and he had great influence in the transition from reconstruction prejudice to the recovery of party consolidation in Tennessee.

[*Who's Who in America*, 1912–13; *Biog. Directory of the Am. Congress* (1928); D. M. Robison, *Bob Taylor and the Agrarian Revolt in Tenn.* (1935), the best study of Taylor's career; P. D. Augsburg, *Bob and Alf Taylor* (1925); J. P., A. A., and H. L. Taylor, *Life and Career of Senator Robert Love Taylor* (1913); DeLong Rice, *"Old Limber," or the Tale of the Taylors* (1921); *Notable Men of Tenn.* (1905), ed. by John Allison; *Robert Love Taylor . . . Memorial Addresses Delivered in the Senate and the House of Representatives* (1913); memorial and obituary notices in *Nashville Banner*, Apr. 1, and *Nashville Democrat*, Mar. 31, Apr. 1, 1912.]   W. C. B.

TAYLOR, ROBERT TUNSTALL (Jan. 16, 1867–Feb. 21, 1929), physician, was born in Norfolk, Va. One month later he was brought to Baltimore, Md., where he lived for the remainder of his life. The son of Robertson Taylor, a coffee merchant, and Baynham Baylor (Tunstall) Taylor, he was accorded many cultural and social advantages. After preparatory education in private schools he entered the Johns Hopkins University and received the B.A. degree in 1889. Following in the footsteps of his maternal grandfather, Dr. Robert Tunstall, of Norfolk he began the study of medicine and graduated from the University of Virginia in 1891. He was married to Florence Templeman, of Baltimore, on Oct. 6, 1891, and began the practice of medicine. A newly acquired interest in orthopaedic surgery led him to devote a year to post-graduate work in this specialty at Harvard, 1894–95, and at Columbia, 1895. When he returned to Baltimore he founded the Hospital for the Relief of Crippled and Deformed Children, the first of its kind in the city. Through this institution he helped to bring the problem of the handicapped child to the attention of the public. His efforts led to the growth of this hospital so that, under the name of The James Lawrence Kernan Hospital and Industrial School, it assumed a major rôle in the hospitalization of Baltimore's crippled children. His zeal manifested itself in the organization of public school facilities for the handicapped. He was likewise instrumental in the development of a service for standard pasteurized milk in the city.

Taylor's enthusiastic efforts were in large part responsible for the opening in 1901 at the University of Maryland of the first orthopaedic department in a medical school in Maryland. He was appointed associate professor of orthopaedic surgery for the 1901–02 session and the following year was promoted to the professorship. He remained head of the department until his death. Concurrently he was orthopaedic surgeon to the St. Joseph's, the Women's, the St. Agnes' hospitals, and consultant to the West Baltimore General Hospital. From time to time he conducted clinics in various communities throughout the state. During the World War he served in the medical corps of the United States Army at Fort Myer, Va., and in the surgeon-general's office in Washington, D. C., as major. Later he became lieutenant-colonel with instruction and examining duties, chief of the orthopaedic service at Fort McHenry, and, later, consultant to the United States Veterans Bureau in Baltimore.

A pioneer in his community in the field of orthopaedics he helped to bring to the attention of the public the existence of a handicapped group of children and to develop a sympathetic interest. Through his teaching he was able to influence the development of orthopaedic surgery wherever his students entered into practice. He wrote two books in the field: *Orthopaedic Surgery for Students and General Practitioners* (1907), and *The Surgery of the Spine and Extremities* (1923). His value as a teacher was enhanced by the skilful technique he displayed in his operative clinics. Articles written by him on surgical tuberculosis, traumatic conditions, such as fractures, infantile paralysis, and new operative procedures, helped to enrich the literature of a new field. The illness that attended the last few years of his life did not deter him from carrying on his work with his characteristic vigor until the day of his death. He was survived by his wife. Richard Lucien Page [*q.v.*] was his great-uncle.

[Personal acquaintance; information from the family; *Who's Who in America*, 1928–29; obituary article, *Bull. of the School of Med., Univ. of Md.*, Apr. 1929; *Baltimore Sun*, Feb. 22, 1929.]   I. W. N.

TAYLOR, SAMUEL HARVEY (Oct. 3, 1807–Jan. 29, 1871), educator, was born at Londonderry, N. H., the son of Captain James Taylor and Persis (Hemphill) Taylor. At fourteen he was largely responsible for the conduct of two extensive farms, and he seemed destined for a life of hard manual labor until a fall weakened his physique and made him decide to follow an intellectual life. Entering Pinkerton Academy in his native town, he prepared himself in two years to enter the sophomore class at Dartmouth, whence he graduated with honors in 1832. For the next five years he studied at the Andover Theological Seminary, from which he graduated in 1837, taught at Phillips Academy, Andover, and at Dartmouth, and occupied his Sundays with preaching. On Dec. 8, 1837, he married Caroline Persis Parker. In the same year he became the sixth principal of Phillips Academy, a position he held for nearly thirty-four years.

His strong personality left its stamp enduringly upon the school. His word was law, his position that of an autocrat to whose will even the trustees deferred. Under his guidance Phillips Academy prospered, its numbers more than doubled, and its standards of scholarship and conduct improved until it reached into the far West and South and even to foreign countries for its students. In the classroom, where at times Taylor taught as many as seven different subjects, his stern and domineering manner made him the terror of shy and sensitive boys, but those who had the strength to stand up under his merciless questioning, his emphasis upon absolute accuracy of memory in the smallest detail, learned the delight and the value of thorough scholarship. Taylor was not an innovator, and the curriculum of Latin, Greek, and mathematics he devised remained unchanged throughout his long administration despite the altered entrance requirements of the colleges. Between 1843 and 1870 he published five textbooks exemplifying his theories: *Guide for Writing Latin* (1843), from the German of J. P. Krebs; *Grammar of the Greek Language* (1844) and *An Elementary Grammar of the Greek Language* (1846), both from the German of Raphael Kühner; *Method of Classical Study* (1861); and *Classical Study; Its Value* (1870). While they were models of accuracy, these showed little breadth of vision or literary appreciation. For many years, 1852–71, he was an editor of *Bibliotheca Sacra*. The spiritual health of his pupils was always a matter of vital import to Taylor. In addition to frequent church services and prayer meetings, he fostered with what to many would seem mistaken zeal the hysterical revivals common in Andover at the time, in which youngsters still in their teens were "converted." On the stormy morning of Jan. 29, 1871, while hastening to meet his Sunday Bible class, he fell dead in the entry of the Academy building. He was survived by his three sons. In both his virtues and his faults he was representative of that Puritan New England where Phillips Academy was founded. His sternness, his accuracy, his dislike of frivolity and hatred of evil, his confidence in religious conversion, his absolute trust in his own infallibility were all qualities of the old, strict Puritan code which has passed away.

[C. M. Fuess, *An Old New England School* (1917), contains a thorough analysis of Taylor's personality and accomplishments. See also D. G. Annis and G. W. Browne, *Vital Records of Londonderry, N. H.* (1914); John Albee, *Three Memorials* (1878); *A Memorial of Samuel Harvey Taylor, Compiled by His Last Class* (1871), from which an address by E. A. Park was reprinted in *Bibliotheca Sacra*, Apr. 1871, and in *Cong. Quart.*, Jan. 1872; death notice in *Boston Transcript*, Jan. 31, 1871.]
            S. H. P.

TAYLOR, STEVENSON (Feb. 12, 1848–May 19, 1926), marine engineer, was born in West Houston Street, New York City, the son of Hugh and Alice (MacWhinney) Taylor. He attended public elementary schools and the New York Free Academy, now the College of the City of New York, and as an apprentice entered the employ of Fletcher, Harrison & Company, proprietors of the North River Iron Works, in 1864. After the usual training in shops and drawing room with outside work in the installation of machinery, he became chief draftsman for the firm about the time he reached his majority and continued in charge of the drawing room and work of design until 1883, when the concern became a corporation under the style of W. & A. Fletcher Company and Taylor was made vice-president. Henceforth he was the active head of the business until 1904, when he disposed of his interest and resigned. During this period he was responsible for designing the machinery for such notable side-wheel steamboats as the *Pilgrim* (1883) of the Fall River Line, the first iron steamboat built on Long Island Sound, and her sister ship, the *Puritan*.

In 1904 he was appointed receiver of the United States Shipbuilding Company, and in the same year became vice-president of the Quintard Iron Works. It was while holding this office that he made the designs and took the contract for the steamer *Commonwealth*, for the Fall River Line, which when put into service was the "largest and most magnificent steamship built for service on inland waters" (E. K. Chatterton, *Steamships and Their Story*, 1910, p. 263). In 1916, having severed his connection with the Quintard works the year before, he was chosen president of the American Bureau of Shipping for the inspection and registration of hulls and machinery of ships. Under his wise and capable management the standing of the American bureau was raised until it became the equal of any of the registration societies. After ten years of service here, having attained his seventy-eighth year, he wished to retire, but was persuaded to continue his connection, with the title of chairman. This relation lasted the few remaining months of his life. During the World War he was appointed, Apr. 2, 1917, a lieutenant commander in the United States Naval Reserve Force (later promoted commander) and rendered valuable service as a member of the board charged with the rehabilitation of seized German vessels and subsequently as a member of the board of appraisal of vessels commandeered by the government. For this latter work he was specially fitted by his judicial temperament as well as by his long experience.

Taylor was a very active member of a number of engineering associations. He was a charter member, one of the few honorary members, and twice president (1910–12, 1916–18) of the Society of Naval Architects and Marine Engineers, and for many years was a trustee, and for three years (1913–15) president, of the Engineers Club of New York. During nearly forty years he gave much time and effort to the management of Webb Institute of Naval Architecture, founded by William H. Webb [q.v.] as a school of collegiate grade for the gratuitous instruction of young men as naval architects and marine engineers, and also as a home for aged mechanics in the trades of shipbuilding and marine engineering and their wives or widows. Taylor was one of the original trustees, and upon Webb's death in 1899 succeeded him as president. He undertook the task as a labor of love, with no compensation of a financial character, and it was probably that part of his life work in which he took the most satisfaction.

Taylor was of medium height and build, with hair snow white from an early age and a rosy complexion. He was always one of the most popular men in any organization, had remarkable skill in composing differences, and was an ideal presiding officer. On Sept. 10, 1874, he married Alma L. Partridge, who died in 1918. He died eight years later, at his home in New York, survived by a daughter and two sons.

[*Who's Who in N. Y.*, 1924; *Who's Who in Engineering*, 1925; *Trans. Soc. of Naval Architects and Marine Engineers*, vol. XXXIV (1926); *Trans. Am. Soc. Mech. Engineers*, vol. XLVIII (1926); *N. Y. Times*, May 20, 1926.]   W. M. M.

TAYLOR, WILLIAM (May 2, 1821–May 18, 1902), evangelist, missionary, bishop of the Methodist Episcopal Church, was born in Rockbridge County, Va. His father, Stuart Taylor, came of Revolutionary stock, and his mother, Martha (Hickman), of an old Delaware family. In his tenth year he had a profound religious experience, which was renewed in 1841. As a result he entered the Methodist ministry, being admitted on trial to the Baltimore Conference on Mar. 15, 1843, ordained deacon in 1846, and elder in 1847. For fifty-three years he traveled and toiled as no other man of his denomination, becoming a missionary evangelist to all lands. He was endowed with a physical frame and vitality that were equal to every demand: "I am six feet high, weigh 207 pounds," he wrote on a photograph, Mar. 14, 1881, "and lifted at one raise 760 lbs. in my fifty-ninth year." In addition to bodily strength, he also had a voice of unusual melody, range, and power, and a commanding personality.

His evangelistic work began in the market house of Georgetown, D. C. In 1848 he was appointed to California under the missionary society of his church and arrived in San Francisco, via Cape Horn, in September 1849, when it was still a city of tents. To the "forty-niners" he preached for seven years. Standing on a pork or whiskey barrel in the Plaza he could be heard by 20,000 people at a time. His work of saving souls carried him into brothels and saloons. He built his own home and his own chapel. From 1856 to 1861 the cities of the United States and Canada, East and West, were his field. In the latter year he sailed for Australia by way of England. After preaching seven months in England and Ireland he visited Asia Minor, Syria, Palestine, Egypt, and Ceylon. For three years he labored in Australia, Tasmania, and New Zealand, where he added thousands to the membership of the Wesleyan Methodist churches. During all this time he derived support for himself and family from books which he published. From Australia in 1863 he sent seeds of the eucalyptus tree to a California horticulturist, and from these seeds came the eucalyptus trees on the Pacific Coast. In 1866 he was in South Africa working with colonists and Kaffirs; the following year, in England and Scotland. In 1869 he was back in Australia. In 1870 he went to India, where he spent seven years preaching to Anglo-Indians and expanding and organizing the work of the Methodist Episcopal Church among them. Here he developed the "Pauline System" of support for missionaries. They were to depend upon contributions from their converts and the communities in which they worked, and if such contributions proved insufficient, they, like Paul, were to labor with their own hands. One of the results of his activities was the organization of the South India Conference. In 1877 and 1878 he was in Peru and Chile, where he organized a system of self-supporting schools, conducted by missionaries; Coquimbo, Chile, became the center of this remarkable school system.

In 1884, having retired from the "itinerant ministry" that he might pursue his evangelistic work independent of ecclesiastical oversight, he went from South America as a lay delegate of the South India Conference to the General Conference in Philadelphia, and was there elected, at the age of sixty-three, missionary bishop for Africa. For twelve years he poured missionaries into this Continent—men and women willing to trust God and the people they served for daily bread, and to receive their salary in full after their arrival in the heavenly Jerusalem (Davies, *post,* p. 106). Africa, however, proved unusually difficult for his self-supporting missionaries, and his great strength began to break under the burdens he carried. In 1896, at the age of seventy-five he was relieved of his responsibilities by the General Conference. He had been married, Oct. 21, 1846, to Isabelle Anne Kimberlin, and three of their sons grew to maturity. His last years were spent quietly in Southern California with his family, from whom he had been separated again and again for years at a time.

In many ways Taylor was the outstanding man in his denomination. His imagination has been compared with that of Cecil Rhodes, and his energies matched his imagination. His firm belief that "God had taken William Taylor into a peculiar partnership" filled him with "the intrepidity and assurance of an apostle" (J. M. Buckley in *Christian Advocate,* June 12, 1902). He was saved from the fevers of fanaticism by a rugged common sense and an abundant humor. His writings include *Seven Years' Street Preaching in San Francisco* (1857); *California Life, Illustrated* (1858); *Model Preacher* (1859); *Infancy and Manhood of Christian Life* (1867); *Christian Adventures in South Africa* (1868); *Reconciliation; or, How to be Saved* (1875); *Four Years' Campaign in India* (1875); *Our South American Cousins* (1878); *Pauline Methods of Missionary Work* (copyrighted 1879); *Election of Grace* (1880); *Letters to a Quaker Friend on Baptism* (1880); *Ten Years of Self-Supporting Missions in India* (1882); *Story of My Life* (1895); *Africa Illustrated* (1895); *Flaming Torch in Darkest Africa* (1898). He died in Palo Alto, Cal.

[Files of the Board of Foreign Missions of the Methodist Episcopal Church; *Christian Advocate,* May 29, June 5, 12, 1902; *Indian Witness,* July 27, Oct. 12, 1921; *Who's Who in America,* 1901–02; *San Francisco Call* and *San Francisco Chronicle,* May 19, 1902; G. F. Arms, *Hist. of the William Taylor Self-Supporting Missions in South America* (copr. 1921); Edward Davies, *The Bishop of Africa* (1885); O. von Barchwitz-Krauser, *Six Years with Bishop Taylor in South America* (1885); J. H. Paul, *The Soul-Digger; or, Life and Times of William Taylor* (copr. 1928).]

O. M. B.

TAYLOR, WILLIAM LADD (Dec. 10, 1854–Dec. 26, 1926), illustrator, was born at Grafton, Mass., the son of William H. and Anna Maria (Darling) Taylor. His education in the public schools of Worcester, Mass., was supplemented by a course in mechanical drawing, and for a time he had employment as a draftsman, but found the work exacting and sought restored health in Colorado. Deciding to become an artist, he studied at the newly established Art Students' League of New York, and in 1881

moved to Boston, "with more ambition than pennies" (Robinson, *post,* p. 167), and established a small studio on School Street. Having won some success as an illustrator, he was soon enabled to go to Paris, where in 1884–85 he registered as a pupil of G. C. R. Boulanger and Jules-Joseph Lefebvre. As an art student and young artist he was remarkable for the seriousness and conscientiousness of his work—characteristics which remained with him. Among his earliest important illustrations were those made for the *Woods and Lakes of Maine* (1884) of Lucius L. Hubbard, whom Taylor accompanied in his adventurous wanderings. By 1888, when he married Mary Alice Fitz, of Norfolk, Va., he had become one of the most popular of American illustrators. He and his wife settled at Wellesley, Mass., where Taylor set up his studio. In it were made almost countless illustrations, notable both for competent documentation and esthetic content.

Taylor became a favorite illustrator of the *Ladies' Home Journal,* called upon year after year for paintings, suitable for reproduction, of historical, literary, and sentimental subjects. Behind these lay careful and elaborate first-hand studies. Taylor never drew from imagination details which he could secure through travel or by other means. Toward his New England themes he accumulated a great collection of costumes and other antiques. His Bible pictures were based on drawings from Near-Eastern bas-reliefs and other similar documents. He avoided the usual run of studio models, and utilized accommodating friends and neighbors who seemed to him typical. His pictures devoted to the nineteenth century in New England, reprinted in his *Our Home and Country* (1908), have been justly acclaimed as "an historical record in pictorial form of a period of enormous importance" (Downes, *post,* p. xvi). Files of the *Ladies' Home Journal* may be valued by collectors very considerably because of Taylor's drawings. Especially important among these are the series, "Those Days in Old Virginia," the illustrations to accompany Longfellow poems, and the Bible Series, most of them reprinted in *Our Home and Country.*

Leading at Wellesley a life uneventful and somewhat apart from that of other professional artists, Taylor worked incessantly until his last year upon many commissions. He belonged to the Boston Art Club, but he was not usually represented at its exhibitions. Many of the originals of his works were shown to interested visitors at the Curtis Publishing Company, Philadelphia. Personally reticent and somewhat austere, he had few of the qualities usually attributed to the artistic temperament. He has been described as "an agreeable and gentlemanly person, common-sensed in his views of affairs, pleasant in conversation and . . . well informed in literature" (Robinson, *post*, p. 172). Though never of robust health, he was devoted to outdoor sports as he was to horses and woodcraft.

[*Who's Who in America*, 1926–27; F. T. Robinson, *Living New England Artists* (1888); W. H. Downes, in Taylor's *Our Home and Country* (1908); *Mentor*, Dec. 1920; *Ladies' Home Jour.*, Mar. 1916, Aug. 1926, p. 28; death notice in *Boston Transcript*, Dec. 27, 1926.]

F. W. C.

TAYLOR, WILLIAM MACKERGO (Oct. 23, 1829–Feb. 8, 1895), Congregational clergyman, was born in Kilmarnock, Scotland, the son of Peter and Isobel (Mackergo) Taylor. His father was a shopkeeper, and the boy grew up in a home where Scotch sagacity, piety, and zest for theological discussion prevailed. Having received his preliminary education in the local academy, he entered the University of Glasgow, from which he graduated in 1849. His training for the ministry he received at the Divinity Hall of the United Presbyterian Church, Edinburgh. Finishing his course there in 1852, he was licensed to preach by the United Presbytery of Ayrshire on Sept. 14, of that year. He was ordained at Kilmaurs, a town about two miles from his birthplace, June 28, 1853, and was pastor there until called, in 1854, to the recently formed United Presbyterian Church of Derby Road, Bootle, a suburb of Liverpool. On Oct. 4, 1853, he had married Jessie, daughter of John and Mitchell (Gregg) Steedman of Kilmarnock. Bootle, situated at the mouth of the Mersey, was the loading place for ships, and Taylor's parishioners were chiefly from the families of those that the activities of a seaport had called thither. For sixteen years he labored among them, building up a substantial church, and gaining in Liverpool and beyond a reputation as a preacher and public speaker of unusual powers.

In the spring of 1871 he came to the United States and for ten Sundays supplied the pulpit of the Church of the Pilgrims, Brooklyn, of which Dr. Richard Salter Storrs, 1821–1900 [*q.v.*], was pastor. So impressed by his preaching were some of his hearers that they proposed building a great tabernacle for him in New York, if he would consider settling there (*Harper's Weekly*, July 18, 1874). In November 1871, however, Dr. Joseph P. Thompson [*q.v.*] relinquished the pastorate of Broadway Tabernacle, New York, and Taylor was immediately invited to be his successor. He accepted the invitation, and on Apr. 9, 1872, was formally in-

stalled. His ministry in this connection continued until 1892, when he was stricken with paralysis. Resigning on Oct. 27, he was made pastor emeritus, and died somewhat more than two years later, survived by six of his nine children.

He was a typical Scotchman of rugged character, conservative theology, analytical mind, and keen discernment. As a preacher he took rank in public esteem along with his noted neighbors, Beecher, Storrs, and John Hall [*qq.v.*]. He was a powerful expositor of the Scriptures and their practical application, a strong advocate of the written sermon, which he himself could make picturesque and glowing. His published works number more than forty, among them being *David King of Israel* (1875); *Elijah the Prophet* (1876); *The Ministry of the Word* (1876), Lyman Beecher Lectures at Yale; *Moses the Lawgiver* (1879, 1894); *The Gospel Miracles in Their Relation to Christ and Christianity* (1880), lectures at Princeton; *John Knox* (1885); *The Parables of Our Saviour Expounded and Illustrated* (1886); *The Scottish Pulpit from the Reformation to the Present Day* (1887), Lyman Beecher Lectures; *The Christian in Society* (1891); *At the End of Twenty Years* (1892); *Contrary Winds and Other Sermons* (1899); *The Limitations of Life and Other Sermons* (1904). From October 1876 to June 1880 he was editor-in-chief of *The Christian at Work*. He took an active part in the missionary activities of the Congregational churches, being a corporate member of the American Board of Commissioners for Foreign Missions (1872–95), and president of the American Missionary Association (1872–95) and of the Congregational Church Building Society (1885–95). He was also a trustee of the University of the City of New York and of Mount Holyoke College, and a manager of the Presbyterian Hospital, New York.

[W. I. Addison, *A Roll of the Grads. of the Univ. of Glasgow* (1898); S. H. Ward, *The Hist. of the Broadway Tabernacle Church* (1901); *The Congregational Year-Book, 1895* (1896); *Outlook* (N. Y.), Feb. 16, 1895; *Congregationalist*, Feb. 14, 1895; *N. Y. Tribune*, Feb. 9, 1895.]

H. E. S.

TAYLOR, WILLIAM ROGERS (Nov. 7, 1811–Apr. 14, 1889), naval officer, was born at Newport, R. I., son of Capt. William Vigneron Taylor [*q.v.*] and Abby (White) Taylor. Through the influence of his father, who spoke of him at sixteen as "a very fair French and Latin scholar" with "some knowledge of rigging and drafting" gained at the Boston Navy Yard (letters, Personnel Files, Navy Department Library), he was made midshipman Apr. 1, 1828. He was in the *Hudson* on the Brazil station,

1829–32. After brief study at the naval school in New York he became passed midshipman (1834), and then joined the *Peacock* on a cruise to the East Indies, 1835–36. When his ship grounded on Mazeira Island, Arabia, Sept. 21, 1835, he commanded a cutter which was sent to Muscat for aid and to convey thither Edmund Roberts [*q.v.*], the United States diplomatic agent (see correspondence, Roberts MSS., vol. IV, Library of Congress). The boat was at sea five days and was pursued for several hours by pirates.

Made lieutenant in 1840, Taylor was on coast survey duty for some time, then on the Brazil station. During the Mexican War he was in the *St. Mary's* at the attack on Tampico and later in command of an 8-inch gun on shore at the siege of Vera Cruz. He was promoted commander in 1855. During this decade his work was largely at Washington in ordnance, in connection with which he attained some reputation, as evidenced by Admiral Du Pont's characterization of him later as "an admirable ordnance officer" (H. A. du Pont, *Rear Admiral Samuel Francis du Pont*, 1926, p. 288). In July 1862 he was made captain and assigned to the steam sloop *Housatonic* on the Charleston blockade. Here he was at various times senior officer, notably on Jan. 31, 1863, when the blockaders were attacked by the Confederate rams *Chicora* and *Palmetto State* (see his report, *Official Records, post*, vol. XIII, pp. 587–88). He was Admiral Dahlgren's fleet captain during the operations against Morris Island, July 10–19, 1863, and afterward until he was invalided home on July 24. In May of the next year he reported to the *Juniata* at Philadelphia and commanded her during the first attack on Fort Fisher, Dec. 24–25, 1864, in which she was hulled six or seven times and lost five killed and eight wounded from the bursting of a Parrott rifle. Apparently at this time he had not fully recovered from his illness of the preceding year, for his fellow captain, Charles Steedman, in a letter of Jan. 6 speaks of his "extremely nervous temperament" and adds, "Poor Taylor has gone home completely broken down physically" (A. L. Mason, *Memoir and Correspondence of Charles Steedman*, 1912, p. 397).

After the war he was made commodore (1866), and rear admiral (1871). He commanded the northern squadron of the Pacific fleet (1869–71), was president of the examining board (1871–72), and had command of the South Atlantic station from May 1872 until his retirement for age Nov. 7, 1873. His death from paralysis occurred at his home in Washington, D. C., and he was buried in the Congressional Cemetery.

He was married Apr. 30, 1840, to Caroline, daughter of Gold S. Silliman of Brooklyn, N. Y. (*Newport Mercury*, May 16, 1840), and was survived by two daughters.

[W. S. W. Ruschenberger, *A Voyage Round the World* (1838); *War of the Rebellion: Official Records* (*Navy*), esp. 1 ser. III, XIII, XIV; L. R. Hamersly, *The Records of Living Officers of the U. S. Navy and Marine Corps* (4th ed., 1890); *Washington Post*, Apr. 16, 1889; *Army and Navy Jour.*, Apr. 20, 1889.]

A. W—t.

TAYLOR, WILLIAM VIGNERON (Apr. 11, 1780–Feb. 11, 1858), naval officer, was born at Newport, R. I., son of James and Mary (Vigneron) Taylor, and a descendant of Dr. Norbent F. Vigneron who came to Newport from Artois, France, in 1690. Both his parents belonged to the Society of Friends. From the local schools and from reading in the library of his uncle, William Vigneron, a successful seaman and merchant, he attained a good foundation of learning. At about eighteen he went to sea, and soon rose to mate and captain in the merchant service.

In the War of 1812 he was among the numerous seamen who joined the navy at Newport under Lieut. O. H. Perry [*q.v.*], his warrant as sailing-master being dated Apr. 28, 1813. His actual entry, however, was considerably earlier, for on Feb. 21, 1813, he left Newport for Sackett's Harbor, Lake Ontario, in charge of a detachment of fifty sailors. On Mar. 30 he joined Perry on Lake Erie, where, with Lieut. Daniel Turner, he had special supervision of the rigging, equipping, and arming of Perry's squadron. According to his fellow officer, Usher Parsons (*post*, p. 18), he was "more experienced than any one on the station in the duties of seamanship." In the battle of Lake Erie, Sept. 10, 1813, he was sailing master of the flagship *Lawrence*. Though wounded in the thigh, he kept the deck, and remained in the battered *Lawrence*—which had twenty-two killed and sixty-one wounded of her complement of 103—when Perry shifted his flag to the *Niagara*. The log of the *Lawrence*, largely written by Taylor, is preserved by the Newport Historical Society. With other officers in the action he received the thanks of Congress and a sword, and on Dec. 9, 1814, he was promoted to lieutenant. After the battle he returned to Erie, Sept. 23, in the *Lawrence*, which had been made hospital ship of the squadron and was then sent to Lake Ontario with dispatches. Shortly afterward he returned to Newport. In the protracted controversy between Perry and his second-in-command, Jesse D. Elliott [*q.v.*] over the conduct of the Lake Erie action, Taylor was naturally a strong partisan of Perry, his affidavit before the Rhode Island legislature in June 1818 being characterized by Elliott's biographer as "a prolix narrative . . . from a warm friend of one party and a decided enemy of the other" (*A Biographical Notice of Com. Jesse D. Elliott*, 1835, p. 217). At the close of 1814 he was engaged in fitting out the *Java* under Perry at Baltimore, and he sailed in her to the Mediterranean in 1815. From 1816 to 1823, partly because of recurrent trouble from his wound, he was on leave or nominal duty at Newport.

During the ensuing quiet naval period up to the Mexican War his sea service included a Mediterranean cruise in the *Ontario*, 1824–26; service on the Brazil station, 1829–30; and in the late thirties, command of the sloops *Erie* and *Warren* in the Gulf. He was made captain Sept. 8, 1841, and late in 1847 took the ship-of-the-line *Ohio* around Cape Horn for operations on the Mexican west coast, where he remained until the latter part of 1848, after the close of the Mexican War. Owing to age and declining health, this was his last sea service. He was placed on the reserved list Sept. 13, 1855. His funeral was in Trinity Church, Newport, which he had joined a few years before his death, and his burial was in the Island Cemetery. He was married Dec. 31, 1810, to Abby, daughter of Capt. Thomas White of Newport, and had seven children, three of whom died young; a son, William Rogers Taylor [*q.v.*], became a naval officer; another, Oliver Hazard Perry Taylor, rose to a brevet captaincy in the army and was killed May 17, 1858, in Indian warfare in Washington Territory.

[Usher Parsons, *Brief Sketches of the Officers Who Were in the Battle of Lake Erie* (1862), pub. also in *New England Hist. and Geneal. Reg.*, Jan. 1863; L. M. Mayer, "The Log of the Lawrence," *Bull. of the Newport Hist. Soc.*, Apr. 1923; *Newport Advertiser*, Feb. 17, 1858; Commandants' and Captains' Letters, Navy Dept. Lib.]   A. W—t.

TAYLOR, ZACHARY (Nov. 24, 1784–July 9, 1850), soldier and twelfth president of the United States, was born at Montebello, Orange County, Va. His ancestor, James Taylor (d. 1698), migrated from Carlisle, England, and settled on the Mattapony River in the sixteen-thirties. A son, James Taylor, served on Gov. Spotswood's staff, accompanied him on the expedition to the Blue Ridge, and purchased land on the Rapidan River. Zachary Taylor (1707–1768), son of the second James and grandfather of the future president, married Elizabeth Lee, established "Meadow Farm" plantation, and acquired twenty-six slaves. One of their four children, Richard (17.?–1829), married Mary Strother, received a degree at William and Mary, became lieutenant-colonel of a Virginia regiment in the American Revolution, served in the Virginia Assembly, and settled at "Hare Forest" estate. The third of their nine children, Zachary, was born a short time before the family migrated to Jefferson County, Ky., in the spring of 1785. There Richard established a plantation on the Muddy Fork of Beargrass Creek, acted as collector of the port of Louisville under appointment from Washington, served as a delegate in the constitutional convention of 1792, and represented his county in the legislature. Zachary received his only formal education from a tutor, Elisha Ayres of Connecticut, who declared that his pupil displayed qualities of stability, firmness, and studiousness. During the formative years in Kentucky, he assisted his father on the plantation.

Although Taylor saw brief service as a volunteer in 1806, his military career of forty years did not actually begin until two years later with an appointment as first lieutenant in the 7th Infantry. He reported to Gen. James Wilkinson at New Orleans but an outbreak of yellow fever forced him temporarily from the service. He was promoted captain in 1810, and the following year his company was placed under Gen. William Henry Harrison, governor of Indiana Territory, who assigned him command of Fort Knox. His company, numbering not more than fifty men, was soon transferred to Fort Harrison which he successfully defended against 400 Indians, Sept. 4, 1812, and as a result he was brevetted major. The following year he recruited, mustered, and inspected troops in Indiana and Illinois Territories, and assisted in the defense of the frontier from Indiana to Missouri. In August 1814, he ascended the Mississippi to destroy Indian villages at the mouth of Rock River; failing in this he returned to the mouth of the Des Moines and erected Fort Johnson. From December until the close of the War of 1812 he was again in command at Fort Knox as major, but when the army was disbanded on June 15, 1815, he was retained as captain. He declined the service but in 1816 Madison restored his former rank and ordered him to join the 3rd Infantry at Green Bay, Wis. Two years in command at Fort Winnebago were followed by a year's furlough which he spent in Kentucky. On Apr. 20, 1819, he was appointed lieutenant-colonel of the 4th Infantry and ordered to report at New Orleans. Four regimental transfers in as many years left him in the 1st Infantry where he remained for an uneventful decade. In 1822 he built Fort Jesup on the Louisiana frontier; in

1824 he served first as recruiting officer at Louisville and later on a board at Washington, headed by Gen. Winfield Scott, designed to perfect the militia organization. In 1827–28 he was again in the Southwest with headquarters at Baton Rouge, and from 1829 to 1832 in the Northwest at Fort Snelling where he acted as Indian "superintendent."

On April 4, 1832, at the age of forty-seven, Taylor was promoted colonel, given command of the 1st Regiment, and stationed at Fort Crawford (Prairie du Chien). In the Black Hawk War he commanded 400 regulars under Gen. Henry Atkinson [q.v.] and received custody of the captured Black Hawk, whom he sent to Jefferson Barracks in the charge of Jefferson Davis. His regiment was ordered to Fort Jesup in 1837, but while descending the Mississippi he received instructions dated July 31 directing him to take command of the field force in Florida. In December he set out from Fort Gardner with 1100 men, followed the Seminoles into the Everglades, defeated them in a desperate battle at Lake Okeechobee on the 25th, and captured much valuable property. For this achievement he was brevetted brigadier-general and soon thereafter (May 1838) superseded Gen. Thomas S. Jesup in command of the department. Dividing his men into several detachments he gave each a limited district to patrol, and he armed white settlers to defend themselves against assault; as a result of this policy, there were numerous skirmishes but no drawn battles. After he had served two years in Florida without accomplishing his major object, his request to be relieved of the command was reluctantly granted, Apr. 21, 1840. He was then transferred to the Southwest with headquarters at Baton Rouge. A year later he was ordered to Fort Gibson to relieve General Arbuckle, and after a brief visit of inspection he established himself and family at Fort Smith, Ark. Although he looked upon the new assignment as a mark of confidence, he accepted it reluctantly as he had hoped to continue at Baton Rouge for some time to create a sufficient competence to support himself and family in retirement. He received little cooperation from Indian agents, but with few exceptions he kept the southwestern frontier quiet during the next three years.

In May 1844 Taylor was ordered to Fort Jesup and, in anticipation of the annexation of Texas, he was directed a few months later to have his command ready to take the field on the slightest notice. Instructions from Marcy, dated May 28, 1845, ordered him to correspond with Texan authorities and repel invasion of the state after it approved annexation. On June 15 he was directed to prepare to depart for the new frontier, and a month later he left New Orleans for Corpus Christi at the mouth of the Nueces where he soon collected an army of about 4,000 men. He was ordered to advance to the Rio Grande on Jan. 13, 1846, and two months later he established a base at Point Isabel and entrenchments opposite Matamoras. On May 8 he met the Mexicans under Gen. Arista at Palo Alto and defeated a force three times the size of his own army, a victory for his artillery. The following day he was again successful at Resaca de la Palma, using artillery, dragoons, and infantry. Because of lack of preparation and insufficient troops he did not cross the Rio Grande at once, and when he did General Arista had abandoned Matamoras. As soon as Polk received official dispatches of the two engagements, he promoted Taylor major-general by brevet. In the states there was almost universal commendation of the American commander. The administration lacked confidence in him, but as it distrusted Scott also, Taylor was officially designated commander of the Army of the Rio Grande.

By the middle of June thousands of volunteers were arriving at Point Isabel but without adequate supplies or transportation into the interior, and many of them had to be disbanded without seeing service. A month later Taylor established a base at Camargo at the mouth of the San Juan. With Saltillo as a goal he departed in September with 6,000 men divided equally between regulars and volunteers, and on the 21st he attacked Monterey. After three days of skirmishing in which bayonet assaults predominated, the Mexican army, somewhat larger than the American, capitulated, and an eight weeks' armistice was arranged subject to the approval of the respective governments. Although Taylor cited cogent reasons for the lenient terms accorded the Mexicans, he was severely criticized by the administration and five days before the end of the armistice he received orders to terminate it. The situation might have served as a pretext for superseding him had it not been for his growing popularity at home. The publication of his letter of Nov. 5 to General Gaines in the *New York Morning Express*, Jan. 22, 1847, defending the Monterey armistice and attacking the administration for lack of support, increased the tension between President and commander.

Meanwhile, Gen. Scott had been commissioned to lead an expedition against Mexico city and empowered to draw upon Taylor's army for a part of his troops. When Taylor received a communication to that effect he was disgruntled and evaded a meeting with his superior officer (Smith, *post*, I, 356, 358, 362, 540–43). Although he was advised to concentrate his remaining force at Monterey and act entirely on the defensive, he disobeyed orders by attempting to defend a line 400 miles long and thus, according to Polk, invited attack (Polk, *Diary*, II, 452; see also 433, 438, and Smith, I, 373). Advancing southward, he received word that Santa Anna was marching on him with 20,000 troops, while he had a fourth of that number. At Buena Vista, Feb. 22–23, the American army defeated the Mexicans and thus ended the war in the northern provinces. The battle was fought for the most part by volunteers, some of whom fled from the field, but it was to the small number of regular artillery that Taylor ascribed a large measure of responsibility for success. However, the victory "was due primarily to Taylor's prestige, valor and gift of inspiring confidence" (Smith, *post*, I, 395). Reluctantly Taylor remained in Mexico until November 1847, convinced that Polk, Marcy, and Scott had plotted to break him down, though he later absolved the Secretary of War from implication (Taylor to Col. J. P. Taylor, Jan. 19, 1848, in Taylor Papers). Largely unfounded as the charge was, the belief increased that he had been victimized by an administration that was jealous of his growing popularity.

Taylor's Whiggism antedated the Mexican War. He registered disapproval of Andrew Jackson and criticized the army patronage of the thirties. He believed the Whig victory of 1840 most timely, professed a deep interest in the success of Harrison's administration, recommended numerous military appointments, and regretted the breakup of the cabinet in 1841. He confessed in 1847 that he had never voted for president, but had he done so in 1844 he would have cast his ballot for Henry Clay (Fry and Conrad, *post*, p. 324). His victories early in the war convinced Whig politicians of his availability as a candidate in 1848. Popular meetings, some of them spontaneous and others inspired by leaders, assembled in the summer of 1846 to applaud his victories. As early as May of that year Thurlow Weed [*q.v.*] began to labor for his nomination (H. A. Weed, ed., *Autobiography of Thurlow Weed*, 1884, pp. 571–73). Of more significance was the indorsement of John J. Crittenden [*q.v.*], lifelong friend of Clay and universally respected for sound judgment and honest conviction. Taylor himself wrote numerous letters to soldiers, public men, and editors, much to the discomfiture of the politicians. Whether he realized it or not, there was political wisdom in his correspondence. He must have written fifty times that he was not a candidate for the presidency and doubted his qualifications for the office, but if the people spontaneously called him he would accept. He would not be the candidate of a party nor would he reach the office through any agency of his own. If called to the highest office, he would serve the people honestly and faithfully; if not he would be neither mortified nor disappointed. Especially did his letter of May 18, 1847, to the editor of the Cincinnati *Signal* (published in *Niles' National Register*, July 3, 1847, p. 288) agitate newspaper comment as its "no-party" doctrine divided Whig leaders.

Upon vital issues before the country, Taylor expressed himself too freely to please the politicians. In private correspondence with Jefferson Davis (July 27, Aug. 16, 1847, Taylor Papers), and in public letters of Apr. 22 and Sept. 4 to Capt. J. S. Allison (*Niles' National Register*, July 8, 1848, p. 8; Sept. 27, 1848, pp. 200–01), he stated his views on current problems. The national bank was a dead issue, he said, and there would be no surplus revenue from the sale of public lands to distribute. Congress was the proper authority to decide between a protective tariff and direct taxation to defray the cost of the war. Internal improvements would continue regardless of what party controlled Congress or what man was president. The executive office should return to the position of a coordinate branch of the government; the veto power should be used to protect the Constitution but sparingly for other purposes. No more territory should be taken from Mexico than that already held in the northern part. The Wilmot Proviso was "a mere bugbare" agitated to produce excitement, and would soon disappear. Although he did not believe Congress would permit slave states to be admitted from territory acquired from Mexico, he felt that the South should resort to arms if necessary to protect their rights in states where slavery already existed. He had no sympathy for extremists in either section. In the first "Allison" letter, which was widely printed, he explained his political position: "I AM A WHIG, *but not an ultra Whig*. If elected I would not be the mere President of a Party. I would endeavor to act independent of party domination. I should feel bound to administer the government untrammeled by party schemes" (*Niles' National Register*, July 8, 1848, p. 8).

Meanwhile, Henry Clay's silence led politicians to believe that he would be a candidate; his visit to Philadelphia and New York in the summer of 1847 was ominous; and his announcement of a Whig platform in his Lexington speech of Nov. 13 placed him definitely before the country. When discussion of a Whig nominating convention began early in 1847, Taylor expressed opposition, viewing the movement as a plot of the politicians to defeat him. Nevertheless, he finally concluded that he would not dictate to the people how he should be nominated, and if the Whigs named him without pledges he would accept. He would not withdraw from the contest, however, if neither major party nominated him. When the Whigs met in Philadelphia on June 7, 1848, he led the field on the first ballot and was nominated on the fourth over Clay, Scott, and Webster. Since no platform was adopted, reliance had to be placed on the hazy statements of the candidate. On Sept. 4, he wrote a second "Allison" letter which explained the history of his candidacy, his consistency in accepting the Whig nomination, his freedom from party pledges, and the non-partisan character of his administration if elected (*Niles' National Register*, Sept. 27, 1848). His victory over Lewis Cass [*q.v.*] in November was promoted by divisions in the New York Democracy and by the support of Taylor Democrats, largely making good the defection of anti-slavery Whigs to the Free Soil party and Van Buren. He carried exactly half of the states, seven in the North and eight in the South. In his brief inaugural address of Mar. 5, 1849, he advocated efficient military and naval establishments, friendly relations with foreign powers, capacity, fidelity, and honesty as qualifications for office-holding, the encouragement of agriculture, commerce, and manufactures, and congressional conciliation of sectional controversies (Richardson, *post*, V, 4–6). The Washington *Daily Union* (Mar. 6, 1849) observed that the address consisted of noncommittal platitudes, and noted an ultra-Whig spirit of federalism; Whig papers applauded its moderation, simple style, and strict adherence to Whig principles.

Although Taylor did not discuss cabinet making openly until after his election, he had informed Davis that should he be chosen, he would compose it entirely of Whigs. The party leaders had accepted Taylor largely upon the indorsement of Crittenden, and it was generally understood that the latter would accept the premiership. Emphasizing the President's inexperience in civil affairs and his unacquaintance with political leaders and methods, both Democrats and Whigs warned the Kentucky statesman that as he would be held responsible for the success of the administration, he should consent to head it. But as he had just been elected governor of Kentucky he declined a place in the cabinet, and John M. Clayton [*q.v.*] of Delaware was appointed secretary of state. Of the seven ministers four were from slaveholding states. Taylor expected his cabinet to be "harmonious, honorable, patriotic, talented, & *hard working*" (A. T. Burnley to Crittenden, Jan. 12, 1849, Crittenden Papers). Though it measured up to his specifications in some respects, in others it was decidedly inferior. It was harmonious and industrious, but it contained no man of outstanding ability, a scandal broke during its brief tenure, and worst of all it made no effort to conciliate the legislative branch. Clayton promised that he would "be as independent of Congress as a wood-sawyer" (Clayton to Crittenden, Aug. 23, 1849, Crittenden Papers). Before Taylor had been in office a month many individuals, including the Secretary of State, were urging Crittenden to hasten to Washington to set the Whig household in order, and by the time he faced his first and only Congress, dissension and discord existed among party leaders and rumors of cabinet reorganization were rife. Democratic papers asserted that in making appointments and forming policies, the President had only one vote in the cabinet council and that the ministers constituted a regency. Nonpartisan declarations during the campaign led to charges of proscription by both Democratic and independent papers. Although Taylor may have entertained idealistic notions on the subject of appointments and removals, he had concluded by May 1849 that it was necessary to fill all offices with his own partisans. As the *National Intelligencer* opposed Taylor's nomination and disagreed with many of his political views, a new official organ, *The Republic*, was established with Alexander C. Bullitt and John Sargent as editors. A. T. Burnley of Kentucky, an enthusiastic Taylor partisan during the campaign, owned a third interest in the paper. A prospectus appeared on Apr. 14 pledging it to support the "liberalizing" campaign doctrines. Friction soon developed between the cabinet and the official organ, and as a result there was little intercourse and no cooperation between the two. Outside of the cabinet the President's most intimate advisers were Burnley and Orlando Brown, commissioner of Indian affairs.

By 1849 Taylor's attitude toward the Wilmot Proviso experienced serious modification. In letters to Davis he said in July 1847 that it "amounts to nothing" (Going, *David Wilmot*, pp. 234–35); in April 1848 that nature had excluded slavery from the new Southwest. Soon after his inauguration it was apparent that he would not veto the Proviso should a bill containing it be presented to him. In a public speech at Mercer, Pa., in August 1849, while he was touring Pennsylvania and New York ostensibly to acquaint himself with the material needs of the people but in reality for political effect, he declared that Northern people *"need have no apprehension of the further extension of slavery"* (*Pittsburgh Daily Gazette,* Sept. 3, 1849). Hoping to prevent sectional agitation of the question, he dispatched an emissary, Thomas Butler King, to counsel the Californians to form a state constitution and apply for statehood, and inhabitants of New Mexico were similarly encouraged. In his message to Congress, Dec. 4, 1849, Taylor recommended that both be admitted into the Union if they presented governments republican in form (Richardson, V, 18–19). In special messages to the House and Senate, Jan. 21 and 23, 1850 (*Ibid.,* V, 26–30), he again urged the unconditional admission of California, and suggested statehood for New Mexico in order that the boundary dispute with Texas could be settled by the Supreme Court. Five months later he recommended that the United States maintain possession of the disputed territory until the boundary was established (*Ibid.,* V, 47–48).

Meanwhile, Southern representatives led by Alexander H. Stephens [*q.v.*] organized a filibuster to prevent a vote on the admission of California and to insist that all proposals affecting the Mexican cession be combined in a single measure. In April delegates from a Southern caucus had called upon the President to warn him of the loss of Southern Whig support if he persisted in his plan to admit California and New Mexico as states and continued his hostile attitude toward Texas; and Stephens and Robert Toombs called on him in July, as they had earlier, threatening secession (A. C. Cole, *The Whig Party in the South,* 1913, pp. 166–67). Taylor was obstinate, and when Secretary of War George W. Crawford [*q.v.*] refused to revoke an earlier order recognizing the Rio Grande to its source as the Texan boundary, Taylor himself signed the order to prevent a cabinet rupture. Before the separate measures known as the Compromise of 1850 passed, Taylor had died. On July 4 he attended a ceremony connected with the building of the Washington Monument. He felt the heat, drank much cold water, and afterward ate cherries and drank iced milk. That night he was attacked by cholera morbus and fever, from which he died July 9. He had decided, however, a few days before his death, to

reorganize his cabinet. The "Galphin claim" brought the matter to an issue as three members were implicated in what appeared to be a scandal. Crawford had a pecuniary interest in the claim, and upon Attorney General Reverdy Johnson's opinion, William Meredith, secretary of the treasury, paid it without investigating its merits. According to Weed, who says the President sought his counsel, all members were to be superseded, with diplomatic posts for those not involved (*Autobiography of Thurlow Weed,* pp. 589–93).

Although Taylor's administration muddled through foreign relations with only a fair degree of success, Clayton performed more creditably as a diplomat than as a politician. The President was unacquainted with diplomatic procedure, but he followed the trends of foreign affairs closely, and several times his dominating influence either encouraged Clayton's own tactlessness or seriously embarrassed the Secretary of State. His arbitrary attitude in the Poussin affair might have led to serious trouble with France had not negotiations taken a fortunate turn (Bemis, *post,* VI, 18–31); his uncompromising position on claims against Portugal was unwarranted and unfair; his stand in supporting Clayton, over the advice of other cabinet members in demanding the release of alleged filibusters captured by a Spanish vessel on the coast of Mexico, may have been unnecessarily bold. In general Clayton had a free hand in negotiating the treaty of 1850 with Bulwer, the most significant achievement of the administration in foreign affairs.

On June 18, 1810, Taylor was married to Margaret Mackall Smith (1787–1852), descendant of a prominent Maryland family. Of their six children, two died in childhood; the three daughters who survived, Ann Mackall, Sarah Knox, and Mary Elizabeth, married army men: Robert C. Wood, Jefferson Davis, and William Bliss. Their only son, Richard Taylor [*q.v.*], became lieutenant-general in the Confederate army. Taylor owned sundry tracts of land in Jefferson County, Ky., but in 1840 he established his residence at Baton Rouge and purchased a cotton plantation, "Cypress Grove," near Rodney, Miss., forty miles above Natchez. The latter proved a bad investment as the river overflowed and ruined his crops nearly every year in the forties. Taylor was muscular and stocky and in early years possessed an iron constitution that won for him the sobriquet of "Old Rough and Ready" in the Seminole War. He seldom appeared in full military dress, and he preferred the discussion of agricultural prospects to military achievement. Although his experience prior to the Mexican War had been limited to frontier fighting, there is evidence of ability to comprehend larger problems. Dissatisfied with the military establishment of the Jackson period, he submitted to a member of Congress an elaborate and meritorious plan for army reorganization. In 1841, while stationed at Fort Smith, he worked out a practical plan for the defense of the frontier from Missouri to Louisiana. He placed little reliance in volunteers but freely criticized West Point graduates. His letters were legible and fairly well composed considering his slender education, but it was fortunate that he had an intelligent, well-informed and loyal adjutant-general, Major Bliss, whose skilled pen colored official dispatches with the glamor necessary to promote Taylor's reputation. Without political background or experience, his practical wisdom, common sense, honest simplicity, and resolute purpose served him well during his brief public career, but were insufficient to produce the leadership demanded by the crisis of 1850. He looked to George Washington as a model, and admiring contemporaries convinced themselves of many analogies existing between the warrior of the Revolution and the hero of Buena Vista.

[The latest biography is O. O. Howard, *General Taylor* (1892). The principal contemporary accounts, many of which contain letters and military reports, are: C. F. Powell, *Life of Major-General Zachary Taylor* (1846); An Officer of the U. S. A., *Life and Public Services of Gen. Z. Taylor* (1846); Henry Montgomery, *The Life of Major General Zachary Taylor* (1847); J. R. Fry and R. T. Conrad, *A Life of Gen. Zachary Taylor* (1847); *Taylor and his Generals* (1847); John Frost, *Life of Major General Zachary Taylor* (1847, reprinted with slight modifications and varying titles as late as 1887); *The Life and Public Services of Major General Zachary Taylor* (1847); *The Life of Gen. Zachary Taylor, and a History of the War in Mexico* (1847). Of the manuscript sources, the Zachary Taylor, John J. Crittenden, Henry Clay, and John M. Clayton Papers, in the Lib. of Cong., are most pertinent. The Deed and Will Books of Orange County, Va., Jefferson County, Ky., Jefferson County, Miss., and East Baton Rouge Parish, La., contain land transfers, wills, etc. Copies of the family genealogical records are deposited in the courthouse at Orange, Va. *Some Eminent Sons of Orange* (1919), contains a sketch of Taylor by Daniel Grinnan. Valuable published sources are: *Letters of Zachary Taylor from the Battlefields of the Mexican War. Reprinted from the Originals in the Collection of Mr. William K. Bixby, of St. Louis, Mo.* (1908), with introduction by W. H. Samson; Mrs. Chapman Coleman, *The Life of John J. Crittenden . . . Correspondence and Speeches* (2 vols., 1871); J. D. Richardson, *A Compilation of the Messages and Papers of the Presidents* (1897), vol. V; M. M. Quaife, ed., *The Diary of James K. Polk* (4 vols., 1910). There are valuable notes in Mary W. Williams, "John Middleton Clayton," in S. F. Bemis, ed., *The American Secretaries of State and Their Diplomacy*, vol. VI (1928); and J. H. Smith, *The War With Mexico* (2 vols., 1919). See also R. M. Johnston, *Leading American Soldiers* (1907).]

W. H. S—n.

TAZEWELL, HENRY (Nov. 27, 1753–Jan. 24, 1799), lawyer, judge, senator, son of Littleton and Mary (Gray) Tazewell, was born in Brunswick County, Va., of which county his father was the clerk. His grandfather, William Tazewell, had emigrated from England to Northampton County c. 1715, but his ancestor Nathaniel Littleton, a descendant of Sir Thomas Littleton, the author of the *Tenures,* had been sheriff of Accomac County in 1636. The line of descent exhibits a procession of lawyers and court officers that imposed almost a hereditary compulsion upon the careers of Henry Tazewell and his son, Littleton Waller Tazewell [*q.v.*]. After a course at William and Mary, which he finished in 1770, Tazewell studied law in the office of his uncle, John Tazewell, later a judge of the general court. In January 1774, he married Dorothy (or Dorothea) Elizabeth Waller, daughter of Benjamin Waller, later presiding judge of the court of admiralty. Tazewell then began the practice of law in his native county of Brunswick, and the following year, after a severe contest, was elected to the General Assembly.

Revolution was in the air; but though Tazewell had raised and been commissioned captain of a troop of cavalry, he was of the element that still hoped for conciliation. As the author of resolutions in this sense, he was the object of a hasty attack by Jefferson in the Assembly of 1775, but met it with a manly independence that won him for life the high regard of that statesman. (For evidences of their later friendship, see A. A. Lipscomb, ed., in *The Writings of Thomas Jefferson,* IX, 1903, pp. 308, 365.) The revolutionary convention of 1776 was unanimous in its declaration of independence; and Tazewell became a member of the important committee named to frame a constitution and bill of rights for the state.

He represented Brunswick in the General Assembly until 1778, when he removed to Williamsburg, and was almost immediately elected to represent that borough in the same body, and continued to do so until his election to the old general court in 1785. The tribute was the more notable in that his practice had been subjected to severe interruptions by the removal of the capital to Richmond and the frequent closing of the courts in Williamsburg as the result of military operations. His state-wide reputation and popularity were established and enhanced by his service on the reorganized general court, created in 1788, the judges of which "rode the circuits" into which the state was divided. The next year he became the chief justice of the general court, and in 1793 was appointed to the court of appeals. Meanwhile he had served as one of the revisors of the law, the revision of 1792 being in principal part the work of his hands. On the simultaneous retirement of James Monroe and John Taylor of Caroline from the United States Senate, each of them requested Tazewell to stand for his place. Choosing Taylor's, he was elected by a large majority for the unexpired term and took his seat on Dec. 29, 1794. Tazewell had been opposed to the ratification by Virginia of the federal Constitution, and his views brought him, on entering the Senate, into opposition to the administration and the Federalist majority. In keeping with the Virginia position, he opposed the ratification of the Jay treaty. But notwithstanding these circumstances, he was, on Feb. 20, 1795, elected president *pro tempore*, and reëlected the following December. Reëlected in 1798 for the full term, he contracted a severe cold in traveling to Philadelphia to resume his duties, and died of pleurisy a few days after arrival in that city. He was buried there in Christ Church yard.

It has been said that Tazewell's posthumous reputation has been overshadowed by that of his distinguished son; but it was rather his being cut off in mid-career that has narrowed for posterity the place that he undoubtedly held among his contemporaries. Never defeated in a political contest, he was probably the most popular Virginian of his day, and this without surrender of strong opinions strongly held. Gifted and genial, he maintained a dignity that impressed without offending, and achieved general recognition of his ability while avoiding all appearance of asserting it. Ambition was cloaked in dedication to the public service. Never has any other Virginian achieved at so early an age so impressive a series of political and judicial honors.

[The most important source is the account (41 closely written pages) in the manuscript "Sketches of his Own Family," written by Gov. L. W. Tazewell in 1823, two copies of which are in the possession of descendants in Norfolk, Va. Printed sources include H. B. Grigsby, *The Va. Convention of 1776* (1855), a brief notice, inaccurate in some respects; *The History of the Va. Federal Convention of 1788* (2 vols., 1890–91), and *Discourse on the Life and Character of the Hon. Littleton Waller Tazewell* (1860). D. G. Tyler, "Henry Tazewell," *Proc. Va. State Bar Asso. . . . 1928,* vol. XL, follows Grigsby. See also R. B. Tunstall, "Henry Tazewell," in A. W. Weddell, ed., *A Memorial Volume of Va. Historical Portraiture* (1930); a thumb-nail sketch in 4 *Call's Va. Reports,* pp. xxiii–xxiv; and, for genealogical data, *Va. Mag. of Hist. and Biography,* Jan. 1910, pp. 20–23.]

R. B. T.

TAZEWELL, LITTLETON WALLER (Dec. 17, 1774–May 6, 1860), lawyer, senator,

governor of Virginia, son of Henry Tazewell [*q.v.*] and Dorothy Elizabeth (Waller) Tazewell, was born in Williamsburg, Va. His mother's death in 1777 and his father's many public employments led to his being placed under the tutelage of his maternal grandfather, Judge Benjamin Waller. To the intimate relation between them, terminated by Judge Waller's death in Tazewell's twelfth year, he attributed "whatever worthy of imitation there may be in any part of my character" ("Sketches of His Own Family," *post*). From his twelfth to his fifteenth year he was under the personal instruction of Chancellor George Wythe, with whom for a time he made his home. In his eighteenth year (1791) he graduated B.A. from William and Mary—a degree then of such difficulty that his was one of very few conferred by the college for many years. After completing his legal studies in the office of John Wickham in Richmond, Tazewell obtained his license in May 1796. Brilliant, handsome, an adept in manly sports, he was already a conspicuous young man.

From 1798 to 1800 he represented James City County in the House of Delegates, and in the latter year was elected to Congress to succeed John Marshall. Remaining but one session (Nov. 26, 1800–Mar. 3, 1801), he removed to Norfolk in 1802 and married Anne Stratton Nivison, daughter of one of its leading lawyers. They had several children. The ravages of war and fire had brought about in Norfolk an approach to pioneer conditions, which combined with the disturbance of its commerce by the country's unsettled foreign relations during the Napoleonic wars to produce a rich field for the lawyer. To the routine of civil and criminal work were added cases involving admiralty and international law. As early as 1805 William Wirt describes Tazewell as at the head of the local bar (J. P. Kennedy, *Memoirs of the Life of William Wirt,* 1856, vol. I, 126). But about the year 1822 Tazewell withdrew from general practice, though he appeared occasionally in noteworthy cases. One of the most famous cases in which he took part, was that of *The Santissima Trinidad* (7 *Wheaton,* 283).

He served in the General Assembly from 1804 to 1806 and again in 1816–17, being elected on the latter occasion without his knowledge and during his absence from the city. In 1807 he was the spokesman of the city in its spirited defiance of the British fleet after the attack on the *Chesapeake* by the *Leopard*, conducting negotiations with Capt. Sir Thomas Hardy, of Trafalgar fame (*Calendar of Virginia State Papers,* vol. IX, 1890, pp. 568 ff.). But in general his part during his professional career was that of a thoughtful and detached observer, with a notable indifference to party lines. By inheritance and principle an anti-Federalist, he nevertheless opposed many important policies of Jefferson's administration, notably the Embargo of 1807 and the Non-Intercourse Act, favoring rather a declaration of war against both Great Britain and France. He opposed the election of Madison, and also the War of 1812, deeming that the time for action had passed; but when war was declared he loyally supported it. Monroe appointed him in 1821 as one of the commissioners under the eleventh article of the treaty of 1819 with Spain.

In 1824 Tazewell was elected to fill the vacancy in the United States Senate caused by the death of John Taylor of Caroline, whom his father had likewise succeeded upon Taylor's resignation from the Senate thirty years before. Relishing debate and excelling in it, he took place with the parliamentary giants of the day and was recognized as one of the leaders of a group opposing President Adams (B. C. Clark, *John Quincy Adams*, 1932, p. 241). As a member (later chairman) of the committee on foreign affairs, he drafted the report against the Panama mission. Later he published in the *Norfolk Herald* a carefully written series of articles subsequently reprinted in England as *A Review of the Negociations between the United States of America and Great Britain, Respecting the Commerce of the Two Countries* (1829). Reelected in 1829, he became president *pro tempore* on July 9, 1832, but resigned shortly thereafter, alleging the pressure of personal affairs. It is probable that more lay behind. He had supported Jackson for the presidency, and had been offered successively the posts of secretary of war and minister to Great Britain, both of which he had declined. But one whose state-rights views were so instinctive that he habitually referred to Virginia as his "country" could not brook the imperious leadership of the toaster of "Our Federal Union." He opposed nullification, but more strongly still he opposed coercion; and Jackson's proclamation of Dec. 10, 1832, drew from him a weighty reply (*Norfolk and Portsmouth Herald*, Dec. 28, 1832–Jan. 30, 1833; reprinted in 1888 as *A Review of the Proclamation of President Jackson*).

During his senatorial term he had served as a member of the notable constitutional convention of 1829–30, in which he spoke not often, but always impressively. Significant as evidence of contemporary estimation was his membership on the important committee of seven appointed to draft the new constitution. On Jan. 7, 1834, he was elected governor of Virginia. The times were stormy. The movement for abolition was growing; federal encroachments were increasing; and the request of the General Assembly that the governor forward instructions to the Virginia senators on the expunging resolution brought the climax. On Feb. 22, 1836, he declined to forward the resolutions, and on Mar. 30 resigned, without explanation (Letter to Wyndham Robertson, Va. State Library). For nearly twenty-five years longer he enjoyed in Norfolk the retirement he had repeatedly sought. Indisputably its first citizen, he was the recipient of local veneration that passed almost into apotheosis.

Tazewell's fame must rest largely on the estimate of his contemporaries. He can claim the paternity of no enduring policy. Such of his writings as have been collected from newspapers and periodicals, while accurate and substantial, are inescapably the work of a lawyer who could or would not disguise the lawyer's heavy hand. His legal arguments, mostly in local courts, are almost wholly lost. Yet of his contemporary reputation there can be no doubt. John Randolph of Roanoke held him "second to no man that ever breathed" (W. C. Bruce, *John Randolph of Roanoke*, 1922, I, 461). William Wirt placed him, as a lawyer, first in Southern estimation, as Webster was in Northern (J. P. Kennedy, *Memoirs of the Life of William Wirt*, II, 121). John Marshall and Spencer Roane are said to have agreed, perhaps for the only time in their lives, that he was "unsurpased . . . by any competitor of his day" (Grigsby, *post*, p. 113). Hugh Blair Grigsby, in his memorial discourse, has added corroborative testimony of other eminent contemporaries. The stress is on his intellectual powers. The only shadow is itself a tribute to his genius for dialectics: a suggestion that the massive and versatile intellect so loved triumph for its own sake as at times to be unheeding of the ultimate right.

But it is noteworthy that his contemporaries repeatedly indulged in discussions of his self-effacement and doubts as to his career. Coldness, lack of broad human sympathy, perhaps a little of the public suspicion that dogs the path of brilliancy, are all put forward to account for Tazewell's failure to take and hold the place to which they felt him entitled. Undoubtedly there is lack of human appeal, not to speak of the "saving element of common sense," in logical processes so severe as to lead a public man to oppose, as did Tazewell, the celebration of George Washington's centenary because it savored of "man worship" (*Register of Debates in Congress*, 22 Cong., 1 Sess., col. 297). Appearing rather awe-inspiring for a democratic society, he made no effort to alter the impression. Unlike his father, to whom we may believe that the implications of the new republic were thoroughly congenial, Tazewell was an extreme individualist, wholly unaffected by trends of social thought. In him the English ancestors reasserted themselves. In a non-elective legislative body, like the House of Lords, freed from the importunity of constituents, he would have left an impress on the times in which he lived. But no urgency of desire impelled him to the compromises, even had he been capable of them, ordinarily required for repeated elections; and the daily legislative grind would have brought to him a tedium not easily endured. He keenly felt the duty to serve, if called upon; he may have secretly hoped for the call; but he would not invite it. What his friends viewed as a career of negations and abnegations was in fact a life, indifferent to official place, in which duty formed the sole impelling motive.

[Tazewell's own manuscript, "Sketches of His Own Family" (referred to in the sketch of Henry Tazewell), is the best account up to his twenty-second year, where it ends. Considerable manuscript material is in the possession of descendants in Norfolk, some in the Univ. of Va. Lib., and his correspondence as governor is in the Va. State Lib. The principal secondary source is H. B. Grigsby, *Discourse on the Life and Character of the Hon. Littleton Waller Tazewell* (1860), a work displaying both the advantages and the disadvantages of intimate personal knowledge. Its appendices contain valuable contemporary estimates, of which that by Wirt should be compared with a striking and intimate letter from him to Francis W. Gilmer, Mar. 16, 1820, in the Lib. of the Univ. of Va. Brief sketches are Richard Walke, in *Va. Law Register*, Nov. 1898, p. 409; R. A. Brock, *Virginia and Virginians* (2 vols., 1888); L. G. Tyler, in *Hist. of Va.* (6 vols., 1924), vol. II, ch. 7; and R. B. Tunstall, "Littleton Waller Tazewell," in A. W. Weddell, ed., *A Memorial Volume of Va. Hist. Portraiture* (1930).]   R. B. T.

TEALL, FRANCIS AUGUSTUS (Aug. 16, 1822–Nov. 16, 1894), editor, was born at Fort Ann, Washington County, N. Y., the fifth of the eight children of Horace Valentine and Sarah Buyss (Shaw) Teall and a great-grandson of Oliver Teall, a druggist, who emigrated from England to New Haven about 1723. Horace Valentine Teall was a minister of the sect founded by Abner Jones [*q.v.*], but, persuaded by the arguments of William Miller [*q.v.*], confidently awaited the second Advent in the early forties. Francis, meanwhile, attended schools at Rhinebeck and Schenectady, learned the printer's trade, and went to New York in 1841 to seek larger opportunities. There, on one of his first jobs, he worked beside Walt Whitman at the composing-case and was later advanced to the proof-reader's desk. Toward the close of 1844 he joined the staff of George Hooker Colton's *American Review: A Whig Journal*; years afterward he recalled how, after passing the final proofs of "The Raven" for the February 1845 issue, he had, as a matter of routine, dropped Poe's manuscript into the wastebasket. He was employed on the *New York Recorder* during the editorship of Martin Brewer Anderson [*q.v.*], who remembered him gratefully and in 1875, as president of the University of Rochester, conferred on him the honorary degree of A.M. Teall was married about 1850 to Orcelia Shaw of West Troy, N. Y., by whom he had a daughter and three sons. In 1853 he became editor of the Huntington *Long Islander*. His next position of importance was on the *New York Tribune,* where the astonishingly broad and exact scholarship that he concentrated on proof-reading soon won the admiration of his associates.

When George Ripley and Charles Anderson Dana [*qq.v.*] contracted in 1857 to edit the *American Cyclopædia* for D. Appleton & Company, they engaged Teall to take charge of the proofs. Not only did he read critically every line of both editions of the *Cyclopædia*, but he also contributed a number of articles and performed other editorial duties. In 1882 he published an American edition, much annotated, of William B. Hodgson's *Errors in the Use of English.* Over a period of many years he gathered great stores of material for a treatise on punctuation and for a vast dictionary of proper names, but neither work was ever completed. Among printers and publishers he was held to have raised proof-reading to the rank of a learned profession, and many anecdotes were told to illustrate his omniscience and his passion for accuracy and consistency. On the organization of the staff of the *Century Dictionary* in 1882, William Dwight Whitney and Benjamin Eli Smith [*qq.v.*] inevitably chose him to supervise the proofs. He also wrote the preliminary definitions of most of the common words as far as the letter M, and remained with the *Dictionary* until its completion. After his wife's death in 1887 he made his home with his son in Bloomfield, N. J., where he died. As the result of a broken hip he was an invalid for the last year of his life.

[James Boughton, *Bouton-Boughton Family* (1890); D. P. Worden, *Descendants of Oliver Teall and Allied Families* (1922); *Evening Post* (N. Y.), Nov. 16, 1894; *N. Y. Daily Tribune*, Nov. 17, 1894; *Appletons' Ann. Cyc. . . . 1894* (1895).]   G. H. G.

TEASDALE, SARA (Aug. 8, 1884–Jan. 29, 1933), poet, was born in St. Louis, Mo., the youngest child of John Warren Teasdale and Mary Elizabeth (Willard) Teasdale, both of whom had soldier-ancestors in the Revolutionary War. Being a shy and sensitive child, never strong, she was tutored at home and later attended a private school nearby, from which she was graduated in 1903. She began to write verse in school. In 1905 she made a first visit to Europe and the Near East which enriched her imaginative background. Upon her return in 1907 William Marion Reedy [*q.v.*] introduced her in *Reedy's Mirror* with "Guenevere," a blank-verse monologue of about seventy lines. Soliloquies by Sappho, Helen, Beatrice, and other far-off heroines soon followed, to be collected in her first book, *Sonnets to Duse and Other Poems* (1907), a further exhibit of her girlish imaginary loves, for she had never seen the Italian actress when she wrote the nine poems in her honor. This book and *Helen of Troy and Other Poems* (1911) offered a mere hint of the lyric talent which was to develop under a richer experience of life and a closer study of her medium. Except for two or three winters in New York from 1911 to 1913, she lived in St. Louis with her parents until her marriage to Ernst B. Filsinger, Dec. 19, 1914. Her husband's business as an exporter soon called him to New York, where for years they lived happily together. Gradually, however, the two were separated; the wife's frail health made her more and more a recluse, and the husband's business required long absences abroad. At last, Sept. 5, 1929, they were divorced.

Meanwhile, Sara Teasdale had published four other books of original poems, in addition to two compilations, *The Answering Voice: One Hundred Love Lyrics by Women* (1917), and *Rainbow Gold* (1922), an anthology of poems for children. In *Rivers to the Sea* (1915) there is evidence of the beginning of a hardening process which was shaping the girl into a woman and her enthusiastic outpourings into poems—poems of a finished and delicate, if narrow, technique. In *Love Songs* (1917) and in the more austere *Flame and Shadow* (1920) she expressed her sensitive reactions to life with the economy of phrase and the simple lyric intensity of a matured art. In *Dark of the Moon* (1926) her technique became still more subtle, her choice of words more exact and distinguished, and her rhythms more delicately harmonized. In all these books she used the simplest lyric forms—usually two or three quatrains of three- or four-footed iambic lines, each quatrain emphasized by a single rhyme. In June 1932 she went to London for research work toward a biographical study of Christina Rossetti, whose "Christmas Carol"— "In the bleak mid-winter Frosty wind made moan"—had first inspired her, as a child, with

a love of poetry. There an attack of pneumonia prostrated her, and at her desire she was taken back to New York. Her recovery, which was slow and incomplete, led to sleeplessness and an overwrought nervous condition. On the morning of Jan. 29, 1933, she was found dead, apparently as the result of an overdose of a sleeping-draft. Her body was cremated. Her last book, *Strange Victory* (1933), which was published after her death, shows her characteristic emphasis upon the inviolateness, the essential aloofness of the human soul amid perishable things and fugitive emotions. All her poems, which bear a record of spiritual experience and growth, are intimately personal and confessional, from the love songs which serve as an "answering voice" for the countless masculine poems of love in English, to the later lyrics which present with impassioned intensity her rather stark philosophy, her courageous outlook upon the mystery of life and death.

[*Who's Who in America*, 1932–33; "Sara Teasdale," pamphlet printed in 1927 by the Macmillan Company; Louis Untermeyer, *American Poetry Since 1900* (1923); Harriet Monroe, *Poets and Their Art* (1926); *New Republic*, and *Commonweal*, Feb. 15, 1933; obituary in *New York Times*, Jan. 30, 1933; information from John Hall Wheelock and from Sara Teasdale's sister.]
H. M.

TECUMSEH (Mar. 1768?–Oct. 5, 1813), Shawnee chief, was the brother, usually said to be the twin brother, of Tenskwatawa [*q.v.*], the Prophet. His name is more properly spelled Tikamthi or Tecumtha. The place of his birth and the circumstances of his youth are not surely known, although it has been claimed that the remnant of his tribe maintain a valid tradition that he was born at the great springs near Old Chillicothe, now Oldtown, Ohio (Galloway, *post*, p. 108). His mother may have been a Creek but more probably was a Shawnee, and there seems to be no adequate evidence of any admixture of white blood in his veins. His father, Pucksinwa, also a Shawnee chief, was killed at the battle of Point Pleasant in 1774. By the time the boy reached adult life he had attained distinction as a warrior; and, from the testimony of his hereditary enemies, the white settlers, it is clear that he had established a remarkable reputation for mercy and humanity, that he had set his face against the torture of prisoners and other cruel practices of border warfare, and that his word was trusted on both sides of the frontier. Early in 1805 he and his brother, with a group of followers, were living in a Delaware village at the west fork of the White River, now in Indiana. Later in the year they removed to Greenville, Ohio. In 1808 they were forced by the white settlers to take themselves farther into the Indian country, within the present state of Indiana. With the permission of the Potawatomi and the Kickapoo they settled on the Wabash near the mouth of the Tippecanoe at a place afterward known as Prophet's Town. For many years white observers, both American and British, recognized only the importance of the Prophet, and as late as August 1810 William Henry Harrison [*q.v.*], then governor of Indiana Territory, referred to Tecumseh as "the Prophet's brother" ("Messages," *post,* I, 460, 470).

Nevertheless, it is clear that Tenskwatawa's religious revival was only an episode in the history of religious revivals, whereas Tecumseh developed a philosophy and a program that threatened to stop the westward thrust of American agricultural settlement. His argument was logical and eloquently defended. He maintained, with historical justification, that no sale or cession of Indian land could be valid without the consent of all the tribes assembled, since the Indians owned the land in common and no particular region belonged to any tribe. Before the white man came each tribe roamed wherever it willed, restrained only by the exigencies of the situation or the location of more powerful tribes; century by century the homelands of almost every tribe shifted and changed. Moreover, he pointed out that at the making of the treaty of Greenville in 1795 the United States government had negotiated with all the tribes assembled and had guaranteed to all the tribes together the title to unceded land. It was only later that frontier leaders saw the implications of such a precedent and set to work to mend matters. Harrison wrote that, when he became governor of Indiana Territory, he "at once determined, that the community of interests in the lands amongst the Indian tribes, which seemed to be recognized by the treaty of Greenville, should be objected to" ("Messages," *post,* II, 639; for Tecumseh's theory see *Ibid.,* I, 460, 465–66; McAfee, *post,* p. 9; Drake, *post,* pp. 121, 124, 231–32).

Tecumseh sought to combine the tribes into a confederacy to prevent land cessions and to develop Indian character and stamina against the temptation offered by the white settlers. To this end he visited the various tribes and brought more and more of them within the scope of his plans. Also he was increasingly successful in his efforts to persuade his immediate followers at Tippecanoe, the "Prophet's Town," to stop drinking the white man's rum, to establish themselves in an agricultural life, and to live on what they earned. On Aug. 7, 1811, Harrison, his worst enemy, wrote: "The implicit obedience

and respect which the followers of Tecumseh pay to him is really astonishing and more than any other circumstance bespeaks him one of those uncommon geniuses, which spring up occasionally to produce revolutions and overturn the established order of things. If it were not for the vicinity of the United States, he would, perhaps, be the founder of an Empire that would rival in glory Mexico or Peru. No difficulties deter him" ("Messages," *post,* p. 549). His was a simple program, but it was the beginning of adaptation to civilization. He hoped that the Indians might be unmolested by the white people for a little while and might find a way to escape decadence and destruction.

To support his theory and his program he looked to the aid of British arms and British diplomacy. Hard pressed by the Napoleonic wars, British officials in Canada steered an uneasy course, trying to keep the Indians from actual warfare without running any risk of losing their support in case Great Britain went to war with the United States. Out of such a troubled situation Tecumseh expected to obtain much. From the documents, the orders, and the reports of the period, it is difficult to determine what promises were made, openly and by implication, and what hopes were nourished in his heart. In 1816 Robert Breckinridge McAfee [*q.v.*] wrote that Tecumseh had believed he could, with British aid, drive the Americans south of the Ohio River, and that "from the *sine qua non* advanced by the British commissioners in the negotiation at Ghent, it would appear, that the British ministry had indulged a delusion not much less extravagant" (McAfee, *post,* pp. 14–15; see Public Record Office report of confidential board, CO, 42:150, and letter of Cochrane to Bathurst, July 14, 1814, WO, 1:141). The existence of a powerful Indian confederation such as the one destroyed at Tippecanoe would have lent point to the British proposals for the international guarantee of an Indian buffer state in the old Northwest. Tecumseh's purpose was to avoid war with the United States "until he should effect a combination strong enough to resist them, or until the expected war with Great Britain should commence" (McAfee, *post,* p. 15). In the years from 1803 to 1811, during which Harrison negotiated with individual tribes one treaty of cession after another, some fifteen in all, Tecumseh constantly took his troubles to the British officials in Canada for advice and sympathy; and he constantly received supplies of arms, ammunition, and clothing from the royal warehouses. After a stormy scene at Vincennes in August 1810 in which he defied Harrison and threatened violence, Tecumseh again visited his British friends in Canada and bore witness to his gratitude for aid from his "Father" the British: "You, Father, have nourished us, and raised us up from Childhood. We are now Men, and think ourselves capable of defending our Country" (Public Record Office, CO, 42:143).

However, he hesitated on the brink of a war unsupported by British arms. A little later he had gone south to tighten the bonds of his confederacy. Tall, straight, and lean, with a light copper complexion, he was a magnificent figure of a man as he traveled from tribe to tribe in the south, making a profound impression and winning many adherents to his cause. He reminded the Indians that "Our fathers, from their tombs, reproach us as slaves and cowards. I hear them now in the wailing winds" (Claiborne, *post*, p. 59); and he foretold, with great effect, the appearance of a comet flaming in the sky. In spite of the delay caused by the able opposition of such leaders as Pushmataha [*q.v.*], he appeared to be on the highroad to the fulfillment of his plans. The imminence of war between the United States and Great Britain gave him further cause to expect success.

The battle of Tippecanoe, into which his brother, the Prophet, allowed himself to be maneuvered in Tecumseh's absence, was disastrous to his hope of a powerful confederacy, of sustained British aid in return for his military support, and of an international guarantee to Indian tenure of territory on which to work out an adjustment to a changing world. When he went south he had cautioned his brother on no account to allow himself to be drawn, unprepared, into a battle (Drake, *post*, pp. 156, 221, 234, Tupper, *post*, p. 191). The drought of the summer of 1811, by ruining the crops and driving away the game, increased the difficulties of the situation, as did the continued glutting of the fur market with no outlet in war-stricken Europe. The confederacy that had been so near realization melted away in his very grasp. The provisions carefully husbanded against a time of need were destroyed. The bravest of his warriors were scattered. At an Indian council in May 1812 he defied any "living creature to say we ever advised anyone, directly or indirectly, to make war on our white brothers . . . Governor Harrison made war on my people in my absence . . . had I been at home, there would have been no blood shed at that time" ("Messages," *post*, II, 52, 51).

With no time to repair his fortunes before the War of 1812 was upon him, he and a few followers entered the British army, in which he received the rank of brigadier-general. He en-

couraged Sir Isaac Brock in his decision to attack Detroit at once and, after the capture of the fort, was active in rallying some of his old warriors to the victorious British cause. He fought with great courage at the River Raisin (Brownstown), Fort Meigs, and Fort Stephenson, trusting that at long last British aid would not fail him; but, when, after Perry's victory on Lake Erie, he apprehended Brig.-Gen. Henry A. Procter's purpose to burn Amherstburg and Detroit and to retreat eastward, he saw the ruin of all his hopes. In a scathing speech he reviewed the course of British friendship, blowing now hot and now cold according to the changing interests of imperial policy: "You always told us, that you would never draw your foot off British ground; but now, father, we see you are drawing back . . . We must compare our father's conduct to a fat animal, that carries its tail upon its back, but when affrighted, he drops it between his legs and runs off . . . You have got the arms and ammunition . . . sent for his red children, if you have an idea of going away, give them to us. . . . Our lives are in the hands of the Great Spirit. We are determined to defend our lands, and if it be his will, we wish to leave our bones upon them" (*Weekly Register, post,* Nov. 6, 1813, p. 175). Reluctantly, distrusting Procter thoroughly, he covered the British retreat as far as Moraviantown, where, at the Battle of the Thames, he fell. He remained a tradition of glory to his own people and a bone of contention to a generation of American politicians intent on making political capital out of his destruction.

[Files of the Office of Indian Affairs, Washington, D. C.; papers in Public Record Office, London; "Governors Messages and Letters. Messages and Letters of Wm. H. Harrison," *Ind. Hist. Colls.* (2 vols., 1922), ed. by Logan Esarey; Moses Dawson, *A Hist. Narrative of the Civil and Mil. Services of Maj.-Gen. Wm. H. Harrison* (1824); R. B. McAfee, *Hist. of the Late War in the Western Country* (1816), reprinted with index (1919); John Richardson, *Richardson's War of 1812* (1902) with notes by A. C. Casselman; J. F. H. Claiborne, *Life and Times of Gen. Sam. Dale* (1860); F. B. Tupper, *Family Records: Containing Memoirs of Maj.-Gen. Sir Isaac Brock* (1835); Benj. Drake, *Life of Tecumseh* (1841); W. A. Galloway, *Old Chillicothe* (1934); James Mooney, "The Ghost Dance Religion," *14th Ann. Report of Bureau of Ethnology,* pt. 2 (1896); *Weekly Register* (Niles), Oct. 9, 23, 1813, Nov. 6, 1813, Apr. 9, 16, 1814.]   K. E. C.

TEDYUSKUNG (c. 1700–Apr. 19, 1763), Delaware chief, was born in New Jersey east of Trenton, the son of a well-known Delaware Indian called "Old Captain Harris." His name was spelled in many different ways, of which the more important are Tadeuskund, Tedyuskung, Teedyuskung, and even Detiuscung and Deedjoskon. He was also sometimes referred to as Honest John. About 1730 he migrated with those of his tribe who, defeated by the Iroquois and crowded by the white settlers, settled in the forks of the Delaware River, near Easton, Pa., and ten years later were living in the Wyoming region between the forks of the Susquehanna. Touched by the preaching of the Moravian missionaries, with his wife, Elizabeth, he became a member of the Indian Christian settlement of Gnadenhuetten on the Mahoning River, after some hesitation was baptized by John Christopher Cammerhoff [*q.v.*], and took the name of Gideon. In 1754 he became a Delaware chief and turned his back on any further attempt to reconcile himself to the clash between European and Indian culture by adopting a religion of submission. Instead he chose war. In spite of the earlier successes of Shikellamy [*q.v.*] and the support given to the Iroquois pretensions by William Johnson, Conrad Weiser, and George Croghan [*qq.v.*], he was in a large measure successful in asserting Delaware independence of the Iroquois. He denounced as frauds all the cessions of Delaware lands by the Iroquois; and, in the hope of bringing about some readjustment, he espoused the cause of the English colonists against the French and against the Indian resentment that burst into flame as the news of Braddock's defeat spread through the Indian country. He favored the mission of Christian Frederick Post [*q.v.*] to the Ohio Indians in 1758 and, with Post, was largely responsible for British success at Fort Duquesne and for the ultimate failure of French arms.

He shared the curse of his people in being unable to resist the temptation of strong drink. At important councils between his tribe and the white government, he was reported as being drunk every night. Conrad Weiser said that "though he is a Drunkard . . . yet he is a man that can think well" (*Pennsylvania Archives, post,* I ser., vol. III, p. 68), and another contemporary wrote "but he is really more of a Politician than any of his Opponents, whether in or out of our proprietary Council; and if he could be kept sober, might probably soon become Emperor of all the neighbouring Nations" (Thomson, *post,* p. 183). He seems to have been able to transact the business of each day with a head clear enough to baffle the provincial officials. Nevertheless his weakness must have played its part in the final failure to make good the Delaware protests against undoubted fraud in land cessions. It was also the immediate cause of his death. His house in Wyoming was set on fire, probably by some Iroquois for revenge, and he was burned to death in a drunken stupor.

[John Heckewelder, "An Account of the Hist., Manners, and Customs of the Indian Nations," *Trans. of the . . . Am. Philosophical Soc.,* vol. I (1819), and in *Hist. Soc. of Pa. Memoirs,* vol. XII (1876) ; W. C. Reichel, *Memorials of the Moravian Church,* vol. I (1870), esp. pp. 217–28, 265; "The Jour. of Christian Frederick Post," in Charles Thomson, *An Enquiry into the Causes of the Alienation of the Delaware and Shawanese Indians from the British Interests* (1759, reprinted 1867) ; esp. app.; Edmund De Schweinitz, *The Life and Times of David Zeisberger* (1870) ; *Pa. Archives,* esp. I ser. vols. II–IV (1853) ; *Minutes of the Provincial Council of Pa.,* vols. VII–VIII (1851–52) ; J. S. Walton, *Conrad Weiser* (1900).]

K. E. C.

TELFAIR, EDWARD (*c.* 1735–Sept. 19, 1807), merchant, member of the Continental Congress, governor of Georgia, was born on the Telfair estate at "Town Head" in Scotland. Having received his formal education in the Kirkcudbright grammar school, he entered a commercial house, and at the age of twenty-three came to Virginia as its agent. About 1766 he settled in Georgia where, two years later, he represented St. Paul's Parish in the Commons House of the Assembly. He identified himself, thereafter, with the city of Savannah, although for a time he lived in Burke County and at "The Grove" near Augusta. In Savannah he formed numerous business partnerships, the firms becoming the principal commercial houses in colonial Georgia, dealing largely in European and East India goods, and also selling some slaves. Telfair engaged also in ship-building and accumulated large land holdings, especially after the Revolution. So successful were his businesses that when he died he left a fortune, which, with the extinction of the family in 1875, was devoted to the establishment of the Telfair Academy of Arts and Sciences and other benefactions in Savannah.

Though prosperous in business and honored by appointment to various commissionerships in the colony, Telfair joined the Liberty Boys, on the rise of discontent in 1774, and became one of the most prominent rebels during the next two years. He was present at the various Tondee Tavern meetings in 1774, was a member of the committee appointed to receive donations for the Boston sufferers, attended the first three provincial congresses, was a member of the original council of safety, and a leader of the mob which broke open the royal powder magazine in Savannah. He was also appointed assistant commander of the up-country militia and was a member of the committee to arm the state, yet, in June 1776, he was listed in a group described as dangerous to the liberties of America. Whether the petty spite of enemies or a temporary relapse in patriotism was responsible (William Telfair, a brother, and Basil Cowper, both business associates, remained loyal to the king), he was soon back in the rebel ranks, with patriotic fervor never again to be questioned. In 1780 and 1781, his name was in the lists attainted for high treason by the restored British authority in Savannah, and from this time forth he remained a bitter enemy of the British. He was a member of the Continental Congress from 1777 to 1783.

At various times from 1781 to 1784 he was justice and assistant justice for Burke County, and in the year 1783 he held the following positions: Indian commissioner to treat with the Creeks and Cherokees, commissioner to adjust the boundary dispute with South Carolina, and representative in the legislature from Burke County. In 1785 he was reëlected to the legislature and the next year he was elected governor. During his one-year term he showed great vigor in dealing with the Indians and with South Carolina in the boundary dispute. In 1788 he was a member of the convention which ratified the federal Constitution, in 1789 he was a member of the legislature from Richmond County, and became the first governor under the new Georgia constitution of 1789. As governor he came into conflict with the United States over the Indian question precipitated by the Treaty of New York, and over the *Chisholm* vs. *Georgia* case (2 *U. S.*, 419), which he pushed forward into such a burning issue that it led to the Eleventh Amendment. He was reckless in his dealings with the state's public lands, illegally signing warrants for as much as 100,000 acres to one person. On May 18, 1774, he was married to Sally, a daughter of William Gibbons [*q.v.*]. They had three sons and three daughters.

[W. J. Northen, ed., *Men of Mark in Ga.*, vol. I (1907); A. D. Candler and C. A. Evans, eds., *Georgia* (1906), vol. III; W. B. Stevens, *Hist. of Ga.*, vol. II (1859); *Biog. Dict. of the Am. Cong., 1774–1927* (1928); U. B. Phillips, *Ga. and State Rights* (1902); A. D. Candler, ed., *Revolutionary Records of the State of Ga.* (1908), vols. I–III; *Colonial Records of the State of Ga.* (1907–11), vols. X, XI, XIX, pt. 2; George White, *Hist. Colls. of Ga.* (3rd ed., 1854); *Am. State Papers, Indian Affairs*, vol. I (1832); E. C. Burnett, ed., *Letters of Members of the Continental Cong.*, vols. III, V, VI (1926–33); *Ga. Hist. Quart.*, Mar., June 1917, *Ga. Gazette*, 1774, 1775, 1783–1791; *Columbian Museum & Savannah Advertiser* and *Republican and Savannah Evening Ledger*, Sept. 22, 1807; *Augusta Chronicle*, Sept. 26, 1807; manuscript letter-book covering most of the year 1786, Lib. of the Ga. Hist. Soc. in Savannah, and other manuscripts relating to the governorship, Dept. of Archives and Hist., Atlanta.]

E. M. C.

TELLER, HENRY MOORE (May 23, 1830– Feb. 23, 1914), lawyer, United States senator, secretary of the interior, the eldest son of John and Charlotte (Moore) Teller, was born on a farm in Allegany County, N. Y. He was a descendant of Wilhelm Teller, who settled in Albany in 1639 and later moved to New York. Henry attended rural schools in the vicinity of his home and the academies at Rushford and Alfred, N. Y. Subsequently he taught school, read law in the office of Martin Grover at Angelica, N. Y., and was admitted to the bar at Binghamton in 1858. Immediately thereafter he moved to Morrison, Ill., where he practised law and engaged in politics. Three years later he went to Colorado and established a law office at Central City.

During the Civil War period he became one of the leading figures of Colorado. He was an unconditional unionist, a major-general of the militia, and took an active part in raising troops and preparing Denver for the defense against threatened Indian attacks. After the war he devoted his energies to his legal practice and business enterprises, serving as attorney for numerous corporations and as president of the Colorado Central Railroad (1872–76), and building the territory's largest hotel.

When Colorado was admitted into the Union in 1876, Teller was elected to the United States Senate as a Republican, serving until Apr. 17, 1882, when he resigned to accept the position of secretary of the interior in the cabinet of President Arthur. He was again elected to the Senate in 1885 and served four terms, the first two as a Republican; the third as an Independent Silver Republican; and the fourth as a Democrat. His most spectacular legislative activities were aimed at the remonetization of silver, and his fight against the repeal of the Sherman Silver Purchase Act in 1893 probably marked their climax. His most notable speeches were those of September 1893 (*Congressional Record*, 53 Cong., 1 Sess., pp. 1348, 1385, 1419) when he attempted to convict the bankers of bringing on the panic, and that of Oct. 26 (*Ibid.*, pp. 2838–50) on the evils of the appreciation of money on the gold standard.

In the field of national politics his bolt from the Republican Convention of 1896 over the silver question was an event of outstanding significance. For a few weeks following, he was a candidate for the Democratic nomination for president, and the agitation back of his campaign stimulated the drift in the convention to Bryan. The Republican bolters organized the Silver Republican party, and during the campaign this group supported the Democratic nominee, an alliance that was repeated in 1900. After the latter campaign Teller announced himself a Democrat. Although traditionally an expansionist, at the outbreak of the war with Spain in 1898 he secured the adoption of the Fourth, or Teller

Resolution (*Congressional Record*, 55 Cong., 2 Sess., p. 3954), which pledged the United States to an independent Cuba. Teller voted against a similar pledge regarding the Philippines, but the Administration's policy of crushing the Aguinaldo government brought forth a devastating attack from him in February 1902 (*Ibid.*, 57 Cong., 1 Sess., pp. 1574, 1640, 1682). He manifested a like opposition to Theodore Roosevelt's policy toward Panama. Teller's later years in the Senate were taken up with perfecting legislation regarding public lands, Indians, reclamation, and the monetary system. When he retired from the Senate in 1909, he retained his place on the National Monetary Commission, on which he served until it was disbanded in 1912.

In personal appearance he was a moderately tall, slender man, almost always dressed in the conventional black frock coat of a senator of the eighties. His most striking feature was a shock of stiff dark hair which he unsuccessfully tried to comb straight back. His beard was full and his upper lip smooth shaven. Rather puritanical in his tastes and outlook, he was cosmopolitan in his friendships. He was not an orator but in the opinion of his contemporaries ranked among the more effective debaters in the Senate. Rather retiring by nature, he was usually willing to let his Colorado colleague assume the burden of debate and floor leadership. His fight over the silver question began as a defense of local interests, but as its relation to the larger struggle between the debtor and creditor classes became clearer to him, he tended more and more to align himself with the weaker groups in society. Certain reforms, unpopular at the time, such as woman's suffrage, always had his support, but after 1890 he was found with considerable regularity supporting discriminating income taxes, the government regulation of large-scale business, and laws for the protection of native interests against those of a distant government.

On June 7, 1862, he married Harriet M. Bruce of Cuba, N. Y., by whom he had three children. He died in Denver.

[*Biog. Dir. Am. Cong.* (1928); *Cong. Record*, 67 Cong., 4 Sess., pp. 3589–3601; T. F. Dawson, *Senator Teller: A Brief Account of His Fifth Election to the U. S. Senate* (1898); Teller MSS., State Museum, Denver, Colo.; Elmer Ellis, "The Public Career of Henry Moore Teller," unpublished MS. in Univ. of Iowa Lib.; W. F. Stone, *Hist. of Colo.*, vol. II (1918); *Who's Who in America*, 1912–13; *Rocky Mountain News* (Denver), Feb. 23, 1914; *N. Y. Times*, Feb. 24, 1914.]   E. E—s.

TEMPLE, OLIVER PERRY (Jan. 27, 1820–Nov. 2, 1907), lawyer and author, was born near Greeneville, Greene County, Tenn., the son of James and Mary (Craig) Temple, and a descendant of William Temple, a native of England who was living in Goshen, Pa., in 1721. While a student at Greeneville College in 1838 Oliver volunteered as a soldier to aid regulars under Gen. Winfield Scott [*q.v.*] in his work of pacifying the Cherokee Indians then being moved beyond the Mississippi. In 1841 he entered Washington College, Washington County, Tenn., and was graduated with the class of 1844. He at once entered the field of politics, delivering speeches throughout his congressional district in behalf of Henry Clay [*q.v.*], candidate for the presidency. Subsequently he read law in Greeneville under Robert J. McKinney, and in 1846 was admitted to the bar. In July of the following year he was the Whig candidate for Congress against Andrew Johnson [*q.v.*], and in a campaign of three weeks, by dexterous attacks on his opponent's record he cut Johnson's usual majority of about 1500 to 314 votes.

In 1848 Temple ren.oved to Knoxville, where he practised law in partnership with leaders of the East Tennessee bar. He was appointed in 1850 one of the commissioners to negotiate with the Indian tribes of Texas, New Mexico, and Arizona. On Sept. 9, 1851, shortly after his return to Knoxville, he was married to Scotia C. Humes, of that city. He took a leading part in the Southern Commercial Convention held in Knoxville in 1856, as proponent and advocate of resolutions against the reëstablishment of the slave trade. In 1860 he was a delegate to the National Union Convention, held at Baltimore, and aided in the nomination of John Bell [*q.v.*] as candidate for the presidency; subsequently, as a Bell and Everett elector, he canvassed his congressional district. In November of the same year he made the first speech in Tennessee, after Lincoln's election, in behalf of the Union, and in December he planned a meeting of East Tennessee Unionists at Knoxville to consolidate the sentiment of that section against secession. The following year he stumped East Tennessee for the Union cause, and took a leading part in the Greeneville Convention of June 17, 1861, which declared for a separation of East Tennessee from the state of Tennessee. In July 1866, he was appointed one of the chancellors of Tennessee by Gov. W. G. Brownlow [*q.v.*], and continued as such until September 1878. He then returned to the bar but after 1881 devoted his attention to his large estate.

When more than seventy-five years old he turned to authorship. His first production was *The Covenanter, the Cavalier and the Puritan* (1897). This was followed by *East Tennessee and the Civil War* (1899), and *Notable Men of*

Tennessee, published in 1912, after his death. He wrote in a vigorous and interesting, though not graceful style, and drew copiously from his own rich store of reminiscences.

His contribution to the progress of transportation and agriculture in East Tennessee was considerable. He was one of the originators of the Knoxville & Ohio Railroad; a director of the East Tennessee & Georgia Railroad Company, and president of the first macadam turnpike company in his section of the state. Before the Civil War he was a member of the state board of agriculture, and in 1872 he was the prime mover in the organization of the East Tennessee Farmers' Convention. For many years he was active as a trustee of the University of Tennessee, and for a period served as chairman of the board. His work for the institution was directed principally toward the development of the agricultural department. After his death the Farmers' Convention built Temple Hall on the experimental farm of the University, in his honor.

[W. S. Speer, *Sketches of Prominent Tennesseans* (1888); biog. sketch by Temple's daughter, Mary B. Temple, in his *Notable Men of Tennessee* (1912); William Rule, *Standard Hist. of Knoxville, Tenn.* (1900); T. W. Humes, *The Loyal Mountaineers of Tenn.* (1888); W. T. Hale and D. L. Merritt, *A Hist. of Tennessee and Tennesseans* (1913), vols. II, III, VII; *Who's Who in America,* 1906–07; *Nashville Banner,* Jan. 30, 1904; *Journal and Tribune* (Knoxville), Nov. 3, 1907.]   S. C. W.

TEMPLE, WILLIAM GRENVILLE (Mar. 23, 1824–June 28, 1894), naval officer, was born in Rutland, Vt., the son of Robert and Charlotte Eloise (Green) Temple, and a descendant of Robert Temple, who was born in Ireland and emigrated to Boston, Mass., in 1717. Appointed midshipman on Apr. 18, 1840, he made his first cruise in the *Constellation* around the world, 1840–44. Then, after service in the Home Squadron, he studied six months ashore until his promotion to passed midshipman, July 11, 1846. He was wrecked in the *Boston* on Eleuthera Island (Bahamas), Oct. 5 following, and subsequently had charge of the sick men sent to Norfolk in the schooner *Volant.* Returning to the Gulf of Mexico in the steamer *Scourge,* he participated in the chief naval events of 1847 in the Mexican War, including the siege of Vera Cruz; the capture of Alvarado, Mar. 31, where he and two men occupied the town for a day after the *Scourge* had taken it unassisted (thus upsetting Commodore Matthew Calbraith Perry's plan for a grand-scale operation); and the occupation of Túxpan and Tabasco. His "Memoir of the Landing of the United States Troops at Vera Cruz in 1847," dated Mar. 23, 1852, but first published in P. S. P. Conner's *The Home Squadron under*

Commodore Conner in the War with Mexico (1896), shows keen professional interest and ability. His duty in the next decade, save for a Mediterranean cruise in 1852–55 and an assignment as flag lieutenant in the Pacific Squadron in 1859–61, was in coast survey work, ranging from New York harbor to Florida. In the Civil War he first commanded the steamer *Flambeau,* sent in November 1861 to cut off blockade runners at Nassau. His work there was not aggressive enough to satisfy the American consul at Nassau (*War of the Rebellion: Official Records, Navy,* 1 ser., vol. XI, 1901, p. 532), but Flag Officer Samuel Francis Du Pont [*q.v.*] spoke approvingly of it (R. M. Thompson and Richard Wainwright, *Confidential Correspondence of Gustavus Vasa Fox, Assistant Secretary of the Navy,* vol. I, 1918, p. 102). On Jan. 22, 1862, he was invalided north. After seven months' ordnance duty in New York he commanded the *Pembina* on the Mobile blockade until November 1863, and was then made flag captain of the East Gulf Squadron. A year later he took command of the side-wheeler *Pontoosuc,* which was in the first line of Admiral David Dixon Porter's fleet in both attacks on Fort Fisher, Dec. 23–25, 1864, and Jan. 13–15, 1865. His report of the first attack, revealing the ineffective use of Gen. B. F. Butler's landing forces, was forwarded by Porter with the comment, "Important as a matter of history, and tells the whole story" (*Ibid.,* vol. XI, 1900, p. 287). Porter included him in recommendations for promotion (*Ibid.,* p. 455). After participating in Virginia waters in the closing operations of the war, he was detached May 25, 1865. He was made commander, Mar. 3, 1865; captain, Aug. 28, 1870; commodore, June 5, 1878; and rear admiral, Feb. 22, 1884, just before his voluntary retirement on Feb. 29.

His post-war service included ordnance duty at Portsmouth, N. H. (1866–69); an assignment as escort to King Kalakaua of Hawaii during his visit to the United States, Dec. 11–28, 1874, for which he was made knight commander of the order of Kamehameha I; service as chief of staff in the European Squadron (1871–73), with a subsequent leave of eighteen months in Europe, as captain of the New York navy yard (1875–77), and as member of the retiring board (1879–84). His death from apoplexy occurred in Washington, where he resided after his retirement, and his burial was in the Congressional Cemetery. He was married Oct. 7, 1851, to Catlyna, daughter of Gen. J. G. Totten, but had no children. As suggested by his frequent staff assignments, he was an officer of unusual ability and striking personality. A relative describes him as "the beau ideal of a handsome man, very tall and very large, celebrated for his wit and gifts as a raconteur."

[Temple Prime, *Some Account of the Temple Family* (1894); L. H. Hamersly, *Records of Living Officers of the U. S. Navy and Marine Corps* (4th ed., 1890); E. L. Temple, *The Vermonter*, vol. XXVIII, no. 12 (1923); obituaries in *Army and Navy Jour.*, June 30, and *Evening Star* ('Washington, D. C.), June 29, 1894.]

A. W—t.

TEN BROECK, ABRAHAM (May 13, 1734–Jan. 19, 1810), soldier, jurist, was born in Albany, N. Y., the tenth child of Dirck Ten Broeck and his wife, Grietja (Margaret) Cuyler. He was a descendant of Wessel Ten Broeck who came to New Netherland with Peter Minuit in 1626. His marriage on Nov. 1, 1763, to Elizabeth, the daughter of Stephen Van Rensselaer, united him with one of the most influential families in upper New York. His father, in addition to holding municipal offices and serving as commissioner of Indian affairs, was a prominent merchant and dealer in furs. Abraham prepared for a business career under the tutorage of his brother-in-law, Philip Livingston [*q.v.*]. By 1752, however, he was back in Albany and soon relinquished mercantile pursuits, for in 1761 he became a member of the colonial assembly and thereafter remained in public life almost continuously until his death. He was a stanch defender of popular rights, and in 1775, still holding his seat in the colonial assembly, he voted approval of the course of the merchants in signing the Association as recommended by the Continental Congress. An ardent patriot, he was a deputy in the New York Provincial Congress 1775–77 and served on the Committee of Safety. He was a member of the convention which in 1777 framed the first constitution for New York State.

With the outbreak of the Revolution and the passage of the new militia law he helped to draft, Ten Broeck, who had held commissions in the colonial militia, was made brigadier-general, first of the Albany and Tryon County militia, and subsequently of the Albany County militia only. At his headquarters in Albany, a strategic center, he was constantly confronted with the dilemma of obeying orders to reinforce the Continental troops and responding to the appeals of the alarmed inhabitants on the western and northern frontiers that the militia be allowed to guard their own homes. His task was further complicated by the lack of equipment and supplies. Zeal for his country's cause was tempered with a caution and practical-mindedness that won him the respect and confidence of his superior officers. His outstanding military achievement was his participation at the most critical moment

in the battle of Bemis Heights in 1777, which resulted in the forced retreat of General Burgoyne. Ill health following an accident compelled him to resign his commission in 1781.

Ten Broeck had acquired a wide acquaintance with the law from his committee work in the colonial and the provincial assembly, where he had helped to revise old laws and draft new ones relating not only to military affairs but also to questions of currency, taxation, land titles, and other civil matters; his land and other business interests had familiarized him with the application of the laws. He had been a justice in various colonial courts, and with the relinquishment of his military duties in 1781 he returned to the judicial field to act for thirteen years as first judge of the court of common pleas of Albany County. From 1779 to 1783 and from 1796 to 1799 he was mayor of Albany.

As an influential resident of a key city in one of the leading colonies and states, he rendered able service to his state and country during the late colonial, the Revolutionary, and the early national periods. He died at the age of seventy-five years. He and his wife had five children.

[G. E. B. Jackson, *Gen. Abraham Ten Broeck* (1886); Emma Ten Broeck Runk, *The Ten Broeck Geneal.* (1897); M. K. Van Rensselaer, *The Van Rensselaers of the Manor of Rensselaerswyck* (1888); F. B. Heitman, *Hist. Reg. of Officers of the Continental Army* (1914); *Jour. of the Votes and Proc. of the Gen. Assembly of the Colony of N. Y. from 1766 to 1776* (1820); *Jour. of the Provincial Cong., Provincial Convention . . . of the State of N. Y., 1775–1776–1777* (2 vols., 1842); *Pub. Papers of George Clinton . . . Military* (1899–1914); *Docs. Relating to the Colonial Hist. of the State of N. Y.*, vol. XV, *State Archives*, vol. I (1887); *Calendar of Hist. MSS. Relating to the War of the Revolution in the Office of the Secretary of State, Albany, N. Y.* (2 vols., 1868); correspondence in New York State Library, Albany.] E. L. J—en.

TEN BROECK, RICHARD (May 1812–Aug. 1, 1892), the first American horseman to assert the prowess of his country on the English turf, was born at Albany, N. Y., the son of Richard Ten Broeck. He was, according to his own account, a grandson of Henry Bicker of Philadelphia, an officer of Pennsylvania troops during the Revolution, and of Col. Dirck Ten Broeck of Albany, likewise a Revolutionary officer. In 1823 the boy saw the famous match race between Eclipse and Henry at the Union Course on Long Island. In 1829 he was admitted to the United States Military Academy at West Point, but left the following year and went South. Here he began the long racing career which continued with some interruptions until he retired in 1887.

When about thirty-five years old Ten Broeck became the partner of the veteran William R. Johnson [*q.v.*], "the Napoleon of the Turf," in racing on Southern tracks. In 1853 he purchased an obscure colt by Boston out of Alice Carneal, and in a series of bold matches and interstate stake races which attracted nation-wide attention scored a succession of brilliant victories that made its name, Lexington, one of the greatest in American turf history. Convinced by this horse's unexampled feat of running four miles in 7:19¾ that American racehorses and training methods excelled those of the mother country, Ten Broeck in 1856 went to England with a quartet of representative runners, one of which was Lecomte, the only horse that ever won a heat from Lexington, and another Pryor, that had beaten Lecomte. Undismayed by the fact that Lexington had to be left behind because he had become blind, and that Lecomte was found to be too unsound to race again, Ten Broeck offered on his arrival to run an American horse at four-mile heats for $25,000 a side against any English thoroughbred that could be produced. This challenge excited widespread and anxious interest in England and the warmest national enthusiasm in all sections of the United States. It was not accepted. The American four-milers were only moderately successful when racing under the British system of dash races at shorter distances, yet Ten Broeck's Prioress scored a sensational victory in the Cesarewitch Stakes, outlasting her competitors, while Starke, half-brother to her and to Lecomte, won the Goodwood Cup and the Bentinck Memorial Plate—the latter at four miles and a quarter, the longest race in England. Ten Broeck remained in England about ten years, winning with English and American horses almost $200,000 in purses, stakes, and matches.

His subsequent career in America was not noteworthy. Financial stress and mental infirmity came upon him in old age, and the last years of life drew to a gloomy close in a lonely little home called "The Hermitage," near Menlo Park, in California. Always a man of quick temper, he had fought several duels, parted from two wives, and at the time of his death driven away his only servant. His second wife, whom he married late in life when she was the widow of H. D. Newcomb of Louisville, Ky., applied unsuccessfully in 1888 for an examination as to his sanity, so eccentric had he then become. Yet one who knew him in his prime wrote in the New York *Sun* when he died: "Mr. Ten Broeck was a genial, well beloved companion, an honest, enthusiastic horseman, and the most intrepid gambler that ever backed a racehorse, bucked the tiger, or bluffed on a pair of deuces." An article of his, "Some Personal Reminiscences, Incidents, and Anecdotes," appeared in the *Spirit of the Times* for Dec. 27, 1890.

[Emma Ten Broeck Runk, *The Ten Broeck Geneal.* (1897); C. E. Trevathan, *The Am. Thoroughbred* (1905); "The American Horses in England," a series of articles in *Porter's Spirit of the Times* in 1857; *Spirit of the Times,* Aug. 6, 1892; *Sun* (N. Y.), Aug. 2, 1892; *N. Y. Herald,* Aug. 2, 1892; letter from Maj.-Gen. Wm. D. Connor, Supt. U. S. Mil. Acad.]

G. C. G.

TENÉ-ANGPÓTE [See Kicking Bird, d. May 3, 1875].

TENNENT, GILBERT (Feb. 5, 1703–July 23, 1764), Presbyterian clergyman, was the eldest of the four sons of William [*q.v.*] and Catharine (Kennedy) Tennent, all of whom were educated by their father and entered the ministry. Of these Gilbert and the second born, William [*q.v.*], were the most distinguished; John died in his middle twenties while pastor of the church at Freehold, N. J.; Charles, the youngest, was pastor of the congregation at Whiteclay Creek, Del., for twenty-four years, and then of the church at Buckingham, Md., until his death. Gilbert was born in County Armagh, Ireland, and was about fourteen years old when the family emigrated to America. From his father he seems to have received a good grounding in the classics, some knowledge of Hebrew, a thorough understanding of the theological problems of the day, and an excellent mental discipline. Yale College conferred the honorary degree of A.M. upon him in 1725.

His early religious experience was a troubled one, but at length he was brought to a sense of saving conversion. Not convinced of his spiritual fitness for the ministry, however, he studied medicine for a year, but at length, May 1725, presented himself to the Philadelphia Presbytery as a candidate for licensure and successfully passed the examination. In December of the same year he was called to the church in Newcastle, Del., but after preaching there for a short time left abruptly. Both the church and the Newcastle Presbytery complained of his action to the Synod, which administered a rebuke. About this time he seems to have assisted his father in the newly established "Log College," but in the fall of 1726 he accepted a call to New Brunswick, N. J., and was ordained there by the Philadelphia Presbytery. The inhabitants of this region, especially the Dutch, had been aroused by the evangelistic labors of the Dutch Reformed pastor, Theodorus Jacobus Frelinghuysen [*q.v.*]; but the English-speaking people were as sheep without a shepherd. Tennent's task was to gather them together and minister to them. Some of the Dutch gave encouragement by contributing to his support. Although Frelinghuysen seems not to have been favorable to his coming, a warm friendship later sprang up between them. Frelinghuysen permitted Tennent the use of the buildings in which the Domine was accustomed to preach, and occasionally the two would address the same congregation, the one in Dutch, and the other in English (*Ecclesiastical Records: State of New York,* vol. IV, 1902, pp. 2557, 2667, 2587, 2588). Undoubtedly Tennent's natural evangelistic tendencies were strengthened by this association. From the beginning of his ministry his appearance, voice, and manner of preaching made a marked impression on his hearers; but he grieved that he could count so few converts. After a serious illness, during which Frelinguysen wrote him an encouraging letter, his zeal increased. His searching examinations into the experiences of professing Christians—which brought him much unpopularity and abuse—convinced him that many of them had not been converted, and he now preached with great vividness on sin, retribution, repentance, and the need of a conscious inner change. As a result many were aroused to a more vital interest in religion, both in the region about New Brunswick and on Staten Island, where he also labored. As time went on, other ministers of his spirit, some of whom had had their zeal kindled by his father in the "Log College," settled in the vicinity. Thus the Tennents and their associates became one of the sources of the Great Awakening, which had its consummation during the visit of George Whitefield [*q.v.*] to America in 1739–40.

Upon his arrival in the Middle Colonies, Whitefield soon formed an intimate relationship with the Tennent group. He visited New Brunswick and preached for Gilbert on Nov. 13, 1739, recording in his journal (*post*) under that date: "Here we were much refreshed with the Company of Mr. Gilbert *Tennent,* an eminent Dissenting Minister. . . . He and his Associates are now the burning and shining Lights of this Part of *America.*" Tennent accompanied him to New York, and Whitefield, hearing him preach there, wrote in his journal, Nov. 14, "never before heard [I] such a searching Sermon. He went to the Bottom indeed, and did not daub with untempered Mortar. . . . Hypocrites must either soon be converted or enraged at his Preaching. He is a Son of Thunder, and I find doth not fear the Faces of Men." In the later summer and fall of 1739 Tennent made an evangelistic tour in South Jersey and westward into Maryland, his labors meeting with notable success. When in November 1740 Whitefield returned from New England, he was accompanied by Daniel Rogers, a tutor at Harvard, who brought to Tennent a message from several New England ministers requesting that he come thither and continue the great work which Whitefield had begun. Persuaded by Whitefield to accept, he reached Boston toward the middle of the following month. The effect of his preaching upon the masses was even greater than that of Whitefield. After Whitefield, wrote the Rev. Timothy Cutler [*q.v.*] in disgust, "came one Tennent, a minister impudent and saucy; and told them all they were *damned, damned, damned!* This charmed them; and in the dreadfullest winter I ever saw, people wallowed in the snow night and day for the benefit of his beastly braying" (John Nichols, *Literary Anecdotes of the Eighteenth Century,* 1812, II, 547). The theme of his first sermon was "The Righteousness of the Scribes and Pharisees," and during his stay he was unsparing in his condemnation of religious formalism; he brandished the terrors of God before the eyes of sinners, and he boldly summoned his hearers to repentance and newness of life. Those unfriendly to him ridiculed his personal appearance and unpolished manners; some deplored the uncharitableness of his denunciations; the hardheaded Cutler resented the financial loss to the city, declaring that Whitefield and Tennent "carried more money out of these parts than the poor could be thankful for" (*Ibid.*); but no one could deny the power of his preaching. One of the Boston ministers testified that about 600 persons concerned for their souls had visited him in three months' time; another reported 1,000 or more. Before leaving New England Tennent preached in some twenty other Massachusetts and Connecticut towns, almost always with like effect.

He returned to the Middle Colonies shortly before the meeting of the Synod at Philadelphia in May 1741, at which occurred the famous schism. In the events leading up to this unfortunate occurrence Tennent had played a prominent part. The ecclesiastical procedure of the more conservative majority of his Presbyterian associates, and the sincerity of their religious pretentions as well, had been attacked by him with unseemly virulence. These conservatives had had no deeply emotional religious experiences, and attached little importance thereto; they were insistent that candidates for the ministry should be men of good character, of sound theology, and adequately trained, but they did not seek for evidences of their conversion and call; they placed emphasis on conformity to the standards rather than on essential orthodoxy, and were inclined to enforce strict obedience to the decrees of the Church. In the judgment of Tennent they were

Scribes and Pharisees—hypocrites; and since he felt it his duty to expose them and to awaken the Church from its "carnal security," it was inevitable that he should come into violent conflict with the Synod. In 1737 that body passed an act forbidding members of one Presbytery to preach without formal invitation to a congregation within the bounds of another Presbytery. In the heat of the revival, the evangelical group felt justified in disregarding this rule. In 1738 the Synod passed a resolution to the effect that candidates for the ministry before being taken on trial must either present a diploma from some European or New England college, or a certificate of satisfactory scholarship from a committee of the Synod. Tennent viewed the action as a blow at his father's "Log College," and also as tending to keep devout and capable men out of the ministry. The New Brunswick Presbytery, organized in 1738, of which Tennent was the leading spirit, ignored this requirement in the case of John Rowland, an alumnus of the "Log College." At the meeting of the Synod in 1739, the presbytery was adjudged to be very disorderly" and admonished to avoid such action in the future. Tennent and others of the presbytery then presented an "Apology for Dissenting from Two Acts or New Religious Laws Passed at the Last Session of the Synod." When the Synod met the following year Tennent and Samuel Blair [q.v.] presented formal papers charging many of their brethren with unsoundness in some of the principal doctrines of Christianity and with being strangers to a knowledge of God in their hearts. When asked to name individuals and produce evidence, they admitted that they had not investigated the reports they had received or discussed the matter with those they condemned. Soon afterward Tennent preached his notoriously abusive "Nottingham Sermon," printed under the title, *The Danger of an Unconverted Ministry, Considered in a Sermon on Mark VI. 34, Preached at Nottingham in Pennsylvania, March 8, anno 1739, 40* (1740). This sermon, which vividly portrayed the majority of ministers as plastered hypocrites, having the form of godliness but not its power, was widely circulated and did much to precipitate the schism of 1741. At the Synod of that year a written protest was offered by certain ministers and elders arraigning the Tennent party for disregarding the authority of the Synod and for other disturbing and unwarranted actions, and denying the right of the offenders to sit in that judicatory. The outcome of the matter was that Tennent and the other members of the New Brunswick Presbytery, finding themselves in a minority, withdrew, and a division of the Presbyterian Church occurred which lasted seventeen years. Tennent immediately published *Remarks upon a Protestation Presented to the Synod of Philadelphia, June 1, 1741* (1741). Not long afterward he made an attack upon the Moravians, preaching several sermons against them in New York which were published under the title, *The Necessity of Holding Fast the Truth Represented in Three Sermons . . . Relating to Errors Lately Vented by Some Moravians . . .* (1743). The fact that in these sermons he seemed to condemn views and practices he had formerly approved called forth from the Rev. John Hancock (1719–1744) of Braintree *The Examiner, or Gilbert against Tennent* (1743), published under the pseudonym Philalethes. To this Tennent replied in *The Examiner, Examined; or, Gilbert Tennent, Harmonious . . .* (1743).

In 1743 he removed to Philadelphia to take charge of a newly organized Presbyterian church composed of Whitefield sympathizers. His career here, which lasted until his death, was less spectacular. He labored hard to build up his congregation and to secure funds for a church edifice. In his dress and in his manner of preaching he became more conventional. As time went on he displayed evidences of regret for his earlier contentiousness, working for a reunion of the Presbyterian Church, and publishing in 1749, *Irenicum Ecclesiasticum, or a Humble, Impartial Essay upon the Peace of Jerusalem.* He was, however, a sturdy opponent of Quaker pacifism, issuing in 1748 two sermons entitled: *The Late Association for Defence Encourag'd, or, the Lawfulness of a Defensive War,* and *The Late Association for Defence Farther Encouraged, or, Defensive War Defended; and Its Consistency with True Christianity Represented.* His published discourses on other subjects were numerous. With the establishment of the College of New Jersey he became one of its trustees, and late in 1753 went to England with the Rev. Samuel Davies [q.v.] to solicit funds for the institution. His first wife died about 1740 and in 1741 he married Cornelia (De Peyster), widow of Matthew Clarkson; she died Mar. 19, 1753, and subsequently he married Mrs. Sarah Spofford. Three children survived him. He was buried beneath the middle aisle of the Second Presbyterian Church, Philadelphia, but his body was later removed to the cemetery at Abington, Pa. Among the leaders of the Great Awakening he ranks with Jonathan Edwards and Whitefield.

[Archibald Alexander, *Biog. Sketches of the Founder and Principal Alumni of the Log Coll.* (1851); W. B. Sprague, *Annals Am. Pulpit*, vol. III (1858); Richard Webster, *A Hist. of the Presbyt. Church in America*

(1857); Charles Hodge, *The Constitutional Hist. of the Presbyt. Church in the U. S. A.* (1851); Thomas Murphy, *The Presbytery of the Log Coll.* (1889); C. H. Maxson, *The Great Awakening in the Middle Colonies* (1920); H. L. Osgood, *The Am. Colonies in the Eighteenth Century*, vol. III (1924); *The Gen. Assembly's Missionary Mag.*, May 1805; *A Continuation of the Rev. Mr. Whitefield's Journal from His Embarking after the Embargo* (1740); Samuel Finley, *The Successful Minister of Christ, Distinguished in Glory* (1764); *Jour. of the Presbyt. Hist. Soc.*, passim.]

H. E. S.

TENNENT, JOHN (*c.* 1700–*c.* 1760), physician, author, was born in England. He appeared first in the colony of Virginia about 1725, and five years later married Dorothy Paul. A son, John Tennent, living in Caroline County, Va., unsuccessfully petitioned the Virginia Assembly in 1760 for assistance in securing a medical education as a recognition of his father's medical contributions and later served as a surgeon in the Continental Army. The elder Tennent appears to have settled first in Spotsylvania County. He acquired property in Fredericksburg and in Prince William County as well. By 1735 he was in Williamsburg, where a year later William Parks [*q.v.*] published Tennent's *Essay on the Pleurisy*. This little publication contained the author's experience in the therapeutic use of rattlesnake-root and gained for him widespread notoriety. He learned of the plant from "a Nation of *Indians,* called the *Senekkas,*" and reasoning "that this Root must be of general Use in Coagulations and Viscidities of the Blood"—a theory he adopted in the treatment of pleurisy and 'peripneumony'—he so employed it; "my Success was so great," he claimed, "that I did not lose above four or five Patients in an Hundred, tho' other Practitioners lost two Thirds" (*A Brief Account of the Case of John Tennent, M.D.,* see Blanton, *post,* p. 125).

In 1737 he returned to London, made himself known to the leading physicians of the town and did his best to popularize the use of his rattlesnake-root. The next year he was back in Virginia, where a controversy had been raging in the *Virginia Gazette* over his plan of treatment. Although the House of Burgesses paid him £100 at this time for having made public his discovery, he was not satisfied with his reception. "Meeting with Ingratitude from the Colony where I resided," he wrote, "I came over to settle in *London* in the Year 1739" (*Ibid.,* p. 125). On Nov. 8, 1741, he was married to a Mrs. Hanger, "a Widow Lady from Huntingdon" (*Ibid.,* pp. 124, 127). His subsequent career was not a happy one. *Detection of a Conspiracy . . . The Singular Case of John Tennent,* published by him in London in 1743, is a defense of questionable conduct. It reveals a man "with hopes of making one Day a Figure in the Medical World," chagrined over the fact that a large portion of the medical profession in Virginia and Great Britain refused to recognize the virtues of his discovery (*Ibid.,* p. 126). He ended by fraternizing with the notorious quack Joshua Ward, stooped to the "foolish step in having kept one Mrs. Carey under the name of Mrs. Tennent," and was finally brought to trial at the Old Bailey for bigamy (*Ibid.,* p. 127). From this predicament he was rescued by no less a person than Sir Hans Sloane. In a letter of thanks written in April 1740, Tennent intimated his intention of going to Jamaica, but nothing is known of his later years.

Besides the broadsides, . . . *Singular Case of John Tennent, M.D.,* and *A Brief Account of the Case of John Tennent, M.D.,* he published anonymously *Every Man His Own Doctor* (2nd edition, 1724), purporting to offer "a Plain and Easy Means for Persons to cure themselves" by medicines grown chiefly in America; *A Reprieve from Death* (London, 1741), containing objections to the use of vinegar and other acids on board His Majesty's ships in the treatment of epidemic fevers of the West Indies; *An Epistle to Dr. Richard Mead, Concerning the Epidemical Diseases of Virginia, Particularly, a Pleurisy, and Peripneumony* (Edinburgh, 1738), elaborating a fantastic theory of disease and expanding the therapeutic uses of snake-root for gout, rheumatism, dropsy, and many nervous disorders; *Physical Enquiries* (1742), discussing the constitutional effects of change of climate and giving his views concerning the irregular practice of medicine; and, finally, *Physical Disquisitions* (London, 1745).

[*A Brief Account of the Case of John Tennent, M.D.*; W. B. Blanton, *Med. in Va. in the Eighteenth Century* (1931); H. A. Kelly, article in H. A. Kelly and W. L. Burrage, *Am. Medic. Biog.* (1920); *William and Mary Quart.*, July 1923; *Jour. of the House of Burgesses, Va.,* 1727–40, 1758–61; *Va. Gazette* for 1736, Nos. 6, 9, 10, 14, 31; *Ibid.* for 1737, Nos. 45, 50, 72; Park's *Va. Gazette,* Aug. 6, 1736.]
W. B. B.

TENNENT, WILLIAM (1673–May 6, 1746), Presbyterian clergyman, founder of the "Log College," was born in Ireland. On July 11, 1695, he graduated from the University of Edinburgh (*A Catalogue of the Graduates . . . of the University of Edinburgh,* 1858, p. 151), and on May 15, 1702, married Catharine, daughter of Rev. Gilbert Kennedy, a prominent Scotch Presbyterian. Tennent was ordained deacon in the Church of Ireland on July 1, 1704, and priest on Sept. 22, 1706. He is said to have been chaplain to an Irish nobleman but never to have had a parish, possibly because of non-conformist tendencies.

In middle life, sometime between 1716 and 1718, with his wife, four sons, and a daughter, he emigrated to Philadelphia, drawn to this particular city, perhaps, because here resided his wife's cousin, James Logan [q.v.], a prominent Pennsylvania official. On Sept. 17, 1718, the Synod of Philadelphia acted upon a petition from Tennent requesting that he be admitted to the Presbyterian ministry. In a statement of his reasons for leaving the Established Church he affirmed his belief that the Episcopal form of church government was "anti-scriptural," and expressed his objection to the Church's "conniving at the practice of Arminian doctrines inconsistent with the eternal purpose of God, and an encouragement of vice" (statement printed in Archibald Alexander, *Biographical Sketches of the Founder and Principal Alumni of the Log College,* 1851, p. 15). Admitted to the Presbyterian fellowship, he lived in East Chester, N. Y., from Nov. 22, 1718, to May 1, 1720, and then accepted a call to the church in Bedford, which he served until August 1726 (C. W. Baird, *History of Bedford Church,* 1882, p. 47f.), though apparently in 1721 he preached for a brief period in Bensalem, Bucks County, Pa. In the fall of 1726 he became pastor at Neshaminy, Pa., where he remained until his death. Soon after beginning work there, he took charge, also, of a congregation at Deep Run, to which he ministered until 1738.

Tennent was well educated, a faithful pastor, a teacher of unusual ability, and withal a man of genuine piety and evangelistic zeal. His significance in American church history lies in the fact that he trained for the ministry and imbued with his own spirit a notable group of men who became religious and educational leaders, and that indirectly he gave impetus to the creating of educational institutions. After living on a farm between Neshaminy and Bensalem, said to have been given him by James Logan, he bought in 1735, perhaps through the financial assistance of Logan, 100 acres of land on the road from Philadelphia to New York. Here he lived and in 1736 erected his famous "Log College," though he had earlier been giving instruction to his sons and possibly to others. The Presbyterians insisted upon an educated ministry, and the fact that candidates in that region could be properly fitted for the work only by going to New England or abroad made it difficult to increase the supply. The "Log College" was an attempt to meet this condition. Here Tennent's three younger sons, William [q.v.], John, and

Charles, all of whom entered the ministry, continued their training; the eldest, Gilbert [q.v.], destined to be one of the chief agencies in the Great Awakening, was ordained about the time of its establishment. Here, too, such men as Samuel Blair and Samuel Finley [qq.v.] were trained. Both conducted academies of their own and Finley became president of the College of New Jersey.

The "College" was not without its detractors, however; in fact the title was given it in a spirit of derision. Many thought the training it offered, however good, inadequate, and in 1738 the Philadelphia Synod decreed that all candidates without diplomas from the Old World universities, Harvard, or Yale must be approved by a commission of the Synod. This edict the recently formed Presbytery of New Brunswick, made up largely of "Log College" men, opposed and disregarded. The feeling between the two parties was intensified by the fact that the Tennents were aggressively evangelistic and welcomed Whitefield and his methods. The elder Tennent went to Philadelphia to visit him in 1739, and in November of that year Whitefield spent several days at Neshaminy, writing in his journal (*post*), under date of Nov. 22, a description of the "College" and its founder. He also preached extensively in the bounds of the New Brunswick Presbytery, giving the weight of his approval and support to its members. Thus the spirit and work of Tennent contributed greatly to strengthen the "New Side" cause and helped to bring about the schism of 1741 in the Presbyterian Church.

Tennent continued his teaching until his death in 1746, at which time the "Log College" ceased to exist; but that same year its supporters united with others in organizing the College of New Jersey.

[In addition to sources cited above, see Richard Webster, *A Hist. of the Presbyt. Ch. in America* (1857); E. H. Gillett, *Hist. of the Presbyt. Ch. in the United States of America* (1864), vol. I; W. B. Sprague, *Annals Am. Pulpit,* vol. III (1858); Thomas Murphy, *The Presbytery of the Log College* (copr. 1889); Elias Boudinot, *Memoirs of the Life of the Rev. William Tennent* (1807, many later editions), a biog. of the younger William; D. K. Turner, *Neshaminy Presbyt. Ch.* (1876); *Jour. of the Presbyt. Hist. Soc.,* June 1902, June 1904, June, Sept. 1912, Sept., Dec. 1913, Sept. 1914, Sept. 1915, Sept. 1919, Oct. 1927; C. H. Maxson, *The Great Awakening in the Middle Colonies* (1920); George Whitefield, *A Continuation of the Rev. Mr. Whitefield's Journal, from His Embarking after the Embargo* (1740).]   H. E. S.

TENNENT, WILLIAM (June 3, 1705–Mar. 8, 1777), Presbyterian clergyman, was the second of the four sons of William [q.v.] and Catharine (Kennedy) Tennent, being about two years younger than his brother Gilbert [q.v.]. He was born in County Armagh, Ireland, and was brought to America as a boy by his parents. He received his classical education in his father's "Log College" at Neshaminy, Pa., and then studied theology under Gilbert, who had become pastor of the church in New Brunswick, N. J.

During his residence there he narrowly escaped being buried alive. Under the strain of intense mental application his health broke and one day, while conversing in Latin with his brother, he became unconscious. Soon every indication of death was present, the body was laid out, and arrangements made for the funeral. In the meantime, fortunately, a physician, a close friend of Tennent, arrived and thought he detected a faint sign of life. Rather against the judgment of Gilbert, who said it was foolish to try to resuscitate one who was "cold and stiff as a stake," the funeral was postponed. Efforts to revive him were unsuccessful, however, and people were assembling for the obsequies when suddenly he gave unmistakable evidence of life. In about a year's time he had entirely recovered, except that memory of his past life was entirely gone and he could not even read or write. Under instruction he was gradually brought back to his former state of mind. During his unconsciousness, he affirmed, he had had the experience of being with a host of happy beings, surrounded by inexpressible glory, engaged in acts of joyous worship. Other extraordinary experiences came to him later, which modern medical science would probably attribute to physical rather than to supernatural causes. The accounts of some of them, as for example that of his "miraculous" escape from being convicted of perjury, will hardly bear critical scrutiny (see H. W. Green, "The Trial of the Rev. William Tennent," *Biblical Repertory and Princeton Review*, July 1868).

As soon as he was sufficiently recovered he was licensed to preach. His brother John died on Apr. 23, 1732, and the following year William was called to succeed him as pastor of the church at Freehold, N. J., and was ordained by the Philadelphia Presbytery on Oct. 25, 1733. Here he ministered until his death nearly forty-four years later. Indifferent to material things, he became somewhat embarrassed financially and a friend, Isaac Noble, a New York merchant, advised him to get a wife "to attend to his temporal affairs, and to comfort his leisure hours by conjugal endearments." He replied that he did not know how to go about it. Accordingly, his friend told him that he had a sister-in-law to whom he would introduce him—Catharine (van Burgh), widow of John Noble. Tennent went

to New York to see her and within a week, Aug. 23, 1738, they were married. The union proved a happy one; of their children, three sons grew to maturity.

In spite of various peculiarities, Tennent had the character and gifts that made him one of the leading Presbyterian ministers of his day. One in whose home he visited described him as "tall —of large frame, but spare, and of a long thin visage," adding, "He wore a white wig" (S. J. Forman, in Sprague, *post*, p. 62). His manners were pleasing and he was capable of a facetiousness that was delightful. Few were better judges of horses or could excel him in horsemanship. He was noted for the ingenuousness of his faith, his firmness of character, independence, and courage. His preaching had more power than grace of form, but students at the College of New Jersey would walk twenty miles to hear him in his own pulpit. Like the other Tennents he was a friend of Whitefield and a promoter of revivals. He probably sympathized in general with his brother Gilbert, but he was free from the disagreeable qualities of the latter and he was a peacemaker rather than a controversialist. Calls came to him from near and far to settle disputes. His keen judgment of men, tact, and skill in dealing with people in doubt or trouble made him eminently successful as a pastor. He took an active interest in John Brainerd's Indian mission. To his many other labors he added teaching, and such men as Alexander Mac-Whorter [*q.v.*] profited by his instruction. Upon the establishment of the College of New Jersey he became one of its trustees. He died in his seventy-second year and was buried beneath his church.

[Elias Boudinot, *Memoirs of the Life of the Rev. William Tennent* (1807), originally published in *The General Assembly's Missionary Mag.*, Mar. 1806; W. B. Sprague, *Annals Am. Pulpit*, vol. III (1858); Archibald Alexander, *Biog. Sketches of the Founders and Principal Alumni of the Log. Coll.* (copr. 1851); Thomas Murphy, *The Presbytery of the Log Coll.* (copr. 1889); Richard Webster, *A Hist. of the Presbyt. Ch. in America* (1857); *Pa. Mag. of Hist. and Biog.*, Apr. 1883, pp. 113, 114.]   H. E. S.

TENNEY, CHARLES DANIEL (June 29, 1857–Mar. 14, 1930), missionary, educator, and diplomat in China, was born at Boston, Mass. His father, the Rev. Daniel Tenney, was a descendant of Thomas Tenney who emigrated from Yorkshire, England, to Salem, Mass., in 1638, and settled at Rowley, Mass., the following year; his mother, Mary Adams (Parker), claimed descent from Gov. Thomas Dudley [*q.v.*]. Reared in a Congregationalist family, Tenney reached young manhood during a period of foreign missionary fervor in New England. He graduated from Dartmouth College in 1878 (taught for a year in an academy at Atkinson, N. H., and completed the divinity course at Oberlin Theological Seminary in 1882. In the same year he proceeded to his first missionary post, in the province of Shansi, China, under the auspices of the American Board of Commissioners for Foreign Missions. He was accompanied by his wife, Anne Runcie Jerrell of Bridgeton, N. J.; of their marriage on Mar. 29, 1882, three sons and two daughters were born.

Retiring from the mission field, Tenney moved in 1886 to the "treaty port" of Tientsin, then seat of the Viceroy Li Hung-chang. Here he at once established intimate relations with the great Chinese statesman by becoming tutor to his sons, and the same year was instrumental in establishing the Anglo-Chinese School, an institution for Chinese students, of which he remained the principal from 1886 to 1895. Concurrently with his other activities, he was vice-consul and interpreter to the American consulate at Tientsin from Mar. 6, 1894 to June 30, 1896. In 1895 he was selected by the Chinese government as the first president of the newly organized Imperial Chinese University at Tientsin (after 1900 designated Peiyang University). He served in this capacity until 1906.

The Boxer outbreak of 1900 interrupted his educational work. During the siege of Tientsin, Tenney and Herbert C. Hoover, then in charge of the reorganization of the Kaiping coal mines, devoted themselves to the relief of numerous Chinese and their families who had thrown in their lot with the beleaguered whites. Among these was a young American-trained Chinese, T'ang Shao-yi, who was to become one of China's eminent statesmen. Following the relief of Tientsin by an international column, Tenney served as Chinese secretary of the Tientsin provisional government from 1900 to 1902, earning the gratitude of the local Chinese populace for his determined stand against unnecessary harshness of treatment at a moment when the many outrages of the Boxers were still fresh in the minds of the armies of occupation.

The University was occupied by German troops during the Boxer troubles, and in 1902, on his own responsibility as its administrative head, Tenney made a special journey to Germany to obtain an indemnity for the seizure of the plant. He was successful in his mission, and the institution was rebuilt on a new site. From 1902 to 1906 he was also superintendent of high and middle schools in Chihli, making inspection tours throughout the metropolitan province. His labors in this connection resulted in a de-

velopment of the school system which placed Chihli in an advanced position in that respect among the "eighteen provinces." When he retired as president of Peiyang University in 1906, he was appointed director of Chinese government students in America, which position he held until 1908, making his headquarters at Cambridge, Mass., and establishing in various American universities successive groups of Chinese students. In 1907–08 he was lecturer on Chinese history at Harvard.

Following his retirement in 1908 from his lengthy service to China, Tenney accepted the appointment of Chinese secretary to the American Legation at Peking. In 1909 he was designated one of the three American delegates to the joint International Opium Commission convened at Shanghai. In 1912, when Nanking assumed importance as the capital of the revolutionary government, he was assigned by the American government to that post with title of consul; but owing to the illness of his wife, he resigned in 1913 and returned to the United States. The following year (May 1, 1914) he was reappointed Chinese secretary of the American Legation at Peking. In 1919 he was advanced to secretary of legation, class I, and counselor of legation, serving as chargé d'affaires ad interim at Peking from September 1919 to July 1920. He returned to the United States on leave in October of the latter year and retired from the diplomatic service, Mar. 1, 1921, to make his home at Palo Alto, Cal. In 1923 he revisited China, and while at Peking in 1924 suffered a severe illness from which he never recovered, remaining an invalid until his death, six years later, at Palo Alto.

Tenney's life left its impress directly upon a multitude of Chinese students. In the rôle of educator, his character, scholarship, thoroughness, and administrative ability made his example of singular importance; and the fact that his influence was exerted not through the usual alien missionary institution but directly under the viceroys Li Hung-chang and later Yüan Shih-k'ai, gave it a unique independence and authority. His publications, which were incidental to his educational work, enjoyed wide popularity in the Chinese school curriculum; they included a series of English lessons (1890), an English grammar (1892), and a geography of Asia (1898). His contribution to American diplomacy during the final decadence of the Manchu imperial house, the revolution, and the World War must be identified with the events of the terms of successive American ministers; in the diplomatic correspondence of the Peking legation between the years 1908 and 1919 it is virtually impossible to distinguish the actual handiwork of Tenney, but it may be accepted as certain that particularly through his wide personal acquaintance among the highest Chinese officials, he exercised a determining influence upon Sino-American relations. The Chinese government bestowed successive decorations upon him, from the order of the Double Dragon, Third Class, No. 1, in 1895, to the *Chiaho* order, Second Class, awarded in 1921, by the republican government.

[Tenney's private papers are in the possession of his family, from whom much of the foregoing information has been obtained; personal memories of surviving associates in China have also been drawn upon. Printed sources include M. J. Tenney, *The Tenney Family* (1904); issues of the *Register of the Department of State*, especially that for 1922; *Who's Who in America*, 1928–29; *N. Y. Times*, Mar. 16, 1930; *China Weekly Review*, Mar. 22, 1930.]   E. M. G.

TENNEY, EDWARD PAYSON (Sept. 29, 1835–July 24, 1916), Congregational clergyman, educator, and author, was born at Concord, N. H., the son of Rev. Asa Peaslee and Mary (Tenney) Tenney. His parents were cousins and descendants of Thomas Tenney of Yorkshire, England, who came to Salem, Mass., in 1638. Edward prepared for college at Pembroke Academy and entered Dartmouth in 1854, remaining one year. In 1858 he graduated from Bangor Theological Seminary, and then made a trip around the Horn to California. Here he remained about a year, doing some editorial work for *The Pacific* of San Francisco, becoming interested in the College of California, and writing the first of a long series of articles championing the cause of frontier education. Returning East, he was ordained a Congregational minister at West Concord, N. H., on Oct. 19, 1859. For some two years he was pastor of a church in the little mining town of Central City, Colo., near Denver. Thereafter he spent a decade on Cape Ann, Massachusetts, in study, meditation, writing and in correcting the astigmatism and inconsistencies in what he called his "hasty" education.

In 1876 a former pupil of his father's, Prof. E. N. Bartlett, then secretary of the two-year-old Colorado College at Colorado Springs, called Tenney's attention to the precarious condition of that institution. Its assets then consisted of a little frame building, twenty-five preparatory, normal, and special students, and the prayers of pioneers impoverished by the panic of 1873. That same year he assumed the presidency, his salary being provided out of his own private income. His love for the Rocky Mountain region, and his belief in the salutary influence of

a college on the frontier were the inspiration of eight years' service in that post. He poured his enthusiasm into a famous booklet, *The New West as Related to the Christian College* (1878), reprinted in 1880 under the title, *Colorado and Homes in the New West*. This work extolled Colorado as a refuge for those desiring new health and Colorado College as an American mainstay and buttress on a polyglot frontier. It secured for the institution the support of the American College and Education Society, and it inspired the local sacrifice necessary to raise the $10,000 which secured the $20,000 offered tentatively by Eastern friends. This money saved the college. During Tenney's administration strengthened faculty gathered together a library of some 6,000 volumes, and secured the erection of Palmer Hall, the first substantial building on the college campus. His belief in educational institutions as safeguards of American civilization on the Rocky Mountain frontier led him to found academies at Santa Fé, N. Mex., and at Salt Lake City.

Giving up his work in Colorado in 1884, he returned to Massachusetts. During his residence in this state he served churches at Assonet, Burlington, Ayer, Braintree, and Lowell. He devoted much time to writing and his publications include *The Silent House* (1876); *Coronation* (1877); *Agamenticus* (1878); *Constance of Acadia* (1886); *The Triumph of the Cross* (1895); *Dream of My Youth* (1901); *Contrasts in Social Progress* (1907); *Looking Forward into the Past* (1910). He was twice married: first, Dec. 1, 1860, to Sarah J. Holden, who died Nov. 23, 1861; second Dec. 8, 1862, to Ellen Weeks, by whom he had two children.

[M. J. Tenney, *The Tenney Family* (1904); M. D. and E. R. Ormes, *The Book of Colorado Springs* (1933); *The Congregational Year-Book for 1916* (1917); *Who's Who in America*, 1916–17; *Boston Transcript*, July 25, 1916; I. H. Kerr MSS., Colorado Coll.]   A. B. H.

TENNEY, TABITHA GILMAN (Apr. 7, 1762–May 2, 1837), novelist and compiler, was born in Exeter, N. H., the daughter of Samuel Gilman and his second wife, Lydia (Robinson) Giddings (or Giddinge) Gilman. Her father, a descendant of John Gilman who emigrated from England to Hingham, Mass., in 1638, was a member of a family that had provided many public servants for New Hampshire. Her mother was an educated and forceful woman, and Tabitha's upbringing was Puritanical, bookish, and secluded. She acquired familiarity with intellectual and gentlewomanly accomplishments, and a code of behavior in which a virtuous common sense predominated. In 1788 (intention recurded, Sept. 6, 1788) she married Samuel Tenney (1748–1816), who had just resumed a residence in Exeter that had been interrupted by his service as a surgeon in the Continental Army for the duration of the Revolution. Instead of returning to medical practice, however, he devoted his energies to politics, and his wife was able to spend several winters in Washington during his terms as congressman (1800–07). In 1801 she published the two-volume novel, *Female Quixotism: Exhibited in the Romantic Opinions and Extravagant Adventures of Dorcasina Sheldon,* upon which her claim to remembrance chiefly rests. Sometime prior to this, possibly in 1799 (see bookseller's advertisement in *Newburyport Herald,* Newburyport, Mass., May 7, 1799) she edited a volume called *The Pleasing Instructor,* an anthology of selections from poets and classical writers for the education of young women, of which no copy is known to exist. The collection was especially recommended "For Female Academies, Schools, &c.," and, as the author's aim was "to blend instruction with rational amusement," she included only those "pieces which . . . tend either to inform the mind, correct the manners, or to regulate the conduct."

Female Quixotism is a satire on prevailing literary tastes, and a minor declaration of American intellectual independence. It purports to be the biography of a young woman, in other respects charming and lovable, whose mind has become corrupted by a too-constant diet of current novels and romances. Dorcasina Sheldon, like her prototype, the Spanish knight-errant, forms her grandiose conceptions of existence from the literary extravagances of her day, and her tragedy lies in their lack of correspondence to the world of actuality. The analogy to the book's great model is skilfully and not too slavishly handled, the conception is clever and humorous, but the plot falters in execution and is marred by the repetitious narration of absurd and wearisomely similar events in the career of the heroine. Moreover, the book is written as an object lesson to similar misguided females, and, though the moral is a healthy one, it is too much in evidence for a work of art. In the character of the Irish adventurer, who occupies the major portion of volume one, there is excellently portrayed a type of charlatan from whom the United States suffered much in its infancy. The whole is a plea to American girls to accept the responsibilities of normal living and to give over their affectations, their day dreams, and their preoccupation with foreign romantic sentimentality,

and it commemorates an interesting phase in the intellectual fashions of the early Republic.

Tabitha Tenney was left a widow in 1816, and apparently had no children. The last twenty years of her life she spent in Exeter, occupied with fine needlework and acts of charity quite after the fashion she had recommended to her erring heroine. Some proverbial examples of her reputation for goodness have been preserved (Duyckinck, *post*). She died at Exeter after a brief illness.

[The days of birth and death are taken from Arthur Gilman, *The Gilman Family* (1869). See also M. J. Tenney, *The Tenney Family . . . 1638–1904* (1904); C. H. Bell, *Hist. of the Town of Exeter, N. H.* (1888); S. A. Allibone, *A Crit. Dict. of Eng. Lit.* (1871); E. A. and G. L. Duyckinck, *Cyc. of Am. Lit.* (2 vols., 1855); *Newburyport Herald and Country Gazette* (Newburyport, Mass.), May 7–21, 1799; *Exeter News Letter,* May 9, 1837; death notice in *New-Hampshire Statesman and State Jour.* (Concord), May 13, 1837.]

J. H. B—h.

TENNEY, WILLIAM JEWETT (1811– Sept. 20, 1883), editor, was born at Newport, R. I., the second of the six children of Caleb Jewett and Ruth (Channing) Tenney, and the sixth in descent from Thomas Tenney, a Yorkshireman, who arrived at Salem, Mass., in December 1638 and settled the following spring in Rowley. The month and day of his birth are unrecorded, but he was baptized in the First Congregational Church, Bristol, R. I., July 2, 1811. His father, a classmate of Daniel Webster at Dartmouth College, was a Congregational clergyman of some note. Tenney entered Yale College from Wethersfield, Conn., in 1827 and graduated with the class of 1832. His movements during the next twenty years are somewhat obscure. He began the study of medicine and was connected in 1835 with the Retreat for the Insane at Hartford. At one time he was an instructor on a naval vessel. He is supposed to have migrated to western New York and thence to Ohio; it is certain that he studied law and was admitted to practice. In 1839 he married Elizabeth M. Benton, by whom he had three sons and a daughter. The great event of his inner life was his conversion to Catholicism, which seems to have estranged him from his family and from the friends of his earlier years, but the date of his conversion is also unrecorded. About 1840 he went to New York City and turned journalist, being employed on the *New York Journal of Commerce,* the *Evening Post,* Freeman Hunt's *Merchants' Magazine,* and the *Mining Magazine.* In 1853 he joined the staff of D. Appleton & Company as reader and editor and remained with the company until his death thirty years later.

Tenney's chief accomplishment was *Appletons' Annual Cyclopædia*, which he edited from its inception until his death, when Rossiter Johnson took his place. For the years 1861–1901 it provides a unique summary of events and statistics, especially valuable for its accuracy and comprehensiveness. A by-product of the *Cyclopædia* was Tenney's *Military and Naval History of the Rebellion in the United States* (1865). The only other book to which he put his name as author was *A Grammatical Analyzer* (1866); the great bulk of his literary labor was expended on the writings of others. His most notable collaboration of this sort was on Jefferson Davis' *Rise and Fall of the Confederate Government* (1881). The Appletons had contracted for the work in 1875, but by January 1880 less than half of the first volume existed even in rough draft. Tenney was then sent to "Beauvoir" to replace Davis' original collaborator and brought the work to a conclusion in three or four months. For some years he made his home in Brooklyn, where he was at one time a judge of a criminal court, thereby acquiring the title by which he was always known. Later he lived in Elizabeth, N. J., where he was president of the board of education and, during President Buchanan's administration, collector of the port. His first wife having died, he married Sarah, daughter of Orestes Augustus Brownson [*q.v.*], in 1873. She was the author of a novel, *Marian Elwood, or How Girls Live* (1859), and of a biography, *Life of Demetrius Augustine Gallitzin* (1873). She died in 1876 after the birth of their second daughter. In 1883 Tenney's own health declined. He returned from a visit to "Beauvoir" in good spirits and apparently in restored health, but died unexpectedly at his boarding house in Newark, N. J.

[J. N. Arnold, *Vital Record of R. I.*, VIII (1896), 410; M. J. Tenney, *The Tenney Family* (1904); F. C. Jewett, *Hist. and Geneal. of the Jewetts of America* (1908); E. E. Salisbury, *Biog. Memoranda . . . of the Class of 1832 in Yale Coll.* (1880); *Obit. Record Grads. Yale Coll.* (1884); *N. Y. Daily Tribune*, Sept. 22, 1883; *Appletons' Ann. Cyc. . . . 1883* (1884); J. C. Derby, *Fifty Years Among Authors, Books and Publishers* (1884).]
G. H. G.

TENSKWATAWA (Mar. 1768?–1834?), Shawnee prophet, is believed to have been born at the great springs near Old Chillicothe, now Oldtown, Ohio (Galloway, *post*, p. 108), and to have been the twin of his brother Tecumseh [*q.v*]. His mother was sometimes said to be a Creek, and his father, Pucksinwa, was a Shawnee chief who was killed at the battle of Point Pleasant in 1774. About November 1805 he announced himself to be a prophet and assumed the name of Tenskwatawa instead of his original one of

Lalawethika. The white people usually referred to him as the Prophet. He was also sometimes called Elskwatawa. The history of his ministry is typical of the long line of such religious revivalists as Skaniadariio, Smohalla, and Wovoka [*qq.v.*]. He appeared in a time of great peril and was said to have shown indifference to religious ideas in his earlier life and to have been roused only by heavenly visions seen in a death-like trance. When he foretold the eclipse of the sun in 1806 his following increased rapidly. He also attacked witchcraft and in witch burnings rid himself of several of his most menacing enemies. He worked on the emotions of his followers by the practice of mystic rites, and he preached a reactionary doctrine of primitive ways nearer to the "Master of Life," the necessity of giving up alcoholic liquor and of again becoming self-supporting. To that end he sought a return to the use of primitive clothing of skin and furs and of the firestick for making fire; he forbade intermarriage with the whites; and he advocated the ancient custom of common possession of all property. At what time his religious revival merged with Tecumseh's political program it is impossible to say, as it is impossible to measure what part he played in that program. During most of the time even close observers assumed, erroneously, that the greater share of responsibility lay on the Prophet's shoulders.

Of middle height, blind in one eye, but possessing great personal magnetism, he gave a false sense of ability and power. He seems really to have been a vain, boastful man who preferred to have others do his fighting for him. In 1811, left by Tecumseh with the strict injunction to avoid war, he was unable to maintain as favorable a situation as his brother left. Perhaps because he was unduly persuaded by hotheads or because he wished to create a diversion for those discontented with his administration, he allowed himself to be maneuvered by William Henry Harrison [*q.v.*] into the battle of Tippecanoe on Nov. 7, 1811. During the progress of the fighting he is reported to have kept himself apart, in a safe place, busy with incantations and prophecies, and, from time to time, encouraging his warriors to believe that Harrison's army was just on the point of yielding to his magic. When the battle was over, disastrously, his own prestige was gone, as was the great hope of Indian confederation. He took no part in the fighting of the War of 1812. He received a pension from the British government and was in Canada until 1826, when he returned to Ohio. Later he lived near Cape Girardeau, Mo. In 1832 he was living in what is now Wyandotte County, Kan., where George Catlin [*q.v.*] knew him and painted his portrait.

[Consult James Mooney, "The Ghost Dance Religion," *14th Ann. Report of Bureau of Ethnology*, pt. 2 (1896); Benj. Drake, *Life of Tecumseh* (1841); George Catlin, *Letters and Notes on the . . . North American Indians* (1841), vol. II; *Am. State Papers: Indian Affairs*, vol. I (1832); W. A. Galloway, *Old Chillicothe* (1934); see also bibliog. of sketch of Tecumseh.]   K. E. C.

TERESA, MOTHER (*c.* 1766–Sept. 9, 1846), foundress of the Visitation Order in the United States, was born in Ireland and spent her childhood in Kilkenny. Her family name was Lalor; she was christened Alice. The girl's unusual piety seems to have attracted the attention of Bishop Lanigan, a local prelate, and he relied on her to help him in the foundation of a community of Presentation nuns in his diocese. This project did not meet with the approval of the family, however, and when one of Alice's sisters married an American merchant named Doran the girl was persuaded to accompany the couple to America. She intended nevertheless to return to Ireland later to cooperate with Bishop Lanigan in his projected foundation. On the boat she formed a deep friendship with two women, both widows, a Mrs. McDermott and a Mrs. Sharpe, who like her were eager to become nuns. The three friends landed in Philadelphia on Jan. 5, 1795. In accordance with an agreement they had made that they would seek out a priest and would regard him, whoever he should be, as their spiritual director and would follow his guidance implicitly, they went to the Reverend Leonard Neale [*q.v.*], a man of unusual character and ability, afterwards archbishop of Baltimore. Upon his advice they rented a house, and there Alice Lalor lived with her two friends in a sort of unofficial religious community. They busied themselves with good works and performed notable service during the yellow fever epidemic that swept through Philadelphia in 1797–98.

When in 1798 Father Neale was transferred to Washington as president of Georgetown College, he invited the little community to follow him. They arrived in 1799 and for a time lived with some Poor Clares who had been exiled from France. Afterwards they opened a school, and in 1804, when the Poor Clares returned to their native country, they were able to purchase the tiny convent belonging to the latter. From the beginning Alice Lalor and her companions had looked upon themselves as a religious community, but they had lacked any formal ecclesiastical authorization. Though Archbishop John Carroll [*q.v.*] urged Neale, now a bishop, to merge his community with the Sisters of Charity, and oth-

ers advised them to adopt the Ursuline rule or unite with the Carmelite nuns, who had already been established at Port Tobacco, Md., Neale was anxious that they should become Visitation nuns, and in spite of great practical difficulties, he succeeded in winning the approval of Rome. On Dec. 28, 1816, the sisters were admitted to solemn vows and became fully accredited Visitation nuns. Mother Teresa resigned her post as superior in 1819 and lived as a simple member of the community for twenty-seven years. During that time she saw the foundation of other houses in Mobile, Ala. (1832), in St. Louis, Mo. (1833), and in Baltimore, Md. (1837). When she died in 1846 she was buried with Archbishop Neale in the crypt of the convent which owed its existence to them.

[See G. P. and Rose Hawthorne Lathrop, *A Story of Courage; Annals of the Georgetown Convent of the Visitation of the Blessed Virgin Mary* (1895); J. B. Code, *Great Am. Foundresses* (1929); *Cath. Encyc.*, vol. VIII (1910); and obituary in *U. S. Cath. Mag. and Monthly Rev.*, Oct. 1846. There is a short contemporary account of Mother Teresa's life in MS. in the archives of the Visitation Academy of Georgetown.]

P. H. F.

TERHUNE, MARY VIRGINIA HAWES (Dec. 21, 1830–June 3, 1922), author, writer on household management, better known as Marion Harland, was born in Dennisville, Amelia County, Va., the daughter of Samuel Pierce and Judith Anna (Smith) Hawes. Her father, a descendant of early New England settlers, was a man of education who, through reverses in fortune, had become a country storekeeper. Virginia was taught at home by tutors and governesses, learned to use her father's well-chosen library, and at thirteen was sent for a year to Hampden Sidney, Va., a college town where she heard the table talk of scholarly men and had a glimpse of social life. In 1844, when the family moved to Richmond, she began contributing to the weekly newspaper. In 1853 her story, "Kate Harper," appeared in the *Southern Era* under the pseudonym of Marion Harland (*Marion Harland's Autobiography*, 1910, p. 240). Her first novel, *Alone*, which was also her best and most famous, was written when she was sixteen, though it was not revised for publication until 1854. From that time on she contributed fiction to numerous popular women's magazines and wrote a series of novels, over twenty-five in number, of which the most popular were *True as Steel* (1872), *Nemesis* (1860), *His Great Self* (1892), *A Gallant Fight* (1888), *Judith* (1883), *Dr. Dale* (1900), and *The Hidden Path* (1859). Her fiction in general is of a mild, pleasant type, often with a marked moral or religious tone. Many of her stories are set in the South in the days before the Civil War. Her marriage on Sept. 2, 1856, to the Rev. Edward Payson Terhune (Nov. 22, 1830–May 25, 1907), who later became widely known, carried her to the country parsonage of Charlotte Court-House, Va., where she served her novitiate at practical housewifery. Her struggles with the blind culinary guides then available led to the preparation of *Common Sense in the Household: A Manual of Practical Housewifery,* which she with difficulty persuaded Scribners to publish in 1871. The volume ran through numerous editions in a short time and continued to sell for many years. This, the first intelligently prepared cook book, the first attempt to dignify housewifery as a profession, dimmed her reputation as a novelist and doomed her to life work in the field of domestic economy. She was swamped with orders for newspaper and magazine articles, syndicate paragraphs, and editorial work. She conducted departments for children in *Wide Awake* (1882–83) and *St. Nicholas* (1876), and edited *Babyhood* (1884–86); she established a magazine, the *Home-Maker* and edited it for two years (1888–90); she edited a department of the *Chicago Daily Tribune* for six years (1911–17), and she produced in addition numerous books on home management and cooking, as well as several on home life. It was not literature, she knew. "But," she said, "it is Influence."

In her husband's successive city parishes— Newark, N. J. (1859–76), Springfield, Mass. (1879–84), and Brooklyn (1884–95)—she found time for much church and charitable work, and for distinguished literary friendships, without neglecting home or children or relaxing her literary pace. It is said that she systematized her work and never hurried. In 1876, her lungs being threatened, the family went abroad for two years. This trip and another in 1897 resulted in several travel books, *Loiterings in Pleasant Paths* (1880), *Where Ghosts Walk* (1898), and four biographical studies, *Charlotte Brontë at Home* (1899), *William Cowper* (1899), *John Knox* (1900), and *Hannah More* (1900). In 1893 the *Christian Herald* sent her to the Holy Land, her letters to it appearing later under the title, *The Home of the Bible* (1895). Lecture tours preceded and followed this trip. Even in her old age she remained indefatigable. At seventy an accident crippled her wrist. She mastered the typewriter. At eighty-nine she went blind. She mastered the difficult art of dictation, writing through an amanuensis her last novel, *The Carringtons of High Hill* (1919). She collaborated with each of her children who reached maturity: with Christine Terhune Herrick in

The National Cook Book (1896), with Virginia Terhune Van de Water in *Everyday Etiquette* (1905), and with Albert Payson Terhune in *Dr. Dale.* Her autobiography appeared in 1910 under the title of *Marion Harland's Autobiography.* She died in New York of old age. Of her six children, a son and two daughters survived her.

[In addition to *Marion Harland's Autobiog.* (1910), see *Who's Who in America,* 1922–23; Mary H. Wright, *Mary Virginia Hawes Terhune* (1934); Frances E. Willard and Mary A. Livermore, *A Woman of the Century* (1893); obituary in *N. Y. Times,* June 4, 1922.]

M. B. H.

TERRELL, EDWIN HOLLAND (Nov. 21, 1848–July 1, 1910), lawyer, diplomat, was born in Brookville, Ind. His parents were Rev. Williamson Terrell, a Methodist minister, and Martha Terrell, the daughter of James Jarrell of Kentucky. His grandfather, Capt. John Terrell, moved to Kentucky from Virginia in 1787 and won distinction in the early Indian campaigns under Josiah Harmar, Arthur St. Clair [*qq.v.*], and Anthony Wayne. His first American ancestor was William Terrell (or Tyrrell), who came from England to Virginia as a crownlands agent, according to family tradition, about the middle of the seventeenth century. Terrell was valedictorian of his class at Asbury (later De Pauw) University, where he received the degree of A.B. in 1871. Two years later he received the degree of LL.B. from Harvard, and spent the following year in Europe, studying international law and modern languages. He became a member of the firm of Barbour, Jacobs, and Terrell in Indianapolis in 1874. In 1877 he moved permanently to San Antonio, Tex., established a law office, and quickly became closely identified with the political, professional, and business life of the city. He was a delegate to the Republican National Conventions of 1880, 1888, and 1904, and was a member of the Republican state executive committee of Texas from 1894 to 1900.

On Apr. 1, 1889, President Harrison appointed Terrell envoy extraordinary and minister plenipotentiary to Belgium, where he served with distinction throughout the Harrison administration. With Henry Shelton Sanford [*q.v.*] he represented the United States at the Brussels International Slave Trade Conference, 1889–90, and signed the General Act for the repression of the African slave trade. He was also United States delegate to the Brussels customs tariff conference of 1890, and signed the convention concerning the formation of an international union for the publication of customs tariffs, July 5, 1890. The same year he was made a member of the *Commission Technique* to revise the tariff provisions of the Berlin Treaty of 1885 under the General Act of Brussels, and on Jan. 24, 1891, he concluded with Leopold II a treaty of commerce, amity, and navigation between the United States and the Congo Free State. In 1891 he also succeeded in persuading the Belgian government to modify greatly the quarantine restrictions which barred American live stock from the Belgian market. Early in 1892, at the request of Secretary of State James G. Blaine, he returned to Washington and aided in persuading the Senate to consent to the ratification of the slave trade treaty. Returning to Brussels, he served as United States commissioner at the International Monetary Conference of 1892, of which he was elected vice-president, and delivered the response to the address of welcome made by the Belgian prime minister. In 1893 he retired from the diplomatic service. In October of that year he was made a grand officer of the Order of Leopold. Returning to San Antonio, he again took an active part in political, business, and civic affairs. On Aug. 17, 1874, he married Mary Maverick, daughter of Samuel A. Maverick, one of the founders of the Republic of Texas. She died in Brussels in 1891, leaving six children. On Feb. 7, 1895, he married Lois Lasater of Corpus Christi, Tex., daughter of Albert Lasater. They had three children. Terrell died in San Antonio after an illness of two years. He was survived by five children of his first marriage and one child of his second.

[See J. H. Tyrrell, *A Geneal. Hist. of the Tyrrells* (n.d.), and *The Geneal. of Richmond and William Tyrrell or Terrell* (n.d.); E. H. Terrell, *Further Geneal. Notes on the Tyrrell-Terrell Family* (2nd ed., 1909); *Who's Who in America*, 1910–11; *A Twentieth Century Hist. of Southwest Tex.* (1907), vol. I, pp. 339–40; and obituary in *Daily Express* (San Antonio), July 2, 1910. Terrell's diplomatic correspondence is in the archives of the Dept. of State, Washington, D. C.; part of it has been printed in *Papers Relating to the Foreign Relations of the U. S. . . . 1891* (1892).]   I. L. T.

TERRY, ALFRED HOWE (Nov. 10, 1827–Dec. 16, 1890), soldier, was a descendant of Samuel Terry who settled in Springfield, Mass., in 1650. Born in Hartford, Conn., the eldest son of Alfred and Clarissa (Howe) Terry, he entered the Yale Law School in 1848, but on admission to the bar the following year left without graduating. He was clerk of the superior court of New Haven County, 1854–60. Soon after the outbreak of the Civil War he was commissioned colonel of the 2nd Connecticut Militia, a three months' regiment, and participated in the first battle of Bull Run. On the expiration of his service, he returned to Connecticut, and with Joseph R. Hawley [*q.v.*] soon raised the 7th Connecticut Volunteers for three years or the duration of the war. Terry was commissioned colonel and Haw-

ley lieutenant-colonel. This regiment took part in the capture of Port Royal, S. C., in November 1861 and subsequently in the bombardment, siege, and capture of Fort Pulaski, Ga., Apr. 10–11, 1862. On Apr. 25 Terry was promoted brigadier-general of volunteers. After the attempted advance on Charleston across James Island had been turned back by the repulse at Secessionville, June 16, he was stationed for some months at Hilton Head, taking part in the action at Pocotaligo Bridge, S. C., Oct. 22. On Oct. 29, 1862, he was placed in command of the forces on Hilton Head.

To supplement the naval operations of Rear Admiral Samuel Francis du Pont [*q.v.*] off Charleston, in the summer of 1863 the army under Gen. Quincy Adams Gillmore [*q.v.*], in cooperation with Rear Admiral John A. Dahlgren [*q.v.*], conducted a siege of Battery Wagner, Morris Island, S. C. Terry's command was sent on a diversion up the Stono River to James Island, whence it soon returned and advanced along Morris Island to reënforce the siege. Later in 1863, Terry was transferred to the Army of the James under Gen. B. F. Butler, and during 1864 was engaged mainly in operations against Richmond and Petersburg. On Aug. 26, 1864, he was brevetted major-general of volunteers.

After the failure of Butler's expedition against Fort Fisher, N. C., in December 1864, Grant assigned the same task to practically the same military forces under Terry, adding only one small brigade and a siege train which was not used. On Jan. 15, 1865, the fort was taken by a series of assaults after severe bombardments by the fleet under Rear Admiral David D. Porter [*q.v.*]. Terry's report, dated Jan. 25, 1865, is the most detailed and comprehensive description of that action (*War of the Rebellion: Official Records, Army*, 1 ser. XLVI, pt. 1, pp. 394–400). He was advanced as of Jan. 15, 1865, to brigadier-general in the regular army and received the thanks of Congress with particular reference to the capture of Fort Fisher. Following that supreme accomplishment of his military career, he occupied Wilmington, N. C., in cooperation with J. M. Schofield [*q.v.*] and soon thereafter started with the X Corps to join Gen. William T. Sherman, then coming up from Georgia. A junction was made near Goldsboro, N. C., and for a time Terry and his corps served under Schofield in the Army of the Ohio. On Apr. 20, 1865, he was commissioned major-general of volunteers.

After the war Terry was mustered out of the volunteer service, and in 1866, as a regular officer, assumed command of the Department of

Dakota, with headquarters at St. Paul and later at Fort Snelling, Minn. In 1869 he was transferred to the Department of the South, but in December 1872 was returned to the Northwest, where he continued at the head of the Department of Dakota during the exploration of the Black Hills in 1874 and the Sioux war, taking the field in personal command of the expedition from Fort Abraham Lincoln on the Missouri River in Dakota to the Yellowstone-Big Horn region of Montana in the summer of 1876. The disaster to the force under Gen. George A. Custer [q.v.] at the Little Big Horn, June 25, 1876, led to a controversy as to whether or not Custer had disobeyed or exceeded Terry's order of June 22, but Terry never made any statement on that point, preferring (it is generally believed) to accept responsibility and criticism rather than create an issue (see Hughes, post). His assignments to the Northwest covered the most important period of railroad construction and development in the present North and South Dakota and Montana. On Mar. 3, 1886, he was advanced to the full rank of major-general, and on Apr. 9 was placed in command of the Division of the Missouri, with headquarters at Chicago. He was retired for disability, Apr. 5, 1888.

Terry was a member of several boards and commissions, notably the Indian Commission created by Congress in 1867 to treat with the Plains Indians. He was the ranking officer in the attempted negotiations with Sitting Bull in the fall of 1877, and a member of the board of army officers appointed in 1878 to review the court martial and sentence of General Fitz-John Porter [q.v.]. Terry was a thorough student of the science and art of war. He was about six feet in height, straight, vigorous and active. A conspicuous trait was his ability to cooperate with superiors, equals, or subordinates. He never wrote for publication outside of numerous official reports of a high order. He was one of very few Civil War volunteer officers who reached the highest permanent rank in the regular army; for a considerable time he was the first general officer on the army list not a West Point graduate. After retirement, he returned to New Haven, where he died. He was unmarried. A full length portrait of him hangs in Memorial Hall, Connecticut State Building, Hartford.

[Stephen Terry, *Notes of Terry Families in the U. S. A.* (1887); *Record of Service of Conn. Men . . . during the War of the Rebellion* (1889); Stephen Walkley, *Hist. of the Seventh Conn. Vol. Infantry* (1905); A. D. Osborne, *The Capture of Fort Fisher by Maj. Gen. Alfred H. Terry and What It Accomplished* (New Haven Colony Hist. Soc., 1911); *War of the Rebellion, Official Records (Army)* and *(Navy)* both, for operations along the Atlantic Coast; F. B. Heitman, *Hist.*

Reg. and Dict. U. S. Army (1903), vol. I; *Battles and Leaders of the Civil War* (4 vols., 1887–88). D. D. Porter, *The Naval Hist. of the Civil War* (1886); *Personal Memoirs of U. S. Grant*, vol. II, (1886) and *Memoirs of Gen. Wm. T. Sherman* (2 vols., 1875); J. M. Schofield, *Forty-six Years in the Army* (1897); N. A. Miles, *Personal Recollections* (1896); R. P. Hughes (Terry's brother-in-law), "The Campaign against the Sioux in 1876," *Jour. of the Military Service Inst.*, Jan. 1896; *General Orders*, Hdqrs. Army, Washington, Dec. 16, 1890; *Army and Navy Jour.*, Dec. 20, 1890; *Harper's Weekly*, Dec. 27, 1890; *Sun* (N. Y.), Dec. 17, 1890.]   R. B.

TERRY, DAVID SMITH (Mar. 8, 1823–Aug. 14, 1889), soldier, California jurist and political leader, was born in Todd (then part of Christian) County, Ky. His great-grandfather, Capt. Nathaniel Terry (d. 1780), of Halifax County, Va., was a man of considerable prominence. His grandfathers, Nathaniel Terry and David Smith, had been officers in the Revolutionary War, and the latter served under Andrew Jackson in the War of 1812. While he was still a boy, his parents, Joseph R. and Sarah (Smith) Terry, removed to Mississippi, where they separated. Subsequently, Mrs. Terry and her sons settled in Texas. Although only thirteen years of age, Terry served as a volunteer in the war for Texan independence but did not participate in any actual fighting (Potts, *post*, p. 297). In the Mexican War he served as a lieutenant in a company of Texas Rangers and participated in the battle of Monterey. In December 1849, Terry became a resident of Stockton, Cal., where he engaged actively in the practice of law. In 1852 he married Cornelia Runnels, a niece of Governor Runnels of Mississippi. In 1855 he accepted the nomination of the Know-Nothing party for the office of associate justice of the California supreme court and was elected to that place when the new party, in an astonishing political upset, swept the state. In 1856 he rashly went to San Francisco to aid in organizing resistance to the Vigilantes, who were in extra-legal control there. When Sterling A. Hopkins, one of the agents of the Vigilance Committee, while endeavoring to arrest illegally one Reuben Maloney, also sought to disarm Terry, a scuffle ensued in which Terry seriously wounded Hopkins in the neck with a bowie knife. Terry was immediately taken into custody by the Vigilance Committee, but, when Hopkins recovered, was released after undergoing an imprisonment of several weeks.

Resuming his place on the supreme court, he became chief justice in the October term 1857. In 1859 he affiliated himself with the Gwin or Southern branch of the Democratic party in California but, because of his Know-Nothing record, its convention refused him a renomination to the supreme court. He made, however, before the state convention of the faction, a vigorous speech in which he assailed Senator David Broderick [*q.v.*], the leader of the other Democratic faction, as a follower of the negro, Frederick Douglass [*q.v.*], rather than one of Stephen A. Douglas [*q.v.*]. Incensed by this attack, Broderick denounced Terry, as a "miserable wretch" and as a dishonest man and judge (Potts, p. 309).

When Broderick refused to retract these intemperate and unjustified statements, Terry challenged him to a duel which Broderick accepted, the seconds naming pistols, with which Broderick was an expert shot, as the weapons. The duel was fought on Sept. 13, 1859, and resulted in Broderick's receiving a fatal wound after having fired prematurely. To allay unwarranted rumors as to the conduct of the duel, Congressman Joseph C. McKibben, Broderick's second and political follower, testified that there was "no perceptible difference in the weapons" (San Francisco *Daily Alta California*, Sept. 18, 1859, evidence at coroner's inquest; Wagstaff, *post*, pp. 20, 207–08). Before this tragic affair, Terry filed his resignation as chief justice, and he afterward went through the formality of a trial for murder, being speedily acquitted. In 1863 he joined the Confederate forces and was wounded at Chickamauga and later commanded a regiment and a brigade in Texas. Upon the collapse of the Confederacy, he was for a time in Mexico, but in 1869 returned to California and resumed the practice of the law at Stockton. In 1878 he was elected to the California constitutional convention.

In 1884 Terry became involved, as one of the attorneys for the plaintiff, Sarah Althea Hill, in the notorious William Sharon divorce case. After lengthy proceedings, judgment was rendered for her in the trial court. On Jan. 7, 1886, while an appeal from this judgment was pending, Terry, whose first wife had died Dec. 24, 1884, married his client. The supreme court of California at first approved the decree of the lower court, but later changed its position. In the meantime, the federal court had decreed the documents, on which the plaintiff relied, to be fraudulent and had ordered their surrender and cancellation. Sharon died and the heirs had to revive the suit to have the decree carried out. When Justice Stephen J. Field [*q.v.*], acting as circuit justice, announced the decision of himself and Judges Sawyer and Sabin, a violent court room scene was precipitated by Mrs. Terry, which resulted in the imprisonment of both herself and her husband for contempt of court. After his release from this imprisonment, Terry threatened physical harm to Field. Because of this, the

Attorney General of the United States had David Neagle assigned to Field as his bodyguard. On Aug. 14, 1889, while Field and Neagle were having breakfast at the railroad eating house at Lathrop, Cal., Terry approached Field and struck him twice and was thereupon shot and killed by Neagle, who was immediately arrested and imprisoned on a charge of murder. From such imprisonment and charge he was freed by the federal courts, the Supreme Court of the United States holding that he was justified in his act, which was performed as a federal officer.

Terry was buried at Stockton and both its bar and the bar of Fresno adopted resolutions laudatory of his character. While he was a man of rash judgment and violent impulses, his honesty was as unquestionable as his courage and his ability as a judge, lawyer, and political leader was not inconsiderable. Much of a derogatory nature that has been written of his career will not bear critical scrutiny. For the duel with Broderick, he cannot, according to the standards of the day, justly be blamed; and for his final offense he paid tragic penalty.

[In this article the Broderick duel is interpreted and the attack on Field described somewhat differently than in the sketches of these men in earlier volumes of this work. It is possible that Broderick's premature firing may have been due to nervousness, and it seems unfair to say that at the time of the attack on Field, Terry was "already known as the assassin of Broderick." It would appear that Terry did not specifically threaten to "shoot" Field, and the tragedy occurred, not in a dining-car, but in a station restaurant.

Sources are: A. E. Wagstaff, *Life of David S. Terry* (1892); H. H. Hagan, "A California Saga," *Commercial Law League Journal*, Nov. 1929; C. S. Potts, "David S. Terry," *Southwest Review*, Apr. 1934; T. H. Hittell, *Hist. of California*, vols. III, IV (1897); H. H. Bancroft, *Hist. of California*, vols. VI (1888), VII (1890); Jeremiah Lynch, *The Life of David C. Broderick* (1911); James O'Meara, *Broderick and Gwin* (1881); *Stephen J. Field Arrested for Conspiracy and Murder of the Hon. David S. Terry* (1889), a violent pro-Terry pamphlet; S. J. Field, *Personal Reminiscences of Early Days in California* (privately printed, 1893); C. B. Swisher, *Stephen J. Field. Craftsman of the Law* (1930); E. G. Waite, in *Overland Monthly*, Oct. 1889, pp. 434–42; *Daily Examiner* (San Francisco), beginning Sept. 4, 1884, and Aug. 15, 1889; 26 *Federal Reporter*, 337; 36 *Federal Reporter*, 337, 419; 128 *U. S. Reports*, 289; 135 *U. S.*, 1; 7 *Pacific Reporter*, 456, 635; 8 *Pacific*, 614, 709; 9 *Pacific*, 187; 16 *Pacific*, 345; 22 *Pacific*, 26, 131.]   H. H. H.

TERRY, ELI (Apr. 13, 1772–Feb. 26, 1852), inventor, pioneer clock manufacturer, the eldest of ten children of Samuel and Huldah (Burnham) Terry, was born at East (later South) Windsor, Conn. He was a descendant of Samuel Terry who emigrated from England to Springfield, Mass., in 1650. Equipped with but a smattering of a common school education, at the age of fourteen he began his clockmaker's apprenticeship. For the succeeding six years (1786–92) he worked for a number of clockmakers in his native state, among them Daniel Burnap of East Windsor and possibly Timothy Cheney of East Hartford. In 1793, a year after making his first clock (still in existence in 1923), he settled in Plymouth, Conn., and set himself up in the business of making and repairing clocks, engraving on metal, and selling spectacles. In his clockmaking he used the simple hand tools of the day and made but one or two hang-up clocks at a time, under orders. Having little difficulty in disposing of his wares, about 1800 he decided to increase his production by using water power to drive his tools, and about three years later he began, with two or three apprentices, to turn out ten to twenty clocks at a time. This enterprise, much ridiculed by Terry's neighbors and fellow clockmakers, was the first clock factory in America. In 1807 he obtained a contract for making four thousand wood clocks at four dollars apiece, sold his original water power factory, bought a large mill with water power in another part of Plymouth, and with Seth Thomas [q.v.] and Silas Hoadley established the firm of Terry, Thomas & Hoadley. The four thousand clocks having been completed in three years and sold at a good profit, Terry sold out to Thomas & Hoadley (1810) and established a business of his own at Plymouth Hollow. He concentrated his attention on one-day shelf clocks with wooden works rather than on uncased grandfather clocks, and in the course of the succeeding four years designed a number of different styles, making as many as several hundred clocks of each pattern. It was not until 1814 that he devised a clock that completely satisfied him—his "perfected wood clock." This shelf clock, which was called the "pillar scroll top case," was made entirely of wood. It immediately took the popular fancy and in the course of the succeeding ten years "drove out all other clocks for a time" (Milham, *post*, p. 352). With the help of his sons Terry gradually increased the production of these clocks to ten or twelve thousand a year, selling them at fifteen dollars each, and by 1825 is said to have accumulated a fortune of about a hundred thousand dollars.

In the course of his life he patented in the neighborhood of ten improvements in clocks, among them one issued on Nov. 17, 1797, for an "equation" clock, which showed both apparent and mean time. In addition to manufacturing the popular shelf clock he made brass clocks of fine quality which were sold to watchmakers as regulators. He built, too, a number of tower clocks which were of novel design. Terry was twice married, first on Mar. 12, 1795, to Eunice Warner of Plymouth (d. Dec. 15, 1839), and second to Mrs. Harriet Ann (Pond) Peck of

Plymouth in October 1840. He was the father of eleven children, nine by his first marriage and two by his second. At the time of his death in Plymouth, in the part of the town known as Terryville, he was survived by the two sons of his second marriage, and two daughters and three sons of his first.

[Stephen Terry, *Notes of Terry Families* (1887); H. R. Stiles, *The Hist. and Genealogies of Ancient Windsor, Conn.*, vol. II (1892); Henry Terry, *Am. Clock Making, Its Early Hist., and Present Extent of the Business* (1870); P. R. Hoopes, *Conn. Clockmakers of the Eighteenth Century* (1930); Francis Atwater, *Hist. of the Town of Plymouth, Conn.* (1895); W. I. Milham, *Time & Timekeepers* (1923); Mrs. N. Hudson Moore, *The Old Clock Book* (1911); J. T., in *Sci. Am. Supp.*, June 15, 1889; death notice in *New Haven Daily Palladium*, Feb. 28, 1852; *Subject-Matter Index of Patents for Inventions Issued by the U. S. Patent Office from 1790 to 1873* (1874), vol. I, compiled by M. D. Leggett; Patent Office records.]　　　C. W. M—n.

TERRY, MARSHALL ORLANDO (June 21, 1848–Oct. 11, 1933), physician, was born at Watervliet Center, N. Y., the son of William Henry and Sarah (Burke) Terry. In 1850 the family moved to Ohio, settling first at Plymouth and later in Ashtabula. Here young Terry attended the local high school and academy, after which he entered the Homoeopathic Hospital College of Cleveland, where he received the degree of M.D. in 1872. After a short period of practice in Akron, Ohio, he removed to Utica, N. Y., in 1873. The several succeeding years were largely occupied in postgraduate study of ophthalmology in New York City and abroad. In addition to practising this specialty, he developed a high degree of skill as a general surgeon and also practised internal medicine. He served as head of the surgical staff of the Utica Homoeopathic Hospital from 1895 to 1905 and was an attending surgeon for the Utica General Hospital. In 1880 he was appointed surgeon to the 4th Brigade, New York National Guard, with the grade of major, and in 1895 he was promoted to the position of surgeon-general of the state troops with the grade of brigadier-general. He served throughout the Spanish-American War on active duty under his state commission. Beginning with the supervision of the medical service of the state camp, he was later commissioned to investigate the care of New York troops in federal camps, with special reference to the cause of the high incidence of typhoid fever, at that time epidemic in these camps. His report to the governor, in which he held that the prevalence of flies was a major factor in the spread of the disease, aroused a storm of discussion and criticism, and resulted in the appointment by the government of the so-called Shakespeare board for the thorough investigation of the camp epidemics. He was offered the appointment of division chief surgeon of volunteers by President McKinley, but his duties to the state troops prevented his accepting it. He perfected a litter, a field operating case, and an ambulance, and developed a medical and surgical field chest. He retired from practice in Utica in 1905, and in the same year married Mrs.. A. M. McGregor of Mamaroneck, N. Y. He became interested in the development of Fort Myers, Fla., where he became the owner of a large hotel, and was instrumental in the construction of a sea-wall and of a boulevard connecting the city with Puntarassa, eighteen miles distant on the Gulf of Mexico. For many years he maintained a summer home at Mamaroneck and a winter home at Fort Myers. His wife dying in 1912, he subsequently married Mrs. Adabelle R. Merritt of Berkeley, Cal. During this later years he divided his residence between New York City and Coronado, Cal., where he died of pneumonia. He was buried at his boyhood home at Ashtabula, Ohio.

Military medicine was Terry's abiding interest. He joined the Association of Military Surgeons of the United States in 1895, soon after its organization, and maintained an active membership for the remainder of his life. He wrote numerous journal articles on topics relating to military medical service, and during the World War he published for free distribution *The Soldier's Medical Friend: A Gift to the Surgeons of the United States Government and their Allies* (1917). This handbook was largely a collection of reprints of previous journal articles, which he considered would be useful to the military surgeon. He was a member and one-time president of the state association of medical officers and of the state homoeopathic medical society, and a member of the American Institute of Homoeopathy. He had a high conception of his civic duties, and was much interested both in public and in private philanthropies.

[*Who's Who in American Medicine* (1925); *Who's Who in America*, 1932–33; *Military Surgeon*, Nov. 1933; obituary in *N. Y. Herald-Tribune*, Oct. 13, 1933.]
J. M. P—n.

TERRY, MILTON SPENSER (Feb. 22, 1840–July 13, 1914), Methodist clergyman and educator, was born in Coeymans, N. Y., the son of John and Eliza (McLaughlin) Terry. He was christened Milton Seaman but when he became a young man adopted Spenser as his middle name. His father was a Hicksite Quaker, mystical in temperament; his mother was of Scotch descent, practical and energetic. The son inherited the spirituality of the father and the practical common sense of the mother. He was the youngest of eleven children. Books were a luxury in the

Terry home, but the Bible, Milton, and Shakespeare held first place. At fifteen, young Terry could recite whole books of *Paradise Lost* from memory. He was eager for an education in the schools but was hindered by lack of means from completing any course. From 1857 to 1859 he attended the New York Conference Seminary at Charlotteville, N. Y., leaving to teach school and obtain needed funds. He planned a college course, which circumstances made impossible, and finally spent a year (1862–63) in the Yale Divinity School instead. Thereafter he studied day and night by himself, read assiduously, and soon attained a reputation for unusual scholarship. He acquired nine languages, ancient and modern, besides his own.

He had joined the Methodist Episcopal Church at the age of eighteen and been licensed to preach on Jan. 28, 1860. Having been admitted to the New York Conference, he was ordained deacon in 1864, and elder in 1866. During his active ministry, which lasted until 1884, he served churches in Delhi, N. Y., Peekskill, Poughkeepsie, and New York City. From 1879 to 1883 he was presiding elder of the New York district. In 1884 he was made head of the department of Hebrew and Old Testament exegesis and professor of Christian doctrine at the Garrett Biblical Institute, Evanston, Ill.

In 1887 he attended lectures at the University of Berlin under Dillmann, Weiss, Kaftan, and Pfleiderer, and there learned something of the newer approach to the Bible through the higher criticism. With growing knowledge he revised many of the conclusions of his earlier years and then stood courageously and consistently for all he had come to believe valid and true. It was his fortune to bear the brunt of a large part of the opposition these newer views encountered in the Church to which he belonged. He had the courage of his convictions and in the days of heated controversy he always could be depended upon to represent the best scholarship of his day with calmness, clearness, and unfailing courtesy. He survived the years of stress and strain and lived to see most of the issues for which he contended in peaceful possession of the field. Meanwhile, he had become a recognized authority in the theological field. His three major works, *Biblical Hermeneutics* (1883), *Biblical Apocalyptics* (1898), and *Biblical Dogmatics* (1907), established his reputation as a sound and progressive thinker and some of his lesser works, notably *Moses and the Prophets* (1901) and *Primer of Christian Doctrine* (1906), were read more widely and created more commotion in the church than the larger books. Other writings include three volumes in D. D. Whedon's *Commentary on the Old Testament,* as well as *The Sibylline Oracles* (1890), *The Prophecies of Daniel Expounded* (1893), *The Song of Songs Analyzed* (1893), *Rambles in the Old World* (1894), *The New Apologetic* (1897), *The New and Living Way* (1902), *The Mediation of Jesus Christ* (1903), *Baccalaureate Sermons and Addresses* (1914). He also contributed many articles to theological magazines. He was a delegate to three General Conferences of the Methodist Episcopal Church (1880, 1896, 1904), and to two Methodist Ecumenical Conferences (1891, 1911).

On May 15, 1864, he was married to Frances O. Atchinson of Hamden, N. Y. While sojourning in California with his wife in 1914, he preached one Sunday night on Jacob's vision of the ladder reaching to heaven and of the angels ascending and descending upon it and, returning to his home in Los Angeles, he died on Monday morning with little warning or pain.

[Stephen Terry, *Notes of Terry Families* (1887); memoir by Terry's daughter in his *Baccalaureate Sermons and Addresses* (1914); *Garrett Biblical Institute Bull.,* Terry Memorial Number, Nov. 1914; *Who's Who in America,* 1914–15; *Los Angeles Times,* July 14, 1914; information regarding baptismal name and name of mother from Terry's daughter, Miss Minnie Terry.]
D. A. H.

TESTUT, CHARLES (c. 1818–July 1, 1892), journalist, poet, and physician, was born in France. He was in New York in November 1839 and assisted at the birth of a new French newspaper, *L'Indicateur.* After it died, almost stillborn, he moved to Pointe-à-Pitre on the island of Guadeloupe. Testut lost his small fortune of 85,000 francs when the terrible earthquake of 1843 completely destroyed that city; but he escaped with his wife and daughter to a ship in the harbor, and it eventually landed him in New Orleans, La., bare of all possessions except a broken trunk, an old mattress, and fifteen cents in cash. During the next few years he supported his family by writing for the Creole newspapers until he had saved enough money to buy a weekly of his own, *Le Chronique.* He immediately augmented it by a "literary supplement" which contained serialized romances based on Louisiana history. Many of these he wrote himself, and he later collected them in two volumes under the title *Las Veillées Louisianaises* (1849). In 1850 he went to Mobile and launched a bilingual paper called the *Alabama Courrier,* but it soon failed and he returned to New Orleans. For the rest of his life he was ridden by an irresistible urge to found newspapers; they multiplied like mushrooms and died like flies. Among the ones he or-

ganized were *La Semaine de la Nouvelle Orléans* in 1852, *L'Equité* in 1871, *La Lanterne* in 1873, *La Semaine Littéraire* in 1876, and *Le Journal des Familles* about 1888 (changed in 1890 to *Le Journal du Peuple*).

He wrote poetry as well as prose, and in 1849 published his first book of verses, *Les Échos.* This was followed two years later by a second volume of poetry, *Fleurs d'Été.* In 1850 he brought out a collection of short criticisms of the local writers, under the title *Portraits Littéraires,* and in 1852–53 a series in parts of Creolized dime novels called *Les Mysteres de la Nouvelle-Orléans.* These were full of counterfeiters, seducers, and noble heroes. They first appeared as "literary supplements" to *La Semaine.* His most interesting novel was *Le Vieux Salomon,* which he wrote in eighty-nine consecutive evenings while on a visit to New York in 1858. It resembled *Uncle Tom's Cabin,* and told the story of a wise old African of Guadeloupe who helped two young slaves to get married. Unfortunately after the ceremony their master lost his fortune and the young couple were sold and shipped to New Orleans. Their new master tried to seduce the wife and treated the husband with the greatest brutality. Knowing the feeling of the South towards this sort of abolition propaganda, Testut did not dare publish it until 1872, when he serialized it in *L'Equité* before bringing it out in book form. Even then, however, it created a great deal of animosity, a feeling he fanned by openly advocating the cause of the former slaves in his editorials. With a consummate aptitude for antagonizing his friends and subscribers, he wrote a series of slurring attacks against Pope Pius IX, which enraged all the Catholics in New Orleans, and published a defense of Free Masonry which certainly did nothing to placate them. Finally a number of editorials affirming his implicit belief in spiritism deprived him of his remaining readers and *L'Equité* died of starvation. With a temperament such as Testut's he could never make money. Inevitably he became a penniless old man and during his latter years was kept alive by a group of generous women who took turns in bringing him food each day. When he died in July 1892, they paid for his funeral.

[E. L. Tinker, *Les Écrits de Langue Française en Louisiane aux XIXe Siècle* (1932); Ruby Van A. Caulfeild, *The French Lit. of La.* (1929); letter by Testut, in *Le Courrier* (New Orleans), Mar. 14, 1843; *L'Abeille de la Nouvelle Orléans,* July 2 (obituary), 3, 1892.]
E. L. T.

TEUSLER, RUDOLF BOLLING (Feb. 25, 1876–Aug. 10, 1934), surgeon, founder of St. Luke's Hospital, Tokyo, was born in Rome, Ga., the son of Rudolf and Mary Jefferson (Bolling)

Teusler; his father was of German descent. Part of his childhood was spent in Wytheville, Va., but in 1884 Richmond became his home. His preliminary education was received in Gordonsville Academy and in private schools. At the early age of seventeen he entered the Medical College of Virginia, where he was graduated in 1894. After visiting hospitals in Baltimore, Montreal, and Quebec, he began practice in Richmond, and almost immediately joined the faculty of the Medical College of Virginia as assistant professor of pathology and bacteriology. Beginning in 1894, he also served in the city dispensary of Richmond and as assistant surgeon and later as surgeon in the 1st Regiment of Virginia Volunteers, Infantry. On July 21, 1898, he married Mary Stuart Woodward, by whom he had four children.

In 1900 he went to Tokyo, Japan, under the Domestic and Foreign Missionary Society of the Protestant Episcopal Church and there, in the service of that Society, entered upon the career which brought him distinction and which was ended only by his death. On his arrival he discovered the hospital building and equipment placed at his disposal to be hopelessly inadequate. He thereupon closed the establishment and gave himself to the study of the language and to making contacts with Japanese. Later, having formulated plans which seemed to him adapted to the situation, he opened a small hospital which, under the name of St. Luke's, was to achieve a place in Japan of unique importance. He combined single-hearted unselfishness with indomitable perseverance, resourcefulness, personal charm, rare gifts as an organizer, and marked skill as a surgeon. For years he served as physician to the foreign embassies in Tokyo and devoted the large income which came to him from these appointments and from other private practice to the enlargement and work of the hospital. He was a pioneer in Japan in public health methods, the professional training of nurses, preventive medicine, and child welfare. He also supervised the Hospital of St. Barnabas in Osaka. From 1918 to 1921 he interrupted his life in Tokyo to serve in Siberia with the Allied Forces as commissioner of the Red Cross. The fire following the earthquake which devastated so much of Tokyo in 1923 destroyed St. Luke's, but the staff of physicians and nurses displayed great heroism in ministering to the sufferers from the disaster. A few months later a second, improvised hospital was also destroyed by fire. Undaunted, Teusler seized the opportunity to realize a project for a greatly enlarged building. This had been proposed as early as 1912 and part of the necessary

money had already been collected. Large additional funds were now obtained, mainly from the United States, and in the heart of Tokyo a model plant was erected, which included what was said to be the largest X-ray equipment in the Far East and provision for a college for nurses, the first of its kind in Japan. The Japanese government gave official recognition and assistance, the Emperor served as patron and made a substantial contribution, help came from private Japanese sources, and in June 1933, only a little over a year before Teusler's death, the new building of St. Luke's International Medical Centre was formally dedicated. In recognition of his services Teusler was, at different times, decorated with the Russian Order of Saint Vladimir, the Czechoslovakian War Medal, and the (Japanese) Order of the Rising Sun.

[*Who's Who in America*, 1934–35; *Spirit of Missions*, Aug. 1933, Sept. 1934; files of the department of foreign missions of the National Council of the Protestant Episcopal Church; *Japan Chronicle* (Kobe), Aug. 16, 1934.]
         K. S. L.

TEVIS, LLOYD (Mar. 20, 1824–July 24, 1899), capitalist, was born in Shelbyville, Ky., and was the son of Samuel and Sarah (Greathouse) Tevis. His father was a prominent attorney in his county, and for a time circuit court clerk. Finishing his formal education at eighteen, Tevis read law under his father, and for nearly two years assisted him in his clerk's office. After a further brief period of law study and work at a neighboring county seat, he took a position as salesman with a wholesale dry goods company in Louisville, Ky. He rose rapidly to a high place in the counting room, and when the firm failed he was appointed assignee. He displayed such ability in this position that he was offered a place in the Bank of Kentucky—all this before he was twenty-five. He left the bank shortly to enter the office of an insurance company in St. Louis. In the spring of 1849 he joined the gold rush to California, crossed the plains in a covered wagon, and tried his luck for nine months in the diggings. But having little success there, and being in any case more disposed towards a commercial and financial career, he went to Sacramento and as a beginning found a place in the county recorder's office. Saving a portion of his salary, he made within a few months his first investment in land, buying a lot for $250. In October 1850 he and a recent acquaintance, James Ben Ali Haggin [*q.v.*], set up a law office together in Sacramento. This noted partnership, which endured until Tevis' death, forty-nine years later, became, as years went on, more and more a partnership for business and finance rather than law. The association between the two men was cemented by the fact that they married sisters, daughters of Col. Lewis Sanders, a prominent ex-Kentuckian, Tevis' wife being Susan G. Sanders, whom he married on Apr. 20, 1854.

By 1853 Haggin & Tevis found their interests too large to be handled in Sacramento, and so removed to San Francisco. There Tevis became identified with some of California's greatest business undertakings. He was one of the principal owners of the California Steam Navigation Company and one of the early projectors of telegraph lines throughout California. He conducted the negotiations by which the State Telegraph Company was taken over by the Western Union, and it is said that his profits and commissions on the deal amounted to $200,000. He was the leading projector of the California dry dock and the California market in San Francisco; one of the promoters of the Southern Pacific Railroad and its president, 1869–70; president and principal owner of the Pacific Ice Company, and one of the early manufacturers in California of illuminating gas. In 1868, while the Central Pacific Railroad was being built, Tevis led the way in organizing the Pacific Express Company to take over the express business on the line and threaten the East-and-West supremacy of Wells, Fargo & Company, then operating the Overland Mail stage line, which was soon to be rendered obsolete by the railroad. Wells, Fargo stock declined greatly in price, and Tevis and his associates bought quantities of it. Wells, Fargo & Company was finally forced to buy the Pacific Express Company in 1869 at an enormous figure, the Tevis faction becoming the controlling element in the older company. Joint operation was begun in 1870, and Tevis served as president from 1872 to 1892. He was a large stockholder in the Spring Valley Water Company, the Risdon Iron Works, and the Sutro Tunnel at Virginia City, Nev. He owned at one time 1,300 miles of stage-coach line in California, as well as streetcar lines in San Francisco, thousands of acres of ranch lands, and enormous herds of cattle and sheep. He was one of the pioneers in reclaiming tule or swamp lands in central California. He was owner or part owner of gold and silver mines in California, Nevada, Utah, Idaho, and South Dakota. These included the Homestake mine in the Black Hills and the Ontario in Utah, in both of which he had George Hearst [q.v.] for a partner. Tevis, Haggin, Hearst, and Marcus Daly [q.v.] owned the great Anaconda copper properties in Montana. The Hearst share was sold to an English syndicate in 1897, and two years later (May 1899) the others sold their holdings to a syndicate headed by John D. Rockefeller. Tevis is said to have received $8,000,000 for his share. He died in San Francisco, survived by his wife, three sons, and two daughters.

[See article on Old Sacramento in *Morning Call* (San Francisco), Nov. 12, 1882; Alonzo Phelps, *Contemporary Biog. of California's Representative Men*, vol. I (1881); *California . . . Fifty Years of Progress* (1900), p. 210; G. T. Marye, *From '49 to '83 in Cal. and Nev.* (1923); and obituaries in *San Francisco Chronicle*, *San Francisco Call*, and *Examiner* (San Francisco), July 25, 1899. For Tevis' testimony concerning the sales of the Pacific Express Company, see *Sen. Exec. Doc. 51*, 50 Cong., 1 Sess., pt. VII, pp. 3114–39. Information about Tevis' parents was supplied by Mrs. Jouett T. Cannon, secretary of the Ky. State Hist. Soc., and by Ludie J. Kinkead, curator of the Filson Club, Louisville, Ky.]   A. F. H.

THACHER, EDWIN (Oct. 12, 1839–Sept. 21, 1920), civil engineer, was born at De Kalb, St. Lawrence County, N. Y., the youngest of four children and the only son of Dr. Seymour and Elizabeth (Smith) Thacher. Both his parents were of New England stock and his father was for almost a half century one of the leading physicians of St. Lawrence County. During Edwin's childhood the family moved to Hermon, in the same county, where they made their home. Thacher entered Rensselaer Polytechnic Institute at Troy, N. Y., in September 1860, and was graduated with high honors as a civil engineer in 1863. After a brief experience with the Cedar Rapids & Missouri River Railroad he was drawn into Civil War service and from 1864 until the end of the conflict acted as assistant engineer of the United States military railroads, being attached to the Department of the Cumberland with headquarters at Nashville, Tenn. In 1866 he accepted a position at Louisville, Ky., in connection with the construction of the Cincinnati branch of the Louisville, Cincinnati & Lexington Railroad.

Two years later he changed from general railroad work to the important related field of bridge construction, becoming in 1868 assistant engineer of the Louisville Bridge Company, then building the Fourteenth Street Bridge over the Ohio River at Louisville. This change marked the turning point in his career, for his later work was entirely of a structural type and it was in the structural field that his reputation was achieved. He remained with the Fourteenth Street Bridge until it was completed and opened for traffic; then resigned, and in August 1870 became assisting and computing engineer of the Louisville Bridge & Iron Company. After nine years in this connection, he became computing engineer for the famous old Keystone Bridge Company of Pittsburgh, Pa., one of the elements in the early career of the great American steel master, Andrew Carnegie. Thacher was made chief engineer about 1883, but in 1887 resigned to become chief engineer, and later receiver, for the Decatur Bridge & Construction Company at Decatur, Ala. Late in 1889 he severed this connection and began his career as a consulting engineer in Louisville, Ky. In 1894 he moved to Detroit, Mich., to become a partner in the firm of Keepers & Thacher and in 1901 became associated with William Mueser in the Concrete Steel Engineering Company, New York City. This last association continued until his retirement in 1912.

Thacher's particular interest in the calculations of structural design was reflected in his invention of the Thacher cylindrical slide rule, which he patented in 1881, and in the many tables for such work which he prepared. His most important contribution to his profession, however, was his pioneer work in the introduction of reinforced concrete construction in the United States. As early as 1889 he became interested in concrete-steel construction and in 1899 his firm built the concrete-steel arch over the Kansas River at Topeka. This was the most famous of his arches of this type, and, while completely eclipsed by modern works, was a notable bridge in its day. Another of his contributions was the "Thacher bar," one of the first of the so-called deformed bars used in reinforced concrete construction—later a standard type of reinforcing. He was a frequent contributor to the *Transactions* of the American Society of Civil Engineers, of which he was elected a member in 1869. On Apr. 22, 1872, he was married at Indianapolis, Ind., to Anna Elbertine Bartholomew, who died in 1905. He died fifteen years later at his home in New York City, survived by his only child, a daughter.

["Memoir of Edwin Thacher," *Trans. Am. Soc. Civil Engineers*, vol. LXXXIV (1921); *Who's Who in America*, 1920–21; H. B. Nason, *Biog. Record of the Officers and Grads. of the Rensselaer Polytechnic Inst.* (1887); *N. Y. Times*, Sept. 23, 1920.]   J.K.F.

THACHER, GEORGE (Apr. 12, 1754–Apr. 6, 1824), congressman and jurist, was born in Yarmouth, Mass., tenth of the eleven children of Lieut. Peter and Anner (Lewis) Thacher, and a descendant of Ant[h]ony Thacher who came to New England in 1635. He was prepared for college under the direction of Timothy Hilliard, the minister at Barnstable. He graduated from Harvard in 1776, and, except for one cruise on a privateer during the Revolution, he spent the three years thereafter studying law with that famous Cape Cod instructor, Shearjashub Bourne (letter, Apr. 12, 1794, Massachusetts Historical Society). The confused land titles and rapidly

growing settlements in Maine offered at that time special inducements to young lawyers, and thither he removed, settling finally in 1782 at Biddeford, where he succeeded to the practice of James Sullivan. After his election by the Massachusetts legislature in 1787 as delegate to the Continental Congress he was elected by the District of Maine as a Federalist to every Congress from 1789 until his retirement in 1801, when he accepted an appointment as associate judge of the supreme judicial court of Massachusetts. He held this office until his resignation in January 1824.

As a member of Congress he was faithful in attendance, although his long absences from home irked him. Not a partisan by nature—he once wrote, "Parties are not necessary to the existence or support of political liberty" (*Ibid.*, May 11, 1796)—he was not especially active in Congress, although on occasion he spoke his mind in no uncertain terms. He did not believe a bill of rights necessary. He favored assumption of state debts, and was reconciled to the Potomac Bill. He opposed attempts to prevent Quaker anti-slavery petitions being read in Congress (*Annals of Congress*, 5 Cong., 2 Sess., p. 658), and he again defended the right of petition when he urged the reference of the petitions of certain free blacks (*Ibid.*, 6 Cong., 1 Sess., p. 232). When the Mississippi Territory Bill came up in Congress, Mar. 23, 1798, he moved to strike out the words "excepting that slavery shall not be forbidden." He defended Matthew Lyon [*q.v.*] in the Griswold-Lyon fight, but objected to the expulsion of either. Though an ardent champion of the rights of Americans and strongly anti-French, he believed that peace should be preserved. With less than his usual judgment, he advocated making the Sedition Act permanent (*Ibid.*, 5 Cong., 3 Sess., p. 2902).

The political support which he gained in his district because of his intellectual power, his integrity, and his natural gift for friendship was sometimes challenged by current reports of his irreligion. A deist, he advocated cheerfulness in religion; he did not believe in the existence of a soul apart from the body; he was a "mortal enemy to the Devil and all such Notions." "Religion," he wrote, "heretofore destroyed the pleasures of Life and made the world a state of misery" (letters, Feb. 22, 1789, and May 16, 1790, Massachusetts Historical Society Collections). He was a follower of Joseph Priestley [*q.v.*], whom he met while in Congress. He was sympathetic to Unitarian beliefs and was one of the founders of the Second Church in Biddeford. He was a great reader both in the classics and in contemporary books on religion, history, and education. In temperament he was more judge than politician. Of his judicial duties, in which his talent for weighing questions came to the fore, he wrote, "This Judge business is more agreeable than I had apprehended" (*Ibid.*, June 17, 1801). When Maine was separated from Massachusetts in 1820, he moved, somewhat unwillingly, to Newburyport in order that he might continue in office, but on his retirement he returned to Biddeford, where he died shortly after. He married on July 21, 1784, Sarah, the daughter of Samuel Phillips Savage of Weston, Mass. He was survived by his wife and nine of their ten children.

[See J. R. Totten, "Thacher-Thatcher Geneal.," *N. Y. Geneal. and Biog. Record*, Apr. 1910–Apr. 1913; D. W. Allen, *Geneal. and Biog. Sketches of the Descendants of Thomas and Anthony Thacher* (1872), which is not entirely accurate; Lawrence Park, *Maj. Thomas Savage of Boston and his Descendants* (1914); *Biog. Dir. Am. Cong., 1774–1927* (1928); William Willis, *A Hist. of the Law, the Courts and the Lawyers of Me.* (1863); George Folsom, *Hist. of Saco and Biddeford* (1830); death notice in *Eastern Argus* (Portland, Me.), Apr. 13, 1824. One coll. of Thacher's papers, mostly letters to his wife, is in the possession of the Mass. Hist. Soc.; another, composed of letters to him—some of which are printed in *Hist. Mag., and Notes and Queries*, Nov., Dec. 1869 —is in the Boston Pub. Lib.; a third, less important, is in the Me. Hist. Soc. Until about 1815 he spelled his name Thatcher.]   R. E. M.

THACHER, JAMES (Feb. 14, 1754–May 23, 1844), physician, patriot, historian, was born in Barnstable, Mass., the third son of John and Content (Norton) Thacher. The Thacher (often spelt Thatcher) family were of English stock, and James was a descendant of Ant [h] ony Thacher who came to America in 1635. They were honest, hardworking people of more than average distinction. Thacher's father was a poor farmer and consequently could give his son scant education. Without academic training the boy was apprenticed at the age of sixteen to Abner Hersey, the leading physician in Barnstable, an eccentric, hard-headed, morose man, greatly respected for his medical skill. Five years of work with Hersey, without leisure for social intercourse, gave young Thacher a sound knowledge of practical medicine. He was about to begin to practise for himself at the age of twenty-one when the events in Boston of the summer of 1775 stirred the young Whig, and in July, after examination by the medical board of the Provincial Congress sitting in Watertown, he was appointed surgeon's mate to the military hospital in Cambridge.

His medical ability, in spite of his lack of training, was soon appreciated. In February 1776 he was promoted to serve as assistant to David Townsend, in Asa Whitcomb's regiment at Prospect Hill and in Boston just after the evacuation by the British. He also went with Townsend to Ticonderoga, taking part in the retreat, which he vividly describes. A long service in the General Hospital at Albany was followed by another period in the field, first with the 1st Virginia Regiment, November 1778 to June 1779, and later with his old friend Townsend in a Massachusetts regiment under Col. Henry Jackson. During this latter period he took part in the ill-fated Penobscot expedition, spent a miserable winter in New Jersey, and witnessed the execution of Major John André, of which he wrote an excellent account in his diary, and in the *New England Magazine*, May 1834. The year 1781 found Thacher acting as surgeon to a select corps of light infantry, under Col. Alexander Scammell [*q.v.*]; he was present at the siege of Yorktown and the surrender of Lord Cornwallis. He retired from the army on July 1, 1783. His diary, *A Military Journal during the American Revolutionary War*, carefully kept from 1775 to 1783, was published in 1823, with a second edition in 1827, and was reprinted as *Military Journal* in 1854 and 1862 and as *The American Revolution* at least six times from 1856 to 1862. It gives a good picture of the spirit of the army, especially under the adverse circumstances of hunger, fatigue, and cold, and provides detailed descriptions of men and events almost unequaled by any of his contemporaries. He was a keen observer of the habits of his fellow-soldiers and, for a young country boy untrained in narration, his *Journal* must be considered a remarkable historical document. Unfortunately, Thacher failed to give many details of his hospital experiences, except in regard to smallpox inoculation, which he carried out on a large scale.

He began the practice of medicine and surgery in Plymouth in March 1784, well qualified, for his time, by his long experience in the army, and he soon established himself as the leading physician of the county. Students came to him for their apprenticeship and rumors that "dissecting material for his demonstrations was obtained from a neighboring church-yard" interrupted instruction for a time (Brewster, *post*, p. 573). Medical writing was begun under difficult circumstances and books soon began to appear, so that Thacher's name came to be known in the thirteen states and even in Europe. His reputation as a man of exceptional worth was well deserved, for to Thacher we owe not only an account of the Revolution, as noted above, but also the first American medical biography. This book, the product of his later years, when deafness was a serious handicap to his practice, has preserved for posterity the names of many physicians that otherwise might have been lost. The *American Medical Biography* (1828), a substantial volume in two parts, is the chief source-book of the period; nearly always accurate, reasonably judicious, and strictly impartial, Thacher did not hesitate to draw exact pictures of his contemporaries, few of which we would care to change a hundred years later. Other works by Thacher are *The American New Dispensatory* (1810, fourth edition, 1821), a sound application of American pharmacopœial principles; *Observations on Hydrophobia* (1812), a good summary of the disease, showing Thacher's extensive reading in spite of his isolation; *American Modern Practice* (1817; second edition, 1826), an early textbook of medicine in this country; *The American Orchardist* (1822, second edition, 1825) ; *A Practical Treatise on the Management of Bees* (1829), useful compilations for farmers; *An Essay on Demonology, Ghosts, and Apparitions* (1831), dealing with Salem witchcraft; and *History of the Town of Plymouth* (1832; second edition 1835).

Thacher's place as an historian of the Revolution is secure. His *Military Journal* was highly praised by John Adams (see preface to the second edition), and many writers have paid tribute to his portraits of Washington, Lafayette, Steuben, and other generals as they appeared in the field. As a practitioner he was sufficient for his time and place; his influence, through his numerous books, was wide-spread, for his *Dispensatory* and his *Practice* received immediate recognition in the United States and soon replaced the English textbooks used previously. He trained many students in medicine and for forty years was without a medical rival in Plymouth. He was married to Susannah Hayward of Bridgewater, Mass., on Apr. 28, 1785. Two of their six children survived him at his death. He was a member of the American Academy of Arts and Sciences, the Massachusetts Medical Society, the Pilgrim Society of Plymouth, and the French Society of Universal Statistics. For many years he was an active member in the First Church of Plymouth. His interest in the town was evidenced by his importation of many rare fruit trees and shrubs. Harvard College granted him an honorory M.D. degree in 1810. Small of stature, light and agile in movements, Thacher was fond of social intercourse, yet regularly studious. His patriotic spirit and sterling integrity endeared him to many; his well-disciplined mind and productive

antiquarianism led to literary endeavors of enduring worth.

[Letters, manuscript biography by his daughter, portrait, and other material, in the Boston Medical Library; J. R. Totten, data on the Thacher-Thatcher family, *N. Y. Geneal. and Biog. Record*, Apr. 1910–Oct. 1913, particularly Jan. 1912, and Oct. 1913; D. W. Allen, *Geneal. and Biog. Sketches of the Descendants of Thomas and Anthony Thacher* (1872) ; S. W. Williams, *Am. Medic. Biog.* (1845) ; article by N. S. Davis in S. D. Gross, *Lives of Eminent Am. Physicians and Surgeons* (1861) ; J. B. Brewster, *Boston Medic. and Surgical Jour.*, June 11, 18, 1891, and J. A. Spalding, *Ibid.* June 19, 1919 ; *Medic. Communications, Mass. Medic. Soc.*, vol. VII (1848), vol. XV (1892); *Quincy Patriot*, June 1, 1844.] H. R. V.

THACHER, JOHN BOYD (Sept. 11, 1847–Feb. 25, 1909), author, bibliophile, public servant, was born at Ballston Spa, N. Y., the son of George Hornell Thacher and his wife, Ursula Jane, the daughter of David Boyd. He was a direct descendant of Peter Thacher, 1651–1727 [*q.v.*]. His early education was acquired under private tutors. He entered Williams College in 1865 and was graduated, *cum laude*, in 1869. He at once began at the bottom in the Thacher Car Wheel Works, at Albany, N. Y., learned the trade of a molder, attended business school in the evenings, and when thoroughly acquainted with the business was taken into the firm, a connection he maintained until his death. On Sept. 11, 1872, he was married to Emma, the daughter of George Curtis Treadwell, of Albany, who survived him. There were no children.

In his own city and state, he was best known through his political activities and his many public services. Following a dozen years of strenuous attention to his business, he became, in 1882, a member of the Albany Board of Health, which he had helped to organize. He served as state senator from 1884 to 1885. As mayor of Albany, 1886–88, 1896–98, he gave the city two clean, vigorous, business administrations. He was named by President Harrison a member of the World's Columbian Exposition Commission, and became chairman of the committee of awards. Governor Hill made him a member of the analogous New York State Commission. In 1896, Thacher, always a Democrat, was nominated by that party for the governorship of New York, but he roused the indignant wrath of most of his political colleagues by declining to run on a free-silver platform with which he was distinctly out of sympathy.

Thacher was a singularly active and versatile man, indefatigable in advancing the interests and welfare of the capital district. As senator he vigorously sponsored laws for prison and housing reforms; he was influential in financing a new capitol building; and against party advice and public criticism he carried through to adoption by the New York legislature and the federal Congress a measure restoring Ex-President Grant to the retired list of generals. During his first term as mayor, Albany celebrated her bicentennial anniversary, an affair which permitted Thacher to exploit all his zeal and enthusiasm as well as his interest in scholarship and historical research. The management of a successful winter carnival in February 1888, the procurement of a public market square, a much-needed public hall, and a new union station, were typical of his municipal achievements. A lasting memorial to his constant and generous thought for his community is the John Boyd Thacher Park, a scenic mountain and forest tract of 400 acres, which Mrs. Thacher, in fulfillment of her husband's plan and purpose, gave to the people of the state of New York in 1914.

Thacher's private life, as author and bibliophile, was equally fruitful and distinguished. A foremost and discriminating book collector, he assembled one of the two dozen existing complete sets of the signatures of the signers of the Declaration of Independence. His nearly nine hundred *incunabula* are a notable enrichment of the Library of Congress. He was long prominent as a Free Mason and gave an exceptional Masonic library to the Albany lodge. He left important collections on the French revolution and on Columbus and his voyages. As a writer, he made worthy contributions to early American history: *Christopher Columbus* (three volumes, 1903–04), *The Continent of America* (1896), and *The Cabotian Discovery* (1897). To a vivid, magnetic personality, there were joined in Thacher many lovable traits. He was simple and unaffected in behavior, quick in sympathy and unostentatious benevolence, a liberal patron of arts and letters, a genial, many-sided, and accomplished scholar.

[*Who's Who in America*, 1908–09; biographical sketch by F. W. Ashley and a bibliography of works in *Lib. of Cong. Cat. of the John Boyd Thacher Coll. of Incunabula* (1915); J. R. Totten, genealogical data on the Thacher-Thatcher family, *N. Y. Geneal. and Biog. Record*, Apr. 1910–July 1918; W. P. Boyd, *Hist. of the Boyd Family* (1912), p. 440; J. H. Manning, ed., *N. Y. State Men*, vol. VI (1912–15); *Albany Evening Jour.*, Feb. 25, 1909.]   J. I. W.

THACHER, PETER (July 18, 1651–Dec. 17, 1727), theologian, clergyman, was born in Salem, Mass. He was the youngest son of the Rev. Thomas Thacher, who came to America in 1635, and Eliza (Partridge) Thacher. A direct descendant of the first Peter Thacher to take the cloth in Sarum, England, during the time of the Puritan ascendancy, he inherited a tendency to the ministry. In 1671 he graduated from Harvard College, where his social position had been unusually advantageous owing to the friendship between his father and President Chauncy. After his graduation he became a tutor in the college, numbering Cotton Mather among his charges. On June 15, 1674, he was appointed a fellow. He appears to have extended his interests beyond theology, for contemporaries refer to his skill in medicine and civil law. During a visit to England in 1676 he manifested great interest in medical practice.

Upon his return he accepted a call to Barnstable, where he preached until invited to the Milton parish. He records in his journal how he was escorted out of Barnstable in September 1680 by fifty-seven horsemen, to make the journey to Milton; after nine months' trial he accepted the post and was installed on June 1, 1681. Here he continued until his death. His journal (printed in Teele, *post*, pp. 641–57), which was begun in Barnstable in 1679 and kept for the better part of three years, attests to his scholarship. He began each day by reading three chapters in the Greek version of the New Testament. On Nov. 21, 1677, he married Theodora, daughter of the Rev. John Oxenbridge, and by her had nine children. She died on Nov. 18, 1697, and on Dec. 25, 1699, he married Susannah, widow of the Rev. John Bailey (or Bayley). She bore him one son, and died in 1724. A few months before his own death he married a second cousin, Elizabeth (Thacher) Gee, widow of Joshua Gee, of Boston. That Thacher was prosperous is indicated by the disposal, in his will, of an unusually large number of slaves. His Milton home was built in an Indian cornfield, which later came to be known as "Thacher's Plain." He acquired enough knowledge of the Indian language to propagate the gospel among the natives in Milton and Ponkapoag. A further example of his missionary work is found in a *Letter*, published in 1721 in the form of a broadside (Harvard College Library), to procure funds for the erection of a church in Providence. Owing to his widespread activity he was proposed, in the draft of the college charter for 1723, as vice-president of Harvard under John Leverett, but failing health forced him to decline. After forty-six years of service as pastor of the Milton church, he died on Dec. 17, 1727.

In theological teaching, he followed the Calvinistic doctrine with slight modification. Among his sermons, *Unbelief Detected and Condemned* (1708) and *The Alsufficient Physician* (1711) best characterize the orthodoxy of his theological belief. To *A Sermon Occasioned by the Late Great Earthquake* (1728), by John Danforth, verses in memory of his brother, the Rev. Samuel Danforth, and Thacher are appended, characterizing them as

"Careful that Christ's Sheep should never feed On Arian, Popish, or Arminian Weed" (reprinted in Emery, *post*, I, 187–91).

Another pamphlet, entitled *An Essay Preached by Several Ministers of the Gospel ... Concerning the Singing of Psalms* (1723), written by Thacher in collaboration with the Danforths, justifies psalm-singing in church, an important issue in Thacher's time. The authors defend the practice, but stipulate that "Irregular, Jarring, Disorderly Singing becomes not the House and Worship of God" (reprint in Emery, I, 272). Such scattered sermons as were published are scarcely representative testimony to the work of a preacher, who, although he lacked the luster of the succeeding Thachers, labored well in the Milton parish for nearly half a century.

[D. W. Allen, *Geneal. and Biog. Sketches of the Descendants of Thomas and Anthony Thacher* (1872); A. K. Teele, ed., *The Hist. of Milton, Mass., 1640 to 1887* (n.d.); *Register of Marriages in Milton, Mass., from the Diary of Rev. Peter Thacher, 1686–1727* (1883); "Harvard College Records," *Pubs. of the Colonial Soc. of Mass.*, vols. XV, XVI (1925); J. L. Sibley, *Biog. Sketches of Grads. of Harvard Univ.*, vol. II (1881), which quotes liberally from Cotton Mather, *The Comfortable Chambers Opened* (1727), a sermon delivered at Thacher's funeral; S. H. Emery, *The Ministry of Taunton* (2 vols., 1853); W. B. Sprague, *Annals of the Am. Pulpit*, vol. I (1857), pp. 196–97.]   E. H. D.

THACHER, PETER (Mar. 21, 1752–Dec. 16, 1802), Congregational clergyman, was the eldest son of Oxenbridge Thacher, Jr., and Sarah (Kent) Thacher, and a great-grandson of the Rev. Peter Thacher, 1651–1727 [*q.v.*]. His father, who had given up the ministry to become a lawyer, represented Boston in the General Court and in 1764 defended Colonial rights in a publication entitled *The Sentiments of a British American* (Corey, *post*, p. 655). Peter was born in Milton, Mass., whither his parents had gone to escape the smallpox epidemic then raging in Boston. He received his early education in Master Lovell's school, and entered Harvard in 1766, where he was graduated with highest honors in 1769. For a few months after his graduation he was master of the Chelsea grammar school, at a salary of six pounds a quarter, but having preached for some months at the Congregational Church in Malden, Mass., he was ordained and installed as its pastor on Sept. 19, 1770. A few weeks later, Oct. 8, he married Elizabeth (Hawkes), widow of Zachariah Poole, by whom he had ten children. It is said of him that "his voice was peculiarly melodious,

and in his public devotions his fluency and fervor were so impressive, that he seldom failed to produce general admiration and applause" (Allen, *post*, p. 19). The theology of his early years seldom departed from Calvinism. He was among the few to be praised by George Whitefield, who referred to him in prayer as the "young Elijah" (Eliot, *post*, p. 280). As the years advanced, he became less rigid and more charitable to other denominations and beliefs, with the exception, perhaps, of the Episcopalians. He was one of those who opposed the coming of bishops to America, although he based his objections more on civil than ecclesiastical grounds.

Throughout the Revolution he was a zealous, outspoken champion of the cause of freedom. At the outbreak of hostilities he enlisted for military duty, but his services as an orator and adviser were in such great demand that he stayed behind. On Mar. 5, 1776, he gave an address in the Old South Church in Boston which awakened such enthusiasm that he was called to repeat it in Watertown in the afternoon. It was subsequently published under the title *An Oration Delivered at Watertown ... to Commemorate the Bloody Massacre at Boston: Perpetrated March 5, 1770* (1776). Its spirit is indicated by the following extract: "The legislature of Great Britain is totally corrupt; her administration is arbitrary and tyrannical; the people have lost their spirit of resentment; and like the most contemptible of animals, *bow their shoulders to bear and become servants unto tribute.*" As a result of this address, the Provincial Congress declared that Thacher should have "beating orders," or a certificate which endowed him with recruiting powers, for the sea-coast defense of Massachusetts. He was also made chaplain to the General Court, a post which he held until his death. He has been credited (Corey, *post*, p. 765) with the authorship of the Malden resolutions to its General Court representative, which promised that if the Continental Congress declared America "to be a free & Independent Republick, your constituance will Support & Defend the measure to the last Drop of their Blood & the last Farthing of Their Treasure." That he penned these words, however, has not been definitely established. When a convention met in 1780 to form the Massachusetts constitution, Thacher was the Malden delegate. He was opposed to Massachusetts having a governor and later to his being given the title of "Excellency."

At his own request, he was dismissed from the Malden pulpit on Dec. 8, 1784, and on Jan.

12 of the following year was installed as pastor of the Brattle Street Church in Boston. The University of Edinburgh conferred the degree of D.D. upon him. In 1787 the Society for the Propagation of the Gospel among the Indians at Boston was incorporated by the Massachusetts General Court, and four years later Thacher became its secretary. He also served as secretary of the Society for Promoting Christian Knowledge. He was a trustee of the Humane Society, a member of the Charitable Fire Society and of the American Academy of Arts and Sciences, and a proprietor of the Town Library in Boston. In 1790 a group of five men under the informal direction of Jeremy Belknap [q.v.] met to form an historical society for Massachusetts. Thacher was one of this group, and when the Massachusetts Historical Society was formally instituted in 1791, he was influential in its origin and design, serving on its Select Committee until his death in 1802. In that year pulmonary tuberculosis forced him to seek a milder climate, and at his physician's order he sailed to Savannah, where, six weeks after leaving Boston, he died.

Between 1776 and 1800 he published twenty-two sermons, which included funeral eulogies for Governors James Bowdoin and Increase Sumner (1791, 1799), John Hancock (1793), and Washington (1800). His *Observations upon the Present State of the Clergy of New England* (1783), while ostensibly composed to deprecate the delayed payment of New England ministers, also gives renewed expression to his hatred of tyranny.

[For a list of Thacher's sermons, see William Emerson, *A Sermon on the Decease of the Rev. Peter Thacher, D.D.* (1803). Other sources include *A Report of the Record Commissioners . . . Containing the Boston Town Records, 1770–1777* (1887); A. M. Baldwin, *The New England Clergy and the Am. Revolution* (1928); *Proc. Mass. Hist. Soc.*, vol. I (1879); John Eliot, in *Mass. Hist. Soc. Colls.*, 1 ser., vol. VIII (1802); *New England Hist. and Geaneal. Reg.*, Apr. 1854; D. W. Allen, *Geneal. and Biog. Sketches of the Descendants of Thomas and Anthony Thacher* (1872); D. P. Corey, *The Hist. of Malden* (1889); W. B. Sprague, *Annals of the Am. Pulpit*, vol. I (1857); S. K. Lothrop, *A Hist. of the Church in Brattle Street* (1851).]   E..H. D.

THACHER, SAMUEL COOPER (Dec. 14, 1785–Jan. 2, 1818), theologian, author, was born in Boston, the sixth son of Peter Thacher, 1752–1802 [q.v.], and Elizabeth (Hawkes), widow of Zachariah Poole. From the Public Latin School he went to Harvard in 1800, and was graduated with highest honors in 1804. The most important influence in his early life was the friendship and tutelage of William Ellery Channing [q.v.]. After his graduation, he began to teach. In 1805 he was the acting headmaster of the

Latin School and would probably have continued happily in that position had not the illness of his close friend, the Rev. Joseph Stevens Buckminster [q.v.] of the Brattle Street Church, Boston, intervened. Buckminster, who suffered from epilepsy, was ordered abroad by his physicians, and as he needed a companion-nurse, Thacher volunteered to accompany him. The two spent the greater part of 1806 in Europe. Thacher's letters during this trip are of general interest. Paris he found "the centre of . . . everything but goodness"; at St. Cloud he had a sight of Napoleon. Traveling in desultory fashion, he visited many libraries and universities on the Continent.

In 1808 he became librarian of Harvard College. John T. Kirkland [q.v.], pastor of the New South Church in Boston, was called to the presidency of the College in 1810, and although Thacher had not been prominent as a theologian, his interest in theology and his wide knowledge of the subject brought about his nomination to the vacant pastorate. On May 15, 1811, he was formally installed. In his sermon on this occasion he voiced professedly Unitarian sentiments, expressing "a belief of the principles of natural religion, and a general acceptance of the truths of Christianity." Subsequently he developed the system of the single personality of God, and some of his discourses, notably *An Apology for Rational and Evangelical Christianity* (1815) and *The Unity of God* (Liverpool 1816, Boston 1817), are among the ablest sermonic defenses of Unitarianism which up to that time had appeared in America. He had inherited tubercular tendencies, and from 1814 until his death, his work was constantly impeded by ill health. At the request of his parishioners he went to England to consult the King's physician in 1815, never to return. After a brief rally he had a series of hemorrhages and the physician dispatched him immediately to Capetown. Here he found that some of his speculations on the dignity of the human race had never received so severe a rebuke as when he looked in the face of a Hottentot (*Sermons*, "Memoir," pp. li–lii). Here, also, he failed to make a recovery. On June 25, 1817, he returned to London, after a stormy voyage of three and one-half months which robbed him of the little strength he had left. He was sent immediately to France, and on Jan. 2, 1818, died at Moulins.

He was a member of the Anthology Club, and made frequent contributions to the *Monthly Anthology*, which he edited from November 1805 to May 1806. With William E. Channing, Charles Lowell, and Joseph Tuckerman, he helped to found, in 1813, *The Christian Disciple* (later *The Christian Examiner*). He wrote a memoir of Joseph S. Buckminster, prefixed to the first collection of Buckminster's sermons (1814), and one of William Emerson (*Collections of the Massachusetts Historical Society*, 2 ser., vol. I, 1814). Among his other publications may be mentioned *On the Evidence Necessary to Establish the Doctrine of the Trinity* (1828), the substance of which, under a somewhat different title, was first appended to James Yates's *A Vindication of Unitarianism* (1816). A collection of Thacher's discourses, *Sermons ... with a Memoir by F. W. P. Greenwood*, appeared in 1824.

[In addition to the memoir of Thacher mentioned above and his writings, see D. W. Allen, *Geneal. and Biog. Sketches of the Descendants of Thomas and Anthony Thacher* (1872); G. W. Cooke, *Unitarianism in America* (1902); W. B. Sprague, *Annals of the Am. Unitarian Pulpit* (1865); S. A. Eliot, *Heralds of a Liberal Faith* (1910), vol. II.]   E. H. D.

THACHER, THOMAS ANTHONY (Jan. 11, 1815–Apr. 7, 1886), classicist, college administrator, was born in Hartford, Conn., the son of Peter and Anne (Parks) Thacher. His first American ancestor on his father's side was Thomas Thacher who emigrated from England to Massachusetts in 1635, and later became minister of the Old South Church in Boston; on his mother's side he was descended from the Rev. Thomas Buckingham of Saybrook, one of the founders of the Collegiate School of Connecticut, since known as Yale College. He had his preparatory training at the Hopkins Grammar School, Hartford, and graduated from Yale with the class of 1835. For a short time he held a temporary teaching position in New Canaan, Conn., and then went to a school in Georgia, which was later to become Oglethorpe University. In all he spent three years teaching in two academies in Georgia, returning to Yale College on Dec. 1, 1838, to take the position of tutor. He was appointed assistant professor of Latin and Greek in 1842 and one year later the title was restricted to Latin and he was given a year's leave of absence for study in Europe. This year was eventually extended to two years and from 1843 to 1845 he studied in Germany and Italy. While in Berlin he instructed the Crown Prince of Prussia, and his cousin, Prince Frederick Charles. Six years after his return to Yale he was made professor of Latin. He was long a trustee of Hopkins Grammar School in New Haven and for several years a member of the state board of education. He was on the committee for building the Yale Art School, serving with President Noah Porter and Pro-

fessor Daniel C. Gilman [*qq.v.*]. On Sept. 16, 1846, he married Elizabeth Day, the daughter of President Jeremiah Day [*q.v.*] of Yale. She died on May 18, 1858, leaving five sons, and on Aug. 1, 1860, he married her cousin Elizabeth Baldwin Sherman, who with three sons and one daughter survived him. Both wives were granddaughters of Roger Sherman [*q.v.*].

Thacher was identified with Yale College more closely than any of his contemporaries. President Timothy Dwight (*post*, p. 352) said of him, "His influence with the Faculty and the Corporation equalled or even surpassed that of any other College officer." This extraordinary position was due not primarily to his scholarship, although he had the reputation of being a sound and thorough scholar, but to his keen interest and constant activity in the management of college affairs both faculty and undergraduate. Before the day of deans, Thacher did much of the work which a dean would perform today. He was known as one of the best disciplinarians that the college ever had and yet he retained the devotion and affection of undergraduates to an extraordinary degree. As an undergraduate he had been "exuberant in spirit," and one who was a student under him in Yale writes of "Tutor Thacher, the florid and fiery, of perpetual youth and enthusiasm." He and Prof. Theodore Dwight Woolsey [*q.v.*] were the first advocates at Yale of graduate instruction in non-technical fields and he himself was one of the first classicists to go abroad for the advancement of his scholarship. This scholarship was never very productive. He edited Cicero's *De Officiis* in 1850, and largely as a result of his work with Karl Zumpt in Berlin he published in 1871 *A Latin Grammar for the Use of Schools*, a translation of the work of Johan Nikolai Madvig. Aside from these productions, a few slight essays and book reviews in the *New Englander* comprise his professional output. A teacher always, rather than an investigator, he seems even to have had a slightly suspicious attitude toward those who gave too much time to research. Even in his teaching he was possibly too much of a disciplinarian and was sometimes thought to stick too rigorously to the grammar. To his work as administrator, Thacher brought exceptional qualifications and in this line lay his great achievements. As a teacher he contributed his share to the department's prestige while, with his strong convictions and fearless courage, his energy in raising and administering funds, his interest in people, his wide acquaintance with Yale alumni, and his devout and conscientious character, he played a larger rôle in the building of modern Yale than that of any one of his contemporaries.

[D. W. Allen, *Geneal. and Biog. Sketches of the Descendants of Thomas and Anthony Thacher* (1872); T. T. Sherman, *Sherman Geneal.* (1920); *Obit. Record, Grads. of Yale Coll.*, 1886; *Biog. and Hist. Record of the Class of 1835 in Yale Coll.* (1881); W. L. Kingsley, *Yale Coll.: A Sketch of Its Hist.* (1879); Timothy Dwight, *Memories of Yale Life and Men* (1903); J. L. Chamberlain, *Universities and Their Sons, Yale Univ.* (1900); Noah Porter, in *New Englander and Yale Review*, May 1886; *New Haven Evening Register*, Apr. 7, 1886; files in the secretary's office, Yale Univ.] C. W. M—l.

THATCHER, BENJAMIN BUSSEY (Oct. 8, 1809–July 14, 1840), author, editor, and lawyer, was born at Warren, Knox County, Me. He was the son of Sarah (Brown) and Samuel Thatcher and a first cousin of Henry Knox Thatcher [*q.v.*]. His father, a graduate of Harvard and a descendant of Samuel Thatcher who was admitted freeman at Watertown, Mass., in May 1642, served as representative to the General Court of Massachusetts, as congressman, and as sheriff of Lincoln County, Me. Benjamin attended Warren Academy, of which his father was a founder, and in 1826 was graduated from Bowdoin College. After studying law in Boston, he was admitted to the bar, and nominally practised law until his death. His deepest interest was in writing, however, and perhaps his greatest mistake in life was "an overestimate of literature as a profession and source of reputation" (Cleaveland and Packard, *post*, p. 357). He became a prolific author, contributing critical articles and verse to the leading magazines, especially the *North American Review* and the *Essayist*. In 1833 he edited the *Colonizationist and Journal of Freedom*, the organ of the Young Men's Colonization Society, of which he was corresponding secretary. Upon the lecture platform he constantly urged that African colonization should be supported "as offering the most effectual and unexceptionable proposal for promoting the welfare . . . of our fellow-men now held in bondage" (*Colonizationist*, April 1833, p. 11). To further this project he wrote a *Memoir of Phillis Wheatley* (1834), and a *Memoir of S. Osgood Wright* (1834), the Liberian missionary. He strove continually to restrain the more extreme reformers in his society, and to prevent the colonizationists from being identified with William Lloyd Garrison [*q.v.*] and the abolitionists. In 1834 he abandoned the *Colonizationist* in the belief that a magazine was not an effective vehicle for his cause. Despite the failure of the American Colonization Society, his faith in the Liberian venture never wavered, and he increasingly devoted

more time and energy to the work of the local Massachusetts organization (*Colonizationist*, April 1834, pp. 357, 384). In 1836 he was forced to go abroad to recover his health. In England he contributed an article on "Atlantic Steam Navigation" to the *Quarterly Review* of June 1838—sufficient evidence of his reputation as an author—and on his return to America published in the reviews sketches of his travels, with intimate vignettes of eminent people whom he had visited. His health, never robust, became increasingly poor, and in 1840 he died, it is said, from overwork (Cleaveland and Packard, *post*, p. 357).

Thatcher was prominent in philanthropic work in Boston, and wrote occasional verse to aid charity. His "Prayer for the Blind," printed on a piece of satin (5" x 8"), was widely sold for the benefit of the Institution for the Blind. He numbered most of the prominent authors of America among his friends. He was best known for his *Indian Biography* (2 vols., 1832), which received flattering comment in the journals (*North American Review*, April 1833, p. 472) and was the first work of its kind to seek accuracy of portrayal. In general, his writings were ephemeral, and have little interest for the present-day reader. Among his more important works are seven articles in the *North American Review*, the first of which appeared in April 1832; *Indian Traits* (2 vols., 1833), in Harper's Family Library; *Traits of the Tea Party* (1835); and *The Boston Book* (1837), a local literary anthology. He is said to have left an unpublished manuscript of his travels. His portrait, painted in England, now hangs in the Bowdoin Gallery.

[G. T. Little, *Geneal. and Family Hist. of the State of Me.* (1909), vol. III, pp. 1491–93; Nehemiah Cleaveland and A. S. Packard, *Hist. of Bowdoin Coll.* (1882); R. W. Griswold, *The Biog. Ann.* (1841); *Colonizationist and Jour. of Freedom*, Apr. 1833–Apr. 1834; obituaries in *Boston Daily Advertiser* and *Daily Atlas* (Boston), July 15, 1840.] C. B—h.

THATCHER, GEORGE [See THACHER GEORGE, 1754–1824].

THATCHER, HENRY KNOX (May 26, 1806–Apr. 5, 1880), naval officer, was born at Thomaston, Me., at "Montpelier," the seat of his grandfather, Gen. Henry Knox [*q.v.*]. Descended from Deacon Samuel Thatcher, born in England, who was admitted freeman in Watertown, Mass., in 1642, he was the second of eight children of Ebenezer and Lucy Flucker (Knox) Thatcher and a first cousin of Benjamin B. Thatcher [*q.v.*]. His father was a lawyer and a graduate of Harvard. After attending the Boston schools, Henry was admitted, on July 1, 1822, as a cadet at the United States Military

Academy, West Point, where he remained less than a year. Preferring the navy, he was appointed midshipman, Mar. 4, 1823, and in September was ordered to the Washington navy yard to join the "mosquito fleet" of Commodore David Porter [q.v.], which was preparing to operate against the West India pirates. From 1824 to 1827 he was attached to the *United States* of the Pacific squadron, the flagship of Commodore Isaac Hull [q.v.].

Promoted passed midshipman on Mar. 23, 1829, while serving on board the *Independence,* stationed at the Boston navy yard, he made a cruise in the West Indies in 1831 as acting master of the *Erie* and in 1834 made a second cruise there as a lieutenant of the *Falmouth,* a rank to which he had been promoted on Feb. 28, 1833. In 1839–41 he was attached to the *Brandywine* of the Mediterranean Squadron, and in 1847–50 to the *Jamestown* of the African Squadron. His shore assignments during this period were to the receiving ship *Ohio* and to duty as inspector at the Boston navy yard. In 1851–52 he commanded the storeship *Relief* of the Brazil Squadron and in 1854–55 he served as executive officer of the Naval Asylum, Philadelphia. When in the last-named year he was made commander, he was advanced eighty-seven numbers by reason of the Naval Efficiency Act of 1855. In 1857–59 he commanded the *Decatur* in the Pacific.

The outbreak of the Civil War found him serving as the executive officer of the Boston navy yard, from which office he was detached in November 1861 to take command of the corvette *Constellation,* fitting out at Portsmouth, N. H., for special duty in the Mediterranean. After his promotion as of July 16, 1862, to commodore, desiring active war service, he hastened home and on Aug. 26, 1863 was assigned to the *Colorado* of the North Atlantic blockading squadron. From December 1864 to January 1865 he commanded the first division of Admiral David D. Porter's fleet and for his attack on Fort Fisher, N. C., was highly commended by the admiral for his share in the Union victory. Appointed acting rear-admiral, he was ordered on Jan. 24, 1865 to take command of the West Gulf blockading squadron in succession to Admiral Farragut. Cooperating with the army in the reduction of Mobile, Thatcher on the surrender of that city pursued the Confederate fleet up the Tombigbee River and received its surrender, an operation for which he was congratulated by the Navy Department. Later his naval force took possession of Sabine Pass and the defenses of Galveston. On the consolidation of the two squadrons in the Gulf of Mexico, Thatcher commanded the combined fleet

known as the Gulf Squadron, with the *Estrella* as his flagship. From 1866 to 1868 he commanded the North Pacific Squadron, with the *Pensacola* as his flagship. Promoted rear-admiral from July 25, 1866, he was retired in that grade on May 26, 1868. In 1869–70 he was port admiral at Portsmouth, N. H.

Thatcher resided at Winchester, Mass., maintaining a summer home at Nahant. On Dec. 26, 1831 he had married Susan C. Croswell of Plymouth, Mass. He died of a disease of the kidneys at Boston, leaving an adopted daughter, the child of a sister, but no children of his own. In 1918 a torpedo-boat destroyer was named for him.

[Bureau of Navigation, Record of Officers, 1818–88; Navy Registers, 1824–68; G. H. Preble, *Henry Knox Thatcher* (1882), repr. from *New Eng. Hist. and Geneal. Reg.,* Jan. 1882; Henry Bond, *Geneals. of the Families and Descendants of the Early Settlers of Watertown, Mass.* (1860); Cyrus Eaton, *Hist. of Thomaston, . . . Me.* (1865), vols. I, II; *Boston Transcript,* Apr. 6, 1880; *Army and Navy Jour.,* Apr. 10, 1880; *Ann. Report of the Secretary of the Navy,* 1865; *Official Records of the Union and Confed. Navies in the War of the Rebellion,* vols. X, XI, XV, XX–XXII; J. T. Headley, *Farragut and Our Naval Commanders* (1866), pp. 426–34.]　　　　C. O. P.

THATCHER, MAHLON DANIEL (Dec. 6, 1839–Feb. 22, 1916), a pioneer merchant, banker, and financier of Colorado, was the second and most widely known of three brothers who were all significant in the early history of that state. Like his brothers, he was born at New Buffalo, Perry County, Pa., a son of Henry and Lydia Ann (Albert) Thatcher. Their father had moved West from New Jersey to the Susquehanna, where he was successively a canal blacksmith, a school-teacher, and a storekeeper; their mother was the daughter of a Pennsylvania farmer of remote Swiss ancestry who had been also a justice of peace and a maker of "grandfather" clocks. The family migrated further westward gradually, following the developing railroads, and the boys received their education in the schools and academies of a succession of Western Pennsylvania towns. The eldest brother, John Albert Thatcher (Aug. 25, 1836–Aug. 14, 1913), set out for Missouri at the age of twenty-one, and in 1862, with a partner and a stock of merchandise, drove across the plains from Nebraska City, Neb., to Denver, Colo. The following year he opened the first general store in Pueblo, then a village of frame and adobe buildings, eight days by wagon south of Denver and hundreds of miles from the nearest railroad. Mahlon joined him here in 1865; for some time he had been a partner in his father's store at Martinsburg, Pa., and when he started West he invested $2,900, the proceeds of the sale of his interest in that business, in a stock of goods bought in Philadelphia, New

York, and Boston. A year later Frank G. Bloom, another clerk from Henry Thatcher's store, settled in Trinidad, Col., where he became a lieutenant of the Thatchers and married their sister, Sarah.

Under the style of "Thatcher Brothers, Merchants," the brothers built up a lasting reputation for honesty and reliability. Gradually, the safe in their store at Pueblo became a repository for funds of cattlemen and miners. In 1871, as "Thatcher Brothers, Bankers," they transferred the banking part of their growing business to a new brick building. Mahlon Thatcher now made a trip to Washington and obtained a charter (1871) for the First National Bank of Pueblo, providing a capital of $50,000. This bank became his chief interest, and he was president from 1889 until his death. John, meanwhile, conducted the outdoor part of their joint activities, especially the cattle and horse ventures in which they were involved. Talking and trading horses with ranchers and miners, he gathered the gossip about men's business and credit. He was known personally to more people than his brother and was popular, while Mahlon was taciturn and less approachable. The reputation of both was that of shrewd dealers, but of established honesty; they kept out of politics and out of lawsuits. They were equal partners in all their principal ventures, including the bank.

Despite the loss and suffering of the critical winter of 1878–79 and the panic of 1893 which paralyzed most western communities, the Thatchers accumulated large fortunes. Their cattle and horse enterprises came to include immense ranches in New Mexico, Colorado, South Dakota, and Canada. In 1911, on the death of David H. Moffat [q.v.], Mahlon took over control of the First National Bank of Denver, the largest bank of the state; he also operated an important trust company in Denver, controlled two Pueblo banks besides the parent institution, and banks in at least six other Colorado cities. His holdings spread ultimately to nearly forty banks. He was heavily interested in electric power in California, beet-sugar manufacturing on a large scale, cement, firebrick, smelting, and sometimes in mining. He built a huge house, "Hill Crest," set beside his brother's "Rosemount" on the highest hill in Pueblo. At his death in 1916 he was perhaps the most important banker in the mountain states and a national financial figure. On Aug. 1, 1876, he had married Luna Ada Jordan of Pueblo, who bore him six children; a son and three daughters survived him. John's death had come three years before. Their sons succeeded them in the chief institutions.

Mahlon and John Thatcher were conspicuous leaders in the period of the "empire builders" in the mountain states. Their wealth became greater and was more stable than in the case of most such leaders, their influence was more permanent in finance, but their public and civic activities were less notable. The youngest brother, however, Henry Calvin Thatcher (Apr. 21, 1842–Mar. 20, 1884), who in 1866 opened a law office in Pueblo, was an important member of the state constitutional convention of 1876 and in that year was elected on the Republican ticket one of the three judges of the first state supreme court. He drew by lot the shortest of the terms and by virtue of this fact became chief justice, in which office he served three years.

[H. H. Hain, *Hist. of Perry County, Pa.* (1922); W. F. Stone, *Hist. of Colorado*, vols. II, III (1918); Frank Hall, *Hist. of the State of Colorado*, vol. IV (1895); *Hist. of Colorado* (1927), vol. V, "Biographical"; *Who's Who in America*, 1914–15; and for H. C. Thatcher, 7 *Colorado Reports*, xvii, and *Denver Republican*, Mar. 21, 1884; obituaries of John and Mahlon, respectively, in *Rocky Mountain News* (Denver), Aug. 15, 1913, and Feb. 23, 1916; *Denver Post*, Aug. 15, 1913, Feb. 23, 1916; *Denver Tribune*, Mar. 21, 1884, and *Pueblo Chieftain*, Aug. 15, 1913, Feb. 23, 1916.]

J. G. R—s.

THATCHER, ROSCOE WILFRED (Oct. 5, 1872–Dec. 6, 1933), agricultural chemist, experiment station director, and college president, was born on a farm at Chatham Center, Ohio, the son of Charles Phelps and Lida Elizabeth (Parkard) Thatcher. His parents moved to Nebraska in 1885 and settled on a prairie farm near Gibbon. In 1892 he entered the University of Nebraska, where he worked his way through the preparatory and collegiate departments. After receiving the degree of B.S. in chemistry in 1898, he taught in a high school for a year, spent two years as assistant chemist at the Nebraska agricultural experiment station, and then accepted a similar position at the Washington State Agricultural Experiment Station, where he later served as chief chemist (1903–07) and as director (1907–13). During the latter period he was also professor of agricultural chemistry at the State College of Washington. During his connection with the Washington station he published in its bulletins a number of important papers upon the chemistry of forage crops, insecticides, soils, fertilizers, and upon the composition and milling properties of Washington wheats. From 1913 to 1917 he served as professor of plant chemistry in the University of Minnesota. In 1917 he was appointed dean of the School of Agriculture and director of the Minnesota experiment station. During this period he reorganized and greatly strengthened the department of agricultural chemistry at the University; at the same time he conducted researches upon forage and cereal crops, insecticides, apples, and dairy products. In 1921 he became director of the New York agricultural experiment station at Geneva, and in 1923 director of the Geneva and Cornell agricultural stations, which were united at that time. In 1924–25 he served as a member of the conference on agricultural legislation called by President Calvin Coolidge. His broad interests in agronomy, organization of agricultural research, and agricultural education induced him to accept in 1927 the presidency of the Massachusetts Agricultural College at Amherst, which in 1931 became the Massachusetts State College. He discharged the administrative duties of this position with great ability. He instituted a new system of freshman dormitories, made important revisions in the curriculum of studies, enlarged opportunities for staff members to do post-graduate study, and entered upon a five-year building program of remodeling and construction which he did not live to carry through to completion. His health, which on previous occasions had shown signs of breaking, had become seriously impaired, and after a temporary leave of absence he was finally obliged in 1932 to resign the presidency of the college. Following a period of rest he resumed his connection with the college in April 1933 as research professor of agricultural chemistry. He began a study of the rôle of the lesser known chemical elements in plant growth, but his work was cut short by an attack of cerebral hemorrhage from which he died in his laboratory on Dec. 6, 1933. He was survived by his wife, Nellie Elizabeth Fulmer of Gibbon, Neb., whom he had married on Aug. 25, 1896, and one daughter.

Thatcher's wide experience in all branches of agricultural chemistry together with his rare gifts as an administrator and organizer made him a leader in the fields of agricultural research and education. He was the author of many bulletins, addresses, and reports. In 1921 he published his *Chemistry of Plant Life*. He was president of the American Society of Agronomy in 1912, of whose *Journal* he was assistant editor from 1913 to 1919, and editor from 1920 to 1927. He was president of the American Society for the Promotion of Agricultural Science in 1919. His reports as chairman of the committee on experiment station organization and policy (1921–23), and as a member of the committee on publication of research for the Association of Land Grant Colleges were most valuable. He was a fellow of the American Association for the Advancement of Science and a member of the American Chemical Society, serving the latter

as chairman of the committee in charge of the Frasch bequest for agricultural research.

[*Who's Who in America*, 1932–33; *Bull. Mass. Agricultural Experiment Station*, Mar. 1934; *Experiment Station Record*, Mar. 1934; *Jour. Am. Soc. of Agronomy*, Dec. 1933; *School and Society*, Dec. 16, 1933; *Mass. Collegian*, Dec. 7, 1933; obituary in *Evening Star* (Washington, D. C.), Dec. 7, 1933.]   C.A.B.

THAW, WILLIAM (Oct. 12, 1818–Aug. 17, 1889), capitalist, philanthropist, was born in Pittsburgh, Pa. His parents, John and Elizabeth (Thomas) Thaw, were natives of Philadelphia and his father was of Scotch-English and Quaker ancestry. John Thaw had removed to Pittsburgh in 1804 to take a position as chief clerk in the Pittsburgh branch of the Bank of Pennsylvania at Philadelphia. William attended the local schools and the Western University of Pennsylvania (now the University of Pittsburgh). At sixteen he traveled through the Ohio Valley on horseback making collections for the Bank of the United States, and thereafter the improvement of transportation facilities was a dominant interest in his career. In 1835 he was employed in the forwarding and commission house of McKee, Clarke & Company and in 1840 he went into partnership with Thomas S. Clarke, his brother-in-law.

The firm of Clarke & Thaw took over the Pennsylvania & Ohio Canal Line and did a large business in receiving and forwarding merchandise by river and canal. Between 1840 and 1859 Thaw had interests in over 150 steamboats operating on various lines, the most famous of which was the Pittsburgh & Cincinnati Packet Line. Realizing the futility of attempting to compete with transportation by rail, he and his partner disposed of the canal line in 1855. The following year he joined the firm of Leech & Company, freight agents of the Pennsylvania Railroad Company, and in 1857 he and Clarke formed the firm of Clarke & Company to take charge of the freight business west of Pittsburgh. He had a large share in promoting the rapid extension of the railroad to St. Louis, which proved a definite advantage to Northern interests during the Civil War. Having helped to devise the first system of through freight transportation over different lines, he took charge in 1864 of the resultant Union Line, later the Star Union Line, and managed it until 1873, when he turned his attention to the internal and financial affairs of the Pennsylvania Railroad Company, of which he served as director from 1881 to 1889. In 1871 he was elected vice-president of the Pennsylvania Company, a corporation chartered in 1870 to manage the lines controlled by the Pennsylvania Railroad Company north and west of Pittsburgh, and of the Pittsburgh, Cincinnati & St. Louis Railway Company; in 1884 he was made a vice-president of the Chicago, St. Louis & Pittsburgh Railroad Company. He also served as director of the Atlantic & Pacific Ship-Railway Company and of the International Navigation Company, in connection with which he furthered the establishment of the Red Star Line. His fortune, estimated at between eight and twelve million dollars, was invested largely in railroad holdings and transportation companies and in coal lands in Westmoreland and Fayette counties, Pennsylvania.

Thaw's wide interests and philanthropic activities made him a force in his community. He avoided publicity and ostentation, but he gave largely to charity organizations, churches, and individuals, and to schools in various parts of the country. One of his chief concerns was to make Pittsburgh an educational center; to further this end he devoted time and money to the Western University of Pennsylvania. Motivated by a desire to advance the frontiers of knowledge, he substantially supported Samuel Pierpont Langley [q.v.] in his work at the Allegheny Observatory, his scientific expedition to California in 1881, and his study of the laws governing flight. He also gave financial aid to John A. Brashear [q.v.]. In 1841 he married Eliza Burd Blair of Washington, Pa., who died in 1863, and in 1867 he married Mary Sibbet Copley of Pittsburgh. He was over the average in height and had an unusual combination of mental and physical powers and great force of character. Survived by ten children—five by each marriage—he died in Paris, France, of a heart attack.

[Thaw Papers in the Hist. Soc. of Western Pa.; *In Memoriam William Thaw* (1891); *William Thaw, a Biog. Sketch* (1911); *Encyc. of Contemporary Biog. of Pa.*, vol. I (1889); George Reed, *Century Cyc. of Hist. and Biog. of Pa.* (1904), vol. I; H. W. Schotter, *The Growth and Development of the Pa. Railroad Company* (1927); *The Pa. Company: Charter with Supplements* (printed for the officials), vol. I (1875); *Pittsburgh Chronicle Telegraph*, Aug. 17, *Pittsburgh Post*, Aug. 19, *Pittsburgh Commercial Gazette*, Aug. 19, 31, *Presbyterian Banner*, Aug. 21, and *Harper's Weekly*, Sept. 7, 1889; *Pittsburgh Leader*, Dec. 12, 1886; *Mag. of Western Hist.*, Oct. 1885; *Gazette Times* (Pittsburgh), Oct. 21, 28, 1917.]   S. J. B.

THAXTER, CELIA LAIGHTON (June 29, 1835–Aug. 26, 1894), poet, was born in Portsmouth, N. H., the daughter of Thomas B. and Eliza (Rymes) Laighton. Her father, a descendant of one of the oldest Portsmouth families, was a successful dealer in lumber and West India goods, editor of the *New-Hampshire Gazette,* and a member of the state legislature. Disappointed in his expectation of being elected to the governorship, he had himself appointed keeper of the lighthouse at the Isles of Shoals,

and in October 1839 removed with his wife and children to the keeper's cottage on White Island, determined never again to set foot on the mainland. Except for the decayed fishing village of Gosport on Star Island, the Shoals were practically uninhabited when the Laightons came. Celia and her two younger brothers had no playmates but sky and ocean. Their education, however, was carried on by their parents with the assistance of chance visitors such as John Weiss and Levi Lincoln Thaxter. The latter spent an entire winter at the lighthouse as tutor to the lonely children. The long seclusion of the family was broken in 1848 when Laighton opened a summer hotel on Appledore Island, the first of its kind on the Atlantic coast. It soon attracted many visitors, including among the earliest Lowell and Henry David Thoreau, and became noted as the summer haunt of artists and men of letters. The poet Whittier and the painters William Morris Hunt [qq.v.] and Childe Hassam, among many others, were constant visitors and close friends of the Laightons.

Meanwhile Thaxter had spent a second winter at the Shoals and had fallen in love with his pupil. With her parents' consent Celia was married at Appledore on Sept. 30, 1851. For some time she continued to live with her family, while her husband occupied himself with the pastoral care of the fisher-folk on Star Island and the study of Browning's poetry, his lifelong passion. Three sons were born in the course of seven years, the eldest a mental defective who required his mother's care for the remainder of her life. The youngest son, Roland Thaxter [q.v.], became a professor of botany at Harvard. About 1860 the Thaxters removed to Newtonville, Mass. In her inland surroundings Mrs. Thaxter pined for the sea; a poem expressing her homesickness reached Lowell's hands through the mediation of a friend and without the author's knowledge appeared in the *Atlantic Monthly* for March 1861 with the title "Land-Locked." Thereafter Mrs. Thaxter was a frequent contributor of poems, sketches, and children's stories to various magazines. Her first volume, *Poems* (1872), was followed by the notable prose sketches called *Among the Isles of Shoals* (1873), which had appeared serially in the *Atlantic.* Later, among others, came *Drift-Weed* (1879), *Poems for Children* (1884), *Idyls and Pastorals* (1886), and *An Island Garden* (1894), with illustrations by Childe Hassam.

The death of her father in 1866 brought Mrs. Thaxter back to Appledore to care for her mother, who survived until 1877. Her two brothers continued to manage the hotel, and Mrs. Thaxter spent at least a part of each year in a nearby cottage. Her garden was famous for its splendor of poppies, and her living-room became a salon where the finer spirits of the summer colony delighted to gather. Her spontaneous appreciation of poetry and painting, her deep passion for music, and her childlike joy in nature endeared her to many friends. In 1880 the Thaxters moved to Kittery Point, Me., and in the autumn of the same year Mrs. Thaxter visited Europe, met Robert Browning, and indulged herself in a long rapture of picture-galleries and concerts. At home once more she settled into the quiet routine of a literary life, spending the summers at the Shoals and the winters in Boston or Portsmouth. Her husband died in 1884 and was honored by an epitaph from his favorite poet. Ten years later Mrs. Thaxter died suddenly at Appledore and was buried there. In 1895 a selection from her letters, *Letters of Celia Thaxter,* was edited by her friends Annie Adams Fields [*q.v.*] and Rose Lamb, who also prepared the final edition of her *Poems* (1896).

[The date of birth is from the Laighton family Bible; the date of marriage from the town records of Kittery, Me. See *Rymes Geneal.: Samuel Rymes of Portsmouth, N. H., and His Descendants* (1897); Oscar Laighton, *Ninety Years at the Isles of Shoals* (1930); Annie Fields, *Authors and Friends* (1896); Aubertine W. Moore, "The Story of the Isles of Shoals," *New England Mag.,* July 1898; John Albee, *Ibid.,* Apr. 1901; Celia Thaxter, *The Heavenly Guest* (1935), which contains recollections by various friends; *Appletons' Ann. Cyc.,* 1894; obituary in *N. Y. Times,* Aug. 28, 1894.]
G. F. W.

THAXTER, ROLAND (Aug. 28, 1858–Apr. 22, 1932), botanist, was born in Newtonville, Mass., the youngest son of Levi Lincoln Thaxter, lawyer, scholar, authority on the work of Robert Browning, and Celia (Laighton) Thaxter [*q.v.*], and a descendant of Thomas Thaxter of Hingham, Mass. He attended the Boston Latin School, the private school of Joshua Kendall in Cambridge, and was graduated from Harvard in 1882 with A.B. degree, *magna cum laude.* Although interested chiefly in botany and entomology, he started work at the Harvard Medical School in 1883, but after one year, through receiving the Harris fellowship, he was enabled to enter the Graduate School of Arts and Sciences, where he concentrated on cryptogamic botany under William G. Farlow [*q.v.*], published the first of his famous mycologic papers, and received in 1888 the degrees of M.A. and Ph.D. On June 8, 1887, he was married to Mabel Gray Freeman of Springfield, Mass. With their four children, they made up an unusually congenial family; it was the great sorrow of Thaxter's life that his eldest son died in the flower of his youth.

Thaxter's first position, as mycologist at the Connecticut Agricultural Experiment Station, led him into the practical field of mycology in relation to agriculture and, although he was primarily interested in pure research, his contributions to plant pathology were numerous and valuable. In 1891, he returned to Harvard as assistant professor of cryptogamic botany under Professor Farlow; in 1896 he assumed the full responsibilities of teaching and research in this field; in 1901 he was made full professor; and in 1919, at his own request, he was retired from active academic work, became professor emeritus, and devoted himself to his own research and to the administration as honorary curator of the Farlow Herbarium and Library. During his forty years of teaching, nearly one thousand students passed through his courses or worked under his guidance toward higher degrees. A thorough and exacting teacher, his training left a lasting impression even upon men who went no further in scientific fields. By transmitting his knowledge, ideals, and methods to a large number of younger men, he developed, in a sense, a school which has contributed notably to the progress of botany.

It is for his research, however, that he is renowned. His greatest work is his *Contribution Towards a Monograph of the Laboulbeniaceae,* which appeared as *Memoirs of the American Academy of Arts and Sciences* (5 volumes, 1896–1931), and stands out as one of the greatest single pieces of work in the whole field of mycology. Had he never published another paper this monograph would have gained him preëminence. Yet in addition, in more than eighty papers, shorter but of similar excellence, he added notably to our knowledge of the structure, development, and relationship of each of the major groups of fungi. He traveled widely in the course of his investigations, studying fungi intensively in many tropical as well as temperate regions, and as a result his familiarity with the fungi, not only as laboratory specimens but also as living organisms in their habitats, was phenomenal. Without question he had the widest and yet most intimately detailed knowledge of the fungi of any mycologist of his time.

He was a fellow of the American Academy of Arts and Sciences, the American Philosophical Society, the National Academy of Sciences, Phi Beta Kappa, the American Association for the Advancement of Science, and other learned or technical societies. He served as president of the New England Botanical Club, the American Mycological Society, and the Botanical Society of America. He was an honorary member of the Russian Mycological Society, the Linnean Societies of London and of Lyons, the Royal Botanical Society of Belgium, the Royal Academies of Sweden and of Denmark, the Botanical Society of Edinburgh, and the Academy of Science of the Institute of France. He was the only American botanist of his time on whom honorary membership was conferred by the British Mycological Society and the Deutsche Botanische Gesellschaft. From 1907 until his death he was the American editor of the *Annals of Botany*. In recognition of his earlier work on the *laboulbeniales* he was awarded the *Prix Desmazières* by the French Academy.

Tall, well built, of great dignity, poise, and self-restraint, austere, devoted to his work, yet with a dry sense of humor and a reserved kindliness, he had a keen appreciation of beauty, was an accomplished musician, a scholarly and discriminating reader, an unequaled draughtsman of exquisite, accurate botanical illustrations. His death was a severe loss to botany.

[*Who's Who in America*, 1932–33; J. M. and Jaques Cattell, ed., *Am. Men of Sci.* (4th ed., 1927); W. H. Weston, biographical notes in *Mycologia*, Mar.–Apr. 1933, in *Phytopathology*, July 1933, and in the *Berichte der Deutsche Botanische Gesellschaft* (in press); G. P. Clinton, in *Proc. Am. Acad. Arts and Sciences*, vol. LXVIII (1933); *Class of 1882, Harvard Coll., 7th Report of the Secretary*. The human and delightful narrative of Thaxter's uncle, Oscar Laighton, *Ninety Years at the Isles of Shoals* (1930), yields revealing glimpses of Thaxter's parents. See also death notice in *Boston Evening Transcript*, Apr. 23, 1932.]

W. H. W., Jr.

THAYER, ABBOTT HANDERSON (Aug. 12, 1849–May 29, 1921), painter, was born in Boston, Mass., the son of Dr. William Henry and Ellen (Handerson) Thayer. The American progenitor of the family was Thomas Thayer, an early settler of Braintree, Mass. Dr. Thayer was a Harvard graduate, an army surgeon during the Civil War, a lecturer at Vermont Medical College, and a practitioner at Keene, N. H., and later in Brooklyn, N. Y. Abbott Thayer lived in the country near Keene until he was about eighteen years old, with a three-year period (1863–66) at the Chauncy Hall School in Dorchester, Mass., established by his paternal grandfather, Gideon French Thayer [q.v.]. From an early age he drew and painted birds, dogs, and horses, and the animals of the menageries he frequented. He is said, in fact, to have made something of a profession of canine and equine portraiture, charging from ten to fifty dollars apiece before his school days were over. After some informal art instruction in Dorchester, he attended the classes of H. D. Morse in Boston, of J. B. Whittaker in Brooklyn, and of L. E. Wilmarth in New York. By 1869 he had opened a studio in Brooklyn. On June 5, 1875, he married Kate Bloede of Brooklyn, and left for Paris with the intention of specializing in animal painting. After a short period at the École des Beaux-Arts in the Lehmann studio, however, he entered the atelier of Jean Léon Gérôme, and gradually turned his attention to portraits and figure painting, with occasional landscapes. Returning to America in 1879, he opened a studio in New York, was chosen president of the young Society of American Artists, and for the next ten years or more lived in the Hudson River towns, going to New Hampshire for the summer vacations. Two daughters and a son were born to the Thayers, and they with Mrs. Thayer became admirable models. Thayer was elected an Academician in 1901, and in 1909 became a member of the American Academy of Arts and Letters. He won numerous important prizes—among them gold medals at the Pennsylvania Academy of the Fine Arts (1891), at Paris (1900), at the Pan-American Exposition, Buffalo (1901), and at the Carnegie Institute, Pittsburgh (1920); the Elkins Prize, Pennsylvania Academy (1895), the Thomas B. Clarke Prize, National Academy (1898), and the Saltus Medal, National Academy (1915). When mental illness blighted the career of his wife, Thayer's whole outward life changed. After her death he married, on Sept. 3, 1891, her close friend Emeline B. Beach of Peekskill, N. Y. About 1901 he moved to New Hampshire, where he lived at the foot of Mount Monadnock and became more and more hermit-like in his habits, his communion with nature for long hours expressing itself in his growing interest in the coloration of animals. During his later career he made three trips to Europe. He died at Monadnock, his ashes being cast from the top of the mountain he had loved and painted so grandly. Memorial exhibitions of his works were held at the Metropolitan Museum, New York, at the Corcoran Art Gallery, Washington, and the Carnegie Institute, Pittsburgh, and of his coloration models at the Brooklyn Museum.

Thayer's paintings are varied in subject and in technique, with the ideal figures and landscapes supplying the masterpieces. "Caritas" in the Boston Museum of Fine Arts, "Virgin Enthroned" and "Angel," Gellatly Collection, and "Virgin" in the Freer Collection, Washington, represent the first group; "Winter Sunrise, Monadnock," Metropolitan Museum, dominates the second. The boy's head from the "Virgin Enthroned" is probably unsurpassed. The serene magnificence of "Figure—Half Draped" in the Gellatly Collection, from the New York studio days and long forgotten; "Roses," in the Worcester Museum; the "Lady in Green Velvet," in the Addison Gallery, Andover, Mass.; the promising mural, "Florence Protecting the Arts," at Bowdoin College; "Capri," in the Freer Collection, and the Stevenson memorial in the Albright Art Gallery, Buffalo, also demand listing. Worthy of note, too, are the earliest "Winged Figure" at Smith College, the startling sincerity of the "Self-Portrait" at the Corcoran Gallery, the "Baby Asleep," Thayer's own favorite "Boy and Angel," the "Mary," where a light blue strip in the background is inexplicable but absolutely right, and the "Seated Angel" of the Freer Collection, with its haunting dedication to Kate Bloede Thayer.

Like Thomas Dewing, Thayer idealized women; like Winslow Homer [q.v.] he realized his figures on canvas directly and sincerely. Unlike many of his contemporaries, however, he was free from the control of French technique. Originality was the very basis of his style. With an almost mystic consciousness of his mission he felt compelled to make visible the beauty of spirit he saw in the person, in the natural object—such qualities as dominating purity or love of truth that demanded a painter's interpretation. To gain monumentality he exaggerated light and shadow, and placed his colors in large, simple masses. His color range was limited—dark green, wine, pure blue, and purple, usually resolved into white. The whites—sometimes luminous, sometimes flat, but always suggestive—are as essentially part of Thayer's vision as the wings of his humane angels. The sense of outside guidance under which he worked may also explain the lack of finish so often met with in his pictures. He painted until he said as well as he could what he had to say; then he stopped. (His article, "'Restoration'; the Doom of Pictures and Sculpture," in *International Studio*, March 1920, is a vigorous expression of his objection to any modification by others of work which has left an artist's hands as finished.) Yet "Passenger Pigeons" illustrates the perfection of finish he could achieve when he cared to, and the sculpturesque rather than fabricated drapery of his figures, with its value relation to the head the essence of its perfection, indicates how far he was willing to go to express rather than to exploit. His letters, with their molten, illuminating metaphors, make clear that his personality was not that of the eccentric, much less that of the poseur, but that of one whose utter sincerity knew only originality.

Thayer's experiments in the protective coloration of animals dominated a large part of his later career. The essential theory of "Thayer's Law," as it came to be known, was that "animals are painted by nature darkest on those parts which tend to be most lighted by the sky's light, and vice versa" (*Annual Report . . . of the Smithsonian Institution . . . 1897*, 1898, p. 477), the upper colors, when seen from below, tending to disappear in the blue of the sky, the lower in the brown of the earth. In addition to writing articles on the subject which appeared in *Popular Science Monthly*, December 1909 and July 1911, and in the *Scientific Monthly*, December 1918, Thayer made many illustrations for *Concealing-Coloration in the Animal Kingdom* (1909), an exposition of his theories written by his son, Gerald H. Thayer. The interested public varied in its reception of the theory, to Thayer absolutely irrefutable. On one side was such a voluble critic as Theodore Roosevelt, who, with more vigor than acumen, denied the validity of the whole point of view. On the other side were an increasing number of naturalists who realized the fundamental significance of the discoveries, but thought Thayer went too far in his belief that the new theories largely replaced those of mimicry and of warning colors. The application of Thayer's law to camouflage devices in the World War is a matter still controverted, but there is little doubt that England, France, and Germany studied *Concealing-Coloration* in an effort to devise ways of concealing arms and movements, and that his theories had a general influence upon the designs used. Another aspect of his interest in the study of animals is seen in the Thayer Fund, raised through a period of years to protect seabirds of the Atlantic coast. These efforts at protection led to the passing of Audubon laws by eleven states, and were influential in the organization of the National Association of Audubon Societies. More poetically, one likes to speculate on the lover of sea-gulls who was fond of providing his figures with wings.

To those who knew and loved the man, he was primarily a great soul; Dewing and George De Forest Brush among the painters, George Grey Barnard and Daniel Chester French among the sculptors, and a whole company of young people, among them Rockwell Kent, William James, Louis Agassiz Fuertes [q.v.] and Richard S. Meryman, testify to one effect. French wrote Mrs. Thayer at the death of his friend, "A soul the like of which I believe does not exist on earth has flown . . ." A country minister found the man who hated both clergymen and undertakers strangely Christlike. Thayer continually expressed himself with unconscious kindliness, generosity, and humor, and he was a man who attracted worshippers. He loved the primitive; he adored Stevenson and the old sagas, he cared nothing for outward comforts, he knew all weathers. He collected bird feathers and anything which seemed to him beautiful. He was of slight build, of nervous temperament, penetrating in his glance, with a voice of fine timbre. He was marked above all by an earnestness, a passion for beauty which could reveal the strength of womanhood, the hush of the angelic, or the mysterious assurance of a mountain mass lit by the rising sun. He was always the crusader—always intense, always awkward, always followed. In a day when sentiment is taboo in painting, the sincerity of the man disarms the critic.

[The chief center for the study of Thayer's work is Washington, D. C., where he is admirably represented in the Freer Coll., the Nat. Gallery of Art, to which the Gellatly Coll. was bequeathed, and the Corcoran Gallery of Art. For biog. and crit. material see *Who's Who in America*, 1920–21; Nathaniel Pousette-Dart, *Abbott H. Thayer* (1932), with bibliog.; E. H. Blashfield, *Commemorative Tribute to Abbott Handerson Thayer* (1922); cats. of the memorial exhibitions at the Metropolitan Museum of Art, N. Y., the Corcoran Gallery (1922), and the Brooklyn Museum (1922), and of the exhibition at the Carnegie Institute (1919); Royal Cortissoz, *Am. Artists* (1923), Samuel Isham, *The Hist. of Am. Painting* (1927 ed.); Suzanne La Follette, *Art in America* (1929); Catherine B. Ely, in *Art in America*, Feb. 1924; Maria O. Dewing, in *Internat. Studio*, Aug. 1921; Homer Saint-Gaudens, *Ibid.*, Jan. 1908; memorial issue, *Arts*, June–July 1921; and obituary in *N. Y. Times*, May 30, 1921. Other information has been supplied by R. S. Meryman. The line of Thayer's descent is shown in Bezaleel Thayer, *Memorial of the Thayer Name* (1874). A number of his letters are in the possession of Royal Cortissoz, New York. For comment on Thayer's theories of coloration and his work for bird protection, see *Nature*, May 12, 1921, and *Bird-Lore*, July 1921.]   W. S. R.

THAYER, ALEXANDER WHEELOCK (Oct. 22, 1817–July 15, 1897), biographer of Beethoven, United States consul at Trieste, was born at South Natick, Mass., the son of Dr. Alexander and Susanna (Bigelow) Thayer, and a descendant of Thomas Thayer who was in Braintree, Mass., by 1647. The younger Alexander attended Phillips Academy at Andover, Mass., and entered Harvard College, from which he graduated in 1843. He studied at the Harvard Law School, and received the degree of bachelor of laws in 1848. For several years he was employed in the college library at Harvard. In 1849 he went abroad and spent more than two years in Europe, studying the German language and corresponding with American newspapers. He also commenced gathering data for a life of Ludwig van Beethoven, a project which he had conceived while a student at Harvard, and which became the principal undertaking of his life. At first he intended merely to make an English translation of Anton Felix Schindler's biography of Beethoven, but as he came into possession of fresh material he decided to continue original researches and write an entirely new work.

In 1852 he returned to New York, and for a time was on the staff of the *New York Tribune*. He also became one of the contributors to *Dwight's Journal of Music,* published in Boston. His duties in New York proved so detrimental to his health that he returned to Germany in 1854, and sought Beethoven data in the Royal Library at Berlin. Because of continued ill health and straitened finances he came back to America in 1856 and was employed in cataloguing the extensive music library of Lowell Mason [*q.v.*]. Two years later, chiefly through Mason's financial assistance, he was able to return to Europe. In Breslau he examined the Lansberger collection of Beethoven autographs; he consulted the archives of libraries at Prague, Vienna, and Bonn; he journeyed to Paris on a fruitless search for documents on the history of Bonn (Beethoven's birthplace); and in London he secured the reminiscences of Charles Neate, George Hogarth, and Philip Potter, Englishmen who had known Beethoven personally. On subsequent occasions he consulted Anselm Hüttenbrenner, Caroline van Beethoven, Ignaz Moscheles, Gerhard von Bruening, and other relatives or associates of Beethoven.

Thayer completed the first volume of his work in 1856. To Hermann Deiters, whom he had met in Bonn, he entrusted the editing and translation of the manuscript into German, and the first volume, published by Weber of Berlin, did not appear until 1866, the second was issued in 1872, and the third in 1879. The three volumes covered all but the last ten years of Beethoven's life. Thayer never finished the last volume; a malady which caused severe headaches prevented his final writing of the notes he had arranged in chronological order. After his death in Trieste, Deiters undertook to revise the first three volumes and complete the work. He died before the task was finished, and Hugo Riemann completed it, the biography appearing in five volumes between the years 1901 and 1911. In the meantime, Henry E. Krehbiel [*q.v.*], the American music critic, had been preparing an English version in three volumes, based on Thayer's original manuscript in English. The World War prevented the original plans for the publication of Krehbiel's work, and it was not issued until, subsidized by the Beethoven Association, it appeared under the title *The Life of Ludwig van Beethoven* in 1921.

In order to support himself, Thayer had entered the diplomatic service. According to several accounts, including a report of the United States consul at Trieste in 1897, he took a small post in the legation at Vienna in 1862, but the

Department of State has no record of this appointment. On Nov. 1, 1864, President Lincoln, on recommendation of Senator Charles Sumner, appointed Thayer consul at Trieste, and he retained this position until Oct. 1, 1882. As a consul he succeeded in modifying and improving commercial relations between the merchants of Trieste and those in American ports, and for this service was decorated by the Emperor of Austria with the Iron Cross, third class.

Thayer's biography of Beethoven has become the standard work on the subject. It is fair in its judgments, and makes no attempt to idealize its subject or to present a critical estimate of Beethoven's music; it deals with the composer as a man, and relates the facts of his life. Thayer also edited *Signor Masoni: and Other Papers of the Late I. Brown* (Berlin, 1862), and was the author of *Ein kritischer Beitrag zur Beethoven-Literatur* (Berlin, 1877); and *The Hebrews and the Red Sea* (Andover, Mass., 1883). He never married.

[For sources see Bezaleel Thayer, *Memorial of the Thayer Name* (1874); G. B. Howe, *Geneal. of the Bigelow Family of America* (1890); H. E. Krehbiel, "Alexander Thayer and His Life of Beethoven," *Musical Quart.*, Oct. 1917; *Musical Courier*, July 21, 1897; *Grove's Dict. of Music and Musicians* (3rd ed., 1928), vol. V; *New England Hist. and Geneal. Reg.*, Jan. 1883, p. 84; *N. Y. Tribune*, July 20, 1897. The Dept. of State has in its archives a report from the consul at Trieste, following Thayer's death in 1897, which contains biog. material.]
J. T. H.

THAYER, AMOS MADDEN (Oct. 10, 1841–Apr. 24, 1905), jurist, teacher of law, was a descendant of Thomas Thayer who emigrated from Braintree, Essex, England, to Braintree, Mass., before 1647. The son of Ichabod Thayer, a farmer, and Fidelia (La Due) Thayer, he was born at Mina, Chautauqua County, N. Y. After attending Westfield Academy he entered Hamilton College, graduating in 1862. From August of that year until August 1865 he was in the Federal military service, first as a second lieutenant of the 112th New York Volunteers and eventually as chief signal officer of the Department of the Susquehanna, with the brevet rank of major.

In 1866 he moved to St. Louis, Mo., where, after studying law for two years in the office of a maternal uncle, he was admitted to the bar. In 1876, as a Democrat, he was elected judge of the circuit court of St. Louis and in 1882 was reelected, but resigned in 1887 to accept appointment by President Cleveland as federal judge for the eastern district of Missouri. In 1894 he was elevated to the position of federal circuit judge for the eighth circuit. Meanwhile, in 1890, upon the urging of William Gardiner Hammond [*q.v.*], he had become a teacher at the Law School of Washington University, St. Louis. From this time until his death he helped in the important work of changing typical American legal education from an apprentice system into a university process.

As a federal judge, Thayer made a deep and favorable impression on the lawyers of his generation by reason of his patience, impartiality, thorough study of facts, and especially his ability to adjust the doctrine of *stare decisis* to the changing needs of society. His written opinions, generally short and concise, can be found in volumes 30 to 134 of the *Federal Reporter*. The two most notable are those in *Hopkins* vs. *Oxley Stave Company* (83 *Fed. Rep.*, 912) and *United States* vs. *Northern Securities Company* (120 *Fed. Rep.*, 721), both involving the law of conspiracy. In the first of these cases (1897) the common law of conspiracy was made effective by injunction against members of a labor union. In the latter case (1903) the statutory law of conspiracy in interstate commerce was made effective by injunction against an impressive group of railroad corporations and prominent financiers. Thayer's opinion was afterwards affirmed by the United States Supreme Court (193 *U.S.*, 197). Thayer published for the use of law students *Jurisdiction of the Federal Courts* (1895) and *A Synopsis of the Law of Contract* (1897). His address before the American Bar Association on the Louisiana Purchase (*Report*, 1904) presented the orthodox constitutional justification for the federal policy adopted in developing the vast territory ceded to the United States by France in 1803.

In 1880 Thayer married Sidney Hunton Brother, who with one daughter survived him.

[Bezaleel Thayer, *Memorial of the Thayer Name* (1874); Adin Ballou, *Hist. of the Town of Milford, Mass.* (1882), p. 1057; Wm. Hyde and H. L. Conard, *Encyc. of the Hist. of St. Louis* (1899), IV, 2250; *Who's Who in America*, 1903–05; *In Memoriam: Amos Madden Thayer, 1841–1905* (1905), proceedings of the federal courts in St. Louis, May 13, 1905; *Report of the . . . Am. Bar Asso.*, 1905; *St. Louis Globe-Democrat*, Apr. 25, 1905.]
T. W.

THAYER, ELI (June 11, 1819–Apr. 15, 1899), educator, originator of the Emigrant Aid Company, congressman, was born in Mendon, Mass., the eldest child of Cushman and Miranda (Pond) Thayer, and a descendant of Thomas Thayer, an early settler of Braintree, Mass. Cushman Thayer was a farmer and later kept a store. Eli was educated somewhat irregularly, with interludes for school teaching and working in his father's store; but by the autumn of 1840, having finished his preparation at the Worcester Manual Labor High School (later Worcester Academy), he was able to enter Brown University. Here, delayed again by teaching, he graduated as salutatorian of his class in 1845. A position awaited him at his old school in Worcester, and from 1847 to 1849 he was principal. On Aug. 6, 1845, he married Caroline M. Capron, by whom he had five daughters and two sons.

On Goat Hill, in an undeveloped part of Worcester, where he had been purchasing land since 1845, Thayer erected between 1848 and 1852 a large "castle," completely machicolated and with four-story round towers at its ends. This was the site of the Oread Collegiate Institute, a school for young women which Thayer established, and the residence of Thayer and his family for the greater part of fifty years. One of the pioneers in the history of education for women, he made provision in the institution for collegiate instruction. Three departments were established, primary, academic, and collegiate, the last offering a four-year course closely modeled on that of Brown and leading to the diploma of *Oreas Erudita*. Thayer himself retained the active headship—including the instruction in Latin and mathematics—for only a few years, and thereafter the Institute, which under his own guidance had flourished, soon lost much of its college emphasis and became a young ladies' seminary more close to the usual type.

Entering public life, Thayer held one or two municipal offices, and in 1852 was elected to the General Court as a Free Soiler, serving in 1853-54. There his chief effort was directed to securing a charter of a bank of mutual redemption. Its purpose was to redeem the bills of New England banks—its stockholders being such banks as cared to subscribe—and thus to enable country bankers to escape the tyranny of the Suffolk Bank in Boston. The charter was granted in 1855, though the institution did not begin operation till sometime later. Meantime, Thayer embarked on the great enterprise of his life, that of promoting organized emigration. In the spring of 1854, while the Kansas–Nebraska bill was pending, he interested a number of influential people in the cause of making Kansas free by colonization, and within six weeks (Apr. 26, 1854) obtained a charter for the Massachusetts Emigrant Aid Company. The charter was thought to be defective and was given up, and a voluntary organization took its place, under the name New England Emigrant Aid Company, chartered Feb. 16, 1855. Thayer always believed in the scheme as an investment, though many of his associates did not. Throughout various changes of organization and until its work was largely done (1856), he remained by far its most energetic promoter and for a period was paid a commission for the sums obtained through his efforts. His early enlistment of Horace Greeley and the *New York Tribune* in support of the movement gave it great aid. For over two years Thayer spent most of his time traveling in New England and New York on the business of the company.

In 1856 he was suddenly drafted as Republican candidate for Congress in the Worcester district, and served two terms, 1857-61. His position in Congress was unusual. So great was his enthusiasm for company colonization of new lands that he came to regard the method as almost a panacea. It was his belief that free men, backed by investors and preceded by efficient agents to form "receiving stations," would suffice to create free and prosperous communities, and that the question of slavery—or, in the case of Utah, polygamy—would soon disappear. Even the border states, he thought, might be brought to freedom by this means, and in 1857-59 he worked hard in connection with the founding of Ceredo in western Virginia. Filibustering in Central America, he was convinced, could be stopped by the same means. All his very witty and genially satirical congressional speeches were directed to this theme, the implications of which formed a sort of popular-sovereignty doctrine which made him totally uninterested in congressional action about slavery in the territories. This most unorthodox Republicanism was anathema to many of Thayer's constituents, and when in 1859 he swung a decisive though small group in the House to vote for the admission of Oregon, his political fate was sealed. As a delegate at the Chicago Convention his support of Lincoln rather than of Seward was a further count against him. In 1860 he was forced to run as an independent and was defeated. A painful episode of these years was Thayer's contact with John Brown, who visited him at the Oread, asked for arms to defend the free settlers of Kansas, and received all Thayer had. These arms were used at Harpers Ferry, and Thayer was always very bitter about the deception that had been practised on him (*Boston Herald*, Aug. 22, 1887).

Thayer's subsequent life was not a happy one. He served as a treasury agent in 1861-62, obtained some support at Washington for a plan of military colonization of Florida, and in 1864-70 was land agent in New York for Western railroad interests. Returning to Worcester, he was a candidate for Congress on the Democratic ticket in 1874 and 1878. In 1887 he entered on a period of vigorous newspaper controversy with the Garrisonian abolitionists, whom he condemned whole-heartedly as disunionists and as having added nothing but disloyalty to the national struggle against slavery. He felt that his efforts in securing Kansas for freedom were not properly recognized. His speeches in Congress appear in *Six Speeches, with a Sketch of the Life of Hon. Eli Thayer* (1860). He was the author of *The New England Emigrant Aid Company, and Its Influence, through the Kansas Contest, upon National History* (1887), also printed in *Collections of the Worcester Society of Antiquity* (vol. VII, 1888), and of *A History of the Kansas Crusade, Its Friends and Its Foes* (1889), in which he expressed his feelings regarding the part he played in that movement.

[A manuscript life of Thayer by his friend F. P. Rice, with a collection of clippings, is in the Harvard Coll. Lib.; Thayer Papers and clippings are at Brown University, and other clippings, in the American Antiquarian Society; the Kans. State Hist. Soc. has much material on the Emigrant Aid Company. Other sources include: Bezaleel Thayer, *Memorial of the Thayer Name* (1874); G. O. Ward, *The Worcester Acad.* (1918) and sketch of Thayer in *Worcester Acad. Bull.,* June 1917; M. E. B. Wright, *Hist. of the Oread Collegiate Institute . . . 1849–1881* (1905); F. P. Rice, *The Worcester of Eighteen Hundred and Ninety-eight* (1899); R. V. Harlow, in *Am. Hist. Rev.,* Oct. 1935; S. A. Johnson, in *New England Quart.,* Jan. 1930; *Boston Transcript,* Apr. 15, 1899; *Worcester Evening Gazette,* Apr. 15, 1899; *Worcester Sunday Telegram,* Apr. 16, 1899.]   H. D. J.

THAYER, EZRA RIPLEY (Feb. 21, 1866–Sept. 14, 1915), professor of law, was the brother of William Sydney Thayer [*q.v.*], and the son of James Bradley Thayer [*q.v.*], a distinguished legal scholar and professor in the Harvard Law School. His mother, Sophia Bradford (Ripley) Thayer, was the daughter of Rev. Samuel Ripley and a cousin of Ralph Waldo Emerson. Thayer was born in Milton, Mass., but in 1874, when his father turned from practice to teaching law, the family moved to Cambridge. Very early the son's marked ability was evident. He led his class in the Cambridge High School, where he began his preparation for college; and after a year in Athens studying Greek under Prof. W. W. Goodwin [*q.v.*] and further preparation at Hopkinson's School in Boston, entered Harvard in 1884 and was graduated in 1888. Here, also, though taking part in athletic sports and in college societies, he led his class, as he did in the Harvard Law School, from which he was graduated in 1891.

He then spent a year in Washington as secretary to Justice Horace Gray [*q.v.*] of the United States Supreme Court and upon returning to Boston entered the office of the firm of which Louis D. Brandeis, afterwards a justice of the same high court, was a member. Thayer became a partner of the firm in 1896, under its later name of Brandeis, Dunbar & Nutter. In 1900 he gave up that association to become a member of Storey, Thorndike, Palmer & Thayer.

He was highly successful as a practitioner, and also gave his time freely to work of the Boston, Massachusetts, and American bar associations. He was a member of the committee of the last-named body which drafted the national code of legal ethics, and he had a large share in this work.

His distinction as a student had led, immediately after his graduation, to an offer of an assistant professorship in the Harvard Law School, but he declined the offer and when tendered full professorship in 1902, on his father's death, again refused to exchange the life of a practitioner for that of a teacher and scholar. In 1910, however, on the death of Dean James Barr Ames [*q.v.*], when urged to take the direction of the Law School, he consented, though with some hesitation, to do so. After the new work was once undertaken, he threw himself into it with characteristic conscientious thoroughness, cutting off all connection with practice. From similar motives, when offered an appointment in 1913 to the supreme judicial court of Massachusetts, he declined because he felt that having undertaken to give himself to the Law School he was bound to persist in his work there. As an administrator and director of the policy of the school, Thayer achieved immediate success. Equal success in his new work as a teacher and scholar was evidently sure to follow after a brief novitiate. Undoubtedly overwork caused by conscientious devotion to the task he had undertaken led to his suicide, by drowning, in 1915. In person, Thayer was handsome and attractive, with great social gifts. He continued to the end of his life the love of Greek and the reading of Greek authors as well as of English classics. This gave an intellectual charm without pedantry to his conversation. On June 23, 1898, he married Ethel Randolph Clark of Pomfret, Conn., who with three children survived him.

[*The Centennial Hist. of the Harvard Law School* (1918); *Harvard Law Review,* Nov. 1915; *Harvard Grads. Mag.,* Dec. 1915; *Harvard Coll. Class of 1888, Secretary's Report,* no. 8 (1920); *Ezra Ripley Thayer; An Estimate of His Work as Dean of the Harvard Law School; a Sketch of His Life, and Reprints of Certain of His Writings* (Harvard Law School Asso., 1916); *Proc. at the Meeting of the Bar in the Supreme Judicial Court of Mass., in Memory of Ezra Ripley Thayer, July 7, 1916* (1916); *Who's Who in America,* 1914–15; *Boston Transcript,* Sept. 16, 1915.]   S. W.

THAYER, GIDEON FRENCH (Sept. 21, 1793–Mar. 27, 1864), educator, was born in Watertown, Mass., the son of Zephion and Susannah (Bond) Thayer. He was a descendant of Thomas Thayer who was in Braintree, Mass., as early as 1647. In his early boyhood his parents removed to Brookline, Mass., where he had his first schooling. Within a few years both parents died, and Gideon was adopted by Gideon French, a tallow merchant of Boston, whose name he bore. A period of schooling in Boston was followed by his apprenticeship, at fourteen, to a retail shoe-merchant, with whom he remained for six years. Throughout this time he studied privately to prepare himself for teaching. In 1814 he was appointed usher in the South Writing School of Boston, where he acquired a reputation for his instruction in penmanship. To augment his salary he conducted an evening school for apprentices. A severe hemorrhage of the lungs in 1818 forced him to withdraw from teaching, and at the expense of sympathetic friends he was sent to New Orleans. Returning two years later, he took up his residence in Milton, Mass. He married, Aug. 27, 1821, Nancy Pierce, daughter of Rufus and Elizabeth Pierce of Milton, by whom he had three sons and a daughter. In 1820 he established a private school in Boston, where two innovations which proved popular with his students were the installation of gymnastic apparatus and his practice of taking the boys to the Boston Common for exercises and games during periods of recess. In lectures to schoolmasters he stressed the importance of a well-balanced program of mental, moral, and physical instruction. The school succeeded so well that he was able in 1828 to secure sufficient credit for the purchase of a site and the erection of a school-building on Chauncy Place (later Chauncy Street). This was the famous Chauncy-Hall School. Among his first pupils was Francis Parkman [q.v.], the historian. A noteworthy feature of the school was its departmental plan of instruction, with competent teachers in charge of the various courses of study. William Russell [q.v.] was the instructor in elocution. Singing by note was introduced in the school, as a general exercise, some years before it appeared in the public schools. Thayer was invited frequently to lecture on the work of the school, and to give addresses on educational topics before various teachers' associations. One of his lectures, delivered in 1840 before the American Institute of Instruction, entitled "On Courtesy, and its Connexion with School Instruction" (*Common School Journal*, Dec. 15, 1840), was reprinted in pamphlet form by Horace Mann and distributed to all the schools in Massachusetts; over fifty thousand copies were also printed and circulated by Henry Barnard [qq.v.], in whose journal Thayer was publishing a series of articles, later separately printed as *Letters to a Young Teacher* (1858).

In 1831 he removed from Milton to Quincy, Mass. There he was influential in establishing the first high school (1852) and in organizing a lyceum for the encouragement of cultural interests in the community. He was one of the organizers of the American Institute of Instruction, serving as its first recording secretary (1830–31) and as president (1849–52). His name also appears among the founders of the American Association for the Advancement of Education, the Massachusetts State Teachers' Association, and the Norfolk County Teachers' Association. In 1848 he was one of the editors of the *Massachusetts Teacher*; and from July 1851 to April 1852 he edited the *Quincy Patriot*, a weekly journal devoted to the arts and sciences, a venture in which he lost a considerable sum of money. He was one of the organizers of the Boston public library, a member of the Boston Common Council (1839, 1844–48), and president of the Boston Dispensary (1840–46). He withdrew from the Chauncy-Hall School in December 1855, leaving it in the charge of Thomas Cushing, who had been his partner since 1840. On Jan. 1, 1856, he became president of the Quincy Fire and Marine Insurance Company (later the Prescott Insurance Company). He resigned in 1860 because of ill health and retired to Keene, N. H., where he died. One of his grandsons was Abbott Handerson Thayer [q.v.] the artist.

[Bezaleel Thayer, *Memorial of the Thayer Name* (1874); Thomas Cushing, *Hist. Sketch of Chauncy-Hall School* (1895), and "Memoir of Gideon F. Thayer," *New Eng. Hist. and Geneal. Reg.*, Apr. 1865; *Am. Jour. of Educ.*, Mar. 1858, June 1865; obituary in *Boston Transcript*, Mar. 28, 1864.]
R. F. S.

THAYER, JAMES BRADLEY (Jan. 15, 1831–Feb. 14, 1902), professor of law, was born in Haverhill, Mass., the second son of Abijah Wyman and Susan (Bradley) Thayer, and a descendant of Thomas Thayer who was an early settler of Braintree. During his boyhood the family moved to Northampton. Since his father did not greatly prosper, young Thayer, besides going to school, worked in various ways—doing chores, setting type in a printing office, and helping in a physician's office. With the aid of friends he entered Harvard College in 1848, and was graduated with distinction in 1852, being the class orator on Commencement day. After a brief period of teaching, he entered the Harvard Law School in 1854, having made up his mind "after infinite distraction, to study law rather than divinity, toward which I had had a strong inclination" (Thayer, quoted by Hall, *post*, p. 350).

In December 1856 he was admitted to the Boston bar and on Apr. 24, 1861, married Sophia Bradford Ripley. For the next thirteen years he made his home in Milton. In 1865 he became a partner of Peleg W. Chandler [q.v.] and George

O. Shattuck, leading Boston lawyers of the time. During the following years he contributed to Bouvier's *Dictionary of Law* and to the *American Law Review*, and in 1870 was chosen editor of the twelfth edition (1873) of Kent's *Commentaries*. He secured for the last-named work the aid of Oliver Wendell Holmes, Jr., and eventually Thayer's part in the undertaking was limited to some revision. He kept up his interest in Greek and Latin, and published elaborate reviews of a number of Greek and Latin translations. Somewhat later he also printed privately *Letters of Chauncey Wright* (1878); *A Western Journey with Mr. Emerson* (1884), recounting the events of a trip to California of a small party in which Thayer was included; and *Rev. Samuel Ripley of Waltham* (1897), a short biography of his father-in-law. In all his writings his mastery of a style exact, flexible, and distinguished is noticeable.

In 1874, having previously refused a Harvard professorship of English, he accepted the professorship in the Harvard Law School which he held for the remainder of his life. This period witnessed great changes in the school resulting from Dean Langdell's introduction of the case system of study and teaching. Langdell, Thayer, John C. Gray, and James Barr Ames [*qq.v.*], together laid the foundation for the future success of the method, and of the school. Aside from this contribution, Thayer's reputation rests on his work in constitutional law and in the law of evidence. On both subjects he became recognized as the leading scholar in the United States. He set himself first to find the causes of the disorderly and unreasoned condition of the law of evidence, as a preliminary step to rationalizing and restating the subject. In *A Preliminary Treatise on Evidence at the Comman Law* (1898), a portion of which, in substance, had been issued in 1896, under the title, "Development of Trial by Jury," he was the first to show the various steps in the early development of the English trial by jury, and the dependency of the rules of evidence on this development. The elaborate treatise on the modern law of evidence, to which the *Preliminary Treatise* was intended as an introduction, was never written, although materials for it were assiduously collected for more than twenty years. It was left for Thayer's pupil, J. H. Wigmore, to erect the superstructure (Wigmore, *A Treatise on the System of Evidence in Trials at Common Law*, 4 vols., 1904–05).

In regard to constitutional law, to which Thayer also devoted himself, he early adopted and always upheld the view that no legislative act should be held unconstitutional unless it was so beyond a reasonable doubt; and further, that the function of a constitution is to lay down in general terms broad fundamental principles. As early as 1859 he wrote a vigorous criticism of a provision in the Kansas constitution prohibiting the manufacture and sale of intoxicants. Constitutions, he said, "were not made to be codes of laws, or to embody the opinion of a momentary majority" (quoted by Hall, p. 366). During his professorship, besides the *Preliminary Treatise on Evidence*, he published *Select Cases on Evidence at the Common Law* (1892, 1900); *Cases on Constitutional Law* (2 vols., 1895), and *John Marshall* (1901), a brief biography. After his death his son edited a volume of his shorter papers under the title *Legal Essays* (1908).

As a citizen and neighbor Thayer neglected no duties. He urged reforms of the tariff and of the methods of granting corporate franchises. The treatment of the Indians by the national government engaged his interest, and with others he was instrumental in securing the passage of the Dawes Bill of 1887 to provide for allotment of lands to the Indians in severalty. Before enactment of the law, and afterwards to insure its proper administration, he wrote articles and delivered addresses (see especially the *Atlantic Monthly*, March 1888, October and November 1891). On questions of local as well as of national politics, his tongue and pen were always at the service of what he deemed a righteous cause. His early inclination towards divinity furnishes a correct indication of his subsequent devotion to the Unitarian church. In 1900 President McKinley offered him a position on the Philippine Commission, but his age compelled him to decline.

Thayer was of distinguished appearance and fine manners, receiving a ready welcome in any society in which he found himself. He died at his home in Cambridge, after an illness of a single day, survived by his widow, two daughters, and two sons, Dr. William Sydney Thayer and Ezra Ripley Thayer [*qq.v.*].

[J. P. Hall in W. D. Lewis, *Great Am. Lawyers*, vol. VIII (1909); *Harvard Law Review*, Apr. 1902; *Proc. Mass. Hist. Soc.*, 2 ser., XVI (1903); *Pubs. Col. Soc. of Mass.*, vol. VII (1905); *The Centennial Hist. of the Harvard Law School* (1918); Grace W. Edes, *Annals of the Harvard Class of 1852* (1922); *Am. Law Review*, Mar.–Apr. 1902; Bezaleel Thayer, *Memorial of the Thayer Name* (1874); *Who's Who in America*, 1901–02; *Boston Transcript*, Feb. 15, 1902.]

S. W.

THAYER, JOHN (May 15, 1758–Feb. 17, 1815), Roman Catholic missionary, fourth son of Cornelius and Sarah (Plaisted) Thayer, was born in Boston, Mass. He was a descendant of Richard Thayer, an early settler of Braintree. Despite an irregular education, he received an honorary degree of A.B. from Yale College in 1779. Licensed but not ordained a Congregational minister, Thayer preached from various pulpits and served as chaplain at Castle William under John Hancock (1780–81) until he went to Paris, where Benjamin Franklin brusquely declined his services as a personal chaplain. As a result of theological controversies with priests in France and in Rome, and a reputed miracle of which he had first-hand knowledge, he entered the Roman Catholic Church (May 25, 1783), and studied theology at the College of Navarre and at Saint-Sulpice in Paris. Ordained, June 2, 1787, by the archbishop of Paris, he was lionized by ecclesiastics as the first converted American divine, who had grand plans for the conversion of his fellow Puritans. In the year of his ordination there appeared *The Conversion of John Thayer . . . Written by Himself*. After two years in the London mission, Thayer set forth for Boston, where his arrival (Jan. 4, 1790) and early activities attracted numerous notices in the New England press. On the whole "John Turncoat," as he was called, was not badly received by native Americans, although the rather tolerant Ezra Stiles confided a harsh estimate of his guest to his *Literary Diary:* "Commenced his Life in Impudence, Ingratitude, Lying & Hypocrisy, irregularly took up preach^g among the Congregationalists, went to France & Italy, became a Proselyte to the Romish Church, & is returned to convert America to that Chh . . . of haughty insolent & insidious Talents" (*The Literary Diary of Ezra Stiles*, 1901, vol. III, p. 416).

In Boston, his tactless zeal, his uncompromising Puritan spirit, his uneasiness under ecclesiastical restraint, and his egotism prevented any degree of success. Soon in conflict with Abbé Louis de Rousselet, who was supported by the French members of the congregation, he was placed in temporary control (1791) by Bishop John Carroll [q.v.]. About this time he engaged in embittered disputations with two ministers, George Leslie and John Gardner, which were later reprinted (Boston, 1793; Dublin, 1809). When in 1792 he was succeeded by Dr. Francis Anthony Matignon [q.v.], he continued as a roving missionary who held Catholic services for the first time in the chief New England towns. For this courageous work he had real talents; his friend William Bentley described him as "a real Dreadnought in adventures" (*The Diary of William Bentley*, vol. IV, 1914,

p. 363). In 1793 he was in Alexandria, Va., where he held services and prepared to build a church. When his pronounced anti-slavery views as well as his excessive zeal destroyed his popularity, he sought an assignment to assist William O'Brien, O.P., of St. Peter's Church, New York, but it was denied (1796). Thayer once more visited Hartford and other New England towns, and Quebec. One of his noteworthy sermons was *A Discourse, Delivered . . . on the 9th of May 1798, a Day Recommended by the President for Humiliation and Prayer Throughout the United States* (1798). A year later he was assigned to assist Stephen Theodore Badin [q.v.], whose missionary field covered Kentucky. Despite conflicts over slavery, Thayer throve on the frontier until in 1803, somewhat to his ordinary's relief, he retired under a cloud to Limerick, Ireland.

Apparently he was happy in Ireland. Aside from brief excursions to England and the continent (as to La Trappe in France, 1807), he remained a missionary in Limerick, where he was considered "a priest of edifying piety and ascetic life," until his death. Thayer was not idle. He did his share in giving an impulse to emigration from the south of Ireland to America and urged Irish priests to volunteer for the missions. Determined to establish a convent in Boston, he collected several thousand dollars, vainly applied to Dublin and London convents for volunteers, and finally trained his own postulants. After his death his legacy enabled several postulants to go in 1817 to Three Rivers, Quebec, and on the completion of their novitiate to establish (1819) a house in Boston, the nucleus of the famous Ursuline Convent in Charlestown which was burned by a nativist mob in 1834.

[In addition to Thayer's *The Conversion of John Thayer* (1787), see Percival Merritt, "Sketches of the Three Earliest Roman Cath. Priests in Boston," *Pubs. Colonial Soc. Mass.*, vol. XXV (1924), in which fugitive notices in newspapers, letters, and memoirs have been brought together in critical and documented form. See also *U. S. Cath. Hist. Mag.*, vol. II, no. 7 (1889); T. E. Bridgett, *A New England Convert* (1887); James Fitton, *Sketches of the Establishment of the Church in New England* (1872); *Am. Mag.*, Sept. 1788, p. 738; Peter Guilday, *Life and Times of John Carroll* (1922); J. J. Dillon, *The Hist. Story of St. Mary's, Albany* (1933); R. H. Clarke, in *Am. Cath. Quart. Rev.*, Jan. 1904; and Bezaleel Thayer, *Memorial of the Thayer Name* (1874).]   R. J. P.

THAYER, JOHN MILTON (Jan. 24, 1820– Mar. 19, 1906), lawyer, soldier, politician, was born at Bellingham, Mass., the youngest of nine children of Capt. Elias Thayer and his wife, Mrs. Ruthe T. Staples, and a descendant of Thomas Thayer who settled at Braintree before 1647. He was reared upon a farm and educated in a district school. After some experience as a rural teacher he attended Brown University from which he was graduated with honor in 1841. He then read law in Worcester, was admitted to the Worcester County bar, and practised until about 1854. During this time he became a lieutenant of the Worcester Light Infantry, and, for a while, was editor of the *Worcester Magazine and Historical Journal*. In the spring of 1854 he made an exploratory expedition to Nebraska and in the autumn moved with his family to Omaha where he acquired land and engaged in farming. In the following year he was admitted to the bar in Nebraska. Indian troubles arose and he was commissioned the first brigadier-general of the territorial militia. He led expeditions against the Pawnee Indians in 1855 and 1859, and at the outbreak of the Civil War was commissioned colonel of the 1st Nebraska Volunteers. He served with distinction with the army of the West throughout the war and returned home at its conclusion, having been brevetted major-general of volunteers.

His political career began in the territorial council of 1860. He was a member of the constitutional conventions of 1860 and 1866 and was elected one of the first United States senators from Nebraska on the Republican ticket. He served from 1867 to 1871. In the reconstruction contests he was an ardent and active radical. He served on various committees: Military Affairs, Indian Affairs, Patents and Patent Office, and Enrollment of Bills. He was an ardent supporter of President Grant's administration. His best work in Congress was relative to Indian affairs. Of this subject he had first-hand knowledge and offered realistic solutions in contrast to the idealism of his fellow radicals from the Northeast. President Grant appointed him governor of Wyoming Territory, 1875–79. On his return to Nebraska he became especially active in the G.A.R. and acted in the capacity of state commander—a position yielding much publicity. He was elected governor on the Republican ticket in 1886 and reëlected two years later. Although not a candidate for reëlection in 1890 he brought suit against Gov. James E. Boyd on the grounds that the latter was not a citizen of the United States and secured a decision from the Nebraska Supreme Court that left him in the governorship until this decision was reversed by the United States Supreme Court in 1892 (143 *U. S.*, 135). Thayer's career as governor was not distinctive. His imposing personal appearance, his military experiences, and his willingness to conform to the demands of his party were his primary assets. In the con-

tests between the anti-monopolists and the railroads he occupied a neutral position.

At the expiration of his governorship, he retired to live in Lincoln. The federal government voted him a liberal pension. His wife, Mary Torrey Allen, to whom he had been married in Sterling, Mass., on Dec. 27, 1842, and four of his six children preceded Thayer in death.

[*Who's Who in America*, 1906–07; *Biog. Directory of the Am. Cong., 1774–1927* (1928); *Vital Records of Bellingham, Mass.* (1904); G. F.. Partridge, *Hist. of the Town of Bellingham* (1919); H. L. Adams, *Worcester Light Infantry* (1924); J. S. Morton, *Illustrated Hist. of Nebr.*, vols. I (1905), III (1913); T. W. Tipton, *Forty Years of Nebr.*, Proc. and Colls., Nebr. State Hist. Soc., 2 ser., vol. IV (1902); *Congressional Globe*, 40 and 41 Cong., 1867–1869; *War of the Rebellion: Official Records* (see Index); R. D. Rowley, "Judicial Career of Samuel Maxwell," Masters thesis, Univ. of Nebr., 1928; for date of marriage, *Mass. Spy* (Worcester), Jan. 11, 1843; *Nebr. State Jour.* (Lincoln), Mar. 20, 1906.]   J. L. S.

THAYER, JOSEPH HENRY (Nov. 7, 1828–Nov. 26, 1901), Congregational clergyman and New Testament scholar, was born in Boston, Mass., the son of Joseph Helyer and Martha Stevens (Greenough) Thayer. He was a descendant of Richard Thayer an early settler of Braintree, Mass. The foundation of his scholarly career was laid by a thorough classical education at the Boston Latin School and at Harvard College, from which he was graduated in 1850. After tutoring and travel in Europe he entered Andover Theological Seminary and completed the course there in 1857. He was resident licentiate at Andover the following year and in 1858–59, acting pastor of a church in Quincy, Mass. On Dec. 29, 1859 he was ordained pastor of the Crombie Street Church in Salem. For a brief period (1862–63) he served as chaplain of the 40th Massachusetts Volunteers. In 1864 he began a long career as teacher of the New Testament, serving as professor of sacred literature at Andover Theological Seminary (1864–82), as lecturer in the Harvard Divinity School (1883–84), and as Bussey Professor of New Testament Criticism and Interpretation (1884–1901). On Nov. 30, 1859 he married Martha Caldwell Davis, by whom he had five children. One of his daughters became the wife of Caspar René Gregory [*q.v.*], and another, the wife of Theodore W. Richards [*q.v.*].

Thayer's main interest was in the Greek language of the New Testament, though he read widely in the whole New Testament field and held positive views on theological problems that were controversial in his time. He accepted the newer methods of Biblical criticism that were causing much alarm and through his teaching and writing commended them by his own genuine religious piety and by his evident sincerity in striving for truth and accuracy. As a teacher his work was marked by conscientiousness and enthusiasm; as a scholar, by industry, accuracy, and self-effacing modesty.

Only two small books were published as exclusively his own, *The Change of Attitude Towards the Bible* (1891) and *Books and Their Use* (1893). He wrote many articles and reviews and was content to put his time and learning into editing and translating the works of others. His *Greek-English Lexicon of the New Testament, being Grimm's Wilke's Clavis Novi Testamenti, Revised and Enlarged* (1887) is an example. Though nominally a translation it was richly supplemented, having received for some twenty years the full benefit of the accuracy and learning of Thayer's mind. When published it represented the full fruition of international scholarship to that date, and a new standard in New Testament lexicography. His hope that his work might be lasting rather than ephemeral is well fulfilled in this achievement. Earlier, 1869 and 1873, he had published translations from the German of the New Testament grammars of B. Winer and Alexander Buttmann.

While the revision of the English New Testament published in 1881 was being made Thayer served as a member and secretary of the American Committee. Here again his own learning was merged with that of others, but he more than anyone else bore the burden of recording the work of the committee and later of preparing and carrying through the press the American edition published in 1901. In his presidential address before the Society of Biblical Literature and Exegesis in 1895 he proposed an American school for Oriental study and research in Palestine. The idea met hearty approval from other scholars and was realized by the founding of the American School of Oriental Research in Jerusalem. At the time of his death he was recognized as the dean of New Testament scholars in America.

[C. J. H. Ropes, in *The Biblical World*, Apr. 1902, and in *Am. Jour. of Theology*, Apr. 1902; C. H. Toy, in *Proc. of the Am. Acad. of Arts and Sciences*, Aug. 1902; *Congregationalist and Christian World*, Dec. 7, 1901, portr.; *Harvard Grads. Mag.*, Mar. 1902, portr.; *Who's Who in America*, 1901–02; Bezaleel Thayer, *Memorial of the Thayer Name* (1874); *Boston Transcript*, Nov. 27, 1901.]   H. J. C.

THAYER, NATHANIEL (Sept. 11, 1808–Mar. 7, 1883), financier, philanthropist, was was born in Lancaster, Mass., seventh of the eight children of the Rev. Nathaniel and Sarah (Toppan) Thayer. His father, minister of the only church then existing in Lancaster, was of a branch of the Thayer family that traced its New England ancestry to Richard Thayer, an early settler of Braintree, Mass. In the intervening generations the family developed a tendency towards the ministry, several of Dr. Thayer's relatives having been like him Congregational clergymen and graduates of Harvard, while a collateral branch produced Father John Thayer [*q.v.*], who was converted in France in 1783, and had the distinction of being the first priest of a regularly organized Roman Catholic church in Boston.

Nathaniel Thayer, Jr., was educated in the academy of his native town, but he chose commerce instead of the ministry as a career. In 1829, when he was but twenty-one years old, he was listed in the Boston directory as already a partner in a firm engaged in the West India trade, an apprenticeship as a clerk in other establishments having preceded his attainment of a partnership at such an early age. About 1840 he became associated with the banking house established by his brother, under the firm name of John E. Thayer & Brother, and on the death of John in 1857 Nathaniel became the senior member and principal director of the business. The organization of which the Thayer brothers laid the foundation became prominent in American business, and it amassed for Nathaniel one of the largest fortunes acquired by any New Englander of his day. Its operations were principally connected with the building of railroads and the organizing of manufacturing and other corporations of large capital. Thayer's fortune, though considerable even in his early career, became notable during the expansion following the Civil War. By the late sixties his benefactions for charitable and educational purposes had made him conspicuous. In 1866 he was chosen an overseer of Harvard College, and in 1868 became one of the board of fellows. Membership in this small and select administrative body is usually restricted to graduates, but, though Thayer could not qualify in this respect, he had an hereditary interest in Harvard that made him a desirable official. Until his resignation in 1875 he was the dominant factor in the financial management of the College. His largest individual gifts were made to it, although he gave away much more than their total in smaller donations to churches, hospitals, libraries, and persons in need. In behalf of Harvard's department of zoölogy he assumed the expense of the Agassiz expedition to Brazil in 1865; he built a dining hall for the students, an herbarium for the department of botany, and a dormitory called Thayer Hall in memory of his brother. These undertakings, with many smaller gifts, involved an outlay of at least $250,000, and made him one of the institution's most munificent patrons up to that time.

Although he never held public office, he exerted considerable personal influence on the community in which he lived in addition to that resulting from his business activities and philanthropies. On June 10, 1846, he married Cornelia Paterson, daughter of Stephen Van Rensselaer of Albany, N. Y., and grand-daughter of Stephen Van Rensselaer [q.v.], the eighth patroon. With six of their seven children she survived her husband. He died in Boston and was buried in Mount Auburn Cemetery.

[H. S. Nourse, *The Birth, Marriage, and Death Reg. . . . of Lancaster, Mass.* (1890); *New England Hist. and Geneal. Reg.*, Jan.–Oct. 1883; G. E. Ellis, *Memoir of Nathaniel Thayer, A.M.*, reprinted from *Proc. Mass. Hist. Soc.*, 2 ser. II (1886); S. E. Morison, *The Development of Harvard Univ. Since the Inauguration of President Eliot, 1869–1929* (1930); *Boston Transcript*, Mar. 7, 1883; *Boston Post*, Mar. 8, 1883.]   S. G.

THAYER, SYLVANUS (June 9, 1785–Sept. 7, 1872), military engineer, educator, the son of Nathaniel and Dorcas (Faxon) Thayer, was born at Braintree, Mass., where his ancestor, Richard Thayer, had settled in the second quarter of the seventeenth century. He pursued a classical course at Dartmouth College, from 1803 until the early part of 1807, when he entered the United States Military Academy; here he was graduated in 1808, and commissioned second lieutenant in the corps of engineers. For the next few years he was engaged as an assistant in the design and construction of fortifications on the coast of New England and New York. During the War of 1812 he saw service on the Canadian frontier and at Norfolk, Va., and received the brevet of major. In 1815 he was sent by the government to Europe to study military schools, armies, and fortifications, and after nearly two years abroad returned to the United States thoroughly equipped for what was to be his next assignment to duty.

On July 28, 1817, at the age of thirty-two, he was appointed superintendent of the United States Military Academy at West Point, which position he held until relieved at his own request, July 1, 1833. During his first years there he was fortunate in having the enthusiastic support of John C. Calhoun [q.v.], then secretary of war. When Thayer took command, he found the Military Academy in a chaotic condition, without system or regularity in its administration. He at once held examinations, dismissed the incompetent, and made the idle work. He promptly organized the cadets into companies officered by members of their own body and appointed an officer of the army as commandant of cadets responsible for their tactical instruction and soldierly discipline. He classified them according to their proficiency in studies, divided classes into small sections for more thorough instruction, required weekly class reports showing progress, and greatly improved the curriculum according to a well digested program. He also established the system of summer encampments. The diploma now became evidence of the completion of the full course of studies, and a high standard of honor and efficiency was maintained. Commendation, official and unofficial, of Thayer's superintendency came from all quarters. As early as 1826 General Scott recommended him for the brevet of colonel "for the highest development and effect" given the Military Academy, to which, "for more than eight years he has devoted his great attainments and most unwearied zeal and application to its duties." Scott added: "It is believed that he has at length given the school an excellence equal to the most celebrated in the world" (Cullum, *Biographical Sketch, post,* pp. 22–23). The Academy, hardly more than a secondary school when Thayer took charge, claimed before he left a number of able and distinguished professors and was offering instruction of college grade in several fields. Thayer was truly the "Father of the Military Academy," as he was affectionately known to its graduates, and probably had a greater influence on their character and through them on the United States Army than any other of its distinguished sons.

After his relief from the superintendency and until his retirement, June 1, 1863, he was engineer in charge of the construction of fortifications at the entrance of Boston Harbor and of the improvement of harbors on the New England coast. He was also a member of various special engineer, artillery, and ordnance boards. From 1858 to 1863 he was on leave of absence because of broken health. On June 1, 1863, he was retired from the Army, having been brevetted brigadier-general the year before "for long and faithful service."

Thayer's interest in education did not end with his superintendency of West Point. After his retirement he established (1867) and endowed the Thayer School of Engineering of Dartmouth College, drawing up the entrance requirements, planning the curriculum, and appointing the first director—a graduate of West Point. He also provided a fund for a public library in Braintree, Mass., and in his will provided for another scientific academy to be located in Braintree or

Quincy. Because of unfortunate investments, however, some of his plans could not be carried out. He was a member of the American Academy of Arts and Sciences and the American Philosophical Society of Philadelphia, and received several honorary degrees. After his retirement he made his home at Braintree, Mass., where he died. He never married.

[G. W. Cullum, *Biog. Sketch of Brig.-Gen. Sylvanus Thayer* (1883), address delivered at the unveiling of a statue of Thayer at West Point, June 11, 1883; G. W. Cullum, *Biog, Reg. Officers and Grads. U. S. Mil. Acad.* (3rd ed., 1891), vol. I; Bezaleel Thayer, *Memorial of the Thayer Name* (1874); L. B. Richardson, *Hist. of Dartmouth Coll.* (1932), vol. II; *Army and Navy Jour.*, Sept. 14, 1872; *Boston Transcript*, Sept. 7, 1872.]   G. J. F.

THAYER, THOMAS BALDWIN (Sept. 10, 1812–Feb. 12, 1886), Universalist clergyman, editor, author, was born in Boston, Mass., the son of Benjamin and Catherine (Davis) Thayer and a descendant of Richard Thayer, an early settler of Braintree. Thomas received his early education in the public schools of Boston and at the Boston Latin School. He was tutored in the studies of the freshman year at Harvard, by F. R. Leverett, master of the Latin School from 1828 to 1831, and then taught in Hawes Grammar School and later in a preparatory school for boys established by Leverett. While teaching he supplied Universalist churches, and in December 1832 was ordained by the Boston Association of Universalists. The following year he became pastor of the First Universalist Society in Lowell, Mass.

He seems to have entered the ministry with the fervor and zeal of a missionary. Theological disputations were the fashion and were carried on uncompromisingly. Thayer quickly took a leading position in the warfare against the doctrine of eternal punishment. He fought with his pen with even greater vigor than with his voice. Assisted by the Rev. Abel C. Thomas, he established and edited (1841–42) *The Star of Bethlehem,* a journal devoted to Universalist propaganda. During the same period he and Thomas wrote and published the *Lowell Tracts,* five of which are credited to Thayer—"What is Universalism?", "Scripture Doctrine of the Devil," and "Truth and Reason Against Creeds" being the best known. He also assisted Thomas in publishing the *Lowell Offering,* the articles in which were written by the mill girls of Lowell. In 1845 he accepted a call to Brooklyn, N. Y. He now became less militant, partly because his spare time was devoted to editing *The Golden Rule and Odd Fellows' Family Companion,* a fraternal publication. In 1851 he returned to his first charge in Lowell, and in March 1853 he married Mrs. Sarah Athena Peck, daughter of Samuel H. Harris of Methuen, Mass., by whom he had a daughter. In 1859 he left Lowell to become pastor of the Shawmut Avenue Universalist Church in Boston, with which he remained until he retired from the active ministry in 1867.

His earliest polemic was *Christianity against Infidelity* (1836) which was reissued in considerably enlarged form in 1849. One of his most successful and influential works was *The Bible Class Assistant, or Scriptural Guide for Sunday Schools* (1840). It was a pioneer work in the direction of more sensible and illuminative methods of Biblical instruction, and passed through many editions. In 1855 he copyrighted *The Origin and History of the Doctrine of Endless Punishment,* and in 1862, *Theology of Universalism.* He was a frequent and forceful contributor to the *Universalist Quarterly,* of which he became editor in 1864. With the exception of a few months' absence on a tour of Europe and the Far East he conducted this journal until his last illness. In it are found his most lasting contributions to the literature of Universalism. He was also the author of much verse which, however, is not available in collected form. Thayer was an overseer of Harvard from 1858 to 1864 and again from 1865 to 1871. He died in Roxbury (part of Boston), Mass.

[Bezaleel Thayer, *Memorial of the Thayer Name* (1874); G. H. Emerson, in *Universalist Quart.,* July 1886; *Autobiog. of Rev. Abel C. Thomas* (1852); J. G. Adams, *Fifty Notable Years* (1882); Richard Eddy, *Universalism in America* (2 vols., 1884–86); *Universalist Reg.,* 1887; *Christian Leader,* Feb. 18, 1886; *Boston Daily Advertiser,* Feb. 13, 1886.]   C. G.

THAYER, WHITNEY EUGENE (Dec. 11, 1838–June 27, 1889), organist, composer, was born in Mendon, Mass., the son of Perry and Charlotte (Taft) Thayer, and a descendant of Thomas Thayer, an early settler of Braintree, Mass. He began the study of music at an early age, but he did not consider it seriously as a profession until he came under the influence of John Knowles Paine [q.v.], and was chosen with Paine, Benjamin J. Lang [q.v.], and others to play at the dedication of the organ in Boston Music Hall on Nov. 2, 1863. In 1865 he went abroad to study organ and counterpoint with Haupt and composition with Wieprecht. The following year he made a concert tour of Europe and a trip to England where he played at Westminster Abbey and at St. Paul's in London. When he returned to Boston, he immediately became active as an organist and teacher, and, until he went to New York in 1881, he occupied the organ-lofts successively of the Arlington Street, Hollis Street, Old First Unitarian, and New

England Churches in Boston, and the Harvard Church in Brookline. He was also active as a recitalist on the organ, and in 1868 inaugurated a long series of concerts in Boston, the first free organ concerts to be given in the country. He gave many others, in America and abroad. When Ole Bull, the violinist, made his American tour, Thayer was his official pianist. In 1875 he opened a private organ studio in Boston, said to be the first of its kind in the United States. From 1881 to 1886 he was organist of the Fifth Avenue Presbyterian Church in New York City, and then played for a season at Holy Trinity Episcopal Church in Harlem, after which he retired to devote the remaining twelve years of his life to teaching and composition.

As a teacher Thayer exerted a strong influence. He was one of the early teachers of George W. Chadwick, and his many pupils numbered such musicians as Edward Fisher, Walter C. Gale, Gerrit Smith, J. Warren Andrews, and Sumner Salter. Throughout his life he sought to bring about an improvement in church music and to raise the standards of taste. In addition to his many lectures, he preached his doctrines in the pages of the two magazines he edited at various times while in Boston, probably between 1870 and 1881,—the *Organist's Journal and Review,* and the *Choir Journal and Review.* He also conducted the Boston Choral Union and the New England Church-Music Association. His talents were recognized in his own time by the award of a Doctor of Music degree from Oxford University, for the composition of his "Festival Cantata" for soli, eight-part chorus and orchestra. Among his other compositions were a Mass in E flat, a Fugue for the organ, five organ sonatas, variations for two performers on the organ on the Russian national hymn, many shorter pieces for the organ, and solo and part songs. His most ambitious educational publication was *The Art of Organ Playing Complete in Five Parts* (1874), and his *Vest Pocket Harmony Book* (1883).

On Oct. 8, 1862, Thayer was married to Elizabeth Davis Eaton, of Worcester, Mass. She and three of their five children survived him when he died, by his own hand, at Burlington, Vt. For some time before his death he had been mentally unsound. The family home "Mt. Ida" at Newton provided a place of happy diversion for Thayer, and it was there that he indulged especially his great interest in philosophical speculation and in astronomy.

[In view of his contemporary prominence Thayer is surprisingly neglected by writers on American music. He is omitted from the standard books on the subject by Ritter, Hughes, and Howard, and L. C. Elson, in *The Hist. of Am. Music* (rev. ed., 1925), gives him only casual and perfunctory mention. See, however, *Grove's Dict. of Music and Musicians, Am. Supp.* (1930), an article by his daughter, Louise Friedel Thayer, in *Am. Organist,* Aug. 1933, and two articles by Sumner Salter in the *Musician,* Dec. 1912, and by J. W. Andrews, in the *Am. Organist,* Mar. 1932. For names of his parents see *Vital Records of Mendon, Mass.* (1920); for ancestry, L. T. Ojeda, *Catálogo Biográfico de la Casa de Thaye de Braintree* (1904), p. 51; and, for obituary, the *N. Y. Times,* June 28, 1889.]

J. T. H.

THAYER, WILLIAM MAKEPEACE (Feb. 23, 1820–Apr. 7, 1898), clergyman, editor, and writer, was born and died in Franklin, Mass. His father, Davis Thayer, merchant and early manufacturer of straw hats, was a descendant of Thomas Thayer, freeman of Braintree, Essex, England, who received title of lands at Braintree, Mass., soon after its first settlement. His mother, Betsey (McKepiece) Thayer, of limited education and unsatisfied literary longings, aroused in him a desire for education and a professional life. He began attending the district school when he was four. Before he was fifteen he was studying at the Franklin academy. In 1843 he received the A.B. degree from Brown University. He taught school in Attleboro, South Braintree, and Franklin, Mass., and studied theology with the Rev. Jacob Ide of West Medway, Mass. In 1844 he was licensed to preach by the Mendon conference of orthodox churches, but he did not at once give up teaching, which he considered a useful preparation for preaching. On Oct. 19, 1845, he married Rebecca W. Richards, the daughter of Calvin Richards of Dover, Mass., by whom he had five children. He began preaching at Edgartown, Martha's Vineyard, Mass. In 1849 he accepted the pastorate of the Congregational Church at Ashland, Mass., which he held until 1857 when he was forced to give up preaching because of throat trouble. He continued to the end of his life to preach occasionally in neighboring churches.

In 1858 he extended his educational and religious work beyond the bounds of school room and church. From 1858 to 1862 he was editor of *The Home Monthly* to which he and many of his ministerial friends were prolific contributors. He was editor successively of the *Nation,* 1864–68, and *Mother's Assistant,* 1868–72. He was twice a member of the Massachusetts General Court, in 1857–58 and in 1863–64. He was also secretary of the Massachusetts State Temperance Alliance from 1860 to 1876. He never ceased writing from his early school days until his death. While still at the academy he began publishing his compositions in local temperance and religious papers. He frequently wrote funeral hymns and occasional verse. In 1853 he published *The Gem and Casket,* and the following year *Life at the Fireside.* In *The Poor Boy and Merchant Prince . . . the Life of . . . Amos Lawrence* (1857) and *The Poor Girl and the True Woman . . . Life of Mary Lyon* (1857), he hit upon a form of biography that proved a popular way to point morals and to preach the gospel of virtue and success. Among his early biographies were *The Bobbin Boy* (1860), *The Pioneer Boy and How he Became President* (1863); among the later ones was *A Youth's History of the Rebellion* (4 vols., 1864–65), which gave a partisan and contemporary account of the Civil War. In the last decade of his life he published *Success and its Achievers* (1891), later published as volume III of *Ethics of Success* (3 vols., 1893–94), a series of school readers, *Turning Points in Successful Careers* (1895), *Men Who Win* (1896) and *Women Who Win* (1896). After his death the *Unfinished Autobiography of William M. Thayer* was privately printed by his son (n.d.). He traveled through the West once, to describe which he wrote *Marvels of the New West* (1887), but otherwise his experiences and associations were confined to his native state. He limited his reading to books he considered inspirational and ruled out novels as not contributing to intellectual strength. From his reading he compiled many notebooks of facts and incidents and others of his random thoughts, from which he later drew for illustrative material in his writing. His work was didactic and depended for its interest largely upon anecdote and incident.

[*Autobiography, ante*; Bezaleel Thayer, *Memorial of the Thayer Name* (1874), pp. 184, 222, 332, 432; *Hist. Cat. of Brown University* (1895); *N. Y. Tribune,* Apr. 8, 1898.]
V. L. S.

THAYER, WILLIAM ROSCOE (Jan. 16, 1859–Sept. 7, 1923), biographer, historian, was born in Boston, Mass., the son of Frederick William and Maria (Phelps) Thayer. He was descended on both sides from a straight English and New England ancestry; his paternal ancestor, Thomas Thayer, was an early settler of Braintree, Mass. Frederick William Thayer, a prosperous shipping merchant, had business connections in England and there became so much interested in the work of the Liverpool banker-historian of Italy, William Roscoe, that he gave his name to his own son. Thus from earliest childhood the thoughts of the boy were turned toward the history of the country which next to his own was to be the ruling interest of his mature life.

He attended St. Paul's school at Concord,

N. H., for three years, and was then taken to Europe, where he remained two and a half years, most of the time under the care of an exceptionally gifted private tutor. Entering Harvard College in 1877, he was graduated in due course. Meanwhile a change in the family fortunes had made it necessary for him to seek gainful occupation. From the very beginning of his conscious life he had shown more than ordinary capacity for writing in both prose and verse, and he at once accepted a very humble position as "space writer" for the *Boston Sunday Budget.* This experience led to an engagement on the *Philadelphia Evening Bulletin,* where he served an apprenticeship of four years, writing literary, musical, and dramatic criticism and editorials upon all subjects except politics.

In the autumn of 1885 a modest inheritance from his mother made it possible for him to give up the unsatisfying routine of journalism and return to his studies and literary ventures. As a preliminary he spent a year in the Harvard Graduate School, receiving his master's degree in 1886. After another year in Europe he settled in Cambridge and accepted an appointment as instructor in English at Harvard (1888–89), hoping that by performing the "chore-work" of theme correcting "I might eventually have an opportunity of testing my ability in a more congenial course" (*Letters, post,* p. 63). In this hope he was disappointed. The appointment was not renewed, and alluring offers from other places did not attract him.

His marriage, Nov. 24, 1893, to Elizabeth Hastings Ware of Cambridge, member of a notable family of scholars and divines, strengthened Thayer's purpose to go on with the historical study and writing for which he had long been steadily preparing. His devotion to the University continued unabated. He was chosen as editor of the new *Harvard Graduates' Magazine* and continued in that capacity for twenty-three years (1892–1915). He was twice elected to the board of overseers (1913–19 and 1920–23). The Harvard Union owed its origin to him, and it was largely through his persistent advocacy that it was founded and began its beneficent service.

Thayer's interest in Italian history began early to center about the period of the *Risorgimento,* the struggle for unity and independence. The first fruit of this interest was *The Dawn of Italian Independence* (2 vols., 1893), a survey of the preparatory stages. For the central figure of his work he chose Cavour as the chief constructive agent about whom he might group the other elements, both radical and reactionary, that contributed to the final result. With his ardent love of liberty and hatred of tyranny there could be no question of "impartiality" in his treatment of the subject, yet he was equally far from blind admiration of his hero. His two volumes, *The Life and Times of Cavour,* published in 1911, at once placed him in the front rank of biographical historians. The appreciation of the Italian government was shown by his nomination to membership in the Order of the Crown of Italy and in the Order of Saints Maurizio & Lazzaro with the title of *Commendatore,* the highest civic honor in the gift of that country. In 1905 he had published *A Short History of Venice.*

Work on the Cavour was interrupted for four years by a serious nervous disorder which he faced with unflinching courage and overcame at last by persistent occupation within the limits of his strength. Upon its completion he turned with renewed energy to a new field of study in preparation for *The Life and Letters of John Hay* (2 vols., 1915). Four years later he published *Theodore Roosevelt; an Intimate Biography* (1919), and in 1920, *The Art of Biography.* In 1918–19 he was president of the American Historical Association. Meanwhile, his affection for Italy had developed in him an equal detestation of Bismarckian Germany. The events of 1914 roused him to intense hostility and he gave himself wholeheartedly to the task of stirring American opinion to the point of war. His pamphlets, *Germany vs. Civilization* (1916) and *The Collapse of Superman* (1918), and his letters to men of political importance indicate his point of view during this period. He died in Cambridge, at the age of sixty-four, survived by his wife and one daughter.

[*The Letters of William Roscoe Thayer* (1926), ed. by C. D. Hazen; *Who's Who in America,* 1922–23; J. F. Rhodes, *Commemorative Tribute to William Roscoe Thayer* (1924); Bezaleel Thayer, *Memorial of the Thayer Name* (1874); Owen Wister, "William Roscoe Thayer," *Harvard Grads. Mag.,* Dec. 1923; *Twenty-fifth Anniv. Report . . . Class of 1881 of Harvard Coll.* (1906); *Harvard Coll. Class of 1881, Fiftieth Anniv.* (1931); *Boston Transcript,* Sept. 8, 1923; personal acquaintance.]   E. E—n.

THAYER, WILLIAM SYDNEY (June 23, 1864–Dec. 10, 1932), physician, was born in Milton, Mass., the eldest son of Sophia Bradford (Ripley) and James Bradley Thayer [*q.v.*], and the descendant of Thomas Thayer who emigrated from Braintree, England, to Braintree, Mass., before 1647. His brother was Ezra Ripley Thayer [*q.v.*]. He graduated from Harvard College in 1885 and in 1889 from the Harvard Medical School. After serving as interne in the Massachusetts General Hospital, he studied under Paul Ehrlich and others in Berlin and Vienna. On his return to America, he practised for a short time in Boston and in November 1890 became a member of the house staff of William Osler [*q.v.*] in the Johns Hopkins Hospital and was resident physician there for seven years. He became professor of clinical medicine in the Johns Hopkins Medical School and, later, professor of medicine and physician-in-chief to the hospital. In 1921 he was made professor emeritus of medicine. Throughout his career he was prominent in medical research, teaching, organization, and practice. He investigated the blood in leukaemia, typhoid fever, and malaria, and he made numerous contributions to knowledge of the circulatory system, including publications upon the third heart sound, heart murmurs, bacterial endocarditis, heart block, angina pectoris, and arteriosclerosis. He published several volumes, including: *Lectures on the Malarial Fevers* (1897), *America—1917 and Other Verse* (1926), and *Osler and Other Papers* (1931). He inspired younger men to engage in research work, and many men were grateful to have been his pupils. As a teacher he laid great stress upon the accuracy of physical examinations and set an example of painstaking work himself. Skilled, too, in the use of the methods of the clinical laboratory, he drilled his students rigorously in their application to the study of patients. He insisted upon the keeping of most careful clinical records from the time of admission until the discharge of each patient; such records became very valuable later for statistical analyses. With William George MacCallum he held regular clinical-pathological conferences with regard to fatal cases, at which the clinical studies made during life were compared with the findings at autopsy. His students were urged, too, to make use of the library and were taught the importance and the technique of studies of the bibliography of the maladies that came under observation. A linguist himself, he encouraged his students to learn to read and to speak two or three foreign languages. As a consulting practitioner in medicine, he was much sought after because of his vast experience, his soundness of judgment, and his powers of inspiring confidence. A brilliant diagnostician, he was also a competent therapist, emphasizing always the adoption of the simpler methods of physical and mental treatment.

In 1917 he and his friend Frank Billings of Chicago were made members of the American Red Cross Mission to Russia, for which in 1918 he received the distinction badge of the Red Cross of Russia. While he was absent, in August 1917, his wife, Susan Chisolm (Read) Thayer, to whom he had been married on Sept. 3, 1901, died in Baltimore after a long invalidism. She left no children. He served successively as major, colonel, and brigadier-general of the medical corps in the World War and, during 1918–19, acted as chief consultant of the American Expeditionary Force in France. For these services he received the Distinguished Service Medal of the United States in 1919 and a commandership of the Legion of Honor in France in 1928. He was made fellow of many foreign medical academies and honorary member of a large number of scientific associations in this country and abroad. He was president of the American Medical Association, 1928–29. He served as a trustee of the Carnegie Institution of Washington and for two terms as a member of the board of overseers of Harvard University. Numerous honorary degrees were conferred upon him. He accepted invitations to deliver the Bright Lecture in London in 1927, the Gibson Lectures at Edinburgh in 1930, and the Frank Billings Lecture in Chicago in 1932. In May 1927 the "William Sydney Thayer and Susan Read Thayer Lectureship in Clinical Medicine," providing for one or more lectures annually at the Johns Hopkins, was endowed by a group of their friends. Physically he was of average height, slender in later life, and healthy until some three years before his death, when he began to suffer from anginal attacks. He died suddenly from a heart attack while visiting in Washington.

[L. F. Barker, "Wm. Sydney Thayer," *Science*, Dec. 30, 1932; *Harvard College Class of 1885 Secretary's Report*, no. 2–9 (1889–1925); *Who's Who in America*, 1932–33; Bezaleel Thayer, *Memorial of the Thayer Name* (1874), esp. pp. 184, 587, 590, 621; *N. Y. Times*, Dec. 12, 1932.]   L. F. B.

THÉBAUD, AUGUSTUS J. (Nov. 20, 1807–Dec. 17, 1885), Roman Catholic priest and educator, was born of an aristocratic family of wealth in Nantes, France, which was then still under the shadow of Carrier's terrorism. Its ruined churches depressed the spiritual and precocious child, who read tolerably well at four years of age and who progressed so rapidly under tutors in private schools that he was well advanced when he entered the local *petit séminaire* which accommodated candidates for the priesthood and young aristocrats who held aloof from Napoleonic foundations. Thereafter he studied theology in the Grand Seminary of Nantes, and on ordination to the priesthood he was named *vicaire* of St. Clement's Church in his native town. In 1835 he entered the Jesuit novitiate at Rome, completed a course of higher studies in the Roman College, and studied science at the Sorbonne in Paris (1836–38). In the meantime he took

his final vows in the Society on Dec. 3, 1837. Acquainted with the shortage of priests in America through the appeals of visiting prelates from the United States and the reports in the *Annals of the Propagation of the Faith,* Thébaud petitioned successfully to be sent on the American missions and arrived in New York, Dec. 18, 1838. His first assignment was at St. Mary's College, Marion County, Ky., where he taught chemistry and in 1846 presided as rector. When the Jesuits withdrew from the institution because of an apparent lack of episcopal appreciation (1846), and assumed control of St. John's College, Fordham, N. Y., on the invitation of Bishop John J. Hughes [*q.v.*], Thébaud went to St. John's, and served as rector and director of the diocesan seminary until he became pastor of St. Joseph's Church in Troy (1852–60). A tolerant man of tactful approach, he moderated nativist antagonism and established friendly relations with Episcopalian leaders and the Presbyterian employers of Irish labor. He was loved by the Irish for his dispatch of Jesuits to care for the stricken immigrants at Grosse Isle, Canada, in 1847. In accordance with the policy of his society, he was transferred frequently. He was rector and professor in Fordham (1860–63, 1874–75), pastor at Troy, N. Y. (1863–69, 1873–74), professor and preacher at a Jesuit institution and at St. Mary's Church in Montreal, pastor at Hudson City, N. J. (1870–73), and teacher and pastor at St. Francis Xavier's College and Church in New York City (1875–85). He died at Fordham and was buried in the college cemetery.

As a missionary, lecturer, distinguished preacher, and an associate of prelates, Thébaud became widely acquainted with the country, and undertook a serious study of immigration and social problems. He was a faithful observer, and his books and numerous essays on current religious, historical, and educational problems, published in Catholic magazines, have historical value. Two of his most valuable articles are those on "Superior Instruction in our Colleges" (*American Catholic Quarterly Review,* Oct. 1882) and "Freedom of Worship in the United States" (*Ibid.,* Apr. 1885). His books include *Gentilism* (1876), *The Church and the Gentile World at the First Promulgation of the Gospel* (2 vols., 1878), *The Church and the Moral World* (1881), and *The Irish Race in the Past and Present* (1873). In addition to *Louisa Kirkbride* (1879), an ephemeral novel of New York life, he left two valuable manuscript memoirs which were edited by C. G. Herbermann as *Forty Years in the United States of America* (1904), with a biographical sketch by T. J. Campbell, S. J., and *Three-Quarters of a Century* (2 vols., 1912–13).

[For biog. materials see Thébaud's own writings; Woodstock Letters; J. T. Smith, *The Cath. Church in N. Y.* (1905); B. J. Webb, *The Centenary of Catholicity in Ky.* (1884); rev. of *Gentilism,* in *Month and Cath. Rev.* (London), Apr. 1876; "Father Thébaud and His Critics," *Ibid.,* June, July 1876; obituaries in *Sun* (N. Y.), Dec. 18, *N. Y. Times,* Dec. 20, and *N. Y. Freeman's Jour.,* Dec. 26, 1885.]   R. J. P.

THEOBALD, SAMUEL (Nov. 12, 1846–Dec. 20, 1930), ophthalmologist, was born in Baltimore, Md., the son of Dr. Elisha Warfield Theobald and Sarah Frances (Smith) Theobald. His mother was a daughter of Dr. Nathan Ryno Smith [*q.v.*], and after the death of his father when he was five Theobald lived with his grandfather. He was educated at the preparatory school of George Carey, studied in his grandfather's office, and at the same time pursued his medical course at the University of Maryland, from which he received the degree of M.D. in 1867. On Apr. 30, 1867, at Bristol, R. I., he married Caroline Dexter de Wolf, by whom he had two daughters and one son. In 1870, after working with his grandfather for several years, he went abroad for eighteen months to specialize in ophthalmology and otology. In Vienna he studied the eye with Ferdinand von Arlt, Eduard Jaeger, and the ear with Leopold Maximilian Politzer; later he worked with William Bowman, George Critchett, and Jonathan Hutchinson at the Royal London Ophthalmic Hospital. In 1871 he returned to Baltimore to practise his specialties. He was the leading spirit in establishing the Baltimore Eye and Ear Dispensary in 1874, and in 1882, together with some colleagues, he founded the Baltimore Eye, Ear, and Throat Charity Hospital, with which he kept up an active association until within a few years of his death. From 1889 to 1925 he was ophthalmic surgeon to the Johns Hopkins Hospital; from 1896 until 1912, clinical professor of ophthalmology and otology in the Johns Hopkins School of Medicine; from 1912 to 1925, clinical professor of ophthalmology; from 1925 until his death, professor emeritus of ophthalmology.

In spite of a very large private and hospital practice, he was a prolific and forceful writer. A collection of one hundred and eighteen reprints of his articles covers a wide range of subjects of ophthalmological and otological interest. Those on the eye include descriptions of instruments that he devised, surgical procedures, clinical discussions, case reports, discussions of the relation of diseases of the eye to general disease, studies in the prevention of blindness, and reports upon new medicines and apparatus. His genius is

memorialized by his method of treating closure of the tear ducts and by his invention of lachrymal probes, which he described in 1877. He introduced boric acid to ophthalmologists ("Boric Acid; A New Remedy in Eye Diseases," *Medical Record,* Feb. 7, 1880), and in 1884, shortly after the discovery of the anesthetic properties of cocain, he wrote concerning his clinical experience with this drug. In 1892 he described the use of the electro-magnet for removing metallic particles from the eye. In 1906 he published his *Prevalent Diseases of the Eye,* an eminently practical volume of over five hundred pages. In addition to his articles on ophthalmological subjects, he wrote several papers upon the ear. He was keenly interested in the activities of medical societies, and served as president of the Medical and Chirurgical Faculty of Maryland (1900) and as president of the American Ophthalmological Society (1910). Throughout his career he took time for the courtesies of life, and he possessed to a rare degree the gift of friendship. Slightly but strongly built, he was exceedingly good to look upon. He was a skilful surgeon and a painstaking ophthalmologist, who held the esteem of the entire medical profession and whose patients became his friends and ardent admirers.

[See *Who's Who in America,* 1930–31; Harry Friedenwald, in *Archives of Ophthalmology,* Mar. 1931, and *Trans. Am. Ophthalmological Soc.,* vol. XXIX (1931); W. H. Wilmer, in *Bull. School of Medicine, Univ. of Md.,* May 1931, and *Am. Jour. of Ophthalmology,* Apr. 1931; obituary in *N. Y. Times,* Dec. 21, 1930. Information has been supplied by Theobald's daughter, Mrs. J. W. Williams, and by Dr. J. M. H. Rowland. A large collection of reprints of articles by Theobald is in the possession of the lib. of the Medical and Chirurgical Faculty, Baltimore, Md.]   W. H. W.

THEUS, JEREMIAH (*c.* 1719–May 18, 1774), portrait painter, was born, it is believed, in Switzerland. About 1739 his parents with their three sons joined the colony of Swiss and German immigrants then lately settled in Orangeburg County, S. C. (Salley, *post,* p. 81). One son, the Rev. Christian (or Christianus) Theus, became a celebrated and effective preacher in South Carolina. What training in art Jeremiah may have had is unknown. By 1740 he was painting in Charleston, for he advertised, Aug. 30, 1740, in the *South Carolina Gazette:* "Jeremiah Theus, Limner, gives notice that he is removed into Market Square, near Mr. John Laurens, Sadler, where all Gentlemen and Ladies may have their pictures drawn, likewise Landscapes of all sizes, Crests and Coats of Arms for Coaches and Chaises. Likewise for the convenience of those who live in the country he is willing to wait on them at their respective Plantations." Four years later, Nov. 5, 1744, he inserted a notice in the *Gazette* "to all young Gentlemen and Ladies inclinable to be taught the Art of *Drawing*" that he would open an evening school at his house in Friend Street, where "every Branch of that Art" would be taught "with the greatest Exactness" (*South Carolina Historical and Genealogical Magazine,* October 1930, p. 315). Thus began a career during which Theus made likenesses of many men and women of the southern colonies.

In connection with an exhibition of colonial portraits at the Copley Gallery, Boston, about forty canvases by Theus were listed (*Boston Evening Transcript,* June 1, 1917), some of them previously mistaken for works by John Singleton Copley [*q.v.*]. Several portraits were of the South Carolina Huguenot connection, with whom Theus was evidently intimate: Samuel Prioleau and his wife, Mr. and Mrs. Gabriel Manigault, Peter Porcher, Mrs. Thomas Cordes, and others (A. H. Hirsch, *The Huguenots of Colonial South Carolina,* 1928, p. 163). Among his portraits of Jewish sitters were those of Mr. and Mrs. Manuel Josephson (Hannah R. London, *Portraits of Jews by Gilbert Stuart and Other Early American Artists,* 1927). A not inept characterization of Theus' artistry is that of Dunlap (*post,* vol. I, p. 31), who says that, though the faces were painted with great care, "he had not the art to give grace and picturesque effect to the stiff brocades, enormous ruffles, and *outre* stays and stomachers of our grandmothers; or the wigs, velvet coats, and waistcoats . . . of our grandfathers. His pictures were as stiff and formal as the originals, when dressed for the purpose and sitting for them." The characteristic concealment of the sitter's hands may indicate a weakness in his powers, but his drawing was accurate, his coloring good, and the likenesses unmistakably true (Wilson, *post,* p. 142).

Theus married, Jan. 13, 1741/42, Elizabeth Catherine Schaumlöffel, who died Nov. 8, 1754, leaving three sons and two daughters. Late in life he married Mrs. Eva Rosanna Hilt, who bore him two sons and two daughters. He accumulated a sizable fortune, his estate including a house at Broad and Mazyck streets (destroyed by fire in 1861), and a pew in the south gallery of St. Michael's Church, Charleston. Doubtless many of his portraits, unlisted, the artist's name unknown to the owners, still hang in plantation houses.

[According to J. H. Morgan, *Early Am. Painters* (1921), p. 9, Theus sometimes signed his name Theüs. See also Robert Wilson, in *Year Book, 1899, City of Charleston, S. C.,* App., p. 137; A. S. Salley, Jr., *The Hist. of Orangeburg County, S. C.* (1898); William Dunlap, *A Hist. of the Rise and Progress of the Arts of Design in the U. S.* (3 vols., 1918), ed. by F. W. Bayley, and C. E. Goodspeed.]

F. W. C.

THIERRY, CAMILLE (October 1814–April 1875), Louisiana poet, was born in New Orleans, the son of a Frenchman from Bordeaux and his octoroon mistress. Camille at first had private tutors but when he was older went to day school. He was preparing to go to a college in Paris when his father died, leaving him a small fortune. What decided him to change his mind no one knows, but he remained in New Orleans and went into business. Being entirely unfitted for its drudgery, however, he soon gave it up. Once free from its restraint he made frequent trips to Paris, where he lived in a spectacularly dissipated fashion and wasted his patrimony. In 1855, convinced by these visits that he could no longer bear the intellectual and social isolation imposed upon him in New Orleans because of his color, he placed all his affairs in the hands of his agents, Lafitte, Dufilho & Company, and went to Paris to live. There he frequented literary circles and continued his tempestuous career for some years until, suddenly tiring of it, he withdrew to Bordeaux, where he lived the life of an anchorite. He had written a good deal of French verse, and as early as 1843 his "Idées" was published in *L'Album Littéraire* of New Orleans. When Armand Lanusse in 1845 was preparing his anthology of French verse written by Louisiana men of color, he included in *Les Cenelles,* as he called it, fourteen of Thierry's poems, twice as many as those of anyone's else, which goes to show that Thierry was regarded as one of the leading poets of his race. His verses were especially admired for their quality of freshness and gentleness, although a note of bitterness born of racial discrimination crept into his later poetry, which clearly showed the inspiration of Charles-Hubert Millevoye and Lamartine.

In 1873 his Louisiana agents became bankrupt, and Thierry lost both the rents they had collected and the capital he had invested in their firm. Leaving his retreat in Bordeaux, he sailed for New Orleans to attempt to straighten out his affairs. But he was more a poet than a business man, and so he was persuaded to transfer all title in his real estate to his agents, who had reembarked in business, upon their promise to pay him an annuity of fifty dollars a month for the rest of his life. He returned to Bordeaux and, collecting all his fugitive poems, published them there at his own expense in a small volume called *Les Vagabondes,* which appeared in 1874. Shortly after this Lafitte, Dufilho & Company failed again, Thierry's annuity was discontinued, and he was left practically penniless. This shock was too much for him, and in April 1875 he died in Bordeaux. His verses were so popular that for years after his death they were reprinted from time to time in the Creole press of Louisiana.

[E. L. Tinker, *Les Écrits de Langue Française en Louisiane aux XIXe Siècle* (1932), and *Les Cenelles: Afro-French Poetry in Louisiana* (1930), reprinted from the *Colophon*, pt. III; R. L. Desdunes, *Nos Hommes et Notre Histoire* (1911); Armand Mercier, in *Comptes Rendus de l'Athénée Louisianais*, Jan. 1, 1878, p. 135; Ruby Van A. Caulfeild, *The French Lit. of La.* (1929).]   E. L. T.

THOBURN, ISABELLA (Mar. 29, 1840–Sept. 1, 1901), missionary and educator, was born at St. Clairsville, Ohio, the daughter of Matthew and Jane Lyle (Crawford) Thoburn, and a sister of James M. Thoburn [q.v.]. She attended the public schools, and in her fifteenth year entered the Female Seminary of Wheeling, Va. (now W. Va.). After a period of teaching she returned to the Wheeling institution, now become a college, for further study, and subsequently spent a year in the Cincinnati Academy of Design. During the Civil War she gave herself freely to organizing relief groups and sewing circles, collecting supplies, feeding passing troops, and nursing the wounded in the hospitals. Teaching in Wheeling, W. Va., Newcastle, Pa., and West Farmington, Ohio, prepared her further for what was to be her life career.

In 1869 her brother James, then in India, convinced that because of their home responsibilities the wives of missionaries could not be depended upon to meet the demands of women's work, wrote a letter to his sister which he closed with these words: "The women of India need you. How would you like to come and take charge of ... a school, if we decide to make the attempt?" By return steamer Isabella replied that she would "come just as soon as a way was opened" (Thoburn, *post*, p. 34). That same year the Woman's Foreign Missionary Society of the Methodist Episcopal Church was founded in Boston, Mass., and under its auspices, on Nov. 3, accompanied by Dr. Clara A. Swain [q.v.], she sailed for India, arriving in Bombay on Jan. 7, 1870. The city of Lucknow in Oudh became the center of her activities. Into the education of the girls and young women of India she threw herself with zeal and courage. On Apr. 18, in Aminabad bazaar, she began a school with six girls and herself the only teacher, while a Christian youth guarded the group with a stout bamboo. From a day school it developed into a boarding school, then into a high school, and finally into a college for women—now the Isabella Thoburn College, the women's college of Lucknow University. Buying the beautiful estate of the Ruby Garden

(Lal Bagh) with its seven acres from a Mohammedan nobleman of the old kingdom of Oudh, she erected her buildings. The college that came into being was for Indian and Eurasian, Hindu, Mohammedan, and Christian alike; no religious or racial prejudice was to mar its peace and fellowship.

She was in America in 1880–81, and again from 1886 to 1891. During this latter period she was closely associated with the new Deaconess movement in the Methodist Episcopal Church, and herself became a graduate deaconess. She assisted Lucy Rider Meyer in the Chicago Training School, and was the founder in Cincinnati, Ohio, of the Elizabeth Gamble Deaconess Home and Training School, and of the Christ Hospital. Returning to India, she continued her educational activities. In 1899 she came back to the United States, accompanied by Lilavati Singh, one of her graduates and teachers, seeking funds. The two Christian women made a deep impression upon the Ecumenical Conference held in New York in 1900. That same year she returned to India and on Sept. 1, 1901, died of Asiatic cholera in Lucknow. The Isabella Thoburn College and the Lal Bagh High School remain her perpetual memorials. She also founded the Girls' High School in Cawnpore (1874), and helped in establishing the Wellesley School for girls in Naini Tal (1891). For years she edited the *Rafiq-i-Niswan* (*The Woman's Friend*), a paper that went into non-Christian *zenanas* and Christian homes. She also wrote and published in 1899 a life of Phoebe Rowe, one of her teachers and friends.

[Files of the *Indian Witness, Heathen Woman's Friend,* and *Woman's Missionary Friend*; W. F. Oldham, "Isabella Thoburn," in *Effective Workers in Needy Fields* (1902); J. M. Thoburn, *Life of Isabella Thoburn* (1903); B. T. Badley, *Visions and Victories in Hindustan* (2 vols., 1932); *Christian Advocate*, Oct. 17, 1901; *Northwestern Christian Advocate*, Sept. 11, 1901.]   O. M. B.

THOBURN, JAMES MILLS (Mar. 7, 1836–Nov. 28, 1922), missionary bishop of the Methodist Episcopal Church, was born in St. Clairsville, Ohio. He was the seventh child of Matthew Thoburn (originally Thorburn) and Jane Lyle (Crawford), Irish immigrants (1825) from counties Down and Antrim. On their way to Ohio the four-story brick building of Allegheny College at Meadville captured their imagination, and to this college in later years they sent all five of their sons. James entered in 1851; for two years he taught school at Loydsville, Ohio; then returned to graduate in 1857. While he was teaching, religious difficulties by which he had been disturbed became clarified, and he entered the ministry of the Methodist Episcopal Church, being admitted on trial to the Pittsburgh Conference in 1858.

Feeling called to missionary service, he was sent to India in 1859 by the Missionary Society of his Church, after ordination under the auspices of the New England Conference. His first appointment was Naini Tal, a hill station in the Himalayas (Kumaon Division, United Provinces). Preaching each Sunday to British troops in a formal "parade-service," he made a discovery: "I found," he said, "I could give the people God's message a great deal more effectively in thirty minutes than in sixty" (*My Missionary Apprenticeship*, p. 72). In time he became known as the best preacher of his church in India. On Dec. 16, 1861, he married Sarah Minerva (Rockwell), widow of J. R. Downey; she died on Oct. 30, 1862, leaving him a son. Thoburn returned to America with his motherless child in October 1863, and was tempted strongly to remain and organize a school for preparing missionaries, but the frank questioning of his sister Isabella [*q.v.*] as to the nature of his "call" sent him back to India in 1865. The North India Conference appointed him to Pauri (Garhwal), a remote station in the Himalayas, where for over two years he had few returns for his labors but much time to brood over big ideas. He was sent next to the thickly populated plains of the upper Ganges Valley, serving at Moradabad (1868), Sambhal (1869), Rae Bareilly (1870), and Lucknow (1871–73). During these years he matured rapidly and became intimately associated with the problems occasioned by the influx of converts from the depressed classes, the opening of work among Indian women by unmarried women missionaries from America, and the expansion of religious activities throughout India in consequence of the evangelistic meetings of William Taylor [*q.v.*].

On Taylor's insistence Thoburn left Lucknow in 1874 to shepherd, without salary from the Missionary Society, the little group of Taylor's converts in Calcutta, and until 1888 he was associated with missionary enterprise in that city. On one of the busiest streets he built, and later rebuilt, a church, which was filled twice every Sunday. "It is the strangest church I ever saw," one person remarked. "It seemed to me that all the bad people in Calcutta were there" (*My Missionary Apprenticeship*, p. 319). Sailors, soldiers, Europeans, and Asiatics were in the congregation. In religious work among Europeans and Anglo-Indians, Thoburn became the outstanding figure in India. All the time, however, he was dreaming of farther India, and in 1879

he began work in Rangoon; in 1884–85 with William F. Oldham he was in Singapore founding a church; in 1885 he was appointed general evangelist. The General Conference of 1888 elected him missionary bishop for India (later Southern Asia), and until his retirement in 1908 he performed the duties of this office with notable skill and power, being the acknowledged missionary leader in his denomination. In America he won innumerable friends for his far-flung missions; on the field his "singular blend of the mystical enthusiast and the clear-seeing practically-minded man" (Oldham, *post*, p. 17) gave him great effectiveness. The years of his administration witnessed a remarkable growth both in number of converts and in extent of territory occupied. Soon the Methodists were in almost every great city of India, in Baluchistan, in Java, in Sumatra, and in British Borneo. When the Philippines were opened in 1898 Thoburn was first on the field. After his retirement he settled in Meadville, Pa. Allegheny College honored him by a jubilee celebration in 1909, which brought fitting recognition to his career. When he died he was buried in the college plot. His second wife, whom he married in Philadelphia, Nov. 11, 1880, was Dr. Anna Jones of Kingston, Ohio. At the time of their marriage she was preparing for medical missionary work, and in 1882 she joined her husband in India; she died in 1902. Of Thoburn's five children three grew to maturity.

In spite of his numerous activities, Thoburn was continually busy with his pen. In 1871, with James H. Messmore, he started a small paper to which he contributed and which developed into the *Indian Witness,* official organ of the Methodist Episcopal Church in India. He was also the author of a number of books, among which may be mentioned: *My Missionary Apprenticeship* (1887); *Missionary Addresses before Theological Schools* (1887); *India and Malaysia* (1892); *The Deaconess and Her Vocation* (1893); *Light in the East* (1894); *The Christless Nations* (1895), Graves Lectures at Syracuse University; *The Church of Pentecost* (1901); *Life of Isabella Thoburn* (1903); *The Christian Conquest of India* (1906); *India and Southern Asia* (1907). To the *Western Christian Advocate* he contributed "Wayside Notes: An Autobiography," published between Jan. 4 and Dec. 27, 1911, and to the *Northwestern Christian Advocate,* "How Christ Came to India," published between Jan. 3 and Apr. 24, 1912.

[Files of the Board of Foreign Missions of the Methodist Episcopal Church; files of *Indian Witness; Christian Advocate,* Apr. 22, 1909; *Western Christian Advocate,* Apr. 21, 1909; *Northwestern Christian Advo-*

cate, Dec. 6, 1922; *World Wide Missions*, Dec. 1904; W. F. Oldham, *Thoburn—Called of God* (1918); B. T. Badley, *Visions and Victories in Hindustan* (2 vols., 1932); W. H. Crawford, *Thoburn and India* (1909); *Who's Who in America*, 1908–09; *N. Y. Times*, Nov. 29, 1922.]
                 O. M. B.

THOMAS, ALLEN (Dec. 14, 1830–Dec. 3, 1907), Confederate soldier, diplomat, was born in Howard County, Md., the son of Allen and Eliza Bradford (Dall) Thomas. He was a descendant of Tristram Thomas, born in England, who settled in Talbot County, Md., in 1666. Tristram's father, Christopher, had been in Maryland in 1637–38, but returned to England and came back to Maryland in 1664. The elder Allen Thomas, a physician and farmer, was a leading man in the neighborhood, a member of the legislature for several terms, and once a presidential elector. The son entered Princeton as a sophomore in 1847 and graduated in 1850. He studied law under John S. Tyson in Ellicott City, Md., was admitted to the bar, and practised for several years in Howard County, but following his marriage, Jan. 8, 1857, to Anne Octavie Marie, daughter of Michel Doradu Bringier of New Orleans, he removed to Louisiana and became a planter, retaining, however, his family estate, "Dalton," in Maryland. His wife, through her sister's marriages, was a sister-in-law of Duncan F. Kenner, Richard Taylor [*qq.v.*], and Horr Browse Trist, brother of Nicholas P. Trist [*q.v.*]. Thomas had four sons.

At the beginning of the Civil War he organized a battalion of infantry, of which he was appointed major. It was later expanded into the 28th Louisiana Regiment (some official records call it the 29th). Thomas was elected its colonel and was appointed in October 1862 with rank antedated to May 3. He served during the Vicksburg campaign, notably at the battle of Chickasaw Bluffs, and during the subsequent siege, commanding his regiment and at times a brigade. After the surrender of Vicksburg he was paroled and carried the report of Gen. John C. Pemberton [*q.v.*] to President Davis. Subsequently, he was put in charge of collecting other paroled prisoners and reorganizing them west of the Mississippi. Appointed brigadier-general, Feb. 4, 1864, to the place vacated by Gen. Henry W. Allen [*q.v.*], who had resigned upon his election as governor of Louisiana, Thomas was assigned to the command of a brigade of troops from that state, then stationed at Alexandria, La. He served with it until Polignac's departure for France, when he succeeded to the command of the division. He surrendered and was paroled at Natchitoches, La., on June 8, 1865.

Again he became a planter at New Hope on the Mississippi River. He was a presidential elector in 1872 and in 1880, voting for Greeley and Hancock; in 1876 he declined nomination for Congress. He was a member of the board of supervisors of Louisiana State University in 1882, and from 1882 to 1884 was professor of agriculture in that institution. Following a term of service as coiner of the mint in New Orleans during Cleveland's first administration, he removed in 1889 to Florida, which remained his home till near the end of his life. In January 1894 he was commissioned consul at La Guayra, and in July of the next year took over the legation at Caracas as envoy extraordinary and minister plenipotentiary to Venezuela. His tenure of office covered the period of controversy over the boundary of British Guiana. There is nothing in his dispatches to the state department, however, to suggest that he was consulted as to American policy toward Great Britain, or that he had any influence upon President Cleveland's vigorous action in defense of Venezuela's rights. Resigning after the change of administration, he left the legation in June 1897 and returned to Florida. Some ten years later he removed to a plantation which he had bought at Waveland, Miss., and there he died. He was buried in the Bringier family vault at Donaldsonville, La.

[R. H. Spencer, *Thomas Family of Talbot County, Md.* (1914); C. A. Evans, *Confederate Mil. Hist.* (1899); A. B. Booth, *Records of La. Confederate Soldiers and La. Confederate Commands* (1920); *War of the Rebellion: Official Records* (*Army*); S. C. Arthur and G. C. H. de Kerniou, *Old Families of La.* (1931); *New Orleans Picayune* and *New Orleans Times-Democrat*, Dec. 4, 1907, valuable for facts but inaccurate as to several dates; *Princeton Alumni Weekly*, Jan. 22, 1908; papers in U. S. State Dept. archives.]
       T. M. S.

THOMAS, AMOS RUSSELL (Oct. 3, 1826–Oct. 31, 1895), homoeopathic physician, teacher of anatomy, was born at Watertown, N. Y., the son of Azariah and Sarah (Avery) Thomas. He was a descendant of Evan Thomas who emigrated from Wales to Massachusetts in 1640. He spent his early life on a farm, where much of his spare time was occupied by reading. He was educated in the common schools and in the Jefferson County Institute, and in 1846 he began teaching in the schools of western New York. On Sept. 26, 1847, he married Elizabeth M. Bacon of Watertown, by whom he had a son and a daughter. In 1850 he entered business in Ogdensburg, N. Y., but found it distasteful and soon abandoned it. Meanwhile his study of an Indian skull so aroused his interest in anatomy that he arranged to study medicine, and in 1852 under the preceptorship of Dr. S. Potter of Syracuse, N. Y., he entered the Syracuse Medical College, from which he graduated in February 1854. He then moved to Philadelphia and entered Penn Medical University, where he was later professor of anatomy (1856–66). For some years he was lecturer on artistic anatomy in the Philadelphia Academy of the Fine Arts (1856–70) and in the Philadelphia School of Design for Women (1863–71). During the Civil War he served as a surgeon and was assigned a post in charge of a ward at the Armory Square Hospital, Washington, D.C. On being mustered out, he returned to Philadelphia. He had become interested in homoeopathy, and in 1867 he accepted the position of professor of anatomy in the Hahnemann Medical College of Philadelphia, which he held until his death. From 1874 until 1895 he served with great interest and enthusiasm as dean of the college and it was largely through his efforts that funds were raised for a new college building.

His publications include *A Practical Guide for Making Post-Mortem Examinations and for the Study of Morbid Anatomy, with Directions for Embalming the Dead and for the Preservation of Specimens of Morbid Anatomy* (1873); *The Diseases of the Pancreas, and their Homoeopathic Treatment* (1882), with several collaborators; *A New Preparation of the Nervous System* (1889), which contains a description of a unique dissection of the entire nervous system in the museum of Hahnemann Medical College; *History of Anatomy* (1893); and *Genealogical Records and Sketches of the Descendants of William Thomas of Hardwick, Mass.* (1891). In addition to these, he was the author of numerous papers on general medicine published in various homoeopathic journals, and in the transactions of the American Institute of Homoeopathy and of the Homoeopathic Medical Society of Pennsylvania. He was editor of the *American Journal of Homoeopathic Materia Medica* (1871–76) and co-editor of the *Hahnemannian Monthly* (1877–78). In 1887 he was president of the Homoeopathic Medical Society of Pennsylvania. He was a member of a number of scientific, historical, and art associations. He died in Philadelphia, survived by his son.

[A. R. Thomas, *Geneal. Records . . . of the Descendants of William Thomas of Hardwick, Mass.* (1891); L. B. Thomas, *The Thomas Book* (copr. 1896); T. L. Bradford, *Hist. of the Homoeopathic Medic. Coll. of Pa., the Hahnemann Medic. Coll. and Hospital of Pa.* (1898), and "Biogs. of Homoeopathic Physicians," vol. XXXI, in the lib. of the Hahnemann Medic. Coll.; H. A. Kelly and W. L. Burrage, *Am. Medic. Biogs.* (1920); *Hahnemannian Monthly*, Oct. 1892, Dec. 1895; *Pacific Coast Jour. of Homoeopathy*, Jan. 1896; obituary in *Pub. Ledger* (Phila.), Nov. 1, 1895.]

C. B—t.

THOMAS, AUGUSTUS (Jan. 8, 1857–Aug. 12, 1934), dramatist, was born in St. Louis, Mo., the son of Elihu Baldwin and Imogene (Garrettson) Thomas. Between grade and high school in St. Louis he served as a page boy, first at the Missouri state capitol (1868) and then in the House of Representatives at Washington (1870–71). While in Washington he was caught by Gen. Benjamin Franklin Butler [q.v.] making a caricature of that statesman. Butler (who had a huge cranium) took his hat and jammed it down over the boy's head to the shoulders, remarking, "When you can fill that hat, young man, you make caricatures of General Butler" (*The Print of My Remembrance*, 1922, p. 50). Young Thomas followed most of the debates, and laid the foundation of a lasting interest in public affairs and public speaking. Beginning at fourteen he worked in the St. Louis railroad yards, with evening study and practice in drawing, acting, and playwriting. For a time he was a reporter on the *St. Louis Post-Dispatch* (1885). In 1887 he worked in Kansas City as a newspaper man, and the next year returned to St. Louis, where he was staff artist on a newspaper. But in the meantime, between jobs, he had made a stage version of Mrs. Frances Hodgson Burnett's story, "Editha's Burglar," and with this and an improvised vaudeville program he and several other stage-struck young people, including Della Fox, had attempted to tour the Middle West. They made two trips, in fact, but secured more adventure than cash. The experience fixed Thomas in his determination to become a playwright, however, and with several play scripts in his bag he set out for New York in 1888. Failing to sell the plays, he took a job as business assistant to Julia Marlowe, and then as "press agent" to the so-called thought reader, Washington Irving Bishop. A year later he sold *The Burglar* to Maurice Barrymore [q.v.], and in 1891 attracted wide attention with *Alabama*, produced by the Palmer stock company.

After this success his road was easy. Among his better known plays produced in the nineties were *In Mizzoura* (1893), *Colonel Carter of Cartersville* (1892), *The Capitol* (1895), *Colonel George of Mount Vernon* (1895), *Chimmie Fadden* (1896), *The Hoosier Doctor* (1897), and most successful of all, *Arizona* (1899). Nearly all these plays, it will be noted, belonged to the local-color school. After the turn of the century Thomas inclined to farce comedy for a time, and in rapid succession wrote *The Earl of Pawtucket* (1903), *The Other Girl* (1903), *Mrs. Leffingwell's Boots* (1905), and *De Lancey* (1905). In 1907 he produced *The Witching Hour*, which was based on his experiences with Bishop many years before, and which was in a much more serious vein than his previous work.

This drama proved extremely popular. Thomas followed it with two others in the same general vein, *The Harvest Moon* (1909), and *As a Man Thinks* (1911). The last remains probably his best play, both in technique and substance. He wrote a dozen or fifteen more plays, the best known being *The Copperhead* (1918), but never again reached the level of popularity or achievement which marked his work in the late nineties and the first decade of the new century. In all, he wrote or adapted nearly seventy plays.

He was president of the National Institute of Arts and Letters (1914–15), a member of the American Academy of Arts and Letters, and a recipient of its medal for drama (1913). From 1922 through 1925 he acted as executive chairman of the Producing Managers' Association, and during that time made a vain effort to found a national theatre. He took a life-long interest in public speaking and debate, and was in constant demand as an after-dinner speaker because of his wit, and as a speaker for the Democratic party. It was frequently noted that his curtain speeches at the first nights of his plays seemed sometimes to have more style and substance than the plays. This was perhaps because he was reared in the old-fashioned theatre of melodrama and sheer entertainment, and was quite unaffected by the "new drama" which came in during the nineties. (He makes no reference to it whatever in his autobiography, *The Print of My Remembrance,* 1922). His descriptions of securing local color for his "State" plays, like *Arizona* and *Colorado,* disclose painstaking trips to the chosen scenes, but no stirring of dramatic interest in what lay below the surface. It was only his reflections on the telepathic feats of Bishop that prompted him, in *The Witching Hour* and *As a Man Thinks,* to probe below surfaces. Technically, his plays were well put together, and because of their theatrical expertness and local color were important in their day in helping to free the American stage from bondage to Europe and in solidifying the dramatist's craft in America. As president of the American Dramatists' Association from 1906 to 1911, also, Thomas was able by his shrewdness and force of character to exert a great influence. But, in spite of his successes, his plays (with the possible exception of *As a Man Thinks*) did little to further the development of playwriting or to inspire younger writers to tackle more significant and less "theatrical" themes. Considering his wide acquaintance with the American scene and with the leading men of the day, his interest in political questions, his keen mind and sharp wit, it is curious that he was so little affected by the new drama which

was being born around him, and apparently made so little effort to put his best powers into his plays.

Thomas was a moderately tall, sturdy man, both democratic and dignified, with a square, smooth-shaven face, a generous mouth set in parentheses, and a pugnacious chin. He had a rather slow, clear-cut speech in public, and a masterly technique for making his incisive wit and epigram tell to the full. After coming to New York, he lived most of his life in New Rochelle, near his intimate friend, Frederic Remington [*q.v.*], but passed a few years early in the twentieth century in Paris, and the last two years of his life near Nyack, where he died. He was survived by his wife—Lisle Colby of St. Louis, sister of Bainbridge Colby, whom he had married on Aug. 16, 1890,—a daughter, and a son.

[In addition to *The Print of My Remembrance,* see *Who's Who in America,* 1934–35; A. H. Quinn, *A Hist. of the Am. Drama from the Civil War to the Present Day* (2 vols., 1927); Burns Mantle, *Am. Playwrights of Today* (1929); W. D. Howells, in *North Am. Rev.,* Mar. 1901; preface to *The Witching Hour,* and other plays by Thomas, Samuel French edition; Locke Theatre Coll. in N. Y. Pub. Lib., and Theatre Coll. in Harvard Univ. Lib.; obituaries in *N. Y. Times, N. Y. Herald Tribune,* and *St. Louis Post-Dispatch,* Aug. 13, 1934.]

W. P. E.

THOMAS, CALVIN (Oct. 28, 1854–Nov. 4, 1919), German scholar, was born in a log cabin at Lapeer, Mich., the son of Stephen Van Rensselaer Thomas and Caroline Louisa (Lord) Thomas, who had not long before emigrated from the state of New York. Stephen Thomas was a sturdy and enterprising young farmer who fought under Burnside and Stoneman in the Civil War, and won a captaincy in the 10th Michigan Cavalry. Later he became a lawyer and attained some prominence in politics. The bracing life of early farming days offered the son a wholesome opportunity for all-round development. At eleven years he had not only become something of a naturalist and hunter, but had won great renown as a young spelling prodigy. Ready for college at fourteen, two years before he could be admitted, he entered the University of Michigan in 1870 as the youngest of his class, specializing in Latin and Greek, and graduating in 1874 as valedictorian. After three years of teaching at the high school in Grand Rapids, he went in 1877 to Leipzig for further study of the classics. Before the year was out, however, he was called back to his university to teach Greek; but, owing to certain exigencies, he was almost at once given full-time work in German and was made professor in 1886.

From this point on, his career as teacher and scholar was one of steady progress. During the next ten or fifteen years he contributed upward of one hundred articles and reviews to various journals, especially to the *Nation*. But he soon began to concentrate on the subject of Goethe. In 1888 he published *Goethe's Torquato Tasso* and within the next ten years made a notable contribution to scholarship in his brilliantly edited *Goethe's Faust* (2 vols., 1892–97), one of the greatest literary commentaries in the English language. His other publications include his widely used *A Practical German Grammar* (1896), *The Life and Works of Friedrich Schiller* (1901), *An Anthology of German Literature* (1907), and *A History of German Literature* (1909). Finally came the work upon which he bestowed some of his most loving care and labor, his *Goethe* (1917). A complete enumeration of his edited texts, reviews, and addresses would make a list many times as long. Thirteen of his papers were published by his colleagues in 1924 under the title *Scholarship, and Other Essays.* As consulting editor (1909) of the *New Standard Dictionary*, he wrote each of the twenty-six articles on the history of the letters of the alphabet and their phonetic values. For a time he was an enthusiastic spelling reformer and a member of the Simplified Spelling Board. He was also one of the founders of the Modern Language Association of America and its president for 1896–97. In 1896 he was called to Columbia University as Gebhard Professor of Germanic Languages and Literatures, where the wide range of his scholarship, his tolerance and wisdom, no less than the warm glow of his sympathy and sense of humor, endeared him to his students and colleagues alike. He was married first, on Mar. 25, 1880, to Mary J. Sutton of Lapeer, who died in the same year, and again, on June 16, 1884, to Mary Eleanor Allen of Grand Rapids, by whom he had two sons.

[*Who's Who in America*, 1918–19; B. A. Hinsdale, *Hist. of the Univ. of Mich.* (1906), ed. by I. N. Demmon; W. A. Braun, biog. introduction to *Scholarship, and Other Essays* (1924); obituary in *N. Y. Times*, Nov. 5, 1919; Thomas' unpublished autobiog. notes.]

W. A. B.

THOMAS, CHARLES SPALDING (Dec. 6, 1849–June 24, 1934), senator, lawyer, was born on a plantation near Darien, Ga., the son of William Brownell and Caroline Baldwin (Wheeler) Thomas, Connecticut Yankees who had moved into the South. His father died during his early boyhood. Charles was sent to a private school where discipline was strict but instruction good, and during the final months of the Civil War he served in the Confederate army. After Appomattox his mother returned to Connecticut and later moved to Michigan, where after her death

Charles attended the University of Michigan, graduating in law in 1871. Since Georgia offered no prospects for the future, he migrated to Denver, Col., in the same year.

Denver in 1871 was a small city with limited opportunities, but Thomas quickly won success as a criminal lawyer. In 1875 and 1876 he was city attorney; in 1873–74 and again from 1879 to 1890 he was a partner of Thomas M. Patterson [*q.v.*]. Following the rush of 1879 to Leadville, he built up a solid reputation as one of the leading mining lawyers of the state. His most famous case, the Del Monte-Last Chance case (171 *U. S.*, 55), resulted in the settlement of several difficult and important points in the interpretation of mining law. In 1885 he returned to Denver to be associated with several partners until he retired from active practice in 1927. He was noted as one of the keenest and most fearless attorneys in Colorado.

Thomas entered early upon a political career that witnessed many vicissitudes. He was too frank and critical to be a conventional party man. In 1882 he was state chairman of the Democratic party and from 1884 to 1896, a member of the Democratic National Committee. He was an unsuccessful candidate for the House of Representatives in 1884, but his greatest political ambition was to be elected United States senator. A candidate for that office in 1889, he was defeated by Edward O. Wolcott [*q.v.*]. In 1894 he ran for the governorship without hope of election; in January 1895 he was again a candidate for the senatorship, but received only three votes in the joint session of the legislature. In 1898 he was elected governor by the silver fusionists, and when his term was drawing to a close (1900–01) he once more entered the senatorial race, but withdrew when he found that the majority of the Democrats were pledged to Thomas M. Patterson. At last, in 1913, he realized his ambition when he entered the Senate to complete the term of Charles J. Hughes. He was elected for a full term in 1914, but in 1920, persuaded by friends to run as an independent candidate, he went down to overwhelming defeat.

Thomas was in Washington, as he had been in Colorado, a non-conformist. He opposed the Treaty of Versailles, the League of Nations, the soldiers' bonus, and the demands of the railroad brotherhood and profiteering capitalists. He was an ardent bimetallist, even after his party had abandoned the cause. He served as special counsel for the Korean Commission while the United States watched in apathy the actions of Japan. A lawyer, he denounced the conservatism and venality of the bar; a politician, he poured out his scorn upon time-serving congressmen and party leaders. He opposed the "New Deal" of President Franklin D. Roosevelt. One of his last acts, at eighty-four, was to defy the presidential proclamation against the hoarding of gold (*New York Times*, May 4, 5, 1933).

Thomas was married, Dec. 29, 1873, to Emma Fletcher of Kalamazoo, Mich., by whom he had five children. He died in Denver after writing "A Salute to Death" in which he explained his refusal to give allegiance "to any man-made religion either revealed or otherwise."

[The brief sketch in vol. V, "Biographical," accompanying J. H. Baker and L. R. Hafen, *Hist. of Col.* (1927), is reasonably accurate; the account of Thomas' legal work in the *Rocky Mountain Law Review,* Apr. 1931, has merit; the privately printed *Closing Events in the Last Years of the Career of Charles S. Thomas* (Denver, 1934), contains reprints of newspaper biographies and other pertinent material. See also *Who's Who in America*, 1932–33; *Portr. and Biog. Record of the State of Col.* (1899); W. N. Byers, *Encyc. of Biog. of Col.* (1901); *Biog. Dir. Am. Cong.* (1928); *Rocky Mountain News* (Denver), June 25, 1934.] J. F. W.

THOMAS, CHRISTIAN FRIEDRICH THEODORE (Oct. 11, 1835–Jan. 4, 1905), musician, conductor, was born at Esens, Germany, the eldest child of Johann August Thomas, the *Stadtpfeifer,* or chief town musician of Esens, and his wife Sophia, the daughter of a physician at Göttingen. The boy showed his talent for music when he was only two years old. His father gave him a few violin lessons, and according to the *Memoirs* of Mrs. Thomas (*post*) he seemed to be recalling something he had known before whenever he was taught anything in music. In 1845 the household emigrated to New York, for the meager income of the *Stadtpfeifer* was not enough to support the growing family. In New York, matters were not much better and it was necessary for Theodore to play his violin for dances, weddings, in theatres, and sometimes in saloons, where he passed his hat for the coins of the generous.

In 1850 Thomas took a concert trip through the South, unaided and alone. When he came to a town he would tack up a few posters announcing a concert by "Master T. T.," the remarkable prodigy. Then he would stand at the door and sell tickets until he decided that all who were coming had arrived. At this point he would rush backstage to change his clothes, and then appear before the audience with his violin. When Louis Antoine Jullien came to America in 1853, Thomas was chosen as one of the first violins of the orchestra. He was disgusted with Jullien's antics and showmanship, but he gained his first idea of the symphony from this conductor. In 1854 he was elected a member of the Philharmonic Society of New York, and in the following

year he joined William Mason, 1829–1908 [*q.v.*], in the series of Mason-Thomas chamber music concerts which were given at Dodworth's Hall, next to Grace Church, Broadway, for a number of years. During the season 1857–58 he appeared in New York and on tour as a violin soloist with several famous artists, among them Carl Formes and Sigismund Thalberg. In 1858 he became a member of the orchestra for the opera at the Academy of Music.

In December 1860 Carl Anschütz, conductor of the opera at the Academy, was suddenly unable to appear one evening, and Thomas was called to take his place. He conducted Halévy's *Jewess,* a score he had never seen before, so well that the retirement of Anschütz became permanent and Thomas was made conductor. Conducting was a revelation to him; he found that he could play on an orchestra as he could on a great instrument, and from that time his mission in life became the development of a taste for orchestral and symphonic music throughout the United States. He continued as an operatic conductor in New York, at the same time giving chamber music concerts, as well as recitals with Carl Wolfsohn, in Philadelphia. In 1862 he organized an orchestra of his own, which gave its first concert in Irving Hall, New York, on May 13. Thomas soon realized that only a permanent orchestra could achieve the results he wanted. In 1862 he was made alternate conductor with Theodore Eisfeld of the Brooklyn Philharmonic Society, and four years later he became its sole conductor. During 1863 he continued his own orchestral concerts at Irving Hall, and on Dec. 3, 1864, he began his symphony *soirées.* In 1865 he was appointed musical director of the New York Institution for the Blind. In the following year he commenced his famous summer concerts at Terrace Garden, and two years later he moved them to the Central Park Garden. By 1867 Thomas was able to guarantee his men a full season's engagement, and his orchestra was permanent in the sense that its members were not engaged in other pursuits. His concerts in New York were not well enough attended to support the orchestra, so in 1869 Thomas took his men for a tour, discontinuing the New York concerts until a committee of prominent citizens asked that they be resumed. They were accordingly continued from 1872 to 1878.

In 1873 Thomas was invited to organize and conduct the music festivals in Cincinnati, which came to be biennial, and in 1876 he conducted the Philadelphia Centennial concerts. The latter led to financial disaster; they were poorly attended, and finally the sheriff put a stop to them and sold

Thomas' music library at auction. Although he could have evaded his debts by voluntary bankruptcy, Thomas paid every cent he owed during the following twelve years. By this time Thomas had received several offers to conduct the New York Philharmonic, but he had previously declined them because acceptance would have compelled him to abandon his own orchestra. In 1877, however, the directors renewed the offer and agreed to let him continue his own concerts. He arranged that the programs of his own orchestra would be lighter in character than those of the Philharmonic, to avoid competition.

In 1878 Thomas left New York to assume the directorate of the College of Music in Cincinnati. He immediately clashed with the backers of the school when he concluded that they intended the institution to be a commercial enterprise, rather than one which would fulfil his own ideals as an educational center. He accordingly returned to New York in the spring of 1880 and again became the conductor of the Philharmonic Society. The orchestra at this time was distressed financially, and its playing was **mediocre**. In his first season as its conductor, Thomas brought it to artistic heights far beyond any of its former achievements, and the attendance accordingly increased. The players were engaged on a co-operative basis, and they made more money. From this period Thomas became something of a storm center. The Symphony Society of New York was organized in 1878, and Leopold Damrosch [q.v.] was appointed its conductor. Musical New York was soon divided into Thomas and Damrosch factions, and, while the two conductors might have remained at peace had they been allowed to arrange matters themselves, their followers urged them to bitter rivalry.

In 1885 Thomas was induced to accept the directorship of the American Opera Company (first performance in January 1886), thinking that its wealthy sponsors would continue to back it even though its first seasons showed a deficit. He accordingly employed all his resources to present opera as finely as it could be given, and it was generally agreed that he had done so; but after the first season, and a resulting loss, the sponsors left the company to founder, and Thomas, merely a salaried employee, was blamed for the unpaid debts of the company. This tragedy was followed by several years in New York, and on tour with his own orchestra, before it disbanded in 1888, journeying to small cities which had never heard an orchestra before, and where later there were permanent orchestras for which Thomas originally planted the seeds. In 1891 he received an offer to go to

Chicago, to conduct an orchestra whose existence would be guaranteed by a group of public-spirited citizens. He was not eager to leave New York, but he saw an opportunity to realize his ideals. He accordingly accepted, and conducted the Chicago Symphony Orchestra for the next fourteen years, until his death in Chicago in 1905.

In 1893 Thomas acted as music director for the World's Fair in Chicago. He planned an all-summer series of programs, designed to show the world what America had accomplished musically, and to show America the music of the world. The plans for the festival offered one of the most comprehensive schemes that had ever been presented in the country. Thomas arranged for an orchestra of over a hundred players, and for an exposition chorus. He invited the leading soloists of the world to appear in the concert hall, and asked the foremost orchestras of the world to give concerts. He again became the storm center in a controversy between artistic ideals and commercial interests. The exhibitors of musical instruments made a rule that no instruments not exhibited at the Fair should be used in the concert hall. Paderewski had already been engaged as a soloist, and since Steinway & Sons had not rented exhibit space the exhibitors sought to prevent Paderewski from using his own Steinway piano. Thomas insisted that there be no interference with Paderewski, and the exhibitors accused the conductor of being in the pay of instrument manufacturers. Even though the charges were disproved and attempts to force Thomas' resignation were fruitless, he incurred the enmity of those who controlled the exposition. Finally the panic of 1893 necessitated curtailment of expenditures for music, so Thomas resigned, and though he was asked to resume his duties at the Fair when matters improved he declined the invitation.

Thomas was an able conductor, yet it was as a musical missionary that he accomplished his greatest work, by taking his orchestra through the country and cultivating a taste for the best in music. As a program maker he was shrewd. Rather than conceiving a program as a single unit, he concerned himself with series of programs, planned to elevate the public taste progressively and gradually. At first he would select lighter pieces to play between heavier selections—melodious compositions chosen for their relation to the more substantial works with which they were paired. Thomas knew that if he could enable his hearers to recognize the themes of a symphony, they would grow eventually to like it. Consequently, when he played a movement of a symphony, he would follow it with a waltz or light overture in which the themes had some relation to those of the symphony. Eventually he found his audiences prepared to listen to an entire symphony, without the interruption of other pieces between its movements.

Thomas was married twice—in 1864 to Minna L. Rhodes, who died Apr. 4, 1889. She bore him three sons and two daughters. His second wife was Rose Fay, whom he married May 7, 1890, and who survived him without issue.

[C. E. Russell, *The American Orchestra and Theodore Thomas* (1927), is excellent in its appreciation of the importance of Thomas in the growth of American culture, and in its understanding of him as an epic figure. His second wife, Rose Fay Thomas, published in 1911 her valuable *Memoirs of Theodore Thomas*. G. P. Upton edited *Theodore Thomas, A Musical Autobiography* (2 vols., 1905) ; the biographical material, written by Thomas himself, is meager and reticent, but the second volume is invaluable because it contains all of his programs. For an obituary, see *Chicago Daily Tribune*, Jan. 5, 1905.] J.T.H.

THOMAS, CYRUS (July 27, 1825–June 26, 1910), ethnologist, entomologist, was born at Kingsport, Tenn. His father, Stephen Thomas, was of German descent, and his mother, Maria (Rogan) Thomas, was of Irish parentage. Cyrus received a village school education and attended the academy at Jonesboro, Tenn. In his formative period, filled with ambition and in perfect health, he studied medicine, law, theology, and natural history, and occupied several teaching and official positions before he found his major pursuit in anthropology. Of his earlier studies entomology was his chief interest, especially on the economic side, and he wrote in this period thirty-eight valuable scientific papers among which was his *Noxious and Beneficial Insects of the State of Illinois, Sixth to Eleventh Reports of the State Entomologist, 1877–1882.* In 1882 the Bureau of American Ethnology called for his services. He had already done some work on the mounds (see *Ancient Mounds of Dakota, Geological Survey of the Territories for 1873*), and for the Bureau he pursued the study of the mound areas of the United States for several field seasons, directing a large force in plotting and excavating the mounds, the collections being placed in the National Museum. A review of this work was published as the twelfth annual report of the Bureau in 1894 under the title *Report on Mound Explorations.* A number of his papers on the aspects of the mound question appeared in various bulletins and journals. He did much to controvert the general belief that the mound builders were a mysterious ancient race by proving that the remains are those of American Indians.

In the interim of seasonal field expeditions he pursued the study of the Maya culture, begin-

ning as early as 1881 when he published several papers. The more important of these are *A Study of the Manuscript Troano, Contributions to North American Ethnology,* volume IV (1882) ; *Notes on Certain Maya and Mexican Manuscripts, Third Annual Report of the Bureau of American Ethnology* (1884) ; *Aids to the Study of the Maya Codices, Sixth Annual Report* (1888) ; and *The Maya Year, Bulletin No. 18, Bureau of American Ethnology* (1894). Papers by him on *Mayan Calendar Systems, Numeral Systems of Mexico* and *Central America* are to be found in the nineteenth and twenty-second Bureau reports, published in 1900 and 1904. His work on the Maya subject has emerged from the fray of controversy and he is acclaimed as a pioneer in this difficult field. He also found time to produce works of a more general character : *The Indians of North America in Historic Times* (1903), second volume of the History of North America Series and, with William J. McGee [*q.v.*], *Prehistoric North America* (1905), the nineteenth volume of the Series.

Thomas was possessed of tireless energy and an individuality that brushed aside all obstacles to his mental growth. His first wife was Dorothy Adeline Logan, the sister of John A. Logan [*q.v.*], to whom he was married on June 13, 1853. After her death he was married to Viola L. Davis on Apr. 20, 1865. They had six children. Thomas held many positions of trust. He was clerk of Jackson County, Ill., 1850–53, and later in charge of the schools of DeSoto, Ill. From 1865 to 1869 he was minister of the Evangelical Lutheran Church in that town. He was principal founder of the Illinois Natural History Society in 1858, professor of natural sciences in an Illinois normal school, 1873–75, state entomologist of Illinois, 1874–76, and member of the United States Entomological Commission, 1876–77. He was member of many scientific societies. At his death he was survived by three daughters.

[*Who's Who in America,* 1910–11 ; Cyrus Thomas, *Geneal. Descendants of Gabriel Thomas, John Thomas, etc.* (1905) ; *Am. Anthropologist,* Apr.–June 1910 ; personal recollections of the author.] W. H.

THOMAS, DAVID (June 11, 1762–Nov. 27, 1831), Revolutionary soldier, member of Congress, New York politician, was probably descended from John Thomas who came to Massachusetts from London about 1635 and settled at Marshfield. He was born in Pelham, Mass., the son of David Thomas and Elizabeth (Harper), his second wife. After participation in 1777 in expeditions of Massachusetts troops for the relief of Rhode Island, the boy was apprenticed to a shoemaker in Worcester, but in 1781 reëntered the army, serving with the 3rd and 5th Massachusetts regiments and ultimately reaching the rank of sergeant.

Shortly after the war he went to Salem, N. Y., where his father's sister had her home. Here, in 1784, he married Jeannette Turner, his aunt's daughter, and entered vigorously into the life of the community. For some years he kept a tavern in partnership with his brother-in-law. In 1793 he was elected to the Assembly and immediately evinced Republican orthodoxy by moving for the election of the Assembly from single-member districts, a principle embodied fifty-two years later in the constitution of 1846. He was again elected to the Assembly in 1798 and in 1799. Meanwhile, he was active in the state militia and in 1805 attained the rank of major-general, in command of the 3rd Division.

In 1800 he was elected to Congress from the seventh New York district. He served four terms, maintaining fairly consistent regularity as a supporter of the Jefferson administration. On Mar. 29, 1806, he moved a resolution for an amendment to the federal Constitution providing for the choice of presidential electors by districts within the states. On Feb. 17, 1808, he resigned his seat to accept the office of treasurer of the state of New York. This position he held until Feb. 10, 1810, when Federalist control of the legislature turned him out, but he was elected to the same position by a new legislature in 1812. He achieved a wide acquaintance among the figures in New York's political life and developed a reputation for great sagacity in political diagnosis and manipulation. He also became prominently identified with the cause of DeWitt Clinton [q.v.]. Under these circumstances, his acceptance in 1811 of the position of agent for the Bank of America in its application for a charter exposed him to savage attack. During the summer of that year he traveled over the state in the campaign to get legislators committed to the cause of the Bank before the beginning of the session of 1812. He was subsequently indicted for attempted bribery of a state senator, and was tried, Sept. 17-18, 1812 (*New York Gazette & General Advertiser*, Sept. 25, 1812). The trial aroused intense popular interest, since the affair was regarded as a political prosecution. Though he was acquitted, his canvass for reëlection to the treasurership in February 1813 resulted in defeat. This experience seems to have led to his determination, in the prime of life, to retire not only from politics but also from residence in the state.

His first wife had died in 1795, leaving one daughter, and on Jan. 15, 1800, he had married Mary Hogeboom of Claverack, N. Y. They separated, Thomas arranging for her to live with her sister in Troy, N. Y., while he went to his sister in Providence, R. I., where he spent his remaining years.

[*Biog. Dir. Am. Cong.* (1928); W. H. Hill, *Hist. of Washington County, N. Y.: The Gibson Papers* (1932); J. D. Hammond, *The Hist. of Political Parties in the State of N. Y.* (1842), I, 115, 263, 300–17; D. S. Alexander, *A Political Hist. of the State of N. Y.*, I (1906), 190–94; *Military Minutes of the Council of Appointment of N. Y.*, vol. I (1901); *Providence Patriot*, Nov. 30, 1831.]
        C. W. S.

THOMAS, DAVID (Nov. 3, 1794–June 20, 1882), iron manufacturer, was born at Tyllwyd, in the parish of Cadoxtan, Glamorganshire, Wales, the only son of David and Jane Thomas, who gained a poor livelihood at farming. Both parents were deeply religious, belonging to the "Independent" community at Maesyrhaf Chapel, and they gave David strict training. He attended school first at Alltwen, but his progress was so rapid that he was sent to a more advanced school at Neath at the age of nine. Beginning in 1812, he was employed at the Neath Abbey iron works, where he acquired a thorough knowledge of blast furnaces as well as technical training in building mining machinery and Cornish pumping engines. After five years here he was made general superintendent of the Yniscedwyn Iron Works, which three years later was acquired by George Crane.

This plant was erected on the only bed of anthracite coal in Great Britain, but no method had yet been devised to use this fuel in the smelting of iron ore. For years both Crane and Thomas tried to utilize the anthracite without success, two expensive experiments terminating in absolute failure. In 1836, however, their opportunity came when they read about the hot-blast invention of James Beaumont Neilson (see sketch of Neilson in *Dictionary of National Biography*). As a result Thomas went to Scotland, where the hot-blast method was already being employed, and returned with permission to use this patented process. Work was started immediately on the construction of a furnace and it was blown in February 1837 with such successful results that world-wide attention was at once focused upon the plant. Within a short time the Lehigh Coal & Navigation Company of Pennsylvania reached an agreement with Crane and Thomas by which the latter signed a generous contract to construct and operate similar furnaces on the Lehigh River, the plant to be called the Lehigh Crane Iron Company. Thomas was hesitant about going to the United States, but his ambitious wife urged him to accept the position. In May 1839, after he had spent four months in purchasing machinery, he set sail with his family from Swansea to Liverpool and thence to New York. They arrived in Allentown, Pa., July 9, 1839.

Construction of the blast furnace was begun almost immediately and was carried to completion in the face of great odds. It was necessary to have the blowing cylinders built in the United States, and none of the few foundries in existence had ever made machinery of such large size. Thomas suffered a severe illness in the autumn of 1839 which prevented him for a time from overseeing the actual construction. He found it hard to secure experienced labor, and the ores and fuels with which he was supplied were of unknown and varying constituents. Nevertheless, his indomitable energy, activity, courage, and tenacity enabled him to overcome all these difficulties and on July 4, 1840, the first furnace of the Lehigh Crane Iron Company produced four tons of good foundry anthracite iron. Small amounts of anthracite iron had been manufactured a year or two earlier, but Thomas' Catasauqua furnace was the first of all the early anthracite-iron manufacturing establishments to be permanently successful from both the engineering and the commercial standpoint. For this reason and because he subsequently became identified with the manufacture of anthracite pig-iron on a more extensive scale than any of his contemporaries, he has been justly called "the father of the American anthracite-iron industry."

While Thomas did not develop any new basic principles in the smelting of iron ore, he was directly responsible for many improvements, among which were the erection of higher and larger furnaces and better and more powerful blast machinery, and the use of steam instead of air for making the blast. In 1854, he and several others organized the Thomas Iron Company at Hokendauqua, Pa. Although he did not take an active part in the management of this enterprise for several years, because he maintained his connection with the Lehigh Crane Company, he took an active interest in its affairs even to the extent of indorsing and filing a personal bond guaranteeing the money borrowed by the Company during the financial panic of 1857. He was principally interested in other manufactories, including the Lehigh Fire-Brick Company and the Catasauqua Manufacturing Company, and for a great part of his declining years was president of the latter concern. He took much interest in the political, financial, religious, and charitable affairs of Catasauqua, where he lived until his death. He was president of the Catasauqua & Fogelsville Railroad and a director of the Lehigh

Valley Railroad Company. He was elected first president of the American Institute of Mining Engineers because it was felt that he was "the man whose name would do more than any other name to unite in support of our new enterprise the enthusiasm of science with the experience of practice" (*Transactions, post,* XI, 15). Thomas' wife was Elizabeth, daughter of John Hopkins, a native of Gilvendre, South Wales. Five children were born of this union; the three sons all became connected with the iron industry.

[*Trans. Am. Inst. Mining Engineers,* vols. I (1874), III (1875), XI (1883) ; William Firmstone, "Sketch of Early Anthracite Furnaces," *Ibid.,* III (1880) ; Samuel Thomas, "Reminiscences of the Early Anthracite-Iron Industry," *Ibid.,* vol. XXIX (1900) ; *Iron Age,* June 22, 29, 1882; *Hist. of the Lehigh Valley Railroad Company* (1872) ; *The Thomas Iron Company, 1854–1904* (1904) ; C. R. Roberts and others, *Hist. of Lehigh County, Pa.* (1914), vols. I, III ; J. M. Swank, *Hist. of the Manufacture of Iron in All Ages* (2nd ed., 1892) ; *Bull. Am. Iron and Steel Asso.,* June 28, 1882; *Public Ledger* (Phila.), June 22, 1882.]   H. S. P.

THOMAS, EDITH MATILDA (Aug. 12, 1854–Sept. 13, 1925), poet, was born at Chatham, Ohio, the daughter of Frederick J. and Jane Louisa (Sturges) Thomas. Her father's family, originally Welsh, had moved to Ohio from New York; her mother was a native of Connecticut. Her father, a school-teacher and farmer, moved from Chatham to Kenton soon after 1854, and thence to Bowling Green, Ohio, where he died in 1861. Soon after her father's death Edith was taken by her mother to Geneva, Ohio, and in 1872 she was graduated from a normal school there. She then spent a short, dissatisfied period at Oberlin College, following which she taught school for several months. Unhappy in this work, she learned, and for a short while practised, the trade of typesetting. At the normal school she had succeeded in having a class in Greek organized, and her eager study of the language and its literature stimulated her in a way that was profoundly to influence her poetry, which as a student she had begun submitting to Geneva and Cleveland newspapers. She also became a disciple of Keats, perceiving in his poetry that sensuous yet spiritual love of beauty which she herself felt. Her desire to give herself to poetry had been whetted by an uncle, James Thomas, a romantic adventurer, who had made her gifts of books and who in 1881 took her to New York. There he presented her to Anne Charlotte Lynch Botta, who in turn sent her to Helen Hunt Jackson [*qq.v.*]. The latter read her poetry, thought it excellent, and secured publication of some of it in the *Century*.

After her mother's death (1887), Edith Thomas moved to New York. Her first book, *A New Year's Masque and Other Poems,* had been published in 1885, and her verse had begun to appear in the pages of *Scribner's*, the *Atlantic Monthly*, *Harper's*, the *Nation*, the *Critic*, the *Independent*, the *Outlook*, and several metropolitan newspapers. Sponsored by Richard Watson Gilder [*q.v.*] and others, she won the friendship of some of the most prominent writers of the day. For a decade after her removal to New York she made her home with Dr. and Mrs. Samuel Elliott, at whose house she met such men as Charles Anderson Dana, Parke Godwin, and Edwin Booth [*qq.v.*]. For a while she helped prepare the *Century Dictionary*. In 1908 she became a reader for *Harper's Magazine*, under Henry Mills Alden [*q.v.*], and continued in this work until her death. She wrote several books of a pedestrian sort, among them a series of books for children, called the Children of the Seasons Series (1888). She also wrote one book of prose, nature-sketches, *The Round Year* (1886). Representative volumes of her verse are *Lyrics and Sonnets* (1887), *The Inverted Torch* (1890), *In Sunshine Land* (1895), *The Dancers, and Other Legends and Lyrics* (1903), and *The Flower from the Ashes* (1915).

She was a frail little woman who preferred a nunlike seclusion. She made many friends, but only those who came to recognize the quiet, reserved manner as one which concealed a consuming passion for poetry really appreciated her personality, her work, or her refined intelligence. Her muse was remote, unimpassioned, classical; she was "more Greek than American" (F. L. Pattee, *A History of American Literature since 1870*, 1915, p. 341). Her verse is characterized by painstaking craftsmanship, genuine lyric feeling, and an excellent sense of rhythm, but it made little appeal to the public because of its pervading spirituality, and has had little influence upon later writers.

[See *Who's Who in America*, 1920–21; Jessie B. Rittenhouse, in *Selected Poems of Edith M. Thomas* (1926); R. H. Stoddard, in *Book Buyer*, Mar. 1888, pp. 56–57; *N. Y. Times*, Sept. 15 (obituary), 16, 1925; for critical analyses of Edith Thomas' poetry, see *Atlantic Monthly*, Mar. 1885, pp. 418–21, Dec. 1890, pp. 844–45, and *Dial* (Chicago), Nov. 1886, pp. 158–60, Feb. 1888, pp. 249–50.]　　　　　H. S., JR.

THOMAS, FRANCIS (Feb. 3, 1799–Jan. 22, 1876), congressman from Maryland and governor, was born at "Montevue" near Petersville, Frederick County, Md., the seventh child of John and Eleanor (McGill) Thomas, and the descendant of Hugh Thomas who emigrated from Wales to Pennsylvania about 1702. He matriculated at St. John's College, Annapolis, but turned directly to the study of law, when classes closed temporarily at that institution. Opening an office in Frederick after admission to the bar in 1820, he soon became one of the leading lawyers in western Maryland. His record before 1841 was a succession of triumphs. In 1822, as a stripling of twenty-three and a Democrat, he won election to the state assembly from a Federalist section on the issue of legislative reapportionment. He appeared as a successful candidate for the same position in 1827 and 1829, and even won the speakership of the house in his last term. The manner in which he handled the house led to his being made congressional candidate the next year. For ten years, 1831–41, he sat in Congress, where his eloquence and parliamentary skill made him an active participant in most of the important legislation. As chairman of the judiciary commitee, he became a defender and friend of Jackson. For a brief period, 1839–40, he was president of the Chesapeake and Ohio Canal Company and also found time to lead a revolt for popular election of state senators in Maryland. Though temporarily unsuccessful, this ultimately brought reorganization of the legislative department. It was during his congressional campaign of 1840 that he became involved in a duel with William Price. His nomination and election for governor in 1841 ushered in the most tempestuous period of his life. His marriage to Sally Campbell McDowell, the daughter of Gov. James McDowell [*q.v.*] of Virginia on June 8, 1841, had united the forty-two-year old bachelor to a twenty-year old girl. Discord manifested itself in a few weeks. They were divorced after an unusually unsavory scandal during which he issued a pamphlet, *Statement of Francis Thomas* (1845), setting forth, entirely without reserve, the details of the courtship, marriage, and estrangement. Ten years later his wife married John Miller, 1819–1895 [*q.v.*], a Presbyterian clergyman. The quarrel and divorce involved Thomas in a libel suit and led him to wild charges against John Carroll Le Grand, whom he had just appointed judge. Ultimately, it cost him his possible opportunity of being president because of the bitterness of his father-in-law in the convention of 1844.

He did not allow his domestic difficulties to interfere with his duties as governor. His chief contribution was to save the state from repudiation, although it was heavily involved in debt for internal improvements. After his governorship he led the life of a recluse until the Civil War, emerging only to fight, in the constitutional convention of 1850–51, the system of representation whereby the small slave-holding counties held power over the populous western counties, and to run unsuccessfully in 1853 as an independent candidate for Congress. At the outbreak of the Civil War he enlisted a volunteer regiment of 3,000, though he left the command to younger men, and inspired union sentiment in western Maryland with his eloquence. In 1861 he returned to Congress as a Unionist and served until 1869. During Reconstruction he whole-heartedly supported the extreme Radicals. Upon his retirement from Congress, he was appointed in 1870 internal revenue collector for Maryland. He resigned to accept the post of minister to Peru, where he served from 1872 to 1875. The remaining year of his life he occupied with law practice and with sheep-raising on a large tract of land near Frankville. He was killed by an engine of the Baltimore and Ohio railroad.

[M. P. Andrews, *Tercentenary Hist. of Md.* (1925), vol. I; E. S. Riley, *A Hist. of the General Assembly of Md.* (1905); C. W. Sams and E. S. Riley, *The Bench and Bar of Md.* (1904); J. W. Thomas and T. J. C. Williams, *Hist. of Allegany County, Md.* (1923), vol. I; T. J. C. Williams, *Hist. of Frederick County* (1910), vol. I; L. E. Blauch, "Education and the Md. Constit. Convention, 1850–51," *Md. Hist. Mag.*, June 1930; *N. Y. Herald*, Apr. 8, 1845; *Inquirer and National Gazette* (Philadelphia), Nov. 13, 1845; *Baltimore Amer. and Commercial Advertiser* and *Sun* (Baltimore), Jan. 24, 1876.]   E. L.

THOMAS, FREDERICK WILLIAM (Oct. 25, 1806–Aug. 27, 1866), journalist and novelist, was the son of Ebenezer Smith and Ann (Fonerden) Thomas, and a descendant of Evan Thomas, a Welshman who emigrated to Massachusetts in 1640. Ebenezer Thomas, born in Massachusetts, learned the printing trade in the shop of his distinguished uncle Isaiah [*q.v.*] and as a young man went to Charleston, S. C., where he became a bookseller. He also had business interests in Providence, R. I., and there Frederick William, eldest of eight children, was born. After two years (1807–09) on a farm near Baltimore, Md., the family returned to Charleston, where E. S. Thomas was for some years editor of the *City Gazette*. Injured by a fall as a child and later permanently lamed by another injury, Frederick was sent to live with relatives in Baltimore, where his family joined him in 1816. He was admitted to the bar in 1828 and began the practice of law in Baltimore, but in 1831 he followed his father to Cincinnati, assisted him there in the editing of the *Commercial Daily Advertiser,* and resumed the practice of law. For the next ten years, a citizen of Cincinnati, he combined literary and journalistic work—including six months as editor of the *Democratic Intelligencer*—with extensive travel, chiefly in the Middle West. For some years

after 1841 he held a clerkship in the Treasury Department in Washington, for which he also collected a library. In 1847–48 he was professor of rhetoric and English literature in the University of Alabama; in 1850, after some journalistic work in Kentucky, he entered the ministry of the Methodist Episcopal Church in Cincinnati, and achieved some success as preacher and lecturer. After practising law for a time in Cambridge, Md., he became in 1860 literary editor of the *Richmond Enquirer* and was later a member of the staff of the Columbia *South Carolinian.* His death, caused by typhoid fever and complications, occurred in Washington, D. C.

In 1833 he published a descriptive poem of considerable length called *The Emigrant.* A song entitled, " 'Tis said that absence conquers love," which was set to music and enjoyed a wide popularity, appeared in a Cincinnati paper in the same year, and in 1840 another song, "Oh blame her not, her love was deep," was printed in Baltimore. His first novel, *Clinton Bradshaw; or the Adventures of a Lawyer* (2 vols., 1835), was published anonymously in Philadelphia. This was followed in 1836 by *East and West,* credited to the author of *Clinton Bradshaw,* and in 1840 by *Howard Pinckney: a Novel* (2 vols.). His other books were *The Beechen Tree, a Tale Told in Rhyme* (1844); *Sketches of Character, and Tales Founded on Fact* (1849), a volume of essays; *An Autobiography of William Russell* (1852), a novel; and *John Randolph, of Roanoke* (1853).

Thomas is remembered as a loyal friend and correspondent of Edgar Allan Poe [*q.v.*], whom he first met in Philadelphia in 1840. He is described by a contemporary as five feet nine inches tall and compactly built, his hair black and wavy, "worn long and negligently about his temples" (*Southern Literary Messenger, post,* p. 301). Because of his childhood injury he could not walk without a cane. His literary work was in the mode of the time and won some critical approval, his fiction being regarded as imitative of Bulwer-Lytton.

[The dates of birth and death are from the Thomas family Bible, which, with a portrait and some correspondence, is in the lib. of the Am. Antiquarian Soc. See also E. S. Thomas, *Reminiscences of the Last Sixty-Five Years* (1840), vol. II, pp. 46–47; F. W. Thomas' letter, Aug. 3, 1841, in J. A. Harrison, *The Complete Works of Edgar Allan Poe* (1902), vol. XVII, pp. 95–100; W. T. Coggeshall, *The Poets and Poetry of the West* (1860), p. 185; *Southern Literary Messenger,* May 1838, pp. 297–301; memoir in 1872 ed. of *The Emigrant;* R. L. Rusk, *The Lit. of the Middle Western Frontier* (1925), vol. I, pp. 296–97; and death notice in *Daily Nat. Intelligencer* (Washington, D. C.), Aug. 30, 1866.]   J. C. F—h.

THOMAS, GEORGE (*c.* 1695–Dec. 31, 1774), colonial governor of Pennsylvania and Delaware, son of Col. George Thomas and Sarah (Winthrop) Thomas, was born and educated in Antigua in the British West Indies. He was a member of the Assembly of Antigua, 1716–17 and 1721–28, being speaker in 1727–28, and a member of the council of the Leeward Islands from 1728 to 1738. In 1737 he was in England and appeared before the Board of Trade and Plantations to give information on the problem of suppressing the contraband trade in the West Indies. In the summer of that year he was appointed deputy governor of Pennsylvania and the Lower Counties on the Delaware, but because of the opposition of Lord Baltimore, who claimed proprietary rights in the Lower Counties, the appointment was not confirmed by the Crown until the following February. He arrived in Philadelphia on June 1, 1738.

Thomas' administration as governor of Delaware was uneventful, but in Pennsylvania he soon became involved in a bitter quarrel with the Assembly over financial and military affairs. In 1738–39 he refused to approve a bill for the emission of paper currency until provision had been made for the payment of the proprietary rents at the old rate of exchange. In this connection he wrote a communication to the Board of Trade a copy of which was obtained surreptitiously by Richard Partridge [*q.v.*], the colonial agent, and sent to Philadelphia, where it was printed by Benjamin Franklin. (*A Letter to the Lords of Trade,* 1740). Shortly after this dispute was settled, war broke out between Great Britain and Spain. Thomas urged the Assembly to provide funds for local defense and the support of the Pennsylvania troops who were to participate in the expedition against the Spanish West Indies. They replied that war was contrary to Quaker principles, that the colony was not really in danger, and that troops could be raised without a vote of the Assembly. This episode gave rise to a series of recriminations, in the course of which the Assembly withheld the Governor's salary and he refused to sign their bills. The controversy was intensified after France entered the war in 1744, but Thomas finally admitted defeat, and his relations with the Assembly were friendly during the latter part of his administration. He was more successful in dealing with the Indians. Conferences were held with the Shawnees and the Delawares and important treaties were concluded with the Iroquois Confederacy at Philadelphia in 1742 and at Lancaster in 1744. Delegates were sent to the conference at Albany in 1745.

He relied to a large extent on the advice of Conrad Weiser [*q.v.*] and accepted the policy of recognizing the suzerainty of the Six Nations over the Indians of Pennsylvania. This caused some friction with the local tribes, but the neutrality of the Iroquois was secured and as a result the back country was rapidly settled. Thomas also acted as a mediator in a quarrel between the Iroquois and the governments of Maryland and Virginia.

In 1747, his health failed and he sailed for England about the first of June (*Pennsylvania Gazette,* June 4, 1747). He was governor of the Leeward Islands from Jan. 25, 1753 until Dec. 18, 1766. In 1765, after the Stamp Act went into effect, he wrote to England that the stamps had been seized and the distributor forced to resign at St. Kitts, but Antigua remained quiet and loyal. He sailed for England in June 1766 and was created a baronet on Sept. 6 of that year. After his retirement he settled in England and acquired the manors of Yapton and Ratton in the county of Sussex. He died in London in his eightieth year and was buried in the parish church at Willingdon, Sussex. Thomas was married, Apr. 18, 1717, to Elizabeth King (*c.* 1700–Sept. 24, 1763), daughter of Capt. John King of Antigua. They had two sons and three daughters.

[V. L. Oliver, *The Hist. of the Island of Antigua* (3 vols., 1894–99); *Jour. of the Commissioners for Trade and Plantations, 1734/5–1741* (1930), *1741/2–1749* (1931), *1749/50–1753* (1932); *Acts of the Privy Council of England, Colonial Series,* vol. IV (1911); *Minutes of the Provincial Council of Pa.,* vols. IV–VI (1851–52); *Votes and Proceedings of the Assembly of Pa.,* vols. III–IV (1754, 1774); G. P. Donehoo, *Pennsylvania, a Hist.,* vol. I (1926); W. T. Root, *The Relations of Pa. with the British Government, 1696–1765* (1912); obituary in *Gentleman's Magazine* (London), Jan. 1775; character sketch, *Ibid.,* Sept. 1775.]
           W. R. S.

THOMAS, GEORGE CLIFFORD (Oct. 28, 1839–Apr. 21, 1909), banker, philanthropist, and collector, was born in Philadelphia, Pa., the son of John W. and Sophia Kezia (Atkinson) Thomas. On his father's side he was the grandson of John Thomas who emigrated from Wales prior to 1802; his mother's ancestors came to Maryland with Lord Baltimore. After graduating from the Episcopal Academy, he worked six years as a clerk for his father, a dry-goods merchant with banking connections. In 1863 his financial aptitude attracted the attention of Jay Cooke [*q.v.*], whose banking house Thomas entered, and there proved himself a quick pupil, working hard to promote the flotation of government war loans. When Cooke rearranged his partnerships, Jan. 1, 1866, he included Thomas with a share of 5% and assurance of $3000 annually, although the young man brought no property into the firm and was then possessed of not more than $3000, his savings from his salary as clerk. The next year, Nov. 26, Thomas married Ada Elizabeth, daughter of J. Barlow Moorhead, a brother of Cooke's partner, William G. Moorhead, and a prominent Pennsylvania iron master.

Thomas rapidly became Cooke's right-hand man in Philadelphia, but the latter's failure in 1873 unfortunately absorbed all of Thomas' small fortune. By December following, however, he was forming a new banking and brokerage connection, known first as Joseph M. Shoemaker & Company, and later as Thomas & Shoemaker. The steady success of this house attracted the interest of another prominent financier, Anthony J. Drexel [q.v.], and on Jan. 1, 1883, Thomas was admitted to partnership in the local firm of Drexel & Company, in the New York firm of Drexel, Morgan & Company, and in the Paris firm of Morgan, Harjes & Company. Again, he became a strong asset to the houses with which he was connected, and from Dec. 31, 1894 he served for ten years as the senior resident partner in the Philadelphia firm. Through these connections with the leading American bankers he contributed to the directive genius which placed the control of United States transportation in banking hands.

While Thomas' business career differed little from that of other successful financiers of his generation, he won some claim to notice through his avocations—church work, philanthropy, and the collection of rare objects. As early as 1868 he began employing his talent for organization in building up the Protestant Episcopal Church. For many years he was superintendent of the Sunday School connected with the Church of the Holy Apostles, and he gave much time and thought to the training of teachers and the advancement of religious education. He set up the machinery for the annual financing of the Church's missions and schools, serving as treasurer of the Board of Missions. As wealth grew he and his wife became known, not alone for the generosity of their public benefactions, but particularly for the private aid which they bestowed. Donations for parish chapels, parish houses, a gymnasium, and a nurses' home on the one hand, were matched by quiet help to students and hard-pressed families on the other. In his later years he became known to agents abroad and at home as a discriminating purchaser willing to pay the large prices exacted for rare things. His collections included Shakespeare folios; many autographs, including those

of the signers of the Declaration of Independence; and William Penn's original "Charter of Liberties to the people of the State of Pennsylvania." In the room where these treasures were kept, he installed a pipe organ, whereon he played with skill for his own relaxation. He died in Philadelphia, survived by his widow, two sons, and a daughter.

[L. B. Thomas, *The Thomas Book* (copr. 1896); J. W. Jordan, *Encyc. of Pa. Biog.*, vols. X (1918), XVI (1927); E. P. Oberholtzer, *Phila., a Hist. of the City and Its People* (n.d.), vol. IV, and *Jay Cooke; Financier of the Civil War* (1907), vol. II; *In the Matter of Jay Cooke & Company, Bankrupts, in the District Court of the U. S. for the Eastern District of Pa.* (1875); *Spirit of Missions*, May, June 1909; *Cat. of the More Important Books, Autographs, and MSS. in the Lib. of George C. Thomas* (1907); *Autograph Letters and Autographs of the Signers of the Declaration of Independence in the Possession of George C. Thomas* (1908); *Phila. Inquirer* and *North Am. Press* (Phila.), Apr. 22, 1909; information from Drexel & Company.]
J. P. N.

THOMAS, GEORGE HENRY (July 31, 1816–Mar. 28, 1870), soldier, was born in Southampton County, in southeastern Virginia, the son of John and Elizabeth (Rochelle) Thomas. The family, on his father's side, was Welsh and English; on his mother's, French Huguenot. He received his early education in the local Southampton Academy and began the study of law, serving meanwhile as deputy to his uncle, James Rochelle, clerk of the county court. Through the influence of this uncle he received an appointment to the United States Military Academy, entered in 1836, and was graduated in 1840, number twelve in a class of forty-two members. Among his classmates were William T. Sherman and Richard S. Ewell [qq.v.]. He received his commission as second lieutenant in the 3rd Artillery, then on field service in the Florida War. He remained in Florida for two years, and received the brevet rank of first lieutenant for gallantry in action against the Indians; then he served in several Southern garrisons, receiving his promotion to the substantive grade of first lieutenant in 1844. The following year he was assigned to Bragg's light battery with Taylor's force in Texas, and served throughout Taylor's Mexican campaign. He was brevetted captain and major for gallantry at Monterey and Buena Vista. He again served in Indian troubles in Florida, and then was an instructor in artillery and cavalry at West Point, 1851–54, being promoted, meanwhile, to the rank of captain.

Upon relief at the Academy he went with a detachment of his regiment via Panama to California, and to Fort Yuma, where he served for a year. He then accepted a commission as major in the newly raised 2nd (later designated as the 5th) Cavalry, and joined at Jefferson Barracks,

Mo. In this regiment, Albert S. Johnston was colonel, Robert E. Lee lieutenant-colonel, and William J. Hardee the other major; in it served many other officers who later became famous, including the Federal general George Stoneman, and the Confederate generals John B. Hood, Fitzhugh Lee, and Earl VanDorn [qq.v.]. He served with the new regiment in Texas, and on garrison and exploration duty. On one of his exploring expeditions he was wounded in the face by an Indian arrow. On Nov. 1, 1860, he was granted a twelve months' leave of absence and was in the East at the outbreak of the Civil War.

In spite of his Southern birth, Thomas decided to remain with the Union army, and on Apr. 14 he joined his regiment at Carlisle, Pa. In April he became a lieutenant-colonel, and in May a colonel. He commanded a brigade in the opening operations in the Shenandoah Valley. On Aug. 17, 1861, he was made brigadier-general of volunteers and assigned to duty in Kentucky, organizing new troops. In November 1861, he assumed command of the 1st Division, Army of the Ohio, and won the small but decisive action of Mill Springs on Jan. 19, 1862. His command was then withdrawn to Louisville and took part in Buell's advance to Nashville and to Pittsburg Landing. Here, on Apr. 25, 1862, he was promoted major-general of volunteers, and commanded the right wing of Halleck's army in the advance to and capture of Corinth. He remained in command of the garrison at that place until June 22, when, with his own division, he was reassigned to Buell's army with which he served during the campaign against Bragg in Kentucky. Buell's retreat to Louisville caused dissatisfaction in Washington, and on Sept. 29 Thomas received orders to supersede him. Thomas declined the command, pointing out that Buell had already issued orders for the offensive, and served as Buell's second in command in the Perryville operations in October.

On Oct. 30 General Rosecrans replaced Buell. Thomas, although he had declined to supersede Buell himself, protested against serving under Rosecrans, a former junior; but the president antedated Rosecrans' commission to make him senior, and Thomas promptly acquiesced and served under him loyally. The command was several times reorganized, and was finally designated the Army of the Cumberland; Thomas' own command became the XIV Army Corps, one of three corps in the army. This corps he commanded at Stones River (Dec. 31–Jan. 3), and in the Tullahoma campaign in June and July

1863, which pushed Bragg out of Tennessee. Early in September, Rosecrans crossed the Tennessee River and maneuvered Bragg out of Chattanooga as he had out of the Tullahoma lines. In this process his army became widely extended, and Bragg, having been reënforced by Longstreet's corps from Virginia, made an effort to cut him off from Chattanooga. He succeeded in concentrating in time, and took position on Chickamauga Creek. Of this line, Thomas' corps formed the left, or northern flank.

The battle of Chickamauga began on Sept. 19 but the heaviest fighting came the next day. Bragg's attack came first upon Thomas' position, which was reënforced progressively by parts of other corps. Toward noon, a gap opened on Thomas' right through an erroneous movement by a division not at the time engaged, and Longstreet penetrated the lines. Thomas' right was violently bent back, and all the troops south of that point were driven in disorder across Missionary Ridge, where they took the road to Chattanooga. Rosecrans, whose headquarters were behind the right wing, was carried to the rear by what seemed the rout of his whole force. Thomas, however, was still in the field with over half the army. His line was bent into horseshoe shape, but not broken; and here he stood all day, earning his title, "the Rock of Chickamauga." After dark, he drew off to Rockville, five miles to the north, and he retired unmolested to Chattanooga. For this service he was promoted brigadier-general in the regular army on Oct. 27, 1863.

The situation at Chattanooga was critical. The army was in a state of siege, its supply being so reduced as to place it in a starving condition. All the energy of the North was turned toward its relief, active operations elsewhere being suspended. Grant was given supreme command in the West, and directed upon Chattanooga his own old Army of the Tennessee, now under Sherman; Hooker was sent by rail from Washington with two corps of the Army of the Potomac; Rosecrans was relieved from command of the Army of the Cumberland, and Thomas put in his place. Grant's first telegram to him directed that Chattanooga be held "at all hazards." Thomas replied, "We will hold the town till we starve"—which seemed not a mere rhetorical expression, for the men, to use their own language, were on "half rations of hard bread and beef dried on the hoof" (see Van Horne, post, p. 156). By the use of Hooker's command, a new and direct line of supply was opened; and when Sherman finally assumed his position on Nov. 23, after having been delayed by bad weather, Grant was ready to undertake a general offensive. As a first move, Thomas made a reconnaissance in force on Nov. 23, which cleared up the question of Bragg's strength and position, and secured favorable ground for the decisive action, but which also served to put Bragg on his guard. On the following two days was fought the battle that forced Bragg back from Chattanooga. Thomas' right, under Hooker, seized Lookout Mountain; the rest of his army carried Missionary Ridge.

Operations during the winter were of minor character, but in May 1864 Sherman's Atlanta campaign began. In this campaign, Thomas' Army of the Cumberland constituted over half of Sherman's entire force. It was constantly engaged, was in every offensive move, and bore the brunt of the only serious Confederate counter-stroke—Hood's attack at Peachtree Creek, Ga., on July 20. Troops of this Army received the surrender of Atlanta and were first to enter the city. Thomas now suggested that his army be detached from Sherman's command, and sent on a march to the sea. When it was decided that Sherman's main force should make this movement, it became necessary to form a new army to oppose Hood in the west; Thomas was designated to command it, and was ordered to Nashville in October. The nucleus of his force, 35,000 men, was furnished from Sherman's army, but it was necessary to collect another 35,000 by drawing in detachments, even from beyond the Mississippi, and by bringing new troops from the north. Hood began his advance northward late in November. Thomas kept his entire field force, under Schofield, in front of Hood, delaying him. This force, having held out so long as almost to be cut off, finally took position at Franklin, vigorously checked Hood there on Nov. 30, and then withdrew into Nashville. General Grant insisted strongly upon an immediate offensive by Thomas' whole force, but the latter insisted that he was not yet strong enough to gain a decisive victory, and that nothing less should be considered. On this point he remained firm, although his fitness for independent command and even his loyalty, were seriously questioned. It is a moot question whether Thomas did not seriously jeopardize the success of the campaign as a whole by his insistence. On Dec. 9 Grant directed that he be relieved, and Schofield put in his place; but meanwhile Thomas reported himself ready to move, and the order was suspended. A violent storm, with snow and ice, caused another delay. Grant then dispatched General Logan with orders to supersede Thomas; and he himself started from the James

River for Nashville on Dec. 15. But before either arrived, Thomas had moved. In a two days' battle, Dec. 15–16, he fully vindicated his plan of action, and administered so severe a defeat to Hood that his army played no further important part in the war. He was promoted to the rank of a major-general in the regular army and on Mar. 3, 1865, received the thanks of Congress.

He remained in command in this region for the rest of the war, and for some years after. In 1868 President Johnson sent his name to the Senate for promotion to the brevet ranks of lieutenant-general and general, but, believing that the purpose of these promotions was to use him as an instrument for displacing General Grant in command of the army, he declined, saying that the honor was too great for his services since the war, and came too late to be acceptable for war service. In the same year he was strongly urged to become a candidate for the presidency, but he refused to allow his name to be used. In June 1869, he assumed command of the Military Division of the Pacific, at San Francisco, Cal., where he died of apoplexy, leaving a widow but no children. He was buried at Troy, N. Y., the home of his wife, Frances Lucretia Kellogg, to whom he had been married on Nov. 17, 1852.

Thomas was a man of fine presence—six feet in height and weighing about 200 pounds. He was studious in his habits, deliberate but decided in action, and fastidious to the point of exasperation. He is said to have remarked to a less tidy officer, "The fate of an army may depend on a buckle" (B. A. Liddell Hart, *Sherman,* 1930, p. 257). He was respected by his superiors and beloved by his subordinates; at the same time, his deliberateness was often looked upon as sluggishness, and his Southern birth sometimes led to suspicion of lukewarmness. Even his various nicknames are indicative of his dominant traits of character: as a cadet, he was called "Old Tom"; as an instructor, "Slow Trot"; and in the Army of the Cumberland, "Pap Thomas." His military reputation, however, may rest upon the judgments of two superiors. Sherman, although sometimes impatient at Thomas' deliberateness, remarked on one occasion, "I wish Old Thom was here! he's my off-wheel horse" (W. F. G. Shanks, *Personal Recollections of Distinguished Generals,* 1866, p. 58). And Grant writes (*Personal Memoirs,* volume II, 1886, p. 525), that although Thomas could hardly have conducted the offensive operations of the Atlanta campaign as Sherman did, he could have handled Johnston's problem in that campaign to perfection; that his dispositions were always good, and that he could not be driven from a point he was given to hold.

[Letters filed with the manuscript "Reports of General Officers," Old Records Division, Adjutant-General's Office, War Dept.; G. W. Cullum, *Biog. Reg.* . . . *Officers and Grads., U. S. Mil. Acad.* (1891); T. B. Van Horne, *The Life of Major-General George H. Thomas* (1882); Henry Coppée, *General Thomas* (1893); R. W. Johnson, *Memoir of Maj.-Gen. George H. Thomas* (1881); Timothy Hopkins, *The Kelloggs in The Old World and The New* (1903), vol. I; *Morning Bull.* (San Francisco, Cal.), Mar. 29, 1870; *N. Y. Tribune,* Mar. 30, 1870.] O. L. S., Jr.

THOMAS, ISAIAH (Jan. 19, 1749 o.s.–Apr. 4, 1831), printer, historian of the press, founder of the American Antiquarian Society, was born at Boston, Mass., the son of Moses and Fidelity (Grant) Thomas and great-great-grandson of Evan Thomas who came to Boston from Wales in 1640. Isaiah's grandfather, Peter Thomas, was a local merchant of some ability and means, but his father was an unsuccessful dabbler in many occupations. He died in 1752, leaving a penniless widow and five children who, with the aid of friends and a small shop, managed to escape poverty. With but six weeks of indifferent schooling Isaiah began at the age of six his real education before the type cases of a printing office. In 1756 he was apprenticed to Zechariah Fowle of Boston, an ignorant and shiftless printer and peddler of ballads and chapbooks, by whom he was misused. Having learned much of his trade from one of Fowle's short-time partners, Samuel Draper, and from another local printer, Gamaliel Rogers, Thomas took over, while still in his early teens, the management of Fowle's shop. By the age of seventeen he was considered an excellent printer. He read much, wrote plain English with a dash of satire, and attempted occasional verses to fill out a column. Tall, handsome, always neatly dressed, he made many friends in the trade and among the men of substance of the town.

In 1766 Thomas had a "serious fracas" with his master and left Boston secretly for Halifax, whence he hoped to reach London in order to perfect his knowledge of printing. He found immediate employment with the *Halifax Gazette* but soon got into trouble because of his opposition to the Stamp Act, returned via Portsmouth, N. H., to Fowle's shop in Boston, and secured a final release from his unexpired apprenticeship. He then started south with the hope of reaching England by way of the West Indies. After various adventures he found himself in Charlestown, S. C., where he worked for a time on the *South Carolina and American General Gazette.* He failed to reach England or to establish a business

of his own and finally, in the spring of 1770, returned to Boston. He became Fowle's partner in July, established the *Massachusetts Spy,* which was destined to live until 1904, soon bought out his partner, and made his paper famous for its support of the liberties of the people. He was in constant conflict with the royal government and every effort was made to suppress his fearless and dangerously successful Whig newspaper.

The British occupation of Boston in 1775 finally drove him from the city. Escaping with his press and type on the night of Apr. 16, Thomas sent his equipment before him to Worcester while he, two nights later, joined Paul Revere and others in alarming the countryside. As a minute-man he took part in the skirmishes at Lexington and Concord and on the 20th arrived in Worcester; here he reëstablished his newspaper and did the official printing for the patriots of the colony. In the spring of 1776 Thomas leased his paper and moved to Salem, where he made an unsuccessful attempt to carry on the printing business; he returned to Worcester in the spring of 1778 and resumed publication of the *Spy.* These were trying days for the young printer but by the end of the war his business was on a firmer footing and he began the publishing of books.

Thomas was the leading publisher of his day. His printing establishment in Worcester eventually employed 150 persons and included seven presses, a paper mill, and bindery. Many of his former apprentices were sent out as his partners to establish other newspapers and bookstores. He had branches in Boston, Walpole, Brookfield, Portsmouth, Windsor, Newburyport, Baltimore, and Albany and employed a line of messengers connecting his various establishments. In 1774–75 for fifteen months Thomas published the *Royal American Magazine,* in 1786–88 the *Worcester Magazine,* and from 1789 to 1796 the *Massachusetts Magazine.* In 1771 he published his first almanac (Ezra Gleason, *The Massachusetts Calendar, or an Almanack for . . . 1772*), the title of which was changed to *Thomas's New England Almanack* in the issue for 1775; the last to bear his name appeared in 1822.

As a book publisher Thomas was notable for the beauty of his typography and the popularity and importance of the books published. His more than 400 titles included a handsome folio Bible, the first printed in English in the United States, and many other religious volumes. His scores of educational works included Caleb Alexander's Greek grammar, the first written and published in America, Nicholas Pike's arithmetic, the first dictionary printed in America, William Perry's, of which he sold 54,000 copies, and fourteen editions and 300,000 copies of Perry's spelling book. He was the first American publisher to do extensive printing from musical type. Blackstone's *Commentaries* came from his press as well as many other works in law, medicine, and agriculture. He reprinted the best English literature of his day and issued the first edition of *The Power of Sympathy* (1789), attributed to William Hill Brown and earlier to Sarah Wentworth Apthorp Morton [*q.v.*], the first novel by a native American.

He is still famous for his more than a hundred children's books of which he published tens of thousands of copies. Of these his first American edition of *Mother Goose's Melody* (1786), is the most famous but he also printed inexpensive but attractively illustrated editions of the *New England Primer, The History of Little Goody Twoshoes, The Pilgrim's Progress,* and *Travels of Robinson Crusoe.* He may be regarded as the greatest early publisher of juveniles in the country. Franklin called him "the Baskerville of America," and an examination of the products of his busy presses bears out this high praise from the only other American printer of his day who had anything like his success as a publisher.

By 1802 Thomas had become rich and so was able to retire in favor of his son and devote the rest of his life to scholarship. His personal library, perhaps the best in the country in the field of American history, furnished the source materials for *The History of Printing in America* (2 vols., 1810), which is still (1935) the recognized authority on the subject. Realizing the need for a national society for the preservation and study of the materials of American history, Thomas founded and, on Oct. 24, 1812, incorporated the American Antiquarian Society of which he became the first president. His gifts to the society, including books, manuscripts, building, land, and endowment, amounted to $50,000. Thomas was the first printer and the first postmaster of Worcester (1775–1801), the first in Massachusetts known to have read the Declaration of Independence to a public gathering (July 24, 1776), the first master of the first Masonic lodge in Worcester and later master of the Grand Lodge of Massachusetts. He received the honorary degree of A.M. from Dartmouth in 1814 and that of LL.D. from Allegheny College in 1818. He was apparently a member of every learned society in America. His personal friends included Washington, Franklin, the Adamses, Jefferson, Hancock, and many of the other leaders of his time.

One of his old friends, Gov. Levi Lincoln of Worcester, has left this picture of Thomas in his later years: "With a strong and vigorous mind and a cultivated intellect, enterprise, energy and industry, in early life, gave him wealth, and possessed of this, he lived in courtly style, and with beneficent liberality. . . . In his person, he was tall and slender, stooping somewhat in his gait. His address was courteous, his conversation frank, but something conventional, and his attention to appearance and dress singularly precise and studied. He was a public spirited citizen, generous in his contributions to all worthy objects, and a most efficient co-operator with others in promoting the growth, improvement and prosperity of the place." Thomas was married three times: first, Dec. 25, 1769, in Charlestown, S. C., to Mary, daughter of Joseph and Anne Dill of Bermuda, from whom he was divorced in 1777; second, May 26, 1779, in Boston, to Mary Fowle (d. Nov. 16, 1818), daughter of William and Rebecca (Bass) Thomas and widow of Isaac Fowle; third, Aug. 10, 1819, in Boston, to Rebecca Armstrong (1757–1828), daughter of John and Christian (Bass) Armstrong, a cousin of his second wife. Two children by his first wife survived, Mary Anne and Isaiah.

[Thomas' original diaries, business papers, and correspondence, a virtually complete collection of works from his press, including newspapers, periodicals, books, pamphlets, and broadsides, at Am. Antiquarian Soc., Worcester, Mass.; C. L. Nichols, ed., "Extracts from the Diaries and Accounts of Isaiah Thomas from the Year 1782 to 1804 and His Diary for 1808," in *Proc. Am. Antiquarian Soc.,* n.s., vol. XXVI (1916); B. T. Hall, ed., "The Diary of Isaiah Thomas, 1805–1828," in *Trans. and Colls. Am. Antiquarian Soc.,* vols. IX, X (1909); Isaiah Thomas, *History of Printing in America* (2nd ed., enlarged, in *Trans. and Colls. Am. Antiquarian Soc.,* vol. V (1874)); same as separate (1874, 2 vols.); B. F. Thomas, "Memoir of Isaiah Thomas," in *Trans. and Coll. Am. Antiquarian Soc.,* vol. V (1874), pp. xvii–lxxxvii; Levi Lincoln, *Reminiscences of the Original Associates of the Worcester Fire Society* (1862), pp. 32–33; C. L. Nichols, *Isaiah Thomas, Printer, Writer & Collector* (1912), with bibliography of imprints; C. L. Nichols, *Bibliography of Worcester, 1775–1848* (2nd ed., 1918); C. L. Nichols, "The Portraits of Isaiah Thomas with Some Notes upon his Descendants," in *Proc. Am. Antiquarian Soc.,* n.s., vol. XXX (1921), pp. 251–77; J. T. Buckingham, *Personal Memoirs* (2 vols., 1852); Annie Russell Marble, *From 'Prentice to Patron: The Life Story of Isaiah Thomas* (1935); L. N. Richardson, *A Hist. of Early Am. Magazines* (1931).] R. W. G. V.

THOMAS, JESSE BURGESS (1777–May 3, 1853), United States senator, territorial judge, was born in Shepherdstown, Va. (now W. Va.), the son of Jesse and Sabina (Symmes) Thomas. Through his mother he claimed descent from Lord Baltimore. In 1799 he was studying law with his brother at Washington, Mason County, Ky., where he also served as county clerk until 1803. An early marriage ending with the death of his wife in that year led him to leave Kentucky, and he began practising law in Lawrenceburg.

Indiana Territory. He was soon elected (1805) to the lower branch of the territorial legislature, where he served as speaker for three years. In 1805 he was appointed captain of militia in Dearborn County by Gov. William H. Harrison. On Dec. 2, 1806 he married Rebecca (Mackenzie) Hamtranck, widow of Col. Hamtranck and mother of John Francis Hamtranck [q.v.].

In 1808 Thomas was elected as delegate to Congress to fill a vacancy, thanks largely to the support of Illinoisans who desired division of Indiana Territory. He kept his preëlection promise to work for this end, and was successful before the end of the session in March 1809 (*Annals of Congress*, 10 Cong., 2 Sess., pp. 339, 1095). Realizing that "the service he had rendered the Illinoisans was fatal to his further political aspirations in Indiana" (Snyder, "Forgotten Statesmen," *post*, p. 515), he shrewdly obtained from President Madison appointment to one of the three federal judgeships in the newly created territory of Illinois. Removing thither, he served continuously as federal judge until 1818, winning a reputation for ability and fairness.

As a delegate from St. Clair County, Thomas was chosen president of the first constitutional convention of Illinois in 1818 (R. V. Carpenter, in "The Illinois Constitution Convention of 1818," *Journal of the Illinois State Historical Society*, October 1913). He was one of the first United States senators from the state of Illinois, serving until March 1829. His most important senatorial action occurred in 1820 during the debate over slavery and the admission of Missouri into the Union. Although not a slaveholder himself, he believed in the institution and favored its establishment in Illinois. During the congressional deadlock relative to the admission of Missouri and Maine, however, he introduced an amendment prohibiting slavery north of the line 36° 30' except for the section included in the proposed state of Missouri. This amendment was embodied in the famous "Missouri Compromise" (*Annals of Congress*, 16 Cong., 1 Sess., p. 427). Thomas' support of his friend William H. Crawford [q.v.] for the presidency in 1824 led to alienation from his party, which was largely composed of Jackson followers. He therefore refused to stand for reëlection at the expiration of his term and left Illinois for Mount Vernon, Ohio, where his wife had considerable property. In 1832 he saw service in the Black Hawk War. His last participation in politics was the nomination of his friend William H. Harrison [q.v.] for the presidency in 1840.

Always interested in business (in 1817 he had set up the first wool-carding machine in Illinois), he now turned his attention to the management of his wife's property with such success that he accumulated a moderate fortune. He assisted in organizing St. Paul's Episcopal Church, at Mount Vernon, of which he was a member. After the death of his wife in 1851 his mind became deranged and he committed suicide on the night of May 3, 1853, dying childless. Jesse Burgess Thomas, 1832–1915 [q.v.], a Baptist minister, was his grand-nephew.

Thomas was better as a politician than as a judge or lawyer. Despite nine years on the federal bench, his knowledge of the law was superficial and his primary interest was politics. His "quickness of perception, clear intellect, sound judgment, and knowledge of human nature, constituting strong common sense" (Snyder, *op. cit.*, p. 516) were invaluable to him as a politician. He was considered "tricky" by some contemporaries, yet won a reputation for fairness and justice for which there must have been considerable basis.

[N. N. Hill, *Hist. of Knox County, Ohio* (1881); J. M. Palmer, *The Bench and Bar of Ill., Hist. and Reminiscent* (1899); Charles Robson, *The Biog. Encyc. of Ill. of the Nineteenth Century* (1875); J. F. Snyder, *Adam W. Snyder, and His Period in Illinois Hist., 1817–1842* (1903) and "Forgotten Statesmen of Illinois," *Trans. Ill. State Hist. Soc. for the Year 1904* (1904); L. B. Thomas, *The Thomas Book* (copr. 1896); *Biog. Dir. Am. Cong.* (1928); *Commercial Register* (Sandusky), May 6, 1853.]　E. B. E.

THOMAS, JESSE BURGESS (July 29, 1832–June 6, 1915), Baptist clergyman, son of Jesse Burgess and Adeline Clarissa (Smith) Thomas, was descended from English ancestors who settled in Maryland in the middle of the seventeenth century. Several of the family were distinguished members of the legal profession; his father was a judge of the supreme court of Illinois; his great-uncle, another Jesse Burgess Thomas [q.v.], had been a federal judge in Illinois Territory and one of the state's first senators. Young Jesse graduated from Kenyon College in 1850, studied law, and was admitted to the bar in 1852. Later, feeling an obligation to prepare for the ministry, he entered Rochester Theological Seminary, but withdrew after a year to engage in mercantile business, and soon returned to the law. After five years more of practice, however, he decided definitely for the ministry and in 1862 was ordained at Waukegan, Ill., becoming pastor of the local Baptist church. His gifts of eloquence and leadership recommended him to the Pierrepont Street Baptist Church, Brooklyn, N. Y., where he served four years, a period followed by a few months in the First Baptist Church, San Francisco, and a longer term as pastor of the Michigan Avenue Baptist Church, Chicago. In 1874, the Pierrepont Street and First Baptist churches of Brooklyn having merged, he was called to be pastor of the united congregation. Here he remained for fourteen years.

A natural orator, logical in thought, incisive in utterance, picturesque in style, kindly of heart, and of winsome personality, he was one of several Brooklyn ministers—including Henry Ward Beecher, Richard S. Storrs, and T. De Witt Tallmage [qq.v.]—who were nationally renowned as preachers. In theology he was conservative; when it seemed as if the higher criticism and the arguments of the scientists threatened his cherished beliefs, he spoke strongly of his convictions in the pulpit and on the lecture platform, and wrote books to express his opinions more amply.

In 1888 Thomas left the pastorate to become professor of church history in the Newton Theological Institution, Newton Center, Mass. After seventeen years of teaching he became professor emeritus, serving as minister-at-large. He was also nominally pastor emeritus of his old church in Brooklyn, in which city he died.

His publications included *The Old Bible and the New Science* (1877); "Significance of the Historic Element in Scripture," in Joseph Cook's *Christ and Modern Thought* (1881); *The Mould of Doctrine* (copyright 1882); *Some Parables of Nature* (1911); and *The Church and the Kingdom, a New Testament Study* (1914). He was married, May 30, 1855, to Abbie Anne Eastman of Ottawa County, Mich., and had five sons and three daughters; four of his children died young.

[Wm. Cathcart, *The Baptist Encyc.* (1881); *Who's Who in America*, 1914–15; L. B. Thomas, *The Thomas Book* (copr. 1896); *Watchman-Examiner*, June 17, 1915; *Standard*, June 26, 1915; *Brooklyn Daily Eagle*, June 7, 1915; *Sun* (N. Y.), June 8, 1915.] H. K. R.

THOMAS, JOHN (Nov.9,1724–June2,1776), Revolutionary soldier, great-grandson of John Thomas who came to Massachusetts in 1635 as a fourteen-year-old orphan, was born in Marshfield, Mass., the son of John and Lydia (Waterman) Thomas. After studying medicine in the office of Dr. Simon Tufts of Medford, he practised for a short time at Green Harbor, then went to Kingston, Mass., where he resided for the rest of his life except when absent on military duty. On Mar. 1, 1746, he was authorized by Governor Shirley to practise "Chirurgery and Medicine" in the army and in the following year he served under General Waldo in Nova Scotia. In February 1755 he was commissioned lieutenant and surgeon's mate and empowered to enlist volunteers in the province; later the same year he

participated in Winslow's descent upon Acadia; and in 1759–60 he served in Nova Scotia and in the expedition dispatched to Canada under Amherst. During the next fifteen years he was principally occupied in practising his profession at Kingston. In 1770 Governor Hutchinson appointed him a justice of the peace.

At the outbreak of the Revolution he was chosen (Feb. 9, 1775) by the Provincial Congress of Massachusetts one of five general officers, on May 19 was commissioned lieutenant-general of the state troops, and on June 22, elected brigadier-general by the Continental Congress. Learning that his Continental commission was antedated by those of William Heath and Seth Pomeroy [qq.v.] who had previously served under his command in the Massachusetts forces, he decided to resign, but Washington, who held him in high esteem, appealed to him in an earnest and eloquent letter (W. C. Ford, *The Writings of George Washington*, vol. III, 1889, pp. 39–43) to subordinate personal considerations to the common interest, and Thomas consented to remain. During the winter of 1775–76, he was in command at Roxbury, the most important post in the American siege lines. Washington directed him to occupy Dorchester Heights, overlooking both the harbor and town of Boston, and on the night of Mar. 4, accompanied by about 3,000 picked men, several pieces of artillery, and 360 ox teams laden with entrenching materials, he seized and fortified this strategic site. Howe planned an attack, but a violent storm delayed the movement and enabled Thomas to render his position impregnable. As a result the British were obliged to evacuate Boston.

In the meantime disaster had overtaken the American arms in Canada. In a futile assault upon Quebec on the night of Dec. 31, 1775, Montgomery had been killed and Arnold had been wounded; sickness and desertion were decimating the Patriot ranks. Chosen by the Continental Congress to take charge of this discouraging situation, Thomas was promoted to the rank of major-general on Mar. 6, 1776, and ordered north. Arriving before Quebec on May 1, he found that of a force of some 1,900 men, only about 1,000 were fit for duty; there were only 150 pounds of powder and less than a week's provisions; a large British fleet laden with supplies and reënforcements was approaching Quebec. Thomas summoned a council of war at which it was unanimously decided to retreat, and the army accordingly fell back to Sorel. Shortly thereafter Thomas died of smallpox and was buried near the fort at Chambly.

He had married in 1761 Hannah Thomas of

Taunton, daughter of Nathaniel Thomas, who although bearing the same name as her husband was not related to him. They had two sons and a daughter. John Thomas was a man of commanding presence, six feet tall and well proportioned. Washington commended him (Ford, *op. cit.*, III, 16) as "an able good Officer."

[Milton Halsey Thomas, Esq., Columbia Univ. Library, has compiled a manuscript bibliography of material relating to General Thomas. The General's diaries (1748–60), orderly books, commissions, many of his letters and personal belongings, and a portrait by Blythe are in the possession of the Mass. Hist. Soc. His diary of the expedition to Acadia is published in *New Eng. Hist. and Geneal. Reg.*, Oct. 1879. Arthur Lord has contributed biographical sketches to *Proc. Mass. Hist. Soc.*, 2 ser. XVIII (1905), and *Bostonian Soc. Pubs.*, vol. XII (1915). A sketch by Milton Halsey Thomas appeared in the *Boston Sunday Globe*, May 31, 1925. See also *Vital Records of Kingston, Mass.* (1911); M. A. Thomas, *Memorials of Marshfield* (1854); Peter Force, *Am. Archives*, 4 and 5 ser. (9 vols., 1837–53); Jared Sparks, *Corresp. of the Am. Revolution* (4 vols., 1853); J. H. Smith, *Our Struggle for the Fourteenth Colony* (2 vols., 1907); Charles Coffin, *The Life and Services of Major General John Thomas* (1844).]   E. E. C.

THOMAS, JOHN JACOBS (Jan. 8, 1810–Feb. 22, 1895), pomologist, author, editor, was born at Ledyard, Cayuga County, N. Y., the son of David and Hannah (Jacobs) Thomas, and a descendant of David Thomas who is said to have emigrated from Wales with William Penn in 1699. His father, a Quaker, was a self-taught engineer active in the construction of the Welland Canal and of the Erie Canal from Rochester to Buffalo; he was also the author of *Travels through the Western Country in the Summer of 1816* (1819), and a pioneer fruit-grower and nurseryman of central New York. John Jacobs Thomas early demonstrated unusual ability in a wide range of rural activities. For some thirty years he conducted nurseries successively at Palmyra, Macedon, and Union Springs, N. Y., and it is recorded that each tree he sold was allowed to bear fruit first to be sure that it was true to name. Although he had only the education afforded by the neighborhood district school, he early acquired a clear style of expression. He was assistant editor of the *Genesee Farmer* from 1838, an editor of the *New Genesee Farmer and Gardeners' Journal*, 1840–41, and associate editor of the *Country Gentleman* from its foundation in 1853 until shortly before his death in 1894, his editorials in the *Cultivator* and the *Country Gentleman* constituting the most varied and extensive series of discussions of rural topics written by an American during that period. His *Farm Implements and Machinery* (1854) and a series of nine volumes entitled *Rural Affairs* (1869–81), of which he was editor, covered a wide range of topics of interest to practical farm-

ers. He developed skill as an artist, and illustrated his published articles and books with cuts from his own drawings. He invented several tools and implements, one of which, the smoothing harrow, came into extensive use throughout the eastern and northern states. He was active in the formation of the American Pomological Congress (later the American Pomological Society), and served as the first president of the large and influential Western New York Horticultural Society, organized in 1855.

In 1846 he published *The Fruit Culturist,* a paper-covered volume of some two hundred pages devoted primarily to practical instruction in the nursery propagation and commercial growing of temperate climate fruits. In 1849 this was expanded into *The American Fruit Culturist,* in which the content was trebled and the information condensed, systematized, and generously illustrated. Although it was preceded by the publications of many other able pomologists, it marks the beginning of systematic pomology in America. The most comprehensive of the earlier fruit books—*The Fruits and Fruit Trees of America* (1845), by Andrew Jackson Downing [*q.v.*]—was essentially encyclopedic in character, with little attempt at systematization of varietal description and no effort to classify varieties in such way as to facilitate the identification of unknown sorts. Thomas gave careful attention to the selection and use of terms in his descriptions of varieties, and covered not only the characteristics of the fruits themselves but habit of growth, characteristics of bark, bud, leaf, and flower, productiveness, hardiness, etc., as well. For each of the major fruits he developed a "Synopsis of Arrangement" which, though artificial in character, constituted a convenient guide to the identification of the varieties included in the book. Adopted by agricultural colleges as a standard text in horticultural courses, the book was important in the advancement of technical pomology and in the training of pomologists, as well as in the development of amateur and commercial fruit growing. It went through many editions during Thomas' life, and after his death was revised and enlarged (1897) by W. H. S. Wood.

Thomas married Mary Slocum Howland, Aug. 23, 1838, at North Street Brick Meeting House, near Union Springs, N. Y. He died in Union Springs, where he had lived for nearly forty years, survived by his wife and four of their seven children. He was a man of singular gentleness and sweetness of character, with a kindly, humorous, somewhat square face and alert eyes. Because of a lameness in one foot he went on crutches. For many years his study was near his garden and his orchard, to which he made frequent daily visits and where he conducted numerous experiments.

[Sources include W. T. Lyle, *The Thomas Family* (1908); L. H. Bailey, *Standard Cyc. of Horticulture*, vol. III (1915), pp. 1599–1600; W. H. S. Wood, in J. J. Thomas' *Am. Fruit Culturist* (1897 ed.), pp. v–vi; *Cultivator and Country Gentleman*, Feb. 28 (reprint of obituary in *Union Springs Advertiser*), Mar. 7, 1895; correspondence with David Fairchild, Paul H. Fairchild, and Mrs. Emily Thomas. For David Thomas, see U. P. Hedrick, *Peaches of N. Y.* (1917), pp. 55–56, n.]   W. A. T.

THOMAS, JOHN WILSON (Aug. 24, 1830–Feb. 12, 1906), railway executive, was descended from a pioneer family which had settled on a farm on the Cumberland River near Nashville, Tenn., during the latter part of the eighteenth century. James Thomas, his father, after marrying Ellen Meneese, left the farm to enter the saddlery business in Nashville, and there John was born and grew to manhood. After attending preparatory schools in Nashville and at Georgetown, Ky., he entered Union University, Murfreesboro, Tenn., where he graduated in 1851 with the highest honors in his class. He served as instructor in that institution from 1851 until ill health forced his resignation in 1854, and then operated a hotel at Murfreesboro until 1858, when he became local agent for the Nashville & Chattanooga Railroad. In this position he played an important part in the transportation of Confederate troops during the early months of the Civil War, and in 1863 he was made custodian of the rolling stock and records of the road. In order to save this property from the Federal forces he took all movable materials to Augusta, Ga., and later to Wilmington, N. C.

After the close of the war his promotion was rapid. He became auditor and paymaster in 1865, division superintendent in 1868, general superintendent of the enlarged system which became the Nashville, Chattanooga & St. Louis Railway in 1872, general manager in 1883, and president in 1884, which position he held until his death. In his work as an executive he quickly gained a reputation for honesty and integrity which won the respect of his business associates, while his spirit of sympathy and good will toward the employees of his company made him one of the most popular and most beloved railroad executives of his time. These qualities, combined with his energy and efficiency, enabled him to place his road in a leading position in Southern transportation development.

His most important service to his state, aside from his railroad activity, was rendered as president of the Tennessee Centennial and International Exposition which was held in Nashville in 1897. Serving without salary, he directed the organization, managed the finances, and acted as host with such success that the Exposition closed free from indebtedness. He was an active worker in church circles, and among his outstanding contributions in that field were the organization and financing of the Monteagle Sunday School Assembly as an intellectual and recreational center in the Cumberland Mountains. Records show that during the later years of his life he was the most liberal man in Nashville in his support of charitable organizations; but while his gifts were large they were always made unostentatiously, and it is believed that at the time of his death he was a comparatively poor man.

He was twice married; first, in 1852, to Elizabeth Thomas of Murfreesboro, who died in 1886; and second, May 14, 1891, to Evalina DeBow of Nashville. A son and a daughter were born of the first marriage; the son survived his father, who died in Nashville in his seventy-sixth year.

[*Nashville American*, Feb. 13, 1906; *Nashville Banner*, Feb. 12, 1906; Herman Justi, *Official Hist. of the Tenn. Centennial Exposition* (1898); *John W. Thomas: A Memorial* (1906), a collection of addresses delivered at the various mass meetings held in his honor after his death.]   W. C. B.

THOMAS, JOSEPH (Sept. 23, 1811–Dec. 24, 1891), lexicographer, educator, and physician, was born at Ledyard, Cayuga County, N. Y., the son of David and Hannah (Jacobs) Thomas, and a brother of John Jacobs Thomas [*q.v.*]. After attending Rensselaer Polytechnic Institute at Troy, N. Y., where he received the degree of A.B. in 1830, he entered the senior class at Yale College (1832) to pursue a classical course but left almost immediately because of illness. In 1833–34 he taught Latin and Greek at Haverford College. He then entered the School of Medicine of the University of Pennsylvania, and took the degree of M.D. in 1837 with a thesis on the pulse. Although he lived in Philadelphia during the remainder of his life, and took further courses at the same institution in subsequent years, he seems not to have practised medicine for long, turning instead to his earlier training in classical languages and in literature as the means for a career. He returned to Haverford College as professor of elocution in 1852–53, but again remained for only one year. Between 1854 and 1871 he was associated with J. B. Lippincott and Company of Philadelphia as compiler and editor of a series of reference books: *A New and Complete Gazetteer of the United States* (1854); *Lippincott's Pronouncing Gazetteer: a Complete Geographical Dictionary of the World* (1855), both with Thomas Baldwin; *A Comprehensive Medical Dictionary* (1864); and a *Universal Pronounc-*

ing Dictionary of Biography and Mythology (2 vols., 1870). In 1852 he also prepared *The First Book of Etymology,* based on that of James Lynd, an elementary text for use in schools. In order to improve his knowledge of the pronunciation of Oriental proper and place names, he took a rapid tour of Egypt and Palestine in 1852–53. The record of this trip, *Travels in Egypt and Palestine* (1853), displays considerable antiquarian knowledge. In 1857 he made a similar trip to India to study Sanskrit and remained for fourteen months.

About 1866, through his friendship with Edward Parrish [*q.v.*], he became identified with the founding of Swarthmore College and with other activities of the Society of Friends, although he himself was not at that time a member. During 1865 and 1866 he delivered numerous lectures in Philadelphia, most of them under the auspices of the Friends' Social Lyceum, on ancient philosophy and philosophers, and on topics dealing with travel, education, and literature. At the laying of the cornerstone of Swarthmore College on May 10, 1866, he made an address in which he stressed the advantages of a liberal education for leadership in a democracy, and of higher education for women. During 1874–75 he gave the first series of lectures on English literature at Swarthmore, and was professor of English there until 1887, when he retired. His attainments as a scholar led to his election to membership in the American Philosophical Society. He died, unmarried, in Philadelphia.

His knowledge of Latin, Greek, and many other foreign languages made it possible for him to become one of the authorities of his day on etymology and the principles of pronunciation, and he did much to clarify the confusion of usage in works of reference. He emphasized the historical derivation of word meanings, and the use of phonetic re-spelling and native pronunciation of foreign place and proper names, made increasingly important in gazetteers and dictionaries by the decline of classical and linguistic training in the schools. As an authority he was invited to contribute the pronouncing vocabularies of biographical and geographical names to the 1867 edition of Webster's *An American Dictionary of the English Language,* unabridged. His contributions to education were not as specific or as original as those to lexicography, but were none the less consistent and courageous. His advocacy of modernized liberal studies for men and women alike was radical doctrine for his day, and his courses in English literature were in accord with the best practices of the present. He was a man of commanding presence, admired and respected by those who knew him.

[W. T. Lyle, *The Thomas Family* (1908); H. B. Nason, *Biog. Records . . . of the Rensselaer Polytechnic Institute* (1887); E. H. Magill, *Sixty-five Years in the Life of a Teacher* (1907), pp. 159–62; H. A. Kelly and W. L. Burrage, *Am. Medic. Biogs.* (1920); manuscript diary of Edward Parrish in the possession of a descendant; minutes of the board of managers of Swarthmore Coll.; W. I. Hull, "A Hist. of Swarthmore Coll.," in MS.; alumni records, Univ. of Pa.; prefaces to Thomas' reference works; obituary in *Pub. Ledger* (Phila.), Dec. 25, 1891.]   R. E. S.

THOMAS, LORENZO (October 1804–Mar. 2, 1875), soldier, was born in New Castle, Del., the son of Evan and Elizabeth (Sherer) Thomas. There was a military tradition in the Thomas family and in 1819 Lorenzo entered the United States Military Academy. At his graduation in 1823 he stood seventeenth in his class and was made a second lieutenant in the 4th Infantry. Subsequently he rose to the rank of major (1848) in this regiment. Except for service as quartermaster in the Seminole War (1836–37), his early duties were mostly of a routine nature. He was appointed assistant adjutant-general at Washington in 1838, with the rank of brevet major, and remained there almost continuously until 1846, when he joined the volunteer division of Maj.-Gen. William O. Butler [*q.v.*] as chief of staff during the Mexican War. "For gallant and meritorious conduct" at Monterey he was brevetted lieutenant-colonel, Sept. 23, 1846. At the close of the war he returned to his duties as assistant adjutant-general at Washington and continued in that capacity until designated as chief of staff to Lieut.-Gen. Winfield Scott in 1853. Upon the resignation of Col. Samuel Cooper [*q.v.*], the adjutant-general of the army, Thomas was promoted to a colonelcy and put in charge of that office, Mar. 7, 1861. Five months later he was made adjutant-general and given the rank of brigadier-general.

Like other bureaus of the War Department, when the Civil War came, the office over which Thomas presided proved hopelessly inadequate in equipment and personnel and gradually had to be expanded. Meanwhile, he was subjected to sharp criticism from some of the zealous war governors because he seemed too slow in furnishing state quotas and other necessary information. There apparently was considerable laxity and inefficiency in his bureau and many persons surmised that he was "lukewarm" regarding the war, but there was no sound basis for this suspicion. In what was probably an effort to be rid of him, Secretary Stanton ordered him to the Mississippi Valley in March 1863 to organize negro regiments. This work, together with arranging for the exchange of prisoners and the consolidation of depleted regiments, kept him occupied until the end of the war. He was brevetted major-general on Mar. 13, 1865. The next year Stanton sent him on an inspection tour of the provost marshal general's office and in 1867 on an extended inspection tour of the national cemeteries.

While he was engaged in the latter work the difficulties between President Johnson and Stanton came to a head, and the President, desiring to have a "rightminded" man in the adjutant general's office, directed Thomas on Feb. 13, 1868, to resume full charge of the bureau. On Feb. 21, Johnson dismissed Stanton, appointed Thomas secretary *ad interim,* and requested him to take possession of the department. The selection was unfortunate, for the Adjutant-General proved to be a vain and garrulous person. When he publicly boasted that he would oust the Secretary by force if necessary, Stanton ordered his arrest for violation of the Tenure of Office Act. Although immediately admitted to bail and discharged within a week, the General failed to displace the recalcitrant Secretary, the contest between them degenerating into opera bouffe. Thomas' testimony and his naïveté in the impeachment trial of the President effectively dispelled the charge that he and Johnson had conspired forcibly to eject Stanton and helped to win for the President an acquittal. After the adjournment Thomas resumed his inspection duties, but was retired from active service on Feb. 22, 1869. He died in Washington six years later.

[G. W. Cullum, *Biog. Reg. Officers and Grads. U. S. Mil. Acad.* (3rd ed., 1891); F. B. Heitman, *Hist. Reg. and Dict. U. S. Army* (1903), vol. I; *War of the Rebellion: Official Records (Army)*; *Diary of Gideon Welles* (1911), vol. III; *Trial of Andrew Johnson* (1868), vol. I; G. C. Gorham, *Life and Public Services of Edwin M. Stanton* (1899), vol. II; Frank Leslie's *Illustrated Newspaper,* Nov. 25, 1865; *Army and Navy Journal,* Mar. 6, 1875; *National Republican* (Washington), Mar. 3, 1875; bibliog. of article on Edwin M. Stanton.]   A. H. M.

THOMAS, PHILIP EVAN (Nov. 11, 1776–Sept. 1, 1861), railroad pioneer, was born at "Mount Radnor," Montgomery County, Md., the third son of Evan and Rachel (Hopkins) Thomas. When he went to Baltimore to work, the town had a population of only 15,000. In 1800 he began business for himself as a hardware merchant. On Apr. 20, 1801, he was married to Elizabeth George of Kent County, Md. He was already prominent as president of the Mechanics' Bank when the means by which Baltimore might retain its important trade with the "Ohio country" came under anxious discussion. The National Road had been Baltimore's link with the extending settlements in the Ohio and Missis-

sippi valleys, and had contributed to make the city the third in the Union by 1827. But the Erie Canal had been opened in 1825, and the "Pennsylvania system of public works," connecting Philadelphia with Pittsburgh, had been begun the following year. The speed and cheapness of transportation which these offered threatened to draw off western trade to New York and Philadelphia. Maryland and Virginia joined in reviving the project of the Chesapeake and Ohio Canal, designed to run from Georgetown to the Youghiogheny. Thomas was made a Maryland commissioner in this undertaking, but withdrew after a year, convinced that the canal could do nothing commercially for Baltimore. Interested by an account of the newly completed Darlington and Stockton Railroad in England, he immediately began to investigate the railroad as a means of solving the transportation problem, and in February 1827, with George Brown, 1787–1859 [*q.v.*], he called a meeting of business men at which he explained the superiority of railroads over canals. The call of a second meeting the same month declared it would "take under consideration the best means of restoring to . . . Baltimore that portion of the western trade which has recently been diverted from it by the introduction of steam navigation and by other causes" (Hungerford, *post,* vol. I, p. 19). Within a week Thomas, as chairman of a subcommittee on definite plans, reported in favor of a "double railroad" to the Ohio. Progress thereafter was rapid. The Maryland act to charter the Baltimore and Ohio Railroad was approved Feb. 28, 1827, and the actual incorporation took place Apr. 24. Except for the Mohawk and Hudson Railroad, chartered two months earlier, the Baltimore and Ohio thus became the first railroad chartered in the United States to carry passengers. Thomas was made president and a director. Charles Carroll [*q.v.*] of Carrollton laid the first stone, July 4, 1828. Thomas was unfaltering in overcoming the many difficulties which presented themselves once the first enthusiasm had died down—the delays in payment of Baltimore's subscription, the hostility of the Chesapeake and Ohio directors, the discord over the route of the road, the unexpected costs of excavation in the first westward miles, the designing of a locomotive which would go around curves, the refusal of Congress to remit the import duty on scrap iron for the tracks. When he resigned the presidency in 1836, the road had reached Harpers Ferry and the chief mechanical problems had been solved.

Like his father and his first ancestor in America, Philip Thomas, who came to Maryland from Wales about 1651, Thomas was a Quaker. He took active part in protecting the Indians of New York against the taking of their reservations by land speculators, and for this the Senecas made him "Chief Sagouan" (Bountiful Giver) and constituted him their representative in Washington. He was president of the Mechanical Fire Company, the first president of the Maryland Bible Society, and advanced $25,000 that the state might begin the erection of the Washington monument in Baltimore. He was a stout man, clean-shaven, with high forehead, prominent nose, and a pleasant expression. He died in Yonkers, N. Y., while on a visit to his daughter some years after his retirement from business. He was survived by five daughters and two sons.

[L. B. Thomas, *The Thomas Book* (copr. 1896); P. E. Thomas, *Proc. of Sundry Citizens of Baltimore . . . for Intercourse between that City and the Western States* (Baltimore, 1827); G. W. Howard, *The Monumental City* (1873–76), pt. 2; Edward Hungerford, *The Story of the Baltimore and Ohio Railroad, 1827–1927* (1928), vol. I; obituaries in *Sun* (Baltimore), Sept. 2, and *Baltimore American and Commercial Advertiser*, Sept. 3, 1861. The mural painting, "Builders of the Baltimore and Ohio," Baltimore and Ohio Building, Baltimore, shows Thomas at the extreme left.]

B. M.

THOMAS, PHILIP FRANCIS (Sept. 12, 1810–Oct. 2, 1890), secretary of the treasury, congressman from Maryland, and governor, was born in Easton, Talbot County, Md., and figured in Maryland politics for more than half a century. He was the son of Maria (Francis) and Tristram Thomas, a prominent physician, and a descendant of Tristram Thomas who settled in Talbot County in 1666. After attending the Easton academy he studied at Dickinson College for two years, until his college course was abruptly terminated by a youthful prank. He then returned home to read law in the office of William Hayward and was admitted to the bar in 1831. Defying the political affiliations of his family and neighbors in this Whig stronghold, he declared himself, unsuccessfully, as Democratic candidate for the state legislature in 1834. Undaunted by defeat, he offered himself again in 1836, when he advocated reapportionment of representation in the state Assembly, a most unpopular measure on the Eastern Shore, and yet again in 1837. In 1838, however, he piled up a majority greater than that accorded the governor. In 1838 he was named congressional candidate and defeated his veteran opponent, James Alfred Pearce [*q.v.*]. For personal reasons he declined a renomination and resumed his law practice. He accepted, however, appointment as judge of the Eastern Shore land office court.

His prominence in the Assembly, to which he returned in 1843 and 1845, won him the Democratic nomination for governor in 1847 and suc-

cess at the polls. In his inaugural address he undertook a campaign to replace the seventy-year-old constitution by one more modern. It was at this time that the directors of the Baltimore and Ohio Railroad offered him the presidency of the road, even urging him to name his own salary. He declined the portfolio of the navy offered by Pierce because of the inadequacy of the salary but soon accepted the post of collector of the port at Baltimore. When a change in administration lost him that position, he practised law for a time in St. Louis, Mo. President Buchanan offered him, first, the governorship of Utah Territory, then the secretaryship of the treasury, and, finally, the humble post of commissioner of patents, which he accepted. Within a few months he resigned in order to enter the cabinet finally as secretary of the treasury, but he felt obliged to retire within a month, with the southern members of the cabinet. Though he took no part in the Civil War, it is known that his sympathies were with the Confederacy and that his only son joined the southern army. This attitude cost him a seat in the federal Senate, for, when the conservatives obtained control of the Maryland legislature, to which he had returned in 1867, and chose him senator, he was denied his seat on the charge of disloyalty. The vote of a Democrat against Johnson's impeachment seemed so necessary that Thomas urged immediate choice of a democratic candidate who could not be challenged. However, his loyalty was not questioned when he was elected to the House of Representatives in 1874. After a single term in Congress, he returned once more in 1878 to the Maryland Assembly in the hope of being elected to the federal Senate but was defeated in caucus. He made his final unsuccessful attempt at the coveted senatorship by allowing himself to be returned to the assembly of 1884. On Feb. 5, 1835, he was married to Sarah Maria Kerr. After her death in 1870 he was married, Jan. 29, 1876, to Clintonia (Wright) May. Of his thirteen children, three daughters survived him.

[M. P. Andrews, *Tercentenary Hist. of Md.* (1925), vol. IV; H. E. Buchholz, *Governors of Md.* (1908); Oswald Tilghman, *Hist. of Talbot County, Md.* (1915); E. S. Riley, *A Hist. of the General Assembly of Md.* (1905); R. H. Spencer, *Thomas Family of Talbot County, Md.* (1914); *Baltimore American* and *Sun* (Baltimore), Oct. 3, 1890.]

E. L.

THOMAS, RICHARD HENRY (Jan. 26, 1854–Oct. 3, 1904), religious leader, physician, and author, was born in Baltimore, Md., son of Dr. Richard Henry and Phebe (Clapp) Thomas, and a descendant of Philip Thomas who emigrated from Wales and settled on Chesapeake Bay in 1651. His parents were members of the

Society of Friends. He was a sickly child, though mentally keen, sensitive, and imaginative. He entered the sophomore class in Haverford College in 1869 and received the degree of B.A. in 1872. After three years at the University of Maryland, where he received the degree of M.D. in 1875, he studied in London (1876), at the Johns Hopkins University (1876–77) as a special student in biology, and in Vienna (1880–81). He was professor of the diseases of throat and chest in the Woman's Medical College of Baltimore from 1882 to 1893, and at two different periods was dean of the faculty. He prepared many medical papers for this institution, and was a beloved and effective teacher. Early in life he showed a profound interest in religion, and before he finished his medical studies he had begun to be a public interpreter of the Quaker faith and ideals. Recorded a minister of the Society of Friends in 1883, he became one of the foremost ministers in that Society in his generation, and a leading interpreter of its principles both in America and England. On Mar. 28, 1878, he married in London Anna Lloyd Braithwaite, daughter of J. Bevan Braithwaite, who was one of the most distinguished English Quakers. One daughter was born of this union. Traveling extensively with his father-in-law in England, Europe, and America, Thomas concentrated his interest on the interpretation of Christianity to meet the challenges of modern science and criticism. His preaching came to many in England and America as a solvent of doubt, and he helped many of the youth of his generation to adjust their religious faith to the new discoveries of the age. He was a clear and effective advocate of methods of peace as a solution for international controversies. For several years he was president of the Peace Association of Friends in America.

He possessed a poetical gift and wrote poetry throughout his life, much of which was published in contemporary periodicals. His writings include one volume of collected poems, *Echoes and Pictures* (London, 1895); a novel, *Penelve* (1898); and *The History of the Society of Friends in America* (1894), with his brother, Allen C. Thomas, in which he interpreted the original Quaker message and treated the history of the two American "separations." He wrote a striking paraphrase translation of the medieval hymn, "Veni Sancte Spiritus," which was praised by the poet Whittier. He was joint editor and founder of the *Interchange*, a periodical. Two of his most important essays were printed in the third volume of *Present Day Papers* (5 vols., 1898–1902) under the title "Fides et Spes Medici." He died in Baltimore. His reminis-

cences were printed after his death in *Richard H. Thomas, M.D., Life and Letters* (1905), edited by his wife. His greatest single characteristic was his religious influence on other lives, made very evident in the numerous letters written to him.

[In addition to Thomas' reminiscences, see L. B. Thomas, *The Thomas Book* (copr. 1896); *Who's Who in America*, 1903–05; *Biog. Cat. . . . Matriculates of Haverford Coll.* (1922); death notice in *Sun* (Baltimore), Oct. 4, 1904.]　　　　　　　R. M. J.

THOMAS, ROBERT BAILEY (Apr. 24, 1766–May 19, 1846), founder, editor, and publisher of the *Farmer's Almanack*, was born at Grafton, Mass., the son of William and Azubah (Goodale) Thomas. Both his father and his grandfather were men of some education; the grandfather, William Thomas, emigrated from Wales about 1718 and about 1720 settled in Marblehead. Young Thomas grew up in Sterling (later West Boylston), Mass., where his father was a farmer and a schoolmaster. Although it was intended that he should go to Harvard, he preferred self-education, which consisted of reading all the books in his father's library. Among these was James Ferguson's *Astronomy Explained* (1756), which first gave him the idea of "calculating an Almanack." But at sixteen he realized that he lacked the necessary mathematical background for astronomical computations, so he temporarily followed in his father's footsteps and became a school-teacher. He left this occupation almost immediately to become an apprentice bookbinder, and at twenty-four took the first step toward his goal. He had been studying mathematics and astronomy; now he hired a printer, N. Coverly, to print a thousand copies of a spelling book—William Perry's *The Only Sure Guide to the English Tongue; or, New Pronouncing Spelling Books* (1790),—bound them himself, and sold them to the country schools. With the profits he paid his tuition in and attended a mathematics school in Boston run by Osgood Carleton, an almanac-maker. In 1792, when Carleton retired, he stepped into the breach with an almanac of his own—shrewdly titled *The Farmer's Almanac . . . for the Year of Our Lord 1793* (1792). It was afterwards called *The Farmer's Almanack*, and later *The Old Farmer's Almanack*.

This was a success from the start, mainly because Thomas knew his audience, an intelligent group of well-to-do farmers. His realization of the intelligence of his readers led him into an unprecedented and heretical departure from the science of almanac-making—the omission of the *Homo Signorum* (Man of the Zodiac). He considered astrology quackery, and thought the stars followed their courses with no influence on the life of man. Consequently, he omitted the conventionalized figure of the naked man surrounded by the zodiacal signs, which were connected by arrows to the organs of the body each had under its especial care. The zodiac signs themselves he did not omit. With characteristic shrewdness, however, he translated them into the terms of the farmer's daily life. Gemini, the Twins, were no longer Castor and Pollux, but two farmers walking through a field of wheat. In Thomas' *Almanack* all questions of the day were touched upon: slavery, the Indian wars, witchcraft, the morality of the theatre, and the condition of the post roads. These discussions were larded with agricultural advice, poetry, and philosophical comment, homely epigrams and pointed wit, some culled from the classics but more being of Thomas' own production. Among maps of the traveled roads between Quebec and Savannah, too, there might appear stanzas of doggerel exuding the patriotic zeal of the new Union, or an imposing list of the "First-line ships of the American Navy," thrillingly set down in order of their complement of guns, for in those feverish days patriotic material never failed to arouse interest.

On Nov. 17, 1803, Thomas married Hannah Beaman of Princeton, N. J. By this time the *Almanack* was ten years along the road of success. It was sold in Boston, Salem, New York, and Philadelphia, but the bulk of the sales was in the backwoods reached by itinerant pack pedlars, whose books formed the literary "circulating" libraries of the day. Thomas' accounts show that in the decade 1820–30 more than 200,-000 copies were sold by these men to outlying readers. In 1837, by popular demand, Thomas ran a woodcut of himself—a Pickwickian, round-faced character, as healthy and hearty as the *Almanack* itself. A memoir of his life appeared in the *Almanack* in the years 1833–37 and 1839. In the spring of 1846, putting aside a proof sheet of his *Almanack* for 1847, and remarking that his eyes were dim "from reading such a quantity of fine print," Thomas went to his room, lay down, and in a little while quietly died. He had no children. In his will he entrusted further publication of the *Almanack* to two nephews, in whose hands it stayed until 1904.

[The date of death is from *Vital Records of West Boylston, Mass.* (1911). See also G. L. Kittredge, *The Old Farmer and His Almanack* (1920) and H. M. Robinson, "The Almanac," *Bookman,* June–July 1932.]

H. M. R.

THOMAS, SETH (Aug. 19, 1785–Jan. 29, 1859), pioneer clock manufacturer, was born at Wolcott, Conn., the son of James and Martha (Barnes) Thomas. His father was an immigrant from Scotland. Thomas had a very meager education consisting of intermittent attendance at the district school, and at an early age began his apprenticeship as a carpenter and joiner. Upon completing this he worked for a number of years building houses and barns, generally in the country and towns near his home, although occasionally he went as far afield for work as New Haven, where he spent some time in the construction of Long Wharf. About the time this work was completed, Eli Terry [q.v.] at Plymouth, Conn., was ready to begin his unusual venture of making clocks at a wholesale rate. He needed both craftsmen and financial help, and suggested to Thomas—who, though he had very little money, was a skilful wood-worker— that he join him and Silas Hoadley in the undertaking. Between 1807 and 1810 the firm of Terry, Thomas & Hoadley was busily engaged in making four thousand clocks. In the first year they made and fitted up the necessary machinery to be operated by water power; in the second year they made one thousand clocks, and in the third year, three thousand. These were all "hang-up" or "wag-on-the-wall" clocks, usually without cases, the purchasers depending upon local cabinetmakers to make the grandfather cases if they were desired. In this undertaking Thomas did the joiner work, and fitted the wheels and different clock parts together. Upon the completion of this job in 1810, Thomas & Hoadley purchased Terry's interest in the firm and for two years continued making clocks in partnership.

In 1812 Thomas sold out to Hoadley and began a clock factory of his own in Plymouth Hollow. While he was not an inventive genius, he was an excellent mechanic and a keen business man, and from the beginning of this undertaking he was successful. Two years after he began operations he boldly paid Terry one thousand dollars (an unheard-of price at the time) for the manufacturing rights of the latter's popular shelf clock, and was soon making and selling as many clocks as Terry. As his business developed Thomas built a mill for rolling brass and making wire at Plymouth Hollow, and operated it in conjunction with the clock factory. Finally, in 1853, he established the business on a firm foundation by organizing the Seth Thomas Clock Company, with a capital of seventy-five thousand dollars. Thomas was twice married: first, on Apr. 20, 1808, to Philena (or Philinda) Tuttle (d. Mar. 12, 1810) of Plymouth, and second, on Apr. 14, 1811, to Laura Andrews of Plymouth, who with three sons and three daughters survived him.

His son Seth (1816–1888) carried on the business and enlarged it. Shortly after Thomas' death at Plymouth the town was divided by act of the legislature, and the western portion, which contained the Thomas factory, was made into a new town, named Thomaston in his honor.

[Samuel Orcutt, *Hist. of the Town of Wolcott (Conn.) from 1731 to 1874* (1874); Francis Atwater, *Hist. of the Town of Plymouth, Conn.* (1895); W. I. Milham, *Time & Timekeepers* (1923); Mrs. N. H. Moore, *The Old Clock Book* (1911); Henry Terry, *Am. Clock Making, Its Early Hist., and Present Extent of the Business* (1870); death notice in *Columbian Weekly Reg.* (New Haven), Feb. 5, 1859.] C. W. M—n.

THOMAS, THEODORE [See THOMAS, CHRISTIAN FRIEDRICH THEODORE, 1835–1905].

THOMAS, THEODORE GAILLARD (Nov. 21, 1831–Feb. 28, 1903), obstetrician and gynecologist, was born on Edisto Island, near Charleston, S. C. His father, the Rev. Edward Thomas, a priest in the Episcopal Church, was a descendant of Samuel Thomas, an Anglican clergyman, who came to America about 1700; his mother, Jane Marshall (Gaillard), was the daughter of Judge Theodore Gaillard, descendant of a Huguenot refugee who fled from France and settled in Charleston after the revocation of the Edict of Nantes. Thomas entered the College of Charleston at the age of fourteen. In 1852 he graduated from the Medical College of South Carolina, and in this same year left New York, sailing on a coasting vessel as a common sailor. After serving as an interne at Bellevue Hospital, he spent six months at the immigrant's hospital on Ward's Island. His training here was supplemented by a year in Paris and several months at the Rotunda Hospital, Dublin. He returned to the United States in 1855 to begin the practice of his profession in New York, and was soon taken into partnership by Dr. John T. Metcalfe. With Dr. William Donaghe he started a "quiz class" which proved so successful that he was soon appointed adjunct to the clinic of obstetrics in the medical department of the University of the City of New York. In 1855 he was made professor of obstetrics, but resigned this post in 1863 to accept an appointment at the College of Physicians and Surgeons, where he succeeded to the chair of obstetrics in 1865. In 1879 he was transferred to the chair of gynecology and in 1881 became professor of clinical gynecology in which capacity he continued to teach until his retirement as professor emeritus in 1890. From 1872 to 1887 he was also attending surgeon to the Woman's Hospital. After 1879 he devoted himself entirely to gynecology, serving on the staffs of several hospitals and attending to private practice as late as 1900.

His contributions to his profession were varied. He was one of the first to distinguish the cervix and body of the uterus as different organs. He played a principal part in disproving the inflammatory nature of chronic metritis, as well as in putting a stop to the wide-spread custom of alarming patients about ulcers. He was the inventor of many surgical instruments and the originator of many new methods in surgery, most notably, perhaps, the operation of laparo-elytrotomy. He was the first to remove a small ovarian tumor by cutting through the vagina. As early as 1867 he suggested and used an incubator. Although a careful operator, he was rapid and deft and not afraid of progress. He was willing to try antiseptic surgery in its pioneer days. With the orator's rich voice and an impressive style, he had few peers as a clinical lecturer, enlivening his discourses with a variety of phrase and illustration. His writings were fluent but exact. The chapters on chronic cervical and chronic corporeal endometritis in his *Practical Treatise on the Diseases of Women* (1868) made that textbook famous. It was translated into twelve languages and went through many editions, a classic of its kind. He wrote numerous medical articles and was the author of *A Contribution to the History of the Huguenots of South Carolina* (1887), which includes notes about his own ancestors. He was a member of many medical societies, was founder and president of the New York Obstetrical Society, and third president (1879) of the American Gynecological Society.

Thomas was married twice: first to a cousin, Mary Gaillard, and second, in 1862, to Mary Theodosia Willard, daughter of John Hart Willard and grand-daughter of Emma (Hart) Willard [*q.v.*]. He had four sons and one daughter. His sister, Jane, became the wife of Dr. Edwin Samuel Gaillard [*q.v.*]. Thomas was a man of great culture, a born leader, and one who brought confidence and cheer into the sick room. He was kind, generous, and hospitable, and his friendship and advice were sought by many. He was a handsome, well-groomed man, of robust build and medium height. Physically alert, he was known to be an excellent horseman. He died suddenly of rupture of the aorta at Thomasville, Ga.

[*Yearbook of the Medic. Asso. of the Greater City of N. Y.* (1903); *Trans. Am. Gynecol. Soc.*, vol. XXVIII (1903); *Addresses at the Dinner given to Dr. T. Gaillard Thomas on His Seventieth Birthday* (1901); William Gaillard, *Hist. and Pedigrees of the House of Gaillard* (1872); L. B. Thomas, *The Thomas Book* (copr. 1896); *S. C. Hist. and Geneal. Mag.*, Apr. 1903; *Who's Who in America*, 1901–02; H. A. Kelly and W. L. Burrage, *Am. Medic. Biogs.* (1920); John Shrady, *The Coll. of Phys. and Surgeons, N. Y., A Hist.* (n.d.), vol. II; *Am. Jour. Obstetrics*, Apr. 1903; *N. Y. Jour. of Gynecol. and Obstetrics*, Dec. 1891; *N. Y. Times*, Mar. 4, 1903.]   G. L. A.

THOMAS, WILLIAM WIDGERY (Aug. 26, 1839–Apr. 25, 1927), lawyer, politician, diplomat, was born in Portland, Me., the son of William Widgery and Elizabeth White (Goddard) Thomas. After his graduation from Bowdoin College in 1860, he studied law until he was appointed a carrier of diplomatic dispatches in 1862. He then served successively as vice-consul-general at Constantinople, acting consul-general at Galatz, Moldavia, and consul at Gothenburg, Sweden. In 1865 he resigned and in the following year completed his legal studies at Harvard, whereupon he established his residence at Portland and became active in politics. He served as commissioner of public lands for Maine (1869), as a member of the commission of immigration (1870–73), as a member of the Maine House of Representatives (1873–75), and as a member of the upper house of the state legislature (1879).

During his residence at Gothenburg, Thomas had acquired a deep attachment for Sweden and a great admiration for its people (he learned to speak fluent Swedish and translated into English Viktor Rydberg's masterpiece *The Last Athenian*, 1869), and in 1870 he played an important part in the establishment of the Swedish settlement in Aroostook County, Me. As a member of the commission of immigration appointed to find means of attracting settlers to increase the declining population of Maine, he went to Gothenburg in May 1870, embarked on an extensive advertising campaign in the newspapers, commissioned agents armed with circulars to visit the northern provinces, and himself visited many parishes. On July 23, 1870, with Thomas as their leader, a party of some fifty immigrants arrived at a spot in the woods destined to be known as New Sweden. The advertising campaign in Sweden continued, and from time to time new immigrants came, until at the end of a decade Maine's Swedish colony boasted a population of almost eight hundred. In 1883, as a reward for his services to the Republican party, he received the appointment of minister to Sweden and Norway, and served under four presidents (1883–85, 1889–94, 1897–1905). He was married on Oct. 11, 1887, to Dagmar Törnebladh (d. 1912), a Swedish noblewoman. In 1892 he published a bulky volume, *Sweden and the Swedes* (which was also published in Sweden), a description of the country and the customs of the people, with some account of his experiences as a diplomat. After his retirement as a diplomat

he lived in Portland. His ability to deliver speeches in Swedish made him a valuable stump speaker in states like Minnesota and Illinois, and he continued to hold a position of prominence in Maine. The genial founder of the Swedish colony was always a welcome visitor there, and was present on a number of ceremonial occasions. He was married a second time, on June 2, 1915, to Mrs. Aina Törnebladh. He had two children by his first marriage, and one adopted son.

[See *Who's Who in America*, 1926–27; *Biog. Rev. . . . of Cumberland County, Me.* (1896); Sidney Perham, *Address of Gov. Perham to the Legislature of the State of Me., Jan. 1871* (1871); W. W. Thomas, *Reports of the Board and Commissioner of Immigration, 1870* (1871); E. H. Elwell, *Aroostook: with some Account . . . of the Colony of Swedes, Settled in the Town of New Sweden* (1878); *Celebration of the Decennial Anniversary of the Founding of New Sweden, Me.* (1881); *The Story of New Sweden* (Portland, 1896); and obituary in *Portland Press Herald*, Apr. 26, 1927. Advertisements and news items about the Swedish colony appeared in *Amerika* (Gothenburg), June 30, 1870, June 14, 1871; *Öresunds-Posten* (Öresund), Mar. 20, Apr. 14, 1871; *Hemlandet* (Chicago), Mar. 11, 1873; *Nya Verlden* (Gothenburg), Apr. 3, 1873. In the papers of John Lind at Minneapolis are two letters from Thomas, Dec. 17 and 26, 1888, with reference to his diplomatic appointment.]   G. M. S.

THOMES, WILLIAM HENRY (May 5, 1824–Mar. 6, 1895), author, was born in Portland, Me., the child of Job and Mary (Lewis) Thomes. The family shortly afterwards moved to Boston, and there both parents died. The orphan, reared by a guardian, did not take well to schooling, and in October 1842 shipped on the *Admittance* in the California hide-trade. His experiences are related with essential accuracy in his *On Land and Sea* (1883), and are comparable to Richard Henry Dana's as described in *Two Years before the Mast*. The ship arrived in Monterey, Mar. 4, 1843, and after numerous voyages up and down the coast sailed from San Diego, Jan. 25, 1846. Shortly before this, however, Thomes had deserted or, according to a less likely story, had arranged by a ruse to be left behind. The chief authority for his life in the next year is his *Lewey and I* (1884), which even he admitted to be largely fiction. It is probable, however, that he was knocked about considerably, saw some military service during the conquest of California, and left California in December 1846. By way of Mazatlán and England Thomes returned to Boston. There he served as printer and reporter on the *Boston Daily Times* for about a year, and also married. His wife seems to have been the daughter of Capt. Peter Peterson, his old master on the *Admittance* (Bancroft, *post*). But he got the gold-fever, and joined the Boston and California Joint Stock Mining and Trading Company, which sailed on the *Edward Everett* in

January 1849 and arrived in San Francisco on July 6. Although not an officer, Thomes had risen to be of some importance in the company, and was assigned to remain with the ship. After the break-up of the company in August, he mined at Bidwell's Bar, with some success for a while; but finally, broken in health and almost penniless, he returned to San Francisco. There he served as caretaker of a ship. In 1851 he sailed for the Hawaiian Islands, and after some months' residence there, visited Guam, the Philippines, China, and finally the gold mines of Victoria. Of his activities during these three years little can be determined. He made some money, probably by keeping a store at Ballarat, and returned to the United States by way of the Cape of Good Hope early in 1855.

After a short time in New Orleans he returned to Boston, and for several years was a reporter for the *Boston Herald*. He was also married again, to Frances Ullen. About 1860 he became a member of Elliott and Thomes, publishers of the *American Union*, a weekly magazine. For this he wrote *The Gold Hunters' Adventures; or, Life in Australia* (1864), a long tale of lurid adventure. Its success encouraged him to its sequel, *The Bushrangers* (1866), and his profession was established. His other books were *The Gold Hunters in Europe* (1868), *The Whaleman's Adventures* (1872), *Life in the East Indies* (1873), *A Slaver's Adventures* (1872), *Running the Blockade* (1875), *The Belle of Australia* (1883), *The Ocean Rovers* (1896), and *Daring Deeds* (n.d.). With the exception of *On Land and Sea,* which contains vivid and accurate descriptions of early California, his books are of no literary or historical importance; they are little removed, indeed, from the dime-novel. Partial figures, however, indicate a sale of over half a million copies by 1895.

In later life Thomes was a member successively of Elliott, Thomes and Talbot, and Thomes and Talbot. Publications of these firms included the *Flag of our Union,* and *Ballou's Monthly.* Thomes lost heavily in the fire of 1872 but otherwise was highly successful in business. His activities included politics, Masonry, and collecting. In 1888 he organized, and became president of, the Society of California Pioneers of New England, and in 1890 he was the leader of its elaborate excursion to California. He died suddenly of heart-failure.

[In addition to Thomes's autobiographical books, see his "The Reminiscences of a Gold Hunter," *Ballou's Monthly Mag.,* Sept. 1882, reprinted in *Alta California* (San Francisco), Oct. 22, 29, 1882; O. T. Howe, *Argonauts of '49* (1923); Nicholas Ball, *The Pioneers of '49* (1891); H. H. Bancroft, *Hist. of Cal.,* vol. ʿi (1886), Pioneer Register and Index; obituary in *Boston Evening Transcript,* Mar. 7, 1895. A manuscript statement by Thomes is in the Bancroft Lib., Berkeley, Cal. The names of Thomes's parents and information about his second marriage were supplied by Clarence H. Carter, of Boston.]   G. R. S., JR.

THOMPSON, ALFRED WORDSWORTH (May 26, 1840–Aug. 28, 1896), landscape, figure, and historical painter, was born in Baltimore, Md. His parents are said to have been of Maryland and Virginia stock, their ancestors early settlers on the tributaries of Chesapeake Bay. Thompson was educated in Baltimore, and, though he began the study of law in his father's office, he turned to art before coming of age. At the time of John Brown's raid he went to Harpers Ferry, and made drawings of the places of interest and a likeness of Brown, whom he visited in prison. He opened a studio in Mulberry Street, Baltimore, just before the Civil War began. Many of the war pictures which appeared in *Harper's Weekly* and the *Illustrated London News* during the first year of the war were his. In 1861 he went to Paris, where he was a pupil successively of C. G. Gleyre, Émile Lambinet, A. Pasini, Adolphe Yvon, and finally of Antoine Barye, the sculptor, under whose tutelage he studied the anatomy of the horse. In 1864–65 he worked at the École des Beaux-Arts, and in the same year he sent to the Salon his first picture, "Moorlands of Au Fargis." To make a painting of the great Gauli glacier he climbed in the company of three mountaineers to a desolate place ten thousand feet above sea-level, surrounded by snow and ice. Later he made some extensive tours on foot through the Eifelwald in Germany, along the banks of the Rhine and the Danube, and through the rugged regions of the Tyrol and Bohemia. One of his trips was a six months' walk from Heidelberg to Calabria in the south of Italy. He walked through Sicily and climbed to the summit of Mount Etna. At a later period he made several visits to Corsica and Sardinia on mule-back.

In 1868 he returned to America and opened a studio in New York, where he soon received a gratifying measure of recognition. He was one of the first members of the Society of American Artists. After his election as an Academician in 1875, he regularly sent pictures to the annual exhibitions of the National Academy. To the Centennial Exhibition, Philadelphia, 1876, he sent "On the Sands, East Hampton" and "Virginia in the Olden Time," and to the Paris Exposition of 1878 his "School-house on the Hill." Among the best known of his works are "Annapolis in 1776," in the Albright Art Gallery, Buffalo, N. Y.; "The Parting Guests," owned by the New York Historical Society; "Old

Bruton Church, Virginia, in the Time of Lord Dunmore," in the Metropolitan Museum, New York; and "Washington Reviewing the Troops, 1777." In his later years he made occasional voyages to France, and traveled in Spain, Morocco, and Asia Minor, his zeal for fresh subjects leading him to wander in many lands. In the early part of his career the scenery of Italy engaged his attention; later he turned to the delineation of American landscape and life; and finally he ventured into the realm of history. He painted a few scenes from the Revolutionary period, or the one just preceding it, "with a smoothness and skill of handling recalling that if he worked under Gleyre, he was also a pupil of Pasini" (Samuel Isham, *The History of American Painting*, 1905, p. 349). He died at Summit, N. J., aged fifty-six. He was survived by his widow, whose name is said to have been Pompella or Pumpelly.

[*Boston Globe*, May 7, 1873; G. W. Sheldon, *Am. Painters* (1879); S. G. W. Benjamin, *Our Am. Artists* (1879); Clara E. Clement and Laurence Hutton, *Artists of the Nineteenth Century* (1879), vol. II; Edward King, in *Monthly Illustrator*, May 1895; *Cat. of Am. Paintings Belonging to William T. Evans* (1900); *Illustrated Cat.: Paintings in the Metropolitan Museum of Art, N. Y.* (1905); *Reports . . . U. S. Commissioner . . . Paris Universal Exposition, 1878* (1880), vol. I, p. 389; obituaries in *N. Y. Tribune*, Aug. 29, and *Sun* (Baltimore), Aug. 31, 1896.]   W. H. D.

THOMPSON, ARTHUR WEBSTER (May 8, 1875–Nov. 9, 1930), railroad and utilities executive, was born at Erie, Pa., the son of Sheldon Elisha and Barbara LaVerne (Webster) Thompson. He grew up in Meadville, Pa., and after preparing in the local schools entered Allegheny College, where he was graduated with the degree of civil engineer in 1897. His father had been in the employ of the Santa Fé railroad and while Arthur was still an undergraduate he spent one summer as a rodman on location work for the Bessemer & Southwestern road, and another in the locomotive shops of the Erie Railroad at Meadville. For a brief period after his graduation he worked as instrument man on the Pittsburgh & Lake Erie, but within a short time, Aug. 7, 1899, he went to the Baltimore & Ohio as chief of a party of surveys.

With the Baltimore & Ohio he spent most of his extremely active life. In a space of a little less than twenty years he headed its most important and diverse departments—engineering, operation, traffic, and commercial development. At the age of twenty-eight, he was superintendent of one of the most important divisions of the road; at thirty-five, he was its general manager; and a year later he became its vice-president in charge of operation. At the beginning of the

World War he was senior vice-president, in full charge of operating, traffic, engineering, and commercial development. The final weeks of the war brought governmental control of the entire railroad system of the United States. In the new order of things, Thompson was made federal manager in charge of a large group of roads, of which Baltimore & Ohio was the most important. He established headquarters at Pittsburgh and kept traffic moving steadily against almost insuperable odds and difficulties.

His work at Pittsburgh brought him to the personal attention of numerous capitalists and industrial leaders, with the result that on Feb. 1, 1919, he abandoned steam railroading and became the president of the Philadelphia Company, which owned and operated the street railroads and the lighting systems and other utilities of Pittsburgh. His record here maintained the high level that he had set at Baltimore; hardly a half dozen years had passed before, in 1926, he was made president of one of the outstanding utilities of the country—the United Gas Improvement Company of Philadelphia. This post he resigned, shortly before the time of his death. Personally he did not approve the "high financing" of the period.

He was a man of keen wit, great kindliness, and a charm that made almost everyone associated with him his friend. His homes were veritable treasure houses of the many things that interested him, and he gathered about him men of every thought and shade of opinion. Intensely democratic, he was nevertheless a good disciplinarian, and an excellent executive. He was married, June 29, 1905, to Marion Dinwiddie Gordon, daughter of Judge Robert H. Gordon, of Cumberland, Md., who with two sons survived him. He died in Pittsburgh.

[T. W. Morris, "Biog. Sketch of Arthur W. Thompson" and P. H. Utech, "Reminiscences of Arthur Webster Thompson," MSS. in possession of author; W. H. and M. R. Webster, *Hist. and Geneal. of the Gov. John Webster Family of Conn.* (1915); E. A. Smith, *Allegheny—A Century of Education* (1916); *Railway Rev. and Outlook*, Aug. 1919; *Who's Who in America*, 1930–31; *Public Ledger* (Phila.), Nov. 10, 1930.]   E. H.

THOMPSON, BENJAMIN (Mar. 26, 1753– Aug. 21, 1814), better remembered by his title, Count Rumford, physicist, organizer, and philanthropist, the only child of Benjamin and Ruth (Simonds) Thompson, was born in Woburn, Mass., where his ancestor, James Thompson, had settled in 1642. His paternal grandfather, in whose house he was born, was Capt. Ebenezer Thompson; his maternal grandfather had performed distinguished service in the French and Indian Wars. His father died in November

1754, and his mother in 1756 married Josiah Pierce, Jr., of Woburn. A small inheritance from his grandfather was used toward the support and education of the boy. He attended school in Woburn, Byfield, and Medford. His writing was clear and spelling accurate, and he early showed an aptitude for drafting and mathematical studies. His guardians, realizing that he was not likely to develop into a thriving farmer, apprenticed him on Oct. 14, 1766, to John Appleton of Salem, a warehouseman and dealer in British goods, with whom he remained for about three years. He seems to have performed his duties satisfactorily but to have been more interested in tools, mechanical devices, and other scientific matters. He studied algebra, geometry, astronomy, and higher mathematics with the Rev. Thomas Barnard of Salem, and carried on experiments and scientific discussions and correspondence with his lifelong friend, Loammi Baldwin, 1744–1807 [q.v.], of Woburn. In October 1769 he commenced the study of the French language at Boston and began to keep a boyish notebook which still survives and shows the breadth of his early interests.

In 1771 he commenced the study of medicine with Dr. John Hay of Woburn, and while continuing with him, contrived to attend the lectures of Professor John Winthrop at Harvard. He taught school for a short time, first probably at Bradford, Mass., and later at Concord, N. H., where he met and, about November 1772, married, the wealthy widow of Col. Benjamin Rolfe, Sarah (Walker) Rolfe (Oct. 6, 1739–Jan. 19, 1792), daughter of the Rev. Timothy Walker. On their wedding tour the couple visited Portsmouth, where Thompson's fine appearance on horseback, his courtly manner, and his new family connections so impressed Governor Wentworth that he at once commissioned him to a majorship which happened to be vacant in the 2nd Provincial Regiment of New Hampshire. The appointment aroused the jealousy and resentment of experienced junior officers who were qualified for promotion. Throughout his life Thompson seems to have neglected no opportunity for his own advancement. He knew how to ingratiate himself with men of powerful position, and incurred the enmity of those of lesser rank.

For two years after his marriage, Thompson devoted himself chiefly to farming his wife's land and to conducting experiments with gunpowder. Their only child, Sarah, was born Oct. 18, 1774, in the Rolfe mansion; her parents separated in May of the following year and never saw one another again. Thompson's indebtedness to Governor Wentworth committed him in a manner to the British or Loyalist side in the Revolutionary War, though he seems at first to have had no strong inclination toward one side or the other. In the summer of 1774 he was summoned before a committee of the people of Concord to answer to the charge of "being unfriendly to the cause of Liberty," but was discharged for lack of evidence. He was publicly threatened at Concord and sought refuge at Woburn, where he was again tried on a similar charge with similar result. He mingled with the patriots of Medford, Cambridge, and Charlestown, and applied for a commission in Washington's army but was refused, probably because of the disapproval of the officers from New Hampshire. He then definitely chose the British side. Leaving Woburn on Oct. 13, 1775, he embarked on the British frigate *Scarborough* at Newport. The vessel proceeded to Boston and lay in the harbor until after the town had been evacuated by the British forces in March 1776, then proceeded to England with dispatches. On reaching London, Thompson quickly secured the favor of Lord George Germain, secretary of state for the colonies, was given a position in the Colonial Office, and was soon appointed to a sinecure, the secretaryship of the Province of Georgia. He continued his experiments on gunpowder, sent a paper on cohesion to the Royal Society, became acquainted with its president, Sir Joseph Banks, and in 1779 was elected a fellow of that body. In September 1780 he was made under-secretary of state for the Northern Department, and later, probably in 1781, was commissioned lieutenant-colonel in the British army for service in America. In March 1782 he was engaged in action near Charlestown, S. C.; he then served on Long Island until April 1783, where he commanded a regiment and built a fort for winter quarters near Huntington. In August of that year, after his return to England, he was made colonel of the King's American Dragoons.

Having retired from active service on half pay, with the King's permission to leave England, he set out in September 1783 for a tour of the Continent. At Strasbourg he met Prince Maximilian des Deux Ponts, field-marshal of France, who gave him a letter of introduction to his uncle, the Elector of Bavaria. The latter, impressed with Thompson's abilities, invited him to enter his services in a half military, half civil capacity, and Thompson returned to England to secure the permission of the King. The King approved and on Feb. 23, 1784, conferred on him the honor of knighthood (the original parchment is in the possession of the American Academy of Arts and Sciences). Sir Benjamin returned at once to Munich, where he was made colonel of cavalry and general aide-de-camp and in 1788 major-general, privy councilor of state, and head of the war department. On request of the Elector, the King of Poland conferred on him the Order of Saint Stanislaus. He was elected to the academies of Berlin, Munich, and Mannheim. In 1791 the Elector of Bavaria, being at the time Vicar of the Empire, made him a count of the Holy Roman Empire, with the Order of the White Eagle; Thompson chose the title Count Rumford after the old name of Concord, N. H. He improved the living conditions of the soldiers of the Bavarian army, their homes, food, clothing, and the use of their leisure, abolished beggary in Munich, established workhouses, and devised methods and equipment for the preparation of wholesome food cheaply on a large scale. In 1790 he converted a large tract of waste land on the outskirts of Munich into the Englisches Garten, where, in 1795, upon his return to England, the citizens erected a monument in recognition of his services. He continued his scientific experiments—on gunpowder, on the transmission of heat, on the absorption of moisture by various substances. He concluded that the large part of the heat of a hot body cooling in air is lost by radiation, and showed by his experiments on the boring of cannon and the friction of metal surfaces that heat is a mode of motion.

In the fall of 1795 he returned to England in order to renew his friendships with men of science, to read papers before the Royal Society, and to publish the first volume (1796) of his *Essays, Political, Economical, and Philosophical* (3rd ed., 2 vols., 1798; 5th ed., 3 vols., 1880; vol. IV added, 1802). He visited Ireland for two months in the spring of 1796, installing important improvements in the workhouses and hospitals of Dublin, and in a church, a steam-heating system. He was elected honorary member of the Royal Irish Academy of Dublin and of the Society for the Encouragement of Arts and Manufactures. His improvements in heating and cooking equipment aroused much interest in England. He installed non-smoking and more efficient fireplaces in more than 150 houses of London, among them those of Lord Palmerston, Sir Joseph Banks, and the Marquis of Salisbury. Rumford Roasters came into extensive use in Great Britain and the United States. He presented £1000 at this time to the Royal Society for the establishing of a Rumford prize and medal for "the most important discovery, or useful improvement—in any part of Europe during the preceding two years, on Heat or on Light," and

$5,000 to the American Academy of Arts and Sciences (of which he had been elected a foreign honorary member May 29, 1789), for the most important discovery in the same fields "in any part of the Continent of America, or in any of the American Islands." His letters offering these funds were both dated July 12, 1796. The first award of the Royal Society's Rumford Medal was made in 1802 to Count Rumford himself.

He had previously sent for his daughter, Sarah, to whom he seems to have sent money regularly; she joined him in London, and in midsummer, 1796, accompanied him to Munich. Here, as head of the council of regency, he was able to prevent the French and Austrian armies from entering the neutral city. He did important service in feeding and sheltering the large Bavarian force which was quartered there. The Elector made him head of the department of general police of Bavaria, and later sent him to London as minister plenipotentiary of Bavaria to Great Britain. On arriving there in September 1798, he was informed that being a British subject he would not be accepted as the minister of another nation. Disappointed and relieved of his diplomatic and political duties, he remained for a time in London devoting himself to humanitarian and scientific activities. His daughter returned to America late in the summer of 1799. He had some intention of joining her there and was offered through Rufus King, the American minister, both the inspectorship of artillery in the United States Army and the superintendency of the Military Academy, but was kept in London by the affairs of the Royal Institution. This organization, incorporated in January 1800 under the patronage of the King, was the direct outcome of Rumford's published *Proposals for Forming by Subscription in the Metropolis of the British Empire, a Public Institution for Diffusing the Knowledge and Facilitating the General Introduction of Useful Mechanical Inventions and Improvements, and for Teaching, by Courses of Philosophical Lectures and Experiments, the Application of Science to the Common Purposes of Life* (1799). He personally supervised the construction of the Royal Institution's building on Albemarle Street, lived there himself, and secured for the Institution the services of Humphry Davy.

His life in London was not altogether happy. He was not able to carry out his plans arbitrarily and without resistance as he had done in Bavaria, and he quarreled with the managers of the Royal Institution. In October 1801 he visited Munich, where he helped plan the organization of the Bavarian Academy of Arts and Sciences, and in the same month visited Paris for the first time. Here he was cordially received, found his work well known, and met Madame Lavoisier, widow of the chemist. In May 1802 he left England, never to return. He visited various places in Europe, especially Munich and Paris, and on Oct. 24, 1805, married Madame Lavoisier (Marie Anne Pierrette, née Paulze). Their life together was not happy; Thompson loved flowers and tranquility, while his wife loved neither of these but wanted dinner parties and entertainments to such an extent that he found it difficult to entertain his own friends in the quiet way he enjoyed. They separated amicably on June 30, 1809, and the terms of the marriage contract were respected as regarded their joint property. Thompson then sent to America for his daughter, and in the late autumn of 1811 she came to live with him at Auteuil, near Paris, in a house which he had rented. Here he spent much time in walking and in cultivating a flower garden. He had been elected a foreign associate of the Institute of France in 1803, attended its meetings, and from that time onward read many papers and demonstrated experiments before the Institute. He also transmitted papers to the Royal Society of London and published in its *Philosophical Transactions*. Some of these studies appeared in his *Philosophical Papers* (1802), projected as a two-volume work, of which only one volume was issued. He studied the traction of broad and of narrow wheels, favored the former, and rode about Paris in the only carriage in the city which was equipped with broad-rim wheels. He developed his calorimeter and photometer, made improvements in lamps and illumination, and described the drip coffee pot in a fascinating essay, *Of the Excellent Qualities of Coffee, and the Art of Making It in the Highest Perfection* (1812). By temperament he was not adapted to genial companionship, and he had few friends among the French men of science. He lived a lonely life and died at Auteuil during a temporary absence of his daughter. A natural son, born the year of Thompson's death, became an officer in the French army; a natural daughter had died some time before, in childhood. Thompson's will, executed Sept. 28, 1812, made a bequest to Harvard College for the establishment of a professorship, "in order to teach by regular courses of academical and public Lectures, accompanied with proper experiments, the utility of the physical and mathematical sciences for the improvement of the useful arts, and for the extension of the industry, prosperity, happiness, and well-being of Society." His daughter returned to America, and died Dec. 2, 1852, in the chamber in which she was born. The American Academy of Arts and Sciences and Harvard College at present share the expense of caring for his grave at Auteuil.

[G. E. Ellis, *Memoir of Sir Benjamin Thompson, Count Rumford, with Notices of His Daughter* (1871), published by the Am. Acad. of Arts and Sci. in connection with *The Complete Works of Count Rumford* (4 vols., 1870–75); T. E. James, "Rumford and the Royal Institution: A Retrospect," *Nature*, Sept. 19, 1931; H. B. Jones, *The Royal Institution: Its Founder and Its First Professors* (1871); F. K. Möhl, *Die vorläufer der heutigen Organisation der öffentl. Armenpflege in München, insbesondere: Das Armeninstitut des Grafen Rumford* (Erlangen, 1903); R. W. Hale, "Benjamin Thompson: Count Rumford: His Romantic Career in Statesmanship and Science," *Technology Review*, Nov. 1931; J. A. Thompson, *Count Rumford of Mass.* (1935); Leander Thompson, *Memorial of James Thompson* (1887); Allen French, *Gen. Gage's Informers* (1932); L. D. Einstein, *Divided Loyalties: Americans in England during the War of Independence* (1933); W. F. Rae, in *Dict. Nat. Biog.*; *Gentleman's Mag.*, Sept., Oct. 1814; *Times* (London), Aug. 29, 1814.]   T. L. D.

THOMPSON, CEPHAS GIOVANNI (Aug. 3, 1809–Jan. 5, 1888), painter, was born at Middleboro, Mass., a son of Cephas and Olive (Leonard) Thompson, and a descendant of John Thomson, a Welshman who emigrated to New England before 1623. He was a brother of Marietta and Jerome B. Thompson [*q.v.*], both of whom attained celebrity as artists. The elder Cephas Thompson (1775–1856) was a self-taught portraitist whose permanent home was at Middleboro, but who was accustomed winters to make painting tours of the cities from New York to New Orleans. Among his famous sitters were John Marshall, Stephen Decatur, and David Ramsay. Taught and encouraged by his father, Cephas Giovanni at eighteen set up for himself at Plymouth. He later drew from the antique at the Boston Athenaeum, and he made many portraits at Providence. In 1837 he took a studio at New York. There, a handsome little man, with engaging smile and good manners, he became a favorite in the literary and artistic coterie of which William Cullen Bryant, Fitz-Greene Halleck, and Henry T. Tuckerman [*qq.v.*] were prominent figures. He married in December 1843 Mary Gouverneur Ogden, daughter of Samuel Gouverneur Ogden, a prominent New York merchant. They had two sons and a daughter. They lived during brief periods at New York, Boston, and New Bedford, and in 1852 went to Rome, where for seven years Thompson painted portraits and copied old masters. His intimacy at this time with the Hawthorne family, also resident at Rome, is of familiar record. Nathaniel Hawthorne accorded him high praise as "earnest, faithful and religious in his worship of art" (Arvin, *post*, p. 265), and it was Julian

Hawthorne's opinion that no other artist in Rome "could paint as well as Mr. Thompson," whose color, even though "he had never learned how to draw correctly ... redeemed all and made his pictures permanently valuable" (Hawthorne, *post*, p. 262-63). This judgment has not been confirmed; Thompson's works have little value, though many of them are of historic importance as portraits of celebrities.

He returned in 1859 to New York, where for many years he painted portraits, some of them quite elaborate family groups (Tuckerman, *post*, p. 491). In 1861 he was elected an associate of the National Academy of Design. He kept up his friendships with authors and through his sister-in-law, Anna Cora Ogden Mowatt [*q.v.*], he had a large acquaintance with actors. Several of his portraits were acquired by the New York Historical Society; his likeness of Chancellor James M. Matthews, by the University of the City of New York (later New York University). In 1887 the aged artist was appointed United States inspector of life preservers at New York, a post which he filled faithfully almost to the day of his death. He died at his home, 8 East Eighty-fifth St. A follower of Swedenborg, he was buried from the Church of the New Jerusalem.

[C. H. Thompson, *A Geneal. of Descendants of John Thomson, of Plymouth, Mass.* (1890); W. O. Wheeler, *The Ogden Family in America* (1907); Thomas Weston, *Hist. of the Town of Middleboro, Mass.* (1906); Clara E. Clement and Laurence Hutton, *Artists of the Nineteenth Century* (1884); H. T. Tuckerman, *Book of the Artists* (1867); Julian Hawthorne, *Hawthorne and His Circle* (1903); Rose Hawthorne Lathrop, *Memories of Hawthorne* (1923); *The Heart of Hawthorne's Journals* (1929), ed. by Newton Arvin; death notice in *N. Y. Times*, obituary in *N. Y. Tribune*, Jan. 7, 1888.]

F. W. C.

THOMPSON, CHARLES OLIVER (Sept. 25, 1836-Mar. 17, 1885), engineer, educator, was born at East Windsor Hill, Conn., where his father, Rev. William Thompson, was a professor in the Theological Institute of Connecticut. He was a descendant of Anthony Thompson, who came to Boston in 1637 and later was one of the founders of New Haven, Conn. Charles's mother was Eliza Butler, whose ancestors were among the pioneer settlers who established Hartford, Conn. Young Thompson entered Dartmouth College in 1854 and four years later, having taken high rank, was graduated with the degree of A.B. For six years he had a varied experience in teaching and engineering practice. Until 1864 he was principal of the Peacham Academy at Peacham, Vt., but used his vacation periods in the practice of surveying and civil engineering. From 1864 to 1868 he was principal of the Cotting High School at Arlington, Mass. Here

he established a reputation which led to his being called to Worcester in February 1868 as principal of the new Worcester County Free Institute of Industrial Science (later Worcester Polytechnic Institute). He spent the summer of 1868 abroad, studying European technical schools. Upon his return in November, he put into effect at Worcester what were then considered rather radical innovations in American technical education. "In all the great schools that began before 1868," he said in after years, "there were collections of apparatus and models, drawing-rooms and laboratories for the proper teaching of practical science, but there was no workshop worthy of the name. The mechanical arts were the last to be recognized in schools of engineering. The first school to embody in the course a thoroughly equipped and genuine workshop was the Free Institute at Worcester, Mass., in 1868" (*Transactions American Institute of Mining Engineers, post,* p. 193). Thompson was thus a pioneer in the introduction of shop practice in engineering teaching. He even planned to have the articles made by the students in the shops compete in the open market with those produced by commercial manufacturers. He thus sought a solution of the still important problem of the relation of engineering education to engineering industry by bringing industry into the technical school. His scheme has since been largely abandoned in advanced engineering schools, in favor of sending students to industrial works to secure this training; but to Thompson belongs the credit of being the first to emphasize this important feature in engineering education.

The great success of the Free Institute led to its director receiving many offers from other institutions. These he refused until, in 1882, he had the opportunity to become the first president of Rose Polytechnic Institute at Terre Haute, Ind., Chauncey Rose [*q.v.*], the founder of this school, having decided after making a careful survey of the field that Dr. Thompson was the person best fitted to establish the institution. It was opened on Mar. 7, 1883, but Thompson was destined to do no more than organize it and start it on its career, for he died at Terre Haute almost exactly two years later.

He published several papers on teaching and manual training, which include *Hints Toward a Profession of Teaching* (1867); *The Modern Polytechnic School* (1883); *Manual Training in the Public Schools* (n.d.); and "A Review of the Reports of the British Royal Commissioners on Technical Instruction" (*Circulars of Information of the Bureau of Education,* no. 3, 1885). He was a member of a number of societies, including the American Association for the Advancement of Science and the American Institute of Mining Engineers. On May 14, 1862, he married Maria, daughter of Dr. Horace and Elizabeth (Dickinson) Goodrich of Ware, Mass., who with their two sons and a daughter survived him.

[*Memorials of the Families of Mr. James Thompson and of Dea. Augustus Thompson of Goshen, Conn.* (1854); L. W. Case, *The Goodrich Family* (1889); *Proc. of the Am. Antiquarian Soc.*, n.s., vol. III (1885); *Trans. Am. Inst. Mining Engineers*, vol. XIV (1886); *Indianapolis Jour.*, Mar. 18, 1885.]   J.K.F.

THOMPSON, DANIEL PIERCE (Oct. 1, 1795–June 6, 1868), author, lawyer, was born at Charlestown, Mass., the son of Daniel and Rebecca (Parker) Thompson. On his father's side he was descended from James Thompson, who settled in Massachusetts before 1632; on his mother's he was apparently descended from Ezekiel Cheever [*q.v.*], seventeenth-century educator (Flitcroft, *post*, p. 317). In 1800 his father, being unsuccessful in business, moved to a small farm at Berlin, Vt. Thus Daniel grew up in a frontier settlement in which there was neither a library nor an adequate school. At sixteen, however, he chanced upon a volume of English poetry, and this book opened a new world to him. He worked hard on the farm, studied and later taught in the district schools, saved money, and finally, after a winter's residence at the Randolph-Danville Academy at Danville, Vt., entered Middlebury College with advanced standing. While in college he contributed a number of poems and essays to periodicals. After his graduation in 1820, he went to Virginia (probably Culpeper County), where he remained for three or four years as a tutor in a wealthy family. During this period he studied law, obtained an interview with Thomas Jefferson ("A Talk with Jefferson," *Harper's New Monthly Magazine*, May 1863), and was admitted to the bar.

Returning to Montpelier in 1823 or 1824, Thompson began the practice of law, and soon became prominent in the political and cultural life of Vermont. He served as judge of probate for Washington County (1837–40; 1841–42), clerk of the county court (1844–46), and secretary of state for Vermont (1853–55). He compiled *The Laws of Vermont . . . Including the Year 1834* (1835), was one of the founders of the Vermont Historical Society, and during 1840 served as secretary of the state education society. He took part in the anti-Masonic controversy to the extent of publishing, in the guise of "A Member of the Vermont Bar," *The Adventures of Timothy Peacock, Esquire* (1835), a satirical novel concerned with "the amusing adventures of

a Masonic Quixot." In the same year he wrote for the *New England Galaxy* a story called "May Martin, or the Money Diggers," which won a prize of fifty dollars, and thus encouraged him to continue with the writing of fiction as an avocation. Originally a Jeffersonian Democrat, Thompson later became active in the Liberty party, editing from 1849 to 1856 the *Green Mountain Freeman*, a weekly paper identified with the anti-slavery movement. In 1856 he joined the Republicans because they were making opposition to the extension of slavery the chief issue in their presidential campaign. He was well known as a lyceum lecturer. On Aug. 31, 1831, he was married to Eunice Knight Robinson, by whom he had six children.

Thompson's claim to recognition is based mainly on his achievement as a historical novelist in the school of Cooper. Through his fiction he probably did more than any other person to popularize the early history of Vermont. Local tradition represents him as wandering through the country with his fishing rod, stopping at intervals to chat with some old settler by the roadside. He would spend hours listening to stories about Ethan Allen, Seth Warner, and Colonel Stark; and he kept careful notes of all he heard. Influenced by Scott and Cooper, he blended history with romance in a half dozen novels of adventure, of which the best known is *The Green Mountain Boys* (1839). This book deals with the land-grant controversy between New York and New Hampshire, and with such incidents of the Revolution as Ethan Allen's capture of Fort Ticonderoga and the battle of Hubbardton. Its popularity is evidenced by the sale of fifty editions before 1860 and sixty editions by 1900. A sequel, *The Rangers*, appeared in 1851. Another novel, *Locke Amsden* (1847), deserves mention for its truthful record of frontier life, its autobiographical significance, and its interest to the student of American education. Among his other publications are *Gaut Gurley* (1857), *The Doomed Chief* (1860), *History of the Town of Montpelier* (1860), and *Centeola* (1864). An old-fashioned Yankee with a keen sense of humor, Thompson possessed genuine narrative ability, but fell far short of Cooper in imaginative power.

[See Leander Thompson, *Memorial of James Thompson* (1887); E. A. and G. L. Duyckinck, *Cyc. of Am. Lit.* (2 vols., 1855), which contains a brief autobiog. memoir; *Biog. Encyc. of Vt.* (1885), pp. 256–60; D. F. Wheaton, in *Vt. Hist. Gazetteer*, vol. IV (1882), pp. 69–72; obituary in *Burlington Times*, June 9, 1868. The dates of Thompson's public offices are from J. M. Comstock, *A List. of the Principal Civil Officers of Vt.* (1918). The only full biog. is J. E. Flitcroft, *The Novelist of Vt.* (1929), which contains Thompson's unfinished novel, "The Honest Lawyer."]   J.E.F.

THOMPSON, DAVID (Apr. 30, 1770–Feb. 10, 1857), explorer, geographer, fur-trader, was born in London, England, the son of David and Ann Thompson. His family was of obscure Welsh lineage and, before moving to London, used the name ApThomas. When David was three years of age his father died, leaving the mother and several children in abject poverty. The Grey Coat School, then a charity school for boys, admitted the lad when he was seven years of age and he spent the next seven years under strict religious discipline and tutelage. When he was fourteen he was apprenticed to the Hudson's Bay Company for seven years of service in the fur-trade in North America, and was landed at Fort Churchill on the inhospitable west shore of Hudson Bay to begin his career. As far as it is known, he never returned to England.

He received his first training under Samuel Hearne, the explorer, and Philip Turnor, surveyor for the Company, who guided the young man in his passionate study of mathematics and instructed him in the use of the sextant, compass, and astronomical instruments. His field service began in 1789, and for twenty-five years, first with the Hudson's Bay Company and later with the North West Company, he kept daily journals and field notes of his travels, which took him more than 50,000 miles and covered almost every lake and stream in western Canada. Thompson's work was practically unrecognized until about 1900, and only after the publication of some of his documents in 1916 under the title *David Thompson's Narrative of his Explorations in Western America,* volume XII of the *Champlain Society Publications* was he generally recognized as one of the greatest land geographers of the English race. Because of Thompson's groundwork on the Peace River district, Fraser named the largest tributary of the Fraser River for him. Thompson discovered a new route to Lake Athabasca; located by survey the Mandan Indian villages on the Missouri River in the winter of 1797–98; marked the crossing of the forty-ninth parallel by the Red River, and during conditions of almost impossible travel in the spring of 1798, surveyed the most northerly source of the Mississippi, and the course of the St. Louis River to Lake Superior. In 1807 he crossed the Canadian Rockies and discovered the source of the Columbia River. In 1808–10, he penetrated the Kootenai, Pend Oreille, and Clark Fork (Flathead) country of Washington, Idaho, and Montana. In 1811 he surveyed the Columbia River from source to mouth; he placed on the map main routes of travel within 1,200,000 square miles of Canadian territory and 500,000 square miles of the United States. The trading posts he established on the Kootenai, Pend Oreille, and Spokane rivers in the United States antedated the establishment of Astoria by John Jacob Astor, 1763–1848 [q.v.], by several years.

After his retirement from field service in 1812, he devoted two years to drawing a large map, five and a half by ten and a half feet, of the northern part of the United States and Canada, using his own surveys and those of other explorers including Lewis and Clark. It is still preserved in the archives of Ontario, and is remarkable for its accuracy, detail, and extent. From 1816 to 1826 he was in charge of the British commission for establishing and marking the boundary between Canada and the United States from its crossing of the St. Lawrence River west to the angle of Lake of the Woods. After ten more years of public and private surveying, he retired to live in Williamstown, county of Glengarry, and then in Longueuil.

In June 1799 he was married to Charlotte Small, the half-breed daughter of Patrick Small, who bore him seven sons and six daughters. Financial reverses reduced him to extreme poverty in his old age and he was forced finally to sell the precious instruments that had served him so well. He was buried in the Mt. Royal Cemetery in Montreal. Washington Irving is said to have offered to buy Thompson's journals but the old man refused to sell, and probably thus denied to the world a sequel to Irving's *Astoria.*

[Journals and note-books in the archives of Ontario; J. B. Tyrrell, ed., *Jour. of Samuel Hearne and Philip Turnor, Champlain Soc. Pubs.,* Toronto, vol. XXI (1934); C. N. Cochrane, *David Thompson the Explorer,* Canadian Men of Action Series, No. II (1924); T. C. Elliott, "The Discovery of the Source of the Columbia River," *Oregon Hist. Soc. Quart.,* Mar., June 1925; L. J. Burpee, "Some Letters of David Thompson," *Canadian Hist. Rev.,* June 1923, and also *Canadian Mag.,* Jan. 1926; S. F. Bemis, "David Thompson, Explorer," *Sunset,* Mar. 1923; F. W. Howay, in *Queen's Quart.,* Aug. 1933.]   T. C. E.

THOMPSON, DAVID P. (Nov. 8, 1834–Dec. 13, 1901), contractor, banker, public official, was born at Cadiz, Ohio. His father, a mill-owner, was of Irish descent; his mother, of Scotch. David's schooling was such as was afforded by the village and he was early apprenticed as a blacksmith. He earned his way to Oregon with the immigrant train of 1853 by driving a flock of sheep, arriving at Oregon City with his capital reduced to twenty-five cents. Here he worked as a wood cutter, blacksmith, and surveyor's assistant, becoming in a few years a United States deputy surveyor for Oregon and Washington. He ran the base line of Oregon across the Cascades to the Blue Mountains, and the Columbia Guide Meridian north to the Big

Bend of that river. In 1869 he surveyed the Dalles-California military wagon road and in 1872 surveyed and alloted lands to the Indians of the Grande Ronde Reservation.

In the meantime he engaged in numerous business and construction enterprises. He built the first railroad in Oregon—a horse railroad around the Willamette Falls, between Oregon City and Canemah. The road yielded dividends of $48,000. From 1866 to 1868 he was president and manager of the Oregon City Woolen Manufacturing Company. He was a member of the Willamette Falls Canal and Locks Company, which built, and opened on Jan. 1, 1873, the canal around the Willamette Falls, and he served as president of the Oregon Construction Company, which built most of the lines of the Oregon Railway & Navigation Company, of which he was a vice-president and director. He secured profitable contracts (1872–78) to carry mail through the Pacific Northwest. In 1880 he organized the Portland Savings Bank, of which he became president; he was also president of the Commercial National Bank of Portland and a director in many other financial institutions.

During these years he was one of the leaders of the Republican party in his state and for the most of the time a public official. He served as state senator (1868–72); as governor of Idaho Territory (1875–76); as representative in the Oregon legislature (1878–79, 1889–90); as mayor of Portland (1879, 1881). In 1890 he was the Republican candidate for governor but was defeated by Sylvester Pennoyer [q.v.]. From November 1892 to April 1893 he was minister to Turkey, succeeding in that position another resident of Oregon, Solomon Hirsch. For ten years he served as regent of the University of Oregon. Unlike most bankers he campaigned for free silver (1895–96) and served as chairman of a bimetallic conference held at Salt Lake City in May 1895. He was married in 1861 to Mary R. Meldrum of Salem, Ore., by whom he had three children.

[*Morning Oregonian* (Portland), Oct. 5, 1888, Dec. 14, 1901; H. H. Bancroft, *Hist. of Washington, Idaho, and Montana* (1890); H. W. Scott, *Hist. of the Oregon Country* (1924), vols. II, III; *Oregon Native Son and Hist. Mag.*, May 1899; *Papers Relating to the Foreign Relations of the U. S. . . . 1893* (1894); *Who's Who in America*, 1899–1900.]   R. C. C.

THOMPSON, DENMAN (Oct. 15, 1833– Apr. 14, 1911), actor and playwright, was born in a log cabin near Girard, Pa., the son of Capt. Rufus Thompson and Anna Hathaway (Baxter), daughter of Dr. Henry Baxter of Swanzey, N. H. He was named Henry Denman, but later used only his middle name. His parents had moved to Pennsylvania from Swanzey, where his paternal forebears had been established for some four generations, and during the boy's teens they returned to that place. In 1850 Denman went to Boston, where he worked first as a chore boy with a circus and later got a job as a super with Charlotte Cushman. During the next few years he drifted to various cities, nearly always in some minor capacity in a theatrical troupe. It was not until the middle of the decade, when he became a member of the Royal Lyceum Company in Toronto, that he secured any worthwhile training. With this company he remained for several seasons, playing a variety of parts, including Uncle Tom in *Uncle Tom's Cabin*. In 1862 he went to England, hoping to play Salem Scudder in the London production of *The Octoroon*, but he failed to secure the rôle and returned to Toronto, where he remained until 1868.

During the next seven years he led the wandering life of a minor actor; he had found no place in the theatre which brought him distinction. In 1875, however, he evolved a brief sketch, in two scenes, based on his boyhood observation of rural Yankee types (and, it must be confessed, also on innumerable other Yankee sketches), in which he played the part of an old New Hampshire farmer on a trip to Boston. This sketch was first tried in Pittsburgh, in February 1875, and met success. In Chicago, J. M. Hill suggested that he expand it into a full-length play. Hill became his manager, and at Haverley's, Chicago, in 1877, a three act comedy was presented called *Joshua Whitcomb*, after the name of the old farmer. For the next nine years it was acted under that title, undergoing numerous changes, and being worked over by at least one collaborator—George W. Ryer. In September 1878 it was acted at the Lyceum Theatre, New York, and it later ran for two seasons at the Fourteenth Street Theatre. On Apr. 5, 1886, at the Boston Theatre, an augmented version, in four acts, now called *The Old Homestead*, was presented, and it was this play which Thompson continued to act almost to the end of his life, carrying it all over the country and making it one of the best known dramas on the American stage. Conservative estimates set its earnings at $3,000,000. Thompson became completely identified with this play, and never again acted any other character. His kindly old face as Josh Whitcomb was as familiar to Americans in the nineties as the Statue of Liberty. Asked why he played no new parts, he replied, "My ambition's satisfied, and bein' so, it's gone." Although it was a crude and sentimental affair, *The Old Homestead* had a homely flavor of veracity in

its leading character, and plenty of broad comedy. The more sophisticated laughed at rather than with the play, but with Thompson acting it its appeal to the masses was enormous.

On July 7, 1860, Thompson married Maria Ballou, who died in 1904. They had three children. After his success, he remodeled an old house in West Swanzey, N. H., where he made his home thenceforth, and where he died. His last appearance in New York was at the City Theatre, in September 1910. Thompson was the author of one or two other plays and sketches, notably *The Sunshine of Paradise Alley* (with George W. Ryer) in 1896, but it is entirely on *The Old Homestead* and especially on his impersonation of the old Yankee farmer, Joshua Whitcomb, that his reputation rests. Asked in later years what he thought of Ibsen, he replied, "Funny, but I never saw an Ibsen play nor a baseball game; them's two things I've escaped" (*Current Literature*, June 1911, p. 650). In person, he was of medium size, inclined to stoutness in later years, with a round, genial face framed in white hair; he looked at all times far more the shrewd but kindly Yankee farmer than the actor.

[J. J. Brady, *The Life of Denman Thompson* (1888); *Who's Who in America*, 1910–11; E. S. Stearns, *Geneal. and Family Hist. of the State of N. H.* (1908), vol. III; Benj. Read, *The Hist. of Swanzey, N. H.* (1892); W. W. Walsh, "Reminiscences of Denman Thompson," *New Eng. Mag.*, Sept. 1910; *Theatre*, May 1911; *Current Literature*, June 1911; *Boston Transcript*, Apr. 14, 1911; *Concord Evening Monitor* (Concord, N. H.), Apr. 14, 1911; *N. Y. Times*, Apr. 15, 1911; theatre collections, N. Y. Pub. Lib. and Harvard College Lib.] W. P. E.

THOMPSON, EGBERT (June 6, 1822–Jan. 5, 1881), naval officer, was born in New York City, the son of Egbert and Catherine (Dibble) Thompson, a nephew of Smith Thompson [*q.v.*], and a descendant of Anthony Thompson, who came to Boston in 1637. Egbert was appointed midshipman Mar. 13, 1837. After a year's cruise in the *Independence*, he experienced unusual and trying duty, first in the Wilkes Exploring Expedition, 1838–42, in the Antarctic and South Seas, and next in the brig *Somers*, commanded by Capt. Alexander S. Mackenzie [*q.v.*], at the time of the alleged mutiny led by Midshipman Philip Spencer, which resulted in Spencer's execution. Thompson's testimony at Mackenzie's court martial (*Proceedings, post*, pp. 185–88) revealed that he had once had an altercation and scuffle with Spencer, and though small of stature had bested him; also that, while not implicated in Spencer's intrigues, he had been the only officer to bid him farewell at his death, and had been moved to tears. He was executive of the schooner *Bonita* during the Mexican War, participating in the capture of Tabasco, Tampico, Vera Cruz, and Tuxpan. Subsequently, he was in the *Michigan* on the Great Lakes, 1847–50; in the *Decatur*, Home Squadron, 1851–52; and in the *St. Louis*, African Squadron, 1855–58.

During the Civil War, he served on the *Powhatan* in the Gulf and in January 1862 joined Foote's Mississippi flotilla at Cairo. Commanding the gunboat *Pittsburg*, he participated in the attack on Fort Donelson, Feb. 13, in which his vessel was struck forty times and narrowly escaped sinking. Before dawn on Apr. 7 following (two nights after Commander Walke's similar exploit in the *Carondelet*), he ran the heavy batteries at Island No. 10, Mississippi River, to aid Polk's army below. In operations that same morning to support Polk's crossing of the river, Thompson, according to Walke (*post*, p. 152), executed the latter's orders very tardily, and "at a distance astern throwing shell in a dangerous proximity over our bow." Walke's criticism is weakened by his general tendency to monopolize credit, but it undoubtedly worked against Thompson's subsequent advancement. The Navy Department, upon Foote's report, included both vessels in its official thanks for hazardous service. After joining in the action of May 10 against the Confederate river flotilla, and in the capture of Fort Pillow on June 6, the *Pittsburg* remained at the latter point, and on June 16 returned to Cairo for overhaul. Thompson's later river service was uneventful. He went ashore in October, and in 1863–64 was at the Philadelphia naval rendezvous. He was made commander, dating from July 16, 1862, but only after an appeal from the advisory board's adverse report, in which he declared himself the only instance of an officer "commended for a daring and heroic act" and then passed over. From October 1864 until the close of the war he commanded the *Commodore McDonough* and later the *Cimarron* on blockade duty, being senior officer at Stono Inlet and for a time in May at Charleston.

Made captain in 1867, he commanded the *Dacotah*, Pacific Squadron, 1866–67, and then, as stated in an obviously inspired article in the *Chicago Tribune* (quoted in Walke, *post*, p. 79), "was sent . . . with his scars and his ironclads to rust away" at the Mound City (Ill.) Naval Station. His last command was the *Canandaigua*, 1871–72. He was retired for physical disability Jan. 5, 1874, and lived subsequently in Washington, occupied till his death in vain efforts to secure restoration. He was survived by his wife, Emily B. Thompson, and a daughter, Kate, wife of Capt. Edward Lloyd, U.S.A.

[W. B. Thompson, *Thompson Lineage* (1911); *Proc. of the Naval Court Martial in the Case of Alexander Slidell Mackenzie* (1844); Henry Walke, *Naval Scenes and Reminiscences* (1877); *War of the Rebellion: Official Records* (Navy); *Petition of Lieut. Egbert Thompson. U.S.N. against the Action of the Late Advisory Board* (1862); L. R. Hamersly, *The Records of Living Officers of the U. S. Navy and Marine Corps* (3rd ed., 1878); *Army and Navy Journal*, Jan. 8, 1881, and Jan. 13, 1894 (death of his wife).]   A. W—t.

THOMPSON, HUGH MILLER (June 5, 1830–Nov. 18, 1902), bishop of the Protestant Episcopal Church, was born at Londonderry, Ireland, the eldest son of John T. and Annie (Millar) Thompson. At the age of six he was brought to the United States and attended the public school at Caldwell, N. J., and later an academy at Cleveland, Ohio. Deciding to enter the ministry of the Protestant Episcopal Church, in 1849 he walked from Cleveland to Nashotah, Wis., and enrolled as a student at Nashotah House. On June 6, 1852, he was ordered deacon by Jackson Kemper, bishop of Wisconsin, and was ordained priest by the same bishop at Portage, Wis., on Aug. 31, 1856. His early ministry was spent as a missionary in Wisconsin and Illinois. He served successively at Grace Church, Madison, Wis., and the Church of the Nativity, Maysville, Ky.; at Portage, Baraboo, Elkhorn, Kenosha, and Milwaukee, Wis.; and at Galena, Ill. For one year he was rector of St. James's, Chicago, and in 1872 he became rector of Christ Church, New York, where he attracted large congregations. For several years he was rector of Trinity Church, New Orleans. He combined his rectorship at Kenosha with the chair of ecclesiastical history at Nashotah House, and founded Kemper Hall, a school for girls. In 1853 he married Caroline Berry, by whom he had a son and a daughter; his wife died in 1857 and on Oct. 25, 1859, he married Anna Weatherburn Hinsdale, by whom, also, he had a son and a daughter.

Late in 1882 he was elected bishop coadjutor of Mississippi and was consecrated in New Orleans on Feb. 24, 1883. Four years later, on the death of William Mercer Green, senior bishop, Thompson became diocesan bishop and served until 1902. He had an unusual combination of gifts; he was an excellent teacher, and had a natural aptitude for metaphysics, large attainments as a scholar, and popular gifts as a preacher. Doctrinally he was a high churchman with a strong antipathy to the Anglo-Catholic movement and extreme ritualism. He used his pen with good effect in church journalism. From 1860 until its consolidation with the *Churchman* in 1871, he was editor of the *American Churchman*, published in Chicago, and subsequently he edited the *Church Journal,* published in New York. He had the knack of making the commonplace interesting, and his comments on current events were shrewd and shot through with sound common sense. Many of his editorials were widely copied and in 1872 selections from them were published under the title of *"Copy": Essays from an Editor's Drawer.* The volume passed through many editions and had a wide circulation in England. In 1897 he published *More "Copy"; a Second Series of Essays from an Editor's Drawer.* Among his other writings were *Unity and Its Restoration* (1860); *First Principles* (1869); *Absolution* (1872); *The World and the Logos* (1886), Bedell Lectures; *The World and the Kingdom* (1888), Paddock Lectures; *The World and the Man* (1890), Baldwin Lectures; *The World and the Wrestlers: Personality and Responsibility* (1895), Bohlen Lectures. Bishop Thompson died at Jackson, Miss., at the age of seventy-two.

[Jours. of the Diocese of Miss., 1883–1903; *Who's Who in America*, 1901–02; *Churchman* and *Living Church*, Nov. 22, 1902; *Weekly Clarion-Ledger* (Jackson, Miss.), Nov. 20, 27, 1902.]   E. C. C.

THOMPSON, HUGH SMITH (Jan. 24, 1836–Nov. 20, 1904), educator, governor of South Carolina, was born at Charleston, S. C., the son of Agnes (Smith) and Henry Tazewell Thompson. Waddy Thompson [*q.v.*] was his uncle. His youth was passed in poverty on his father's farm in Greenville District. He entered the Citadel Academy at Charleston in 1852, where he graduated, four years later. On Apr. 6, 1858, he married Elizabeth Anderson, the daughter of Thomas Boston Clarkson, and taught at the Arsenal Academy in Columbia. In 1861 he returned to the Citadel, where until 1865 he taught French and belles-lettres and served in the Confederate Army as captain of a company of cadets of that academy in the defense of the Charleston harbor and the coastal region of South Carolina. Immediately after the war he became principal of the Columbia Male Academy, a position he held until 1880. His unusual ability as a teacher and disciplinarian raised this school to a position of preëminence among the educational institutions of South Carolina. His success as an educator, coupled with his engaging personal qualities, facilitated his entrance into public life. His handsome physique, mellow voice, and ease of speech made him a popular orator. In 1876 he became the Democratic candidate for state superintendent of education and in the canvass of that year aided Wade Hampton [*q.v.*] in winning the election for his party. He was state superintendent of education from May 1877 until December 1882. His conduct of this office was brilliantly constructive. The plans for universal education drawn up by his Radical predecessors were put into operation by him. He reformed the educational administration, spent wisely the funds he had at his disposal for the benefit of both whites and blacks, and in a series of moving addresses and reports largely removed from the public mind the prejudices against universal public education. In 1880 he established summer teachers' institutes, and the following year directed the foundation of a state teachers' association.

In 1882 the Democrats nominated him for governor. Being easily elected for two terms, he served in that office from December 1882 until his resignation three and one half years later. His conduct of the governorship was efficient but unsensational. He promoted tax reform, rigid economy, and education. In June 1886 President Cleveland appointed him assistant secretary of the treasury. In the summer of 1887 he resolutely anticipated and averted a seasonal monetary stringency by releasing an unusually large treasury surplus to purchase federal bonds in the market over and above the annual sinking fund requirements. From 1889 to 1892 he was a member of the civil service commission on the appointment of President Harrison. In this capacity he cooperated with his fellow-commissioner, Theodore Roosevelt, in carrying out the intentions of the Pendleton act. During the last twelve years of his life he was comptroller of the New York Life Insurance Company. He died in New York City and was buried in Trinity Church Yard, Columbia, S. C., leaving behind him the memory of one who had discharged with efficiency as many important public trusts as have been held by any South Carolinian since the Civil War.

[H. T. Thompson, *Establishment of the Public School System of S. C.* (1927); *Cyc. of Eminent and Representative Men of the Carolinas* (1892), vol. I; A. D. Mayo, in *A Report of the Commissioner U. S. Bureau of Education . . . 1904*, vol. I (1906), pp. 1031–39; *Confederate Veteran Camp of N. Y. Memorial on the Death of Comrade Hugh Smith Thompson* (1905?); *News and Courier* (Charleston, S. C.), and *N. Y. Times*, Nov. 21, 1904; information from his son Waddy Thompson, Atlanta, Ga.]   F. B. S.

THOMPSON, JACOB (May 15, 1810–Mar. 24, 1885), congressman from Mississippi, secretary of the interior, secret agent of the Confederate government, was born at Leasburg, Caswell County, N. C., of English and Dutch stock. Nicholas Thompson, his father, went to North Carolina from Virginia as a humble tanner but by his own diligence as well as by his marriage to Lucretia Van Hook had acquired wealth. As a thank offering for his success, Nicholas decided to make a minister of his studious, quiet and rather ugly third son, Jacob, who could not summon courage to oppose his stern father until he was a student in the University of North Carolina. From that institution he graduated in 1831, and there he remained for eighteen months as a tutor. He read law in Greensboro and was admitted to the bar in 1835. Possibly because he had disagreed with his father, he chose to begin his career in a distant region and with his next elder brother, James Young Thompson, a physician, settled at the booming town of Pontotoc in north Mississippi. Later he removed to Oxford, Miss., where he married Catherine, the daughter of Paton Jones, a wealthy planter. They had one son. Both brothers prospered, and Jacob soon entered politics. In 1837 he was one of the leaders in the fight of the new counties of his section for immediate representation in the state legislature. The same year he was defeated for the attorney-generalship of the state, but he was soon elected to Congress, where he attained some prominence and was for a time chairman of the committees on public lands and Indian affairs. After six terms, Mar. 4, 1839–Mar. 3, 1851, he was defeated by a temporarily powerful combination of Whigs and Union Democrats. In the spring of 1845 an executive appointment to the Senate was sent him by Gov. A. G. Brown, but Robert J. Walker, to whom the commission was intrusted, did not deliver it and thereby caused a small political tempest in Mississippi. After playing an important part in the Democratic conventions of 1852 and 1856, he was appointed secretary of the interior in 1857. He reorganized this department to increase its efficiency and seems to have had considerable influence over President Buchanan. He resigned because of his state-rights views, when the *Star of the West* was sent to Fort Sumter.

Serving with the Confederate forces until the fall of Vicksburg, he became chief inspector of the army under Pemberton. In the autumn of 1863 he was elected to the legislature of Mississippi. In 1864 he and C. C. Clay [*q.v.*] were sent to Canada as secret agents of the Confederacy. From that base he cooperated with the "Sons of Liberty" of Ohio, Indiana, and Illinois until convinced that this organization would not take up arms against the Union. After that he sought to free thousands of Confederate soldiers imprisoned near the Great Lakes and to encourage the hoarding and export of gold from the North so as to damage its financial strength. He even abetted plans for burning several northern cities, including New York (*Official Records, post,* ser. 1, vol. XLIII, pp. 930–36). An attack against Saint Albans, Vt., by revengeful, escaped Confederate prisoners focused the fear and hatred of northern patriots on him. He, however, disclaimed any share in that episode. Being thus in the limelight when Lincoln was assassinated, it was natural that he should have been charged with complicity in that crime. A large reward was offered for his capture. With his wife, who joined him in Canada, he lived there and in Europe for several years. Certainly not earlier than the summer of 1868 he returned to Oxford. Soon after this he settled permanently in Memphis. In 1876 he was for a short time brought out of private life when, as a political move to divert attention from the Belknap scandals, he was sued for a large sum stolen from the Indian funds of the department of the interior during his administration. Though the money had indeed been stolen, he had at the time been judged innocent by a congressional committee, and, as soon as the election of 1876 was over, the case was dismissed at the cost of the government. He died in Memphis.

[Letters and papers in Lib. of Univ. of N. C., and in Lib. of Cong.; J. F. H. Claiborne, *Miss. as a Province, Territory and State,* vol. I (1880), the fullest account, based on notes furnished by Thompson for that purpose; P. G. Auchampaugh, *James Buchanan and His Cabinet* (1926); *War of the Rebellion: Official Records (Army),* ser. 1, XLIII, part 2, ser. 2, VIII; D. Z. Oldham, *Life of Jacob Thompson,* MS., a thesis in the lib. of the Univ. of Miss.; J. F. Bivins, "Life and Character of Jacob Thompson," *Pubs. of the Hist. Soc. of Trinity College,* ser. 2 (1898); letter in J. F. H. Claiborne, *Life and Correspondence of John A. Quitman* (1860), II, pp. 62–65.]   C. S. S.

THOMPSON, JAMES MAURICE (Sept. 9, 1844–Feb. 15, 1901), Indiana poet and author, better known as Maurice Thompson, was by traditions and temperament a Southerner. His paternal ancestors, a family of Scotch-Irish extraction, had been pioneers in the South since the seventeenth century. His father, the Rev. Matthew Grigg Thompson (married Diantha Jaeger), was a Baptist minister who was living at Fairfield, Ind., at the time of Maurice's birth, but who shortly moved to Missouri, to Kentucky, and finally, about 1854, to a plantation in the Coosawattee valley of north Georgia. Here the son's education, directed by a mother of unusual gifts and by such tutors as a schoolless region afforded, was almost evenly divided between the study of books and the study of nature, both of which remained lifelong passions ("The School in the Woods," *St. Nicholas,* October 1879). At seventeen Thompson entered the Confederate army, and served for three years with loyalty and distinction. After the war, which left the family

destitute, he studied both civil engineering and law in Calhoun, Ga., until the rigors of Reconstruction drove him to try his fortune in the North. In 1868, quite penniless, he drew up at Crawfordsville, Ind., to work as civil engineer on a railroad there building. In the same year he married Alice Lee, daughter of John Lee, his employer, and settled permanently at Crawfordsville. Civil engineering he soon relinquished (1871) in favor of law, and for thirteen years he was a practising lawyer whose avocation was literature. In 1884 he turned to literary work alone. He was a state legislator in 1879, and for two terms (1885–88) creditably filled the position of state geologist.

In the South he had contributed verse and prose to *Scott's Monthly Magazine* (Atlanta, Ga.) and other literary publications (J. W. Davidson, *The Living Writers of the South,* 1869, pp. 558–67); in 1871 the *New York Tribune* and in April 1873 the *Atlantic Monthly* introduced him to the East. His reputation was speedily increased by a series of magazine articles on archery, a sport which he and his brother, Will Henry Thompson (1848–1918), were the principal agents in reviving (R. P. Elmer, *Archery,* 1926, pp. 112–14), and soon his stories, poems, and sketches, published in all the leading periodicals, contributed to a reputation for letters that grew to be the most commanding of his generation in the Middle West. For the last twelve years of his life he was non-resident literary editor of the *Independent.* After his first book, dialect sketches called *Hoosier Mosaics* (1875), he published several books on archery, a number of books for juvenile readers, three collections of nature sketches—*By-Ways and Bird Notes* (1885), *Sylvan Secrets, in Bird-Songs and Books* (1887), and *My Winter Garden* (1900) —, a number of books of fiction, and two of poems, *Songs of Fair Weather* (1883) and *Poems* (1892). It is on the poems that his most enduring fame will probably rest. As critic, he was notably the militant and uncompromising opponent of the rising tide of realism. (See his papers in the *Critic* and the *Independent,* and *The Ethics of Literary Art,* 1893). His strong romantic bias found expression in his own fiction. In addition to three or four unimportant novelettes, he wrote *A Tallahassee Girl* (1881), *His Second Campaign* (1883), *At Love's Extremes* (1885), all sentimental novels of Southern life and character; *The King of Honey Island* (copyright 1892), an historical romance of the same region, and *A Banker of Bankersville* (copyright 1886), a study of Indiana village life. No signal success attended any of these performances until *Alice of Old Vincennes* (copyright 1900), an historical romance of the George Rogers Clark expedition of 1779, brought him at the very end of his career nation-wide popularity. Retiring by nature, he shrank from any kind of publicity, refusing repeated offers of editorial position and lectureships. Though lithe and athletic, he was not robust of constitution, and regularly spent the winters in the South. He died of pneumonia at his home, Sherwood Place, Crawfordsville. He was survived by his wife, two daughters, and a son.

[Scattered autobiog. material is to be found in Thompson's accounts of his hunting and exploring experiences. See also *Who's Who in America*, 1899–1900; W. M. Baskervill, *Southern Writers*, vol. I (1897), pp. 89–136; Meredith Nicholson, *The Hoosiers* (1900); Mary H. Krout, in *Independent*, Feb. 21, 1901, which also has a poem by James Whitcomb Riley and an editorial; obituaries in *N. Y. Times, Indianapolis Sentinel*, Feb. 16, and *Indianapolis News*, Feb. 15, 16, 1901. Information on the family was supplied by Thompson's daughter, Mrs. Albert Blair Ballard of Tampa, Fla. A thesis on Thompson was prepared by George A. Schumacher at the Univ. of Va., 1934.]   F. H. R.

THOMPSON, JEREMIAH (Dec. 9, 1784–Nov. 10, 1835), merchant and ship-owner, was born of Quaker parentage at Rawdon, Yorkshire, a cloth-manufacturing village midway between Leeds and Bradford. His father, William Thompson, was the eldest of seven brothers engaged in the manufacture of woolen cloths. In 1798, shortly after the opening of the Leeds and Liverpool canal across the Pennine range, the youngest of these brothers, Francis Thompson, came to New York to represent the family business, and in 1801 Jeremiah followed, presumably to assist him. In the course of his business activities in New York, Francis entered into an informal association with Isaac Wright, a Quaker merchant of New York (whose daughter he married), and with Benjamin Marshall [*q.v.*]. In 1807 Francis and Isaac Wright became joint owners of the fast-sailing transatlantic ship, *Pacific*. In 1807 William Thompson had manufactured the first cloth made from Australian wool at the family mill at Rawdon. The product was highly esteemed, and it is probable that the employment of this wool in later years was a powerful influence in promoting the cloth trade of the Thompsons in New York.

Jeremiah seems to have begun business on his own account in 1815, when his name first appears in the New York directory. At that time he also became a joint owner with Francis Thompson, Benjamin Marshall, Isaac Wright, and his son William Wright, in the *Pacific*. The *Pacific* was employed in regular trade with Liverpool and in 1816 her owners placed the *Amity*, and in the spring of 1817 the *Courier*, in the same service. In October 1817 these five men

announced the organization of a line of American packets to make regular sailings from New York and Liverpool on a fixed day in each month. This idea of regular monthly sailings, with strict adherence to the advertised day of departure, is attributed to Jeremiah Thompson. The Liverpool line began service in January 1818, with the *Pacific, Amity, Courier,* and a fourth and new ship, the *James Monroe*. For some years it continued operations with difficulty, in the face of business depression; but in 1822, the practice of regular sailings was copied by other firms, and the "Old Line of packets," as it was termed, doubled its fleet to provide regular sailings twice a month.

During the next few years Thompson's commercial and shipping business greatly expanded. He participated in the formation of packet lines from New York to Belfast and to Greenock, and from Philadelphia to Liverpool. In 1827, he was designated the largest ship-owner in the United States and the most extensive cotton dealer in the world, with an annual purchase in the United States of about 150,000 bales. At the end of September 1827, however, the Liverpool house to which he consigned his cotton refused to accept his bills, with the result that he and his brother William (his partner in England) were compelled to suspend payments. He became insolvent in 1828, and all his interests in shipping were sold. Francis Thompson seems also to have failed at about the same time.

The absence of a bankruptcy law in New York State at that time appears to have made it impossible for Thompson ever to secure a release from his debts and to regain an independent position in business; yet it may be conjectured that he had a share in the formation in 1828 of a short-lived Union line of packets for steerage passengers only, and in 1831 of an emigrant packet office, both of which conducted their business at 273 Pearl Street, his own business address. This emigrant agency, which was headed by his cousin Samuel Thompson (previously Francis Thompson's partner), led in the later years to the formation of the Black Star line of packets and of the Guion line of steamships, and also had brief connections with the Cunard line. Thompson died in New York City; he never married. The preëminence of New York among the Atlantic seaports was ascribed by Matthew F. Maury [*q.v.*] in 1839 largely to Thompson's establishment there of shipping service on a regular schedule.

[Records of the New York meeting, Society of Friends; *Boston Commercial Gazette*, Nov. 19, 1827; *New-England Palladium*, Nov. 30, 1827; *New York Commercial Advertiser*, Dec. 1, 1827, Nov. 11, 1835; J. A. Scoville. *The Old Merchants of N. Y. City*, vol.

IV (1866), vol. V (1870); C. P. Wright, "The Packet Ships of N. Y." (unpublished thesis, Harvard Univ. Lib.); *N. Y. Daily Advertiser*, Nov. 12, 1835; *Herald* (N. Y.), Nov. 13, 1835; M. F. Maury, "Direct Trade with the South," in *Southern Lit. Messenger*, Jan. 1839.]
C.P.W.

THOMPSON, JEROME B. (Jan. 30, 1814–May 1, 1886), painter, was one of three artist children of Cephas Thompson, portrait painter, of Middleboro, Mass., and Olive (Leonard) Thompson. His father, who thought that one artist in the next generation would be enough, gave his instruction only to Cephas Giovanni [q.v.]. Encouraged, however, by his sister Marietta, who had learned to paint miniatures, Jerome painted in the attic at Middleboro a likeness of a cousin, a divinity student. When he discovered this, his father in anger smashed both canvas and easel, whereupon Jerome left home with his sister and set up for himself in Barnstable as sign and ornamental painter. An interesting anecdote is also recorded of the young painter's facility in making a likeness in five minutes on a wager (Thompson, *post*, p. 141). One of his early sitters was Daniel Webster, who had a house at Marshfield. Having saved a little money from his sign-painting and portraiture, Thompson went with his sister to New York, where both met with considerable success, she as a miniaturist, he as a depictor of rustic scenes, usually combining landscape and figures. He first appeared in New York directories in 1835. He was married twice: on Mar. 23, 1839, to Maria Louisa Colden, and on Apr. 19, 1876, to Marie May Tupper, an artist. He had one son. In 1852 he went to England, where he studied the pictures of Turner and Hogarth and painted portraits of several of the nobility. Upon his return he conducted a farm at Mineola, L. I., gaining distinction as a gardener as well as artist. He was a deeply religious and moral man, keeping regularly a "Book of Advice" for his own edification.

He made many sketches and studies in the Massachusetts Berkshires and Vermont, and in the far West. Some of his paintings of historic, literary, and sentimental subjects were used as "copy" for lithographic and chromolithographic reproduction, as were his "The Old Oaken Bucket," "Home, Sweet Home," "Scenes of My Childhood," "Coming through the Rye," and "Woodman, Spare that Tree." A long and somewhat amusing criticism of his picture, "The Hay Maker," was contributed by "Amateur" to *A Critical Guide to the Exhibition at the National Academy of Design* (1859). After his death, which occurred at "Mount Jerome," his country place at Glen Gardner, N. J., the National Academy of Design, of which he had been elected an associate in 1851, paid him a glowing tribute as "a most excellent and worthy man, deservedly honored in his life and sincerely mourned in his death" (*Ibid.*, p. 142). It is conceivable that there may at some time be a rediscovery of the merits of Jerome Thompson as a painter; at this writing (1935) he is well-nigh forgotten except by collectors of old lithographs.
[C. H. Thompson, *A Geneal. of Descendants of John Thomson, of Plymouth, Mass.* (1890); Thomas Weston, *Hist. of the Town of Middleboro, Mass.* (1906); Clara E. Clement and Laurence Hutton, *Artists of the Nineteenth Century* (1884); death notice in *N. Y. Times*, May 3, 1886.]
F.W.C.

THOMPSON, JOHN [See THOMSON, JOHN, 1776–1799].

THOMPSON, JOHN (Nov. 2, 1802–Apr. 19, 1891), New York publisher and banker, was born in the town of Partridgefield (now Peru), Berkshire County, Mass. He was a son of Amherst and Sarah (Clarke) Thompson, and a descendant of James Thompson who emigrated to Salem, Mass., in 1630, later moved to Charlestown, and in 1642 settled in Woburn. John's boyhood was spent on a mountain farm, and his early education was obtained in neighboring schools and at Harley Academy. For a time he taught a select school at Albany, N. Y., and then associated himself with the firm of Yates & McIntyre, which was engaged in promoting a lottery for the benefit of Union College.

Thompson seems to have been fairly successful in selling lottery tickets, but in 1833 he appeared in New York City, where he opened a brokerage office in Wall Street on a capital of $2,000. His contact with the financial world revealed to him an opportunity which he was quick to improve. The fact that an increasing number of state banks were circulating currency in every part of the country made it next to impossible for bankers or merchants in the East either to detect counterfeits or to know the actual value at a given time of any form of bank paper issued in the West or South. Thompson believed that reliable information on these matters would be welcomed by the business community, even if the cost of acquiring it should be relatively high. Accordingly, in 1842 he began the periodical publication of *Thompson's Bank Note and Commercial Reporter*, which not only pointed out differences between the actual and the spurious issues of particular banks, but gave quotations of discount rates on currency and a record of actual rates of exchange throughout the country. It thus presented facts not otherwise obtainable by the individual except at great expense, and it attained a large weekly circulation.

In the course of the Civil War Thompson, through his publication, attracted the attention of Secretary Chase and readily obtained a hearing on legal-tender and national bank policies. In 1863 soon after the establishment of the system of national banks, he received the charter for the First National Bank in New York City. He and his sons, Samuel and Frederick, originally owned the entire capital stock of $300,000. Most of the city's banks, operating under state charters, were distrustful of Secretary Chase's policies and looked with disfavor on his national banking system. Consequently, for some time Thompson's institution could not get clearing-house privileges and was chiefly engaged in the marketing of United States bonds. In 1873, the year that Jay Cooke [q.v.] failed, George F. Baker and Harris C. Fahnestock [q.v.] bought a controlling interest in the First National on condition that Thompson retain the presidency (article on George F. Baker, *New York Times,* May 3, 1931). Four years later, at the age of seventy-five, he withdrew and with his two sons founded the Chase National Bank, of which for a short time, after the death of his son Samuel in 1884, he was president. In his latter years he became erratic on questions of money and finance. The Chase Bank admitted in 1887 that its venerable founder was "a strong advocate of silver," and articles by him appeared, with others by Thurlow Weed and Edwards Pierrepont in *The Silver Dollar of the United States and Its Relation to Bi-Metallism* (1889), but he did not live to see the "sixteen-to-one" agitation of the next decade. In 1829 he had married Electa Ferris, who with a son and a daughter survived him.

[Leander Thompson, *Memorial of James Thompson . . . and of Eight Generations of His Descendants* (1887) ; *Vital Records of Peru, Mass., to the Year 1850* (1902) ; B. J. Lossing, *Hist. of N. Y. City* (1884), pp. 733–35 ; E. P. Oberholtzer, *Jay Cooke* (1907), I, 344 ; W. T. Hardenbrook, *Financial N. Y.,* pt. 3 (1897), p. 267 ; *N. Y. Herald, N. Y. Times,* and *N. Y. Tribune,* Apr. 20, 1891.]　　　　　　　　　W. B. S.

THOMPSON, JOHN BODINE (Oct. 14, 1830–Sept. 4, 1907), educator and clergyman, was born at Readington, N. J., the son of Joseph and Ann (Post) Thompson. He was the great-grandson of John Thomson, a Scotch emigrant who settled in Hunterdon County, N. J., married Juda Bodin (Judith Bodine), a descendant of the early Huguenot settlers, and about 1777 joined a group that undertook settlement in the Shamokin country of Pennsylvania. When he was killed in an Indian attack of 1778, his widow accomplished the feat of walking back to New Jersey, wheeling their only son and the family Bible in a small cart. There she reared the boy, also called John, to a place of influence and responsibility. He changed the spelling of the

family name. Her grandson, Joseph, was one of the leading citizens of central New Jersey, a teacher, surveyor, farmer, and for over thirty years county judge of either Hunterdon or Somerset county courts. John Bodine Thompson was his eldest son. When a mere boy he taught in a rural school and in 1851 was graduated from Rutgers College. He was active in the mid-century movement to improve the educational system of New Jersey, led by Richard S. Field [q.v.]. As agent of the New Jersey Teachers' Association from 1856 to 1859, he traveled up and down the state, delivering addresses and organizing teachers' institutes and urging the establishment of high schools and normal schools. He also advocated school libraries and the social use of school houses and libraries by the community, and he was among the first to urge summer schools.

Meanwhile he had entered the Theological Seminary of the Reformed Church in America at New Brunswick, was graduated in 1858, and was licensed to preach. On Apr. 5, 1859, he was married to Hannah Garrigues Reeve. They had two sons. He held pastorates at Metuchen, N. J., 1859–66, and at Tarrytown, 1866–69, Saugerties, 1869–71, Peekskill, 1873–74, and Catskill, 1874–84, in New York. During a long vacation, 1871–73, he went to Europe, where he supplied the pulpit of the American Protestant Church at Florence and studied at Tübingen University, still at the height of its fame as a seat of liberal theology. In company with Alessandro Gavazzi, the leader of the Free Italian Church and in his time one of the greatest of the Italian orators, he returned to the United States and was helpful in obtaining contributions for that movement. Religiously he was a liberal, philosophically a Hegelian, and he believed that the doctrine of the Trinity ought to be formulated in more philosophical terms. A large and dynamic man, he was an inspiration to those with whom he came in contact, and especially to young men and women in the formative years. Many of these later regarded his influence as the intellectual and moral background of their lives. From 1884 to 1888 he was minister of the First Presbyterian Church at Berkeley, Cal., where he became close friend of Joseph LeConte [q.v.]. He was also professor in the Presbyterian Theological School at San Francisco. He published voluminously, addresses such as *The Evolution of the American College* (1894), bits of family description as *John Thomson and Family* (1889, also in J. F. Meginness, *Otzinachson: A History of the . . . Susquehanna,* 1889, vol. I), and such other contributions as the chapter on "The Middle of the

Century" in David Murray's *History of Education in New Jersey* (1899). He was chairman of the committee responsible for *Reformed Church ... Hymns* (1869). He died in Trenton, N. J.

[E. T. Corwin, *A Manual of the Reformed Church in America* (4th ed., 1902) ; *The Acts and Proc. of the ... General Synod of the Reformed Church in America ... 1908* (n.d.) ; J. P. Snell, *Hist. of Hunterdon and Somerset, N. J.* (1881), pp. 491–93 ; M. C. Stuart, *Zes Maanden in Amerika* (1875), vol. II, pp. 66–74 ; *Cat. of the Officers and Alumni of Rutgers College* (1909) ; *Marriage Records of Hunterdon County, N. J.*, vol. I (1918) ; *Daily True American* (Trenton, N. J.), Sept. 6, 1907 ; information from his nephew, James Westfall Thompson, Berkeley, Cal.]   K. E. C.

THOMPSON, JOHN REUBEN (Oct. 23, 1823–Apr. 30, 1873), editor and poet, was born in Richmond, Va., the son of John Thompson of New Hampshire and Sarah (Dyckman) Thompson of New York. He attended schools in Richmond and in Easthaven, Conn. He was a student at the University of Virginia from 1840 to 1842, read law in the office of James A. Seddon [*q.v.*], and returned to the law class of the university, where he received the degree of Bachelor of Laws in 1845. For two years he practised law in Richmond. His father, then a prosperous merchant, purchased for him *The Southern Literary Messenger,* the editorship of which Poe had surrendered just ten years before. Thompson was owner and editor from 1847 to 1853, when he disposed of the ownership to his printers and continued as editor until he was succeeded in 1860 by George W. Bagby. The period of Thompson's editorship was that of the magazine's greatest influence and reputation. The acknowledged representative of the South, it printed especially the work of its leading writers. In 1854, with John Esten Cooke acting for him on the *Messenger,* Thompson sailed for his first visit to Europe. His travel sketches were printed in 1856 by Derby & Jackson, with the title, *Across the Atlantic,* but the whole edition was destroyed in a New York fire, except for one volume, now at his own university. Thompson left the *Messenger* in 1860 to become—for only a few months —editor of a weekly publication of Augusta, Ga., the *Southern Field and Fireside.* When Virginia seceded, his pen became one of the readiest in the Confederacy. In addition to his duties as assistant secretary of the Commonwealth of Virginia, he helped edit, while they were printed, the *Richmond Record* and *The Southern Illustrated News,* and he contributed to the *Index,* spokesman of the Confederacy in England. When his health failed, he resigned his office and in July 1864 ran the blockade to England, where he was the chief writer on the *Index* until the fall of the Confederacy. In England his influence

was especially favorable to the South because of his wide friendship among celebrated writers. He had known Bulwer-Lytton, Thackeray and the Brownings on his earlier visit to Europe and among the many friends of the later period were Tennyson and Carlyle. After the defeat of the South, he maintained himself for a time in England by newspaper work and by preparing for *Blackwood's Edinburgh Magazine* from the notebooks of Major Heros von Borcke the "Memoirs of the Confederate War for Independence" (Sept. 1865–June 1866 and published in two volumes in 1866). In September 1866 he returned to America. He was American correspondent for the London *Standard* and lectured, besides writing for other papers. In April 1867 he left Virginia for New York and, after one or two temporary engagements, was appointed by William Cullen Bryant to the literary editorship of the New York *Evening Post.* He held that position until the development of tuberculosis forced him to seek rest in Colorado in 1873. He died in New York and was buried in Hollywood Cemetery in Richmond.

His importance is chiefly as an influence upon his own times and as the author of a considerable body of verse, most of it "occasional," that was accepted by his contemporaries as perfectly expressing the Southern sentiment of the decades following the Civil War. He was looked upon as the poet consecrated to the traditions of Virginia. Five or six of his poems are memorable for their own worth. Among those that have been best known are "Music in Camp," "The Burial of Latané," "Lee to the Rear," "Ashby," and "The Window-Panes at Brandon." His collected *Poems* were first published in 1920, edited by John S. Patton, with an excellent biographical sketch. Of his lectures, which were popular in his lifetime, *The Genius and Character of Edgar Allan Poe* was privately printed in Richmond in 1929.

[Some letters in Lib. of Cong. ; sketch by W. G. McCabe, in *Lib. of Southern Literature*, vol. XII (1910) ; biog. introduction in *Poems of John R. Thompson, ante* ; J. R. Miller, Jr., "John R. Thompson : His Place in Southern Life and Literature," manuscript dissertation, 1930, Univ. of Va. Library ; E. A. and G. L. Duyckinck, *The Cyc. of Am. Lit.* (1875), vol. II ; manuscript minutes of the Faculty, Univ. of Va., 1845 ; *Evening Post* (N. Y.), May 1, 3, 1873.]   J. S. W.

THOMPSON, JOSEPH PARRISH (Aug. 7, 1819–Sept. 20, 1879), Congregational clergyman, editor, author, was born in Philadelphia, Pa., the son of Isaac and Mary Anne (Hanson) Thompson, and a descendant of John Thompson who emigrated from London to Stratford, Conn., in 1635. His father was a druggist. Thompson graduated from Yale College in 1838, studied for the ministry at Andover and New Haven, and, as a favorite pupil of Nathaniel W. Taylor [q.v.], was drawn early into an influential circle of clergymen. In consequence he was ordained, Oct. 28, 1840, as pastor of the Chapel Street Church (later the Church of the Redeemer) at New Haven and was called thence in 1845 to the Broadway Tabernacle, New York, one of the strategic outposts of New England Congregationalism. To this large and discriminating congregation he ministered successfully for a quarter-century. He was one of the conspicuous leaders of the home missionary movement in his denomination, was the instigator of the Albany Congregationalist Conference of 1852, and worked unceasingly to arouse public opinion in behalf of the negro slaves. He made two visits to Europe, Palestine, and Egypt, and acquired some esteem as an Egyptologist. While still in New Haven he had helped Leonard Bacon [q.v.] to found the New Englander, and he wrote frequently for it and for Bibliotheca Sacra. With Bacon, Richard Salter Storrs, and Joshua Leavitt [qq.v.] he was a member of the editorial board of the Independent from its organization at the close of 1848, but as the result of differences with the proprietor, Henry Chandler Bowen [q.v.], he resigned in 1862. During this period he published some fifteen books, besides numerous pamphlets, sermons, lectures, and contributions to periodicals and reference works. He wrote well, and evidently with ease. Among his books were memoirs of the younger Timothy Dwight (1844), David Hale (1850), David Tappan Stoddard (1858), and Bryant Gray (1864); Egypt Past and Present (1856); Love and Penalty, or Eternal Punishment consistent with the Fatherhood of God (1860); Man in Genesis and in Geology (1869); The Theology of Christ from His Own Words (1870); and Home Worship (1871). He had no new ideas and was a thorough scholar in no department of knowledge, but he readily assimilated ideas and information from all sides and presented them in an intelligible form, he served no cause or institution perfunctorily, and his capacity for work was awe-inspiring. He was married twice: on May 5, 1841, to Lucy Olivia Bartlett of Portsmouth, N. H., who bore him five children and died in 1852; and on Oct. 25, 1853, to Elizabeth Coit Gilman of New York, a sister of Daniel Coit Gilman [q.v.]. By her he had one son, William Gilman Thompson [q.v.]. Two of his sons fought in the Civil War; the elder, John Hanson, died in the service and was commemorated by his father in The Sergeant's Memorial (1863). Thompson himself

was a delegate of the Sanitary Commission with Sherman's army.

In 1871 his health broke down, and with scant hope of future usefulness ahead of him he resigned his charge. William Mackergo Taylor [q.v.] became his successor. His congregation and some personal friends presented him with $70,000. He removed to Germany and established himself in Berlin, where he worked desultorily on a monograph on the Hebrews in ancient Egypt. As his health improved he appeared in society, preached frequently, and soon became an active publicist, devoting himself to the complicated ecclesiastical problems of the Reich, and to strengthening comity between the United States and Germany. He lectured in England, Scotland, Germany, Switzerland, France, and Italy; published several volumes, including Church and State in the United States (1873), The United States as a Nation (1877), and The Workman: His False Friends and His True Friends (1879); interested himself in international law; attended conventions of all kinds and delivered numerous occasional addresses. He spoke German and French readily. He kept alert mentally to the last, in spite of pain, headaches, partial paralysis, and the humiliation of an attempt to blackmail him. He died of an apoplectic stroke and was buried in the graveyard of the Jerusalem Church in Berlin. His brother-in-law edited a posthumous volume of American Comments on European Questions (1884).

[Arthur Gilman, The Gilman Family (1869); Biog. Record of the class of 1838 in Yale Coll. (1879) and Supplement (1889); Obit. Record Grads. Yale Coll. . . . June 1880 (1880); Broadway Tabernacle Church: Its Hist. and Work (1871); Susan H. Ward, The Hist. of the Broadway Tabernacle Church (1901); obituary in N. Y. Daily Tribune, Sept. 22, 1879; obituary and editorial in Phila. Press, Sept. 22, 1879; Independent, Sept. 25, 1879 (editorial); Leonard Bacon, Ibid., Oct. 2, 1879; G. W. Gilman, Ibid., Oct. 16, 1879; W. H. Ward, Ibid., Dec. 10, 1908.]   G. H. G.

THOMPSON, JOSIAH VAN KIRK (Feb. 15, 1854–Sept. 27, 1933), coal operator, banker, was the son of a Scotch-Irish father and a German-Dutch mother, Jasper Markle and Eliza (Caruthers) Thompson. Born on a farm near Uniontown, Fayette County, Pa., he was educated in the local schools and at Washington and Jefferson College, Washington, Pa., from which he graduated in 1871. In November of the same year he began to work in the First National Bank of Uniontown, an institution that Jasper Thompson had been instrumental in organizing and the presidency of which he held. The son advanced rapidly to the positions of teller and cashier, and in 1889, at the death of the elder Thompson, he became president. He served in this capacity for the next twenty-five years, at the same time carrying on another activity that his father had started in a small way—speculation in coal lands. He reputedly bought lands at from $30 to $100 an acre and sold them at from $170 to $2,850 an acre. Most of the coal under Greene and Fayette counties passed through his hands, as well as that under several thousand acres in the other counties of southwestern Pennsylvania and in West Virginia. At the peak of his career, with a fortune that was conservatively estimated at seventy million dollars, he was believed to control more than half of the coking coal in Pennsylvania and was known as the largest individual owner of coal lands in the country.

His bank was believed to be as prosperous as he was. It paid regular semi-annual dividends of eleven per cent. in addition to special ones. After 1903 it was housed in an eleven-story "skyscraper," the only such building in a town the size of Uniontown (7,500) in the country. It paid no interest on deposits, and carried a surplus of more than a thousand dollars for every hundred dollars of capital stock. When, however, Thompson refused to sell coal to the large steel interests except on his own terms, his troubles began. Early in 1914 he found himself blocked both in making sales and in getting extensions of credit. His bank was involved, because a large part of its supposed surplus was out in direct and indirect loans to him, and on Jan. 18, 1915, it was forced to keep its doors closed. After fruitless efforts to reëstablish himself, Thompson sold out in 1919 to the Piedmont Coal Company for a reported sum of five and a half million dollars, retaining only his home. For the rest of his life he continued to hope to "put through a deal," but only became more involved. Between 1926 and 1930 he faced charges of embezzlement for mismanagement of the estates of Emma Messmore and John A. Niccolls, and in December 1930, served a few days in jail for contempt of court, being released because of ill health.

Previous to the failure of the bank, Thompson was a dominating influence in Uniontown, and took an active interest in the town's welfare. Friendly, cheerful, and a tireless worker, he inspired a faith that was akin to religion. A number of his fellow townsmen became wealthy through opportunities he opened to them, and none lost a penny through deposit in his bank. His home, "Oak Hill," was lavishly furnished and housed a large library. He served as a trustee of Washington and Jefferson College from 1889 until his death, and in 1901 he contributed $100,100 to its endowment. From 1900 to 1915 he was president of the Presbyterian Banner

Publishing Company. On Dec. 11, 1879, he married Mary Anderson, who died in 1896, and on Aug. 11, 1903, he married Mrs. Blanche A. Gardner Hawes, who divorced him in 1912. On Dec. 14, 1929, he married Mrs. Rose Maloney of Pittsburgh. By his first wife he had two sons. He died in Uniontown.

[J. W. Jordan and James Hadden, *Geneal. and Personal Hist. of Fayette and Greene Counties, Pa.* (1912); scrapbooks on Uniontown kept by James Hadden, in Carnegie Lib., Pittsburgh; *N. Y. Times*, Jan. 19, 22, 1915, June 14, 1919, May 5, 1927, Apr. 14, 1929, Dec. 18, 1930, Sept. 28, 1933; *Pittsburgh Post-Gazette*, Sept. 1933; *Who's Who in America*, 1918–19.]   M. S.

THOMPSON, LAUNT (Feb. 8, 1833–Sept. 26, 1894), sculptor, was born at Abbeyleix, Queens County, Ireland, and came with his widowed mother to the United States in 1847. They made a home in Albany, N. Y., where he soon found a place in the office of Dr. James H. Armsby. In 1848 Erastus Dow Palmer [*q.v.*], who had made a portrait bust of Dr. Armsby, accepted Launt as a studio boy, doubtless because of the striking talent shown in his drawings of bones and muscles, made at the doctor's office. During the nine years he spent as assistant to Palmer, a kindly, conscientious master, Thompson developed into a capable young sculptor, expert in all studio processes, especially clay modeling and marble carving. In 1857, thus equipped, he set up a studio for himself in New York City, where he promptly met recognition, at first for ideal medallion heads in Palmer's vein and soon afterward for more original productions not only in relief but also in portrait busts and statues. He was made an associate of the National Academy of Design in 1859, and a full member in 1862. Three years later Thomas Bailey Aldrich described for young readers (*Our Young Folks*, Dec. 1865) his visit to Thompson in the famous Tenth Street studio building, where the sculptor was at work on the plaster cast of a colossal statue of Napoleon I, almost ready for the bronze. On the walls were many medallions, portrait or ideal, the subjects of the latter including Elaine and other heroines from the *Idyls of the King*. "Morning Glory," the profile of a child with a flowery fillet, became a popular work. There were three life-size busts, representing the "Rocky Mountain Trapper," Edwin Booth as Hamlet, and the poet William Cullen Bryant. Thompson's carefully studied head of Bryant, of which there is a copy in the Metropolitan Museum, New York, has remained for sculptors the authentic source portrait of the poet.

The "Trapper" and the Napoleon I were

shown in 1867 at the Paris Exposition, after which the sculptor spent some months in Rome, Italy. The Napoleon has been praised as an example of "dignified monumental art," "self-contained in every line" (Taft, *post*, p. 235), and irreproachable in modeling. Equally sculptural in conception, though less pleasing in detail, is Thompson's bronze statue of Abraham Pierson, the younger, erected on the campus of Yale University in 1874. In September 1869 Thompson married at Schenectady, N. Y., Maria L. Potter, daughter of Bishop Alonzo Potter [*q.v.*]. Six years later he went to Italy for a prolonged stay, from which he returned to New York in 1881. During his Albany years the Palmers must have felt a true esteem for the young sculptor, for they gave his name to their son, Walter Launt Palmer [*q.v.*]. Thompson learned many things from his generous elder, but not the secret of orderly living. He was endowed, it has been said (*Ibid.*, p. 236), "with an intuitive grasp of the sculptural side of things, and with an artistic conscience, which seems the more remarkable when contrasted with his erratic life." His influence on early monumental art in America was undoubtedly good. He died at Middletown, N. Y.

In the grounds of the Old Soldiers' Home, Washington, D. C., is his bronze figure of Gen. Winfield Scott, founder of the home. His "bewhiskered standing figure" of Admiral Samuel Francis Du Pont was for some time at the center of Du Pont Circle, Washington, but was removed in 1921 to Delaware. Other statues by Thompson are the Gen. John Sedgwick, West Point, N. Y. (1869); the Charles Morgan, Clinton, Conn. (1871); and the bronze equestrian figure of Gen. Ambrose E. Burnside, Providence, R. I. (1887), the last important work from his studio. Among his excellent portrait busts are those of James Gordon Bennett, Robert B. Minturn, Stephen H. Tyng, Capt. Charles H. Marshall, Charles L. Elliott, and S. F. B. Morse.

[Lorado Taft, *The Hist. of Am. Sculpture* (1903); H. T. Tuckerman, *Book of the Artists* (1867); Charles Moore, *Washington Past and Present* (1929), p. 242; *Rand-McNally Guide to Washington* (1925); obituary in *N. Y. Tribune*, Sept. 27, 1894.]   A—e. A.

THOMPSON, MARTIN E. (*c.* 1786–July 24, 1877), architect, first appears in the New York directory in 1816 as a carpenter. He may have been a pupil of Josiah R. Brady, the architect, for among the drawings in the New York Historical Society is one of the Merchants' Exchange, credited in the handwriting of a contemporary to J. R. Brady and M. E. Thompson. In any case, he was commissioned in 1822–23 to design the second Bank of the United States on Wall Street, later the United States Assay Office

(1854–1915), its lovely façade now serving as the south front of the American wing of the Metropolitan Museum of Art. In 1824 he was called on for a design for the Merchants' Exchange, completed in July 1827 and burned in the great fire of 1835. In beauty and richness the building had no peers in the city. It was dignified, simple, and commodious, and the Exchange Room, 85 by 55 feet, with rounded ends and a screen of columns, was well proportioned and impressive. It is shown in one of the Pendleton lithographs of New York. By 1827 Thompson had formed a partnership with Ithiel Town [*q.v.*]. Their office at 32 Merchants' Exchange soon became an artistic center, and was opened as an "Architectural Room" to those who wished to consult Town's magnificent library of architectural books and engravings (*The Picture of New-York*, *post*, p. 376). The effect on Thompson was to convert him at once to the Greek Revival. In their combined work—especially in the Church of the Ascension (1828) on Canal Street, and in the brick tower and spire of St. Mark's in the Bowery (still standing, 1935)— Town may have had a great part, though Minard Lafever in *The Young Builder's General Instructor* (Newark, 1829) gives Thompson the credit for the Church of the Ascension, and a Mr. Morris in the *New York Mirror*, Mar. 1, 1828, in praising the St. Mark's steeple for its beauty and its omission of such "pretty things" as the common brazen weathercock, mentions only Thompson's name. In 1826 Thompson was one of the thirty founders of the National Academy of Design. Both he and Town exhibited there regularly until about 1833. Their partnership seems to have ended in 1828, for in 1829 Thompson exhibited several designs alone. He was the designer of the Columbia Grammar School (begun 1829), the façades of the houses on the Murray Street lots of Columbia University, and the noted house of Robert Ray, 17 Broadway, burned in the great fire of 1845 (*New York Mirror*, July 26, 1845). In 1839 he received the second premium in the competition for the Ohio capitol at Columbus (diary of Alexander Jackson Davis, Metropolitan Museum of Art, New York). He made several plans for the enlargement of the City Hall. From May 1847 to January 1850 he served as street commissioner of New York City. He lived on East Eleventh Street, 1844–53, and on West Twelfth, 1853–64. After the death of his wife, Mary (who was born in New York City and died there, Feb. 9, 1864, at the age of seventy-five), he seems to have left New York and retired to Glen Cove, L. I., where he died. Besides being one of the founders of the National Academy of Design he was a member of the General Society of Mechanics and Tradesmen from 1822 on.

As a designer Thompson ranks high. The second Bank of the United States is gracious, restrained, delicate, rather in the English tradition, as was the Ray house. The Merchants' Exchange was more original, more daring, more powerful; the recessed portico was a new note, its cupola was unusually effective, and its large Exchange Room both delicate and monumental. The St. Mark's spire is markedly original in conception in its avoidance of the orders, the Columbia Grammar School was well massed, and the plans for the City Hall extensions reveal great planning ability. The Columbia houses are simple and straightforward, and give stylistic support to the assumption that Thompson was probably the architect of many of those dignified houses built in the northern part of Greenwich Village in the forties and fifties.

[*The Picture of New-York, and Stranger's Guide to the Commercial Metropolis of the U. S.* (N. Y., 1828), pub. by A. T. Goodrich; *Proc. and Docs. of the Board of Assistant Aldermen,* vols. XXXIV–XXXVII (N. Y., 1851); Thomas Earle and C. T. Congdon, *Annals of the General Soc. of Mechanics and Tradesmen . . . 1785 to 1880* (1882); I. N. P. Stokes, *The Iconography of Manhattan Island,* vols. III–VI (1918–28); *Memorial of St. Mark's Church in the Bowery, N. Y.* (1899); death notice in *N. Y. Tribune,* July 25, 1877; vital statistics of N. Y. City; cats. of exhibitions, Nat. Acad. of Design; drawings, estimates, etc., in the "Columbiana" Coll., Columbia Univ. Lib.; minutes of the board of trustees, Columbia Univ., 1826–30; MSS. in Columbia Univ. Lib.; City Hall plans, McComb Papers, N. Y. Hist. Soc.; information from Mrs. Charles Curran, librarian of the Nat. Acad. of Design.]   T.F.H.

THOMPSON, MAURICE [See THOMPSON, JAMES MAURICE, 1844–1901].

THOMPSON, RICHARD WIGGINTON (June 9, 1809–Feb. 9, 1900), lawyer, politician, author, was born in Culpeper County, Va., the son of William Mills Thompson, a merchant and lawyer, and Catherine Wigginton (Broadus) Thompson. His great-grandfather, the Rev. John Thompson, born near Belfast, Ireland, emigrated to Virginia in 1739. His mother was the daughter of Maj. William Broadus, an officer of the Revolution. Thompson received a "good English and classical education." When twenty-two years old he left Virginia and after a short residence in Louisville, Ky., settled in Lawrence County, Ind., where he taught school, worked in a store, and studied law at night. Coincident with his migration he sloughed off most of the political and cultural viewpoints that had been the heritage of his Virginia birth and took on those predominant in his adopted community. In 1834 he was admitted to the bar and began the practice of law at Bedford. For four terms,

1834 to 1838, he was a member of the Indiana legislature; and in 1840 and again in 1846 he was elected to the Senate. In 1843 he moved to Terre Haute. On May 5, 1836, he married Harriet Eliza Gardiner (d. Mar. 25, 1888), who bore him eight children. On several occasions Thompson was a presidential elector, first on the Whig and later on the Republican ticket. Presidents Taylor, Fillmore, and Lincoln made him proffers of offices, but he declined. He was active in the secession controversies and during the Civil War served as provost marshal for the Terre Haute district. He was a delegate to Republican National Conventions in 1868, 1876, and 1892, and in the last named nominated Benjamin Harrison for the presidency. In 1877 he was appointed secretary of the navy in the Hayes administration (appointment confirmed, Mar. 10, 1877). It has been affirmed that this was the only major appointment made by Hayes that was "dictated entirely by political considerations and it was the only bad one" (Eckenrode, *post,* p. 242). While holding this post he took the chairmanship of the American Committee of the Panama Canal Company at a salary of $25,000 yearly, thinking this no bar to his retaining his post in the cabinet, whereupon Hayes notified him "that his resignation (unoffered) had been accepted" (*Ibid.,* p. 303). Extremely partisan in politics, intolerant in religion, a lobbyist for railroads, Thompson was throughout his active life a figure about whom angry controversy swirled. Few of his contemporaries among public men were so frequently attacked on ethical grounds. Apart from politics and law the major interests of Thompson's life were speechmaking and writing, and to these he devoted himself tirelessly whenever opportunity offered. His published writings include two volumes of historical essays, *Recollections of Sixteen Presidents* (1894), of considerable literary and historical merit; *The History of Protective Tariff Laws* (1888), a work of special pleading; and two volumes of polemics against the Catholic Church, *The Papacy and the Civil Power* (1876) and *The Footprints of the Jesuits* (1894), written, it has been said, while Thompson was "manifestly inspired by an undue fear of the Pope's protruding his official sway into American political life" (Bowers, *post,* p. 273).

In his personal relations Thompson was "a man of benevolence and unassuming manners," and throughout his life had hosts of friends, among them many who were at times his outspoken critics. In his old age the people of his state applied to him the affectionate designation of "the Grand Old Man." He loved children and never let pass an opportunity to be in their company. In his habits he was temperate, except in respect to smoking; for fifty years prior to his death he smoked an average of twenty cigars a day. He died in Terre Haute, Ind.

[See *Who's Who in America*, 1899–1900; *Richard W. Thompson Memorial* (copr. 1906); *Biog. Dir. Am. Cong.* (1928); Charles Lanman, *Dict. of the U. S. Cong.* (1869); *A Biog. Hist. of Eminent and Self-Made Men . . . of Ind.* (2 vols., 1880); G. W. Taylor, ed., *Biog. Sketches . . . of the Bench and Bar of Ind.* (1895), which contains a rather florid eulogy; Logan Esarey, *A Hist. of Ind.*, vol. II (1918); Charles Roll, *Ind., One Hundred and Fifty Years of Am. Development* (1931), vol. V, pp. 461–62; Francis Curtis, *The Republican Party . . . 1854–1904* (2 vols., 1904); H. J. Eckenrode, *Rutherford B. Hayes* (1930); C. G. Bowers, in *Green Bag*, June 1900; obituaries in *Sun* (N. Y.), Feb. 10, and *Sunday Sentinel* (Indianapolis), Feb. 11, 1900. Other sources include family information supplied by Thompson's daughter, Mrs. D. W. Henry, of Terre Haute, Ind.; correspondence with Ind. Hist. Soc.; and a letter written by Thompson in 1894, published in the *Culpeper Exponent*, Jan. 5, 1922, which deals with his ancestry and his early life in Va.] W. E. S—a.

THOMPSON, ROBERT ELLIS (Apr. 5, 1844–Oct. 19, 1924), educator, economist, was born of Scotch-Irish parents, Samuel and Catherine (Ellis) Thompson, near Lurgan, County Down, Ireland. As a child he attended the local country school and the Donaghloney Presbyterian Church. His father, driven by economic distress in Ireland, sold his freehold farm and came to Philadelphia in 1857. The boy attended successively the Hancock, Harrison Grammar, and Central High schools, completed his preparation for college at Faires' Classical Institute, and graduated from the University of Pennsylvania (A.B., 1865) with the highest honors. He had long planned to enter the ministry, and after graduating from the Reformed Presbyterian Seminary, Philadelphia, in 1867, was licensed to preach, and seven years later was ordained. After supplying vacant churches as far west as Illinois in 1867–68, he returned to the University as instructor in Latin and mathematics, and after three years was invited to give the newly established course in social science, being appointed professor in 1874. He became the first dean (1881–83) of the Wharton School of Finance and Economy, and continued to teach political economy after he was given (1883) the Welsh Professorship of History and English Literature. He had served in 1872–74 as librarian, was chaplain in 1889–91, and lectured widely on ethics and the social sciences in university extension courses.

Meanwhile, as an editor of the *Penn Monthly*, 1870–81, he was intimately associated with the Philadelphia protectionist group, including Henry C. Carey [*q.v.*], who became Thompson's economic mentor. On relinquishing this post he became an editor (1880–91) of the *American*, a weekly similarly devoted to economics, politics, and literature. He was on the staff of the *Irish World* from 1884 and of the *Sunday School Times* from 1892 to the end of his career. He was an editorial contributor to *Stoddart's Encyclopædia Americana* (4 vols., 1883–86), published as a supplement to the ninth edition of the *Encyclopædia Britannica*. The varied and voluminous reading and ready writing thus done added to his influence, his wealth of illustration, and his literary facility. His first book, *Social Science and National Economy* (1875), which he used as a text with his classes, enjoyed popularity elsewhere. Written with the encouragement of Joseph Wharton [*q.v.*], it was a talented exposition and vigorous defense of the position of the nationalist school of political economy, founded primarily upon the teachings of Carey but marked by Thompson's own personality. With him the nation became, and remained to the end of his life, not only an economic, political, and cultural entity, but an ordinance of God. His own nature fitted in with the buoyant views of the school; he attacked the Ricardian theory of rent and the Malthusian principle of population with more than academic ardor. His method was always in the main inductive, the result gaining much from aptness and concreteness of observation. After a pamphlet on *Hard Times and What to Learn from Them* (1877), came his *Elements of Political Economy* (1881), a revision of his earlier work. An active advocate of a high tariff policy in the Blaine-Cleveland campaign of 1884, he was invited the next year to give lectures at Harvard which were subsequently published under the title *Protection to Home Industry* (1886), an arsenal of persuasive argument. He gave similar lectures at other institutions.

Suddenly, in 1892, his connection of twenty-four years with the University of Pennsylvania was severed. He considered himself forced out. It is probable that his differences with Provost William Pepper [*q.v.*] were occasioned by conflict with younger members of the Wharton School faculty recently returned from German universities. He declined the presidency of Lake Forest College, and discouraged a movement to make him professor of Christian sociology in Princeton Theological Seminary—a consequence of his Stone lectures delivered there and published as *De Civitate Dei—The Divine Order of Human Society* (1891), in which, as in other of his writings on social ethics, he espoused national will to social improvement as against the controlling influence of economic materialism.

Thompson represents as well as anyone the unsuccessful struggle of national economic optimists against the rising tide of reformers, mainly socialists, who thought in international terms and preached class cleavage instead of a harmony of economic interests. In Thompson the moralist frequently threatened to hamper the economist.

In 1894 the second half of his career opened with his election to the presidency of the Central High School of Philadelphia. His early misgivings as to his executive capacity were banished by his brilliant success in greatly enlarging the school and enriching its instruction and influence. His cordial and intimate contacts with pupils and faculty produced an enthusiastic loyalty to him which was manifested on many occasions. He retired from the headship of the Central High School in 1920 in accordance with the new Retirement Act, after a vigorous protest by himself and many alumni and faculty members had failed, but he continued for a time his teaching of ethics and economics. He died in Philadelphia after a lingering illness. Thompson was twice married: in 1874, to Mary E. Neely who died July 8, 1894, and on Aug. 18, 1910, to her sister, Catherine Neely, who with two daughters and a son of his first marriage survived him. He was a large, heavy man, with bald head, drooping eyelids, and an engaging smile. His salient characteristics were conviction, spiritual, mental, and physical vigor, and personal magnetism. To the end of his life he wrote with a quill pen in very large characters, expressive of his positive temperament.

[Richard Montgomery, *Robert Ellis Thompson, a Memoir* (1934); *Who's Who in America*, 1924–25; L. R. Harley, *Confessions of a Schoolmaster and Other Essays* (1914); J. H. Bossard, "A History of Sociology at the University of Pennsylvania," in *Gen. Mag. and Hist. Chronicle* (Univ. of Pa.), April–July 1931; F. S. Edmonds, *Hist. of the Central High School of Phila.* (1902); *Public Ledger* (Phila.), Oct. 20, 1924.]

B. M.

THOMPSON, SAMUEL RANKIN (Apr. 17, 1833–Oct. 28, 1896), educator and scientist, was born at South Shenango, Crawford County, Pa. He was the son of William and Mary (Latta) Thompson, of Scotch and Irish descent. His early life was spent on his father's farm. In 1848, after three months at an academy in Greenville, he began teaching in Clarion County, Pa. From 1848 to 1856 he taught school in the winters and worked on the farm in the summers, with the exception of a year (perhaps 1854–55) in Nebraska, where he worked in a sawmill at Rockbluff. In his spare time he prepared himself for college entirely by home study; he often plowed with book tied to the plowhandle. He entered Westminster College at New Wilmington,

Pa., in 1856, and by alternate teaching and studying he finished with the class of 1860. At commencement time, however, he was serving as superintendent of schools for his home county, so it was not until 1863 that he could return to receive the degree of A.B. He received the degree of A.M. in 1881 from Westminster. He was superintendent of schools for Crawford County, Pa., 1860–65; professor of natural sciences and vice-principal of the state normal school, in Edinboro, Pa., 1865–67; and organizer and principal of the Pottsville, Pa., high school, 1868. He left Pottsville to organize a state normal school at Marshall College, Huntington, W. Va., which he conducted until 1871. In September 1871 he was elected professor of theoretical and practical agriculture at the University of Nebraska and began his work there in September 1872. He was the first dean of the College of Agriculture, which opened for the year 1872–73, and served in that position until December 1875. He was principal at the Nebraska State Normal School, Peru, 1876–77; superintendent of public instruction for Nebraska, 1878–81; superintendent of public schools, Lincoln, Nebr., for six months in 1882; and professor of agriculture at the University of Nebraska once more, with the added chair of didactics, 1882–84. In 1884 he returned to Westminster College as professor of physics and remained there until his death. At Rockbluff, Nebr., in 1859, he married Lucy Gilmour. They had one daughter, who died while a student in college, and whose memorial is the Mary Thompson Science Hall at Westminster College.

Thompson was an ambitious, talented, hardworking, and scholarly man, an influential pioneer in educational organization in three states. In Nebraska he organized the state weather service, started farmers' institutes, incorporated into the public school system some excellent features, and secured important school legislation. He was six feet, three inches tall, slender, of pleasant address and scholarly bearing, and his alert face with its bright blue eyes suggested his eager mind. In later life his white hair and full white beard gave him a prematurely venerable appearance. Restless, roving, and adventurous, he wrote little, preferring to teach, to travel, to plan, and to perform. The historical sketch of Westminster College in *A History of Higher Education in Pennsylvania* (1902), edited by C. H. Haskins and W. I. Hull, is from his pen. A report he wrote as dean of the University of Nebraska College of Agriculture, printed in the chancellor's report for 1874, reveals some of his ideas and ideals.

[R. P. Crawford, *These Fifty Years: a Hist. of the Coll. of Agriculture of the Univ of Nebr.* (1925); *Ann. Report: Nebr. State Board of Agriculture . . . 1896* (1897); *Pa. School Jour.*, Dec. 1896, pp. 292–93.]

J. I. W.

THOMPSON, SEYMOUR DWIGHT (Sept. 18, 1842–Aug. 11, 1904), jurist, was born in Will County, Ill., of English and Scotch-Irish ancestry, the son of Seymour and Betsy (Mc-Kee) Thompson. His father, a Presbyterian clergyman, had been compelled by the loss of his voice to give up the ministry and was endeavoring as a farmer to support a large family. In 1855 the Thompsons moved to a farm in Fayette County, Iowa, where in 1858 the father and a younger son were burned to death in a prairie fire. The survivors returned to relatives in Illinois. Seymour now undertook to support himself and to prepare for college. Without a permanent home, he managed to secure a fair education by attending Clark Seminary at Aurora, and Rock River Seminary at Mount Morris, working meanwhile as farm laborer, peddler, and grammar school teacher.

Ready for college when the Civil War began, he went back to Iowa and enlisted, May 21, 1861, in the 3rd Regiment of that state. He was made a first sergeant, Sept. 4, 1862, and in 1866 was mustered out of military service at Memphis, Tenn., with the rank of captain. He took part in the battle of Shiloh and the siege of Vicksburg, and witnessed the riotous burning by Union soldiers of Holly Springs, Miss. In 1864 he published *Recollections with the 3rd Iowa Regiment* an unromantic presentation of actual warfare. After the war he remained in Memphis for five years, making his living as a policeman, as a balloonist, as a court clerk, and, after he was admitted to the bar in 1869, as a self-educated lawyer. In 1872 he moved to St. Louis, where he soon attracted the attention of John Forrest Dillon [*q.v.*], then United States circuit judge. Dillon appointed Thompson to a fairly lucrative position as master in chancery, and in 1874 founded the *Central Law Journal* with himself as editor and Thompson as associate editor. In 1875 Thompson became editor of the publication and served in that position until 1878. From 1883 until his death, he was principal editor of the *American Law Review*. From 1880 to 1892 he was a judge of the St. Louis court of appeals, and from 1892 to 1898 practised law in St. Louis, although chiefly engaged in authorship. Thereafter until his death he maintained a law office in New York City for consulting work and also a residence in the suburbs, though he still claimed St. Louis as his legal domicile.

Thompson was a successful practitioner and a sound judge, but his distinction rests chiefly on his many widely read treatises, which, although designed primarily for the busy lawyer, were more than mere compilations of statutes and court decisions, since they contained vigorous and constructive criticism of law as announced by judges or established by statute. His more important works were *A Treatise on Homestead and Exemption Laws* (1878), *The Law of Negligence in Relations Not Resting in Contract* (2 vols., 1880), *A Treatise on the Law of Trials* (2 vols., 1889), and *Commentaries on the Law of Private Corporations* (7 vols., 1895–99). This last work was the most extensive legal treatise on a single topic ever published in the English language up to the time of Thompson's death (Lawson, *post*, p. 174). Several of Thompson's works have appeared in amplified posthumous editions. He was a hard and rapid worker in the tasks of authorship but generally had earnest pupils as assistants. In January 1865 he married Lucy A. Jennison, who with three sons and two daughters survived him. He died in East Orange, N. J.

[Thompson's judicial opinions appear in 9–53 *Mo. Appellate Reports.* For biog. data, see A. J. D. Stewart, *The Hist. of the Bench and Bar of Mo.* (1898); *Am. Law Rev.*, Sept.–Oct. 1904; *Central Law Jour.*, Sept. 16, 1904; J. D. Lawson, in *Proc. . . . Mo. Bar Asso. . . . 1904* (1905); *Report . . . Am. Bar Asso.*; *Chicago Legal News*, Oct. 20, 1904; *N. Y. Times*, Aug. 13, 1904; information from a son and a daughter.]

T. W.

THOMPSON, SMITH (Jan. 17, 1768–Dec. 18, 1843), jurist, was born in the town of Amenia (Stanford), Dutchess County, N. Y., the son of Ezra and Rachel (Smith) Thompson. His father was a descendant of Anthony Thompson who arrived in Boston in 1637 and subsequently settled at Milford in the New Haven colony. Smith Thompson graduated from the College of New Jersey (Princeton) in 1788, and studied law in Poughkeepsie under James Kent [*q.v.*], supporting himself meanwhile by teaching school. He was admitted to the bar in 1792 and practised for a time in Troy, but returned to Poughkeepsie in 1793 when Kent went to New York City. In 1794 he married Sarah, daughter of Gilbert Livingston of Poughkeepsie, a member of the powerful Livingston family, and thereafter he was affiliated with the Jeffersonian Republicans of the anti-Burr faction in New York. He was elected to the state legislature in 1800 and represented Dutchess County in the constitutional convention of 1801. The same year he was appointed district attorney for the middle district but his appointment as associate justice of the supreme court of New York on Jan.

8, 1802, prevented his serving. In 1807 the Council of Appointment offered him the mayoralty of New York City, but he declined it, remaining on the bench. On Feb. 25, 1814, he was made chief justice in place of Kent, who became chancellor.

In November 1818 Thompson was appointed secretary of the navy by Monroe. He assumed his duties Jan. 1, 1819, and served until Aug. 31, 1823, when he resigned to accept appointment to the associate justiceship on the Supreme Court left vacant by the death of Henry Brockholst Livingston [q.v.], a position for which both Kent and Van Buren were strongly urged. Thompson debated accepting the appointment for some time because of his poor health, the low salary, and his lack of judicial experience in fields outside the common law, but mainly because he thought the Republicans might nominate him for the presidency in 1824. Finally convinced that he had no chance for the nomination against John Quincy Adams and William H. Crawford, he accepted the judicial appointment and remained on the Court until his death. His judicial duties did not quiet his political ambitions, however. In 1828 he allowed himself to be nominated for the governorship of New York by a badly divided National Republican party and ran against Martin Van Buren [q.v.] in one of the bitterest and most spectacular campaigns the state had seen. He was sharply criticized by his Jacksonian opponents for running for political office without resigning from the Court, and was defeated by a vote of 136,794 to 106,444.

On the Supreme Court Thompson joined the group which had already begun to pull away from the strong nationalism of Marshall. The death of his daughter prevented his taking his seat in February 1824 until after the arguments in *Gibbons* vs. *Ogden* (9 *Wheaton,* 1) had been heard, and he did not participate in the decision. Had he done so he would probably have disagreed with Marshall, since in 1812 he had rendered a decision in the New York court of errors upholding the power of the state to create the steamboat monopoly (*Livingston* vs. *Van Ingen,* 9 *Johnson,* 507, at p. 563). He dissented in *Brown* vs. *Maryland* (12 *Wheaton,* 419), in 1827, in which the Court held void a state license tax on imports in the original package, and in the same year he helped overrule Marshall in *Ogden* vs. *Saunders* (12 *Wheaton,* 214), writing a strong concurring opinion upholding the validity of a state bankruptcy law. He dissented in 1830 from Marshall's decision in *Craig* vs. *Missouri* (4 *Peters,* 410), holding certain state certificates void as bills of credit, and wrote a concurring

opinion in the later case (1837) of *Briscoe* vs. *Bank of Kentucky* (11 *Peters,* 257), upholding the note issue of a state-owned bank. He concurred in a separate opinion in *Mayor of New York* vs. *Miln* (11 *Peters,* 102), 1837, holding valid certain state regulations affecting foreign and interstate commerce, and although personally a bitter opponent of slavery, in 1842 he expressed his agreement with *Prigg* vs. *Pennsylvania* (16 *Peters,* 539), upholding the federal Fugitive Slave Act. He dissented with Story in *Charles River Bridge* vs. *Warren Bridge* (11 *Peters,* 420), 1837, and also dissented in *Cherokee Nation* vs. *Georgia* (5 *Peters,* 1), 1831. The most notable case in which Thompson spoke for the Court was that of *Kendall* vs. *United States* (12 *Peters,* 524), 1838, upholding the right of the federal courts to require a cabinet officer by *mandamus* to perform a ministerial duty. Thompson's oral opinion in this case contained a paragraph vigorously rejecting the theory attributed to Jackson that the president under his power to see that the laws are faithfully executed may enforce his own interpretation of the Constitution by extending protection to his subordinates when they violate the acts of Congress or the mandates of the courts. This paragraph was expunged at the request of Attorney-General Benjamin F. Butler [q.v.], who denied that such a theory had been urged in argument. It is significant as a judicial repudiation of a theory of executive independence generally supposed to have been held by Jackson and Lincoln (see Warren, *post,* II, 317 ff.). Thompson wrote the opinion of the Court in eighty-five cases, few of which related to constitutional matters. He wrote eleven dissenting opinions and five concurring opinions.

In 1836, after the death of his first wife, Thompson married her cousin Eliza, daughter of Henry Livingston. Two sons and two daughters were born of the first marriage and one son and two daughters, of the second. Egbert Thompson [q.v.] was his nephew. In 1813 he was made one of the regents of the University of the State of New York. He was a strong Presbyterian and a vice-president of the American Bible Society. He was small in stature, reserved in manner and speech, but kind and affable upon close acquaintance. He died in Poughkeepsie in his seventy-sixth year.

[Thompson's opinions in the Supreme Court appear in 9 *Wheaton* to 16 *Peters,* inclusive. Biog. material appears in *Law Reporter,* Jan. 1844; A. B. Street, *The Council of Revision of the State of N. Y.* (1859); Charles Warren, *The Supreme Court in U. S. Hist.* (1922), vol. II, *passim*; H. L. Carson, *The Supreme Court of the U. S.* (1891); D. S. Alexander, *A Political Hist. of the State of N. Y.,* vol. I (1906); Alden Chester, *Courts and Lawyers of N. Y.* (1925); W. B.

Thompson, *Thompson Lineage* (1911); *N. Y. Herald,* Dec. 20, 1843, and *N. Y. Tribune,* Dec. 20, 1843, which gives incorrect date for death.]   R. E. C.

THOMPSON, THOMAS LARKIN (May 31, 1838–Feb. 1, 1898), editor, congressman, diplomat, son of Robert Augustine and Mary (Slaughter) Thompson, was born in Charleston, Va. (now W. Va.). His father and grandfather, Philip Rootes Thompson, were both members of Congress. His great-grandfather, John Thompson, was an Irish Presbyterian minister who came to America in the eighteenth century. At twelve the boy went to work in the office of the *West Virginian* at Charleston. In 1853–54 he attended Buffalo Academy in Putnam County. The next year he went to San Francisco, where he worked on the *San Francisco Herald* until 1858, except for an interlude in 1855–56 when, at the age of seventeen, he established the *Petaluma Weekly Journal and Sonoma County Advertiser* at Petaluma, Cal. The two years following he worked in the San Francisco post office. In 1859 he married Marion Satterlee, daughter of Judge William Satterlee of San Francisco; of this union one son and four daughters were born. Thompson published the *Sonoma Democrat* (Santa Rosa, Cal.) from 1860 to 1868, and the *Solano Democrat* (weekly) and the *Vallejo Daily Independent* at Vallejo, Cal., for the ensuing five years. In 1871 he again purchased the *Sonoma Democrat* and in 1873 settled permanently in Santa Rosa. He was a delegate to the Democratic national conventions of 1880 and 1892. From 1882 to 1886 he was secretary of state of California. He was elected in 1886 to the Fiftieth Congress, where he served on the rivers and harbors and invalid pensions committees.

In 1893 Thompson was appointed by President Cleveland envoy extraordinary and minister plenipotentiary to Brazil. On his arrival at Rio de Janeiro, Aug. 25, a diplomatic situation of the most difficult kind confronted him. The capital of the four-year-old republic was seething with revolutionary ferment, which burst into actual civil war when the Brazilian navy revolted on Sept. 6 and threatened to bombard the city. American property and lives were jeopardized, and South Americans and Europeans jealously watched for evidence of interference in the internal politics of Brazil by the United States. Thompson determined to protect American interests and to preserve as impartial an attitude as possible. During the six months that elapsed before the surrender of the revolutionists the United States minister, working in harmony with other members of the diplomatic corps, maintained a friendly attitude toward the national government without allowing himself to become committed to its support. He refused to become involved in the revolutionary movement even to the extent of announcing American neutrality, which would have given the revolting party the status of belligerents. At the same time, through his cooperation with United States naval officers, American commerce was protected and continued with practically no interruption throughout the whole period. Disastrous shelling of the capital was also prevented. A less rigidly maintained position on the part of the minister might have resulted in a different outcome of the conflict, but the announced intention of the revolutionists to establish a monarchy precluded either popular or official sympathy in the United States. As it was, many of the leading American newspapers of the day wrongly accused Thompson of favoring the revolutionists. Many evidences of good will for the United States in Brazil followed the termination of the naval revolt; in connection with the presidential inauguration ceremonies on Nov. 15, 1894, the cornerstone of a monument to the memory of James Monroe and the Monroe Doctrine was laid in Rio de Janeiro. Thompson resigned in 1897, but before his return home he had negotiated and signed an extradition treaty for the United States with Brazil (ratified 1903). For many years he had been suffering from an ear infection, and following his return to his home in Santa Rosa, Cal., his health failed rapidly. On Feb. 1, 1898, while temporarily deranged, he took his own life. His wife and all five of his children survived him.

[R. T. Green, *Geneal. and Hist. Notes on Culpeper County, Va.* (1900); J. P. Munro-Fraser, *Hist. of Sonoma County* (1880); W. J. Davis, *Hist. of Political Conventions in Cal.* (1893); *Biog. Dir. Am. Cong.* (1928); *Papers Relating to the Foreign Relations of the U. S.,* 1893, 1894, 1895, 1897; L. F. Hill, *Diplomatic Relations between the U. S. and Brazil* (1932); *San Francisco Chronicle,* Feb. 2, 1898; *Examiner* (San Francisco), Feb. 2, 1898.]   I. L. T.

THOMPSON, WADDY (Sept. 8, 1798–Nov. 23, 1868), congressman from South Carolina, diplomat, was born in Pickensville, south of the present town of Easley, S. C., the son of Waddy Thompson, a distinguished lawyer and a successful local politician, and Eliza (Blackburn) Thompson, both natives of Virginia. He was the uncle of Hugh Smith Thompson [*q.v.*]. Young Waddy was graduated from South Carolina College, now the University of South Carolina, in 1814. He afterward studied law in the private offices of two South Carolina lawyers and was admitted to the bar in 1819. After practising for five years in Edgefield, where he married Emmala Butler, the daughter of William Butler,

1759–1821 [q.v.] and the sister of Andrew and Pierce M. Butler [qq.v.], he removed to Greenville. In 1826 the Greenville District elected him to the state legislature and he served in that body until 1830, when he retired because he was not in accord with the Union sentiment of his constituency. He was then chosen by the legislature as solicitor for the Western District. Opposed to the tariffs of 1824 and 1828, he became an ardent Nullifier and was made a brigadier-general in the forces organized to defend his state against Federal interference, an office that he held until 1842. In 1835 he was the successful Whig candidate to fill the vacancy in Congress caused by the death of Warren R. Davis, and he continued to represent the Greenville District in that capacity until 1841 despite the vigorous opposition of John C. Calhoun, who had gone over to the Democratic party and wished to carry the state with him. Although no candidate announced against Thompson for the campaign of 1840, he decided to retire from the political arena.

Early in 1842, however, the Whig administration appointed him as minister to Mexico. His appointment to the post might have appeared unwise, for his career in Congress had been conspicuous for his hostility to John Quincy Adams with respect to anti-slavery petitions, and for his advocacy first of the recognition and then of the annexation of Texas. Nevertheless, his mission met with a considerable degree of success. He obtained the release of some three hundred prisoners, citizens of the United States in the main, who had been captured during the desultory war between Mexico and Texas; made some progress in the settlement of claims; persuaded the Mexican government not to exclude American immigrants from California; obtained minor commercial concessions; and at one time set in motion negotiations that appeared to promise the peaceful acquisition of California. He won the respect and friendship of the Mexicans and returned to the United States in 1844 an ardent friend of Mexico. Two years later he published his *Recollections* (1846) of his mission, a calm, judicious volume still cited by historians.

Returning to Greenville he resumed his legal practice and accumulated a small fortune in South Carolina and Florida real estate. After the death of his first wife, he married in 1851 Cornelia Jones of Wilmington, N. C., who with their one son survived him. Soon after 1852 he built on the top of Paris Mountain, really a hill about 2,000 feet above sea level, a luxurious house equipped with almost every known convenience and filled with books, paintings, and curios. He might have reëntered politics, if he

had not been too honest to trim his sails to the popular breeze. Disapproving the war with Mexico and doubting the expediency of secession, he preferred to retire to private life. As the result of the Civil War, he lost his fortune. Early in 1867 he removed to Madison, Fla., where he still owned a plantation. His death occurred during a visit to Tallahassee.

[Much of Thompson's personal correspondence was destroyed by fire in 1901; the remainder appears to be in the hands of Waddy Thompson, Atlanta, Ga.; his diplomatic correspondence may be found in the state department archives and his speeches in the *Congressional Globe*; a few letters are in the Lib. of Cong.; see also H. T. Thompson, *Waddy Thompson, Jr.* (rev. ed., 1929); G. L. Rives, *The U. S. and Mexico* (2 vols., 1913); J. M. Callahan, *Am. Foreign Policy in Mexican Relations* (1932); *Charleston Daily Courier*, Nov. 27, 1868.]

J. F. R.

THOMPSON, WILEY (Sept. 23, 1781–Dec. 28, 1835), congressman from Georgia, Indian agent, was born in Amelia County, Va., the son of Isham and Elizabeth (Williams) Thompson. His father, a soldier of the Revolution, removed to Wilkes, now Elbert County, Ga. Educated in the county school, there, Wiley soon rose to local prominence and was appointed by the legislature to be commissioner of the Elbert County academy in 1808. He served in the War of 1812, was elected in 1817 major-general of the 4th Division of Georgia militia, and resigned in 1824. In 1819 he served on a commission to determine the boundary line between Georgia and East Florida (Gov. William Rabun to Secretary of War, Feb. 19, 1819, Georgia Department of Archives and History, Atlanta). He was a member of the state Senate from 1817 to 1819, when he resigned. He served in the federal House of Representatives from 1821 to 1833. As chairman of the committee of military affairs he obtained payment of Georgia militia claims of 1793 and 1824. A bitter opponent of protection, he expressed the view that the South would "be driven to the necessity of resistance" and, while he loved the Union, that "he 'would go with him who goes the farthest' in an effort to stave off oppression" (*Register of Debates*, 21 Cong., 2 Sess., col. 573; 22 Cong., 1 Sess., col. 3733).

In close accord with Jackson on Indian removal, he was appointed as agent of the Seminole Indians in Florida. Instructed to superintend the removal of the Indians on the Apalachicola and Chattahoochee rivers under the treaties of Payne's Landing of 1832, and Fort Gibson of 1833, he won the friendship of some of the chiefs and in 1834 led John Blount and Davy Elliott, with their bands, to New Orleans, where he paid them $8,000 of their allowance in cash. This action was approved by Elbert Herring, then commissioner of Indian affairs. In council after his return, he found some of the chiefs unwilling to emigrate. He made clear Jackson's determination that they go, but Osceola [q.v.] led a group that threatened resistance. Thompson then ordered the sale of liquor and ammunition to the Indians and the purchase of their slaves stopped, and he asked for troops to aid in removal. Jackson approved the order forbidding trade and ordered Gen. Duncan L. Clinch with troops to Florida. On July 8, 1834, Thompson was appointed "superintendent of emigration" and was to continue also as Seminole agent. In a council of 1835 he agreed that the Seminole should be transported by water in one body, rather than overland in three annual parties, as the earlier treaties had provided. When Osceola was still hostile and interrupted the council, Thompson harshly rebuked him and removed him and four other disgruntled chiefs, an action that General Clinch termed as judicious handling of the difficulty. Jackson, however, forbade the removal of chiefs, believing it would arouse hostility, and the press condemned Thompson's action as highhanded and tyrannical. Osceola, still obdurate, later visited Fort King and used abusive language toward Thompson and the United States government because of the forced removal and the seizure of his young wife as a slave. Thompson warned him and then put him in chains but finally released Osceola, who pretended to be penitent and returned a few days later with seventy-nine recalcitrants who appeared to agree to emigrate. However, with a band of sixty warriors Osceola lay in wait for two days near Fort King. As Thompson and Lieut. Constantine Smith were walking, the band attacked and shot Thompson dead, and then scalped him. He was buried at Fort King but later his wife, formerly Mrs. Ellington, had his body removed to Elberton, Ga., where it was buried on his estate.

[Biog. Dir. Am. Cong. (1928); J. T. Sprague, The Origin, Progress, and Conclusion of the Fla. War (1848); C. M. Brevard, "A Hist. of Fla.," Fla. State Hist. Soc. Pubs., no. 4, vol. I (1924); Army and Navy Chronicle, Jan. 21, Feb. 18, Mar. 31, Apr. 7, 1836; Niles' Weekly Register, Jan. 30, 1836, Nov. 4, 1837; Hist. Colls. of the Ga. Chapters, D.A.R., "Records of Elbert County," vol. III (1930); Daily Savannah Republican, Jan. 9, 11, 20, 1836.]   F. M. G.

THOMPSON, WILL LAMARTINE (Nov. 7, 1847–Sept. 20, 1909), writer of sacred and secular songs, was born in Beaver County, Pa., one of seven children of Josiah and Sarah (Jackman) Thompson. His grandfather, William Thompson, had emigrated to Pennsylvania from Ireland. His father was a merchant and a banker, and served for two terms in the state legislature of Ohio. His father's family were all musical, and, after attending the public schools of East Liverpool, Ohio, and Mount Union College, Alliance, Ohio, Thompson began the serious study of music in 1870 at the Boston Music School. Later he studied at the Boston Conservatory of Music and then went to Leipzig, Germany. One of his earliest compositions was a *Schottische* which he named for his home town, "Liverpool"; another was a song, "Gathering Shells from the Seashore," written in 1872. When his price of one hundred dollars for this and three other compositions was refused by a Cleveland publisher, he undertook the management of the sales for himself, the song having been published in New York. It was introduced upon the stage by the Carncross and Dixey Minstrel Company of Philadelphia, and its popularity became so great that the presses were kept running day and night for several months to meet the demand. Thompson's financial returns from it ran above one thousand dollars during the first year. About 1875 he organized a music publishing business and store at East Liverpool, Ohio.

Some of his other popular secular songs are "Drifting with the Tide," "My Home on the Old Ohio," and "The Old Tramp," which during the financial troubles of 1876–77 was on everyone's lips—"I'm only a poor old wanderer, I've no place to call my home." His humorous mode is illustrated by "My First Music Lesson" and "My Sweetheart and I Went Fishing"; among his other compositions are the "Protective Tariff March," "God Save Our Union," a patriotic song, and "Come Where the Lilies Bloom." It is perhaps by his sacred songs that he will be longest remembered, for these have been introduced into many hymn books. The best known is "Softly and Tenderly Jesus Is Calling," which has been translated into many languages. "There's a Great Day Coming" (1903), "Golden Years Are Passing By" (1879), "Jesus Is All the World to Me," "Lead Me Gently Home," and "The Sinner and the Song" are his, both words and music, and he wrote the music for "Break the News Gently to Mother" (1878), the words of which were by Allie E. Wardwell of East Liverpool.

Thompson made his home at East Liverpool, where he established a music store. He later became president of the Thompson Music Company, Chicago. He married Elizabeth Johnston at Wellsville, Ohio, on Apr. 23, 1891. He died in New York at the end of a summer spent abroad with his wife and son. Among the books he published are *Enduring Hymns* (n.d.), *The New Century Hymnal* (copyright 1904), and *The Young People's Choir* (n.d.).

[H. B. Barth, *Hist. of Columbiana County, Ohio* (1926), vol. II, pp. 453–55; *Hist. of the Upper Ohio Valley* (1891), vol. II, pp. 362–65; *Who's Who in America*, 1908–09; C. B. Galbreath, in *Ohio Archaeological and Hist. Quart.*, July 1905; *Musical Million*, Oct. 1909; *Classmate*, Dec. 13, 1913; J. H. Hall, *Biog. of Gospel Song and Hymn Writers* (copr. 1914); C. H. Gabriel, *Gospel Songs and their Writers* (1915), which gives incorrect dates of birth and death; obituary in *Ohio State Jour.* (Columbus), Sept. 21, 1909.]

F. J. M—f.

THOMPSON, WILLIAM (1736–Sept. 3, 1781), Revolutionary soldier, was born in Ireland. Emigrating to America, he settled on a farm near Carlisle, Pa., where he became a surveyor and justice of the peace. During the French and Indian war, he was commissioned captain of a troop of horse and participated in the expedition led by John Armstrong, 1717–1795 [q.v.], against Kittanning. He took part in the work of settling the western boundary of Pennsylvania and in locating lands granted by the king to officers serving in the war.

On July 12, 1774, at a meeting of the freeholders from several townships of Cumberland County, called to denounce the closing of the port of Boston, he was elected member of a committee of correspondence; and later, in May 1775, he served upon the provincial committee of safety. When the news of the battle of Bunker Hill reached Pennsylvania, he was placed in command of a battalion of riflemen raised in the southeastern counties, designated at first as the 2nd Pennsylvania Regiment but later as the 1st Continental Infantry. Marching promptly to Boston, it won credit as the first body of men to reach that point from the South. It constituted a crack corps, the privates being unusually "stout and hardy; many of them exceeding six feet and remarkable for the accuracy of their aim." They were dressed in "white frocks, or rifle shirts, and round hats" (James Thacher, *A Military Journal during the American Revolutionary War*, 1823, pp. 37–38). During the siege they were posted on Prospect Hill. On Nov. 9, 1775, they repulsed an attack upon Lechmere Point, for which Thompson was thanked by Washington in general orders (J. C. Fitzpatrick, *The Writings of George Washington*, vol. IV, 1931, p. 79). On Mar. 1, 1776, he was promoted to the rank of brigadier-general and was presently ordered to Canada in charge of a detachment of about 2,000 men, comprising the regiments of Poor, Paterson, Greaton, and Bond. General Sullivan, commanding the American forces on the St. Lawrence, directed him to attack Three Rivers. On the night of June 7, he crossed the stream a few miles above the town, hoping to surprise the foe at dawn, but owing to the treach-

ery of a guide, his men got lost in a swamp and were repulsed while he was made prisoner.

On Oct. 25, 1780, he was exchanged for Baron Riedesel. Prior to this, however, he was placed on parole and returned to Pennsylvania. Here he became involved in a controversy with Thomas McKean [q.v.], then serving as a member of Congress, whom he accused of hindering his exchange. He submitted a memorial to Congress in which he referred to McKean in such opprobrious terms that, on Nov. 23, 1778, that body voted that he was "guilty of an insult to the honor and dignity of this house, and of a breach of privilege" (W. C. Ford, *Journals of Continental Congress*, vol. XII, 1908, p. 1151). He was summoned before Congress and tendered an apology. McKean sued him for libel and was awarded £5,700 damages, which he released, since he only desired to see the law and the facts settled (see Peeling, *post*). Thompson died and was buried in Carlisle. His energy, fearlessness, and pugnacity admirably qualified him to occupy high command in an army whose plight was often desperate.

[The Pennsylvania Historical Society possesses manuscript letters of Thompson. Consult also J. H. Peeling, "Life of Thomas McKean," Ph.D. thesis, n.s., Univ. of Chicago; J. T. Scharf and Thompson Westcott, *Hist. of Philadelphia* (1884), vol. I; *Pa. Mag. of Hist. and Biog.*, Apr. 1883, July 1911; *Centennial Memorial of the Presbytery of Carlisle* (2 vols., 1889); J. H. Smith, *Our Struggle for the Fourteenth Colony* (1907), vol. II; E. C. Burnett, ed., *Letters of Members of the Continental Cong.*, vols. I–IV (1921–28); S. W. Parkinson, *Memories of Carlisle's Old Graveyard* (1930); *Pa. Gazette and Weekly Advertiser*, Sept. 12, 1781.]

E. E. C.

THOMPSON, WILLIAM BOYCE (May 13, 1869–June 27, 1930), miner, financier, philanthropist, was born at Virginia City, then a Montana mining camp of ebbing fortunes. He was the elder son of William Thompson, a native of Canada who had lived in the United States since 1853, and of Anne (Boyce), a Missourian of Virginian ancestry. His father, a carpenter by trade, arrived in Virginia City at the height of the gold excitement of 1863; during the territory's pioneer stage he did considerable building and also operated lumber mills. In 1880 he moved his family to Butte, Mont. Stimulated mentally by the principal of the Butte high school, a young Englishman from Balliol College, Oxford, William elected at eighteen to go East to Phillips Exeter Academy in New Hampshire because Daniel Webster had studied there. His father was beginning to develop gold, silver, and copper mining claims in Montana, and in 1889, without graduating, the son went from Exeter to the School of Mines of Columbia University. After one year, however, he returned to

Montana as superintendent of an unsuccessful silver mine. For a time he was secretary of a lumber company of his father's, for a time a coal dealer in Helena. In 1897 he returned to Butte, where he dealt in real estate, mines, and insurance, and recovered a considerable amount of copper from the Butte ore dumps. He was among the first to see the possibilities of working low-grade ores with improved machinery on a large scale, thus utilizing claims that had been abandoned as unprofitable. When, after years of experimentation, he believed he had the technical key to successful mass production he interested capital in his projects.

After a brief attempt to sell mining stocks in New York City (1899), he spent five years developing a copper mine in Arizona. Returning to New York in 1904, he opened a broker's office, operating on the Curb; he was one of the few men dealing in copper stocks in Wall Street who knew at first hand the actual conditions of existing and prospective mining properties. The Nipissing silvermine, which he launched in 1906, laid the foundation of his great fortune. Into Inspiration Copper Company in Gila County, Ariz., he put $17,000,000 before a dollar was taken out, but the first year the mine was operated it showed a net profit of $20,000,000. He became interested in mining properties in all parts of the world and his investments yielded large returns. He was active in politics as a Republican, and was a director of the Federal Reserve Bank of New York for six years (1914–19). Becoming intensely interested in Robert Kennedy Duncan [q.v.] and his scheme of industrial fellowships, he provided thirty-six temporary fellowships in the Mellon Institute, Pittsburgh.

At the beginning of the World War, Thompson bought a considerable interest in Bethlehem Steel and during the conflict entered many other fields which gave him bountiful returns. He was a leader in securing funds for Herbert Hoover's Belgian relief work, and was instrumental in promoting the passage of the first "daylight saving" law. In 1917, having offered to pay the expenses of the American Red Cross mission to Russia, he was sent with that expedition as business manager and after the withdrawal of Dr. Franklin Billings, became its leader. He labored, though vainly, to secure aid from the United States for the Kerensky régime and contributed a million dollars to finance a propaganda campaign designed to keep the Russian army fighting on the Eastern front. After the overthrow of Kerensky, he urged recognition and aid of the new Soviet government by the Allies.

Upon his return to the United States, he be-

came a promoter of Theodore Roosevelt, whom he had opposed in 1912 and 1916, as a candidate for the presidential nomination; after Roosevelt's death in January 1919, Thompson headed the Roosevelt Memorial Association (1919–24). At the Republican National Convention of 1920 he supported Leonard Wood, then Will Hays, but as chairman of the party's ways and means committee raised Harding's campaign fund. His reward for this service was appointment as a United States commissioner to attend the celebration of the centenary of Peru's independence, and as a member of an advisory council connected with the Washington Conference on the Limitation of Armament (1921–22).

Thompson's lifelong interest in vegetable growth was manifested in his personal direction of the planting of his extensive estate "Alder," at Yonkers, N. Y., and of his estate near Superior, Ariz. In 1919 he organized the Farm and Research Corporation for the investigation of plant life. In 1923, after some revision of the plans, the title of this foundation was changed to Boyce Thompson Institute for Plant Research; a liberal endowment was provided; suitable buildings were erected at Yonkers and dedicated in 1924; and before Thompson's death the Institute had already made important advances in botanical experimentation. He also established the Boyce Thompson Southwestern Arboretum in Arizona and gave large sums of money to Phillips Exeter Academy. The bulk of his large estate was left to his wife, Gertrude (Hickman) Thompson, whom he had married on Feb. 6, 1895, and to their daughter.

[Hermann Hagedorn, The Magnate: William Boyce Thompson and His Time (1935); Who's Who in America, 1930–31; Inspiration Consolidated Copper Company: Reports, 1915, 1916; Bessie Beatty, "Gold and Fool's Gold," Asia (N. Y.), Aug. 1918; The Roosevelt Memorial Asso. . . . Report, 1919–21, 1921–22, 1923, 1924; J. M. Coulter, "Boyce Thompson Institute for Plant Research," Scientific Monthly, Aug. 1926; Contributions from Boyce Thompson Institute for Plant Research, Inc., vol. I (1929), containing addresses at the opening of the Institute; N. Y. Times, June 28, July 4, 1930; memorandum from William Crocker, Esq., director of the Boyce Thompson Institute for Plant Research, Apr. 3, 1933.]   W. B. S.

THOMPSON, WILLIAM GILMAN (Dec. 25, 1856–Oct. 27, 1927), physician and pioneer in industrial hygiene, was born in New York City, the son of Joseph Parrish Thompson [q.v.], and his second wife, Elizabeth Coit Gilman. Daniel Coit Gilman [q.v.] was his uncle. He received his early education in private schools and the Hopkins Grammar School, New Haven, Conn., with one year of study in Karlsruhe, Germany. He was graduated from Yale with the Ph.B. degree in 1877 and proceeded to the College of

Physicians and Surgeons in New York City. His work here was interrupted by the death of his father in Europe. He crossed the sea at once and spent a year studying at the medical departments of King's College, London, and the University of Berlin. He returned to the United States and received the M.D. degree from Columbia in 1881. In 1885 he won the Joseph Mather Smith prize for his essay, "Structure of the Heart Valves," and the Harsen prize for his essay, "Photography of the Living Heart in Motion." He served for eighteen months as interne of the New York Hospital, and then was appointed visiting physician to the Bloomingdale Asylum at White Plains, N. Y., and at the New York Cancer Hospital. In 1887 he became visiting physician of the New York Hospital and the Presbyterian, serving the former for seven years and the latter for twenty-five. He was made "quiz master" at the College of Physicians and Surgeons in 1884–85, and in 1887 became professor of physiology at the University of the City of New York. He held this chair until 1898. From 1898 until 1916 he served as professor of medicine at Cornell University Medical College in New York City and was then made professor emeritus.

He introduced important changes in the methods of teaching physiology, and was one of the first physicians in America to develop clinical research along with laboratory investigation. When the Loomis Laboratory, the first institute of experimental medicine in America, was opened in 1888, he was made director. He knew the value of clinical research and spent much of his life in the study of disease at the bedside. On his retirement from Cornell, he plunged into the work for which he has become best known—reeducation in connection with war and industrial diseases. For many years he was chairman of the Industrial Hygiene Division of the New York Labor Department, organized to carry out a scientific study of hygienic conditions in industries. During the World War he organized a functional reëducational clinic, and from that developed the Reconstruction Hospital, of which he was the founder. Under his direction chronic patients and incurables were taught to do constructive and interesting work.

A dynamic man of untiring energy, he devoted his life to his work and left little time for hobbies. He was forceful and progressive, remarkable for his affability in spite of the fact that among his associates he had few intimate friends. He held offices in the New York Botanical Society and the Garden Club, and was a member of many medical societies in New York. He was considered an authority on foods, and his *Practical Dietetics* (1895) went through many editions. He wrote numerous medical articles which were published in medical journals, newspapers, and textbooks (for bibliography, see Shrady, *post*). He was co-editor, with A. L. Loomis, of *System of Practical Medicine by American Authors* (4 volumes, 1897–98), and author of *Training-Schools for Nurses* (1883), *Text-book of Practical Medicine* (1900), and *Occupational Diseases* (1914). He was married on Aug. 11, 1887, to Harriet Howard Pomeroy, daughter of John Norton Pomeroy [q.v.], whom he survived by a few months. He died of heart disease.

[*Who's Who in America*, 1926–27; Ledyard Bill, *Hist. of the Bill Family* (1867); F. W. Chapman, *Coit Family* (1874); John Shrady, ed., *The Coll. of Physicians and Surgeons, A Hist.* (1903–04?), vol. I; J. J. Moorhead, Address at the Unveiling of a Memorial Tablet to Dr. Thompson at the Reconstruction Hospital, May 16, 1933; *N. Y. Times*, Oct. 28, 31, 1927.]

G. L. A.

THOMPSON, WILLIAM OXLEY (Nov. 5, 1855–Dec. 9, 1933), Presbyterian clergyman, university president, the eldest of ten children of David Glenn Thompson and Agnes Miranda (Oxley) Thompson, was born in Cambridge, Ohio, and spent his early years there, in New Concord, and in Zanesville. His paternal grandfather was a native of the North of Ireland; his father was a shoemaker and farmer who served in the Civil War. William's elementary education was interrupted by the war and limited by the short term of the rural schools; when not studying he worked as a farm hand at eight dollars per month. In 1870 he entered Muskingum College but was able to attend only at intervals, between periods of laboring on the farm and teaching school. It took him eight years to complete the course, but he graduated first in his class in 1878. He subsequently taught for a time in the academy at Indiana, Pa.

In early life Thompson had determined to be a missionary, and accordingly he entered the Western Theological Seminary (Presbyterian), Allegheny, Pa., from which he graduated in 1882, again with honors. In the same year he married Rebecca Jane Allison and accepted an appointment to a Presbyterian mission church in Odebolt, Iowa, being ordained at Fort Dodge on July 13, 1882. In Odebolt, a town of some six hundred, his genius as a leader of religious and community activities manifested itself, his interests extending into every community within the traveling range of his team. In 1885 he removed to Longmont, Colo., where for six years he served as pastor of the local Presbyterian church and president of the newly established Synodical

College. In 1886 his wife died, leaving one daughter, and in October 1887 he married Helen Starr Brown of Longmont, who bore him two sons. After her death in 1890 he sought a return to Ohio, and in 1891 was elected president of Miami University at Oxford. On June 28, 1894, he married Estelle Godfrey Clark, a member of the faculty of Oxford College for Women.

His success at Miami was such that in 1899 he was called to the presidency of Ohio State University, where he served until his retirement, as president emeritus, in 1925. During his administration the University grew from a local college of some 1,200 students to an institution comprising all the higher educational activities —undergraduate and graduate—of a modern state university, with an enrollment of some 12,-000. He was an acknowledged leader in the field of education: he was president of the Association of American Agricultural Colleges and Experiment Stations, 1903–04; president of the Ohio Education Association, 1905–06; president of the National Association of State Universities, 1910–11.

Meanwhile, his interest in religious activities continued. His devotions at the college chapel exercises made lasting impressions upon his students. He conducted weekly convocation at the Ohio State University for many years after the number of students made it impossible to hold a general chapel exercise. He was a dominant figure in various religious bodies, special minister to numberless congregations in the Middle West, baccalaureate speaker in colleges and high schools, president of the Ohio Sunday School Association 1897–1902, moderator of the General Assembly of the Presbyterian Church in the United States of America in 1927. He also participated in civic life with enthusiasm. In Oxford he served on the village council; in Columbus, on the Board of Education. He was chairman of the United States agricultural commission sent to Europe to make observations on the food supply in England, France, and Italy in 1918, and chairman of the United States Anthracite Coal Commission in 1920. He was president of the Midland Mutual Life Insurance Company of Columbus, Ohio, from 1905 to 1925.

Thompson was a natural leader, endowed with an admirable physique, boundless energy, and a pleasing voice. He possessed great dignity without imperiousness; his eloquence was uncontrolled by rhetorical rules. He was simple in his habits, frank in conversation and debate, sympathetic toward misfortune. His friends among the simple and poor were as dear to him as those

in positions of influence. Upon his death he was acclaimed as Ohio's first citizen.

[J. J. Burns, *Educ. Hist. of Ohio* (1905); *Ohio Archæol. and Hist. Quart.,* Jan. 1934; *Who's Who in America,* 1932–33; T. C. Mendenhall, *Hist. of the Ohio State Univ.,* vols. I–III (1920–26); *Alumni Cat., Miami Univ.* . . . *1809–1909* (n.d.); *Columbus Evening Dispatch,* Dec. 9, 1933; *Ohio State Journal* (Columbus), Dec. 11, 13, 1933; *Ohio State Univ. Mo.,* Dec. 1933.]

H. C. M.

THOMPSON, WILLIAM TAPPAN (Aug. 31, 1812–Mar. 24, 1882), editor and humorist, was born in Ravenna, Ohio. His father, David Thompson, was a settler from Virginia; his mother, Catherine (Kerney) Thompson, had been born in Ireland. He presumably attended school in the small schoolhouse he mentions as existing in Ravenna in 1816; but he was orphaned in his early teens and thrown on his own resources in Philadelphia, where acquaintances of his father befriended him. After working in the office of the *Daily Chronicle,* Philadelphia, he was appointed assistant (1830) to James Diament Westcott, secretary of the territory of Florida, under whom he studied law for several years. By 1835, however, he had turned again to journalism, this time in Augusta, Ga., where he was associated with Augustus Baldwin Longstreet [*q.v.*] in issuing the *States Rights Sentinel.* For a few months in 1836 he served with an Augusta militia unit in the campaign against the Seminoles in Florida. On June 12, 1837, he was married to Carolina A. Carrié of Augusta. In the spring of 1838 he founded in Augusta a literary journal, the *Mirror,* which in 1842 he merged with the *Macon Family Companion* under the composite title of the *Family Companion and Ladies' Mirror.* Though the new periodical was discontinued in 1843 for lack of patronage, the humorous letters of "Major Jones" which Thompson began in one of its last issues attracted immediate attention, and a small collection of them was published locally as *Major Jones's Courtship* (1843), afterwards enlarged and republished in Philadelphia. Later appeared *Major Jones's Chronicles of Pineville* (1843) and *Major Jones's Sketches of Travel* (1848). From 1843 to 1845 Thompson controlled the *Miscellany,* a weekly published in Madison, Ga., but left in the latter year to assist the poet, Park Benjamin [*q.v.*], with the *Western Continent,* a weekly in Baltimore, Md. Benjamin withdrew from the partnership after a few months, and Thompson continued the publication alone until 1850. At this time he returned to Georgia and founded the *Savannah Morning News,* which he edited until the time of his death and of which he made one of the strongest newspapers of the state. During the sectional struggle preceding the Civil War he stoutly defended the institution of slavery. He not only wrote editorials in support of the Southern cause, but launched a volume of fictional propaganda, *The Slaveholder Abroad* (1860), full of excerpts from British newspapers designed to show that free England engendered more crime and true slavery than the South. During the Civil War he labored to maintain the morale of his fellow citizens, and in 1864 served as a volunteer soldier. He took an active part in local, state, and national politics. In 1868 he was a delegate to the National Democratic Convention and in 1877 a member of the convention which shaped a new constitution for Georgia. He died in Savannah, survived by his wife and several children. His writings include an unpublished farce, "The Live Indian"; a body of sketches, *John's Alive* (1838), published after his death; and a dramatization of *The Vicar of Wakefield*. He also edited W. A. Hotchkiss' *A Codification of the Statute Laws of Georgia* (1845).

Thompson was a dignified and somewhat retiring man, but an excellent raconteur, a ready conversationalist, a kindly friend. He was independent in his judgments and uncompromising in support of what he considered right. As an editor he was handicapped by sectional prejudices, but he succeeded in keeping the *Morning News* free of petty journalistic squabbling and steadfastly honest in reporting facts. His humorous volumes dealing with Major Jones not only entertained two or three generations of American readers but retain some permanent value as a record of provincial society.

[See L. L. Knight, *Standard Hist. of Ga. and Georgians* (1917), vol. III, p. 1762, vol. VI, p. 3277; J. D. Wade, *Augustus Baldwin Longstreet* (1924); Jennette Tandy, *Crackerbox Philosophers in Am. Humor and Satire* (1925); W. M. Clemens, *Famous Funny Fellows* (1882); autobiog. articles in Thompson's *John's Alive* (1883); obituary in *Savannah Morning News*, Mar. 25, 27, 1882. Information has also been supplied by Thompson's granddaughter, Mrs. T. Fletcher Smith, of Quitman, Ga.; Ruth Blair, State Historian of Ga., Atlanta; and William Harden of the Ga. Hist. Soc., Savannah.]

J. H. N.

THOMPSON, ZADOCK (May 23, 1796–Jan. 19, 1856), historian, naturalist, mathematician, was born at Bridgewater, Vt., the second son of Capt. Barnabas Thompson, a farmer, who was one of the earliest settlers in Windsor County, and Sarah (Fuller) Thompson. He was a descendant of John Thomson who was brought from Wales to Plymouth about 1622. His education came slowly—he was twenty-seven when he graduated from college—for he had to work his way almost from the beginning. He did farm work (as little of it as possible, disliking it intensely), wrote and peddled his own almanacs and gazetteers, and taught school. He graduated from the University of Vermont in 1823, and the next year, Sept. 4, 1824, married Phebe Boyce, by whom he had two daughters. Appointed tutor at the University of Vermont in 1825, he taught and wrote extensively in Burlington until 1833, edited a magazine, the *Iris,* and the *Green Mountain Repository,* and conducted astronomical observations for his own gazetteers and for *Walton's Vermont Register and Farmer's Almanack.,* Between 1833 and 1837 he filled teaching positions in Canada, first in Hatley and then in Sherbrooke. His *History of the State of Vermont, from Its Earliest Settlement to the Close of the Year 1832* (1833) had appeared just before he left Vermont, and in 1835 he published a *Geography and History of Lower Canada,* which went through several editions. In the same year he was ordained deacon in the Protestant Episcopal Church.

Returning to Burlington, Thompson taught in a boys' school at Rock Point and began the preparation of his most important work, *History of Vermont, Natural, Civil and Statistical* (1842). After more than ninety years it is still an indispensable book of reference on a wide variety of Vermont topics, including the involved and dramatic story of Vermont during its turbulent days of conflict, independence, and final statehood. The wealth of information it contains affords impressive evidence of Thompson's versatility, thoroughness, scientific conservatism, and perspicacity. Relatively few additions or corrections have been found necessary. The section on natural history contains a very adequate list of rocks, fossils, and minerals, including the commercial rock products of the state. Thompson himself had built up a private cabinet of over three thousand specimens, widely known and visited. He described with much detail and accuracy, chiefly because he examined most of them personally, over a hundred and fifty species of birds, forty-eight fishes, thirty-five Amphibia and reptiles, fifty mammals, and over four hundred species of plants. He tells of the fossil elephant unearthed at Mount Holly, the fossil whale from Charlotte, and in the Appendix, published in 1853 and bound with the third edition of the work, he carefully describes the catamount (one of the last in the East) caught in Manchester in 1850 and the seal taken on the ice of Lake Champlain in the next year. The book abounds in excellent illustrations.

Thompson was appointed assistant state geologist in 1845, professor of chemistry and natural history in the University of Vermont in 1851 and state naturalist of Vermont in 1853. In 1851 by.

the assistance of friends he was enabled to make a trip abroad, and in the following year published the journal of his travels. Various books besides those named above came from his busy pen, but there remains to mention his only lucrative venture in publication, a school book called *The Youth's Assistant in Practical Arithmetick* (1825). This was popular, at least with school trustees, since it ran into fourteen editions and printings. Thompson lived most frugally in a tiny frame house facing the University, and died of "ossification of the heart." A tall, lean Yankee, kindly and mild-mannered, beloved and trusted by a very wide circle of friends, he enjoyed an enviable position in the community, and holds a high place among the early naturalists and historians of the United States. Hampered by illness and poverty, he nevertheless left behind him a remarkable record as a doggedly determined worker, a keen and careful observer in many fields, a clear and prolific writer, a notable contributor to and recorder of the history of his state.

[See C. H. Thompson, *A Geneal. of Descendants of John Thomson, of Plymouth, Mass.* (1890); Augustus Young, *Preliminary Report on the Natural Hist. of the State of Vt.* (1856); *Hist. Mag.*, Oct. 1858, p. 301, reprinted from *Walton's Vermont Register for 1857*, and Feb. 1859, pp. 48–49; G. H. Perkins, *Report of the State Geologist on . . . Certain Areas of Vt. . . . 1901–1902* (1902); W. H. Crockett, *Vermonters: a Book of Biogs.* (1931); M. D. Gilman, *The Bibliog. of Vt.* (1897); and obituary in *Burlington Sentinel*, Jan. 24, 1856. First editions and MSS. of Thompson's writings are in the lib. of the Univ. of Vt.]   H. F. P—s.

THOMSON, CHARLES (Nov. 29, 1729–Aug. 16, 1824), secretary of the Continental Congress, was born in County Derry, Ireland, and came to America when he was ten years of age, one of six orphaned children set ashore at New Castle, Del. The mother had died in Ireland; the father, John Thomson, died on shipboard within sight of the American shores. Charles was ere long enabled to enter the academy of Dr. Francis Alison [*q.v.*] at New London, Chester County, Pa., and after leaving the academy conducted a private school for a few years. In 1750, through his acquaintance with Benjamin Franklin, he received an appointment as tutor in the Philadelphia academy, and subsequently (1757–60) he was master of the Latin school in what ultimately became the William Penn Charter School. In 1760 he turned from teaching to the mercantile trade, in which he appears to have prospered.

Meanwhile, because of his reputation for fairness and integrity, he was chosen by the Indians to keep their record of proceedings at the treaty of Easton (1757), and in the following year he was adopted into the Delaware tribe, with a name meaning "man who tells the truth." An outcome of these relations with the Indians was *An Enquiry into the Causes of the Alienation of the Delaware and Shawanese Indians from the British Interest,* published in London in 1759.

Having long taken an active part in Pennsylvania politics, during the decade preceding the Revolution Thomson was in the forefront of all the colonial controversies with Great Britain, and in all of them the politician in him seems to have dominated the merchant. By the time, therefore, that the crucial days of May 1774 arrived, he had become an adept in politics according to the most approved Pennsylvanian standards, as is evinced by his own account of the neat maneuver by which Pennsylvania was brought into substantial accord with the Massachusetts proposals and the way was prepared for the assembling of the Continental Congress (*Collections of the New York Historical Society: Publication Fund Series,* vol. XI, 1879, pp. 274–86).

Thanks to Joseph Galloway, leader of the Pennsylvania conservatives, Thomson was prevented from being chosen a delegate to the Congress, but he was the very man in Philadelphia with whom John Adams, busily probing the minds of all and sundry on the vital questions involved, would wish to have, as he did have, "much conversation." "This Charles Thomson," Adams wrote, "is the Sam Adams of Philadelphia, the life of the cause of liberty, they say" (C. F. Adams, *The Works of John Adams,* vol. II, 1850, p. 358). Galloway was surprised as well as chagrined when this Charles Thomson, whom he characterized as "one of the most violent of the Sons of Liberty (so called) in America" (*Pennsylvania Magazine,* October 1902, p. 310), was chosen by Congress to be its secretary. Following the adjournment of Congress at the end of October, Thomson was characteristically conspicuous in the Pennsylvanian political scene, and on the reassembling of Congress in May 1775 he was again chosen secretary.

It is as secretary of the Continental Congress that Thomson is best known. For nearly fifteen years he sat at the secretarial table, listening to the debates, minuting the birth-records of a nation. As year succeeded year, delegates came and delegates went, but Charles Thomson, the "perpetual secretary," remained. The great drama of the American Revolution as enacted on the stage of the Continental Congress he beheld from its beginning to its consummation as did no other man. Although Congress from time to time prescribed some of the duties of the secretary, occasionally laid new tasks upon him, and even now and then sought to "regulate" the secretarial functions, the office was from the first to the last conducted much as Thomson was pleased to conduct it.

As the chief surviving link between the old government and the new he was chosen to notify General Washington of his election to the presidency; yet, to his great mortification, he was given no part in the inaugural ceremonies. His hope that he might be continued in a similar or appropriate office under the new dispensation was likewise doomed to disappointment. Accordingly, on July 23, 1789, he transmitted to President Washington his resignation of the office of secretary of the Continental Congress and of the custodianship of its records. Retiring to his estate at "Harriton," near Philadelphia, he devoted the next twenty years to making translations of the Septuagint and the New Testament, translations that have been pronounced both scholarly and felicitous. They appeared in 1808 in four volumes under the title *The Holy Bible, Containing the Old and New Covenant, Commonly Called the Old and New Testament*. He also published *A Synopsis of the Four Evangelists* (1815).

Thomson was twice married. His first wife, Ruth Mather, daughter of John Mather of Chester, Pa., died about 1770. His second marriage, which took place on Sept. 1, 1774, four days before he was elected secretary of Congress, was to Hannah Harrison, daughter of Richard Harrison of Maryland. She died Sept. 6, 1807.

[For sources see L. R. Harley, *The Life of Charles Thomson* (1900), with bibliography; J. F. Watson, "Biographical Memoir," in *Hist. Soc. of Pa. Colls.*, vol. I (1853); J. F. Watson, *Annals of Phila.* (1830); *Pa. Mag. of Hist. and Biog.*, Oct. 1891, pp. 327–35, Jan. 1892, p. 499, July 1909, pp. 336–39; *Pa. Archives*, 1 ser., vol. III (1853); *N. Y. Hist. Soc. Colls. . . . for 1878* (1879); C. J. Stillé, *The Life and Times of John Dickinson* (1891); W. B. Reed, *Life and Correspondence of Joseph Reed* (1847); C. H. Lincoln, *The Revolutionary Movement in Pa., 1760–1776* (1901); A. M. Schlesinger, *The Colonial Merchants and the American Revolution, 1763–1776* (1918); A. H. Smyth, *The Writings of Benjamin Franklin* (10 vols, 1905–07); E. C. Burnett, *Letters of Members of the Continental Cong.*, vols. I–VII (1921–34). The Lib. of Cong. has, besides official papers, two vols. of private papers, a small body of miscellaneous papers, and a part of the translation of the New Testament; the Hist. Soc. of Pa. has a letter-book of Thomson (1784), and a few other Thomson manuscripts; the Lib. Company of Phila., Ridgway Branch, has some letters, chiefly to John Mifflin.]

E. C. B.

THOMSON, EDWARD (Oct. 12, 1810–Mar. 22, 1870), first president of Ohio Wesleyan University, editor, bishop of the Methodist Episcopal Church, was born in Portsea, a suburb of Portsmouth, England, the fourth of thirteen children. His father, Benjamin Thomson, was a dry-goods merchant; his mother, Eliza Moore, a woman of education and attainments. In 1817, because of financial reverses, the father sought a new business location, first going to southern France and thence to America (1818), finally settling in Wooster, Wayne County, Ohio, where he opened a drug store. Here young Thomson received his early education and manifested such an interest in books that he neglected play. In 1828 he entered Jefferson Medical College in Philadelphia, and after a year's study passed the examinations which admitted him to medical practice. He opened an office at Jeromeville, Ohio, a small village near Wooster. While he was engaged in practice his interest in religion was awakened by the preaching of Russell Bigelow, an eloquent Methodist circuit rider, whom he heard at a camp-meeting, where he had been called to make a professional visit. This interest grew until in December 1831 he united with the Methodist Episcopal Church and the next year, July 1, was licensed to preach. In the fall of 1832 he was admitted on trial to the Ohio Conference and assigned as junior preacher on the Norwalk circuit.

His rise to a place of influence in the Methodist Episcopal Church was rapid. He served at Sandusky and Cincinnati, and at the latter place took a full course of lectures at the Cincinnati Medical College, from which he received the degree of M.D. In 1836 he was appointed to Detroit, and on July 4, 1837, married Maria Louisa, daughter of the Hon. Mordecai Bartley [q.v.]. In 1838 Thomson was appointed principal of Norwalk Seminary, and four years later was chosen president of Ohio Wesleyan University, then in process of establishment. From 1844 until he took up his duties as president in 1846 he edited the *Ladies' Repository* at Cincinnati. His presidency covered the formative years of the institution's life and at the time of his retirement in 1860 the college was well established, with four buildings and a student body of about five hundred.

Thomson was a strong anti-slavery man, and this fact together with his recognized literary abilities led to his selection in 1860 as editor of the *Christian Advocate and Journal* in New York, the chief Methodist organ in the United States. This important post he filled admirably during the years of the Civil War, conducting the paper on a high patriotic plane. He represented the North Ohio Conference in the General Conference from 1840 until in 1864 he was elected bishop. He was sent immediately to visit Methodist missions in the Orient, and later published a two-volume work entitled *Our Oriental Missions* (1870). His other published works include: *Essays, Educational and Religious* (1855, 1856, 1857); and *Evidences of Revealed Religion*

(1872). He died at Wheeling, W. Va., while on his way to preside over the Eastern conferences. His first wife died in 1863, and on May 9, 1866, he married Annie E. Howe, who with a son and daughter by his first wife and a son by the second survived him.

[Thomson's *Our Oriental Missions* contains biog. sketch; see also Edward Thomson, Jr., *Life of Edward Thomson, D.D., LL.D.* (1885); E. T. Nelson, *Fifty Years of Hist. of the Ohio Wesleyan Univ., 1844–1894* (1895); *The Biog. Cyc. and Portrait Gallery . . . of the State of Ohio* (n.d.), vol. VI; T. L. Flood and J. W. Hamilton, *Lives of Methodist Bishops* (1882); *The Biog. Encyc. of Ohio* (1876); *Christian Advocate* (N. Y.), Apr. 7, 1870; *Cincinnati Commercial*, Mar. 23, 1870; MSS. in library of Ohio Wesleyan Univ.]
W. W. S.

THOMSON, EDWARD WILLIAM (Feb. 12, 1849–Mar. 5, 1924), editor, author, poet, was born in Toronto, Canada. He was the son of William and Margaret Hamilton (Foley) Thomson, and a member of one of the Loyalist families which removed from the United States to Canada after the Revolution. He was educated in the public schools and at Trinity College School, Weston, Ontario. Before he was sixteen, influenced by his hatred of slavery and his boyish admiration for the character of Abraham Lincoln, he left home to enlist in the Union army during the Civil War. He served in both the 3rd and the 5th Pennsylvania Cavalry during the Virginia campaigns of 1864 and 1865. On his return to Canada he enlisted in the Queen's Own Rifles, and saw service with them during the Fenian raids of 1866. For a number of years (1868–79) he was a civil engineer, and was employed in the construction of the Carillon Canal, around the rapids of the Ottawa River. He discovered, however, a taste for writing and a bent for journalism, and joined the staff of the Toronto *Globe,* one of the most influential of Canadian newspapers. He served the *Globe* as chief editorial writer from 1879 to 1891. In the latter year he moved to Boston, Mass., where he was for twelve years one of the editors of the *Youth's Companion.* After leaving the *Companion,* he was Canadian correspondent of the *Boston Evening Transcript,* resident in Ottawa, but traveling much about the country in the preparation of his articles. During these years he practised independent journalism as well, contributing numerous articles to magazines and newspapers in the United States and Canada. Always a political liberal of the old school, he took a deep interest in Canadian politics. He was the friend of many public men of the Liberal party, and was especially intimate with Sir Wilfred Laurier, long the premier of the Dominion.

Thomson's first work in fiction was *Old Man*

Savarin and Other Stories, published in 1895; this was followed by *Walter Gibbs, the Young Boss* (1896) and *Smoky Days* (1901). More important in a literary way were his contributions to poetry, which were limited in quantity but of no little excellence. They included *Between Earth and Sky* (1897) and *The Many Mansioned House and Other Poems* (1909), published in the United States and England as *When Lincoln Died, and Other Poems* (1909). His verses show considerable imaginative and emotional power. Those that deal with the Civil War reflect his early admiration for Lincoln, which only strengthened with the years; it was always a sentimental satisfaction to him that his birthday was the same as Lincoln's. He also made a metrical version of M. S. Henry's translation of the medieval French romance, *Aucassin and Nicolette,* delicately rendered in a verse form as nearly as possible that of the original poem (1896). He was a fellow of the Royal Society of Canada, and of the Royal Society of Literature of the United Kingdom. He was married in March 1873 to Adelaide (d. 1921), daughter of Alexander St. Denis. He died in Boston, Mass., survived by his only child, a son.

[*Who's Who in America,* 1918–19; W. S. Wallace, *The Dict. of Canadian Biog.* (1926); H. J. Morgan, *The Canadian Men and Women of the Time* (2nd ed., 1912); Archibald MacMurchy, *Handbook of Canadian Lit. (English)* (1906); obituary in *Boston Transcript,* Mar. 7, 1924; personal acquaintance, and private information.]
H. S. C—n.

THOMSON, FRANK (July 5, 1841–June 5, 1899), president of the Pennsylvania Railroad, was born at Chambersburg, Franklin County, Pa., the son of Alexander and Jane (Graham) Thomson. His grandfather, Alexander Thomson, emigrated from Scotland in 1771 and established himself in the Cumberland Valley. His son, Frank's father, became a lawyer and took a prominent part in the political life of his day. He represented his district in Congress, 1824–26, and in 1828 was chosen judge of the Sixteenth Judicial District of Pennsylvania. He was also professor of jurisprudence in the law school of Marshall College, the school at that time being located at Chambersburg.

Frank Thomson entered Chambersburg Academy at an early age, but left at seventeen, putting an end to his formal schooling. He chose railroading as his career at the suggestion of Thomas A. Scott [*q.v.*], who was at that time general superintendent of the Pennsylvania Railroad Company. His first appointment was that of machinist's apprentice in the Altoona shops. The Pennsylvania, through the purchase of the state works, had acquired a variety of equipment which had been in service on the Philadelphia & Columbia and the Portage railroads, and there was need of a plan, adapted to the conditions of a modern standardized railroad, that would unify the construction and repair of locomotives. To this problem Thomson gave his principal attention during the early part of his service. He was also occupied with appliances for the burning of coal, both anthracite and bituminous, on locomotives, with car lighting, improvements in braking devices, and similar mechanical problems concerned with improved efficiency in transportation. The Pennsylvania road, under the influence of Scott and others, was taking a progressive attitude toward the introduction of better appliances in all processes of transportation and the Altoona shops provided Thomson with a schooling in applied mechanics which for that period was unequaled.

When, at the outbreak of the Civil War, Vice-President Scott was called to Washington and made assistant secretary of war in charge of military transportation, he took Thomson, then twenty years of age, as one of his assistants. For three years he was engaged in restoring and keeping open service interrupted by the enemy, and in building new lines of railroad and telegraph for the rapid transfer of troops. In the year 1864 he returned to the Pennsylvania as superintendent of the eastern division of the Philadelphia & Erie, which had recently come under Pennsylvania control. For a short period he managed the Oil Creek Railroad during the oil excitement in 1866. In 1873 he became superintendent of motive power and in 1874 was made general manager of the entire system east of Pittsburgh and Erie. In 1882 he was made second vice-president, in 1888 first vice-president, and on Feb. 3, 1897, he became president.

In his capacity as superintendent of motive power and rolling stock, he devoted his attention to the work of practical railroad construction and also laid the foundations of the system that has since produced the standard Pennsylvania engines. Later, as general manager east of Pittsburgh, he introduced many advanced methods of roadway maintenance, particularly methods for the establishment of solid roadway and standard track and systems of track inspection. He introduced superior standards of equipment, planned picturesque stations and ornamental grounds, and was largely instrumental in the establishment of block-signal systems and other operating improvements. He was also responsible for introducing the high grade of discipline which has since prevailed. In his capacity as second and first vice-president, as a direct representative of the president, he was in position to make effective the reforms that he had earlier instituted.

Although his entire business life was passed in the service of the Pennsylvania Railroad, his career as president which followed closely on the panic of 1893 and was uneventful, lasted only two years and four months. He was married on June 5, 1866, to Mary Elizabeth, daughter of Benjamin Clarke. Thomson died in Merion, Pa., survived by three children.

[J. E. Watkins, "Hist. of the Pa. Railroad Company, 1846–96," incomplete MS. in possession of the Pa. Railroad Company, Phila.; W. B. Wilson, *Hist. of the Pa. Railroad* (1899), vol. II; H. W. Schotter, *The Growth and Development of the Pa. Railroad Company* (1927); *A Biog. Album of Prominent Pennsylvanians*, vol. III (1890); Ernest Spofford, *Encyc. of Pa. Biog.*, vol. XVII (1928); *Public Ledger* (Phila.), June 6, 1899.]

F. H. D.

THOMSON, JOHN (Nov. 3, 1776–Jan. 25, 1799), orator and political writer, who gained a measure of distinction in his fragment of life by his spirited and talented espousal of Jeffersonian thought in politics, was the son of a prominent physician of Petersburg, Va., Dr. John Thomson, and his wife Anne. The early death of his father in 1785 left the boy under the guardianship of his mother, but with a comfortable patrimony. When he was about fourteen he entered the College of William and Mary and shared in college oratorical contests. On leaving college in 1792 he studied law in Petersburg with the help of the library and the advice of his loyal and admiring friend, George Hay, the son-in-law of James Monroe [q.v.]. Thomson learned with phenomenal speed and retentiveness and began to practise law when he was still in his teens. With rather melancholy and thoughtful countenance, grace of manner, and kindly consideration for others, the young attorney soon became popular in Petersburg and the surrounding county of Dinwiddie and gained an unusual practice for so young an advocate. Six feet tall, loosely put together, blue-eyed, he might well have come from the same physical stock as Jefferson; certainly the two were akin in political faith. Thomson voiced his opinions in the press under the popular classical signatures of Cassius, Gracchus, and Curtius, and his writings were widely copied by Republican papers. His style has been caustically criticized by Henry Adams as "stilted and artificial" (*Gallatin, post*, p. 46), but even this critic recognized his unusual promise and conceded that he echoed party feeling.

In August 1795 he attacked Jay's treaty in a speech of biting invective before a meeting of the inhabitants of Petersburg. He revealed in his caustic criticisms, not only the temper of the Virginia Republicans toward the treaty, but remarkable knowledge of the history of his country for one less than twenty years old. This speech gave him prestige among party leaders. Three years later when John Marshall had voiced his views on the Alien and Sedition Acts in his so-called "Answers" (*Times and Virginia Advertiser*, Oct. 11, 1798), Thomson joined the general press attack on him in a series of five letters under the signature Curtius.

Thomson was the leader in a coterie of talented young Republicans in southside Virginia which included his dissipated, ill-fated, but well-loved brother William and John Randolph of Roanoke. Randolph and John Thomson esteemed each other with deep friendly affection and mutual intellectual admiration. Thomson called Randolph "a brilliant and noble young man" (Garland, *post*, I, 73) and Randolph declared that Thomson had held the first place in his heart and the first rank in the intellectual order. Thomson's untimely death as the result of pleurisy caused keen regret in the ranks of his party. Albert Gallatin, who knew him only from his writings and influence, esteemed him as "one of the brightest geniuses of Virginia and the United States" (quoted by Adams in *Gallatin*, p. 227), and keenly regretted his loss as a severe blow to the Republican interest. A partial collection of Thomson's writings was published in *Letters of Curtius . . . to Which is Added a Speech . . . on the British Treaty* (Richmond, 1804). It contains a short sketch of his life, probably by George Hay.

[Printed sources include: Henry Adams, *The Life of Albert Gallatin* (1879), and *John Randolph* (1883); A. J. Beveridge, *The Life of John Marshall* (1919), II, 126–29, 395–96; Powhatan Bouldin, *Home Reminiscences of John Randolph* (1878); W. C. Bruce, *John Randolph of Roanoke* (1922); H. A. Garland, *The Life of John Randolph of Roanoke* (2 vols., 1850); *William and Mary Coll. Quart.*, July 1895, p. 106, Apr. 1919, p. 237. The wills and inventories of the estates of Dr. John Thomson and his son John are in Will Book No. 1 in the Court House at Petersburg, Va.; a manuscript sketch by C. T. Lassiter, "John Thomson of Petersburg and the Genesis of Republican Institutions in the United States," in private hands, contains data not otherwise available.] M. H. W.

THOMSON, JOHN (Oct. 25, 1853–June 1, 1926), inventor, manufacturer, oldest son of Alexander Thomson, a farmer, and Elizabeth (Hay) Thomson, was born in Fochabers, Morayshire, Scotland. In 1854 the family emigrated to the United States and settled on a farm at Marion, Wayne County, N. Y. Here Thomson spent his youth and obtained a common-school education. At the age of sixteen he left home and went to Rochester, N. Y., where he found employment in a jewelry store and devoted his spare time to the study of mechanical, civil, and electrical en-

gineering. These studies in combination with the intricate and delicate work of watch and clock repair developed his natural bent for mechanics as well as his inventive talent, and in 1877 he obtained his first patents, all for improvements in watches, including two escapements, a regulator, and a stem-winding device. About 1880 he moved to Brooklyn, where he continued his inventive work and by 1884 had obtained several patents on mechanical movements such as a ratchet and pawl and a differential screw.

He had meanwhile begun to give particular attention to improvements in water meters and printing presses. The first of his patented improvements of the former, devised between 1883 and 1885, he assigned to a manufacturer in Brooklyn, while the first of his inventions in the latter field—an intermitting circular feed motion, perfected in 1887—he assigned to the Colt Patent Fire Arms Manufacturing Company, Hartford, Conn. He now went to Hartford and in the next three years, as an employee of the Colt company, made additional improvements which resulted in the production of the Thomson Printing Press. In the meantime, he also obtained ten patents for improvements in water meters, including his basic patent of the disk water meter, Dec. 20, 1887.

Leaving the Colt company about 1890, he organized in Brooklyn the John Thomson Press Company and the Thomson Meter Company, both of which organizations he directed until shortly before his death. The Thomson Press became standard equipment in some 15,000 job-printing plants throughout the country while some 20,000,000 Thomson disk-type water meters were put into service in the United States and abroad. Besides looking after his manufacturing interests Thomson was a registered patent attorney and was retained in a number of important patent cases. He was awarded in all some 350 patents—for his improvements in printing presses and water meters, and also for a number of improvements in electric furnaces, for a process for refining metallic zinc, and for the manufacture of zinc oxide. To exploit the last two inventions he organized the Electric Zinc Company of London, England. Because of his wide experience and practical knowledge in the electrical field, he was at one time chief engineer of the Primary Electrical Subway Commission of New York, which undertook the construction of the first underground conduit for telegraph and telephone wires in that city. He was an active member of a number of clubs and technical societies both in New York and London, and was president of the Engineers' Club of New York,

1898–1901. In 1887 he married Alice Elizabeth McKee of Canandaigua, N. Y., who with two sons and a daughter survived him. He died in Brooklyn.

[*Inland Printer,* July 1926; *Brooklyn Daily Eagle, N. Y. Times, N. Y. Herald Tribune,* June 2, 1926; correspondence with family; Patent Office records.]

C. W. M—n.

THOMSON, JOHN EDGAR (Feb. 10, 1808– May 27, 1874), third president of the Pennsylvania Railroad, was born in Springfield Township, Delaware County, Pa., son of John and Sarah (Levis) Thomson and descended from Quaker forebears said to have come from England with William Penn. His father, a civil engineer, was connected with the construction of important public works of the time, among them the Delaware & Chesapeake Canal. He has been credited with planning for Thomas Leiper [*q.v.*] what was probably the first experimental railroad in the United States. John Edgar had little formal schooling, but from early years he was the constant companion of his father and through parental instruction gained a sound foundation of engineering training which he diligently perfected by reading, observation, and experience. Through his father's influence he became a member of the state's engineer corps which was at the time making preliminary surveys for a rail line from Philadelphia to Columbia. He was soon made assistant engineer, and in 1830, when the line of the Camden & Amboy Railroad was located across the state of New Jersey, Thomson was placed in charge of an engineering division.

The caliber of the man is shown by the fact that as soon as these duties were completed, he made a trip to Europe to study the new form of transportation which George Stephenson's genius was making possible and to familiarize himself with European and especially English civil and mechanical engineering practice. Returning in 1832, he was appointed chief engineer of the Georgia Railroad which was just being chartered to build a line from Augusta to Atlanta. He remained with this company for fifteen years, meanwhile becoming widely recognized as an authority on engineering practice.

The Pennsylvania Railroad was incorporated in 1847 to build a line from Harrisburg to Pittsburgh that would do away with the inefficient Allegheny Portage Railroad and the slow-serving canals, and place the railroad system of the state on a par with the Baltimore & Ohio to the south and the New York Central to the north in the struggle for western business. It was a critical time in the commercial development of Pennsylvania, and the directors of the company appointed Thomson as their chief engineer to handle this vital competitive problem. With characteristic energy he set himself to find the most favorable location for the project. When the Portage Railroad was built engineers had declared a road without inclined planes to be impossible of operation in that mountainous territory. The location of the Horseshoe Curve and the construction of a road with practicable grades was Thomson's answer to this pessimistic prophecy and constituted the high point in his career as a railroad engineer. The last link in the through line between Philadelphia and Pittsburgh was completed early in 1854 by the elimination of the Portage Railroad and the completed road was formally opened for traffic in February of that year.

Meanwhile, in 1852, Thomson had been made president, and thus placed in position to use his growing influence in securing the funds necessary to the completion of the western extension. The connecting roads east of the mountains from Lancaster to Philadelphia belonged to the system of state works begun a quarter century earlier. These the state had several times attempted to dispose of, but without success. Finally, in 1857, the entire system of state works, consisting of 278 miles of canals and 117 miles of railroad, together with real estate and rail equipment, was put up at auction. Thomson offered $7,500,000, and the property came into the possession of the Pennsylvania.

A through connection with the headwaters of the Ohio was not the limit of Thomson's ambitions, however. He saw clearly that the railroad of the future would be the one that could pick up freight at point of origin and deliver it in its own cars on its own rails at final destination. He had advocated for years before he became president the extension of the road west of Pittsburgh. His policy had resulted by 1856 in the consolidation of various western lines into the Pittsburgh, Fort Wayne & Chicago Railway. This company was formally leased to the Pennsylvania in 1869 and in 1870–71 the Pennsylvania Company, one of the first of the holding companies, was created to take over the properties west of Pittsburgh which were developing into large northwest and southwest systems.

The growth of traffic from the West made the necessity of a terminal in New York Harbor imperative, a project long contemplated. Thomson's negotiations resulted in a long-time lease, in 1871, of the properties of the United Companies of New Jersey, comprising 456 miles of railroad and 65 miles of canal. In 1869 an independent line from Baltimore to Washington was decided upon and by 1873, through the acquisition of a one-sixth interest in the Southern Railway Security Company, a connection which gave access to all points in the Southern states had been effected. Thomson took great interest in the establishment of Philadelphia as a transatlantic port and was instrumental in the creation of the American Steamship Company in 1870 under the patronage of the Pennsylvania Railroad.

Up to the time of his death, Thomson was thus almost continuously engaged in important construction projects that were to render the Pennsylvania Railroad safe from competitive attack. Furthermore, from the sixties on, the Pennsylvania was a leader in insisting upon high standards of operating practice and a pioneer in the introduction of improved equipment and devices of various kinds. Thomson's career was coincident with the pioneer and construction stage of railway development in the United States. He was associated with the movement in its beginnings and lived to see the Atlantic and Pacific connected by rail, while his keen vision as to the future place of railroads in the industrial life of the country was in process of rapid realization during his service as chief engineer and president of the Pennsylvania. His ability as a financier was shown in his handling of the affairs of three different railroads under panic conditions—the Georgia Railroad in 1837, the Pittsburgh, Fort Wayne & Chicago in 1857, and the Pennsylvania in 1873. The dividend record of the Pennsylvania Railroad was unbroken from the establishment of the through line between Philadelphia and Pittsburgh to the close of his career.

Although he was taciturn and abrupt in manner, and inclined to action on his own initiative without consultation with others, his judgment was greatly respected and his services were sought in various capacities outside of the railroad business. He aided the cause of many civic projects in Philadelphia. He was a member of the Park Commission and rendered valuable service in the extension of Fairmount Park. One of the early steel companies organized by Andrew Carnegie [q.v.] was known as the J. Edgar Thomson Steel Company.

Thomson was married late in life to Lavinia Frances Smith; they had no children of their own, but adopted a daughter. He died in Philadelphia in his sixty-seventh year. By his will he left his estate in trust, the income to be employed to educate and maintain the daughters of railroad men killed in the discharge of their duties. This foundation, known as St. John's Orphanage, is still serving its purpose in Philadelphia.

[J. E. Watkins, "Hist. of the Pennsylvania Railroad Company, 1846–96" (1898), incomplete and not printed, in possession of Pa. R.R. Co., Phila.; W. B. Sipes, *The Pa. Railroad* (1875); W. B. Wilson, *Hist. of the Pa. Railroad Company* (2 vols., 1899); H. W. Schotter, *The Growth and Development of the Pa. Railroad Company* (1927); *Ann. Reports . . . Pa. Railroad*, 1847–74; *Mag. of Western Hist.*, Aug. 1888; *Penn Monthly*, July 1874; *Press* and *Public Ledger* (both of Phila.), May 29, 1874.]   F. H. D.

THOMSON, MORTIMER NEAL (Sept. 2, 1831–June 25, 1875), humorist, known as "Q.K. Philander Doesticks, P.B.," was born in Riga, Monroe County, N. Y., the elder of two sons of Edwin and Sophia Thomson. The Thomsons were prominent old settlers there, the grandfather, Joseph Thomson, having held minor public offices. In 1841 the family moved to Ann Arbor, Mich., where the father set up in the practice of law. Thomson matriculated at the University of Michigan in the fall of 1849, but was expelled during the winter because of membership in a secret society. Subsequently he tramped—playing at times, it is thought, with various strolling stock companies—to New York City, where he became a clerk in a jewelry store and rapidly explored the gayeties of Gotham. His first humorous letter, "Doesticks on a Bender," a hilarious sketch of a trip to Niagara, won immediate popularity and was copied widely by the newspapers of the country. In rapid succession (Sept. 22, 1854–May 30, 1855) there followed a series of twenty-nine humorous letters, most of them appearing in the *Detroit Daily Advertiser,* others in the *New York Tribune* and the *Spirit of the Times* (New York). These letters, collected and published as *Doesticks: What He Says* (1855), made "Doesticks" a national figure. In 1855 Thomson joined the staff of the *New York Tribune,* writing police-court sketches (later published as *The History and Records of the Elephant Club,* 1856) in a way they had never before been done, and a series of feature articles on fortune tellers (*The Witches of New York,* 1859). With Thomas Nast [q.v.] he covered such special assignments as the famous Heenan-Morrissey prize fight, Oct. 20, 1858, and reported dramatically and with devastating effect the great auction sale of slaves held in Savannah in 1859. When William Allen Butler's famous poem, "Nothing to Wear," aroused New York, Thomson was offered one dollar a line for a parody. In less than a week he had produced a poem of eight hundred lines, a satire on snobbery called *Nothing to Say* (1857), which was probably more popular than the original. The popularity of "Doesticks" had already been considerably enhanced by the tremendous sale of an earlier piece of parody in verse, *Plu-ri-bus-tah,* *a Song That's-by-No-Author,* which had appeared in May 1856. With this book-length mock-heroic, precipitated by the wave of interest in Longfellow's *Hiawatha,* he achieved a national hit, taking telling hits at American follies, especially American love of money. Although it was probably begun as parody, it soon achieved independent position on its own merits as social satire.

In addition to regular staff duty on the *Tribune,* Thomson ventured in 1858 to edit the *New York Picayune,* the best comic weekly of the day. Later he became dramatic critic for the *Tribune* and wrote a play, *The Lady of the Lake* (1860), a travesty of Scott's poem. During the Civil War he served as staff reporter for the *Tribune,* as well as chaplain to a regiment. He was twice married. His first wife, Anna H. Van Cleve, an old friend, whom he married on Oct. 24, 1857, died in childbirth late in 1858, leaving a son. In July 1861, while home on leave, he married again, this time Grace Eldridge, daughter of Sara Payson Willis Parton [*q.v.*]. Again his happiness was short-lived, for his second wife died twenty days after the birth of their daughter. After the war Thomson continued the humorous lectures he had begun in 1859. For a short time he was an associate editor of the *Minneapolis Tribune,* but in 1873 he returned to New York to become an editor of *Frank Leslie's Illustrated Weekly.* In this position he continued until his death. The Ring Lardner of his day, he brought to American humor terse, vigorous, quick-moving phrases and vivid slang, and became the most popular American humorist writing in the period before that of Charles Farrar Browne [*q.v.*].

[Thomson's name is sometimes spelled Thompson. See Fletcher D. Slater, "The Life and Letters of Mortimer Thomson," 1931, unpublished thesis in the lib. of Northwestern Univ.; obituaries in *N. Y. Times, N. Y. Tribune,* and *N. Y. Herald,* June 26, 1875.]

F. J. M—e.

THOMSON, SAMUEL (Feb. 9, 1769–Oct. 4, 1843), botanic physician, originator of the Thomsonian system of medical treatment, was born in Alstead, N. H., the son of John and Hannah (Cobb) Thomson. His father was a struggling pioneer farmer, who put his son to work on the farm when he was five, though he had been lame from birth. At ten the boy had one month's schooling. He took a great dislike to farm work, and from his earliest years spent most of his time in the fields and woods. Here he became interested in herbs and their medical uses. One especially impressed him because of its peculiar effect in producing vomiting and profuse perspiration. It was *lobelia inflata,* and later he was to use it extensively in his career of healing,

claiming its medical properties as his own discovery. At the age of twenty-one he assumed charge of the family farm, and on July 7, 1790, married Susan Allen, who bore him eight children. Soon after his marriage his wife became ill, and when the regular physicians failed to perform a cure he employed two root doctors, under whose ministrations she rapidly recovered. His confidence in the curative properties of herbs thus strengthened, he began to use them, first in his own family and then among the neighbors. Calls for his services increased and at length, formulating a system, he devoted himself wholly to medical practice, his activities extending over all eastern New England. He soon incurred the enmity of the regular school physicians, who persecuted him for the rest of his life. He became involved in many law suits, was charged with murder on at least one occasion (see *Commonwealth* vs. *Thompson,* 6 *Tyng* 134) and was once confined for six weeks in a loathsome prison. The trials in which he was involved created a considerable sensation in their day.

His theory of disease was based on the assumption that all ills are produced by cold and that any treatment which increases inward heat will hasten recovery. Although he used many other vegetable remedies, his method in general consisted in prescribing *lobelia* followed by Cayenne pepper. Usually the vapor bath was also employed. So great was his success that he decided to obtain a patent for his process. One was granted on Mar. 3, 1813, and a revised patent on Jan. 28, 1823. He also conceived the idea of selling rights to practise his system, and societies were formed in all parts of the country, including the Middle West. Most of the agents whom he employed proved dishonest, and his life was made miserable by their misdeeds. He published *A Brief Sketch of the Causes and Treatment of Disease* (1821); *A Narrative of the Life and Medical Discoveries of Samuel Thomson* (1822); *New Guide to Health: or Botanic Family Physician* (1822); and *Learned Quackery Exposed* (1824). Having had no educational advantages, in writing his books he wisely accepted aid from others. A number of short-lived journals, exponents of his system, were issued, among them the *Botanic Sentinel* (later called *Philadelphia Botanic Sentinel and Thomsonian Sentinel*), 1835–40, and the *Thomsonian Recorder,* started in Columbus, Ohio, in 1832, which was later (1837) called the *Botanic-Medical Recorder* and lasted until 1852.

Although most of the regular school of physicians were jealous of Thomson's success, he was treated with much kindness by such practitioners as Benjamin Rush of Philadelphia, Benjamin Waterhouse of Harvard, and William Tully [*qq.v.*] of Yale. Without question he was sincere, and he exhibited great courage in withstanding the persecutions of his opponents. The significance of his work lies not in any contribution to medical science but in the strong influence that he created against the prevailing practice of his day, in which bleeding, calomel, and opium were the ruling remedies. His residence in his later years was Boston, Mass., where, at his home on Salem Street, he died.

[In addition to Thomson's own writings, see Samuel Robinson, *A Course of Fifteen Lectures Demonstrating Thomson's New Method of Medical Practice* (Columbus, Ohio, 1830) ; J. W. Comfort, *The Practice of Medicine on Thomsonian Principles* (1843) ; *Bull. of the Lloyd Lib. of Botany, Pharmacy and Materia Medica*, no. 11, Reproduction Series, no. 7 (1909) ; Alexander Wilder, *Hist. of Medicine . . . in the Nineteenth Century* (1901) ; J. M. Ball, in *Annals of Medic. Hist.*, June 1925 ; F. R. Packard, *Hist. of Medicine in the U. S.* (2 vols., 1931) ; H. A. Kelly and W. L. Burrage, *Am. Medic. Biogs.* (1920) ; obituary in *Boston Daily Advertiser*, Oct. 5, 1843.]   A. N. A.

THOMSON, WILLIAM (Jan. 16, 1727–Nov. 2, 1796), Revolutionary soldier, known as "Old Danger," is said to have been born in Pennsylvania, and to have moved with his Scotch-Irish parents, Moses and Jane Thomson, during the 1730's to settle in Amelia Township, S. C. He had the usual frontier education and became an expert rifleman. Beginning life by planting with his father, William Thomson was a trader to the Cherokee Indians probably until the outbreak of the Cherokee War, when, as major commandant of the Rangers, he rendered important services for which the Assembly voted him a gratuity. After the war, having received a number of land grants, he planted indigo, and was active in local affairs as justice of the peace, enquirer and collector of taxes, commissioner for building the parish church, representative in the Assembly, and colonel of the Orangeburg militia. In the disturbances between the Regulators and Scovilites, he was one of the leaders who averted bloodshed, and when courthouses were finally built in the backcountry, he became the first sheriff of Orangeburg. In 1772, he was also a commissioner for adjusting the boundary with North Carolina.

At the opening of the Revolution, he was placed on the General Committee and became a member of the first Provincial Congress. When William H. Drayton [*q.v.*] carried the Continental Association into the backcountry, Thomson as lieutenant-colonel-commandant supported him with the militia, and was one of the witnesses to Drayton's treaty with the Loyalists on Sept. 16, 1775. Under Col. Richard Richardson,

he served in the "Snow Campaign" of that year against the Loyalists, and was in command of the party that captured Robert Fletchall. His dispersal of Patrick Cunningham's followers at the great Cane Brake was supposed at the time to have shattered the king's party in South Carolina. His greatest service was rendered at the battle of Fort Moultrie in June 1776, when with 700 Rangers he blocked the British attempt to land on the east end of Sullivan's Island. For this he received the thanks of Congress. When the Rangers became the third regiment of South Carolina continentals, he was promoted to the rank of colonel, and served under Robert Howe [*q.v.*] in the defense of Savannah. In 1778 he resigned from the continental service and commanded the Orangeburg militia. He was also elected to the state Senate and served there intermittently until the close of his life.

Upon the surrender of Charlestown, he was paroled, and his plantation became a fortified British post. Accused of having broken his parole, he was imprisoned in a dungeon for several months in Charlestown. Upon his exchange in June 1781, he joined Greene and is said to have served in an advisory capacity without a command. After the war, he returned to his devastated plantation and resumed planting, but is said to have been overgenerous to friends who involved him in financial losses. In March 1783, he secured an act establishing upon his plantation the market town of Belleville, which, however, never developed. In the South Carolina convention of 1788, he voted for ratification of the federal Constitution. In the state constitutional convention of 1790, he opposed a movement to return to Charleston as the state capital. In 1795, he was defeated for Congress by Wade Hampton, and the following year he died at Sweet Springs, Va., where he had gone for his health. Amiable, energetic, and without brilliance, he contributed to the Revolutionary party the stabilizing influence of his solid dependability and common sense. On Aug. 14, 1755, Thomson was married to Eugenia Russell. They had twelve children, four sons and eight daughters.

[Thomson's Order Book and other documentary material are in A. S. Salley, *Hist. of Orangeburg County* (1898). His correspondence is in R. W. Gibbes, *Doc. Hist. of the Am. Revolution* (1855) ; "Journal of the Council of Safety . . ." in *Colls. of the S. C. Hist. Soc.*, vol. II (1858) ; "Papers of the First Council of Safety . . ." in *S. C. Hist. and Geneal. Mag.*, Jan. 1900–Oct. 1902. Sketches are in *Ibid.*, Apr. 1902, and in Joseph Johnson, *Traditions and Reminiscences Chiefly of the Am. Revolution in the South* (1851). See also John Drayton, *Memoirs of the Am. Revolution* (2 vols., 1821), Wm. Moultrie, *Memoirs of the Am. Revolution* (2 vols., 1802), and Edward McCrady, *The Hist. of S. C. in the Revolution* (1902).]   A. K. G.

THOMSON, WILLIAM McCLURE (Dec. 31, 1806–Apr. 8, 1894), missionary in Syria, was born at Spring Dale, Ohio, near Cincinnati, son of the Rev. John Thomson. He graduated at Miami University in 1828, studied for two years, 1829–31, in Princeton Theological Seminary, and on Oct. 12, 1831, was ordained by the Presbytery of Cincinnati. In October 1832, having married Eliza Nelson Hanna on June 6, he sailed for Syria under appointment of the American Board of Commissioners for Foreign Missions. The Syria mission was then but ten years old. Reaching Beirut in February 1833, Thomson lived there until April 1834, when he moved to Jerusalem. In May, while he was traveling to Jaffa, the peasants rebelled against the rule of Mohammed Ali Pasha of Egypt, who had seized Palestine, and Thomson was imprisoned as a spy. His wife's experiences during the violent warfare around Jerusalem resulted in her death in July, soon after her husband's release. He returned to Beirut in October 1834, with his infant son, William Hanna Thomson, who later became a distinguished physician of New York. In Beirut he preached and taught, opening a boys' boarding-school in 1835, the first in the Turkish Empire, and on Aug. 3 of that year he married Mrs. Maria Abbot, widow of a British consul in Syria. He also traveled much in the country, seeking new missionary fields. In 1843 he moved to a station which he had helped to establish at Abeih in the Lebanon. Here in 1845 there was savage fighting between the Druses and the Maronite Christians, and at risk of his life, Thomson obtained opportunity for the Maronites to escape to Beirut. Thither he, too, went in 1846. In this early period of the Syria mission he was a great source of courage, wisdom, and organizing ability. His kindliness and ability to enter into the life of the natives won the confidence of the conflicting elements of the Syrian population and brought him commanding influence.

On his return to Syria in 1850 after a furlough at home, he went to live at Sidon in order to manage a station at Hasbeiyeh, where he had been a pioneer; in these places he worked until 1857. During another visit to America he published *The Land and the Book* (2 vols., 1858). In 1859 he settled at Beirut, where he lived for the remainder of his service. After the destructive war between the Druses and Maronites in 1860 he was adviser to Lord Dufferin, representative of the allied powers in the reorganization of the government of the Lebanon. In 1870 the Syria mission was transferred to the Presbyterian Board of Foreign Missions, under which Thomson served until 1876. Thereafter, he lived for some time in New York, preparing the second edition of *The Land and the Book* (3 vols., 1880–85). In 1890 he removed to Denver, where he died, survived by his son and two daughters.

Thomson's *The Land and the Book* is a description of Palestine and southern Syria in the form of journals of travel, with constant reference to the Bible. The first edition had an extraordinary circulation. It was republished in England and more copies were sold than of any previous American book except *Uncle Tom's Cabin*. The second edition, more than twice the size of the first and much improved, at once attained great popularity. Thomson had traveled widely and repeatedly in Palestine and Syria, and had studied the topography and the ancient buildings and sites, using the best archeological helps available. His appreciation of natural beauty and power of description were unusual; he knew the life of the people in all its aspects, and spoke their languages; he was minutely familiar with the Bible, and well read in the writers on Palestine, ancient and modern. These qualifications, with an easy graceful style, produced a book of unique appeal. It fulfilled in high degree its purpose of elucidating the Bible and greatly increased knowledge of Palestine in the English-speaking countries. Furthermore, it preserved faithful descriptions of Palestinian life while it was as yet little affected by western civilization.

[*Biog. Cat. of Princeton Theological Sem.* (1933); records of Miami Univ.; reports of Am. Board of Commissioners for Foreign Missions, 1833–70; reports of Presbyt. Board of Foreign Missions, 1870–90; *Missionary Herald*, Mar. 1842, Feb., June, Oct. 1843, June, Nov., Dec. 1844, Apr., June, Oct., Dec. 1845; H. H. Jessup, *Fifty-Three Years in Syria* (1910); J. S. Dennis, in *Church at Home and Abroad*, June 1894.]

R. H. N.

THORBURN, GRANT (Feb. 18, 1773–Jan. 21, 1863), seedsman, author, the son of James and Elizabeth (Fairley) Thorburn, was born near Dalkeith, Scotland, amid scenes made famous by Sir Walter Scott in *The Heart of Midlothian*. His mother died when he was two and a half years of age, and he says that it was the carelessness of a nurse that caused him to be dwarfed in stature, and to have short, feeble legs. His father was a maker of nails by hand, and, notwithstanding his handicap, Grant learned the trade and became expert at it, claiming on one day to have made 3,222 nails between 6 A.M. and 9 P.M. In 1792 he took part in a radical agitation for parliamentary reform, and was imprisoned on a charge of high treason, but was later released with a warning. To escape the odium which he believed he had incurred, he set sail for New York City, and landed in June 1794. He immediately found work as a nailer; met very soon a charming girl, Rebecca Sickles, and was married to her in June 1797. With his wife as shopkeeper he set up a small business in notions in his home and continued his nail-making. Rebecca died in 1800, leaving her husband with a young child. "Thinking it more creditable and wise to marry a wife than to hire a housekeeper," wrote Thorburn later, "I again entered into that state in 1801" (*Lawrie Todd, post,* p. 60). This wife, Hannah Wortemby, lived until 1852.

The invention of the nail-cutting machine deprived Thorburn of an occupation, and he started a small grocery business in his home. Having painted some flower pots one day to encourage their sale, it occurred to him that some growing plants in them might also be attractive to customers. He became interested in plants (which he had never noticed before), and after buying a number of them from a gardener, he began to have inquiries for the seed. It was thus that Thorburn, about 1803, became the first seedsman of any consequence in America, and came to found a business that functioned for more than a century. An English seed catalogue fell into his hands, and after studying it he issued one of his own in 1812, *The Gentleman and Gardener's Kalendar for the Middle States of North America,* the first in American history. He continued issuing these catalogues and manuals at intervals throughout his career. In 1808 he purchased a farm in New Jersey to grow his own seed, but it failed after he had sunk all his earnings into the venture, and he spent a time in debtors' prison. In 1816 he made a fresh start as a seedsman, and was soon on his feet again, prospering from that time on.

Thorburn now indulged his liking for mingling with prominent and intellectual people of all casts of thought, and jeopardized his standing with his church by cultivating an acquaintance with Thomas Paine. He also took to writing. A popular novel of the time, *Lawrie Todd* (1830), by John Galt, was said to have been founded on his life-story, and he assumed Lawrie Todd as a pen name. He wrote many articles and sketches for newspapers and magazines, displaying in them a mixture of naïveté, keen observation, and whimsical or bitter humor. Some of these were published collectively under the title *Sketches from the Note-book of Lawrie Todd* (1847). His principal works were *Forty Years' Residence in America* (1834); *Fifty Years' Reminiscences of New-York* (1845); *Men and Manners in Great Britain* (1834); *The History of Cardens and Carver* (1847); *Laurie*

Todd's Notes on Virginia; with a Chapter on Puritans, Witches and Friends (1848); and an autobiography, *Lawrie Todd, Life and Writings of Grant Thorburn* (1852). He spent the last eight years of his life in New Haven, Conn., where he died. On June 12, 1853, at the age of eighty, he was married to his third wife, Maria ——. His business was carried on by his sons and grandsons.

[Manuscript genealogical notes of the Thorburn family; Thorburn's autobiography, with a supplement, *Grant Thorburn in his Golden Age* (1863); J. A. Scoville, *Old Merchants of N. Y. City* (1863); *N. Y. Herald,* Jan. 25, 1863.]   A. F. H.

THOREAU, HENRY DAVID (July 12, 1817–May 6, 1862), essayist, poet, transcendentalist, was born in the town of Concord, Mass., of a varied ancestry which, on his mother's side, ran back to the Loyalist Jones family of Weston, Mass., and to the Scotch Dunbars of New Hampshire. It was these Dunbars that Henry Thoreau most resembled, having a romantic imagination like that of his grandfather Asa Dunbar, a love of nature and an unconventionality like that of his mother, and an inventiveness and whimsical humor like that of his favorite uncle Charles Dunbar. On his father's side the family derived directly from the Isle of Jersey and remotely from the city of Tours, from which place-name the family name seems to have originated. Henry's father, John Thoreau, was a grandson of Philippe Thoreau of St. Helier, Jersey, and eldest son of John Thoreau, Jersey sailor and adventurer, who in 1772 settled in Boston and began a successful mercantile career, retiring in 1800 to Concord. There his son John, the father of the author, became storekeeper and pencil manufacturer and "remembered more about the worthies (and unworthies) of Concord village . . . than anyone else" (Thoreau's "Journal" for Feb. 3, 1859, *Writings,* Walden ed., XVII, 437). John Thoreau on May 11, 1812, married Cynthia Dunbar, a native of Keene, N. H., and a woman of rare independence of spirit, vivacity, and with a deep love for the out-of-doors unusual at that time. Thoreau was born at the home of his maternal grandmother Mrs. Jonas Minott, widow of Asa Dunbar, on the Virginia Road northeast of the village, and, except for short periods in early childhood in Boston and Chelmsford, Mass., resided in Concord during his entire life, enlarging the town in his imagination until it became a microcosm holding within its borders the phenomena of the world.

His mother and his uncle Charles Dunbar introduced him to the countryside when he was very young, and he took a normal boyish delight in hunting, fishing, and country sports. At college and later as tutor he longed for his native fields and wrote homesick letters about them. In company with his brother he became, after college, a naturalist without rod and gun. His early maturity was made notable by daily exploration of familiar haunts, where he contemplated nature with a wise passiveness that owed something to Wordsworth and something to the Oriental mystics, who were ever attractive to him. The ecstasy of pantheism characterized his journalizing about nature during his first fifteen years out of college. Later in life his nature observation, perhaps under the influence of his friends Louis Agassiz and Thaddeus W. Harris [*qq.v.*] and perhaps as a result of his own middle age, became more objective and scientific. His interest in nature is too early and too nearly a passion to be treated lightly even in thinking of him as more than a naturalist.

He was named David Henry for his uncle David Thoreau who died in Concord in August 1817. After retaining the original order of names until his graduation from college, Thoreau reversed them, assigning no reason for the change. He prepared for college at Concord Academy and entered Harvard in August 1833. At college he submitted himself to the restricted curriculum of the day, entered little into the undergraduate life, went to chapel in a green coat "because the rules required black," and found solace in resorting to the alcove of the college library in which were the writings of the English poets, particularly those of the seventeenth century. In 1834 he began keeping a journal, a practice continued until the end of his life; and in 1835, between terms, he taught school at Canton, Mass., and boarded at the home of Orestes A. Brownson [*q.v.*], who taught him to read German. During his college course he was granted a scholarship in the form of the income from a Chelsea (Mass.) estate and with some difficulty collected the rents himself, as Emerson had done fifteen years earlier. Thoreau felt particularly the influence of two teachers: Edward T. Channing, who taught him to write English sentences, and Jones Very [*q.v.*], who taught him Greek and introduced him to the poetry of the English mystics. He emerged from Harvard in August 1837 far from the top of his class but perhaps the best-read member of the group.

College having prepared him for no occupation, he turned school teacher and for a fortnight in September 1837 taught the town school of Concord, where he sought discipline through moral suasion much as Bronson Alcott had done in Boston a few years before. A member of the school committee so objected to the absence of the ferule that the next day Thoreau, to make whipping absurd, whipped half a dozen surprised pupils and that night resigned his school. During the rest of that year he helped his father in what had become the family industry of pencil making. Early in 1838 he wrote to his brother John, then teaching in Staunton, Mass., proposing that they migrate westward and try teaching in Kentucky. Later they decided to open a private school in their father's house, John in charge and Henry teaching Latin, Greek, French, and mathematics. The next year they moved the school to the old Academy building, and the brothers continued teaching until the spring of 1841, introducing "field trips" for nature instruction, an innovation in American education. John perhaps caught the imagination of more pupils, but Henry's nature lore and thoroughness remained long in the memories of those whom he taught.

It was while they were teaching, during the first half of September 1839, that the Thoreau brothers made their thirteen-day vacation voyage down the Concord River and up the Merrimack as far as Concord, N. H., a pastoral journey not memorable in itself, but immortalized by Henry in his first book. On Apr. 11, 1838, Thoreau delivered the first of his almost annual lectures to the Concord Lyceum, the first one being on the subject of "Society." Later in the year, in December, he wrote his essay "Sound and Silence" and followed it in July 1840 with his rhapsody on courage, refused for the *Dial* by Margaret Fuller but printed in 1902 under the title *The Service*.

Early in 1841, in the full tide of success, the Thoreau brothers announced their school would close because of John's ill health. Henry went to live in the Emerson home, where during a two-year intimacy their long friendship began, a friendship cemented early by keen bereavements, Thoreau's brother dying on Jan. 11, 1842, and Emerson's son Waldo sixteen days later. Their sorrow drew them together and the next few years marked the height of their friendship. It was about this time that Thoreau was disappointed in his brief love affair with Ellen Sewall, and his friendship for her brother Edmund was broken off when the boy went with his parents to live in Scituate, Mass. Years later Thoreau put into the first chapter of his *Walden* a reference to his loss of "a hound, a bay horse, and a turtle-dove"; Edmund Sewall, John Thoreau, and Ellen Sewall. But the residence in the Emerson home brought gains also, for Thoreau began meeting with the group now known as the Transcendental Club and became acquainted with F. H. Hedge, A. Bronson Alcott, James Freeman

Clarke, George Ripley, Margaret Fuller, and Elizabeth Palmer Peabody [*qq.v.*]. In the Emerson household he turned his facile hand to all things from gardening and fence-mending to writing essays and poems, and during Emerson's absence edited the April 1843 number of the *Dial*. In May 1843 he became tutor in the home of his Concord patron's brother, William Emerson. The year on Staten Island constituted Thoreau's longest residence outside of Concord. He published "A Walk to Wachusett," a record of a July 1842 expedition, in the *Boston Miscellany* (January 1843) and while tutoring he translated "The Seven Against Thebes" but did not seek to publish it. In New York he made his acquaintance with the sea and with William Henry Channing, Lucretia Mott, Henry James, Sr., and Horace Greeley [*qq.v.*], and sought out publishers in a generally unsuccessful effort to sell articles to the magazines.

As early as Dec. 24, 1841, Thoreau, in his journal, had expressed a desire to "go soon and live away by the pond." It is not surprising, therefore, to find him upon his return to Concord early in 1844 again turning his thoughts toward this project. His friend Stearns Wheeler had lived in a hut at nearby Sandy Pond in 1841–42 and Thoreau had visited him and lived there perhaps as long as six weeks at one time; moreover, Ellery Channing had written to him on Mar. 5, 1845: "I see nothing for you in this earth but that field which I once christened 'Briars'; go out upon that, build yourself a hut, and there begin the grand process of devouring yourself alive. I see no alternative, no other hope for you. . . . Concord is just as good a place as any other" (*Writings*, Walden ed., VI, 121). Thoreau had some private business to transact, chiefly the writing of his book, *A Week on the Concord and Merrimack Rivers*; in the same month in which Channing had told him to build a hut he began a small house on Emerson's land on the northwest shore of Walden Pond. As Henry S. Salt has said: "Walden was, in fact, to Thoreau what Brook Farm was to others of the transcendentalists—a retreat suitable for philosophic meditation, and the practice of a simpler, hardier, and healthier life" (*Life of Thoreau*, 1896, p. 65).

Thoreau took up residence at the Pond July 4, 1845, and remained there until Sept. 6, 1847. During the summer of 1845 he was arrested for non-payment of poll tax, as Alcott had been in 1843. Both were protesting against slavery as it became a political issue in the Mexican War, and both chose "civil disobedience" as the most effective form of protest. Thoreau spent but one night in jail, the tax, much to his disgust, being paid by one of his aunts. Thoreau told the story of his jailing in his essay "Resistance to Civil Government" (later called "Civil Disobedience" and "On the Duty of Civil Disobedience") in Elizabeth Peabody's short-lived periodical *Æsthetic Papers* (1849), and retold it at the close of the chapter "The Village" in *Walden*. It may well be that the jailing episode, bringing into high relief Thoreau's extension of Jefferson's definition of good government to its ultimate conclusion—anarchy as far as any existing government was concerned—is the most significant incident of his twenty-six months at Walden Pond, for much of the life there has been misunderstood and exaggerated. Viewed as an experiment, these years with their dependence upon the home pantry and the Emerson dinner table become meaningful. Thoreau tried his theories, he gained two years of youthful leisure, he wrote a book, he declared himself on the matter of an individual's duties to his government, and he returned to the village mature and certain of himself. He did not, in spite of his own satisfaction with the experiment, urge his scheme on others as the ideal way of life. He had, however, settled one matter so thoroughly to his satisfaction that he was willing ever after to preach the doctrine of simplification without specifying that the simplifying should be in the Walden mode or in any particular mode except one which each individual should fit to his own life.

On Sept. 6, 1847, Thoreau moved back to his father's house in the village. He brought with him the first draft of his book, *A Week on the Concord and Merrimack Rivers*, a series of comments upon life and literature gleaned from his journals of ten years and strung on the thread of narrative telling the story of the boat trip of the two brothers in September eight years before. He brought back new journals to be reaped in the preparation of *Walden* six years later. "He was a student when he came to Walden; when he returned to Concord he was a teacher" (Salt, *Life*, 1896, p. 84). He began, in the early autumn of 1847, his second residence in the home of Emerson, where he lived for a year while Emerson was in Europe. The *Week* had found no publisher, though Emerson had, on Aug. 6, 1847, solicited the aid of W. H. Furness in getting it published in Philadelphia, saying that "Thoreau is mainly bent on having it printed in a cheap form for a large circulation" (H. H. Furness, ed., *Records of a Lifelong Friendship . . . Ralph Waldo Emerson and William Henry Furness*, 1910, p. 61). Thoreau, after adding to the book (the section on friendship, according to

Alcott's diary, having been written as late as January 1848), finally published his first book at his own risk in the spring of 1849. Slightly over 200 copies were sold, and in 1853 three-quarters of the original thousand copies came back to the author. He salved his wounded spirit by commenting on the lack of sale, "It affects my privacy less, and leaves me freer" ("Journal," Oct. 28, 1853, *Writings,* XI, 460). The six years between the return from Walden Pond and the receipt of the unsold books had also contributed to Thoreau's freedom. Early in 1849 he returned to his father's "yellow house reformed" on Main Street and lived there during the remainder of his life.

One will not well understand Thoreau unless he places him in the midst of the Thoreau family, for that family life was as delightful and as intimate as that of their neighbors the Alcotts. None of the Thoreau children married or left home. Mrs. Thoreau shared with Mrs. Alcott the rare ability to create a rich home life out of simple materials. The family business of pencil making was a home industry, practised in a lean-to of the house, participated in by all, and managed after the father's death Feb. 3, 1859, by Sophia and Henry and made more profitable by the latter's inventiveness. Henry made himself useful in many other ways and became the "handy man" of Concord but was more dependent upon the *esprit de corps* of home life than the family was dependent upon him, more dependent than he or his first biographer, Emerson, would willingly admit. He was happy only when he was fulfilling his early wish expressed in a letter from Staten Island to his mother in 1843: "Methinks I should be content to sit at the back door in Concord, under the poplar tree, henceforth forever" (*Writings,* VI, 99).

Between the publication of the *Week* (1849) and that of *Walden, or Life in the Woods* (1854) Thoreau's friendships multiplied and the poet Ellery Channing replaced Emerson in the center of his acquaintance. In 1849 he came to know Harrison G. O. Blake of Worcester, Mass., with whom he maintained a long correspondence and to whom his sister bequeathed his manuscripts and journals. He toured Cape Cod on foot late in 1849, spent a week in Canada in 1850, went in 1853 on his second journey into Maine. Four of his posthumous books derive in part at least from these expeditions: *Excursions* (1863), *The Maine Woods* (1864), *Cape Cod* (1865), and *A Yankee in Canada* (1866). In the midst of these happy journeyings he made one sad trip as emissary from Concord to Fire Island beach near New York, where July 19, 1850, Margaret Fuller

Ossoli with her husband and son had been drowned in a shipwreck—a melancholy rummaging among the flotsam on the beach.

For five years after the return from the pond Thoreau lived ecstatically. He found keen delight in his daily walks about Concord and in the rarer, more ambitious trips into farther fields. It is the period of his friendship with the Emerson children, the berrying parties, the period of the formation of friendships, the years when one book was on the market (a drug there, to be sure) and when the next was in process of composition. He thought of himself as a poet and late in the period feared that his observation "is from year to year becoming more distinct and scientific" ("Journal," Aug. 19, 1851, *Writings,* VIII, 406). One turns from these five free years to 1852, the year which has been called "the noon of his life" (Odell Shepard, ed., *The Heart of Thoreau's Journals,* 1927, p. 106), when his most fruitful journalizing was done. He became interested in more individuals while his opinions of society became steadily more critical. He discovered a kindred youthful spirit in Emerson's seventy-seven year old aunt, Mary Moody Emerson, and a lively companion in Ellery Channing. He had become involved in the slavery question a second time on Oct. 1, 1851, when he put a fugitive slave on the train for Canada. His growing distrust of society would seem to coincide with his increasing interest in a slavery issue that was rapidly reaching a crisis and in an industrialism that had begun in New England to reproduce the evils of the factory system of old England. The problem of labor is generously discussed in the 1853 journal in entries which were brought together in the posthumously published "Life Without Principle" (*Atlantic Monthly,* October 1863). Though he was suspicious of reformers, Thoreau's excitement over slavery grew to white heat during the notorious Anthony Burns extradition in 1854, while he filled his journal with a denunciation of government which later in the year he delivered as a speech, "Slavery in Massachusetts," at an anti-slavery rally in neighboring Framingham (*Writings,* IV, 387–408). These concerns of 1853 have a place in his book *Walden,* finished during that year and published Aug. 9, 1854.

Walden confused the critics, for the book exhibited many of the paradoxes of its author. Seemingly parochial in its comments on the social condition of Concord, it has universal social criticism in it. With a reputation for being harmless natural history, it strikes blows at all the superficialities of society and government. Those qualities are also the qualities of Thoreau, who was at once as harmless and as devastating as the book, and as disarming to the commentators and critics.

After the publication of *Walden* Thoreau's life is anticlimactic. He became the scientific observer rather than the nature poet, working indefatigably upon his Concord herbarium, his weather records, and his ethnological study of the Indian. He became a lyceum lecturer with indifferent success outside of Concord. He began to finish life, making a last trip to Cape Cod in 1855, a last journey to Maine in 1857. Ill health in the form of tuberculosis began to close in upon him. In October 1854 he became acquainted with his one foreign friend, the donor of his extensive Oriental library, Thomas Cholmondeley. At Christmas 1854 he made his first visit to his Quaker correspondent Daniel Ricketson [*q.v.*] of New Bedford, and formed a lasting friendship which was recorded by the latter's children, Anna and Walton, in *Daniel Ricketson and His Friends* (1902). The third of the new friends was John Brown of Osawatomie [*q.v.*], whom he met in the home of Emerson in March 1857. To these new friends, Emerson added two names of late acquaintances who made a profound impression on Thoreau: Joe Polis, his Indian guide in Maine, and Walt Whitman, whom he met in New York in November 1856.

Thoreau's life burned out in a great enthusiasm, a defense of John Brown, who had been arrested at Harpers Ferry on Oct. 16, 1859. Thoreau was the first American to make public utterance in defense of Brown. He spoke in Concord Vestry on Sunday night, Oct. 30, against the protests of his townsmen, having to ring the bell with his own hands and to open the door with the key which the fearful vestrymen had dared neither to give nor refuse him and so had left it where he could find it. In "A Plea for Captain John Brown" (*Writings*, IV, 409–40; first printed in James Redpath, *Echoes of Harper's Ferry*, 1860), Thoreau rose to new heights of incisiveness in avowing his approval of Brown's action, and eulogized the man so magnificently that he was heard, as Emerson wrote, "by all respectfully, and by many with a sympathy that surprised themselves" (*Atlantic Monthly*, Aug. 1862, p. 242). On Nov. 1 he read the same lecture in Boston, and the *Liberator* (Nov. 4, 1859) commented on his enthusiasm. He spoke again a month later at the Concord service in commemoration of Brown's death. Thoreau regarded the John Brown affair as a touchstone which brought out the true nature of the American government. It became also the touchstone of his own nature, for his misanthropic reputation sloughed off

when he rose to defend a martyr, and his antisocial position among his neighbors gave way to a respect among many for one in the van of social justice.

In December 1860 he caught cold which led to a bronchial infection aggravated by his insistence on keeping a lecture engagement. After that, tuberculosis made rapid progress. In the spring of 1861 he made a fruitless journey, accompanied by Horace Mann, Jr., to Minnesota in search of health. He observed in semi-invalid fashion the vast new region of the Great Lakes and the Mississippi and went 300 miles beyond St. Paul to witness a gathering of the Sioux at Redwood. But the zest was gone. He returned to Concord weaker than when he had left, made one brief visit to New Bedford in August 1861, and then went to his room. The months of illness became so normal to him that he said he enjoyed the experiences of the sickroom as he had previously enjoyed those of the world of nature. He feverishly edited manuscripts which he left for his sister Sophia to publish. He weakened until the effort of holding the pages was too great for him; and then, at nine in the morning of May 6, 1862, he uttered the words of his beloved wilderness, "moose" and "Indian," and died. His funeral was held May 8, 1862, from the first parish church with a eulogy by Emerson (printed in enlarged form in the *Atlantic Monthly*, August 1862, and as a preface to Thoreau's *Excursions* in 1863) and with burial in the New Burying Ground in Concord. Some years later the body was moved to a new family lot in Sleepy Hollow Cemetery, on the ridge near the places where his friends Hawthorne, Emerson, Alcott, and Channing were to be buried.

Thoreau published but two books and a few magazine articles during his lifetime. From the huge mass of manuscript left at his death his sister published the volumes already mentioned. In 1865 Emerson presented a stoical Thoreau in his editing of *Letters to Various Persons*, enlarged in 1894 as *Familiar Letters of Henry David Thoreau*. His friend H. G. O. Blake edited selections from the journal as *Early Spring in Massachusetts* (1881), *Summer* (1884), *Winter* (1888), *Autumn* (1892). His poems, edited by H. S. Salt and F. B. Sanborn, were published as *Poems of Nature* (1895). The Riverside edition of his works (11 vols., 1894) was superseded by the Walden edition of *The Writings of Henry David Thoreau* (20 vols., 1906), fourteen volumes of which contain virtually all of the extant journal with the exception of two years between April 1843 and July 1845 and a few unimportant nature records. In 1902 his early essay on bravery was published under the title of *The Service*; and in 1905 the Bibliophile Society published his 1843 essay *Sir Walter Raleigh* and a two-volume record of his travels called *First and Last Journeys of Thoreau.* The same society published an enlarged and garbled *Walden* (1909) containing 12,000 rejected words not included in the original edition and badly edited by F. B. Sanborn. There have been some slight additions to the Thoreau canon since 1909, but nothing of great consequence except possibly the themes he wrote in college which, with changes, were included in Sanborn's biography of 1917. Some manuscript, including his notes for a history of the American Indian, remains unpublished, but it does not contain any considerable addition to Thoreau literature.

Thoreau's powerful influence upon later literature, both English and American, is more due to his style than even his admirers have realized. It is a nervous style, usually staccato, though often expanding in poetic passages of complex rhythm, the style of an exhorter who does not "pull his punches," and directly in the tradition of the most characteristic American writing, journalistic and otherwise. It has the pith and force of a man who, more concerned with incisive thought than with sustained argument, cares more for his sentences than for his essays as a whole. Even his descriptions depend more upon a single vivid image than upon a continuity of phrase. At his finest he is one of the best writers, if not the best, of American prose, but just as he wrote often from notes of uneven pitch, so he must be read in excerpts in order to be most impressive.

Of his books, only *Walden* is really organized; the rest are either journals padded with reflections or left as lean and specific narrative, or fragmentary essays made from crystallizations of his thought. *A Week on the Concord and Merrimack Rivers,* which has usually shared the reputation of *Walden,* is memorable now chiefly for the nature studies which were to give him his first eminence in literature. *The Maine Woods* is the same kind of book minus both the literary criticism of the *Week* and the social purpose of *Walden.* His observations of nature, which were lifelong, are characterized, not so much by their accuracy, in which others have exceeded him, as by a characteristic tension that gives them at their best an almost unequaled force and is felt in his style. Thoreau was teetering always between the transcendental and the scientific view of nature. From the first came his deep perceptions of spirit manifest in form which gives to simple, almost trivial, observations upon a flower,

a cloud, a tree, a bird, a significant and often a passionate expression. To the latter is due the careful thoroughness of his study, as of one who looks and looks again at the same thing. If he saw sometimes too much with the inner eye, the accuracy of his words never fails. As he grew older the transcendental seems to have been overborne in him by the very mass of his observations collected in his tireless rambles, until in his later journals the poet is almost lost in the sense of duty of a routine naturalist. Curiously enough, although he is supposed to be the fountain head of American nature writing, Thoreau actually stands apart from the American tradition in that he was unsentimental, and unromantic except in the expansiveness of his transcendentalism. He had a passion for nature which became articulate, and this is very American, but the Concord swamps and fields and the Maine woods were never merely picturesque to him, or sentimentally "wild" and emotionalized in that vein, as with Audubon, Burroughs, Muir, and with the nature fakers.

Walden, though uneven, is his one real book, and for that reason his greatest achievement, although most of its chapters can be duplicated, and some of them excelled, in his other writings. But it was not the nature writing of *Walden* which made it a textbook of the British Labor party, and read throughout the world. Thoreau's sojourn at Walden Pond was an experiment. He bought lime in the village to plaster the cabin he built there, but before he used it gathered a bushel of clamshells on the shores of nearby Fair Haven Bay and burnt them to a double handful of lime. His bean and potato planting, his baking in the ashes, his hunting and fishing, were likewise experiments, all intended to prove that certain transcendental doctrines of simplicity could be practised if need be, and, even more important, that a civilized man could make himself independent of the commercialism and the industrialism of New England. Thoreau has often been called anarchistic or anti-social. It would be more accurate to describe him as one who, urging conscience above government and being determined to rely upon himself before relying upon others, proposed to obey a set of laws which he regarded as more fundamental than those enforced by his particular state. Some of these he deduced from the tested experience of the ages— some were local to his own prejudices. Inevitably this brought him into conflict with both the ideals and the practice of his neighbors. The greed of many, the low and unsatisfactory nature of the values that nearly all sought in experience, inspired an attack which was nothing new in philosophy but which gained freshness and force when made by a man who found his greatest happiness in walking over the land they bought and sold. His perception of the lacks and dangers of the recent industrialism of New England was, however, both new and cogent. Like Carlyle, he saw politics as economics and current economics as spiritual diminution. But he was concrete where Carlyle was cloudy, specific where Carlyle was rhetorical, and a cool-headed Yankee where Carlyle lost his poise in universals and in the admiration of the dubiously great. Size never impressed Thoreau. A Yankee again, he argued for the practicality of the supposedly impractical. Only the grosser wrongs, like slavery, or an occasional esotericism from the Orient, drove him toward rhetoric. Thus *Walden* is a complete report of an experiment in thinking and living, with the definite design of arguing for true values against false and with abundant illustrations drawn from nature of the true; it is an attempt to demonstrate that civilized man can escape the evils of competition, and to show that a nature lover has his own passions worth describing for a world delivered over unto artifice. Its extraordinary influence is due to this organic purpose, excellently expressed, and to its highly important themes, of which, ironically, that furthest from his philosophic purpose though nearest to his heart, joy in nature, gave the book its position as a classic for youth.

The philosophy of his famous essay on civil disobedience is all implicit in the later *Walden*. This is the classic of individualism in its inevitable conflict with government, but, again, implies a state based upon laws in conformity with Thoreau's conception of what is noblest and most worthily human. It is a mistake, however, to define Thoreau as a social philosopher. He was, essentially, a man of letters, an essayist in the best sense, with a touch of the prophet. He was not a reformer, for he distrusted group action, but rather belongs with Walt Whitman as one who, having put his own definition upon morality, exhorted to the moral life. Both men are at the heart of the persistent American tradition of perfectibility, although Thoreau is on the pessimistic, Whitman on the optimistic side.

Thoreau was not a scientist in any true sense (though a good naturalist), not an important philosopher, but an admirable critic of everything except literature, where, in spite of some fine sayings, he was limited by the narrow range of his emotions. It was his own literary skill, however, that made him the best interpreter of the American environment of woods, swamps, meadows, fauna and flora, and weather, to the domesticated Europeans who were his fellow Americans. It was to know the soil, as the English know theirs, that he waded marshes and sought the wisdom of the Indians in the Maine woods. He would seem to be assured of permanence in English literature, partly for his style, though certainly not for any power over form beyond the sentence or, rarely, the paragraph, but still more as a germinal influence completely articulate for ideas which keep recurring in every culture and always search out their best translator into words. He is one of those writers whose particular job is to relate the best of man to the possibilities of his environment. And here he is a landmark in the vital thread of American literature—the conflict between ideals of living and methods of making a living. The environment he described was conditioned by Concord; but few writers in English have been so often clear, lofty, eloquent within such narrow limits of experience. It was a natural, though not inevitable, contribution of rural New England to world literature.

[F. H. Allen, *A Bibliography of Henry David Thoreau* (1908), is definitive up to that year; it may be supplemented by the bibliography in *The Cambridge Hist. of Am. Literature*, vol. II (1918), and R. W. Adams, *A Thoreau Checklist, 1908–1930* (1930). There are numerous full-length biographies. W. E. Channing, *Thoreau, the Poet-Naturalist* (1873; new ed. 1902), gives a personal appraisal. F. B. Sanborn, *Henry D. Thoreau* (1882), enlarged into *The Life of Henry David Thoreau* (1917), is rich in family history and Concord lore but opinionated. Henry S. Salt, *The Life of Henry David Thoreau* (1890), revised as *Life of Henry David Thoreau* (1896), remains the most accurate and complete biography, not superseded by Léon Bazalgette, *Henry Thoreau, Bachelor of Nature* (1924), J. B. Atkinson, *Henry Thoreau, the Cosmic Yankee* (1917), and Mark Van Doren, *Henry David Thoreau; a Critical Study* (1916). F. B. Sanborn, *The Personality of Thoreau* (1901), and Edward Waldo Emerson, *Henry Thoreau as Remembered by a Young Friend* (1917), are particularly valuable studies which emphasize the kindly humanness of their subject. Thoreau has been the subject of a myriad of shorter studies among which, outside the histories of American literature, the reader will find the following valuable: Norman Foerster, "Thoreau," in *Nature in American Literature* (1923); J. R. Lowell, "Thoreau" in *My Study Windows* (1871); H. S. Canby, "Henry David Thoreau," in *Classic Americans* (1931), a study of Thoreau's social thinking.]

R. W. A.
H. S. C—y.

THORNDIKE, ASHLEY HORACE (Dec. 26, 1871–Apr. 17, 1933), scholar, was born in Houlton, Me., the son of the Rev. Edward Robert and Abby Brewster (Ladd) Thorndike. He prepared for college at the Roxbury Latin School, Boston, and in 1893 graduated A.B. from Wesleyan University, where he came under the influence of the distinguished literary scholar, Caleb T. Winchester [*q.v.*]. During the next two years he was principal of the Smith Academy in Hatfield, Mass., where he met Annette Marian Lowell, who became his wife on June 21, 1899. They had four children. In 1895 he went to Harvard University for graduate study, took the A.M. degree in 1896, and the Ph.D. in 1898, at the same time acting as instructor in English in Boston University. For four years, 1898–1902, he was instructor and associate professor in Western Reserve University, and for the next four, professor in Northwestern University. In 1906 he was called to Columbia University, where he taught till his death. Among his colleagues there were his two brothers, Edward L. Thorndike, psychologist, and Lynn Thorndike, historian. He received many honors and distinctions. He was president of the Modern Language Association in 1926–27, and of the Shakespeare Association of America from 1923 till his death; was vice-president of the National Institute of Arts and Letters; and in 1927 gave the annual Shakespeare lecture of the British Academy, published as *Shakespeare in America* (1927).

These facts, while they suggest correctly enough a highly successful academic career, give little indication of either the quality of Thorndike's mind or the range of his influence. Something of these may be gathered from his writings. His doctoral dissertation, *The Influence of Beaumont and Fletcher on Shakspere* (1901), was a work of marked originality which has affected the whole course of Shakespearean criticism in the last thirty years. Barrett Wendell [*q.v.*] had been emphasizing for some years the typical and contemporary elements in Shakespeare's work, and it was probably a suggestion from him that led Thorndike to the specific investigations in which he showed Shakespeare as taking up and developing the methods and devices of his contemporaries rather than originating them. His volume on *Tragedy* followed in 1908, giving evidence of a finely balanced literary judgment. From 1913 to 1915 he edited in collaboration with William A. Neilson The Tudor Shakespeare, with a fortieth volume on *The Facts about Shakespeare* (1913). *Shakespeare's Theatre* (1916) is a compendious account of the scholarship on a subject that had been growing rapidly and to which he made substantial contributions. In his *English Comedy* (1929) he produced a companion study to his *Tragedy* of twenty years before. Though it is as a student of the Elizabethan drama that Thorndike is most widely known, his literary interests were very extensive. He acted for many years as literary adviser to a large publishing house; and from the reading of hundreds of manuscripts he obtained an insight into the intellectual currents of his own time, such as could not have been obtained from published books alone, and exercised an influence, as great

as it was unobtrusive, on literary production. *Literature in a Changing Age* (1920) and *The Outlook for Literature* (1931) deal penetratingly with the place of books in modern culture. In the writing and editing of textbooks for the teaching of English at all stages, he was prolific. These run from his *Elements of Rhetoric and Composition* (1905) through *Everyday English* (2 vols., 1912–13, with F. T. Baker), *The Minor Elizabethan Drama* (2 vols, 1910) for Everyman's Library, an edition of *The Maid's Tragedy* (1906) in the Belles-Lettres Series, *A History of English Literature* (1920 with W. A. Neilson), to those of more general interest as his revision, with John W. Cunliffe, of *The Warner Library of the World's Best Literature* (30 vols., 1917).

Alongside this activity in the production of books went his life as a busy university teacher. For over a quarter of a century, he was the guide and adviser of a great stream of young men and women engaged in the graduate study of English, and these students carried on his influence in scores of colleges throughout the United States. The characteristic of the training he gave them, as of his own writing, was the combination of a profound respect for facts with a lively interest in their significance. He did not allow the weight of his erudition to crush his interest in general truths, and he retained, as too few scholars do, a sense of the emotional values of the literary documents with which he dealt. Many people depended on him for aid and counsel, for his judgments were sound and his sympathies ready. Externally, he was a man of large physique with a mass of hair which early turned white, and a deliberate manner which masked the quickness of his mind, as his humor and appearance of ironic detachment masked his warmth of feeling.

[Family and personal sources; *Who's Who in America,* 1932–33; *Columbia Univ. Quart.,* June 1933; *N. Y. Times,* Apr. 18–20, 1933.]   W. A. N.

THORNDIKE, ISRAEL (Apr. 30, 1755–May 8, 1832), sailor, merchant, was born in Beverly, Mass., the son of Andrew and Anna (Morgan) Thorndike. He was descended from John Thorndike, one of the original settlers of Ipswich, but does not seem to have been born to much in the way of material possessions, for his lack of education is noted by his contemporaries. He must have gone to sea as a youth, as, on Oct. 30, 1776, he was commissioned commander of the schooner *Warren,* was later first lieutenant of the brig *Tyrannicide,* and commander of the ship *Resource,* all privateers (see *Massachusetts Soldiers and Sailors of the Revolutionary War,* vol.

XV, 1907, p. 691). As the harbor of Salem and Beverly was not controlled by the British during the Revolution, he was able to make valuable captures with these and other ships, and at the close of hostilities to keep vessels in operation at a time when American shipping was practically reduced to the Salem-Beverly fleet. He became an active partner of the shipping firm of Brown and Thorndike, which his brother-in-law, Moses Brown, had established in 1777, and which he conducted alone after Brown's retirement in 1800. This firm took a very conspicuous part in the trade with China and the Orient that originated in Salem and was later expanded from Boston. Before he was thirty-five years of age his part in the Revolution, his financial prominence, and his personal influence made him one of the leading men in the state.

From 1788 to 1814 he was thirteen times elected to the state legislature, seven times to the lower, and six times to the upper branch; he was member of the constitutional conventions of 1788 and 1820; and a presidential elector in 1812 and 1816. In 1810 he changed his residence from Beverly to Boston, where he was already so well known that he was elected to the state Senate from his new constituency in 1812. He continued his extensive business with the Orient, invested largely in manufacturing and other business enterprises, and his mansion became a political and social center. One of his dinner-parties in 1812 was renowned because the famous "Gerrymander" drawing that gave a new word to the English language was exhibited at his home soon after its origin (New-England Historical and Genealogical Register, Oct. 1873, Oct. 1892). He contributed freely for public purposes sums then considered large, and in 1818 purchased the library of Professor Ebeling of Hamburg, Germany, a valuable collection of Americana, and presented it to Harvard College. As this was his largest public gift, although he left an estate of $1,500,000, and the outlay was only $6,500, he cannot be considered a pioneer in philanthropy, but he was a sturdy patriot in the Revolution, and he influenced the economic development and politics of Massachusetts for the first half-century of independence.

His oratory was more conspicuous for its substance than its form, but his mastery of fact was often made use of by legislative colleagues of more eloquence for whom he collected material. On Oct. 31, 1784, he was married to Anna Dodge, of Salem, who died in 1817. They had twelve children, three dying in infancy. He died and was buried in Boston, but his body was transferred to Mount Auburn Cemetery in 1896.

[Memorial Biog. of the N.-E. Hist. and Geneal. Soc., vol. VI (1905); Josiah Quincy, The Hist. of Harvard Univ. (1840), vol. II; E. M. Stone, Hist. of Beverly (1843); Thomas Bridgman, The Pilgrims of Boston (1856); obituary articles in N.-E. Mag., June 1832, and Boston Daily Advertiser and Patriot, May 10, 23, 1832.]   S. G.

THORNE, CHARLES ROBERT (c. 1814–Dec. 13, 1893), actor and manager, was born in New York City of a merchant family. His father may have been Thomas W. Thorne. If the date which is generally given for his birth is correct, his precocity was remarkable, for on Apr. 23, 1829, billed as "a young gentleman in this city," he made his "first appearance on any stage" as Octavian at the Park Theatre, New York (Odell, post, vol. III, p. 395). On Apr. 28 he played the difficult rôle of Pierre in Otway's Venice Preserved, and on Apr. 30 had a benefit. In December 1830 he acted Pythias to Thomas Hamblin's Damon at the Bowery, and later played the title rôle in Pizarro. The same year he married Maria Ann Mestayer, who was of a well-known theatrical and circus family. This is enough, even in those days of juvenile prodigies, to cause some wonder; however, it should be noted that one of his sons was later to exhibit a similar precocity. On May 4, 1831, Thorne appears as "proprietor" of the Chatham Theatre. The New York Mirror of June 11, 1831, praises his Pizarro as displaying "force and expression," though wanting "study, practice, and observation." November 1831 found him and his wife at the new theatre on Richmond Hill. During the next few years, like most other actors save those at the Park, Thorne drifted from one house to another and took part in an unbelievable number of plays. In February 1835 he was back at the Bowery, playing Glaucus in The Last Days of Pompeii, which ran from Feb. 9 to Mar. 7, a New York record at that time. In June 1836 he was at the Franklin on Chatham Square; in November he supported James Henry Hackett [q.v.] at the Bowery in Horse-Shoe Robinson and later the elder James Wallack in Sardanapalus. On Nov. 27, 1837, he played Wellborn to the elder Booth's Sir Giles Overreach in A New Way to Pay Old Debts at the Olmypic. On Dec. 18, 1837, he was again at the Bowery, where on Jan. 2, 1838, he rode the "fiery, untamed steed" in Mazeppa. In the late summer of 1838 he managed the little Olympic and in February 1840 took over the Chatham, where he enjoyed success for two years but failed the third. His failure has been attributed (Odell, post, vol. IV, p. 647) to lack of any sustained policy; his seasons were hodge-podges.

From this time on his New York appearances grew fewer, and the intervening gaps represent tours made by Thorne and his wife, or attempts at management in other cities. He acted, Feb. 19, 1844, in *Thérèse* and *The Swiss Cottage* at the Bowery Amphitheatre; on Dec. 4, 1848, he and his wife acted *Don Cæsar de Bazan* at Chanfrau's National; at the ill-fated Astor Place opera house, Feb. 22, 1851, he and Chanfrau had a benefit (in the midst of opera); and from Aug. 30, 1852, till Sept. 14, he attempted to manage that house, without success. Beginning Aug. 1, 1853, he attempted to manage a season at the St. Charles. Finally, in 1874, he rented old Niblo's from A. T. Stewart for three years at $35,000 a year, and attempted to create "an American Drury Lane." In 1847, between New York engagements, he and his wife managed the old Boston Theatre on Federal Street, and for a brief time the Howard Athenaeum. In 1849 they went to California; again in 1853 they toured to San Francisco, and thence to the Orient and around the world, being absent many years on an adventurous if not very profitable tour. In 1880 they celebrated their golden wedding. In 1883 a letter from Thorne to Albert Marshman Palmer, asks for a benefit; "No doubt," he writes, "I will be Edwin's [his son's] next care after he pays his debts." Ten years later he died in San Francisco.

Thorne was chiefly notable as one of the early American-born actors and managers, who had courage to adopt the stage as a career. He was good-looking and graceful, and his rather round, healthy face was expressive. But his training was haphazard, gained chiefly in the cheaper Bowery theatres where romantic and melodramatic rant was most appreciated, and his artistic intelligence as a manager does not seem to have been conspicuous. He contributed little to the development of a native drama or style of acting. He and his first wife (d. 1881) had five children, among them Charles Robert [*q.v.*]. In 1883 he married the widow of James Stark, an actor.

[E. D. Barbour, *Geneal. Record of John Thorne* (1913); G. C. D. Odell, *Annals of the N. Y. Stage*, vols. III–VI (1928–31); *Music and Drama*, Oct. 21, 1882; theatre colls. in Harvard Coll. lib. and N. Y. Pub. Lib.; obituary notice in *San Francisco Chronicle*, Dec. 16, 1893.]   W. P. E.

THORNE, CHARLES ROBERT (1840–Feb. 10, 1883), actor, was born in New York City, son of Charles Robert Thorne [*q.v.*] and Maria (Mestayer) Thorne. In 1847 he went to school in Boston, where his parents were playing. He was a student at St. John's (later Fordham) College, 1854–57, and is said to have been a "clerk" with his grandfather Thorne on Wall Street. In 1854, according to his own statement, he acted with his father in San Francisco, and

soon afterwards went to Australia with his parents. It is certain that a C. Thorne was at the Bowery, New York, in September 1857, and "C. R. Thorne, Jr.," was a full-fledged member of Joseph Jefferson's company at Laura Keene's Theatre, New York, May 16, 1860, and played Captain de Boots in *Our American Cousin*, July 23, 1860. In September 1860 he supported Mr. and Mrs. Barney Williams in New York, and then (like many other American actors when the Civil War began) he left the East. He played at McGuire's in San Francisco, quarreled with Edwin Forrest, and set out to find his father and mother in China. The year 1866 found him as leading man at the Boston Theatre, where he remained three years. Touring followed, and in 1871 he joined the Union Square Theatre company in New York, one of the best in the country, where for many years he enjoyed a great measure of popular success. Here he received good training, especially by Dion Boucicault [*q.v.*] in *Led Astray*, and a large salary. Physically, he was of a ruddy but athletic type, looking a bit like a young hunting squire, and as the heroes of the domestic melodramas characteristic of the period he cut a great dash. He had a sonorous voice, which he made much use of. As one critic said after his appearance in 1880 as Sardou's *Daniel Rochat*, his style did not "lend itself to expressions of subtlety." But he could suggest suppressed power, and audiences found him "sympathetic" and good to look at. In 1874 with Stuart Robson [*q.v.*], he played *Led Astray* in London. In 1878 he acted in Bronson Howard's *The Banker's Daughter*. His last days were unfortunate. Late in 1882 he left the Union Square to be made a star in *The Corsican Brothers*, by John Stetson, the famous and eccentric Boston manager. The play opened at Booth's Theatre, New York, early in 1883 to a crowded and expectant house, but Thorne disappointed the audience by his acting, and the production was violently criticized. It quickly developed, however, that Thorne was not well. His illness accentuated by disappointment and the flaming success of young Richard Mansfield [*q.v.*] in *A Parisian Romance* at the Union Square where he had so long been regnant, he broke down completely and soon afterwards died. His funeral, at which the "cloud-capped towers" passage from *The Tempest* and a telegram from Robert Green Ingersoll [*q.v.*] were read for all ceremony, raised a teapot tempest difficult now to understand, and poor Thorne was widely branded "atheist."

Thorne's first wife was a Miss Calder of Boston, whom he married early in 1859. After his wife secured a divorce in Indiana, Thorne married Mary (Smith) Brown of Philadelphia. He was survived by his wife and a daughter of his first marriage. Of him one critic said, "His instincts are mock-heroic, bully-boy instincts, but he knows better." He never knew quite enough, however, or had the ambition to overcome these instincts thoroughly; he was too handsome and easy-going, perhaps. Another critic remarked, after the funeral, "Thorne didn't know enough to be an atheist"—which was another way of saying that he lacked the mental equipment required of the best actors.

[The date of Thorne's birth is given variously as Mar. 10 and June 11, 1840. See E. D. Barbour, *Geneal. Record of John Thorne* (1913); G. C. D. Odell, *Annals of the N. Y. Stage*, vol. VII (1931); records of Fordham Coll.; *N. Y. Times, N. Y. Daily Tribune*, Feb. 11, 13, 1883; theatre colls. in lib. of Harvard Univ. and N. Y. Pub. Lib. The quotations are from newspaper clippings in the Harvard coll.] W. P. E.

THORNTON, HENRY WORTH (Nov. 6, 1871–Mar. 14, 1933), railroad manager, son of Henry Clay and Millamenta Comegys (Worth) Thornton, was born in Logansport, Ind. He prepared for college at St. Paul's School, Concord, N. H., and was graduated from the University of Pennsylvania in 1894, with the degree of B.S. He began his railroad service in that year as a draftsman in the office of the chief engineer of the Southwest system of the Pennsylvania Railroad and advanced rapidly in that department to the position of engineer of maintenance of way. In 1901 he became a division superintendent and in 1911, after several promotions, was appointed general superintendent of the Long Island Railroad. His work was of such character that it attracted the attention of Samuel Rea [q.v.], then president of the Pennsylvania Railroad, and in 1914, when asked by Lord Claude Hamilton, chairman of the board of the Great Eastern Railway of England, to suggest a man for the general managership of that property, Rea recommended Thornton, who was elected to the position a few months before the outbreak of the World War.

When Great Britain entered the war and the Great Eastern was called upon to perform an important part in the transportation of troops and military supplies, Thornton's ability and resourcefulness in adapting the service of his railway to meet the emergency, his tact in relations with railway and governmental officers and the public, and his exceptional powers in inspiring the confidence and loyalty of the workers, quickly overcame the initial prejudice against him as an alien. He was made a member of the national committee of general managers appointed to administer the British railways for the government. In 1916 he was appointed deputy director

of inland water transportation, with rank of colonel in the Royal Engineers. In 1917 he became assistant director general of railway movements in France, representing the director and army council in negotiations with the French, Italian, and American governments. Later in that year he became deputy director general of railway movements, with rank of brigadier-general, and in 1918 he was made inspector general of transportation and advanced to the rank of major-general. His military service completed, he returned to the management of the Great Eastern Railway and on several occasions served also on the National Wage Board in arbitration proceedings, as well as on a committee to investigate the operations and finances of the Metropolitan Water Board of the City of London. In 1919 he was gazetted Knight Commander of the Order of the British Empire. He was honored also by decorations from the United States, France, and Belgium.

Thornton became a naturalized British subject in 1919, evidently intending to remain in England, but when steps were taken in 1922 to consolidate all of the English railways into four systems there was some uncertainty as to his position. It was then that the Canadian National Railways, just created in Canada by the amalgamation of a large number of separate railways, sought his services, and in October 1922 he became chairman of the board and president of that large system. The properties brought together as a nationalized system to compete with the strong and well organized Canadian Pacific Railway were typically weak and had little in common. The task of welding them into a coherent and unified whole was one of major proportions. Many of the separate units were bankrupt and in poor physical condition when acquired, and the morale of employees was distinctly low. During his ten years as chief executive Thornton succeeded in welding the properties together, creating an efficient operating organization, and establishing a high degree of *esprit de corps*. While he was unable to satisfy all shades of political opinion or to make the system earn enough in net income to pay interest charges on all of the government obligations incurred in the acquisition of the properties, he raised the net revenue (exclusive of the interest charges) from $2,000,000 in 1922 to almost $60,000,000 in 1928, and brought the quality of public service to a high standard.

With the depression in 1929, however, the Canadian National deficits increased and political opposition became intensified. The government then in power was not of the same political faith as that which had called Thornton from England in 1922. Criticism was focussed upon him personally and fault was found with his policies, especially those which called for expenditures which in his far-sighted view he believed would be ultimately justified by improved service. Despite constantly increasing criticism and political pressure he held to his task, but in July 1932 finally resigned when the opposition became so strong as to impair his usefulness. After his retirement he returned to New York. The strain had told upon his health, and he died of pneumonia following an operation at the age of sixty-one.

On June 20, 1901, Thornton married Virginia Dike Blair of New Castle, Pa. A son and a daughter were born to this marriage, which was ended by divorce in 1926. In September of that year he married Martha Watriss of New York City. In his youth Thornton was an athlete and a member of the football team of his college. Of imposing stature, he was a commanding figure, and he carried himself as a leader of men. One of his outstanding characteristics was his liberal attitude in relations with organized labor, especially in the creation of cooperative committees of shopmen. His death occurred a few days before the scheduled date for a dinner to be given him in New York City by organized labor as a testimonial of confidence and respect.

[*Who's Who in America*, 1930–31; *Travel*, May 1914; *Forum*, Dec. 1922; *Current Opinion*, Jan. 1923; *Canadian Mag.*, Apr. 1924; *Outlook*, June 4, 1924; *Collier's*, Apr. 4, 1925; *Sat. Eve. Post*, July 6, 1929; *Canadian Forum*, Sept. 1932; *Ann. Reports of the Canadian National Railway System*, 1922–32; *N. Y. Times*, July 28, Aug. 31, Sept. 11, 12, 14, 1926, Mar. 15, 1933.]
W. J. C.

THORNTON, JESSY QUINN (Aug. 24, 1810–Feb. 5, 1888), Oregon pioneer, was born near Point Pleasant, Va. (now W. Va.), a descendant of an English immigrant who came to Virginia in 1633. His parents moved to Champaign County, Ohio, when he was an infant. He received a good education. Choosing the law for a profession, he spent nearly three years in London as a student, and on his return continued his preparation in the office of John H. Peyton of Staunton, Va. After his admission to the bar in 1833 he attended law lectures at the University of Virginia. In 1835 he opened a law office in Palmyra, Mo., and in the following year edited a newspaper in that town. On Feb. 8, 1838, at Hannibal, Mo., he married Mrs. Nancy M. Logue, and three years later moved to Quincy, Ill. Their health failing, in 1846 he and his wife set out for Oregon, overtaking on the way the California-bound ox-train of Col. William Henry Russell [*q.v.*] and arriving in the Salem neighborhood in November.

Thornton at once came into public notice, and on Feb. 9, 1847, Gov. George Abernethy [*q.v.*] appointed him judge of the supreme court of the provisional government. In October he was delegated to proceed at once to the national capital and press the demand of the people for the organization of a territory. Making the trip by water, he arrived in Washington in May 1848, and was soon joined by Joseph L. Meek [*q.v.*], who, with similar instructions, had traveled by land. With the support of President Polk, Thornton worked tirelessly against a hostile, or indifferent, majority in Congress, and was successful in obtaining the passage of an act establishing the territorial government of Oregon on Aug. 14, the last day of the session. A disagreement with the President lost for him, however, a reappointment as judge. While in Washington he wrote *Oregon and California in 1848*, which was published early the following year, in two volumes, in New York; a second edition appeared in 1855.

Returning to Oregon, he was appointed Indian sub-agent for the region north of the Columbia, but soon gave up the post. He then resumed the practice of law and became active in politics. In 1864–65 he represented Benton County in the legislature. For some years he lived in Oregon City, later in Albany and Portland, and from 1871 in Salem. His later years were spent in poverty. He died in Salem, and was buried there in the Methodist churchyard. He was survived by his wife.

Thornton was one of the leading figures in early Oregon, and his work was important and useful. Into the act establishing the territory he succeeded in incorporating a provision doubling the amount of land ordinarily set aside for school purposes, and thus made possible the rapid expansion of educational facilities in the young community. He was a voluminous writer. For the meeting of the Oregon Pioneer Association of 1874 he expanded the sketch of the provisional government given in his book, and for the meeting of 1878 he prepared an account of the emigration of 1846. Both articles are printed in *Transactions* of the Association. He was also the author of a series of political articles in the *New York Tribune* under the pen-name of Achilles de Harley, and he wrote many letters for the local press. Much of his writing is bitterly critical of some of his contemporaries, and though late in life he made partial amends for this censoriousness, he set in motion controversies that continued long after his death.

[H. H. Bancroft, *Hist. of Ore.*, vol. I (1886); H. W. Scott, *Hist. of the Ore. Country* (6 vols., 1924); C. H. Carey, *Hist. of Ore.* (1922); Portland *Morning Oregonian*, Feb. 7, 1888; information from J. Neilson Barry, Portland, Ore.]   W. J. G.

THORNTON, JOHN WINGATE (Aug. 12, 1818–June 6, 1878), historian, was born at Saco, Me., the son of James Brown and Eliza (Gookin) Thornton. His father, a descendant of Thomas Thornton who emigrated to New England in 1663, was a shipping merchant with a lively interest in water power and the promotion of railroads; his mother contributed poems to the *Southern Literary Messenger* and the *Christian Mirror*. After graduating from the Harvard law school in 1840, Thornton practised law in Boston, living first at Brookline, later at Winthrop, in the winters and at Oak Hill, Scarboro, Me., in the summers. He was a typical antiquarian, a founder of the New England Historic Genealogical Society in 1844 and of the Prince Society in 1858. Author of many books and pamphlets, he corresponded with the leading antiquaries of his time, maintaining traditions of old-fashioned politeness. In his fervid and didactic family letters he referred to his wife as "my lady." In his quaintly formal journal covering May 1850 to July 1851, he noted "what would be of permanent interest, of pleasure, or use in retrospect"; he thanked God for the abolition of the slave trade; he animadverted on things literary, political, and legal. His catholicity of mind admitted in 1850 that everything might be possible in physical science "except aerial navigation." In the winter he haunted bookstores, collecting rare Americana, documents, and letters written by famous people. His office at 20 Court St. was a gathering place where men like the historian, John S. Barry, came for consultation with him during the preparation of books and papers.

His separate publications were *A Genealogical Memoir of the Gilbert Family* (1850); *Lives of Isaac Heath and John Bowles, Elders of the Church, and Principal Founders of the Grammar School in Roxbury, and Rev. John Eliot, Jr., Preacher to the Indians, and First Pastor of the Church in Newton* (1850); *Mementos of the Swett Family* (1851); *The Landing at Cape Anne* (1854), one of his most valuable works; *Ancient Pemaquid* (1857); *Peter Oliver's 'Puritan Commonwealth' Reviewed* (1857); *The First Records of Anglo-American Colonization* (1859); *The Pulpit of the American Revolution; or the Political Sermons of the Period of 1776* (1860); *Colonial Schemes of Popham and Gorges* (1863); *D'Amerie, Emery, Amory* (1869); and *The Historical Relation of New England to the English Commonwealth* (1874).

In addition, he wrote many fugitive papers, some of them so controversial in tone that they distressed his friends. His part in the rediscovery of the manuscript of Governor William Bradford's history, "Of Plimoth Plantation," then in the Fulham Library, bringing in the names of Barry, Drake, Charles Deane [*q.v.*], and Nathaniel Bradstreet Shurtleff [*q.v.*], makes good reading (*Proceedings of the Massachusetts Historical Society*, Nov. 1881, pp. 118–20). While abroad in 1872 he ferreted out and obtained for the Maine Historical Society the invaluable Trelawny papers relating to the fishing station at Richmond Island.

He was of a "manly and generous nature," amiable, loyal to his obligations, deeply religious, with a mind "evenly poised and well regulated" (Amory, *post,* p. 273). He had an open, friendly countenance, curly hair, and a generous beard. He loved flowers and the open sea, and his letters show with what eagerness he looked forward to his summers at Oak Hill. He married at Roxbury, Mass., May 31, 1848, Elizabeth Wallace Bowles, daughter of Stephen Jones Bowles. Their son, Henry Thornton Thornton, to whom the father was passionately attached, died at the age of ten; a daughter Elizabeth died at Lexington, Mass., in 1931. Two other daughters, Elizabeth and Agnes, did not survive infancy. Thornton died at Oak Hill in Scarboro, Me.

[See J. W. Thornton, *Thornton Family* (1850); T. C. Amory, in *New England Hist. and Geneal. Reg.*, July 1879, reprinted as *Memoir of John Wingate Thornton, with a List of his Publications* (1879); and obituary in *Boston Transcript*, June 8, 1878. Thornton's journal, 1850–51, and family letters and pictures, 1866–76, are in the Boston Athenaeum; four bound vols., of correspondence, pamphlets, notes, portraits, and clippings, and two bundles are in the possession of the New England Hist. Geneal. Soc., Boston.]   C. K. B.

THORNTON, MATTHEW (*c.* 1714–June 24, 1803), physician and Revolutionary patriot, was born in Ireland. There is some uncertainty as to the date of his birth. He was of Scotch-Irish extraction and his parents, James and Elizabeth (Jenkins) Thornton, emigrated to America about 1718, settling first in Maine and later in the neighborhood of Worcester, Mass., where Matthew received his early education and began to study medicine. He completed his studies in 1740 and began to practise in Londonderry, N. H., where there was a vigorous Scotch-Irish colony whose members and descendants played such a prominent part in New Hampshire history. He resided here until 1779, was married to Hannah Jack about 1760, was successful in his profession, took an active part in the affairs of this somewhat contentious community, and brought up a family of five children. In 1745 he took part in the Louisbourg expedition and his name appears as "under-surgeon" in the roster of the New Hampshire contingent. For some time he held a commission as colonel of militia under the royal government.

In 1758 his name appears in the records as member of the legislature from Londonderry and for the next thirty years he was an outstanding figure in provincial and state politics. From Jan. 17, 1760, when he waited on Gov. Benning Wentworth with a legislative address expressive of gratitude for recent victories and "fresh zeal for his Majesty's service," until June 8, 1775, when he delivered to that governor's successor a denunciation of the "unconstitutional and tyrannical Acts of the British Parliament," Thornton's career was a chronicle of revolutionary progress in that part of New England. Prominent in the agitation against the Stamp Act he advanced steadily in the confidence of the revolutionary party and when the break came was elected president of the provincial congress of 1775 and chairman of the committee of safety that organized resistance and exercised general powers of government in the first stages of the war. His address to the people under the date June 2, 1775, is a model plea for order, self-restraint, and vigorous cooperation in the emergency.

During the war, while governmental organization was in more or less confusion, he held a variety of important places, speaker of the house, member of the council, and president of the constitutional convention. In 1776 he was chosen an associate justice of the superior court, holding office until 1782. It was a period when "separation of powers" had not been fully achieved and when legal training was not a prerequisite to service on the bench. In 1776 he was elected to the Continental Congress and although he did not take his place until November, he was in time to acquire immortality by affixing his signature to the Declaration of Independence. He served about one year as delegate and returned to resume service in state affairs. In 1780 he established his home in Merrimack County. He had given up professional work but continued to be active in political affairs for some years, serving in the newly organized state Senate, 1784–86. His last years were spent on his Merrimack farm where he enjoyed the standing of a rural Nestor who had well served the councils of the state in the critical quarter-century, 1763–89. He died in Newburyport, Mass., while visiting his daughter, but his body was interred near his home in Merrimack. Thornton, N. H., was named in his honor.

[Thornton's private papers and a manuscript biographical sketch by a contemporary, William Plumer, are in the archives of the N. H. Historical Society at Concord. See also C. T. Adams, *The Family of James Thornton* (1905); E. L. Parker, *Hist. of Londonderry* (1851); C. H. Woodbury, "Matthew Thornton," *Proc. N. H. Hist. Soc.*, vol. III (1902); *N. H. State Papers*, vols. XVIII (1890), XX–XXII (1891–93); *Provincial Papers*, vols. VI (1872), VII (1873); *N. H. Hist. Soc. Colls.*, vol. VII (1863); John Sanderson, *Signers to the Declaration of Independence*, vol. V (1823); W. H. Bailey, "Matthew Thornton," *Granite Monthly*, Mar. 1892.]

W. A. R.

THORNTON, WILLIAM (May 20, 1759–Mar. 28, 1828), architect, inventor, and public official, was born on the little island of Jost van Dyke in the community of the Society of Friends centering at Tortola in the Virgin Islands. His father is believed to have been also named William; his mother was Dorcas Downing Zeageus (or Zeagurs). He was sent to England at the age of five, and from 1781 to 1784 attended the University of Edinburgh, where he studied medicine; his degree of M.D., however, he received from Aberdeen University on Nov. 23, 1784 (diploma in Thornton Papers, Library of Congress). After a period in Paris he returned to Tortola (1786) and then came to the United States, being in New York in 1787, and becoming an American citizen in Delaware, Jan. 7, 1788. He soon made Philadelphia his headquarters. He did not practise medicine, and seems to have had some small means and to have been well received. In 1789 he achieved his first public distinction. The Library Company of Philadelphia offered as a prize a share in the Company for the best design for its new building on Fifth Street. Thornton writes in an autobiographic fragment, "When I travelled I never thought of architecture. But I got some books and worked a few days, then gave a plan in the ancient Ionic order, which carried the day." The building, one of the finest in the country in its time, stood until 1880. From 1778, if not earlier, to 1790 Thornton was associated with John Fitch [*q.v.*] in his experiments with steamboats operated by paddles. Fitch had demonstrated his first boat on the Delaware in 1787; his second, in which Thornton had a share, made a trip of twenty miles in 1788. For his third, the *Thornton,* it would appear that Thornton advanced much of the cost and made fruitful suggestions. It made a speed of eight miles an hour, and is said to have been run regularly on the Delaware as a packet boat and to have covered some thousand miles before it was retired in the winter of 1790. After Fulton's success Thornton published in 1814 his *Short Account of the Origin of Steam Boats,* vindicating Fitch's and his own contributions.

On Oct. 13, 1790, Thornton married Anna

Maria Brodeau, then sixteen years of age, and took her to Tortola for two years. While there he learned of the competition for the public buildings in the new federal city of Washington, and wrote the commissioners in July that he would bring his plans to the United States. Delayed by illness, he arrived at the beginning of November, to find that no decision had yet been reached as to the design of the Capitol. Of those first received that of Étienne Sulpice Hallet [*q.v.*], a French professional, had been most favored, and he had been retained to prepare further studies, while certain other competitors were invited to revise their designs according to new data. It was obvious at once to Thornton that the design brought with him from the West Indies (the drawings are preserved by the Library of Congress and the American Institute of Architects) would not be acceptable, and he undertook a new one. In its preparation he was much influenced by a glimpse of one of Hallet's designs submitted the previous October. The new design was still unfinished on Jan. 31 when it was recommended by President Washington in terms which assured its adoption. This followed early in March. Thornton received as premium a lot in the new city (No. 15 in Square 634) and five hundred dollars. The drawings of this design appear to have been destroyed by Thornton at a later period, but from the manuscript description which accompanied them, and other evidence, it is possible to reconstruct its essential provisions.

Since Thornton was not an architect by profession, nor a builder, there was no idea of employing him to supervise the erection of the Capitol, and Hallet was retained for the task. He and the contractors in Washington at once raised numerous structural and practical objections to the design, some of which, aimed at defects and inconsistencies arising from Thornton's lack of experience, appear to have been justified. At a conference with the President and with Jefferson, the secretary of state, held in July 1793, a revised plan prepared by Hallet—"considered," Jefferson wrote (*Documentary History of the ... United States Capitol, post,* pp. 26–27), "as Dr. Thornton's plan rendered into practicable form"—was adopted, subject to certain modifications left for future decision. The foundations were begun in accordance with this plan, but in the modifications undertaken differences of opinion arose which resulted in Hallet's dismissal, June 28, 1794. James Hoban [*q.v.*], architect of the President's House, remained in charge of the erection of the Capitol. On Sept. 12, 1794, Thornton was appointed one of the commissioners of the city, and shortly removed his residence

there from Philadelphia. He considered that he had a mandate to restore the form of the Capitol to conformity with his designs. The progress made rendered this not entirely practicable, and he prepared revised designs determined, in considerable measure, by the work already performed, but returning to some of the principal features of his design which had been abandoned. A complete reconciliation of the two designs was not feasible, and many problems regarding the central portion of the structure remained unsolved. A further confusion had been threatened by the proposition of George Hadfield [*q.v.*], who was appointed superintendent in 1795, to substitute an attic for Thornton's basement, but Thornton was successful in constraining Hadfield to follow his directions. The north wing had been constructed in accordance with Thornton's ideas by the time Congress removed to Washington in 1800, and the exterior of the south wing, constructed later, necessarily conformed with it. Thornton's idea of a great central rotunda was also adhered to by later architects of the building. In May 1802 the board of commissioners of the city was abolished by Congress, and Thornton had henceforth no official connection with the work on the Capitol. This, however, did not prevent him from continuing to concern himself with it. The elder Benjamin Henry Latrobe [*q.v.*], whom Jefferson appointed in 1803 to the new post of surveyor of the public buildings, was, like Hadfield, keenly alive to certain difficulties in the design, and proposed changes which Thornton was quick to oppose. He addressed a printed letter "To the Members of the House of Representatives of the United States," Jan. 1, 1805, and a pamphlet war ensued, from which Latrobe, supported by President Jefferson, emerged embittered but victorious, remaining in charge of the work until after the outbreak of the War of 1812.

Thornton's designs in architecture were not limited to those already mentioned. For George Washington he supervised the erection, in 1798–99, of two houses on North Capitol Street between B and C Streets. For John Tayloe he built in 1798–1800 a fine house, the Octagon, still standing (1935), now the headquarters of the American Institute of Architects. It was distinguished by the circular rooms at the corner, in one of which, while the house was occupied by Madison after the burning of the White House in 1814, the Treaty of Ghent was signed. In 1800 Thornton made for Lawrence Lewis, who had married Washington's adopted daughter, Eleanor Custis, a design for Woodlawn, which appears to have been followed in this fine mansion in Fairfax County, Va. The same year he appears to have given Bishop John Carroll [q.v.] a plan for the cathedral in Baltimore, but Latrobe's design was followed. Homewood in Baltimore, a Carroll house, may possibly follow a design of Thornton's. Beginning about 1812 Tudor Place in Georgetown was erected from his designs. Mrs. Thornton says in her diary that her husband was the architect of Brentwood in the District of Columbia, and that he gave a plan for the house of Mr. Dobson in Stokes County, N. C., in 1805. The Octagon, Tudor Place, and Brentwood show a plastic and spatial variety and mastery rarely found in America before their time. In 1817 Jefferson outlined to Thornton his plan for the University of Virginia and requested suggestions for the fronts of the pavilions, as "models of taste & good architecture, & of a variety of appearance" (letter quoted in Fiske Kimball, *Thomas Jefferson, Architect,* 1916, p. 75). Thornton supplied two sketches, from one of which Pavilion VII was built (*Ibid.,* pp. 75–76, 187, fig. 212).

At the close of Thornton's service as a commissioner in May 1802, Jefferson appointed him clerk in the State Department, in charge of patents—the first functionary specially assigned to this matter. He is credited (*Daily National Intelligencer,* Sept. 7, 1814) with having saved the Patent Office from destruction on the capture of Washington in 1814. As superintendent of patents he continued in charge of the Patent Office until his death, Mar. 28, 1828 (G. W. Evans, "The Birth and Growth of the Patent Office," *Records of the Columbia Historical Society,* vol. XXII, 1919, 105–24). His own wide curiosity and inventiveness admirably fitted him for this position. A memorandum in his papers lists eight patents of his own between 1802 and 1827, dealing with improvements in boilers, stills, firearms, and other devices.

Thornton's interests and activities were astonishingly varied. He drew and painted with facility. Miniatures by him and his copy of Stuart's profile portrait of Washington survive, as do the manuscripts of three unpublished novels (Thornton Papers, Library of Congress). The Magellanic gold medal of the American Philosophical Society was awarded to him in February 1793 for his *Cadmus: or, a Treatise on the Elements of Written Language,* published the same year. Appended was an "Essay on the mode of teaching the Surd or Deaf, and consequently Dumb to speak." This last Dr. Alexander Graham Bell [q.v.] calls the first work upon the education of the deaf actually written and published in America, and says its suggestions "certainly

have not received that attention from practical teachers of the deaf that their importance deserves" (*Association Review,* Apr. 1900, pp. 113–15). Thornton's Quaker antecedents and humanitarianism also led him, as early as 1788, to strive for the freeing of slaves through African colonization. In 1791, when at Tortola, he was endeavoring to send blacks to Sierra Leone at the time of the second negro settlement there under the presidency of Henry Thornton, and his pamphlet *Political Economy: Founded in Justice and Humanity,* published in 1804, advocated the abolition of slavery. In later years he was active in the American Colonization Society. Thornton was concerned also in the effort to found a national university in Washington. Following Washington's gift of stock in the Potomac Company to further the enterprise, announced in 1795, the Commissioners set aside a site, and memorialized Congress to authorize the acceptance of contributions. In later years Thornton's sympathies were enlisted by the liberation of South America. In 1815 he published a tract, *Outlines of a Constitution for United North & South Columbia,* a grandiose dream of union, proposing a capital city near Panama, "where a canal may be made from sea to sea, by locks" (p. 8). To his many other vocations Thornton added those of soldier and magistrate. He became a lieutenant and captain of militia, a justice of the peace, and a commissioner in bankruptcy. His business enterprises, from the raising of merino sheep and the breeding of race horses to steamboats and gold mines—he issued a sanguine prospectus of the North Carolina Gold Mine Company in 1806—were uniformly unsuccessful, but his straitened means never prevented him from mingling in the best society, in which he was a general favorite. He assiduously cultivated the acquaintance of persons of distinction, and enjoyed the friendship of the Earl of Buchan, of Franklin, Rittenhouse, Washington, Jefferson, Volney, Trumbull, John Randolph, and particularly of the Madisons.

The best personal characterization of Thornton is the one published just after his death by William Dunlap [q.v.]: "He was a scholar and a gentleman—full of talent and eccentricity—a Quaker by profession, a painter, a poet, and a horse-racer—well acquainted with the mechanic arts. . . . He was a 'man of infinite humour'—humane and generous, yet fond of field sports—his company was a complete antidote to dullness" (*History of the Rise and Progress of the Arts of Design in the United States,* vol. II, 1918 ed., p. 8). He died in Washington and was buried in the Congressional Cemetery.

[Many papers of Thornton and his wife, including a number of studies for the Capitol and other buildings, particularly Tudor Place, are in the Lib. of Cong.; certain drawings for private buildings were in the possession of the late Glenn Brown, Esq., of Washington, D. C.; other papers are at the office of public buildings and grounds, and in the office of the superintendent of the Capitol. Many of the personal papers in the Lib. of Cong. were published by A. C. Clark, in *Records of the Columbia Hist. Soc.*, vol. XVIII (1915), and a memorial to Thornton published by the Columbian Institute after his death is quoted. For contemporary allusions see J. P. B. de Warville, *Nouveau Voyage dans les États-Unis de l'Amérique Septentrionale, fait en 1788* (3 vols., 1791); *Autobiog., Reminiscences and Letters of John Trumbull* (1841); and *Letters of Horatio Greenough to His Brother, Henry Greenough* (1887). See also Glenn Brown, in *Architectural Records*, July–Sept. 1896, pp. 53–70, *Hist. of the U. S. Capitol*, vol. I (1900), pp. 81–88, with portrait, and *The Octagon* (1917?), pp. 16–25, the biog. sketches to be used with a certain caution; *Documentary Hist. of the ... U. S. Capitol* (1904); W. M. Watson, *In Memoriam: Benjamin Ogle Tayloe* (1872), pp. 97–101; W. B. Bryan, *A Hist. of the Nat. Capital* (2 vols., 1914–16); Gaillard Hunt, "William Thornton and Negro Colonization," *Proc. Am. Antiquarian Soc.*, Apr. 1920; death notice in *Daily Nat. Intelligencer* (Washington), Mar. 29, 1828. The degree of Thornton's responsibility for the design of the Capitol has been reconsidered, with many additional docs., by Fiske Kimball and Wells Bennett, in *Art Studies: Medieval, Renaissance and Modern*, vol. I (1923). For the Octagon, see Brown, *The Octagon*; for Woodlawn and Tudor Place, W. R. Ware, *The Georgian Period* (3 vols., 1899–1902); for Brentwood, H. F. Cunningham and J. A. Younger, *Measured Drawings of Georgian Architecture in the District of Columbia, 1750–1820* (1914). The Gilbert Stuart paintings of Thornton and his wife in the T. B. Clarke coll., have been frequently reproduced.]

F. K.

THORNWELL, JAMES HENLEY (Dec. 9, 1812–Aug. 1, 1862), Presbyterian clergyman, president of the South Carolina College, was born in Marlboro District, S. C., the son of James and Martha (Terrel) Thornwell. His father, an overseer on the plantation of Christopher B. Pegues, died in 1820, leaving the family in straitened circumstances, but James Henley managed to enter the old-field school at Level Green, where his diligent study won him the patronage of two prominent citizens of the nearby town of Cheraw, who assumed the burden of his education. After two years at the Cheraw Academy, in December 1829 he entered the junior class of the South Carolina College, then passing through a turbulent period of opposition to the religious liberalism of the president, Thomas Cooper [*q.v.*]. In 1831 Thornwell graduated at the head of his class. While teaching at Sumterville in 1832 he experienced an emotional conversion, joined the Presbyterian Church, resolved to be a minister, and two years later entered the Andover (Mass.) Theological Seminary. Finding the theology of this institution too liberal for his conservative views, he soon withdrew and after a few months at Harvard returned to South Carolina in October 1834, repelled alike by the New England climate and mental attitude.

Licensed to preach by the Harmony Presbytery of the Synod of South Carolina, Nov. 28, 1834, he served as pastor of several churches in Lancaster District, and on Dec. 3, 1835, married Nancy White, the daughter of Col. James H. Witherspoon, a prominent citizen of Lancaster and former lieutenant governor of the state. In 1837 Thornwell's orthodoxy, learning, and effective preaching resulted in his election to the professorship of metaphysics in the South Carolina College by the faction which four years before had ousted Cooper from the control of that institution. Resigning in 1840 to become pastor of the Columbia Presbyterian Church, he returned the following year as chaplain and professor of sacred literature, holding these positions, with the exception of a short interval as pastor of the Glebe Presbyterian Church in Charleston, until 1851, when he was elected to the presidency of the college. In this connection his work was notably successful. His *Letter to Governor Manning on Public Education in South Carolina* (1853) quieted the strong party in the state that was advocating sectarian education at the expense of secular instruction, and his orthodox preaching and teaching, together with his persuasive personality, did much to remove what was left of the "blatant infidelity" that Cooper had implanted. He never found the atmosphere of the college wholly congenial, however, feeling that he should devote his entire time to religious activities. Accordingly, he resigned in 1855 to become professor of didactic and polemic theology at the Presbyterian Theological Seminary at Columbia, a position which he held until his death seven years later.

Thornwell's activities as an educator were overshadowed by his achievements as a preacher and controversialist. Although unprepossessing in appearance and inclined to pedantry, he combined rigorous logic and emotional fervor in an effective manner. In 1847 he founded at Columbia the *Southern Presbyterian Review*, a powerful exponent of his views. Between 1837 and 1860 he attended ten of the annual assemblies of his denomination, serving as moderator in 1847. In these he opposed the participation of the church in such secular affairs as the slavery controversy and temperance reform. When the assembly of 1861 adopted resolutions indorsing the Federal government he induced the Synod of South Carolina to indorse political secession and was a leading spirit in the organization of the Presbyterian Church in the Confederate States of America. He was the author of an "Address to All the Churches of Jesus Christ throughout the Earth," a brilliant exposition of the viewpoint of the Southern Presbyterian separatists.

A political moderate before 1860, he championed the formation of the Southern Confederacy after the election of Lincoln. His article on "The State of the Country" (*Southern Presbyterian Review,* January 1861) was published as a pamphlet and won wide acclaim as a cogent defense of the Southern point of view, and in a widely circulated address to the Southern soldiers, *Our Danger and Our Duty* (1862), he drew a dire picture of the fate he felt would overtake the South if the North were victorious. His premature death, due to consumption, aggravated by overwork and the excitement of war, prevented the execution of a comprehensive treatise on theology which he contemplated preparing. Most of his addresses and sermons are preserved in *The Collected Writings of J. H. Thornwell* (4 vols., 1871–73), edited by J. B. Adger and J. L. Girardeau.

[B. M. Palmer, *The Life and Letters of J. H. Thornwell* (1875); T. H. Law and others, *Centennial Addresses . . . Commemorating the Birth of J. H. Thornwell* (1913); H. A. White, *Southern Presbyterian Leaders* (1911); Maximilian La Borde, *Hist. of the S. C. Coll.* (1874); E. L. Green, *A Hist. of the Univ. of S. C.* (1916); Alfred Nevin, *Encyc. of the Presbyt. Church in the U. S. A.* (1884); *Southern Presbyterian Rev.,* Oct. 1862; *Charleston Daily Courier,* Aug. 2, 1862.]

F. B. S.

THORP, JOHN (1784–Nov. 15, 1848), machinist, inventor, was the son of Reuben and Hannah (Bucklin) Thorp, and was born presumably in Rehoboth, Mass., where his father was engaged at his trade of coach-builder. Practically nothing is known of Thorp's life until he was twenty-eight years old, when he obtained his first patent (Mar. 28, 1812; renewed, Jan. 28, 1843) for a hand- and water-loom. Presumably he had learned the machinist's trade and had worked in the textile mills in Rhode Island; certainly he had developed a marked inventive ability. His loom had an ingenious shedding motion, an automatic take-up, a novel picking motion, and a clever protective device. To acquire the funds to engage in further invention Thorp worked at his trade in various establishments in New England, and while in Taunton, Mass., acquired his second patent (Oct. 14, 1816) for a power loom. This was issued jointly to him and Silas Shepard, a textile manufacturer, who probably retained Thorp during the period of development of the invention. For the next twelve years nothing is known of him. He probably was prosperous, for his two inventions yielded him, if not financial independence, at least a reputation as a skilled machinist, and therefore the

highest pay of all artisans of his day, namely $1.50 to $1.75 a day.

On Nov. 25 and Dec. 31, 1828, Thorp, then living in Providence, R. I., and engaged in his own machinist business, received three patents for improvements in spinning and twisting cotton, now called "ring spinning." These are the basic patents of the continuous method of spinning now (1935) employed for more than one hundred million of the one hundred and sixty million cotton spindles in the world, and increasingly employed for the spinning of other textile raw materials. The inventions involved fundamentally the use of a ring and traveler, or hook, and were wholly novel in the art of both hand and machine spinning with respect to the control of the wind and twist of the thread. It is believed, too, that they are the only spinning inventions, with one exception, of the era of transition from hand to machine cotton manufacture that were not adaptations of earlier hand methods or derived directly therefrom. Thorp may have had an agreement with the Fletcher brothers of North Providence, R. I., to help meet the cost of developing these inventions, for they immediately adopted them in their braid manufacturing business and early in 1829 issued jointly with Thorp a warning against the purchase or use of the inventions without their consent (advertisement in *Manufacturers' and Farmers' Journal,* Mar. 9, 1829). Thorp was also granted a patent for a netting machine (Nov. 20, 1828), the principle of which is still in use. During 1829 Thorp and the Fletchers made and sold his ring-spinning equipment to other manufacturers, and Thorp obtained four more patents, including one for a narrow fabric loom (patented Dec. 22, 1829) which was probably the first gang loom operated by power. His arrangement with the Fletchers continued only about a year, after which he worked independently. Sometime in the thirties he established himself as a machine builder in Providence, and later in North Wrentham, Mass. He apparently continued in this until his death. On Sept. 27, 1844, he secured a patent for improvements on his original ring-spinning invention. Thorp received very little financial reward for his great inventions and no honor until 1928, when a memorial tablet was placed in the old Slater Cotton Mill at Pawtucket, R. I., by the National Association of Cotton Manufacturers. He married Eliza A. Williams of Providence on Aug. 18, 1817, and died without issue, outliving his wife. His place of burial is unknown.

[For a biog. sketch of Thorp which includes a discussion of the place and date of his birth, see C. H.

Clark, in *Trans. Nat. Assoc. of Cotton Manufacturers* (1928), pp. 72–94. See also *Textile World*, Apr. 14, May 5, 1928; *Textile American*, Apr. 1928; *Fibre and Fabric*, Apr. 28, 1928; *Evening Bulletin* (Providence, R. I.), Apr. 26, 1928.]   C. W. M—n.

THORPE, THOMAS BANGS (Mar. 1, 1815–Sept. 20, 1878), author, artist, humorist, was born in Westfield, Mass., the son of the Rev. Thomas Thorpe. At the age of sixteen he painted a picture illustrating Washington Irving's "Bold Dragoon" which, after exhibition at the New York Academy of Fine Arts, was hung in Irving's home in Tarrytown. In 1833 Thorpe matriculated at Wesleyan University, Middletown, Conn., but because of delicate health left in his junior year for Louisiana, where he remained until 1853. The years in Louisiana marked the period of his greatest productivity. At once at home in the South, he soon won the genuine love and admiration not only of rough backwoodsmen but also of Southern statesmen. In his Baton Rouge studio he divided his time between brush and pencil. Sketches and vivid paintings of life on the prairies, portraits of such famous personages as Jenny Lind, Joseph Walker, and Zachary Taylor, filled his studio. His masterpiece, the full-length portrait of President Taylor, was purchased by the state legislature and the House of Representatives.

The same talent for careful observation and accurate portrayal that made him a fine painter of scenery rendered him a descriptive writer of power and distinction in American literature. R. W. Griswold's evaluation of Thorpe in his *Prose Writers of America* (1847) is excellent: "He has a genuine relish for the sports and pastimes of southern frontier life, and describes them with remarkable freshness and skill of light and shade. No one enters more heartily into all the whims and grotesque humours of the backwoodsman, or brings him more actually or clearly before us" (p. 546). The first of Thorpe's realistic sketches to achieve international acclaim, *Tom Owen, The Bee-Hunter* (later used by Thorpe as a pseudonym) was translated into French, Italian, and German, and was published and praised in the best English periodicals. Decidedly the most humorous and critically the most important of all Thorpe's stories was the "Big Bear of Arkansas" which first appeared in the New York *Spirit of the Times*, Mar. 27, 1841. In this tall tale Thorpe achieved the first great piece of genuinely "Western" humor; in addition to telling a good story he sustained a continuous and racy exaggeration that marked a new phase in American humor. Representative of his local color descriptive work are "The Prairies of Louisiana," "Wild Turkey Hunting," "Water-

craft of the Backwoods," etc. Many of these were later collected under the titles *Mysteries of the Backwoods* (1846), and *The Hive of the Bee-Hunter* (1854).

Thorpe had a great fondness for politics: he held minor offices and frequently "stumped" for his friends, particularly for Taylor. His speeches and writing show a thorough knowledge of statesmen and politics of his day. He conducted a number of Whig newspapers in Louisiana either alone or with associates: in 1843, the Concordia *Intelligencer*; in 1845, the New Orleans *Commercial Times*; in 1846, the New Orleans *Daily Tropic*; in 1847, the Baton Rouge *Conservative*; in 1850, the Batesville *Eagle*. He was with General Taylor at Matamoras in 1846 and his books, *Our Army on the Rio Grande* (1846), *Our Army at Monterey* (1847), and *The Taylor Anecdote Book* (1848), grew out of these experiences. In 1853 he returned to New York City where he contributed frequently to many prominent periodicals. In 1860 he was co-proprietor and co-editor of the New York *Spirit of the Times*. During the Civil War he served as staff officer to Gen. B. F. Butler with rank of colonel of volunteers (1862), and was surveyor of the port of New Orleans. After the war he was city surveyor in New York, and chief of the warehouse department of the New York Custom House from 1869 until his death.

Thorpe's other published works are: *The Master's House* (1854); *Lynde Weiss, An Autobiography* (1852); *A Voice to America* (1855); *Reminiscences of Charles L. Elliott* (1868). His stories appeared in two anthologies to which they gave titles, *The Big Bear of Arkansas* (1845), collected and edited by William T. Porter [*q.v.*], and *Colonel Thorpe's Scenes in Arkansaw* (1858). Thorpe was married but little is known of his wife.

[R. W. Griswold, *Prose Writers of America* (1847); New York *Spirit of the Times*, 1840–60, especially for July 27, 1850, and Sept. 28, 1878; *Alumni Record of Wesleyan University* (6th ed., 1931); A. N. DeMenil, *Literature of the La. Territory* (1904); *N. Y. Times*, Sept. 21, 1878.]   F. J. M—e.

THRASHER, JOHN SIDNEY (1817–Nov. 10, 1879), editor, author, adventurer, was born at Portland, Me. After receiving a good education in the United States, he moved with his parents in 1832 or 1833 to Cuba, where he was destined to win notoriety. In this island he acquired considerable worldly experience, as a clerk (until 1847) in the mercantile house of Tyng & Company, ship-brokers and commission merchants; as a revolutionary agitator and propagandist assisting Narciso López and others from 1848 to 1851; and as a partial editor of the **Cu-**

ban-owned commercial and anti-Spanish paper, *El Faro Industrial de la Habana,* from August 1850 to September 1851. As a result of this editorial activity, he was tried by court martial on Oct. 16, 1851, imprisoned by the Spanish authorities, and sent to serve eight years at hard labor at Ceuta on the north coast of Africa. From this embarrassment he was freed, by the beginning of 1852, through the intervention of the American minister and his wife at Madrid, and he promised never to return to any Spanish possession. A year later, 1853, he presented to the State Department—though he never pressed it— a claim against Spain for a sum which he felt represented the extent of damage to his Cuban periodical and the cost of the balm for his wounded pride and reputation.

In the middle of 1852 he was back in New York, but he soon went to New Orleans where he actively aided John A. Quitman [*q.v.*] and the Cuban filibusters and vociferously declared for Cuban annexation to the United States. He remained there until 1855, when he again returned to New York. Using his journalistic experience in Cuba and New Orleans, he was able to obtain a position on the *New York Herald,* for which paper he traveled in Mexico and South America until 1859. During the Civil War he was connected with the Southern Associated Press, with headquarters at Atlanta. By this time he had married Rebecca Mary, widow of Michel Branamour Menard [*q.v.*], founder of Galveston, Tex.

Thrasher's chief reputation rests upon his writing and his editorial work. Besides the Cuban paper already mentioned he was connected as editor or contributor with the *Beacon of Cuba, DeBow's Review,* and the *Picayune* of New Orleans; with the *New York Herald,* Leslie's *Ilustración Americana,* and *Noticioso de Nueva York* of New York City; with the *Civilian* of Galveston; and probably with other periodicals. He was also author of several pamphlets in Spanish and English, including *Cuba and Louisiana* (1854) and *A Preliminary Essay on the Purchase of Cuba* (1859). At New York in 1856 he translated and edited in a garbled fashion Alexander von Humboldt's essay on Cuba, under the title *The Island of Cuba,* omitting the arguments against slavery which so offended his own pro-slavery views. This led in 1865 to a brief journalistic tilt with Von Humboldt.

As an itinerant editor, author, and general adventurer, Thrasher seems not to have been entirely honest in dealing either with his friends or with his enemies, but as a pro-slavery protagonist of the purchase of Cuba, his sincerity

and his enthusiasm cannot be questioned. To his numerous other interests he added in later life a study of spiritualism, and he finally forsook his Baptist faith for this new adventure. He died after a stroke of apoplexy, and was buried in Magnolia Cemetery, Galveston.

[Fernando Ortiz, ed., *Ensayo político sobre la Isla de Cuba por Alejandro de Humboldt* (Havana 1930), vol. II; Herminio Portell Vilá, *Narciso López y su Época,* vol. I (Havana 1930); R. G. Caldwell, *The Lopez Expeditions to Cuba, 1848–1851* (1915); Vidal Morales y Morales, *Iniciadores y Primeros Mártires de la Revolución Cubana* (1901, repr. in 3 vols., 1931); J. F. H. Claiborne, *Life and Correspondence of John A. Quitman* (1860), vol. II; A. C. Quisenberry, *Lopez's Expeditions to Cuba, 1850 and 1851,* being Filson Club Pub. no. 21 (1906); José Gutierrez de la Concha, *Memorias Sobre el Estado Politico, Gobierno y Administración de la Isla de Cuba* (1853), pp. 226–27, 282; *House Ex. Doc. 14,* 32 Cong., 1 Sess.; *Senate Ex. Doc. 5,* 32 Cong., 1 Sess.; documents listed in L. M. Pérez, *Guide to the Materials for Am. Hist. in Cuban Archives* (1907), pp. 70, 71; and *Galveston Daily News,* Nov. 11, 12, 1879.]
A. C. W.

THROOP, ENOS THOMPSON (Aug. 21, 1784–Nov. 1, 1874), jurist, congressman, governor of New York, was the eldest child of George Bliss Throop and Abiah (Thompson). His father, son of John and Mary (Throop) Bliss, had been adopted by a maternal uncle, the Rev. George Throop of Johnstown, N. Y.; there was a tradition that their ancestor, William Throope, who settled in Barnstable, Mass., before 1666, was a son of Col. Adrian Schoope or Scrope, one of the regicides (Fitch, *post*). After the Revolution, George Bliss Throop married the daughter of Enos Thompson, who had moved from New Haven to develop a tract of wild land in Dutchess County, N. Y. The young couple purchased land at the sale of confiscated Loyalist estates, and established a home in Johnstown, and here Enos Thompson Throop was born. The death of his father in 1794 seriously interfered with the boy's schooling, but four years later he obtained permission to enter the law office of George Metcalf, a friend of his mother and at that time district attorney for Montgomery, Albany, Saratoga, and Schoharie counties. Metcalf arranged for Throop to study law, and personally instructed him in the classics. He was admitted to the bar in January 1806. The ensuing March he began to practise at Poplar Ridge, N. Y., but soon removed to Auburn, where he became a partner of Judge Joseph Richardson. This partnership continued until the junior partner, in 1811, was appointed county clerk.

Throop now became very active in politics. A member of the Republican party of that day, he supported the administration's war policy, and in 1814 was elected to Congress largely on that issue. In 1816, however, he was defeated for reelection because of his support of the act to change the pay of members of Congress from six dollars per day to eighteen hundred dollars per annum. He thereupon resigned, and returned to his law practice. In 1823 he was appointed circuit judge—a position which he held until 1828. In that year his friend of long standing, Martin Van Buren [q.v.], who was seeking the governorship, persuaded him to become candidate for lieutenant governor. Both men were elected, and consequently, when in March 1829 Van Buren was appointed secretary of state by President Jackson, Throop became acting governor. In 1830 he was elected to the governorship, but in 1832 he refused to be a candidate for reëlection. He appears to have made this decision primarily because of protests which his opposition to the construction of the Chenango Canal aroused in certain localities. It was through his efforts as governor that the first state insane asylum was founded in New York. In 1833 President Jackson appointed him naval officer at the port of New York, and in 1838 President Van Buren appointed him chargé d'affaires to the Kingdom of the Two Sicilies. In this capacity he served until 1841, devoting his chief efforts to obtaining a better market for American products, particularly tobacco. He returned to the United States in 1843, and until 1846 resided at "Willowbrook," his home near Auburn. He later acquired a large estate in Michigan, where he engaged successfully in farming, but eventually sold this property and spent his last years in New York City and at "Willowbrook." He was married, July 14, 1814, to Evelina Vredenburgh, daughter of Col. William J. Vredenburgh of Skaneateles, N. Y.; they had three children, all of whom died in infancy.

[Cornelia Williams (Mrs. E. T. T.) Martin, *The Old Home* (1894) and "Sketch of the Life of Gov. Throop" in *Cayuga County Hist. Soc. Colls.*, no. 7 (1889); L. M. Sears, "The Neapolitan Mission of Enos Thompson Throop, 1838–1842," in *N. Y. State Hist. Asso. Quart. Jour.*, Oct. 1928; Winchester Fitch, "The Throope Family and the Scrope Tradition," *N. Y. Geneal. and Biog. Record*, Apr. 1905, Jan. 1906; E. S. Martin, *Some Account of Family Stocks Involved in Life at Willowbrook* (1933); J. S. Jenkins, *Lives of the Governors of the State of N. Y.* (1851); C. Z. Lincoln, *State of N. Y.: Messages from the Governors* (1909), vol. III; *N. Y. Herald*, Nov. 2, 1874.]   R. W. I.

THROOP, MONTGOMERY HUNT (Jan. 26, 1827–Sept. 11, 1892), jurist, was born in Auburn, N. Y., the son of George B. Throop and Francis (Hunt). His education was acquired in Cazenovia Academy, in Geneva and Naples while his uncle Enos Thompson Throop [q.v.] was in the diplomatic service, and at Hobart College, which he left before graduation. He studied law in the office of his uncle Ward

Hunt [q.v.], was admitted to the bar in 1848, and practised in Utica in partnership with Hunt until 1856, at which time he became a partner of Roscoe Conkling [q.v.], who had been a fellow student in Auburn. In spite of temperamental and political differences between the two men this partnership lasted until 1862. Throop played the part of the office lawyer while Conkling presented the arguments orally in trial court. The former, however, frequently argued on appeal cases in which his partner had appeared in the lower court. In 1864 Throop moved to New York City, where he continued his practice. He appears to have had no political ambitions and never ran for public office, but he took a keen interest in the turbulent political controversies of his day. He was a stanch Democrat, rather of the type of Samuel Nelson or Jeremiah S. Black [qq.v.] who found himself unable to justify what he deemed the excesses of the Republicans, but who desired the preservation of the Union and believed that that end might have been achieved by peaceful means. In March 1864 he published a volume, *The Future: A Political Essay,* written late in the preceding year, giving his views on the war and reconstruction. It is a temperate but forceful attack upon what Throop regarded as the unconstitutional practices and policies of the Lincoln administration as well as the presidential and congressional plans for reconstruction then being shaped and discussed. He did not advocate the abandonment of the war but he protested vigorously against the use of coercive measures in the conquered sections of the South and urged that the existence of war does not suspend the ordinary guarantees of the Constitution. He advocated the calling at the close of the war of a national constitutional convention to adjust the governmental system to radically changed conditions, in part by devising a plan for eliminating the ruinous spoils system and by redrawing the line of demarcation between the powers of the federal and state governments so as to prevent the undue expansion of national power at state expense.

In 1870 Throop was made chairman of a commission to revise the New York statutes. This task, of which he performed the major part, occupied seven years and determined the future direction of his interests; it was brought to completion by the publication, in 1877, of *The Code of Civil Procedure of the State of New York,* which superseded *The New Revision of the Statutes of the State of New York: Code of Remedial Justice,* issued in 1876. The rest of Throop's life was devoted to legal authorship and the editorship of codes and compilations of statutes and decisions. His chief publications in these fields were: *A Treatise on the Validity of Verbal Agreements* (1870), projected as two volumes, of which only one was published; various editions of *The Code of Civil Procedure,* with notes; *The New York Justice's Manual* (fourteen annual issues, 1880–93); the seventh edition (1882) of *The Revised Statutes of the State of New York,* frequently reprinted; *Digest of the Decisions of the Supreme Judicial Court of the Commonwealth of Massachusetts, from 1884 to 1886* (2 vols., 1887); and *A Treatise on the Law Relating to Public Officers and Sureties in Official Bonds* (1892).

Throop moved to Albany in 1880 and made his home there until his death. He was peculiarly fitted for his labor in the field of legal scholarship. Throughout the greater part of his life he was almost totally deaf, but he was intellectually alert, a tireless worker, and a thorough linguist. He was an accomplished scholar in the field of medieval Latin and was widely read in history and belles-lettres. On June 22, 1854, he married Charlotte Williams Gridley of Utica. Two sons were born to them, of whom one died in boyhood. Throop's death was due to apoplexy.

[W. D. Edmonds, "Memorial of Montgomery H. Throop," *Asso. of the Bar of the City of N. Y.* . . . *Twenty-fourth Ann. Report* (1894), also printed separately; *Proc. N. Y. State Bar Asso.* . . . *1892* (1893); *N. Y. Geneal. and Biog. Record,* Jan. 1906; *Albany Evening Journal,* Sept. 12, 1892; *N. Y. Times,* Sept. 12, 1892.]   R. E. C.

THULSTRUP, BROR THURE (Apr. 5, 1848–June 9, 1930), artist and painter, known in America as Thure de Thulstrup, was born in Stockholm, Sweden, of a prominent family. He was the son of Carl Magnus Thulstrup, a soldier, a member of the Swedish ministry, and for a time secretary of naval defense, and Hedvig Kristina (Akrell) Thulstrup. His education and his early experience were essentially those of a soldier. Graduating from the National Military Academy in Stockholm at the age of twenty, he went to Paris, where in 1870 he became an officer in the French Foreign Legion. He saw service in Algeria and later in France during the war with Germany in 1871, through which, after being advanced to the rank of captain, he served to the end. Although now a veteran and by inheritance and tradition inclined to army life, he began to study drawing in the French capital, giving particular attention to topographical engineering, and it was in pursuit of this work that he emigrated to Canada in the early seventies. A thorough master of line, the possibilities of color and the temptations of paint and canvas

drew him into the field of creative art. In the latter he always claimed that he had no master, belonged to no school, and was self-taught. Since the United States presented a better chance for his artistic endeavors, he moved to Boston and thence to New York, where, on June 3, 1879, he married Lucie Bavoillot. There were no children.

A close student of military history, he naturally turned in that direction in his paintings. He was scrupulously careful about the correctness of equipment, collecting from every available source the proper uniforms for his models; his work, never haphazard, was correct to the smallest detail. He painted numerous pictures of American battlefields, one of his earliest subjects being Pickett's charge at the battle of Gettysburg. The illustrated weeklies of New York soon found out the value of this painter-illustrator, whose work was dependable and always done on time. For a time on the staff of the *Daily Graphic* (New York), he subsequently became a free lance; for many years hardly an issue of *Frank Leslie's Illustrated Weekly Newspaper* or *Harper's Weekly* came out without some of his drawings, or black and white water-colors. Without hesitation he undertook to do illustrations that involved so many figures, so much composition and detail that the task would have appalled most artists. Gifted not only with imagination but with superb health, he could labor for as much as fifteen hours at a stretch. Taking up color again after this period of strenuous and remunerative endeavor, he produced and exhibited a series of historical paintings of American colonial days that later, reproduced in color, had a large, popular sale. In 1898 appeared a book of reproductions, *Drawings by Thulstrup and Others,* and a year later *Outdoor Pictures,* drawings by Thulstrup alone. He illustrated several books, among them Arthur Conan Doyle's *The Refugees* (copyright 1893).

He was saddened by the death of his wife in 1915 (*Vem Är Det?, post*) and as time drew on his eyesight began to fail in a great measure. The market for illustration disappeared, photographic reproduction taking its place; but he maintained a courageous attitude, and held the stanch loyalty and affection of his friends. Elected to the Players' Club of New York in 1889, in his loneliness he found there welcome and comfort. He was a member of the Society of Illustrators, the American Water Color Society, the John Ericsson Society of Swedish Engineers, and a knight of the Order of Vasa, Sweden. He died at St. Luke's Hospital, New York. For the nine years preceding his death he had lived at the Episcopal Home for Old Men and Aged Couples.

[For the names of Thulstrup's parents, see *Svenskt Biografiskt Handlexikon* (1876) and *Nordisk Familjebok* (1933). Other sources include *Who's Who in America*, 1930–31; *Vem Ar Det?*, 1929; *Svenskt Porträttgalleri*, vol. XX (1901), with portrait; P. H. G., Jr., in *Book Buyer*, Sept. 1895; *Players' Bull.*, June 15, 1930; obituary in *N. Y. Times*, June 10, 1930; personal acquaintance.]   J.B.

THUMB, TOM [See STRATTON, CHARLES SHERWOOD, 1838–1883].

THURBER, CHARLES (Jan. 2, 1803–Nov. 7, 1886), inventor, manufacturer, teacher, was born at East Brookfield, Mass., the son of the Rev. Laban and Abigail (Thayer) Thurber. After attending the local public schools, Thurber was sent to Milford Academy, and subsequently prepared for college in Bellingham, Mass., under a private tutor. At the age of twenty he entered Brown University and graduated in 1827 with the degrees of A.B. and A.M. With the opening of the school year in the autumn of 1827 he returned to Milford Academy as a teacher, in which capacity he served for four years. He then accepted the principalship of the Latin Grammar School in Worcester, Mass., which he retained for eight consecutive years, relinquishing it only when the pressure of outside business required his full attention. Three years prior to giving up his school work, Thurber entered into partnership with his brother-in-law, Ethan Allen, to manufacture firearms in Worcester. Because of Thurber's mechanical ability this partnership proved to be a most effective one. Within three years after it was formed, on Aug. 26, 1843, a patent (No. 3,228) was granted him for a hand printing machine which proved to be the first invention that approximated a typewriter in the modern sense of the word. It was a type-wheel machine and suggested the first principle of the movable carriage in that the letter spacing was effected by the longitudinal motion of a platen, a principle which is the feature of all modern machines. Furthermore, it incorporated a way of turning the paper when a line was completed, as in the present-day machine. Thurber's typewriter did excellent work, but its action was too slow for practical use. Furthermore, the business world was not ready for a writing machine, and none was manufactured. In 1845 Thurber obtained a second patent, No. 4,271. This was for a writing machine rather than a typewriter, for it was intended for the use of the blind and was designed to perform the motions of the hand in writing. Thurber called it a "Mechanical Chirographer." Allen & Thurber's principal business, however, was pistol manu-

facture, and the firm continued in this until 1856, when it was dissolved, Thurber retiring from active work.

During his active career he had served as county commissioner (1842–44), and had been elected a member of the Massachusetts Senate for one year (1852–53). He was also a member of the board of trustees of Brown University for over thirty years, from 1853 until his death. He married Lucinda Allen, sister of Ethan Allen, immediately after his graduation from college. His wife, by whom he had two daughters, died in Worcester in 1852, and some time later Thurber married Mrs. Caroline (Esty) Bennett. From the time of his retirement until his death he lived in Norwich, Conn., Brooklyn, N. Y., and Germantown, Pa. He died in Nashua, N. H.

[C. G. Washburn, *Industrial Worcester* (1917); Charles Nutt, *Hist. of Worcester and Its People* (1919), vol. II; E. W. Byrn, *The Progress of Invention in the Nineteenth Century* (1900); records of the Am. Antiquarian Soc., Worcester, Mass., Brown Univ., and the U. S. Nat. Museum; obituary in *Boston Transcript*, Nov. 9, 1886.]   C. W. M—n.

THURBER, CHRISTOPHER CARSON (May 19, 1880–May 31, 1930), social worker, was born in Norwich, Conn., the son of Charles Francis and Annie Elizabeth (Cragg) Thurber. After attending the Norwich Free Academy, he entered Trinity College, Hartford, in 1899, but left after one year to do settlement house social work in Danbury, N. H. Thence he went to Canada to work for seven years introducing improved methods of caring for the mental and physical welfare of lumbermen in the woods. From 1910 to 1912 he was employed by the Young Men's Christian Association to do similar work among the soft-coal miners of Pennsylvania and West Virginia. In 1912 he became superintendent of the Home for Homeless Boys at Covington, Va. When the United States entered the World War in 1917, he left this position for work in the army camps with the Red Cross, which eventually made him director of its hospital work in the South, with headquarters at Greenville, S. C. When the war ended, he became social director of the United States Public Health Service at the same place.

In 1921 he joined the Near East Relief organization and was appointed head of an orphanage of three thousand boys at Sivas in Eastern Turkey. After the defeat in 1922 of the Greek army in Anatolia by the Turkish forces under Mustafa Kemal Pasha, Thurber took in four thousand additional boys who had become orphans during the deportation and exchange of the Anatolian Greeks. For eight months he contrived to provide food and shelter for his boys, despite the meagerness of his funds and the suspicions of the local government. On one occasion he was arrested by Turkish authorities and so severely bastinadoed that thereafter he always walked with a limp. Eventually he led five thousand of the orphans on foot across the Pontic Mountains to the Black Sea coast. Thence they were taken on American battleships to Constantinople and housed in the Selimiye Barracks, made famous by Florence Nightingale during the Crimean War. While working there among eleven thousand typhus-stricken refugees, Thurber himself contracted the disease, but survived to become director of the Constantinople unit of the Near East Relief. Invalided home in 1924, he underwent three surgical operations and spent nearly a year in hospitals, but was nevertheless able during two years to address more than eleven hundred meetings on behalf of the relief organization, which in 1926 sent him back to Athens as director of its work in Greece. In addition to regular duties connected with administering the orphanages and training the orphans in trades and farming, he undertook the establishment of three working-boys' homes for orphans who had left the institutions and were earning their own living. His single-hearted devotion to his ideal of service, especially during a severe epidemic of dengue fever, his unstinted labors on behalf of Greek refugees, and his engaging personal qualities gained the respect and affection of the Greek people to a remarkable degree. The government of Greece, which had bestowed upon him three decorations, including the Cross of War and the Golden Cross of the Order of the Saviour, buried him with all the honors of a general after a state funeral service in the Cathedral of Athens.

[*Trinity Coll. Bull.*, n.s., vol. XXVII (1930), pp. 68–69; obituaries in *N. Y. Times*, June 3, and in *Hestia* (Athens), June 2, 1930; copies of letters and biog. data furnished by the Near East Foundation of New York, N. Y.]   W. L. W., Jr.

THURBER, GEORGE (Sept. 2, 1821–Apr. 2, 1890), botanist, horticulturist, author, editor, was born in Providence, R. I., the son of Jacob Thurber, a business man, and Alice Ann (Martin) Thurber. For a time he attended the Union Classical and Engineering School of Providence, but was in the main self-educated. He early took up pharmacy, first as an apprentice, then as a proprietor in partnership with Joshua Chapin. He soon developed an interest in chemistry, and for a time he held a lectureship in this subject with the Franklin Society of Providence. Turning to botany for the sources of vegetable drugs, in time he became intimately associated with such emi-

nent scientists as Asa Gray, George Engelmann, John Torrey, and Jean Louis Rodolphe Agassiz [*qq.v.*]. Plant study became an absorbing passion, and he eagerly seized the opportunity, presented in 1850, to serve as botanist, quartermaster, and commissary on the survey of the boundary between the United States and Mexico. For several years he pursued the fascinating, sometimes perilous business of collecting the native flora along the Mexican border. His herbarium assembled there, comprising many species new to scientists, formed the basis of Gray's "Plantae Novae Thurberinanae" (*Memoirs of the American Academy of Arts and Sciences*, n.s., vol. V, 1855). Among the new plants named for their discoverer was the cactus *Cereus thurberi*, subsequently cultivated in the desert regions of North Africa. Thurber held a position in the United States Assay Office in New York (1853–56), was lecturer in botany and *materia medica* at the College of Pharmacy in New York (1856–61, 1865–66), and also lectured on botany at Cooper Union. The New York Medical College in 1859 conferred on him the degree of M.D. In the same year he was appointed to the chair of botany and horticulture at Michigan State Agricultural College (later Michigan State College). In 1863 he returned to New York to become editor of the *American Agriculturist*. Establishing his home on a small farm, "The Pines," near Passaic, N. J., he cultivated an experimental garden which furnished abundant material for the columns of his journal. His unsigned "Notes from the Pines" for years were conspicuous in horticultural literature for the extent and accuracy of their botanical information. His series entitled "The Doctor's Talks," noted for charming simplicity of style, was designed to instruct young people on scientific subjects. Under his editorship the *American Agriculturist* exerted a vigorous progressive influence upon agriculture and horticulture. He gave much attention to the exposure of business and professional frauds. In 1885 ill-health forced him to relinquish the active direction of the journal, but he continued to contribute regularly to its columns up to the time of his death. He died in Passaic, survived by a brother and three sisters, with one of whom he had shared his home. He never married.

He was one of the earliest exponents of agricultural botany. His specialty was the grasses; he collected many specimens and long cherished the ambition, unhappily never realized, to publish a monograph on American grasses. He revised William Darlington's *Agricultural Botany* (1847) under the new title *American Weeds and Useful Plants* (1859), contributed botanical articles to Appleton's *The American Cyclopedia* (16 vols., 1873–76) and the section on grasses to the *Botany* (1880) published by the Geological Survey of California, and supervised the editing of hundreds of rural books published by Orange Judd [*q.v.*]. He was president of the Torrey Botanical Club (1873–80), a life member of the American Pomological Society, a corresponding member of the Academy of Natural Sciences of Philadelphia, and an active member of the New York Academy of Sciences. In 1880, on a trip abroad, he visited many European botanists and horticulturists, and in 1886 he was made a corresponding member of the Royal Horticultural Society of London.

[C. P. Wimmer, *The Coll. of Pharmacy of the City of N. Y.* (1929); W. J. Beal, *Hist. of the Mich. Agricultural Coll.* (1915); *Semi-Centennial Celebration of Mich. State Agricultural Coll.* (1908), ed. by T. C. Blaisdell; L. H. Bailey, *Cyc. of Am. Agriculture*, vol. IV (1912), and *Standard Cyc. of Horticulture*, vol. III (1915); *Garden and Forest*, Apr. 9, 1890; *Am. Agriculturist*, May 1890; *Botanical Gazette*, May 1890; H. H. Rusby, in *Bull. Torrey Botanical Club*, Aug. 12, 1890; obituary in *N. Y. Tribune*, Apr. 4, 1890; information from F. S. Kedzie, Mich. State Coll.]

C. R. W.

THURMAN, ALLEN GRANBERRY (Nov. 13, 1813–Dec. 12, 1895), representative and senator from Ohio, was born in Lynchburg, Va. His father, Pleasant Thurman, was a minister of the Methodist Church; his mother, Mary Granberry (Allen) Thurman, was the daughter of Nathaniel Allen, of Edenton, N. C., the nephew and adopted son of Joseph Hewes [*q.v.*]. In 1819 his parents removed to Chillicothe, Ohio, where Thurman lived until he removed permanently to Columbus in 1853. His education was largely directed by his mother, who was a cultured woman. Thurman attended the Chillicothe academy and in early life acquired a knowledge and fondness for French literature that was rare in his day. When eighteen years of age, he assisted in land surveying and at twenty-one became the private secretary to Gov. Robert Lucas [*q.v.*]. He had already begun the study of law with his uncle, William Allen, 1803–1879 [*q.v.*]; and at Columbus he continued his legal studies with Noah H. Swayne [*q.v.*]. In 1835 he was admitted to the bar and returned to Chillicothe, where he soon formed a partnership with his uncle. For ten years he rode the circuit. As a lawyer he was studious, painstaking in the preparation of his cases, logical in the presentation of his arguments, quick to discover the vulnerable points in those of his adversary, and aggressive. He practised largely in the higher state and federal courts and as early as 1851 was recognized throughout the state as one of its foremost lawyers. On Nov. 14, 1844, he married Mrs. Mary A. Tompkins, the daughter of Walter Dun of Fayette County, Ky. One of their daughters married Richard C. McCormick [*q.v.*]. The same year, 1844, he was nominated and elected as the Democratic candidate for representative to Congress. While a member of the House, he served on the judiciary committee, supported the administration's conduct of the Mexican War, made a vigorous speech in behalf of the claims of the United States to Oregon for 54° 40', and voted for the Wilmot Proviso. At the end of his term in Congress, he declined to be a candidate for renomination. He practised law until 1851, when he was elected associate justice of the state supreme court under the new constitution. He was chief justice from Dec. 4, 1854, to Feb. 9, 1856. His mind was instinctively judicial, and the decisions he rendered are notable for their clarity of expression, forceful language, and accurate statements of law. At the expiration of his term, he refused a renomination and resumed his law practice in Columbus.

He took a prominent part in the discussions growing out of the slavery controversy. He opposed the repeal of the Missouri Compromise and advocated non-interference by the federal government, so far as slavery in the territories was concerned. He was against the Lecompton constitution for Kansas and supported Stephen A. Douglas for president in 1860. Although he never accepted the doctrine of secession, he questioned the wisdom of employing coercion against a state that had already left the Union. He wanted to preserve the Union; but he believed that an appeal to arms would destroy the Union forever. Throughout the Civil War, he was one of the leaders of the "Peace Democrats" who opposed the federal administration's arbitrary arrests, suspension of the *habeas corpus,* and infringement of the freedom of the press. In 1867 the Democratic party nominated him as its candidate for governor of Ohio against Rutherford B. Hayes. The campaign was fought over the question of negro suffrage and attracted national attention. Hayes was elected by a majority of fewer than 3,000; but the legislature was Democratic; and Thurman was elected by this body to the federal Senate. It was due to Thurman's political strategy that the Democrats elected William Allen as governor in 1873, carried the legislature, and returned Thurman to the Senate.

During his twelve years of service in the Senate he was the recognized leader of his party in the Senate. The "Old Roman," as he was called, was a doctrinaire, strict constructionist, partisan Democrat of the Jeffersonian school. He won for himself a national reputation for his judicial fairness and skill in debate, especially upon questions of constitutional law. Upon entering the Senate he was appointed to the judiciary committee and, when his party obtained a majority in the 46th Congress, he was made its chairman and was also chosen president *pro tempore* in April 1879, owing to the illness of the vice-president, William A. Wheeler. Thurman also rendered valuable service as a member of the committee on private land claims. He is best remembered for his attacks on the constitutionality of the Civil Rights Bill, his opposition to all inflationary measures, and as the author of the Thurman Act relating to the Pacific railroads. He was a member of the electoral commission of 1877 and voted to seat Tilden. In 1881 he was an unsuccessful candidate for reëlection to the Senate. Upon his retirement, President Garfield appointed him one of the American representatives to the international monetary conference at Paris. He traveled extensively in Europe and shortly after his return home he was selected, with Thomas M. Cooley and Elihu B. Washburne [*qq.v.*], to arbitrate the great trunk line railroad companies' difficulties about differential rates. He was a presidential candidate in the Democratic conventions of 1876, 1880, and 1884; and the unsuccessful candidate for vice-president on the Democratic ticket with Grover Cleveland in 1888. He died in Columbus.

[W. U. Hensel and G. F. Parker, *Life and Public Services of Grover Cleveland and Allen G. Thurman* (1888); J. G. Blaine, *Twenty Years of Congress* (2 vols., 1884–86); *Biog. Cyc. and Portrait Gallery of Ohio*, vol. I (1883); E. O. Randall and D. J. Ryan, *Hist. of Ohio* (1912), vols. IV, V; R. C. McGrane, *William Allen* (1825); *Cincinnati Times-Star*, Dec. 12, 1895; Papers in Lib. of Cong., and in Lib. of Arch. and Hist. Soc., Columbus.]   R. C. M.

THURSBY, EMMA CECILIA (Feb. 21, 1845–July 4, 1931), singer, voice teacher, was born in Brooklyn, N. Y., the daughter of John Barnes Thursby, a rope manufacturer of New York City, and his wife, Jane Ann (Bennett) Thursby. John Barnes Thursby was the grandson of the John Thursby who came to New York in 1796 and founded the first rope manufactory in America. Emma Thursby entered the Moravian Seminary at Bethlehem, Pa., with the class of 1857. In 1859 her father died, and it became necessary for her to help toward the support of the family. She accordingly began vocal study under Julius Meyer, a pupil of Mendelssohn, and later with Achille Errani. She rapidly developed a soprano voice of remarkable range—from middle C to F above the staff. From 1865 to 1868 she was engaged as soprano soloist at Plymouth Church in Brooklyn. In 1873 she went abroad for instruction with Lamperti, in Milan, and with San Giovanni, and returned to America to study for a time with Madame Rudersdorff before making her début as a concert singer in 1875 at the Bedford Avenue Church in Brooklyn. For this concert she engaged the services of Patrick S. Gilmore [*q.v.*] and his band. Gilmore was so impressed with Thursby's singing that he engaged her for his summer concerts in New York and for a tour through the United States. Engagements at the Church of the Divine Paternity and at the Broadway Tabernacle in New York followed. At the Tabernacle she came to the attention of Maurice Strakosch, concert manager and brother-in-law of Adelina Patti. He persuaded her to appear in concerts and oratorios under his management and she remained under his direction for seven years.

She appeared in concert with the London Philharmonic on May 22, 1878, and for almost a year sang at the Crystal Palace, the Popular Concerts, and with Leslie's Choir. From London she went to Paris, where her début created a sensation, and then toured the French provinces. In France she received the most flattering offer of her career, a proposal that she appear at the Paris Opéra on her own terms. Thursby, like Jenny Lind, was prejudiced against the opera and the theatre, and it is said that she had promised her friends at Plymouth Church never to be an opera singer. According to a family tradition these same friends were disappointed that she had not accepted the offer when she returned to America expecting approval.

In 1879 she was in America again, appearing with the Norwegian violinist, Ole Bull, on his last American tour. In 1880–81 she toured the Continent, returning to America at the end of 1882. In 1883 she toured the United States and Canada, and during her last full season was the principal soloist for Theodore Thomas [*q.v.*] and his orchestra. Thereafter Thursby appeared in concert at less frequent intervals. She began a scientific investigation of methods of voice training and in 1898 commenced her active career as a vocal teacher. She was the first teacher of Geraldine Farrar and acted as sponsor and adviser to the younger singer throughout Farrar's entire career. Thursby made a tour of China and Japan in 1903 and then definitely retired as a concert artist. Her voice, like Jenny Lind's, has become something of a tradition. She was one of the first American singers to win an international reputation after having won first laurels at home and she was considered one of the greatest Mozart interpreters of her time. Until the year of her death in New York City, her apartment in Gramercy Park was a salon for the gathering of the most brilliant figures in the musical world.

[Records and documents supplied by the family; *Who's Who in America*, 1901–02; *Hist. of Plymouth Church, 1847–1872* (1873); "The Biography of Emma Thursby," reprint from the *Ladies Home Jour.*; Edmund Kennedy, "Emma Thursby: Speranza," *Musical Digest*, Sept. 1930; *Musician*, Aug. 1931; *N. Y. Times*, July 5, 1931.]   J. T. H.

THURSTON, LORRIN ANDREWS (July 31, 1858–May 11, 1931), lawyer, editor, official of Hawaii, a descendant of Daniel Thurston who settled in Newbury, Mass., between 1635 and 1638, was born in Honolulu, the son of Asa Goodale and Sarah (Andrews) Thurston. His grandfathers on both sides—Asa Thurston and Lorrin Andrews [*q.v.*]—were American missionaries. His early education was obtained at a private school and at Oahu College in Honolulu. He then studied law as a clerk in the office of the attorney general of Hawaii; was admitted to practise in the lower courts in 1878; spent two years in sugar plantation work; in 1880 went to New York and studied for two years at Columbia Law School. Returning to Hawaii in 1883, he was admitted to practice before the supreme court and formed a law partnership with W. O. Smith. In 1886 and 1892 he served in the Hawaiian legislature as an elected member. Interested in politics only for its bearing on the problem of good government, he sought a legislative seat only when the need of reform was acute. His convictions that if reform could not be accomplished in any other way revolution must be the remedy, and that the Hawaiian Islands must some day be a part of the United States, serve to explain his political career from 1885 to 1898.

The few reform members of the legislature of 1886—capable and earnest men, of whom Thurston was one of the most active—were unable to drive out the corruption and maladministration which prevailed under the premiership of Walter M. Gibson [*q.v.*], and the revolution of 1887 followed in due course. As one of the leaders in the movement Thurston helped to draft the new constitution, curtailing the royal prerogative, and was appointed minister of the interior. The reform ministry remained in office until 1890 and was then forced out, partly by dissensions among its own members and partly by a rising tide of native Hawaiian opposition zealously fostered by King Kalakaua. During 1890–92 the royalist party grew and old abuses crept back. The legislative session of 1892 was a repetition of that of 1886. In the spring of 1892 Thurston visited Washington to sound out opinion on the subject of annexation, conditioned on its being accomplished by peaceful means with the acquiescence of Queen Liliuokalani, who had succeeded to the throne; but at the close of the year he believed neither annexation nor the end of the monarchy to be near at hand. Liliuokalani's attempted *coup d'etat* in January 1893 precipitated the revolution which dethroned her. Thurston was admittedly the outstanding leader in the revolution. He drafted the proclamation of the provisional government and headed the commission sent to Washington to negotiate for annexation. In May 1893 he was appointed Hawaiian envoy to the United States, a post which he held for two trying years. He did not possess a diplomatic temperament and the ill-concealed hostility of President Cleveland and the Secretary of State, Walter Q. Gresham, led him into a breach of diplomatic etiquette which brought a request for his recall. He helped in framing the constitution of the Republic of Hawaii in 1894 and was a member of the commission that negotiated the second treaty of annexation in 1897. He energetically opposed the idea of declaring Hawaiian neutrality during the Spanish-American War.

After annexation had been consummated, Thurston withdrew from political life and resumed his private business career. In 1898 he became principal owner and editorial director of the *Honolulu Advertiser,* which he built up to metropolitan standards. He was enthusiastically devoted to the development of the latent resources of Hawaii, was one of the earliest promoters of the pineapple industry and the tourist business, and both in office and out advocated the building of roads and harbor facilities. There was hardly a public question on which he did not write vigorously and pertinently. In his championship of any cause, he was not much concerned about conciliating opposition, but simply strove to overpower it by the weight of argument. Examples of his numerous contributions to the press are, "The Sandwich Islands: The Advantages of Annexation" (*North American Review*, March 1893), "The Growing Greatness of the Pacific" (*Ibid.*, April 1895), and *A Hand-book on the Annexation of Hawaii* (n.d., *circa* 1897). In 1904 he edited a volume of Hawaiian constitutions and related documents under the title *The Fundamental Law of Hawaii*. His last important public service was in bringing forward (1926) and advocating the cause of a civil government for American Samoa. Thurston was twice married: first to Margaret Clarissa Shipman of Hilo (Feb. 21, 1884), and some years after her death, to Harriet Potter of St. Joseph, Mich. (Apr. 5, 1894). He was survived by his second wife, a son of his first marriage, and a son and a daughter of the second.

[Sources include Brown Thurston, *Thurston Geneals.* (1880); *Who's Who in America*, 1930–31; *Men of Hawaii* (1921); *Oahu College Directory* (1916); G. F. Nellist, *The Story of Hawaii and Its Builders* (1925); A. A. Greene, in *Honolulu Advertiser*, July 2, 1931; obituary, *Ibid.*, May 12, 1931; *Foreign Relations of the U. S., 1894*, App. II (1895); *Sen. Report 227*, 53 Cong., 2 Sess.; Hawaiian legislative records, 1886–92; correspondence in Hawaiian archives and in U. S. State Dept. Certain papers of Thurston have been announced for early publication.]   R. S. K.

THURSTON, ROBERT HENRY (Oct. 25, 1839–Oct. 25, 1903), engineer, educator, was born in Providence, R. I., eldest of three children of Robert Lawton Thurston [*q.v.*] and Harriet (Taylor) Thurston. The father was one of the pioneer steam-engine builders of the country and the son, during his early years, spent much time in his father's shops. Persuaded by his high-school principal, Edward H. Magill [*q.v.*], to take a college course in preparation for engineering as a learned profession, he matriculated in Brown University at sixteen and graduated in 1859 with the degree of Ph.B. and a certificate in civil engineering. In the fall of that year he entered the drafting room of his father's firm in Providence and a year later went to Philadelphia as their representative. Here he published his first technical paper, "On the Economy Resulting from the Expansion of Steam" (*Journal of the Franklin Institute*, March 1861). Not very successful in a business way in Philadelphia, he returned to Providence, but within a few months, on the outbreak of the Civil War, volunteered for service as an engineer in the navy, and after examination was appointed a third assistant engineer.

On Aug. 25, 1861, he was called to active service in the U.S.S. *Unadilla*, fitting out at the Brooklyn Navy Yard for duty on the Southern blockade. He was subsequently assigned as a member of the prize crew to the *Princess Royal*, a merchant steamer taken by the *Unadilla* in an attempt to run the blockade, and later, successively, to the *Chippewa*, the *Maumee*, the *Pontoosuc*, and the *Dictator*. In the meantime he had, on examination, been promoted to the rank of second assistant engineer, which rank he held until July 1865, when on examination he was promoted first assistant engineer.

After the close of the war, following a brief delay on waiting orders during which time he married (Oct. 5, 1865) Susan Taylor Gladding, he was assigned in December 1865 to the Naval Academy as assistant professor in the department of natural and experimental philosophy. Upon the death of Prof. A. W. Smith a few months later, he became head of the department. While at Annapolis he devised a successful magnesium lamp for signaling, made a study of friction and lubrication, and contributed several papers to the *Journal of the Franklin Institute*. Two of these, "Steam Engines of the French Navy" (September 1868) and an account of the British ironclad *Monarch* (April 1870), prepared at the request of the editor, Henry Morton [*q.v.*], gave Morton such a conception of his capacity that in 1871, as president of the newly founded Stevens Institute of Technology, Hoboken, N. J., he called Thurston to help with the organization of that institution as professor of mechanical engineering. Meanwhile, in 1870, on leave of absence from the Naval Academy, Thurston had visited Great Britain to investigate for Rhode Island interests certain metallurgical processes in Wales, and upon his return he published in the *Journal of the Franklin Institute* (January, March, April, May 1871) a series of papers on "Iron Manufactures in Great Britain," which further enhanced his reputation.

After accepting the call to Stevens but before leaving Annapolis, he drew up a plan for a four-year course of instruction in mechanical engineering, designed as preparation for entrance into practice. This plan, dated July 1871, he circulated among engineers all over the country asking for criticism, and it subsequently became the basis for the curriculum at Stevens Institute. The work at Stevens was largely pioneer in character, and precedents and guides were few and uncertain in value. One of his first new measures was the inauguration of a small mechanical laboratory, formally organized in 1875—the first in the country. Seeing an opportunity to combine the training of students in research with the accomplishment of researches of commercial value, he began at once to accept commissions from business firms to assist them in solving problems. The income from this commercial work was applied directly to the purchase of additional equipment for the laboratory and for the shop courses which he inaugurated in 1878. His experience as a boy in his father's shop in Providence had impressed on his mind the importance to an engineer of a practical knowledge of the tools and processes of the machine shop. Both the mechanical laboratory and the shop courses had formed part of his original plan for his course of instruction; he realized them as soon as he could (see his articles, "On the Necessity of a Mechanical Laboratory: Its Province and Its Methods," *Journal of the Franklin Institute*, December 1875, and "Instruction in Mechanical Engineering," *Scientific American Supplement*, Apr. 19, 1884). For his laboratory he designed an "autographic recording testing machine" for testing materials in torsion, and a machine for testing lubricants, both of which he patented. Feeling the need of textbooks for the course on structural materials, one of his fundamental courses, he used the laboratory to gather findings which were ultimately incorporated in *The Materials of Engineering* (3 vols., 1883–84), abridged under the title, *A Text-Book of the Materials of Construction, for Use in Technical and Engineering Schools* (1885).

Thurston's personal energy and his bold and striking measures at Stevens attracted the attention of leaders in engineering and industry and he was soon called upon to serve on important commissions and juries. Thus he was a member of the committee to test steam boilers at the American Institute exhibition of 1871 (*Annual Report*, 1872, p. 66) ; in 1873 he was a member of an international jury and also a United States commissioner at the Vienna exposition, and he was subsequently appointed to edit *Reports of the Commissioners of the United States to the International Exhibition Held at Vienna, 1873* (4 vols., 1876), for which he wrote "Report on Machinery and Manufactures," included in Vol. III. He served as a member of a government commission to experiment with steam-boiler explosions (1871–76), and in 1875 was appointed secretary of the important United States Board to Test Iron, Steel, and Other Metals. Much of the work of the latter board was carried on under his direction in the laboratories of Stevens Institute, and it was in connection with some of these investigations, while studying the physical properties of the alloys of copper and tin, copper and zinc, and copper, tin and zinc, that he developed the three-coördinate solid diagram, exhibiting at a glance any specified physical quality of any relative combinations of these three constituents—a form of diagram which has since become standard for purposes of this character. This device he described at a meeting of the American Association for the Advancement of Science in 1877 (*Proceedings*, vol. XXVI, 1878).

During these years his zeal for work began to outrun his physical and nervous endurance, and between 1876 and 1880 he was forced to accept a part-time schedule. From 1878, some months after the death of his wife, until 1880, he was incapacitated by a breakdown, but regained his health, and during the remaining twenty-three years of his life he lost no time from serious illness. His first wife left one daughter. On Aug. 4, 1880, he was married a second time, to Leonora Boughton of New York. Two daughters were born of this marriage.

In 1885 he resigned his post at Stevens Institute to accept a call by the trustees of Cornell University to undertake as Director the reorganization of Sibley College as a high-grade college of mechanical engineering. He was given full responsibility, including control of appointments, equipment, and instruction, and proved fully worthy of the trust imposed. Under his administration the number of candidates for the degree of M.E. increased from sixty-three in 1885 to 885 in 1903, and the faculty from seven to forty-three. He was successful at once in establishing a department of experimental engineering, a great elaboration of the pioneer mechanical laboratory courses at Stevens. During his eighteen years as director of Sibley College he taught the courses in thermo-dynamics and steam-engineering. He saw the possibility of a great engineering school at Cornell and gave his unremitting efforts to its realization.

In addition to his regular work at the University, he found time to serve as member of the New York state commissions on voting machines and on the selection of a firearm for the National Guard, and of the United States commissions on postal-pneumatic service and on safe and vault construction. He was a member of the leading engineering and scientific societies of America and Europe, notably of the American Society of Civil Engineers from 1871 and of the American Institute of Mining Engineers from 1875; he took a leading part in organizing the American Society of Mechanical Engineers in 1880, and was its first president, serving for two terms; he was three times a vice-president of the American Association for the Advancement of Science.

In his own researches on the reciprocating steam engine, Thurston gave much thought and study to the losses arising from the reaction between the steam and the iron of the cylinder— losses arising from what may be called the cycle of the cast iron, parallel to and at the expense of that of the steam; and many of his papers and certain inventions relate to this phase of engineering. Always a voluminous writer, he was the author of a number of exhaustive treatises and contributed a very large number of papers, on a wide range of subjects, to the transactions of numerous engineering and scientific societies.

He possessed in remarkable degree the capacity for rapid and intensive work; the flow of his ideas was often too rapid for expression. A list of his books and more important papers comprises works on the materials of engineering construction, works on the steam engine and steam boiler, and works of historical, biographical, or philosophical character. His principal publications, most of which went through a number of editions, were: *A History of the Growth of the Steam-Engine* (1878) ; developed from popular lectures at Stevens Institute; *Friction and Lubrication: Determinations of the Laws and Coefficients of Friction by New Methods and with New Apparatus* (1879) ; *The Materials of Engineering* (3 vols., 1883–84), previously mentioned; *Stationary Steam Engines, Especially as Adapted to Electric Lighting Purposes* (1884) ; *A Treatise on Friction and Lost Work in Machinery and Millwork* (1885) ; *A Text-Book of the Materials of Construction, for Use in Technical and Engineering Schools* (1885), mentioned above; *Steam-Boiler Explosions, in Theory and in Practice* (1887) ; *A Manual of Steam-Boilers; Their Design, Construction, and Operation* (1888) ; *Heat as a Form of Energy* (1890) ; *Reflections on the Motive Power of Heat* (1890), a translation of *Réflexions sur la Puissance Motrice du Feu* (1824), by M. L. S. Carnot; *A Handbook of Engine and Boiler Trials, and of the Indicator and Prony Brake* (1890) ; *Robert Fulton, His Life and Its Results* (1891) ; *A Manual of the Steam-Engine: For Engineers and Technical Schools* (2 vols., 1891) ; *The Animal as a Machine and a Prime Motor, and the Laws of Energetics* (1894). He was also editor for the subjects comprehended under "Engineering" for the *Universal Cyclopædia* and contributed to the *Century Dictionary*, with collaboration in certain fields, the definitions in general technology, "including all branches of the mechanical arts."

It was not, however, through books and papers that his greatest influence was exerted. Hundreds of engineers who passed under his personal instruction, being touched by his loyalty to scientific truth and his high ideals of life and service and carrying into after life the inspiration of his example, were the most influential contribution to his profession of this pioneer in the domain of engineering education.

In his personality and bearing Thurston was gracious, sympathetic, and kindly. His judgments on technical questions were rapid; on matters involving the human element he was likely to be more deliberate in reaching a conclusion. He had the ability to present scientific results with great clearness. As an administrator he had organizing ability of a high order; he respected individuality and did his best to make use of the distinctive capabilities of his subordinates; he was cordial and generous; gave credit liberally, and had the gift of friendship. Under storm and stress he was always cheerful; an appearance of failure never discouraged him. Little, and shaggy of head and beard, with bright, dark eyes,

great personal dignity, and quick, energetic movements, he was affectionately known on the campus as "Bobby" and his steam-engine courses, as "Bobbyology." He died suddenly and peacefully while friends were gathering to celebrate his sixty-fourth birthday, in the midst of his labors and in full possession of his normal strength and mental activities, with apparently many years of fruitful labor yet before him.

[Thurston's autobiography (MS.), written for his family; W. F. Durand, *Robert Henry Thurston* (1929) and memoir in *Ann. Report . . . of the Smithsonian Inst. . . . 1903* (1904) ; *Trans. Am. Soc. Mech. Engineers*, vol. XXV (1904) ; *Trans. Am. Inst. Mining Engineers*, vol. XXXV (1905) ; *Who's Who in America, 1903–05* ; F. M. Bennett, *The Steam Navy of the U. S.* (1896) ; *Morton Memorial: A Hist. of the Stevens Inst. of Technology* (1905), ed. by F. DeR. Furman; W. T. Hewett, *Cornell Univ.: A Hist.* (1905), vol. II ; *N. Y. Tribune*, Oct. 26, 1903 ; personal acquaintance.]   W. F. D.

THURSTON, ROBERT LAWTON (Dec. 13, 1800–Jan. 13, 1874), pioneer manufacturer of steam engines, was born on his father's farm at Portsmouth, R. I., the youngest son of Peleg and Ruth (Lawton) Thurston. He was a descendant in the sixth generation from Roger Williams [*q.v.*], founder of Rhode Island, and in the fifth, from Edward Thurston who was living in that colony as early as 1647. After obtaining a good schooling, he began learning the trade of machinist in the local shop of Pelham & Walcott, having shown since his early boyhood an unusual mechanical talent. In the course of his apprenticeship, about 1821, he attracted the attention of John Babcock, Sr., who was engaged in experimental work on steam boilers. The latter persuaded young Thurston to assist him, and together the two built an experimental steam engine and a "safety tubular boiler" of Babcock's invention, and placed them in a small boat designed for use at Slade's Ferry near Fall River. This apparatus gave such a satisfactory performance that the partners undertook the design and construction of two large steamboats and between 1826 and 1828 completed the *Babcock* and the *Rushlight* for use on the Providence-New York run. The machinery for the former was of their own construction, while that for the latter was built by James P. Allaire [*q.v.*].

After the death of Babcock in 1827, Thurston was employed for a time by the Fall River Iron Company and assisted in the construction of the Annawan mill. His thoughts, however, were wholly taken up with steam-engine building and in 1830 he went to Providence where, in partnership with John Babcock, Jr., he formed the Providence Steam Engine Company for the manufacture of steam engines and power machinery of all kinds. This is said to have been the first establishment for the manufacture of steam engines in New England and the third in the United States. The undertaking was successful from the start, primarily because of the intelligence and practical experience of the partners. In 1838 Babcock retired and the firm became Robert L. Thurston & Company, the business of which Thurston continued to direct alone. Early in the forties, a boiler explosion destroyed several of his factory buildings and several months later came a fire which completely destroyed the plant. Between these two disasters, in 1845, he reorganized the company as Thurston, Green & Company, and soon after the fire rebuilt the plant. One of the first acts of the new company was to purchase the invention of Frederick E. Sickels [q.v.] of the "drop cut-off" for steam engines, which they incorporated in their engines; they were the first manufacturers in either Europe or America to build a standard form of expansion steam engine. Thurston, however, continued to be unfortunate in monetary matters and in 1854 the company was reorganized again as Thurston, Gardner & Company and began the manufacture of the steam engine invented by Noble T. Greene which long remained a favorite form in the field of automatic cut-off steam engines. Thurston brought suit against George H. Corliss [q.v.] for infringement of the Sickels patent and after a long drawn-out trial won a decision, but on appeal the United States Supreme Court decided in favor of Corliss. Although the cost of this lawsuit was extremely heavy, Thurston carried on, but the heavy losses which his company incurred at the beginning of the Civil War, coupled with his advancing age, caused him to retire in 1863 from active participation in the business. He was twice married: first, in 1827, to Eliza Stratton of Portsmouth, who died July 10, 1828. On Jan. 5, 1839, he married Harriet Taylor, daughter of William and Elizabeth (Bailey) Taylor of Little Compton, R. I., who with three children survived him. His elder son, Robert Henry Thurston [q.v.], won great distinction in the profession of mechanical engineering.

[Providence Daily Journal, Jan. 14, 21, 1874; Brown Thurston, Thurston Geneals. (1880); C. M. Thurston, Descendants of Edward Thurston (1868); W. F. Durand, Robert Henry Thurston (1929); Scientific American, Mar. 7, 1874; R. H. Thurston, The Hist. of the Growth of the Steam Engine (1878).] C. W. M—n.

THWAITES, REUBEN GOLD (May 15, 1853–Oct. 22, 1913), librarian and editor, was born in Dorchester, Mass., the son of parents recently from Yorkshire, England, William George and Sarah (Bibbs) Thwaites, and he was educated in the public schools of Massachusetts.

Then going to Wisconsin in 1866, he worked on a farm, taught school, and put himself through a course of college studies. Before the age of twenty he was on the staff of the Oshkosh Times and was sent to report the convention at Baltimore in 1872 that nominated Horace Greeley. His desire for college training led him to Yale University in 1874, where he supported himself as a newspaper correspondent, while studying advanced courses in history and economics. In 1876 he became managing editor of the Wisconsin State Journal, the leading Republican newspaper at Madison, Wis. There he worked for a decade acquiring a wide acquaintance in the state and a thorough technique in the art of printing, typography, and proof reading that was valuable to his future career.

His fondness for history took him often to the rooms of the State Historical Society of Wisconsin, presided over by Lyman C. Draper [q.v.]. Draper recognized the promise of the young journalist, invited him to become assistant secretary, and on his own retirement at the close of 1886 recommended Thwaites as his successor. He was unanimously elected and assumed his duties on Jan. 1, 1887. The new secretary's first care was to enlarge the society's usefulness by building up its manuscript collection and making it available to the scholars of the University of Wisconsin. He visited the descendants of the French pioneers and obtained many of their papers; then in 1891 the society inherited the vast collection of the Draper Manuscripts. Thwaites arranged seminar rooms for the use of Frederick Jackson Turner, where Turner gathered advanced students for research in the history of the West, now made available in these manuscript sources. It was soon evident that the society must have a larger place than the rooms it had occupied in the Capitol. Thwaites obtained the enthusiastic support of the state's leaders for a joint library building for the state historical society and the university upon the lower campus of the university. To this building he gave such care and attention that it may be called his monument. Dedicated in 1900, the historical library has amply fulfilled its purpose.

Impressed with the need of a new edition of the Jesuit Relations, he collected and translated these, with a corps of assistants, until from 1896 to 1901 there appeared seventy-three volumes of Jesuit Relations and Allied Documents. This edition with its fine annotations and translations established his reputation as one of the best historical editors of his day. Continuing his editorial work he brought out the Original Journals of the Lewis and Clark Expedition (8 vols.,

1904–05) ; Hennepin's *New Discovery* (1903) and Lahontan's *New Voyages* (1905), two volumes each with bibliographies; *Early Western Travels,* annotated reprints in thirty-two volumes (1904–07) ; the Draper Series (with L. P. Kellogg) from his manuscript material, *Documentary History of Dunmore's War* (1905) ; *The Revolution on the Upper Ohio* (1908) ; *Frontier Defense on the Upper Ohio* (1912). During all these years he produced a yearly volume of the society's *Proceedings* and a biennial volume of the *Collections,* containing source material for the history of the state. As an author he wrote along the lines of his editorial work, bringing out *Father Marquette* in Appletons' Life Series and *Daniel Boone* (both in 1902) ; *A Brief History of Rocky Mountain Exploration* (1904) ; *France in America* (1905) for the American Nation Series. He wrote in 1891 *The Colonies* for the Epochs of American History Series, and several books on Wisconsin history, of which *Wisconsin* (1908) in the American Commonwealth Series remains the standard. His love of nature and travel served as a basis for *Historic Waterways* (1888) ; *Our Cycling Tour in England* (1892) ; *Afloat on the Ohio* (1897).

In addition to editorship and authorship, he was much in demand for lectures, and his executive ability was enlisted for professional service. In 1900 he was president of the American Library Association, and he served the American Historical Association in many capacities. He was a delightful host and guest, a great friend, a lover of nature and of human nature. His wife, Jessie Inwood (Turville) Thwaites, whom he married in 1882, supplemented him in all his activities. They had one son.

[F. J. Turner, *Reuben Gold Thwaites, a Memorial Address* (1914), with bibliog. of writings; *Who's Who in America,* 1912–13 ; *Review of Reviews* (N. Y.), Dec. 1913 ; *Outlook,* Nov. 8, 1913 ; *Wis. State Jour.* (Madison), Oct. 23, 1913.]
          L. P. K.

TIBBLES, SUSETTE LA FLESCHE [See BRIGHT EYES, 1854–1903].

TIBBLES, THOMAS HENRY (May 22, 1838–May 14, 1928), journalist, social reformer, was the son of William and Martha (Cooley) Tibbles and was born in Washington County, Ohio. It is said that he ran away from home at the age of six and that he was picked up by a party of emigrants who took him to western Missouri. In 1856 he appears to have been a member of John Brown's company in Kansas. According to the legend he was once captured by Quantrill's men and hanged, though friends arrived in time to save his life. He returned to Ohio and for a time attended Mount Union College at Alliance.

In 1861, at Freedom, Pa., he married Amelia Owen. During the Civil War he served on the plains as a guide and scout, and had some employment as a newspaper correspondent. After the war he became an itinerant Methodist preacher, though later he joined the Presbyterians and still later the Unitarians. In 1873–74 he was employed as a reporter on the *Omaha Daily Bee* and in 1876–79 on the *Omaha Daily Herald* (subsequently the *Morning World-Herald*). It was while engaged with the latter paper that he took part in an episode that brought him into general notice. A party of thirty-four homesick Poncas, led by their chief, Standing Bear, had left their new reservation in the present Oklahoma and after a terrible mid-winter journey had arrived among the friendly Omahas late in March 1879. They were arrested by the military, under orders to return them to the reservation. Tibbles, with a fellow reporter, enlisted the help of two attorneys, and on Apr. 30, after a trial in the Federal District Court, the Poncas were freed (*United States ex rel. Standing Bear* vs. *Crook, 25 Federal Cases,* 695). Tibbles, arranging with Standing Bear and with Francis La Flesche and his sister Susette, or Bright Eyes [*q.v.*], of the Omahas to plead the cause of the Indians before the people, conducted a speaking tour which inspired a nation-wide movement in their behalf. His first wife had died in 1879. In 1881, on the Omaha reservation, he married Bright Eyes.

Tibbles was, from their beginning, a zealous supporter of the National Farmers' Alliance and the People's (Populist) party. In 1895, at Lincoln, he took charge of the *Independent,* a weekly organ of the movement, which became nationally influential. In 1904 he was the party's candidate for vice-president. From 1905 to 1910 he edited a weekly newspaper, the *Investigator,* and then returned to the *World-Herald,* where his last newspaper work was done. His wife died on May 26, 1903. At Ute, Iowa, Feb. 24, 1907, he was married to Ida Belle Riddle, who, with two daughters, survived him. He died at his home in Omaha.

Tibbles was an indefatigable writer and besides his newspaper work published three books —*Ponca Chiefs* (1880) ; *Hidden Power* (1881), and *The American Peasant* (1892). He was active also as a stump speaker for the People's party, and as a lecturer on social questions and Indian welfare. He was a large man, somewhat expansive in manner, who made many friends, and who was highly respected for his integrity and for his courageous espousal of unpopular causes.

[Who's Who in America, 1920–21; C. Q. De France, in Nebr.Hist.Mag.,Oct.–Dec.1932; obituaries in N. Y. Times, Morning World-Herald (Omaha), and Nebr. State Jour. (Lincoln), May 15, 1928; information from Ida B. Riddle Tibbles.]　　　　　　　　W. J. G.

TICHENOR, ISAAC (Feb. 8, 1754–Dec. 11, 1838), lawyer, politician, and jurist, was born in Newark, N. J. Little is known of his parentage and early life. He was graduated at the College of New Jersey (Princeton) in 1775, began the study of law in Schenectady, N. Y., and soon afterward entered the commissary service of the Continental Army. The course of his duties took him to Bennington, Vt., in 1777 and he settled at that place, where he maintained a residence throughout the rest of his long life.

The organization of the new state of Vermont, accompanied as it was by disputes with neighboring states and some internal dissension, offered opportunity for political leadership and constructive service. Tichenor served in the legislature from 1781 to 1785, being speaker in 1783–84. Between 1782 and 1789 he served as agent to the Continental Congress for several sessions and in 1790 was appointed a commissioner for the settlement of boundary and land-title difficulties with New York. He was a member of the council from 1786 to 1791 and of the supreme court from 1791 to 1796, serving as chief justice for two years and resigning to enter the United States Senate.

His service in the latter body was of short duration (Oct. 18, 1796–Oct. 17, 1797), since in 1797 he was elected governor of Vermont. In this capacity he served continuously for eleven years (1797–1807), although the Federalist party to which he belonged was losing ground and in the last part of his service he was usually confronted by Republican legislatures. He was reported by contemporaries to be most attractive personally, his charming manners winning him the somewhat uncomplimentary nickname of "Jersey Slick." His messages to the legislature are free from the monotonous pessimism and vindictiveness of many Federalist documents of the era; if they are overloaded with wise saws and governmental truisms, they also contain sound admonitions concerning economy and the retirement of the public debt. While Tichenor lamented the unfortunate "progress and violence of party spirit" the state under his régime was prosperous and well governed. After a year's enforced retirement, he was reëlected governor for the term 1808–09, his election recording Vermont's bitter opposition to the Embargo, but condemning local instances of violence and disorder which had characterized that opposition. In his message of this year he urged a revision of the criminal code and a humane administration of the newly founded state's prison.

He was not in the political foreground during the War of 1812 but in 1815 was elected to the United States Senate for a six-year term. Voting for the most part with the Federalists who still remained in the Capitol, he played no prominent part in national affairs. His last years were spent at Bennington. His wife, Elizabeth, died there in 1815, and he left no children.

[La Fayette Wilbur, Early Hist. of Vt. (4 vols., 1899–1903); Records of the Gov. and Council of the State of Vt., vols. III (1875), IV (1876); Hiland Hall, The Hist. of Vt. (1868); Governor's Messages in Jour. of the Gen. Assembly, 1797–1807, 1808–09; A. M. Hemenway, The Vt. Hist. Gazetteer, I (1868), 174–75; Isaac Jennings, Memorials of a Century ... Bennington (1869); Biog. Dir. Am. Cong. (1928); J. M. Comstock, A List of the Principal Civil Officers of Vt. (1918); Daughters of the Am. Rev. Mag., Nov. 1916; Boston Daily Advertiser, Dec. 19, 1838.]　　　　　　W. A. R.

TICHENOR, ISAAC TAYLOR (Nov. 11, 1825–Dec. 2, 1902), Baptist clergyman, educator, missionary secretary, was born in Spencer County, Ky., the son of James and Margaret (Bennett) Tichenor. He was a descendant of Martin Tichenor, said to have been of French extraction, who was in New Haven, Conn., as early as 1644, and was later one of the settlers of Newark, N. J. Martin's great-grandson, Daniel, grandfather of Isaac, moved from New Jersey to Kentucky in 1790. At the age of fifteen Isaac entered the Taylorsville academy, where he was under two able teachers, Moses and David Burbank, graduates of Waterville College, Maine, and there did work that would have admitted him to the junior class of a college. An attack of measles, however, left him with physical infirmities which troubled him for a long time. When he was sufficiently recovered, he engaged in teaching and was for three years connected with the Taylorsville academy, the last year as principal.

In the meantime, at the solicitation of local Baptists, he had begun to preach, and his effectiveness soon won for him the title "boy orator of Kentucky." In 1847 he became agent for the American Indian Mission Association and while traveling about in its interest he was called to the Baptist church in Columbus, Ky., where in 1848 he was ordained. He served here until 1850, then traveled and preached in Texas, was in charge of the church at Henderson, Ky., for a short time, and on Jan. 1, 1852, began a sixteen-year pastorate at the First Baptist Church, Montgomery, Ala. For two years during the Civil War he served as chaplain of the 17th Alabama Regiment—not confining himself strictly to his prescribed duties, for he acquired reputation as a sharpshooter and at the battle of Shiloh went to the front of his regiment and rallied the wavering lines. In 1868 he resigned his church and for some three years lived on his plantation in Shelby County, Ala., engaging more or less in evangelical work. He accepted a call to the First Baptist Church, Memphis, Tenn., in 1871, but the following year returned to Alabama to be the first president of the State Agricultural and Mechanical College, located at Auburn.

During the ten years he was at the head of this institution he laid a broad and firm foundation for its subsequent development. He studied the agricultural, mineral, and manufacturing resources of the state, and in his numerous addresses awakened its people to a greater appreciation of them. He prophesied the industrial development which has since taken place and labored to prepare the way for it. Throughout this period he continued to maintain a position of leadership in the councils of the Southern Baptists, and in June 1882 he resigned his collegiate position and became secretary of the Home Missionary Board of the Southern Baptist Convention, the headquarters of which were at Atlanta, Ga.

For eighteen years he carried on the work of this office with a statesmanship that resulted in great constructive achievements. At the outset his activities did much to preserve for the Southern Convention its natural field, which was being encroached upon by other more aggressive and better equipped Baptist bodies. He inaugurated extensive work west of the Mississippi, took possession of Texas, insisted that the Convention provide its own Sunday school literature and arranged for its publication, initiated educational projects in the mountain regions, and grappled with problems created by growing industrial centers. In 1899 he retired from active work and was made secretary emeritus. His health soon failed and after protracted suffering he died at Atlanta.

He was four times married: first, Dec. 16, 1853, to Monimia C. Cook, who died Feb. 9, 1860; second, in April 1861, to Emily C. Boykin, who died Sept. 7, 1864; third, in October 1865, to Lulah Boykin, who died in 1869; and fourth, to Mrs. Eppie Reynolds McCraw, who died in 1878. By each he had children, four of whom survived him.

[J. S. Dill, *Isaac Taylor Tichenor: The Home Mission Statesman* (1908), contains some of his writings; see also R. B. Teachenor, *A Partial Hist. of the Tichenor Family in America* (1918); J. M. Carroll, *A Hist. of Texas Baptists* (1923); *Annual of the Southern Bapt. Conv.,* 1903 (n.d.); *Religious Herald* (Richmond, Va.), Dec. 4, 8, 1902; *Atlanta Jour.,* Dec. 2, 3, 1902.]

H. E. S.

TICKNOR, ELISHA (Mar. 25, 1757–June 22, 1821), educator, merchant, was born in Lebanon, Conn., the son of Col. Elisha and Ruth (Knowles) Ticknor. His earliest education was obtained on his father's farm and in the local district school; later he was sent to the academy conducted by Nathan Tisdale in Lebanon, where he acquired a fair mastery of the classical languages. In 1774, his parents removed to Lebanon, N. H. For the next five years, Ticknor assisted his father in developing his new farm, continuing, in periods of leisure, his preparation for college, and teaching in near-by district schools. Graduating from Dartmouth College in 1783, he was appointed master of Moor's Charity School, Hanover, N. H., but withdrew from this position to open a private school in Boston in October 1785. On Mar. 5, 1788, he was appointed principal of the South Writing School, in Boston. At the end of six years he resigned because of ill health, and in 1795 he ventured into business as a grocer. Within a short time he had acquired a sufficient fortune to enable him to devote himself to the cultivation of his various civic and intellectual interests. On May 23, 1790, he married Elizabeth (Billings) Curtis, widow of Dr. Benjamin Curtis of Boston and daughter of Elijah and Elizabeth (Hartshorn) Billings of Stoughton, Mass. The only child of this marriage was George Ticknor [*q.v.*], who, according to his own letters, received most of his really worthwhile preparation for college from his father.

While he was principal of the South Writing School, Ticknor published a grammar entitled *English Exercises* (1792) which was widely used in the schools of Massachusetts. In 1798, he was one of the organizers of the Massachusetts Mutual Fire Insurance Company; and in 1816 he founded, with his friend James Savage [*q.v.*], the Provident Institution for Savings in the Town of Boston, one of the first savings banks in the United States. He was elected selectman of Boston in 1815. Throughout the period of his business life he took an active interest in the work of the public schools. In 1805 he suggested an important innovation in the school system, the establishment of free schools for children under seven years of age. At that time, the town regulations, under which the grammar schools admitted only those who were able to read, virtually excluded from higher education all children whose parents could not provide for their preliminary instruction. Ticknor urged the importance to the town of reducing illiteracy among its citizens and continued to press his suggestion until in 1818 the town of Boston established its first primary school. From 1818 to 1821 he served as a member of the Primary

School Committee Among his activities after his retirement from business was an attempt to establish the popularity of the merino sheep in New England. He imported and kept a large flock on his father's farm, in Lebanon, N. H. For some years his counsel on educational matters was sought by President Eleazar Wheelock of Dartmouth, and he died, as the result of a paralytic stroke, while visiting a member of the Dartmouth faculty in Hanover.

[Wm. Allen, *The Am. Biog. Dict.* (3rd ed., 1857); *Am. Jour. Educ.*, V, 335 (1858), XXVIII, 796 (1878); *Life, Letters, and Journals of George Ticknor* (2 vols., 1876), ed. by G. S. Hillard; *Reports of the Record Commissioners of the City of Boston*, vols. XXV (1894) and XXVII (1896), containing Selectmen's Minutes, 1776–98, vol. XXX (1903), containing Boston Marriages, 1752–1809, and vol. XXXVII (1906), containing Boston Town Records, 1814–22; Justin Winsor, *The Memorial Hist. of Boston*, vol. IV (1881); J. M. Hunnewell, "The Ticknor Family in America," 1919, typescript in Lib. of Cong.; *Boston Daily Advertiser*, June 25, 1821.]   R. F. S.

TICKNOR, FRANCIS ORRAY (Nov. 13, 1822–Dec. 18, 1874), poet, physician, was born at Fortville, Jones County, Ga., son of a Connecticut physician, Dr. Orray Ticknor, who had settled in Savannah and there married Harriet Coolidge of Norwich Town, Conn. He was a descendant of William Ticknor who was in Scituate in 1646. After Dr. Ticknor's death in 1823, Mrs. Ticknor removed to Columbus, Ga., where she reared and educated her three children. Francis, after completing his schooling in Massachusetts, studied medicine in Philadelphia and New York, spent a year (1842) in Norwich Town, received the degree of M.D. at the Philadelphia College of Medicine in 1843, and, returning to Georgia, began to practise at Shell Creek, Muscogee County. On Jan. 18, 1847, he married Rosalie Nelson, daughter of Thomas Maduit Nelson of Virginia, an officer in the War of 1812 and subsequently a member of Congress. He and his wife had six sons and two daughters. About 1850 he settled at "Torch Hill," seven miles south of Columbus, and followed the busy existence of a country doctor, finding time nevertheless for such major passions as the cultivation of fruits and flowers (with infrequent articles thereon for the *Southern Cultivator*) and the writing of poetry, such minor ones as music and drafting. The verses which he contributed to newspapers or obscure periodicals won him some local reputation before the war years which saw his nature deepen and his poetic powers develop; but he was careless of literary fame, and, although certain of his pieces had found a place in the anthologies of Southern war poetry, it was five years after his death before an incomplete collection of his work appeared in volume form.

This posthumous publication shows the range of his poetic interests to have been essentially that of his Southern colleagues, but, despite their unevenness and other occasional limitations, even the conventional lyrics about roses and humming-birds reveal a feeling for artistic structure, a graceful prosody, an incisive and effective turn of phrase which are well above the average of the day and which furnish ground for the assumption that with more leisure, more criticism, more encouragement, Ticknor might readily have secured a considerably higher place among the American poets. As it was, he reached full stature only in his poems on martial and chivalrous themes, with their simple and direct narrative, dramatic intensity, and noticeable compactness of style. "Little Giffen," based on an actual incident during Ticknor's supervision of the Confederate hospital work in Columbus, and easily his best-known poem, can bear comparison with any other American heroic ballad, yet such war verses as "The Virginians of the Valley" and "Loyal" (his tribute to General Cleburne) are not markedly inferior to it. His grand-daughter (Michelle C. Ticknor, *post*, p. 152) attributes to him the authorship of the anonymous "The Barefooted Boys," one of the most spirited and memorable of all the Civil War poems, but does not undertake to prove Ticknor's title to this tremendously powerful lyric which may well have come from his pen. Genial, humane, unselfish, he died in middle life, partly in consequence of his unremitting devotion to duty. The epitaph which he wrote for the title character in his humorous poem, "The Farmer Man," further sums up his own career: "He read the Bible, loved his wife . . . loved God, his neighbor, and his home." Posterity has unduly neglected his work, as did his generation, yet various poets whose names are better known might have learned much from him.

[J. M. Hunnewell, "The Ticknor Family in America," 1919, typescript in Lib. of Cong.; biog. sketch by Michelle C. Ticknor, in *The Poems of Francis Orray Ticknor* (1911); P. H. Hayne, in *Poems of Frank D. Ticknor, M.D.* (1879), ed. by Kate M. Rowland; *Lib. of Southern Lit.*, vol. XII (1907); *Cambridge Hist. of Am. Lit.*, vol. II (1918); S. A. Link, *Pioneers of Southern Lit.* (1899), vol. I, pp. 89–115; Sarah V. Cheney, "Francis Orray Ticknor," 1934, MS. in Duke Univ. lib.; obituary in *Savannah Daily Advertiser*, Dec. 22, 1874.]   A. C. G., Jr.

TICKNOR, GEORGE (Aug. 1, 1791–Jan. 26, 1871), educator and author, was born at Boston. He was the son of Elisha [*q.v.*] and Elizabeth (Billings) Ticknor, the widow of Benjamin Curtis, and was a descendant of William Ticknor who came from England to Massachusetts in or before 1646. William Davis Ticknor [*q.v.*] was a cousin. His father, who graduated from Dartmouth College in 1783, was a teacher before becoming a successful man of business in Boston. George's mother had also been a teacher. He was fitted for college in the home circle and received a certificate of admission to Dartmouth before he was ten years old, after an examination which, in later life, he termed "perhaps a farce." He did not enter Dartmouth until he was fourteen, but he was then admitted as a junior.

Graduating in 1807, Ticknor continued with a private tutor the study of Latin and Greek, which he had begun to cultivate at an early age. After reading law in an office for three years, he was admitted to the bar in 1813, but he realized very soon that the law had no real attraction for him and that the ancient classics had a potent hold on his fancy. As the family fortune left ample opportunity for the purpose, it was decided that he should go to Europe for study. After a journey through the Mid-Atlantic states he made a visit to "Monticello," where he was cordially received by former President Jefferson. The latter may then have told him, as he later wrote, about the plans which eventually took form in the University of Virginia. Ticknor set sail for England in 1815. Among his fellow passengers was Edward Everett [q.v.]; these two scholarly youths were probably the first to go from the United States to German institutions of learning for the express purpose of obtaining a university training more advanced than that possible at home.

Ticknor's first visit to Europe lasted four years, and it took him to England, the Netherlands, Germany, France, Switzerland, Italy, Spain, and Portugal. Inspection of the pages of the *Life, Letters, and Journals of George Ticknor* (2 vols., 1876; new ed., 1909) reveals the ease with which this American student penetrated into the aristocratic, literary, scientific, and generally scholarly circles of the different European centers to which his travels led him. Among the scholars, scientists, and men of letters who received him were A. von Humboldt, Byron, Châteaubriand, Humphry Davy, Mme. de Staël, Miss Edgeworth, Goethe, A. W. and F. Schlegel, Scott, Wordsworth, Southey, J. H. Voss, and F. A. Wolf. With many of these notable personages he maintained a correspondence after his return to the United States, and no few of them he saw again on the occasion of later visits to Europe.

At the University of Göttingen, then the leading institution of higher learning in Germany, Ticknor remained in residence for twenty months (1815–17) attending lectures, reading assiduously, and forming invaluable personal relations with his various teachers. He ardently applied himself to the acquisition of a practical command of German and a good knowledge of its literature, but was not overimpressed with the worth of German philosophy. Greek also claimed his serious attention in this center of philological activity, and he would probably have continued his devotion to it but for the invitation which came to him before the end of 1816 to enter upon the duties of the recently founded Smith professorship of French and Spanish at Harvard College, with an added professorship of belles-lettres. "Here," he says in a letter to his father of Nov. 9, 1816, "is at once a new subject of study proposed to me, to which I have paid no attention since I have been here, and which I have not taken into the plan of my studies and travels in Europe. If I am to be a professor in this [Spanish] literature, I must go to Spain" (*Life*, I, 117). His formal letter of acceptance of the post at Cambridge was written by him at Rome on Nov. 6, 1817, so that he spent a year in consideration of the proposal. From April to August 1817 he was in Paris, eagerly improving all opportunities of augmenting his knowledge of French and its literature; and from early October to the end of the spring of 1818 he visited various cities of Italy, spending most of his time in Rome, where he took private lessons in Italian. He passed some four months of 1818 in Madrid and made no little progress in Spanish under the guidance of some able tutors, among whom was the Orientalist J. A. Condé. Then, after a few weeks in Portugal, he sailed for England, en route for his native land. On Aug. 10, 1819, he was inducted into the professorship which he was to hold until 1835.

Interpreting broadly his functions as a professor of belles-lettres, Ticknor proposed to President John Thornton Kirkland [q.v.] a program of lectures which would have permitted him to cover ancient as well as modern literatures, but he was obliged to restrict his attention in large measure to the French, Spanish, and Italian domain. Within this field he found enough to enlist his best endeavors, and, in spite of the coldness and even declared opposition of colleagues committed to a stereotyped curriculum allowing little scope for the teaching of modern foreign languages and their literatures, he won and maintained the interest of a considerable body of the students. Certain of his lectures, framed for the purpose, attracted a notable audience from without the walls of the college. On Sept. 18, 1821, Ticknor married Anna Eliot, a daughter of Samuel Eliot, a prosperous merchant of Boston.

Her fortune, added to that which he had inherited from his father, allowed him to live in ease and elegance for all the rest of his life; but he avoided ostentation, spent his money rather in the acquisition of a large and useful library than in pompous display, and contributed generously to private and public charities.

Dissatisfied with the state of education in Harvard College and encouraged by a few colleagues and alumni, Ticknor proposed certain changes in the curriculum to the governing bodies, the Corporation and the Board of Overseers. "We are neither a university—which we call ourselves," he said in 1823, "nor a respectable high school—which we ought to be" (*Life,* I, 359). He proposed, among other things, a division of the college into departments grouping related studies. The majority of his colleagues, after a brief period of unwilling experimentation on their part, rejected his innovations, but he triumphed to the extent of receiving permission to continue them for his own courses in modern languages. Thus he began a departmental system which was to develop fully under his wife's nephew, President Charles W. Eliot [*q.v.*], and was to be reflected eventually in all the higher institutions of learning in the United States.

In 1826 Ticknor was appointed a member of the Board of Visitors of the United States Military Academy at West Point. Sooner or later he became identified with a number of enterprises of a more or less public nature, such as the Massachusetts General Hospital, certain banking and insurance companies, and the Boston Primary School Board, of which his father had been a founder. His home life was happy. Although two children, a girl and a boy, died at a tender age, two daughters remained to gladden the household. In January 1835, he wrote to a friend: "I have substantially resigned my place at Cambridge, and Longfellow is substantially appointed to fill it. . . . I have been an active professor these fifteen years, and for thirteen years of the time I have been contending, against a constant opposition, to procure certain changes which should make the large means of the College more effectual for the education of the community. In my own department I have succeeded entirely, but I can get these changes carried no further. As long as I hoped to advance them, I continued attached to the College; when I gave up all hope, I determined to resign" (*Life,* I, 399–400).

Released from his professorial duties, Ticknor planned to go to Europe for a prolonged visit, and, accompanied by his wife and his two little girls, he landed at Liverpool, June 25, 1835. The details of this stay abroad are revealed in a manuscript journal of some 1700 quarto pages. The journal of his first visit is no less bulky. This second visit occupied full three years, during which he had the pleasantest of relations with old and new friends, and began an acquaintance with Prince (later King) John of Saxony, which was highly appreciated by that devotee of Dante. At home again by June 1838, Ticknor was to spend the ensuing period in the writing of his *History of Spanish Literature,* for which his earnest studies during his professorial career had well fitted him. He had the advantage of the constant advice of his friend, the historian Prescott, who had profited in no small degree by the counsel which Ticknor had given him when he was writing his *History of the Reign of Ferdinand and Isabella* (1838). With unflagging ardor Ticknor labored for some ten years on the elaboration and coordination of the material entering into his famous work. Having assembled a representative Spanish library through his own efforts and those of foreign friends, he had at hand a goodly array of documents on which to base his estimate of Spanish letters. To an English friend, Sir Charles Lyell, he wrote when the book was finished: "You know our reading public in the United States, how large it is, as well as how craving and increasing; so that you will be less surprised than others that I have prepared my book as much for *general* readers as for scholars" (*Life,* II, 253.)

The first edition of the book was published by Harper & Brothers, New York, in the latter part of 1849; at the same time John Murray brought out a small edition in London. The reception given to the work was immediately favorable both at home and abroad, and the sales exceeded the author's expectations. No captious criticism of recent times can detract from the fact that in it, for the first time, there was produced a truly scholarly survey of the whole range of Spanish letters from their inception to the early nineteenth century. Nothing at all comparable in merit had hitherto appeared in Spain; the accounts given by the German Bouterwek and the Swiss Sismondi, the most considerable antedating his, pale to insignificance in its light. It blazed the way for the investigations of Spanish literature which were carried on so energetically after the midpoint of the nineteenth century, and it remains a monument of American scholarship. Ticknor's other writings are of ephemeral or minor value, but this book shines in no reflected glory and has a brilliancy of execution which suffices to fix permanently its creator's fame. The defects in it which the greatest of Spanish literary critics, Menéndez y Pelayo, indicated (Jaime Fitzmaurice-Kelly, *Historia de la literatura Española . . . con un estudio preliminar por Marcelino Menéndez y Pelayo,* 1900, pp. xiii–xiv) were natural at a time when many original documents that later came to light were unknown. Again, they are to be explained in part as due to the fact that Ticknor, trained as a student of the ancient classics, was largely autodidact in so far as modern literature is concerned, and in part to the no less patent fact that, dealing with an essentially Catholic literature, Ticknor, the New England Protestant, though no intellectual bigot, could not always appreciate at their full worth many of the leading religious writers of Spain. After nearly a century of brilliant literary accomplishment in Spain the *History of Spanish Literature* is somewhat antiquated. Its treatment of the medieval period and of the Renaissance calls for correction and addition; on the other hand, its story of the course of Spanish authorship in the rationalistic eighteenth century retains much of its original worth.

The first edition was followed by one of 1854; then came a third edition, that of 1863, in which Ticknor availed himself of the additions and corrections provided by his European translators and critics. During the remaining eight years of his life he added the supplementary notes and changes which were printed in the definitive edition issued in 1872, shortly after his death. The work was translated and published with critical notes in Spanish (4 vols., 1851–56), German (1852; 2 vols., 1867), and French (3 vols., 1864–72). In 1850, Hawthorne made a visit to Ticknor which he thus recorded : "He has a fine house, at the corner of Park and Beacon Streets, perhaps the very best position in Boston. . . . Mr. Ticknor has a great head, and his hair is gray or grayish. You recognized in him at once the man who knows the world, the scholar, too, which probably is his more distinctive character, though a little more under the surface. . . . Methinks he must have spent a happy life (as happiness goes among mortals) writing his great three-volumed book . . .; writing it, not for bread, nor with any uneasy desire of fame, but only with a purpose to achieve something true and enduring" (*Passages from the American Note-Books of Nathaniel Hawthorne,* 1868, pp. 151–53).

Ticknor became one of the founders of the Boston Public Library in 1852 and, four years later, passed fifteen months in Europe, engaged in the purchasing of books for it with funds provided chiefly by a benefactor, Joshua Bates [*q.v.*].

He presented 2400 volumes to the library in 1860 and a few hundred additional volumes in succeeding years. Finally, by his will, he bequeathed to it his invaluable collection of books relating to the Spanish peninsula, stipulating that not a volume was ever to leave the precincts of the library building.

In 1859 Ticknor undertook the preparation of a biography of his close friend, the historian Prescott; it appeared as the *Life of William Hickling Prescott* (1864). His other writings comprise: a *Syllabus of a Course of Lectures on the History and Criticism of Spanish Literature* (1823); *Outlines of the Principal Events in the Life of General Lafayette* (1825); *Remarks on Changes Lately Proposed or Adopted in Harvard University* (1825); *The Remains of Nathaniel Appleton Haven, with a Memoir of His Life* (1827); *Remarks on the Life and Writings of Daniel Webster* (1831); a *Lecture on the Best Methods of Teaching the Living Languages* (1833); and various articles in the *North American Review* and other periodicals.

The last part of Ticknor's life was uneventful and happy, cheered by the company of his wife, children, grandchildren, and many friends. He died on Jan. 26, 1871, in his eightieth year. He had been elected to numerous learned societies and had received several honorary degrees.

[*Life, Letters and Journals of George Ticknor* (2 vols., 1876), the ed. referred to in this article; new ed., with introduction by Ferris Greenslet (1909); *Proc. Mass. Hist. Soc.,* vol. XII (1873), pp. 13–29; vol. XX (1884), pp. 384–91; C. H. Hart, *Memoir of George Ticknor, Historian of Spanish Literature. Read before the Numismatic and Antiquarian Soc. of Philadelphia, May 4, 1871* (1871); W. H. Milburn, "George Ticknor and a Glimpse of Boston Society in 1854," *Quart. Review of the M. E. Church, South,* April 1893; *Briefwechsel König Johanns von Sachsen mit George Ticknor herausgegeben von Johann Georg, Herzog zu Sachsen, im Verein mit E. Daenell* (Leipzig and Berlin, 1920); George Ticknor's *Travels in Spain,* ed. by G. T. Northup (1913); *George Ticknor: Letters to Pascual de Gayangos* (1927); O. W. Long, *Thomas Jefferson and George Ticknor. A Chapter in American Scholarship* (1933); *Catalogue of the Spanish Library and of the Portuguese Books bequeathed by George Ticknor to the Boston Public Library,* by J. L. Whitney (1879); *Boston Daily Advertiser,* Jan. 27, 1871; correspondence in private hands.] J. D. M. F.

TICKNOR, WILLIAM DAVIS (Aug. 6, 1810–Apr. 10, 1864), publisher, was born in Lebanon, N. H., the son of William and Betsey (Ellis) Ticknor. An ancestor, William Ticknor, had emigrated from England and settled in Massachusetts as early as 1646. The boy's educational opportunities were confined to those offered by the village school; and at the age of seventeen, with a sum of money derived from the sale of sheep which he had raised on his father's farm, he went to Boston to seek his fortune. There he found employment in the broker-age office of an uncle, Benjamin Ticknor. And there, five years later, his bookish tastes as well as his marked aptitude for business prompted him to establish himself as a publisher and seller of books. The firm which he founded, and in which James Thomas Fields [q.v.] early became a junior partner, was variously known in Tick-nor's lifetime as Allen and Ticknor (1832–33), William D. Ticknor and Company (1833–49), Ticknor, Reed, and Fields (1849–54), and Tick-nor and Fields. In addition to taking over the *Atlantic Monthly* Ticknor's house published, with financial success, the works of many of the leading contemporary writers of England and America: Tennyson, Browning, DeQuincey, Leigh Hunt, Hawthorne, Emerson, Thoreau, Longfellow, Holmes, Whittier, Lowell, and others. During these years, too, Ticknor was the directing genius of "the old Corner Book-store," which was the favorite rendezvous of the literary men of Boston, Cambridge, and Con-cord.

In his busy career as publisher, Ticknor found time for his family, for public service, and for friendships. He married on Dec. 25, 1832, Eme-line Staniford Holt, who bore him seven chil-dren, five of whom survived their father. He was a public-spirited citizen prominent in many civic and educational enterprises, and an active member of the Baptist Church. An unimpeach-able integrity was his leading trait; as an in-stance, for which he should receive especial honor, one may cite the fact that at a time when piratical publication flourished in both England and America Ticknor was among the first in America to insist upon full payment for the works of English authors. Tennyson in a letter to the son of the publisher in 1889 rightly praised Ticknor as "one who gave so honorable an example to his countrymen of justice in the highest sense" (Caroline Ticknor, *post*, p. 3).

His notable friendship with Nathaniel Haw-thorne [q.v.] began about 1850 and continued without interruption until death. Their rela-tions can be traced in details in the numerous letters (about one hundred and fifty altogether) written by the author to his publisher. Ticknor often accompanied Hawthorne on journeys: to Washington in 1853, shortly after the inaugura-tion of Franklin Pierce; to Liverpool in the same year, Ticknor returning to America after having spent about three months in England and on the Continent; and to Washington again in 1862, when the two men saw Lincoln and visited the scene of Bull Run. During these years of friendship, and particularly while he was abroad,

Hawthorne trusted his publisher implicitly with the management of his business affairs. On Mar. 28, 1864, Ticknor, apparently robust, set out with Hawthorne on a southward journey in the hope of reviving the latter's failing health. In Philadelphia Ticknor was suddenly stricken with pneumonia and died on Apr. 10; and Haw-thorne's death, which occurred little more than a month later, was doubtless hastened by the shock of the loss of this true and faithful friend.

[J. M. Hunnewell, "The Ticknor Family in Amer-ica," 1919, typescript in Lib. of Cong.; H. W. Boyn-ton, *Annals of Am. Bookselling, 1638–1850* (1932); *Letters of Hawthorne to William D. Ticknor, 1851–1864* (2 vols., 1910, privately printed); Caroline Tick-nor, *Hawthorne and His Publisher* (1913); H. M. Ticknor, in *Memorial Biogs. of the New-England Hist. Geneal. Soc.*, vol. V (1894), pp. 396–403; obituaries in *New England Hist. and Geneal. Reg.*, Oct. 1864, pp. 381–83, and in *Boston Transcript*, Apr. 11, 1864.]
R. S.

TIDBALL, JOHN CALDWELL (Jan. 25, 1825–May 15, 1906), soldier, of Scotch-Irish and Welsh descent, was born in Ohio County, Va. (now W. Va.), the son of William and Maria (Caldwell) Tidball. He graduated from the United States Military Academy in 1848, was appointed brevet second lieutenant, 3rd Ar-tillery, and saw service against the Seminoles, in New Mexico, in the exploration of a route to California, with the Coast Survey, and with the Harpers Ferry expedition to suppress John Brown's raid in 1859.

After the outbreak of the Civil War he took part in the expedition to Fort Pickens, Fla., April–July 1861. Promoted captain in May, he returned to Washington in command of Battery A, 2nd Artillery. He served in the Manassas campaign, and his battery, with that of Henry Jackson Hunt [q.v.], covered the withdrawal of the Union forces from Centreville into the de-fenses of Washington. In September he or-ganized his battery to operate with cavalry. He was in all of the battles of the Peninsular cam-paign; after the battle of Mechanicsville, May 27, 1862, he supported Porter's withdrawal to Gaines's Mill, where he checked the Confederate envelopment and again assisted the withdrawal. During this campaign, to avoid causing an alarm, Tidball initiated the custom of having "Taps" sounded at a soldier's burial, in lieu of firing vol-leys.

In the Maryland campaign of 1862 he served with the cavalry division. At Boonsboro, and repeatedly at Antietam, the fire of his battery was a decisive factor, while in the pursuit of the enemy and subsequent cavalry operations he again rendered valuable service. He participated in Stoneman's raid on Richmond (Apr. 13–May

2, 1863) and in the operations in northern Virginia culminating in the battle of Chancellorsville (May 2–4). Experience had taught massed employment of artillery and in June 1863 Tidball was assigned to command a brigade of horse artillery. He ably supported the cavalry corps throughout the Gettysburg campaign. In August, he was appointed colonel of the 4th New York Volunteer Artillery (foot), and assigned to the defenses of Washington.

Reassigned to the Army of the Potomac in March 1864, to command the artillery of the II Corps, he was conspicuous for skill and gallantry at Spotsylvania and the North Anna (May 1864). In July he was appointed commandant of cadets at the Military Academy, but in October rejoined the Army of the Potomac as chief of artillery, IX Corps. On Mar. 25, 1865, when a Confederate force surprised and captured Fort Stedman, a key point in the Union lines before Petersburg, Tidball by a prompt concentration of artillery fire paralyzed the attack and enabled the infantry to recapture the position. A week later he directed the artillery preparation and support of the final assault on Petersburg.

After the war, having received brevets of major-general of volunteers and brigadier-general, United States Army, he reverted to his Regular Army rank of captain. There followed service on the West Coast and in Alaska. He was promoted major in 1867, and was superintendent of artillery instruction at Fort Monroe from 1874 to 1881. During this period he compiled the *Manual of Heavy Artillery Service* (1880). Other writings of his were "The Artillery Service in the War of the Rebellion" (*Journal of the Military Service Institution,* at intervals, July 1891–November 1892) and various official reports included in the *Annual Report* of the secretary of war. He was promoted lieutenant-colonel, 1882, and colonel, 1885. From 1881 to 1884 he served as aide-de-camp to General Sherman, and from 1883 to 1888, as commandant of the Artillery School. He was retired for age, Jan. 25, 1889.

Tidball was an officer of martial appearance and austere manner, back of which was a nature rich in humor and affability. He was twice married: first, in 1853, to Mary Hunt Davis, and after her death, to Mary Langdon Dana in 1870. He was survived by two sons and two daughters.

[J. A. Caldwell, *Hist. of Belmont and Jefferson Counties, Ohio* (1880) ; J. H. Calef, "A Distinguished Horse Artilleryman," *Jour. of the Military Service Inst.,* July-Aug. 1908; *Ann. Reunion Asso. Grads., U. S. Mil. Acad.* (3rd ed., 1891), vol. II ; T. F. Rodenbough, *The Army of the U. S.* (1896) ; *Battles and Leaders of the Civil War* (4 vols., 1887–88) ; *War of the Rebellion:*

Official Records (Army) ; H. C. Kirk, *Heavy Guns and Light* (1890) ; *Memoirs of Gen. W. T. Sherman* (1891); *Who's Who in America,* 1906–07 ; *Army and Navy Jour.,* May 19, 1906 ; *Newark Evening News,* May 16, 1906.]   T. F. M.

TIEBOUT, CORNELIUS (1777–1832), line and stipple engraver, was born in New York City, the son of Tunis and Elizabeth (Lamb) Tiebout and a descendant of Jan Tibout [*sic*] who came to America before 1656 and in 1660 joined the church in New Amsterdam. As a lad, Cornelius was apprenticed to John Burger, a goldsmith in New York City, and he is said to have begun his experiment in engraving before he was out of his indentures. What is probably his earliest piece of work—a plan of New York —is dated 1789, but before he completed his apprenticeship he had engraved maps, portraits, and subject plates for the *New York Magazine* and for John Brown's *Self-Interpreting Bible.* In 1793 he went to London, where he received training in engraving in line and stipple under James Heath. While he was in the British capital (1795), he engraved and published a stipple portrait of John Jay which has been characterized as "probably the first really good portrait engraved by an American-born professional engraver" (Stauffer, *post,* pp. 271–72).

Having acquired the practical knowledge he needed, Tiebout returned to New York in November 1796, and in partnership with his brother Andrew set up in business as an engraver. On Apr. 20, 1799, he married Esther Young, who bore him two sons and a daughter. Later that year he removed to Philadelphia, which was his home for the following quarter century. He had already made portrait plates for some of William Dunlap's translations from Kotzebue and was now engaged by booksellers to furnish plates, but he also engraved portraits in quarto and in folio. Conspicuous among his larger plates were those of Rembrandt Peale's Thomas Jefferson, a full length, and "View of the Water Works at Centre Square," after the picture by Barralet. Tiebout also engraved plates for Benjamin Tanner [*q.v.*]. A small stipple plate, printed in color, after Sir Joshua Reynolds' "Hope," was another of his early accomplishments. Some of his work is to be found in Mathew Carey's Family Bible (1803–05) ; in the *Port Folio* (1812) ; in William Gibson's *Institutes and Practice of Surgery* (1824) ; and in many of the volumes of William Mavor's *Historical Account of Celebrated Voyages* (1802–03).

In 1817 Tiebout joined Benjamin Tanner and Francis Kearny [*q.v.*] in exploiting Henry S. Tanner's patent (1815) for engraving ornaments on banknotes to make them difficult to counterfeit. The banknote company of Tanner, Kearny & Tiebout existed until 1822, when it succumbed. According to one account (Dunlap, *post*), Tiebout accumulated considerable property but lost most of his savings through investment in a blacking manufactory. He is said to have gone to Kentucky about 1825, where he died, apparently in 1830. His last published plate, a stipple of a picture entitled "Lion and Horse," appeared in *The Casket* for May 1830. In 1928 he was represented in the exhibition of One Hundred Notable Engravers at the New York Public Library.

[William Dunlap, *A Hist. of the Rise and Progress of the Arts of Design in the U. S.* (1834), vol. II; W. S. Baker, *Am. Engravers and Their Works* (1875); D. M. Stauffer, *Am. Engravers upon Copper and Steel* (1907); Mantle Fielding, *Am. Engravers upon Copper and Steel* (1917); *One Hundred Notable Am. Engravers* (N. Y. Pub. Lib., 1928); *The Ancestry and Posterity of Cornelius Henry Tiebout of Brooklyn* (1910).]

J. J.

TIEDEMAN, CHRISTOPHER GUSTAVUS (July 16, 1857–Aug. 25, 1903), professor of law, legal writer, was born in Charleston, S. C., the son of Otto and Caroline Amelia Tiedeman. His childhood and youth were spent in the city of his birth, where he completed his secondary and college education, graduating from the College of Charleston with the degrees of A.B. and A.M. in 1876. The following spring he went to Germany where he attended successively courses at the Universities of Göttingen and Leipzig, coming under the influence of Rudolf von Ihering, Wilhelm Roscher, and Emil Albert Friedberg. On his return to the United States, in the autumn of 1878, he matriculated at the Columbia Law School, being graduated LL.B. the following spring. After a short period of practice, first in Charleston, then in St. Louis, he accepted in 1881 an assistant professorship of law in the University of Missouri; he was made full professor in 1882 and retained that position until 1891. The Phi Delta Phi Legal Fraternity chapter at Missouri bears his name. During this period of his life, in 1885, he married Helen Bruce Seymour. He became a professor at the law school of the University of the City of New York in 1891, remaining with this school until June 1897, when he resigned to pursue his literary activities. When he had completed the text he was then writing, he accepted the position of dean of the Law School of the University of Buffalo, in which capacity he served from May 1902 until his death in 1903.

Successful as Tiedeman was as a teacher, he was probably better known for his writings on legal subjects. Publishing his first text in the early years of his incumbency at the University of Missouri, he continued his literary labors unremittingly, either in revising editions or in preparing new treatises and texts. These were: *An Elementary Treatise on the American Law of Real Property* (1884; 4th ed. 1924); *A Treatise on the Limitations of Police Power in the United States, Considered from both a Civil and Criminal Standpoint* (1886); *A Treatise on the Law of Commercial Paper* (1889); *The Unwritten Constitution of the United States* (1890); *A Treatise on the Law of Sales of Personal Property* (1891); *A Treatise on Equity Jurisprudence* (1893); *A Treatise on the Law of Municipal Corporations in the United States* (1894); and *A Treatise on State and Federal Control of Persons and Property in the United States* (1900), a second edition of his earlier work on the limitations of the police power. He also edited *Selected Cases on Real Property* (1897) and prepared a student's textbook under the title, *A Treatise on the Law of Bills and Notes* (1898). In addition he was a frequent contributor to the legal periodicals of the day.

In all his writings Tiedeman displayed a clarity and accuracy that made his works very popular. By 1897 texts of his were used in thirty-six law schools. Personally he was well liked. He was, in the words of a successor at the University of Buffalo, "a most cultured and thorough gentleman in every sense of the word." He was survived by his wife and four children.

[*Buffalo Express*, Aug. 26, 1903; *Gen. Alumni Cat., N. Y. Univ., 1833–1906* (1906); *Publisher's Weekly*, Sept. 5, 1903; *Who's Who in America*, 1903–05; *The Brief* (Phi Delta Phi), first quarter, 1904; J. F. Tucker, "The Law School of the Univ. of the City of N. Y.," *Intercollegiate Law Jour.*, Dec. 1891.]

L. M. S.

TIERNAN, FRANCES CHRISTINE FISHER (July 5, 1846–Mar. 24, 1920), author, was born at Salisbury, N. C., the daughter of Col. Charles Frederic and Elizabeth (Caldwell) Fisher. Her father was an Episcopalian, her mother a Roman Catholic; she followed the religion of her mother and was confirmed in the Catholic Church by the Rt. Rev. James Gibbons, at the time vicar apostolic of North Carolina. She was educated at home in the mountain town where her family had lived since the earliest settlement. Her youth was saddened by the death of her father, a Confederate officer, who was killed in 1861 at the battle of Manassas. For years she lived in the old home, a columned gray house in a setting of cedars and oaks, with a maiden aunt as her companion. Visits to Asheville were the chief break in her routine of walking, driving, and writing, for she avoided most social relations. She was devoted to her religion and had the Church of the Sacred Heart built on a portion of the family land.

Her first novel, *Valerie Aylmer* (1870), was published under the pseudonym of Christian Reid. Others followed rapidly until she had written nearly fifty. Representative novels of her early period are *Morton House* (copyright 1871), which describes Christmas on a plantation; *A Daughter of Bohemia* (1874); *A Question of Honor* (1875); *The Land of the Sky* (1876), whose scene is western North Carolina; *Bonny Kate* (1878); and *Hearts of Steel* (1883). On Dec. 29, 1887, she married James Marquis Tiernan of Maryland and went with him to Mexico, where he was engaged in mining developments. There she lived most of the time until his death in January 1898, when she returned to Salisbury. Many of her novels of this period have Mexican settings and characters, and make use of Mexican history and legends. Among them are *A Cast for Fortune* (copyright 1890); *Carmela* (1891); *A Comedy of Elopement* (1893); *A Little Maid of Arcady* (1893); *The Land of the Sun* (1894); *The Picture of Las Cruces* (1896); *The Man of the Family* (1897); and *Fairy Gold* (1897). Her later books include *Under the Southern Cross* (1900), a drama, which shows her passionate devotion to the Confederacy and her belief in the right of secession; *A Daughter of the Sierra* (1903); *Princess Nadine* (1908), later dramatized; *The Light of the Vision* (1911); *The Wargrave Trust* (1912); and *A Far-Away Princess* (1914). In 1909 she was awarded the Laetare medal by Notre Dame University. She died at Salisbury. Her fiction has been described as "pellucidly pure" in style, with some dramatic quality and wit in dialogue; yet it lacked real humor and depth of intellectual perception, and, because of its author's aloofness from life, was without wide appeal (Egan, *post*, p. 18).

[*Who's Who in America*, 1920–21; *Cath. Encyc.*, Supp. I (1922); Eleanor C. Donnelly and others, *A Round Table of the Representative Am. Cath. Novelists* (1887); *Ave Maria* (Notre Dame, Ind.), Apr. 17, 1920; Maurice F. Egan, in *America*, Apr. 24, 1920; *Charlotte Observer* (Charlotte, N. C.), June 1, 1909, and Mar. 25, 1920.]   S. G. B.

TIERNEY, RICHARD HENRY (Sept. 2, 1870–Feb. 10, 1928), Roman Catholic priest and journalist, sixth child of Richard Tierney who came from Thurles, Ireland, and his wife, Bridget Shea, who was brought as a child to America from County Clare, was born at Spuyten Duyvil, New York, where his father was a superintendent in Johnson's Iron Foundry. Reared in a family of eight children, attending local schools at Kings Bridge and St. Francis Xavier's College, New York, from which he was graduated in 1892, Tierney was a good student and a superior athlete of powerful physique. He

was received as a candidate for the Society of Jesus by Provincial Thomas J. Campbell, and made his novitiate in Frederick, Md. Following a period of study at Woodstock, and of teaching in Gonzaga College, Washington, and Holy Cross College, Worcester, Mass., he returned to Woodstock for his theological studies, and was ordained priest by Archbishop John Farley, June 27, 1907. On completion of his tertianship at Linz, Austria, in 1909, he was assigned to teach philosophy and education at Woodstock; an outcome of this experience was his stimulating manual, *Teachers and Teaching* (1914). He had already sent numerous contributions to Catholic magazines, and in January 1914 he joined the editorial staff of the Jesuit weekly, *America,* of which he became controlling editor some two months later.

Through the pages of *America* Tierney became in some minds "the journalistic spokesman of the Catholic Church in the United States" (Talbot, *post,* p. 54). The journal reflected its editor—a man of exceptional ability, abrupt in manner, self-confident, by some considered arrogant, caustic in speech, and liberal in his views. He inevitably made enemies; at times his weekly worried some of the leaders of the Catholic Church—though it received full patronage from Archbishop Patrick Hayes—because of its aggressiveness in controversial matters. Neutral in the World War until the entry of the United States, *America* was a target for both German and Allied propagandists. The champion of the Church in Mexico in the days of Carranza and Villa, it instituted the Mexican Fund for refugees and stoutly opposed the Mexican policy of the Wilson administration. He spoke trenchantly on the Irish question, accepted the Free State despite attacks by extremists, fought Mayor John Purroy Mitchel [*q.v.*] in the New York charities investigation, opposed prohibition although he was personally a total abstainer, and waged a fight against what he regarded as a dangerous federal control of education. At times he may have been irritating, but he was frank in his courageous espousal of an issue. After the World War, he promoted relief work in Europe, especially in Austria. On three occasions, he received papal briefs in commendation of his services as a Catholic leader. Prior to his retirement as the result of a paralytic stroke in 1925, he served in 1922 as a delegate to the International Sodality Conference in Rome, and in 1923 as a delegate to the General Congregational of his Society in Rome. He died at St. Vincent's Hospital, New York, after three years of invalidism.

[F. X. Talbot, *Richard Henry Tierney, S.J.* (1930), a sympathetic study; *Who's Who in America, 1926–27*; *N. Y. Times*, Feb. 12, 1928.]　　　　R. J. P.

TIFFANY, CHARLES LEWIS (Feb. 15, 1812–Feb. 18, 1902), jeweler, the son of Comfort and Chloe (Draper) Tiffany, was born in Killingly, Conn., a descendant of Humphrey Tiffany who was in the Massachusetts Bay Colony in 1660. The boy first attended a district school and then spent two years at an academy at Plainfield, Conn. Meanwhile his father organized a small cotton-manufacturing company, and near his mill started a general store which the boy Charles was set to manage at the age of fifteen. The mill prospered, Comfort Tiffany bought out his partners, and the firm became C. Tiffany & Son. Charles had some more snatches of education at schools near by, then entered the office with his father. In 1837 he followed his schoolmate, John B. Young, to New York City, and the two opened a small stationery and notion store on a thousand dollars capital, loaned by Comfort Tiffany. Their total sales for the first three days amounted to $4.98. They were opposite the City Hall, which was considered rather far uptown. By 1839 they were selling mostly glassware, cutlery, porcelain, clocks, and jewelry. In 1841 the firm became Tiffany, Young & Ellis, and they rented the adjoining room, more than doubling their space. Jewelry, Bohemian glass, porcelain, and similar goods now became their specialties. They had established a reputation for selling articles of beauty and taste, and they strove to better it. Finer grades of English jewelry, and then Italian and Roman jewelry were sought by Young, now the European buyer; they issued an annual catalogue; and in 1848 they began manufacturing jewelry, the revolutionary movements in Europe that year enabling them to buy diamonds at very low prices. During the next few decades they bought some historic gems, the relics of royal and noble houses of Europe—the collection of the Hungarian Prince Esterhazy, for example, and the crown jewels of the Second French Empire. In 1850 a branch was established in Paris, and in 1868 one in London. In 1853 Young and Ellis retired from the firm, and, with the admission of new partners, the business was reorganized under the name of Tiffany & Company, and so continues eighty years after. In 1858 Tiffany procured a large section of the first Atlantic cable which was left after the laying, cut it into short pieces, and made them into souvenirs which were so popular that a detail of police was required to keep the throng of buyers in order. At the outbreak of the Civil War, for a time his store became a depot for military sup-

plies. The New York house gradually moved uptown until it erected its own building on Fifth Avenue. Incorporated in 1868, the company became the greatest jewelry company on the continent, and at Tiffany's death was capitalized at $2,400,000.

For half a century Tiffany was considered the leader of the jewelry trade in America. He was one of the founders of the New York Society of Fine Arts, a patron of the Metropolitan Museum of Art, and a member of the National Academy of Design. France made him a Chevalier of the Legion of Honor (1878) and the Czar of Russia conferred on him the medal Praemia Digno. His company had more than twenty foreign monarchs among its customers. He married Harriet Olivia Avery Young, sister of his first partner, on Nov. 30, 1841. She died on Nov. 6, 1897. Tiffany died in Yonkers, N. Y., survived by four of his six children.

[N. O. Tiffany, *The Tiffanys of America: Hist. and Geneal.* (1901); *Who's Who in America*, 1901–02; G. F. Heydt, *Charles L. Tiffany and the House of Tiffany & Company* (1893); *N. Y. Times*, Feb. 16, 19, 1902; obituaries in *N. Y. Tribune*, *N. Y. Herald*, Feb. 19, 1902.]　　　　A. F. H.

TIFFANY, KATRINA BRANDES ELY (Mar. 25, 1875–Mar. 11, 1927), civic worker, social reformer, was born in Altoona, Pa., the daughter of Theodore N. Ely and Henrietta (Brandes) Ely. Her father, chief of motive power of the Pennsylvania Railroad, was not only an able engineer but a man of great cultivation, a descendant of William Ely who went from the West Indies to Connecticut in 1670. Her maternal grandfather, Dr. Charles von S. Brandes, a Hanoverian, emigrated to America in the 1830's and settled in Erie, Pa., where he is said to have been the outstanding physician and surgeon of a large region. From him Katrina Ely absorbed an especial devotion to liberal ideas and unpopular causes. Educated by tutors and in private schools in Detroit and Bryn Mawr, she entered Bryn Mawr in 1893, where she became at once an outstanding personality by reason of her personal beauty, her boyish spirit of adventure, her athletic skill, her fine intellect, and her love of people. At Bryn Mawr, under such teachers as Franklin Giddings, she developed the absorbing interest in civic, political, and philanthropic undertakings which were to characterize all her later life. She received the degree of A.B. in 1897. On June 24, 1901, she was married at Bryn Mawr to Charles Lewis Tiffany, son of Louis C. Tiffany [*q.v.*].

In New York, where she went to live, she interested herself immediately in city politics, and when woman's suffrage came to the fore she devoted much of her time and her money to it. She became president of the College Women's Equal Suffrage League and recording secretary of the Woman Suffrage Party of New York; she was one of the foremost women speakers and debaters on suffrage, and traveled extensively through the state of New York throughout the suffrage campaign. Later she allied herself more closely with the Democratic party in the state of New York, and more than once took the stump for its candidates. But her interest in party politics did not preclude her enthusiastic support of the New York League of Women Voters, of which she was a regional director at the time of her death. She was a member of the executive board of the Foreign Policy Association (1918–27), one of the founders of the Woodrow Wilson Foundation and a contributor to its prize fund, an enthusiastic worker in the cause of world peace, and a strong supporter of the League of Nations. Soon after her marriage she interested herself in the New York Intercollegiate Bureau of Occupations, which sought to find positions other than teaching for women college graduates. It was largely through her efforts as chairman of the finance committee that the bureau became the important and outstanding institution of its kind in the United States, and served as a model for numerous others. For many years she was a trustee of the New York Infirmary for Women and Children, and treasurer of the Sunnyside Day Nursery. She died in New York, survived by her husband. She had no children. Her friends speak of her sincerity and utter simplicity, of "the cheerful gallantry with which she ... would challenge the inertia or the selfishness of society," of the fact that always "she put truth in the first place."

[M. S. Beach, *The Ely Ancestry* (1902), ed. by G. B. Vanderpoel; *The Hist. of Woman Suffrage*, vols. V–VI (1922), ed. by Ida H. Harper; *Woman's Who's Who of America*, 1914–15; *Bryn Mawr Alumnae Bull.*, Apr. 1927; *News Bull.* (Foreign Policy Asso.), Mar. 18, 1927; *Weekly News of the N. Y. League of Women Voters*, Mar. 18, 1927; obituary and editorial in *N. Y. Evening Post*, Mar. 11, 12, 1927; obituaries in *N. Y. Times* and *World* (N. Y.), Mar. 12, 1927; letters in the possession of Gertrude Ely, Mrs. Tiffany's sister; letters from friends.] L. K. M. R.

TIFFANY, LOUIS COMFORT (Feb. 18, 1848–Jan. 17, 1933), artist, glass-maker, philanthropist, was born in New York City and was the son of the jeweler, Charles Lewis Tiffany [*q.v.*], and Harriet Olivia (Young) Tiffany. The boy was simply reared, and his formal education took him only through the secondary schools. He early began to show his natural bent by haunting art galleries and studios of leading artists in New York, and presently took up serious study under the latter—first with George Inness and Samuel Colman [*qq.v.*], later under Léon Bailly in Paris. His first work was in oil and water color. He was accepted in 1871 as an associate of the National Academy of Design. His early training with Inness turned him towards landscape only for a brief time; as years passed, human figures became more and more prominent in his landscapes, and presently the figure was his chief concern. He had an oriental love of color, which was intensified by a visit to the Near East in his youth. Although a member of the American Water Color Society and a participant in its exhibitions for many years, he early in life aroused much acrimonious debate among its members by his advanced methods. In 1877 he and other artists, such as Wyatt Eaton, John La Farge, and Augustus Saint-Gaudens [*qq.v.*], who felt that the National Academy of Design was too narrow and unprogressive, organized the Society of American Artists.

He had already begun to turn his attention to other media than paints. In 1875 he began experimenting with stained glass, and in 1878 established a glass-making plant of his own, the first of several, his factory being destroyed by fire no less than three times. He invented a process of his own for staining glass. Instead of producing a much-leaded mosaic of different colored pieces of glass, or painting the color upon the surface and burning or fusing it in—processes hitherto prevailing in Europe—he worked his pigment directly into the glass and produced draperies or other shadings by forcing a pot-metal glass, while in a molten condition, into wrinkles or folds. He designed several famous windows, but his largest work in this medium was the glass curtain for the National Theatre in Mexico city, a creation weighing many tons, depicting the florid landscape near the city, with its two volcanoes in the background. Having much colored glass left over from such work, he utilized it in the production of vases, bric-à-brac, cigarette boxes, ornamental plaques, wall and floor tiling. This beautiful product, to which he gave the name of Favrile glass, brought him his greatest popular reputation. Between 1893 and 1926 he received numerous prizes and medals, among them the Grand Prix and a gold medal at the Paris Exposition of 1900. He was a Chevalier of the Legion of Honor, and an honorary member of the Imperial Society of Fine Arts of Tokyo, and of the Société Nationale des Beaux Arts of Paris. He also gave no little attention to the designing of jewelry, rugs, and textiles. He owned at one time and another four notable homes, for which he designed grounds, buildings, decoration, and furnishings. In 1919 he established the Louis Comfort Tiffany Foundation for art students, deeding to it his eighty-acre estate and buildings at Oyster Bay, Long Island, as well as his entire collection of paintings, glass, and other art objects, and a $1,000,000 endowment. He built additional studios and living quarters, and every summer thereafter during his lifetime invited artists from all parts of the country to work there. He was vice-president and a director of both Tiffany & Company, jewelers, and the Tiffany & Company Safe Deposit Company. On May 15, 1872, he married Mary Woodbridge Goddard (d. Jan. 22, 1884), by whom he had two sons and two daughters. On Nov. 9, 1886, he married Louise Wakeman Knox (d. 1904), by whom he had one son and four daughters. He died in New York City, survived by a son and a daughter of his first marriage, and three daughters of his second.

[N. O. Tiffany, *The Tiffanys of America: Hist. and Geneal.* (1901) ; *Who's Who in America*, 1932–33 ; L. C. Tiffany, *The Art Work of Louis C. Tiffany* (1914) ; Ethel Syford, in *New England Mag.*, Sept. 1911, pp. 197–208; *International Studio*, Dec. 1906, pp. xxiii–xlii ; Samuel Howe, *Ibid.*, Feb. 1908; H. H. Saylor, *Ibid.*, Dec. 1908 ; Charles De Kay, *Ibid.*, Oct. 1920, pp. lxxviii–lxxxi ; J. K. Mumford, in *Arts and Decoration*, Feb. 1921 ; obituaries in *N. Y. Herald Tribune, N. Y. Times, Sun* (N. Y.), Jan. 18, 1933.]   A. F. H.

TIFFANY, LOUIS McLANE (Oct. 10, 1844–Oct. 23, 1916), surgeon, was born in Baltimore, Md., the son of Henry and Sally Jones (McLane) Tiffany, and a descendant of Humphrey Tiffany who was in Massachusetts in 1660. His maternal grandfather was Louis McLane [*q.v.*]. Tiffany obtained his academic education at Cambridge University, England, receiving the B.A. degree from Emmanuel College in 1867. He was graduated from the University of Maryland School of Medicine in 1868, with the degree of M.D. It was customary at the time for medical students to enter the offices of professors as office students, and Tiffany became an office student of Nathan R. Smith [*q.v.*]. The influence of this association was lifelong. The year after his graduation he began to teach as demonstrator of anatomy and became professor of operative surgery in 1874, succeeding Christopher Johnston as professor of surgery in 1880. He retained this position until the year before his retirement in 1903.

Tiffany entered upon the practice of surgery in the pre-antiseptic days ; he promptly accepted Lister's principle but often questioned the method employed. In the disinfection of the skin he laid great stress on the mechanical effects of soap and water, but did not deny the value of chemical disinfectants. He was always a be-liever in clean hands, clean field, and clean surroundings. He practised and taught the advantage of sharp rather than blunt dissection, believing that the vitality of the tissues was thus better preserved and the dangers of tension in a wound reduced. Drainage was an important part of his technique and in his early days must have contributed largely to his good results. He was ambidextrous, using the knife first in one hand then in the other—a maneuver that gave a decided flourish to his operations. In many fields he was a pioneer ; he is credited with performing the first nephrolithotomy in America, and excised the Gasserian ganglion for trifacial neurology a few months after Frank Hartley [*q.v.*] and F. Krause had performed the same operation almost simultaneously in New York and in Germany. He also performed the first successful gastro-enterostomy in Baltimore in October 1892.

A considerable number of papers in the surgical literature came from Tiffany's pen. As a member of several professional societies, he took an active part in the proceedings and discussions. He was at different times president of the Baltimore Medical Association, the Medical and Chirurgical Faculty of Maryland, the Southern Surgical and Gynecological Association, and the American Surgical Association, and was an honorary fellow of the American College of Surgeons. A man of distinguished appearance, tall, of splendid proportion, with a commanding manner and address, he was an impressive figure in any company. Socially he was a delightful companion but in dispute he was an opponent to be dreaded. For many years he dominated surgical thought as well as surgical practice in Maryland. In August 1871 he was married to Madeline, the daughter of M. Woolsey Borland, of Boston. They had two children, one of whom survived him. After the death of his wife he was married, in January 1879, to Evelyn May Bayly, the daughter of Thomas H. Bayly, 1810–1856 [*q.v.*].

[*Who's Who in America*, 1916–17 ; N. O. Tiffany, *The Tiffanys of America: Hist. and Geneal.* (1901) ; Frank Martin, biographical sketch in H. A. Kelly and W. L. Burrage, *Am. Medic. Biog.* (1920) ; *Hospital Bull., Univ. of Md.*, 1914; *Medic. Annals of Md.* (1899) ; *Trans. Am. Surgical Asso.*, vol. XXXVI (1918) ; *Jour. Am. Medic. Asso.*, Oct. 28, 1916 ; Baltimore *Sun*, Oct. 24, 1916.]   A. M.

TIFFIN, EDWARD (June 19, 1766–Aug. 9, 1829), first governor of Ohio, was born in Carlisle, England. His parents, Henry and Mary (Parker) Tiffin, with their five children emigrated in 1784 and settled near Charles Town, Va., now in Jefferson County, W. Va. He studied medicine in England, then attended Jefferson Medical College in Philadelphia, and began practice in Charles Town. In 1789 he married Mary, the daughter of Robert Worthington, a wealthy land-owner of the neighborhood. They had no children. He and his wife became ardent Methodists, and he was ordained a lay preacher by Bishop Asbury in 1792. In the spring of 1798 Tiffin and his brother-in-law, Thomas Worthington [q.v.], with their families and several negroes, whom they had recently manumitted, removed to Chillicothe, Ohio. If he removed to Ohio with political ambitions, he acted opportunely for the Virginia Military District became a political unit that determined Ohio's political history for more than a decade. Short of stature with heavy body and light limbs, a large head, and round, florid face, he was remarkable for his animation and energy; and from 1798, when St. Clair appointed him prothonotary of the territorial court of common pleas, until his death he was constantly in public office. In 1799 and 1801 he was a member of the territorial legislature, and served as speaker in both sessions. Contemporary correspondence points to Tiffin as the leading spirit in the internal organization of the "Chillicothe Junto" that successfully opposed St. Clair. As president of the constitutional convention in November 1802 he determined the membership of committees and was able to prevent any concerted action on the part of the Federalists.

Elected governor almost without opposition in the subsequent state election and reëlected two years later, he took office in March 1803. The constitution of 1802 gave little authority to the governor, but as leader of Ohio Jeffersonians, he exerted considerable influence. Although English-born, he urged that English common-law crimes, as such, should not be recognized by Ohio courts. The requisite legislation was enacted, and hence in Ohio all crimes are, of necessity, statutory. In his second administration he displayed such energy in directing the efforts to capture Aaron Burr's flotilla that his activity was publicly praised by Jefferson. He was elected to the federal Senate on Jan. 1, 1807, to fill the place of Worthington, whose term was about to expire but resigned after adjournment in March 1809. He supported the measures of the administration, including the embargo policy, and served on a number of committees having to do with Western problems; and his advice seems to have carried weight. In July 1808 his wife died. On Apr. 16 of the following year he married Mary Porter, who had recently removed to Ohio from Delaware. Four daughters and a son were born to this second marriage. Although he seems to have desired to retire to his farm and to

his medical practice he could not keep out of politics. He served as speaker of the state House of Representatives in the sessions of 1809–10 and 1810–11. In the controversy involving the right of the state courts to nullify acts of the state legislature on the grounds of unconstitutionality, being a thorough-going Jeffersonian, he was a party to the passage of the "sweeping-resolutions" by which the conservative court was ousted.

When in 1812, Congress created a general land office to be administered by a commissioner, Madison, apparently without solicitation, appointed him to the position. He entered into his new duties with characteristic energy; he brought order out of the chaotic records and surveys and was able, in December 1813, to present a creditable report to the Thirteenth Congress. When the British invaded the capital, he was sufficiently far-sighted to remove his records to a place of safety. However, he longed for his home in Ohio and with the consent of Madison exchanged positions, in the fall of 1814, with Josiah Meigs, surveyor-general of the Northwest and carried on the routine of this office almost to the day of his death. He grew old among his friends who continued to respect his political opinions, his skill as a physician, and his sincerity as a Methodist exhorter. Tiffin, Ohio, was named in his honor.

[Tiffin MSS. in Ohio State Lib., Columbus, and Western Reserve Hist. Soc. Lib., Cleveland; W. E. Gilmore, *Life of Edward Tiffin* (1897); C. G. Comegys, *Reminiscences of . . . Edward Tiffin* (1869); W. T. Utter, "Judicial Review in Early Ohio," *Miss. Valley Hist. Rev.*, June 1927 and "Ohio and the English Common Law," *Ibid.*, Dec. 1929; W. Lang, *Hist. of Seneca County* (1880); *Scioto Gazette* (Chillicothe), Aug. 12, 1829.]
W. T. U.

TIGERT, JOHN JAMES (Nov. 25, 1856–Nov. 21, 1906), clergyman, editor, elected a bishop of the Methodist Episcopal Church, South, six months before his death, was born in Louisville, Ky., the son of John and Mary (Van Veghten) Tigert. His father was a pump maker. Carefully reared by his Methodist parents, the boy obtained his early education in the schools of Louisville, and in 1875 matriculated at the newly opened theological school of Vanderbilt University, Nashville, Tenn. Completing his studies there in two years, he received license to preach in 1877 and the same year joined the Louisville Conference of the Methodist Episcopal Church, South.

For four years he served small churches near his native city, continuing, also, his studies in the Baptist Seminary of Louisville. In 1881 he returned to Vanderbilt as instructor in sub-collegiate courses and candidate for the degree of master of arts. Here he began to show that enormous capacity for work which was to characterize his entire career. His hours during this period were regularly from seven o'clock one morning to one the next. In 1884, having obtained his master's degree, he was appointed professor of philosophy in the University. This relation continued six years. Meanwhile, he had become much interested in history and English, developing a lucid and robust style of writing. In 1885 he published a textbook on logic.

Tigert gave up his professorship in 1890 to engage again in the work of the active ministry. Assigned to a pastorate in Kansas City, Mo., he remained there four years. During this time he continued his studies and wrote much. In 1892 he was the fraternal delegate of his Church to the General Conference of the Methodist Episcopal Church. His address on that occasion, "A Voice from the South," and the personal contacts incident to the visit resulted in a series of friendships with the leaders of the sister denomination which continued throughout his life.

Elected in 1894 to the position of Book Editor, he devoted twelve years to editing, revising, annotating, writing, and publishing books, mainly theological. At the same time, 1894–1906, he edited the *Quarterly Review of the Methodist Episcopal Church, South*, known also during this period as the *Methodist Quarterly Review*. For its columns he wrote voluminously and established contacts with numerous scholars and writers throughout the world. His reviews of books were widely read and had much influence. The list of his published volumes grew; among them were *The Preacher Himself* (1889), *Theism; a Survey of the Paths that Lead to God, Chiefly in the Light of the History of Philosophy* (1901), and *The Christianity of Christ and His Apostles* (1905). In 1894 he published his most important work, *A Constitutional History of American Episcopal Methodism*, and later compiled and edited, with a historical introduction, *The Doctrines of the Methodist Episcopal Church in America as Contained in the Disciplines of Said Church from 1788 to 1808* (2 vols., 1902).

In the General Conference of 1906, such was the esteem in which he had come to be held, that on the first ballot he was elected to the episcopacy. In November of that same year, some six months later, having presided at but a single annual conference, he went to Indian Territory to prepare for another. There while taking one day a hurried wayside luncheon he accidentally swallowed a small bone. It lodged in his throat in such a way that a physician when called was unable to locate and remove it. Blood poisoning followed and within two weeks, at the city of Tulsa, four days short of his fiftieth birthday, he died. On Aug. 28, 1878, he was married to Amelia McTyeire, daughter of Bishop H. N. McTyeire [*q.v.*], then president of Vanderbilt University, by whom he had three sons and three daughters. Tigert was a large, vigorous man, of great vitality, rarely ill, never tired. In the pulpit and on the platform he was an impressive figure. His voice was powerful, though a little harsh, his vocabulary was affluent, and his sermon themes invariably human and spiritual.

[*Who's Who in America*, 1906–07; *Methodist Quart. Rev.*, Jan. 1907; *Christian Advocate* (N. Y.), Nov. 29, 1906; *Christian Advocate* (Nashville), Nov. 30, 1906; *Nashville American*, Nov. 22, 1906; personal acquaintance.]
                              G. B. W.

TIKAMTHI [See TECUMSEH, 1768?–1813].

TILDEN, SAMUEL JONES (Feb. 9, 1814–Aug. 4, 1886), governor of New York, presidential nominee, corporation lawyer, was born at New Lebanon, N. Y., the fifth child of Elam Tilden and Polly Younglove Jones. He was descended from Nathaniel Tilden of Tenterden, Kent, who emigrated to New England in 1634 and settled in Scituate, Mass. His father, Elam Tilden, storekeeper, postmaster, and a man of political consequence in his community, was a friend of Martin Van Buren and Silas Wright. During the long ascendency of the Albany Regency, it was not uncommon for Van Buren, Wright, William L. Marcy, Edwin Croswell [*qq.v.*], and others to repair to the Tilden home for conferences. Elam's stock of goods included patent nostrums and drugs. His interest in these dubious specifics amounted to an obsession and led to a morbid interest in his own health. His painstaking descriptions of "symptoms" to Samuel created one of the strangest bonds of sympathy which has ever existed between father and son. These, then, were Samuel Tilden's patrimony: a genuine patriotism, a devotion to the Democratic party based upon tradition and also upon intimate acquaintance with Democratic leaders, and a morbid and introspective interest in his physical health. It may almost be said that he was nurtured on the Constitution and that the writings of Thomas Jefferson were his *Mother Goose*. Certainly his precocity and early environment robbed him of his childhood and, in so doing, perhaps stunted the development of certain social characteristics which would have eased his later life and made him more comprehensible to his contemporaries.

Tilden's formal education was sporadic and disjointed. He spent little time in the village school because of his uncertain health, but was given some private tutoring at home and for a short time attended an academy at Williamstown, Mass., which he left, too, for reasons of health. Following this experience he remained at home for a period of two years and then went in 1832 to New York, where he hoped to continue his preparatory studies and at the same time have access to a higher order of medical skill than was available in his native village. In New York he lived with an aunt, a Mrs. Barnes, who eked out a precarious living by keeping a fashionable boarding house. Tilden found the boarding house atmosphere uncongenial, and much of his time was irritatingly consumed in business transactions for his impractical aunt and his exacting father. He did manage to take a few lessons in elocution and to do a little tutoring. On one of his visits to his home during this period he wrote an article defending President Jackson's veto of the bill for the recharter of the United States Bank. This paper, written by a boy not yet out of his teens, was published by the Democratic party and distributed throughout New York state. On one of these visits to New Lebanon, too, it was decided that he should enter Yale. There was a lengthy discussion of this prospect, as there was of every problem affecting any member of the Tilden family. (For Samuel's own state of mind see a letter written to his father from New York in June 1833, Bigelow, *Life*, I, 31–32.) He entered Yale in June 1834, but left after one term never to return. The diet in commons and the climate were obnoxious, and all connection with this institution was terminated until 1875 when he was given the honorary degree of LL.D. and enrolled with the class of 1837. He returned home and shortly thereafter resumed his residence in New York. He attended the University of the City of New York (later New York University) spasmodically but was concerned mainly for several years with the writing of political treatises, the most noteworthy being a series written for the old *New York Times* (Mar. 23–May 12, 1837) over the pseudonym "Jacksonis Amicus" in which he defended President Van Buren's threat to veto any bill aimed at the abolition of slavery in the District of Columbia (*Writings*, I, 41–54); and two letters for the *Daily Albany Argus* (Sept. 28, Oct. 20, 1837) signed "Crino" and supporting Van Buren's call of a special session of Congress to recommend the establishment of the Independent Treasury. Tilden entered the law school of the University of the City of New York with the first class in 1838 and took the three-year course. At the same time he served a clerkship in the law office of John W. Edmonds [*q.v.*].

He was admitted to the bar at the May term of the supreme court in 1841, and immediately hung out his shingle at No. 11 Pine Street in New York City.

Once launched upon his legal career, Tilden's life became more purposeful and consistent and there was a noticeable decline in "symptoms." The death of his father in 1842 was a severe shock and severed his closest tie with his early life. He entered earnestly into the practice of law, was named corporation counsel of New York City in 1843, and rapidly became a commanding figure in the New York Democracy. The Van Buren-Wright faction of the New York Democracy was demoralized by the nomination of Polk in 1844 and their instinctive reaction was to oppose Polk and by defeating him in New York cause him to lose the election. Tilden at this juncture intervened with temperate counsel and suggested that his friends could place Polk under obligation by saving the state for him and thus the election. Silas Wright, much against his will, was induced to run for governor and to aid in the campaign. Tilden with John L. O'Sullivan [*q.v.*] undertook the establishment and publication of the *New York Morning News*. The state was saved for Polk, but in New York affairs Polk fell under the influence of Marcy and others who were opposed to the Wright faction, and his distribution of federal patronage to Marcy's friends signalized the definite split in the New York Democracy. Marcy led the group known as Hunkers (later Hardshells), who were closely aligned with the Southern Democrats because of their complacent attitude towards the extension of slavery, while Wright, Van Buren, Azariah C. Flagg, Benjamin F. Butler (1795–1858), Tilden and others led the opposition group dubbed Barnburners (later Softshells). This latter faction was committed to free-soil principles, and carried within it the germ of the later Republican party. Tilden did not follow the revolt to that extreme but this schism in the party resulted in his practical divorcement from Democratic leadership until after the Civil War. It is true that at the special request of Governor Wright he served a term in the state legislature in 1846 during which he presented a lucid analysis of the anti-rent disturbances (*Writings*, I, 188–220); that as a member of the constitutional convention of 1846 he distinguished himself in framing legislation to improve state finance; and that he was an unsuccessful candidate for the attorney-generalship in 1855. These activities enriched his political experience without adding appreciably to his political stature.

In his disappointment with the trend of politics Tilden turned his attention and energies to the development of his law practice. He gained his first real prominence at the bar in the case of *Giles* vs. *Flagg,* arising out of frauds in connection with the votes for the comptrollership of New York City in 1855 (*New York Tribune,* Apr. 2–7, 23–25, 1856). In this case he was associated with Charles O'Conor and William M. Evarts in the defense of Azariah C. Flagg. Tilden was given a conspicuous rôle and the resultant publicity added great lustre to his reputation. In 1857 he conducted another spectacular trial involving the murder of Dr. Harvey Burdell and the fraudulent claim of his housekeeper and suspected murderess that by virtue of a secret marriage she was entitled to a widow's third in his estate. In both of these cases Tilden was handicapped by lack of evidence in favor of his own clients and built his arguments on the inconsistencies in the testimony of opposing witnesses.

Following these suits Tilden engaged in a maze of cases of a complex nature, among the most notable of which were *Pennsylvania Coal Company* vs. *The President, Managers and Company of the Delaware and Hudson Canal Company,* and *The Cumberland Coal and Iron Company* vs. *Sherman, Dean and Postley* (O. L. Barbour, *Report of Cases . . . in the Supreme Court of the State of New York,* XXIX, 1860, p. 589; XXX, 1860, p. 553). His peculiar genius, however, seemed to be adapted to that type of litigation and advice incident to the reorganization of railroads. He himself stated that at one time or another more than half of the great railway companies north of the Ohio and between the Hudson and Missouri rivers were his clients. It was in connection with the refinancing and reorganization of railroads and in the acquirement of certain mining interests that he laid the foundation for his enormous fortune which was later augmented as a result of shrewd financing during the period of unstable money which resulted from the Civil War. At his death he possessed one of the largest personal fortunes in America.

Tilden's attitude during the Civil War was one of detachment. He opposed the election of Lincoln and disapproved of the war from the beginning. In a letter to Judge William Kent, printed in the New York *Evening Post* a week before the election of 1860, he pointed out the salient fact that a victory of the Republican party would amount to a practical disfranchisement of the whole South and predicted that it would lead to dire consequences (*Writings and Speeches,* I, 289–330). When war was actually declared Tilden was called to Washington by Secretary of War Stanton (Bigelow, *Life,* I, 169). At that time he advised Stanton to call out the full military strength of the North immediately and by sheer force of superior numbers to crush the uprising by a swift and devastating stroke. Following this early visit to Washington, Tilden took little part in wartime activities. He rather devoted his energies to encouraging the Democratic party in the maintenance of a "constitutional opposition" to the threat of tyranny inherent in the powerful, centralized government at Washington. He favored President Johnson's liberal reconstruction policy, supported him in his efforts to circumvent the savage onslaughts of the Radicals in Congress, and was a not infrequent caller at the White House.

Tilden was elected from New York City as a delegate to the state constitutional convention of 1867, and the year previous he had succeeded Dean Richmond as chairman of the Democratic state committee, a position which he held for the eight years following. It was in this latter capacity that he prosecuted his titanic labors to oust the "Tweed ring" from New York City. Under the dominance of the predatory and unscrupulous William M. Tweed [*q.v.*] the "ring" controlled city politics absolutely, its insidious influence extended even into the state government, and, fortified by a charter made to its measure, it appeared impregnable. In the face of what many leaders believed to be political suicide, Tilden commenced his fight for good government. It is true that in 1870 the *New York Times* instituted a campaign to expose the rogues in the city government, organizing in 1871 the Committee of Seventy to assist in the movement. None the less, the dissipation of the "ring" was justly regarded as Tilden's personal triumph. He went to the legislature in 1872 to lead the battle for adequate legislation with which to combat the situation in the city, and his legal talent and persistent devotion to the mass of intricate details resulted in the production of the judicial proof which finally convicted the guilty persons. The system adopted by him in tracing misappropriated municipal funds to private bank accounts was closely analogous to that employed by him in the Flagg and Burdell cases. In taking the leading part in the smashing of the "Tweed ring" Tilden was responsible also for reforming and purifying the state judiciary, securing an investigation of certain suspect judges by the Bar Association of the City of New York, which he was partly instrumental in organizing, and the impeachment of two judges. A third judge resigned to escape punishment.

Tilden was active in the campaign of 1868, in which Horatio Seymour was defeated for the presidency, and also in that of 1872 in which, fantastically, Horace Greeley was the Democratic presidential nominee. Tilden's influence in politics was becoming more and more potent within his party, and his valiant fight for reform had made him a national figure. It was logical, therefore, that he should be the Democratic candidate for governor of New York in 1874. He was elected by a plurality of 50,000 over Gov. John A. Dix [q.v.]. During his two years as governor he did heroic work in the arena of state affairs, not however without an occasional gesture to the national gallery. He was swept into office as a champion of reform and reform was the constantly recurring theme in his governmental symphony. He brought about a substantial reduction in state taxes and expenditures as a result of the discovery and elimination of frauds and of economies in administration. His most spectacular stroke for reform was the shattering of the "Canal ring," a group of politicians in both parties bound together by the common ties of dishonesty and avarice, who had grown wealthy and powerful through control of the enormous sums expended in repairing and extending the state canal system. Tilden exposed the fraudulent device of revised estimates under which the "ring" cloaked its predatory activities and then undertook an arduous speaking campaign throughout the canal counties of the state exhorting the electors to return honest men to the legislature to break the power of the "ring" and to support the campaign to exterminate fraud (*Writings*, II, 98–116, 214–33, 296–305). His determined effort to reform municipal financing was frustrated because of one obnoxious item in the proposed amendment to the state constitution which was to give it effect. In his first message to the legislature, he advocated the resumption of specie payments by the national government, and the next week protested, in a special message, against the action of General Sheridan under whose orders a squad of United States soldiers entered the legislature of Louisiana and removed five of its members (*Writings*, II, 60–62, 80–84). His intrepid leadership and championship of reform movements had attracted the attention and fired the imagination of the whole country, and his nomination for the presidency on the Democratic ticket was almost inevitable. When the National Democratic Convention met at St. Louis June 27, 1876, Tilden was nominated on the second ballot. His nearest rival, Thomas A. Hendricks [q.v.], who held "soft-money" views, was named for vice-president. The Re-

publicans nominated Rutherford B. Hayes [q.v.] of Ohio.

The campaign was one of exceptional bitterness. The Democrats made savage onslaughts against the waste and extravagance in the Grant administration and their speeches were liberally sprinkled with intimations or outright charges of graft and corruption against men closely identified with the national administration. The Republicans, resorting to the waving of the "bloody shirt," accused the opposition party of rebel sympathies; attempted to stigmatize Tilden's connection with the railroads and to make an issue of his frail health; and imputed fraud in connection with his personal income tax returns. Because of his bad health and his absorption in his duties as governor, he himself manifested such a secretive aloofness that the campaign committee thought him indifferent (Nevins, *post*, pp. 305–19). On Nov. 7, 1876, a majority of approximately 250,000 of the voters indicated their preference for Tilden, and to this day it is uncertain whether this majority was so distributed as to signify election as well as preference by the people of the country. Following conflicting reports on the morning of Nov. 8, it became apparent from the returns that Tilden was assured of 184 electoral votes and Hayes of 163. The still-doubtful states of Oregon, Louisiana, South Carolina, and Florida, with a total of 22 electoral votes, were claimed immediately by the Hayes managers. There ensued an invasion of the South by representatives of both parties who betook themselves to the scenes of dispute. These "visiting statesmen" of both parties were involved in a frenzied welter of probing, cajoling, and bargaining, of plot and counterplot, and the actual circumstances which governed events must have been even more obscure at that time than they are today. The dispute was finally resolved by the creation of an Electoral Commission resulting from a compromise. It came about, partly through force of unforeseen circumstance, that this body had a majority of one in favor of the Republicans. By a strict party vote the commission declared that Hayes had carried all doubtful states. Tilden claimed his constitutional right, acquiescing in the compromise only as an escape from civil war, and always maintained stoutly that he was wrongfully deprived of the presidency.

Following the disputed election Tilden's political activity was restricted, but he remained to the end of his life a significant figure in national politics. In 1877, accompanied by John Bigelow, he took a trip to England, his previous trip having been made alone in 1873. This peaceful interlude was followed in 1878 by a feverish period in which he was involved in the investigation of the "Cipher Despatches." These were concerned with some questionable negotiations of the "visiting statesmen" of the Democratic party about which Tilden disclaimed any personal knowledge. Also, beginning shortly after his nomination in 1876 and continuing intermittently for approximately five years, he was plagued by a personal income tax investigation set in motion by the government, an effort which spent itself eventually in futility. In 1879 he purchased "Greystone," a magnificent estate at Yonkers, where he spent the remainder of his days. In 1880 and again in 1884 he was mentioned for the presidential nomination but he persisted in his refusal to be seriously considered, basing his refusal on his advanced age and physical infirmities. While Tilden supported the policies of the Cleveland administration, the personal relationship between the two men was none too cordial. In his last years Tilden's infirmities were such that he became almost a recluse and his time was spent mainly in reading and in collecting books for his large library.

Tilden died at the age of seventy-two, a bachelor. In his will he provided that the bulk of his estate, involving some six million dollars, should be administered by a Tilden Trust whose object should be the establishment of a free library for the City of New York. Proceedings were brought by certain of the Tilden heirs to break the will and finally the clause establishing a Tilden Trust was declared invalid by the New York Court of Appeals for indefiniteness of subject (130 *New York Court of Appeals,* 29). The vote of the court was four to three. According to a settlement with the heirs, the Tilden Trust was finally established with a capital of approximately three million dollars and in the end the cherished dream of Tilden to establish a free library for New York City was realized, largely through his generosity and instrumentality.

In appearance Tilden in the prime of life was a man of unimpressive mien. Of medium stature, slight build, nervous and awkward in his movements, he attracted little attention in a group of men. His face was round and boyish, his eyes were large and blue, his hair was a chestnut color, his broad brow of the intellectual type, and his voice weak. Throughout his life he was afflicted with a feeble constitution which curtailed his social contacts. Although inordinately secretive, exasperatingly dilatory, and extremely non-committal, he possessed extraordinary power of concentration, had a logical and analytical mind, was endowed with a marvelous, well-stored

memory, and was favored with a remarkable command of language. It was not his personality but his intellect that made him an outstanding corporation lawyer, a sagacious financier, and a political leader for half a century.

[In addition to the contemporary newspapers and magazines, which devoted considerable space to Tilden's reform activities, his accomplishments as governor and his presidential candidacy, there appeared in 1876 two campaign biographies, a semi-official one by T. P. Cook, and another of less value by W. M. Cornell. John Bigelow, *The Life of Samuel J. Tilden* (2 vols., 1895), presents a full but perhaps too apologetic interpretation. The same author's *The Writings and Speeches of Samuel J. Tilden* (2 vols., 1885), and *Letters and Literary Memorials of Samuel J. Tilden* (2 vols., 1908), form the best printed collection of Tilden's papers. His messages to the legislature are found in C. Z. Lincoln, *State of N. Y. Messages from the Governors* (1909), vol. VI. On the election of 1876, see the *Congressional Record*; *Proceedings of the Electoral Commission . . . 1877* (1877); "Presidential Elections Investigations" (5 vols., 1879), *House Miscellaneous Doc. No. 31,* 45 Cong., 3 Sess.; P. L. Haworth, *The Hayes-Tilden Disputed Presidential Election of 1876* (1906), a full study with Republican leaning; A. M. Gibson, *A Political Crime* (1885), inspired and financed by Tilden and presenting his side of the case; Allan Nevins, *Abram S. Hewitt, with Some Account of Peter Cooper* (1935), containing fresh material on the campaign and election. Contemporary writers of both political parties supply additional information. See also D. S. Alexander, *A Pol. Hist. of the State of N. Y.,* vols. II, III (1906–09); obituaries in *N. Y. Times,* Aug. 5, 1886, and other papers. The large collection of personal papers of Tilden, which he preserved with care, are in the N. Y. Pub. Lib., but under the full authority of his will they are to be thoroughly sorted out by the executors before leaving their custody. A new interpretation of his life, based on the study of his papers, is in preparation by A. C. Flick.]   A. C. F.

TILESTON, THOMAS (Aug. 13, 1793–Feb. 29, 1864), printer, merchant, ship-owner, was descended from another Thomas Tileston who crossed from Cheshire to settle in Dorchester, Mass., in 1634. The younger Thomas was born in Boston, second of the numerous children of Lemuel and Mary (Minns) Tileston. He attended the public schools until thirteen, when the family finances led him to become a printer's devil with the firm of Greenough & Stebbins for thirty dollars a year and board. He chose this trade in the hope of absorbing an education and soon revealed literary ability. When the firm moved to Haverhill, Mass., and acquired the *Merrimack Intelligencer,* Tileston became its editor. At twenty-one he supervised the printing of a revised American edition of the King James version of the Bible and soon bought an interest in the firm. On Apr. 11, 1820, he married Mary Porter of Salem (Nov. 30, 1797–Nov. 9, 1879). They had one son, who died in childhood, and eight daughters.

In 1818 Tileston had joined the swarm of New Englanders who were seeking fortunes in New York City just as it was clinching its leadership over the rival American ports. Haverhill had become an active manufacturing center during the War of 1812, but needed an outlet for its shoes and other products. Tileston formed a partnership with Paul Spofford (Feb. 18, 1792–Oct. 28, 1869), who had started as a country storekeeper, to sell these Haverhill wares on commission. They began by sending these to the West Indies, South America, and Southern ports, and in turn imported coffee, sugar, and other products of those regions. This trading, as in the case of Preserved Fish and Charles Morgan [*qq.v.*], led to ship-owning, which soon overshadowed their other business. Their yellow house flag with its blue cross appeared over a steadily increasing flotilla. About 1822 Spofford & Tileston became agents for a line of coasting packets to Boston. For their southern trade they chartered vessels at first but soon bought several brigs and schooners, and later built two excellent packets for the Havana trade. In 1846 they built for the New York-Charleston run the *Southerner,* followed in 1847 by the *Northerner.* These have been called "our two first coastwise steamships" (Morrison, *post,* p. 445), the earlier New England steamboats evidently being excluded from that category. Spofford & Tileston later added to their steam fleet the *Marion, Columbia, James Adger,* and *Nashville,* as well as the fast excursion steamer *Leviathan.* They were among the first to send ships to California during the gold rush. When Edward Knight Collins [*q.v.*] started his famous line of subsidy steamships in 1850, Spofford & Tileston purchased the sailing packets of his "Dramatic Line," later adding the *Webster, Calhoun, Clay,* and *Orient.* Though they were inferior to the Collins and Cunard steamships, these sailing packets, like those of Charles Henry Marshall [*q.v.*], were operated well into the 'sixties. The firm's southern business, like Charles Morgan's, was seriously interrupted by the Civil War. The Confederates made a privateer of the *Nashville;* the *James Adger* was bought for the naval blockading force; and the other steamships were diverted from Charleston to Havana. The firm refused to transfer any vessels to British registry.

Tileston was also a prominent figure in New York financial circles. He was president of the Phoenix Bank from 1840 until his death, and was a founder (1829) and director of the Atlantic Insurance Company. He was an organizer and for nine years chairman of the New York Clearing House. As early as 1846 his fortune was estimated at $300,000 and Spofford's at $200,000. He was a gifted speaker and a tireless worker. His evenly balanced mind, his sa-

gacity, and his promptness helped to account for his success. His portrait, showing a full, cleanshaven face, bears a superficial resemblance to that of Stephen A. Douglas. He remained active and progressive to the end, and was described, just before his death, as "'Young America on the shoulders of seventy years' experience'" (*Hunt's Merchants' Magazine,* Feb. 1864, p. 90). He died very suddenly of heart trouble at his home on Fourteenth Street in New York.

[Mary W. F. Tileston, *Thomas Tileston, 1793–1864* (1925), with geneal. tables; *Hunt's Merchants' Mag.,* Feb., Apr. 1864, with portrait; George Wilson, *Portrait Gallery of the Chamber of Commerce of the State of N. Y.* (1890); J. H. Morrison, *Hist. of Am. Steam Navigation* (1903); F. L. Griswold, *The House Flags of the Merchants of N. Y.* (1926), reprinted in *Clipper Ships and Yachts* (1927); M. Y. Beach, *The Wealth and Biog. of the Wealthy Citizens of N. Y.* (1846); *N. Y. Tribune,* Mar. 1, 1864.]   R. G. A—n.

TILGHMAN, EDWARD (Feb. 11, 1750/51–Nov. 1, 1815), lawyer, was born at Wye, Queen Anne Co., Md., the second son of Edward and Elizabeth (Chew) Tilghman. He was the cousin of William and Tench Tilghman [*qq.v.*], and the great-grandson of Richard Tilghman, a physician who emigrated to Maryland in 1661 from Kent County, England, on the *Elizabeth and Mary.* His father was high sheriff of his county, member of the provincial assembly for many years and one time speaker, officer in the Maryland militia, and a member of the Stamp Act Congress. In 1767 he graduated from the College, Academy, and Charitable School of Philadelphia, now the University of Pennsylvania. On June 24, 1772, he was admitted to study at the Middle Temple in London. During his two years abroad he attended regularly the courts of Westminster Hall, taking extensive notes of the arguments in chancery before the leading jurists, which he later used to advantage before courts as a lawyer. His days in London were spent in serious study and hard work. Upon his return to America he married on May 26, 1774, his first cousin, Elizabeth, the daughter of Benjamin Chew [*q.v.*]. The youngest of their four children became the mother of William Henry Rawle [*q.v.*]. The same year he was admitted to the Philadelphia bar, where he continued to practise until his death. Although the Tilghman family in colonial days enjoyed many favors from the Crown, at the outbreak of the Revolution Edward, like his father, threw his lot with the colonials. In 1776 he enlisted as a private soldier with the Philadelphia associators and later the same year at the battle of Long Island was a brigade major attached to Lord Sterling.

However, he soon returned to Philadelphia to continue his practice as a lawyer.

It was in the field of law that he gained distinction. A biographer, also a leading lawyer, credits him with having possessed "the most accurate legal judgment of any man of his day" at the Philadelphia bar (Binney, *post*, p. 51). His severe and rigid training so imbued him with legal principles that he seemed to seize the true result on some perplexing legal question before he had time to prove it. In the field of contingent remainders and executory devices he was recognized as an authority. In addition to being well versed in the law, he was also an advocate of surpassing powers. There was little ornament in his speech; he commanded attention rather by the weight of what he said than how he said it. A wary tactician in managing a case, eloquent in language, a faultless logician, he was highly feared by opposing lawyers. Judges had deep confidence in his opinions and respected his plain and direct reasoning. Before juries his sense of shrewdness, occasional pleasantry, and constant air of sincerity were almost indomitable. He had a persistent aversion to authorship and public office. In 1806 he was proffered the chief justiceship of the supreme court of Pennsylvania by Governor McKean, but he declined the honor and recommended his cousin, William Tilghman, for the post. He was rather short in stature, spare of flesh and delicate, but well proportioned. Possessed of a buoyant spirit and a sharp wit, his cheerfulness invariably brought a luminous circle about him on all occasions. Neither jester nor satirist, he quoted English and Latin poetry frequently and with ease, and he demonstrated the utmost simplicity in dress and manner. Unlike his colleagues he never wore black at the bar nor powdered his hair. His last years of life were darkened by lack of health and the loss of all of his property.

[Horace Binney, *The Leaders of the Old Bar in Philadelphia* (1859) and in *Pa. Mag. of Hist. & Biog.*, Apr. 1890; *Ibid.*, July 1916; J. H. Martin, *Martin's Bench & Bar of Phila.* (1883); *Md. Hist. Mag.*, Dec. 1906; E. A. Jones, *Am. Members of the Inns of Court* (1924); B. A. Konkle, *Benj. Chew* (1932); *Relfs' Phil. Gazette and Daily Advertiser*, Nov. 2, 1815.]　　J. H. P.

TILGHMAN, MATTHEW (Feb. 17, 1718–May 4, 1790), Revolutionary leader, member of the Continental Congress, the son of Richard and Anna Maria (Lloyd) Tilghman, was born in Queen Anne County, Md. His paternal ancestry has been traced to Richard Tilghman, a civilian of Snodland, Kent County, England, in the fifteenth century. His grandfather, Richard Tilghman, a surgeon, arrived in Maryland in 1661 on the *Elizabeth and Mary*. For transporting to the province twenty persons of British descent he received a grant of one thousand acres of land. He built the Tilghman "Hermitage" in Queen Anne County, continued the practice of his profession, and acquired other lands by purchase. His son Richard, Matthew Tilghman's father, joined two large landholding families by marrying the daughter of Philemon Lloyd and became prominent in public life as a representative of Talbot County in the Maryland Assembly and as a member of the governor's Council. Matthew Tilghman was the youngest of nine children. His early education was under the direction of Hugh Jones [*q.v.*], and at the age of fifteen he was adopted by his cousin, Matthew Tilghman Ward, who endowed him with the riches of experience and influence acquired from long public service, and a large estate at Ward's Point (now Tilghman's Point) in Talbot County.

Tilghman entered public life in 1741 as captain of a troop of horse organized for protection from Indian incursions on the Eastern Shore. The same year he was appointed an associate justice of the Talbot County court. He was promoted to a justice of the quorum in 1749, continued in that capacity until 1769, and was the presiding justice from 1770 to 1775. He took a seat in the Maryland Assembly in 1751, as a representative of Talbot County, served until 1758, represented Queen Anne County in 1760 and 1761, was returned by Talbot County in 1768, and served until the Revolution. In 1773 and 1774 he was speaker of the Assembly. In recognition of his high standing, the lord proprietor, in July 1768, issued commissions appointing him to a seat in the Council and agent to direct the collection of his territorial revenue. But Tilghman declined. Although a large landholder, he had at no time been friendly to the proprietary interests, and since the British Parliament had undertaken to tax the colonies he cast his lot with the popular cause against both Parliament and proprietor. In June 1768 he served on a committee of the Assembly to draft a remonstrance to the king against the Townshend Acts. He signed the non-importation agreement, adopted on June 22, 1769, as a further protest against those Acts. He presided over the Maryland Conventions, 1774–76, which formed the Association of the Freemen of Maryland, adopted a provisional government with a council of safety and committees of observation and correspondence, and chose delegates to the Continental Congress. He was chairman of the committee of correspondence for Talbot County, was president of the council of safety, and headed every Maryland delegation to the Continental Congress from September 1774 to December 1776. Tilghman was one of the Maryland delegates who first expressed themselves openly in favor of independence and recommended a session of the Maryland Convention with a view to the removal of its restrictions in that particular. He presided over that session and the restrictions were removed, but he was not present in Congress when the Declaration of Independence was passed or when it was signed.

The few remaining years of his public life were devoted chiefly to the organization and operation of a government for the State of Maryland. He was chosen president of the convention that met at Annapolis on Aug. 14, 1776, to draft the first constitution of the state, and served as chairman of the committee elected by that body to prepare "a declaration and charter of rights, and a form of government." He was elected in December 1776 to a seat in the state Senate for a term of five years, was reëlected in September 1781, and for a time served as its president. While senator, he voiced his opposition to the confiscation of British property, and, as president of a special council, afforded military protection to property on the Eastern Shore. Immediately following the declaration of peace in 1783, he closed his public career, retired to "Bayside," his estate in Talbot County, where he resided until his death from a paralytic stroke. On Apr. 6, 1741, he was married to Anna Lloyd, the daughter of James Lloyd, and to them were born three sons and two daughters. The younger daughter, Anna Maria, became the wife of her cousin, Tench Tilghman [q.v.], aide-de-camp of General Washington.

[Christopher Johnston, "Tilghman Family," *Md. Hist. Mag.*, June–Dec. 1906; Oswald Tilghman, *Hist. of Talbot County, Md.* (2 vols., 1915); H. F. Powell, *Tercentenary Hist. of Md.* (1925), vol. IV; *Archives of Md.*, vols. XI, XIV, XLVII (1892, 1895, 1930); *Proc. of the Conventions of the Province of Md. . . . 1774, 1775 and 1776* (1836); *Md. Jour. and Baltimore Advertiser*, May 18, 1790.]   N. D. M.

TILGHMAN, RICHARD ALBERT (May 24, 1824–Mar. 24, 1899), chemist, the fourth son of Benjamin and Anna Maria (McMurtrie) Tilghman, was born in Philadelphia, Pa. He was of the sixth generation from Richard Tilghman, and a grandson of Edward Tilghman [q.v.]. He studied at the University of Pennsylvania, graduating with the B.A. degree in 1841. While in college, he became interested in chemistry and physics. As the laboratory facilities were very meager, he was compelled to seek practical experience in the private analytical laboratory of James C. Booth [q.v.], under whom his active interest in research was sustained and directed. His first scientific paper, presented be-

fore the American Philosophical Society in 1847, was entitled "On the Decomposing Power of Water at High Temperatures" (*Proceedings of the American Philosophical Society*, vol. IV, 1847), and dealt with the question of the hydrolysis of hydrated and anhydrous inorganic salts when exposed to water vapor at elevated temperature. This was the first systematic study of hydration, and was later rewritten to include the action upon fats by water at elevated temperature and various pressure conditions. A hydrolysis was effected, by means of which a pure fat acid and glycerine were obtained. The acid was of high grade and the method was sold to the Price Patent Candle Company of London.

At the time of Tilghman's early activity, the chemical industries in America were not well developed and he did much of his work in Scotland, where he completed a method for the production of caustic soda, based upon hydrolysis, that met with some commercial application. His first practical work was concerned with the manufacture of potassium dichromate and his method was adopted by the Baltimore Chrome Works. The production of gas from coal, and the use of gas as a smokeless, dustless fuel in surface evaporation in chemical operations next absorbed Tilghman, but his idea was somewhat in advance of the time and did not receive the notice it deserved. He also proposed to convert coal into gas at the mines and then pipe it to the market, a suggestion that has since been repeated but not yet put into practice. He spent two years evolving a method, later known as the "sulphite process," for the manufacture of paper pulp. The method was not commercially successful at the time, but his patents covered all the basic principles. With a brother, Benjamin Chew Tilghman, he developed the "sand blast" process for shaping objects made of hard, brittle materials, and manufactured chilled iron shot for sandblasting machinery. He was also a director in the George Richards and Company, Ltd., manufacturers of machine tools, and in the Tilghman Sand Blast Company at Broadheath near Manchester, England.

In 1860 he was married to Susan Price Toland, the daughter of Robert and Rebekah Toland. He lived a quiet life, interested only in his work and his home. The fact that he had much trouble with his eyes, owing to an explosion, led to his avoidance of public affairs. A long and painful illness terminated his scientific and business activities a number of years before his death. He was survived by his wife, two sons, and three daughters.

[Isaac J. Wistar, biographical article in *Proc. Am. Phil. Soc., Memorial Volume* (1900); *Trans. Am. Phil. Soc.*, vol. X, n.s. (1853); Dingler's *Polytechnisches*

Jour., vols. CVI, CXXXVIII (1847, 1858); *Public Ledger* (Philadelphia), Mar. 25, 1899.]   O. L. S.

TILGHMAN, TENCH (Dec. 25, 1744–Apr. 18, 1786), Revolutionary soldier, was a descendant of an ancient family of Kent, England, and a great-grandson of Richard Tilghman, who emigrated to Maryland in 1661. He was the eldest son of James Tilghman, a Provincial Counselor of Pennsylvania, and Anna, the daughter of Tench Francis [*q.v.*], a brother of William, and a cousin of Edward Tilghman [*qq.v.*]. He was born at "Fausley" in Talbot County, Md., and was graduated from the College, Academy, and Charitable School of Philadelphia (now the University of Pennsylvania), in 1761. He entered upon a mercantile career in Philadelphia, but liquidated his business at the approach of the Revolution. He acted as secretary and treasurer, in 1775, to the Continental Congress commissioners to the Six Nations, and his private diary, supplementing his official minutes of these proceedings, is a valuable record of Indian character and the social life of Albany and vicinity—the frontier of the period. He was adopted by the Onondagas, but sagely noted that the customary bowls of punch that he furnished may have been the reason for this complimentary ceremony. On his return to Philadelphia he became captain of an independent company which joined the Flying Camp in 1776. In August he joined the military "family" of General Washington as a volunteer and served continuously as aide-de-camp until the end of the war.

The amount of secretarial work, in addition to military duties, that he performed for Washington was prodigious. Washington's letters to and about Tilghman constitute a most unusual acknowledgment of friendship, of valued services, and a high eulogy of patriotic devotion. Washington successfully urged Congress to grant Tilghman a regular commission of lieutenant-colonel and aide, in place of his volunteer appointment, in these words: "He has been a zealous Servant and slave to the public, and a faithful assistant to me for near five years, great part of which time he refused to receive pay. Honor and gratitude Interest me in his favor, and makes me sollicitous to obtain his Commission" (Papers of George Washington, Letter to Sullivan, May 11, 1781). His selection to carry to the Continental Congress the announcement of the surrender of Cornwallis was the highest military honor in the gift of the commander-in-chief. He was given a horse, properly caparisoned, and a sword, by Congress, on Oct. 29, 1781, in recognition of his services.

Tilghman was married on June 9, 1783, to his cousin, Anna Maria Tilghman, daughter of Matthew [*q.v.*]. After the war he entered into a business association with Robert Morris [*q.v.*], but the hardships encountered during the war caused his death two years later. He was survived by his widow and two daughters. Washington referred to him as a pillar of the Revolution and as having left "as fair a reputation as ever belonged to a human character ..." (Washington Letter Book, volume VII, p. 130, Letter to Jefferson). He was buried in St. Paul's churchyard in Baltimore. The best portrait of Tilghman was painted by Peale, and hangs in the State House at Annapolis.

[Papers of the Continental Congress and the George Washington Papers, Library of Congress; S. A. Harrison, *Memoir of Lieut. Col. Tench Tilghman* (1876), containing his diaries of 1775 and 1781, with certain correspondence; Oswald Tilghman, *Hist. of Talbot County, Md.* (2 vols., 1915); information furnished personally by Harrison Tilghman, of Easton, Md.; Christopher Johnston, "Tilghman Family," *Md. Hist. Mag.*, June–Dec. 1906; *Md. Jour. and Baltimore Advertiser*, Apr. 21, 1786.]   J. C. F—k.

TILGHMAN, WILLIAM (Aug. 12, 1756–Apr. 29, 1827), jurist, was born at "Fausley" in Talbot County, Md., the son of James and Anna (Francis) Tilghman. He was the cousin of Edward Tilghman, the nephew of Matthew Tilghman, the brother of Tench Tilghman, and the grandson of Tench Francis [*qq.v.*]. He was the great-grandson of Richard Tilghman, a physician who emigrated from England to Maryland in 1661. His father, also a lawyer, sat in the Maryland Assembly and, after moving to Philadelphia about 1762, was secretary of the proprietary land office. The boy entered the College, Academy, and Charitable School of Philadelphia, now the University of Pennsylvania, in 1763 and in 1769 entered the college department, from which he was graduated in 1772. For the next four years, 1772 to 1776, he read law in the office of Benjamin Chew [*q.v.*]. In the Revolutionary War, both he and his father were loyalist and late in 1776 retired to the family estate in Maryland. He lived quietly reading law and classical literature and in 1783 was admitted to practice in Maryland. He first entered public life as a member of the Maryland Assembly, 1788, 1789, and 1790. A silent adherent of the federal Constitution rather than an enthusiastic supporter of it, he was a delegate to the Maryland convention for ratification. In 1791 he became a member of the Maryland Senate, but in 1793 he resigned and removed to Philadelphia, where he was admitted to the bar on Sept. 1, 1794. On July 1 of that year he had married Margaret Elizabeth, the daughter of James Allen. They had one daughter. On Mar. 3, 1801,

President Adams appointed him one of the "midnight judges," chief judge of the third circuit court. When this court was abolished in 1802 he resumed his law practice until his appointment in 1805 as president judge of the court of common pleas for the district embracing Philadelphia and the surrounding counties, and he also became a judge of the Pennsylvania high court of errors and appeals. In 1806 he was commissioned chief justice of the Pennsylvania supreme court, over which he presided until his death. As a judge he was careful to remain aloof from the bitter partisanship of Pennsylvania politics. During his tenure the judges of the supreme court prepared for the legislature a report of the English statutes in force in Pennsylvania (see *Digest of Select British Statutes,* 2nd ed. 1817). His chief contribution as a jurist was the incorporation of the principles of scientific equity with the law of Pennsylvania.

His *Address Delivered before the Philadelphia Society for Promoting Agriculture* (1820), of which society he was an active member, reflects his keen interest in agriculture and his experiments on the family estate in Maryland. He was one of the early advocates of a line of canals between the Susquehanna and Alleghany rivers. A firm believer in the development of home industry, for the last ten years of his life he refused to wear any article of cloth not made in the United States. He was president of the American Philosophical Society from 1824 until his death and a trustee of the University of Pennsylvania from 1802 until his death. Slight of frame, unpretentious in manner, his gentle and amiable disposition commanded high respect from members of the bar. He was the author of *An Eulogium in Commemoration of Doctor Caspar Wistar* (1818), which was delivered before the American Philosophical Society. He died in Philadelphia.

[John Golder, *Life of . . . William Tilghman* (1829); Horace Binney, *A Eulogium upon . . . Wm. Tilghman* (1827) and in 16 *Sergeant and Rawle's Pa. Reports,* 439–56; D. P. Brown, *The Forum,* vol. I (1856); J. H. Martin, *Martin's Bench & Bar of Philadelphia* (1883); Oswald Tilghman, *Hist. of Talbot County, Md.* (1915), vol. II; B. A. Konkle, *Benj. Chew* (1932); *Am. Phil. Soc. Proc.,* "Memorial Vol." I (1900), p. 192; *Univ. of Pa., Biog. Cat. of the Matriculates of the College* (1894); *Md. Hist. Mag.,* Dec. 1906; *Pa. Mag. of Hist. and Biog.* (July 1877, Apr., Oct. 1893); *National Gazette* (Philadelphia), Apr. 30, May 1, 1827.]

J. H. P.

TILGHMAN, WILLIAM MATTHEW (July 4, 1854–Nov. 1, 1924), frontier peace officer, known as "Bill" Tilghman, was born in Fort Dodge, Iowa, the son of William Matthew and Amanda (Shepherd) Tilghman, and a descendant of the Richard Tilghman, of England, who settled in Maryland in 1661. In 1856 the family moved to a farm near Atchison, Kan. His father and elder brother served in the Civil War, leaving the boy as the main support of the mother and four children. He early became an expert in the use of firearms. At the age of sixteen, with three other boys, he made a successful trip to the buffalo country, then thronging with hostile Indians, and in the following year adopted the Fort Dodge (Kan.) region as his home. He became a noted buffalo hunter, was at times a scout operating from Fort Dodge, and at a later time a cattleman. In 1877 he served as a deputy sheriff of Ford County under "Bat" (William B.) Masterson [q.v.], and was for a time marshal of Dodge City. In 1878 he was married to Flora Kendal and started a stock ranch on the Arkansas River. He was one of the participants in the spectacular settlers' race that marked the opening of Oklahoma, on Apr. 22, 1889, and obtained a good location in the present Guthrie. In 1891 he took up a claim at Chandler, which he developed into a fine farm. In the same year he was appointed a deputy United States marshal, and though a Democrat, continued to hold the office for about twenty years. The region was for a number of years overrun by outlaw gangs, and it was largely through Tilghman's efforts that they were broken up or exterminated.

In 1910 he was elected to the state Senate, but in the following year he resigned to become chief of police of Oklahoma City, a post he retained for two years. After the death of his first wife, by whom he had four children, he was married on July 15, 1903, to Zoe Agnes Stratton, of an old pioneer family. By the second marriage he had three children. In 1915 he superintended the making of a moving picture, "The Passing of the Oklahoma Outlaws," which for several years he exhibited. He had retired from active business when, in August 1924, the citizens of Cromwell, a "boom" oil town, asked him to become marshal. He accepted, and three months later was assassinated on the street. His body was taken to Oklahoma City, where it lay in state in the capitol, and his funeral was largely attended. His wife and several children survived him.

Tilghman was of powerful build, five feet eleven inches in height. His manner was gentle, he was generous, kindly, and notably fond of children. He had many devoted friends. In personal habits he was abstemious. He was a student and possessed an exceptional knowledge of Western history and a fluent command of the Spanish language. His reputation for courage is not exceeded by that of any other frontiersman of his time, and his skill with a revolver was uncanny. It was in answer to a question by President Theodore Roosevelt, who had eagerly sought his acquaintance, that he explained that the secret of his survival from so many desperate encounters was his ability to fire a sixteenth of a second before the other man, and that this shade of advantage was due to the fact that he represented the law (see Macdonald, *post*, pp. 64–65).

[Information from Mrs. Zoe A. Tilghman, of Oklahoma City; H. R. Stratton, *A Book of Strattons*, vol. II (1918); J. B. Thoburn, *A Standard Hist. of Okla.* (1916), vol. III; A. B. Macdonald, *Hands Up!* (1927); *Muskogee Daily Phoenix*, Nov. 2, 1924.] W. J. G.

TILLMAN, BENJAMIN RYAN (Aug. 11, 1847–July 3, 1918), governor of South Carolina and United States senator, was born in Edgefield County, S. C., the youngest of the seven sons of Sophia (Hancock) and Benjamin Ryan Tillman. His ancestors, both paternal and maternal, had settled in South Carolina before the Revolution. His father, a farmer who supplemented his income by using his house as an inn for stage passengers, died in 1849; two brothers were killed in war; one died of fever; two others were killed in personal encounters; and in 1856 Tillman's brother George, who had become a lawyer and politician at Edgefield Court House, killed a bystander in a gambling feud and as a consequence served two years in jail. Ben aided his mother in the management of her many slaves, studied in a local private school, and in 1861 entered Bethany, a rustic academy near his home. An apt student of English and Latin, he left school in 1864 to join the Confederate army, but was prevented from carrying out his plan by an illness which incapacitated him for two years and resulted in the loss of his left eye. On Jan. 8, 1868, he married Sallie Starke of Elbert County, Ga., by whom he had seven children. Tillman and his wife lived on a four-hundred acre estate adjoining his mother's property, and for the next seventeen years he gave most of his time to wresting a meager living from his red lands. He participated in the Hamburg and Ellenton Riots of 1876, and aided in the Democratic triumph of that year by frightening prospective colored voters away from the polls. In 1880 he ardently championed the political ambitions of Gen. Martin Witherspoon Gary [*q.v.*] in the Edgefield County Democratic convention, and in 1882 was an inconspicuous figure in the state convention of his party. Up to this time no one dreamed that he was destined to have a conspicuous political career. Careless in manners, unattractive in personal appearance, and possessed of a rasping voice and irascible disposition, he was not even liked by his neighbors.

But in 1885, moved by his reverses as a farmer, he forced himself on the attention of the people of South Carolina. In a speech on Aug. 6 at Bennettsville, he aroused the enthusiasm of the farmers by bluntly asserting that their interests were being betrayed by lawyers and merchants, and by demanding that the state undertake a system of agricultural education. This address was followed by a series of masterful letters to the Charleston *News and Courier* in which he caustically arraigned the rulers of the state and urged the farmers to organize. Although the personal character of his indictments aroused bitter opposition, he was able to organize the Farmers' Association, and in 1886 almost captured control of the state government. Fresh stimulus was given to his agitations by the death of Thomas Green Clemson [*q.v.*] in April 1888, who left a site and an endowment for a proposed state agricultural college. During the following summer, Tillman so awakened the rural masses that he was almost able to name the Democratic nominee for governor, and was able to force the governor and legislature to accept the Clemson bequest. Convinced that he was the only man who had "the brains, the nerve and the ability to organize the common people against the aristocracy" (*News and Courier*, Mar. 28, 1890), Tillman in 1890 became the farmers' candidate for the Democratic nomination for governor. The result of the canvass, which created almost unparalleled excitement, was the nomination of Tillman by the state Democratic convention of August 1890, and his election by a great majority over Alexander C. Haskell, an independent Democrat, in the following November. Tillman was easily reëlected in 1892 after a canvass as turbulent as that of 1890. He served as governor from Dec. 4, 1890, to Nov. 27, 1894.

For a number of years Tillman was complete master of the political fortunes of South Carolina. At his dictation distinguished men long in office—Wade Hampton (1818–1902), Samuel McGowan [*qq.v.*], and Judge William H. Wallace—were replaced by his partisans. When the legislature of 1890 refused to do his exact bidding, he stigmatized it as "dead, rotten driftwood" on "the tide which swept from the mountains to the seaboard" (*Ibid.*, Dec. 30, 1891), and the voters in 1892 enthusiastically gave him a legislative body thoroughly obedient to his will. In 1894 he defeated Matthew Calbraith Butler [*q.v.*] for United States senator, and made John Gary Evans, the youthful nephew of Gary, his successor as governor. The following year, in the face of bitter opposition, he was able to secure a convention which rewrote the constitution of the state as he bade. Moreover, he accomplished constructive reforms. Clemson College was opened in 1893, and two years later Winthrop College, a state controlled normal and industrial school for women. The state railroad commission was given power to fix rates; taxes were equalized and expenditures for public education increased; representation in the legislature was reapportioned and congressional districts were redrawn so as to discriminate against the negroes. The most radical innovation of the Tillman administration was the establishment in 1893 of the state dispensary, a public monopoly over the sale of alcoholic beverages. Tillman also wrote into the constitution of the state a provision for educational and property qualifications that legally disfranchised the negroes. Having aroused the political consciousness of the white masses, he made more effective their participation in politics by securing in 1896 the primary method of nominating state officers.

On his election to the Senate Tillman achieved national notoriety as an extreme champion of Southern agrarianism. "Send me to Washington," he had yelled at the frantic mobs responsible for his election, "and I'll stick my pitchfork into his [Cleveland's] old ribs !" (*Chronicle*, Augusta, Ga., June 18, 1894). The maiden effort of "Pitchfork Ben," as he was now called, was a coarse indictment of Cleveland. Aspiring to the Democratic nomination for president in 1896, he ruined his chances by his violent speech before the national convention. Dark and savage-featured, snapping his jaws together, his hands high above his head, and hissing out a denunciation of Cleveland, he failed to touch the multitude; the nomination went to William Jennings Bryan [*q.v.*]. Tillman followed his efforts at the Democratic convention by a series of addresses in the Senate denouncing the policies of the Republicans. Although he favored naval expansion and the war with Spain, he opposed the annexation of Hawaii and the Philippines, and Roosevelt's Panama policy. Charging that the "armor trust" was making excess profits out of the government, he advocated the establishment of government shops for the manufacture of armor plate for battleships (*Congressional Record*, 54 Cong., 2 Sess., pp. 2556–60). Although this move was defeated, he had succeeded in exposing before an interested public the machinations of the steel magnates. He also presented to the nation the views of Southern extremists on the race question in a series of addresses in the Senate and on the Chautauqua platform. He justified lynching in cases of rape and the use of force in disfranchising the negro, and advocated the repeal of the Fifteenth Amendment. Toward President Roosevelt he developed a hatred similar to that he had manifested toward Cleveland. This was induced by the President's withdrawal in 1902 of an invitation to a White House state dinner after Tillman had engaged in a personal altercation with John L. McLaurin on the floor of the Senate. Tillman accused Roosevelt of hypocrisy in dealing with the trusts and of dictatorial ambitions. In retaliation the President published documents intended to show that the senator, while trying to forestall alleged illegal purchases of public lands in Oregon, was using his official influence to effect advantageous purchases of Oregon lands for himself. Although fraud was not proved, these disclosures were embarrassing for a professed champion of the public interest against private greed. Personal aversion for the President did not, however, prevent Tillman from championing administration measures which he favored. The most constructive act of his legislative career was the steering of the Hepburn Rate Bill, an administration measure, through the Senate.

After his elevation to the Senate he continued to be a powerful factor in South Carolina politics. With little difficulty he secured his reëlection in 1900, 1906, and 1912; until his death he was able to control the state's vote at the national Democratic conventions; and his advice was always sought by the political leaders of the state. Largely through his influence his nephew, Lieutenant-Governor James H. Tillman, was acquitted in 1903 of the assassination of N. G. Gonzales, an editor who was the impassioned foe of Tillmanism. After engaging on Feb. 22, 1902, on the floor of the Senate in a fist fight with John L. McLaurin, his colleague and former friend, he demonstrated his power by forcing the retirement of McLaurin to private life. But after 1902 his influence in South Carolina affairs gradually declined. A growing conservatism, stimulated by the gratification of personal ambitions, led him to view complacently the return of traditional influences in politics. His irascible disposition led to quarrels with old friends without the gain of more than the stimulated affections of former enemies. In 1908 and 1910 paralytic strokes deprived him of the ability to harangue the people. In 1902 Duncan C. Heyward, a member of an old low-country family, was elected governor. The state dispensary, Tillman's pet institution, grew corrupt, and was abolished by the legislature in 1907; and state-wide prohibition was adopted in 1915. A Tillman-created state supreme court in 1910 decided against him in a contest with his daughter-in-law, a member of the aristocratic Pickens family, for the possession of his two infant grandchildren. In 1912 he was unable to prevent the reëlection of Coleman L. Blease, a Tillman partisan with whom he had quarreled. Tillman is remembered for his constructive achievements, notably Clemson and Winthrop colleges, and the advance of white democracy, but he is also remembered for having overturned honored traditions and for arousing bitter passions. When South Carolinians want to recall a hero from the immediate past, they more often think of Wade Hampton than Ben Tillman.

[See *Who's Who in America*, 1918–19; F. B. Simkins, *The Tillman Movement in S. C.* (1926), which summarizes Tillman's early career; Thornwell Haynes, *Biog. Sketch of Gov. B. R. Tillman of S. C.* (copr. 1894); *Benjamin Ryan Tillman . . . Memorial Addresses . . . in the Senate and House of Representatives* (1919); J. C. Hemphill, ed., *Men of Mark in S. C.*, vol. I (1907); J. B. Knight and August Kohn, in Yates Snowden, *Hist. of S. C.* (1920), vol. V, pp. 101–03, reprinted from *News and Courier* (Charleston), July 4, 1918; files of the *News and Courier*, 1885–1918, and *State* (Columbia, S. C.), 1891–1918; *Independent*, Feb. 27, 1902, p. 527, July 12, 1906, pp. 68–70, Jan. 21, 1909, p. 115; Zach McGhee, in *World's Work*, Sept. 1906; *Current Lit.*, Feb. 1909, pp. 118–21; obituary in *Lit. Digest*, July 27, 1918, pp. 32–36. The Tillman Papers are in the lib. of the Univ. of S. C.]   F. B. S.

TILTON, EDWARD LIPPINCOTT (Oct. 19, 1861–Jan. 5, 1933), architect, born in New York City, was the son of Benjamin White and Mary (Baker) Tilton, and a direct descendant of John Tilton, who emigrated to Lynn, Mass., from England between 1630 and 1640. He was educated in private schools in Mount Vernon and Chappaqua, N. Y. (1870–80), and studied architectural drawing with a private tutor (1879–80). In 1880, after experience in business, first with the firm of R. R. Haydock and later with Corlies, Macy and Company, he entered the offices of the architects McKim, Mead & White. The following year, on their advice, he went to Paris for three years at the École des Beaux Arts. He returned to New York in 1890 and in 1891 formed a partnership with William A. Boring, the firm at first being Boring, Tilton & Mellen, later Boring & Tilton. Long interested in archaeology, in 1895, through William Robert Ware [*q.v.*], Tilton was appointed architect to the group sponsored by the American School of Classical Studies in Athens to excavate the Argive Heræum. Boring and Tilton's first important commission was that for the United States immigrant station on Ellis Island, won by competition and completed in 1900. Largely because of its efficient solution of this complicated problem, the firm was awarded a gold medal at the Paris Exposition of 1900. Other important works of the firm are Tome Institute, Port Deposit,

Md., the Seamen's Institute, New York City, and the Town Hall, East Orange, N. J. After the withdrawal of Boring in 1915 to become director of the Columbia University School of Architecture, Tilton associated himself with Alfred M. Githens, the firm name in 1921 becoming Tilton and Githens.

The public library at Mount Vernon, N. Y., built in 1910, was the first of a long series of buildings with which Tilton's name is especially connected, and the modern public library form (with ground-floor stack space and reading-room above) is in no small measure due to his logical analysis of library problems. His views on control of books and readers, efficiency and directness of service, and open cheerfulness of effect are fully expressed in his "Library Planning" (*Architectural Forum*, Dec. 1927) and "Library Planning and Design" (*Ibid.*, June 1932). During the World War Tilton designed over sixty libraries and over thirty theatres for various army camps and cantonments. Characteristic examples of his work are the public libraries at Somerville and Springfield, Mass., and especially the more recent McGregor Public Library (1925) of Highland Park, Mich., and the Wilmington, Del., library (1930), awarded the Gold Medal of the American Institute of Architects. In the last two the stack and service floor is sunk into the ground in order to secure entrance to the reading-room floor from the street. Both are also characterized by an original handling of classic motives, the wings becoming almost all glass on the sides, with a more solid central entrance. Other important libraries designed by Tilton are the Knight Memorial Library, Providence, R. I., the library of Emory University, Atlanta, Ga., several branch libraries in Washington, D. C., and the library of Girard College, Philadelphia, Pa. In addition, Tilton served as consulting architect to many libraries, and Tilton and Githens were associated with Clyde and Nelson Fritz in the Enoch Pratt Free Library of Baltimore, Md. Notable works of other types include the Central High School, Johnstown, Pa., the Museum of Fine Arts and the Museum of Natural History at Springfield, Mass., and the county administration building for Bergen County, N. J.

Tilton's work is remarkable for its careful study of practical requirements. He was a classicist in taste, inspired in his early work by the Italian Renaissance and in his later by the work of ancient Greece and Rome, but he was never the copier or the unthinking plagiarist, and in his novel and charming buildings at Highland Park and Wilmington achieved a new synthesis of classic detail and modern needs. He was a man of wide and scholarly interests, and a charming speaker. He was one of the organizers of the Society of Beaux Arts Architects, and for twenty-five years treasurer of the fund for the Paris prize; a member of the Architectural League; a fellow of the American Institute of Architects; a fellow of the Archaeological Institute of America, and its treasurer at the time of his death. In religion he was a Quaker. In addition to his architectural articles he was the author of *The Architecture of the Small Library* (Lansing, Mich., 1911), and "The Architecture of the Argive Heræum" in *The Argive Heræum* (2 vols., 1902–05), by Sir Charles Waldstein and others. He married Mary Eastman Bigelow of Mount Vernon, N. Y., on June 5, 1901, and had a son and a daughter. He died in Scarsdale, N. Y., survived by his wife and his son.

[F. T. Tilton, *Hist. of the Tilton Family in America*, vol. I, no. 1 (1927); *Who's Who in America*, 1932–33; *The Works of Edward Lippincott Tilton* (N. Y., n.d.); I. N. P. Stokes, *The Iconography of Manhattan Island*, vol. V (1926); *Am. Art Ann.*, 1933; obituaries in *N. Y. Times*, Jan. 6, *N. Y. Herald Tribune*, Jan. 7, 1933; information from W. A. Boring and C. E. Tilton.]

T.F.H.

TILTON, JAMES (June 1, 1745–May 14, 1822), army surgeon, was born on a farm in Kent County, Del., at that time a part of Pennsylvania. All records of his parents have been lost, but he is said to have been descended from John Tilton who emigrated to Lynn, Mass., between 1630 and 1640 (Tilton, *post*). His mother, left a widow, sent him to Nottingham Academy at Nottingham, Md. Later after studying with a local physician he entered the newly created medical department of the College of Philadelphia and was given the degree of B.M. with the first class from that school in 1768. His graduation thesis was on respiration. He settled for practice in Dover, Del., but returned to his old school to obtain the degree of M.D. in 1771 with an essay entitled *"De Hydrope."* The outbreak of the Revolutionary War found him a medical practitioner in Dover and a lieutenant of infantry in the local militia. With the organization of the Delaware Regiment in 1776 he was appointed regimental surgeon. He served with the regiment through that year in the battle of Long Island, at White Plains, at Trenton, and until it was virtually wiped out at the battle of Princeton on Jan. 2, 1777. From that time until October 1780 he was in charge of hospitals at Princeton, Trenton, and New Windsor, Md. He wrote scathing reports upon the condition of these hospitals and of the system which made it possible. He devised and later established a hos-

pital group of small well-ventilated log huts, each to accommodate but six patients. A great decrease in hospital mortality followed this innovation. In 1780 he was promoted to senior hospital physician and surgeon, and in this capacity he operated a hospital at Williamsburg, Va., during the Yorktown campaign. With the close of hostilities he returned to his practice at Dover. In the meantime he had been offered and had declined the chair of materia medica in his old medical school, reorganized as the medical department of the University of Pennsylvania in 1779. He served one term (1783–85) in the Continental Congress and several as a member of the state House of Representatives. From 1785 to 1801 he occupied the position of government commissioner of loans for Delaware.

Giving up the active practice of medicine, he bought a farm in the hill country adjoining Wilmington and varied the work of cultivation of his fields by an occasional essay on some agricultural subject. In February 1813, while the country was at war with Britain, he published a small treatise entitled *Economical Observations on Military Hospitals: and the Prevention and Cure of Diseases Incident to an Army.* It was dedicated to Gen. John Armstrong [*q.v.*], secretary of war, and embodied his observations during the Revolutionary War, and repeated his former recommendations regarding the construction and administration of military hospitals. Probably as a result of this book, he was offered the position of physician and surgeon-general of the army, an office created by a reorganization of the staff departments under an act of Mar. 13, 1813. Immediately upon taking office he made a tour of inspection along the northern frontier, where he found such a contempt for all sanitary measures and such direful results as to tax to the utmost his administrative ability. His efforts to remedy these defects and to rehabilitate the medical and hygienic service of the army resulted in the publication of the *Regulations for the Medical Department* issued in general orders of December 1814. This, the most important result of his administration, defined clearly for the first time the duties of medical officers and other sanitary personnel. His office was terminated by an act of Congress of June 1815.

While still in office he developed a malignant tumor of the leg, which materially affected his usefulness to the military service and which resulted in an amputation at the knee in December 1815. Despite his seventy years he withstood the pre-anaesthetic agonies of this operation with stoical fortitude. He passed the remainder of his days in his stone mansion overlooking Wilmington, occupied with the care of his orchard and garden. Physically he was of unusual height and of spare build. He was of a jovial disposition, and though a bachelor he was fond of company. He was exceedingly eccentric in his habits, and in his medical practice was a warm advocate of the use of mercury for practically all acute disease.

[F. T. Tilton, *Hist. of the Tilton Family in America*, vol. I, nos. 1–7 (1928–29); James Thacher, *Am. Medic. Biog.* (1828), vol. II, pp. 129–40; H. E. Brown, *The Medic. Dept. of the U. S. Army* (1873); J. E. Pilcher, *The Surgeon Generals of the Army of the U. S.* (1905), with portrait; F. R. Packard, *Hist. of Medicine in the U. S.* (2 vols., 1931); J. T. Scharf, *Hist. of Del.* (1888), vol. I; Elizabeth Montgomery, *Reminiscences of Wilmington* (1851), pp. 53–57; obituary in *Del. Gazette* (Wilmington), May 17, 1822.]   J. M. P—n.

TILTON, JOHN ROLLIN (June 8, 1828–Mar. 22, 1888), landscape painter, was born at Loudon, N. H., the son of Daniel Tilton. He began his career at a time when there was little opportunity for study and little encouragement for the painter; what knowledge and skill he gained were of his own getting. After a common-school education, he went to Rome in 1852, and lived in Italy for over thirty-five years, traveling again and again to its famous places, visiting the Alps, the Rhine, Spain, Greece and its islands, Egypt, and Switzerland, specializing in pictures of places famous for their historical associations. His studio in the Barberini Palace in Rome was for years a favorite resort for American and English tourists, who were eager to buy pictures of the places they had visited and enjoyed. Many of his landscapes found their way into the collections of the British nobility and gentry. He exhibited "The Palace of Thebes" at the Royal Academy, London, 1873, and his "Lagoons of Venice" and "Komombo" at the Centennial Exhibition, Philadelphia, 1876. He also sent his work to the National Academy, New York, and to the Boston Athenaeum. His "Venetian Fishing Boats" and "Rome from Mount Aventine" belong to the Corcoran Gallery, Washington, D. C. In addition to many medals and honors, he received much extravagant praise on both sides of the Atlantic. The *London Daily News* solemnly announced that he was "the first American painter since Benjamin West to receive special commendation from the President of the Royal Academy" (*The Corcoran Gallery of Art: Catalogue of Paintings*, 1920, p. 90). H. T. Tuckerman found "a ghostly charm" in one of his pictures of the Alps, and went into raptures over some other indifferent performances which he characterized as "most faithfully and artistically rendered," "very attractive,"

"charming," "greatly admired in Rome" (Tuckerman, *post*, p. 558).

Tilton was a prominent example of the American artists who have won fame for themselves by persevering industry. He studied life and nature in many countries, and his paintings of Naples and Venice, of Greece and Egypt were as well known in England and all over Europe as they were in his own country. His wife, Caroline Tilton, published some translations from the Italian. There were two children. Tilton died in Rome. In the winter of 1889, about a year after his death, a sale exhibition of his oil paintings and watercolors was held at the gallery of Leonard & Company, Boston, the collection being composed of two hundred and ninety-six works belonging to his estate; all but thirteen of these were watercolors.

[Tilton's name is given in the records of Loudon, N. H., as John B. Rollins Tilton. For biog. material see H. T. Tuckerman, *Book of the Artists* (1870); J. D. Champlin, Jr., and C. C. Perkins, *Cyc. of Painters and Paintings*, vol. IV (1887); *Atlantic Monthly*, Mar. 1869, Feb. 1881; *Standard* (London), Feb. 5, 1874; *Times* (London), Jan. 8, 1878; *New England Mag.*, Nov. 1895; *Boston Transcript*, Jan. 26, 1889; intro., cat. of sale of Tilton's paintings, Boston, 1889; obituary in *N. Y. Times*, Mar. 24, 1888. Information has been supplied by the registrar of vital statistics and the N. H. Hist. Soc., Concord, N. H.]   W. H. D.

TILTON, THEODORE (Oct. 2, 1835–May 25, 1907), editor, was born in New York City, the son of Silas and Eusebia (Tilton) Tilton. His father kept a store. Both his parents were strict Advent Baptists, and brought the boy up in a religious atmosphere. From the public schools he went to the Free Academy (later the College of the City of New York), where he was a student from 1850 to 1853. He gained some newspaper experience reporting for the *New York Tribune*, and came under the notice and influence of Greeley himself. Ardent, impressionable, devoted to evangelical Christianity, abolition, and other causes, and fluent of speech and pen, he attracted attention both by his tall handsome figure and his impetuous energy. Immediately after leaving school he declined a place on the *New York Herald* because it involved Sunday work, and joined the *New York Observer*, a Presbyterian weekly, instead. One of his regular assignments was to take down in shorthand the sermons of Henry Ward Beecher [*q.v.*]; and on Oct. 2, 1855, he married Elizabeth Richards, a Sunday school teacher of Plymouth Church in Brooklyn, Beecher performing the ceremony. In the following year he quarreled with the *Observer* for its lukewarm attitude toward slavery, and owing in part to the good offices of the Rev. George B. Cheever [*q.v.*], a leader of the religious anti-slavery party in New York, became managing editor of the *Independent,* the Congregationalist journal of Henry C. Bowen [*q.v.*].

In this post he at once made a notable reputation. It is little exaggeration to say that, taking more and more of the control from Bowen and his aide Joshua Leavitt, he temporarily "developed into one of the really great editors of the country" (Hibben, *post,* p. 170). The *Independent* had been distinctly sectarian, its chief contributors clergymen; Tilton made it a journal of broad appeal, numbering Elizabeth Barrett Browning, Whittier, Lowell, Garrison, Seward, and Kossuth among its writers. Losses were converted into profits. He also arranged for the regular publication of Beecher's sermons, thus increasing the preacher's audience and income. The association between the two men became closer than ever. Tilton acted as superintendent of Plymouth Sunday School, and he, Bowen, and Beecher were called "the Trinity of Plymouth Church." When the Civil War fell with ruinous effect on Bowen's mercantile business, Beecher came to his aid late in 1861 by assuming the editorship of the *Independent,* while Tilton remained in his old place. The two used the journal aggressively in the fight for emancipation and a more vigorous prosecution of hostilities; but the arrangement lasted only a year, and when Beecher went to England to plead the Northern cause, Tilton succeeded him as editor-in-chief, holding the place until 1871. He not only kept the *Independent* a successful family magazine but made it an organ of political power, taking a "radical" stand throughout the war and Reconstruction; its circulation increased so remarkably that in 1865 Bowen offered him a partnership. To his house in Livingston Street, Brooklyn, frequently came such famous figures as Greeley, Wendell Phillips, Sumner, Henry Wilson, and Gerrit Smith. Immediately after the close of the war he became one of the most popular figures on the lyceum platform, while he also blossomed out as a writer of musical but unoriginal verse, *The King's Ring* and *The Sexton's Tale, and Other Poems* appearing in 1867. He attracted much attention when he went to Washington to labor for Johnson's impeachment, and when he threw himself into the woman's suffrage cause. His wife for a time edited *Revolution,* a suffragist journal, and both were prominent in the Equal Rights Association. In 1870 he assumed an additional burden in the editorship of the Brooklyn *Union,* also owned by Bowen. He was a national figure.

But this promising career was totally disrupted by the great Beecher scandal. In the summer of 1870 Elizabeth Tilton confessed to her husband intimate relations with the pastor of Plymouth Church. The exact degree of intimacy was disputable, Tilton and his friends being convinced of adultery while Beecher first believed himself accused merely of "making improper solicitations" (*Tilton* vs. *Beecher, post,* III, 50). At first Tilton resolved to shield his wife and keep the matter secret; but unfortunately neither could forget. In a short time several members of the woman's rights group, including Victoria Woodhull [*q.v.*], of whom Tilton had become a blind admirer, knew all about it; so did others in Plymouth Church who did everything in their power to keep the peace and suppress the scandal. Henry Bowen in alarm decided to dismiss Tilton from the *Independent* and the Brooklyn *Union;* he had just described him in a signed article in the *Independent* as "bold, uncompromising, a master among men" (Dec. 22, 1870), but now declared him guilty of moral lapses and unsafe in judgment (Hibben, *post,* p. 248). Beecher acquiesced in this proceeding while asking through an intermediary for Tilton's forgiveness and writing: "I humble myself before him as I do before my God" (*Ibid.,* p. 257). Tilton's friend Frank Moulton came to the rescue by enabling him to start a new magazine, the *Golden Age,* but it proved weak. In April 1872 he sued Bowen for breach of contract. Meanwhile, his charge against Beecher, though not openly pressed, was the subject of smouldering gossip.

Full publicity was ultimately inevitable. On Nov. 2, 1872, *Woodhull and Claflin's Weekly* printed the charges in full. Beecher, unable longer to maintain a dignified silence and forced to try to clear his name, appointed a committee of members and stockholders of Plymouth Church to investigate. It completely exonerated him, as later did a group of Congregational ministers. Under Frank Moulton's restraining hand Tilton had played a longsuffering rôle, trying to shield Beecher while assailed by Beecher's friends; but now his patience was exhausted. On July 20, 1874, he appeared before Plymouth Church and formally lodged a charge of adultery against Beecher. In this crisis the distracted Elizabeth Tilton decided to leave her husband and children and stand by her pastor. Tilton, deserted by his emotional wife, condemned by thousands of Beecher's admirers as a slanderer, charged by Beecher himself with blackmail, found his position desperate. The result was his suit against Beecher for criminal conversation, with damages of $100,000 demanded. Hearings began Jan. 11, 1875, in Brooklyn City Court, lasted 112 trial days, and resulted in a hung jury and a division of public opinion that still persists.

The case left Tilton completely ruined in fortune and reputation. He had sold his share of the *Golden Age* in 1874, and lived by writing and lecturing. In 1883 he left the country never to return, traveling in England and Germany and finally settling in Paris. Books and articles brought him small sums, and he long lived on a pittance on the Île St. Louis, writing poetry and playing chess at the Café de la Regence. Though four years after the trial his wife recanted and declared her husband's charges true (*New York Times*, Apr. 16, 1878), he was never reconciled with her. Among his later books were a wildly improbable romance, *Tempest Tossed* (1874); ballads called *Swabian Stories* (1882); *Great Tom, or the Curfew Bell of Oxford* (1885); *Heart's Ease* (1894); and *Sonnets to the Memory of Frederick Douglass* (1895). Tilton's death in Paris resulted from pneumonia; four children lived to maturity.

[Paxton Hibben, *Henry Ward Beecher: An Am. Portrait* (1927); Lyman Abbott and S. B. Halliday, *Life of Henry Ward Beecher* (1887); Emanie Sachs, *The Terrible Siren* (1929); *Theodore Tilton* vs. *Henry Ward Beecher* (1874); *The Great Brooklyn Romance; All the Documents in the Famous Beecher-Tilton Case, Unabridged* (1874); L. P. Brockett, *Men of Our Day* (1868); *Evening Post* (N. Y.), May 25, 1907; *N. Y. Tribune* and *N. Y. Herald*, May 26, 1907; J. E. Stillwell, *Hist. and Geneal. Miscellany*, vol. V (1932).]
A. N.

TILYOU, GEORGE CORNELIUS (Feb. 3, 1862–Nov. 30, 1914), amusement park owner and inventor, son of Peter Augustus and Ellen (Mahoney) Tilyou, was born in New York City. His father, a descendant of a pioneer Huguenot family of New York, was a hotel proprietor at Coney Island, the neighboring seaside amusement resort, and thither the family removed when George was three years old. The boy received a part of a common-school education. At fourteen his business career may be said to have begun. That was in 1876, when many inland American visitors to the Centennial Exhibition at Philadelphia went on to New York and down to Coney Island, just for a look at the Atlantic Ocean. George Tilyou set up a stand near his father's hotel, and as souvenirs of their ocean visit sold to these inlanders little boxes of sifted beach sand and bottles of sea water. In the course of one busy excursion day he earned enough money to enable him to enjoy a trip to the Centennial. At seventeen, with a capital of $2.50 invested in business cards, he began a successful career as a Coney Island real-estate operator. He laid out the Island's famous Bowery, a carnival amusement street barred to wheeled vehicles, and built Tilyou's Surf Theatre, the first

show-house of importance at the resort. In 1897 he founded his famous Steeplechase Park, which expanded until it covered nearly twenty acres. Twice it was wrecked by fire, and each time restored on a greater and more gorgeous scale.

Tilyou originated most of the fun-making devices used in his amusement enterprises, their various objects being to give the patron nervous thrills as he was whirled or tumbled about, shot down steep slopes, and made to undergo weird experiences in dark chambers, or to subject him unexpectedly to the laughter of others and then give him his turn to laugh at those who followed him. Among the devices which Tilyou patented, built, or perfected were the Human Roulette Wheel, the Human Pool Table, the Bounding Billows, the Earthquake Floor, the Blow Hole, the Eccentric Fountain, the Razzle Dazzle, the Third Degree Regions, the Electric Seat, the Hoodoo Room, the California Bats, the Funny Stairway, the Barrel of Love, the Aerial Thrill, and others. He believed in and always purveyed clean amusements. He became a reformer in politics and was instrumental in the overthrow of John Y. McKane, the notorious political boss under whose rule Coney Island had taken on a distinctly rowdy tone. During this reform movement Tilyou was elected a justice of the peace. In addition to his Coney Island park, he operated at one time or another similar large concessions at Atlantic City, Asbury Park, N. J., Rockaway Beach, N. Y., Revere Beach, Mass., Bridgeport, Conn., St. Louis, and San Francisco, several of these being likewise christened Steeplechase Park. He married Mary Elizabeth O'Donnell of New York in 1893, and she, with three sons (who continued his great amusement business) and two daughters, survived him.

[H. I. Hazelton, *The Boroughs of Brooklyn and Queens, Counties of Nassau and Suffolk, Long Island, N. Y.* (1925), vol. II; *Hist. of Coney Island, List and Photographs of Main Attractions* (1904); *Brooklyn Daily Eagle, Brooklyn Times, World* (N. Y.), *N. Y. Times, N. Y. Herald, N. Y. Tribune, Sun* (N. Y.), and *Coney Island Times*, Nov. 30, 1914; files of the last-named paper.]
A. F. H.

TIMBERLAKE, HENRY (1730–Sept. 30, 1765), soldier, was born in Hanover County, Va., the son of Francis and Sarah (Austin) Timberlake, and the grandson of Joseph Timberlake who emigrated from England to Virginia. After receiving a fairly adequate education, he joined the Patriot Blues for the campaign of 1756 against the French and Indians under George Washington. In 1758 he was appointed to a cornetcy of horse in the regiment of William Byrd III and was in the John Forbes campaign against the French at Fort Duquesne.

Timberlake

He served in 1759 under John Stanwix, who placed him in command of Fort Burd, or Fort Necessity, in Pennsylvania. In the spring of 1761 he was ordered to join the regiment of Colonel Byrd against the Cherokee, then besieging the British Fort Loudoun on Little Tennessee River, and he marched with Adam Stephen to the Holston River. After the peace of Nov. 19, 1761, the Cherokee requested that an officer visit them, and Timberlake, then an ensign, volunteered for this mission, to be accompanied by Thomas Sumter [q.v.]. The twenty-two-day journey to the Indian towns was made by skiff down the Holston and up the Little Tennessee. Timberlake made notes of the courses of these rivers and executed an excellent map of the streams, showing, also, the locations of the towns of the Overhill Cherokee.

After three months with the Cherokee, they returned to Virginia, where they were placed in charge of Outacity [q.v.] and two of his warriors to make a visit to England. In London the Indians drew large crowds to see them, the aristocracy included. Entertained sumptuously at Vauxhall Gardens and other leading resorts, the Cherokee and the two young Virginians were admitted to audience by the King. Timberlake is said to have received a lieutenant's commission as a reward for his services. He married in London and returned to Virginia. In 1764 he conducted overseas a second group of Cherokee warriors. Falling into financial difficulties, he sought to recoup by writing and publishing the *Memoirs of Lieut. Henry Timberlake,* which was published in London in 1765. There he recorded his experiences in the French and Indian War and his observations of the customs and ceremonies of the Cherokee. The book ever since its appearance has been considered by ethnologists as dependable source material. A German translation appeared in J. T. Köhler's *Sammlung neuer Reise-Beschreibungen,* vol. I, pt. 2 (1769), and a French translation by J. B. L. J. Billecocq was published in Paris *Voyages du lieutenant Henri Timberlake* (1796); the poet Robert Southey drew largely from the book in the preparation of his epic, *Madoc* (1805). Timberlake died in London, seemingly before his book came from the press, certainly before he could have profited from its sale.

[*Lieut. Henry Timberlake's Memoirs* (1927), ed. by S. C. Williams, with bibliog. references; bibliog. in sketch of Outacity for London visit of 1762; "The Official Records of Robert Dinwiddie," *Va. Hist. Colls.,* n.s., vol. IV (1884); *Annual Register . . . 1765* (1766), pp. 65–66; *Gentleman's Mag.,* Oct. 1765, p. 491; information from Wade H. Fleischer, Northport, N. Y.]

S. C. W.

Timby

TIMBY, THEODORE RUGGLES (Apr. 5, 1822–Nov. 9, 1909), inventor, was born in Dutchess County, N. Y., the son of George W. and Sarah (Johnson) Timby, formerly of Pittsfield, Mass. He grew up on his father's farm, attending the local common schools. During his teens he is said to have invented a form of floating dry dock. As early as 1841 he exhibited at the War Department, Washington, a model and plans for a revolving battery for coast defense, suggested to him by the circular form of Castle William on Governors Island in New York Harbor. He seems also to have conceived of a similar structure for ships of low freeboard. On Jan. 18, 1843, he filed a *caveat* covering the invention of the revolving turret for use on land or water. It appears that in the spring of the same year he sent a model to China by Caleb Cushing [q.v.], the United States minister, and in June exhibited a model to President Tyler and his cabinet. During the fifties he urged the revolving battery on Emperor Napoleon III, but the idea seems nowhere to have received effective recognition until, in 1861–62, it was utilized by John Ericsson [q.v.] as a distinctive feature of his first Monitor. After the *Monitor* had proved successful, Timby, then a resident of Worcester, Mass., was granted two patents on July 8, 1862 (No. 35,846 and No. 35,847), for a revolving battery tower and a revolving tower discharging guns by electricity. In September he received another patent for a revolving battery tower. Ericsson's associates in the business of building Monitors for the government acquired these patents almost at once and thus quieted all claims of infringement. In later years a controversy followed as to credit for the idea of the revolving turret or battery tower, Ericsson arguing that the idea of a revolving fort long antedated the nineteenth century and thus was one of the concepts of military engineering which belonged as common property to the engineering practice of the time, while supporters of Timby pointed to his early *caveat* as proof that credit should go to him. It seems clear that the honor of first publicly urging this form of gun housing on governmental authorities belongs to Timby, while the honor of first using the idea in actual construction belongs to Ericsson, who may or may not have known of Timby's design. In 1857 and 1862 Timby received patents for a barometer; in 1869 he patented a turbine water wheel, and in 1871, a gun carriage; he also devised a process of printing terrestrial globes in colors and a process for quickly ripening coffee. His inventions seem to have brought little financial return, however, and his family was supported in part by the friends who memorialized Congress and the New York legislature in his behalf. During his later years, as a resident of Brooklyn, N. Y., he occupied himself with literary avocations, publishing several small volumes of poems and essays, including *Bridging the Skies* (1883), *Beyond* (1886), *Stellar Worlds and Other Didactic Literature* (1896); *Lighted Lore for Gentle Folk* (1902). In 1844 he married Charlotte M. Ware. He died in Brooklyn.

[*N. Y. Herald*, June 7, 1843; *N. Y. Weekly Evening Post*, June 7, 1843: "The Revolving Tower and Its Inventor," *Harper's New Monthly Mag.*, Jan. 1863; James Parton, *People's Book of Biog.* (1868); W. C. Church, *The Life of John Ericsson* (1890), vol. II; *Famous Am. Men and Women* (1895), ed. by Stanley Waterloo and J. W. Hanson, Jr.; F. M. Bennett, *The Monitor and the Navy under Steam* (1900); Alfred King, "Theodore R. Timby," *Successful American*, Jan. 1902; *Am. Shipbuilder*, Oct. 23, 1902; *Memorial of the Patriotic League of the Revolution to the Fifty-Seventh Cong.* (1902); *Who's Who in America*, 1908–09; Helen Woods, "Timby the Forgotten," *Harper's Weekly*, Feb. 11, 1911; *What Authorities Say about Timby and the Revolving Turret* (1912); *Brooklyn Daily Eagle*, Nov. 10, 1909.]   W. F. D.

TIMKEN, HENRY (Aug. 16, 1831–Mar. 16, 1909), inventor, manufacturer, son of Jacob Timken, a prosperous German farmer, was born near Bremen, Germany. He was one of seven children, and three years after the death of his mother, when he was seven years old, his father emigrated to the United States and settled in St. Louis, Mo. A year later he bought a tract of farm land near Sedalia, Mo., and there young Timken grew up, doing his share of the farm work and attending the country school. He disliked farming, however, and when he was sixteen years old he went to St. Louis and apprenticed himself to one of the leading carriage and wagon manufacturers.

Upon completing his apprenticeship he worked as a journeyman wagon maker for a while and in 1855 established his own carriage factory in St. Louis. That same year he married Fredericka Heinzelmann. His business was successful and within a year or two, in partnership with his father-in-law, he established a branch factory at Belleville, Ill. In 1860, however, afflicted with the gold fever, Timken deliberately gave up his business and went to Pikes Peak to seek his fortune. Six months' prospecting convinced him that carriage manufacturing was more profitable, and returning to St. Louis, he engaged again in that enterprise. Its fortunes were considerably affected during the Civil War by Timken's military services in the home guard, and in the 13th Regiment of the Missouri Militia, in which for three years he was a captain. In 1864, moreover, his plant was destroyed by fire. This he rebuilt after the war and operated it success-fully until 1887, when he retired and established his home at San Diego, Cal. Seven years later, however, he reëntered the carriage-making business in St. Louis and erected there a model factory, which he conducted in association with his two sons until 1897. He then retired again to his home in California and lived there until his death.

Timken possessed a bent for invention and secured during his life thirteen patents, all but two of which pertained to carriage or wagon improvements. On Nov. 27, 1877, he was granted Patent No. 197,689 for a carriage spring which he introduced to the carriage trade through his own vehicles in 1878. This "Timken Spring" was an immediate success and carried his name and fame over all the world. Demands for it became so great that his carriage plant gradually became a spring-manufacturing plant and yielded him a handsome fortune. The two patents which were not for carriage or wagon improvements were issued June 28, 1898, and were for a tapered roller bearing, which has come into very wide use in recent years and has also done much to make his name widely known. For the production of this product he organized the Timken Roller Bearing Axle Company, with himself as president, and erected a plant at Canton, Ohio, but left the active management to his two sons. During 1896 and 1897 he was president of the Carriage Builders' National Association, at that time the largest and oldest trade association in the country. Besides his manufacturing interests he was the owner of extensive agricultural lands in Kansas and citrus groves in California. His greatest pleasures in his later years were derived from these interests and from travel. He died at the age of seventy-eight years in San Diego and was survived by five children.

[William Hyde and H. L. Conard, *Encyc. of the Hist. of St. Louis* (1899), vol. IV; *Carriage Monthly*, Oct. 1895, Apr. 1909; *Los Angeles Daily Times*, Mar. 17, 1909; Patent Office records.]   C. W. M—n.

TIMM, HENRY CHRISTIAN (July 11, 1811–Sept. 5, 1892), musician, conductor, was born in Hamburg, Germany. He received his musical education from Albert Gottlieb Methfessel (known principally as a composer of part-songs for men's voices), and Jacob Schmitt, and made his début abroad in 1828. In 1835 he emigrated to New York and immediately became active in the city's musical life. He made his first American appearance in a concert at the Park Theatre, and at once gained popular favor. His next venture was an unsuccessful concert tour of New England, after which he returned to New York and became second horn player at the Park Theatre. Later he went South for six months as conductor of a traveling opera troupe. He remained in Baltimore for a time, where he had a position as church organist and gave some concerts with Signora Velané and the baritone, Giuseppe De Begnis. Upon his return to New York, he became trombone player and chorus master of Charles Edward Horn's opera company, which was about to open the National Opera House with *The Pilgrim of Love*. The theatre burned a few months later and Timm secured a position as organist of St. Thomas's Church. Later he became organist at All Souls', where he played for almost eighteen years. He was one of the early members of the Philharmonic Society of New York (founded in 1842), assistant director in its third and fourth seasons, vice-president in its fifth, and president from 1848 to 1863 (seventh to twenty-first seasons inclusive). He died in Hoboken, N. J.

Timm often appeared as piano soloist with the Philharmonic. The New York correspondent of *Dwight's Journal of Music* called him "the most elegant of our pianists" (May 1, 1852), and on another occasion (Nov. 20, 1852) he wrote: "How finely that gentleman plays you need not be told. The deeply melancholy character of the music (Hummel's piano concerto in B minor) was admirably conveyed in the performance of both pianist and orchestra, and was doubly effective from its contrast to the Symphony" (Beethoven's 8th). The same magazine was less flattering in another account: "Later in the evening he (William Scharfenberg) and Mr. Timm played a Grand Duo of Mendelssohn's. . . . It was effective but not striking." William Mason, the pianist, perpetuated the tradition that Timm had such a perfect technique that he could play scales with a full wine glass on the back of each hand without spilling a drop (*Memories of a Musical Life*, 1901, p. 58). As a composer, Timm wrote a Grand Mass for soli, chorus, orchestra, and organ; a number of part-songs; and transcriptions for two pianos of classical works. As an editor, he prepared several editions of works from the standard repertoire.

[In addition to the contemporary sources cited above, see H. E. Krehbiel, *The Philharmonic Soc. of N. Y.* (1892) ; J. T. Howard, *Our Am. Music* (1931); Theodore Baker, *A Biog. Dict. of Musicians* (1900) ; *Musical America*, Feb. 24, 1917; F. L. Ritter, *Music in America* (1883) ; *N. Y. Tribune*, Sept. 6, 8, 1892.]
J. T. H.

TIMON, JOHN (Feb. 12, 1797–Apr. 16, 1867), Roman Catholic prelate, the second of ten children of James and Margaret (Leddy) Timon, immigrants from County Cavan, was born in Conewago, Pa. In 1802 the Timons removed to Baltimore, where the father, who had served apprenticeship to a draper, carried on a successful dry-goods business. Later, they went to Louisville (1818) and finally to frontier St. Louis (1819), where they prospered until the hard year of 1823. John completed his theological studies in the Lazarist seminary at The Barrens. He accompanied John Mary Odin [*q.v.*] of the seminary on missionary circuits through Missouri and into the Indian country, and an intense lifelong friendship between the two resulted. Ordained in June 1825 by Bishop Joseph Rosati [*q.v.*] of St. Louis as a priest of the Congregation of the Mission (Vincentians or Lazarists), he continued in the seminary as a teacher until assigned to the missions of the Southwest with the log church at Cape Girardeau, Mo., as a center. Though a retiring, sensitive little man, hardly five feet in height, his zeal for souls enabled him to brave bigoted hostility and dangerous journeys on horseback over the wild country even into Texas.

Appointed visitor general of the Vincentians in 1835, he handled the community's business, effected a compromise in its conflict with Rosati over properties, built a permanent foundation at Cape Girardeau, refused Archbishop Eccleston's offer of Mount St. Mary's College at Emmitsburg, Md., and visited Europe in 1837 to secure missionaries, one of whom was Michael Domenec, later bishop of Pittsburgh. Refusing an appointment as coadjutor bishop of St. Louis, Timon accepted the more arduous position of prefect-apostolic of Texas with Odin as his vice-prefect. Letters of Cardinal Fransoni, which he transmitted to Acting President David G. Burnet [*q.v.*] were regarded as a papal recognition of Texan independence. Within the space of a few years, he made visitations in Texas and Indiana, journeyed through the Colorado region, represented his community in ecclesiastical councils, aided in founding the first conference of the Society of St. Vincent de Paul in St. Louis (1844), and revised the rules of the Lorentine Sisters. Few priests in the Mississippi Valley were as well known, and in 1847 Pius IX selected him for the new diocese of Buffalo, concerning the creation of which he was quite ignorant. Consecrated in New York on Oct. 17 by Bishop Hughes who regarded him as the humblest man he had ever known but rather lacking in force, Timon lost no time in undertaking his new burdens.

His most annoying problem was removed when the rebellious trustees of St. Peter's Church succumbed before an interdict. A prelate who would give his clothes to beggars and carry destitute babies to orphanages was naturally a founder of eleemosynary institutions. Among those he established were three orphanages, including one for German children; a hospital under the Sisters of Charity; Providence Lunatic Asylum; a home for mutes; a Magdalen asylum; and the first American Catholic institution for unmarried mothers. With more vigor than success, he urged the right of inmates of county institutions to have the service of a priest and to be freed from attendance at Protestant exercises (see *Buffalo Daily Republic,* June 5, 1858). As an educator, he established Niagara Seminary under the Lazarists (1848) and St. Joseph's College in Buffalo (1849), which was unsuccessful until assigned to the Christian Brothers (1861); aided the Franciscans at Allegany; and promoted the American College in Rome. Despite Know-Nothing threats, he dedicated his Cathedral of St. Joseph in 1855, for which he made collections in Europe and in Mexico. During the Civil War he was an ardent militarist who favored waging the war with sufficient energy to enforce an early peace and who took active steps to end the local draft riots (see *United States Catholic Historical Society, Historical Records and Studies,* vol. I, 1900, pp. 189–90). In 1862 he published *Missions in Western New York and Church History of the Diocese of Buffalo.*

Timon attracted non-Catholic attention by his unostentatious piety, charity, and civic interest. His self-sacrificing spirit was apparent in his death from erysipelas contracted during a visit to the hospital. Bishop Francis P. Kenrick [*q.v.*] preferred him for the see of Baltimore and when he himself was translated to Baltimore urged Timon for Philadelphia. He exerted a marked influence in Rome as a papal prelate and as an invited guest on various occasions.

[C. G. Deuther, *The Life and Times of Rt. Rev. John Timon* (1870); R. H. Clarke, *Lives of the Deceased Bishops of the Catholic Church in the U. S.,* vol. II (1888); *Cath. Encyc.*; J. E. Rothensteiner, *Hist. of the Archdiocese of St. Louis* (1923); F. E. Tourscher, *The Kenrick-Frenaye Correspondence* (1920); files of *Western New York Catholic,* especially Apr. 1867; *N. Y. Freeman's Jour.,* Apr. 27, 1867; *Catholic World,* Apr. 1871; *Buffalo Commercial Advertiser,* Apr. 17, 1867.]

R. J. P.

TIMOTHY, LEWIS (d. December 1738), printer, was the son of a French Protestant who had taken refuge in Holland at the revocation of the Edict of Nantes. In Holland he learned the printing craft and married Elizabeth ——. He arrived in America in September 1731 with his wife and four children (*Pennsylvania Archives,* 2 ser., vol. XVII, 1890, pp. 29, 31, 32),

and by October had settled in Philadelphia, advertising himself in the *Pennsylvania Gazette* of October 14, 1731, as "Mr. Louis Timothée, Master of the French Tongue." In June 1732 he was connected in an editorial capacity with Benjamin Franklin's *Philadelphische Zeitung,* the first German-language newspaper in America. In November 1732, some time after the demise of the very short-lived *Zeitung,* he became librarian of the Philadelphia Library Society. In 1733 he was working for Franklin as a journeyman printer. On Nov. 26, 1733, there was effected a partnership agreement between Franklin and Timothée whereby the latter was to conduct a printing business at Charlestown, S. C., as successor to Thomas Whitmarsh, Franklin's former partner in Charlestown, who had died the preceding September. On Feb. 2, 1734, Timothée revived the *South-Carolina Gazette,* which had ceased publication on the death of Whitmarsh. In April 1734 the printer anglicized the spelling of his name to Lewis Timothy.

Timothy was the printer of the most ambitious and important production of the colonial press of South Carolina, the two-volume collection of *The Laws of the Province of South-Carolina* (1736), compiled by Nicholas Trott, LL.D. The printing of this work, of about eight hundred pages, was Timothy's principal occupation from December 1734 until early in 1737 (see McMurtrie, "The First Decade," *post,* p. 442, for a discussion of the date). In its production the printer was generously subsidized by the provincial government. In addition to the monumental *Laws,* Timothy has left record of only some eighteen pieces of printing, other than the issues of his newspaper, for the five years of his activity at Charlestown; of these printed works, only eight are now known from surviving copies. They include legislative acts, tracts on the smallpox, an almanac, a sermon, an essay on currency, and *A Collection of Psalms and Hymns* (1737), the earliest Wesley collection (McMurtrie, "A Bibliography of South Carolina Imprints," *post*).

Timothy died in December 1738 and was buried on the thirtieth of that month (A. S. Salley, Jr., *Register of St. Philip's Parish, Charles Town, S. C., 1720–1758,* 1904, p. 174). He was survived by his widow, Elizabeth Timothy, and six children, of whom one, his son Peter, became his active successor in the printing business. Benjamin Franklin, in his *Autobiography,* said of Lewis Timothy and his wife: "He was a man of learning, and honest but ignorant in matters of account; and, tho' he sometimes made me remittances, I could get no account from him, nor any satisfactory state of our partnership while he lived. On his decease, the business was continued by his widow, who, being born and bred in Holland, where, as I have been inform'd, the knowledge of accounts makes a part of female education, she not only sent me as clear a state as she could find of the transactions past, but continued to account with the greatest regularity and exactness every quarter afterwards, and managed the business with such success, that she not only brought up reputably a family of children, but, at the expiration of the term, was able to purchase of me the printing-house, and establish her son in it" (Smyth, *post*, vol. I, pp. 344–45).

When Lewis Timothy died, just five years of the six-year partnership agreement with Benjamin Franklin had expired. "At the expiration of the term," Peter Timothy became the owner of the business and so continued, with some interruptions, until 1781. In that year he was taken prisoner by the British to St. Augustine and was drowned at sea. In addition to his printing, he was active in public affairs, especially during the Revolutionary War. His widow, Ann Timothy, continued the printing business until her death in September 1792, and was succeeded then by her son, the happily named Benjamin Franklin Timothy, with whom the Timothy dynasty of printers seems to have ended.

[In addition to Benjamin Franklin's account of Timothy, A. H. Smyth, ed., *The Writings of Benjamin Franklin*, vol. I (1905), pp. 345 ff., see *Pa. Mag. of Hist. and Biog.*, Jan. 30, 1906, pp. 104–06, which contains the partnership agreement between Franklin and Timothy; D. C. McMurtrie, "The First Decade of Printing in the Royal Province of S. C.," *Trans. Bibliog. Soc.* (London), 2 ser., vol. XIII (1933), and "A Bibliog. of S. C. Imprints, 1731–1740," *S. C. Hist. and Geneal. Mag.*, vol. XXXIV (1933), nos. 11–30; Isaiah Thomas, *The Hist. of Printing in America* (2nd ed., 1874), vol. I, p. 342, vol. II, p. 170; and A. H. Hirsch, *The Huguenots of Colonial S. C.* (1928), pp. 239–42.]

D. C. M.

TIMROD, HENRY (Dec. 8, 1828–Oct. 6, 1867), poet, was born in Charleston, S. C., of racially varied, middle-class stock. His paternal grandfather, Heinrich Dimroth, emigrated to Charleston from Germany in 1765, and, after amassing property as a merchant tailor, set up as a planter. His third wife was his Scotch-Irish housekeeper, Susannah Hargan; their son, William Henry, a bookbinder of uncommon character and intellect who achieved local recognition through his literary abilities, died in 1838 as a consequence of his services in the Seminole War, leaving his family in straitened circumstances. From him Henry Timrod inherited poetic temperament and a vein of impracticality; from his English-Swiss mother, Thyrza Prince, to whom "a walk in the woods . . . was food and drink, and the sight of a green field was joy inexpressible,"

the sensitive city-born child derived his deeply seated love of nature. A normally active boy, despite his slightness and his bookish inclinations, he was educated in the Charleston schools, where began his life-long intimacy with Paul Hamilton Hayne [*q.v.*]; although modest, diffident, and slow of speech, he proved ambitious and quick to learn. At eighteen he entered Franklin College (later the University of Georgia), in Athens, where he applied himself diligently to belles-lettres and the classics, in his leisure hours composing verses to the face of "every pretty girl" whom he met. Temporary ill-health and chronic want of means forced his withdrawal after two years, and, returning to Charleston, he began to read law in the office of James L. Petigru [*q.v.*]. He was not long, however, in realizing how unsuited he was to the law; abandoning it, he renewed his classical studies in order to qualify as a college professor. When no professorship offered, he taught school for a term at Bluffton, subsequently accepting employment as tutor on a Carolina plantation.

For a decade and more the shy and abstracted young poet lived in this cloistered fashion, faithfully if none too effectually instructing his charges, yet finding opportunity to feed "his muse with English song," to commune with nature, or to write verses for the *Southern Literary Messenger* and other periodicals. During his holidays he hastened to Charleston to fraternize —sometimes too convivially—with the little group of litterateurs who clustered about William Gilmore Simms [*q.v.*], joining with them in 1857 to launch the short-lived but valuable *Russell's Magazine*, to which he contributed numerous poems and occasional prose articles. In 1860 Ticknor & Fields published a small collection of his poems, but although favorably received by discriminating readers, North and South, the volume was speedily obscured by the stress of events. Timrod's disappointment was soon engulfed by his tremendous emotion at the approach of hostilities between the sections, a feeling foreshadowed in his memorable nature lyrics, "Spring" and "The Cotton-Boll." In February 1861 he wrote his elaborate and impressive ode, "Ethnogenesis"; he followed this with a series of impassioned and fervent war poems which strongly stirred the South and focussed attention upon him as "the laureate of the Confederacy." From the beginning he had been an artist, self-controlled, careful of form, studious of the exact word, the felicitous phrase; now that he had something other than mid-century commonplaces to say, his powers ripened. "A Cry to Arms," "Carolina," "Carmen Triumphale," "Charleston," and others not only proved popularly effective, but struck a firmer and stronger note than had appeared in his earlier work.

During the first year of the war he remained in Charleston, his health rendering him unfit for military service. On Mar. 1, 1862, he enlisted in Company B, 30th South Carolina Regiment, and was detailed as a clerk at regimental headquarters. After Shiloh he joined the Confederate Army of the West as correspondent of the *Charleston Mercury,* but neither his constitution nor his temperament was adapted to camp life, and he was compelled to withdraw; in December he was discharged from the Confederate service as suffering from incipient tuberculosis. On top of this, the project of certain Charleston admirers late in 1862 of bringing out in England an elaborate illustrated edition of his poems was allowed to lapse, to the "unspeakable disappointment" of Timrod, who saw fame and competence once more elude him. For a brief period, however, the tragedy that was never distant from him lagged behind. In January 1864 he moved to Columbia to become part proprietor and associate editor of the *South Carolinian;* married a month later (Feb. 16, 1864) Kate Goodwin, the English "Katie" of his pleasing and distinctive love lyric, whose brother had married Timrod's sister Emily; and found his happiness brought to a climax by the birth of a son on Christmas Eve. Then, just a year and a day after his marriage, Columbia was burned, and Timrod, his livelihood destroyed, was reduced to abject poverty. Ill, unworldly, inadequately equipped to support even his own small family, he saw added to this household his mother, his widowed sister and her four children. In October died his son, Willie, his "single rose-bud in a crown of thorns," plunging the poet into a grief from which he never recovered. His health began to fail rapidly, accelerated by the lack of medicines and proper food. Not until December did he obtain employment, on a newspaper; at the end of four months he had received nothing for his editorial labors. He sought vainly to establish a girls' school in Columbia; his efforts to market poems in the North were equally abortive. Writing to Hayne in March 1866 he summed up his story for the preceding year as "beggary, starvation, death, bitter grief, utter want of hope" (Hayne, *post,* p. 45). Only through the gradual sale of their belongings and the generosity of similarly impoverished neighbors could his household find sustenance, yet there is no querulousness, no morbidity in his letters: "We have eaten two silver pitchers," he continues, "one or two dozen silver forks, several sofas, innumerable chairs,

and a huge—bedstead!" Small wonder that the desperate poet should exclaim of his verse that he "would consign every line of it to eternal oblivion, for—*one hundred dollars in hand!*" An exhausting clerkship in the governor's office lasted merely a few weeks; an invitation to visit a Northern publisher had to be declined for lack of railroad fare. His visit, in April, to Hayne's home in the Georgia pine barrens served as a welcome anodyne, but was followed shortly by a painful and dangerous operation; while still suffering from its effects he completed his exquisite Magnolia Cemetery "Ode," perhaps the most perfect and enduring of his compositions. In August he visited Hayne again; hemorrhages commenced soon after his return to Columbia; a month later he died. For ten years his grave remained unmarked, although efforts of Hayne, Simms, and other faithful friends to perpetuate his fame eventually bore fruit. In 1873 Hayne (even before collecting his own verses) edited *The Poems of Henry Timrod,* prefacing them with a sympathetic memoir; in 1884 appeared an illustrated edition of "Katie"; and in 1899 the activities of the Timrod Memorial Association (founded 1898) in promoting the standard "Memorial Edition" effected a mild but fairly widespread revival of interest in the man and his work.

Both the restricted range and the small body of his product place Timrod definitely among the lesser gods of song. Yet he was the most representative and, barring Sidney Lanier [*q.v.*], the ablest Southern poet of his century. He knew better than most of his contemporaries what poetry was, just as he surpassed most of them in taste and sheer lyrical power; and, a masterly artificer, he devoted time and patience to the polishing of his measures. His style is regularly crystal-clear, chastened, natural, extraordinarily quotable; if the thought lacks profundity, it is straightforward and sane, showing a "genial breadth" rather than provincialism—even his most fiery war songs soften at the end into a prayer for peace. His address at Columbia, 1863, for the benefit of the Soldiers' Hospital reveals his conviction that the sources of poetry could not be reduced to the element of beauty alone, but that to this must be added power and truth ("A Theory of Poetry," *Independent,* Mar. 28, Apr. 4, 11, 1901; *Atlantic Monthly,* Sept. 1905); there are other aspects of his theory in his essay, "The Character and Scope of the Sonnet" (*Outlook,* July 23, 1904), although his own attempts at this form, while often extravagantly praised, are for the most part mediocre and well below his best work. Vicissitudes of fortune hampered his genius and occasionally affected his writing;

at times he followed too closely in the footsteps of Wordsworth or Tennyson; otherwhiles the conventionalities of the plantation tradition led him into oversweetness or a too pronounced didacticism. In the handful of singularly beautiful pieces, however, in which he succeeded in turning "life's tasteless waters into wine" and by which he will be remembered and measured, he made a valuable and permanent contribution to American literature. His ideals, his intense imagination and playful fancy, his spirituality, his wholesomeness, his unmistakable sincerity, even his sentiment, were characteristic of the finer qualities of his section, as was his own high-minded and heroic nature. It was one of the ironies of American literature that so gentle and childlike a spirit should have been the outstanding poet of the Confederacy; it was more than ironic that his output should have been so reduced by tragic circumstance and premature death.

[Timrod's name was entered in his father's day books as Henry H. See G. A. Cardwell, Jr., "The Date of Henry Timrod's Birth," *Am. Lit.*, May 1935; Paul H. Hayne, in *The Poems of Henry Timrod* (1873); H. T. Thompson, *Henry Timrod, Laureate of the Confederacy* (1928), with bibliog.; G. A. Wauchope, *Henry Timrod: Man and Poet* (1915); H. E. Shepherd and A. S. Salley, in *Southern Hist. Asso. Pubs.*, Oct. 1899; W. P. Trent, *William Gilmore Simms* (1892); obituary in *Charleston Daily Courier*, Oct. 9, 1867.]

A. C. G., Jr.

TINCKER, MARY AGNES (July 18, 1831–Nov. 27, 1907), novelist, was born at Ellsworth, Me., the daughter of Richard and Mehitabel (Jellison) Tincker. Educated in the public schools of Ellsworth and at Bluehill Academy, Bluehill, Me., she began teaching at the age of thirteen in the public schools of Ellsworth; later she taught in a Roman Catholic parochial school. At fifteen she began writing and contributed sketches, anonymously, to local newspapers and to magazines. At twenty she embraced the Catholic faith, an action which was profoundly to influence all her later work. She became a volunteer nurse in 1863 and worked in military hospitals in Washington for a short time. Returning to Boston, she began again her anonymous contributions to periodicals, mainly *Harper's Magazine* and *Putnam's Monthly Magazine*. Her first published book, *The House of Yorke*, appeared in 1872, after having been serialized in the *Catholic World* from April 1871 to June 1872. The setting of the story is her home, Ellsworth, during the Know-Nothing times of 1854–55; the atmosphere and the philosophy of the novel are decidedly religious. From 1873 to 1887 she lived in Italy. After that period she lived almost uninterruptedly in Boston until her death,

which occurred in Dorchester, frequently contributing sketches and short stories to magazines, notably the *Catholic World*. She was in poor health all the latter years of her life, doing her writing under serious physical handicaps. She had been a precocious child of wilful temperament, now gay, now melancholy, adjectives which fittingly describe contrasting moods in her novels. In her twenties, when her writings began to reach a larger and more appreciative audience, she felt a strong urge to leave what she thought to be a cramping environment. This feeling, with the personal renaissance caused by her religious ideas, served thoroughly to transplant her in thought from New England to Rome. It would be difficult to overestimate the influence which her religion had upon her writing or her life.

She published eleven novels and books of sketches, among them *By The Tiber* (1881), *Aurora* (1886), *Two Coronets* (1889), *San Salvador* (1892), and *Autumn Leaves* (1899), which contains some verse. Her novels were highly praised by contemporary reviewers for their rich imagination and Christian spirit. The most popular of these, *Signor Monaldini's Niece* (1879), is, indeed, characterized by delicate descriptive touches which serve pleasingly to recreate the atmosphere of Rome, but whatever charm she possessed as a novelist lay in her ability to describe atmospheric lights and shadows, and not in any especial stylistic or imaginative excellence. In this novel appears her one strong social protest, that against the conventional restriction of woman's freedom, especially the freedom of the unmarried woman. In general, her work has had little influence upon later novelists and is well-nigh forgotten.

[There are no adequate biog. sketches. Information has been supplied by Adah A. Tincker of Cambridge, Mass., a relative. Some data may be found in *Who's Who in America*, 1906–07; J. F. Kirk, *A Supp. to Allibone's Critical Dict. of Eng. Lit.* (2 vols., 1891); death notice in *Boston Transcript*, Nov. 30, 1907. Reviews are to be found in *Cath. World*, June 1872, *Nation*, Mar. 13, 1879, and June 9, 1881, and *Lit. World* (Boston), Sept. 27, 1879, and Dec. 12, 1885. The date of birth is from Louise Royal of Belfast, Me., a niece.]

H. S., Jr.

TINGEY, THOMAS (Sept. 11, 1750–Feb. 23, 1829), naval officer, was born in London, England, the son of a Church of England clergyman. In youth he served in the British navy with officer's rating, as evidenced by an order (copy in Personnel Files, United States Navy Department Library) from Admiral John Byron, R.N., July 31, 1771, giving him command of twenty-two men at Chateau Bay, Labrador. Not long thereafter he left the British service (according to family tradition because of differences with a fellow officer), and in 1778 he was master of the brig *Lady Clausen* in trade from Saint Croix, Virgin Islands, to Europe. He was married at Saint Croix, Mar. 30, 1777, to Margaret, daughter of William Murdoch of Philadelphia. Following the Revolution he commanded vessels in the American merchant service, living after 1783 in Philadelphia, and after about 1797 in Kingston, N. J. At the opening of naval warfare with France he was made captain in the American navy, Sept. 3, 1798, senior of five captains added that year, and during the next winter he commanded the *Ganges* and two smaller vessels cruising in the Windward Passage. Here he captured numerous prizes, including the *Vainqueur* (8 guns), taken after a ninety-mile chase. When the British frigate *Surprise* sought to examine his crew for British seamen, he peremptorily refused the demand, declaring the flag a sufficient protection. He had already assured his crew that he would resist search "while he was able to stand at quarters" (Letters, 1798–99, *post*, p. 49). Benjamin Stoddert, secretary of the navy, in a letter of Mar. 7, 1799, informed him that the president highly approved his action. From June until late in the following autumn, after the departure of Commodores Thomas Truxtun and John Barry [*qq.v.*], he was senior officer in the West Indies. On Jan. 22, 1800, he was appointed by Secretary Stoddert, as "being a man of understanding and having seen the navy-yards of England" (Hibben, *post*, p. 25), to lay out and command the new Washington navy yard. Though twelfth in the captain's list and thus not among the nine retained in the Peace Establishment of 1801, he remained superintendent of the Washington yard till 1803, was then temporarily "financial agent," and on Nov. 23, 1804, was recommissioned captain and made commandant of the yard and naval agent —the only instance of the combined functions. In these duties he continued until his death. Until 1814 his yard was the chief naval depot and construction base. Tingey was an indefatigable worker, carrying on the official correspondence largely in his own hand, slow to admit error and quick to defend himself, but never shirking responsibilty. His rules for government of the yard (1808) were adopted for all similar stations on the coast. At the British invasion of Washington in 1814 he received orders, based on a cabinet consultation, to burn the yard, and accordingly set fire to the buildings and shipping at 8:20 P.M., Aug. 24, just as the Capitol was fired by the British. He returned next morning at nine, being, as he wrote to his daughter (Sept.

17, 1814), "the last officer who quitted the city after the enemy had possession . . . and the only one to venture in" next day. The establishment was valued at $678,210 and the loss at $417,745.

Highly respected and of genial, kindly nature, Tingey was prominent in Washington social life, a school trustee in 1805, head of the vestry of Christ Church, and an incorporator of its cemetery (now the Congressional Cemetery), in which he was buried. He was a close friend of Commodore John Rodgers [*q.v.*] and his second in negotiations (1806) for a duel—happily averted—with Capt. James Barron [*q.v.*]. By his first marriage he had three daughters who lived to maturity, one of them the mother of the naval officers Thomas Tingey Craven and Tunis A. M. Craven [*qq.v.*]. He was married, second, Dec. 9, 1812, to Ann Bladen Dulany; and third, May 19, 1817, to Ann Evelina Craven. He died in Washington.

[G. W. Allen, *Our Naval War with France* (1909); F. W. Hackett, in *Proc. U. S. Naval Institute*, Mar. 1907; H. B. Hibben, "Navy-Yard, Washington . . .," in *Sen. Exec. Doc. 22*, 51 Cong., 1 Sess.; W. B. Bryan, *A Hist. of the Nat. Capital*, vol. I (1914); Margaret B. Smith, *The First Forty Years of Washington Society* (1906); C. O. Paullin, *Commodore John Rodgers* (1910); obituary in *Daily National Intelligencer* (Washington), Feb. 24, 1829; correspondence, etc., in Navy Dept. Lib., including Letters and Communications to Comm. Thomas Tingey, 1798–99, Letters and Communications from Mordecai Booth, Aug. 22–Sept. 10, 1814, and Log of the Washington Navy Yard, 1822–30; family data from Lewis D. Cook of Philadelphia.]
A. W—t.

TINGLEY, KATHERINE AUGUSTA WESTCOTT (July 6, 1847–July 11, 1929), theosophist, was born in Newbury, Mass., the daughter of James P. L. Westcott and his wife, Susan Ordway (Chase). Her father, a shipwright, became an officer in the Civil War, and later a hotel proprietor in Newburyport. She was descended from Stukely Westcott, one of the associates of Roger Williams in the founding of Providence Plantations. According to theosophical accounts, she was subject in her childhood to religious visions. She was educated in the public schools and by private tutors and is also reported to have spent two years in a convent in Montreal. While still a young woman, she was married three times: her first husband, Richard Cooke, was a printer; her last, Philo Buchanan Tingley, to whom she was married on Apr. 25, 1888, was a stenographer. Until she was past forty her life was spent in almost total obscurity, but at about that time she emerged in New York City as a spiritualist medium who was also engaged in mission work on the East Side, having thus combined two of the major interests of her life—occultism and philanthropy.

A third major interest—personal power—was soon to be gratified.

She was brought into the theosophical movement by William Quan Judge [q.v.], Outer Head of the Theosophical Society in America, over whom she acquired extensive influence. Immediately after Judge's death in 1896, a meeting of the "Esoteric Section" was held in New York City, at which extracts were read from an alleged secret diary of Judge, referring to the remarkable occult powers of a mysterious disciple whom he appointed as his successor. A report of this meeting was sent out by the members of a new "Advisory Council," who also claimed appointment by Judge, and in this report the Society was informed that the identity of the Outer Head would not be made known until a year had passed. Although the papers of Judge on which this action was said to be based were never exhibited, the coup d'état passed unchallenged. The new Outer Head was variously described as "Promise," "the Veiled Mahatma," "the Light of the Lodge," and "the Purple Mother," but long before the year was out it was an open secret that the person chosen was Katherine Tingley. At the annual Theosophical Convention in April 1896, she secured the election of E. T. Hargrove (the man chiefly instrumental in putting her forward as Outer Head) as president of the Society, and raised a large sum of money to found a "School for the Revival of the Lost Mysteries of Antiquity." Soon after, she duplicated this success by getting many thousands of dollars from her followers to send a group of "Crusaders" under her leadership on an eight months' trip around the world. After their return, a rift developed between Mrs. Tingley and Hargrove. At the annual convention in April 1898 she unseated the latter by obtaining the adoption of a new constitution which merged the Theosophical Society in a new organization called the Universal Brotherhood and vested absolute power in her as its "Leader and Official Head." This action led to numerous schisms, but she retained control of the central body until her death.

Her abilities lay mainly in the field of organization. During the Spanish-American War she established an emergency hospital for sick and wounded soldiers at Montauk Point, L. I., and was furnished transportation and assistance by the United States government for hospital work in Cuba. In 1904 she led a second theosophical crusade around the world. In addition to the international headquarters at Point Loma, Cal., which included the School of Antiquity, the Theosophical University, Râja Yoga College, a Greek theatre, and a home for orphan children, she erected a children's summer home at Spring Valley, N. Y., a theosophical institute at Newburyport, Mass., three schools in Cuba, seven theosophical centers in Europe, one in England (at Fleet in Hampshire), and Swedish theosophical headquarters on the island of Visingsoe in Vetter Lake, Sweden. In 1925 she received the Medal of Honor of the German Red Cross. She edited the Century Path, a weekly, from 1907 to 1911, when it was superseded by the Theosophical Path, of which she was editor until 1929; she also edited the Râja Yoga Messenger, a bimonthly, from 1912 to 1929, and published a number of fugitive pamphlets of little importance.

Charges of immorality brought against her institution at Point Loma were answered by Mrs. Tingley through successful libel suits, but in 1925 a verdict against her of $100,000 was upheld by the California supreme court for alienating the affections of Dr. George F. Mohn, a theosophist, from his wife, Irene M. Mohn (Mohn vs. Tingley, 191 California, 470). Thenceforth Mrs. Tingley resided chiefly in Europe, where she lectured every year in Paris and Berlin. On her way to Berlin in June 1929 she suffered serious injuries in an automobile accident near Osnabrück in Westphalia, and though she recovered sufficiently to permit her return to her home at Visingsoe in Sweden, she died there a few days after arrival.

[Vital Records of Newbury, Mass. (1911); R. M. Tingley, The Tingley Family (1910); J. C. and G. W. Chamberlain, Seven Generations of the Descendants of Aquila and Thomas Chase (1928); R. L. Whitman, Hist. and Geneal. of the Ancestors and Some Descendants of Stukely Westcott (1932); J. J. Currier, Hist. of Newburyport (1906), II, 393; Lilian Whiting, Katherine Tingley, Theosophist and Humanitarian (1919); The Theosophical Movement, 1875–1925 (1925); E. T. Hargrove, An Occultist's Life, May 17, 1896, eulogistic pamphlet; E. T. Hargrove, E.S.T., Mar. 1, 1898, denunciatory pamphlet; N. Y. Tribune, May 18, 1896; Theosophy, passim, 1896–97; A. L. Cleather, H. P. Blavatsky as I Knew Her (Calcutta, 1923); N. Y. Times, July 12, 1929; Theosophical Path, Aug. 1929; Who's Who in America, 1928–29.]   E. S. B—s.

TIPTON, JOHN (Aug. 15, 1730–August 1813), soldier, frontier politician, was born in Baltimore County, Md., the son of Jonathan and Elizabeth Tipton and the uncle of John Tipton [q.v.]. When he was about twenty years of age he removed to Frederick County, Va., with his father, and settled on Cedar Creek. Sometime before 1753 he was married to Mary Butler, who bore him nine sons. After her death in 1776, he was married on July 22, 1779, to Martha (Denton) Moore, the widow of Dr. James Moore. They had about six children. From John Tipton's numerous progeny stem many of the Tiptons whose names appeared in almost every frontier community of the Shenandoah Valley, the transmontane districts of North Carolina, Tennessee, Ohio, and Indiana. Tipton's services in Virginia extended over a period of more than thirty years. He was instrumental in founding Woodstock, in Dunmore (later Shenandoah) County, was a vestryman and justice of the peace in Beckford Parish, cooperated with John Peter Muhlenberg [q.v.] in organizing the Revolutionary meeting at Woodstock, June 16, 1774, and signed the resolutions drawn up on that day. He served under Andrew Lewis [q.v.] in Dunmore's War and participated in the battle at Point Pleasant in October 1774, became a member of the committee of safety and correspondence and a recruiting officer for his county, and served as a member of the Virginia House of Burgesses from 1774 to 1781. He represented Dunmore County at the Virginia Convention at Williamsburg on May 6, 1776, supported four or five sons as Revolutionary soldiers, and acted as lieutenant-colonel of militia, commissioner, and high sheriff of Shenandoah County during the war.

Late in 1783 he removed to the Watauga settlement in North Carolina (later part of Tennessee), where, after some vacillation, he soon crystallized his political views in opposition to John Sevier [q.v.], and the "State of Franklin." His election from Washington County to the North Carolina Assembly in 1785 precipitated the first conflict with Sevier, then governor of the State of Franklin, and Tipton, as colonel of the Washington County militia, and justice of the court, followed it up by strenuous punitive measures. The two men became bitter and implacable enemies. Innumerable opportunities for clashes rose out of a chaotic situation in which two sets of courts, two sets of local officials, and two "officially" authorized bodies of militia tried to function. Armed raiding parties, first from one side and then the other, carried off the court records and official papers of the opposition, and for three years the community was in a state of civil war. Tipton's side was clearly in the minority; when the petition of William Cocke [q.v.], representing Franklin's case for separate recognition, was refused in the North Carolina Assembly, Franklinites hanged Tipton in effigy. Upon one occasion the two leaders met, and, after long and spirited argument, Tipton finally set upon Sevier, and, as an early historian so quaintly put it, "began to annoy him with his hands clinched..." (Haywood, post, p. 161). A compromise arranged by Evan Shelby [q.v.] on behalf of the conciliatory North Carolina government failed, and strife subsided, with Tiptonites victorious, only after a pitched battle in 1788 at Tipton's fortress-like home near Jonesboro.

The adoption of the federal Constitution brought about the final collapse of the State of Franklin; but Tipton's enthusiasm for a central government was bounded by state lines, and he voted against adoption in the Assembly. His tactics, those of a strong, self-reliant, ambitious, hot-headed, unrelenting dispenser of justice, were nowhere popular, although his long record testifies to the fact that his neighbors respected him highly. Sevierites were ultimately elected to all offices in the Washington district, but Tipton's great native ability and his experience were once more made use of when Tennessee became a territory; he represented his county in the first assembly in 1793, and in 1794 and 1795. He helped to draft the constitution, when Tennessee became a state in 1796, and was a senator in the first and second state legislatures. This was his last public service. He and Sevier were among the first trustees of Washington College at Salem in 1795. He died at his home on Sinking Creek at the age of eighty-three.

[C. B. Heinemann, "Tipton Family" (1934), typescript, Lib. of Cong.; Selden Nelson, "The Tipton Family of Tenn.," *East Tenn. Hist. Soc. Pubs.*, no. 1 (1929); S. E. Massengill, *The Massengills, Massengales and Variants* (1931); N. K. Reid, "Sketches of Early Indiana Senators—(IV) John Tipton," *Ind. Mag. of Hist.*, Dec. 1913; J. W. Wayland, *A Hist. of Shenandoah County, Va.* (1927); S. C. Williams, *Hist. of the Lost State of Franklin* (rev. ed., 1933); John Haywood, *Civil and Pol. Hist.-. . . . of Tenn.* (1823); J. G. M. Ramsey, *The Annals of Tenn.* (1853); *State Records of N. C.*, vols. XVIII (1900), vols. XX-XXII (1902-07); H. E. Carr, *Washington Coll.* (1935); *Tenn. A Hist.* (1933), ed. by P. M. Hamer, vol. I.] M. S. E.

TIPTON, JOHN (Aug. 14, 1786–Apr. 5, 1839), soldier, senator, was born in Sevier County, Tenn., the son of Joshua and Jennett (Shields) Tipton, and a nephew of John Tipton [q.v.]. The family had migrated from Maryland to eastern Tennessee, where Joshua Tipton was killed by Indians in 1793. Fourteen years after his death his widow, with four children, moved to Harrison County, Indiana Territory, where one of the sons operated a ferry across the Ohio River. John Tipton received no formal education, and learned to read and write with meager facility only when he became justice of the peace in 1810. At that time Indiana Territory was on the Indian frontier and Tipton belonged to a company of riflemen that saw service at the battle of Tippecanoe. For several years thereafter he commanded a troop of rangers which harassed the Indians away from the Ohio River frontier. In 1822 he was elected major-general of the 2nd Division of Indiana Militia. Meanwhile, 1816–19, he served as sheriff of the county, and then represented his county in the state assembly until 1823. He was appointed one of the two surveyors to run the Indiana-Illinois boundary line in 1821.

On Dec. 22, 1823, he was appointed Indian Agent for the Fort Wayne district of Northern Indiana, and negotiated important Indian treaties in 1826, 1828, and 1836. He speculated widely in the cheap lands of the state and was a prolific founder of county seats on sites adjacent to generous holdings of his own. In 1831 he was appointed to fill out an unexpired term in the United States Senate, and in 1833 was elected for a full term. In politics he was a Democrat, being a close friend of Jackson and a frequent visitor at the "Hermitage." His senatorial career was not spectacular, since he was not a fluent speaker and was never as adept in the intricacies of national intrigue as in the rough and tumble of local frontier politics. He was hostile to the abolition of slavery, championed Michigan's fight for the "Toledo strip," and took a moderate part in all discussions of Indian and military affairs.

In appearance he was of medium height, sinewy, small featured, with a low wrinkled forehead, and stern grey eyes. His stiff sandy hair stood erect in the Jacksonian manner. He was married about 1818 to his cousin, Jeanette Shields, by whom he had three children. After her death, he was married, in April 1825, to Matilda Spencer, and had three children by this marriage. He completed his senatorial term in March 1839, and died the following month at his home in Logansport, Ind. He was a typical frontier politician, a hard-drinking, hard-hitting Indian fighter, and an adroit land speculator. His "journal" was published in the *Indianapolis News* of Apr. 17, and May 5, 1879, and reprinted in the *Indiana Magazine of History*, volume I, numbers 1 and 2, 1905.

[No adequate account of Tipton exists in printed form, but the Indiana Historical Commission has in preparation a two-volume edition of his letters with a generous biographical preface. For this sketch the author consulted a collection of more than 8,000 original Tipton documents and photostats housed in the Indiana State Library, Indianapolis, Ind. See also, C. B. Heinemann, "Tipton Family" (1934), typewritten manuscript, Lib. of Cong.; *Biog. Direct. Am. Cong.* (1928); M. W. Pershing, *Life of Gen. John Tipton and Early Ind. Hist.* (n.d.); N. K. Reid, "Sketches of Early Indiana Senators—(IV) John Tipton," *Ind. Mag. of Hist.*, Dec. 1913; *Ind. Democrat*, Apr. 17, 1839.]

G. A. B.

TISQUANTUM [See Squanto, d. 1622].

TITCHENER, EDWARD BRADFORD (Jan. 11, 1867–Aug. 3, 1927), experimental psychologist and leader of the "structuralist" school, was born at Chichester, England, son of Alice Field (Habin) and John Titchener, of a family

that in several centuries had displayed unusual ability. His early school training was obtained in the Prebendal School at Chichester and at Malvern College. From 1885 to 1889 he was at Brasenose College, Oxford, where he was senior scholar in classics and philosophy, and senior Hulme exhibitioner; in 1889–90 he was research student in physiology. He received the degree of B.A. in 1890. The next two years he spent in Wilhelm Wundt's psychological laboratory at Leipzig, and there in 1892 he won his doctorate. After a short time as extension lecturer in biology at Oxford, in the autumn of 1892 he accepted an assistant professorship of psychology in Cornell University; three years later he became Sage Professor of Psychology. In 1894 he received the degree of M.A. from Oxford. In the same year he became American editor of *Mind*, a position he held through 1921; in 1895 he joined Edmund Clark Sanford as associate editor of the *American Journal of Psychology*. On June 19, 1894, he married Sophie Kellogg Bedlow of Portland, Me., who had been studying history at Cornell. In the summer of 1896 he made his only return to England and the Continent.

During the first eight years of his career at Cornell he published a number of translations: with J. E. Creighton, *Lectures on Human and Animal Psychology* (1894), from the German of Wundt; *Outlines of Psychology* (1895), from Oswald Külpe; with W. B. Pillsbury, *Introduction to Philosophy* (1897), from Külpe; and, with J. H. Gulliver, *Ethics* (1897), from the first volume of Wundt's *Ethik*. He also published two textbooks, *An Outline of Psychology* (1896) and *The Primer of Psychology* (1898). The point of view of these books is orthodoxly Wundtian: the subject matter of psychology is mental processes, and its method analysis by introspection of these processes into elements and attributes. In 1898 he defended the Wundtian type of psychology as "structural" against the "functional" type then coming to the fore, especially at the University of Chicago, which dwelt on the significance of various mental reactions for welfare rather than on the introspective analysis of mental states ("The Postulates of a Structural Psychology," *Philosophical Review*, Sept. 1898).

His most important work, *Experimental Psychology* (2 vols., 1901–05), was a milestone in the progress of psychology. Each volume consisted of two manuals, one for the student, the other for the instructor. The first volume, "Qualitative," dealt with experiments not involving exact measurement; the second, "Quantitative," with more precise psycho-physical work; the student's manuals gave carefully tested directions for experimenting, while the instructor's manuals were mines of erudition on all possible points, historical and theoretical, relating to the interpretation of the experiments. It is characteristic of his loyalty to England (he never gave up his British citizenship) that he presented these books to Oxford for the degree of D.Sc., which he won in 1906. In 1904 he published a translation of the first volume of Wundt's *Grundzüge der physiologischen Psychologie.* Later appeared *Lectures on the Elementary Psychology of Feeling and Attention* (1908); *Lectures on the Experimental Psychology of the Thought-Processes* (1909); *A Textbook of Psychology* (2 vols., 1909–10), dedicated to the memory of his Oxford teacher in physiology, Sir John Burdon Sanderson; and *A Beginner's Psychology* (1915). In 1909 he became research professor in the graduate school, and in 1917 declined a call to succeed Hugo Münsterberg [*q.v.*] at Harvard. He delivered the Lowell Institute lectures, never published, at Boston in 1911. From 1921 to 1925 he was editor of the *American Journal of Psychology.* The last ten years of his life were relatively unproductive; he was, however, working on a systematic psychology, to be his *magnum opus,* but his death from a brain tumor, after only a few days' illness, came before it was far advanced. His wife, a son, and three daughters survived him. In 1929 some introductory material for his unfinished work appeared, edited by a colleague, under the title of *Systematic Psychology: Prolegomena.*

Titchener's personality was a dominating one. It has been pointed out that his attitude towards his junior colleagues and his students was modelled after the autocracy of Wundt at Leipzig (Boring, *post,* p. 492). Because the American Psychological Association refused to expel one of its members for a mild plagiarism from one of Titchener's translations, he attended only one of its meetings after 1895, and formed a group of his own. It was a point of personal privilege that caused him to relinquish the editorship of the *American Journal of Psychology* in 1925. Yet in his letters he was unassuming, reasonable, and kind. As a lecturer he was unequaled. He could hold an ordinary popular audience spellbound through an hour's discourse on the measurement of sensations. He was versatile—a scholarly amateur of music (he was actually professor of music at Cornell, 1896–98, before its department was organized), a connoisseur of coins. But, although he wrote a classic book on experimental psychology, he made no important experimental discovery. And although he was a

penetrating, if not always illuminating, critic of theory, he made no major contribution to it. So far as his writings show, the most noteworthy change in his views on method as time went on was an inclination towards the use of "phenomenological observation" as a substitute for introspection (see "The Schema of Introspection," *American Journal of Psychology,* October 1912, and "Experimental Psychology, a Retrospect," *Ibid.,* July 1925), but he was not the author of this new method. The originality of his mind was apparently not equal to its remarkable grasp, versatility, and acuteness. But it may truly be said of him that his high conception of psychology as pure science has made his work, and that of his pupils, the strongest bulwark against the flood of applied psychology, educational psychology, and mental testing that has threatened in America to obliterate the science. He held a number of honorary degrees, and was a member of numerous important scientific and philosophical societies.

[*Who's Who in America,* 1926–27; *Brasenose Coll. Reg., 1509–1909* (1909), vol. I, p. 682; E. G. Boring, in *Am. Jour. of Psychology,* Oct. 1927; *Cornell Alumni News,* Aug. 1927, pp. 495–96; obituary in *N. Y. Times,* Aug. 4, 1927; personal acquaintance.] M. F. W.

TITCOMB, JOHN WHEELOCK (Feb. 24, 1860–Jan. 26, 1932), fish culturist and conservationist, was born in Farmington, N. H., the son of George Alfred and Mary Elizabeth Lemist (Lancaster) Titcomb. He was educated in the public schools and at Phillips Exeter Academy, from which he graduated in 1880. During the succeeding thirteen years he was in the employ of the Howe Scale Company at St. Johnsbury, Vt. In 1891 he was appointed one of the fish and game commissioners of the state of Vermont, and in 1894 he assumed in addition the superintendency of the federal fish hatchery at St. Johnsbury. On Dec. 22, 1896, he was married to Martha Ross of St. Johnsbury, by whom he had a son and a daughter. In 1902 he went to Washington as chief of the division of fish culture of the United States bureau of fisheries, and in this position showed himself to be an efficient and progressive administrator. A year later, at the request of the Argentinian government, he spent a number of months in South America establishing a fisheries service in the Argentine and successfully introducing American fishes. The Peruvian government later requested his services for a similar purpose, but for some reason the trip was not made. When his services with the bureau of fisheries ended in 1909, he returned to Vermont, and again assumed the duties of state fish and game commissioner. From 1916 to 1921 he was state fish culturist for New York.

He intermittently accepted private commissions as well, in the somewhat unusual character of consulting fish culturist. He entered the employ of the state of Connecticut in 1921, and in 1922 became superintendent of its board of fisheries and game. In this position, which he occupied until his death, he achieved real success in demonstrating the possibility of maintaining fishing and hunting in a state having a limited area and a large population. He was president of the American Fisheries Society, 1899–1900 and 1926–27, its librarian for a number of years, and an officer and active participant in the American Game Conference sponsored by the American Game Association. He was always prominent in deliberations having a bearing upon the conservation of wild life, and the vigor with which he supported his own views at times engendered unjustified opposition. He died in Hartford, Conn., survived by his two children.

Titcomb was a fairly prolific writer, most of his work being of a technical, though not strictly scientific nature. Government publications under his authorship comprise six titles, and he wrote extensively for the official reports of the states with which he was connected, and for the transactions and proceedings of the societies in which he had a membership. He also contributed occasional articles to sportsmen's magazines. Among his outstanding publications were a government pamphlet on *Aquatic Plants in Pond Culture* (1909) and a report on a biological survey of Lake George, N. Y. His first consideration was for the welfare of wild life rather than the desires of would-be exploiters of game and fish, and he deserves recognition as a successful conservation administrator during an era when, all too frequently, positions of this nature were political spoils, and were filled by men who had little conception of their responsibilities and limited ability for meeting them.

[The maiden name of Titcomb's mother was Seaverus, but she was known by her stepfather's name. See *Who's Who in America*, 1930–31 ; *Trans. Am. Fisheries Soc.* (1932) ; official records and reports, U. S. Bureau of Fisheries, and fish and game depts. of N. Y., Vt., and Conn. ; obituary in *Hartford Times*, Jan. 27, 1932 ; information from Titcomb's colleagues and from his daughter.]   M.C.J.

TOBANI, THEODORE MOSES (May 2, 1855–Dec. 12, 1933), composer, was born in Hamburg, Germany, the son of Josef Tobani and Marianne (Wède) Tobani. He began the study of the violin at three years of age. In his boyhood he was taken to New York by his family and for a time attended the Rivington Street School in that city. The boy's musical talent was so remarkable that after a few years in America the family returned to Germany so that Theodore could have the best instruction in music. He is said to have studied composition in Germany under V. Bermuth. In 1870 the Tobanis came once more to America, and the fifteen-year-old Theodore became a violinist at Simpson's Theatre in Philadelphia (*New York Herald Tribune, post*). Two years later, in 1872, he was engaged as first violinist at the Arch Street Theatre in Philadelphia, but he soon left for New York and for six years played at Wallack's Theatre. After that he held positions at the Grand Opera House, the Bijou Opera House, Daly's Theatre, and the Thalia Theatre, all in New York.

It was as a composer and an arranger that Tobani was best known. He composed altogether 5,480 original pieces, some under his own name and others under the pen-names "Theodore Moses," "Florence Reed," and "Andrew Herman," and his orchestrations of the works of other composers were widely distributed and performed. His own compositions were of a semiclassic variety that were never too difficult for the abilities or the comprehension of average performers. They were generally marked by a wistful sentimentalism and pathos which found a ready response when they were written and for several decades later. His first composition (1877) was entitled "The Telephone Galop" because of the interest in the new invention then coming into use. For a piano gavotte called "The Little Nestling" (1883), which was performed 1,100 times during the run of a single play, he received only thirty-five dollars, but in the case of his most popular work, "Hearts and Flowers," he was more fortunate. He received a royalty on every copy sold, and the sale ran into the millions, though the figure 23,000,000 which is sometimes given (*New York Herald Tribune, post*) is a great exaggeration. "Hearts and Flowers" was first published in 1893 as a piano piece, simple enough to be played by those of the most modest attainments. Soon it was transcribed in arrangements for solo instruments and combinations of all sorts, and its popularity became international. It was particularly useful as incidental music to pathetic moments in the theatre, and today whenever those producing a revival of a late nineteenth- or early twentieth-century melodrama seek to be authentic, they select "Hearts and Flowers" for the orchestra to play during sad scenes. Others of Tobani's popular works were "Echoes from the Metropolitan Opera House," "The Spanish Patrol," "Moonlight on the Hudson," "Land of My Dreams," "The White Squadron," "Crack Regiment Patrol," and two Hungarian fantasias. He was the composer of several marches, "The Patriot," "The United States," "Manhattan," and others. His last published composition, "Just a Gem," was issued in 1917, just before the beginning of the "jazz era." Tobani was a genial sort of person with a kindly humor. A distinctive feature of his appearance was a spreading moustache that remained black when his hair became grey. At the time of his death at Jackson Heights, L. I., he was still busy composing, at work on an "Old World Symphony" and a suite, "The Battle of the Marne." His wife, Helena Tobani, died some years before him. He was survived by five daughters and three sons.

[*Metronome*, Apr. 1906; *Musical Courier*, Dec. 23, 1933; *Musical America*, Dec. 25, 1933; obituaries in *N. Y. Times*, Dec. 13, and *N. Y. Herald Tribune*, Dec. 14, 1933; information from Tobani's family.]

J.T.H.

TOBEY, EDWARD SILAS (Apr. 5, 1813–Mar. 29, 1891), merchant, capitalist, was born in Kingston, Mass., the only child of Silas and Betsey (Fuller) Tobey. He was a descendant of Thomas Tobey who was in Sandwich by 1644. His father was a sea captain who died in 1817, and in 1823 his mother married Capt. Phineas Sprague, senior member of the Boston shipping firm of Phineas and Seth Sprague. Tobey became a clerk in the office of the firm in 1827, after having received the usual education of those days in the public schools of Boston and Duxbury. In 1833 he was made a partner, but though he remained one for thirty-three years, his business activities extended far beyond the affairs of the firm. He became an officer of several steamship companies, one of them developing into the Fall River Line; treasurer of the United States Insurance Company and of the Russell Mills, a cotton-duck factory in Plymouth, Mass.; and director of commercial and savings banks in Boston. During the Civil War he was prominent because of his knowledge of shipping and finance. In 1861 Gov. John Albion Andrew of Massachusetts appointed him to a committee to devise defenses for Boston Harbor, and Secretary Salmon P. Chase [*qq.v.*] made him a member of an advisory group to formulate a financial policy for the United States government; in 1863 Secretary Edwin M. Stanton appointed him to a board to discuss means of destroying the Confederate iron-clad *Merrimac*, and he was conspicuous in other ways because of being president of the Boston Board of Trade (1861–63) and of the Boston Young Men's Christian Association.

After the war he continued his connection with commercial and religious organizations. Some of his speeches on public questions were published to give them wider currency: *The Industry of the South* (1865), *American Shipping Interests* (1871), and *The Boston Hydraulic Protector Against Fire* (1873). He was a trustee of Bradford Academy (1863–75) and of Dartmouth College (1863–70), and he indorsed and enlisted support for the founding of the Massachusetts Institute of Technology. He was a member or officer of many bodies concerned with the propagation of religion or the investigation of American history, being himself an orthodox Congregationalist with five generations of American ancestors. In 1866 he was elected to the Massachusetts Senate, serving one term there; in 1869 he was appointed to the board of commissioners of Indian affairs; and in 1875 he was appointed postmaster of Boston (appointment confirmed, Dec. 13, 1875), an office he held until December 1886. However, his distinction arose not so much from the public offices he held as from his wide range of influence in activities for public safety or welfare. On Apr. 5, 1841, he married in Boston Hannah Brown Sprague, his stepfather's daughter, by whom he had ten children. He moved from Boston to Brookline in 1883, and died there, survived by his wife, three sons, and four daughters.

[R. B. Tobey and C. H. Pope, *Tobey (Tobie, Toby) Geneal.* (1905); J. S. Pond, *Bradford: a New England Academy* (1930); obituaries in *Boston Herald, Boston Transcript*, Mar. 30, 1891, and *Brookline Chronicle*, Apr. 4, 1891.]

S.G.

TOD, DAVID (Feb. 21, 1805–Nov. 13, 1868), governor of Ohio, diplomat, and capitalist, was born near Youngstown in Trumbull, later Mahoning, County, Ohio, the son of George Tod [*q.v.*] and Sarah (Isaacs) Tod. Reared on his father's farm, "Brier Hill," he went to the neighborhood schools and later to Burton Academy in Geauga County. He read law in the office of Powell Stone of Warren and was admitted to the bar in 1827. From 1830 to 1838 he was Democratic postmaster at Warren, though his father was affiliated with the Whig party. For one term, 1838–40, he represented in the state Senate a district normally Whig. He became the unsuccessful Democratic nominee for governor in 1844 and again in 1846. Accepting an appointment as minister to Brazil in 1847, he remained there until 1851. His tact and good sense soon cleared away the misunderstandings with that government; but his efforts to stop the African slave trade to Brazil, largely in the hands of Americans, ended in failure because his own government would take no action. Amassing a fortune in the coal and iron business, he was an important figure in the business affairs of

Youngstown; and business interests, rather than politics, occupied his attention through the 1850's. He began to ship coal to Cleveland by canal from his "Brier Hill" mines in 1841 after having personally convinced steamboat owners of its value as fuel. He soon became interested in iron manufacturing and was one of the founders of Youngstown's great iron industry. He was also one of a group of six promoters who built the Cleveland and Mahoning Valley Railroad, and he served as president of the road from 1859 to his death.

In the Democratic convention of 1860 he appeared as a Douglas delegate, was elected first vice-president of the convention, and after Caleb Cushing [q.v.] withdrew assumed the chair. When the Civil War began, his active espousal of the Union cause led to his nomination for the governorship by the Union party, and he was easily elected. He had to deal with such matters as draft evasion and resistance, the activities of the Peace Democrats, the excitement over the Vallandigham arrest, the defense of Cincinnati against Kirby-Smith's threatened invasion in September 1862, and the raid of John H. Morgan across the Ohio in July 1863. His vigorous actions and forceful utterances gave offense in some quarters but stamped him as an executive of energy and decision. He was especially watchful over the welfare of the disabled and wounded soldiers, but in making promotions of officers he incurred some criticism. However, the system, rather than the governor, was principally at fault. When he was defeated for renomination by John Brough, he supported the ticket, though deeply disappointed at the result. He was inclined to blame the national administration for his defeat, and perhaps this was a consideration in causing him to refuse Lincoln's offer of the secretaryship of the treasury in 1864 after Chase's resignation, though he gave the condition of his health and his business affairs as reasons. He was chosen as one of the Republican presidential electors in 1868 but died soon after the election from a stroke of apoplexy. He was survived by his widow, Maria (Smith) Tod, to whom he had been married on June 4, 1832, and by six of his seven children.

[Letters and papers in archives of department of state, in Ohio Arch. and Hist. Soc. Lib., Columbus, Western Reserve Hist. Soc. Lib., Cleveland, and in Lib. of Cong.; G. B. Wright, *Hon. David Tod* (1900) and in *Ohio Arch. and Hist. Pubs.*, vol. VIII (1900); Samuel Galloway, *Eulogy on Ex-Gov. David Tod* (1869); J. G. Butler, *Hist. of Youngstown* (1921), vols. I, III; E. H. Roseboom, "Ohio in the 1850's," thesis in Widener Lib., Harvard Univ.; E. A. Holt, *Party Politics in Ohio, 1840–1850* (1931) and in *Ohio Arch. and Hist. Quart.*, July 1929; G. H. Porter, *Ohio Politics During the Civil War* (1911); L. F. Hill, *Diplomatic Relations between the U. S. and Brazil*

(1932); Whitelaw Reid, *Ohio in the War* (1868), **vol.** I; *Herald* (Cleveland), Nov. 16, 1868.]　　E. H. R.

TOD, GEORGE (Dec. 11, 1773–Apr. 11, 1841), jurist, was born in Suffield, Conn., the son of David and Rachel (Kent) Tod. His father was an emigrant from Perthshire, Scotland. His brother was John Tod and his son David Tod [qq.v.]. Upon graduating from Yale College in 1795 he entered the Litchfield Law School conducted by Tapping Reeve [q.v.]. On Sept. 18, 1797, he was married to Sarah Isaacs, the daughter of Ralph Isaacs, a Yale graduate and merchant of some means, and, admitted to the bar that year, began practice in New Haven. In 1800, after a preliminary visit, he removed to Youngstown, Ohio, where he lived until his death. In August 1800 he was appointed prosecuting attorney of Trumbull County in the Northwest Territory. In the contest that ended in Ohio's statehood he was not active, apparently distrusting the "Republicanism" of the "Chillicothe Junto." He rose rapidly in the esteem of his neighbors and represented them in the state Senate, 1804–06. In January 1807 he was elected judge of the state supreme court by the legislature, a position he had held since the previous April by an interim appointment. In 1807 he and Samuel Huntington [q.v.] upheld the decision of a district court declaring unconstitutional an act of the legislature to grant jurisdiction to magistrates in civil suits involving as much as fifty dollars. This was held by the court to impair the right of jury trial. The state legislature, dominated by Jeffersonians, regarded the decision as a challenge. An attempt was made to remove Tod by impeachment, which failed in 1809 by the narrow margin of one vote and established the doctrine of judicial review in Ohio. The next year the legislature removed him by a strictly political maneuver, when his enemies were able to interpret the constitutional provision for a term of seven years as meaning that his term should close on the seventh anniversary of statehood, that is in 1810.

During 1810–12 he served two terms in the state Senate. In the War of 1812 he saw active service in northern Ohio as major of the 19th Infantry and later as lieutenant colonel of the 17th Infantry in the regular army. In February 1816 he was elected by the legislature as presiding judge of the 3rd district circuit court of appeals, a position he filled with distinction until his retirement to private practice at the end of 1829. Such decisions of his as were printed indicate a lucid, well-trained mind. In politics he was nominally a Jeffersonian and later a Whig but had the conservative inclinations that characterized so many transplanted New Englanders. He took an active interest in the improvement of agricultural methods in the state but was unable to make a financial success of his own farm. It remained for his son David to exploit the coal that underlay the farm. His old age was uneventful, his last political activity being in behalf of the candidacy of Harrison in 1840. He died at his home "Brier Hill," near Youngstown, survived by his widow and five children.

[Papers in Western Reserve Hist. Soc. Lib., Cleveland; some letters and papers in Ohio State Lib., Columbus, and in Lib. of Cong.; F. B. Dexter, *Biog. Sketches of the Grads. of Yale College*, vol. V (1911); *Western Law Monthly*, Aug. 1863; W. T. Utter, "Judicial Rev. in Early Ohio," *Miss. Valley Hist. Rev.*, June 1927; F. W. Bailey, *Early Conn. Marriages*, vol. VII (1906), p. 27.]   W. T. U.

TOD, JOHN (November 1779–Mar. 27, 1830), congressman from Pennsylvania, was born in Suffield, Hartford County, Conn., the son of Rachel (Kent) and David Tod, an emigrant from Scotland. He was the brother of George Tod and the uncle of David Tod [*qq.v.*]. He attended the common schools of Connecticut, and, while still a youth, lived for a time in New York. He studied law in the office of his brother George and about 1802 removed to Bedford, Pa., where he practised very successfully. During 1806 and 1807 he was clerk to the county commissioners of Bedford County. From 1810 to 1813 he sat in the state House of Representatives and was speaker twice. From 1814 to 1816 he was a member of the state Senate, in which he was president for a time. His record in the legislature was one of cooperation with the Democratic majority. Like many of his colleagues from the western counties he urged the adoption of more extensive programs for the construction of roads and canals and for the promotion of manufactures. In 1817 he married Mary R. Hanna. They had three daughters.

He was elected by the Democrats to Congress, where he served from Mar. 4, 1821, until his resignation in 1824. He was a ready debater with a lofty conception of his obligations to his constituents. A member of the committee on military affairs, he was an advocate of an extensive military establishment and in 1822 vigorously urged larger appropriations for fortifications and the ordnance department. If necessary he would have abolished all military bands in favor of appropriations for these branches of the service on the theory that it was "better to part with our fiddlers, than our laborers" (*Annals of Cong.*, 17 Cong., 1 Sess., col. 1632). In 1822, when it was proposed to increase the number of congressmen in the reapportionment bill, he denounced

the idea as "an heretical and pernicious innovation in American politics, supported by no reason, nor recommended by any experience" of the American people. To increase the membership would bring in a "legislative rabble" and would be like increasing a club of debaters ten times over "because speeches are reproductive of speeches, and the more is said the more there remains to say" (*Ibid.*, cols. 926, 930). During 1823–24 he was chairman of the house committee on manufactures and in this capacity worked indefatigably for higher duties and for a wide extension of the protective list. In the debates on the tariff of 1824 he urged higher duties as a military necessity to encourage manufactures for the nation's needs in case of war. Pointing to the danger and disgrace of habitual reliance upon foreign nations for the daily necessaries of life, he saw in the tariff a means of utilizing natural resources, especially hemp, glass, lead, and iron, of finding a market for the raw products of the farmer, and of preventing money from being drained out of the country by foreign nations—a scheme that he thought would, in the final analysis, reduce the cost of commodity prices instead of increase them. He declared that all the devastations and losses of the War of 1812 were nothing compared with the devastations and losses of manufacturing capital under the tariff of 1816 (*Ibid.*, 18 Cong., 1 Sess., col. 1473). In 1824 he was appointed president judge of the 16th judicial district of the state. On May 25, 1827, he was appointed associate justice of the state supreme court. He died in Bedford, Pa.

[W. H. Egle, *Notes and Queries, Hist. and Geneal. . . . 1900* (1901), pp. 39–41, 47–51; *Hist. of Bedford, Somerset, and Fulton Counties* (1884); *Biog. Directory Am. Cong.* (1928); *Niles' Weekly Register*, Apr. 3, 1830; *The Register of Pa.* (ed. by Samuel Hazard), Apr. 10, 1830.]   J. H. P.

TODD, CHARLES STEWART (Jan. 22, 1791–May 17, 1871), lawyer, soldier, diplomat, son of Thomas [*q.v.*] and Elizabeth (Harris) Todd, was born near Danville, Ky., then a part of Virginia. His father in his later years was associate justice of the United States Supreme Court. After attending Transylvania University (Lexington, Ky.), Charles entered the College of William and Mary and was graduated in 1809. He then studied law with his father in Washington, and later with James Gould and Tapping Reeve [*qq.v.*] in Litchfield, Conn. Admitted to the bar in 1811, he began the practice of law in Lexington, Ky.

On the outbreak of the War of 1812 he volunteered, and was made acting quartermaster in the advance of the left wing of the Northwestern Army. He served on Gen. William H. Har-

Todd

rison's staff, his courage and intelligence winning him steady promotion until in March 1815 he was inspector general with the rank of colonel. When the army disbanded he resumed the practice of law at Frankfort, Ky. On June 16, 1816, he married Letitia Shelby, youngest daughter of Gov. Isaac Shelby [q.v.] of Kentucky; twelve children were born to them. He was secretary of state under Gov. George Madison for a short time in 1816 until the latter's death. In 1817 and 1818 he represented Franklin County in the Kentucky legislature.

In February 1820 President Monroe appointed Todd diplomatic agent in Colombia, where he was to observe conditions with a view to guiding the United States government in its recognition policy; promote friendly relations between the two countries; press for the settlement of American claims against Colombia; and work for the withdrawal of discriminating tariffs against the United States. He carried out his duties in a conscientious manner, was friendly, but also realistic and unsentimental. Becoming convinced that Pedro Gual, Colombian secretary for foreign affairs, was unfairly prejudicing Colombian opinion against the United States, he appealed directly to acting-President Santander and other prominent Colombian officials. Gual was furious. He attacked Todd's integrity and wanted him recalled. Todd gained the confidence of the Colombian people, however, and President Monroe offered him an appointment as secretary of legation in Colombia in 1823. This he declined, and retiring to a farm in Shelby County, Ky., became active in agricultural affairs. As a commissioner to the Presbyterian General Assembly he sustained the Old School when the separation of 1837 took place.

In the presidential campaign of 1840 Todd supported General Harrison, making speeches, writing a campaign biography in collaboration with Benjamin Drake (*Sketches of the Civil and Military Services of William Henry Harrison*, 1840), and publishing the *Cincinnati Republican*. He accompanied Harrison to Washington for his inauguration, and was closely associated with him until his death. President Tyler appointed him minister to Russia on Aug. 27, 1841, which post he held throughout the administration. No outstanding issue arose during his residence at St. Petersburg. In 1846 he retired to his farm in Shelby County where he raised blooded stock and wrote numerous articles for magazines and newspapers. He refused to become candidate for governor in 1848, but took an active part in the presidential campaign in behalf of Taylor. In 1850 he was appointed one

Todd

of three commissioners to treat with Indian tribes on the Mexican border and drew up the final report. He became interested in the development of Texas resources, and was for a time a Texas railroad official. In his later years he was an editor of the Louisville *Industrial and Commercial Gazette*. At the beginning of the Civil War he offered his services at Washington, but they were declined. He died of pneumonia at the home of his son-in-law, Judge Posey, in Baton Rouge, La.

[For sources, see G. W. Griffin, *Memoir of Col. Chas. S. Todd* (1873); T. M. Green, *Hist. Families of Ky.* (1889); J. R. Witcraft, *The Virginia Todds* (1913); *The Biog. Encyc. of Ky. . . . of the Nineteenth Century* (1878); Lewis Collins, *Historical Sketches of Ky.* (1850); Lewis and R. H. Collins, *Hist. of Ky.* (1874); *Louisville Commercial*, May 20, 1871 (editorial); H. M. Wriston, *Executive Agents in Am. Foreign Relations* (1929). A few personal letters are in the manuscripts division, Lib. of Cong.; diplomatic correspondence is preserved in the archives of the Department of State; selections from Todd's official correspondence while diplomatic agent in Colombia are printed in W. R. Manning, *Diplomatic Correspondence of the U. S. Concerning the Independence of the Latin-American Nations* (1925).]   I. L. T.

TODD, ELI (July 22, 1769–Nov. 17, 1833), physician, a descendant of Christopher Todd who settled in New Haven in 1638, was born in New Haven, Conn., the son of Michael and Mary (Rowe) Todd. His father, who was in the West India trade, died in 1774, leaving a large estate, and thereafter, until he was eight years of age, Eli lived with his great-uncle, the Rev. Jonathan Todd of Guilford, Conn. He prepared for college with the Rev. Elizur Goodrich of Durham, entered Yale College in 1783, and graduated with honor in 1787.

After a voyage to Trinidad, where he suffered an almost fatal attack of yellow fever, he returned to New Haven and studied medicine for two years with Dr. Ebenezer Beardsley. Before he was twenty-one he was practising medicine in Farmington, Conn. There he achieved distinction and was commended by the governor of the state for his courage and devotion during the epidemic of "spotted" fever in 1808, when nearly all those unaffected fled from the town in panic. He spent four years practising in New York, but was persuaded to return to Farmington in 1816. In 1820 he moved to Hartford, where he became the most distinguished consulting physician in the city.

Todd was an early member of the Connecticut Medical Society, of which he was elected vice-president in 1823 and president in 1827 and 1828. In 1812, he was made a member of the society's official committee to investigate the condition of the mentally ill, who were misunderstood and abused. The interest thus aroused was renewed in 1821, and in 1822, largely through his initiative and leadership, a Society for the Relief of the Insane was incorporated. Because his father and a sister had suffered from mental illness, Todd had a special interest in this field. When the movement for a public asylum was begun, he became the leader, and in 1824 was instrumental in raising money to build the Connecticut Retreat for the Insane at Hartford. He became its first superintendent when it opened, Apr. 1, 1824.

The humane Quaker methods used by William Tuke in York, England, were known to Todd, and he instituted the same methods at the Retreat, giving to the institution "a character for the comfort and care of its members not surpassed in this or in any other country" (Woodward, *post*). He was the first to realize the necessity of trained nurses and attendants in the mental hospital, and believing alcoholism to be a form of mental disease, recommended that it be treated as such, and suggested the organization of a home for inebriates. The influence of Todd and the Retreat which he organized was felt throughout America and many countries in Europe. He refused offers of the position of superintendent in Bloomingdale Asylum, New York, and in the Massachusetts State Lunatic Asylum, Worcester, but remained superintendent of the Retreat at Hartford until his death in 1833. Todd was a man of charming personality —sympathetic, understanding, courageous, and of a friendliness which inspired unusual confidence. On Aug. 9, 1796, he married Rhoda Hill, who died in 1825. Three years later, in November 1828, he married her sister, Catherine Hill, who survived him.

[Unpublished material collected by Dr. Henry Barnard, and certain Todd MSS., including "Medical Diary No. 1, 1819" and notes on the spotted fever epidemic, in the files of the Hartford Retreat; C. W. Page, "Dr. Eli Todd and the Hartford Retreat," *Am. Jour. of Insanity*, Apr. 1913, and separately reprinted; W. H. Rockwell, "Biographical Sketch of the Late Eli Todd, M.D.," *U. S. Medic. and Surgic. Jour.*, vol. I (1834); H. A. Kelly and W. L. Burrage, *Am. Medic. Biogs.* (1920); *Boston Medic. and Surgic. Jour.*, Apr. 20, 1836; F. B. Dexter, *Biog. Sketches Grads. Yale Coll.*, vol. IV (1907); J. E. and G. I. Todd, *The Todd Family in America* (1920); *The Seventieth Ann. Report ... of the Retreat for the Insane* (1894); S. B. Woodward, 'Dr. Eli Todd," in S. W. Williams, *Am. Medic. Biog.* (1845); *Columbian Register* (New Haven), Nov. 30, 1833.]   C. C. B.

TODD, HENRY ALFRED (Mar. 13, 1854– Jan. 3, 1925), Romance philologist, editor, was born at Woodstock, Ill., the son of a distinguished Presbyterian divine, the Rev. Richard Kimball Todd, and Martha (Clover) Todd, both of New England descent. His early education was directed by his father. In 1876 he was graduated from the College of New Jersey (later Princeton University), where for the next four years he taught French. In 1880 he went abroad to continue his studies, first at Paris, then at Berlin, where he followed the courses of Adolph Tobler, at that time the chief German authority on Old French syntax. Going thence to Rome, he worked for one semester under Ernesto Monaci, a leading philologist of Italy, after which he passed to the Central University of Madrid in order to attend, during one semester, the courses of the literary critic Marcelino Menéndez y Pelayo. Returning to Paris in 1882, he spent a year studying Romance philology and literature, as well as Sanskrit, under Gaston Paris, Paul Meyer, Arsène Darmesteter, and Abel Bergaigne. During this time he was commissioned by the Société des Anciens Textes Français—the first American to receive that honor—to edit for its series an Old French text, *Le Dit de la Panthère d'Amours* (Paris, 1883), by Nicole de Margival.

From 1883 to 1891 he was instructor in Romance languages at Johns Hopkins University, Baltimore, where he was awarded the degree of Ph.D. in 1885. During this time he collaborated with A. Marshall Elliott in founding and editing *Modern Language Notes,* of which the first number appeared in January 1886, and in organizing the Modern Language Association of America (1883). He later served as treasurer of the Association (1886–91), member of the editorial committee (1894–95), member of the executive council (1893, 1908–11), and president (1906). On July 30, 1891, he married Miriam, daughter of John S. Gilman, a banker of Baltimore. The following autumn he was called to Leland Stanford University as professor of Romance languages and head of the department. Two years later (1893) he became professor of Romance philology at Columbia University, a chair that he held until his death. He was one of the chief organizers of the celebration held in March 1894 to commemorate the centenary of the birth of Friedrich Christian Diez, the founder of Romance philology; in collaboration with Adolphe Cohn, he founded and edited until his death the Columbia University Studies in Romance Philology and Literature; and in 1909, with three colleagues, he founded at Columbia the *Romanic Review,* a quarterly journal devoted to research in Romance philology and literature, the first of its kind to be established in the United States. With Raymond Weeks, he continued joint editorship of the *Review* until his death. He was a life member of the Institut Français aux États-

Unis; president of the committee on courses and lectures of the Institut; president of the French Union, university branch of the Institut, from 1917; and vice-president of the council of administration of the Musée d'Art Français. In 1919 he was sent to France by the United States government as a member of the *mission de rapprochement*. He died in New York City, survived by his wife, two daughters and a son.

He was author of nearly one hundred books, articles, and book reviews. His chief publications include the following editions of Old French manuscripts: "Guillaume de Dole" (*Publications of the Modern Language Association of America,* vol. II, 1886); "La Naissance du Chevalier au Cygne" (*Ibid.,* vol. IV, 1889), a French poem of the twelfth century; "La Vie de Sainte Catherine d'Alexandrie" (*Ibid.,* vol. XV, 1900); "The Old French Versified Apocalypse of the Kerr Manuscript" (*Ibid.,* vol. XVIII, 1903); "An Unpublished Fourteenth-Century Invocation to Mary Magdalen" (*Studies in Honor of A. Marshall Elliott,* vol.I, n.d.); and, in collaboration with F. C. Ostrander, *Li Romans dou Lis* (1915). After his death his colleagues, friends, and pupils issued the *Todd Memorial Volumes: Philological Studies* (2 vols., 1930), edited by John D. Fitz-Gerald and Pauline Taylor.

[*Who's Who in America,* 1924–25; J. D. Fitz-Gerald, in *Todd Memorial Vols.,* vol. I (1930), with bibliog.; T. F. Crane, in *Romanic Rev.,* July–Sept. 1925; obituary in *N. Y. Times,* Jan. 4, 1925.]　　J. L. G.

TODD, JOHN (Oct. 9, 1800–Aug. 24, 1873), Congregational clergyman, author, was a descendant of Christopher Todd, who came to Boston from England in 1637, and was one of the settlers of the New Haven colony. He was born in Rutland, Vt., where his parents Dr. Timothy and Phoebe (Buel) Todd had recently settled. The father died when John was six years old; the mother, who became insane at his birth, lived for many years without recovering her reason. The boy spent his youth in various places and at length lived for a number of years in Charlestown, Mass., attending school in Boston. At the age of eighteen he entered Yale, where, in spite of scant preparation, poverty, and constant ill health, he was graduated in 1822 with honors. While a student of theology at Andover, he began to preach at Groton, Mass., and was called to the pastorate by the orthodox portion of the church. His rejection by the parish led to the formation of a new church, where he was ordained Jan. 3, 1827. Here he continued till 1833, when he removed to Northampton, Mass., to assume the pastorate of a newly established church,

which he persuaded his people to name the Edwards Church, in honor of his favorite New England divine. After a pastorate of three years, he was called to a recently organized Congregational church on Clinton Street, Philadelphia, which was the first church of that order in the city. At the dedication of its new building he preached a sermon, published under the title *Principles and Results of Congregationalism* (1837), which contained such strictures on the other denominations as to cause much feeling. The new enterprise was successful at first, but dissensions and the business depression of the time ultimately caused its failure, and in 1842 Todd was settled over the First Congregational Church in Pittsfield, Mass., where he remained till his death.

When he went to Pittsfield, he was in the full maturity of his powers, and he at once assumed a position of leadership in western Massachusetts and far beyond, both within and without his denomination. In his theological positions he never swerved from the Calvinism of Edwards; but his preaching was seldom doctrinal and his sermons were made attractive by his vivid imagination, apt illustration, and quaint earnestness of speech. The membership of his church was increased by frequent revivals, of which he was an earnest promoter. He was a constant advocate of temperance and a stanch supporter of foreign missions. The Berkshire Medical Society made him an honorary member; he was one of the founders of Mount Holyoke Seminary, and for many years a trustee of Williams College.

He became widely known through his numerous publications. As a student he had written much for periodicals and while at Andover he had been offered two editorships. His *Lectures to Children* (1834) achieved immediate success; 200,000 copies were issued, and it was translated into five foreign languages. His better known and most influential work, *The Student's Manual* (1835), was circulated and translated even more widely, over 150,000 copies being sold in London alone. Among his other books were *The Sabbath School Teacher* (1837); *Truth Made Simple* (1839); *Serpents in the Doves' Nest* (1867); *Woman's Rights* (1867). Of the last two, the former was highly commended by the medical profession and the latter bitterly attacked for its criticism of a rising movement. He was a constant contributor to magazines and periodicals and wrote many sketches, stories, and question books for Bible students. While always solemn in the pulpit, he possessed rare social gifts and was much in demand as an after-dinner speaker. On Mar. 11, 1827, he married Mary Skinner Brace of Newington, Conn., who survived him with five of their nine children.

[J. E. and G. I. Todd, *The Todd Family in America* (1920); *Obit. Record Grads. Yale Coll.*, 1874; *John Todd: The Story of His Life, Told Mainly by Himself* (1876), ed. by J. E. Todd; R. H. Cooke, "Rev. John Todd, D.D.," in *Colls. of the Berkshire Hist. and Sci. Soc.*, vol. III (1899); J. E. A. Smith, *The Hist. of Pittsfield* (1876); Caleb Butler, *Hist. of the Town of Groton* (1848); Mark Hopkins, *A Sermon Delivered at the Funeral of Rev. John Todd, D.D., Aug. 28, 1873* (1873); *Congregationalist*, Aug. 28, 1873; *Pittsfield Sun*, Aug. 27, Sept. 3, 1873; *Berkshire County Eagle*, Aug. 28 and Sept. 4, 1873; *Springfield Daily Republican*, Aug. 25, 1873.]　　　　　　　　　　　F.T.P.

TODD, MABEL LOOMIS (Nov. 10, 1856–Oct. 14, 1932), author, and first editor of Emily Dickinson's poems and letters, was born in Cambridge, Mass., the daughter of Eben Jenks and Mary Alden (Wilder) Loomis, and a descendant of Joseph Loomis who emigrated in 1638 to Dorchester. Her father, by profession a mathematician and astronomer, was by temperament a poet-naturalist, a friend of Thoreau, Whitman, Burroughs, and Joaquin Miller. After attending private schools in Washington and Boston, and spending one year in Washington society, Mabel Loomis married on Mar. 5, 1879, David Peck Todd, a brilliant young pupil of Simon Newcomb [*q.v.*], then attached to the United States Nautical Almanac Office. They had one daughter. In 1881 her husband was appointed professor of astronomy and director of the observatory at Amherst College, where Mrs. Todd, young, vivacious, beautiful, with buoyant energy, gave herself without stint to the enrichment of her surroundings. She taught music and painting in two private schools for girls, sang in the village church, and made her home a center for lovers of music and literature. With William Austin Dickinson, treasurer of the college, she worked effectually to promote the tasteful development of both public grounds and private estates; through him also she came to know his secluded poet-sister Emily [*q.v.*]. The Boston Authors' Club originated in her house, and she took a leading part in founding several other clubs, including the Mary Mattoon Chapter of the Daughters of the American Revolution, and the Amherst Historical Society, for which she obtained permanent headquarters and the nucleus of a valuable historical collection. For the college she secured the gift of Observatory House, where she and her husband made their home from 1898 to 1917, and she was instrumental in raising funds for a new observatory. After 1890 she was increasingly in demand as lecturer on astronomy, literature, travel, or local history. She accompanied her husband on as-

tronomical expeditions to Japan (1887, 1896), Tripoli (1900, 1905), the Dutch East Indies (1901), Chile (1907), and Russia (1914), sending back accounts of her experiences for publication in the *Nation*, the *Century*, and other magazines. In 1887 she was the first woman to climb Fuji-san on foot, and on her second trip to Japan she made a pioneer collection of Ainu artifacts, now in the Peabody Museum, Salem. Her publications include a work of popular science, *Total Eclipses of the Sun* (1894); two books of travel, *Corona and Coronet* (1898) and *Tripoli the Mysterious* (1912); *Footprints* (1883), a novelette; *A Cycle of Sonnets* (1896), edited for her friend Clara E. H. Whitton-Stone; an edition of J. D. Steele's *Popular Astronomy* (1899); and *A Cycle of Sunsets* (1910).

Her most memorable service to American letters was begun about 1886–87 when she undertook to prepare for publication the poems of Emily Dickinson. Twelve hundred or more lyrics were found, some of them "copied" with variant readings puzzlingly indicated in the margin, others obscurely scrawled on odd scraps of paper. Mrs. Todd performed single-handed the arduous task of transcribing and arranging these chaotic papers, a work calling for the most sympathetic and conscientious interpretation of the writer's intention. With Col. Thomas Wentworth Higginson [*q.v.*], she brought out two series of *Poems by Emily Dickinson* in 1890 and 1891, and was alone responsible for a third series in 1896. Meanwhile she had collected and edited the *Letters of Emily Dickinson* (2 vols., 1894), enlarged in 1931. Mrs. Todd's correspondence with her co-editor reveals the care she took to establish an accurate text, comparing each poem in proof with the original manuscript and sometimes resisting, though not always with success, Higginson's impulses to "correct" what Emily had written. Her years of hard work brought Emily Dickinson triumphantly before the world and saved the larger portion of the poet's writing from possible loss or slovenly editing. An alienation from the Dickinson family after Austin's death in 1895 unfortunately prevented Mrs. Todd from completing the work and postponed for many years the publication of the remaining poems.

In 1913 she suffered a cerebral hemorrhage, which resulted in a partial paralysis of the right hand. In Florida, where she spent the winters after 1917, she continued to found organizations for social betterment, to write articles, to lecture, and to encourage all efforts toward culture in the youthful city of Miami. Until the day she died from a second cerebral stroke as she was preparing to leave her summer home on Hog Island, Me., her tireless industry was unchecked. On her gravestone in Wildwood Cemetery, Amherst, a carved panel of Indian pipes commemorates her friendship with Emily Dickinson, for whom she originally painted the flowers, and her invaluable services as the poet's editor and earliest interpreter.

[Much autobiog. material is to be found in Mabel Loomis Todd's writings. See also Elias and Elisha S. Loomis, *Descendants of Joseph Loomis in America* (rev. ed., 1908); J. E. and G. I. Todd, *The Todd Family in America* (1920); *Who's Who in America*, 1932–33; M. L. Todd, in *Amherst Graduates' Quart.*, May 1918; Millicent T. Bingham, in *Amherst Record*, Nov. 9, 1932; obituaries in *N. Y. Times*, Oct. 15, and *Springfield Sunday Republican*, Oct. 16, 1932. On the editing of Emily Dickinson's papers, see the prefaces to *Poems of Emily Dickinson* (1891) and *Letters of Emily Dickinson* (1894, 1931); M. L. Todd, in *Harper's Mag.*, Mar. 1930; and manuscript letters in Galatea Coll., Boston Pub. Lib.]   G. F. W.

TODD, SERENO EDWARDS (June 3, 1820–Dec. 26, 1898), agriculturist, journalist, author, was born on his father's farm near Lansingville, Tompkins County, N. Y. He was the seventh child of Josiah Todd, a descendant of Christopher Todd who emigrated from England to Boston, Mass., in 1637 and the following year moved to New Haven, Conn.; his mother, Lucretia (Ingersoll), was the daughter of David and Sarah (Parsons) Ingersoll of Vermont and the great-grand-daughter of Jonathan Edwards [*q.v.*]. Sereno received some education in the rural schools near his home and while working on the farm borrowed and read many books. The Bible he read through annually for over twenty years. In the academies of Groton and Cayuga near by he acquired a little knowledge of the classics. In 1844 he married Rhoda Peck of Greenwich, Conn., and settled on a farm of his own in Tompkins County. Here he remained until 1860, when he sold his land and moved to Auburn, N. Y., where he worked as a mechanic in the implement factory of D. M. Osborne & Company.

While at Auburn he began to contribute to the agricultural press, particularly to Luther Tucker's *Country Gentleman*. Soon he came to be known as an authority on agriculture, and for a time was one of the advisers of Gov. Alonzo B. Cornell [*q.v.*]. In 1865 he became associate editor of the *American Agriculturist* and moved to New York City. The following year he took charge of the agricultural and live-stock department of the *New York Times*. Later he was editor of the home department of the *New York Observer*, editorial writer for *Hearth and Home*, and agricultural editor of the *New York Tribune*, under Horace Greeley. He also held a posi-

tion on the *New York Herald* and edited the *Practical Farmer*. In 1881 his health failed and he retired to a small farm near Orange, N. J., where he lived until his death seventeen years later.

Recognizing that a vast acreage in New York and adjoining states was in need of drainage, he became a stanch advocate of underdraining and patented, Nov. 12, 1872, a power ditching machine for laying title. He stressed the necessity of systematic and economical management, improved methods of cultivation, and better care of live stock. His earliest book was *The Young Farmer's Manual*, the first volume of which was published in 1860 and the second in 1867. In 1868 he published *The American Wheat Culturist* and about the same time issued a privately printed volume later published in enlarged form as *Todd's Country Homes and How to Save Money* (1870). His growing prominence caused Harper & Brothers to engage him to write *The Apple Culturist* (1871), and he is said to have published a book of verse entitled *Rural Poetry and Country Lyrics*.

After the death of his first wife, who left three children, he married, Mar. 19, 1887, Dora Amanda Peterson, by whom he had two sons.

[J. E. and G. I. Todd, *The Todd Family in America, 1637–1919* (1920); L. H. Bailey, ed., *Cyc. of Am. Agriculture*, vol. IV (1909); *Newark Evening News*, Dec. 27, 1898; city directories of Auburn, N. Y., for 1862–63 and 1863–64; S. P. Mead, *Ye Hist. of Ye Town of Greenwich . . . Conn.* (1911); correspondence with a son, David Peck Todd.]   R. H. A.

TODD, THOMAS (Jan. 23, 1765–Feb. 7, 1826), associate justice of the Supreme Court, was born in King and Queen County, near Dunkirk on York River, Va. He was the youngest son of Richard and Elizabeth (Richards) Todd, and a descendant of Thomas Todd who settled in Norfolk County, Va., in 1669. When Thomas was eighteen months old his father died, and although he left a sizable estate, by the law of primogeniture it descended to the eldest son, William, who afterwards became high sheriff of Pittsylvania County, Va. The mother died when Thomas was eleven, having accumulated a considerable estate after her husband's death through managing a boarding house in Manchester. This inheritance enabled the boy to acquire a good elementary education, including a substantial knowledge of Latin, but through his guardian's mismanagement he was soon left without financial resources.

After serving as a soldier for six months during the latter part of the Revolutionary War, he went in 1786 to Danville, Ky. Here he made his home with Judge Harry Innes [*q.v.*], a cousin of his mother, earning his keep by teaching the judge's daughters. At that time the people of Kentucky, then a part of Virginia, were holding numerous conventions for the purpose of devising plans whereby a separation from the parent state might be effected. At the most of these Todd served as clerk. Having studied law evenings by the light of a fire, he began practice, having as capital a horse, saddle, bridle, and thirty-seven and a half cents. At the end of his first term of court he had not only paid his expenses, but had acquired in addition bonds for two cows and calves. He served as clerk of the federal court for the district of Kentucky until the organization of Kentucky as a state in 1792, and then as clerk of the court of appeals until 1801. For some years, beginning in 1792, he was clerk of the Kentucky House of Representatives. In 1801 he was appointed by Gov. James Garrard [q.v.] a judge of the court of appeals, which position he held until 1806, when he was elevated to the chief justiceship. The opinions of the judges of this court were then rendered anonymously, but it is known that many of the decisions dealing with land titles and other property subjects were rendered by Todd. These laid the foundation for the land law of Kentucky. On Mar. 3, 1807, Todd was commissioned by President Jefferson as an associate justice of the United States Supreme Court. Jefferson had asked the representatives in Congress from the states included in the newly created western circuit—Ohio, Kentucky, and Tennessee—to submit nominations, and Todd was either the first or second choice of each (Warren, post, I, 299–300).

Though Todd during the nineteen years that he was a member of the Supreme Court rendered not over a dozen opinions, there is ample evidence that his judgment—especially on cases involving land laws—was highly regarded by his colleagues. Most of his time and strength while a justice were devoted to traveling the western circuit, the hardships of which task contributed to his ill health and ultimately to his death. Although of the political faith of Jefferson he was of Marshall's constitutional school, and consistently concurred with his chief in cases involving constitutional doctrine. The only instance of any consequence when he seems to have differed with Marshall was in the Dartmouth College case, and absence from court when the decision was rendered prevented a dissent. His ability and integrity were held in high esteem by Marshall, Story, and others of their kind. He was patient, candid, modest to a marked degree, and known for his many acts of benevolence. Physically, according

to one account (*Western Monthly Magazine, post,* p. 402), his body was "finely proportioned" and his dark face was a "model of beauty and intelligence."

In 1788 Todd married Elizabeth Harris; five of their children lived to maturity, one of whom was Col. Charles Stewart Todd [q.v.], a soldier in the War of 1812 and later minister to Russia. A year after the death of his first wife in 1811, Judge Todd married Lucy Payne, sister of Dolly Madison [q.v.] and the widow of Maj. George S. Washington. Two sons and a daughter were born to this marriage.

[T. M. Green, *Historic Families of Ky.* (1889); J. R. Witcraft, *The Va. Todds* (1913); *Western Mo. Mag.,* July 1836; H. L. Carson, *The Hist. of the Supreme Court of the U. S.* (1902); Charles Warren, *The Supreme Court in U. S. Hist.* (1926); A. J. Beveridge, *The Life of John Marshall,* vol. IV (copr. 1919); G. W. Griffin, *Memoir of Col. Chas. S. Todd* (1873); *Daily Nat. Intelligencer* (Washington), Feb. 20, 21, 1826.]   G. W. G.

TOLAND, HUGH HUGER (Apr. 16, 1806– Feb. 27, 1880), surgeon, was born on a plantation at Guilder's Creek, S. C., the fourth child in a family of ten. His father, John Toland, who had emigrated from Ireland, became a wealthy planter and banker, and held a high place in his community; his mother, Mary (Boyd) Toland, of Scotch descent, was a remarkable woman of considerable executive ability. A precocious child, sent to school at four years of age, he soon distinguished himself in studies and athletics. After acquiring a good English education he began to study medicine under the tutelage of a distinguished physician, Dr. George Ross. In 1828 he was graduated in medicine at the head of a class of one hundred and sixty from Transylvania University in Lexington, Ky. After two years of practice in Pageville, S. C., and a winter in Lexington, where he studied French and worked in the dissecting room, he spent two and a half years in Paris under Guillaume Dupuytren, Jacques Lisfranc, and Philibert Joseph Roux. There he met a notable group of American students — George Washington Bethune, Henry Ingersoll Bowditch, Oliver Wendell Holmes of Boston, and William Wood Gerhard, William Pepper [qq.v.], and Joseph Peace of Philadelphia. Although in 1833 he returned to Pageville to resume practice, he soon moved to Columbia, where he married Mary Goodwin, who lived only a few years. Soon he became a dominant surgical leader in his community. His success in operating for the relief of clubfoot and strabismus, and in the use of the lithotomy forceps spread beyond his state, and in 1841 arrested the attention of James Marion Sims [q.v.] of Montgomery, Ala. In 1844 he married Mary Avery, who bore him two daughters.

In 1852, after the discovery of gold in California, he set out for the West. Three days after the arrival of his party his wife died at Stockton. Bringing one of the first quartz mills into the state, Toland bought the Gwin mine in Calaveras County, and tried his luck at mining, but after three months he realized that mining was neither to his taste nor to his profit, and sold out. Saddened by the death of his wife and discouraged by the loss of part of his fortune, in 1853 he moved to San Francisco and gave himself over wholeheartedly to his profession. He was soon appointed chief surgeon to the Marine Hospital and later a member of the staff of the county hospital. For twenty-seven years, even to the day of his death, he played a leading rôle in the practice of surgery, being widely known as the "great surgeon of the Pacific Coast." In 1860 he married Mrs. Mary B. (Morrison) Gridley of San Francisco, by whom he had one son. Four years later he founded at his own expense the Toland Medical College in San Francisco, becoming its president and professor of surgery. The latter position he held until his death. In 1873 he placed the buildings, equipment, and land unconditionally in charge of the regents of the University of California, and they became an integral part of the institution. He died suddenly in 1880, survived by his widow, a stepson, and a son.

Although his teaching and his enormous practice occupied most of his time, he wrote seventy-one articles (mostly discussions of case reports), a large number of which were published in the *Pacific Medical and Surgical Journal,* and a textbook on surgery. His contributions were criticized by some of his contemporaries, but they reveal good judgment, versatility, and sincerity. His lack in style was compensated for by a straightforward description of surgical procedures. Of his surgical ability there can be no doubt. He was a good diagnostician, and for his day a capable and rapid operator. His operations ran the gamut of general surgery. Best known for his lithotomies, he operated for stone in the bladder sixty-four times with a mortality of only two. He popularized the method of Antyllus of the double ligature for the prevention of secondary hemorrhage, and ligated the subclavian artery three times, the brachial six times, the femoral eight times, and the external iliac ten times. Having a thorough knowledge of the fundamental principles of plastic surgery, he performed many operations of this character (see "Rhinoplastic Operation," *Pacific Medical and Surgical Journal,* no. 5, 1863, and

"Skin Grafting," *Western Lancet,* San Francisco, Mar. 1874). His knowledge of bone regeneration was unusual for that period, and his comprehensive article on this subject, "On the Reproduction of Bones" (*Pacific Medical and Surgical Journal,* no. 1, 1858), is illuminating today. Among his other important papers were "Movable Cartilages in the Knee Joint—Operation—Cure" (*Ibid.,* no. 12, 1858), "Two Successful Cases of Ligation of the Femoral Artery for Secondary Hemorrhage" (*Western Lancet,* San Francisco, Aug. 1877), and "Case of Penetrating Gunshot Wound of Abdomen" (*Ibid.,* Oct. 1877). He was a commanding figure, tall, erect, dignified, and deliberate, with an industry, perseverance, and determination that remind one of the indomitable John Hunter.

[Toland's name, which often appears as Hugh Hughes Toland, and the date and place of birth are from the inscription on his tombstone, given in Henry Harris, *California's Medic. Story* (1932), p. 366. See also J. D. B. Stillman, *Cal. Medic. Gazette,* Aug. 1870; H. H. Bancroft, *Chronicles of the Builders of the Commonwealth,* vol. VII (1892); A. B. Stout, in *Trans. Medic. Soc. of the State of Cal.* (1880); W. H. Mays, in *San Francisco Western Lancet,* Apr. 1880; R. A. McLean, in *Western Lancet,* Dec. 1880, highly eulogistic; Emmet Rixford, in *Trans. Am. Surgical Asso.,* vol. XLVI (1928); obituary in *Call* (San Francisco), Feb. 28, 1880.]   E. L. G.

TOLMAN, HERBERT CUSHING (Nov. 4, 1865–Nov. 24, 1923), Greek and Indo-Iranian scholar, author, and clergyman, was born at South Scituate (later Norwell), Mass., son of James Turner Tolman and Mary Thomas (Briggs) Tolman. The earliest of the Tolman family in America was Thomas Tolman who came from England before 1640 and settled at Dorchester, Mass. Of Tolman's mother's line in America the first was Walter Briggs who settled in Scituate, Mass., in 1643. Tolman attended grammar school in Hanover, to which the family removed when he was a boy, and high school at Rockland, Mass. In 1884 he entered Yale University. There he distinguished himself in Greek, Latin, and Sanskrit, and in 1888 received the degree of B.A. with high honors. In 1890 he received the degree of Ph.D. at Yale and became assistant to Prof. William Dwight Whitney [*q.v.*]. On Aug. 26, 1891, he married Mary Belden Wells, who with an adopted daughter survived him. He was instructor in Latin (1891–92) and assistant-professor of Sanskrit (1892–93) at the University of Wisconsin; professor of Greek and Sanskrit (1893–94) at the University of North Carolina; and professor of Greek at Vanderbilt University (1894–1923). During his last ten years at Vanderbilt he served as dean of the College of Arts and Science. He also taught for many years in the summer sessions of the George

Peabody College. Numerous honorary degrees were conferred upon him. He studied at the University of Berlin in 1896, at the University of Munich in 1905.

During his years of teaching and administrative duties he was remarkably active in productive scholarship. He published *Eight Books of Cæsar's Gallic War* (1891), with W. R. Harper; *A Grammar of the Old Persian Language* (1892); *The Gospel of Matthew in Greek* (1892), with Alexander Kerr; *A Guide to the Old Persian Inscriptions* (1893); *Greek and Roman Mythology* (1897), with K. P. Harrington, based on Hermann Steuding's *Griechische und Römische Mythologie*; *Herodotus and the Empires of the East* (1899), with J. H. Stevenson; *The Art of Translating* (1901); *Mycenaean Troy* (1903), with G. C. Scoggin; *Ancient Persian Lexicon and the Texts of the Archaemenidan Inscriptions Transliterated* (1908); and a *Cuneiform Supplement* (1910) to the latter. To Tolman should be assigned also the Vanderbilt Oriental Series of nine volumes, for, aside from his own contributions, the whole series found its inspiration in him. In 1912 he was lecturer for the Archaeological Institute of America. He was associate editor of *The World's Progress* (10 vols., 1911). He was a frequent contributor to such periodicals as the *American Journal of Philology*, the *Journal of the American Oriental Society*, and the *American Journal of Archaeology*. The wide recognition of his scholarship was attested by his being invited to contribute to the Madressa jubilee volume published in Bombay in 1914, for which he wrote "The Grave of King Darius at Naksh-i-Rustam."

In addition to his work in ancient languages, Tolman published three books on religious themes: *Urbs Beata* (1902), *"Via Crucis"* (1907), and *Christi Imago* (1915). The last of these consisted of articles written for the *Living Church*, of which he was devotional editor in 1914–15. Though reared a Congregationalist, he became a member of the Protestant Episcopal Church and studied theology while at the University of Wisconsin; in 1895 in Milwaukee he was ordained deacon and priest. While never rector, he served frequently in the pulpit and had temporary charge of churches both in the United States and abroad. From 1904 he was an honorary canon of All Saints' Cathedral, Milwaukee. Tolman was distinguished for the diversity of his gifts; he was described after his death as "a scholar of rare attainments, a teacher by instinct and by training, an administrator of courage and courtesy, a preacher of eloquence and power."

[Jedediah Dwelley and J. F. Simmons, *Hist. of the Town of Hanover, Mass.* (1910); *Who's Who in America*, 1922–23; *Yale Univ. Obit. Record* (1924); *In Memoriam: Herbert Cushing Tolman* (privately printed, 1926); obituaries in *Living Church*, Dec. 1, 1923; *Evening Tennessean and American* (Nashville), Nov. 24, 26, *Nashville Banner*, Nov. 25, and *Nashville Tennessean*, Nov. 25, 1923; information from Mrs. Tolman.]
E. L. J—on.

TOME, JACOB (Aug. 13, 1810–Mar. 16, 1898), merchant, banker, and philanthropist, was born in Manheim Township, York County, Pa., the son of Christian and Christiana (Badger) Thom or Tome. He attended the district schools, and, when he was only sixteen, on his father's death, he went to work on a farm in York County. For the succeeding seven years he held various jobs in the vicinity, even teaching a country school for a season in spite of his meager education. In 1833 he went to Port Deposit, Md., where he made his home for the remainder of his life, except for a brief stay in Philadelphia that winter to study banking. The next year he was engaged as a clerk in a lumber dealer's office. In 1835 David Rinehart, a lumber merchant from Marietta, Pa., proposed a partnership, though Tome had nothing but labor to invest, and on Rinehart's death in 1851 the original capitalization of $5,000 had been multiplied many times. Tome continued to make money in lumber by forming a partnership with John and Thomas C. Bond in 1855. Since Port Deposit was equally well placed for a steamship line, Tome in 1849 organized, with others, a company that ran steamers between Baltimore and Port Deposit. In 1865 a line between Baltimore and Fredericksburg was established. He also interested himself in railroads and continued to profit in both these fields the rest of his life. His success in the field of banking was even more striking. Establishing the Cecil Bank at Port Deposit in 1850 with a capitalization of $25,000, two decades later he owned banks at Elkton, Hagerstown, Md., and Fredericksburg, Va., with a total value of millions. He also owned stock in many other banks of Maryland. His real-estate holdings in Cecil County alone at the time of his death were estimated at one million dollars. His letters are scarce, but such as have been found of a business nature depict an extremely busy yet sagacious man, terse, direct, very strict in his banking methods, and making his point in spite of the handicap of a meager education with the telltale misspellings and grammatical mistakes (Creswell Papers, Library of Congress).

In the political world he was not quite so successful. As a reward for patriotic unionism, he was elected to the Maryland Senate in 1863 and again the following year, gravitating naturally to the chairmanship of the finance committee. In 1871 he was put up by the Unionists as a candidate for governor; but he was defeated by the Democratic candidate, William Pinkney Whyte. His name is best remembered today by the founding of the large school, the Jacob Tome Institute, later the Tome School for Boys at Port Deposit, incorporated in 1889 and opened in September 1894. He contributed largely to the support of Dickinson College at Carlisle, Pa., and was on the board of trustees for many years. He gave to other charities and built the Tome Memorial Methodist Episcopal Church at Port Deposit. At Port Deposit he married, on Dec. 6, 1841, Caroline M. Webb, an aunt of John A. J. Creswell [q.v.]. After her death he married on Oct. 1, 1884, Eva S. Nesbitt, of the same place. His children all died in infancy.

[*Sun* (Baltimore), Mar. 17, 1898; *Appletons' Ann. Cyc. . . . 1898* (1899); J. T. Scharf, *Hist. of Md.* (1879), III, 714.]
                                                    C.W.G.

TOMKINS, FLOYD WILLIAMS (Feb. 7, 1850–Mar. 24, 1932), Protestant Episcopal clergyman, was born in New York City, the son of Floyd Williams and Eliza (Dunham) Tomkins. He received his early schooling at the Charlier French Institute, New York, and entered Harvard in 1868, graduating in 1872. While in college he supported himself in part by services as an organist; he was always fond of music, and composed several hymns. He graduated from the General Theological Seminary, New York, in 1875, was ordered deacon, and married Ann Maria Grant Cutter. The following year he was ordained priest. After missionary work in Colorado, Wyoming, and the Middle West (1875–83), he returned East and became rector of St. James Church, Keene, N. H., where he remained less than two years. From 1884 to 1888 he was minister in charge of Calvary Chapel, New York City. Thereafter until his death he was rector of important churches in various dioceses: Christ Church, Hartford, Conn. (1888–91); St. James, Chicago (1891–94); Grace, Providence, R. I. (1894–99); and the Church of the Holy Trinity, Philadelphia (1899–1932), where his most notable work was done.

For more than thirty years he was one of the most prominent religious and civic leaders of Philadelphia and one of the best known Episcopal clergymen of the country. This prominence was not the result of any ecclesiastical offices that he held, though he was frequently a delegate to the General Convention of the Episcopal Church; nor can it be attributed to any superlative gifts that he possessed, though he was well equipped for his work both by nature

and by training; it was rather the result of an apostolic zeal dominating him completely and finding expression in whatever he undertook. To its demands he was able to respond with seemingly inexhaustible physical energy, for he was a man of large frame and great endurance, capable of carrying out a daily program of activities that few could equal. His warm evangelistic fervor and his absolute sincerity gave power to his preaching; he was invited to college pulpits and frequently summoned to conduct special services in different parts of the country. He held to the old faith and to the old ways, pleading for loyalty to the Bible, whatever men might say about it, and for the strict observance of the Sabbath, resigning as a director of the Sesquicentennial Exposition, Philadelphia, when the board decided to open it on Sundays. He was active in various organizations, a member of the Civil Service Reform Association and of the Pennsylvania Prison Society, a trustee of the Divinity School of the Protestant Episcopal Church, Philadelphia, and for ten years he served as chaplain of the 1st Regiment, Pennsylvania National Guard. In 1924 he was an honorary vice-president of the World Sunday School Association, meeting at Glasgow.

In the midst of his religious and civic activities he found time for much writing. He contributed to religious periodicals, and for years furnished Sunday School lessons for the Philadelphia *Public Ledger*. His books were published not to display learning, nor to bring renown to the author, but solely to give spiritual aid and inspiration. Like his preaching they glow with fervor and faith, and are eminently practical and helpful. Among them are *Following Christ* (1901), *My Best Friend* (1901), *Beacons on Life's Voyage* (1903), *The Faith and Life of a Christian* (1909), *Helps Toward Nobler Living* (1909), *Prayers for the Quiet Hour* (1910), *Sunshine on Life's Way* (1913). He died of pneumonia in his eighty-third year, survived by a son and three daughters.

[*Harvard Coll.: Class of 1872: Eleventh Report of the Secretary, 1917–1924* (n.d.); *Public Ledger* and *Philadelphia Inquirer*, Mar. 25, 1932; *Who's Who in America*, 1930–31.]
                                                    H. E. S.

TOMLINS, WILLIAM LAWRENCE (Feb. 4, 1844–Sept. 26, 1930), teacher of music, was born in London, England, the son of William and Sarah (Lawrence) Tomlins. He began his career as a choir boy in London, and during that period of service was a pupil of George Alexander Macfarren and Eduard Silas. At the age of fifteen he became organist and choirmaster of a London church and at seventeen began conducting oratorio. At eighteen he was made a government inspector and examiner of music teachers in the public schools of England, in the department of theory and harmony. In 1864 he was made one of the examiners of the Tonic Sol-Fa College in London. He married Mrs. Elizabeth (Stripp) Squire in 1868.

Tomlins came to America in 1870, settling in Brooklyn, N. Y. There he attracted the attention of the Mason & Hamlin Company for his remarkable mastery of the harmonium, and in 1875 that concern sent him to Chicago to demonstrate their orchestral organ. Remaining in Chicago, he became during that same year conductor of the Apollo Club, then a male chorus, which in 1876 was changed to a mixed chorus. Tomlins was its conductor for twenty-three years. He began in 1883 to organize classes of school children for choral singing and in this type of work specialized for many years, producing astonishing results. In 1893 he had charge of choral singing at the World's Columbian Exposition, Chicago, for which he trained a chorus of twelve hundred children. Five years later he resigned his position as conductor of the Apollo Club in order to devote his entire time to his work with children. In 1903 he established in Chicago the National Training School for School Music Teachers and in the same year was engaged by the Chicago board of education as instructor of music teachers in the grade schools. Returning to England in 1906, he carried on his work with children for two years, in four different centers, with notable success. He then came back to America and thereafter until nearly the end of his life spent most of his time lecturing and illustrating his ideas throughout the country.

In his teaching of children, Tomlins' original purpose was simply to establish in early life normal habits of musical expression so as to facilitate later musical studies. In time, however, he came to believe that the act of singing is capable of influencing the character of the singer by liberating the moral and spiritual faculties, and thenceforth he endeavored to stimulate the inner life through breathing, rhythm, the song voice, and "a vital, reverent attitude toward the Human Spirit, Nature, and God." Profoundly religious, though not in any orthodox sense, since he could not bring his philosophy within the limits of any creed, he made a definite effort, as part of his instruction, to awaken his pupils to spiritual values. His system became known as "The Tomlins Idea."

Tomlins was the author of *Children's Songs and How to Sing Them* (1884) and editor of *The Laurel Song Book* (1901). He died in his eighty-seventh year at the home of a daughter in Delafield, Wis.

[*Music*, May 1892, June 1898; *Musician*, Dec. 1930; *Music Supervisors Journal*, Oct. 1930, May 1932; *Grove's Dict. of Music and Musicians*, Am. Supp. (rev. ed., 1930); W. J. Baltzell, *Baltzell's Dict. of Musicians* (rev. ed., 1914); *N. Y. Times*, Sept. 28, 1930; unpub. archives of the Apollo Musical Club; information as to certain facts from a daughter, Miss Christine Tomlins.]   D. A. C.

TOMLINSON, EVERETT TITSWORTH (May 23, 1859–Oct. 30, 1931), author, educator, and Baptist minister, was born at Shiloh, Cumberland County, N. J., the son of the Rev. George Edwin Tomlinson, a prominent Seventh-Day Baptist minister, and his wife, Amanda P. Titsworth. After graduating from the high school in Westerly, R. I., he was a student at Williams College from 1875 to 1877, and in 1881 became principal of the high school in Auburn, N. Y. In 1883 he returned to New Jersey as headmaster of the Rutgers College Preparatory School, a position he held for five years. During this period he published Greek and Latin school texts that were widely used. So successful was he as a teacher that William Rainey Harper [*q.v.*] twice tried to persuade him to accept the principalship of the preparatory school of the new University of Chicago. From 1888 to 1911 he was pastor of the Central Baptist Church in Elizabeth, N. J., resigning that position at last because of the pressure of his literary activities, although he continued to live in Elizabeth. He was one of the executive managers of the American Baptist Board of Education (1898–1912), a member of the board of managers of the American Baptist Home Mission Society (1899–1920), and executive secretary of the Ministers and Missionaries Benefit Board of the Northern Baptist Convention (1911–26). His work in the last capacity has been called the "crowning achievement of his life" (Wright, *post*, p. 3). When he assumed office, the organization was without funds; when he resigned, it had assets of $18,000,000. After his resignation he continued to serve as advisory secretary. He died of heart disease at his home in Elizabeth. He was survived by his wife, the former Anna Miranda Greene, and two sons, his only daughter having predeceased him.

Tomlinson was well known as a writer of books for boys, most of them historical, with the Revolutionary period, the Indian wars, and the Civil War as backgrounds. All his books—and by 1927 he had over a hundred volumes to his credit—went into several editions, and the total sales passed the two million mark. His best known books are *Three Colonial Boys, a Story of the Times of '76* (1895), *Camping on the St. Lawrence, or On the Trail of the Early Discoverers* (1899), *The Fort in The Forest, a Story of the Fall of Fort William Henry in 1757* (1904), *The Young Rangers, a Story of the Conquest of Canada* (1906), *Four Boys in the Yellowstone* (1906), *Four Boys in the Land of Cotton* (1907), *Four Boys on the Mississippi* (1908), *Mad Anthony's Young Scout, a Story of the Winter of 1777–78* (1908), and *Pioneer Scouts of the Ohio* (1924). His own times he used, less successfully, as the setting for *Ward Hill at College* (1899), *The Winner* (1903), *Winning His Degree* (1905), and other stories of American college life. In *Elder Boise* (1901) he attempted, also less successfully, a serious novel. Because he understood boys and girls thoroughly, he did not adopt a condescending attitude towards them. In "The Historical Story for Boys" (*Papers and Proceedings of the Thirty-first Annual Meeting of the American Library Association,* 1909, pp. 270–74) he expressed his belief in the need for accurate use of historical material and in the necessity of maintaining the point of view of a boy. As an historian, he believed that the War of 1812 had been unduly neglected. Although as an historical writer he found it necessary to devote considerable attention to armed conflict, he has expressly stated that he had "no desire to glorify war." He also wrote *A Short History of the American Revolution* (1901), *Young Americans in the British Isles* (1909), a travel-book, and *The Story of General Pershing* (1919). His last work, *The First Twenty Years of the Ministers and Missionaries Benefit Board of the Northern Baptist Convention* (1932), was finished a week before his death.

[*Who's Who in America,* 1930–31; P. C. Wright in Tomlinson, *The First Twenty Years* (1932); *Ann. of the Northern Baptist Convention,* 1932; obituaries in *N. Y. Times, N. Y. Herald Tribune,* Oct. 31, 1931; prefaces to Tomlinson's books; private information.]

H. S. R.

TOMOCHICHI (1650?–Oct. 5, 1739), Indian chief, was born among the lower Creeks, possibly at Apalachicola on the west bank of the Chattahoochee almost directly across the river from Columbus, Ga., in what is now Alabama. Among the various spellings of his name are Thamachaychee, Tomochachi, or even Bocachee. Owing to some unexplained difficulty he left his home after 1721 and with a few Creeks and Yamassee settled at Yamacraw on the Savannah River. He was living there when James Edward Oglethorpe [*q.v.*] and the first Georgia colonists landed in 1733 and began the settlement of Savannah some four miles downstream. With Mary Musgrove, the half-breed wife of a Carolina trader, as interpreter, he came to an understanding with Oglethorpe and signed the formal treaty on May 21, 1733. Shortly afterward he was reconciled to the other Creek tribes and helped to negotiate a similar treaty with them. The next year, with his wife Scenawki and several other Indians, he accompanied Oglethorpe to England. There he was received by the King at Kensington and by the Archbishop of Canterbury at Lambeth Palace. His portrait, painted by William Verelst, was hung in the room of the Georgia trustees at London and in 1735 an engraving from the painting was published as the frontispiece in Samuel Urlsperger's *Ausführliche Nachricht von den Saltzburgischen Emigranten.* Having seen the sights of London like many a later American tourist, Eton, Windsor, the Tower, Greenwich, and Hampton Court, where crowds of the curious gathered in the great gardens to see him and the other Indians, he sailed for Georgia in October 1734 laden with gifts and mementos, which he distributed among his friends at home with notable generosity. His visit was valuable in advertising Georgia and enlisting British opinion in favor of the colony; and in the remaining years of his life he continued to be friendly to the white settlers and to use his influence in easing those adjustments between the two races which made the early years of colonization exceptionally peaceful for Georgia. Numerous anecdotes bear witness to his possession of a philosophic religious sense that continued to be critical of the Christianity of the Europeans about him and withstood the ministrations of John Wesley and George Whitefield. He died secure in the peace of his forefathers, calmly and benevolently. According to his wish his body was taken down the river to Savannah, where it was buried with distinguished military honors in Percival Square, later the Court House Square.

[C. C. Jones, *Hist. Sketch of Tomo-chi-chi* (1868) and *Hist. of Ga.* (1883), vol. I; T. M. Harris, *Biog. Memorials of James Oglethorpe* (1841); A. S. Gatschet, *A Migration Legend of the Creek Indians* (2 vols., 1884–88); *The Colonial Records of the State of Ga.,* vol. IV (1906), XXI (1910), ed. by A. D. Candler; *London Mag.,* June 1734, p. 605, Mar. 1735, p. 162; *Gentleman's Mag.,* June 1734, p. 329; Aug. 1734, pp. 449, 450; Sept. 1734, p. 505, Oct. 1734, p. 571, Mar. 1740, p. 129.]

K. E. C.

TOMPKINS, ARNOLD (Sept. 10, 1849–Aug. 12, 1905), educator, the son of Henry and Delilah (Williams) Tompkins, was born on a farm eight miles south of Paris, Ill. He received his early instruction in nearby schools, worked on his father's farm, and taught school winters. In September 1868 he matriculated at Indiana University, but overwork forced him to withdraw the following spring. Entering Butler University in 1870 he was again obliged to abandon his studies on account of illness. For two years he taught near Paris and in 1872 became principal of a two-room school at Grand View, Ill. Here on Dec. 23, 1875, he married his associate teacher, Jennie, daughter of John and Martha (Butler) Snyder. To prepare for larger opportunities they alternated in attending the Indiana State Normal School at Terre Haute, one of them teaching while the other was in attendance.

Graduating in 1880, they went to Worthington, Ind., where Tompkins had been appointed superintendent of schools. Two years later he was elected superintendent in Franklin, Ind. He had definite theories as to what a school should be, introduced ⌐ system of instruction conforming to them, and in 1883 published *A Graded Course of Study for the Franklin Public School.* This brought him to the attention of schoolmen elsewhere, and in 1885 he was called to take charge of the English department in the normal school of De Pauw University; four years later he became dean of the school. In 1889 Indiana University conferred upon him the degree of A.B. Resigning his position at De Pauw in 1890, he became head of the department of English in the Indiana State Normal School. Here his insistence on greater freedom in the institution brought him into conflict with the officials, and in 1893 he withdrew and entered the University of Chicago, where he remained as a student until 1895. He spent the years 1895–99 at the University of Illinois as professor of pedagogy. In 1899 he was chosen president of the Illinois State Normal University, but remained there only a year, during which time, however, he instituted a complete reorganization of the course of study, making it more flexible and adaptable to students of different degrees of preparation. Called to the presidency of the Chicago Normal School in 1900, he held the position until his death, which occurred at his country home, in Menlo, Ga.

Tompkins believed that the ideal school as he conceived of it was the objective of all educational practice and while he advocated freedom in the employment of method, he considered any method that failed to contribute to the realization of his ideal was thereby discredited. His philosophy is embodied in his publications, which include *The Science of Discourse* (1889), *The Philosophy of Teaching* (1893), and *The Philosophy of School Management* (1895). These works were widely read by teachers and used in training schools. He also published *Literary Interpretations; or a Guide to the Teaching and Reading*

of Literature (1896). He was metaphysical in his thinking, but had abilities in presentation that made him a popular lecturer. His theories, together with his inflexible attitude in advocating them, brought him much criticism and made it difficult for him to get along well with his associates.

[*Arnold Tompkins* (1905), pamphlet issued by the faculty of the Chicago Normal School; *Semi-Centennial Hist. of the Ill. State Normal Univ., 1857–1907* (1907); *The Semi-Centennial Record of the Univ. of Ill.* (1918); *School and Home Education,* Sept. 1905; *Who's Who in America,* 1903–05; *Chicago Tribune,* Aug. 15, 1905; date of death from a daughter.]

R. F. S.

TOMPKINS, DANIEL AUGUSTUS (Oct. 12, 1851–Oct. 18, 1914), engineer, manufacturer, and a leading figure in the industrial development of the South, was born and reared on a cotton plantation in Edgefield County, S. C., the son of DeWitt Clinton Tompkins and his wife, Hannah Virginia (Smyly). From his father he derived mental curiosity, imagination, and eloquence; from his mother, practicality, ingenuity, and moral fervor. At sixteen, having passed through old-field schools and the Edgefield Academy, he entered the University of South Carolina, an institution almost wrecked by the Civil War but holding to its tradition of intellectual independence and honorable conduct. Though he did well in his classes, Tompkins found the literary training uncongenial. In the carpenter and blacksmith shops on the plantation he had developed his mechanical aptitude, and what he valued most at the University was his friendship with Gen. Edward Porter Alexander [*q.v.*], profesor of mathematics, who had been chief engineer in Lee's army. Under Alexander's urging, the boy after two years entered the Rensselaer Polytechnic Institute at Troy, New York, to study mechanical engineering. Thus suddenly transferred, he found himself in his element, and during four happy years stood high in his studies and upon his graduation with the degree of C.E. in 1873 was elected grand marshal, the chief office in the gift of the students.

During his vacations he had supplemented his theoretical training with practical work in the mills and machine shops of Troy. Here he came to know Alexander Lyman Holley [*q.v.*], who was introducing the Bessemer process of steel making into America, and he spent the year after his graduation as draftsman in Holley's office in Brooklyn. On going to Europe, Holley got work for Tompkins under John Fritz [*q.v.*] at the works of the Bethlehem Iron Company in Pennsylvania. Here Tompkins insisted upon getting away from the drawing board to perfect himself as a practical machinist, and at the end of five years was a principal reliance of Fritz, who was the instrument of his going to the Schwerte Iron Works in Westphalia, Germany, to set up American machinery. On his return after a year abroad, Bethlehem recognized his importance to the community by electing him a burgess; he had always taken active part in civic affairs, particularly in promoting a building and loan association. He determined, however, to go back to the South, where both discouragements and opportunities were greater, and after two years devoted to construction work in Missouri, in March 1882 he hung out his sign in Charlotte, N. C.: "D. A. Tompkins, Engineer, Machinist, and Contractor."

His beginning was small enough—repairing piping in the local steam laundry, surveying for the streets of the town. He soon secured the agency for the Westinghouse engine, and worked incessantly not only to introduce his engine into such plants as existed, but also to encourage the establishment of new plants which would use his services. In the midst of apathy and poverty, he strove to bring the industrial development of the North to the prostrate South. R. M. Miller, a cotton commission merchant of Charlotte, backed him with capital. Tompkins soon saw the possibilities in cotton-seed oil manufacture; realizing that the mills being bought up by the American Cotton Oil Company were antiquated, he organized the Southern Cotton Oil Company with the assistance of Richard H. Edmonds, editor of the *Manufacturers' Record*, and designed and built eight new mills scattered through the South, in six months in 1886. Many others followed. Tompkins was the complete promoter, furnishing information, incentive, plans, equipment, buildings, and even capital where necessary. He had seen the old South of exclusive agriculture destroy itself in economic exploitation, political strife, and civil war; he held with a tenacious affection and faith to what was good in the old régime, but now demanded that the bad—poverty, unskilled and languid labor, ignorance, sectionalism—should be replaced by thrift, manufactures, education, and national participation. He made innumerable speeches and wrote for every paper that would print his articles—his burden always being that manufactures must supplement agriculture, that the injuries worked by slavery must be done away by industrial enterprise.

He next promoted a wide and successful campaign for the spinning and weaving of cotton, putting forward a plan whereby any community could start a factory and pay in the capital in instalments. Others—such as William Gregg, Francis Warrington Dawson, and Henry Pinckney Hammett [*qq.v.*]—had preceded Tompkins in advocating cotton manufacture in the South, but Tompkins was technically equipped to bring the program to realization. In his industrial crusade self-interest was mixed with public spirit, but the latter was never a cloak for the former. In the interpretation of its economic history, he told the South unpalatable truths, for he was given to straight thinking and candor. He was constantly pointing out the advantage to the South of increasing the value of its raw materials by adding brains and skill to them in manufacturing processes; he published an ingenious little book comparing the value of cotton in the raw state with its value as worked up into various fabrics (*Cotton Values in Textile Fabrics*, 1900). He was himself the president of three cotton mills, and was interested in many more.

Tompkins realized that the economic recovery of the South rested ultimately upon improved education, and to this cause he gave statesmanlike devotion. Particularly he inspired the founding and guided the work of textile schools connected with the state agricultural and mechanical colleges in North and South Carolina and was instrumental in establishing those of Mississippi and Texas. He wrote volumes which served as texts in these institutions and as handbooks for practical mill men. In his own extensive shops at Charlotte he had apprenticeship courses for boys still attending school.

Many of Tompkins' speeches, on every subject from road building to trained nursing, were published in pamphlet form, while the *Charlotte Daily Observer*, of which he was chief owner for a quarter of a century, served him as a mouthpiece. His principal publications were *Cotton Mill Processes and Calculations* (1899); *Cotton Mill Commercial Features* (1899); *Cotton and Cotton Oil* (1901); and *History of Mecklenburg County and the City of Charlotte from 1740 to 1903* (2 vols., 1903). He received national recognition, among other ways, by appointment on the United States Industrial Commission which reported in 1902; here and in subsequent utterances he represented the capitalist interest in an ingenuous manner: he wanted to substitute proprietor paternalism for restrictive labor legislation and trade unionism; on these matters he really lacked information, his own good intent blinding him to the more selfish designs of others. His strong nationalism was thoroughly wholesome, though his protectionism and imperialism were undiscriminating.

Though fond of the society of women, he never married. His last years, spent at his summer home at Montreat, N. C., where he died, were resolutely cheerful in spite of paralysis. He always gave generously to charities and education; his native town of Edgefield, S. C., has a public library built in his honor.

[G. T. Winston, *A Builder of the New South, being the Story of the Life Work of Daniel Augustus Tompkins* (1920); Broadus Mitchell, *The Rise of Cotton Mills in the South* (1921), and "Some Southern Industrialists," in *Va. Quart. Rev.*, Jan. 1929; *Who's Who in America*, 1914–15; H. B. Nason, *Biog. Record of the Officers and Grads. of the Rensselaer Polytechnic Inst., 1824–1886* (1887); *Charlotte Daily Observer*, Oct. 19 1914; date of birth from Winston, supported by family Bible.]   B. M.

TOMPKINS, DANIEL D. (June 21, 1774– June 11, 1825), governor of New York, vice-president of the United States, was born at Scarsdale, Westchester County, N. Y., the son of a Revolutionary patriot, Jonathan G. Tompkins, and of Sarah (Hyatt), and a descendant of John Tompkins who settled at Concord, Mass., in 1640. Named simply Daniel, he is said to have adopted the middle initial "D" to distinguish himself from a schoolmate of the same name. Tompkins was graduated from Columbia College in 1795. He took up the practice of law in New York City and entered politics as a Republican, was a member of the state constitutional convention in 1801 and of the Assembly in 1803, and was elected to Congress in 1804 but resigned to accept appointment as an associate justice of the New York supreme court. This office gave him a wide acquaintance in the state, and his gracious manner, affability, and broad human sympathy made him a popular favorite. He was spoken of affectionately for years as the "farmer's boy." About 1797 he married Hannah Minthorne, by whom he had seven children; this marriage may have aided him politically, for his wife's father, Mangle Minthorne, was a prominent Republican of New York City.

In 1807 Tompkins was selected by the Clinton faction as their candidate for governor to oppose the incumbent, Morgan Lewis [*q.v.*]. He was elected in that year and reëlected in 1810, 1813, and 1816, serving continuously for almost ten years. Though he had won the governorship with the support of DeWitt Clinton [*q.v.*], he soon became Clinton's most able antagonist in state politics. His administration was marked by loyalty to the measures of the government in Washington, including the Embargo of 1807 and the War of 1812, and by liberal reform measures in the interest of the common people of the state. With varying success he urged improvements in the state's school system, liberalization of its criminal code, more humane treatment of negroes and Indians, the complete abolition of slavery, and a reform in the militia system designed to make wealth bear a larger share in the burden of defense. A militia law such as he desired was passed late in 1814, over the bitter protests of the propertied classes (Van Buren, *post*, pp. 55–57), but too late to be of service in the War of 1812. A law which extinguished slavery in the state on July 4, 1827, was passed at his request in 1817. His democratic attitude is suggested by his remark, in a message opposing the multiplication of banks, that "the less wealthy part of the community ... are generally the most moral, upright and useful members thereof" (*State of New York: Messages from the Governors*, 1909, II, 698). In the spring of 1812 he took the extraordinary step of proroguing the legislature in a vain effort to block the chartering of the Bank of North America.

Tompkins' powers were strained to the utmost during the War of 1812, when, as commander-in-chief of the New York militia, it fell to him not only to supply troops and equipment for the defense of the New York frontiers, but to perform many duties which should have devolved upon officers of the United States. Handicapped by an inadequate staff, a vicious militia system, insufficient funds, a hostile Assembly (till the fall of 1814), and the incompetence of the United States army officers, he probably handled the tasks of war in his area as successfully as any man could have done. Declining an appointment as secretary of state in the fall of 1814, he accepted instead command of the Third Military District, embracing southern New York and eastern New Jersey. New York City was in a panic at the prospect of a British attack. Tompkins succeeded in putting some 25,000 troops in the field about New York City alone and in borrowing, partly on his personal credit, large sums of money for the pay of New York and New Jersey troops and even for the defense of New England and the maintenance of the Military Academy at West Point. For these services he was ill requited. It is not surprising that in the press of his business vouchers had been lost and accounts had fallen into confusion. At the close of the war he was unable to account for all the money that had passed through his hands, and though his integrity was unquestioned and the value of his service recognized, he was technically in default to both New York and the United States. Charges were made against him (Archibald McIntyre, *A Letter ... to Daniel D. Tompkins*, 1819) against which he published a defense (*A Letter to Archibald M'Intyre*, 1819). Eventually the New York legislature balanced his accounts (1820) and Congress, upon President Monroe's recommendation, authorized the payment to him (1823–24) of over $95,000 for losses which he had incurred in the public service (*Annals of Congress*, 18 Cong., 1 Sess., pp. 788, 828, 1906, 2697, and *passim*), but unfortunately, before these settlements were made, the question of his accounts had been dragged into politics when Tompkins ran again (unsuccessfully) for the governorship in 1820. These financial troubles darkened his last years. He impressed contemporaries as a man broken in health and prematurely aged by overwork and worry, grieving his friends by his intemperance. He served as vice-president of the United States from 1817 to 1825, but was absent much of the time from his post; in 1821 he presided over the state constitutional convention. He died at his home on Staten Island in his fifty-first year.

[Edward Tompkins, Jr., *A Record of the Ancestry and Kindred of the Children of Edward Tompkins, Sr.* (1893); *Public Papers of Daniel D. Tompkins* (3 vols., 1898–1902), ed. by Hugh Hastings; *State of N. Y.: Messages from the Governors* (1909), vol. II; J. D. Hammond, *The Hist. of Political Parties in the State of N. Y.* (2 vols., 1842); D. S. Alexander, *A Political Hist. of the State of N. Y.*, vol. I (1906); "The Autobiography of Martin Van Buren," ed. by J. C. Fitzpatrick, *Ann. Report of the Am. Hist. Asso. . . . 1918*, vol. II (1920); P. J. Van Pelt, *An Oration, Containing Sketches of the Life, Character, and Services of the Late Daniel D. Tompkins* (1843); J. L. Jenkins, *Lives of the Govs. of . . . N. Y.* (1851); Robert Bolton, *The Hist. . . . of the County of Westchester* (2nd ed., 1881), II, 223; *Columbia Univ. Quart.*, Dec. 1906; *N. Y. Evening Post*, June 13, 1825.]   J. W. P.

TOMPKINS, SALLY LOUISA (Nov. 9, 1833–July 25, 1916), hospital head and the only woman to hold a commission in the Confederate States army, was born at "Poplar Grove," Mathews County, Va., of prominent lineage, daughter of Christopher and Maria (Patterson) Tompkins, and grand-daughter of Col. John Patterson who was brevetted by Washington at Monmouth. After her father's death, her family removed to Richmond, where Miss Tompkins devoted freely her time and ample means to philanthropic enterprises. When the Confederate government appealed to the people of Richmond after the first battle of Manassas (Bull Run) in July 1861 to open their homes to the wounded, she obtained the use of Judge John Robertson's residence, fitted it up at her own expense, and maintained it as a hospital until June 13, 1865. The institution found many willing helpers, but to the demure, diminutive, and frail young woman who flitted from bed to bed, medicine chest strapped to her side and Bible in hand, fell the responsibility of directing the hospital routine and procuring the necessary drugs and food. The

building was none too large or well adapted to hospital purposes, and often there were few medicines save whisky and turpentine to supplement cleanliness and careful nursing, but the register shows 1,333 admissions between Aug. 1, 1861, and Apr. 2, 1865, with only seventy-three deaths (Freeman, *post*, p. 47)—despite the fact that the authorities, having early noted that her hospital returned a larger number of patients than any other, sent her many of the most desperate cases. When an executive order placed all hospitals under government control, rather than lose the efficient chief of the Robertson Hospital and in recognition of her invaluable work, President Jefferson Davis had her commissioned a captain in the Confederate service, Sept. 9, 1861 (*Ibid.*, p. 14). She returned her pay to the government, but retained the rank that she might issue orders and draw supplies to augment her own liberality in behalf of the sick and wounded soldiers. To the end of her long life she was known as "Captain Sally."

Lacking beauty, she was of dignified and forceful presence, and it was an earnest of her strength of personality and character that after the war she received numberless offers of marriage from men of all ranks in the army. In later years she gave liberally of her means and personal service to the work of the Protestant Episcopal Church, until financial disaster compelled her to become a guest in the Home for Confederate Women, Richmond, upon its establishment. An honorary member of R. E. Lee Camp, Confederate Veterans, at her death she was buried with full military honors. The chapters of the United Daughters of the Confederacy at Gloucester and Mathews Court House, Va., were named in tribute to her.

[Douglas S. Freeman, *A Calendar of Confederate Papers* (1908); *Confederate Veteran*, Feb. 1908, p. 72, and Nov. 1916, p. 521; M. P. Andrews, *The Women of the South in War Times* (1920); Mary N. Stanard, *Richmond, Its People and Its Story* (1923); *William and Mary College Quarterly*, Jan. 1905; obituaries in *News-Leader* (Richmond), July 26, and *Richmond Times-Dispatch*, July 26, 27, 1916.]   A. C. G., Jr.

TOMPSON, BENJAMIN (July 14, 1642–Apr. 10 (?), 1714), author, educator, the son of the Rev. William and Abigail Tompson, was born in Quincy, Mass., then a part of Braintree, five years after his father emigrated from England to the colonies. His mother died shortly after his birth, and he was brought up chiefly in the household of Thomas Blanchard, a neighbor, who moved from Braintree to Charlestown, where Tompson probably studied with John Morley, the local schoolmaster. He graduated at Harvard College in 1662 and, until his father's death in December 1666, lived with him in Braintree. In the next year he married Susanna Kirtland, who bore him nine children. The same year he succeeded Robert Woodmansey as master of the "free school," now the Boston Latin School. In January 1670/71 Ezekiel Cheever [q.v.] replaced him, and Tompson taught in Cheever's former position in Charlestown until Nov. 7, 1674. He seems to have had no regular employment again until 1679, when he began teaching in Braintree. He continued in this work until 1699. He taught in Roxbury, at what is now the Roxbury Latin School for three or four years, and then resumed his place in Braintree, probably in 1704, and kept it till 1710. Throughout his life he labored as physician as well as pedagogue, and his interest in medicine grew with the years. The writing of verses, too, took a share of his time. There were printed before his death: *New Englands Crisis* at Boston in 1676 and *New-Englands Tears for Her Present Miseries* at London in 1676, two volumes of verse on King Philip's War, much of the contents being identical; *A Funeral Tribute* to Gov. John Winthrop of Connecticut, a broadside printed in Boston in 1676; *The Grammarians Funeral,* an elegy on Robert Woodmansey, printed as a broadside, probably in Boston, in 1708; "Upon the Elaborate Survey of New-Englands Passions from the Natives," prefixed to William Hubbard's *A Narrative of the Troubles with the Indians* (1677); "Upon the Very Reverend Samuel Whiting" and "Celeberrimi Cottoni Matheri," both in Cotton Mather's *Magnalia* (1702); *A Neighbour's Tears ... on ... Mrs. Rebekah Sewall* in Boston in 1710; and "The Translation by Death of ... Mr. James Allen," in Benjamin Wadsworth, *Death is Certain* (1710). These, and his other verses, left in manuscript, have been collected in H. J. Hall, *Benjamin Tompson ... His Poems* (1924), except for two which are included in K. B. Murdock, *Handkerchiefs from Paul* (1927).

It is only as a verse-writer that Tompson is remembered, and it is only among his New England contemporaries that he has distinction. He handled couplets competently and is at his best in satire, but his work lacks any truly poetic quality. He displays, however, some signs of literary training and a constant effort to conform to the literary fashions of his time. His writing is of interest because it represents the cultivated standard of achievement in verse in New England in the late seventeenth century, and particularly because it concerns itself specifically for the most part with native material—Indian wars and Puritan divines, colonial fashions, attitudes,

and standards. Subject rather than style makes Tompson's verse a minor landmark in American literary history.

[Hall, *ante,* for best recent biog., bibliog., and critical account; Murdock, *ante,* for correction of Hall's erroneous ascription of one short poem to Tompson, for certain additional material on the Tompson family, and on the poetic background of the colonies in the time; J. L. Sibley, *Biog. Sketches of Grads. of Harvard Univ.,* vol. II (1881); M. C. Tyler, *A Hist. of Am. Lit.* (1879) for critical comment; other references in Hall and Murdock, *ante.*]   K. B. M.

TONDORF, FRANCIS ANTHONY (July 17, 1870–Nov. 29, 1929), seismologist, Roman Catholic priest, was born in Boston, Mass., the son of Joseph and Louise (Musler) Tondorf. After graduating from the Boston College High School he entered the Society of Jesus and spent the next five years in classical studies at the novitiate in Frederick, Md. In spite of his later activities in other fields, his services as a Latin scholar and his skill in the construction of Latin verse in lapidary style were in frequent demand. In 1893 he went to Woodstock College at Woodstock, Md., where he spent two years in the study of philosophy and in 1895 received the degree of A.B. In the years 1895 to 1898 he taught a variety of subjects at Loyola College, Baltimore, and at St. John's College (later part of Fordham University), Fordham, N. Y. At the end of this time he was sent to Johns Hopkins University for graduate work in mathematical physics. There he also did work in general biology and osteology (1898–99) and attended lectures in geological physics (1899–1900). Unfortunately he was not able to stay to finish his work for the doctorate, possibly because he was needed to teach the classics at Fordham the following year. Returning in the fall of 1901 to Woodstock College, he spent three years in the study of theology, was ordained priest, and then was sent to Georgetown University, Washington, D. C., where he remained, except for one year at Poughkeepsie and another at Fordham, until the time of his death. There he was professor of physics (1904–15), professor of biology (1912–29), and at various times also held professorships in astronomy, geology, German, and other subjects. He received the degree of Ph.D. from Georgetown University in 1914.

At Georgetown he founded the Georgetown seismological observatory, which was put into operation in January 1911. Besides carrying on the routine work of the observatory as director (1909–29), he found time to write a large number of popular articles on seismology and to give lectures on the subject, and in this way contributed very materially to the development of seismology in the United States. From 1916 to 1929 he prepared and published for the observatory *The Registration of Earthquakes and Press Dispatches on Earthquakes.* In the fall of 1924 he made a study of the cause of failure of road surfacing, which he showed to be the transverse vibration of traffic. As a seismologist he was widely consulted. From 1913 to 1924 he lectured on physiology at the Georgetown University School of Medicine. As head of the department of physiology he was a most vigorous champion of experimental medicine against the anti-vivisectionists. He published *A Vindication of Vivisection* (1920), to which a supplement was issued in 1922, and once appeared before a Senate committee (Nov. 4, 1929) to testify on the subject. His other publications include *Anniversary Tribute to George Martin Kober* (1920) and *Frank Baker . . . Professor of Anatomy . . . an Appreciation* (1923). He was a fellow of the American Association for the Advancement of Science and of the Royal Astronomical Society, and a member of numerous other scientific associations. He has been described as having "an almost boyish spirit of simplicity."

[*Who's Who in America*, 1928–29; ann. cats. of the Md.-N. Y. Province of the Soc. of Jesus, and of Georgetown Univ.; records of Johns Hopkins Univ.; *Bull. Seismological Soc. of America*, Dec. 1929, pp. 245–46; *Cath. World*, Jan. 1930; obituary in Woodstock Letters, Oct. 1931, and *Evening Star* (Washington), Nov. 29, 1929; personal recollections.]

F. W. S.

TONER, JOSEPH MEREDITH (Apr. 30, 1825–July 30, 1896), physician, writer, collector, was born in Pittsburgh, Pa., the son of Meredith and Ann (Layton) Toner, descendants of early Irish settlers in that state. He attended the Western University of Pennsylvania, Pittsburgh, and Mount St. Mary's College, Emmitsburg, Md. After two years' study under Dr. John Lowman at Johnstown, Pa., he spent the winter of 1849–50 at Jefferson Medical College, Philadelphia, then for three months attended the Vermont Medical College at Woodstock, from which he received a medical degree in 1850. After periods of practice at Summit and Pittsburgh, and at Harpers Ferry, Va., he settled in Washington, D. C., in 1855. In the meantime he had obtained the degree of M.D. from Jefferson Medical College in 1853.

For many years thereafter he was one of the capital city's leading practitioners, though his strong bent toward historical and literary pursuits caused him virtually to abandon medical practice during his later years. In 1861 he aided the Sisters of Charity in founding Providence Hospital, which he long served as attending physician. He inspired the founding of St. Joseph's Orphan Asylum, and was its physician, in which capacity he served also St. Vincent's Female Orphan Asylum and St. Ann's Infant Asylum. He was on the board of directors of Garfield Hospital and of Columbia Hospital, and for years was consultant and member of the board of managers of St. Elizabeth's Hospital. He took a leading part in the local medical societies and was chosen to the presidency of the American Medical Association in 1873 and to that of the American Public Health Association in 1874.

It is, however, as a writer and collector that Toner is best known. His first book, *Maternal Instinct,* appeared in 1864, and his other early writings, mainly professional, discussed the necessity for vaccination, yellow fever, public health problems, and vital statistics. Later he turned his attention to medical history and biography. He wrote *Contributions to the Annals of Medical Progress and Medical Education in the United States before and during the War of Independence* (1874), *Annual Oration before the Medical and Chirurgical Faculty of Maryland . . . Contribution to the Medical History and Geography of Maryland* (1875), *The Medical Men of the Revolution* (1876), and *Address on Medical Biography* (1876). Subsequently he concentrated his research upon the career and writings of George Washington. He edited *Washington's Rules of Civility and Decent Behavior* (1888), *Journal of My Journey over the Mountains . . . 1747–8* (1892), *The Daily Journal of Major George Washington in 1751–2, Kept while on a Tour . . . to the Island of Barbadoes* (1892), *Journal of Colonel George Washington . . . in 1754* (1893), describing his part in the ill-fated Braddock expedition. He also published "Wills of the American Ancestors of George Washington" (*New England Historical and Genealogical Register,* July 1891); *George Washington as Inventor and Patron of the Useful Arts* (1892), an address; "Some Account of George Washington's Library and Manuscript Records" (*Annual Report of the American Historical Association . . . 1892,* 1894); and "Washington in the Forbes Expedition of 1758" (*Records of the Columbia Historical Society,* vol. I, 1897). He left in manuscript an uncompleted biographical dictionary of deceased American physicians.

Toner's collection of books and pamphlets was the work of years. He began collecting generally, though with an especial interest in medical, historical, and biographical material. Later becoming keenly interested in early American physicians, he sought to build up a library as complete as possible of books, pamphlets, and journals to cover America's contribution to medical history. In 1882 he turned over twenty-seven thousand volumes, together with related pictures, charts, and medals, to the Library of Congress, which has kept his collection intact. He made a subject index of the contents of all American medical journals up to 1870. In 1868 he started a library for the American Medical Association in the Smithsonian Institution; when the collection had reached six thousand volumes and had outgrown its quarters, it was transferred to the Newberry Library in Chicago. In 1871 he founded the Toner Lecture Fund for the Smithsonian Institution which for a number of years provided semi-annual lectures upon medical and scientific progress. He also donated medals for scientific research performed by students of Jefferson Medical College and the medical school of Georgetown University. He was repeatedly offered teaching positions in medical schools, but always set them aside. In 1894 he participated in the founding of the Columbia Historical Society and was chosen its first president. Though a bachelor, he maintained a spacious home on Louisiana Avenue where, among his collections, he dispensed a warm and far-reaching hospitality. His Washington's Birthday receptions were famous. A sympathetic contemporary describes him as the soul of geniality, without brilliancy or depth of learning, but eminent in sincerity of purpose and industry. He died unexpectedly while visiting at Cresson, Pa., and was buried in the family plot at Derry, Pa.

[A. R. Spofford, in *Ann. Report . . . Smithsonian Inst. . . . 1896* (1898); M. F. Morris, in *Records of the Columbia Hist. Soc.*, vol. I (1897); Thomas Antisell, *Biog. Sketch of Joseph M. Toner, M.D.* (1878); C. S. Busey and others, in *Nat. Medic. Rev.*, Dec. 1896; *Evening Star* (Washington, D. C.), Aug. 1, 1896.]
J. M. P—n.

TONTY, HENRY de (1650–1704), lieutenant of La Salle, explorer, and founder of the first settlements in the Mississippi Valley, was born probably at Paris, son of Lorenzo de Tonti, originator of the tontine form of life insurance, who had fled from Naples after taking part in an insurrection. Tonty's mother was Isabelle de Liette (or Desliettes), and he was the eldest of three children, all of whom later came to New France. Henry entered the French army at the age of eighteen and, serving in Italian waters, lost his right hand in the explosion of a grenade. He replaced it with a metal hand, which he wore covered with a glove, and which he sometimes used with great effect upon rebellious Indians; from this he was known as "the man with the iron hand." Tonty was introduced by Prince de Conti to the explorer Robert Cavelier. Sieur de la Salle [*q.v.*] in 1678, when the latter was seeking assistance in France for his exploration projects in North America. Tonty immediately enlisted in La Salle's service, and thenceforth gave him a loyalty and devotion that were La Salle's greatest aids in carrying out his plans. After their arrival in Canada they went at once to La Salle's seigniory at Fort Frontenac on Lake Ontario; thence Tonty was detailed to the Niagara River to superintend the building of La Salle's ship, the *Griffon,* the first sailing vessel on the upper Great Lakes. Tonty went in advance at the time of sailing and was taken on board at the Detroit River. Thence he and La Salle sailed for Michilimackinac, where Tonty again left ship, coasting down the east shore of Lake Michigan to join La Salle at the St. Joseph River. Together they advanced into Illinois and in the winter of 1679–80 built Fort Crèvecœur on Lake Peoria. In the spring La Salle found it necessary to return to Fort Frontenac, and Tonty was left in command in the Illinois country. There his men soon deserted; he was unable to complete his fort; and the summer was filled with difficulties of every sort. Yet he never despaired, and when in the autumn a war party of Iroquois Indians entered the Valley breathing vengeance upon the Illinois, he fearlessly visited their camp to protest their raid upon French-allied Indians. He was seriously wounded, but escaped with his life. Then, finding he could not calm the storm, with five companions he retreated through the Wisconsin woods, living upon roots and gleanings from the deserted Indian villages. Toward the end of the year 1680 he finally reached Green Bay and safety (L. P. Kellogg, "A Wisconsin Anabasis," *Wisconsin Magazine of History,* Mar. 1924, pp. 322–39). After recruiting his health and recovering from his wound, he left for Michilimackinac, which he reached in June 1681 just too late to meet his cousin Daniel Greysolon Duluth [*q.v.*]. La Salle, arriving the next day, was overjoyed at finding Tonty, who he feared had perished in Illinois. Together they returned thither once more, built Fort St. Louis on the Illinois, and gathered there a settlement of French and Indians. In the spring of 1682 they explored the Mississippi, finding its mouth and there taking possession of the whole Valley for France (*Wisconsin State Historical Society Collections,* vol. XI, 1888, pp. 33–35). In the spring of 1683 La Salle left for France to prepare to colonize Louisiana. Tonty never saw his chief again. In France La Salle secured a captaincy for his faithful lieutenant left in Illinois.

It was 1686 before Tonty could undertake a voyage to join La Salle; that year he went down the Mississippi without finding any trace of his leader, and returned unsuccessful. The next year he was called upon by Governor Denonville of New France to lead his Indian forces against the Iroquois. At Fort des Sables he also met his cousin Duluth and returned west with him in the autumn of 1687 (Pease and Werner, *post*, pp. 190–92). At his post in Illinois he found Jean Cavelier, brother of La Salle, and Henri Joutel [*q.v.*], neither of whom revealed to him the fact of La Salle's death. In March 1689 he was still unaware of it, as one of his letters shows (Margry, *post*, vol. III, p. 564), but in September of that year one of his men, whom he had left to found a settlement in Arkansas, brought him news of his beloved leader's assassination. He started south in December to try to find the colonists La Salle had left, but returned unsuccessful. For a decade longer he remained in Illinois, bringing settlers, trade goods, and missionaries from Canada. He was respected and beloved by all, and was the true founder of Illinois. In 1700, hearing of the settlement made by Pierre le Moyne, Sieur de'Iberville [*q.v.*], near the mouth of the Mississippi, he asked permission to join the new colony, and for four years gave his valuable services to Louisiana in exploration and in conciliation of the Indians. He died near Mobile, probably from yellow fever. He never married, and left his property to his younger brother Alphonse.

Tonty's exploits have not been as much noticed as they deserve. He wrote two brief memoirs of his experiences, one covering the years 1678–83 (see Margry, *post*, vol. I), the other covering the years 1678–91 (see Kellogg, *Early Narratives*, *post*, for a translation, and Pierre Margry, *Relations et Mémoires Inédits pour Servir à l'Histoire de la France dans les Pays d'Outre-Mer*, 1867). A later memoir published under his name in 1697—*Dernières Découvertes dans l'Amérique Septentrionale de Monsieur de la Salle par Chevalier de Tonti*—he declared spurious. He was a modest person, not given to boasting of his undertakings. He has been regarded only as a faithful lieutenant of La Salle; in fact he was himself a great explorer and an able administrator who succeeded where La Salle failed. He secured the respect and confidence both of the Indians and of his men; he was popular with the missionaries of every group; and his courtesy and consideration enabled him to accomplish his ends. As La Salle wrote of him to the Prince de Conti: "His honorable character and his amiable disposition were well known to you; but perhaps you would not have thought him capable of doing things for

which a strong constitution, an acquaintance with the country, and the use of both hands seemed absolutely necessary. Nevertheless his energy and address make him equal to any thing" (quoted in Francis Parkman, *La Salle and the Discovery of the Great West*, 1869, pp. 117–18).

[Tonty's letters and memoirs are to be found in Pierre Margry, *Découvertes et Etablissements des Français dans l'Ouest et dans le Sud de l'Amérique Septentrionale* (6 vols., 1876–86), vol. I, pp. 573–616. vol. III, pp. 551–64, vol. V, pp. 36–38, 62–66; P. G. Roy, ed., *Bulletin des Recherches Historiques*, Jan. 1900, p. 31, Nov. 1931, p. 704, Jan. 1933, p. 62; I. J. Cox, ed., *Journeys of La Salle* (1905), vol. I, pp. 3–61; and L. P. Kellogg, ed., *Early Narratives of the Northwest* (1917), pp. 283–334. See also Benjamin Sulte, "Les Tonty," *Proc. and Trans. Royal Soc. of Canada*, vol. XI (1894), sec. 1, pp. 1–31; H. E. Legler, "Chevalier Henry de Tonty," *Parkman Club Pubs.*, vol. I, no. 3 (1896); C. W. Alvord, *The Illinois Country* (1920); J. C. Parish, *The Man with the Iron Hand* (1913); L. P. Kellogg, *The French Régime in Wis. and the Northwest* (1925); T. C. Pease and R. C. Werner, "The French Foundations, 1680–1693," *Ill. State Hist. Lib. Colls.*, vol. XXIII (1934).]   L. P. K.

TOOLE, EDWIN WARREN (Mar. 24, 1839–May 17, 1905), lawyer, was born at Savannah, Andrew County, Mo., the eldest of ten children. Joseph Kemp Toole [*q.v.*] was a younger brother. Their grandfather, Benjamin Porter, was a soldier in the American Revolution; their parents, Edwin and Lucinda (Porter) Toole, natives of Kentucky, moved to Missouri in 1837. Edwin Warren attended local schools at Savannah and then entered Masonic College, Lexington, Mo., where he graduated in 1860. He began the study of law, but in 1861 enlisted in the Confederate service and became a lieutenant. He was wounded at the battle of Pea Ridge and soon after retired from the army. In 1863 he went to Denver, Colo., and thence to that part of the Territory of Idaho which in 1864 became Montana Territory.

He settled in Virginia City at a time when there was no recognized law, and his first task was to help formulate a system of law for the mining camps. His practice extended to every community in Montana and his reasoning aided much in bringing the decisions of local courts into harmony with each other. In 1865 he moved to Helena which was his home for the rest of his life. In 1871 the Southern Democrats in Montana, over his protest, nominated Toole for delegate to Congress; the Irish Democrats were angry at the defeat of the incumbent, James M. Cavanaugh, and many of them voted for the Republican candidate. Toole was defeated and thenceforth gave his whole attention to the law, making himself preëminent in this profession and maintaining his position of leadership until his death.

He was an expert in legal logic and a compelling advocate before a jury; his appeal to the court was made attractive by a rich voice under perfect control. His greatest case was probably that of *Barden* vs. *Northern Pacific Railroad Company* (154 *U. S.*, 288–349). This suit was over rights claimed by the railway to minerals under the land in its Congressional grant. The grant had reserved minerals, but the Northern Pacific contended that the reservation applied only to mineral lands known to be such at the time. Toole appeared for the State of Montana, and his argument that the mineral reservation was perpetual was upheld by the courts and caused the railroad the loss of about 80,000 square miles of mineral land.

Many of Toole's important cases depended upon the "apex" law, which gave persons holding mining claims the right to follow veins of ore under land belonging to others. In the case of *Montana Company* vs. *St. Louis Mining and Milling Company* (9 *Montana*, 288; 152 *U. S.*, 160), decided in 1890, Toole upheld the law against charges of unconstitutionality. The "apex" law as he expounded it was seized upon by Frederick A. Heinze [*q.v.*] in his fight to control the copper mines of Montana; Toole became his attorney and guided him through his long fight with W. A. Clark and Marcus Daly [*qq.v.*].

Toole's practice was varied and extensive. He appeared in 228 cases in the territorial supreme court, in 169 cases in the supreme court of the state, and in twenty cases in the United States Supreme Court, and was of counsel in many others. His income from his practice was large and for many years he invested profitably in mines and real estate. He gave liberally to organized charities and to anyone who asked for help. He gave his legal services without charge to poor clients and carried a case for one of them against the Northern Pacific to the Supreme Court of the United States. He had many friends and admirers but few intimates. He was never married, and aside from his legal activities he lived almost a recluse. He was a member of no organizations except the United Confederate Veterans and the Democratic party.

[C. P. Connolly, in *Mag. of Western Hist.*, June 1891; *Progressive Men of the State of Mont.* (2 vols., n.d.); Wm. Wallace, in *Contributions to the Hist. Soc. of Mont.*, vol. VI (1907); *Soc. of Mont. Pioneers, Constitution, Members, and Officers*, vol. I (1899); Tom Stout, *Montana* (1921), I, 430, 433; *Proc. Mont. Bar Asso., 1903–14* (n.d.); *Helena Independent*, May 16–18, 1905; *Montana Daily Record* (Helena), May 17–18, 1905; *Butte Miner*, May 17, 18, 1905; *Anaconda Standard*, May 18, 20, 24, 1905.]   P.C.P.

TOOLE, JOSEPH KEMP (May 12, 1851–Mar. 11, 1929), governor of Montana, the ninth

child of Edwin and Lucinda (Porter) Toole and brother of Edwin Warren Toole [*q.v.*], was born at Savannah, Mo. He attended school at St. Joseph, and later entered Western Military Institute, at Newcastle, Ky., where he was graduated in 1868. He studied law in the office of Webb & Barber for a year, and in 1869 went to Helena, Mont. Here he continued his legal preparation in the office of his brother Edwin, was admitted to the bar in 1872, and became his brother's partner.

Toole soon entered politics and became leader of the Montana Democrats. From 1872 to 1874 he served as district attorney. In 1881 he was elected to the territorial council, and, although a new member, was made president of that body. There he began a campaign to secure statehood for Montana and was influential in calling the constitutional convention of 1884 and in drafting the constitution of that year, which Congress refused to recognize. He was elected territorial delegate to the Forty-ninth and to the Fiftieth Congress, serving from Mar. 4, 1885, to Mar. 3, 1889. He continued his efforts to secure statehood for Montana and was active in support of the omnibus bill of 1889 providing for the admission of North and South Dakota, Montana, and Washington as states of the Union. After the enabling act for Montana was passed he became a member of the convention of 1889 that drafted the state constitution and was influential in securing the insertion of guarantees for social and civil rights. He was unsuccessful, however, in his effort to have the legislature free to decide the question of woman's suffrage.

Toole was elected the first governor of the new state and served from Nov. 8, 1889 to Jan. 1, 1893. Since the first legislature was deadlocked, he was obliged for a time to run the state on credit. To the second legislature he submitted an extensive program of administrative organization. He recommended state provision for higher education and further support of public schools, and championed the claims of miners to the minerals underlying the land grant of the Northern Pacific Railway. Refusing to seek reelection, in 1893 he resumed the practice of law. Soon, however, he was engaged in a fight to have the state capital located permanently at Helena, and in 1896 he actively supported Bryan's candidacy for president. In 1900 he was again elected governor and was reëlected in 1904, serving from Jan. 7, 1901, to Apr. 1, 1908, when he resigned on account of ill health. In 1903 the governor called the legislature in special session to provide means to reopen the mines at Butte which had been closed by the Amalgamated

Copper Company as a protest against the domination of the courts by Frederick A. Heinze [q.v.]. He supported many political and social reforms and in 1905 the initiative and referendum were adopted.

In addition to possessing unusual political talents, Toole had much personal charm. He was handsome, had attractive manners, and could adapt his conversation and interests to all types of people. Endowed with a deep, rich voice, as a public speaker he aroused the emotions of his hearers to a high pitch. He had a genius for organization and was a successful administrator. An invalid during the last twenty years of his life, he lived most of the time in California; yet his great popularity in Montana survived and his opinion on public affairs was often sought. On May 7, 1890, he married Lily, daughter of Gen. William S. Rosecrans [q.v.]; they had three sons.

[Who's Who in America, 1928–29; Biog. Dir. Am. Cong. (1928); Tom Stout, Montana (1921), vol. I; R. G. Raymer, Montana (1930), vol. I; Montana Standard, Mar. 12, 1929; Helena Standard and Lewiston Democrat-News, Mar. 12, 1929.]   P. C. P.

TOOMBS, ROBERT AUGUSTUS (July 2, 1810–Dec. 15, 1885), better known as Robert Toombs, senator, Confederate secretary of state, was a talented, forthright, and high-hearted public servant. Given his quality and circumstances, his career must have seemed to him in the main a matter of course, the more so because of its close parallel to that of his lifelong intimate friend, Alexander H. Stephens [q.v.]. Toombs was born in Wilkes County in the uplands of eastern Georgia, the fifth child of Robert Toombs, who had been a major in the Revolution and was now a well-to-do cotton planter, and the latter's third wife, Catherine Huling. As a lad he attended the University of Georgia, but withdrew in sequel to an escapade and completed his education in the North, graduating at Union College, Schenectady, N. Y., in 1828. Admitted to the bar in March 1830, he soon acquired a lucrative practice, which was intermitted rather than interrupted by legislative service. Part of his accumulating wealth was invested in a plantation and its corps of slaves in southwestern Georgia, but his home was always in the village of Washington in his native county, where life had a serenity not often disturbed by the storms in public affairs. In 1830 he married Julia DuBose, and they had three children.

Elected to the Georgia legislature in 1837, Toombs had half a dozen annual terms of service (1837–43, except for 1841) in that assembly during a time of severe economic depression. He promptly made himself an outstanding member on the Whig side, insisting upon sound finance in all its aspects, urging the creation of a supreme court for the state, but concerning himself little with federal questions. In 1844 he was elected to Congress, taking his seat at the close of the next year during a lull in the strife between the sections. For two sessions he was an unobtrusive member, speaking only to deprecate projects of aggression by the United States whether directed against Great Britain or Mexico, and to indorse moderate protectionism in the tariff. In this phase of his career he was more a conservative Whig than a champion of the South. As always, he was a careful student of public accounts, an advocate of regular procedure, and a watchdog of the treasury. Increasingly his terse phrasing, his robust eloquence, and his familiarity with current business won him a hearing when he took the floor, while his conviviality, salty comments, and hearty laughter warmed his welcome in a widening circle.

The Southern disquiet at the Wilmot Proviso did not at once bring Toombs into the sectional fray, for he pinned his faith to benign rule by his party. But when Taylor as a Whig president became, under Seward's influence, "a Southern man with Northern principles," and the crisis of 1850 was culminating, Toombs became a leader in the aggressive defense of the South. His "Hamilcar speech," demanding a share in the territorial opportunity, was but one of a series by him which became famous throughout the South: "Deprive us of this right and appropriate this common property to yourselves, it is then your government, not mine. Then I am its enemy, and I will then, if I can, bring my children and my constituents to the altar of liberty, and like Hamilcar I would swear them to eternal hostility to your foul domination. Give us our just rights, and we are ready, as ever heretofore, to stand by the Union, every part of it, and its every interest. Refuse it and I for one will strike for Independence" (June 15, 1850, Congressional Globe, 31 Cong., 1 Sess., p. 1216).

Toombs did much in Congress to procure the compromise measures of 1850; and upon the close of the session he, with Stephens and Howell Cobb, canvassed Georgia to procure a ratification of them. When they were ratified by a convention of the state he led the delegates to launch a Constitutional Union party with the maintenance of the compromise measures as its cardinal policy. This party prevailed in Georgia for several years and elected Toombs to the United States Senate. When it dissolved because of lack of response in other states, Toombs with some reluctance joined the Democrats. He gave mild approval to the Kansas-Nebraska Act as "a measure of peace, equality and fraternity" ("Correspondence," p. 342), and then sought to terminate the ensuing disorders by a bill of his own in 1856 providing for the prompt admission of Kansas as a state with whatever constitution a new convention might adopt after a thoroughly policed election of delegates (*Congressional Globe,* 34 Cong., 1 Sess., p. 1439). This bill was adopted by the Senate, against Republican opposition, but was killed in the House. The question of slavery in the territories persisted—trivial in itself because no region remained into which slavery could economically be thrust, but portentous as a touchstone of sectional doctrine and prestige.

Believing that control of the government by the Republican party would menace the security of the Southern régime, Toombs advocated harmony among the Democrats; but when they split in the campaign of 1860 he supported the "Breckinridge and Southern rights" ticket as a gesture of trenchant antagonism to the Republicans. Upon Lincoln's election he considered secession imperative unless, most improbably, the Republicans would sanction guarantees of Southern interests. Having spoken to this effect in Georgia, he supported Crittenden's compromise in the Senate committee of thirteen. Upon the rejection of this by the Republican members he sent broadcast through the press a telegram (Dec. 23, 1860) to his "fellow-citizens of Georgia" urging them to elect secessionists as delegates to a convention already scheduled ("Correspondence," p. 525). Himself chosen among these, he made a farewell speech to the Senate, Jan. 7, 1861 (*Congressional Globe,* 36 Cong., 2 Sess., p. 268), answering the question "What do these rebels demand?" Hastening to Milledgeville where the Georgia convention sat, he took a principal part in the proceedings and wrote the address which the convention adopted to justify its ordinance of secession (*Journal of the Public and Secret Proceedings of the Convention of the People of Georgia,* 1861). As a matter of course he was chosen as one of the delegates from Georgia to meet those of the other seceding states at Montgomery, Feb. 4, to launch a Southern union.

At Montgomery, Toombs was doubtless disappointed at not being made president of the Confederacy when its provisional constitution had been adopted; and he accepted the secretaryship of state with some reluctance, realizing that his talents lay rather in finance. But for the time being his vigor found varied outlets in shaping the permanent constitution and in dashing

about on semi-military errands as well as in writing diplomatic instructions and giving cabinet counsel. His advice, as when he opposed the authorization of Beauregard to reduce Fort Sumter and when he recommended heavy taxation rather than complete reliance upon credit for the conduct of the war, often came to naught. As months passed he grew contemptuous of Jefferson Davis; and subordination in an idle office became unbearable. He therefore applied for a military commission, and in July 1861 was given command of a Georgia brigade on the Virginia front, though still retaining membership in the Confederate Provisional Congress till near the end of the year.

As a general Toombs wanted to fight; and when superior commanders adopted a defensive policy he tried to debate the question and then censured their inaction and that of the government which supported them. It was presumably not merely in private that he said that the epitaph of the Confederate army should be "died of West Point," and of Davis, "We shall get our independence but it will be in spite of him" ("Correspondence," pp. 577, 592). In short, he showed the defects of a political, temperamental brigadier. When at the battle of Malvern Hill his commanding officer, D. H. Hill, reproved him for his tactics with an implication of cowardice, Toombs replied with a challenge to a duel. It was of course declined with an additional reprimand. But on the field of Antietam, where his brigade stanchly held the stone bridge and an enemy bullet shattered his left hand, Toombs proved his bravery and a degree of capacity. In recognition he virtually demanded promotion; and when this was not forthcoming he resigned his commission, saying publicly that he would no longer hold it "under President Davis with advantage to my country, or to you [the brigade], or with honor to myself" (*Ibid.,* p. 612).

Now for a time Toombs had nothing to do but expose the errors and oppressions of the government, censuring the draft of troops, the impressment of supplies, the suspension of *habeas corpus,* and especially the continued reliance upon credit and the partial repudiation of paper currency. With the purpose of making some of his policies effective he sought election to the Confederate Senate, which in a previous year he had declined; but in this candidacy he was defeated. Sherman's advance against Atlanta then gave him a bit of military service again as a divisional adjutant and inspector-general in the Georgia militia; but no glory or contentment was to be had in handling that nondescript array. The collapse of the Confederacy found Toombs at ome, where he stayed until a detail of Federal troops approached his house with an order for his arrest. Thereupon, in May 1865, he became a fugitive, finding his way through New Orleans and Havana to London. When the fervor for punishing "rebels" had passed he returned home in 1867, but he never applied for pardon as a means of regaining citizenship of the United States under the Reconstruction laws. He nevertheless rebuilt a large law practice and resumed a strong influence in the public affairs of the state.

In this phase of his career Toombs was a tribune of the people, opposing whether at the bar or on the rostrum the rapacity of corporations and the plunderings of the Carpet-bag government. Avoiding the perfervid in order not to give ammunition to the vindictive wing of Republicans at the North, he steadily strove to hamper and overthrow Radical rule. For a time he saw salvation in the Democratic party alone; but in 1877 he welcomed the program of President Hayes and censured the Northern Democrats for their criticisms: "They fear it may 'split the party.' So much the better if it does. It certainly needs sifting and cleansing. . . . They do not want redress but grievances to complain of. While that may be fun for the children it is death to the frogs. I hope Hayes will put honest men in office at the South and care not a copper for their politics" (*Ibid.*, p. 727). In the same year his labors to reform and modernize the constitution of Georgia bore fruit. He dominated the convention of 1877 which repudiated the Carpet-bag bonds, diminished the prospective effects of negro suffrage, improved the judiciary system, and provided for the control of corporations. At the same time he resisted the inclusion of specific laws in the constitution, saying: "All this convention has to do is to establish a few fundamental principles and leave these other matters to the legislature and the people, in order to meet the ever varying affairs of human life" (Phillips, *post*, p. 271). Two years later he lent a guiding hand in legislation to create a commission to regulate railroad rates (*Ibid.*, p. 272).

Cataracts now began to darken Toombs's eyes, and a domestic affliction to depress his buoyant spirit; his wife died in September 1883, after suffering from a malady of the brain. His indulgence in liquors became habitual, though he had long known that what was moderation for others was excess for him; and he grew negligent of his affairs as well as of his dress. He was now loved not for what he was but for what he had been. When death ended the decrepitude,

his name was already one to conjure with among Georgians.

[P. A. Stovall, *Robert Toombs* (1892); U. B. Phillips, *The Life of Robert Toombs* (1913), containing frequent quotation of speeches; J. C. Reed, *The Brothers' War* (1905), in large part an appreciation of Toombs; U. B. Phillips, ed., "The Correspondence of Robert Toombs, Alexander H. Stephens, and Howell Cobb," in *Annual Report of the Am. Hist. Asso. for the Year 1911*, vol. II (1913); A. C. Cole, *The Whig Party in the South* (1913); R. H. Shryock, *Georgia and the Union in 1850* (1926); obituary in *Atlanta Constitution*, Dec. 16, 1885.]

U. B. P.

TOPLIFF, SAMUEL (Apr. 25, 1789–Dec. 11, 1864), news-dealer, author, was born in Boston, Mass., the son of Samuel and Mindwell (Bird) Topliff, and a descendant of Clement Topliff who settled in New England between 1635 and 1637. His father was a sea-captain, with a fatal inclination to indorse other men's notes, so that the younger Samuel's life was spent, when he was at home from his voyages as supercargo, in straightening out the family finances. When his father was murdered at sea in a mutiny in 1811, the support of the family devolved upon him, and he forsook the sea and his employer, William Gray, a merchant. Joining Samuel Gilbert, he took charge of the books at "Mr. Gilbert's Marine and General Newsroom," then in the Exchange Coffee House in Boston. In 1814 he succeeded Gilbert and changed the name to the Merchants' Reading Room. Two years later he formed a short-lived partnership with Elkanah Cushman, the father of Charlotte Cushman [*q.v.*], selling West Indian goods on Long Wharf. Meanwhile he was selling foreign news from his correspondents to the Boston, New York, and Philadelphia papers, and the nearer New England journals. For this reason Melville E. Stone [*q.v.*] characterized him as the forerunner of the Associated Press (*M. E. S. His Book*, 1918, p. 292). In 1820 he erected a ninety-two-foot signal staff on an island in Boston harbor by which the approach of vessels could be signalled from far down the harbor, and he had two boats which brought news and bills of lading. In the same year he added the Merchants' Hall Reading-Room to his own. In 1824 his brother Benjamin became his partner. For the *New England Galaxy*, Jan. 12, 1821, he wrote the story of Pitcairn's Island and the mutiny of the *Bounty*. The year 1828, and part of 1829, he spent in making the "grand tour" of Europe. He visited Lafayette at Lagrange and met again in Paris his old friend John Cheverus [*q.v.*], archbishop of Bordeaux. His letters home about his adventures have been published as *Topliff's Travels* (1906).

Topliff married in Providence, R. I., on Dec.

2, 1829, Jane Sisson Blackstock (d. 1860), the daughter of a Scotch merchant of Boston, formerly of New York. On the roof of their house in Washington Square, Fort Hill, overlooking the harbor, was a telescope, and a constant watch was kept to augment Topliff's news-gathering facilities. He and his wife were very social, and their chafing-dish and venison dinners were well known. They had five sons and three daughters. In 1830 the Reading Room and the Boston Post Office shared space in the old State House (then called the City Hall). Later the basement was fitted up for the Reading Room. Here it remained until the Topliffs sold out in 1842. When it closed one newspaper commented that "it has sustained the reputation of the best news-room in the country, and it has become as much identified with the merchants of Boston as State Street itself." Topliff served on the Boston City Council (1844–49), was elected alderman in 1855, and in March offered an ordinance for the erection of the first public library. He later refused to run for the state Senate because of his timidity in public speaking. On his death he was characterized as "not only indefatigable in procuring intelligence of every kind, but . . . remarkably accurate" (*Topliff's Travels, post*, p. 30).

[The fullest account of Topliff is given in *Topliff's Travels: Letters from Abroad in the Years 1828 and 1829 by Samuel Topliff* (1906), ed. by Ethel S. Bolton. Other sources are E. S. Bolton, *Clement Topliff and his Descendants in Boston* (1906); Abel Bowen, *Bowen's Picture of Boston* (2nd ed., 1833); obituary in *Boston Transcript*, Dec. 12, 1864; *Sunday Herald* (Boston), Dec. 3, 1911; and Topliff family papers in the possession of the writer.]   E. S. B—n.

TORBERT, ALFRED THOMAS ARCHIMEDES (July 1, 1833–Aug. 29, 1880), soldier, diplomat, was born at Georgetown, Del., the son of Jonathan R. and Catharine (Milby) Torbert. His father was a farmer, a Methodist local preacher, and a bank cashier. After attending the local schools, Alfred entered the United States Military Academy in 1851 and was graduated and appointed brevet second lieutenant of infantry on July 1, 1855. During the next five years he served on the frontier, participating in operations against Indians in New Mexico and in Florida, 1856–57; in the Utah expedition, 1857–60; and in the march to New Mexico, 1860–61; he was promoted second lieutenant in 1856, and first lieutenant, Feb. 25, 1861.

At the outbreak of the Civil War he was assigned to mustering duty in New Jersey; on Sept. 16, 1861, he was appointed colonel of the 1st New Jersey Volunteers, and nine days later, captain in the Regular Army. He commanded his regiment in the Peninsular campaign and took part in the siege of Yorktown, and the battles of

West Point, Gaines's Mill, and Charles City Cross-roads. In the second Manassas and Maryland campaigns he commanded a brigade of the VI Corps and was wounded at the battle of Crampton's Gap but rejoined his brigade in time to be present at Antietam. After the battle of Fredericksburg, where he rendered efficient service in covering the withdrawal of the VI Corps across the Rappahannock, he was promoted brigadier-general of volunteers, as of Nov. 29, 1862, and retained command of the same brigade during the Chancellorsville and Gettysburg campaigns.

In April 1864, Torbert was assigned to command the 1st Cavalry Division, which in the Richmond campaign, together with the division commanded by Gen. David M. Gregg [*q.v.*] under Sheridan, covered the left of the army in its successive turning movements. During these operations Torbert defeated opposing Confederate forces at Hanovertown, Matadequin Creek, and Cold Harbor. In Sheridan's Trevilian raid, June 5–21, 1864, Torbert defeated the cavalry division of Gen. Wade Hampton [*q.v.*] at Trevilian Station, but suffered a repulse the next day at Mallory's Ford. In the operations before Petersburg he was engaged in a successful action at Darbytown, July 28, 1864.

In August, Torbert was ordered to join Sheridan's Army of the Shenandoah, and on arrival he was appointed chief of cavalry of the middle military division. During the next four months he maintained contact with the Confederate forces in the Shenandoah Valley and carried out Sheridan's policy of devastation. At the battle of Winchester, Sept. 19, 1864, Torbert's envelopment of the Confederate left secured the victory. He defeated the cavalry under Gen. Thomas L. Rosser [*q.v.*] at Tom's Brook, Oct. 9, and when the army was surprised at Cedar Creek, Oct. 19, Torbert's cavalry and Getty's infantry division were the only units that continued resistance until Sheridan arrived and rallied the disordered forces. In December he conducted a cavalry raid to break up the railroads in western Virginia, but did not accomplish that object. Having previously been several times brevetted for meritorious service, on Mar. 13, 1865, he was brevetted major-general, United States Army.

On Jan. 17, 1866, he married Mary E. Curry of Milford, Del., and on Oct. 31 of that year resigned from the service. In April 1869 he was appointed United States minister to Salvador. He was transferred as consul general to Havana in December 1871, and to Paris in December 1873, resigning in 1878 to engage in a business enterprise in Mexico. In August 1880 he sailed from New York on the steamer *Vera Cruz* in connection with this venture and was drowned when the vessel was wrecked off the Florida coast. His chivalrous conduct in this disaster befitted his gallant career.

Torbert as a subordinate commander was stanch, sure, and victorious. On independent cavalry missions requiring the utmost initiative and audacity he was less successful. His genial and steadfast character was evinced by the esteem in which he was held by his military associates, by the dependability of his troops, and by his popularity in public and private life.

[U. S. Census Records of Sussex County, Del., 1840–1850; G. B. Hynson, *Hist. Etchings of Milford, Del., and Vicinity* (1899); *Hist. and Biog. Encyc. of Del.* (1882); G. W. Cullum, *Biog. Reg. Officers and Grads. U. S. Mil. Acad.* (3rd ed., 1891); *Reunion of the Asso. Grads. of the U. S. Mil. Acad.*, 1881; *Personal Memoirs of Gen. P. H. Sheridan* (2 vols., 1888); *War of the Rebellion: Official Records* (Army); *Battles and Leaders of the Civil War* (4 vols., 1887–88); *Papers of the Hist. Soc. of Del.*, no. 57 (1922); *Daily Gazette* (Wilmington, Del.), Sept., Oct. 1880; *Harper's Weekly*, Oct. 15, 1864; *Army and Navy Jour.*, Sept. 18, Oct. 2, 1880.]   T. F. M.

TORRENCE, JOSEPH THATCHER (Mar. 15, 1843–Oct. 31, 1896), iron manufacturer, was born in Mercer County, Pa., the son of James and Rebecca Torrence, natives of that state. He left home at the age of nine to live with a distant relative. For three years he worked for a blast-furnace operator at Sharpsburg, Pa., then went to Brier Hill, Mahoning County, Ohio, where he learned the blacksmith trade. Until the outbreak of the Civil War he worked around the blast furnaces in this region, becoming an assistant foreman. In August 1862 he enlisted in the 105th Ohio Infantry, but was wounded at the battle of Perryville, Ky., in October, and in January retired from service. He later joined the volunteer forces raised for the pursuit of the Confederate raider John Hunt Morgan [q.v.].

After leaving the military service he entered the employ of Reis, Brown & Berger of New Castle, Lawrence County, Pa., operators of rolling mills, blast furnaces, and coal mines. After some five years in charge of the sale of their furnace products, he resigned to go South as an expert rebuilder of iron works. In 1869 he went to Bridgeport, Ill., to build a furnace for the Chicago Iron Company; the following year he became connected with the Joliet Iron & Steel Company; and in 1874 he settled in Chicago as consulting engineer for the Green Bay & Bangor Furnace Company.

From this time forward he was identified with the Chicago region. He was one of the organizers of the Joseph H. Brown Iron & Steel Company, which about 1881 was sold to the Calumet Iron & Steel Company. He purchased a half interest in the rolling mills at Evansville, Ind., in 1884, and the following year moved the business to Hammond, Ind. In 1886 he helped organize the Chicago & Calumet Terminal Railway Company, the beginning of the elaborate system of belt lines which now surround Chicago. About this time he secured title to 1,000 acres of land in Lake County, Ind., on which the town of East Chicago was developed; he was active in securing a congressional appropriation for the improvement of the Calumet River. Another of the enterprises he promoted was the Chicago Elevated Terminal Railway Company, begun in 1890, to bring main line railroads into the city without grade crossings; he was a pioneer in this work of track elevation.

In 1874 Torrence was commissioned colonel of the 2nd Regiment of the Illinois National Guard, and from 1876 until his resignation in 1881, was brigadier-general. During the riots accompanying the railroad strikes of 1877, he was made civil and military dictator of the city and county and succeeded in restoring order without great loss of life or serious property damage. A Republican in politics, he toured through many states in company with Gen. John A. Logan [q.v.] during the Blaine-Logan campaign of 1884.

On Sept. 11, 1872, Torrence married Elizabeth Norton, daughter of Judge Jesse O. Norton of Chicago. They had one child, a daughter. Torrence survived his wife five years, dying in Chicago at the age of fifty-three. He was a man of large physique and capable of great endurance. His expert knowledge of the iron and steel business together with much native sagacity and foresight enabled him to become wealthy, while because of his vision and practical force he left his mark upon the Chicago region.

[*Encyc. of Biog. of Ill.*, vol. I (1892); Joseph Kirkland, *The Story of Chicago*, vol. I (1892); A. T. Andreas, *Hist. of Chicago*, vol. III (1886); A. W. Tourgée, *The Story of a Thousand* (1896); *Chicago Sunday Tribune*, Nov. 1, 1896.]   E. A. D.

TORREY, BRADFORD (Oct. 9, 1843–Oct. 7, 1912), ornithologist, author, was born in Weymouth, Mass., a son of Samuel and Sophronia (Dyer) Torrey. He was a descendant of Lieut. James Torrey who emigrated from England and settled at Scituate, Mass., soon after 1640. He was educated in the public schools of his native town. After graduating from high school, he worked for a time in a local shoe-factory and taught school for several years. He then went to Boston and, after brief connection with two or three business houses, was for sixteen years employed in the office of the treasurer of the American Board of Commissioners for Foreign Missions. From boyhood a lover of nature and an attentive observer of wild life, it was not until these years in Boston that he became especially interested in the study of birds, and then in putting the results of his observation into literary form. His first published writing was an article, "With the Birds on Boston Common," which appeared in the *Atlantic Monthly* in February 1883. Two years later his first book, *Birds in the Bush,* was published. In 1886 he found highly congenial employment as one of the editors of the *Youth's Companion.* He was a member of the staff until 1901; his work was the selection and preparation of the entertaining miscellany pages for which that popular weekly was famous. In this occupation he found leisure for continual observation of bird life, not a little travel, and the writing of a succession of essays, sketches, and books, all dealing in the most charming way with his experiences in the fields and woods. The titles of his published volumes are: *A Rambler's Lease* (1889), *The Foot-path Way* (1892), *A Florida Sketch Book* (1894), *Spring Notes from Tennessee* (1896), *A World of Green Hills* (1898), *Everyday Birds* (1901), *Footing it in Franconia* (1901), *The Clerk of the Woods* (1903), *Nature's Invitation* (1904), *Friends on the Shelf* (1906), which was a book of literary criticism, and *Field Days in California* (1913). He was also the sympathetic editor of the fourteen volumes of the journal of Henry David Thoreau [*q.v.*] which were published in the twenty-volume Walden edition in 1906.

Torrey was not a scientifically trained ornithologist and received no academic recognition. He was, however, as many ornithological authorities have testified, a singularly faithful and accurate field observer, whose careful work has added much to the knowledge of the habits and characteristics of native American birds. He became perhaps the foremost authority on humming-birds during his lifetime. His books are as far as possible from being handbooks of ornithology. Torrey was first of all an essayist, and his writing has the discursive fluency and whimsical humor of the true essayist. His style is graceful, unassuming, almost conversational. He takes his reader delightfully into his confidence, and reveals to him a personality of rare gentleness and charm. He writes not of birds alone, but of nature in all its aspects of beauty, and his books are as attractive to the general reader as to the bird lover to whom they are primarily addressed.

Torrey was never married. His circle of acquaintance was not large, for he lived much by himself, but his friends found in him a rare and sympathetic personality, and a character of unusual gentleness and purity. In his last years he moved, partly for reasons of health, to California. He lived near Santa Barbara, much of the time a solitary life, reminiscent of Thoreau's, in a cabin of which he was the sole occupant. He died Oct. 7, 1912, in a hospital in Santa Barbara.

[F. C. Torrey, *The Torrey Families and Their Children in America* (2 vols., 1924–29); *Who's Who in America,* 1912–13; F. H. Allen, in *Auk,* Jan. 1913; obituaries in *Boston Transcript* and *Evening Post* (N. Y.), Oct. 8, 1912; personal acquaintance, letters, and private information.]   H. S. C—n.

TORREY, CHARLES TURNER (Nov. 21, 1813–May 9, 1846), abolitionist, was born in Scituate, Mass., where his ancestor, James Torrey, had settled soon after 1640. His parents, Charles Turner Torrey and Hannah Tolman (Turner), were first cousins, grandchildren of the Rev. Charles Turner; they both died of tuberculosis in their son's infancy, and he was brought up in the home of his maternal grandfather, Charles Turner, Jr., a substantial citizen and sometime member of Congress. Torrey was prepared for college at Phillips Academy, graduated at Yale (A.B., 1833), and after a few months of teaching entered Andover Theological Seminary in 1834. Here he became an abolitionist and organized a students' antislavery society, but because of failing health withdrew from the seminary and completed his theological training at West Medway under the Rev. Jacob Ide, whose daughter, Mary, he married on Mar. 29, 1837. Two children were born of this union.

Torrey was licensed to preach by the Mendon Association, Oct. 25, 1836, and on Mar. 22 following was ordained and installed as pastor of the Richmond Street Congregational Church of Providence, R. I., but was not successful as a minister either here or at the Harvard Street Congregational Church in Salem, where he served from January 1838 to July 1839. His interest in anti-slavery politics soon encroached upon his pastoral duties. Sharing in the rising irritation against William Lloyd Garrison [*q.v.*] and his heresies regarding Sabbath observance, civil government, and the rights of women, Torrey organized the conservative abolitionists of Massachusetts in a revolt against Garrison's leadership. In the fall of 1838, the conservatives founded the *Massachusetts Abolitionist,* with Torrey as editor, and a few months later they seceded from Garrison's society, organized the Massachusetts Abolition Society, and appointed Torrey as their agent. In this capacity he was not successful. "It was exceedingly difficult for him to labor with others, either as a pastor, a lecturer, or an editor," remarked a colleague (Lovejoy, *post*, p. 87). He shortly resigned, and in 1841 went to Washington as freelance correspondent.

While reporting the notorious "Convention of Slaveholders" at Annapolis, Md., in January 1842, Torrey was identified as an abolitionist and on Jan. 14 arrested. The case immediately attracted national interest. The anti-slavery congressmen employed a Boston lawyer to be his counsel, and two Maryland lawyers, T. S. Alexander and Joseph M. Palmer, acted for him without compensation. After four days of widely publicized proceedings, Torrey was freed (Jan. 19). Made momentarily famous by this episode, he was appointed editor of the *Tocsin of Liberty*, later the *Albany Patriot*, but was unsuccessful in this position and after a few months relinquished its editorial care.

"An exceedingly vain, trifling man, with no wisdom or stability," as a fellow abolitionist characterized him (T. D. Weld to his wife, Jan. 18, 1842; *Letters, post*, II, 896), Torrey was unable to sustain these recurrent stresses of notoriety and failure. Moving to Baltimore, he made grandiose plans to engage in business, and at the same time he helped escaping slaves from Virginia and Maryland across the border. Inevitably he was arrested, and once more figured in a notorious trial (Nov. 29–Dec. 1, 1844). This time, however, although defended by the distinguished Reverdy Johnson [*q.v.*], he was convicted and sentenced to six years at hard labor in the Maryland state penitentiary. Once in the jail, his mind gave way, and tuberculosis, long latent in his constitution, caused his death little more than a year after his imprisonment. His body was removed to Boston, and at a great public funeral he was honored as a martyr to the anti-slavery cause.

[J. C. Lovejoy, *Memoir of Rev. Charles T. Torrey* (1847), by a brother of Elijah P. Lovejoy [*q.v.*], the first anti-slavery martyr; *N. Y. Evangelist*, Jan., Feb. 1842; *Letters of Theodore Dwight Weld, Angelina Grimké Weld, and Sarah Grimké* (2 vols., 1934), ed. by G. H. Barnes and D. L. Dumond; W. P. and F. J. Garrison, *William Lloyd Garrison* (4 vols., 1885–89); *Massachusetts Abolitionist*, vol. I; *Biog. Notices Grads. Yale Coll.* (1913); F. C. Torrey, *The Torrey Families*, vol. I (1924); Jacob Turner, *Geneal. of the Descendants of Humphrey Turner* (1852); *The Sun* (Baltimore), May 11, 1846.]
G. H. B.

TORREY, JOHN (Aug. 15, 1796–Mar. 10, 1873), botanist and chemist, was born and died in New York City. His earliest American ancestor, Capt. William Torrey of the parish of Combe St. Nicholas, Somerset, emigrated to America 'n 1640 and settled in Weymouth, Mass.

His father and grandfather were soldiers of the Revolution serving in the vicinity of New York and settled there at its close. His father, Capt. William Torrey, one of the original members of the Society of the Cincinnati, married Margaret Nichols. John was the second of their ten children. About 1810 William Torrey was appointed fiscal agent of the state prison at Greenwich (later Greenwich Village). Here came—imprisoned for debt, it is said—Amos Eaton [*q.v.*], enthusiast in the natural sciences; he took a fancy to John and inspired him with an interest in science that gave direction to his life work. Much of Torrey's earlier scientific work was in mineralogy, but he must have been at the same time a careful student of botany. He was one of the group of young men at the College of Physicians and Surgeons who, under the stimulating leadership of their professor, Samuel Latham Mitchill [*q.v.*], in February 1817 established the Lyceum of Natural History, forerunner of the New York Academy of Sciences. On May 5 a committee of three was appointed to prepare a catalogue of the plants growing near New York, and on Dec. 22, 1817, *A Catalogue of Plants Growing Spontaneously Within Thirty Miles of the City of New York* (1819) was presented to the Lyceum. Most of the work is shown to have been done by Torrey, and it has always been called "Torrey's Catalogue."

Meanwhile, in 1818, Torrey had received the degree of M.D. from the College of Physicians and Surgeons, and had begun the practice of his profession in his native city, but his real interests lay in other fields. During the next few years he gave special attention to the plants of the northeastern United States, and his published scientific papers and correspondence soon spread his fame. At about this time began the long series of government explorations of the West. Members of these expeditions, as a part of their official duties, collected plants, and nearly all of these, for many years, were turned over to Torrey for study and report. The thoroughness of his pioneer work upon these collections has been amply demonstrated by the studies of later generations of botanists. His first publications in this field were his report on the plants collected by David Bates Douglass [*q.v.*] near the source of the Mississippi in 1820 (*American Journal of Science and Arts*, vol. IV, no. 1, 1821) and his reports on the collection made by Edwin James [*q.v.*] in 1820 (*Annals of the Lyceum of Natural History*, vol. I, nos. 1, 2, 1823; vol. II, nos. 4–5, 1826, nos. 6, 7–8, 1827). Late in 1823 was issued the first part of the first book bearing Torrey's name as sole author, *A Flora of the Northern and Middle Sections of the United States.* Two other parts completed the first volume, but the preparation of an intended second volume was prevented by the pressure of other demands upon his time, and by his growing dissatisfaction with the Linnean artificial system of classification then in general use. A small work, however, issued in 1826 under the title, *A Compendium of the Flora of the Northern and Middle States,* supplied in concise form descriptions not only of the plants actually treated in the first volume, but of those intended for inclusion in the projected second one. On Apr. 20, 1824, Torrey married Eliza Shaw of New York, and they went to live at West Point, where he had been appointed professor of chemistry, mineralogy, and geology in the United States Military Academy. Three years later he returned to New York City as a professor of chemistry at the College of Physicians and Surgeons; in this position he was active until 1855, and he continued as professor emeritus for the remainder of his life. In 1830 he accepted the professorship of chemistry and natural history at the College of New Jersey (later Princeton), which he held concurrently with his professorship in New York for nearly twenty-five years.

It was in 1834 that Asa Gray [*q.v.*] came from western New York to New York City, where he was librarian of the Lyceum and in charge of its buildings and collections for a year, and studied plants with Torrey. The latter was so impressed with the younger man's ability that he invited him to become his associate in the preparation of a work on the *Flora of North America,* of which seven parts, comprising all of one volume and most of another, appeared from 1838 to 1843. Meanwhile Torrey's work upon this publication was more or less hampered by his acceptance in 1836 of an appointment as state botanist, resulting in the preparation of a *Flora of the State of New York* (2 vols., 1843). The necessity of studying the western plant collections, pouring in in increasing numbers every year, finally caused the abandonment of Torrey and Gray's *Flora,* but Torrey continued active botanical study and publication. He reported on the plant collections of Joseph Nicholas Nicollet's explorations of 1836–39, Frémont's first expedition of 1842 and his second of 1843–44; W. H. Emory's military reconnaissance of 1846–47; the Mexican Boundary survey of 1848–54; Howard Stansbury's exploration of the Great Salt Lake region in 1849–50; Lorenzo Sitgreaves' expedition down the Zuñi and Colorado rivers in 1851; R. B. Marcy's exploration of the Red River in 1852; various expeditions connected

with the Pacific Railroad surveys of 1853–55, including those of E. G. Beckwith, J. W. Gunnison, John Pope, A. W. Whipple, R. S. Williamson, and J. G. Parke; and J. C. Ives's exploration of the Colorado in 1857–58. All of these appeared in the official reports of the expeditions. In spite of these labors he did not neglect monographic work. His monograph of the *Cyperaceae* appeared as early as 1836; his revision of the *Eriogoneae,* in collaboration with Gray, as late as 1870. And throughout his career he was building up his botanical library and herbarium until they became among the most valuable in America; these he transferred to Columbia College about 1860, and in 1899 Columbia deposited them with the newly established New York Botanical Garden. Many of the specimens are accompanied by Torrey's pencil sketches illustrating their structure as shown by his careful dissections.

In 1839 Torrey was elected a foreign member of the Linnean Society of London, and in 1841 a member of the American Academy of Arts and Sciences. In 1863 he was one of the corporate members of the National Academy of Sciences. When the Assay Office was established in New York in 1853, Torrey accepted an appointment as United States assayer, resigning from the Princeton faculty in 1854, and retiring from active work as a professor at Columbia. He continued in this position for the remaining twenty years of his life. Much of his time, however, continued to be devoted to botanical study. His position as assayer opened the way for occasional travel. He visited California, by way of Panama, in 1865, on a confidential mission for the Treasury Department and was able to see for the first time in their natural surroundings various plants that he had made known to science by herbarium study many years before. He spent part of the winter of 1871–72 in Florida, and the next summer visited California for the second time. On his way east he ascended Torrey's Peak in Colorado, which had been named in his honor several years previously. Within a year after his return to New York he suffered an attack of pleurisy, from the effects of which he never recovered, and a few weeks later, in his seventy-seventh year, he died. He was survived by three daughters and one son.

No account of Torrey would be complete without some reference to his remarkable personality, which endeared him to all who knew him. It was characterized by integrity, sagacity, and studiousness, but above all by a certain ingenuousness and genial friendliness, which increased with age. His early encouragement of

Asa Gray has already been mentioned, and his influence upon the careers of other young botanists was extremely helpful. Late in his life a group of young men gathered about him and established a botanical society named, even during his lifetime, the Torrey Botanical Club. This organization, dating from 1867, established in 1870 the *Bulletin of the Torrey Botanical Club*, the first botanical monthly in America; it was largely instrumental in the establishment of the New York Botanical Garden, and today occupies an honored place among the scientific societies of the world. It is a fitting memorial of Torrey the man.

[F. C. Torrey, *The Torrey Families . . . in America* (2 vols., 1924–29); *Bull. Torrey Botanical Club*, Mar.–Aug. 1873, Oct. 1900; *Asa Gray, Sci. Papers* (1889), vol. II; T. S. Hunt, in *Proc. Boston Soc. Nat. Hist.*, Mar. 19, 1873; W. J. Youmans, *Pioneers of Sci. in America* (1895); Marcus Benjamin, in *Proc. Am. Asso. for the Advancement of Sci.*, vol. XLVIII (1889); *Botanical Gazette*, Feb. 1883; *Proc. Linnean Soc.* (London), 1872–73; H. L. Fairchild, *A Hist. of the N. Y. Acad. of Sciences* (1887); death notice in *N. Y. Times*, Mar. 11, 1873.]   J. H. B—t.

TOTTEN, GEORGE MUIRSON (May 28, 1809–May 17, 1884), engineer, son of Gilbert and Mary (Rice) Totten, was born in New Haven, Conn. After attending schools in his native town, including the Hopkins Grammar School, in 1824 he entered Norwich Military Academy at Norwich, Vt., which later became Norwich University. Graduating in 1827 during the era of canal building, he at once secured a position as assistant engineer on the Farmington Canal, afterwards used as part of the roadbed of the New Haven & Northampton Railroad. He served in a like capacity on the Juniata Canal in Pennsylvania (1828–31), and on the Delaware & Raritan in New Jersey (1831–35). By this time the railroad was rapidly superseding the canal as the principal means of transportation and in 1835 Totten was employed to assist in the construction of a road from Reading to Port Clinton, Pa.; subsequently he was engaged in similar work in Virginia; in Pennsylvania in connection with the Sunbury & Danville R. R. (1837–40); and in North Carolina in connection with the Gaston & Raleigh (1840–43).

In 1843 his first South American commission took him to the harbor of Cartagena in Colombia, where he built the Canal del Dique to connect that harbor with the Magdalena River. Associated with him in this enterprise was another pioneer engineer of the United States, John C. Trautwine [*q.v.*]. In 1850, also in association with Trautwine, he became identified with the construction of the Panama Railroad, conceived at the time of the California gold rush of 1849,

when the only methods of getting to the West were to go "the Plains across, the Horn around, or the Isthmus over." As engineer-in-chief of this work Totten spent some twenty-five years on the Isthmus, working under the worst possible conditions as to health and compelled to endure great hardships and privations. When Ferdinand de Lesseps became president of the Panama Canal Company in 1879, Totten was asked to remain on the Isthmus as chief, and the only American member, of De Lesseps' staff. Later he went to Venezuela on railroad work near Carácas, served as consulting engineer in connection with the first Panama Canal project, and on many other canal and railroad works.

Generally known as Colonel Totten, he received numerous honors and was recognized as one of the foremost members of his profession. He was made a member of the American Philosophical Society, Jan. 17, 1851; Napoleon III is said to have presented him with a ring and Gen. Guzman Blanco, president of Venezuela, gave him a gold medal. He was married at Pottsville, Pa., July 12, 1835, to Harriet Seely of Sunbury, Pa., who with two daughters survived him.

[W. A. Ellis, *Norwich Univ.* (1911), vol. II; "The Panama Railroad," *Harper's New Mo. Mag.*, Jan. 1859; *Engineering News*, May 24, 1884; *N. Y. Times*, May 17, 20, 1884.]   J. K. F.

TOTTEN, JOSEPH GILBERT (Aug. 23, 1788–Apr. 22, 1864), soldier, scientist, and engineer, for whom Fort Totten in New York Harbor was named, was born in New Haven, Conn., the son of Peter and Grace (Mansfield) Totten. His mother died when Joseph was three years old and his father shortly afterward was appointed vice-consul at Santa Cruz in the West Indies. The guardianship of the boy thus fell upon his uncle, Jared Mansfield [*q.v.*], a Yale graduate who was selected in 1802 as the first professor of mathematics at the United States Military Academy. Here Joseph became a cadet, in November 1802, and was graduated and commissioned a second lieutenant of engineers, July 1, 1805, the tenth graduate of West Point. As a cadet he had been outstanding in scholarship, industry, "gentlemanly deportment," and popularity. Immediately upon his graduation he was made secretary to his uncle, who had been appointed surveyor general of the Northwestern Territory, in charge of the first systematic survey of the new states of the Union. In order to pursue the requisite explorations, Totten resigned from the army Mar. 31, 1806, but was reappointed to the same rank and corps two years later. He was promoted first lieutenant July 23, 1810, and captain July 31, 1812.

From the time of his return to the service, he

acted as assistant engineer of the harbor defenses of New York City, with special supervision of Fort Clinton at Castle Garden, and of the defenses of New Haven, New London, and Sag Harbor. At the beginning of the War of 1812, he was made chief engineer of the army on the Niagara frontier, where he rendered conspicuous and active service in harbor and fortress defense, winning the brevet of major, June 6, 1813. For gallant conduct at the battle of Plattsburg he was brevetted lieutenant-colonel, Sept. 11, 1814. There followed more than two decades of service on various engineering boards, in the planning and erection of coast defenses, and the execution of river and harbor improvements, during which time he was promoted major in 1818, lieutenant-colonel in 1828, and colonel, Dec. 7, 1838. With the last commission he was simultaneously made chief engineer of the army and inspector of the United States Military Academy, both of which posts he held uninterruptedly for over a quarter of a century, until his death. When Gen. Winfield Scott [q.v.] undertook the southern campaign in the Mexican War, he took Totten with him as chief engineer and member of his "Little Cabinet." Totten originated the detailed and successful plan of operations at Vera Cruz, and was brevetted brigadier-general as of Mar. 29, 1847, for "gallant and meritorious conduct" at the siege. He was also one of the commissioners at the capitulation.

In 1851 when the Lighthouse Board was legally established, Totten became a member, serving until 1858 and again from 1860 till his death. In this capacity he was instrumental in establishing and maintaining a system of lighting by Fresnel lenses. His name is particularly associated with the lights at Seven-Foot Knoll, off Baltimore, and Minot's Ledge off Cohasset, Mass., difficult works to which he devoted all his energy and talents. For these contributions alone, according to a colleague, Gen. John G. Barnard [q.v.], he is entitled to recognition among the Smeatons, Stevensons, and Brunels as one of the great engineers of the age ("Memoir," post). Between 1851 and 1855 he conducted a series of experiments on the effects of firing heavy ordnance from casemate embrasures. He was chosen as a member of the New York state commission on the improvement and preservation of New York Harbor, and to a similar capacity with the Massachusetts commission on Boston Harbor. In 1859–61 he made a reconnaissance of the Pacific Coast in order to determine its state of defense. During the Civil War he continued to be chief engineer of the army and on Mar. 3, 1863, was made a brigadier-general. He was active in supervising the defensive works around Washington and was a member of the commission to examine them. He was president of the retiring board for disabled officers in 1861 and a member of the board appointed to regulate and fix the heavy ordnance (1861–62). One day before he died he was brevetted a major-general by Congress "for long, faithful and eminent service."

In addition to his reports on national defenses and his essays on ordnance, he published *Essays on Hydraulic and Common Mortars and on Lime-Burning* (1838), a translation from the French, with added notes of his own, which aided engineering progress materially. His studies in conchology were rewarded by having two shells —the *gemma* and *succinea tottenii*—named for him. In 1829 he was awarded the honorary degree of A.M. by Brown University. He was a regent of the Smithsonian Institution from its establishment in 1846 until his death, and in 1863, a corporator of the National Academy of Sciences.

In 1816 he married Catlyna Pearson of Albany, New York, who bore him three sons and four daughters. Before the close of the Civil War he died suddenly of pneumonia, survived by two daughters. The order of the Secretary of War announcing his death stated that "his military career of more than half a century has been one of continued usefulness and distinguished services."

[J. G. Barnard, "Memoir of Joseph Gilbert Totten," in *Nat. Acad. Sci. Biog. Memoirs*, vol. I (1877), and *Eulogy on the Late Bvt. Major Gen. Joseph G. Totten* (1866); G. W. Cullum, *Biog. Reg. Officers and Grads. U. S. Mil. Acad.* (3rd ed., 1891), vol. I; J. H. Smith, *The War with Mexico* (2 vols., 1919); W. A. Ganoe, *The Hist. of the U. S. Army* (1924); F. B. Heitman, *Hist. Reg. and Dict. U. S. Army* (1903); *Army and Navy Jour.*, Apr. 30, 1864; *Daily National Intelligencer* (Washington), Apr. 25, 1864; Records, Old Files Section, Adjutant General's Office, Washington.]
W. A. G.

TOU, ERIK HANSEN (Oct. 11, 1857–Nov. 14, 1917), missionary, the son of Hans and Helga Serine (Eriksen) Andersen, was born near Stavanger, Norway. After completing his early schooling, he worked as a miller in Tou mill near his home; hence his surname Tou. In 1881 he went to Minneapolis, Minn., to learn more about mills, intending to return to Norway later. Disheartened at the poor prospects for employment, he became a student in Augsburg Seminary, and was graduated with the B.A. degree in 1886, and the degree in theology in 1889. In 1889 he was married to Caroline Elisabeth Knudsen, of Fulton, Iowa, and took up missionary work in Madagascar. They were first stationed at Tulear and St. Augustine, 1889–90, and then in Manasoa, on the southwest coast. They were the first missionaries in the region south of the Onilahy River, occupied by the Tanosy tribe.

Tou preached at two main stations and thirteen substations, established a school, in which Malagasy and French were taught, a theological seminary, and two foundling asylums, which were converted to orphanages when the French government took full possession of the island. He advocated, and finally saw realized, a free dispensary and the teaching of scientific agriculture at his station. Much of the flourishing Christian life in southwest Madagascar owed its beginnings to his efforts. He faced an almost impossible task in the midst of an immoral, grossly superstitious tribe, yet, after a few years he claimed that Christianity had done more for the Tanosy than had three hundred years of partial contact with European civilization. The climate was unhealthful, and financial support entirely inadequate. Three of his children and his wife died on the island. In a fascinating book, *Den lutherske Frikirkes Hedningemission paa Madagaskar* (1898), he related his earlier experiences on the island. His later experiences were detailed in articles for the press, and were published in the *Lutheraneren, Luthersk Kirkeblad, Folkebladet, Gasseren,* and, occasionally, in *Skandinaven,* and *Visergutten.* He also wrote for these papers on theological themes and great missionaries of the past, and translated into Norwegian *The Miracles of Missions* (1891), by A. T. Pierson. At his death he left seven volumes of diaries. Other diaries, antedating these, along with records and books, were consumed when his home was destroyed by fire in Madagascar.

With his health much impaired, Tou left Madagascar in 1903 after his marriage to his second wife, Alida Olen, of Benson, Minn., who had worked as a deaconess at Manasoa. He was missionary pastor in Pukwana, S. Dak., from 1904 to 1909, and at Napoleon, N. Dak., until his death. His hardships were many in these sparsely populated regions of extreme summer heat and winter cold. Hard travel, loneliness, poverty, and exposure, shortened his life. He was a faithful pastor and an able expounder of the Scriptures. In the United States he again gathered a valuable working library and his correspondence was extensive. From 1915 he was editor of *Gasseren.* A short time before he died he was made a member of the Lutheran Board of Missions of the Lutheran Free Church. His wife and three children survived him.

[Diary in the possession of the writer; annuals of *Den norsk danske lutherske Konferents, Den forenede norsk lutherske Kirke i Amerika, Augsburgs Venner,* *Den norsk lutherske Frikirke;* Lars Lillehie, *Augsburg Seminary and the Luth. Free Ch.* (1928); obituaries in *Napoleon Homestead* (Napoleon, N. Dak.), and in *Folkebladet* (Minneapolis, Minn.), Nov. 21, 1917.]

J. O. E.

TOUCEY, ISAAC (Nov. 15, 1792–July 30, 1869), governor of Connecticut, congressman, senator, and cabinet official, was born in Newtown, Conn., the son of Zalmon and Phebe (Booth) Toucey (or Tousey). He was a descendant of Richard Toucey who came from England to Saybrook, Conn., about 1655 and whose grandson, Thomas, was the first Congregational minister of Newtown. After a common-school training, Isaac studied law with Asa Chapman, who later became a judge of the supreme court of errors. Admitted to the bar in 1818, Toucey practised law in the city of Hartford, which was thereafter his place of residence.

From 1822 to 1835 he was state's attorney for Hartford County. In the latter year he became a member of Congress, serving as such until Mar. 3, 1839. He did not speak often, or ever at great length, his most sustained effort being a plea, Sept. 29, 1837, for the postponement of payments on the surplus distribution bill (*Register of Debates in Congress,* 25 Cong., 1 Sess., pp. 1133–35). At the close of his second term, he resumed his practice in Hartford, and again served as state's attorney, 1842–44. In 1845 he was the unsuccessful Democratic candidate for governor; the following year, there being no choice by the people, he was chosen governor by the legislature; in the election of 1847 he was defeated. He had displeased those interested in local railroads by vetoing a bill authorizing the construction of a bridge over the Connecticut River at Middletown, and had aroused ill feelings by declaring that there was a great deal of bribery practised in connection with state elections.

Shortly after his governorship he again became connected with national affairs, serving as attorney-general in Polk's cabinet from June 1848 to March 1849, and for a short time during that period, in the absence of Buchanan from Washington, acting as secretary of state. In 1850 he was elected to the upper house of the Connecticut legislature, and in 1852 was again a member of the lower house. In the latter year he was elected to the United States Senate, and served from May 12, 1852, to Mar. 3, 1857. Here he was more prominent than he had been in the House. In August 1852, while condemning the "higher law" theory embraced by Seward and Sumner, he asked for the enforcement of the fugitive-slave act because it was the law, and because Northern opposition to it amounted to nullification (*Congressional Globe*, 32 Cong., 1 Sess., App., pp. 1121–22). Two years later he supported the Kansas-Nebraska bill, on the ground that the Missouri Compromise had placed an unconstitutional limitation on states to be admitted from the northern part of the Louisiana Purchase (*Ibid.*, 33 Cong., 1 Sess., App., pp. 313–15). For this stand Toucey was criticized by the *Hartford Times,* a Democratic paper which had usually supported his policies as congressman and as governor.

In 1857 President Buchanan chose Toucey as secretary of the navy. His sympathies were more or less with the South, and he was suspected, perhaps unjustly, of so disposing of the country's naval forces in 1860 as to aid the South in the movement toward secession (See *House Journal,* 36 Cong., 2 Sess., pp. 359, 466–69; *House Report, No. 87,* same session; Report of the Secretary of the Navy in *Senate Executive Document, No. 1,* 37 Cong., 1 Sess.). Toucey's sympathetic attitude toward the South incited some members of the Connecticut legislature to remove his portrait from the gallery of ex-governors, and a resolution providing for the replacement of the portrait, offered in the state Senate in 1863, was defeated. One achievement of the much maligned secretary has received unstinted praise: he supervised the naval expedition to Paraguay, December 1858, consisting of a force of some nineteen vessels and 2,500 men, which was financed with such economy as to be completed without a special congressional appropriation. After his retirement from the cabinet Toucey passed the remainder of his life in Hartford. During the Civil War he supported the cause of the North. In private life he was a likeable man, reserved though not distant in contacts with others. He had a striking personal appearance, somewhat resembling that of Andrew Jackson. His declining years were troubled by the feeble health of his wife, Catharine Nichols, whom he had married Oct. 28, 1827; they had no children.

[Index to Barbour Coll. of Conn. Vital Records, State Library, Hartford; *Biog. Dir. Am. Cong.* (1928); J. H. Trumbull, *The Memorial Hist. of Hartford County, Conn.* (1886), vol. I; W. D. Shipman, "Isaac Toucey," 36 *Conn. Reports,* 587–88; J. B. Moore, *The Works of James Buchanan* (12 vols., 1908–11); *U. S. Democratic Rev.,* Oct. 1859; *Hartford Daily Courant,* July 31, 1869.]   J. M. M.

TOULMIN, HARRY (Apr. 7, 1766–Nov. 11, 1823), clergyman, educator, territorial district judge, was born at Taunton, Somersetshire, England. A ministerial bent in the youth, inherited perhaps from his father, the Rev. Joshua Toulmin (see *Dictionary of National Biography*), was strengthened by intimacy with Joseph Priestley [*q.v.*]. Most of his education, however, was acquired in the book store kept by his mother, Jane (Smith) Toulmin, although he also attended Hoxton Academy. While serving as minister in Monton and Chowbent, Lancashire (1786–92), he aroused popular disapproval because of his Unitarian leanings. Influenced by this feeling and by an interest in America gained from extensive reading, he published, in 1792, three pamphlets favoring emigration to America (Jillson, *post*). A few months later, he accompanied Priestley to the United States, where he became acquainted with Jefferson. The latter and Madison furnished him with letters of introduction, commending him as an instructor of youth "in classical knowledge and other branches of liberal education" (Madison Papers, Library of Congress). Thus armed, he went to Kentucky, where, in February 1794, he was elected president of Transylvania University. Despite opposition, he held the office for two years, and then for eight years was secretary to the Commonwealth of Kentucky. During this period he compiled *A Collection of the Permanent and Public Acts of the General Assembly of Kentucky* (1802), and with James Blair prepared *A Review of the Criminal Law of the Commonwealth of Kentucky* (2 vols., 1804–06). In 1806 he published *The American Attorney's Pocket Book,* and in 1807, *The Magistrates' Assistant,* which may have first appeared as early as 1801.

In 1804 Toulmin was appointed judge of the superior court for the eastern, or Tombigbee, district of Mississippi Territory (later part of Alabama). Thenceforth he was permanently identified with this region, without losing touch with influential friends or former background. Through letter, personal counsel, and legal procedure he sought to restrain lawless borderers and to allay the fears of jealous Spaniards by securing the remission of imposts at Mobile and by softening the resentment aroused by these exactions. In this double task he was only partially successful (Cox, pp. 176, 222, 293). Nor did he fare better in 1807 with Burr's mysterious following; he merely succeeded in arresting a few of that conspirator's associates and in remanding them for trial elsewhere. His purpose was to keep Burr away from the restless settlers on the Tombigbee. He found himself roundly abused—unjustly he thought—as a tool of Gen. James Wilkinson (cf. *Indiana Magazine of History,* December 1929, p. 274).

In 1810 Toulmin's law-abiding course experienced its most severe tests. Insurrection broke out in West Florida and self-appointed leaders of the Tombigbee district hastened to organize the Mobile Society for the purpose of occupying the nearby Spanish holdings. Toulmin, prompted both by President Madison and by Gov. David Holmes [qq.v.], bestirred himself to forestall the attempts. While he supported the claim of the United States to the Mobile region and sympathized with those who protested against Spanish exactions there, he sought in a masterly charge to the grand jury, Sept. 16, 1810, to restrain his fellow citizens from using force and to impress upon them their responsibility for the maintenance of peace. His efforts contributed to break up these illegal attempts but thereby made him extremely unpopular (Cox, pp. 444–54; National Intelligencer, Nov. 7 and 13, 1810).

In the following month, Toulmin was still further hampered in his efforts to preserve order by the presence of Reuben Kemper [q.v.]. The latter represented the convention that had wrested Baton Rouge from Spanish control and now sought to incorporate Mobile in the embryo state of West Florida. Toulmin's purpose was to keep the American population above the line from helping Kemper. He also hoped to induce the Spanish authorities to deliver Mobile to the American government (American Historical Review, July 1897, pp. 701–02). In neither task did he gain his immediate end. At a critical period in Kemper's movements, however, by arresting that obstreperous leader, he contributed to the defeat of another filibustering project. For this service, Kemper characterized him as a "base Devil, filled with deception and Bloody Rascality" (Cox, p. 470), but later congressional reports failed to support this prejudiced opinion (American State Papers, Miscellaneous, vol. II, 1834, pp. 162, 184, 443), while most of the "good elements" of the community appreciated his efforts to uphold a high standard of legal procedure.

Toulmin retained his judgeship until 1819 and during this period did much to straighten out the land claims and other legal tangles in the region. He also edited The Statutes of the Mississippi Territory (1807). In 1819 he was a prominent member of the convention that formed a constitution for Alabama, and four years later he compiled A Digest of the Territorial Laws of Alabama (1823). Thus he linked his name with three formal state codes. He was twice married, and left children.

[Printed sources include A. J. Pickett, Hist. of Ala. (1851), vol. II; I. J. Cox, The West Florida Controversy (1918); W. P. Jillson, A Transylvanian Trilogy (1932), reprinting Toulmin's pamphlets favoring emigration, with a bibliog. of his writings and of references; Official Letter Books of W. C. C. Claiborne (6 vols., 1917), ed. by Dunbar Rowland; Robert Peter, Transylvania Univ. (1896), being Filson Club Pub.

No. 11; Daily National Intelligencer (Washington), Dec. 13, 1823. Unpublished letters of Toulmin's occur in the papers of Jefferson, Madison, and John Breckinridge, and the West Florida Papers, in the Lib. of Cong.; in the Miss. Territorial Archives and the Proc. of the Exec. Council of Miss. Territory, Dept. of State, Washington; and in Claiborne Letters E, Miss. Dept. of Archives and Hist. According to Jillson (op. cit.), a manuscript account of the Toulmin family is preserved at Transylvania Univ.]   I. J. C.

TOULMIN, HARRY THEOPHILUS (Mar. 4, 1838–Nov. 12, 1916), Confederate officer, jurist, was born in Mobile County, Ala., the son of Theophilus Lindsay and Amante E. (Juzan) Toulmin. He was a grandson of Judge Harry Toulmin [q.v.], a prominent figure of frontier days. After obtaining his preparatory education in the private schools at Toulminville and Mobile, he entered the University of Alabama in 1852. Although he left this institution in his sophomore year, he resumed his studies in 1856 at the University of Virginia, where he devoted a year to law. Subsequently he became interested in the Civil Law and attended a course of lectures at the University of Louisiana (now Tulane University), studying in the office of a local attorney at the same time. This interest was short-lived for one year later, in 1860, he returned to Mobile where he studied in the office of Col. Robert H. Smith and was admitted to practice before the Alabama bar. The outbreak of the Civil War interrupted his work, and soon after its commencement he was fighting as a private in the Conferedate army. He quickly rose from the ranks and by the end of the war held a commission as colonel. During the course of hostilities he was wounded three times, took part in numerous battles, and participated in the campaigns of Dalton and Atlanta.

When peace was restored he resumed practice with Colonel Smith. In 1868 he was chosen presidential elector and two years later was elected for a two-year term to the Alabama legislature. In the meantime, on May 4, 1869, he married Mary Montague Henshaw. In 1874 he again ran for office and was elected for a six-year term as judge for the sixth judicial circuit of Alabama. In 1880 he was reëlected to the same position (although the circuit was somewhat realigned and was then known as the first circuit) but in 1882 resigned to return to his practice. Upon the creation of the federal Southern District of Alabama in 1886, President Cleveland appointed him district judge. His nomination was confirmed by the Senate Jan. 13, 1887, and on Jan. 31 he took the oath of office. He remained in this office until his death.

During his long career on the bench he earned for himself the affection and esteem of the bar, as shown by the genuine expressions of respect vouchsafed him on the occasion of the announcement of his contemplated resignation, a resignation forestalled by death. His decisions were seldom reversed by the upper courts and were at one time complimented by William Howard Taft. Among the first to use the injunction in labor disputes, he applied it in 1893 to prevent striking shop employees from interfering with strike-breakers in the Louisville & Nashville Railroad strike.

It had been an ambition on the part of Toulmin to be a federal judge, and he took pride in his long service. A little over a month prior to his death, on making known his plans to resign, he said: "I am happy that my early ambitions have been realized and I trust that my stewardship will bear the light of day" (*Mobile Register,* Oct. 4, 1916, p. 1). He died in Toulminville, a quarter-mile from his birthplace; his wife survived him.

[See *Who's Who in America*, 1916–17; T. M. Owen, *Hist. of Ala. and Dict. of Ala. Biog.* (1921), vol. IV; *Memorial Record of Ala.* (1893), II, 606; T. W. Palmer, *A Reg. of the Officers and Students of the Univ. of Ala.* (1901); *Mobile Register*, Oct. 4, Nov. 13, 14, 1916; *Montgomery Advertiser*, Nov. 13, 1916. The first three references give year of birth as 1838, the last three, as 1835.]   L. M. S.

TOUMEY, JAMES WILLIAM (Apr. 17, 1865–May 6, 1932), forester, teacher, was born in Lawrence, Mich., the son of Dennis and Mary (Buckley) Toumey. His youth was spent on his father's farm and his early education was in the local schools. He prepared for college at the high school in Decatur, Mich., but taught school for some years before entering the Michigan Agricultural College, from which he graduated in 1889.

He was appointed instructor in botany at the Michigan Agricultural College in 1890. In 1891 he was called to the University of Arizona, where he remained until 1898, having advanced to a professorship in botany. At the same time he also held the position of botanist in the Arizona State Agricultural Experiment Station, and served as acting director of the Station in 1897–98. While in Arizona he made notable investigations in the fields of botany and entomology, with special work on the date palm and on the cacti. He visited England in 1899 to assist in arranging the collection of cacti at Kew.

In 1899 he was appointed superintendent of tree planting in the division of forestry, United States Department of Agriculture. The following year the Yale School of Forestry was established and Toumey became one of the two regular members of the staff. From 1910 to 1922 he served as dean and during this period he materially enlarged the endowments, physical facilities, and forest properties of the institution. Because of his scholarly attitude and his vigorous personality he played a prominent part in formulating a program of forest education and in building the scientific foundations of the practice of forestry in America. In 1922 he retired from the deanship in order to devote his entire efforts to teaching and research. He possessed exceptional ability to inspire research activities in others and directed basic studies in plant physiology and in ecology as affecting the growth and development of trees and forests. He gave a new emphasis to the importance of soil moisture as one of the factors governing the survival of young trees in the forest.

Toumey was widely known among scholars both in the United States and abroad. His books, *Seeding and Planting in the Practice of Forestry* (1916), revised by Toumey and Clarence F. Korstian in 1931, and *Foundations of Silviculture upon an Ecological Basis* (1928), are standard works. He initiated a series of scientific bulletins at the Yale School of Forestry and he wrote extensively for forestry journals and other periodicals. His writings cover a wide range of subjects, including forestry articles of a popular nature, and though they were dominantly of a scientific character, they include discussions on applied silviculture, forest taxation, watershed protection, forest economics, and public forest policy. Toumey was twice married: first, June 17, 1897, to Constantia H. Blake of New Haven, who died in 1904 leaving a son; second, in 1908, to Nannie Trowbridge of New Haven.

[For sources, see *Science*, June 3, 1932; *Yale Forest School News*, July 1932; *Journal of Forestry*, Oct. 1932; *Who's Who in America*, 1932–33; J. M. and Jaques Cattell, *Am. Men of Sci.* (1927); *Alumni Cat. No. Mich. State Coll. Bull.* (1931); J. M. Cattell, *Leaders in Education* (1932); *N. Y. Times*, May 7, 1932; *New Haven Journal Courier*, May 9, 1932. A list of Toumey's writings is filed at the Yale Univ. Lib.]   H. S. G—s.

TOURGÉE, ALBION WINEGAR (May 2, 1838–May 21, 1905), Carpet-bagger, author, the first and only surviving child of Valentine and Louisa Emma (Winegar) Tourgée, was born in Williamsfield, Ohio. His father was of French Huguenot, his mother of German Palatine descent. At the age of nine he removed with his family to Kingsville, Ohio, and later he lived for two years with a maternal uncle in Lee, Mass. Afterward he attended Kingsville Academy until he entered the sophomore class at the University of Rochester in 1859. He withdrew in January 1861 to teach at Wilson, N. Y., and on Apr. 19 enlisted in the 27th New York Regiment; in

1862, however, he was awarded the B.A. degree. At the first battle of Bull Run he received a spinal wound from which he never entirely recovered, and he said that he there lost the sight of his left eye, but there is considerable evidence that this misfortune had resulted from an accident in boyhood (Dibble, *post*, p. 21). He began to read law, but in July 1862 was commissioned a lieutenant in the 105th Ohio Regiment; at the battle of Perryville he was again injured in the spine. In January 1863 he was captured at Murfreesboro, Tenn., and, according to his own account (Chicago *Daily Inter Ocean*, Feb. 15, 1890), was confined for four months in Confederate prisons. Exchanged, he returned to Ohio and on May 14, 1863, married Emma Lodoiska, the daughter of Harmon and Mary Corwin Kilbourne, who, with one daughter, survived him. Returning to his regiment, he was present at Tullahoma, Chickamauga, Lookout Mountain, and Missionary Ridge. Twice during his military service he was placed under arrest for virtual insubordination, and on Dec. 6, 1863, he resigned and returned to the study of law; he was admitted to the bar of Ohio in May 1864. He taught a short time in Erie, Pa., meanwhile writing for a newspaper, and in the fall of 1865 removed to Greensboro, N. C., where he practised law and organized a nursery company which soon failed.

In 1866 he definitely entered politics. At the Southern Loyalist convention at Philadelphia he attracted widespread attention by a speech notable at once for venom and inaccuracy. In January 1867 he founded the *Union Register*, devoted to Radical policies with respect to the "poor, misguided, and mismanaged South." This paper was forced to suspend in June. In the proceedings of the so-called "carpet-bag" convention of 1868 in North Carolina he took an active and prominent part. He sought vainly to secure the repudiation of the ante-bellum debt of the state, and was instrumental in securing the insertion in the new constitution of a provision for the codification of the whole law in imitation of New York and Ohio; in 1868, with V. C. Barringer and W. B. Rodman, he prepared *The Code of Civil Procedure of North Carolina, to Special Proceedings*. In 1868 also he was elected a judge of the superior court; he served for six years.

As a judge Tourgée was a bitter political partisan, seeking at all times the larger financial rewards and opportunities of a place in Congress, and converting the bench into a stump. But with respect to causes that had no political implications, he became one of the best judges of the Carpet-bag régime. He was utterly careless in attendance upon courts and won the enmity of the mass of the white people, who doubted his honesty, but, by his personal courage, he excited admiration. He was one of the larger beneficiaries of the corrupt Littlefield and Swepson "ring" for services never publicly named (Hamilton, *Reconstruction*, pp. 430–31). He was one of the most brilliant of the Carpet-baggers in the South, but the mature judgment of many of his contemporaries in North Carolina was that he was unstable and unreliable. In public matters he was not so much immoral as unmoral, while his private life was above reproach.

He served without distinction in the convention of 1875, and the following year became pension agent at Raleigh. In 1878 (Mar. 18–May 28, in Greensboro *North State*) he published anonymously the "C" Letters, which are important in North Carolina political literature, and are marked by a brilliance not often found in his writings. In the same year he was defeated for Congress and the following year he went to New York. In the winter he was for a few months in Denver, and in 1881 he purchased a house in Mayville, N. Y., which was thenceforth his home.

Tourgée made money in a number of ways during Reconstruction, but lost it in hopeless ventures. Constantly dabbling with journalism, he finally attempted more pretentious literary work. In 1874, *Toinette*, which had been written some years before, was published under the pseudonym "Henry Churton." It was later published as *A Royal Gentleman* (1881) under his own name. Other works followed in rapid succession. Besides *A Digest of Cited Cases in the North Carolina Reports* (1879), these were chiefly novels and collections of contributions, chiefly political, to newspapers and magazines. He was for two years (1882–84) editor and chief contributor of a weekly magazine, *Our Continent*, which failed, taking all his savings; he was a regular contributor to the Chicago *Daily Inter Ocean*; he collaborated in an unsuccessful play, based upon the best-known of his novels; and he delivered several hundred public lectures. In 1895 he established in Buffalo *The Basis: A Journal of Citizenship*, which died a year later. The sale of his books steadily declined, and his income had almost reached the vanishing point when President McKinley appointed him consul at Bordeaux, where he remained in declining health until his death. In 1903 he was appointed consul-general at Halifax but never accepted the post.

In spite of the volume of his published work, Tourgée's reputation as a writer rests largely upon one book, *A Fool's Errand* (1879), and that, perhaps, more because it was the first literary effort to deal with Reconstruction than because of its inherent merit, though it has undoubtedly a certain power. None of his other works can be compared with it in quality or popularity. Five of his other novels, *Figs and Thistles* (1879), *Bricks Without Straw* (1880), *A Royal Gentleman* (1881), *John Eax and Mamelon* (1882), and *Hot Plowshares* (1883), dealt directly or indirectly with Reconstruction. All of his novels are conventionally romantic, show little originality, and lack literary finish. His political articles, reflecting the author, are dogmatic and egotistical.

[*Who's Who in America*, 1903–05; *Jour. of the Constitutional Convention of the State of N. C. . . . 1868* (1868); *North Carolina Standard*, 1866–70; *The Sentinel* (Raleigh, N. C.), 1865–74; R. F. Dibble, *Albion W. Tourgée* (1921), containing complete bibliog. of writings; J. G. de R. Hamilton, ed., *The Correspondence of Jonathan Worth* (2 vols., 1909); J. G. deR. Hamilton, *Reconstruction in N. C.* (1914); A. W. Tourgée, *The Story of a Thousand* (1896); Frank Nash, in S. A. Ashe, ed., *Biog. Hist. of N. C.*, IV, 1906, pp. 440–49; obituary in *N. Y. Times*, May 22, 1905.]

J. G. deR. H.

TOURJÉE, EBEN (June 1, 1834–Apr. 12, 1891), musician, founder of the New England Conservatory of Music, was the son of Ebenezer and Angelina (Ball) Tourjée, of Warwick, R. I. The Tourjée family was of Huguenot descent, long settled in Rhode Island. On his mother's side Tourjée was of the Balls of Block Island. At the age of eight he was employed in a local calico mill. Later, having obtained work at the Harrisville, R. I., cotton factory owned by Gov. Elisha Harris, he attracted the attention of his employer by exceptionally beautiful singing in a church choir, and in his fourteenth year he so effectively played the organ at the wedding of one of the governor's daughters that he was given opportunity for regular instruction in music at Providence and in academic subjects at the East Greenwich Seminary. In 1851, holding a clerkship in a Providence music store, he edited and published the *Key-Note,* which later became the *Massachusetts Music Journal* (Samuel, *post,* p. 1). In 1853 he visited Boston, seeking support for a conservatory of music, but received no encouragement. Thereupon, with almost no capital, he opened at Fall River, Mass., a school which exemplified for the first time in New England the conservatory system of teaching. It quickly enrolled upwards of five hundred pupils, but as it failed to pay its way Tourjée presently removed to Newport, R. I., where he combined private teaching and organ playing. He there married, in October 1855, Abbie I. Tuell. She died in October 1867. His second marriage, in 1871, was to Sarah Lee of Auburndale,

Mass., who with two sons and two daughters survived him. In 1861 he was chosen music director at the East Greenwich Seminary. At the time of the Civil War he gave enthusiastic service as musical organizer of enlistment rallies. Midway during the war he studied music for a short time in Germany. By 1864 the musical department at East Greenwich had outgrown the seminary, and Tourjée reorganized it as the Musical Institute of Providence (later the Providence Conservatory of Music).

In 1867 he transferred his activities to Boston, where in association with Robert Goldbeck he opened the New England Conservatory of Music almost simultaneously with the Boston Conservatory of Music, directed by Julius Eichberg [*qq.v.*]. Tourjée's ability as an organizer became nationally known when he served as first assistant to Patrick Sarsfield Gilmore [*q.v.*] in the management of two great peace jubilees in Boston, 1869 and 1872. His conservatory, meantime, had a rapid growth. Its first class was graduated in 1870. In 1882 Tourjée transferred the school from rented quarters in the Music Hall to the former St. James Hotel, Franklin Square, which he bought, incurring a debt of about $250,000. An indefatigable worker, who inspired the best efforts of other musicians, Tourjée struggled in his last years under intolerable financial burdens. The school was large, its gross income was increased by supplementary activities, such as summer excursions to Europe which he and Mrs. Tourjée successfully conducted, and yet the deficits persisted. When he sought state aid, such as had been granted to the Massachusetts Institute of Technology, he met with rebuffs, even though the Conservatory had been incorporated as a non-profit-making institution. A frail man, never robust, he became an invalid and directed the school from a wheel chair. Shortly before his death, which occurred in Boston, a directory committee was appointed subject to the final authority of a board of trustees, a plan of management that was continued at the New England Conservatory in later directorships. A bust of Tourjée by W. A. J. Claus is at the Conservatory.

[The best biog. account is that of Elizabeth I. Samuel, in *New England Conservatory Rev.,* June 1913, based on notes supplied by Clara Tourjée Nelson and Lizzie Tourjée Estabrook. See also Nicholas Ball, *Edward Ball and Some of His Descendants* (1891); G. M. Stutsman, in *Musical America,* Aug. 1934; H. M. Dunham, in *The Life of a Musician* (1913); F. W. Coburn, in *Lowell Courier-Citizen,* May 21–June 20, 1934; obituaries in *Boston Daily Globe* and *Boston Transcript,* Apr. 13, 1891. In the lib. of the New England Conservatory of Music are many data.] F. W. C.

TOUSARD, ANNE LOUIS de (Mar. 12, 1749–May 8, 1817), soldier, was born in Paris, the son of Gen. Charles Germain de Tousard, Knight of Malta, and his wife, Antoinette de Poitevin de la Croix. Upon graduating from the Artillery School at Strasbourg, he was commissioned in 1769 a second lieutenant in the Royal Artillery Corps. After the outbreak of the American Revolution, upon the recommendation of Benjamin Franklin, Silas Deane, American commissioner to France, promised the young officer the grade of captain if he would serve in the American army. Tousard, accordingly, joined the Du Coudray expedition, which arrived at Portsmouth, N. H., on Jan. 25, 1777, but Congress refused to confirm the rank promised by Deane. Tousard later joined Lafayette as aide, serving in the ill-fated Canadian campaign, and in the battles of Brandywine and Germantown. In an engagement in Rhode Island on Aug. 28, 1778, he captured a field piece from the English, sustaining a severe wound in his right arm, which was amputated at his request in order that he might the more speedily return to duty. Congress brevetted him a lieutenant-colonel for his gallantry and voted him a life pension of thirty dollars a month (Oct. 27, 1778).

Following his return to France on account of his wound, he was made a Chevalier of St. Louis and awarded the cross of that order, July 3, 1779, and on Apr. 5, 1780, was commissioned major in the Provincial Regiment of Toul. In January 1784, he was made a member of the Society of the Cincinnati, and in July of that year was commissioned lieutenant-colonel of the Regiment du Cap and went to Santo Domingo, where he served brilliantly against the negro uprising. Here he married, in January 1788, Maria Francisca Regina (Joubert) St. Martin, widow of a rich planter.

When the civil commissioners who had been sent to Santo Domingo by the National Convention of France clashed with Colonel Cambefort of the Regiment du Cap and ordered his arrest, Tousard, on Oct. 19, 1792, announced that his regiment would not permit the deportation of its colonel. He was thereupon accused of counter-revolutionary principles, of correspondence with revolted slaves, and of resistance to orders, and with Cambefort was arrested and shipped to the "bloody prisons of l'Abbaye" in France, where the two remained until they were released on Feb. 4, 1793, through the intercession of the American minister. Tousard then joined his wife and children in the United States, whither they had gone for safety. His wife died at Wilmington, Del., in July 1794, and the next year he married Anna Maria Geddes. Reinstated in the United States Army in February 1795, he was

commissioned major of the 2nd Artillery, and became its colonel five years later. During the intervening period he planned and superintended the building of fortifications at Fort Mifflin, Pa., at West Point, N. Y., and at Newport, R. I. He was promoted, Dec. 1, 1800, to inspector of artillery, and the following year moved to West Point where he remodeled the garrison as a military school. In 1802 he went back to Santo Domingo and served under the ill-fated General Leclerc, but returned to France the same year and retired to Soissons on a pension of 2000 francs granted him by the Emperor.

In 1805 he was sent back to America as sub-commissary and chancellor of commercial relations at New Orleans, and was later moved to Philadelphia as vice-consul. In 1809 he was transferred to Baltimore to protect Elizabeth Patterson Bonaparte [q.v.], wife of Jerome Bonaparte, and her son, and in 1811 he was ordered to New Orleans as consul *ad interim*. He occupied this position until July 1816, when he was relieved by Petry and returned to France. He died in Paris less than a year later.

While he was in prison in 1793 Tousard wrote a pamphlet in his own defense, *Tousard, Lieutenant-Colonel du Régiment du Cap, à la Convention Nationale* (1793), which was translated into English, and appeared in Philadelphia under the title, *Justification of Lewis Tousard Addressed to the National Convention of France* (1793). His only other literary venture was the *American Artillerist's Companion* begun in 1795 at the instigation of General Washington, in two volumes (1809–13), with an added volume of plates executed with his left hand.

[Personal letters and documents in the Hist. Soc. of Pa. (Phila.), in the Lib. of Cong., and in the possession of Tousard's descendants; A. B. Gardiner, *The Order of the Cincinnati in France* (1905); F. B. Heitman, *Hist. Reg. of Officers of the Continental Army* (1893) and *Hist. Reg. and Dict. U. S. Army* (1903), vol. I; L. G. M. duB. de Contenson, *La Société des Cincinnati de France* (1934); Dunbar Rowland, *Official Letter Books of W. C. C. Claiborne* (1917), vol. VI.]   E. L. T.

TOUSEY, SINCLAIR (July 18, 1815–June 16, 1887), head of the American News Company, was born at New Haven, Conn., the son of Zerah and Nerissa (Crane) Tousey, and a descendant of Richard Tousey who settled in Saybrook in 1679. Having lost his parents in early childhood, he had very limited schooling and at the age of ten years went to work in a cotton factory in central New York. Later he was bound out to a farmer in the same section. Becoming dissatisfied, he walked back to Connecticut, and worked first as a farm hand and then as an apprentice to a carpenter. Afterwards he sought to make a fortune by going to New York City, where he began as a grocery clerk. After working as a carrier boy for the *New York Herald,* he became a news agent in New Haven for the *New York Transcript,* and then circulation promoter in Philadelphia for the New York *Sun.* When the opportunities in this field seemed to him still too limited, he went to the Middle West as an agent for a patent medicine company; in 1836 he appears in Louisville, Ky., city directory in that capacity. He is said to have established in Louisville a short-lived penny daily newspaper, the *Daily Times* (*Appletons' Annual* and *Frank Leslie's Chimney Corner, post*), the first of its kind west of the Alleghanies. From 1840 to 1853 he operated a farm in New York but in 1853 he entered the firm of Ross, Jones, and Tousey, wholesale news agents and booksellers, in New York City. Seven years later, through the retirement first of one and then of the other of his partners, he became the sole proprietor of the business, which had grown in volume until it amounted, it is said, to a million dollars a year. At the outbreak of the Civil War he enlisted in the 14th New York Regiment of Volunteer Engineers and served until 1863. In 1864 he published *Life in the Union Army,* an account in verse of the difficulties and hardships of the soldiers, which, together with a long introduction in prose, was frankly critical of army officers and of the War Department. Early in 1864 his business was combined with that of some other companies engaged in the same field to form the American News Company, of which he became president, a position that he continued to fill until his death twenty-three years later.

Tousey joined the Republican party at its inception and took an active part in the anti-slavery agitation. During the draft riots in New York City he had fences and sidewalks placarded with posters bearing the words, "Don't Unchain the Tiger," by which he hoped to warn the rioters against an aroused public opinion. Besides his activities against slavery, his humanitarian interests included membership in the societies for the prevention of cruelty to animals and children, and the chairmanship of the executive committee of the Prison Association, to which he devoted much time and effort. Letters he wrote to his family and friends during a six-months' tour through Europe in 1867–68 were published as *Papers from over the Water* (1869). His letters to newspapers and his articles in magazines he published privately in 1871 under the title *Indices of Public Opinion, 1860–1870.* He was married first to Mary Ann Goddard, second to Amanda Fay. He died in New York, survived by his second wife and four sons of his first marriage.

[T. C. Rose, *The Tousey Family in America* (1916); intro. to Tousey's *Life in the Union Army* (1864); *Frank Leslie's Chimney Corner,* Feb. 24, 1866; obituaries in *Appletons' Ann. Cyc.,* 1888, *N. Y. Times, N. Y. Tribune,* and *N. Y. Herald,* June 17, 1887; information from Tousey's grandson, Sinclair Tousey, Esq., of Garden City, L. I.]   W G. B.

TOWER, CHARLEMAGNE (Apr. 17, 1848– Feb. 24, 1923), diplomat, was born at Philadelphia, Pa., the son of Charlemagne and Amelia (Bartle) Tower, and the descendant of John Tower who emigrated from Hingham, England, to Hingham, Mass., in 1637. After attending the public schools at Pottsville, Pa., he entered Phillips Exeter Academy, graduated from Harvard College in 1872, and spent four years in travel and study in Europe and the Near East. Two years after his return to America he was admitted to the bar, in 1878, and practised in Philadelphia until his father's extensive interests in the Vermilion Range iron ore fields in Minnesota took him to Duluth in 1882. He became president of that road and a director of the Minnesota Iron Company, both of which had been largely financed by his father. The Towers sold a large part of their interests in 1887, and he returned to Philadelphia, where he was active in business, especially coal mining and finance, until 1891. On Feb. 8, 1888, he married Helen Smith of Oakland, Cal. He published *The Marquis de LaFayette in the American Revolution* (2 vols., 1895), and he served as a vice-president of the department of archaeology and palaeontology of the University of Pennsylvania and as trustee from 1896 to 1899.

When McKinley became president, Tower's wealth, reputation for learning, and Republican politics made him a logical candidate for diplomatic honors. His appointment on Apr. 1, 1897, as minister to Austria-Hungary, the first of three major diplomatic appointments, launched him upon a diplomatic career that was useful and creditable but by no means brilliant. During his short two years of service at Vienna, June 1, 1897, to Feb. 9, 1899, he was largely concerned with obtaining the release from military service of naturalized American citizens of Austro-Hungarian birth. In this he was generally successful. On Jan. 12, 1899, he was appointed ambassador to Russia, where he served from his arrival on Mar. 16, 1899, to November 1902. He negotiated, although he did not sign, an agreement with Russia to submit to arbitration on the claims of American sealing vessels that had been seized in the Bering Sea by Russian cruisers. His representations to Russia on behalf of the "Open

Door" in Manchuria were less successful (*Foreign Relations, post*, 1902).

Relations between Germany and Venezuela were approaching the breaking point when he received his appointment as American ambassador at Berlin on Sept. 26, 1902. As soon as he reached his post in December he was instructed by the secretary of state, John Hay, to protest to the German government against the measures it was taking to force Venezuela to pay the German claims and to preserve the rights of the United States in case of blockade of Venezuelan ports. Although some of the most important of the Venezuelan negotiations, which led finally to the submission of the dispute to the new Hague Tribunal, took place in Washington, a major portion of the discussions were conducted through Tower at Berlin. He also negotiated with the German foreign office regarding the obligation of a naturalized American citizen born in Alsace to perform military service in Germany. Although Germany would not admit that the Bancroft treaties of 1868 applied to natives of Alsace-Lorraine, then a part of France, he persuaded the foreign office to declare its readiness to negotiate a new treaty to include natives of Alsace-Lorraine. Other troublesome issues between the United States and Germany, such as the tariff question, were settled at Washington. He resigned on June 8, 1908, and returned to Philadelphia. He was a grand officer of the Legion of Honor of France; he was honored with the grand Cordon of the Order of St. Alexander Newski of Russia; and he received numerous honorary degrees. In 1914 he published *Essays Political and Historical*. He died in Philadelphia.

[*Papers Relating to Foreign Relations of the United States*, 1897–1908; *Harvard College Class of 1872. Third Report* (1878) and *Tenth Report* (1917); *Who's Who in America*, 1922–23; sketch of father and family in *The Charlemagne Tower Collection of American Colonial Laws* (1890), comp. by C. S. R. Hildeburn; *Tower Genealogy* (1891), comp. under direction of Charlemagne Tower; W. W. Folwell, *Hist. of Minn.* (4 vols., 1921–30); Jeanette Keim, *Forty Years of German-American Pol. Relations* (1919); *N. Y. Times*, Feb. 25, 1923.]
E. W. S.

TOWER, ZEALOUS BATES (Jan. 12, 1819–Mar. 20, 1900), soldier and engineer, was of English ancestry, a lineal descendant of John Tower who came to America from Hingham, England, in 1637 and settled in Hingham, Mass.; his parents were Nichols and Ann (Bates) Tower of Cohasset, Mass., where he was born. After his school days he entered the United States Military Academy, graduated at the head of his class in 1841, and was commissioned second lieutenant in the corps of engineers. Prior to 1846 he was engaged principally on the construction of the fortifications at the entrance of Hampton Roads, Va.

In the Mexican War he was on the engineer staff of General Scott and took part in all the operations of Scott's army from the siege of Vera Cruz to the capture of the city of Mexico. His duties were mainly the dangerous tasks of reconnoitering the positions of the enemy and of leading columns of attack. For gallant and meritorious service he received the brevets of first lieutenant, captain, and major, United States Army. He was wounded in leading the storming column at Chapultepec, Sept. 13, 1847. After the war he was superintending engineer on the coast defenses of Portland and Portsmouth, and of harbor works on the New England coast; from 1855 to 1858 he was in charge of the defenses of San Francisco, where he also constructed the custom house and appraiser's store.

Early in 1861 he was directed to assume command of Fort Barrancas, near Pensacola, Fla., but when he reached Fort Pickens, on a nearby island, the state troops were already in possession of Barrancas. As a volunteer he assisted in organizing the defenses of Fort Pickens and Santa Rosa Island and in repelling the attacks made by the Confederates in October 1861, and aided in making the works proof against the bombardments of Confederate batteries later in the year. For these services he received the brevet of lieutenant-colonel, United States Army, and was commissioned brigadier-general of volunteers. In Pope's Virginia campaign in 1862 he commanded a brigade and took part in the battles of Cedar Mountain and Manassas and in the engagement at Thoroughfare Gap. In the second battle of Manassas, he was so badly wounded that he was incapacitated for further field service. For this campaign he received the brevets of colonel and brigadier-general, United States Army. He recovered sufficiently to return to duty in June 1864, and in July became superintendent of the United States Military Academy. In September of the same year, however, the unsatisfactory condition of the field defenses of Nashville, Tenn., gave the War Department grave concern and Tower was sent to take charge of them; later, at General Sherman's request, he was also made inspector general of fortifications for the Division of the Mississippi. By organizing the quartermaster and railroad employees he was able so to strengthen the fortifications that when Hood appeared in their front with his army he dared not venture an attack. Under the protection of these works General

Thomas was enabled to organize his forces for the attack that destroyed Hood's army. For his services in the war Tower received the brevets of major-general of volunteers and major-general, United States Army.

From 1866 until his retirement, Jan. 10, 1883, as one of the senior officers of the corps of engineers he was an active member of many boards convened to consider projects of river and harbor improvement and of coast defense. After his retirement he lived at Cohasset, Mass., where he died. He never married.

[Charlemagne Tower, *Tower Geneal.* (1891); G. W. Cullum, *Biog. Reg. Officers and Grads., U. S. Mil. Acad.* (3rd ed., 1891); *Thirty-first Ann. Reunion, Asso. of Grads., U. S. Mil. Acad.* (1900); *Memorial of the Mass. Commandery, Mil. Order of Foreign Wars* (1900); *War of the Rebellion: Official Records* (*Army*); *Army and Navy Jour.*, Mar. 24, 1900; *Boston Transcript*, Mar. 21, 1900.]   G. J. F.

TOWLE, GEORGE MAKEPEACE (Aug. 27, 1841–Aug. 9, 1893), journalist, author, lecturer, was born in Washington, D. C., the only son of Nathaniel Carter and Eunice (Makepeace) Towle. His parents moved to Boston in his childhood, and he attended the public schools there, and Lawrence Academy, Groton, and Day's Academy, Wrentham, Mass. He was graduated from Yale in 1861, studied at the Harvard Law School, and received the degree of LL.B. in 1863, qualifying as a member of the Suffolk County, Mass., bar on Nov. 14, 1862 (Davis, *post*, vol. I, p. 344). He practised law in Boston till 1865, when he became associate editor of the *Boston Post,* and in 1866 he published the first of his many books, a popular work called *Glimpses of History.* In 1866 he was appointed United States Consul at Nantes, France, and in August 1868 was transferred as commercial agent to Bradford, England, where he remained till 1870. In Europe he acquired a command of French that he utilized as a translator of Jules Verne and other popular writers in that language, and gained a knowledge of European politics of which he made literary use. One of his many prominent friends was Charles Dickens, to whose periodical, *All The Year Round,* he contributed many articles on American affairs. In 1870 he published a book, *American Society* (2 vols.), in London.

On returning to Boston in 1870, he acted as correspondent for the London *Athenaeum,* and contributed American notes to the London *Graphic* from 1871 to 1876. He also wrote for a wide variety of American publications. He was managing editor of the Boston *Commercial Bulletin* (1870–71) and foreign editor of the *Boston Post* (1871–76), and he was connected at various times with the *Youth's Companion* and with most of the Boston newspapers as contributor or editor. He published more than twenty volumes, among them *A Brief History of Montenegro* (1877), *Pizarro* (1879), *Beaconsfield* (1879), *Marco Polo* (1880), *Ralegh, His Exploits and Voyages* (copyright 1881), *Drake, The Sea-king of Devon* (1883), *Heroes and Martyrs of Invention* (1890), *Literature of the English Language,* vol. I (1892), and other books on topics of general interest or contemporary prominence. He became known for his ability to present his matter effectively in speech as well as in print. For the Lowell Institute of Boston he gave a series of four lectures on "Famous Men of our Day" (1880–81), eight lectures on "Foreign Governments" (1886–87), and six on "The Era of Elizabeth" (1890–1901), all of which with others of a similar nature, he delivered before many other audiences. In Brookline, where he lived, he served as moderator of the town meeting. He was a member of the Massachusetts Senate in 1890 and 1891 as a Republican, and he took a prominent part in it until illness restricted his activities and prevented his seeking reëlection.

He was physically somewhat striking, having a florid complexion and sweeping side-whiskers of the Dundreary variety; in addition, he was emphatic as well as fluent in his speech, and, perhaps because of his residence in Europe, more effusive in manner than most American men. On Sept. 16, 1866, he was married in Paris to Nellie Lane of Boston, who survived him. He died in Brookline after a long illness culminating in paralysis of the brain, and was buried in Mount Auburn Cemetery. He had no children.

[Published accounts of Towle, which are often erroneous, include *Obit. Record Grads. Yale Univ.* (1900); W. T. Davis, *Professional and Industrial Hist. of Suffolk County, Mass.* (1894), vol. I, p. 344; *Boston Morning Jour.,* Jan. 7, 1891; obituaries in *Boston Herald, Boston Transcript,* Aug. 11, 1893, and *Chronicle* (Brookline, Mass.), Aug. 12, 1893.]   S. G.

TOWLER, JOHN (June 20, 1811–Apr. 2, 1889), writer on photography, college professor, was born at Rathmell, Yorkshire, England, son of George Towler of Sheepwash (baptismal register, Giggleswick parish). Supposedly he prepared at the Giggleswick Grammar School for St. John's College, Cambridge (where he may have been the John Towler, "priest," registered as a non-resident ten-year man, 1836–46), but he received no degree at Cambridge. He went to Karlsruhe, Germany, as "private teacher of his vernacular tongue" (preface to J. L. Hilpert, *A Dictionary of the English and German, and the German and English language,* 1846, vol.

II, p. xiv, of which Towler was co-editor), and there he translated Schiller's poetry and German war-songs into English verse. His edition of *Don Carlos* appeared at Karlsruhe in 1843, and his *Meine Jugendzeit* in the same year. After coming to America, in 1850 he joined the faculty of Hobart College, Geneva, N. Y., where he was professor of modern languages, mathematics, and natural philosophy (1852–68), and professor of civil engineering, chemistry, mathematics, and modern languages (1868–82). In 1855 he received the degree of M.D. from Geneva Medical College, and from 1853 to 1872 served as its dean. In addition to natural philosophy, civil engineering, chemistry, and modern languages, he taught medical jurisprudence, anatomy, pharmacy, and toxicology. He was United States consul at Trinidad, 1882–86, and then retired to do literary work at Orange, N. J. He died at St. Cloud, Orange, N. J. By his first wife, whom he probably married in England, Towler had two sons, who were students at the Geneva Medical College in 1855. By his second wife, Caroline Lili Kaiser, he had two daughters. Towler's red-lined military cloak and long white hair made him a striking figure, and his convivial disposition insured his popularity with friends and students.

Except for his *Guide to a Course of Quantitative Chemical Analysis* (1871), from the German of K. F. Rammelsberg, Towler's American writings were chiefly on photography. He edited *Humphrey's Journal of Photography and the Allied Arts and Sciences* (1862–70) and its annual, the *American Photographic Almanac* (1864–67), besides contributing monthly articles (1868–72) to the *Philadelphia Photographer*. His books on photography were *The Silver Sunbeam* (1864), *The Porcelain Picture* (1865), *Dry Plate Photography; or the Tannin Process* (1865), *The Negative and the Print; or the Photographer's Guide* (1866), and *The Magic Photograph* (1866). Of these books, *The Silver Sunbeam* is the longest and the most important. Photography was in its infancy at the time, and the book probably contributed much to the rapidly increasing use of photographic processes. It presented an introductory history of photography, followed by descriptions of all the known processes, with full directions and formulae. Perhaps the most popular photographic manual of its time, it reached its ninth edition in 1879, and was translated into French, German, Italian, and Spanish. Towler made contributions of his own to photography as well. Among other things he devised a "sky diaphragm" for controlling the influx of light into the camera (E. L. Wilson, *Wilson's Quarter Century in Photography,* 1887, p. 192), and he is credited with being the first proponent of sodium biochromate for photographic use (J. M. Eder, *Ausführliches Handbuch der Photographie,* vol. II, pt. 2, vol. IV, pt. 2, 1893, where many of his chemical formulae are also quoted).

[See Cambridge Univ. Calendars; *Gen. Cat. of Officers, Grads., and Students, 1825–1897* (1897), Hobart Coll.; J. H. Monroe, *A Century and a Quarter of History; Geneva . . . to Nineteen Hundred and Twelve* (1912); obituary in *Gazette* (Geneva), Apr. 5, 1889, which contains some errors. Other sources include memoir in MS. in the lib. of Hobart Coll.; manuscript diary of Mrs. Martha Pope of Geneva; letters from the Rev. G. W. Dresser of Giggleswick, the Rev. A. D. Barker of Rathmell, F. P. White, Esq., of St. John's Coll., Cambridge, and Caroline Towler Smith, Towler's daughter.]

W. H. S—h.

TOWN, ITHIEL (Oct. 3, 1784–June 13, 1844), architect, was born at Thompson, Conn., the son of Archelaus Town, a farmer, and Martha (Johnson) Town. He was a descendant of William Towne who was in Salem, Mass., as early as 1640. Ithiel's father died when the boy was eight years old. During his youth he worked at house-carpentering and also taught school. Adventuring to Boston finally, he there acquired a knowledge of architecture in a school conducted by Asher Benjamin [q.v.], an architect and prolific writer of books on the subject. Little is known of Town's activities during these early years, although he is said, while in Boston, to have contrived a plan for the relief of the Old State House. The important work with which his career began was the construction of Center Church on the New Haven Green. In its construction Town showed familiarity with classical examples of architectural design, and ability both as a designer and as an engineer. He constructed the spire as a unit, on the level and within the tower; when finished, it was raised by an ingenious "windlass and tackle" of his own devising to position on the top of the tower in two and one-half hours. He employed unusual architectural refinements, such as proportioning the orders in the tower so that they would appear of the correct classic proportions when viewed from the pavement below, and giving a slight inward inclination to certain panels in the tower to insure "spring." He was next commissioned, 1814, to design and build Trinity Church, also on the New Haven Green. This was executed in seam-faced local trap rock, with delicate parapets and pinnacles of woodwork, in the Gothic taste, bordering the roof and surmounting the square tower.

His reputation now established, he was called upon to design many public buildings: for New

Haven, a state capitol building and a general hospital; for New York City, the custom house on Wall Street; for Hartford, Christ Church. Other designs of his were those of the state capitol buildings in Indianapolis, Ind., and Raleigh, N. C.; he also designed a number of dwelling houses. During 1827–28, he worked in partnership with Martin E. Thompson [q.v.] of New York. In the exhibitions of the National Academy of Design for those years, Town and Thompson exhibited a number of designs made in common, including "Front Elevation of New Boston Theatre" (1827) and "Design for the Church of the Ascension on Canal Street, New York City" (1828). The diary of Alexander J. Davis [q.v.], in the Metropolitan Museum, reveals that the beautiful, old, Greek-revival asylum building, still standing in the grounds of the Cathedral of St. John the Divine, was designed by Town. About 1829 Town and Davis formed a partnership with offices in New York, and their names are associated in many designs. Though he always maintained his home in New Haven, Town's career is even more associated, both professionally and socially, with New York, where he doubtless found more congenial companionship than in the ultra-religious, academic atmosphere of his home town. His selection by Samuel F. B. Morse as one of the two representatives of architecture, in the founding of the National Academy of Design, shows persuasively Town's outstanding position at that time as a designer and as a man of superior culture.

On Jan. 28, 1820, he was granted a patent for a truss bridge, and from that time forward he was the best known bridge-builder in the country. (See *A Description of Ithiel Town's Improvement in the Construction of Wood and Iron Bridges*, New Haven, 1821.) His returns from this kind of work seem to have been greater than from his work as an architect; from 1820 until his death he apparently had ample funds. He thus possessed the means to gather together in his New Haven residence what for many years was the finest collection of choice books relating to architecture and the fine arts assembled in the United States. The fame of this collection is fully supported by the five catalogues issued after his death for its sale in Boston, Washington, and New York. He traveled extensively in Europe with Morse in 1829–30, envisaged transatlantic steamship navigation, and contributed an unsigned article on the subject to the *American Railroad Journal* of Nov. 24, 1832 (reprinted by J. P. Wright in *Atlantic Steam-ships*, 1838). In 1835 he published *The Outlines of a Plan for Establishing in New York an Academy*

and Institution of the Fine Arts (1835). He also wrote on mathematics and the building of schoolhouses, and published *A Detail of Some Particular Services Performed in America . . . 1776–1779* (1835), founded on manuscript material he bought in England. To him has recently been given credit for designing the very charming obverse of the medal struck in 1838 to commemorate the two-hundredth anniversary of the foundation of New Haven. The greatly inferior reverse of the medal was done by Hezekiah Augur [q.v.]. Town died in New Haven and was buried in Grove Street Cemetery, where his grave is marked by a marble headstone as simple as he was modest and unassuming. He never married, but had a daughter who lived with him and bore his name.

[*Vital Records of New Haven, 1649–1850* (1917), pt. II, p. 803; E. E. Towne, *The Descendants of William Towne* (1901); E. H. Knight, *Knight's Am. Mechanical Dict.*, vol. III (1876); L. C. H. Tuthill, *Hist. of Architecture* (1848); William Dunlap, *Hist. of the Rise and Progress of the Arts of Design in the U. S.* (1834), vol. II; G. D. Seymour, *Researches of An Antiquary, New Haven* (n.d.), and *The Residence and Library of Ithiel Town* (1930), and article in *Art and Progress*, Sept. 1912; archives of National Academy of Design, N. Y.; Rexford Newcomb in *Architect*, Feb. 1929; J. F. Kelly, "Early Connecticut Churches" (MS.); E. F. and E. B. Peters, *Peters of New England* (1903).]

G. D. S.

TOWNE, BENJAMIN (d. July 8, 1793), printer, journalist, was born in Lincolnshire, England, and learned the printer's trade before coming to America. While he was a journeyman printer in Philadelphia in 1766, Joseph Galloway [q.v.] considered placing him, with an apprentice, in charge of a newspaper which he was establishing, but William Goddard [q.v.] was finally selected for this position, and Towne served as a journeyman under Goddard on the *Pennsylvania Chronicle, and Universal Advertiser*. In May 1769, financed by Galloway and his partner, Thomas Wharton, Towne became half-owner and a partner in this enterprise. A public quarrel among the partners brought about revelations which did not help the reputations of any of the four men involved and which ended, in 1770, Towne's connections with the *Chronicle*.

Towne opened a printing house of his own in 1774 and published the first issue of the *Pennsylvania Evening Post*, a tri-weekly, on Jan. 24, 1775. This was the first evening newspaper printed in Philadelphia and the only newspaper that continued to be published in that city through the Revolutionary War. Towne changed sides twice during the war in order to continue publication without moving out of Philadelphia. He started as an ardent Whig and Patriot and succeeded in driving his Royalist competitor,

James Humphreys [*q.v.*], out of business, but the first issue published by Towne after the British army occupied the city in September 1777 shows that he had become a Royalist and was ready to abuse the "Rebels." He published a pro-British paper for seven months, and then the British evacuated the city. He was proscribed for high treason by the Supreme Executive Council of Pennsylvania (proclamation of June 15, 1778; *Pennsylvania Archives*, 4 ser., III, 680), but by this time the fortunes of war had made him a Patriot again, and four days before his proscription was announced he resumed publication with an issue that left no doubt of his new sentiments. The treason charge was dropped (*Ibid.*, 6 ser., XIII, 477), and he published his paper undisturbed. His conduct had made him no permanent friends, however, and his clients apparently changed to other newspapers as these were reëstablished in Philadelphia. The *Evening Post* gradually declined in importance and size and finally died, the last issue that has been located being that for Oct. 26, 1784. Towne made a desperate attempt to revive the dying sheet by changing it to a daily in 1783, but this change resulted after a few weeks in decreasing regularity and frequency of publication.

Little is known of the last years of Towne's life. He is thought to have died poor and there is evidence that he himself hawked the last issue of his paper about the streets, calling "All the news for two coppers." It seems probable, however, that he continued as a job printer after the failure of his newspaper. The census records for 1790 list eight individuals with the firm of "Benjamin Towne & Co. (printer)" and this firm disappears from the Philadelphia city directory with the death of Towne. He died at his home in "Sixth Street near Arch Street" and his remains were interred the following evening "attended by a respectable number of citizens; and most of the typographical profession in Philadelphia."

[Consult: Isaiah Thomas, *The Hist. of Printing in America* (2nd ed., 2 vols., 1874); C. S. Brigham, "Bibliog. of Am. Newspapers," in *Proc. Am. Antiq. Soc.*, n.s., XXXII (1923), pp. 152, 155; *Pa. Archives*, esp. 3 ser., XIV and XVI (1897), 4 ser., III (1900), and 6 ser., XIII (1907); *Minutes of the Supreme Exec. Council of Pa.*, XII (1853), 319, 325; Lorenzo Sabine, *Biog. Sketches of the Loyalists of the Am. Rev.* (1864), vol. II; *Editor and Publisher*, Mar. 17, 1934. The Works of the Rev. John Witherspoon (1802), IV, 397, contains the "Recantation of Benjamin Towne" which was never signed by Towne; William Goddard, *The Partnership: or the Hist. of the Rise and Progress of the Pa. Chronicle &c* (1770), is prejudiced, but the most complete account of the quarrel; the explanations of both sides in the dispute appear in advertisements in the *Pa. Journal* *and the Weekly Advertiser*, July, Aug., and Sept. 1770; *The Mail* (Phila.), July 11, 1793, contains an obituary notice. The best file of the *Pa. Eve. Post* is held by the Am. Antiq. Soc. The Phila. Lib. Company and the N. Y. Pub. Lib. have almost complete files of the *Pa. Chronicle*.]   C. M. T.

TOWNE, CHARLES ARNETTE (Nov. 21, 1858–Oct. 22, 1928), lawyer, congressman, was born in Oakland County, Mich., the son of Charles Judson and Laura Anne (Fargo) Towne, and a descendant of William Towne who came from England and settled in Salem, Mass., about 1640. Charles attended local schools until he was ready to enter the University of Michigan in 1875. His progress through college was delayed by ill health and the necessity of earning his living, so that it was not until 1881 that he was graduated. Subsequently, he became a clerk in the department of public instruction at Lansing, read law, and was admitted to the bar on Apr. 16, 1885. After practising in Marquette, he went in 1890 to Duluth, Minn., and five years later became a member of the law firm of Phelps, Towne, & Harris.

Although he had declined a nomination for Congress in 1888 (E. E. Towne, *post*, p. 268), his political career really began in 1894, when he was elected to Congress on the Republican ticket from the Duluth district. An ardent proponent of free silver, he refused the nomination by the regular Republicans in 1896 and ran as an independent, being defeated by a small margin; again, in 1898, he was similarly defeated; in 1900 he refused to be a candidate. During this period he was generally recognized as the leader of the Silver Republicans and was chairman of their national committee from 1897 to 1901. Although a close associate and friend of William J. Bryan [*q.v.*], Towne felt that he could aid the silver cause more effectively by not affiliating himself with the Democratic party. Bryan evidently hoped that Towne would be selected as vice-presidential candidate in 1900 by Democrats, Populists, and Silver Republicans, but, while he was chosen by the two last named, the Democrats turned to a more moderate candidate, Adlai Stevenson [*q.v.*]; whereupon, Towne declined the other two nominations (*Review of Reviews*, August 1900). When Senator Cushman K. Davis [*q.v.*] died, Governor Lind appointed Towne to fill the vacancy until the legislature could elect a successor. That body, however, turned to Moses E. Clapp, and Towne's term lasted only from Dec. 5, 1900, to Jan. 28, 1901.

In 1901 he removed to New York City, where he made his home for the rest of his life. He was a delegate to the Democratic National Convention in 1904, and represented New York in the Fifty-ninth Congress (1895–97). In 1907 he was asked to be personal adviser to the King of Korea, but, as he later declared, "By the time I reached the King of Korea, there was no longer a Korean question. It was a Japanese question, —Japanese and American" (*Michigan Alumnus, post*, p. 94). This brief Korean experience no doubt colored his views thereafter, for he retained a persistent apprehension concerning Japan's future course with respect to the United States. Before leaving Duluth, Towne had become interested in oil properties; this interest continued for the rest of his life and drew him into other financial undertakings. At the same time he continued to practise law, being for a time associated with B. F. Spellman. During the World War he was an active supporter of President Wilson and was a frequent speaker on patriotic occasions. His final excursion into politics was in 1928, when he made an extensive speaking tour in support of Alfred E. Smith, the Democratic candidate for the presidency. Towne died in Tucson, Ariz. He was married twice: first, Apr. 20, 1887, to Maude Irene Wiley of Lansing, who died in 1915; second, Mar. 3, 1917, to Mrs. Alice Reinhart Elkin of New York. He had no children.

[*Who's Who in America*, 1916–17; E. E. Towne, *The Descendants of William Towne* (1901); *Biog. Dir. Am. Cong.* (1928); *The Outlook*, Oct. 13, 20, 1900; *The Forum*, Nov. 1900; *Review of Reviews* (N. Y.), June, Aug. 1900; *The Nation*, Aug. 17, 1916; *N. Y. Times*, Mar. 4, 1917; *News Tribune* (Duluth), Oct. 24, 1928; *Minneapolis Journal*, Oct. 23, 1928; *Mich. Alumnus*, Dec. 1907.]   L. B. S.

TOWNE, HENRY ROBINSON (Aug. 28, 1844–Oct. 15, 1924), engineer, manufacturer, son of John Henry Towne [*q.v.*] and Maria R. (Tevis) Towne, was born in Philadelphia, Pa. He was a direct descendant of William Towne who emigrated from Yarmouth, England, and settled at Salem, Mass., about 1640. Educated in private schools, he was in his first year at the University of Pennsylvania when the Civil War began, and he thereupon entered the drafting room of the Port Richmond Iron Works, one of his father's companies. He worked there for nearly two years. In 1863 he was put in charge of the erection of machinery made for the Federal government in the navy yards of Boston, Portsmouth, and Philadelphia. From 1864 to 1866, he superintended the erection and installation of all the machinery in the monitors *Monadnock* and *Agamenticus*, both designed by John Ericsson [*q.v.*].

In 1866 he went to Europe, where he traveled and studied engineering under the tutelage of Robert Briggs, an American engineer, and took a special course in physics at the Sorbonne, Paris. Towne and Briggs made numerous engineering investigations; the results of one of these, connected with the transmission of power by belts, they published later in the *Journal of the Franklin Institute* (January 1868). Returning to Philadelphia in 1867, Towne entered the mechanical shops of William Sellers & Company, and while working there was introduced by his father in the summer of 1868 to Linus Yale [*q.v.*] of Shelburne Falls, Mass., who had gone to Philadelphia seeking capital and business management for the manufacture of locks of his invention. Soon afterwards Towne's father brought about the formation of the Yale Lock Manufacturing Company, with Yale as president and Towne as manager. The new company immediately selected a site in Stamford, Conn., and began the erection of a modest factory. The enterprise was but three months old, however, when Yale suddenly died, leaving Towne, then only twenty-four, to carry the burden alone. He conducted the business successfully for many years, relinquishing the presidency of the company in 1916 to become chairman of the board of directors, in which capacity he served until his death.

Towne's great success was due to the fact that he perceived the production advantage in Yale's pin-tumbler lock, which Yale himself considered a minor invention. The tumbler mechanism was contained in a small cylinder separate from the bolt-work case and bulkier part of the lock. This fact permitted, as Towne realized, thousands of locks to be made by quantity production methods, all alike except for the tumbler cylinder, so that any cylinder set to any combination might be added to any bolt case to make the complete lock. Furthermore, the small flat key used offered an advantage over the larger, bulkier key of the ordinary bolt lock. From the day of the founding of the original company, reorganized in 1883 as the Yale & Towne Manufacturing Company, the enterprise had a wide influence on the lock and hardware industry of the United States. In 1876 there was added the manufacture of chain blocks, electric hoists, and later, for a time, large cranes and testing machines. Towne was, in fact, the pioneer builder of cranes in the United States, organizing a department for their manufacture in 1878, and developing a large business, which he sold in 1894 to the Brown Hoisting Machine Company of Cleveland, Ohio. He also undertook, in 1882, the building of the Emery testing machines, which he continued until 1887, when he sold this branch of the business to William Sellers & Company of Philadelphia.

Towne possessed the unique combination of engineering ability and technical training with executive capacity and foresight. He was among the first industrialists of the United States to extend the scope of the engineer to include the economics of engineering and the essential union of production and management. He was an influential member of the American Society of Mechanical Engineers and its president in 1889–90; for five years (1908–13) he was the energetic head of the Merchants' Association of New York; he was a director of the Federal Reserve Bank of New York (1914–19); president of the Morris Plan Company (1914–18); and a director in a number of other banking and industrial institutions. He contributed numerous short papers to technical journals, and was the author of *A Treatise on Cranes* (1883), and *Locks and Builders Hardware* (1905). In his last years he was active in endeavoring to provide a technical museum for New York City. The project was not realized during his lifetime, but he bequeathed a large sum of money, from which gift resulted the establishment in 1926 of the New York Museum of Science and Industry. On Mar. 12, 1868, he married Cora E. White, and at the time of his death in New York was survived by a son.

[E. E. Towne, *The Descendants of William Towne* (1901); *Who's Who in America*, 1924–25; *Trans. Am. Soc. Mechanical Engineers*, vol. XLVI (1925); J. W. Roe, *English and Am. Tool Builders* (1926); A. A. Hopkins, *The Lure of the Lock* (1928); J. L. Chamberlain, *Universities and Their Sons: Univ. of Pa.* (1902), vol. II; J. W. Jordan, *Encyc. of Pa. Biog.*, vol. VII (1916); *N. Y. Herald Tribune*, Oct. 16, 1924.]

C. W. M—n.

TOWNE, JOHN HENRY (Feb. 20, 1818–Apr. 6, 1875), engineer and philanthropist, was born in Pittsburgh, Pa., the eldest son of Sarah (Robinson) and John Towne, a successful business man. He was a descendant of William Towne who emigrated to Salem, Mass., from Yarmouth, England, about 1640. He received the greater part of his education at the Chauncey Hall School, Boston, and his engineering training from the firm of Merrick & Agnew, Philadelphia, Pa. In 1836 he became a junior partner in the firm of Merrick (see Samuel Vaughan Merrick). In 1843 he married Maria R. Tevis, the daughter of Joshua Tevis, a prominent Philadelphia merchant. They had three children, one of whom was Henry Robinson Towne [*q.v.*].

After the partnership was dissolved in 1849, he engaged in private engineering projects, building gas works in particular, two of which were constructed at New Bedford and Savan-

nah. In 1861 he became a partner of the I. P. Morris & Co., the firm's name being changed to I. P. Morris, Towne & Co. This company owned the Port Richmond Iron Works, a concern with a national reputation for the construction of all sorts of heavy machinery. He was by this time considered an engineer of unquestioned ability, and he became the firm's chief engineer. During the Civil War, he produced the engines for the *Monitor, Monadnock, Agamenticus, Lehigh,* and *Sangamon,* and for the *Itasca, Sciota, Pushmataha,* and *Antietam.* Other engineering achievements included the engines for the federal mint, two huge Cornish Bull pumping engines for the Buffalo water works, and blowing machinery for the manufacture of anthracite iron for such well known firms as the Thomas Iron Company of Hokendauqua, Pa., and the Lehigh Crane Iron Company of Catasauqua, Pa. Small-sized machinery was also built, but the concern's reputation was based upon its ability to construct the finest kind of large and heavy machinery. He died in Paris during a European trip taken, on the advice of physicians, to recover his health.

His life was centered mostly on his engineering works, and he was interested in few outside activities. In 1856 he was appointed a director and vice-president of the North Pennsylvania Railroad Company, later leased to the Philadelphia and Reading Railroad Company. He resigned these offices in 1858, but, while he was connected with the railroad for only a short time, he had been faced with a few of its worst construction, operating, and financial problems. He also held a directorship in the Philadelphia and Reading Railroad Company between 1862 and 1864. He joined the Franklin Institute in 1835, listing his occupation as a machinist, and became a life member in 1842. In his will he provided for the University of Pennsylvania Hospital, of which he was a director, the Pennsylvania Academy of the Fine Arts, and the Academy of Natural Sciences of Philadelphia. To the University of Pennsylvania, of which he was a trustee, he left his residuary estate as an endowment fund for payment of salaries in the department of science. The trustees, as one means of perpetuating his memory, created the Towne Scientific School of the University of Pennsylvania, in which most of the university's engineering courses are given.

[Minutes of the board of trustees of Univ. of Pa., and of managers of Philadelphia and Reading Railway Co.; records of Franklin Institute; *General Cat. of the Southwark Foundry and Machine Co.* (1896), p. 3; *Univ. of Pa., Its Hist. . . . with Biog. Sketches* (2 vols., 1901–02); E. E. Towne, *The Descendants of Wm. Towne* (1901); George Morgan, *The City of Firsts*

(1926), p. 268; E. T. Freedley, *Philadelphia and Its Manufactures ... in 1867* (1867), pp. 338–42; *Pa. Gazette* (Univ. of Pa.), May 15, 1931; *Press* (Philadelphia), Apr. 8, 9, 1875.]   H. S. P.

TOWNS, GEORGE WASHINGTON BONAPARTE (May 4, 1801–July 15, 1854), congressman from Georgia and governor, was born in Wilkes County, Ga., the son of John and Margaret (George) Hardwick Towns, both natives of Virginia. He attended the county academy and began the study of medicine in Eatonton, Ga., but was forced to give it up, when thrown from his horse and seriously injured. He studied law in Montgomery, Ala., and was admitted to the bar in 1824. Returning to Georgia in 1826, he settled in Talbot County, where he practised law. He served in the lower house of the state legislature, 1829–30, and in the Senate, 1832–34. He was a bitter opponent of protective tariff and of federal aid to internal improvements. While opposed to protection, he also opposed the call of a southern convention and abhorred nullification. He attended the Georgia nullification convention of 1832 and played a leading part in obtaining the resolution asking South Carolina to retrace her steps.

He was elected to Congress in 1834 as a Union Democrat but resigned on Sept. 1, 1836. Re-elected he served from 1837 to 1839, when he dropped "Bonaparte" from his name. A man of marked business ability, genial nature, attractive manners, and public popularity, he attained great success at the bar and made a good deal of money. His second wife also brought him a fortune and greatly enhanced his social position. He was a man of principle, although timid and inclined to postpone difficulties; and he was a good fighter once he entered an encounter. He was again elected to Congress in 1846 but was not re-elected to succeed himself. He championed military and naval preparedness, defense against the Indians, the interests of the United States in Texas, and the removal of the Cherokee, while opposing protective tariff, federal aid for internal improvements, the Second Bank of the United States, the "American system," and the Wilmot Proviso. In 1847 he defeated Gen. Duncan L. Clinch for governor, and renominated by acclamation he defeated Edward Y. Hill in 1849. During his administration he led the fight for the amelioration of the slave code, obtained the adoption of the *ad valorem* system of taxation and the completion of the Western and Atlantic railroad; and he advocated the use of poll taxes, the revenue from the state railroad, and other revenue for common schools with the hope that Georgia might soon boast that she had no illiter-

ate. He was a stanch supporter of the Mexican War and had, by 1849, become an extreme "fire eater." He obtained from the legislature power to call a state convention, if Congress should pass the Wilmot Proviso or any similar legislation. He called the convention that adopted the "Georgia platform," which became the position of the entire South. He also appointed the Georgia delegation to the adjourned Nashville convention, and he wrote the inscription, "The Constitution as it is, the Union as it was," for Georgia's stone in the Washington monument. Retiring from the governorship, he moved from Talbotton to Macon, Ga., and renewed his law practice. He also ran a cotton plantation with a large number of slaves. He died in Macon. He was married twice: first to the sister of John W. Campbell of Alabama, and second to Mary Jones, the daughter of John Winston Jones [*q.v.*], by whom he had seven children.

[S. F. Miller, *The Bench and Bar of Ga.* (1858), vol. II; *Biog. Directory of Am. Cong.* (1928); R. H. Shryock, *Ga. and the Union in 1850* (1926); Herbert Fielder, *A Sketch of the Life and Times and Speeches of Joseph E. Brown* (1883); L. B. Wylie, *Memoirs of Judge Richard H. Clark* (1898); *Augusta Chronicle*, July 18, 1854; *Federal Union* (Milledgeville, Ga.), July 13, 1847.]   F. M. G.

TOWNSEND, EDWARD DAVIS (Aug. 22, 1817–May 10, 1893), soldier, was born at Boston, Mass., the son of David S. Townsend, an army officer of the War of 1812, and Eliza Gerry, the daughter of Elbridge Gerry [*q.v.*]. He was a descendant of Thomas Townsend who settled in Lynn, Mass., about 1637. He was educated at the Boston Latin School, attended Harvard College for one year, and was graduated from the United States Military Academy at West Point in 1837, as a second lieutenant, 2nd Artillery. He served in the Florida war, and later assisted in removing the Cherokee Indians to what is now Oklahoma. In 1846, he transferred to the adjutant general's department, and for the next fifteen years served on the Pacific coast, and at Washington, D. C. During the winter of 1860–61, he was consulted as to the defense of Southern forts. He recommended that, as the forts were in no condition to resist attack, a nominal defense be made, stipulating only for honorable terms and a free passage to the North for the defenders.

When Lincoln became president, Townsend, now a lieutenant-colonel, became adjutant-general to Winfield Scott [*q.v.*], commander-in-chief. Bowed with age, Scott left the direction of affairs largely to Townsend. President Lincoln frequently visited Scott's office, and formed a lifelong friendship with Townsend. Townsend was responsible for many measures taken in 1861 for the defense of Washington and for the organization and discipline of the newly raised troops. Upon Scott's retirement, Nov. 1, 1861, he became senior assistant in the adjutant-general's department. On Mar. 23, 1862, he became adjutant-general, a position equivalent to what would now be chief-of-staff. In daily contact with the president and the secretary of war for the next three eventful war years, he quietly and efficiently carried out their orders. Wherever possible he effaced himself. He had an expert knowledge of files and office work; he was faithful and reliable, and closely supervised his important department. At the end of the war he was brevetted major-general for his services.

After the war, Townsend issued an order to collect all war papers and by this order was responsible for founding that vast collection published later as the *War of the Rebellion: Official Records.* In 1868, during the difficulties between President Johnson and Secretary Stanton, and the impeachment of the former, Townsend handled a serious situation at the War Department with unusual tact. In 1869, he was appointed adjutant-general by President Grant, after having acted in this capacity for seven years. An improved system of military prisons occupied much of his attention during his term. He retired in 1880, and lived in Washington until his death. He possessed strong religious ideas, and some literary ability, publishing two books, the *Catechism of the Bible—the Pentateuch* (1860), and *Judges and Kings* (1862). In 1884 he published *Anecdotes of the Civil War,* a discreet work with little information in it. He was interested in collecting political papers and heirlooms, and was a member of the Society of the Cincinnati. On May 9, 1848, he was married to Ann Overing Wainwright, a sister of Richard Wainwright, 1817–1862 [*q.v.*]. She, with four of their five children, survived him at his death in Washington.

[A biography is now in preparation by Annette Townsend. Important papers are in the possession of Mrs. Townsend Phillips, N. Y. See Annette Townsend, *The Auchmuty Family of Scotland and America* (1932); G. W. Cullum, *Biog. Reg. . . . U. S. Mil. Acad.* (1891); Samuel Breck, biographical article in *Ann. Reunion, Asso. of Grads., U. S. Mil. Acad.* (1893); *Evening Star* (Washington, D. C.), May 11, 1893.]

C. H. L.

TOWNSEND, GEORGE ALFRED (Jan. 30, 1841–Apr. 15, 1914), journalist and author, was born in Georgetown, Del. His father, Stephen Townsend, who combined carpentry with the profession of itinerant Methodist preacher and at an advanced age gave up both for the study of medicine, and his mother, Mary (Mil-

bourne) Townsend, were both descendants of families long resident in Virginia and Maryland. His first fourteen years were spent in various small towns of Maryland, Pennsylvania, and Delaware, where between 1850 and 1854 he studied in the academic departments of Washington College, Chestertown, Md., and Delaware College, Newark. After 1855 the family was permanently settled in Philadelphia. There Townsend finished his studies at the Central High School, from which he was graduated in 1860. He plunged at once into the newspaper world, first with the *Philadelphia Inquirer,* then with the *Press.* In 1861 he began his connection with the *New York Herald,* which he served first as Philadelphia agent and later as war correspondent. Towards the end of 1862 he went to England, where by lectures and articles, notably in the *Cornhill,* he persuasively advocated the cause of the northern states. On returning to America he became war correspondent for the New York *World,* in which appeared his most vivid reportorial work. His accounts of the final battles and of Lincoln's assassination won him an almost nation-wide recognition. In December 1865 he married Bessie E. Rhodes of Philadelphia, and soon thereafter went abroad to report for the *World* the events of the Austro-Prussian War. After settling in Washington in 1867, he began to contribute, as he continued to do for some forty years, to the *Chicago Tribune,* the *Cincinnati Daily Enquirer,* and many other papers (amounting, in the end, to nearly a hundred), a frequent letter of from two to four columns under the signature of "Gath"—a humorously conceived pseudonym, utilizing his initials, and ironically suggesting the Biblical prohibition concerning the downfall of the mighty, "Tell it not in Gath, publish it not in the streets of Askelon." These letters were mainly occupied with politics and the advocacy of Republicanism, but they included also very perspicacious comments upon almost every event of major importance, and are now peculiarly interesting for their often satirical animadversions upon the social life of the time. Their fearlessness, kindly humor, and wise judgments brought to them a large following, and made of their author one of the most important journalists of the reconstruction era. He assisted Donn Piatt [*q.v.*] in organizing the *Capital* in 1871, but, originally a co-editor of that useful weekly, he was forced by the pressure of his other work to resign after a few weeks.

Washington remained the center of his activities, except for the twelve years following 1880 which he spent in New York, though he lived also for long periods at a country house, built on the battlefield of Crampton's Gap, South Mountain, Md., which he called, with the village that grew up around it, Gapland. He traveled widely both in America and abroad, and gave many popular lectures. The latter half of his life was taken up quite as much with the production of books as with newspaper work. He had always been interested in pure literature and had tried his hand, not very successfully, at a play, *The Bohemians,* as early as 1861, but the majority of his books before 1880 were frankly journalistic. They included such revampings of his ephemeral writings as *Campaigns of a Non-Combatant* (1866), *The New World Compared with the Old* (1869), *Lost Abroad* (1870), *The Mormon Trials at Salt Lake City* (1871), and *Washington, Outside and Inside* (1873), and such hasty venturings into biography as *The Life and Battles of Garibaldi* (1867) and *The Real Life of Abraham Lincoln* (1867). In 1880, however, appeared *Tales of the Chesapeake,* a collection of stories notable for their admirable use of local color. This was followed by a novel, the best of his books, *The Entailed Hat* (1884), a tale involving the kidnaping of free negroes in the days before the war in Delaware and the border counties of Maryland, and remarkable for its careful reconstruction of the period and its vivid presentation of local characters. Its sequel, *Katy of Catoctin* (1886), was less painstakingly executed and was deservedly less popular. Among his varied productions, *Mrs. Reynolds and Hamilton* (1890), deserves mention as one of the first romantic picturings of the great Federalist. His poems are less important. Such volumes as *Poems* (1870), *Poetical Addresses of George Alfred Townsend* (1881), and *Poems of Men and Events* (1899), while showing considerable vigor and a wide range of knowledge, are the works of a prose craftsman unhappily essaying verse. He was an invalid for the last ten years of his life, and died of general debility at the home of his daughter in New York. He was survived by his daughter and a son.

[Biog. material may be found in Townsend's contributions to such newspapers as the *Chicago Tribune,* and in many of his books, notably in *The Entailed Hat.* See also *Who's Who in America,* 1914–15, and obituaries in *N. Y. Times, Evening Jour.* (Wilmington), and *Wilmington Morning News,* Apr. 16, 1914. The Pub. Archives Commission of Del. has supplied certain facts, as have also various of Townsend's friends.]

C. D. A.

TOWNSEND, JOHN KIRK (Aug. 10, 1809–Feb. 6, 1851), ornithologist, was born in Philadelphia, the son of Charles and Priscilla (Kirk) Townsend. He came of an intellectual and cultivated family of Quaker ancestry; a brother, Edward, was distinguished for his philanthropic work, especially in connection with prisons; while two sisters, Hannah and Mary, were writers. John was educated at the famous Quaker boarding school at Westtown, Pa., where much attention was given to the natural sciences. This training, together with close association with his cousin William P. Townsend and Ezra Michener [*q.v.*], both of whom became local ornithologists, may have been the origin of his passionate interest in birds. He spent much of his early life at West Chester, Pa., collecting specimens, and in the course of preparing them became a skilful taxidermist. On one of these early field trips he secured the unique specimen later named Townsend's Bunting by John James Aubudon [*q.v.*] and still preserved in the United States National Museum.

At the age of twenty-five, with the naturalist Thomas Nuttall [*q.v.*], Townsend joined the overland expedition to Oregon under Nathaniel J. Wyeth [*q.v.*], traveling with a wagon train from Independence, Mo., which point they left on Apr. 28, 1834, to Fort Vancouver, where they arrived on Sept. 16. The following year he visited the Hawaiian Islands, and shortly after his return to Fort Vancouver assumed the duties of surgeon to the post; these he performed from late September until the middle of the following March, in the absence of a regular post surgeon. In December 1836 he sailed for home by way of Cape Horn, but at Valparaiso was overtaken by a severe illness which delayed his arrival at Philadelphia until Nov. 13, 1837. On the overland journey and at several places in the Pacific he had assembled valuable collections of birds and mammals. His new birds from the Oregon country were described by himself in the *Journal of the Academy of Natural Sciences of Philadelphia* (vol. VII, pt. 2, 1837; vol. VIII, pt. 1, 1839) and later pictured in the last volume (1844) of Audubon's *Birds of America,* while his mammals were described and pictured by Audubon and John Bachman [*q.v.*] in their *Viviparous Quadrupeds of North America* (3 vols., 1845–49). In 1839 Townsend published *Narrative of a Journey across the Rocky Mountains to the Columbia River,* a valuable contribution to the history of early exploration in western North America. It was reprinted in part by R. G. Thwaites in *Early Western Travels* (vol. XXI, 1905). Townsend also conceived the idea of preparing a work on the birds of the United States and actually published one part (*Ornithology of the United States of North America,* 1840), now one of the rarest of American ornithological treasures. Lack of financial support and the appearance of the octavo edition of Audubon's *Birds* discouraged him, however, and he abandoned his undertaking.

In 1842 he was in Washington engaged in securing and mounting birds for the National Institute, a sort of forerunner of the National Museum, with its collections housed in the Patent Office, but this position was only temporary and in 1845 he was back in Philadelphia studying dentistry, although he probably never practised. Hoping to restore his health, which had begun to fail, he planned to sail early in 1851 as naturalist on a naval vessel bound around the Cape of Good Hope, but his condition rapidly became worse and he had to abandon the plan. He died, in Washington, in February 1851.

Townsend was elected a member of the Academy of Natural Sciences of Philadelphia in September 1833 and a life member shortly before he died. He was a fluent writer as well as an excellent ornithologist, but was overshadowed in his special field by the dominating personality of Audubon. As it is, he will always be remembered for the discovery of many of the birds and mammals of the northwestern United States, not a few of which bear his name. He married Charlotte Holmes of Cape May Courthouse, New Jersey, whose sister, Harriet, later married William Baird, brother of the ornithologist Spencer F. Baird [*q.v.*]. The Townsends had one son.

[Witmer Stone, "John Kirk Townsend," *Cassinia,* no. VII (1903); J. W. Jordan, *Colonial Families of Phila.* (1911), vol. II; F. H. Herrick, *Audubon the Naturalist* (2 vols., 1917); W. H. Dall, *Spencer Fullerton Baird* (1915); death notice in *Daily Nat. Intelligencer* (Washington, D. C.), Feb. 7, 1851; letters from relatives.]

W. S.

TOWNSEND, LUTHER TRACY (Sept. 27, 1838–Aug. 2, 1922), author, Methodist minister, educator, was born at Orono, Penobscot County, Me., son of Luther K. and Mary True (Call) Townsend, both natives of New Hampshire. In his early boyhood he attended various public schools in central New Hampshire, but at twelve, because of his father's death, he was forced to go to work. At sixteen he had become a fireman on a locomotive. In 1855, however, after spending a year at the New Hampshire Conference Seminary at Tilton, he entered Dartmouth College and in 1859 received the degree of A.B. Three years later he completed the regular course at the Theological Seminary, Andover, Mass. He then enlisted with the 16th New Hampshire Volunteers, XIX Army Corps, and served as private and adjutant in the Department of the Gulf, taking part in some of the severest battles of the Southwest. At the expiration of the period of enlistment he was offered a colonelcy but declined it. He was ordained deacon in the Meth-

odist Episcopal Church on Apr. 10, 1864, and elder on Apr. 1, 1866. From 1864 to 1868 he served churches in Watertown, Malden, and Boston, Mass., attracting wide attention by his ability as a preacher. Though he read his sermons, he did so with such perfect art that he seemed to be speaking extemporaneously. In 1868 he became professor of Hebrew and New Testament Greek in the Boston Theological Seminary (later Boston University School of Theology), transferring in 1870 to the department of church history, and in 1872 to the department of practical theology. Few teachers of practical theology have made a more marked impression than he upon his students; his class lectures were rich in content, admirably organized, and unusually stimulating. In 1893 he resigned in order to devote himself to literary work. Throughout his life, however, he remained active as a preacher and lecturer, serving leading churches in different parts of the country for limited periods of time. In 1897–98 he was associate editor of the *Baltimore Methodist.* He was married on Sept. 27, 1865, to Laura C. Huckins of Watertown, Mass., who died in 1917. He had three daughters, only one of whom survived him. He died in Brookline, Mass. He was somewhat short of stature, dark-skinned, with rather boldly chiseled features, wavy hair and beard, and large dark eyes, overhung with noticeable eyebrows. His appearance was dignified and impressive.

It was as the author of books on a variety of subjects that he was best known. Among them are *The Chinese Problem* (1876), *The Art of Speech* (2 vols., 1880–81), and *Clerical Politics in the Methodist Episcopal Church* (1892). But for the most part he dealt with theological topics. His first and perhaps most widely read book was *Credo* (1869). Others are *Lost Forever* (1875), *Bible Theology and Modern Thought* (1883), *The Story of Jonah* (1887), *The Collapse of Evolution* (1905), and *New Theologies Only Bubbles* (Boston, 1906). As these titles suggest, he was an ardent champion of the older authoritarian type of theology. He read widely and had rare gifts of popular exposition, but he made no significant contribution to theological thought. It is as an effective popular apologist for the traditional evangelical theology that he is chiefly to be remembered.

[*Who's Who in America,* 1920–21; *Gen. Cat. of the Theological Seminary, Andover, Mass.* (1908); L. T. Townsend, *Hist. of the Sixteenth Regiment, N. H. Volunteers* (1897); *Zion's Herald,* Aug. 9, 1922, and *Christian Advocate* (N. Y.), Sept. 7, 1922; M. C. McEldowney, "Life of Luther Tracy Townsend," MS. in the lib. of Boston Univ. School of Theology, containing letters from former students and friends; death notice in *Boston Transcript,* Aug. 2, 1922.] A.C.K.

TOWNSEND, MARY ASHLEY (Sept. 24, 1832–June 7, 1901), author and poet, was born in Lyons, N. Y., the daughter of Catherine Van Winkle and her second husband, James G. Van Voorhis. She attended the district school, and later the academy, in Lyons. She was a frail child, and, perhaps because other pleasures were denied her, became devoted to reading early in life. She is reported to have written a good deal in her extreme youth, but to have burned this juvenile literature while still a child. On Nov. 8, 1853, she was married to Gideon Townsend of Fishkill, N. Y. After a short stay in Lyons, they moved first to Clinton, Iowa, and then, in 1860, to New Orleans, where Mr. Townsend had extensive interests in real estate, banking, and mercantile activities.

Mrs. Townsend's writings had begun to appear in print before her marriage, her first efforts being published in the Fishkill, N. Y., *Standard* in 1850. While visiting a married sister in New Orleans, she began to write for the New Orleans *Delta,* a newspaper. She signed her first contributions "Xariffa," the name under which she was to attract a wide circle of friendly readers. Under the name "Mary Ashley" she wrote for the New Orleans *Crescent.* When she went to New Orleans to live she wrote for the *Delta* a series of essays called "Quillotypes." Another series, also uncollected, was called "The Crossbones Papers." During the winter of 1881 she contributed letters to the New Orleans *Picayune* describing her travels in Mexico. She wrote one novel, *The Brother Clerks,* published in New York in 1857. The scene is laid in New Orleans; the plot is melodramatic, the characterization feeble, and the emotional effects are not always happy. Although the book had some success, the author made no further efforts in extended fiction, but employed her talents more happily in verse.

Her first volume of verse, *Xariffa's Poems,* was published in Philadelphia in 1870. This was largely made up of her newspaper poems, and included her popular success, "Creed," first printed in the *Picayune,* Nov. 1, 1868. *The Captain's Story,* published in Philadelphia in 1874, attracted a good deal of attention. The theme dealt with a supposedly white man who discovered that his mother was a mulatto, and the subject was handled with skill and restraint. Oliver Wendell Holmes praised this poem highly. *Down the Bayou and other Poems,* published in Boston in 1882, was dedicated to Holmes. *Distaff and Spindle,* a collection of sonnets, appeared in 1895.

Easter Sunrise, illustrated by A. Molinary, was the only one of her poems to be published separately in New Orleans. Her verse, widely popular at the time of publication, is sincere and competent rather than inspired.

Mrs. Townsend entered fully into the social and literary life of New Orleans. She was one of the founders of the Quarante Club, and president for seven years. With Mary E. Moore Davis [*q.v.*] she edited an illustrated magazine called *Arts and Letters,* published in New Orleans during 1887. She was frequently called upon to write occasional poems. She enjoyed excellent health, and was noted as a gracious hostess and a brilliant conversationalist. Her husband and her three daughters came first in her life. French and Spanish literature, music, and art, were her chief cultural interests. She was injured in a railway accident in the spring of 1901, and died shortly afterwards at Galveston, Tex., at the home of one of her two surviving daughters.

[*Who's Who in America,* 1899–1900; information from the family; Ella Rightor, critical essay in *Lib. of Southern Lit.,* vol. XII (1907); *New Orleans Daily Picayune,* and *Times-Democrat,* June 8, 9, 1901.]
R. P. M.

TOWNSEND, MIRA SHARPLESS (Sept. 26, 1798–Nov. 20, 1859), philanthropist, the daughter of Jesse and Joanna (Townsend) Sharpless, both descendants of early Pennsylvania settlers, was born in Philadelphia and educated at the Select School. A talent for writing became evident in her youth. Her poems were published in contemporary newspapers and magazines; letters written in her early twenties to her cousin, Edward Darlington, showed shrewd observation and a sense of humor; while the journal kept in her later years is a valuable commentary on the experiences of a public-spirited woman in the middle of the nineteenth century.

On Jan. 23, 1828, Mira Sharpless married Samuel Townsend, a prosperous and philanthropic merchant of Philadelphia. They had six children, of whom four died in infancy. Though a Friend all her life, she did not wear plain dress. Doubtless the dignity and distinction of her personality were enchanced by the handsome silks and fine laces in which her taste found expression. For some years she devoted herself to her family and her hospitable home where, during Yearly Meeting Week, as many as fifty Friends would be entertained. As time passed, however, she developed a strong sense of duty toward the unfortunate and the friendless. In 1847 she helped promote a public meeting of women to consider the abolition of capital punishment. At a later meeting of this group, she proposed a plan that led to the formation of the Rosine Association, which founded the Rosine Home, a place for the reformation, employment, and instruction "of unfortunate women who had led immoral lives" (*Public Ledger,* Philadelphia, May 10, 1931). This is said to have been the first institution of the kind run entirely by women (*Ibid.*). The project attracted wide attention and soon led to the establishment of similar homes in other cities. As she came to believe that this charity was more than local in its character, she took the extreme step of going to Harrisburg in 1854 with a friend, Mrs. Sophia Lewis, and petitioning the legislature for an appropriation of $3,000 for the aid of the Rosine Association. The charm of manner of the two women and their sincere devotion to their cause impressed the legislators so favorably that the bill was easily passed. Until her death Mira Townsend remained treasurer of the Rosine Home and a member of its board of managers. A result of her experiences was a volume entitled *Reports and Realities from the Sketch Book of a Manager* (privately printed, 1855). She served as vice-president of the American Female Guardian Society of New York and some of her verse appeared in its semi-monthly publication, the *Advocate and Family Guardian.*

Together with her sister, Eliza Parker, she founded the Temporary Home, still (1936) in existence, of which she became secretary and a manager. This was "a transient boarding house for respectable women out of employment . . . and where also destitute children can be taken care of until suitable homes can be procured." She was instrumental in bringing the House of the Good Shepherd to Philadelphia, for she believed that Catholic girls could be better cared for by their own church. Among other movements that enlisted her sympathies were those concerned with inebriety and slavery. A room in her home was set aside for those whose friendlessness seemed to require her hospitality, while girls needing such encouragement were employed in her service. She seems to have been indefatigable in her care for the wretched, whether these were suffering from misfortune, oppression, or moral unfitness. "The prison and alms houses," she wrote, "houses of ill-fame and the Rosine and Temporary Homes are my familiar haunts." She died at Philadelphia and was buried in Fair Hill Cemetery.

[Joseph Sharpless, *Family Record of the Sharples Family* (1816) ; Gilbert Cope, *Geneal. of the Sharpless Family* (1887) ; J. T. Scharf and Thompson Westcott, *Hist. of Phila.* (1884), vol. II; Troth Papers, vol. I, and Cope Collection, Family Data, vols. LXXII and LXXXI, in Geneal. Soc. of Phila.; *Chester County Times,* Nov. 1859; *Public Ledger* (Phila.), May 10, 1931; *Phila. Daily News,* Nov. 22, 1850: family papers.]
A. L. L.

TOWNSEND, ROBERT (Oct. 21, 1819–Aug. 15, 1866), naval officer, son of Isaiah Townsend and Hannah (Townsend) Townsend, was born in Albany, N. Y. He was a descendant of both John and Henry Townsend, brothers who settled in Oyster Bay before September 1661. He entered Union College in 1834, but was appointed a midshipman in the navy, Aug. 4, 1837. The following year he was sent in the *Ohio* to the Mediterranean, where he remained for two years. He attended the naval school at Philadelphia for one year, and was warranted passed midshipman on completion of his course. The opening of the Mexican War found him on the brig *Porpoise,* attached to the squadron of Commodore David Conner [*q.v.*] off the coast of Mexico. In this vessel he participated in the expedition against Tampico (Nov. 14, 1846) and assisted in the capture of a Mexican schooner, the *Ormigo.* He also took part in the siege and occupation of Vera Cruz and San Juan d'Ulúa. After the capitulation of Vera Cruz, he was permitted by his commanding officer to join the army temporarily. He served with it for six months, taking part in the march on Mexico city and its capture. He saw but little active service after the war, and resigned from the navy, Apr. 7, 1851.

Possessed of ample means, he lived in retirement in Albany until 1861, when he offered his services to his government. Appointed acting lieutenant in September, he was assigned to the *Harriet Lane* of the Potomac flotilla. Three months later he was ordered to the *Miami* on blockade duty off North Carolina. The following summer he was reinstated in his regular position in the navy, with the rank of commander. He was now given command of the *Miami,* and rendered most efficient service in patrolling Albemarle and Pamlico Sounds. In July 1863 he was transferred to the *Mississippi* and given command of the steam iron-clad *Essex,* in which he participated in the siege and capture of Port Hudson. As a division commander under Admiral David Dixon Porter [*q.v.*], he also participated in the Red River expedition and in subsequent operations on the Mississippi. Just before the close of the war he was given command of the *Wachusett,* with orders to sail by way of the Cape of Good Hope and join the East India Squadron off the Chinese Coast. On the coast of China he rendered valuable service in protecting the lives of American missionaries and consuls, without injury to the prestige of the native authorities. He died on his ship off Chin-Kiang-Fu of congestion of the brain due to the excessive heat. Three weeks before his death he had been promoted to the rank of captain. Though a man of scholarly tastes, and devoted to his home and family, he did not hesitate to volunteer his services when they were needed. He proved himself a highly capable officer, very popular with his subordinates. He married Harriet Monroe of Syracuse, N. Y., in 1850, and had one son and two daughters. He was the owner of the most valuable private library in Albany.

[Margaret Townsend, *Townsend-Townshend, 1066–1909* (1909); *War of the Rebellion: Official Records (Navy)*, 1 ser., vols. III–IV, VI, VIII–X, XIX, XXI, XXV–XXVII; G. F. Emmons, *The Navy of the U. S.* (1853), p. 82; Joel Munsell, *Colls. on the Hist. of Albany*, vol. III (1870); G. R. Howell and Jonathan Tenney, *Bi-Centennial Hist. of Albany County, N. Y.* (1886); *Cat. of the Sigma Phi* (1927); obituaries in *Albany Evening Jour.*, Oct. 18, 20, and *Army and Navy Jour.*, Oct. 27, 1866; manuscript letter and reports in Navy Dept. Archives; manuscript log of the *Wachusett*, 1865–66; U. S. Navy Dept. Registers, 1837–51, 1861–66.]   L. H. B.

TOWNSEND, VIRGINIA FRANCES (1836–Aug. 11, 1920), author, was born in New Haven, Conn., a descendant of Thomas Townsend who emigrated to Massachusetts from England in the seventeenth century. She was the daughter of James and Hulda (Smith) Townsend of New Haven, Conn. During her childhood she was debarred from active life by frequent illnesses, and as a result found her greatest pleasures in books. Before she was seventeen she began contributing stories and poems to the ladies' magazines of the time, notably the *Ladies' Repository* of Cincinnati. At the age of twenty, in 1856, she became associate editor of the *Lady's Home Magazine* published by Timothy Shay Arthur [q.v.]. She continued this connection until 1872, supplying the paper regularly with serials, poems, articles, and stories for children, all designed, in accordance with the policy of the magazine, to elevate, inform, and entertain. Her popularity with the readers of the periodical is attested by the fact that for ten years after she ceased to be named as associate editor, she continued to contribute historical sketches and travel articles. In 1857 she published her first book, *Living and Loving*, made up of previously printed stories, and embellished with her portrait engraved by John Sartain [q.v.]. During the next three decades she wrote over a score of popular books for girls. Some of these appeared in the Maidenhood Series, others in the Breakwater Series. Characteristic titles are *Amy Deane* (1862), *Janet Strong* (1865), *Only Girls* (1872), *That Queer Girl* (1874), *Lenox Dare* (1881), *A Boston Girl's Ambitions* (1887). Besides these tales she published three works "out

of love and reverence for the past"—*The Battlefields of Our Fathers* (1864); *Life of Washington* (1887), "a woman's way of looking at George Washington"; and *Our Presidents* (1889).

After 1865 she made her home in Massachusetts. In that year she accepted an invitation to act as teacher of rhetoric in the Family School for Young Ladies conducted by Dioclesian Lewis [q.v.] in Lexington, an institution designed to "secure the symmetrical development of body, mind, and heart." There she enjoyed a pleasant association with girls from many parts of the United States and became increasingly interested in writing books for their entertainment. Some years later, when Dr. and Mrs. Lewis established a sanitarium in Arlington Heights, she became a member of their household. She resided with them until 1881, and afterwards with their successors. She lived a quiet and uneventful life during her later years, reading, walking, writing, and occasionally staying for months in Boston to be near old friends. She died in Arlington and was buried in Mt. Auburn Cemetery.

[L. C. Moulton, "Sketch of Virginia Frances Townsend," *Arthur's Home Mag.*, Sept. 1858; *Cat. and Circular of Dr. Dio Lewis's Family School . . . 1865* (1865); C. H. Townshend, *The Townshend Family* (4th ed. 1884); *Who's Who in America*, 1912–13; date of death from Arlington town records.]   B. M. S.

TOY, CRAWFORD HOWELL (Mar. 23, 1836–May 12, 1919), Orientalist and teacher, was born in Norfolk, Va., the eldest of a family of nine children. His father, Thomas Dallam Toy, a man of influence in the community and of reputation as a scholar, was of English descent. His mother, Amelia Ann (Rogers) Toy, was the grand-daughter of a Revolutionary officer. Crawford prepared for college at the Norfolk Academy and graduated from the University of Virginia in 1856. After teaching English for three years at the Albemarle Female Institute in Charlottesville, he studied theology for one year at the Southern Baptist Theological Seminary in Greenville, S. C., with the intention of becoming a missionary in Japan. The Civil War put an end to this plan, and in October 1861 he entered the Confederate service, first as private in artillery and then as chaplain in infantry. Captured at Gettysburg in July 1863 and exchanged in December, he again entered the army, serving until the summer of 1864. After the war he taught Greek for a year in the University of Virginia, and then spent two years in Germany studying theology and the Semitic languages at Berlin. In 1869 he was made professor of Old Testament interpretation in the Southern Baptist Seminary, which in 1877 removed from Greenville, S. C., to Louisville, Ky.; and during the ten years of his service he earned a wide reputation as teacher and scholar. In May 1879 he resigned his chair because of his inability to accept the doctrine of inspiration of the Scriptures which there and then was insisted upon. Removing to New York, he acted as literary editor of the *Independent* until, in 1880, he was called to Harvard as Hancock Professor of Hebrew and other Oriental languages. He became professor emeritus in 1909. In 1888 he married Nancy, daughter of the Rev. R. M. Saunders of Norfolk, Va. They had no children.

At Harvard Toy ranked as one of the foremost members of the faculty and became widely known through his publications. His *Quotations in the New Testament* appeared in 1884, and in 1890 his *Judaism and Christianity*, a sketch of the progress of thought from the Old Testament to the New. These books show Toy's sound scholarship, the clearness and simplicity of his literary style, and the qualities always characteristic of his work: moderation, independence with modesty, and a remarkable freedom from prejudice. His *A Critical and Exegetical Commentary on the Book of Proverbs* (1899) and *Introduction to the History of Religions* (1913) were achievements for which he was especially fitted by his breadth of view and his didactic habit of mind. The latter work was in the field which absorbed his attention in his later years. He founded a club for the study of the history of religions; and when a volume of essays by his pupils, colleagues, and friends was presented to him after his retirement, it was entitled *Studies in the History of Religions* (1912). He originated two other learned societies at Harvard: the Biblical Club, which met in Boston and included in its membership professors in neighboring institutions, and the Semitic Conference, designed mainly for advanced students. Among Toy's more important publications in the Biblical field were two volumes in the Polychrome Bible series, each entitled *The Book of the Prophet Ezekiel*: the one, a critical edition of the Hebrew text, with notes; the other, a new English translation. These appeared in 1899. He also published valuable articles in the *Encyclopaedia Biblica*, the *Encyclopaedia Britannica*, and the *Jewish Enycyclopedia*, of which he was one of the editors. His contributions to learned journals covered a wide range of subjects. A brief popular *History of the Religion of Israel* (1882) went through many editions.

[*Who's Who in America*, 1918–19; D. G. Lyon, in *Harvard Grads.' Mag.*, Dec. 1919, pp. 266–69, with portrait; S. E. Morison, *The Development of Harvard University, 1869–1929* (1930), with portrait; bibliog.

in *Studies in the Hist. of Religions* (1912); obituary in *Boston Transcript*, May 13, 1919.]   C.C.T.

TRACY, BENJAMIN FRANKLIN (Apr. 26, 1830–Aug. 6, 1915), lawyer, soldier, secretary of the navy, was born near Owego, N. Y., of Irish descent. His grandfather, Thomas Tracy, after living in Vermont and Massachusetts, became one of the first settlers in the southern tier of counties of New York. Benjamin was reared on a farm and was educated at Owego Academy, where Thomas C. Platt [*q.v.*] was a fellow student. After studying in the office of N. W. Davis of Owego, Tracy was admitted to the bar in 1851. Two years later he was elected district attorney of Tioga County as a Whig. In 1854 he organized the Republican party in the county. He was reëlected district attorney in 1856. As an assemblyman, in 1862, he urged full support of the national government in the Civil War.

In the summer of 1862 he recruited two regiments and became colonel of the 109th New York Volunteers. In the Wilderness campaign, though ordered to the rear on account of physical exhaustion, he continued to lead his regiment until the condition of his health forced him to relinquish his command. His gallantry earned for him the brevet rank of brigadier-general and years afterward the Congressional Medal of Honor. During the last months of the war he was colonel of the 127th Regiment (colored troops) and commander of the military prison and recruiting camp at Elmira, N. Y.

In 1866 President Johnson appointed him district attorney for the eastern district of New York, where by a series of able prosecutions he broke up illicit distilling. He drafted the safeguarding provisions of the internal revenue act of 1868, under which federal collections were increased fourfold. In 1873 he resumed his private practice in Brooklyn; he defended Henry Ward Beecher [*q.v.*] in the suit brought against him by Theodore Tilton [*q.v.*] and was unusually successful in cases involving the law of public officers. As a judge of the court of appeals, 1881–82, he rendered decisions on the validity of marriages contracted in other states (90 *N. Y. Reports*, 603) and on the liability of elevated railroad companies for damages for the stoppage of light and air (90 *N. Y. Reports*, 122) which still (1936) stand.

In 1889 he received from President Harrison the appointment as secretary of the navy, which has usually been interpreted as a sop to Thomas C. Platt, though Tracy had the indorsement of both the principal factions of the Republican party of New York. He entered at once on a program for the building of a powerful navy, and during his administration the *Iowa, Indiana, Massachusetts, Oregon,* and *Brooklyn* were completed or authorized. He organized the naval militia, created the board of construction to correlate the work of various bureaus, and did much to abolish political corruption in appointments and the purchase of supplies at the navy yards. In the cabinet he was responsible for several official interpretations of international law, including the right of asylum in the Barrundia case (see J. B. Moore, *A Digest of International Law,* 1906, II, 851), neutral rights and duties in the Chilean revolution (*Ibid.,* II, 1107–08), and the right of property in seals which became the basis of one of the questions put up for arbitration by the United States in the Bering Sea controversy (see Tracy, in *North American Review,* May 1893).

After his retirement he was counsel for Venezuela in the boundary arbitration with Great Britain. He was chairman of the commission of 1896 which formulated the charter of Greater New York. At Platt's insistence, he became the regular Republican nominee for mayor in 1897, but was defeated by a large majority. His principal avocation was the breeding of trotting horses on his Tioga County farm. In person he was unusually handsome. He had keen powers of analysis, good judgment, and great executive ability. In 1851 he married Delinda E. Catlin; she and their younger daughter lost their lives in the burning of their Washington home in February 1890; a son and a daughter survived him.

[*Who's Who in America,* 1914–15; *The New International Yearbook, 1915* (1916); W. B. Gay, *Hist. Gazetteer of Tioga County, N. Y.* (n.d.); L. W. Kingman, *Our Country and Its People* (n.d.); H. R. Stiles, *The Civil . . . Hist. and . . . Industrial Record of the County of Kings and the City of Brooklyn* (copr. 1884); G. O. Seilhamer, *Hist. of the Republican Party* (n.d.); *N. Y. Times* and *N. Y. Tribune,* Aug. 7, 1915; J. D. Long, *The New Am. Navy* (1903); D. S. Alexander, *Four Famous New Yorkers* (1923); *The Autobiog. of Thomas Collier Platt* (1910); H. F. Gosnell, *Boss Platt and His N. Y. Machine* (copr. 1924); *Hist. of the Bench and Bar of N. Y.,* vol. II (1897); *Bench and Bar,* Jan. 1915.]   E. C. S.

TRACY, JOSEPH (Nov. 3, 1793–Mar. 24, 1874), Congregational clergyman, editor, author, was born in Hartford, Vt., the son of Joseph and Ruth (Carter) Tracy, and a descendant of Stephen Tracy who came to Plymouth, Mass., in 1623. After graduation at Dartmouth in 1814 and a period of teaching at Albany, N. Y., and Royalton, Vt., he began the study of the law. When nearly ready for admission to the bar, he changed his life-purpose and turned to the study of theology, with Asa Burton [*q.v.*] of Thet-

ford, Vt., as his preceptor. Ordained June 26, 1821, he assumed the double pastorate of Post Mills and West Fairlee, Vt. In 1829 he became editor of the *Vermont Chronicle,* which immediately took rank as one of the ably edited journals of the country. In 1834 he became editor of the *Boston Recorder,* and the following year, of the *New York Observer.* Appointed secretary of the Massachusetts Colonization Society in 1842, he continued in this office for the remainder of his life, becoming, also, in 1858, director of the American Colonization Society. The outstanding work of his career was in connection with the colonization movement, the object of which was a Christian republic of colonized Africans in Africa. He was active in founding the Trustees of Donations for Education in Liberia, and was chosen as secretary at its first meeting, Jan. 15, 1851. To his energetic measures is largely due the founding of Liberia College, the first missionary college in Africa. For many years he wrote the annual reports of the Massachusetts and American colonization societies, and he also prepared the *Memorial of the Semi-Centennial Anniversary of the American Colonization Society* (1867), containing a comprehensive account of the rise and progress of the colonization movement.

His principal published works are *History of American Missions to the Heathen* (1840); *The Great Awakening; a History of the Revival of Religion in the Time of Edwards and Whitefield* (1842); *Colonization and Missions; a Historical Examination of the State of Society in Western Africa* (1844). In addition, he published several missionary maps and occasional sermons and was a frequent contributor to the press.

Tracy had a clear and logical mind, an unusual memory, and a vast store of knowledge. His literary style was crisp and incisive and he had no superior as a controversialist; yet he was modest and unpretending, with a native delicacy of feeling that kept him from giving offense. While conservative in his theological positions, he was always charitable toward those of opposed beliefs. On June 9, 1819, he married Eleanor, daughter of Rev. Azel Washburn of Royalton, Vt., who died Feb. 14, 1836. Of their eight children, seven survived their parents. His second wife, whom he married June 3, 1845, was Sarah C. Prince of Beverly, Mass., who survived him. He died in Beverly.

[E. E. Tracy, *Tracy Geneal.* (1898); *Vital Records of Beverly, Mass., to . . . 1849* (1907); G. T. Chapman, *Sketches of the Alumni of Dartmouth Coll.* (1867); *Congregationalist,* Apr. 2, 1874; *Boston Traveller,* Mar. 25, 1874; E. A. Lawrence, *Address at the Funeral of Dr. Joseph Tracy* (1874); *Fifty-Eighth Ann. Report* of the Am. Colonization Soc. (1875); E. M. W. Love-joy, *Hist. of Royalton, Vt.* (1911), pp. 321, 330, 1015; *Boston Transcript*, Mar. 26, 1874.] F.T.P.

TRACY, NATHANIEL (Aug. 11, 1751–Sept. 20, 1796), merchant, philanthropist, patriot, one of the financiers of the Revolution, was born in Newbury (now Newburyport), Mass., the eldest son of Capt. Patrick Tracy, who had migrated to Massachusetts from Ireland as a youth, and his second wife, Hannah Gookin. He was graduated from Harvard College in 1769 and received the M.A. degree in 1772. He commenced business in Newburyport with his brother-in-law, Jonathan Jackson, and in 1775 fitted out a fleet of privateers which sailed out of Newburyport in August. Between 1775 and 1783 he sent to sea twenty-four cruisers manned by 2800 men and captured 120 sail of vessels with 2225 prisoners of war. During the same period, as the principal owner, he sent out 110 merchant vessels, all but thirteen of which were either captured or lost before the end of the war. The chief service of his cruisers was in capturing ammunition and supplies intended for the British army; his merchant vessels with their cargoes were worth $2,733,300. The 120 vessels that were captured were sold for $4,000,000. In spite of his wealth, which was considerably increased early in the war, he died in virtual bankruptcy due to the fact that as the war continued his fleet was almost entirely captured or destroyed. Of his cruisers only one remained in 1783. He was further reduced by the failure of several enterprises, particularly by a contract to furnish masts for the marine of France, and as one of the principal creditors of the Spanish merchant Gardoqui. He contributed $167,000 in cash, as well as clothing and food to the government. In addition to Jackson, he was associated in business with his brother, John Tracy, another brother-in-law, Joseph Lee, and a cousin, Capt. Nicholas Tracy.

Among his homes was the brick mansion in Newburyport (now the public library) built for him by his father upon his marriage, and in which he entertained Washington and Lafayette, the Vassall house in Cambridge, now known as the Craigie or Longfellow house, once the home of the poet, and the Spencer-Pierce farm in Newbury, to which he retired and where he died. During his affluence he is said to have owned so many houses that he could travel from Newburyport to Philadelphia and sleep under his own roof every night. He served as deputy to the Massachusetts General Court, 1781–82, as a state senator in 1783. He was a charter member of the American Academy of Arts and Sciences. On Feb. 28, 1775, he was married to Mary Lee, the daughter of Col. Jeremiah and Martha (Swett) Lee, of Marblehead. She, with several of their eleven children, survived him. Charles, James, 1777–1867, and Patrick T. Jackson [*qq.v.*] were his nephews.

[T. A. Lee, "The Lee Family of Marblehead," *Essex Institute Hist. Colls.*, Jan. 1916–July 1917, and "The Tracy Family of Newbury," *Ibid.*, Jan. 1921; S. C. Paine, C. H. Pope, *Paine Ancestry* (1912); J. E. Greenleaf, *Geneal. of the Greenleaf Family* (1896); T. A. Lee, biographical sketch in *Harvard Grads. Mag.*, Dec. 1916; J. J. Currier, "*Ould Newbury*" (1896); Marquis de Chastellux, *Travels in North-America* (1787), vol. II; F. L. Bullard, *Hist. Summer Haunts* (1912); *Columbian Centinel* (Boston), Sept. 21, 1796.] R.L.J.

TRACY, URIAH (Feb. 2, 1755–July 19, 1807), representative and senator from Connecticut, was born in that part of Norwich which is now Franklin, Conn., the son of Eliphalet and Lucy, or Sarah (Manning), Tracy. He was the descendant of Thomas Tracy who emigrated from England to Massachusetts and in 1660 was one of the proprietors of Norwich. After graduation from Yale College in 1778, Uriah read law with Tapping Reeve [*q.v.*], was admitted to the bar in 1781, and began to practise in Litchfield, Conn. A man of sober carriage, a devout Christian, and a stout Federalist, he won reputation as one of the state's most eminent and successful lawyers. A clever politician with a keen knowledge of men, an attractive speaker gifted with satire and humor, and an impetuous debater, he was honored by his community with an appointment as state's attorney for Litchfield County, election to the General Assembly, 1788–1793, and promotion in the militia to the rank of major-general. Meanwhile, he made a good marriage to Susan, or Susannah, the daughter of Isaac and Eunice (Gillett) Bull of Hartford, by whom he had a son and four daughters. He became the father-in-law of James Gould, Samuel Howe, and Theron Metcalf [*qq.v.*].

He was elected a representative to Congress, where he served from Mar. 4, 1793, until he was elected to the Senate in October 1796 as the successor of Jonathan Trumbull. An associate and confidant of the outstanding Federalists, Hamilton, Ames, Morris, Rufus King, and Adams, he was a man of influence in the party's counsels and one of its shrewdest politicians. He attracted attention in a speech against the resolution for an amendment of the machinery for the election of the president and vice-president (*Mr. Tracy's Speech in the Senate . . . Dec. 2, 1803,* 1803; reprinted in Williston, *post,* and Moore, *post*). His brochure, *Reflections on Monroe's View of the Conduct of the Executive as Published in the Gazette of the United States under the Signature of Scipio* (1798), once ascribed to

Hamilton, was an able, cynical, partisan criticism that had force as a campaign document. Long an ill man, he died of dropsy in Washington.

[Letters and photostats in Lib. of Cong.; letters in George Gibbs, *Memoirs of the Admr. of Washington and John Adams* (2 vols., 1846) and in *The Life and Correspondence of Rufus King*, vol. IV (1897), ed. by C. R. King; speeches in Frank Moore, *Am. Eloquence*, vol. I (1857), and E. B. Williston, *Eloquence of the U. S.* (1827), vol. II; F. B. Dexter, *Biog. Sketches of the Grads. of Yale College*, vol. IV (1907); *Biog. Directory Am. Cong.* (1928); *Encyc. of Conn. Biog.* (1917), vol. I; P. K. Kilbourne, *Sketches and Chronicles of the Town of Litchfield, Conn.* (1859); G. H. Hollister, *The Hist. of Conn.* (1855), vol. II; E. E. Tracy, *Tracy Geneal.* (1898); *Conn. Jour.* (New Haven), July 29, Aug. 5, 12, 1807; *Conn. Courant* (Hartford), July 29, 1807.]
                                               R. J. P.

TRAETTA, FILIPPO [See TRAJETTA, PHILIP, *c.* 1776–1854].

TRAIN, ENOCH (May 2, 1801–Sept. 8, 1868), merchant, shipowner, was born probably in Weston, Mass., the son of Enoch and Hannah (Ewing) Train, and a descendant of John Traine who came from England in 1635 and settled in Watertown, Mass. After the death of his father in 1805 his mother married Capt. Levi Bishop of Windsor, Vt. (*Town of Weston: Births, Deaths, and Marriages*, 1901).

During the second quarter of the nineteenth century, Train became one of Boston's most active merchants. He seems to have made a specialty of the Baltic trade, but he also had business connections in South America. His particular distinction, however, comes from the fact that in 1844 he established a line of sailing packets between Boston and Liverpool. Ever since the formation of the Black Ball line in 1817, New York had had a virtual monopoly of the packet service. The only successful outside rival was the Cope line from Philadelphia. Near by Train had as a competitor the Cunard line, which had been maintaining regular steamship service between Liverpool and Boston since 1840. Bostonians were openly skeptical about Train's venture. The most of his earlier ships were criticized as slow; frequently, moreover, the lack of adequate eastbound cargoes in Boston led him to sacrifice regularity of sailings—an essential packet feature—and send his ships to Southern ports for cotton cargoes. He made a shrewd move in 1844, however, when he commissioned Donald McKay [*q.v.*] to build the *Joshua Bates* and then persuaded him to move his shipyard from Newburyport to East Boston. About this time young George Francis Train [*q.v.*], a kinsman, became associated with Enoch as a clerk; later he was Liverpool manager, and finally a partner. During the next nine years McKay built for the Train line the *Washington Irving,*

Anglo-Saxon, Ocean Monarch, Anglo-American, Parliament, Daniel Webster, Staffordshire, Chariot of Fame, and *Star of Empire.* Some of these were clipper ships and at least one, the *Staffordshire,* was diverted from the Liverpool run for a voyage to California and Calcutta. McKay's masterpiece, the *Flying Cloud,* was built for the Trains, but was sold by them to Grinnell, Minturn & Company of New York for $90,000, double the contract price. Altogether, the line owned or chartered at least twenty-four different ships.

The immigration which followed the Irish famine of 1846 gave the line a great impetus and Train aggressively encouraged the bringing of immigrants to Boston, widely distributing advertising in Europe. By arrangements with European and American railroads, through rates from foreign cities to the interior of America were offered. The Train line also did a business, amounting it is said to $1,000,000 a year, in sending remittances from the immigrants in America to their old homes. The line derived its popular name from the "white diamond" which appeared on the red house flag; the ships also carried a large black "T" on their foretopsails.

Two of the Train ships, the *Anglo-Saxon* and *Staffordshire,* were lost off Cape Sable; the *Ocean Monarch* was burned near Liverpool with a loss of 400 lives, and with the general slump in American shipping about 1854 many of the ships found their way into British hands. In 1855, Train was one of the leading incorporators of the Boston & Europe Steamship Company, which never materialized, and the panic of 1857 seems further to have increased his business difficulties.

Train is credited with being one of Boston's public-spirited citizens and his name is associated with the development of Fenway Court. He resided on Mount Vernon Street, Beacon Hill. His first wife was Adeline, daughter of Silas and Nancy Tobey Dutton. Their daughter, Adeline Dutton Train Whitney [*q.v.*], was a well known writer of stories and verse. Train's second wife, whom he married in January 1836, was Almira Cheever (*New England Historical and Genealogical Register,* April 1884, p. 188). His portrait shows a narrow, thoughtful, dignified face, with a high forehead. He died at Saugus, Mass., and was buried in Mount Auburn Cemetery, Cambridge.

[Henry Bond, *Geneals. . . . of the First Settlers of Watertown* (1855), I, 607; R. C. McKay, *Some Famous Sailing Ships and Their Builder, Donald McKay* (1928); G. F. Train, *My Life in Many States and in Foreign Lands* (1902); C. C. Cutler, *Greyhounds of the Sea* (1930); S. E. Morison, *The Maritime Hist. of Mass.* (1921); *Some Merchants and Sea Captains of*

Old Boston (State Street Trust Company, 1918); information in regard to dates of birth and death from supt. of Mount Auburn Cemetery.]　R. G. A—n.

TRAIN, GEORGE FRANCIS (Mar. 24, 1829–Jan. 19, 1904), merchant, promoter, author, was born in Boston, the only son of Oliver and Maria (Pickering) Train, and a descendant of John Traine who settled in Watertown, Mass., in 1635. Oliver was a merchant who moved from Boston to New Orleans, and whose last traceable act was to send his son back to Boston by sea and alone, the child's mother and his three sisters having been victims of a yellow fever epidemic. Train was finally delivered to his maternal grandmother in Waltham, and on her farm he lived until he was fourteen, attending the district school and, for three months only, an academy in Framingham. In 1843 he left his home to escape being apprenticed and found employment in a grocery store in Cambridge. A year or more later a relative, Enoch Train [q.v.], called to inquire about him, and the next day George betook himself to his visitor's shipping-office in Boston and demanded employment there. His insistence overrode all objections, and he was soon actively engaged in the management of the business.

Enoch Train had established a packet line to Liverpool and had recently commissioned Donald McKay [q.v.] to build a ship for him. Commissions for other ships followed and young Train acquired some prominence in connection with them. It was he, according to his own account, who ordered for the firm, in 1848, the building by McKay of the famous *Flying Cloud,* which the Trains sold at a huge profit. In 1850 he was sent to England as manager of the Liverpool office. Three years thereafter he went to Melbourne, Australia, where he established a shipping firm, and is said to have earned commissions amounting to $95,000 in the first year. He now began to show an increasing tendency to become associated with the sensational and spectacular. Leaving Australia in 1855, he toured the Orient, the Levant, and Europe, establishing connections in Paris with the entourage of Queen Maria Cristina of Spain, from whose banker he later secured funds to build the Atlantic and Great Western Railroad in Ohio. On his return to America in July 1856, the *New York Herald* printed many columns by him, and during the next eighteen years he wrote extensively, producing such books as *Young America in Wall Street, Young America Abroad, in Europe, Asia, and Australia,* and *An American Merchant in Europe, Asia, and Australia,* all published in 1857, and *Spread-Eagleism,* a collection of his speeches with press accounts of the writer and his books, which appeared in 1859. In addition, he issued innumerable pamphlets, leaflets, and fugitive pieces. In the late fifties and early sixties he was in England seeking capital for American railroads, and endeavoring to promote the construction of street railway lines in Liverpool, London, and Staffordshire; after the outbreak of the Civil War he also made stirring speeches in behalf of the Union.

His return to Boston in 1862 was signalized by his being put in jail—one of numerous such experiences—for disturbing a public meeting. He continued to attract attention by his financial undertakings and other spectacular activities: he espoused the Fenian cause; built an elaborate villa in Newport; announced himself a candidate for the presidency in 1869 and made speeches in his own behalf for the next three years except when otherwise engaged; joined the French Communists in 1870 and was expelled from France; and the same year made a trip around the world in eighty days. He championed the cause of Victoria Woodhull [q.v.] after her arrest for the character of her published charges against Henry Ward Beecher [q.v.], and printed in his paper, *The Train Ligne,* passages from the Bible demonstrating that Victoria's language was well within Biblical limits. This publication resulted in his arrest for obscenity, and he was confined in the Ludlow Street Jail for several months, refusing to avail himself of means of release. Against his protest, his counsel entered the defense of insanity, on which he was discharged. A sheriff's jury then found him sane and not subject to confinement in an asylum. The case is of interest historically, because it marked the beginning of the campaign against obscenity carried on by Anthony Comstock [q.v.].

After the above episode in his career, Train's status was somewhat equivocal, and his business activities were curtailed. He still attracted notice from time to time, however, by trips around the world and sensational lectures. In his last years he seldom spoke to any adult, but lived quietly and frugally at the Mills Hotel in New York, spending much of his time among children. His autobiography, *My Life in Many States and in Foreign Lands* (1902), shows a willingness on his part to claim full credit for the success of any enterprise with which he was at all connected. In spite of his eccentricities and mad escapades—he styled himself the "Champion Crank"—Train was a man of no small ability nor unimportant achievements. That his influence on American shipping and

British street railways was considerable is recognized. In his sensational performances, moreover, there was an element of practical joking that gave them a touch of humor and satire. He was tall and dark, and once humorously designated himself an octoroon. On Oct. 5, 1851, at Louisville, Ky., he married Wilhelmina Wilkinson Davis, who died in 1879; they had four children, two sons and a daughter surviving him. He died in New York City.

[In addition to Train's autobiography, see *Who's Who in America*, 1903-05; D. C. Seitz, *Uncommon Americans* (1925); Heywood Broun and Margaret Leech, *Anthony Comstock* (1927), pp. 108-14; *Bookman*, Mar. 1904; *Outlook*, Jan. 30, 1904; *Harper's Weekly*, Feb. 6, 1904; *Times* (London), Jan. 20, 1904; *Sun* (N. Y.), Jan. 20, 1904; *Evening Post* (N. Y.), Jan. 19, 1904.]
S. G.

TRAJETTA, PHILIP (c. 1776–Jan. 9, 1854), musician, composer, was born in Venice, Italy, the son of Tommaso Michele Francesco Traetta, an eighteenth-century Italian composer who wrote thirty-four operas and was successively *maestro di capella* to the princesses on appointment of Don Filippo, Infante of Spain and Duke of Parma; principal of the Conservatorio dell' Ospedaletto in Venice; and *maestro di corte* by appointment of Catherine II of Russia. Trajetta's mother was a Swedish lady whom his father met in St. Petersburg (*Dwight's Journal of Music, post*, p. 130). After his father's death in 1779 Philip's mother placed him in charge of the Jesuits at the Public Studies of Venice, and the boy's education was directed by this group until he was thirteen. Later he was instructed in music by Fedele Fenaroli and a certain Perillo, who gave him a thorough training in counterpoint and fugue. His inherited talents were looked upon at that time purely as a cultural accomplishment, and the boy expected to follow a military career as a profession. His teachers, however, felt that he should continue his musical studies in Naples with Niccolo Piccinni, the prolific opera composer whose followers and admirers waged the historic controversy with the admirers of Gluck. His friendship with Piccinni, who was suspected of republicanism, led him into political difficulties and cost him the influence he needed to have his works produced. He subsequently joined the patriot army that fought against King Ferdinand IV. When this army was defeated, he was captured, charged with being an enemy and with writing the patriot hymns, and thrown into a dungeon from which he found no escape for eight months. His release was accomplished at last through secret influence, and, provided with a German passport, he sailed for America.

In the winter of 1799 he settled in Boston and immediately became occupied as a musician. There he is believed to have written and published *Vocal Exercises* and a "Washington's Dead March." In 1816–18 he appears in New York city directories as "Philip Tragetta, professor of music." He is said to have composed two cantatas, *The Christian's Joy* and *The Prophecy*, and an opera, *The Venetian Maskers*, in New York. After this he became a theatrical manager in Southern cities, introducing to the public a young singer and actress announced as his daughter, Eliza Trajetta, but according to a contemporary account not related to him (*Ibid.*). It is said that Lorenzo Da Ponte [*q.v.*], opera promoter and former librettist to Mozart, brought Trajetta to New York to become a composer for the Manuel García company which in 1825 gave that city its first hearing of Italian grand opera, but that the plan never materialized because the company had disbanded before Trajetta reached New York. Trajetta is said then to have returned to the South and to have lived in comparative seclusion in the mountains of Virginia, enjoying frequent visits from ex-presidents Madison and Monroe, "who held him in high esteem" (*Ibid.*). He was later persuaded by a friend and former pupil, U. K. Hill (F. L. Ritter, *Music in America*, 1883), who appears in Philadelphia city directories as a professor of music, to settle in Philadelphia, probably about 1828, and to establish in the following year the American Conservatorio. He presumably remained in Philadelphia until his death. Others of his works are said to be the oratorios, *Jerusalem in Affliction* (1828), *Daughter of Zion* (1829), both produced in Philadelphia, and the cantatas, *The Nativity* and *The Day of Rest* (1845). He also wrote *An Introduction to the Art and Science of Music* (1829) and *Rudiments of the Art of Singing* (2 vols., 1841–43).

[Trajetta's name sometimes appears in its Italian form of Filippo Traetta. The most complete account of his career and his work appears in *Dwight's Jour. of Music*, Jan. 28, 1854, which reprints an obituary article from the *Evening Bull.* (Phila.). See also death notice in *Phila. Daily News*, Jan. 11, 1854; *Grove's Dictionary of Music and Musicians, Am. Supp.* (1920); and Theodore Baker, *Biog. Dict. of Musicians* (1900). The date of his birth is given in *Dwight's Jour.*, as Jan. 1776, in Grove and Baker as Jan. 8, 1777. The date of his going to Phila. is given by Grove and Baker as 1822.]
J. T. H.

TRAUBEL, HORACE L. (Dec. 19, 1858–Sept. 8, 1919), author, was born in Camden, N. J., the fifth of the seven children of Maurice Henry and Katherine (Grunder) Traubel. He sometimes referred to himself as a "half-breed": his mother, whose home was in Philadelphia, came of Christian parents; his father was a

German Jew who had emigrated to the United States in early manhood and was by trade a printer, engraver, and lithographer. As a boy Horace was shy, puny, and studious. He left school when he was twelve years old, and for the next thirty-two years was successively a newsboy, errand boy, printer's devil, helper in his father's stationery shop, compositor, lithographer, newspaperman, factory paymaster, and bank clerk. After 1902 he was a free-lance journalist. His family became acquainted with Walt Whitman a short time after the poet came to live in Camden in 1873. As Horace grew to manhood he became Whitman's close friend, visiting him every day during his last years and ministering in innumerable ways and with complete fidelity to the old man's comfort and contentment. Whitman made Traubel one of his literary executors, the other two being Richard Maurice Bucke, a Canadian alienist, and Thomas B. Harned, a Camden lawyer, who had married Traubel's sister Augusta.

Meanwhile, Traubel had founded a monthly paper in Philadelphia, the *Conservator*, the first number of which was issued in March 1890. He continued to edit and publish his paper until June 1919. It yielded him a scanty and uncertain income, which he eked out with miscellaneous journalism. All his life he endured poverty heroically that he might be able to say his say about men, books, and ideas. Profoundly influenced by Whitman, he went beyond Whitman in his social thinking, becoming a Marxian socialist and an ardent supporter of Eugene V. Debs [*q.v.*]. He never took an active part in politics, and his communism was more religious, at bottom, than political or economic. His separate publications were *Chants Communal* (1904), translated into German by Otto Eduard Lessing as *Weckrufe* (1907); *With Walt Whitman in Camden* (3 vols., 1906–14); *Optimos* (1910); *Collects* (1915). He edited, also, various writings by or about Whitman and *The Dollar or the Man?* (1900), a volume of cartoons by Homer Calvin Davenport [*q.v.*]. During the latter years of his life he was praised extravagantly by a coterie of disciples, but outside that group his writings were little read. He was the platitudinizer of the American Socialist movement, performing for it a literary function such as Frank Crane [*q.v.*] was performing for more orthodox Americans. His *With Walt Whitman in Camden*, a diary—beginning Mar. 28, 1888—of his visits to Whitman, is neither dull nor unimportant, but it exasperates at times by its merciless record of Whitman's every remark, however casual or commonplace. About three-fifths of the manuscript remains unpublished, though excerpts from it have been printed in various periodicals.

In person Traubel was short and stocky, with blue eyes, mobile, sensitive features, and a great shock of wavy hair. He radiated kindliness and good cheer; to know him was to love him and to wish that he were as great a poet and prophet as his adorers believed. On May 28, 1891, he married Anne Montgomerie of Philadelphia, who with a daughter survived him. During the last months of his life he made his home with his friend David Karsner in New York. He died at Bon Echo, Ontario, of a heart ailment that had afflicted him for several years, and was buried in Camden.

[*Who's Who in America*, 1916–17; *Die Lese* (Stuttgart), Feb. 1913; Mildred Bain, *Horace Traubel* (1913); W. E. Walling, *Whitman and Traubel* (1916); David Karsner, *Horace Traubel* (1919); O. E. Lessing, "Horace Traubel," Jan., Feb. 1920, and "Ein unbekannter Prophet: Horace Traubel," in *Brücken über den Atlantik* (Leipzig, 1927); H. S. Saunders, "Complete Index to the Conservator," typescript, 1920, Lib. of Cong.; *N. Y. Times* and *Pub. Ledger* (Phila.), Sept. 10, 1919. A card in the Union Cat. at the Lib. of Cong. gives Traubel's middle name as Logo; the initial appears in Whitman's will.]

G. H. G.

TRAUTWINE, JOHN CRESSON (Mar. 30, 1810–Sept. 14, 1883), engineer, was born in Philadelphia, Pa., the son of William and Sarah (Wilkinson) Trautwine. As a youth he showed a marked fondness for the sciences, particularly physics and mineralogy, and a part of his education was acquired under the direction of the meteorologist James P. Espy [*q.v.*]. When eighteen years of age, Trautwine entered the office of William Strickland [*q.v.*], the most prominent civil engineer and architect of his day in Pennsylvania. While receiving his technical training here, he performed services in connection with the construction of the Delaware Breakwater and the erection of various public buildings, including the United States Mint.

The development of railroad systems, which was just then beginning, offered special opportunities for a young engineer, and Trautwine was quick to take advantage of them. In 1831 he secured a position on the Philadelphia section of the Columbia Railroad, and was employed on various less important works until 1835, when he was appointed assistant engineer of the Philadelphia, Wilmington & Baltimore Railroad. In 1836 he became chief engineer of the Hiwassee Railroad, then being projected between points in Tennessee and Georgia, and in 1838 established his residence in Knoxville, Tenn., with his bride, Eliza Ritter, daughter of Jacob Ritter, Jr., of Philadelphia. The financial difficulties of the times having seriously affected the construction of this railroad, in 1843 Trautwine returned to Philadelphia.

The following year he sailed for New Granada (Colombia), South America, where for five years he was engaged with George M. Totten [*q.v.*] in the construction of the Canal del Dique, connecting the Magdalena River with the harbor of Cartagena. At the expiration of that time he went back to Philadelphia, where he was employed for a brief period in surveying work, but late in 1849 left for the Isthmus of Panama to make surveys, in association with Totten, for the Panama Railroad. These he carried on successfully in a tropical region which presented the most difficult problems and innumerable perils to health and life. A copy of the map of the Isthmus which he prepared appeared in the *Journal of the Franklin Institute* (January 1871).

He returned to Philadelphia in 1851, but in April of the year following went back to the Isthmus to seek an inter-oceanic canal route. He spent several months in ascending the Atrato River to its source and in exploring its principal tributaries. Crossing the divide between the Atrato and the San Juan, he descended the latter river to the Pacific, later recrossing the range at several points to locate the lowest section of the divide. He finally decided upon a canal route from the Atrato River at Vigia Cubarador, to Cupica Bay on the Pacific Ocean as "the least inadvisable." In the summary of his report published in the *Journal of the Franklin Institute* (March–May, July–November 1854) he says: "I have crossed it [the Isthmus] both at the site of the Panama Railroad and at three other points more to the South. From all I could see, combined with all I have read on the subject, I cannot entertain the slightest hope that a ship-canal will ever be found practicable across any part of it." In Trautwine's time the causes of malaria and other tropical diseases were unknown, and for this reason it is probable that a canal across the Isthmus could not then have been constructed. His own work, in the face of these and other perils was one of the most difficult and dangerous undertakings upon which an engineer could venture.

In the succeeding years Trautwine was engaged in varied important enterprises. While doing engineering on the Coal Run Railroad in Pennsylvania, he lost an arm, but the loss in no wise lessened his activity. He surveyed the Lackawanna & Lanesboro Railroad (1856); surveyed a route for an inter-oceanic railway in Honduras (1857); planned a system of docks for Montreal (1858), and a harbor for Big Glace

Bay, Nova Scotia (1864); and served as consultant on various engineering problems. After 1864 he appears to have taken life less strenuously, his health having undoubtedly been affected by his previous labors. In 1871 he published the first edition of his justly famous *Engineers' Pocket Book,* a work which was immediately received with unbounded favor by the engineering profession the world over and held its own in competition with other handbooks of similar character for many years. In addition to his reputation as an engineer, he was held in high esteem as a mineralogist, his collection of minerals being one of the best in the country. He died in Philadelphia, survived by two sons.

[*The Jour. of the Franklin Institute,* Nov. 1883; *Phila. Press,* Sept. 15, 1883; "The Panama Railroad," *Harper's New Mo. Mag.,* Jan. 1859.]   F. L. G.

TRAVIS, WALTER JOHN (Jan. 10, 1862– July 31, 1927), champion amateur golfer, was born in Maldon, Victoria, Australia, the son of John Walter and Susan (Eyelet) Travis, and the eldest child in a family of five children. He came of a distinguished family in England and was a direct descendant of Lord Bishop Travis whose tomb is in the Anglican Cathedral at Chester, England. He was educated at a public school and at Trinity College in Melbourne, Australia, and at the age of twenty-three was sent to New York as manager of the New York office of McLean Bros. & Rigg, an Australian importing firm. He was moderately successful in business and, taking a strong liking to the United States, he not long afterwards became a naturalized citizen.

It was in the autumn of 1896 that he first began to play golf, a rather new game in the United States at that time but one that was quickly growing in favor. In 1897 he played in and won his first tournament at Meadowbrook, L. I. He improved rapidly in his skill at the game and within three or four years was the outstanding amateur golf player of the country. He won the national amateur championship of the United States in 1900, 1901, and 1903, and was particularly noted for his skill in putting. His success was considered remarkable in view of the fact that he did not take up the game until he was in his thirty-fifth year, and it is generally recognized that those who are trained to the game from early youth have a great advantage in acquiring correct form and natural swings. To make up for his handicap in such matters, he studied out a plan of play based on the mechanics of the golf swing as they fitted his own physical powers. He wanted to win. He had a keen competitive spirit and a dogged persistence in contests on fairway and green. By unflagging determination and arduous practice he developed a game that, while it was not beautiful to watch, was devastating to his rivals. They hit longer shots from the tee and through the fairway, but the "Old Man," as he came to be called, always hit the ball on a direct line from the tee to the pin, and his putting was deadly. He had no rival in that respect. He became the outstanding amateur player of the United States and capped his career by going to England in 1904 and winning the British amateur championship at the famous Sandwich course, the first time any representative of American golf had performed such a feat. British golfers were startled by the accuracy of his putting and many of them claimed that his success on the greens was due to the "Schenectady" or "mallet-headed" type of putter he used. This led to a formal ruling in Great Britain, that made this type of putter illegal, but the ruling was not accepted in the United States.

Stocky in stature, stern of countenance, and serious in demeanor when on the links, Travis continued in competition for many years, winning many sectional titles though he never again won a national amateur title. He gave up other pursuits and devoted himself entirely to golf, played in tournaments, wrote a book entitled *Practical Golf* (1901), edited and published a golf magazine, *The American Golfer* from 1908, and had a distinguished career as a golf-course architect. He was afflicted with bronchial asthma in later years and died in Denver, Colo., where he had gone for relief. He was married to Anne A. Bent at Middletown, Conn., on Jan. 8, 1890. She, with a daughter and a son, survived him. He was buried at Manchester, Vt.

[Family records and personal acquaintance; A. H. Bent, *The Bent Family in America* (1900); Grantland Rice, "The Marvel of Walter J. Travis," *Am. Golfer*, Sept. 1927; *The Golfer's Year Book* (1930); *N. Y. Times*, Mar. 18, 1917, Aug. 1, 1927.]   J.K.

TRAVIS, WILLIAM BARRET (Aug. 9, 1809–Mar. 6, 1836), commander of the Texas troops at the Alamo, the eldest son of Mark Travis and Jemima (Stallworth) Travis, was born near Red Banks, Edgefield County, S. C. In 1818 the Travis family removed to Alabama and settled in Conecuh County, where the ten children were given such schooling as their father's means and the frontier state afforded. William Barret studied law in the office of Judge James Dellett at Claiborne, and before his twentieth birthday was admitted to the bar and had set up his own law office. While preparing for his profession he had to earn his living by teaching school. On Oct. 26, 1828, he was married to Rosanna Cato, one of his pupils. Two children were born to them, but the marriage was not a happy one, and Travis, in 1831, left his wife and went to Texas. A reconciliation was never effected and they were divorced in November 1835.

In Texas, Travis settled at Anahuac, the legal port for Galveston Bay and the headquarters of a military garrison commanded by Colonel Bradburn, a Kentuckian in the Mexican service. Bradburn was arbitrary and offensive in his relations with civilians, and by opposing him Travis soon found himself a foremost leader of the "war party," a faction of Texans ever ready to assert their rights and to maintain them by force if necessary. In October 1832, he removed to San Felipe, where he set up a law office and was appointed secretary of the ayuntamiento. He became an ardent leader in local politics. When, in 1835, Santa Anna sent troops to regarrison the fort at Anahuac, abandoned since 1832, Travis raised a company of volunteers and captured and disarmed the Mexican soldiers. Though the mass of the settlers repudiated his action, seeking to avoid trouble with Mexico, they were soon driven to resistance and the Texas revolution began.

During the siege of San Antonio by the Texans in the fall of 1835 Travis performed valuable service in commanding a scouting company. In December he was appointed major of artillery, but was shortly afterward transferred to the cavalry with the rank of lieutenant-colonel. Ordered to reinforce the Alamo, which the Texans had taken in December, he reached San Antonio with twenty-five men—all that he was able to enlist—on Feb. 3, 1836. Ten days later the garrison passed under the joint command of Travis and James Bowie [*q.v.*], Travis commanding the regulars and Bowie the volunteers. Discord developed between the commanders and the breach was hardly healed when the Mexican forces under Santa Anna arrived on Feb. 23. On the next day Bowie was stricken with typhoid-pneumonia and from that date until the final massacre on Mar. 6, Travis, at the time only twenty-seven years of age, was in full command. Probably all of the 188 men who fought under his orders died without asking for quarter after a desperate struggle. Travis was apparently a man of charming personality and had unusual powers for making friends with men of all conditions. As a lawyer he was fairly well-trained. As a politician he was practical, astute, and youthfully ambitious. He was six feet tall and weighed about 175 pounds. Contemporaries spoke of him as "the gallant Travis," and the adjective in its best sense describes him.

[The fullest treatments of the life of Travis are two graduate theses (manuscript) in the Library of the University of Texas: Ruby Mixon, "William Barret

Travis, His Life and Letters" (1929), and Amelia Williams, "The Siege and Fall of the Alamo" (1931). See also Army Papers; Comptroller Military Service Records, nos. 652, 5926; Governor and Council Papers —all manuscript collections in the Texas State Library; *Tex. State Hist. Asso. Quart.*, Jan. 1901; Henderson Yoakum, *Hist. of Tex.* (2 vols., 1856); John Henry Brown, *Life and Times of Henry Smith* (1887); E. C. Barker, *The Life of Stephen F. Austin* (1925); Amelia Williams, "A Critical Study of the Siege of the Alamo and of the Personnel of its Defenders," *Southwestern Hist. Quart.*, Apr. 1933–Apr. 1934, especially Oct. 1933.]

A. W—s.

TRAYLOR, MELVIN ALVAH (Oct. 21, 1878–Feb. 14, 1934), banker, was born in Breeding, Ky., the son of James Milton and Kitty Frances (Hervey) Traylor. His grandparents, Methodists and Jeffersonian Democrats, had moved to Kentucky from Virginia. The family was poor and Melvin, the eldest of seven children, began ploughing and harvesting corn and tobacco at the age of eight. He attended the country schools until he was fifteen, receiving the equivalent of a sixth-grade education. At sixteen he entered the high school at Columbia, Adair County, where he stayed four months, and then taught school at Leatherwood Creek for two years. In 1896 he campaigned for Bryan. Two years later he went to Hillsboro, Tex., fifty-five miles from Fort Worth, where he studied law, passing the bar examination in 1901. For the next four years he practised law and was also city clerk (1901) and assistant county attorney (1904–05) of Hill County. He started his banking career by acting as cashier of a bank at Malone, Tex., from 1905 to 1907. He then became cashier and later vice-president of the Citizens' National Bank in Ballinger, Tex., and when this was consolidated with the First National Bank he was elected president of the new institution. Most of the depositors were farmers and cattlemen and Traylor mastered the farm and cattle-loan business. In 1911 the Stock Yards National Bank of East St. Louis, Ill., made him vice-president and three years later he was given a similar appointment at the Live Stock Exchange National Bank at the Chicago Stock Yards. He was soon made president of the bank and also of the Chicago Cattle Loan Company (1914–19). During the World War he organized the local campaign for the Treasury certificate of indebtedness, and by that time was recognized as one of the outstanding bankers of Chicago.

Traylor was made president of the First Trust and Savings Bank in 1919 and at the same time vice-president and director of the First National Bank. Six years later he was president of the latter institution. These two banks and the Union Trust Company were consolidated in 1928 under the name of the First-Union Trust and Savings Bank, Traylor continuing as president of the combined institution. In 1931 the Foreman-State National Bank (itself a consolidation) with its affiliated group was absorbed, and the First National became the largest bank in Chicago. Traylor was a man of broad interests, an excellent golf player (president of the United States Golf Association, 1928) and greatly interested in higher education. He was president of the Illinois Bankers Association (1923–24), vice-president (1924–26) and president (1926–27) of the American Bankers' Association, president of the Shedd Aquarium Society, and trustee of Northwestern University, of Berea College, and of the Newberry Library. He was also director in various important corporations.

In 1929 Traylor represented the United States, together with Jackson Reynolds, in organizing the Bank for International Settlements at Basel. His point of view as a financier appears most clearly, perhaps, in a speech which he delivered before the International Chamber of Commerce in Washington, on May 5, 1931, and from which he gained great publicity ("The Human Element in Crises," *Pamphlets on the Economic Crisis of 1929*, vol. IV, 1931, no. 15). He said that financial leaders must take large responsibility for the crash, and proposed as remedies the abolition of the daily settlement and the daily call-money rate, the abolition of floor trading, and the limitation of trading to cash when the amount involved was less than $10,000. "This country," he said, "cannot afford again the wreck and ruin of people of small means which followed the last crash." He was mentioned as a Democratic candidate for the presidency of the United States in 1932. At the time of his death in Chicago, on Feb. 14, 1934, he was chairman of the committee on drought relief for Illinois and of the national committee to plan aid for the drought-ridden farms in the whole country. His wife, Dorothy Arnold (Yerby) whom he had married on June 8, 1906, and two children survived him.

[*Melvin A. Traylor, Homespun American* (privately printed, 1932), a pre-convention biography; "Dr. Traylor's Prescription," *Literary Digest*, May 23, 1931; Frazier Hunt, "The Mountaineer Boy who went Places," *Popular Mechanics Mag.*, Apr. 1933; *Business Week*, June 24, 1931; *Colliers*, Feb. 13, 1932; L. W. Burnham, "Melvin Traylor," *Rev. of Reviews*, Mar. 1932; *Who's Who in America*, 1932–33; *Who's Who in Finance Banking and Insurance*, 1931–32; *N. Y. Times, Chicago Daily Tribune, Chicago Daily News*, Feb. 15, 1934.]

E. L. B.

TREADWELL, DANIEL (Oct. 10, 1791–Feb. 27, 1872), inventor, Rumford Professor at Harvard, was descended from Thomas Treadwell who settled at Ipswich, Mass., in 1638. Born on his father's farm at Ipswich, the son of Capt.

Jabez and Elizabeth (Dodge) Treadwell, Daniel was left motherless at two and orphaned at eleven. Living with a guardian, he attended school until he was fourteen, and was then apprenticed to his eldest brother, who had just set up as a silversmith. After the failure of this brother two years later, Treadwell completed his apprenticeship in Boston with Capt. Jesse Churchill and continued as Churchill's partner for four years. A youth of studious tastes, as soon as he moved to Boston, where a library was available, he commenced a course of reading in history and the English poets.

Although Treadwell became an able silversmith, he cared less for his trade than for experimenting with machinery. Accordingly, when the War of 1812 ruined his business, he zealously went to work with a friend to devise a screw-making machine. Completed in about a year, although in imperfect form, it was put into successful operation in a mill at Saugus, Mass., but with the return of imported screws to the market at the close of the war, this business declined. Treadwell next devised a successful nail-making machine, but was compelled by ill health to seek a less strenuous occupation, and studied medicine for a year and a half with Dr. John Ware [q.v.].

Returning to his mechanical experiments, he centered his attention on the printing press, and by an ingenious application of levers and the "toggle joint" he produced a press in which a treadle operated by the weight of the printer took the place of the laborious hand-lever. He also invented a means of printing on both sides of paper without shifting the sheet. He was unsuccessful in his effort to introduce his press into England in 1819–20, but on his return to Boston, with the financial aid of friends, began to manufacture his presses. Later he applied steam power to the operation of his press, patenting a power printing press on Mar. 2, 1826. "Treadwell's Power Press" was soon installed in all the larger cities of the Atlantic Coast. It was at first used wholly in book printing, but in 1829 was introduced into newspaper work by the Boston Daily Advertiser. In this year Treadwell relinquished the business, having made a profit of some $70,000.

Meanwhile, he had made a study of rope making and in 1828 completed a machine for spinning hemp. For the greater part of the next eight years he devoted his time to developing machines for this purpose, securing four basic patents between 1831 and 1835. In 1833, after it had successfully demonstrated his method of manufacturing rope, the company which he organized

was merged in a larger corporation. The "Gypsey," as his machine was called, attained world-wide use, and seventy-six of the machines were still in operation fifty years after they were built.

Treadwell's brief period of medical study with Dr. Ware had brought him into a group of Boston's scientific men; in 1823 he was elected a fellow of the American Academy of Arts and Sciences, and from that year until 1826, with his preceptor and Dr. John W. Webster [q.v.], he edited the Boston Journal of Philosophy and the Arts. Chosen vice-president of the Boston Mechanics' Institute in 1827, he began to give a course of lectures on the steam engine and other practical subjects, adapted to the needs of the working man. He became president of the Institute and was awarded the honorary degree of A.M. by Harvard College in 1829, and in May of that year presented a report "On the Practicability of Conducting Transportation on a Single Set of Tracks" to the Massachusetts Railroad Association, describing a system of turnouts he had devised; this system was later adopted by three New England railroads.

In 1834 he accepted the call of Harvard College to the post of Rumford Professor and Lecturer on the Application of Science to the Useful Arts, and in 1835 went to England to observe processes and gather equipment for his lectures, of which he gave about two a week for the next ten years. He served on two commissions (1825; 1837) appointed to investigate the practicability of a water supply for Boston, and on one (1835–36) to examine the state standards of weights and measures; in 1837 he supervised the construction of Gore Hall, to house the Harvard library, and devised a method of heating that building. The Cambridge Scientific Club was organized at his house in 1842. From 1833 to 1839 he was recording secretary of the American Academy of Arts and Sciences, and from 1852 to 1863 a vice-president.

In the later thirties Treadwell turned his attention to an improved cannon. In 1841 he filed in the United States Patent Office a caveat which described a method of cannon construction consisting of building up a series of steel rings welded together and reinforced by bands, and in 1842 organized the Steel Cannon Company to manufacture four small pieces ordered by the United States. He was unsuccessful, however, in seriously interesting any government in his product, and this disappointment, together with his conviction, evidenced in a lawsuit against Robert P. Parrott [q.v.] about 1863, that the latter had appropriated his idea, so preyed on his mind that he never regained interest in his earlier activities and for the last ten years of his life lived more or less in retirement in his home in Cambridge, Mass. In his will he made generous gifts to the American Academy of Arts and Sciences and other educational institutions of Boston and provided liberally for the public library of Ipswich. He was survived by his wife, Adeline (Lincoln), daughter of Dr. Levi Lincoln of Hingham, whom he married on Oct. 6, 1831; they had no children.

[T. F. Waters, *Augustine Heard and His Friends* (1916); W. A. Robbins, *Thos. Treadwell of Ipswich, Mass. and Some of His Descendants* (1906); Patent Office records; *Boston Daily Advertiser*, Feb. 28, 1872; *Boston Morning Journal*, Feb. 29, 1872.]

C. W. M—n.

TREAT, ROBERT (1622?–July 12, 1710), colonial governor, was born at Pitminster, Somerset, England, the second son of Richard and Alice (Gaylard) Treat, or Trott. His exact date of birth is unknown; if his epitaph is correct, he was at least two years old at the time of his baptism on Feb. 25, 1624/25. The family emigrated to America and by 1639 was settled at Wethersfield, Conn., where Richard Treat rose to a position of prominence. Although only a youth, Robert took part in the settlement of Milford in 1639–40. Because many early records of the town and of the New Haven Colony are lost, the first steps in his public career cannot be traced. By 1653 he was being regularly elected deputy from Milford to the General Court of the colony and in the following year was chosen lieutenant and chief military officer of the town. From deputy he advanced to magistrate in 1659 and was annually reëlected until 1664, when he declined to serve. In the vain struggle to prevent the absorption of the New Haven Colony by Connecticut under its charter of 1662 Treat took a fairly active part, and, although he represented Milford in the General Assembly of Connecticut in 1665, he remained for some time unreconciled to the union and determined to emigrate. He became the leader of the group from the former New Haven Colony that settled Newark, N. J., and from 1667 until 1672 was deputy from that town to the Assembly of East Jersey. He also served as magistrate and recorder of Newark. But eventually he returned to Milford and was chosen an assistant of Connecticut in 1673. In the meantime his military capacities were gaining recognition. In 1661 he had become captain of the Milford train band and on his return from Newark was promoted to major. In the summer of 1675 he was appointed commander in chief of the Connecticut troops operating against King Philip. Although too far away at the time to prevent attacks upon Northfield and Springfield,

Mass., he took an active part in the defeat of the Indians at Hadley. In the following winter campaign in Rhode Island he again commanded the Connecticut contingent and distinguished himself in the successful attack upon the Indian stronghold. He lacked conventional military training, yet he proved an adept leader in Indian warfare. The colony rewarded his services in May 1676 by electing him deputy-governor, and after the death of William Leete in April 1683 he advanced to the governorship.

His first problem was the settlement of a boundary dispute with New York, which resulted in the loss by Connecticut of the town of Rye. Soon a more serious threat to the colony appeared with the creation of the Dominion of New England. Connecticut refused to admit the validity of the writs of *quo warranto* issued against its charter in 1685 and 1686, and, when Sir Edmund Andros reached New England, Treat followed as long as possible a policy of postponement and delay. But resistance was futile, and at a meeting in Hartford, Oct. 31, 1687, Andros assumed authority over Connecticut. For the second time Treat found a government of which he was an important member absorbed by a more powerful neighbor. Although appointed to the council of the Dominion, he took little part in its administration. Upon the overthrow of Andros at Boston in 1689 Connecticut restored its government under the charter, which, owing largely to Treat's wise management, had never been legally invalidated. He continued as governor until 1698, carrying on the conservative traditions of the colony. In 1692, when Gov. Benjamin Fletcher of New York claimed superior authority over the Connecticut militia, Treat and the Assembly sent Fitz John Winthrop to England to gain recognition of their military independence. The successful accomplishment of this mission brought Winthrop great popularity, and in 1698 he was elected governor. The aging Treat stepped down to the deputy-governorship, where he continued to serve until 1708, two years before his death.

In 1647 or before, he married Jane Tapp, the daughter of Edmund Tapp, one of the leaders in the settlement of Milford. She died in 1703, survived by seven of their eight children. Two years later, on Oct. 24, 1705, he married Elizabeth (Powell) Hollingsworth Bryan, the daughter of Michael Powell of Boston and widow of Richard Bryan, a Milford merchant. Her death occurred in the spring of 1706. According to the standards of seventeenth-century Connecticut, Treat was a wealthy man. He became a large landholder and was an owner or part owner of saw and fulling mills in Milford. Pious and orthodox, he was highly respected in the community, yet gained a reputation for good nature and humor in personal contacts as well as for firmness and wisdom in public affairs.

[Milford Land Records, I, Town Clerk's Office, Milford, Conn.; *Records of the Colony or Jurisdiction of New Haven from May 1653 to the Union* (1858); *The Public Records of the Colony of Conn.*, vols. I–V (1850–70); Records of the Town of Newark, New Jersey, in *N. J. Hist. Soc. Colls.*, vol. VI (1864); Benjamin Trumbull, *A Complete Hist. of Conn.* (1818), vol. I; G. H. Hollister, *The Hist. of Conn.* (1855), vol. I; I. M. Calder, *The New Haven Colony* (1934); E. R. Lambert, *Hist. of the Colony of New Haven* (1838) with several legendary episodes of Treat's early career; J. H. Treat, *The Treat Family* (1893) with "Life and Character of Gov. Robert Treat," by Henry Champion; G. H. Ford, "Robert Treat: Founder, Farmer, Soldier and Statesman," *Papers New Haven Colony Hist. Soc.*, vol. VIII (1914).]

L. W. L.

TREAT, SAMUEL (Dec. 17, 1815–Aug. 31, 1902), jurist, law teacher, son of Samuel Lancton and Lydia (Sheldon) Treat, was born in Portsmouth, N. H., being descended through Gov. Robert Treat [*q.v.*] of Connecticut, from the Treat (Trott) family of Somerset, England. After receiving a good education in the public high school at Portsmouth and teaching there for one year, he entered Harvard College, where he received the degree of A.B. in 1837. While teaching for four years in private schools, first at Jamaica Plain, Mass., and afterwards at Geneseo, N. Y., he studied law under practising lawyers. In 1841 he went to St. Louis and was admitted to the Missouri bar. Before 1843 he was recognized as an influential member of the Democratic party in that state. Treat himself attributed his early prominence to an encounter with the state leader of the Whig party, Henry Sheffie Geyer [*q.v.*]. The latter had publicly disparaged New Englanders, of whom there was a considerable group in Missouri—some Democrats and some Whigs; Treat publicly defended New England and was afterwards regarded as the political champion in Missouri of that section. Sent as a delegate to the National Democratic Convention of 1848, he was elected secretary. He was also a delegate to the national railroad convention of 1849, held at St. Louis, and introduced the resolution which resulted in a formal petition that the federal government build a telegraph line and railroad from the Missouri River to the Pacific Ocean.

In 1849 Treat became judge of the St. Louis court of common pleas. He served in this capacity until 1857, when he was appointed federal district judge for eastern Missouri by President Pierce. A competent, hard-working, urbane, courageous, respected trial judge, he remained on the bench until failing sight forced his retire-ment in 1887. He maintained his home in St. Louis until his death, though he spent much of his time in later years with a daughter in Rochester, N. Y., where he died.

In the judicial history of Missouri Treat stands out as the chief expert in admiralty, a branch of federal law significant locally in his time because of the great though temporary importance of steamboating on the Mississippi and Missouri rivers. The advent of the Civil War, with St. Louis becoming a fortified camp and half of Missouri a huge battle ground, brought to his tribunal novel and delicate questions. After the war, by charges to grand juries and by fearless handling of criminal trials, he combatted the spirit of lawlessness which undoubtedly prevailed in Missouri during the era of the outlaw Jesse James [*q.v.*] and the so-called "whiskey ring" of St. Louis. Of his published opinions the most widely cited is *In re McDonald* (16 *Fed. Cases, 17*), decided in May 1861, upholding the jurisdiction of federal courts at that particular time to issue writs of *habeas corpus* to military authorities (see also *American Law Register*, September 1861, pp. 661–95).

In 1853 Treat became one of the incorporators and original directors of Washington University, St. Louis; in 1867, cooperating with Henry Hitchcock [*q.v.*], he helped to organize the law school of that university, and for twenty years he was a member of its faculty as professor of admiralty law. On Aug. 21, 1841 he married Caroline Bryan of Geneseo, N. Y., who with one daughter survived him.

[Sources include: Treat Papers, Mo. Hist. Soc., Jefferson Memorial, St. Louis; J. H. Treat, *The Treat Family* (1893); J. L. Chamberlain, *Universities and Their Sons*, vol. V (1900); Wm. Hyde and H. L. Conard, *Encyc. of the Hist. of St. Louis* (1899), vol. IV; *Proc. of the St. Louis Bar on the Retirement of Samuel Treat* (1887); *Am. Law Rev.*, Mar.–Apr. 1887, Sept.–Oct. 1902; C. C. Allen, "The St. Louis Law School," *Green Bag*, July 1889; *St. Louis Republic*, Sept. 2, 1902; *St. Louis Globe-Democrat*, Sept. 2, 1902. The extension of federal admiralty jurisdiction to the Mississippi River is described in *The Hine* vs. *Trevor* (1866), 71 *U. S.*, 555.]

T. W.

TREAT, SAMUEL HUBBEL (June 21, 1811–Mar. 27, 1887), jurist, was born in Plainfield, Otsego County, N. Y., the son of Samuel and Elsie (Tracy) Treat and a descendant of Matthias Treat, who was a freeman of Wethersfield, Conn., in 1657. After spending most of his early life on his father's farm, young Treat studied law at Richfield, N. Y., where he was admitted to the bar in 1834. Seeking a field for practice, he turned to the West, and journeyed, most of the way on foot, to Springfield, Ill., where shortly before Stephen T. Logan and Stephen A. Douglas [*q.v.*] had settled, to be followed within a few years by Abraham Lincoln.

Treat's rise in the practice in Springfield was rapid, and by 1838 he had more cases on the circuit court docket than any other lawyer. In the following year he was appointed judge of the circuit court, which office he resigned in 1841 to accept appointment as justice of the supreme court of Illinois. He served on the supreme bench for fourteen years, during the last seven as chief justice. In 1855 he resigned to accept the offer tendered him by President Pierce of a federal judgeship for the newly created southern district of Illinois. This position he held for the remainder of his life, a period of thirty-two years.

Treat's opinions are characterized by exact and terse expression, many of them not exceeding a page in length. He was a lover of books and collected one of the finest libraries in the state. With Walter B. Scates and Robert S. Blackwell he compiled and annotated *The Statutes of Illinois* (2 vols., 1858). From early life he was an active and devoted member of the Protestant Episcopal Church; it is said that he never entered a church of another denomination except on public occasions when his presence was necessary. He was a stanch Democrat throughout life but aside from the performance of his judicial duties took little part in public affairs. In appearance he was tall and straight and in later life walked with a slow and dignified step, seldom stopping to greet acquaintances. He was, however, always courteous, quiet, and unostentatious. Though he was regarded as eccentric and had but few intimate friends, his integrity, legal ability, and unusual power to grasp and appraise facts were respected by all. So closely did he attend to his judicial duties that his private affairs suffered, and at his death they were found in a much neglected condition. The only recreation he is known to have cared for was chess, a game which he sometimes played with Lincoln.

In 1837 he married Ann Bennett of Jacksonville, Ill., but they had no children. When he died his only close relative was a married sister.

[*Chicago Legal News*, Apr. 2, 1887; J. H. Treat, *The Treat Family* (1893); John Moses, *Illinois, Hist. and Statistical*, I (1889), 431, 445; *Albany Law Jour.*, Apr. 16, 1887; *Green Bag*, May 1891; Newton Bateman and others, *Hist. Encyc. of Ill.* (1925), vol. I; U. F. Linder, *Reminiscences of the Early Bench and Bar of Ill.* (1879); J. M. Palmer, *The Bench and Bar of Ill.* (1899), I, 35; A. J. Beveridge, *Abraham Lincoln* (1928), I, 212, 506; *Am. Law Rev.*, May–June 1887; *Chicago Tribune*, Mar. 28, 1887.]   G. W. G.

TREE, LAMBERT (Nov. 29, 1832–Oct. 9, 1910), jurist, diplomat, was the second son of Lambert and Laura Matilda (Burrows) Tree, of Washington, D. C. Two of his great-grandfathers were Revolutionary officers, and both his grandfathers fought in the War of 1812; his father was a postal official in the capital for sixty years. With a background of brilliant social and official life, Lambert Tree grew to manhood. Early schooling under private tutors was followed by two years of law study in the office of James Mandeville Carlisle [*q.v.*] and a year in the law department of the University of Virginia. In 1855 he was admitted to the Washington bar, and the same year moved to Chicago, Ill., where he soon became junior member of the firm of Clarkson & Tree. He met and formed a lasting friendship with Abraham Lincoln, then a practising lawyer.

In 1864 he was elected president of the Chicago Law Institute, and in 1870, judge of the circuit court of Cook County. One of his first duties was to conduct an investigation into charges of corruption of Chicago city officials, which he pressed with such vigor, sincerity, and effectiveness that a dangerous political ring was broken up. Reëlected without opposition, he resigned in 1875 because of ill health and traveled for three years in Europe. Before his return Illinois Democrats nominated him for Congress, but the overwhelming Republican majority in his district made his race hopeless, and four years later he was again defeated. He was delegate-at-large from Illinois to the National Democratic Convention in 1884. In an exciting contest for a seat in the United States Senate in 1885 he lost to John A. Logan [*q.v.*] by one vote.

In July 1885 President Cleveland appointed him minister resident of the United States in Belgium, where one of his first official duties was to present notes announcing United States recognition of the new Congo Free State government. On March 15, 1886, he signed the conventions for the international exchange of official documents, parliamentary, scientific, and literary publications. The rank of the United States representatives in Belgium was raised in 1888, and Tree was made envoy extraordinary and minister plenipotentiary. To King Leopold's expression of gratification the Belgium foreign minister added, "Mr. Lambert Tree during his residence here has won universal good will" (*Papers Relating to the Foreign Relations of the United States, 1888*, pt. 1, p. 50). Late in the same year Tree was appointed envoy extraordinary and minister plenipotentiary to Russia, but resigned after a few weeks at St. Petersburg. He was made a grand officer of the Belgian Order of Leopold and an officer of the French Legion of Honor.

As Democratic member of the United States delegation to the International American Monetary Commission (Washington, 1891), he succeeded in preventing a resolution favoring a common double monetary standard for the Americas. His loyalty to the principle of monometalism led to his breaking with the Democratic party in the free silver campaign of 1896. He was an incorporator of the American Red Cross Society and one of the organizers of its Illinois branch, president of the Illinois Historical Library Board, vice-president of the Chicago Historical Society, and life trustee of the Newberry Library. On Nov. 24, 1859, he married Anna Josephine Magie, only daughter of Haines H. Magie, pioneer Chicago merchant. Two sons were born to them, one of whom died in infancy. Lambert Tree died in New York City, a few days after his 122nd transatlantic voyage.

[J. G. Leach, *Some Account of the Tree Family* (1908); J. S. Currey, *Chicago* (1912), IV, 30–35, and *The Makers of Illinois* (1913), II, 367–71; *Encyc. of Biog. of Ill.*, vol. I (1892); Paul Gilbert and C. L. Bryson, *Chicago and Its Makers* (1929); John Moses and Joseph Kirkland, *The Hist. of Chicago, Ill.* (2 vols., 1895); J. M. Palmer, *The Bench and Bar of Ill.* (1899), I, 492–94; *Who's Who in America*, 1910–11, and previous volumes; *Chicago Daily News*, Oct. 10, 1910; *Chiacgo Daily Tribune*, Oct. 10, 11, 1910; *Chicago Record-Herald*, Oct. 10, 11, 1910; *Papers Relating to the Foreign Relations of the U. S., 1885–89* (1886–90); official correspondence in the archives of the Dept. of State.]   I. L. T.

TREMAIN, HENRY EDWIN (Nov. 14, 1840–Dec. 9, 1910), soldier and lawyer, the son of Edwin Ruthven and Mary (Briggs) Tremain, was born in New York City. He was a descendant of Joseph Truman, who settled in New London, Conn., in 1666. After preliminary education in the public schools he attended the College of the City of New York and was graduated with the B.A. degree in 1860. He then entered Columbia University Law School, but his course was interrupted by service in the Civil War and he received the LL.B. degree in 1867. In April 1861 he enlisted as a private in the 7th New York State Militia. On the return of the regiment from Washington, he resigned to recruit the 73rd New York Volunteers in which he was commissioned first lieutenant in August 1861. Under McClellan and Pope he participated in the Virginia campaigns of the Army of the Potomac and was mentioned for gallantry at Williamsburg and Malvern Hill. Taken prisoner while leading a counter attack at the second battle of Bull Run, he was confined in Libby Prison for a short time. He resumed duty as aide-de-camp to Daniel E. Sickles [*q.v.*], and rendered notable staff service in the battles of Fredericksburg, Chancellorsville, and Gettysburg. He was

also a favorite staff officer of Joseph Hooker [*q.v.*]. In 1864 he accompanied Sickles to the West to inspect all armies in the field. Upon his return he rejoined the Army of the Potomac, and participated as a staff officer in all battles to Appomattox. He was appointed captain in 1862, major and aide-de-camp in 1863, and brevetted lieutenant-colonel on Mar. 13, 1865, "for gallant and meritorious service." He became a colonel in June and a brigadier-general in November 1865. For conspicuous gallantry at the battle of Resaca, on May 15, 1868, when he rode between two brigades of Union troops that were firing into each other, he was awarded the Congressional Medal of Honor. He served in South Carolina until his discharge in 1866.

Immediately after his return to New York in 1868 he began his career at the bar. He was unsuccessful in his candidacy for justice of the court of common pleas in the following year, but maintained an active interest in politics and public law. As special counsel to the United States marshall in 1870 he prosecuted violations of the election laws, and participated in attacks upon the "Tweed ring." From 1873 to 1877 he was first assistant United States attorney in New York, and thereafter appeared as counsel in the federal courts in cases involving revenue law violations. He joined Joshua T. Owen in 1872 in establishing the *New York Law Journal,* a daily devoted to news of the courts. He served as editor for two years, but relinquished the post because of the pressure of his legal duties. He showed deep interest in the associations made by the War. He was president of the Society of the Army of the Potomac, 1902, colonel of the Veterans of the 7th N. Y. N. G., and president of the III Army Corps Union. He was twice president of the National Republican Club and, from 1870 to 1874, president of the alumni association of the College of the City of New York. Besides many papers on law, tariff, and taxation he wrote: *Last Hours of Sheridan's Cavalry* (1904); *Two Days of War* (1905); *Sectionalism Unmasked* (1907); and *Fifty Papers, Addresses and Writings* (1909). He was married to Sarah Brownson, of New York City, on June 1, 1869. They had no children.

[*Who's Who in America*, 1910–11; E. M. Treman, M. E. Poole, *The Hist. of the Treman, Tremaine, Truman Family in America* (1901), vol. I; H. E. Tremain, *A Family Geneal.* (privately printed, 1908); F. B. Heitman, *Hist. Reg. . . . U. S. Army* (1903); *Am. Decorations . . . 1862–1926* (1927); *N. Y. Times*, Dec. 11, 1910.]   D. A. R.

TREMAINE, HENRY BARNES (July 20, 1866–May 13, 1932), manufacturer of mechanical musical instruments, was born in Brooklyn,

N. Y., the son of William Burton Tremaine, and Emeline Cornelia (Dodge) Tremaine. He was a descendant of Joseph Truman who settled in New London, Conn., in 1666. He was educated in the public schools of Brooklyn and at about sixteen entered the employ of Hastings & Company, paper merchants of New York City. In 1888 he joined the Aeolian Organ and Music Company, of which his father was manager, a firm which in 1887 had acquired the business of the Mechanical Orguinette Company. The product of the company was a small mechanical organ, played by a crank that turned a paper music-roll. Tremaine saw immediately that, though the promoters of the organette were offering it as a toy, it had possibilities as a musical instrument, and he accordingly proposed that a better instrument be introduced which would appeal to adults as well as children. In 1890 he succeeded his father as manager. In 1894 he acquired the sales rights of the Vocalion organ, and in the same year a mechanical device for playing it, the Orchestrelle. In 1895 the name of the company was changed to the Aeolian Company, and three years later Tremaine was elected president. When in 1896 the pianola, a mechanical device for playing the piano, was invented, Tremaine acquired it for the Aeolian Company. This led to the formation of the Aeolian, Weber Piano and Pianola Company in 1903. Subsequent activities of the firm included the manufacture of phonographs and records (1913–25), and the development of the Duo-Art (1914), a device similar to the pianola, but one which automatically reproduced the expression and nuances of living pianists in its performance.

Tremaine's ability to anticipate changes in taste was shown not only by his development of mechanical musical instruments but also by his choice of locations for the firm in New York City. He seemed to know what sections would become fashionable shopping centers. When he joined the firm at 831 Broadway, the owners had difficulty in paying the rent. Tremaine insisted that they move (1891) to West Twenty-third Street, where the rent was higher, and the same intuition guided him in subsequent moves. He also gave his business an international aspect by the establishment of foreign branches —London (1898), Berlin (1901), Australia (1905), and Paris (1907)—and furthered musical activities by establishing concert halls in the United States and abroad. Although he labored under severe handicaps of health and during his active career was forced to be absent for more than half of his usual working hours, he possessed a remarkable faculty for judging situations and solving problems in absence. In November of 1930 he resigned the presidency of the Aeolian Company, and became chairman of its board of directors. He died suddenly in Washington, D. C. He was married to Maud Aline Cooke of New York City, Apr. 2, 1890, and had two daughters and a son. He was awarded several foreign decorations, among them the Order of Leopold, the Order of Philip the Magnanimous (Belgium), 1922; the Order of St. Gregory the Great (papal), 1923; and the Order of the Crown of Italy, 1926; he became a member of the Legion of Honor in 1927.

[See E. M. Treman and M. E. Poole, *The Hist. of the Treman, Tremaine, Truman Family in America* (2 vols., 1901); *Who's Who in America*, 1932–33; "The Development of the Player-Piano," booklet issued by the Aeolian Company; obituaries in *Music Trades*, May 1932, and *N. Y. Times*, May 14, 1932. Information has been supplied by relatives of Tremaine and by members of the staff of the Aeolian Company.]   J. T. H.

TRENCHARD, STEPHEN DECATUR (July 10, 1818–Nov. 15, 1883), naval officer, son of Capt. Edward Trenchard, United States Navy, and Eliza (Sands) Trenchard, was born in Brooklyn, N. Y. He was a descendant of George Trenchard who came to America with the followers of William Penn. At the age of eleven, intending to become an Episcopal clergyman, he enrolled at Kenyon College, Gambier, Ohio, an institution conducted by Bishop Philander Chase [*q.v.*]; but on Oct. 23, 1834, he entered the navy as a midshipman. His studies under the Bishop made a lasting impression on him, however, and throughout his career he was known in the service as a deeply religious man. In 1840, after one year's study at the naval school in Philadelphia, he was warranted a passed midshipman. The next four years he served in the Mediterranean, at the end of which time he was assigned to the coast survey. On this duty his ship, the brig *Washington,* was nearly wrecked off the coast of North Carolina and the captain and ten seamen were drowned. The following spring, the brig having been repaired, he sailed with her under Lieut. Samuel Phillips Lee and joined Commodore Perry's squadron off Vera Cruz. The *Washington* took part in the expedition against Tabasco in June 1847, but on July 4 was ordered back to coast-survey duty. Commissioned lieutenant the same year, he was occupied mainly in coast-survey work until 1857. On Aug. 14, 1856, while in command of the *Vixen,* he rescued the sinking British bark *Adieu* off Gloucester, Mass. For this action he was presented with a sword by Queen Victoria, and with a chronometer by the owners and underwriters. He sailed with the *Powhatan* (East India Squadron) on her diplomatic cruise to China and Japan (1857–60). On this cruise Trenchard was Commodore Tattnall's flag-lieutenant, accompanying him on his visit to the British Admiral Hope, and participating in the British action on Peiho River, China, June 25, 1859, where he was wounded.

At the outbreak of the Civil War, he was assigned to the command of the *Keystone State* (Apr. 19, 1861), and three days later arrived at Hampton Roads, where he witnessed the burning of the Norfolk Navy Yard. He assisted in saving the *Cumberland* from capture, and brought off Commodore Paulding and the marine garrison. Three months later he was transferred to the steamer *Rhode Island* with orders to transport supplies to the blockading squadrons. After eighteen months of this arduous duty, his ship, armed for cruiser warfare, was assigned to blockade duty. While towing the original *Monitor* (Dec. 31, 1862), the *Rhode Island* ran into a heavy storm. The *Monitor* foundered, but owing to Trenchard's vigilance and expert seamanship, most of her crew was saved. He was then ordered to cruise off Havana and Key West, keeping a sharp lookout for the Confederate raiders, *Alabama* and *Florida*. Late in 1864 he joined Admiral Porter's great fleet at Hampton Roads and participated in both attacks on Fort Fisher, his men assisting in landing the heavy siege guns and mortars for the army.

He was commissioned captain in 1866, commodore in 1871, and rear admiral in 1875. In 1876 he commanded the North Atlantic Squadron. After the disputed Hayes-Tilden election of that year, he assembled a large fleet at Washington to prevent disturbances. He retired July 10, 1880. He was a strict disciplinarian but was conceded, even by his enemies, to be a highly upright, humane man. He made an admirable record in the Civil War and in the second attack on Fort Fisher played a distinguished rôle. He married Ann O'Connor Barclay in 1848, and had one son, Edward Trenchard, an artist.

[*Army and Navy Jour.*, Nov. 17, 1883; G. F. Emmons, *Navy of the U. S.* (1853); L. R. Hamersly, *The Records of Living Officers of U. S. Navy* (1890); C. C. Jones, *The Life and Services of Commodore Josiah Tattnall* (1878); E. S. Maclay, *Reminiscences of the Old Navy; from Journals and Private Papers of . . . Rear-Admiral Trenchard* (1898); *N. Y. Times*, Nov. 16, 1883; *War of the Rebellion: Official Records* (*Navy*); Edward Trenchard, transcript of his father's Civil War record, in Office of Naval Records, Navy Dept.; *The Report of the Supt. of the U. S. Coast Survey*, 1847, 1856; U. S. Navy Dept. archives; Navy Registers, 1834–80; *American Ancestry*, vol. VI (1891).]

L. H. B.

TRENT, WILLIAM (Feb. 13, 1715–1787?), Indian trader and land speculator, was born probably in Philadelphia, Pa., the son of Mary (Coddington) and William Trent who had emigrated from Scotland and become a prominent citizen and officeholder, first in Pennsylvania and later in New Jersey. In 1746 the younger Trent was appointed captain in the Pennsylvania troops raised for an expedition against the French in Canada, and he spent several months in 1746 and 1747 on the New York frontier north of Albany. He attended councils with the Indians at Logstown in 1752, at Easton in 1757, and at Fort Pitt in 1759. While at Logstown in 1752 he was directed by the Virginia commissioners to proceed with Andrew Montour to Pickawillanee, a village of the Twightwee, or Miami, Indians, with presents. He kept a journal of the expedition, which is available in published form (*post*). About this time he was married to Sarah Wilkins. They had six children. He lived in Lancaster and in Carlisle, Pa., and from 1768 to 1784 his home was in Trenton, N. J., where he was a vestryman in the St. Michael's Episcopal Church. In 1754, acting upon the authority of Governor Dinwiddie of Virginia, he raised a force and undertook the construction of a fort at the forks of the Ohio. When, in his absence, the post was captured by the French before its completion and renamed Fort Duquesne, he was blamed (*The Writings of George Washington,* vol. II, 1834, ed. by Jared Sparks, p. 47). In 1758 he accompanied John Forbes's successful expedition against Duquesne, which later became Fort Pitt. During these years, he had also been engaged in the Indian trade. About 1749 he had formed a partnership with George Croghan [*q.v.*], a connection that lasted five years or more. In 1754 he and his associates suffered heavy losses from French and Indian depredations along the Ohio. About 1760 he became a member of the Pennsylvania trading firm of Simon, Trent, Levy & Franks, being stationed at Fort Pitt. Again Trent and his partners suffered severe losses during Pontiac's uprising.

Many years were spent by Trent and others in endeavoring to obtain restitution for the losses of 1754 and 1763, and out of these efforts grew his career as a land speculator. At the treaty of Fort Stanwix in 1768, along with Samuel Wharton and George Morgan [*qq.v.*], he obtained from the Six Nations, by way of compensation, a grant of a vast tract along the upper Ohio that became known as "Indiana." Early in 1769 he accompanied Wharton to England, to try to obtain royal confirmation of the grant. The Indiana enterprise was merged with the larger Vandalia project, involving a still greater extent of territory and the participation of many prominent Englishmen and Americans. The royal authorization was never obtained, and early in 1775 he returned to America, where he endeavored to make good the Indiana claim by establishing the principle of the validity of titles obtained from the Indians by private purchase. Meetings of the Indiana Company were held, and in 1779 he presented its claims before the Virginia Assembly, but without success. He then directed his efforts toward Congress and during the period 1779 to 1783 presented several memorials relating to both the Indiana and Vandalia projects, but to no avail. The enterprise failed and after 1783, little more is heard of Trent. In 1784 he removed to Philadelphia, where he died.

[*Journ. of Captain William Trent from Logstown to Pickawillany, A.D. 1752* (1871), ed. by A. T. Goodman, including biog. sketch; E. F. Cooley, *Geneal. of Early Settlers of Trenton* (1883); Hamilton Schuyler, *A Hist. of St. Michael's Church, Trenton* (1926); C. A. Hanna, *The Wilderness Trail* (2 vols., 1911), also with text of journ.; Gratz papers and manuscript "Opinions Regarding the Grant to Wm. Trent, 1775" in possession of Hist. Soc. of Pa.; *Case*, rare pamphlet in N. Y. Pub. Lib., relating to grant to Trent and other traders, probably printed in London about 1770; *Minutes of the Provincial Council of Pa.*, vol. VIII (1852), esp. pp. 382, 383; *Jours. of the Continental Cong.*, vols. XV (1909), XVIII (1910), XX–XXI (1912), XXIV (1922); A. T. Volwiler, *George Croghan and the Westward Movement* (1926); Max Savelle, *George Morgan, Colony Builder* (1932); date of death from statement concerning date of will in Cooley, *ante*, p. 289.]
                                              W. E. S—s.

TRESCOT, WILLIAM HENRY (Nov. 10, 1822–May 4, 1898), historian, diplomat, was born in Charleston, S. C., the son of Henry and Sarah (McCrady) Trescot. After attending private schools in his native city he graduated from the College of Charleston in 1841. He read law under his uncle, Edward McCrady, and was admitted to the bar in 1843. In 1848 he married Eliza Natalie Cuthbert and devoted the next four years of his life to the practice of law, the management of his wife's estate on Barnwell Island near Beaufort, S. C., and the study of the history of American diplomacy. He was small in stature and noted for the instability of his opinions; but he was impressive in manners and brilliant and voluble in conversation and public speech. His historical works are marked by forcible summaries, calmness of tone, and the elegance of style popular in his generation. He first attracted attention in 1849 by a pamphlet entitled *A Few Thoughts on the Foreign Policy of the United States*. To the controversial literature provoked by the Omnibus Bill of 1850 he contributed *The Position and Course of the South* (1850), an excellent summary of the Southern social and economic view. Two years later his

illuminating *Diplomacy of the Revolution; an Historical Study* (1852) appeared. The same year he was appointed secretary of legation in London. The following year he wrote *A Letter to Hon. A. P. Butler . . . on the Diplomatic System of the United States* (1853), which is still regarded as a valuable contribution of the history of that subject. Returning to South Carolina in 1854, he published his most pretentious and original work, *The Diplomatic History of the Administrations of Washington and Adams* (1857).

In June 1860 he was appointed assistant secretary of state. When South Carolina seceded the following December he resigned, but, remaining in Washington until February as the unofficial adviser of the South Carolina authorities, he played an important part in the negotiations over the Charleston forts. He urged the necessity of caution upon the state authorities and strove with some success to postpone a crisis by endeavoring to prevent the federal government from reinforcing the forts. His "Narrative and Letter" (published with notes by Gaillard Hunt, *American Historical Review*, Apr. 1908) is his own account of those difficult days. During the Civil War he served on the staffs of Gov. Andrew Magrath and of Gen. Roswell S. Ripley and was a member of the Executive Council of South Carolina, an important local body. From 1862 to 1866 he represented Anderson District in the legislature. There he delivered a series of memorial eulogies which, notably the *Memorial of the Life of J. Johnston Pettigrew* (1870), excited wide comment. During the summer of 1861 he acted as an intermediary between the Confederate government and the British and French consuls at Charleston in their effort to obtain the adherence of the Confederate government to the Declaration of Paris respecting privateering (see his *Confederacy and the Declaration of Paris*, 1918, reprinted from the *American Historical Review*, July 1918).

Intermittently for twenty-five years after the war he labored with notable success in Washington as the agent of South Carolina for the recovery of lands seized and taxes levied under the direct tax act of Congress. In 1866 he refused to become a candidate for the federal Senate. Although not affiliated with the Radical party in South Carolina, as an attorney for the Blue Ridge Railroad he defended before the state tax-payers convention of 1871 the scheme to have the state indorse the bonds of that dubious venture. He was one of the counselors for the United States government before the Halifax fishery commission in 1877. Three years later, with James B. Angell and John F. Swift [*qq.v.*], he was sent to China to arrange for the modification of the Burlingame treaty concerning Chinese immigration. The following year he concluded a treaty with the Colombian minister in Washington regulating American rights in the Isthmus of Panama. Later in 1881 Blaine sent him to South America to warn Chile against making excessive demands on Bolivia and Peru as the result of her victories in the War of the Pacific; but when he arrived in Chile he learned that Blaine had resigned and that his original instructions had been published and reversed in order to discredit Blaine's policies. The mission was accordingly a failure. In order to compensate him for this undeserved humiliation he was appointed, along with Ex-President Grant, in 1882 to negotiate a commercial treaty with Mexico. The treaty was approved by the Senate but was never put into operation because of the opposition of the House of Representatives to its free sugar provisions. His last diplomatic service was as a delegate to the Pan-American conference of 1889, in which he participated actively. Shortly afterward he retired because of lack of health to his home in Pendleton, S. C., where he died, survived by his widow and five children.

[Letters in Lib. of Cong.; R. M. Betts, "William Henry Trescot," manuscript biog. in lib. of Univ. of S. C.; biog. sketch by Gaillard Hunt in *Am. Hist. Rev.*, Apr. 1908; R. W. Simpson, *Hist. of Old Pendleton District* (1913); *Appletons' Ann. Cyc. . . . 1898* (1899); W. P. Trent, *Southern Writers* (1905); *Lib. of Southern Lit.*, vol. XII (1907); *News and Courier* (Charleston), May 5, 1898, Aug. 30, 1903; *State* (Columbia), May 5, 6, 1898; information from son, Edward A. Trescot, Pendleton, S. C.]   F. B. S.

TREVELLICK, RICHARD F. (May 1830–Feb. 15, 1895), labor leader, was born on St. Mary's, one of the Scilly Islands. He became a ship's carpenter, worked in a Southampton shipyard, and later, as a seaman, visited Africa, India, China, and the Antipodes. As a youth he became known among his fellows as a debater, agitator, and advocate of the eight-hour day for workers. In Auckland, New Zealand, in 1852, and in Melbourne, Australia, in 1854, he attained prominence in controversies raging about this subject. His wanderings brought him at length, in 1857, to New Orleans, La., where he worked at his trade and became president of the ship carpenters' and caulkers' union, in which rôle he led a successful fight for the nine-hour day.

On the outbreak of the Civil War he settled in Detroit, and in 1864 became the first president of the Detroit Trades' Assembly. That same year he was a delegate to the Louisville Convention which set up the short-lived International

Industrial Assembly of North America. In 1865 he was made president of the International Union of Ship Carpenters and Caulkers. He represented the Detroit Trades' Assembly and the Michigan Grand Eight Hours League at the congress of the National Labor Union in 1867, and in that year was elected a delegate to the International Workingmen's Association, meeting at Lausanne, Switzerland, but could not attend because of lack of funds. In 1869, 1871, and 1872 he served as president of the National Labor Union, the leading labor organization of the day. When, in 1872, it split into two sections, he attended the meetings of both factions. Later he carried on organization work for the Knights of Labor.

Paying his own expenses, Trevellick in 1868 led one of the first successful labor lobbies, pushing through Congress an act instituting the eight-hour day for federal workmen, mechanics, and laborers. With William H. Sylvis and Andrew C. Cameron [*qq.v.*], he led an agitation against subsequent efforts to make proportionate wage reductions. Trevellick also led the fight against the blacklist, from which he himself suffered seriously. He opposed the importation of Chinese labor under contract, and, in 1870 capitulated to the majority in the National Labor Union when it accepted the California idea of complete exclusion of Chinese. He espoused the unpopular idea of abolishing the color-line then generally drawn in labor unions against negro workers. As a leader in the National Labor Union he advocated the relief of the working classes from capitalist exploitation. The collapse of organization after organization never undermined his belief in the general principle of organized labor struggle. With the decline in unionism under employers' attacks after the crisis of 1873, however, he fell under the influence of the Greenback movement, and thenceforth advocated relieving industrial depression by means of inflationary price-boosting schemes. He helped establish the Greenback Party and was a delegate to the convention of 1876 which nominated Peter Cooper [*q.v.*] for the presidency; he also served as temporary chairman of the convention of 1878 at Toledo which formed the National Greenback Labor Party, and as chairman of the convention of 1880 which nominated James B. Weaver [*q.v.*].

His energy was boundless. In 1867–68 he toured the West, making 270 addresses to labor audiences and organizing forty-seven unions. In 1869 he spent 169 days on the road, especially in the industrially backward South and the Pennsylvania anthracite fields. In 1870 he covered sixteen states and helped to establish 200 local unions and three state organizations. His vision may have been narrower than that of Sylvis, but his sense of the need for combined industrial and political activity, his ability for organization, and his oratorical powers made him one of the first great labor agitators of America. In every major industrial center of the country his black beard, fierce eyes, and ringing phrases were well known to workers. He was married, and was survived by four of his five children. He died in Detroit.

[Obadiah Hicks, *Life of Richard F. Trevellick* (1896), which gives day of birth as May 20; J. R. Commons and others, *Hist. of Labour in the U. S.* (1918), vol. II; G. E. McNeill's *The Labor Movement* (1887); T. V. Powderly, *Thirty Years of Labor* (copr. 1889); *Detroit Jour.* and *Evening News* (Detroit), Feb. 15, 1895, which give day of birth as May 2.]   H. S.

TRIMBLE, ALLEN (Nov. 24, 1783–Feb. 3, 1870), governor of Ohio and agriculturist, was born in Augusta County, Va., the son of James and Jane (Allen) Trimble and the grandson of John Trimble who with three brothers emigrated from the north of Ireland early in the seventeenth century and settled at Staunton, Va. When only eleven months old, Allen was taken by his parents to their new home, near the present Lexington, Ky. The father, accompanied by Allen, visited Ohio in 1801 and in 1802 to select lands, and in 1804 he built a cabin in what is now Highland County, Ohio. When he died in the autumn of 1804, Allen removed the family to the new home the next year. In 1808 or 1809 he was appointed clerk of the common pleas court for Highland County and county recorder. At this time he removed to Hillsboro, the county seat. In the second war with Great Britain he served as a colonel in a successful expedition against the Indians of the upper Wabash and Eel rivers for the relief of the garrison at Fort Wayne. Later he commanded a battalion of militia, which was, however, disbanded almost at once. He served in the Ohio House of Representatives, 1816–17, and in the Ohio Senate, 1817–25, of which he was speaker for seven consecutive years. Owing to the resignation of Gov. E. A. Brown to become a federal senator, Trimble served as acting governor in 1822. In this position he appointed a committee on the common schools, whose work established the substantial basis for Ohio's school system. He was defeated in the election for governor in the autumn of 1822 and in 1824. In the legislative session of 1824–25 he was chosen as one of the first canal fund commissioners, authorized to negotiate a loan for building the newly planned Ohio canal system, but resigned in 1825. In 1826 he was elected governor over three opponents by an overwhelming majority. He was authorized by the legislature to select a half million acres of land granted by Congress for canal purposes, and in the summer of 1827 he went with a companion to the Maumee and Sandusky river valleys to examine the region. A supporter of Henry Clay, he was again chosen to the governorship as an Adams-Clay partisan in 1828, although the Ohio Jacksonian electoral ticket was successful in November. Retiring from public life in 1830, he continued to participate in the plans of the National Republican party in Ohio and later in those of the Whig party. A lover of the Union, he became a candidate of the American party for governor of Ohio in 1855, apparently hoping that this organization might help to offset a too ardent sectionalism.

He was instrumental in the establishment of the Ohio State Board of Agriculture, and he served as its president, 1846–48. He was a pioneer in Ohio in the importation of British horses and cattle to improve the domestic breeds. Although modest and apparently guileless, he could be firm and self-reliant when occasion demanded. He found religious satisfaction in the Methodist faith, which he embraced in 1828. He was married twice, in January 1806 to Margaret McDowell, who died in 1809, and to Rachael Woodrow on Jan. 10, 1811. His widow, four sons, and a daughter survived him at his death in Hillsboro.

[Letters in the McArthur Papers, Lib. of Cong.; *Autobiog. and Correspondence of Allen Trimble* (1909) and in *Old Northwest Geneal. Quart.*, July 1906–Jan. 1909; *Biog. Encyc. of Ohio of the 19th Cent.* (1876); E. H. Roseboom, "Ohio in the 1850's," in Widener Lib., Harvard Univ.; *Highland Weekly News* (Hillsboro), Feb. 10, 1870.]   F. P. W.

TRIMBLE, ISAAC RIDGEWAY (May 15, 1802–Jan. 2, 1888), soldier, engineer, was born in Culpeper County, Va. In 1805 his father, John Trimble, moved to Kentucky, and through Isaac's uncle, David Trimble, congressman from Kentucky, the youth received an appointment to the United States Military Academy. Graduating in 1822, he was commissioned a second lieutenant in the artillery. His principal service as a subaltern was on the survey of a road from Washington to the Ohio River. About this time the development of railroads in the United States offered an attractive field to young West Point graduates and many resigned from the army to engage in this work, among them six members of Trimble's class, including himself. His own resignation took effect May 31, 1832, and for three years he was assistant engineer on the Boston & Providence Railroad.

Thereafter, he was chief engineer successively of the Baltimore & Susquehanna Railroad, the Philadelphia, Wilmington & Baltimore, and the Philadelphia & Baltimore Central, and from 1859 to 1861 general superintendent of the Baltimore and Potomac Railroad.

At the beginning of the Civil War he took an active part in obstructing the movement of Union troops to Washington by burning bridges north of Baltimore. In May 1861 he went to Virginia and received a commission as colonel of engineers in the state troops. On Aug. 9, 1861 he was commissioned brigadier-general in the Confederate service and in September was charged with the construction of batteries on the Potomac River to prevent the passage of United States vessels. In 1862 he was assigned to the command of a brigade in the Army of Northern Virginia and was charged with the removal of the stores from the depot at Manassas Junction when the army was withdrawn to meet McClellan on the Peninsula. Trimble's brigade remained on the Rappahannock as a part of Ewell's division. It took part in Jackson's famous operations in the Shenandoah Valley in 1862 and did conspicuous service in the battles of Winchester and Cross Keys. After this campaign it took part in the Seven Days' battles in the vicinity of Richmond.

In the campaign against Pope's army in northern Virginia in 1862, Trimble's command saw action in the battle of Cedar Mountain, the engagement at Hazel Run, and in Jackson's march around Pope to Bristoe Station on the Orange and Alexandria Railroad. Jackson reached this station at dark after a forced march of some twenty-five miles under an August sun. The Union depot of supplies at Manassas Station was about seven miles away, but Jackson was unwilling to order his infantry to proceed any farther that night. When, however, Trimble volunteered to take part of his brigade and advance on Manassas, Jackson gladly acquiesced, and the depot was captured at dawn of Aug. 27 by Trimble assisted by J. E. B. Stuart's cavalry. In the battle of Manassas that followed Trimble was so seriously wounded that he was unable to perform field service for many months. In October of that year when Jackson was promoted to command a corps he recommended that Trimble be commissioned major-general and placed in command of his old division. Trimble returned for duty in 1863 just as the Gettysburg campaign opened, and on June 18 was assigned by General Lee to the command of the troops in the Shenandoah Valley. He led his troops in this campaign as far north as Carlisle, Pa., where he received orders to return. On the second day at Gettysburg he was assigned to the command of a division in Hill's corps, of which the commander, Gen. William D. Pender, had been seriously wounded. With two brigades he took part in the third day's attack in support of Pettigrew's division on Pickett's left. In this engagement he was seriously wounded, lost a leg, and was left a prisoner when the Confederate army retreated. The Union authorities, remembering the part he had played early in the war in obstructing troop movements and fearing his influence in the important border state of Maryland, did not permit his exchange until February 1865. He was on his way to join Lee when the latter surrendered at Appomattox. After the war he made his home in Baltimore, where he died. "Of all the soldiers whom Maryland furnished to the Southern Cause, General Trimble performed the most distinguished services, obtained the highest rank, and won the greatest name" (*Nineteenth Annual Reunion of the Association of Graduates of the United States Military Academy, 1888,* p. 68). He was twice married: first, to Maria Cattell Presstman of Charleston, S. C., who died in 1855; second, to her sister, Ann Ferguson Presstman. By his first marriage he had two sons, who survived him.

[G. W. Cullum, *Biog. Reg. Officers and Grads. U. S. Mil. Acad.* (3rd ed., 1891); *Nineteenth Ann. Reunion . . . Asso. Grads.*, cited above; *War of the Rebellion: Official Records* (*Army*); *Southern Hist. Soc. Papers,* vol. XXVI (1898); G. F. R. Henderson, *Stonewall Jackson and the Am. Civil War* (1898); *Army and Navy Jour.*, Jan. 7, 1888; *Sun* (Baltimore), Jan. 3, 1888.]

G. J. F.

TRIMBLE, ROBERT (1777–Aug. 25, 1828), jurist, the son of William Trimble, was born in Augusta County, Va. While still very young he was taken by his parents to Clark County, Ky., where his father acquired a patent to 700 acres of frontier land. Here Robert grew to manhood, clearing ground, cultivating crops, hunting wild game, and fighting Indians. From early boyhood he appears to have been a leader among his fellows, excelling in physical as well as mental activities. In the spring of 1795 he entered Bourbon Academy in Bourbon County, from which institution, a year later, he was compelled to withdraw because of illness. After teaching for a short period he became a student in Kentucky Academy in Woodford County. Upon completing his course there, he began reading law, first under George Nicholas [q.v.] and later under James Brown [q.v.], afterwards minister to France.

In 1800 Trimble entered upon the practice of his profession at Paris, Bourbon County, and thereafter maintained a residence in that town. His practice was uninterrupted, except for one term, 1802, in the state legislature, until the governor made him a judge of the court of appeals in 1807. This position he resigned two years later because the emoluments were insufficient for the support of himself and his family, and for the same reason he declined the chief justiceship of the court in 1810, and another offer of a justiceship in 1813. In the meantime his practice and reputation as a lawyer were growing, and by 1815 he was appearing in most of the important cases arising in his section of the state. From 1813 to 1817 he also served as district attorney and in this capacity was a courageous and vigorous prosecutor. In the latter year he gave up his practice to accept the tender by President Madison of the federal district judgeship for Kentucky, in which position he served until May 9, 1826, when, upon the nomination of President Adams, he was confirmed by the Senate as an associate justice of the Supreme Court of the United States, succeeding his friend and fellow Kentuckian, Thomas Todd [q.v.]. Though a Jeffersonian politically, as a district judge Trimble had insisted upon the supremacy of the federal over the state law. For this reason he was opposed for confirmation as a Supreme Court justice by Senator Rowan of Kentucky, but much to the satisfaction of Marshall and Story, the opposition was able to muster but five votes as against twenty-seven in Trimble's favor. On at least two occasions he was importuned unsuccessfully to become a candidate for the United States Senate, and was twice offered but declined the professorship of law at Transylvania University.

His service on the nation's highest tribunal was curtailed by his untimely death to the brief period of two years, but the vigor, clarity, and statesmanlike quality of the opinions rendered by him during that time mark him as a jurist of high order. Though nearly always in accord with Marshall on constitutional doctrine, he differed with him in the case of *Ogden* vs. *Saunders* (12 *Wheaton*, 212), wherein Trimble wrote one of his ablest opinions, holding that a state insolvency law was not an impairment of the obligation of a future contract between citizens of that state. Marshall dissented. Trimble also thought, contrary to the view of the Chief Justice and a majority of the Court, that such a law could be made to apply constitutionally to the rights of creditors who were citizens of another state. He was married soon after he began the practice of law and had a large family.

Trimble County, Ky., was named in his honor. He died at Paris, Ky.

[Obit. by Joseph Story, in *Columbian Centinel* (Boston), Sept. 17, 1828, reprinted in "Memoir of Judge Trimble," *Am. Jurist*, Jan. 1829, and in *Ky. Law Jour.*, Sept. 1882; H. L. Carson, *The Hist. of the Supreme Court of the U. S.* (1902); Charles Warren, *The Supreme Court in U. S. Hist.* (1922); *Autobiog. and Correspondence of Allen Trimble, Gov. of Ohio* (1909); Lewis and R. H. Collins, *Hist. of Ky.* (1874); *Western Citizen* (Paris, Ky.), Aug. 30, 1828.]   G. W. G.

TRIPP, BARTLETT (July 15, 1842–Dec. 8, 1911), jurist and diplomat, was born at Harmony, Me., the son of William and Naamah (Bartlett) Tripp. After attending the common schools and several academies he taught school and went to Waterville (later Colby) College from 1857 to 1860. His first acquaintance with the West came in 1861 on a trip to California, in the course of which he taught at Salt Lake City, Utah, and worked as engineer on the Central Pacific Railroad. In 1863 he married Ellen M. Jennings of Garland, Me., who died in 1884 leaving one daughter. In 1867 he studied at the Albany Law School of Albany, N. Y., and for two years practised law in Augusta, Me. He then returned to Dakota Territory, with which he had been impressed on his western trip, and practised at Yankton, which was his home the rest of his life. On Nov. 6, 1887, he married Maria Janet (Davis) Washburn, the sister of Cushman K. Davis [q.v.]. His service as a member of the Yankton school board, an incorporator of Yankton College in 1881, and as a member of the board of regents of the University of South Dakota indicate his constant interest in education. A prominent member of the Dakota bar, he served as president of the bar association, was in 1875 made a member of the commission for codifying the laws of the territory (*The Revised Code of 1877*, 1877), and in 1903 served on a similar commission for the codification of the laws of the state (*The Revised Codes, 1903*, 1903). In his later years he became a lecturer in law at the University of South Dakota. Although a Democrat he presided in 1883 over the first territorial constitutional convention, which was strongly Republican in composition. Two years later President Cleveland made him chief justice of the territorial supreme court, and he served from 1885 to 1889. When the legislature of the state of South Dakota met to choose a federal senator in 1891 he seems to have been near to election as the Democratic candidate. The election was, however, settled by a kind of compromise, and James H. Kyle [q.v.] was named.

Tripp's services to the federal government began with his arrival in Vienna on June 1, 1893, as minister to Austria-Hungary to succeed Frederick D. Grant. During the four years before he resigned on June 18, 1897, he was called upon to protest to the Austro-Hungarian government the seizure of numerous naturalized American citizens, natives of Austria-Hungary, for performance of military duty. One of the most important of these cases was that of John Benich in which Tripp persuaded the Austrian government to admit that its administrative officers should accept American passports as *prima facie* evidence of citizenship. Olney was able to say in 1896, in the only annual report ever made by a secretary of state, that friction with Austria-Hungary over citizenship cases had recently diminished greatly. In April 1899 Tripp was made the American member of the Samoan commission that was to undertake provisionally the government of the Samoan Islands then on the brink of civil war. Upon their arrival in the islands on May 13, the British and German members chose Tripp chairman. The report of the commission was rendered in July and his own able report to the secretary of state on Aug. 7, 1899. He urged the importance of Pango-Pango harbor to American interests, and it may be significant that when the islands were partitioned later in the same year the United States received Pango-Pango. After his return to the United States he published *My Trip to Samoa* (1911). He died at Yankton.

[A collection of photographs of events in Samoa during 1899 in the archives of state department; *Who's Who in America*, 1899–1900, 1910–11; obituary in *Report of . . . the S. D. Bar Asso. . . . 1912* (1912); Doane Robinson, *South Dakota* (1930), vol. I; G. W. Kingsbury, *Hist. of Dakota Territory* (1915), vols. II–IV, ed. by G. M. Smith; *Daily Argus-Leader* (Sioux Falls), Dec. 8, 1911.]   E. W. S.

TRIPP, GUY EASTMAN (Apr. 22, 1865–June 14, 1927), industrialist, son of Alonzo K. and Abbie F. (Yeaton) Tripp, was born in Wells, Me.; his father was an attorney. Guy attended the district school in Wells and later, South Berwick Academy, working in a grocery store summers to secure needed funds. When he was eighteen, a friend found a place for him as clerk in the office of the Eastern Railroad at Salem, Mass.; at twenty-five, he was employed by the Thomson-Houston Electric Company as its storekeeper in Boston and subsequently became traveling auditor. In this capacity he visited and studied many public-utility plants, attracting attention by his keenness in appraising the value and possibilities of such properties.

In 1897 he joined the staff, as auditor, of Stone & Webster, then a young engineering firm beginning to build and operate public-service plants. He rapidly rose to the vice-presidency of both of the two corporations into which, for engineering and management purposes, the business of the firm was divided. When in 1910 the firm was called upon to aid in the reorganization of the Metropolitan Street Railway Company of New York, Tripp acted as its representative. He became chairman of the reorganization committee, and at the auction of the railway's properties in December 1911, he bought them in for the bondholders for about $12,000,000. His masterly handling of the intricate task of reorganizing this company led in January 1912 to his being chosen chairman of the board of directors of the Westinghouse Electric & Manufacturing Company, a position which he continued to hold until his death. Under his direction the company enjoyed great prosperity, increasing its varied business in all countries of the world. During the participation of the United States in the World War, Tripp was one of the most prominent of all civilians in patriotic service. In January 1918 the government selected him as chief of the production division of the ordnance department with the rank of major, but within ten months he was made a brigadier-general and assistant to the chief of ordnance of the United States Army. Upon his resignation, Nov. 21, 1918, the Distinguished Service Medal was conferred upon him. Thereafter, he continued to cooperate with the War Department in plans for industrial preparedness for possible war. He was for some time a member of the advisory board of the New York ordnance district, and for several years president of New York Post, Army Ordnance Association. In 1923–24 he made a trip around the world to study business conditions bearing upon the great foreign trade of the Westinghouse concerns, and during his visit to Japan he was decorated by the Emperor with the Second Class Order of the Sacred Treasure, the highest honor that Japan confers upon a private citizen.

During the latter years of his life, he spent much time studying the future possibilities of electric development in the United States, believing that power is to be perhaps the greatest factor in progress. He spoke and wrote much on the subject, and worked out in detail an elaborate plan for a great electric system to operate all railroads, street transportation, factories, farms, and homes in the entire country. Among his published monographs are *Proposed Antitrust Legislation* (1914), a speech before the Chamber of Commerce of the United States; *Water Power and Statesmanship* (1923), reprinted from the *New York Times*, Mar. 11, 1923; *Super-Power as an Aid to Progress* (1924); *Electric Development as an Aid to Agriculture* (1926). He was a director of nearly a dozen Westinghouse corporations, besides radio companies, banks, and other concerns. On Aug. 25, 1887, he married Mary Elaine O'Connell of Salem, Mass., who with three daughters survived him. He died in New York City.

[*Who's Who in America*, 1926–27; *Am. Mag.*, Nov. 1919; *N. Y. Times, N. Y. Herald Tribune*, and *Sun* (N. Y.), June 15, 1927; *Industrial Management*, July 1927.]   A.F.H.

TRIPPE, JOHN (1785–July 9, 1810), naval officer, was born in Dorchester County, Md. He was a direct descendant of Henry Trippe, prominent soldier and legislator, who migrated from England to Dorchester County in 1663. His paternal grandfather, John Trippe, married Elizabeth Noel, and, according to a son's account, had twenty-one children. One son, William, the father of John, was married to his cousin, Mary Noel, and to this union were born three children. It is not clear what academic training John received, but the superior quality of his official communications to the navy department, after he had reached maturity, suggests that his formal schooling had by no means been neglected. When hostilities occurred between the United States and France, he was residing at Easton, Md. On Apr. 5, 1799, he entered the navy as a midshipman, and during the next two years made extended voyages on the *United States* and the *Experiment*. After the settlement of difficulties with France, he was transferred to the *President* and sent to the Mediterranean, whither a squadron had been dispatched to check the aggressions of the Barbary powers, particularly Tripoli. In 1802 he received a furlough to make a voyage in the merchant service. The following year he was ordered to the *Vixen* as acting-lieutenant, and, on Aug. 3, 1803, sailed for Tripoli, where he joined Commodore Edward Preble's squadron.

In the subsequent assaults upon the enemy, Trippe displayed courage of the highest order. While in command of Gunboat No. 6, Aug. 3, 1804, he ran alongside one of the largest of the enemy boats and boarded her with only ten companions, his own boat falling off before others could follow. There were thirty-six of the enemy, led by a Tripolitan over six feet in height, who, it was said, had sworn upon the Koran that he would never surrender (Goldsborough, *post*, p. 224). Trippe, who was undersized but exceedingly agile, now engaged in a desperate hand-to-hand conflict with this man. His own pike broke, and he was forced to grapple with his antagonist. Both fell; but Trippe, after receiv-

ing a total of eleven wounds, finally killed the Tripolitan commander with the latter's own saber. Meanwhile the Americans under Trippe's command subdued the remaining Tripolitans. Some of his wounds were serious, but he nevertheless participated in subsequent attacks. For his outstanding services he received the thanks of Congress, and was voted a sword. He returned to the United States in November 1805.

His later activities included service in the Mediterranean in 1806, duty at Charleston, S. C., relative to the enforcement of embargo legislation in 1808, a mission to Holland on board the *Enterprise* to transact business pertaining to commercial relations in 1809, and the beginning of a voyage to New Orleans in 1810. Near Stirrup Key, on June 24, 1810, Trippe's vessel, the *Vixen*, was fired upon by the British warship, *Moselle*. The *Vixen* was immediately cleared for action, but an engagement was averted when the British commander tendered a written apology for his action. Trippe died at Havana. He was unmarried. Two United States vessels have been named after him: a sloop-of-war and a destroyer.

[Manuscript records, Archives Section, Naval Records and Library, Washington, D. C.; family papers and records collected by E. C. Trippe under the title: "Manuscript Genealogical Records of the Trippe and Allied Families," 1928, at the Lib. of Cong. Useful secondary works are G. W. Allen, *Our Navy and the Barbary Corsairs* (1905); J. H. Brown, *Am. Naval Heroes* (1899); Charles Gaylord, *Am. Naval Battles* (1837); and C. W. Goldsborough, *U. S. Naval Chron.* (1824).]   R.W.I.

TRIST, NICHOLAS PHILIP (June 2, 1800– Feb. 11, 1874), diplomat, was born in Charlottesville, Va., the son of Hore Browse and Mary (Brown) Trist and the descendant of Nicholas Trist who emigrated from Devonshire, England, and died in Louisiana in 1784. He was educated at the United States Military Academy at West Point, although he did not graduate, and in the law office of Thomas Jefferson, whose granddaughter, Virginia Jefferson Randolph, he later married. This family connection and a friendship with Andrew Jackson Donelson, the nephew of Andrew Jackson, established while the two were at West Point, were destined to be influential in his career. He possessed a keen conscience and a high sense of honor. In 1827 he refused to profit by conciliating Jackson, whose campaign biographer wished him to allow Jefferson's name to be used in behalf of the "Hero of New Orleans." Trist thought that Jefferson, if living, would not have allowed his influence to be thus employed. His first appointment, a clerkship in the state department, resulted from Henry Clay's desire to comfort the mother of Trist's wife,

Martha Jefferson Randolph, who was harassed by debt. It was obtained several months before the inauguration of President Jackson; but, doubtless owing largely to the influence of Andrew Jackson Donelson, he retained the post under the new administration, and during a brief period in 1829 appears indeed to have been private secretary to the President. His relationship with Jackson soon developed into mutual admiration. In April 1833 he was commissioned as consul to Havana, a position he held until July 1841. Owing to conditions in Cuba and the character of American shipowners, captains, sailors, and residents in Havana, the duties of this post were heavy and often irritating. Although the consul acted with his usual industry and high regard for duty, he was accused of failure to support the rights of American citizens, of cruelty to American captains, of truckling to the Spanish authorities, and of connivance in the slave trade. An investigation made by Congress and the state department failed to sustain these charges in 1840 (see *House Report 707, 26 Cong., 1 Sess., 1840*), although it seems to have revealed that citizens of the United States were illegally engaging in the negro traffic. Trist's recall in 1841 was due to partisan politics rather than to any doubt as to his faithful performance of his functions.

Shortly after Polk's inauguration, Trist was called back to the state department as chief clerk; and occasionally, in Secretary Buchanan's absence, he acted as head of the department. The Mexican War soon brought him the greatest opportunity of his public career. Early in 1847 he was sent as special agent to negotiate a treaty of peace. Upon his arrival in Mexico he had an initial quarrel with Gen. Winfield Scott. The general's suspicious nature and the failure of the war department to keep its commander informed of the administration's policy were mainly responsible for the unpleasant episode, and Scott and Trist soon became warm friends. Trist was eager to bring his negotiations to a successful and speedy conclusion in order to save Mexico from collapse and anarchy, but Polk and his cabinet gradually came to regret that they had offered such mild terms. On one occasion Trist allowed his eagerness to induce him to agree to a boundary not warranted by his instructions. His motive was to avoid the termination of negotiations, but his conduct proved too much for the feeble endurance of an administration already irritated by the initial quarrel with Scott and perhaps not unwilling to demand severer terms of peace. In November 1847 he accordingly received his letter of recall. This action by his su-

periors was followed by general consternation in Mexico and pressure on the part of British and Mexican diplomats to have him proceed with his negotiations. The American agent, although knowing that to stay would end his career, soon decided, nevertheless, to yield to pressure in Mexico, and on Feb. 2, 1848, he signed a treaty in strict compliance with his original instructions. The pact was reluctantly received by an embarrassed administration in Washington and finally accepted by both governments. Trist had done what he conceived to be his duty, and Polk dared not refuse to accept the result.

Trist then settled down to unsuccessful legal practice, observing political developments from a distance. He denounced the dogmas of Calhoun, opposed secession, voted for Lincoln, and received from President Grant in 1870 an appointment as postmaster at Alexandria, Va. There he died four years later.

[Trist Papers, 44 vols., in Lib. of Cong.; archives of the state department; L. M. Sears, "Nicholas P. Trist, a Diplomat with Ideals," *Miss. Valley Hist. Rev.*, June 1924; J. H. Smith, *The War with Mexico* (2 vols. 1919); G. L. Rives, *The U. S. and Mexico* (2 vols. 1913); J. S. Reeves, *Am. Diplomacy under Tyler and Polk* (1907); information from Mrs. Harry R. Burke, Rosemont, Alexandria, Va.]
                                              J.F.R.

TROLAND, LEONARD THOMPSON (Apr. 26, 1889–May 27, 1932), psychologist, physiologist, physicist, engineer, inventor, was born in Norwich, Conn., the son of Edwin and Adelaide Elizabeth (O'Brien) Troland. On his father's side he was, it is said, of Dutch ancestry. Graduating in 1912 from the Massachusetts Institute of Technology with the degree of B.S. in biochemistry, he took up the study of psychology under Hugo Münsterberg [*q.v.*] in Harvard University, obtaining the degree of A.M. in 1914 and that of Ph.D. in 1915. As Sheldon Traveling Fellow, he spent the following year in the Nela Research Laboratory of the General Electric Company, Cleveland, Ohio, where he undertook his first researches in physiological optics (flicker and heterochromatic photometry, after-images, Purkinje phenomenon). On his return to Harvard in 1916 one of his first enterprises was an investigation of telepathy in the psychology laboratory, which gave negative results. Already the articles which he contributed to various scientific journals had begun to attract notice. His first book, *The Nature of Matter and Electricity, an Outline of Modern Views,* written in collaboration with D. F. Comstock, appeared in 1917. During the World War Troland was employed by the United States navy in the development of submarine acoustical apparatus. At the same time he was a member of the committee of the National Research Council on vision and aviation psychology, and in 1921 as a member of the Council's committee on physiological optics he wrote a learned monograph on *The Present Status of Visual Science* (1922). From instructor in psychology in Harvard University (1916–22) he was promoted to the rank of assistant professor (1922–29); he later became lecturer on psychology. During these years of ceaseless activity Troland gave advanced courses in psychology in Harvard, lectured on physiological psychology, psychology of motivation, and other subjects, and, most important of all, organized and conducted with consummate skill a series of novel and far-reaching experiments in the psychology and physiology of vision which brought him into prominence in a wide field of pure and applied science, and made his name known in Europe as well as in America. He was an active member of many learned societies and in 1922–23 president of the Optical Society of America. His *The Mystery of Mind* (1926) was followed soon afterwards by *The Fundamentals of Human Motivation* (1928). In addition he contributed nearly forty articles to various scientific journals, besides writing long chapters in several handbooks of psychology.

Troland's university work in pure science was, however, only one part, perhaps the smaller part, of his varied scientific activities. From 1918 to 1925, in addition to his other employments, he was closely associated with the scientific engineering firm of Kalmus, Comstock and Westcott in Boston; at the same time he was also chief engineer of the Technicolor Motion Picture Corporation of California, which maintained an office in Boston chiefly in order to employ Troland's services without compelling him to sever his connection with Harvard. In 1925 he was made director of research, an office which he continued to hold for the rest of his life. He not only developed and improved the old two-color process of color photography, but invented and perfected the modern multicolor process in all its details. He devised nearly all the photographic and mechanical apparatus for colored motion pictures, the patents being issued in his name. Towards the end of 1929 the Boston office of the Technicolor Corporation was closed, and Troland was induced, though with reluctance, to resign his chair in Harvard and move to California in order to be near this organization. At this time (1930) he must have been very much overworked. Two volumes of his *magnum opus, The Principles of Psychophysiology*, had just been published—the first (1929)

on the problems of psychology and on perception, the second (1930) on sensation—and he was then at work on the third volume (1932) on cerebration and action. (The manuscript of the fourth and last volume on the ultimate theory of mind and matter was finished before Troland died but has not yet, 1936, been published.) His constitution was naturally strong and robust, but in California his health gave way under the strain of his incessant labors, and he was advised by his physician to take a rest. Going to Hollywood with his wife for a vacation, he stood one day (May 27, 1932) on the edge of a cliff near the summit of Mount Wilson, posing for a kodak picture. Suddenly he lost his balance and fell headlong into the rocky chasm; he was killed instantly. He was survived by his wife, Florence Rogers Crockford, whom he married on June 28, 1924; there were no children.

Troland was almost equally at home in physics, physiology, and psychology; he was conversant with the problems of biophysics and biochemistry; and withal he was an engineer, mechanical as well as electrical, of extraordinary ability. He had little art of expression either as writer or speaker, although his mind was too clear and logical ever to leave in doubt the meaning he sought to convey. His intellectual powers almost instantly impressed everybody who came into contact with him; it has been said of him that "the theoretical scientists respected him because of his technological achievements, while technologists admired him for his vast fund of theoretical knowledge" (Roback, *post,* pp. 26–27). Affable and courteous in manner, Troland mingled easily with his comrades and yet was a solitary, aloof from all, *facile princeps* among his peers.

[*Who's Who in America,* 1932–33; *Who's Who in Engineering,* 1931; A. A. Roback, in *Sci.,* July 8, 1932; J. P. C. Southall, *Jour. Optical Soc. of America,* Oct. 1932; J. B. Beebe-Center, in *Am. Jour. Psych.,* vol. XLIV (1932); obituary in *N. Y. Times,* May 28, 1932; letter from Dr. E. F. McCarthy, closely associated with Troland at Harvard.]   J. P. C. S.

TROOST, GERARD (Mar. 15, 1776–Aug. 14, 1850), geologist, was born at Bois-le Duc, Holland. His parents, Everhard Joseph Troost and Anna Cornelia van Haeck, were of but limited means, yet he was educated at the universities of Leyden and Amsterdam, devoting himself especially to chemistry, natural history, and geology. From the former institution he received the degree of doctor of medicine and from the latter that of master in pharmacy. He practised as a pharmacist at Amsterdam and at The Hague. He served in the army as a private soldier and later as a health officer and was twice wounded. In

1807, Louis Napoleon, King of Holland, sent him to Paris for further scientific study. There he became a pupil of René Just Haüy and attained the remarkable skill in mineralogy and crystallography that characterized his later work. Between 1807 and 1809 he traveled widely in Europe, collecting minerals for the cabinet of the King of Holland. He was a pupil, probably during this period, of Abraham Gottlob Werner.

In 1809 he was appointed on a Dutch scientific commission to Java, but was captured, taken to a French port, released on his identity becoming known, and proceeded to Paris, where he was made a corresponding member of the Museum of Natural History of France. Early in 1810 he sailed for Philadelphia. The Kingdom of Holland was soon after annexed to the French Empire. Troost then abandoned the idea of going to Java and decided to become an American citizen. He soon established a pharmaceutical and chemical laboratory in Philadelphia and in 1812 was one of the seven founders of the Academy of Natural Sciences in Philadelphia, which for five years he served as its first president.

In 1811 he became interested in establishing at Cape Sable, Md., the first manufactory of alum in the United States. This venture failed within a few years, causing Troost heavy losses. In 1821 he became professor of mineralogy in the Philadelphia Museum and in 1821–22 was professor of pharmaceutical and general chemistry in the Philadelphia College of Pharmacy. Between 1821 and 1825 he made a geological survey of the environs of Philadelphia for the Philadelphia Society for Promoting Agriculture, publishing the results in 1826.

In 1825 he joined William Maclure, Thomas Say, Robert Dale Owen, and C. A. Lesueur [qq.v.] in the "boat-load of knowledge" which floated down the Ohio to Robert Owen's community at New Harmony, Ind., but, disappointed he moved in 1827 to Nashville, Tenn., with the large collections in natural history and geology which he had spent twenty years acquiring. While in Philadelphia he had made frequent scientific excursions into New Jersey and New York, and from New Harmony had visited the Missouri lead mines. From Java alone he had over 400 species of mounted birds. Later he acquired so much more material that his museum at Nashville became the most notable west of the Appalachians. His meteorites have since been acquired by Yale University.

From his election early in 1828 until his death, Troost was professor of geology and mineralogy, and for most of that time of chemistry and natural philosophy, also, in the University of Nash-

ville; from 1831 to 1850 he was also state geologist of Tennessee and did much to make known the mineral resources of that state. Becoming interested in Indian archeology, he made extensive collections from Tennessee mounds and graves. His last important work, a monograph on the crinoids of Tennessee, remained unpublished for many years but was at length reworked and published by the Smithsonian Institution (Elvira Wood, *A Critical Summary of Troost's Unpublished Manuscript on the Crinoids of Tennessee,* United States National Museum Bulletin 64, 1909).

Troost was a member of many of the learned societies of both Europe and America and was a frequent contributor to their publications. His interests ranged over practically all the known sciences. The bibliography of his writings (Glenn, *post,* pp. 90–94) contains articles on geology, natural history, chemistry, ethnology, mineralogy, and crystallography. Kindly and courteous, he had the polish that characterized the literary and scientific circles in which he moved in Paris; he was an excellent teacher, a good classical scholar, and widely read in science; he was probably most able in chemistry and mineralogy. Because of the long delay in publishing his work on fossil crinoids he lost much of the honor prompt publication would have brought him.

He was twice married: first, Jan. 14, 1811, to Margaret Tage, who died Aug. 3, 1819; and second, to a Mrs. O'Reilly. He left two children, both of the first marriage.

[Philip Lindsley, "The Life and Character of Professor Gerard Troost, M.D." (discourse, Oct. 2, 1850), in *The Works of Philip Lindsley,* vol. I (1859); L. C. Glenn, "Gerard Troost," in *Am. Geologist,* Feb. 1905; H. G. Rooker, "A Sketch of the Life and Work of Dr. Gerard Troost," in *Tenn. Hist. Mag.,* Oct. 1932; *The First Century of the Phila. Coll. of Pharmacy* (1922); G. P. Merrill, *The First One Hundred Years of American Geology* (1924); *Popular Science Monthly,* June 1894; *Nashville True Whig,* Aug. 17, 1850.]

L. C. G.

TROTT, BENJAMIN (c. 1770–c. 1841), portrait painter in miniature and oil, was born probably in Boston, Mass. He first set himself up as a painter in 1791 in New York. Several years later he moved to Philadelphia, which was his headquarters for many years, to make miniatures after the portraits of Gilbert Stuart [q.v.]. With his friend Elkanah Tisdale he lived in Albany for a time about 1796 (Dunlap, *post,* vol. I p. 354). He devoted 1805 to a horseback tour of the "western world beyond the mountains" (*Ibid.,* vol. II, p. 99). In 1812 he exhibited at the Pennsylvania Academy, receiving glowing attention from the press. He was painting in Charleston,

S. C., in 1819. Following an obscure marriage made in Philadelphia he went to Newark, N. J., in 1823 to obtain a divorce, and lived there painting for several years. The three years following 1829 he spent in New York because, as Dunlap says, he felt he had lost his public in Philadelphia. In 1833 he moved to Boston. His last residence was in Baltimore, where he went in 1839; he appears in the Baltimore directory for 1840–41 as "B. Trott. Portrait and **miniature** painter. Office cor. St. Paul and Fayette Streets."

William Dunlap [*q.v.*] says Trott "was of the full medium height, thin, with a prepossessing countenance" (*Ibid.*, vol. II, p. 101). He lived his life as a man with a grievance, his sense of inferiority centering about the painter's technical problems. Possibly from being self-taught, he lacked the authority of a system and always imagined other painters possessed secrets he did not know. Dunlap once saw him experimenting on a miniature by Walter Robertson, half obliterating it in his efforts to discover the secret of its brilliance, making his way "beneath the surface like a mole, and in equal darkness" (*Ibid.*, vol. II, p. 98). He refused to exchange miniatures with Edward Greene Malbone [*q.v.*], suspecting some mischievous plan. Yet he was a close friend of David Edwin [*q.v.*], the engraver; he won the confidence and admiration of Stuart, who is said to have enjoyed his blunt and caustic manner; and he is said twice to have shared a house with Thomas Sully [*q.v.*] in Philadelphia (*Ibid.*, vol. II, p. 100). Dunlap's analysis of Trott's personality is confirmed by examples of the artist's work, such as the Joseph Anthony miniatures, which show him insecure in his method and lacking in confidence.

His earliest style is unknown. The first examples known, which date from 1795, were painted with broad free strokes, with studied concentration on the face, with attractive and lifelike color. Much of the ivory was left showing through, and the backgrounds as a rule were light. The characteristics by which any of Trott's best miniatures may be recognized are those which prevail in this period. It is likely that Stuart's influence upon his style was a determining one, but he evolved from this a manner of his own which is distinguished by his talent for characterization. He gave nearly all his sitters the same easy half-front pose and eliminated any but the most necessary details of costume. One flaw fairly common to his drawing was the lengthening of the neck line; the elongated collar is very nearly a Trott signature. By 1819 the principal change in his style is a broader stroke and more slapdash application. The painterly quality which distinguishes his work from that of the earlier miniaturists, with their engraver technique, became extremely marked in this period. From then on his powers began to decline. In 1828 his stroke was smaller and much constrained. Trott achieved fine clear color, profiting from frequent chemical experiment. Though his transitions and combinations of color were not so subtle as Malbone's, the effect of naturalness is much the same. Like Malbone he is unmistakably American in his palette. The works of Trott from his best period, around 1805, compare favorably with fine miniature painting in England and France. In his own country half a dozen of his miniatures are excelled only by Malbone's. About fifty of his miniatures have been identified but none of his oil portraits. Among his sitters were Nicholas Biddle, Robert Morris, Charles Wilkins, and Sally Waln.

[Almost the only source for Trott's life is William Dunlap, *A Hist. of the Rise and Progress of the Arts of Design in the U. S.* (3 vols., 1918), ed. by F. W. Bayley and C. E. Goodspeed. H. B. Wehle and Theodore Bolton, *Am. Miniatures, 1730–1850* (1927), contains the best modern account and reproduces many of the miniatures. See also *Cat. of an Exhibition of Miniatures . . . 1720–1850* (1927), *Metropolitan Museum of Art*; and Jean L. Brockway, in *Antiques*, Aug. 1931, where miniatures not in Wehle and Bolton are reproduced.]
J. L. B.

TROTT, NICHOLAS (Jan. 19, 1662/63–Jan. 21, 1739/40), South Carolina jurist, was appointed, by the Lords Proprietors, naval officer and attorney-general of that part of the Province of Carolina which lay south and west of Cape Fear, Feb. 5, 1697/98, and arrived at Charlestown (Charleston) on May 3, 1699. An English lawyer of great learning, he can probably be identified with the Nicholas Trott, Jr., who was attorney-general in Bermuda, 1696–97, but should not be confounded with Governor Nicholas Trott of the Bahamas, who appears to have been his cousin. This governor, who was removed from office, married a daughter of Thomas Amy, one of the proprietors and, becoming one himself, made Nicholas Trott of Carolina his deputy. The latter, elected a member of the Commons House of Assembly in 1700, was made speaker. However, the House being dissolved by Governor Blake, Trott was arrested and held to bail for seditiously denying and disowning the governorship of Blake on the ground that he was without commission; Chief Justice Moore found this a sufficient reason for Trott's arrest, but the electors of the province disregarded it and elected him a member of the new Commons House by the highest vote cast for any one. Nominated again for speaker, he failed of election. The record of proceedings, however, reveals Trott as the aggressive leader of the faction in the province which ruled it for the twenty years following it. A man of great learning and unwearied industry, a sincere supporter of the Church of England and the proprietary government, he rose to the office of chief justice (Mar. 5, 1702/03) and to membership in the Council. In 1714 the proprietors gave him the exclusive right to appoint the provost marshal of the province, and made his presence necessary for a quorum of the Council and his consent necessary to the ratification of its acts; but in 1716 this grant of extraordinary power was revoked on protest from the Assembly.

Upon the overthrow of the proprietors' government, it has been claimed that he retired from public life, thereafter devoting himself exclusively to legal and historical pursuits, but as late as 1729 he claimed the office of chief justice. He had published *Clavis Linguæ Sanctæ* in 1719, and *The Laws of the British Plantations in America, Relating to the Church and the Clergy, Religion and Learning,* in 1721. As early as 1714, Trott was engaged on his monumental work, *The Laws of The Province of South Carolina* (2 vols. in one, 1736), the publication of which was refused by the provisional government most unreasonably. In the last year of his life he devoted himself to his explication of the original Hebrew text of the New Testament, finishing one folio. After the death of his wife, Jane, who was buried Feb. 23, 1726/27, he had married, on Mar. 4, 1727/28, her sister, Sarah (Cooke) Rhett (*Register of St. Philip's Parish,* pp. 23, 158). The latter was the widow of Col. William Rhett and the mother of William Rhett, who had married Trott's daughter Mary.

[J. H. Heyward, *Nicholas Trott. A Sketch* (n.d.), which is too eulogistic; A. S. Salley, Jr., "Judge Nicholas Trott," *State* (Columbia, S. C.), Mar. 18, 1923, the best account, quoting obituary in *S. C. Gazette,* Feb. 2, 1740; A. S. Salley, Jr., *Register of St. Philip's Parish, Charles Town, S. C.,* 1720–1758 (1904); *S. C. Hist. and Geneal. Mag.,* Jan. 1903, July 1920; Edward McCrady, *The Hist. of S. C. under the Proprietary Government* (1897), and *The Hist. of S. C. under the Royal Government, 1719–1776* (1899), fairer to Trott in the latter than in the former; J. B. O'Neall, *Biog. Sketches of the Bench and Bar of S. C.* (1859), vol. I, a brief, unfavorable account with a reprint of a charge to the grand jury; *Calendar of State Papers. Colonial Series, America and West Indies, 1699–1702, 1712–15, 1719–20* (1908–33).]

T. D. J.

TROUP, GEORGE MICHAEL (Sept. 8, 1780–Apr. 26, 1856), representative and senator from Georgia, governor, son of George and Catherine (McIntosh) Troup, was born at McIntosh's Bluff on the Tombigbee River in that part of Georgia that became Alabama. His father was born and educated in England, served as an officer in the British army, but spent his later years as a successful merchant in Georgia. His cousin was William McIntosh [*q.v.*], a Creek chief. About 1782 Troup was taken by his father to "Belleville," the home near Savannah, Ga., where he grew up. Tutored at home, he later studied at Erasmus Hall, Long Island, N. Y., where he was prepared for college by Peter Wilson [*q.v.*]. He graduated from the College of New Jersey (Princeton) in 1797. He studied law in Savannah and was admitted to the bar. Probably in 1801 he was elected to the state legislature and reëlected twice from Chatham County. In 1804 he removed to Bryan County but returned to Savannah within a year or two. Elected to the federal House of Representatives, he served from Mar. 4, 1807, to Mar. 3, 1815. A consistent supporter of the Jeffersonian program, he won the confidence of the Democratic administrations. He was a bitter opponent of the Yazoo claims and the recharter of the federal bank. He supported the Embargo as a resistance measure and voted against its repeal. Ready for war in 1807, in 1809 he opposed non-intercourse because he believed New England favored compromise; and as a vigorous advocate of preparedness he was willing to incur a debt up to a billion dollars to build a navy and raise an army. He was elected to the federal Senate and served from Nov. 13, 1816, until he resigned on Sept. 23, 1818.

Defeated as the Crawford candidate for governor in 1819 and 1821, he was elected in 1823 and reëlected in 1825. He advocated public education, a state supreme court, a state program of roads, canals, and railroads, a state penitentiary, combining hard labor and solitary confinement, and the repeal of the law for the sale of free persons of color. His most conspicuous work as governor, however, had to do with the Creek Indian controversy (see sketch of William McIntosh). He openly defied President Adams' orders and called upon the people of the state to stand by their arms in defense of the sovereign power of the state, and thereby secured the cession of all the Creek lands.

Again elected to the federal Senate he served from Mar. 4, 1829, until November 1833, when he resigned. Continuing to be a strong State-Rights Democrat, he voted against the bonus bill, the tariff, and the bank recharter. He upheld the right of nullification but thought South Carolina unwise in acting alone. He urged legislative remonstrance against the tariff, and Southern non-consumption as a remedy. In 1830 he openly advocated secession if the federal policy of aggression was not abandoned. He attended the State-Rights convention at Milledgeville in 1832 and was nominated for the presidency. He accepted but refused a similar nomination by South Carolina. He retired from the Senate in 1833 to devote his time to the care of his six plantations; but he was consulted by the State-Rights party on all important issues and gave his views in public letters that were generally accepted by the press and the people. He favored annexing Texas in 1844 and opposed the compromise of 1850. Lack of health prevented his attending the Nashville Convention, but he wrote a public letter advocating military schools, arsenals, armories, and powder manufactories as the only means whereby Southern rights could be safeguarded. He was married, first, on Oct. 30, 1803, to Anne St. Clare McCormick, the daughter of James McCormick of Louisville, Ga., who died the next year. On Nov. 8, 1809, he was married to Anne Carter, the daughter of George Carter of Alexandria, Va. They had six children. He died and was buried at his plantation "Rosemont" in Montgomery County, Ga.

[*Biog. Directory Am. Cong.* (1928); E. J. Harden, *The Life of George M. Troup* (1859); L. L. Knight, *Georgia's Landmarks, Memorials and Legends* (2 vols., 1914) and *Reminiscences of Famous Georgians*, vol. II (1908); *Men of Mark in Ga.*, vol. II (1910), ed. by W. J. Northen; George White, *Statistics of the State of Georgia* (1849); C. S. Wylly, *Annals and Statistics of Glynn County, Ga.* (1897); *Times and Centinel* (Columbus, Ga.), May 7, 9, 1856.]   F. M. G.

TROUP, ROBERT (1757–Jan. 14, 1832), soldier, jurist, and agent of the Pulteney estate, was probably the son of Robert Troup, commander of the privateer *Sturdy Beggar* (see *New York Historical Society Collections*, Publication Fund Ser. vol. XXX, 1898), who married, May 22, 1737, Elinor Bisset (*Names for Whom Marriage Licenses Were Issued . . . Province of New York*, 1860). This Robert, who died in 1768, mentioned a son Robert in his will (*Archives of the State of New Jersey*, 1 ser. XXXIII, 1928, p. 438). Graduating from King's College in 1774, Troup studied law, first in the office of Thomas Smith of Haverstraw, N. Y., and subsequently under John Jay [*q.v.*]. At the beginning of the Revolution he obtained a lieutenancy in the Continental Army, then stationed on Long Island. Shortly afterward he was appointed aide-de-camp to Brig-Gen. Timothy Woodhull. When Howe prepared to capture New York, Troup with three other officers was captured at Jamaica Pass while attempting to reconnoiter the enemy (Aug. 27, 1776). After a period of confinement in the prison ship *Jersey* and in the Provost Prison, New York City, he was exchanged (Dec. 9, 1776) and joined the army in New Jersey. On Oct. 4, 1777, he was promoted to a lieutenant-colonelcy "as a reward of his merit and services in the American army" (*Journals of the Continental Congress*, vol. IX, 1907, p. 770), and attached to the staff of Gen. Horatio Gates. He participated in the battle of Stillwater and was present at the surrender of Burgoyne (Oct. 17, 1777). In February 1778 Congress created the board of war, of which Troup was appointed secretary. When the board was dissolved (1779), Congress made him secretary to the board of treasury (May 29, 1779–Feb. 8, 1780). Returning to civil life, he completed his law studies with William Paterson [*q.v.*], one of his fellow students being Aaron Burr [*q.v.*]. Troup practised law at Albany and New York, was elected to the state Assembly, and in 1796 was appointed judge of the United States district court of New York.

In 1794 he became interested in land speculation and invested a considerable portion of his fortune in western New York. Charles Williamson [*q.v.*], agent for the Pulteney interests in this region, was spending large sums for improvements designed to attract settlers, and for a while Troup had visions of handsome profits. The lands failed to sell readily, however, and some of those who bought were not able to make payments. In 1800 Sir William Pulteney became uneasy and requested Williamson's withdrawal from the agency. Since Williamson held the lands in his own name, Troup was employed to facilitate the transfer and between December 1800 and March 1801 he secured a series of deeds conveying the Genesee Tract to Sir William and his associates. Pulteney now offered the agency to Troup and for the next thirty years his name was intimately connected with the Genesee country, during which time a large portion of the Pulteney lands were sold and settled. In 1814 he became a permanent resident of Geneva, although he still spent much of his time at Albany, where he assisted or hindered legislation which might affect his special interest. Keenly watchful of western welfare, he was one of the early promoters of the Erie Canal (*A Letter to the Honorable Brockholst Livingston . . . on the Lake Canal Policy of the State of New York*, 1822).

A friend to strong central government, Troup gave valuable help in the campaign to secure the adoption of the Federal Constitution in New York. He was a warm personal friend of Alexander Hamilton; in fact, few enjoyed more intimate acquaintance with the prominent men of his day. He was a conservative in politics with small liking for republicanism or Republicans. The more he saw of "the progress of Jacobinism," the more he realized the need of setting up a college for the training of the clergy of the Episcopal Church (C. R. King, *post*, V, 37; Troup to King, June 1, 1807). He therefore gave his support to the founding of Geneva (later Hobart) College. He died in Laight Street, St. John's Square, New York City.

[Troup Papers, Rochester Hist. Soc.; Pulteney Papers, Canandaigua Hist. Soc.; Rufus King Correspondence, N. Y. Hist. Soc.; C. R. King, ed., *The Life and Correspondence of Rufus King* (6 vols., 1894–1900); Geneva *Gazette*, Hobart College; G. S. Conover, "Kanadesaga and Geneva" (MS., Hobart College); G. S. Conover, *The Genesee Tract* (1889); L. C. Aldrich, *Hist. of Ontario County, N. Y.* (1893), ed. by G. S. Conover; R. H. Greene, "King's College and its Earliest Alumni," *N. Y. Geneal. and Biog. Record*, Apr. 1896; Orsamus Turner, *Hist. of the Pioneer Settlement of Phelps and Gorham's Purchase and Morris' Reserve* (1851); *Memoirs of Long Island Hist. Soc.*, vol. III (1878); A. C. Parker, *Charles Williamson, Builder of the Genesee Country* (1927); Morgan Dix, *A Hist. of the Parish of Trinity Church in the City of New York* (4 vols., 1898–1906); D. R. Fox, *The Decline of Aristocracy in the Politics of N. Y.* (1919); P. D. Evans, "The Pulteney Purchase," *Quart. Jour. of the N. Y. State Hist. Asso.*, Jan. 1922; John Schuyler, *Institution of the Soc. of the Cincinnati . . . N. Y. State Soc.* (1886), pp. 313–14; *N. Y. Evening Post*, Jan. 14, 16, 1832.]
J. G. V–D.

TROW, JOHN FOWLER (Jan. 30, 1810–Aug. 8, 1886), printer, bookseller, and publisher, was born in Andover, Mass., the son of Lieut. John Trow and Martha (Swan). He was graduated from Phillips Academy, Andover, Mass., with the class of 1831, and entered the employ of his brother-in-law, Timothy Flagg, of the printing concern of Flagg & Gould, later the Andover Press. Here he acquired a knowledge of printing in the oriental languages, for the firm, having received a donation of Greek and Hebrew type, was doing such printing under supervision of members of the Andover Theological Seminary faculty. On Apr. 14, 1832, Trow established the *Nashua Herald* at Nashua, N. H., with S. J. Bard as editor and himself as printer. The newspaper was not successful, however, and was discontinued on July 11, 1832.

Removing to New York City in 1833, he first appears in the city directories as a printer in 1834. In that year he formed a partnership with John T. West under the firm name of West & Trow, which continued until 1837. Thereafter he seems to have conducted the business alone until 1844, when he became associated with Jonathan Leavitt and carried on a book shop as well as his printing establishment. This connection was broken in 1849. In 1866 the firm of John F. Trow & Company, printers and publishers, was formed; for most of the time from 1873 to his death Trow was an official of the Trow City Directory Company, and from 1877, of Trow's Printing & Bookbinding Company.

He is best remembered for his publication of *Trow's New York City Directory*, compiled until 1878 by Henry Wilson, which was first issued in 1852–53. The John Doggett, Jr. and Charles R. Rode series of New York directories, begun in 1842, were being published when the Wilson-Trow directory was launched, but after the issue of 1854–55 this series was discontinued, leaving Trow's alone in the field. It continued under its original name until 1925, many years after Trow's death. In 1847 he began printing and publishing *Wilson's Business Directory of New York City*, which appeared annually thereafter until 1884, when it became *The Trow City Directory Co.'s (Formerly Wilson's) Business Directory of New York City*. Another publication, first issued by John Doggett, Jr., and later printed by Trow, was *Wilson's New York City Co-partnership Directory*.

In his directories Trow advertised himself as a printer and stereotyper, doing every type of book and job printing. In 1853 he issued a volume entitled *Specimen Book of the Letterpress, Stereotyping, and Wood-cut Printing Establishment of John F. Trow, 49 Ann Street, New-York*. He is credited with being one of the first to introduce electrotyping into the printing business, and honors were conferred upon him for the excellence of his work. He published the *New York Citizen and American Republican*, later *New York American Republican*, a daily paper, from Jan. 1, 1844, to its discontinuance in 1845. He was also the author of *Alton Trials: of Winthrop S. Gilman, Who Was Indicted . . . for the Crime of Riot Committed on the Night of the 7th of November, 1837* (1838). On Aug. 12, 1834, Trow married Catharine Swift, daughter of Dr. Nathaniel and Sarah Abbott Swift of Andover, Mass., and they had five children, four of whom survived him. His death occurred at the home of a daughter in Orange, N. J.

[*Vital Records of Andover, Mass.* (1912); E. E. Parker, *Hist. of the City of Nashua, N. H.* (1897); Harrison Ellery, *The Memoirs of Gen. Joseph Gardner Swift* (1890); manuscript records of the Trow family; records of Phillips Acad., Andover, Mass.; *N. Y. Herald*, Aug. 9, 1886.]
A. J. W.

TROWBRIDGE, AUGUSTUS (Jan. 2, 1870–Mar. 14, 1934), physicist, was born in New York City, the son of George Alfred and Cornelia Polhemus (Robertson) Trowbridge, and a descendant of Thomas Trowbridge who came to Dorchester, Mass., about 1636. Augustus entered Columbia University in 1890, but left in 1893 to take a position with the World's Columbian Exposition at Chicago. On Sept. 20 of that year he married Sarah Esther Fulton of New York. After finishing his work at the Fair, he went to Germany, where he studied physics at the University of Berlin, receiving the degree of Ph.D. in 1898.

Returning to the United States soon thereafter, he became instructor in physics at the University of Michigan, leaving there in 1900 to accept the position of assistant professor at the University of Wisconsin; three years later he was promoted to a full professorship. In 1906 he accepted a similar position at Princeton, which he held until his resignation shortly before his death. In 1928 he became dean of the graduate school and fulfilled the duties of that office with notable success from that time until June 1932, when failing health compelled him to relinquish it. During his lifetime he carried on important research work and published between twenty and thirty articles, some of them in collaboration with other scholars, which appeared in various scientific publications. His studies were chiefly in the field of radiations, including the theory and behavior of the coherer.

In 1903 as a member of the International Congress of Applied Chemistry in Berlin, he began that phase of his activities for which his career was chiefly noted, those of an able administrator and director of organizations for the advancement of science. He was secretary of the physics section of the International Congress of Arts and Sciences, St. Louis, in 1904; a member of the National Academy of Sciences and in 1921 chairman of its division of physics; and chairman of the division of physical sciences and member of the research fellowship board of the National Research Council, 1920–21. In 1925 he obtained leave from Princeton in order to go to Paris as the director for science of the International Education Board of the Rockefeller Foundation, in which connection he was charged with the distribution of many millions of dollars, designed to restore the scientific institutions of Europe and to revive scientific work. His service in behalf of the advancement of science abroad was later recognized by his appointment as a Knight of the Order of St. Olav (Norway).

During the World War he was attached, 1918, to the staff of General Pershing as a member of the intelligence department, with the rank of lieutenant-colonel. His principal work was with the flash and sound ranging service of the army, the function of which was to locate the position of enemy guns either from the flash when fired, if that could be seen, or from the report. The French had devised a method of such location which the British had developed, and all the information acquired was put at Trowbridge's disposal. With the aid of this, American officers, through the incorporation of automatic devices, were able to develop, in the Palmer Physical Laboratory, equipment by which an enemy's gun at its normal range could be located within forty to forty-five seconds after it was fired. At the end of the war Trowbridge's services were recognized by the award of the Distinguished Service Medal (United States), the Distinguished Service Order (Great Britain), and appointment as an officer of the Legion of Honor (France).

Trowbridge combined an unusual knowledge of the world and its peoples with a gift for languages. The combination made it possible for him to carry on readily the conferences required by the negotiations of the International Education Board, and while in the military service, to act as a liaison officer for the staffs of the allied armies. After resigning his professorship at Princeton in June 1933, he went to Europe, hoping to benefit his health, but died in Taormina the following March, survived by his wife and two sons.

[F. B. Trowbridge, *The Trowbridge Geneal.* (1908); *Who's Who in America*, 1932–33; *Princeton Alumni Weekly*, Mar. 23, 1934; *N. Y. Times*, and *Evening Star* (Washington), Mar. 15, 1934.]　　　H. M.

TROWBRIDGE, EDMUND (1709–Apr. 2, 1793), jurist, son of Thomas Trowbridge by his second wife, Mary (Goffe), was born in Cambridge, Mass. He was a descendant of Thomas Trowbridge of Taunton, Somerset, England, who came to Dorchester, Mass., about 1636 and about 1638 moved to New Haven, Conn. Down into middle life Edmund bore the name Goffe, after his uncle, Col. Edmund Goffe, whose adopted child and heir he was. About 1766 he appears to have resumed his surname of Trowbridge. He graduated from Harvard in 1728 and subsequently became prominent at the Massachusetts bar. Commissioned attorney-general in 1749, he held this office until his appointment as judge of the superior court in 1767. In 1759 John Adams referred to him as commanding "the practice in Middlesex and Worcester and several other counties," adding, "He had power to crush, by his frown or his nod, any young lawyer in his county" (*Works, post,* IV, 6). Isaac Parker [q.v.], later chief justice of the Massachusetts superior court, characterized him as "perhaps the most profound lawyer of New England before the Revolution" (Warren, *post,* I, 51).

While Trowbridge's arguments before the superior court do not appear to have met with more than average success, his skill as a special leader is evinced by the forms of his pleadings which were incorporated into later books of practice.

His opinions on the bench were notable for their impartiality and penetration. His disagreement with the rule laid down by the majority on an earlier occasion in *Baker* vs. *Mattocks* (*Quincy*, 69, at p. 74), to the effect that the province statute of 1692, by which lands descended to all the children, did not extend to estates tail but left them as at common law, was an example of clear thinking and in accord with earlier precedent (cf. R. B. Morris, *Studies in the History of American Law*, 1930, pp. 96–97). His colleague, Thomas Hutchinson [*q.v.*], who was not a professionally trained lawyer, appears to have leaned heavily upon him for legal advice. In 1765 they issued a joint opinion in which they denied that justices of the peace were empowered to grant writs of assistance, but conceded the legality of the latter when issued by the superior court (*Quincy*, 439). A moderate conservative and attached to Hutchinson at this time, Trowbridge refused spiritedly to enter a *nolle prosequi* against the Berkshire rioters in 1766 (Adams, *post*, II, 204). His fairness and impartiality were manifest in the Boston Massacre trial in 1771. An expert in real property law, Trowbridge wrote a tract on mortgages, one of the few known colonial studies in private law (appended to 8 *Massachusetts Reports*; 1818). While borrowing much from Coke on Littleton and from Bacon's *Abridgment*, he was quite critical of Mansfield's contributions to this subject.

On the eve of the Revolution Trowbridge was a moderate sympathizer with the Loyalist point of view, and on this account was dropped from the Council in 1766 (Adams, II, 195). Nevertheless, he expressed strong resentment at the appointment in 1771 of Foster Hutchinson to the probate court, manifesting a traditional Puritan hostility to the judicial powers of the Anglican Church (*Ibid.*, II, 284). Again, in 1774, he was frank to concede that, in the light of the English Constitution, the Massachusetts House of Representatives had the power to impeach the judges, asserting that this power was "essential to a free government" (*Ibid.*, II, 331; X, 239). Somewhat gloomy in manner and a notorious hypochondriac, Trowbridge counted among his large circle of friends such Revolutionary leaders as John Adams and Joseph Hawley. Surrounded by relatives and associates active in the Patriot cause, he maintained a strict neutrality during the conflict. He received an offer of safe conduct from the Committee of Public Safety and retired from his Cambridge home, taking up his residence with the Parsons family in Byfield, whither he took his famous law library, probably the finest in New England at that time. Here The-

ophilus Parsons [*q.v.*] studied with him and gained the legal foundation for his later career. Among other leaders of the bar who studied law in his office were James Putnam and his nephew and heir, Francis Dana [*q.v.*]. On Mar. 15, 1737/38 Trowbridge married Martha, daughter of Jonathan Remington; there were no children. He died at Cambridge at the age of eighty-four.

[F. B. Trowbridge, *The Trowbridge Geneal.* (1908); Theophilus Parsons, *Memoir of Theophilus Parsons* (1859); Lorenzo Sabine, *Biog. Sketches of Loyalists of the Am. Revolution* (1864), II, 362–64; L. R. Paige, *Hist. of Cambridge, Mass.*, 1630–1877 (1877), pp. 671, 672; W. T. Davis, *Professional and Industrial Hist. of Suffolk County, Mass.* (1894), I, 216; Emory Washburn, *Sketches of the Judicial Hist. of Mass.* (1840); C. F. Adams, *The Works of John Adams*, vols. II (1850), IV (1851), X (1856); Charles Warren, *Hist. of the Harvard Law School* (1908), I, 51, 129; John T. Morse, "Bench and Bar in Boston," in Justin Winsor, *The Memorial Hist. of Boston*, vol. IV (1881).]

R. B. M.

TROWBRIDGE, JOHN (Aug. 5, 1843–Feb. 18, 1923), physicist, educator, was born in Boston, the son of John Howe Trowbridge and Adeline (Richardson) Whitney Trowbridge, and a descendant of Thomas Trowbridge who came from Somersetshire, England, to Dorchester, Mass., about 1636. Though at his birth the family was in comfortable circumstances, a reverse of fortune compelled John while still a youth to use his considerable artistic talent as a means of earning money, and he painted a number of pictures which found a ready sale. Graduating from the Lawrence Scientific School of Harvard University in 1865, with the degree of S.B., he taught mathematics at Harvard for a time, served in the physics department of the Massachusetts Institute of Technology, 1868–70, and then returned to Harvard as assistant professor of physics. Ten years later he became full professor, and from 1888 until his retirement in 1910 was Rumford Professor of Science and director of the Jefferson Physical Laboratory.

One of the first of American teachers to encourage students in original research in physics, Trowbridge was largely responsible for changing the method of instruction of the Harvard department from the old system of set lectures, demonstrations, and textbook assignments, to the modern plan of laboratory practice, research, and encouragement of constructive thought. Imbued with the spirit of progress, he possessed vision and furthermore had the ability to recognize and give scope to the capabilities of other men. Keeping abreast of developments elsewhere, he planned for, worked for, and finally in 1884 secured for Harvard a physics building with genuine laboratory features, though the first director of this laboratory was his senior, Prof. Joseph

Lovering [*q.v.*]. It was under Trowbridge's influence and guidance, however, that the Jefferson Laboratory gradually acquired a physical equipment and a working staff which made it notable. This achievement, together with the assistance he gave to younger investigators, must be regarded as his great contribution to the progress of science.

Trowbridge was an associate editor of the *American Journal of Science* from 1880 to 1920, and published therein numerous brief contributions, including notices of work done by others. He also published often in the *Proceedings* of the American Academy of Arts and Sciences (Boston), of which he was president from 1908 to 1915. He was interested particularly in spectrum analysis and the conduction of electricity through gases, and many of his papers were contributions in these fields. In 1910 he retired from the directorship of the Jefferson Laboratory and from the Rumford Professorship.

Trowbridge was quiet and gentle, almost melancholy in manner, and except when he encountered intentional opposition was generous, almost too yielding; in the face of opposition, however, he could display considerable tenacity. His sense of humor was ordinarily concealed, but could not be ignored, and he was by nature quite as much an artist as a man of science. He wrote easily, producing besides his scientific papers a number of books combining fiction and science, which he illustrated with pencil sketches of his own. His published volumes include *The New Physics* (1884); *The Electrical Boy; or the Career of Greatman and Greatthings* (1891); *Three Boys on an Electrical Boat* (1894); *What is Electricity?* (1896); *The Resolute Mr. Pansy* (1897); and *Philip's Experiments; or Physical Science at Home* (1898). He married, June 20, 1877, Mary Louise, widow of Thomas W. Gray and daughter of Seth Turner Thayer. There were no children of this marriage. Trowbridge survived his wife sixteen years, dying in Cambridge in 1923.

[E. H. Hall, "Biog. Memoir of John Trowbridge" (1931), with portr. and bibliog., in *Nat. Acad. Sci., Biog. Memoirs*, vol. XIV; *Science*, June 1, 1923; *Am. Jour. Sci.*, June 1923; S. E. Morison, *The Development of Harvard Univ. . . . 1869–1929* (1930); F. B. Trowbridge, *The Trowbridge Geneal.* (1908); *Who's Who in America*, 1922–23; *Boston Transcript*, Feb. 19, 1923; personal acquaintance.]   E.H.H.

TROWBRIDGE, JOHN TOWNSEND (Sept. 18, 1827–Feb. 12, 1916), author, was born on his father's farm in Ogden Township, Monroe County, N. Y., the eighth of the nine children of Windsor Stone and Rebecca (Willey) Trowbridge, and seventh in descent from Thomas

Trowbridge of Somerset, England, who emigrated to Dorchester, Mass., about 1636. Except for weak eyes he was a healthy boy, fond of hunting, fishing, ball playing, and kite flying, but his real business, even then, was with literature. A list of foreign words and phrases in his spelling book tantalized his imagination, and the brief extracts from the poets in Goold Brown's grammar exercised a charm that he never forgot. A cousin bequeathed him her French grammar, dictionary, and reader, and with them he taught himself French. A few years later he taught himself to read Latin. By the age of thirteen he was writing verse. Five Byronic stanzas by him on "The Tomb of Napoleon" were printed in the *Rochester Republican* when he was sixteen years old, and while attending the academy at Lockport, 1844–45, he contributed the newscarriers' New Year address to the *Niagara Courier*. After a brief experience as a school teacher in Du Page County, Ill., and at Lockport, he went to New York in 1847, at the age of twenty, determined to make a career as a writer. His confidence was justified. He had a gift for story-telling and was practical, industrious, and quick to learn. Mordecai Manuel Noah [*q.v.*] gave him kindly advice and helped him to find a publisher for his first stories. He was fortunate in other ways also, especially in his friendship with a French family, in whose household he lived the greater part of a year. Boston, however, was still the literary center of the country, and thither he removed in 1848. It remained his headquarters for the rest of his long life.

After a few years of journalism and hack writing for Benjamin Perley Poore [*q.v.*] and some lesser men, Trowbridge began his literary career with a novel, *Father Brighthopes* (1853), which he published over the pseudonym of Paul Greyton. Its success resulted in a series of related stories and the eventual abandonment of the pseudonym. Fifty years later he closed his career, formally but not quite completely, with a volume of collected poems (*The Poetical Works of John Townsend Trowbridge*, 1903), and an autobiography, *My Own Story* (1903). During the half century intervening, he wrote with remarkable steadiness, neither idling nor overworking, producing in all some forty volumes of fiction; a few plays adapted from his novels; several volumes of verse; a descriptive work, *The South: A Tour of its Battlefields and Ruined Cities* (1866), and some miscellaneous matter. He contributed constantly to *Our Young Folks*, the *Atlantic Monthly*, and the *Youth's Companion* and occasionally to other magazines. He was a contributing and consulting editor of

Our Young Folks, 1865–70, and managing editor, 1870–73. The genre that he made peculiarly his own was a boys' story sufficiently mature in substance to be about equally interesting to adults. Few American novelists have had so large and loyal a public. He himself regarded his fiction as good journeyman's work but thought that he would be remembered for his poetry.

He was married twice: on May 9, 1860, to Cornelia Warren of Lowell, who died Mar. 23, 1864; second, on June 4, 1873, to Sarah Adelaide Newton of Arlington. He had two children by the first marriage, one dying at birth, and three by the second. He was a discriminating admirer of Walt Whitman and a sane friend. Of other Boston men of letters, he was on especially friendly terms with Holmes and Longfellow. He twice made extended visits to Europe. His home, from 1865 until his death, was in Arlington, Mass., eight miles from Boston. He died there in his eighty-ninth year.

[**In** addition to Trowbridge's autobiog., see *Who's Who in America*, 1914–15; F. B. Trowbridge, *The Trowbridge Geneal.* (1908); A. E. Winship, "Authors as I Have Known Them: J. T. Trowbridge," *Jour. of Educ.*, Mar. 16, 1916; *N. Y. Times*, Feb. 13, 1916.]

G. H. G.

TROWBRIDGE, WILLIAM PETIT (May 25, 1828–Aug. 12, 1892), engineer, scientist, educator, was born in Troy, N. Y., a descendant of Thomas Trowbridge who settled in New Haven, Conn., early in the seventeenth century, and the son of Stephen Van Rensselaer and Elizabeth (Conkling) Trowbridge. His early education was obtained in rural schools, but at the age of sixteen years he was able to fulfil the requirements for entrance to the United States Military Academy, where he stood at the head of his class throughout the four-year course. Graduating in 1848, he was made brevet second lieutenant of engineers. During the last year of his course, he had acted as assistant professor of chemistry, and after his graduation he spent two years in the astronomical observatory, preparing himself for service in the United States Coast Survey; he was commissioned second lieutenant on Nov. 30, 1849. His first assignment was on the Atlantic coast, where he was engaged in the execution of the primary triangulation of the coast of Maine; subsequently, he was engaged in surveys of the Appomattox and James rivers in Virginia.

Proceeding to the Pacific coast in 1853, he was occupied during the succeeding three years in conducting astronomical, tidal, and magnetic observations along the coast from San Diego to Puget Sound. He was promoted to a first lieutenancy in the corps of engineers on Dec. 18, 1854; but, upon returning from the West in

1856, he resigned from the army to accept a professorship of mathematics in the University of Michigan. In the course of a year, however, he was persuaded to accept a permanent appointment as assistant superintendent of the Coast Survey. The *Reports of the Superintendent of the Coast Survey, Showing the Progress of the Survey During the Years 1857–1861* (1858–62) reveal the nature of Trowbridge's employments at this period. They cite observations on the winds of the Pacific coast; arrangement of Gulf Stream observations; investigation of the laws of motion governing the descent of the weight and line in deep-sea soundings; a review of the origin, cost, and progress of foreign geodetic surveys; description of an apparatus devised by Trowbridge for determining ocean depths and obtaining specimens of the bottom; results of experiments made with an instrument, also devised by Trowbridge, to register depths in soundings, and distance as a log at sea. In 1860 he was selected to install the self-registering instruments of the permanent magnetic observatory established at Key West for the purpose of recording the variations in the direction of the magnetic needle, and also the intensity of the earth's magnetic force in terms of the fundamental units of space, mass, and time.

The following year preparations for warfare became of concern to his office, and, by recourse to the official records, he produced detailed descriptions of the harbors, inlets, and rivers of the coasts of the Southern states for the use of the navy; this task finished, he proceeded to execute a hydrographic survey of Narragansett Bay in relation to the project to establish a navy yard there. Soon after the beginning of the Civil War, he was placed in charge of the army engineer agency at New York City for supplying materials for fortifications, and for constructing engineering equipage for armies in the field; at the same time he was superintending engineer of the construction of the fort at Willets Point, of the repairs to Fort Schuyler, and of the works on Governors Island.

In 1865 he accepted the vice-presidency of the Novelty Iron Works, New York City, which position he held until 1871, when he became professor of dynamic engineering in the Sheffield Scientific School at Yale; from 1877 to the close of his life he was professor of engineering in the School of Mines of Columbia College. He lent impetus to the advancement of engineering education and to the application of science in place of empiricism in engineering. While at Yale, he served as a member of the New Haven board of harbor commissioners, as a commissioner for the building of the capitol at Hartford, and as adjutant-general of Connecticut; while at Columbia, he was a member of the commission to examine and report upon the construction of the capitol at Albany. He was the author of designs for a cantilever bridge across the East River at Blackwell's Island, N. Y. (see his *Proposed Plan for Building a Bridge across the East River at Blackwell's Island*, 1868), and of treatises entitled *Heat as a Source of Power . . . An Introduction to the Study of Heat Engines* (1874), and *Turbine Wheels* (1879), besides important contributions on various subjects to the *Transactions of the New York Academy of Sciences*.

From 1878 to 1884 he was councilor of the New York Academy of Sciences, and from 1885 to 1889, a vice-president; he was also prominent in the American Association for the Advancement of Science, and a member of the National Academy of Sciences. On Apr. 21, 1857, he was married, in Savannah, Ga., to Lucy, daughter of Samuel Breck and Theresa (Halsey) Parkman. He died in New Haven, Conn., survived by his wife and six children.

[F. B. Trowbridge, *The Trowbridge Geneal.* (1908); *Twenty-fourth Ann. Reunion, Asso. Grads. U. S. Mil. Acad.* (1893); G. W. Cullum, *Biog. Reg. Officers and Grads. U. S. Mil. Acad.* (3rd ed., 1891); *Nat. Acad. Sci. Biog. Memoirs*, vol. III (1895); *New Haven Evening Reg.*, Aug. 13, 1892.]　　　　G.W.L.